P9-AFF-641

WITHDRAWN
JUN 2 7 2024
PROPERTY OF:
DAVID O. McKAY LIBRARY
BYU-IDAHO
REXBURG ID 83460-0405

FEB 2 6 2002

WHO'S WHO IN THE ARAB WORLD

2001 - 2002

Fifteenth Edition
(Thoroughly revised and completed)

Published since 1966

Publishers
PUBLITEC PUBLICATIONS
Gedeon Bldg., 139-141 John Kennedy Street
P.O.Box 166142 — Beirut — Lebanon
Fax 961-1-493330 - e-mail:mecico@dm.net.lb

Distributed exclusively in the United States and Canada by
Gale Group Inc.,
27500 Drake Road
Farmington Hills, MI 48331-3535, U.S.A
Telephone: 1-800-877-GALE, FAX: 1-248-699-8076

Distributed exclusively throughout the rest of the world by
K.G.Saur Verlag GmbH & Co; KG.
A Gale Group Company
Postfach 701620, D-81316 München,
Telephone: (089) 76902230, FAX: (089)76902250

Publitec Publications Ref.: ISBN 2-903188-17-3
ISSN 0083-9752

Founded in 1963

●

The title and general layout of

WHO'S WHO IN THE ARAB WORLD

are duly rcgistered at the Ministry of National Economy of the Lebanese Republic (Property and Patents Office) in conformity with the provisions of Article 161 of Decree No. 2385 of 17th January 1924

●

Copyright No. 370
dated March 16th 1966

●

All rights of reproduction, adaptation, translation in all countries are reserved to

PUBLITEC PUBLICATIONS

Publisher : Charles G. Gedeon

CONTENTS

PART I

— BIOGRAPHICAL SECTION

PART II

PART III

SURVEY OF THE 19 ARAB COUNTRIES

PART IV

OUTLINE OF THE ARAB WORLD

N.B. Lebanon in surveyed in a separate publication under the title of:

WHO'S WHO IN LEBANON

The 16th edition of this biographical dictionary 2000-2001 is available in one hardbound volume

●

Revised and Published every other year

FOREWORD

This is the fifteenth edition of WHO'S WHO IN THE ARAB WORLD published every other year since more than 30 years. It is definitely the reference book of the Arab countries, available at present in more than 170 countries of the world.

It is published this year after important events in the Middle East and North Africa, namely the continued but lengthy implementation of the Declaration of Principles on Palestinian Self-Rule in the Occupied Territories signed by Israel and the PLO in 1993, the recognition of the Palestinian Authority as the legitimate representative of the Palestinians by the Israeli government, the continued U.S. efforts to inject fresh momentum into the stalled Middle East process, with some significant improvement during the Camp David meeting in year 2000, the U.S. Secretary of State Madeleine Albright further visit to Israel and the Palestinian self-rule areas in early June 2000 as part of a wider tour of the Middle East region, the death of a heart attack on June 10, 2000 of President Hafez al-Assad of Syria and the nomination on June 27, 2000 of his 34 years son Bashar, as new president of Syria, the Government changes in Jordan, the recuperation by Lebanon, on May 20, 2000 of the occupied part of its South, when the Israeli troops departed their self declared security zone, some 6 weeks before the scheduled date of July 7, 2000, the U.N. Secretary General, Kofi Annan visit to Lebanon on June 19-20, 2000 to ascertain that the U.N. Resolution 425 has been implemented, the release by Israel of Lebanese prisoners, the death on April 6, at the age of 96, of Habib Bourguiba, 1st President of Tunisia, the four day visit on June 4, 2000 of President Abdelaziz Bouteflika of Algeria to France, in spite of the continued but reduced cycle of violence in Algeria, the continued U.N. Sanctions in Iraq, in spite of some humanitarian improvements, etc.

There is no doubt that a peace agreement between all the parties to the Arab-Israel conflict could lay the foundation to a remarkable economic development in that region of the world. It might take some further time to occur, particularly in respect to the Jerusalem problem, but seemingly all parties concerned have no other choice than to move inevitably in that direction.

Our 15th edition of WHO'S WHO IN THE ARAB WORLD is 3 books in 1, thus comprising 4 distinct parts:

— The first part includes about 6000 biographical notices (It is a WHO'S WHO book by itself).

— The 2nd Part includes some institutions in the Arab World.

— The 3rd Part is a methodical and concise study of the 19 Arab countries, from the following standpoints: Geography, History, Constitution, Governments, Accredited Embassies, Economy, Commerce, Banks, Transports, Radios, TV, Press, Statistics, etc. with the exception of Lebanon which has its own WHO'S WHO IN LEBANON, published separately and which should be considered as Volume II of the WHO'S WHO IN THE ARAB WORLD. If one is interested in the Arab World, he should consider having both volumes, particularly that LEBANON is considered again as the gate to the Middle East.

— The 4th Part deals with certain particularities of the Arab World and in particular the conflicts inherent to the troubled region which remains the largest reservoir of petroleum in the world.

The people we have selected in our WHO'S WHO IN THE ARAB WORLD have generally a touch of ambition or genius, and have left their mark in their own field of activity. Some have led, a meaningful life and been an inspiration to others. Our entrants are nearly all of Arab nationality, or are Arab expatriates with a good record of achievements, or are foreigners with an offical status, present in the Arab countries. Their answers to the questionnaires we have sent them are not edited for clarity or space, and nicknames and pen names are reproduced as they stand, bearing in mind that if some biographical notices are missing, we cannot force these personalities to fill them and return them to us.

WHO'S WHO IN THE ARAB WORLD was first published in Beirut, at a time when the notion of WHO'S WHO was practically non existent. Persuading prospective entrants to fill in the questionnaire sent to them for the background of their biographical notices was quite a job. They were doubtful of the purpose they were intended to serve. Some went so far as to suspect that the data would be used by parties working against them, while a certain number of potential entrants refused to fill the questionnaires, either because they did not want to show that they occupied senior positions well above the level of their academic qulifications, or because they preferred to remain unknown for personal reasons. Nevertheless, since then, the concept of WHO'S WHO has changed and is now entering more and more the mind and the customs of the Arabs. However, we cannot force anyone to complete his questionnaire and return it to us. We cannot even force him to update his biographical notice.

This year, as ever, we wish to express our gratitude to the numerous individuals, firms and organizations who have provided us with new or revised information for inclusion in this 15th edition and have turned the WHO'S WHO IN THE ARAB WORLD into a must, a unique and acknowledged authority on the Arab World.

Charles G. Gedeon

TRANSCRIPTION OF ARABIC NAMES

The Arabic Language is used over a vast area. Though the written language and the script are standard throughout the Middle East, the spoken language and also the pronunciation of the written signs show wide variations from place to place. This is reflected, and even exaggerated, in the different transcriptions in use in different countries.

Arabic names occurring in the historical and geographical sections of this book have been rendered in transliteration i.e. it is based on the writing, which is standard throughout the Arab world.

Consonants:

d — represent two Arabic letters. The second, or emphatic d, is transliterated d. It may also be represented, for some dialects, by dh and by z, e.g. Qadi, qahdi, qazi.
dh — in literary Arabic and some dialects pronounced like English th in this. In many dialects pronounced z or d.
gh — A strongly guttural sometimes written g, e.g. Baghdad, Bagdad.
h — represents two Arabic letters. The second more guttural h, is transliterated h, e.g. Husain, Husein.
j — as English; in john, also represented by dj and g. In Egypt this letter is pronounced as a hard g. and may be thus transcribed (with u before and i) c.g. Najib, Nadjib, Nagib, Naguib, Ncguib.
kh — as ch in Scottish loch, also sometimes represented by ch and h, e.g. Khalil, Chalil, Halil.
q — a guttural k, pronounced farther back in the throat. Also trancribed k,k, and, for dialects, g, e.g. Waqf, Wakf, Wagf.
s — represents two Arabic letters. The second, emphatic s, is transliterated, s. It may also be represented by c, e.g. Salih, Saleh, Caleh.
t — represents two Arabic letters. The second, emphatic t, is transliterated t.
th — in literary Arabic and some dialects pronounced as English th in through. In many dialects pronounced t or s, e.g. Thabit, Tabit, Sabit.
w — as in English, but often represented by ou or u, e.g. Wadi, Vadi, Oued.
z — represents two Arabic letters. The second, or emphatic z, is transliterated z. It may also be represented for some dialects, by dh or d, e.g. Hafiz, Hafidh, Hafid.
A glottal stop, as in Cockney «li'l bo'ls». May also represent the sound transliterated, a deep guttural with no English equivalent.

Vowels

The Arabic script only indicates three short vowels, three long vowels, and two diphthongs, as follows:

a — as in English hat, and rendered e, e.g. balad, beled, emir, amir; with emphatics or gutturals usually pronounced as u in but, e.g. Khalifa, Baghdad.
i — as in English bit. Sometimes rendered e, e.g. Jihad, Jehad.
u — as in English good. Often pronounced and written o, e.g. Muhammad, Mohammad.
In some Arabic dialects, particularly those of North Africa, unaccented short vowels are often omitted altogether, and long vowels shortened, e.g. Oued for Wadi, bled for balad, etc.
a — Long a, variously pronounced as in sand, dart and half.
i — As ee in feet. In early books often rendered ee.
u — As oo in boot. The French transcription ou is often met in English books, e.g. Mahmud, Mahmood, Mahmoud.
ai — Pronounced in classical Arabic as English i in hide, in colloquial Arabic as a in take. Variously transcribed as ai, ay, ei and ê, e.g. sheikh, shaikh, shaykh, etc.
aw — Pronounced in classical Arabic as English ow in town, in colloquial Arabic as in grow. Variously rendered aw, ew, au, ô, av, ev, e.g. Tawfiq, Taufiq, Tevfik, etc.

LIST OF ABBREVIATIONS

Acad.	Academy
accred.	accredited
A.D.C.	Aide-de-camp
Admin-Gen.	Administrator-General
ADMA	Abu Dhabi Marine Areas
ADOCO	Abu Dhabi Oil Company
ADPC	Abu Dhabi Petroleum Company
AFDB	African Development Bank
Amb.	Ambassador
AMINOIL	American Independent Oil Company
AMOSEAS	American Overseas Petroleum Ltd
AOC	Arabian Oil Company
AOF	Afrique Occidentale Française (French West Africa)
API	American Petroleum Institute
Aramco	Arabian-American Oil Company
A.R.E.	Arab Republic of Egypt
Ass.	Assembly
Asscn.	Association
Assoc.	Associate
Asst.	Assistant
Ave.	Avenue
B.A.	Bachelor of Arts
BAPCO	The Bahrain Petroleum Company Ltd
bbl(s)	Barrel(s)
BD	Bahrain Dinars
Bd.	Board
B.Lit(t)	Bachelor of Letters
Blvd.	Boulevard
B.P.	Boîte Postale (Post Office Box)
BP	British Petroleum
B.Sc.	Bachelor of Science
B.S.T.	British Standard Time
CA	Chargé d'Affaires
cap.	capital
Capt.	Captain
CENTO	Central Treaty Organisation
CFP	Compagnie Française des Pétroles
Chair.	Chairman
Cie.	Compagnie (Company)
C-in-C.	Commander-in-Chief
Co	Company
Comm.	Commission
Commdr.	Commander
Commdt.	Commandant
Commr.	Commissioner
Conf.	Conference
Contrib.	Contributor; Contribution
CPA	Compagnie des Pétroles d'Algérie
CREPS	Compagnie de Recherche et d'Exploration de Pétrole du Sahara
Del.	Delegate; Delegation
Dem.	Democratic
dep.	deposits
Dept.	Department
Devt.	Development
Dir.	Director
Div.	Division
Dr.	Doctor
ed.	Educated
Edn.	Edition
Educ.	Education
EEC	European Economic Community
EFTA	European Free Trade Association
ERAP	Entreprise de Recherches et d'Activités Pétrolières
est.	estimate(d)
Exec.	Executive
Extra.	Extraordinary
f.	Founded
FAO	Food and Agriculture Organisation
FCM	Federation of Muslim Councillors
Fed.	Federation; Federal
FLOSY	Front for the Liberation of Occupied South Yemen
f.o.b.	Free on Board
ft.	feet; foot
gal.	gallons
G.D.P.	Gross Domestic Product
Gen. Man.	General Manager
G.H.Q.	General Headquarters
G.O. -in-C	General Officer Commanding-in Chief
Gov.	Governor
Govt.	Government
GUPCO	Gulf of Suez Petroleum Company
ha.	hectares
H.E.	His Eminence; His Excellency
Hist.	Historical
H.M.	His (or Her) Majesty
H.Q.	Headquarters
IAEA	International Atomic Energy Authority
IATA	International Air Transport Association
IBRD	International Bank for Reconstruction & Development
ICAO	International Civil Aviation Organisation
ICATU	International Conference of Trade Unions
IDA	International Development Association
IFC	International Finance Corporation
ILO	International Labour Organisation
IMF	International Monetary Fund
Inc.	Incorporated
incl.	included; including

Ind.	Independent
INOC	Iraq National Oil Company
KFAED	Kuwait Fund for Arab Economic Development
KNPC	Kuwait National Petroleum Company
KOC	Kuwait Oil Company
LL.B.	Bachelor of Laws
M.A.	Master of Arts
Maj.	Major
Maj.-Gen.	Major-General
M.B.E.	Member of the British Empire
M.D.	Doctor of Medicine
MEA	Middle East Airlines
Mgr.	Monseigneur; Monsignor
Mil.	Military
Min.	Minister, Ministry
M.P.	Member of Parliament
M.Sc.	Master of Science
n.a.	not available
Nat.	National
NATO	North Atlantic Treaty Organisation
NLF	National Liberation Front (People's Democratic Republic of Yemen)
NUP	National Unionist Party (Sudan)
OAPEC	Organisation of Arab Petroleum Exporting Countries
O.A.U.	Organisation for African Unity
O.B.E.	Officer of the (Order of the) British Empire
OECD	Organisation for Economic Co-operation & Development.

PART I

BIOGRAPHICAL SECTION

A

ABAAKIL (Najim), Moroccan banker. **Born** in 1934 in Morocco. **Career:** Former President and Director General, Banque Marocaine pour l'Afrique et l'Orient; Vice President, Algemene Bank, Maroc; former President and Director General, Chamber of Commerce and Industry, Casablanca; Vice President, Federation of the Chambers of Commerce and Industry, Morocco; former Vice President, Union of the Arab Chambers of Commerce and Agriculture. **Addr.:** Casablanca, Morocco.

ABAHSAIN (Abdulaziz, Ibrahim), Saudi businessman. **Born** in 1917 at al-Shaiger, Saudi Arabia. **Son** of late Sheikh Ibrahim Abahsain. **Career:** Together with his (late) brother Saleh Abahsain, established business in 1945 as the first electrical contractor in the Eastern Province of Saudi Arabia, incorporated the Abqaiq Electric Supply Co. for the distribution of electricity in Abqaiq community in 1953, now has a joint Venture in Electrical Contracting since 1980; Operated one of the nation's pioneer Pipeline Contr ting Company (1953-78); formed a joint Venture with Hood Corp. of USA in 1978 to expand pipeline contracting (1978-89) and also with Majestic Contractors Ltd. Canada (1984-89); also has Joint Venture with a Lebanese Construction Co. since 1978 for Civil, architecture & Design works; in 1965 began Road Construction work, which has its Head Quarters in Riyadh, now completing major government & private projects throughout Saudi Arabia; is in Joint Venture with a prominent UK Company for the service & maintenance of Valve Actuators- Abahsain Rotork Controls Arabia Ltd. was formed 1984; in 1981 formed a Joint Venture with T. J. Cope Inc. USA for the manufacture of Cable Trays & Cable Support Systems; had a Joint Venture with a US Company for the manufacture of Fire Proofing Materials and enclosures (1981-89); in 1981 formed a Joint Venture with Holland's ESBD concrete bonding Company and later with USA's Adhesive Engineering Co. Ltd. (1981-88); in 1988 entered into dealership for Saab Cars from Sweden; Dealer in Construction and Heavy Equipment, materials related with the Petro-Chemical Industry, Power Generation & Distribution, Construction & Earth Moving, Chemicals & Industrial Gases & Laboratory Chemicals, representing well over 40 well known manufacturers world-wide. Also became stockist & whole sale traders in Food Stuff. Has branches in Riyadh, Jeddah and most recently in Medina. One of major Suppliers to ARAMCO, SCECO, SWCC, PETROMIN, ROYAL COMMISSION besides others. **Addr.:** ALKHOBAR: King Abdulaziz Str., P.O.Box 209, Alkhobar 31952,Tel.: 864-2025, Fax: 895-1542, Telex: 870026 BASAIN SJ., Saudi Arabia. RIYADH: al-Kharj, Kilo 9, P.O.Box 42127, Riyadh 11541, Tel.: 495-0104, Fax: 495-4900, Telex: 404-689 SAHERD SJ., Saudi Arabia. JEDDAH: Sary Str., P.O.Box 1300, Jeddah 21431, Tel.: 682-0944, Fax: 683-3124, Telex: 603309 BASAIN SJ., Saudi Arabia.

ABAHUSAYN (Mansur, Muhammad), Saudi Arabian businessman. **Born** in 1942 in Saudi Arabia. **Son** of Muhammed Aba-Husayn. **Married**, three sons. **Educ.:** American University of Beirut, University of Arizona, University of California. **Dipl.:** B.S., M.S., Ph.D. **Career:** Professor of Agriculture, University of Riyadh (1972-1975); Director General of Development in the Ministry of Agriculture and Water, Saudi Arabia (1975); Assistant Deputy Minister, Deputy Minister (1976); President, Harad Agricultural and Animal Production Company (1979). Aba-Husayn Consulting Engineers and Aba-Husayn Dev. Co. (1981). Represented Ministry of Agriculture and Water in the Saudi US Joint Economic Commission (1975) and in the Arab-European Dialogue (1976). Chairman of: Saudi Dutch Potato Development Program, al-Faisal Settlement Project, al-Hasa Irrigation and Drainage Authority, Saudi Arabian Agricultural Bank. **Publ.:** Over ten scientific publications. **Sports:** Table tennis and fishing. **Hobby:** reading. **Prof. Addr.:** Aba-Husayn Consulting Engineers, P.O.Box 26668, Riyadh 11496, Telephone 4789052 and 4778836.

ABALKHAIL (Abdul Rahman Abdullah), Saudi diplomat. **Dipl.:** B.A. (Arabic and Eastern Languages). **Career:** Diplomatic Attaché, later Third Secretary, Saudi Embassy, Cairo; Second Secretary, Saudi Embassy, Beirut; Ambassador, Saudi Embassy, Cairo; General Manager, Ministry of Finance; First Counsellor, Ministry of Foreign Affairs; ex-Minister of Labour and Social Affairs; authorized member of the Board, Arab Cement Company Ltd., Medina Press Organization; President of the Advisory Social Security Board; Chairman of Board of General Social Affairs Conferences of UN Agencies; attended Arab Ministers of Social Affairs, Conferences. **Addr.:** Jeddah, Saudi Arabia.

ABALKHAIL (Mohamad Ali, Sheikh), Former Saudi minister of Finance. **Born** in 1935 in Buraidah, Saudi Arabia. **Dipl.:** B.A. (Public Administration), Faculty of Commerce, Cairo University, 1956. **Career:** Began professional career with the Ministry of Communications; was entrusted with the establishment of the Institute of Public

Administration (1961); Director General, the Institute of Public Administration, (1962-63); Deputy Minister of Finance and National Economy (1964) Vice Minister of Finance and National Economy, (1970); Minister of State for Finance and National Economy and Member of the Council of Ministers (1971); Minister of Finance and National Economy (1975-1995); Chairman of the Board, Saudi International Bank (London), Public Investment Fund, Institute of Public Administration, Pension and Retirement Fund, Saudi Fund for Development; Chairman (Saudi Side) Saudi Arabia-U.S. Joint Commission on Economic Cooperation, Saudi Arabian-German Joint Commission on Economic and Technical Cooperation, Saudi Arabian SINO Permanent Joint Committee on Economic and Technical Cooperation; member of the Board of Directors, Supreme Consultative Council of Petroleum and Minerals, Royal Commission for Industrial Estates in Jubail and Yanbo, Saudi Arabian-Yemeni Coordination Council. **Honours**: King Abdulaziz 2nd Class Sash; Republic Medal 2nd Class, Egypt; Niger Medal Leader Status, Niger; Pakistan Crescent Medal (Two Medals); Leopold II Sash, Belgium; along with several other medals and sashes from Spain, Republic of China, Indonesia, Luxembourg, Zaire, West Germany, Sudan, Togo, France and Spain. **Hobbies:** Reading, indoor sports. **Address:** Riyadh, Saudi Arabia.

ABALKHAIL (Sulaiman, Dr.), Kuwaiti banker. **Born** in 1951 in Kuwait. **Son** of Saleh Abalkhail. **Educ.:** Kuwait University and California (U.S.A.) Citibank Training Centre, Athens, Greece. **Dipl.:** B.Sc., U.S.C.; M.A.; M.P.A.; Ph.D. **Career:** Consultant; Accounts Officer, Gulf International Bank, Bahrain; Assistant Vice-President, United Gulf Bank, Bahrain; General Manager, Arab European International Trading Co. (SAK), Safat, Kuwait. **Member:** Bankers Club, Bahrain. **Addr.:** P.O.Box 23074, Safat, Tel.: 2421390-94, Kuwait.

ABAZA (Mohamed Magid, Hussain), Egyptian administrator. **Born** in 1935 in Cairo, Egypt. **Married,** 1 son, 1 daughter. **Educ.:** Cairo University; American University of Cairo. **Dipl.:** B.A., M.Sc. in Business Administration. **Career:** District Sales Manager for North of England, Egypt Air (1966-72); Regional Sales and Marketing Director for Middle East, Sheraton Hotels (1972-82), Regional Sales and Marketing Director for Middle East, Oberoi Hotels International (1982-). **Hobby:** Sport. **Member:** Gezira Sporting Club, Automobile Club, Egyptian National teams for handball and squash. **Prof. Addr.:** 4 Ahmad Pasha Street, Garden City, Tel.: 400204, 409091, Telex: 92558, Cairo, Egypt. **Priv. Addr.:** 17 Aziz Abaza Street, Zamalek, Cairo, Egypt.

ABAZA (Mohamed Maher), Egyptian engineer and politician. **Born** in 1930. **Educ.:** Faculty of Engineering. Postgraduate studies in Germany and Sweden. **Career:** Worked on Aswan Dam project, participated in laying down of High Dam electric Power grids. Former head of electricity authority; Under-Secretary Ministry of Electricity (1974-82); Minister of Electricity and Energy (since 1982-1999). **Addr.:** Cairo, Egypt.

ABAZA (Sami, Abdallah), Egyptian politician. **Born** in 1934 at Minia al-Kamh, Egypt. **Married,** three children. **Educ.:** Higher Institute for Commercial Cooperation. **Career:** Chairman Minia al-Kamh town (1964-67); Public Relations Manager, Madhareb al-Sharqiyah Company (1963); Director General of Madhareb al-Sharqiyah Company. **Member:** of the People's Assembly (since 1968), Chairman of the Youth Committee of said assembly (1971-76), Chairman of the Cultural, Information and Tourism Committee of said assembly (since 1976). Represented Egypt in delegations to Ireland, USA, France, Italy and many other European countries. Secretary General of Egypt Party in Minia al-Kamh, Assistant Secretary General for the National Democratic Party for Sharqiyah Governorate. **Member:** of the Board of Directors of Zamalek Sporting Club. Chairman of the Board of "Sawt Baladna" magazine. **Prof. Addr.:** 427 Ramsis Street, Cairo, Tel. 31718. **Priv. Addr.:** Minia al-Kamh, Sharqiyah Governorate, Tel. 833133.

ABAZA (Sarwat), Egyptian lawyer and writer. **Born** on June 28, 1927. **Educ.:** Farouq Secondary School, Cairo University. **Career:** Lawyer (1950-54), Editor al-Masri daily newspaper (1952-54), Editor al-Kahira (1954-55), Publishing Consultant (1956-57), Member of Committee on Fiction, Supreme Council for Arts, Literature and Social Sciences; Deputy Speaker at Majlis Ash-Shura (since 1986). **Publ.:** "Ibn Ammar" (1954), "al-Hayat Lana" (1955), "Harb men Alayam" (1956), "Alayam al-Khadra" (1958), "Zhekriat Baida" (1961), "Hayat Alat al-Hayat", "Houna Yamil al-Mizan", etc... **Awards:** State Prize for Fiction (1959): State Decoration Grade I for Literature. **Priv. Addr.:** 5, an Nadi Street, Maadi, suburb of Cairo, Egypt.

ABBAD (Abdul-Muhsin, bin Hamad, al), Saudi academic. **Born** in 1933. **Educ.:** al-Azhar University (seat of Muslim learning and philosophy), Cairo, Egypt. **Dipl.:** M.A. (Prophet's Traditions). **Career:** Lecturer, Sidirah Religious Institute; teacher at the Faculty of Islamic Law, Islamic University (Medina, Saudi Arabia) since 1973. **Publ.:** Author of a number of several verified editions of groups of the prophet's tradition. **Prof. Addr.:** The Islamic University, Tel.: 24045. Medina. **Priv. Addr.:** Tel. 21368, Medina, Saudi Arabia.

ABBADI (Abdul Muhsin, al), Egyptian academic. **Born** in 1924 in Alexandria, Egypt. **Married,** three children. **Educ.:** Alexandria University, London University, University of Michigan. **Dipl.:** B.S. in Chemistry, Ph.D. in Synthetic Pharmaceutical Organic Chemistry, Fellowship at University of Michigan. **Career:** Demonstrator, Chemistry

Department, Faculty of Science, Alexandria University (1947); Lecturer, Chemistry Department, University College for Girls, Ain Shams University, Egypt (1953); Lecturer, Chemistry Department, Faculty of Education, Baghdad University, Iraq (1958-59); Assistant Secretary General of the Science Council, Cairo, Egypt (1960); Head of the Synthetic Organic Chemistry Unit, National Research Center, Cairo (1960-64); Assistant Professor, Chemistry Department, University College for Girls, Ain Shams University (1961); Assistant Professor, Chemistry Department, Faculty of Science and Faculty of Agriculture, Baghdad University, Iraq (1964-66); Professor, Chemistry Department, University College for Girls, Ain Shams University February (1969), Chair. Professor of Organic Chemistry Faculty of Science, Tanta University, Egypt October (1969); Chairman of the Chemistry Department, and Head Deputy Dean of Faculty of Science (1969) and Acting Dean of Faculty of Education (1972) at the Tanta University; Dean of Faculty of Science, Sana'a University, Yemen Arab Republic (1974-79); Acting President (1975) and later Consultant (1979-80) at the above mentioned university. Head of Chemistry Department, Faculty of Science, Sana'a University (1981-89). Professor of Organic Chemistry, Faculty of Education, Sana'a University (1992-1996). **Publ.:** Many research articles of organic chemistry. **Sport:** tennis. **Hobbies:** reading and traveling. **Prof. Addr.:** Emaret Mecca, 11th Floor, 45, 15 May Square, (behind Sidi Gaber Rail-way Station), Smuha, Alexandria-Egypt.

ABBADI (Beshir, Ahmad B.), Sudanese engineer. **Born** in October 1936 at Omdurman (Sudan). **Son** of Ahmed B. Abbadi (Teacher) **and** Mrs. née Fatima Amir Beshir. **Married** on 1st December 1966 to Miss Huda Mohd. Logmen, 5 children: Shihab, Hassan, Ahmed, Nada, Nuha. **Educ.:** Wadi Siedna Secondary School, University of Khartoum, Northwestern University. **Dipl.:** B.Sc. (Eng.) 1st class Honours, University of Khartoum; M.S. and Ph.D. Northwestern University (U.S.A.). **Career:** Lecturer, Faculty of Engineers, University of Khartoum (1966-69); Chairman Sudan Airways (1969-70); Minister of Transport and Communications (1971-77); Chairman Kenana Sugar Co. (1977); Chairman University of Khartoum (1975); Minister of Industry (1977-79); **Member:** Sudanese Engineers' Association; the Central Committee of Sudanese Socialist Union; member of Political Bureau (1975-80). **Medals and Decor.:** The Constitution Medal, Decoration of el-Neilan (1st Order), Decoration of the Republic (1st Order). **Sports:** Basketball and squash. **Hobby:** Reading. **Addr.:** Khartoum, Sudan.

ABBADI (Hassan Bin al-Hassan), Moroccan agricultural engineer and former minister. **Born** on December 4, 1943 in Temara, Morocco. **Married**, 1 son, 3 daughters. **Educ.:** Ecole d'Agriculture de Meknes, Morocco; Ecole Nationale Supérieure Agronomique de Montpellier, France; University of Montpellier, France; **Dipl.:** Higher Certificate in Rural Economy. **Career:** Senior Engineer, Ministry of Agriculture (1973); Senior Lecturer, Enseignement Supérieur Agronomique (1974) Head of Development Service (1975); Deputy in the Moroccan Parliament (1977-82) (1983-92); Member, Association of Agronomy Engineers; Member, Science Council, Moroccan Review of Public Finance and Economy; Various positions in local government and agricultural administrations; Minister of Labour (1985-1992). **Publ.:** Viticulture du Maroc. **Priv. Addr.:** Km1, Route Sidi Yahia, Temara, Morocco.

ABBAS (Abbas, Khudhayer), Iraqi lawyer and registered patent attorney. **Born** in 1922 in Diyala, Iraq. **Son** of Khudayer Abbas **and** Mrs. Abbas. **Educ.:** Baghdad University, Iraq; Saint Francis Xavier University, Canada, Swansea University College, Wales, UK; The National Recreation School, New York, U.S.A. American University of Beirut; Kuwait Institute of Economic and Social Planning in the Middle East. **Dipl.:** LL.B, Social Leadership Diploma, Social Policy Course Certificate, Certificate in Community Recreation, Certificate in Farm Management, Post Graduate Diploma in Comprehensive Development Planning. **Career:** Civil Servant, in Iraqi Government; Ministry of Foreign Affairs, Ministry of Labour and Social Affairs (1973). **Publ.:** several articles on community works and manpower planning and other subjects in the field of intellectual property. **Member of:** The Bar Association, the Journalists Union, the Deaf and Dumb Society, the Association of Social Science and Ex. mem. of Human Rights; the Union of Authors and Writers. **Sport:** Swimming. **Hobby:** Art, Literature (Poetry & Travel). **Addr.:** P.O.Box 3289, al-Sadoon, Baghdad, Tel. Office 7183223, Tel. Resid. 5413169, Telfax: 964-1-7183223.

ABBAS (Esmat, Seif al-Dawla), Egyptian lawyer. **Born** on August 20, 1923 at Egypt. **Married**, 2 sons, 1 daughter. **Educ.:** Cairo University, Egypt; Paris University, France. **Dipl.:** LL.B. (1946), LL.D. (1957). **Career:** Lawyer in Cairo Syndicate of Lawyers, Cairo; Member, Union of Arab Lawyers. **Publ.:** Bases of Arab Socialism (1965); The Way to Democracy (1970); The Student Movement (1971); Arab (1983). **Hobbies:** Sculpture and drawing. **Member:** Gezira Sporting Club. **Prof. Addr.:** 22 Qasr al-Nil Street, Cairo, Egypt. **Priv. Addr.:** 40 al-Masaha Street, Dokki, Giza, Egypt.

ABBAS (Mohamad, Hamza), Jordanian economist. **Born** in 1928 in Jerusalem. **Son** of Hamza Abbas **and** Mrs. Abbas. **Married. Educ.:** Colorado State College and University of Wisconsin, USA. **Dipl.:** B.A. in Business Administration (1950); M.A. and Ph.D. in Economics (1950-53). **Career:** Economist, Government of Jordan, Amman (1954-56); Chief, Economic Division, UN Relief and Works Agency for Palestine Refugees in the Near East (UNRWA), Beirut (1956-58); Project Officer, UNDP, New York (1959-62); Chief Programme Coordinator, Food and Agriculture Organisation (1962-65); Deputy Chief, Operations Service, FAO, Rome (1965-68); Senior Officer, Land and Water Development Division FAO, Rome (1969-78); Former Assistant Director General, Economic and Social Policy Dept. (since 1978). **Member:** of the Society for International Development. **Hobby:** Music. **Prof. Addr.:** Amman, Jordan.

ABBAS (Salih, Mohammad), Yemeni politician. **Born** in 1934. **Married**, five children. **Educ.:** General. **Career:** Assistant Director General of the Arab Affairs Office, UN, New York (1954); 1st Secretary, Yemeni Legation to Saudi Arabia (1955); Director, Minister's Office, member and Secretary of the Technical Committee, Ministry of Education (1960), Director, Hodeida Schools (1962); Administrative Inspector, Department of Education, Hodeida Province (1962); Assistant Secretary General, Council of Ministers (1962-65); Secretary General, Council of Ministers with rank of Minister (1965). **Member** of Yemeni Cultural Association. **Sports:** Tennis, Table tennis, swimming. **Hobbies:** Arabic literature and history. **Priv. Addr.:** Tel. 533135, Sana'a, Republic of Yemen.

ABBASI (Sajid, Ali), Pakistani banker. **Born** on December 1939 in Peshawer, Pakistan. **Son** of Sultan Mahmood Abbasi (Lawyer). **Married** on October 14, 1967, in Peshawar to Mrs. Rahilat Abbasi, five children: Amin (1968), Majid (1970), Zahid (1972), Shahla (1974) and Pakiza (1978). **Educ.:** Peshawar University. **Dipl.:** B.A. Economics (1960); State Bank of Pakistan's Officers Course. **Career:** Senior Vice President, United Bank Ltd. (Pakistan) (1963); Chief Manager, Bank of Oman, Peshawar; Director and General Manager, Commercial Bank of Oman, Ruwi, Sultanate of Oman; General Manager, BCCI (Oman Region); At present working as Director and Deputy General Manager of National Bank of Oman. **Sports:** Hockey, tennis. **Hobbies:** Reading, music, tourism. **Member:** Seeb Novotel, Muscat, Oman; Peshawar Club, Peshawar, Pakistan. **Credit Cards:** American Express; Visa Card. **Prof. Addr.:** National Bank of Oman Ltd. (S.A.O), P.O.Box 3752 Ruwi, Tel.: 708692, Muscat, Sultanate of Oman. **Priv. Addr.:** Tel.: 561906, Muscat, Sultanate of Oman.

ABBASSI (Izzedine), Tunisian businessman. **Born** in 1920 in Tunis. **Married**, 5 children. **Dipl.:** diploma from the national Higher School of Mines, St. Etienne. **Career:** Engineer, Government Department of Public Works; Member of the Administrative Commission of the General Union of Tunisian Workers; Minister of Public Works in the first Bourguiba Government (1956); Minister of Industry and Transport (1957-61); Manager of Compagnie des Phosphates et des Chemins de Fer de Gafsa (1961-65); President and Director General of "el-Bouniane" (government controlled commercial and industrial group) (1966); Director General, Mining and Iron Ore Group, SOMTEMI and Société Djebel Djerissa (1968-69); Director General, Office Nationale des Mines (1969-74); Businessman (since 1984). **Addr.:** Tunis, Tunisia.

ABBO (Bakri, Hassan), Sudanese official. **Born** in 1933 at El-Obaid, Sudan. **Son** of Hassan Abbo **and** Mrs. Abbo. **Married**, with four children. **Educ.:** Syracuse University, Syracuse, USA. **Dipl.:** M.A. in Business Administration. **Career:** Industrial Relations Officer at the Ministry of Labour, Sudan (1957); Administration and technical Depts., Industrial Bank of Sudan (1961); Deputy Managing Director of said bank (1970); Labour Expert on secondment from Sudan Government to United Arab Emirates, Ministry of Labour (1972); professional positions in ADMA-OPCO, Abu Dhabi (1977); Head of Government and Employee Relations of said organisation (1982). **Sport:** Tennis. **Hobbies:** Travel, photography. **Addr.:** Khartoum, Sudan.

ABD (Hamed, al), Egyptian university professor. **Born** on November 28, 1928 in Gunzur, Nile Delta. **Married** Dr. N. Seif (Associate Professor of Education, Cairo). **Educ.:** Aïn Shams University, University of Cairo, Institute of Education, London University. **Dipl.:** Bachelor of Science, B.Ed. (1952), Master of Arts (1961), Doctor of Philosophy (1964). **Career:** Teacher in Germany and United Kingdom (1957-1963); Research Investigator, Institute of Education (London University, 1964); Associate Professor of Psychology, Assiout Teachers' Training College in Egypt; Professor of Educational Psychology, Makerere University (Kampala, Uganda, 1965-1971); Associate, British Psychological Association; Foreign Affiliate of the American Psychological Association, East African Academy, Egyptian Psychological Society. **Publ.:** Author of various articles, abstracts and research reports, including contributions to the E.T.S. International News-letter, Princeton (1968, 1969, 1970) and J. of Multivariate Analysis of Behavior (1970). **Awards:** Carnegie Travel Grant (1967), Commonwealth Foundation Grant (1969), Nuffic Grant (1970). **Addr.:** Cairo, Egypt.

ABD (Medhat, Mohammed, al), Egyptian engineer. **Born** on May 13, 1938 in Cairo, Egypt. **Educ.:** Aïn Shams University. **Dipl.:** B.Sc. in Architectural Engineering (1959). **Career:** Design Section Manager and Manager of all Regional Branches, el-Abed Egyptian Cooperative Contracting Co. (1959-65); Consultant Engineer and General Contractor in Kuwait, the Middle East and the Far East (1966-73); self-employed private contractor in Egypt (1973); Founder and Director, al-Mohandiss Engineering Office (1974-); Founder, Chairman and Managing Director, Cairo Specialist Hospital (1974-); Founder, Chairman, Amal Tourism Group of Companies (1976-). **Hobbies:** Tennis, shooting, music and drawing. **Addr.:** 4 Hassan Sabri Street, Zamalek, P.O.Box 91, Cairo, Egypt.

ABD (Omar, el), Egyptian investment banker. **Born** in 1942 in Egypt. **Son** of Abdel Hamid Ibrahim el-Abd (retired banker). **Educ.:** Alexandria University. **Dipl.:** B. Comm. (1966). **Career:** Vice President in Corporate Finance at Salomon Brothers; Director of Treasury and Investments at the Arab Monetary Fund; Vice President at Harris Bank in Chicago; former Director of International Project Finance for the First Boston Corp., directing all First Boston's advisory and financing activities for projects located outside the United States. **Work:** Advising governments on project financing and financial strategy and as such during past years he advised among others: The Ministry of Finance of Republic of Korea in the establishment of the Korea Fund; the Ministry of Finance, Central Bank and National Energy Corp. of the Republic of Trinidad and Tobago; the National Bank of Abu Dhabi in connection with long term strategic planning; and Sumer Bank of Turkey. **Member** of the Board of Directors of Turkish American Business Council, Washington D.C. **Sport:** Squash. **Hobby:** Classical music. **Clubs:** Union Club, New York. **Addr.:** New York, U.S.A.

ABD RABBO (Yassir), Palestinian politician. **Born** in 1944 in Palestine. **Career:** member of Palestine Liberation Organisation (PLO) Executive Committee; representative of the Popular Democratic Front of the Arab Nationalist Movement. Left Popular Front for the Liberation of Palestine (PELP) (1968-1969) to form PDFLP. Participated in the DFLP delegation to Moscow (1975). Head of PLO Information Department (1977-); Minister of Culture and Information in Palestinian Cabinet (Sept. 1999-). **Addr.:** P.L.O. Tunis, Tunisia.

ABDA IBRAHIM (Fahmi, Abdul Hamid), Egyptian artist. **Born** on February 1, 1939 in Cairo, Egypt. **Married,** 2 sons, 1 daughter. **Educ.:** Cairo Academy of Fine Arts. **Dipl.:** B.Sc. in Graphics (1962). **Career:** Deputy Controller of Animated Cartoons and Special Effects; Egyptian Television, later Controller and Director; Professor of Animated Cartoons, Cairo Academy of Fine Arts, Egypt. **Awards:** Several merit awards from the Ministry of Information, the Arab Broadcasting Federation, from the Academy of Fine Arts, Paris Television and the Egyptian Broadcasting Federation. **Hobbies:** Music, songs and poetry. **Prof. Addr.:** al-Masakin al-Iktisadiyah, Block 4, Madkhal 2, al-Kanater al-Khyriyah, Egypt.

ABDAL (al-Sharif Sharaf Nasser, al), Saudi former official. **Born** in 1943 in Mecca, Saudi Arabia. **Dipl.:** B.A. (Architecture), M.A. (Architectural Design). **Career:** Demonstrator, King Saud University (1970-72); Lecturer (1975-78); Deputy Mayor of Mecca for Technical Affairs; **Member**, Makkah Cultural Club, al-Wehda Sport Club; participated in a solar energy conference held in Italy, 1977. Now retired. **Publications:** several articles in local newspapers. **Hobbies:** Reading, sports. **Home Addr.:** Tel. 5420192, Mecca, Saudi Arabia.

ABDALAQUI (Aissa), Algerian official engineer. **Born** on December 5, 1941. **Married,** 4 children. **Educ.:** Agronomy engineer. **Career:** Director, Institute of Agricultural Technology in Mostaganen; Director, National Office for Forestry and Agrarian Revolution; Minister of Agriculture; General Secretary, Secretary of State for Forestry and Regional Planning (1977-84); Deputy Minister of the Environment and Forests (1984-86). **Addr.:** Algiers, Algeria.

ABDALLA KHODJA (Kamil), Algerian economist. **Born** at Constantine, Algeria. **Educ.:** Degree in Economics. **Career:** Member of the Provisional Executive (1962); Director, later Director General of Planning, Ministry of Finance; Secretary of State for National Plan (1970); participated in drafting and implementation of Four-Year Plan (1969-73); Secretary of State for Planning (1977); Practical Experience of Economic Planning in Morocco. **Participated** in Economic Study Commission of National Liberation Front (FLN). **Addr.:** Ministry of Planning, Tel. 780323, Telex 52516, Algiers, Algeria.

ABDALLAH (Abdul Aziz), U.A.E. bank manager. **Born** in 1950 in Dubai, U.A.E. **Son** of Mohamed Saeed Abdalla. **Married** in 1976. **Educ.:** High School and banking courses in England. **Career:** Clerk, Officer and Branch Manager, British Bank of the Middle East, Dubai (1964-77); Commercial Manager, Union Bank of the Middle East (1977-); Director, al-Ahliyah Printing Press, Dubai. **Member:** al-Ahli Club. **Hobby:** Football. **Addr.:** Dubai, U.A.E.

ABDALLAH (Abdul Melik, Muhammad), Yemeni physician. **Born** in 1942 in Yemen. **Married,** 3 children. **Educ.:** Ain Shams University, Cairo. **Dipl.:** B.Sc. (Medicine); Diploma in Public Health, Gynaecology and Obstetrics. **Career:** General Practioner, Jumhuriyah Hospital in Taiz; Medical Section, Taiz Province; World Health Organization (WHO) Representative in Taiz; Director of Nasser Hospital; Ministry of Health (1975-). **Hobby:** Reading. **Addr.:** Tel.: 2502, Sanaa, Republic of Yemen.

ABDALLAH (Abdul Rahman), Sudanese politician and diplomat. **Born** in 1933 at Abu Hamad. **Educ.:** Khartoum University College, School of Administration, New York University. **Career:** Joined Ministry of Interior, Sub-Maamour (1956); Inspector, Tokar District, later of Kassala Province; joined Halfa People's Settlement Commission (1959); Director, Inst. of Public Administration (1963-65); Director, UN African Administration Training and Research Inst., Morocco (1965); Director, National Inst. of Public Administration, UN, Libya; Former chairman, Sudan Public Service Council, Kenana Sugar Project, Sudan; Former member, Sudan Supreme Judicial Council of Sudan Commission of resettlement of population made homeless by the Aswan Dam; Deputy Minister of Local Government (August 1971); Minister of Public Service and Administrative Reform (1971-77); of Industry & Mining (1977), of Communications (1977-78); of Transport (1978); Deputy Director and officer-in-charge, Div. of Devt. Administration, UN Dept. of Tech. Co-operation, New-york (1979-80). Member, Executive Bureau, Sudanese Socialist Union, Assistant Secretary-General (1978-79); Permanent Representative of Sudan to the UN (1980-86) **Addr.:** Khartoum, Sudan.

ABDALLAH (Abdulsami), Egyptian artist, caricaturist. **Born** in Egypt. **Married**, three children. **Educ.:** Teachers Training College, Cairo, Egypt. **Career:** Caricaturist, worked for "Rose al-Yusuf" magazine (1946); "al-Gumhuriyah" newspaper, Head of Technical Department (1964); "al-Musawwar" (1965). **Act.:** Exhibited at the Formalism Art Exhibition (1963, 1966). **Publ.:** "Black and White" collections of short stories (1963, 1972). **Member:** Zamalek Club. **Sport:** Walking. **Hobbies:** Music and theatre. **Addr.:** Dar el-Hilal, 16 Sharia Mohamed Ess al-Arab, Tel. 50836, Cairo, Egypt.

ABDALLAH (Abdulwahab), Sudanese economist. **Born** in 1927 in Khartoum, Sudan. **Son** of Abdel Wahab Elsheikh. **Married** in 1971, 1 daughter and 1 son **Educ.:** Faculty of Arts, Khartoum; St. Andres, Scotland. **Dipl.:** Diploma in Arts, with distinction, M.A. Economics (Hons); Fellow of the Economic Ass. Institute of the World Bank (1958-59). **Career:** Under-Secretary, Ministry of Finance and Economics, Sudan (1962-67); Founder and Chairman, Sudan Shipping Line; Founder and Chairman, Institute of Public Administration; Under-Secretary, Ministry of Industry and Mineral Resources (1967-70); Founder and Chairman, Industrial Planning Corporation; Founder and Chairman, Institute of Industrial Research; Consultant, UNIGO (1970-71); Senior Industrial Development and Field Advisor in Middle East (1971-80); Kuwait and whole of the gulf area including Saudi Arabia, and Yemen; Managing Director, Emirates and Sudan Investment Co., Khartoum (1980). **Publ.:** A number of papers and research works in Economics and Industrial Development. **Member:** Board of the Public Electricity and Water Corporation, Emirates and Sudan Investment Co. Khartoum, Sudanese Economists' Association, Arab Economists' Association. The Cultural Centre of the Sudan. **Hobbies:** Gardening, swimming, painting and music. **Addr.:** P.O.Box 7026, Khartoum, Tel.: 79687, 73245, Sudan.

ABDALLAH (Ahmadou, Ould), Mauritanian diplomat. **Born** in 1940 in Birié par Aioun-el-Atrouss (Eastern Mauritania). **Son** of Ahmed Ould Abdallah (scholar and landowner). **Married** in Paris to Miss Rosemarie Delay (psychologist), 1 child. **Educ.:** Koran school (1949); Rosso College (1954); Lycée Van Volenhoven, Dakar, Senegal (1961); Faculty of Law and Economics, Grenoble University, France (1961-62); Institute of Political Science, Paris (1966); Faculty of Law & Economics, la Sorbonne, Paris. **Dipl.:** B.Sc. (Economics) - B.A. (Political Science) - M.Sc. (Economics). **Career:** Director of Industrialisation, Ministry of Industry, Nouakchott (1968-70); Managing Director of State Corporations since 1968; Director, Société Minière de Mauritanie (SOMIMA) (1969); seconded to the International Bank of Reconstruction and Development (IBRD), Washington (1970); Minister of Commerce and Transport (1971-72); Ambassador to Washington (1973). **Publ.:** "Investir en Mauritanie" (1970), "Les Possibilités de l'Industrie Animale en Mauritanie" (1970). **Member:** Parti du Peuple Mauritanien (PPM), Party suspended in 1978 following Military Coup. **Addr.:** Nouakchott, Mauritania.

ABDALLAH ASSHAIKH (Hassan, Shaikh), Saudi Arabian politician. **Born** in 1932. **Educ.:** Sharia College of Mecca; al-Azhar University, Cairo, Egypt. **Career:** Member, Judicial Supervisory Committee; Vice-President, Judicial Supervisory Committee; Minister of Education and Health (1962); Minister of Higher Education (1975); Director, Council of Arts, Sciences and Literature; Chancellor, University of King Abdel Aziz, University of Riyadh, Islamic University of Imam Mohammed Ibn Saud, Islamic University (Medina); Director, Archaeological Department. **Publ.:** "Our turn in the Struggle" (Arabic); "Brave Ideas"; "Dignity of the Individual in Islam". **Prof. Addr.:** Ministry of Higher Education, Riyadh, Saudi Arabia.

ABDALLAH AWAD AHMAD (Ahmad), Yemeni legal advisor. **Born** on 13 February 1939 in Aden. **Son** of Awad Ahmed Awad (on pension) **and** Mrs. Mariam Abdulla Awad. **Married** on 28 June 1970 in Aden to Miss Bilquis Mohmad Hamoud, 3 daughters: Mona (1971), Salwa (1973) and Layla (1977). **Educ.:** Elementary School at Mualla (Aden), Gasid Secondary School at Tanta (Egypt); Faculty of Law, University of Alexandria (Egypt). **Dipl.:** High Secondary School Certificate, LL.B. **Career:** Legal assistant in the State Legal Office, Sana'a (1968); General Manager of the State Legal Office, Sana'a (1969); Deputy of the Legal Office (with the status of Deputy-Minister) (1970); Deputy to Legal Advisor of the Presidency and Council of Ministers; Deputy of the State Legal Office (status of a minister) (1975); Part time lecturer in the Faculty of Sharia and Law, University of Sana'a (1970-75); Part time member for the Yemeni Ports General Corporation (1975-79); Editor of the Sharia and Law Bulletin (1974); President of the Appellate Committee of Taxation; member of the People's Constitutional Assembly (Yemen Parliament); former Secretary of the Constitutional Committee in the People's Constitutional Assembly. **Sports:** General athletic exercises and occasionally swimming. **Hobbies:** Reading, mental exercises and house gardening. **Credit Card:** American Express. **Prof. Addr.:** State Legal Office, P.O.Box 1292, Sana'a, Tel. 2752 or 4297, Yemen. **Priv. Addr.:** Abdulla Awad Ahmad, P.O.Box 364, Sana'a, Tel. 2511, Republic of Yemen.

ABDALLAH (Ibrahim, A.), Jordanian executive. **Born**

in 1923 in Palestine. **Married**, six children. **Educ.:** Arab University of Beirut, Lebanon. **Dipl.:** B.A. in Commerce and Business Administration (1965); Diploma in Credit, Cooperative and Management. **Career:** Teacher in Palestine (1941-46); Cooperative Officer, Palestine (1946-48); Jordan Government Teacher (1949-58); Deputy General Manager, Jordan Central Cooperative Union (1960-66); Cooperative and Credit Expert FAO, Iraq (1966-71); Cooperative and Credit Expert and Project Manager, Afghanistan (1971-77); Regional Credit, Cooperative and Marketing Officer, Jordan (since 1977); Secretary General Near East, North Africa Regional Agricultural Credit Association (NENARACA) (since 1977). **Publ.:** "Management of Agricultural Loans" (1982); many studies and lectures on Agricultural Credit and Cooperative Theories. **Prof. Addr.:** P.O.B. 35286, Tel. 668632, Amman, Jordan. **Priv. Addr.:** Tel. 668372, Telex, 21835 ALOUN JO., Amman, Jordan.

ABDALLAH (Ismail-Sabri), Egyptian economist. **Born** in 1924 at Mallawi, Egypt. **Educ.:** Khedive Ismail School, Cairo; Faculty of Commerce, Cairo University; Sorbonne University, Paris. **Dipl.:** Ph.D. **Career:** Lecturer, Alexandria University (1951-54); Cairo University (1954-56); Adviser, Economic Development Organisation (1957-59); Chief Editor, Dar el-Maarif Publishing House (1965-69); Director General, Institute of National Planning (1969-71); Deputy Minister of Planning (1971); Minister of State for Planning (1972-74); Minister (1974-75); Deputy Chairman of Board, Société Egyptienne d'Economie Politique, de Statistique et de Législation (1972); Secretary General, Scientific Conference of Egyptian Economics; member, Advisory Board, UN African Institute of Development and Planning, Dakar (1971-76); member, UN Arab Institute of Planning, Kuwait; founding member and Chairman Third World Forum (1975-); Board member, Council for the Development of Economic and Social Research in Africa (1980). **Publ.:** "Economie et Structure Economique" (1952), "Lectures in Economics" (Arabic) 1954; "The Organisation of the Public Sector" (Arabic) (1969), "Confrontation with Israel" (Arabic) (1969), "Towards a New Economic World Order" (Arabic) (1976); "Development Pattern and Life Style in West Asia" (UN Publication) (1980); "The International Monetary System in Crisis" (Dag Hammarskjold Foundation) (1980); "La Gise" (IFDA-Dossier) (1981). **Decor:** Order of the Republic (first class) 1974); Order of Merit, (France) (1975). **Prof. Addr.:** 39 Dokki Street, Tel.: (2)989641, Telex: 93919 CADSA, Cairo, Egypt.

ABDALLAH (Jalal Mohamed Salih), Iraqi academic. **Born** in 1932 in Kirkuk, Iraq. **Educ.:** B.Sc. in Chemistry; Ph.D.; FRSC. **Career:** Demonstrator, University of Baghdad (1962); Assistant Professor, University of Baghdad, Baghdad (1968); Professor, University of Baghdad, Baghdad (1973); Dean of the College of Sciences, Saddam University for Engineering and Science. **Member** of the Iraqi Academy of Sciences (since 1979), the Jordanian Academy of Arabic languages (since 1980). **Publ.:** numerous researches published in international professional journals; several chemistry textbooks published by the Ministry of Education. **Editor** of the Iraqi Journal of Sciences. **Prof. Addr.:** P.O.Box 47077, Jadiriyah, Baghdad, Iraq. **Addr.:** Hayy al-Bunuq, 4202/6/5, Tel. 8829680, Baghdad, Iraq.

ABDALLAH (Jellal, Bin), Tunisian painter. **Born** in 1921 in Tunisia. **Married. Career:** Painter, miniaturist. **Work:** Linking traditional Arab art with modern trends derived from Mediterranean classical arts; revived and created Arab theatrical stage design as set designer for the Tunis Theatre (1957-60); painted the mural decorations for the Maison de Tunisie, Cité Universitaire, Paris (1953); designed ceramics for the Palais des Congrès, Bizerta and mosaics for Lycée Ibn Khaled and other buildings; exhibited at Venice Biennale, Alexandria Biennale, etc. **Medals:** Silver Medal for the Tunisian Pavillion, Brussels (1958); Officer of the Order of the Tunisian Republic; Commander of the Order of Cultural Merit. **Awards:** Cannes Festival prize for design of film "Roger Mauge"; Moscow prize for design of "Sidi Bousaid". **Addr.:** 55 Ave. President Kennedy, Tel.: 270705, Sidi Bousaid, Tunisia.

ABDALLAH (Rahmatalla), Sudanese diplomat. **Born** in 1922. **Educ.:** Trinity College, Cambridge. **Dipl.:** M.A. **Married** in 1954 to F.I. Allam, 4 children: Mohammad, Tarik, Amir and Aliya. **Career:** Ministry of Education, Khartoum (1944-53); Social Development Officer; Assistant General of the Sudan Gezira Board (1953-56); Ambassador to India (1956-60), to Nigeria (1960-61); Minister of National Education (1964-65); Deputy Under-Secretary of State, Ministry of Foreign Affairs (1965-68); Ambassador to France (1968-70); and concurrently to the Netherlands, Switzerland and Spain; Ambassador to Zaire (1970-71); Sudan Permanent Representative at UN., also Representative at Security Council (1972-74). Personal Envoy of the Government to a meeting of the African Heads of State; attended many international conferences (UN-OAU- League of Arab States). **Publ.:** "The Black Sultanate in Sudan". **Member:** Rotary club. **Prof. Addr.:** Ministry of Foreign Affairs, Khartoum. **Priv. Addr.:** P.O.Box 446, Khartoum, Sudan.

ABDALLAH (Seif, Abbas), Kuwaiti diplomat. **Born** on March 22, 1949. **Married**, 1 son, 3 daughters. **Educ.:** Indiana University, USA. **Dipl.:** M.A. in General Management (1969), Ph.D. in Political Science (1973). **Career:** Kuwaiti Delegate at UNESCO, Paris (1975); Cultural Attaché, Kuwaiti Embassy, Paris (1976); Manager of Cultural Relations with Spain, Ministry of Education; Manager, Personal and Student's Affairs, University of Kuwait (1976-80); Cultural Manager and Consultant, Office of the University of Kuwait, Kuwaiti Embassy, Washington D.C.

(1980-); Member of the Board of Directors, Arabic Studies Centre, Georgetown University, USA. **Publ.:** "A Trip into International Politics" (1975), "General Planning in Kuwait" (1975), "Kuwait, the Arab Island and Morocco" (1984). **Hobbies:** Tennis, fishing and camping. **Prof. Addr.:** University Office, Embassy of Kuwait, 3500 international Drive NW, Washington DC 20008, USA.

ABDALLAH (Taha Ibrahim, al), Iraqi statesman. **Career:** Minister of Irrigation (1969); **member** of the State Planning Council (1969), member of the Supreme Agricultural Council (1972); President of Baghdad University (1974-1980); Minister of Planning (1980-1982); Professor, Baghdad University (1982-). **Prof. Addr.:** Baghdad University, Jadiriyah, Baghdad, Iraq.

ABDALLAHI (Sidi Moktar Ould Sheikh), Mauritanian statesman. **Born** in 1937 at Aleg (Middle Mauritania). **Son** of Mohamad Abdallahi Ould Sheikh Abdallahi (relegious leader). **Married** to Miss Khattou mint Boukhary (secretary). **Educ.:** Primary school in Aleg (1946-1950); Rosso College (1951-54); Teacher Training College, Senegal (1955-57); Faculty of Science, Dakar, Senegal (1958-60); Faculty of Science, Grenoble University, France (1961-63); Faculty of Law and Economics, Paris (1964-67). **Dipl.:** Baccalaureat (1957), B.Sc. (Economics 1967). **Career:** Director of Planning, Ministry of Planning, Nouakchott, Mauritania (1968); Deputy Governor of the African Development Bank (1969); Governor of the United Bank (1972); Member of the Development Committee; Member of executive councils of various economic associations and public enterprises; Minister of Industrial Development (1971-72); Minister of Planning & Industrial Development (1972-75); Minister of State for National Economy (1975-77); Minister of Planning and Mines (1977); Minister of Rural Development (1978); Economic Adviser for Kuwait Fund for Arab Economic Development (1982-86); Minister of Hydraulics and Energy (1986). Presently, Chairman, Société Nationale, Industrielle et Minière (SNIM). **Prof. Addr.:** SNIM, P.O.Box 42, Nouakchott, Mauritania.

ABDEL AHAD (Pierre, Mgr. Gregorius Butros), Syrian, Bishop of Syrian Catholics in Jerusalem. **Born** on June 28, 1930 in Aleppo, Syria. **Son** of Karim Abdel Ahad **and** Mrs. née Eugenie Tashash. **Educ.:** Charfeh Seminary, Harissa, Lebanon. **Dipl.:** Licence in Philosophy and Theology. **Career:** 1954 Ordained Priest; 1954 to 1965 Professor, Treasurer and Director of Syrian Catholic Seminary at Charfeh Harissa; 1965-1977 Parish Priest in Bethleem; 1977- Patriarchal Vicar General for the Syrian Catholic Church in Jerusalem, Palestine and Jordan. **Other Information:** 1974 Founder of Saint Joseph Pilgrim House in Bethleem; 1974 Constructor of Saint Joseph School in Bethleem; 1986 Constructor of Saint Thomas Church in Jerusalem; 1986 Founder of St. Thomas Pilgrim House in Jerusalem. **Sports Practised:** Volley-ball. **Hobby:** Chess. **Prof. Addr.:** Jerusalem Chaldean Str. No. 6, Tel./Fax: 00972 2 6284217, 00972 2 6282657, Amman, Jordan. and Syrian Catholic Church, P.O.Box 510393, Amman, Jordan.

ABDEL AZIZ (Mahmoud), Egyptian Chairman, National Bank of Egypt. **Born** on January 10, 1940 in Egypt son of Abdel Aziz, married, 2 daughters and 3 grandsons. **Educ.:** Schools and Universities attended: B. Com. (Accountancy) Cairo University, Egypt (1961). **Career:** Bank of Alexandria (Formerly Barclays 1961-67); Central Bank of Egypt (Banking control Dept. 1967-78); General Manager, National Bank of Egypt (1978- June 1992), then Chairman (June 1992 - present) **work:** Chairman National Bank of Egypt, Chairman Commercial International Bank; Chairman Banking and Finance Committee - Egyptian Businessmen's Association, Chairman Union of Arab Banks, Chairman Bank's Association of Egypt. **A member of the following:** -Production and Economic Affairs Council - National Specialized Councils, American Chamber of Commerce, Cairo, Economic Research Bureau - Academy of Scientific Research and Technology, Business Advisory Council - IFC, Supreme Council for Exporting - chaired by the President of the Arab Republic of Egypt, Board of the Faculty of Commerce - Cairo University, Board of the Centre for Economic and Financial Research and Studies - Faculty of Economics and political Sciences - Cairo University, The Economic Research Forum, Leading Committee for following up the Private Sector Promotion Programs in Egypt, Committee of Infrastructural, Economic and Environmental Development Priorities of the Project for liaison of Egyptian American Universities - Supreme Council of Universities, Board of Commerce Club, Master Card International Board of Directors of the Middle East and Africa Region, Board of Trustees - Egypt's International Economic Forum. The Egyptian Council for Foreign Affairs. **Awards:** The Banker of the Year for 1994, according to a poll by, World Today (Al Alam Al Youm) Newspaper, Awarded the Banker's Achievement Award for the Year 1997 granted by the Arab Bankers Association of North America, The Foreign Manager of the Year 1999 - granted by Mannheim Unternehmer Forum, Management Berater ans VWD.

ABDEL SALAM (Mohamed El-Hosseiny), Egyptian Engineer-General. **Born** on April 25, 1930 at El-Menofia-Sirs El Layan. **Son** of Abdel Salam Mohamed El-Tech **and** Mrs. née Fatma Osman Ismaeel. **Married** on January 1, 1958 in Cairo, to Liela el-Najjar, 3 children: Mahmoud (28/12/1958), Ossama (22/2/1960), Omar (7/12/1965). **Educ.:** El Bagerer Primary School - Shebin El Kom Secondary School, Cairo University, School of Military Engineers Egyptian Armed Forces, School of Military Engineers British Army, Staff College of Nasser Academy in the Egyptian Armed Forces. **Dipl.:** BSc Civil Engineering, Diploma Military Engineering Egyptian Armed Forces, Diploma Advanced Military Engineering British Army, Egyptian Staff College diploma, Nasser Academy Diploma Fellowship, Computer Diploma Faculty of Engineers, Cairo University, **Career:** Engineer, Officer in the Corps of Engineers of the Egyptian Armed Forces 1952-1982; He Occupied Various Commanding Positions in His Military Career. Retired in 1982 when he was Chief of Staff of the Engineering Organization of the Egyptian Armed Forces; Chairman of Board of Nile Company for Road Construction 1982-1983; Chairman of Board of National Authority for Tunnels 1983-1998; Technical Consultant for the Egyptian Minister of Transport & Telecommunication 1998-. **Other Information:** He Introduced and Constructed Lines 1 & 2 of the Cairo Underground Metro System. President of the Egyptian Tunnelling Society. Member of Board of the International Tunnelling Association (ITA). Member of Board of the Egyptian Society of Engineers, Civil Engineering Society, Member of Board of the Academy of Science. **Medals & Decorations:** Evacuation 1955 - Independence 1957 - Republic 1988 - Army Day 1959 - 10th Anniversary of Revolution 1962 - Training 1971 - duty First Class 1972 - Rcpublic Second Class 1974 - Republic First Class 1982 -25th Anniversary of October War 1998 - French Legion d'Honneur Degree Chevalier 1989 - French Legion d'Honneur Degree Officier 1998. **Sports Practiscd:** Speedo Ball - Tennis Table. **Hobbies:** Music - Reading. **Clubs:** Heliopolis Sport Club - Zohour Sport Club - Naser City Sport Club - Army Clubs. **Credit Cards:** Visa - Master Card. **Prof. Addr.:** Ministry of Transport - 105 Kasr El Einy Street, Cairo, Egypt, Tel. 3555868. and P.O.Box 466, 11794 Cairo, Egypt. **Priv. Addr.:** 17 Sabri Abu Alam Str., Heliopolis, Cairo, Egypt.

ABDELBARI (Abdalla), Egyptian journalist and businessman. **Born** on 25 April 1924, at Okda, Delta, Sharkieh, Egypt. **Married,** 3 children: Afaf (1950), Mohamed (1954), Raouf (1956). **Educ.:** Egyptian Primary and Secondary Schools, Fouad 1st University (now Cairo University, Giza, Egypt). **Qualifications:** B.A. English Language and Literature. Faculty of Arts, Cairo University (1947); M.A. Journalism, Institute of Journalism, Faculty of Arts, Cairo University (1949). **Career:** Reporter, Al-Misry Newspaper (1948); Traffic Officer MISRAIR (now EGYPTAIR) (1948); Copywriter, Société Egyptienne de Publicité (1948), Head of Section Technique, S.E.P. (1948); Manager, S.E.P. and Fondé de Pouvoirs and Director of Production (1951); General Manager, S.E.P. (1952); Advertising Director, Akhbar El Yom Publishing House (1954); Advertising Director, Al-Ahram Organization (1964); Managing Director, Pyramid Advertising Agency (1964); General Advertising Director and elected Member of the Board, Al-Ahram Organization (1968); General Manager, appointed Member of the Board, Al-Ahram Organization, Managing Director, Pyramid Advertising Agency (1974); appointed Managing Director per interim & assuming the board responsibilities of Al-Ahram Organization (1978); Chairman of the Board Al-Ahram Organization (1979 to 1984); Thereafter Consultant to the board todate. Chairman, Al-Ahram Investment Co. (1980); Member of the Board of Directors, National Bank for Development (1980); Founder, under the late President Sadat, of the National Democratic Party group of newspapers; Chairman, Mayo National Publishing House (publishers of: Mayo Newspaper, The National Democratic Party Newspaper, Al-Lewa-Al-Islami Newspaper, Shabab Biladi Newpaper (1980); Chairman, Al-Ahram International S.A., Geneva (1983); Chairman, Al-Ahram International P.L.C., United Kingdom (1983); Vice-President S.I.C.E.P. (Joint Venture of Al-Ahram & French-Arab Investors manufacturers of Bic products for the Arab World (1976); President I.A.A. Egyptian Chapter (1977); Founder of the Al-Ahram Employees Fund 1979, and its life honorary Chairman; Appointed President S.I.C.E.P. (1979); Chairman of the Egyptian Co. for Commerce and Services (affiliated to the Egyptian Expatriots Co. for Investment & Development; presently, President, Egyptian Chapter, International Advertising Association. **Member:** Committee of the Egyptian Businessmen's Association, The Committee of the Egypt - U.S. Business Council; The Committee of the German Business Council, Member of the Supreme Press Council and Deputy Chairman of its Financial and Economic Committee since 1980 to date; Member or the Writer's Association. **Dccor:** Different decorations and medals from various countries of the world. **Sports:** Tennis, Football, Hockey, Fencing, Swimming, Golf. **Hobby:** Classical Music, Chess. **Member:** Gezira Sporting Club, National Club, Automobile Club, The Graduates' Club. **Prof. Addr.:** Al-Ahram Organization, Al Galaa Str., Tel.: (202) 5747045, 5747411, Cairo, Egypt. **Priv. Addr.:** 20, El Montazah Str., Tel.: (202) 3404725, 3404751, Fax (202) 3407498, 3409046, Zamalek, Cairo, Egypt.

ABDELCHAFI (Haidar), Palestinian politician. **Born** in Gaza, Palestine in 1919. **Educ.:** in Beirut, Lebanon. **Dipl.:** M.D. General Surgery. **Career:** in various hospitals in Palestine and since 1972 head of the Red Crescent Organisation in the Gaza strip and a Private clinic. Following Israeli occupation in 1967, imprisoned (1967) and later expelled to Lebanon (1970); Returned to Gaza following the International Red Cross intervention; head of the Palestinian delegation to the Peace Conference on the Middle East held in Madrid on 30/10/1991. **Addr.:** Gaza, Palestinian Occupied territories.

ABDELHAKIM (Muhammad, Subhi), Egyptian academic. **Born** on June 4, 1928 in Cairo, Egypt. **Married**, 3 daughters. **Educ.:** Cairo University. **Dipl.:** M.A. in Geography (1954), Ph.D. (1958). **Career:** Professor, Cairo University (1970-), Deputy, Faculty of Arts (1972-73), Dean, Faculty of Arts (1975-79), Vice President (1979-80); Head, Advisory Committee Council (1980). **Publ.:** "The Population, Geography and Demography" (1963), "The Arab Country, Population, Land and Mines" (1968), "The City of Alexandria" (1958), "Studies in the Geography of Egypt" (1957). **Decor:** Order of the Republic for Sciences and Arts (1st Class), Egypt (1964). **Award:** Merit Award, Colombia (1981). **Member:** el-Ma'adi Sporting Club. **Addr.:** 45 Street 104, el-Ma'adi, Cairo, Egypt.

ABDELHAMID (Abdel Latif), Sudanese diplomat. **Born** on January 1, 1938 in Dongola, Sudan. **Married,** 3 daughters. **Educ.:** University of Khartoum; University of Sorbonne, Paris. **Dipl.:** B.A. in Economics; History; State Doctorate in Literature and Humanities; Dip. in International Relation; Dip. in French Language & Italian Language. **Career:** Diplomat in Nigeria (1961-65); Italy (1965-66); Chad (1971-73); United Kingdom (1973-74); France (1978-79); Ambassador in Lebanon (1980-81); United Arab Emirates (1981-87); Sudan's Ambassador to Kenya (1990-1995). **Publ.:** Ph.D. Thesis "The Mahdism in The Sudan" in French. **Hobbies:** Reading, swimming and tennis. **Prof. Addr.:** Ministry of Foreign Affairs, Khartoum, Sudan.

ABDELJABER (Tayseer, Mohamad), Jordanian economist. **Born** in 1940 in Jordan. **Married** Four children. **Educ.:** University of Southern California, USA. **Dipl.:** Ph.D. in Economics. **Career:** Director, Economic Research Department, Central Bank of Jordan (1970-1972); Director, Economic Department, Ministry of Foreign Affairs, Amman (1973-74); Economic Expert, UNECWA, Beirut, Lebanon (1975-76); Secretary General, National Planning Council (1977-79); Under Secretary, Ministry of Labour (1979-84); Minister of Labour (1984-85); Chairman of Board of Trustees of Arab Consult Center (1985-88); former Under-Secretary General and Executive Secretary of the UN Economic & Social Commission for Western Asia (ESCWA) (1989-1993). Director, Arab Consulting Center (1993-97). Commissioner, Jordan Securities Commission, (1997-).. **Member of:** the Board of Directors, Vocational Training Corporation and Social Security Corporation, the Jordan Economists Association, the American Economic Association; Secretary General, Jordanian Businessmen Association; President, Institute of Management Consultants of Jordan; member, World Affairs Council; member, Arab Thought Forum. **Publ.:** "Studies in Arab Economical Integration" (1972) in Arabic, "Jordan's Experience and Policies in Reverse Transfer of Technology" UNCTAD Report, numerous studies in various journals and magazines in Arabic and English; column writer in daily "Jordan Times" and Ad-Dustor. **Medals:** Order of the Jordanian Star; Knight of the Order of the Republic of China. **Sports:** Tennis. **Hobby:** Gardening. **Addr.:** P.O.Box 926550, Tel.: 5530866, Amman, Jordan, and Tel.: 5534250, Fax: 5536714.

ABDELJAWWAD (Taha, Said Omar), Bank General Manager. **Born** on February 8, 1944 at Jerusalem. **Son** of Said Omar (contractor) **and** Mrs. Alia Omar. **Married** on October 1, 1976 at Jerusalem to Miss Abdel-Al, 5 children: Said Omar (19.7.77), Alia Omar (11.2.79), Rasha Omar (27.4.82), Mohammad Omar (6.9.84), Miss Ala'a Omar (August 1992). **Educ.:** M.B.A. from George Washington University, U.S.A.; Rasheediah High School Jerusalem from 1956 THRU 1962; B.Sc. Degree Beirut Arab University, Beirut-Lebanon from 1963 THRU 1968; Computer Program from El-Centro College Dallas, Texas, From 1971 THRU 1972; MBA from George Washington University, USA From 1975 THRU 1976. **Career:** Joined Citibank N.A., Doha Branch as Ex. Trainee in 1980. In 1981 promoted to Branch Manager. 1984 promoted to Resident Vice-President. In February 1987 promoted to Officer-in-Charge of Citibank Doha Branch. In September 1987 Joined Al Ahli Bank of Qatar as Branch Manager. In 1989 promoted to DY. General Manager and in June 1990 became General Manager. **Sport:** Football. **Hobby:** Reading. **Credit Card:** Mastercard. **Prof. Addr.:** Al Ahli Bank of Qatar, P.O.Box 2309, Doha, Qatar, Tel.: 326611.

ABDELKHALEK (Mohamed, Lutfi), Egyptian geologist. **Born** on February 3, 1927 in Cairo, Egypt. **Married,** 1 son, 1 daughter. **Educ.:** Faculty of Science, Cairo University. **Dipl.:** B.Sc. (1949), M.Sc. (1953), Ph.D. (1957). **Career:** Head, Geology Department, Faculty of Science, Cairo University (1974) and (1979); Vice-Dean, Faculty of Science, Cairo University (1980), Dean (1981); Member, Geological Society of Egypt, Egyptian Academy of Sciences, Academy of Scientific Research and Technology. **Award:** Award for Sciences and Arts, 1st degree (1982). **Hobbies:** Tennis and shooting. **Priv. Addr.:** 20 Aanab Street, Dokki, Cairo, Egypt.

ABDELLAH (Slaheddine), Tunisian diplomat. **Born** in Kairouan, Tunisia. **Married** three children. **Educ.:** University of Lyon, France. **Dipl.:** B.A. in History, Diploma in Political Studies. **Career:** Secretary in Tunisian Embassy in Cairo (1957); Chargé d'Affaires, Tripoli, Libya (1958), Counsellor, in Rabat Morocco (1959-1960), Director of the Department of Asia and Africa, Ministry of Foreign Affairs, Tunis (1960-68); Minister Plenipotentiary, Tunisian Embassy in Washington D.C., USA (1965-68); Ambassador to Addis Ababa, Nairobi, Dar es-Salam, Kampala, and Permanent Representative of Tunisia at the OAU (1968-70); Ambassador to Beirut, Amman, Damascus, Baghdad (1970-73); Secretary of State for Information (1974); Ambassador to Cairo and Permanent Representative of Tunisia at the Arab League (1975-78); Ambassador to Rabat (1978-84); Ambassador Diplomatic Adviser (1985-86); Ambassador representative of Tunisia to the Arab League (1986-1989); Director General for Political Affairs (1990); Ambassador to the Russian Federation (1990-1992); Ambassador to Egypt (1993); Ambassador Permanent Representative of Tunisia to the United Nations (1994-). **Decor.:** Grand Cordon de l'Ordre du Cèdre, Lebanon, (1973); Grand Officier de l'Ordre de l'Indépendence, Tunisia, (1974); Grand Officier de l'Ordre de la République Tunisienne, (1974); Grand Cordon de l'Ordre de la République, Egypt, (1978); Grand Cordon du Wissam Alaouite, Maroc (1985). **Sports:** Swimming, Golf. **Hobbies:** Arabic poetry and literature, history. **Prof. Addr.:** 40 East 71st Street, New York, NY 10021, USA.

ABDELLATIF (Fawzi, Hussain), United Arab Emirates diplomat. **Born** on April 18, 1942 in Sharjah, UAE. **Married,** 1 son. **Educ.:** Jordan University; Diplomatic Course, UN Institute for Training and Research in Abu Dhabi and United Nations. **Dipl.:** B.A. in Economics and Commerce (1971). **Career:** 3rd Secretary, UAE Delegation to UN (1972); Minister Delegate, Ministry of Foreign Affairs (1975); Ambassador to Zaire (1975-84); **Hobbies:** Writing, Arabic poetry, hunting, swimming, riding, travel, chess, backgammon. **Prof. Addr.:** Ministry of Foreign Affairs, P.O.Box 1, Abu Dhabi, UAE. **Priv. Addr.:** P.O.Box 1219, Dubai, United Arab Emirates.

ABDELMAGED (Muhammad, Reda), Egyptian businessman. **Born** on March 15, 1943 in Egypt. **Married,** 1 son, 1 daughter. **Educ.:** Cairo University, Egypt. **Dipl.:** B.Sc. in Commerce (1966). **Career:** Director, ICL Company, Egypt (1966-75); Director General of Misr Iran Bank for Development, Egypt (1978-81), General Manager and Director, Misr Iran Touristic and Office Buildings Company (1981-). **Hobbies:** Rowing and Squash. **Member:** Heliopolis Club, University of Cairo Rowing Club. **Prof. Addr.:** P.O.Box 227, Giza, Egypt. **Priv. Addr.:** 8, Salah Salem Avenue, Heliopolis, Cairo, Egypt.

ABDELMAGUID (Abbas), Sudanese agricultural engineer. **Born** in Khartoum (Sudan). **Married,** with children. **Educ.:** Primary education in Damar; secondary education in Wadi Sina; Faculty of Agriculture, Khartoum University; London University; University of California (USA) (1958-60). **Dipl.:** B.A., M.A. (Soil studies) (1960). **Career:** Served in the Ministry of Agriculture, Development of the South Division, Blue Nile Province; Agriculture and Irrigation Directorate, Kordofan (1961-67); Director, Rural Development (1967- March 1968); Director, Mechanised Farming Department (1968-70); Commissioner, Gezira Project (March 1973-74); Commissioner, Northern Kordofan Province (1974-Aug. 1975); Minister of State for Agricultural Production (1975). **Addr.:** Khartoum, Sudan.

ABDELMOUMENE (Mohamed), Algerian Neurophysiologist. **Born** on April 10, 1937 at El Kala, Algeria. **Son** of Abderrahman Abdelmoumene **and** Mrs. Ragaya Nassane. **Married** on April 8, 1972 in Algiers to Sakina Benkhelil, 4 children: Selma; Amina; Ludmilla, Jasmine. **Educ.:** Faculty of Medicine, Paris, France (1962); Faculty of Sciences, University of Paris, France (1966); University of Algiers (1968). **Dipl.:** Doctorate in Medicine (M.D.); Diplôme d'Etudes Appronfondies de Neurophysiologie; Aggregation of Physiology. **Career:** Scientist, Physiology Dept., Faculty of Medicine and Pharmacy, Algiers (1968-1970); Director, Institute of Medical Services, Algiers (1970-1977); «Dean» (1970-1972); Scientist, Neural Mechanisms Section, National Institutes of Health, Bethesda, Md, USA (1977-1980); Professor of Physiology, Institute of Medical Services, University of Algiers (1980-1982); Chief, Office of Research Promotion and Development, Office of the Director-General, World Health Organization (1983-1988); Deputy Director-General, World Health Organization (1988-1993); Special Representative of Director-General for Near Eastern Affairs, WHO and Director of Health, United Nations Relief Works Agency (UNRWA) for Palestine Refugees in the Near East), Vienna, Austria (1993-1997); Deputy Commissioner-General of UNRWA (1997- to date). **Awards:** Doctor Honoris Causa, University of Louvain, Belgium (1988); Public Health Medal, Ministry of Health of Tunisia (1991). **Sports:** Swimming. **Hobbies:** Music, Reading; Cultural and Social Activities. **Member:** Int'l Association for the Study of Pain; Society for Neurosciences, International Brain Research Organization (IBRO-UNESCO). **Prof. Addr.:** UNRWA, P.O.Box 700, A-1400 Vienna, Austria, Tel.: 21131 (Ext: 4391/4392. **Priv. Addr.:** 8 James Fazy, 1201 Geneva, Switzerland, Tel.: 7411544.

ABDELNABI (Hafiz, Abdel Ghani), Former Jordanian politician. **Born** in 1924 in al-Khalil, Palestine. **Married,** 5 sons, 4 daughters. **Educ.:** Cairo University. **Dipl.:** B.Ch. (1951). **Career:** Financial Secretary, Jordan Universities' Union (1953-60); Member, al-Khalil Local Council (1954-56), Member, Jordanian Representatives Council (1956-61) and (1967); Manager, Society of the Friends of the Diseased, al-Khalil (1976-); Private practice at a clinic in al-Khalil (1953-). **Addr.:** Occupied West Bank.

ABDELNOUR (Amine Fakhry), Egyptian businessman. **Born** on July, 1916 in Cairo. **son** of late Fakhry Bey ABDELNOUR (Former Deputy of Upper Egypt). **Married** to Daughter of late Amine Pasha GHALI (Former Minister of Finance), two sons. **Educ.:** Paris University, Sorbonne, France, International Marketing Institute, Harvard Business School. **Career:** Assistant General Manager, Comptoir des Ciments (1953-61); General Delegate, Banque de L'Union Europeennne (1970-98), General Delegate, Groupe Credit Industriel et Commercial (1984-98); Advisor Groupe Schneider (1984-); Advisor Groupe Lafarge (1999-); Member Egyptian Bank Association; Advisor to Commerce Exterieur Français. **Publ.:** Note Personnel sur le Golfe Persique (1953) in French. **Decor.:** Order of the Nile (2nd class), Egypt (1951), Order of the Star, Ethiopia (1959); Order of St. Silvester, Vatican City (1967); Order of St. Gregory the Great, Vatican City (1973); Commandor of Legion of Honour, France (1989). **Member:** Caritas International, Coptic Archeology Society. past-President of Cairo Rotary Club. Egyptian Businessmen Association. Club d'Affaires Franco-Egyptiennes. **Prof. Addr.:** 3 Ahmed Nessim, Giza, Tel.: 3610586 - 3610591, Egypt. **Priv. Addr.:** 8 El- Saleh Ayoub st., Zamalek, Cairo, Tel.: 3404185, Egypt.

ABDELNOUR (Ziad, Khalil), Financier, Owner & Director of Companies. **Born** on January 8, 1961 in Beirut. **Son** of Khalil Abdelnour (Industrialist & Politician) **and** Mrs. Rose (Salha) Abdelnour. **Married** on December 23, 1983 in USA to Nada Sahyoun, 2 children: Karl (1986), Mark (1990). **Educ.:** The Wharton School of Finance, University of Pennsylvania, USA, American University of Beirut, College Notre Dame de Jambour. **Dipl.:** MBA in Finance/ Investment Banking (Wharton). B.S. in Economics (AUB). **Career:** Trainee, Relationship Management, The Chase Manhattan Bank, New York (1982-1983); Senior Vice President, Lehman Bros International New York (1984-1986); Managing Director, Drexel Burnham Lambert, New York (1986-1990); General Partner, Laidlaw International NYC (1990-1992); Founding Partner and Director, INTERBANK/ PRIVATE CAPITAL HOLDINGS, NYC (1992- Pres.). **Publ.:** Published a Number of Articles on Mergers, Acquisitions and Cross Border Financing Techniques in a Variety of Magazines in the US, Europe and the Middle East. Naturalized US Citizen. Active Fundraiser for a Number of Educational, Political and Business Organizations. **Awards:** Listed also in: WHO'S WHO in the World, WHO'S WHO in America, WHO'S WHO in the Arab World, WHO'S WHO in Finance and Industry. **Sports:** Skiing, Horseback Riding. **Hobbies:** Fundraising, Public Speaking, Foreign Affairs. **Member:** Former President, Arab Bankers Association of North America, Executive Director, United State Committee for a Free Lebanon. Fellow Member, Council on Foreign Relations, Center for Middle East Peace & Economic Cooperation. Board Member, Middle East Forum. **Credit Cards:** Amex Platinum, Citibank Visa Gold. **Priv. Addr.:** in NYC: 300 East 56th Street 14D, New York, NY 10022, Tel.: (212) 319-3984 in Beirut: P.O.Box 90/1228, Tel.: (01)885-956, or (01) 202-145, Lebanon. Email: Ziad@i-2000.com.

ABDELRAHMAN (Ibrahim, Hilmi), Egyptian politician. **Born** 1919 in Egypt. **Married. Educ.:** Cairo University, Egypt; London University, UK, Edinburgh University, UK; Cambridge University, UK. **Dipl.:** B.Sc., Ph.D. in Astrophysics. **Career:** Assistant Professor, Cairo University (1942-52); Secretary General, Council of Ministers (1953-58), Secretary General, Supreme Science Council (1956-58); Secretary General, Atomic Energy Commission, Egypt (1955-59), Secretary General, National Planning Commission, Egypt (1957-60), Director, Institute of National Planning, Egypt (1960-63); Industrial Development Commissioner, UN, New York (1963-66); Executive Director, United Nations Industrial Development Organisation, Vienna, Austria (1967-74); Technological Adviser to the Prime Minister, Egypt (1974); Minister of Planning and Administrative Development (1975-76). **Publ.:** "National Planning Memoirs", "Academic Studies in Astrophysics"; Numerous publications on industrial development. **Hobbies:** Music, photography, astronomy and farming. **Addr.:** Cairo, Egypt.

ABDELRAHMAN (Mohamed Jalal, Abdel Hamid), Egyptian legal adviser. **Born** on January 1, 1927 in Aysut, Egypt. **Married**, 2 sons. **Educ.:** Cairo University. **Dipl.:** LL.B. (1946), Diploma in Public Law (1948). **Career:** Government Lawyer, Legal Proceedings Management (1948-55); Adviser to the Deputy Chairman of the State Chamber (1955-); President, Judicial Committee, Arab Organisation for Manufacturing (1976-); Member of the Board, International Institute for Management Science (1983-). **Hobbies:** Sports, travelling and reading. **Member:** Gezira Sporting Club, al-Ahly Club, Automobile Club. **Addr.:** 39 Iraq Street, Mohandiseen, Dokki, Giza, Egypt.

ABDELRAHMAN (Nasrat, Salih), Jordanian academic. **Born** on October 16, 1934 in Jordan. **Married**, 2 sons, 2 daughters. **Educ.:** Cairo University. **Dipl.:** M.A. in Arabic (1969), Ph.D. (1972). **Career:** School Teacher in Jordan (1958-62), Teacher in Qatar (1962-67), Teacher in Libya (1967-68); Professor of Arabic, University of Jordan. **Publ.:** "Ancient Arabic Poetry from a New Critical Perspective" (1975), "The Struggle Against the Romans until the Fourth Century AD", poem (1977), "Recent Developments in Criticism" (1980). **Prof. Addr.:** Faculty of Arts, University of Jordan, Amman, Jordan.

ABDELWAHAB (Mohamed, Farag), Egyptian engineer and former minister. **Born** on September 5, 1932 in Cairo, Egypt. **Married**, 2 children. **Educ.:** Ain Shams University, Egypt. **Dipl.:** B.Sc. in Mechanical Engineering (1954). **Career:** Chairman, Helwan Diesel Engine Company 1965-83), Chairman, Nasr Motor Company (1983-84); Minister of Industry (1984-1990). **Awards:** Order of Merit (5th Class) in 1959; (1st Class) in 1980. **Medal:** Medal of Science and Arts (1st Class) in 1984. **Addr.:** 4 Mohammad Zeki al-Said Street, Masr al-Jadida, Cairo, Egypt.

ABDELWAHAB (Shamseldin), Sudanese executive. **Born** in 1949 in Elkamlin, Sudan. **Son** of Abdelmageed Abdelwahab (retired civil servant) **and** Mrs. Khadija Syd Ahmed. **Married** on November 22, 1977 to Ishraga Seifeldin, three children: Talal (1979), Wisam (1982) and Mohamed (1986). **Educ.:** Hantoub High Secondary School; University of Khartoum, Sudan; University of Kent Canterbury, U.K. and University of Bradford, U.K. **Dipl.:** B.Sc. (Business Administration 1973); Graduate Diploma Management Science; MBA. **Career:** Marketing specialist in Sudan (1973-76) and an I-L-O unit in Sudan; District Manager for Sudan Airways in Sana'a, Yemen (1976-80), in Libya (1985-87); Regional Manager for Europe, based in London (1987-88); Actually Vice President Corporate Planning and Investment, he is assigned for all the functions and strategic planning policy making researches and investment projects selection. **Member** in the Business Administration Society in Sudan. **Hobbies:** Music, viewing video films (scientific ones) and theatre. **Prof. Addr.:** Sudan Airways, P.O.Box 253, Khartoum, Tel.:

(00249 11) 472372, Fax: (00249 11) 472377, Sudan. **Priv. Addr.:** Tel.: (00249 11) 560267, Omdurman, Sudan.

ABDELWAHED (Hosni, Saad), Egyptian judge. **Born** on December 15, 1946. **Educ.:** Cairo University; Paris Law School, France. **Dipl.:** Postgraduate Diploma in Law and Administrative Sciences (1974), Doctor of Administrative Law (1948). **Career:** Assistant District Attorney, Cairo (1969-76), District Attorney, (1976-77); Judge, South Cairo Court (1977-78), Head, Court of Urgent cases (1978-79), Head, Court of Zagazig (1979-81), Court of North Cairo (1981-83), Court of South Cairo (1983); Lecturer, Faculty of Law, Cairo University (1984); Member, Egyptian Society for Political Economics and Legislation. **Publ.:** "Execution of Administrative Orders" (1984). **Hobbies:** Reading, travel and table tennis. **Member:** Hunting Club, al-Ahly Club. **Prof. Addr.:** 90B Ahmed Orabi St., Mohandiseen, al-Agooza, Giza, Egypt.

ABDERRAZAK (Mohamad, Larbi), Tunisian journalist. **Born** in 1936 at Tunis, Tunisia. **Son** of Larbi Abderrazak **and** Mrs. Abderrazak. **Married** four children. **Educ.:** University of Paris. **Dipl.:** Ph.D. **Career:** Teacher (1959); Assistant Director, Tunisian Radio and Television (1966); Director of National Guidance, Ministry of Information (1970); Assistant Director of Political Affairs in the prime Minister's Office (1971); Assistant Professor Faculty of Literature, Tunis (1972); Director of "al-Amal" newspaper of the Socialist Destour Party (1972); Deputy in the National Assembly (1974); Vice President of Tunis Municipality; Administrator, Counsellor of the Tunisian Government. **Medals:** Officer of the Order of Tunisian Independence, Grand Officer of the Order of Tunisian Republic, Grand Officer of Cultural Merit, Director of a youth cultural center. **Sports:** Gymnastics, tennis. **Hobbies:** Literature, music, painting. **Addr.:** Tunis, Tunisia.

ABDI (Abdelhaq, el), Moroccan banker. **Born** in 1937 in Fes, Morocco. **Married,** 2 children. **Educ.:** High Certificate of Commercial Studies (1958); Diploma of Higher Commercial Education (1960); Institute of Social and Economic Development (1961); Formation at the Paris Chamber of Commerce (1968); Seminary at World Bank on Management of Development Banks (1983); Various Formations and Seminaries in Morocco and Foreign Countries. **Career:** Recruitment at Credit Populaire du Maroc (November 1961); Banking formation at Banque Regionale d'Escompte et de Depots in Paris, in study and appreciation of credit files dept. (Nov. 1961- Oct. 1962); Deputy Manager, Banque Populaire de Rabat (Oct. 1962- Febr. 1964); On mission in different departments at Credit Populaire de France (Nov. 1964- Dec. 1965); Manager Banque Populaire de Casablanca (Dec. 1965- Dec. 1968); Secretary General, Crédit Populaire du Maroc, at the same time Responsible for management of other departments in the bank (Jan. 1969- Nov. 1972); Deputy General Manager (November 1972); General Manager (1988-). Member of the Board of: Banque Chaabi du Maroc, Paris; Arab Bank Maroc; Maroc Assistance; Institut Hautes Etudes de Management (HEM). **Addr.:** Crédit Populaire du Maroc, 101, Boulevard Zerktouni, P.O.Box 10622, Tel.: 20.25.33, 27.62.81, Telex: BANCEPO 21 723, Fax: 2.19.32, Casablanca 20170, Morocco.

ABDILLAHI (Mohamed, Barkat), Djbouti Deputy at the National Assembly. **Born** on December 14, 1947 in Djibouti. **Educ.:** Diploma in Law. **Career:** National Police (1968-1970); Military at French Army (1970-1977) and at National Army (1977-1980). Elected Deputy at the National Assembly (18.12.1992- to date); Appointed Minister of Civil Service and Administrative Reform (19.04.1997); Appointed Minister of Youth, Sports and Cultural Affairs (1.11.1997); Appointed Minister of Trade and Industry (28.12.1998). **Prof. Addr.:** National Assembly, P.O.Box 138 Djibouti, Djibouty.

ABDIN (Kamal, Hafiz), Saudi academic. **Born** in 1927 in Cairo (Egypt). **Educ.:** Secondary and Higher. **Dipl.:** B.A. (Economics & Political Science). **Career:** Director of Personnel, Ministry of Petroleum and Mineral Resources; Advisor and Director of Public Relations and Information, Ministry of Petroleum and Mineral Resources; Director of Industrial Information, Industrial Development and Research Centre; Director, Organisation and Management Department, King Abdul Aziz University, Jeddah (Saudi Arabia); Administrative Consultant King Abdul Aziz University, Jeddah. **Addr.:** Jeddah, Saudi Arabia.

ABDOULKADER (Ali Dini), Djibouti Deputy at the National Assembly, and Lawyer. **Born** in 1951 at Tadjourah. **Educ.:** University Graduate. **Career:** President of the Bar Association. Member of FRUD and UNECAS. Elected Deputy at the National Assembly (19.12.1997- to date). Secretary-Rapporteur of the Legislation Commission and General Administration of the Republic and member of the Permanent Commission. Vice-President of the Supreme Court of Justice. **Prof. Addr.:** National Assembly, P.O.Box 138 Djibouti, Djibouti.

ABDOULKADER (Mohamed, Daoud), Djibouti Deputy at the National Assembly. **Born** in 1936 at Tadjourah. **Career:** Accountant. Retired in 1990 as Assistant Manager from CFPA; 1st Special Agent at "Cercle of Tadjourah"; Member of "Union Democratique Afar"; Member of "Union Nationale pour l'Independance"; Secretary rapporteur of the Commission of National Defence and Member of Foreign Affairs Commission; Elected Deputy at the National Assembly (19.12.1997- to date). **Prof. Addr.:** National Assembly, P.O.Box 138 Djibouti, Djibouti.

ABDOWANI (Sadek), Omani Publisher and Editor-in-Chief of Al Usra Magazine. **Born** in 1947. **Son** of Hassan Ali Abdowani **and** Mrs. Fatima Ahmed. **Married** in 1962 in Kuwait to Siddika Hussain Hassan, 3 children: one daughter Kefah (1963), two sons Hassan (1969), Qabas (1978). **Educ.:** Kuwait Kefan Secondary School; Beirut Arab University; Kuwait University. **Dipl.:** BA in Arts, History Section, Preliminary M.A., Kuwait University. **Career:** Diplomat (1972-75); Charge d'Affaires & Permanent Representative of Oman to UNIDO, Vienna (1975-77); Executive Secretary to Council of Agriculture, Fisheries & Industry, Oman (1979-81); Assistant Secretary General, The Shoura Assembly, Oman (1981-94); **Publ.:** Author of Short Stories Published 1990. **Medals:** Medals Awarded as President of Volley Ball Association (1985-89); Certificate of Thanks from H.M. Sultan Qaboos as Scholar on History Research; Certificate of Merits as Good Serviceman to the Shoura Assembly, 1991. **Sports:** Table tennis, swimming. **Hobbies:** Reading, writing. **Member:** president of Volley Ball Association (1985-89). **Credit Card** Visa. **Prof. Addr.:** Al-Usra Magazine, P.O.Box 440, PC 114 Mutrah, Tel.: 794922, 794923, Fax: 795348, Sultanate of Oman. **Priv. Addr.:** Qurum, Tel.: 561345, Sultanate of Oman.

ABDU (George), Egyptian banker. **Born** in 1924 at Tanta, Egypt. **Son** of Mr. Lutfi Abdou (Engineer). **Married** in 1952, 2 sons. **Educ.:** American University. **Dipl.:** B.A,; M.A. **Career:** Accountant and Branch Manager, Barclays Bank D.C.O. (1943-47); General Manager, International Division, Bank of Alexandria (1957); Director, Mahauds National Food Products (Schweppes). **Member:** International Bankers' Association Inc. Washington, USA; National Sporting Club, Cairo; Shams Club, Cairo. **Addr.:** 49, Kasr al-Nil Street, Tel.: 911999, Cairo.

ABDU (Mohamed, O.), Saudi leading singer and composer. **Born** in 1939 in Mecca, Saudi Arabia. **Dipl.:** Ship Building Diploma. **Career:** Proprietor and Director of Musical Arts and Electronics Est., founded in 1975; has composed and performed many famous songs and anthems since 1960. **Hobbies:** Reading classical poetry, arabic literature. **Addr.:** Musical Arts and Electronics Est., Nuzla Yamania, Tel. 6367165, Jeddah, Saudi Arabia. Telephone: Office 636-6165, Jeddah.

ABDULAAL (Abdul Halim Reda, Prof. Dr.), Egyptian academic. **Born** on January 9, 1933 in Alexandria, Egypt. **Married** to Soad Abdul Megid in August 1943, Cairo, Egypt, 2 children: Wael Abdul Halim Reda (28 Sept. 1969); Rania Abdul Halim Reda (23 March 1973). **Educ.:** B.Sc. of Social Work, Higher Institute of Social Work, Alexandria, (June 1963); Master Degree in Social Work, Community Organization Major (1972); Ph.D. in Social Work, Specialization in Community Organization, Faculty of Social Work, Helwan University, Cairo, Egypt. **Career:** Field instructor (October 1963); Lecturer (1972); Associate Professor (July 1978); Professor (December 1984); Vice-dean (1985); Dean, (January 1987); former Dean, Faculty of Social Work, Helwan University, Cairo, Egypt. **Work Abroad:** Qatar University (1977-78); United Arab Emirates University (1980-84). **Field Experiences:** Supervising C.D. projects in rural areas; Conducting C.D. project in an rur-urban area, (el-KOUM el-AKHDAR) Giza Governorate, Egypt: Supervising coordination Work in Giza Federation of Social Welfare agencies; Working in an urban-fringe area, (Mounib). **International Field Experiences:** Co-Investigator of "Doctoral Program Project", in collaboration with H.E.W., U.S.A. (1974-76); Co-Investigator of "Boulak Eddakrour Research Project", in collaboration with H.E.W. (1974-76); Co-Investigator of "Youth Training Project", in collaboration with H.E.W. (1978-80), (The aforementioned Projects were conducted by the Faculty of Social Work, Helwan University, Cairo Egypt and H.E.W., U.S.A.); Field Officer of Boulak Eddakrour Development Project (1972-77), conducted by: - Faculty of Social Work, Helwan University, Cairo, Egypt, - UNICEF, - Giza Governorate, "It was a comprehensive developmental Project of an urban transitional area"; A Field training program for two months (July-August, 1977), in the U.S.A., organised and financed by H.E.W. It included visiting several outstanding schools of Social Work and various Social Welfare Agencies; Resource Person for planning post-graduate studies (Master in Social Work) for Khartoum University, Sudan (January 1990). **International Conferences Attended:** International Federation of Social Workers Conference, Nairobi, Kenya (July 1974); African Conferences on Planned Parenthood, Lusaka, Zambia (September 1978); Conference on Scientific Cooperation between Egypt and Jordan, Akaba, Jordan (May 1985); Arabian Seminar on After-Care services, Riyadh, Saudi Arabia (July 1986); United Nations Conference on Juvenile Delinquency, Beijing, China (October 1988). **Research Work:** Community Organization in industrial settings, M.S.W., thesis (1972); Stimulating Citizen participation for the development of urban unplanned areas (1976); The Role of Community Organization in the Economy of Developing countries (1977); Developing a Practice Theory for Community Organziation application in Egypt (1979); The Stance of Community Organization Method in Developmental Social Work (1979); Measuring Accountability of Social Services (1980); Supervising Field Work in Community Development Projects (1980); The Community of Social Welfare Organizations (1982); The Integrated practice-model of Community Development (1984); **Publ.:** The Role of Social Work in Labour Force Policy (1979); Contemporary Social Work (1985); Fundamentals of Community Organization (1986); Social Work Research (1987); **Present Duties:** As Dean, the present duties are being conducted: Planning and implementing the Faculty's educational policy, as chairman of the Faculty's Board; Managing the administrative activities of the Faculty; Directing Staff-Development actions, as part of human-resources development; Liaison activities, between the Faculty and other cooperating organizations; Member of the Council of Helwan University; Member of the Sectorial Council of Social Sciences, stemmed from the supreme Council of the

Egyptian Universities; Member of the Sectorial Council of Non-Governmental Higher Institutes of Social Work in Egypt; Member of Certificates Validation Committee, Supreme Council of Egyptian Universities; President of the Annual Conference on the Science of Social Work since 1987. **Sports:** Football, Walking. **Hobby:** Picnics. **Member:** Heliotedo Club, Flowers Club, Egyptian Association of Social Workers, African Association of Social Work Education. **Priv. Addr.:** Munshiet el-Bakry, Awhady Street, No.5 Flat 10, Tel.: 2575814, Cairo, Egypt.

ABDULAKHAR (Ahmad, Mustafa), Egyptian politician. **Born** in 1925 at Sohag, Egypt. **Son** of Mustafa Abdul Akhar **and** Mrs. Abdul Akhar. **Educ.:** Cairo University. **Dipl.:** B.A. in Agriculture. **Career:** Ministry of Agriculture (1950-1957); **Member** of the Sohag Arab Socialist Union (ASU) Committee (1963-1967); Secretary of the Sohag ASU Committee (1968); elected to the People's Assembly (1969-1971); elected Secretary for Membership, Finance and Administration (1971); Chairman of Sohag People's Council, re-elected to People's Assembly (1971); Deputy Minister in the Presidency (1973); Governor of Giza (1974). **Addr.:** Cairo, Egypt.

ABDULAZIZ (Munir Bashir), Iraqi artist, official. **Born** in 1930 in Mosul (Northern Iraq). **Son** of Bashir Abdul Aziz (carpenter) **and** Mrs. nee Karima Gergis. **Married** in 1965 in Budapest to Irene Dazho Bashir, 2 children: Saad Munir Bashir (1966); Omar Munir Bashir (1970). **Educ.:** Graduate, Institute of Fine Arts, Baghdad; Higher Studies in Music Research and Composition, Hungary. **Career:** Vice-President, International Music Council, UNESCO; Director, International Society for Music Education; Member, Executive Committee, International Music Council; President, National Music Committee of Iraq; Secretary General, Academy of Arab Music; Art Director-General, Babylon International Festival; Editor-in-Chief, al-Qithara Review, Arab Music Review, Music and Children Review; Art Consultant and Director-General, Department of Music, Ministry of Information and Culture, Iraq. Give Lectures at: University of Geneva, Switzerland; of Oxford, Britain, of Cambridge, Britain; of Humboldt, Germany; of Copenhagen, Denmark; of Tokyo, Japan; University of Qatar, Qatar; of Yarmouk, Jordan; of Shiraz, Iran; of Sorbonne, France; of Budapest, Hungary. Founded Centres for Children's Music Education in Iraq; Organised bands for contemporary Iraqi Music; Made many long playing as well as laser compact records; Performed sole Ud at more than 44 countries since 1954. **Awards:** Honorary Member, Higher Committee for Music, Egypt; Life-time Honorary Member, International Music Council, UNESCO; Order of Culture, Commander, France; Order of Civil Merit 1st Class from H.M., King Juan Carlos of Spain; Fellow Ribbon, University Murcia, Spain; Order of Culture and Arts, Poland; Order of Independence from H.M. King Hussein of Jordan; Order of Culture 1st Class, Cuba; United Nations Peace Insignia, International Peace Organisation, Sweden; Charles Crow Prize for best disc, France; Disque Academique Prize, France; Gold Key of the City of Yokohama, Japan; Certificate of Ambassador, Iraqi-Spanish Friendship Society; Honorary Citizen of various foreign countries; Picasso's Gold Medal; Chopin Medal, Poland; Franz Liszt Medal and Bela Bartok Medal with Higher Diploma, Hungary; Villa-Lobos Medal, Brazil; Czecholovaki Medal, Soviet Union. **Prof. Addr.:** Ministry of Information and Culture, Tel.: 5531798, Iraq. **Priv. Addr.:** Amiriya, Mahalla 626, Zuqaq 28, House 17, Tel.: 5561212, Baghdad, Iraq.

ABDULAZIZ (Zeinab, Mustafa), Egyptian Academic. **born** on January 19, 1935 in Alexandria, Egypt. **Widow,** Onc son. **Educ.:** Cairo University. **Dipl.:** M.Sc. in French Literature; Ph.D. in French Literature and Culture (1974). **Career:** Head, Translation Department, Egyptian Antiquities Registration Centre (1963-74); Professor, Culture and History of Art, Faculty of Human Sciences, Al-Azhar University (1985-); Head, French Department, Faculty of Arts, Menoufia University (1995); **Member:** Founder Member, Syndicate of Egyptian Plastic Artists; Egyptian Writers Union **Publ.:** In Islam: "John Paul II and Islam" Dar al-Kods (1994); Five Years Plan of John Paul II", Dar al-Kods (1994); "Articles from René Junot (Sheikh Abdel Wahed Yahya), Dar al-Ansar (1996); "Hamlat Al-Mounafikih Al-Fransis" Dar al-Nahar (1998); In Culture and History of Art: "Yawmiyat Fanan", Dar al-Maaref (1971); "Voltaire Romantic" (1980); "Modern Art Game" (1984); "Humanity in Van Gogh Art" (1993). Translated several foreigh books and Articles into Arabic and attended several conferences and seminars. Active in several arts movements and expositions since 1955. **Hobby:** Music. **Member** of Gezira Sporting Club. **Address:** 23 Sharia Hamadan, Flat 1001, Giza, Cairo, Tel. 5739791, Egypt.

ABDULBAKI (Murtada Said), Iraqi politician. **Born** in 1941 in Ramadi. **Educ.:** Higher Teachers' Training Inst. and University of Baghdad; College of Law and Politics. **Career:** School teacher, Fallouja (1966-67); member of Revolutionary Command Council (1968); Chairman Kurdish Affairs Bureau and Peace Committee (1968); member of World Peace Committee; Minister of Labour (1970-71); Minister of Economy (June- Oct 1971), Minister of Foreign Affairs (1971-74); Ambassador to U.S.S.R. (1974-75). **Addr.:** c/o Ministry of Foreign Affairs, Baghdad, Iraq.

ABDULFATTAH (Abdallah, Mahmoud), Egyptian statesman. **Born** in 1918 in Minufiyah, Egypt. **Married** four children. **Educ.:** Cairo University, Egypt; Cairo Military Academy. **Dipl.:** B.Sc. in Mechanical Engineering (1949). **Career:** Assistant to the Minister of War for Technical and Financial Affairs with the rank of General, supervising the technical institutes and organisations within the armed forces; Secretary to the Higher National War Committee chaired by the late President Sadat; Minister of State for Cabinet Affairs (Secretary to the Cabinet) (1973); Minister of State for Presidential Affairs (1974); Minister of State for Cabinet Affairs and Control (1975). **Member** of the Higher Arms Procurement and Reduction Committee (1975); Attended many of the meetings in Aswan with Dr. Kissinger (1974); accompanied the late President Sadat to the ensuing inter Arab meetings. **Former President** of the Armed Forces Club, Dean of the Engineers Syndicate (1973-74). **Addr.:** General Trade Union for Engineers, 90 Galaa Street, Cairo, Egypt.

ABDULGADER (Mohamad Abdul Aziz, Major General), Sudanese politician and army officer. **Born** in 1929 in Omdurman, Sudan. **Married** four children. **Educ.:** Military Academy, Khartoum; Staff courses in the UK and USA. **Career:** Lieutenant Colonel (1963); Military Attaché, Addis Ababa, Ethiopia; promoted to Colonel (1965); Headquarters (1966); Commander of the Sudanese Battalion to Egypt (1967); Headquarters (1968); Senior Staff Officer, South of Sudan (1969); Deputy Chief of Staff, Headquarters, Sudan (1970); Chief of Staff (1971-72); Sudanese Ambassador to Uganda (1972-1973); Governor of Kassala Province (1973). **Addr.:** Ministry of Defence, Khartoum, Sudan.

ABDULGADER (Zain al-Abdin Mohamad Ahmad), Sudanese politician. **Born** on May 7, 1940 at Tuti, Sudan. **Married,** children. **Educ.:** Omdurman Military Academy (1959); course in parachuting in U.K. (1962); Paratroopers Training Center Course in U.K. (1969); course of Company's Commander, Jebeit (1968). **Career:** Commissioned 2nd Lieutenant (1959); 1st Lieutenant (1964); Colonel (1968); Minister of Animal Protection and Production (1970); Assistant Prime Minister for Agricultural Sector (1971); Minister of Communication (1971); Minister of Communications and Transport (1971); Minister of Transport (Oct. 1971- Oct. 1972); Minister of Youth and Sports (1975). **Member** of the Political Bureau, Assistant General Secretary of the Sudanese Socialist Union (SSU) for Popular Organisations, now dissolved following coup in 1989. **Sports:** Football, swimming. **Hobbies:** Poetry and music. **Addr.:** Khartoum, Sudan.

ABDULGHAFFAR (Hashim Hassan), Saudi physician. **Born** in 1932 in Mecca, Saudi Arabia. **Dipl.:** D.D.S., M.S.D., F.T.C.D. **Career:** Director of Students Health Centre, Ministry of Education, (1959-62); Director General of Students Health Services, Ministry of Education (1962-65); Deputy Minister, Ministry of Health (1965-76); Fellow of International Dental College; member of American Academy of Oral Roentgenology, Executive Council, World Health Organization (WHO), Geneva; attended several medical conferences. **Honour:** Commander of Order of Cedar of Lebanon. **Publications:** Articles in American Journal of Dental Research. **Addr.:** P.O.Box 2121, Tel. 4012626, Riyadh, Saudi Arabia.

ABDULGHAFFAR (Mansour Mahmoud), Saudi civil servant. **Born** in 1936 at Yanbu, Saudi Arabia. **Dipl.:** Received general education, supplemented by training courses at the Institute of Public Administration, London and Ireland. **Career:** Member of Customs Committe of Western Region Customs; Director general of Customs Administration and general director of Jeddah Islamic Sea Port Customs. **Honour:** Medal of Japanese Customs Department. **Publications:** Lectures on Customs organization and precedure delivered at the Institute of Public Administration, Jeddah Islamic Sea Port Customs, Tel. 6431748 (Office), and 6719128 (Home), Jeddah, Saudi Arabia.

ABDULGHAFUR (Adil, Salim), Iraqi academic and physician. **Born** in 1935 in Baghdad, Iraq. **Married** three children. **Educ.:** College of Medicine, Baghdad; Fellow of the Royal College of Physicians and Surgeons of Canada; Fellow of the American College of Cardiology. **Dipl.:** M.B., Ch.B., FRCP, FACC. **Career:** Consultant cardiologist and Chief of Cardio-Pulmonary Laboratory, Veterans Administration Hospital, Dayton, Ohio, USA (1970); Secretary General, Iraqi Cardio-Thoracic Society (1975); Former Chairman, Department of Cardiology, Medical City Teaching Hospital of the College of Medicine, Baghdad University, Baghdad (since 1980). **Publ.:** Editor of the Journal of the Faculty of Medicine, Baghdad (1973); numerous publications in scientific and medical journals in English, French and Arabic. **Member** of the Hunting Club of Baghdad. **Sports:** Jogging, swimming, Tennis. **Hobbies:** Reading, travel, painting and music. **Addr.:** Baghdad, Iraq.

ABDULGHANI (Abdul Aziz, Major), Yemeni Politician. **born** on July 4, 1939 in Haifan, Republic of Yemen. **Married** to Aceya Hamza in 1966, 6 children: Mohammed, Hanan, Omar, Osama, Walid, Bassam. **Educ.:** B.A. In Economics, Colorado College (1962); Masters Degree in Economics, University of Colorado (1964); Ph.D (Hon;) , University of Colorado (1978). **Career:** Teacher, Belquis College, Aden (1964-1967); Minister of Health (1967-1968); Director, Yemen Bank for reconstruction & Development (1968); Minister of Economy (1968-1971); Chairman, Yemen Oil Company (1971); Governor, Central Bank of Yemen (1971-1975); Lecturer, Politics & Economics, Faculty of Law, Sanaa University (1972-1974); Prime-Minister of Yemen (1975-1980); Member of the Command Council (1975-1978); Vice-President of Yemen (1980-1983); Member of the Consultative Council (1978-to present); Member of the Permanent Committee, People General Council (PGC) (1982); Chairman, Supreme Council for Reconstruction of Earthquake Affected Areas (1983); Prime-Minister of Yemen (Nov. 1983-May 1990); Member of the Presidential Council of Yemen (May 22, 1990); Assitant Secretary-General to the PGC (1990); Member of the World Bank Council of Advisers for the Middle East & North Africa (1993); Prime Minister of Yemen (Oct. 1994); Chairman of the Consultative Council (May 1997). **Member:** Yemeni Economic Society (Y.E.S.);

Arab Economists Union; Arab Thought Forum. **Medals:** Sash of Mareb; Sash of El Fateh; Decoration of Unity. **Hobbies:** Swimming and hiking. **Prof.Addr.:** Office of the Presidential Council, Tel. 276777-9, Fax: 274147, Sanaa, Yemen. **Priv.Addr.:** P.O.Box 2661, Tel. 247754. Fax: 263024, Sanaa, Yemen.

ABDULGHANI (Mohamad Ben Ahmad, Colonel), Algerian politician. **Career:** Served in French Armed Forces; during Revolution served in Oran Wilaya; Commander, First Military region (Algiers) (1962-65); Commander, Fourth Military Region (1965-67); President, Revolutionary Court, Oran (1969); Promoted Colonel (June 1969); Commander, Fifth Military Region (Constantine); Member, Revolutionary Council; Minister of the Interior (1976-8 March 1979); Prime Minister and Minister of Interior March 8, 1979; Prime Minister (1982-85); Minister counsellor to the Presidency (1986- September 1989). Presently member of the Political Bureau of the FLN. **Addr.:** Algiers, Algeria.

ABDULHADI (Samir, Naim), Jordanian engineer. **Born** in Jerusalem in 1942. **Son** of Naim Abdulhadi (former Minister) **and** Mrs. Samira Abdulhadi. **Married** to Malak Abdulhadi in 1965 in Cairo. **Educ.:** Friends Boys School, Ramallah (1950-1959); American University of Beirut (1959-1964). **Dipl.:** Bachelor of Engineering (Civil) AUB (1964). **Career:** Engineer Chief Engineer Contracting Co., Tripoli, Libya (1964-1968); Head of Design Section, Ministry of Housing, Tripoli, Libya (1968-72); Associate General Manager, Consolidated Engineering Co. Khatib & Alami, Dubai, UAE (1972-now) **Member** of UAE and Jordan Engineers Association. **Sport:** Tennis. **Credit Cards:** American Express, Visa. **Prof. Addr.:** P.O.Box 5091, Tel. 222203, Dubai, UAE. **Priv. Addr.:** P.O.Box 5091, Tel.: 06/522535, Dubai, UAE.

ABDULHAFEZ (Mahmoud), Egyptian former minister. **Born** in December 1919 in Assiout. **Married** 2 children. **Educ.:** Cairo University, University of London. **Dipl.:** Doctor in Engineering (1950). **Career:** Professor, Ain Shams University (1950), Secretary General of the Ministry of Housing and Construction (1963), Minister of Housing and Construction (March 1973). **Addr.:** Cairo, Egypt.

ABDULHAKIM (Tariq), Saudi civil servant and composer. **Born** in 1920 in Taif, Saudi Arabia. **Educ.:** Received military education. **Career:** Held wide-ranging positions within the ranks of the Saudi Arabian Army, retired lieutenant-general; head of the Army Music School; Art Director of Army Music Department; Deputy Chairman of Saudi Arts Society, Riyadh (1968), General Supervisor, Music and Songs Department, Ministry of Information (1975); Manager, Public Relations and Administration, Abdul Latif Jameel Co.; General Manager, Popular and Folk Arts Department, the General Presidency of Youth Welfare, Riyadh; member, Arab League Music Department and Paris Society of Melodists; conducts wide range of activities in the field of music. **Honours:** Received numerous medals and badges in appreciation of his artistic talents and contributions to folk songs and music. **Publications:** Numerous books on Arabic music and ancient Arabic musical instruments; writes and introduces several radio programmes. **Address:** Department of Popular and Folk Arts, Youth Welfare Authority, Tel. 4771062 (office) and 4647504 (Home), Riyadh, Saudi Arabia.

ABDULHALIM (Ahmad), Sudanese statesman. **Born** in 1933 at Wad Medani, Sudan. **Married** four children. **Educ.:** Alexandria University. **Dipl.:** B.Sc. in Economics and Political Sciences; Postgraduate Diploma in Librarianship, London. **Career:** Assistant Librarian, University of Khartoum, Sudan (1958-64); Director, School of Extra-Mural Studies, University of Khartoum (1964-69); Under Secretary, Ministry of Youth, Sports, Social Affairs and Religious Affairs (1969-71); Deputy Minister of Culture and Information (1971-72); Minister of Culture and Information (1975-76); Chairman of the Board of Directors, Dar al-Ayyam for Printing and Publishing; Assistant Director General, Arab Educational Cultural and Scientific Organisation, Director, Khartoum Institute of Arabic Language. **Member** of the Political Bureau, Sudanese Socialist Party, SSU (1972-1979); Leader of the People's Assembly (1973-75); Assistant Secretary General Sudan Socialist Union (Party dissolved in 1989). **Publ.:** Books and articles on Education, Arabic and Islamic bibliographies, literary criticism and other Subjects. **Decor.:** Order of Dastour; Order of the Republic, 1st Class; order of the Yemen Republic; Order of the Lion, Senegal; etc. **Prof. Addr.:** Khartoum International Institute for Arabic Language, P.O.Box 26, al-Duyum al-Shargia, Khartoum, Sudan.

ABDULHALIM (Mohammad), Sudanese politician. **Born** in May 1927 in Cairo (Egypt). **Married,** children. **Educ.:** Secondary school and Military Academy, Cairo (Egypt). **Career:** Commissioned (1948); served with Egyptian armed forces until 1958; editor "Sot el-Shabab"; transfered to Sudan armed forces (1958); deputy legal adviser (1961); registrar of societies and trade unions; Director, Labour Department (1964); Manager, Misr Bank (1964-69); Minister of State (October 1969); Minister of the Treasury (July 1970- April 1972). **Addr.:** Khartoum, Sudan.

ABDULHAMID (Abdulwahab, Mahmoud, Dr.), Yemeni diplomat. **Born** in Taiz, Yemen in 1940. **Educ.:** University of Cairo; University of Prague, Czechoslovakia. **Dipl.:** Ph.D. in Economics. **Career:** Ambassador to France; Deputy Minister of Economy (1969); Diplomat to U.K. (1973-74); Minister of Economy (1974-75); Reappointed Minister of Economy, Trade and Supply (1988-90); Minister of Electricity and Water (May 1990-1993). **Addr.:** Sanaa, Republic of Yemen.

ABDULHAMID (Fikry), Egyptian law court judge and counsellor. **Born** on 20 September 1926, in Alexandria. **Educ.:** Faculty of Laws, Alexandria University. **Dipl.:** LL.B. (1951). **Career:** Joined the Public Prosecutor's Office, Akhmime, Upper Egypt, then Public Prosecutor in the State Security (1956); appointed counsellor, Court of Appeal, Asyout and Mansourah; President of Zagazig Primary Court; Public Attorney, South Cairo Public Prosecutor's Office; First Public Attorney and Judicial Inspector General of the State Public Prosecution; President of South Cairo Primary Court, Governor of Gharbiyeh Governorate (1982). Cairo, Egypt.

ABDULHAMID (Shafie), Egyptian diplomat. **Born** in 1927 in Cairo, Egypt. **Married** three children. **Educ:** Cairo University. **Dipl.:** B.A. in Law and Political Economics. **Career:** Consul, Egyptian Embassy, Paris (1950-55); 1st Secretary, UN Mission (1956-60); Deputy Director, International Organisation (1960-64); First Counsellor, New York (1964-69); Minister Plenipotentiary (1972); Director of Legal Affairs (1973); Ambassador to Vatican (1974); Rapporteur of the UN for the Law of the Sea and later Vice President of the Conference of the UN for the Law of the Sea; Ambassador to West Germany (1984-85). **Medals:** Order of the Egyptian Republic; Order of the Great Merit, Egypt; Order of the Magna Cruce of PIUS IX. **Member** of the Circolo degli Scacchi, Rome; the Gezira Sporting Club, Cairo; the Tahrir Club, Cairo. **Sport:** Tennis. **Addr.:** Ministry of Foreign Affairs, Cairo, Egypt.

ABDULJABBAR (Adnan Ibrahim), Saudi businessman. **Born** in 1947. **Dipl.:** B.Sc. (Architecture); diploma in radio engineering. **Career:** Director-General, Talal Establishment. **Member** of Mecca Chamber of Commerce and Industry; member of Mecca Cultural Club; agent of AEG Co. for Traffic Lights and Road Signs. **Hobbies:** Sports, travel. **Addr.:** Talal Establishment P.O.Box 1356, Tel. 35858, Mecca, Saudi Arabia.

ABDULJABBAR (Ahmad Khalil, Sheikh), Saudi Arabian diplomat. **Born** on 25 December 1921 in Mecca, Saudi Arabia. **Married** on 31 December 1945 to Miss Ina'am Araf Pharaon, 3 daughters: Maha, Rima and Lina. **Dipl.:** B.A. American University of Beirut, Lebanon (1943); M.A., Georgetown University of Washington, USA (1953). **Career:** Worked at the Royal Court of H.M. King Abdul-Aziz (1943-45); Participated as a member of the Saudi Arabian Delegation to the founding of the United Nations in San Francisco (1945); First Secretary, Saudi Arabian Embassy, Washington, Promoted as counsellor in 1952 and served as well at the U.N. (1946-55); Appointed assistant to the Head of Cabinet of Presidency of the Council of Ministers for Political Affairs with a rank of an Ambasador (1955-60); Ambassador of Saudi Arabia to Japan and Nationalist China (1960-63); Ambassador of Saudi Arabia to the Federal Republic of Germany (1964-65); Ambassador of Saudi Arabia to Italy (1966-77); Ambassador Permanent Representative to the United Nations and specialized agencies in Geneva (since 29/8/1977); Participated as a member of the Saudi Arabian Delegation to the regular General Assembly sessions (1977-79); Head of the Saudi Arabian Delegation to the Law of the Sea Conference (1978-79); Head of the Saudi Arabian Delegation to the Second Session of the Interim Committee of the United Nations Negotiating Conference on a common fund under the Integrated Programme for Commodities (1979); Head of the Saudi Arabian Delegation to the United Nations Conference on an International Code of Conduct of the transfer of technology (1979); Head of the Saudi Arabian Delegation to the United Nations Ad Hoc Intergovernmental Working Group to review the Economic Consequences of the Existence or lack of a genuine link between vessel and flag of Registry (1980). **Work:** Published poems in Arabic and English which were translated to French, German and Italian; wrote articles in several magazines (al-Adib, al-Makshouf, Pegasus and al-Mustakbul). **Awards:** King Abdul-Aziz Medal of Distinction from H.M. King Faysal (1973); Grand Cross from the President of Italy (1973); George 1st Medal from the King of Greece (1952). **Prof. Addr.:** The Permanent Mission of the Kingdom of Saudi Arabia, 32, Chemin des Colombettes, Tel. 34.57.60, 1202 Geneva, Switzerland.

ABDULJABBAR (Fahad Abdallah), Saudi academic. **Born** in 1940 at Al-Majma'ah, Saudi Arabia. **Dipl.:** B.S., M.B., DTM & H, DRCOG, MRCOG. **Career:** Lecturer (1975-77), then Assistant Professor (1977-80), Obstetrics and Gynaecology Department, King Saud University; Vice Dean, College of Dentistry, King Saud University; ex-member, Recruitment Committee and Examination Board, College of Medicine; General Secretary of 5th Saudi Medical Conference (1980); presently, member of King Saud University Council and Chairman of the Examination Control Committee; Adviser to the Ministry of Health Tender Drug Committee (1977-78); Adviser since 1978, National Guard Health Department; Vice-Dean and Associate Professor, Obstetrics and Gynaecology Department, College of Medicine, King Saud University. **Publications:** Several research paper on Obstetrics and Gynaecology. **Hobby:** Reading. **Address:** P.O.Box 2925, College of Medicine, King Saud University, Tel. 4781985 (Office) and 4916053 (Home), Riyadh, Saudi Arabia.

ABDULJAWAD (Ghazi, M.), Saudi banker. **Born** on Sept. 15, 1949 in Jeddah, Saudi Arabia. **Married,** three daughters. **Educ.:** Lewis & Clark College, Portland, Oregon, U.S.A.; Fletcher school of law & Diplomacy; Tufts University, Medford, Mass., U.S.A.; Rice University, Houston, Texas, U.S.A. **Dipl.:** B.A. Political Science; M.A. International Relations; Post Graduate Studies; Credit Training Programe, Chase Manhattan Bank, New York, N.Y. USA. **Career:** Director of External Relations Dept., Ministry of Education, Riyadh, Saudi Arabia (1972-74); Deputy Educational Attache of the Saudi Arabian

Educational Mission to the United States and Canada (1975-78); Assistant General Manager, Western & Southern Regions, Saudi Investment Banking Corporation (1978-84); Assistant General Manager, Banking Assets and Liabilities Gulf International Bank, BSC (1984- 31/7/85); General Manager, Gulf International Bank, BSC (1/8/85-). **Memberships and Association:** Chairman, Bankers' Society of Bahrain; Arab Bankers' Associations, London; International Counsellor to the Institute of Bankers (London). **Prof. Addr.:** Gulf International Bank, Al-Dowali Building, 3 Palace Avenue, P.O.Box 1017, Tel.: 534000, Telex: 8802 DOWALI BN, Fax: 522633 S.W.I.F.T.: GULFBHBM, Manama, Bahrain.

ABDULKADER (Abdulrahman Abdulmohsen, al), Saudi civil servant. **Born** in 1939 at Mubarraz, al-Ahsa, Saudi Arabia. **Dipl.:** B.A. **Career:** Manager of Organization and Methods, Petromin, Riyadh (1972); Director General, Civil Service Bureau (1976); Vice-President for Service Development, Civil Service Bureau; member of Board of Directors, Institute of Public Administration. **Address:** Civil Service Bureau, Tel. 4034090 (Office), and 4645984 (Home), Riyadh, Saudi Arabia.

ABDULKADIR (Yahia), Egyptian diplomat. **Born** in 1920 in Alexandria. **Educ.:** Cairo University. **Dipl.:** LL.B. **Career:** Ministry of Foreign Affairs, Secretary then Counsellor, Egyptian Embassies to Yugoslavia, Sudan, Italy; Ambassador to Saudi Arabia (1964-68); Ambassador to Yugoslavia (1968-71); Chairman, Egyptian Radio and TV (1971); Ambassador to USSR (1971-74); Ambassador to Greece (1974-77). **Medals:** Egyptian order of the Republic; Order of the Yugoslavian Flag with Cordon; Egyptian Order of Merits; Great Cross of Greek Order of the Phoenix. **Priv. Addr.:** 1095 Cornish al-Nil Street, Garden City, Cairo, Egypt.

ABDULKARIM (Bakri, Musa, Dr.), Sudanese Information Specialist. **Born** on August 19, 1954 in Singa Town, Sudan. **Son** of Musa Abdulkarim, (Forests Ranger) **and** Mrs. née Amna Ahmad Mohamed Ali. **Married** on July 1980 to Ihsan Osman Mohamed Khair, Five children, 4 sons and a daughter: Osman, Amin, Hunayda, Musamih and Mohriz. **Educ.:** Singa Primary School; Dinder Intermediary School; Sinnar Secondary School; University of Khartoum and University of Wales, UK. **Dipl.:** 1978: Bachelor of Science (Honours) in Economics, University of Khartoum; 1980: Postgraduate Diploma in Library Science, University of Wales, UK.; 1981: Masters of Information Science, University of Wales, UK.; 1997: Ph.D in Information Management, University of Wales, UK. **Career:** 1981-1983: Deputy Librarian, University of Gezira, Sudan; 1983-1987: Chief Librarian, University of Gezira, Sudan; 1987-1990: Deputy Librarian, Sultan Qaboos University, Muscat, Oman; 1990- to date: Chief Librarian & Examinations Officer, Etisalat College of Engineering, Sharjah, UAE. **Other Information:** Published 8 articles about information services, information management, manuscripts and libraries; Member of the Sudan National Committee for UNESCO (Subcommittee on social sciences), 1984-1987; Certified Technical Translator. Resident in the USA since 1996. **Sports:** Swimming and Walking. **Hobbies:** Travel and antiques collecting. **Associations:** Member of the Special Libraries Association; the British Library Association. **Credit Card:** Visa Card (National Bank of Abu Dhabi) **Prof. Addr.:** P.O.Box 980, Sharjah, United Arab Emirates, Tel.: 971 6 355355, Fax: 971 6 378987, e-mail: bakri@ece.ac.ae. **Priv. Addr.:** Apt. 203, 81 Orange Street, New Haven, CT 06510, USA, Tel.: (203) 624 5445.

ABDULKARIM (Ibrahim), Bahraini Politician. **Born** in 1940. **Educ.:** in Bahrain, and at Baghdad University, Iraq. **Dipl.:** B.A. (Economics) (1965). **Career:** Superior, Personnel Relations, Bahrain Petroleum Company (BAPCO); Director, Economics Affairs, Ministry of Finance and National Economy; Director, Oil and Economy (1971); Parliamentary Secretary, Ministry of Finance (1972); Deputy Minister of Finance (1973-76); Minister of Finance (1976); former Governor, Islamic Development Bank, Jeddah, Saudi Arabia. Presently, Chairman, Gulf International Bank. **Prof. Addr.:** P.O.Box 1017, 3 Palace ave. Al-Dowali Bldg., Manama 317, Bahrain, Tel.: 534000, Fax: 522633.

ABDULKARIM (Omar Ibrahim, al), Saudi engineer. **Born** in 1938. **Dipl.:** M.A. (Civil Engineering). **Career:** Lecturer, Faculty of Engineering, King Saud University; member, American Society of Civil Engineers; Consultant to Saudi Development Fund; co-designer, Central Library, King Saud University, former Deputy Minister for General Projects, Ministry of Education. **Hobbies:** Reading, sports. **Addr.:** Riyadh, Saudi Arabia.

ABDULKARIM (Tayih), Iraqi politician. **Born** in 1933 in Iraq. **Educ.:** Teachers Training College, Baghdad University, Mustansiriyah University, Baghdad. **Dipl.:** B.A., English Literature (1959); LL.B. (1969). **Career:** Deputy Governor, Basra Governorate, Ministry of Interior (1963); Ambassador to Sudan (1969); Under Secretary, Ministry of Education (1970); Minister of Oil (1974-82); President, Iraq National Oil Company (1977). **Member of:** Regional Leadership, Arab Baath Socialist Party (1970); Chairman, Economic Affairs Bureau, Revolutionary Command Council; Chairman Arab Affairs Bureau, Revolutionary Command Council; member of Revolutionary Command Council (1977). **Addr.:** Baghdad, Iraq.

ABDULKHALIQ (Mustafa, Dr.), Yemeni lawyer, politician. **Born** in 1945 in Yemen. **Educ.:** Baghdad University, Baghdad, Iraq. **Dipl.:** LL.B. **Career:** Magistrate; Secretary of Aden Municipality and Prosecutor of the People's Court in the First Governorate; Secretary to the Yemen- USSR Friendship Association (1970); Minister of

Justice and Waqfs (1971-73); Ambassador to USSR (1973-74); Member of People's Supreme Council; former President of the Supreme Court. **Addr.:** Aden, Republic of Yemen.

ABDULLA (A. Saudi), Libyan Banker. **Born** on March 20, 1937 Tripoli/Libya. **Married** in 1961 to Mrs. Awasha Aborubia, 5 children: **Educ.:** Commercial College (1957); Accountancy Diploma (1955). **Career:** Joined Central Bank of Libya in 1958 and remained there until May 1972 at which time appointed Chairman & General Manager of the Libyan Arab Foreign Bank until February 1980, and was appointed President & Chief Executive of Arab Banking Corporation in Manama, Bahrain. **Present Profile of Activities:** Owner of ASA - Consultants, Manama, Bahrain (since Sept. 1994); Vice-Chairman of Arab International Bank, Cairo, Egypt (since July 1974); Member of the Board of Directors of the Housing Bank, Amman, Jordan; Director of IVECO N.V. Amsterdam (Netherlands) (Fiat Subsidiary) since May 1979; **Previous Profile of Activities:** Director of Union de Banques Arabes et Françaises -UBAF, Paris, France (from August 1970 until December 1979); Executive Director of UBAf Bank Ltd., London, U.K. (from March 1972 until December 1980); Chairman of UBAE Arab Italian Bank, Rome, Italy (from November 1972 until April 1982); Chairman & General Manager of Libyan Arab Foreign Bank, Tripoli, Libya (from May 1972 until February 1980); Director of UBAN Arab Japanese Finance Ltd., Hong Kong (from July 1974 until December 1980); Director of UBAF Arab American Bank, New York, U.S.A. (from April 1976 until February 1977); Director of Fiat S.P.A., Turin, Italy (from March 1977 until May 1982); First Vice-Chairman of Arab Insurance Group, Manama, Bahrain (from May 1980 until February 1982); Director of Institute of International Finance, Inc. Washington D.C., U.S.A. (from September 1983 until September 1984); Chairman of Banatlantico Zurich, A.G., Zurich, Switzerland (from April 1985 until February 1991); Chairman of the Supervisory Board: ABC-Daus & Co. GmbH Frankfurt, Germany (from April 1984 until April 1993). Deputy Chairman, President & Chief Executive of Arab Banking Corporation (B.S.C.), Manama, Bahrain (from 1980- May 1994); Chairman of the Arab Financial Services Company, Manama Bahrain (from Oct. 1982 until 1994); Chairman of Banco Atlantico S.A., Madrid, Spain (from March 1984 until 1994); Chairman of Arlabank International E.C., Manama, Bahrain (from April 1984 until 1994) and First Vice-Chairman (October 1977- March 1984); Chairman of ABC Investment & Services Co. E.C., Manama, Bahrain (from December 1985 until 1994); Executive Chairman of ABC International Bank Plc, London, U.K. (from February 1991 until 1994); **Merits and Distinctions:** Great Cross of the Civil Merit granted by His Majesty, The King of Spain, (July 1977); President's Gold Medal granted by the President of Italy (September 1977); Award of «The Most Innovative Banker of the Year» by International Herald Tribune (September 30, 1980); «Banker of the Year 1981» by the Board of Editors of Institutional Investor; Banking Achievement Award for «Distinguished Lifetime Achievement & Pioneering Contributions to Banking» by the Arab Bankers Association of North America («ABANA») (on May 29, 1991); The Grand Medal of the Republic of Tunis, granted by H.E. The President of the Republic (1993); Award of "The Banker of the Arab World", Granted by the Union of Arab Bank (1993). **Sports practised:** Basketball, Tennis. **Prof. Addr.:** ASA-Consultants, P.O.Box 11544, Manama, Bahrain, Tel.: 537277, Fax: 537040.

ABDULLA (Mohamad Fahmi Omar), Egyptian administrator. **Born** on March 6, 1928 in Egypt. **Married,** 2 sons. **Dipl.:** LL.B. **Career:** held several positions with the Egyptian Broadcasting Authority. **Medals:** Medal of Sport (1974), Medal of the Republic (1981). **Decor.:** Order of Merit (1984) Egypt. **Member:** Gezira Sporting Club, Automobile Club, Zamalek Club. **Addr.:** 40 Jamiat al-Dowal al-Arabiyah, Dokki, Cairo, Egypt.

ABDULLATIF (Ahmad), Saudi banker. **Born** in 1935 in Jeddah, Saudi Arabia. **Educ.:** B.Sc. Economics, American University, Cairo (1957); extensive training with the IMF, Washington DC, USA in Commercial banks in New-York USA and India. **Career:** Managing Director, Riyad Bank, Saudi Arabia; Deputy Governor, Foreign Investments, Saudi Arabian Monetary Agency; Director General of Foreign Investments Divisions (SAMA); Director of Banking Control Division (SAMA); contributed to the formulation of the Banking Control Law in Saudi Arabia; was first Bank Controller; helped established and run the Saudi Institute for Public Educational voluntary organization to fight illiteracy. **Associations (Current):** Chairman of the Board of Directors, National Industrialization Company, Saudi Arabia; Chairman of the Board of Directors, Banco Saudi Espanol, Madrid, Spain; Deputy Chairman, Saudi Swiss Bank, Geneva, Switzerland; Director, the National Company for Cooperative Insurance, Saudi Arabia; Director, Saudi International Bank, London, U.K.; Board Trustee, The Arab Institute for Banking Studies, Amman, Jordan. **(Previous):** Board member, Gulf International Bank, Bahrain, Board member, Inter-Arab Guarantee Corporation-Kuwait. Board member Real-Estate Fund-Riyadh. **Founder member**, the Arab Bankers Association, London, U.K. **Publ.:** Commentaries broadcast by The Saudi English Broadcasting Station. **Hobby:** Reading. **Addr.:** Riyad Bank, Old Airport Road, P.O.Box 22622, Riyadh 11416, Tel.: 01-4010028, Saudi Arabia.

ABDULLATIF (Hussaini, al), Former Egyptian Minister. **Born** on June 23, 1920 in Awlad Moussa. **Married,** 7 children. **Educ.:** Cairo University. **Dipl.:** Bachelor of Arts (Architecture, 1945). **Career:** Engineer, served in the Egyptian Army, Minister of Transports (1973). **Addr.:** Cairo, Egypt.

ABDULMAHMUD (Fatma), Sudanese physician. **Born** in Sudan. **Married,** two children. **Educ.:** University of Sudan, University of Moscow. **Dipl.:** M.D. (1967); M.A. in Public Health (1967). **Career:** Ministry of Health (1967-69); Deputy Minister, Social Affairs Department (1972); Minister of State for Social Welfare (1975); Minister of Social Affairs (1976). **Prof. Addr.:** Khartoum, Sudan.

ABDULMAJEED (Adnan Abdulrahman), Saudi businessman. **Born** in Mecca in 1948. **Married,** three children. **Career:** Ministry of Information (1960-70); Saudi Arabian Airlines (1970-73); Owner of Saudi International Corporation for Marketing; Owner of Saudi International Trade and Industry Fair Organisation; Former **Vice President** of Third World Fair Organisation Association, Algiers (1967). **Hobbies:** Bowling, chess. **Addr.:** P.O.Box 4571, Tel. 6672056, 6671691, 6671692, Jeddah, Saudi Arabia.

ABDULMAJEED (Amin, Abdel Razzaq), Saudi civil servant. **Born** on 10/12/1936. **Married:** 4 children, 1 son and 3 daughters. **Educ.:** Certificate in Commerce- Technical Institute, Beirut; Diploma in Accountancy and Bookkeeping, Beirut: Advanced English Course- Pitman Institute, London. **Career:** Various Positions in Zakat and Income Tax Department which ended by Assistant Director- Zakat & Income Tax Department in 1957; Then joined Saudi Arabian Airlines as Staff Manager for 9 months; Then Manager- Public Relations; In 1979 promoted to Executive Representative- External Affairs (Gen. Mgr. Level); Currently General Manager- Arab Affairs (Saudia)- Participant in various GCC Airlines Committees; Participant in various AACO Committees; Member of Executive Staff of Yemen Airways as Director- Joint Affairs Coordination (Kingdom of Saudi Arabia holds 49% and Yemen Arab Republic 51% of Yemen Airways). **Publ.:** Author of "Poor Bachelor" (covering short Stories in Arabic); Novelist & Column writer in various Saudi Arabian newspapers; Writer of Articles to Saudi Television & Radio. **Sports:** Swimming and walking. **Hobbies:** Writing, reading and listening to soft music. **Member:** Jeddah Municipal Council; Jeddah Literary Club; Ex. Chairman of "Rabie" 1st Class Sports Club. **Prof. Addr.:** P.O.Box 620, CC-071, Jeddah, 21231; Tel.: 686-2337 (Office), 642-5261 (Home), Kingdom of Saudi Arabia.

ABDULMAJEED (Mahmoud, Hamed), Egyptian legal adviser. **Born** in 1921 Mansoura, Egypt. **Son** of Hamed Abdul-Majeed. **Married** in 1953, 3 children, **Educ.:** Cairo and Alexandria University, Egypt. **Dipl.:** LL.B. (1944), LL.M. (1945). **Career:** Advocate in Private Chambers, Egypt (1944-46); Advocate, Tax Division, Ministry of Finance, Egypt (1946-48); Attorney General's Office, Egypt (1948-54); Judge, High Court, Egypt, (1953-65); Chief Prosecutor, Attorney General's Office, Kuwait (1965-68); Legal Advisor, National Bank of Kuwait S.A.K. (1969-91). **Publ.:** Research work on Taxation, Criminal and Commercial Law. **Hobbies:** Tennis and Music. **Member:** Sports, Clubs, Kuwait and Egypt. **Addr.:** Cairo, Egypt.

ABDULMAJEED (Yahia), Sudanese politician. **Born** in 1926 in Omdurman, Sudan. **Married. Educ.:** Omdurman, Sudan; Gordon Memorial College; Imperial College, London, UK. **Dipl.:** Civil Engineering; Diploma in Hydrology. **Career:** Part-time lecturer, Khartoum University; training with British companies specialized in the construction of irrigation projects; Ministry of Irrigation; Under-Secretary, Ministry of Irrigation (1969); Secretary, Sudanese Engineering Society (1963-65); Minister of Irrigation and Hydro-Electric Power (1971); Minister of State for Irrigation (May 1973- July 1974); Minister of State for Irrigation and Hydro-Electric Power (1975-77); Minister of Irrigation and Hydro-Electric Power (September 1977-79). **Member:** British Association of Engineers; International Committee for Hydraulic Law. **Addr.:** Khartoum, Sudan.

ABDULMALEK (Anouar), Egyptian research professor and writer. **Born** on 23 October 1924 in Cairo (Egypt). **Son** of Me. Iskandar Abdel-Malek (Lawyer and Diplomat) **and** Mrs., née Alice Amnens Zaki Ibrahim. **Married** one daughter; Nadia-Alice (1961). **Educ.:** College de la Sainte-Famille, Cairo (1929-40); The British Institute, Cairo (1940-44); Faculty of Arts, Ain Shams University, Cairo (1950-54); Faculty of Arts, University of Paris- Sorbonne and Ecole des Hautes Etudes (1960-69). **Dipl.:** B.A. Hons. (Philosophy), Ain Shams University, Cairo (1954); Dr. Sociology, University of Paris- Sorbonne (1964); Dr. es-lettres, University of Paris-Sorbonne (1969). **Career:** Banking (1940-46); journalism (1950-59); Research Professor in Sociology, Centre National de la Recherche Scientifique, Paris (since 1960); Adjunct Professor, Ecole des Hautes Etudes en Sciences Sociales; Project Coordinator, The United Nations University, Tokyo (since 1978), Visiting Professor: University of Ain Shams and Institute of Louvain, Sociological Institute (University of Uppsala), University Candido Mendes (Rio de Janeiro), El-Colegio de Mexico (Mexico), Instituto de Estudios Internationales (Universidad de Chile, Santiago). **Works:** Participated to more than 60 scientific meetings, symposia and congresses; Wrote hundreds of articles, essays, translations,... **Member of:** The Executive Committee of I.S.A., Société Française de Sociologie, Association Internationale des Sociologues de Langue Française; Former Vice-President, International Sociological Association (1970-74); Egyptian Philosophical Society; Egyptian Sociological Association; International Institute for Strategic Studies; International Political Science Association. **Sports:** Walking, swimming. **Hobbies:** Music, travel, opera, cinema, theatre, Ballet. **Member:** Al-Shams Sporting Club, Heliopolis (Cairo); The International House of Japan (Tokyo). **Priv. Addr.:** 17 Avenue d'Italie, Apt. 194, 75013 Paris, Tel.: 588-8713, France and 13, El-Badr Street, Heliopolis, Cairo, Egypt.

ABDULMEGUID (Abdel Razzak, Dr.), Egyptian economist and former minister. **Born** on May 4, 1931 in Alexandria, Egypt. **Educ.:** Faculty of Commerce, Alexandria University; Birmingham University, UK.; Oxford University, UK. **Dipl.:** B.Com., M.Sc. (Economics) (1955), Ph.D. (Economics) (1957). **Career:** Director, Regional Planning, Aswan Governorate; visiting Professor, Texas University, USA; Director, Research Department, Bank of Alexandria (1963); appointed Expert, Ministry of Planning, Cairo; Deputy Director, Foreign Investment Authority (April 1977); seconded to the United Nations in December 1977 where he served as Assistant Secretary General, Developing Countries Division; Minister of Planning (1978). **Publ.:** Author of 24 books on the Social and economic aspects of different Egyptian Governorates; on Planning and Economic Development on the Banking System in the Middle East and on Balanced Development. **Addr.:** Cairo, Egypt.

ABDULMEGUID (Adli), Egyptian economist. **Born** in 1929 in Egypt. **Educ.:** University of Wisconsin, USA. **Dipl.:** Ph.D. in Economics (1956). **Career:** Assistant Professor, Alexandria University, Egypt (1956-59); Lecturer, University of Khartoum, Sudan (1959-62); UN Adviser to Sudanese Ministry of Economy (1962-65); Chief of Investments and Export Promotion, UN Industrial Development Org. (UNIDO) (1965-75); Chief of Egyptian Economic Mission in New York (1975). **Addr.:** Cairo, Egypt.

ABDULMEGUID (Ahmad Esmat, Dr.), Egyptian diplomat. **Born** in 1923, in Alexandria, Egypt. **Married** 3 sons. **Dipl.:** B.A. (Law), Alexandria University (1944); Political Science Diploma (Paris); Ph.D. (International Law), University of Paris (1951). **Career:** Attaché and Third Secretary, Embassy of Egypt, London (1950-54); Head, United Kingdom Affairs Desk, Ministry of Foreign Affairs, Cairo (1954-57); Member of the Egyptian Delegation negotiating the British evacuation from the Suez Canal, leading to the Anglo-Egyptian Agreement (1954-1956); Member of the Egyptian Delegation negotiating with the French Government the conclusion of the Zurich Agreement (1957); Counsellor, Permanent Mission of Egypt to the European Office of the United Nations, Geneva (1957-61); Member of the Egyptian Delegation to the Disarmament Committee (1962); Assistant Director, Legal Department, Ministry of Foreign Affairs, Cairo (1961-63); Minister Plenipotentiary, Embassy of Egypt in France, Paris (1963-67); Director of Cultural Affairs and Technical Assistance Department, Ministry of Foreign Affairs, Cairo (1967-69); Secretary General of the Committee of Cultural Relations and Technical Assistance of the Arab Republic of Egypt (1969); Chairman of the Egyptian Delegation to the United Nations Conference on the Law of Treaties (Vienna 1969); Official Spokesman of the Egyptian Government and Head of Information Organization, Cairo (1969-70); Ambassador of Egypt to France, Paris (1970); Minister of State for Cabinet Affairs, Cairo (1970-72); Ambassador Extraordinary and Plenipotentiary, Permanent Representative of Egypt to the United Nations, New York (until 1983); Chairman of the Group of 77 at the United Nations (1972-73); Chairman of the Preparatory Committee for the World Food Council (1974); Founding Member of the United Nations University (1974-75); Chairman of the Arab Group for the Introduction of Arabic as a working language at the United Nations (1974); Chairman of the Egyptian Delegation to the United Nations Conference on the Law of the Sea (1973, 1976, 1977, 1978, 1979, 1981, 1982); Member of the United Nations Group of Governmental Exports on the implementation of the declaration of the strengthening of International Security (1980); Chairman of the Cairo Preparatory Conference for Geneva Peace Conference (1977); Deputy Prime Minister and Minister of Foreign Affairs of Egypt (1984-91); elected on 15/5/1991 Secretary General of the League of Arab States. **Awards:** Ordre du Mérite, Government of France (1967); Decoration from the Government of France (1967); Decoration from the Government of Yugoslavia (1969); First Class Decoration from the Arab Republic of Egypt (1970); Grand Croix from the Government of France (1971). **Member:** Egyptian Society of International Law in Cairo. **Prof. Addr.:** League of Arab states, Tahrir Square, P.O.Box 11642 Cairo, Egypt.

ABDULMUNIM (Abdul Qadir, El Sayed), Sudanese businessman. **Born** in 1920 in Sudan. **Married** five children. **Educ.:** American University of Cairo, Egypt. **Dipl.:** B.A. in Business Administration. **Career:** Member of the Board of Mineral Water Co. Ltd.; Chairman of the Board of Sudan Batteries Co. Ltd.; Owner and director of two commercial companies. **Member of:** Khartoum Municipal Council; the Board of al-Khartoum Bank Ltd.; of the Building Insurance Co.; Chairman of the board of al-Jazira Commercial Co. Ltd. **Hobbies:** Reading, social activities. **Prof. Addr.:** P.O.Box 44, Tel. 70100/196, Khartoum, Sudan. **Priv. Addr.:** Tel. 71888, Khartoum, Sudan.

ABDULMUNIM (Mohamad), Egyptian journalist. **Born** in 1937 in Cairo, Egypt. **Educ.:** Cairo University. **Dipl.:** B.A. in English Literature. **Career:** Officer, Armed Forces (1957-68); Military Correspondent, al-Ahram newspaper and sub-editor (since 1968). Press Adviser to President Mubarak (1989-94); Managing Editor Al-Ahram newspaper (1994-); Chairman and Chief Editor Rose al Yussif Weekly magazine (1998- to date). **Publ.:** "October 6th: First Electronic Warfare", "Hawks of Peace", "A Wolf in the Sun's Disk". **Sports:** Tennis, swimming. **Hobby:** Billiards. **Addr.:** 7 Ibn Marwan Street, Dokki, Tel. 3488058, Cairo, Egypt.

ABDULNABI (Hidayat), Egyptian journalist. **Born** in 1948 at Heliopolis, Egypt. **Educ.:** American University in Cairo, Egypt; Fletcher School of Law and Diplomacy, Hedford, USA. **Dipl.:** B.A. in Economics and Political Science; M.A. in International Relations (1975). **Career:**

Researcher, Al-Ahram newspaper (1971-74); Graduate Assistant, American University in Cairo (1974-75); Script writer, TV and radio programmes (1975-77); Diplomatic Reporter, al-Ahram newspaper (1974-77). **Sports:** Tennis, swimming. **Prof. Addr.:** al-Ahram Newspaper, al-Galaa Street, Tel. (02) 745666, ext. 122, 242, Cairo, Egypt.

ABDULNOOR (Yusef, The Rev.), Egyptian church minister. **Born** on April 5, 1933 in Egypt. **Son** of The Rev. Abdul Noor Michael Abdul Noor **and** Mrs., née Amera Abu al-Faras. **Married** to Soad Abdul Noor in Cairo on August 27, 1964, 3 daughters: Amera, Mona & Amani. **Educ.:** American College, Asiyut (Upper Egypt); Evangelical Theological Seminary, Cairo (Egypt); New York Theological Seminary. **Dipl.:** B.D.- M.Div.- M.A. (Religious Education). **Career:** Pastor, The Arab Congregation; The National Evangelical Church, Kuwait (1959); President of the National Evangelical Church in Kuwait (1963). **Member:** Executive Committee, The Middle East Council of Churches. **Prof. Addr.:** P.O.Box 80, Tel. 433230, Safat, Kuwait. **Priv. Addr.:** P.O.Box 80, Tel. 438498, Safat, Kuwait.

ABDULNOUR (Mounir, Amin Fakhry), Egyptian economist. **Born** in 1945, in Cairo (Egypt). **Son** of Amin Fakhry Abdel-Nour. **Married** in 1976, 2 children. **Educ.:** Cairo University, Faculty of Economics and Political Science; American University, Cairo. **Dipl.:** B.Sc. Statistics (1976); M.A. Economics (1970). **Career:** Representative in Egypt and the Middle East, Banque de l'Union Européenne (1970-75); Vice-President, American Express Middle East and American Express Bank (1976-80); Managing Director, Egyptian Finance Company (1980); Director, Industrie du Froid S.A.E. **Member:** Economic, Law and Research Society of Egypt; Cairo Rotary Club; Gezira Sporting Club. **Hobbies:** Travel and Sport. **Addr.:** 4 Ibn Zanki Street, Zamalek, Tel.: 651116, 807510, 811070, Cairo, Egypt.

ABDULQADIR (Gaguig, Salih), Moroccan academic. **Born** in 1948 in Morocco. **Married** two sons. **Educ.:** Education and Psychology. **Career:** Teacher (1965); Inspector of Education (1974); Professor of Psychology (1976); Publisher of Al-Tarbiya wa-l Ta'lim (since 1982). **Publ.:** Textbooks for primary schools (1980); Textbooks in Mathematics (1982). **Hobbies:** Reading in psychology, literature. **Prof. Addr.:** P.O.B. 35, Ya'cub Al-Mansur, Rabat, Morocco.

ABDULQADIR (Mardhy al-Tayib), Sudanese politician. **Born** in 1927 in Sudan. **Married,** five sons. **Educ.:** Teachers' Institute, Bakht al-Redha (1946); Sudanese Military College (1948); Camberley Staff College, UK; training courses in Pakistan and USA. **Career:** Second Lieutenant (1950); Colonel, Sudanese Army; Director of Sudanese Military Intelligence; Military Attaché, Sudanese Embassy to USA (1966-67); Military Attaché, Sudanese Embassy to UK (1968-69); retired (1969); Governor of Darfur Province (1973-74); Governor of District of North Darfur (1974); Chairman of the Board of Darfur General Transport Company (1976). **Member of:** Committee for Resettlement of Refugees of Southern Sudan, First Constituent Assembly. **Chairman of:** The National Defence Committee and 10th Constitutional Law Committee; Secretary of Sudanese Socialist Union (SSU); Party now dissolved following coup in 1989. **Medals:** Long Service Medal; Order of the Two Niles, 2nd Class; Order of the Constitution. **Hobbies:** Reading poetry, history and biographies of military commanders and politicians. **Addr.:** North Darfur Province, Tel. 2001, el-Fasher, Sudan.

ABDULQADIR (Mohamad al-Fousi), Saudi academic. **Born** in 1941 in Medina, Saudi Arabia. **Dipl.:** B.A. (Shari'a); M.A. Edinburgh University, Ph.D. (Principles of Islamic Jurisprudence). **Career:** Lecturer, Assistant Professor, member of Shari'a Department Council of Umm Al-Qura University; Head of Islamic Law Department, Faculty of Sharia, Umm Al-Qura University; Faculty of Shari'a Council, Mecca Cultural Club; member of Conference of Muslim Students Association of U.S.A. and Canada, Muslim Students Society of Britain and Ireland, Educational Festival, India (1975). **Publ.:** The Traditional View of Malik Ibn Anas, Life and Works (M.A. thesis), Maliki Legal Doctrine in the West (Ph.D. Dessertation). **Addr.:** Faculty of Shari'a, Umm Al-Qura University, Tel. 5564770, Saudi Arabia.

ABDULRAHEEM (Muddathir), Sudanese academic and diplomat. **Born** on July 19, 1932 at Ad-Daman (Sudan). **Married** in 1958 to Moira Elizabeth Miller, one daughter, 3 sons. **Educ.:** Wadi Seidna Secondary School; Faculty of Arts, University of Khartoum; University of Nottingham, England; University of Manchester, England. **Dipl.:** B.A. (Honours). Ph.D. **Career:** Lecturer in government, University of Manchester, England (1960-65); Head, Department of Political Science, University of Khartoum (1965-70); Visiting Professor, Makarere University, Uganda (1970-71); UNESCO senior expert in public administration and social science; Seconded as head, Human Resources Development Programme, CAFRAD, Tangiers (Morocco) (1971-74); Professor of International Relations and Modern History, University of Rabat (October 1974- June 1975); Ambassador to Finland, also accredited to Norway and Sweden (1975). **Publ.:** Author of "Imperialism and Nationalism in the Sudan: A study in constitutional and political development (1899-1956)" (Clarendon Press, Oxford, 1969), "Human Rights in theory and Practice" (Dar Elkheyr, Beirut, Lebanon 1970), "The Problem of the Southern Sudan: Its Nature and Development" (Aldar Alsudanyya, 1971). **Member:** International Political Science Association. **Sports:** Horseriding, swimming and tennis. **Hobbies:** Music, poetry, travelling. **Addr.:** Ministry of Foreign Affairs, Khartoum, Sudan.

ABDULRAHMAN (Faisal, Mohamad), Sudanese statesman. **Born** in 1934 at Omdurman (Sudan). **Married**, with children. **Educ.:** Primary and secondary education locally; higher education at Hantoub (1945); Faculty of Law, Khartoum University. **Dipl.:** LL.B. **Career:** Judge, appointed to various courts (1962); attached to the International Labour Organisation (ILO), Geneva (Switzerland) becoming ILO Deputy Director; Minister of State for Presidential Affairs (April 1974). **Addr.:** Khartoum, Sudan.

ABDULRAHMAN (Farouk, Mohamad), Sudanese economist. **Born** in 1948 at Wad Medani, Sudan. **Son** of Mohamed Abdulrahman (merchant) **and** Mrs., née Bakhita Abdelgadir. **Married** in 1976 in Omdurman to Miss Faiza, two sons. **Educ.:** Wad Medani Secondary School, Aligar University, England; Bradford University, England. **Dipl.:** B.A., M.A. also Statistics, Islamic Economic Studies. **Career:** Inspector, Ministry of Finance and Economic Planning (1974); Project Officer, Sudan Development Corp. (1975); Senior Economist, Sudan Development Corp. (1982); Manager, Research and Promotion, Sudan Development Corp. (1983); Chairman Kasala Fruit Processing Co. (KFPC). **Member** of Board of Karani Investment Co. **Publ.:** Financial Analysis, Preparation of Feasibility Studies, Research Work in Connection with Project Analysis, Project Indentification, Evaluation and Investment Promotion. **Medal:** Position Medal, M.A. Economics at Aligah University, India. **Sport:** Football. **Hobbies:** Chess and Fishing. **Prof. Addr.:** P.O.Box 710, Tel. 47754, Khartoum, Sudan. **Priv. Addr.:** Tel. 55721, Omdurman, Sudan.

ABDULRASHID (Khondkar), Bank adviser. **Born** in 1927 in Dacca, India. **Son** of Khondkar Muhammad Mustafa Abdul-Rashid. **Married** in 1954, 2 children. **Dipl.:** B.A. (Hons.) (1945); CAIIB. **Career:** Joined Imperial Bank of India and State Bank of India (1948-62); Pakistan Industrial Credit and Investment Corporation Ltd. Karachi, Pakistan (1963-75); Deputy Managing Director Pakistan Industrial Credit and Investment Corp. Ltd. Bangladesh (1967-71); Deputy Governor, Bangladesh Bank (Central Bank) (1972-75); Chairman & Managing Director, Sonali Bank (1975-81); Consultant, (Short term assignment) World Bank (1981); Adviser, Bank of Oman Ltd., Dubai. **Member:** Fellow, International Bankers' Association, Washington; Fellow, Institute of Bankers, Bangladesh. **Addr.:** Karachi, Pakistan.

ABDULRAZZAQ (Saud Abdul Aziz, Muhammad), Kuwaiti businessman. **Born** in 1918. **Married,** 2 sons. **Educ.:** Received education in Kuwait. **Career:** Public Health Administration (1953-61); Member, Constituent Assembly (1962); National Assembly Member (1963-67); Deputy Speaker, National Assembly (1963-65); President and Speaker, National Assembly (1965-67); Chairman, al-Ahli Bank of Kuwait (1967); Businessman in Bombay and Kuwait (since 1982); Partner, Dasma General Trading & Contracting Est. **Prof. Addr.:** P.O.Box 2379, Safat, Kuwait.

ABDULSALAM (Ibrahim), Egyptian lawyer and banker. **Born** in 1935 in Cairo, Egypt. **Son** of Mohamed Abdel-Salam. **Married** in 1959, 1 son. **Educ.:** Cairo University; and Paris. **Dipl.:** Licence in Law (1957); Diploma in Public Law (1962); Diploma in Administration Sciences (1962); B.A. (Licence es-Lettres) (1966); Diploma in Public Administration (1969). **Career:** Lawyer, Cairo (1957-58); Assistant Manager, Fox Corporation (1958-59); General Department for Legislations and Researches (1959-64); Central Department for Inspection and Follow-up (1964-65); General Department for Researches (1965-70); General Department for External Relations (1970-71); Public Administration Expert, Civil Service Agency, Yemen Arab Republic (1971-75); Assistant General Manager, Administrative Affairs, Misr Iran Development Bank, Cairo. **Member:** Guezira Sporting Club, Tewfikeya Tennis Club. **Addr.:** 2 Maamal el-Sokkar Str., Apt. 24, Garden City, Tel.: 92480, Cairo, Egypt.

ABDULSALAM (Jasem M.), Kuwaiti Professor of Parasitology, Kuwait University. **Born** in 1947 in Kuwait. **Son** of Mohammad Abdul-Salam **and** Mrs. née Zamzam Al-Awadhi. **Married** to Muna Al-Taqi, 5 children: Nour, Amal, Yousef, Dhuha and Ahmad. **Educ.:** B.A., North Texas (1970); M.S., North Texas (1973); S.M., Harvard (1975); D.Sc., Harvard (1979). **Career:** Assistant Professor (1979); Associate Professor (1988); Professor of Parasitology, Kuwait University (1990- present). **Other Information:** Dean Graduate Studies; Member University Council; Member Board of Trustees, KISR; Director Research Department, KFAS. **Prof. Addr.:** Kuwait University, Faculty of Science, Department of Zoology, P.O.Box 5969, Safat, Code No. 13060, Kuwait. **Priv. Addr.:** P.O.Box 488, Safat, Kuwait.

ABDULSALAM (Mohamad, bin Ibrahim bin), Saudi educator, diplomat. **Born** in 1934 in Saudi Arabia. **Educ.:** Faculty of Art. **Dipl.:** B.A. (Arabic Language and Literature). **Career:** Primary school teacher; Director of a secondary school; Head of Professional (Technical) Board, Ministry of Education; Chief, Education Mission of Saudi Arabia to Algeria and the Cultural Attaché in Algeria; Saudi Arabian Cultural Attaché, Morocco. **Attended** several conferences on Islamic Philosophy. **Prof. Addr.:** Embassy of the Kingdom of Saudi Arabia, 6, Residence Minaret Bldg. (near Cinema Royal), Tel. 21329, Rabat. **Priv. Addr.:** Tel. 52228, Rabat, Morocco, and P.O.Box 8, Riyadh, Saudi Arabia.

ABDULSALAM (Othman Hashim), Sudanese economist and former minister. **Born** in 1937. **Educ.:** in the USA. **Dipl.:** Economics Degree, University of Chicago, USA. **Career:** Economic Commision for Africa (ECA), Addis Ababa, Ethiopia (1962-67); African Institute for Economic

Development and Planning, Dakar, Senegal (1968-69); Sub-Regional Office of UN Economic Commission for North Africa (1971-74); former Deputy Chairman, Sudan Development Corporation SDC; Minister of Industry (1979). **Addr.:** Khartoum, Sudan.

ABDULWAHAB (Ahmad, Sheikh), Saudi official. **Born** in 1923 in Mecca, Saudi Arabia. **Educ.:** Received general education supplemented by extensive experience in diplomatic ceremonial and protocol. **Career:** When the late King Faisal was Viceroy of Hijaz territory, he was chosen as Chief of Protocol at the Viceroy's Court; he later became Chief of Protocol at the Royal Court after King Faisal acceded the Throne in 1964; accompanied the late King Faisal in all his State visits to Arab, European, Asian, African and American States; accompanied the late King Khalid in similar State visits. **Addr.:** The Royal Cabinet, Riyadh, Saudi Arabia.

ABDULWAHAB (Ali, Mohamad), Egyptian academic. **Born** on November 10, 1941 at Sohag (Upper Egypt). **Son** of Mohammed Abdel Wahab. **Married** in February 1974 to Miss Mona Raafat, 2 children: Hind and Ossama. **Educ.:** General Education Secondary School, College of Commerce. **Dipl.:** Baccalaureat, M.BA. (Business Administration), Ph.D. (Sociology) from University of Massachusetts (USA). **Career:** Assistant Professor of Management, College of Commerce, Ayn Shams University, Cairo, Egypt. **Publ.:** Several studies in specialised journals. **Books:** "Personnel Management" (2 vols), "Human Behaviour in Management", "How to Deal with your Boss", all published by Ayn Shams University Press; (in print) "Training and Development", Published by Institute of Public Administration, Riyadh, Saudi Arabia. **Sports:** Track sports. **Hobby:** Picnics. **Club:** Ayn Shams University club. **Prof. Addr.:** College of Commerce, Ayn Shams University, Cairo (Egypt) and I.P.A., P.O.Box 205, Riyadh, Saudi Arabia. **Priv. Addr.:** 10 Hussein Bin Ali Street, Heliopolis, Egypt.

ABDULWASIE (Abdul Wahhab Ahmad), Saudi minister. **Born** in 1929 in Jeddah, Saudi Arabia. **Dipl.:** B.A. (Commerce), University of Cairo; Diploma (Tax Accounting), Higher Institute of Taxation, Alexandria. **Career:** Assistant Director of the Budget, Ministry of Finance and National Economy (1954); Director General of Financial Affairs, Ministry of Education (1955); Director General of Education (1959); Assistant Deputy Minister for Education Affairs (1963); Deputy Minister of Education (1964); Minister of State and President of the Control Board (1971); Minister of Pilgrimage and Endowments (1975 to July 1993); Advisor to the Royal Court with Ministerial rank as (from July 1993). **Founder member**, Daghestani and Abdul-Wahab Accounting Office; **Member** of the following: Equestrian Club, Makkah Literary Club, Okaz Press and Publishing Organization, Supreme Council of Higher Education, Supreme Council of Hajj (Pilgrimage) Affairs, Transportation Higher Committee; member of the Board of Trustees, Palestine Studies Foundation, Lebanon; member of Board, Islamic Cultural Foundation, Geneva; member Civil Service Council, the Supreme Council for the Universities, King Saud University Supreme Council, Higher World Council of Mosques; attended various international conferences relating to education, the combatting of illiteracy, Mosques and general Islamic affairs, Palestine studies; part-time Lecturer, College of Commerce, King Saud University. **Honours:** King Abdulaziz Sash, Second Class; Tunisian Republic Medal, First Class; Golden Star Medal, First Class, Republic of China; Medal of Merit with the title of Datu, First Class, State of Sabah, Malaysia; Indonesian Republic Medal, First Class; Medal of Merit, First Class, Kingdom of Belgium, awarded during the visit of H.M. late King Khalid Ibn Abdulaziz to Belgium; Medal of Merit with the title of Datu, First Class, State of Sarawak, Malaysia; Republic of the Philippines Medal, with the title of Datu First Class; Honorary Degree of Doctorate of law, Republic of China University; medal of Merit with the title of Datur, State of Sarawak Malaysia. **Publications:** Our Schools and Education (in Arabic); Education in the Kingdom of Saudi Arabia (in both Arabic and English); Personnel Management; several other school textbooks in mathematics and bookkeeping. **Hobbies:** Reading, walking. **Address:** The Royal Court, Riyadh; and Tel.: 4785222 (Home), Riyadh, Saudi Arabia.

ABDUNNADI (Ahmad, Mahmoud), Egyptian lawyer and landowner, former Governor. **Born** in Egypt. **Son** of Mahmoud Abdunnabi. **Educ.:** Secondary and Higher. **Dipl.:** Licentiate of Law, Faculty of law (Cairo University). **Career:** Joined Ministries of the Interior and the Foreign Affairs, Former Governor of Alexandria City. **Addr.:** Cairo, an-Nil Street, Farid al-Atrach Bldg., Gezireh, Tel. 805170, and Alexandria Moaskar ar-Roumani Street, Mahroussa Bldg., Rushdy Pasha Station, Tel. 65054, Cairo, Egypt.

ABDURRAHMAN (Ali, Shaikh), Sudanese lawyer and statesman. **Born** in Sudan. **Educ.:** Islamic studies. **Career:** Former Judge of Religions Courts: member of Parliament since 1953; Minister of Justice (1954-55); Minister of Education (1955-56); Minister of the Interior (1956-58); Minister of Agriculture, then of Commerce (1958); President of the People's Democratic Party (1956-67); Vice-President of Democratic Unity Party since 1967; Deputy Prime Minister and Minister of Foreign Affairs (1968-70). **Addr.:** Khartoum, Sudan.

ABDURRASSOUL (Ahmad, Ahmad), Egyptian radiochemist. **Born** on March 4, 1929 in Alexandria. **Son** of Ahmad Abdurrasoul **and** Mrs., née Raoufah Ghoneim. **Educ.:** University of Alexandria, Johannes Gutenberg University (Mainz, Germany), National Institute of Management Development. **Dipl.:** Bachelor of Science (1949),

Master of Science (1955), Doctorate (1960), Degree in research Development (1964). **Career:** Demonstrator Chemistry, University of Alexandria (1949); Research worker Max-Planck Otto Hahn Institute for Radiochemie, Mainz (1956-1960); Lecturer, Nuclear Chemistry, Egypt Atomic Energy Establishment (1960); Associate Professor since 1964; Visiting Research Fellow Institute for Atomenergy, Kjeller, Norway (1962); Staff Radioisotope Production Laboratory, Inchass (1962-64), Member of Egyptian, Chemical Society. **Publ.:** Author of publication on production of a series of radionuclides in high chemical and radiochemical purity for medical applications; Developed analytical schemes based on nuclear activation to solve medical and biochemical problems, particularly disposition of anti-Bilharzial antimonial drugs; purity control of reactor materials, scintillation for successive and other induced nuclear reactions. **Prof. Addr.:** Egypt Atomic Energy Office, Cairo. **Priv. Addr.:** 19 Abdul Aziz Fahmi Street, Heliopolis, Cairo, Egypt.

ABDURRAZZAQ (Muhamad, Abdurrazzaq), Egyptian physician. **Born** on April 23, 1928 in Cairo. **Son** of Abdurrazzaq Abdurrazzaq **and** Mrs. Fathia Abdurrazzaq. **Married** on September 6, 1958 to Miss Leila Hasaballa, 2 children: Omar and Rawia. **Educ.:** Cairo University. **Dipl.:** Bachelor of Medicine, Master of Chemistry , Doctor in Medicine. **Career:** Professor and associate professor, international and nuclear medicine, Cairo University since 1954; Head, Medicine research Atomic Energy Establishment (1964-65); Staff Medicine Unit Regional Radioisotope Centre (1963-66); Member of the Egyptian Medicine Association, Society of Nuclear Medicine. **Publ.:** Author of research and studies on use of radioisotopes in study hemodynamics and blood flow to different regions in normal states and in hepatosplenic bilharziasis. Effect drugs on hemodynamics of liver and kidneys, photo-canning of liver in bilharziasis. **Addr.:** Cairo University, Faculty of Medicine, Cairo, Egypt.

ABED (Hamza, Mohamad), Saudi civil servant. **Born** in 1926 in Medina city (Saudi Arabia). **Educ.:** Faculty of Arts, Cairo University, Teacher Training College. Cairo. **Dipl.:** B.A. (Arabic language and Literature), B.A. (Education) (1954). **Career:** Inspector- General, Ministry of Education (1954-56); Director, Personnel Department, Ministry of Education (1956-62); Director- General of Education (1962-65); Director- General of Culture, Ministry of Education (1965-73); contributed to the Committee for setting textbooks and curricula (1966-77); attended UNESCO Conference, Paris (1962); UNESCO Conference, Geneva (1960); Education Counsellor, Saudi Education Bureau, Cairo (Egypt). **Publ.:** Author of a number of school textbooks. **Sports:** Tennis and swimming. **Hobbies:** Reading and music. **Prof. Addr.:** Office of the Education Adviser, 1, 26 July Square, Muhandessin City, Dokki District, Tel. 814158 Cairo. **Priv. Addr.:** Tel. 803599, Cairo, Egypt.

ABERKANE (Muhammad), Algerian diplomat. **Born** on November 7, 1934. **Married**, 3 children. **Educ.:** Rutjers University, USA; Pennsylvania University, USA. **Dipl.:** B.A. in Economics, M.A. in Economics. **Career:** Adviser, Algerian Embassy to the USA; Assistant Director for Economics, Culture and Social Affairs, Ministry of Foreign Affairs, then Chief of Western Europe and North America Department at said Ministry. **Prof. Addr.:** c/o Ministry of Foreign Affairs, Algiers, Algeria.

ABID (Ali), Tunisian artist, caricaturist. **Born** in 1938 in Tunis, Tunisia. **Married** nine children. **Educ.:** General. **Career:** Caricaturist for several Tunisian newspapers. Now exclusive caricaturist of "Dialogue" magazine. **Act.:** Held various exhibitions: in Tunis (1972); in Cite Internationale des Arts, Paris, France (1974); International Salon of Humour, Bordighera, Italy; annual participant International Salon of Caricature, Montreal, Canada. **Member:** National Union of Plastic and Graphic Arts. **Award:** 1st Prize for the Ali Riahi Festival from La Marsa Commune. **Hobby:** Graphic arts. **Addr.:** Dialogue Magazine, Tel. 264899, Tunis, Tunisia.

ABO HASSAN (Atalla, A.), Saudi academic. **Born** on 10 October 1944 at Rabigh. **Dipl.:** Ph.D. (Forestry), U.S.A., 1976. **Career:** Demonstrator, King Saud University (1969-70); Head of Cultural Committee, Faculty of Agriculture, (1976-78); Associate Professor and Chairman, Plant Production Department, Faculty of Agriculture, King Saud University. **Member:** Saudi Biological Society, Society of American Foresters, American Society for Range Management, Society of Sigma XI, American Wild Life Federation, Growth Regulators Working Group; member of the Council of Faculty of Agriculture since 1977; member Agriculture Research Centre since 1977; member, King Saud University Council (1979); Chairman, Farm Committee; Director, Experimental Farm; Supervisor, University Campus Nursery Farm; member of the Information Committee of Muslim Scientists' 1st Conference; member of the Committee of 2nd Arab Conference for Food Technology, Faculty of Agriculture, Riyadh, 1976. **Publ.:** several research articles published in al-Faisal and al-Sharq magazines; has participated in several radio talks in his field of specialization. **Hobbies:** Reading, sports. **Address:** Faculty of Agriculture, Plant Production Department, King Saud University, Tel. 4358744 (office) and 4811000 Ext. 2210 (Home), Riyadh, Saudi Arabia.

ABOUAMMAR (Yasser), Palestinian Engineer, President of the Executive Committee of the P.L.O. See **ARAFAT (Yasser).**

ABOUDI (Mohamad Ibn Nassir), Saudi secretary general of Islamic Call. **Born** in 1926 at Buraida, Saudi Arabia. **Educ.:** Secondary School Certificate. **Career:** Secretary of Public Library, Buraidah (1944); Teacher, Buraidah School (1944); Headmaster, Mansouriah School, Buraidah (1948); Director of Scientific Institute, Buraidah, (1952); Secretary General of the Islamic University, Medina (1973); Secretary General of Islamic Call. **Member:** Literary Club, Riyadh, Advisory Council for Research and Ifta' (Islamic Decisions); member of Board, Islamic University; member, the Selecting Committee for King Abdulaziz Prize; member of Board, Plants Dictionary; member of Board, Gassiem Literary Club; member of the Preparatory Board of the Islamic Call. **Attended** the First Conference of Saudi Men of Letters; Conference of Islamic Information, Conference of Mosque Message, and various local and international conferences. **Honours:** Medal of Literature Merit awarded by King Abdulaziz University. **Publ.:** several books comprising more than 20 vols. including Dictionary of Gassiem Province (6 vols.); Common Proverbs in Najd (5 vols.); In Green Africa; Exhaltation of Qur'anic Peace; News on Abil Aynaa Al-Yamani, Madagascar Land of Lost Muslims. **Addr.:** General Secretariat of the Islamic Call, Oleisha, 37 Ohod Street, Tel. (Office), and 4036174 (Home), Riyadh, Saudi Arabia.

ABSY (Salim, R.), Bahraini diplomat. **Born** in 1925 in Bahrain. **Married**, 2 sons and 1 daughter. **Educ.:** School of Oriental and African Studies, London, UK. **Dipl.:** in legal Translation. **Career:** school master (1943), journalist (1956), translator (1954-71), Director of the Prime Minister's Office in Bahrain (1976), Ambassador of Bahrain to Jordan (1977-81), Ambassador to Iraq (1981) and presently in the Ministry of Foreign Affairs. **Sports:** Swimming. **Hobbies:** history, politics and social affairs. **Medals:** al-Hussain Bin-Ali Medal. **Priv. Addr.:** P.O.Box 1040, Manama Bahrain.

ABU-AMER (Mohamed, Zaki, Dr.), Egyptian Politician. **Born** in March 1946. **Educ.:** Ph.D., Criminal Law, Alexandria University. **Career:** Head, Law Graduates Society; Member, Medicine and Law Board of Directors; Dean, Faculty of Law, Alexandria University (1991); Secretary General, National Democratic Party (NDP) in Alexandria (1992); Member, Shura Council (1992); Minister of State for Administrative development (1993 Oct.1999) **Address:** Cairo, Egypt.

ABUAALI (Saeed Atiyah), Saudi academic. **Born** in 1940 in Ghamid, Saudi Arabia. **Dipl.:** B.Ed. (English), Faculty of Education, Mecca; M.Ed. (Curricula), Wisconsin University; Ph.D. (Curricula and School Administration), North Colorado University. **Career:** Primary School Teacher; Primary School Director; Director of Teachers' Training Institute; Demonstrator, King Abdulaziz University; Assistant Professor of Education, King Abulaziz University; General Director of Education in the Eastern Province; member Curriculum Development; attended the Arab Education Vice-Ministers' Conference. **Publ.:** Articles and research in the fields of education and sociology. **Hobbies:** Reading, swimming. **Addr.:** General Directorate of Education in the Eastern Province, Tel. 8268212 (Office), 8269946 (Home), Damman, Saudi Arabia.

ABUALELA (Ali Hassan), Saudi Former civil servant. **Born** in 1924. **Educ.:** Received secondary school education. **Career:** Clerical jobs, Ministry of Finance and Ministry of Interior; Assistant Director then Director, Administrative Affairs, Ministry of Interior; Director, Bureau of the Deputy Minister of Interior; Acting Chief, Jeddah Municipality (1953); Administrative Adviser, Makkah Governorate; Secretary to the Higher Committee for Pilgrims and Higher Committee for Transportation; Director of General Administrative Affairs; member of Mecca Municipal Council; Chairman of "Tawaf" Ministry of Pilgrimage; Former Director General, Claims Department, Mecca Governorate. **Member**, Committee for Freeing Poor Prisoners; member, Mecca Welfare Society, Mecca Charity Fund Committee. **Publ.:** Buka-Ulazhar (weeping flowers), collection of poems. **Hobbies:** Travel, reading. **Addr.:** Mecca Governorate, Tel. 5748981 (Office), 5421511 (Home), Mecca, Saudi Arabia.

ABUALHAMAYEL (Habib, I), Saudi Academic. **Born** in 1950 in Jeddah, Saudi Arabia. **Dipl.:** M.S. (KFUPM) King Fahd University of Petroleum & Minerals (1975), M.S. University of Colorado at Boulder (1980), Ph.D. (Mechanical Engineering) University of Colorado at Boulder, (1981). **Career:** Assistant Professor Mechanical Engineering Department, KFUPM (1981) Associate Professor, Mechanical Engineering Department, KFUPM (1989); Chairman, Mechanical Engineering Department, KFUPM (1986-91); Director, Summer Program, KFUPM (1994 & 1995); Dean, College of Engineering Sciences, KFUPM (1994- present). **Specialization:** Thermal Sciences and Combustion. Member, International Combustion Institute; Member, ASME Saudi Arabian Chapter. **Hobbies:** reading, sports. **Address:** P.O.Box 1889, King Fahd University of Petroleum & Minerals, Dhahran, 31261, Saudi Arabia. Tels: Office 9663-860-2574; Home 9663-860-6272.

ABUALI (Sultan), Egyptian politican. **Born** in 1937 in Egypt. **Educ.:** Harvard University. **Dipl.:** Ph.D. **Career:** Worked at stock exchange in Alexandria (1955-65); Fellow, Institute of National Planning (1965-67); Kuwaiti Fund for Development (1963-69); Deputy Chairman, Investment Authority (1984); Minister of Economy and Foreign Trade (1985). **Addr.:** Cairo, Egypt.

ABUALSAMH (Abdallah, A.), Saudi businessman. **Born** in 1935, in Mecca, Saudi Arabia. **Son** of Abdulzaher Abul-Samah. **Married** in 1963, 4 children. **Educ.:** Cairo University; Syracuse University, U.S.A. **Dipl.:** B.A. (Journalism) (1959); M.A. (Radio & T.V.) (1966). **Career:** Head, Public Relations Dept., Ministry of the Interior; Direction of the Administration, Ministry of Petroleum; General Manager, Jeddah TV Station; Direction of the

Administration, Ministry of Information; Director-General, Saudi News Agency; Deputy Chairman, Board of Directors, Industrial Services Co.; Executive Manager, Westinghouse Industry Services Co. (1973-76); Manager, National Commercial Bank, Dammam (1976-79); Deputy Managing Director, al-Bank al-Saudi al-Fransi, Jeddah (1979); Boards Member and Management Consultant for Western Province (Al-Bank-Al-Saudi Al-Fransi (1988). **Member:** Arab Bankers Association, London. **Hobbies:** Reading and travelling. **Addr.:** P.O.Box 1, Tel.: (02) 6515151, Telex: 601168 SAFJ SJ, Jeddah, Saudi Arabia.

ABUASSALI (Dib), Syrian banker. **Born** in 1932 in Syria. **Educ.:** University of Paris, France. **Career:** Manager, Arab Unity Bank; Manager, Commercial Bank of Syria (1967-73); Chairman and General Manager, Commercial Bank of Syria (1973). **Addr.:** Damascus, Syria.

ABUATLAH (Mohamad Wafik, Dr.), Egyptian barrister. **Born** on January 28, 1934 in Cairo, Egypt. **Married** to Miss Nagat Taysear Kassar (reference assistant to the UN Information Center, Cairo), 2 children: Nagla'a and Walid. **Educ.:** Faculty of Law, Ain Shams University (1952-57); Higher Institute of Economic and Political Sciences, Cairo University (1958-59). **Dipl.:** LL.B. (Ain Shams University); LL.M. (Political Science); Ph.D. (Faculty of Law, Cairo University, 1971, subject: "Regulations of the Use of Space, Airspace and Outerspace"). **Career:** Lawyer; Researcher in the Legislative Department, National Assembly; Member of the Consultation and Legislation Department, National Assembly; Technical Secretary of the Legislative Committee, National Assembly; Researcher in the Technical Secretariat, Egyptian Congress Preparatory Committee; Technical Secretary, Egyptian National Congress reportery committee; Technical Secretary, Political Organization Committee of the Social Union; Assistant Manager of the Constitutional and Legislation Branch, National Assembly; Director of the Legislations Department, National Assembly; Member of the Egyptian Constitution Committee; Member of the Arab Republic Union Constitution; Member of the Technical Committee for pursuing the establishment of the Arab Republic Union units; Technical Director, Misr-Libya Unity (Oct. 1972 May 1973); General Secretary, Supervision Committee of Misr-Libya Unity (May 1973-Oct. 1973); General Secretary, Technical Secretariat, Misr-Libya Unity (Oct. 1973- July 1978); General Secretary, Committee of Registering Egypt's History; Legal Adviser to the Vice-Prime Minister of the Social Development (Dec. 1977- July 1978); Barrister; Delegated Professor in Cairo and Ain Shams Faculties of Law; Legal Adviser to the Arab British Helicopter Company and some other joint-venture companies. **Member:** Egyptian International Law Association, Board of the Egyptian Political Science Association, Egyptian Association of the Political Economical Legislations and Statics, the I.L.A. (London); David Davies Memorial Institute of the International studies (London), Trustees of Space (London), correspondent member of the International Group of the Human Rights (Berlin- G.D.R.), Board Member of the Group of the Faculty of Law Graduates (Ain-Shams University); Vice Chairman, Board Member of the U.N. Association. **Publ.:** Participated in the preparation of the Arabic Encyclopedia of International Constitutions (issued by the National Assembly); issued the first volume of the Human Rights Encyclopedia, published the "Regulations of Space", which was translated into several Languages; published a comparative study of "Multilateral Agreements of Airspace"; published the first issue of the comparative study of the "Specialized National Councils"; published an issue about the institutions of the Arab Republic Union; issued two volumes of the constitutions and parliament Encyclopedia. **Prof. Addr.:** 11, el-Zobeir Ebn el-Awam St. el-Sadat, Misr el-Kadima, Cairo. **Priv. Addr.:** 11, Abd el-Rahman el-Barkouky St., el-Manial, Tel. 845837-843792, Cairo, Egypt.

ABUBAKR (Abdul Hamid Ali), Egyptian businessman. **Born** on September 23, 1923 in Cairo, Egypt. **Married,** 2 sons, 1 daughter. **Educ.:** Cairo University, Egypt; Harvard University, USA. **Dipl.:** B.Sc. in Civil Engineering. **Career:** Secretary General, Petroleum Institute, Ministry of Petroleum; Secretary General, Suez Canal Authority; former Chairman of the Board of several oil companies. **Awards:** Order of Merit (1st Class) and several other awards. **Hobbies:** Tennis and swimming. **Member:** Gezira Sporting Club. **Priv. Addr.:** 10 Giblay Street, Zamalek, Emaret Leebone, Cairo, Egypt. **Prof. Addr.:** al-Ghais al-Tabiei Enterprises Co., 2 Maidan Kasser al-Dobar, Garden City, Cairo, Egypt.

ABUBAKR (Ali, bin Saad), Saudi academic. **Born** in 1940 in Saudi Arabia. **Educ.:** Faculty of Education, Riyadh University; Wisconsin University; University of Northern Colorado, USA. **Dipl.:** B.A., M.A., Ph.D. (Education). **Career:** School teacher; Riyadh Intermediate School; Palestine Intermediate School (Riyadh); Civil Servant, Department of Publications, Public Relations and Archaeology, Ministry of Education; Assistant Lecturer, Faculty of Education, Riyadh University; now Assistant Professor of Education in the said university. **Prof. Addr.:** Faculty of Education, Riyadh University, Riyadh, Saudi Arabia.

ABUBASHA (Hassan), Egyptian politician. **Born** in 1923 in Egypt. **Married. Educ.:** Police Academy. **Career:** Held various posts in police force; Deputy Director of State Security Investigation Department (1971), Director (1975); First Assistant to Minister of Interior (1978); Minister of Interior (1982); of Local Government (1985); presently Member of the Political Bureau of the National Democratic Party. **Addr.:** Cairo, Egypt.

ABUDAWOOD (Ismail Ali, Sheikh), Saudi banker.

Born in 1335H (1916), in Jeddah, Saudi Arabia. **Educ.:** High School Certificate and private education. **Career:** President, Chamber of Commerce & Industry, Jeddah; President, Ismail A. Abudawood Establishment, Jeddah; President, Mohammed Ali Abudawood for Trade & Industry, Jeddah; Chairman, Modern Industries Co. Jeddah; Chairman, Modern Industries Co., Dammam; Chairman, Modern Products Co., Jeddah; presently Chairman, Riyadh Bank, Saudi Arabia. **Addr.:** Riyadh Bank, P.O.Box 22621, Riyadh 11416, Tel.: 4013030, Telex: 407490 RYDX SJ., Fax: 4040090, Saudi Arabia.

ABUDAYEH (Saad Salim), Jordanian academic. **Born** on Sept. 11, 1947 in Ma'an, Jordan. **Married,** 3 daughters. **Dipl.:** M.A. in General Management, Ph.D. in International Relations. **Career:** Consul, Embassy of Jordan in Egypt (1978-82); Professor, Yarmuk University, Amman (1982-); Chairman, Political Science Department, Jordan University; Member of the Arab Historians 1984; Member Arab Organization for Political Science; Member of Jordan Union Writer; Secretary for Jordan Pakistan Friendship Association. **Publ.:** 22 books about Jordan and Arab Foreign Policy: Ma'an, A Study on the place, Decision Taking in Jordan Foreign Policy; Arab Issues; The Arab and the Turks after 1923; the Diplomacy of Desert; the History of the Arab Legion; Jordan Political Thought... etc. **Hobbies:** Walking and Reading. **Prof. Addr.:** P.O.Box 926075, Telefax: (9626)5345758, Amman 11110, Jordan.

ABUEMMA (Abdulrahman Mohammad), Saudi University Professor. **Born** in 1950 at Al'ula. **Dipl.:** B.Sc. (Mathematics); Ph.D. (Probality and Statistics). **Career:** Research Assistant (Demonstrator), King Saud University (1973); Assistant Professor (1978), Associate Professor (1987) and Professor (1991), Faculty of Sciences, King Saud University; Head of Statistics Department, Vice-Dean of College of Graduate Studies (1983-1987), Vice-Dean, College of Science (1988-1992), Dean since 1993, King Saud University, Riyad; elected member, International Statistical Institute of Statistics; member, Bernoulli Statistical Society, Statistics and Institute of Mathematical Statistics (U.S.A.), member of the editorial board of three International Journals in Statistics. **Publ.:** a wide range of papers in scientific journals and conferences. **Addr.:** Faculty of Science, King Saud University, P.O.Box 2455, Tel.: 4676266, Riyadh 11451, Saudi Arabia.

ABUFURAYWAH (Musa, Ahmad), Libyan statesman. **Son** of Ahmed Abu Furaywah **and** Mrs. Abu Furaywah. **Career:** Director General, Ministry of Planning; Minister of Planning (1976-77); Secretary for Planning, General People's Committee (1977-80); former Secretary of the General People's Committee for Economy and Light Industries (1980). **Addr.:** Tripoli, Libya.

ABUGARBIA (Bahjat), Palestinian politician. **Born** in 1925 in Hebron, Palestine. **Career:** Former Member of the Baath Party in Syria; Member of first Palestine Liberation Organization Executive Committe (1964); formed Popular Struggle Front (PPSF) together with Dr. Samir Ghosha, PSF representative, Central Committee of the Palestine Resistance Movement (later PLO) in 1970; Elected Member of PLO Executive Committee following PPSF affiliation to Fatah in July 1971; PSF joined Arab Liberation Front (ALF) PFLP and PFLP General Command (PFLP-GC) in the Rejection Front in 1973; Owner of a printing press in Jordan (1984-). **Addr.:** Amman, Jordan.

ABUGHARIB (Ali Haidar, Y.), Egyptian physician. **Born** in 1923 at Sohag, Egypt. **Married,** six children. **Educ.:** Cairo University, Egypt (1943-51); London School of Hygiene and Tropical Medicine, London University, UK (1955-56); Calcutta University, India Institute of Public Health (1958-61). **Dipl.:** M.B., B.Ch., D.Sc. **Career:** Superintendent, Provincial Government Hospitals, Ministry of Health, Cairo (1952-55); Lecturer, High Institute of Public Health, University of Alexandria, Egypt (1956-58); Team Leader, World Health Organisation (WHO) Cholera Control Team, Inter Regional HQ, stationed in Calcutta and Manila; Team Leader, WHO Intercountry Communicable Diseases Control Team, Western Pacific Region, Manila, Philippines (1967-71); Regional Adviser for Communicable Diseases Control, WHO Regional Office for Africa, Brazzaville, Congo (1971-74); Regional Adviser and Chief, Communicable Diseases Control, WHO Regional Office for Africa, Brazzaville, Congo (1974); Director of Disease Prevention and Control, African Region of WHO (since 1979); Consultant National Academy of Sciences, Medical Centre, Washington D.C. (1963) (temporary honorary assignment for co-authorship of a publication). **Winner** of the National Prize on Medical Research for 1963 by the High Council of Medical Research, Ministry of Scientific Research, Cairo. **Member** of the Egyptian Public Health Association; Fellow of the Royal Society for Tropical Medicine, London, UK. **Publ.:** numerous articles on research and control of tropical diseases and health problems, in English, French, German, in medical periodicals in USA, England, India, Germany and Egypt. **Member of:** Alexandria Sporting Club and Clayman Sporting Club, Brazzaville, Congo. **Sports:** swimming, running, riding. **Addr.:** World Health Organisation, P.O.B. 6, Tel. 813860/5, Brazzaville, Congo.

ABUGHAZALA (Dawud, Sulaiman), Jordanian civil servant. **Born** on December 1, 1932 in Amman. **Married. Educ.:** American University of Beirut, Lebanon; London University, UK; **Dipl.:** diploma in politics and history (1935); LL.B. (1940); Lawyers Association Permit (1942) from Lincoln's Inn, London, UK. **Career:** Judge in Palestine (1948-51), Jerusalem Appeal Courts (1951-52), judge seconded to khartoum High Court (1956-59); Director General of Aqaba Port Authority (1959-61); Governor of Jerusalem (1961) and (1963-65); Minister of Communications (1962); Ambassador to Spain (1966); Ambassador to

Iran (1967); Member, Court of Cassation (1971); Now retired. **Awards:** Order of Holy Sepulchre (1st class); Independence Medal (1st class); Star of Jordan (2nd Class). **Priv. Addr.:** Shmessani, Tel.: 667468, Amman, Jordan.

ABUGHAZALA (Field Marshal Mohamad Abdul Halim), Egyptian military commander and politician. **Born** in 1930 at Al-Bihaira, Egypt. **Married**, five children. **Educ.:** USA Army War College, War College of Egypt. **Dipl.:** M.A. in Economics, M.A. in Military Science. **Career:** Commander of Artillery Brigade (1968), Commander of Artillery Division (1969); Commander of the Artillery of the 2nd Field Army (1972); Chief of the Artillery Corps. (1972); Director of the Military Intelligence and Reconnaisance Department (1974); Defence Attaché, Washington, USA (1976); Chief of Staff of the Egyptian Armed Forces (1980); Minister of Defence and Military Production (1981); Chief of Defence Staff (1980); Commander in Chief of the Egyptian Armed Forces (since 1981); Minister of Defence and Military Production (1981); Field Marshal (1982); Deputy Prime Minister and Minister of Defence and Military Production (1982 to 1993); Assistant to the President of Egypt (since 1989 to present). **Publ.:** "Soviet Military Strategy"; "History of the Art of War" (five volumes); "The Guns Opened Fire at Noon"; "The October War"; "Mathematics and Warfare". **Decor.:** Order of the Republic, 1st Class; Order of the Star of Honor; The Memorial Order of the UAR Establishment; The Liberation Order; The October 6th Medal; Medal of the 20th Anniversary of the Revolution; Medal of Long Service and Exemplariness, 1st Class; Medal of the 10th Anniversary of the Revolution; The Army Day Medal; The Muhammad Ali Memorial Medal; The Distinguished Service Ribbon; The Training Ribbon; The Victory Ribbon; The Independence Ribbon; The Evacuation Ribbon. **Sports:** Tennis, basketball, soccer. **Hobbies:** Reading, chess. **Addr.:** Presidency of the Republic, Heliopolis, Cairo, Egypt.

ABUGHAZALA (Fouad), Former Egyptian Minister of Industry. **Born** in 1925, Cairo. **Educ.:** Faculty of Engineering, Cairo University. **Dipl.:** B.Sc. (Mechanical Engineering). **Career:** Appointed to the Board of Directors, Steel Projects Company (1960); Chairman of the Board of Directors, Egyptian Metal Structures Company (1968); Director, War Factory 333; Deputy Chairman, Iron and Steel Complex (1976-78); Chairman, Iron and Steel Complex (1978-82); Minister of Industry (1983). **Decor.:** Merit Medal (A.R.E.); Presidency Medal (1965); Medal of Merit (1st class) in 1968; French Medal of Merit (awarded for his services to metallurgy). **Addr.:** Cairo, Egypt.

ABUGHAZALA (Hani, Fouad), Saudi engineer. **Born** in 1943 in Jeddah (Saudi Arabia). **Dipl.:** B.Sc. (Civil Engineering). **Career:** Civil Engineer, Municipalities Agency; Head, Technical Department, Abha Municipality, then Vice-President of the said Municipality; now Director of Town-Planning and Engineering Administration, Southern Province. **Hobbies:** Reading and travel. **Prof. Addr.:** Town-Planning Office, Tel. 6352, Abha, Saudi Arabia.

ABUGHAZALA (Hayfa, Shaker), Jordanian educator. **Born** in 1945 in Yafa, Palestine. **Married**, 3 children. **Educ.:** Jordan University, Jordan Jesuit University. **Dipl.:** M.A. in Educational Guidance, Ph.D. in Education. **Career:** Member, Psychological Guidance Department, Ministry of Education; Head, Educational Guidance Department, Ministry of Education (1981-); Secretary, Union of Jordanian Women. **Publ.:** "Effective Teaching" (1981), "An Approach to Education" (1983), "Educational Measures" (1983), "A Guide for the Educator" (1985). **Hobbies:** Writing and Reading. **Prof. Addr.:** Ministry of Education, P.O.Box 9796, Amman, Jordan.

ABUGHAZALEH (Talal), Jordanian public accountant and consultant. **Born** on April 22, 1938 in Jaffa, Palestine. **Married** to Nuha Salameh in 1963 in Beirut, Lebanon, 4 children: Luay, Qusay, May, Jumana. **Educ.:** American University of Beirut (Lebanon). **Dipl.:** BB.A. (Bachelor of Business Administration-Honors) (1960). **Career:** Audit Clerk in a accounting firm (1960); Audit Manager (1965); Partner (1970); Deputy Chairman (1971); Chairman Elect. (1972); Founder of Talal Abu-Ghazaleh & Co., TAG (Public Accountants) (1973); Founder of TMP Agents (Trade Marks and Patents Registration 1972); Founder of Talal Abu-Ghazaleh Associates, TAGA (Management & Industrial Consultants) (1974); Chairman of Price Waterhouse Abu-Ghazaleh & Co. PWAG (Public Accountants and Management Consultants (1974-80); Founder of Arab International Projects Co., AIPC (Projects & Investment Banking Advisory Services (1978); Chairman of the Board of Directors of Talal Abu-Ghazaleh International (TAGI, UK) holding company for the group operating firms TAG, TAGA, TMP, AIPC, incorporating 29 branch offices in the Arab World, Sponsor: The Talal Abu Ghazaleh Graduate School of Business and Management at the American University of Beirut (1978); Member of the Board of Trustees of the American University of Beirut (1979); Representative, ASPIP, observer at the World Intellectual Property Organization (WIPO), Geneva (1987); Representative ASCA at the UN, Intergovernmental Working Group of Experts of International Standards of Accounting and Reporting (ISAR), New York (1989); Representative, The Arab Society for the Protection of Industrial Property, (ASPIP), consultative status, at the U.N. Economic and Social Council, N.Y. (1989); Chairman, Steering Committee for the Newly Industrialized and Developing Countries Affairs, International Accounting Standards Committee (IASC) (1989); Representative, The Arab Society of Certified Accountants, (ASCA) consultative status at the U.N. Economic and Social Council, N.Y. (1991); Chairman of: Abu-Ghazaleh for Legal Services (ABLE) (Legal Services); Abu-Ghazaleh for Intellectual Property; Abu Ghazaleh Projects Co.; Abu Ghazaleh Consulting Co.; Al-Dar Consulting Co. (ADCO) (Project

Management and Financial Consultancy); The First Project Management Co. (FBMC) (Project Management Consultants); Talal Abu-Ghazaleh International Management, Inc. (TAGIMI) (Management Consultants); Al-Dar General Trading Co. (ADTCO) (Business Advisors). TAGI is listed with the World Bank Register of accredited auditors and consultants. He has conducted seminars and speeches in various international forums "Doing Business" in the Middle East, covering accounting, consulting, intellectual property, business, taxation and strategy. Appointed Chairman, Intergovernmental Working Group of Experts on International Standards of Accounting and Reporting – New York (1993-1994). **Member:** Member of the Council/International Federation of Accountants (IFAC), U.S.A. (1992); Member of the Board, International Accounting Standards Committee (IASC), London (1987-1990); Member of the Board, International Auditing Practices Committee (IAPC), New York (1987-1990). Founding Member, Arab Non-Governmental Organizations Committee, Cairo (1990); Member, International Policy Board, Grant Thoronton International, Chicago (1990); Member of the Chartered Institute of Arbitrators - UK; Founder and present chairman of the Arab Management Society (AMS), New York (1989); Founder and present chairman of the Arab Society for the Protection of Industrial Property (ASPIP), Munich (1987); Board Member of University of Houston, Center for Applied Technology (1986); Founder member of Federation of Consultants of Islamic Countries, Istanbul (1986); Member of the Arab Thought Forum (1985); Founder and Board Member of the Egyptian International Business Center in Cairo (1985); Founder and present chairman of the Arab Society of Certified Accountants (ASCA), London (1985); Chairman of the First Arab International Accountancy Conference, Government of Keck Center for International Strategic Studies in Los Angeles (1984). **Intellectual Property and Legal Services:** Member of the Founders Committee – The International Society of Arab Arbitrators, London (1991); Member of Arbitration System of the Euro – Arab Chambers of Commerce (since 1991); Guest Lecturer at Georgetown University, Washington D.C. (1988-1990); President, The Arab Society for the Protection of Industrial Property (ASPIP), Munich (since 1987). **Publ.:** Member of the Supervisory Board of the following magazines: Protection of Industrial Property, Jordan; Trademark World, UK; Patent World, UK; al-Inmaa al-Arabi, Jordan; Copyright World, UK; Arab Certified Accountants, Jordan Author: "Taxation in the Arab Countries; The Abu-Ghazaleh English-Arabic Dictionary of Accounting and "Trademark Laws in the Arab Countries". Member of the Editorial Board of the following magazines: World Intellectual Property Report, U.S.A.; The trademark Reporter, Jordan. **Honors and Awards:** Doctor of Humane Letters, The Canusius College of Buffalo, New York (1988); Decoration of the Republic of Tunisia, Tunis (1985); Chevalier de la Legion d'Honneur, France (1985); Appreciation Certificate and Coat of Arms of the Kuwaiti Association of Accountants (1982); The Gulf Mercury International Award by Prime Minister of H.H. Sheikh Khalifa bin Salman al-Khalifa, State of Bahrain (1978); Decoration of Independence by H.M. King Hussain, Jordan (1967). **Sports:** Swimming and Tennis. **Member:** Several Profession and Business Associations. **Prof. Addr.:** Talal Abu-Ghazaleh International, Cairo Office, 23 Wadi el-Nil Str., Mohandesseen City, P.O.Box 55 Mohammed Farid 11518, and P.O.Box 96 Imbaba 12411, Tel.: 3462951, 3479952, Fax: 3445729, Cairo, Egypt.

ABUHAJAR (Abdul-Wahab, Abdul Rahman (Bou Hadjar), Formerly Saudi Arabian airlines executive. **Born** on Oct. 20, 1933, in Jeddah, Saudi Arabia. **Son** of: Abdul-Rahman Mohammed **and** Mrs., Habibah Mohammed (el-Gharraz). **Married** on March 22, 1972 to Miss Elham Ibrahim el-Gharraz, 3 children: Ahmed, Alaa and Amal. **Dipl.:** Baccalaureate, Mecca (1952); B.A. in Sociology and Economics, Cairo University (1957). **Career:** Clerk, Arab Bank Ltd., Jeddah (1/12/1951- 20/10/53); Secondary School Tutor and Jeddah District Supervisor, Ministry of Education, Jeddah (1957-58); Systems Head office Manager, Riyadh Bank, Jeddah (1958-62); Director General, Printing, Press & Publ. Corp., Jeddah (1963-64); Corporate Secretary General, Saudi Arabian Airlines, Jeddah (1964-92); Managing Director to Saudi Institute of Popular Education (Girls' School), Jeddah (National Benevolent Institution) (12/8/1957- 22/8/1977). **Member:** Saudi Arabian Airlines Sport Club, Jeddah; American Association of Individual Investors (AAII) Chicago, Illinois, U.S.A.; Institute of Directors (IOD), London, U.K.; Fortune Book Club, Camp Hill, PA. U.S.A. **Publ.:** Author of some articles. **Addr.:** Ibn Battoutah St., al-Nuzlah, P.O.Box 42203, Jeddah 21541, Tel. (02)689-2652, (02)687-7146, Saudi Arabia, and c/o Saudi Airlines, BRD-DIR-C.C. 111 JED, P.O.Box 620, Jeddah 21231, Saudi Arabia.

ABUHAMAD (William, Youssef), Engineer. **Born** in 1926 in Haifa, Palestine. **Son** of Youssef Abu-Hamad (civil contractor) **and** Mrs. Najla Habiby. **Married** in 1961 in Beirut, Lebanon to Leila Habayeb, three sons: Bassam, Wassim and Issam. **Dipl.:** Degree in Mechanical Engineering. **Career:** Project Manager, Mothercat Co. Ltd. (1951-72); In 1972 established "Mechanical Contracting and Services Co. WLL" (mechanical & civil contractors; Refinery and Petrochemical construction & shutdown maintenance; Real estate development and construction); Founder/Chairman, Delmon Development Corporation, U.S.A.; Executive Director/Partner, Mechanical Contracting & Services Co. WLL, Bahrain and Industrial Services Co. WLL. **Sports:** Swimming, **Hobby:** Playing bridge (cards). **Credit Card:** American Express; Visa Card; Master Card. **Prof. Addr.:** M.C.S.C.; P.O. Box 5238, Tel.: 623723, Telex: 9275 MCSC BN, Manama, Bahrain. **Priv. Addr.:** Tel.: 591144, Manama, Bahrain.

ABUHAMDAN (Jamal), Jordanian writer and administrator. **Born** in 1944 in Amman, Jordan. **Educ.:** Licence in Law. **Career:** Broadcaster and Producer in Cultural Section of Jordan Radio (1966); Lawyer (1969); Information and Publications Manager for ALIA (Royal Jordanian Airlines) (since 1969); Writer. **Publ.:** "The Second Exodus", a political essay (1967), Beirut; several short story collections and plays; "Love Poems of the World", translated with introduction, Beirut; collection of children's stories; political and literary articles in Lebanese and Jordanian press. **Member:** of Jordanian Writers Association; founding committee member of Arab Theatre Federation. **Hobbies:** travel, writing. **Priv. Addr.:** Tel. 71405, Amman, Jordan.

ABUHASSAN (Khaldum, Abdul Rahman), Jordanian businessman. **Born** in 1940 in Amman, Jordan. **Son** of Abdul Rahman Abu Hassan **and** Mrs. Abu Hassan. **Married**, four children. **Educ.:** American University of Beirut, Lebanon; University of Denver, Colorado, USA. **Dipl.:** B.A. and M.A. in Business Administration. **Career:** Chairman, General Manager, Jordan Insurance Co. Ltd.; Deputy General Manager, Jordan Insurance Co. Ltd., Jordan Gulf Bank, Jordan Public Mining Co. Ltd., Jordan National Committee, International Chamber of Commerce. Deputy Chairman, Jordan Paper and Cardboard Co. Ltd.; President, Amman Chamber of Industry. **Prof. Addr.:** P.O.Box 1800, Amman, Jordan.

ABUHUSSEIN (Hassan Hamza al-Marzouqi), Saudi civil servant. **Born** in 1936, in Mecca, Saudi Arabia. **Dipl.:** B.Sc. (Accountancy); M.A. (Public Administration). **Career:** Chief Financial Analyst, Ministry of Finance; Director of Planning Bureau of Agriculture Directorate; Director of General Administration, Ministry of Planning; Director of Private Secretariat of Minister of Pilgrimage; Director of Religious Affairs and Libraries Department; deputized for the Minister of Planning on the Board of the Industrial Research and Development Center; Director General of Endowments, Mecca; Supervisor of Islamic Orientation Magazine; attended several FAO conferences; on Economy, Makkah; Conference on The Message of the Mosque; Conference of Islamic World Affairs, Sri Lanka; the 3 conferences of Ministers of Awqaf and Islamic Affairs. **Addr.:** Directorate of Endowments, Tel. 5434300, 5426702 (Office); and 5739716, 5438600 (Home), Mecca, Saudi Arabia.

ABUISMAIL (Ahmad), Egyptian economist, politician. **Born** in 1915 in Egypt. **Educ.:** Cairo University, Birmingham University, UK. **Dipl.:** B.Comm. (1937); Ph.D. in Economics (1942). **Career:** Professor and Dean of Economics, Cairo University; Director of State Railways and the Maritime Transport Organisation; elected to the People's Assembly (1971); Chairman of the Planning and Budget Committee; appointed to the National Council for Production and Economic Affairs (1974); Minister of Finance (1975-76). **Act.:** Accompanied the late President Sadat of Egypt to the Salzburg meeting with President Ford (1975); formerly, Chairman, Cairo Far East Bank. **Prof. Addr.:** 104 Corniche el-Nil, P.O.Box 757, Cairo, Egypt.

ABUISMAIL (Tewfick), Egyptian politician **Born** in 1929 in Dakahliya Governorate, Egypt. **Educ.:** Military Academy, Faculty of Commerce, Cairo University. **Dipl.:** Military Academy diploma Bachelor of Commerce (1960), B.Sc. (Marketing) (1965). **Career:** Joined Shell Petroleum Company, Cairo (1966); Executive, Ministry of Tourism; Commercial Attaché, Egyptian Embassy, Federal Republic of Germany until 1970; elected member of the People's Assembly (1976); assigned to the Presidency of the Republic (1981); Minister of Tourism and Civil Aviation until 2 September 1982 following Cabinet reshuffle. **Addr.:** Cairo, Egypt.

ABUJABER (Farah), Jordanian businessman. **Born** in 1919 in Salt, Jordan. **Married**, 4 sons, 2 daughters. **Educ.:** Accountancy in Amman, International Relations in Beirut, Lebanon. **Career:** Loans Manager, Board of Development; Member of Parliament (1947-); Member of Parliament third Period (1958); Member of Parliament last Period from 1967 to 1987; Kentucky Colonel, U.S.A.; Deputy Sheriff in Gaines Ville, Florida, U.S.A.; General Manager and Proprietor, Jordan Marble Company. **Medals:** Medal of the Sacred tomb from the Patriarch of Jerusalem; Medal of Colonel from the last King of Greece. **Member:** King Hussein Club, Amman. **Prof. Addr.:** Ibn al-Roomi Street, Jabal Amman, P.O.Box 172 Amman, Jordan.

ABUJABER (Kamel S.), Jordanian Professor. **Born** in 1932 in Amman, Jordan. **Son** of Mr. Saleh Abu Jaber (landowner) **and** Mrs. Aneeseh Zorob. **Married** in 1957 at Corning, N.Y. (U.S.A.) to Miss Loretta Pacifico, 2 children: Dr. Linda M.D. (1961), Nyla (1965). **Educ.:** B.A. (1960), Syracuse University, U.S.A.; Ph.D. (1965), Syracuse University, U.S.A. (Political Science); Post-Doctoral studies in Oriental Studies at Princeton University (1962-1963). **Career:** Lecturer, Syracuse University (1965); Assistant Professor, University of Tennessee (1965-1967); Associate Professor, Smith College (1967-1969); Associate Professor, University of Jordan (1969-1971); Professor, University of Jordan (1971-1972); Dean, Faculty of Economics and Commerce (April 1972-May 1973); Minister of National Economy, Jordan Cabinet (May 1973-November 1973); Dean, Faculty of Economics and Commerce (1973-1979); Professor, University of Jordan (1979-1980); Director, Queen Alia Jordan Social Welfare Fund (1980-1982); President, Council of Consultation, Technical Services and Studies Center, University of Jordan (1982-1984); Director, Strategic Studies Center, University of Jordan (1984-1985); Professor, Jordan University (1985); Visiting Professor, Emory University-Carter Center Atlanta, GA.

(Jan-May, 1989); Minister of Foreign Affairs, Jordan Cabinet (Oct. 1991- May 1993); Senator, Jordanian Upper House of Parliament (1993-). **Biography Recognition:** Who's Who in the Arab World; The International Who's Who in the Arab World; Contemporary Authors; Dictionary of International Biographies; The International Who's Who of Intellectuals; The International Directory of Distinguished Leadership; The International Who's Who of Contemporary Achievement; 5.000 Personalities of the World; The International Book of Honour. **Work and Publ.:** Editor, «Journal of Arab Association of Political Science»; Editorial Board: «Al-Nadwah», Amman, Jordan; «International Third World Studies Journal And Review», Omaha, Nebraska; Editorial Board: «International Third World Studies»; Academic: Adviser Board, «Institute on Comparative Political & Economic Systems», Georgetown University, Washington, D.C.; Member Bd. of Trustees and Secretary General, Royal Society, for the Conservation of nature (since 1977). Member Bd. of Trustees and Secretary General, Jordan World Affairs Council (since 1978); HAYA Children's Center (since 1985); Counsellor for West Asia of the International Union for Conservation of Nature (since 1991). **Books:** Author of: «The Arab Ba'th socialist Party: History, Ideology and Organization», Syracuse, Syracuse University Press, (1966) (English); «United States of America and Israel», Cairo, Mh'had al-Buhuth wa al-Dirasat al-Arabiyyah (1971) (Arabic); «Israeli Political System», Cairo, Ma'had al-Buhuth wa al-Dirasat al-Arabiyyah (1973) (Arabic); «The Jordanians and the People of the Jordan», Published in Amman, Royal Scientific Society (1980); «Economic Potentialities of Jordan», Tokyo, Institute of Developing Economics (1984); «Political Parties and Elections In Israel», Amman, Dar al-Anwar (1985) (Arabic); «The Palestinians: People of the Olive Tree», Amman, Jordan, Institute for M.E. Studies (1993); **Contributor Co-Author:** Co-Author of «Government and Politics of the Contemporary Middle East», Homewood, Dorsey Press (1970), (Editor, Tareq Ismael); «Concise Encyclopaedia of the Middle East», Washington, Public Affairs Press (1973) (Editor, Mehdi Heravi); «Modern Socialism», New York, Harper Torch Books, (1968) (Editor, Massimo Salvadori); «The Arab-Israeli Confrontation», 1967 Evanston, North western University Press (1969) (Editor, Ibrahim Abu Lughod); «The Jordan Five Year Economic Development Plan (1976-1980) (with others); «The Beduins of Jordan: A People in Transition», Amman, Royal Scientific Society Press (1987); «The Five Year Planned Development of the Balqa - Amman Regions» (1981-1985), Amman (1980); «The Beduins of Jordan» in The Future of Pastoral Peoples, Ottawa (1981) (Eds. J.G. Galaty, D. Aronson and P.C. Salzman); «Social Change in Jordan» Contemporary Mediterranean World, New York Preager (1983) (Editor, C.G. Pinkele and A. Pollis); «The Iran-Iraq War: Regime Security and Regional Security» Mohammad Ayoob, ed., London, Croom Helm (1986); «Jordan (Several articles on Jordan)», London, Middle East Economic Digest Book (1983); «Jordan's View of the Regional Factors Affecting Peace in the Middle East», in Political and Economic Trends in the Middle East, Boulder, Westview Press (1985); «The nature of the State in the Middle East», Exeter (1987); «Middle East Institutions: The Concept of the State», Tokyo, International University of Japan. The Institute of Middle Eastern Studies Publications (1989); «Jordan and the Middle East Crises». London, Published by SOAS (1990); «Strategic Studies and The Middle East: A View From the Region» In, The Contemporary Study of the Arab World, eds. E.L. Sullivan and J.S. Ismael, Ed The University of Alberta Press (1991); «Middle East Conflicts: The Religious Factor». Leeds, to be published by the Center for Arab Gulf Studies, University of Exeter (1990); «The Hashemite Kingdom of Jordan» in T.Y. Ismael and J.S. Ismael ed.. Politics and Governments of the Middle East and North Africa, Miami, Florida, International University Press (1991); «The Teaching of Political Science in Jordan», to be published by the International Political Science Association (1990); «Security and Development: The Case of Jordan», to be published by McGill University (1990); «Iraq: An Emerging Regional Power?» C. Davis, ed. After The War, Iran Iraq and The Arab Gulf, London, Cavden Publications (1990); «The Arab-Israeli and the Iran Iraq Conflicts; a View From Jordan», in Politics and the Economy in Jordan, ed. by R. Wilson, London and New York, In Jordan, ed. by R. Wilson, London and New York, Center for Near and Middle Eastern Studies (1991); «The Role of Germany in the Formation of the New World Order» Amman, Arab Thought Forum (1993); «Strategic Studies and the Middle East: A View From the Region», E.L. Sullivan and J.S. Ismael, eds., The Contemporary Study of the Arab World, Edmonton, The University of Alberta Press (1991). **Awards and Honours:** Jordan Order of the Star, First Class (Kawkab order) (1976); Fellow, Aspen Institute for Humanistic Values (1978); Honorary Doctorate, University of Buenos Aires, Argentina (1980); Silver medallion, Queen Alia social Welfare Fund (1981); Honorary Member, Jordanian Arab University Women's Alumni (1984); Swedish Royal Order of the Polar Star, Commander (1989); Order of the Sacred Tomb, First Class, Orthodox Patriarchate of Jerusalem and the Holy Land (1992). **Hobby:** Reading. **Prof. Addr.:** Jordan Institute for Middle East Studies, P.O.Box 5407, Tel.: 814526, Amman. Jordan.

ABUJABER (Raouf, Sa'd), Jordanian businessman. **Born** in 1925 in al-Salt, Jordan. **Son** of Sa'd Farhan Abujaber **and** Mrs. née Bassima Jurji Kawar. **Married** in 1962 to Mireille Gabriel Seikaly, 3 children: Bassima, Ziad and Marwan. **Educ:** Bishop's School, Amman, American University of Beirut, B.B.A. 1964 Jordan University M.A. Modern History 1984 Oxford University D.Phil. Modern History 1987 **Career:** Partner (Holding Company) Sa'd Abujaber & Sons; Underwriter at Lloyds; President, United Insurance Co. Ltd., General Manager, General Investment Co. Ltd., Honorary Consul-General of the

Netherlands, Amman, Jordan, and Dean of Honorary Consular Corps, President Arab Orthodox Society President YMCA Jordan, Member Higher Education Council. **Award's:** Officer and Commandor of the Netherlands Order of Orange Nassau. **Publ.:** "Pioneers over Jordan" London 1989 and over fifty articles and Papers. **Hobbies:** Collection of rare books, rare coins and swords and daggers. **Prof. Addr:** P.O.Box 312 Tel: 5625161/2/3, 5637967, Telex 21323 JO. Fax: 5628167 Amman Jordan, **Priv. Addr:** Zahran Str. Tel: 5642635, 5634460 Amman Jordan.

ABUKHADER (George, Nicola), Palestinian businessman. **Born** on February 7, 1939 in Cairo, Egypt. **Married,** 3 Children: Isabelle, Nicola and Shireen. **Educ.:** Terra Santa College, Amman-Jordan; American University of Beirut, Lebanon. **Dipl.:** B.B.A. **Career:** Businessman involved in the automotive spare parts trade since 1960; also Chairman of the Abu Khader Group of Companies including Nicola Abu Khader & Sons Co., Auto parts, Motor Vehicle Trading Co. Ltd., MMC buses and Trucks and others. **Sports:** Soccer, Tennis, Swimming and basketball. **Hobby:** Travelling. **Clubs:** Rotary Club, Orthodox Club, Amman, Sport City Club, Royal Automobile Club. **Member:** The Orthodox Educational Society (Amman); Board of the Orthodox Club, Amman. **Credit Card:** American Express. **Prof. Addr.:** P.O.Box 739 Amman 11118, Tel.: (962-6) 402-2141, Fax: (962-6) 402-2147, e-mail: akgedp@go.com.jo Amman-Jordan.

ABUKHADRA (Faisal), Saudi businessman and banker. **Born** in 1934 in Jaffa, Palestine. **Son** of Hilmi Abu-Khadra. **Married,** 2 children. **Dipl.:** Bachelor of Arts (Economics). **Career:** President, Overseas Development Promotion; Representative of Petroleum and Civil Engineering Companies, Highways Maintenance, Construction in Saudi Arabia and the Middle East; Banque des Affaires Franco-Arabe SA (BAFA); President, Orbit Establishment (Riyadh, al-Khobar, Jeddah; Beirut, Paris). **Hobbies:** Horse Races, Breeding of Arabic Race Horses, Farming. **Member:** Racing Club (Beirut), Racing Club (Paris), Golf Club (Beirut). **Addr.:** Jeddah, Saudi Arabia.

ABUKHADRA (Yusef, Rabah), Lebanese Banker. **Born** on February 1, 1947 in Yafa. **Married,** 3 sons. **Education:** American University of Beirut, Lebanon; Michigan State University, USA. **Diplomas:** B.A. (in Business Administration); M.A. (in Business Administration). **Career:** started as Trainee at Citibank in Beirut (1970-71); Assistant Middle East Representative at Baring Brothers & Co. of London, and Lombard Odier & Cie of Geneva (1971-75); Manager of Arab Company for Trading Securities, Kuwait (1975-78); Manager at Morgan Stanley (London and New York) (1978-83); Executive Director of Arabian Investment Banking Corporation (INVESTCORP) (since 1983). Founder Member of Arab Bankers Association UK; Member of the Management Committee, INVESTCORP Bank (1983-). **Professional Address:** INVESTCORP International Limited, 48 Grosvenor Street, London W1Y 6DH, England. **Private Address:** 48 Chelsea Square, London SW3 6LH, England.

ABUKHASHABA (Abdelmalik Abbas), Saudi academic. **Born** in 1945 in Mecca, Saudi Arabia. **Dipl.:** in Mechanical Engineering. **Career:** Director, Central Workshop for the Industrial Area in Riyadh (1971); Chief of Design Department, Industrial Studies and Development Centre, Riyadh (1978); Director, Administration Department, Faculty of Engineering, King Abdulaziz University and Assistant Professor of Mechanical Engineering since 1980; Vice Chairman, Mechanical Engineering Department, Faculty of Engineering, King Abdulaziz University. **Publ.:** Several individual and joint research topics on metal cutting, material behaviour, wear, planning, manufacturing techniques, computer techniques along with other general topics. **Addr.:** King Abdulaziz University, Faculty of Engineering, P.O.Box 9027, Tel. 6870248 (Office), 6680793 (Home), Jeddah, Saudi Arabia.

ABUKHEIR (Osman, Haga), Sudanese legal adviser. **Born** in 1945, at Shendi, Sudan. **Son** of Haga Abu Kheir from Gali Tribe. **Married** in 1976, 4 sons. **Educ.:** University of Khartoum. **Dipl.:** LL.B. (1971). **Career:** Legal Practice (1971-72); Judiciary ultimately provincial judge (1972-81); Legal Adviser, Industrial Bank of Sudan (on secondment) (1977-81); Permanent Appointment in 1981. **Hobbies:** Reading, swimming and music. **Addr.:** Industrial Bank of Sudan, P.O.Box 1722, Tel. 71984, 71208, Khartoum, Sudan.

ABUKURAH (Abdulghani, Abdallah), Jordanian engineer. **Born** on April 4, 1935 in Amman (Jordan). **Son** of Abdullah Abdo (businessman) **and** Mrs., née Jamila Murad Abukurah. **Married** to Afrah Abukurah in 1961, Amman (Jordan), 5 children: May, Abdullah, Ghassan, Khaled and Zeid. **Educ.:** Islamic College (Amman); American University in Beirut (Lebanon); Stuttgart Technical School (Germany). **Dipl.:** B.Sc. (Civil Engineering). **Career:** General Manager, Alia Royal Jordanian Airlines (1963-67); President ACE, Jordan till 1975; Chairman and President, Sigma Consulting Engineers (1975-83); now President, Engineering Consortium Consulting Engineers and Architects. **Clubs and Societies:** Royal Automobile Club, Secretary general for Islamic Educational Society. President of Jordanian Austrian Friendship Society, Member of World's Affairs Council, Member of s.o.s. **Awards:** Order of Independence, Jordan. **Credit Card:** American Express, Visa, Master Card. **Prof. Addr.:** P.O.Box 2177, Tel. 663554, 660029, 667029, 604382, Amman, and Abdulghani Abukurah Engineering Consortium, Amman, Jordan **Priv. Addr.:** P.O.Box 2177, Tel. 669920, Amman, Jordan.

ABUL (Hamad, Abdallah), Bahraini businessman. **Born** on December 26, 1939 in Muharraq, Bahrain. **Mar-**

ried, 2 sons, 2 daughters. **Educ.:** International College, Beirut, American University of Beirut. **Dipl.:** B.A. in Economics (1965). **Career:** International Auditor and Head of Internal Auditing, Abu Dhabi, Ministry of Finance (1965-70); Head of the Department of Economic Studies, Bahrain Chamber of Commerce and Industry (1970-72); Member of Parliament, Bahrain (1972-75); Proprietor of Zenj Establishment (1975-); Chairman, Bahrain Light Industries Co. (1980-); Member of the Board of Directors of Bahrain Chamber of Commerce and Industry (1985-). **Prof. Addr.:** P.O.Box 236, and P.O.Box 267, Manama, Bahrain.

ABUL-HAMAYEL (Mohamad A., Dr.), Saudi Manager of the Water Resources and Environment Division of the Research Institute and an Associate Professor in the Chemical Engineering Department of the King Fahd University of Petroleum and Minerals, Dhahran, Saudi Arabia. **Born** on 2 February 1947. **Dipl.:** He received a PhD degree in Chemical Engineering from Oklahoma State University in 1979. He has earned MS and BS degrees in Chemical Engineering from the University of California at Santa Barbara and Arizona State University respectively in the years 1973 and 1970. **Carrer:** Dr. Abul-Hamayel has been associated with the King Fahd University of Petroleum and Minerals since 1979. He is an Associate Professor since 1984 in the Chemical Engineering Department. Prior to Joining the Water Resources and Environment Division, Research Institute, Dr. Abul-Hamayel was Director of the Information Technology Center, KFUPM. His responsabilities included selecting, directing and developing technical and administrative staff. He has also supervised the financial and human resources systems, material management and student information systems. His research activities have also included studies on heat transfer, computation, and energy utilization. Dr. Abul-Hamayel has participated in studies which were conducted for government organizations such as, Technical Education, Rail Road Organization, Ministry of Health, Ministry of Higher Education, Ministry of Foreign Affairs, Islamic University in Madina, Hassa Irrigation and Drainage Authority, GCC Security Center, and GCC Training Center. Dr. Abul-Hamayel is the author and co-author of numerous research papers and technical reports. His main publications are in the areas of systems management, networking, computation, heat transfer, energy utilization and environment. He is a member of the American Institute of Chemical Engineers (AICHE), and Association of Computing Machinery. **Mailing Address:** KFUPM P.O.Box 1483, Dhahran 31261, Saudi Arabia, Tel.: 966-3-860-3232(O); 966-3-8600(R) & E.mail: hamayel @dpc.kfupm.edu.sa.

ABULATTA (Abdul Azim Abdallah), Egyptian politician, engineer. **Born** in 1925 in Egypt. **Educ.:** Alexandria University, Egypt. **Dipl.:** B.Sc. and M.Sc. in Irrigation Studies. **Career:** Deputy Director of Irrigation Works; Deputy Engineer in charge of Uganda Dam; Technical Secretary to the Minister of Works; Director of the High Dam Office in Moscow; Under Secretary for the High Dam (1964); Deputy Chairman of the Land Reclamation Authority (1970); Chairman of Land Development Projects Authority; Minister of Irrigation (1975); Minister of Ariculture and Irrigation (1976); Minister of Irrigation (1977). **Addr.:** Cairo, Egypt.

ABULEISH (Ezzat, Ibrahim), Egyptian. Professor of Anesthesiology. **Born** on 28 January 1931 at Sharkia (Egypt). **Son** of Ibrahim Abouleish (Landlord) **and** Mrs., née Aziza Ibrahim Sakr. **Married** in Cairo on 8 January 1959 to Miss Atiya Saleh, 3 children: Hassan (1961), Amr (1963), Reda (1972). **Educ.:** Amir Farouk Primary School (Cairo), Tawfikia Secondary School (Cairo), Ain-Shams University (Cairo). **Dipl.:** M.B. CH.B. (Bachelor degree of Medicine and Surgery), D.A. (Diploma of Anesthesiology), D.M. (Diploma of Internal Medicine), M.D. (Medical Doctorate, Anesthesiology). **Career:** Instructor, Assistant Professor, Associate Professor: Ain Shams University (1957-68); Instructor, Case Western Reserve University (1968-70); Assistant Professor to Professor, University of Pittsburgh (1970-82); Professor of Anesthesiology, Professor of Obstetrics & Gyn., University of Texas, Houston; Medical Director of Obstetric Anaesthesia at Hermann Hospital, Houston (1983- to present). **Work:** Published three books in Anesthesiology, several chapters in books, many medical articles. **Sports:** Swimming, tennis, racquet ball. **Hobby:** Photography. **Member:** UHCLC Club at Clear Lake, Texas. **Prof. Addr.:** Anesthesiology Dept., University of Texas, Houston 77030, USA, Tel. (713) 792-5566. **Priv. Addr.:** 16518 Brook Forest Drive, Clear Lake, Houston, Texas 77059, USA, Tel.: (713) 488-1388.

ABULELA (Saad), Sudanese businessman. **Born** in 1920 in Sudan. **Married**. **Educ.:** General. **Career:** Managing the AbulEla Trading Corp. and the AbulEla Group of Companies. Partner of his brother Abdul Salaam AbulEla. **Member** of the Advisory Board to Radio Omdurman (1954); composer and an authority on Sudanese Music. **Addr.:** Abulela Bldg., Abbas Square, P.O.Box 121, Tel. 70020, 71173, 42968, Khartoum, Sudan.

ABULFARAJ (Ghalib Hamza), Saudi Businessman **Born** in Madinah in 1931. **Diploma:** B.A. **Career:** Technical Expert, Ministry of Health; Secretariat of the Royal Court; Technical Advisor, General Directorate for Broadcasting and Press; Director General, Directorate for Press and Publications; Editor in Chief "UMM AL-QURA" newspaper; Editor in Chief "THE BROADCASTING MAGAZINE"; Editor in Chief "WEEKLY NEWS LETTER" (the first English newspaper in Saudi Arabia); Former Editor in Chief, "AL MADINAH" daily newspaper; Former Editor in Chief, "AL BILLAD" daily newspaper; Chaired the Saudi Delegation to the Council of Information Ministers at the Arab League; President, Saudi International Company for trading, Industry and Agencies. **Publications:** More than twenty novels and short stories including "From My Country", "Big House", "Red Devils", "Love is not Enough", "Strangers without Homeland", "The Lost Years", "See you Tomorrow", "The Green Demonstration", "And so Beirut is Burned", "A Woman and not Remains", "Bare Faces", "Hearts Sick of Travelling Around", "Colored Papers", "Lost Around", "Drums are beaten", "Years with Him", "No Sun over the City", "Nothing Prevents Love". **Honors:** Awards from Egypt, Lebanon and Tunisia. **Address:** P.O.Box 15157 Jeddah 21444, Fax: (966 2) 667-2700, Saudi Arabia.

ABULGASIM (Mohamad Ibrahim, Major), Sudanese politician. **Born** in 1937 at Omdurman, Sudan. **Married. Educ.:** Military Academy (1961) with rank of 2nd Lieutenant; posted to Al-Obeid; parachute course at Aldershot, UK. (1962); assisted in the setting up of a paratroop unit in Khartoum. **Career:** Minister of Local Governments (1969); Minister of Interior (1970); Assistant Prime Minister for Services; Minister of Health (1971) played important part in the establishment of the Sudanese Socialist Union (SSU); appointed Joint Deputy Secretary General of SSU (1973) Deputy Secretary General SSU (1974); Minister of Agriculture, Food and Natural Resources. Member of the Revolutionary Command Council (1969). **Addr.:** P.O.Box 285, Khartoum, Tel. 70895, Sudan.

ABULHAGGAG (Yusif, Ibrahim), Egyptian academic. **Born** on October 15, 1919 in Luxor, Egypt. **Married,** 1 son, 3 daughters. **Educ.:** Cairo University, Cairo; London University. **Dipl.:** B.A. in Geography (1944), Ph.D. in Physical Geography (1954). **Career:** Junior Geologist, in American Oil Companies in Egypt (1944-48); Assistant Lecturer and Demonstrator in Geography, Cairo and Aim Shams Universities (1948-51); Lecturer, then Professor, Ain Shams University (1955-74); Director of Middle East Research Centre, Ain Shams University (1974-77); Dean, Faculty of Arts, Ain Shams University (1977-78), Part-time Professor (1984-); Held teaching positions in Wisconsin University, Waterloo Lutheran, Riyadh, Baghdad and UAE Universities; Chairman of the Department of Geography, United Arab Emirates University, al-Ain, UAE. **Member,** The Institute of British Geographers (1951-54), the Association of American Geographers (1968-72), Member of the Board of Egyptian Geographers Society (1973-78), the National Committee of Environmental Problems, Academy of Scientific Research and Technology, Cairo, the Nasser's Lake Project (1976-78). **Publ.:** articles in the Bulletin of the Society of Geographers, Egypt. Various books in Arabic on the Physical, regional and economic geography of the Middle East and Africa. **Addr.:** 9 Murad St., Flat 9, Giza, Egypt.

ABULHASAN (Abdulrasul, Yousef), Kuwaiti businessman, **Born** in 1941 in Kuwait. **Son** of Yousef Yacoub Abul-Hasan. **Married** in 1968, 3 children. **Educ.:** Oregon State University, USA; University of Utah, USA. **Dipl.:** M.S. (1966); M.B.A. (1969). **Career:** Banking Control Supervisor, Ministry of Finance (1966); Director, General Budget (1969); Manager, Banking Supervisor Department, Central Bank of Kuwait (1979-76); former Director, United Gulf Bank EC, Manama, Bahrain. **Member:** Kuwait Economic Society; Kuwait Graduate Society. **Addr.:** Kuwait City, Kuwait.

ABULJADAYEL (Anwar, As'ad), Saudi businessman. **Born** in 1917 in Jeddah, Saudi Arabia. **Educ.:** al-Falah Secondary School, 1931. **Career:** Supervisor of Works, Alwaziriyah (1932); Clerk, Ministry of Finance, Riyadh (1935), Customs Office in al-Hejaz, Jeddah (1936); Chief Clerk of Customs Office; Assistant Director, Jeddah Customs Office, later Director, Secretary General, al-Hejaz Customs till 1953; resigned and started private business, import and distribution of furniture, jewellery, wheats and food-stuffs; has established cold storage units and an ice factory, a car service station, automatic bakeries, a biscuit factory and a fleet of transport trucks. **Publ.:** Writes daily articles in al-Madina daily newspaper titled Istraa' Intibahi (Attracted my Attention) and daily articles titled Maa al-Ahdath (With the Events) in al-Bilad daily newspaper. **Hobbies:** Reading, picnics, travel. **Addr.:** P.O.Box 72, Tel. 6479200 (Office) and 6659717 (Home), Jeddah, Saudi Arabia.

ABULJADAYEL (Nizar Anwar), Saudi businessman. **Born** in 1948 in Jeddah, Saudi Arabia. **Dipl.:** B.Sc. (Civil Engineering). **Career:** Owner of Nizar Abul Jadayel Establishment for Contracting, Real Estate and Government Contracts. **Hobbies:** Horse-breeding, hunting, reading. **Addr.:** N. Abul Jadayel Villa, Khalid Ibn al-Walid Street, Tel. 6655538 (Office) and 6653258 (Home), Jeddah, Saudi Arabia.

ABULKHAIR (Kamal, Hamdi Mahmoud), Egyptian academic. **Born** on December 16, 1922 in Cairo, Egypt. **Married,** 1 daughter. **Educ.:** Ain Shams University. **Dipl.:** B.Com. (1947), Graduate Diplomas in Organization and Management (1953), in Marketing (1954) in Stock Exchange Cotton Studies (1955), Ph.D. in Cooperatives Organization and Management (1960). **Career:** Teacher, Faculty of Commerce, Ain Shams University, Professor of Business Administration; Consultant at the Presidential Office for Economic Research (1961); Dean, High Institute of Cooperative and Managerial Studies (1961); Member of the Supreme Council for Reorganization of the Cooperative Movement (1968); Consultant to the Cooperative Committee, Central Committee of the Arab Socialist Union. Member, Higher Cooperative Supreme Council of Agriculture; Vice-Chairman, Egyptian Society for Cooperative Studies, Congress of the Arab Socialist Union (1962). **Publ.:** "Principles of Organization and Management" (1961), "The Development of the Cooperative Movement in the UAR" (1962), "Consumer's Cooperative

Structure" (1970), "The Development of Cooperative Thought" (1970), "Cooperative Application in Great Britain" (1970), "Towards Sound Cooperative Movement in the UK" (1962). **Decor.:** Order of the Republic (2nd Class), Egypt (1982). **Hobbies:** Travelling, reading and music. **Priv. Addr.:** 15 Abou El Feda Street, Zamalek, Cairo, Egypt.

ABULKHAIR (Mohamad, Nour), Saudi academic. **Born** in 1936 in Mecca (Saudi Arabia). **Educ.:** Faculty of Arts. **Dipl.:** B.A. (Geography), B.A. (Education). **Career:** school teacher; Inspector, Ministry of Education; Assistant to Director, Al-Thagr Model Schools; represented Saudi Arabia at the Tunis Conference on Problems of Education. **Publ.:** Author of a number of text-books. **Hobbies:** Reading and music. **Prof. Addr.:** al-Thagr Model Schools, Tel. 281188, Jeddah. **Priv. Addr.:** Tel. 22965, Jeddah, Saudi Arabia.

ABULMAGD (Ahmad, Kamal), Egyptian politician. **Born** in 1930 in Cairo, Egypt. **Married,** 5 children. **Educ.:** Cairo University, Egypt; Law Studies, University of Paris, France; Constitutional Law in London. **Career:** Lecturer, University of Michigan, USA; held various teaching posts in Cairo; Cultural Counsellor, Embassy to USA (1966); Member, Provisional Secretariat of the Arab Socialist Union (ASU) (1971), ASU Secretary for Youth (1971); Minister of State for Youth (1972); Chairman, ASU Committee (1973); Minister of State for Cabinet Affairs during October War (1973); Minister of Information (1974-75); ASU Secretary for Ideology (1975-82); Professor of Law, Ain Shams University, Cairo. **Addr.:** Cairo, Egypt.

ABULNAJA (Abdallah, Siraj), Saudi geologist. **Born** in 1939 in Mecca (Saudi Arabia). **Educ.:** Faculty of Science. **Dipl.:** B.Sc. (Geogory), M.Sc. (Geology). **Career:** Geologist; Director, Geological Department (1971-75); Joined the General Organisation of Geology and Natural Resources; Board member, Centre of Applied Geology; attended Second Arab Conference of Mineral Resources, Conference of General Geological Studies; now Director-General, Technical Affairs Division, Directorate General of Mineral Resources. **Prof. Addr.:** Directorate - General of Mineral Resources, Tel. 33133 Jeddah. **Priv. Addr.:** Tel. 51912, Jeddah, Saudi Arabia.

ABULNASR (Mahmoud), Egyptian diplomat. **Born** on June 23, 1931 in Cairo, Egypt. **Married,** 2 children. **Educ.:** Faculty of Law, Cairo University; Institute of Higher International Studies, University of Paris. **Dipl.:** Bachelor of Laws; Graduate, University of Paris. **Career:** attached to the Egyptian Embassy to France (1955-56); Consul, Egyptian Consulate in Genoa (Italy) (1957-59); moved to Egyptian Embassy to Albania (1959-61); Member, Permanent Mission of Egypt in New York (1964-68); Head, Human Rights section, International Organisation Department, Ministry of Foreign Affairs, Cairo (1969-71); Counsellor, Deputy, Permanent Representative of Egypt, Geneva (Switzerland). **Member** UN Committee on elimination of all forms of racial discrimination since 1971. **Member:** Bar Association, Egypt (1952-54). **Prof. Addr.:** 72, rue de Lausanne, CH-1202, Geneva, Switzerland.

ABULNOUR (Mohamed el-Ahmadi), Egyptian politician. **Born** in Egypt in 1932. **Educ.:** Theological Faculty, al-Azhar University. **Dipl.:** M.A., Ph.D. **Career:** Teacher, al-Azhar Institutes (1957-63); Reader, Theological Faculty (1963); teacher and head of al-Tafsir section of Faculty for Girls (1973); Prof. of al-Hadith (1981); later Dean, Faculty for Girls; Vice President Muslim Youth Socs; Minister of Wakfs (1985-86). **Publ.:** Several works on al-Tafsir and al-Hadith. **Addr.:** Cairo, Egypt.

ABUMAIZER (Mohamad, Abdulmuhsin), Palestinian politician. **Born** in 1933. **Educ.:** Law, LLB. **Career:** Worked as a journalist, editor of both a Syrian and a Lebanese newspaper (1960s); worked as Fatah representative in Algeria and Iraq (1969) and France (1968). Member of Fatah Central Committee (1973); expelled by Israelis from West Bank (1973); Head of Palestinian National Front (PNF) in Occupied Territories (1974); elected to PLO Executive Committee as Representative of PNF (1974). Participated in PLO delegation to Moscow (1974); PLO spokesman and head of Pan-Arab and Returnees Affairs Department; member of Occupied Homeland Affairs Department (1977); Member of the Executive Committee and Head of Palestine Liberation Organisation (PLO) Department of National, Pan-National and Returnees Affairs. Sometime member of the Baath Party. **Member:** Higher Islamic Committee in Arab Jerusalem. **Publ.:** "La Palestine Libérée", Paris, (1968). **Addr.:** Tunis, Tunisia.

ABUMILHA (Abdallah Saeed), Saudi businessman. **Born** in 1943 at Mushait. **Dipl.:** B.A. (Accountancy, Business Administration). **Career:** Director, Financial Affairs, Asir Governorate; owner and General Manager, Southern Establishment for Trading and Contracting; Chairman, Southern Welfare Society; member of the Board, Southern Province Cement Company; President of Abha Chamber of Commerce and Industry, Southern Region; founding member of Asir Journalist Establishment. **Honours:** Certificate of Ideal Citizenship awarded by H.R.H. Prince Khalid al-Faisal Abdulaziz. **Hobby:** Sports. **Addr.:** P.O.Box 8, Tel. 2246509 (Office) and 2246795 (Home), Abha, Saudi Arabia.

ABUMILHA (Mohamad Abdulaziz), Saudi official. **Born** in 1936. **Dipl.:** M.A. (Business Administration). **Career:** Assistant Director, Land Records Department, Ministry of Municipal and Rural Affairs; Director of Inspection Department; Director General, Organization and Programming; Director General of Municipal and Rural Affairs, Southern Region, Abha; member of Board,

Manarat Schools, Asir Region. **Hobby:** Reading, **Address:** General Directorate of Municipal and Rural Affairs, Southern Region, Tel.: 2246280 (Office) and 2242926 (Home), Abha, Saudi Arabia.

ABUNAGA (as-Sayed), Egyptian businessman. **Born** in Egypt. **Educ.:** Secondary and Higher. **Dipl.:** Doctorate in Business Adminsitration. **Career:** Former Lecturer on Business Administration in Alexandria (Egypt); former Chairman and Board Director of "al-Maaref" Printing and Publishing House, Cairo; Board Director of "al-Ahram" newspaper. **Hobby:** Reading. **Member** of the Gezira Sporting Club. **Addr.:** "Dar al-Maaref", 1119, Corniche Road, Maspero, Tel.: (02) 777077-87, Cairo Egypt.

ABUNAWAR (Ali, Abdulqader), Jordanian military. **Born** in 1925 in Salt. **Educ.:** School of War, Staff School of Great Britain. **Dipl.:** From both aforesaid schools. **Career:** In the Jordanian active army, First chief of the Jordanian army staff following the departure of Glubb Pasha (March 1st, 1956) and the arabisation of the Jordanian Royal Forces; Instigator of a conspiracy against King Hussain (1957); Exiled in Egypt, Returned to Jordan (1964) with the consent of King Hussain; Attaché to the Ministry of Foreign Affairs with rank of Ambassador (May 1970); Appointed as Personal Representative of H.M. King Hussain of Jordan (October 9, 1970), Jordanian Ambassador to France (March 1971). **Addr.:** Amman, Jordan.

ABUNAWAR (Ma'an), Jordanian statesman. **Born** on July 26, 1926 in Jordan. **Widower** of Vivian Ann Richards, 9 Children: Leith (1951) Aubeida (1954), Tariq (1957), Rajhdah (1960), Jihed (1961), Zain (1964), Mai (1965), Miriam (1967), Lora (1971). **Educ.:** Salt Secondary School, London University, UK. **Dipl.:** Diploma in World Affairs (1963). **Career:** Joined Jordanian Army (1943); Colonel, Infantry Regiment Jordan Arab Army, (1956); Commander, 1st Infantry Brigade (1957-63); Counsellor, Jordanian Embassy to England (1963); Director, Jordan Civil Defence (1964-67); Director, Jordan Public Security (1967-69); Assistant Chief of Staff, General Affairs (rank of Major-General) (1969-72); Editor, al-Aksa (military weekly); Minister of Culture and Information (August 1972-March 1973); Ambassador to England (1973-76); Mayor of Amman (1976); Minister of Public Works (1979); Minister of Culture and Youth and of Tourism and Antiquities (1980-85). **Awards:** Star of Jordan, 1st Class. **Hobbies:** Music, theatre, reading, television, cinema, museums. **Addr.:** Amman, Jordan.

ABUOBEID (Awad Muhsen), Jordanian diplomat. **Born** in 1938 in Irbid, Jordan. **Married** 2 sons, 2 daughters. **Educ.:** John's Hopkins University, USA. **Dipl.:** B.A. in Sociology, Diploma in Diplomacy and International Affairs. **Carrer:** Head of Section, Ministry of Social Affairs (1961); Diplomat, Embassy of Jordan to Canada, France, USA, USSR, Kuwait, Morocco and Syria (1963-83); Director General, Prime Minister Office, Jordan (1984); Ambassador of Jordan to Algeria (1985-86). **Medal:** Jordan Medal of Independance (1963). **Hobbies:** Travelling and reading. **Prof. Addr.:** c/o Ministry of Foreign Affairs, Amman, Jordan. **Priv. Addr.:** P.O.Box 950519, Amman, Jordan.

ABUODEH (Adnan, Said), Jordanian statesman. **Born** in 1933 in Nablus, Jordan. **Son** of Said Abu Odeh **and** Mrs. Abu Odeh. **Married** five children. **Educ.:** Teachers College, Amman; Damascus University. **Dipl.:** B.A. in English Literature. **Career:** Teacher in Jordan (1954-56); Teacher in Kuwait and Trucial States (1959-66); Officer in General Intelligence Service (1966-70); Minister of Culture and Information, and of Tourism and Antiquities (1970-72); Secretary General of the Arab National Union (1972-73); Chief of Royal Cabinet (1973); Minister of Culture and Information (1973-74); member of the Senate (1974-76); Minister of Culture and Information, and President of the Executive Bureau for the Affairs of the Occupied Territories (1976-79); member of the Senate (1979); member of the National Consultative Council (1980); Minister of Information (1980-83); Minister to the Royal court (1984-1990). **Member** of the Board of Trustees of Jordan Universities; and the World Affairs Council. **Publ.:** numerous articles and papers on the Middle East and Israel published in professional journals. **Decor.:** Order of Independence; Order of the Jordanian Star. **Sport:** Cycling. **Hobbies:** Reading, Arabic literature, history, poetry, philosophy. **Prof. Addr.:** The Royal Court, Amman, Jordan.

ABUQURA (Ahmad, Salih), Jordanian statesman and physician. **Born** in 1918 in Salt, Jordan, **Son** of Salih Abu Qura **and** Mrs., Abu Qura. **Married**, five children. **Educ.:** Syrian University, London University, Harvard University, Boston, USA. **Dipl.:** B.A. in Medicine; specialisation in Radiology in UK and USA. **Career:** Director of Radiology Section, Amman Hospital (1951-56); Minister of Health (1965-66); Minister of Social Affairs and Labour (1966); Secretary General of Jordanian National Red Crescent Society (1962-63). **Decor.:** Independence Medal, 3rd Class; Order of the Star of Jordan, 1st Class; Order of Tunisian Republic; Grand Knight of the Order of the Italian Republic; Bernadotte Medal of International Red Cross Committee. **Addr.:** P.O.Box 147, Tel.: 73141, Amman, Jordan.

ABURABAH (AbdulRahman), Jordanian official. **Born** in 1932 at Ramallah, Jordan. **Married**, seven children. **Dipl.:** B.A. in Education and Psychology; M.A. in Tourism and Transport; Ph.D. in Tourism. **Career:** Ministry of Tourism, Amman; Secretary General, Arab Organisation of Tourism, League of Arab States (1967); Under Secretary, Ministry of Tourism, Amman (1973-74). **Publ.:** Editor in Chief of "Arab Tourism"; several works on Tourism. **Hobby:** Folklore. **Addr.:** Arab Organisation for Tourism, P.O.Box. 2354, Amman, Jordan.

ABURAS (Sadek Amin), Yemeni Politician. **Born** in 1950 in Barat al-Inan. **Married,** four daughters, four sons. **Educ.:** B.Sc., Military Service, Yemeni Military Academy (1976). **Career:** Chairman, Planning Committee (1979-81); Financial and Administrative Committee (1981-82); Yemeni Cooperative Development Association, Board Vice President, Agricultural Cooperative Development Credit Bank (1982-85); Secretary General, Assistant of the Confederation of the Yemeni Development Association (1985-88); Secretary General, The General Union of the Gulf Association for Cooperative Development (1988-93); Board Chairman, Yemeni Association for Marketing Agricultural Products; Chairman, Yemeni-Soviet Friendship Association; Member, People's Constituent Assembly; Member, Yemeni Parliament; Minister of Agriculture and Water Resources (1993-94); Minister of Civil Service and Administrative Reform (1994-May 1997); Minister of Local Administration (May 1997-to date). **Address:** Ministry of Local Admistration, P.O.Box 198, Sanaa, Yemen.

ABURASHID (Abdul Razzag Rashid), Saudi official. **Born:** Mecca, 1941. **Son** of Rashid Abdulrashid. **Dipl.:** B.Sc. (Geology of Mining). **Career:** Geological expert; member of Royal College of Mining, U.K.; Director of Concessions Department, Mineral Resources, Ministry of Petroleum and Mineral Resources. **Publ.:** some research papers. **Hobby:** Football. **Addr.:** Jeddah, Saudi Arabia.

ABURIJAL (Ali Ahmed), Yemeni statesman. **born** in 1932 In Sanaa, Yemen. **son** of Ahmed ABU RIJAL. **Career:** Clerk, Ministry of Waqf (1948-1957); Supervisor at the Hospital of Sanaa (1958); Principal, Industrial School (1958-1962); General Manager, Ministry of Public Works (1962-1968); Under-Secretary, Ministry of Public Works (1968-1976); Governor of Sanaa (1976-1977); Governor of Hodeidah Provice (1977-1982). Member, the People's General Congress and of the Permanent Committee of the People's General Congress, Chairman, Municipal Council of Sanaa (1982-1985); Deputy Director, Presidential Office (1983-1991); Head, National Center for Archives (1991-till today) **Add.:** P.O.Box 1162 Sanaa, Republic of Yemen.

ABUSAID (Ahmad), Yemeni statesman. **Born** in North Yemen southern district. **Married** to Irene Abu Said (French). **Career:** opened a private school in Ta'iss, North Yemen; Deputy Minister of Economy (May- September 1964); Finance Minister (April- July 1965); Minister of the Treasury (November - December 1967); Counsellor, with ministerial rank, for economic and financial affairs (Sept. 1968 - March 1969); Minister of State for the Presidency (April - July 1969); Deputy Prime Minister (1969-70); Minister of Economy (May- July 1971); Minister of State for Development (1971-72); Minister of Communications (March- June 1974); minister of state for public services (1975-76); appointed by Decree as Government supervisor of the Water Company (1977). **Addr.:** Sanaa, Republic of Yemen.

ABUSALIM (Mohamad, Ibrahim), Sudanese academic. **Born** in 1928 in Halfa District, Sudan. **Married** seven children. **Educ.:** Khartoum University College. **Dipl.:** Ph.D. in History. **Career:** Assistant Archivist (1955); Civil Service (1957); Director of Central Records Office with rank of Under Secretary; Visiting Professor of History University of Khartoum, Sudan (1976); Headed many State Boards and Committees including the Committee of Re-distribution of Sudan's Provinces. **Publ.:** "Calender of Mahdi's Proclamations", "Cultural Movements in the Mahdist Period", "History of Khartoum", "Some Funj Land Certificates", "The Fur and the Land", "The Mahdists and the Land", "Documents from 18th Century Sennar" (in English), "Memo of Osman Digna", Collection of Poems of Tawfic Salih Gibril", etc. **Chairman and member** of the Sudanese Philosophical Association; Chairman of the Sudanese Historical Society; former Secretary General of Arab Branch of International Council on archives, member of the Board of the Faculty of Arts, Faculty of Social and Economic Studies, Institute of African and Asian Studies, University of Khartoum. **Hobbies:** History, archives, English and Arabic literature. **Sports:** Swimming, indoor activities. **Prof. Addr.:** National Records Office, P.O.B. 1914, Tel. 71995, Khartoum, Sudan. **Priv. Addr.:** Tel. 79100, Khartoum, Sudan.

ABUSAQ (Mohamad, Othman), Sudanese politician. **Born** in 1938 in Sudan. **Married** two sons. **Educ.:** University of Khartoum, University of Aberdeen, UK; University of Edinburgh, UK. **Dipl.:** B.A. in History and Arabic; M.A. in History and Politics; Ph.D. in Islamic Political Thought. **Career:** Secondary school teacher (1961-62); Teacher, Training Institute (1965); Lecturer, Department of Political Science, University of Khartoum (1965-74); Secretary for Thought and Propagation, Sudanese Socialist Union (SSU) Party dissolved following Coup in 1989, (1974-80); Minister of State for Culture and Information (1977-80); Minister of Culture and Information (1980). **Publ.:** Conference papers, pamphlets on ideology and SSU institutions. **Sport:** Swimming. **Hobbies:** Indoor games, political thoughts. **Prof. Addr.:** Khartoum, Sudan.

ABUSAUD (Alawi Nuri), Saudi academic. **Born** in 1943 in Mecca, Saudi Arabia. **Dipl.:** B.A., M.P.A., Ph.D. **Career:** Liaison Officer between the English Department and the University Administration, King Abdulaziz University (1971); Assistant Professor and Chairman, Department of Public Administration, Faculty of Economics and Administration, King Abdulaziz University; member, the American Society of Public Administration (ASPA) and the American Political Science Association (APSA). **Publ.:** Administrative Development and Planning in Saudi Arabia (Ph.D. thesis). **Hobbies:** Swimming, volleyball, reading.

Addr.: Department of Public Administration, Faculty of Economics and Administration, King Abdulaziz University, Tel. 6892376 (Office), 6711106 (Home), Jeddah, Saudi Arabia.

ABUSHAAR (Hind, Ghassan, al), Jordanian academic. **Born** on December 16, 1949. **Educ.:** University of Jordan. **Dipl.:** M.A. (History) (1980). **Career:** Teacher at Ajloun Facutly; Headmaster of al-Zarkaa Secondary School for Girls. **Publ.:** Historical documentary (1984) as well as collections of short stories (1982) and (1984). **Member:** Jordan Writer's Union. **Hobbies:** Reading, oil painting, gardening. **Prof. Addr.:** P.O.Box 84, Al Zarkaa, Tel.: 986513, 981578, Jordan.

ABUSHAMA (Faisal, Tageldine), Sudanese university professor. **Born** on June 14, 1935, in Khartoum. **Son** of Tageldine Abushama **and** Mrs., née Amina al-Moubarak al-Mahmoud. **Married** in April 1966 to Miss Faiza Hasab el-Rassoul, 4 children: Khalid, Muna, Ashraf and Mubarak. **Educ.:** Universities of Khartoum and London. **Dipl.:** Bachelor of Science, Master of Science, Doctor in Philosophy (Zoology). **Career:** Assistant (1960-65), then Assistant-Professor (1968), then Professor and Dean of the Faculty of Science (University of Khartoum) (1970); Dean of Graduate College (1978); Deputy Vice-Chancellor (1979-83); Professor of Zoology and Head Dept. of Zoology, Kuwait University (1983-90); Professor of Zoology, University of Khartoum (1990- to date). **Publ.:** Author of more than 43 studies and papers published in Arabic and English. **Sports:** Football, swimming and horseriding. **Hobbies:** Reading, Music and Theatre. **Prof. Addr.:** Zoology Department, Faculty of Science, Khartoum University, P.O.Box 321, Khartoum, Sudan. **Priv. Addr.:** Tayif, Block 23 House No. 27, Khartoum, Sudan.

ABUSHAWARIB (Mujahid Yehya, Brig. General), Yemeni politician. **Born** in 1930 in Khamr, Republic of Yemen. **Educ.:** Military. **Career:** Governor and Military Commander of the Province of Hajja (after Civil War); Member, Command Council and Deputy Commander in-Chief (June 1974-75); resigned from Command Council and Governership of Hajja (June 1975); Deputy Prime-Minister and Minister for Internal Affairs (1979- May 1990); Deputy Prime Minister for Internal Affairs (May 1990- Oct. 1994); Presently adviser to the President. **Addr.:** Presidential Office, Sanaa, Republic of Yemen.

ABUSHERIF (Bassam), Palestinian politician. **Educ.:** American University of Beirut. **Career:** Member of Popular Front for the Liberation of Palestine (PFLP) and official spokesman of the PFLP. Editor of "al-Hadaf" newspaper. Wounded by letter bomb in "al-Hadaf" office (1972) **Addr.:** Tunis, Tunisia.

ABUSINEINA (Amin), Sudanese politician. **Born** in 1933 in Sudan. **Married** four children. **Educ.:** Cairo University, Egypt; London University, UK. **Dipl.:** B.Sc. (1959); Ph.D. (1963). **Career:** Senior Lecturer, University of Khartoum (1960-69); Project Manager, FAO (1971-74); Ambassador to UN, Geneva (1974-75); Deputy Minister of Industry (1975-76); Minister of State for Industry (1976-77); Minister of State for Agriculture, Food and Natural Resources (1977). **Publ.:** Many articles in international journals. **Medals:** Order of the Republic, 2nd Class, Sudan. **Hobbies:** Music, bridge, politics. **Priv. Addr.:** Tel. 73306, Khartoum, Sudan.

ABUSITTA), Palestinian politician, independent member of the Palestine Liberation Organization (PLO), Executive Committee and Head of PLO Occupied Homeland (1964); re-elected to the Executive Committee chaired by Yasser Arafat (1969); appointed member of the six-man General Secretariat (1970); remained member of the new Executive Committee (1971); re-elected member of the PLO Executive Committee (1973). **Member** of the PLO delegation to Moscow, led by Yasser Arafat (1974). **Addr.:** Tunis, Tunisia.

ABUSOLAIMAN (Abdul Wahhab Ibrahim), Saudi academic. **Born** in 1936. **Dipl.:** Ph.D. (Comparative Jurisprudence). **Career:** Secondary school teacher, (1959-66); Demonstrator, Faculty of Shari'a (Islamic Law) Mecca (1966); Dean, Faculty of Shari'a, (1970-72); Chairman, Western Region Customs Appeal Committee and Manuscript Committee, King Abdulaziz University; member, Pilgrimage Islamic Orientation Board. **Honours:** King Abdulaziz University Medal of Merit (First Order) (1972); University Medal awarded to Deans of the Faculty of Shari'a on the occasion of the twenty-fifth anniversary of the Faculty (1974). **Publ.:** some research articles published in academic journals: al-Tashri'e al-Islami Fil Qarn al-Rabie Ashar (Islamic Legislation in the fourteenth Century); al-Fiqhul Islami, Mashkilohu wa Wasa'ilu Tatweerih (Islamic Jurisprudence, Problems and Ways of Development); Necessiry and Its Effect on Islamic Law; Muhammad Ibn Abdul Wahhab; characteristics of his jurisprudential thoughts and other related articles; co-edited, Codification of Hanbali Law. **Hobbies:** Reading, excursions. **Addr.:** Faculty of Shari'a, Umm al-Qura University, Tel. Home 5436956, Mecca, Saudi Arabia.

ABUSOLAIMAN (Jamil, Ahmad Mohamad), Saudi diplomat. **Born** in 1930 in Mecca (Saudi Arabia). **Educ.:** Faculty of Letters. **Dipl.:** B.A. (Arabic Language and Literature). **Career:** Schoolmaster (1955); Assistant Inspector-General, Ministry of Education (1957); Director-General, Primary Education; Director-General, Teachers' Training Institutes (1959); Director-General, Educational Planning; Cultural Attaché, Embassy of the Kingdom of Saudi Arabia, to Mauritania (1974). **Publ.:** Author of a number of text books. **Hobbies:** Gardening & reading. **Prof. Addr.:** c/o Ministry of Education, Riyadh, Saudi Arabia. **Priv. Addr.:** Tel. 61275, Riyadh, Saudi Arabia.

ABUSSINN (Tayeb, Ali Ahmad), Sudanese writer. **Born** in 1940. **Son** of Ali Ahmad Aboussinn **and** Mrs., née Boushriya Ali Moustapha. **Married** in 1967 to Miss Nawal Abdallah Junaidali, 2 children: Hala and Mazen. **Educ.:** Khartoum University. **Dipl.:** Bachelor of Arts (1964), Master of Arts (1972). **Career:** Teacher (1975), Writer. **Publ.:** Author of several booklets and studies. **Hobby:** Swimming. **Priv. Addr.:** Khartoum, Tel. 34364, Sudan.

ABUSSUUD (Abdulaziz, A.), Saudi former President & Chief Executive Officer. **Born** on August 5, 1940, Saudi Arabia. **Married,** three children. **Languages:** Arabic and English. **Educ.:** Bachelor of Business Administration from the American University of Beirut in 1971; Three Course Diplomas in Management and Insurance. **Career:** Joined Arab Commercial Enterprises (ACE) in al-Khobar (1961). Transfered to Establish ACE Dammam with another Senior Colleague in 1964. Continued in ACE Dammam in various capacities until 1966, and thereafter left on an educational leave to pursue his Academic Career, until he rejoined ACE in Beirut in 1971. After a short stay in ACE Abu Dhabi and Dubai during 1971-72 as Acting Manager, he was sent to Muscat to start ACE Oman. On Completion of this Assignment, he was sent to Bahrain in late 1973 to establish ACE Bahrain. In 1978 became Regional Manager of ACE Bahrain and U.A.E., thereafter held various titles until he became Senior Vice President - Gulf and Eastern Province of Saudi Arabia in 1986. Continued in this capacity until he was elevated to the position of Senior Group Vice President - Broking and Agencies in January 1988. Appointed President and Chief Executive Officer of ACE Group (September 1989). **Member:** of the Board of Directors of American Express, Saudi Arabia and of the Chartered Insurance Institute, London. **Hobbies:** Reading, Travelling and Swimming. **Prof. Addr.:** c/o Arab Commercial Enterprises Ltd., P.O.Box 667, Riyadh 11421, Saudi Arabia, Tel.: 4774070, Telex: 401091 ACERYD SJ, Fax: 4772377, E-mail: aceho@ace.ins.com.

ABUSSUUD (Aziz, Ali), Saudi businessman. **Born** in 1942 in Qatif, Saudi Arabia. **Son** of Ali Abussuud. **Married,** two sons. **Educ.:** American University of Beirut, Lebanon. **Dipl.:** B.A. in Business Administration, Diplomas in Management, Marine Insurance and Risk Management. **Career:** Joined Arab Commercial Enterprises Group of Companies, al-Khobar, Saudi Arabia (1962): Progressed to Senior Vice President Post: Claims Manager and Assistant Company Manager, Dammam (1964-66): Visiting Manager, Abu Dhabi, Dubai (1971-72); Manager (1972-73) Oman; Manager (1973-78) Bahrain; Regional Manager, Bahrain and United Arab Emirates (1979-80); Regional Manager, Bahrain, Qatar and United Emirates (1980-81); Assistant Vice President for Bahrain, Qatar, Oman & United Arab Emirates (1981-82), Regional Vice President, Gulf (1982-85); Senior Vice President Gulf and Eastern Saudi Arabia (Since 1985); **Member** of the Chartered Insurance Institute, London. **Hobby:** Reading. **Prof. Addr.:** Arab Commercial Enterprises, P.O.Box 781, Awal Bldg., Apartment No. 205, 232 Government Avenue, Manama 315, Tel.: 251656, State of Bahrain.

ABUTALEB (Fathi,), (Field Marshal) Jordan. **Born** on May 14, 1934 in Amman-Jordan. **Married,** 3 sons, 1 daughter. **Educ.:** High School Amman-BA Management. Master's management and Military Sciences. **Military Educ.:** Tank Tech officers Course at the School of Tank Technology, U.K. 1957. All Arms Tactical Course U.K. 1963. Armour Advance Course, Fort Knox, USA. 1968 Joint Command and Staff College Course in India 1966; Royal College of Defence Studies U.K., 1976, Senior Management Course at the Naval Post graduate school Monterey, USA. 1979. **Career:** Held various positions in the Army Armoured Formations, from officer to Brigade, and Division Commanders; Assistant Military Attaché in London (1970-71). Defence Attaché, Washington D.C. (1971-73); Director of Intelligence; Assistant Chief of Staff for Intelligence (1979-81); Chief of Staff of the Jordan Armed Forces 1981; and after the Reorganization of forces, became (CHAIRMAN OF THE JOINT CHIEFS OF STAFF) until April 1993. As a field Marshal at present adviser for all Defence and Security Matters to The King and the Government of Jordan. **Awards:** All Jordanian Decorations from first Degree. American, British, French, some European Countries High Military Decorations. **Prof. Address:** Field Marshal. Fathi Abu Taleb, P.O.Box 850182, Amman 11185, Jordan.

ABUTALEB (Mohamad, Gamal), Egyptian engineer. **Born** in 1943 in Egypt. **Son** of Gamal Abutalib. **Married. Educ.:** Civil Engineering, Ain Shams University, Cairo, Egypt; Sheffield University, England. **Dipl.:** B.Sc. in Civil Engineering (1965); M.Sc. in Engineering (1971); Ph.D. in Engineering (1974). **Career:** Field Engineer with the Arab Contractors Egypt and Iraq (1966-69); Research student, Sheffield University, England (1969-74); Geotechnical Engineer Grade II (1974) and Grade III (1975) at McClelland Engineers, London; Project Engineer (1977), Senior Engineer, Consulting Engineering Office CEO, Soil Division, Saudi Arabia (1978), Chief Engineer (1979). Chartered Engineer. **Member of:** the Institution of Civil Engineers UK (1976), American Society of Civil Engineers (1979), the Institution of Engineering Profession, Egypt. **Publ.:** Many articles in professional journals. **Hobbies:** Reading, bridge, photography. **Sport:** Squash. **Prof. Addr.:** c/o CEO-Soil Division, P.O.Box 1736, Alkhobar, Saudi Arabia, Tel. Dammam 8321676. **Priv. Addr.:** Tel. 8646616, ext. 132, Al-Khobar, Saudi Arabia and 8 Mossdale, Chevely Park, Belmot, Durham, UK, Tel. 038548773.

ABUTALEB (Sufi Hassan), Egyptian professor and politician. **Born** on January 27, 1925 at Fayoum, Egypt. **Educ.:** Cairo University Law School; Faculty of Law, Paris & Rome Universities. **Career:** Professor of Law, Cairo

University (1952-58); Chairman, History and Philosophy of Law Department (1958-65); Legal Adviser, University of Assiut (1965), University of Cairo (1967); Joined Arab Socialist Union (1962), Secretary General (1964); Lecturer in Law, Beirut Arab University (1970-72); Professor of Law, Cairo University (1972); appointed Vice-President (1973); President (1975-78); elected member for Fayoum, People's Assembly (Oct. 1976); Joined Arab Socialist Party (Nov. 1976); Founder of National Democratic Party (1978); member Higher Ministerial Committee for Egyptian-Sudanese Political and Economic Federation; elected Speaker, People's Assembly (1978-84); member of the Board of Directors, Islamic Studies Institute, Cairo, Conference on Islamic Education, Mecca; has lectured at several American Universities. **Publ.:** Arab Society (1965); Studies in Arab Nationalism; The Legal Status of Women in the Arab Countries (in French) and many others. **Addr.:** The People's Assembly, Cairo, Egypt.

ABUTALEB (Youssef Sabry, Gen.), Egyptian former minister. **Born** in 1929 in Cairo. **Educ.:** Military Academy, Cairo; specialisation studies in the United States of America and the Soviet Union. **Dipl.:** Military Academy diploma. **Career:** appointed Governor of Sinai North in May 1980, following evacuation of Sinai Peninsula, under the terms of the Egyptian- Israeli Peace Treaty; Minister of Popular Development (1982); Minister of Defence and Military Production (1990-1991). **Addr:** 5, Ismail Abaza Street, Kasr el-Aini, Cairo, Egypt.

ABUZAID (Ahmad, Muhammad), Egyptian judge. **Born** on July 22, 1933 in Cairo, Egypt. **Educ.:** Ain Shams University, Cairo. **Dipl.:** LL.B. (1954). **Career:** Justice, Court of Cassation, Ministry of Justice (1980-84), Deputy Chief Justice (1984), Elected to the People's Assembly (Deputy speaker since Dec. 1995). **Member:** Hunting Club. **Addr.:** 14 al-Manial Str., Masr al-Qadeema, Cairo, Egypt.

ABUZAID (Hikmat), Egyptian politician and academic. **Born** in 1923 at Assiut, Egypt. **Educ.:** Cairo University, University of Edinburgh, UK; University of St. Andrews, UK; London University, UK. **Dipl.:** B.A. in Literature; M.A. in Education; Ph.D. in Educational Psychology. **Career:** Teacher in several secondary schools in Egypt; lecturer in Psychology, College for Women, University of Ain Shams, Cairo; Minister of Social Affairs (1962-65); Professor at Cairo University. **Member of:** the Egyptian National Peace Council; alternate member of the Arab Socialist Union (ASU) Central Committee (1968); Secretary of Art and Literature Committee; member of the ASU Secretariat General (1970); member of the General Committee of the Citizens War Committees (1970); National Council for Services and Social Affairs. **Medals:** Lenin Peace Prize. **Prof. Addr.:** Cairo University. Cairo, Egypt.

ABUZAID (Leila), Moroccan writer. **Born** in 1950 at al-Ksida, Morocco. **Dipl.:** Licence in English, Diploma in Journalism. **Career:** Journalist (1970); Correspondent for television and radio (since 1973); member of the Council for the Ministry of Information, for the Council of the Prime Minister. Correspondent for the BBC. **Member** of the Higher Council for Relief and Development. **Publ.:** "Social Problems in the USA" (1974); "Women's Situation in Morocco" (1975); "Communism" (1976); "The British Life and Society" (collection of short stories) (1979). **Sports:** Swimming. **Hobbies:** Reading, travel, journalism. **Addr.:** Rabat, Morocco.

ABUZAID (Ma'Moon, Awad, Major), Sudanese Army Officer and politician. **Born** on December 6, 1939 at Omdurman (Sudan). **Married** with children. **Educ.:** Military Academy (Khartoum). **Career:** spokesman, Sudan Revolutionary Command Council (1969-71); Head, National Security Service of Sudan (1969-71); Minister of State for Cabinet Affairs (1969-71); Secretary-General, Sudan Socialist Union (October 1971- May 1972). **Awards:** Order of Bravery (Sudan); Order of Loyal Son of Sudan; Grand Cordon, Order of Menelik (Ethiopia). **Sports:** Swimming, tennis and horseriding. **Hobby:** Reading. **Addr.:** P.O.Box 1850, Khartoum, Sudan.

ABUZAID (Mohamad, Hamdi), Egyptian diplomat. **Born** in 1919 in Egypt. **Married** to Fatima Said in 1942, two children. **Educ.:** Egyptian Air Force Academy; RAF Navigational Course at Hamble, UK (1951). **Career:** Pilot (1949-60); retired at the rank of Group Captain; appointed **Member** of First Revolutionary Council (1952); Director of the Office of Asian Affairs in the Presidency (1960-62); Ambassador to Yugoslavia (1962-68); Ambassador to Mexico (1968-73); Head of the Western European Department, Ministry of Foreign Affairs (1973-74); Ambassador to Syria (1974-75); Minister of Civil Aviation (1975-76); Ambassador to USSR (1976-79). **Prof. Addr:** Ministry of Foreign Affairs, Giza, Cairo, Egypt. **Priv. Addr.:** 31 Mazhar Street, Zamalek, Cairo, Egypt.

ABUZAID (Mustafa Fahmi), Egyptian statesman. **Born** in 1928. **Son** of Fahmi Abu Zaid. **Married**, three children. **Educ.:** Cairo University, Egypt. **Dipl.:** LL.B. **Career:** member of Faculty of Law; Lecturer, Alexandria University, Egypt, Professor and Head of Department of Constitutional and Administrative Law; seconded as Professor and Head of Department of General Law at Arab University of Beirut, Lebanon (1968); Prosecutor General with ministerial rank; Minister of Justice (1974-75). **Member** of the Committee of the Arab Socialist Union (ASU); elected member of the Central Committee of the ASU Reorganisation, elected member of the National Assembly. **Addr.:** Cairo, Egypt.

ABUZAID (Omar, Mustafa), Jordanian businessman. **Born** in 1931 in Jaffa, Palestine. **Married,** three sons.

Career: Chairman of the Board and General Manager of Mustafa Abu Zaid and Sons Co. Ltd.; Amman; Chairman of the board of Contruction Equipment and Machinery Co. Ltd.; United Arab Building Materials Co. Ltd. **Member of:** the Board of Directors of Amman Chamber of Commerce, Council of Jordan Federation of Chambers of Commerce (1974-78). Major shareholder and board member of Ready Mix Cement Industries Co. Ltd., Alhilal Trading Co. Ltd., Amman. **Clubs:** member of several. **Addr.:** P.O.Box 435, Tel. 641228, Telex 21641 JO, Amman, Jordan.

ABUZAID (Othman, Mahmud), Egyptian journalist; resident in Qatar. **Born** in in 1933 at Kafr al-Shaikh, Egypt. **Son** of Mahmud Abu Zaid. **Married,** three children. **Educ.:** Faculty of Arts, Cairo University. **Dipl.:** B.A. in Journalism. **Career:** Journalist, Middle East News Agency (1959); Director of Gulf Area, Middle East News Agency (1966); Director and Editor, The Qatar News Agency (1975); Adviser to the Qatari News Agency (1980). **Publ.:** several papers and articles on the Middle East. **Medals:** Ordre du Chevalier, Morocco; awarded the Prize of Production, Egypt. **Sports:** Jogging, swimming. **Addr.:** Qatar News Agency, P.O.Box 3299, Tel. 322725, Doha, Qatar.

ABUZAID (Salah), Jordanian statesman. **Born** in 1923. **Educ.:** Syrian University, Syracuse University, USA. **Dipl.:** Honorary Diploma in Radio and Television. **Career:** Teacher in Irbid (1943); Government Official in Arab National Bank (1946-50); Publicity Officer in Statistics Department (1950-53); translator at Jordanian Development Board (1953-55); Chief Clerk at Department of Press and Publications (1955-57); Director of Amman Broadcasting Service (1958-59); Assistant to Director General of Jordanian Broadcasting Service (1959-60) Director General of Jordanian Broadcasting Service (1961-62) and of Press and Publications Department (1962); Director General of National Guidance and Information Department (1963); Minister of Information (1964-65 and 1967); Minister of Information and Tourism and Antiquities (1967-68); Ambassador to UK (1969-70); Personal Advisor to HM King Hussain (1971-72); Foreign Minister (1972); Senator (1973-74); Minister of Culture and Information (1974-76); Ambassador to Court of St. James, London (1976-78); Chairman and director, the Arab Information Centre for Public Relations (1980); Chairman and Director, The Arab International Center for Counselling and Public Relations, The AIC for Tourism and the AIC for Publishing, Printing and Distribution. Retired from Government service (1978). Established in 1980 "the Arab International Centre" for Counselling and Public Relations, for Tourism, for Publication, Printing and distribution and for arts. He is the Chairman and General Manager. **Publ.:** "Al Hussain Bin Talal" (1958). **Medals:** Arab Renaissance Medal; Star of Jordan; Cedar of Lebanon; various other medals. **Addr.:** P.O.Box 5105, Tel. 667576, Amman, Jordan.

ABUZINADA (Abdul Wahab), Saudi executive. **Born** in 1943. **Dipl.:** B.A. (English). **Career:** Secretary, Jeddah Chamber of Commerce and Industry; Director of Public Relations, National Advertising Agency; Director of Public Relations, International Markets Agency; Assistant Director, Jeddah Chamber of Commerce and Industry; member of Board, Saudi Agency for International Trade and Industry. **Publ.:** Poems, articles and short stories published in local newspapers. **Hobbies:** Swimming, excursions. **Addr.:** Jeddah Chamber of Commerce and Industry, Mina Road, P.O.Box 1264, Tel. 6424824 (office) and 6431059 (Home), Jeddah, Saudi Arabia.

ABUZINADA (Abdulaziz Hamid), Saudi academic and conservations. **Born** in 1941 in Jeddah, Saudi Arabia. **Qualifications:** B.Sc., Univ. Riyadh, (1963); M.Sc., Univ. Minnesota, USA (1967); Ph.D. (Microbiology), Univ. of Durham, England (1971). **Career:** Demonstrator, Botany Department, (1964-65); later Instructor (1967-68); Lecturer, (1971-78); Vice Dean, Faculty of Science, (1974-76); Chairman, Department of Botany (1976-78); Associate Prof. (1978-1983) full Professor (1983-1986) in the Faculty of Science, King Saud University; Founder member (1974-present) and President (1974-1991), of the Saudi Biological Society, Secretary General, Saudi National Commission for Wildlife Conservation and Development, (1986-present). Attended several conferences relating to the Arabization of Science. **Member:** Board of Directors, Drainage and Irrigation Authority and the Agricultural Research Council, Ministry of Agriculture; Editorial Committee, Saudi Biological Society (since 1972); Research Centre, Faculty of Science (1978-80); King Saud University Council (1974-79), Consultative Committee for the Higher Commission of Educational Policies, Ministry of Education (since 1975); Consultative Committee for Agriculture, Ministry of Agriculture (since 1975); National Working Group for Science (since 1979); Council of the School of Graduate Studies (1978-80); Chair, Regional Advisory Concil of the Internat. Union for Cons. of Nature (IUCN) (1994-); Vice Chair Species Survival Commission, IUCN (1993-); Chair, Arabian Plant Specialist Group, IUCN (1996-); Internat. Union of Biological Sciences, IUBS (1990-); Executive Council, IUBS (1991-1994); Bonn Convention on Migratory Species (Chair of Standing Committee 1997-); **Awards:** recipient of The World Conservation Union, CNPPA Fred Packard Award for National Parks (1992); Certificate of Appreciation from Friends of the Earth (1991); Certificate of Appreciation from Greenpeace International (1991); The British Institute of Biology and the American Association of the Pathology of Botany (1992); Distinguished Service Award, Dept. of Plant Pathology. Univ. of Minnestota (1992); Distinguished Leadership Award, American Biographical Institute (1993); The Senckenbergische Naturforschende Gesellschaft Award, Univ. of Senckenberg, Germany (1993); Certificate of Appreciation, The Wildlife Society of the USA (1993); Certificate of Appreciation, Saudi

Environmental Society (1997); **Publ.:** a wide range of articles published in Arab and International academic journals; authored and co-authored several text books in Arabic; translated into Arabic "Aspects of Microbiology II. Biotechnology Principles", pub. Nostrand Reinhold (UK), 1987; **Addr.:** Secretary General, National Commission for Wildlife Conservation and Development, P.O.Box: 61681, Riyadh 11575, Saudi Arabia. Tel.: 966 1 441 8700, Fax: 966 1 441 0797.

ACCAD (Rifaat), Syrian former official. **Born** in 1922 in Damascus. **Married**, three children **Educ.:** Secondary and Licentiate in Law, Damascus University (1949), specialized in Banking, Belgium (1955). **Career:** Director, European Arab Bank Ltd., UK; Director, European Arab Holdings, Luxembourg; Director, European Arab Bank, Germany; Chairman and Governor, Central Bank of Syria, Damascus (1978-84). **Publ.:** Articles and research papers. **Hobby:** Basketball. **Addr.:** Damascus, Syria.

ACHRAOUI (Hanane), Palestinian Politician. **Born** in 1946 in Nablus, Palestine. **Educ.:** Charlottown University, Virginia, U.S.A. (1970). **Career.** Head of the English Department, Birzeit University, West Bank, (1973); Spokeswoman of the Palestinian Delegation in Madrid, Spain (1991); Founded the Human Rights Association (1993); Minister of Higher Education at the Palestine Cabinet (1996) then resigned in 1998; Deputy at the Palestinian Parliament (1999-). **Addr.:** West Bank, Palestine.

ADASANI (Mahmoud, Khaled, al), Kuwaiti engineer. **Born** on January 31, 1934 in Kuwait. **Son** of Khaled Sulaiman al-Adasani **and** Mrs. Badriya Sayyid Muhammad al-Rifai. **Married** to Kadriya Almula, on August 31, 1961, 3 children: Rula, Reema and Sulaiman. **Educ.:** International College (Beirut), University of Southern California (Los Angeles). **Dipl.:** Bachelor of Science, Petroleum Engineer, (June 1958). **Career:** Assistant Petroleum Engineer, Kuwait Oil Company, Ahmadi, Kuwait (1958-60); Petroleum Engineer, Kuwait Oil Company, Ahmadi, Kuwait (Feb.-July 1960); Member of Board of Directors, Kuwait Oil Company, London, U.K. (1960-75); Technical Assistant, General Oil Affairs Department, Ministry of Finance and Oil, Ahmadi (August 1960-63); Director of Technical Affairs, Ministry of Finance and Oil Ahmadi (1963-66); Assistant Under-Sercretary for Oil Affairs, Ministry of Finance Oil, Ahmadi (1963-66); Assistant Under-Secretary for Oil Affairs, Ministry of Finance and Oil, Kuwait, (1966-75); Under-Secretary, Ministry of Oil, Kuwait (1975); Direction of Kuwait Metal Pipeline Company, Kuwait (1970-79); Kuwait Representative at Executive Bureau of the Organization of Arab Petroleum Exporting Countries (OAPEC) (1975); Chairman, Petroleum Resources Conservation Board (1976); OPEC Governor for Kuwait (1976); Head of Kuwait side at Kuwait Saudi Permanent Joint Committee (1975); Member, Kuwait Engineering Society (1962 till present); Businessman since 1982. **Remark:** Headed Governmental Delegations to: Arab Petroleum Congress, Baghdad (1967), Represented Kuwait as Delegate at: The Second Arab Summit Conference, Alexandria, The Third Arab Summit Conference, Alexandria, The Third Arab Summit Conference, Casablanca, The non-Aligned Congress (Cairo), Various meetings of OPEC in Geneva and Vienna. **Publ.:** "Oil of Kuwait (Facts and Figures)" (1970); "The Greater Burgan Field" (1965); "North Kuwait Oil Fields" (1967). **Sport:** Water skiing. **Priv. Addr.:** P.O.Box 3242, Tel. 28967, Kuwait.

ADASANI (Mohamad, Yusuf, al), Former Kuwaiti Speaker of National Assembly. **Born** in 1925 in Kuwait. **Son** of Yusuf Adassani (Merchant) **and** Mrs., née Moussa Abdelwahab Rifai. **Married** in October 1957 to Miss Badria Abdurrahman al-Omar, 7 children: Waël, Wassel, Nizar, Wafa', Ayman, Yusuf and Ahmad. **Educ.:** al-Mubarakiya School, Kuwait. **Career:** Businessman; Elected Deputy of Kuwait (1963 and 1967); President, Kuwait Municipality (1964-66); Ambassador to Saudi Arabia (1967-70); Ambassador to Somalia (1968-70); Ambassador to Lebanon (1970-75); Minister of Planning (1976) and re-appointed on February 15, 1978; Minister of Public Works (1978-80); Speaker, Majlis al-Umma (National Assembly) (1981 until dissolved July 1986). **Addr.:** Kuwait City, Kuwait.

ADAWI (Mohamad, Hamza, al), Egyptian Banker. **Born** in 1934 in Cairo, Egypt. **Son** of Hamza al-Adawi. **Married** in 1960, 2 sons. **Dipl.:** Bachelor of Commerce. **Career:** Manager, Documentary Credits Department, National Bank of Egypt (NBE) (1965-76); General Manager, NBE (1976-78); Board Member, NBE (1977-78); General Manager and Board Member, Suez Canal Bank (1978-81); Managing Director, Suez Canal Bank, Cairo (1981); Director, International Shoe Co. SAE; Ismaila Tourist Co. SAE and Suez Canal Company for Trade and Development SAE. **Member:** Arab Banker's Association, Rotary Club of Egypt, Gezira Sporting Club, National Sporting Club, Automobile and Touring Club of Egypt. **Hobbies:** Reading, swimming and tennis. **Addr.:** 11, Mohamed Sabry Abou Alam Street, Tel. 751133, Cairo, Egypt.

ADDAILAMY (Yahia, Abdullah), Yemeni Banker. **Born** on December 22, 1936 at Yemen. **Son** of Abdullah H. Addailamy (Gov. Administrator). **Married** in 1954 in Sanaa, Republic of Yemen, 6 children. **Educ.:** Primary, Zabid, Republic of Yemen; Preparatory, Tripoli, Lebanon; Secondary, Cairo, Egypt, University: Dublin University, Dublin, Ireland. **Dipl.:** BA Eco., MA. **Career:** Director General, Ministry of National Economy (1963-1965); Department General Manager, The Yemen Bank (1965-1969); General Manager, (1970-1973); General Manager, Yemen Petroleum Co. (1974); Chairman, The Yemen Bank, (1975-1978); London Representative (1980-1988); Emigrants BR. (1989-Mid 1991); Department General

Manager (July 1991-11 Feb. 1992); General Manager (12 Feb. 1992-); Chairman of Yemen Bankers Association (Sept. 1993-). Member of the Union of Arab Banks/ Beirut Oct. 1993. **Sports:** Tennis, Swimming, Travelling. **Hobbies:** Photography, Gardening. **Credit Cards:** Amex, Visa, Mastercard. **Prof. Addr.:** Yemen Bank for Reconstruction and Development, H/O, P.O.Box 541, Tel.: 271626, Sanaa, Republic of Yemen. **Priv. Addr.:** P.O.Box 12038, Sanaa, Republic of Yemen.

ADDOKHAYEIL (Hamad Bin Nasser, Dr.), Saudi Academic. **Born** in 1364H corr. 1945G at Al Magma City, K.S.A. **Dipl.:** Bachelor degree in Arabic Language Sciences, Arabic Language College, Riyadh (1389H, 1969G), Master Degree, Arabic Literature and Critique , Arabic Language College, Al Azhar University, Cairo (1394H, 1974G); Doctorate, Arabic Literature (Ph.D), Arabic Language College, Mohammed Bin Saud Islamic University, Riyadh (1402H, 1982G) with Honour Grade First Class. **Career:** Member, Instructive Department of Arabic Language, Al Imam Mohammad Bin Saud Islamic University; Was in charge of Administration of Teaching Arabic Language for non spoken Arabic Language Institute for six years (Riyadh); in charge of Presidential of Literary Section in Arabic Language College; Member of Higher Board of Arabic in Pakistan; Member of recent Literary Group in Cairo; Reviewed a number of books and literature, history works for a number of parties; Supervised on many Bachelor, Master and Decorate Researches and contribute in discussing many of them inside the University and outside of it; participate in many Scientific and Cultural Committees; also participated in stand activities in Cultural Clubs in S. A.; has constant participation in the media (press and broadcast); took part in number of Seminars and scientific Cultural Conference sharing with specialized Researches; Shared in writing episodes of learning Arabic Language for non spoken Arabic Language in Al Imam Mohammed Bin Saud Islamic University; Shared in writing curriculums of Arabic Language in the intermediate stage in Ministry of Education **Publ.:** Issued seventeen books and thirteen instructional books. **Prof.Addr.:** P.O.Box 6687, Riyadh 11452, Tel.: 2585340, Fax: 4935505, Saudi Arabia. **Priv. Addr.:** Tel. 4915452, Saudi Arabia.

ADEL (Fouad Rachad, al), Syrian diplomat, politician, lawyer, writer and poet. **Born** in 1922 in Damascus. **Educ.:** Specialist from Paris University in Labour Laws and Social Problems (1951); Licentiate of Law from the Syrian University (1947). **Career:** Minister of Social Affairs and Labour, Syria (1961); Deputy of Damascus (1961); Minister of Culture and Information (1962-63); Senior Adviser of Ministry of Labour in Saudi Arabia since 1964. **Publ.:** Author of "al-Mahzoun", "al-Mackakel al-Igtimaiyah", "Roua"; Poetry: "The Social Justice" (1969), "My Nation between two wars" (1973). **Addr.:** Baghdad Street No. 57, Damascus, Syria.

ADEL (Omar, Abdulhamid), Sudanese UN Official. **Born** on July 27, 1923 in Dongola. **Educ.:** Sudan Schools and Kings College, London University, Hendon Police College (London). **Dipl.:** Bachelor of Law, Diploma in International Affairs, Diploma in Criminal Investigations. **Career:** Entered Government Service (1942); Customs Officer (1945-48); Joined Sudan Police (1948); Studied in England (1952-54); Barrister-at-Law, Gray's Inn (1955); Superintendent of Police (C.I.D.) (1955); Private Secretary to Supreme Council of Republic (1956); Ambassador to Italy, Austria and Albania (1956-59); Permanent Representative to United Nations (1959-64); Appointed by United Nations Secretariat to supervise elections in Cook Islands (1965); Elected Chairman of the First Political and Security Committee U.N. (1962); Head and member of several Sudanese Delegations to International Organizations all over the World; Consultant for implementation of United Nations General Assembly and Security Council Resolutions on Non Self-Governing Territories (1965-66); Resident Representative of United Nations Development Programme (UNDP) in Iraq (Oct. 1966-71); Special Consultant to the Administration, UN Development Programme (UNDP), New York (1972-79); Resident Representative, Iraq, UNDP (1972). **Awards:** Grand Cross Order of Saint Silvestro, Holy See; many foreign decorations from Ethiopia, Italy, Panama, Bolivia, Paraguay. **Addr.:** Khartoum, Sudan.

ADEN (Mohamad, Ali), Somali Politician. **Born** in 1939 in Bargaal village, Iskushuban District, Somalia. **Married**, with children. **Educ.:** elementary and intermediate education in Bargaal; secondary education in Mogadishu. **Career:** Teacher (1960-65); Chairman, Teachers' Union (1965-69); Secretary, General Confederation of Somali Labourers (1966-69); Regional Education Director of Benadir (1970- Dec. 1974); Secretary of State for Labour and Sports (1974 July- 1976); Minister of Education (July 1976- May 1988); Minister of Marine Transport, Ports and Fisheries (June 1988-90). **Member:** Somali Socialist Revolutionary Party (SSRP) Central Committee since July 1976. **Addr.:** Mogadishu, Somalia.

ADEN (Mohamed), Djibouti executive. **Born** on October 15, 1936 in Tadjourah, Djibouti. **Son** of Cheikh Aden (Moslem Judge) **and** Mrs, Koyna Omar. **Married** on November 17, 1971 to Miss Annick Fouillade, 7 children: Omar (1957), Ali (1960), Hemeda (1961), Louback (1963), Hasna (1965); Zeinab (1966) and Houssein (1970). **Educ.:** Primary and secondary education in Djibouti; Faculty of law, Paris. **Dipl.:** LL.B.; Diplome de l'Institut des Hautes Etudes d'Outre-Mer, Paris. **Career:** Assistant to Head of Administrative Affairs, then Head and Inspector and Technical Counsellor at the Ministry of Interior; In charge of Moslem affairs. Currently President of Banque pour le Commerce et l'Industrie (Mer Rouge), Djibouti; First Vice President of the Djibouti International Chamber of Commerce and Industry as well as Director of several public and semi-public companies. **Sport:** Horse riding. **Hobbies:** Fishing, bridge, tennis and golf. **Member:** Espadon Club, affiliated to I.G.F.A., Nautical Clubs. Former President of Rotary Club. **Credit Card:** American Express. **Prof. and Priv. Addr.:** P.O.Box 2122, Tel.: 35.08.57 (Off.), 351036 (Res.), Djibouti, Republic of Djibouti.

ADHAM (Abbas Yahya Mohamad), Saudi businessman. **Born** in Jeddah, 1932. **Educ.:** Received general education. **Career:** Government employee; Accountant, Ministry of Communications; member of Mecca Chamber of Commerce and Industry; owner, Talal Establishment for Architecture and General Contracting. **Addr.:** Talal Establishment, P.O.Box 1356, Tel. 35858, Mecca, Saudi Arabia.

ADI (Abdel Karim), Syrian politician and lawyer. **Born** in 1931 in Hama, Syria. **Married**, with children. **Educ.:** Law Faculty, Damascus University, Syria. **Dipl.:** LL.B. **Career:** Ministry of Education; Governor of Deir al-Zor; Director-General, Public Consumption Organization; Member, Baath Regional Command (since November 1970); Member, People's Council (February 1971); Minister of Supply and Internal Trade (April 1971-75); Minister of State for Foreign Affairs (August 1976-79); Minister of Presidential Affairs (1980-86). **Addr.:** Damascus, Syria.

ADIB (Abdul Hary), Egyptian artist, scenarist. **Born** in 1928 at Mahallat Kubra, Egypt. **Married**, three children. **Educ.:** Drama and Theatre Institute. **Dipl.:** B.A. **Career:** firm scenarist (since 1967), one of the first film producers and cinema writers in Egypt. **Member** of the Cinema Association at the Chamber of the Cinema Industry. **Publ.:** short stories and screenplays for 120 Egyptian feature films of which the most important "Bab al-Hadid" (1957); "Um al-Arusa". **Sports:** Swimming, walking. **Hobbies:** Cinema and stage, reading contemporary and classical literature. **Addr.:** 36 Sharif Street, Tel. 43780, Cairo, Egypt.

ADLI (Ibrahim), Syrian UN official. **Born** in 1921 in Damascus, Syria. **Married. Educ.:** Damascus University, Syria; American University, Washington D.C., USA. **Dipl.:** LL.B., M.A. in Law and Ph.D. in Economics. **Career:** Head of Income Tax Department, Ministry of Finance (1952-54); Director of Internal Revenue, Ministry of Finance (1954-58); Director of Personnel, Ministry of Finance (1958-60); Director General, Pension and Insurance Fund, Syrian Government (1960-62); Chairman of the Board and Director General, Banque de Syrie et d'Outre-Mer, Damascus (1962-63); Resident Representative, UN Development Programme, UNDP, Kuwait (1966-72); Resident Representative, UNDP, Libya (1972-78); Resident Representative, UNDP, Riyadh, Saudi Arabia (1978); Resident Co-ordinator, UN Systems Operational Activities for the Development of Saudi Arabia (since 1981). **Publ.:** several articles on economics and finance in professional journals. **Medals:** Syrian Order of Merit. **Addr.:** UNDP, P.O.Box 558, Riyadh, Saudi Arabia.

ADOU (Abbate, Ebo, Dr.), Djibouti deputy at the National Assembly, and M.D. **Born** in 1951 in Dikhil. **Educ.:** Medical Education, Paris (1980). **Career:** Medical Practician. Director of Public Health (1985-1989); Doctor (1989-1997); **Member:** of "Association pour l'Avenir des Jeunes du Territoire" in 1969; Association des Etudiants Afar, France (1973), Union Nationale des Etudiants des Côtes Afar-Somali, Paris (1975); Member of FRUD, Spokesman of FRUD. Elected Deputy at the National Assembly (19.12.1997- to date). Commission Member for Social Development, Environment Protection, Finance Commission, Economy and Planning. **Prof. Addr.:** National Assembly, P.O.Box 138 Djibouti, Djibouti.

ADWAN (Mohammad Affash, Dr.), Jordanian diplomat. **Born** in 1943 in Shuneh, Jordan. **Son** of Affash Adwan and Mrs. Sheima Saud. **Married** in 1978 in California, U.S.A. to Natasha Razmenkov, one child, Raya (June 16, 1987). **Educ.:** Islamic Scientific College, High School; California State University (San Jose); University of Colorado, Boulder. **Dipl.:** B.A, M.A., Ph.D.; Leadership & Management, University of Pittsburgh; Development, Claremont Graduate School. **Career:** Vice-President, Jordan Valley Authority (1977-82); Director, Office of Her Majesty Queen Noor al-Hussein (1982-85); Ambassador of Jordan to Spain (1985-89); Ambassador of Jordan to the U.S.S.R. (1990-1992); Ambassador (non-resident) to Finland and Poland (1990-1992); Chief of Royal Protocol (8.8.1992-14.10.1993); Minister of Tourism and Antiquities (14.10.1993-1995). **Awards:** Jordan's Independence Decor, First Order Spain's Grand Cross. **Sports:** Horseback riding, swimming. **Hobbies:** Reading, chess. **Members:** World Affairs Council, Amman; American Political Science Honor Society. **Priv. Addr.:** Tel.: 813266, Amman, Jordan.

ADWOK (Luigi, Bong Gicomeko), Former alternate assistant secretary general, Sudanese Socialist Union (SSU). **Born** on March 24, 1929 at Agodo, Kodok District. Upper Nile Province. **Son** of a Shilluk Chief. **Educ.:** Lul primary School; Bussere Intermediate School; Rumbek Secondary School. **Dipl.:** Intermediate Teacher's Training College, Bakht Er Ruda (1954). **Career:** schoolmaster (1952-57); member, Constituent Assembly (1958); Headmaster, Tembura Intermediate School (1963-64); member, Supreme Council of State (Dec. 1964- June 1965); re-elected (June 1965) but resigned in protest against Government policy at the time. **Member**, Central Executive Committee, Southern Front Party (1964-67); member, Constituent Assembly (1967-69); appointed member, Sudan Research Unit (1969); sat on Preparatory Committee, Sudanese Socialist Union (SSU); Minister of Works (1971); appointed Commissioner for Upper Nile Province

(Nov. 1971); appointed member for Education, High Executive Council for the Southern Region (April 1971); Acting Assistant Secretary General, Sudanese Socialist Union (Feb. 1972); Alternate Assistant Secretary General, SSU, since May 1974 until Party dissolved following Coup in 1989. **Addr.:** Khartoum, Sudan.

AFIF (Ahmad, Jaber), Yemeni statesman. **Born** in 1930 in Sana'a. **Educ.:** High School, Sana'a. **Career:** Director of Schools, Hodeida Province (1952-56), Under-Secretary for Education (1956-58), Director Sana'a Hospital (1958-60), Under-Secretary for Health (1960-63), Ambassador to Lebanon and Syria (1963-69), President of Council of Petroleum Co. (1969), Minister of Education (1970). **Priv. Addr.:** ar-Rayani Street, Sanaa, Republic of Yemen.

AFIFI (Hilmi al-Bar, Major-General), Egyptian military commander. **Born** in 1922 in Egypt. **Married** three children. **Educ.:** graduated from Egyptian Military Academy (1942). **Career:** commissioned in artillery; attended course at Middle East Anti-Aircraft School, Haifa; served in Egyptian antiaircraft units in Suez Canal Zone; course at Egyptian Staff College (1956); attended Air Defence Course at Soviet Air Defence Academy Odessa, USSR; Chief of Staff of Air Defence Command, October 1973 War; attended Farnborough Air Show, UK in 1974; Commander of Air Defence (1975). **Addr.:** Ministry of Defence, Cairo, Egypt.

AFIFI (Kamil, Faeq, al), Jordanian surgeon. **Born** in 1942 in Nablus, Jordan. **Married,** 1 son, 2 daughters. **Educ.:** University of Zurich, Switzerland, Hand Surgery Unit, Derby, UK (1981). **Career:** Surgeon and Hand Surgeon, al-Bashir Hospital, then at a Private Clinic (1983-); Fellow, Swiss Orthopaedic Association, English Orthopaedic Association, Associate Member, British Hand Surgery Association. **Hobbies:** Reading and tennis. **Prof. Addr.:** P.O.Box 926592, Amman, Jordan.

AFIFI (Nawal, Mohammad), Egyptian physician. **Born** on June 11, 1936 in Cairo, Egypt. **Married,** 2 sons. **Educ.:** Cairo University; Postgraduate Studies in Immunology and Cytology at Hopital St. Louis, Lyon Institute, Paris; Hopital St. Antoine, Paris. **Dipl.:** M.Sc. in Medicine and Clinical Pathology. **Career:** Clinical Demonstrator (1962-64); Lecturer, Cairo University (1964-69) and (1972-74), Assistant Professor, Cairo University (1974-79), Professor of Clinical Pathology, the British Society for Allergy and Clinical Immunology, the International Blood Transfusion Society and the American Blood Bank Association. **Hobbies:** Reading and music. **Member:** Shooting Club, Yachting Club, Gezira Sporting Club. **Prof. Addr.:** Clinical Pathology Department, Faculty of Medicine, Cairo University, Egypt. **Priv. Addr.:** 13 Ahmed Abdel Aziz Street, Aguza, Cairo, Egypt.

AFRA (Saad, Abdallah), Egyptian diplomat. **Born** in 1924 in Alexandria, Egypt. **Son** of Abdullah Afra. **Married. Educ.:** Cairo University. **Dipl.:** B.A. in Law; M.A. in Political Sciences. **Career:** Army Officer; Director of Egyptian Information Service (1957-60); joined Ministry of Foreign Affairs, rank of ambassador (1960); Ambassador to Poland (1962-68); Director, East European Affairs (1968-70); Under Secretary of State, Ministry of Foreign Affairs (1970); Ambassador to Yugoslavia (1971-74); Under Secretary of State, Ministry of Foreign Affairs (1975-79); Ambassador to Greece (1979-83). **Addr.:** Ministry of Foreign Affairs, Cairo, Egypt.

AGEEB (Osman A.A.), Sudanese Agronomist. **Born** On January 1, 1939 at El Affad-Sudan. **Son** of Ahmed A. Ageeb (Merchant) **and** Mrs. Misk El Yemen Abdelkarim. **Married** on January 23, 1973 in Wadmedani to Agba Dawelbait, five children: Muntasir (1975), Moataz (1977), Tayseer (1979), Sahar (1981), Soha (1984). **Educ.:** Hantoub Secondary School 1954-1958, University of Khartoum- School of Science 1958-1960, University of Khartoum - School of Agriculture 1960-1963 (B.Sc), University of Nottingham, U.K., Sutton Bonington, School of Agriculture, U.K., 1965-1968, Ph. D (Agronomy). **Career:** 1963-1965 Assistant Research Scientist, Gezira Research Station; 1968-1973 Research Scientist, Abunaam Research Station; 1973-1979 Senior Research Scientist, Hudeiba Research Station; 1979-1982 Associate Professor; 1982-Professor; 1985-1990 National Coordinator Wheat Research; 1990-1993 Deputy Director Agricultural Research Corporation; 1993-1998 Director General, ARC, Sudan; 1999-2002 Representative of Near East and North Africa in Consultative Group on International Agricultural Research (CGIAR). **Decorations:** Tothill Prize 1963 (Best Student). **Sports Practised:** Walking. **Hobby:** Sight Seeing. **Clubs and Associations:** Gezira Club, Agricultural Society, Environment Society. **Prof. Addr.:** P.O.Box 126, Wadmedani, Sudan, Tel.: (249-511) 42226, Fax: (249-511) 43213. **Priv. Addr.:** Same as Above, Tel.: (249-511) 43216, Sudan.

AGEEL (Abdullah, O.), Saudi businessman. **Born** on August 16, 1934, in Bombay, India. **Educ.:** Fallah Scholl, Jeddah; Randolph Macon College, Virgina, USA. **Dipl.:** B.A. (in Economics). **Career:** Government work with Supreme Planning Council and Ministry of Information; Business consulting Representative; became one of two Saudi Members of New York Stock Exchange; Representative of agricultural business and product companies in Saudi Arabia; Owner of "Abdullah Ageel Establishment" in Jeddah. **Hobbies:** Fishing, swimming and Islamic culture. **Prof. Addr.:** King Abdul Aziz Street, Alireza Bldg., Jeddah 21411, Jeddah, Saudi Arabia.

AGEEL (Abdulrahman Mohammed), Saudi academic. **Born** in 1943 in Jizan, Saudi Arabia. **Educ.:** King Saud University, Riyadh, Saudi Arabia; College of Pharmacy, Wayne State University, Detroit, Michigan, U.S.A.; College of Pharmacy, University of Arizona, Tucson, AZ,

U.S.A. **Dipl.:** B.S. in Pharmacy (1965); M.S. in Pharmacology (1970); Ph.D. in Pharmacology (1974). **Career:** Prof. of Pharmacology, Principal & Co. Investigator in Folk & Khat projects respectively; Head: Dept. of Pharmacology, College of Pharmacy, King Saud University, Riyadh for 10 Years; Assistant Editor in Poisonindex, U.S.A.; On Editorial Board of Saudi Pharmaceutial Journal and Pakistan Journal of Pharmacology; Founder & Former Director, Drug & Poison Information Center, College of Pharmacy, King Saud University, Riyadh; Part-time consultant, a Chairman & a member of several committees in the Ministry of Health of Saudi Arabia; Superviser of the Audiovisual Unit, & Cell Culture Laboratory, College of Pharmacy, King Saud University, Riyadh (formerly); **Conferences:** Attended numerous conferences in the Kingdom and in different countries of the World. **Research:** Published many papers in different areas of Pharmacology, in Folk Medicine & in Khat. **Books:** Co-author of several books on Narcotics, Drug Education, Medical Terminology, Folk Medicine & Management of Poisoning. **Membership:** The Saudi Pharmaceutical Society; Drug Information Association, U.S.A.; American Association of Poison Control Centers; International Federation of Pharmacy (FIP-Associate Member); Collegium International Neuropsychophama Collegium; Pharmaceutical Society of Japan; European Association for the Study of Diabetes (EASD); The Alumini Association, University of Arizona, U.S.A.; The Rhochi Society (Pharmaceutical Honor Society), Wayne State University, U.S.A. **Addr.:** Dept. of Pharmacology, College of Pharmacy, King Saud University, P.O.Box 2457, Riyadh 11451, Saudi Arabia.

AGGAD (Omar, Abdul-Fattah), Saudi bank director and businessman. **Born** in 1927 in Palestine. **Son** of Abdul-Fattah Aggad. **Married** in 1960, 4 children. **Educ.:** Manchester University, Birmingham College of Technology. **Dipl.:** B.Sc. (Electrical Engineering); Industrial Administration Diploma. **Career:** Director of: Saudi British Bank, Riyadh, Saudi Arabia; Arabian Investment Banking Corp.; Smith Barney, Inc. Chairman: Saudi Plastic Products Co. (Sappco), and a Director of its subsidiaries: Sappco-Dammam; Arabian Plastic Manufacturing Co. (Aplaco); Sappco-Texaco Insulation Products Co. (Saptex); Director, Prefabricated Building Co. (Mabes); Director, Arabian Technical Contracting Co. (Artec); Director, Aluminium Products Co. (Alupco); Director, Health Water Bottling Co. (Nissah); Director, Steel Products Co. (Stepco); Saudi International Petroleum Carriers (Sipca); Arabian Ductile Pipe Co. (Adipco) and Hygienic Paper Factory (Fine); Director, Arab Investment Co. Luxembourg and Switzerland; Chairman, Saudi Continental Insurance Co., Riyadh. **Hobby:** Social Service. **Member:** Equestrian Club and several professional and social institutions. **Honours:** Man of the Year Award (Middle East Money) (1985); Man of the Month Award (Saudi Business Magazine) (1984 April). **Addr.:** P.O.Box 2256, Tel. 01-476-7911, Fax: 01-476-7895, Telex 200276 AGGAD, Riyadh 11451, Saudi Arabia.

AGOUMI (Abdelwahab), Moroccan artistical counsellor at the Ministry of Culture. **Born** on 10 October 1918 at Fez, Morocco. **Son** of Hachem Ben-Mohamed Agoumi (late) **and** Mrs., née Zoubida Berrada. **Married** in 1955 in Algers to Miss Yasmina Makaci, 2 children: Amal (1956) and Adil (1957). **Educ.:** Ecole Coranique, Ecole Agoumi, Lycée Moulay Idriss at Fez; Université Karaouine (Fez); Conservatoire Fouad 1er (Cairo); Ecole Normale (Paris); Ecole de Musique (Compostela). **Dipl.:** Culture of Music; Harmonisation and Orchestration, Composition. **Career:** Choir (Marly le Roy); Singer, Composer, Director of the Conservatoire; Head of the Music Section, Ministry of Culture; Artistical Counsellor, Ministry of Culture, Ministry of Social Affairs; research on folklore and theory of the Andalusian music; has recorded, in Paris, records. **Decor.:** Exceptional decoration awarded by H.M. late King Hassan II. **Sports:** Horseriding, swimming. **Hobbies:** Scrabble, cross words. **Member:** Union de l'Amitié Maroco-Soviétique, Société d'Editeurs et Compositeurs (Paris). **Prof. Addr.:** Ministry of Social Affairs, Tel. 70090, Rabat. **Priv. Addr.:** 12, Avenue Ibn Toumerfe, Tel. 330-89, Rabat, Morocco.

AHERDANE (Mahjoubi), Moroccan former Minister. **Born** in 1921. **Married. Educ.:** Azrou-College, Dar el-Beida Military School (Meknes). **Dipl.:** of Officer (1940). **Career:** Fought in Europe during World War II; Caid of Oulmes (1949); participated in the independence fights and member of the National Committee of the Resistance; Governor, Province of Rabat; Secretary-General of the "Movement Populaire" (1957-86); Minister of Defence (1961-64); Minister of Agriculture (1964); Participated in the formation of "Front pour la Défense des Institutions Constitutionnelles (FDIC)" (1963); elected at the Chamber of Counsellors (Province of Rabat) (1963); Minister of Defence (1966-67); Minister of State (1977); Minister of State for the P.T.T. (October 1977); member of Parliament; Minister of State for co-operation (1982) Minister of State (Nov. 1983). Presently Leader of "Mouvement Nationale Populaire". **Hobbies:** Painting and poetry. **Addr.:** Mouvement Nationale Populaire, Rabat, Morocco.

AHMAD (Abdallah, Awadh), Yemeni lawyer. **Born** in 1939 in Aden. **Son** of Awadh Ahmad. **Married**, three daughters. **Educ.:** Law College, University of Alexandria, Egypt. **Career:** Director, Legal advviser's Office (1968); Assistant Legal Adviser (1970); Deputy Legal Adviser to the Revolutionary Council and to the Council of Ministers; Chairman of the Central Appeal Committee for arbitration on tax disputes (1977); member of the People's Constitutional Council (1978); member of the Supreme Judicial Council (1979). **Publ.:** Two articles in "Sharia and Law" magazine (1973). **Hobbies:** Reading, history, law, music, theatre. **Addr.:** legal Office for the State, P.O.Box 1292, Sanaa, Republic of Yemen.

AHMAD (Ahmad, Mohamad), Egyptian official. **Born** in 1921 in Cairo, Egypt. **Son** of Mohamed Ahmad. **Married**, seven children. **Educ.:** B.Sc. in Military Science (1945); Licence in Journalism (1960). **Career:** Army Officer (1945); teacher, Army Education Corps (1949); Private Secretary to late President Nasser (1952); Deputy Adviser and Private Secretary to late President Nasser (1970); Minister of Local Administration (1970); Minister of Presidential Affairs (1971); Deputy Prime Minister (1971); Minister of Presidential Affairs (1971); Deputy Prime Minister (1971); Secretary General, Federation of Arab Republics' Presidential Council (1971); Acting Head of the Federation Council of Ministers (1976). **Head** of the Egyptian Olympic Committee; Head of the Egyptian Football Union; Chairman, al-Hurriya School, Bab al-Louq, Cairo. **Medals:** Flag Decoration of Yugoslavia, 3rd Class (1960); Order of the Throne, 2nd Class, Morocco (1960); Order of the Two Niles, 2nd Class, Sudan (1960); Order of the Star, 2nd Class, Afghanistan (1960); Star of Ethiopia, Commando Class (1962); Order of Maarib, 3rd Class, Yemen Arab Republic (1964); Order of Merit, 2nd Class, Tunisia (1965); Alawi Medal, 1st Class, Morocco (1965); Order of the Flag Golden Crown, Yugoslavia (1965); Order of Stitoto Commando Class, Pland (1965); Order of Merit Grand Officer Class, Mauritania (1976); Order of Merit Commando Class, Brazzaville, Congo (1969); Order of the Two Niles, 1st Class, Sudan (1969); Medal of National Merit Commando Class, Central African Republic (1970); Order of the Flag, 1st Class, Hungary (1970). **Addr.:** 5 Ibrahim Naguib Street, Garden City, Cairo, Egypt.

AHMAD (Ahmad, Sulaiman, al), Saudi administrator. **Born** in 1953 in Majmaah, Saudi Arabia. **Married. Dipl.:** B.A. in Public Administration, Diploma in Educational Administration. **Career:** Director of Personnel Affairs, Ministry of Higher Education, Budget and Planning Department; Director General, Adminstrative and Financial Affairs, Ministry of Higher Education; Assistant Under Secretary, Ministry of Higher Education (1985-); Supervisor, Office of "al-Majalla al-Arabia" magazine. **Prof. Addr.:** Ministry of Higher Education, Riyadh 11153, Saudi Arabia. **Priv. Addr.:** Sulimania, P.O.Box 58255, Riyadh, Saudi Arabia.

AHMAD (Ahmad, Sulaiman Mohamad), Sudanese diplomat. **Born** in 1923 at Wad Medani, Sudan. **Son** of Sulaiman Ahmad. **Married. Career:** Lawyer; Minister of Agriculture in the First Transitional Government formed after the October 1964 Revolution; Minister of Agriculture in Third Transitional Government (1965); Ambassador to USSR; Minister of Economics and Foreign Trade; transferred to Ministry of Industry and Mining (1970); Minister of Justice (1971); Ambassador to UK (1973-75). **Addr.:** Ministry of Foreign Affairs, Khartoum, Sudan.

AHMAD (Hassan Omer, Dr.), Sudanese legal counsellor. **Born** in 1935 in el-Duiem, Sudan. **Son** of Omer Ahmed (Senior Government Official) **and** Mrs. al-Risala Mohamed. **Married** in 1965 in Khartoum to Wafa Beshir, six children. **Educ.:** Faculty of Law, University of Khartoum, Sudan; Law School, University of Chicago, U.S.A.); Oxford University, U.K., Harvard University Law School, U.S.A. **Dipl.:** LL.B. (Khartoum, 1959); M.G.L. (Chicago, 1960); B.C.L. (Oxford, 1963); S.J.D. (Harvard, 1970). **Career:** Lecturer, Senior Lecturer, Reader at the University of Khartoum, Sudan (1960-69); Senior Legal Officer, United Nations, New York and UNEP (Nairobi, 1970-76); Attorney General (Ministry of Justice), Republic of Sudan (1976-78); Badea Legal Council (since 1979) Former , Legal Adviser to the Supreme Council of State. **Medals:** The Two Niles Order, First Class, Republic of the Sudan. **Hobbies:** Swimming, reading. **Member:** American Club, Khartoum; Gezira Club, Cairo. **Credit Cards:** American Express. **Prof. Addr.:** P.O.Box 2640 Khartoum, Sudan Tel.: 70600. **Priv. Addr.:** Manshiya, Khartoum, Sudan, Tel.: 79428.

AHMAD (Ibrahim, Mohamed Ahmad), Sudanese businessman. **Born** in 1920 in Khartoum, Sudan. **Son** of Mohamed Ahmad. **Married**, four children. **Educ.:** Gordon Memorial College (1956); Diploma in Commerce and Accounting, National University, Cairo, Egypt (1956). **Career:** Government employee (1937-48); Audit Assistant, Russell and Company, Chartered Accountants (1937-48); Audit Assistant, Russell and Company, Chartered Accountants (1948-55); Manager, I.I. Zahman Enterprise (1955-67); Director, Abulezz Contracting Company, Tripoli, Libya (1967-68); Sudan Employers Consultative Association (1968); Managing Director, Tahir Commercial Agencies (manufacturers' representatives, commission agents, imports and exports, government tenderers); Managing Director, Sudan Market and Trade. **President** of Port Sudan Rotary Club (1964-65). **Hobbies:** Gardening, motor cars. **Addr.:** P.O.Box 1758, Tel.: 71381, Khartoum, Sudan.

AHMAD (Khalid, Mohamad), United Arab Emirates journalist. **Born** in 1950 in Dubai, United Arab Emirates. **Son** of Mohamed Ahmad. **Educ.:** Journalism, Cairo University, Egypt (1973-74). **Career:** 3rd Secretary, Diplomatic Service, Ministry of Foreign Affairs; former Chief Editor of "al-Ittihad" and "Akhbar al-Imarat al-Arabiya" published by Ministry of Information. **Member:** of the Board of UAE Press and Publishing Organisation. **Sports:** Football. **Hobbies:** Travel, hunting. **Addr.:** Abu Dhabi, United Arab Emirates.

AHMAD (Laila Nadine Abdulaziz), Egyptian academic. **Born** in 1940 in Cairo Egypt. **Educ.:** Cambridge University, UK. **Dipl.:** B.A. in English (1958-61); Ph.D. in English (1966-71). **Career:** Assistant Lecturer, Ain Shams University, Cairo (1962-63); Assistant Lecturer, Al-Azhar University, Women's College, Cairo (1963-65); Inspector of English Language Teaching in the United Arab Emirates, and Adviser to Ministry of Education on English Language Teaching Development, Ministry of Education, United Arab Emirates; Associate Professor, Chairman of Department of Foreign Languages, University of the United Arab Emirates. **Member:** of the British Society for Middle Eastern Studies. **Publ.:** "E.W. Lane and English Ideas of the Middle East in the Nineteenth Century" (1976). **Addr.:** 27 Marlowe Road, Cambridge, Tel.: 63805, UK.

AHMAD (Mohamad, Abdel Magid), Sudanese economist. **Son** of Abdel Meguid Ahmed (Economist) **and** Mrs., née Hussna Mohamed Yousif. **Married** in 1952 to Fatma Abdelgadir Omer, four children: Hussam, Sawsan, Tarif and Muna. **Educ.:** Gordon Memorial College; Khartoum University; University of Aberdeen (Scotland); London School of Economics. **Dipl.:** B.A., M.A. (Economics), M.A. (International Relations). **Career:** Inspector of Finance, Ministry of Finance (1955-56); Diplomatic Officer (1956-65); Ambassador to Belgium (1965-70); Under-Secretary of Economics and Trade (1971-72); Commissioner of Planning (1972-74); Chairman and Managing Director of SDC since 1974. **Awards:** National Order of Merit (Yugoslavia); Order of Nilain (Sudan), May 1976. **Hobby:** Reading. **Prof. Addr.:** 69, Africa Road, P.O.Box 710, Telex: 2427 SDC SD, Khartoum. **Priv. Addr.:** No.11 Block 16, Riyad Area, Khartoum, Sudan.

AHMAD (Obeid, bin Issa), U.A.E official and businessman. **Born:** UAE national. **Son** of Issa Ahmed. **Married** in 1979. **Dipl.:** B.A., AUB. **Career:** Director General, Sharjah Municipality; Member, Board of Directors, several local companies; Director, Investbank, Sharjah, UAE. **Member:** International Club of Sharjah. **Addr.:** P.O.Box 1885, Tel. 356201, Sharjah, United Arab Emirates.

AHMAD (Othman I., al), Saudi official. **Born** in 1942 in Saudi Arabia. **Dipl.:** M.Sc. **Career:** Trainer and Instructor at the Institute of Public Administration (1969-1971), Director General of Employment, Central Civil Service Bureau (1971-74); Assistant Vice President and later Vice President, Civil Service Bureau; Deputy Secretary General of the Arab League (1981) Member of the Shura Council "Parliament" (1998-); has participated in several conferences and symposia on manpower development and personnel management. **Publ.:** several research papers on the Civil Service and manpower in the public sector. **Addr.:** P.O.Box 1222, Tel. 4027452 (Office) and 4641413 (Home), Riyadh, Saudi Arabia.

AHMAD (Saad Mohamed), Egyptian politician. **Born** in 1931 in Egypt. **Career:** Active in labour and trade union movement for over 30 years. President Cultural Committee for Coca-Cola Co.; President General Labour Union for Gaseous Water, General Union for Foodstuffs Industries, Egyptian Labour Federation; Secretary of Cultural Affairs, General Labour Federation; Minister of State for Manpower and Vocational Traning (1978). **Addr.:** Cairo, Egypt.

AHMAD (Sayyid, Saadidin), Egyptian academic. **Born** on January 24, 1944. **Son** of Saadidin Ahmad. **Married**, 1 son, 1 daughter. **Educ.:** Leonardo da Vinci Institute (1967). **Dipl.:** B.A. in Photography. **Career:** Teacher of Photography, Leonardo da Vinci Institute (1967-73), Professor (1973-76); Head, Department of Drawing, Consultant Artist, IEOC (1976-78), Professor of Photography, Ministry of Education, Libya (1978-80), Artist, Ministry of Culture, Egypt (1980-). **Decor:** Gold Medal, Ena Tourning, Milan, Italy (1967), Gold Medals, Alexandria International Biennale (1976 and 1982). **Hobbies:** Classical music, poetry and reading. **Priv. Addr.:** 71 Hosny Metwaly Khalaf, al-Harani, Tel.: 757995, Giza, Egypt.

AHMADI (Mohamad Bin Mussa, al), Moroccan academic. **Born** in 1951 in Morocco. **Married. Educ.:** Diploma of Higher Studies in Public Law; Diploma in International Relations, Geneva, Switzerland; Ph.D. in Law. **Career:** Lecturer, Faculty of Law, University of Casablanca, Morocco; Lecturer, National School of Public Administration; Participated in conferences on the Law of the Sea and on the Refugees. **Publ.:** Articles and papers on the Law of the Sea and the other legal subjects published in professional journals. **Sports:** Swimming, tennis. **Addr.:** 10 Rue du Mont Ventoux, Tel. 250148, Casablanca, Morocco.

AHMED (Ougoureh, Kifleh), Djibouti Deputy at the National Assembly, and Official. **Born** on November 18, 1955 at Dikhil. **Educ.:** Secondary. **Career:** Employee at Aistrict of Dikhil, in French Army, National Polic;e, Employee at UNICEF; Manager/Hospital of Balbala. Member of FDLD (1979-1983), AROD (01.01.1991-8.8.1991) and FRUD (8.8.1991); Member of Directorate of FRUD; Executive Member (Chief of Staff between-1 Oct. 1991- 19 March 1992); Head of Military Affairs Department (19.03.1992- 26.08.1992); Head of Education and Civil Affairs Department (26.08.1992- 12.02.1993); Principal element of the National Reconciliation; General Secretary of FRUD; Minister of Agriculture and Energy (8 June 1995-23 Dec. 1997); Minister of Civil Service and Administrative Reform (28 Dec. 1997- to date); Elected Deputy at the National Assembly (19.12.1997- to date). **Prof. Addr.:** National Assembly, P.O.Box 138 Djibouti, Djibouti.

AIDI (Osman), Hydraulic Engineer, President of Companies, Responsible of Professional Organisms, President of International Hotels Union. **Born** on October 4, 1931 in Damascus, Syria. **Son** of Mounif Aidi (Doctor, Rector of University) **and** Mrs. née Chahira Chichakly. **Educ.:** College Ulmieh Watanieh (Damascus, Syria), American University of Beirut (Lebanon). Ecole d'ingenieurs hydrauliciens de l'Institut Polytechnique of Grenoble, Faculty of Sciences (Sorbonne, Paris). **Dipl.:** Hydraulic Engineer, Engineer-Doctor ès Sciences. **Career:** Member of Sciences Academy in Syria; Member of several Government Committees of Plannification concerning Dams, Irrigation, Drainage, Energy and Oil. Professor, Faculty of Engineers (Aleppo and Damascus. Presiden-Director General of "Editions Orientales" (1958-66) Beirut; President and Administrator of various Construction Companies, Public Works, Touristic Development, and Hostelry including Groupe Royal Monceau and Société Louison Bobet (Thalassothérapie) in France, U.A.E., Plaza Houston U.S.A., Chain Chame Palaces & Hotels in Syria; Founder/ Member of the Board, Banque de la Méditerranée, Beirut then in Paris (1974-1982); President, Inter-Arab Union for Hostelry and Tourism (since 1993); Consultant and Administrator of "Association Internationale de l'Hôtellerie" (1994); President of "Unions Professionelles Inter-Arabes (since 1994); Vice-President of "Association Internationale de l'Hôtellerie et de la Restauration"; President "Organisation de tourisme euro-méditérranéenne; Member of the Board, University of Balamand (Lebanon), American University of Beirut (Lebanon); Member of Advisory Committee for the Middle-East, Nort Africa (Mena) of World Bank. **Works:** "Aménagement de la Vallée de l'Oronte et de ses Barrages" (1956), "Historique des aménagements et constructions des barrages dans le monde arabe antique" (1958), "Contribution a l'Etude des diffuseurs courts de revolution" (1960), "Etude sur l'Aménagement de la vallée de l'Euphrate et de son barrage (1962). **Decor.:** Officer, Legion of Honour (France), Grand Officer of Merit (Syrian Republic), Officer Order of Cedar (Lebanon), Grande Médaille des Saint-Cyril et Methode (Bulgaria). **Dist.:** Grande Médaille de vermeil de la Ville d Paris. **Sports Practised:** Swimming. **Prof. Addr.:** Hotel Royal Monceau, 37 av. Hoche, 75008 Paris. Cham Palace, P.O.Box 2209, Damascus, Syria. and Hazmieh/Mar Takla, P.O.Box 2986 Beirut (Lebanon). **Priv. Addr.:** Les Floralies, 1 av. de Grande Bretagne, Monaco.

AINI (Mohsen), Yemeni diplomat. **Born** in 1932, Sana'a Yemen. **Educ.:** Cairo University of Paris. **Married,** four children. **Career:** Schoolmaster, Aden, Democrate Republic of South Yemen; Minister of Foreign Affairs, Sanaa, Yemeni Republic (1962); Permanent Representative to UNO (1962-65), (1965-66) and (1967-69); Ambassador to USA (1963-65) and (1965-66); Ambassador to USSR (1968-70); prime Minister (1970-72); Ambassador to UK (1973-74); Prime Minister (June 1974- Junuary 1975); Ambassador to France (1975-76). Permanent Representative to the United Nations (1980-81); Ambassador Extraordinary and Plenipotentiary to the Federal Republic of Germany (1981-84); Ambassador to U.S.A. (1984). **Prof. Addr.:** Ministry of Foreign Affairs, Sanaa, Republic of Yemen.

AISHA (Lalla, H.R.H. Princess), Moroccan Royal Princess, eldest daughter of late King Mohamed V and sister of King Hassan II of Morocco. **Born** in 1930. **Married,** two daughters. **Educ.:** Privately in Islamic and modern subjects. **Career:** First public appearance (1945); first public speech at girls school inauguration in Sale (1947); announced the Sultan's idea that Moroccan women should play a part in national life. Leader of Moroccan Delegation to Arab Women's Congress in Damascus (1957); visited Syrian front lines; Moroccan Ambassador to UK (Morocco's first woman ambassador) (1965-69); Ambassador to Italy (1969-72). **Work:** Has promoted female emancipation. **Award:** Appointed Honorary Colonel of the Syrian Army. **President** of National Mutual Aid; Played prominent part in measures for the relief of Agadir (1960); Honorary President of the National Union of Moroccan Women (since 1969). **Addr.:** Palais Royal, Rabat, Morocco.

AISSA (Brahim), Algerian diplomat. **Born** in 1935, in Algeria. **Married. Educ.:** Diploma in Economic Science, Prague School of Economics, Czechoslovakia (1963). **Career:** Embassy to Guinea (1963-65); Embassy to Bulgaria (1966-68); Department of International Organisation, Ministry of Foreign Affairs (1968-72); Delegate, International Labour Conference; Counsellor, Permanent Mission of Algeria, UN, Geneva, Switzerland (1972-1975); Minister-Counsellor of Algerian Embassy to Tripoli, Libya (1975-1977); Sub-Manager of Multilateral cooperation at the Ministry of Foreign Affairs, Algiers (1977-1979); Sub-Manager for the Arab League at the Ministry of Foreign Affairs, Algiers (1979-1982); Ambassador to Niger (1982-86) also non resident Ambassador to Ouagadougou (Upper volta) (1983-1984); Ambassador to Warsaw (Poland) (1986-89); Director General of Arab Countries (1989-1993); Ambassador to Lebanon (1993-1994); Ambassador to the Sultanate of Oman (1994-1995). **Publ.:** "Le Commerce Extérieur de l'Algérie et les Problèmes de sa Nationalisation" (1963). **Addr.:** Ministry of Foreign Affairs, 1, Rue Ibn Batran, (Le Golf), Algiers, Algeria.

AIT-MESSAOUDENE (Said), Algerian politician army officer. **Born** in 1933 in Algeria. **Educ.:** Trained in various countries and qualified as fighter pilot; Course at Aeronautical Division of Moscow Military Academy. **Career:** Major in Air Force at Officers Flying School, Salon, France (1955); Commander of Air Force; Counsellor for Aviation Affairs in Presidency, Director General of Air Algerie (1968); Minister of Posts and Telecommunications (1972-77); Minister of Public Health (1977-80); Minister of Light Industries (1980-1985). **Member** of National Liberation Army (ALN), led Algerian military missions to China, Iraq and USSR during War of Independence. **Addr.:** Algiers, Algeria.

AIYOUTY (Yassin, al), Egyptian academic. **Born** in 1928 in Sharqiya, Egypt. **Married. Educ.:** Teachers Institute, Cairo; State Teachers College, Trenton, New Jersey,

USA; Rutgers University, New Brunswick, New Jersey, USA; New York University, USA. **Dipl.:** Teachers Institute Diploma (1948); B.S. (1953); M.A. History (1954); Ph.D. Political Science (1966). **Career:** Teacher, Cairo (1948-52) Department of Public Information, UN, Geneva and New York (1958-62); Officer in charge, Radio and Visual Services (Arabic), UN New York (1962-64); Special Assistant to the Executive Director UN Institute for Training and Research (UNITAR) (1964-70); Deputy Director of Training (UNITAR), (1970-71); Political Officer, Department of Political and Security Council Affairs, UN, New York (1971-73); Senior Political Affairs Officer and later Principal Officer and Secretary of AUN Council for Namibia, Department of Political Affairs, Trusteeship and Decolonisation UN (since 1973); Professor of African and Middle Eastern Studies, State University of New York, Stony Brook, USA. **Member of:** the Egyptian Society of International Law, the American Political Science Association; fellow of the African Studies Association USA, the Middle East Studies Association for North America. **Publ.:** "Refugees South of the Sahara, an African Dilemma" (1970); "The UN and Decolonisation - The Role of Afro Asia" (1971); "Africa and International Organisation" (1974); "The Organisation of African Unity After Ten Year - A Comparative Perspective" (1975 and 1976); Many articles in English and Arabic newspapers and Journals. **Medals:** New York University Founders Day Award (1966). **Sports:** Walking, cycling, gymnastics. **Hobby:** Fishing. **Prof. Addr.:** Department of Political Affairs, Trusteeship and Decolonisation, UN, UN Plaza, Tel. (212)7541234, New York, NY 10017. **Priv. Addr.:** 2 Peter Cooper Road, New York, NY 10010, USA.

AJAJ (Safuh, Galib), Jordanian businessman. **Born** in 1929 in Jordan. **Married,** five sons. **Career:** Chairman of the Board and General Manager, al-Zahra Manufacturing and Trading Company and al-Nasr Company for Plastic Manufacture; owner of a factory for the production of leatherwear goods. **Member** of the Board of Amman Chamber of Commerce and Industry (1972-76). **Sport:** Swimming. **Hobbies:** Reading and riding. **Prof. Addr.:** King Talal Street, P.O.Box 2441, Tel. 23626, 38091, Factory 92291, Amman, Jordan. **Priv. Addr.:** Tel. 814887, Amman, Jordan.

AJLAN (Abdallah Mohammad, al), Saudi educator. **Born** in 1934 at Al-Burah. **Dipl.:** Ph.D. **Career:** Held wide-ranging positions as a teacher, soldier, warehouse employee, Secretary to the President of Girls' Education, warehouse Director; Secretary General, Girls' Colleges; Director, Girls' Education, Taif; General Director, Girls' Colleges; Vice President, Girls' Colleges; delivered several lectures at different universities; participated in various panels on the university and public levels; participated in the conferences for the Preparation of Teachers (Mecca), the Islamic Fi'qh Committee (Riyadh) and Sheikh Muhammad Ibn Abdul-Wahab Week (Riyadh). **Publ.:** various preparatory school textbooks. **Hobby:** General reading. **Prof. Addr.:** Girls Colleges Presidency agency, Salam Street; Tel. 4029129, Riyadh, 11113 Saudi Arabia. **Priv. Addr.:** Tel. 4633827, 4633841, Riyadh 11113, Saudi Arabia.

AJLAN (Mohamad Ibn Abdallah, al), Saudi academic. **Born** in 1938 at Huraymla, Saudi Arabia. **Dipl.:** B.A. (1962); M.A. (1977) and Ph.D. (1981); Shari'a (Islamic Law). **Career:** Teacher, Riyadh Islamic Institute (1962); Vice Dean, Islamic Law College (1969); President, Academic Council, Imam Muhammad Ibn Saud Islamic University; Vice Rector, Imam Muhammad Ibn Saud Islamic University (1976); Secretary General, Conference of Islamic Jurisprudence; active participant, the Week of Islamic jurisprudence in Tunis, a symposium on Islamic Legislation in Libya and an Islamic Propagation (Da'wa) Education Conference, India. **Publ.:** Editor-in-Chief for 8 years of al-Da'wa al-Shari'yya magazine, published by Imam Muhammad Ibn Saud Islamic University; a paper on the Judiciary of Grievances and a thesis on the Evidence of Legal Rules according to the Juristic Fundamentals of al-Shatibi and another thesis entitled; "Some light on Imam Ibn Hanbals Doctrine". **Hobby:** Reading. **Addr.:** Tel.: 4355081 (Home), Riyadh, Saudi Arabia.

AJLOUNI (Kamel, Prof.), Jordanian academic. **Born** on 1st March 1943 in Sarih, Jordan. **Son** of Salah Ajlouni. **Married,** 4 children: Sachir (1969, Leith (1973), Heitham (1974), Hibah (1979). **Languages:** Arabic, English, German. **Educ.:** Rashidiah College, Jerusalem, Palestine (June 1955 - May 1958); Hussein College, Amman, Jordan (June 1958 - May 1960); Studien Kollege (General Science), University of Heidelberg, West Germany (1st May 1961 - 30th April 1962); Medical School, University of Heidelberg, West Germany (1st May 1962 - 11th December 1967) Date of Graduation (State Examination), 11th December 1967 (Magna Cum Laude) Doctor of Medicine, University of Heidelberg, 16th February 1968 (Cum Laude). **Certifications:** M.D., 1967 Doctor der Medizin (Anatomy; (1968); ECFMG 112-470-0 (12th February 1969); FLEX (11th June 1974); American Board of Internal Medicine (19th June 1974); Fellowship of the American College of Physicians (1975). **Training:** Rotating Intership, University of Heidelberg, Stuttgart City Hospital, West Germany (1st January 1968 - 31st December 1968); Internal Medicine Residency, St. Ursula Hospital, Boppord, Rhein, West Germany (1st January 1969 - 31st October 1969); Straight Intership, Medicine, Mercy Hospital, Buffalo, New York, U.S.A. (1st November 1969 - 31st December 1970); Residency, Medicine, Mercy Hospital, Buffalo, New York, U.S.A. (1st January 1971 - 31st December 1971); Residency, Medicine, The Medical College of Wisconsin, Milwaukee, U.S.A. (1st 1972 - 31st December 1972); Chief Medical Resident, Medical College of Wisconsin, Milwaukee (1972-73); Fellowship, Endocrine, The Medical College of Wisconsin, Milwaukee (1st July 1973 - 30th June

1975). **Medical Education:** Fellowship RTTC, Shiraz, Iran (1977); Fellowship Department of Medical Education, Dundee, U.K. (1978); Workshop on Educational Planning in Amman, Jordan (1978); workshop on Educational Planning and Evaluation in Damascus, Syria (1978); Worshop on Active Medical Education Centers on Medical Education in Khartoum, Sudan (1979); Workshop on Curriculum Development in Riyadh, Saudi Arabia (1979); Workshop on System and Problem Oriented Medical Education, Masstricht, Holland (1979); Workshop on curriculum Planning and Design in Riyadh, Saudi Arabia (1980); Workshop in American University of Beirut on Basic Medical Sciences (1980); Temporary Consultant for WHO on Medical Education (1978 and 1980); Workshop on Teaching and Teaching Effectiveness Amman, Jordan (1981). **Academic Positions:** Clinical Instructor of Medicine, Medical College of Wisconsin, U.S.A. (1972-73); Clinical Instructor of Medicine + Endocrinology, Medical College of Wisconsin (July 1973-75); Appointed Assistant Professor, January 1975, Medical College of Wisconsin, Starting 1975-76; Assistant Professor of Medicine, University of Jordan (1975-79); Associate Professor of Medicine (1979-83); Associate Professor of Physiology (1979); Professor of Medicine-Endocrinology (1983). **Academic Administrative Positions:** Vice-Chairman of Medicine (1976-78); Chairman of Medicine (1978-82); Director, Jordan University Hospital (January 1978 - October 1978); Assistant Dean, University of Jordan Medical School (1978-82); Vice-Dean, Chairman of Department of Medicine (1983-84), Chief of Staff, Jordan University Hospital (1983-84). **Academic Committees:** Chairman of Curriculum Committee Faculty of Medicine (1977 - September 1980); Chairman of Examination Committee (1977-81); Member of the Academic Committee for Evaluation of Academic Achievement, University of Jordan (1979-81); Member of the Pan Arab Highest Council for Medical Speciality Boards (1978-85); Member of the Executive Council of Arab Medical Speciality Boards (1978-84); Vice-Chairman of Pan Arab Board of Internal Medicine (1980-81); Member of the Highest Medical Council in Jordan (1978- present); Member of the Temporary Council for Planning High Education Plan (1980-85); Member of the Society for World Affairs; Member of the Pan Arab Hospital Accreditation Committee; Member of the Supervisory Committee for Licencing Examination in Jordan; Member of the Curriculum Committee of the Pan Arab Board of Internal Medicine; Member of the Examination Committee of the Pan Arab Board of Internal Medicine (1979-86); Member of the Committee for Scientific Counselling, Jordan University; Member of the Committee for Uniting the Educational Programmes in the Arab World, Jordan University; Member of the Governing Board of Hamad General Hospital, Doha, Qatar (1981-83); President of the Arab Board for Internal Medicine (1983-84); Member of the Scientific Editorial Board of "Majallat al-Tabib" (French Journal); Editor-in-Chief for the Jordan Medical Journal (1979-86). **Public Offices:** Minister of Health of Jordan (11.1.1984 - 6.4.85); President of the Jordan Medical Council (1984 and 1985); President of the Jordan University of Science and Technology (1986- present). **Publ.:** K. Ajlouni, Untersuchunger uber das Yoshida - Ascites - Sarkom der Ratte im Zusammenhang mit dem Freund - Kaminerischen Phaenomen. Universitat Heidelberg, February 1968 (Inauguration Thesis), K. Ajlouni & T. Branigan, Pacemaker Therapy in Acute and Chronic Heart Block, Mercy Hospital Bulletin, Buffalo, New York, 1970., K. Ajlouni & G.B. Theil, Mithramycin Effect on Calcium Phosphate and Phosphorus and Parathyroid Hormone in Osseous Paget's Disease. Clin. Res. 21:883, 1973, K. Ajlouni & T.D. Doeblin: The Syndrome of Hepatitis and Aplastic Anemia. Brit. J. Haem. 24:345-355, 1974. K. Ajlouni, M. Kern, J. Tures, T.C. Hagen & G.B. Theil, Thiothixene Induced Hyponatraemia. Arch. Int. Med. 134:1103-1105, 1974. K. Ajlouni, W. Millman, J.A. Libnoch & G.B. Theil, Hyperphosphatemia and Hypocalcemia in Myeloproliferative Disorder. Ann. Int. Med. 81:99-100, 1974. K. Ajlouni & P.S. Rosenfeld, Treatment of Hypercalcemia Drug Therapy 4:103-111, 1974. K. Ajlouni & T.C. Hagen, Growth Hormone Response to Oral Glucose in Stable and Hypoglycemia Prone Diabetics 23:351, 1974. A.R. Guansing, Y. Leung, K. Ajlouni & T.C. Hagen, The Effect of Hypoglycemia on TSH Release in Man. Clinc. Res. 22:599A, 1974. K. Ajlouni & T.C. Hagen, The Effect of Calcium on Growth Hormone Release in Man. Clin. Res. 22:615A, 1974. K. Ajlouni, D.R. Martinson & T.C. Hagen, The Effect of Glucose on the Growth Hormone Response to L-Dopa in Diabetic and Normal Subjects. Clin. Res. 22: 616A, 1974. A.R. Guansing, Y. Leung, K. Ajlouni & T.C. Effect of Hypoglycemia on TSH Release in Man. J. Clin Endocrin. Metab. 40:755-758, 1975. K. Ajlouni & T.C. Hagen, The Effect of Acute Hypercalcemia on Growth Hormone Release in Man. J. Clin, Endocrinol. Metab. 40:780-782, 1975. T.C.Hagen & K. Ajlouni, Growth Hormone Response to Oral Glucose in Stable and Hypoglycemia - Prone Diabetics. Proc. Soc. Exp. Biol. Med. 149:223-226, 1975. K.R. Shetty, K. Ajlouni, P.S. Rosenfeld & T.C. Hagen, Protracted Vitamin D Intoxication. Arch. Int. Med. 135:186-188, 1975. K. Ajlouni & T.C. Hagen, The Effect of Glucose on Growth Hormone Response to L-DOPA in Diabetic and Normal Subjects. Diabetes 24: 633-636, 1975. Y. Leung, A.R. Guansing, K. Ajlouni, T.C. Hagen, P.S. Rosenfeld & J.J. Barboriak, The Effect of Hypoglycemia on Hypothalmic Thyrotrophin Releasing Hormone (TRH) In The Rat. Endocrinology 97:380-384, 1975. K. Ajlouni & G.B. Theil, The Effects of Mithramycin on Calcium. Phosphorus and Parathyroid Hormone Metabolism in Osseous Paget's Disease. Am. J. Med. Sci. 296:13-18, 1975. A. R. Guansing, Y. Leung, K. Ajlouni & T.C. Hagen, Hypoglycemia, A Non-Thyrotrophin Relesasing Hormone (TRH) Mediatd Stimulus To Prolactin Release (PRL) in Rats. Clin. Res. 23:236A, 1975. K. Ajlouni, D.R. Matinson & T.C.Hagen, Failure of Acute and Chronic Hyperglycemia in Suppressing The Growth Hormone

Response of L-DOPA in Diabetics. 24:407, 1975. A.R. Guansing, Y. Leung, K. Ajlouni, L. Murk, J. Chakravarty & T.C. Hagen, Nyctohemeral Variation in Hypothalmic (HTH) Thyrotrophin-Releasing Hormone (TRH) Content in Rats. Clin. Res. 24:272A, 1976. R.V. Bamrah, K. Ajlouni, W.H. Squires, C.V. Hughes, P. Rosenfeld & F.E. Tristani, Aortic Regurgitation and Pigmentation - Unusual Features of Noonan Syndrome. Am. J. Med. Sci. 271:211, 1976. K. Ajlouni, Glucagon in Diabetes. J.M.J., 1976. K. Ajlouni, A.J.Sill & T.C. Hughes, Glucoregulation of Prolactin Secretion. Diabetes 25:351, 1976. J.A. Libnoch, K. Ajlouni, W. Millman, A.R. Guansing & G.B. Theil, Acute Myelofibrosis with Malignant Hypercalcemia. Am. J. Med 62:432-438, 1977. K. Ajlouni & M. Tarawneh, Review of Thyroid Function Tests. J.M.J. Vol. 12, No. 2, 60-69, 1977. K. Ajlouni, Diagnosis and Treatment of Endocrine Causes of Short Stature. J.M.J. Vol. 13, No.1, 36-44, 1978. G.B. Theil & K. Ajlouni, Effect of Mithramycin on Hydroxyproline Metabolism in Paget's Disease. Journal of Lab and Clinical Medicine. Vol. 90, No.5, 803-809, 1977. B. Varke, A. Funahashi, K. Ajlouni & S.H. Tsung, Protease Inhibitor System and Pulmonary Function Sudies in Klinefelter's Syndrome. (American Review of Respiratory) Disease. Vol. 130, No.14, 1976. K. Ajlouni et. al., Consultant for Chapter Drug Affecting Calcium Metabolism in the AMA Drug Evaluation Book. 3rd Edition, Year 1977. Science Publisher Inc. S.H. Tsung. & K. Ajlouni, Immune Competence in Patients with Klinefelter's Syndrome (The American Journal of the Medical Sciences), Vol. 275, No. 3, 311-317, May-June 1978. W. L. Millman, K. Ajlouni, M. G. Hekhman & G. B. Theil, Hypercalcemia, Metastatic Calcifications and Cardiac Abnormalities. Wisconsin Medical Journal, Vol. 77, S91-S94, Sept. 1978. K. Ajlouni et. al., Hyperthyroidism in Jordan. J.M.J. 14:1, 17-23, 1980. K. Ajlouni et. al., Management of Diabetes Insipidus, J.M.J. 14:1, 55-62, 1980. K. Ajlouni, Habab & Tarawneh, Malaria ad Thyphoid Concomittant Infections, Brief Communication. J.M.J. 14:1, 105-108, 1980. K. Ajlouni & T.C. Hagen, Growth Hormone and Prolactin Abnormalities in Diabetics. Proceeding Arab Emirates Medical Journal, Vol. 1, No.2, 53-58, 1980. K. Ajlouni & M. Khatib, The Effect of Glucose on Growth Hormone Response to Diazepam. Clinical Research, Vol. 28, No.2, 384, 1980. K. Ajlouni & M. Khatib, The Effect of Growth Hormone TSH and Prolactin Response in Normal Subject. Hormone Research, Vol. 13:160-164 (1980). K. Ajlouni & M. Khatib, The Effect of Acute Hypercalcemia on Prolactin Release in Normals. Clinical Research, October, 1980. K. Ajlouni & M. Khatib, The Effect of Acute Hypercalcemia on Prolactin Release in Normal Subjects. Hormone Metabolic Research, Vol.13, No.5, 281-284, 1981. K. Ajlouni & M. Khatib, The Effect of Hyperglycemia on GH Response to Diazepam in Diabetics. Clinical Research, October 1980. T.C. Hagen, K. Ajlouni, D.R. Martinson & A. J. Sill, Glucoregulation of Prolactin Secretion. J.M.J. Vol.15, 45-52, 1981. K. Ajlouni & Dawani, The Use of Mono-Component Insulin in the Treatment of Insulin Resistance. J.M.J. Vol.15, No.1, 95-100, 1981. K. Ajlouni & S. Dahabrah, Hyper Pseudo Pseudo Hypo Parathyroidism, Kuwaiti Medical Journal. 15, (3), 185-189, 1981. K. Ajlouni et, al., Thyroid Disorders in Jordan-Abstract, Procedings of American Thyroid Association Meeting, October 1981. K. Ajlouni, The Growth Hormone Response to Diazepam in Diabetic Subjects. Journal of Endocrinological Investigation. 5: 157-159, 1982. K. Ajlouni et, al., Intestinal Obstruction and Pregnancy. J.M.J. 16, 2: 169-172, 1982. K. Ajlouni et. al., Non-Secretary Tumor of the Islet Cells of the Pancreas. J.M.J. 16, 2: 158-162, 1982. K. Ajlouni et. al., 11-B Hydroxylase Deficiency with Pulmonary Stenosis and Skeletal Abnormalities. J. Endocrinol. Invest. 7: 129, 1984. K. Ajlouni, The Failure of Diazepam to Affect Growth Hormone Prolactin in Acromegalis. Hormone-Research 18: 186-190, 1983. T.C. Hagen, A.M. Lawrence, K. Ajlouni & Thad Hagen, Chronic Propranolol Administration Impairs Glucagon Release During Insulin-Induced Hypoglycemia in Normal Men. J. Endocriol & Metab 59: 622-624, 1984. K. Ajlouni et. al., Primary Empty Sella Syndrome with Panhypopituitarism in a Child. Helv. Paed. Acta, 39: 473-479, 1984. K. Ajlouni et. al., Absence of the Pectoralis Major and Dextro Cordia without Skeletal Abnomalities - A Variant of the Poland Syndrome. J.M.J. Nov. 1986. M.A. Arnaout, R. Amari, K. Ajlouni, D. Martinson, T. Garthwaite, & T.C. Hagen, Different PRL and GH Responses to Vasoactive Intestinal Peptide in Patients with Hyperprolactinemia. Clinical Research, Vol.34, No.4 1986. K. Ajlouni, N.A. Sliman, A. Najdawi, M.M. Abu-Hajir, & M.A. Arnaout, Effect of Exposure to the Altitude of 300 Meters Below Sea-Level on Testosterone, Luteinzing Hormone, Follicle-Stimulating and Prolactin in Man. J. Endocrinol. Invest. 11: 621-623, 1988. M. A. Arnaout, K. Ajlouni & I. Jalal, Effect of Different Glibenclamide Formulas on Blood Levels of Immunoreactive Insulin and Glucose in Noninsulin-Dependent Diabetics. Current Therapeutic Research, Vol.44, No.6, 1988. T.K. Daradkeh & K. Ajlouni, The Effect of Neuroleptics on Prolactinoma Growth in a Jordanian Schizophrenic Girl. Acta Psychiatr. Scand., 77: 228-229, 1988. K. Ajlouni, Sheehan's Syndrome - A Review with Emphasis on the Hypothalamic - Pituitary Function, Journal of the Kuwait Medical Association, 22 (3): 219-224, 1988. M. A. Arnaout, A. S. Awidi, A. M. el-Najdawi, M. S. Khateeb & K. M. Ajlouni, Arginine-Vasopression Modulates Endothelial Associated Proteins in Thyroid Disease, Acta Endcrinologics, (in press). **Awards:** The German Academic Exchange Service Scholarship Award (May 1964 - February 1969); Abdul Hamid Shuman Prize for the best Arab Young Researcher (1983). **Member:** American Diabetes Association; American Federation for Clinical Research; Fellow, American College of Physicians; American Endocrine Association; Jordan Society of Internal Medicine; Arab Association for Advancement of Medical Sciences; New York Academy of Science; American Society for Bone and Mineral Research; Jordan Medical Association; Member of Jordan

Medical Licencing Board; Editor-in-Chief, Jordan Medical Journal (1978-86). **Prof. Addr.:** Jordan University of Sciences and Technology, P.O.Box 3030, Tel.: 295111 Ext. 2720, Telex: 55545 Just Jo, Irbid, Jordan. **Priv. Addr.:** Tel.: 828888, Jordan.

AJOU (Abdul Ghani, Ahmad, al), Saudi businessman. **Born** on January 10, 1935. **Son** of Ahmed Said al-Ajou **and** Mrs. nee Rauhiya al-Hariri. **Married**, seven children: Marwan (Vice-President), Maher (Vice-President), Moin (Manager), Maha, May, Mona and Shirene. **Career:** Proprietor, Chairman of Board of el-Ajou Group (el-Ajou Corp., al-Jeel Medical Co., Ardico-Unysis Co., National Glass & Mirror Factory, Saudi Ribbon Factory), **Member:** Numerous International Clubs. **Credit Cards:** Major International Cards. **Prof. Addr.:** Abdul Ghani el-Ajou Corporation, P.O.Box 78, Riyadh 11411, Tel. 404717, Fax: 4560134, Saudi Arabia.

AJROOSH (Mohamad al-Saad, al), Saudi executive. **Born** in 1930 at Onaizah, Saudi Arabia. **Dipl.:** B.A. (Law), Ain-Shams University; Certificate of Diplomatic Training, UN Centre for Training and Research. **Career:** Assumed several government and diplomatic posts; Attaché, Saudi Embassy, Ethiopia (1955); Attaché, Saudi Embassy, Iran (1959); Director General, Mecca Governorate (1962); one of the founders of Al-Madina to the UN (1965-70); transferred to the Saudi Embassy, Kuala Lumpur (1971-74); then to the Ministry of Foreign Affairs Headquarters; Director General, Yanbu Cement Co. (1974); member of Board, Dar-el 'Ilm Press. **Publ.:** newspaper articles. **Hobbies:** Photography, reading, swimming. **Addr.:** Tel.: 6872198 (Home), Jeddah, Saudi Arabia.

AJROOSH (Saleh al-Ali, al), Saudi executive. **Born** in 1931 in Mecca, Saudi Arabia. **Dipl.:** Licence (Sociology). **Career:** Financial Representative, Ministry of Finance (1958-64); Head of Riyadh Water Department (1973); presently Director General, al-Jazeerah organization for Press, Printing and Publishing; member, the Saudi Arabian Olympic Committee and its Executive Bureau; Fund Secretary, the Saudi Arabian Olympic Committee; member and Treasurer, Arab Federation for Sports; **Addr.:** P.O.Box 354, Tel. 4030934 (Office) and 4763755 (Home), Riyadh, Saudi Arabia.

AKALWIN (Natali, Olwak), Sudanese academic. **Born** in the Upper Nile Province, Shilluk, Sudan. **Educ.:** University of Khartoum, Sudan; London University, UK; Oxford University, UK. **Dipl.:** LL.B., LL.M., D.Phil. **Career:** Regional Minister for Regional Administration and Legal Affairs, Southern Region (1973); Senior Lecturer in Law at the University of Khartoum, Sudan. **Publ.:** D.Phil. thesis in Shilluk Customary Law. **Addr.:** University of Khartoum, P.O.Box 321, Khartoum, Sudan.

AKASHEH (Farid Abdallah), Jordanian physician retired. **Born** in 1921 at Karak, Jordan. **Son** of Abdullah Salim Akasheh (deceased lawyer) **and** Mrs., née Anestas Abo Akleh (deceased). **Married** in 1945 in Damascus to Miss Antoinette B. Fares, six children: Bassam, Ibtisama, Taghrid, Zeid, Hakam, Hussein. **Educ.:** Secondary in Jordan Government schools; St. Joseph University (FFM), Beirut; Post Graduate Studies: Wayn State University, Detroit, USA; St. Andrews University, Dundee, Scotland. **Dipl.:** Doctorat d'Etat Français; Fellow American College of Surgeons; Fellow Royal College of Obstetricians and Gynaecologists. **Career:** Medical Officer, Ministry of Health, Jordan (1949-52); Senior Medical Officer (1952-56); Director and Chief Surgeon, Government Maternity and Gynaecology Hospital, Amman (1957-65); Minister of Social Welfare and Labour (1967); Minister of Health (1972-73); Private Practice. **Medals:** 2nd Order Jordan Star (from King Hussein of Jordan) (1963); 1st Order Cross of the Holy Land (from the Greek Orthodox Patriarch in Jerusalem) (1963); 1st Order Star of Jordan (from King Hussein of Jordan) (1967). **Hobbies:** Classical Music, chess, reading political books and journals. **Member:** Jordan Medical Association; Royal College of Obstetricians and Gynaecologists, London; American College of Surgeons, USA. **Credit Cards:** American Express; Access, Visa. **Priv. Addr.:** Jabal Amman, P.O.Box 2173, Tel. 4641943, Amman 11181, Jordan.

AKBI (Abdulghani), Algerian diplomat. **Born** on March 20, 1933. **Dipl.:** diploma in Law. **Career:** Governor of Saido, Aures, Setif, Oran; Ambassador to Italy; Governor of Constantine; Permanent Algerian Delegate FAO; General Secretary in the Ministry of Internal Affairs; Minister of Commerce (1979); Member FLN Committe (1979); Ambassador to Tunisia (1980-84). **Prof. Addr.:** c/o Ministry of Foreign Affairs, Algiers, Algeria.

AKHATARZADEH (Mohamad), Bahraini merchant/hotelier. **Born** on July 3, 1937 in Manama, Bahrain. **Married** to Mrs. Fakhri, four children: Flora, Fareed, Faud and Mona. **Educ.:** Up to GC O level in England. **Career:** 1955 up to present, Managing Director of Moon Plaza Hotel, Moon Supermarket and Moon Stores. **Sports:** Tennis, football and all sports. **Member:** Skal Club; Chain Club. **Credit Card:** American Express, Visa Card. **Prof. Addr.:** P.O.Box 26218, Tel.: 729005, 727278, Bahrain.

AKHDAR (Farouk, M.), Saudi official. **Born** in 1939 in Jeddah, Saudi Arabia. **Dipl.:** Ph.D. (Economics), University of California. **Career:** Economic Analyst, Ministry of Finance (1958-69); Lecturer, University of Petroleum and Minerals, (1969-74); Director, Technical Office, Ministry of Planning (1974-75); Secretary General, Royal Commission for Jubail and Yanbu; member of the Board of Trustees, Arab Thought Forum, Amman, Jordan; member of the Board, Society for Economists Interested in Resources and Environmental Affairs, Washington, U.S.A., the Saudi Arabian Unified Electric Co. of the Western Region; has represented the Kingdom of Saudi Arabia at many international conferences and scientific seminars held in U.S.A., Britain, Spain, Belgium, Bahrain and the Emirates. **Honours:** Orders of Merit, U.S.A. Korea and Belgium. **Hobby:** Writing. **Addr.:** The Royal Commission for Jubail and Yanbu, P.O.Box 5964, Tel. 4010365 (Office) and 4039515 (Home), Riyadh, Saudi Arabia.

AKHRAS (Mahmoud, al), Jordanian librarian. **Born** on January 9, 1927 in Jerusalem. **Married**, two children. **Educ.:** education in England. **Dipl.:** ALA and FLA in Librarianship (1965) and (1975). **Career:** Teacher at the Ministry of Education, Jordan (1949-52); Secretary in the Scholarship Committee (1953-56); Head of Libraries Division, Ministry of Education, Jordan (1958-61), (1964-68) and (1968-79); Librarian, University of Jordan (1962-64); Library Expert, Saudi Arabian Ministry of Education (1966-68); Expert at the Department of Documentation and Information, Arab League Educational, Scientific and Cultural Organisation (1979-89). **Publ.:** "Classifications" (in Arabic (1965); "Library and Research" (1969); "Manual of School Libraries" (1972); "Palestine-Jordan Bibliography 1900-75" (1976); Chief Editor of "Arab Magazine for Information", Tunisia (1980). **Award:** Jordanian State Prize in Research (1977). **Member:** British library Association; Jordan Library Association. **Hobby:** reading. **Addr.:** Amman, Jordan.

AKHRAS (Mohamed, Chafic), Economist. **Born** on July 10, 1929 at Homs, (Syria). **Son** of Abdul Maula Akhras (Businessman) **and** Mrs. née Asma Akhras. **Married** On March 28, 1953 to Miss Pierette Solana, 5 children: Rami, Rima, Samia, Amal and Sami. **Educ.:** College des Pères Jésuites d'Homs, Faculty of Law (Paris). **Dipl.:** Licence in Law, Doctor ès Sciences Economiques, Diploma from Institute of Political Studies, Paris. **Career:** General Secretary of Planning and Economic Affairs at the Presidency of the United Arab Republic (1951-61); Director General of Economic Development Organization in Syria (1961-1962); President-Director General, Banque Omayad, Damascus (Syria) (1963-1967); Head of Finance and Industrial Political Department at the United Nations for Industrial Development, (ONUDI) in Vienna (Austria) (1968-1971); Vice-President-Director General, Bank Al Mashrek, Beirut, (Lebanon) (1971-1973), Founder and President, Saudi Bank Group (1973-1988; Founder and President, Arab Finance Group (1974-1992); Founder of Center for Economic Financial and Social Research and Documentation (1992); President of Investment and Finance SA (since 1992). **Hobbies:** Music, Reading. **Sports Practised:** Swimming, Tennis. **Priv, Addr,:** 37 Av. Foch, 75116 Paris, France.

AKIL (Fakher, Hussain), Syrian professor, writer. **Born** in 1919 in Kafar Takharim, Aleppo. **Son** of Hussain Akil. **Educ.:** American University of Beirut, London University. **Dipl.:** Bachelor of Arts, Master of Education, Doctor of Psychology. **Career:** Professor in Damascus Secondary Schools (1945-55), Professor of Psychology at the Faculty of Education, Damascus University since 1956, Advisor at UNESCO. **Publ.:** Author of several scientific and pedagogy studies in Arabic and English, e.g. "Psychology" (1955). **Member** of the Psychological Society (England). **Addr.:** Sahet Al-Najmeh, Tel. 228824, Damascus, Syria.

AKIL (Nabih, Hussain), Syrian academic. **Born** on August 1, 1929. **Married**, 1 son, 2 daughters. **Educ.:** Damascus University, Syria; London University, UK. **Dipl.:** B.A. in History (1951), Ph.D. in Islamic History (1960). **Career:** Head, History Department, Faculty of Arts, Damascus University (1969-75), Dean (1973-77) and (1980-82), Dean, College of Education, University of United Arab Emirates (1977-79); Vice Chancellor of Damascus University (1982); Assistant Secretary General, Union of the Arab Universities (1985); Deputy Chairman, Committee of Historians', Damascus University, Editorial Board Member of Historical Studies in Damascus University; former Editor in Chief, Damascus University Magazine. **Publ.:** "Tarikh al Arab al-Qadeem Wa Asr al-Rasoul", "Khilafat al-Rashideen", "Khilafat Bani Omaya", "Studies in Byzantine History", "The Byzantine Empire", "Studies in Arab Society", "Introduction to History". **Medal:** Medal of the Kawkab, King Hussain of Jordan. **Decor.:** Order of Arts and Letters, France (1981). **Member:** Arab Historians Union and the International Association for Byzantine History. **Prof. Addr.:** Damascus University, Damascus, Syria. **Priv. Addr.:** Jadet Shakib Arslan, Abou Rommana, Building No.54, Damascus, Syria.

AKKAD (Ruwaid Ahmad), Saudi educator. **Born** on 17 October 1943 in Mecca, Saudi Arabia. **Dipl.:** B.Sc., M.Sc., Ph.D. **Career:** Drilling Engineer, Aramco, then Production Engineer; Instructor and later Assistant Professor, University of Petroleum and Minerals; Assitant Professor and Dean of Student Affairs, University of Petroleum and Minerals; member, Society of Petroleum Engineers (U.S.A.), Swedish Centre for International Relations, Pi Epsilon Tau Tet Honor Society for Petroleum Engineers; participant, the 10th Arab Petroleum Conference; member of Saudi National Committee for the International Petroleum Conference; member of the Islamic Charity Fund. **Publ.:** "Energy and What We Should Know About It", "Energy and the Leading Role of Saudi Arabia" (Public Lecture). **Addr.:** Tel.: 8606235 (Home), Dhahran, Saudi Arabia.

AKROUSH (Anwar, Atallah), Jordanian official. **Born** in 1934 in Jordan. **Son** of Atallah Akrush. **Married**, three children. **Educ.:** University of Damascus, Michigan University, USA. **Dipl.:** Licence in Literature (1968); Master of Science, Librarianship. **Career:** Librarian of the State Library of Tourism; Librarian of the British Council Library, Amman, Jordan; part time lecturer, University of Jordan. **President**, Jordan Library Association; Director, Yarmouk University Library. **Publ.:** articles on library sciences. **Addr.:** Yarmouk University Library, P.O.Box 566 Irbid, Jordan.

AKWAA (Ismail, Ali), Yemeni diplomat. **Born** in 1920. **Married**, 2 sons, 1 daughter. **Career:** 1st Secretary, Yemen Legation, Moscow, USSR; Minister Plenipotentiary and Cultural Attaché, Cairo, Egypt; Ambassador, Ministry of Foreign Affairs; Minister of Information (1968-69). **Publ.:** in several scientific Arabic magazine, also research papers in history, criticism and genealogy and literature. **Addr.:** P.O.Box 227, Sanaa, Republic of Yemen.

AKWAA (Mohamad Ali, al, Brig.), Yemeni army officer. **Born** in 1933, Sana'a. **Educ.:** Secondary School; Military College, Sana'a. **Career:** Participated in the liberation movements against the last three Imams of Yemen; Free Yemeni Revolution of 1948; held several posts in military and civil service, including Assistant Military Commander of Taiz District; Head of Criminal Investigation Department; head, National Security Department; Chief of Staff, Army Operations; head, South Yemen Relief Office attached to the Presidency; Minister of the Interior (1973-74). **Addr.:** Bir El-Azab, Sana'a, Republic of Yemen.

AL-AGBARI ALI (Mohamed, Othman), Yemeni agricultural engineer. **Born** on December 12, 1948 in Yemen. **Son of** Othman Ali (Chief Cook) **and** Mrs. **Hamama** Ismail. **Married** in 1977 to Miss Sabah Ahmed, five children: Dunya, Ayid, Riem, Asma and Ahmed. **Educ.:** University of Leipzig in the German Democratic Republic (1968 and 1975). **Certif.:** B.Sc., M.Sc. in Agricultural Science and Economics. **Career:** General manager of Yemen General Livestock Corporation (1977), Deputy Chairman of the Consumption Society of Public and Joint Corp. (1978); Board Member of Grain storage Corporation and Livestock Corporation (1978-79), Present occupation General Manager of the Foreign Loans Department at the Cooperative and Agricultural Credit Bank (Yemen) Fellowship: of the Economic Development Institute in Washington, (U.S.A) **Sports:** Swimming, football and tennis. **Hobbies:** Reading of ancient history, arts and travelling. **Credit Card:** American Express. **Prof. Addr.:** Cooperative and Agricultural Credit Bank, P.O.Box 2015 or 2850 Sana'a, Republic of Yemen. Telefon: Private (967-1-417101), Telefax: Office (967-1-219236).

AL-AMAD (Mohamad, Abdul Ghani), Jordanian journalist. **Born** in 1930 in Salt, Jordan. **Married. Dipl.:** B.A. in Political Science and Economics (1955). **Career:** Bank Manager (1962-71); Director, al-Rai newspaper (1972-75); Chief Editor, Jordan Times (1975); presently, Director General Jordan Press Foundation. **Prof. Addr.:** Jordan Press Foundation, P.O.Box 6710, Amman, Jordan.

AL-DARWISH (Yousuf, Jassim), Qatari Chairman of the Board of Directors, AL MAHA HOLDINGS W.L.L. **Career:** A well known businessman and investor in the State of Qatar and other G.C.C. & Middle East countries. Also, Chairman of a number of subsidiaries and affiliated companies and maintains connections with the Commercial & Economic communities and associations. **Address:** P.O.Box 405, Doha-Qatar, Tel.: (974) 672244/ 333333, Fax: (974) 672526/ 333399.

AL-HAZMI (Ahmad Saad), Saudi academic. **Born** in 1950 at Hail, Saudi Arabia. **Dipl.:** Ph.D. in Plant Pathology (Nematology), North Carolina State University, U.S.A. (1981). **Career:** Professor, Faculty of Agriculture, King Saud University. Member: Society of Nematologists, American Phytopathological Society, Saudi Biological Society, Pakistan Society of Nematologists, Arab Society for Plant Protection, Afro-Asian Society of Nematologists, participated in several conferences on Nematoloty, plant pathology and biological control of agricultural pests. Author of the textbook (in Arabic) "Introduction To Plant Nematology". **Member:** Honour Society of Agriculture (Sigma, Gamma, Delta). **Addr.:** Department of Plant Protection, Faculty of Agriculture, P.O.Box 2460, Riyadh 11451, Saudi Arabia.

AL-HUSSEIN (Queen Noor, H.M.), nee Lisa Najeeb Halaby. **b.** 23 August 1951; **m.:** late King Hussein I of Jordan (1978), four children. **Educ.:** B.A. in Architecture and Urban Planning from Princeton University (1974). **Career:** (1974-1978) Architectural and urban planning projects in Australia, Iran and Jordan; Founded in Jordan: (1979) the Royal Endowment for Culture and Education, the annual Arab Children's Congress, (1980), the annual international Jerash Festival for Culture and Arts (1981), the Jubilee School, a secondary school for outstanding scholarship students (1984), the Noor Al Hussein Foundation, a non-profit non-government organization, that initiates national projects in education, women and community development, children's health and welfare, culture and heritage (1985), the National Music Conservatory (1986); Chair; National Task Force for Children, Advisory Committee for the United Nation's University International Leadership Academy, Amman; Patron of the General Federation of Jordanian Women, the National Federation of Business and Professional Women's Clubs as well as various environmental, cultural, sports and national development organizations. **International commitments:** The Jordan Society, Washington D.C. (1980); Patron of the International Union for the Conservation of Nature and Natural Resources (1988); Founding member of the International Commission on Peace and Food (1992); President of the United World Colleges (1995); Director of The Hunger Project; President and Patron of the British Society of the St. John Ophthalmic Hospital in Jerusalem; member of the General Assembly of the SOS-Kinderdorf International and a member of the International Council of the Near East Foundation et al. **Awards:** Queen Noor has been awarded numerous honorary doctorates in international relations, law and humane letters as well as international awards and decorations for her efforts to promote environmental conservation and awareness, economic and social development of women, children and communities, cross cultural exchange, international understanding and world peace. **Recreation:** skiing, horseback riding, tennis, gardening, reading and photography. **Addr.:** Royal Palace, Amman, Jordan

AL-KHALIFA (Mohammed, Saleh, Prof. Dr.), Saudi academician. **Born** in 1947 at Qassim, Saudi Arabia. **Dipl.:** Ph.D. (Zoology, Entomology). **Career:** Demonstrator, College of Science. King Saud University (1971-1972); Assistant Professor (1977); Associate Professor (1981); Professor since 1988 and Vice-Dean and Dean of Librar-ies, King Saud University (1982-1984 and 1984-1985). **Member:** Saudi Biological Society, Royal Microscopical Society (U.K.), Entomological Society of America (U.S.A.) and African Association of Insect Scientists (AAIS). **Publ.:** Over forty scientific articles and five books. **Addr.:** Zoology Department, College of Science, King Saud University, P.O.Box 2455, Tel.: 4675750, Riyadh 11451, Saudi Arabia.

AL-KHOWAITER (Soliman Hammad), Saudi academic. **Born** in 1947 at Onaizah, Saudi Arabia. **Dipl.:** B.Sc., Ph.D. (Physical Chemistry). **Career:** Demonstrator, Department of Chemistry Faculty of Science, King Saud University (1972-73); Assistant Professor (1979-84) and Associate Professor (1984-1994); Vice Dean of Continuing Education and Community Service Centre, King Saud University (1983-85); Head of the Chemistry Department, Faculty of Science, King Saud University (1988-90), and presently Director of Petroleum & Petrochemicals Research Institute, King Abdulaziz City for Science and Technology. **Publications:** Five books and several scientific papers in Physical Chemistry and Catalysis. **Hobbies:** reading, research in the field of chemistry and catalysis. **Prof. Addr.:** Petroleum & Petrochemicals Research Institute, King Abdulaziz City for Science and Technology, Riyadh, Saudi Arabia, Tel.: 4813797, Fax: 4813755.

AL-MAHAYNI (Mohamad Khaled Dr.), Syrian Minister of Finance. **Born** on May 30, 1943 in Damascus, Syria. **Son** of Saleem Al-Mahayni (financial and agricultural business) and Mrs. née Weedad Araman. **Married** to Falak Sakkal in 1966, 2 sons: Salim and Tarek, 2 daughters: Suzan and Rima. **Educ.:** Ph.D. in Economics. **Career:** Various public financial and Economic positions in Syria (1961 to date); Auditor (1970 to date); Finance Director of Various industrial Public enterprises (1964-77); Director, Debt Fund and Information, Ministry of Finance (1979-80); Director, Public Enterprises Affairs (1981-84); Deputy Minister of Finance (1984-87); Governor, International Bank for Reconstruction and Development (IBRD), World Bank, Washington DC (1987 to date); Minister of Finance, Syrian Ministry of Finance (1987 to date); Governor, Arab Bank for Economic Development in Africa (BADEA) (1989 to date); Professor, Faculty of Economy, Damascus University (1992 to date). **Publication/Articles:** Methology of the General Budget of the State in the Syrian Arab Republic (1994); Supplementary Policies for Financial Planning (Presentation and Analysis) (1995); Government Accounting (1996); Public Finance and Tax Legislation (1999). **Memberships:** Committees: Member of the specialized Ministerial Committees and the Cabinet; Permanent Committees of the Uniform Accounting system (1987 to date). **Hobbies:** Reading and Computer. **Prof. Addr.:** Ministry of Finance, Jule Jamal Street, P.O.Box 13136, Tel.: (963) (11) 2239624 and 2216605, Telex: (492)-411932 FINASY SY, Fax: (963) (11) 2224701, E-mail: mof@nct.sy, Damascus, Syria **Priv.Addr.:** Mezze, Villat Sharkie, Boukaii Building, Second Floor, Damascus, Syria.

AL-MUAAMMAR (Faisal Abdurahman), Administrator, educator. **Born** in Sedous Riyadh, Saudi Arabia on January 11, 1959. **Educ.:** B.A University of Riyadh (1982); M.A. in Management, Webster University (1985); Library Development Planning & Management of Libraries, International Graduate Information studies School, University College of Wales (1993). **Career:** Deputy of the National Guard for Educational and Cultural Affairs and Supervisor General of King Abdulaziz Public Library, Riyadh (1996-); Director General, King Abdulaziz Public Library (1987-1996); Director, Training, National Guard, Riyadh (1985-1987); **Member:** Board of Governors, King Abdulaziz Historical Research Center; Board of Governors, King Abdulaziz Society for Talented Persons; International Federation of Library Associations and Institutions (IFLA); International Federation for Information and Documentation (FID); Board of Directors, Fondation du Roi Abdulaziz Al-Saud pour les Etudes Islamiques et les sciences Humaines, Casablanca, Morocco; British Society for Middle Eastern studies, Durham; Board of International Advisors, School of Library and Information Science, University of Wisconsin, Milwaukee USA. Organizer: "Islamic World Information Sources", Symposium (1999); "Rare Photographs Exhibition on al-Quds", Exhibition (1998); "Rare Books Exhibition" (1996); "Al-Andalus: Centuries of Upheavals and Achievments", Conference (1993); "Role of the Citizens in Safeguarding the Achievement and Developments of the Country", Conference (1991); "psychological Warfare", Conference (1991); "Children Right between Theory and Application", Conference (1990); The Relations Between Libraries and Information and Their Effects on qualifications Program", Symposium (1990); "Saudi Arabia in Focus", Photographic Exhibition (1990); "Women and Reading", Conference (1989); "Methods of Cooperation and Documentation", Conference (1988). **Prof. Addr.:** King Abdulaziz Public Library, Khurais Road, P.O.Box 86486 Riyadh 11622, Tel,:

4911280, 4911300, 4914397, Fax: 4911949, 4913481, E-mail: kapl@anet. net.sa.

AL-MUBARAK (Issam), Saudi Diplomat. **Born** on October 4, 1962 at Riyadh, Saudi Arabia. **Son** of Hamed Al-Mubarak **and** Mrs. Hassa. **Married** on March 1987 to Miss Manal, three children: Badr (20/09/1990) & Faisal (18/01/1995) and Nouf (27/09/1998). **Educ.:** Financial Sciences and Math, King Saud University (1983). **Dipl.:** Economical Studies, Bormoth College (1983-1984). **Career:** Responsible of the International Affairs, Foreign Trade Department, Ministry of Trade; Several Stages of Studies in the Diplomatic Institute at the Ministry of Foreign Affairs and the General Administration Institute; Participated in several bilateral and International conferences Locally and Internationally; Commercial Attaché to Saudi Arabia at the United Nations since 1987 to 30/07/1999; Presently, Director General of Foreign Trade Department since 1/8/1999 to date, Ministry of Commerce, Riyadh, Saudi Arabia. **Sports:** Football, Swimming. **Hobbies:** Reading, Travelling. **Credit Cards:** Eurocard, Mastercard. **Prof. Addr.:** 11595 Riyadh, P.O.Box 62774 Saudi Arabia. Tel.:(01)4056420, Fax: (01)4080791.

AL-MULLA (Hasan Eisa), Lawyer & Legal Consultant, **Born:** in 1943 in Al-Khobar, Saudi Arabia. **Education:** Cairo University, P.H.D. **Career:** Owns Dr. Hasan Al Mulla (Lawyers & Legal Consultants) established in Riyadh, Kingdom of Saudi Arabia in 1981. It is one of the known Law firms in Saudi Arabia and the GCC Countries. The Firm is staffed with attorneys and lawyers from various countries, and its services cover all GCC States, with Global associated law offices. Vice Chairman of Saudi National Committee of ICC, Riyadh; Vice Chairman of Legal Consultants Committee, at Riyadh Chamber of Commerce; Chairman of GCC Commercial Arbitration Centre, Bahrain. Board member of Saudi Automative Services Company; Board member of Saudi Advanced Industries Company. EX-General Counsel, Saudi Industrial Development Fund; EX-Board member of Saudi American Bank. EX member of I.C.C. Court of Arbitration. **Areas of Practice:** Agency & Franchise, Construction & Engineering Companies, Collection, Foreign Investments & Joint Venture, Intellectual Property, Labour, Litigation, Arbitration and Commercial & Banking Dispute Settlement, Trademarks & Patents. **Publication:** People Participation in Public Administration; Several Articles in Saudi Magazines and Newspapers" **Address:** Wadi Al Thumama Street, Sulaimaniyah, Riyadh, P.O.Box 15185, Riyadh 11444. Tel.: 4655477 - Fax: 4616155 E-mail: almulla@zajil.net;utmp almulla@zajil.net.

Al-MULLA (Najeeb, Abdulla), Kuwaiti merchant. **Born** on August 2, 1941 in Kuwait. **Son** of Abdalla Saleh Al Mulla (Former Secretary of State and merchant) **and** Mrs. Badriya Al Ghuneim. **Married** to Wafeeqah Al Thaqeb on March 1962, 4 children: **Education:** Victoria College, Alexandria (1948-50), Taunton School, Somerset, England (1950-57), Aberdeen Private School, Scotland (1958-59), Lycée Jaccard, Lausanne (1959-60). **Career:** Joined the Family business in 1960 and was appointed as General Manager of the Al Mulla Group of Companies in 1966, became Chairman of the Group in 1969. Al Mulla Group, established in 1938, is a leading business conglomerate in the State of Kuwait with wide ranging interests in Trading, Engineering, Manufacturing, Consumer Financing and Services. The Group is Professionally managed and has a multinational work force of over 4500 employees. The Group's Trading activities include dealerships for automobiles and heavy equipment-Chrysler, Mitsubishi and Kato with allied support and service facilities; office equipment and consumer durables with leading agencies for White Westinghouse, Minolta, Sharp, Oki, Zanussi. In Engineering, the Group offers complete electro-mechanical services for projects and is a leader in the fields of air conditioning, electrical, plumbing, fire fighting, operation and maintenance services. Group business in the Service Sectors include Auto Rental & Leasing, Travel & Cargo, Insurance agency and brokerage, Security and Environmental Services and consumer Financing. **Sports:** Martial Arts, Squash, Tennis & Swimming. **Credit Cards** Diners, Visa, Mastercard, American Express. **Professional Address:** Al Mulla Group of Companies, P.O.Box 177 Safat, 13002 Safat, Kuwait, Tel.: 244 5040, Telefax: 242 3069.

AL-NABOODAH (Saeed, Juma), United Arab Emirates Businessman. **Born** in 1934 in Dubai. **son** of Juma Al Naboodah. **Career:** Former Member to the Federal National Council and Chairman of the Legal Committee for the U.A.E.; Member of the Dubai Municipality Board; Board Member of: The Arab-British Chamber of Commerce; The Arab-U.S.A. Chamber of Commerce; The Arab-Italian Chamber of Commerce; President: Development Board Government of Dubai; Dubai Chamber of Commerce and Industry; Al Naboodah Group (Private); Vice-President, The National Bank of Dubai. **Address:** P.O.Box: 1200, Dubai, U.A.E.

Al-NAJJAR (Mustafa, Abdelkader), Ex, Secretary-General of Association of Arab Historians (1984-1998); Presently: Director of Arab Gulf Developmental Studies at Qatar Univ., Qatar. **Born** in 1936 in Basrah, Iraq. Married, 2 sons, 3 daughters. **Educ.** Ain Shams University, Cairo. **Dipl.:** M.A (Hons.), Ph.D. **Career:** Junior Lecturer, History Department of Basrah University, Iraq (1969-71) Lecturer (1973-77); Director of Arab Gulf Study Centre, Basrah (1979-1984); Member of the Consultative Committee, Ministry of Foreign Affairs; Member of several Historical, scientific and archaelogical societies and organization; contributed to numerous national and international conferences and symposia; Member of the National Assembly (1984-1988); Professor, Al-Mustansiriyah University, Baghdad, Iraq; **Publ.:** Co-author of "Arab Gulf Contemporary History" (1984), as well as numerous research papers, books and articles on the history of the Arab Gulf, Arabian Province and Arabian Peninsula. Medals of estimation, Basrah University (1982), Medal of the Union of Arab Historian, Baghdad (1986). **Hobbies:** football, swimming. **Private Address:** Hai Al-Shammasia, Adhamiya, Mahalla 318, Zuqaq 25, House 9, Baghdad, Iraq.

AL-RAHMAH (Abdullah Nasser Dr.,), Saudi Academic. **Born** on December 20th, 1943, at Al-Rass, Qassim. **Dipl.:** B.Sc. King Saud University (1969); Ph.D. (Mycology), Glasgow University (1975). **Career:** Demonstrator, Botany and Microbiology Department, College of Science, King Saud University (1969-71); Assistant Professor, same Department (1975-1977); Associate Professor, same Department (1977-1986); Professor, Same Department (1986-); Voice Dean of University Library (1978-1980); Head of the Department of Botany and Microbiology. K.S.U., (1985-1987); Council: Member of College of Science Council (1985-1987); Member of Editorial Board of Journal of College of Science, K.S.U., (1983-1985); Member of Center for Desert Studies Council, K.S.U. (1987-1993); Member of British Mycological Society. Arabian Plant Protection Society; Member of Saudi Biological Society; Member of Second Conference on Mycology, Florida, Third Conference on Plant Pathology, Geneva and other local and International Scientific Conferences to which be Submitted work papers. **Honours and Awards:** Award of 14th Kuwaiti Exhibition book in the field of Scientific book Authoring (1988). **Publications:** More than 50 Research papers on Mycology and Plant Pathology Published in Arab and International Scientific Journals. Authors of some Arabic books on Mycology. **Hobbies:** Reading, Excursions, Photography. **Address:** Botany and Microbiology Department, College of Science, King Saud University, P.O.Box 2455, Riyadh 11451, Saudi Arabia. Tel.: 4675824; 4675835 (Office) Fax: 4675833 Riyadh.

AL-SAHEAL (Yosif Ali), Saudi academic. **Born** in 1955. **Dipl.:** Ph.D. Genetics and plant breeding Department of Botany King Saud University. **Member** in many scientific society, Est., and assign as General Manager at Gassim agril. company and TAIBA INVESTMENT for real estate development company. Dean College of agril. and Vet. Medicine in Gassim Branch K.S.U. **Hobbies:** Photography, Sports. **Address:** Botany Dept. Faculty of Science King Saud University, Tel.: 4675876, P.O.Box 2455, Riyadh 11451, Saudi Arabia.

AL-SHALLAL (Abdullah ben Ali Dr.,), Saudi senior civil servant. **Born** in 1945 in al-Gasab. **Qualification:** PHD. in Arabic Grammar (1987). **Career:** Successfully clerk, Secondary School teacher; General Supervisor of Arabic language at the Ministry of Education; Was delegated to work as a Supervisor of Arabic in Bahrain (1976); now Chairman of Arabic language department at the Ministry of Education since 1980. **Publication:** Explanation of (Al-Tohfa Alwardia by Ibn Al-Wardi) 1990. Explanation and Documentation of (Sharh Shawahed sharh Al-Tohfa Al-Wardia by Abdulkadir Al-Baghdadi); Documentation of (Alkhasassa fee Tayseer Alkholasa by Ibn Al-Wardi). Also participated in writing many "Arabic" school textbooks. **Address:** P.O.Box 17455, Riyadh 11484, Saudi Arabia.

AL-SHOBAILY (Abdulrahman Saleh), Saudi. **Born** in 1944, Saudi Arabia. **Dipl.:** Ph.D. (Mass Communication), Ohio State University 1971. **Career:** Former Director General, Saudi Arabian Television Department, Ministry of Information; Director General, Information Department, King Saud University; Assistant Director of Programmes, Riyadh Broadcasting Service (1965-66); Director of Programmes, Riyadh Television Service (1966-68); Deputy Minister for Higher Education, Ministry of Higher Education; Member, Al-Shura (Consultative) Council, S.A., Member, High Council on Information, Saudi Arabia; Professor, Mass Communication Department, King Saud University, Riyadh. **Publications:** Ph.D. thesis on Mass Media in Saudi Arabia; 4 books on media. **Address:** P.O.Box 843, Tel. 4763227, Riyadh, 11421 Saudi Arabia.

AL-TAWAIL (Mohammed, A.), Saudi President, Al-Tawail Management Consulting & Training. **born** on September 5, 1944 in Saudi Arabia. **Son** of Abdulrahman Al-Tawail and Mrs. Monirah Al-Bawardi. **Married** in 1970 in Riyadh to Monira al-Guwaiz, 4 children: Mona, Ghadah, Gassan, Monther **Educ.:** B.A Economics and Politics, King Saud University (1967); M.A. in Public Administration, University of Pittsburgh, USA (1970); Ph.D. in Public Administration, University of Pittsburgh. USA (1974). **Career.** Expert in Public Administration, Institute of Public Administration (IPA) (1967-74); Director General, Institute of Public Admistration (IPA) (1978-95); President, Al-Tawail Management Consulting & Training (AMT) (1996-to date). **other Information:** President, International Institute of Administrative Sciences, Brussels-Belgium (1986-89); president, Executive Council of Arab Organization for Administrative Development (1979-83); chairman, Board of Directors, Saudi National Shipping Company (1987-92). **Awards:** Distinguished Graduate, University of Pittsburgh (1986). **Sports.** Swimming, Jogging. **Hobby:** Reading. **Prof. Addr.:** Al-Tawail Management Consulting & Training, P.O. Box 9171 Riyadh 11413, Saudi Arabia, Tel.: (996) 1 4790116; Fax: (966) 1 4790157; E Mail: altawail@sps.net.sa; web Site: www.altawail.com.

AL-WATARY (Hussein, Ali), Yemeni Businessman. **Born** in 1926 in Sana'a, Yemen. **Son** of Ali Al Watary. (Sanaani Tribe). **Married** in 1943, 3 sons, 4 daughters. **Career:** Chairman, Alwatary Trading & Agricultural Development Co (YSA).; Alwatary Industrial & Trading Corporation Ltd. **Member of Board of Directors:** Yemen Bank for Reconstruction & Development, Sana'a, Yemen.

President: Federation of Yemen Chambers of Commerce & Industry, Sana'a Chamber of Commerce. **Member:** Arab-Belgium Chamber of Commerce. **Hobby:** Social Welfare Activities. **Address:** P.O.Box 61/2207, Sana'a. Tele: 272998, 272024 - Fax: 271992, 272040 - Telex: 2268 A/B WATARY YE, Sana'a, Republic of Yemen.

AL-YOUSEF (Mohammed bin Musa Abdullah), Omani Administrator, **Born** in 1948 in Muttrah, Oman. **Son** of Musa bin Abdullah Al-Yousef. **Married**, five children. **Education:** Fellow of the Chartered Institute of Certified Accountants, U.K. M.Sc. in Development Planning and Administration from the University of Bristol. Now reading for Ph.D. in University College London. **Carrer:** Accounts Clerk, Petroleum Development Oman (1966-67); Auditor, Whinney Murrey and Co. (1967-71); Treasury Accountant Petroleum Development Oman (1971-72); Joined the Government service in 1972, as Director of Accounts and Treasury (1972-74); Director General of Finance (1974-75); Undersecretary of Finance (1975-88); Secretary General, Development Council and Supreme Committee for Town Planning with the rank of Minister (1989-93). Minister of State for Development Affairs since 1994. **Member of:** Financial Affairs Council, Development Council, Board of Governors of Central Bank of Oman, Supreme Committee for Town Planning, Supreme Committee for Vocational Training and Labour; Chairman of Oman Development Bank of Oman National Insurance Co. **Address:** Ministry of Development, P.O.Box 881, Muscat, Postal Code 113, Sultanate of Oman, Telephone. 698830, Telefax 696285, Telex 5384 DEVELOP ON.

ALABBAS (Ebrahim Ahmed Abdulnabi), United Arab Emirates businessman **Born** in 1949 in Dubai. **Married,** 4 sons and 5 daughters. **Educ.:** University of Beverly Hills, USA. **Dipl.:** B.Sc. **Career:** Chairman, Al Abbas Group (AL Abbas Trading Company, Al Abbas Technical Supplies And Services, International Office Supplies, Hadi Enterprises, Publilink Advertising, National Medical Supplies, Al Abbas Interior Environments, Al Abbas International LLC, Al Abbas Travels, Abba Electronics LLC, Mega Sports LLC, Food and Life LLC). **Address:** Al Abbas Building, Khalid Ibn Al Walid Road, P.O.Box 327, Tel.: 3521000, Fax: 3521200, E-mail: group@alabbas.com, website: http://www.alabbas.com.

ALAKI (Madani, Abdulkader), Saudi Minister. **Born** in 1940 in Jizan, Saudi Arabia. **Dipl.:** Ph.D. (Business Administration). **Career:** Assistant Professor and Vice Dean, Faculty of Economics and Administration (1972-77); Assistant Deputy Minister, Ministry of Transportation (1979); Associate Professor, and later Professor, Faculty of Economics and Administration; Dean, Faculty of Economics and Administration, King Abdulaziz University; Alumni member, University of Arizona; member, Information Management System Society, USA; former member of the Board of Directors, Saudi National Gas Company and Saudi Public Transportation Company (SAPTCO); member of the Board of Directors, Saudi Retirement Fund (1974); Participant member, the Conference of Arab Ministers for Higher Education, Algiers; Minister of State (since Aug. 1995). **Publ.:** Management Functions; Organization Functions; Business Administration in Saudi Environment; Manpower Development; Management: Functions and Decision-Making Analysis (books). **Hobbies:** reading history books, music. **Addr.:** King Abdulaziz University, Faculty of Economics and Administration, P.O.Box 9031, Tel. 6892376 (Office) and 6879751 (Home), Jeddah, Saudi Arabia.

ALAKI (Mohamad, Abdul Kader), Saudi diplomat. **Born** on July 15, 1932 in Saudi Arabia. **Educ.:** Faculty of Political Science, Cairo University. **Dipl.:** B.Sc. (Econ. & Political Science). **Carrer:** shool headmaster; joined the Ministry of Foreign Affairs; 20 years' foreign service at Saudi missions in the Hashemite kingdom of Jordan, Switzerland, Guinea, Japan, UN and France: formerly chargé d'Affaires, Embassy of the Kingdom of Saudi Arabia to the Republic of Korea. **Publ.:** Co-founder of "al-Madina" Arabic language newspaper, and editorialist. **Hobbies:** Reading, travel & music. **Sports:** swimming & tennis. **Prof. Addr.:** Ministry of Foreign Affairs, Riyadh, Saudi Arabia.

ALALWAN (Faisal, Mansour, al), Bahraini Executive. **Born** on December 21, 1949 in Bahrain. **Son** of Mansour Abdulla Al-Alwan (merchant) And Mrs. Dana Awal Al Zeera. **Married** on May 1, 1980 in Bahrain to Wedad E. Al-Mansour, four children: Manahil (1981), Naseem (1984), Basma (1990) and Hawra (1993). **Educ.:** Bahrain Higher Secondary School, Bahrain and Teachers Training College, Bahrain; Executive Management-Diploma, College of Business and Management, University of Bahrain (1988-1990); Citibank Normal Operations Course - 6 months (1976); Citibank I.T.P.S. Computer (1977); Citibank Selling Skills (1978) Citibank Intermediate Management (1979); Citibank Financial and Credit Course - 6 months (1980): Euromoney Projet Financing (1982); Bahrain Bankers Training Center; Sovereign Lending (1985); Capital Market Course (1988). **Career:** School teacher with the Ministry of Education where he taught Mathematics and English (1967-1971); Started as a Platform Clerk with the Citibank and in a span of ten years, rose to be the Manager of the Bahrain Marketing Unit (1971-1981): Joined Saudi National Commercial Bank, Bahrain as Senior Marketing officer (1981-1983; Joined Bahrain Middle East Bank, Bahrain as Vice President and Head of the Middle East Marketing Unit (1983-1984); Was invited by Saudi European Bank S.A. to join their Bahrain Management Team as Vice President and General Manager (1984-1990) and presently General Manager of the Arab Investment Company S.A.A (1990 to date). **Sports:** Tennis, Squash and swimming. **Hobby:** Reading. **Member:** Bahrain Bankers Society, Bahrain. **Credit Card:** Visa and

Master Card. **Priv. Addr.:** P.O.Box 5442. Tel. 224998, Mobile: 9608884, Manama, Bahrain.

ALAM (Mohammad, Maqbool), Pakistani banker. **Born** on November 2, 1948 in Karachi, Pakistan. **Son** of late Badrul Huda **and** late Mrs. Meher Bano. **Married** on August 2, 1977 in Karachi to Qudsia, three sons: Salman (1978), Zeeshan (1980) and Daanish (1984). **Educ.:** Government College of Commerce; Chittagong University. **Dipl.:** B.Com.; Diploma Associate of the Institute of Bankers in Pakistan (D.A.I.B.P) (1975). **Career:** Started banking career in July 1969; Joined United Bank Limited, Pakistan, and worked as departmental head in various branches. Later worked in the international division. In 1975 transferred to Yemen and worked there till year 1980. Joined Bank of Oman Ltd. in 1981 and worked with this bank in U.A.E., Egypt, Kenya and as country manager in Khartoum and Bahrain. Presently Chief of the O.B.U. in Bahrain and Looking after the interests of the bank in Saudi Arabia and Bahrain. **Decor.:** Allied Bank Ltd., Pakistan, Prize for standing second and securing second highest mark in first attempt in D.A.I.B.P. Exam. **Sports:** Cricket and jogging. **Hobbies:** Reading books, playing cricket and sightseeing. **Credit Card:** Visa. **Prof. Addr.:** Bank of Oman Ltd.; King Faisal Road, Ground Floor, P.O.Box 20654, Tel.: 257858, Telex: 9565 BOL BK BN Manama, Bahrain. **Priv. Addr.:** Al-Zamil Garden No. 2, House No. 745, Tel: 694349, Budaiya, Bahrain.

ALAMI (Driss, Ben Aomar, el), Moroccan statesman. **Born** in May 18, 1917 in Moulay Idriss du Zerhoun. **Son** of Aomar el-Alami. **Educ.:** Primary and secondary studies in Meknes, Military Academy of Meknes (1935-39). **Career:** Officer, Participated in the Second World War with the French Army (1939-45); joined Moroccan Army (1954); Governor of the Province of Meknes (1956-58); Commander, Royal Military Academy of Ribat al-Khaïr (1958-60); Commander of the Royal Gendarmery (1960-61); Governor of Casablanca (1961-64); General of the Royal Armed Forces (1964-67); Major-General of the Royal Armed Forces (1967-70); Minister of Postal Administration (1970-77); Chairman and President of Royal Air Maroc (1977). **Addr.:** Casablanca, Morocco.

ALAMI (Fawaz, Abdulssatar, al), Saudi academic. **Born** in 25 June 1946 in Mecca, Saudi Arabia. **Son** of Abdulssattar al-Alamy (Dentist) **and** Mrs., née Aziza al-Ghori. **Married** in 1973 to Miss Basila Ahmad al-Homoud. **Educ.:** B.Sc. (Chemical Physics), University of Kent, England (1970); M.Sc. (Solid State Technology), Institute of Technology, England (1972); Ph.D. (Solid State Technology), Institute of Technology, England (1976). **Career:** King Abdulaziz University: Assistant Professor, Physics Department (1976-77); Head of Physics Department (1977-78); Associate Dean, College of Engineering (1978-79); Dean, Institute of Meteorology & Arid Lands Studies, (1979). **Member:** The British Institute of Physics (1974). **Publ.:** "The Growth of the Layer Compound Series Sn xZr and X-ray Analysis", "The Pendelofens Technique", "Thermal Expansion of Layer Compounds", "Chemical Decomposition of Layer Compounds" and "Growth Parameters and X-ray Analysis of Some Transition Metal Dichalcogenides". **Sports:** Swimming. **Hobby:** Chess. **Prof. Addr.:** King Abdulaziz University, P.O.Box 1540, Jeddah, Saudi Arabia.

ALAMI (Muhammad, Ahmad al-Idrissi), Moroccan academic. **Born** in 1947 in Rabat, Morocco. **Married,** 2 sons, 1 daughter. **Educ.:** University of Paris, France. **Dipl.:** Ph.D. in Law (1972). **Career:** Teacher, University of Morocco (1970-71); Consultant, Ministry of Information; Principal of the Higher Institute of Journalism (1971-). **Publ.:** "Law Manual" (1974), "Commercial Law" (1975). **Decor.:** Order of Merit, King Hassan of Morocco in 1982. **Hobbies:** Reading, music and sport. **Prof. Addr.:** Higher Institute of Journalism, Charia Maa Aima, Rabat, Morocco.

ALAMI (Muhammad, Yahia, Abdel Raouf, al), Egyptian broadcasting executive. **Born** on July 5, 1941 in Zakazik, Egypt. **Married,** 1 daughter. **Educ.:** Ain Shams University. **Dipl.:** LL.B. (1962); Diploma in Cinema and Television Directing, BBC, United Kingdom (1972). **Career:** Producer, Egyptian Televison (1980-82), Assistant Chief, Channel One (1982), Deputy Video Production Manager (1983-). **Decor.:** Egyptian Order of the Republic for Sciences and Arts (1st Class) in 1983; Order of Artistic Merit, Egypt (1982). **Prof. Addr.:** Television Broadcasting Corporation of Egypt, Maspiro, Cairo, Egypt. **Priv. Addr.:** 34 Abdel Moneim Riad Str., Dokki, Cairo, Egypt.

ALAMI (Mundir), Moroccan financial and administrative manager. **Born** in 1939, in Rabat, Morocco. **Son** of Hassan Alami. **Married** in 1962, 4 children. **Educ.:** Cairo University, Michigan University. **Dipl.:** B.Com., Computer Studies. **Career:** Financial and Budgeting Controller, Ministry of Public Works; Chief Accountant, Ministry of Public Works (1962-74); Financial and Administrative Manager, Kuwait International Contracting Company (1974-79); Financial and Administrative Manager, Consortium Moroc-co- Koweitien de Développement, Casablanca (since 1979); Member of the Board, Farah Maghreb, Sicopar, Safir, Promoconsult. **Hobbies:** Reading, flowers and horticulture. **Sports:** swimming and tennis. **Addr.:** 46, Avenue des F.A.R., Tel.: 313185, 312074, Casablanca, Morocco.

ALAMI (Zuheir), Palestinian consultant. **Born** in Gaza, Palestine in 1935. **Son** of Yusef Alami (Merchant) **and** Mrs. Zakkia Shaath. **Married** to Nadia Achour in 1972, four children. **Educ.:** Cairo University; University of Texas, Austin, Texas. **Dipl.:** B.Sc. in Civil Engineering from Cairo University; M.Sc. and Ph.D. in Civil Engineering from University of Texas. **Career:** Assistant and Associate Professor of Engineering at A.U.B. (1962-75); Visiting Lecturer of School of Architecture at Arab University of

Beirut (1966-71); Partner in the Consulting Engineering Firm "Khatib and Alami", (since 1964); **Credit Cards:** American Express, Visa. **Prof. Addr.:** P.O.Box 14-6203, Beirut and P.O.Box 688, Sharjah **Priv. Addr.:** Beirut Tel.: (1)785903, Sharjah, Tel.: 5248434.

ALAMOUDI (Abdallah), Saudi Attorney at Law. **Born** on 19 Aprit 1950. **Son** of Hussein Alamoudi-Land Lord **and** Mrs. Khadija Alamoudi. **Married** on 5 July 1971 in U.A.E. to Carmen Alamoudi, 3 children: Ismael, Gabreil and Rayan. **Educ.:** Jeddah K.S.A. Alshaty Secondery School - Lyon, Faculty Catholique, Université Lyon, Courses in French - Cairo, Egypt, Faculty of Law, Cairo University - U.S.A. Chicago Kent Law School, Chicago, ILL. U.S.A. **Dipl.:** Licence of Law - Juris Doctor. **Career:** Associated with Gibson, Dunn & Crutcher (1982-1987). **Work:** Attorney at Law. **Other Information:** Translation Licence. **Sports:** Swimming & Walking. **Hobby:** Modern Arts. **Member:** CAFDA. **Credit Card:** Mejor Card. **Prof.Addr.:** P.O.Box 2186 Jeddah 21451, Tel.: 6607775, 6611171, Saudi Arabia. **Priv. Addr.:** Alhamra Dist., Tel.: 6690459, Jeddah, Saudi Arabia.

ALAOUI MDAGHRI (Driss), Moroccan Former Minister. **Born** on 21 June 1944 at Fès, Morocco. **Son** of Abdelouahed Alaoui Mdaghri **and** Mrs., née Fatima Zohra Alaoui Belarbi. **Married** to Mrs Zineb Fassi Fihri, 4 Children from first mariage (Mehdi, Meriem, Ali, Fatima Zohra) and one child with Zineb Fassi Fihri (Amina). **Educ.:** Université Mohammed V, Rabat; Universite de Nice, France. **Dipl.:** Doctorat d'Etat (Law); Diplôme d'Etudes Approfondies en Sociologie. **Career:** Head of Department, State Tobacco Company (1967-73); Director, Maghreban Center of Administrative Studies and Research, Alger (1973-75); Director, Tadla's National Sugar Mill (1975); Director, Higher Institute of Trade and Management (ISCAE), Casablanca (1976-82); Director, Islamic Center for Development of Trade (since 1982), subsidiary organ of the Organization of the Islamic Conference. Since 1989, member of the Moroccan Cabinet: Secretary of State for Foreign Affairs in charge of the Maghreb Arab Union -UMA- (1989-90); Minister of Energy and Mines (1991-93); Minister of Youth and Sports (1994); Minister of Communication (1995-99). **Publ.:** Thesis on the Control of Public Entreprises (Le contrôle des entreprises publiques); "Droit et Gestion des Entreprises Publiques au Maroc"; A book about "Casablanca"; various studies and articles; poems. Founder and member of various associations. **Decor.:** Chevalier de l'Ordre du Trône. Légion d'honneur (Commandeur). **Sports:** Tennis. **Hobbies:** Reading and Science Fiction. **Addr.:** Rabat, Morocco.

ALAQEEL (Adnan H., Prof.), Kuwaiti Director General of Kuwait Institute for Scientific Research. **Born** on March 16, 1945 in Kuwait. **Son** of Sayed Hashim Al-Aqeel **and** Mrs. née Amena Al-Rasheed. **Married** on January 5, 1950 in Kuwait to Mrs. Farida Shehab, 6 children; 5 boys and one girl, Zaid, Hamid, Imad, Abdullah, Abdul Aziz, and Shaikhah. **Educ.:** Kuwait University (1970); Durham University (1974). **Dipl.:** Ph.D. in Differential Geometry. **Career:** Director General of KFAS (1978-1984); Dean of Kuwait University (Dec. 1989-8/2/1992); Director General of Kuwait Institute for Scientific Research (KISR) (29/2/1992- to present). **Other Information:** Associate Editor, J. Prog. Math.; Member of the Editorial Board of T.S.I. Journal. **Awards:** First Class Honors in Math., Kuwait University (1970), Prize of His Highness The Amir of the State of Kuwait for the First Student in Kuwait University (1970); Academic Mission of the University (1970-1974); Prize of Scientific Achievement from Kuwait Foundation for the Advancement of Sciences (1989). **Credit Cards:** Visa. **Prof. Addr.:** Director General, Kuwait Institute for Scientific Research, P.O.Box 24885, 13109 Safat, Kuwait. **Priv. Addr.:** Al-Faiha, Section 1, Str. 14, House 10, Tel.: 2523633, Kuwait.

ALARRAYED (Jalil, Ebrahim, Dr.), Education & Administrative Consultant and University Professor of Education. **Born** on 26 January 1933 in Bahrain. **Son** of H.E. Mr. Ebrahim Arrayed (Ambassador) **and** Mrs. Fatima Arrayed. **Married** on 27 November 1958 to Miss Jalila al-Moosawi, 3 children: Lamya (1960), Iyad (1963), Anmar (1967). **Educ.:** American University of Beirut (Lebanon, 1950-54), Leicester University (U.K. 1960-61, 1963-64), Bath University (U.K. 1972-74). **Dipl.:** B.A. (Chemistry), American University of Beirut (1954); M.Ed. (Science Education), Leicester University (1964); Ph.D. (comparative Science Education and Management of Curriculum Development), Bath University (1974). **Career:** Bahrain Government Department of Education: Science & Math. Teacher (1954-59), Science Inspector (1959-66); Bahrain Men's Teacher Training College, Principal (1966-74)) Bahrain Ministry of Education, Under-Secretary (1974-82); Rector, Bahrain University College, (1982-87); Vice President, Academic affairs, University of Bahrain (1987-91). The Arab Bureau of Education for the Gulf States: Executive Council member (Bahrain representative) (1975), Deputy Chairman (1978-79), chairman (1979-80); The Council for Higher Education in the Gulf States, Member (Bahrain representative) (since 1976), Bahrain University College of Arts, Science and Education, Board of Trustees, Member (1979-86). **Work:** Over 60 articles and papers on educational issues in general and science and higher education in particular; has contributed in the International Encyclopedia of Higher Education (U.S., 1977) and the Encyclopedia of Higher Education (U.K., 1992). Research Students representative on the Board of Studies of University of Bath School of Education (1973-74); has taken part in several regional and international conferences on educational reform, held at ministerial and at expert levels, and chaired several of their committees; Invited by UNESCO and by ALECSO to serve as consultant to some of their specialised seminars on strategies of curriculum reform at regional and at inter-Arab levels; Deputy Chairman, first conference of Arab Educators (Baghdad, June 1975) Chairman, UNESCO/ ALECSO Seminar on Planning and Management of Curriculum Development in Arab States (Cairo, Nov. 1976); Deputy Head of Bahrain Delegation to the 36th Session of the International Conference on Education (Geneva, Sept. 1977); Deputy Chairman, Second Conference of Arab Educators (Baghdad, June 1978); Deputy Chairman, UNESCO Seminar on "Aims of Education in Arab States. A Future outlook" (Cairo, October 1978); Head of Bahrain Delegation to the 37th Session of the International Conference on Education (Geneva, July 1979); Deputy Chairman, the International Congress on Planning and Management of Educational Development (Mexico, 1990); The International Institute of Educational Planning (IIEP) Council of Consultant Fellows, Member (1984-92); Bahrain Ministry of Education prize (for Academic Achievement (1975). American Biographical Institute (ABI), Commemorative Medal of Honor (1988), and World Decoration of Excellence (1989); Bahrain Government annual State Award for Distinguished Professional Service (1992). **Sports:** Table Tenis. **Hobbies:** Chess, reading and listening to music. **Member:** The Association for Science Education (U.K.); The Institute of Management, (U.K.). Fellow; The Institute of Administrative Management (U.K.), Member; The Indian Institute of Public Administration. Life Member; The International Biographical Association, Life Fellow; International Association of University Presidents, Life Member; The International Council on Education for Teaching (U.S.A.) Life Member. **Priv. Addr.:** P.O.Box 26165, Tel.: 400919, Manama, Bahrain.

ALASAAD (Abdul Karim Mohamad), Saudi academic. **Born** in 1930 at Burqah. **Dipl.:** B.A. Shari'a (Islamic Law), Azhar University (1951); Diploma for Arabic Language Teaching, Azhar (1952); B.A. (Arabic Language), King Saud University (1968); M.A. (Arabic Grammar) (1973) and Ph.D. (Arabic Language Grammar and Eloquency) (1975), Ein-Shams University, Egypt. **Career:** School teacher (1952-65); member of Technical Board for Intermediate Education, Ministry of Education (1965-70); Assistant Professor, Arabic Language Department, Faculty of Arts, King Saud University; Associate Professor, then Professor, Faculty of Arts, King Saud University, Riyadh. **Publ.:** Ph.D. thesis: Abu al-Erfan Muhammad Ibn Ali al-Sabban, Gramatical Works; edits educational books for intermediate schools and Teacher's Preparatory Institutes; Bayt al-Nahou wal Mantek wa Ouloum al-Shariah (Ed. 1982); Ahadith fi Tarikh al-Balagha wa fi baad Kadayaha (Ed. 1985); al-Hashiah al-Asriah ala Sharh Shouzour al-Zahab, 3 volumes (Ed. 1989); al-Wassit fi Tarikh al-Nahou al-Arabi (Ed. 1991); contributes articles to al-Darah al-Saudia, Arab Saudia; Dar King Abdul Aziz Magazine, Riyadh; Faculty of Arts Magazine, King Saud University, Riyadh; Defence Magazine, Riyadh; National Guards Magazine, Riyadh; al-Faysal Magazine, Riyadh; al-Arab Magazine, Riyadh. **Addr.:** P.O.Box 548, Riyadh 11421, Saudi Arabia, Tel.: (Home) 4646555, Saudi Arabia.

ALASKAR (Fahd Ibrahim), Saudi General Directore (Special Programmes). **Born** in 1954 in Saudi Arabia. **Educ.:** M.Sc., Degree in Libraries & Information Sciences, Western Michigan University, U.S.A.; M.A.T. in Education, Western Michigan University, U.S.A. **Dipl.:** Diploma in English Language Studies, BA Degree in Geography, Imam Mohamed Bin Saud Islamic University, Saudi Arabia. **Career:** General Director of Special Programmes of the I.P.A.; Director of Information Services Department at I.P.A.; Staff Member & Consultant, I.P.A.; Libraires Studies Programmes Coordinator; Director of the Central Library at I.P.A.; Vice President of International Association of Information and Documentation in Public Administration. **Other Information:** Secretary General of Arab Regional Branch of the International Council on Archives (ARBICA). **Awards:** Silver, Golden Medal & Shield of I.P.A.; Shield from King Abdul-Aziz Research Centre. **Associations:** Saudi Geographical Association. **Credit Cards:** Visa, Master Card. **Prof. Addr.:** Institute of Public Administration (I.P.A.), P.O.Box 205, Riyadh 11141, Saudi Arabia. **Priv. Addr.:** P.O.Box 8681, Riyadh 11492, Saudi Arabia.

ALAWI (Ali Jaber), Yemeni geologist. **Born** on January 1, 1942 in Sanaa, Yemen Arab Republic. **Married,** 3 sons, 3 daughters. **Educ.:** Mining Institute of Ostrava, Czechoslovakia. **Dipl.:** M.Sc. (1966). **Career:** Technical Director, Ministry of Public Works (1966-67); Technical Manager, Yemen Oil Company (1967-68); General Director of Geological Survey, Aden (1968-76), Director General, Geological Survey Board (1976-84); General Secretary, Supreme Council for Oil and Mineral Wealth (1984); President, Syndicate of Yemeni Engineers (1984); President, South Yemeni Engineers; Chairman, First Society of Housing in Sanaa. **Publ.:** "Brief Summary of Geology and Exploration Activities in Yemen Arab Republic" (1978). **Prof. Addr.:** P.O.Box 81, Sanaa, Republic of Yemen.

ALAWI Bin Abdullah (Yusif Bin), Omani Minister. **Born** in Salalah in 1942. **Married. Educ.:** Eucated in Oman and finished his Secondary education from Egypt; continued University Studies in the field of political Science in the UK. **Career:** Second Secretary, Omani Diplomatic Rank (1972); posted in Oman's Embassies In Cairo and Beirut; Ambassador to Lebanon (1973); Under Secretary, Ministry of Foreign Affairs (1974); Minister of State for Foreign Affairs (1982); Minister Responsible for Foreign Affairs (1997-). **Address:** P.O.Box 252, Muscat 113, Tel.: 699532, Fax: 699531, E-mail: mfaoman@omantel.net.om, Sultanate of Oman.

ALAWI (Hamid), Moroccan painter. **Born** on June 21,

1937 in Fès. **Educ.:** Academy of Fine Arts of Casablanca (1954), specialisation in Paris (1960-64) and Louvre (1965). **Career:** Painter, Participated to several art exhibitions in Morocco, France, Switzerland, Germany, etc... Dir. Inox Maroc. **Addr.:** Fès, Morocco.

ALAWI (Moulay Abdallah), Moroccan businessman. **Born** in 1932 in Casablanca, Morocco. **Married**, 4 children. **Educ.:** Institute of Higher Studies, Rabat. **Dipl.:** Postgraduate, National School of Administration. **Career:** Deputy, Ministry of Youth and Sports (1955); Principal Private Secretary (1956-58); joined Mobil Oil Group in 1958; Principal Private Secretary to the Prime Minister (1964); Commercial Director, Mobil Oil (1965); Director General, Mobil Oil, Morocco (1974-); Director, Atlas Sahara SA (1978-), Mobil Exploration, Morocco (1982-); Director, Petrocab (cabotage Maritime); Director, Compagnie d'Entreposage Communautaire; Treasury of Ajyal Association; Founder Member of Ajyal Association; Committee Member, International Chamber of Commerce. **Hobbies:** Tennis and swimming. **Prof. Addr.:** 23 Allal Ben Abdallah Street, Casablanca, Morocco. **Priv. Addr.:** 1 Allee de Mimosas, Casa Anfa, Casablanca, Morocco.

ALAWI (Moulay Abdel Hafid), Moroccan statesman and businessman. **Born** in 1918 in Morocco. **Married. Educ.:** Qarawiy in University, Fez, Morocco. **Career:** entered Habous Administration, served at Fez and Rabat; Inspector of Habous at Meknes; visited H.M. the late King Mohamed V during HM's exile in Madagascar; on return of HM the King to Morocco was appointed Pasha of Meknes; Governor of Meknes (January 1959); Minister of Saharan and Mauritanian Affairs (January 1965); Saharan Affairs following Maroccan recognition of the Islamic Republic of Mauritania; Chamberlain to HM the King; President, Famab S.A., Bachet S.A., Somadu, Sommi; Minister of Royal Protocol (1988). **Addr.:** Casablanca, Morocco.

ALAWI (Moulay Ahmad), Moroccan statesman. **Born** in Morocco. **Educ.:** Secondary and Higher. **Career:** Head of the Press Service (1957); Minister of Handicraft, Mines, Industry and Commerce (1966-68); Minister of Tourism (1968); President, Maroc Soir S.A., Hertz, U.g.c., Secretary General, Arab Organization for Mineral Resources, Rabat, Morocco; Minister of State (1982-1999). **Prof. Addr.:** Rabat, Morocco.

ALAWI (Moulay Mustafa Belarbi), Moroccan former Minister of Justice. **Born** in 1923 in Fès, Morocco. **Married. Educ.:** School for Higher Education, Rabat. **Dipl.:** Degree in Law. **Career:** joined Driss Mohammed in nationalist activities in Atlas Mountains; Director, Cabinet of the Minister of the Interior, after independence; Political Affairs Director, Ministry of the Interior (1959-60); Political Affairs Director, Ministry of Islamic Affairs (1965); Governor of Casablanca in 1971; Ambassador to Italy (1977-82); Minister of Justice (1982-1994). **Decor.:** Order of Massira; Morocco; Officer of the Order of Merit; Commander of the Order of the Throne, Morocco (1972). **Addr.:** Rabat, Morocco.

ALBANAWI (Ismail Mohammad), Saudi businessman. **Born** in 1934 in Jeddah, Saudi Arabia. **Educ.:** Secondary. **Career:** Businessman; Owner and Managing Director, AlBanawi Agencies, AlBanawi Chalets and AlBanawi Garden Equipt. **Hobbies:** Swimming, fishing. **Prof. Addr.:** AlBanawi Agencies, P.O.Box 84, Tel.: (02)6600200, Jeddah 21411, Saudi Arabia. **Priv. Addr.:** Tel.: 6654295, Jeddah, Saudi Arabia.

ALBARRAK (Saad Abdallah, al), Saudi academic **born** in 1948 at Mobarraz. al-Ahsa. **Dipl.:** Ph.D. **Career:** Professor, Major Soils, Minor Soils Morphology and Classification; Vice-President for Higher Studies and Scientific Research,; Chairman, Scientific Council (since 1996), King Faisal University. Member American Society of Agronomy, the Saudi Biological Society. **Hobby:** reading. **Addr:** Faculty of Agricultural Sciences and Food, King Faisal University, P.O.Box 380, Tel.: 5812520, Fax: 5801819, al Ahsa Saudi Arabia.

ALEBRAHIM (Ahmad, A.), Kuwaiti Diplomat. **Born** on January 26, 1944 in Kuwait. **Son** of Abdul Karim Al-Ebrahim (Businessman) **and** Mrs. Fateema Al-Zukir. **Married** in 1984 in Kuwait to Najibah Al-Otaibi, 4 children: Fateema (F. 04.11.1984), Abdul Karim (M. 22.03.1986). Hamed (M. 22.05.1994), Nawal (F. 09.10.1995). **Educ.:** B.A. Economics, from the University of California (USA) 1970, Alumni of the Georgetown University (Washington)/ Advanced course at Fortham University (NY) 1972-1973. **Dipl.:** B.A. Economics, University of California (USA) 1970, Alumni of the Georgetown University (Washington)/ Advanced course at Fortham University (NY) 1972-1973, Master of International Politics, Université Libre de Bruxelles (Brussels) 1997. **Career:** Appointed at the Ministry of Foreign Affairs in June 1970, in the Political Department; Member of the Permanent Mission to the UN in New York, 1971; 1974-1988: Until his nomination as Ambassador Extraordinary and Plenipotentiary to Belgium, His Excellency held the following positions: -Deputy Director of the Economic Section of the Ministry of Foreign Affairs; -Responsible for all UNCTAD, North/South and South/ South negociations; Deputy Director of the Department of Europe at the Ministry of Foreign Affairs; Since 13.10.1988: Ambassador Extraordinary and Plenipotentiary to the Kingdom of Belgium; since 24.01.1989: and Dean of the Arab Diplomatic Corps since September 1997. Head of Mission to the European Communities and since 12.10.1989: Ambassador Extraordinary and Plenipotentiary to the Grand-Duchy of Luxembourg; Commemorative emblem awarded by the Supreme Headquarter Allied Powers Europe (SHAPE), 4 June 1991; Commemorative plate awarded by the SHAPE British troop which took part in the Gulf war, on the occasion of the end of the war, 4 June 1991. European Merit Gold Medal confered to His Excellency by the European Merit Foundation (Grand-Duchy of Luxembourg) on 04.11.1995. **Sports:** Squash, walking, swimming. **Prof. Addr.:** Embassy of Kuwait, 43 Av. F.D. Roosevelt, 1050 Brussels, Belgium, Tel.: (322) 6477950.

ALESSA (Sheikh Abdulaziz, Hamad), Saudi businessman. **Born** in 1924. **Son** of Hamad A. Alessa. **Career:** Co-Founder of Hamad A. Alessa and Sons Co. (1947) and of Alessa Industries (1973); Vice Chairman of Saudi Lime and Bricks Company; Vice Chairman of Saudi Businessmen in Chamber of Commerce; President and Chairman of the Board of Hamad A. Alessa and Sons Company and of Alessa Industries. **Credit Cards:** American Express; Visa. **Prof. Addr:** Hamad A. Alessa and Sons Co., P.O. Box 2091, Riyadh 11451, Tel.: 4039295, Riyadh, Saudi Arabia.

ALFI (Mahmoud Amr, al), Egyptian architect. **Born** in 1939 in Egypt. **Married**, 1 daughter. **Educ.:** Cairo University, Egypt. **Dipl.:** B.Sc. in Architecture (1963). **Career:** Owner of Amr el-Alfy Consulting Office (1965); Designer, Mena House Oberoi Hotel, Cairo (1972-84). **Hobbies:** Farming and landscaping. **Member:** Gezira Sporting Club, Automobile Club. **Addr.:** 7 Boston Street, Cairo, Egypt.

ALFRAIH (Mohammed A.), Saudi businessman. **Born** in 1934 in Onaizah (Saudi Arabia). **Son** of Abdulrahman Alfraih. **Married** in 1969 in Riyadh, Saudi Arabia. **Educ.:** Elementary & Secondary in Saudi Arabia; Faculty of Arts, Cairo University. **Dipl.:** Bachelor of Arts (1953). **Career:** Deputy Director of Administration, Ministry of Education, Saudi Arabia; Cultural Attache, Saudi Embassy to Syria & Lebanon (1957-61); Director General Minsitry of Education, Riyadh (1961-63); Managing Director & General Manager, Riyadh Electric Co. (1963-65); General Manager, Yamama Cement Co., Riyadh (1965-70); Chairman, Riyadh Chamber of Commerce and Industry (1975-81); Set up his own firm under style "Eastern Corporation" in 1965; Managing Director & General Manager of Eastern Corporation since 1965; Chairman AlBank AlSaudi Al-Hollandi (1980-89). **Member:** Board of Directors of the Following: Saudi Ceramic Co., Riyadh; al-Alamiya Insurance Co. England; al-Alamiya for Commerce & Service, Jeddah; Nissah Health Water Bottling Co. Ltd., Riyadh; Montazah Tabarka Co., Tunisia. **Credit Cards:** American Express; Euro Card; Visa Card; Access. **Addr.:** Eastern Corporation, P.O.Box 792, Riyadh 11421, Tel.: 401-0051, Fax: 4015368, Telex: 404267 EASTRA SJ, Saudi Arabia.

ALFURAIH (Ali Abdallah), Saudi academic. **Born** in 1949 at Al-Bakiriah, Qassim province, Kingdom of Saudi Arabia. **Dipl.:** B.Sc., Ph.D. (Geology). **Career:** Instructor, Lecturer, Assistant Professor, Associate Professor, then Professor of Geology, Faculty of Science, and Chairman of the Geophysical-Seismological Observatory, King Saud University; Member of the Saudi Society for Earth Sciences, The British Micropalaeontological society, The Palaeontological Association, London. **Publ.:** Thirty one research articles on geology. **Hobbies:** Swimming, shooting. **Addr.:** Department of Geology, Faculty of Science, King Saud University, P.O.Box 2455, Riyadh 11451, Saudi Arabia. and P.O.Box 85262, Riyadh 11691, Tel.: 4676201, Saudi Arabia.

ALGHANIM (Ali Mohammed Thunayan), Kuwaiti businessman. **Born** in 1937 in Kuwait. **Married:** 5 children. **Education:** Bachelor's degree in Mechanical Engineering from University of Hanover in West Germany. **Career:** Founder and Owner of Ali Alghanim & Sons Group of Companies (Ali Alghanim & Sons Automotive Co., Ali Alghanim & Sons General Tranding Company, Ali Alghanim & Sons Trading & Contracting Group Co., Ali Alghanim Sons General Trading & Contracting Co., Ali Alghanim General Trading & Contracting, Mechanical Engineering & Contracting Company, Ali Alghanim & Sons Trading & Investment Company, Alghanim Wormald Safety & Security Equipment Company); Partner and Chairman of the Board of National Paper Company; Deputy Chairman of Public Authority for Industry, Vice President of Public Institution for Social Security, Member of Kuwait Chamber of Commerce & Industry and Member of the Board of Industrial Development Committee. **Postal Address**: M/S. Ali Alghanim & Sons Group of Companies, P.O.Box 21540, Safat 13076, Kuwait.

ALGHANIM (Dalal Abdulla Thunayan), Kuwaiti Businesswoman, bank executive. **Born** in 1947 in Kuwait. **Daughter** of Abdulla Al-Ghanim **and** Mrs. née Ruqayah Al-Qatami. **Education:** Al-Jazaeer Secondary School for girls. American University of Beirut (B.A. in Fine Arts, 1975). Syracuse University, U.S.A. (M.A. in Public Relations, 1981). **Career:** Public Relations & Advertising Officer (1976-80), Commercial Bank of Kuwait; Assistant Manager, Public Relations & Advertising (1981-82), Commercial Bank of Kuwait; Manager, Public Relations & Advertising (1983-85), Commercial Bank of Kuwait; Senior Manager, Marketing, Commercial Bank of Kuwait (1985-88); Assistant General Manager, Marketing, Commercial Bank of Kuwait (1988-90); Assistant General Manager, Marketing, Construction & Property Management & Administrative Services, Commercial Bank of Kuwait (1991- present). **Duties:** Develops and implements marketing strategies and programmes to enhance the Bank's business both domestically and internationally. Upgrades the Bank's corporate image through publications, corporate identity and other related activities. Responsible for all the Bank's property, fixed assets (their maintenance), vital records, archives, stationery & printing. **Publ.:** Publishes articles regularly on cultural matter in Kuwait. **Sports:** Squash and swimming. **Hobbies:** Reading and travelling. **Member:** Kuwait Women's Society, Gulf

Marketing Association, American Management Association, Gulf Advertising Association, Member in Al-Futtat Sports Club (Kuwait), Board Member in Kuwait Olympic Committee (NOC). **Credit Cards:** Visa, American Express. **Professional Address:** The Commercial Bank of Kuwait, P.O.Box 2861 Safat, 13029 Safat, Kuwait, Tel.: 2468179. Fax: 2434856. Telex: 22004 CBK KT. **Private Address:** P.O.Box 21635. Tel.: 255337.

ALGOSAIBI (Ghazi), Saudi Diplomat. **Born** on March 2, 1940 at Al-Hasa, Saudi Arabia. **Son** of Abdul Rahman Algosaibi **and** Mrs. Fatma Algosaibi. **Married** in 1968 to Sigrid Presser, 4 children: 3 sons and one daughter. **Educ.:** University of Cairo, South California and London. **Career:** Assistant Professor, King Saud University, Riyadh (1965), then Professor and Head of Political Science and Dean, Faculty of Commerce; Director, Saudi Railways (1974); Minister of Industry and Electricity (1975), Minister of Health (1982); Ambassador to Bahrain (1984); to U.K. and Ireland (1992-1994); Ambassador to Bahrain (1994-). Numerous decorations. **Publ.:** The Gulf Crisis: An Attempt to Understand; 10 collections of essays and 10 collections of poems. **Hobbies:** Swimming, fishing, table Tennis. **Prof. Addr.:** Embassy of Saudi Arabia, Juffair, Bldg. 1450, Rd. 4043, Area 340, P.O.Box 1085, Manama, Bahrain.

ALHASHIM (Dhia, Dawod, al), Arab-academic. **Born** in 1941 in Baghdad, Iraq. **Married,** 1 daughter. **Educ.:** University of Baghdad, Iraq; University of California, Los Angeles, USA; University of Missouri, Columbia, USA. **Dipl.:** B.A., M.B.A, Ph.D. **Career:** Assistant Professor, University of Baghdad (1965-68); Assistant Professor, California State University, Northridge, USA (1970-72); Associate Professor, Florida International University, Miami, USA (1972-74), California State University, Northridge, USA (1974-76); Visiting Professor of Accounting, University of California, Los Angeles, USA (Summer Quarters 1975: 1980); Chairman, American Accounting Association, International Accounting Section (1979-80); Director, International Accounting Studies Centre, California State University, Northridge, USA (1976-87); Director, Center for International Business, California State University, Northridge (1988 to present). Professor, California State University, Northridge, USA (1977-); **Publ.:** numerous research papers, articles and books on National and International accounting. **Decor.:** Certificate of Appreciation, US National Association of Accountants; Certificate of Appreciate, US Internal Revenue Service. **Hobbies:** travelling, reading, swimming. Middle Eastern affairs. **Prof. Addr.:** School of Business Administration and Economics; California State University, Northridge, California 91330-8245, USA.

ALHEGELAN (Faisal Abdul Aziz, Sheikh), Saudi Arabian diplomat. **Born** on October 7, 1929 in Jeddah, Saudi Arabia. **Son** of Sheikh Abdul Aziz Alhegelan (Businessman) **and** Mrs. née Fatima al-Eissa. **Married** in August 1961 to Nouha Tarazi, 3 sons: Khaled (1962), Hisham (1963) and Omar (1966). **Educ.:** Faculty of Law, Fuad University, Cairo. **Dipl.:** Diploma in Law. **Career:** Ministry of Foreign Affairs, Jeddah (1952-54); served Embassy in Washington, D.C. (1954-58); Chief of Protocol in Ministry (1958-60); Political Adviser to H.M. King Sa'ud (1960-61); Ambassador to Spain (1961-68); to Venezuela and Argentina (1968-75); to Denmark (1975-76); to U.K. (1976-79); to U.S.A. (1979-83); President of the Saudi Delegation at the Special Session of the General Assembly of the United Nations (1980); Minister of State and member Council of Ministers (Saudi Arabia) (1984-85); Minister of Health (1984-95) since 1996 Ambassador to France; Chairman Board of Directors, Saudi Red Crescent Society (1984-); President of the Association for the fight against the nicotine-poisoning (1985-1995). **Decor:** Order of King Abdulaziz; Gran Cruz Cordon of Order of Isabela la Catolica (Spain); Gran Cordon, Order de Libertador (Venezuela); Grande Official, Order Riobranco (Brazil); May Grand Decoration (Argentina); Knight Grand Cross of the British Empire (U.K.). **Hobbies:** Bridge, golf. **Addr.:** S. Exc. Sheikh Faisal ALHEGELAN, Ambassadeur du Royaume d'Arabie Saoudite. Ambassade d'Arabie Saoudite, 5, Av Hoche, 75008 Paris, France, Tel.: 47.66.02.06, Fax: 40.44.25.76.

ALI (Abdulaziz Mohamad), Sudanese engineer. **Born** in 1942 in Medani, Sudan. **Married,** two children. **Educ.:** B.S. in Civil Engineering; M.Sc. in Structures. **Career:** Worked for Sudan Government (1966-75); Resident Engineer, Sharjah Sport Center (1975-78); Chief Structural Engineer, Public Works Department, Abu Dhabi (1978). **Member:** of Institution of Civil Engineers, UK. **Hobbies:** Reading, painting, walking. **Addr.:** Khartoum, Sudan.

ALI (AbdulHalim Mohamad), Egyptian diplomat. **Born** in 1932 in Egypt. **Son** of Mohamed Ali. **Single. Educ.:** Alex Andria University; Cairo University; Amesterdam University. **Dipl.:** B.Comm. (1955); Marketing (1968); European Integration (1975). **Career:** Egyptian Economic Representative (since 1959); served in Egyptian embassies in: Burma, Soviet Union, Sri Lanca, Belgium, German Democratic Republic, Brazil, USA. **Medals:** Officer of the Order of Leopold (Belgium), 1982. **Sports:** Squash, ping pong, tennis. **Hobbies:** Chess, travel. **Member of:** Internationl Club (Washington); Gezira Club (Cairo). **Credit Cards:** American Express. **Prof. Addr.:** Ministry of Foreign Affairs, Cairo, Egypt.

ALI (Abdullah, M.), Kuwaiti Economist. **Born** in 1937 in Kuwait. **Married,** 1 son, 1 daughter. **Dipl.:** B.Sc. in Mathematics and Statistics (1962), M.A. in Economics (1965); **Career:** Assistant to Chief of Statistical Department, Ministry of Education, Kuwait (1961-62); Teacher, Shuwaikh Secondary School (1962-63); Lecturer in Statistics, North Dakota, USA (1964-65), Lecturer in Statistics and National Accounts, Kuwait Institute of Economic and Social Planning (1966-69); Co-Director, Kuwait Institute of Economic and Social Planning (1971-72); General Director, the Arab Planning Institute (1972-). **Publ.:** "Balance of Payments of Kuwait" (1965-66 to 1967-68), "National Accounts of Kuwait" (1965-66 to 1967-68). **Hobbies:** Reading and theatre. **Member:** Kuwait Cine Club. **Prof. Addr.:** The Arab Planning Institute, P.O.Box 5834, Safat, Kuwait.

ALI (Ahmad, Mohamad), Saudi former President, Islamic Development Bank. **Born** in 1932 in Medina City, Saudi Arabia. **Son** of Mohamad Ali **and** Mrs. Amina Ali. **Married** to Miss Ghada Mahmood Masri, 5 children (4 daughters and 1 son). **Educ.:** B.A., Cairo University, Cairo; (1957); M.A., University of Michigan, Ann Arbor, USA. (1962); Doctorate in Public Administration, fiscal Management, State University of Albany, USA (1967). **Dipl.:** B.A. (1957); M.A. (1962); Doctorate in Public Administration (1967). **Career:** Appointed Director of the Scientific and Islamic Institute, Aden (1958-59); Acting Rector of King Abdul Aziz University, Jeddah (1967-72); Deputy Minister of Education for Technical Affairs (1972-75); President of the Islamic Development Bank (1975-1996). **Membership of Boards of Academic Institutions:** King Abdul Aziz University Council, Jeddah; King Saud University, Riyadh; Oil and Minerals University, Dhahran; Islamic University, Medina; Imam Mohamed Ben Saud University, Riyadh; administrative Board of the Saudi Credit Bank and Administrative Board of the Saudi Fund for Development. **Other Information:** Published Many articles and working papers on Islamic economics and banking and education. **Hobbies:** Cycling; walking. **Addr.:** Jeddah, Saudi Arabia.

ALI (Fathi, Mohamed), Egyptian politician. **Born** in Egypt. **Dipl.:** Ph.D. **Career:** Deputy Dean, Faculty of Commerce, Ain Shams University (1978); member of Board of several banks; Adviser, Central Bank of Egypt (1978-84); Minister for Higher Education (1985-86); **Publ.:** Many studies in the field of higher education. **Addr.:** Ministry for Higher Education, 4 Sharia Ibrahim Nagiv, Cairo (Garden City), Egypt.

ALI (Hassan, Ali bin), Qatari businessman. **Born** on November 29, 1943 in Doha (Qatar). **Son** of Ali bin Ali (businessman) **and** Mrs., née Mariam. **Married** in July 1967 to Mona Nizar Fakhoury, Beirut (Lebanon), 3 children: Wael, Nadia and Khalik. **Educ.:** Broumana School, Lebanon; Concord School, Turnbridge Wells (UK.); Victoria Technical College, London. **Dipl.:** B.Com. **Career:** General Manager, N.A.S.A.L.I. (1969-74); Proprietor and General Manager, Elemee (1973-76); AEG Showroom (1973); Gulf Supustromeck Piling, Ready Mix, Lighting Showroom; Genereal Manager, Reliant Elec. Mech. & Trading, Pepsi Cola, Block Making Machine; Director, Binalli Contracting. **Sports:** tennis and table tennis. **Member:** Doha Senior Staff Club. **Credit Card:** American Express (Golden). **Prof. Addr.:** P.O.Box 2863, Tel.: 328526-26195, Doha, Qatar, **Priv. Addr.:** Tel.: 32565/8, Doha, Qatar.

ALI (Hussain, al), Kuwaiti, Deputy general manager and chief auditor of the National Bank of Kuwait. **Born** in 1942 in Kuwait. **Son** of Abdul Khader Al Ali. **Married** in 1961. 5 children. **Educ.:** B.Sc. in Commerce and Economics (1977); and B.Sc. in Banking (1979); High Diploma in Financial Planning (1979). **Member** of Institute of Internal Auditors, UK; and Fellow Member of the Association of Certified Public Accountants, England; Tuck Executive Program for high potential executives (1989). **Career:** Joined National Bank of Kuwait (1962); worked in all the departments in Head Office and Branches; Branch Manager (1970-76); Auditor (1976-80); Chief Auditor since 1980. **Hobbies:** Reading and Swimming. **Addr.:** Kuwait City, Kuwait.

ALI (Ibrahim, Ali), Djibouti Deputy at the National Assembly. **Educ.** Secondary. **Career:** Employee of ONAC; President of ALCD Association; Member of FRUD. Elected Deputy at the National Assembly (19.12.1997- to date). Secretary-rapporteur for the Social Development, Environment Protection Commission and Member of the Commission of Foreign Affairs, Member of the Supreme Court of Justice. **Prof. Addr.:** National Assembly, P.O.Box 138 Djibouti, Djibouti.

ALI (Idriss, Arnaoud), Djibouti Deputy at the National Assembly. **Born** in 1945 at Ali-Sabieh. **Educ.:** Psychology Diploma. **Career:** Air-Djibouti (02.01.1980- 14.06.1982); Chief of personel (14.06.1982- 20.12.1982); Head of Administrative and Labour Relations Department (20.12.1982- 14.11.1983); Head of Foreign Relations Department (15.11.1983- 31.03.1985); Head of Financial and Administrative Department (1.04.1985- 22.04.1986); Assistant General Manager in addition to the function of the Head of Financial and Administrative Department (24.04.1986- 01.03.1990); Director General by interim (1.03.1990- 31.01.1991); Director General of Air-Djibouti. Technical Consultant at the Ministry of National Education. Member of Executive Committee of RPP. Elected Deputy at the National Assembly (19.12.1997- to date). President of Permanent Commission and Member of National Defence. **Prof. Addr.:** National Assembly, P.O.Box 138 Djibouti, Djibouti.

ALI (Kamal Hassan, General), Egyptian politician, army officer. **Born** in 1921, in Egypt. **Married,** two children. **Educ.:** Attended military courses in USSR; Bovington, UK; Lulworth, UK and Nassir Academy. **Career:** Positions in the Army from Tank Squadron Commander to Director of Armour; Assistant Minister of War with responsibility for training and development (1975); Minister of Defence and Commander in Chief of Egyptian

Armed Forces (1978-80); Deputy Prime Minister and Minister of Foreign Affairs (1980-84); Prime Minister (1984-85); presently Member of the Political Bureau of the National Democratic Party and former Chairman, Egyptian Gulfbank. **Addr.:** Cairo, Egypt.

ALI (Mohamed, Yusuf, al), Qatari businessman. **Born** in 1941 in Qatar. **Married. Educ.:** University of Colorado, USA. **Dipl.:** Electrical Engineering diploma; practical training in UK. **Career:** Former Chairman of Qatar National Cement Co.; now Director of Qatar Electricity Department; association with Qatar Trading Company; Arab **Co-Chairman** of Science and Technology Subcomittee in Euro-Arab Dialogue. **Addr.:** Qatar Trading Co., P.O.Box 51 and 116, Doha, Qatar, Arabian Gulf.

ALI (Mohammad, J., al), Qatari Managing director, Al-Jazeera Satellite Channel. **Born** in 1954 in Doha, Qatar. **Son** of Jasim Al-Ali. **Married,** Seven children: Khloud, Amna, Jasim, Ahmed, Shaikha, Reem, Aisha. **Educ.:** Qatar University. Bachelor of Arts (BA), Sec. Education and Arts Dept./ History Branch. **Career:** 1975-1979 Work for Qatar TV as (Programme Coordinator; Assistant director of Programmes, Head of Coordination Department, Programme Director); 1980-1988 Head of Programmes, Qatar TV; 1989-1992 Work in Sharja (UAE) to launch TV in Sharja; 1992-1995 Assistant TV Director, Qatar TV; 1996-Now Member of Board & Managing Director, JSC (Jazeera Satellite Channel). Many Training Courses in the Fields of TV programmes & Management in Japan, UK, Germany and USA. **Medals and Decorations:** Special Medal from Qatar Minister of Information (1994); Medal of the Qatari Al-Watan Newspaper (1999); Medal From the Arab States Broadcasting Union for Drama (1995). **Sports Practised:** Tennis, Gymnastics, Football, Swimming. **Hobbies:** Reading, Travel. **Clubs:** Local Social Clubs in Qatar. **Credit Cards:** Golden Visa, Master Card. **Prof. Addr.:** P.O.Box 23123 Doha, Tel.: +974-885666, Fax: +974-885333. Doha, Qatar, E-mail: jazeera@aljazeera.net.qa.

ALI (Moulay, H.R.H. Prince), Moroccan businessman, former diplomat. **Born** in 1924 in Marrakech, Morocco. Cousin of HM King Hassan II. **Married,** one child. **Educ.:** In Marrakesh and Lycée Lyautey, Casablanca. **Career:** President National Sugar Company (COSUMAR) (since 1966); arrested by Protectorate Authorities on political charges at time when HM King Mohamed V was sent into exile; joined HM the King in voluntary exile in Madagascar until returning to Morocco; accompanied HM the King on state visits to US and France (1963); Director of several commercial companies in Casablanca; Ambassador to France (1964-66); former President, Société de Banque et de Crédit S.A. **Medals:** Decorated by General de Gaulle as Grand Officer of the Légion d'Honneur. **Addr.:** Casablanca, Morocco.

ALI (Salah Omar, al), Iraqi diplomat. **Born** in 1937 in Tikrit, Iraq. **Married,** 4 sons. **Educ.:** Mustansiriya University, Iraq. **Dipl.:** LL.B. (1974). **Career:** Held various positions at the Ministry of Education and the Ministry of Municipalities (1958-68), Member of the Revolutionary Command Council; Minister of Information (1968-70); Ambassador to Sweden (1972-76), Spain (1976-78), United Nations (1978-82). **Medals:** Medal of Merit, 1st Order, Sudan; Medal from King of Spain. **Hobbies:** Sports and reading. **Prof. Addr.:** Ministry of Foreign Affairs, Bagdad, Iraq.

ALI (Souleiman, Miyir), Djibouti Deputy at the National Assembly. **Born** in 1961 in Djibouti. **Educ.:** Certificate from "Institut International d'Etudes Sociales de Genève" (Switzerland). **Career:** Assistant Manager of SMI/CPS (1982-1991), Director of CPS/SMI (1991-1997); Member of Central Committee of RPP; Former Member of Various Associated Movements to ONG: Elected Deputy at the National Assembly (19.12.1997- to date); President of Legislation Commission, General Administration of the Republic and Member of Permanent Commission. **Prof. Addr.:** National Assembly, P.O.Box 138 Djibouti, Djibouti.

ALI (Wijdan, H.R.H. Princess), Jordanian art historian, painter. **Born** in 1939 in Baghdad, Iraq. **Daughter** of Sherif Fawaz Muhana (architect) and Sherifa Nafaa Jamil. **Married** in 1966 in Amman to HRH Prince Ali Bin Nayef, four children. **Educ.:** Sisters of Nazareth, Amman (1957), Beirut University College (1957-61). **Dipl.:** B.A. in History (1961). (SOAS) University of London; Ph.D. in History of Art (1993). **Career:** First woman to enter Jordanian Foreign Service (1962); First woman to represent Jordan at the UNÉGeneral Assembly, New York (1962) and at E.C.O.S.O.C. Geneva (1962), resigned in 1966 to marry; Took up painting as a career (since 1964); Had exhibitions in London, West Berlin, Washington D.C., Madrid, Karachi Assilah-Morocco, Tunis, Moscow and Amman. **Publ.:** "Taarif Bil Fan al-Islami" Dar al-Bashir lilnashr Jordan (1988) (Arabic); "Contemporary Art from the Islamic World" Scorpion Publishing Ltd. London (1989); Started writing (1982) and working on a series of 3 books "Introduction to Islamic Art" by Islamic Art Foundation. (English) (1989); "The Status of Islamic Art in the Twentieth Century" in Muqarnas (1992); "An Overview of Arab Art" in "Forces of Change: Artists of the Arab World" International Council of Women in the Arts, Washington DC (1994); "What is Islamic Art?" (English) Al al-Bayt University, Mafraq (1996) Editor and Contributor to "The Dictionary of Art", Macmillan, London (1996); "Modern Art in Jordan" (Arabic) The Royal Society of Fine Arts, Amman (1996); "Modern Art in Jordan" (English The Royal Society of Fine Arts Amman (1997); "Modern Islamic Art: Development and Continuity" (English) The University Press of Florida, USA (1997); Development of Islamic Art" (Arabic) Occasional Papers Series, Jordan

Institute of Diplomacy, Amman (1998); "Challenges of Peace Support into the 21st Century" (English) The Jordan Institute of Diplomacy (seminar papers) (1999); "Arab Contribution of Islamic Art" (English) the American University of Cairo Press (1999); "Islamic Art Resources in Central Asia and Eastern and Central Europe" (Arabic & English" Editor with Khalid Deemer (seminar papers), Al al-Bayt University, Isesco and the Royal Society of Fine Arts (under publication) **Membership:** The Journal of the Royal Institute for Religious Studies, Amman (1998); Centre for World Dialogue, Nicosia : Member of Board of Governors (1998); Premi International Catalunya, Barcelona: Member of the Jury (1998); Prize for Mediterranean Young Writers, Genoa: President of the Jury Committee (1998); L'Accademia del Mediterraneo, Naples: Member (1998); International Council for Philosophy and Humanistic Studies , Paris: Vice-President (1997); International Congress of Asian and North African Studies (ICANAS), Budapest: Advisory Member of the Board (1997); Mc Mullen Museum, Boston: Board member (1997); Fondazione Laboratorio Mediterraneo, Napoli: Founding Member (1996); Standing International Committee of Forum Civil Euromed, Barcelona: Member (1995); International Research Center for Islamic History, Culture and Arts (IRCICA), Istambul: Member of Board of Governors (1995); World Arts Council, Geneva: Founding Member (1990-94); Arab Thought Forum, Amman: Amman (1986). **Sports:** Horse Riding and Swimming. **Hobby:** Travels to exotic places. **Member** of Board of Governors International Center of Islamic Studies, London. President, Royal Society of Fine Arts, Amman. Member of Arab Thought Forum, Amman; World Affairs Council, Amman. **Credit Cards:** American Express, Visa **Addr:** P.O.Box 850746 Amman 11185, Jordan; Tel./Fax: (00962) 5934400.

ALI (Zailaie, Ali), Saudi scientist. **Born** in 1939 in Jazan (Saudi Arabia). **Dipl.:** B.Sc. (1967), D.R.C. (1971), M.Sc. (1973). **Career:** Director of Chemical Laboratories, Ministry of Petroleum and Mineral Resources. **Publ.:** Author of a number of research papers, including "Uses of X-ray Fluorescent Solution Techniques", "Analysis of Silica and Alumina by Atomic Spectrometry". **Member:** Arab Association of Analytical Chemists, Cairo (Egypt); Association of British Chemist, Glasgow (Scotland). **Priv. Addr.:** Tel. 25242, Jeddah, Saudi Arabia.

ALIER (Abel), Sudanese statesman. **Born** in 1933 in Borr District (Upper Nile Province). **Married** in 1970 to Siama Fatma Bilal, one daughter. **Educ.:** primary and secondary at Borr; Faculty of Law, Khartoum University, until 1959; School of Advanced Legal Studies, London University (1961-64). **Dipl.:** LL.B., LL.M., Research Fellow (Law Studies); M.A. Law. **Career:** Barrister-at-Law; District judge at El-Obeid and Wadi Madani and Khartoum (1964-65); attended the Round Table Conference on the Southern question as an active member of the Southern Front; Member, Constitutional Commissions (1966-68); re-elected Member for Borr, National Assembly (1968); Minister of Housing (May- Oct. 1969); Minister of Supply and Internal Trade (Oct. 1969- June 1970); Minister of Southern Affairs (July 1970- July 1971); Minister of Public Works (July 1971-77); led the seven-man Khartoum team to the Addis Abeba negotiations with Southern Sudan (Feb. 1972); President, High Executive Council for the Southern Region (April 1972); Discussed in Bonn, Federal Republic of Germany the opening of iron ore sources in the Red Sea and copper and zinc deposits (1974). **Member:** Sudan Law Association; Internationl Law Association. **Hobbies:** music and reading. **Sports:** tennis and athletics. **Addr.:** Khartoum, Sudan.

ALIKHAN (Abbas, Abdullatif), Kuwaiti academic. **Born** on March 15, 1943 in Kuwait City. **Married,** 5 children. **Educ.:** B.S., M.S., and Ph.D. Petroleum and Natural Gas Engineering, (1967, 1970, 1973), Pennsylvania State University, U.S.A. **Career:** Assistant Dean College of Engineering and Petroleum, Kuwait University (1977-80); Director, Summer Program Office, Kuwait University (1978-82); Director, Symposia and Cultural Affairs, Kuwait Foundation for the Advancement of Sciences (1985-Present); Coordinator, Arab School on Science and Technology (1980-82) and Chairman of the Kuwait Office (1995- Present); Advisor, Director General, Kuwait Institute for Scientific Research (1979-82); Kuwait Contact Officer, Federation of Arab Scientific Research Councils (1980-82); presently Assistant Professor Engineering Department. **Work:** Teach Petroleum Engineering Courses, Established: College of Engineering and Petroleum, Kuwait University; Petroleum Engineering Department, Kuwait University; Summer Program, Kuwait University. **Member:** SPE of AIME, Kuwait Society of Engineers. **Credit Card:** Visa. **Prof. Addr.:** Petroleum Engineering Department, Kuwait University, P.O.Box 5969, 13060 Safat, Tel.: (965) 4836058/4836059, Fax: (965) 4849558, Kuwait. **Priv. Addr.:** P.O.Box 6676, Hawali, Tel.: (965) 5331155/5330055, Safat 32041, Kuwait.

ALIREZA (Abdallah Abdulghaffar), Kuwaiti businessman. **Born** in 1918 in Saudi Arabia. **Married,** four children. **Educ.:** St. Xavier's, Bombay, India. **Career:** President of the Alireza Group of Companies, with extensive interests in the Middle East and other countries. **Prof. Addr.:** The Alireza Group of Companies, P.O.Box. 60 and P.O.Box 106, Safat, Kuwait, Tel.: 4816836, 4840161, Telefax: 4831030, 4810270.

ALIREZA (Abdallah, Ahmad Y.Z.), Saudi businessman. **Born** in 1944 in Jeddah, Saudi Arabia. **Married,** 3 children. **Educ.:** Falah School and Hailebury College, UK; Whittier College, USA. **Dipl.:** B.A. in Political Science, M.A. in Public Administration. **Career:** Director, Alireza Haji Abdullah and Company Ltd.; Saudi Cable Co. **Prof. Addr.:** P.O.Box 8, Jeddah 21411, Saudi Arabia.

ALIREZA (Abdallah, Mohamad), Saudi official. **Born** in 1940 in Jeddah, Saudi Arabia. **Educ.:** in UK and University of California, Berkeley, USA. **Career:** Head of International Marketing, General Petroleum and Mineral Organisation (since 1971); Ministry of Petroleum; Chairman of ARGAS, the Saudi Official Geological Service (1970-72); Director, Haji Abdullah Alireza & Co. Ltd. **Prof. Addr.:** P.O.Box 8, Jeddah, Saudi Arabia.

ALIREZA (Ahmad, Yusuf Zainal), Saudi businessman. **Born** in 1916 in Saudi Arabia. **Married,** five sons. **Career:** President of Hajji Abdullah Alireza Co. Ltd.; Chairman, International Mechanical & Electrical Contracting Co. Ltd.; Laing Wimpey Alireza Ltd., P.O.Box. 8, Jeddah, Saudi Arabia.

ALIREZA (Ali Abbas), Saudi businessman. **Born** on March 21, 1916 in Jeddah (Saudi Arabia). **Son** of Haji Abbas Alireza (merchant) **and** Mrs. nee Fatema Ali Alireza. **Married** to Fatma Abdulrahim Alireza, two children: Nourjehan Alireza and Salah J. Alireza, B.C.L. Barrister-at-law, (King's Inn). **Educ.:** St. Xavier's High School and College, Bombay, Bombay University; Berlin University. **Dipl.:** B.Sc. (Economics), B.Com.; Languages: Arabic, Persian, Urdu (Hindi), French, English, German, Italian, Spanish, and Russian. **Career:** in Business as Alireza & Sons, Bahrain. **Member:** Chamber of Commerce Bahrain. **Credit Cards:** Visa, American Express. **Prof. Address:** P.O.Box 79, Tel: 214358/ 223612/ 214359, Telex: 9185 REZALI BN, Fax. 210013, Manama, Bahrain.

ALIREZA (Ali, Ibrahim), Saudi businessman. **Born** on July 14, 1950. **Educ.:** Roosevelt University, Chicago, USA; University of Sussex, United Kingdom. **Dipl.:** B.A. in Political Science, M.A. in International Relations. **Career:** President, Transcontinental Corporation for Trading and Transportation. **Hobbies:** Tennis, swimming and classical music. **Prof. Addr.:** P.O.Box 7101, Jeddah, 21462, Saudi Arabia.

ALIREZA (Fahd, Mohamad Abdallah), Saudi scientist. **Born** on December 25, 1946. **Educ.:** Advanced University studies. **Dipl.:** B.Sc. (Business Administration (1967), M.A. (Business Administration) (1969). **Career:** in various shipping and commercial enterprises; now Managing Director of International Chemical Industries. **Member:** Jeddah Chamber of Commerce: International Business Fraternity; Board of International Chemical Industries and Trade Marketing Company; Jeddah Electricity Company, Ltd.; Saudi Shipping Company; Reza Institution for Trade Marketing. Development and Investment. **Sports:** Swimming and tennis. **Hobbies:** chess and travel. **Prof. Addr.:** Alireza Compound, Kilo 5, Mecca Road, P.O.Box 1555, Tel.: 6533424, Jeddah 21441, Saudi Arabia.

ALIREZA (Faisal Ali A.), Saudi executive. **Born** in 1947. **Dipl.:** M.A. (Public Administration). **Career:** Assistant Director, International Chemical Industries and Trade Co.; Member of Board, Reza Establishment for Marketing and Development. **Hobbies:** music, swimming, tennis. **Addr.:** P.O.Box 1555, Jeddah 21441, Saudi Arabia.

ALIREZA (Hisham, Ahmad Y.Z.), Saudi businessman. **Born** in Jeddah. **Educ.:** Wellington College, UK, University of Berkeley, USA. **Career:** worked for Charterhouse Group, Morgan Stanley Inc. in New York and Paris. Actually Chairman of Arabian Bulk Trade Ltd. and Saudi Bulk Transport; Chairman, Dar Alfikr Schools; Executive Director, Xenel Industries in Jeddah. **Hobbies:** Tennis, architecture, design and photography. **Prof. Addr.:** P.O.Box 2824, Jeddah and P.O.Box 2194, Alkhobar 31952, Saudi Arabia.

ALIREZA (Hussein, Ali), Saudi businessman. **Born** in 1931 in Saudi Arabia. **Educ.:** University California, Berkely (USA). **Dipl.:** B.A., M.A. (Economics). **Career:** President of Haji Hussein Alireza & Co. Ltd.; General agent for Mazda motor cars; Hawker Siddeley Power Plant Ltd., Lister Engines, Goodyear Tyres; Board member: Saudi Arabian Airlines Corporation (Saudia); Saudi American Bank; former Board member: Jeddah Chamber of Commerce. **Sports:** Diving and fishing. **Prof. Addr.:** P.O.Box. 40, Tel.: 6423509, Jeddah and Adil Khashogji Bldg. Airport Road, P.O.Box. 833, Tel.: 477 4770, Riyadh. **Priv. Addr.:** Tel.: 6432330, Jeddah, Saudi Arabia.

ALIREZA (Khalid, Ahmad Y.Z.), Saudi businessman. **Born** in 1948 in Jeddah. **Educ.:** Wellington College, UK; University of California, Berkeley, California, USA. **Dipl.:** B.Sc. and M.E. in Industrial Engineering and Operational Research. **Career:** Executive Director, Xenel Industries Ltd.; Member of the Board of Jeddah Chamber of Commerce and Saudi Arabian Standards Organisation; Chairman, AMI Saudi Arabian Ltd., Saudi Cable Co. Ltd., Hidad Ltd. **Prof. Addr.:** P.O.Box 2824, Jeddah 21461, Saudi Arabia.

ALIREZA (Mahmoud, Y.Z.), Saudi leading businessman. **Born** in 1929 in Jeddah, Saudi Arabia. **Dipl.:** Matriculation (1949); B.A., University of California, Berkeley (1954); Harvard Law School (1954); Postgraduate Diploma in Law (1957); King's College, London University. **Career:** Partner Director and Chairman of the Supervisory Board of his conglomerate family firm Haji Abdullah Alireza and Co. Ltd.; Chairman of Arabian Petroleum Supply Company (APSCO), member of original Board of Founders of the Red Sea Club, under the chairmanship of H.R.H. Prince Muhammad al-Faisal. **Hobbies:** Underwater fishing, hunting, bridge, photography. **Addr.:** P.O.Box 8, Jeddah 21411, Tel.: 6472233. Saudi Arabia.

ALIREZA (Mohamad, Ahmad Y.Z.), Saudi engineer. **Born** in 1942 in Saudi Arabia. **Married,** 3 children. **Educ.:** Haileybury College, UK; Cornell University, USA. **Dipl.:**

M.Sc. in Civil Engineering. **Career:** Chairman, Xenel Industries Ltd. and Director in numerous Associated Companies. **Prof. Addr.:** P.O.Box 2824, Jeddah 21461, Saudi Arabia.

ALIREZA (Sheikh Ali, Abdallah), Saudi Arabian diplomat. **Born** on 12 May 1921. **Educ.:** Falah Schools, Mecca; Victoria College, Alexandria, Egypt; Berkeley University, California. **Dipl.:** B.Sc. (Petroleum Engineering and Business Engineering). **Married**: in 1943, to Huguette Misk, 5 children: Hamida, Faisal, Tarek, Nadia, Ghassan. **Career:** Business Manager, Haji Abdullah Alireza & Co. (1945); Technical Adviser to Saudi Arabian Delegation to UN Conference, London (1946); Financial Adviser to H.E. Sheikh Abdullah Suleiman; Minister of Finance; Member, Saudi Arabian Delegation to U.S. (1946); Alternate Representative to UN Conference, New York (1946); Liaison Officer between late King Abdel Aziz Al-Seoud and Anglo-American Fact-Finding committee on Palestine (1946); Counselor (1st class) with Prince Saud al-Saud, Crown Prince of Saudi Arabia during State Visit to US, UK, and Egypt (1947); Adviser to H.R.H. Prince Faisal al-Saud, Saudi Arabian Minister of Foreign Affairs (1947); Minister Plenipotenciary and Delegate to UN; Minister without portfolio; Member, official Delegation led by H.R.H. Prince Faisal to Greece (1953); Member, Delegation that represented H.M. the King of Saudi Arabia at the Coronation of H.M. Queen Elizabeth II (1953); Minister of State and Delegate to the Bandung Asian-African Conference (1955); Member, Delegation led by Crown Prince Faisal to India and Pakistan (1955); Member of the Board of Directors, Saudi Arabian Monetary Agency (SAMA) (1972); Ambassador to USA (1975-79). **Awards:** Holder, Grand Order and Sash of the Phoenix; Cross of Leopold II (Belgium). **Addr.:** Jeddah, Saudi Arabia.

ALJASSIM (Ahmed, Abdulaziz), Kuwaiti diplomat. **Born** in Kuwait in 1938. **Educ.:** Cairo University (B.A. Political Science 1963). **Married** in 1963 to Myryam al-Mutawa, three children: one son & 2 daughters. **Career:** Acting Consul general, New York and member of Kuwait delegation to the United Nations (1963-67); Councellor of Kuwait Embassy in Baghdad, Iraq (1967-73); Ambassador to Muscat, Sultanate of Oman (1974-77); Ambassador to Islamabad, Pakistan (1978-79) Ambassador to Iran (1979-83); Ambassador to Tripoli, Libya, concurrently accredited to Lagos as non resident Ambassador (1983-85); Ambassador to Damascus, Syria (since 1985 to present); From January to May 1989. Special Envoy of the Chairman of the six Committee of the Arab League to Lebanon, Concurrently Non-Resident Ambassador to Lebanon since January 1991 to 1992. **Addr.:** Kuwait City, Kuwait.

ALJASSIM (Sulaiman, Moosa, Dr.), United Arab Emirates Director (Higher Colleges of Technology). **Born** on January 15, 1954 at Fujairah, U.A.E. **Son** of Moosa Al-Jassim **and** Mrs. Maryam Sulaiman. **Married** in 1978 at Fujairah to Amina Al-Jassim, 5 children: Manal (1.1.1979), Abeer (25.2.1980), Alya (24.1.1982), Faisal (27.1.1985), Maitha (23.12.1987). **Educ.:** Teachers Diploma, Kuwait (1971), Public Administration Certificate, The Public Administration Institute, Cairo (1972), Certificate of Diplomacy, Oxford University, U.K. (1975), B.A. Administration Sciences, U.A.E. University (1986), Mphil, Arabic and Islamic Studies, Exeter University, U.K. (1987), Ph.D., Exeter University, U.K. (1990). **Career:** Teacher, Khor Fakkan School (1971); Minister Plenipotentiary in the Diplomatic Corp, Ministry of Foreign Affairs (1972-1990); Member of delegation to the UN 32nd session of the General Assembly, UAE Delegation to the United Nations (1975); Chief of Emiri Court of His Highness Shaikh Hamad Bin Mohammad al-Sharqi, Ruler of Fujairah and Member of the Supreme Council, Emiri Court, Fujairah (1975-1986); Managing Editor, Journal of Social Affairs, U.A.E.; Director of Community Relations and Manpower Development, Higher Colleges of Technology, Abu Dhabi (1990- to present). **Memberships:** Member, UAE Constitution Preparation Committee; Chairman, UAE Consumption Co-operative Union; Assistant General Secretary, Arab Cooperative Union; Member, Board of Directors, National Bank of Fujairah; Member, Board of Directors, Fujairah National Insurance Company. **Publ.:** Dissertation: National Workforce of the UAE Weekly column in daily newspaper Al-Khaleeg Theatre plays. **Sports:** Swimming, Travelling. **Hobbies:** Music, Reading and Writing (National Workforce of the UAE Weekly column in daily newspaper Al-Khaleeg Theatre plays). **Member:** Co-operative Union, Sociology Association. **Credit Cards:** Visa. American Express. **Prof. Addr.:** Higher Colleges of Technology, P.O.Box 25026, Tel.: 971.2.341153, Abu Dhabi, United Arab Emirates.

ALKHALDI (Awwad), Jordanian diplomat. **Born** on November 21, 1932 in Jordan. **Son** of Mohamed al-Khaldi (deceased) **and** Mrs. Ayida al-Khaldi. **Married** on July 27, 1961 in Irbed, Jordan, to Fatima al-Khaldi, 6 children: Ghaleb (1956), Randa (1959), Khaled (1962), Nasser (1966), Sa'ed (1968), Eman (1975). **Educ.:** Royal Military Academy Sandhurst - U.K., Command and General Staff College - U.S.A., Royal College of Defence Studies - U.K. **Dipl.:** B.A. Military Sciences, Master Degree Military Science and Strategical Studies. **Career:** Army Officer: Lieut. to the Rank of General-Jordan Army; Inspector General-Jordan Army; Defence Adviser to H.M. king Hussein of Jordan. Chief of Staff United Arab Emirates Armed Forces. Defence Adviser to H.E. The President of the United Arab Emirates; Ambassador of Jordan to the Hellenic Republic of Greece; Ambassador of Jordan to the French Republic, Paris. **Decor:** al-Kawkab 1rst Class/ Jordan; al-Istiklal 1rst Class/Jordan; al-Nadwa 2nd. Class/ Jordan; Order of Merit/France. Other decorations from: Iraq, Egypt, Greece, Japan, and Spain. **Sports:** Tennis, Horse Riding, Shooting. **Credit Cards:** American Express and Nat West Visa. **Prof. Addr.:** Ministry of Foreign Affairs, Amman, Jordan.

ALKHEREIJI (Abdullah al-Mohamad, al), Saudi academic. **Born** in 1943 in Medina, Saudi Arabia. **Dipl.:** Ph.D. (Sociology). **Career:** Advisor to Ministry of Labour and Social Affairs; Chairman, Department of Sociology, and Professor of Sociology, King Abdulaziz University, Jeddah; member of Middle East Conference on Sociological Sciences, Alexandria, Egypt. **Publications:** Books on Contemporary Sociology, Social Development, Family Sociology, Economic Sociology, Social Change, Demography, Developmental Experiments in the Arab World, Social Control, Islamic Social Structure and Social Research Methods. **Prof. Addr.:** King Abdulaziz University, Department of Sociology, Tel.: 00966-2-695-2599, Fax: 00966-2-691-2689, Jeddah, Saudi Arabia.

ALLAF (Ibrahim, Khalil, al), Saudi educationalist. **Born** in 1931 in Mecca, Saudi Arabia. **Educ.:** Cairo University, Egypt. **Dipl.:** B.A. in Arabic Language, Literature and Islamic Study. **Career:** Teacher and Assistant Principal, Mecca Educational Institute, Mecca (1953); Director of the News Department at the Minsitry of Information, Jeddah (1975); Inspector General, Ministry of Education (1957); Director Public Libraries Department at the Ministry of Pilgrimage and Wakfs (1962), Cultural Adviser (1965); Supervisor of Muslim World League Library, Mecca (1975-77); retired in 1977 devoting time to historial, political, literary and Islamic studies. **Publ.:** four collections of poetry. **Awards:** Certificate of Merit, Dictionary of Internationl Biography, Cambrige (1976); Certificate of Merit, Marquis Publications (1978-79). **Hobbies:** travelling, reading and writing (poetry); **Member:** Mecca Cultural Club. **Priv. Addr.:** Shubaika Quarter, Allaf bldg., Tel.: 24288, Mecca, Saudi Arabia.

ALLAHOUM (Abdelmajid), Algerian diplomat. **Born** in 1934. **Married,** 4 children. **Dipl.:** B.Sc. in Political Science. **Career:** Schools and Instruction Director, Ministry of Education (1963-65); Director of Protocol to the President (1977-79); Member of the FLN Central Committee (1979); Minister of Tourism (1979-84); Ambassador to the USSR (1984). **Prof. Addr.:** Ministry of Foreign Affairs, Algiers, Algeria.

ALLAM (Mohamed, Abdel Khalek), Egyptian educator. **Born** in Cairo, Egypt in 1921. **Son** of Abdel Khalek Allam. **Married** with three children. **Educ.:** Ohio State University and Indiana University. **Dipl.:** Teachers' Diploma (1944); M.A. in Physical Education (1949); Ph.D. in Health and Safety Education (1955). **Career:** Teacher in secondary school; Professor, Higher Institute of Physical Education for Men, Supreme Council for Youth Welfare; Director General, American University in Cairo, Dean of Records and Admissions; actually Vice President for Student Affairs, American University in Cairo. Consultant to Arab Universities. **Awards:** Honorary Doctor's Degree of Laws from Indiana University, USA (1979), Honorary Doctor's Degree from Soka University, Japan (1991). Decoration of Sports, First Degree. **Sports:** Tennis, swimming, diving and gymnastics. **Hobby:** walking. **Member of:** Indiana University International Council in USA, The Egyptian National Council on Education, Gizira Club, Shooting Club, Automobile Club, American Association for Foreign Student Advisors. **Prof. Addr.:** AUC, 113, Sharia Kaser El Aini, P.O.Box 2511, Tel.: 3542964, Fax: 355-7565, Telex: 92224 AUCAI UN, Cairo, Egypt. **Priv. Addr.:** 640, Street 14, Mokattam, Cairo, Egypt.

ALLAWI (Abul Salam Abdul Rahman), Iraqi Banker. **Born** in 1924 at Basrah, Iraq. **Married,** 3 children. **Educ.:** Banking, Finance and Accounting. **Dipl.:** B.A. (Baghdad), MBA (AUB). **Career:** More than twenty years experience in Accounting Banking & Industrial Management; Consultant for five years; Lecturer, Baghdad University & Mustansseryah University; former Director General, Industrial Bank of Iraq (1978); former Director, The Central Bank of Iraq; chairman of two industrial companies; Member of the Board, Iraqi Federation of Industries; Member of the Board, Iraqi Union of Accountants and Auditors; Associate, British Institute of Bankers. **Member:** The Iraqi Hunting Club, Baghdad; Al-Mansour Club, Baghdad. **Addr.:** Baghdad, Iraq.

ALLOUACHE (Merzak), Algerian film director. **Born** on October 6, 1944 in Algiers. **Son** of Omar Allouache **and** Mrs. Fatma Allouache. **Married** in 1962 to Lazib Anissa, one daughter. **Career:** Worked in National Institute of Cinema, Algiers; Institute of Film, Paris; then worked as adviser, Ministry of Culture, Algiers Algeria. Films include: Our Agrarian Revolution (documentary 1973); Omar Gatlato, Les aventures d'un heros, L'homme qui regardait les Fenetres (1982). **Awards:** Silver Prize, Moscow Festival; Tanit D'or Prize, Carthage (1979). **Addr.:** Cite des Asphodeles, Bt D15, 183 Ben Aknoun, Tel.: 793360, Algiers, Algeria.

ALLOUBA (Naela, Hassan), Egyptian Businesswoman. **Born** on August 5, 1928 in Cairo, Egypt. **Married,** 3 daughters. **Educ.:** Cairo University. **Dipl.:** B.Sc, in Journalism (1970). **Carrer.:** Owner Of N.A.H.A.L Trading Co and Associate of Al-Barari Tourism Co. **Member Business Ass.** Member of Egyptian Businessmen's Ass. and Chairperson of its Export Committee (1981); Egyptian-Scandinavian Business Council; The German Arab Chamber of Commerce & Industry; Club d'Affaires Franco-Egyptien; The Egyptian Tunisian Council; The Egyptian Moroccan Council; The Egyptian Jordanian Council; Folllow-up Committee for the recommendations of the First Arab Businessmen's Conference; participates in numerous economic commercial conferences. **Publ.:** Local and international publishes economical and social articles in local and international press and participates in several press interviews and T.V. meeting to discuss and study economical and social problems. **Decor.:** Named ideal mother of Arab Republic of Egypt (1958); Granted Golden Medal of Excellence first grade, President of Egypt (1972); Appreciation Medals from Cairo and Guiza Governorates (1972); Regional Medal of Guiza Governorate (1996); Appreciation Certificate and Medal on Egyptian Woman's Day for the Women's role in economic development (March 1997); Identified as one of the fifty leading women entrepreneurs of the world (1998); Award of Excellence from the German-Arab Chamber of Commerce in Cairo (Special Recognition for her remarkable achievements as pioneer Businesswoman -1998); Appreciation Certificate on Egyptian Women's Day, Guiza Governorate, from Ministry of Social Affairs, for Women's social care and economic development (March 1999). **Member:** The Automobile Club, Gezira Sporting Club and Maadi Sporting Club. **Addr.:** 16 Sherif Pasha Street, Cairo, Egypt.

ALMA'I (Zaher Awwal, al), Saudi Academic. **Born** in Assir, in 1934. **Dipl.:** B.A. (Islamic Law), Riyadh University; M.A. (Interpretation of Koranic Science) al-Azhar University, Cairo, Egypt; Ph.D. (Interpretation of Holy Koran), al-Azhar University, 1973. **Career:** Teacher, Abha Islamic Institute; Director of Najran Islamic Institute; Lecturer, Faculty of Islamic Law, Imam Mohamed Ben Saud Islamic University, member of university council and university Supreme Council; represented the university in the Arab Universities Union Council meeting, Iraq and the Saudi Cultural Week, Morocco; former Dean of University Libraries, Islamic University of Imam Mohamed Ibn Saud, Riyadh. **Publ.:** "al-Alma'iyat" (collection of poetry), Beirut 1972; "Ma'a al-Mufasirin wal Mustashriqin" (Orientalists and Interpreters of Koran), Beirut. **Hobbies:** reading, swimming. **Addr.:** Imam Mohamed Ben Saud University, Riyadh, P.O.Box. 4124. Tel.: 4766096 (Office) and 4760454 (Home), Riyadh, Saudi Arabia.

ALMARAYATI (Abid A.), Arab-American Academic, Professor Emeritus The University of Toledo. **Born** in 1931 in Baghdad, Iraq. **Married**, 1 son. **Educ.:** College Freshman, Tripoli, Lebanon (1948-1949); B.A., Bradley University, Peoria, Illinois (1949-1952); M.A., Bradley University, Peoria, Illinois (1952-1954); Ph.D., New York University (1954-1959). Majors for B.A.: Political Science, Sociology; Minor: Economics and for M.A.: Political Science, Minors: Economics, Sociology; Fields of Specialization for Ph.D.: International Organizations, International Relations, International Law, International Administration, the Near East. **Career:** United Nations Intern, (Summer 1954); Secretary, Delegation of Iraq, 10th Session, United Nations General Assembly (1955); Secretary, Delegation of Yemen, 11th, 12th, 13th and 14th Sessions, United Nations General Assembly (1956-1960); Instructor, Department of Government, University of Massachusetts (1960); Technical Assistance Officer, Division of Economic and Technical Assistance, International Atomic Energy Agency, Vienna, Austria (1960-1962); Associate Professor, State University College of New York (1962 - Feb. 1964); Research Fellow, Harvard University, (Feb. 1964 -June 1965); Lecturer and International Education Consultant, American Institute for Foreign Trade, Glendale, Arizona (Part-time position held simultaneously with his position at Arizona State University (Sept. 1965-1968); Associate Professor, Arizona State University (Sept. 1965-1968); Professor Emeritus. Former Director, Center for International Studies; Former Professor and Chairman, Department of Political Science, University of Toledo (1968- to present). Research and Lecturing, Soviet Academy of Sciences and International Research and Exchange Board under the United States-U.S.S.R. Educational Exchange Program (Summer 1974); Outstanding Teacher, University of Toledo (1981-82); Visiting Professor, University of Kuwait (1982-83) and The Institute for Public Administration, Riyadh, Saudi Arabia (1985-86) academic Year; Guest Lecturer, Summer 1990, He gave lectures at Universities in Australia and New Zealand (Victoria University, University of Otago, Curtin University of Technology, Victoria College, University of Western Australia, Philipps College, Victoria University of Technology, as well as many radio, television appearances and public lectures); Visiting Professor Beijing Foreign Studies University, Spring Quarter 1991 with additional Lectures to Beijing University, Fudan University, Shanghai Institute for International Studies, Foreign Affairs College. **Non-teaching Activities Since 1965: (a partial list).** Chairman, Committee on International Education N.Y. State College; Chairman, Conference Committee on Nonwestern Studies, N.Y. State College; Advisor-Foreign Service, Arizona State University; Advisor, International Relations Club, Arizona State University; Faculty Consultant, Arizona State University, Center for Latin American Studies; Member, Graduate Committee, Arizona State University; Conference Committee, 19th Annual Conference, Middle East Institute; Speaker to civic organizations; Commentator, radio and television programs in the United States and abroad; Liaison Officer with the United States Committee for the United Nations University; Member, Board of Trustees, Toledo Council on World Affairs; Discussant, The Middle East Institute Conference on the Middle East and the United Nations (1965); Discussant, The Rocky Mountain Social Science Association, Annual Meeting (1968); Panelist, Challenges to Middle Eastern Political Development, Middle East Conference, Bowling Green State University (1969); Participant, Scholar-Diplomat Seminar, U.S. Department of State (1971); Moderator, Panel on Teaching Civilization in Universities, Comparative Civilization Conference, Richmond, Kentucky (1972); Discussant, Peace Science Society (April 1973); Panelist, Oil and Politics in the Middle East, Conference, University of Houston (1973); Consultant, Committee on International Relations, Group for Advancement of Psychiatry; Primary Discussant, «The Psychological Impact of the Seventeen Day War», Department of State (1974). The summary was published in 1975. Moderator, Annual Meeting, Foundation for Student Communications (1973); Chairperson, Panel, 1976 Annual Meeting, International Studies Association; 1976 Duquesne History Forum; Panel, «Educational Development in the OPEC Countries», Comparative and International Education Society, Midwest Regional Meeting (1976); Panel, 1977 Annual Meeting, Midwest Political Science Association. **Professional Activities:** In Conjunction with his professional activities, He has participated in professional associations as officer, panel chairman, discussant, or consultant including the following: Association of Student Education; Middle East Studies Association of North America; Member, Board of Consultants, Constitution Associates; Member, Board of Directors, World Association of Former U.N. Interns and Fellows; Popular Cultural Association; Midwest International Studies Association; International Studies Association; Association for Advancement of Policy; American Cultural Association; Institute for Oriental Studies, Moscow and St. Petersburg; Arab Political Thought Forum, Amman, Jordan; Business Administration Association; Gulf Center for Strategic Studies, London; Institute for Psychiatry and Foreign Affairs; Group for the Advancement of Psychiatry. **Membership in Professional Organizations:** International Studies Association; American Political Science Association; The Middle East Institute; The Middle East Studies Association of North America; Phi Kappa Phi. **Nonteaching Activities at the University of Toledo: (a partial list).** Chairman, Departmental Executive Committee (1972); Chairman, Arrangements Committee, 1972 Conference, Center for International Studies; Department Representative, Council of the College of Arts and Sciences; Member: Discipline Committee, Committee on Middle East Studies, Committee on Asian Studies, Committee on European Studies, Committee on Latin American Studies; Chairman, Committee on International Relations; Secretary, Committee on International Education; Coordinator, International Education Club; Chairman, Council on University College; Member, International Student Affairs Advisory Committee; Chairman, Policy Committee, Center for International Studies; Recipient, Key to the Golden Door Award, Toledo, Ohio (1984). **Directory Listings:** Who's Who in the Arab World; International Who's Who in Asian Studies; Who's Who in the West; Personalities of the West and Mid-West; Dictionary of International Biography; Contemporary Authors; International Who's Who in Community Service; International Scholars Directory; Creative and Successful Personalities; National Social Directory; Who's Who in American Men of Science; Community Leaders of America; The Writers Directory; Who's Who in the Midwest; Men of Achievement. **Research Grants and Fellowships:** Research Associate, University of Denver, Graduate School of International Studies (1966-1968); Faculty Research Grant, College of Arts and Sciences, The University of Toledo (1969-1971); Faculty Research Fellowship, The University of Toledo, (Summer 1971); American Friends of the Middle East-Grant-in-Aid; Arizona State University-Research Grant; American Philosophical Society-Fellowship; New York State University Research Foundation-Grant-in-Aid; Carl and Lily Pforzheimer Foundation-Fellowship; Ella Lyman Cabot Trust-Fellowship; Rockefeller Foundation-Fellowship. **Publications:** Books: A Diplomatic History of Modern Iraq. New York: Robert Speller & Sons, Inc. (1961); Middle Eastern Constitutions and Electoral Laws. New York: Frederick A. Praeger, Inc., (publishers 1968); With contributors, The Middle East: Its Governments and Politics. MA: Duxbury Press (1972); Editor, International Relations of the Middle East and North Africa, Cambridge, MA: Schenkman Publishing Company, Inc. (1985); In Progress, United Nations Enforcement Action: The Case of Iraq, A Comparative Study. Also, studies on the United Nations and the Middle East. **Articles and Papers:** «The Kuwait Question», Foreign Affairs Reports (July 1966). This study was submitted under the title «The Case of Kuwait Before The United Nations», Annual Meeting, Popular Cultural Associations (1982); «The Problem of Oman», Foreign Affairs Reports (September 1966); «Aden and the United Nations», India Quarterly (October 1966); «The Question of Yemen, Part I», Foreign Affairs Reports (December 1966); «The Question of Yemen, Part II», Foreign Affairs Reports (January 1967); «United Nations Observers Group in Lebanon, Part I», Foreign Affairs Reports (May 1967); «United Nations Observers Group in Lebanon, Part II», Foreign Affairs Reports (May 1967); «The Anglo-Iranian Oil Problem», The National Chengchi University Journal, Vol. XV, (May 1967); «Iraq's Participation in International Organizations», Middle East Forum, Vol. XLIII, No. 4 (1967); «Syrian-Lebanese Questions», Pakistan Horizon, Vol. XXI, No. 2, Second Quater (1968); «Modern Iraq», Middle East Forum, Vol. XXVI, No. 2 (April 1969); «The United Nations and Inter-Arab Conflicts». Paper presented at the 1969 Annual Meeting of the Middle East Studies Association of North America; «United Nations Oberver's Group in the Arab States». Paper presented at the 1971 Annual Meeting of the Middle East Studies Association of North America; Contributor-Concise Encyclopedia of the Middle East. Edited by Medhi Heravi, Public Affairs Press, Washington, D.C. (1973); «Proposal for an International University». Hearings before the Subcommittee on Education of the Committee on Labor and Public Welfare, United States Senate, 89th Congress, 2nd Session. A revised version was submitted to the Annual Meeting, Popular Cultural Association (1982); «Psychological Factors in the Arab-Israeli Conflict». Paper presented before the Joint meeting of the Middle East Institute and The Institute for Psychiatry and World Affairs in April, 1972, Washington, D.C. This Paper was published as a monograph by the Middle East Institute in 1974; With J. Lindeen and S. Jutila, «Manpower Policies in Selected Arab States; Problems and Opportunities». Paper presented before the 1978 Annual Meeting of the Middle East Studies Association of North America; Consultant, Group for the Advancement of Psychiatry, Self-Involvement in the Middle East conflict, Publication No. 103, Vol. 10 (1979); Contributing editor, Imam Mohammad Chirri, The Brother of the Prophet Mohammad, Islamic Center of Detroit (1980); Al Hawadeth. June 13,20, July 4, 11 Editions. Proceedings of conference, Institute for Strategic Studies, London (1986); «The Iraq-Kuwait Dispute and the United Nations», a paper presented before the 1993 Annual Conference, the International Studies Association. **Reviews of Books and Articles:** Abstracts for some of the previously mentioned articles have been published in Peace Research Abstracts and Current Thought on Peace and War. **Research Proposals:** «Psychological and Cultural Factors in the Iraq/Iran War»; «Shiism: A Study in Religion and Politics»; «United Nations Enforcement Action: The Case of Iraq, A Comparative Study»; «United Nations Enforcement Action: The Case of Iraq Compared with United Nations Humanitarian Peacemaking in the Former Yugoslavia and Somalia»; Newspaper and magazine articles and commentaries. **Other Information:** Selected for Who's Who in America. **Prof. Addr.:** Political Science Department, University of Toledo, 2109 Terrace View West, Toledo, OH 43607, U.S.A., Tel.: (419) 531-7283 (Home), (419) 530-4529 or 530-4151 (Office).

ALMOAYED (Tariq, Abdul Rahman), Bahraini former Minister of Information. **Born** in 1943. **Son** of Abdul Rahman Khalil Almoayed. **Married** to Layla Almoayed, 4 children. **Educ.:** in Bahrain; University of London, UK. B.Sc. Economics; Graduate in Political Economy (1967). **Career:** After his studies in the UK, Joined his family in their business, Member, Constituent Assembly (1972); Minister of Information, (1973-1995). **Addr.:** P.O.Box 253, Tel.: 780888, Manama, Bahrain.

ALMOAYYED (Farouk, Yousuf), Bahraini businessman. **Born** in 1944 in Bahrain. **Son** of Yousuf Khalil Almoayyed (businessman) and Mrs. Aisha Ahmed Almoayyed. **Married** in 1973 in Bahrain to Miss Fadia Fahad Algosaibi, four children: Ms. Mashael, Mr Mohammed, Ms. Hala and Master Yousuf. **Educ.:** Loughborough College, England. **Dipl.:** B.E. in Mechanical Engineering. **Career:** Vice-President of Bahrain Consultative Council; Chairman Y.K. Almoayyed & Sons, B.S.C. (c); Chairman of Almoayyed International Group, Almoayyed Computers, Almoayyed Commercial Services, Almoayyed Trading & Contracting, Almoayyed Electronics, Apple Centre, Bahrain, Chairman of Ashraf Brothers w.l.l., Bahrain; Chairman of Bahrain Duty Free Shop Co., Bahrain; Deputy Chairman of Bahrain Hotels Company (Gulf Hotel), Bahrain; Managing Director of Algosaibi Travel Agency, Bahrain; Deputy Chairman of National Bank of Bahrain; Director of Arab Banking Corporation, Bahrain; Director of International Bank of Asia, Hong Kong; **Member:** Rotary Club of Manama; **Sports:** Tennis, Squash. **Hobbies:** Boating, fishing. **Prof. Addr.:** Y.K. Almoayyed & Sons B.S.C. (c), P.O.Box 143, Manama, Bahrain, Tel.: (0973)211211, Fax: 211222.

ALMOHANDIS (Ahmed A., Prof.), Saudi academic. **Born** on 21 December 1948 in Medina, Saudi Arabia. **Dipl.:** B.Sc., M.Sc., Ph.D. (1977). **Career:** Laboratory Chemist, Aramco, Ras Tanura (1970); Laboratory Instructor, King Saud University (1970-72); Head of the Cultural Society, Faculty of Science, King Saud University; Fellow of the Geological Society, U.K.; Assistant Professor of Mineralogy, King Saud University (1977-); Visiting Scientist, Smithsonian Institution, Washington, D.C. U.S.A. (1980); Vice Dean of Student Affairs (1984-1986); Vice-Dean, College of Science (1992-1995); Chairman, Geology Dept. (1990-1992); Chairman, Astronomy Dept. (1994-1995); Vice Director, Translation Centre, King Saud University (1997-); Director, Translation Centre (1997-now); Associate Professor of Mineralogy and Petrology (1987-); Professor of Mineralogy and Petrology (1992-); Vice-Chairman of Saudi Society for Earth Sciences. **Member:** Mineralogical Society, U.K., the American Mineralogical Society, U.S.A., Saudi Arabian Society for Advancement of Art and Culture. **Publications:** several articles dealing with scientific and educational matters, published in professional journals and magazines. **Hobbies:** reading, writing, driving, travel. **Prof. Addr.:** Prof. A.A. Almohandis, Department of Geology, College of Science, King Saud University, P.O.Box 2455, Riyadh 11451, Saudi Arabia. **Priv. Addr.:** Tel.: 4676203. 4676212, Riyadh, Saudi Arabia.

ALOUNI (Habib), Tunisian executive. **Born** in 1931 at Kairouan, Tunisia. **Career:** At the Ministry of Finance (since 1958); Director of Insurance Section at the Ministry of Finance (1967-71); Principal private secretary at the Ministry of Finance (1973-74); Principal private secretary at the Ministry of Defence (1974-78); General secretary of the Defence Ministry (1974-78); Elected representative of civil servants in the Commission Paritaire (since 1961); President of the Civil Servants Society (1967-74). Founding **member** and Secretary General of Prevention Routiere Tunisienne (1961-75); Vice president of the Federation Europeenne d'Epargne et de Credit pour le Logement (1982-84); President of the Municipal Council of the city of Kairouan (1980-85); Chairman and General Manager of Caisse Nationale D'Epargne Logement. **Addr.:** Tunis, Tunisia.

ALOUSI (Khalil, Ibrahim Akif, al), Iraqi physician. **Born** in 1923 in Baghdad, Iraq. **Married**, two sons. **Educ.:** M.B., Ch.B., Ph.D. in Pathology. **Career:** Pathologist, Professor of Pathology, College of Medicine, University of Baghdad, Iraq; Head of Department of Pathology; retired from the University (1975); private practitioner in pathology. Founding **member** of Iraqi Cancer Association. **Publ.:** "Aids to Pathological Histology" (1969) in English; many research papers in medical journals in Arabic and English, **Sports:** Swimming, horseriding. **Addr.:** al-Alousi

Laboratory, Rass al-Qarih, Rashid Street, Tel.: 889224, 4437227, Baghdad, Iraq.

ALQASSIM (Abdul Rahman Abdul Aziz), Saudi academic. **Born** in 1932 in Najd. **Dipl.:** Ph.D. (Comparative Law). **Career:** Former University staff member; Assistant Professor and Chairman, Department of Law, Faculty of Commerce, King Saud University. Now Lawyer. **Publications:** al-Islam Wa Tadwean al-Ahkam (Islam and Codification of Provisions); Islamic Judiciary System, a Comparative Study (Ph.D. dissertation); Jurisprudence and Prosecution; Confirmation of Evidence in Jurisprudence. **Hobby:** reading. **Address:** Dar al-Qassem for Defence and Legal Consulting, P.O.Box 500 Riyadh 11411, Saudi Arabia. Tel.: 4767045- 4767037- 4767336.

ALSALAMI (Mohamed Abdullah, Sultan), United Arab Emirates Chairman. **Born** on December 25, 1960 in Dibba, Fujairah, U.A.E. **Son** of Abdullah Sultan Alsalami (Chairman). **Married** in 1988 in Dibba to Maryam Al Mansoori, 2 children: Mashael, Aisha. **Educ.:** Indiana State University (1984). **Dipl.:** BS in Political Sciences. **Career:** Director, Department of Industry & Economy, Fujairah, U.A.E. (1984-86); Chairman, Department of Civil Aviation, Fujairah, U.A.E. (1986-); Vice-Chairman, Fujairah Aviation Centre, Fujairah, U.A.E. (1986-); Chairman, Fujairah National Catering Est., Fujairah U.A.E. (1989-); Vice-Chairman, Port of Fujairah, Fujairah, U.A.E. (1984-). **Other Information:** Board of Directors-Al Fujairah Insurance Co.; Member, Federal National Council, Abu Dhabi, U.A.E. (1987-); Executive Member, Emirates Insurance Association, Abu Dhabi, U.A.E. (1988-); Member, Airports Council International (ACI-Asia Region). **Member:** Chairman, Dibba Sports Club, Dibba, Fujairah, U.A.E. **Credit Cards:** American Express, Diner's Club, Mastercard. **Prof. Addr.:** P.O.Box 977, Fujairah, United Arab Emirates. **Priv. Addr.:** Tel.: (971-9) 226381, Fujairah, United Arab Emirates.

ALSALEH (Abdul Aziz Abdul Rahman), Saudi Faculty professor. **Born** in 1948 in Al-Gassab, Saudi Arabia. **Dipl.:** B.Sc. (Science), Ph.D. (Cell Biology). **Career:** Professor of Cell Biology. Specialized in DNA technology, cell cultures and effect of drugs on cell chromosomes. Head of Zoology Department for two years (1984-1985). He has published books in Arabic. **Hobbies:** Painting, poem and writing in local news papers. **Address:** Zoology Department, Faculty of Science, King Saud University, Riyadh, P.O.Box: 2455 Saudi Arabia.

ALSALLAL (Mohammad, Saad), Kuwaiti Ambassador and Consul General. **Born** on March 1, 1949 in Kuwait. **Son** of Saad Al-Sallal (Businessman) **and** Mrs. Ruqaia Al-Sallal. **Divorced,** 3 children: 1 son, Feras Al-Sallal (1976) and 2 daughters: Dalal Al-Sallal (1981), Hussa Al-Sallal (1981). **Educ.:** University of Leningrad/ St-Petersbourg. **Dipl.:** Master's Degree in Economic. **Career:** Attaché at the Ministry of Foreign Affairs (12.9.1974); Third Secretary, Kuwait Embassy in Beirut (5.4.1975 to 22.12.1975); Second Secretary, Kuwait Embassy in Brazil (7.5.1977 to 27.1.1980); First Secretary, Kuwait Embassy in Moscow (28.1.1980 to 31.12.1981); In 1985 assigned to the Cooperation Council of the Arab Gulf States; Counsellor, Kuwait Mission to the United Nations, New York (9.7.1985 to 10.9.1992); Participated in many Conferences of the Non-aligned Movement and the Group of 77; From 1991 non-resident Ambassador to Ecuador; Since 2.10.1992 Ambassador, Permanent Representative, Kuwait Mission Geneva and Consul General of the State of Kuwait, Geneva; 1982-1984 joined the International Organization Department at Ministry of Foreign Affairs. **Sports:** Swimming. **Hobby:** Reading. **Credit Card:** American Express. **Prof. Addr.:** Permanent Representative, Kuwait Mission Geneva, 2, Avenue Ariana, 1202 Geneva, Tel.: 022/734 96 00. **Priv. Addr.:** Chemin du Ruth, 1223 Cologny/CE, Tel.: 022/736 81 50. Ambassador of the State of Kuwait, Madrid, from 1.3.1996.

ALSAUD (Alwaleed Bin Talal Bin Abdulaziz, al, H.R.H. Prince), Saudi entrepreneur, chairman of Kingdom Holding Company; chairman of United saudi bank; chairman of Azizia-Panda United; chairman of Rotana Video & Audio Visual Co.; chairman of Al Azizia Commercial Investment Co.; Chairman of Fairmont Hotel Management Co. **Born** in Riyadh; Saudi Arabia. **Son** of Prince Talal Bin Abdulaziz Alsaud. **Divorced,** two children: Prince Khalid Bin Alwaleed Bin Talal (1979), Princess Reem Bint Alwaleed Bin Talal (1982). **Educ.:** Menlo College, California (1979), Syracuse University, New York (1985). **Dipl.:** B.Sc. in Business Administration, Menlo College; M.Sc. from Syracuse University. **Career:** chairman of Kingdom Holding Company, Riyadh; chairman of United Saudi Bank. **Other Information:** biggest shareholder in Citicorp, New York, owning 8,3% of Capital. Owns 25% of Four Seasons * Regent Hotels, 25% of Disneyland Resort and Theme Park-Paris, 10% of Saks Fifth Avenue, 30% of Arab Radio and Television Broadcasting Co. (ART), 3% of Ballast Nedam, 5% of Mediaset, 10% of Canary Wharf-London, 5% of Trans World Airlines (TWA), 5% of Norwegian Cruise Lines (NCL), 5% of Apple Computers, 2% of Planet Hollywood, 3% of Saatchi & Saatchi Advertising, 7% of the fashion house Donna Karan International, 30% of MOVENPICK Hotels and Resorts, 6% of Daewoo Corporation, 3% of the Malaysian automobile manufacturer Proton, 5% of News Corporation's preferred shares, 5% of Netscape, and 1% of Motorola, 3% of Hotel Properties Limited-Singapore, 50% of Nile Plaza Complex-Cairo, 5% of Palestine Development & Investment Company PADICO, 5% of Jerusalem Development & Investment Company JEDICO. **Prof. Addr.:** Kingdom Holding Company, P.O.Box 8653, Riyadh 11492, Tel.: + 96614881111, Fax: +96614811954, Telex: 405270 NETC SJ, Saudi Arabia.

ALSHALAN (Ghaleb), Jordanian Businessman. **Born** on December 15, 1953 in Amman, Jordan. **Son** of Adnan Alshalan-Businessman **and** Mrs. Intisar Alsaoudi. **Married** on July 25, 1975 in Amman to Monavar Sabri Bahbahani, 2 Children: Rula (4/11/1979), Adnan (11/3/1984). **Educ.:** Terra Sancta College-Amman; American University of Beirut. **Dipl.:** Bachelor of Business Administration. **Career:** Since Graduation in 1975, Worked in Different family owned Businessman and Established new ones. Today on the Board of Directors of many Companies Ranging in Activity from Trade to Manufacturing, to Finance, to Telecommunications, in Different Countries. **Sports Practised:** Tennis & Squash. **Hobbies:** Travel & Reading. **Clubs and Associations:** World Affairs Council, Businessmen Associations in Jordan-Lebanon-Egypt. **Credit Cards:** American Express, Diner's Club, Visa. **Prof. Addr.:** Amman, P.O.Box 1428, Tel. 96265924111, **Priv. Addr.:** Amman, Tel.: 96265925889, Jordan.

ALSHAREEF (Fehied Fahad), Saudi Acting Governor of General Electricity Corporation. **Born** on 1.10.1948 in Medinah, Saudi Arabia. **Married,** four children. **Education:** MA (Economics) from USA-1975. **Career History:** Economic Researcher, Saudi Consulting House (ISDC) (1970-76); Director General of Minister's Office, Ministry of Industry & Electricity (1976-81); Assistant Deputy Minister for Financial & Administration Affairs, Ministry of Industry & Electricity (1981-83); General Director, Financial & Administrative Affairs, Ministry of Health (1983); Vice Governor of General Electricity Corporation (1983- till-date); Acting Governor, Electricity Corp. (1997). Chairman, Saudi Consolidated Electric Co. for Eastern Province (SCECO East). **Membership:** Saudi Handicapped Charitable Association, Saudi Economic Association. **Member:** Saudi Management Association; Member of the Board and Chairman, Finance and Administration Committee, G.C.C. Cigre, Doha, Qatar; Member of Higher Committee, G.C.C. Cigre, Doha, Qatar; The Charitable Foundation for Orphans Custody in Makkah al Mukkaramah. **Awards:** Order of Merit from Moroccan and Spanish Govts. **Address:** The General Electricity Corporation, P.O.Box: 88227, Riyadh 11662, Saudi Arabia.

ALSHOWIMAN (Salim Showiman), Saudi Professor. **Born** in 1947, at Qassim. **Degree:** Ph.D. (Chemistry, U.K.), **Career:** Assistant Professor, Chemistry Department, King Saud University; Head of the Department, Director of the Research Center, then Professor, same department. **Publications:** 38 papers and 7 books. **Hobbies:** reading, travel. **Address:** Chemistry Department, College of Science, King Saud University, P.O.Box 2455, Riyadh-11451, Saudi Arabia.

ALSIBAI (M. Hisham N.), Saudi physician. **Born** in 1943 in Mecca, Saudi Arabia. **Dipl.:** Ph.D. (Obstetrics and Gynaecology). **Career:** Vice-Dean, Student Affairs; Acting Dean, Student Affairs; Vice-Dean, Academic Affairs; Dean, College of Medicine and Medical Sciences; Chairman, Department of Obstetrics and Gynaecology; Professor of Obstetrics and Gynaecology; has attended several conferences related to his field of interest, national and international; member, the Society of Obstetricians and Gynaecologists of West Germany, the Arab Board of Medical Specializations. **Publications:** several articles in local and international medical journals. **Hobbies:** photography, reading. **Address:** King Fahd Hospital of the University, Tel. 8943600. **Priv. Addr.:** Tel. 8649771, Al-Khobar, Saudi Arabia.

ALSUGAIR (Mohammad Abdullah), Saudi Economist. **Born** on December 16, 1937 at Qassim, Saudi Arabia. **Married,** 5 children. **Educ.:**Lebanese University, Beirut, Lebanon; University of California, Los Angeles, California. **Dipl.:** B.A. Business Administration (1960), M.A. Economics. **Career:** Deputy Minister of Finance and National Economy for Budget and Organization (1972-1980); Vice-Chairman and Managing Director of the Saudi Fund for Development (1980- present). **Other Informations:** Has Been Board Member of several Institutions such as: The High Commission for the Development of Riyadh (1975-1977); The Saline Water Conversion Corporation (1974-1980); The Grain Silos and and Flour Mills Organization (1972-1980); The Electricity Corporation of Saudi Arabia (1976-1980); Chairman of the Board of National Shipping Company, Capital 2 Billion Saudi Riyals (1980-1983). **Sport:** Swimming. **Hobby:** Reading. **Member:** Equestrian Club-Riyadh. **Prof. Addr.:** Saudi Fund for Development, P.O.Box 50483, Riyadh 11523, Saudi Arabia. Tel.: 4640292.

ALTAYYIB (Abdul-Hamid, J.), Saudi Academician. **Born** on 14 March 1946 at Al-Ahsa. **Dipl.:** B. Sc., M. Sc., Ph. D. (Civil Engineering). **Career:** Research Assistant, University of Petroleum and Minerals and Texas Tech University (1972-1980), Assistant Professor, February 1980; Chairman Department of Civil Engineering, University of Petroleum and Minerals (1981-1983); Associate Professor, May 1985; Manager, Materials and Building Technology Section at the Research Institute of King Fahd University of Petroleum and Minerals, since September 1985; Professor of Civil Engineering at King Fahd University of Petroleum and Minerals, since June 1993; member of a number of professional organizations such as ACI, ASCE, NACE. **Sports:** tennis and swimming. **Address:** Research Institute, King Fahd University of Petroleum and Minerals, Dhahran 31261, Saudi Arabia. Tel. 966-3-860-3474. Fax 966-3-860-3996.

ALTHIGA (Reda Seraj, A.), Saudi engineer and businessman. **Born** in 1946 in Jeddah, Saudi Arabia. **Dipl.:** Ph.D. Systems Engineering. **Career:** Director, Fadlu-Rahman National Press, Jeddah (1963-66); Assistant Professor (1975-80); Associate Professor University of Petroleum and Minerals, Dhahran (1980-86); Reservoir Engineer

Aramco (1974); Chairman, Systems Engineering department U.P.M, (1976-77); Dean, College of Graduate Studies (1978-84); Founder and President of Saudi Computer Industries; First Computer Manufacturer in the Arab world (since 1984); Chairman of the Board of Saudi EMC (a joint Venture between Realtime Engineering & Data Analysts & EMC Controls Incorporated, a U.S. Process Control manufacturer (a division of REXNORD automation) (since 1986). **Member:** of the Academic Board of the Gulf Technical College, Bahrain, and of UPM Applied Research Institute; Regional Director, Eastern Province, Saudi Royal Computer Society. **Publ.:** Many scientific studies and articles in specialized journals, wrote seven books on computer technology and Arabic computer languages and computers as well as many reference and technical manuals. **Sports:** Swimming. **Hobbies:** chess, reading, computers. **Addr.:** Saudi Computer Industries, P.O.Box 14087, Jeddah 21424, Saudi Arabia.

ALTORKI (Khaled N., H.E.), Saudi Diplomat, **Born** on February 8, 1928 in Mecca, Saudi Arabia. **Son** of Nasser Al Torki (businessman) **and** Mrs. Munira Al Torki. **Married** in 1952 in Jeddah to Mrs. Khadija Al Torki, 3 children: Dr. Nasser Al Torki, Miss Maha Al Torki, Miss May Al Torki. **Educ.:** Different Institutes in Saudi Arabia and Egypt. **Career:** Entered the Chancery of the Viceroy (1945); Started the Diplomatic career in different Arab Countries (1946); Consul General in Cairo (1961-1962); Counsellor and then Minister Plenipotentiary in the Saudi Embassy in Rome (1963-1970), Ambassador of Saudi Arabia in Italy (1977). After being appointed Ambassador (1973) he participated in different missions and conferences in Arab and Islamic Countries (Arab League - Islamic Conferences...) as well as at the United Nations. Saudi Arabian Ambassador in Malta (1981) and presently Ambassador in Italy and Malta. **Awards:** King Abdulaziz Decoration (Excellent Grade); Cavaliere di Gran Croce of the Italian Republic. **Credit Cards:** American Express, Diner's Club. **Prof. Addr.:** Ministry of Foreign Affairs, Jeddah, Saudi Arabia.

ALTWAIJRI (Abdulaziz Othman, Al, Dr. H.E.), Saudi Director General Of the Islamic Educational, Scientific and Cultural Organization (ISESCO).Secretary General of the Federation of the Universities of the Islamic World (FUIW). **Born** on April 3, 1950 in Riyadh-Saudi Arabia. **Son** of Othman Abdulaziz Al Twaijri and Mrs. Hussa Saleh Al Jamil **Married** in 1969 in Riyadh to Fatima Faris Al Jamil, 5 Children: Nizar, Majid, Ahmed, Nawaf, Reem. **Educ.:** Dar-Al-Tawhid (Taif-Saudi Arabia), King Saud University (Riyadh-Saudi Arabia), University Of Oregon (U.S.A.) **Dipl.:** Secondary School Certificate (Taif-1969), B.A. in the English language and History (Riyadh-1974), M.A. in Applied linguistics (Oregon 1977), Ph.D. in Curriculum and Instruction linguistics (Oregon 1981) **Career:** Chairman of Muslim Student Association (Oregon, 1977-1981), Director of Islamic Center (Oaregon, 1978-1981), Assistant Professor at King Saud University (Riyadh, 1982-1985), Deputy Director General for Culture, ISESCO, 15 September 1985; Unanimously elected Director General of the Islamic Educational, Scientific and Cultural Organization-ISESCO-by The Fourth General Conference, held in Rabat from 28 to 30 November 1991; Unanimously re-elected Director General of the Islamic Educational, Scientific and Cultural Organization by ISESCO's Fifth General Conference, held in Damascus on 27-30 november 1994; Unanimously re-elected Director General of the Islamic Educational, Scientific and Cultural Organization-ISESCO-, for two new three-year periods, by the Sixth General Conference of ISESCO, held in Riyadh, on 6-8 December 1997; Secretary General of the Federation of the Universities of the Islamic World; **member** of the Board of Trustees of: the Islamic University in Niger; the Islamic University in Uganda; the Islamic University in Pakistan; the Islamic University in Bangladesh; Member of the Royal Academy of Islamic Civilization Researches (al-Bayt Institutions), Amman, Hashemite Kingdom of Jordan; Member of the Advisory committee of the Arab-Islamic Civilization Encyclopaedia; Executive Director of "Islam Today". an Islamic academic Journal; and "AL JAMIA" Journal. **publ.:** Author of Numerous educational and cultural studies and articles published in leading magazines. **here are some of his intellectual and cultural contributions: Books:** "Dialogue for Coexistance" (Arabic); "On the civilizational building of the Islamic world (Arabic, English and French). **Studies:** Situation of the Islamic world and strategy for the future. (Arabic, English, and French); Social sciences and ISESCO's role in their development in the Islamic world. (Arabic, English, and French); Women in Islam and their position in the Islamic society-(Arabic, English, and French); Economic Human Rights in Islam. (Arabic, English, and French); ISESCO and the Islamic World's educational, Scientific and cultural prospects. (Arabic, English, and French); Child Delinquency: "The Problem and the Solutions". (Arabic, English, and French); Cultural development from an Islamic perspective, (Arabic, English, French and Russian); The Muslim Ummah, in the face of Civilizational Challenge, (Arabic, English, and French); Human Rights in the Light of the Islamic Teachings. (Arabic, English and French).**Medals**: Was awarded the Commander Order Decoration of the Green Crescent Distinction from the Federal Islamic Republic of Comoros in 1992; was awarded the first class Science and Arts Decoration from the Arab Republic of Egypt in 1998; Certificate of Excellence from OIC-Jeddah; Gold Medal from Egyptian Council of Shura. **Sports:** Gymnastics-Swimming. **Hobbies:** Reading, travels. **Prof, Addr.:** ISESCO, P.O.Box 2275- C.P. 10104, Avenue Attine, Hay Ryad-Rabat, Morocco, Tel.: 715285, 715294, 715305, 713266/67, 715298, 772433. Telex: 32645/31844 M-Fax: 777459, 772058, 715321 E-mail ISESCO: cid@isesco.org.ma.

ALWAN (Hamia), Iraqi politician and former journalist. **Born** in 1930 in Babylon Governorate. **Educ.:** American University in Beirut. **Career:** Served Ministry of Finance for several years; arrested several times for political activity; Editor in Chief and Publisher al-Shaab newspaper, served in State Organisation of Commerce; Director General of Information (1968); Minister of State for Presidential Affairs (1968); Minister of Culture and Information (1969); of Youth (1970); Head of Iraqi-German Friendship Association (1972); Minister of Information (1972); Head of Executive Bureau, General Federation of Iraqi Youth (1974); Minister of State (1974-76); Head of Bureau of Vice Chairman of Revolutionary Command Council with rank of Minister (1976-77); Minister of State for Foreign Affairs (1977). **Addr.:** c/o Ministry of Foreign Affairs, Karradat Mariam, Baghdad, Iraq.

ALWAN (Muhammad, Hassan), Iraqi former diplomat. **Born** in 1923 in Baghdad, Iraq. **Married**, 2 sons. **Educ.:** American University of Beirut; Fordham University, New York. **Dipl.:** B.A., M.A. in International Relations and Organizations, MBA in Management and International Finance. **Career:** Chief of Bills Department at the Rafidain Bank, Baghdad (1948-49); Attaché, Iraqi Ministry of Foreign Affairs (1949); Third Secretary, Embassy to Syria (1949-51); Vice Consul, Khorramshahr, Iran (1951-54), Second secretary, Embassy to Iran (1954-55), first secretary, Embassy to USA (1955-60); Director of International Organizations and UN Department (1960-61); Chargé d'Affaires, Embassy to Yugoslavia (1961-63), Embassy to Nigeria (1963-64), Counsellor, Embassy to Lebanon (1964-66), Director General, UN and International Organizations Department (1967-71); Ambassador, Permanent Representative to the UN European Office, Geneva, Switzerland (1971-72); Representative at the UN General Assembly Sessions (1957-71); Head of Iraqi Delegation to UNCTAD in 1971; Member, UN Advisory Committee for Administrative and Budgetary Questions (1971-73). Participated in several world conferences. **Publ.:** "Algeria before the United Nations" New York (1959), "The Dynamics of Neutralism in the Arab World", San Francisco (1964). **Decor.:** Order of St. Silvestro, Holy See; Knight of American Redemption, Government of Liberia. **Hobbies:** Travelling, swimming and tennis. **Addr.:** Baghdad, Iraq.

ALWANI (Abdul Wahed, Al), Bahraini Editor in Chief. **Born** on June 15, 1959 in Bahrain. **Son** of Essa al-Alwani **and** Mrs. née Zainab Al Sabodi. **Married** on March 5, 1988 in Bahrain to Mariam Ali Ahmad, 4 children: Essa, Zainab, Fatima, Amina. **Edu.:** Al Khamis Elementary Hoora Secondary School, Kuwait University. **Dipl.:** Marketing-Ticketing, B.A. Degree in Business Administration - Jan. 1981. **Career:** Editor in Chief, Fanar Publishing. **Awards:** Received a Lot of Awards, Plaques from Various Conferences and Seminars. **Hobbies:** Sports, Reading, Travelling. **Associations:** Many Associations. **Credit Cards:** American Express, Visa, Master Card. **Prof. Addr.:** P.O.Box 10131 Manama, Bahrain, Tel.: 213900, H. 2429 RD. 3949 Block 939 Bahrain.

AMAD (Hani Subhi, al), Jordanian librarian. **Born** in 1938 in Salt, Jordan. **Married** to Intesar Bashiti in 1968, four children. **Educ.:** Salt Secondary School; Cairo University and in U.S.A. **Dipl.:** M.A., Ph.D. **Career:** Librarian, University of Jordan Library (1963-74); Director (1983-); Librarian, Faculty of Arts and Human Sciences, University of Mohamed V, Rabat (1974-76); Director General Culture and Arts Dept., Amman (1977-78); Assistant Professor Faculty of Arts, University of Jordan (1979-); Assistant Dean (1981-83); President, Jordan Library Association (1984-85); President, Jordanian Writers Union (1987). **Publ.:** Jordan Folk Songs (1969); Jordan Folk Proverbs (1978); Cultural Policy in Jordan (1980); Studies in Biographical Sources (1981); Jordan Folk Elegies; Lamentation (1984); Director of Notables in the Southern Region of Bilad Ash Sham (1985); Literature of Writing and authorship among Arabs: a general view (1986); Principles of methodology in Arabic authorship extracted from introductions (1987); "Arab Character in the biography of Princess that al-Himmah" (1988). **Hobbies:** Reading and doing research. **Addr.:** Amman, Jordan.

AMAMI (Salahiddin, al), Tunisian engineer. **Born** in 1936 in Sfax, Tunisia. **Married** three children. **Educ.:** Institut National Agronomique de Paris (1959-62). **Career:** Researcher and Principal Engineer, Laboratory of Bioclimatology, Tunis (1962-64); Head of the Laboratory of Bioclimatology (1962-74); Tunisian counterpart for FAO Projects (1963-67); Chief Engineer (1971); Director of the Center of Research of Rural Engineering and of Project CATID (since 1974); General Engineer (1979). **Publ.:** Many articles published in professional journals and magazines. **Hobby:** History of agriculture in the Mediterranean. **Prof. Addr.:** P.O.Box. 10, Ariana Tel.: 231634, Tunisia. **Priv. Addr.:** 74 Avenue de l'Afrique el-Menzah 5, Tel.: 231139, Tunis, Tunisia.

AMAMOU (Mohamed), Tunisian Diplomat. **Born** on October 7, 1933 in Kairouan (Tunisia). **Married**, 2 children. **Career:** Diplomat and specialist in Arab and Islamic affairs, former general consul in Paris, former ambassador to Zaïre, Lebanon, Jordan, Syria, Morocco and Portugal. Former member of the Tunisian government as Secretary of State for Maghreb affairs; former minister advisor to president Ben Ali, Maghreb representative to the Madrid Peace Conference on the Middle East, and since October 1991, Secretary General of the Arab Maghreb Union (Offices in Rabat, Morocco). **Prof. Addr.:** Arab Maghreb Union, 27, Avenue Agdal-Rabat, Tel.: 772682, 772668, Fax: 772693, Telex: 36 4 88M, Rabat, Morocco.

AMAR (Ahmad Ben), Mauritanian politician. **Born** in 1926 at Aleg (Mauritania). **Son** of Sidi Mohamed Ould

Amar (chief of the Torkoz tribe). **Married:** Khatou mint Denahi, 5 children. **Educ.:** Koran school of Boutilimit (1936); Higher Studies at Boutilimit (1942-44), William Ponty Teacher's Training School. **Dipl.:** Teacher's diploma; secondary education certificate (1964). **Career:** Director of Education (1967); Minister of Justice (1968); Minister of Health and Labour (1970); Minister of Interior (1971); Minister of Primary Education and Religious Affairs (1972- Aug. 1975) **Awards:** Order National Merit of Mauritania. **Member:** Parti du Peuple Mauritanien (PPM); Bureau Politique du PPM, Party suspended following Coup in 1978.

AMARA (Adel, Mohamed), Egyptian surgeon. **Born** in 1931 in Cairo. **Married,** 3 children. **Dipl.:** Diploma in Surgery (1963), Doctorate in Surgery (1973). **Career:** Assistant Professor of Surgery; Member, Egyptian Surgeons Association. **Publ.:** Several articles in "Azhar Medical Journal", "Tanta Medical Journal", "Egyptian Journal of Surgery". **Hobby:** Tennis. **Member:** Gezira Sporting Club. **Priv. Addr.:** 7 Mahmoud Azmi Street, Zamalek, Cairo, Egypt.

AMEEL (Mohamad Iben Saleh, al), Saudi official. **Born** in Al-Rus, 1932. **Dipl.:** B.A. (Arabic Language). **Career:** Teacher; Inspector; Director, Intermediate Education; Director, Primary Education; Director, Planning and Budget; Director-General, Intermediate Education, Ministry of Education; member of Endowments Supreme Council; member of Board, Saudi Real Estate Co.; attended Islamic Education Conferences in Mecca and in India; Assistant to Deputy Minister of Finance for Administrative Affairs, Ministry of Finance. **Addr.:** P.O.Box 2677, Tel.: 23422, Riyad, Saudi Arabia.

AMEIR (Ahmad, Mohamad bin), Omani businessman. **Born** in 1933 in Muscat, Sultanate of Oman. **Married,** two children. **Career:** Chairman of Bin Ameir Est. for Commerce and Contractors; Chairman of Establishment of Oman Contractors; Chairman of the International Company for Insecticides; formerly Chairman of the Chamber of Commerce and Industry, Oman. **Hobby:** Arabic Poetry. **Addr.:** P.O.Box 5157, Tel.: 701973, 701495, Ruwi, Muscat, Oman.

AMER (Hamad, Hassanein), Egyptian chemical engineer. **Born** on December 26, 1924 in Cairo. **Son** of Hassanein Amer **and** Mrs., née Khadiga Sulaiman. **Married** on June 18, 1953 to Miss Hoda Hamad Sulaiman, 2 children: Hassanein and Hannifa. **Educ.:** Cairo University, Stanford University. **Dipl.:** Bachelor of Science in Chemical Engineering with distinction (1946); Master of Science in Petroleum Engineering (1948), Doctor of Philosophy in Chemical Engineering (1955). **Career:** Teaching Assistant Chemical Engineering Department, Cairo University (1946); Petroleum Engineer, Mines and Fuels Administration, Ministry of Commerce and Industry (1953); Construction Engineer, Government Petroleum Refinery, Suez (1953-54); Production Superintendent (1954-57); General Manager (1958-62); Manager Refining Manufacturing Section, Egyptian General Petroleum Corporation (1962-64); Manager Director Organic Chemical Industries Company (1964-66); Manager Director, The Gulf of Suez Petroleum Company (1966). **Publ.:** Author of research in vapor, liquid equilibria. **Award:** Presidencial Order (4th Class). **Member:** of several chemical Associations. **Prof. Addr.:** 1097, Corniche an-Nil Street, Cairo. **Priv. Addr.:** 11, Ibn Zanki, Zamalek, Cairo, Egypt.

AMER (Hussain, Qassim), Yemeni banker. **Born** in 1944 in Hodeidah, Yemen. **Married,** 2 sons. **Educ.:** Cairo University, Egypt. **Dipl.:** B.Sc. in Management. **Career:** Director General, Cooperative and Agricultural Credit Bank, Sanaa (1982- to date). **Prof. Addr.:** P.O.Box 2015, Sanaa, Republic of Yemen.

AMERI (Abdul Qadir, Braik, al), Qatari diplomat. **Born** on November 25, 1943 in Doha. **Married,** two sons. **Educ.:** Beirut Arab University, Lebanon; Institute of Law, Political and Administrative Sciences Faculty, University of Algeria. **Dipl.:** LL.B.; Diploma of Graduate studies in General Law. **Career:** Employed with the Qatar Petroleum Company for eight years; 3rd Secretary at the Qatari Foreign Ministry (1972); Ambassador to Algeria (1974); non-resident Ambassador to Mauritania (1974); Ambassador, Ministry of Foreign Affairs, Qatar (1979); Ambassador to USA (1980). **Hobbies:** Reading, music. **Prof. Addr.:** Ministry of Foreign Affairs, Doha, Qatar.

AMEUR (Makin), Tunisian artist painter. **Born** on April 5, 1937 in Sfax. **Educ.:** Fine Arts School of Tunis. **Dipl.:** Diploma of the said School, Laureate of the Tunisian Government (1959). **Career:** Artist Painter, Contributed to several Art Exhibitions in Tunisia, France (1959) and Italy (1964), Teacher at Bab Djedid School. **Works:** "Landscapes". **Dist.:** Tunis Prize (1958). **Addr.:** Tunis, Tunisia.

AMEZIANE (Ahmed), Moroccan Former Minister of Youth and Sports. **Born** on December 12, 1946 at Béni-Tadjit (Figuig). **Son** of Assou Ameziane and Mrs. Fatima Ameziane. **Married** on July 1976 to Mrs. Zoulikha BENALI, 3 children: Naoual 18 year old; Nabil 15 year old, Imane 8 year old. **Educ.:** - Marquette University. Milwaukee Winsconsin - Universite Libre de Bruxelles. Bruxelles-Belgique. **Dipl.:** Ph.D Educational Administration, Doctorate in Physical Education and Sport. **Career:** Minister, (1995-98); Deputy, since October, 1993; Director of Royal Institute of Training Staff at the Ministry of Youth and Sport 1986-1991; Director of Moulay Rachid Center of Sports 1978-1982; Professor at Regional Training School 1976-1978; Professor at the Secondary School since 1968. **Sports:** Track and field - Soccer - Hand-ball. **Addr.:** 5, Rue Cadi Dinia, Pinède-Rabat-Morocco, (Tel.: 75.06.62 - 75.20.33).

AMIN (Abdul Fattah Mohamad), Iraqi former minister. **Born** in 1932, Salaheddin Governorate, Iraq. **Educ.:** College of Commerce and Economics, Baghdad University (1955). **Career:** Ambassador to Lebanon (1969); Under-Secretary, Ministry of Economy (1973); Member, Baath Party Regional Command (1974); Minister of State without Portfolio (23 January 1977- September 1977); Minister Local Administration (1977-81); Minister of Youth Affairs (1989- March 1991). **Addr.:** Baghdad, Iraq.

AMIN (Amin, Abdul Latif, al), Sudanese diplomat. **Born** on May 30, 1931 in Khartoum, Sudan. **Married,** 2 sons. **Educ.:** Cairo University, Egypt; London School of Economics, London. **Dipl.:** B.Sc. in Agriculture (1957); Diploma in International Relations. **Career:** Assistant Inspector, Soil Department, Agricultural Research Corporation, Sudan (1957-60); 3rd Secretary, Ministry of Foreign Affairs, Khartoum (1960-61); Chargé d'Affaires, Embassy of Sudan, Greece (1961-63); Consul General, Embassy of Sudan, Egypt (1964-66); First Secretary, Embassy of Sudan in India (1966-68); Counsellor, Sudan Embassy in Uganda (1968-71), in London (1971-72), Chargé d'Affaires, Sudan Embassy, USSR (1972-73); Director, East European Department, Ministry of Foreign Affairs, Khartoum (1973-74); Director, Minister's Office, Ministry of Foreign Affairs (1974-75), Director General, Political Affairs Department, Ministry of Foreign Affairs (1975-76); Sudan Ambassador to Nigeria (1976-78); Ambassador to Scandinavian Countries (1978); Represented Sudan in several congresses and conferences. **Publ.:** papers for discussion, "Ideology in Soviet Foreign Policy, Brinksmanship in Foreign Policy". **Hobbies:** Squash, folklore music, swimming and mini golf. **Addr.:** Ministry of Foreign Affairs, Khartoum, Sudan.

AMIN (Hassan B.), Saudi academic. **Born** in 1949 in Mecca, Saudi Arabia. **Dipl.:** B.Sc., Ph.D. (Chemistry). **Career:** Demonstrator, Faculty of Science, King Saud University; Associate Professor, Department of Chemistry, Faculty of Science, King Saud University since 1978; representative of Chemistry Department, Equipment Committee, Faculty of Science. **Publ.:** several research papers in Physical Organic Chemistry, **Addr.:** Faculty of Science, King Saud University, Tel.: 4675891 (Office), and 4648519 (Home), Riyadh, 11451, Saudi Arabia.

AMIN (Mahmoud), Egyptian petroleum geologist. **Born** in 1920 in Cairo, Egypt. **Married** in 1945, three children. **Educ.:** Cairo and London Universities. **Dipl.:** Ph.D. **Career:** Deputy General Manager of Exploration and Production, General Petroleum Corporation (1958-68); Chairman Western Desert Petroleum Corporation (1968-75); Assistant Secretary General OAPEC (1975-79); Petroleum Consultant (1979-). **Publ.:** Economics of Petroleum Resources, about 25 scientific papers on geology and petroleum, about 100 articles on petroleum. **Prof. Addr.:** 20 Mohamed Hassan Street, Heliopolis, Cairo. **Priv. Addr.:** 391 Horyia Street, Apart. 802, Alexandria, Egypt.

AMIN (Mohamed, Ahmad), Egyptian diplomat. **Born** in Cairo, Egypt. **Married,** 3 sons, 1 daughter. **Career:** Commentator, Egyptian Broadcasting System (1950-62); Editor and then Editor in Chief, "Egyptian Gazette" (1950-59); Editor in Chief, National Publication House, Cairo (1959-62), Middle East News Agency, Cairo (1962); Manager, Middle East News Agency, London, UK (1962-67); Counsellor, Information Department, Cairo (1967-69); Press Counsellor, Permanent Mission of Egypt to the UN, New York, later Minister Plenipotentiary for Press and Information (1969-79); represented Egypt at the UN General Assembly in 1978; Member of the Centre for the Study of the Presidency, New York, USA, of the Academy of Political Science, New York, USA; Member of the Press Syndicate, Cairo, Egypt. Under Secretary of State, Department of Information, Ministry of Foreign Affairs, Cairo (1979-). **Publ.:** "Nationalism not for Sale" (1961), "Egypts Quest for Peace" (1971); numerous articles in Egyptian as well as foreign newspapers. **Prof. Addr.:** Ministry of Foreign Affairs, Department of Information, Cairo, Egypt.

AMIN (Muhammad Jassim, al), Iraqi diplomat. **Born** in 1930 in Baghdad, Iraq. **Married,** 4 children. **Dipl.:** B.Sc. in Mathematics. **Career:** Teacher of Physics and Mathematics at Iraqi Secondary schools (1955-63); Cultural Attache, Embassy of Iraq to Egypt (1963-64); Teacher in Morocco at the Iraqi School (1965-68); Vice Governor of Baghdad and Mosul (1969-70); General Director of Administrative Affairs, Ministry of Information, Iraq (1970-77); Director, Iraqi News Agency in Beirut; Director General of Information, Ministry of Information; Minister of Information; Editor in Chief of "al-Thawra" newspaper; Ambassador of Iraq to the United Arab Emirates (1978-80). **Hobbies:** Peotry and litterature. **Prof. Addr.:** Ministry of Foreign Affairs, Baghdad, Iraq.

AMIN (Nafisa, Ahmad, al), Sudanese politician. **Educ.:** Teacher Training College, Omdurman, Sudan; Domestic Science at Hull, United Kingdom. **Career:** Teacher in Teachers Training College; elected Executive Council Member of the Blue Nile Province; held office in the former Women's Union in the Blue Nile Province, later President of Sudan Socialist Union; Active in the anti-illiteracy campaign, in adult education schemes and in the setting up of health centres and kindergartens; Member, Khartoum Cheshire Homes Committee; Deputy Minister of Sports and Social Affairs, of Youth Affairs (1971-72); President of the Sudan Womens union (1972) Member of the Peoples Assembly (1974). **Addr.:** Khartoum, Sudan.

AMIN (Nasseh, Hussain), Egyptian academic. **Born** on May 21, 1924 in Cairo. **Married,** 1 son. **Educ.:** Cairo University. **Dipl.:** M.B. B.Ch. (1947), Diploma in Biochemical Analysis (1950) and in Bacteriology (1951),

M.D. in Haematology (1953). **Career:** Kasr al-Aini Hospital, Cairo (1948), Demonstrator in Clinical Pathology (1949-53), Assistant Professor of Clinical Pathology (1961), Professor (1968), Head of Clinical Pathology Department (1981-); life member, Society of Haematology (1973-), Society of Clinical and Biochemical Pathology (1973-). **Member:** Executive Member, Cairo Automobile Club; Member of Egyptian Shooting Club, Gezira Sporting Club. **Prof. Addr.:** 5 Talaat Harb Street, Cairo, Egypt. **Priv. Addr.:** 20 Montazah Street, Zamalek, Cairo, Egypt.

AMIN (Omaima), Egyptian academic and professor of music. **Born** on March 18, 1934 in Cairo, Egypt. **Married** to D. Reda Kamel (Head of the Dept. of Architecture, Faculty of Engineering, Cairo Univ.), 3 children: Eng. Randa Reda Kamel (Ass't Teacher Faculty of Engineering & Technology); Eng. Ruwaida Reda Kamel; Ramy Reda Kamel (Demonstrator Faculty of Music Educations). **Educ.:** High Institute of Music Teachers, Garden City, Cairo; Jacques Dalcroze Institute, Paris. **Dipl.:** High Institute of Music Teachers, Bachelor of Music; Jacques Dalcroze Institute, High Certificate in Specialization, equivalent to the Egyptian Doctoral Degree. **Career:** Dean, Faculty of Music Education, Helwan University; Professor of Solfeggio, Eurhytmics and Improvisation, Faculty of Music Education, Helwan University, 1956 to 1992. **Work:** Member of State Councils on Musical Arts; Member on International Society of Music Education; Member of Committees related to the Administration of Helwan University, Organizing Music Programs for the Faculty of Music Education and Academy; Setting Up a Recording Studio, and a Center for Community Music Program. **Publ.:** Text Books on Solfeggio, On Eurhythmics and Music Games for Faculty of Music Book: "Theory of Music to be Sung" and Cassette for Children; Books on Music for Kindergartens and Nursery Schools. **Awards:** Five Monetary Prizes for being the first of the Graduating Class in 1956. **Hobbies:** Reading, Music, Cooking. **Prof. Addr.:** Faculty of Music Education, 27 Ismail Mohamed Str., Zamalek, Tel.: 3403750, Cairo, Egypt. **Priv. Addr.:** 17 Bahgat Aly Str., Zamalek, Cairo, Egypt.

AMIN (Samir), Egyptian economist. **Born** in Cairo, in 1931. **Educ.:** Cairo secondary Schools; University of Paris. **Dipl.:** Ph.D. (Economics). **Career:** Senior Economist, Economic Development Organisation, Cairo (1957-60); Technical Adviser for Planning to Government of Mali (1960-63); Prof. of Economics, Universities of Poitiers (France), Paris and Dakar (Senegal); Director of Third World Forum- African Office, Dakar, Senegal. **Publ.:** "Trois expériences africaines de développement, Mali, Guinée, Ghana" (1965); "L'économie du Maghreb" (1967); "Le développement du capitalisme en Côte d'Ivoire" (1968); "Le monde des affaires Sénégalaises" (1968); "Maghreb in the Modern World" (1970); "L'accumulation à l'échelle mondiale" (1970); "L'Afrique de l'ouest bloquée" (1970); "Le développement inégal" (1973); "La Nationalité" (1976); "Class et Nation dans l'histoire" (1979); "l'Economie Arabe Contemporaine" (1980); "L'Avenir du Maoisme" (1983); "La Deconnexion" (1985); "Azma al-Moujtama al-Arabi" (Le Caire- 1985). **Priv. Addr.:** Forum du Tiers Monde, P.O.Box 3501, Dakar, Senegal.

AMIN (Tigani Muhammad, al), Sudanese official. **Born** in 1934 in al-Obeid, Sudan. **Married**, 2 sons. **Educ.:** Cairo University, Egypt; Rostock University, Germany. **Dipl.:** B.Sc. in Agriculture, Ph.D. in Entomology, Diploma in Nematology. **Career:** Head of Entomology Section and Senior Scientist, the Agricultural Research Corporation, Sudan (1970-78); Assistant Professor (1976), Professor of Entomology (1978), National Coordination for Entomology Research (1978-80); Director, Gezira Agricultural Research Station (1980-). **Member** of FAO/UNEP Panel of Experts on Integrated Pest Control, German Agricultural Society, Plant Protection Teams of the Arab Agricultural Organization, Egyptian Entomological Society and others. **Publ.:** published numerous research papers in professional Sudanese and foreign journals. **Hobbies:** Poetry and literature. **Prof. Addr.:** P.O.Box 126, Wadi Medani, Sudan.

AMIRI (Hassan Ali, al), Iraqi politician. **Born** in 1941 in Baghdad, Iraq. **Career:** Under Secretary, Ministry of Municipalities (1973); Member, Arab Baath Socialist Party Regional Leadership (1974), Member of the follow-up Committee (1974); Head of the Revolutionary Command Council Public Organisations Bureau (1974); Vice Chairman, Higher Agricultural Council (1974); Minister of Internal Trade (1976), Acting Minister of Trade (1977); former member of the Revolutionary Command Council. **Prof. Addr.:** P.O. Box 6012, Baghdad, Iraq.

AMIRI (Yusif Muhammad Salih, al), United Arab Emirates businessman. **Born** in 1948 in Abu Dhabi, UAE. **Married,** 1 daughter. **Educ.:** courses on the British Postal System. **Dipl.:** Diploma in English. **Career:** Assistant Marketing Manager, Abu Dhabi Telephone and Telegraph Company; General Manager, Amiri Establishment. **Hobbies:** Hunting, reading and swimming. **Prof. Addr.:** P.O.Box 2666, Abu Dhabi, United Arab Emirates.

AMLY (Abdul Kader, al), Egyptian meteorologist. **Born** on May 2, 1926 in Mansura, Egypt. **Married. Educ.:** Faculty of Science, Alexandria University, Egypt; Imperial College of Science and Technology, London, UK. **Dipl.:** B.Sc. in Physics and Maths; Diploma in Meteorology, M.Sc. in Meterology. **Career:** Egyptian Meteorological Department (1948-50); Aviation Forecaster (1953); Lecturer, Meteorological Department, Aeronautical Meteorology (1953-56); Officer, Meteorological Department, International Affairs, Egypt (1956-64); Technical Officer for Africa, World Meteorological Organization, Geneva, Switzerland (1964-67); Representative, Regional Officer for Africa, World Meteorological Organization, Geneva

(1968). **Publ.:** "Meteorology for Aviation". **Hobby:** Meteorology. **Prof. Addr.:** World Meteorological Organization, 41 Avenue Guiseppe Motta, CH-1211, Geneva 20, Switzerland.

AMMAR (Abdulhamid), Tunisian diplomat. **Born** in 1935 in Sousse, Tunisia. **Married,** four children. **Educ.:** Sadiki College, Tunis; Faculty of Law, Sorbonne, University of Paris, France. **Career:** Secretary General of the Tunisian Students Union (1962-63); Secretary General of the Destour Party Youth Organisation (1964); Secretary General of the Destour Party Franco-Tunisian Friendship Organisation, Les Amis de la France (1964); member of the Economic and Social Council and Director of Youth and Sports (1965); Director of Foreign Relations for the Socialist Destour Party; Vice President of the Municipality of Sousse; Ambassador to Zaire (1969-71); Ambassador to Senegal, Ivory Coast, Sierre Leone and Mauritania (1972-76); Ambassador to USSR (1976-84); Minister of Foreign Affairs (1985-88). **President** of the Union Tunisienne de la Jeunesse (1965). **Addr.:** Ministry of Foreign Affairs, Tunis, Tunisia.

AMMAR (Ferdjani Ben Hadj), Tunisian politician. **Born** in 1916 in Tunis. **Married,** three children. **Son** of Ben Hadj Ammar. **Career:** Active member of the Neo Destour (since 1935); Minister of National Economy in the first Bourguiba Government (1965); member of Union Tunisienne de l'Industrie du Commerce et de l'Artisanat and represented Tunisia on several missions abroad; first Vice President of the National Assembly (1964); President of the Tunisian Group of the Interparliamentary Union. **President** of the Comité Nationale de la Solidarité Sociale and the Co-ordinating Committee for Flood Relief (Autumn of 1969); Director of the Destour Socialist Party (1972); President of Union Tunisienne de L'industrie, du Commerce et de l'Artisanat (1984-88). **Addr.:** Tunis, Tunisia.

AMMAR (Moncef, Belhadj), Tunisian politician. **Born** on September 21, 1931 in Beni Khiar, Tunisia. **Married,** 2 daughters. **Dipl.:** LL.B. **Career:** Head of the Office of the Minister of Finance (1970); Secretary General of Finance (1971); Secretary General of the Government (1973); Secretary General of the Government and the Minister responsible for the relations with National Assembly; Vice President, National Assembly; Minister Delegate attached to Prime Minister responsible for Civil Service and Administrative Reform (April 1980- December 1980). **Awards:** Grand Cordon, Order of the Tunisian Independence; Grand Officer, Order of Tunisian Republic; various Foreign Decorations. **Addr.:** Tunis, Tunisia.

AMMARI (Nabih, Ayoub), Jordanian chemical consultant. **Born** in 1933 in Amman, Jordan. **Son** of Ayoub Awad Ammari, Army Officer **and** Mrs. Hana Nimer Ayoub. **Married** to Mary Dalia Mazelis in 1967 in USA, two children. **Educ.:** Al-Asbaliah Elementary School (1942-49); Islamic Educational College (1949-53); Oklahoma City University (1954-60); East Texas State University (1972-76). **Dipl.:** B.A., B.Sc., M.Sc., Ed.D. **Career:** Analytical Chemist (1957-60); Research Chemist (1960-72); University Instructor (1972-76); Business Executive (1977-78); Consultant (since 1978). **Publ.:** "Selected Synthetic Studies of Aliphatic Dithioacids and their Reactions with Thionyl Chloride and Sulfure Oxychloride". **Decor.:** Honorary Colonel Certificate from the Honorable Raymond Gary (1957); The President's Award from the Perkin Elmer Corp., (both in 1981 and 1985). **Sports:** Swimming and walking. **Hobbies:** Reading, travelling and writing proses in Classical Arabic. **Member:** of the American Chemical Society (full member). **Credit Cards:** American Express and Diner's Club. **Prof. Addr.:** P.O.Box 2462, Amman, Jordan. **Priv. Addr.:** P.O.Box 5329, Amman, Jordan.

AMMARI (Shabib, Farah), Jordanian economist. **Born** in 1941 in Ma'an, Jordan. **Son** of Farah H. Ammari **and** Mrs. Rasmieh Issa Ammari. **Educ.:** University of Cairo, B.Sc. in Political Science and Economics; Michigan State University, M.Sc. in Economics; University of Southern California, M.A. and Ph.D. in Economics. **Career:** Acting Director, General Planning Dept., Ministry of Planning, Amman (1968-69); Teaching Assitant Responsible of Teaching Classes at U.S.C., Los Angeles, California (1980-84); Senior Lecturer at U.S.C. in Los Angeles, California, California State University at Long Beach, California, Pomona Pomona, California (1985-86); General Manager, Jordan Management and Consultancy Corp., Amman, Jordan (1987); Managing Director, Jordan Industrial Investment Corp. and member in the Board of Directors of Finance and Credit Corp., Amman and Jordan Sulphochemicals Corp., Amman. **Hobby:** Reading. **Credit Cards:** A/X, Diner's, Visa. **Prof. Addr.:** Jabal Amman, Behind Ammar Centre Park, Tel.: 639714, Amman. **Priv. Addr.:** Shmeisani, Tel.: 606773, Amman, Jordan.

AMMASH (Salih, Mahdi), Iraqi diplomat. **Born** in 1924 in Baghdad, Iraq. **Married,** four children. **Educ.:** Military College, Staff College, Baghdad, Iraq. **Career:** Army Officer (1954); Chief of Army Intelligence (1958); Director of Air Force Operations (1963); Minister of Defence (1963); General Commander of the Joint Syrian-Iraqi Army (1963); Minister of the Interior (1968); member of the Revolutionary Command Council (1968); Deputy Prime Minister, Vice President of the Republic and member of the Revolutionary Command Council (1970); Ambassador of Iraq to USSR (1972); Ambassador of Iraq to France (1974); Ambassador of Iraq to Finland (1975). **Member** of both the Regional and the National Leaderships of the Arab Baath Socialist Party (1963-73). **Publ.:** "The Military Unity"; "The Successful Commandership"; "Men Without Leadership"; "From Zi-Qar to Qadisia"; "Qutaiba Bin Muslim"; "The Evaluation of 5th June Defeat"; "The Strategic Points in the Arab Fatherland"; "Moscow the Capital of Ice"; "The Civil Popular Defence". **Medals:** Military Ordeer of Rafidain, 2st Class; many other Iraqi decorations. **Sports:** Tennis, swimming. **Hobby:** Reading, writing, horseriding. **Priv. Addr.:** 54/29/332 Al-Rabi District, Adhania, Tel.: 4438187, Baghdad, Iraq.

AMMAWI (Ahmad, al-), Egyptian Politician. **Born** In July 1932. **Married,** three sons. **Educ.:** B.A. law (1968); **Career:** Head, General Trade Union Federation (1987); Member of Board, International Labor Association; Assistant Secretary General, Arab Labor Association; Member Socialist Union Secretariat; Head, Syndicate Committee (1966); Secretary and then Chairman, General Syndicate for Chemicals; Member, Founding Committee of National Democratic Party (NDP); Minister of Manpower and Employment (1993 to date). **Address:** Ministry of Manpower and Employment, Sheikh Rihan, Bal el-Louk, Cairo, Egypt.

AMOUDI (Muhammad Said), Saudi official. **Born** in 1940 in Mecca, Saudi Arabia. **Married,** 4 children. **Educ.:** Faculty of Literature, Cairo University, Egypt. **Dipl.:** B.A. **Career:** Head of Department, Ministry of Pilgrimages, Saudi Arabia (1964-69); Director (1969-76); Managing Director (1976-80); Director General (1980-84); Under Secretary (1984-) and editor of "Hajj" periodical. **Hobbies:** Scientific research and reading. **Prof. Addr.:** Ministry of Pilgrimages, Omar Ibn Khattab Str., Riyadh 1183, Saudi Arabia.

AMR (Mahmoud), Egyptian journalist and diplomat. **Born** on 18 January 1923 in Assiut (Egypt). **Son** of Ahmed Amr **and** Mrs., née Fatima el-Imam. **Married** on 18 January 1951 in Cairo to Miss Seyada Ismail, 3 children: Yehia, Ahmed and Amr. **Dipl.:** Graduate of Teacher Training Programme, British Institute (Cairo); Bachelor of Science, Iona College (New York) Graduate Work in International Relations at same college Later obtained a Ph.D. from California. **Career:** Local News Editor, Assistant Editor-in-chief, Editorial writer, Egyptian Gazette (1950-59); Editor-in-chief of: The Arab Observer (Weekly Magazine), The Scribe (Monthly Magazine) (1959-62); Deputy Editor-in-Chief Middle East News Agency (1962); United Kingdom Manager, Middle East News Agency, London (1962-67); Counsellor, Information Department, Cairo (1967-69); Commentator, Egyptian broadcasting System (1950-62); Advisor and Representative, Egyptian Delegation to the General Assembly (the 24th to the 33rd Sessions) (1969-78); Minister Plenipotentiary (Press and Information) (1976-79); Chief at the Foreign Affairs Sector, Department of Information, Cairo (1971-1982); Consultant, Mass media Trust and Adviser to the Government of Zimbabwe on Media Affairs, his duties included the training of Journalists and Press Officers (1982-1987); Head of the Department of Public Information and Chief Lecturer, Institute of Mass Communications, Zimbabwe (1987-1990) Consultant, Government of Zimbabwe (1993-1999) Cairo. **Works and Publ.:** Contributed Features and Articles to: Reuters News Agency, Cairo Calling (Weekly), Al-Hilal (Monthly), Bourse Egyptienne (Daily); Rendered into English a number of Short Stories which were published in Cairo Calling and Broadcast by the Egyptian Broadcasting System; Rendered into Arabic a number of Short Stories which were published by Al Thagafa, a leading literary magazine; Attended at least 30 seminars and symposia between 1950 and 1962, Author of two books in English: New Era for Arabs (1960) and Nationalism not for Sale (1961). **Awards:** Recipient of the Key to the City of Memphis, Tennesse, USA (Summer 1981); Permanently inscribed upon the Roll of Honour of "Men and Women of Distinction" in recognition of his "outstanding services and achievements", International Biographical Centre (IBC) of Cambridge, England. **Member:** The Academy of Political Science, New York; Centre for the Study of the Presidency, New York; The Press Syndicate, Cairo; United Nations Association, Cairo; Top Management Group, Cairo. **Prof. Addr.:** and **Priv. Addr.:** 2, Kubbeh Street, Roxy, Heliopolis, Tel.: 2580747, Cairo, Egypt.

AMRANI (Mohammed Raja), Moroccan academic. **Born** on August 31, 1948 in Fes, Morocco. **Son** of Mohamed Jawad Amrani (deceased) **and** Mrs. Meryem Mikou. **Married** in 1977 in Rabat to Ghyslaine el-Fihry, 2 children: Kenza (8.4.1979), Jaafar (29.11.1982). **Educ.:** Faculty of Law, Rabat; Panthéon Sorbonne, Paris I. **Dipl.:** Institute of Business Administration, Paris (I) Cycle L.4; Doctorat d'Etat in Economical Sciences, Paris I (1976) **Career:** Assistant Professor then Lecturer at the Faculty of Law of Casablanca and Professor at the Faculty of Law of Rabat; Director of Economical Sciences Department (1983-85 and 1985-89); presently Professor, Faculty of Law, Universite Mohamad V. **Other Information:** Former Vice President of the Moroccan Organization for Human Rights. **Sports:** Swimming. **Prof. Addr.:** Avenue des Nations Unies, Agdal, Rabat, Morocco, and Université Mohamad V, Faculty of Law, P.O.Box 721, Rabat, Morocco. **Priv. Addr.:** 5 Lots Dhar Temaa Souissi, Tel.: 754095, Rabat, Morocco.

AMRAWI (Omar, Abdul Aziz), Moroccan engineer. **Born** in 1945 in Fez, Morocco. **Married,** 4 children. **Educ.:** Ecole Polytechnique, Paris, Ecole Nationale Supérieure des Mines, Paris, France. **Career:** Research Engineer, National Economic Development Bank (1969-72); Director of Exploitation; Trade and Cooperation, Bureau de Recherches et de Participation Minières (1973-80); Director of Industry, Ministry of Industry (1980-83); Administrator Managing Director, Berliet-Maroc (since 1983-); Administrator, Renault-Maroc; Member of the Board Arab Federation of Engineering Industries; President of the Moroccan Automobile Industry Association (1985-87); President of Groupement du poids lourd et de la carrosserie. **Addr.:** Berliet, Maroc, Tarik Al-Rabat, Ain Sebaa, P.O.Box 2624, Tel.: 212-2-733290, 792107, Fax: 73.10.42, Casablanca, Morocco.

AMRI (Abdul Rahman Omar, al), Saudi M.D. **Born** in 1934 in Taif, Saudi Arabia. **Dipl.:** M.B.B. Ch. **Career:** M.D., Physician, Assistant Director, Jiyad Hospital, Mecca (1960); Director, King Faisal Hospital, Taif (1963); Director of Health School, Mecca (1965); Director of General Hospital, Jeddah (1966); Director of Health School, Jeddah (1973); owner, AMRI Clinic; member, Jeddah Literary and Cultural Club; member of Board, Okaz Organization, Jeddah Cultural and Arts Society; Editor of the Medical Section, Okaz daily; attended the 6th Annual Saudi Medical Meeting, Jeddah (1981); offers medical services for Women's Welfare Society, Dar al-Hanan School. **Publ.:** regular contribution and weekly medical articles in Okaz daily since 1966, Min Ajli Sihattik (For Your Health); in addition to several scientific articles. **Hobby:** literature. **Addr.:** Bab Makkah, Mously Building, Tel.: 642-4550 (Office) and 651-0779 (Home), Jeddah, Saudi Arabia.

AMRI (Bakor, al), Saudi academic. **Born** on January 27, 1940 in Mecca, Saudi Arabia. **Dipl.:** M.A. (Foreign Affairs) 1971; Ph.D. (Political Science) 1973. **Career:** Third Secretary, Conference Department, Ministry of Foreign Affairs; Vice-Consul, New York, (USA); Adviser to Saudi Delegation at UNO, New York; Director, Saudi Public Relations Bureau, New York (USA); Current: Legal Adviser, Islamic Development Bank; Adviser to World Muslim League on African Affairs, Consultant to Ministry of Foreign Affairs: Chairman of Co-ordination Committee, World Muslim League Conference on Islam in Africa; Current: Professor of Political Science and Assistant Dean, Faculty of Economics and Public Administration, King Abdul Aziz University, Jeddah, Consultant Tabuk Province. **Publ.:** Author of 2 university textbooks and numerous articles. **Hobbies:** reading and travel. **Addr.:** King Abdul Aziz University, P.O.Box 9031, Jeddah, Saudi Arabia.

AMRI (Hussain, al), Yemeni diplomat. **Born** in 1943 in Sanaa, Yemen. **Educ.:** Damascus University, Syria; Cambridge University, UK. **Dipl.:** Ph.D. **Career:** Ministry of Foreign Affairs (1962); served in Yemen Arab Republic to Syria (1970); Permanent Under Secretary, Ministry of Foreign Affairs (1975); Minister of Agriculture (1986). **Addr.:** Sanaa, Republic of Yemen.

AMRI (Youssef, al), Saudi academic. **Born** in Medina, in 1938. **Dipl.:** B.A. (Business Administration), Riyadh University; M.A. (Business Administration), Michigan State University; Ph.D. (Accounting and Economics and Finance), Arizona University. **Career:** Official in charge of administrative affairs, Ministry of Defence and Aviation (1956-66); Accountant, PETROMIN; General Supervisor, Finance Department, King Abdulaziz University; member of teaching staff (1976); attended International Accounting Conference, Munich (1977); Assistant Professor, Faculty of Economics and Administration, King Abdul Aziz University. **Publ.:** Ph.D. thesis on Saudi Primary Schools Budget. **Addr.:** Faculty of Economics and Administration, King Abdulaziz University, P.O.Box 9031, Jeddah, Saudi Arabia.

ANAM (Abdul Jabbar Hail Said), Yemeni businessman. **Born** in 1944 in Taiz, Yemen. **Married**, 6 children. **Educ.:** Faculty of Economics and Political Science, Cairo University, Egypt; Private courses in Management and Finance. **Dipl.:** B.Sc. **Career:** Director, Hail Said Anam Company (1969-75), District Director (1975-84); Chairman, Yemen Chamber of Commerce (1977-84); General Director of Industrial Management, Hail Said and Partners Company (1984-); Managing Director, Middle East Trading Co., and Director in several other industrial and trading companies. **Prof. Addr.:** Mujamma Street, P.O.Box 5302, Taiz, Republic of Yemen.

ANAM (Ali Mohamad Said), Yemeni politician. **Born** in 1925 in Yemen. **Married**, 9 children. **Career:** Businessman; Minister of Health (1962); member of the Presidential Council (1963); Chairman of the Board, Yemeni Bank for Construction and development (1964-65); Minister of State (1965-66); participated in the movement of liberation from the Imam's regime; member of the Consultative Council (1972-75); Vice Chairman and Manager, Hail Said Company, largest Yemen private company; Chairman of the Board, Yemeni Company for Industry and Commerce: Chairman of the Board, Oil and Soap Co. **Publ.:** "Industry and Commerce Magazine". **Medals:** Order of the Nile, 1st Class, Egypt. **Hobbies:** Reading, Arabic and Yemeni music and songs. **Addr.:** Mujamma Street. P.O.Box 5302, Taiz, Republic of Yemen.

ANANI (Jawad, Ahmad, al), Jordanian economist. **Born** in 1943 in Halhul, Jordan. **Son** of Ahmad Anani. **Married**, four children. **Educ.:** B.A. in Economics, American University of Cairo, AUC, Cairo (1967); M.A. and Ph.D. in Economics in USA (1970, 75). **Career:** Director of Research, Central Bank of Jordan (1975-77); Under Secretary, Ministry of Labour (1977-79); Director General, Social Security Corporation (1979); Ministry of Supply (1979-80); Minister of Labour (1980-1985). **Member of:** the American Economists Association, the Jordanian Higher Education Council, the International Affairs Association, Jordan, the Olympic Committee of Jordan. President of the Board of the Cultural Organisation for Children. **Publ.:** "Pooling of Reserves among Arab Common Market Countries" (1974), in English, many articles on economic subjects published in various magazines. **Medals:** Order of the Jordanian Star (1981). **Sports:** Tennis, Volley-ball (President of the Volley-ball Union). **Hobbies:** Reading, music. **Addr.:** Amman, Jordan.

ANBAR (Ahmad, Hassan), Saudi musician and composer. **Born** in 1940 in Jeddah (Saudi Arabia). **Educ.:** Conservatoire. **Dipl.:** Diploma of music (violin). **Career:** Saudi radio and TV Services, and Ministry of Information, member of Saudi Arabian Arts Society; Attended Fraternity Festivals in Algeria, Tunisia, Kuwait, Bahrain and Abu Dhabi. **Publ.:** Author of a number of musical compositions and songs. **Hobbies:** Reading and music. **Prof. Addr.:** Ministry of Information Building, Tel.: 6426222/38 (Office) and 642-3225 (Home), Jeddah, Saudi Arabia.

ANBAR (Faisal, A.), Saudi executive. **Born** in 1946 in Medina, Saudi Arabia. **Dipl.:** M.Sc. (Petroleum Engineering). **Career:** Petroleum Engineer, Ministry of Petroleum and Mineral Resources, (1969-73) Chief, Petroleum Engineering Department, same Ministry; Contracts Manager, Petroline; General Manager, Planning, Petroline; General Manager, Operation and Maintenance, Petromin Services Rabigh, attended conferences and seminars related to the Oil Industry. **Hobbies:** Personal computer application, photography. **Addr.:** P.O.Box. 5250, Tel.: 6600123 (Office) and 682-1669 (Home), Jeddah, Saudi Arabia.

ANBARI (Abdul Amir Ali, al), Iraqi administrator. **Married,** 1 son, 2 daughters. **Educ.:** Harvard Law School. **Dipl.:** LL.M., Doctorate of Juridical Science. **Career:** Director of Legal Department, Iraqi National Oil Company (1968-69), OPEC (1970-71); Deputy General Director of Oil Affairs, Ministry of Oil (1972-74); Director General (1975-77), Senior advisor (1978-79); Chairman and President, Iraqi Fund for External Development (1979-85); Ambassador, Director General, Multilateral International Economic Relations, Ministry of Foreign Affairs (1985); Ambassador to the Court of St. James (1985-87), to the USA (1987-90); Permanent Representative of Iraq at the United Nations (1991-1994); Member with the rank of judge, OAPEC Judicial Tribunal (1980-); Board Member of the International Development Law Institute (1984-). **Publ.:** several articles on International Economic Corporation, Oil and legal Development. **Hobbies:** Swimming and reading. **Addr.:** Baghdad, Iraq.

ANBARI (Saleh Abdul Muhsen, al), Saudi civil servant. **Born** in 1931 in Damascus. **Dipl.:** B.A. (Economics and Public Administration), King Abdulaziz University. **Career:** Attaché, Royal Embassy of Saudi Arabia, Tunis (1963-66); 3rd Secretary, Royal Embassy of Saudi Arabia, Kabul (1966-68); Director of Foreign Ministry Bureau, Dammam (1970-73); Chargé d'Affaires, Libya (1974-77); Director of African Affairs Department, Ministry of Foreign Affairs. **Hobby:** Watching football. **Addr.:** P.O.Box. 6731, Tel.: 69-0900 (Office) and 665-4004 (Home), Jeddah, Saudi Arabia.

ANBATAWI (Munzer, Fayek), Jordanian lawyer. **Born** in 1929 in Nablus, Palestine. **Married. Dipl.:** Licence in Law (1953), Doctorate in International Law (1962). **Career:** Ministry of Justice, Tripoli, Libya (1953-56); Barrister and Civil Magistrate in Jordan (1957-58); Advisor, Political Department, Ministry of Foreign Affairs, Kuwait (1963-64); General Manager, Palestine National Fund, Jerusalem (1965), Institute for Palestine Studies in Beirut, part-time Lecturer in International Law, Arab University of Beirut, Lebanon (1965-68); Professor and Head of Political Science Department, Jordan University (1968-75); Member of Human Rights Centre (1976-); Secretary of Human Rights Committee, United Nations, Geneva (1977-84), Chief Advisory Services Unit (1984-). **Publ.:** "Palestinian Documents" (1965), "Reflection on Israeli Propaganda Policy" (1968), "Duties of Third Parties in Contemporary Wards" (1971), "Role of Intellectuals in the Promotion of Human Rights" in Al-Mustaqbal Al-Arabi Magazine, Beirut (1983). **Hobbies:** Reading and swimming. **Addr.:** Geneva, Switzerland.

ANGAWI (Fouad, Abdulhameed), Saudi businessman. **Born** in 1936 in Mekka, Saudi Arabia. **Son** of Abdulhameed Angawi. **Educ.:** Cairo University and London University. **Dipl.:** B.A. Arabic literature; Public Relations Diploma. **Career:** Assistant Director General of Press Affairs; Director General of Publication, Ministry of Information; Director General of Housing, Director General of Public Relations, King Abdulaziz University, Jeddah. **Attended** conferences of Arab Ministers of Information in Cairo, Beirut, Tunis, Rabat. Six Jumbori-Greece (1963); Janifo Jakarta. **Act.:** Ex-member of: Alwihda Sport Club; al-Nasr Sport Club; ex Vice President of al-Ahli Sport Club; Mutawwif-Mekka (guide to pligrims during performance of Hajj); ex-Chairman of First Hajj Corp., ex-Chairman, Iranian Hajj Organization; Consultant to the Minister of Hajj; Director of Hajj and Umrah Training Centre. **Publ.:** "La Dhilla Taht Algabal" (No Shadow at the Mountain Foot), a historical novel about Mekka; short stories "Scattered Days"; "Sand and Blood" a historical novel about Ottoman Empire; "The Pelotte" Makkah, Hajj and Tawafa: Two volumes (historical and documentary). **Hobbies:** Reading, writing, sport, travel, classical music. **Addr.:** P.O.Box. 2723, Saudi Arabia, Tel.: 6715160, 6723560, mobile: Tel.: 055668861, Jeddah, 21461.

ANI (Abdullah Najim, al), Iraqi academic. **Born** on October 14, 1939 in Iraq. **Married,** 4 children: 2 daughters and 2 sons. **Educ.:** University of Baghdad, Iraq; University of California, USA, University of Nebraska, USA. **Dipl.:** B.Sc., M.Sc., Ph.D. in Soil Science and Soil Physics. **Career:** Lecturer, University of Baghdad (1970), Assistant Professor, University of Baghdad (1976-77); Professor, University of Baghdad (1988); Chairman of Soil Science Department, University of Baghdad (1974-87). **Publ.:** Numerous papers in English and Arabic in professional journals; Editor of "Water Requirements of Crops and Trees in different Ecological Region in the Arab World"; Author of Elements of Soil Sciences"; translated "Fundamentals of Soil Science", into Arabic. **Hobbies:** Swimming, painting, poetry, gardening. **Prof. Addr.:** Department of Soil Science, College of Agriculture, University of Baghdad, Abu Gharib, Iraq. **Priv. Addr.:** Hay Al-Adl, 645/36/15, Baghdad, Iraq.

ANI (Badri, Ahmad, al), Iraqi academic. **Born** in 1933 in Iraq. **Married**, 3 children. **Educ.:** Teachers College, Baghdad, Iraq; University of Pennsylvania. **Dipl.:** M.A., M.Sc., Ph.D. **Career:** Teacher (1957); Research Assistant, University of Pennsylvania (1961-62); Lecturer, University of Baghdad (1962); Deputy Head of Botany Department, Faculty of Sciences, University of Baghdad (1965); Deputy Dean for Students Affairs, Faculty of Sciences (1965); Assistant Professor, University of Baghdad (1967); Deputy Head, Biology Department (1974), Head of Biology Department (1975-76); Associate Professor (1976), Professor (1977); participated in many international conferences; Member, American Botanic Sciences Association, Iraqi Biology Society as well as Member of several other committees and associations; Head of Biology Department, Faculty of Sciences, University of the United Arab Emirates (1978-90). **Publ.:** published numerous articles in professional journals, several books. **Hobbies:** Jogging, swimming, travelling and writing. **Addr.:** Abu Dhabi, United Arab Emirates.

ANI (Tahir, Tawfiq, al), Iraqi politician. **Career:** Secretary, Revolutionary Command Council (1968), Secretary General (1969); Under Secretary, Ministry of Works and Housing (1973); Member of Arab Baath Socialist Party Regional Leadership (1974), Member of the follow-up Committee (1974); Minister of State, Member of Regional Leadership (1974); President, Higher Agricultural Council (1975), President, High Committee for Public Services (1976); Minister of Industry and Minerals (1979-83). **Addr.:** Baghdad, Iraq.

ANIS (Ibrahim), Egyptian philologist and member of the Academy of the Arabic Language. **Born** in 1960 in Cairo. **Educ.:** London University. **Dipl.:** Bachelor of Arts (Honours), London University (1939), Doctor of Philosophy (1941). **Career:** Lecturer, at Jordan University in Amman, actually member of the Academy of the Arabic Language. **Publ.:** Author of "The music of Poetry", "Secrets of Language", "The future of the Arabic Language", and a large number of research works and specialised liguistic studies. **Prof. Addr.:** 26, Murad Street, Giza, Cairo, Egypt. **Priv. Addr.:** 22, Dokki Street, Giza, Tel.: 800713, Egypt.

ANNAB (Ziad Radhi), Jordanian politician. **Born** in 1927 at Kerak, Jordan. **Married**. **Educ.:** Collège des Frères, Ramallah; American University of Beirut, Lebanon; Toledo University, USA. **Dipl.:** B.A. (1950); Certificate for Economics Planning Studies (1953); study mission to IMF on Problems of Monetary Policies. **Career:** Attached to Ministry of National Economy (1951); Assistant Under-Secretary, Ministry of Economy (1965); General Manager, Industrial Development Bank (1966); member, Board of Tourist Authority; member, committee for encouragement of investment; Member, Board of Jordanian Phosphates Company; Chairman, Jordan Cement Factories Co. Ltd.; Marriott Amman Hotel; Minister of Industry and Trade (April 27, 1989- end 1990). **Awards:** Star of Jordan (3rd Class). **Member:** Royal Jordanian Automobile Club. **Addr.:** Zahran Str., Jebel Amman, P.O.Box 1982, Tel.: 42216119, Amman, Jordan, and P.O.Box 610, Amman, Jordan.

ANQAI (Abdallah Aqil), Saudi Academic. **Born** in 1939 in Mecca, Saudi Arabia. **Dipl.:** Ph.D. Cambridge University. **Career:** Assistant Professor, Associate, then Professor of Medieval Islamic History, Faculty of Arts, King Abdul Aziz University, Jeddah. **Publ.:** «The Mahmil»; «The Arab Civilization»; «Makkah during the reign of Qatadah»; «The Caliphate»; «The Kiswah of the Kabah in Mamluk Times»; «The Historian Taqi al-Din al-Fasi». **Addr.:** Faculty of Arts, King Abdul Aziz University, P.O.Box 40939, Jeddah 21511, Saudi Arabia.

ANQARI (Faisal Mohamad, al), Saudi businessman. **Born** in 1952 in Jeddah, Saudi Arabia. **Dipl.:** B.A. (International Law and Political Science). **Career:** Director, Financial Department, Saja Trading Co. (1975-77); President, Saja Trading Co. since 1977; Expert in import-export regulations and procedures; Chairman of Wid for Projects Ltd., Yanbu; Seven Pharmacy (a chain of pharmacies); al-Nabaa' Co.; owner of al-Jude Pharmacy; Vice Chairman, Board of Directors, United Maintenance and Operations Company, Riyadh; and member of several welfare and sports clubs. **Hobbies:** Flying, hunting, swimming. **Addr.:** Saja Trading Co., P.O.Box 2289, Tel.: 665-1211, 669-2989 (Office) and 651-5870, 651-4531 (Home), Jeddah, Saudi Arabia.

ANQARY (Ibrahim, Abdallah, al), Saudi former Minister and Diplomat. **Born** in 1938 in Saudi Arabia. **Educ.:** Secondary school education and university. **Dipl.:** B.A. **Career:** Director of the Bureau to the Minister of Education; joined the Ministry of Foreign Affairs and served as an official at the Saudi Embassy in Washington; Director General, Ministry of the Interior; later Deputy Minister of Interior; served as Minister of Information; represented the Kingdom at several regional and international conferences; Minister of Labour and Social Affairs; Minister of Municipal and Rural Affairs (1983-1992). **Addr.:** Riyadh, Saudi Arabia.

ANQARY (Khalid Ibn Mohamad al-, Dr.), Saudi Politician. **Born** in 1952. **Educ.:** Ph.D. Geography, University of Florida, USA (1981). **Career:** Assistant professor, King Saud University (1981-83); Deputy Minister, Municipal, and Rural Affairs (1983-84); Minister, Municipal and Rural Affairs (1990); Minister of Higher Education

(1991-to date). **Address:** Ministry of Higher Education, King Faisal Hospital Street, Main Ministry, Riyadh 11153, Saudi Arabia.

ANSARI (Ali, Ahmad, al), Qatari statesman. **Born** in 1916 in Qatar. **Son** of Ahmad Mohamad al-Ansari (merchant) **and** Mrs. Maryam al Ansari. **Married** with 12 children. **Educ.:** General Secondary Education Certificate, Bahrain; enrolment at College of Law in Cairo University; enrolment at Berlitz Institute for Foreign Languages in Cairo (1953-55). **Career:** Various administrative posts in Saudi Arabia (1930-46); Director of Customs in the Oil Area in Qatar (1946-53); General Director of Immigration, Passports and Nationality in Qatar (1955-70); Minister of Labour and Social Affairs in the State of Qatar (1970-1992). **Act.:** Head of Arab Ministerial Follow-up Committee for resolutions and activities of UNFPA (May 1975); member of Executive Board for UICW in Geneva (1977). **Medals:** UAR Republic Medal (1975); U.N. World Peace Emblem (1976); Medal of Lebanese Islamic Welfare Associations (1976); Medal of Sultanate of Oman (1977); Medal of Islamic Republic of Pakistan (1978); Medal of Republic of Venezuela (1979); Medal of Republic of Italy (1979); Medal of "PIO Manzu" International Center on the Habitant in Italy (1983); Medal of Republic of Korea (1983). **Member:** Six Continents Club, Clipper Club (life membership). **Credit Cards:** American Express, Diners, Visa. **Priv. Addr.:** P.O.Box 48, Tel.: 423683, 422645, Doha, Qatar.

ANSARI (Faisal, al), Iraqi army officer. **Born** in 1933 in Iraq. **Educ.:** Military Academy, Cairo. **Career:** Joined the Iraqi Army; Promoted General, Commander of the 2nd division, Commander in Chief of the Army (February 1968- December 1968); Former member of the Supreme Council of Defence. **Addr.:** Baghdad, Iraq.

ANSARI (Jasem Mohamad Ali, al), Saudi academic. **Born** in 1948 in Dammam, Saudi Arabia. **Dipl.:** B.Sc., and Ph.D. (Mechanical Engineering). **Career:** Demonstrator, Mechanical Engineering Department (1972-73); Assistant Professor, Mechanical Engineering, University of Petroleum and Minerals; member of ASME, ASHRAE: member of the Technical Committee on Thermal Energy Storage of ASHRAE; has attended several conferences on Thermal Energy Storage. **Sports:** tennis. **Addr.:** Mechanical Engineering Department, UPM, Tel.: 8602548, (Office) and 8606619 (Home), Dhahran, Saudi Arabia.

ANSARI (Nasser, Abdallah, al), Saudi senior civil servant. **Born** in 1935 in Mecca, Saudi Arabia. **Educ.:** Secondary and Higher. **Dipl.:** B.A., M.A. (Community Development and Educational Planning), 1974. **Career:** served for 20 years in the field of education; Secretary General of Prince Fawaz Project; member of Islamic Centre, (USA); attended the International Conference on the Elimination of Illiteracy, Teheran (Iran) (1965); initiated the first literacy project in Aljoaf area, Cooperative Housing and Development Society project; Model village project, Prince Fahad project for Social Solidarity; authorised member of the Board, Prince Fawaz Project for Co-operative Housing. **Publ.:** Author of a number of textbooks. **Hobbies:** Reading and travel. **Prof. Addr.:** P.O.Box 6015, Prince Fawaz Project for Cooperative Housing, Kilo 3, Mecca Road, Tel.: 27396, Jeddah, Saudi Arabia.

ANSARI (Salem, Hassan, al), Qatari businessman. **Born** in Qatar. **Son** of Hassan al-Ansari. **Educ.:** Secondary and Higher. **Career:** Chairman, Salem Hassan al-Ansari & Sons; Salem Furniture, Dar al-Thakafa Printing, al-Thakafa Library. **Addr.:** P.O.Box 4355, Doha, Qatar.

ANSI (Abd al-Karim), Yemeni Qadi (religious judge) and statesman. **Born** in 1920, in Tarca. **Career:** State Minister for South Yemen Affairs (1963); Minister of Information (Feb.- April 1964); Minister of Wakfs (religious endowments) (4 May 1964- 27 Dec. 1964); resigns his post in protest against President Sallal's policy; Minister of Education (April- July 1965); arrested in Cairo by the Egyptian authorities on 19 September 1966; released, 8 Aug. 1967 and returned home; Minister of State for Presidential Affairs (April 1969- July 1969); Counsellor to the Republican Council; following the coup d'état of 13 June 1964 he is one of two Qadis to retain their government post; Governor of Taez (1971); Minister for Presidential Affairs (January- August 1971); Adviser on Legal Affairs to the President (1973); Minister of State (June 1974- January 1975). **Member:** Zaydit tribe. **Addr.:** Sanaa, Republic of Yemen.

ANSI (Saudi Salim Hassan, al), Omani former diplomat. **Born** in 1949 in Salalah, Sultanate of Oman. **Married,** 2 daughters. **Educ.:** University of Beirut. **Dipl.:** B.A. in Sociology (1972). **Career:** Director of Social Services Department (1974); Head of Press Department at the Ministry of Information (1975); Director of Electricity Board (1975); Director in the Sultan's Diwan (1975); First Secretary, Embassy of Oman in Tunis (1976), Consul General, Sultanate of Oman in Karachi (1977); Head, Research and Studies Department, Ministry of Foreign Affairs, Oman (1978); Ambassador Plenipotentiary and Extraordinary, Sultanate of Oman in Djibouti (1980-81); Ambassador of Sultanate of Oman, Kuwait (1982-84); Permanent Representative of Sultanate of Oman to United Nations (1984-85). **Publ.:** various articles in several magazines; "Development in Oman" (1973) in Arabic. **Hobbies:** Reading, writing, music, tennis and swimming. **Member:** History Society of Oman. **Addr.:** Muscat, Oman.

ANTAKI (H.E. Mgr. Paul), Egyptian Archbishop. **Born** in 1927 in Cairo. **Educ.:** College des Frères (Cairo), Collège des Pères Jésuites (Cairo), Greek Catholic Seminary of Sainte Anne, Jerusalem (1945-49). **Career:** Ordained to the Priesthood (1950); Vicar in Alexandria (1951-54);

Principal of the Patriarchal College of Cairo (1954-57); Patriarchal Vicar in Alexandria (1957-67); Superior of Rayak Institute (1967-68); Sacred Archbishop and Patriarchal General Vicar in Egypt and the Sudan since December 1st, 1968. **Resid.:** Greek Catholic Patriarchate, 16 Daher St., Tel.: 905790, Faggalah, Cairo, Egypt.

ANWAR (Mohamad Samih), Egyptian diplomat. **Born** on December 10, 1924 in Cairo, Egypt. **Son** of Ahmed Fouad Anwar. **Married** in 1953 to Miss Omayama Soliman Hazza, 2 children: Tarek and Laila. **Educ.:** Cairo University, Cairo. **Dipl.:** Bachelor of Law (1945). **Career:** Joined Ministry of Justice (1946-54); First Secretary, Ministry of Foreign Affairs (1946-54); First Secretary, Ministry of Foreign Affairs (1954); appointed to Egyptian Embassy of USSR (1957), and UK (1963); Ambassador to Kuwait (1966); Under-Secretary, Ministry of Foreign Affairs (1968); Ambassador to Iran (1970); Minister of State for Foreign Affairs (1974); Ambassador at the Ministry of Foreign Affairs (1975); Ambassador to UK (1975). **Awards:** Egyptian Order of the Republic, 2nd Class; Egyptian Order of Merit, 1st Class; Order of Hamayoun, 1st Class, Iran; Order of the Flag, Yugoslavia. **Sports:** Rowing, Tennis. **Addr.:** c/o Ministry of Foreign Affairs, Cairo, Egypt.

AOUFI (Mahfud), Algerian banker. **Born** in 1930 in Algeria. **Educ.:** University of Grenoble, France and Lausanne, Switzerland. **Dipl.:** in Law and Economics. **Career:** General Treasurer of Algeria (1965); Assistant Director of the Treasury and Credit (1967); Secretary General in the Ministry of Finance, until Oct. 1977; Chairman and Managing Director, Algerian Development Bank; Governor, Central Bank of Algeria (1981-82), Director General (1982). **Addr.:** Algiers, Algeria.

AOUIDJ (Farid), Tunisian official. **Born** in 1934 in Tunis. **Married** 3 children. **Educ.:** Sadiki College, Tunis; Paris, France (political and economic studies). **Career:** Deputy Director, Ecole Nationale d'Administration in Tunis; Director of Ports; Head of Cabinet in the Ministry of Post, Telephones and Telegraphs; Head of Cabinet and Director of the Central Administration, Ministry of Planning; Secretary General, Tunis Municipality. **Prof. Addr.:** Tunis Municipality, Tunis, Tunisia.

AQEEL (Youssef Ibrahim Alsolaima, al), Saudi businessman. **Born** in 1941 in Taif, Saudi Arabia. **Dipl.:** B.Sc. (Business Administration). **Career:** Chief of Projects Division, Saline Water Conversion Corporation; Director General, Technical and Projects Affairs; Saline Water Conversion; former Deputy Governor, Saline Water Conversion Co.: Chairman, Al-Bayda Development Est.; President, Saudi Marketing and General Contracting Corporation; member of constituent committee for the Eastern Region Electric Co., International Desalination Council; member of Board of IDEA (International Desalination and Environmental Association); attended Desalination Conference, Cairo, International Desalination Organization Conference, Florida, U.S.A. **Hobby:** Fishing. **Addr.:** P.O.Box 7356, Tel.: 6713008 (Office) and 6511755 (Home), Jeddah, Saudi Arabia.

AQRAWI (Hashim, Hassan), Iraqi politician. **Born** in 1926 in Iraq. **Career:** Teacher; member of the Kurdish Democratic Party KDP (1951); member of the KDP Central Committee (1959); member of the KDP Executive Committee (1970); Governor of the Dohuk (1970) Minister of Municipalities and Rural Affairs (1974); member of the Kurdistan Legislative Assembly (1974); first Chairman of the Kurdish Executive Council (1974); Secretary, Kurdistan Democratic Party (1976); Minister of State (1977-1991). **Member** of the High Committee of the National Progressive Front. **Addr.:** Baghdad, Iraq.

AQUILINA (Nelly, Joseph), Egyptian free-lance journalist. **Born** on February 14, 1927 in Cairo. **Daughter of** Joseph Aquilina (Former chartered accountant) **and** Mrs., Adèle Kemeid. **Married** in 1970. **Educ.:** Mère de Dieu Convent School, Cairo, La Sorbonne, France (1946-48) and specialisation in Journalism. **Dipl.:** Secondary Education Certificate (1945), Degree in Journalism. **Career:** Between 1946 and 1956 made a very successful career in International journalism as Managing-Proprietor of "Orient Presse" news agency, Cairo; Cairo Correspondent of "Agence Parisienne de Presse" (Paris) and a number of other world press organisations including "France-Illustration", once an authoritative and widely-circulated French periodical, "copyright" trustee in Egypt for several French press media; Contributed no less than 200 articles, special reports and features to different French, Canadian, and British papers and magazines, some of which were commissioned by the Ministry of Foreign Affairs in Cairo and initially published in the Cultural and Information Bulletin of the said Ministry. **Hobby:** Special Interest in interior decoration. **Priv. Addr.:** 44, Talaat Harb Pasha Street, Tel.: 53886 and 47712, Cairo, Egypt.

ARAB (Hussein Ali), Saudi leading man of letters. **Born** in 1920 in Mecca, Saudi Arabia. **Dipl.:** Diploma of Higher Religious Institute, Mecca. **Career:** Sub-editor, Sawtul Hijaz newspaper; sub-editor Umm al-Qura official newspaper; official member, Viceroy's Court; Secretary-General, Ministry of the Interior; Deputy Minister of the Interior; ex-Minister of Pilgrimage and Endowments; contributed to various social, literary and political activities; member of the Board, Makkah Printing and Information Establishment; member of Makkah Cultural Club; member of First Conference of Saudi Men of Letters, King Abdulaziz University; Shareholder in some cement and electrical companies. **Publ.:** several articles on politics, sociology and literature. **Hobbies:** reading poetry, studying Koranic interpretations. **Addr.:** Zahra, Tel.: 5424024 (Office) and 5446670 (Home), Mecca, Saudi Arabia.

ARABI (Abdulmu'ti, al), Egyptian military. **Born** on October 3, 1925. **Married,** 2 children. **Educ.:** Military Academy. **Career:** Egyptian Officer, Promoted General, Commander-in-Chief of the Naval Forces (July 1967-September 1969); Secretary General, Ministry of Naval Transports then Minister of the said Ministry (March 1973). **Addr.:** Cairo, Egypt.

ARABI (Isam), Syrian executive. **Born** in 1934 in Damascus. **Married** in 1974, 2 sons. **Dipl.:** LL.B. **Career:** Administrative and Legal Affairs, Real Estate Bank, Damascus, Syria. **Hobbies:** Reading, Travel and Sports. **Addr.:** P.O.Box 2337, Tel.: 118602-3, Telex: 19171 A/B REBANK, Damascus, Syria.

ARABI (Mahmoud, Adil), Egyptian businessman. **Born** on February 5, 1936. **Married. Dipl.:** B.A. in Commerce and diploma in Higher Marketing Studies. **Career:** Director, Egyptian Cotton Office in Geneva, Switzerland; Deputy General Manager of United Arab Emirates Trading Company, Abu Dhabi, U.A.E. **Hobbies:** Reading, tennis. **Prof. Addr.:** P.O.Box 4171, Tel.: 44819, Abu Dhabi, U.A.E.

ARABI (Nizar Ahmad, al), Saudi executive. **Born** in 1941 in Mecca, Saudi Arabia. **Dipl.:** M.A. (Clay Mineralogy), Wichita State University, Kansas USA; Ph.D. (Geophysics), al-Azhar University, Cairo, Egypt, 1966. **Career:** Assistant Lecturer, King Abdulaziz University, Jeddah (1966); Geophysicist at Iraq National Oil Co.; head of team of seismologists, Iraq National Oil Co.; supervisor of implementation of contracts for seismological survey carried out by foreign companies working in Iraq and contracted by the Iraq National Oil Co.; member of the Iraqi Geological Society (1971-75); attended several conferences on geology and geophisics in U.S.A. (1966-71); Executive Vice President, Tihama Branches Affairs; Chairman, Tihama DAW Co. West Germany. **Publ.:** studies on clay minerals. **Addr.:** P.O.Box. 4681, Tel.: 4771000, Riyadh, Saudi Arabia.

ARADI (Mohamad Darwish), Kuwaiti administrator. **Born** in 1930. **Married. Educ.:** Primary and Intermediate in Kuwait; secondary in Baghdad and Higher in Cairo, Egypt. **Dipl.:** B.A. in Commerce and Economics, Cairo University, Cairo (1958). **Career:** Director of Labour Bureau in Security Department in Ahmadi (1958-59); Director, Investigation Department (1960-62); Secretary to HH the Amir; Grand Chamberlain to HH The Amir (1962-65); Director, Kuwait National Industries Company and Kuwait Automotive and Trading Company. **Addr.:** Safat, Kuwait.

ARAFA (Abdulghani, Kamel), Syrian physician. **Born** in 1922 in Damascus. **Son** of Kamel Arafa. **Educ.:** Faculty of Medicine, Syrian University and University of Paris. **Dipl.:** Doctor in Medicine, specialisation in Chest diseases. **Career:** Civil servant attached to the Ministry of Health, Chief Physician of Ibn an-Nafiss Sanatorium. **Member** of the Antituberculosis Medical Association **Publ.:** Author of "Le diagnostic tuberculeux". **Addr.:** Damascus, Syria.

ARAFA (Mohamad Abdallah), Saudi academic. **Born** in 1935 at Al-Ola, Saudi Arabia. **Dipl.:** B.A. Shari'a (Islamic Law); M.A. Shari'a. **Career:** Director of Religious Institute, al-Majma'ah (1960-63); Director, Religious Institute Jeddah (1964-68); Vice Dean, Faculty of Arabic Language and Social Sciences, (1979-74) and later Dean (1975), Imam Muhammad Ibn Saud Islamic University; attended several conferences within the Kingdom and abroad; praticipated in television and radio programmes. **Honour:** a Sash awarded by Imam Muhammad Ibn, Saud Islamic University in recognition of efforts devoted to the First Islamic Geographic Conference. **Publ.:** book, Women's Rights in Islam; articles in specialised magazines. **Hobbies:** reading, travel. **Addr.:** P.O.Box. 3169, Tel.: 477-3749 (Office), and 403-5674 (Home), Riyadh, Saudi Arabia.

ARAFAT (Walid, Najib), Jordanian academic. **Born** in 1921 in Nablus, Palestine. **Son** of Najib Arafat. **Married,** two sons. **Educ.:** B.A. in English, Latin, Arabic (1947) in London; Ph.D. in Arabic (1952). **Career:** Lecturer in Arabic, School of Oriental and African Studies, University of London (1951-61); Reader in Arabic, University of London (1961-72); Professor and Director of the Institute of Arabic and Islamic Studies, University of Lancaster (founded by Professor Arafat with financial support from the University of Kuwait). **Publ.:** Many articles and papers in English and Arabic on Islamic science, culture, Arabic literature and criticism, comparative literature etc. in many journals and magazines; "Diwan of Hassan Ibn Thabit" 2 volumes in Arabic (1971). **Work:** Many talks in the BBC Arabic Service. Fellow of RAS, **member** of Council of BRSMES of the Council and Executive Committee of SRTH of Great Britain and Northern Ireland; of the Board of Religion and Theology, CNAA. **Hobbies:** Gardening, reading, writing, literature in general, development of Islam. **Sport:** Walking. **Addr.:** Institute of Arabic and Islamic Studies, Landsdale College, University of Lancaster, Lancaster LAl 47N, UK.

ARAFAT (Yasser), ("Abu Ammar"), Palestinian leader. **Born** in 1929 in Jerusalem. **Son** of Abdurraouf Arafat. **Married** in January 1992 to Suha Tawil, one daughter: Zahwa. **Educ.:** Cairo University. **Dipl.:** Of Engineer: **Career:** President of the League of Palestinian Students (1952-56), Formed "al-Fath" movement (1956), Engineer in Egypt (1956) and Kuwait (1957); Founded "Al-Fath" organization; Chairman of al-Fath Central Committee and of the P.L.O. Executive Committee (1969); Commander-in-Chief, Palestinian High Command (1971); addressed UN General Assembly in November 1974; evicted from Beirut with 10,000 of his militia men following seven weeks of Israeli land, air and sea bombardment in September 1982; set up new head-quarters in Tunis, Tunisia, and his militia men were offered sanctuary in seven Arab countries; Chairman of the Executive Committee of the P.L.O. (since 1968); Leader of the Fath movement and Commander of its Forces (since 1968). Elected Chairman of the Palestinian Self Rule West Bank and Gaza. **Addr.:** Chairman's office, West Bank and Gaza.

ARAIM (Mahmoud, Ahmad), Jordanian businessman. **Born** in 1922. **Married**, 2 sons, 1 daughter. **Educ.:** Iraqi Military College and Iraqi Staff College. **Career:** former Army Officer; Director General, Jordanian Establishment for Trading and Engineering Equipments. **Decor.:** several Iraqi and Jordanian decorations. **Hobbies:** walking, hunting, swimming, music, history, poetry, literature and military strategic studies. **Prof. Addr.:** P.O.Box 6136, Amman, Jordan.

ARAJI (Ali, Mouhieddine, al), Iraqi civil engineer. **Born** on August 9, 1926. **Educ.:** Iraqi primary and secondary school and Durham University (England). **Career:** Civil engineer (1951-53); Government Oil Refineries Administration (GORA) (1953-54); Iraq Petroleum Company at Kirkuk and Pipeline stations (1954-57); Plant engineer and chief construction coordinator at Dora Refinery, Goverment Oil Refineries Administration (1957-59); Civil and offsite engineer Kellogg International Corporation, London (1959-62); Director of Projects (1962-64); Director General, Oil Planning and Construction Administration, Ministry of Oil (1964). **Addr.:** Baghdad, Iraq.

ARASHI (Qadi, Abdul Karim, al), Yemeni politician. **Career:** former Minister for Local Government and the Treasury; Speaker of the Constituent People's Assembly (since 1978) and since July 1988 Speaker of the Consultative Council; Chairman Provisional Presidential Council (June- July 1978); Vice President Yemen Arab Republic (July 1978- May 1990); member of the Presidential Council of the Republic of Yemen (May 1990- Sept. 1994). **Addr.:** Sana'a, Republic of Yemen.

ARASHI (Yahya, Hussain Ahmad, al), Yemeni former minister. **Born** in 1947. **Married**, 2 children. **Educ.:** Studies in social development and labour education. **Career:** Teacher (1961-62); National Guard (1962-63); Director, Hodeida Province Office (1964-65); Director, Al-Alfi Hospital Hodeida (1966); Organization Director General, Hodeida Province (1967); Director General, Social Affairs and Labour Organization (1968-69); Director of Taxation Department (1970-73); Director, Yemeni Bank for Construction and Development (1973-74); Head, the Central Organization for Auditing and Accountancy (1974-75); Minister of Culture and Information (1976); Minister of the State for Unity Affairs (1986- May 1990); Minister of Culture and Tourism (1993-1999). **Publ.:** "A Study of Social Development in Yemen". **Decor.:** Order of the Republic, Egypt. **Hobbies:** Volley-ball, chess, Yemeni social, cultural and political history. **Addr.:** Sanaa, Republic of Yemen.

ARDHAOUI (Amor), Tunisian diplomat. **Born** on February 24, 1933 at Djerba (Tunisia). **Married**, with 2 children. **Educ.:** University of Toulouse, France. **Degrees:** Political Sciences; International Studies. **Career:** appointed to Tunisian embassies to Ethiopia, Morocco, Sweden, U.S.A., Canada; Director of African Department, Tunis (1971-72); Attaché to Presidential Cabinet, Carthage, Tunisia (1972-73); Deputy Permanent Representative to U.N. New York (1973-74); Deputy Director of Intern. Cooper. Tunis (1979-80); Ambassador to Nigeria (1980-81); Ambassador to Togo (1981-84). **Priv. Addr.:** 3, Rue Houcine Bouzaiane, Megrine- Coteaux, Tunisia.

ARFAJ (Abdul Latif, Mohamad, al), Saudi Arabian businessman. **Born** on 1 September 1954 at al-Hassa, Saudi Arabia. **Son** of Mohammed al-Arfaj (Businessman). **Married** on 10 June 1978 at al-Hassa, 2 children: Noora (1978) and Sultan (1980). **Educ.:** Hofuf Secondary School, Hofuf- Saudi Arabia; Riyadh University, Riyadh- Saudi Arabia. **Dipl.:** B.Com. (Riyadh University, 1977), Diploma in Business Administration (Arab University, Beirut). **Career:** Director, A.M. Arfaj Trading Corporation, Moj Decoration General Service Co., With branches all over Saudi Arabia and dealing in import and trading. **Medals:** Gold Medal, Riyadh University, Riyadh; Silver Medal, Sunset Boat Club, al-Khober. **Sports:** Fishing and boating. **Hobby:** Tourism. **Member:** Aleigir Boat Club, al-Hassa (Saudi Arabia). **Prof. Addr.:** P.O.Box 2531, Alkhobar 31952, Saudi Arabia. **Priv. Addr.:** Hofuf, Tel.: 032-26610 and 032-21625, Saudi Arabia.

ARFAWI (Farid), Moroccan bank director. **Born** in 1941 in Tangier, Morocco. **Son** of Driss Arfawi. **Married** in 1970, 2 children. **Educ.:** Université de Paris. **Dipl.:** Licence Political Sciences; Diplôme d'Etudes Supérieures de Doctorat (Sciences Economiques). **Career:** Joined Banque Marocaine du Commerce Extérieur (BMCE) (1967); appointed Head of Economic Studies and Marketing Department; director, International Division; BMCE (1971); helped establish BMCE's branch in Paris (1972). **Member:** Golf Club d'Anfa and Golf Club of Mohammedia; A.N.M.A. **Addr.:** 26, Hay Erraha, Anfa Superieur, Casablanca, Morocco.

ARIAN (Abdallah, al), Egyptian diplomat. **Born** in 1920 in Egypt. **Educ.:** Cairo University, Egypt; Harvard University, Boston, Mass. USA; Columbia University, New York, USA. **Dipl.:** LL.B. and Ph.D. **Career:** Assistant District Attorney, Buhairah Governorate (1942-43); Lecturer in Law, Cairo University (1943-45); Assistant Professor of International Law and International Organisations, Institute of Public Administration, Cairo

(1959-61); Professor of International Law, Division of Legal Studies, Institute of Arab Higher Studies, Cairo (since 1959); Counsellor, Office of the President (1955-56); Counsellor and Legal Advisor, Permanent Mission to UN (1957-59); Director, Department of Legal Affairs and Treaties, Ministry of Common Affairs and Treaties, Ministry of Common Affairs (1959-68); Ambassador and Deputy Permanent Representative to UN (1968-71); Ambassador to France (1971-74); Permanent Representative to UN Office, Geneva, Switzerland (1974). **Member:** of International Law Committee, (1957-58, 1961-65, 66); Delegate to various UN and Organization of African Unity (OAU) conferences and several sessions in UN General Assembly. **Publ.:** Several books and articles on international law and the United Nations. **Addr.:** Ministry of Foreign Affairs, Cairo, Egypt.

ARIF (Awni al Din), Iraqi physician. **Born** in 1925 in Baghdad, Iraq. **Married. Educ.:** Faculty of Medicine, Baghdad University, Baghdad, Iraq; School of Public Health Administration, Columbia University, New York, USA; Oklahoma Medical School, USA; National Communicable Diseases Center, Atlanta, USA. **Dipl.:** M.B., Ch.B. (1944-50); MPH (1958-59); Certificate in Preventive Medicine (1959); Certificate in Communicable Diseases and Statistics (1959); Board of Public Health and Preventive Medicine Degree (1967). **Career:** Military service (1950-51); Medical clinician and teacher, Faculty of Medicine, Baghdad University (1951-58); Fellow, School of Public Health, Columbia University, New York (1958-60); Medical Officer, WHO, Geneva (1960-66); Director General, Preventive Medicine Service, Ministry of Health, Iraq (1966-69); Representative of Libya, Regional Office for East Mediterranean, WHO, Libya (1969); Fellow of American Public Health Association. **Member:** of Supreme Scientific Research Board, Iraq; Medical Research Board, Baghdad University; Iraqi Medical Association; Red Crescent Society, Baghdad; Iraqi Children's Protection Society. **Publ.:** Many Books on Preventive medicine and Diseases. **Club.:** Mansour Club, Baghdad. **Sports:** Tennis, golf, swimming. **Hobbies:** Bridge, fishing, health administration, health planning, epidemiology. **Addr.:** Baghdad, Iraq.

ARINAN (Hamad, Mohamad), Saudi academic. **Born** in 1944 in Mecca (Saudi Arabia). **Married**, with children. **Educ.:** Faculty of Arts, King Abdul Aziz University; St. Andrews University (U.K.). **Dipl.:** B.A., M.A., Ph.D. (Islamic History). **Career:** Lecturer, King Abdul Aziz University (1967); Lecturer, Faculty of Arts, King Abdul Aziz University; Vice-Dean of Faculty of Arts, King Abdulaziz University (1973-75); Member of Translation Seminar, Kuwait (1973); now Assistant Professor of History, Faculty of Arts, King Abdul Aziz University, Jeddah (Saudi Arabia). **Publ.:** Author of "Bedouin Settlement in the Kingdom of Saudi Arabia". **Priv. Addr.:** Jeddah, Saudi Arabia.

ARMANAZI (Ghayth, Najib), Syrian diplomat. **Born** in 1943 in Damascus, Syria. **Son** of Najib Armanazi. **Married,** three children. **Educ.:** University of Colorado, USA; University of London, UK. **Dipl.:** B.A. in Economics; M.A. in Area Studies. **Career:** Information Assistant, League of Arab States, London (1967-70); Editor, Institute for Palestine Studies, Beirut, Lebanon (1971-74); Information Counsellor, Embassy of the United Arab Emirates, London (1974-1986) General Manager, Arab Bankers Association (1986-1991); Editor in Chief of Quarterly Review "Arab Affairs", London (1986-1991); Presently, Head of the London Mission of the League of Arab States. Occasional Contributor to several Arab and British publications including. The Guardian, The Daily Telegraph, The Independent, The World Today, Al Hayat. Broadcaster and Commentator on Arab and Middle Eastern affairs. **Sports:** Tennis, squash, swimming. **Hobbies:** Theatre, Music, Archaeology and the Arts. **Member** of London Diplomatic Association; of the Association of Economic Representatives, London. **Prof. Addr.:** 52 Green Street, London W1Y 3RH. **Priv. Addr.:** 22 Campden Hill Court, London W8, 7HS.

ARMOUTI (Ismail, Naza, al), Jordanian economist. **Born** in 1931 in Amman, Jordan. **Son** of Nazal Armouti. **Educ.:** Baghdad University, Iraq; London University, UK. **Dipl.:** B.Sc. Political Science; Managerial Economics Diploma (1965). **Career:** Chief of Trade Department, Ministry of Economy (1969); Director of Companies and Commercial Registration (1969-76); Minister of Interior for Municipal and Village Affairs (1976). **Publ.:** "Arab Common Market" (1969); "Theory of Arab Economic Integration" (1975). **Addr.:** Amman, Jordan.

ARMOUTI (Mohamad, Nazzal, al), Jordanian businessman and former diplomat. **Born** on July 16, 1924 in Amman. **Son** of Nazzal Ahmad al-Armouti **and** Mrs. Hamdeh Hamdan Abou-Shuwaina. **Married** to Souad Omar Ma'ani in 1949, 9 children: Mazin, Sultan, Intissar, Maysoun, Nazzal, Omar, Zein, Alia and Sabah. **Educ.:** Second Secondary School of Amman, Second Secondary School of Salt, Syrian University (Damascus), Exeter University (U.K.). **Dipl.:** Bachelor in Laws (1946), Diploma in Public Administration (1959). **Career:** Chief Clrek, Chief Justice Dept. (1947); Secretary General, Ministry of Interior (1948); Secretary General Parliaments, Both Houses of Senates and Representatives (1950); Inspector General, Income Taxes Dept. (1952); legal Adviser, Minister of Finance (1954); Governor of the following Governorates respectively; Irbid, Ma'an, Hebron, Karak, Nablus and Salt (1955-61); Under Secretary, Ministry of Interior (1961); Jordanian Ambassador to Libya, Tunisia and Algeria (1965); to Kuwait (1967-71); Head of Political Department, Ministry of Foreign Affairs (1971); retired (1971); Chairman, Jordan Gulf Bank, Jordan (1989). **Awards:** Jordanian 1st Bank Istiklal (Independence), 1st Bank Kawkab (Star), Syrian 1st Rank Istihkak, Grand Cross,

Silver Knights Organization (Papal), Grand Decoration of Holy Sepulchre (Greek Orthodox). **Sports:** Tennis and Table Tennis. **Hobbies:** Reading, hunting and particularly Bird's Shooting. **Member** of Gazelle, Hubara, Sheraton, Unity (Kuwait). **Priv. Addr.:** Jabal Nazzal, P.O.Box. 357, Tel.: 64085, Amman, Jordan.

ARNAOUT (Zaki Mahmoud), Egyptian Engineer. **Born** in 1928. **Married**, 1 son 1 daughter. **Career:** First Under Secretary of State, Ministry of Land Reclamation (1983-1988); Chairman of the Board of Directors: General Authority for Agricultural Development Projects (74-76) & (82-83) and General Land Reclamation Company (76-78); Consultant, Center for Arab Development Studies and Consultancy (78-82) & (1988-); Board Member, Science Research Academy (1983-1985); Member, Egyptian Syndicate of Engineers (1949-). **Decor.:** Egyptian Order of Republic, Order of Merit. **Hobby:** Tennis. **Member:** El Nasr Sporting Club. **Addr.:** 36 el-Sheikh Mahmoud Abou el Oyoun, Heliopolis, Cairo, Egypt. and Centre for Arab Development Studies and Consultancy, 14 Naquib Fawzi Rammah Str., Madinet Al Mohandeseen, P.O.Box 149 Dokki, Cairo, Egypt.

AROP (Justin, Yac), Sudanese physician. **Born** in Bahr al-Ghazal, Sudan. **Son** of Yac Arop. **Educ.:** M.B., B.Sc. in Sudan; postgraduate training in obstetrics and gynaocology in UK. **Career:** Practice as gynaecologist in Wau Civil Hospital; appointed Regional Minister of Health and Social Welfare (1973); responsible in collaboration with WHO for implementation of Primary Health Care Programme in Sudan; Member of Parliament of the People's Regional Assembly, Juba (1978); Regional Minister of Agriculture, Food and Natural Resources (1979). **Sports:** Basket-ball. **Hobbies:** Music and hunting. **Addr.:** Juba, Sudan.

ARRAR (Sulaiman, Atallah), Jordanian politician. **Born** on October 8, 1934 at Maan, Jordan. **Married. Educ.:** in Egypt and Morocco. **Dipl.:** Licence in Law (1961); Diploma in Civil Law, Law College, Rabat. **Career:** Attaché, Jordanian Embassy, Saudi Arabia (1961-67); Attaché, Jordanian Embassy, Algeria and Morocco (1967-72); Governor, Ministry of Interior (1971-72); Director-General of al-Ittihad (1972); General Manager and Chief Editor, al-Rai (1972); Minister of Interior (July 1976), reappointed in (June 1978), and again in (July 1980); former Speaker of the House of Representatives, Amman. **Awards:** Star of Jordan, 3rd Class. **Prof. Addr.:** P.O.Box. 6710, Amman, Jordan.

ARRAYED (Jawad, Salim), Bahraini politician. **Born** in 1940 in Manama, Bahrain. **Son** of Salim Al-Arayed. **Married. Educ.:** LL.B. and LL.D. from Universities of Cairo, Leeds and London. Read for English Bar. **Career:** First Bahrain Public Prosecutor (1969); Member of State Council, with responsibilities for Labour and Social Affairs (1970); Minister of Labour and Social Affairs (1972); Minister of State for Cabinet Affairs (1972-82); Minister of Health (1982 to June 1995); Minister of State (June 1995-). **Addr.:** Manama, Bahrain.

ARRAYID (Jalil, Mansour), Bahraini academic. **Born** in 1944 in Manama, Bahrain. **Married. Educ.:** Arab University of Beirut, Lebanon; Institute of Arab Research and Studies; Cairo University, Egypt. **Dipl.:** M.A. in Arabic Literature. **Career:** Primary teacher, intermediary and secondary schools, Professor at the institute of Tutors, Bahrain; Lecturer, University College of Bahrain; Coordinator, Faculty of Arabic Language and Islamic Studies, University College of Bahrain. **Publ.:** published in "Al Mawaqif" Bahraini paper (1973); several articles on Bahraini Arab Heritage Three Hundred Years ago; "The History, Function and Cultural Influence of Bahraini Journalism" (1979); Assisted in school books editing for the intermediary Bahraini schools. **Hobbies:** Reading, collecting antiques and photography. **Prof. Addr.:** Arabic Language and Islamic Studies Department, University College of Bahrain, P.O.Box 1082, Bahrain.

ARTEH GHALIB (Omar), Somali politician. **Born** in 1930 in Hargeisa (Somalia). **Married**, 9 Children. **Educ.:** Primary School at Hargeisa; Secondary education at Sheikh and Higher education at St. Paul's College of education, Faculty of Bristol University (Eng.) Cheltenham (England). **Career:** Teacher (1946-49); headmaster of various elementary schools (1949-54); Vice-Principal, Sheikh Intermediate School (1954-56); Principal, Gabileh Intermediate school (1958); Education officer in charge of Adult Education (1959); Assistant District Commissioner for Hargeisa (1960); District Commissioner for Erigave (1961); First secretary, somali Embassy to USSR (1961-62); seconded to UN to represent Somalia on the Special Committee South-West Africa (1962-63) where he served as rapporteur and later as Acting Chairman; Counsellor, Permanent Mission to UN, New-York (1963-64); Political Adviser, Ministry of Foreign Affairs (1964-65); Somali Ambassador to Ethiopia (1965-68); resigned from Civil Service and stood for elections (1968); elected member of Parliament (March 1969); Secretary of State for Foreign Affairs (Oct. 1969, May 1976); Chairman, OAU Liberation Committee (1973-74); Presidential Adviser for Foreign Policy: Adviser, Social and Political Commission of the Presidency; Minister of Higher Education & Culture (July 1976); Minister at the Presidency (1978-80); Prime Minister (1991). **Work:** attended almost all OAU Council of Ministers (1972-74); widely travelled throughout the world, in Particular Africa, Asia and the Middle East. **Publ.:** Author of "Back from the Lion of Judah". **Awards:** has been decorated by many african and world leaders. **Addr.:** Mogadishu, Somalia.

ASFAHANI (Mohamad Hussein), Saudi businessman. **Born** in 1920 in Jeddah, Saudi Arabia. **Educ.:** Secondary

School Certificate. **Career:** Owner, Dar al-Asfahani Printing Press, Jeddah; Member, Saudi Trade Delegation to Sudan (1963); Chamber of Commerce Delegation to Far East (1975); has been involved in the modernization of the local printing industry. **Addr.:** P.O.Box. 497, Tel.: 682-0107, 682-2958 (Office) and 669-2000, 699-3000 (Home), Jeddah, Saudi Arabia.

ASFOUR (Khalil Mohamad Ibrahim), Jordanian statesman. **Born** in 1924 in Amman, Jordan. **Son** of Ibrahim Asfour. **Married,** two children. **Educ.:** Diploma in Public Administration, Holland. **Career:** Arab Legion (1941); Prime Minister's Office (1958); Official in National Assembly (1958-75); Secretary General to National Assembly, now retired. **Medals:** Order of the Star of Jordan, 3rd Class, Jordan. **Member of:** King Hussain Club, the Royal Automobile Club. **Hobbies:** Sport, music. **Addr.:** Amman, Jordan.

ASFOUR (Walid Mithkal), Jordanian businessman, former Minister of Industry and Trade. **Born** on December 10, 1932 in Amman, Jordan. **Son** of Mithkal Asfour (Businessman, deceased) **And** Mrs. Zakieh Asfour. **Married** in 1984 in Amman to Janet Asfour, 3 children: Jude, Marian, Faysal. **Educ.:** Bishop's School, Amman; American University, Beirut; University of Tennessee, U.S.A. **Dipl.:** High School B.A. M.A. **Career:** Businessman (1959); President, Amman Chamber of Industry (1962-80); Deputy Mayor of Amman (1977); Member, Jordan Consultative Council (1978); Minister of Industry and Trade (1980-84); Chairman Directors Committee, Jordan Gulf Bank (1989-1992); Minister of Energy and Mineral Resources (1993); Chairman Royal Jordanian Airline (1997); Mithkhal, Shawkat and Sami Asfour Co., P.O.Box 26 Amman, Jordan; President, Royal Automobile Club. **Awards:** Kawkab 2nd Degree, Jordan; Kawkab 1st Degree, Jordan; Dasgrosse Siberne, Austria. **Sports:** Walking. **Hobby:** Reading. **Member:** Arab Thought Forum, The Queen Alia Jordan Social Welfare Fund; World Affairs Council. **Credit Card:** American Express. **Prof. Addr.:** P.O.Box 26, Tel. 623301, Amman, Jordan. **Priv. Addr.:** Swaifih, Tel.: 819399, Amman.

ASGAH (Nasser Abdallah, al), Saudi academic. **Born** in 1946 at Gassiem. **Dipl.:** Ph.D. **Career:** Demonstrator, Faculty of Science (1971); Lecturer (1977); Assistant Professor, Faculty of Science, King Saud University; member of Saudi Biological Society, King Saud University; member of Saudi Biological Society, Faculty of Science Council, 1981. **Publ.:** research works and a book in preparation. **Addr.:** Faculty of Science, King Saud University, Tel.: 481-1000 Ext. 2344 (Home), Riyadh, Saudi Arabia.

ASHANU (Abdullatif Bin), Algerian economist. **Born** in 1943 in Algeria. **Educ.:** Economic Studies, Political Economic Studies, Director, Research Center for Applied Economics, National Organisation of Scientific Research, Ministry of Higher Education, Secretary General, Association of Third World Economists (1976); President, Committee of Economic and Social Affairs, National Liberation Front Party, FLN. **Addr.:** 20 Rue Shahid Khalif Mutafa Bin Aknoum, Tel.: 784292, 786154, Algiers, Algeria.

ASHEMIMRY (Nasir Mohamad), Saudi businessman. **Born** in 1947. **Dipl.:** B.A. Texas, USA; Diploma in Techniques of Modern Management. **Career:** Pilot, Saudi Arabian Airlines, Jeddah; Supervisor, Boeing 737; owner, Ashemimry Trading, Contracting and Industry, Jeddah; member, Jeddah Chamber of Commerce; participant, Arab American Businessmen's Conference, Atlanta, Georgia. **Publ.:** an article published in Middle East Business, November 1978. **Hobbies:** Flying, swimming, hunting. **Addr.:** P.O.Box 3472, Palestine Street, Tel.: 6603260, 6603735 (Office), Jeddah, Saudi Arabia.

ASHMAWY (Mohamad Ahmad), Saudi businessman. **Born** in 1935 in Jeddah, Saudi Arabia. **Educ.:** Victoria College, Egypt, Concord College, USA, Pitman College, England. **Career:** Secretary to Sheikh Ahmed Ashmawy; Director General, the Saudi Arabian Markets Corporation; Chairman, Saudi Arabian Markets Corporation; Chairman, Peninsular Aviation Services Co. Ltd.; one of the founders of Tihama Co., co-publisher of Who's Who in Saudi Arabia and member of Tihama Control Board. **Hobbies:** reading, tourism, sports, aviation, interior decoration. **Addr.:** the Saudi Arabian Markets, King Abdulaziz Street, Tel.: 6423034, 6423140 (Office), and 6423034, 6423606 (Home), Jeddah, Saudi Arabia.

ASHMAWY (Mohamad, Said, al), Egyptian judge. **Son** of Mohamad Ashmawy. **Born** in 1932 in Egypt. **Educ.:** Cairo University, Egypt; Harvard Law School, USA. **Dipl.:** B.A. Law (1954); Technical Program in Investment Stimulation diploma (1978). **Career:** Assistant District Attorney, Alexandria (1954); District Attorney (1956); Judge (1961); Chief prosecutor (1971); Chief Prosecutor, Middle Cairo District (1974); Counsellor of State for Legislation (1977); High Court Judge (1978); Chief Justice of the High Court, Chief Justice of the Court of Assize, Chief Justice of the High Court of Security of State (1981). **Publ.:** "Mission of Existence" (1958), (1977 in Arabic); "History of Existentialism" (1963 in Arabic); "Conscience of the Age." (1968, 1979 in Arabic); "Harvest of the Mind" (1974 in Arabic); "Roots of Islamic Law-Shari'a" (1978 in Arabic) (an English translation under publication); "Spirit of Justice" (1982); numerous articles in Egyptian daily newspapers. **Member** of the Syndicate of Egyptian Writers. **Sport:** Tennis. **Hobbies:** Writing, travel, classical music. **Addr.:** 9 Gezira Al-Street, Apt. 19, Zamalek, Tel.: 650522, Cairo, Egypt.

ASHOOR (Mohamad Saleh Jamil), Saudi academic, **Born** in Makkah, in 1942, **Educ.:** B.S. In public administration from the University Of Maryland Masters and Ph.D. in Library & Informatiton Sciences from the University of Pittsburgh **Career:** Dean of Library Affairs, KFUPM, Dhahran, Saudi Arabia for 17 years (1979-96); Currently Professor of Library and Information Science at the same University. **Publ.:** Contributed more than 25 research papers to national and international professional journals and is the author or co-author of 4 books on Library and information science and library education. Taught at various universities in Saudi Arabia; Served as an information consultant to the University of Kuwait, the University of Qatar and the Ministry of Planning in Saudi Arabia; Initiated short courses as part of the continuing education project at the library of KFUPM; Served on the Board of the Congress of Muslim Librarians and Information Scientists (COMLIS) for many years; Served the Arabian Gulf Chapter of the Special Librarians Association in a presidential capacity (1992-95); Currently Consultant to the Saudi Ministry of Health on establishing a national medical library. Also writing a book on guidelines for planning an electronic library in the gulf region. **Addr.:** KFUPM Library, Dhahran 31261, Saudi Arabia, Tel.: (03)860-3000 (Office), (03)860-6414 (Home), Fax: (03)860-3018, Saudi Arabia.

ASHOOR (Saif al-Deen Ahmad), Saudi publisher. **Born** in 1918 in Mecca, Saudi Arabia. **Educ.:** Secondary school and English literature education. **Career:** Director, Time Office, the Arabian American Oil Company (Aramco), Dhahran, (1939-45); Arabic-English Translator, Aramco, Dhahran (1946-49) and New York, (1950-55); Supervisor, Arabic Division, Public Relations Department, Aramco, Dhahran (1956-66); Publisher, Saudi Economic Survey magazine since 1967. **Publ.:** a regular contributor to local newspaper; author of the Arabic fiction "Latagul Weda'a" (Do not say goodbye). **Hobbies:** reading history and English literature. **Addr.:** P.O.Box 1989, Tel.: 6514952 (Home), Jeddah 21441, Saudi Arabia.

ASHRAF (Anwar), Bahraini businessman. **Born** in 1933 in Bahrain. **Married**, three children. **Career:** Managing Director, Ashraf Brothers. **Sports:** Table tennis, cricket, swimming. **Hobby:** Chess. **Addr.:** Ashraf Brothers, P.O.Box 62, Manama, Bahrain.

ASHRAM (Fouad Salim Mohamad), Saudi executive. **Born** in 1944 in Jeddah, Saudi Arabia. **Dipl.:** B.A., M.P.A. **Career:** Manager, Jeddah Central Mail; Assistant General Manager for Financial and Administrative Affairs, Saudi Telephone, Jeddah District; Manager, Saudi Telephone, Mecca District; General Manager, Jeddah post office. **Addr.:** Jeddah, Saudi Arabia.

ASHTAL (Abdalla Saleh, al), Yemeni diplomat. **Born** on October 5, 1940 in Addis Ababa, Ethiopia. **Married** to Viviane Eshoo al-Ashtal, two children, one son, one daughter. **Educ.:** Menelik II Secondary School, American University of Beirut and New York University. **Career:** Assistant Director, Yemeni Bank for Reconstruction Development, Sanaa (1966-67); member Supreme Peoples's Council, Hadramout Province (1967-68); General Commandant Yemeni National Liberation Front (1968-70); Political Adviser, Permanent Mission to UN (1970-72), Senior Counsellor (1972-73), Permanent Representative (1973-); Non Resident Ambassador to Canada (1974-), to Mexico (1975-79), to Brazil (1985-); Permanent Representative to U.N. (1994-). **Addr.:** Permanent Mission of the Republic of Yemen to the United Nations, 413 East 51st. Street, New York, N.Y. 10022.

ASHY (Abdul-Ghany Mahmood), Saudi Civil Servant. **Born** in 1930, in Mecca, Saudi Arabia. **Dipl.:** High Diploma in Administration. **Career:** Director, Press and Publication Administration, Eastern Province; Chairman, Examination Board, Personnel Department; member of Board, al-Yamamah Press Organization; attended the Conferences of Arab Ministers of Health; Secretary-General, Arab Red Crescent. **Hobby:** Reading. **Addr.:** P.O.Box 2947, Tel.: 6422535 (Office) and 6442257 (Home), Jeddah, Saudi Arabia.

ASHY (Mohammed Ahmad Abdullah), Saudi Academic. **Born** in 1946 Mekkah, Saudi Arabia. **Dipl.:** B.Sc. King Saud University Riyadh, 1968; Ph.D. (Chemistry) Sheffield University, U.K., 1973. **career:** Professor of Analytical Chemistry, King Abdulaziz University, Jeddah (1984); Vice-Dean, Faculty of Science, K.A.U. (1974-1979); Dean, Faculty of Science, K.A.U. (1979-1982); Dean, Library Affairs, K.A.U. (1986-1990); Deputy Minister, Ministry of Haj, Saudi Arabia (1990-1995). **Member** of number of Scientific Societies. **Hobbies:** reading, travel, Social activities, gardening. **Addr.:** Faculty of Science, P.O.Box 9028, Jeddah 21413, Saudi Arabia.

ASKALAN (Abdulkader), Jordanian bank executive. **Born** in 1937 in Nablus, Jordan. **Son** of Ahmed Askalan **and** Mrs. Munira Askalan. **Married** in 1962, four daughters. **Career:** Arab Bank Ltd. (since 1958); now General Manager Oman Arab Bank. **Sports:** Tennis. **Credit Cards:** American Express, Diners, Visa. **Prof. Addr.:** Oman Arab Bank, P.O.Box 5010, Postal code 112 Ruwi, Tel.: 700161, Muscat, Sultanate of Oman.

ASKALANI (Ahmad, Hatem), Egyptian physician. **Born** in 1934 in Cairo, Egypt. **Married**, 1 son, 1 daughter. **Educ.:** Cairo University, Egypt. **Dipl.:** M.B., B.Ch.; Diploma of General Surgery; Masters Degree, Doctors Degree in Obstetrics and Gynaecology. **Career:** Intern, Cairo University Hospitals (1959-60), then Resident, Obstetrics and Gynaecology (1961-63), Clinical Demonstrator (1963-65); Tutor in Obstetrics and Gynaecology at the Faculty of Medicine, Al-Azhar University (1967-70), Associate Professor (1970-75), Professor of Obstetrics and Gynaecology (1975-). Chairman, OB/Gyn. department, Faculty of Medicine, Al Azhar University (1989). **Member:** Egyptian Obstetrics and Gynaecology Society, Fertility Care, Egyptian Medical Society. **Publ.:** numerous research papers on obstetrical and gynaecological subjects published in international periodicals; Author of an obstetrics and gynaecology text book (1972). **Member:** Automobile Club, Gezira Sporting Club. **Prof. Addr.:** 1 El-Cherifein Street, Bab El-Louk, Cairo, Egypt. **Priv. Addr.:** 8, Nadi E1 Seid Street, Dokki, Cairo, Egypt.

ASKARI (Hussein Mohamad Hussein, al), Saudi executive. **Born** in 1937 in Tabuk. **Educ.:** Secondary School Certificate. **Career:** Teacher, Primary School, Ministry of Education; News Administration, Ministry of Information; attended several Arab League Information Conferences; former Director-General of Jeddah Broadcasting Service Presently, Secretary General, Islamic States Broadcasting Organization (ISBO). **Hobbies:** Swimming, fishing. **Prof. Addr.:** Islamic States Broadcasting Organization, P.O.Box 6351, Jeddah 21442, Tel.: (2) 6721121, Fax: (2)6722600, Saudi Arabia. **Pri. Addr.:** Tel.: 6653378 (Home), Jeddah, Saudi Arabia.

ASNAJ (Abdallah, Abdulmajid, al), Yemeni politician. **Born** in 1934 in Aden. **Son** of Majid al-Asnaj. **Married** in 1966 to Miss Nadira Abdallah al-Asnaj, 3 children: Menal (1969), Muhammad (1971) and Mufat (1973). **Educ.:** secondary education. **Career:** Reserve army officer; works for Aden Airways (1951-62); Secretary-General, Federation of Aden Trade Unions (1962); imprisoned for one year by the British military authorities (1962-63); Chief of the Political Bureau of FLOSY (Front for the Liberation of South Yemen), the political rival of NLF (National Liberation Front) which seized power in South Yemen, following the evacuation of British forces from Aden; seeks sanctuary in North Yemen, early in 1968; Foreign Minister of YAR (Aug.- Sept. 1971); Minister of Economy, YAR (Sept. 1971- 28 Dec. 1972); Minister of Communications (22 June 1974- 16 Jan. 1975); Minister of Foreign Affairs (1975-79). **Publ.:** Author of "Yemeni Workers' Struggle". **Addr.:** Sanaa, Republic of Yemen.

ASSAAD (Assaad, Samaan), Egyptian banker. **Born** in 1931 in Cairo, Egypt. **Son** of Samaan Assad. **Married,** three children. **Educ.:** Cairo University, Egypt; Brussels University, Belgium. **Dipl.:** B.A. in commerce (1954); M.A. (1958). **Career:** Central Exchange Control, National Bank of Egypt (NBE) (1948); Assistant Inspector, Credit Control Department, NBE (1956); Assistant Manager, Main Branch, NBE (1960); Manager, National Bank of Abu Dhabi (NBAD) (1968); General Manager NBAD (1975); Chief Executive, NBAD (1979); President, Abu Dhabi International Bank, USA; Director, UBAF, Arab American Bank, New York. **Sports:** Swimming, tennis. **Hobby:** Chess. **Addr.:** P.O.Box. 4, Tel.: 335262, Abu Dhabi, United Arab Emirates.

ASSAAD (Omar Abdul Mohsin), Saudi physician. **Born** in 1920 in Medina, Saudi Arabia. **Dipl.:** M.D., B.M. (General Surgery). **Career:** Physician for Saudi Arabian Missions in Cairo; member of Medical Syndicate, Cairo Clinical Society, Faculty of Medicine, Cairo University; former Director General of Medical Department, King Abdulaziz University; Associate of American Surgical Colleges; contributed to preliminary studies for the establishment of the Faculty of Medicine, King Abdulaziz University; member of Arab Medical Conferences, Cairo, American Surgeons Conference, Miami Beach, U.S.A. **Publ.:** medical and surgical research papers. **Hobbies:** reading religious and literary works. **Addr.:** 6651661 (Home), Jeddah, Saudi Arabia.

ASSAAD (Rashid Mohamad), Saudi TV producer and director. **Born** Cairo, 1942. **Dipl.:** B.Sc. (Commerce), Riyadh University; Diploma in Movie Directing, RCA Institute, New York. **Career:** Director, TV Station, Jeddah; Coordination Manager; Executive Manager; Head of News Desk, same station; produced three TV serial plays; directed several TV dramas and variety shows for Saudi TV; first Saudi TV director. **Hobby:** Travel, chess. **Addr.:** Kaki Building, Tel.: 46010, Jeddah, Saudi Arabia.

ASSAD (Mohamad, Qussay Walliyuddin), Saudi scientist and educationist. **Born** in 1937 in Cairo (Egypt). **Married,** with children. **Educ.:** Faculty of Science. **Dipl.:** B.Sc. (Geology). **Career:** Geologist; Assistant Director, then Director, Geological Department; Director, Technical Affairs; Director-General for Projects, Ministry of Mining and Mineral Resources; former Deputy Minister of Mining and Mineral Resources; also Vice-Chairman of the Arab Company for Geophysics and Surveys; attended several conferences in Saudi Arabia and abroad dealing with geology, mining survey, nuclear power and solar energy. **Member:** American Federal Geological Society. **Publ.:** Author of a textbook on geology for secondary schools. **Sports:** Swimming, walking. **Hobbies:** reading and travel. **Priv. Addr.:** Tel.: 20523, Jeddah, Saudi Arabia.

ASSAD (Nassereddine, Mohamad, al), Jordanian politician. **Born** on December 14, 1922 in Aqaba. **Son** of Mohamad al-Assad **and** Mrs. Amina al-Assad. **Married** in 1946 (Cairo) to Awatif al-Assad, 4 children: Bishr, Wail, Sulafa and Tarif. **Educ.:** Arab College (Jerusalem), Cairo University. **Dipl.:** Matriculation (1941), Intermediate (1941), Bachelor of Arts (1947), Master of Arts (1951), Doctor of Philosophy (1955). **Career:** Secondary School Teacher: Jerusalem, Libya, Cairo (1947-54); Cultural Attaché, League of Arab States, Cairo (1954-59); Dean, Faculty of Arts and Education, University of Libya, Benghazi (1959-61); President, University of Jordan, Amman (1962-68); Deputy Director, Cultural Department, League of Arab States, Cairo (1968); Minister of Higher Education (27 April 1989- Nov. 1989). **Publ.:** Author of "Sources of Pre-Islamic poetry and their historical value" (4th Edition, 1970), "Singing and Singing girls in Pre-Islamic Arabia" (2nd Edition, 1968), "Divan Qais Ibn al-Khatim" (2nd Edition, 1967), "Literary Modern Trends in Palestine and Jordan" (1957), "Modern Poetry in Palestine and Jordan" (1960). **Awards:** Istiklal Decoration, First Rank (Jordan). **Hobbies:** Travels and Composing Poetry. **Addr.:** Amman, Jordan.

ASSAD (Shuja' Mohammad, al), Jordanian official. **Born** in 1928 in Aqaba, Jordan. **Son** of Mohammed al Assad. **Married. Educ.:** Wayne State University, USA; Chicago University USA; American University in Cairo, Egypt. **Dipl.:** Blitt (1951); M.A. and Higher Studies in Economics diploma (1958-59). **Career:** Assessor at the Income Tax Department (1952-56); Registrar of Trade Names and Patents, Ministry of National Economy (1958-64); Head of Industry Department, Head of Commercial Department; Assistant Director General of Passports (1964-65); Assistant Director General of Tourism (1965-71); Director General Statistics Department (1971-79); Regional Adviser on Census, United Nations Economic Commission for Western Asia ECWA, Beirut - Lebanon (1979-1982); Director of Cooperative Institute (1983-1988). **Addr.:** P.O.Box 5314, Tel.: 41894, Jabal Amman, Amman, Jordan.

ASSADI (Bashir, Ahmad, Dr.), Sudanese engineer. **Born** in 1936 at Omdurman (Sudan). **Married** to Ruda M. Logan, 4 children. **Educ.:** Primary education at Omdurman; Wadi Sayedna secondary school (1961); Faculty of Science, Khartoum University; North-Western University, Evanston, Illinois (USA) 1961-66. **Dipl.:** B.Sc. (Honours) 1961, M.Sc. (Engineering) 1963, Ph.D. (Mechanical Engineering) 1966. **Career:** Lecturer in engineering, Khartoum University (1966-68); Sudan Railway Board of Directors (1968); Chairman, Sudan Airways Board of Directors (1969); Head, Department of Mechanical Engineering, Khartoum University (Oct. 1971); Head, African Air Transport Association (1971); Minister of Communications (Oct. 1971- May 1973); Minister of Transport and Communications (May 1973). **Publ.:** "Technical Education in Sudan" (1966). **Prof. Addr.:** Khartoum, Sudan.

ASSAF (Ibrahim Ibn Abdulaziz, al, Dr.), saudi Politician **Born** in 1949. **Educ.:** B.A., Economics and Political Science, King Saud University, Riyadh; M.A., Economics, Denver University Colorado, USA; Ph.D., Economics, Colorado State University, Fort Collins, USA. **Career:** Lecturer in Economics (1971-82); Associate Professor, Head of Department of Administrative Sciences, King Abdulaziz Military College, Riyadh (1982-86); Alternate Advisor to Saudi Development Fund (1982-86); Alternate Saudi Executive Director, International Monetary Fund (1986-89); Saudi Executive Director, Executive Board, World Bank Group (1989-95); Vice Governor, Saudi Monetary Agency (June-October 1995); Minister of State and Member of Council of Ministers (Oct. 1995-Jan. 1996); Minister of Finance and National Economy (Jan. 1996-to date). **Address:** Ministry of Finance and National Economy, Airport Road, Riyadh 11177, Saudi Arabia.

ASSAILAN (Abdulrahman, Nasser), Saudi administrator. **Born** on 10 August 1947 in Taif, Saudi Arabia. **Son** of Nasser Abdulrahman Assailan (Businessman) **and** Mrs., née Noor Ahmed Halawany. **Married** on 17 August 1971 in Mecca to Selma, 4 children: Nada (1/8/1974), Wa'il (20/8/1977), Dena (20/2/80), Majed (23/8/1982) and Mushari (31/12/84). **Educ.:** St. Louis University, USA; Indiana University, USA. **Dipl.:** Certificate of Performance, Indiana; B.S. Management Science (1973); M.S. Education Management (1978). **Career:** Training Manager, Ministry of Education (1973-76); Manager of Riyadh District, Saudi Arabian Food Est. (S.A.F.E.) (1979-80); Director of Training Dept., Saudi Consolidated Electric Company, Central Region (1980-81); Vice President Affairs Saudi Consolidated Electric Company, Central Region (1982-present). **Work:** Guiding and coordinating the work of five departments: Personnel, Customers Affairs, PR, Training, Administrative Affairs: Representative of Saudi Arabia in the Committee of Human Resource Development of "Gulf Cooperative Council". **Sport:** Soccer. **Hobby:** Fishing. **Credit Cards:** American Express. **Addr.:** Riyadh, Saudi Arabia.

ASSALI (Kamil, Jamil), Jordanian historian. **Born** in Jerusalem in 1925. **Son** of Jamil Assali. **Married**, four children. **Educ.:** University of London; Jerusalem Law Classes; Humboldt University, Berlin, GDR. **Dipl.:** B.A. (1950); Law Diploma (1951); Ph.D. (1967) **Carrer:** Teacher at schools and colleges; Broadcaster; Director General, University of Jordan Library (1968-83); Since 1983 researcher on the history and heritage of Jerusalem at the University of Jordan. **Publ.:** Author of seven books on Jerusalem: "Islamic Institutions of Learning in Jerusalem", "Some Islamic Monuments in Jerusalem", "Jerusalem Historical Documents" I and II, "The Heritage of Palestine", etc.; **Medals:** Deutsche Friedensmedaille (GDR Peace Council), Prize of the Kuwait Foundation for the Advancement of Science (1982). **Prof. and Priv. Addr.:** P.O.Box 950226, Tel. 662539, Amman, Jordan.

ASWADY (Fateh Abdurahman, al), Yemeni bank assistant deputy general manager. **Born** in 1942 in Dubaa, Yemen Arab Republic. **Son** of Abdurrahman (From al-Aswady Tribe). **Married** in 1964, 8 children. **Dipl.:** B.Sc. Economics. **Career:** Head of the Economics Administration, Ministry of Economy (1966-67); Deputy Minister and Head of Monetary Control Authority, Minister of Economy (1967-71); General Manager, Tobacco & Matches Co. (1971-73); General Manager, Foreign Trade Co. (1973-74); Chairman and General Manager, Cement Corporation (1974-76); Chairman, Tobacco & Matches Co. (1967-78); Manager, Yemen Bank for Reconstruction and Development (1979-80); Assistant Deputy General Manager, Yemen Bank for Reconstruction and Development (1980-81). **Hobbies:** Reading and swimming. **Addr.:** P.O.Box 541, Tel.: 73177, 71320, Sanaa, Republic of Yemen.

ATA (Ahmad, Sayed), Egyptian university professor of applied art. **Born** on 23 February 1933 in Cairo. **Son** of Sayed Mohamad Ata **and** Mrs., née Raqiyah Ibrahim. **Married** to Miss Ingrid Eisermann, 2 daughters. **Educ.:** Abdin Primary School; Rod el-Farag Secondary School; Faculty of Applied Art (1951-56). **Dipl.:** Secondary Education Certificate; Diploma of Applied Art (1956), Ph.D. (1966) following scholarship specialisation in the Soviet Union, Italy and the Federal Republic of Germany (1958-66). **Career:** Assistant & Demonstrator, Faculty of Applied Art, Helwan University (1956-58); Lecturer in Applied Art, Helwan University (1966-71); Deputy Professor of Applied Art (1971-76); Full Professor of Applied Art since 1977; Also active partner in Pierre Genoud Interior Decoration Office since 1968. **Works:** participated in the planning design and execution of a number of important projects, both in Egypt and abroad, including building and furnishing of the Hall of the Executive Council, Arab Socialist Union; The new building of the People's Assembly (Egyptian Parliament), Cairo; Sheraton Hotel, Cairo; Meridien Hotel, Cairo; Rest House of the President of the Republic Mersa Matrouh, Egypt; Egyptian Armed Forces Saff building, Cairo; Offices of the Japanese CITO Company Garden City, Cairo; Offices of the Essential Oils Company, Cairo; Al Ahram Newspaper building; President Hotel, Zamalek, Cairo; Kuwaiti Girls' Hostel, Cairo; El Nabila Hotel, Zamalek, Cairo; the Aviation Council of Canada, etc. **Sports:** Football and swimming. **Hobbies:** architecture, modern applied art, interior decoration. **Prof. Addr.:** Pierre Genoud Office, 28 Tallah Harb, Abu Regayla Building, Tel.: 44083 & 979208; also Faculty of Applied Art, Helwan University. **Priv. Addr.:** 9 El-Gazaer street, El-Omramyah, Tel.: 852832, Pyramids District, Cairo, Egypt.

ATALAH (Ahmad A.), Saudi academic. **Born** in 1950 in Medina, Saudi Arabia. **Dipl.:** Ph.D. **Career:** Research Assistant, State University of New York at Buffalo; Assistant Dean, Faculty of Medicine, King Abdulaziz University, Jeddah. **Publ.:** presented and published several papers in the 3rd and 4th International Prostaglandin Conferences, Florence, 1975, 1979; has done extensive research in his field. **Addr.:** King Abdulaziz University, Faculty of Medicine, P.O.Box 9029, Tel.: 6882057 (Office) and 6881821 (Home), Jeddah, Saudi Arabia.

ATALLA (Munir, Hanna), Businessman/Merchant. **Born** in 1933 in Jerusalem. **Son** of Hanna Atalla (Lawyer) **and** Mrs. Milly née Halaby. **Married** in 1955 in Amman to Miss Odette Wadie Zumot, four children. **Education:** American University of Cairo (1948-1950); American University of Beirut (1950-53). **Dipl.:** B.A. in Economics. **Career:** Analyst at the Economic Research Institute, AUB (1953-54). Chairman and Shareholder of The Near East Group of Companies. The Near East Group of Companies operate in the following fields: Electronic, Avionics, Aviation. Power and Petrochemical Equipment, Water and Special Engineering Projects. Communications. Energy. Dubbing of foreign films and documentaries into Arabic & distribution thereof. Real Estate. **Founder of the following companies:** Projects & Trading Co.; Communication Development Corporation; Jordan Canning Industries; Grosvenor Int.'l Management (London); Nest U.S.A. - USA. **Others:** Past President of Amman Rotary Club (1975-1976). Active member of the Orthodox Club. Member of Haya Art Center. Member of Jordanian Scandinavian Friendship Association. Member of Jordanian Businessmen Association. Member of the Jordanian American Friendship Society. Past Member of Harvard University Institute. Member of IoD "Institute of Directors". Member of the Board of Trustees of the Royal Academy of Aeronautics in Jordan. **Hobbies:** Gardening, Aviation. **Address:** P.O.Box 1838, Amman 11118, Jordan, Tel.: +962 6 593 1013, Fax: +962 6 593 0664.

ATALLAH (Fouad, Naguib), Senior science master in charge of the Preparatory Division, College de la Sainte Famille, Cairo (Egypt). **Born** on June 19, 1936 in Cairo. **Son** of Naguib Atallah (railway engineer) **and** Mrs., née Lily Moghabghab (cousin of Patriarch Moghabghab). **Married** to Hoda William Tadros in June 1965, 2 daughters: Lily and Samia. **Educ.:** English School, Heliopolis (1943-52); Faculty of Science, Ayn Shams University (1935-58). **Dipl.:** Egyptian Baccalaureat (science) 1953; B.Sc. (geology and chemistry) 1958; M.Sc. 1962. **Career:** appointed junior teacher of science, College de la Sainte Famille, in 1958; and worked his way up to mastership of the Preparatory Division; member of the Central Synod, Anglican Church of Egypt and North Africa. **Publ.:** M.Sc. thesis "Effect of phenylazides on maleimides", subsequently published in "Tetrahydron" Journal of organic chemistry; The thesis was one of the papers tabled before the Chemistry Conference, London (1964). **Awards:** received Proficiency in teaching award in 1970. **Hobbies:** classical music and reading. **Sport:** Swimming. **Club:** al-Shams Heliopolis. **Priv. Addr.:** 26 Atallah street, Ayn Shams, Tel.: 869229, Cairo. **Prof. Addr.:** College de la Sainte Famille, 1, el-Maksy street, Tel.: 900411, Cairo, Egypt.

ATALLAH (Ibrahim, Abdel Rahman), Egyptian businessman. **Born** on October 23, 1920 in Port Said, Egypt. **Married**, 4 daughters. **Educ.:** Cairo University, Egypt. **Dipl.:** B.Sc. in Mechanical Engineering (1944). **Career:** Chairman of the Board of Directors, al-Nasr Steam Boiler Co. (1971-73); Deputy Minister of Industry (1973-78), Minister (1978-80); Chairman, Mohandiseen Food Co. (1981-83); Member, Engineers Union (1944); Chairman, International Exploitation Co. (1983-); Member of the Board of Port Said Industrial and Commercial Co.

(1984-). **Hobbies:** Tennis and swimming. **Member:** Cairo Automobile Club, Cairo Rotary Club. **Addr.:** 41 al-Kader al-Sharif, al-Mohandiseen, Cairo, Egypt.

ATALLAH (Mursi), Egyptian journalist. **Born** in 1943 at Gharbiyah Province, Egypt. **Educ.:** Diploma in English and Hebrew; Higher Diploma in Information; B.Sc. Agricultural Science. **Career:** Secretary, Editorial Board, al-Ahram weekly (since 1976). **Publ.:** "October War from Operations Duty". **Sports:** Football, tennis. **Prof. Addr.:** al-Ahram Newspaper, al-Galaa Street, Tel.: 59010, Cairo, Egypt.

ATALLAH (Nasri, Fuad), Jordanian official. **Born** in 1934. **Married,** three children. **Educ.:** Dover College, UK; Georgetown University, Washington D.C., USA (1961); Research Fellow at the Center for International Relations, Harvard University, USA; Massachusetts Institute of Technology, USA (1972). **Career:** Jordanian Foreign Service (1961); Attaché, Jordanian Embassy to USA (1961-68); Assistant Chief of the Royal Protocol (1968-71); Secretary to HM King Hussein of Jordan (1971-72); Private Secretary to HM the King (1972-74); Adviser to the Minister of Tourism (since 1975), Appointed Director General of Tourism, Ministry of Tourism, Jordan (1985-1994). **Sports:** Cricket, squash. **Addr.:** P.O.Box 224, Tel.: 642311/6, Telex: 21741 TOURIS JO, Fax: 648465, Amman, Jordan.

ATALLAH (Tharwat Taha, Gen.), Egyptian Governor, Governorate of Fayoum. **Born** on 28 August 1925. **Educ.:** Police Force Academy, and Faculty of Law, Cairo University. **Dipl.:** Graduate officer (1947) and LL.B. (1961). **Career:** appointed Commander, Utilities Police Force, then Inspector at the Ministry of the Interior; appointed deputy director of Cairo Security (1971) then Director of Cairo Security (August 1978); appointed Governor, Sohag Governorate (15 May 1980), now Governor, Fayoum Governorate since May 1982. **Addr.:** Fayoum Governorate, Egypt.

ATARI (Bassam), Jordanian executive. **Born** in 1940 in Jordan. **Son** of Mohammed and Zakeyyah Atari. **Married** to Kora Julia in 1966 in Cairo, Egypt, four children. **Educ.:** Ain Shams University, Syracuse University, USA. **Dipl.:** B.A., Ain Shams University, Higher Diploma in Financial Controllership, Syracuse University, USA (1968). **Career:** Auditor in the Government Auditing Bureau (1968-69); Auditor and subsequently head of Internal Auditing Division, Central Bank of Jordan; Head of the Administration Dept. and then Deputy General Manager of the Housing Bank (since 1974); also was seconded to the Omani Housing Bank as General Manager (1979-80). **Medals:** Jordanian Independent II, decorations. **Hobbies:** Reading, minor sports. **Member** of A.M.A. Jordan Royal Automobile Club. **Credit Cards:** American Express and Visa Card. **Priv. Addr.:** Tel. 664443, Amman, Jordan.

ATASSI (Safwan), Syrian executive. **Born** in 1930 in Homs, Syria. **Son** of Mohamad Atassi (director of Homs Municipality) **and** Mrs. Mozafar Atassi. **Married** in 1971 in Damascus to Miss Antoinette Kalashe, five children (out of two marriages). **Educ.:** University of Damascus. **Dipl.:** LL.B. **Career:** Lawyer (1951-55); banking (since 1955), now manager of National Bank of Ras al-Khaimah, Dubai. **Hobbies:** Bridge. **Member:** Dubai Bridge Association. **Prof. Addr.:** National Bank of Ras al-Khaimah, P.O.Box 1536, al-Maktoom Street, Tel.: 226291, Dubai. **Priv. Addr.:** Al-Shargan, Tel.: 357404, Sharjah.

ATEEQI (Abdul Rahman Salem, al), Kuwaiti politician. **Born** on 5 April 1928. **Son** of Salem al-Ateeqi **and** Mrs. Na'aimah. **Married** to Miss Balqees al-Zuhair. **Educ.:** Studied in al-Mubarekia School (Secondary). **Career:** Occupied various posts until Secretary General of Police (1952); Director General, Health Department (1959); Kuwait's Delegate at the United Nations (1961); Kuwait's Ambassador to Washington D.C. (1961); Under-Secretary of Foreign Affairs (1963); Minister of Finance and Oil (1967-75); Minister of Finance (1975-81); Governor, Islamic Development Bank, Jeddah; Governor, Kuwait Fund for Arab Development, Kuwait; Chairman, Gulf organization for the Development of Egypt (GODE) Appointed as Adviser to H.H. The Amir of Kuwait (1981); Chairman of Arab Investment Banking Corp. (INVESTCORP) Bahrain; Chairman, Bahrain Middle East Bank. **Credit Cards:** Diners Club. **Hobbies:** Reading. **Prof. Addr.:** P.O.Box 848, 13009 Safat, Kuwait, Tel.: 833741/ 813993. **Priv. Addr.:** House No.11, Area 2, Kuresh St., al-Noozha, Kuwait.

ATEEQI (Salah, al), Kuwaiti bank officer. **Born** in 1951, in Kuwait. **Son** of Saif Al-Ateeqi. **Married** in 1977, 2 children. **Educ.:** B.Sc. Economics, University of Kuwait. **Career:** Financial Officer (1974-76), Assistant Manager Porfolio Department (1976-78), Manager Secondary Trading Department (1978-81), Kuwait Investment Co., Kuwait; Manager, Investment Dept. (1981-1983); Head of Research Dept. in the Trading Section (since 1983); Kuwait Finance House, P.O.Box 19031 Khaitan, Kuwait; Owner of Arabian Sea General Trading Est. (founded in 1985). **Addr.:** P.O.Box 54445, Kuwait City, Kuwait.

ATIYAH (Ahmed Mamdouh), Egyptian former minister. **Born** in 1923. **Educ.:** Faculty of Law, Cairo University. **Dipl.:** LL.B. Doctorate degree in Islamic law. **Career:** Magistrate (1952); Counsellor of Supreme Court; Minister of Justice (1978); President of the Constitutional Court (1979); Minister of Justice (1982-87). **Addr.:** Cairo, Egypt.

ATIYAH (Ghassan, Rayih), Iraqi administrator. **Born** on February 18, 1940 in Baghdad, Iraq. **Married,** 2 sons. **Educ.:** American University of Beirut; Edinburgh University, UK. **Dipl.:** B.A. (1963), Ph.D. (1968). **Career:** Director of the Centre for Palestine Studies in Baghdad (1970-74); Assistant Professor, Baghdad University (1972-80);

Counsellor, Permanent Mission of Iraq to the United Nations, New York (1974-76); Director General of the Information Department, League of Arab States; Tunis, Tunisia (1980-84); Managing Director, Laam Ltd. Publications and Research (1985-). **Publ.:** "A Political Study", Arab Institute for Research, Beirut (in English); "Israel in Africa" (in Arabic 1973); "The Palestine Question and the United Nations", Baghdad (1976). **Prof. Addr.:** London, United Kingdom.

ATIYAH (Khalid Bin Abdallah, Sheikh), Qatari politician. **Born** in 1939 in Qatar. **Career:** Minister of Public Works (1970-89); financial interests in several companies. **Addr.:** Doha, Qatar.

ATIYAH (Muhammad, Muhammad), Egyptian cardiologist. **Born** on April 15, 1922 in Gharbia, Egypt. **Married**, two sons. **Educ.:** Cairo University, Egypt; American College of Physicians, USA. **Dipl.:** Doctor of Medicine; Honorary Fellow, American College of Physicians. **Career:** Lecturer of Cardiology, Ain Shams University (1951-60), Assistant Professor (1960-67), Professor (1967-80), then Chairman of Cardiology (1977-80); Secretary General of the Egyptian Society of Cardiology (1970-); Fellow of the International Society of Angiology (1967); Private physician to late President Sadat (1970-81); Fellow of the American College of Chest Physicians (1981); Medical Consultant to the Presidency of Egypt (1980-); Private physician to President Hosny Mubarak of Egypt (1981-). **Publ.:** Several research papers on cardiology in various journals in Egypt, Italy, Austria and USA. **Decor.:** State Science Award, Government Academy (1972); Medal of Science and Art (1974); Officer of the Legion of Honour, France (1974); Decoration of the Egyptian Republic (1983) as well as other decorations from Saudi Arabia, Kuwait, Jordan, Austria, Japan, Iran, West Germany, Bulgaria and Romania. **Hobbies:** Tennis, shooting. **Prof. Addr.:** Private Clinic, 11 Falaky Square, Tel.: 740389, Cairo, Egypt.

ATIYAT (Talal Mohammed Ismail), Jordanian banker. **Born** on December 28, 1952, Amman, Jordan. **Son** of Mohammed Ismail Atiyat (Ex. Minister of Finance) and Mrs. Fatemah Atiyat. **Educ.:** Harvard University; Ottawa University. **Dipl.:** Master of Business Administration; International Law. **Career:** Director of Marketing Banking, Co-operative Bank of Jordan. **Member:** International Institute of Administrative Science; Member, International Consumer Protection Society. **Credit Cards:** American Express; Diner's Club; Master Card. **Prof. Addr.:** The Co-operative Bank, P.O.Box 1343, Tel.: 665171-4, Telex: JO 21835, Amman, Jordan. **Priv. Addr.:** P.O.Box 930008, Amman, Jordan.

ATIYEH (George, Nicholas), Arab American administrator. **Born** in 1923 in Lebanon. **Son** of Nicholas H. Atiyeh (lawyer) **and** Mrs., née Mary Bisharah. **Married** in 1954 in Puerto Rico to Miss Daisy Roper, three children. **Educ.:** American University of Beirut, Beirut; University of Chicago. **Dipl.:** B.A., M.A., Ph.D. **Career:** Professor, University of Puerto Rico (1954-61); Chairman, Dept. of Humanities, University of Puerto Rico (1961-67); Head, Near East Section, Library of Congress, Washington D.C., USA. (1967-). **Publ.:** Author of several books and articles. **Member of:** Advisory Board of Editors, Middle East Journal; Advisory Council, Center for Contemporary Arab Studies, Georgetown University, Washington D.C.; Advisor Council, al-Furqan Islamic Heritage Foundation, London, U.K. **Member** of National Advisory Board, Arab-American Affairs Council, Washington D.C. **Sport:** Walking **Hobby:** Reading. **Clubs:** Middle East Studies Association. **Credit Cards:** American Express, Visa. **Priv. Addr.:** 4301 Bushie Ct. Tel.: (703) 256-4828; Alexandria, Va, 22312, USA.

ATRACHE (Taha, al), Syrian Civil Engineer. **Born** on August 8, 1938 at Harasta, Syria. **Son** of Shafik al-Atrache "Trading Business" **and** Mrs. née Fatima Omeir. **Married** on July 23, 1966 in Damascus to Zahira Al Hakim, 2 Children: Muhanad (1968), Ihab (1971). **Educ.:** Preparatory & Secondary in Tajhiz School in Damascus, Civil Eng, Construction: 12-1958 to 07-1964 Cairo University, Cairo-Egypt. **Dipl.:** Sanitary Eng. Diploma - Delft University in the Netherlands. **Career:** 1964-1973: Ministry of Municipal & Rural Affairs; 1973-1976: Public Est. for Exploitation of Euphrates Basin; 1976-1981: General Co. for Irrigation Works; 1981-1986: Public Est. for Land Reclamation "General Manager": 1987-1990: Ministry of Irrigation "1st Technical Adviser of Minister"; 1990 1998: Work for a Private Co. (Water & Construction Projects) in UAE; 1998-2000: Adviser at Prime Ministry - since March 2000 **"Minister of Irrigation". Other Information:** Participation in many Courses - Study Tours - Conferences held in and outside Syria about Irrigation - Land Reclamation - Water supply and Sanitary Eng., Presentation of Papers to these Conference. **Awards:** Medal presented by H.E. President Al-ASSAD in the Celebration held for outstanding Workmen in Workers Day. **Sports Practised:** Swimming - Walking. **Hobbies:** Reading - Sports Practising. **Associations:** Order of Syrian Engineers. **Prof. Addr.:** Damascus - Ministry of Irrigation, Tel.: (+011) 2228571, Syria. **Priv. Addr.:** Damascus - Adawi Inshaat Health Inst. Square, Al-Mughrabi Bldg., Tel.: (+011) 4457440, Syria.

ATTAF (Ahmed), Algerian Politician. **Born** in 1954 in Ain Defla. **Married,** 3 children. **Educ.:** Graduate of E.N.A. (Ecole National d'Administration) (1975); Degree, Political Sciences. **Career:** Diplomat since 1977; Secretary to Algeria's Permanent Mission to the UN (1979-82); Director of International Political Affairs, Ministry of Foreign Affairs (1984-89); Ambassador to Yugoslavia (1989-92) and India (1992-94) Attended numerous International Conferences; Founding Member, National Institute of Global Strategy Studies, Secretary of State for Maghreb

Affairs and Cooperation (1994-95); Minister of Foreign Affairs (1995-Dec. 1999). **Publicatiton:** Author of articles and studies in scientific journals. **Address:** Algiers, Algeria.

ATTAR (Abdul Wahab, Abdul Salam), Saudi academic. **Born** in 1940 in Mecca, Saudi Arabia. **Married**, with children. **Educ.:** Faculty of Commerce, Cairo University; University of Southern California (USA). **Dipl.:** B.Com. (1967), M.Sc. (Economics), Ph.D. (Economics). **Career:** Assistant Director, Planning Department, Supreme Planning Board (1969-71); Director-General, Research Department, Central Planning Organisation; member of Board of Higher Social Security Committee, Saudi Credit Bank, Supreme Council for Science, Arts and Literature, Central Committee for Community Development and Higher Committee for the Development of Rural Areas; attended Third Regional Conference of Ministers of Education and Ministers in charge of Economic Planning in the Arab States, Morocco (1974), Conference of Social Experts, Tripoli, Libya (1970), Conference of Population Policies, Cairo (1975), Conferences of Arab Ministers of Social Affairs, Khartoun (Sudan), and Cairo (Egypt), 1975; now Under-Secretary of State for Social Affairs, Ministry of Labour and Social Affairs, Riyadh, Saudi Arabia (1982); Minister of Planning (Since August 1995). **Hobby:** Reading. **Prof. Addr.:** P.O.Box 1358, Riyadh, 11182 Saudi Arabia.

ATTAR (Mohamad Said, al, Dr.), Yemeni economist and former minister. **Born** on 26 November 1927, in Djibouti. **Married**: four children. **Educ.:** Ecole Pratique des Hautes Etudes à la Sorbonne; Institut d'Etudes du Développement Economique et Social (I.E.D.E.S.), Université de Paris (1958-60). **Career:** Research I.E.D.E.S. (1960-62); Director-General, Yemen Bank for Reconstruction and Development (1962-65); President (1968-71); Minister of Economy (1965, 1967-68); President, Econ. Comm. (1965-66); President, Board, Yemen Bank and Econ. High. Comm. (1966-68); Minister of Foreign Affairs (1967-69); Vice-President, High Committee for Planning; member Int. Association of Sociology; Permanent Representative to UN (1969-71, 1973-74); Deputy Premier for Financial Affairs; Minister of Economy (1971); Executive Secretary UN. Economic Commission for Western Asia (ECWA) (1974); Special Adviser to government on the Economic Plan (1981-83); Deputy Prime Minister, Minister of Development and Head of the Central Planning Organization (1984- May 1990); Minister of Industry of the Republic of Yemen since May 24, 1990; Deputy Prime Minister and Minister of Industry; and Minister of Oil and Mineral Resources (1995-99). **Publ.:** "L'Industrie du Gant en France" (1961); "L'Epicerie à Paris" (1961); "Etude sur la croissance économique de l'Afrique Occidentale" (1962); "Le Marché Industriel et les projets de l'Arabie Seoudite" (1962); "Le Sous-Développement Economique et Social du Yemen" (Perspectives de la Révolution Yémenite) (1964). **Addr.:** Sanaa, Republic of Yemen.

ATTAR (Mohamad Siraj), Saudi businessman. **Born** in Mecca, in 1924. **Educ.:** Received commercial education in Cairo. **Career:** Member of Board of Jeddah Chamber of Commerce and Industry, Saudi National Electric Power Co., Jeddah; member of Saudi Economic Delegation to Algeria; Head of Trade Delegation to Italy; member of Saudi Chamber of Commerce and Industry Delegation to the Conference of Chambers of Commerce and Industry Federation, Abu Dhabi; member of similar delegation to similar conference in Tunis; member of Saudi Trade Delegation to Korea; Honorary Consul of Mexico, Jeddah. **Hobbies:** Reading, travel. **Addr.:** Gabel Street, Sharbatli Building, 4th Floor, Flat No. 49, P.O.Box 1765, Tel.: 26241, Jeddah, Saudi Arabia.

ATTAR (Nawzad Ahmad Amin, al), Iraqi academic. **Born** in 1941 at Sulaimaniya, Iraq. **Son** of Ahmad Amin Attar. **Married**, three children. **Educ.:** University of Baghdad, Royal College of Surgeons of England, UK; Royal College of Surgeons of Edinburgh, UK. **Dipl.:** M.B., Ch.B., D.S., FRCS. **Career:** Director of the General Teaching Hospital, Sulaimaniya, Iraq (1976-78); Dean of the College of Medicine, University of Salahuddin, Iraq (1978-82); Dean, College of Medicine, University of Mosul, Iraq. **Sport:** Tennis. **Hobby:** Gardening. **Prof. Addr.:** College of Medicine, University of Mosul, Iraq.

ATTAR (Omar Saddiq), Saudi businessman. **Born** 1929. **Educ.:** Secondary School Certificate. **Career:** President of Saddiq and Muhammad Attar Co.; member of International Air Transport Association (IATA), American Society of Travel Agents (ASTA), Pan American, TWA; Honorary Consul-General of Norway. **Sport:** Swimming. **Addr.:** P.O.Box 439, Tel.: 6423437, 6423244 (Office) and 6651309 (Home), Jeddah 21441, Saudi Arabia.

ATTAS (Amin Akil), Saudi official. **Born** on 14 December 1935 in Mecca, Saudi Arabia. **Dipl.:** B.Com. (Accountancy). **Career:** Accountant, Saudi Arabian Monetary Agency (1957); Assistant Director General, Alms and Income Tax Department (1960-65); Director General, Alms and Income Tax Department (1965-71); member of the Board of Secretariat-General, African Islamic Centre, Khartoum, Sudan; member of Board, Islamic Welfare Society, Riyadh; Deputy Chairman of Board, Welfare Society, Mecca; member of Board, al-Eiman (faith) Schools. **Addr.:** P.O.Box 1030, Tel.: 5434260 (Office), and 5422983 (Home), Mecca, Saudi Arabia.

ATTAS (Faisal, al), Yemeni official. **Born** in 1938. **Career:** Governor of the Fourth Governorate (1969-70); Governor of the Fifth Governorate; Former Member of the People's Supreme Council; Permanent Secretary at the Ministry of Public Works, and later at the Ministry of

Communications. **Prof. Addr.:** Ministry of Communications, Sanaa, Republic of Yemen.

ATTAS (Haidar, Abu Bakr, al), Yemeni politician. **Born** in 1939 in Al-Haraida, People's Democratic Republic of Yemen. **Educ.:** B.Sc. Electronics, Cairo (1966). **Career:** In the Administration, Head of Public Works Department in the Fifth Province; Minister of Works (April 1969-75); Minister of Communications (December 1975-79); Member of Central Committee (March 1975); Minister of Construction (December 27, 1979), Prime Minister (Feb.1985- Jan.1986); President of the People's Democratic Republic of Yemen (since 24/1/1986), and Chairman of its Supreme People's Council (Jan. 1986-May 1990); Prime Minister of the Republic of Yemen (since May 1990 May 10, 1994). **Addr.:** in exile.

ATTAS (Hussein Ibn Hashim, al), Saudi businessman. **Born** in 1922 in Jeddah, Saudi Arabia. **Educ.:** Secondary School Certificate. **Career:** Has been in hotel business for 35 years; owner of al-Attas Hotel, al-Haramain Palace Hotel, al-Haramain Hotel, al-Attas Holiday Beach Hotel, (Obhor), al-Attas Tourist and Travel Agency, al-Attas Trading and Contracting, al-Attas Oasis Decoration and Furniture Centre, Montana Pastries, al-Attas Operations and Maintenance; Chairman of Board, Saudi Limousine; Founding member Arab National Bank, Jeddah. **Hobbies:** Swimming, reading. **Addr.:** al-Attas, P.O.Box 1299, Tel.: 6420211 (Office), and 6657630 (Home), Jeddah 21431, Saudi Arabia.

ATTEYEH (Abchir, Hassan), Djibouti Deputy at the National Assembly, and Businessman. **Born** in 1969 at Ali-Sabieh. **Career:** Member of the Federation of Party RPP at (Ali-Sabieh). General Secretary of the Bus and Truck-Drivers Syndicate; Treasurer of the first Sports Association of Ali-Sabieh; Elected Deputy at the National Assembly (19.12.1997- to date). Commission Member for the Environment Protection, Finance Commission, Economy and Planning. **Prof. Addr.:** National Assembly, P.O.Box 138 Djibouti, Djibout.

ATTIGA (Ali, Ahmad), Libyan economist. **Born** in 1931 in Libya. **Educ.:** University of Wisconsin and University of California (USA). **Dipl.:** Bachelor of Science, Master of Science, Doctor of Philosophy. **Career:** Assistant Economic Adviser of National Bank of Libya (1959-60); Director of Research (1960-64); Under-Secretary Ministry of Planning and Development (1964); Member of the Supreme Council for Petroleum Affairs (1964); Minister of Development and Planning (1968-69); Minister of Economy (June 1969); General Manager, Libya Insurance Co. (1970-73); Chairman (1973); Chairman, National Investment Co. (1971-73), Libya Hotel and Tourism (1971-73); Chairman and General Manager, National Drilling Co.; Secretary General, Org. of Arab Petroleum Exporting Countries (OAPEC) (1973-82); Member, Board of Directors, Arab Reinsurance Co., Beirut. **Publ.:** "The Impact of Oil on the Libyan Economy 1956-1969" (1974). **Addr.:** Tripoli, Libya.

AUDA (Abdulmalik Ali Ahmad), Egyptian academic. **Born** in 1927 at Dakahliya, Egypt. **Son** of Ali Ahmad Auda. **Married**, two sons. **Educ.:** Cairo University, Egypt. **Dipl.:** B.A. Political Science (1951); Ph.D. Political Science (1956). **Career:** Lecturer (1957); Professor (1962); Professor of Political Science and Economics, College of Political Science, Cairo University (1967); Dean of the College of Information, Cairo University; Assistant Editor of Al-Ahram newspaper (1971-74). **Member of:** the Journalists Association, the African Political Science Association, the International Association of Information. **Prof. Addr.:** Al-Ahram, Al-Galaa Street, Cairo, Egypt.

AULAQI (Mohamad Farid, al, Shaikh), Yemeni politician. **Born** in 1929. **Son** of Farid al-Aulaqi. **Educ.:** Aden Protectorate College for Sons of Chiefs, Government Secondary School, Aden and Queen's College, Oxford. **Career:** Joined Protectorate Government Service as Assistant Political Officer (1950); Political Officer (1956-59); Minister of Finance, Federation of South Arabia (1959-63); Minister of External Affairs (1963-63); Minister of External Affairs (1963-67). **Addr.:** Aden, Republic of Yemen.

AUMAIR (Ali, Mohamad), Saudi publicist. **Born** in 1936 at Fazan (Saudi Arabia). **Career:** Notary Public, Chief Clerk of a Law Court; Secretary, Under-Secretary of State, then Director, Information and Publicity Office, Ministry of Communications; Managing Editor "al-Jazirah" daily newspaper; Editor "al-Bilad" newspaper; Secretary, Board of Directors, al-Bilad Press Organisation; now Administrative Manager al-Bilad Press and Publishing Organisation, Jeddah, Saudi Arabia. **Member:** Literary Club, Jeddah. **Prof. Addr.:** al-Bilad Press Organisation, P.O.Box 6340, Tel.: 32191, Jeddah, Saudi Arabia. **Priv. Addr.:** Tel.: 2273, Jeddah, Saudi Arabia.

AWAD (Ali, Gamaledin, Dr.), Egyptian lawyer. **Born** in 1929 in Egypt. **Son** of Gamaledin Awad. **Married** in 1957, 2 children. **Dipl.:** Doctor in Law (1953). **Career:** Director, Central Bank of Egypt; Attorney-at-Law; Vice Dean and Professor, Cairo University, Faculty of Law. **Member:** Société d'Economie et de Législation d'Egypte; Société Egyptienne de Droit International; Hunting Club, Cairo. **Publ.:** On banking law, maritime law, society law. **Hobbies:** Music and reading. **Addr.:** 48, Giza, Tel.: 980165, Cairo, Egypt.

AWAD (Ali, Mohamed), Djibouti Deputy at the National Assembly, and Contrator-Businessman. **Born** on september 19, 1951 in Djibouti. **Career:** Contractor-Businessman. Member of Central Committee of RPP. Elected Deputy at the National Assembly (18.12.1992- to date);

President of the National Defence Commission and Commission Member of Legislation and General Administration of the Republic. **Prof. Addr.:** National Assembly, P.O.Box 138 Djibouti, Djibouti.

AWAD (Fahmi, Ibrahim), Egyptian academic surgeon. **Son** of Ibrahim Awad. **Born** in 1924 in Cairo, Egypt. **Educ.:** Cairo University, Egypt; London University, England. **Dipl.:** Bachelor of Veterinary Medicine, Ph.D. Veterinary Medicine. **Career:** Assistant, Cairo University (1948); Scholarship to England (1949-54); Lecturer at the Veterinary College (1955); Head of Diagnosis Department in Sudan (1956-61); Assistant Professorat Veterinary College (1962); Visiting Professor, Nigeria (1968); Head of Department and Assistant Dean (1970); Assistant Director of the FAO (1977); Professor and Head of Veterinary Medicine Department; Consultant to the State Company for Meat and Dairy Products; Consultant to the Arab Pharmacutical Co.; Assistant Director of FAO Project for the Middle and Far East, **Secretary** General of the Veterinary Trade Unions. **Member** of the Royal College of Veterinary Surgeons. **Publ.:** Many papers in veterinary medicine. **Clubs:** member of the South Cairo Rotary Club; member of Al-Maadi and Al-Yakht Sports Clubs. **Addr.:** 12 Street No. 14, Maadi, Cairo, Egypt.

AWAD (Fouad, Hashem, Dr.), Egyptian bank executive. **Born** on August 11, 1928 in Suez, Egypt. **Son** of Hashem Awad **and** Mrs., née Fatma el Derestawy. **Married** on March 25, 1978 to Miss Maha el Sebaay, three children: Azza, Ola and Hisham. **Educ.:** Faculty of Economics and Political Science, Cairo University, Cairo; Leeds University, U.K. **Dipl.:** B.Comm. (honours Economics), (1949); M.A. (Economics, Manchester) (1954); Ph.D. (Economics, Leeds) (1956). **Career:** Professor of Economics, Faculty of Economics and Political Science, Cairo University, Egypt (1971); Head Department of Economics, Institute of Arab Research and Studies, Egypt (1974); Board of Directors, Misr Bank, Minister of Economy and Foreign Trade (1982); Member, International Finance Corporation (IFC) (since Febr. 1990-); Presently Chairman, Union Arab Bank for Development and Investment, Cairo, Tel.: 766926. **Publ.:** Publications include "Economics of Money and Monetary Stability" (1960); "Foreign Trade and National Income" (1965); 12 articles, most recent: Industrial policies in UAR (1971). **Medals:** The First Grade of the order of Merit. **Sports:** Tennis, Squash. **Hobbies:** Music, Reading. **Member:** El-Shams Club, Automobile Club, (honorary membership in all clubs). **Prof. Addr.:** Union Arab bank for Development and Investment, 8, Abdul Khalek Tharwat St., Cairo, P.O.Box 826 Cairo, Tel.: 766934, 766926, Egypt. **Priv. Addr.:** 1 Hussein Kamel, el-Nozha, Heliopolis, Tel.: 2455487, 2432822, Cairo, Egypt.

AWAD (Karamalla), Sudanese politician. **Born** in 1926 in Sudan. **Educ.:** Institute of Social Studies, The Hague, Netherlands; University of Manchester, England. **Dipl.:** Diploma of the Social Studies Institute, M.A. Economics. **Career:** Administration Office, Sudan (1949-53); Assistant District Commissioner (1954-55); Lecturer, Public Administration, University of Khartoum (1955-57); Head of Department of Public Law and Administration, University of Khartoum (1958-66); Governor, Bahr al Ghazal Province (1966-69); Under Secretary, Ministry of Local Government (1969-72); Deputy Minister and Governor, Red Sea Province (1973-75); Minister of State, Secretary of Sudan Socialist Union (1975-77); member of the Central Committee of the Sudan Socialist Union (since 1977 Until its dissolution following Coup in 1989); presently Chairman, People's Cooperative Bank. **Addr.:** P.O.Box 922, Khartoum, Sudan.

AWAD (Khalafalla Amir, Gen.), Sudanese army commander. **Born** in 1932. **Educ.:** Military Academies; Flying course in UK, Royal Air Force Staff College Course, UK. **Career:** Second in Command, Sudan Air Force (1964); Colonel, Cammanding Officer, Air Force (1966); Brigadier, Major General, Chief of Staff (1972); Served ex-officio as Chairman of Sudan Airways; Minister of Defence and Commander in Chief (1973); General (1974); Adviser of Military and Aviation Affairs, Presidency of the Republic (1974). **Addr.:** Khartoum, Sudan.

AWAD (Mohamad Hadi), Yemeni Diplomat. **Born** on May 5, 1934. **Married** in 1956 to Adela, one son and three daughters. **Educ.:** Murray House College of Education. **Dipl.:** Education Certificate. **Career:** Schoolmaster (1953-59); Education office (1960-62); Chief Inspector of Education (1963-65); Vice-Principal, Al-Shaab College (1965-67); Permanent Representative to the League of Arab States; Ambassador to the United Arab Republic, also accredited to Sudan, Libya, Lebanon and Iraq (1968-70); Permanent Secretary, Ministry of Foreign Affairs (1970-73); Ambassador of the People's Democratic Republic of Yemen (Aden), to the Court of St. James since 1973, to Sweden and Spain (1974-80), and to Denmark, Portugal and the Netherlands (1975-80); Ambassador to Tunisia and Permanent Representative to the Arab League (1980-1990); Director of Western Europe Department, Ministry of Foreign Affairs, Sanaa (1990-). **Prof. Addr.:** Ministry of Foreign Affairs, Sanaa, Republic of Yemen. Permanent Address: P.O.Box 19262, Sanaa, Republic of Yemen.

AWAD (Mohamad, Hashim, Dr.), Sudanese economist. **Born** on April 15, 1935 in Khartoum North, Sudan. **Son** of Mohamad Ahmad Awad (Civil Servant and Wartime Officer) **and** Mrs., née Fatima Mohamed Majid. **Married** in 1939 to Gillian Mary Hashim, Nottingham (UK), 3 children: Tarig, Imam and Ahmed el-Rayah. **Educ.:** Al-Izba Primary School (1942-45); Khartoum Bahri Intermediate School (1946-49); Khaor Taggat Secondary School (1950-53); University of Khartoum (1954-58); London School of Economics (1958-64). **Dipl.:** B.A., B.Sc. Economics (Honours), Master in Economics, Ph.D. in Economics. **Career:** Assistant lecturer in economics, University of Khartoum (1958-64); Lecturer (1964-74); Head of Economics Department (1973-74); Member of National Assembly (1974-77); Controller of the N.A. (1975-77); Minister of Cooperatives (1977-79); presently Chairman, Islamic Cooperative Development Bank. **Member:** Political Bureau, Sudanese Socialist Union. **Sport:** Soccer. **Awards:** Order of Nilain (1st class); Order of the Republic (1st class). **Hobbies:** Drawing cartoons, writing novels; composing poetry. **Association:** Member of Arab Economicst Association (1977-78); Sudanese Economists Association. **Prof. Addr.:** P.O.Box 62, Khartoum, Sudan. **Priv. Addr.:** 21 Haiz el-Matar, Tel.: 81722, Khartoum, Sudan.

AWADALLAH (Ahmad, Moustapha), Egyptian companies director. **Born** in Egypt. **Educ.:** Secondary and Higher. **Dipl.:** Bachelor of Commerce, Financial Studies Diploma. **Career:** General Manager and Representative of Economic Development Organization at Eastern Co.; Director, Middle East Agricultural Co. (Misr and Sudan), and Clothing and Equipment Co. **Member** of the Board of the Association of Accountants and Auditors of Egyptian Region of Egypt. **Addr.:** 409, Ramses Street, Cairo, Egypt.

AWADALLAH (Babakr), Sudanese politician. **Born** on March 2, 1917 in Sudan. **Married**, 3 children. **Educ.:** Secondary and Higher. **Dipl.:** Licentiate of Laws. **Career:** Lawyer; President of the 1st Chamber of Sudan (1954); Patriot, Member of the Revolutionary Council after the Coup d'Etat against General Abboud (October 8, 1964); President of the Supreme Higher Court (1965); Former Prime Minister (May 1969- October 20, 1969) after the Coup d'Etat against Presidents al-Azhari and Muhammad Mahgoub; Vice-President of the Revolutionary Council and Minister of Foreign Affairs and Justice (October 1969); Vice-President of the Republic (1970-72). **Resid:** Khartoum, Sudan and Cairo, Egypt.

AWADI (Abdul Karim), Syrian politician. **Born** in 1936 in Hama, Syria. **Married. Educ.:** Law Faculty, Damascus University, Syria. **Dipl.:** in Law. **Career:** joined Ministry of Education; Governor of Deir Zor; Director General, Public Consumption Organisation; Member, Baath Regional Command (1970-); elected Member of People's Council (1971-); Minister of Internal Trade and Supply (1971-75); Minister of State for Foreign Affairs (1976-80); Minister of State for Presidential Affairs (1980-85). **Addr.:** Damascus, Syria.

AWADI (Abdul Rahman Abdulla, al, Dr.), Kuwaiti physician and director of Regional Organisation for Protection of Marine Environment (ROPME). **Born** on December 18, 1936 in Kuwait. **Son** of Abdalla Mohamad Hadi al-Awadi (Businessman) **and** Mrs. Mariam Sharif al-Awadi. **Married** in 1969 to Dr. Sadika A. al-Awadi, 5 children: Abdulla (1970), Ahmad (1973), Omar (1975), Mohammad (1978), Fatima (1982). **Educ.:** Secondary School in Kuwait (1954); B.Sc. Faculty of Science, American University of Beirut, Lebanon (1958); M.D., Faculty of Science, University of Aberdeen, Scotland, U.K. (1963); M.P.H., School of Public Health, Harvard University, Boston, U.S.A. (1965). **Career:** Resident Physician, Ministry of Public Health Hospitals, Kuwait (1963-65); Raporteur, Planning Committee for the same Ministry (1965); Registrar in Medicine, Ministry of Public Health Hospitals, Kuwait (1966-69); Assistant Director, Preventive Services Dept., same Ministry (1969-70); Director of Preventive Services, Ministry of Public Health, Kuwait (1971-75) grade of Assistant Under Secretary; Minister of Public Health, (1975-83); Minister of Public Health and Minister of Planning, (1983-87); Minister of Planning (1987-90); Minister of State for Cabinet Affairs (1990 - April 1991). Chairman of the Executive Bureau, of the Council of Arab Ministers of Health (1976-87); Chairman of the Higher Committee for Environment Protection, (1975-80); Chairman of Environment Protection Council, (1980-87); Acting Executive Secretary, of Regional Organisation for the Protection of the Marine Environment (ROPME) (1981-91) and since Oct. 1991 Executive Secretary of the same Organization; Secretary General, Arab Centre for Medical Literature (ACML) since 1983. **Professional Activities: Acted as:** Member of WHO Executive Board for two terms, (1966-69 and 1980-83); Member of the Consultative Committee to the Regional Director of East Mediterranean Region, (1978-79) and since 1984; President of the International Commission for the Prevention of Alcoholism and Drug Dependency, 1979 and 1986; Vice President of the ICPA (1980-85); President of the 33rd Session of WHO General Assembly, (1980); Member of the Global Advisory Committee on Medical Research (1980-83); Chairman of WHO Experts Committee on Smoking Control Strategies in Developing Countries, (1982); Chairman of the Technical Discussions of the 35th WHO on Alcohol Consumption and Alcohol Related Problems, (1982); Vice-President of the International Council on Alcohol and Addictions, (1982); Member of the WHO Expert Advisory Panel on Public Health Administration since 1983; **Member:** WHO Advisory Council on HIV and AIDS since 1991; WHO Director General's Council on the Earth Summit Action Programme for Health and Environment since 1993; WHO-Global Advisory Group on Expanded Programme on Immunization since 1993; WHO Tuberculosis Programme of the coordination Advisory and Review Group since 1993; Harvard School of Public Health Environment Council since 1993; Harvard School of Public Health Visiting Committee since 1994; WHO Certification Commission for Global Polio Eradication (1995); WHO Regional Technical Advisory Group for the Expanded Programme of Immunization May 1995; Chairman, WHO International Commission for the Certification of Dracunculiasis Eradication since 1997; President, The Medical Foundation of Dr. Nassib Berbir, Beirut, Lebanon. **Activities in the Field of the**

Environment: the National Level: 1) Chaired the Steering Committee for the Human Environment Project (1970-72), a project co-sponsored by both the WHO and ILO. The broad based committee was the nucleus of the Council entrusted later with looking after the environment in Kuwait. 2) In his capacity as the Director of the Preventive Services, Ministry of Public Health, he developed the Occupational Health Section. The Section was entrusted with monitoring air and water pollution problems resulting from the industrial activities. The Section was later turned to the Occupational Health and Environment. 3) Took an active part in the development of the environment legislation, promoting research in the field of the environment legislation, promoting research in the field of the environment and support of the activities of all the relevant organisations represented in the Environment Protection Council. **At the Regional Level:** 1) Promoted the activities of the Ministries of Health in the Arabian Gulf States in the area of protection of the environment. Established the role of the health authorities in this respect. Helped develop the infra-structure in the Arab Gulf States for looking after the environment. This covered drafting of legislation, developing the manpower, provision of training and integrated work plans for protection of the environment. This was further development in the context of the Gulf Cooperation Council (GCC) countries. A general policy for protection of the environment was adopted by the Heads of the States of the GCC countries. Strategies and Work plans in cooperation with the regional and international organizations is being developed and implemented. 2) Coordination of the activities of the ROPME. This covers the areas of public education, research, information and setting emergency plans for combating pollution oil etc. **Arabian States:** The League of the Arab States showed an interest in the field of the protection of the environment. The first meeting of the Ministers responsible for the protection of the environment was held in Tunis under the Chairmanship of Dr. al-Awadi in 1986. At his advice a steering board was established to set strategies for protection of the environment determining the areas in which cooperation between the States would be fruitful. This will cover work plans, promoting research and invertigations and manpower development. **Publ.:** The Study of Allergy in Kuwait - Part I: Prevalence and Role of Environment Factors. Ministry of Public Health Publication (1973); Study of Non-Fatal Home Accidents in Kuwait. al-Awadi A., and el-Desouky M. Ministry of Public Health Publication (1973); Epidemiology of Injuries resulting from Traffic Accidents in Kuwait. Paper Presented in First Traffic Accident Conference for the Arab Gulf States (1981); Blood Pressure and Epidemiology of Hypertension in Kuwait (1981); Pharmaceuticals for Developing Countries-Needs and Problems from the Respective Developing Countries. Presented at the APHA 110th Annual Meeting, (1982); Murine Typhus in Kuwait in 1978. WHO Bulletin, 60 (2) 283-289, (1982); Smoking Control Strategy in the Developing Countries. Presented at the 5th World Conference on Smoking and Health - Winnipeg, Canada (1983); Health Impacts of Urbanization and Development (1983); Epidemiology of Accident Injuries in Kuwait. A Series of Public Health Reports (Editor:) Pre-School Children; Children; Elderly People; Home; Sports: Occupation; Traffic. **Founding Member and Member of:** Kuwait Medical Association (KMA) Journal (Chief Editor); Kuwait Red Crescent Society (Secretary General 1966-75 and Vice-President since 1975); Kuwait Society for Smoking and Cancer Prevention (President since its establishment in 1980); Kuwait Association for Handicapped welfare (Vice-President since 1975); Kuwait Environment Protection Society (Chairman 1974-78); Kuwait Graduate Association; Kuwait Ham Radio Amateur Association (President); Kuwait Kidney Transplant Society (President since 1984); Islamic Organization for Medical Sciences (President since 1984); Kuwait Heart Foundation. Very active in international health and environment affairs at all levels, in regional and international organizations. **Honorary Degrees and Awards:** Honorary Fellow, Royal College of Medicine, Ireland (1977); Honorary Doctor of Law, Si-Chand Bon University, Korea (1977); Honorary Fellow, Royal College of Surgeons & Physicians, Glasgow (1982); Honorary Member, American Public Health Association (1982); Certificate of Recognition, by Egyptian Medical Syndicate (1986). Fellow, Royal College of Physicians, Edinburgh (1994); Jointly awarded the United Arab Emirates Health Foundation Price for 1997, through the Executive Board of the World Health Organization; Selected as one of the ten Arab Personalities from Euro-Arab Co-operation Center (Cairo); Selected as Gulf Co-operation Council Environment Personality for the year 1998. **Hobbies:** Walking, Jogging, Swimming, Photography and Agriculture. **Member:** Kuwait Medical Association; Kuwait Red Crescent (Sercretary General 1966-75). **Credit Cards:** Visa, American Express, Diners Club Card. **Prof. Addr.:** Regional Organization for the protection of the Marine Environment (ROPME), P.O.Box 26388, Safat 13124, Kuwait, Tel.: 5312140-4, Fax: 5335243/ 5324172, e-mail: ropme@qualitunet.net. **Priv. Addr.:** Dahia Abdullah Al-Salem, P.O.Box 38034, Dahia 72251, Kuwait., Tel.: 2549494, Fax: 2527688.

AWADI (Abdul Salam A., al), Kuwaiti businessman. **Born** in 1947, **Married,** 5 children. **Educ.:** B.S. in Economics and Polictical Science, Cairo University (1970); Post-Graduate Studies, International Economy & Development, University of Aberdeen, U.K. (1973). **Career:** Economic Researcher, Prime Minister's Office (1970-72); Deputy Director, Economic Dept., Prime Minister's Office (1973-74); Representative of the Prime Minister's Office at the Commission for Oil and Petroleum Sales, Ministry of Oil (1975-76); Member of the High Council for Housing, Kuwait (1982-86); Deputy Chairman & Managing Director, al-Ahli Bank of Kuwait (KSC) (since May 1986-). **Directorships:** Member of Board of Directors, Pearl Investment Co. (Bahrain) (1979); Member of Board of Directors, United Gulf Bank (Bahrain) (1980); Member of Board of Directors, Kuwaiti French Bank (Paris) (1980); Member of Board of Directors, Pearl Holdings S.A. (Luxembourg) (1980); Chairman of the Kuwait General Investments Co. (Geneva) (1986); Member of Board of Directors, Insititute of Banking Studies (Kuwait) (1986); Deputy Chairman of Industrial Bank of Kuwait (Kuwait) (1987-90); Acting Chairman & Managing Director of the Industrial Bank of Kuwait (Kuwait) (1987-88); Member of Board of Directors, Arab General Investments Co. "Shua'a" (Dubai) (1989); Member of Board of Directors, ALUBAF Arab International Bank (London) (1989-90). **Membership of Professional Organizations:** Member of the Arab Bankers Association (London) (1982). **Addr.:** AlAhli Bank of Kuwait (KSC), P.O.Box 1387 Safat, 13014 Safat, Tel.: 2444444, 2443443, Fax: 2424557, 2421130, Telex: 22067, Kuwait.

AWADI (Badria Abdullah, al, Dr.), Kuwaiti lawyer. **Born** in Kuwait in 1944. **Daughter** of late Abdullah Mohd. Hadi al-Awadhi **and** Mrs. Mariam al-Awadhi. **Single. Educ.:** Cairo University, University College, London. **Dipl.:** LL.B., LL.M., Ph.D. in International Law. **Career:** Lecturer of International Law, Faculty of Law and Sharia (1975-77); Head of the Department of International Law, Faculty of Law and Sharia (1977-79); Assistant Professor (1979); Dean of Faculty of Law and Sharia (1979); Dean of Faculty of Law (1982); Legal Consultant, Regional Organization for the Protection of the Marine Environment (1982), Co-Ordinator Tech. and Admin. (1984). **Medals:** United Nations Environment "Global 500 Roll of Honour". **Credit Cards:** VISA, Diners. **Prof. Addr.:** R.O.P.M.E., P.O.Box 26388, 13124 Safat, Kuwait. **Priv. Addr.:** 6, Ibn al-Abbas Street, Block 2, al-Dahyya, Kuwait.

AWADI (Mohamad Siddiq), Saudi academic. **Born** in 1927 in Medina, Saudi Arabia. **Dipl.:** Ph.D. (Persian Language). **Career:** Teacher, Secondary School; Chief Inspector Administrative Staff, Directorate of Education, Jeddah; Assistant Professor, King Saud University; Associate Professor, Faculty of Arts, King Saud University. **Publ.:** The Letter 'A' in the Persian Language (research). **Hobby:** Reading books on linguistics. **Addr.:** Faculty of Arts, King Saud University, Tel.: 4811000 Ext. 2239 (Home), Riyadh, Saudi Arabia.

AWAR (Arif, Mahmoud, al), Lebanese contractor and engineer. **Born** on 18 March 1918 at Kornayel, Lebanon. **Son** of Mahmoud S. al-Awar **and** Mrs., née Anisah Sabra. **Married** in 1950 in Lebanon to Miss Aida Basheer, 4 children: Nadim, Janan, Nada, Joumana. **Educ.:** I.C. Beirut; American University of Beirut; University of Mich. Ann, Arbor, Mich. USA; University of California, Berkeley, Calif. USA. **Dipl.:** B.A. Engineering, AUB; B.Sc. Engineering, University of Mich.; M.Sc Engineering, University of California. **Career:** Instructor, School of Engineering, American University of Beirut (1941-42); Manager of al-Awar & Co. SAL (Engineers & Contractors) Beirut since 1942; General Manager, SAURABIA Contractors Ltd., Saudi Arabia. **Work:** Civil engineering construction. **Sport:** Walking. **Credit Card:** American Express. **Prof. Addr.:** P.O.Box 6248, Tel.: 6515716, 6515968, Jeddah, Saudi Arabia; Tel.: 366880-81, 366811, Beirut, Lebanon. **Priv. Addr.:** Tel.: 6710286, Jeddah; Tel.: 808452, Beirut.

AYAD (Mohamad, Abdel Fattah), Egyptian expert in radiation protection and professor in Atomic Energy Est. Cairo. **Born** on July 5, 1930 in Kenah (Upper Egypt). **Married** to Dr. Siham Tewfick on September 9, 1965, one son: Amr. **Educ.:** Mohamed Aly Primary School; Khediviah Secondary School. **Dipl.:** Baccalaureat; B.Sc., M.Sc., Ph.D. (Physics) (London). **Career:** Teacher in Government Schools, Cairo; Demonstrator, Faculty of Science, Ain Shams University, Cairo; Professor, of Health Physics, Atomic Energy Est. (A.E.E.), Cairo (1983); obtained IAEA training in Health Physics on IAEA program in 1962. **Member:** Institute of Physics, London, (1974); Institute of Acoustics, London (1976). **Distinction:** Awarded Diploma of Imperial College of Science and Technology, London, (UK). **Publ.:** Author of over 56 research papers and covered over a wide range of spectrum from phonons to photons, i.e. ultrasonic wave propagation and gamma ray penetration in biological system and effects due to interactions. Ultrasonic cavitation and Ultrasonic Hæmolysis in blood to differentiate different types of anæemia; Study of neutron attenuation in simulated tissue; equivalent material had been accomplished since 1962 at INDIA; the publications are including. "Detailed Record of the Exposed Occupational Workers, 1961"; "Record on Exposure of workers of the A.R.E. Atomic Energy Establishment"; "Thermal Neutron Diffusion length in tissue Equivalent Media"; "Scattered Radiation in U.A.R. Van de Graff main hall"; "The Hæemolysis of Blood by ultrasound"; "Electromagnetic Radiation During Ultrasonic Caviation"; "Some Observations on Cavitation"; "The Effect of Gamma radiation on the Infra red Spectrum of Polyethymethacrylate"; "Response of Liquid Scintillator to Nuclear Radiation and Ultrasonic Waves"; "Testicular Dose underlying Hodjkin's radiotherapy treatment"; "Lung Scan in Bronchial Carcinoma"; "Guidance for Assessment and Handling of Radiation Exposure and Radiocontamination Cases from Nuclear Installations"; "Water Requirements and Total Body Water Estimation as affected by Species, Pregnancy and lactation using tritiated Water", "Inter-comparison between Radiation Medical Exposure and Radiation occupational Exposure in the Atomic Energy Est. of Egypt" (publ. March 1982), "Heavy Particle Beams in Tumour Radiotherapy", "Risk Assessment of Ionizing Radiation Energy in Diagnostic Radiology", "Dose Estimation Assessment in case of a Nuclear Reactor Accident"; "Internal Contamination Assessment with Regard to Sr-90, Cs-137 and Cs-134 Nuclei during Reactor Accident"; "Patient Exposures and Radiation Risks in

Saudi Diagnostic Radiology"; "Radiation Occupational Exposure at King Saud University"; "Study of the Developed Shielding Material for Radiation". **Hobbies:** Travelling and reading **Prof. Addr.:** Atomic Energy Agency, 3 Ahmed El Zamer Str., P.O.Code 11787, Cairo, Egypt. **Priv. Addr.:** 30 Road No.11, Flat 403, Maadi, Tel.: 5199711, Cairo, Egypt.

AYAD (Shukri), Egyptian academic. **Born** in 1921 in Egypt. **Educ.:** Cairo University, Egypt. **Dipl.:** B.A. and Ph.D. in Arabic Literature. **Career:** Teacher; journalist; diplomat; Associate Professor of Modern Arabic Literature at Cairo University; Cultural Counsellor, Embassy to Brazil; Assistant Editor of "al-Majalla" magazine, Cairo. **Publ.:** has translated into Arabic works of fiction and criticism; Two short story collections; "Experiments in Literature and Criticism" (1967), a collection of essays in Arabic, "The Short Story in Egypt" (1968). **Prof. Addr.:** Faculty of Arts, Cairo University, Cairo, Egypt.

AYADI (Mohammed, el), Moroccan academic and researcher. **Born** in 1948 in Rabat, Morocco. **Son** of Ahmed el-Ayadi (deceased) **and** Mrs. née Fatma Maani. **Married** on December 25, 1970 in Rabat to Laila Boumediane, 2 children: Charif, Loubna. **Educ.:** Lycée Mohammed V in Rabat; University Mohammed V in Rabat; La Sorbonne Nouvelle in Paris. **Dipl.:** Licence ès-Lettres (in Philosophy), C.E.A. (in sociology), DEA (in Islamology), Doctorate 3rd cycle (in Social Sciences). **Career:** Teacher of Philosophy, Casablanca (1972-175); Inspector of Philosophy, Casablanca (1975-78); Student at the Sorbonne, Paris (1978-83); Teaching Philosphy of History and Islamic civilisation at Hassan II University (1983- to present); Teaching and Chairing the Department of History, Hassan II University. **Sports:** Football, Tennis, Swimming. **Member:** Historians Association, Study Group of Social and Religious History. **Credit Card:** Diner's Club. **Prof. Addr.:** Faculté des Lettres et des Sciences Humaines I, Hay Inara, P.O.Box 8507, Tel.: 213965, Casablanca, Morocco. **Priv. Addr.:** 300. Bd. Bordeaux, Appt. No.3 Casablanca 20000, Morocco.

AYAR (Hamad Mubarak, al), Kuwaiti businessman. **Born** in Kuwait. **Career:** Minister of Social Affairs and Labour (1971-75); Minister of Housing since 1975; reappointed on February 16, 1978; Businessman since 1982. **Work:** involved in the Ardiah housing development plan (initial building of over 3,000 houses); and a plan to build over 51,000 new houses to help solve housing shortage: Chairman, Mubarak al-Ayar Co. **Addr.:** Mubarak al-Ayar Co., P.O.Box 20718, Safat, Kuwait.

AYARI (Chedly), Tunisian economist. **Born** on August 24, 1933 in Tunis. **Son** of Sadok **and** Fatouma Chedly. **Married** in 1959 to Elaine Vatteau, three children. **Educ.:** Secondary, university, College Sadiki, Institut de Hautes Etudes. **Dipl.:** LL.B. and Ph.D. in economic sciences (1961). **Career:** Head of service at Société Tunisienne de Banque (1958); Assistant lecturer at the Faculty of Law in the University of Tunis (1959); Economic adviser in Tunisia's permanent mission at the UN, participating in the 15th, 16th, 17th, 18th sessions of UN General Assembly (1960-64); Chairman of Industrial Committee of UN (1962); Rapporteur General of the United Nations Conference on Trade and Development (1963-64); Agregate of the economic sciences at the University of Paris (1964); Executive director of the World Bank Group (1964-65); Professor and Dean of the Faculty of Law and Political and Economic Sciences at the University of Tunis (1965-67); Director of the University's Centre for Economic Studies and Research (1967-69); Secretary of State for planning in the office of Prime Minister (1969-70); Minister of National Education, Youth and Sport (1970-71); Ambassador of Tunisia to Belgium, Luxembourg and the EEC (1972); Minister of National Economy (1972-74); Minister of Planning (1974-75); Chairman of the Board of Directors and Director General of Arab Bank for Economic Development in Africa (BADEA) (1982-87). **Act.:** Took part in the resistance as a member of General Union of Tunisian Students; elected member of the Buro and Central Committee of the Socialist Destourian Party (till 1975). **President** of the Tunisian Association of Economists (since 1981). **member** of the UN Committee for Development Planning; founding member of the Dakar Club and Honorary President of the International Association of French Speaking Sociologists. **Publ.:** Author of numerous works and articles of economic theory and practice as well as political essays. **Award:** Honorary doctorate from Aix-en-Provence University, France. **Medals:** Grand Cordon of Tunisian Republic, Grand Cordon of the Order of Tunisian Independence, Grand Officer of the French Legion of Honor. **Addr.:** Rue Tanit, Gammarth, La Marsa, Tunis, Tunisia.

AYIK (Arop Yor), Sudanese politician. **Born** in 1935 in Palo, ten miles south of Malakal Town, Sudan. **Son** of Yor Ayik. **Educ.:** Primary Education at the American Mission School at Doleib Hill (1945-49); Government Intermediate School at Atar (1950-53); Government Secondary School at Rumbek (1954-58); University of Khartoum (1958-62); American University in Cairo (1986). **Dipl.:** B.A. (Arts); M.A. (Teaching Arabic as a Foreign Language - TAFL). **Career:** Teaching Assistant in the Faculty of Arts (Dept. of Arabic), University of Khartoum in 1962; Assistant Student's Warden, University of Khartoum (1964); Minister of Public Works (1966); Director of Education in the Southern Sudan (1970-74); Also Director of Information and Culture after Addis Ababa Peace Accord in 1972; Regional Director of Education (1973-74); elected to the People's Assembly as a member of the Upper Nile Constituency (1974); elected Deputy Speaker (1974); elected Principal of the University of Khartoum (1974); Commissioner for Census (with a status of Deputy Minister) in Southern Sudan (1981); Dean of Students,

University of Juba (1982); Centre Coordinator, University of Khartoum (School of Extra-Mural Studies, 1986) as Supervisor of Teaching Arabic as a second Foreign Language; Member of the Council for the South and Minister of Education (1988); Chairman, National Committee for the reorganization of Education of the displaced pupils and students from the Southern Sudan (1989); Chairman, Shilluk Language Literacy Committee of Shilluk Elders, Khartoum; Centre Coordinator, University of Khartoum (School of Extra-Mural Studies, 1991), as Supervisor of Teaching Arabic as second Foreign Language. **Addr.:** University of Khartoum, School of Extra-Mural Studies, Khartoum, Sudan.

AYOUB (Fouad), Jordanian diplomat. **Born** on August 15, 1944 in Amman, Jordan. **Married** in 1974 to Marie Vernaze, 3 children: Hussein Ayoub, Rakan Ayoub, Lana Ayoub. **Educ.:** California State University; San Francisco Harvard University; Fellow Centre for International Affairs, Harvard (1983-1984); Fellow of Harvard University. **Dipl.:** B.A. and M.A. (Degree in Philosophy), California State University (1974). **Career:** Press Secretary to His Majesty King Hussein (1977-91); Ambassador of Jordan to the Court of St. Jame's (1991), Ambassador of Jordan to the United Kingdom; Member of the Jordanian Delegation to the Madrid Peace Conference (1991); Non-resident Ambassador of Jordan to Ireland (1992); Non-resident Ambassador of Jordan to Iceland (1992); Ambassador of Jordan to Switzerland (Dec. 1999- to present). **Awards:** Commander's Cross, Federal Republic of Germany, (November 5, 1978); Order National du Merit, France (August 1980); Greek Orthopatriarch Decoration (in Greek) (1981); Commandatore, Italy (November 26, 1983); Merito Civil Encomienda de Numero, Spain (March 20, 1985); Bintang Jasa, Indonesia (1986); Istiqlal III, Jordan (1987); Commandeur de l'Ordre du Lion de Finland (1987); Das Grosse Goldene Ehrenzeichen, Republic of Austria (February 26, 1978 and January 22, 1988); Kommendör av Kungl, Nordstjärneorden, Sweden (September 8, 1989); Istiqlal I, Jordan (October 27, 1991); **Hobby:** Reading. **Prof. Addr.:** Embassy of Jordan, Belpstr. 22, Berne 3007, Tel.: (31)254146, Fax: (31)262119, Switzerland.

AYOUB (Ibrahim, Taha), Sudanese diplomat. **Born** on October 20, 1940 in Wadi Halfa, Sudan. **Married**, 3 children. **Educ.:** University of Khartoum, Johns Hopkins University, USA. **Dipl.:** B.A. in Arts, M.A. in International Public Policy. **Career:** Attaché, Ministry of Foreign Affairs, Sudan (1965); Third Secretary, Sudan Embassy in Baghdad, Iraq, and Amman, Jordan (1966-69); 2nd Secretary, Sudan Embassy to Addis Ababa, Ethiopia (1969-71), Consul General of Sudan in Asmara, Eritrea (1971-73); Director of African Department, Ministry of Foreign Affairs, Sudan (1974-75); Ambassador to Ethiopia (1976-77), to Malaysia, Indonesia and Sri Lanka (1977-78); Ambassador to New Delhi (1978-79). **Decor.:** Order from Ethiopia in 1971, from Iran in 1974, from Oman in 1977. **Hobbies:** Arabic poetry, travelling and swimming. **Prof. Addr.:** Ministry of Foreign Affairs, Khartoum, Sudan.

AYOUB (Sami), Jordanian statesman. **Born** in Jordan. **Educ.:** Secondary and Higher. **Dipl.:** Doctorate. **Career:** Joined Ministry of Foreign Affairs; Secretary General of the said Ministry, Minister of Agriculture in the Cabinet of Mr. Bahjat at-Talhouni (October 1967- 24 March 1969), in the Cabinet of Mr. Abdul Moneim ar-Rifaï (March 1969) and in the Cabinet of Mr. Bahjat at-Talhouni (1969-71). **Addr.:** Amman, Jordan.

AYOUBI (Mahmoud, al), Syrian politician. **Born** in 1932. **Married**, 2 children. **Educ.:** University of Damascus. **Dipl.:** Licentiate in Literature. **Career:** School Teacher (1949-64); Director General of Administrative Affairs, Euphrates Office; Under Secretary, Ministry of Education (1963-65); Deputy Minister (1965-67); Assistant General Director, Euphrates Dam Project (1967-68); Minister of Education (1969-March 1971); Member of the Command of the Baath Regional Party (November 16, 1970); Vice-President of the Syrian Arab Republic (1971-72); Prime Minister (1972-76). **Addr.:** Damascus, Syria.

AYOUBI (Mohamad, Zuhair bin Abdul Wahab, al), Saudi senior civil servant. **Born** in 1939 in Medina city. **Dipl.:** LL.B. **Career:** Teacher; TV and Radio Newscaster; Director, Department of Culture, Radio and TV; Director of Programmes, Riyadh Radio Service; Director of Riyadh Broadcasting Service; attended Islamic Conference, Damascus (Syria) 1954; Represented Saudi Arabia at Conference of Federation of Arab Broadcasting Stations, Algiers, Algeria (1973) and at Conference of the Organisation of Islamic States Broadcasting Stations, Riyadh (1975) and Jeddah (1975); former Director-General, Jeddah Broadcasting Service. **Publ.:** Author of "Breakfast Greeting", "For God's Sake" and number of TV programmes of a religious character. **Sports:** Swimming and tennis. **Hobbies:** Reading and music. **Priv. Addr.:** Tel.: 22794, Riyadh, Saudi Arabia.

AYOUBI (Sadik), Syrian politician. **Born** in 1925. **Educ.:** American University, Washington D.C., USA **Dipl.:** Ph.D. in Economics (1951). **Career:** Head of Budget Department, Ministry of Finance (1952-64); Director, Accounting and Consulting Firm, Damascus; returned to government service with economic liberalization programme (1972); Minister of Finance (1976). **Addr.:** Damascus, Syria.

AZAR (Aimé, Joseph), Egyptian university professor. **Born** in 1934 in Cairo. **Son** of Joseph Azar (Professor) **and** Mrs., née Lilie Badaro. **Educ.:** College de la Sainte Famille (1940-52), Faculty of Arts (French Department) of Cairo University (1952-57). **Dipl.:** Secondary Education Certificate (1952), Bachelor of Arts (French Literature) in 1957, Master of Arts (1963) and Doctor of Philosophy (1966).

Career: Professor of French Literature and the History of Art (Egypt). **Publ.:** Author of "Pensée et Art de Maurice Guérin" (Thinking and Art of Maurice Guérin), "Influence de la peinture sur le langue plastique au XIX siècle" (The influence of painting on the plastic language of the XIXth century), "Peinture Moderne en Egypte" (Modern Painting in Egypt and "Frodman Cluzel". **Sports:** Football and Horseriding. **Hobby:** Music (piano), preferably the music of Bach. **Prof. Addr.:** Faculty of Arts, Aïn Shams University, Zamalek, Egypt. **Priv. Addr.:** 30 al-Gezirah al-Worta Street, Zamalek, Tel.: 801191, Egypt.

AZAR (Nasib, Salim), Jordanian judge. **Born** in 1920 at al Husn, Jordan. **Son** of Salim Azar. **Married. Educ.:** Law diploma from Syrian University (1943). **Career:** Amman Public Prosecutor (1948-50); Civil Magistrate, Zerqa (1950-51); Judge of First Court, Kerak (1951-53); Judge of First Court, Jerusalem (1953-55); Judge of First Court, Nablus (1955-57); Judge of First Court, Amman (1957-59); President of the Court of First Instance, Kerak (1959-60); President of Court of First Instance, Jerusalem (1953-55); President of Court of First Instance, Nablus (1955-57), of Amman (1957-59); of Salt (1960-61), of Irbid (1961-63); Appeal Court Judge, Amman (1963-65); Attorney General, Amman (1965-73); Member of the Court of Cassation (since 1973). **Addr.:** Amman, Jordan.

AZAR (Wasef, Y.), Banking Executive. **Born** on August 29, 1936. **Son** of Yacoub Azar **and** Mrs. Asma Azar. **Married** on January 21, 1963 in Amman to Miss Abla Muasher, four children: Khalid, Amal, Suha and Rula. **Educ.:** American University of Beirut, Lebanon; University of Iowa, USA; University of Damascus, Syria. **Career:** Economics Division Head, Statistics Dept. (1964-72); Director, Economic Dept., Royal Scientific Society (1973); Secretary General, National Planning Council (1976); Managing Director, Shair Management Services (1977-78); Director, Department of Statistics (1979); Managing Director, Jordan Pension Fund (1979-82); Managing Director, Jordan Phosphate Mines Co. (1983-92); Vice Chairman-Director General, The Business Bank (1992-97); Managing Director, The Jordan National Bank (1997-). **Directorships:** Amman Chamber of Commerce; First Deputy Chairman Amman Chamber of Industry; Jordan National Shipping Lines; Middle East Ins. Co.; Aqaba Port Authority; Vocational Training Corporation; Civil Service Commission; University of Jordan. **Sport:** Swimming. **Hobby:** Reading. **Member:** World Affairs Coucil; Royal Society for the Conservation of Nature. **Credit Cards:** American Express; Visa Card. **Prof. Addr.:** P.O.Box 3103, Tel.: 688474, Amman, Jordan. **Priv. Addr.:** P.O.Box (1130) Code (11821) Amman, Jordan, Tel.: 5527765.

AZHARI (Naaman, al), Syrian banker. **Born** in Syria. **Educ.:** University of Paris. **Dipl.:** Doctor in Law and Economics. **Career:** since 1951 banking career; Minister of Finance and Planning in Syria (1961-62); living in Lebanon since 1962; Chairman General Manager, Banque du Liban et d'Outre-Mer SAL; former Vice-Chairman, the Lebanese Banking Association. **Publ.:** Author of "L'Evolution du Système Economique Libanais" (1970). **Prof. Addr.:** General Management, Banque du Liban et d'Outre-Mer SAL, P.O.Box. 11-1912, Tel.: 346290, Beirut, Lebanon.

AZHARI (Ryad), Syrian Consul of the Netherlands and Shipping Agent. **Born** on January 6, 1930 in Lattakia, Syria. **Son** of late Azhari Majd el-Dine (Politician) **and** Mrs. Roueiha Zahideh. **Married** in 1957 to Mitrovic Miryana in Yougoslavia, three children, Nada (1958); Yasmina (1961); Lina (1964). **Educ.:** College des Frères, Lattakia, Syria; I.C. of the A.U.B; A.U.B.; **Dipl.:** B.A., M.A. in Political Science. **Career:** Lattakia Port Co. Administration (1956-62); Shipping as from (1962); Consul of the Netherlands (1970-). **Awards:** Medal of the "Oranje-Nassau"; Order in 1981, also "Officier" of the same Order in 1995 Bestowed by H.M. the Queen of Netherlands. **Sports:** Volley Ball, swimming. **Member:** AUB Alumni Club; Archeological Association. **Credit Cards:** American Express, Visa. **Prof. Addr.:** Consul of the Netherlands Baghdad Str. Chkeifeh Bldg., P.O.Box 242, Tel.: 234184, Telex: 451019, 451136 SY, Fax: 221329, Lattakia, Syria, and al-Joumhouriyah Str., Haffar and Hilbaoui Bldg., P.O.Box 3242, Tel.: 221646, Telex: 412425, Damascus, Syria, and Selim Jeanbart Str., Hamed Baki Bldg., P.O.Box 356, Tel.: 330331, Telex: 331526, Aleppo, Syria. **Priv. Addr.:** Baghdad Str., Tel.: 234637, Lattakia, Syria.

AZIZ (Abdelslam, al), Moroccan writer and journalist. **Born** in 1941 at Tetouan, Morocco. **Son** of Hamadi Al-Azir (Merchant) **and** Mrs., née Fatima al-Hadj. **Married** in Tanger to Miss Zohra Amiri, 2 children: Najib (1978), Iman (1979). **Educ.:** Escuela Muley Ismail Primaria, Tetouan: Instituto Marrouqui de Ensenaura Media, Tetouan: University al-Karouin, Fez; Escuela Telefonica, Madrid, **Career:** Teacher, College Ibn Baçal, Bel-Krizi (1962); Press Correspondent, Tanger (1965); Member of the newspaper "al-Anbaa" (1972); Broadcaster at the Moroccan Radio (1975); Attaché, Direction of Royal Records (1975); Press Attaché, National Cooperation (1975); Attaché, Ministry of Social Affairs (1979). **Work:** Author of several novels, studies and social research: Lahib et Horman, Aoulad al-hay al-mouhafez, Hacid al-Ayam, Lahazat Darira, Aourac al-Doufla, Wamazamir Saghira al-Tajriba fi; al-Oujtamaat al-Namiyah, Research paper; collaborating with Moroccan and Arabic newspapers and Magazines. **Sports:** Rambling. **Member.:** Moroccan Writers Association. **Priv. Addr.:** Av. Hassan II, al-Adarissa St. No.2, Rabat, Morocco.

AZIZ (Hassan), Egyptian businessman and industrialist. **Born** in Egypt. **Educ.:** Secondary and Higher. **Career:** President Egyptian Rice Mills, Near East Produce Trading, Vice-President and Director-General Egyptian Plastics and Electrical Industries, Director of The National Starch Co., The North East Africa Trading Co., Montazah and Moqattam Companies. **Member:** Yacht Club, Jockey Club, Automobile Club. **Addr.:** 109, Army Road, Ibrahimiah, Tel.: 73133, Alexandria, Egypt.

AZIZ-OUAZZANI (Kacem), Moroccan Teacher engaged in research. **Born** on March 17, 1934 in Fes. **Son** of Tayeb Aziz-Ouazzani **and** Mrs. Aicha Ben Maajouze. **Married** in 1960 in Meknes to Fatima Kricha, 3 children: Saloua, Mounya, Anas. **Educ.:** University of Carawiin, University Mohamed V, School Dar Al Hadith Al Hassania. **Dipl.:** Baccalaureate from University of Carawiin, Degree of Law from University Mohamed V, Master of Arts from School Dar Al Hadith Al Hassania. **Career:** Teacher in Primary School, then in Secondary School, and now at the University. **Work:** Different articles concerning Islamic studies and Arabic linguistics. **Awards:** Medal of National Merit, Medal of Throne. **Sport:** Jogging. **Hobby:** Tourism. **Prof. Addr.:** Department of Islamic Studies, University Moulay Ismail, Faculté des Lettres et Sciences Humaines, P.O.Box 4009, Meknes, Morocco. **Priv. Addr.:** 16, rue el-Wahabi Ali IM.B., P.O.Box 91, Meknes, Morocco.

AZIZ (Tareq), Iraqi politician. **Born** in 1936 in Mosul, Iraq. **Educ.:** English studies, College of Arts, Baghdad University. **Career:** Member, Editorial Staff, al-Jumhuriyah newspaper (1958); Chief Editor, al-Jamaheer (April 1963); Worked for the Baath press (Syria) (till February 1966); Chief-Editor, al-Thawra (1969); Head, al-Thawra Publishing House; Member, Revolutionary Command Council General Affairs Bureau (1972); Reserve member, Arab Baath Socialist Party Leadership (January 1974); Minister of Information (11 November 1974- 15 October 1977); Member, Baath Regional Leadership (January 1977); Deputy Prime Minister (16 July 1979); Deputy Prime Minister and Minister for Foreign Affairs (24 January 1983- March 1991); Deputy Prime Minister (March 1991-). **Addr.:** Minister's Office, Baghdad, Iraq.

AZIZA (Muhammad, Sadeq), Tunisian academic. **Born** in 1940 in Tunis, Tunisia. **Married,** 1 son. **Educ.:** Paris University, Sorbonne. **Dipl.:** LL.B., M.A. in Literature, Ph.D. in Islamic Studies. **Career:** Chargé de Mission, Ministry of Information and Culture (1970-72); Information Director, Organisation of African Unity in Addis Ababa, Ethiopia (1972-75); Chairman of the International Consultative Council, the International Cultural Centre, Hammamet, Tunisia (1984); President of the Euro-Arab University Association (1985). **Publ.:** "La Calligraphie Arabe", Société Tunisienne de Diffusion (1971), "L'image de l'Islam", Paris (1982), "L'astrolabe de la Mer", Paris (1980), "Le Livre des celebrations" Paris (1984). **Decor.:** Knight of the Order of Arts and Letters, French Ministry of Culture (1985). **Priv. Addr.:** Tunis, Tunisia.

AZIZI (Abdul Aziz Bin Mattar, al, H.E.), Omani Minister of Civil Service. **Born** in 1961 in Dhank, Oman. **Son** of Mattar Salim Al Azizi. **Married** 10 children: 8 sons and 2 daughters. **Educ.:** High School. **Dipl.:** Internal Government - U.K. **Career:** 25 May 1981 Assistant/hri Mayor Office, Oman; 1 September 1987 Mayor Assistant Mahadha, Oman; 15 Sept. 1989 Mayor Assistant Al Buraimi, Oman; 1 August 1990 Mayor Bahla, Oman; 15 July 1991 Mayor Nizwa, Oman; 19 December 1995- Minister - Ministry of Civil Service. **Sports Practised:** Soccer. **Hobbies:** Watch soccer games. **Credit Cards:** American Express, Diner's Club, Visa, Master. **Prof. Addr.:** P.O.Box 3994, Ruwi, P.C. 112, Tel.: (698)698390, Sultanate of Oman.

AZMEH (Abdallah, al, Dr.), Syrian bank manager. **Born** in 1928 in Damascus, Syria. **Son** of Mohamad Fauzi al-Azmeh. **Married** in 1952, 5 children. **Educ.:** The Syrian University; Lausanne University, Switzerland. **Dipl.:** License in Law (1951); Diploma in Graduate Studies (Econ. Inst.) (1958); License in Economic and Commercial Sciences (1958); Ph.D. (Economics and Commerce) (1961). **Career:** Deputy Minister, for Monetary and Banking Affairs. Ministry of Economy and Trade, Syria; Director, Public Debt Fund, Ministry of Finance, Syria; Member, Banking Advisory Council; Division Head, Arab Bank, Damascus; Director of Finance, General Organization of Electricity, Syria; Director of Economic Affairs, Ministry of Petroleum and Electricity; Director, Bureau of Petroleum Marketing; Member, Finance and Banking Committee, Council of Ministers; Adviser, Bureau of Audits; Member, Administrative Committee for the General Organisation of Electricity; Deputy Chairman, Administrative Committees of Industrial, Petroleum Organisations; Chairman, Board, General Authority of Free Zones; Chairman, Board, Postal Saving System; Certified Public Accountant; Vice-President, Syrian Economic Association, Lecturer, Financial Planning, Institute of National Planning; Member of the Board, Union des Banques Arabes et Européennes (UBAE) Rome; **General Manager** Union des Banques Arabes et Européennes SA; Member of the Board, Arab Bank for Economic Development in Africa; Member, Council of Money and Credit, Central Bank of Syria. **Addr.:** Damascus, Syria.

AZMEH (Aziz, Malak), Syrian academic. **Born** in July 23, 1947 in Damascus, Syria. **Educ.:** Tubingen University, West Germany; Oxford University, UK. **Dipl.:** M.A., Ph.D. in Islamic History and Culture. **Career:** Adviser and Consultant to various Arab and International Educational and Cultural Organizations; Lecturer at Arab and Western Universities (1978-); fellow of British Society of Middle East Studies; Member of the Arab Philosophical Society; Member of the National Conference of University Professors; Member of the Arab Club (London); former Chairman of the Arab Human Rights Organization, UK Branch; Professor of Islamic Studies, University of Exeter (1985-). **Publ.:** "Ibn Khaldoun in Modern Scholarship", London

(1982), "Historical Writing and Historical Culture", Beirut (1983); "Ibn Khaldoun An Essay", London (1983); "Arabic Thought and Islamic Societies", London (1986); "Arabs and Barbarians", London (1991); "Secularism", Beirut (1992); "Islams and Modernities" (1993). **Awards:** Recipient of the Republican Order of Merit, Tunisia, to Services and Arab Culture. **Prof. Addr.:** Department of Arabic and Islamic Studies, University of Exeter, Old Library, Prince of Wales Road; Exeter EX4 4JZ, Tel.: (0392)264028, 263263, Telex: 42894 EXUNIV G, United Kingdom.

AZMEH (Issam), Jordanian bank manager. **Born** in 1928 in Amman, Jordan. **Son** of Abdel Azmeh. **Married** in 1954, 3 children. **Educ.:** B.A. in Law and Economic Sciences. **Career:** Manager, Arab Bank (Overseas) Ltd., Geneva; President, Arab Swiss Chamber of Commerce and Industry. **Hobbies:** Arabic history, swimming, tennis and skiing. **Addr.:** Arab Bank (Switzerland) Limited, P.O.Box 5281, Talacker 21, CH 8022, Zurich, Switzerland.

AZRAQ (Abdulwahab, al), United Arab Emirates lawyer. **Born** in 1919, in Aleppo, Syria. **Married,** eight children. **Educ.:** LL.B., Damascus University, Syria and Paris University, France. **Career:** Secretary, Syrian Chamber of Deputies; Director General of the Military Court; Director General of Syrian Customs; First Attorney in the Civil Court; Head of Administration of Syrian Government Affairs; member of the Syrian Higher Council for Science and Law; Lecturer in the Institute of Commerce and Law; Attorney General in the United Arab Emirates. **Addr.:** Attorney General's Office, P.O.Box 753, Tel.: 45765, 43737, Abu Dhabi, United Arab Emirates.

AZZABI ALI (Ridha), Tunisian engineer. **Born** on September 17, 1932 in Tunis, Tunisia. **Married:** one son. **Educ.:** Graduated in Mathematics and Physics, Sorbonne, University of Paris, France; postgraduate studies in Petroleum Engineering, France. **Career:** Chief Engineer of the Bizerta Oil Refinery (1963-64); Chief City Engineer of Tunis (1964-69); Governor of Nabeul (1969-71); Director of the National Tourist Office (1971-74); Director General of the District of Tunis, Ministry of the Interior (1975); Head of Public Works Planning (1976); Vice-President, Syndicate of Tunisian Contractors (1980); Mayor of Marsa, Tunis (1982-85); Vice-President, Institut Arabe des Chefs d'Entreprises, and the National Exporters Federation (1985); Member, Executive Committee, Arab Union of Contractors (1983-86); Chairman, Cie. Méditerranéenne de Travaux (C.O.M.E.T.R.A.) (1988); P.D.G. Industries Chimiques du Fluor. **Decor:** Officer of the Order of the Republic (1968). **Sports:** Football. **Member:** President of National Football Federation (1969). **Addr.:** Tunis, Tunisia.

AZZABI (Ayyad, Muhammad), Libyan official. **Born** in 1936 in Tripoli, Libya. **Career:** Director, Commercial Agencies Department; Ministry of Economic Affairs in late 1960s; Study Fellowship, Jesus College, Oxford, United Kingdom (1968-69); Ministry of Industry (1969); Under Secretary, Secretariat of the General People's Committee for Industry; has led Libyan economic team in negotiations for union with Egypt. Director of National Oil Company (1970). **Addr.:** Tripoli, Libya.

AZZAM (André-Mounir, Afif), Egyptian journalist. **Born** in 1945 in Cairo. **Son** of Afif Azzam (Professor) **and** Mrs., née Adeline Alfred Atallah. **Educ.:** College de la Sainte Famille (1948-62), Faculty of Arts, Cairo University (1964-67). **Dipl.:** Secondary Education Certificate (1963), Bachelor of Arts (French Literature 1967). **Career:** Press Reporter on the staff of the French News Agency (Cairo, 1968-76), then entered the "development" field in a private organisation working in rural areas in Upper-Egypt where he specialised in external relations, information, setting up of projects, arts and crafts and economic development projects. **Sports:** Walking, Swimming and Tennis. **Hobbies:** Crafts and old things and monuments. **Prof. Addr.:** The Christian Association of Upper-Egypt for Schools and Social Promotion 85 A, Ramses Avenue, Cairo, Tel.: 752381- 754723. (Egypt). **Priv. Addr.:** 13, Hegaz Street, Heliopolis, Cairo, Tel.: 864277, Egypt.

AZZAWI (Hikmat, Ibrahim, al), Iraqi politician. **Born** in 1934 in Iraq. **Educ.:** College of Commerce and Economics. **Career:** Reserve Lieutenant (1957-58); Central Bank (1958-63); First Superintendent, Central Bank (1963); Auditor, Directorate of Stores and Warehouses, Directorate of Marketing, State Company for Electrical Instruments and Equipment (1966-68); Director General and Chairman of Government Purchasing Board (1968); Chairman, General Establishment of Trade (1969); Member of Board of Directors, Central Bank (1969); Under Secretary in the Ministry of Economy (1969); Minister of Economy (1972-76); Minister of Foreign Trade (1976-77); Minister of State for Kurdish Affairs (1977); Governor, Central Bank of Iraq (1985-89). **Member** of Iraqi Baath Party (1977); member of Iraqi Economists Association. **Addr.:** Baghdad, Iraq.

AZZI (Abderrahmane), Algerian Professor at the Institute of Information and Communication, University of Algiers, Algeria. **Born** on August 18, 1954 in Beni-Ourtilane, Bedjaia, Algeria. **Married,** 2 children. **Educ.:** University of Algiers, North Texas State University, Denton, Texas, USA. **Dipl.:** B.A. in Journalism at the University of Algiers; M.A. in Journalism at North Texas State University; M.A. and Ph.D. in Sociology at North Texas State University. **Career:** Editor of the Annales de l'Université d'Alger (1990-1933); Vice-Chancellor in charge of Higher Education of the University of Algiers, (1990-1993); presently Professor at the Institute of Information and Communication, University of Algiers, Algeria. **Publ.:** Author of many publications on mass media and communication.

Sport: Footing. **Hobbies:** Reading and travelling. **Prof. Addr.:** ISIC, 11 Doudou Mokhtar, Ben Aknoun, Algiers, Algeria.

AZZI (Bah'a Ibn Hussein), Saudi consultant. **Born** in 1933 in Medina, Saudi Arabia. **Dipl.:** B.A. (Economics and Political Science), King Saud University; Ph.D., UWIST, United Kingdom. **Career:** Assistant General Manager Administration Department, Royal Saudi Air Force; Economic Researcher, Petromin; Administrative Manager, SAFCO, Petroship; Managing Director, Petronal; Presided over a Petromin team for Rabigh Refinery; member, Arab Club in Britain, Arab Horse Society of Britain; former member of the Board, SAFCO, Petronal; former member, Executive Committee, Petroship; former alternate member of the Board, AMPTC. **Publ.:** "Shipping and Development in Saudi Arabia", (in English) and "The Arabs to where and the world to where", in Arabic. **Hobbies:** Home design, construction, farming, Arab horse breeding. **Addr.:** P.O.Box 7880, Tel.: 6711649, 6711650 (Office), and 6655026 (Home), Jeddah, Saudi Arabia.

AZZIMAN (OMAR), Moroccan Academic and Minister of Justice. **Born** on October 17, 1947 at Tetouan, Morocco. **Son** of Mhamed Azziman (Professor, retired) **and** Mrs. née Rkia Lebbadi. **Married** to Ijlal Bennani born in Tanger (Morocco) 17/09/1954, 3 children: Zineb (09.05.75), Amine (22.02.80), Ali (05.12.86). **Educ.:** Colegio del Pilar (Tetouan), Lycée Gouraud (Rabat), Lycée Descartes (Rabat), Faculty of Law (Rabat), Université de Paris (France) Université de Nice (France). **Dipl.:** Licence in Private Law, diploma "Etudes Supérieures en droit des Affaires", Doctorat d'Etat in private Law, **Career:** *University Career in Morocco:* Professor, Faculty of Law, Université Mohammed V-Agdal-Rabat since 1972; Professor, Ecole Nationale d'Administration Publique-Rabat; Professor at the Académie Militaire; Member of Jury of "Concours d'agrégation de droit privé"; Titular of the Chair UNESCO for Human rights since 1996. *Abroad:* Visiting Professor, Faculty of Law of Tunis (Tunisia), Algiers, (Algeria); Visiting Professor to IREMAM (Aix-en Provence-France), IMA in Paris and IDLI (Rome-Italy); Correspondent at the "Institut international pour l'Unification du Droit Privé" (Rome) since 1990. **Other activities:** Consultant Lawyer at the Bar of Rabat since 1972; Member of the Higher Council of "Système euro-Arabe de conciliation et d'arbitrage"; Member of "Comité Averroès pour le rapprochement des peuples espagnole et marocain"; Representative of Morocco at the Annual sessions of the United Nations Commission for Commercial Law (1988-1993); Member of several diplomatic missions in Central and Latin America; Member of the conciliation commission for the settlement of various problems related to the struggle against discrimination in Education in UNESCO (1995); Legal Adviser of National Council of the Order of Engineers since 1996; Expert-consultant jurist at the Ministry of Privatization (Project of PNUD, 1992-93); Member of the experts commission of the Ministry of Finance for the preparation of insurance code (1991); Member of the Hispano-Moroccan commission for the juridical studies of the project for the detroit of Gibraltar. *Political:* Minister delegate to the Prime Minister in charge of Human Rights (1993-1995), President delegate to the "Fondation Hassan II pour les Marocains" residents Abroad (since 1997), **Minister of Justice (since 1997). Other Information:** Permanent Member of the "Académie du Royaume du Maroc" since 1996. **Publications:** "Etudes sur les structures juridiques des Banques au Maroc", these de 3ème cycle, Paris 1972; "Edude sur la profession libérale au Maroc, collection de la Faculté des sciences juridiques, économiques et sociales: - Rabat 1980; "Droit des obligations", Volume 1, le contrat, Editions le Fennec, 1995; Participation collective works in articles for national and foreign magasines; Editing for synthesis, colloquies and seminars; Director, co-director and scientific director of several national & international reviews. **Awards:** Knight of Order of the Throne (Morocco), 1995; Grand Cordon of the Order of Merit, Portugal Republic, 1998; Commander, Legion of Honor, French Republic, 1999. **Sports practised:** Walking. **Hobby:** Reading. **Association:** *in Morocco:* Founder/Member and former President of "Organisation Marocaine des Droits de l'Homme (OMDH); Founder/Member and Member of the Scientific Committee of "Groupe d'Etudes et de Recherches sur la Mediterranée" (G.E.R.M.); Founder/Member and Vice-President of the Association "AFAK" for the development and citizenship. *Abroad:* Founder/Member and Member of the Board of "Association Maghrébine des Juristes Universitaires" (Tunisia); Founder/Member of "Cercle de Sociology et Nomologie Juridiques (France); Member of "Association Internationale de Droit Economique" (Belgium); Member of "Instituto di studie e programmi per il mediterranee (Italy). **Professional Address:** Ministry of Justice, Place Mamounia, P.O.Box 1015, Rabat-Morocco, Tel.: (00 212 7) 730708/721589.

AZZOUNI (Mustafa Kamal Salem, al), Egyptian businessman. **Born** in 1922 in Alexandria, Egypt. **Married,** 2 sons. **Educ.:** Armed Forces Staff College, Cairo University. **Dipl.:** M.Sc. in Military Sciences. **Career:** Chief of Strategic Planning Department at the Armed Forces General Headquarters (1955-62); Professor, Academy of Postgraduate Studies, Armed Forces General headquarters; Under Secretary of State, Central Agency of Organisation and Administration, at the Presidency of the Arab Republic of Egypt; Under Secretary of State, Managerial Efficiency Evaluation Sector; Chief Executive Officer and Chairman of Universal Agencies Company. **Decor.:** Several military decorations. **Hobbies:** Hunting, fishing, geology, exploration. **Member:** Gezira Sporting Club, Armed Forces Club. **Prof. Addr.:** 197 26th July Street, Appt. 33, Agouza, Giza, Greater Cairo, Egypt. **Priv. Addr.:** 4 El-Sad Al-Aly Street, Apt. 30, Dokki, Giza, Egypt.

AZZOUZ (Amar), Algerian politician. **Born** in 1934. **Married. Dipl.:** B.A. in Sociology. **Career:** Member of the FLN Civil Organisation, Technical Adviser to the Wilaya; Assistant Director for Social Service, Ministry of Works and Social Affairs; Deputy National Popular Assembly, General Secretary, Sub-Committee on Mass Party Organisations, FLN, Deputy Minister of Works; Director General, National Office of Manual Work; Director of Employment and Human Resources, Then Secretary General, Ministry of Works and Social Affairs. **Addr.:** Algiers, Algeria.

B

BAALASSANE (Mamadou), Mauritanian politician. **Born** in 1936 in Maghama (Southern Mauritania). **Son** of Bâ Alassane (Marabout). **Educ.:** Primary education at Maghama, Rosso College, Lycée Faidherbe of Saint-Louis; Teacher's Training School William Ponty, Dakar, Senegal (1953); Ecole Normale Supérieure, Saint Could, France (1961-62); Faculty of Human Studies and Letters, Sorbonne, Paris (1969-70). **Dipl.:** B.A. (Philosophy). **Career:** Schoolmaster at Bababé (1958-59), Deputy Inspector of Primary Education at Kaédi (1962-63); Inspector of Primary Education at Rosso (1966-67), at Aioin-el-Atrouss (1958); Minister of Youth and Sports (Dec. 1973- Aug. 1975); Minister in charge of Administrative Affairs at the PPM Secretariat (1975- June 1976); Minister of Information and Tele-communications (June 1976). **Member:** Parti du Peuple Mauritanien (PPM), and of Bureau Politique du PPM (Party of PPM suspended following coup in 1978). **Addr.:** Nouakchott, Mauritania.

BAASHER (Taha, Ahmad), Sudanese international officer. **Born** on June 2, 1922 in Suakin, Red Sea (Sudan). **Married**, with children. **Educ.:** Kitchner School of Medicine, Khartoum Sudan (1942-48), Institute of Psychiatry, University of London (1954-56). **Dipl.:** M.D., B.Sc. (Psychiatry), DPM. **Career:** Senior Psychiatrist, Sudan (1957-69); Minister of Labour, Khartoum (1969-70); Minister of Health, Khartoum (1970-71); Regional Adviser in Mental Health, Regional Officer for the East Mediterranean, World Health Organisation (WHO), Alexandria, Egypt since 1972. **Publ.:** "Survey of Mental Health in Wadi Halfa" (1961), "Some aspects of the history of the treatment of mental disorders in the Sudan" (1963), "The Influence of culture on psychiatric manifestations" (1963), "Treatment and Prevention of Psychosomatic Diseases" (1965), "Psychiatric Study in Sudanese Children" (1968), "Problems of Psychiatric cure in developing countries" (1968). **Awards:** Fellow, Royal College of Psychiatry (1973). **Member:** World Federation of Mental Health, Association of Psychiatrists in Africa, Sudanese National Association for Mental Health, Arts Society, Alexandria, (Egypt). **Sports:** Tennis, swimming. **Hobbies:** History, literature. **Prof. Addr.:** WHO, P.O.Box 1517, Tel.: 30090, Alexandria, Egypt. **Priv. Addr.:** 55, rue Ahmed Zulficar, Laurens, Ramleh, Tel.: 30090, Alexandria, Egypt.

BABA (Kamal, Tawfic, al), Syrian politician. **Born** in 1940 in Aleppo, Syria. **Married**, 2 sons. **Educ.:** in East Germany. **Dipl.:** Degree in Electrical Engineering (1965). **Career:** Director of Electricity, Kamishli Region, Syria (1965-66), Northern Region (1977-84); Minister of Electrical Resources (1984 to June 1994). **Addr.:** Damascus, Syria.

BABBAH (Mohamade, Ould), Mauritanian politician. **Born** in 1935 in Akjout (Western Mauritania). **Married**, with Lahbiba, 3 children. **Educ.:** In the purest Muslim tradition and its classical humanism, Koran school in Boutlimit (1945-49), University of Beirut, Lebanon (1960-61); Sorbonne (Paris) for the preparation of Ph.D. Arab philology (1962-64); University of Dakar (Senegal), for studies in French philology (1967-68). **Dipl.:** B.A. (Arabic Language, 1969), Ph.D. (Philology) and diploma of higher studies (1970). **Career:** Inspector of Primary Arab Education (1961-62); professor, Lycée National of Nouakchott (1964-65); Inspector of Studies, Lycée National of Nouakchott (1965-66); Principal, Lycée National of Nouakchott (1966-70); Professor, Ecole Normale Supérieure, Nouakchott (1970-71); Minister of Technical and Vocational Training and Higher Education (1971-73); Minister of National Education (Dec. 1973- Aug. 1975); Minister of Fundamental Education (1975). **Publ.:** several research papers. **Member:** Mauritanian Youth Association, Parti du Peuple Mauritanien (PPM), (Party suspended following Coup in 1978); Mauritanian Students Association. **Hobbies:** Literature, Moorish history. **Addr.:** Nouakchott, Mauritania.

BABLI (Rafic, Muhammad, al), Egyptian architect. **Born** in 1932 in Banha, Egypt. **Married. Educ.:** Cairo University. **Dipl.:** B.Sc. in Architecture. **Career:** Architect, Popular Housing Company (1957-62); Private Practice (1962-). **Member:** Gezira Sporting Club. **Prof. Addr.:** 1 Talaat Harb Square, Cairo, Egypt. **Priv. Addr.:** 22 Taha Hussein St., Zamalek, Cairo, Egypt.

BACCOUCHE (Hedi), Tunisian politician. **Born** on January 15, 1930. **Educ.:** Secondary. **Dipl.:** Licencié-ès-Lettres, Sorbonne (France), Institute of Political Sciences (Paris). **Career:** President, Federation of Neo-Destour (France and Europe); Secretary-General of the Tunisian Youth; Deputy Director, Destourian Socialist Party; Governor of Bizerta and Sfax; President, Director, Social Security in Tunis; Minister of Social Affairs and Labour (Sept. 1987), Prime Minister (Nov. 1987- April 1989); Presently Ambassador to Algeria. **Awards:** Recipient of distinctions from Morocco, Niger, Finland, Roumania, Jordan, Lebanon and Tunisia. **Addr.:** Tunis, Tunisia.

BACHIR EL BOUHALI (Mourad), Moroccan General Director of the Office for Industrial Development (O.D.I.). **Born** on November 29, 1951 in Rabat, Morocco. **Married**, 3 children. **Educ.:** University of Bordeaux, France. **Dipl.:** Master of Business and Administration, Bordeaux; Doctorate of Management, Bordeaux. **Career:** Assistant Professor in the University of Bordeaux (1979); Chargé de Mission in IDI, France (1980); Central Bank of Morocco (1983); General Director of the Office for Industrial Development (1984- present). **Sports:** Tennis, Jumping, Hunting. **Addr.:** Office for Industrial Development, 10 Rue Ghandi, P.O.Box 211, Tel.: 70.66.30, Rabat, Morocco.

BACHIRI (Mohamed, Mamoun), Moroccan engineer. **Born** in 1948 in Berkane, Morocco. **Married**, 2 sons. **Educ.:** Ecole Mohammadia d'Ingenieurs, Rabat; Institut Portuaire d'Etude et de Recherche, le Havre, France. **Career:** Divisional Head of Public Works, Berkane (1969-76); Deputy Head of Ports in Morocco, Ministry of Public Works (1976-83); President of the Association des Ingenieurs de l'Ecole Mohammadia, Founder/Editor in Chief of the "el-Handassa al-Watania" Revue (1980-84); Regional Manager, Tensift District, Ministry of Equipment (1983); President in 1987 and life Member of the National Council, Social Works Foundation at the Ministry of Equipment (1985); Director of Planning for the "Formation Professionnelle" (1984-); in 1991 President du Groupe pour l'Investissement et le developpement "G.I.D." - Société Holding au Capital de 15 Millions de DH. Constituée par 300 Ingenieurs et Hauts Cadres. **Addr.:** Rabat, Morocco.

BADAWI (Abdel Halim), Egyptian diplomat. **Born** on July 26, 1930 in Egypt. **Married,** 2 sons. **Educ.:** Cairo University. **Career:** Joined Egyptian Foreign Service (1951); posts at Egyptian Embassies in London, Yaounde, Cameroun (1953-61); Minister Counsellor, London (1974-76); Counsellor, Egyptian Mission to UN, New York (1966-71); Deputy Permanent Representative (1976-78); Permanent Representative (1986-89); former Ambassador to Portugal; Assistant to Minister of Foreign Affairs, Cairo (1982-86). **Addr.:** Ministry of Foreign Affairs, Tahrir Square, Cairo, Egypt.

BADAWI al-MOULASSAM (Yacoub, al), Pen name of **OUWAIDAT**, Jordanian Writer, Journalist. **Born** in Jordan. **Educ.:** Privately. **Career:** Writer, journalist, contributed to several newspapers, including "Ad Dad" (edited in Aleppo). **Publ.:** Author of several books, e.g. "Islam Napoleon" (1937), "Al-Qafila al Mansiya" (1940), "An Natiqoun bid Dad fil Amerikiyyatain" (1946 and 1956), "A Sira'am Taawon fi Falistine" (1947), "Fawzi al-Maalouf" (1948), "Dik al-Jinn al-Homsi" (1948), "Ibrahim Toukane" (1957), "Arar ash Shaer" (1958), "Ours wa Ma'tam" (1959), "Sulaiman al-Boustani" (1963), "Issa Iskandar al-Maalouf" (1964), "Shoukri Sha'sha'a" (1964), "Alwane ala Tabaq" (1965), "Fathallah Sakkal" (1967), "Antara", "Aboul Qassem ach-Chabbi", "Walieddine Yakan", "Ayya Zamane", "A'lam al-Adab fi Falistine" (Manuscripts). **Addr.:** Amman, Jordan.

BADAWI (Hussein, Saad, el), Egyptian emeritus professor, faculty of medicine, Alexandria, Egypt. **Born** on June 23, 1922 in Alexandria, Egypt. **Son** of Saad el-Badawi (Director Arab League) **and** Mrs. Nefisa née Bakir. **Married** in 1946 in Alexandria to Zahra Shourbagy, 2 children: Tarek (1947), Daher (1949). **Educ.:** University of Alexandria. **Dipl.:** MB BCH, M.D. General Medicine (1949). **Career:** Lecturer in Medicine (1949); Assistant Professor (1959); Professor (1964); Physician Cardiology; presently Emeritus Professor, Faculty of Medicine, Alexandria. **Other Information:** President, Pan African Society of Cardiology; Professor, Alexandria Medical Association. **Sports:** Tennis. **Hobby:** Travel. **Member:** Egyptian Society of Cardiology; Alexandria Medical Association; Pan African Society of Cardiology. **Credit Cards:** Alexandria Sporting Club; Yacht Club. **Addr.:** 10 Abany Pacha Str., Zizenia, Alexandria, Egypt.

BADAWI (Mohamed Badawi Ismail), Egyptian journalist. **Born** on February 12, 1934 in Egypt. **Educ.:** Cairo University. **Dipl.:** B.A. in Journalism. **Career:** Head of Studies Department, "al-Akhbar" newspaper, Cairo; Assistant Editor-in-Chief, "al-Etihad" newspaper, Abu Dhabi, UAE; formerly Managing Editor of "al-Wafd" newspaper, Cairo. **Publ.:** "Sectarian Strife" - "Origins and Causes", "Victims and Martyrs from Islamic History". **Hobbies:** Chess and reading. **Addr.:** 3 el-Moayed Street, Roxy, Heliopolis, Cairo, Egypt.

BADAWI (Mohamed, Mustafa), Egyptian academic residing in United Kingdom. **Born** in 1925 in Alexandria, Egypt. **Married,** 1 son, 3 daughters. **Educ.:** Alexandria University, Egypt, London and Oxford. **Dipl.:** B.A., M.A. and Ph.D. **Career:** Research Fellow at Alexandria University, Egypt (1947-54); Lecturer (1954-60); Professor of English (1960-64); Lecturer, Brasenose College (1964-1992); Fellow of St. Antony's College (1967-); Visiting Professor, University of Kuwait (1973), University of Alexandria (1977); Lecturer at Oxford University; (1964-92); Member of the Committee of Correspondents for the Annual Bibliography of "Shakespeare Quarterly", Washington DC, USA (1961-80); UNESCO Expert on modern Arabic Culture (1974); Advisory Board Member, Cambridge History of Arabic Literature 1970-); Co-founder and Editor of the "Journal of Arabic Literature" Leiden (1970-96); Awarded King Faisal International Prize in Arabic Literature (1992). **Publ.:** "An Anthology of Modern Arabic Verse" (1970), "Coleridge; Critic of Shakespeare" (1973), "A Critical Introduction to Modern Arabic Poetry" (1975), "Background to Shakespeare" (1981); "Modern Arabic Literature and the West" (1985); "Modern Arabic Drama in Egypt" (1987); "Early Arabic

Drama" (1988); "The Cambridge History of Arabic Literature: Modern Arabic Literature", Ed. (1992); "A Short History of Modern Arabic Literature" (1993) as well as several books in Arabic. **Hobbies:** Music, comparative literature and theatre. **Prof. Addr.:** St. Antony's College, Oxford, OX2 6JF, United Kingdom.

BADDOU (Abderrahman), Moroccan politician. **Born** in 1925 in Meknes. **Educ.:** Juridical & administrative studies at Institut des Hautes-Etudes Marocaines, Rabat. **Career:** Active member of the Nationalist Movement in Rabat and other cities; excluded from Moroccan educational establishment in 1944 following his participation in manifestations asking for independence; arrested and imprisoned for political reasons in 1952; following became an active member of the Executive Committee of the Istiqlal Party; occupied senior functions at the Ministry of Justice for several years; elected deputy of Meknes (1963); reintegrated Ministry of Justice (1965); Ambassador to Saudi Arabia (1968) and to Lebanon (1971); Again Ambassador to Saudi Arabia (1972-75); represented Morocco in several international conferences; appointed Secretary of State for Foreign Affairs (1977). **Decor:** Order of His Majesty King Khaled Ibn Abdelaziz of Saudi Arabia (1st Category). **Addr.:** Rabat, Morocco.

BADER (Ali Abdul Rahman Rashid, al), Kuwaiti banking executive. **Born** in Kuwait 1949. **Son** of Abdul Rahman Rashid al-Bader. **Married** to Salwa A. Razzak Mahmoud al-Razouqi, five children. **Educ.:** Cairo University, Michigan State University. **Dipl.:** B.Sc. (Commerce); M.BA. **Career:** General Manager, Kuwait Real Estate Bank (till March 1987); Chairman and Managing Director of the Bank of Kuwait and the Middle East (1987). Also former Chairman of Arab African International Bank in Cairo. **Addr.:** Kuwait City, Kuwait.

BADIB (Ali Abdul Razzak), Yemeni politician. **Career:** former Ambassador to Democratic Republic of Germany; Ambassador to Rumania (1974-74); Minister of Culture and Tourism and Acting Minister of Information (1975); Member of Political Bureau of the Yemen Socialist Party; Deputy Prime Minister (1982). **Addr.:** Aden, Republic of Yemen.

BADKOOK (Mohamad Mohamad), Saudi businessman. **Born** in Jeddah, 1916. **Educ.:** B.Sc., Agriculture. **Career:** School teacher (1933-37); worked in the Ministry of Agriculture as Agricultural Engineer; Representative of the Ministry of Agriculture, the Western Province; Deputy Minister of Agriculture (1960-65); owner of Kilo-10 Garden Restaurant; former member of al-Yamamah Press Organization; attended the Conference on Agriculture and Nutrition, Cyprus (1951) and the Agriculture Fair, USSR (1957); contributed to several welfare associations. **Honour:** Silver medal from H.E. Mayor of Jeddah City. **Publ.:** some dialectic poems published in local newspapers. **Hobbies:** travel, reading. **Addr.:** P.O.Box 221, Tel.: 643499, (Office) and 6871603 (Home), Jeddah, Saudi Arabia.

BADOUL (Said Ibrahim), Djibouti Speaker/ President of the National Assembly. **Born** in 1944 at Gagadé (Dikhil). **Son** of Ibrahim Badoul (Notable) **and** Mrs. née Mariam Hassan. **Married,** on 5/8/1975, 8 children: Fatoum, Mariam, Mirah, Mohamed, Ibrahim, Fatouma, Abdoulkader, Arafat. **Educ.:** Secondary Studies. **Career:** Elected Deputy at the Chamber of Deputies (17 Nov. 1973); Member of the Opposition Parliamentarians (1975-1977); Elected Deputy at the National Assembly (1979-21 Nov. 1993); Elected **President** of the National Assembly (22 Nov. 1993- to date). **Member** of the National Reconciliation Mission. **Medals:** two times (Médaille du 27 Juin, Fête Nationale, (Commander). **Prof. Addr.:** Tel. 350172, and National Assembly, P.O.Box 138, Djibouti. **Priv. Addr.:** Tel.: 357140, Djibouti.

BADR ELDIN (Hamed Mohamed), Egyptian banker. **Born** on July 26, 1934 in Cairo. **Son** of Mohamed Badr el-Din. **Married,** one son. **Educ.:** Ain Shams University; Cairo University. **Dipl.:** B.Comm. (1954); Institute of Bankers, Cairo (1959); Post Graduate Diploma in Finance (1969). **Career:** Barclays Bank D.C.O.; Bank of Alexandria (from 1955 to 1973); Arab African Bank, Cairo (1965-66); Masraf Al-Goumhouria, Tripoli (1971-73); Arab African Bank H.O., Cairo (1973-81); General Manager, Delta International Bank (January 1991-1992); and Member of Board of Directors & Executive Committee, Misr Finance Investment Co. (1981 to date). **Member:** El-Shams Club; El-Ahly Club. **Priv. Addr.:** Sheikh Mohamed Salama Street, Nozha, Heliopolis, Cairo, Egypt.

BADR (Faiqah Mohamad, Mrs.), Saudi academic. **Born** in Mecca in 1949. **Dipl.:** B.A. (Education and Psychology); M.A. (Psychology). **Career:** Former lecturer and Director Students' Affairs, Umm al-Oura University; member of the Board of Umm al-Qura Welfare Society, Mecca; regular writer, Sayidaty, a weekly women's magazine; Lecturer, Faculty of Arts, King Abdulaziz University, Jeddah. **Member:** al-Faisaliyah Welfare Society. **Hobbies:** Reading, travel. **Addr.:** Faculty of Arts, King Abdulaziz University, Tel.: 6717726 (Office) and 6718955 (Home), Jeddah, Saudi Arabia.

BADR (Fayez Ibrahim), Saudi politician. **Born** in Mecca in 1936. **Educ.:** Primary, Preparatory and secondary at Falah School, Mecca, B.Com., Cairo University, M.A. and Ph.D. (Economics), University of Southern California, U.S.A. **Career:** Adviser to the President of the Central Planning Organization, Vice President of Central Planning Organization; Deputy Minister of Planning; member of the Royal Commission for the Development of Jubail and Yanbu Industrial Zones; supervised the formulation of the Kingdom's First Development Plan, (1970-75) and the Second Development Plan (1975-80); Chairman, Seaports

Authority, Riyadh; under Dr. Badr's administration, Saudi ports have achieved an international standard of efficiency; has presided over several conferences and symposia on ports and navigation in the U.K., France and the Gulf Region; Minister without portfolio (1986-1995). **Publ.:** numerous articles, research papers and specialized reports. **Hobbies:** reading, swimming. **Prof. Addr.:** Seaports Authority, P.O.Box 5162, Riyadh 11188, Saudi Arabia.

BADR (Hamoud Abdel Aziz, al), Saudi academic. **Born** in Alzilfi in 1939. **Educ.:** Ph.D. (Public Relations and Education). **Career:** Secretary General of the Shoura Council (1993-to present); Professor of Education and Public Relations (1988-1993); Chairman of Saudi Society for Education & Psychology; Former Vice-President, King Saud University, Riyadh (1976-88); Former journalist al-Yamama newspaper, (1964-65); Director of Foreign Relations and Conferences' Department, Ministry of Labour, (1963-64); Dean of Adminissions and Registration, King Saud University, Riyadh, (1975-76); President, Marakh Club at Alzilfi, (1973-75); President, Saudi Gymnastics Federation; member, Arab College Registrars and Accreditation Organization, American College Registrars and Accreditation Organization (ACRAO); member of the Board. Institute of Public Administration. **Publ.:** al-Bilad Newspaper, Material and Layout; the 80 Years of the Saudi Press (a chapter of a book published in 1961); Public Relations in King Saud and King Abdulaziz Universities; Public Relations Basics and Application (in Arabic); This is Islam (in Arabic) as well as several research papers on Education and Communication (in Arabic). **Hobbies:** reading, swimming. **Prof. Addr.:** P.O.Box 263, Tel.: 4881837, Riyadh. **Priv. Addr.:** Tel.: 476-7215, Riyadh, Saudi Arabia.

BADR (Mansour Ibrahim Yusuf), Saudi businessman. **Born** in 1944. **Educ.:** B.A. (International Relations). **Career:** Chairman Mansour Group of Companies. Aide to Minister of Planning, Ministry of Planning, (1972-75); Chairman, Board of Directors, Mansour-General Dynamics Ltd., Saudiphic Construction Company, Mansour Travel and Tourism and United Advertising Company. **Addr.:** P.O.Box 3362, 4643989, Riyadh, 11471 Saudi Arabia.

BADR (Mansour, Mohamed), Libyan politician. **Born** in 1931 in Libya. **Married. Educ.:** Extensive military training in Turkey and UK for army. **Career:** Joined Libyan Armed Forces (1954); Army officer, First Commanding Officer of Libyan Navy on its foundation (1962); Chairman of the Marine Transport Corp.; Minister of Marine Transport (1974-77); Secretary of Marine Transport, General People's Committee (1977). **Addr.:** Tripoli, Libya.

BADR (Mohamed, Abdel-Latif), Egyptian University Professor. **Born** in Cairo, Egypt. **Son** of Abdel-Latif Badr (Geographist, Teacher) **and** Mrs. Esmat Al-Mofty. **Married** on August 1968 at Alexandria, Egypt, to Samira El-Sissi, 2 children: Ali (December 1, 1972), Mai (October 1, 1978). **Educ.:** Ain Shams University, Cairo, Egypt 1960-1965 (B. Sc.; Electrical Engineering); Ain Shams University, Cairo, Egypt 1966-1969 (M.Sc. Program); Polytechnical Institute of Leningrad, USSR 1970-1975 (Ph.D. Program); University of Calgary, Canada 1980-1982 (Post Doctor Fellow). **Dipl.:** B. Sc. Ain Shams University (1965), M. Sc. Ain Shams University (1969), Ph.D. Polytechnical Institute, Leningrad (1974). **Career:** Part-Time Professor, American University in Cairo (1983-1988); Associate Professor, Ain Shams University (1979-1984); Professor of Electrical Engineering, Ain Shams University, since 1984; Head of Department of Electrical Engineering, Qatar University, since 1989. **Work:** Teaching, Research Work, Consultancy. **Other Information:** Expert in Power System Analysis and Control, Computer Applications in Power Systems, Automatic Control Systems. **Awards:** Honors of Graduation. **Sports:** Swimming, Scouts. **Hobbies:** Electric Model Trains, Arabic Literature. **Member:** Senior Member IEEE. **Prof. Addr.:** Qatar University, P.O.Box 2713, Tel.: (0974) 892092, Doha, Qatar. **Priv. Addr.:** Al Sadd Str., Darwish Bldg., Tel.: (0974) 441589, Doha, Qatar.

BADR (Zaki, Maj. Gen.), Egyptian former minister. **Born** 28 February 1926 in Menoufiyeh. **Educ.:** Police Force Academy. **Dipl.:** Graduated from Police Force Academy in 1946. **Career:** Joined the Police Force where he worked his way up to Director of Criminal Investigations; Director of Galiyoubiyeh Security, then Director of Public Security, Ministry of the Interior; Assistant to the Minister of the Interior, Central Zone; Governor, Asiyut Governorate (1982); Minister of the Interior (1988-89). **Addr.:** Cairo, Egypt.

BADRAH (Abdul Rasheed Ahmad), Saudi businessman and industrialist. **Born** in 1927 in Mecca, Saudi Arabia. **Career:** Chairman and General Manager of Badrah Saudi Factories, Jeddah; Has been working in the sweets and biscuits industry for the last 20 years; his factories have a production capacity of 12,000 tons of sweets and 12,000 tons of biscuits; Established housing units for factory workers. **Member** of Jeddah Chamber of Commerce. **Addr.:** Badrah Saudi Factories, P.O.Box 1678, Tel.: 6430255, Jeddah 21441, Saudi Arabia.

BADRAKHAN (Ali, Ahmad), Egyptian film director. **Born** on 25/4/1946 in Cairo, Egypt. **Position:** Director of "Feature Films and Children Films Department" in Egyptian Film Center. Professor of "Film Directing" in Cinema High Institute. Consultant for the National Center for Child Culture. **STUDIES AND QUALIFICATIONS:** B.A. of Cinema High Institute - Egypt in 1967; Training scholarship in Italy at "RED" and "TCINI TCITA" studios in 1967/1968; Member of jury committees of several national and international festivals, last one is Damascus International Film Festival 1991. **PROFESSIONAL WORKS:**

Worked as an assistant film director in 17 films during the period 1963-1970. Most important films are: "Sayed Darwish", Director Ahmed Badrakhan; "Nadia", Director Ahmed Badrakhan; "El nas w'alnil, People and the Nile", Director Youssef Chahine; co-production "Egypt-Soviet Union" "Al'ikhtyar, The Choice", Director Youssef Chahine; "Al'Asfour, The Sparrow", Director Youssef Chahine; "El-Fallah El-Fasieh, The Fluent Farmer", Director Shadi Abdel Salam. **FILM DIRECTOR: A. FEATURE FILMS: 1973** "El-hob Al'lazi Kan, The Past Love" Starring: Soa'd Hosni, Mahmoud Yasin & Mahmoud El-Meligi. The best film in 1973 from "Egyptian Cinema Critics Association". Represented Egypt in "Tashkand Festival" Soviet Union, 1974. **1975** "Al-Karnak" Starring: Soa'd Hosni, Nour El-Sherif & Kamal El-Shenawy. The best film in 1975 from the Ministry of Culture. The best film-directing from "Film Society", beside six prizes in different branches. Represented Egypt in "Belgrade Festival" Yugoslavia in 1976. **1977** "Shaieni wa Shaielak, Live and let others live" Starring: Mohamed Awad & Nesrin. **1978** "Shafieka & Metwali" Starring: Soa'd Hosni Ahmad Zaki, Mahmoud Abdel Aziz, Ahmed Mazher & Gamil Rateb. The best film from the Ministry of Culture. The Bronze Tanite Prize from "Carthage Festival" Tunisia 1978. The first prize from "Nantes Festival" France 1980. The best film from "Egyptian Cinema Critics Association" and "Film Society". Representd Egypt in "New Delhi Festival" India in 1981. **1981** "Ahel El-Kemma, Top People" Starring: Soa'd Hosni, Nour El-Sherif & Ezzat El-Alaili. The best film from the Ministry of Culture. Represented Egypt in "Locarno Festival" Switzerland in 1981. "Torino Festival" Italy in 1981. "Oscar" Competition America in 1982. "Montreal Festival" Canada in 1984. "Poitiers Festival" France in 1988. The best film from "Egyptian Cinema Critics Association" and "Film Society". **1986** "Al-gou'a, The Hunger" Starring: Soa'd Hosni, Mahmoud Abdel Aziz & Yousra. The best film-production from the Ministry of Culture. **1991** "El-Raie wa Al-nissa'a, The Shepherd & Women" Starring: Soa'd Hosni, Ahmed Zaki & Yousra. The best film from "Alexandria Int'l Film Festival". The best film from "Alexandria Festival" beside four prizes (acting, music, editing). The best film-directing from "National Festival for Feature Films". 5 Prizes (production, acting, music, photography) from "National Festival for Feature Films". Represented Egypt in "Nantes Festival" France 1991. **1995** "The Third Man" Starring: Ahmed Zaki, Laila Elwy, Mahmoud Hemida. **DOCUMENTARY FILMS: 1976** "The International Match" Produced by the High Council for Youth and Sports. **1982** "Beach of Palm Trees" Produced by the Egyptian Film Center. "Soldiers of Well-Being" Produced by the Ministry of People's Development. **1983** "Exodus from Beyrout" Produced by PLO. "Is Any Body There" Produced by Arab League. **1984** "Am Abbas, The Inventor" Produced by Egyptian Film Center. Represented Egypt in: "Cinema of Reality" France 1987. "Leipzig Festival" Germany 1988. The best film from "Ismailia Festival" Egypt 1988. **Resident:** 7 Studio Al-Ahram St., Giza, Egypt, Telephone Home: 865284, Office: 5852177.

BADRAN (Adnan, M., Dr.), Jordanian academic. **Born** on December 15, 1935 in Jerash, Jordan. **Son** of Mohammed Badran (Judge) and Mrs. Fareza Badran. **Married** to Maha Muwalla in August 1969 in Amman, 5 children: Serine, Samir, Raid, Dana and Samer. **Education Record:** Ph.D. 1963, Michigan State University, East Lansing, Mich. USA.; M.Sc. 1961, Michigan State University, East Lansing, Mich. USA.; B.Sc. 1959, Oklahoma State University, Stillwater, Okla, USA. **Employment History:** Currently Deputy Director-General of UNESCO and ADG/SC (1993-); Also, currently Secretary-General of the Third World Academy of Sciences (TWAS); Assistant Director-General for Science (ADG/SC, UNESCO, Paris (1990-1993); Minister of Education in Jordan (1989), Minister of Agriculture (1988-1989), Secretary-General of the Higher Council for Science and Technology (1986-1987); President of Yarmouk University (1976-1986) and Dean of the Faculty of Science University of Jordan (1971-1976); Professor of Biology at the University of Jordan, Yarmouk University and Jordan University for Science and Technology (1966-1986); Senior Research Plant Physiologist and Biochemist at the United Fruit Research Laboratories, U.S. and Central America (1963-1966). Research Assistant at the Michigan State University (1960-1963). **Activities:** Most of his career was spent in teaching (molecular, cell and plant physiology and plant biochemistry) and research in the field of plant phenols and enzymes catalytic oxydation of phenolic compounds, ethylene biogenesis and environmental control and management of higher education and science and technology policy. A large part of his career was spent in establishing the faculty of Science (Departments of biology, chemistry, physics, geology, mathematics) at the University of Jordan and the Marine Science Centre on the Red Sea (Aqaba) and Managing the Faculty of Science of 75 Ph.D staff, 150 technical staff, 1,200 undergraduate and 80 graduate students. Also managing the Premedical, Prenursing schools, at the Faculty. Also, great part of his career was spent in establishing the new Yarmouk University and the Campus of the Jordan University of Science and Technology and managing the University (15,000 undergraduate and graduate students, 750 Ph.D faculty, 2,500 technical and administrative staff). Another considerable part of his career was spent in the development of biological curricula. Member of Board of Trustees of five public and private universities. Vice-President, General Conference UNESCO (1989). He is the author of biology textbooks at national level (Jordan and Oman) and at regional level (Arab Region) (15 textbooks). Another part of his career was spent in science and technology policies, strategies and funding research priorities in the developing countries, in particular Middle-East. He is a joint author of the book "Strategy for the development of science and technology in the Arab World", 1987. **Books and papers published:**

Seventy scientific papers and books in biology and related sciences. Also articles on higher education, author of the book "At crossroads: Education in Middle East" (1989), science and technology policy. Four patents on controlled atmosphere and enzyme work. **Affiliations and Honours:** Honorary Doctorate 1981 Jungkyunwan University, Seoul, Republic of Korea; Al-Nahda Medal; 2nd class; Yarmouk Khalid Bin Walid Medal, Alfonso the tenth Medal, Spain; Hall of Fame Alumni Award, Oklahoma State University, USA. Member of the Executive Board International Association of Universities (IAU) 1984, President of Middle East Chapter of International Association of University Presidents (IAUP) (1986), ICSU, IUBS, bioscience networks, Royal Conservation Society, Presidential fellow of Aspen, World Affairs Council, National Parks, Who's Who in the Arab World, Third World Academy. Honorary President of the Renewable Energy Network. **Prof. Addr.:** 7, place de Fontenoy, 75352 Paris 07 SP, France, Tel.: (33.1) 45 68 10 00, Fax: (33.1) 45 67 16 90.

BADRAN (Ibrahim Mohammed-Said), Jordanian engineer. **Born** in 1939. **Married,** 4 children. **Educ.:** Cairo University, Egypt; London University, UK. **Dipl.:** B.Sc. in Electrical Engineering. Ph.D. in Electrical Engineering. **Career:** Professor of Electrical Engineering at Tripoli University, Libya (1971-74); Planning Manager, Jordan Electricity, Authority (1978-80) Deputy Minister, Ministry of Industry and commerce (1984-1985, 1990-1991) Deputy minister, Ministry of Energy and mineral resources (1985-1990). Advisor to the Prime ministry since 1991. Executive Director of Noor Al-Hussein Foundation (August 1995 to date). Member of the Board of Trustees of Univ. of Philadelphia, Amman, Jordan. Member of the Jordanian Academy of Arabic Language. Ex. Member of the Board of Directors of Petrol Refinery Co. and Jordan Electricity Authority and Natural Resources Authority and Faculty of higher studies of Univ. of Jordan Ex. Chairman of Middle East Regional isotope Centre, Cairo Egypt. **Publ.:** «Studies in the Arab Mind» (1974), «Problems of Science and Technology» (1978). «Dictionary of Scientists and Inventors» (1978). Energy Resources in Jordan» (1985). «Nuclear Energy and Chernobil Incident» (1987). History and Progress in the Arab World 1991, On Thought, Culture and Progress, 1992. **Hobbies:** Gardening, table tennis, writing and reading. **Prof. Addr.:** Noor Al-Hussein Foundation, P.O.Box 926687, Amman, Jordan.

BADRAN (Mudar Mohamad), Jordanian politician. **Born** in 1934 in Jerash, Jordan. **Married. Educ.:** Damascus University, Syria. **Dipl.:** B.A. in Law (1957). **Career:** 1st Lieutenant in Public Security (1957); Assistant Legal Adviser to Armed Forces (1957); Military Representative (1962); Defence Attorney in the Military Court (1962-65); Assistant Chief of Jordanian Intelligence (1968-70); Major-General, retired on pension (1970); Secretary-General, Royal Court (1970-71); National Security Adviser of His Majesty (1971-72); Minister in the Royal Court (1972); Member of Executive Council of Arab Nations (1972); Deputy Head of Executive Office of Occupied Territories Affairs (1972-73); Minister of Education (1973-74); Minister of Defence; Minister of Foreign Affairs, Prime Minister (July 1976- Dec. 79); Minister of Foreign Affairs (1976-79); Prime-Minister, Minister of Defence (1980-87); reappointed Prime Minister and Minister of Defence (Dec. 1989 - June 1991). **Awards:** 4th Class, Independence Medal; 3rd Class, Renaissance Medal; 1st Class, Independence Medal (1972). **Addr.:** Jabal Webdeh, Tel.: 22784, Amman, Jordan.

BADRAWI (Alaeddin, Hussein), Egyptian economist. **Born** on November 7, 1939 in Egypt. **Married,** 3 children. **Educ.:** Cairo University; London University. **Dipl.:** B.A. in Political Science, M.Sc. in Economics. **Bareer:** Manager of Morgan Crucible (1974-75); Director, Commercial Union (1975-77), Beyer Peacock (1977-80); Private Banking Advisor, Hong Kong Bank (1980-). **Hobbies:** Squash and tennis. **Member:** Hurlingham Club, London. **Prof. Addr.:** 45 Hanover House, Regents Park, London, United Kingdom.

BADRI (Muhammad A., al), Egyptian statistician. **Born** on November 16, 1920 in Cairo. **Educ.:** in Cairo, Egypt; University of London, UK. **Dipl.:** B.Sc. in Mathematics (1941-45); Ph.D. in Statistics (1946-48); DIC (Diploma of Imperial College) in Statistics (1948). **Career:** Statistician in the Ministry of Social Affairs, Egypt (1948-52); Professor of Statistics and Demography, Cairo University (1952-62); UN Expert in India (1959-62); Chief of Projections Section and of Estimates, UN Secretariat (1965-72); Assistant Director of the Population Division, UN Secretariat (1972-80); Member, International Union for the Scientific Study of Population, International Statistical Institute and the Population Association of America; Director, Cairo Demorgraphic Centre (1980-). **Publ.:** various articles on statistics and population published in several international magazines and journals (in Arabic, Japanese, Enghlish, Korean, Hungarian) as well as books on statistics, philately. **Prof. Addr.:** 109 Kasr al-Aini Street, Cairo Demographic Society Building, Tel.: 30571, Cairo, Egypt.

BAFAQIH (Fadhl, Abdallah), Saudi senior civil servant. **Born** in 1940 in Saudi Arabia. **Married,** children. **Educ.:** Faculty of Commerce and training course in some British Factories, top management training course under Petromin. **Dipl.:** B.Com., B.I.B.M. (Bachelor of Industrial Business Administration). **Career:** Bureau Manager, Governor of Petroleum and Minerals General Corporation; Administrative Assistant, Iron and Steel Plant Project, later Commercial Director member Board of Petromin Lubricating Oil Plants; Vice-Chairman of Executive Committee, Iron and Steel Plant; member of Board of Directors, Arab Iron and Steel Association; attended first Arab Iron and Steel Association Conference, Tunis, Tunisia (1973), Second Conference, Riyadh (1974); now Director-General of Iron and Steel Plant. **Prof. Addr.:** Petromin Iron and Steel Plant, Tel.: 32699, Jeddah. **Priv. Addr.:** Tel.: 53003, Jeddah, Saudi Arabia.

BAGADER (Abubakr Ahmad), Saudi academic. **Born** in Mecca in 1950. **Educ.:** Ph.D. in Education and Sociology, University of Wisconsin, U.S.A. **Career:** Assistant Professor, Sociology Depratment, Faculty of Arts, King Abdulaziz Univeristy; Chairman, Cultural Committee, King Abdulaziz University, (1979-82); Chairman, Department of Islamic Studies (1980); Assistant Director, Institute of Muslim Minorities Affairs Club (IMMA), (1979); Assistant Director, Institute of Muslim Minorities Affairs Club (IMMA), (1979); Assistant Secretary General of World Assembly for Muslim Youth (WAMY), (1980); active member, Jeddah Literary Guild, American Sociology Association, American Adult Education and other educational societies; member of the Board, Faculty of Arts, King Abdulaziz University; has attended various conferences and symposia on Islam: Islam from Morocco to Indonesia, Washington D.C., Islam in Western media, Italy, Islamic Sociology, Indonesia, Ibn Sina, Malaysia. **Honours:** Honorary membership of several societies in the fields of education and sociology. **Publ.:** Literary and Social Change in Saudi Arabia; Urbanization in the Middle East; Islamization of the Social Science; articles in local newspapers. **Hobbies:** Reading, classical music. **Prof. Addr.:** P.O.Box 8856, Tel.: 6884490, Jeddah. **Priv. Addr.:** Tel.: 6892031, Jeddah, Saudi Arabia.

BAGHAJATI (Adnan), Syrian statesman. **Born** in 1934 in Damascus. **Educ.:** Damascus University. **Dipl.:** Licence ès-Letters from the said University. **Career:** Held key positions in the Ministry of Education; Managed the "as-Sawra" newspaper (July 1st, 1968- June 30, 1969); Vice-Minister of Education; Minister of State for the Council of Ministers in the cabinet of General Hafez al-Assad (1970). **Addr.:** Damascus, Syria.

BAGHDADY (Abdul Kareem Ahmad), Saudi academic. **Born** in Mecca in 1942. **Educ.:** Secondary School Certificate. **Career:** Director of Public Affairs, Umm al-Qura University, Mecca; Head of the Office of the University Chancellor; Former employee, Youth Welfare Department; Secretary, Personnel Department, Director of Public Relations, Umm al-Qura University, Mecca. **Addr.:** Umm al-Qura University, Tel.: 5564770, Mecca, Saudi Arabia.

BAGHDADY (Bakr Ahmad), Saudi businessman. **Born** in Mecca in 1934. **Educ.:** B.A. (Law), Cairo University. **Career.:** Former contracts and regulations auditor; patent expert, secretary and legal adviser, Arab and Foreign Trade Agreements Committee; member of Commercial Court; Chairman of Committee on Contravention of Bills of Exchange Regulations; member of Anti-Israel Arab Boycott Saudi Investigation Committee; member of Board, Al Sharq Establishment. **Hobbies:** Reading, swimming. **Addr.:** Ministry of Commerce Branch, King's Street, Dammam, Saudi Arabia.

BAGHIR (Ahmad, Mohamad, Gen., el), Sudanese army officer and former minister. **Born** on April 5, 1927 at el-Sofi, Gedaref District (Eastern Sudan). **Married**, with five children. **Educ.:** Kassala Primary school; Omdurman Commercial school; Faculty of Arts, Khartoum Branch, University of Cairo; military training in England and Egypt; and Staff College, Camberley (England). **Dipl.:** B.A. and Military Sciences degree. **Career:** Commissioned in Sudan Armed Forces (1950); served on the General Staff of the Infantry School at Omdurman; Instructor, Infantry school (1957); Chief of Staff, Southern Command at Juba (Oct. 1958- July 1959); Military Governor, Upper Nile Province (1959); Military Attaché, Sudanese Embassy, London (Aug. 1960-65); Commander, Bahr El Ghazal Garrison, Western Command (1965); Promoted Brigadier, and Commandant of Omdurman Military College (Oct. 1967); Director, Training. & Chief of Staff, Southern Command (Jan. 1968); First Deputy Chief of Staff, Armed Forces (Dec. 1969- June 1970); Minister of Interior (Oct. 1971-73); Vice-President (1972); Minister of Interior (1975). **Awards:** 25th May medal; Bravery Medal (1st class); Independence Medal; Long and Excellent Service Decoration; Lenin Centenary Medal. **Member:** Council, University of Khartoum; National Council for the Eradication of Water & Grass. **Prof. Addr.:** Khartoum, Sudan.

BAGHLAF (Ahmad Omar), Saudi academic. **Born** in 1943. **Educ.:** B.Sc. (Chemistry- Geology), King Saud University. M.Sc., Ph.D. (Chemistry), Manchester University, England. **Career:** Chairman, Chemistry Department, Faculty of Science, King Abdulaziz University; Geologist, Mineral Resources Department, Jeddah; Demonstrator, Faculty of Education, Umm al-Qura University, Mecca; Lecturer, Chemistry Department, King Abdulaziz University. **Member** of the Chemical Society, U.S.A. and England. **Publ.:** scientific research on transition metal halides and sulphur-halides and their complexes and methanol as a carbon source in single cell proteins. **Prof. Addr.:** P.O.Box 8106, Jeddah. **Priv. Addr.:** Tel.: 6312527, Jeddah, Saudi Arabia.

BAGHLI (Ibrahim, Taher, al), Kuwaiti director of antiquities and museums. **Born** in 1942 in Kuwait. **Son** of Taher al Baghli. **Married** in 1969 in Kuwait to Miss Zahra Ahmed al Baghli, seven children. **Educ.:** Bachelor of Arts in History, Baghdad University (1968). **Career:** Director, Kuwait National Museum. **Publ.:** Guide of Kuwait National Museum. **Hobbies:** Excavation in archaeology and picnicing. **Credit Cards:** American Express, Diner's. **Prof. Addr.:** Kuwait National Museum, P.O.Box 193 Safat, Tel.: 2432020. **Priv. Addr.:** House-2, Str. 25, Rumathiya, Tel.: 5633415, Kuwait.

BAH (Abdallah, Ould), Mauritanian politician. **Born** in 1935 at Boutilimit (Western Mauritania). **Son** of Ahmedou ould Bah (scholar). **Married** to Yahmettou mint El Mokhtar, 1 child. **Educ.:** Médersa (Koran school) in Boutilimit (1944-45); French and Arab studies (1947-48); Rosso College (1948-49); Lycée van Vollenhoven, Dakar, Senegal (1952-55); studies in medicine in France (1959-1963); practical course in cardiology, France (1966-67). **Dipl.:** B.A. & M.D. **Career:** Chief physician of the medical centre of the first region (Oriental Hodh) (1964); physician in the 1st region (1967-68); Director of National Health Services (1968-71); Minister of Health and Social Affairs (1971- Aug. 1975); Minister of National Defence (1975). **Member:** Parti du Peuple Mauritanien, and of the Bureau Politique National du PPM (Party suspended following Coup in 1978). **Addr.:** Nouakchott, Mauritania.

BAHABRY (Mohamad Sultan), Saudi official. **Born** in 1945. **Dipl.:** M.Sc. (Geology). **Career:** Geologist, Bureau Manager for Director General of Mineral Resources; Assistant Director of Concessions Department, Mineral Resources Directorate; member of Geological Conference, Japan, Minerals Conference, England. **Hobbies:** reading. **Addr.:** Mineral Resources Directorate, Tel.: 33133, Jeddah, Saudi Arabia.

BAHAEDDIN (Ahmad), Egyptian journalist. **Born** in 1927. **Married. Educ.:** Faculty of Law, Cairo University. **Career:** Editorial staff of "Rose el-Youssef", Editor in Chief of "Sabah el-Kheir" magazine, "Akhbar al-Yom" (1959-64), Editor, "Akhir Saa" (1961); appointed Chairman of Dar al Hilal in 1964; Editor in Chief of "al-Mussawar" (1964-70); Chairman of "Rose el-Youssef Publishing House" (1968-69), Press Syndicate (1968-69); Editor in Chief of "al-Ahram" (1974-75); Chairman of the Union of Arab Journalists (1976-78). **Publ.:** Various books about Egyptian and Arab history and politics. **Hobbies:** Reading and travelling. **Addr.:** 11 Hargon Street, Dokki, Cairo, Egypt.

BAHAEDDIN (Hussein, Kamel, Dr.), Egyptian Politician. **Born** on September 18, 1932 in Charkieh. **Married,** one child. **Educ.:** Bachelor of Medicine and Surgery (1954); Ph.D., Pediatrics, University of Cairo (1959). **Career:** Professor then Head, Pediatrics Department, Cairo University; Secretary General then Head, Egyptian Pediatrics Society; Member, Permanent Council, World Pediatrics Union; Director, New Pediatrics Hospital (1983); Adviser, International Pediatrics Association (1983-to date); Adviser, Middle East and Mediterranean Federation of Pediatric Societies (1987); Minister of Education (1991-to date). **Decor:** World Health Organizations Pediatrics Prize, First Arab and African Physician (1989). **Address:** Ministry of Education, Sharia al-Falaki, Cairo, Egypt.

BAHAFZALLAH (Ahmad Abdul Kader, Dr.), Saudi academic. **Born** on January 1, 1941 in Al Khobar, Saudi Arabia. **Education:** Ph.D., Geology, 1976, Bristol University, U.K. **Career:** Member of the Teaching Staff of the Faculty of Earth Sciences, King Abdul Aziz University, Jeddah, since 1976; Presently ASSOCIATE PROFESSOR at the Faculty; SUPERVISOR-GENERAL of Manarat International Schools, Western Region, Jeddah, since 1979; Dean of Student Affairs, King Abdul Aziz University, 1976 to 1980; Executive Director, Research Institute of Muslim Minority Affairs, King Abdul Aziz University, 1977-78; Secretary General, Technical Office of the University Design & Planning, King Abdul Aziz University, 1980 to 1982; Secretary General of the WORLD ASSEMBLY OF MUSLIM YOUTH, Riyadh, from the beginning of 1978 upto 1981. **Conferences:** Attended as a participant member: The First International Conference on Islamic Economics, Makkah Al-Mukkaramah, 1976; The International Conference on Muslim Minorities, London, 1978; The 9th Conference of Foreign Ministers of Islamic States, Dakkar, 1978; The 10th Conference of Foreign Ministers of Islamic States, Fez, Morocco, 1979; The 11th Conference of Foreign Ministers of Islamic States, Islamabad, 1980; The 12th Conference of Foreign Ministers of Islamic States, Baghdad, 1981; Besides the above, also attended a number of national, regional & international seminars, meetings and conferences. **Member** of the British Micropalaeontological Society, U.K. **Member** of the American Association for the Advancement of Science, U.S.A **Publications:** Over 10 Publications in the field of Geology as follows: Bahafzallah, A.A.K., 1979, Recent Benthic Foraminifera from Jeddah Bay, Red Sea, Saudi Arabia, N.Jb. Geol. Palaont. Mh., Vol. 7, pp. 385-398; Bahafzallah, A.A.K., 1984, Recent Foraminifera from the Red Sea, Farasan Islands, Saudi Arabia, Proc. Symp. Coral Reef Environment, Red Sea, pp. 198-215; Bahafzallah, A.A.K., Basahel, A.N., Mansour, H.H., and Omara, S, 1983, Geologic Mapping and Stratigraphy of the Sedimentary Sequence in Haddat Ash-Sham Area, Northeast Jeddah, Saudi Arabia, Arab Gulf J. Scient. Res., Vol. 1, No. 2, pp. 423-442; Bahafzallah, A.A.K., and El-Askary, M.A., 1981, Sedimentary and Micro-Paleontological Investigations of the Beach Sands around Jeddah, Saudi Arabia, Bull. Fac. Earth Sci., K.A.U., Vol. 4, pp. 25-42; Bahafzallah, A.A.K., Jux, U., and Omara, S., 1981, Occurence of Prototaxites in Saudi Arabia, Bull. Fac. Earth Sci., K.A.U., Vol. 4, pp. 43-55; Bahafzallah, A.A.K., Jux, U., and Omara, S., 1981, Stratigraphy and facies of the Devonian Jouf Formation, Saudi Arabia, N. Jb. Geol. Palaont. Mh., Vol. 1, pp. 1-18; Bahafzallah, Gazzaz, M.A., Moufti, R.H., Sejiny, M.J., Gama, T.H., 1989, Bibliography of Earth Sciences for the Kingdom of Saudi Arabia, King Abdulaziz University, 119 pages; Basahel, A.N., Bahafzallah, A.A.K., Jux, U., and Omara, S., 1982 Age and Structural Setting of a Proto-Red Sea Embayment, N. Jb. Geol. Palaont. Mh., Vol. 8, pp. 456-468; Basahel, A.N., Bahafzallah, A.A.K., Mansour, H.H., Omara, S., 1983, Primary Sedimentary

Structures and Depositional Environments of the Haddat Ash-Sham Sedimentary Sequence, Northwest Jeddah, Saudi Arabia, Arab Gulf J. Scient. Res., Vol. 1, pp. 143-156; Basahel, A.N., Bahafzallah, A.A.K., Omara, S., and Jux, U., 1984, Early Cambrian Carbonate Platform of the Arabian Shield, N. Jb. Geol. Palaont. Mh., Vol. 2, pp. 113-128. **Hobbies:** Working for the cause of Islam and humanity as well as Islamic & International Education; Reading, Gardening, Travelling, Soccer, Athletics, Arts, Antiques, Wildlife & Nature. **Professional Addresses:** Present (Postal Address): - DR. AHMAD BAHAFZALLAH, Supervisor-General, Manarat International Schools, Western Region, P.O.Box 40513, (Al-Amir Met'ab Street), Jeddah-21441, Saudi Arabia. Office Phone: 6700224, 6719732, Office Fax: (9662) 6719859. **Associate Professor,** Faculty of Earth Sciences, King Abdul Aziz University, P.O.Box 1744, Jeddah-21441, Saudi Arabia. Office Phone: 6952319.

BAHAR (Abdul Aziz, Ahmad, al), Kuwaiti businessman and financier. **Born** in 1929. Member of a longestablished merchant family. **Educ.:** in Kuwait and Lebanon. **Dipl.:** B.A. (American University of Beirut) (1953). **Married** to Mariam al-Rifai, 5 children: Adnan, Iman, Maha, Ahmad and Ibtisam. **Career:** Director General, Housing Department, Ministry of Finance (1956-61); member Kuwait-Saudi Arabia Neutral Zone Boundary commission (1961); Director general, Kuwait Fund for Arab Economic Development (FKAED) (1961-62); Director, Kuwait Chamber of Commerce and Industry (1962-72); Chairman, Kuwait National Industries (1963-65); Chairman, Kuwait Foreign Trading Contracting and Investment Company (1965-73); Director, Rifbank (1967-74); Chairman, Commercial Bank of Kuwait (1965-78); Director, United Bank of Kuwait Ltd., London (1975-78); Deputy Chairman, Commercial Bank of Dubai (1970-78); Director, Kuwait Metal Pipe Industries (1965-67); Member, Industrial Development Committee (1963-65); Director, Arab Trust Co. (1975-78); Chairman, Kuwait Insurance Co. (1965-67); Chairman, Arab European Financial Management Co. SAK, since 1978; Chairman, Kuwait Investment Co. (since 1980); Honorary Consul for the Republic of Costa Rica; Director of Central Bank of Kuwait (1980), Member, Board of Directors, Bank of Bahrain and Kuwait (1981). **Member:** International Banking Association; Advisory Committee to American College in Switzerland; Kuwait Economists Society; trustee of Kuwait University (1966-70). **Prof. Addr.:** P.O.Box 460, Safat, Kuwait.

BAHAR (Abdullatif, A.R., al), Kuwaiti official. **Born** in 1940 in Kuwait. **Educ.:** Victoria College, Alexandria, Egypt from 1951 to 1956; Shuwaikh Secondary School, Kuwait; Keele University, UK. **Dipl.:** B.Sc. in Economics and Political Institutions from 1959 to 1963. **Career:** General Manager: Kuwait Public Transport Corporation from 1963 to 1966; Director General, Office of H.H. the Crown Prince and Prime Minister from 1967 to date; represented Kuwait at several conferences. **Addr.:** Office of H.H. the Crown Prince and Prime Minister, P.O.Box 4, Safat 13001, Kuwait City - State of Kuwait. Tel.: 2430777, 2441900.

BAHAR (Ali Hamed, Al), Kuwaiti General Manager. **Born** on July 25, 1962 in Kuwait. **Son** of Hamed al Bahar (Businessman). **Married** to Nusaibah Bodai, 2 children: Hamed (14.3.1990), Bader (10.2.1997). **Educ.:** Bachelor of Science in Business Administration (1987). **Career:** General Manager, Kuwait Insurance Company (1994-1997); Deputy General Manager, Kuwait Insurance Company (1991-1994); Manager, National Bank of Kuwait (1988-1990). **Credit Card:** Diner's Club. **Prof. Addr.:** Kuwait Insurance Company, P.O.Box 769, Safat-13008, Kuwait, Tel.: 2462794. **Priv. Addr.:** Tel.: 4819593, Kuwait.

BAHAR (Basel, K.), Iraqi businessman. **Born** in 1939, in Baghdad, Iraq. **Son** of Kadum Bahar **and** Mrs., née Farida Hashim. **Married** in 1967 to Miss Muna Akram, five children. **Educ.:** Oklahoma State University, USA. **Dipl.:** B.A. in Business Administration. **Career:** Started in the family business; moved to UAE (1968); Wholesale Manager, Allied Enterprises (1968-71); Al-Otaiba Group of Companies dealing with Avis Rent-A-Car, Brunswick Bowling Equipment, Xerox Emirates, Foodservice Equipment, Medical Equipment, Nashua Office Equipment, etc. (since 1971). **Sport:** Swimming. **Hobby:** Reading. **Member:** al-Nasr Club. **Credit Cards:** American Express, Master Card, Diners Club, Eurocheque. **Prof. Addr.:** P.O.Box 5009 Tel.: 661575, Dubai, UAE. **Priv. Addr.:** Villa No.2938 Mushrif Area, Rashidiya, Tel.: 886162, Dubai, UAE.

BAHAR (Mohamad Abdulrahman, al), Kuwaiti banker. **Born** in 1920. **Married**. **Career:** Chairman, National Bank of Kuwait; Chairman, Kuwait Shipping Agents Association; Director, Chamber of Commerce & Industry; Agent for Caterpillar, Unilever, Lipton Tea, Rowntree-Mackintosh, Hapag Lloyd, Jugolinija, General Electric, 3M, Hermes, John Tann, Hunter Douglas, Sponsor of English School in Kuwait. **Addr.:** Abu Bakr Street, P.O.Box 148, Safat 13002, Tel.: 2433881, Telex: 22068 KWT, Kuwait.

BAHARETH (Abdul Rahman Saleh), Saudi businessman. **Born** in Mecca in 1937. **Educ.:** B.Sc. (Political Science), Boston University, U.S.A. **Career:** Began his career as a government official, Protocol Department, Ministry of Foreign Affairs (1964-67-72); Charge d'Affaires, Saudi Embassy in Jakarta (1972-74); Sales Manager, Saudi Arabian Fertilizers Co. (1974-77); owner of Logeen Commercial Exhibition; Owner of General Trading Company; Owner of International Decor Center. **Member:** Dammam Chamber of Commerce; attended several international conferences on fertilizer production and marketing. **Hobbies:** travel, sports. **Addr.:** P.O.Box 665, Khobar, Saudi Arabia.

BAHARETH (Mohamad Saleh), Saudi businessman. **Born:** Mecca in 1926. **Educ.:** Teaching certificate from Mecca Teachers' Institute. **Career:** Clerk at the Minister's Office, Ministry of Finance; later Assistant Director and then Director of the Minister's Office; now member of Jeddah Administrative Council; Chairman, Jeddah Society for memorization of the Qura'n; member of Mecca Society for the Qura'n; Chairman, Jeddah Subsidiary Council of Endowments; member of the Higher Council for Endowments; member of the Board, Bin Ladin Organization; Chairman, Consulting Committee, the Melli Iranian Bank, Jeddah; Assistant Director, the Saudi Arabian Company for Dry Batteries; member, Board of Directors, the Saudi Arabian Company for Edible Oils and Fats; member, the Organization for the Propagation of Islam, Khartoum, Sudan. Chairman of Bahareth Organization, Jeddah. **Hobbies:** memorization of the Qura'n, general reading. **Prof. Addr.:** P.O.Box 404, Tel.: 6445101, Jeddah. **Priv. Addr.:** Tel.: 6658057, Jeddah, Saudi Arabia.

BAHARNA (Hussain Mohamad, al), Bahraini former minister. **Born** on December 5, 1932 in Manama, Bahrain. **Son** of Mohamad Makki **and** Mrs. Zahra Sayed Mahmood (al-Tabatabai), al-Baharna. **Married** on July 12 1966 to Fawqiyah Ahmad Adli, 3 children: Adel, Ebtihal, Eman. **Dipl.:** LL.B. (Baghdad University, 1953); Diploma Law, University of London, 1956); M. Litt., Ph.D. in Pub. International Law (Cambridge University (England), (1961). **Career:** Legal Adviser, Kuwait Ministry of Foreign Affairs (1962-64); Legal Adviser, Analyst Arabian Gulf Affairs, Arabian American Oil Co., Dhahran, Saudi Arabia (1965-68); Legal adviser, Bahrain Ministry of Foreign Affairs (1969-70); Bahrain Government (1970-71); also member, Bahrain Council of State, Pres. Legal Com. (1970-71); Minister, for Legal Affairs, (1972-1996); member, Drafting Com. Constn. Fedh., Arabian Gulf Emirates (1970-71); Legal Adviser, Member Bahrain Del. to UN General Assembly (1970-71); Chairman, Bahrain Delegation to 3rd UN Conference on Law of the Sea (1979-82); Special Envoy of League Arab States to North American States and Japan (1974); Member, Bahrain Bar (1953-54); Member, Lincoln's Inn, London (1955-57); lectr. in field; Member, Brit. Inst. Internat. and Comparative Law; Member American Soc. International Law. **Member:** Univ. Grads., Urubah. **Publ.:** Author of "The Legal Status of the Arabian Gulf States" (1968, 2nd rev. edit., 1978); "Legal and Constitutional Systems of the Arabian Gulf States" (1974); also articles. **Addr.:** Minister's office, Legal Affairs Govt. House, P.O.Box 790, Manama, State of Bahrain.

BAHARNA (Taqi, Mohamad, al), Bahraini businessman. **Born** in 1930 in Manama, Bahrain. **Son** of Mohamad Makki Albaharna (businessman). **Married** in 1959. **Educ.:** Bahrain and Baghdad Schools. **Career:** in business since 1948; Ambassador of the State of Bahrain, Cairo (Egypt) (1971-74); also Head of Bahrain delegation to the League of Arab States, Cairo; business activity only since 1974. **Member:** Secretary-General, Gulf States Chambers of Commerce Federation (1970-71); Member of Supreme Council of Tourism (1985); Member, Board Director of Bahrain Stock Exchange Market; Member, Board Director of Bahrain Chamber of Commerce & Industry. Chairman, Al-Ahlia Insurance Co. BSC. **Award:** decoration by President Anwar Sadat of Egypt (1974). **Sports:** swimming and tennis. **Hobbies:** reading, chess and home movie. **Clubs:** Local clubs. **Credit Card:** American Express, Master & Visa Cards. **Prof. Addr.:** Sadiq & Taqi Albaharna, P.O.Box 179, Tel.: 253816, Manama. **Priv. Addr.:** Bab el-Bahrain Road, Tel.: 253239, Manama, Bahrain.

BAHJAT (Hussein, Hassan), Egyptian businessman. **Born** in 1927 in Cairo, Egypt. **Married**, 1 son, 1 daughter. **Educ.:** Ecole Hôtelière Lausanne, Switzerland. **Career:** held various positions in Swedish hotels (1953-61); Manager of own chain of restaurants in Stockholm, Sweden (1961-80); Member of the Board of Swedish Hotel and Restaurants Association; Promoter in real estate, Marbella, Spain (1980). **Hobby:** Golf. **Addr.:** Cairo, Egypt.

BAHNASSAOUI (Mohamad, Kamel, al), Egyptian judge. **Born** in Egypt. **Educ.:** Secondary and Faculty of Law, Fouad 1st University (Cairo). **Dipl.:** Licentiate of Law, Criminology Diploma. **Career:** Judge Court, Public Prosecutor, Director of Justice Courts Service and Technical Secretary at Ministry of Justice, President Court of Appeal. **Publ.:** Author of "Our Daily life and its Relationship to the Law", "Woman's Crown" (in Arabic), "The Invoice Journey", "Life and Court Philosophy". **Member** Gezireh Sporting Club, Magistrate Club, Philatelists Association. **Addr.:** 127, Army, Road, Alexandria, Egypt.

BAHNASSI (Afif), Syrian Professor of History of Art and Architecture, University of Damascus. **Born** on April 17, 1928 in Damascus. **Son** of Ahmed Rafik Bahnassi **and** Mrs. née Mekieh el Oushe. **Married** on October 27, 1972 to Maysoun Jazairi, 5 children: Ayad (1960), Anas (1973), Yola (1974), Kinan (1978), Omar (1981). **Educ.:** Secondary School, Damascus; Education Institute, Damascus; Faculty of Law, University of Damascus; Ecole du Louvre, Paris; Sorbonne University, Paris. **Dipl.:** Licence in Law, Damascus; Diploma in History of Art, Paris; Doctorate in Modern Art, State Doctorate, and Ph.D. of Islamic Art from Sorbonne University, Paris. **Career:** Director of Department of Fine Art (1958-1971); General Director of Antiquities and Museums (1972-1988). **Work:** Writer of 45 books and Dictioneries, Painter, and Professor, History of Art and Architecture. **Other Information:** Chairman and Member of many Institutions and committees. **Medals:** 12 Medals, Commandor of the Order of Arts and Letters from Syria, Germany, France, Italy, Bulgaria, Poland, Denmark, Belgium...; First Prize in Islamic Architecture 1991 ICO Award, Jeddah. **Sport:** Running. **Hobbies:** Painting, Sculpture. **Member:** First President of Association of Fine Art, Member of Union of Arab Writers. **Prof. and Priv. Addr.:** 34 Gazzi St., Rawda, Tel.: 3334554, Damascus, Syria.

BAHNINI (Hadj Mohamed), Moroccan former Minister of State. **Born** in 1914 in Fes. **Educ.:** Primary and Secondary in Fes and at Lycée Gouraud of Rabat. **Dipl.:** B.E.J.A.M., LL.B., licence ès-letters. **Career:** Secretary Central Maghzen; Judge, Moroccan High Court; Professor, Imperial College (where he taught to HM. King Hassan II); Director, Imperial Cabinet (1950); resigned in 1951; Judge delegate to Meknes till 1952); resigned in 1951; Judge delegate to Meknes till 1952; later exiled in the south by French Authorities, then following H.H. King Mohamed V return from exile, became Secretary General of Government; Minister of Justice, Mr. Abdallah Ibrahim's Cabinet (December 1958); re-appointed in his functions in May 1960 in HM Mohamed V cabinet, presided by HRH Maulay Hassan; Minister of Administrative Affairs and Secretary General of Government (May 1965); Minister of Defence and Secretary General of Government (Oct. 1970- August 1971); Minister of Justice (August 1971); Vice Prime-Minister, Minister of Justice and Secretary. General of Government (13 April 1972); Minister of State (20 November 1972- April 1974); Minister of State for Cultural Affairs (April 1974- Dec 79); Minister in charge of T.R.H. Princes and Princesses, and Minister of State for Cultural Affairs (Jan. 1980- Oct. 1982); Minister of State (1982-1992). **Awards:** Several Moroccan and foreign decorations. **Addr.:** Rabat, Morocco.

BAHR (Ali, Abdulrahman, al), Yemeni banker. **Born** in 1929 in Yemen. **Son** of Abdulrahman Bahr. **Married. Educ.:** M.A. in Economics, USA. **Career:** Director of Administration of Loans and Grants (1972); Lecturer, College of Economics, Sana'a University (1974); Deputy Minister of Economy (1974); Deputy Governor for the Yemeni Bank in IBRD World Bank; Member of the Board of: the Central Bank, the Yemeni Bank, the Electricity Corp.; former, Chairman of Housing Credit Bank. **Publ.:** M.A. Thesis "Factors Affecting the Rate of Unemployment"; "Interests and Recreations". **Sports:** Volleyball, swimming, tennis. **Hobbies:** Reading, classical Arabic poetry. **Addr.:** Sanaa, Republic of Yemen.

BAHRI (Jamaleddin, Mohamed), Egyptian surgeon. **Born** on April 23, 1916 in Kena, Egypt. **Married,** 1 son, 2 daughters. **Educ.:** Cairo University, Egypt. **Dipl.:** M.B., B.Ch. and M.D. in General Surgery. **Career:** Demonstrator, Lecturer and Assistant Professor in General Surgery, Cairo University (1942-53); Consultant Plastic Surgeon of the Egyptian Army (1948-); Professor of Plastic Surgery, Cairo University (1962-); President of the Egyptian Society of Plastic Surgery (1962-); Chairman of the Surgical Department, Cairo University (1971-76); Member of French, American and British Societies of Plastic Surgery. **Publ.:** "Surgery in Egypt" (1972), Egypt, co-author of "Treatment of Burns" (1973), Italy; "Cancer of the Bladder" vol. 2 (1984), USA. **Decor.:** Physicians Syndicate Shield (1977). **Medal:** Medal of the Republic; President of Egypt (1976). **Member:** Automobile Club, Gezira Sporting Club. **Prof. Addr.:** 176 Tahrir Street, Cairo, Egypt. **Priv. Addr.:** Nile Hospital, 23 Abdel Aziz Alseoud, Rodah, Cairo, Egypt.

BAID (Ali, Salim, al), Yemeni politician. **Born** in 1940 in Yemen. **Son** of Salim Baid. **Educ.:** Engineering in Cairo. **Career:** Active in National Liberation Front (NLF); Minister of Defense (1967-68); Foreign Minister (1968-71); Minister of State to the Presidential Council (1971); Minister of Planning (1973-75); Minister of Local Government Affairs (1975); **Member** of the NLF Political Bureau, Head of Economic Affairs, NLF Political Bureau (1975); Secretary-General of the Central Committee of the Yemen Socialist Party. Former Vice-President of the Republic of Yemen and former Member of the Presidential Council. **Addr.:** In exile.

BAIDAR (Hamud Mohamed, Lieutenant Colonel), Yemeni diplomat, army commander. **Born** in 1932 in Yemen. **Son** of Mohamad Baidar. **Educ.:** Sana'a Military College. **Career:** Took part in the leadership of the Free Officers Movement to overthrow the monarchy and led to the creation of Yemen Arab Republic on 26 September 1962. Chief of Staff of Republican Forces (1962-67); Officer, Commander of Military College at Rawdah (1968-75); Assistant to the Chief of Staff, Minister of the Interior; member of the Command Council and Governor of Ibb (till 1976); Ambassador of Yemen Arab Republic to Algeria (since 1976 to 1993). **Addr.:** Ministry of Foreign Affairs, Sanaa, Yemen.

BAJOUDA (Hassan, Mohamad), Saudi academic. **Born** in 1940 at Ta'if (Saudi Arabia). **Married,** children. **Dipl.:** B.A., M.A., Ph.D. (Arabic Language and Literature). **Career:** Lecturer in Arabic; Head of the Arabic Language Department, King Abdul Aziz University (1968-73); Vice-Dean of the Faculty of Sharia (Islamic Law) (1970-73); attended Saudi Men of Letters Conference, Mecca; also the Conference on the Role of the University, Mecca and Beirut (Lebanon); Supervisor of Arabic Postgraduate Studies, Umm al-Qura University. **Publ.:** Produced authentic editions of the collected works of Abdullah bin Rawaha and Abu Qais bin al-Ashat; "Meditations around the Yassin verses in the Koran" Maryam, al-Israa, al-Furqan, al-Aadiat, Annaziaat, al-Haqqah, Arrad, Muhammad, al-Fatiha, al-Ahzab, al-Baqarah and "The Objective Unity of the Yusuf Verses in the Koran" in manuscript, an authentic edition of the collected works of Uhaiha Bin al-Jullah al-Awsi al-Jahili; "The Role of the University in preserving the Islamic Heritage". **Sport:** Swimming. **Hobby:** Reading. **Prof. Addr.:** Faculty of Arabic Language, Umm al-Qura University, University of King Abdul Aziz, Mecca Branch, Tel.: 22515, Saudi Arabia.

BAJUBEER (Abdalla, A.), Saudi advertisor. **Born** in 1945 in Jeddah, Saudi Arabia. **Educ.:** Received general education. **Career:** Sports Editor of "Okaz" daily newspaper; Editor of "Okaz" supplements and special issues; "Okaz" Special Representative in Europe; Deputy Editor of "Okaz" (1964-77); represented "Okaz" and "Saudi Gazette" daily newspapers in international conferences held in Europe and Canada (1974-76); Director General, Saudi Advertising; member, Foreign Journalists' Association and the International Advertising Association. **Publ.:** Majed Ibn Abdulaziz, Prince of Makkah, 1980; Editor, The Saudi Arabia Trade Directory; editorials and feature articles in various newspapers; weekly columnist for "Okaz" daily newspaper. **Hobbies:** Reading, sports. **Prof. Addr.:** P.O.Box 6557, Tel.: 6650380, 6602286, Jeddah. **Priv. Addr.:** Tel.: 6651707, Jeddah, Saudi Arabia.

BAKALLA (Mohammad, Hasan), Saudi academic. **Born** on January 1, 1946 in Mecca, Saudi Arabia. **Son** of Hasan Mohammad Bakalla **and** Mrs. Aisha Ahmad (Lamfun). **Married** on July 30, 1968 to Miss Brenda Lilian Richardson in London. **Educ.:** Department of Arabic, College of Arts, King Saud University; University College, London; School of Oriental & African Studies, University of London. **Dipl.:** B.A., King Saud University (1964); Diploma in Linguistics, London (1968); M. Phil., University of London (1970); Ph.D., University of London (1973). **Career:** Teaching Assistant, King Saud University (1964-65); Lecturer, King Saud University (1974-75); Assistant Professor, King Saud University (1976-78); Associate Professor, King Saud University (1979-82); professor (1983- to present); Head, Phonetics Laboratory, King Saud University; Curator, Folklore Museum. King Saud University; Deputy Dean, Arabic Laguage Institute, King Saud University. **Sports:** Football, Table Tennis. **Hobbies:** Philately, Photography, Reading, Numismatics, Travel. **Member:** Acoustical Society of America, American Association of Teachers of Arabic, Arabic Islamic International Schools Federation (Saudi Arabia), International Association for the Melody Programmed Therapy of Speech (France), International Linguistics Association (USA), International Phonetic Association (London); International Society of Phonetic Sciences (Norway), Linguistic Society of America, Linguistc Society of the Philippines, Literary Club of Riyadh and Saudi Arabian Association for Culture and the Arts (Riyadh), Middle East Studies Association of North America, Phonetic Society of Japan, Riyadh Linguistic Circle, Royal Asiatic Society (London), Royal Philological Society (London), Society of Saudi Dialects and Folklore (Riyadh). **Credit Cards:** American Express, Diners Club, Access. **Prof. Addr.:** Phonetics Laboratory, College of Arts, King Saud University, Riyadh. **Priv. Addr.:** P.O.Box 1771, Riyadh, 11141, E-Mail: mbakalla@ksu.edu.sa Saudi Arabia.

BAKDASH (Hisham, Zaki), Syrian academic. **Born** in 1934 in Damascus, Syria. **Son** of Zaki Bakdash. **Married,** two children. **Educ.:** Damascus University, Syria; University of California, Los Angeles, USA. **Dipl.:** M.D. (1959); Residency and Fellowship in Neuro-surgery (1962-69), diploma, American Board of Neurological Surgery (1969). **Career:** Associate Professor, American University of Beirut (1971); Assistant Professor of Neuro-surgery, Damascus University (1974-78); Professor, Damascus University (since 1979); Chief Neuro-surgeon, Damascus University Hospital; Professor and Chairman, Department of Neuro-surgery, Damascus University; Chairman of the Examination Committee of Specialists in Neuro-surgery, Ministry of Health, Syria (since 1970); Secretary of the Scientific Committee of Damascus Medical Association (1977-79); founding **Member** of the Alumni Club of UCLA, University of California, USA (1978); member of the American Association of Neurological Surgeons (1970); Fellow, American College of Surgeons. **Publ.:** Many papers on Neuro-surgery in professional journals in USA (1969-70); Arab Medical Journal (1970-79); text book in Neuro-surgery, in Arabic. **Hobbies:** History, travelling. **Addr.:** Jisr Abiad, Damascus, Syria.

BAKHIT (Bassam, Salim), Jordanian engineer. **Born** in 1936 in Salt, Jordan. **Son** of Salim Bakhit. **Married,** two children. **Educ.:** B.Sc. in Soil Mechanics, University of Arizona, USA (1960). **Career:** Owner, Chairman of the Board and Managing Director of General Enterprise Co. Ltd.; involved in the construction and building of major Jordanian Cement Factory (1960-63); member of the Planning Council (1961-68); of Municipality of Amman (1961-64). **Medal:** Order of Independence, Jordan. **Sport:** Swimming. **Priv. Addr.:** Tel.: 812374, Amman, Jordan.

BAKHIT (Mohammad, Adnan Salameh, al), Jordanian President of AL al-Bayt University. **Born** on January 15, 1941 at Mahas, Jordan. **Son** of Salameh Al-Bakhit (Farmer) **and** Mrs. née Rasmieh Al-Khatib. **Married** on January 10, 1985 in Jordan to Mrs. Hayat Al-Asmar. **Educ.:** B.A. in Arts (History), American University of Beirut (1963); Diploma of Education, American University of Beirut (1963); M.A. in Islamic History, American University of Beirut (1965); Ph.D. in Islamic History, School of Oriental and African Studies, University of London (1972); Full Professor at the Department of History-Faculty of Arts, University of Jordan (1983- present). **Dipl.:** Ph.D. in Islamic History from the School of Oriental and African Studies, University of London. **Languages:** Arabic, English and Turkish. **Career:** Teaching and Research Assistant at the American University of Beirut (1963-1966); Teaching and Research Assistant at the Department of History-Faculty of Arts, University of Jordan (1966-1967); Visiting Professor at Princeton University (1977-1978); Dean of Academic Research at the University of Jordan and Editor-in-Chief of Dirasat Scientific Journal (1984-1989); Administrative Superior of the University of Jordan Library (1984-1989); Chairman of the Committee on Scholarly Work Translation at University of Jordan (1984-

1989); Director for the Strategic Center at the University of Jordan (1985-1989); Member of the Council of the Center for Strategic Studies (1988-1989); Member of Conferences/ Symposia Committee at the University of Jordan (1989-1990); Member of the Golden Jubilee Committee at the University of Jordan; He was also a member to 23 other committees as well as Rapporteur; Vice-President for the Planning and Community Services (1989-1990); Professor of History at the Faculty of Arts of the University of Jordan (1966-1991); Vice-President for Humanities, Faculty at the University of Jordan (1990-1991); President of Mu'tah University (1991-1993); President of Al al-Bayt University (1993- present). **Supervision of Academic Theses:** M.A. Theses (1980-1993); Ph.D. Theses (1989- present). **Conferences/Seminars:** Attended 80 Conferences and Seminars Held in different countries in the World (1975-1993); in addition he has delivered a number of lectures at various institutions/universities inside and outside Jordan, and was member of the Madrid Peace Conference. **Publ.:** He has published numerous books, written articles in well-established academic journals worlwide, and edited and supervised academic research. He submitted numerous papers at international conferences worldwide. **Medals and Decorations:** Al-Quds (Jerusalem) Decoration for Arts and Culture (The Palestine Liberation Organization); The University of Jordan Silver Medal; The Arab Historian Decoration (Union of Arab Historians); Jordan Independence Medal First Grade; Jordan State Prize for Social Sciences. **Sports:** Jogging. **Hobby:** Reading. **Prof. Addr.:** President of Al al-Bayt University, P.O.Box 772, Tel.: and Fax: 840150, Al-Jubaiha, Amman, Jordan.

BAKHOTMAH (M. Saleh), Saudi official. **Born** in 1939, **Dipl.:** B.A. (Economics), University of Cairo. **Career:** Attaché, Ministry of Foreign Affairs; Consul of the Kingdom of Saudi Arabia in Cairo; attended Islamic Foreign Ministers Conference, Jeddah 1975, the 62nd Session of the Arab League 1977; First Secretary, Ministry of Foreign Affairs. **Publ.:** social and cultural articles, poetry, in local newspapers and mangazines. **Hobby:** reading. **Addr.:** Ministry of Foreign Affairs, Tel.: 21322, Jeddah, Saudi Arabia.

BAKHREBAH (Saleh Abdallah), Saudi educator. **Born** in 1946 at Al-Grain (Southern Arabia). **Dipl.:** Ph.D. (Civil Engineering - Structures). **Career:** Assistant Professor and Supervisor of University Projects, KFUPM (1973-74); Assistant Professor and Dean of Business and Technical Affairs, KFUPM (1975-78); Secretary General of the University (1978-89); Associate Professor, KFUPM, since 1980; presently Vice Rector for Applied Research. **Member:** American Society of Civil Engineers, American Concrete Institute, Taux, Beta Pi, Chi Epsilon. **Publ.:** several technial papers on shell analysis and applied research. **Hobbies:** reading, music, photography, travel. **Sports:** Scuba Diving, wind surfing, sailing, skiing. **Prof. Addr.:** KFUPM, Box. 162, Tel.: 8602200, Dhahran 31261, e-mail: bakhreba@kfupm.edu.sa. **Priv. Addr.:** Tel.: 8606296, Dhahran, Saudi Arabia.

BAKHSH (Abdalla Taha), Saudi businessman. **Born** in 1935, in Mecca, Saudi Arabia. **Educ.:** Univesity of Southern California. **Dipl.:** M.A. Business Administration. **Career:** Chief Accountant, Zakat Administration. **Career:** Chief Accountant, Zakat Administration (1958); Branch Manager, Zakat Administration, Riyadh (1967); Owner, Traco Corporation and Bakhsh Corporation; Member Chamber of Commerce, Mecca; former Director, Saudi Bank, Paris; Union Bank of the Middle East Ltd., Dubai; Beirut-Riyadh Bank, Lebanon; Chairman, Arab Finance Corporation, Luxembourg. **Member:** Mecca Charity Society. **Addr.:** Bakhshab Bldg., King Abdulaziz Str., P.O.Box 459, Jeddah 21411, Saudi Arabia.

BAKHSH (Abdul Rahman, Taha, Dr.), Saudi physician and businessman. **Born** on 10th November, 1936, in Mecca, Saudi Arabia. **Degree: M.B.B.Ch, 1962; D.E.U.S., D.S., M.B.A. F.R.C.S. London (1970), U.S. Career:** Intern & Registrar, Department of Surgery of Urinary Tract, at al-Dimerdash Hospital, Ain-Shams University, Cairo; Owner and Manager: Bakhsh Hospital, Dar al-Shifa Hospital & Bakhsh Clinic (opened in 1985) and Jazira Hospital, Jeddah and Makka Medical Center, Member of Board of Director. **Member** of British Urological Surgery Association (F.R.C.S), London (1970), American International College of Surgeons; **attended** the conference of Urinary Tract Surgery, London, 1971; Director-General National Health Service Co.; **Hobbies:** Reading, travel; **Professional Addr.:** Dr. Abdul Rahman Taha Bakhsh Hospital, Prince Fahad Street, P.O.Box 6940, Jeddah 21452, Saudi Arabia. Tel.: 6510555.

BAKHSH (Adnan, Taha), Saudi businessman. **Born** in 1950 in Mecca, Saudi Arabia. **Son** of Taha Bakhsh (Jeweller). **Married** on November 15, 1974, one daughter. **Educ.:** Victory College (Cairo); Brummana National School (Lebanon); Whittier College (U.S.A.). **Career:** Proprietor of International Bakhsh Corporation (Inbacorp) (Transport, Catering and Catering Equipment Division); Adnan Trans World L.T.D.; Raniah Fashion and Inbacorp France; Board member: H.B. Services Ltd. and Tatco. **Sports:** Parachute diving. **Prof. Addr.:** P.O.Box 5609, Tel.: 6517163- 651959, Jeddah 21432. **Priv. Addr.:** Palestine Road, Villa Adnan Bakhsh, Jeddah, Saudi Arabia.

BAKIR (Mona, Mohamed), Egyptian lawyer & registered patent attorney. **Born** on September 29, 1953 in Cairo, Egypt. **Married,** 3 children. **Educ.:** Cairo University, Egypt. **Dipl.:** LL.B. **Career:** Member, the United States Trademark Association, the Chartered Institute of Patent Agents, the Institute of Trademark Agents (ITMA), Association Pour la Protection de Propriété Industrielle au

Moyen Orient; Director of Mohamed Bakir Office (since 1976 to 1983). **Hobby:** Riding. **Member:** Gezira Sporting Club, Hunting Club. **Prof. Addr.**: 13 Dr. Mahmoud Azmi Street, Tel.: 3402592, Facs. 2023403828 G II & III AUTOM, Telex: 22838 DOUDA UN, Zamalek, Cairo, Egypt.

BAKJAJI (Sabah el-Deen, Dr.), Syrian, former minister of state for planning affairs. **Born** in 1930 in Deir el-Zor, Syria. **Son** of Shukri Bakjaji **and** Mrs. Najiyeh Ali Bey. **Married** to Lucienne Reding in 1965 in Belgium, 4 children: Rima B (1967, Brussels-Student), Nadia B (1966, Brussels-Student), Kinda B (1969, Damascus-Student), Wael (1973, Damascus-Student). **Educ.:** Licentiate's degree in mathematical sciences-Damascus University-Faculty of Sciences (1954-55); Secondary schools teaching aptitute-Damascus University-Education Fac. "Teachers' High Institute" (1955-56); Actuarial Sciences Institute Certificate in act. sciences Louvain University (Belgium 1962); Preparation certificate for Actuarian and Doctorate (1963); State Doctorate in actuarial sciences (Louvain 1967). **Works:** Sthocastical process applicable in pension funds studies - in french - Louvain 1967 - Publication of Louvain Univ. (#150P); Financial Mathematics - in Arabic - Damascus 1970 + Publications of Damascus Univ. "Univ. Book" (#400P); Collection of Actuarial Mathematics - 2V - Mathematics of composed interest - Publications of al-Mukayed Printing - Damascus 1971 - Reference book (#500P); Collection of Acturial Math. - 3V - Mathematics and Statistics of Insurance - Publications of Damascus Univ. 1976 - Univ. Book; Collection of Actuatial Math. - 4V - Statistical Math. - Publications of Damascus Univ. (1967-77); First edition - Univ. Book (#350P) (1982-83); Second edition, Operational Researches - Pub. of Damascus Univ. (1981-82) Univ. Book (#400P); Electronic data processing (Informatics), Pub. of Damascus Univ. (1981-82) - Univ. Book (#400P); Informatics - Arab Faculty of Post - Arab States League (1985); Economics of Transport - Arab Faculty of Post - Arab States League (1985); Electronic Data processing (Fortran and Basic) 1986-87 Univ. Book; Operational researches and Informatics (1986-87) - Univ. Book. **Researches (Manuscrits):** Book dealing with the possibility of employing the lattices (trellises) in actuarial studies (#200P) Paris 1979-80 - Direction of Univ. self assignment. Mathematical bases to be adopted in organisation and management of insurance and reinsurance companies Paris 1979-80 (#150P) Direc. of Univ. self-assignment. **Articles:** Education and sciences articles - "SAWT-EL-FARAT" magazine (1957-60) Series of articles on Economics, Planning and Insurance (#15P) published in Syrian revue of economics. Period 1969-76; Series of articles on Researches and strategies (#10Art) Pub. in "Military Thought" Trimestrial magazine published by the Head Quarters Academy and Political Administration in Damascus, period 1973-79. **Lectures:** Lecture in Aleppo Univ. by invitation from the faculty of Econ. Sciences, on "The mathematical equations of the Existence", (27 April 1974); Lecture in the Cultural Centre of the teachers Association in Damascus, on "the Matrixes and their use in the social and demographical studies, and their mathematical transformations", Spring 1970. **Studies and Advices:** Establishment of the mathematical bases to the investment acts and participation in the finishing of its project for the Popular Credit Bank in Damascus (1969); Establishment of the acturial tables for the singking of the fundamental loans according to the alternatives adopted by the Ministry of Economy for the fundamental Bank (1970); Participation and finishing of the promulgation of the decrees related to the previous services of the workers and their inclusion in the law of the social insurance in Syria, (1969-70); Establishment of the actuarial study related to the creation of the Social Integration Fund of the Association of Teachers in Syria. Establishment of the actuarial study concerning the creation of the Pension Fund of the Association of journalists in Syria, (1978). **Membership in Committees and Administration Councils:** Member of the adm. council of the Arab Union Company for the Reinsurance, period 1974-78; Member of the Committee of the high instruction planning in Syria, year 2000, period 1976-78. Regional Command-High Instruction Board; Member of the Consultative Committee of the Economical Board in the Regional Command, (1976-78); Member of the Executive Sub-Board of the Association of Teachers in Damascus Univ. (1969-77); Member of the Committees of: prices, taxation amendment... for the Ministry of Finance, period 1974-76. **Univ. Committees:** Member of the Committee of the Univ. self-assignment, 1978-79, 81-82; Member of the Com. for the creation of the middle-institute of Trade in Damascus Univ.; Member of the Council of discipline of the Professors in the Baath Univ. (1982-83); Member of the Com. of the Univ. Titles Equavalence - High instruction Board in Syria (1982-83); Member of the Com. for the establishment of the statute for the creation of the High Institute for Administrative development: (1982-83); Member of the Com. of claims in Damascus Univ. (1982-83); Member of the Com. for the starting of the Computer Centre in Damascus Univ. (1981-82); Member of the Com. of studying the project of creation of the High Institute of Informatics (1981). **Functions and Missions:** Elementary school - teacher in charge, (1949-50); Mathematics teacher in secondary school in Deir el-Zor (1956-60); Director of the Actuarial and statistic-Establishment of Social Insurance in Damascus, (1967); Professor and Intendant of the Faculty of Trade (1967-68, 73); Dean of the Trade Faculty (1973-76); Head of the Statistics Department (1976-79); Dean of the Economy and Trade Faculty 1981-82, 1983... Minister of State for Planning Affairs until 1992. **Univ. Missions Abroad:** Professor in visit for high studies - Constantine Univ. (Algeria) 1977-78, 1 month; Mission for scien. research in Paris, for the Univ. year 1980-81; Mission-visit to the Universities in the U.S.A., 1983 1 month. **Non Univ. Mission:** Actuarial study for the Arab Fund for Econ. and Soc. development, May 1983. **Sports:**

Swimming. **Hobbies:** Reading and Composing Books. **Priv. Addr.:** Mazen-Western Villas, Ghazawi 12, Tel.: 663039, 248835, Damascus, Syria.

BAKOUR (Yahia), Syrian academic, Director General-AOAD. **Born** on February 20, 1938 in Banias, Syria. **Son** of Mustafa Mohamed Bakhour **and** Mrs. Shafica née Adra. **Married** in 1964 in Lattakia, Syria to Miss Fatma Imam, three children: Firas, Shighaf, Rawan. **Educ.:** Banias highschool, University of Alexandria, Egypt; University of Meissen; Germany. **Dipl.:** B.Sc. in Agricultural Engineering, University of Alexandria (1963); Diploma in Agricultural Economics University of Totshental, Germany (1971), Ph.D. in Agricultural Economics Meissen University (1974). **Career:** Head, Agricultural Cooperation Dept., Lattakia, Syria (1966-68); Director General Agricultural Cooperation Directorate, Ministry of Agriculture and Agrarian Reform, Damascus (1968-74); Associate Professor, Faculty of Agriculture, Damascus University (1973-77); Director of Regional Office in Damascus, Arab Organisation for Agricultural Development (1974-1993); Chairman of Agricultural Engineers Syndicate in Syria (since 1971); Secretary General Arab Agricultural Engineers Union (since 1980); Chairman, Syrian National Committee for Man and the Biosphere (since 1981); Council Coordinator, International Man and Biosphere Bureau (UNESCO) (since 1982); Director General, Arab Organization for Agricultural Development (since 1993-); Agric. Cooperative Dept., Ministry of Agriculture, Syria. **Member** Arab Experts Committee for Cooperation (Arab League) (1969-75); Member of Arab Society for Economic, Social and Agric. Sciences. **Director** General of Arab Organization for Agricultural Development and the Executive Board of Arab Agricultural Engineers Union. **Medals:** Awarded Medals and Decorations at Home Country and at Regional and International Levels, Several honours from government authorities. **Sports:** Swimming. **Hobbies:** Reading, chess. **Member** of Association of High Studies. **Prof. Addr.:** Arab Organization for Agricultural Development, P.O.Box 474, Khartoum, Sudan, Tel.: (249-11-) 472176-183, Fax: (249-11-) 471402, **Priv. Addr.:** the same.

BAKR (Abdallah Yusuf), Saudi engineer. **Born** in 1948 in Jeddah, Saudi Arabia. **Dipl.:** B.Sc. (Civil Engineering) (1972); completed the higher training course for Executive Management, King Abdulaziz University. **Career:** Civil engineer, Municipality Office, Engineering Department, Ministry of the Interior (1972); Director, Engineering Department, King Abdulaziz University; member of the Third Arab Engineers Conference in Tunisia; member of the Housing Co-operative Society, Jeddah. **Hobbies:** Sports, football. **Prof. Addr.:** Engineering Department, King Abdulaziz University, Tel.: 6879033, Jeddah. **Priv. Addr.:** Tel.: 6427337, Jeddah, Saudi Arabia.

BAKR (Abdul Razzag Yusuf), Saudi academic. **Born** in 1940. **Dipl.:** Ph.D. (Geology), University of Leeds, U.K. (1973). **Career:** Geologist, Ministry of Petroleum and Mineral Resources, Jeddah (1966-69); former Chairman, Department of Geology, Faculty of Science, King Abdulaziz University; member, International Centre of Seismological Studies, UNESCO National Hydrological Committee and King Abdulaziz University Council. **Hobby:** Football. **Addr.:** Jeddah, Saudi Arabia.

BAKR (Babikir, Abdallah), Sudanese former president Court of Appeal. **Born** on January 9, 1920 in Gedaref, Sudan. **Son** of Abdallah Bakr. **Educ.:** London Memorial College. **Career:** Nazir Dar Bakr, Gedaref District, President Court of Appeal (Dar Bakr and Doka Courts); Member of Gedaref South Rural Council; President Education Committee; Member of Finance Committee; President of Health Committee; Member of Official Affairs, Agricultural Committee; Member of the People Assembly; Member of the Judiciary of Khartoum People Assembly; Member of the Fundamentals of the Sudanese Society. **Member:** Ahli Sports Club, Doka Club, Gedaref Club. **Addr.:** P.O.Box 278, Gedaref, Sudan.

BAKR (Bakr, Abdallah), Saudi academic. **Born** on January 1, 1938 in Taif, Saudi Arabia. **Son** of Abdullah Mohamad Bakr (Businessman) **and** Mrs., née Aisha Mohamad Hassan Magraby. **Married** on August 8, 1965 in Taif to Miss Fakhriyah Salah Ramadhan, 7 children: Osama, Maha, Wael, Zahia, Abdullah, Hani Ahmed. **Educ.:** University of Texas (1959-63), Stanford University (1965-67), USC (1968-70). **Dipl.:** Bachelor of Petroleum Engineering (1963), Master of Business Administration (1967), Doctor of Business Administration (1970). **Career:** Petroleum Engineer, Aramco (1963-64); Assistant to the Dean of College of Petroleum & Minerals (1964-66); Executive Assistant to the Governor of PETROMIN (1966-70); Dean of the College of Petroleum & Minerals (1970-74); Rector, King Fahd University of Petroleum & Minerals (1974- present); Member of Riyadh University Board, King Faisal University Board, King Abdul Aziz University Board, University of Petroleum & Minerals Board, Imam Mohammad Ibn Saud University Board, Islamic University Board, Qatar University Board of Regents, Member, University of Bahrain; Member, Board of Trustees, United Nations University, Tokyo, Japan (until 1990); Chairman, Committee on finance & Budget, U.N. University, Japan (Until 1990); Advisory Group Member, UN Institute of Training and Research, New York; Council Member, International Social Prospects Academy, Geneva, Switzerland; Member, Center for Research on the Muslim Contribution to Civilization, Doha, Qatar; International Association of Science and Technology for Development (IASTED) Canada, Arab University Presidents Association; President, KFUPM Foundation. **Sport:** Swimming. **Hobbies:** Photography, reading and music. **Member:** American Management Association (AMA); American Management Association of Engineers

(AMAE). **Prof. Addr.:** King Fahd University of Petroleum and Minerals (KFUPM), P.O.Box 274, Dhahran 31261, Saudi Arabia, Tel.: (03)860-2000.

BAKR (Ibrahim), Palestinian- Jordanian politician, lawyer. **Born** in 1924 in Nazareth. **Married** with children. **Educ.:** Jerusalem Law College, graduated in law. **Career:** Practiced law in Ramallah later in Jerusalem till the June War of 1967; actively involved in political life of Jordan, before and after June War 1967 (imprisoned several times); expelled by Israelis from West Bank of the Jordan (1967); practised law in Amman. **Member** of the Palestine National Council, Palestine Liberation Organisation (since 1968); Vice Chairman of PLO Executive Committee (1969), resigned (September 1969); Independent member of the Central Committee of the PLO (1970); member of the six man General Secretariat; resigned from PLO (1971). **President** of the Jordanian Bar Association (1977); Member of the Palestine National Council and the Palestine Central Council of the PLO; re-elected President of the Jordanian Bar Association (1979). **Prof. Addr.:** P.O.Box 6981, Tel.: 42471, Amman, Jordan. **Priv. Addr.:** Tel.: 44112, Amman, Jordan.

BAKR (Ibrahim, Salih), Saudi diplomat. **Son** of Salih Bakr. **Educ.:** University of Columbia, New York; Georgetown University, Washington D.C., USA. **Dipl.:** In Political Sciences. **Career:** Foreign Ministry (1948-53); Consul and member of Saudi Arabian Delegation to UN, New York (1953-57); 1st Secretary, Egypt (1958-59); Counsellor, Chargé d'Affairs, Ghana, (1962-64); Minister Plenipotentiary, Chargé d'Affaires, UK (1965-66); Ambassador, Head of Western Department, Foreign Ministry (1966-68); Ambassador to Indonesia (1968-74); Ambassador to Iran (1975-80); Ambassador to Venezuela (since 1981); represented the Kingdom of Saudi Arabia at several conferences and meetings. **Publ.:** Articles in "Yawmiyat al-Bilad". **Medals:** King Abdul Aziz Order of Merit; and several other decorations from Iran, Morocco, Jordan, Egypt; Indonesia. **Addr.:** Saudi Arabian Embassy, P.O.Box 62565, Avenida Principal de la Floresta, con Fco. de Miranda-Edif. Sucre, 6 Piso la Floresta, Telex 23146, Caracas 1060 A, Venezuela.

BAKR (Kamel, Mohamad al-Wali Ismaïl, al), Sudanese university professor. **Born** on April 4, 1918 in Khartoum. **Son** of Mohamad al-Wali Ismaïl al-Kardafani **and** Mrs., née Umm Koulthoum Ali Abouzaid. **Married** on August 1, 1960 to Miss Nafissa Mudthir Ali al-Bouchi, 5 children: Wafa', Mohamad Iqbal, Issam and Hicham. **Educ.:** Universities of Cairo and London. **Dipl.:** Bachelor of Arts (Arabic Literature), Diplomas in Education, Islamology and Psychology, Doctor of Philosophy. **Career:** Professor Aïn Shams University (1953-54); al-Azhar University (1953-54); Director General, Religions Affairs Department (1955-64); Rector, Umdurman University (1965-69). **Publ.:** Author of several books and studies. **Hobbies:** Reading and Poetry. **Priv. Addr.:** al-Imtidad al-Jadid, Khartoum, Sudan.

BAKR (Mohamad, Abdul Karim), Saudi official. **Dipl.:** B.Sc. (Civil Engineering), Massachusetts Institute of Technology (1971); M.Sc. (Civil Engineering), Stanford University (1972). **Career:** Director of Industrial Sector, Ministry of Planning (1972-76); Director General of Saudi Ports Authority since 1976; supervised the preparation of the Saudi Arabian Second Industrial Development Plan (1975/76- 1979/80); member of the Technical Committee, Supreme Petroleum Council, Saudi-U.S. Industrial Cooperation team, International Conference on Energy and Raw Materials, Paris, 1974. **Publ.:** Energy and Development: a Case Study (M.I.T. Press, 1973). **Sport:** Swimming. **Addr.:** P.O.Box 5162, Tel.: 4760600, Riyadh, 11188, Saudi Arabia.

BAKR (Mohamad, Abdulrahman, al), United Arab Emirates politician. **Married. Educ.:** Islamic Studies. **Career:** Chairman of Audit and Accounting Department; Ambassador to Syria (1973); Minister of Justice and Islamic Affairs and Waqfs (1977-84). **Addr.:** Abu Dhabi, United Arab Emirates.

BAKR (Mohamad, Bakr), Egyptian governor, Suez Governorate. **Born** in 1930, Cairo. **Married**, two sons and one daughter. **Educ.:** Military Academy. **Dipl.:** Military Sciences Diploma (1949). **Career:** sent on study mission in the Soviet Union where he attended "Fronz" College (1962); attended Nasser Staff College (1978); led the VIIIth field infantry batallion at Suez during the war of attrition with Israel; Director of Operations, Third Army Corps (1971); head of Operations Division, Armed Forces; now Governor, Suez Governorate since May 1982. **Addr.:** Governate of Suez, Egypt.

BAKR (Rasheed, el-Tahir), Sudanese politician. **Born** in 1930 at Karkoj, Blue Nile Province (Sudan). **Married**, with children. **Educ.:** Elementary Education in Karkoj; Intermediate Education in Omdurman; Secondary Education at Hantub; Faculty of Law, Khartoum University. **Dipl.:** LL.B. (1958). **Career:** Private Law Practice; resisted the former military regime and consequently served a five-year term of imprisonment, (1958-64); Minister of Animal Wealth and Justice (Oct. 1965); Sudanese Ambassador to Libya (1972); Member of the Political Bureau, Sudanese Socialist Union (SSU) and Secretary, Farmers' Union in the SSU (1972); Assistant Secretary-General of the Sectoral Organisations of the SSU (Jan. 1974); Speaker, People's National Assembly, (May 1974); Minister of Animal Resources then Minister of Justice (short period in 1974); returned to Law practice (Oct. 74); Vice-President and Prime-Minister (Aug. 1976-79); Chief of Parliament (1979). **Addr.:** Khartoum, Sudan.

BAKR (Saleh Ibn Rashid, al), Saudi educator and

official. **Born** in 1920 at Hail, Saudi Arabia. **Dipl.:** B.A. (1963). **Career:** Primary school teacher (1938); Assistant Director (1942); Director, (1953); Director of Intermediate School (1955); Director of Secondary School (1957); Central Inspector (1959); Director of Education, Abha Region (1961); Director of General Warehouses, Ministry of Education, (1963); Director General, Personnel Department (1965); Deputy Director General of General Administration (1968); Director General of Capital Model Institute (grade of Deputy Minister); Participant member of conferences, symposia and meetings related to career; acted as Secretary General of Regional Education Committee; participated in creating World Muslim Youth Assembly; Head, Committee for Recruitment of non-Saudi Teachers, 1968. **Hobbies:** reading, travel, hunting. **Addr.:** Tel.: 4765750 (Home), Riyadh, Saudi Arabia.

BAKR (Seraj, al), Kuwaiti businessman. **Educ.:** University of Wisconsin, USA. **Dipl.:** Political Sciences and International Economics. **Career:** Direct Investments Department, Kuwait Foreign Trading Contracting & Investment Company (KFTCIC); Assistant Manager, New Issues Department, Kuwait International Investment Company (KIIC) (1979); Arab Latin American Bank, Peru; Director, Kuwaiti- Egyptian Shoes & Leather Products Co., Cairo, Egypt; Board Member, International Transport Equipment Co., Kuwait. **Addr.:** P.O.Box 22792, Tel.: 420762, 438273-9, Safat, Kuwait.

BAKRI (Maawiya, Mahmoud, al), Jordanian physician. **Born** in 1936 in Irbid, Jordan. **Married**, 2 sons. **Educ.:** Diploma of Obstetrics and Paediatrics. **Career:** Resident Obstetrician (1961-62); Doctor, Refugees Relief Agency (1963-65); Paediatrician and Obstetrician, Ministry of Health (1966-74), Head of Maternity and Childhood Centres (1974-); Board Member of Education, Ministry of Education (1980-84); Member of the Board of Irbid Development (1985-). **Hobbies:** Reading and travelling. **Member:** Associate Member, Jordanian Arab Youth Club; Chairman, Arab Female Academics Club (1982-). **Addr.:** Dahiat Al-Atibba, Number 9, P.O.Box 6202 Amman, Jordan.

BAKRI (Mustafa, Abdelbaki, al), Egyptian administrator. **Born** on October 30, 1924 in Cairo, Egypt. **Married**, 3 children. **Educ.:** London University, UK; Ecole Hôtelière de la Société Suisse des Hôteliers de Lausanne, Paris. **Dipl.:** B.Sc. in Economics; Diploma in Hotellery. **Career:** Manager of Cecil Hotel in Alexandria, Egypt (1948-54); Upper Egypt Hotels Company, Luxor and Aswan, Egypt (1954); Société Hôtelière de Montazah, Alexandria (1954-56); Hilton International, New York, USA (1956-59); Assistant General Manager, Nile Hilton in Cairo (1959-66); General Manager, Kuwait Hilton, Kuwait (1966-73); Member, Association des Anciens Elèves, Ecole Hôtelière de Lausanne; Vice Chairman, Hyatt International Corporation (Middle East and Africa) (1973-). **Publ.:** "International Cook Book" (1964). **Decor.:** Order of Merit (2nd Class), Egypt (1963). **Prof. Addr.:** 11 Sayed Abdel Wahed, Mohandiseen, Cairo, Egypt.

BAKRY (Mustafa, Mohamed), Egyptian physician. **Born** in 1939 in Cairo, Egypt. **Married**, 2 sons. **Educ.:** Cairo University, Egypt; also studied in London, England. **Dipl.:** MBBCH, DA, FFARCS. **Career:** Clinical Demonstrator and Internship Residence, Cairo University Hospital (1964-69); Anaesthetist and Registrar, St. Mary's Hospital, Charing Cross Hospital, Moorfields Eye Hospital, London, UK (1969-73); Senior Registrar Anaesthetist at St. George's Hospital, London (1973-74); Consultant Anaesthetist, Falkoping General Hospital, Sweden (1975-84); Head of Intensive Care Unit and Consultant Anaesthesist, Assalam International Hospital, Cairo (1984-). **Award:** National Sports Merit Award, Egypt (1959). **Hobbies:** Reading, music, sports and photography. **Prof. Addr.:** Assalam International Hospital, Cairo, Egypt. **Priv. Addr.:** 49 Giza Street, Giza, Egypt.

BALBAA (Chafiq), Egyptian university professor. **Dipl.:** Bachelor of Science (Agriculture), Doctor of Philosophy, Doctor in Chemistry. **Career:** Lecturer, Pharmacognosy (1951); Assistant Professor (1958); Professor of Crude Drugs (1964); Head, Pharmacognosy Department, Cairo University; Dean, Faculty of Pharmacy (1966). **Member** of Sigma Xi., Rho Chi, Phi Sigma, Gamma Sigma Epsilon, Egyptian Pharmaceutical Society, Egyptian Chemical Society, Egyptian Botanical Society, Tawfikieh Tennis Club, Cairo University Staff Club. **Publ.:** Medicinal Plan Constituents and 65 papers in the field of Pharmacognosy and Phytochemistry. **Awards:** Holder of the Newcomb Memorial Award for the Best research paper published in 1954 in the U.S.A. in the field of pharmacognosy. **Addr.:** Cairo, Egypt.

BALEELA (Mustafa, M.), Saudi consultant in architecture. **Born** in 1941 in Medina, Saudi Arabia. **Dipl.:** Doctorate (Urban Planning), University of Rome (1969); Ph.D. (Architecture), University of Pennsylvania. **Career:** Lecturer (1969); Secretary (1975), Acting Chairman (1976) and later Associate Professor (1979) Department of Architecture, King Saud University; Founder and President, (1980); EDCO Environmental Design and Consulting Centre; active in Planning, Architectural, Engineering Consultancy and the organization of conferences, seminars and public lectures; member, Institutes of Architecture in Italy and U.S.A., the International Society of Housing and Real Estate Fund; Government Representative for Saudi Government Center; Representative of the Council on Tall Buildings and Urban Habitat (UNESCO); active in the Preservation of architectural heritage; first saudi citizen to attain a Ph.D. in Architecture. **Publ.:** Design for Livability. **Hobbies:** Reading, jogging. **Prof. Addr.:** P.O.Box 51087, Tel.: 4656106, Riyadh 11543. **Priv. Addr.:** 4642675, Riyadh, Saudi Arabia.

BALGHONAIM (Saad Suliman Mohamad), Saudi academic. **Born** in 1948 in Hofuf, Saudi Arabia. **Dipl.:** B.A. and M.A. (Economics). **Career:** Director of Student Affairs, (1975-76); Director Administrative Affairs, College of Education, King Faisal University.; Vice-Dean, Student Affairs, King Faisal University, al-Ahsa (1981); Vice President, Head, Retail Banking, Eastern Province, Saudi American Bank, Alkhobar, Saudi Arabia (1982-1987); Treasirer, Saudi Consolidated Electric Company in the Eastern Province (1988- Present). **Publ.:** Agricultural Development in Saudi Arabia (M.A. thesis). **Hobbies:** Reading, writing, swimming, photography. **Addr.:** P.O.Box 5190, Dammam, 31422, Saudi Arabia, Telephone No. 858-6228. **Priv. Addr.:** P.O.Box 333, Alkhobar, 31952, Saudi Arabia.

BALI (Slaheddine), Tunisian statesman. **Born** on July 29, 1926 in Tunis, Tunisia. **Widower,** 3 children. **Educ.:** in Tunisia and France. **Dipl.:** Licence in Law (French and Tunisian); two diplomas for Higher Studies for the French Doctorate of Law. **Career:** Inspector of Finance (1949); Magistrate (1954); Republican Prosecutor, Permanent Military Tribunal (1957); Acting Colonel, Director of the Central Administration and Head of the Office of the Secretary of State for National Defence (1966); Secretary-General, Ministry of National Defence (25 February 1971); Permanent Secretary, National Defence Council (1971-73); Minister of Justice (1973-80); Minister of National Defence (1980-88); President of the National Assembly (1989). **Awards:** Grand Officer, Order of the Tunisian Republic; Knight, Order of Tunisian Independece; Commemorative Medal for the Battle for the Evacuation of Bizerta; Grand Cordon, Order of Egypt; Grand Officer, Order of Merit, Federal Republic of Germany; Commander, Alaouite Medal; Commander, Order of Iran. **Secretary- General,** Tunisian Olympic Committee; Vice-President, Tunisian Federation of Equestrian Sports: President of the Rugby Federation; President, Nautical Sports Federation; Head of the Tunisian Delegation and of the Liaison Office for Africa in the International Council for Military Sports. **Sport:** Shooting and Modern Pentathlon. **Addr.:** Tunis, Tunisia.

BALKHAIR (Yarub Abdullah), Saudi executive. **Born** in 1946 in Makkah, Saudi Arabia. **Dipl.:** B.Sc. (Film Production). **Career:** Former accountant and personnel executive, Aramco; during his under-graduate study in England he produced seven films; Manager of Public Relations for Europe and the Americas, Saudi Arabian Airlines; General Manager Public Relations, Saudi Arabian Airlines; Editor-in-Chief of its inflight magazine, «Ahlan Wasahlan»; and Member of the Board of Directors of World Aerospace Education Organisation. **Hobbies:** photography, reading and amateur radio. **Prof. Addr.:** P.O.Box 620, Jeddah 21231, Saudi Arabia. Tel.: 6862349, Fax: 6862006.

BALKHY (Hassan Omar), Saudi academic. **Born** in 1939 in Mecca, Saudi Arabia. **Dipl.:** M.A. (Economics) (1968); M.A. (Statistics), (1970); Ph.D. (Economics) (1973). **Career:** Head of Petroleum Research Section, Petromin, Riyadh, (1964-65); Assistant Professor, Department of Economics, King Abdulaziz University (1973-78); Vice President of Jeddah Municipality (1978-81); Chairman, Economics Department, Faculty of Economics and Administration, King Abdulaziz University; member American Economic Association, American Statistical Association and the Econometric Society; attended Conference on the Organization of Central Administration in Arab States, Riyadh (1975). **Publ.:** The Cost of Redistributing Income through Trade Policy, 1974. **Addr.:** Jeddah, Saudi Arabia.

BALKIS (Mahmoud, Jamal), Jordanian aviation official. **Born** in 1939 in Amman, Jordan. **Married,** 3 children. **Educ.:** Cranwell Royal Air Force College, UK (flying instructor); Royal Air Force, UK; Chinese Armed Forces University, Taiwan. **Career:** A.D.C. to his Majesty King Hussain (1967-68); Operations and Training Director, Royal Jordanian Air Force (1972-78); Deputy Chairman, Jordan Hotels and Tourism Company; President of ALIA, Royal Jordanian Airline (1984). **Hobbies:** Reading, music and sports, flying. **Member:** Anglo-Jordanian Society, Royal Jordanian Gliding Club, Imperial Falcon Club. **Prof. Addr.:** P.O.Box 302, Amman, Jordan.

BALLAL (Musa, Awad), Sudanese diplomat. **Born** on January 20, 1931 at El-Fasher (Western Sudan). **Married** to Alawia Yusif Mustafa, 3 children. **Educ.:** Primary and intermediate education at el-Fasher; Hantoub Secondary School; Faculty of Arts, University of Khartoum, until 1956; University of Pennsylvania, USA (1967-69). **Dipl.:** Economics and Geography (1956), where he worked in the industrial relations section and trade union registration, until 1964; Director, Management Development and Productivity Centre, Khartoum; Deputy General Manager, Industrial Development Corporation (1965-67); Secretary General, Industrial Production Corporation (1970); Secretary General, Higher Council of Public Sector Corporations (1970-71); Minister of Supply (Oct. 1971- Oct. 1972); Minister on Industry and Mining (Oct. 1972- Oct. 1973); Minister of Industry (Oct. 1973- Jan. 1975); Ambassador, Ministry of Foreign Affairs (Jan. 1975); Ambassador to the Federal Republic of Germany (June 1975-78); Ambassador, State of Kuwait (1978-80); Ambassador to Tunis and Permanent Representative to Arab League (1980-84). **Publ.:** "Industrialisation and Social Progress in the Rural Areas of Sudan" (1971), "The Problems of Industrialisation in Southern Sudan" (1971). **Sports:** Motoring and tennis. **Hobbies:** Gardening and photography. **Prof. Addr.:** Ministry of Foreign Affairs, Khartoum, Sudan.

BALTO (Omar, Mohamad), Saudi civil servant. **Born** in 1937 in Mecca city, Saudi Arabia. **Married,** children. **Educ.:** Faculty of Commerce, King Abdul Aziz University.

Dipl.: B.Com. (Accountancy). **Career:** Accountant, Income Tax Department; Financial Representative, Ministry of Finance; now Director of Financial Department, Mineral Resources Directorate, Jeddah. **Prof. Addr.:** Mineral Resources Directorate, Tel.: 52981, Jeddah, Saudi Arabia.

BAMASHMOUS (Mohamad Ahmad), Saudi academic. **Born** in 1945. **Dipl.:** Ph.D. (Educational Management), Kansas University, U.S.A. **Career:** Lecturer, Faculty of Education, Umm al-Qura University, Assistant Professor, later Acting Vice Dean, (1974); member of Conference on Open School Primary Education, Conference on University Administration; his doctoral research formed part of the master plan for higher education in the State of Kansas, U.S.A. **Hobby:** reading. **Priv. Addr.:** Tel.: 5425732, Mecca, Saudi Arabia.

BAMOGADDAM (Abdalla Ali), Saudi businessman. **Born** in 1940. **Career:** Owner and President of al-Eqtessad Establishment in Riyadh, Jeddah and Dammam (specialized in importing and selling all kinds of office furniture, Diazo Plan Printer copier machines, micro films and computers); Partner in other firms including insurance and sensitive paper factory in Lebanon, U.A.E. and Saudi Arabia. **Prof. Addr.:** P.O.Box. 32, Tel.: 4633331, Telex: 201367 AL-FRAT SJ, Riyadh 11411, Saudi Arabia.

BAMUFLEH (Salem), Saudi civil servant. **Born** in 1924 in Mecca city, Saudi Arabia. **Married**, children. **Educ.:** Faculty of Commerce, Cairo University. **Dipl.:** B.Sc. Accountancy (1950). **Career:** Joined Government service; Chief Accountant, Mecca Health Department; Director-General of Administration, Ministry of Agriculture and Water Resources; Adviser to the Ministry of Agriculture; Director-General, Insect Control Department; attended many international conferences, notably those of the Food and Agriculture Organisation (FAO) Rome (Italy); now Director-General of Agricultural Research Centre, Jeddah. **Hobbies: Fishing and Travel. Prof. Addr.:** Agricultural Research Centre, Tel.: 27777-27840, Jeddah City. **Priv. Addr.:** Tel.: 56127, Jeddah, Saudi Arabia.

BAMUJALLY (Ahmad ben Mohsin), Saudi businessman. **Born** Jeddah, in 1952. **Educ.:** received training courses in Business Administration in London. **Career:** Manager of Bamijally Co. for Trade and Industry; major dealer in perfumery and cosmetics. **Hobbies:** horse riding, music. **Addr.:** P.O.Box 112, Tel.: 22984, Jeddah, Saudi Arabia.

BAMUJALLY (Mohsen Mujally Ahmad), Saudi businessman. **Born** in 1929, **Educ.:** received general education at el-Falah School, Jeddah. **Career:** Businessman, Canned Dairy Products and Soft drinks dealer. **Hobbies:** Horse riding, watching football and wrestling match. **Addr.:** P.O.Box 112, Jeddah 21411, Tel.: 6474236, 6474484, 6470855, Telex: 401696 WADI SJ, Saudi Arabia; and P.O.Box 963, Dammam, Tel.: 8348658, 8339704, 8341149, Dammam, Saudi Arabia.

BANAJAH (Mohamad Said), Saudi auditor. **Born** in Jeddah, in 1931. **Educ.:** Secondary School Certificate. **Career:** Warehouse Manager, Hussein Aeouini & Co. (1949-56); Assistant Stores Accountant, Saudi National Co. for Electric Power (1956-58); Fuel Controller, Saudia (1958-62), Supervisor, Property Department (1961-62), Sales and Interline Accountant (1962-65), Assistant to Financial Adviser (1966-67), Assistant to General Manager for Revenue and Financial Affairs (1965-66), Revenue Manager (1967-68), Assistant General Auditor (1968-71); General Auditor, Saudia Saudi Arabian Airlines Corporation. **Publ.:** articles in Saudia's monthly magazine al-Jinah al-Akhdar (Green Wing). **Hobby:** Reading. **Addr.:** Jeddah, Saudi Arabia.

BANAJAH (Samir Hamid), Saudi civil servant. **Born** in 1940 in Jeddah, Saudi Arabia. **Dipl.:** B.Com., Faculty of Commerce, Cairo University (1966); M.B.A., University of Michigan (1970). **Career:** Taught at the Faculty of Economics and Administration, King Abdulaziz University (1971-74); Director of Planning and Budgeting; Director of Projects Department; Director of Purchasing and Tenders Department, financial Controller at King Abdulaziz University Director General of Posts since 1976. **Honour:** Grand Cordon of the Order of the Brilliant Star (Taiwan, Republic of China). **Hobbies:** philately, reading. **Addr.:** Directorate General of Posts, Tel.: 4769550, Riyadh, Saudi Arabia.

BANAWI (Ali Mohamad), Saudi businessman. **Born** in 1929 in Jeddah, Saudi Arabia. **Educ.:** General Certificate of Secondary School, Jeddah; attended several seminars on management and Industry. **Career:** Entire career has been in the private industrial sector; Chairman, Banawi Industrial Group; represented Saudi Arabia in the Arab Union for Paper Industries, the Arab League; involved in many social and charitable activities. **Publ.:** several articles about industry and development in Saudi Arabia. **Hobbies:** Hunting, swimming, reading, fishing. **Prof. Addr.:** P.O.Box 8281, Tel.: 6674074, Jeddah. **Priv. Addr.:** 6674057, Jeddah, Saudi Arabia.

BANBI (Hamdi Ali, Abdelwahab, al-), Egyptian Politician. **Born** on October, 4, 1935 in Asyut. **Married,** Two children. **Educ.:** B.Sc., Petroleum Engineering, Cairo University (1958); M.Sc., Petroleum Engineering, Tulsa University, USA (1961); Ph.D. Petroleum Engineering, Texas A&M USA (1963). **Career:** Field Production Engineer, Assistant Manager, Compagnie Oriental de Pétroles d'Egypte (1963-65); Assistant Professor, Al-Azhar University, Cairo (1966-68); Senior Reservoir Engineer and Deputy Chairman, Western Desert Petroleum Corp. (1968-77),; Chairman and Managing Director, Gulf of Suez Petroleum Corp. (1977-88); Chairman, Egyptian General

Petroleum Corp. (1988-91); Adviser, Ministry of Petroleum (1977-91); Minister of Petroleum and Mineral Resources (1991-93); Minister of Petroleum (Oc. 1993-Oct.99). **Publ:** Author of numerous publication on Petroleum Engineering. **Address:** Cairo, Egypt.

BANDAK (Mazen, al), Palestinian Journalist. **Born** in 1934 in Bethlehem, Palestine. **Married. Educ.:** al-Rashidiyah College, Jerusalem; Cairo University. **Dipl.:** Licence in Law. **Career:** Journalist, writer and publisher; General Manager, "Dar al-Kuds" publishing, printing and distribution house, Beirut, Lebanon. **Publ.:** "Israel: Mujtamaa Askari" (1969), "al-Harb al-Thalitha" (1972), "Quusat al-Naft" (1974), "al-Mukawama al Falastiniya"; Numerous articles in various magazines and newspapers in Arabic. **Hobbies:** History, fiction, music, theatre and walking. **Member:** Egyptian Journalists Association; Palestinian Writers and Journalists Union. **Addr.:** Amman, Jordan.

BANGASH (Ibrahim Abdallah), Saudi official. **Born** Jeddah, in 1933, **Educ.:** received secondary school education. **Career:** Vice-President of United Bureau of Pilgrims' Agents; has vast experience in the business of guiding pilgrims, providing facilities, accommodation and guidance to pilgrims arriving by sea; acts as agent for pilgrims of all nationalities except those from Pakistan and Java; travels all over the Islamic world to arrange group pilgrimages; President of Pilgrim's Agents Association; Director, Pilgrims Distribution Board; Chief Agent for guiding pilgrims. **Hobbies:** reading, travel. **Addr.:** Centre for Pilgrims Arriving by Sea, Tel.: 22495, Jeddah, Saudi Arabia.

BANGASH (Mohamad Ali), Saudi official. **Born** in Jeddah, in 1932. **Educ.:** Secondary School Certificate. **Career:** Contributes largely to the organization of pilgrims' accommodation, facilities and transport inside the holy places during the pilgrimage season; one of the major organizers of pilgrim guidance in the Islamic holy land, **Hobbies:** reading. **Addr.:** Airport, Pilgrims' City, Tel.: 24770, 480/33, Jeddah, Saudi Arabia.

BANNA (Bandali), Jordanian banker. **Born** in 1937 in Jaffa, Palestine. **Son** of Michael Banna. **Married** in 1974, 4 children. **Educ.:** Intermediate Bookkeeping, London Chamber of Commerce. **Career:** Chief Accountant, Development Bank of Jordan (1957-67); Comptroller, Central Bank of Jordan (1967-78); Comptroller, Petra Bank, Amman (1978-80); Assistant Manager, foreign Relations Dept., Syrian Jordanian Bank (1980-1982); Since 1982 Manager & Owner of Banna Travel & Tourism Co., Amman. Jordan. **Hobbies:** Swimming and Travelling. **Member:** Greek Orthodox Club, Amman. **Addr.:** P.O.Box 5237, Tel.: 644763 (Office), 651664 (Res.), Telefax: 962 6 651663, Amman 11183, Jordan.

BANOOB (Samir Nagib), Egyptian-American physician. **Born** in 1937. **Married**, 2 children. **Educ.:** Medical degree, University of Alexandria, Egypt; School of Public Health, Johns Hopkins University, USA. **Dipl.:** M.D., Diplomat of Internal Medicine, Diplomat of Public Health, Ph.D. in Health Administration. **Career:** Specialist in Internal Medicine in the Navy Hospital, later Director of Medical Division, Ports Department (1962-69); Director of Medical Services, Ministry of Maritime, Alexandria (1969-74); Consultant to the World Bank and to the General Secretariat of Health in the Gulf States, on health information and planning, Director of Office for National Health Planning, Ministry of Public Health; Kuwait (1974-82); Visiting Professor at the International Health Department, John Hopkins School of Hygiene and Public Health (1980-); Professor of Health Policy and Management and Director of the International Health Programs, College of Public Health, University of South Florida, USA (1983-). **Member**, Egyptian Medical Association, American Public Health Association and President of its international Health Section, Consultant on major assignments in more than 46 countries with governments, the World Health Organization and its regional offices, UNICEF, World Bank, UNDP, the United States Agency for International Development, and the United Nations Institute of Aging, is a consultant for Health Planning, Health Manpower Development, and Hospital Management for the Secretariat General of Health for the Arab Gulf Countries (1980-), Consultant to state and local health agencies in the USA (1983-). **Publ.:** Authored more than 35 articles that were published in the most reputable International and American Scientific journals, presented more than 100 papers in major International Conferences including the World Health Organization and the American Public Health Association meetings, and authored extensive major consultancy reports and government documents. **Addr.:** University of South Florida, College of Public Health, 13201 Bruce B. Downs Blvd. MDG 56 Tampa, Florida 33612/3805, USA.

BANYAN (Abdallah Saleh, al), Saudi executive. **Born** in 1937 in Riyadh, Saudi Arabia. **Dipl.:** Ph.D. **Career:** Director General of Planning and Social Studies Department, Ministry of Labour and Social Affairs; Associate Professor, Sociology Department, King Saud University; Managing Director & member of the Board, Saudi Ericsson Communications Co. Ltd.; Executive Director US, Saudi Arabian Business Council; Board member of National Bank; participated in several conferences of the Arab League, UN and other international organizations. **Publ.:** Saudi Students in U.S.A., a Study of Cross Cultural Education and Attitude Change; Child and City; Personality and Social Change in Saudi Arabia. **Prof. Addr.:** P.O.Box 27582, Riyadh 11427, Tel.: 4762554, **Pri. Addr.:** P.O.Box 146, Riyadh 11371, Tel.: 4933642, Saudi Arabia.

BARAJA (Abdallah Saleh), Saudi businessman. **Born** Shahar, in 1942. **Educ.:** Secondary School Certificate;

business administration training. **Career:** Former Sales Manager of Modern Supplies Corporation, Jeddah; later Sales Manager of International Products Corporation, Mecca, al-Sulaiman Co., Riyadh, Haji Abdullah Alireza and Co., al-Khobar; Riyadh Branch Manager, Alissayee Trading Co.; member of Riyadh Chamber of Commerce; agent for Peat Marwick Mitchell & Co.; Proprietor and General Manager, General National Corporation (Public Relations and Representation), Riyadh. **Addr.:** P.O.Box 4226, Tel.: 28183, Riyadh, Saudi Arabia.

BARAKAT (Abdallah, Hussein), Yemeni politician. **Born** on January 26, 1936 in Sanaa Y.A.R. **Married:** four children, three sons, one daughter. **Educ.:** Military College, Sanaa (1950); Police College, Cairo, Egypt. **Dipl.:** M.A. in Law, Cairo University, Egypt (1958). **Career:** Army Officer (1960); Assistant Head of Security, Taiz (1961); Minister of Agriculture (1965-66); Minister of the Interior (1967-71); Ambassador to Algeria (1971-74); Minister of Youth and Social Affairs, Deputy Prime Minister for Internal Affairs (1975); Director, Head of State's Office (1976). **Publ.:** "Neutrality, Non-Alignment and Positive Neutrality"; The Straits and their International Significance. **Decor:** Order of the Nile, 2nd Class, Egypt (1975). **Sports:** Tennis, Table-Tennis, Football. **Addr.:** Airport Street, Ring Road, Tel.: 2795, Sanaa, Republic of Yemen.

BARAKAT (Ahmad Kaid), Yemeni politician. **Born** on January 1, 1934 in Sanaa, Republic of Yemen. **Son** of Kaid Ismail Barakat, **Married** in 1960 to Khadijah Rufaat, two sons, Bashar (1961), Barash (1966), and one daughter, Bushra (1970). **Educ.:** Primary education in Yemen and Lebanon (1941-49); Secondary education in Egypt (1949-52). **Dipl.:** B.Sc. University of Birmingham, UK; Diploma, Imperial College, London, UK (1953-59). **Career:** Worked with several American and European companies in the field of petroleum and mineral exploration (1959-63); General Director, Ministry of Public Works (1963-64); Private employment with Arab establishment in Sanaa; Director, Kuwaiti Aid, Office, Dubai (1964-69); Minister of Foreign Affairs (1969-70); Personal Representative of the President; Secretary General, Republican Council; Head of the General Election Commission (1970-71); Minister of Information and Culture (1971); Ambassador Extraordinary and Plenipotentiary to the Federal Republic of Germany and non-resident Ambassador to Belgium, the Netherlands, Switzerland, Austria; Head of the Y.A.R. Mission to the E.E.C. (1972-77) Minister of Oil and Mineral Resources, Member of the Peoples' Constituent Assembly (1978-80); Ambassador to Japan (1981-83); Minister of Economy and Industry (1983-86); Member of the Peoples' Constituent Assembly (1986-87); Chairman, Board of Directors, International Bank of Yemen (1987-90); Vice Minister of Oil; Chairman of Yeminco (Yemen Oil and Mineral Resources Corporation) (1990-92); Chairman of Yemen Airways Corporation (1992-95); Headed and took part in different social activities as Chairman of: Sanaa Cooperative Society; Yemeni-German Friendship Society; Yemen Water Protection Society; Member, Board of Trustees: 1) The International Campaign for the Preservation of the Old City of Sanna, 2) Al Afif Cultural Foundation. **Authored and published a number of books on:** Progress, Development, Democracy, the phenomenon of Defamation, Petroleum and Mineral Resources in Yemen as well as novels and short stories. **Hobbies:** Writing, Music (Classical and Folk), popular poetry, folklorew, swimming, gardening, cross-country running, gymnastics. **Addr.:** P.O.Box 16916, Sanaa, Yemen Republic.

BARAKAT (Gamaleddine), Egyptian diplomat. **Born** in 1921 in Egypt. **Educ.:** Cairo University, Academy of International Law, The Hague and Orient College, Oxford. **Dipl.:** Licentiate of Law, Diplomas of International Law. **Career:** Third secretary of the Egyptian Embassy, London (1950-52); Political Bureau, Ministry of Foreign Affairs (1953-55); Consul General in Aleppo, Syria (1955-58); Counsellor, Washington (1958-60); Head of Service Training Department, Ministry of Foreign Affairs (1961-63); Member of Organization of African Unity Expert Committee, Addis Abeba (1963-64); Egyptian Ambassador to Uganda (1964-68), to Burundi (1967-68), to Finland (Oct. 1968-1973); Assistant to the President's Adviser on National Security (1973-74); Head of Cultural Relations and Techn. Co-Operation Dept., Ministry of Foreign Affairs (1975); Ambassador to Iraq (1976-77); Director Institute of Diplomatic Studies, Foreign Ministry, Cairo (1979-80). **Publ.:** Author of "Status of Aliens in Egypt" (1949), "Lectures on Diplomacy and Diplomatic Terminology in Arabic" (1962). **Awards:** Order of Merit (Egypt, 1958), Order of the Republic (1964), Order of the Lion, Finland (1973). **Priv. Addr.:** 55, Hegaz St., Heliopolis, Cairo, Egypt.

BARAKAT (Ghaleb, Zaki), Jordanian tourism and travel Counsellor. Former minister, ambassador, international civil servant. **Born** on September 20, 1927 in Jaffa. **Son** of late Zaki Barakat **and** Mrs., née Fatmeh Barakat. **Married** in 1959 to Jalia Barakat, in Amman, 3 children: Sireen, Salwa and Zaki. **Educ.:** Bishop Gobat School, Jerusalem; American University of Beirut, Beirut. **Dipl.:** B.B.A. (Honours) (1949). **Career:** Press Attaché to Tourism Department (1952-54); Tourist Attaché, Jordanian Embassy, Rome (1954-60); Director-General of Tourism Authority (1960-72); Under-Secretary, Ministry of Tourism and Antiquities (1967-72); Minister of Tourism and Antiquities (1967-72); Minister of Tourism and Antiquities, and Chairman of Jordan Tourism Authority, and Chairman of Jordan Hotels and Rest-Houses Corporation (1972-79); Lecturer, Faculty of Economics and Commerce, University of Jordan, Amman (1967-79); Special Envoy of World Tourism Organisation (1980); Ambassador/ Permanent Representative of Jordan to the United Nations, Geneva, (1980-85); Member of the UN Commission on Human Rights, Geneva (1980-85); Assistant Director General of the International Labour Organisation (ILO) Geneva, responsible for ILO activities in the Arab Region (1986-90); now, Tourism and Travel Counselor. **Decorations:** Jordan, Belgium, the Vatican, Rumania and Mexico. **Sport:** Swimming. **Member:** Royal Automobile Club, Jordan; Honorary President Skal Club, Jordan, American University of Beirut Alumniclub of Jordan; American Biographical Institute, Raleigh, USA. Fellow, International Biographical Centre, Cambridge; World University Roundtable, Benson Az. USA. **Priv. and Prof. Addr.:** P.O.Box 9064, Amman, 11191, Jordan.

BARAKAT (Mohamad Rushdi), Egyptian Diplomat. **Born** on August 4, 1936 in Cairo. **Married. Educ.:** Ain Shams University, Cairo; Cairo University, Cairo al-Azhar University, Cairo; Budapest University, Hungary. **Dipl.:** B.A. (Commerce) (1974); Ph.D. (Economic Sciences) (1979); **Career:** joined Ministry of Economy (1960); Commercial Attache, Embassy of Egypt in India (1961-65); 1st Secretary of Commercial Affairs, Egyptian Embassy in Budapest, Hungary (1974-78); Commercial Adviser, Egyptian Embassy in Washington D.C. USA (1980). **Hobbies:** Swimming, squash, tennis. **Addr.:** Ministry of Foreign Affairs, Cairo, Egypt.

BARAKATI (Ghali Ghazi, N., al), Saudi academic. **Born** in 1943 in Baghdad. **Dipl.:** Ph.D. (Solid State Physics). **Career:** Demonstrator, King Abdulaziz University, Mecca (1973); Assistant Professor and Chairman, Department of Physics, Umm al-Qura University since 1980; Consultant to Kindico Consulting Engineers, Jeddah. **Publ.:** "The Electronic Properties of as-Se Glassy Alloys" (Ph.D. thesis). **Hobbies:** electronic circuitry, photography, fishing. **Addr.:** Department of Physics, Umm al-Qura University, P.O.Box 715, Tel.: 5564770 Ext. 219, Mecca, Saudi Arabia.

BARGASH (Mohamad), Moroccan banker. **Born** in 1928 in Rabat, Morocco. **Married,** 2 children. **Educ.:** Licencié en Droit, Diploma, Ecole des Sciences Politiques, Paris. **Career:** Chief of Cabinet of the Deputy Prime Minister in the first Moroccan Government after independence (1956); then Director of the Cabinet of the Minister of Defence; First Counsellor, Moroccan Embassy to France; Director of Credit, Bank of Morocco; Deputy Governor, Bank of Morocco (1964); Head of National Advancement and Planning, Royal Cabinet (1965); Minister of Development (1966); Minister of Agriculture (1967); Deputy Governor, Bank of Morocco (1969); President, Banque Nationale pour le Développement Economique (1972); presently Chairman, Société Générale Marocaine de Banques, Rabat; Counsellor, Groupement Professionnel des Banques du Maroc; Chairman, Cie Industrielle de Travaux du Maroc; Société Nationale d'Investissements and many other Companies. **Addr.:** 55 Blvd. Abdelmoumen, Casablanca, Morocco.

BARGES (Barges, Hamoud, al), Kuwaiti administrator. **Born** in 1931 in Kuwait. **Married,** 6 children. **Educ.:** Institute of Hospital Administrators in UK (1974). **Career:** Assistant Under-Secretary for Administration, Ministry of Public Health (1964-69), for Health Affairs (1969-71), Assistant Under-Secretary for Administration and Financial Affairs (1971-73), Under Secretary (1973-76); Secretary General, Kuwait Red Crescent Society (1969-); Member of Petroleum Information Committee for the Arab Gulf States, State of Kuwait Planning Committee, ALESCO Committee, High Board of Information for the State of Kuwait; President, Federation of Arab News Agencies (1979-81), (1984-86); Chairman and General Director, Kuwait News Agency (1976). President, Kuwait Red Crescent Society (1995-). **Publ.:** Many analyses and articles on political and social subjects in national and other Arab newspapers. **Decor.:** Honorary Degree, Columbia Pacific University, USA; Cyril and Methodius Order (1st Degree), USSR. **Hobbies:** Fishing, sports, travelling and reading. **Member:** Hunting and Equestrian Club, Kuwait Sporting Club. **Priv. Addr.:** P.O.Box 59, Safat, Kuwait.

BARGOUD (Georges, Zaki), Egyptian ophtalmologist, Ex-Director, Organon Scientific Bureau, Cairo (Egypt). **Born** on September 13, 1931, in Cairo, Egypt. **Married** to Azar Linda Boulos; 4 children: 1 daughter and 3 sons. **Educ.:** College of the Christian Brothers; Faculty of Medicine, Ayn Shams University, Abbassiyah District, Cairo. **Dipl.:** D.O.M.S. (Ophtalmology). **Career:** Ex-Director of Ophtalmologic Hospitals in Cairo, Ministry of Public Health, now Ophtalmologist (Private Practice) and Ex-Director, Organon Scientific Bureau, Cairo now retired. **Hobbies:** Music, cinema, travelling and reading. **Prof. Addr.:** Organon Scientific Bureau, 36, Sherif Street, Tel.: 974478, Cairo. **Priv. Addr.:** 3, Ghornata Street, Heliopolis, Tel.: 2582258, Fax: 2580502, e-mail: BARGOUD-S@AOL.COM, Cairo, Egypt.

BARKOUKY (Mohamed Adel, El), Egyptian Chairman and Managing Director of Alexandria Commercial and Maritime Bank. **Born** on January 1, 1932 at Kafr el Sheikh, Egypt. **son** of Moghazy El-Barkouky - President of Court of Appeal **and** Mrs. née Neemat Zakaria Nassef. **Married** on July 26, 1961 in Alexandria to Hanaa Ahmed el Barkouki, 4 children: Mohamed (18/9/1962), Omar (20/1/1964), Nivine (24/9/1968), Rasha (23/1/1976). **Educ.:** Faculty of Law - Cairo University. **Career:** *Previously:* Lawyer until 1962; Promoted in Marine Transportation field since 1962 until Being the Chairman of Alexandria Company of Maritime Agencies in March 1978; Chairman of Public Sector Organization of Marine Transportation; Board Member of National Marine Company & of Arab Union of Marine Transportation, Chairman of Arab Bridge Maritime Co. & of Alexandria Maritime Chamber, Member of Technical Consultant Committee of Harbours. *Now:* Chairman & Managing Director of Alexandria Commercial & Maritime Bank, Alexandria from 18/6/1991 till now; Member of National Council of Production & of Technology & Science Research Academy; Board Member of Consultancy & Research Center of Maritime Transportation Sector & of Egyptian Trading Chamber. **Sports Practised:** Tennis. **Hobbies:** Economic and Marine Studies, Agriculture, Horses and Tennis. **Clubs:** Smouha Club and Yacht Club. **Credit Cards:** Visa. **Prof. Addr.:** Alexandria Commercial and Maritime bank, 85, El Horreya Str., P.O.Box 2376, Alexandria 21519, Egypt.

BARO (Abdoulaye), Mauritanian educationist. **Born** in 1935 at Boghé, Southern Mauritania. **Son** of Mamdou Daouda Baro (judge). **Married** to M'Bengue Diaw, 3 children. **Educ.:** Sorbonne, Paris where he studied language and literature (1956-61). **Dipl.:** Licence ès-Lettres (B.A.). **Career:** Schoolmaster at Rosso College teaching French language and literature (1961-64); examiner, Rosso Lycée (1964); Director, National School of Administration (1966); High Commissioner for Technical Education, formation of cadres and Civil Service (1968); Minister of Civil Service and Labour (1971- Aug. 1975); Minister of State for Social Promotion (Aug. 1975- January 1977); Minister of State for Rural Promotion (January 1977). **Member:** Parti du Peuple Mauritanien (PPM); Bureau Politique du PPM (Party suspended following Coup in 1978). **Hobbies:** Reading, chess. **Addr.:** Nouackchott, Mauritania.

BAROOM (Abdallah Mohamed), Saudi businessman. **Born** 1936. **Educ.:** received general education. **Career:** Has run his own business since his career in 1956; runs a number of successful business enterprises; member of the Board of OKAZ daily newspaper; Saudi Metal Co. (manufactured reinforced concrete bars); Red Sea Insurance Co.; former Chairman, Trans-Arabian Investment Bank E.C; founding member of Arab National Bank, several contracting companies (Bilmat Saudi Arabia Est., Saudi Steel Reinforcements Ltd.); various hotels worldwide; participated in a project of credit facilities for low income citizens for building private houses; founder of a Saudi Sea transportation line; participated in the establishment of several local industries; attended several economic conferences in the Middle East and Europe. **Hobby:** Travel **Addr.:** Baroom Center, Hail Street, P.O.Box 1346, Jeddah 21431, Saudi Arabia. His business has representative offices in Asia, Europe and U.S.A.

BARROU (Mohamad), Moroccan director. **Born** on 25 May 1925 in Midelt, Morocco. **Son** of Embarek Barrou (farmer) **and** Mrs. Itto Bent Mohamad. **Married** on 3 July 1958 in Rabat to Miss Rita Manjra, 4 children: Nadia, Omar, Nizar, Abdelkarim. **Educ.:** Ecole de Midelt. **Career:** Worked in banking sector (1941); Caïd (1957); Political deportee by the Protectorat for eight years; Political refugee for twelve years (Independence); member of the board of companies (1976). **Prof. Addr.:** 5 Bd. Abdellah B. Yacine, Tel.: 304257, Casablanca, Morocco. **Priv. Addr.:** 9 Rue de Beziers C.I.L., Tel.: 362779, Casablanca, Morocco.

BARRY (Abdelrahman), Sudanese bank manager. **Born** in 1940 in Khartoum, Sudan. **Son** of Ali Barry (Galli Tribe). **Married** in 1970, 5 children: 4 sons, 1 daughter. **Educ.:** University of Cairo, Egypt. **Dipl.:** B.Comm. (1965). **Career:** Joined Ottoman Bank; Manager, Unity Bank, Khartoum; member, Sudan Economic Society; member, local Football Associations. **Publ.:** Articles in Sudanese Press on banking and foreign Exchange operations. **Hobbies:** Sports, Tennis and football. **Member:** el-Neil Sports Club. **Addr.:** Unity Bank, P.O.Box 408, Tel.: 71332, Khartoum, Sudan.

BARRY (Zain Aladdeen), Saudi academic. **Born** on 7 May 1949, in Medina, Saudi Arabia. **Dipl.:** Ph.D. (Economics). **Career:** Adviser, Ministry of Planning; Professor, Department of Economics, King Saud University; member, Western Economic Association. **Prof. Addr.:** Department of Economics, King Saud University, Tel.: 4354400 Est. 135, Riyadh. **Priv. Addr.:** Tel.: 4811000 Est. 2460, Riyadh, Saudi Arabia.

BASAHEL (Ahmed Nasir), Saudi academic. **Born** in 1939. **Dipl.:** B.Sc., Ph.D. (Geology). **Career:** Demonstrator (1963-67); Assistant Lecturer (1968-69); Lecturer (1969-71); member of National Geological Committee; Fellow of The Geological Society of Britain; Assistant Professor and Dean of Science and Mathematics Centre, Riyadh University. **Publ.:** Precambrian Correlation on the Geology of Saudi Arabia, Egypt and Sudan; Geological Map; General Geology. **Hobby:** excursions. **Addr.:** Department of Geology, Faculty of Science, Riyadh University, Tel.: 36110, Riyadh, Saudi Arabia.

BASAHY (Abdallah Yahia), Saudi academic. **Born** in 1943 at Sabia. **Dipl.:** Ph.D. **Career:** Demonstrator, Lecturer and then Assistant Professor, Botany Department; Head, Botany Department, Faculty of Science, King Saud University; Vice Dean of Student Affairs; member, Saudi Biological Society; member of several committees. **Publ.:** various books and articles. **Hobbies:** Tourism. **Prof. Addr.:** Botany Department, Faculty of Science, King Saud University, Tel.: 4781374, Riyadh. **Priv. Addr.:** Tel.: 4013755, Riyadh, Saudi Arabia.

BASALAMAH (Abdullah, Hussain), Saudi Physician. **Born** on September 27, 1936 in Mecca. **Dipl.:** M.D. (1965); MRCOG (1971); FRCOG (1981); FACS (1973); **Career:** Obstetrician and Gynaecologist at the Central Hospital in Riyadh (1965-70); Assistant Professor of Obstetrics and Gynaecology, Faculty of Medicine, Riyadh University (1970-84) then Vice Dean (1973-74); Dean, Faculty of Medicine and Allied Sciences of King Abdul Aziz University in Jeddah (1974-80), then Professor and Chairman of its Obstetrics and Gynaecology Department (since

1980); President of Arb Board OBS/GYNAE (1984-). **Publ.:** numerous articles in various medical journals (in Arabic) on childbrith and care; several books. **Hobbies:** Mountaineering, reading, fishing. **Prof. Addr.:** King Abdul Aziz University, Faculty of Medicine, P.O.Box 9029, Tel.: 6871193/5, Jeddah, Saudi Arabia. **Priv. Addr.:** Tel.: 6659707, Jeddah, Saudi Arabia.

BASALEEM (Mohamad, Ali), Saudi senior civil servant. **Born** in 1941 at Makalla, Saudi Arabia. **Married**, with children. **Educ.:** Faculty of Economics and Political Science, Riyadh University; American University in Beirut (Lebanon). **Dipl.:** B.Com. and B.B.A. (Bachelor of Business Administration). **Career:** Accounting clerk, Jeddah Electric Company (1957-58); Technical Supervisor and Secretary, al-Asfahani Printers, Jeddah (1958-68); Press Manager, Mecca Printing and Information Organisation (1965-66); Purchase Agent, Technical Division, Saudia; Personnel Procedure Analysis Supervisor, Saudia; now Manager of Personnel Department (Saudia), Saudi Arabian Airlines Corporation. **Prof. Addr.:** SAUDIA, Personnel Department, Airport Road, Tel.: 25222, Ext. 284, Jeddah City. **Priv. Addr.:** Tel.: 21492, Jeddah, Saudi Arabia.

BASERAIN (Mohamad Abdul Rahman), Private legal and religious adviser. **Born** Jeddah, in 1933. **Dipl.:** B.A. (Civil Law). **Career:** Has been working in the field of legal and judical consultancy for 20 years; also runs a real estate and contracting business. **Hobby:** Arabic literature. **Addr.:** Souq al-Nada, Tel.: 28688, Jeddah, Saudi Arabia.

BASHAIREH (Ahmad Suleiman), Jordanian academic. **Born** in 1934 in Kofr-asad, Irbid, Jordan. **Married**, 4 children. **Educ.:** Cairo University, B.Sc.; Indiana University, U.S.A. **Dipl.:** M.Sc. in Education, Ph.D. **Career:** Teacher (1959-63); Supervisor of Mathematics at the Ministry of Education (1964-65); Principal, Amman Demonstration School (1965-66); Director of Beit Hanina Institute of Public Administration (1966-67); Member of Mathematics Curricula in the MOE (1967); Director of Huwara Teachers College (1967-68); Director of Amman Teachers College (1968-72); Cultural Counsellor in Pakistan (1972-74); Director of Education Department at the Royal Scientific Society (1974-78); Director of General Education (1978-80); Member of Education Council (1982-87); Director of Examinations (1982-85); Secretary General of the MOE (1986-87); Member of the Faculty of Science Council and of University Council, Jordan University (1986-87); Director General of Orphans Fund Development and Administration Corporation (1987-88); Secretary General of the MOE (1987-). **Member** of the Higher Education Council (1987-); Member of the Faculty of Education Council, Jordan University (1987-). **Publ.:** Arabic translation of SMP, school mathematics projects, co-author of other education books; co-author of some children reading books. **Hobbies:** Travelling, reading, chess and music. **Member:** Founder Member of Jordan Road Safety Association, Islamic studies Association, Science and Technology Club, Arab Culture Associations. **Prof. Addr.:** Ministry of Higher Education, Amman, Jordan.

BASHARY (Ahmad, Adel, el), Egyptian banker. **Born** in 1956 in Cairo, Egypt. **Son** of Adel Ahmad el-Bashary (ship's master). **Married** in 1979, two children. **Educ.:** The Maret School, Washington D.C., George Washington University, Washington D.C., the American University of Cairo, Egypt. **Dipl.:** B.A. and B.Sc. **Career:** Vice President and Secretary to the board of directors, ALUBAF Arab International Bank, Bahrain. **Sports:** Diving, fishing. **Hobbies:** Photography, hunting. **Member** of the Egyptian Hunting and Fishing Club, Alexandria, Egypt; Holder of all major **Credit Cards. Addr.:** Manama, Bahrain.

BASHEER (Tahseen, Mohamad), Egyptian diplomat. **Born** on April 5,1925 in Alexandria, Egypt. **Son** of late Dr. Mohamad Basheer, D., **and** Mrs. Aziza Khalil. **Dipl.:** B.Sc. (Political Economy) Alexandria, Egypt (1950); Graduate work at Princeton and Harvard Universities; M.A. (Political Economy) Harvard (1955); awarded the Commercial Bank Prize for Political Economy (1950); awarded the Ahmed Abdel Wahab Prize for Political Economy. **Career:** Instructor in Political Economy, Department of Economics, Faculty of Commerce, Alexandria University (1950-56); Held many other positions in students activities in Egypt and the USA; chairman of the Middle East studies Society, University of Alexandria (1949-50); one of the Founding members and former President of the Organization of Arab Students in the U.S.A. (1952-55); Former Member of Executive Committee of the All African Students Union of the Americas (1954-55); Spokesman and Information Officer for the Egyptian Permanent Mission to the UN (1956-57); Acted as spokesman at the Second African Summit Conference (July 1964); Member of the UAR Delegation to the Second Arab Summit Conference, Alexandria (September 1964); Member of the UAR Delegation to the Non-Aligned Conference, Cairo (1964), also worked as Spokesman of the UAR Delegation; Acting Director of the league of Arab States Office, London (1965-66); Senior Staff Member of the Arab States Permanent Delegation to UN, New-York (1966-68); Lecturer on International Affairs and Arab problems in the Institute of Diplomatic Affairs, Ministry of Foreign Affairs, Cairo (1969, 1970, 1971); Member of the UAR Delegation to the Permanent Committee of Information, Arab league (1970) and Head of the UAR Delegation to the Committee (1971); Member of the UAR Delegation to UN General Assembly Session (1970); Counsellor (Press Affairs) UAR Embassy, London (1969-71), and Director of the Egyptian Information Centre, London; Official Spokesman of Egypt (1970) (under president Nasser); Spokesman of the Cairo Conference on the Palestinians (September 1970); Official Spokesman of Egypt (May 1971- March

1972) (under President Sadat) with rank of Minister Plenipotentiary, Ministry of Foreign Affairs; Director of the Press and Information Department Ministry of Foreign Affairs, and spokesman for the same Ministry (1972); Representative of the Arab league (Observer, The Peace Committee Conference on the Middle East, Helsinki, August 1973); Representative of the Arab league, The Congress on Peace & Progress, Moscow (1973); Aid to the Secretary-General of the Arab league, Cairo (1973); Official Spokesman and Member of the Egyptian Delegation to the Geneva Peace Conference (December 1973); Acting Presidential Counsellor on Press Affairs (During the October War) (October 1973-74); Spokesman of the Egyptian Delegation to Arab Summit Conference, Algiers (November 1973); Spokesman of the Egyptian Delegation to Arab Summit Conference, Rabat (October 1974); Spokesman of the Egyptian Delegation to the African 12th Summit Conference, Kampala (July 28, 1975); Member of the Egyptian Delegation to the UN (1975); Spokesman of the Egyptian Delegation to Salzburg Conference, between President Sadat-President Ford, Salzburg (May 1975); Presidential Press Affairs, with the title of Ambassador at the Foreign Office (November 1974- April 1976), in his capacity worked as Official spokesman for President Sadat and the Egyptian Delegation during official conferences and state visits to USA, Europe and many Arab countries; Permanent Representative to the league of Arab States and Ambassador at the Foreign Office (since September 1976). **Work:** Fellow, Center for International Affairs, Harvard (currently); T.V. and Radio appearances on major World Networks; Press interviews and commentry on Middle East and third World problems; Faculty Member of the Salzburg Seminar (February 1979); Ambassador to Canada (1984-85); Lectured widely on Arab, African and UN problems, to World African Conferences, UN Associations, Universities (such as Harvard, Princeton, Yale, Oxford and Air War College, etc.); published articles on International Affairs in both Arabic and English. **Decor.:** Egyptian order of Merit, First Degree (March 1978); Egyptian Order of the Republic, Second Degree (1973); Officer, Order de la légion d'Honneur, France; Grande Décoration d'Honneur, France; Grande Décoration d'Honneur en or avec plaque, Austria; King Abdulaziz Order, Second Degree, Saudi Arabia (1976); la Cordecoration del Aquila Azteca En El Grado Encomiendo, Mexico (September 1976). **Priv. Addr.:** 1, Ibn Marwan Street, Apt.63, Dokki, Giza, Tel.: 3612029, 3487831, Cairo, Egypt.

BASHIER (Mustafa, Bedawi, Dr.), Sudanese Surgeon. **Born** in July 1934 in Omdurman, Sudan. **Son** of Bedawi Bashier. **Married,** Four children. **Educ.:** B.V.Sc. Veterinary Science, University of Khartoum, Sudan (1961): M.Sc. Dairy Science, Kansas State University, Manhattan, USA (1966). **Career:** Assistant Livestock Officer Range and Livestock Center, Darfur (1961-64); Chief Livestock Officer, Animal Improvement Centre, Um Benein (1966-70); Chief Livestock Officer and Director, Ranch and Research Centre, Darfour (1970-72); Head of Animal Breeding Section, Administration of Animal Production and Research, Ministry of Agriculture - Khartoum (1973-75); Assistant Director, Animal production and Research Administration, Ministry of Agriculture (1975-77); Assistant Commissioner for Animal Resources, Blue Nile Province-Damazine (1977-78); Chairman and Managing Director, Animal Production Public Corp. Ministry of Agriculture (1978-84); General Manager, Seliet Food Production Company Ltd. (1984-88); Executive Director, Arab Company for Agricultural Production and Processing-Dairy Unit (1988-90); General Manager, Um Benein Scheme for Animal and Agricultural Production (1998-99). Member Manager, Veterinary and Farm Supplies Company Ltd. (1991-98); Member, Peoples Assembly (1992-93); General Manager, Um Benein Scheme for Animal and Agricultural Production (1998-99). Member the Technical Committees that reviewed, summarized and evaluated the following Studics and Rcports: Hunting Report (1972); Study of the Arab Company for Economic and Social Development (1975); Savannah Dvelopment Project Phase II (1976); Agrar Working paper for the Feasibility Study and mechanized Farming in Southern Darfour and Southern Kordofan and Bahr Elgazal Provinces (1976); Uffot Kordagali project for producing Brinemeat, Dairy Products and Grains (1977); Blue Nile Agricultural Project U.S. AID (1978); Steering committee for Gazira Rehabilitation and Modenization Project (1981-82). Also he was a Member the Boards of Directors of: Mechanized Farm Cropping Corporation; New Hylfa Agricultural Corporation; The Arab Sudanese Company for Livestock Development; Khartoum Dairy Production Company Ltd. **Activities and Publications:** Factors that affect the non-return in Artificial Breeding with Reference to certain Climatic Influences, Kansas (1966); Inbreeding and Hybridization; The Effect of the Month of Highest Yield, Maximum Initial Yield and Persistency on the Production of a Herd of Kenan at Um benein Centre (1968); Causes of Caulling cows at Um Benein Centre (1970); Animal Production Development at Al-Fonj (1970); Al-Ghazala Farm (1973); Centre for Cattle Improvement and Meat Production in Sudan (1975); etc. Presently, Associated professor, College of Veterinary, University of Bahr El-Ghazal, Khartoum. **Medals:** Order of the Constitution (1973). **Sports:** Walking. **Hobby:** Music. **Addr.:** P.O.Box 10739, Tel.: 385510, 225680, Fax: (249-11) 223015, E-mail: ubggal@sudan.net, Khartoum, Sudan.

BASHIN (Yusuf Abdul Rahman), Saudi architect. **Born** in Jeddah in 1941. **Dipl.:** Degree in Architecture and Town Planning. **Career:** Director, Compensation Department, Jeddah Municipality, (1972); Director, Engineering Department, (1974); Director of Jeddah Town Planning Department, (1973-76); Principal Architect, Jeddah Municipality; member of al-Ittihad Football Club. **Hobbies:** reading books about history, politics, adventure.

Addr.: P.O.Box 2763, Tel.: 6445212 (Office) and 6512274 (Home), Jeddah, Saudi Arabia.

BASHIR (Ali, Abdul Rahman, al), Jordanian lawyer. **Born** in 1930 in Salt, Jordan. **Married**, 3 sons, 2 daughters. **Educ.:** University of Nebraska, USA. **Dipl.:** Licence in Law, Diploma in Public Law. **Career:** Head of Income Tax Department, Ministry of Finance, Ministry of Justice, Civil Magistrate, Public Prosecutor, Assistant Attorney General; President, Income Tax Court of Appeal; Member of the Court of First Instance; Judge to Kuwait for 6 years; Governor of Kerak, of Irbid and Amman. **Decor.:** Egyptian Order of Merit (1st Class); Honorary Citizenship from Governor of Nebraska, Honorary Citizenship of Oakland, California. **Medals:** Independence Medal (1st class), King Abdul Aziz al-Saud Medal (1st class). **Hobbies:** Walking and hunting. **Addr.:** Jabal Amman, Amman, Jordan.

BASHIR (Haifa, Malhis, al), Jordanian academic. **Born** on April 29, 1931 in Nablus, Palestine. **Married**, 6 sons. **Educ.:** Jordan University, Jordan; Jerusalem Women's Training College, Israel. **Dipl.:** B.Sc. in Nursing. **Career:** Teacher at the Ministry of Education (1962-71); President, White Beds Association (1971-83); President, General Federation of Jordanian Women (1983-); Member of the National Consultative Council (1984-). **Award:** from the Italian Cultural Centre, Rome, Italy (1977). **Member:** Arab-Austrian Friendship Association. **Prof. Addr.:** P.O.Box 922126, Amman, Jordan. **Priv. Addr.:** P.O.Box 9028, Amman, Jordan.

BASHIR (Mohamad, Omar), Sudanese academic, writer. **Born** in 1926 in Sudan. **Son** of Omar Bashir. **Educ.:** University of Khartoum, Sudan; Queen's University, Belfast; Linacre College, Oxford, UK. B.A. and other degrees. **Career:** Secretary General, Round Table Conference on Southern Sudan (1964-65); Counsellor, Ministry of Foreign Affairs; Academic Secretary and Principal, University of Khartoum; Professor, Institute of African and Asian Studies, Sudan. **Publ.:** "The Southern Sudan: Background to Conflict", London (1968); "Educational Development in Sudan", London (1969); "Revolution: Nationalism in the Sudan", London (1974); "The Southern Sudan From Conflict to Peace", London (1975); "Terramedia - Themes in Afro-Arab Relations", London (1982). **Prof. Addr.:** University of Khartoum, Institute of African and Asian Studies, P.O.Box 321, Tel.: 77044, Khartoum, Sudan.

BASHIR (Mohamed, Ali, Lieutenant General), Sudanese Army Commander. **Born** in 1932 in Sudan. **Educ.:** Military Academy. **Career:** Infantry Officer (1956), Western Command (1964-68); 6-month course in USA; Promoted to GHQ as Deputy to the Director of Organisation, Brigadier and Foreign Relations Director (1970); Director, Armaments Division (1971); Member of military delegation to UK; Armoured Corps Commander as Major General (1971), Chief of Staff (1973), Lieutenant General (1974); Minister of Defence and Commander in Chief of the Armed Forces (1976). **Prof. Addr.:** Khartoum, Sudan.

BASHIR (Taha, Ahmad), Sudanese psychiatrist and statesman. **Born** on June 2, 1922 in Suakin. **Son** of Ahmad Bashir (Businessman) **and** Mrs. Khadiga Muhammad. **Married** to Sayda Muhammad Bashir on November 29, 1964, one child, Rashid. **Educ.:** Gordon Memorial College, Faculty of Medicine (Khartoum), London Post-Graduate, Institute of Psychiatry. **Dipl.:** Diploma of Psychological Medicine (London). **Career:** Medical Officer, Ministry of Health, Sudan (1949); Senior Medical Officer (1951); Psychiatrist (1955); Senior Psychiatrist (1958); Minister of Labour (1969-70); Minister of Health (1970-71); Regional Health Advisor to WHO, Egypt (1972-). **Dist.:** Graduate Prize of Medicine and Prize of Surgery. **Sport:** Tennis. **Hobbies:** History, philosophy, sciences, photography and travelling. **Member** of World Psychiatric Association, World Federation for Mental Health. **Addr.:** P.O.Box 1517, Alexandria, Egypt.

BASHRAHEEL (Mohamad Saleh), Saudi businessman. **Born** Mecca, in 1928. **Educ.:** received general education. **Career:** Auditor, Ministry of Finance (1949); Accountant, Ein al-Aziziah Water Co., Mecca, later Chairman Purchasing Committee, Secretary to Director-General; Treasurer, Ein Zibaidah Water Co.; Owner-Manager of Abla Trading and Contracting Corporation, Mecca, dealing in foodstuffs. **Hobby:** Travel. **Addr.:** Aziziah, Tel.: 27742, Mecca, Saudi Arabia.

BASILIOUS (Nagi, Moussa), Egyptian artist. **Born** on December 12, 1949 in Cairo, Egypt. **Educ.:** High Institute of Leonardo da Vinci, Cairo; Faculty of fine Arts, Helwan University. **Dipl.:** B.A. and Postgraduate Diploma in Painting. **Career:** Graphic Designer, Egyptian Television (1973-75); Member, The National Association of Fine Arts (1976), the Cairo Atelier (1977). Graphic Designer and Scene Painter, Egyptian Television (1977-83), Painter and Designer (1983-). **Publ.:** participated in several cultural exhibitions (1971-78), has given one-man exhibitions since (1977-). **Decor.:** Ministry of Culture (1979), Fine Arts Association (1976). **Medal:** Photography, electronics and reading. **Prof. Addr.:** 26 July Street, No.28, Flat No. 24, Cairo, Egypt.

BASINDWAH (Mohamad, bin Salem), Yemeni politician. **Born** in 1927 in Aden. **Married** to Khadigah Salim, 5 children. **Educ.:** Secondary and Higher. **Career:** City Councellor, Aden Municipality (1953-58); elected member of the legislative Council (1958); served in the medical services (1959-61); Minister of Health (1961-62); Minister of Posts and Immigration (1962-63); Finance Minister (1963); Editor-in-Chief "al-Nour" newspaper, also Secretary-General of the Front for the Liberation of South Yemen (FLOSY); went to the Yemen Arab Republic (North Yemen) in 1965 where he was appointed Minister of Social Affairs and Labour (March 1974- June 1974); following the coup d'Etat of June 13, 1974, he was offered the post of Minister of State in September 1975; two years later he was offered and accepted the portfolio of socio-economic development in charge of the Central Planification Office (1977-79); Adviser to the press; and Deputy Prime Minister (1979-); Permanent Representative to UN (1985-89); Minister of Foreign Affairs. (1991); Minister of Information (1994-95); Presidential Adviser (June 1995-). **Medals:** order of Independence from HM king of Jordan; order of the Republic 1st class, Egypt. **Hobbies:** Arabic Literature, Travelling. **Addr.:** Sanaa, Republic of Yemen.

BASMAEIL (Saeid Mohamad), Saudi academic. **Born** in 1947 in Mecca, Saudi Arabia. **Dipl.:** B.SC., M.Sc., Ph.D. (Animal Production and Nutrition). **Career:** Demonstrator, Faculty of Agriculture, King Saud University, (1970-72); Chairman, Working Group (Animal Resources) at Saudi Arabian National Centre for Science and Technology, (SANCST), (1980-82); Biological Society, Saudi Arabia member of the faculty of Agriculture Council, King Saud University (1979-82); Director Agriculture Research Centre (1983-1987); Associate Professor and Head of Animal Production Department, King Saud University (1989-1993); participated in Animal Production and Nutrition conferences in Europe; contributed to the Faculty of Agriculture Animal Production Extension Service and Agricultural Show. **Publ.:** Scientific papers Secondary School Biology 7 Book 1986, Camel Research Production (Current Interist). **Prof Addr.:** Department of Animal Production, Faculty of Agriculture, King Saud University, P.O.Box 2460, Tel. 4678482, Riyadh 11451, Saudi Arabia.

BASRAWY (Mohamad Said), Saudi diplomat. **Born** on 8 December 1931 in Mecca, Saudi Arabia. **Dipl.:** B.Sc. (Economics and Political Science), Cairo University (1957). **Career:** Former junior diplomat Ministry of Foreign Affairs, later Political Attaché; Political Attaché, Saudi Embassy in Cairo; Saudi Consul-General, New York for seven years; Head, Department of Arab Affairs, Ministry of Foreign Affairs, Jeddah; later Head, Department of Islamic Affairs; Saudi Ambassador to Turkey; Executive Secretary, Agreements Committee; member of the Saudi Arabian delegation to the Arab league meetings, Ministry of Defence meetings and Third Islamic Summit Conference; member of the Saudi Arabian delegation to the UN General Assembly and First and Second Islamic Summit Conferences. **Honours:** King Abdulaziz Medal, Excellent Grade; Independence Medal, Second Grade. **Hobbies:** Reading, photography. **Prof. Addr.:** Ministry of Foreign Affairs, Tel.: 6437033, Jeddah. **Priv. Addr.:** Tel.: 6825572, 6825069, Jeddah, Saudi Arabia.

BASRI (Driss), Moroccan former minister. **Born** on November 8, 1938 at Settat. **Dipl.:** Licence in Public Law, dipl. of Higher Studies (Political Sciences), thesis of Doctorate (3rd cycle) (1975). **Career:** Chief of Police, Rabat Regional Security; member, cabinet of General Director National Security; administrator- director of General Affairs and Authority personnel, Ministry of Interior; Assistant Professor, Faculties of Law of Rabat and Casablanca; Head, General Direction of the territory surveillance attached to the Ministry of Interior (January 1973); Secretary of State for the Interior (April 1974); Secretary of State for the Interior (October 1977-79); Ministry of the Interior (March 1979- 1982); Minister of Interior and Information (1986-Feb.1995); Minister of the Interior (1995-1999). **Addr.:** Rabat, Morocco.

BASRI (Taha, Yassin Hassan, al), Iraqi official. **Born** on 1 July 1939 at Mikdadiyah, Iraq. **Son** of Yassin Hasan al-Basri (retired) **and** Mrs. Nathima Ahmad. **Married** on 21 July 1968 in Baghdad to Sual al-Basri, 3 children: Nawfal (23/9/1969), Suhair (25/2/1971), Ahmed (9/5/1977). **Educ.:** Mikdadiah Primary and Intermediate Schools, Khalis Secondary School, Iraq; University of Baghdad, College of Education (Foreign Languages Department); two years after college: Course in Educational Psychology. **Career:** English Language teacher (1960-63) (1964-67); Deputy Editor-in-Chief, Baghdad Observer (1968-69); Director-General and Chairman of Iraq News Agency (1973-76); Under Secretary, Ministry of Culture and Information (1976-78); Director General and Chairman, Iraqi News Agency (1979-89). **Sports:** Tennis, Swimming. **Hobby:** Reading. **Member:** Iraqi Hunting Club, Iraq Journalist Union. **Priv. Addr.:** Khadra Quarter, Tel.: 5555130, Baghdad, Iraq.

BASSAM (Abdul Aziz, Sulaiman, al), Bahraini landlord investment, merchant and manufacturer. **Born** in 1941 in Manama (Bahrain). **Son** of Sulaiman Bassam **and** Mrs. Nora Bassam. **Married** in 1966 to Fatma Bassam, Basra (Iraq), three children: Nabeel, Ghada and Noora. **Educ.:** Cairo University (Egypt). **Career:** In business and industry (manufacturing aluminium doors, windows, banisters, and cutting and fixing glass and ice plant), and Investment in shares and bonds. **Sport.:** Soccer. **Hobby:** Stamp collecting. **Prof. Addr.:** Bassam Aluminium, Industrial area, P.O.Box 26699 and P.O.Box 177, Tel.: 727049, Cable: ALBASSAM, Manama, Bahrain. **Priv. Addr.:** Goffol, Tel.: 250228, Manama, Bahrain.

BASSAM (Abdul Hamid, Abdul Rahman, al), Saudi economist. **Born** on November 25, 1951 in Bahrain. **Married. Educ.:** Michigan State University, USA. **Dipl.:** M.A. in Economics, Ph.D. **Career:** Adviser, Ministry of Commerce, Riyadh (1981-83); Member, American Economic Association (1977-), American Association of University Professors (1977-), National Tax Association (1977-); Senior Economics Executive, Gulf Cooperation Council, Riyadh (1983-). **Publ.:** several economic articles in the field of International Economics and Economic Theory published in specialized journals. **Member:** Michigan State

University Faculty Club, USA; Equestrian Club, Riyadh. **Prof. Addr.:** Gulf Cooperation Council, P.O.Box 7153, Riyadh 11462, Saudi Arabia.

BASSAM (Abdullah al-Ali, al), Saudi businessman. **Born** Unaizah, in 1920. **Educ.:** Secondary School Certificate, Iraq. **Career:** Former employee, Ministry of Finance, Jizan; now deals in foodstuffs, textiles, refrigerators, washing machines, household goods, foreign exchange; former member of the Chamber of Commerce; owner of al-Bassam Trading and Contracting Corporation. **Addr.:** al-Bassam Building, Bab Mecca, P.O.Box 193, Tel.: 22260, Jeddah, Saudi Arabia.

BASSAM (Ibtissam, al, Mrs.), Saudi academic. **Born** in 1948 in Mecca, Saudi Arabia. **Dipl.:** B.A. (English Literature) (1967); M.A. (English Literature) (1970); Ph.D. (Education). **Career:** Head of the English Department, Girl' College of Education, Jeddah (1975-78); Dean, Girls' College of Education, Riyadh; member of the Council of Faculty of Arts for Girls, Riyadh; member of the Council of Higher Institute for Social Service, Riyadh; participated in various seminars and panels in charitable societies and universities. **Publ:** articles in the fields of arts and education. **Hobbies:** reading, learning foreign languages, travelling. **Prof. Addr.:** Girls' College of Education, Malaz, Tel.: 4789126, 4760274, Riyadh, Saudi Arabia.

BASSAM (Khalid Suleiman, al), Bahraini businessman. **Born** in 1956. **Married** in 1979. **Educ.:** Kuwait University, Kuwait. **Dipl.:** B.S. degree; Proficiency in English Language. **Career:** Administrative Manager, Pearl Investment Co.; Director, Pearl Investment Co.; Private Business in Real Estate & Shares. **Hobbies:** Tennis and Swimming. **Member:** Alahli Sports Club, Bahrain. **Addr.:** P.O.Box 5809, Tel.: 246570, 232574, 232573, Manama, Bahrain.

BASSAM (Mohamad Ali, Abdul Amir Ali, al), Iraqi mathematician, educator. **Born** on December 7, 1923 in Baquba. **Son** of Abdul Amir Ali al-Bassam **and** Mrs., née Sadika Khadem. **Married** on June 21, 1944 to Miss Sabiha Ismaïl Hakki, 5 children: Wael, Nudhar, Nael, Ali and Rafiq. **Educ.:** Baghdad University, Texas University. **Dipl.:** Bachelor in Science (1944), Master of Arts in Pure Mathematics (1948), Doctor of Philosophy (1951). **Career:** Assistant Professor, Huston - Tillotson College, Texas (1951-53); Assistant Professor, Texas Lutherian College (1951-53); Assistant Professor, University of Baghdad (1953-59); Associate (1961-64); Visiting Professor, American University of Beirut (1965). **Publ.:** Contributed articles and papers of original research to numerous international publications. **Member:** American, Indian and London Mathematical Societies, American Mathematics Association, Mathematical Society (France). **Addr.:** Baghdad, Iraq.

BASTI (Abderraouf Mohamed), Tunisian Secretary General of the Arab States Broadcasting Union (ASBU). **Born** on August 19, 1947 in Tunis, Tunisia. **Son** of Mohamed Basti **and** Mrs. née Essia Turki. **Married** on August 7, 1972 in Tunis to Hayet Kallel, 4 children: Bochra, Jawhar, Aya and Mohamed. **Educ.:** Primary and Secondary Studies at Sadiki School (Tunis). 1966-1970: University of Literature and Human Sciences (Tunis). 1967-70: Drama Students Institute. **Dipl.:** 1966: Baccalaureate - 1970: Master's Degree in Arab Literature and Language - Complementary Diploma in French and English Literature (Specialized in Drama). **Career:** 1970-1973: High School Teacher; 1974-1979: In charge of the following duties at the Tunisian Ministry of Culture: Director of Studies at the Arts·Drama Institute, Director of the International Festival of Hammamet, Director of Carthage International Festival; 1979-1981: Director of Television at the Tunisian Rad. and TV. Est.; 1981-1989: Director of Programme Department at the Arab States Broadcasting Union (ASBU); 1989: Acting Secretary General of ASBU - 1990: Elected Secretary General of ASBU by its General Assembly-Nominated by the President of the Tunisian Republic, member of the High Communication Council as from 1988. Has been appointed as Expert by the UNESCO and entrusted to conduct case-studies. **Published** a number of Studies about information and communication. **Awards:** 1969: Prize for the best directed play at Istambul International Student Drama Contest - (Order of Cultural Merit - Order of Independence: Awarded by the President of The Tunisian Republic). **Sport:** Swimming. **Prof. Addr.:** P.O.Box 250 Tunis Cedex 1080 Tunisia, Tel.: (216. 1705530). **Priv. Addr.:** Cite Tanit Sidi Daoud La Marsa, Tunis, Tel.: (216 1779409).

BASTOS (Mohamed), Moroccan engineer and Head Architect. **Born** in 1946 in GOULMIMA, Morocco. **Married. Dipl.:** Diploma in Civil Engineering (E.M.I./RABAT) Architect/Ecole Spéciale d'Architecture, PARIS - FRANCE-. **Career:** Head Engineer, Technical Office of Agadir Public Works Department (1970-1975); Head of Public Equipment Division at the Ministry of Equipment of Architects and Town Planners and of the Association of Engineers of the Mohammadia Engineering School; Secretary General, Compagnie Générale Immobilière (1980); Managing Director, Moroccan Society for Coordination and Ordonnance (1983-1991). **Award:** Wissam Reda (exceptional class) - Morocco - The Aga Khan Award for Architecture (Dar Lamane Housing Community - 4.000 Units - CASABLANCA). **Prof. Addr.:** 42 Chareh Al-Alaouiyines, Tel.: 212.772.48.74 Rabat, Morocco. **Priv. Addr.:** 181 Ambassador, Souissi, Rabat, Morocco.

BASUNBUL (Islam, A.), Saudi engineer. **Born** in 1949 in Mecca, Saudi Arabia. **Dipl.:** B.Sc., M.Sc., Ph.D. (Civil Engineering). **Career:** Lecturer, University of Petroleum and Minerals (1973); Former Associate Professor, Civil

Engineering University of Petroleum and Minerals; member of ACI. **Priv. Addr.:** Tel.: 8605434, Dhahran, Saudi Arabia.

BATANI (Mohammed, Abdullah, Al), Yemeni Minister of Insurance and Social affairs. **Born** in 1946 at Abian, Republic of Yemen. **Son** of Abdullah Mohammed al-Batani **and** Mrs. née A'aminah Nasir Hasan. **Married** in 1971 to Fatima Mohammed Hadi, 4 children: Widad, Waeel, Wisam, Waddah. **Career:** Teacher, then attended Ministry of Interior (Police Sector) where promoted to Brigadier and finaly appointed Minister of Interior in 1986. In 1986 left the Post. In 1993 appointed Minister of Insurance and Social Affairs and Labour, When the Ministry has been diveded, Continued to be **Minister of Insurance & Social Affairs** only. **Medals and Decorations:** Medal of Liberation's Struggle, Decoration of Sincerity and of 30th November. **Sports Practised:** Swimming, Walking. **Prof. Addr.:** Sanaa, Ministry of Insurance, Tel.: 967(1)262809, Yemmen. **Priv. Addr.:** Sanaa, Tel.: 967(1)267769, Yemen.

BATAWI (Mustafa, Amin, el), Egyptian health expert. **Born** on February 17, 1932 in Cairo (Egypt). **Educ.:** Faculty of Medicine, Cairo University; Graduate School of Public Health, University of Pittsburgh (USA). **Dipl.:** M.D., D.Sc. and MHP **Career:** Health Officer Ministry of Public Health, Cairo (Egypt); Lecturer, Faculty of Medicine, Alexandria University; Professor, Department of Occupational Health (Egypt); Interregional Adviser, Occupational Health, International Labour Office (ILO), Bangkok; Chief Medical Officer, Occupational Health, World Health Organization (WHO) (1970). **Publ.:** author of "Occupational Health in Developing Countries"; "Monitoring of Workers' Health"; "Early Detection of Health Impairment"; "Psycho-Social Factors at Work". **Awards:** Honorary member, International Society for Agricultural Health. **Clubs:** Rotary club. **Hobbies:** Painting, drawing. **Sports:** Boating and gymnastics. **Addr.:** Cairo, Egypt.

BATAYNEH (Arif S., Dr.), Former Jordan Minister of Health. **Born** in 1933 in Barha/Irbid, Jordan. **Married** in 1947 in Haifa/Palestine to Mrs. Haifa Fahoum, 4 children: Alaa' (1969), Nasreen (1970), Nadin (1973), Mohammad (1976). **Educ.: General Education:** Jordan: Irbid Secondary School-Jordan (1940-1944), Beir-Zeit College - Palestine (1944-1947). Pre-Medical Education: Lebanon: American University of Beirut, Pre-Medics "Intermediate Certificate" (1951-1953). **Medical Education:** England: Westminister Medical School, University of London (1953-1960), Degree: MRCS; LRCP (1960). **Dipl.:** Diploma of Gynaecology and obstetrics 1965, Royal College of OB/GYN London; MRCOG, 1967, Royal College of OB/GYN London; FRCOG, 1979, Royal College of OB/GYN London. **Languages:** Arabic, English. **Present Position:** Director of Royal Medical Services Senior Obstetrician and Gynaecologist/King Hussein Medical Centre. **Career:** Chairman of OB/GYN: King Hussein Medical Centre (1975-1990); Chief of Staff, King Hussein Medical Centre (1978-1980); Director, King Hussein Medical Centre (1980-1990); Director, Royal Medical Services (1990-1991); Minister of Health (1991-1993); Member of Jordanian Parliament (1993- until now); Minister of Health (1994-99). **Other Information: Professional Training:** Internship at Army Base Hospital (1960-1961). **Surgical Training:** General Surgery/Army Base Hospital (1961-1964). **Gynaecology and obstetrics Training:** Senior House Officer: Bellshill Hospital-Scotland (Feb. 1964- Feb. 1965); Registrar (OB/GYN): Amercham Hospital - England (Jan. 1965 - Jan. 1966); Registrar (OB/GYN): London Hospital - Mile End - London (Feb. 1966- July 1967). **Postgraduate Certification:** Fellow in Laparoscopy, Gynaecological and Onchology Department at Johns Hopkins Hospital and the Memorial Hospital for Cancer and Allied Diseases- New York (Aug. 1971- Aug. 1972). **Professional Posts:** Gynaecology and Obstetric Specialist, Army Base Hospital (1967-1969); 1st Specialist (OB/GYN) Army Base Hospital (1970-1975); Consultant (OB/GYN) King Hussein Medical Centre (Aug. 1975); Consultant and Chairman of (OB/GYN) Dept. King Hussein Medical Centre (Sept. 1976-1990); Consultant and Senior Gynaecologist and Obstetrician King Hussein Medical Centre Sept. 1991. until the Present time; Clinical Associate Professor: Jordan University of Science and Technology. **Professional Organizations:** Jordan Medical Association; Jordan OB/GYN Society; British Medical Council. (Permanent Registration); Arab Board for Medical Specializations - Chairman of OB/GYN Scientific Council 1989- Present; Member of the Jordan Medical Council (Jordan Speccialty Board); Member of the Jordan University Medical School Council; Examiner: Gynaec. & Obst., Jordan Speccialty Board; Examiner: Gynaec. & Obst., Arab Board of Higher Studies; Examiner: Royal College of Obst. and Gynaec. England. **Special Scientific Missions:** General Secretary of 1st Arab - Italian OB/GYN Conference Rome (May 1988); Lecturer: Anti Coagulant Protocols in Pregnant Women following Open Heart Surgery; Visiting Professor at King Faisal Specialist and Research Centre (Jan. 1990); Lectures: High Risk Pregnancy, Pre-Term Labour, Pre-Mature Rupture of Membranes; Syrian Society of OB/GYN 1989; Lecture: Pregnancy after Open Heart Surgery; Pan-Arab Medical Union Meeting - Jordan 1983; Lecture: Review of 1100 Cases of Laparoscopies Performed at King Hussein; Iraq Medical Association (Pan-Arab Medical Union Meeting) 1989; Lecture: Safe Motherhood. **Publications:** A. Batayneh, C. Dihmis "Non-Radio Opague Renal Calculi" Jordan Medical Journal 1964; O. Oumeish, a. Batayneh, S. Farraj "Some Aspects of Impetigo Herpetiformis" Archives of Dermatology, Vol. 118 February, 1982; A. Batayneh, J. Bashiti "Pregnancy Following Open Heart Surgery" under Publication. American Journal of OB/GYN - Green Journal. **Honours and Awards:** Jordanian Kawkab Medal of the 2nd Order; Jordan Nahda Medal of the 2nd Order;

Jordanian Istiqlal Medal of the 2nd Order; Istihkak Askary Medal of the 1st Order. **Hobbies:** Reading, Travelling, Swimming and Farming. **Priv. Addr.:** Tel.: 839920, Amman, Jordan.

BATTERJEE (Abdul-Ilah H.), Saudi citizen, **Born** in 1945 in Jeddah, Kingdom of Saudi Arabia. **Dipl.:** B.Sc. (Public Health); M.Sc. (Health Administration); Diploma, (Public Administration), Pittsburgh, USA. **Career:** Administrative Assistant, Marion Country General Hospital, Indiana, U.S.A. (January-August 1972), Director, Public Hospitals and Health Care Units, Ministry of Health (MOH), Riyadh (1972-1975), Director, Organization and Management (Five Hospitals Project), Ministry of Health; Riyadh (1975-1977), Director, Department of Organization and Management, MOH, Riyadh (1975-1977), Director of Organization and Management, MOH, Riyadh (1977-1979), General Manager (Organization and Management, MOH, Riyadh) (1979-1983), Vice-President (Comptroller), Saudi Medcenter Limited, Riyadh (March 1983-June 1983), General manager/Chief Executive Officer, Saudi Medcenter Limited, Riyadh (1983-1986), Project Director, King Fahad Armed Forces Hospital, Jeddah, Wittikar Saudi Arabia Ltd (April 1987-November 1987), Senior Vice-President, Project, American Medical International (AMI) Saudi Arabia Ltd., Jeddah; Assigned Project Director for Security Forces Hospital, Riyadh and Company Project Management for King Fahad Military Medical Complex in Dhahran (1987-1990), Senior Vice-President, Special Projects, AMI Saudi Arabia Ltd, Jeddah (1990-1991), Treasurer, Health Care Executives Association, Jeddah [Resolved] (January 1992-January 1993), Senior Vice-President and Mobilization Team Leader, King Khalid National Guard Hospital, Jeddah (May 1993-July 1993), Senior Vice-President, Special Projects and Business Development, AMI Saudi Arabia Ltd, Jeddah (1991-1993); **Memberships:** Member, the International Hospitals Federation and Indiana University Alumni Association; member, Board of Directors, the Saudi Red-Crescent Society (1978-1979); Liaison Officer, Baha General Hospital and Jizan New Central Hospital, member, Board of Directors, Saudi Health Care Executives Association (1977-1993); **Hobbies:** Reading, trave, **Prof. Address:** P.O.Box 3270, Jeddah 21471, Kingdom of Saudi Arabia, Tel.: 009662-02-682-1685.

BATTERJEE (Abdul Jaleel Ibrahim), Saudi businessman. **Born** on March 1, 1921 in Jeddah, Saudi Arabia **Son** of late Ibrahim H. Batterjee **and** Mrs., née Khadijah Sabir. **Married** in 1942, 5 children: Abdul Majeed, Adel, Sobhi, Khalid and Walid. **Educ.:** al-Falah School, Jeddah, Saudi Arabia. **Career:** Founder of Batterjee National Pharmacies; President of Saudi Arabian National Development Co (SAND); President of Computer Analysis and Programmers (CAP); President of Fibracan Saudi Arabia. **Sports:** Football and walking. **Prof. Addr.:** P.O.Box 2550, Tel.: 6693423, 6693426, 6672054, Telex: 401253 SANOHO SJ, Jeddah, Saudi Arabia.

BATTERJEE (Abdul Majeed), Saudi senior executive. **Born** on July 14, 1944. **Son** of Abdul Jaleel Batterjee. **Married** on June 3, 1969 in USA, 3 children: Rana, Modi and Majid. **Educ.:** Whittle College (USA). **Dipl.:** BBA (Bachelor of Business Administration). **Career:** Acting Manager Corporate Regulations, Saudi Airlines: General Manager "al-Huda Drug Stores" (1973-75). **Hobbies:** Reading and painting. **Prof. Addr.:** P.O.Box 2550, 6033, Tel.: 55960/55961, Telex: 40488 SAINDJED SJ, Jeddah, Saudi Arabia.

BATTERJEE (Abdul Raoof Ibrahim), Saudi businessman. **Born** in 1920 in Jeddah, Saudi Arabia. **Educ.:** General education. **Career:** Chairman of the board Batterjee National Pharmaceutical owner of Batterjee Internation Establishment owning 5 factories for Cement Blocks, Plastic materials, Snacks and Chips and Aluminium fabrication. In addition to a commercial division for Hospital supplies, baby lines, household wares and disposables. **Hobby:** travel. **Prof. Addr.:** P.O.Box 2, Tel.: 6602933, Fax: 6611204, Saudi Arabia.

BATTERJEE (Elham Abdul-Raoof, Mrs.), Interior designer. **Born** in 1949 in Jeddah, Saudi Arabia. **Dipl.:** B.Sc. **Career:** Interior Designer Office (1975); runs a private interior design business; member of Welfare societies. **Hobbies:** designing, listening to music. **Addr.:** Bani Malik, P.O.Box 5853, Tel.: (Home) 6711036, Jeddah, Saudi Arabia.

BATTERJEE (Shahir Abdul Raouf), Saudi programmer. **Born** 1948. **Dipl.:** B.Sc. (Mathematics). **Career:** Member of Batterjee International Corporation; attended IATA (International Association of Travel Agents) Conferences; Computer programmer, Saudia-Saudi Arabian Airlines Corporation since 1970. **Hobbies:** philately, coin collection, poetry and literary readings. **Addr.:** P.O.Box 5853, Jeddah, Saudi Arabia.

BATTERJEE (Sobhi, A.), Saudi engineer and senior executive. **Born** on February 3, 1950 in Saudi Arabia. **Son** of Abdul Jaleel Batterjee (President Sand Ltd.) **and** Mrs., née Thoraia Nazer. **Married** to Dalal Alfadil on July 13, 1972 in Jeddah (Saudi Arabia), 1 child: Mckary S. Batterjee. **Educ.:** Kansas University (USA); Colorado University (USA). **Dipl.:** B.Sc. (Electrical Engineering) (1972) and M.Sc. (Electrical Engineering) (1973). **Career:** Site Engineer, Head Office I.A. Juffali and Bros (1973); General Manager, E. & M. Division of Saudi Arabian National Development Company (Sand) and present Board Member; Board member of Computer Analysis and Programmers (CAP) and of Fibracan Saudi Arabia. **Awards:** Thou Beta Phi, Honorary Academic Society. **Sports:** Football and walking. **Credit Cards:** American Express. **Prof. Addr.:** P.O.Box 2550, Tel.: 55960, 56208, 55961, Telex

40488 SANDJED SJ. Jeddah, Saudi Arabia. **Priv. Addr.:** Tel.: 53016, 56972, Saudi Arabia.

BATTIKHI (Anwar Munir, Dr.), Jordanian President/ The Hashemite University, Zarqa. **Born** on October 10, 1946 in Amman, Jordan. **son** of Munir Othman Battikhi (Private business) and Mrs. Munaoer Hassan Battikhi **Married** to Sahar mahmoud Alaeddin, born in Damascus, Syria, currently Assist. General Manager,ÉArab Land Bank, 2 children: Amer (1976), Ala'a (1980). **Educ.:** American University of Beirut, Lebanon; Iowa State University, USA. **Dipl.:** B.Sc. (Soils & Irrigation) American University, Beirut (1963-67); M.Sc. Soils (Major) Irrigation (Minor) American University, Beirut (1967-69); Ph.D. (Soil Physics) Iowa State University, USA. (1974-77). **Career:** 1967-69: Graduate/Research Assist. American Univ. of Beirut; 1969-72: Assistant Director, Wadi Dhuleil Irrigation Project, Jordan; 1972: Director, East Ghor Canal Project, Jordan 1972-73: Director, Wadi Dhuleil Irrigation Project, Jordan 1973-74: Lecturer, University of Jordan; 1977-82: Assist. Prof., Dept. of Soils & Irrigation, Univ of Jordan; 1982-84: Head, Dept. of Soils & Irrigation, Univ. of Jordan; 1984-85: Sabbatical Leave to Dept.of Agri. & Irrigation Eng., College of Eng., Utah State Univ Logan Utah, USA; 1984-86: Assoc. Prof. of Soil Physics, Univ. of Jordan; 1986-87: Assist. Dean, College of Agric., Univ of Jordan; 1987-89: Assoc. Prof. of Soil Physics, Univ. of Jordan; 1989- now: Prof. of Soil Physics, Univ. of Jordan; 1989-91: Head, Dept. of Soils & Irrigation, Univ. of Jordan; 1991-1994: Director, Center for Consultation, Technical Services and studies, Univ of Jordan; 1994 1997: Dean of Faculty of Graduate Studies, Dean of Academic Research, Univ. of Jordan; (1997-98); Vice president, Jordan University for Science and Technology, Irbid, Jordan; 1998- now: President, The Hashemite University, Zarqa, Jordan.**Teaching Experience**: Soil Physics Lab. Iowa State University. Soil Physics, Univ. of Jordan. Advanced Soil Physics, Univ of Jordan. Soil Water Plant Relationships, Univ. of Jordan. Drainage, Univ, of Jordan. Principles of Irrigation & Drainage, Univ, of Jordan. Fundamentals of Soil Science, Univ. of Jordan. Soil & Irrigation Seminars, Univ, of Jordan. Special Topics in Soil & Irrigation, Univ of Jordan. Major Prof. of 25M.Sc. Graduate Students, Univ of Jordan. Co-advisor or Committee Member for about 30 Graduate Students, Univ. of Jordan. **Conventions, Seminars, and Workshops:** Irrigation Water Use, 1972, Montpelier, France. Communication Seminar, 1977, Michigan State Univ. AID, USA. Soil Science of America Annual Meeting, 1979, Fort Collins, Colorado, USA. Rainfed Agriculture Seminar, 1980, FAO Jordan. Save our Soils Workshop, 1980, IFIAS & UNEP, Sochi, Soviet Union. Plastic use in Jordan Agriculture Workshop, 1981, Univ, of Jordan. Save our Soils Workshop 1982, IFIAS & UNEP, Wagneingen, Netherlands. Irrigated Agriculture in the Arab World Seminar, 1982, AOAD, Khartoum, Sudan. Soil Taxonomy and Agrotechnology Transfer Workshop, 1984, USAID, USDA, Jordan. International Benchmark sites Network for Agrotechnology Transfer. General Meeting, 1984, Maui, Hawaii, USA. Soil Science Society of America Meeting, 1984, Las Vegas, Nevada, USA. Irrigation Systems and Water Use Workshop for Yemenese Engineers, 1985, Amman, Jordan. Highlands Project in Jordan Seminar, 1985, Amman, Jordan. Crop. Modeling and Agrotechnology Transfer Workshop Coordinator, 1985, IBSNAT & ACSAD, Amman, Jordan. Irrigation Systems Workshop for Yemenese Engineers, 1986, UOJ, Amman, Jordan. Muwaqar Project Workshop, 1987, UOJ, Amman, Jordan, Symposium on Rainfed Field Crops and Farming Systems in Jordan and the Neighboring Countries, Sept. 1988, UOJ, Jordan. First Symposium on Horticultural Productin in Jordan and thc Neighboring Countries, 1989, UOJ, Amman, Jordan. Water Use Efficiency in Dry Land Farming, 1989, Ankara, Turkey. Vegetables Production under Irrigation 1989, Marietta, Italy. Nuclear Energy use in Agriculture, 1991, IAEA, Vienna, Austria. Fertigation/ Chemigation Consultation Meeting, 1991, FAO, Cairo, Egypt. Modern Irrigation systems in thc Arab World, 1991, AOAD, Arab League, Morocco. Coordination Meeting with National Center for Research, 1992, Cairo, Egypt. Freshwater Quality and Efficiency in the Arab Region, Meeting, 1993, CEDARE, Cairo, Egypt. College on soil Physics, 1993, Inter. Center of Theoretical Physics. Trieste. Italy. Use of Nuclear Techniques in Agriculture. IAEA. 1994. Visit to the University of Ghent. Ghent. Belgium. Soil Science Society of American Meeting 1994, Seattle, Washington, USA. visit to The Higher Education and Research Centers in France, March 1997. King Abdullah Hospital Steilingation Unit. Visit to European Hospitals (Holland, Spain, Francc, Swcden, Austria and Switzerland). March 1998. Coordination meeting between King Abdullah admministrators Hospital and Mcdical Center Staff, American University of Beirut, Lebanon. June 1998. European-Mediterranean Conference on Heritage Conservation. Napoli, Italy. February 1999. Coordination meetings with 10 American Universities. June 1999. (Washington, Nevada, Iowa State, Iowa. Tulane, Cincinnati, Lousiana State, Oklahoma, Nebraska, and New Orleans). **Councils and Committees Other Duties:** Assistant Dean (1986-1987). Dept. of Soils & Irrigation Head (1982-84), (1989-1991). Soils and Irrigation Dept. Council (1977-now). College of Agric. Council Secretary (1979-80) (1986-1987). University Council Member (1981-1982). Faculty Research Committee (1981-1982) (1986-1991). Dept. Planning and Appoitment Committee Member (1979-1982). Dept. Curriculum Committee Member (1979-1982) (1986-1991). Dept. Graduate Studies Member (1979-1982) (1987-now). Dept. Research Committee Head (1979-1982) (1987-1991). Faculty Building & Space Committee Member (1982-1984). College 10th an University Committee Member (1982-1984). Advisor to Agric. Students Society (1979-1984) (1986-1987). Faculty Committee for Graduate Studies (1982-1984) (1986-1987). Univ. Research Station Committee Member (1977-1978).

University Council Member in Committee of "Univ, and Society" (1981-1982). University Council Member in Committee of "student Affairs" (1981-1982). Teaching and Research Load Faculty Committee (1983-1984). Faculty Curriculum Committee (1986-1987). Faculty Silver Jubilee Committee Member (1986-1987). Faculty Promotion Committee (1989-1994). Faculty Council (1989-1991). Graduate Dept, Council (1989-1991). Graduate Faculty Council (1990-1991). Faculty Tenure Committee (1989-1994). Faculty Space Committee (1989-1992). Water Center Technical Committee (1991-1992). Promotion and Tenure Ship Faculty Committee (1991-1994). Ph.D. Program Faculty Committee, Chairman (1991-1992). Jordan Valley Problems Faculty Committee, Chairman (1991-1992). Ethics Faculty Committee (1991-1992). Department Curriculum Committee, Chairman (1991-1992). Faculty Curriculum Committee (1991-1994). University Journal "Dirasat Editorial Board" (1991-1994). Faculty Appointment and Promotion Committee (1991-1994). Dirasat (University of Jordan Scientific Journal), Editorial Board (1991-1994). Computer Center Board of Directors Member (1991-1994). Center for Consultation, Technical Services and Studies, Board of Directors Member (1991-1994). Department Graduate Studies Committee Member (1992-1994). Public Administration Academy Committee Member (1993-1994). National Center for Agricultural Research and Technology Transfer-Committee on Organization and structure new Strategy (1993-1994). Dean's Council Member (1994-1997). "Dirasat" Journal, Chief Editor (1994-1997). University Research Council, Chairman (1994-1997). University Staff Appeal Committee, Member (1994-1997). Student's Appeal Committee, Member (1994-1997). Graduate College Board Council, Chairman (1994-1997). University Conferences Committee, Member (1994-1997). Yarmouk University Research Board, Member (1994-now). University Curriculum Committee, Member (1994-1997). Acrreditation of Private University Committee Acting, Chairman, Ministry of Higher Studies (1994 now). English School Consulting Committee, Member (1996-now). Model School, Univ. of Jordan Board of Directors, Member (1995-1997). Center for consultation, Technical Service and Studies, Board, Chairman (1995-1997). Jordan Science & Technology Univ. Consult. Center. board of Directors Member (1996-now). Irrigation Agriculture Committee Member, National Center for Agricultural Research and Technology Transfer (1996-now). Jordan Environmental Society, Member (1991-now). Marine Science Station, Univ. Of Jordan Executive Board Member (1994-1997). University Curriculum Committee, Chairman (1997-1998). Staff Promotion Rules Revision Committee, Chairman (1997, 1998). King Abdullah Hospital Equipment Committee, Chairman (1997,1998). University Space Committee, Chairman (1997-1998). Higher Education World Bank Project, Univ. Representative (1997-1998). Shoman Awards Consultation Committee. Member (1997- now). Staff Appealing Board, Chairman (1997-1998). Seminars University Committee, Chairman (1998). Courses Grading Committee, Chairman (1998). Agricultural Center Board, Chairman (1998). Environment Center Board, Chairman (1998). Student's Fund Board Chairman (1998). Center Tenders Committee, Chairman (1998). Employees Appointment Committee, Chairman (1998). Board of Deans, Chairman - The Hashemite University, Zarqa-Jordan (1998-now). Appointment and Promotion Committee, Chairman, Board of Deans, The Hashemite University, Zarqa-Jordan (1998-now). Investment Fund, Chairman, The Hashemite University, Zarqa-Jordan (1999). Society of Friends of Research at Jordanian Universities, Member, Amman-Jordan (1999). University House for Consultation and Studies Company. Board of Directors, Chairman (1999). National Center for Agricultural Research and Technology Transfer Board, Member, Amman-Jordan (1998-now). Donations' Fund, Chairman, The Hashemite University, Zarqa-Jordan (1998-now). Students' Fund, Chairman, The Hashemite University Zarqa-Jordan (1998-now). Students Transfer Committee, Chairman, The Hashemite University, Zarqa-Jordan (1998-now). King Hussein Awards committee, Amman Greater Municipality, Amman-Jordan (1999). Abd el Hamid Shoman Awards Committee, (1998-now). Abd el Hamid Shoman Research Committe (1999). Advisory Board to the Minister of Agriculture (1999). Advisory Committee on Soil and Water for Jordan, Chairman (Ministry of Water and Irrigation) (1999). Advisory Committee on Water Strategy for Jordan. (Ministry of Water and Irrigation) (1999). Advisory Board on Environment Protection in Jordan (Ministry of Tourism) (1999). Committee on Drought and Orchard Trees in Jordan. Natural Center for Agric. Research and Technology Transfer, (1999). Board of Higher Education in Jordan, Member, (1998-now). Academic Committee, Board of Higher Education, Member, (1998-now). **Other Activities:** Advise Undergraduate Students in their Curricula. Advise Graduate and Undergraduate Students in their Seminars. Preparation and Installation of Equipment and other needs of the Soil Physics Lab. Evaluation of the Jordan Valley Agric. Services Program for USAID, 1984. **Scientific Societies:** American Geophysical Union. American Society of Agronomy. International Soil Science Society. Jordanian Association of Agricultural Engineers. **Honorary Societies:** Phi Kappa phi. Gamma Sigma Delta. Sigma XI. **Prizes & Awards** Abdel-El Hamid Showman Awards for best Young Agricultural Scientist in the Arab World, 1986. **Publications:** Abu Awad., A.M. Battikhi and I.O. Ghawi. 1983. Crop Production Functions as Influenced by Irrigation Amounts and Urea Fertilization Rates of Sweet Corn in the Jordan Valley. Dirasat, Vol.X, No. 1, Univ. of Jordan, Ammam, Jordan. Abu Awads., A.M. Battikhi, and I.O. Ghawi. 1987. Nitrate Movement as Influenced by Irrigation Amounts and Urea Fertilizers Rates in the Jordan Valley. Dirasat, Vol. XIII. No. 8, Univ. of Jordan, Amman, Jordan. Battikhi, A.M. and S. Arabiat. 1983. Constraints to the Successful Application of Modern

Technology for Soil conservation in Jordan. Part 1- Environmental Features and Extent of Erosion. Dirasat, Vol.X, No.2, Univ of Jordan, Amman, Jordan. Hawatmeh., N., adn A.M. Battikhi. 1983. Wetting Fronts under a Trickle Source on Two Soils of the Jordan Valley, Dirasat, Vol. X, No.1, Univ of Jordan, Amman, Jordan. Battikhi A.M. 1985. Some Physical Characteristics of the "Ghor-1" Soil Series in the Jordan Valley. Dirasat, Vol.XII No. Univ. of Jordan, Amman, Jordan. Suwwan, M.A., A.M. Battikhi, and O. Judah. 1984. Effect of Soil Moisture Tension on Yield and Quality of Tomatoes (Lycopersicon Esculentum Mill), grown under Plastic House Conditions in the Jordan Valley. Dirasat, Vol.X. No.7. Univ. of Jordan. Battikhi, A.M., O. Judah, and M.A. Suwan. 1985. Irrigation Scheduling of Tomatoes Grown under Drip Irrigation and Green Houses in the Jordan Valley. Dirasat, Vol. XII. No.6. Univ. of Jordan, Amman, Jordan. Battikhi, A.M. 1983. Soil Conservation from Erosion. Royal Jordanian Socicty for conscrvation of Nature and Arab League for Educational, Cultural, and Scientific Organization. Tunisia. (In Arabic). Battikhi, A.M. and Don Kirkham. 1979. Casing and Leak Depths, And Solute Travel Times to Wells. Water Res. Bull. Vol.15. No.4pp 1004-1015. Battikhi, A.M. and Others. 1982. Planting and Improving Palm Tree Grown in Kuwait Arab Org. for Agric. Dev., Arab League. Khartoum, Sudan. (In Arabic). Battikhi, A.M. Optimum Soil Moisture Content for Germination of Barely Seeds in Three Major Soil Series from the Northern Regions of East Jordan. Dirasat, Vol.XIII. May 1986. Univ of Jordan. Amman, Jordan. Ghawi, I., and A.M. Battikhi. 1986. Watermelon (Citullus Lanatus) Production under Mulch and Trickle Irrigation in the Jordan Valley. J. Agron. & Crop Science 156:225-236. Battikhi, A.M., and R.W. Hill. 1986. Irrigation Scheduling and Watermelon Yield Model for the Jordan Valley. J. Agron. & Crop Science. 157: 145-155. Paul Parey Scientific Publishers, Berlin and Hamburg, Germany. Battikhi, A.M. and Ghawi. 1987. Muskmelon Production under Mulch and Trickle Irrigation in the Jordan Valley. Hort. Science. 22(4): 578-581. Ghawi, I., A.M. Battikhi. 1987. Effect of Plastic Mulch on Squash (Cucuribta Pepo L.): Germination, Root Distribution, and Soil Temperature under Trickle Irrigation in the Jordan Valley. J. Agron. & Crop Science. Battikhi, A.M. and I. Ghawi. Cucumber (Cucumis Sativis) Production under Mulch and Trickle Irrigation in the Jordan Valley (In Arabic). Dirasat. Univ. of Jordan, Amman, Jordan. Vol. XIV. 1987. Battikhi, A.M., and R.H. Hill. Vegetable Yield and Irrigation Scheduling Model for the Jordan Valley. Dirasat. Univ. of Jordan, Amman, Jordan. Vol. XIV. 1987. Battikhi, A.M., and I. Ghawi. Squash (Cucurbita Pepo) Production under Mulch and Trickle Irrigation in the Jordan Valley. Dirasat Univ. of Jordan. Vol. XIV. 1987. Saimeh, M.H., and A.M. Battikhi. Replenishment and Depletion of Soil Moisture in the Northern Areas Jordan. I-Soil Series 11. Dirasat. Univ of Jordan. Amman, Jordan. Vol. XII. 1985. Qasem, J., O.M. Judah, and A.M. Battikhi. Water Utilization by Tomato under Drip Irrigation in the Jordan Valley. Dirasat. Univ of Jordan. Amman, Jordan. Vol. XII. 1985. Battikhi, A.M. and M. Saimeh. Replenishment and Depletion of Soil Moisture in the Northern Rainfed Areas of East Jordan. II-Soil. Series 31. Dirasat. Univ. of Jordan. Amman, Jordan. Vol. XIV. 1987. Battikhi A.M., and M.H. Saimeh. Replenishment and Depletion of Soil Moisture in the Northern Rainfed Areas of East Jordan. III-Soil Series 15. Dirasat. Univ. of Jordan. Amman, Jordan. Vol. XIV. 1987. Battikhi, A.M., and R.W. Hill. Irrigation Scheduling and Cantaloupe Yield Model for the Jordan Valley. Agricultural Water Management, 15, 1988, 177-187. Elsevier Sc. Pub. Netherlands. Battikhi, A.M., and I. Ghawi. Effect of Plastic Mulch on Squash (Cucurbita Pepo L.) Yield and Water Consumption under Trickle Irrigation in the Jordan Valley. Dirasat, Vol. XIV, 1987. Number 11.pp 58-72. Univ of Jordan. Amman, Jordan. Safadi, A.S., and A.M. Battikhi. Irrigation Scheduling of Squash under Black Plastic Mulch and Drip Irrigation in the Central Valley. Emirates Journal of Agric. Sc. Al-Ein, Vol.1, 1988. Arab Emirates State. Safadi, A.S., and A.M. Battikhi. Root Growth and Distribution of Squash as effected by Soil Moisture Depletion's under Black Plastic Mulch and Drip Irrigation in the Central Jordan Valley. Dirasat. Vol. XV, 1988. Number 10 pp 30-42. Univ. of Jordan. Amman,Jordan. Muhsen. N., S. Khattari, and A.M. Battikhi. Effect of sewage Sludge on Corn Yield, Water Consumption and some Soil Physical Properties in Jiza. Dirasat, XVI,1989. Number 9. pp 71-86. Univ. of Jordan. Amman, Jordan. Zureiqi, S., and A.M. Battikhi. Yield Response of Plastic House Tomato to Soil Moisture Tension in the Jordan Valley. Dirasat. Vol. 17, Number 3, pp 196-211, 1990, Univ. of Jordan, Amman,Jordan. Kharouf, M.A., and A.M. Battikhi. Soil Moisture Storage and Depletion as Influenced by Fall Tillage Pratices and Fertilizer Rates for Wheat Production in the Mushaqar Region. Dirasat. Vol. 18B. pp 33-47.1991. Kharouf, M.A., and A.M. Battikhi. Effects of Fallow Cultivation Methods on Soil Moisture Conservation and Wheat Production in the Central Highlands of East Jordan. Dirasat. Vol 18B.pp 18-28. 1991. Al-Turshan, M., and A.M. Battikhi. Soil Moisture Conservation for Wheat Production in the Central Highlands of Jordan. Journal of Agronomy and Crop Science 170: 208-213. 1993. Paul Parey Scientific Publishers, Berlin and hamburg, Germany. Zureiqi, S. and A.M. Battikhi. The Effect of Frequency of Nitrogen Fertilizer Application on Growth and Yield of Tomato Grown under Plastic House. Emir. J. Agric. Sci. 1992, 4: 1-13. United Arab Emirate. Battikhi, A.M. Hammad. Comparison between the Efficiencies of Surface and Pressurized Irrigation Systems in Jordan Irrigation and Drainage Systems Journal. Kluwer Pub. Holland. Vol. 8: 109-121-1994. Hammad A.M. Battikhi. Tillage-Residue Management Practices. Soil Moisture, and Crop Yield in Rainfed Areas of Jordan. Dirasat. University of Jordan. Amman, Jordan. Vol. 22B No. 2, pp 445-462, March 1995. Hammad. A.M., and A.M. Battikhi. Tillage- Residue Management Practices and Soil Physical

Properties. Dirasat, University of Jordan. Amman, Jordan. Vol. 22B No.2, pp 413-422, March 1995. Battikhi, A. Ground Water in Jordan: Currentand Future Uses.in "Intergration of Information between Oil Drilling and Hydrogeology of Deep Aquifers. Published by The Inter-Islamic Network on Water Resources Development and Management. Amman, Jordan 1996. Al Deek, I. And A.M. Battikhi. Effect of Irrigation and N-Fertilization (Fertigation) Scheduling on Tomato in the Jordan Valley. Journal of Agron and Crop Science 178: 205-209. 1997. Blackwell Wissenschafts-Verlag, Berlin, Germany. A.M. Mohammad, and A.M. Battikhi. Effect of sewage Sludge on some Soil properties and Barley Yield in Muwaqar Area. Dirasat, Agricultural Sciences, Volume 24, No. 2, pp 204-216, 1997. Univ. Of Jordan, Amman, Jordan. Battikhi, A.M., and A. Suleiman. Uncertainties of Soil Moisture Reading Using Neutron Probe in Vertisols. Dirasat, Agricultural Sciences, Volume 24, No.3, pp 335-345, 1997. Univ. of Jordan, Amman, Jordan. Ankeer A, Hattar B, and A.M. Battikhi. Effect of Nitrogen Fertilizer Forms and Application Methodes on Soil Moisture and Wheat Crop Yield in Vertisols. Dirasat, Agricultural Sciences, Volume 24. No.2, pp 187-192, 1997. Univ. of Jordan, Amman, Jordan. Ankeer A, Battikhi A.M., and S.K. Khattari. Crop Rotation, Tillage Practices and Frequency of Nitrogen Fertilizer Application-Effects on Soil Moisture and Crop Yield on a Vertisol in Jordan. Dirasat, Agricultural Sciences, Volume 24, No.2, pp 224-233. 1997. Univ. of Jordan, Amman, Jordan. Button, R.W., Clarke, J.I., and A.M. Battikhi. Arid land Resources and their Management Jordan's Desert Margin. Kegan Paul International. New York, 1998. A.M. Battikhi, M.s Suifan, and J.T. Al-Bakri. Effect of Tillage and Plant Residue Management Practices on some Physical properties of Vertisols. Dirasat, Agrigultural Sciences, Volume 25, No,3, pp 362-374, 1998. Univ. Of Jordan, Amman, Jordan. Battikhi A.M., and A. Suleiman. Temporal Variation of Infiltration Rate in a Vertisol under Lentil-Wheat Rotation. Accepted, Journal of Agron. And Crop Science 183, 67-70. 1999. Germany. Battikhi, A.M., Suleiman. Effect of Tillage and Plant Residues Management Practices on Shrinkage of a Vertisol. Accepted, Journal of Agron and Crop Science. Germany Vol. 182(4), 217-296. 1999. Battikhi, A.M., and A. Suleiman. Effect of Tillage System on Soil Stenght and Bulk Density of Vertisols. Accepted, Journal of Agron and Crop Science. Germany. 1999. Battikhi A. and S.K. Khattari. Soil Science: Principal and Application, by Hausenbuiller. (Translated into Arabic), 1999. Kevin Tansey, Kevin White, Anwar Battikhi and Andrew Millington. Relationships Between Surface Roughness and Ers-1 Sar Backscatter on Desert Surfaces in Eastern Jordan: Preliminary Results. **Papers Sent for Publication** Tansey, K, White, K, Battikhi, A., and A. Millington. Comparison of Modelled Backscatter Response and ERS-1 Sar Data For Desert Surfaces, The Eastern Badia Of Jordan. Sent for Publication to Journal of Agron and Crop Science. Germany. 1998. Salahat, M. Khattari, S., Battikhi A. Effect of Drip Irrigation Scheduling and Nitrogen Fertiliztion (Fertigation) on Tomato Corp in Jordan Valley. Sent for Publication to Irrigation and Drainage Systems. Journal of Agron and Corp Science. Germany. 1988. A. Battikhi, M. Shatanawi, and M. Omar. influence of Different Water Amounts on Cucumber Yield under Plastic House. Journal of Agron and Corp Science. Germany. 1999. A Battikhi, M. Shatanawi, and M. Omar. Influence of Different Water Amounts applied to Cucumber on Nitrogen Fertilizer Use Efficiency under Plastic House. Journal of Agron and Corp Science. Germany. 1999. A. Abu Sirhan, A Battikhi and B. Snober. Management of Primary Tillage Operation to Reduce Tractor Fuel Consumption. Sent for Journal of Agron and Crop Science. Germany. 1999. A. Abu Sirhan, A. Battikhi and B. Snober. Corp Biological Yield and Soil Moisture Storage under Different Treatments of Primary Tillage. Sent for Journal of Agron and Crop Science. Germany. 1999. A.M. Battikhi and M.A Suwwan. Irrigation Scheduling Inside Plastic Houses. **Studies and Reports** Battikhi, A.M. and Others. Improving of Dates Production. Prosessing and Marketing in Saudi Arabia. Arab Organization for Agric. Dev. 1984. Le Baron, A.D., R.W. Hill and A.M. Battikhi Irrrigation Sector Assessment for Haiti. Water Management Synthesis II Project USAID and Utah State Univ. USA. 1984. Battikhi, A.M., and Others. Towns of Irbid: Watewater Collection. Treatment & Re-use Schemes. Water Authority of Jordan. Assoc. Con.Eng. Contract Agreement. No. 107/85. 1985. Battikhi, A.M. and Others. Storage Facilities on Yabis, Kufrunga, and Kaffrein Wadis in the Jordan Valley, Agriculture Section. Harza Eng. Co. & Arab Tech Consulting Engineers. 1988. Battikhi, A.M., and Others. Kaffrein Dam Extension in the Jordan Valley. Jordan Engineer Co. 1991. Battikhi, A.M., H. Nabulsi, and M. Saudi. National Center for Agricultural Research and Technology Transfer. Strategy on Organization and Structure. 1994. Amman, Jordan. Battikhi A., and Others. Regional Study on Water Supply and Demand Development: Jordan Consulting Engineers, and, GTZ Jordan, 1995. Battikhi A., and Others. Storage Dams in Al-Karak Governorate. Jordan Consulting Engineers. Jordan. 1995. Battikhi A., and others. Wadi Musa Waste Water use in Agriculture. ACE., jordan. 1995. **Prof. Addr.:** Dr. Anwar Battikhi, president, The Hashemite University, Office of the president, P.O.Box 150459 Postal Code 13115, Zarqa, Jordan. **Private Addr.:** Tel.: 962 6 5159917, Jordan.

BAUER (Carl John), American bank executive. **Born** on July 2, 1941 in Saginaw, Michigan, U.S.A. **Educ.:** University of Michigan, Dearborn, Michigan; University of Michigan, Ann Arbor, Michigan. **Dipl.:** B.B.A. (1965); M.B.A. (1966). **Career:** Account Executive, Merrill Lynch, Pierce, Fenner & Smith Inc., Fort Lauderdale, Florida, U.S.A. (1968-71); Assistant Treasurer and District Manager, Fuerth, American Express International Banking Corp., Frankfurt, West Germany (1971-79); Associate

Director of Marketing and Director of Product Development, Commerce Union Bank, Nashville, Tennesse, U.S.A. (1979-82); Senior Manager, Marketing Services Division, The Gulf Bank, Kuwait (1982-85) and Product Development Division (1985-88); Senior Manager, Retail & Private Banking, National Bank of Bahrain (1988-90); Senior Manager, Corporate Planning, National Bank of Bahrain, Manama, Bahrain (1990-1991); Senior Manager, Investment Advisory (1992- Present). **Membership of Professional Organisations:** President-Broward Country Chapter, University of Michigan Alumni Association (1970-71); Instructor of Business Administration, University of Maryland, European Division (1967-68) & (1973-77); American Business & Professional Association Kuwait (1982-88); American Association of Bahrain (1988- to present); Republicans Abroad-Country Chairman, Kuwait (1985-88); Republicans Abroad-Country Chairman, Bahrain (1988-1992); Member at Large, Executive Committee, Washington (1992- Present). **Addr.:** Manama, Bahrain.

BAWARDI (Mohamad al-Saad, al), Saudi engineer. **Born** in 1943 in Shaqra. **Dipl.:** West Germany, M.Sc., U.S.A. **Career:** General Director, al-Nasseriya Electricity; Chairman of the Board, al-Bawardi Consultant Engineers; member of Chamber of Commerce, Riyadh; attended Saudi Engineers meeting; conducted studies for Central Region electricity. **Publ.:** a study and design of a unit which uses solar energy for heating in Saudi Arabia. **Prof. Addr.:** P.O.Box 8080, Tel.: 4782355, Riyadh. **Priv. Addr.:** Tel.: 4768286, Riyadh, Saudi Arabia.

BAWARDI (Saad Abdul Rahman, al), Saudi educational adviser. **Born** in 1930 at Shaqra'. **Educ.:** Dar al-Tawhid Religious Institute. **Career:** Assistant Director for Foreign Scholarships; Ministry of Education; Director, Public Relations Department; General Secretary, Higher Council of Education, Higher Council of Arts and Science and Literature; Educational Attaché, Beirut; Educational Adviser, Saudi Information Affairs, Cairo; owner and Editor-in-Chief, Al-Isha'a (Radiation) magazine, al-Khobar; participated in the Arab Men of Letters Conference, Kuwait. **Publ.:** "The Return Song"; "A Ghost from Palestine", "The Logic of Lunatics"; "Sweet Glimpses"; "Society Gongs"; "The Alarm: or Raid Sirens, Quartets and Morning Chats". **Prof. Addr.:** Saudi Culture Office, Tel.: 705628, 703779, Cairo. **Priv. Addr.:** Flat No. 114, 143 al-Tahrir St., Dokki, Tel.: 846679, Cairo, Egypt.

BAYATI (Mohamad, Abdulhussain, al), Iraqi engineer. **Born** in March 1918 in Baghdad. **Son** of Abdulhussain al-Bayati (retired Printer), **and** Mrs. Zahra al-Bahrani. **Married** in 1953 to Halima al-Khayat, one child: Talib. **Educ.:** Birmingham University (England), Institute of Mechanical Engineers (London). **Dipl.:** Bachelor of Science, (Mechanical Engineering), G.I. Mechanical Engineering (1944). **Career:** Apprentice to Iraqi Railways as Assistant Mechanical Engineer, Central Workshop, Baghdad (1943-45); Mechanical Engineer, Iraqi Railways (1945-50); Works Manager, Brick Fields, Iraq Building Materials Co. (1950-56); Works Manager, Cement Factory, The Euphrates Cement Co. (1956-57); Associate Member of the Institution of Mechanical Engineers (1955); Technical Assistant to the Managing Director, Diesel Trading Co. (1957-58); Lecturer at the Engineering College (1958); Chief Mechanical Engineer, Iraqi Railways (1958-60); Chief Engineer, The National Electricity Administration (1960-67); Head of the Technical Department, The National Electricity Administration (1967-68); now on the boards of management of National Electricity Administration, Baghdad Electricity Service and Estate Industries Co. (representing Industrial Bank of Iraq). **Member** of the Institution of Mechanical Engineers, The Iraqi Engineering Society, The Iraqi Engineers Club, The Iraqi Association for Engineers. **Sport:** Swimming. **Hobby:** Gardening. **Prof. Addr.:** as-Sayyad Building, P.O.Box 2059, Tel.: 81664, Baghdad, Iraq. **Priv. Addr.:** 75/51 Ad-Dawoodi, Tel.: 37598, Baghdad, Iraq.

BAYAZID (Ali Mohamad), Saudi businessman. **Born** in Jeddah in 1949. **Dipl.:** B.Sc. (Commerce), Cairo University. **Career:** Member of Board, H.R.H. Prince Fawwaz Co-operative Housing Project, King Faisal Islamic Bank, UNITEC of Ireland, Spain and Federal Republic of Germany for Trading and Development; owner of Bayazid Establisment for General Trading Contracting and Industrial Maintenance. **Hobbies:** reading, poetry, writing, diving, billiards. **Addr.:** P.O.Box 6049, Jeddah, Saudi Arabia.

BAYOUMI (Hussain, Ali, al), Yemeni official. **Born** in Yemen. **Son** of Ali al-Bayoumi. **Educ.:** Secondary and Higher. **Career:** Former Minister of State, Southern Yemen (ex-Aden) Government; Minister of Civil Aviation and Acting Minister of Agriculture (1965-66); of National Guidance (1966-67); Formed the first Government of South Arabian Federation, General Secretary of the United National Party. **Addr.:** Aden, Republic of Yemen.

BAYOUN (Adnan, Adel), Jordanian Executive. **Born** on February 18, 1927, Amman, Jordan. **Educ.:** Diploma in Law, Diploma in administration and accounting, Diploma in information and shorthand. **Experiences:** Managerial, Financial, Legislative and marketing experiences. **Languages:** Arabic, English. **Career:** Currently, Government retiree; Social Security retiree; Executive manager for the Jordanian Who's Who annual guide; along with a wide range of social curricular activities. Formerly: Employee in the Jordanian house of parliament (1949-1960); Assistant Secretary General in the upper and lower house of parliament (1960-1978); Secretary General for the National Consultative Council (1978-1982); Manager of Export and Marketing in Al-Hussein Industrial city (1982-1986); Assistant Secretary General for the Upper and lower houses of Parliament. **Activities:** Member in government employees union (1956-1959), Member in different committees at the same Union; Member in the administrative committee of Cooperative Society for government employees; Member in the administrative committee of the Savings Cooperative Society; Member in Al-Hussein Housing Estate Society; President of the Arabian Charity Mouasa Society in Amman and Zerqa City; President of the Jordanian Parliament Housing Committee; President of the administrative committee in the Employees House of Parliament Savings Society; Member in King Hussein Club; Member in the United Arab Supreme Council for ancient and accepted Scotch rite; Grand Master for United Arab Supreme Council for Arab Maysons; Founder and member of the Jordanian Chinese friendship Society; Founder and vide President of the Jordanian American friendship Society; Member in the friends diabetic Society; Member in the Jordanian prevention Society against road accidents. Visited lots of countries as a member of parliamentarian delegations and on tours all Arab countries in Asia, Africa, and the Arab Gulf as well as Japan, China, India, Pakistan, Celon, Soviet Union, Hong-Kong, North and South Korea, Iran, Great Britain, France, Italy, Rhodos, Turkey, Philippines and Thailand. **Important Meetings:** Honored to meet, talk and take pictures with all their Majesties and highnesses and excellences of the Hachemite Kingdom of Jordan, and a number of Presidents and Kings from outside Jordan namely: King Faisal, King Juan Carlos, Sultan Qabous Bin Said, Prince Abdul Illah, Prince Rida of Libya, President Gamal Abdel-Nasser, President Anwar Al-Sadat, President Hafez Al-Assad, Kim II Song, Benderenika, Yasser Arafat, Sadam Hussein, Jimmy Carter, Gaafar Al-Numeiry, prince Abdullah Bin Abdul Aziz, Prince Sultan Bin Abdul Aziz, Prince Abdallah Al-Faisal, prince Nayef Bin Abdul Aziz. **Award:** The Jordanian Star (Qauqab) medal 3rd degree. **Addr.:** P.O.Box 17071, Tel.: 666779, Amman, Jordan.

BAZ (Abdulaziz Ibn Nassir Ibn Ali, al), Saudi educater. **Born** in 1933 at Hawtat Bani Tamim. **Educ.:** secondary school education, Religious Institutes (1955); Licence of Shari'a (Islamic Law), Faculty of Shari'a, Riyadh (1959); two Diplomas, Institute of Public Administration. **Career:** Assistant to his cousin, Shaikh Abdulaziz Ibn Abdullal Ibn Baz, (1960); Private Secretary to the Chairman of the Islamic University, Medina (1961); Director, the Office of the Vice Rector of the Islamic University (1969) and the Office of the Rector of the Islamic University, (1973); attended a conference organized by the Islamic University, Deoband, India (1980) on behalf of his cousin General Superviser, Office of the President for Islamic Research, Ifta, Dawa and Guidance Departments; Adviser to the President; Member of the Advisory Board in the said Presidency. **Hobbies:** reading religious books of interpretations of the Holy Qur'an and Prophet Muhammad's Traditions. **Prof. Addr.:** The Presidency of Islamic Research, Ifta' and Propagation Office, Tel.: 4580996, Riyadh, Saudi Arabia.

BAZ (Hussein, Mohamad, al), Egyptian bank manager. **Born** in 1937 in Mansurieh, Egypt. **Son** of Mohamad al-Baz. **Married** in 1968, 3 children. **Educ.:** Alexandria University, Egypt. **Dipl.:** B.Comm. (1957). **Career:** Joined Commercial Bank of Egypt, Alexandria (1957-61); el-Nasr Export & Import Co., Egypt (1961-68); General Manager, el-Nasr Export & Import Co., Kuwait (1968-72); AFARCO-SAK (1972-74); Managing Director, WILLCO Kuwait SAK (since 1980); Director of: WILLCO Kuwait SAK (Oil Company), ARTOC SAK (Investment & Foreign Trading Company), AMVCO Luxembourg (Investment & Financial Co.), el-Shams Hotel & Tourism Co. (Egypt), Misr & Gulf Bank. **Addr.:** P.O.Box 23074, Tel.: 444035, Safat, Kuwait.

BAZ (Mohamad ben Abdul Rahman, al), Saudi official. **Born** al-Hufouf, in 1933. **Dipl.:** B.A. (History). **Career:** Former registrar, Riyadh University; Demonstrator, Riyadh University (1967); Director of Drinking Water Bureau, Ministry of Agriculture and Water (1968); Former Director-General, General Administration for Projects Implementation, Ministry of Agriculture and Water 1975. **Hobbies:** reading, travel. **Addr.:** General Administration for Projects Implementation, Riyadh, Saudi Arabia.

BAZ (Oussama, al), Egyptian diplomat. **Born** in 1931. **Married**, 1 son. **Educ.:** in USA. **Dipl.:** Ph.D. **Career:** Egyptian Foreign Service; Counsellor and Senior Lecturer, Ministry of Foreign Affairs Training Institute; worked in Arab Socialist Union Youth Secretariat following the dismissal of left-wing supporters of Ali Sabri (1971); Deputy Head, Private Office of Foreign Minister Ismail Fahmi (1974); Ambassador, Head of Foreign Ministers Private Office (1975-84); Head, President Mubarak's Office for Political Affairs (1984-). **Prof. Addr.:** President's Office, Cairo, Egypt.

BAZARA (Omar Salim), Yemeni bank manager. **Born** in 1941 in Yemen. **Married** in 1963, 3 children. **Educ.:** University of London, UK; Institute of Bankers (London). **Dipl.:** B.A.; Certificate Part I, Institute of Bankers. **Career:** Joined Central Bank of Yemen; Manager, Foreign Department, Central Bank of Yemen, Sanaa (1970). **Addr.:** Central Bank of Yemen, P.O.Box 59, Tel.: 5215, Sanaa, Republic of Yemen.

BAZIE (Bader, al), Kuwaiti public accountant. **Born** on October 15, 1937 in Kuwait. **Son** of Bazie al-Yassin **and** Mrs. HAYA al-Mutawa. **Married** in Kuwait to Miss Fatima al-Mutawa, 4 children: Bazie, Misha'al, Farah and Basma. **Educ.:** Cairo University, Cairo, Egypt. **Degree:** B.Com., Licensed Auditor, State of Kuwait. **Career:** Accounting, auditing, management consulting and company formation; principal founding partner of Kuwait Auditing Office (January 1963); Asst. Under-secretary for Financial Affairs, Ministry of Finance & Oil, Kuwait (6 July 1969- 31

October 1973); Director of General Budgeting, Ministry of Finance, Oil, Kuwait (4 April 1967- 5 July 1969); In charge of Kuwait Investment Office in London, which handled substantial government funds (25 January 1966- 3 April 1967). **Hobby:** Reading. **Member:** Kuwait Accounting Association. **Credit Cards:** American Express and Diners Club. **Prof. Addr.:** Kuwait Auditing Office, Bader al-Bazie & Co., Kuwait Airways Bldg., 7th floor, al-Hilali Street, Tel.: 2410010, P.O.Box 2115 Safat 13022, Kuwait. **Priv. Addr.:** Dahiat Abdullah Salem, Villa No.20, Sayed Ali Sayed Sulaiman St., Kuwait.

BAZZAZ (Saad Abdulsalam, al), Iraqi diplomat. **Born** in 1950 in Mosul, Iraq. **Son** of Abdulsalam Bazzaz. **Married**, two children. **Educ.:** Baghdad University; Institute of Broadcasting and Television, Baghdad. **Dipl.:** B.A., Politics and Law (1973); Certificate, Cinema Script. **Career:** Writer, Journalist and Television Producer (since 1969); Broadcaster and Editor, Mosul Television (1969-72); Producer, Editorial Secretary, Head of Cultural Department, Director of the 2nd Channel of Baghdad Television (1972-78); Free Lance Editor "Alif Baa" Magazine, Baghdad (1977-78); Assistant Director, Iraqi Cultural Center, London (1979-80); Press Counsellor, Iraqi Embassy, London (1980); Editor in Chief of UR, magazine of Arabic culture, London, in English. **Publ.:** "al-Hijerat" short stories (Beirut 1972) in Arabic; "In Search for the Sea Bird"; "The Story of the Boy and the Girl" short stories (Beirut 1980) in Arabic; "The Future of Broadcasting" (1980), research, Baghdad. **Medals:** Prize of the Best Radio Programme (1975); 2nd Prize of the Union of Arabic Broadcasting Company; 1st Prize from the International Festival of Palestinian Films and Programmes (1977). **Member** of the Union of Iraqi writers and the Union of Iraqi Journalists. **Hobby:** Chess. **Addr.:** Ministry of Foreign Affairs, Baghdad, Iraq.

BEANO (Said), Jordanian Engineer. **Born** in 1928 at Suweileh (Jordan). **Son** of Youssef Beano (farmer) **and** Mrs., née Fatima Bilton. **Married** on January 16, 1961 to Farida Faisal Sultan, in Suweileh, four children: Nadia, Aladdin, Hashim and Mohamed. **Educ.:** Engineering College of Baghdad; University of Washington, Seatle, Washington (USA); Royal College of Science and Technology, Glassgow, Scotland (UK). **Dipl.:** B.Sc. (Civil Engineering) (1950); M.Sc. (Civil Engineering) (1958); Post Graduate diploma. **Career:** District Engineer; Bridge Engineer; Director of Roads, Ministry of Public Works, Amman, Jordan (1950-64); Under-Secretary of State, Ministry of Public Works (1964-76); Minister of Public Works, in Charge of planning, designing, construction and maintenance of all roads outside the city perimeter; also planning, designing and construction of government buildings (1976). **Awards:** Jordan Medals: Alistiqlal Order, al-Kawkab Order; Order of Republic Service Merit (Korea); Gwanghwa Medal (Korea). **Sport:** Soccer. **Hobby:** Photography. **Member:** Jordan Engineers Society; Jordan Roads Society; A.S.C.E. **Priv. Addr.:** Tel.: 32, Suweileh, Jordan.

BEBBOUCHI (Rashid), Algerian academic. **Born** in 1945 in Algeria. **Married**, two daughters. **Educ.:** University of Algiers; University of Orsay, Paris, France. **Dipl.:** B.Sc. (1967); Diploma in Mathematics (1968); Ph.D. in Mathematics. **Career:** Lecturer, University of Algiers (1968-69); Assistant Professor, Centre Universitaire de Savoie, France (1971-73); Assistant Professor, Université d'Oran Es-Senia, Algeria (1973-74); Assistant Professor (1975-81); Director of the Institute of Mathematics, Université d'Oran Es-Senia, Algeria (1975-78); President of the Scientific Council of Mathematics, Université d'Oran Es Senia (since 1979). **Member** of the Mathematics Society of France (since 1971). **Publ.:** Many articles published in international professional journals. **Sports:** Swimming, tennis. **Hobbies:** Travelling, fishing, chess, reading and music. **Addr.:** Oran, Algeria.

BEBLAWI (Hazem, Abdel Aziz, el, Dr.), Egyptian executive. **Born** on October 17, 1936 in Cairo. **Married**, three children: Dina, Karim and Salma. **Educ.:** Faculty of Law, Cairo University; University of Grenoble, France, Fitzwilliam College, University of Cambridge, England, University of Paris, France. **Dipl.:** LL.B. Hons. (1957); Graduate Diploma in Political Economy (1958) and Public Law (1959); Ph.D. Doctorat d'Etat et Sciences Economiques (1964). **Career:** Legal Adviser, State Council, Egypt (1957-60); Scholarship to pursue graduate studies in France and England (1960-65); Faculty of Law, University of Alexandria. Assistant, Associate and then full Professor of Economics (1965) (Seconded to Kuwait since 1974). Senior Economist, The Arab Fund for Economic and Social Development (1974-76); Director, Research Department, Ministry of Finance, Kuwait (1980-83); Chairman, Export Development Bank of Egypt (1983-) and Executive Secretary of ESCWA (Economic and Social Commission for Western Asia). **Other Activities:** Adviser to the Ministry of Planning, Cairo (1966-67); Visiting Professor at the Ecole Pratique des Hautes Etudes, La Sorbonne, Paris (1968); Head of the Economic Unit, Center of Strategic and Political Studies, Al-Ahram, Cairo (1972-73); Visiting Professor at the University of California, Los Angeles (1979); Board Member representing the Government of Kuwait at the French Company, Sipares in Lyon, France (1981); Member of the Editorial Board of the Journal of Arab Affairs, California (1981); Teaching at the Universities of Cairo, Ain Shams, Kuwait, the American University in Cairo and UCLA (1981); Editor of "Finance and Industry", Journal published by the Industrial Bank of Kuwait. **Attended** many International Conferences and Meetings: International Economic Association, Vienna (1962); Arab Economic Association, Baghdad (1965) Paper submitted; Colloque des Economistes Franco-Egyptien, Paris (1966) paper submitted; Seminar on Economic Development, Berlin, East Germany (1967); I.M.F. and I.B.R.D. Seminar for Middle-Eastern Professors of Economics, Washington (1972); Arab Economic Association, Kuwait (1973); Colloque sur les conditions pour le Developpement des Pays Mediterranes Cagliari, Sardigna, Italy (1973), paper submitted; Arab Economic Association, Kuwait (1976) and Iraq (1978); Ad Hoc. Advisory Group on Communication and Information, UNESCO, Paris (Feb. 1980); Represented the Arab Fund in various meetings and conferences (1974-76); Participated in negotiations on behalf of Kuwait with foreign Governments and institutions. **Publ.:** a) **In French:** "La Zone Franc et l'Aide Française de Cooperation", l'Egypte Contemporaine (Jan. 1966); "L'Interdependance Agriculture- Industrie et le Développement Economique": Le Cas de l'Egypte, Edition Cujas, Paris (1968); "La Reforme Agraire et les Coopérations Agricoles en Egypte", Archives Internationales de Sociologie de la Coopération et du Développement Paris (July-Dec. 1968 No. 24). b) **In English:** "The Dollar Crisis, Oil Prices and the Foreign Exchange Risk: The Case for Basket of Currencies as nomeraire", International Journal for Middle East Studies (1980); With E. Shafei "Strategic Options of Development for Kuwait" (1980), The IBK Papers, the Industrial Bank of Kuwait (July 1980); "International Financial Markets: The End of Stability" (Jan. 1981); "The Arab Gulf States Predicament: Individual Gains and Collective Losses", In, Rich and Poor States in the Middle East, ed. M. Kerr, S. Yassin, Western View Press (1981); "Oil Surplus Funds: The impact of the mode of placement, OPEC Fund for International Development", Series No.16 Vienna (1981); "Gulf Foreign Investment Coordination: Needs and Modalities", Arab Gulf Journal (April 1981), U.K.; With R. Fahmi, "The Kuwaiti Stock Market" (1946-1980), the IBK papers (1982); "The Reagan Program and American Economy: An Appraisal in perspective", Finance and Industry, No.2 (1981). c) **many** publications in Arabic, among which Books: "Agricultural Development with special reference to Arab countries" (1967); "International Trade" (1968); "Monetary Theory" (1971); "Principles of Political Economy" (1975). **Articles:** "Towards an Arab Economic Order, 1976", Proceedings of the Arab Economics Association, Kuwait (1976); "Petro surpluses and the structure of the world economy", Oil and Arab Cooperation, OAPEC, Vol. 4 (1978); "OPEC AND LDs attempts to reform the international monetary system", Oil and Arab Cooperation, OAPEC, Vol. 5, No.3 (1979); "An Arab Monetary Unit", Arab Institute For Planning, Kuwait (1978); "Problems of monetary integration between Egypt and Libya", Institute of Arab Studies, Arab League, Cairo (1973); "Oil surplus funds in the service of a new economic order", Finance and Industry, Kuwait (1981). **Awards:** Scholarship from the Egyptian Government (1960-65); Prize for best thesis dissertation, Paris (1964). **Prof. Addr.:** 10 Talaat Harb Street, Tel.: 776331, Cairo, Egypt. **Priv. Addr.:** 117 Al Thawra St., Heliopolis, Tel.: 673570, Egypt, and ESCWA, Riad Solh Sq., P.O.Box 11-8575, Beirut, Lebanon.

BECHRAOUI (Mohamad Taher), Tunisian educator. **Born** on 18 October 1925 in Gabes, Tunisia. **Widower,** 7 children. **Dipl.:** Certificate of Proficiency in Education, Arabic Higher Diploma. **Career:** Bilingual Teacher (1948-63); attached to the Central Administration, Ministry of National Education: Social Action (Scholarship Dept), Pedagogic Department, Direction of Foreign Relations (Technical Cooperation and International Organization) (1964-73); Member, Tunisian Cultural Mission, Alger (1973-74); Teacher in Tunis (1975-79); Retired. **Publ.:** author of poems in Arabic entitled "Cri du Coeur"; also of numerous poems, published in journals and broadcasted on the Radio and the T.V. **Member:** Destourian Socialist Party of Tunis. **Addr.:** 3, Rue Pasteur, La Bardo, Tel.: 222.538, Tunis, Tunisia.

BEDJAOUI (Mohammed), Algerian lawyer. **Born** on September 21, 1929 in Sidi Bel Abbes. **Son** of Benali Bedjaoui and Fatima Oukili. **Married** in 1962 to Miss Leila Francis, two daughters. **Educ.:** University of Grenoble and Institut d'Etudes Politiques, Grenoble. **Career:** Lawyer, Court of Appeal, Grenoble (1951); research worker at Centre National de la Recherche Scientifique (CNRS) Paris (1955); Legal Counsellor of the Arab League in Geneva (1959-62); Legal Counsellor Provisional Republican Government of Algeria in Exile (1958-61); Director Office of the President of National Constituent Assembly (1962); member Delegation to UN (1957, 1962, 1977, 1978-82); Secretary General Council of Ministers, Algiers (1962-63); President Socété Nationale des Chemins De Fer Algeriens (SNCFA) (1964); Dean of the Faculty of Law, Algiers University (1964); Minister of Justice and Keeper of the Seals (1964-70); member, special Rapporteur, International Law Commission (1965-82); Ambassador to France (1970-79); Permanent Representative to UNESCO (1971-79); to UN (1979-82); Vice President UN Council on Namibia (1979-82); member UN Commission of Inquiry (Iran) (1980); President Group of 77 (1981-82); Judge, International Court of Justice (1982-); Head of Algerian Delegation to UN Conference on Law of the Sea (1976-80). **Medals:** Carnegie Endowment for International Peace (1956); Ordre du Mérite Alaouite, Morocco; Order of the Republic, Egypt; Commander Legion d'Honneur (France), Ordre de la Resistance (Algeria). **Publ.:** "International Civil Service" (1956); "Fonction Publique internationale et influences nationales" (1958); "La Revolution algérienne et le droit" (1961); "Succession d'Etats" (1970); "Terra nullius, droits historiques et autodetermination" (1975); "Non-alignement et droit international" (1976); "Pour un nouvel ordre économique international" (1979). **Prof. Addr.:** International Court of Justice, Peace Palace, 2517 KJ, The Hague, Netherlands, Tel.: 392.44.41. **Priv. Addr.:** 39 rue des Pins, Hydra, Tel.: 603089, Algiers, Algeria.

BEHAIRY (Abdul Kader Ali), Saudi University Professor; **born** in 1940 in Makkah, Saudi Arabia. **Edu. and Dipl.:** B.Sc. (geophysics), Riyadh University, Saudi Arabia (1965); M.Sc. (Geochemistry), Wichita State University, USA (1972); Ph.D. (oceanography), Liverpool University,

UK (1975). **Career:** Assistant professor, Department of Marine Science, King Abdulaziz University (1976-80); Associate Professor, Intitution of Marine Science (1980), Professor, Faculty of Marine Science (1984); Supervisor and Scientific Consultant, Oceanographic Museum and Aquarium (1985-); Director, Marine Science Station (1976-77); Chairman, Department of Marine Science (1977-79); Dean, Institution of Marine Science (1979-81); Dean, Faculty of Marine Science, King Abdulaziz University, Jeddah (1982-85). **Member:** Faculty of Marine Science (1985-90); Faculty of Meteorology and Environment Science (1989-95); University Council (1988-94); Committee for Scientific Promotion (1988-96); Secretary of Scientific Council (1989-96); Scientific Council (1989-now); Permanent Committee of Scientific Council's Affairs (1997-now); Planning Comon Research on Red Sea Hot Brines (1977-78); International Oceanographic Commission (IOC), UNESCO (1978-); Comission for Compilation of Scientific Directory On Red Sea; Expert's Commission in FAO; Expert's Commission for Environment Protection; Consultant for General Directorateof Meteorology, Saudi Arabia (1978-); Representative of Kingdom of Saudi Arabia in IOC, UNESCO and in Arab Council for Marine Environment; Represented Saudi Arabia in a number of International Meetings and Conferences connected with Marine Science. **Publ.:** Engaged in Research Activities in Oceanography and published papers in national and International Scientific Journals of Faculty of Marine Science. **Hobbies** and Recreations: Cruising and outdoor games. **Address:** Faculty of Marine Science, P.O.Box 1540. Jeddah 21441, Saudi Arabia.

BEHAIRY (Mamoun, Ahmad), Sudanese Economic Adviser. **Born** in October 1925 in Um Ruaba, Sudan. **Son** of Mr. Ahmad Abdel Wahab Behairy (Administrator) **and** Mrs. Um Beshaeir Ali Dinar. **Married** in 1957 to Miss Soad Sayed Ali Omar, in Khartoum, 5 children: Hind (1958), Ali (1959), Huda (1962), Ahmed (1966) and Salwa (1972). **Educ.:** Wad Medani Primary and Intermediate School; Victoria College, Alexandria; Oxford University. **Dipl.:** B.A. Honours Economics, Politics & Philosophy (1949). **Career:** Inspector of Finance (1950-52); Senior Inspector of Finance (1952-54); Deputy Under-Secretary (1956-58); Director, representing Ministry of Finance and Economy on Board of several companies (1953-59); Chairman, Sudan Currency Board (1956-58); National Technical Planning Commission (1961-63); Alternate Governor, International Monetary Fund (IMF) (1957-62); Minister of Finance and Economics (1963-64); Governor; International Bank for Reconstruction and Development (IBRD), IMF and International Finance Corporation (IFC) (1963-64); President, African Development Bank (ADB) (1964-70); President, Board of Trustees, Special Fund for Southern Region (1972); Minister of Finance, Planning and National Economy (1975-77); Chairman, Sudan Currency Board; Economic Adviser to the Prime Minister; Chairman, Sudan Shipping Line (1982); Chairman, Sudan Islamic Cooperation Development Bank (1983). **Chairman** of the Board of Directors, Gezira University. **Decor.:** Many Medals from various Arab and African countries, and four from the Sudan. **Sport.:** Football, **Hobby:** Reading. **Prof. Addr.:** Sarkis Ismirlian Corporation Ltd., P.O.Box 112, Tel.: 70951, Khatoum, Sudan. **Priv. Addr.:** Tel.: 43674, Khartoum, Sudan.

BEHBEHANI (Abdulmajid, Sayed Hassan), Kuwaiti Businessman. **Born** on March 23, 1940 in Kuwait. **Son** of Sayed Hassan Behbehani (Banker). **Married** on March 18, 1964 to Mrs Najat Behbehani, 5 children - Adnan, Maha, Yasmeen, Anwar and Mohammad. **Educ.:** Secondary and Higher. **Career:** Businessman; Banker; International Real Estate Developer and Investor; **Sport:** Flying (Aircraft) and Yachting. **Prof. Addr.:** P.O.Box 1262, Postal Code 13013, Safat, Kuwait. Tel. 2417975, 2457274. Fax: 2457275, Kuwait

BEHBEHANI (Ahmed Yousef), Kuwaiti businessman. **Born** in 1941 in Kuwait. **Son** of Yousef Behbehani. **Married** in 1978. **Educ.:** Schooling in Kuwait, Diploma in Business Administration from Geneva University, B.A. from Beirut University. **Career:** Vice-Chairman, Morad Yousef Behbehani Group, Kuwait Medical Centre, Chairman and Owner, Ahmed Yousef Behbehani Est. since (1967); Chairman, Dar al-Yaqza, Nawasser Trading & Contracting Co. and AYB SA, Geneva; Vice-President, Behbehani Motors Co.; Director, Kuwait International Investment Co. and Kuwait Hotels Co.; Chairman, Kuwait Journalists' Association and Board Member of Consultants' Board of Ministry of Information.; Editor in Chief, al-Yaqza Weekly Magazine. **Member:** Los Angeles Press Club, American Society of Travel Agents. **Hobbies:** Travel, Sports and Reading. **Addr.:** P.O.Box 567, Safat, 13006 Safat, Kuwait, Tel.: 4831221/551, Fax No. 4831661.

BEHBEHANI (Morad Yousuf), Kuwaiti Businessman. **Born** in 26/12/1919 in Kuwait. **son** of Yousuf Mohmmad Hussein Behbehani, Businessman and Sarah Morad Behbehani. **Married** to Zainab Marafie, 4 children: Malleeha, Ali, Hussein and Sameeha. **Educ.:** passed matriculation and then got into doing business. Circumstances were such that he had to dedicate his entire time to development of Business. **Career:** Started Business at the age of 15 as a merchant dealing in Swiss watches. Expanded operation into various business activities and international investments. Now owns and/or has controlling interest in 13 companies with assets exceeding USD 1.5 billion. Introduced Radio Broadcasting, Television and Air Conditioning Equipments for the first time in Kuwait. **Other Information:** Distributor for many reputed brands in Kuwait. Few of them are: Porsche, Volkswagen, Audi Cars. Carrier Air Conditioning, Ericson Telecommunication, Omega, Piaget, Tissot, Roamer Watches, Toa, Grundig, Sansui, Akai, Samsonite, Leica AG, Swissair, SAS, etc. **Medals and Decorations:** Honorary Consular for Swiss

Government in Kuwait; selected as the "Man of the Year" by American Biographical Institute; Chairman of the Alahli Bank of Kuwait; Arabian Gulf investments (Far East) Hong Kong; Board Member of Kuwait Danish Dairy Co.; Gulf Security; etc. **Sports:** General interests in all. **Hobby:** Closely watches investment market all around the world. **Member:** Hunting and Equestrian Club, Kuwait. **Credit Cards:** American Express, Visa Card, Diner's Club. **Prof. Addr.:** P.O.Box 146, 13002 Safat, Tel.: 4844000. Kuwait. **Private Addr.:** Sha'ab Kuwait.

BEHROOZIAN (Abdul Ghafoor), UAE businessman. **Born** in 1949 in Fujairah, United Arab Emirates. **Son** of Hashim Behroozian (from the Awazi tribe). **Married** in 1971, 3 children. **Educ.:** Graduated in England. **Career:** President, Behroozian Corporation; Chairman, al-Fujairah National Insurance Company, member of leading al-Fujairah Trading Family; Director, Bank Audi Affiliate, Fujairah; Director, Arab International Trust S.A., Luxembourg; former Adviser to the Ruler of Fujairah. **Addr.:** P.O.Box 234, Tel.: 473175, Dubai, United Arab Emirates.

BEHROOZIAN (Hashim), United Arab Emirates administrator. **Born** in 1925 in Fujairah, United Arab Emirates. **Married. Career:** Accountant to the Ruler of Fujairah, Shaikh Hamad Bin Mohamad al-Sharqi. **Addr.:** Amiri Court, P.O.Box 1, Government House, Tel.: 22111, Fujairah, United Arab Emirates.

BEHZAD (Behzad Youssef), Qatari Attorney and Legal Consultant. **Born** on November 15, 1951 in Doha, Qatar; Legal Profession since 1974. Established own law office in 1982. Licensed to practice before all the Courts of Law in Qatar and the G.C.C. countries. **Educ.:** Faculty of Law, Alexandria University, Egypt (LL.B., 1974). **Experience:** Head, Legal Affairs Department, Government of Qatar, Ministry of Justice, 1974-1976; Ministry of Finance and Petroleum, 1980-1982; Legal delegate in Conference Section of the Legal Department, Ministry of Foreign Affairs, Government of Qatar. Representing Qatar in International Conventions, 1977-1980. **Specialization:** Commercial Banking, Company Law, Maritime Law, Insurance, Trade Regulations, Foreign Investments, Property and Real Estate Law, Collection Cases, Estate Planning, Trade Disputes, and Taxation. **Member:** Gulf Consultants, a consortium of non-governmental professionals from Bahrain, Kuwait, Oman, Saudi Arabia, United Arab Emirates, and Qatar, for the Protection of intellectual property; Arab Society for the Protection of Industrial Property (Board Member). **Languages:** Arabic, English. **Associates:** Steven Orlikoff, Attorney-at-Law, 220 East 54th Street, New York NY 10022 USA; telephone 212 826-6747; Szlavik, Hogan & Miller, Inc., International consultants, 1150 Connecticut Avenue, N.W., Suite 303, Washington, DC 20036 USA; telephone 202 862-3900. **Address:** P.O.Box 869, Doha, Qatar, Tel.: (974) 352 333, Fascimile: (974) 352 888, Telex: 4955 (MUHAMI DH).

BEIDAS (Burhan, Said), Advertiser. **Born** on May 5, 1944 at Jaffa. **Son** of Said Beidas (trade) **and** Mrs. Wajiha Dajani-Beidas. **Married** on July 7, 1972 in Beirut to Ikram Shakhshir, 3 children: Reem (1974), Rowan (1983), Moussa (1985). Now married to Nariman Abou Ghazaleh (1990). **Educ.:** Ahliya School, Beirut (1950-1952), English School for Boys, Beirut (1953-1958), Anglican School for Boys, Beirut (1959-1962), American University of Beirut (1963-1966), Texas State University, U.S.A. (1968-1969). **Dipl.:** B.A. (AUB, 1966), MBA (U.S.A. 1969). **Career:** in 1971 acquired an Advertising Agency which was established in (1967); Opened the Second Office in Dubai, U.A.E. (1973) and Bahrain Office (1979); Started in Saudi Arabia Office-Al Khobar (1981) then moved to Jeddah in (1985); Started Kuwait Office in (1986); Opened a Liaison Office (Client Servicing Office) in Long Grove, Illinois, U.S.A. (1989), opened Abu Dhabi Office, U.A.E. (1995) and Started Cairo, Egypt Office in (1996). MADCO GROUP is Highly Specialised Experienced communication Network, covering the entire Middle East, North Africa and Indian Subcontinent. **Services offered:** are full above the line advertising, direct marketing, public relations, BTL and promotions. Madco Group has a Total Staff of 193 professionals in 8 Offices and Consolidated Group Sales Volume in 1996 of US$ 48.5 million. MADCO GROUP is recognised among the Top 5 Network Agencies in the Middle East, servicing well known International and Regional Clients amongst them: Alcatel, Al Mawarid Group, BAT, Casio, Chiquita, DHL, DHL/SNAS, Estee Lauder, German Agricultural Marketing Board (CMA), Goldcorp Australia, Hyundai, Hilton Hotels, ITT Industries, Juma Al Majid Group, Luxottica, Malaysia Airlines, Manitoba, MKS Finance, Nabisco, Royal Mint U.K., Sharp, TDK, Toyota, World Gold Council, etc... **Sports:** Fishing, Swimming, Backgamon, Table Tennis, Bowling. **Member:** International World Trade Club, International Advertising Association, American Business Council, Swiss Business Council, Lebanese Business Council. **Credit Cards:** Visa, American Express. **prof. Addr.:** P.O.Box 161, Tel.: 971-1-694550, Dubai, U.A.E., E-Mail: madco@emirates.net.ae **Priv. Addr.:** Jumeirah, Tel.: 971-4-448706, Dubai, U.A.E.

BEKKA (Abdennour), Algerian diplomat. **Born** in 1935. **Married,** 5 children. **Dipl.:** B.Sc. in Political Science. **Career:** Senior Officer of the National Liberation Army (1958-80); Central Director of the Ministry of National Defence (1965-80); Minister of Post and Telecommunications (1980-82), Minister of Youth and Sports (1982-84); Ambassador to Rumania (1984-). **Addr.:** Ministry of Foreign Affairs, Algiers, Algeria.

BELAID (Abdessalam), Algerian politician. **Born** on July 1928, in Dehemcha, Algeria. **Married,** 6 children, four sons, two daughters. **Educ.:** Grenoble University. **Career:** Former Honorary President of Union Generale des Etudiants Musulmans Algeriens (UGEMA); Instructor, Front de Liberation Nationale (FLN) School, Oujda; Political Adviser in Cabinet of Mr. Ben Khedda (1961); in charge of Economic Affairs, F.L.N.; Provisional Executive (1962); President Director General, Societe Nationale pour la Recherche, la Production, le Transport, la Transformation et la Commercialisation des Hydrocarbures (SONATRACH) (1964-66); retaining the same Post (1965-66); Minister of Industry and Energy (1966-77); of Light Industry (1977-84); President of Special Economic Commission of Central Committee of FLN (1979-81); Chairman, Council, Organisation of Arab Petroleum Exporting Countries (1974); Prime Minister (July 1992-August 1993). **Addr.:** Algiers, Algeria.

BELAID (Slaheddine), Tunisian Politician. **Born** on November 13, 1939 in jemmal. **Married.** one child. **Educ.:** Engineering Diploma, Ecole National des Ponts et Chaussées Paris (1962). **Career:** Engineer, New Port Construction (1962); Assigned to Secretariat of State for Foreign Affairs to work at Economic Commission for Africa (1964); Project Director, Tunisian National Tourism Office (1967); President Director General, SONTRA-GET (1974); Official, Ministry of Public Works and Housing (1988-94); President Director General, Lake of Tunis Development Authority (1994); Minister of Public Works and Housing (Oct.1997-to date). **Address:** Ministry of Public Works and Housing, 10 Boulevard Habib Chrita, Cité Jardins, 1002 Tunis, Tunisia.

BELAIL (Hassan), Sudanese economist, banker. **Born** in 1930 **Married**, three children. **Educ.:** University of Khartoum, University of Pennsylvania, USA. **Dipl.:** B.A.; M.A., Money and Banking. **Career:** Teacher, Secondary School; Official, Sudan State Railways; Government Service, Ministry of Finance and National Economy; Assistant Under Secretary and Director of Taxation; Assistant General Manager, Sudan Commercial Bank (1966); Managing Director, State Cotton Organisation (1970); Chairman and Managing Director, Sudan Commercial Bank (1971); member of the Board of the Union of Arab and French Banks (1971); Deputy General Manager, UBAF Bank Ltd., London; Minister of State for Trade (1973-75); Director, Khartoum Branch of the Arab Investment Co. (1975-80); Governor, Central Bank of Sudan (1980-89); Representative Arab African International Bank. **Prof. Addr.:** P.O.Box 2721, Khartoum, Sudan.

BELAKZIZ (Abdelwahed), Moroccan statesman. **Born** on July 5, 1939 in Marrakesh. **Educ.:** Primary & Secondary in Marrakesh; College Moulay Youssef, Rabat; Faculty of Law, Rabat. **Dipl.:** LL.B.; Dipl. for Higher Learning; University Doctorate from the Faculty of Law & Economical Sciences of Rennes. **Career:** Dean, Faculty of Law (Rabat) and Juridical Studies Centre (Casablanca & Fes) (1966); Secretary General of the University Board & presided the Council of the Association of Arab Universities in Rabat (1975); Ambassador to Iraq (1977-79); Minister of Information, Youth and Sports (March 27, 1979-1983). **Decor:** Ouissam de Chevalier de l'Ordre du Trône. **Addr.:** Rabat, Morocco.

BELAYAT (Abderrahman), Algerian politician. **Born** in 1938. **Married**, 4 children. **Dipl.:** LL.B. **Career:** Chief Inspector, Annaba Academic, Chief of Judicial Section; Administrator, later General Secretary, Governorate of Algier; Deputy, National Popular Assembly (APN) (1977), Vice President of APN; Minister of Construction (1984-86); Minister of Equipment and of National and Regional Development (1987-99). **Addr.:** Algiers, Algeria.

BELGHITI (Mustafa, Muhammad, al), Moroccan diplomat. **Born** on March 7, 1933 in Fez. **Son** of Mohamad al-Belghiti (Industrialist) **and** Mrs., née Radia Guenoun. **Married** on September 24, 1960 to Miss Naïma Larari, 3 children: Ahmad, Ali and Halima. **Educ.:** French Lycées of Casablanca and Paris, University of Paris. **Dipl.:** Bachelor of Laws. **Career:** Attached to the Ministry of Foreign Affairs, Moroccan Ambassador to France (1964-66), Attached to the Ministry of Foreign Affairs Director Manic S.A. **Prof. Addr.:** Rabat, Morocco.

BELGUEDJ (Mourad), Algerian executive. **Born** in 1946 in Constantine, Algeria. **Married** in 1985, one son. **Educ.:** Tufts University and Boston University, Mass. USA; Holborm College, London University; School of Interpreters, Geneva University, Geneva, Switzerland. **Dipl.:** A.M., M.ALD. Ph.D., also M.Sc.; Technical Translator, Conference Interpreter from University of London. **Career:** Translator, Conference Interpreter (1969-70); Head of Energy Economics & Development Planning Sonatrach of Algeria (1977-78); Director of Gas Exports, Sonatrach of Algeria (1978-82); 2nd Professor of Energy Economics, Algiers University (1977-78); President Director General of Algerian National Hydrocarbon Shipping Corp. (SNTM-HYPROC) (since 1982). **Sports:** Swimming, tennis, flying (A&B rated). **Member** of: Algiers/ Oran Flying Clubs. **Prof. Addr.:** P.O.Box 60, Arzew, Algeria.

BELHACHIMI (Ahmad), Moroccan artist. **Born** in 1927 in Casablanca. **Educ.:** Universities of Paris, Cambridge and Washington. **Dipl.:** Bachelor of Arts. **Career:** Artist, Joined King Mohamad V Cabinet, Realised several films and scenarios including "Les affamés", "Le test", "Le rempart de sable", "Prestige", "l'Algérien", "Sourire à la tempête", "le violon" (1959). **Addr.:** Rabat, Morocco.

BELHAJ (Mohamed), Moroccan engineer. **Born** in 1947 in Guercif, Morocco. **Married,** 1 son. **Educ.:** Hassan II Institute of Agronomy, Rabat; Postgraduate studies in Applied Science, Louvain University, Belgium. **Dipl.:** B.Sc. in Physical Chemistry. **Career:** Research Engineer, AIEA, Austria (1974-75); Member, Association of Moroccan Agronomy Engineers, Association of Food Industry Sciences; Senior Lecturer, Rabat University (1976-77); Company Managing Director (1977-). **Hobbies:** Bridge and tennis. **Prof. Addr.:** Rue Maremola 48/4, Kenitra, Morocco. **Priv. Addr.:** Rue Souss No.3, Kenitra, Morocco.

BELHOUCHET (Abdallah), Algerian politician. **Born** in 1923. **Career:** Member of Revolutionary Council (1965-); Member, Political Bureau (1 of 2 Armed Forces Members of the Revolutionary Council to participate in the Political Bureau); Head, First Region (Blida) Ministry (1967-79); Deputy Minister of Defence (1980); General Inspector of the Army later chief of Staff (1984-1991). **Prof. Addr.:** The Political Bureau, Revolutionary Council of the FLN, Emir Abdelkader square, Algiers, Algeria.

BELKACEM (Charif), Algerian statesman. **Born** in Algiers. **Career:** Former Member of Armée de Libération Nationale; Deputy for Tlemcen; Questeur, National Assembly; Minister of National Orientation (1963-64); Minister of Education (1964-65); Member of Revolutionary Council and Director of Information (July 1965); Member of Bureau Politique of F.L.N. (Front de Libération Nationale) in 1965; Member of the Revolutionary Council (1965); Minister of State for Finance and Planning (1968-70); Minister of State (1970-75). **Addr.:** Algiers, Algeria.

BELKHODJA (Hassan), Tunisian statesman. **Born** on March 10, 1916 in Ras Jabal (Bizerta Regions), Tunisia. **Married**, 3 children. **Educ.:** Secondary studies, Lycée Carnot, Tunis; Faculty of Law, Paris. **Dipl.:** Doctorate of Law. **Career:** President of the Association of North African Students, France (1950); Tunisian High Commissioner, France (1955); First Tunisian Ambassador to France, after Independence; Ambassador to Spain (1957); charged by President Bourguiba to establish the National Agricultural Bank (1959); Founder, Tunisian Society of the Dairy Industry; Managing Director, National Tunisian Real Estate Company (15 July 1968) and Managing Director, Tunisian Trade Office (5 April 1969); Minister of Economic Affairs (7 November 1969- June 1970); Administrator, Tunisian Government on the Board of Directors of the Tunisian Banking Society (12 March 1971- 25 September 1974); Minister of Agriculture (1974-80); Minister of Foreign Affairs (April 1980-81). **Awards:** Commander, Order of the Tunisian Republic; Grand Cordon, Tunisian Independence. **President** of "L'Espérance Sportive", Tunis. **Addr.:** Tunis, Tunisia.

BELKHODJA (Mohamed Moncef), Tunisian banker. **Born** on February 12, 1932, in Bizerte, Tunisia. **Son** of Ahmed **and** Omheni Belkhodja. **Married** to Michele Riviere, two daughters. **Career:** Administrator, Chairman and Managing Director, Banque de Development Economique de Tunisie; former Chairman and Managing Director, Banque Nationale de Tunisie; former Executive Director IBRD; former Director of Credit and Banks; Governor, Banque Centrale de Tunisie (1980-86); President, Association of African Central Banks (1985). **Addr.:** Tunis, Tunisia.

BELKHODJA (Nagib), Tunisian artist painter. **Born** on November 25, 1933 in Tunis. **Educ.:** Sadiki College (till 1956), Paris College (1959-61). **Career:** Artist Painter, Contributed to several art exhibitions in Tunisia (1958-63), and France (1959) and (1963). **Works:** "Composition". **Dist.:** Tunis City Prize (1958). **Addr.:** Tunis, Tunisia.

BELKHODJA (Taher), Tunisian statesman. **Born** in 1931 in Tunis. **Educ.:** Ecole Supérieure d'Agriculture, Tunis. **Dipl.:** Agricultural Engineer. **Career:** Member of the Tunisian Delegation of the United Nations General Assembly (1959); Secretary of State at Ministry of Foreign Affairs (1959-60); Director of Foreign Affairs (1960-61); Chargé d'Affaires, Paris (1961); Tunisian Ambassador of Senegal also accredited to Guinea, Mauritania and Ivory Coast (1961-66); Director General, Ministry of the Interior (1967-68); Secretary of State, Youth and Sports (1970-71); Tunisian Delegate to the United Nations Organization (1971-73); Ministry of the Interior (March 1973); dismissed as Interior Minister in December 1977 after disagreeing with the Government's hardline approach to the unrest which led to the January 1978 social and industrial crisis; re-established his political position after the retirement in March 1980 of the then Prime Minister, Mr. Hedi Nouira, and was appointed Tunisian Ambassador to the Federal Republic of Germany; Ministry of Information (1981-84); Lived in exile in France, returned to Tunisia in 1989. **Awards:** Ordre de L'Indépendance, Order de la République Tunisienne and other decorations. **Addr.:** Tunis, Belvedere, Tunisia.

BELLAGHA (Bachir), Tunisian trade-unionist. **Born** in 1920 in Tunis. **Educ.:** Alaoui College, Tunis. **Career:** First Trade Union Post (1945), later attached to Office of Minister of Labour, Elected to Parliament (1957), Secretary General of Union Générale Tunisienne du Travail in 1965, Member of Political Bureau of Destour Socialist Party. **Awards:** Grand Cordon Tunisian Indépendance. **Addr.:** 29, Place Muhammad Ali, Tunis, Tunisia.

BELTAGUI (Mamdouh, Ahmed, al-), Egyptian Politicain. **Born** on April 21, 1939 in Cairo. **Married,** one son. **Educ.:** L.L.B. (1958); Ph.D. Economic Science, Sorbonne University, France (1973); Ph.D., Political Sciences, Sorbonne University, France (1975). **Career:** Assistant Prosecutor Court of Appeals, Cairo (1958-75); Information Plenipotentiary at Egyptian Embassy in Paris (1975-82); Chairman, State Information Service (1982-93); Secretary General, Cairo National Democratic Party (1992); Member, Shura Council (1992); Minister of Tourism (1993-to date). **Address:** Ministry of Tourism, Tourism Tower, Abbasia, Cairo, Egypt.

BELTAGY (Adel S. El), Director General of ICARDA. **Born** on February 26,1944 in Cairo, Egypt. **Son** of ElSayed Tawfik **and** Mrs. Saadat. **Married** to Dr. Alia'a Rafee, 3 children: Samha'a, Mohamed, Moustafa. **Educ.:** 1960-1965 Bsc College of Agriculture, Ain Shams University, Cairo, Egypt; 1966-1968 Msc College of Agriculture, Ain Shams University, Cairo, Egypt; 1970-1974 PhD University of Wales, UK. **Major Research Interest:** Desert Development & Arid Land Agriculture. **Area of Specialization:** Stress Physiology/Adaptive Mechanisms with reference to the role of plant hormones in the adaptive process. Past professional and academic activities include: **Career:** Professor, Arid Land Agriculture (LAB), Faculty of Agriculture, Ain Shams University, Cairo; First Under-Secretary of State for Land Reclamation, Egypt (1987-1991); Director/Board Chairman of Agricultural Research Center, Egypt (1991-1994); Chairman of Executive Board, Arab Center for the Studies of Arid Zones and Dry Lands (ACSAD) (1989-1995); Chairman of the Scientifid Technical Council of the International Sahara and Sahel Observatory (OSS) (1993-present); Secretary General of the International Desert Development Commission (IDDC) (1987-1996); Chairman of the International Desert Development Commission (IDDC) (1996 - present); Director General of ICARDA (1995 - present); Member of the CGIAR Genetic Resources Policy Committee (1994 - present). **SCIENTIFIC SOCIETIES:)** British Plant Growth Regulator Group (Founding Member); American Association for the Advancement of Science (AAAS); International Plant Growth substances Association; Federation of European Societies of Plant Physiology; International Society for Horticultural Science; American Society for Horticultural Science; Society for Experimental Biology, U.K.; Egyptian Society for Horticultural Sciences. **MAJOR WORK EXPERIENCE:** 1995 - Present Director General of the International Center for Agricultural Research in the Dry Areas (ICARDA); 1993-1995 Board Chairman, Agricultural Research Center, Ministry of Agriculture, Egypt; 1991-1993 Director, Agricultural Research Center, Ministry of Agriculture, Egypt; 1990-1991 First Under Secretary of State for Land Reclamation, Agricultural Foreign Relations & Egyptian International Center for Agriculture, Minister's Office, Ministry of Agriculture, Egypt; 1988-1990 Under Secretary of State for Land Reclamation, Minister's Office & Supervisor of Foreign Agricultural Relations, Egyptian International Center for Agriculture, Ministry of Agriculture, Egypt; 1987-1988 Under secretary of State for Land Reclamation, Minister's office, Ministry of Agriculture, Egypt; 1985-1986 Visiting Professor, Biology Department College of Science, San Diego State University, San diego, California, USA; 1976-1995 Lecturer, Associate Professor, Professor, Department of Horticulture, Arid land Agriculture (Lab). Faculty of Agriculture, Ain Shams University, Cairo, Egypt; 1974-1976 Research Associate, Department of Botany and Microbiology, University College of Wales, Aberystwyth, U.K.; 1965-1976 Demonstrator, Assistant Lecturer, Department of Horticulture, ain Shams University, Cairo, Egypt. **PROFESSIONAL AND ADMINISTRATIVE ACTIVITIES:** Vice Chairman, Tropical and Subtropical Committee North Africa) International Horticultural Society (1986-1990); Secretary General of the International Desert Development Commission (IDDC) (1987 - present); Chairman of the International Desert Development Commission (IDDC) (1996 - present); Chairman for the Scientific Technical Council of the International Sahara & Sahel Observatory (1993 - present); Member, Agricultural Council for Land Reclamation, Egyptian Academy of Science (1987-1995); Chairman, Executive Board, Arab Center for the Studies of Arid Zones and Dry Lands (ACSAD), Arab League (1989-1995); Director/ Board Chairman of Agricultural Research Center, Egypt (1991-1994); Member, National Committee for Renewable Energy, Chaired by the Minister of Energy, Egypt (1990-1995); Co-Chairman, Government of Egypt led mission with the World Bank, UNDP, FAO, UNEP and World Food program to develop a report on "An Agricultural Strategy for 1990s". Document of the World Bank, Report No 11083-EGT-September 1992; Member, Research Council, Cairo University (1991-1995); Member, board of Academy of Scientific Research and Technology, Egypt (1991-1995); Member, Committee on Agricultural Research, Egyptian Supreme Council of Universities, Chaired by the Minister of Education (1992-1995); Established the Arid Land Agriculture Lab at Ain Shams University (1981); Developed and supervised multi-disciplinary, experimental research projects in plant stress physiology; Supervised post graduate Masters (17) and Doctoral (16) theses research in plant stress physiology at Ain shams University; Taught numerous University courses at the Graduate and Undergraduate levels; Organized and hosted International Conferences; Represented the Egyptian Government in International and Regional Organizations; Coordinated Mega-Research and Development programs connected with Ain shams University and the Ministry of Agriculture and Land Reclamation, Egypt. **As supervisor of the Under Secretary for Foreign Agricultural Relation (1988-1991)** Initiated, coordinated, and followed up on world-wide agricultural activities between the institutes of the Ministry of Agriculture and Land Reclamation and the International Agricultural Community. Acted as focal and contact point between the sector of agriculture and Land Reclamation with International Organization (i.e. FAO, World Bank, WFC, UNDP). Supervised and coordinated the activities of the Egyptian Documentation and Information Center for Agriculture (EDICA). This center is a computer Information Network System for the retrieval, compilation and dissemination of scientific information from different databases (i.e. AGRIS, CAB, AGRICOLA, BIOSIS) via the BRS & DIALOG system. **As Supervisor General for the Egyptian International Center for Agriculture (1988-1991)** Coordinated training and scholarship programs in different agricultural fields for trainees from Africa, Asia, Latin

America and the Arab World (approx. 1000 trainees/year). **As Under-Secretary and First Under Secretary of State for Land Reclamation (1987-1991):** Responsible for overseeing and following up the activities of the major institutions in Ministry of Land Reclamation including: - GARPAD General Authority for Rehabilitation Projects and Agricultural Development. - PSAAD Public Sector Authority for Agriculture Development. - DRC Desert Research Center. Supervised the Project Preparation Unit (PPU) and the Information and Documentation Center (IDC) activities including designing future projects in land reclamation. Chairman of the National Committee formed at the Minister's Office for Land Reclamation to redraw the initial Land Master Plan (LMP) maps, including land available for reclamation in each Governorate to enhance private sector investments (1988-1989). Initiated and co-ordinated the establishment of several land reclamation projects within the framework of the cooperation program with the Italian Government (approved level of funding 70 million US$). Led the negotiation of a proposal for the development of 215,000 acres in the North Coast of Egypt with Abou-Dhabi Fund (approved level of funding 65 million US$). Initiated a program to support the Young Graduates Project based on protected agriculture in newly reclaimed lands. The main components of this project were the R & D unit for Protected Agriculture, Central Nursery, Mechanization Center and Credit Line. The approved level of funding: - France, 20 million LE credit line (Revolving Fund), 10 million FF plus 7 million LE - EEC, 8.5 million LE Greenhouse construction. Established and directed activities of the MIS, Microfilm and Computer Training Unit. A Central Support Facility for Ministry of Agriculture and Land Reclamation (funded by the World Bank) 1987. Responsible for directing the North Sinai Development Project, (World Bank Project). This effort produced an 18 volume study on suggested land use for 400,000 Feddans. (Estimated total funding requirement 1,45 billion EP 2,5 million US$). **As Director General for the Agricultural Research Center (1991-1993)** His goals as Director for the Agricultural Research Center have been to provide and enabling research environment, especially for junior research workers; modernize the physical infrastructure and optimize the capabilities of the existing human resources; to restructure the ARC toward and interdisciplinary and interdepartmental approach to creating the 5 Year Plans; to Find means and ways of sustainable funding for research from local resources; to optimize the efficiency of utilization of grants from donor countries and to maximize interlinking with information, material and human resources. Towards these objectives, the following activities has been accomplished to date: - Eighteen research programs were developed based on a demand driven, problem solving approach which was interdisciplinary and interinstitutional in nature. These programs catered to the constraints facing agricultural development in Egypt, including crop, fish and animal production. This has involved the Participation of 16 research institutes, 7 central laboratories and 37 experiment station, and a total of 4,000 researches of whom 2,052 are PhDs. - The Establishment of 4 regional agroecological Zones and the Regional Research and Extension Council to implement activities in each zone. The regional councils consists of the Agricultural Research Center with its 37 nation-wide research stations, the Desert Research Center, the Water Research Center and 14 College of Agriculture, 7 Veterinary Schools and the Agricultural Division of the National Research Center. The objective of this council is to implement the 18 national research programs and to enhance appropriate technology transfer to meet the needs of agricultural development in each region. - Establishment of the Research Support Fund at the ARC. Funding sources include levies on given crops and a percentage income of special environmental units and economical units in the Ministry including Aquaculture, Serum and Vaccine, Tissue Culture, Soil Water and Plant Analysis, etc. Donations and grants from individuals, organizations and international parties are also included. These funds are being used to support proposals from junior researchers, international publications, physical infrastructure, books and participation in national and international conferences. The interest generated from an endowment is used to support these activities while the economic base will be enriched over time. - Enhancement & establishment of a Collaborative Research Program and Training Agreement between ARC and USA, Finland, Canada, Italy, France, China, Chile, Germany, Commonwealth countries and International Organizations. **Member** of the External Evaluation Panel for ICARDA, 21/1 to 9/2/1993 and 22/4 to 9/5/1993. Attended numerous conferences, Symposiums and international meetings all over the world. **Author** of more than 100 scientific publications in Egyptian and International Journals. **RESEARCH AND DEVELOPMENT PROJECTS:** 1980-1985 Principle Investigator of the Egyptian/ Norwegian Tomato Project (EGNO) funded by NORAD, Norway and Ain Shams University. 1982-1987 Member of the Steering Committee and Principal Investigator of the New Crops for Arid Land: National Academy of Science (USA) & Egyptian Academy of Science. Project funded by USAID. 1982-1990 Egyptian General Coordinator and Principal Investigator of the Cooperative Arid Land Agriculture Research Program (CALAR) supported by USAID. 1987-1991 Chairman, Coordinating Committee of the Agricultural Development Project in Fayoum, supported by IFAD and executed by World Bank. 1987-1995 National Project Coordinator of Protected Cultivation Project funded by UNDP, FAO. 1988-1995 Supervisor of the Joint Research and Development Project on Composite water holding substances for Arid land, Japan Desert Development Institute, R & D Project funded by Desert Development Institute of Japan. 1989-1995 National Project Coordinator of the Expert Systems for Improved Crop Management Project funded by UNDP/FAO. 1989-1993 Supervisor and Coordinator of the Urban Encroachment Project. National Technical Committee (Ministry of Agriculture. Universities, Institutes and Research Centers). Revised and prepared up-to-date maps (1:2500) from aerial photographs in cooperation with the Egyptian Survey Authority for MOALR planning. 1989-1995 Coordinator, Chairman, Egyptian Steering Committee of the Joint Committee for Remote Sensing for Agriculture and Land Reclamation with members from the Soil and Water Research Institute (ARC) and the Remote Sensing Unit and Desert Research Center (DRC) within MOALR funded by UNDP/ CIDA/France. 1990-1993 Chairman of the Egyptian Steering Committee of the Egyptian-Finnish Project for Agricultural Development (Phase 1) supported by Finida. 1990-1995 Member of the Steering Committee and Egyptian General Coordinator of the Integrated Agriculture Development Project, Maryut Agro-Industrial Complex supported by USAID. 1990-1995 Egyptian General Coordinator of the Desert Greenhouse Research Program (CALAR II) supported by USAID. 1990-1995 National Project Coordinator and Member Governing Board of the National Agricultural Lab (NAGEL) financed by UNDP. 1990-1995 Director General of the National Agricultural Research (NARP), Agricultural Research Center, MOALR. A USAID funded project with a budget of 205 million US$ and 250 million LE, established to enhance the capabilities of the ARC by improving human and Physical infrastructural resources. this project has allowed the ARC to become closely linked with Egyptian Universities, the National Research Center and the Central Administration for Agricultural Extension services. Ties with US agricultural Scientists in the USDA and in universities have been strengthened as a direct result of aspects of NARP, including Collaborative Grants, Collaborative Research Support Programs (RSP), new initiatives and training in Egypt. Collaborative grants amounting to 21 million US$ have emphasized up-to-date research efforts including the use of genetic engineering as a tool, integrated pest management, biocontrol, water use efficiency, irrigation technology, computer expert systems, remote sensing and post harvest technology among many other topics. These efforts have resulted in improved fertilization and irrigation and increased productivity to continue to meet Egypt's most critical agricultural research challenges. New initiatives funding has reached 19 million US$ and has been designed to bring developed technologies to Egypt for adoption into the food production system. These technologies include research programs in aquaculture, biotechnology and recombinant DNA and Vaccine production. NARP out of country training has placed almost 1300 people in education and research institutions int US and other countries for post doctoral, PhD and Masters level work as well as for short term experiences and professional scientific exchange. 1991-1993 Chairman, Egyptian Steering Committee of the Regional Program for Nile Valley. Regional (Egypt-Ethiopia-Sudan) activity coordinated by ICARDA. 1994-present Member of CGIAR Genetic Resources Policy Committee (1994-present). **INTERNATIONAL NETWORK LINKAGES AGRICULTURAL RESEARCH CENTERS AND INSTITUTIONS:** The following list represents countries of cooperation and official visits for all aspects of professional duties: **Europe:** France, Germany, Holland, Norway, United Kingdom, Finland, Austria, Switzerland, Czechoslovakia, Denmark, Greece, Italy, Newzeland, Spain. **America:** USA, Canada, Mexico, Brazil, Chile. **Australia:** Australia. **Africa:** Kenya, Uganda, Tanzania, Ethiopia, Angola, Republic of sierra Leone, Zimbabwe, Republic of Zambia, Ghana, Republic of Burundi, Mali, Rwanda, Tchad. **Asia:** China, Cyprus, India, Japan, Philippines, Sri Lanka, Thailand, Turkey, Indonesia, Iran, Tashkent, Uzbekistan. **Middle East:** Algeria, Lebanon, Jordan, Morocco, Syria, Tunisia, United Arab Emiratesd, Sudan, Palestine, Kuwait, Saudi Arabia, Yemen. **AWARDS & DISTINCTIONS:** 1982 Golden Pen of the International Society for Horticultural Science, 1989 FAO silver medal commemorating the theme of the 1989 cultural policy planning through contributions made to the national programme for New Land Reclamation, vertical agricultural expansion and appreciation for efforts to support all agriculture development projects in the country, 1990 FAO silver medal of World Food Day, 1990 in recognition of the efforts related to the issues of ecological degradation, 1991 FAO silver medal of "Trees for life" for supporting Agroforestation in Egypt specially in Arid Lands, 1992 Certificate of Recognition for contributions to agricultural development in Egypt and the Shield of the University during the celebration of the Golden Anniversary of Alexandria University, 1993 FAO silver medal in recognition of outstanding efforts and support to biological diversity, sustainable development of natural resources and agricultural development, 1994. Awarded a Fellow of the University College of Wales, Aberystwyth, U.K. **Hobby:** Tennis. **Credit Cards:** Amex Card, Visa Card. **Prof. Addr.:** ICARDA, P.O.Box 5466 Aleppo, Syria, Tel.: (963-21-2225517 - 2231330), Fax; (963-21-2225105), 963-21-5741480, E-Mail A. El-Beltagy@cguar.org.

BEN ALI (Zine el-Abidine), Tunisian politician. **Born** on September 3, 1936 in Hamman Sousse, Tunisia. **Married**, 5 children. **Educ.:** Graduate in Electronics, Saint-Cyr Military Academy (France), Chalons-sur-Marne School of Artillery (France); High School of Intelligence and Security (U.S.A.). **Career:** Head of Military Security (1964-74); Military Air and Naval Attache, Rabat, Morocco (1974-77); Member of Cabinet for Minister of National Defence; Director-General, National Security (1977-80); Ambassador to Poland (1980-84); Secretary of State for National Security (1984-85); Minister of National Security (1985); Minister of the Interior (1986-87); Minister of State for the Interior (May-November 1987); Prime Minister & Minister of the Interior (October 1987); **President of the Republic of Tunisia** (November 1987- to date). **Member:** Political Bureau of Parti Socialiste Destourien (PSD) (1986), Deputy-Secretary General of the PSD (June

1986); Secretary General (PSD) (1986); President of the Rassemblement Constitutionnel Democratique (Ex-PSD). **Awards:** Order of Merit of Bourguiba: Grand Maître of Order of Independance, Grand Maître of Order of the Republic, Grand Maître of Order of November 7, 1987, Several Foreign Orders. **Addr.:** Presidency of the Republic, Carthage, Tunisia.

BEN AYED (Abdelssalem), Tunisian Banker. **Born** in 1929 at Sfax, Tunisia. **Married** in 1963, 4 children. **Educ.:** Institute of Political of Science, Paris; Faculty of Law, Paris; Ecole Nationale d'Administration, Paris. **Dipl.:** Political Science, Law Licence (1953); ENA Paris (1956). **Career:** Director of Tunisian Budget (1956-64); Tunisian Ambassador, Federal Republic of Germany (1964-70); Secretary of State, Cabinet Director of the Prime Minister (1970-74); Chairman and General Manager, Union Bancaire pour le Commerce et l'Industrie (UBCI-TUNIS) (1974- to present). **Awards:** Grand officer order of Greman Merit. Grand Cordon Order of French Merit. **Priv. Addr.:** 8 Avenue Habib Bourguiba Salambo, Carthage, Tunisia. **Prof. Addr.:** UBCI, 7-9 Rue Gamal Abdel Nasser, P.O.Box 829, 1000 Tunis, Tel.: 340.644, 245.877, Telex: 14990, 14992, Tunis, Tunisia.

BENABBES TAARJI (Bachir), Moroccan advocate and diplomat. **Born** in 1918. **Married** in 1950 to Miss Khadja Benchakroune, 4 children: Hicham, Houria, Hinde, Dounia. **Dipl.:** Baccalaureat; Licence en Droit (Faculté de Paris); Licence ès Lettres (Sorbonne). **Career:** Advocate at the Bars of Marrakesh (1947) and Casablanca (1952); Director, Cabinet of the Sûreté Nationale (May 1956- June 1957); Governor of City of Marrakesh (June 1957- May 1958); Minister of Labour and Social Affairs (May- December 1958); Ambassador (1959-62); Mayor of the City of Marrakesh (1969); Deputy of Marrakesh (1970); Member, Constitutional Court (1971); Governor of Province of Marrakesh (May- November 1972); Minister of Justice (1972-74). **Member** of Istiqlal Party; presently Chairman, Brasseries du Maroc, **Addr.:** P.O.Box 2660, Ain Sebaa, Morocco.

BENABBES (Yusuf, Dr.), Moroccan physician and diplomat. **Born** on August 15, 1921 in Marrakesh (Morocco). **Educ.:** Marrakesh Secondary school Medical College of Algiers (Algeria) and Paris. **Dipl.:** M.D. **Career:** Joined Public Health Service (1949); Director, several hospitals, then Inspector- General of Health; Minister of Health (1958-61); Minister of Health and Education (1961-62); Minister of Education (1961-65); Mayor of Marrakesh city; President, Provincial Council; Ambassador to United Arab Republic (now Arab Republic of Egypt) (1965-66); Ambassador to Italy (1967-69); to Algeria (1969-70); Minister of Foreign Affairs (October 1970-70); Minister of Foreign Affairs (October 1970- August 1971); Ambassador to Spain (May- September 1972); Ambassador to France since 1972, and non-resident Ambassador to Vatican (1973). **Awards:** Commancer, Order of the Throne (Morocco); Grand Cordon, Order of the Italian Republic; Grand Cordon, Order of the Yugoslav Republic; Grand Cordon, Order of the Nile (Egypt); Grand Cordon, Order of the Hashemite Kingdom of Jordan; Grand Cordon, Order of Liberia; Grand Cordon, Order of Ethiopia; Grand Officer, French Order of Merit. **Hobby:** Cinema. **Prof. Addr.:** c/o Ministry of Foreign Affairs, Rabat, Morocco.

BENABDALLAH (Abdulaziz), Moroccan academic. **Born** in 1923 in Rabat, Morocco. **Married**, seven children. **Educ.:** Degree in Law and Literature, Algiers University (1946); studies in Islamic sciences with a group of Moroccan Ulemas. **Career:** Director of Property Conservation and Engineering Interests (1957); Director of Higher Education and Scientific Research (1958-61); Director of Bureau of Coordination of Arabisation in the Arab World Arab League (since 1962); Professor at Qarawiyin University, Fes, Morocco, Mohammed V University, Rabat and Dar al-Hadith al-Hassaniya; Member of Royal Moroccan Academy and four Arab Academies. **Publ.:** "The Philosophy and Morality of Ibn al Khatib", "Aspects of Maghreb Civilisation" in Arabic; "Moroccan Art in Various Ages" in French and Arabic; "Medicine and Doctors of Morocco", a comparative study of Arabic and foreign texts; "The Geography of the Maghreb"; "The Development of Thoughts and Languages in Modern Morocco" (a series of lectures delivered at the Institute of Arabic Studies in Cairo); "Human and Cultural Encyclopedia of Morocco", ten volumes; "The Blond Country Girl" stories of Moroccan history, Beirut; "Arabization and the Future of the Arabic Language" (lectures delivered in the Institute of Arabic Studies, Cairo; "Towards the Elimination of Illiteracy in the Arab World", in French; Author of forty dictionaries in various fileds in Arabic, French and English. **Other Publ.:** Moroccan Army; Foreign and Moroccan embassies; Monographies of Moroccan cities. **Medals:** Honorary Medal with rank of Knight (1969); Academic Medal (1984); Great Price of Moroccan Merit (1991); Represented Morocco at Islamic and educational conferences; Participated in many international conferences such as UN Conference of Experts on African Affairs. **Hobbies:** Architecture, Andalusian music, philosophy. **Priv. Addr.:** Ryad, Secteur 3, Villa E6, Tel.: 71-00-39, Rabat, Morocco.

BENABDALLAH (Moncef), Tunisian Economist. **Born** on October 21, 1946 in Tunis. **Married**, 3 children. **Educ.:** Licenciate Es-Sciences Mathematics from University of Tunis (1968); Engineering from Ecole Centrale de Paris (1972). **Career:** Principal Engineer, Head of Department at the Management of Production, Société Tunisienne d'Electricité et du Gaz (STEG) Centrale Goulette II (October 1972- January 1975); Chargé de Mission, Technical Advisor and Chief of Cabinet at the Ministry of National Economy (January 1975- December 1977); Director of the Participations and Development at Entreprise Tunisienne d'Activités Pétrolières (ETAP) with rank Deputy Director General (December 1977- April 1979); Director of Industry, Ministry of Industry, Mining and Energy (April 1979-1980); Director of Cabinet, Ministry of National Economy (April 1980- October 1980); President Director General, Agence de Promotion des Investissements (A.P.I.) (October 1980- November 1984); Technical Advisor in charge of Economic Affairs to the Prime Ministry (November 1984- December 1985); President Director General, Agence pour la Maïtrise de l'Energie (A.M.E.) (December 1985- August 1991); President Director General, Société des Ciments d'Enfidah (August 1991- June 1992). **Other Activities:** Administrator State Representative in several Tunisian Public Enterprises (since 1975); Administrator, Banque Centrale de Tunisie (1980-1986); Administrator, Société Tuniso-Saoudienne d'Investissement et de Développement (STUSID) (1981-1985); Administrator, Banque de Tunisie et des Emirats d'Investissemnt (BTEI) (1982-1984); President, Comité Economique Tuniso-Scandinave (since 1984); International Expert in the Energy Field at the Banque Mondiale et du PNUD (since 1986); Advisor, Institut International de la Maïtrise de l'Energie (since 1989). **Medals:** Commander, Order of the Republic (1976); Knight Order of Merit, French Republic (1981). **Addr.:** Société Tunisienne de l'Electricité et du Gaz, 38 Rue Kemal Ataturk, P.O.Box 190, 1080 Tunis Cedex, Tel.: 243.522, 341.311, Fax: (216.1) 349 981, 330 174, 341 401, Telex: 14020, 14744, 13060, 13061 TUNIS, Tunisia.

BENABDELRAZIK (Muhammad, Abdel Aziz), Moroccan official. **Born** in 1926 in Marakesh, Morocco. **Married**, 3 sons. **Educ.:** Faculty of Law, University of Paris, France. **Dipl.:** M.A. **Career:** Manager for handicrafts, Ministry of Commerce and Handicrafts (1956-59), Manager for Commerce (1959-61); General Secretary, Ministry of Commerce and Industry (1961-63), Chargé de Mission, Royal Cabinet (1964-65); General Secretary, Ministry of Commerce and Industry (1965-69); participated in several international conferences and meetings on future planning, economic and energy; General Manager and Director of Société Chérifienne des Pétroles (1969). **Hobbies:** Golf and swimming. **Priv. Addr.:** 6 Rue Cadi Ahmed Moutine, La Pinede, Souissi, Rabat, Morocco.

BENABDERRAZIK (Abderrahman), Moroccan Industrial Engineer. **Born** on Jul 28, 1935 in Marrakech, Morocco. **Son** of Mohamed Ben Driss Benabderrazik (Tradesman) **and** Mrs. Ghita nee Chraibi. **Married** on September 22, 1962 in Marrekech to Khalila Kamili, 3 children: Karim (9 April 1965), Ali (21 February 1968), Amine (28 August 1972). **Educ.:** Etudes Préparatoires Grandes Ecoles (Université de Grenoble); Ecole Nationale Supérieure d'Electricite Mécanique (Nancy-France); Faculté des Sciences, Nancy (France); Institut d'Admininstration d'Entreprises (Dauphine-Paris); **Dipl.:** Diplome Etudes Appronfondies en Chimie Minérale (Nancy-France); Doctorat d'Ingenieur en Metallurgie (Nancy-France); Diplôme de l'Institut d'Administration d'Entreprises (Dauphine-Paris): Doctorat de 3ème Cycle en Gestion (Casablanca-Maroc). **Career:** Engineer Researcher, Institut de Recherches Siderurgiques, France (1963-66); Chief Engineer Projects, Bureau de Recherches Pétrolières et Minières, Maroc (1966-68); Professor Metallurgy (1966-68); Chief Engineer Projects S.E.I. (OCP), France (1968-70); Chief Engineer Projects OCP, Maroc (1970-73); Secretary General, Office pour le Développement Industriel, Rabat (1974-79); Secretary General S.A.M.I.R. (Mohammedia, Maroc), (1980-98) (Refinery); Professor Cycle Supérieur de Gestion, I.S.C.A.E. (Casablanca, Maroc). Member of the Energy Commission at the Paris International Chamber of Commerce (I.C.C.); Town Concillor, Energy Consultant. **Sports:** Swimming, golf. **Hobbies:** Play Luth, Classical Arab Music. **Member:** Secretary General, Association du Grand Atlas - Section de Casablanca. **Addr.:** 45, Blvd. Mohamed V, Mohammedia, Tel.: (03)31.22.60, Morocco.

BENABDESSELEM (Muhammad, Muncef), Tunisian engineer. **Born** in 1943 in Tunisia. **Educ.:** Ecole Centrale des Arts et Manufactures, Paris, France. **Dipl.:** B.Sc. in mathematics. **Career:** Manager of Equipment, District of Bizerte (1972-80), of Tunis (1980-82); Chairman and Managing Director, E.P. Iskam (1982-). **Prof. Addr.:** E.P. Iskam, Rue No.4, Zone Industrielle Charkiya, Tunis, Tunisia.

BENAHMAD (Mohamad), Algerian statesman. **Born** in Algeria. **Career:** Under the name of "Commandant Moussa" played an important role in the Socialist Forces front (F.F.S.) led by Mr. Ait Ahmad; Arrested on July 13, 1964; Sentenced to death by the Criminal Revolutionary Court of Algeria (10 April 1965); Released on August 24, 1966 by President Boumedienne; Member of the Algerian Revolutionary Council (June 1965- October 1969); **Addr.:** Algiers, Algeria.

BENAHMED (Mohamed), Tunisian academic. **Born** on March 28, 1941 in Tunis. **Son** of Abderrahman Ben Ahmed **and** Mrs. née Melika Frourej. **Married** on March 31, 1968 in Tunis to Zeinab Benosman, one child: Melika (May 16, 1971). **Educ.:** College Sadiki (1952-60); Faculty of Science, Tunis 1960-63); Faculty of Science, Paris (1963-66); University of Paris IX (1972-78). **Dipl.:** Doctorat d'Etat in Computer Science (May 1978). **Career: Educational:** Assistant at the Faculty of Science, Tunis (Oct. 1967 - Sept. 1972); Researcher at the Institut de Recherche en Informatique et Automatique (Oct. 1972 - Sept. 1977); Master-Assistant at the Faculty of Science, Tunis (1977-78); Master of Conferences (1978-82); Professor of Higher Education since January 1983. Director of the Department of Data Processing at the Faculty of Science, Tunis (Jan. 1981 - Sept. 1984); Director, Founder of Ecole Nationale des Sciences de l'Informatique (University of Tunis) (Sept. 1984 - Sept. 1990). **Other Activities:** Secretary General of "Union Générale des Etudiants de Tunisie" (UGET) (1966-67); Secretary of Young Scholars (1967-69); Secretary General of Union Tunisienne de la Jeunesse (U.T.J.) (1969-72); Municipal Counsellor to the City of Tunis (1969-72); Editor then Director of "Erraï" Arabic newspaper (1978-82); Editor then Editor in Chief of a French newspaper "Démocratie" (1979-81); Consultant in Data Processing to several Tunisian Companies; Expert, ALECSO (1985-87); Counsellor to three Ministers for Higher Education (1982-87; Expert Consultant to ONUDI (1988-89); Counsellor of the President of "Institut National de la Recherche en Informatique et en Automatique" (France) (Oct. 1990 - May 1991). **Publ.:** "La Passion du Savoir" (1989); "La Flamme et le Cristal" (1991) and many other papers and reports. **Prof. Addr.:** ENSI, 16 Rue 8010, Tel.: 784032, 1002 Tunis, Tunisia. **Priv. Addr.:** 21 Rue du Lycée, el-Menzah 6, Tel.: (216)-1-233.592, Tunisia.

BENAISSA (Hamdan), Tunisian lawyer and economist. **Born** on August 24, 1935 at Midoun, Tunisia. **Married**, 2 children. **Dipl.:** Licence en Droit (School of Law and Economic Science, University of Bordeaux, France); Arts & Language Certificate (School of Letters, University of Bordeaux); Preparation of Doctorate in Economics (School of Law and Economic Science, University of Paris, Sorbonne); LL.M. (New-York University, School of Law); AMP (Graduate School of Business, Harvard University). **Career:** Head, Economic and Financial Division, Ministry of Foreign Affairs, Tunisia (1960-62); Chargé d'Affaires and Economic Counsellor, Tunisian Embassy to France (1962-65); Chargé d'Affairs and Member, Permanent Mission of Tunisia to the UN (New-York (1965-67); Special Assistant to Under-Secretary General, UN (New-York) (1967-72); Department of Political Affairs, Trusteeship and Decolonisation; UN Secretary, UN Council for Namibia (1972-75); Deputy Director in Charge of Middle East, Mediterranean, Europe and Interregional Projects Branch, Department of Technical Cooperation for Development, (1975); also Associate Professor of Management, Pace University, New-York since 1979. **Addr.:** Tunis, Tunisia.

BENAISSA (Hanafi), Algerian academic. **Born** in 1932 in Algeria. **Married**, four sons. **Educ.:** B.A. in Psychology and in English, Ph.D. in Philosophy. **Career:** Head of the Cultural Exchange Service, Ministry of Education (1962-63); Professor, Higher School of Interpretation, University of Algeria (1963-73); Professor of Psychology, Institute of Social Sciences, University of Algeria (since 1973); Editor of "al-Thaqaga" magazine (1975), **Member of:** The Union of Algerian Interpreters; The Union of Algerian Writers. **Publ.:** Many articles published in newspapers and magazines; Translation of several books into Arabic. **Sport:** Swimming. **Hobbies:** Writing, translation, journalism. **Addr.:** Cite Chevally Bt 14B Bouzarah, Tel.: 785561, Algiers, Algeria.

BENAISSA (Mohamed Mohamed), Moroccan Minister **Born** on January 3, 1937 at Asilah, Morocco. **Married** to Mrs. Laila Hajoui-Benaissa (M.A. in Library Science, University of Maryland) and has 5 children: 4 daughters and 1 son. **Educ.:** B.A. in Communications University of Minnesota (1963); Rockfeller Foundation Fellowship for Research in Communications, Colombia University, New York (1964). **Career:** Press Attaché, Permanent Mission of Morocco th the United Nations, New York (1964-65); Information Officer, United Nations Department of Information, New York-USA and Adis Abeba-Ethiopia (1965-67); F.A.O. Regional Information Adviser for Africa, Accra-Ghana (1967-1971); In charge of Development Support Communication, F.A.O. Headquarters Rome-Italy (1971-73); Assistant Director of Information and Publications, F.A.O. Headquarters Rome-Italy (1973-74): Director of the Information Division, F.A.O. Headquarters Rome-Italy (1974-76); Assistant Secretary-General of the UN (on Loan to the UN) World Food Conference New York and Rome (1975); Member of the City Council of Asilah, Asilah-Morocco (1976-83); Member of the Moroccan Parliament and Rapporteur of the Cultural and Information Commission of the Parliament, Rabat-Morocco (1977-83); Founding Member of the Al-Mouhit Cultural Association and of the Asilah International Cultural Festival (1978); International Consultant on Communication Development for UNDP, IFAD and UNFPA Rabat-Morocco (1978-1985); Chief Editor of the Publications "Al-Mithak-Al Watani in arabic and "Al Maghrib" in French (1980-85); Elected Mayor of the City of Asilah, Morocco (1983-92); Re-elected Member of the Moroccan Parliament (1984-92); Minister of Culture (1985-92); Re-elected Mayor of the City of Asilah (1992); Ambassador of Morocco to the USA Washington D.C. (1993-99); Minister of Foreign Affairs and Cooperation (since April 8,1999-). **Publ.:** "Grain de Peau" published in 1974 by shoof publishers in Casablanca; Studies and essays in communication and development for various regional and international Organizations. **Social Activities:** Secretary-general of the Afro-Arab Cultural Forum (Asilah Forum Foundation); Secretary-General of the "Al-Mouatamid Ibn Abbad" Summer University - Asilah, Morocco; Member of several national and international fora and associations. **Addr.:** Ministry of Foreign Affairs and Cooperation, ave. Franklin Roosevelt, Tel.:(7) 762841; Fax: (7) 764679; E-mail: ministere@maec. gov.ma, Rabat, Morocco.

BENALI (Mohamad), Tunisian actor. **Born** in Februry 1932. **Educ.:** Secondary. **Career:** Journalist (1950-1955), Actor, Radio and Theatre, then Television (1955), Cinema (1966), **Member of** Troupe de l'Unité Théâtrale (1948), Troupe du Théâtre Populaire (1954), la Troupe des Etoiles de l'Art (1960), Troupe du Théâtre Populaire (1968), Troupe du Théâtre Républicain. **Publ.:** Author of

17 theatral pieces, 25 television pieces and 35 radio pieces; Publisher, Art Review (1955). **Awards:** 2nd Prize Cinematographic Interpretation, Ministry of Culture (1966). **Addr.:** 9 immeuble Leroud Escellier 2, Cité al-Menzah, Tunis, Tunisia.

BENALLAL (Mohamad), Moroccan academic. **Born** in 1950 in Morocco. **Married**, one child. **Educ.:** Diploma in Accountancy (1968); B.A. in Political Sciences (1971); Doctorat d'Etat, International Law, University of Nice, Nice, France, (1976). **Career:** Professor of International Law and International Relations, Faculty of Law, University of Hassan II, Casablanca, Morocco (since 1976); Juridical Adviser on Legal Problems related to Gibraltar (1980); Director, National School of Administration, Rabat (1981). **Member of** the Moroccan Delegation, UN Conference on the Law of the Sea, New York and Geneva. **Publ.:** "Morocco and the Law of the Sea" (1976, Nice); several articles in university journals. **Addr.:** 7 Rue Tachfin, Tel.: 4240, Tetouan, Morocco.

BENALLAL (Mohamad), Moroccan artist painter. **Born** in 1924 in Marrakech. **Married**, 2 daughters. **Educ.:** Privately. **Career:** Joined Dar Si Saïd Museum (1948), Artist Painter, Contributed to several art exhibitions in Morocco, U.S.A., France, Italy. **Addr.:** Marrakech, Morocco.

BENAMAR (Driss), Moroccan statesman. **Born** in 1928. **Educ.:** Military Academy of Meknes. **Career:** Joined the Moroccan Army, Promoted General (1963), Governor of Casablanca (1964), Commander-in-Chief of the Army (1967), Minister of P.T.T. (1970), Minister of Defence (1972). **Addr.:** Rabat, Morocco.

BENAMAR (Hassib), Tunisian statesman. **Born** in 1924 Tunis, Tunisia. **Married**, four children. **Educ.:** Faculty of Sciences, University of Paris, France. **Career:** Director of Youth and Sports (1958); Secretary General for Youth (1960); Deputy Mayor of Tunis (1963); Governor Mayor of Tunis (1964); Ambassador to Italy (1969); Minister of National Defence (1970); Director of S.A. el-Iskane (Real Estate); Director of S.A. Mercure (bookshop and Publishing); Director of "ar-Rai" weekly newspaper; and Director ""Démocratie" monthly French, Arabic periodical; both since 1984 to present. **Member:** of the Red Crescent; of the Socialist Destour Party Central Committee (1940) and Director of same (1970); of the Association Sauvegarde de la Medina (1964). **Editor** of the "Ech-Chebab" organ of the Higher Committee of Youth suspended in 1985. **Participated** in the creation of the Union of Arab Cities and in preparation of the project to preserve Tunis-Carthage supported by UNESCO. **Addr.:** Tunis, Tunisia.

BENAMAR (Mondher, Mohamad), Tunisian lawyer. **Born** on May 9, 1917 in Tunis. **Son** of Mohamad Ben Ammar (Barrister) **and** Mrs. Fatma. **Married** to Miss Samia in 1947. **Educ.:** Law. **Dipl.:** Licentiate of Law, Paris University. **Career:** Called to the Bar; during Independence War defended Tunisian patriots; at the beginning of Tunisian independence appointed Chief of the Cabinet of the President of the Council, Tunisian Ambassador to Rome (1956), to Bonn (1957); also Tunisian Representative in Brussels, The Hague; Minister of Tourism and Land Development; Minister of Health, Social Affairs, Youth Sports and Tourism (1961-70); Lawyer, Supreme Court of Appeal (since 1970). **Award:** Order on Independence, Tunisian Republic. **Addr.:** Tunis, Tunisia.

BENAMAR (Mustafa), Algerian diplomat. **Born** in 1937. **Married**, 1 child. **Educ.:** University of Algiers. **Dipl.:** B.A.; Degree in Social Sciences. **Career:** Officer of the National Liberation Army (1956); Embassy Secretary, Minister Plenipotentiary, Consul for Central Services, Ambassador to Mali, Ministry of Foreign Affairs (1962-80); Adviser, Ministry of Finance (1981); Vice-President, Committee for Algerian- Iraqi Cooperation; Director General, External Finances (1982-84). **Prof. Addr.:** Ministry of Foreign Affairs, Algiers, Algeria.

BENAMARA (Abdelkader), Algerian executive. **Born** in 1942 in Algiers, Algeria. **Married**, 3 children. **Educ.:** University of Algiers; Michigan State University; George Washington University. **Dipl.:** Degrees in Sociology and Economics, Specialized in International Finance and Development Cooperation. **Career:** Senior Editor, Algerie Press Service, Algiers; Research Officer, Research Department, International Monetary Fund Washington D.C. U.S.A.; Director of Research and Information, OPEC Fund for International Development, Vienna. **Addr.:** P.O.Box 995, A-1011 Vienna, Austria; Tel.: 515 64-0, Telex 1-31734, Fax: 513 92 38.

BENANI (Abdel-Latif), Moroccan banker. **Born** in 1941 in Casablanca. **Married** in 1970; 2 **sons. Educ.:** Polytechnique School & University of Lausanne, Switzerland. **Dipl.:** Degree in Economy and Business Administration; Degree in Law (major in International Law). **Career:** Joined Citibank N.A./Citicorp International (1967-78); Paris, Manila, New York, Casablanca, London, Beirut, Athens, Vice President Citibank N.A. (1975); Assistant General Manager of UBAF, Union de Banques Arabes et Françaises, Paris (since 1978-82); General Manager of ALUBAF Arab Int. Bank Bahrain (1982-83); General Manager of UBAF Paris (1983-87); Managing Director and Founder of CICC Commercial & Investment Credit Corp. Geneva, Switzerland (since 1987), Chairman of Citibank Maghreb, Morocco (since 1977); Chairman & CEO of Digital Media Partners Morocco (since 1995); Former Board and Executive Committee Member of: UBAF Bank LTD. London, UBAE Arab Italian Bank Rome, Arlabank Lima, UBAE Arab German Bank (1979-88). **Publ.:** Articles/Studies on Arab Banking and Finance,

Economic Development issues; Geopolitical Analysis on Arab/Islamic World and on Africa. **Hobbies:** Reading of political, historical and biographical works, classical Music, Collection of Oriental objets d'Art, photography. **Addr.:** 59 Rue du Rhône, 1204 Geneva, Switzerland, Tel.: (4122) 310-2360, Fax: (4122) 781-0783.

BENANI (Abdelhak), Moroccan bank president. **Born** in 1945 in Morocco. **Son** of Hadj Driss Bennani. **Married** in 1971, 2 sons. **Educ.:** Diplome d'Expertise Comptable (B.P.L.G.), Ecole Supérieure de Commerce à Paris. **Career:** President, Wafasalaf, Wafa Systems, Diners Club du Maroc. Wafabank; Vice-President, Wafa Assurance; Director, Sopar, Texnord, Morsew, Société Nouvelle d'Assurances. **Hobby:** Sports. **Addr.:** Wafabank, 163, Avenue Hassan II, Tel.: 224105, Casablanca, Morocco.

BENARAB (Faouzi), Tunisian General Manager/ Chamber of Commerce and Industry of the South. **Born** on September 12, 1956 at Sfax (Tunisia). **Son** of Hamed Ben Arab (retired) **and** Mrs. Zeineb Abida. **Married** on September 1, 1985 to Hedia Abdel kafi, 2 children: Sabrine (4.11.1987), Hana (2.6.1991). **Educ.:** IPSI (Institut de Presse et des Sciences de l'Information). **Dipl.:** Master ès Sciences in Information Option «Economy». **Career:** Centre National d'Etudes Industrielles (CNEI) (1981-1982); Institut National de la Normalisation et de la Propriété Industrielle (INNORPI) (1982-1989); Chamber of Commerce and Industry of South (1990- to date). **Prof. Addr.:** P.O.Box 794, 3018 Sfax, Tunisia, Tel.: 296120. **Priv. Addr.:** Route de Mahdia KMS - Sfax, Tel.: 225063, Tunisia.

BENBARKA (Ibrahim), Moroccan economist. **Born** in 1939 in Rabat, Morocco. **Married**, three children. **Educ.:** University of Damascus, Syria; University of Cairo, Egypt. **Dipl.:** B.A. in Economics (1963); M.A. in Statistics and Research (1966). **Career:** Chief Statistian (since 1967); Secretary, State Office for Regional Planning and Development (1972); Director, Regional Planning and Development (since 1978); Director of Statistics, League of Arab States, Tunisia (since 1981). **Publ.:** Translated "Social Economic Indicators of Morocco", Abdul Malik Cherkaoui; many studies and researches on the economy of Morocco and the Arab World in professional journals. **Medals:** Order of Reda (1971). **Sports:** Swimming, jogging, tennis. **Addr.:** 17 Avenue Abda Aviation, Tel.: 59938, 65136, Rabat, Morocco.

BENBASHIR (Said), Moroccan politician. **Born** in 1935. **Educ.:** Degrees in Law and Political Sciences and Doctorate in Public Law. **Career:** Professor of Law, Morocco; President of the Administrative Council and UN expert at CAFRAD; Director of the National School of Public Administration; organized various conferences on legal questions and public administration and other subjects in Morocco and other African countries; General Secretary of the Association of Moroccan Jurists; Secretary of State for Higher Education and Scientific Research (1977); Minister of Cultural Affairs (1981-83). **Addr.:** Rabat, Morocco.

BENBELLA (Ahmad), Algerian freedom fighter. **Born** in 1916 in Algeria. **Career:** was a leader in the formative years of the Algerian revolution. Drafted into the French Army during World War II, he was decorated for distinguished service in Europe. After returning to Algeria in 1945, he entered politics as an elected municipal councillor in Marnia in 1946. His revolutionary activities began in 1948 when he helped establish the "Organisation Spéciale", a secret para-military organisation. In 1950 he was arrested and imprisoned, but he escaped in 1952 and went to Cairo (Egypt), where he helped lay the foundations for the revolution. During his absence in Cairo, he joined the "Comité révolutionaire pour l'Union et l'Action" in 1954. Two years later he was arrested by the French and spent the duration of the Algerian War in prison. Upon his release in 1962, he began to organise and consolidate his political power. He and his supporters within the provisional government of the Algerian Republic established the Political Bureau, which took control of the revolution. On September 7, 1963 he and Houari Boumedienne (who died in 1978) had either isolated or eliminated all political opposition. Ben Bella's political career came to an end on June 19, 1965 when he was overthrown by Boumedienne in a bloodless coup and imprisoned; released in 1980. Left to France. In 1984 he formed in Paris new Party "Mouvement pour la Démocratie en Algérie" and later a united democratic front with Dr. Hocine Ait Ahmed; presently Leader of Mouvement pour la Démocratie en Algérie. **Medal:** Lenin Peace Medal. **Addr.:** Paris, France.

BENBOUCHTA (Mehdi), Moroccan statesman, businessman. **Born** in 1936 in Fes, Morocco. **Son** of Mahdi Benbouchta. **Married**, three daughters. **Educ.:** Social Sciences and Law Studies, Licence en Droit, College of Law, University of Grenoble, France. **Career:** King's Counsel in the Rabat High Court of First Instance (1960-63); Director, Cabinet of the Prime Minister (1963-65); Chargé de Mission in the Royal Cabinet (1965-66); Under Secretary of State for Youth and Sports (1967); Minister of Youth and Sports (1968); Minister of Labour and Employment and Professional Training (1969); Deputy in Parliament (1970); Vice President of the Chamber of Deputies, President of the Chamber (1971); President, Société Marocaine de Construction Automobile (SOMACA) and several other Companies, (since 1972 to present). **Prof. Addr.:** Société Morocaine de Construction Automobile, Km 12, Autoroute de Rabat, P.O.Box 2628, Telex: 25825, Casablanca, Morocco.

BENBOUZID (Boubakeur), Algerian Minister of Higher Education and Scientific Research. **Born** on 20 March 1954 in Ain Beida, Algeria. **Son** of Zoubir, Agriculturist and Land Owner **and** Mrs. Baza. **Married** on 5

June 1980 in Odessa, to Victoria, on child: Nadia (3.6.1986). **Dipl.:** Masters in Engineering, Doctorat d'Etat in Electronics. **Career:** Institute Director (1986); President Scientific Council of University (1987); Vice-Rector (1989); Rector (1991); President, Rectors Conference (Central Region) (1992); Minister of Higher Education and Scientific Research (1993-96); Minister of National Education (1997-99). **Other Information:** Professor of University, Chief of Chair. **Hobbies:** Football. **Prof. Addr.:** Ministry of Higher Education and Scientific Research, Tel.: 91-10-55, 91-10-64, Algiers, Algeria. **Priv. Addr.:** Villa N°3, Club des Pins, Algiers, Algeria.

BENCHEIKH (Abdulqader), Tunisian writer. **Born** in 1929 in Zaghouan. **Educ.:** Secondary and Higher. **Dipl.:** Doctor of Philosophy, Arabic Literature. **Career:** Professor, Writer and Novelist. **Publ.:** Author of several studies and novels including "Et ma part d'horizon" (in Arabic, published in 1970). **Addr.:** Tunis, Tunisia.

BENCHEIKH (Taleb), Moroccan former Minister of Health. **Born** in 1938 at Zoumi, Morocco. **Son** of Mohamad Bencheikh. **Married** in 1967, 3 children. **Educ.:** Graduate Engineering (Statistics and Economics), ENSAE, Paris; M.Sc., University of Paris; Graduate, Institute of Political Studies, Paris. **Career:** Professor of Political Economy; Director, Statistics Department, Morocco; Ministry of Regional Development and Planning (1974-81); Minister of Economic Affairs (1982-85); Minister of Health (1986-1992); President, Meknes Provincial Council, Morocco. **Hobbies:** Literature, Arts, Tennis, Sailboard, Water-Skiing, Diving and Skiing. **Addr.:** 12, Rue Beni Amir, P.O.Box 178, Rabat, Morocco.

BENCHENEB (Rachid, Mohamad), Algerian Higher Official in French Administration. **Born** on January 9, 1916 in Saint-Eugène (Algiers). **Son** of Mohamad Bencheneb (Faculty Professor) **and** Mrs., née Kateb. **Educ.:** Lycée Bugeaud (Algiers), Faculties of Letters (Paris and Algiers). **Dipl.:** Licentiate in Literature, Doctor in Literature, Diploma in Higher Studies, Diploma in Oriental Languages. **Career:** Professor at Medea College (1941), at Blida College (1944), attached to the French Cabinets in Algeria and France (1944-58), Assistant-Chief Commissioner, Chief-Commissioner General Inspector of Administration in 1959. **Awards:** Knight Legion of Honour (France), Croix de Guerre (1939-45), Officier des Palmes Académiques (France), Officer of Nichan, etc... **Addr.:** 3, Boulevard Emile Augier Paris 16ème, France.

BENCHERIF (Ahmad), Algerian politician. **Born** in 1927 in Algeria. **Career:** Served in French Armed Forces; joined Wilaya IV of National Liberation Army (ALN) (1975); Commander of National Gendarmerie, with rank of Colonel (1962); elected member of National Liberation Front (FLN) Committee (1964); member of Revolutionary Command Council (1965); Minister of Hydraulics, Land Improvement and Environment (1977); member of Politburo (1979); President of FLN Commission of the Supreme Council of Youth; Vice President of the Commission on Higher Education; member of the Central Committee (1979). **Publ.:** "L'Aurore des Mechats". **Addr.:** 10 Rue des Frères Belhafidh, Hydra, Algeria.

BENDARI (Adel, Nader), Egyptian businessman. **Born** in 1935 in Cairo, Egypt. **Married**, 2 children. **Career:** Owner, Electric Wire Factory, Abaseya; Agent, Kidde Company and Fulton Company, USA, Agent, Henry Simon Company, UK, Agent, Stolz SA, France; Member, Lloyds, London; Board Member, Cairo Poultry Company; Chairman, AMAK, Cairo. **Member:** Automobile Club of Egypt, Gezira Sporting Club, Shooting Club. **Prof. Addr.:** 4 Behlar Street, Kasr el-Nil, Egypt. **Priv. Addr.:** 17 Malek el-Swisry Street, Zamalek, Cairo, Egypt.

BENDJEBBOUR (Abdulkarim, Kaddour), Algerian engineer. **Born** on December 28, 1955 in Algeria. **Educ.:** Ecole Nationale des Travaux Publics, Algeria. **Career:** State engineer, LTPO, Oran (1981-82); Teacher of Soil Mechanics at ENIATP, Oran (1982-); participated in various international and national meetings; Head of Geotechnical Department, LTPO, Oran (1982-83), Head of the Technical Department (1983-84), Technical Director, LTPO (Laboratoire des Travaux Publics de L'Ouest) (1984-); Professor, USTO; President of C.O.R.T.; Director of E.P.T.P.; Director of C.T.C. **Prof. Addr.:** P.O.Box 6020, Oran, Algeria. **Priv. Addr.:** Cité du Rond Point BT A5, Bel-Air, Oran, Algeria.

BENFREIHA (Ahmad), Algerian politician. **Born** in 1940. **Married**, 3 children. **Educ.:** University of Algiers; Higher studies, Faculty of Agriculture, Moscow, USSR. **Dipl.:** DES in Biological Sciences; Researcher at the National Institute of Agronomical Sciences. **Career:** Head of Mission, Ministry of Agriculture, later Central Director, Secretary of State for Fisheries (1980-82), Secretary of State for Fisheries and Maritime Transport (1982-84); President, Sub-Commission of the Algerian Revolution of the FLN (1979), Acting Member, Central Committee FLN (1979), Minister of Public Works (1984-87); Minister of Hydraulics, Environment, Forestry and Fishing (1988-89). **Addr.:** Algiers, Algeria.

BENGHASEM (Hamida), Tunisian executive director. **Born** in 1938 at Beni Khaled, Tunisia. **Son** of Mohamed Ben Ghasem. **Married** in 1967, 4 children. **Educ.:** University of Harvard, USA. **Dipl.:** M.Sc. (USA); Statistician (1963). **Career:** Deputy Director of Planning, Tunisia; Abu Dhabi Economic Adviser; UAE Minister of Planning Adviser; Director of Statistics, Arab Monetary Fund; former Executive Director, Arab Monetary Fund; Mayor of Ben Khaled City (Tunisia); President of Cultural Club - E.S.B.K. (Tunisia). **Hobby:** Reading. **Publ.:** "Saving and Government Investment in Tunisia". **Addr.:** Tunis, Tunisia.

BENHABYLES (Abdelmalek), Algerian politician. **Born** in 1921 in Cherreuil, Setif, Algeria. **Married. Educ.:** Graduated in Law. **Career:** started political activities in 1943; Member, Parti Populaire Algérien; member, Central Committee, Mouvement pour le Triomphe des Libertés Démocratiques (1946); Vice-President, Association of North African Students; founder Member, with Belaid Abdessalam of the General Union of Algerian Muslim Students (UGEMA); legal Adviser to UGEMA; member, Commission on Information and Propaganda Fédération de France (1958); Representative, National Liberation Front (FLN) in Damascus, Syria and in Far East (Tokyo); represented Algeria at numerous conferences; following Independence, Head, Ministry of Foreign Affairs, Eastern European Division; Secretary General, Ministry of Foreign Affairs (1963); Ambassador to Japan (1964-67); Ambassador to Tunisia (1967-70)); Assistant Secretary-General, Ministry of Foreign Affairs (1974-77); Minister of Justice (April 1977- March 1979); Secretary of the Presidency (1979). **Addr.:** Algiers, Algeria.

BENHAMIDA (Slahiddine), Tunisian journalist. **Born** in 1934 in Monastir, Tunisia. **Married,** two children. **Educ.:** Journalism and literature in Tunisia. **Career:** Editor in Chief of "al-Amal" newspaper, organ of Neo Destour Party (1960); Director General of Tunis-Afrique Press Agency (1972); Director General of Radio Diffusion Television Tunisienne (1974). Member of the Central Committee of the Destour Socialist Party; Vice-President of the Tunis Municipal Council (1972); member of the Administrative Board of ASBU; presently Managing Director, Société Tunisienne de Diffusion. **Publ.:** "Between the Barada and the Nile" (1961); "From the Happy Yemen to Revolutionary Yemen", a study of the Yemeni Revolution (1962). **Medal:** Commander of the Order of Tunisian Independence (1975); Commander of the Order of Tunisian Republic (1972); Officer of the Legion d'Honneur awarded by the President of the French Republic (1975); Egyptian, Iranian and other decorations. **Member** of Tunisian Writers Union. **Hobbies:** Reading, chess. **Prof. Addr.:** 5 Avenue de Carthage, P.O.Box 440, Tunis, Tunisia. **Priv. Addr.:** 60 rue des Selliers, Tunis, Tunisia.

BENHAMOUDA (Boualem), Algerian politician. **Career:** Minister of Ex Combattants (1965-70); of Justice (1970-80); of Public Works (1977-80); of the Interior (1980-82); of Finance (1982). **Member** of Political Bureau of National Liberation Front; Chairman FLN Committee on Education Training and Culture (1979-80); Presently, Secretary-General, National Front (FNL). **Addr.:** 7, rue du Stade, Algiers, Algeria.

BENHIMA (Ahmad, Taïba), Moroccan diplomat and statesman. **Born** on November 13, 1927 in Safi. **Son** of Taïba Benhima **and** Mrs. née Roquia Benhima. **Educ.:** Universities of Nancy and Paris (1951). **Career:** Ministry of Foreign Affairs, successively Chargé d'Affaires (Paris, 1956-57); Ambassador to Italy (1957-59); Secretary General of Ministry of Foreign Affairs (1959-61); Permanent Representative to United Nations (1961-64); Minister of Foreign Affairs (1964-66); Director Cabinet of King (1966-67); Permanent Representative to United Nations (1967-71). **Addr.:** Rabat, Morocco.

BENHIMA (Mohamad, Taïba), Moroccan statesman. **Born** on June 25, 1924 in Safi. **Son** of Taïba Benhima **and** Mrs. née Requia Benhima. **Married,** 4 children. **Educ.:** Safi Secondary School, Marakesh, Morocco; Nancy College, France. **Dipl.:** Doctor of Medicine. **Career:** Head, Medical Department, Ministry of Health (1954); Head, Ministry of Public Health's Council (1957); Secretary, Ministry of Public Health (1960); Governor of Agadir (1960-1961); Minister of Public Works (1961-62 and 1963-67); Minister of Industry and Mineral Resources (1962-63); Minister of National Education (1965-67); Prime Minister, with overall control of economic policy (1967-69); Minister of Agriculture and Agrarian Reform (1969); Minister of the Interior, Lamrani Government (1972-73); Minister of State for Co-operation and Training (1973-77); Minister of State for the Interior (1977); President of Safi Municipal Council; President, Guy-Moyat S.A., Casablanca. **Decorations:** from governments of Ethiopia, Belgium, Sweden, Tunisia, Egypt, Niger, Liberia, Cameroon, Italy, Libya, France, Ivory Coast. **Addr.:** 79, Avenue Hassan II, Tel.: 224114, Casablanca, Morocco.

BENJELLOUN (Abdel Aziz), Moroccan economist. **Born** in 1933 in Casablanca, Morocco. **Married. Educ.:** in Fez and Casablanca. **Dipl.:** Licenciate in Financial and Commercial Studies, Catholic University of Louvain. **Career:** Manager, Banque Centrale Populaire, Casablanca, Director of the Budgetary Control Board (1986); Presently President, Confection B2L. **Addr.:** 101 Blvd. Mohamed Zertouni, P.O.Box 10622, Tel.: 270540, Casablanca, Morocco.

BENJELLOUN (Ahmed Majid), Moroccan lawyer and politician. **Born** in 1927 in Fez, Morocco. **Educ.:** Institute of Political Science, Paris. **Dipl.:** L en D. **Career:** Public Prosecutor, Marrakesh (1956); Public Prosecutor of Military Tribunal, Meknes; General Counsel, Supreme Court; Public Prosecutor Court of Appeal (1960-64); Minister of Information (1965-67); Secretary General, Ministry of Justice (1967); Minister at the Royal Cabinet (1967-71); of Civil Service (1971-72); of Information (1972-74); Prosecutor General (1974); former Professor Institut des Hautes Etudes Juridiques; Dean, Faculty of Law and Economics, University of Rabat, Ecole Marocaine d'Administration. **Member** Commission for the Drafting of the Penal Code and Penal Procedure Code; has attended numerous international judicial conferences. **Medals:** Order of the Throne and several foreign decorations. **Addr.:** Rabat, Morocco.

BENJELLOUN (Ali), Moroccan statesman and diplomat. **Born** in 1927 in Morocco. **Educ.:** Moulay Idriss College of Fès, Paris Faculty of Law. **Dipl.:** Licenciate of Law. **Career:** Casablanca Court of Justice (1950); Director and Secretary General of Civil Affairs, Ministry of Justice (1950); Chairman of Committees establishing Supreme Court and Nationality Code; Government Lawyer to Common Interests of Conciliation and Arbitration (Geneva, 1957); Moroccan Ambassador to the United States and to Canada (1962-65); Director of the "Office Chérifien des Phosphates" (1965-67); Minister of Justice (1967-68). **Award:** Order of the Throne, Morocco. **Addr.:** Rabat, Morocco.

BENJELLOUN (Othman), Moroccan engineer. **Born** on November 1, 1932 in Casablanca, Morocco. **Married** with Leila Mezzian (ophtalmologist eye surgeon, first woman doctor graduated in 1961), 2 children: Dounia (1951), Kamal (1965). **Educ.:** Mechanical and electrical engineering in Polytechnique of Lausanne, Switzerland; practical training in Holland (1958) at Phillips/ Eindhoven and in Sweden (1959) with major Swedish industries. **Career:** Chairman, Banque Marocaine du Commerce Extérieur SA; Chairman, La Royale Marocaine d'Assurances; Chairman, Goodyear Morocco (tires manufacture); Chairman, I.T.T. Morocco (telecommunications manufacture); Chairman, SAIDA/ STAR-AUTO (General Motors, Volvo and Hino trucks and buses manufacturing plant); Chairman, King Ranch Morocco (Cattle breeding and life stock); Chairman, Moroccan Aluminium Company (Aluminium architectural products); Chairman, Afrique Chimie (Montedison and Degussa Chemicals); Chairman, Condor (consulting and development organization, Rockwell, Westinghouse, American Motors General, Construction of ports and dams); Chairman, L.B.C. (real estate development corporation); Director, CITIBANK (banking); Co-chairman with Dr. Henry Kissinger of the Moroccan-American Foundation under the Honorary Chairmanship of His Majesty the King Hassan II and the President Ronald Reagan; leader of Moroccan industries; created and started several industrial enterprises after Morocco reached its independence in 1956; has promoted substantial U.S. interests in Morocco; Founder of the American Chamber of Commerce in Morocco; Adviser to several private and governmental organizations. **Sports:** Deep-Sea Fishing, Skiing. **Hobby:** Photography. **Addr.:** BMCE, P.O.Box 13425, Casablanca 2000, Morocco.

BENJELLOUN (Tahar), Writer. **Borm** on December 21, 1944 in Fez (Morocco). **Son** of Hassan Benjelloun (Businessman) **and** Mrs. née Fatma Badraoui, 3 children. **Educ.:** College Ibn Al Khatib and Lycée Regnaut de Tanger, Faculty of Letters, Rabat (Morocco). **Dipl.:** Licenciate and Certificate of Aptitude à l'enseignement du second degré (CAPES) in Philosophy, Doctorate, 3rd cycle in Social Psychiatry. **Career:** Professor of Philosophy in Tetouan and Casablanca (Morocco) (1968-71); Sociology Studies at Nanterre (1971-72); Social Psychiatry at Ecole pratique des hautes études (1972-75); Contributor to "Le Monde" newspaper for the Maghreb and Arab Culture in general since 1973); Member of: Mallarme Academy (1976), Higher Council of French Language (since 1989), High Council of francophony, of prix Hassan II. **Publ.:** "Hommes sous linceul de silence (poem, 1971), "Cicatrices du soleil" (Poem and news 1972), "Harrouda" (Novel, 1973), "Le Discours du chameau" (Poem, 1974), "La Memoire future" (Anthology of new poetry in Morocco, 1976), "Les Amandiers sont morts de leurs blessures" (Poems and news), 1976, prix de l'amitié franco-arabe), "Chronique d'une solitude" (Theatre, festival Avignon, 1976), "La Réclusion solitaire" (Novel, 1976), "La Plus haute des solitudes" (Essay, 1977), "Moha le fou, Moha le sage (1978, prix de l'Association des bibliothécaires de france et de Radio Monte-Carlo), "La Mal vie" (film for television, 1978, "A l'Insu du souvenir" (Poetry, 1980), "La Prière de l'absent" (Novel, 1981), "Entretien avec M. Said Hammadi" (1982), "L'Hospitalité française" (1984), "La Fiancée de l'Eau" (theatre play 1984), "L'Enfant de sable (1985), "La Nuit Sacrée" (1987, prix Goncourt), "Jour de silence à Tanger" (1990), "Les Yeux baissés (1991, prix Hemispheres), 'Alberto Giacometti" (1991), "La Remontée des cendres" (poems 1991), "L'Ange aveugle" (1992), "La Soudure fraternelle (essay, 1993), "L'Homme rompu" (1994), "Le Premier amour est toujours le dernier" (1995). Complete Poetry: 1966-1995 (1995), "Rachid, l'Enfant de la télé" (1995), "Les Raisins de la galère" (1996), "La Nuit de l'erreur" (1997). **Dcor.** Knight, Legion of Honour, Arts and letters. **Dist.:** Prix de la Méditerranée (1994). **Prof. Addr.:** Paris. France.

BENKIRANE (Abdulqader), Moroccan film producer and distributor. **Born** on June 27, 1930. **Educ.:** Commercial and Cinematographic production of the following films: "Marie Chantal Contre le Dr. Kah", studies. **Career:** Participated in the "Requiem pour un Agent Secret", "Mission Apocalypse", "Bob Fleming Mission Casablanca", "Attentat Contre les 3 Grands"; Producer, "La Route du Kif". **Addr.:** 10, Avenue des F.A.R., Casablanca, Morocco.

BENKIRANE (Ahmed), Moroccan statesman. **Born** on July, 12, 1927 in Morocco. **Son** of Mokhtar Benkirane (Merchant) **and** Mrs. Malika Bousserghini. **Married** to Leila Lahlou in 1962, 3 children; Kenza, Souad and Saad. **Educ.:** Guessous Institute, Rabat (primary), Muhammad Ben Youssef College, Morocco (secondaires), High School of Commerce of Paris. **Dipl.:** Diploma from the High School of Commerce of Paris. **Career:** Director of the Cabinet of the Minister of Industry and Commerce (1956-57); Under-Secretary of State for Commerce, Industry, Mercantile Marine and Working Classes (1958); Chargé d'Etudes at the Cabinet of the Minister of National Economy and Finance (1965-68); Director, La Caisse de Dépôt et de Gestion (1965-68); Under-Sectetary of State for Commerce, Industry, Mines, Working Classes, Mercantile

Marine and Director General of the Marketing and Export Office (1968-70); Director and Editor of the newspaper "Le Matin" (French language) (1971); Ambassador to Belgium and the EEC (1973). Director of Several Companies. **Award:** Knight, Order of the Throne. **Sports:** Golf and ski. **Member** of "Centre des Jeunes Patrons". **Priv. Addr.:** Evelyne Clopet Street, Anfa, Tel.: 535-46, Casablanca, Morocco.

BENLADEN (al-Fadhl Abdul Kadir Mohamad), Leading businessman. **Born** in Jeddah, in 1932. **Educ.:** Received general education, supplemented by commercial training. **Career:** Chairman of Board of Al-Fadhl Trading and Engineering Corporation; Owner-President of Trading and Shipping Agencies; Chairman of Board of Economic Development Corporation, Electronic Maintenance Services Ltd,; member of Board of al-Fadhl Ben Laden-C & P.B.R.C. al-Fadhl (Saudi) Ltd., Arabian Cement Co., al-Jazirah Bank; member of Chamber of Commerce and Industry, Jeddah, Administrative Council, Jeddah; Honorary Consul of the Republic of Sierra Leone. **Hobby:** study of Arabic literature and history. **Addr.:** P.O.Box 82, Jeddah, Saudi Arabia.

BENLADEN (Salem Mohamad), Saudi businessman. **Born** in Mecca. **Educ.:** Millfield College, U.K. **Career:** Owner and Chairman of Board of several companies; Founding member and member of Board of Saudi Bank, Paris; member of Board of Tihama for Advertising, Public Relations and Marketing Research; his contribution to the Saudi economy is substantial; his vast enterprises are nation-wide and world-wide. **Hobbies:** Reading, travel. **Addr.:** Sheikh Salem ben Laden Mansion, Jeddah, Saudi Arabia.

BENLOUCIF (Mostafa), Algerian politician and military. **Career:** Acting Member, Political Bureau (1984), Promoted to Major General (1984); Personnel Director, Ministry of National Defence, then Secretary General (1980-84); Chief of Staff of the National Popular Army and Deputy member of the Political Bureau of the FLN (1984-87). (imprisoned in February 1993). **Addr.:** Algiers, Algeria.

BENMANSOUR (Noureddin), Moroccan physician. **Born** in 1935 in Morocco. **Married,** 2 daughters. **Dipl.:** Ph.D. in Medicine. **Career:** Professor of Medicine; Director of Avicenne Hospital (1975-78); Director, National Institute of Hygiene (1978-). **Publ.:** numerous articles and medical papers published in professional journals. **Prof. Addr.:** Institut Nationale d'Hygiene, Ibn Batouta Avenue, P.O.Box 769, Rabat, Morocco.

BENMLIH (Fouad), Moroccan economist. **Born** on July 14, 1948 in Tangier, Morocco. **Married. Educ.:** University of Baghdad, Iraq; Higher studies in Paris, France. **Dipl.:** B.Sc. in Economics and Political Sciences; Diplôme d'Etudes Supérieures d'Economie d'Entreprises. **Career:** Director, Banque Centrale Populaire, Morocco; President, Personnel Council of Moroccan Banks, Morocco; Secretary General, Arab Bank, Morocco; Director Arabco, Casablanca. **Publ.:** articles in Arabic and French published in professional journals and newspapers. **Prof. Addr.:** Arabco, 2 rue des Frères Lughérini. Casablanca, Morocco.

BENNANI (Ahmad), Moroccan banker. **Born** on December 12, 1926 in Fes **Career:** Former Governor of Bank al-Maghrib. **Educ.:** Diploma of Higher Commercial Instruction, Licence of Law, Faculty of Paris (France). **Dipl.:** Chartered. **Career:** Director-General, Depot Funds and Administration; Chief of Cabinet (January 1956); Director of Cabinet for Minister of National Defence (November 1956); Secretary-General, Ministry of Finance (1963); Secretary of State, Ministry of Commerce, Industry, Mines and Merchant Marine (1964); General Director, Caisse de Dépôt et de Gestion (1965-66); Secretary of State for Economic Affairs to the Prime Minister (1967-68); Vice-Governor, Bank al-Maghrib (Rabat, 1968); Vice-President, Union des Banques Arabes et Française (1980); Governor, Bank al-Maghrib (1985-89); Vice-President, Banque Nationale de Développement Economique (BNDE), Rabat; Vice-President, Banque Morocaine du Commerce Extérieur (BMCE), Casablanca; Vice-President, Banque Centrale Populaire; Administrator, UBAF Bank Limited, London; Administrator, UBAE Arab American Bank, New-York; Administrator UBAE, Rome; Administrator, Caisse Marocaine des Marchés; Administrator, Compagnie Marocaine de Navigation (COMANAV); Member Council, UBAF (paris); Member Council, UBAF Ltd. (London); Member Council, UBAAB (New York). **Awards:** Officer, Order of the Throne (1970). **Addr.:** Paris, France.

BENNIKOUS (Abdelkader), Algerian international officer. **Born** on January 30, 1923 at Collo, Constantine (Algeria). **Married,** with children. **Educ.:** Faculty of Arts, University of Algiers. **Dipl.:** B.A. (Lit.). **Career:** joined the Algerian Teachers Union (1956); Director, Algerian Trade Union Journal (1964); Secretary, Federation of Teachers (1962-67); Member, Executive Committee, Union Générale des Travailleurs Algériens (1962-69); Vice President, Pan African Trade Union since 1969; Secretary General, Union Générale des Travailleurs Algériens; Workers' Deputy Member, Governing Body of the International Labour Organisation (ILO) Algiers (1971); reelected Secretary-General of UGTA National Congress (1973). **Publ.:** Author of various articles and editorials on labour issues. **Addr.:** Algiers, Algeria.

BENNIS (Abdullatif Mohamad, Bin Salim), Moroccan journalist. **Born** in 1940 in Fes, Morocco. **Son** of Salim Bennis. **Married,** two sons. **Educ.:** University studies in Paris, Moroccan School of Administration. **Dipl.:** In Classical Arabic. **Career:** Secretary Editor "Nation Africaine",

Chief Editor "l'Opinion" daily paper; former Editor in Chief "le Matin" daily paper, former Director "Maroc Soir" daily paper. **Sport:** Tennis. **Addr.:** Casablanca, Morocco.

BENNIS (Abdurrahim), Moroccan biologist. **Born** on 4 April 1927 in Fès, Morocco. **Son** of Abdeslen ben Mohamad Bennis **and** Mrs. Tham Bennis. **Married** on 10 June 1957 in Casablanca to Fatima Nicha Boukharta, 3 children: Ali (1958), Farid (1959); Hassan (1964). **Educ.:** College Moulay Idriss, Fes; Lycée Lyautey, Casablanca; Faculté de Pharmacie, Paris; Faculté de Pharmacie, Inscription Institut de Chimie Biologie Marseille; Instituts Fournier & Pasteur, Paris; C.P.A.E. Faculté de Droit, Casablanca; Institut de Pharmacie Industrielle, Paris. **Dipl.:** Baccalaureat (Mat.); Diploma of Pharmaceutical Chemist; Diploma of Immunology from the "Institut Fournier", Diplomas from the Faculty of law and Institut de Pharmacie Industrielle. **Career:** President, Syndicate of Pharmacists (1958-65); President, Order of Pharmacists (1964-65); Vice-President, Conseil National de la pharmacie (1959-77); Delegate-member of the Board, then Delegate President, Laboratoires de Produits pharmaceutiques d'Afrique du Nord-LAPROPHAN, Casablanca; worked in the industrialization of the Pharmaceutical sector in Morocco; research and marketing of a special range of medicines for Morocco (40 moroccan païent medicines presented in 93 forms). **Sports:** Swimming, tennis. **Hobby:** reading. **Member:** RUC, Golf Club, Club Mohammedia. **Credit Cards:** Diner's Club, Avis, Herts, Europcar, Carte Blanche. **Prof. Addr.:** Laprophan S.A., 21 Rue des Oudaya, Tel.: 24866/55/72, Telex: 25816M, P.O.Box 3047, Casablanca 05. **Priv. Addr.:** Villa Antigua, 26 Rampe d'Anfa, Tel.: 363148, Casablanca, Morocco.

BENNIS (Mohamad), Moroccan engineer. **Born** on August 6, 1932 in Fès. **Educ.:** Baccalaureat, 1st and 2nd parts, M.P.C., Certificate, General Chemistry. **Dipl.:** Chemical Engineering, E.S.C.M. **Career:** with the Cabinet to the Ministry of E.N. (1957-58), Ibid, Ministry of A.E. (1958-59), Economic Counsellor, Mobil Oil (1959-64), Research, O.N.E (1966), Chemical Laboratory official (1969-70); **Member** of the International Chamber of Commerce, Recipient of Distinguished mention for diploma in chemical Engineering (1955). **Addr.:** Casablanca, Morocco.

BENNIS (Mohamad), Moroccan Poet. **Born** in 1948 in Fès, Morocco. **Son** of Abdelwahid Bennis. **Married,** two sons. **Educ.:** Ph.D. and Doctorat of State in Literature in Morocco. **Career:** Teacher of Arabic (1972); Assistant Professor (1980); Professor of Superior Studies (1992); Faculty of Literature, University of Mohammed V, Rabat, Morocco; Director of «Al Thakafa Al-Jadida», Review (1974-1984); Member of «Dar Toubkal» for publishing, Casablanca; Member of «Mawakif», Lebanese Review. **Publ.:** Seven books in Arabic Poetry,, Books of Studies in Contemporary Poetry. **Hobbies:** Poetry, music, painting. **Addr.:** P.O.Box 505, Mohamadia 20650, Tel.: (3) 31.06.13, Morocco.

BENNOUNA (Driss), Moroccan diplomat. **Born** in 1923 in Tetouan, Morocco. **Married**, six children. **Educ.:** Electro-Mechanic Engineering, Madrid, Spain. **Career:** Director of Professional School, Tetouan (1949); Chief Engineer of Production and Distribution of Electrical Energy for Cooperativa Ihmsa and for Electras Marroquies, Tetouan (1949-56); member of the Executive Committee of the Reformist National Party (1950); participated in negotiations for independence with Spain (1956); founding member of the Ministry of Foreign Affairs, Morocco (1956); Counsellor, Moroccan Embassy in Cairo, Egypt (1957-58); Director of Royal Protocol (1959); Head of Royal Protocol (1961); Ambassador, Ministry of Foreign Affairs, Morocco (1967); Under Secretary of State of Royal Affairs and the Chancery (1968); Ambassador of Morocco to Damascus, Syria (1971); Ambassador to Beirut, Lebanon (1974); Ambassador to Syria (1979-1986); Member of the Moroccan delegation to the UN on several occasions; Head of the Morocco-Mauritanian Joint Delegation on the Affairs of Sahara (1975). Envoy of King Hassan of Morocco for special missions to Saudi Arabia, Iran, Spain and Tunis; Participated in international conferences and of Arab League confierences as well as of the Non-Aligned countries. Founding **Member** of the Academy of the Kingdom of Morocco (1978). **Medals:** Officer of the Order of the Throne, Morocco (1963); Grand Cordon of the Order of Independence, Syria (1974); Grand Cordon of the Republic of Egypt (1960), etc. **Sports:** Tennis, Swimming. **Hobby:** Bridge, chess, reading. **Priv. Addr.:** Rabat, Morocco.

BENNOUNA (Mehdi), Moroccan journalist. **Born** on February 22, 1919. **Married**, 4 children. **Educ.:** Primary School, Tetouan (Morocco), Secondary School, Nablus (Palestine), School of Law, University of Fouad 1, Cairo (Egypt, 1940). **Dipl.:** Bachelor of Arts, Journalism (American University) Cairo (1941). **Career:** Chief Editor, Arabic daily Al-Hurriyah, Tetouan (Morocco 1945-47); Founder and Director, Morocco Office of Information, New York (1947-53); Chief Editor, Arabic daily al-Oummah, organ of the National Reformist Party, Tetouan (Morocco) (1954-56); Administrative Secretary-General, 1st Moroccan Parliament (Assemblée Nationale Consultative) (1957-58); Counsellor for Press and Public Relations to King Muhammad V (1958-59); President and General Manager, Maghreb Arab Press News Agency (M.P.A.), and Publisher and Director, La Dépêche (in French), Casablanca (1959); President of the Islamic News Agency (1973); founder and director of a Public Relations office; President, Page Iberica Maroc. **Member** of the Moroccan Reformist Party until 1956. **Publ.:** Numerous newspaper and magazine articles and author of all material published by Moroccan Office of Information (1947-53), "Our Morocco, a true story of a Just Cause" (printed clandestinely in English, in Morocco) (1951). **Awards:** Kinght, Order of the Throne, Morocco (1969), "Décoration d'Honneur et Vaillance" for service in the Congo, Morocco (1962), UN decoration for service in the Congo (1962), various decorations from Tunisia. Egypt, Hashemite Kingdom of Jordan, Lebanon, Iraq and Iran. **Addr.:** Rabat, Morocco.

BENNOUNA (Mohamed), Academic, Director, Cultural Institute. **Born** on April 29, 1943 at Marrakech (Morocco). **Son** of Abdelmajid Bennouna (businessman) **and** Mrs. née Fatima Tazi. **Married** on April 17, 1965 to Miss Isabelle Amet, 3 children: Jaafar, Mehdi, Yacine. **Educ.:** Lycée Lyautey, Casablanca (Morocco), Université Sorbonne Paris I, Université de Nancy. **Dipl.:** Doctorat d'Etat in International Law, Aggregate in Public Law and Political Science. **Career:** Professor, Faculty of Law (1972); Dean, Faculty of Law, Rabat (Morocco) (1975); Ambassador of Morocco to United Nations, New York (U.S.A.) (1985); General Director, Institut du Monde Arabe, Paris (since 1991); Associate Professor of Algiers Universities (Algeria), Tunisia, Nice and Paris. Member "Institut de Droit International". **Publ.:** "le Consentement a l'ingérence militaire dans les conflits internes" (1974), "Le Droit international du développement" (1984). **Sports Practised:** Tennis. **Prof. Addr.:** Institut du Monde Arabe, 1 rue des Fossés Saint-Bernard, 75005 Paris. **Private:** 155 rue de Courcelles, 75017 Paris, France.

BENNOUR (Ahmad), Tunisian politician. **Born** in 1937 in Tunis, Tunisia. **Married** three children. **Educ.:** Sadiki College, Tunis; Higher Studies at the Faculty of Law, Political and Economic Sciences, Tunis. **Career:** Assistant Secretary General, Union Generale des Etudiants de Tunisie (UGET) (1958-62); Ministry of the Interior (1965); first Delegate of the Governorate of Gefsa (1967); Director of Political Affairs at the Directorate General of National Security (1967-68); Governor of Tunis South (1972); Governor of Souss (1973-74); Secretary of State, Ministry of National Defence (1974-80); Director General of National Security, Ministry of the Interior (1980-84); Ambassador to Italy (1985-89). **Member** of the Executive Committee of the Neo Destour Party (1962-65); Director General of the Tunisian Society for the Promotion of Tourism (1969). **Medals:** Commander of the Order of Tunisian Republic; Grand Cordon of the Order of Tunisian Republic; Grand Cordon of the Order of Tunisian Independence; Officer of the order of Tunisian Independence. **Prof. Addr.:** Ministry of Foreign Affairs, Tunis, Tunisia.

BENOSMAN (Lassaad), Tunisian politician. **Born** on February 16, 1926 in Tunis, Tunisia. **Married,** 1 daughter. **Educ.:** Studies in sub-soil resources, Ecole Supérieure des Mines, Paris, France. **Dipl.:** Diploma from l'Ecole Supérieures des Mines. **Career:** Directorate of Public Works (1949); oil exploration (1952-59); Director of Hydraulics and Supply, Ministry of Agriculture (1959); Chief Engineer, Hydraulics and Supply, Ministry of Agriculture (1963); Under-Secretary of State, Ministry of Agriculture (1976); Secretary of State, Ministry of Agriculture (1968); Minister of Public Works (1970-71); Director-General, Tunis Air (1973); Minister of Transport and Communications (November 1973-76); Minister of Supply (1976-80); Minister of Agriculture (1980-85). **Awards:** Commander of the Order of Tunisian Republic. **Addr.:** Tunis, Tunisia.

BENRAHMOUN (Ahmad, Hashemi), Algerian economist. **Born** on September 13, 1942 in Algeria. **Married,** 3 daughters. **Educ.:** Sorbonne, Paris; Centre d'Etudes des Programmes Economiques, Paris. **Dipl.:** M.Sc. and Ph.D. in Economics. **Career:** Société Nationale de Siderurgie (SNS) (1969-73), Commercial Manager (1973-79); Director General, Ministry of Planning and Regional Development (1980-84), Secretary General (1984-). **Prof. Addr.:** Ministry of Planning, Chemin Ibn Badis, el-Biar, Algiers, Algeria.

BENSADDIQ (Mahjoub), Moroccan Union Leader. **Born** in 1925. **Career:** Secretary General Union Morocaine du Travail since (1960 to present); President of All-African Trade Union Federation (1964); Member of Secrétariat Général de l'Union Nationale des Forces Populaires, Secretary General of Royal Air Maroc, Imprisoned for Political Reasons (1967), member of Secretariat General, Union Nationale des Forces Populaires (UNEP); member of Administrative Council of ILO. **Addr.:** Union Marocaine du Travail, 232, Avenue des Forces Armées Royales, Casablanca, Morocco.

BENSAID (Abdussalam), Tunisian architect. **Born** on November 10, 1928. **Married,** 3 children. **Educ.:** Higher National School of Fine Arts, Paris (France). **Member:** Permanent Commission of Civil Buildings of Tunis and Carthage. **Addr.:** 12, Avenue des Etats Unis d'Amérique, Tunis, Tunisia.

BENSAID (Mohamad), Moroccan lawyer. **Born** on 20 January 1934 in Fès, Morocco. **Son** of Abdelkader Bensaid (Merchant) **and** Mrs. Fatima Sefraoui. **Married** on 2 May 1959 to Fassi Fihri Assia, 5 children: Zouheir, Salim, Amine, Nouema and Hatim. **Educ.:** Faculté de Droit, Paris. **Dipl.:** LL.B. **Career:** Chief of Cabinet, Under-Secretary of State for the Interior (1958); Private Secretary, Minister of Public Works (1959); Head of Administrative Services, Office Chérifien des Phosphates (1960-63); Deputy of Fes; Vice-President, Chamber of Representatives (1977-83); Municipal Counsellor, City of Fes (1976-83); Vice-President, Municipal Council, Fes (1983); Member, Commissariat Général de la Route de l'Unité; Member of the Administrative Commission, Union Socialiste des Forces Populaires (USFP) (1962-75); Member, Central Commission, USFP (1975); Member, National Commission for External Relations, USFP; Member, National

Commission for Local Collectivities, USFP; presently, Secretary General of Organisation de l'Action Démocratique et Populaire. **Award:** Silver Medal from "Route de l'Unité". **Member:** Lion's Club. **Credit Card:** Diners' Club. **Prof. Addr.:** P.O.Box 15797, Casablanca, Morocco.

BENSALEM (Abdul Rahman), Algerian former army commander. **Born** in Algiers, Algeria. **Career:** Officer of the French Army; Joined National Liberation Army and spent war years in Algeria with Houari Boumedienne in Morocco; elected Deputy to National Assembly for Annaba (1962); Member of National Liberation Front (FLN), Central Committee (1964); Member of the Commission for National Defence; Member of General Staff (1964); accompanied President Boumedienne to Moscow (1965); Member of Revolutionary Council (1965); Assistant Chief of Staff (1968). **Prof. Addr.:** National Liberation Front (FLN), Place Emir Abdel Kader, Algiers, Algeria.

BENSLAMA (Abderrahim, Abdesalem), Moroccan Consultant Judge at the High Court, Rabat. And a Professor at the National Institute for Judiciary Studies. **Born** on April 14, 1945 in Fez, Morocco. **Married**, 4 children. **Educ.:** Doctorate in Law and Islamic Law, Muhammad University and Quaraouyine University (1985); Diploma in Management Science, Accounting and Commerce. **Former Occupations:** General Secretary of Faculty of Letters, Muhammad University, Rabat (1968-69); President of the Court of First Instance, Sale, (1970-1980); Executive Member, Moroccan Writers' Union (1968-1970), Adviser, Arab Organization for the Prevention of Crime (1980-1985); Consultant Judge (1985). **Membership in Professional Organizations:** Member of the Moroccan Writers' Union; President of the Moroccan Association for Muslim Solidarity; President of the UNESCO Club, Rabat. **Creative Works:** "Morocco before Independence" 1975; "Morocco's Struggle for Freedom and Democracy" 1975; "The Accounting System in Islam" 1980; Language, History and Civilizations" 1975; "A Guide for Judges and Lawyers". **Honors:** The Throne Badge of Honor. The UNESCO Order of Intelligence, 1972. **Hobbies:** Listening to Classical Music - Taking part in Intellectual Conferences - Interest in the Fine Arts - Playing Tennis. **Address:** P.O.Box 351, Rabat, Morocco, Tel.: 711816, Fascimile: 754902, Rabat, Morocco.

BENSLIMANE (Abdel Kader), Moroccan executive. **Born** on February 22, 1932 at Rommani (Morocco). **Son of** Haj Slimane Benslimane (farmer) **and** Mrs., née M'Barka. **Married** to Guenoun Moadhah on September 18, 1966 in Rabat, 3 children: Souad, Omar and Abla. **Educ.:** Primary education at Moulay Youssef College and Lycée Gouraud; Faculty of Law and Political Science, Toulouse University (France). **Dipl.:** Baccalaureat; LL.B. **Career:** Attached to the Cabinet of the Finance Minister (1957-59); Chief, Budget Department, Ministry of Finance (1959-61); Minister-Adviser, Embassy of the Kingdom of Morocco, Paris (France) (1961-63); General Manager, Bureau d'Etudes et de Participation Industrielles; and at the same time, Head, Depারmental Staff of the Minister of Economy and Finance, and Permanent Representative of the Kingdom of Morocco to the Comité Permanent Consultatif du Maghreb-Arabe (Head Office initially in Rabat) (1963-66); Vice-President, Maghreb Committee, Tunis (1966-72); Ambassador to Benelux and EEC, Brussels (1972); Minister of Commerce, Industry, Mercantile Marine, and Mines (1972-74); Minister of Finance (1974-77); President Director-General, National Bank for Economic Development, Rabat (Morocco) (1978); former President and Director General of B.N.D.E. exercises the functions of President for ten associated companies and is a Director on the Board of 24 others; President, Maroc Lumière Industrie. **Awards:** Ouissam of the Throne (Morocco); Commander, Merit Order, France; Commander, Order of the Italian Republic. **Hobbies:** Travelling and reading. **Priv. Addr.:** Lotissement Ambassador, Route des Zaers, Rabat, Souissi, Morocco.

BENSOUDA (Ahmad), Moroccan diplomat. **Born** in 1918 in Morocco. **Educ.:** Secondary and Higher. **Career:** One of the leaders of nationalist movement of Morocco; Director of the periodical "al-Raï al-Aam" (Democratic party periodical); former Under Secretary General, Ministry of Youth and Sports in the Independent Government; Governor of Kenitra (1962); General Director of Radiodiffusion Marocaine (1964); Ambassador Attached to the Royal Cabinet (July 1965-August 1966); Moroccan Ambassador to Lebanon (1966-69); elected Deputy for Larache (August 1970); Ambassador to Lebanon (1972); reappointed to Royal Cabinet (Nov. 1973); Director of Royal Cabinet (April 1975); HM King Hassan II Counsellor (1977 to present); Member of the Moroccan Ulama League; Moroccan Writers Union. **Publ.:** Author of 2 books: Talks of al-Mufti, and a collection of poems; Known for his journalistic humorous articles and oratony skills. Director of Several Companies. **Awards:** 13 decorations. **Addr.:** The Royal Cabinet, Rabat, Morocco.

BENSOUDA (Said si Yahia), Moroccan banker. **Born** in 1934 in Fes, Morocco. **Married**, 2 sons. **Educ.:** University of Paris (1959). **Dipl.:** B.A. in Political Science. **Career:** Member, Moroccan General Economic Confederation, Member of the Exporters Association of Morocco, and, the Chamber of Commerce and Industry; General Manager, Banque Marocaine du Commerce Exterieur (1961-84). **Member:** Vice-President, Royal Gulf Club of Anfa and Mohammedia. **Priv. Addr.:** Route d'Azemmour, Rue 9, Villa Asma 11, Anfa, Casablanca, Morocco.

BENYAGHLANE (Kamel), Tunisian Chairman. **Born** on September 1, 1950 in Tunis. **Son** of Mohamed Ben Yaghlane (Tradesman) **and** Mrs. Mongia Ben Yaghlane. **Married** on August 11, 1971 in Tunis to Radhia Barnat, 3 children: Karim, Nadhim, Marwan. **Educ.:** Superior school, Paris. **Dipl.:** Chemist. **Career:** Chairman, Industrie Pharmaceutique et Cosmétique. **Other Information:** Member of Board JCI. **Award:** Senator JCI No. 47216. **Sport:** Tennis. **Hobbies:** Music and Association. **Member:** JCI + Club Exportateur. **Credit Cards:** Diners. **Prof. Addr.:** Laboratoires Sadep Ariana Tunisie, P.O.Box 151, Cedex 1080 Tunis, Tel.: (216-1) 710536, Tunisia. **Priv. Addr.:** El Menzah 9, Tel. (216-1) 881394, Tunis, Tunisia.

BENYAHMED (Bashir), Tunisian journalist. **Born** in 1928. **Married. Educ.:** Sadiki College, Tunis; Ecole des Hautes Etudes Commerciales, Paris. **Career:** Director, Cabinet of Muhammad Masmoudi (1954); resigned to edit "l'Action" French Language Weekly (1955); Secretary of State for Information (1956) and (1957); resigned to publish "Jeune Afrique", Paris, France. **Addr.:** c/o Rue 2 Mars 1934, Tunis, Tunisia.

BENYAKLEF (Mustafa, Mohamad), Moroccan academic. **Born** in 1942 in Morocco. **Son** of Mohamad Benyaklef. **Married** in 1966 in Rabat to Miss Aita Benyaklef, two children. **Educ.:** University of Paris, France; Michigan State University, USA; University of California (Berkeley), USA. **Dipl.:** Ph.D. in Mathematical Statistics. **Career:** Assistant Professor of Statistics (1971-73); Assistant Director of INSEA (1973-77); Director of INSEA (since 1977) (INSEA, National Institute of Statistics, an institution for higher learning). **Hobbies:** Reading, bicycling. **Prof. Addr.:** INSEA, P.O.Box 6217, Tel.: 709-27, Rabat, Morocco. **Priv. Addr.:** Tel.: 519-93, Morocco.

BENZAKOUR (Fuad), Moroccan bank manager. **Born** in 1947 in Fès, Morocco. **Son** of Mohamad Benzakour. **Married** in 1978, 3 daughters. **Dipl.:** Licence en Sciences Economiques. **Career:** Joined Banque Marocaine du Commerce Extérieur in 1968: Manager, Agadir Branch (1972-75); Manager, Rabat Branch (1975-76); Deputy Manager, Paris Branch (1976-78); Manager, Paris Branch (1978-to present). **Addr.:** B.M.C.E., P.O.Box 326-09, 37 Rue Caumartin, 75427 Paris, France.

BENZAZA (Mustafa), Algerian politician. **Born** on March 11, 1940. **Married,** 5 children. **Educ.:** Higher studies in Pharmacy and Law. **Career:** Member of Central Committee, FLN; Chief of Tighenmi county, then Reliziane; Governor of Jijil/Laghouab; Deputy Minister of Agriculture and Fisheries, (1984). **Prof. Addr.:** Algiers, Algeria.

BENZEKRI (Mehdi, Muhammad), Moroccan engineer. **Born** on July 20, 1944 in Oujda, Morocco. **Married,** 3 children. **Educ.:** Mohammedia Engineering School, Rabat, National School for Bridges and Roads. **Dipl.:** B.Sc. in Civil Engineering. **Career:** Head of Dams, Ministry of Hydraulics (1968-72); Vice President, Moroccan Committee for High Dams (1980); Director of Technical Affairs, Ministry of Equipment (1980-82), Director of Hydraulic Fittings (1982); Vice President, Society of Moroccan Civil Engineers (1983); Member of Moroccan Geological Society (1984); Director C.I.D. (Conseil, Ingenierie et Developpement). **Publ.:** several articles in national periodicals. **Decor.:** Order of Merit (1st Class), Morocco (1985), Order of Satisfaction (1st class), King Hassan of Morocco (1973). **Addr.:** C.I.D., P.O.Box 1340, Rabat, Morocco.

BERNOUSSI (Mohamad), Moroccan politician. **Born** on June 20, 1927. **Educ.:** Degree in Law, Licence ès-Lettres, National School of Administration, Paris (France). **Career:** Controller, Defence Engagements (1960-61); Deputy Secretary-General, Ministry of Finance (1961); Director, General Treasury (Morocco) (1961-70); Director of Cabinet, Ministry of Finance (1955-56); Professor, Moroccan School of Administration, Faculty of Law; Deputy, National Assembly, President, Provincial Assembly; Director-General, National Social Security (Morocco); President, Lions Club (Rabat 1970); Member of the Chamber of Representatives; Head, Financial Commission, Moroccan Parliament; Minister of Public Works and Communications (August 1971); Governor of Tangier (April 1973); Member, Administrative Council, Maghreb Centre of Administration Studies and Research, Algiers; Member, National planning Council. **Publ.:** Author of 2 publications. **Award:** Knight, Order of the Throne. **Addr.:** Avenue Mohammad V, Rabat, Morocco.

BERRABAH (Belkacem), Algerian Chairman and General Manager. **Born** on February 22, 1954 in Algeria. **Son** of Boussad Berrabah (deceased) **and** Mrs. née Tassadit Oussadi (deceased). **Married,** 5 children: Assia, Youcef, Samia, Yasmine, Lynda. **Educ.:** Mechanical Engineering Institute. **Dipl.:** State Engineer. **Career:** Central School, Paris; State of Management, U.E.C.; Chairman and General Manager, Entreprise Nationale des Industries de l'Electromenager. **Hobby:** Reading. **Credit Card:** A. Express. **Prof. Addr.:** Entreprise Nationale des Industries de l'Electroménager, P.O.Box 71A, Chikhi, Tizi-Ouzou, Tel.: 3 21 80 83, Algeria.

BERRADA (Abdeslam), Moroccan agricultural expert. **Born** in 1931 in Fes, Morocco. **Educ.:** Ecole Nationale d'Agriculture de Grignon; Ecole Nationale des Eaux et Forêts, Nancy, France. **Career:** Waters and Forests Administration; Director of Water and Forests Administration (1965); Secretary General, Ministry of Agriculture and Agrarian Reforms (1972-74); represented Morocco at many international and regional conferences; President, Cellulose du Maroc (1972-). **Addr.:** Cellulose du Maroc, P.O.Box 429, Rabat, Morocco.

BERRADA ALLAM (Tayib), Moroccan geologist and executive. **Born** in 1941 in Casablanca, Morocco. **Educ.:** Ecole Nationale des Sciences Geograhiques, Paris, France.

Dipl.: Ing. **Career:** Former Head of the National Land Survey Service, Former Head of the Rabat Land Survey; Member of several technical committees; Active Member, National Association of Topographical Engineers and Association des Géomètres et Entreprises Topographiques; Chairman and General Manager of SETRAT; Director and Manager of SETA; Vice-President, Conseil National de l'Ordre National des Ingénieurs Topographes. **Prof. Addr.:** 4 Rue el-Araich, Rabat, Morocco. **Priv. Addr.:** 25 Houara Street, Administrative City, Rabat, Morocco.

BERRADA (Mohamad, Jadj), Moroccan M.D. **Born** on 25 December 1936 in Casablanca, Morocco. **Son** of Jadj Mohamad Berrada (Director) **and** Mrs. Oum el-Kheir Berrada. **Married** on 15/6/1962 to Miss Raymonde Mouret, 2 children: Ghislane (1965) and Lamia (1970). **Educ.:** Faculté de Médecine de Paris. **Dipl.:** M.D., specialized in Pediatry at the Faculty of Medicine of Paris. **Career:** Intern at Moroccan Hospitals (1961-64); Assistant Physician, Service of Pediatry; Chief Physician, Service des Prématurés et du Service des Nourrissons de la Goutte de Lait, Casablanca (1964 till now). **Member:** Société des Sciences Médicales; Société Marocaine de Pédiatrie, Société Française de Pédiatrie. **Sports:** Golf, Swimming. **Hobby:** Reading. **Member:** Rotary International de Casablanca. **Addr.:** 60 Rue d'Alger, Tel. 27-15-12, 27-98-91, Casablanca. **Priv. Addr.:** Villa La Thibaide, Rue St. Servon, Anfa, Tel.: 365260, Casablanca, Morocco.

BERRADA (Mohamed), Moroccan Ambassador in France. **Born** on November 3, 1944 in Casablanca (Morocco). **Married** on August 7, 1972 to Miss Afaf Bennani, 5 children: Maha, Myriam, Kaoutar, Kenza, Idriss. **Educ.:** Université de Bordeaux, France. **Dipl.:** Diploma from High School of Commerce, Institute of Political Studies, Diploma of Higher Studies in Private Law, Bachelor in Sociology, Doctor d'Etat ès Sciences économiques, Chartered Accountant, Diploma from "Institut d'Administration des Entreprises" (IAE). **Career:** Professor of Economy, Université Hassan II (1968-1986); Head of Economic Science Department, Faculty of Law, Economic and Social Sciences, Casablanca (1979-1986), Minister of Finance (1986-1993); Governor of "Fonds Arabe de Développement" (1986-1993); President, "Assemblées annuelles du Fond monétaire international and of the Banque Mondial (1992); President of Morocco Fund (since 1994); Ambassador of Morocco in France and UNESCO (since 1994). **Works:** "Comptabilité nationale et analyse macroéconomique" (1982), "Comptabilité analytique et le nouveau plan comptable" (1984). **Sports practised:** Volley-ball, golf, tennis. **Prof. Addr.:** Embassy of Morocco, 5 rue le Tasse, 75016 Paris, France.

BESSAIAH (Boualem), Algerian politician. **Born** in 1930 in Algeria. **Career:** Teacher of Arabic Literature (1951-56); Officer in National Liberation Army (1956-62); joined the Ministry of Foreign Affairs (1962); Ambassador to Belgium, Luxembourg and European Economic Community (1963-70); Ambassador to Egypt (1970-71); Secretary General of Foreign Affairs (1971-78); Ambassador to Kuwait (1978-80); Minister of Information (1980-84); Minister of Posts and Telecommunications (1985); Minister of Culture and Tourism (1986- Sept. 1989). **Publ.:** "Etendard Interdit" (1976). **Addr.:** Algiers, Algeria.

BEYAH (Mohamed Khalifa, Ould), Mauritanian Director of Railway and Energy (SNIM). **Born** on October 10, 1959 in Mauritania. **Son** of El Khalifa Ould Beyah **and** Oum el Moumnine. **Married** in 1988 in Mauritania, 4 children: Zouleikha (1988), Khalifa (1990), Sidi Mohamed (1993), Sami (1998). **Educ.:** Ecole Mohammedia des Ingénieurs - Rabat - Morocco, Université de Téchnologie de Compiegne - France. **Dipl.:** Electrical Engineer - 1981 - Morocco, "DEA" Mechanical Engineering - France 1986. **Career:** SNIM = "Société Nationale Industrielle et Minière"; 1981 = Chief engineer in charge of Locomotive Maintenance; 1986 = in charge of Rolling Stocks (Locomotives and Cars); 1988 = Chief of Railway Department; 1989 = Director of Railway and Energy (R & D); 1993 = Director of Railway, Energy and Port. **Sports Practised:** Jogging. **Hobby:** Reading Books. **Prof. Addr.:** Tel.: 222 745174, and SNIM, P.O.Box 42, Nouadhibou, Mauritania. **Home** Tel.: 222 742434, Mauritania.

BIALI (Mohamad, al), Egyptian journalist. **Born** on 24 October 1921 at Biala Egypt. **Son** of Ahmad Osman (General Police Commander of Cairo Fire Brigade). **Married** in London on 8 October 1952 to Miss Adriana Tagliaferri, one daughter; Paula (June 1953- Dr. in economics from Rome University 1978). **Educ.:** American University (Cairo) **Dipl.:** B.A. in Journalism (1945). **Career:** Chief Editor, Akhbar el-Yom Organization (1945); Chief Bureaux London, Bonn, Morocco, Rome, Damascus, North Africa for Akhbar el-Yom, al-Kahira, al-Shaab and then Middle East News Agency (1952); Foreign Correspondent, Rotosei Review (Rome); former Chief Editor, Middle East News Agency and Member of Board of Directors. **Hobbies:** Decoration, Gardening, Engineering and Photography. **Member:** Gezira Sporting Club, Automobile Club Cairo, International Journalist Club London, Egyptian Press Syndicate. World Media Association, N.Y. **Priv. Addr.:** 188 el-Nile Street, Agouza, Tel.: 3464083, Cairo, Egypt.

BIATI (Abdul Jabbar Towfiq Mohammed, Al), Iraqi former Minister of Education. **Born** in 1940 in Iraq. **Son** of Towfiq Mohammed (dead) **and** Mrs., née Sabha Hassa. **Married** in 1966 in Baghdad to Amal Abdul Halim, 4 children: Awis (1967), Towfiq (1969), Anas (1975), Ayman (1981). **Educ.:** Teacher's Training Institute, College of Education-University of Baghdad, University of Pittsburgh, U.S.A., Regional Center for Educational Planning and Administration. **Dipl.:** Certificate in Education, B.A. in Education, M.Ed (Master), Ph.D. (Doctor of Philosophy). **Career:** Elementary School Teacher (1959); Secondary School Teacher (1966); Instructor in Teacher Training Institute (1967); Researcher in Ed. Res. Center-University of Baghdad (1986); Director of Ed. Res. Center (1973); Director General of Curriculum, Ministry of Education (1976). **Other Information:** Head of Ed. Advisers in the Arab Center for Educational Res. (1980), Former Minister of Education. **Medals** of High Deserve. **Sports:** Swimming. **Hobby:** Reading. **Clubs:** Teachers Association, Iraqi Association for Ed. and Psych. Sciences. **Priv. Addr.:** Tel.: 8872943, Baghdad, Iraq.

BIDAWID (Raphael I, H.E. Mgr.), Iraqi Patriarch of Babylon for the Chaldean Rite. **Born** on April 17, 1922 in Mosul, Iraq. **Educ.:** St. Dominique Fathers School and Patriarcal Seminary in Mosul (1933) and Pontifical Urban University in Rome (1936). **Dipl.:** Doctorate in Theology and Philosophy. **Career:** Ordained Priest (1944); Teacher at the Patriarcal College of Mosul (1947); Sacred Bishop of Amadiya in Iraq (1957-1966); Transfered to Bishopric of Beirut (1966-89); Elected on (May 15, 1989) Patriarch of Babylon for the Chaldean Church. **Publ.:** Author of several books including "History of the Christians under the Abbasides". **Note:** Fluent in 12 written and spoken Oriental and European Languages. **Addr.:** Chaldean Patriarcal Residence, Baghdad, Iraq.

BILADY (Atiq Ibn Gaith, al), Saudi writer and publisher. **Born** in 1931 in Mecca, Saudi Arabia. **Dipl.:** Diploma in Journalism and a Certificate from the Language Institute, Riyadh. **Career:** Colonel in the Army until 1977; owner of Dar Makkah for Distribution and Publication; member, Jeddah, Makkah and Taif Literary Clubs. **Publ.:** several books, articles and essays. **Hobbies:** Reading, research. **Priv. Addr.:** Tel.: 5427568, Mecca, Saudi Arabia.

BILAIHID (Abdallah ben Mohamad ben Abdallah, al), Assistant Deputy Governor of Riyadh Governorate. **Born** in 1940. **Dipl.:** M.P.A. (Public Administration). **Career:** Former Director of Organization and Budgeting Department, Ministry of Education; attended several conferences on public administration at home and abroad; Assistant Deputy Governor of Riyadh Governorate. **Publ.:** M.A. dissertation in Public Administration; Introduction to his father's work, Saheehul Akhbar' Amma Fi Bilad-il Arab Min Athar (The Proper History of the The Monuments of Arabia). **Hobby:** Swimming. **Addr.:** Riyadh Governorate (Emirate House), Riyadh, Saudi Arabia.

BILBEISSI (Mo'atasim, Ismail), Jordanian Diplomat. **Born** in 1933 in Amman, Jordan. **Married. Educ.:** American University of Beirut. **Dipl.:** B.A. (Economics) (1954). **Career:** Attached to the Foreign Ministry (1958); Attaché, Jordanian Embassy to Spain (1959); Foreign Ministry, Amman (1959-62); Attaché, Embassy to Lebanon (1962); Assistant Head, Protocol, Royal Court (1969-70); Minister Delegate, Foreign Ministry (1970); Ambassador to Nationalist China (1971-73); non-resident Ambassador to Japan (1971-73); non-resident Ambassador to Turkey (1973-75); Head of Ceremonies Department, Foreign Ministry (1975-76); Director-General of Press and Publications (1976-77); Ambassador to Switzerland (1977-81); Ambassador to Lebanon (1982); Shareholder in Ismail Bilbeisi & Co. **Awards:** Star of Jordan, 3rd Class; Independence Medal, 3rd Class; Order of Holy Sepulchre, 3rd Class; Order of Cedars of Lebanon; Hamayouni Order (Iran). **Addr.:** Ministry of Foreign Affairs, Amman, Jordan, and P.O.Box 213, Amman, Jordan.

BILI (Osman, Sid Ahmad Ismaïl, al), Assumed name ABU MUHAMMAD, sudanese academic. **Born** on December 16, 1930 in Mansourkotti (North Sudan). **Son** of Sid Ahmad Ismaïl al-Bili (deceased July 1971) **and** Mrs. née Um al-Hasan Ibrahim Nabré (deceased April 1979). **Married** on April 24, 1964 to Aminah Hasan Muhammad, 3 children: Umayma (21.5.1956); Muhammad Iqbal (14.2.1969 and Ahmad Bello (19.3.1975). **Educ.:** Wadi Sayyidna Secondary School (Omdurman) (1948-51); University College of Khartoum (1952-56); School of Oriental and African Studies (University of London) (1956-58 and 1960-63). **Dipl.:** Cambridge School Certificate (1951); B.A. General (1956) (University of London); B.A. Hon. (1958) Ph.D. (1963) (University of London). **Career:** Lecturer (1958), Senior Lecturer (1965), Head Dept. of History (1965-70) University of Khartoum, Sudan; Reader (1971), Research professor (1972), full Chair professor (1973), Director N.H.R.S. (1972-77) University of Ahmadu Bello Zaria, Nigeria; Dean Faculty of Arts (1979-80) University of Khartoum; General Secretary, Chairman, Council of Higher Education, Sudan (1980-81, 1982-85) and Minister of Education, Sudan (1982-85); Executive Board member, UNESCO (1984-87); Professor and Director, Documentation and Humanities Research Centre (DHRC) (1985-1995), University of Qatar. Life member, Clare Hall, University of Cambridge, U.K., since 1986 presently, General Supervisor, Centre for Muslim Contribution to Civilization, Qatar. **Awards:** Gold Medal for Arts and Literature, Sudan (1980); Gold Medal for Research, Sudan (1983); The Two Niles Order (1983). **Sports:** Football, Tennis, Swimming and Sprinting. **Hobbies:** Arabic and English Poetry; Classical Music. **Member:** Goats Club (University of London), Life member Clare Hall (Cambridge). **Prof. Addr.:** General Supervisor Center for Muslim Contribution to Civilization, P.O.Box 327 Doha, Qatar. **Priv. Addr.:** 2 Sahat al-Teeb, Khalifa North, P.O.Box 120141, Tel.: 875041, Doha, Qatar. House No. 101 Block 21, Riyad Town, Tel.: 224323, Khartoum, Sudan.

BIN AMIR (Taha Sharif), Libyan politican. **Born** in 1940 in Benghazi, Libya. **Educ.:** Engineering in Germany. **Career:** Under Secretary, Ministry of Communications,

Minister of Communications and Power (1971-75); Minister of State for Revolutionary Command Council Affairs (1975-76). **Addr.** Tripoli, Libya.

BIN SIDDIQ (Mohammed Mustafa), Management Consultant, Saudi Executive. **Born** on August 7, 1949, in Jeddah. **Education:** B.A. (Public Administration) from King Abdul Aziz University, Jeddah Saudi Arabia. **Member of:** American Management Association, British Management Association, British Marketing Association, Alexander & Hemolton Institude, Gulf Marketing Association, Industrial Committee, Member Consultant Offices Committee, Chamber of Commerce Jeddah. Audit Manager, Saudi Airlines, Jeddah 1966-77. Director Logistics, Dallah Avco Trans Arabia Co. Ltd., Jeddah 1977-78, **Director** Marketing 1978. (Member Board of Directors) Assistant General Manager Administration Saudi Industrial Development Co., Board Member & Executive Committee Member - National Spring & Foam Mattresses Mfg. Co. Ltd. (Sleep High), Board Member & Executive Committee Member - SIDC Metal Coating Co. (SMC). **Hobby:** Reading **Address:** P.O.Box 1724. Jeddah 21441, **Fax:** 6716835, Jeddah - Saudi Arabia.

BINALI (Abdul Aziz M. al-Rashid), Bahraini counsellor. **Born** on December 12, 1937 in Bahrain. **Married,** 4 children. **Educ.:** Jowaharlal Nehru University, New Delhi, India. **Dipl.:** M.A., B.A. from the American University of Beirut (AUB), and M.Phil. **Career:** Teacher, Ministry of Education (1960-63); Inspector, Member of the Executive Bureau of Oil Affairs, Ministry of Finance (1963-71), Member of the Constitutional Board (1972-73), Representative of Bahrain in OAPEC and OPEC; Counsellor, General Secretariat of the Gulf Cooperation Council, Riyadh (1982). **Hobbies:** Swimming and reading. **Prof. Addr.:** P.O.Box 7153, Riyadh 11462, Saudi Arabia.

BINOUS (Muhsen)), Tunisian writer. **Born** on October 18, 1932. **Educ.:** College Diploma, Tunis (Tunisia). **Career:** Former Pupil of the Tunisian School of Administration. **Publ.:** Writer and Translator, Journal "Tunis-Soir" (1952-54); Special Correspondent, Moroccan Magazine "Houna Koullou Chai", Editor, Magazines "Le Feu", "L'Art" (1953), Chronicler, Journal "Le Petit Malin" (1967), Past President, Association of Scholastic Youth. **Addr.:** 27, Rue de la Hafsia, Tunis, Tunisia.

BINZAGR (Wahib, Sheikh), Saudi businessman. **Born** in 1934 in Saudi Arabia. **Son of** Said Zagr. **Educ.:** Victoria College, Alexandria, Egypt; University of Durham, UK. **Dipl.:** B.A. (Economics). **Career:** Former Director, Saudi Arabian Airlines (1965-70); Former Mayor of Jeddah, Saudi Arabia; Director, Riyad Bank, Jeddah (1981-); Chairman, Bin Zagr Group of Companies; Chairman, Saudi Cairo Bank, Jeddah, and Al-Alamiya Insurance Co. Ltd., Jeddah. **Member:** Jeddah Chamber of Commerce. **Addr.:** P.O.Box 2374, Jeddah 21451, Saudi Arabia.

BIRIDO (Omer, Y.), Sudanese diplomat. **Born** at Singa, Sudan, in 1939. **Dipl.:** B.A. degree from University of Khartoum, Sudan; M.A. degree in Political Science, Delhi University, India. **Career:** Joined Sudan Ministry of Foreign Affairs in 1963; served in the Embassies of Sudan at New Delhi and London respectively (1963-69); Deputy Director of Consular Department in the Ministry of Foreign Affairs of Sudan (1969-71); Counsellor at Sudan Embassy in Uganda (1971-73); Served at the Sudan Permanent Mission to the United Nations in New York (1973-76); Director of Department of International Organizations and Department of African Affairs respectively in the Ministry of Foreign Affairs of the Sudan (1976-78); Ambassador, Permanent Representative of the Sudan to the United Nations and International Organizations in Geneva (1978-1983); Ambassador and Permanent Representative of the Sudan to the United Nations, New York, U.S.A. (1984-86); Director, Department of International Organizations, Ministry of Foreign Affairs, Khartoum, Sudan (1986-89); Ambassador of Sudan to the Kingdom of Saudi Arabia, Riyadh (1989-1992); First Under Secretary, Ministry of External Relations (1992-95); Ambassador of Sudan to London, UK (1995-98); Director of Political Affairs, The Republican Palace, The Presidency (1998-up to present). **Addr.:** Director of Political Affairs, The Republican Palace, The Presidency, Khartoum, Sudan.

BISHARA (Abdallah, Yacoub), Kuwaiti diplomat **Born** on November 6, 1936 in Kuwait City (Kuwait). **Married,** with children. **Educ.:** Faculty of Arts, Cairo University (1955-59); Balliol College Oxford, UK (1961-62); St. John's University (1972-73). **Dipl.:** B.A. (Lit. & Arts), LL.B. (International Relations), Degree of African Studies. **Career:** Teacher, Secondary schools (Kuwait) (1960-63); Secretary, Kuwaiti Embassy to Tunisia (1963-64); Director, Office of the Minister of Foreign Affairs (Kuwait) (1964-71); Ambassador to Argentina, also accredited to Brazil since 1974; Ambassador, Permanent Representative of Kuwait (New York) (1974-81); Secretary General, Gulf Co-operation Council (1982-1994). **Prof. Addr.:** P.O.Box 7153, Riyadh 11462, Saudi Arabia.

BISHARA (al-Fatih Mohamad Bashir), Sudanese military. **Born** in 1932 in Madinat al Abyadh, Sudan. **Son** of Bashir Bishara. **Married,** seven children. **Educ.:** Various military qualifications; Military College, M.A. in Military Science (1954); British Staff College. **Career:** General (1971); former Deputy Chief of Staff, Sudanese Armed Forces. **Medals:** Independence Medal; May Revolution Medal; Worthiness Medal; Excellent Long Service Medal; Unity Medal; Star of Ethiopia (rank of Commander); German Military Officers' Cross; Egyptian Medal of Merit; Victoria Medal; Yugoslav Medal of Merit. **Member** of the Care for the Handicapped Association; President of the Officers' Club. **Priv. Addr.:** Tel.: 76134, Khartoum, Sudan.

BISHARA (Shehata, Kamel), Egyptian physician. **Born** on September 3, 1930 in Alexandria (Egypt). **Son** of Kamel Bishara **and** Mrs., née T. Gabriel. **Married** to Mona Rashed on November 9, 1967 in Cairo. **Educ.:** Coptic Secondary School (1942-46); Faculty of Medicine, Ain Shams University (1947-53). **Dipl.:** M.D., D.S. diploma of Surgery; Kasr el Ainy, (1957); D.Orth. Diploma of Orthopaedics (1958); F.R.C.S. Edinburgh (1967). **Career:** Head of Orthopaedic Section, Embaba General Hospital, Giza, Cairo (Egypt). **Publ.:** Spotlight on Tibial Shaft Fractures (tabled before the London Orthopaedic Meeting in 1966). **Award:** received the Coptic College Prize. **Hobbies:** Music and reading. **Prof. Addr.:** 80, Goumhouriya Street, Cairo. **Priv. Addr.:** 6, Syria street, Madinet el-Mohandessin, Agouza, Egypt.

BISHI (Ali, Ahmad Nasr, al), Yemeni former Army Commander. **Born** in 1937 in Al-Khuraiba, Second Province, People's Democratic Republic of Yemen. **Educ.:** Koranic School, al-Khuraiba. **Career:** Former Member of the Presidential Council; had training course in USSR (1974); as Commander in Chief, paid official visits to USSR, China and Eastern Europe; Field Commander of National Liberation Front, North West Region; Deputy Minister of Defence and Commander in Chief of the Army; Member of the People's Supreme Council, Member of the Central Committee. **Addr.:** Aden, Republic of Yemen.

BITAR (Muhammad), Syrian economist. **Born** on June 21, 1922 in Damascus, Syria. **Married,** 2 sons, 2 daughters. **Dipl.:** Licence in Law; Licence and Ph.D. in Economics. **Career:** Director of Monetary Control Bureau (1952-54), Director General (1954-56); Director of Control Department and Foreign Relations, Central Bank of Syria, Syria (1956-61); Deputy Governor, Central Bank of Syria (1961-63); Economic Advisor, Algeria (1964); Financial Adviser, Saudi Arabia (1965-71); Adviser of the Technical Assistance of the International Monetary Fund (1971-73); Deputy Director General, later Director General, Union of Arab French Banks (1973-84). **Publ.:** Numerous articles and lectures published in English and French; "The Monetary Union" (1955) in French and Arabic. **Prof. Addr.:** Rue Ancelle Neully-Seine, France.

BITAT (Rabah), Algerian statesman. **Born** in 1927 in Algeria. **Career:** Member of the F.L.N. (Front de Libération Nationale); Imprisoned (1955-62); Former Minister of State, Algerian Provisional Government in Tunis later in Algiers; Member of Political Bureau (in charge of Party organization) (July 1962-63); Deputy Prime Minister (September 1962- May 1963); Third Deputy Prime Minister (May 1963- September 1963); Returned to Algeria (December 1964); Minister of State (July 1965); President of the National Assembly (and Head of State for ashort period of 45 days after Boumedienne's death in (1987) and member of the Political Bureau of the FLN. **Addr.:** Algiers, Algeria.

BOCTOR (Samuel, Matta), Egyptian physician. **Born** on October 1, 1918 in Tanta (Egypt). **Son** of Matta Boctor (Railway Engineer) **and** Mrs. Yasmin Tawadros. **Married** to Massa Sidhom on July 12, 1945, 2 children: Doreen (Mrs. Adel L. Habib) and Amira (Mrs. Magdy I. Boulos). **Educ.:** Zeitoun Primary School, Koubba Secondary School, Cairo University (Faculty of Medicine). **Dipl.:** M.B.B.Ch. (Doctor of Medicine and Surgery), Cairo University, Fellow of the Royal College of Surgeons, Edinburgh, Fellow of the Royal College of Surgeons, England. **Career:** House Surgeon, Qasr al-Einy Hospital (1942), Surgical Resident Registrar (1943-45), Clinical Demonstrator in Surgery, Alexandria University (1945); Lecturer in Surgery, University of Alexandria (1948); Professor of Neurosurgery, University of Alexandria since 1962. **Member:** British Society of Neurological Surgeons (1962); ex-president, Middle East Neurological Society, Beirut (1962); ex-president, Egyptian Society, Neurosurgeons (1968); member of American Association of Neurological Surgeons, USA (1978); member of Congress of Neurological Surgeons, USA (1980). **Sports:** Tennis, golf and swimming. **Hobby:** Music. **Member** of Alexandria Sporting Club, Conservatoire de Musique of Alexandria. **Prof. Addr.:** 28, Ghorfa al-Tougaria Street, Tel.: 22444, Alexandria. **Priv. Addr.:** 18, Aly Zulficar Street, Tel.: 48433, Alexandria, Egypt.

BOGAMI (Tami Hudaif), Saudi official. **Born** in 1936 at Traba. **Dipl.:** Licence in Shari'a (Islamic Law), Diploma in Law. **Career:** Served as secondary school teacher, secondary school principal and later Director of Education; General Librarian (National Library); Legal Counsellor; Secretary General, King Abdulaziz Research Centre; Member, World Assembly of Muslim Youth; former Deputy Minister of Higher Education for Administrative and Financial Affairs. **Hobby:** Reading. **Addr.:** al-Malaz Tel.: 4412286 (office) and 4785217 (Home), Saudi Arabia.

BOGARY (Mohamad Ahmad), Saudi businessman. **Born** Mecca, in 1915, **Dipl.:** Business Administration. **Career:** Import Manager, Omar Ali Bogary and Bros.; honorary Secretary, Mecca Chamber of Commerce 1962-77; founder and owner, Bogary Plastics Factory; Mecca; founder, Saudi Arabian Carpet Factory; member of Mecca Cultural Club; member of Mecca Printing and Information Establishment; attended several economic and business conferences in Pakistan, Lebanon, Egypt, Tunisia and Sudan. **Hobbies:** music, travel, tennis. **Addr.:** P.O.Box 585, Mecca, Saudi Arabia.

BOGHDADI (Abdullatif, Mahmoud, al), Egyptian Wing Commander Air Force, Former Minister and Vice-President, Arab Republic of Egypt. **Born** on September 20, 1917 in Shawa, Dakahlia province. **Son** of Mahmoud al-Boghdadi. **Educ.:** Mansourah Secondary School, Military

College (Cairo), Graduate Air Force College (Cairo). **Career:** Wing Commander, Air Force Palestine War (1948 and 1956), Speaker National Assembly of Egypt, former Minister of War, Minister of State for Economic Planning; Minister of Planning and Minister for Port-Saïd Affairs, Former Vice-President, Arab Republic of Egypt. **Addr.:** al-Ourouba Street, Heliopolis, Cairo, Egypt.

BOGIS (Abdalla Abdul Muttalib), Saudi official. **Born** in 1929 in Mecca, Saudi Arabia. **Dipl.:** B.A. (Education and Psychology) and Licence (Arabic Language). **Career:** Former teacher, Secondary Teacher's Institute, Mecca; General Inspector, Arabic Language, Ministry of Education; General Director, Secondary Education; Director General of Education, Jeddah; Saudi Arabian Cultural Attache, Federal Republic of Germany; member, General Arab Society of the Organization of Arab Tourism, the Supervisory Commission, Islamic Solidarity magazine, Central Committee for Pilgrimage; Chairman the Executive Committee for Transportation; Deputy Minister for Pilgrimage Affairs, Ministry of Pilgrimage and Endowments; member of Board of Directors, the Saudi Arab Bank; member and Vice Chairman, Mecca Literary Club; has attended UNESCO Conferences on the Elimination of Illiteracy and Sociological Sciences; Chairman, the Saudi Arabian delegation to the Conference of Arab Ministers of Tourism, organized by the Arab Organization for Tourism. **Publ.:** Da'watul Haqq (The Call for Truth), a history book; Ba'yna Al-Hadana Wal Rawdah (Batween the Nursery and Kindergarten), a psychology book; a collection of stories for children; several books on Islamic and Arab historical personalities. **Prof. Addr.:** Bureau of the Deputy Minister for Pilgrimage Affairs, Tel.: 5431137, Mecca. **Priv. Addr.:** Tel.: 542642, Mecca, and/or 6600668, Jeddah, Saudi Arabia.

BOKHARI (Abdalla Yahia), Saudi academic. **Born** on 28 February 1944. **Dipl.:** B.Sc. (Architecture); M. (Architecture); M. (Urban Design); Ph.D. (Architecture). **Career:** Architect, Aramco, Dhahran (1970-71); Teaching Assistant, University of Petroleum and Minerals, Dhahran (1971-72); Director of Master Plan Office King Abdulaziz University (1979-80); Vice Dean, Faculty of Engineering, King Abdulaziz University (1979-81); Associate Professor of Architecture and Urban Design, King Fahd University of Petroleum and Minerals, Dhahran (1981-92); General Manager of Archiplan, Architects and Planners, Jeddah; member Cultural and Literary Club, Jeddah, Middle Eastern Studies, USA and United Kingdom; member, Advisory Board to MIMAR for International Islamic Architecture. **Honour:** Jeddah Medal. **Publ.:** "How to build your house in Saudi Arabia", Book; Ph.D. thesis on Jeddah Architecture and Planning; several articles on Islamic Architecture in local and foreign magazines; weekly writer in Jeddah newspapers; writer for a few professional magazines. **Hobbies:** Chess, reading, writing, swimming, classical music. **Prof. Addr.:** P.O.Box 6048, Tel.: 6824808, 6826140, Jeddah, Saudi Arabia.

BOKHARI (Abdul Hameed, M. Zakir), Saudi businessman. **Born** on August 25, 1932 in Jeddah, Saudi Arabia. **Married** in 1952 to Mrs. Zainab Bokhari, daughter of late Abdul Rahman Zakir Bokhari, 4 Children: Mohamed, Hind, Abla and Nada. **Educ.:** al-Falah High School, Jeddah; Nautical Institute Shipping Course, Liverpool, Amsterdam and Gothenburg. **Degree:** Second Mate. **Career: Present Position:** Chairman, Al-Zakir International Group of Companies Inc., P.O.Box 160, Jeddah-21411, Kingdom of Saudi Arabia. **Associate Companies:** Orient Commercial & Shipping Co., Ltd., Saudi Arabia; Saudi Arabian Maritime Agencies Co. Ltd., Saudi Arabia; Mutual Marine Services Al-Mushtaraka Ltd., Saudi Arabia; Marine Services Co. Ltd., Saudi Arabia; Transworld Tourism & Transport Co., Ltd., Saudi Arabia; Sohar Shipping, Transport and Trading Agencies LLC, Sultanate of Oman; Fenkel Oriental Marine Services Co. Ltd., Eritrea; Mutual Business Centre, Egypt, **Business Activities:** Ship Owner, Shipping Agents in all Saudi ports: Handling Bulk - Tanker - LPG Carriers, General Cargo - Containers - Reefers - Passengers/Pleasure Boats - Naval Ships, Liner Service World Wide, Container Storage and repairs, Dry Docking Arrangements/Repairs; Bunkering/Supplies/Chandling; Crew Changes and repatriation; Husbandry/Management; Stevedoring/Tally/Supervision; Tran-Shipment; Custom Brokerage/Forwarding; Trucking; Inspection and Surveys; Protection and Indemnity Clubs Correspondence; General Trading and Commission Agents, Travel and Tourism Agents; Chemical and Lubricants; Marine Engines; Diving Equipment; Swimming Pool. **Member of:** Arab Federation of Shipping; Baltic & International Maritime Conference; International Ship Supplies Association; Major Arab Foreign Joint Chambers of Commerce/Industry & Development; Multiport Ship Agencies Network; International Maritime Bureau; International Marine Purchasing Association; The Federation of National Associations of Ship Brokers and Agents; International Federation of Freight Forwarders Association (FIATA); Elected Member, Multiport Ship Agencies Network, Rotterdam; Board Member of Arab Hellenic Chamber of Commerce & Development, Greece; Chairman, Maritime Committee, Jeddah Chamber of Commerce & Industry; Appointed Member of Special Committee to Persue and Evaluate Performance of the Arab-Foreign Joint Chambers of Commerce and Industry under the Auspices of the Council of Saudi Chambers of Commerce and Industry, Riyadh; Appointed Member of Jeddah Islamic Port Advisory Council; Member of Saudi British Society, London; Member of Saudi Egyptian Joint Committee; Member of Saudi National Committee in the International Chambers of Commerce (ICC), Paris; Vice Chairman National Committee for Transport, Riyadh. **Professional Activities:** Merchant Marine Officer; Nautical Institute of Shipping, Liverpool; Courses in Management, Holland & Sweden; Widely Travelled and Attended a Number of; Conferences and

Symposia, Organised under the Auspices of World Economic Forum (WEF) and other International Trading and Shipping Organisations; Presented Working Papers Based on in-Depth Study of Topics related to trading and shipping Industry; Managing and Operating various Fully/ Partly owned Shipping, Trading and Industrial Companies World-Wide. Mr. Abdul Hameed M. Zakir BOKHARI is a Popular Business Personality in the Kingdom of Saudi Arabia. He is at the Helm of a Number of Al-Zakir Group of Companies. Al-Zakir International Group is a Multi Unit, Multi - Product and Service Group Well Kwnown in the Market. Mr. Zakir BOKHARI has Introduced some changes in the Organisation's Structure with a View to Boosting its Efficiency. He is not a Status Quo Executive. He likes to introduce changes for the Better. He is Equipped with Skills to lead People in his Organisation. Those Who have worked. Closely know well that He quite often Adopts participate Style of decision making. He is Cheerful, Humorous and Courteous in his Interaction with his Colleagues and Friends. **Hobbies:** Shooting and fishing. **Prof. Addr.:** Oriental Commercial and Shipping Co. Ltd., P.O.Box 160, Jeddah 21411, Saudi Arabia.

BOKHARI (Ahmad Mohamad), Saudi academic. **Born** on 10 April 1947, in Jeddah, Saudi Arabia. **Dipl.:** Ph.D. (Chemistry). **Career:** Lecturer (1975); Assistant Professor, Department of Chemistry, King Fahad University of Petroleum and Minerals, Dhahran. **Prof. Addr.:** Department of Chemistry, K.F.U.P.M., Tel.: 8603830, Dhahran. **Priv. Addr.:** Tel.: 8606943, Dhahran, Saudi Arabia.

BOKHARI (Fuad Saleh, Abdul Hajji), Saudi Academic. **Born** in 1943 in Mecca city (Saudi Arabia). **Educ.:** Faculty of Science. **Dipl.:** B.Sc., M.Sc. (Mathematics). **Career:** Demonstrator, Department of Mathematics King Abdul Aziz University; now Lecturer, Department of Mathematics, Faculty of Education, King Abdul Aziz University. **Publ.:** Translated a number of books on modern mathematics. **Sports:** Soccer and table tennis. **Hobby:** Reading. **Prof. Addr.:** Faculty of Education, King Abdul Aziz University, Mecca, Saudi Arabia.

BOKHARI (Nabil Yahya Abdallah), Saudi academic. **Born** in 1942, in Jeddah, Saudi Arabia. **Dipl.:** M.Sc.; Ph.D. (Horticulture), Kansas State University 1973. **Career:** Lecturer, Department of Botany, Faculty of Science, Riyadh University (1965-66); Professor, Department of Plant Production, College of Agriculture, Riyadh University (1973-99); member of American Society of Horticultural Science (ASHS); member of Joint Committee (Faculty of Agriculture and Ministry of Agriculture) for the establishment of a Higher Agricultural Institute. **Publ.:** Some research papers published in the Scientific Journal of the American Society for Horticultural Science; Journal of the Faculty of Agriculture, Riyadh University; series of researches on weed control in onions and potatoes. **Hobbies:** soccer, swimming, travel. **Addr.:** Faculty of Agriculture, Riyadh University, Riyadh, Saudi Arabia.

BONDOGJI (Hussain Hamza), Saudi academic. **Born** in 1936, in Jeddah, Saudi Arabia. **Dipl.:** M.A. (Political Geography). **Career:** Lecturer, Department of Geography, Faculty of Arts, King Saud University; former teaching assistant; member of Geographical Society of Egypt, American Geographical Association. **Publ.:** The State, a study in Political Geography; An Atlas of Saudi Arabia. **Addr.:** Department of Geography, Faculty of Arts, King Abdulaziz University, Jeddah, Saudi Arabia.

BOOLAKY (Ibrahim), British Social Scientist retired, Lecturer in Business Studies. **Born** on July 21, 1937 in Mauritius, British Citizen. **Married** on June 18, 1974 to Jamila Ben Mansour, Tunis One son. **Educ.:** Primary/ Secondary education in Mauritius. 1976-83: Higher studies in Social Sciences & Development Planning in U.K. BA (Hons): Middlesex University; MSc. (Econ): University of London; M. Phil., London School of Economics and Political Science. **Career:** 1957-62: Teacher; 1962-69: Journalist; 1969-75: Director General, Islamic Institute, Mauritius; 1976-83: Press Correspondent/Researcher whilst pursuing higher education in London; 1984-89: Lecturer in Planning and Development, University of Tunis, Tunisia; (1989-1990): Lecturer in Business Studies in London and appointed, since 1991, Lecturer at City & Islington College, Islington, London N7 OSP, Including such subjects as Development Studies and Business European Studies. (1998- to date): Consultant. **Publ.:** Over 25 publications between 1964 and 2000 (mainly literary contributions to journals). These include: Democracy (1964); "La première conférence des organisations islamique à la Mecque" (1974); "Old tools and techniques for a new development strategy for the Muslim World" (1981); "The Feasibility of an Islamic Medical Model for the Muslim World" (1983); "The mathematical geography of Al-Biruni" (1984); "The impact of Islamic medicine on the development of civilization" (1985); "The melody of peace" (1988); "The strategy of the 1.5 million house programme of Sri Lanka" (1991); "Old and Modern Pioneers of Islamic Medical Education (1998)"; "Ibn Khaldun's methods in traditional environment research" (1994). "The Systemic Nature of Islamic Medicine" (1999) and "Islamic Medical Manuscripts Up to the New Millenium" (2000). **Awards:** M.Sc. (Econ) in Development and Planning; B.A. (Hons.) in Social Science, mainly environmental studies. PETC (Teacher's Certificate in Education) from University of London. BTEC D32 & D33 (Award Certificate as Assessor of Students' performance etc.). **Memberships:** FBIM (Fellow of the British Institute of Management) Elected in 1983. FIMS (Fellow of the Institute of Management Specialists) Elected in 1984. Certificate of Merit awarded by the International Biographical Centre in 1997. Member of Convocation, Senate House, University of London (since 1982). **Hobbies:** Reading, travelling, music, swimming, horse-riding & c/affairs. AFRICA WHO'S WHO (1996) & DIRECTORY OF HISTORIANS OF ISLAMIC MEDICINE AND ALLIED SCIENCES (1995). Dictionary of International Biography (1997); Outstanding People of the 20th Century (1998); 2000 Prominent Arabs of the 20th Century (1999); International Book of Honor (1999) and 1000 LEADERS OF WORLD INFLUENCE (2000). **Other Professional activities:** Included attending the International symposium on Islamic Architecture and Urbanism, King Faisal University in Dammam (January 1980); and in April 1983, the International, Symposium on Islamic Art in Istanbul. 36th International Congress on the History of Medicine, Tunis, 1998. **Priv. Addr.:** "Les Tours Blanches", Cité des Juges, Raoued Plage, B.P. 29, 2056 Raoued, Ariana, Tunisia. Tel. and Fax: +216/1/769526.

BOROLOSSY (Abdel Wahab, Ali, el), Egyptian scientist. **Born** on February 8, 1921 in Cairo (Egypt). **Married. Educ.:** Faculty of Medicine, Cairo University (1936-43); School of Pharmacy, University of London (1946-49); **Dipl.:** M.B., B.Ch., Ph.D. (medical science). **Career:** Lecturer, Faculty of Medicine, Cairo University (1946-60); Dean, Faculty of Medicine, Asiyut University (1960-64); Director General, Medical Insurance, Egypt (1964-65); Rector, Asiyut University (1965-68); Minister of Higher Education (1968-71); Minister of Scientific Research, Egypt (1971); Professor, Faculty of Medicine, Cairo University (1971-74); Member, Executive Board, UNESCO, Kuwait. **Publ.:** Author of numerous research papers on pharmacology, chemotherapy, experimental therapeutics; Chief Editor "Essential of Pharmacology and Therapeutics". **Member:** Egyptian Society of Pharmacology and Experimental Therapeutics; Egyptian Chemical Society. **Awards:** Order of the Republic, Egypt; Flag with Star, Yugoslavia. **Member:** Rotary International; Cairo South Club. **Hobbies:** Rotary International; Cairo South Club. **Hobbies:** Travel, tourism, social and youth service. **Prof. Addr.:** Tel.: 811774, UNESCO, Kuwait.

BORSHAID (Isa Abdulla Ibrahim, Al), Bahraini businessman. **Born** on June 11, 1945 in Bahrain. **Son** of Abdulla Al Borshaid (Ship Captain) **and** Mrs. Mariam A. Ibrahim. **Educ.:** Muharraq - Omar Ibn Abdulaziz School; East Riffa Boys School; Middlesex Polytechnic, London. **Dipl.:** Fellow Chartered Institute of Management Accountants; Fellow British Institute of Management. **Career:** Undersecretary, Ministry of Finance and National Economy (1981-1993); Undersecretary, Ministry of Health (1993-1995) First Deputy Chairman, National Bank of Bahrain (1980-1993) Chairman, Bahrain Commercial Facilities Company (1988-1993); Chairman Bahrain Development Bank (1991-1993), Chairman, Awal Commercial Investments C0. W.L.L. (1983) **Prof. Addr.:** Tel.: 530505, P.O.Box 20743, Diplomatic Area, Bahrain.

BOUABID (Maati), Moroccan politician. **Born** on November 11, 1927 in Casablanca. **Educ.:** Secondary, College Moulay Youssef (Rabat) and Lycée Lyautey (Casablanca), Faculty of Law (Bordeaux). **Dipl.:** LL.B. and Licence of Higher Studies (Private Law). **Career:** Participated to the fight for Independence; lawyer in Casablanca since 1955; The King's Prosecutor, Tangier (1956); The King's General Prosecutor, Tangier Court of Appeal (1957); Minister of Labour and Social Affairs (Dec. 1958- May 1960); first President of the Municipal Council of Casablanca and Deputy of the same town to the first Parliament (1963-65); resumed his activities as lawyer in Casablanca; elected five times at the Bar Association of Casablanca and three times its President; Minister of Justice (October 10, 1977); Prime Minister and Minister of Justice (March 22, 1979); Prime Minister (Nov. 83); Minister of State (Nov. 84); presently Leader of the Party "Union Constitutionnelle". **Addr.:** Rabat, Morocco.

BOUAMOUD (Muhammad), Moroccan politician. **Born** in 1928 in Ouajda, Morocco. **Dipl.:** Degree in Classical Arabic and French. **Career:** held various posts in General and Technical Education at the Ministry of Education; worked in the Office of Prime Ministers, and Ministers of PTT and Defence; Minister of Primary and Secondary Education (1974-77); Minister of Professional Training and Labour (1977-84); Member of Parliament; Minister of Transport (1984-1992). **Prof. Addr.:** Rabat, Morocco.

BOUAZIZ (Nasser, Mohamad al-Nouldi), Tunisian producer. **Born** on March 31, 1937. **Son** of Shaikh Mohamad al-Nouldi Bouaziz (Magistrate). **Career:** Typographer (1950-1953), Editor of artistic themes in periodicals, Collaborator in the following Reviews: "Flambeau de l'Art", "Noujoum Al Fann", "Koul Chai Bil Makchouf" (1953-57); Director Administrator, Journal of Pr. Hamadi Dsaziri Known under the Penname of As-Sitar (1960-62); Founder, 3rd Folklore Ballet of Tunis, "Rannat Kholkhal" (1960-62); Founder, "Théâtre African", troup of dramatic artists, dancers and musicians (1962); Founder, Film Society, Maghreb Films; Director, Adahoua al-Madina (weekly paper); Founder, General Union of Arts and Culture (1969); Composer of over 100 melodies; Founder, National Organization of Help for Children affected by poliomyelitis (1972); Founder, Magazine "Children's Protection". **Publ.:** Author of several plays broadcast on the Arab Radio, also of articles in the Army journal. **Addr.:** 23, Rue Albert Samain, al-Omrane, Tunisia.

BOUAZZA (Tayib), Moroccan diplomat. **Born** in 1923 in Morocco. Married, six children. **Career:** Secretary General, Moroccan Trade Unions (1959); President, Social Commission of the National Council; Adviser, Higher Council of Planning; Judge; Ambassador of Morocco to Yugoslavia (1959-61); Ambassador to Scandinavian Countries (1961-65); Head of Africa and Asia Department, Ministry of Foreign Affairs, Morocco (1965-68); Minister

Plenipotentiary (1968-71); Ambassador to Ghana (1971-72); Head of Africa and Asia Department (1972-74); Ambassador to Portugal (1974). **Member** of the Portugese Literature Club. **Medals:** Order of the Moroccan Kingdom; Order of Merit, Nigeria, Liberia, Yugoslavia, Sweden, Norway, Cameroon, Portugal. **Sports:** Horseriding, skiing, swimming. **Prof. Addr.:** Ministry of Foreign Affairs, Rabat, Morocco. **Priv. Addr.:** 33 Hayy al Sa'ada, Tel.: 52878, al-Tayaran, Rabat, Morocco.

BOUCETTA (Dr. Hadj Omar), Moroccan Physician, former Ambassador of Morocco. **Born** on February 13, 1921 in Marrakech, Morocco. **Son** of Ahmed Boucetta (Inspector University) **and** Mrs. née Fatma Benslimane. **Married** on December 1951 at Fès to Aziza née Sebti, 4 children: Fatiha 1954), Fadel (1956), Ahmed Amine (1959), Aziz (1964), (2 lawyers, 1 Architect, 1 Economist). **Studies:** Koranic School in Marrakech, Primary School in Marrakech, Secondary Studies. A) Comprehensive School Sidi Mohammed Marrakech: Secondary Studies Certificate, Arabic Certificate, Physical Training Certificate. B) Comprehensive School Moulay Youssef Rabat: First Part of the General Certificate of Education (Baccalaureat), Diploma of Secondary Studies Ending. C) Secondary School (Fès): Second Part of the General Certificate of Education (Philosophy). **Higher Studies:** ICB (Certificate of Physics, Chemistry and Biology Studies); In Algiers (1st and 2nd years) Faculty of Medicine; Faculty of Medicine in Paris (3rd - 4th - 5th - 6th years); Doctorate in Medicine (1949). **Medical Activities:** Graduate from the Faculty of Medicine of Paris; Non-resident Medical student of the Hospitals (Algiers); Head-Doctor on duty-Hospital Ibn Khatib (Fes); Head-Doctor of the Hospital Drissi (Fes); In charge of the Direction of the Health service of the Royal Armed Forces; Stage in Paris at the Ministry of Defence; Stage of Dermato Venereology organised by the WHO (Rotterdam, Holland) 1954; Founder President of the High Council of the Order of Doctors of Morocco (1958-1962); President of the Regional Council of the Order of Doctors in Casablanca and the south of Morocco; Private Consulting Room in Fes then in Casablanca. **Sporting, Social and Cultural Activities:** Member of the Committee of the Editorial Staff of the Review Medical Morocco; Founder Director of the Magazine Maroc-Sports (1960); President of the MAS of Fes Omnisports (1951-1954); President Founder of the Royal Moroccan Federation of Foot Ball (1956-1962); President-Delegate of the High Committee of Sports (1956-1962); Vice-President of the Moroccan National Olympic Committee (1956-1962); Member of the International Committee for the different Civilizations. (Brussels) 1956-1966; Promoter of the Sporting Complex Moulay Rachid (Rabat) First sporting Complex of Morocco; Member of the National Council of Young (CNJIA). **Diplomatic and Governmental Activities:** Ambassador of Morocco in Lebanon (1962); Ambassador of Morocco in Italy and Greece (1962-1965); Ambassador of Morocco in the Federal Republic of Germany (1965-1967); Ambassador of Morocco in Tunisia (1967-1969); Minister of Youth, Sports and Social Affairs (1969-1970); Several times member of the Moroccan Delegations at the Arab League and at the Summit Meeting of the heads of States of the AUO; In charge of the Moroccan Red Crescent and the National Mutual Aid as Minister of Social Affairs. **Other Activities:** President of the Cement Factory Asmar (Marrakech) C.A.=30 million dollars US; Member of the Cement-Manufacturers' Association of Morocco; Former President of the Municipal Council (Mayor), Ain Chok (Casablanca); Former Vice-President of the District (Vice-Mayor) of the Great Casablanca; Private Consulting Room (Casablanca); Sworn Doctor-Expert approved of by the Courts of Morocco; Controller Doctor at the National Social Security Fund; Doctor-Council of the national Airlines Company Royal Air Maroc; Works Doctor, Company Scif- 600 workers; former Administrator of the Autonomus Management of the Urban Transports of Casablanca; Former Administrator of the Autonomous Management of Water and Electricity Distribution in Casablanca (RAD); Special Administrator of the Civil Estate Company Darkoum (Casablanca). **Published Works (Scientific - Social - And Literary):** 1st Collection of Poems (400 pages) 1984; 2nd Collection of Poems (still in preparation); Essay on the Moroccan Diseased Psychology; Ramadan's Fasting; Nervos Syphilis observed on Moroccan Males; The Moroccan Woman; Her Present-Day condition-Preface to her (evolution); Recklinghausen Disease with recent royal tumor; Some considerations upon our way of lodging in Morocco - (Hygieno and Wenthor); Where do Prophylaxis lead and the treatment of syphilis in Morocco; Essay on the treatment of the diabetes mellitus with Isoniazide; Account of a pilgrimage to Mecca, Religious and socio-medical considerations; Ibn Sina (Avicenne) (His life and Medical Work; Dysentery for Ancient Arabic Doctors; The Moroccan Constitution (Its caracteristics, and originalities); Poems published in newspapers and reviews. **Decorations: Moroccan:** Knight of the Alaouit Ouissam, Officer of the Sport Order, Officer of the Throne Order. **Foreign:** Ribbon decorated with the Star of the Cedar Order (Lebanon); Ribbon decorated with the Star of the Republican Merit (Italy); Ribbon with the Star of St. Georges Order (Greece); Ribbon with a Star (Federal Republic of Germany); Second Ribbon with a Star (Federal Republic of Germany); Commander of the Jordanian Order; Officer of the Nichan Iftikhar (Tunisia); Contagious Diseases Medal (Algiers); Silver Medal of the International Olympic Order. **Credit Cards:** Visa, BNP PARIS. **Addr.:** Rue Teddert Californie, Casablanca, Morocco, Tel.: 244895, 210411, 210593 (Casablanca); 02 112292 (Car); 04 308469 (Marrakech); 03 324945 (Mohammadia, Morocco); 47.56.1936 (Paris); 77.56.13 Marbella (malaga) Spain.

BOUCETTA (Muhamad), Moroccan politician. **Born** in 1925 in Marrakech. **Educ.:** Sidi Mohamed School

(1937), Lycée Moulay Idriss (Fes), Faculty of Law (Sorbonne), Institut des Etudes Supérieures (France). **Dipl.:** in Philosophy, LL.B. **Career:** Represented the Istiqlal party at the congress of anti-imperialist countries (1949); represented same party at the Congress of Arab Students (Lieden), then at the congress of North-African Students (Tunisia) (1950); Lawyer in Casablanca (1951-56); Director, Minister of Foreign Affairs Cabinet (April 1956); assistant Secretary of State for Foreign Affairs (1958); member of the Moroccan Delegation in charge of the ratification of diplomatic relations between Morocco and France and between Morocco and Spain; member of the Moroccan delegation to the U.N.; Minister of Public Affairs and Administrative Reforms (June 1960); also Minister of Justice (June 1960); presided several delegations to Europe and Africa; member, Istiqlal delegations to Europe and Africa; member, Istiqlal Political Commission (1956); member, Istiqlal Executive Committee (1963); Secretary-General, Istiqlal (1974); re-elected in 1978 to present; Minister of State (March 1977); Minister of State for Foreign Affairs and Cooperation (October 1977); deputy to the Parliament (since 1977); Minister of State for Foreign Affairs (Nov. 1981- Nov. 83); Minister of State (Nov. 1983); in his capacity, he represented H.M. King Hassan II to the following international conferences: 9th Arab Summit (Baghdad 1978), 16th African Summit (Monrovia 1979), 19th African Summit (Addis Ababa 1983). **Prof. Addr.:** Secretary General of the Istiqlal Party, 4 Charia Ibnou Toumert, Rabat, Morocco.

BOUCHEMA (Kamel), Algerian politician. **Born** in 1943. **Educ.:** University Studies in Cairo and Algiers. **Career:** Militant in the Civil Organisation of FLN, former Member of Permanent Secretariat; Central Committee, FLN; Assistant National Commissioner in Chief of FLN, National Commissioner, FLN, Party of Bouira Governorate; Minister of Youth and Sports (1985-87). **Prof. Addr.:** Algiers, Algeria.

BOUCHOUCHA (Sadeq), Tunisian pharmacist. **Born** on November 30, 1925. **Married,** 6 children. **Educ.:** Pharmacist's Diploma in Serology, Biological Chemistry and Clinical Biochemistry, Faculty of Montpellier (France). **Career:** Pharmacist, Bizerta, Tunisia (1953); Vice-President, Municipality of Bizerta, Tunisia (1953); Vice-President, Municipality of Bizerta (1957-60), Municipal Counsellor, Bizerta (1960-63). **Awards:** Recipient of distinction in Serology (1953). **Addr.:** 1, Bis Square Command and Bijaoui, Bizerta, Tunisia.

BOUCHOUK (Elmostapha), Moroccan academic. **Born** on July 21, 1947, B.S. Safi, Morocco. **Son** of Abdallah Bouchouk (deceased) and Mrs. Abouche Sbaï (deceased). **Married** in 1978 in Tetouan, Morocco to Habiba Ben Moussa Medkouri, 3 children: Nada, Hajar, Chahrazad. **Educ.:** Faculty of Literature, Fes; Faculty of Literature, Rabat; Université Libre de Bruxelles; Université de l'Etat à Mons (Belgique); Faculty of Psycho-Pedagogy; University of State - Gent (S.I.M.A.). **Dipl.:** Licence ès Lettres; (C.A.P.S.); Diplôme of higher Studies; Post Graduate; Doctorat d'Etat. **Career:** Linguistic, Psycho-Linguistic and Didactic of Arabic Language. **Other Information:** Professor in Mohammad V University, Faculty of Educational Sciences (1977), Rabat, Morocco; Author of: Educational Evaluation; Learning and Teaching Arabic Language (1991) edited in Morocco; 2nd edition (1994) (Arabic) also in Michigan, U.S.A. (Feb. 16. 1993); Survey of Islamic Manuscripts (1991) edited in London (English); Islamic Manuscripts in the World (1992) in London also with other authors and many articles in Moroccan and Arab reviews; Supervision of Scientific papers for Higher Studies diploma, such as Doctorat d'Etat; Supervision of Sessions with UNESCO Cooperation of Arabic educations in Konakry (1990), Madrid (1993), etc. **Sports:** Swimming, Taekwando, Jogging. **Hobby:** Royal Taekwando Federation. **Member:** Royal Moroccan Taekwando Federation (S.G.). **Prof. Addr.:** Faculty of Educational Sciences, Mohammad V University, P.O.Box 1072, Tel.: 774278, Rabat, Morocco. **Priv. Addr.:** 44, Zankat Ouedziz No.1 Agdal, 10.000, Tel.: 770929, Rabat, Morocco.

BOUDALI (Nouri), Tunisia Trade Unionist. **Born** in 1919. **Educ.:** Secondary and Higher. **Career:** Trade Unionist (1936), helped found Union Générale des Travailleurs Tunisiens (with Farhat Hached), Secretary-General (1952-54) and (1965), Middle East Representative to ICFTU (International Confederation of Free Trade Unions) (1954-56), Member of National Assembly, Member of Destour Socialist Party. **Addr.:** Union Générale Tunisienne du Travail, 29 Place Muhammad Ali, Tunis, Tunisia.

BOUDIA (Mohamad), Algerian writer. **Born** on February 24, 1932 in Algiers. **Educ.:** Secondary. **Career:** Writer, member of the "Théâtre National Algérien", Contributor to "Alger-Soir" (Daily newspaper) and "Novembre" (cultural monthly magazine). **Publ.:** two plays "Naissances" and "L'Olivier" (1962). **Addr.:** Algiers, Algeria.

BOUGHALI (Mohamed), Moroccan dean, faculty of arts, Marakech. **Born** in 1944 in Marakech, Morocco. **Son** of Larbi Boughali (Shoemaker) **and** Mrs. Khadija Amane. **Married** in 1969 in Marakech to Fatima Rafik, 5 children: Hicham, Laïla, Yasmina, Sara, Khalil. **Educ.:** Faculty of Arts, Rabat, Morocco; Sorbonne, Paris, France; Faculté des Lettres d'Amiens, France. **Dipl.:** Licence in Philosophy, Doctorate of 3rd Cycle, Doctorat d'Etat ès-Lettres. **Career:** Professor in Philosophy at High School (1967-76); Professor in Psychopedagogy (1976-79); Professor in Philosophy, Faculty of Arts, Marakech (1979-81); presently, Dean, Faculty of Arts, Marakech, Morocco. **Work:** "La Représentation de l'Espace chez le Marocain Illétré" (1974); "Lettre Ouverte à un Arabe" (1982); "La Poétique de Senghor" (1986); "L'Erotique du Language chez

Barthes" (1986); "Sociologie des Maladies Mentales au Maroc" (1988); "Approche d'Yves Bonnefoy" (1990); "Poétique de la Pudeur" (1991). **Awards:** Knight of the Order of the Throne (1990); Medal of Vermeil from the French Academy (1990). **Sports:** Walking. **Hobbies:** Reading, writing, theatre. **Prof. Addr.:** Faculty of Letters, University Cadi Ayyad, Amerchic Square, P.O.Box S 511, Tel.: (4)30.27.42, Marakech, Morocco. **Priv. Addr.:** Faculty of Letters, Tel.: (04)30.43.60, Marakech, Morocco.

BOUH (Robleh, Obsieh), Djibouti Deputy at the National Assembly. **Born** in 1937 in Dikhil. **Career:** Teacher. Founder/Member of PMP in 1960; Organiser Member of Interior Cell of FLCS; Member of Central Committee of RPP; Elected Deputy at the National Assembly (8 May 1977- to date); General rapporteur of Finance Commission. Member of Permanent Commission and Member of Finance Commission, General Economy and Planning; Permanent Delegate of National Assembly to ACP-CEE. **Prof. Addr.:** National Assembly, P.O.Box 138 Djibouti, Djibouti.

BOUHARA (Abdulrazak), Algerian politician. **Born** on December 1, 1934. **Married**, 4 children. **Career:** Military Attaché, Paris (1965); Brigade Commander, National Popular Army (ANP); Mission in Suez (1967); Military Attaché, Moscow, USSR (1968); Ambassador in Hanoi, North Vietnam (1970); Lieutenant Colonel, ANP in 1974; President, Organization Committee of the FLN (1978); Governor of Algiers; Minister of Health (1979-84); Member in charge of Foreign Relations, Permanent Secretariat of the Central Committee, FLN (1984). **Prof. Addr.:** Permanent Secretary of the Central Committee, FLN, Algiers, Algeria.

BOUJBEL (Mohsen, Dr.), Tunisian statesman. **Born** on July 17, 1945 in Beni-Khaled, Tunis. **Son** of Ahmed Boujbel (Farmer) **and** Mrs. Fatma Bennis. **Married** in Beni-Khaled to Miss Souad Ben Slimane, three Children, Inès (1973); Lilia (1977); Ahmed (1981). **Educ.:** University of Tunis; Ecole Nationale de la Statistique et de l'Administration Economique (ENSAE) Paris. **Dipl.:** Master's Degree of Mathematics; Diploma of Statistician Economist. **Career:** In Charge of Agricultural Planning at Ministry of Plan (1971-77); Expert in Fao Roma (1977-78); Director of Planning at Ministry of Agriculture (1979-88); Chairman and Managing Director of National Bank of Agricultural Development (1988); State Secretary of Agriculture (July 1988). **Lord-Mayor** of Beni-Khaled Since 1980. **Decor:** Chevalier de l'Ordre de la République (Nationale Decoration). **Sport:** Joggins. **Prof. Addr.:** 30, Alain Savary Street, Tel.: 680319, 1002 Tunnis Belvedere, Tunisia. **Priv. Addr.:** Jasmin 2, Belvedere II, Menzah 6, Tel.: 236279, Tunis, Tunisia.

BOUKHRIS (Mohamad Ali), Tunisian executive. **Born** on January 21, 1933 at Bekalta (Tunisia). **Son** of Chadli Boukris (former head-master) **and** Mrs. Salam **Dougui. Married** to Nirvah Legros on October 17, 1965, 2 **children:** Alya and Samia. **Educ.:** Lycée Carnot, Tunis (Tunisia); School of Mines, Paris (France). **Dipl.:** B.Sc. (Mining Engineering). **Career:** Manager, Khalaa Djerda Phosphate Mines (1961-63); Manager, Metlawi Mine Workings (1963-68); General Technical Manager, Compagnie des Phospates SFAX GAFSA (1969); Chairman, Compagnie des Phosphates de Gafsa (1969); Chairman, Industries Chimiques Maghrébines (I.C.M.), Société Industrielle d'Acide Phosphorique et d'Englais (S.I.A.P.E.), Gabès Chimie Transport (G.C.T.) (1970-75); Chairman, I.C.M. and G.C.T. (1976); Chairman, I.C.M. S.A.E.P.A. and S.I.A.P.E. (1979). **Awards:** Officer, Order of the Republic. **Prof. Addr.:** 7, Rue du Royaume d'Arabie Saoudite, Tunis, Tunisia. **Priv. Addr.:** Hauts de Gammarth, La Marsa, Tunisia.

BOULARES (Habib), Tunisian Journalist and Writer. **Born** in 1933 at Tunis. **Educ.:** Secondary and higher. **Career:** Journalist, Editor ASSABAH (1955-57); Director Tunis Radio and Television (1962-64); Director and founder of agence Tunis-Afrique Presse (1961-62); Chief of Press of Destour Socialist Party (1964-67); Minister of Information and Culture (1970-71); Minister of Foreign Affairs (1990); Minister of Defence (1991); President of the National Assembly, since October 1991. **Addr.:** National Assembly, Tunis, Tunisia.

BOULOS (Antoine, Abdulmassih), Egyptian physician. **Born** on December 29, 1927 in Cairo. **Son** of Abdulmassih Boulos (Merchant) **and** Mrs. Gamila Massabki. **Educ.:** Maronite Secondary School, Ain Shams University (Faculty of Medicine). **Dipl.:** M.B.B. Ch., (Doctor of Medicine and Surgery), Ain Shams University (1956), Diploma of Physical Medicine (1961). **Career:** First Physical Medicine Specialist in the Middle East, Combines knowledge of Physical culture with physical medicine experience and practice of cure of the crippled and patients needing Physical Therapy treatment, Owner of a Gymnasium for Physical Culture. **Sports:** Physical culture, tennis, squash, etc... **Hobbies:** Physical culture and special interest in Psychology and Mental diseases. **Member** Gezira Sporting Club and Heliolido Club. Honorary member of all Egyptian Clubs. **Remark:** "Mr. World" Winner in France of "Le plus bel Athlete du Monde" (1954), Runner up Class I "Professional Mr. Universe" in London (1960). **Prof. Addr.:** Handicapped Children Hospital, 435, Talaat Harb Street, Cairo, Tel.: 745220, 755476, 755235 (Egypt), Gymnasium: 12, Naguib ar-Rihani Street, Tel.: 78234, Cairo (Egypt). **Priv. Addr.:** 37, Qasr an-Nil Street, Tel.: 78234, Cairo, Egypt.

BOUMAHDI (Ali), Algerian professor and man of letters. **Born** in 1934 in Berrouaghia. **Educ.:** Secondary and Higher. **Dipl.:** Licentiate of letters, Diploma of English higher studies. **Career:** Man of Letters professor of

French language in Algiers. **Publ.:** Author of many studies and articles as well as a novel "Le village des Asphodèles" (in French language, 1970). **Addr.:** Algiers, Algeria.

BOUMIZA (Salem), Tunisian academic. **Born** on May 6, 1943 at Wardanine (Tunisia). **Educ.:** Faculty of Letters, Tunis University. **Dipl.:** B.A. **Career:** Teacher (1969-74); Governor of Mednine (1974-78); Director-General of State Broadcasting and TV Service, Tunis, (1978-84). **Publ.:** Author of "Les Arabes et les Contraintes de la Civilisation", "Discours du Voyageur". **Awards:** Commander, Order of Independence and of the Republic. **Sports:** Football and swimming. **Prof. Addr.:** Tunis, Tunisia.

BOURAOUI (Sadek), Tunisian official. **Born** in 1941 in Sousse, Tunisia. **Educ.:** Studies in Engineering. **Career:** Engineer at the Ministry of Public Works; Director General, State Public Works and Construction Co. (SOMATRA) (1971-73); Director General of National Tourist Office (1973-); Chairman of Tunis Air (1978-79), Chairman of SEREPT Co. for petroleum exploration and research (1979-80), COFIT Co. for Financing and Development of Tunisia and real estate (1980); Chief Executive and Managing Director of National Bank for Tourist Development (1984). **Prof. Addr.:** Tunis, Tunisia.

BOURGUIBA (Habib Junior), Tunisian statesman. **Born** on April 9, 1927 in Paris. **Son** of President Habib Bourguiba. **Married** on December 9, 1954 to Neila Zoviten, 3 children: Mouez (1956), Mahdi (1959), Merian (1963). **Educ.:** Sadiki College of Tunis, Lycée of Dijon, Faculty of Law, Paris and Grenoble. **Dipl.:** First Part of Baccalaureat, Sadiki College (1945); Second Part Philosophy (June 1948); Bachelor of Law (Faculty of Law), Paris-Grenoble (June 1954); **Career:** Lawyer in training (1954-56); Chief of the Cabinet of the Minister of Foreign Affairs (1956); Special Mission to Indonesia and Malaysia (1957); Tunisian Ambassador to Rome (1957-58); Represented Tunis at the Sub-committee for Laos of the Security Council of United Nations (1959); Ambassador to Paris (1958-61); Special Mission to Congo (1960); Ambassador to Washington, Ottawa, Mexico (1961-63); Special Mission to Argentine (1963); General Secretary of the Presidency of Republic (1964-70); in charge of missions at Dar As-Salam to the OAU (February 1964), at Dakar (April 1964), at New Delhi and Middle East (May 1964), at Morocco (June 1964); Elected member of the Central Committee of the Destourian Socialist party at the Congress of Bizerte (1964); Member of the Political Bureau of the Party (November 11, 1964); Assistant General Secretary of same Bureau; Former Secretary of State for Foreign Affairs of Republic of Tunis; Member of the Upper Chamber of Tunisian Parliament; Deputy for Mahdia November 8, 1964; Mayor of Monastir; Minister of Justice (1970); Special Adviser to the President (April 1980); former Chairman and General Manager, Tunisian Bank of Economic Development and Novotel Tunisie; Chairman and Managing Director of numerous companies; President, Export Promotion Centre; Director, Banque Internationale Arabe de Tunisie. **Awards:** Grand Cordon de l'Indépendance et de la République and many other foreign decorations. **Remark:** Participate in all regular and special sessions of the United Nations and the OAU. **Prof. Addr.:** 68 Avenue du 7 Novembre, Tel.: 245600, Tunis, Tunisia. **Priv. Addr.:** Villa Dar Es-Salaam, La Marsa, Tunisia.

BOURI (Abdul Rahman, al-Tohami, al), Moroccan engineer. **Born** on January 10, 1935, in Fez, Morrocco. **Educ.:** in Paris, France (1960); University of Rabat (1968); National School of Management and Economis. Paris (1972). **Career:** Electricity and Water Distribution Manager in Casablanca (1960); Manager of the Planning Department at the Ministry of General Works (1967-69); Deputy of the National Bureau for Drinking Water (1978-80); Arab Representative of the Official Committee for Arab Europeen Discussions (1983); President of the General Council for Supplies (1983); Director C.I.D. (Conseil, Ingenierie et Developpement). **Award:** Order of the Throne, Moroccan Council of State (1983). **Prof. Addr.:** P.O.Box 802, Rabat, Morocco.

BOURICHA (Abdelrazzak), Tunisian academic. **Born** on December 13, 1929 in Sfax, Tunisia. **Educ.:** University of Paris. **Dipl.:** Degree in mathematics. **Career:** Professor of Physical Chemistry (1953-67); Headmaster of a senior School (1967-74); Managing Director and Chairman, Société Industrielle des Articles Métalliques (SIAM), (1974). **Prof. Addr.:** SIAM, Route de Gabes km3, 3028 Sfax, Tunisia. **Priv. Addr.:** Route de Soutera Km4, 3063 Sfax, Tunisia.

BOURJINI (Salah), Tunisian economist. **Born** on January 17, 1938 (Tunis) Civil Status. **Married,** 3 children. **Languages:** Arabic, French, English. **Education:** Diploma Engineer Statistics and Planning, MA and PHD in Economics. **Career:** Engineer Ministry of Planning (1963-67); Professor School of Cooperation (1964-67); Lecturer University of Kansas (1969-72); Professor Faculty of Law and Economics, Tunis (1972-80); Advisor Minister of Economy, Tunis (1972-75); Deputy Director General of International Cooperation Ministry of Foreign Affairs (1976-80); Deputy UN Resident Representative and UN Coordinator Algeria (1980-82); Chief Division for Regional Programme for Arab States UNDP- New York (1982-87); UN Resident Representative and UN Coordinator Iraq (1987-92); UN Resident Representative and UN Coordinator Lybia (1992 till Now). **Member** of Association of American Economists, Member of Tunisian Economists Association. **Medals:** Medal Knight of the Order of Tunisian Republic (1978), Decorated by Tunisian Association of Blinds. **Address and Telephone Nos.** Salah A. Bourjini, UNDP-Tripoli-Lybia, P.O.Box 1608 GR CNTR STA, NY New York 10163-1608, Tel.: 218-21-3330855/52/53/54,

Fax: 218-21-3330856, SATELITE Tel.: 871-1506414, Fax: 871-1506415.

BOUSAIDI (Riad, Abdalla, al), Omani banker. **Born** in 1942 in Zanzibar. **Married**, 4 children. **Educ.:** Prague University, Czechoslovakia. Leeds University, UK (post-graduate sttudies in Economics). **Dipl.:** Degree in Sociology. **Career:** Assistant Manager, Bank of Credit and Commerce, London (1973-77); Contracts and Funds Management Controller, Gulf Air (1977-79); Member of the Board of Directors of Gulf Hotel, Bahrain (1979-81); Corporate Planning Manager, Gulf Air (1980-81); Assistant General Manager, al-Bahrain Arab African Bank (1982); Member of the ISIS Association, UK (1983-), Institute of Directors, UK (1983-); Former Deputy General Manager, Oman Aviation Services Co. SAO. **Hobbies:** Reading, history, swimming and philately. **Addr.:** Muscat, Oman.

BOUSAIDI (Salim, Bin Nasr, al), Omani statesman. **Born** in 1933. **Career:** Petroleum Development (Oman) (1970); attended a series of courses in the UK (1971-72); Director General of Civil Aviation; Under Secretary, Ministry of Communications (1975); Minister of Communications (1978-86); Director, Gulf Air, Bahrain; former Chairman, Oman Arab Bank SAO; Director, Consolidated Contractors Oman LLC; Director, Gulf Hotels Oman Co. SAO; former Chairman, Oman United Insurance Co. SAO. **Addr.:** P.O.Box 4522 Ruwi, Oman.

BOUSNINA (Mongi), Tunisian Academic, Ambassador of Tunisia in France. **Born** on March 4, 1944 in Tunis, Tunisia. **Son** of Abderrazzak Bousnina, **and** Mrs. Bahia. **Married** to Miss Lilia Houidi, 3 children: Sophia (Mrs. Sahbi Fekihj), Mehdi, Emna. **Educ.:** College Sadiki, Tunis (Tunisia), Lycée Henri IV, Paris (France), Ecole Normale Supérieure de Saint-Cloud, Université de Paris I - Pantheon Sorbonne. **Dipl.:** Master of Geographis-History, Doctorate (3rd cycle) in Geography. Doctorat d'Etat ès lettres and Human Sciences. **Career:** Lecturer at Université de Tunis (1970); Director of Cabinet, Minister of National Education, then of Information and Culture, Secretary of State of National Education (1990); Minister of Culture (1991-95); Ambassador in Morocco (1995-96); in France (since 1996). **Works:** "Etude de la croissance urbaine de la banlieue" (Tunisia), "Développement Scolaire et disparités régionales" (Tunisia), "Le Réseau d'éducation prescolaire" (Tunisia), "Le Réseau scolaire tunisien", "Géographie scolaire de l'Algérie", "Croissance régionale de la population tunisienne (from 1956 to 1980); "Les Chances d'accès des jeunes aux différents niveaux d'enseignement" (Tunisia), "Les Relations formation-emploi in tunisia", "Situation et perspectives du secteur de l'information in Tunisia" (1986), "L'Information Culturelle in Tunisia" (1987). **Decor.:** Grand Commander, Order of the Tunisian Republic; Commander, Order of 7 November of the Tunisian Republic and Order Alouite (Morocco). **Hobbies:** Music, Reading. **Member** of Rotary Club (Tunisia). **Prof, and Private Addr.:** Embassy of Tunisia, 25 rue Barbet de Jouy, 75007 Paris, France.

BOUTAIB (Muhammad Ben Mohamed), Moroccan businessman. **Born** on March 25, 1926 in Casablanca, Morocco. **Married**, 5 sons, 1 daughter. **Educ.:** Ecole Professionnelle d'Electricité Camille Mathieu. **Career:** Managing Director and Chairman of Electro-Koutoubia (1962-). **Prof. Addr.:** 100, rue Jaafar Al Barmaki, Casablanca, Morocco; **Priv. Addr.:** 1 Rue Chemin Fleuri Ermitage, Casablanca, Morocco.

BOUTAIBA (Belgasim Saad), Algerian official. **Born** in 1945 in Sidi Aissa, Algeria. **Married**, 3 children. **Educ.:** Ecole Nationale d'Administration, Algiers. **Career:** Administrator, Wilaya of Tiziouzou (1971-73); Vice Director, Wilaya of Annaba (1973-74), Director of Local Regulation and Administration (1974-79); Head Daira of the Wilaya of Tebessa (1980-82), Wilaya of el-Aoumt (1983-84), Wilaya of Sidi Obha (1984); Secretary General, Wilaya of Mostaganem (1984). Active in the FLN party. **Addr.:** Mostaganem, Algeria.

BOUTALEB (Abdelhadi), Moroccan Official. **Born** on December 23, 1923 in Fez, Morocco. **Son** of Mohammad Boutaleb **and** Mrs. Fatima Boutaleb. **Married** in 1946 to Touria Chraibi, 3 children: Majid, Amina, Saad. **Educ.:** Received his BA Law from Al Qarawiine University (1943). **Career:** From 1944 to 1948 he tutored His Majesty King Hassan II, then Crown Prince; In 1948 was a founding member of the Shura and Istiqlal Party and also member of its political bureau until 1959. In the meantime, he was chief editor of Ar-Ra'y al-'Am (Public Opinion) Newspaper; in 1951, he was a member of the Moroccan delegation which raised the question of national independence at a United Nations meeting, at «Palais Chaillot» in Paris; In addition he was a leading resistance member who fought french colonialism when the french drove the late King Mohammed V into exile; From August 1953 to February 1954, he was placed under house arrest in Casablanca, then he went to Paris, heading the Moroccan delegation to stimulate awareness within french parliamentary and political circles about the need for independence. In the process, he held a number of news conferences and provided the french press with his writings; In 1955, he took part in the Aix-Les-Bains negociations pertaining to the country's independence and the return of the late King Mohammed V to his homeland; He was a member of the National Delegation which made the first contact with the late King while in exile in Antserabe in Madagascar, and worked out together a political course of action designed to speed up His Majesty's return to Morocco and the recognition by France of the country's independence. **From 1955 till nowadays:** When the late King eventually returned to his homeland, he held a number of government positions in addition to conducting other political activities. On December 1955, he was appointed by His Majesty the late King Mohammed V Minister of Labour and Social Affairs in the first post-independence cabinet up to October 1956; He was involved in the setting up of the Union Nationale des Forces Populaires (UNFP) party, and became one of its secretaries generals (from 1959 to 1960); Represented Morocco at the Conference of African Peoples Held in Tunis (January 1960); Appointed Ambassador to Damascus (1961) then he became Minister of Information, Youth and Sports; Minister of the Sahara and Mauritania; Minister responsible to the prime minister; government spokesman to parliament; then Minister of Justice; From 1966 to 1969 he became successively Minister of Education, Minister of State and Foreign Minister; Elected President of Parliament (1970); Lecturer at Rabat's Faculty of Law (1971); Appointed Ambassador to Washington and Mexico (1974); Appointed Advisor to His Majesty King Hassan II (1976); Appointed Minister of Information (1978); He has been lecturing at Casablanca's Faculty of Law and Constitutional law and political institutions (from 1979 till 1982); Elected Director General of the Islamic Educational, Scientific and Cultural Organization -ISESCO- Rabat, Morocco (May 1982); Lecturer at Rabat's Faculty of Law, and is still acting as such (Political Regimes in the Third World) (1982); he became member of the Royal Academy for Islamic Civilization Research-Al Albait Foundation- Jordan (October 1982); Admitted to the Royal Academy of Morocco (November 1982); Elected by the Islamic Conference Vice-President of the International Commission for the Preservation of Islamic Cultural Heritage presided over by Prince Fayçal Ibn Fahd (November 1983); Awarded the Supreme Distinction of Merit of the Kingdom of Morocco (March 1990); Appointed advisor to His Majesty King Hassan II (December 1991). **Publ.:** Author of a number of publications in literature, History, Politics and Law, chief among which are: «The vizir of Granada» (from Lissan Eddine Ibnul Khatib); «My course» (a collection of political articles); «Between Arab nationalism and Islamic solidarity»; «From a political to a social revolution»; «Constitutional law and political institutions: A reference book» (2 volumes); «Contemporary world political systems», in Arabic (1981) and French (1986); «The Islamic Revival» (1986); «Outlooks on the Arabic cause», in Arabic (1987) and French (1990); «Memories, Testimonies and Faces» (1993) (2 volumes); «Position of the Islamic World vis-à-vis civilizational dialogue»; Unity of the Islamic world between theory and practice»; «Rule, Authority and the State in Islam»; «Role of Education in the Development of the Islamic world and Promotion of its solidarity»; «Shari'ah, Fiqh and Law»; «The salafiyya as a prospective movement»; «Role of Information in taking up the Challenges facing the Islamic world»; «Democracy and Shurah (Consultation)»; «Human rights in Islam and the spiritual dimension in the Developmental process». **Decor.:** Commander of the Throne of Morocco; Grand Cordon of the Republic of U.A.R. and other decorations from many African and Arabic Countries. **Sports:** Golf, Swimming. **Hobbies:** Music, reading, sports. **Prof. Addr.:** Royal Cabinet, Tel.: 07.77.22.55, Rabat, Morocco.

BOUTALEB (Abdul Hafid), Moroccan politician. **Born** on June 30, 1928 in Fes, Morocco. **Married. Dipl.:** Licence in Law, Degrees in History, Geography and Arts. **Career:** called to the Bar in Casablanca; Member of the Moroccan delegations to negotiate independence agreements with France and Spain; Director of Cabinet, Ministry of Administrative Affairs (1958), Director of Administrative Affairs (1959-60), Director of Royal Cabinet (1964); Under Secretary, Ministry of the Interior (1964); Minister of Labour and Social Affairs (1965), Minister of Public Works and Communications (1968), Minister of Justice (1969); Minister of Labour, Employment and Vocational Training (1969). **Decor.:** from Tunisia, Egypt, Liberia and West Germany. **Addr.:** 8 Rue Tedders, Rabat, Morocco.

BOUTEFLIKA (H.E. Abdelaziz), President of Algeria. **Born** on March 2, 1937 at Tlemcen, Oran, Algeria. **Educ.:** Faculty of Letters, Algiers University. **Career:** Sectional Secretary-General, General Union of Algerian Muslim Students (UGEMA); Commandant, Algerian Resistance in Wilaya 5-Oran, and at Oujda (1956), Member, Central Committee and Political Bureau, National Liberation Front (FLN) (1959-60); Secretary General, National Liberation Army (ALN), General Staff, Ghardimaou, Tunisia; Member, FLN delegations to Guinea and Mali; served in Sahara at time of Independence; spokesman for Late Colonel Boumedienne; Minister of Youth and Sports, first Ben Bella Government; Minister of Foreign Affairs (September 1963); Rapporteur, Council of Ministers, Organization of African Unity (OAU) Dakar, Senegal (1963); Chief Delegate to Second UNCTAD Conference, New Delhi (1968); President, Council of Ministers, OAU, Algiers (1968); Chief of Delegation, UN General Assembly, New-York, USA (1963); Chief Delegate, Economic and Social council (ECOSOC), UN, Geneva (1973); Chief Delegate of Algeria to Third UNCTAD Conference, Santiago, Chile (1972); President, Conference of Ministers of Non-Aligned Countries, Algiers (1972-73); Delegation of Algeria to Summit Conference of Heads of Arab States (1962-73); Chief Delegate, Conference of Ministers of Islamic Countries (1972-74); President, UN General Assembly (1974); Counsellor to the President Benejedid Chadli (1979). Elected President of Algeria on April 15,1999. **Awards:** Several decorations from African Countries. **Addr.:** President Palace, Algiers, Algeria.

BOUTROS-GHALI (Boutros), Egyptian secretary general of the french speaking Association ("Francophone") and former secretary general of the United Nations. **Born** on November 14, 1922 in Cairo. **Son** of Yusuf Boutros-Ghali **and** Mrs. Safeya Mikhail Charobim. **Dipl.:** LL.B., Cairo University (1946); Dipl. of Higher Studies in Public

Law, Paris University (1948); Dipl. of Higher Studies in Economics, Paris University (1948); Dipl. of the Political Science Institute, Paris University (1949); Ph.D. in International Law, Paris University (1949). **Career:** Professor at Cairo University since 1949; Ful-bright Research Scholar, Columbia University, New York (1954-55); Associate Director of the First Dag Hammarshold Seminar; Director of the Centre of research of the Hague Academy of International Law (1967-69); Lecturer on International Law and International Relations in various Universities and Institutes including Columbia University, New York; Princeton University, New Jersey; New Delhi Institute of International Relations, Warsaw Institute of International Relations, Geneva University, Algiers University, Dakar University, Dar Es Salam University, Nairobi University, etc... Participated in Conference of Government Experts on the reaffirmation and development of International Humanitarian Law applicable in armed conflicts, Geneva (May- June 1972); Conference de l'Académie Mondiale pour la Paix, Menton (7-11 January 1974); Conférence Mondiale des Chrétiens pour la Palestine, Geneva (11-14 January 1974); Christian Peace Conference on the Middle East, Cairo, (23-27 April 1974); Conference organized by the Instituto Affari Internazionali on Cooperation and Development in the Mediterranean Area, Milan (3-4 May 1974); United Nations Seminar on the Promotion and Protection of Human Rights of National, ethnic and other minorities, Ohrid (Yugoslavia) (25 June- 8 July 1974); Seminar of the International Relations, Institute of Cameroon, Yaoundé (September 16- 23 1974); Afro-Arab Symposium on Liberation and Development, Khartoun (7-11 January 1976); Seminar on the role of non-alignment in a changing world, India International Centre, new Delhi (April 26-29, 1976); UNESCO Peace Forum on the Social and Human Sciences and the Problem of Peace, UNESCO House, Paris (3-6 May 1976); Arab and American Cultures, a conference sponsored by the American Enterprise Institute for Public Policy Research, Washington D.C. (September 23-24, 1976); Afro-Arab Symposium, Sharjah (U.A.E.) (December 1976); Conférence de l'Académie Mondiale pour la Paix: les guerres civiles (January 1977); International Conference on Development and Stability in the Mediterranean sponsored by the Instituto Affari Internazionali, Athens; Appointed Minister of State for Foreign Affairs (Oct. 1977- May 1991); on November 19, 1977 accompanied President Sadat to Jerusalem on the first leg of a drawn-out diplomatic process designed to establish just and lasting peace between the Arab countries and Israel through negotiations; attended the Camp David Summit meeting between President Sadat, President Carter and Israeli Premier Menahem Begin; Minister of State for Foreign Affairs (1988-91); Deputy Prime Minister for International Affairs and Minister of State for Immigration and Egyptian Expatriates (May 1991- Nov. 1991); Elected Secretary General of the United Nations (Nov. 1991). Presently Secretary General of the Union of Francophony (French Speaking Countries). **Publ.:** Author of "Contribution à l'Etude des Ententes Régionales" (1949), XV Editions A. Pedone, Paris; "Cours de Diplomatie et de Droit Diplomatique et Consulaire", Anglo-Egyptian Library, Cairo; "Les Problèmes du Canal de Suez" (1957); "Egypt and the United Nations" in collaboration with the Carnegie Endowment for International Peace, New York (1957); "Le Principe d'Egalité des Etats et les Organisations Internationales" (1961); "Foreign Policy in a World of Change", Harper and Row, New York (1963); "Contribution à une Théorie Générale des Alliances", Editions A. Pedone, Paris (1963); "L'Organisation de l'Unité Africaine" Librairie Armand Colin, Paris (1969); "Le Mouvement Afro-Asiatique", Presses Universitaires de France, Paris (1969); "Les Difficultés Institutionelles du Panafricanisme", Geneva (1971); "La Ligue des Etats Arabes", Leyden, The Netherlands; "Les Conflits de Frontières en Afrique", Paris (1973); in addition to well over 100 articles on foreign policy problems published in specialised journals. **Priv. Addr.:** 2, Al-Nil Avenue, Giza, Cairo, Egypt.

BOUTROS-GHALI (Youssef, Dr.), Egyptian Minister of the Economy. **Born** on August 20, 1952 in Cairo, Egypt. **Languages:** Arabic, English, French, Italian, Spanish Portuguese. **Academic Degrees:** Ph.D. in Economics, Massachusetts Institute of Technology, Cambridge Mass 1981; B.Sc. in economics, Cairo University, 1974. **Present and Former Positions:** Minister of the Economy (1999-). Minister of State for Economic Affairs; Minister of State for International Cooperation (October 1993- January 1996); Minister of State at the Council of Ministers (April 1993-October 1993); Economic Advisor to the Prime Minister (1986-1993); Economic Advisor to the Governor of the Central Bank of Egypt (1991-1993); Associate Professor of Economics, Faculty of Economics and Political Science, Cairo University (1988-1993); Director of the Center for Economic Analysis, Council of Ministers (1991-1993); Member of the Board of Directors, National Bank of Egypt (1991-1993); Lecturer in Macroeconomic Theory, American University in Cairo (1987-1988); Senior Economist, International Monetary Fund, Washington D.C. (1981-1986); Research Assistant, Massachusetts Institute of Technology, Cambridge Mass (1979-1981); Teaching Assistant, Faculty of Economics and Political Science, Cairo University (1974-1975). **Publications:** "Recent International Developments and the North South Dialogue", in From the Debt Crisis to Sustainable Development G. Vaggi (cd) Macmillan Press, February 1993; "Egypt's 1991 Paris Club Agreement: Theoretical Foundations and Financial Implications" (in Arabic), forthcoming, L'Egypte Contemporaine, Revue Trimestrielle de la Société Egyptienne d'Economie Politique, de Statistique et de Legislation; "Exchange and Monetary Policies, New Tools for New Environment" Business Monthly, May 1991; "The Mechanics of Inflation with an Incomplete Information Set An Attempt at Theory" (in Arabic). Symposium on "Inflation: Problems and Solutions". The Center of Economic and Financial Research and Studies (CEFRS) February 1990 Published in Inflation in Egypt. H. Kheir El Din (ed), CEFRS, Cairo 1991; "Egypt's External Debt Problem: Elements of a Solution". Working Papers in Economics, The Center of Economic and Financial Research and Studies (CEFRS), December, 1989; "An Egyptian Proposal for third World Debt Relief" Internal Working Papers, Council of Ministers, Cairo 1989; "The OAU and Multilateral Aspects of African Debt" Silver Jubilee Celebration of the OAU, Cairo, January, 1988; "The Programs of the International Monetary Fund Theory and Practice" (in Arabic). Symposium on "Structural Adjustment Policies and the Elimination of Economic Constraints". The Center of Economic and Financial Research and Studies, February, 1988; Contemporaine, Revue Trimestrielle de la Société Egyptienne d'Economie Politique, de Statistique et de Legislation, February, 1991; "Credit Markets in Rural Economics. The Invisible Hands", L'Egypte Contemporaine. Revue Trimestrielle de la Société Egyptienne d'Economie Politique, de Statistique et de Legislation, July, 1988; "Private Land Ownership in Hydraulic System: Egypt of the Nineteenth Century". L'Egypte Contemporaine, Revue Trimestrielle de la Société Egyptienne d'Economie Politique, de Statistique et de Legislation, January, 1988; "Fiscal Discipline and Exchange Market Reforms" Aujourd'hui l'Egypte, September 1987; "Dettes du Tiers-Monde: Theorie et Pratique". Aujourd'hui l'Egypte, June 1987; "The Solution to Third World Indebtedness: Rescheduling of Forgiveness", Al Siyassa Al Dawlliya, October 1986; "Foreign Exchange, Black Markets and Currency Substitution". MIT Working Papers, 1984; "Analysis of the Government Financial Management System in Bahrain" (with others). International Monetary Fund, 1982; Labor Force Growth Employment and Earnings in Egypt 1966-1986" The World Bank, 1981; "Essays on Structuralism and Development". Ph.D. Dissertation, Massachusetts Institute of Technology, 1981; "Basic Needs in Macroeconomics: The Case of Egypt" (with L. Taylor) Journal of Policy Modeling, 1980; "Picture of Egypt's Future: A Dynamic Analysis of Sectoral Development" (with R. Eckaus). MIT Working Papers, 1980; "Computable General Equilibrium Models An Application to Egypt" (with others). MIT Working Papers, 1979. **Address:** Minister's Office, Cairo, Egypt.

BOUZIRI (Najib), Tunisian politician. **Born** on September 3, 1925 in Tunisia. **Educ.:** La Sorbonne (Paris) and Higher School of Political Science. **Dipl.:** Licentiate of Law, Diploma of the Institute of Political Studies in Paris, Diploma of Higher Studies in Public Law and Private Law. **Career:** Joined Neo-Destour Party (now Destour Socialist Party) 1941; Member of Central Committee since 1964; Practised Law in France; Member Tunisian Delegation autonomy negotiations (1954-55); Served with Home and Foreign Ministers (1955-56); Chargé d'Affaires in Paris (1956); Director of Cabinet Foreign Affairs Ministry (1957-58); Chargé d'Affaires then Ambassador to Italy (1958-61), to German Federal Republic (1961-64); Secretary of State for Post Telegraph and Telephone (February-November 1964); 2nd Vice-President of National Assembly (1964); Ambassador to U.S.S.R. (March 1965), concurrently to Poland (February 1967) **Member** and Head Delegation to the Conference of the Law of the Seas (Geneva 1960), Member of Tunisian Delegation to the General Assembly of the U.N., Head of Tunisian Delegation to the Conference for Diplomatic relations and immunity (Vienna 1961). **Addr.:** Ministry of Foreign Affairs, Tunis, Tunisia.

BRAHAM (Maloum, Ould), Mauritanian politician. **Born** in 1930 in Mauritania. **Educ.:** Rosso and William Ponty Schools. **Dipl.:** School leaving certificate. **Career:** Teacher, Nema (1951-54); Boutilimit (1954-56); Headmaster, Tidjika and Kiffa (1957-63); Inspector of Primary Education (1963-66); Minister of Foreign Affairs (Feb.-Oct. 1966); Minister of Rural Economy (1966-67); Minister of Commerce, Transport and Tourism (1967-68); Guardian of the Seals and Minister of Justice (1968-73); Minister of Handicrafts and Tourism (1973); former Minister of Justice. **Prof. Addr.:** Nouakchott, Mauritania.

BRAHIMI (Abdelhamid), Algerian politician. **Born** on April 2, 1936. **Married,** 1 child. **Dipl.:** Ph.D. in Economics. **Career:** worked for the resistance forces during war of independence; Governor of Annaba (1963-65); Director, Franco-Algerian Industrial Cooperation (1968-70); Lecturer, Algiers University (1970-73); Sonatrach Representative in the USA (1976-79); Minister of Regional Planning and Development (1979-81); Acting Member of the Political Bureau (1984-88); Prime Minister (1984-89). **Prof. Addr.:** London, U.K.

BRAHIMI (Brahim), Algerian politician. **Born** on January 1, 1935. **Married,** 9 children. **Career:** held various positions at the Ministry of National Defence; Commander of Operational Units on the Suez Canal, Egypt (1967-68); High Commissioner, National Service (1973); Member of the Central Committee, FLN (1979); Secretary of State for Forestry (1979-80); Minister of Hydraulics (1980-84). **Prof. Addr.:** Algiers, Algeria.

BREHRI (Abdelhak), Algerian politician. **Born** in 1940. **Married,** 5 children. **Career:** Rector, Constantine University (1972-77); Member, Central Committee FLN (1979), Vice President, Social and Economic Commission, FLN; Director, Constantine University Research Centre for Study and Realization; Professor, Faculty of Medicine; Minister of Higher Education and Scientific Research (1979), Vice President of Algerian-USSR Friendship Association; Minister of Higher Education (1984-87); Minister of Youth and Sport (1988- September 1989). **Prof. Addr.:** Algiers, Algeria.

BREISH (Abdulmagid), Libyan banker. **Born** in 1951 in Tripoli, Libya. **Son** of Abdussalam Breish. **Married** in

1981. **Educ.:** Tripoli College, and Choueifat School, Lebanon; American University of Beirut; Financial Analysis and Policy, International Monetary Fund, Washington (1977). **Dipl.:** B.A. (1971). **Career:** Libyan Arab Foreign Bank Manager, Equity Participations, Tripoli (1975-77), Assistant to the Chairman (1977-80); Assistant Vice President, Business Development, Arab Banking Corporation, Bahrain (1980-1983); Vice-President, Arab Banking Corporation (1983-84); Director, ABC International Limited, London (1984); former managing Director, ABC Investment and Banking Services Co. EC, Bahrain. **Sports:** Water Sports, Horse Riding and Tennis. **Addr.:** Manama, Bahrain.

BRENI (Ageli), Libyan bank director. **Born** in 1943, Aziza. **Son** of Abdussalam Breni. **Married** in 1973, 3 children. **Educ.:** Benghazi University, Oklahoma State Universiy, USA. **Dipl.:** B.Sc. (Econ.) (1967), M.S. (1977). **Career:** Industrial and Real Estate Bank of Libya (1967-81); Director, Research Dept., Savings and Real Estate Bank Libya since 1981. **Publ.:** Research paper in "Financial Institutions and Industrial Development in Libya" as a part of thesis paper for M.S. **Addr.:** P.O.Box 2297, Tel.: 46031, 41588, Tripoli Libya.

BSEISU (Adnan, Nureddin), Bahraini businessman. **Born** in 1931 in Nablus. **Son** of Noureddin Bseisu. **Married**, 3 children. **Educ.:** American University of Beirut. **Dipl.:** M.A. Economics. **Career:** Assistant Economic Researcher, Economic Research Institute, American University of Beirut (1953-54); Diretor, Economic Research Department, Saudi Arabian Monetary Agency (1954-57); Teacher, al-Maqased College, Beirut (1958-59); Assistant Manager and later Manager, Arab Bank Ltd., Benghazi, Hebron and Bahrain (1959-73); Part time Professor Faculty of Commerce, University of Libya, Benghazi (1959-62); General Manager, Financial Affairs, Gulf Air, Bahrain (1973-80); Adviser, Financial Affairs to the Chief Executive and the Board of Directors, Gulf Air (1981); Assistant General Manager and Chief Executive for Middle East Operations, ARLA Bank (Arab Latin American Bank), Bahrain (1981); served on the Board of Directors of several companies associated with or subsidiaries of Gulf Air (1978-81); Chief Executive, Middle East Consultancy Center, Bahrain. **Member:** Visiting Council, Talal Abu Ghazaleh Graduate School of Business and Management, American University of Beirut; "The Euromarket Institute", Vienna; Financial and Economic Research Committee, Bahrain Chamber of Commerce and Industry; Founder member, Rotary club of Manama (Bahrain). **Publ.:** "Economic Reforms of Mohamed Ali" (B.A. thesis, 1953, AUB); "Monetary Organization in Saudi Arabia" (M.A. thesis, 1958, AUB); several articles relating to Money and Banking in magazines: "Arab Newsweek", "Bahrain Commerce Review", "al-Iktissad Wal Aamal". **Addr.:** P.O.Box 1013, Tel.: 213223, Manama, Bahrain. Fax: 211548, E-Mail: mecon@batelco.com.bh.

BUALLAY (Kassim, Muhammad), Bahraini diplomat. **Born** on March 15, 1942 in Muharraq, Bahrain. **Married**, 4 children. **Educ.:** American University of Beirut, Beirut, Lebanon. **Dipl.:** BBA. **Career:** Superintendent of Bursaries and UNESCO sections, Ministry of Education (1961-70); Member of Bahraini delegation to UNESCO General Conferences in 1966 and 1968. Programme Specialist of the Division of Higher Education, UNESCO, Paris (1970-74); 1st Secretary, Ministry of Foreign Affairs, Bahrain (1974-75); First Chargé d'Affaires, Bahrain Embassy to France (1975-76); First Ambassador to France (1976-79); Director, Economic Affairs Directorate, Ministry of Foreign Affairs, Manama, Bahrain (1979-1987); Ambassador to Tunisia, Algeria and Morocco (1987-1994); Per. Rep. to UN, New York (1994-). **Decor.:** National Order of Merit, France. **Hobbies:** music, théâtre, tennis, swimming. **Member:** Member Alliance Française; Member, La Chaine des Rotisseurs, Bahrain, the Alumni Club. **Prof. Addr.:** Ministry of Foreign Affairs, P.O.Box 547, Manama, Bahrain. & Permanent Mission to the United Nations, Two U.N. Plaza, 25th Floor, New York, N.Y. 10017.

BUALY (Abdul Aziz, Abul Rahman), Bahraini diplomat. **Born** in 1939 in Bahrain. **Married**, 3 children. **Educ.:** University of Baghdad, Iraq; Reading University, UK (graduate studies). **Dipl.:** B.A. **Career:** High School Principal in Bahrain (1969-71); Ministry of Education, then Ministry of Information; Assistant Chief of Protocol at the Ministry of Foreign Affairs; Ambassador to Iran, Ambassador to USA (1967). **Prof. Addr.:** Ministry of Foreign Affairs, Manama, Bahrain.

BUALY (Nassir, Seif, el), Omani former diplomat. **Born** on January 1925 in Dar-es-Salaam, Tanzania. **Married** on 29 February 1957 in Zanaibar to Miss Sharifa al-lamki, 3 children: Ali (1958), Aziza (1959) and Asiya (1962). **Educ.:** College of Arts and Science, Baghdad, Iraq. **Dipl.:** B.A. (Economics) (1954). **Career:** Assistant Inf. Officer (1956-60); Assistant Secretary, Min. of Works and Commerce (1960-63); Principal Sect. Min. of Works and Commerce (1960-63); Principal Sect. Min. of Planning and Development (Sept. 1964- Feb. 1965); Project Economic Analyst (Feb. 1965- Sept. 1968); Senior Admin. (Sept. 1968-70); Director of Information (1971); Director General Information (1972); Ambassador Extraordinary and Plenipotentiary to U.K. (Feb. 1973- May 1980); Head Consular affairs, Ministry of Foreign Affairs, Oman (June 1980); Head of Asian and Australian Affairs (May 1982); former Counsellor at the Sultan Diwan. **Hobbies:** Collection of Books, articles, Refs Stamps, on Oman. **Member** of several clubs and associations. **Credit Cards:** American, Diners Access, Barclay, etc. **Addr.:** Muscat, Oman.

BUANINI (Mohamad, Abdul Salam, al), Moroccan journalist. **Born** in 1929 in Asila, Morocco. **Son** of Abdulsalam al Buanini. **Married**, three children. **Career:** Producer and Director on Paris Radio and Television (1955-64);

Director of Programmes, Moroccan Television in Spain (1964-67); Producer on Moroccan Television (until 1970); Director of Programmes, Moroccan Television (1971); Head of Department and Producer on Moroccan Television; Director of Competitions. **Publ.:** Stories and poetry published in French, Spanish and Arabic magazines. **Member** of Moroccan Writers Union. **Hobbies:** Fishing, poetry, history of civilisation. **Addr.:** 14 Rue Yougoslavie, Rabat, Morocco.

BUBSHAIT (Abdulla, Fouad), Saudi businessman. **Born** on July 22, 1925 in Dammam, Saudi Arabia. **Son** of Abdul Aziz Bubshait (businessman) **and** Mrs. Hessa Yusuf Bubshait is the Mother. **Married** to Mariyam Hassan Sater in 1944 in Bahrain & married to Siham Naqshabandi in 1959 in ALIPO, 10 daughters and 2 sons. **Educ.:** Primary and Secondary in Bahrain. **Career:** Started business in 1947 at Ras Tanura, with contracts for a wide variety of construction projects for corporations such as the Arabian American Oil Company (ARAMCO) and the Trans Arabian Pipeline Company (TAPLINE). Now Abdulla Fouad is a group of companies and joint ventures, covering pipeline contracting, building construction, manufacturing, commercial agencies, medical supply agencies, computer agencies, Toys, educational aids and recreational facilities. **Sports:** Tennis, golf and fishing. **Member:** Aramco Club. **Credit Cards:** American Express, Master Card, Access and Visa. **Addr.:** P.O.Box 257, Dammam 31411, Saudi Arabia, Tel.: (03) 8324400, Fax: (03) 8345722. E-Mail, info@abdulla-fouad.com.

BUBSHAIT (Ahmad, Ibrahim), Saudi executive. **Born** in 1939 at al-Ihsaa, Saudi Arabia. **Educ.:** Faculty of Commerce. **Dipl.:** B.B.A., M.B.A. (Business Administration). **Career:** Training Executive, Aramco (1945-63); Instructor of Accounting and Financial Affairs, Institute of Public Administration (1968-70); Budgeting Executive, Saudi Arabian Airlines Corporation (Saudia) (1972-74); presently Vice-President, Finance and Administration, Saudi Arabian Airlines Corporation. **Publ.:** Author of textbook on Mathematics for the Anti-illiteracy campaign in Saudi Arabia; "Management of Objectives", "Principles of Accounting" and "Financial Mathematics". **Member:** Board of Scholarships Ministry of Education; American Accounting Association; Chartered Auditors Association; American National Accounting Association. **Hobbies:** Reading (particularly classical poetry) and music. **Prof. Addr.:** P.O.Box 620, Tel.: 6860000, Jeddah, Saudi Arabia.

BUDJELLAB (Omar), Algerian physician. **Born** in 1930 in Belcourt, Algeria. **Married**, 3 daughters. **Educ.:** Faculty of Medicine, Sorbonne, University of Paris, France. **Career:** Specialised in cardiology at Franco-Moslem Hospital and qualified as cardiologist; leading cardiologist in Algeria, Mustapha Hospital, Ministry of Public Health (1970-77). **Prof. Addr.:** Ministry of Public Health, Algeria, Algeria.

BUERA (Abubakr, Mustafa), Libyan educator. **Born** in 1941 in Jardinah, Libya. **Married** in 1969 in Benghazi, Libya to Miss Nuria M. Saleh, six children. **Educ.:** University of Libya, University of California, Los Angeles, University of Missouri, Columbia, USA. **Dipl.:** Master's Degree in Business administration (1970); Ph.D. (Business Administration) (1975). **Career:** University professor (since 1970); Chairman, Department of Management (1975-81); Senior Management Adviser, Arab Organisation for Administrative Sciences (1982-84); Chairman, Academic Affairs (1984-85); Dean, Higher Institute for Administrative Sciences (since 1985); Training Director, Arab Organization for Administrative Development (1987-91). **Hobby:** Travel. **Member** of Management Professional Organisation. **Addr.:** P.O.Box 9497, Tel.: (61)28096/ 94359, Benghazi, Libya and Arab Consulting & Training Group, 705-709 Islamic Call Building, P.O.Box 4155, Tel.: 98462, Fax: 94359, Benghazi, Libya.

BUFLASA (Saif Ahmad Muhammad Saif Musbah, al), United Arab Emirates businessman. **Born** in 1945 in Dubai, UAE. **Married**, 1 son, 3 daughters. **Educ.:** Cable and Wireless Institute, Cairo, Egypt; Language studies in United Kingdom. **Career:** Teacher, Ministry of Education, Bahrain; Personnel Department, Shell Company; Customs Official, Abu Dhabi; Secretary, the United Arab Emirates Federal Assembly, Abu Dhabi; Teacher of the Cultural Section, Abu Dhabi Defence Department; Secretary of the Board and Deputy Managing Director of United Arab Emirates Trading Company (a government/public company). **Hobbies:** reading and swimming. **Prof. Addr.:** UAE Trading Co., Abu Dhabi, United Arab Emirates.

BUHUSSAIN (Ahmad, Abdallah), United Arab Emirates Official. **Born** in 1948 in Dubai, United Arab Emirates. **Married**, two children. **Educ.:** Baghdad University, Iraq. **Dipl.:** B.A. in History. **Career:** Head of Cultural Department, Ministry of Education; Administrative Secretary, United Arab Emirates University (1971). **Member:** Executive Committee of the Arab Educational, Scientific and Cultural Organization (1972); Chairman of the Board of the Ahli Club. **Sport:** Table tennis. **Hobbies:** Reading, table-tennis, **Addr.:** Abu Dhabi, United Arab Emirates.

BUKAIR (Abdallah Ahmad), Yemeni physician and former minister. **Born** on March 13, 1941 in Waht, Second Governorate, Republic of Yemen. **Married. Dipl.:** Degree in Medicine, University of Hungary (1963-71). **Career:** Medical Officer, Ministry of Health (1971-73); Director of Health Service, Ministry of Health (1971-79); Minister of Health (1979). **Member:** Executive Board, WHO, Aden; Yemeni Doctors Association. **Hobbies:** Reading and sports. **Addr.:** Aden, Republic of Yemen.

BUKHARI (Dr. Atif Y.), Saudi Assistant Director General/ Regional Representative for the Near East, Food and Agriculture Organization of the United Nations. **Educ.:**

B.Sc. in Agriculture from the University of Cairo (1962); Master's degree (1966); Ph.D. degree in Agriculture from Kansas State University, USA (1972). **Career:** Assistant Professor, Faculty of Agriculture, Riyadh University (1973); Director General, King Faisal Settlement Project (1975); Technical Advisor to the Minister of Agriculture and Water (1978); Ambassador/Permanent Representative to FAO, WFP and IFAD, Rome (1978); Member of the Executive Board and Alternate Governor of IFAD (1978); Member and Chairman FAO Finance Committee, FAO; Committee Member of Food Aid (CFA), Present position since 1990; presently, Assistant Director General/ Regional Representative for the Near East, Food and Agriculture Organization of the United Nations. **Address:** FAO, Near East Regional Office, P.O.Box 2223, Cairo, Egypt.

BULASRI (Muhammad, al-Hussain), Moroccan administrator. **Born** in 1949 in Morocco. **Married**, 2 sons. **Educ.:** Ecole Supérieure des Sciences Sociales, Paris. **Dipl.:** DEA. **Career:** Assistant General Manager, Cooperative Promotion Office (1976-77); Secretary, Moroccan Cooperative for Drug Care; Office Head, Ministry of Social Affairs and Craftwork (1977-79); Director of Social Affairs (1979). **Publ.:** "Agricultural Cooperatives and Economic Social Development", "Studies on the Hamuz Case" (1976). **Addr.:** Rabat, Morocco.

BULTIA (Abdul Latif Miligi), Egyptian politician. **Born** in 1927. **Married. Dipl.:** B.Sc. in Commercial Studies. **Career:** Trade unionist since 1949; elected President of the Misr Insurance Company Union (1952); President of the Insurance Workers' Union (1953); Secretary General, Egyptian Federation of Labour (1961); President, Federation of Labour (1970); Member, International Confederation of the Arab Trade Unions (ICATU) Council; Member, Executive Council of the International Labour Organization; Member of the National Assembly for Helwan (1964) and (1969); Deputy Chairman, All-Africa Trade Unions Federation; elected second Deputy Speaker of the National Assembly (1970); Assistant Secretary for Cairo in the Arab Socialist Union (ASU) and ASU Central Committee (1968); Secretary General of ICATU (1972), visited UK (1968); Minister of Labour (1970), Minister of Manpower (1975), Minister of Manpower and Training (1976); Member of the National Peace Council; Member of the National Democratic Party; Chairman of Local Council, Cairo Governorate (1984). **Addr.:** 1095 Corniche Al-Nile, Garden City, Cairo, Egypt.

BURGAN (Salih Khalil), Jordanian physician, politician and international Civil Servant. **Born** in 1917 in Kerak. **Educ.:** American University of Beirut. **Dipl.:** Doctor of Medicine. **Career:** Physician, Transjordan Frontier Forces (T.J.F.F.) (1943-46); Director of Arab Physicians (T.J.F.F.) (1946-48); private physician at Zerka, Jordan (1948-63); member of Parliament (1961-62), of Senate (1963-69); Minister of Health (1963-64), of Social Affairs and Labour (1966), of Public Health (1966-67), of Social Affairs and Labour and Minister of Interior for Municipal and Rural Affairs (1967-69); Director, International Labour Office, Beirut (1969-77); Assistant Director-General, Geneva (June 1975-96). **Award:** al-Kawkab Medal (First Grade); Grand Knight of the Holy Tomb. **Addr.:** Amman, Jordan.

BURHAN (Hamid, Osman), Sudanese academic. **Born** in 1931 in Sudan. **Son** of Osman Burhan. **Married**, four children. **Educ.:** University of Khartoum, Colorado State University, USA; Arizona State University, USA. BSc Agriculture (1955); M.Sc. in Agronomy (1958); Ph.D. in Agronomy (1963). **Career:** Assistant Inspector of Agriculture (1955-57); Agronomist, Agricultural Research Corporation (1958-65); Senior Agronomist (1965-66); Acting Head, Statistics Section (1965-67); Head, Agronomy and Crop Physiology Section (1966-74); Research Professor of Agronomy (since 1977); Project Manager for UNDP/FAO Wadi Jizan Agricultural Development Project, Saudi Arabia (1975-78); Director General and Chairman of the Board of Directors, Agricultural Research Corporation, Sudan (1978-1981); Professor and Chairman, Crops and Range Dept., College of Agriculture, King Faisal University, Saudi Arabia (1981-1994); Professor of Agronomy, Faculty of Agric., University of Khartoum, Sudan (since 1994-). **Chairman** of several scientific and technical committees in Sudan and other countries. Director FAO Training Center on Statistical Techniques in Agricultural Experimentation, Sudan (1966). **Member** of Honour Society Phi Kappa Phi, USA (1958) and Gamma Sigma Delta, USA (1963). **Publ.:** Research papers and reports on agriculture in "Sudan Agricultural Journal", "Journal of Agricultural Science" Cambridge and other professional magazines in Sudan and abroad. Selected by the International Biographical Centre of Cambridge, England as an International Man of the year for 1996-97. **Sports: Jogging** and football. **Hobbies:** Reading and films. **Prof. Addr.:** P.O.Box 676, Khartoum North, Sudan, Tel.: 313482.

BUSHNAK (Adil Ahmad), Saudi academic and businessman. **Born** in 1947 in Medina, Saudi Arabia. **Dipl.:** Ph.D. in Civil Engineering. **Career:** Lecturer, then Assistant Professor, Faculty of Engineering, King Saud University (1977-84); President and Co-founder, Al-Kawther Co., Jeddah (1984 to present); Director, Saudi Investments Development Centre; Consultant to several government and research organizations. **Publ.:** several technical articles on Transportation of Pilgrims, Decision-Making and Desalination. **Hobbies:** Reading, photography. **Prof. Addr.:** P.O.Box 7771, Tel.: 6360644, Jeddah. **Priv. Addr.:** Tel.: 6370065, Jeddah, Saudi Arabia.

BUZIZI (Mohamed, Jassim), Bahraini hotelier/ businessman. **Born** on December 15, 1945 in Manama, Bahrain. **Son** of Jassim Buzizi **and** Mrs., née Fatima Abdulla.

Educ.: Brighton Technical College, UK. **Dipl.:** In hotels and catering. **Career:** Administration and Public Relations Officer, Kuwait State Office (1970-71); Progressed within the Gulf Hotel from Trainee Manager to Front office Manager, promoted to sales and Public Relations Manager to Director of Sales and Public Relations and from Sept. 1980 promoted to General Manager of Gulf Hotel, March 1990 promoted to General Manager of Bahrain Hotels Company, and in March 1992 he has been appointed Chief Executive of Bahrain Hotels Company to date. **Member:** Skal Club; Hotel Sales; Marketing International. **Credit Cards:** American Express, Visa. **Prof. Addr.:** Bahrain Hotels Company, P.O.Box 580, Manama, Bahrain, Tel.: 726100. **Priv. Addr.:** Tel.: 785444, Manama, Bahrain.

C

CAPOUGI (Hilarion, Bashir, H.E. Mgr.), Syrian Archbishop. **Born** on March 2, 1922 in Aleppo, Syria. **Son** of Bashir Capougi **and** Mrs., née Chafika Rabbath. **Educ.:** Secondary and Philosophy in Aleppo, Theology in St-Anne Seminary of Jerusalem. **Career:** Order of Basilians of Aleppo (1935); Ordained to the priesthood at St-Anne (Jerusalem) on July 20th 1947; Professor at Deir-Ach-Chir Small Seminary (6 years); Principal of An-Nahdat Al-Wataniya School; attached to Deir Ach-Chir Convent; in charge of village parish priests, churches and schools of Damascus (1953-62); Superior of the Basilian Order of Aleppo (July 1962); Raised to the Titular Archbishopric of Caesareum (Palestine); Vicar-General of the patriarchate of Jerusalem (1965); imprisoned and released by the Israeli Government (Nov. 1977). **Works:** Founder of several societies and institutions: the "Flamme" (The Blaze), "Les Colonies de Vacances" (Holiday Camps for Poor Children) etc. **Addr.:** The Vatican, Rome, Italy.

CARAMI (Mohamad, S.), Saudi educator. **Born** in 1946 in Mecca, Saudi Arabia. **Dipl.:** B.A. (Geography) (1966); M.A.T. (Social Studies) (1970) and M.Sc. (Educational Counselling and Guidance) (1972); Oregon College of Education; M.Ed. (Educational Administration) (1972) and Ed.D. (Educational Administration) (1978), University of Cincinnati; Ph.D. (Geography, Urban, Economic and Transportation), University of Kentucky. **Career:** Demonstrator, Faculty of Education, Umm al-Qura University, Mecca; Lecturer and later Assistant Professor, Umm al-Qura University, Mecca; Director, Training Programme Centre, Umm al-Qura University; Assistant Professor, Educational Administration, Umm al-Qura University; member, Committee on Public Services for the City, Mecca Municipality, American Society of Planning Officials, (ASPO), U.S.A., the Association of American Geographers (AAG), U.S.A., the Association of Muslim Social Scientists, National Education Association (NEA), U.S.A., Franklin Geographical Society (FGS), U.S.A.; former member, National Council for Geographic Education (NCGE), U.S.A.; President, the Islamic Association at the University of Cincinnati; Secretary, Organization of Arab Students at the University of Cincinnati and Canada, Muslim Students Association in U.S.A. and Canada, the Association of Arab-American University Graduates (AAUG), U.S.A.; President, the Association for Better Understanding of the Middle East (ABUME), U.S.A.; participated in many academic, educational and scientific conventions; headed King Abdulaziz University Delegation (Sports Group) to visit Omdurman University, Sudan, 1979. **Publ.:** various research papers and articles: The Role of Students' Deanships, presented to Symposium on Students' Deanships of Saudi Arabian Universities, King Abdulaziz University, Jeddah (1979); The Crisis of The Abdulaziz University, Jeddah (1979); The Crisis of The Educational Systems in Contemporary Islamic States, with special reference to Saudi Arabia, a paper presented to the Sixth Annual Convention, the Association of Muslim Social Scientists, Indianapolis (1977); Residential Patterns of Ethnic Groups in Makkah, Saudi Arabia, a paper presented tn the 74th Annual Meeting of the Association of American Geographers, New Orleans (1978); books in preparation: Education in Saudi Arabia, Concepts and Terminology in Geography, Administrative Problems in Saudi Schools. **Hobbies:** stamp and coin collecting. **Prof. Addr.:** P.O.Box 1807, Tel.: 5564770, Mecca. **Priv. Addr.:** Tel.: 5566916, Mecca, Saudi Arabia. Tel.: Office 5564770; Home 5566916, Mecca, Saudi Arabia.

CARPITA (David), Bank Vice-President. **Born** in 1944. **Educ.:** University of Senior Montana, American School of International Management, The Pacific Coast Banking School. **Career:** American Express International Banking Corporation, Germany, Switzerland, Pakistan, and England; Bank of California and Rainer National Bank, Seattle Washington; General Manager and Director Trans-Arabian Investment Bank EC (TAIB), Manama (1982 to date). **Addr.:** Sehl Center, P.O.Box 20485, Tel.: 533334, Manama, Bahrain.

CARTY (John, Alston), American cleric. **Born** on May 6, 1926 at Worcester, Massachussets, USA. **Son** of John A. Carty Sr. **and** Mrs., née Helena Griffin. **Educ.:** Gates Lane Grammar School, Worcester, Mass. (USA) (1932-40); South High School, Worcester (USA) (1940-44); Holy Cross College, Worcester (USA) (1946-48); Weston College, Weston, Mass. (USA) (1951-53 and 1956-60). **Dipl.:** AB in English (1948); M.A. in philosophy (1953); Licentiate in Theology (1960). **Career:** Teacher and administrator, Baghdad College, Baghdad, Iraq (1953-56 and 1961-69); Teacher at College de la Sainte Famille, Cairo, Egypt. **Sports:** Angling and hiking. **Hobbies:** Classical music and reading. **Prof. & Priv. Addr.:** College de la Sainte Famille, Faggalah, Tel.: 900411, Cairo, Egypt.

CATTAN (Khalifa, al), Kuwaiti artist painter. **Born** in 1934 in Kuwait. **Educ.:** Obtained a scholarship for the Fine Arts Faculty of Lister (1958). **Dipl.:** Diploma of Commerce, followed courses at the Faculty of Industry (1962). **Career:** Artist painter, professor of drawing, held 13 exhibitions in Kuwait and foreign countries, and 24 collective exhibitions, Presided the Kuwaiti Association of Fine Arts (1967-70). **Addr.:** Kuwait City, Kuwait.

CHAABAN (Issam, Prof. Dr.), Syrian dentist/ surgeon. **Born** on March 25, 1937 in Syria. **Son** of Mustafa Chaaban (Businessman) **and** Mrs., Fuhmieh Chaaban. **Married** on August 27, 1971 to Miss Rihab Turk, 3 children: Hala (1973), Karim (1978) and Duha (1987). **Educ.:** Dental School, Damascus University (D.D.S.) Syria; Pennsylvania University, Philadelphia, U.S.A. **Dipl.:** Graduate Medical School; M.Sc. in Maxillo-facial Surgery. **Career:** Professor at Damascus University, Syria; Head of Maxillo-facial Department, Dental School (1973-78); Dean of Dental School, Damascus University (1981-86); Currently Chief of Maxillo-facial Department, Al-Tal Hospital, Damascus; Chief of Maxillo-facial Syrian Society. **Sports:** Tennis, squash, swimming. **Hobbies:** Sports, travelling. **Member:** Syrian Dental Association; International Association for Maxillo-facial Surgery. **Credit Card:** American Express. **Prof. Addr.:** Salhieh Street, P.O.Box 2297, Tel.: 2323930, Fax: 2231901, Damascus, Syria. **Priv. Addr.:** Mezzeh, Villa West, Tel.: 6624356, Mobile: 093 214452, Damascus, Syria.

CHAABANE (Sadok), Tunisian Minister of Higher Education. **Born** on February 23, 1950 in Sfax, Tunisia. **Son** of Jilani Chaabane (Agriculturist) **and** Mrs., née Habiba Maalej. **Married** on July 14, 1973 in Tunis to Miss Dalinda Ennouri, 3 children: Skander, Syrine and Yasmine. **Educ.:** Faculty of law and Political Science, Tunis, University of Paris, Sorbonne. **Dipl.:** Doctorate in Public Law; Agregate in Public Law and Political Science. **Career:** Professor (1973-88); Consultant to the Arab League (1979-88); Permanent Secretary of the Party Rassemblement Constitutionnel Democratique (RCD) (1988-89); Secretary of State for Higher Education and Scientific Research (1989). Minister of Justice (1992); presently, Minister of Higher Education. **Sport:** Football. **Decor.:** Order of the Tunisian Republic. **Member:** International law Association. **Prof. Addr.:** Ministry of Higher Education, Ave. Ouled Haffouz, 1005 Tunis, Tunisia. **Priv. Addr.:** Manar 3, M. Jarbou Street, No.30, Tel.: 01239309, Tunisia.

CHAABI (Faisal, Abdullatif, ach), Yemeni statesman. **Born** in the Republic of Yemen. **Son** of Abdullatif ach-Chaabi. **Educ.:** Secondary and Higher. **Career:** Member Executive Committee of NLF; Member of the NLF Delegation to the NLF and FLOSY meetings (1967); Minister of Economy, Commerce and Planning in the 1rst Government after Independence (December 1967). **Addr.:** Aden, Republic of Yemen.

CHAABI (Kahtane, ach), Yemeni Former President of the People's Democratic Republic of Yemen. **Born** in Aden. **Educ.:** Secondary and Higher. **Career:** Statesman, Patriot, Member Executive Committee of NLF, Head of the NLF (National Liberation Front) Delegation to the NLF and FLOSY (Front for the Liberation of occupied South Yemen) meetings (1967), Head of the 1rst State and Supreme Commander of the Armed Forces (December 1967), President of the People's Democratic Republic of Yemen (Nov. 1967- June 1969). **Addr.:** Aden, Republic of Yemen.

CHABAANE (Mahmoud), Tunisian educationalist. **Born** on April 15, 1928. **Educ.:** Sadiki College, Tunis; Ecole Normale d'Instituteurs, High School, University of Southern California (U.S.A.). **Career:** Teacher, Schools' Director, Inspector of Primary Schools, Tunis Regional Inspector of Primary Schools, Tunis. **Member:** Scoutmaster, Tunisian Scouts, Tunisian Nationalist Party, Secretary-General, Young Scholars, President Modern Co-operative Teaching, Secretary-General, Association of School Inspectors. **Publ.:** Author of numerous books on education, children's stories and various articles. **Award:** Gold Knight, Ouissam of Labour; Order of the Tunisian Republic; Ordre du Mérite Libanais. **Addr.:** 2 bis Rue de Cronstadt, Montfleury, Tunis, Tunisia.

CHACCOUR (Yusuf), Syrian army officer. **Born** in 1928 in Homs. **Married**, 4 Children. **Educ.:** Military College (Homs), Specialization in artillery in Chalonssur-Marne, (France 1949) and in the USSR. **Career:** Joined the Syrian Armed Forces; Syrian Consul General to Venezuela and Brazil (1961-64); Director of the Security (1964); Promoted Colonel, then General, then Major General (1970); Chief of Staff of the Syrian Armed Forces (1972); took part in the Arab War against Israel in 1967 and 1973. **Remark:** Fluent in Arabic, French, English, Spanish, Russian and Aramean. **Addr.:** Damascus, Syria.

CHADAREVIAN (Henri), Syrian bank manager. **Born** in 1925 in Aleppo, Syria. **Son** of Dikran Chadarevian. **Married** in 1951, 4 children. **Career:** Banque de Syrie et du Liban, Damascus (1947-56); Banque Centrale de Syrie, Damascus (1956-69); Crédit Populaire d'Algérie, Algeria (1969-74); Manager, Banque du Liban et d'Outre-Mer SAL, Dubai (since 1974). **Sport:** Swimming. **Member:** Leisure Land, Country Club. **Addr.:** P.O.Box 4370, Tel.: 226017, 229877, Dubai, United Arab Emirates.

CHADIRJI (Rifat, Kamil), Iraqi architect. **Born** in 1926 in Baghdad, Iraq. **Married. Educ.:** Diploma in Architecture, Hammersmith School of Arts and Crafts, London. **Career:** Founder, Senior partner and Director of Iraq Consult (since 1952); Section Head, Baghdad Building Department, Waqaf Organisation (1954-57); Director General, Housing Department, Ministry of Planning (1958-59); Head of Planning Committee, Ministry of Housing (1959-63); private practice, Iraq Consult (1963-78); member of Mayor's Council (1958-61); member of

Iraqi Tourist Board (1970-75); Counsellor, Mayoralty of Baghdad (1980-82). **Works:** include Cabinet Ministers' Building, United Arab Emirates, (1978) ; National Theatre Abu Dhabi (1977); al-Ain Public Library, United Arab Emirates (1978). Exhibited at Gulbenkian Hall, Baghdad (1966); University of Khartoum (1966); Ministry of Art and Culture, Accra, Ghana (1966); Middle East Technical University, Ankara, Turkey (1966); Athens Technical Institute, Greece (1966); American University of Beirut (1966); Arab Engineers Conference, Amman, Jordan (1966); Hammersmith College of Arts, London (1966); Ain Shams University, Cairo (1967); Arab Engineers Conference, Kuwait (1975); Kuwait Engineers Union (1975); Iraqi Cultural Center, London (1978); Vienna Technical University, Austria (1978). **Awards:** First Prize for Council of Ministers Building, Baghdad (1975), First Prize for New Theatre, Abu Dhabi (1977); First Price for Council of Ministers' Building, Abu Dhabi (1978) and several awards. Honorary **member** of RIBA; Loeb Fellow, Harvard University. **Hobbies:** Photography, travelling. **Addr.:** Baghdad, Iraq.

CHADLI (Benjedid, Colonel), Algerian former Head of State from Feb. 9 1979 to Jan. 11 1992. **Born** in 1929 in Sebaa, near Constantine in eastern Algeria. **Career:** Fought throughout the campaign against the French; in 1960 he was made commander of the 13th batallion and in June the following year became a member of the general staff of Col. Boumedienne's Army just inside the Tunisian border. As conflicts among the ranks of the guerilla forces grew within Algeria itself Mr. Chadli was sent back to take command of the east of the country where he was taken prisoner by the "Wilaya" 2 guerillas from whom he however succeeded in escaping. In 1963 he was appointed military commander of Constantine and a year later became military commander of the western area of Oran; he retained this latter position until taking charge of military and defence affairs in November 1978 when President Boumedienne became incapacitated by his illness; he had been promoted to the rank of colonel in 1969. In the meantime he had played an important part in the plot which in 1965 overthrew President Ben Bella and brought Col. Boumedienne to power, shortly after which he became a member of the Revolutionary Council. Despite being a senior member of the armed forces Col. Chadli was little known to the Algerian public. It was widely believed, however, that he was a political centrist and a moderate who was unlikely to deviate greatly from the domestic and foreign policies of his predecessor. Col. Chadli was generally regarded as having been a "compromise candidate" of the Army in an effort to end the dissent within the political leadership which had intensified coincidentally with President Boumedienne's illness and subsequent death on Dec. 27, 1978; Reelected for the third time President of Algeria on 22/12/1988 for five Years. Resigned on Jan. 11 1992. **Addr.:** Algiers, Algeria.

CHAFIK (Mohamad, Binali), Moroccan educationalist. **Born** in 1926 in Morocco. **Son** of Binali **Chafik. Married**, eight children. **Educ.:** B.A. in History; **Diploma** in Classical Arabic; Aptitude Certificate in Inspection and Teaching; Cetificate in History of Arts; Diploma in Berber. **Career:** Teacher (1944-52); Teacher at Grammer School (1953-55); Inspector of Primary Education (1955-61); Inspector of General Education (1962-64); Principal Inspector for History and Geography (1965-67); Head of Mission at the Royal Cabinet (1968-69 and 1973-77); Assistant Secretary of State (1970-72); Secretary of State (1972); Director of the Royal College (1977). **Publ.:** "Pensées Sous Developpées" (1972) in French; "A Grammar of Berber" in Arabic; "Ce Que Dit le Muezzin" (1974) and several articles on education published in professional journals and magazines. **Medals:** Wissam Reda, Morocco; Palmes Academiques, France. **Sport:** Walking. **Hobbies:** Reading, gardening. **Addr.:** 42 Cité Saada, Aviation, Rabat, Morocco.

CHAINANI (Vashdev), Indian businessman. **Born** in 1935, Pakistan. **Son** of Menghraj (Sindhi Tribe). **Married** in 1964, 4 Children. **Educ.:** B.Comm. **Career:** Director, Universal Garment Factory; former Director, Dubai Bank Ltd., Dubai, United Arab Emirates; Trustee, Indian High School; Trustee, Indian Sports Club. **Member:** Indian Sports Club; Founder Member, Country Club; Passport Club. **Addr.:** P.O.Box 12654, Tel.: 459397, Dubai, United Arab Emirates.

CHAKER (Abdulmagid), Tunisian politician. **Born** in Tunis. **Educ.:** Seconday and Higher. **Career:** Secretary of State, Ministries of Agriculture (1962-64) and Information (1964-66); Member of Neo-Destour (now Destour Socialist Party); Director until November 1964, Member of Political Bureau (November 1964); Ambassador to Algeria (1966). **Priv. Addr.:** Tunis, Tunisia.

CHAKER (Moncef), Tunisian engineer. **Born** on July 11, 1935. **Married**, 3 children. **Educ.:** Primary School (Sfax); Certificate of Studies and Baccalaureat 2nd part (Tunis); University studies at Bordeaux (France); Engineering Diploma of the Techniques of Rural Equipment, National Engineering School for rural Works and Sanitary Techniques. **Career:** Head of the Subdivision of Industrial Agriculture, Director, Rural Spirit Centre of Research, Treasurer, Destourienne Cell of Agronomic Research; Secretary-General, Treasurer, General Union of Tunisian Students (Sadiki College Section), Third Commission of the International Institute of Refrigeration. **Addr.:** Hadi Saidi Boulevard, Printemps Bldg., No.4, Apt. No.16, Tunis, Tunisia.

CHALABI (Abdul Wahab, al, Dr.), Iraqi academic, physician. **Born** in 1930 in Mosul, Iraq. **Married**, 3 children, one son and two daughters. **Educ.:** University of Istanbul, Turkey; Cairo University, Egypt. **Dipl.:** M.D.,

M.Sc. **Career:** General Practitioner (1960); Physician, Forensic Medicine (1965); Assistant Lecturer (1972); Demonstrator (1976); Assistant Professor of Forensic Medicine (since 1978) and Assistant Professor, Medical Ethics (1987); Head of Section of Forensic Medicine, College of Medicine, University of Mosul. **Publ.:** "Atlas of Forensic Medicine" (1979); Books of Medical ethics (1988); research papers published in professional journals; (Forensic Medicine and Toxicology, "WHO, Emro" with many Prof. s from Arab Countries. 1993). **Sport:** Walking. **Hobby:** Travel. **Member** for the translation of F.M. to Arabic Language in WHO. **Prof. Addr.:** P.O.Box 61, Mosul, Iraq. **Priv. Addr.:** Tel.: 913371, Mosul, Iraq.

CHALABI (Fadhil, J., al), Iraqi oil economist. **Born** in 1929 in Baghdad, Iraq. **Son** of Jafar Mohamad al-Chalabi **and** Mrs. Fatima née al-Uzri. **Married** in 1956 in Baghdad to Miss Abda Bahjat Salih, four children. **Educ.:** B.A. in Law, Baghdad University (1951); post graduate diplomas (DES in Economics), Université de Poitiers (France) (1956, 1958); Doctorat d'Etat in Economic Sciences, Université de Paris (1962). **Career:** Director General of Oil Affairs, Ministry of Oil, Baghdad (1968-73); Permanent Under-Secretary, Ministry of Oil, Baghdad (1973-76); Assistant Secretary General, OAPEC, Kuwait (1976-78); Deputy Secretary General of OPEC, Vienna (1978) (Acting for the Secretary General of OPEC (1983)). **Publ.:** "OPEC and the International Oil Industry: A Changing Structure", Oxford University Press (1980); author of many papers and articles on energy, oil and economic affairs. **Awarded** the "Order of the Liberator - Officer Class" by the President of the Republic of Venezuela (1977). **Sports:** Long walks. **Hobbies:** Music reading (art, history and religion). **Member of:** North-South Roundtable, Islamabad (Pakistan); Society for International Development, Rome; Oxford Energy Policy Club, Oxford; Economists Association, Iraq. **Credit Cards:** American Express, Eurocard. **Addr.:** Baghdad, Iraq.

CHALABI (Hassan, ach), Iraqi university professor and lawyer. **Born** in Iraq. **Educ.:** Secondary and Higher Studies. **Dipl.:** Bachelor of Law. **Career:** Lawyer; Director of the Juridic Department at the University of Baghdad (1965); Member of the Patronage Committee of "Proche Orient, Etudes Juridiques" (Beirut 1967). **Addr.:** University of Baghdad, Baghdad, Iraq.

CHALABI (Raouf), Egyptian politician. **Born** in 1923 in Cairo, Egypt. **Son** of Faiek Chalabi. **Married** in 1950, 5 children. **Educ.:** Collège des Pères Jésuites; Cairo University. **Dipl.:** B.Sc. (Engineering) (1947). **Career:** Vice-President, Banque Crédit Foncier, Cairo; Member of Egyptian Senate (1980). **Member:** Rotary Club, Heliopolis Branch. **Addr.:** 601, Khalifa El-Maamour St., Cairo, Egypt.

CHALABI (Talal, Saleem, al), Iraqi physician, academic. **Born** in 1937 in Baghdad, Iraq. **Son** of Saleem al-Chalabi. **Married,** two daughters. **Educ.:** Baghdad University, Iraq; Royal College of Edinburgh, UK; American College of Surgeons, USA. **Dipl.:** M.B., Ch.B. (1961); FRGS (1969); FACS (1979). **Career:** Consultant Orthopædic Surgeon (since 1974); Head, Department of Surgery, Medical College, Basrah, Iraq (1978-79); Dean, College of Medicine, University of Basrah, Iraq (since 1979). **Publ.:** Articles in the Medical Journal of Basrah University. **Hobby:** Classical music. **Prof. Addr.:** College of Medicine, University of Basrah, Iraq.

CHALHOUB (Michel), Egyptian actor, See **ach-SHARIF (Omar)**.

CHAMI (Hassan), Moroccan Director of Companies. **Born** on April 30, 1938 at Fes, Morocco. **Son** of Mohammed Chami (Notary) **and** Mrs. Khnata Chami. **Married** in Fes in 1965, 2 children: Yasmine Chami (17.05.66); Khalid Chami (05.08.67). **Educ.:** Ecole Nationale des Ponts et Chaussées de Paris. **Dipl.:** in Engineering. **Career:** Engineer-Chief of Department (1961); Manager, Régie d'Aconage Port de Casablanca (1963); Manager, Port de Casablanca (1965); General Manager of Hydraulic (1969); Minister of Public Works (1970); General Manager, Office de Commercialisation et d'Exportation (1972); since 1977: President of Various Industrial Companies (ATLAS, ZENEKA MAROC, FACEMAG, MULTITEX). **Sports:** Tennis, Bicycle. **Hobbies:** Music, Painting. **Credit Card:** Visa. **Prof. Addr.:** 81, Av. Houmane El Fetouaki, Tel.: 22.41.90, Casablanca, Morocco. **Priv. Addr.:** 5, Allée des Farigoules, Tel.: 36.03.15, Casablanca, Morocco.

CHAMLANE (Faisal), Yemeni politician. **Born** in The Republic of Yemen. **Educ.:** Secondary and Higher. **Career:** Statesman; Member of the NLF; Minister of Public Works and Communications in the First Government after Independence (December 1967) Chairman of the Public Corporation for Electric Power (P.C.E.P) (1969-77); former Executive Director, Aden Refinery Company (A.R.C.) (1977). **Addr.:** Aden, Republic of Yemen.

CHAPRA (Muhammad, Umar), Saudi economist. **Born** in 1934 in Bombay, India. **Son** of Mr. Abdulkarim Chapra (businessman) **and** Mrs. Halimabai Tahir Muhammad. **Married** in 1962 to Khairunnisa Jamal Mundia, four children. **Educ.:** MBA, University of Karachi; Ph.D., University of Minnesota, Minneapolis, Minn. USA. **Career:** Teaching assistant, University of Minnesota (1957-60); Assistant Prof., University of Wisconsin, Platteville (1960-61); Senior Economist and Associate Editor, Pakistan Development Review, Pakistan Institute of Development Economics, Karachi (1961-62); Reader in Economics, Central Institute of Islamic Research, Karachi (1962-63); Associate Professor, University of Wisconsin, Platteville, and University of Kentucky, Lexington (1963-65); Economic Adviser, Saudi Arabian Monetary Agency

(1965-1999); Research Advisor Islamic Research & Training Institute (IRTI) of the Islamic Development Bank (IDB), Jeddah, since November (1999-). **Publications:** 8 books and monographs and 52 papers. **Medals:** from the University of Karachi for standing first in the High school examination (1950); Gold Medal for outstanding scholastics from the Sind Government College of Commerce and Economics (1986); King Faysal International Award in Islamic Studies (1989); and Islamic Development Bank award in Islamic Economics (1989). **Prof. Addr.:** Islamic Research & Training Institute (IRTI), Islamic Development Bank (IDB) P.O.Box No. 9201, Jeddah 21413, Saudi Arabia, Tel.: 6466139.

CHARARA (Mohamad), Saudi diplomat. **Born** in 1924 in Medina, Saudi Arabia. **Dipl.:** B.A. in Law and Political Science, King Farouk University (now Alexandria University). **Career:** Worked in Saudi Embassies in Rome and Tokyo; Ambassador and permanent delegate to European office of U.N., Geneva; Ambassador to Belgium and Luxembourg; Ambassador and Head of Saudi Arabian Mission to E.E.C.; Ambassador to Mexico; President of Islamic and Cultural Centre in Brussels; President of Euro-Arab Club in Brussels; member of U.N. General Assembly (1955,57 and 61); member of Saudi Arabian delegation to the Conference of Non-Alignment, Belgrade (1961) and Cairo (1964); President of Saudi Arabian delegation to Economic Cooperation Conference of Developing Countries, Mexico (1976); Ambassador to Mexico (1981). **Honours:** King Abdulaziz Order, First Class (1972); Grand Officer, Order of Leopold II, Belgium; Order de La Couronne, Belgium, Order of Senior Officer, Spain. **Hobbies:** Hunting, golf. **Prof. Addr.:** Ministry of Foreign Affairs, Riyadh, Saudi Arabia.

CHARFI (Abdelmajid Ahmad), Tunisian academic. **Born** in 1942 in Sfax, Tunisia. **Son** of Ahmad Charfi. **Married**, one son. **Educ.:** University of Paris. **Dipl.:** B.A., Ph.D. in Literature, University of Tunis. **Career:** Editor of "Ibla" magazine (since 1972); Editor, "Islamochristiana" (1976); "Trans State Islam" (1995); Head, Arabic Department, Tunis High College of Teachers (1977); Dean, Faculty of Letters and Humanities, Tunis University (1983-1986); Member, Economic and Social Council (since 1993). **Publ.:** "Maqami' as-Sulban"; "ar-Risala al-'Asgadiyya"; "al-Fikr al-islami fi-r-radd 'ala-n-nasara ila nihayat al-qarn 4/10"; al-Islam wa-l-hadatha"; "Labinat". **Addr.:** 9 April 1938 Street, No.94, Tunis 1007, Tunisia.

CHARIF (Abdulhamid, ach), Egyptian statesman and company director. **Born** in Abiar, Kafr az-Zayat Province (Egypt). **Educ.:** Secondary in Cairo and Higher in Montpellier and Paris. **Dipl.:** of Commerce and Finances From Montpellier and Paris (France). **Career:** Former Board Chairman Misr Bank; Former Minister of Finance; Company Director. **Member** of Rotary Club of Cairo, Gezira Sporting Club. **Addr.:** 5, Willcoks Street, Zamalek, Tel.: 807261, Cairo. **Summer Residence:** 22 Horreya Avenue, Tel.: 26831, Alexandria, Egypt.

CHARIF (Saad, Mahmoud), Egyptian university professor. **Born** on July 25, 1924 in Alexandria. **Son** of Mahmoud Charif **and** Mrs., née Raïfa Ali Henno. **Married** on July 21, 1966 to Miss Fadwa Muhammad Khalaf, 2 children: Youmna and Tamer. **Educ.:** University of Cairo. **Dipl.:** Bachelor of Science (Agriculture 1945), Master of Science (Soils 1951), Doctor of Philosophy (Soils 1955). **Career:** Demonstrator (1946), then Lecturer (1957-63), then Associate Professor (1963-71), then Professor (since 1971) of Soils, Aïn Shams University. **Sport:** Tennis. **Hobby:** Music. **Priv. Addr.:** 20, Umar Bakir Street, Heliopolis, Tel.: 868070, Cairo, Egypt.

CHARRAN (Mohamad), Egyptian judge. **Born** on February 10, 1933 at Abou-Hommos, Beheira Governorate (Lower Egypt). **Married** to Amal Abou-Elala on 29 January 1960, 3 children: one daughter and two sons. **Educ.:** Kafr el-Dawar Primary school (1940-1944); Damanhour Secondary School (1945-51); Faculty of Law, Alexandria University (1951-54). **Dipl.:** LL.B. Criminal Law (1963); LL.B. Private Law (1964). **Career:** Joined the Public Prosecutor Office, Alexandria (1954-1964); Judge, Damanhour Law Court (1964-68); Judge, Sohag Law Court (1968-69); President, Kafr el Sheikh Law Court (1970-76); now Law Court counsel since 1976. **Prof. Addr.:** Ministry of Justice, Abbassiyah District, Tel.: 830206, Cairo. **Priv. Addr.:** 16, Sidi Gaber Street, Sporting District, Tel.: 41506, Alexandria, Egypt.

CHATTI (Bourhan Eddine), Syrian economist. **Born** in 1922, in Damascus, Syria. **Son** of Taher Chatti. **Married** in 1953. **Educ.:** LL.B. (1947); Ph.D. (Economics) (1957). **Career:** Inspector of Finance, Ministry of Finance, Syria (1947-51); Assistant Director of Economic Research, Syrian Development Board (1957-59); Director of Plan Implementation, Syrian Ministry of Planning (1959-62); Assistant Secretary General, Ministry of Planning (1962-63); Chief Economic Adviser, Kuwait Planning Board (1963-76); Director, Arab Fund for Economic and Social Development, Regional Programme for Inter-Country Arab Projects (AFESD, UNDP Joint Programme) (1977). **Member:** Kuwait Economic Society, Syrian Economic Association, American Economic Association, Gazelle Club of Kuwait. **Hobbies:** Numismatics, reading, swimming and walking. **Addr.:** P.O.Box 21923, Tel.: 431870, 433860, Safat, Kuwait.

CHATTI (Mohamed Eyad, Dr.), Syrian Politician. **Born** on July 25, 1940 in Damascus. **Married** two daughters. **Educ.:** Medical Diploma, Damascus University (1964); Diploma in Neuropathology, A.F.I.P. (1965); Diploma in Citology, Case Western Reserve University, Ohio (1969); American Board of Pathology (1970). **Career:** Professor of Pathology; Full Member, New York Academy of Science;

Dean, Medical School, Damascus University (1986-87); Member, Consultative Commission for East Mediterranean Region (1987-to date); Chairman of Executive Board, WHO (1993-94); Head, Research Committee, WHO-East Mediterranean Rigion (1995); Minister of Health (1987-to date). **Address:** Ministry of Health, Parliament Street, Damascus, Syria.

CHAYA (Jamil), Syrian politician. **Born** in Syria. **Educ.:** Secondary and Higher. **Career:** Civil Servant; Minister of Supply and Trade (1964); Minister of Information, Tourism and Culture in the Cabinet of Dr. Youssef Zouayen (1966); Ambassador to Brazil (September 1967-69); Ambassador to Italy (1969); Ambassador to USSR (1970-75); Deputy Prime Minister for Economic Affairs (1976-80). **Addr.:** Damascus, Syria.

CHBANI-IDRISSI (Mohamad Lyazid), Moroccan bank executive. **Born** in 1946 in Settat District, Morocco. **Son** of Larbi Chbani-Idrissi. **Married** in 1980. **Educ.:** Engineer and Economist. **Career:** Held several positions, now Director, Credit Department, Caisse Nationale de Crédit Agricole, Rabat (since 1969). **Addr.:** P.O.Box 49, Tel.: 311-77, 348-66, Rabat, Morocco.

CHEBIB (Taleb), Iraqi diplomat. **Born** in Iraq. **Educ.:** Secondary and Higher. **Career:** Minister of Foreign Affairs (1963-66); Director, Arab League Bureau in Paris (1966-67); Ambassador of Iraq to Lebanon (December 1968-April 1969). **Addr.:** c/o Ministry of Foreign Affairs, Baghdad, Iraq.

CHEDLY (Muhammad, Fredj Muhammad), Tunisian politician. **Born** on May 9, 1927 in Kairouan, Tunisia. **Married**, 4 sons, 1 daughter. **Educ.:** Ecole Normale de Tunis. **Dipl.:** M.A. in Arabic Literature. **Career:** Director of Secondary Schools, Ministry of Education (1957-67), Director of Primary School Teaching (1968-70); Chief of Cabinet (1970-71), Chief of Cabinet, Ministry of Culture (1973); President of the National Commission for UNESCO, ISESCO, ALECSO (1983); President of the Tunisian Association for the Preservation of the Palestinian Cultural Heritage (1983); Ministry of Education (1985). **Publ.:** several scholarly books; author of several articles on cultural and educational subjects. **Decor.:** Commander of the Order of the Republic of Tunisia; Chevalier of the Tunisian Order of Independence. **Medal:** Medal for Cultural Achievement. **Priv. Addr.:** 9 Rue Halima Saadia El Manzah VI, Tunis, Tunisia.

CHEIKH (Salem, Muhammad), Tunisian former official. **Born** in 1943 in Tunisia. **Married**, 3 children. **Educ.:** Ecole Nationale d'Administration, Tunisia. **Dipl.:** LL.B. **Career:** Chef de Service, Prime Minister's Office (1974-77), Adviser and Administrator (1974-80), Assistant Manager (1977-78); Manager, Ministry of Higher Education (1979-82); Senior Administrator (1981-83); General Manager of Administration Finance, Agency of Cultural and Technical Cooperation (1983); Public Services Adviser (1984). **Publ.:** "Les Modes de Recrutement", CREA ENA, Tunis. **Decor.:** Order of the Republic, Ministry of Higher Education (1980). **Member:** Lions Club of Tunis; Association des Anciens Elèves (ENA); President, Lions Club of Tunis (1979). **Addr.:** Tunis, Tunisia.

CHEIKHROUHOU (Habib), Tunisian publisher, businessman. **Born** in 1914 in Sfax, Tunisia. **Career:** Chairman and Managing Director, Dar as-Sabah Publishing House, publish "as-Sabah" and "Le Temp" daily newspapers; Chairman and Managing Director: Nour Company (manufacture batteries), STIPCE (manufacture chemical fertilizers), Venus (travel agency), and various other companies; Former Vice President, Municipality of Carthage. Actively **involved** in the Socialist Destour Party. **Medals:** Order of Tunisian Republic; Egyptian Order of Merit and other decorations from Arab and other countries. **Clubs:** Former Secretary General of Sfax Sporting Club; former Director of Najm Theatre Group. **Hobby:** Theatre. **Addr.:** 4 Rue Ali Bach Hamba, Tel.: 340222, Tunis, Tunisia.

CHELLI (Tijani), Tunisian diplomat & businessman. **Born** on March 23, 1931 in Nabeul (Tunisia). **Son** of Hamida Chelli **and** Mrs., née Kaboura Bahroun. **Married** to Chantal Jussiaux in 1962, 3 children: Sophia, Tijani and Malika. **Educ.:** Sadiki College, Tunis (Tunisia); Polytechnic School, Paris (France). **Dipl.:** B.Sc. (Engineering) (1955). **Career:** Engineer, Ministry of Public Works (1959-60), Depuy Chief Engineer of Roads and Bridges (1960); Director of Transport (1961); Director of Sea and Air Transport (1962); Director, National Railways, Tunis (1965-67); Director, Department of Planning and National Economy (September 1967- January 1969); Director, Compagnie Chimique Maghrébines (1969); Minister of Public Works (1969-70); Minister of Economy (1970-72); President Director-General, Investment Promotion Agency since 1973; President General Manager, Banque de Développement Economique de Tunisie. **Awards:** Grand Cordon, Order of the Republic. **Sports:** Swimming and shooting. **Hobby:** Reading. **Prof. Addr.:** 34, rue Hédi El Karray, el-Menzah 1004, P.O.Box 48, Tunis 1080, Tunisia.

CHELLI (Zouhair), Tunisian diplomat. **Born** in 1930. **Married** to Miss Lilia Tounisi in 1954, 3 children. **Educ.:** Sadiki College, Sousse College. **Career:** Ministry of Foreign Affairs, Chief of Division (1956-60); Chief of Cabinet, Secretary of State and Information (1958); Deputy Permanent Representative of Tunis to the Security Council and the United Nations Organization (1960-62); Tunisian Ambassador to Switzerland (1962) and concurrently to Austria (1965); Tunisian Permanent Representative to the European Office of the United Nations Organization, Geneva (1966). **Addr.:** c/o Ministry of Foreign Affairs, Tunis, Tunisia.

CHENOUDA III (Nasri Gayeb, H.H.), Pope and Patriarch of the Coptic Orthodox Church. **Born** in 1923 in Egypt. **Educ.:** Universities of Egypt, Coptic Orthodox Theological College. **Dipl.:** Licentiate in Theology and Philosophy (1949), Bachelor of Divinity (B.D). **Career:** Ordained to the Priesthood, Professor and Journalist, Priest in Dair as-Surian (1954), Secretary of late Pope and Patriarch Cyrille VI (1958-71), Bishop of the Religious Education (1963), Elected 117th Pope and Patriarch of the Coptic Orthodox Church (October 31, 1971), Acting Pope since November 14, 1971; visited Greek and Russian Orthodox Patriarchs, Istanbul (1971); visited the Pope, Vatican (1973). **Publ.:** Author of several books and booklets. **Resid.** Coptic Orthodox Church, P.O.Box 9035, Cairo, Egypt.

CHERQAWI (Abdulmalik), Moroccan economist. **Born** in 1941 in Morocco. **Married**, two children. **Educ.:** B.A. in Economics and Statistics, INSEE, Paris, France. **Career:** Professor, Institute of Statistics, Rabat (1971); Director of Statistics (1972); Director General, Cooperative Office Movement (1972); Secretary General of Planning (1974). **Publ.:** "Indicateurs Socio-Economiques du Maroc", Morocco (1980); articles on social economics published in professional journals. **Medal:** Ouissame Reda. **Sport:** Tennis. **Hobby:** Chess. **Addr.:** Rabat, Morocco.

CHERQAWI (Mohamad), Moroccan statesman and diplomat. **Born** in Morocco. **Career:** Moroccan Ambassador to France (1961-64); Minister of National Economy and Finance (1964-65); Minister of Development (1965-66), of Foreign Affairs (1966-67); President Permanent Consultative Committee of the Maghreb (1964); Minister of National Defence (1967); President Organisation for Afro-Asian Economic Co-operation. **Addr.:** Rabat, Morocco.

CHIBANE (Abdelrahman), Algerian politician. **Born** in 1922. **Married**, 8 children. **Educ.:** Zitouna University, Tunisia. **Career:** Teacher of Arabic Literature; Editor in Chief of "La Resistance Algérienne" and "La Jeunesse Algérienne" Magazines; Member of Constituent Assembly (1962); Director of Diplomatic Mission in Libya; Reporter, National Education Commission, General Inspector for Arabic language and literature, Ministry of Education; Member of Islamic High Council; Minister of Religious Affairs (1980-85). **Prof. Addr.:** Algiers, Algeria.

CHINCHINIAN (Zaven, Rev.), Archbishop. **Born:** in September 1929, Aleppo, Syria. **Son** of Osep Chinchinian. (Trader) and Mrs. Lucy Chinchinian **Educ.:** Seminary of Armenian Patriarchate St. James, Jerusalem. **Diplomas:** In Humanities: Theology, Sociology, Philosophy, Logic, Psychology, History, Comparative Literature, Classics, Patristics. **Career:** Celibate Priest, Jerusalem (1951); Head-Master, Armenian School, Secondary Dept., Jerusalem (1953-55); Director, Printing Press, Armenian Patriarcahte, Jerusalem (1952-56); Patriarcal Vicar and Teacher, Alexandria-Egypt (1957-77); Primate's Vicar in New York, USA (1977-78); Prelate of the Armenian Orthodox Church in Egypt and North Africa (1979-) **Awards:** St. George's Medal of Merits from the Russian Orthodox Church granted in 1982. **Sports:** Horse Riding. **Hobbies:** Classical Music and Writing Articles. **Cards:** Credit Suisse. **Member:** A number of Cultural and Benevolent Unions. **Address:** Armenian Patriarchate, 179 Ramses Ave., Tel,: (20-2) 5901385, Fax: (20-2) 5906671, Cairo, Egypt.

CHIRAZI (Hussain, ach), Iraqi writer and poet. **Born** in 1935 in An-Najaf. **Educ.:** in Karbala'. **Dipl.:** "al-Ijtihad" Diploma (1959), Higher Studies in Theology and Philosophy. **Career:** Writer, Poet, Professor, University of Karbala', Dean of "Ibn Fahd" College for Islamical Studies, Contributed to several periodicals, Arrested for political reasons by the Iraqi Authorities, May 16, 1969. **Publ.:** Author of more than 70 books, studies and Philosophical works, including: "al-Amal al-Adabi", "al-Adab al-Mouwajjah", "Kalimat al-Islam", "Kalimat Allah", "Kalimat al-Rassoul al-A'zam", "Kalimat al-Imam al-Hassan", "al-Iqtissad", "Ilah al-Kawn", "Injazat al-Rassoul", "Ach Cha'er al-Husseiniya", "al-Ichtiqaq", "Rassoul al-Hayat", "Milad al-Qiyada al-Islamiya", "an Nassir al-Awal lil Islam", author of several poems and talks. **Addr.:** Karbala', an-Najaf, Iraq.

CHIRDON (Djama, Aouled), Djibouti Deputy at the National Assembly. **Born** in 1945 in Djibouti. **Career:** Contractor of Public Works; Former President of Contractors Order; Member of RPP; Elected Deputy at the National Assembly (19.12.1997 - to date); Member of the Commission on Foreign Affairs and National Defence. **Prof. Addr.:** National Assembly, P.O.Box 138 Djibouti, Djibouti.

CHOUFANI (Abdulmagid), Moroccan judge. **Born** in Morocco. **Married**, 4 children. **Educ.:** Diploma, National Institute of Judicial Studies; French Language Section (Rabat). **Career:** Teacher, Public Education; Magistrate, since Moroccan Independence (1957). **Member:** President of the Association and Safeguard of Children in Casablanca. **Publ.:** Une Etude sur le Régime des Associations au Maroc and Une Etude sur la Police Judiciaire Marocaine, published by the Royal Police Review. **Addr.:** Regional Tribunal, Casablanca, Morocco.

CHOUFANI (Paul), Bank manager. **Born** in 1946, Jerusalem. **Son** of Michel Choufani. **Married** in 1973, 2 children. **Educ.:** Degree in Law, Degree in Banking Studies. **Career:** General Manager, Investment Bank for Trade and Finance LLC. **Addr.:** P.O.Box 1885, Tel.: 355391/2, Telex: 68083, 68218 A/B EM INVESTBANK, Sharjah, United Arab Emirates.

CHOUFI (Hammoud, el), Syrian politician and diplomat. **Born** in 1935 in Syria. **Married,** three children. **Educ.:** University of Damascus. **Career:** Secretary General Syrian Baath Party (1962-64); Ambassador to Indonesia (1965-70), to India (1970-72); Director American Dept., Ministry of Foreign Affairs (1972-78); Permanent Representative to UN (1978-79). **Publ.:** History of the Sweida Region (1961). **Addr.:** c/o Ministry of Foreign Affairs, Damascus, Syria.

CHOUK (Houcine), Tunisian Politician. **Born** on December 2, 1946 in Nefta. **Married,** three children. **Educ.:** Degree in Mathematics, Science Faculty of Tunis (1969); Diploma in Aeronautical Engineering, Ecole National de l'Aéronautique et de l'Espace, Toulouse, France (1972). **Career:** Engineer, Tunisian Meteorological Service and Tunis-air Airline (1972-75); Navigability Inspectorate, Ministry of Transport and Communications (1975); Director, School of Civil Aviation and Meteorology (1981); President Director General, National Corporation of Interurban Transportation (1987); Tunisian Office of Airports (1990); tunisian Navigation Company (1996); President, Shipbuilders Association of Tunis and Southern France/Tunisia Maritime Association; Minister of Transport (Oct. 1997-to date) **Address:** Ministry of Transport, 13, rue 8006 Cité Monplaisir, 1002 Tunis Tunisia.

CHOURBAJI (Mazhar, Saïd, ach), Syrian barrister, former Deputy. **Born** in 1922 in Damascus. **Son** of Saïd ach-Chourbaji. **Educ.:** University of Damascus, University of Paris. **Dipl.:** Licentiate of Laws, Doctor in Criminal and International Laws. **Career:** Lawyer, Elected Deputy for Ghoula (1954-57); Syrian Representative to several international organizations. **Publ.:** Author of various studies e.g. "Sira' ad-Dimokratiah". **Hobby:** Music. **Addr.:** An-Nasr Street, Tel.: 111563 and 110663, Damascus, Syria.

CHRAIBI (Larbi, Dr.), Moroccan physician and executive. **Born** on September 13, 1921 in Rabat, Morocco. **Married** in 1957 in Rabat to Miss Iraqi Naima, 4 children: Ali, Jawad, Anas, Meriem. **Educ.:** Lycée de Casablanca, Faculty of Medicine, Montpellier, France; Faculty of Medicine of Paris. **Dipl.:** Doctor in Medicine (1950). **Career:** Minister of Health (1963-69); President-Delegate, Société Chérifienne des Pétroles (1969). **Awards:** Ouissam Alaouite. **Sport:** Swimming. **Priv. Addr.:** Cadi Mekki Bitaouri Street, Souissi, Rabat, Morocco.

COUBECHE (Said, Ali), Djibouti President Director General "Ets. Coubeche and Cie". **Born** on March 3, 1917. **Son** of Ali Coubeche **and** Mrs. née Zeinab Mowafi. **Married** in 1941, 2 children: Sami and Magda. **Career:** President Director General "Ets. Coubeche and Cie". **Other Information:** President of the "Chamber Internationale de Commerce et d'Industrie de Djibouti". **Awards:** Officer. Legion d'Honneur Française; Commander, National Order of Merit; Officer, Big Star of Djibouti; Commander, Legion d'Honneur Française; Commander, Big Star of Djibouti. **Clubs and Associations:** President, Club Arabe (1939/59), President, Ecole Franco-Islamique, Member/ Founder of Lions' Club, Djibouti (1966). **Prof. Addr.:** P.O.Box 105, Tel.: 351027, Djibouti, Republic of Djibouti, and Chamber Internationale de Commerce et d'Industrie, P.O.Box 84 Djbouti, Republic of Djibouti.

COUDSI (Michel, Constantin), Former chief account supervisor of the Central Bank of Egypt, Cairo, Egypt. **Born** on June 7, 1919, Cairo, Egypt. **Married** to Nelly Zaki Bargoud on December 7, 1947, 2 daughters. **Educ.:** College of the Christian Brothers, College de la Salle (primary education), Khoronfish College (secondary edution) (1933-37). **Dipl.:** B.Com. **Career:** Accountant, Emile Henrich & Company; Associate editor, "La Patrie" daily newspapers (1938-40); Chief Account Supervisor, Central Bank of Egypt; now Arabic-French Translator, Authorship and Scientific Translation Office, Cairo. **Member** Board member, St.Vincent de Paul Benevolent Society, Paris; Board member, Dominican Fathers, Abbasiah, Cairo. **Hobbies:** Stamp collecting, reading and TV. **Prof. Addr.:** Authorship and Scientific Translation Office, 40 Kasr el-Nil Street, Tel.: 54394, Cairo, Egypt. **Priv. Addr.:** 4 Orabi Square, Flat No.17, Tel.: 975595, Cairo, Egypt.

CUTAYAR (Egidio), Egyptian Banker. **Born** on December 22, 1937 in Alexandria, Egypt. **Married,** 1 daughter: Lara. **Career:** Joined Barclays Bank International (December 1961); Assistant Representative, Milan, Italy (1970); Assistant Manager Banca Barclays Castillini SPA, Milan (1975); Manager, Banca Barclays Castillini SPA, Milan (1976); also Director of Barclays Leasing International, Milan (1978); General Manager, Barclays Bank International, Greece; Board Member of the Hellenic Investment Bank, Vice Chairman of the Loans and Participations Committee of the Hellenic Mutual Fund Management Co. SA, Greece, and member of the Board (1979); Assistant General Manager, Europe Barclays Bank plc, Head Office, London (1986); Senior General Manager, Barclays Bank plc, Milan, Italy, Vice Chairman, Barclays Financial Services Italia SPA, Milan, Italy (October 1986). Joint Managing Director, Banque du Caire Barclays International SAE, Cairo, Egypt since March 1988- present. **Awards:** The title of «Cavaliere» from Italy. **Sport:** Swimming. **Hobbies:** Reading, classical music, operas. **Member:** Board Member of the Italian Chamber of Commerce. Vice President of The Egyptian British Businessmen Association, Board Member of The Egyptian British Friendship Society, Member of The American Chamber of Commerce, Member of The German Chamber of Commerce, Member of The Greek Chamber of Commerce, Member of The Rotary Club, Member of The Gezira Club, Member of the Sakkara Country Club, Member of the "Confrerie de la Chaine des Rotisseurs". **Prof. Addr.:** Banque du Caire Barclays International S.A.E., 12 Midan El Sheikh Youssef, Tel.: (202) 3540686, Cairo, Egypt.

D

DABBAGH (Abdallah E., Dr.), Saudi Geologist and Administrator. **Born** on May 21, 1945 in Taif, Saudi Arabia. **Son** of Eassa Dabbah (Civil Servant, Education) **and** Mrs. Omhany Dabbagh. **Married** with Thuraya Arrayed, 4 children: One boy, 3 daughters, May, Hashim, Noor, Layla. **Educ.:** B.Sc. in Geology, June 1968, American University of Beirut; Ph.D. in Geology (Structural Geology, Metamorphic and Igneous Petrology), October 1975, University of North Carolina at Chapel Hill, U.S.A. **Career:** Administrative Assistant, (Summer Assignment) Raytheon Corp., Jeddah (1964); Research Assistant, College of Petroleum and Minerals, Dhahran (1968-1969); Visiting Lecturer, Princeton University (1975-1976); Assistant Professor of Geology, University of Petroleum and Minerals, Dhahran (1976-1979); Associate Professor of Geology, King Fahd University of Petroleum and Minerals, Dhahran (1980- present); Director, Research Institute (Dean), King Fahd University of Petroleum and Minerals, Dhahran (September 1, 1978- present); Responsible for organization and start up of the Research Institute activities, growing from three members to 350 technical and support Staff. Actively participated in the development of the FIRST FIVE YEAR PLAN of the Research Institute and totally responsible for the implementation of that plan and later plans, including preparation and start up of a 30.000 sq. meters research facility with first-class equipment, instrumentation, and major research programs. The Institute has become a model for application of modern technology in the Saudi Arabian environment, and is an established leading energy center in the area; Leader of scientific team and responsible for planning, design and implementation of the scientific program of Prince Sultan bin Salman, the first Arab astronaut on the US Space Shuttle (51-G) (1985); Member, Board of Directors, Saudi Aramco (1989- present); Member of Executive Committee, Audit Committee and Compensation Committee. **Training:** Summer Training, Raytheon Corp., Jeddah (1964); Field Geology Training Program, Wadi Fatima and Wadi Liyya, College of Petroleum and Minerals and DGMR, nine months (1968-1969); Stanford-NUS Executive Program (August 2-21, 1987) and several other programs in management and planning. **Professional Affiliation:** Board Member, UPM Foundation (1978-1983); Vice-President, UPM Foundation (1983-1986); Board Member, Terraset Foundation (1978-1980); Member, American Association of Petroleum Geologist; Member, Geological Society of America; Member, Sigma Xi Scientific Society; Member, National Association of Geology Teachers; Member, International Desalination and Environment Association; Editorial Board Member, Arab Journal of Scientific Research, Arab Bureau of Education for the Gulf States, Riyadh (1988- present); Member, Water Sciences and Technology Association; Member, The Planetary Society (1990- present); Member, Institute of Electrical and Electronic Engineers (1990- present). **Conferences:** Chairman, speaker and attendee at a large number of international conferences and symposia over the years. Representative of Saudi Arabia in a number of international congresses including the World Petroleum Congresses (1985- present), World Energy Council (1991), and WMO/UNIP Intergovermental Panel on Climate Change (1991). **Awards and Recognitions:** Listed in: Who's Who in the World; Dictionary of International Biography; Men of Achievement; Who's Who in Saudi Arabia; Reference ASIA. Aramco Scholarship for Undergraduate Work at American University of Beirut (1963-1968); Saudi Government Scholarship (University of Petroleum and Minerals) (1969-1975); Best Student Paper at the Geological Society of America meeting 1976, Washington, DC.; Leader of the Skyland Segment in the Brevard Zone Conference Geological Society of America, Southern Section (August 4-12, 1974); King Faisal Medal (1985); and Several other medals from scientific and government organizations in appreciation of the role of the scientific team supporting the First Arab Astronaut, and subject of numerous articles in magazines and newspapers; frequent appearances in televisions interviews. **Current Research Interest:** Evaluation of water resources in Saudi Arabia; Global Climate Change; Sand dunes structure and distribution and their relation to the wind regime in the Eastern Province of Saudi Arabia; Research Management and Planning in Saudi Arabia; Application and adaptation of modern technologies to the environment of Saudi Arabia; Application of Radar imagery in desert regions. **Publ.:** Dabbagh, A.E. and Dunn D.E. (1975) Structural and Metamorphic History of the Skyland and Dunsmore Mountain Quadrangles, Western North Carolina, Geological Society of America, Abstract with Programs, V.7, No. 4, P. 480; Dabbagh, A.E., E.R.T.S.-1 Imagery: Interpretation of Structural Features in the Knoxville Sheet (1975), North Carolina Academy of Science meeting, Durham, N.C.; Kish, S., Fullagor, P., and Dabbagh, E.E., Paleozic Plutonic Activity in the Blue Ridge of North Carolina, S.E. Geological Society of America meeting, Washington, D.C. (March 1976); Dabbagh, A.E., Role of Applied Research in the Industrialization Plan for Saudi Arabia, The Research Institute Model, presented at the First International Area Conference on Saudi Arabia: Energy, Development Planning, and Industrialization, University of Colorado, Boulder (October 15-16, 1980); Nimmo, B., Dabbagh, A.E., and Said, S.A.M., The Solar Program of the Research Institute, University of Petroleum and Minerals, Dhahran, Saudi Arabia, presented at the SOLTECH Conference, Bahrain (November 10, 1980); Dabbagh, A.E., Geologic Map and Mineral Resources of the Skyland Quadrangle, North Carolina, North Carolina Department of Natural Resources and Community Development, Geological Survey Section, GM 193-NE, MRS 193-NE RALEIGH, N.C. (1981). Mineral Resources Summary by McDaniel, R.D.; Akili, W., and Dabbagh, A.E., The Middle East - A Potential Market for Sulpher Asphalts and Concretes, Proceedings of SULPHER-81, Sulpher Development Institute of Canada, P. 61-73 (August 14, 1981); Dabbagh, A.E., and others, The Importance of Applied Research in Water Resources Development in Saudi Arabia, presented in Water Resources Symposium, Ministry of Planning, Riyadh (March 8, 1982); Dabbagh, A.E., Applied Research and Technology Transfer, UPM-RI Model, paper presented at the Second Conference of Scientific Research Leaders in the Arab Gulf Countries, Moharram, 1406 H, Dhahran, Saudi Arabia; Dabbagh, A.E., and Shahrokhi, F. The Image Processing Center at the Research Institute, Symposium on Commercial Opportunities in Space: Role of Developing Countries, Taipei, Taiwan (April 19-24, 1987); Dabbagh, A.E., and others (1987), Evaluation of Underground Water Resources, Long-term Strategic Plan for the Use of Underground Water for Domestic Purposes, report in Arabic, (unpublished), King Fahd University of Petroleum and Minerals, Dhahran, Saudi Arabia; Dabbagh, A.E., Technology Transfer, Application and Innovation: A Working Model, presented at Conference on Industrial Techno-economic Cooperation between the Federal Republic of Germany and the Arab Gulf Region, Wuerzburg (23-25 September, 1987); Dabbagh, A.E., and Nawab, Z., Atlantis-II-Deep Study: Minerals Resources Evaluation, Symposium on Techno-economic Studies of Mining Projects in the Arab World, Arab Organization for Mineral Resources, Rabat, Morocco (March 30-April 8, 1988); Abderrahman, W.A., Dabbagh, A.E., Edgell, H.S.; and Shahalam, A.B., Evaluation of Groundwater Resources in the Aquifer Systems of Three Regions in Saudi Arabia (1988), Sixth IWRA World Congress on Water Resources, Ottawa, Canada; Dabbagh, A.E., Long-term Strategic Plan for the Use of Groundwater for Domestic Purposes in Saudi Arabia, First Saudi Symposium on the Earth Sciences, Jeddah, Saudi Arabia (28-30 January, 1989); Dabbagh, A.E., Satellite Imagery Interpretation of the Rub'Al-Khali and the Proposed Transarabia Expedition, First Saudi Symposium on Earth Sciences, Jeddah, Saudi Arabia (28-30 January, 1989); Dr. A.E. Dabbagh, Technology Transfer in Developing Countries - A Case Study, Thirteenth World Petroleum Congress, Buenos Aires, Argentina (20-21, October 1991). **Credit Cards:** American Express, Gold Card. **Prof. Addr.:** Director, Research Institute, King Fahd University of Petroleum and Minerals, Tel.: (03) 860-3319, Dahran 31261, Saudi Arabia. **Priv. Addr.:** House No. 3015 Doha/ Rafideen Street, Campus, KFUPM, Tel.: (03) 860-6263, Dhahran 31261, Saudi Arabia.

DABBAGH (Abussattar, Yunes), Iraqi university professor. **Born** in 1943 in Mossul. **Son** of Yunes Dabbagh **and** Mrs., née Wahbia Ahmad Malko. **Married** in 1966 to Miss Mona Kharrofa, 2 daughters: Siba and Rand. **Educ.:** London University, Iowa State University. **Dipl.:** Bachelor in Civil Engineering, Master in Agricultural Engineering, Doctor in Civil and Agricultural Engineering. **Career:** Assistant Engineer, University of Mossul (1965-66); Instructor, Iowa State University (1967-70); Head of Agricultural Engineering Department, University of Mossul (1972); Dean of the Engineering College (1972-73). **Publ.:** Author of several scientific studies. **Sports:** Football and Basketball, **Hobbies:** Reading and Travelling. **Priv. Addr.:** Mossul, Tel.: 6855, Iraq.

DABBAGH (Ammar, Tahir, al), Saudi senior civil servant. **Born** in 1937 in Mecca, Saudi Arabia. **Educ.:** Faculty of Commerce, Riyadh University. **Dipl.:** B.Com. (1962), M.A. (Accounting) (1974). **Career:** Director, Financial Companies Department; Director, Department of Companies, Investment and Industrial Affairs, Ministry of Commerce, Jeddah Branch; Acting Deputy Director, Ministry of Commerce; now Director, Industrial Information and Documentation Department, Industrial Development and Research Centre. **Hobbies:** TV and music. **Sport:** Swimming. **Prof. Addr.:** P.O.Box 1267, Tel.: 29010-20900, Riyadh. **Priv. Addr.:** Tel.: 24178, Riyadh, Saudi Arabia.

DABBAGH (Faiza Ibrahim, al, Mrs.), Saudi academic. **Born** in 1938 in Mecca, Saudi Arabia. **Dipl.:** B.A. (1960); Diploma in Education (1961); **Career:** Inspector, General Presidency for Girls' Education (1961-63); Senior Inspector of Art (1963-74); Dean, Girls' College of Education, Jeddah (since 1974); active member of the Faisaliyah Welfare Society; member of Board, Girls' College, Riyadh; Chairman of Board, Girls' College, Jeddah. **Hobby:** Reading. **Addr.:** Girls' College of Education, Baghdadia, Tel.: 642997, Jeddah, Saudi Arabia.

DABBAGH (Hasheem, Salih, al), Saudi physician. **Born** in 1925 in Hadramaut. **Educ.:** Faculty of Medicine. **Dipl.:** M.D. (Tropical Medicine). **Career:** Deputy Assistant Director of Preventive Medicine (1952); Director General, Malaria Eradication Programme (1962); attented several public health and preventive medicine conferences, and symposiums, including the latest at Guy's Hospital, London; Director General, Preventive Medicine Department, Ministry of Public Health (1971-96). **Member:** Saudi Red Crescent Board;

Public Sanitation Board for the Easterm Region. Riyadh, Saudi Arabia.

DABBAGH (Hassan Ali, al), Kuwaiti former diplomat. **Son** of Ali Dabbagh. **Married. Educ.:** B.A., University of London, UK (1949-52). **Career:** Ministry of Education, Kuwait (1952-61); Inspector of Education; Minister Counsellor, Embassy to Egypt (1961-69); Minister Counsellor, Embassy to France (1969-73); Consul General, Switzerland (1973); Permanent Representative of Kuwait, UN, Geneva (1973). **Addr.:** Ministry of Foreign Affairs, Kuwait City, Kuwait. Kuwait Arabian Gulf.

DABBAGH (Hussein, Mohamad Ali, al), Anglo-Arab academic. **Born** in 1929, Jaffa, Palestine. **Son** of Mohamad Ali Dabbagh. **Married,** two children. **Educ.:** London University, UK; Durham University, UK. **Dipl.:** B.A. in Classical Arabic; Ph.D. **Career:** Assistant Lecturer in Arabic (1956-61); Lecturer in Arabic (since 1961); seconded to University of Malaya (1964-66); University of Ibadan, Nigeria (1969-70); Lecturer in English, University of Kuwait (1970-71); visited University of California by invitation (1969); Lecturer in Arabic, Durham University, UK. **Member of:** Association of University Teachers (AUT), Durham; the British Society of Middle Eastern Studies (BRISMES), Council for the Advancement of Arab-British Understanding (CAABU), London. **Publ.:** a translation of Shakespeare Sonnets into Arabic verse published in "Aswat" magazine, London (1961); several poems published in "al-Ra'id al-Arabi" periodical. **Hobbies:** Gardening, watching television, badmington. **Sport:** Tennis. **Addr.:** University of Durham, School of Oriental Studies, Elvet Hill, Durham, UK.

DABBAGH (Riyadh Hamid, al), Iraqi academic, geologist. **Born** in 1946 in Mosul, Iraq. **Son** of Hamid al Dabbagh. **Married,** one son. **Educ.:** University of London. **Dipl.:** B.Sc. in Geology (1968); M.Sc. (1972); Ph.D. (1975); International Seminar of Hydrology, UNESCO, Moscow (1981). **Career:** Assistant Geologist, University of Mosul (1968); Assistant Head of Geology Department, College of Sciences, University of Mosul (1970); Demonstrator, Geology Department (1975); Head of Geology Department (1976-78); Vice President, University of Mosul (1977); presently President of Al Mustansiriya University, Baghdad. **Member** of International Hydrologists Association, the British Geology Society, the Iraqi National Council for International Hydrology Programme, UNESCO, the Iraqi Geologists Society; Head of the Iraqi Geologists Association; Deputy Chairman, Cultural Social Center, University of Mosul. **Publ.:** Numerous articles and researches in professional journals and magazines, translation of two books on hydrology (1979, 1981). **Sports:** Tennis. **Hobbies:** Reading, travelling. **Addr.:** The Presidency of the University of Baghdad, P.O.Box 14022, Waziriya, Baghdad, Iraq.

DABBAGH (Taher, H., al), Saudi academic. **Born** in 1939 in Mecca, Saudi Arabia. **Dipl.:** (Personnel Management and Behavioral Science). **Career:** Held several posts at Petromin, Accounting Department (1964-65) Riyadh; Assistant Professor, Business Administration Department, Faculty of Economics and Administration; Dean, Girls' Higher Education, King Abdulaziz University, Jeddah; **Publ.:** About 40 research articles on industry in Saudi Arabia. **Hobbies:** Swimming, chess. **Prof. Addr.:** King Abdulaziz University, Faculty of Economics and Administration, P.O.Box 9031, Tel.: 6890765, Jeddah. **Priv. Addr.:** Tel.: 6894233, Jeddah, Saudi Arabia.

DABBAGH (Zein el-Abidin), Saudi diplomat. **Born** in 1925. **Dipl.:** B.A. (Political Science), University of Washington (1950); M.A. (International Relations), University of Connecticut (1952); further studies towards Ph.D. (International Law) Under Professor Herbert W.Briggs, Cornell University (completed all requirements except thesis, 1953, 1955). **Career:** Temporary assignment at Saudi Arabian Mission to the United Nations (1952-53); joined Diplomatic Service, Ministry of Foreign Affairs (1955), Third Secretary, Saudi Arabian Embassy, Tokyo, Japan (1957-59); Assistant Deputy Chief, Saudi Arabian Permanent Mission to the United Nations, New York, Saudi Arabian Representative on the Sixth Legal Committee of the General Assembly (1959-64); Counsellor, Ministry of Foreign Affairs; Head, Legal and Conferences Department (1964-66); Minister Plenipotentiary and Charge d'Affaires, Saudi Arabian Embassy, Taipei, Taiwan (1966-73); Ambassador, Political Assistant to the late Foreign Minister Mr. Omar Saqqaf (1973-74); Head of the Legal and Conferences Department since 1975, member of Saudi Arabian delegation to the Japanese Peace Conference, San Francisco, (1951); Deputy Chief, Saudi delegation to the UN Conference for Trade and Development (UNCTAD), Geneva, Switzerland (1964); member of Saudi delegation to the Non-Aligned Conference of Heads of State, Cairo, Egypt (1964); member of Saudi Preparatory Committee for the Non-Aligned Conference of the Heads of State, Algeria (1965); Head, Saudi delegation to the Conference on the Development of Humanitarian Law during Armed Conflict, Geneva, Switzerland (1975); Head, Saudi delegation to the UN Second Conference of the Law of the Sea, Geneva, Switzerland (1975); attended fourteen sessions of the UN General Assembly; member of American Society of International Law; Ambassador to Japan (1976-83); Ambassador to the Netherlands (since 1983). **Hobby:** sports. **Addr.:** Ministry of Foreign Affairs, Tel.: 6651359, Jeddah, Saudi Arabia. Tel.: Office 6651359, Jeddah, Saudi Arabia.

DABBAS (Hanna, E.), Jordanian civil engineer. **Born** in 1947 in Amman, Jordan. **Son** of Emile Hanna Debbas (merchant) **and** Mrs. Mimi née Zarifeh. **Married** in 1972 to Miss Barbara Gregg, one son. **Educ.:** American University of Beirut. **Dipl.:** Bachelor of Civil Engineering.

Career: Project Management, Construction Management, Project Evaluation and Estimation, International Contracting and Investment Co. **Sports:** Basketball, tennis. **Hobby:** Computer Sciences. **Member of:** Royal Automobile Club, Sports City, Engineering Association. **Credit Cards:** American Express, Visa, Access. **Prof. Addr.:** P.O.Box 19170, Tel.: 813781, Amman, Jordan. **Priv. Addr.:** P.O.Box 9330, Tel.: 644551, Amman, Jordan.

DABBAS (Hashem, Ahmad), Jordanian Former Minister of Energy, president of audit bureau for the Government of Jordan. **Born** in Salt in 1929. **Son** of Ahmad Dabbas (agriculture- farming) **and** Mrs. Maha Ahmad Dabbas. **Married**, 7 children: Ihsan (1962), Aida (1964), Anwar (1965), Raouf (1965), Sami (1966), Jamal (1969), Jawad (1973). **Educ.:** Salt Secondary School, Jordan (1949); Faculty of Commerce, Cairo University (1955); Kansas State University, Manhattan, USA (1958); Missouri University, Colombia, USA (1963). **Dipl.:** Bachelor of Commerce, M.A., Dr. Degree of Philosophy in Political Science and Economics. **Career:** Economist, National Planning Council (1964-66); Director General, Statistic Department (1964-70); Under-Secretary, Ministry of Industry and Trade (1966-70-81); Permanent Alternate Governor World Bank, Amman; member of board of Directors of Tourism Authority, of the National Petroleum Company, of the National Petroleum Refinery, of the Greater Amman Commission, of the Retired Army Personnel Agency; Member of the Aqaba Zoning Committee; Assistant Secretary General of Pan-Arab Economist Union; President of the Federation of Jordan Economists (1972 till present); former Chairman of the Syrian Jordanian Industrial Free Zone; former Chairman, Jordan Phosphate Mines Co. Ltd.; Minister of Energy (1996). **Awards:** Independance Decoration (Grade.2); Renaissance Decoration (Grade 1). **Hobby:** Reading. **Sport:** Swimming. **Member:** Al-Hussein Youth City Club. **Priv. Addr.:** P.O.Box 3218, Amman, Jordan.

DABBOUS (Aly Gamal el-Din Tayel), Egyptian bank executive. **Born** in 1924 at Nekla el-Enab, Buheira Province, Egypt. **Educ.:** Cairo University **Dipl.:** B.Com. **Career:** Joined National Bank of Egypt (1946-76). **Chairman:** The Chase National Bank, Egypt till 1983; Chairman & Managing Director, Egypt Arab African Bank (1983-88); Presently Managing Director, Arab International Bank. Member of the Board of Directors of World Trade Center, Egypt. Vice Chairman of International Company for Touristic Investments, Egypt. Vice Chairman Compagnie Arabe de Financement International (CAFI) Luxembourg. **Prof. Addr.:** Arab International Bank, 35 Abdelkhalek Sarwat St., P.O.Box 1563, Cairo, Egypt.

DABBUR (Ali Ibrahim Mohamad), Saudi academic. **Born** in 1939 in Medina, Saudi Arabia. **Dipl.:** B.Sc. (Agriculture), Cairo University, M.A. (Insects), Oklahoma University, Ph.D. (Insects), U.K. **Career:** Head of Insects Department, Ministry of Agriculture (1962-69); Lecturer, Faculty of Agriculture, King Saud University (1970); Assistant Professor (1974); Head of Cultural Activities, Faculty of Agriculture (1974); Head of Social Activities (1975); Associate Professor, Faculty of Agriculture, King Saud University since 1981. **Member:** American Insects Association, Egyptian Insects Society, African Insects Society, American Mosquito Eradication Association; Saudi Biological Society; member of Board, Faculty of Agriculture Council, Research Centre Council. **Publ.:** Insect and Animal Blights in Saudi Arabia, the Spread of Flies in the Kingdom of Saudi Arabia (book). **Prof. Addr.:** Faculty of Agriculture, King Saud University, Riyadh. **Priv. Addr.:** Tel.: 4811000 Ext. 2299, Riyadh, Saudi Arabia.

DABDOUB (Ibrahim, Shucri), Jordanian Banker (CEL). **Born** on August 9, 1939. **Son** of Shucri Dabdoub **and** Mrs. Deik, Mena Dabdoub. **Married** on August 20, 1976 in Betlehem to Elda Al Bandak, 2 children: Tamara, Shucri. **Educ.:** Graduate Of: 1) Middle East Technical University-Ankara, Turkey; 2) Stanford University-California. **Dipl.:** BA & The Senior Executive Program. **Career:** Joined National Bank of Kuwait Jan. 1961. CEO (1983- till present); Deputy CEO (1980-1983); Assistant GM (1974-1980); Head of Credit Department (1969-1974); Assistant to Bank's Secretary (1961-1969); **Other Information:** Director, The Institute of International Finance-Washington; Director, Arab Thought Forum, Amman-Jordan, Director, The Executive Committee of the Institute for Social and Economic Policy in the Middle East-Harvard University; Director, Institute of Banking Studies-Kuwait; Director, Arab Management Centre-Bradford University; Director, Centre for Contemporary Arab Studies-Georgetown University-Washington; Director, International Advisory Board-Council on Foreign Relations-New York; Deputy Chairman, National Bank of Kuwait International Plc; Chairman, NBK Investment Management Ltd.-London; Chairman, NBK Finance S.A.-Geneva; Chairman, NBK (Lebanon)-Beirut. **Awards:** Awarded, the Banker's Achievement Award, by the Arab Bankers Association of North America (ABANA), New York (October 1995). Elected the Arab Banker of the year Award by the Union of Arab Banks (December 1997). **Sport:** Fishing. **Hobby:** Reading. **Prof.Addr.:** National Bank of Kuwait SAK, P.O.Box 95, Safat 13001, Kuwait, Tel.: 24220111.

DADDAH (Abdallahi, Ould), Mauritanian statesman. **Born** in Boutilimit (Mauritania). **Married:** Tukiya, 2 children. **Educ.:** Van Vollehhoven College, Dakar (Senegal); Faculty of Law, University of Paris. **Dipl.:** Baccalaureat; B.Sc. (Econ), 1962. **Career:** Secretary General, Ministry of Foreign Affairs (1962-64); Ambassador to France, also accredited to United Kingdom, Italy and Switzerland (1964-66); Ambassador to United States of America, also accredited Permanent Representative to UNO, New York

(1966-70); Minister of Equipment; Minister of Rural Development (1975). **Member:** Mauritania People's Party (PPM) Party suspended following Coup in June 1978. **Awards:** Commander, Order of Merit. **Addr.:** Nouakchott, Mauritania.

DADDAH (Moukhtar, Ould), Former President of the Islamic Republic of Mauritania. **Born** on December 25, 1924 in Boutilimit, Tarza District (Mauritania). **Educ.:** Medera (Koranic School); Sons of Chiefs' School; Interpreter's School, St. Louis, Dakar (Senegal) and Nice (France); Faculty of Law, University of Paris; National School of Oriental Languages, Paris. **Dipl.:** LL.B., B.A. (Letters). **Career:** Set up Law Practice, Dakar (Senegal) (1955); elected member of Territorial Assembly (1957); Vice-President, Governing Council; Minister of Youth Sports and Education; founded Parti du Regroupement Mauritanien (PRM), 1958); elected member, French National Assembly (1959); Prime Minister and Minister of the Interior (1959); founded Mauritanian People's Party (PPM), 1961; elected President of the Republic (1960); President, Malagasy Common Organization (1965); Chairman, Organization of African Unity (1971); overthrown on July 10, 1978 and put under arrest, later released. **Addr.:** Nouakchott, Mauritania.

DAFAI (Hussain, al), Yemeni Army Officer, Diplomat and Statesman. **Born** in North Yemen. **Educ.:** Secondary and Higher, and Military Academy. **Career:** Commissioned Lt-Col., in the Republican Army; Minister of Labour and Social Affairs in the second Cabinet (31 Oct. 1962- 13 April 1963), and member of the Revolutionary Command Council; War Minister in the 3rd, 4th and 5th Cabinets following the overthrow of Imam Badr, (1963-64); appointed member of Tribal Affairs Commission (29 May 1965); Minister of the Interior (July 1965- September 1966); Arrested by President Sallal on charges of subversion; Ambassador to the Soviet Union until 1966, thereafter serving on the Revolutionary Command Council; Adviser, Political Affairs, to President Al-Hamdi (April 1977) and Minister of State (1977). **Addr.:** Sana'a, Republic of Yemen.

DAFALLAH (Gizouli), Sudanese physician and politician. **Career:** Chairman Alliance of the National Forces (1985, after overthrow of President Gaafar al-Nemery); Chairman Doctor's Union; Prime Minister of Sudan (1985-86). **Addr.:** Khartoum, Sudan.

DAFALLAH (Nazir, Dr.), Sudanese veterinary. **Born** on January 1, 1922 at el-Obeid in Kordofan (Sudan). **Married** in 1952 to Deriya Hassan el-Amin, one daughter, four sons. **Educ.:** Primary and secondary education locally; faculty of Veterinary Science, University of Khartoum (1943-64); Manchester University, England. **Dipl.:** B.Sc. (Veterinary Science) 1946; B.Sc. (Bacteriology) 1952. **Career:** Government Veterinary Officer, Government research laboratories at Khartoum, Malakal and Nyala (1952-54); Research Officer (1955-56); Senior lecturer in bacteriology, University of Khartoum (1956-57); Dean, Faculty of Veterinary Science (1958-62); Deputy Vice-Chancellor, University of Khartoum (1960-62); Vice-Chancellor and Professor of bacteriology (1962-68); Provost of Agriculture and Veterinary Medicine, Ahmadou Bello University, Zaria (Nigeria) (1971-72); Speaker, People's Assembly (1972- Jan. 1974); Participated in Round Table Conference for Southern Sudan; Minister of Health and Social Guidance (July 1974- Jan. 1975); Minister of Health (Jan. 1975-79). **Publ.:** Author of many papers on bacteriology; Chairman, Editorial Board, Sudan Journal of Veterinary Science and Husbandry; Head, Editorial Committee of the International Veterinary Magazine. **Member:** President, Sudan National Scientific Council; FAO International Panel of Experts, Committee for the Campaign against animal sickness (1973); Advisory Panel of Experts on the Emergency Control of Livestock Diseases, Rome; International Committee of Abou Genat Disease; International Bacteriology Society; Skin Diseases Society (USA); Executive Vice-President, Association of African Universities; Administrative Board, International Association of Universities; International Association of University Staff; Chairman, Committee for Developing East Africa University; Chairman, Conference of the South. **Hobbies:** Reading and travelling. **Prof. Addr.:** Khartoum, Sudan.

DAFFA (Ali, A.), Saudi academic. **Born** in 1941 at Onaizah, Saudi Arabia. **Dipl.:** B.A. (Pure Maths). Ohio University (1966); B.Sc. (Maths) Stephen of Austin State University (1968); M.Sc. (Maths) Vanderbilt University (1969); Ph.D. (Maths) Peabody College and Vanderbilt University (1973). **Career:** Assistant Lecturer, Vanderbilt University (1971-72); Assistant Professor, King Fahad University of Petroleum and Minerals (1973-74); Chairman, Mathematics Department, KFUPM (1974-77); Acting Dean, Faculty of Science, KFUPM (1975-77); Dean, Faculty of Science. KFUPM (1977); proofreader, Mathematics History Magazine (Canada); member, American Mathematical Society, British Society for History of Science, International Commission on the History of Science, Association of Muslim Scientists and Engineers, Association of Arab Scientists; honorary member, Iranian Mathematical Association: President, Union of Arab Physicists and Mathematicians. **Publ.:** A large number of books on Science, Mathematics and Islamic subjects since 1977; many articles, studies and papers in addition to broadcasts on Saudi Radio on the subject of Arab and Muslim Scientists and Modern Mathematics in the Programme Hadeeth As-Sharah (1979). **Hobby:** Writing. **Priv. Addr.:** Tel.: 8606292, Dhahran, Saudi Arabia.

DAFFA (Khattab, Omar, al), Qatari statesman. **Born** in 1952 in Doha, Qatar. **Son** of Omar al-Daffa. **Married**, two children. **Educ.:** B.Sc. in Economics and Political

Science, Western Michigan University, USA. **Career:** Financial official, Ministry of Finance and Petroleum; Director of Civil Service Department, Ministry of Finance and Petroleum. **Sport:** Football. **Hobbies:** Poetry and music. **Addr.:** Government House, Civil Service Department, P.O.Box 36, Telephone: 447290, 413572, Telex: 40332 CEVSER, Doha, Qatar, Arabian Gulf.

DAGHESTANI (Nejib, Abu al Alla, al), Syrian engineer. **Born** in 1940 in Damascus, Syria. **Son** of Mohamad Kazem Daghestani. **Divorced** two sons. **Educ.:** Diploma in Civil Engineering, Enfield College of Technology, University of Middlesex, (formerly), UK, (1968); Postgraduate Diploma, Foundation Engineering UK (1969); M.Sc. in Mining and Engineering Geophysics, University of Strathclyde, UK (1972). **Career:** Soil and Foundation Engineer, UK (1968-70); Counterpart to UN/ILO Expert, Ministry of Communications, Syria (1972-74); Civil and Material Engineer, Roads and Bridges, Saudi Arabia (1974-78); Joint General Manager Oman Building and Construction Co. Ltd. (OBCO) Oman (1978-81); Contract's Manager Libya (1981-92); Promotion and Development Manager (Gulf) (1982-85); Independant Development and Investment Consultant (Portugal), (1985-). **Publ.:** Manuals and Articles (Site Investigations). **Sports:** Swimming, Snorkling, Hiking. **Hobbies:** Reading, Music, painting, cinema, theatre. **Priv. Addr.:** P.O.Box 428,8500 Portimao, Portugal.

DAGHISTANI (Abdulaziz, I.)), Saudi academic & economist. **Born** in 1947 in Taif, Saudi Arabia. **Dipl.:** Ph.D. (Economics), University of Houston, Texas (1979). **Career:** Researchers, Department of Economics, King Saud University (1970-72); Associate Professor (1988), same University; Economic Adviser to the Ministry of Pilgrimage and Endowments; Chairman, General Cultural Committee, King Saud University; member, the National Geographic Society, USA; Saudi Economic Association; Western Economic Association, USA. **Publ.:** Economic Development in Saudi Arabia: Problems and Prospects (Ph.D. thesis); Economic and Political Issues, Riyadh (1980); Development and Under-development in Islam and Modern Ideologies (1981); General Manager, Saudi Installment Company (1988-90); President, Economic Studies House (1991-); Publisher & Editor-in-Chief of the Economic World Magazine (1992-). **Addr.:** Economic Studies House, P.O.Box 1661, Riyadh 11441, Tel.: 966-1-462-3444, Fax: 966-1-462-1349, Riyadh, Saudi Arabia, and P.O.Box 8795, Jeddah 21492, Tel.: 669-0993, Fax: 660-4026, Jeddah, Saudi Arabia.

DAGHISTANI (Abdulaziz, Mohamad), Legal accountant. **Born** in 1922 in Medina, Saudi Arabia. **Dipl.:** B.A. (Accounting), Faculty of Commerce, Cairo University. **Career:** Former Deputy President of the Public Control Board (1960-80); Political Attaché, Ministry of Foreign Affairs; First Secretary and Consul Geneal, Saudi Embassy in Cairo; General Director of Financial Affairs, Ministry of Foreign Affairs; Chartered Accountant since 1966. **Hobbies:** Reading, swimming. **Prof. Addr.:** 41 Jarir St., al-Malaz, P.O.Box 3736, Tel.: 4761885, Riyadh. **Priv. Addr.:** Tel.: 4763302, Riyadh, Saudi Arabia.

DAGHISTANI (Ali, Mahmoud Fahmi, al), Egyptian engineer. **Born** on December 1, 1918 in Cairo, Egypt. **Married:** one daughter. **Educ.:** B.Sc. in Engineering, Cairo University, Egypt (1941). **Career:** Chairman, Egyptian Railways Institute (1941-71); Chairman of the Board, Institute of Planning and Transport (1971-78); Minister of Transport (1978-80); Engineering Consultant, Ministry of Supply (1980-83); Chairman of the Board, National Bank of Kefer al-Shaikh (1981-83); Construction Consultant, Ministry of Construction and Land Reclamation (1983-84); Chairman of the Consultative Committee for Construction (1984); Secretary to the Chairman of the Board of Transport, Scientific Academy; Professor of Postgraduate Commercial Transport Studies, College of Commerce, al-Azhar University. **Publ.:** Waque Sikak Hadeed Maste Wa Iqtirahat Tatweraha (1969); Naqel al-Bachâa Ala al-Turuk (1974); al-Naqel Bel-Sikak al-Hadeedeyah (1982). **Decor:** Order of Merit (First Class) Egypt (1968). **Member:** Chairman of the Railway Club, member of Gezira Sporting Club. **Priv. Addr.:** 31 Falah Street, Madinat al-Mohandisseen, Tel.: 755858, 812020, Giza, Egypt.

DAGHISTANI (Fakhreddine, Abdul Hadi), Jordanian engineer. **Born** on December 19, 1936 Jordan. **Married**, 2 sons, 4 daughters. **Educ.:** University of Missouri, USA. **Dipl.:** B.Sc. in Mechanical Engineering, M.Sc., Ph.D. **Career:** Staff Engineer, IBM, Rochester Minnesota, USA (1968-71); Director, Mechanical Engineering Department, Royal Scientific Society, Jordan (1971-76), Vice President (1976-83); Member of the Board of Directors of Natural Resources Authority and Jordan Telecommunications Corporation, Jordan, Board Member of Scientific Council of the Islamic Foundation for Science and Technology, Saudi Arabia, Member of the Board of Trustees of the Royal Scientific Society and the National College for Engineering and Administrative Science, of Directors of the Arab Federation of Scientific Research Councils, Iraq; President, Royal Scientific Society (1984). **Publ.:** "Science and Technology for Development" (1978), "Environment Monitoring for the Arab World" (1981), "Building Codes and Specifications for the Arab World" (1983). **Decor.:** The Great Merit Cross with Star, President of the Federal Republic of Germany. **Hobbies:** research, classical music and reading. **Prof. Addr.:** P.O.Box 925819, Amman, Jordan.

DAGHISTANI (Jafar Abdul Hamid), Saudi banker. **Born** in Mecca, in 1928. **Educ.:** Secondary School Certificate; attended banking courses, London. **Career:** Manager, Riyadh Shop; Director, Accounting and Warehouse

Depot, Juffali Brothers; Director, International Agencies; Director of Chamber of Commerce and Industry, Mecca; member of Board of Chamber of Commerce, Mecca; Arab Banks Union, Beirut; Manager, Riyadh Bank, P.O.Box 160, Mecca. **Hobbies:** Painting, music. **Addr.:** Riyadh Bank, Mecca, Saudi Arabia.

DAGHMAN (Abdulmoula, Khalil), Libyan former rector of university. **Born** in 1930 in Benghazi. **Educ.:** B.A. from Cairo University (1957), M.A. from Boston University (U.S.A) (1960). **Career:** Demonstractor, Faculty of Arts & Education University of Libya (1961-63); Dean, Faculty of Arts & Education (1963); Under Secretary, Ministry of Petroleum Affairs (1964); Dean, Faculty of Arts (1965-76), Rector, University of Libya (June 1967 - Sept. 1969); Ex-Member of the Broadcasting Committee, ex-Member of High Committee for the Preservation of Liberal & Fine Arts. **Addr.:** Benghazi, Libya.

DAHAB (Abdul-Rahman Swar, al, Gen.), Sudanese army officer and politician. **Born** in 1934 in Omdurman. **Married**, five children. **Career:** Joined Sudanese Military Academy (1954); trained at military academies in Jordan, Britain and Egypt; Minister of Defence; Commander in Chief of Sudanese Army (1985); led military coup (April 1985); Chairman, Transitional Military Council (1985-86). **Addr.:** Khartoum, Sudan.

DAHABI (Mahir, Antoun, al), Egyptian journalist. **Son** of Antoun al-Dahabi. **Born** in 1936 in Alexandria, Egypt. **Married**, two sons. **Educ.:** B.A., College of Arts, Press Department, Cairo University, Cairo, Egypt; studied journalism with the Thompson Group, UK. **Career:** Joined "Rose al-Yusif" (1955); Editor "al-Ahram" newspaper (1958-71); Chief of the Editing Technical Department (1971); Assistant to the Editor in Chief "al-Ahram" newspaper (1980); Lecturer Layout Techniques and Journalism, Faculty of Mass Media, Cairo University; Supervisor of "Engineer's Magazine", "Arab Youth" and "Islamic Banks Magazine"; Supervisor of the production of books and publications of some Egyptian publishing houses; collaborated with al-Ahram in the Establishment of Dar al-Kitab al-Gadid publishing House. **Member of:** the Egyptian Press Syndicate, of the International Research Association for Newspaper Technology (IFRA), al-Gazira Club, the Hunting Club, al-Ahli Sporting Club. **Publ.:** Articles in "al-Ahram", books on Arab press. **Addr.:** 7 Abdul Hamid Said Street, Kasr al-Nil, Tel.: 45854, Telex: 92001, 92544, Cairo, Egypt.

DAHABIYEH (Hassan Ahmad Ellayyan), Financial adviser. **Born** in 1948 in Jerusalem. **Son** of Ahmed Dahabiyeh. **Married** in 1976, 2 daughters. **Educ.:** Secondary Education, Jerusalem; Ain Shams University, Cairo, Egypt. **Dipl.:** B.Com. (1970). **Career:** Chartered Accountant, London (1971-74); Accountant, Ernest & Whinney, London (1975-77); Senior Audit Manager, Ernst & Whinney, M.E. (1978-80); General Auditor, Commercial Bank of Kuwait SAK, Kuwait; Director and Financial Adviser in the Board of Directors of the Commercial Bank of Kuwait. **Member:** Institute of Chartered Accountants in England and Wales; Institute of Internal Auditors, U.K. and USA; Institute of Bankers, UK, Arab Bankers Association. **Publ.:** Business articles relating to banking accounting published in the daily local newspaper in Kuwait. **Sports:** Jogging, golf, squash, swimming. **Hobbies:** Music, reading and writing. **Addr.:** P.O.Box 2861, Safat, Tel.: 2468521, 2411001, Telex: 22004 A/B CBK KT, Kuwait.

DAHAISH (Abdullatif Abdallah, ben), Saudi academic. **Born** in 1943, in Mecca, Saudi Arabia. **Dipl.:** B.A. (History), Riyadh University 1967; M.A., Ph.D. (History), University of Leeds, U.K. **Career:** Demonstrator (1967-68); Assistant Professor, Faculty of Sharia; attended the Preparatory Conference of Okaz Festival for the Revival of Classical Arab Poetry; Head of History Department, Faculty of Sharia (Islamic Law). **Publ.:** edited Arabic manuscripts in the University of Leeds, Faculty of Sharia Journal; published articles in British and Italian journals; now editing a reference book on the Mecca Holy Sanctuary decorations, Mecca ancient buildings with illustrations and data (to be published by Faculty of Sharia, Mecca). **Hobbies:** Reading, research. **Addr.:** Faculty of Sharia, Mecca, Saudi Arabia.

DAHAK (Driss, Jelloul, al), Moroccan judge. **Born** in 1939 at al-Kasr al-Kabeer, Morocco. **Married** 2 sons. **Educ.:** Nice University, France. **Dipl.:** LLB. **Career:** Investigating Magistrate, Ministry of Justice (1962-67), General Advocate (1967-68), Public Prosecutor (1968-72), Counsellor for the Minister of Justice, Justice Courts of Appeal (1972-77), Director, Magistrates Institution (1977-85); representative of Morocco to the United Nations for Maritime Law (1973-82); Counsellor to the United Nations for Human Rights, Arab Committee (1982-85); Chairman, Arab Permanent Committee for Human Rights (1984-87); President, Maritime Arbitration Chamber; Secretary General, Organisation Arabe de Defense Social Contre le Crime (1985); Justice, Court of Cassation, Court of Constitution, State Chamber (1985-). Presently First President of Supreme Court in Rabat. **Publ.:** "The Concise Traffic Accidents Law" (1975), "Compulsory Insurance" (1980), "Traffic Law" (1981), "The Concise in law of Fishing" (1986), "Arab Countries and Maritime Law" (1986) in Arabic and French. **Hobbies:** Golf, tennis. **Prof. Addr.:** P.O.Box 1378, Rabat, Morocco.

DAHAMI (Muhammad), Moroccan economist. **Born** on July 1, 1943 in Tinjdad, Morocco. **Married**, 4 sons. **Educ.:** Ecole Superieure de Commerce in Bordeaux, France (1966). **Career:** Assistant Commercial Director (1966-69); Head of Provisions Department, Societe SEFERIF (1969-71); Director General, Societe SEREC (Office of Economical and Commercial Studies (since 1975);

Member of Parliament (1977-); Director of "Bulletin des Decideurs" magazine (1979-); President and Director General of SODIPRESS (1982-). **Publ.:** "Machinisme Agricole au Maroc", Serec (1983). **Hobbies:** Travelling, tennis. **Prof. Addr.:** 10, Place Mohammed V, Tel.: 271016, Telex: 21062, Casablanca 01, Morocco.

DAHHAN (Omaymah Ezzat, al), Jordanian academic. **Born** in 1942. **Educ.:** Ph.D. in Business Administration, Texas University, Austin, USA (1975). **Career:** Professor, Business Department, University of Jordan; Member of the Board of World Women Banking; President of Working Women Club, Jordan. **Publ.:** several articles in business administration in various Arab universities journals, co-author of many research works published by national and international organisations. **Hobby:** Music, Travel, Arts. **Addr.:** Faculty of Business Administration, University of Jordan, Tel.: 843555, Amman, Jordan.

DAHI (Abdel Wedoud Ould), Mauritanian financial administrator. **Born** in 1954 in Atar, Mauritania. **Son** of Mohamed Ould Dahi (deceased) **and** Mrs. Mroum nee Meimah. **Married** to Miss Zeine Bou Hmeida on January 30, 1982 in Nouakchott, 3 children: Houda, Mohamed, Mohamed Lemine. **Educ.:** University Mohamed V (Morocco); Ecole Nationale d'Administration (ENA-Mauritania). **Dipl.:** L.L.B. and Diploma from ENA (Public Finance). **Career:** Director, Housing and Equipment, Ministry of Finance; Director General of Taxes, Ministry of Finance; Director, Internal Trade and Economic Control; Assistant Director General, Societe Nationale d'Assurances et de Reassurances (SNAR). **Hobbies:** Reading, Scrable, TV. **Member:** Rotary Sahel de Nouakchott. **Prof. Addr.:** P.O.Box 1596, Tel.: 52662, Nouakchott, Mauritania. **Priv. Addr.:** Tel.: 51918, Mauritania.

DAHLAB (Saad), Algerian businessman and former diplomat. **Born** in April 1918. **Married**, 4 children. **Educ.:** Secondary and Higher. **Career:** Member of the Committee of Co-ordination and Executive for Front de Libération Nationale (F.L.N.) in Algeria (1956-57); Foreign Minister of "Provisional Government of the Algerian Republic" formed by F.L.N. in Tunisia (1958-61) and (1961-62); Ambassador to Morocco (1963-64); Director General of "Société Berliet Algérie" since 1965. **Publ.:** "Une Etude sur le Régime des Associations au Maroc" and "Une Etude sur la Police Judiciaire Marocaine", published by the Royal Police Review. **Addr.:** Société Berliet Algérie, P.O.Box 15, Rouiba, Algiers, Algeria.

DAHLAN (Mohamad Bakry), Saudi businessman. **Born** in 1941, in Mecca, Saudi Arabia. **Educ.:** received Secondary School Education, Certificate and Diploma from a language institute (England). **Career:** Adminisrative Supervisor, Ministry of Foreign Affairs; Political Attaché, Ministry of Foreign Affairs; Political Attaché, Ministry of Foreign Affairs; member of al-Wihda (Unity) Sporting Club, Mecca; founder of the first factory in Mecca for ready-made clothes 1971; Owner and Director-General of Dahlan Trade and Contracting Est. **Addr.:** Riyadh, Saudi Arabia.

DAHLAN (Rabea Sadiq), Saudi civil servant. **Born** in 1949 in Mecca, Saudi Arabia. **Dipl.:** M.A. (Public Administration). **Career:** Began his career in the private sector, (1970-75); Demonstrator, Faculty of Economics and Public Administration, King Abdulaziz University (1975-76); Lecturer, Faculty of Economics and Public Administration, King Abdulaziz University (1978-79); General Manager of Telephone and Telex Department, Western Region, Ministry of Post, Telephone and Telegraph, Jeddah; (1979-80); General Manager, Saudi Telecom, West Region (1981-); member, Jeddah Literary Club; attended various regional and international conferences on communications; represented the Ministry of Post, Telephone and Telegraph at the 3rd meeting of the Saudi-Canadian Joint Committee in Ottawa, Canada; Vice President of the Authorized Representatives, Conference of the International Union for Wire and Wireless Communication, Nairobi, Kenya. **Hobbies:** Reading, travel. **Addr.:** P.O.Box 6220, Tel.: 6360000 (Office) and Tel.: 6675567 (Home), Jeddah, Saudi Arabia.

DAHLAWI (Hassan, al, Sheikh), Saudi businessman. **Born** on December 20, 1952 in Mecca, Saudi Arabia. **Son** of Mohamed Jamil Mohd. Haroon (former Businessman, President of Mecca Chamber of Commerce). **Married**, 3 children: Mohamed (1985), Abdulaziz (1986) and Rayan (1988). **Educ.:** University of Portland, USA. **Dipl.:** BBA. **Career:** Joined family business in Jeddah, Saudi Arabia; Senior Vice President of M. jamil al-Dahlawi Company, Jeddah, sole agent and distributors of Matsushita Electrica Industrial Co. Ltd., Japan, in the Kingdom of Saudi Arabia, dealing in electronics, telecommunications equipment, electrical, audio visual, home appliances and computers, also in general trading in food and other consumer goods, real estate development, finance, banking, hospitality entreprises, manufacturing and investment and import of grain especially rice. Managing Director, Saudi International Est.; Director of al-Baha Hospital, also Director in National Metal Manufacturing and Casting Co. (Maadaniah); Vice President of International Trading Co. Ltd. and Trans Middle East Company, Saudi Arabia; Director of International Bank of Commerce, Bahrain; Managing Director of General Ceramics (UAE) Ltd., Sharjah, UAE; Director, International Investment and Finance Corp. S.A., UK; Managing Director, Draycott Resources Ltd., UK; Director of St. James's Club, Antigua, West Indies. **Hobbies:** Swimming, boating. **Member:** World Economic Forum, Geneva. **Credit Cards:** American Express; Diners Club; Carte Blanche; Barclays; Hilton; Bank of America Visa. **Prof. Addr.:** M. Jamil Al Dahlawi Co., P.O.Box 1522, Jeddah 21441, Tel.: 6470000, Telex: 601023 SJ, Fax: 6474549, Jeddah, Saudi Arabia.

DAHLAWI (Mohammed Amin, Al, Sheikh), Saudi businessman. **Born** in 1942 in Makkah, Saudi Arabia. **Son** of Mohammed Jamil Mohd. Haroon (Businessman). **Married**, five children. **Education:** Amercian University of Cairo, Egypt. **Diploma:** Graduate/ G.C.C. B.A. (Economics & Political Science from American University of Cairo. **Career:** Joined family business in Jeddah, Saudi Arabia (1963); Chairman and President of M. Jamil Al Dahlawi Company, Jeddah, sole agent and distributors of Matsushita Electric Industrial Co., Ltd., Japan, in the Kingdom of Saudi Arabia, dealing in Electronics, Telecommunications Equipment, Electrical, Audio Visual Home Appliances and Computers, also General Trading in Food and other consumer goods, real estate development, finance, banking, hospitality enterprises, manufacturing and investment; Chairman of Trans Middle East Company, International Trading Co., Ltd. and Al-Baha Hospital, Saudi Arabia; Director of Le Palace Hotel in Tunisia; Chairman of General Ceramic (UAE) Ltd., Sharjah, UAE, Vice Chairman of Montaza Tabaraka, Tunis, Director of Tunisian Real Estate Co. and Jerba Fisheries, Tunis, Dahlawi California Corp., Macca International Ltd. and Miami Freedom Tower, Miami, Director of Tiedmann/Goodnow Int'l Member of the Board of Advisors, Foster Management Co. U.S.A. Chairman of St. James's Club Antigua. **Decoration:** Kentucky Colonel. **Member:** Honours Medal of the Republic of Tunisia, Honorary Consul in Saudi Arabia for the Government of Antigua & Barbuda. Institute of Directors, London; World Economic Forum Geneva, Arab Bankers Association of North America, USA and England, Charter Member of the President's Club of American University, Cairo, **Credit Cards:** American Express; Diners Club, Barclays, Hilton, Bank of America Visa. **Address:** Al-Dahlawi Company, P.O.Box 1522, Jeddah 21441, Tel No: 02-698-0000; Telex: 601023 Dehlwi SJ, Telefax: No. 02-698-1238/ 698-2238, Jeddah, Saudi Arabia. **Hobby:** Swimming. Tennis.

DAHLEH (Seif), Yemeni army officer and statesman. **Born** in Southern Yemen. **Educ.:** Military School for Officers. **Career:** Joined Army Forces, Promoted Colonel, Member of the Front de Libération Nationale (F.L.N.), Minister of Foreign Affairs in the first Government after the Independance, (December 1967). **Addr.:** Aden, Republic of Yemen.

DAHMANI (Hussein), Tunisian bank executive. **Born** in 1934 in Tunisia. **Son** of Salem Dahmani. **Married** in 1960, 4 children. **Educ.:** College Sadiki, Ecole Nationale d'Administration, Faculté de Droit, Faculté de Théologie et des Sciences Religieuses; High Administration. Diploma; Magistrate in Law. **Career:** Financial Controller (1960-64); General Manager, Civil Service Office, Tunis (1964-70); Director, Administration Research Center, Mgluch, Algiers (1971-75); Secretary General, Health Ministry, Tunis (1975-77); President, Société Tunisienne de Diffusion, Tunis (1977-80); Secretary General, Islamic Development Bank (1980). **Member:** Société des Sciences Administratives Tunis. **Hobby:** Old handwritten books. **Addr.:** Tunis, Tunisia.

DAHMASH (Ahmad, Qassim), Yemeni politician. **Born** in Yemen. **Married**, one son. **Career:** Teacher, Islamic Higher Institute, Aden (1961-62); Director of Information, Taiz (1964); 1st Secretary, Yemen Arab Republic Embassy to Somalia (1965); Director of the Prime Minister's Office (1965-67); Under Secretary, Ministry of Information (1968); Director, Printing Corporation, Ministry of Information (1971-76); Head of Commission for Administrative Re-organisation; Minister of Labour, Youth and Social Affairs (1976). **Hobby:** Folk dancing. **Sport:** Walking. **Addr.:** Sanaa, Republic of Yemen.

DAIRI (Sulaiman, Mohamad, al), Jordanian banker. **Born** in 1928 in Jordan. **Married. Educ.:** B.A. in Economics, American University of Cairo, Egypt (1950); Postgraduate studies, London School of Economics (1952-53). **Career:** Jordan Foreign Currency Department (1950-53); Director of Foreign Currencies Department, Jordan Central Bank (1964-65); Director of Research and Statistics, Jordan Central Bank (1965-67); Chief Auditor and Head of Internal Organisation Department of Central Bank (1969-71); Under Secretary, Ministry of Finance (1971-77); Deputy President, Audit Bureau (since 1977). **Addr.:** P.O.Box 921026, Tel.: 640398, Amman, Jordan.

DAJANI (Abdul Salim), Jordanian UN official. **Born** on December 28, 1922 in Palestine. **Educ.:** University of Beirut, Lebanon; Law College, Jerusalem; Suffolk University, Law School, Boston, Massachussets, USA. **Dipl.:** LL.B. **Career:** UN, New York (1950); Programme Office and Acting Chief of Middle East Section of UN Radio and Visual Services Division (1950-57); Various UN functions in Asia, the Pacific region, Africa, Europe and the Middle East; returned to UN Headquarters in New York in 1965; Chief of UN Headquarters in New York in 1965; Chief of UN Public Services (1972), Chief of Centre Services in the External Relations Division (1972); Member of UN Mission to Malaysia; Member of UN Joint Appeal Board and UN Appointments and Promotions Committee (1967-76). **Prof. Addr.:** United Nations, New York, NY 10017, USA.

DAJANI (Ali Taher), Jordanian Administrator, Economist, Journalist. **Born** in 1914 in Jerusalem. **Educ.:** English College, American University of Beirut, B.A. Jerusalem Institute of Financial Studies. **Career:** Assistant Information Officer; Assistant Commissioner of Commerce and Industry until end of the British Mandate in 1948; Director Arab Chamber of Commerce in East Jerusalem (1948-1950); Director, Amman Chamber of Commerce (1950-1954); Controller: The Jordan Electric Power Co., Amman (1955-1962); Founder and Director: Amman

Chamber of Industry (1962-1983); In between Deputy of Jerusalem (1963-1967); Minister of Transport (1965); Member of the Royal Fiscal Commission (1963); Commentator and Writer Ad-Defa'a Newspaper (formerly of Jerusalem), Al Hayat and Daily Star (formerly of Beirut, Al Sharq Al-Awsat Arabic Daily, London (1983-97); Honorary Consul of Japan (1969-1974); Honorary Commercial Representative of Canada (1979-1983); Founder Member and Former President of the Amman Rotary Club; Declared Man of the Year by the Rotary Club (1998); Advisor Amman Chamber of Industry (1988-); Jordanian Employer Delegate to the International Labour and the Arab Labour Organizations; Board Member of the Jordanian Daily Newspaper «Sawt El-Sha'ab». **Publ.:** «Jerusalem Faith and Struggle» (Arabic); «Palestinian Proverbs»; Pilgrimage to Mecca»; «The Economy of Jordan» (English); «Industry of Jordan» (English); «Jordan: a base for Regional Enterprises». **Decors:** Jordan «Al-Kawkab» (Star) 1st Class; Amman Chamber of Industry «Shield on Industry»; Japan: Insignia of the «Sacred Treasure»; Others: Tunis, Italy and the national Republic of China. Correspondent; The Economist Intelligence Unit, Cost of Living Survey. **Addr.:** P.O.Box 830085, Postal Box 11183 Amman, Jordan.

DAJANI (Aziz, Awni), Libyan financial executive. **Born** in 1948 in Cairo, Egypt. **Son** of Awni Dajani. **Single. Educ.:** London University, London School of Economics, Aberdeen University, Accountancy. **Dipl.:** B.Sc. (Economics). **Career:** Accountant, Delloites Haskins and Sells; Credit Analyst, Chase Manhattan Bank; Corporate Finance Executive, Sharjah Group Company, London Office; Director, Aspen Fall Co. N.V.; Director, Al Soukra Co. Ltd., Tunis, Tunisia. **Founder:** Member of Arab Bankers Association, London. **Hobbies:** Skiing, Gliding and Shark-fishing, **Addr.:** 3 Brompton Square, Tel.: 5897638, Telex: 299663, London, SW3, UK.

DAJANI (Jarir, Subhi), Arab-American academic. **Born** in 1940 in Jerusalem. **Married**, 3 children. **Educ.:** American University of Beirut, Lebanon; Stanford Univesity, USA; Northwestern University, USA. **Dipl.:** B.Sc. in Civil Engineering, M.Sc. in Engineering Economics and Construction Management, Ph.D. in Urban Systems Engineering and Policy Planning. **Career:** Resident Engineer, Associated Consulting Engineering, Lebanon, Saudi Arabia and Jordan (1961-66); Transportation and Community Planner, De Lezw Cather & Co., Chicago, Illinois, USA (1968-71); Assistant and Associate Professor of Civil Engineering and Policy Sciences, Duke University, Durham, North Carolina, USA (1971-76); Vice President, Public Systems Associates, Durham, North Carolina (1974-78); Associate Professor of Civil Engineering, Stanford University, Stanford, USA (1976-82); Member of, the American Society of Civil Engineers, the Operations, Research Society of America, American Institute of Planners; Senior Technical Advisor, Abu Dhabi Fund for Arab Economic Development, Abu Dhabi (1982-). **Publ.:** Numerous reports and papers on Infrastructure, Planning and Analysis subjects with emphasis on Land Use, Transportation and Environmental Systems; Co-Author of "Water and Sewer Developments in Rural America: A Study of Community Impacts", Leximgton Books (1975). **Credit Cards:** AMEX, Visa, Mastercard. **Prof. Addr.:** P.O.Box 814, Abu Dhabi, United Arab Emirates.

DAJANI (Nadim, S., al), Jordanian businesman. **Born** on December 1, 1929 in Jaffa, Palestine. **Son** of Salim Mustafa al-Dajani (landlord) and Mrs. Suad al-Dajani. **Married** on November 13, 1958 to Leila Abdul Hamid al Mufti, five children: Salim, Lubna, Maysdon, Basma and Ameer. **Educ.:** Secondary College of the Christian Brothers; Lincoln High School; American University in Cairo. **Dipl.:** B.A. (Industrial Planning and Management), B.Sc. (Accountancy). **Career:** set up business of his own as General Contractor; Chairman, Arab Projects Co. SA Ltd. **Sports:** Horseriding, swimming and tennis. **Hobby:** horseracing. **Clubs:** Hussein Sports Centre; Royal Automobile club; Turf Club. **Credit Card:** American Express. **Prof. Addr.:** Abdali, King Hussein Street, P.O.Box 1318, Tel.: 623133 - 62114 - 65686, Amman, Jordan. **Priv. Addr.:** Djebal Amman, 4th circle, Tel.: 41133 - 44133, Amman, Jordan.

DAJANI (Najmeddin, Dr.), Jordanian economist. **Born** on August 7, 1928 in Jerusalem. **Son** of Izzat Dajani. **Married** in 1965 to Nawal Toukan, 3 children: Rula (1966), Izzat (1967); Farah (1972). **Educ.:** University of Wales, Aberystwyth, UK; University of Wisconsin, Madison, Wisconsin, USA. **Dipl.:** B.A. (Honours); Ph.D. (1957). **Career:** Department of Statistics, Ministry of Economy, Damascus, Syria (1950-52); Economic Analyst, UNRWA, Amman (1952-55); Graduate Student and Research Assistant, University of Wisconsin (1955-56); Economic Analyst, UNRWA (1957-58); Director, Economic Planning and Research (1958-62); Secretary, General Jordan Development Board (1962-64); Vice-President, Jordan Development Board (1964-68); Ambassador to West Germany, Sweden, Denmark, Norway, Luxembourg and EEC (1968-76); Minister of Trade and Industry (November 1967-78 and re-appointed in June 1978-80). **Awards:** First Class, Independence Medal; Commander, Republic of Italy. **Addr.:** Amman, Jordan.

DAJANI (Said, al), Jordanian statesman and attorney-at-law. **Born** in Jerusalem, in 1919. **Son** of Jawdat Said al-Dajani (a leading personality and merchant of Jerusalem, Palestine) and Muhsineh Aref Pasha al-Dajani. **Married** in 1940 to Zeinab Safwat al-Dajani, 3 children; Raja' (1956), Amal (1958), Hana (1960). **Educ.:** Secondary at Jerusalem, Palestine, and Higher at Queens' College Cambridge University, England. **Dipl.:** B.A. Law (1939), M.A. (1941). Former member of the Middle Temple, Inns of Court, London. Certificate of Achievement in Statistics from the International Cooperation Administration, Washington D.C., **Career:** District Governor, Magistrate and Coroner in Palestine and Jordan (1940-52); Assistant Director, Civil Service Commission (1953-56); Assistant under Secretary, Ministry of Interior and Prime Ministry (1956-59); Director of Statistics and Census (1959-62); Did the First Census of Jordan (1961); Director of the Budjet (1962-65); Minister of State, Transport, Tourism & Antiquities and Finance (1965-68), Deputy Chairman of the Board of Directors and Deputy General Manager of the Bank of Jordan (1968-71); Attorney-At-Law and Legal Consultant (since 1973). Established ZERAH International Trading Company and its Managing Director (1974-79). **Medals:** Honorary Citizin of the City of Jacksonville, Florida, U.S.A. (1951), Jordan Renaissance Medal 2nd Class, Jordan Star Medals 2nd & 1st Class, and the I.U.O.T.O. Medal. **Hobby:** Reading, football (soccer) and squash. **Member:** Former President of the Lions Club, Jerusalem, Former Member of the Rotary Club, Amman, Member of the Arab Orphans Society, Haifa-Palestine and Jordan. Member of the Hussein Sports City, Amman, Member of the Six Continents Club and American Express. **Prof. Addr.:** King Hussein Street and P.O.Box 927260, Tel.: 668832/ 662044, Amman, Jordan. **Priv. Addr.:** Shemaisani, Queen Nur Street. Tel.: 662221, Amman, Jordan.

DAJANI (Wafa, Abdul Wafa), Jordanian businessman. **Born** on August 9, 1941. **Son** of Abul Wafa Dajani **and** Mrs. Wafiqa Dajani. **Married** to Fadia Ansari on August 9, 1968, 4 children: Tariq, Lana, Luma and Ziad. **Educ.:** Friends Boys School, Ramallah: American University, Washington DC. **Dipl.:** B.Sc., M.B.A. (Master of Business Administration). **Career:** Managing Director, Wafa Dajani & Son Co.; Director, Near East Tourist Centre; Director, Najjar Bros. & Co.; Director, Wafa Dajani Drugs; Director, Jordan National Bank. **Member:** American Marketing Association; American, Management Association. **Sports:** Football and tennis. **Hobby:** Reading. **Club:** Rotary. **Credit Card:** American Express. **Prof. Addr.:** P.O.Box 33, Telex: 21336, Tel.: 624179, 624170, Amman, Jordan.

DAK (Othman), Sudanese official. **Educ.:** University of Khartoum, Sudan. **Career:** National Council for Research; Acting Director, Economic and Social Research Council (1973-74); Member of the People's Assembly (1974); Minister of State for Local Government (1976-77). **Addr.:** Khartoum, Sudan.

DAKHIL (Fahd Hamid), Saudi academic. **Born** on 2 June 1942 in Jeddah, Saudi Arabia. **Dipl.:** Ph.D. (Civil Engineering). **Career:** Assistant Professor, University of Petroleum and Minerals, Dhahran. (1973-74); Chairman, Civil Engineering Department, KFUPM, Dhahran (1974-75); Dean, College of Engineering Sciences, KFUPM, Dhahran (1975-77); Vice Rector for Graduate Studies and Research, KFUPM, Dhahran; member, American Society of Civil Engineers; member of the Board, Saudi Arabian National Centre for Science and Technology, World Association of Muslim Youths; member, Degree Equivalence Committee, Ministry of Higher Education; Chairman, Islamic Studies Committee at KFUPM. **Publ.:** several research papers on Strength of Materials, Concrete Reinforcements and Deterioration of Concrete in the Gulf Environment, etc. **Hobbies:** Reading, sports. **Addr.:** Dhahran International Airport, P.O.Box 144, KFUPM No. 300, Tel.: 8602200 (Office) and 8606294 (Home), Dhahran, Saudi Arabia.

DAKKAK (Omar, Mohamad), Syrian academic. **Born** in 1927 in Aleppo, Syria. **Son** of Mohamad Dakkak. **Married**, four children. **Educ.:** University of Damascus, Syria, Ain Shams University, Cairo, Egypt; Arabic High Studies Institute, Cairo, Egypt. **Dipl.:** B.A. in Arabic Literature; Diploma in Education; M.A. in Arabic Literature (1966). **Career:** Lecturer, Faculty of Arts, Aleppo University, Syria (1966-72); Vice Dean, Faculty of Arts, Aleppo University (1970-80); Assistant Professor, Faculty of Arts, Aleppo University (1972-77); Professor, Faculty of Arts, Aleppo University (1977-80); Professor, Faculty of Arts, Riyadh University, Saudi Arabia (since 1980). **Member of:** the High Council of Literature, Arts and Social Sciences, Directorate of Arab Scientific Heritage Institute, Aleppo (1978); Central Council of Union of Arab Writers (1977); al-Aksa Committee: the Archælogical Society, al-Adiat; Editor in Chief of the annual archælogical journal "al-Adiat"; Chairman of the Aleppo University Committee for Authorship; Translation and Publication (1973). **Publ.:** Articles in journals on Arab poetry and several books. **Hobbies:** Music, archeology. **Addr.:** P.O.Box 6161, Tel.: 10298, Aleppo, Syria.

DAKR (Rachid, Izzat, ad), Syrian barrister and legal adviser. **Born** in 1920 in Damascus. **Son** of Izzat Dakr. **Educ.:** University of Paris, London University. **Dipl.:** Doctorates of Laws and of Economics. **Career:** Barrister, Leturer in the Damascus Faculty of Law, Legal Adviser to various companies. **Publ.:** Author of several books, including "Le mouvement socialiste et le monde arabe", "Réglementation du fisc en Syrie", "La réforme socialiste et l'impôt sur le revenue en Syrie". **Addr.:** Damascus, Syria.

DAMAX (Abdel Jalil), Tunisian journalist. **Born** on October 10, 1933 in Sfax, Tunisia. **Married**, four children. **Educ.:** studied in the Press Institute. **Career:** Journalists with "Dar al-Sabah", "Le Temps" and "As-Sada" (since 1958), as Staff Correspondent, Sub Editor, Editor in Chief and Director, has made various trips to the Far East, USA, Europe and Africa. **Awards:** Order of Tunisian Republic; Tunisian Order of Cultural Merit; Order of Tunisian Independence. **Addr.:** Tel.: 232816, 256611, Tunis, Tunisia.

DAMLUJI (Faisal, Farouq, ad), Iraqi managing director of companies. **Born** in 1920 in Mossul. **Son** of Farouq ad-Damluji. **Married** to Mona Baroody. **Educ.:** Liverpool University and American University of Beirut. **Dipl.:** Bachelor of Business. Administration. **Career:** Managing Director of National Commercial Co.; Commercial Cosmetics Company (Baghdad); Chairman of the Board, Rubber Industries Co. Ltd., Baghdad. Ltd. **Publ.:** Author of "Some Aspects of Modern Iraq", "The Arabs and the West". **Member** of the Swimming Club, Mansur Club. **Addr.:** 664, Alwiyah, P.O.Box 306, Baghdad, Iraq.

DANA (Hani, Osman, El), Lebanese Banker. **Born** on March 1, 1952 in Beirut, Lebanon. **Son** of Osman El-Dana, Politician **and** Mrs., née Sophie Hoss. **Married** to Susan Serbey, 3 children: Sophia (1/7/1974), Nicole (20/10/1976), Carole (10/10/1996). **Educ.:** Master Business Administration, New York University, U.S.A.; B.A. (Economics), American University of Beirut. Baccalaureate 2nd Part International College, Beirut, Lebanon. **Career:** Executive Director, Member of the Board of Directors, Banque de la Méditerranée. Beirut, Lebanon, 1993-Present; General Manager, Qatar National Bank, (1988-1993); Vice President, Chase Manhattan Bank (1977-1988). **Sport:** Swimming. **Prof. Addr.:** Banque de la Méditerranée, P.O.Box 11-348, Beirut, Lebanon. Tel.: (03)760300.

DANNO (Severius), Iraqi engineer. **Born** on January 21, 1921 in Mossul. **Married** to Miss Cornelia Mary Kendall. **Educ.:** Sheffield University, Liverpool University. **Dipl.:** Doctor of Philosophy, Bachelor of Engineering, Associate Member of Institution of Mechanical Engineers. **Career:** Head of Electrical Engineering Department College of Engineering (Baghdad), Consultant. **Member** of Alwiyah Club. **Hobbies:** Swimming, recorded music, and motoring. **Addr.:** 28, Karradat Mariam, Baghdad, Iraq.

DAOUD (Ali, Mohamed), Djibouti Deputy at the National Assembly, and Minister of Public Health. **Born** in 1950 in Djibouti. **Educ.:** Health Services, Health Public Study, Paris (1973-1976). **Career:** Member of Political Bureau of "Mouvement Populaire de Libération" (1975-1977). Minister of Public Health and Social Affairs since 8 Juin 1995 to date. President of FRUD since 1991 to date. Elected Deputy at the National Assembly (19/12/1997 - to date). **Prof. Addr.:** National Assembly, P.O.Box 138 Djibouti, Djibouti.

DAOUD (Diaeddine), Egyptian statesman. **Born** in 1926 in Egypt. **Educ.:** Secondary and Higher. **Dipl.:** Licentiate of Law. **Career:** Lawyer, Elected Deputy of the National Assembly, Minister of Social Affairs and Minister of State for the National Assembly Affairs (1968), Minister of Information (1970). Presently Chairman of Nasserists Party. **Addr.:** Cairo, Egypt.

DAOUD (Mahmoud, Mohamad, Dr.), Egyptian agronomist. **Born** in 1926 in Gharbiyeh Governorate (Lower Egypt). **Educ.:** Faculty of Agriculture, Alexandria University. **Dipl.:** B.Sc., M.Sc., Ph.D. (Agriculture). **Career:** Lecturer, Faculty of Medicine, Alexandria University; Dean, Faculty of Agriculture, Alexandria University; attended several international conferences on agricultural production; represented Egypt at the Khartoum Conference of Arab Deans of Faculties of Agriculture; led two scientific delegations to the Federal Republic of Germany and Austria; elected secretary to Misr Political Party, Bab Sharky and Sidi Gaber constituencies of Alexandria city; Minister of Agriculture (May 1978- May 80); Minister of State for Agriculture and Food sufficiency (May 80). **Publ.:** several research papers published by Berkeley University (USA); Nuclear Radiation and its impact on Foetus. **Addr.:** Cairo, Egypt.

DAOUD (Moussa, Baragoita), Djibouti Deputy at the National Assembly. **Born** in 1949 at Tadjourah. **Educ.:** Secondary. **Dipl.:** Diploma from Institut National de Nutrition in Tunisia. **Career:** Medical Service of Tadjourah (1965-1992). Elected Deputy at the Chamber of Deputies (1973-1977); Member of Central Committee of RPP and Member of Foreign Relations Commission; Member of Communications and Pringing Commission; President of National Council of ADEPF; President of Annex RPP of tadjourah; Elected Deputy at the National Assembly (18/12/1992 - to date); President of Foreign Affairs Commission and Member of Finance commission, general Economy and Planning. **Prof. Addr.:** National Assembly, P.O.Box 138 Djibouti, Djibouti.

DAOUD (Raafat, Georges), Egyptian interior decorator. **Born** on 23 September 1948 in Cairo (Egypt). **Son** of Georges Daoud (Deputy General Manager, Central Bank of Egypt) **and** Mrs., née Marcelle Terzian. **Married** to Miss Sybil Joseph Farès in February 1978. **Educ.:** French Lycée, Cairo (1955-67); Faculty of Applied Arts, Cairo (1967-72). **Dipl.:** Secondary Education Certificate (1967); B.Sc. (Applied Arts) (1972). **Career:** Joined Furniture Galdy Touny Gallery (1972-74); Interior Architect and Decorator, Pierre Genoud Office (Interior Decoration Consultants) since 1974. **Work:** Participated in the design and layout of Sheraton Hotel, Méridien Hotel, Cairo; Egyptian Armed Forces Staff Officers Headquarters, etc. **Sports:** Horseriding, Tennis, Shooting, Skin Diving and Swimming. **Hobbies:** modern music, drawing, painting and sculpture. **Prof. Addr.:** Pierre Genoud Interior Decoration Office, 28, Talaat Harb Street, Abu Regeila Building, Tel.: 756208 & 746083, Cairo. **Priv. Addr.:** 69 Abu Bakr el-Seddiq St., Heliopolis, Tel.: 818520, Cairo, Egypt.

DAOUDI (Abdel Jawad, Muhammad, al), Moroccan administrator. **Born** in 1939 in Fez, Morocco. **Married**, 3 daughters. **Educ.:** National College for Radio and Electricity; National School for Civil Aviation. **Dipl.:** Degree in

Electrical Engineering. **Career:** Manager of Civil Aviation Department, Ministry of Transport (1967-81), General Air Traffic Manager (1984), Director Sotoram S.A. **Decor.:** Order of Merit (1st Class), Morocco (1985). **Hobbies:** Music, swimming, football. **Addr.:** Rabat, Morocco.

DAOUDI (Riad), Lawer and Legal Advisor. **Born** in 1942 in Damascus, Syria. **Son** of Rachad Daoudi (Editor and Mrs. Adelate Faris. **Married** in 1978 in Paris to Mrs. Viviane Collin, 3 children: Tamim (1981), Karim (1983), Nesrine (1984). **Educ.:** Baccalaureate, Damascus American School (1960); B.A in Law, Damascus Law School (1964) M.A. In Public Law (Diplome d'Etudes Superieures), University of Paris, (1970); Diploma of the Institut des Hautes Etudes Internationales - University of Paris (1973). **Career:** Director, Office of the Minister of Culture, Damascus (1965-66); Assistant at the Department of International law, University of Damascus (1966-78); Instructor (moniteur) in Constitutional and Administrative Law, University of Paris (1974-77); Participant to the United Nations International Law Commission Seminar (1972); Participant to the Research Center of the Hague Academy of International Law (1979); Professor of Public International Law, Faculty of Law-University of Damascus (1978-92); Professor of Public International Law compared with the Principles of Islamic Law, Faculty of Islamic Legislations-University of Damascus (1978-83); Attorney at Law, Member of the Damascus Bar Association (since 1982-); Dean Assistant for Academic Affairs, Faculty of Law-University of Damascus (1980-82); Registrar of the Judicial Tribunal of the Organization of Arab Petroleum Exporting Countries (OAPEC) (1983 since 1991 to date on part time basis); Currently Legal Advisor for the Syrian Ministry of Foreign Affairs (1991-) **Decor.:** Laureat at the Competition of Best Thesis of the University of Paris II for the Year 1987-88. **Sports:** Tennis Swimming. **Hobbies:** Music, Reading. **Addr.:** P.O.Box 20501 Safat 13066, Kuwait.

DAOUR (Muhammad Salah al-Deen), Egyptian diplomat. **Born** on July 22, 1930 in Cairo, Egypt. **Married,** 1 son, 1 daughter. **Educ.:** Cairo University, Egypt. **Dipl.:** B.A. in Political Science, M.A. (1954). **Career:** Vice Consul, Egyptian Embassy, Aleppo, Syria (1955-58), Consul, Egyptian Embassy, Turkey (1960-61), Chargé d'Affaires, Egyptian Embassy, Togo (1962-65); Permanent Member, Egyptian Delegation to all the Organization of African Unity Meetings (1965-68); Head of the Organization of African Unity Section in the Foreign Office (1965-68); Counsellor, Egyptian Embassy in Nicosia, Cyprus (1968-72); Observer, United Nations Associations Conferences, Nicosia, Cyprus (1968-71); Chief of Cabinet, Under Secretary of State, Foreign Office (1972-74); Minister, Egyptian Embassy in Tokyo, Japan (1974-77); Deputy Director of Asian Department in charge of East and South Asia and South Pacific (1977-78); General Consul, Egyptian Consulate in San Francisco, USA (1979-82), promoted to the rank of Ambassador in 1982; Dean, Consular Corps of San Francisco (1982); Ambassador of Egypt to Liberia (West Africa) (1985-89). **Decor.:** Order of Merit, President of Syria (1958); Order of the Republic, Egypt (1958) and (1976); Order of the Rising Sun, Emperor of Japan (1977); Order of Merit, President of Egypt (1982); Knight Great Band of the Liberian Humane Order of African Redemption (1989). **Hobbies:** Swimming and photography. **Member:** Sun and Diplomatic Clubs. **Addr.:** 71 Maqrizi Street, Manshiyat al-Bakri, Cairo, Egypt.

DAQHAN (Omar, Abdullah), Jordanian official. **Born** in 1927 in Amman, Jordan. **Married,** 7 children. **Educ.:** Degree in Civil Engineering. **Career:** Under Secretary Assistant, Ministry of Public Works (1954); General Director, Jordan Hijaz Railway (1956); of Central Water Authority (1964); Director of Geological and Mineral Research (1965); Deputy President and Director General of Natural Resources Authority (1966); Director General, Jordan Phosphate Company (1969); Minister of Agriculture (1970-72); President, Jordan Valley Authority (1972-81); Member, National Consultative Council (1982); formerly Chairman, Arab Potash Co. Ltd. **Addr.:** Amman, Jordan.

DARANDARY (Malik Amin), Saudi engineer. **Born** Medina, in 1922. **Dipl.:** B.Sc. (Aviation Engineering). **Career:** Assistant pilot; pilot of the royal aircraft of the late King Abdulaziz; General Manager of Saudi Arabian Airlines in Amman, Jordan; Aviation Inspector, Saudia; member of several IATA conferences abroad. **Honours:** several Orders of Merit from the late King Abdulaziz; First Badge of Honour from late King Abdullah, King of Jordan. **Addr.:** Jeddah, Saudi Arabia.

DARDANJI (Hayam, Ramzi, al), Jordanian writer. **Born** in 1942 in Yafa. **Married,** 2 children. **Educ.:** Benghazi University, Libya; Cairo University, Egypt. **Dipl.:** B.A., M.A. in Authropology. **Career:** Member of Jordan Writers' Union. **Publ.:** "Songs for the Moon" (1974), "The Scent of Words" (1982), "The Palm Tree and the Storm" (1985). **Hobbies:** Social and cultural activities, reading, table tennis. **Prof. Addr.:** Ibrahim Toukan Street, P.O.Box 910075, Amman, Jordan.

DARDEER (Hassan Mohamad), Saudi businessman. **Born** Medina, in 1939. **Diploma**, Technical School. **Career:** Archivist 1955; accountant, Customs Department; TV and radio comic actor; owner of Abha Agricultural, Industrial, Tourist and Florist Town, Abha; owner of Arts Renaissance Co. for Radio and TV Production; member of Board of National Corporation for Trade, Public Relations and Trade Representation, National Sporting and Cultural Club; founder of first automatic date-packing factory, Medina, first poultry farm for frozen chickens, Medina, first aromatic oil distillery. **Hobbies:** Sport, acting. **Addr.:** Medina, Saudi Arabia.

DARKAZALLY (Maamoun), Syrian bank manager. **Born** in 1941 in Damascus, Syria. **Son** of Abdul Hadi Darkazally (Bani Hamdan Tribe). **Married** in 1971, 1 son. **Dipl.:** Master in Business Law and International Management (1972). **Career:** Public Relations Officer; Student Advisor, Saudi Educational Delegation, New York. Held International Posts, Chase Mahhattan Bank (1970-78); Regional Manager, in charge of the Saudi Arabian Region, Al Saudi Banque (1978-82); Manager, Middle East and Africa (1982-); Chairman of Syrian Community, Doha, Qatar; Former President, Arab Students Club, New York University; Manager, al-Saudi Bank, London (1983). **Publ.:** Author of "The Economic Theory of Islam", "The Foundation of Bayt Almal", "Taxation in Islam", "International Management in the Arab Countries". **Member:** Arab Bankers Association, American Bankers Association and British Institute of Management, Institute of Directors (U.K.), Chartered Institute of Bankers, **Hobbies:** Flying, Tennis and Scuba Diving. **Addr.:** London UK.

DARMAKI (Hamad Bin Sultan, al), United Arab Emirates diplomat. **Born** in 1944. **Married**, four children. **Career:** Secretary to HH the Ruler (1961-68); Under Secretary, Director of Labour and Social Affairs Department; Ambassador of United Arab Emirates to Oman (1972); Assistant Director, al-Ain Municipality; Director, Al-Ahlia Oilfields Development Co. **Sport:** Swimming. **Hobby:** Travelling, **Addr.:** al-Ain, United Arab Emirates.

DARMAKI (Khalifa Mohamad Khalfan, al), United Arab Emirates administrator. **Born** in 1948 in al-Ain, United Arab Emirates. **Married**. **Career:** Director of Commercial Licence Department in al-Ain Municipality; Director of al-Ain Municipality. **Member** of al-Ain Sporting Club. **Sport:** Swimming. **Hobbies:** Hunting, travelling. **Addr.:** al-Ain, United Arab Emirates.

DARMAKI (Saif bin Ali al-Dhab, al), United Arab Emirates businessman. **Born** in 1950 in al-Ain, United Arab Emirates. **Son** of Ali al-Dhab al-Darmaki. **Married**, three children. **Career:** Director of Labour and Social Affairs (1973-76); Director of Antiquities and Tourism, al-Ain; Chairman and Managing Director SEDCO Dubai Ltd. Contracting and Trading Company. **Publ.:** "Majallat al Siyaha"; "Museum Guide", in Arabic and English; "Tourism in the UAE" in Arabic, French, English. **Sports:** Football, table tennis. **Addr.:** P.O.Box 397, Tel.: 829000, Telex: 23311 SEDCO EM, Abu Dhabi, United Arab Emirates.

DARWAZA (Adnan, Abdul Kareem), Jordanian bank manager. **Born** in 1937 in Amman, Jordan. **Married** in 1964, 2 sons, 3 daughters. **Dipl.:** LL.B. **Career:** Arab Bank Ltd., Amman; Branch Manager, Bank of Jordan, Amman; Assistant General Manager, Petra Bank, Amman: General Manager, Jordan Gulf Bank, Amman; Deputy Chairman, Philadelphia Insurance Co., Amman: Chairman, Modern Juice co., Amman; Member of the Board of Banking Institution, Central Bank of Jordan, Amman. **Member:** Jordan Banks Association, Amman, Jordan; Orthodox Club; Hussein Sports City Club. **Hobby:** Chess. **Addr.:** P.O.Box 9989, Tel.: 64110, 64116/9, Telex: 21959 A/B JGBANK JO, Amman, Jordan.

DARWICH (Samir), Syrian businessman. **Born** in 1937 in Damascus, Syria. **Son** of Amin Darwich (electrical engineer) **and** Mrs. Samia née Bernoti. **Married** in 1972 to Miss Ghada Liane, two children. **Educ.:** Collège des Pères Lazaristes and Lycée Franco-Arabe de Damas; Faculté de Droit, Damascus University (1963); Université Saint-Joseph (1964). **Career:** Assistant Editor in several local newspapers (1960-62); Chief Editor of "Bureau des Documentations Syriennes et Arabes" (1962-64); Founder and President of OFA-Edition (1964) and OFA-Holdings S.P.P. (1975) which includes OFA Business Consulting Center and OFA Renseignements Commerciaux. Shareholder in several Arab and European Companies involved in business in the Middle East. **Sports:** Riding (show-jumping), in addition to a large collection of vintage cars. **Positions:** Vice-President, Syrian Equestrian Federation; President, Classic Car Club of Syria. **Addr.:** 67, Shahbandar Square, P.O.Box 451, Damascus, Syria.

DARWISH (Essam, A.), Saudi engineer and businessman. **Born** in 1943 in Taif, Saudi Arabia. **Dipl.:** B.Sc. (Civil Engineering), University of Miami, Florida, U.S.A.; M.Sc. candidate. **Career:** Assistant Lecturer. School of Engineering, University of Petroleum and Minerals; President, Darwish Saudi Arabia, Consultants, Architects, Engineers, Planners; **Hobbies:** Sports, travel. **Prof. Addr.:** P.O.Box 2571, Tel.: 6513738, Jeddah. **Priv. Addr.:** Tel.: 6600649, Jeddah, Saudi Arabia.

DARWISH (Madiha, Ahmad, Miss.), Saudi academic. **Born** in Mecca (Saudi Arabia). **Educ.:** Faculty of Arts, King Abdul Aziz University. **Dipl.:** B.A., M.A. (Modern History), Ph.D. (Middle Eastern Studies). **Career:** Assistant Supervisor and Assistant Teacher, Girls' College, Faculty of Arts, King Abdul Aziz University (1970-76); Deputy dean at the same University (1976-79); Member of Conferences on Workshop Management concerning registration, Beirut, American College for Girls (1970); Attended colloquium on Access and Admission to University Education, American University in Beirut, Lebanon (1970); participated in the International Conference on Saudi Arabian Developments, Duke University, Durham, North Carolina, USA (1979); Attended conference on Omani Studies, Muscat, Oman (1980); Contributed to the establishment of the Girls' College, Department of History, Geography and Sociology Library, Science and English, Faculty of Arts, King Abdul Aziz University, Jeddah; Contributed largely to the field of higher education for girls in Saudi Arabia; considered one of the pioneers of women's education; now Associate Professor of History and Deputy Dean, Faculty of Arts, King Abdul Aziz University, Jeddah. **Publ.:** "History of Saudi State till the First of the Twenty Century" (1980), "Oman in the Eighteenth and Nineteenth Centuries" (1982). **Prof. Addr.:** P.O.Box 2571, Tel.: 6879130, 6879033, Jeddah, **Priv. Addr.:** Tel.: 6653911, Jeddah, Saudi Arabia.

DARWISH (Mahmoud), Palestinian patriot and poet. **Born** in 1941 in al-Barwa, near Akka. **Educ.:** Secondary. **Career:** Patriot, contributed to Palestine Front of Liberation since the war of 1956 and Journalist, Imprisoned (1961, 1965 and 1967), living in Haïfa (June 1967), Editor of "al-Jadid" (monthly magazine), living in Damascus and Beirut; President of the Union of Arab Poets (1982-). **Publ.:** Author of several studies and poems including "Nihayat al-Lail" (1967), "Oiseaux sans ailes" (1960), "Feuilles d'olivier" (1964), "L'Amant de la Palestine" (1966). Member of The PLO Executive Committee (resigned in August 1993). **Addr.:** Tunis, Tunisia.

DARWISH (Mustafa), Egyptian film critic. **Born** in 1928 in Cairo Egypt. **Educ.:** Law, Faculty of Law; Cairo University, Cairo, Egypt (1949); Diploma in Politics and Economics, Cairo University (1950); Diploma in Public Law, Cairo University (1951). **Career:** Adviser to the Council of State; Chief Censor of Arts (1962, 1966-68); Administrative Judge (1969-82). **Sports:** Swimming, cycling. **Hobbies:** Cinema. **Addr.:** 13 al-Boustan Street, Tel.: 740116, Cairo, Egypt.

DAW (Hussain, Talaat), Egyptian official. **Born** in 1922 in Cairo, Egypt. **Son** of Talaat Daw. **Married. Educ.:** Cairo Medical School, Harwell Isotope School, University of Rochester, New York, USA. **Dipl.:** M.B., Ch.B. (1940-46); D.B. (1951-53); training in Radiation Biology and Halth Physics (1955-56). **Career:** Deputy Director, Central Army Laboratory (1953-59); Staff member, Cairo Radiosotope Center (1953-59); 1st Medical Officer, International Atomic Energy Agency (IAEA) (1959-67); Director, Egyptian Atomic Energy Establishment (1969-71); Senior Medical Officer, Radiological, Health and Safety Office, IAEA, Vienna, Austria (1967). **Sports:** Swimming, health physics. **Hobbies:** Chess. **Addr.:** Cairo, Egypt.

DAW (Khalifa, Ali), Libyan academic. **Born** in 1945. **Son** of Ali Dau. **Married,** four children. **Educ.:** B.Sc., MAS, CMA, Ph.D. in Accounting. **Career:** Associate Dean and Head of the Business and Economics Research Center, Faculty of Economics, Garyounis University (1976-78); Dean, Faculty of Economics, Garyounis University and member of the Board of Directors, Central Bank of Libya (1978-79); Assistant Professor of Accounting and Chairman of the Accounting Department (1979-80); **Sports:** Football, tennis. **Addr.:** Benghazi, Libya.

DAWALEH (Youssouf, Moussa), Djibouti Deputy at the National Assembly. **Born** in 1968 at Dire-Dawa. **Educ.:** 2nd year BTS (CICID). **Career:** Manager at Health Service; Head of the "Grande Pêcherie de Djibouti"; President of Alumni Club of CICID; Member of RPP; Elected Deputy at the General Assembly (19/12/1997 - to date); Vice-President of Exchange and Production Commission and Commission Member for Social Development and Environment Protection. **Prof. Addr.:** National Assembly, P.O.Box 138 Djibouti, Djibouti.

DAWANI (Abdul Hussain, Khalil), Bahraini businessman. **Born** in 1937 in Bahrain. **Son** of Khalil Dawani. **Married,** two children. **Educ.:** Diploma in Commercial Studies, Polytechnic of Central London. **Career:** Manager of family real estate business (1957-65); Director of al-Jazira Cold Storage Company; founder of a marine operations company; Director, Khalil Haji Murtatha Dawani and Sons; Chairman, Coastal Marine. **Member** of Rotary Club, Manama, Bahrain. **Sports:** Swimming, riding. **Hobbies:** Reading, fishing. **Addr.:** P.O.Box 26087, Tel.: 712978, Manama, Bahrain.

DAWOUDI (Adib), Syrian former diplomat. **Born** in 1923. **Married** in 1955, to Miss Amal Khartabil, 2 daughters: Rula and Rania. **Educ.:** Damascus University, Paris University (La Sorbonne). **Dipl.:** Baccalaureat, Licentiate of Laws, Doctor of Laws. **Career:** Joined the Ministry of Foreign Affairs since 1942, Secretary to the Ministry of Foreign Affairs during negotiations to establish the Arab League, Cairo (1943-44); served with the Syrian Delegation in Paris (1945-49); Director of Palestine Refugees in Damascus (1952-55); Representative at the Advisory Committee to the United Nations Relief and Works Agency for the Refugees (1953-54); Counsellor and Chargé d'Affaires, Syrian Embassy to London (1955); First Counsellor, Syrian Embassy to India (1957); United Arab Republic First Counsellor to Pakistan (1958); Promoted Minister, Syrian Embassy to Prague (1961); Syrian Ambassador to India (1962-64); Has attended the United Nations Organization Sessions from 1948 to 1962 and Bandung Conference of Afro-Asian countries, now retired. **Award:** Order of the Syrian Merit. **Addr.:** Damascus, Syria.

DAWSARY (Fahad, S., al-Hazzam), Saudi academic. **Born** on 12 November 1942 at Wadi Dawasir. **Dipl.:** Ph.D. (Administration of Higher Education), Arizona State University. **Career:** Assistant for Planning, University of Petroleum and Minerals, Dhahran; Assistant Professor and Director of Administrative Services, UPM, Dhahran; General Manager, Dar al-Youm daily newspaper; member of International Management Association of Higher Education. **Publ.:** contributes regularly to local press. **Hobbies:** chess, horse-riding, music. **Addr.:** Dhahran, Saudi Arabia.

DAY (Stephen, Peter), British former Diplomat, now Consultant Executive. **Born** on January 19, 1938 at Ilford,

UK. **Son** of Frank Day **and** Mrs. Mary Elizabeth née Franklin. **Married** on February 26, 1965 in Aden to Angela Waudby, 3 children: Belinda Mary Hernandez (14.9.1966), Philippa Joy Day Kamoun (28.10.68), Richard Franklin Day (21.10.1972). **Educ.:** Bancroft's School, UK; Cambridge University - MA (Cantab). **Career:** Senior Political Officer, Aden Government (1961-1967); H.M. Diplomatic Service (1967-1993), British Ambassador, Doha (1981-1984); Special Adviser to HRH the Prince of Wales; Ambassador, Tunis (1987-1992); Senior British Trade Commissioner, Hong Kong (1992-1993); Now Chairman of the Palestine Exploration FUND, British-Tunisian Society and the MBI Trust at SOAS; Director Claremont Associates (Middle East Consultancy). **Awards:** C M G. **Hobbies:** Reading, Walking, Family. **Member:** Athenaeum, Doha, Hong Kong. **Credit Cards:** Access. **Prof. Addr.:** c/o MBI INTERNATIONAL, 78 Wiemore St., London WIH OAS, Tel.: 0207/935/5859, UK. **Priv. Addr.:** 92 West End Lane, Esher, Surrey KT10 8LF, Tel. 1372 464138, UK.

DAYOUB (Karim, Robert), Egyptian businessman. **Born** on August 1, 1956 in Cairo, Egypt. **Son** of Robert Dayoub (businessman) **and** Mrs., née Hoda Ghadban. **Educ.:** Collège de la Sainte Famille, Cairo, Egypt (1962-73); Faculty of Engineering, Cairo University (1974-79). **Dipl.:** Secondary Education Certificate (1974); B.Sc. (Mechanical Engineering) (1979). **Career:** Partner and Technical Director, Egyptian Engineering and Automotive Supply Agencies, Cairo and Alexandria; Partner and Technical Director, Robert Dayoub and Sons, Aleppo; Technical Director, Egyptian Engineering Agencies, Cairo; Technical Director, Commercial Engineering Agencies, Damascus. **Sports:** Water skiing, swimming, horseriding, golf, tennis. **Hobbies:** Do-it-yourself, photography, Music. **Member:** Gezireh Sporting Club, Cairo, **Prof. Addr.:** 16-18 Naguib et Rihani Street, Tel.: 913277, 913692, 913853, Telex: 93300 EEA UN, Cairo, Egypt; and 16, 18 Brazil Street, Tel.: 117192, Telex: 31317 CEA SY, Damascus, Syria; and Ibn Khaldoun Street, Tel.: 20374, Aleppo, Syria. **Priv. Addr.:** 18 Saray el Gezira Street, Zamalek district, Tel.: 803130, Cairo, Egypt.

DAYOUB (Raouf, Robert), Egyptian businessman. **Born** on August 27, 1955 in Cairo, Egypt. **Son** of Robert Dayoub (businessman) **and** Mrs., née Hoda Ghadban. **Educ.:** Collège de la Sainte Famille, Cairo, Egypt (1962-74); Faculty of Commerce, Cairo University (1974-78). **Dipl.:** Secondary Education Certificate (1974); Bachelor of Commerce (1978). **Career:** Partner and Director; Egyptian Engineering and Automotive Supply Agencies, Cairo and Alexandria; Partner and Director, Robert Dayoub & Sons, Aleppo (Syria); Director, Egyptian Engineering Agencies, Cairo (Egypt); Director, Commercial Engineering Agencies, Damascus (Syria). **Sports:** Swimming, golf, horseriding, tennis & water skiing. **Hobby:** Painting, **Member:** Gezireh Sporting club, Cairo (Egypt). **Prof. Addr.:** Egypt: 16-18 Naguib el-Rihani street, Cairo, cable: Robday Cairo, Tel.: 913277 - 913853 - 913692; Syria: 16-18 Brazil street, Damascus, Calbe: Tawkilat Damascus, Tel.: 117192; Ibn Khaldoun street, Aleppo, Syria, cable: Tawkilat Aleppo, Tel.: 20374. **Priv. Addr.:** 18 Saraya el-Gezira Street, Zamalek district, Tel.: 803130, Cairo, Egypt.

DAYOUB (Robert, Georges), Egyptian businessman and manufacturers' representative. **Born** on December 12, 1919 in Tantah (Lower Egypt). **Son** of Georges Dayoub **and** Mrs., née Marie Chammas. **Married** to Hoda Ghadban in July 1954, three sons: Raouf, Karim and Rafik. **Dipl.:** Higher Commerce Diploma (1939). **Career:** Partner and Chairman "Egyptian Engineering and Automotive Supply Agencies", Cairo and Alexandria; Partner and Chairman, "Egyptian Engineering Agencies" Cairo and Alexandria; Proprietor and General Manager, "Commercial Engineering Agencies", Damascus (Syria); Partner and Chairman, "Robert Dayoub & Sons", Aleppo (Syria). **Sports:** Swimming, golf, horseriding and tennis. **Member:** Gezireh Sporting club. **Prof. Addr.:** Cairo (Egypt): 16-18 Naguib el-Rihani street, cable: Robday Cairo, Tel.: 913277 - 913853 - 913692. Damascus (Syria): 16-18 Brazil street, cable: Tawkilat Damascus, Tel.: 117192; Aleppo (Syria): Ibn Khaldoun street, cable: Tawkilat Aleppo, Tel.: 20374. **Priv. Addr.:** 18 Saray el-Gezira, cable: Rodbay Cairo, Tel.: 803130, Cairo, Egypt.

DEBBANE (Joe, Alfred), Lebanese Bank Manager. **Born** in 1940 in Beirut. **Son** of Alfred Debbane **and** Mrs., née Marie Aractingi. **Married** in 1966 in Beirut to Miss Renée Hatem. 3 children: Marylène, Claudine and Fred. **Educ.:** St. Joseph University. **Dipl.:** French State Doctorate in Economics-Degree in Law. French and Lebanese Licenciate. **Career:** Central Bank of Lebanon, trainee (1964-66); Economic Adviser to Banks and companies (1967-73); Economics Professor at St. Joseph University (1970-76): Manager Infibank Beirut (1974-76); General Manager, Banque Audi (Suisse) (1977-99), Chairman of the Board as at January 2000. Director and President of Executive Committee, Banque Audi (Luxembourg) SA; Director, Bank Audi (USA)., **Prof. Addr.:** Banque Audi (Suisse) S.A., 2, rue Massot, P.O.Box 384, 1211 Geneva 12, Tel.: 704.11.11.

DEEB (Edward), Lebanese Dentist. **Born** in 1927 in Lebanon. **Son** of Eli Deeb Jr. (businessman) **and** Mrs. Rose née Kattas. **Married,** in 1955 to Miss Marion Nader, six children. **Educ.:** A.A and B.A from UCLA, California (1950); M.A. University of Oregon, USA (1951); D.D.S, University of Southern California (1955); Member of Pierre Fauchard Academy (since 1991); member of American Academy of Pain Management (since 1991); F.A.C.D. (Fellow American College of Dentists); F.I.C.D. (Fellow International College of Dentists). **Career:** Periodontist, Endodontist (since 1955); L.A. County General Hospital Chairman Endo-Periosection (1956-69); Chairman Dental

Attending Staff (1967-69); Lecturer at State National and International Dental Meetings (1956-70); Specialist in periodonitic and Endodontics - Private practice. **Awards:** Oral Pathology award; Honorary Ph.D. Pepperdine University. **Sports:** Football, tennis, golf. **Hobby:** Boating. Member of National and Local Dental Association. **Prof. Addr.:** 10116 Riverside Dr., Suite 301, Toluca Lake, 91602 California, Tel.: (818)7666126. **Priv. Addr.:** 4570 Charmion Ln. Encino, California 91613, Tel.: (818)7830705.

DEEB (Walid, Mohamed), Jordanian academic. **Born** in 1946 in Haifa, Palestine. **Son** of Mohamed Deeb. **Married**, one daughter. **Educ.:** B.Sc. in Mathematics, Jordan University (1970); Ph.D., State University of New York, Albany, USA (1974). **Career:** Assistant Professor (1974-79); Associate Professor, Faculty of Science, University of Jordan (1979-81); Associate Professor, Kuwait University (1981-1986); Professor, Kuwait University (1986-90); Visiting Professor, University of California, Los Angeles (1990-91); Dean, Faculty of Science, Jordan University for Women (1991-93); Professor of Mathematics, Jordan University for Women (1993-present). **Publ.:** Many publications in Mathematics. **Prof. Addr.:** Department of Mathematics, Jordan University for Women, P.O.Box 961343, Tel.:415981, Amman, Jordan.

DEHLAWI (Ahmad Ismail), Saudi businessman. **Born** in 1955 in Mecca, Saudi Arabia. **Dipl.:** Business Administration. **Career:** Managing Director, Ismail Haroon, Dehlawi Establishment, and al-Dehlawi Furnitures. **Prof. Addr.:** P.O.Box 340, Mecca, Saudi Arabia. Mecca 54-25303. **Priv. Addr.:** Mecca, Tel.: 5433881.

DEHLAWI (Ismail Haroon), Saudi businessman. **Born** in 1929 in Mecca, Saudi Arabia. **Educ.:** Received primary School education. **Career:** Partner and Chairman of M. Jamil Haroon Dehlawy Establishment: member of Board, General Commercial Office; President of Ismail Haroon Dehlawy. **Prof. Addr.:** P.O.Box 340, Mecca, Saudi Arabia Tel.: 5425303, 5434027, **Priv. Addr.:** Tel.: 5433881, Mecca, Saudi Arabia.

DEHLAWI (Sami Ismail), Saudi businessman. **Born** in 1952 in Mecca, Saudi Arabia. **Dipl.:** B.A. (Management). **Career:** Member of Board, General Commercial Office; Vice-President, Ismail Haroon Dehlawi Establishment. **Hobbies:** Reading, swimming. **Addr.:** P.O.Box 340, Tel.: 5425303, 5434027, Mecca, Saudi Arabia, and Tel.: 6478914 and 6472992, Jeddah, Saudi Arabia.

DEIF (Chawqi), Egyptian writer. **Born** in Egypt. **Educ.:** Secondary and Higher. **Dipl.:** Doctor in Literature. **Career:** Writer, Journalist, Professor. **Publ.:** Author of more than 30 works eg. "al-Fan wa Mazahibouhou fil Nathr al-Arabi", "al-Fan wa Mazahibouhou fil Shi'r al-Arabi", "Chawqi, Shaer al-Asr al-Hadith", "al-Adab al-Arabi al-Mouasser fi Misr", "at-Tatawwor wal Tajdid fil Shi'r al-Oumawi", "Dirasat fil Shi'r al-Mouasser", "Ibn Zaidoun", "al-Risa", "al-Makamat", "al-Rahalat", "al-Tarjama al-Chakhsiya", "an-Nakd". **Addr.:** Cairo, Egypt.

DEIF (Nazih), Egyptian economist and international civil servant. **Born** on March 4, 1923 in Egypt. **Married**, 4 children. **Educ.:** Faculty of Commerce, Cairo University; University of Chicago U.S.A. **Dipl.:** B.Com., B.Sc. (Economics), M.Sc. (Statistics). **Career:** Elected member of the Expert Group on Industrialisation of United Arab Republic (now Arab Republic of Egypt) (1953-54); Director, Economic Planning Commission (1957-58); Director General, Economic Planning Commission (1958-61); Under Secretary, Ministry of Planning (1961-64); Governor International Monetary Fund (IMF) (1964-66); Minister of Treasury (1964-68); professor, Institute of Statistical Studies and Research, Cairo University (1968); Special Custodian, American University in Cairo (1969-70); Executive Director, IMF (1970); Deputy Chairman and Managing Director, Al-Watany Bank of Egypt. (1979-81); Advisor to Government Administration (1981). **Member:** United Nations Committee for Development Planning (1966); UN Industrial Development Organization (1968); Arab Centre for Industrial Development. **Addr.:** Cairo, Egypt.

DEIFALLAH (Abdullatif), Yemeni army officer and statesman. **Born** in 1928 in Sana'a. **Educ.:** Taez Military School of Officers. **Career:** Joined the Police Service; Member of the Presidency Council of Yemen; Deputy Minister of the Interior; Deputy Minister of Finance; Minister of the Interior; Minister of Finance, Lived in Lebanon (1966-67); Deputy, Commander-in-chief of the Armed Forces (1969). **Addr.:** Sanaa, Republic of Yemen.

DEIFALLAH (an-Nazer), Sudanese university professor and deputy vice chancellor. **Born** in 1922 in Khartoum. **Educ.:** Khartoum and Manchester Universities. **Career:** Government Veterinary Officer (Khartoum, Malakal and Nyala) (1946-50); Research Officer, Ministry of Agriculture (1952-56); Senior Lecturer, University of Khartoum (1956-57); Dean Faculty of Veterinary Science (1958-60); Deputy Vice-Chancellor (1960-68); President of the Round Table Conference for Southern Sudan, member of FAO International Panels of Exports and various foreign societies. **Addr.:** Khartoum University, P.O.Box 321, Khartoum, Sudan.

DEMERDASH (Ahmad, Nour el-Deen Muhammad, al), Egyptian broadcasting official. **Born** on November 13, 1925 in Kafir el-Sheikh, Egypt. **Married**, 2 sons, 1 daughter. **Educ.:** Cairo University, High Institute of Drama, Egypt. **Dipl.:** B.Com., B.A. **Career:** General Manager, Egyptian Television (1961-77); Professor, High Institute of Drama (1968-); General Production Manager, Voice of Cairo for Phonetics (1977-80); Drama Consultant, Egyptian Television (1981); Head of Television Channel One and Deputy, Ministry of Information (1983). **Decor.:** Egyptian Order of Merit (1982) and (1984). **Hobby:** Football. **Member:** Zamalek Club, Gezira Sporting Club. **Addr.:** 33 Midan el-Roda, Manial, Cairo, Egypt.

DENG (Francis Mading), Sudanese politician. **Born** on January 1, 1938. **Son** of Deng Majok of Ngok Dinka (Southern Kordofan, Sudan). **Married** in 1972 to Dorothy Ann Ludwig, 2 children: Donald, Daniel. **Educ.:** Primary in Southern Sudan; Khor Taggat Secondary School, Northern Sudan; University of Khartoum; Yale University, USA; Kings College, London University, UK. **Dipl.:** LL.B. (Honours); LL.M. Yale University; Doctor of Juristic Science, Yale University; Post-Graduate research, Kings College. **Career:** Officer, United Nations Human Rights Officer (1967-72); Adjunct Professor of Legal Anthropology, New York University (1969-70); Lecturer in Law, Columbia University, USA (1971-72); Research Fellow in Law and Modernization, Yale University (1971-72); Ambassador to Scandinavia (1972-74); Ambassador to USA (1974-76); Minister of State for Foreign Affairs (1976-79). **Awards:** Silver Medal Award for Scientific and Literary Works. **Member:** Law, Anthropology and Cultural Associations and Academies. **Publ.:** Tradition and Modernization (Yale 1971-received Herskovitz Award); The Dinka of the Sudan (New-York 1972); The Dinka and their Songs (Oxford 1973); Dinka Folk Tales (1974); Dynamics of Identification (Khartoum 1974). **Hobbies:** writing, nature; collection and translation of oral literature. **Addr.:** Khartoum, Sudan.

DERBAL (AbdelWahab), Algerian, Minister in charge of Relations with the Parliament. **Born** on June 19, 1952 at El-Oued, Algeria. **Son** of Mokhtar Derbal (Imam) **and** Mrs. née Mabrouka Anad. **Married** on March 19, 1982 at Biskra to Atika M'Ziou, 6 children: Asma, Hajer, Mouath, Shanïera, Bouthaina, Soufiane. **Educ.:** Baccalaureate Degree (A. Level) 1973. University of Constantine: Licence in Law (June 1977)/- University of Cardiff, Wales, Acadimia School of English, Bournmouth: Linguistic Formation in English (1978). **Dipl.:** Diploma in International Law and International Relations (Q.U.B., U.K.) (1979) - Master of Law by Research during 2 years (Equivalence of a Doctorate 3rd Degree). **Career:** Professor in Annaba University, January 1982, Joining the National Popular Assembly, June 1997. Lawyer at the Court/ - Member of the National Commission of the Constitution Amemdment (1996) - Member of the National Popular Assembly, Subsequent to the Elections Held in June 1997/ - President of a Parliamentary Group - Member of the Legal Commission - Member of the National Commission for Justice Reform - Member of the Scientific Council in the Institute of Law in Annaba University/ - In charge of Studies and Pedagogy, and Higher Studies. - Participation in Several National meetings and International Conferences. **Sports Pracised:** Football and Basketball. **Hobbies:** Reading and Travelling. **Clubs and Associations:** Football Club of Annaba/ and Association of Socio-Cultural Activities. **Prof. Addr.:** Palais du Gouvernement, Algiers, Tel.: 02/73/26/10, Algeria. **Priv. Addr.:** Club des Pins, Villa No. 160, Tel.: 01508192, Algeria.

DERBAS (Adnan, Muhammad), Palestinian businessman. **Born** on January 5, 1938. **Married**, 3 children. **Educ.:** American University of Beirut, Lebanon. **Dipl.:** B.Sc. in Civil Engineering. **Career:** Consulting Engineer (1960-66) in Saudi Arabia and Lebanon; established his own construction company "Arabconstruct" in Abu Dhabi (1967). **Hobbies:** Swimming, poetry and philosophy. **Prof. Addr.:** P.O.Box 238, Abu Dhabi, United Arab Emirates.

DERHALLY (Abdul Hamid, Said), Saudi civil servant. **Born** on July 23, 1929, in Jaffa. **Son** of Said A. Derhally **and** Mrs., née Wedad R. Al Solh. **Married**, 3 children: Rima (1961), Sa'id (1962), Abeer (1969). **Educ.:** St. Mark's College, University of Grenoble in France. **Dipl.:** High Degree in Commerce (Etudes Supérieures de Commerce), High Degree in Economics and Planning, Diploma of Chief Accountant in French, English and Arabic. **Career:** Interpretor at the Royal Palace, Riyadh (1952-54); Chief of translation and press bureau at the Presidency of Council of Ministers (1954-62); Director General, Public Relations Department, Ministry of Petroleum and Mineral Resources (1962-69); Director General, Planning Organization (C.P.O. title is now changed to Ministry of Planning) (1979); Director General, Ministry of Planning for the Western Region Branch, Jeddah; Participated in Symposiums, Seminars and Conferences as Saudi Arabia Representative Eight Islamic Conference of Ministers of Foreign Affairs, Ninth, Tenth, Eleventh, Twelvth and thirteenth 22-26 August 1982. have participated to the National Economy in preparing: The Annual Economic Report, The First, the Second and the Third Five Year Development Plan of Saudi Arabia, The South West Regional Plan and the Western Regional Plan; contracting various European and American Enterprises, advisor to various committees, Social Organizations and Institutes. **Works and Publ.:** Presented a series special French Informative Program through Saudi Arabia Television and Radio covering the Socio-Economic Development, entitled "Arabic en Marche"; Presented Conferences and Lectures in U.S.A. and Europe; Presented to Grenoble University in France, a paper in French entitled "le Rôle du Pétrole dans le Développement de l'Arabie Séoudite" (1968); Presented a paper in English to Harvard University (USA), entitled "Saudi Arabia Middle East's New Power"; (1975). Published a book in French entitled "Association des Entreprises Nationales et Etrangères dans le Développement de l'Arabie Seoudite" (1980). **Member:** Pilgrimage High Committee; of different joint commissions for economic and technical cooperation; in the Islamic Commission for Economic, Cultural and Social Welfare Affairs of the Organization of the Islamic Conference. **Awards:** Syngrye Medal, Order of the Diplomatic Service Merit of the Republic of Korea (May 3, 1977);

Order of Brilliant Star with Grand Cordon (Republic of China) 12 October 1977); Officer, Ordre National du Mérite (France) (29 November 1977); Syngrye Medal, Order of Diplomatic Service Merit of the Republic of Korea (May 11, 1980). **Sports:** Tennis, Swimming. **Hobbies:** Farming, Reading, Music. **Prof. Addr.:** Jeddah, Saudi Arabia.

DERHAM (Abdulrahman, Bin Saad, H.E., al), Qatari politician. **Born** in 1948 in Doha, Qatar. **Son** of Saad Bin Abdulraham al-Derham **and** Mrs. née Noora al-Mansour. **Married** on February 1972 in Doha to Latifa Hassan al-Derham, eight children: Bothaina (Dec. 1972), Johaina (1975), Saad (1977), Dana (1980), Noora (1983), Mohammed (1986), Haya (1991), Hassan (1993). **Educ.:** Elementary, Preparatory and Secondary Schools in Qatar, American University of Beirut (Enrolment for one year) (1969). **Dipl.:** Qatar General Secondary Certificate, Diploma in Manpower Planning. **Career:** Head of Employment Section (1970-79); Appointed to Establish the Qatar Medical Office in Lebanon (1974); Assistant Director of Labour Department (1979-82); Director of Public Housing Department (1982-89); Minister of Labour, Social Affairs and Housing (1989- July 1995). **Other Information:** Represented the Ministry in Several National Committees, Participated in Many Regional and International Meetings, Conferences, and represented the Government in International events such as the SUMMIT of the NON-ALIGNED STATES (JAKARTA, Sept. 1992), and the WORLD SUMMIT FOR SOCIAL DEVELOPMENT (COPENHAGEN, March 1995). **Sports:** Tennis, Swimming. **Hobbies:** Reading and Sports. **Member:** Doha Club (Social and Sports). **Credit Card:** Diner's Club. **Priv. Addr.:** P.O.Box 1220, Tel.: 674886, 674430, Doha, Qatar.

DERRIJ (Mohamad), Moroccan professor, **Born** in 1949 in Tetouan, Morocco. **Married**, three children. **Educ.:** University of Mohamad V, Free University of Brussels, Belgium. **Dipl.:** B.A. in Philosophy, Diploma of Higher Studies in Education and Psychology; Ph.D. in Educational Psychology. **Career:** Teacher of Philosophy and Islamic Thought in Moroccan schools (1970-75); Lecturer of Pychology, Faculty of Arts, Res (1975-77); Professor of Education, Royal Institute for Youth and Sports (since 1977); Professor of Education, Education Center, Rabat (since 1977); Professor of Education and Psychology, Teachers' Training College, University of Mohamad V, Rabat (since 1977). **Publ.:** "l'Analyse de l'Enseignement", 1st edition (1983), second edition (1986); "L'Enseignement par objectifs" 1st edition (1990); Founding Director of "Psychological and Educational Studies Journal". **Hobbies:** Andalusian Music. **Sport:** Tennis. **Member of:** Moroccan Philosophy Society, Moroccan Society for the Revival of Andalusian Music, President of Educational laboratory Society. **Addr.:** P.O.Box 823, Tel.: 757532, Rabat, Morocco.

DESSUKI (Salah), Egyptian official. **Born** in 1922 in Cairo, Egypt. **Married**, 1 son, 2 daughters. **Career:** Former Governor of Cairo; Ambassador, Ministry of Foreign Affairs; Member, International Institute for Strategic Studies, UK; Chairman of Sinai Hotels. **Decor.:** several international and national decorations. **Hobby:** Tennis. President, Veterans Tennis Federation of Egypt. **Prof. Addr.:** 32 Sabri Abu Alam Street, Cairo, Egypt. **Priv. Addr.:** 34 Ibrahim el-Lakkani Street, Heliopolis, Cairo, Egypt.

DHAFIR (Mohamad Ismail), Saudi academic. **Born** in 1934, **Dipl.:** Ph.D. (Education), Cairo University. **Career:** Educational Supervisor, Preparatory School Education, Ministry of Education; Educational Supervisor, Secondary School Education, Ministry of Education; educational expert, Ministry of Education; Lecturer, King Abdulaziz University; Supervisor of Teacher Training, Secondary School Education; member of first Conference of Teacher Training, Mecca; member, The Message of University Conference, Riyadh; initiated the idea of holding the first Conference of Teacher Training in Saudi Arabia; former Vice-Dean, Faculty of Education, King Abdulaziz University, Mecca branch; former **Dean**, Faculty of Education, King Abdulaziz University, Medina Branch. **Hobby:** Reading, sport. **Addr.:** Medina, Saudi Arabia.

DHAHRI (Ahmad, Saeed, Badi, al), United Arab Emirates director of investment and former Minister. **Born** in al-Ain, United Arab Emirates in 1956. **Son** of Saeed Badi al-Dhahri, government official. **Married**, one child. **Educ.:** Lewis and Clark College, Portland/ Oregon, USA. **Dipl.:** B.A. in International Affairs; Courses in Management of International Liquidity (1983); Preparation of Investment Policy for Multi Currency Investments (1984). **Career:** Deputy Director, Finance and Administration, Abu Dhabi Investment Authority (1982); Manager, Abu Dhabi Investment Authority, Foreign Exchange and Treasury Operations of the Abu Dhabi Investment Authority. **Member of:** the Board of Directors, Abu Dhabi Commercial bank; the Board of Directors, Arab Investment Company, Vice President, General Industry Corporation (Abu Dhabi Government Industrial Body); member of the Board of Directors, Emirates Insurance Company; Minister of Health (1992-May 1995). **Sport:** Horseback riding. **Hobby:** Reading. **Credit Cards:** American Express. **Addr.:** Abu Dhabi, U.A.E.

DHAHRI (Mohamad Ibn Omar Ibn), Saudi legal adviser. **Born** in 1943, in Shagra. **Dipl.:** B.A. (Islamic Law). **Career:** Auditor, General Employees Bureau (1962, 1966); Director of Services, General Administration for Girls' Education (1973); Legal Adviser, Ministry of Municipal and Rural Affairs, Riyadh; member of Riyadh Literary Club; attended First Conference of Saudi Men of Letters, Mecca. **Publ.:** Sharhu Diwan Bin Saqiyyah (Interpreting Bin Saqiyyah's Collection of Poetry), Nadharatun Lahiyad

(Playful Looks), Descartes Baynal Shakhi Wal Yaqeen (Descartes between Scepticism and Certainty), Tahqeeq al-Isharah Wa'l Imal (Interpreting the book of Imitations and Hints), Tareekhu Najd Fi Osour al-Ammiyah (The History of Najd during the Colloquial Epoch), Shia B Bowan (Bowan Quarters), Laylah Fi Garden City (A Night in Garden City). **Hobby:** Reading. **Addr.:** Legal Administration, Ministry of Municipal and Rural Affairs, Riyadh, Saudi Arabia.

DHAHRY (Ali, bin Khalfan, Al, H.E.), U.A.E. Businessman. **Born** on 27.11.1943. **Son** of Khalfan al Dhahry. **Married,** 3 daughters and 4 sons. **Career:** Owner of Ali & Sons Company (Business Consultants, Representatives of Companies, General Trading, Investment, Oilfield Supplies and Services). **Positions previously held:** Member of the Abu Dhabi Executive Council (local Government: 1974-1991), Chairman of Abu Dhabi Civil Aviation Department, Chairman of Abu Dhabi Aviation Co., Chairman of Gulf Air, Chairman of Gulf Aircraft Maintenance Company (GAMCO), Chairman of Al Ahlia General Trading Group. **Other positions previously held:** Director, Abu Dhabi Government Office, Cairo, Egypt (1970-72), Under Secretary for Housing & Purchase, Ministry of Finance (1972-74), Chairman of Abu Dhabi National Foodstuff Co. (1980-84), Deputy Chairman and Managing Director of Emirates Commercial Bank (now known as Abu Dhabi Commercial Bank) (1981-85), Vice Chairman of Emirates Industrial Bank (1982-84), Chairman of the Board of Directors, Al Dhafra Insurance Co. (1982-84). **Awards:** Order of the Egyptian Republic, Decorations from Tunisia, Morocco and Lebanon. **Hobbies:** Sailing and Water Skiing. **Address:** Ali & Sons Co. Bldg., 2nd floor, P.O.Box 915, Tel.: (09712) 723900, Telex: 23900 ABKA, Fax: (09712) 723901, Abu Dhabi, U.A.E.

DHAIFALLAH (Abdullatif, Mohamed, H.E.), Yemeni Diplomat. **Born** in 1933 at Haria Village, Naderah province, IBB Governate Yemen Republic. **Son** of Mohamed Dhaifallah, Village Shiekh **and** Mrs. Zienah Abdullah Al-Hag. **Married two wives:** Nadima Saleh Anqad born in 1940, Sanaa (died) and Lotfia Qaid Anqad born in 1948, 13 children: Fuaad, Amaal (died), Nabil, Ishraq, Kawkab, Tariq, Khaled, Altaf, Fayez, Fairoz, Zienah, Mohamed, and Dhaifallah. **Educ.:** Naderah Village School, Sanaa Secondary School, Lebanon Primary School, Egypt Secondary School. **Dipl.:** Military Academy Certificate, Signal Infantry Certificate. **Career:** Academician teacher in the Armed Forces (1959-1960); Director of Military Signals School (1961-1962); Revolution Command Council Member (1962); Interior Minister (31.10.1962); Interior Minister-Presidential Council/National Security Committee/ Member Ap. 1963; Presidential Council Chairman (25.4.1963); Deputy/Vice/Premier for Health and Agricultural Affairs (3.5.1964); Public Transport and Works Minister (6.1.1965); Public Works and Municipalities Minister (20.4.1965); Public Works Minister (16.4.1966); Army Supreme Committee Chairman Public Works and Transport Minister (18.6.1966); Public Transport Minister (21.12.1967); Deputy/Vice/General Commander; Seige Breaking Expedition Commander and Armed Forces Joint Staff committee Chief and Deputy Chief-in-Command (Hodeidah Governate- 1967, 1969, 1970); IBB/EBB/ Governate Governor; Public Transport Minister (18.9.1971); Public Works Minister (3.3.1974); Deputy Premier for Internal Affairs (1975-1985); Member of Consultative Council for the Republican Presidency (1985); Yemen Republic Ambassador Extraordinary and Plenipotentiary in the Czech and Slovak Republics (1985-); But he truthfully consider his practical and main work is his participating in the Revolution Command (26.9.1962). **Awards:** Egyptian Revolution Medal (1952); Yemen Revolution Medal (1962). **Sports:** Walking and Swimming. **Hobbies:** Reading, Hearing Radio and Watching T.V. **Addr.:** c/o Ministry of Foreign Affairs, Sanaa, Yemen.

DHALI (Seif Ahmad, ad), Yemeni statesman. **Born** in 1931 in Aden. **Educ.:** United Kingdom. **Career:** Joined Aden Public Works Department, Joined Front de Libération Nationale (F.L.N.) (1963); Worked with Mr. Kahtan ach-Chaabi (Former President of Southern Yemen Republic) in Yemen and Arab Republic of Egypt; Head of Political Bureau of the National Liberation Front; Minister of Foreign Affairs (November 1967-68), of Finance (1968-69). **Addr.:** Aden, Republic of Yemen.

DHARIF (Ahmed Juma, al), United Arab Emirates businessman. **Born** in 1946. **Son** of Juma al Dharif. **Married,** six children. **Career:** Development of Housing (1968-71); Inspector of Industrial Section, Ministry of Oil (1971-72); Director and General Manager, National Drilling Company (1973). **Member of** Tourism Club; Technical publications on drilling. **Hobby:** Hunting. **Sport:** Swimming. **Addr.:** Abu Dhabi, United Arab Emirates.

DHUBAIB (Ahmad Mohamad, al), Saudi academic. **Born** in 1935 in Mecca, Saudi Arabia. **Dipl.:** B.A. (Arabic Literature) Cairo University (1960); Ph.D. (Ancient Arabic Literature) Leeds University (1966). **Career:** Lecturer, Arabic Department, King Saud University (1966-70); Assistant Professor (1970-74); Associate Professor (1974-78); Acting Chairman of the Arabic Department (1969-72); Chairman of the Arabic Department)1972-74); Professor of Arabic, King Saud University since 1978; Dean of King Saud University Libraries (1974-80); Secretary General, King Faisal International Prize since 1977; member of the Supreme Council of Information until 1981, the Supreme Council of Antiquities, the Supreme Council of King Saud University (1974-80); founder and Chairman of the Saudi Society of Dialects and Folklore, King Saud University, since 1967; founder of the Museum of Arabian Folklore, King Saud University (1967); member of the High Advisory Committee, Society of Culture and Arts; member of the Advisory Board, Centre for Contemporary Arab Studies, Georgetown University, the Iraqi Academy and the Academy of the Kingdom of Morocco; participated in several regional and international conferences and symposia, including the 27th Congress of Orientalists, Ann Arbor, Michigan, U.S.A. (1967), 29th Congress of Orientalists, Paris (10-22 July 1973), First Conference of Saudi Arabian Men of Letters, Makkah (1974), Conference of the University message, Riyadh (1974), Confernece of International Federation of Library Associations (IFLA), Oslo, Norway (11-16 August 1978), meetings of the Councill of the Union of Arab Universities, Amman (1977), IFLA World Wide Seminar, Seoul, South Korea (May 1976), IFLA Conference, Copenhagen, Denmark (August 1979), First Conference of Saudi Arabian Librarians, Riyadh (May, 1980), meetings and Symposia of the Academy of Morocco since 1980, meetings and annual symposia of the Centre for Contemporary Arab Studies since 1978 and the First Conference of the Royal Academy for Research on Islamic Civilization, Amman (1982). Presently President, King Saud University. **Publ.:** A critical and Comparative Study of the Ancient Arabic Proverbs Contained in Al Maidani's Collection, Leeds (1966); An Authentic, Critical Edition of Kitab al-Amthal of al-Sadusi (book of ancient Arabic proverbs) Riyadh (1970); An Arabic Translation of T.M. Johnstone's Eastern Arabian Dialect Studies, Riyadh (1975); Ala Marafi al-Turath (a collection of critical research papers on Ancient Arabic Heritage) Riyadh (1981); al-A'mash al-Zarif (al-A'mash the Humorist, Biography and collection of witty sayings of the ancient scholar al-A'mash) Riyadh (1982). **Hobby:** Reading. **Prof. Addr.:** The President's Office. King Saud University, P.O.Box 2454, Riyadh 11451. **Priv. Addr.:** Tel.: 4767091, Riyadh, Saudi Arabia.

DHULAYMI (Talal Taha), Saudi executive. **Born** on 10 June 1951 in Dammam, Saudi Arabia. **Dipl.:** B.A. (Economics), AUB (1975), MBA, University of Portland (1978). **Career:** Advertising Manager, Tihama (1975); Vice President for Advertising, Tihama (1976); Executive Vice-President, Tihama Advertising, Public Relations and Marketing Research since 1978; Chief Executive Officer, TMI Advertising since 1987. **Member Of:** American Management Association; Board Director of International Advertising Association (IAA); Founder and Chairman of the Board, Gulf Cooperation Council Advertising Association (GCCAA); and Chairman of the Advertising Committee in Saudi Council of Chamber of Commerce and Industry. **Hobbies:** Reading, travel, swimming. **Prof. Addr.:** TMI Advertising, P.O.Box 13823, Jeddah 21414, Saudi Arabia, Tel.: (02) 6714322. **Priv. Addr.:** Tel.: (02) 6605316.

DIA (Amir), Arab-American academic, physician. **Born** in 1929 in Cairo, Egypt. **Married,** two children. **Educ.:** M.B., B.Ch., Cairo Medical School, Egypt; Internship at Demardash Hospital, Abasia, Egypt. Fellow of the American College of Obstetricians and Gynæcologists; Fellow of the American Fertility Society. **Career:** Instructor in Obstetrics and Gynæcology, University of California, Los Angeles (UCLA), USA (1970); Assistant Professor of Obstetrics and Gynæcology, UCLA (1975). **Publ.:** "Family Planning" (1974); "Laparoscopic Tubal Sterilization" (1974). **Member** of Planned Parenthood Organisation; President of the Egyptian Scholars Association. **Awards:** American Medical Association of Physicians Recognition Award (1974). **Sports:** Skiing, tennis. **Hobbies:** Fishing, travelling. **Addr.:** 2800 Via Campesina, Palos Verdes Estates, Tel.: 3785388, California, USA.

DIA (Dia Azeez), Egyptian artist. **Born** in 1948 in Cairo, Egypt. **Dipl.:** B.A. (Fine Arts, Interior Design), Academy of Fine Arts, Rome, Italy. **Career:** Teacher of Art, al-Thaghr Schools; Master Engineer office design, Saudi Airlines; owner of MAS Establishment for Fine Arts Production; directed several radio and television programmes; produced several art exhibitions and contributed to other artistic activities. **Hobbies:** photography, TV photography, radio and television directing. **Prof. Addr.:** al-Musaideya, opposite Jeddah Secondary School, Tel.: 6863521, Jeddah. **Priv. Addr.:** Tel.: 6675857, Jeddah, Saudi Arabia.

DIAB (Mahmoud), Egyptian dramatist. **Born** in Egypt. **Educ.:** Secondary and Dramatic. **Career:** Dramatist, Professor of drama at the Drama Institute of Cairo. **Publ.:** Author of many plays as "az Zawba'a". **Dist.:** First price ex aequo for the above mentioned play offered by the Inter-Arab drama Board (Cairo, March 1969). **Prof. Addr.:** Drama Institute of Cairo, Cairo, Egypt.

DIAB (Salaheddine, Ahmad), Egyptian engineer. **Born** on January 4, 1944 in Cairo, Egypt. **Married,** 3 children. **Educ.:** Cairo University, Mechanical Engineering Department, Egypt. **Dipl.:** B.Sc. in Engineering. **Career:** Member of the Board of Directors of Picco Company (1975-), National Drill Company (1981), Hong Kong Bank, Egypt (1983). **Hobbies:** Squash, tennis. **Member:** Chivalry Club, Hunting Club, Gezira Sporting Club. **Addr.:** 3 Shareh Shajarat al-Dur, Zamalek, Cairo, Egypt.

DIAGANA (Sidi, Mohamad), Mauritanian statesman, **Born** in 1929 in Kaedi, Mauritania. **Married** to Tandia Dumou. **Educ.:** William Ponty College, Dakar (Senegal). **Dipl.:** baccalaureat. **Career:** School teacher, M'Bagne and Kædi schools (1950-65); Assistant Mayor, Kædi (1960-66); Minister of Health, Labour and Social Services (1965-66); Counsellor, Kædi Municipal Council (1966); Minister of construction, Public Works, Transport, Post and Telecommunication (1966); Minister of Equipment (1966-68); Minister of finance (1968-70); Minister of Industrialisation & Mines (1970-71); Minister of National Defence (1971-75); Minister for the Presidency (1976). **Addr.:** Nouakchott, Mauritania.

DIALDIN (Ali, M.), Saudi geologist. **Born** in 1938 in el-Medina, Saudi Arabia. **Married,** 4 children. **Educ.:** San Diego State University, USA. **Dipl.:** B.Sc. in Geology. **Career:** Teacher, Ministry of Education (1961-68); Industrial Engineer, Aramco (1968-70); then various training, staff positions and administration at Present; General Manager, Training Organization; Member, Arab Society for Training & Management Development (1987-90); Member, International Federation of Training and Development (IFTDO) (1980-). **Prof. Addr.:** P.O.Box 8293 ARAMCO, Dhahran 31311, Saudi Arabia.

DIB (Mohamad), Algerian poet and novelist. **Born** on July 21, 1920 in Tlemcen. **Educ.:** Secondary and Higher. **Career:** Poet and Novelist (In French Language), Began his career with simple poems published in many French reviews as "Les Cahiers du Sud", Started to write Novels in 1952. **Publ.:** Author of "La Grande Maison" (1952), "L'Incendie" (1954), "Le Métier à tisser" (1957), "Un été Africain" (1959), Compilation of Novelettes "Au Café" (1956), Compilation of poems "Ombre Gardienne" (Ireface of Arabon), "Qui se souvient de la mer" (1962), "Cours sur la rive sauvage" (1964), "Le Talisman" (1966). **Addr.:** Algiers, Algeria.

DIB (Mohammad Khalil, al), Egyptian administrator. **Born** in 1919 in Belbis, Egypt. **Married,** 2 sons, 2 daughters. **Dipl.:** B.Sc. in Military Science. **Career:** Head of the Egyptian Delegation to the International Military Sports Council (1960-70); Secretary, then Deputy President Squash Union (1962); elected twice Member of the Executive Committee of the International Military Sports Union (1964) and (1970); Member, Egyptian Olympic Committee (1968); Secretary General, Armed Forces Sports Union; General Manager and Secretary General, Egyptian Football Union. **Decor.:** Sports Decoration (1st Class). **Hobbies:** Swedish exercises, squash. **Addr.:** 3 al-Tahawi Street, Manshiyat al-Bakri, Cairo, Egypt.

DIDI (Hasni Ould), Mauritanian administrator. **Born** in 1945 in Tidjikja, Mauritania. **Son** of Mohamed El Hacen **and** Mrs. Aicha (née Nafe). **Married** in October 1975, four children: Zeinebou (1977), Saca (1981), Sidi Abdallah (1984) and Taleb (1987). **Educ.:** Primary School of Tidjikja; Coppolani College, Rosso; Lycée de Nouakchott; Institut des Hautes Etudes d'Outre-Mer (IHEOM), Paris. **Dipl.:** diploma from IHEOM. **Career:** Director General of Work (January 1967- July 1969); Secretary General (July 1969- October 1971); Governor of Novadhibou (October 1971- December 1974); Minister of Trade and Justice (December 1974- September 1977); Governor of Regions (September 1977- May 1979). Minister of National Education and Higher Learning (1979). **Medals:** from Brazil, Uganda, and France. **Prof. Addr.:** Nouakchott, Mauritania.

DIFRAWY (Mahmoud), Egyptian Banker. **Born** on March 3, 1948 in Alexandria, Egypt. **Son** of Abdelmonsef El-Difrawy - Member of Parliament (retired), Landowner. **Married** on June 30, 1983 at U.S.A. to Shirley Ann Stewart. **Educ.:** Victoria College, Alexandria, Egypt, Rutgers University, New Jersey, U.S.A. **Career:** United Jersey Bank, New Jersey (1971-1981); Citibank (1981-1987); Gulf International Bank, Bahrain (1987-1992); Managing Director & Regional Manager for Middle East. Chase Manhattan Bank, Bahrain (1992- to present). **Prof. Addr.:** The Chase Manhattan Bank, P.O.Box 368, Tel.: 535388, Fax: 535149, Manama, Bahrain.

DIJIBRIL (Abdallah Chirwa), Djibouti Deputy at the National Assembly, and Minister of Defence. **Born** in 1946 at Holl-Holl (district Ali-Sabieh). **Career:** Militant of the LPAI; Member of the Central Committee of RPP; Elected Deputy at the National Assembly (8 May 1977 - to date); President of the Permanent Commission (1993 - 27/03/1996); Minister of National Defence (27/03/1996 - to date). Prof. Addr.: National Assembly, P.O.Box 138 Djibouti, Djibouti.

DILEITA (Abdoulkader, Mohamed), Djibouti Deputy at the National Assembly. **Born** on February 22, 1956 in Djibouti. **Career:** Employee at "EDD". Member of Executive Committee of RPP (treasurer); Elected Deputy at the National Assembly (18/12/1992- to date); President of the Exchanges and Production Commission and Member of the Finance Commission, General Economy and Planning; Member of Supreme Court of Justice. **Prof. Addr.:** National Assembly, P.O.Box 138 Djibouti, Djibouti.

DINI AHMED (Ahmed), Djibouti politician. **Born** in 1932 in Obock. **Career:** Vice President, Territorial Assembly, French Somaliland (now Republic of Djibouti) (1959-60); Minister of Production (1963-64); of Interior (1967-72); joined Ligue Populaire Africaine pour l'Independence (1972); President National Assembly of French Territory of the Afars and the Issas (May-June 1977); of the Republic of Djibouti (June-July 1977); Prime Minister (July-Dec. 1977). **Addr.:** Djibouti, Republic of Djibouti.

DIOP (Mamadou, Amadou), Mauritanian politician. **Born** in 1936 at Vinding, Southern Mauritania. **Son** of Mamadou Diop (farmer). **Married** to N'Date N'Diaye (teacher), 3 children. **Educ.:** Primary School (1945-51); Lycée Van Vollenhoven, Dakar, Senegal (1951-55); University of Dakar, Senegal, (1958-64). **Dipl.:** B.Sc. (physics and chemistry). **Career:** Teacher in secondary schools, Nouakchott, and at the Teacher Training College (1974-76); Principal, Boys' Secondary School (1970-71); Minister of Rural Development (1971- Aug. 1975); Minister of National Education, (Aug. 1975). **Addr.:** Nouakchott, Mauritania.

DIRANEH (Dirir, Miguil), Djibouti Deputy at the

National Assembly. **Born** in 1952 at Holl-Holl. **Educ.:** Diploma from Institut regional d'administration (IRA) Nantes, France. **Career:** Assistant-Director of CPS (2/05/1979 - 31/05/1994); Director of CPS (1/06/1994 - 5/01/1995); Director of SMI (6/05/1995 - 31/03/1997); Member of Executive Committee of RPP; Elected Deputy at the National Assembly (19/12/1997 - to date); Vice-President of National Defence Commission, and Commission Member for the Social Development and Environment Protection. Member of Supreme Court of Justice. **Prof. Addr.:** National Assembly, P.O.Box 138 Djibouti, Djibouti.

DIREIJ (Ahmad, Ibrahim), Sudanese politician. **Born** in 1933 in Darfur Province, Sudan. **Married. Educ.:** University of Khartoum, Sudan; University of Leicester, United Kingdom. **Career:** Ministry of Commerce; worked in Sweden, France and Italy before returning to the Department of Statistics; contested 1965 general election as Chairman of the Darfur Front; Member of the Umma Party; Minister of Labour and Cooperation (1966-67); reelected in 1968 as Leader of the Opposition; Adviser to the Ruler of Umm al-Qawain, United Arab Emirates (1970). **Addr.:** Khartoum, Sudan.

DIWANI (Mustapha Kamal Ibrahim, al), Egyptian diplomat. **Born** in 1930 in Cairo, Egypt. **Married,** 1 son, 1 daughter. **Educ.:** Cairo University, Egypt. **Dipl.:** LL.B., Diploma in Personal Law. **Career:** Director of Protocol Administration, Ministry of Foreign Affairs (1979-80); Ambassador to the Vatican (1980-84); Director of Protocol Administration, Ministry of Foreign Affairs (1984). **Decor.:** Rio Branco, Brazil (1973); Order of Pins IX, Vatican (1984); Grand Croix de l'Ordre Pro Merito Melitensi, Malta (1984). **Medal:** Medal of the Republic of Egypt, 2nd Class (1974), 1st Class (1982). **Addr.:** 35A Abu al-Feda Street, Zamalek, Imara al-Zahra, Cairo, Egypt.

DJAIT (Hichem), Tunisian historian and philosopher. **Born** on December 6, 1935. **Educ.:** Sadiqi College, Tunis (1940-54), Studies in Paris, Ecole Normale Supérieure and Sorbonne, France (1954-62); History Graduate, Sorbonne (1959), History Aggregate (1962); Doctorat d'Etat (1981). **Married,** 2 children. **Career:** Assistant Professor, Tunis (1962-69); Lecturer, La Sorbonne (1970); Professor, Faculty of Social Sciences, Tunis (1981). **Publ.:** Author of numerous articles on Islamic studies and of six books especially "L'Europe et l'Islam"; Numerous press articles. Participation in the arab and international debates. **Addr.:** University of Tunis, Faculty of Social Sciences, Tunis, Tunisia.

DJAMA (Djama, Djilil), Djibouti Deputy at the National Assembly, and Politician. **Born** in 1931 at Ali-Sabieh. **Career:** Elected Deputy at the territorial Assembly (24 Dec. 1958 - Nov. 1963); reelected Deputy at the Chamber of Deputies (17 Nov. 1973); Minister of Public service (1973-1975); Member of Parliamentary Opposition (1975-1977); Minister of National Defence (16 May 1977); Minister of Labour and Social and Social Affairs (18 May 1977-1978); Elected Deputy at the National Assembly (8 May 1977 - to date). President of the Supreme Court of Justice, Commission Member of the Production and Exchanges. **Prof. Addr.:** National Assembly, P.O.Box 138 Djibouti, Djibouti.

DJAZZAR (Sabih), Syrian physician. **Born** in 1923 in Damascus, Syria. **Son** of Wajih Djazzar **and** Mrs. Khayrieh née Zari. **Married** in 1957 to Miss Amal Katibi, three children. **Educ.:** Syrian University, Damascus, Syria; Columbia University, New York; Northwestern University, Chicago; University of Michigan, Ann Arbor. **Dipl.:** PCB (Physics, Chemisary and Biology) (1943); MD (1950); MPH (1952); MS in Hospital Administration (1954); RHA (1955). **Career:** Associate Professor of Anæsthesiology in the Faculty of Medicine, Syrian University, Damascus (1952-53); Director, Damascus General Hospital, Ministry of Health (1955-56); Director General of Health, Department of Civil Defense, Syria and Director General of Public Health Assistance & Hospitals, Central Ministry of Health, Damascus (1956-58); Chairman, Health Planning Committee and Chairman Committee for the Evaluation and Equivalance of Foreign Medical Diplomas, Central Ministry of Health, Damascus (1958-63); World Health Organisation Short Term Consultant for Medical Care and Health Planning, Saudi Arabia (1962-63); PHA-MCH Advisor and Tean Leader of Development of Health Advices Project, Congo-Brazzaville, WHO (1965-69); Head WHO Mission to Togo and Dehomey (Benin); Representative-Lecturer at WHO Regional Training Center of Health Personnel (1969-75); Professor of Public Health and Hospital Administration, School of Medical Assistants, Lome, Togo (1973-75); Acting WHO representative, Ghana, Ivory Coast, Upper Volta, Niger, Mali, Mauritania, Gambia, Nigeria, Gabon, Central African Republic and Tchad (1969-75); Head, WHO Mission to Central Africa Republic and Tchad Program Coordinator, member of Planning Committee for the Creation of the Faculté des Sciences de la Santé de Banquiers and Professor of Public Health, Maternal and Child Health and Hospital Administration at that Faculté (1975-80); member Coordination Program Development Unit, WHO Headquarters, Geneva (1978-84); Special Mission to Southern Sudan on behalf of WHO with Islamic Development Bank (1979). Retired (1985). **Publ.:** "Infant Care", three editions; "Nursing"; "School Health" two editions; 10 academic books for secondary Schools in Arabic. **Member:** Syrian Pediatricians Association; International Public Health Association; Northwestern University Alumni; Columbia University Alumni. **Medals:** Order of Mono (Togo), "Men of Achievement", Cambridge, UK. **Sports:** Pingpong, tennis, walking. **Hobbies:** Translation, writing books, teaching, lecturing. **Credit Cards:** American Express, Eurocard. **Addr.:** Geneva, Switzerland.

DJEBAR (Assia), Algerian university professor, novelist and writer. **Born** on August 4, 1936 in Cherchel. **Educ.:** Ecole Normale Supérieure (Paris). **Dipl.:** Diploma of education. **Career:** Novelist, Writer in French Professor of History at the Universities of Rabat (Morocco) and Algiers (Algeria). **Publ.:** Author of several novels, eg. "La Soif" (1957), "Les Impatients", "Les Enfants du Nouveau Monde" (1962), "Les Alouettes Naïves". **Addr.:** Algiers, Algeria.

DJIBRIL (Abdallah Chirwa), Djibouti Deputy at the National Assembly, and Minister of Defence. **Born** in 1946 at Holl-Holl (district Ali-Sabieh). **Career:** Militant of the LPAI; Member of the Central Committee of RPP; Elected Deputy at the National Assembly (8 May 1977- to date); President of the Permanent Commission (1993-27.03.1996); Minister of National Defence (27.03.1996-to date). **Prof. Addr.:** National Assembly, P.O.Box 138 Djibouti, Djibouti.

DJIBRIL (Ibrahim, Idriss), Djibouti Deputy at the National Assembly. **Born** in 1948 at Obock. **Educ.:** Secondary, Nursing Formation. **Career:** Member of Central Committee of RPP; Minister of Public Works (25 Nov. 1990 - 3 Feb. 1993); Elected Deputy at the National Assembly (18/12/1992 - to date); Minister of Civil Service and Administrative Reform (1/11/1997); became Minister of Agriculture, Livestock and Fisching in charge of Hydraulic Resources (18/12/1997). **Prof. Addr.:** National Assembly, P.O.Box 138 Djibouti, Djibouti.

DJILANI (Hedi), Tunisian executive and deputy. **Born** on February 13, 1948 in Tunis and has studied Medecine in Paris. **Married** 5 children. **Professionnal Responsabilities:** Mr. DJILANI is owner and chairman of several companies mainly in the textile, finance, tourism and real estate sectors. Most of his companies are export-oriented. **Other Responsabilities:** Since 1987: Member of the Board of Directors of the Tunisian Central Bank. Since 1988: President of UTICA, the Tunisian Federation of Private Employers. Since 1989: Member of Parliament; Member of the Central Committee of the Rassemblement Constitutionnel Démocratique (the party in power). President of the Tunisian Committee of the ICC (since 1992); President of the Panafrican Employers' Confederation (May 1993-June 1995); Vice- President of the ILO (International Labor Office) since June 1995. **Decorations:** Commander of Order of the Republic of Italy (since 1990); Commander of Order of 7th November (since 1991); "Médaille d'Or du Travail" in 1992; Commander of Order of the Republic of Tunisia (since July 25, 1992); Member of the French "Legion of Honour" (since 1992); "Grand officier" of the Republic of Tunisia (since September 1994). **Prof. Addr.:** Union Tunisienne de l'Industrie du Commerce et de l'Artisanat, 103, Avenue de la Liberté, 1002 Tunis-Belvedere, Tel.: 785 431, Fax: 802248.

DJOUDI (Hocine), Algerian diplomat. **Born** on May 4, 1930. **Married,** five children. **Educ.:** Montpellier University. **Dipl.:** LL.B. **Career:** Counsellor for Foreign Affairs and Chief Deputy of the Algerian Department of International Organisation (1963); Counsellor, Algerian Embassy to the U.K. (1963-64); at the Permanent Mission to the UN (1964-68); Cousellor, Office of the Minister of Foreign Affairs (1968-78); Ambassador to Spain (1978-79); to Portugal (1979-82); to Mozambique and Lesotho (1982-84); Permanent Representative to the United Nations (1984-91). **Addr.:** Ministry of Foreign Affairs, Algiers, Algeria.

DKRORI (Imad, Abdalla), Egyptian lawyer. **Born** on April 5, 1924 in Benha, Egypt. **Married,** 2 sons. **Educ.:** Cairo University, Egypt. **Dipl.:** LL.B. **Career:** Deputy Attorney General, Ministry of Justice (1948-54), Judge (1954-63), President of Public Prosecution (1963-70), Justice in the Courts of Appeal (1970-75); Legal Adviser and Solicitor (1975-). **Hobbies:** Music, walking, jogging, tennis. **Prof. Addr.:** 39 Qasr al-Nile, Cairo, Egypt. **Priv. Addr.:** 17A Muhammad Madhar Street, Zamalek, Cairo, Egypt.

DOANY (Atallah), Jordanian civil engineer. **Born** in 1929 in Haifa. **Son** of Ibrahim Doany (pastor) **and** Mrs., née Kamleh Hawwa. **Married** to Samia Hissen in 1962, in Beirut (Lebanon), 4 children: Ibrahim, Dina, Ramzi Nasser and Camille. **Educ.:** Bishop Gobat school, Jerusalem; American University in Beirut (Lebanon). **Dipl.:** B.Sc. (Physics, Mathematics), B.A., B.S.C.E. (Civil Engineering). **Career:** American University in Beirut where he served as Supervising Engineer, then Contract Engineer (1952-58), alongside private engineering consulting in Lebanon; Engineering consultant to Getty Oil Co. and others (1958-62); Jordan University chief architect & designer, later Head of Planning and Development Department (1963-73); merged private office Al Muhandes al-Arabi into STIGMA - Consulting Engineers (1975). **Member:** Royal Society of Health (UK); Institute of Architects and Surveyors (UK); Institute of Arbitrators (UK); Institute of Arbitrators (UK); Society for University and College Planning (USA). **Decorations:** Al Istiklal medallion (2nd degree), Hashemite Kingdom of Jordan. **Sports:** Swimming and Shooting. **Hobbies:** Reading, travel and music. **Member:** Shooting club; Royal Society Conservation of Nature; Youth Sports City. **Credit Cards:** American Express, Carte Blanche. **Prof. Addr.:** P.O.Box 20076, Tel.: 63554 - 61031 - 62612, Amman, Jordan. **Priv. Addr.:** Shmeisani, Tel.: 67356, Amman, Jordan.

DORDA (Abu Zeid Umar), Libyan politician. **Career:** Governor of Misurata; Minister of Information and Culture (July 1972- November 1974); Under-Secretary, Ministry of Foreign Affairs (1974-76); Minister of Municipalities (October 1976-77); Secretary of Municipalities, General People's Committee (March 1977); Secretary for Economy (Jan. 1981 - June 1982); Secretary for Land

Reclamation and Land Reform (1982); Secretary General of the General People's Committee (1990). Assistant secretary, General People's Congress (1994) Presently, Permanent Representative of Libya to the United Nations. **Prof. Addr.:** 309-315 East 48th St., New York, NY 10017, Tel.: (212) 752 5775, Fax: (212) 593 4787, USA.

DOUALEH (Aden Warsama), Djibouti Deputy at the National Assembly. **Born** in 1945 in Djibouti. **Educ.:** Technical Education College. **Career:** Technical Assistant Director "Imprimerie Nationale" (1979-1988) then Director (1988-1997). **Member** of PMP, LPAI and RPP. Elected Deputy at the National Assembly (19/12/1997 - to date). Member of the Foreign Affairs Commission, Legislation Commission and General Administration of the Republic, Member of the Supreme Court of Justice. **Prof. Addr.:** National Assembly, P.O.Box 138 Djibouti, Djibouti.

DOUALEH (Houssein, Aden), Djibouti Deputy at the National Assembly. **Born** in 1942 in Djibouti. **Career:** Private Sector/ President of SOGIK. Elected Deputy at the National Assembly (18/12/1992 - to date), 2nd Vice-President (1993 - 7/01/1998); Commission Member of Legislation and General Administration of the Republic. **Prof. Addr.:** National Assembly, P.O.Box 138 Djibouti, Djibouti.

DOUALEH (Youssouf, Dideh), Djibouti Deputy at the National Assembly. **Born** in 1947. **Career:** Assistant Manager at EPH (1993 - 19/12/1997); Member of RPP. President of Association: "developpement de la Jeunesse", "La Soldarité", "Action Communautaires" (1993 - Dec. 1997); Elected Deputy at the National Assembly (19/12/1997 - to date); Member of National Defence Commission, Legislation and General Administration of the Republic. **Prof. Addr.:** National Assembly, P.O.Box 138 Djibouti, Djibout.

DOUEK (Maurice-Haim), Chief Rabbi of Egypt. **Born** in Cairo, **Educ.:** Secondary and ecclesiastical. **Career:** Chief Rabbi of the Jewish Community to the Arab Republic of Egypt. **Awards:** Middle East and Foreign decorations. **Addr.:** 13 Sharia Sabil Al Khazindar, Abbassia, Cairo, Egypt.

DOUIRI (Mohamad), Moroccan politician. **Born** in 1929. **Married**, 4 children: 2 sons and 2 daughters. **Educ.:** in Paris (1945-51). **Career:** Joined Istiqlal Party; leader, Istiqlal Students Group, France; Engineer, Direction des Mines; member and later Head, Provisional Committee of Istiqlal (1952-56); member, Istiqlal Political Commission; member, Executive Committee (1960); Minister of Public Works (1958-60); Minister of National Economy and Finance (1960-62); Director, al-Risala Press, publishing the Journal of "Union Générale des Travailleurs Marocains" (1963); re-elected member, Istiqlal Party Executive Committee (1974); Minister of Supply and National Revival (October 1977-1982); Minister of Planning and Vocational Training (May 1982-85). **Addr.:** Rabat, Morocco.

DOUKHALI (Abdulwahab, ad), Moroccan actor and musician. **Born** on January 2, 1941 in Fes. **Educ.:** Secondary. **Career:** Artist, Actor, Composer, Member of the Moroccan National Group Theatre, Appeared in pictures like "Le Caire la nuit" (1963), "Extase" (1964), "Sable d'Or" (1965); Author of 130 songs; affected by King Hassan II to organize the artistical programme for the Independence Day, Author of several music works, specially for Oum Koulsoum (Egyptian Vocalist). **Addr.:** Rabat, Morocco.

DOURI (Abdulaziz, ad), Iraqi educationalist, former Rector of University. **Born** in 1917 in Baghdad. **Educ.:** Secondary School of Baghdad, University College and School of Oriental Studies, University of London. **Dipl.:** Bachelor of Arts, Doctor of Philosophy. **Career:** Teacher, Assistant Professor and Professor at Higher Training College of Baghdad (1943-48); Director of Translations and Publications in the Ministry of Education (1948-50); Acting Dean and later of University College of Baghdad (1949-60); Professor of Islamic History (1961-65); Rector of Baghdad University (1967). **Publ.:** Author of "Studies on the Economic Life of Mesopotamia in the 10th Century" (in Arabic), "Islamic Institutions" (2 Volumes), "Abbasid History of Early Islam". **Priv. Addr.:** Haibat Khatoum, 2-2-22, Baghdad, Iraq.

DOURI (Izzat, Ibrahim Khalil, al), Iraqi politician. **Born** on July 1, 1942, al-Dour, Governorate of Salahuddin (Iraq). **Son** of Ibrahim Khalil al-Douri (farmer) **and** Mrs. Hamdah Saloum al-Douri. **Married** in 1968 to Jawhar Majeed Khalil al-Douri, 5 children: Hawazen, Ahmad, Ibrahim, Abdallah and Fatimah. **Educ.:** Al-Adamiyah Secondary school, scientific section. **Career:** Editor, Voice of Peasant (1968); Head, Supreme Committee for People's Work (1968-70); Minister of Agrarian Reform (1970-74); Vice-President, Supreme Agricultural Council (1970-71); Minister of Agriculture (1973-74); Minister of Interior (1974). Presently Vice-Chairman, Revolutionary Command Council; and Deputy Regional Command Secretary of the Arab Baath Socialist Party. **Hobby:** shooting **Prof. Addr.:** Arab Baath Socialist Party, P.O.Box 6012, Baghdad, Iraq.

DRISS (Guiga, M.), Tunisian former diplomat. **Born** on August 21, 1924 in Tunisia. **Married**, 4 children. **Educ.:** University education in Algiers and Paris. **Dipl.:** Licence in Law, Agrégé in History and Geograpy. **Career:** called to the Bar and practised Law (1948-52); Head of the Office, Minister of Public Healt (1952); Director, Regional and Commercial Administration, of National Security (1952-63); General Comissioner of Tourism (1963-69); State Secretary for Public Health and Social Affairs (1969) Minister of Public Health (1969), Minister of National Education (1973-76); Ambassador to West Germany (1976); Businessman in London UK (1985). **Decor.:** Grand Cordon of the Order of the Tunisian Republic; Commander of the Order of Tunisian Independence. **Addr.:** Tunis, Tunisia.

DRISS (Rachid), Tunisian former diplomat. **Born** on January 27, 1917 in Tunis, Tunisia. **Married** in 1953 to Jeanine Driss, 1 child **Educ.:** Sadiki School, Tunis; **Career:** Journalist, Youth Group Organizer, Tunisia (1938-42); Representative of Neo-Doustour Party, Egypt, Indonesia & Pakistan; Head, Tunisian Section, North African Liberalization Committee, Cairo (1946-52); Director, al-Amal Party. Newspaper (1955); Chief African-Asian Division, Foreign Affairs Department & Deputy, Constituent Assembly, Tunis (1956-57); Secretary of State for Posts, Telegraph & Telephones (1957-64); Member, National Assembly & Political Bureau of Neo-Detour Party, Tunis (1959); Member, Central Committee, Doustour Socialist Party (1964); Delegate, UN General Assembly, New York (1965-74); Ambassador to USA and Mexico (1964-70); Vice President, Economic & Social Council (ECOSOC) (1970); President ECOSOC, UN (1971); Ambassador, Permanent Representative of Tunisia, New York. Diplomatic Counsellor (1976); Presided the Tunisian Delegation to Buenos Aires, the Conference of the Technical cooperation (CTPD) (1978); Presided a good will mission to Latin America (1978); Messenger of President Bouguiba to President Sarkis of Lebanon and to Yasser Arafat of PLO, to Yemini President to Sultan Kaboos of Oman, to Princes of Bahrain and Qatar, (This mission was for the preparation of the Arab League Headquarters in Tunis 1979) now retired. **Publ.:** "De Bab Souika a Manhattan", "Souvenirs de bureau du Maghred Arab au Gaire", "A l'Aube, la tanterne" **Awards:** Grand Cordon, Order of Independence, Tunisian Republic, **Addr.:** Rue St. Cyprien, 2016 Carthage, Tunisia.

DRISSI QEYTONI (Bennacer), Moroccan engineer. **Born** in 1934 in Fes, Morocco. **Married**, 3 children. **Educ.:** Faculty of Sciences Rabat; Ecole Nationale Supérieure des Télécommunications de Paris, France. **Dipl.:** B.Sc. in Mathematics, B.Sc. in Engineering. **Career:** joined Radiodiffusion Television Marocaine (1962), Assistant Head, Technical Services (1963), Head, Technical Services (1964), Chief Engineer (1972), Technical Director (1974); Director General, Radiodiffusion Television Marocaine (1978-1987). **Decor.:** Officier de l'Ordre du Trône, Morocco (1964). **Addr.:** 14 Lotissement Saada, Aviation, Rabat, Morocco.

DRISSI QEYTONI (Mohamad), Moroccan official. **Born** on December 22, 1929 in Fes, Morocco. **Married,** 2 sons, 2 daughters. **Educ.:** Moroccan School of Administration. **Career:** Vice President, General Economic Confederation; President, Moroccan Association of Textile Industry, President, Federation of Industry; Member of Parliament, President of the Economic Commission; former Director General, "Ste Tisbrod"; former President Delegate "Ste Cofitex". **Decor.:** Chevalier de l'Ordre du Trone, Morocco (1974). **Member:** Rotary Club; active Member of various social societies and organizations. **Addr.:** 45 Rue de Toulouse, CIL, Casablanca, Morocco.

DROOBI (Ala'uddin), Syrian physician, psychiatrist (resident in Australia). **Born** in 1925 in Homs, Syria. **Married**, three children. **Educ.:** American University of Beirut, Lebanon; University of Lausanne, Switzerland; London University. **Dipl.:** B.A. (1947); M.D. (1952); Diploma of Psychological Medicine (1957). **Career:** Senior Consultant Psychiatrist, The Lebanon Hospital for Mental and Nervous Disorders, Beirut (1957-62); Lecturer in Psychiatry, School of Medicine, American University of Beirut (1960-72); President of the Lebanese Society of Neurology and Psychiatry; Senior Lecturer, Department of Psychiatry, Medical School, University of Western Australia; Consultant Psychiatrist, Royal Perth Hospital and Perth Medical Center, Perth, Western Australia. **Member of:** the Royal College of Psychiatrists, US (1973); the Australian and New Zealand College of Psychiatrists, Australia (1974); the Lebanese Association of Physicians; former member of Editorial Board of Lebanese Medical Journal. **Publ.:** articles on psychiatry in professional journals in English. **Hobbies:** Music, travelling, walking. **Priv. Addr.:** 53 Bruce Street, Nedlands, Perth, Western Australia (6009), Tel.: 867728.

DROOBI (Sami, Misbah), Syrian former diplomat. **Born** 1921 in Homs. **Son** of Misbah Droubi. **Educ.:** La Sorbonne (France). **Dipl.:** Doctorate of Law, Licenciate of Philosophy. **Career:** Professor of Philosophy at the University of Damascus (1955-57), Diplomat, Served in the Ministry of Foreign Affairs, Syrian Ambassador to Belgrade (Yugoslavia), Syrian Permanent Representative at the League of Arab States (1965), Syrian Ambassador to Arab Republic of Egypt (January 1967). **Publ.:** Author of several studies translated from French, English and German. **Addr.:** Damascus, Syria.

DUAIJ (Ahmad, Ali, al), Kuwaiti official. **Born** in 1938 in Kuwait. **Educ.:** Kuwaiti Secondary School; University College of North Staffordshire, Keele, UK (BA); Oxford University UK, Post Graduate Studies. **Career:** Kuwait Foreign Ministry (1962); Secretary, Planning Board (1962-63); Director General, Kuwait Real Estate Investment Consortium (1964-75); Chairman and Managing Director, Kuwait Real Estate Investment Consortium, Safat, Kuwait (1975-). Chairman of Yemeni-Kuwait Real Estate Development Company, Sanaa. Head of Government Scholarship Commitee and Member of the Board of Kuwait University, also presently Director General, Kuwait Planning Board. **Member:** Kuwait Economic Society. **Addr.:** P.O.Box 23411, Commercial Area 3, Palestine Street 1, Tel.: 2448260, Telex: 2620, 2849 A/B CONSORT, Safat, Kuwait, and P.O.Box 15, Safat 13001, Kuwait.

DUBAISHY (Ali Ibrahim), Saudi official. **Born** in 1934, at Buraidah. **Dipl.:** B.Sc. (Accounting). **Career:** Accountant, Arab Bank (1957-58); Accountant, Saudi Monetary Agency (1960-62); Director General of Control, Petromin (1966-67); Deputy Governor of Petromin; member of

Executive Committees of Petromin and Riyadh Refinery. **Addr.:** Petromin, P.O.Box 757, Riyadh, Saudi Arabia.

DUDIN (Marwan), Jordanian politician. **Born** in 1936 at Beersheba, Palestine. **Married,** with Children. **Career:** Teacher of English, Jordan; Translator, Arabian America Oil Company (Aramco) (1963-64); Dean of Students, Saudi College of Petroleum and Minerals (1964-67); Director, Commercial Division of Royal Jordanian Airlines ALIA (1968-71); Director-General, Hashemite Broadcasting Service (1971-73); Minister of Information and Culture (August-November 1973); Minister of State at the Prime Minister's Office (1973-74); Minister of Agriculture (1980-84); Manager, Jordan Distribution Agency (Publications), (1984-85); Chairman, general manager; Agricultural Marketing and Processing Co. of Jordan (since April 1985). **Prof. Addr.:** P.O.Box 9936, Amman, Jordan.

DUGHAITHER (Taha Ali al-Rashid), Saudi diplomat. **Born** in 1929 at Sudain. **Dipl.:** B.A. (Political Science), Cairo University (1952); M.A. (Political Science), St. John's University, New York; Ph.D. student (History). **Career:** official, Ministry of Foreign Affairs, (1955-57); Saudi Embassy in Rome (1957-62); Addis Ababa (1962-64); Ministry of Foreign Affairs (1964-65); Saudi Embassy in Djakarta (1965-67); member of Saudi Arabian permanent delegation to UN (1967-73); the Saudi Embassy in Sanaa' (1973); Ambassador to Somalia; attended Oceanography Sciences Conference, Geneva (1958); First Conference of Nonaligned Nations, Belgrade (1961); the 40th session of Arab League Meetings (1964); UN sessions: 22nd, 23rd, 24th, 25th, 26th, 27th and 30th; Islamic Foreign Minister's Conference, Kuala Lumpur (1975); 3rd Nonaligned nations Conference, Colombo; the Regional Refugees Conference, Geneva (1976). **Honours:** Brazilian and Iranian decorations. **Hobbies:** reading, literary criticism, travel, stamp collecting. **Addr.:** c/o Ministry of Foreign Affairs, Jeddah, Saudi Arabia.

DUKHEIL (Abdulaziz, M., al), Saudi economist. **Born** on July 15, 1942 in Medina, Saudi Arabia. **Dipl.:** Ph.D. (Economics). **Career:** Secretary General of the Public Investment Fund, Ministry of Finance (1975); Director General, Economic Rresearch Department (1976); Deputy Minister of Finance for Financial Affairs and Accounts (1978); President, Saudi Consulting Centre for Finance and Investment; member of the American Economics Association, Arab Banker's Association, the American Finance Association; Chairman of the Arab Investment Co., the Real Estate Development Fund, the Gulf Organization for Development in Egypt; member, Arabian Gulf Countries Development Assembly, International Businessmen's Conference. **Publ.:** An Optimum Base for Pricing Middle Eastern oil, (Ph.D. thesis) (1974); Monetary Effects of Denominating Saudi Government Foreign Obligations in Riyals (1981). **Hobbies:** Reading, writing, sports. **Addr.:** P.O.Box 2462, Riyadh 11451, Tel.: 4782525 (Office) and 4762013 (Home), Riyadh, Saudi Arabia.

DURAIB (Saud Ibn Saad, al), Saudi legal adviser. **Born** in 1937. **Dipl.:** M.A. (Islamic Jurisprudence and Principles). **Career:** Clerical and secretarial work; Bureau Manager for Director General, Bureau Manager for Under Secretary, Ministry of Justice, Legal Adviser, Ministry of Justice; former member of Board for the Settlement of Commercial Disputes; member of al-Dawa Islamic Press Organization, Riyadh; attended the Sixth Anti-Narcotic Conference, Riyadh, Conference on the Function of the University. **Publ.:** books: al-Muamalatil Masrafiyyah Wa Mawaqif al-Shariatil Islamizati Minha (Banking Transactions in the Light of Islamic Law), al-Sharikat Fi Fiqhil Islami Wal Qanoun al-Wadhie (Companies as Viewed by Islamic Jurisprudential Study), Muhammad Ibn Abdul Wahab, Hamil Rayatil Islam Fil Qarnil Thani Ashar (Mohamad Ibn Abdul Wahab, Bearer of the Banner of Islam During the Twelfth Century); several contributions to local press; lectures delivered at Umm al-Qura University, Makkah. **Prof. Addr.:** Bureau of the Minister of Justice, Tel.: 4351155, Riyadh, **Priv. Addr.:** Tel.: 4352613, Riyadh, Saudi Arabia.

DUWAIDAR (Salah, Mahmoud), Egyptian executive. **Born** in 1944 in Egypt. **Son** of Mahmoud Dewedar. **Married** in 1968, 1 son, 1 daughter. **Dipl.:** B.Sc. Engineering. **Career:** Senior Project Engineer, Egypt (1965-73); Petroleum Adviser, Libya (1973-74); Petroleum Expert, Kuwait (1974-77); Project and Investment Manager. Arab African International Bank (1978-79); Acting Regional Representative, Arab Multinational Finance Co. S.A., Cairo, Egypt (1979-). **Addr.:** Abdul Khalek Sarwat Street, P.O.Box 1143, Cairo, Egypt.

DWEIK (Abdel Kader), Jordanian Executive. **Born** in 1947. **Son** of Abed Al-Hakeem Dueik. **Married** in 1974, 3 sons, 2 daughters. **Dipl.:** B.Sc., Business Administration. **Career:** Deposit Department, Central Bank of Jordan; Director, Arab Insurance Co. (1981); Assistant Deputy General Manager, The Housing Bank, Amman, Jordan (1985- to present); Director of: Jordan Securities Corp. (1985- to present) and Jordan Cement Co. (1986). **Addr.:** P.O.Box 926691, Amman, Jordan.

DWEIK (Yusuri), UAE Legal Adviser. **Born** in 1935 in Hebron, Jordan. **Son** of Mahmoud Dweik. **Married** in 1960, 2 sons, 2 daughters. **Educ.:** B.A. in Law, M.A. in International Law. **Career:** Lawyer and Civil Judge, Jordan; Chief Justice, Sharjah (1960-75); Legal Adviser to the Ruler of Sharjah, UAE (1975-). **Publ.:** A Book on Islamic Charity (WAKF). **Addr.:** P.O.Box 1, Government of Sharjah, Kiwan al-Emiri, Tel.: 357419, Sharjah, UAE.

E

EBAID (Atef, Mohamed, Dr), Egyptian Politician. **Born** on April 14, 1932 in Gharbiya Governorate. **Married.** Two Children. **Educ.:** Faculty of Commerce, Cairo Universiy B.A. (1952), M.A. (1956) and University of Illinois Ph. D. (1962). **Career:** Member of Arab League Media Policy Coordinating Committee (1970); former Professor of Business Administration, Faculty of Commerce, Cairo University (1962-1984), President International Management Center (1973-1984), Adviser to various Ministries (Electricity, Industry, Higher Education and Housing), and the International Labour Organization in Cyprus, Minister of Public Sector and Minister of State for Administrative Development (1984-Oct. 1999), Prime Minister (Oct. 5, 1999-). **Addr.:** Office of the Prime Minister, Cairo, Egypt.

ECHIGUER (Mohamad, Haddou), Moroccan politician. **Born** in 1932 in Khemisset. **Educ.:** Secondary in Rabat. **Dipl.:** B.A. (Literature). **Career:** Teacher, Khemisset Deputy to the first Moroccan Parliament (1963); Minister of P.T.T. and later of Agriculture and Agrarian Reform (1964); Minister, Royal Cabinet (1966); Minister of National Defence (1967); Member, Chamber of Representatives (1979); Under Secretary of State for the Interior (1970); Minister of Primary Education (1966-72); Minister of National Education (1972-73); Minister of the Interior (1973- February 1977); Minister of Cooperation and Cadre Training (Feb. 1977- April 1977); Minister for Relations with Parliament (April 1977-82); Member of Parliament since 1977. **Prof. Addr.:** Moroccan Parliament, Rabat, Morocco.

ECONOMIDES (Jean), Egyptian company director. **Born** in Cairo. **Educ.:** College of the Christian Brothers (Laureate) French School of Law of Cairo. **Married** to Miss Elly Economides (Bachelor of Science). **Career:** Proxy for "Credit Foncier Egyptien", Director of Textile Fibres Industry, Cultural Director Hellenic Centre of Cairo, Honorary Member of the Christian Brothers Old Boys Association. **Publ.:** Author of "Movable Assets", "Crisis and Belgium", "Egypt and the Marshall Plan", "Investment Companies", "The Problem of Financing in Egypt", "The Egyptian New Regime". **Awards:** Academy Officer, Knight Order of Georges I of Greece. **Member** of Hellenic Centre of the French Friendships, French-Hellenic League of Athens, France-Greece League of Paris, Gezireh Sporting Club. **Hobby:** Chess. **Addr.:** 43, Sharif Pasha Street, Tel.: 43217, Cairo, Egypt.

EFFAT (Ahmad, M.), Egyptian engineer. **Born** in 1920 in Egypt. **Educ.:** M.Sc. in Naval Architecture and Marine Engineering, University of Michigan, USA (1948). **Career:** Marine engineer in Cleveland, Ohio shipyard, USA; technical surveyor, American Bureau of Shipping (ABS); employed by ABS in Japan (1961-63); Technical Director of Alexandria Shipyards, Egypt (1963-67); returned to ABS (1967); returned to Egypt (1969); Minister of Maritime Transport (1972-73); Egyptian Chairman, US-Egyptian Business Council (1975); Professor Faculty Engineering, Alexandria University (1984-). **Addr.:** Alexandria University, 22 el-Geish Street, Alexandria, Egypt.

EFFAT (Kamal-Eddine, Ahmad), Egyptian scientist. **Born** on April 12, 1920 in Beni Suef city, Beni Suef Governorate (Upper Egypt). **Married** in 1952 to Nadia Henry Burns, 3 children: two daughters and one son. **Educ.:** Beni Suef Secondary School (1932-37); Faculty of Engineering, Cairo University (1937-42); Faculty of Science, Birmingham University, UK (1948-53); Argonne National Laboratory, (USA), (1955). **Dipl.:** B.Sc. (Electrical Engineering) (1942), B.Sc. (Honours-Physics) (1950); Ph.D. (Nuclear Physics) (1953); Diploma of Nuclear Science and Engineering (1955). **Career:** Lecturer, Faculty of Engineering, Cairo University (1954); Assistant Professor, Atomic Energy Establishment (1958); Professional Officer, International Atomic Energy Agency (IAEA), Vienna, Austria (1958-60); Director-General, Nuclear Power Project (1965); Director, Atomic Energy Establishment (1975), Chairman, Atomic Energy Establishment, Cairo, Egypt (1977). **Sport:** Swimming. **Hobby:** Bridge. **Priv. Addr.:** 25, Amin Elrasi street, Dokki District, Tel.: 982512, Cairo, Egypt.

EGAL (Mohamed Ibrahim), Somali politician. **Born** in 1928 in Berbera, Somalia. **Son** of Haji Ibrahim Egal **and** Hajia Khadija Mohamed Osman. **Married** to Aasha Saeed Abby (1946) five children. **Educ.:** Koranic School, Sheikh Intermediate School and in U.K. **Career:** Secretary General, Somali National League Party (1958-60); Prime Minister of Somaliland (1960); Minister of Defence, Somali Republic (1960-62); of Education (1962-63); Leader of Parliamentary Opposition (1963-65), resigned leadership (1965); member of Somali Youth Party (1966); Prime Minister and Minister of Foreign Affairs, Somali Republic (1967-69); in detention following coup (1969); released (October 1975); Ambassador to India (1976); rearrested (Oct. 1976) and released (Feb. 1982);

Chairman, Chamber of Commerce, Industry and Agriculture; President, Republic of Somaliland, (since May 1993). **Sport:** Golf. **Hobbies:** Reading and films. **Addr.:** Hargeisa Somaliland.

EKIANE (Abdallah, al), Egyptian diplomat. **Born** in 1920 in Egypt. **Educ.:** Faculty of Law (Cairo University). **Dipl.:** Bachelor of Law (1942), Master of Arts in Political Sciences (1948), Doctor in Philosophy (1951). **Career:** Professor of Internationl Law, Cairo University (1952-61); Director of the Legal and Treaties Department, Ministry of Foreign Affairs (1961-65); Chairman of the Sixth Committee (Legal) of the General Assembly, United Nations (September 1965); Head of Member of the Egypt delegations to numerous international meetings, Organizations, Committees and Commissions all over the world (1953, 1955, 1958, 1961 and 1963); Ambassador of Arab Republic of Egypt to France (1971-74) now retired. **Addr.:** Cairo, Egypt.

EL-ADM (Khaled), Egyptian; Library Consultant and Advanced Information Service. **Born** in 1957 in Alexandria, Egypt. **Son** of Charles El Adm (Auditor & Economical Expert) (deceased in 1961) **and** Mrs. née Mary Khangy. **Educ.:** Girard School - St. Mark's College (French education), Montpellier University BSc. Computer Department, Faculty of Engineering, Alexandria University. **Dipl.:** Library and information network Computer diplomas; Library Science Certificat (GSUSADA). Graduate School of Librarianship. **Languages:** Arabic, French, English, Italian, Esperanto. **Career:** Science Clubs management (1971); Scientific reporter (1973); Management Administration (1974); Project Manager of Scientific firms (1979); Library Science and information, Reference Librarian, Methodology (since 1980- to date). **Other Information:** Organizer of Local and international Congress & Seminars (12 years); Expert in the scientific and Cultural activities (out disciplinary program - Science Clubs) (20 years). **Sports:** Tennis, Volley-Ball, Ping Pong. **Hobbies:** Photography (Landscape out doors), History of the Ancient World. **Member:** IFLA, FID, AVSL, IAOL, ICC, CLR, USS, ANSTU. **Prof. Addr.:** P.O.Box 37, Ibrahimieh (21321), Alexandria, Egypt, Tel.: (0203) 5975238. **Priv. Addr.:** P.O.Box 37, Ibrahimieh, Alexandria (21321), Egypt.

EL-AYED (Ahmad), Tunisian professor. **Born** on May 7, 1934 in Sousse, Tunisia. **Married**, 2 children. **Educ.:** University of Paris (Sorbonne). **Dipl.:** Agrégation de Langue et de Civilisation Arabes. Paris; Specialist of Bilingualism and Developing of Modern Arabic in Tunisia. **Career:** Teacher, High School (1961-65); since 1965: Professor in the University: Bourguiba Institute of Languages; Ecole Normale des Professeurs Adjoints, Ecole Normale Supérieure; Adviser in Secondary Education, Associate Professor in Linguistics Section (Centre of Economic and Social Research); Professor in "Faculté des Lettres" and General Director of Primary Education in Tunisia (1974-78); Consultant and Expert in "Organism of Promotion of Arabic Language and Islamic Culture", (ALECSO: Arab League Educational Cultural and Scientific Organization) Tunis; Director of "l'Institut National des Sciences de l'Education", (1986-1992) Director of "La Revue Tunisienne des Sciences de l'Education" (academic review) and "Le Bulletin Pédagogique", (review for the Primary and Secondary Education in Tunisia). Representative of Tunisia in the Executive Council of ALECSO (1987-1996); Vice President of Lexicology Association in Tunisia, Member of the Board of "Lexicology Review". **Publ.:** Author of books and articles in the field of Arabic lexicography and teaching of Arabic for foreign students; among books are "Cours Pratique d'Arabe littéral" among books with other authors: "Cours Elémentaire d'Arabe", "al-Racid al-Loughawi al-Wadhifi" (for the Primary Schools in Tunisia, Algeria, Morocco, Mauritania 1975) and "al-Racid al-Loughawi al-'Arabi for Arab Countries (ALECSO 1989), "al-Mu'gam al-'Arabi al-Asasi (ALECSO 1989), "Al-Murchid dictionnaire Français-arabe" "Trainer Training Guide (1995); among his articles "Fonds Lexical Commun au Niveau du Maghreb et Enseignement Moderne" (in Aimav Seminar (Tunis 1974), "al-Lugha al-'Arabiya, Ma-Hiya Wa-Kaifa Nanhadu Biha" "Review al-Fikr". Basic Languages English, French and Common Lexical Fund "in Arabic"; ("Review al-Mu'gamiya" Tunis 1985); La Fonction de la Langue arabe et son rayonnement civilisationnel en Afrique dans le passé et le présent" (in "Lisan al-'Arabi, ALECSO, Rabat 1987). **Addr.:** 8. Rue Mohamed Ennakhli, 1009 El Ouardia, Tunis, Tunisia.

EL-AYOUTY (Yassin, al), Egyptian UN principal officer, Dept. of Public Information. **Born** on April 14, 1928 at Kanayat, Zagazig, Sharkia Governorate (Egypt). **Married** one child. **Dipl.:** Diploma Teacher's Institute, Cairo (May 1948); B.S. (Education), State Teachers College, Trenton, New Jersey, USA (June 1953); M.A. (history), Rutgers University, New Brunswick, N.J., USA (June 1954); Ph.D. (International Relations, Organization and Law), New York University, New York City, USA (Feb. 1966); J.D. (Doctor of Jurisprudence), Cardozo School of Law, New York City, USA. **Career:** Teacher of Social studies, Cairo (1948-52); Officer in charge, Radio and Visual Services, UN Dept. of Public Information (DPI), New York (1962-64) and (1983-86), Special Assistant to Executive Director, United Institute for Training and Research (UNITAR) (1964-70); Acting Director of Training, (UNITAR) (1970-71); First Officer, Department of Political and Security Council Affairs, (PSCA), UN (1971-73); Senior Political Affairs Officer, UN (1973-79); Chief of Africa Division, Political Affairs, UN (1979-82); Secretary of UN Council for Namibia (1982-83); Visiting Professor, Political Science, St. Johns University, New York City (1966-72); Visiting Professor, State University of New York at Stony Brook, (SUNY), (1972-97); Professor Emeritus SUNY at Stony Brook; Adjunet Professor of Law, Cardozo School of Law, New York City (1996- to present) Distinguished

Visiting Professor, and Executive Director of the Center for the Study of the United Nations System and the Global Legal Order (SUNSGLO), Law Center, Nova South Eastern University, Fort Landerdak, Florida, USA (1997- to present); Practising Attorney of Law and Special Counsel Spector and Feldman, LLP, Attorneys At Law, New York City, N.Y., USA; writer. **Publ.:** "Refugees South of the Sahara, an African Dilemma" (1970); "The UN and Decolonization: The Role of Afro-Asia" (1971); "Africa and International Organisation" (1974); "The Organization of African Unity After Ten Years- Comparative Perspectives" (1975, 1976); "The Organization of African Unity after twenty years" (1984); "The Organization of Africa Unity after thirty years" (1994); "Government Ethics and Law Enforcement: Toward Global Guideline" (2000); journalistic contributions and editorial and academic consultancies in USA, Europe and Arab World; speakerships on areas of specialization **Special Interest:** War and revolution in Africa and the Middle East; role of International organizations in peace Super-Powers and the third World; and development in Third World; Egyptian external policy. International Law; Domestic U.S. Laws. **Member:** The American Bar Association; The New York State Bar Association; The New Jersey State Bar Association; The Association of Former International Civil Servants; The Real Estate Board of New York. **Awards:** Fulbright Scholar (1952-54); NYU Founders Day Award, (1966). **Sports:** Walking, cycling, gymnastics, table tennis and fishing. **Prof. Addr.:** Spector and Feldman, 800 Second Avenue, 3rd Floor, New York City, N.Y. 10017, USA. **Priv. Addr.:** 2 Peter Cooper Road, Apt. 7-B, New York, City, NY 10010, USA.

EL-BAZ (Farouk), Arab-American space scientist. **Born** in 1938 in Zagazig, Egypt. **Married**: four daughters. **Educ.:** B.Sc. in Chemistry and Geology (1958); M.S. in Geology (1961); Ph.D. in Geology, (1964). **Career:** Instructor, Assiut University, Egypt (1958-60); Instructor, Heidelberg University, West Germany, (1964-66); Geologist, Pan-Am-UAR Oil Company, Egypt, (1966-67) Supervisor, Lunar Science Planning and Lunar Exploration, Bellcomm and Bell Telephone Laboratories, (1967-72); Research Director, Centre for Earth and Planetary Studies, National Air and Space Museum, Smithsonian Institution, Washington D.C., (1973-82); Vice President for Science and Technology, Itek Optical Systems, Lexington, Massachusetts (1982-86); Director, Center for Remote Sensing, Boston University (1986- Present); Adjunct Professor of Geology and Geophysics, University of Utah, USA, (1973-77); Adjunct Professor of Geology Ain Shams University, Cairo (1978-81 and 1995- Present). **Member** of US delegation of experts for joint US/USSR Lunar Cartography, (1973); member of NASA Science Panel; Chief, Surface Processes and Properties Panel, (1974); member of the International Astronomical Union, (1973) US Board of Geographic Names-Estraterrestrial Features, (1975), Task Group of Lunar Nomenclature, Member of landing sites selection committee for Apollo Missions; Chairman of Astronaut Training in lunar observations and photography, (1967-72); Principal Investigator for Earth Observations and Photography of Apollo-Soyuz Mission (1975). Active in twenty professional societies of geological sciences, member of American Friends of the Middle East, Wafa wal Amal Rehabilitation Society, Egypt, Association of Arab American University Graduates. **Publ.:** over 300 scientific papers and research papers; "Coprolites: An Annotated Bibliography" (Geological Society of America 1968); "The Moon Viewed by Lunar Orbiter" (NASA, Washington 1970); "Glossary of Mining Geology" (1971); "Say it in Arabic", New York (1968); "Astronaut Observation from the Apollo-Soyuz Mission", (Smithsonian Institution) (1977); "Space Flight and Man's Destiny" in Arabic, (1977); "Egypt as Seen by Landsat" in Arabic and English, (Cairo, 1979); "Catalogue of Earth's Photographs from the Apollo-Soyuz Test Project", (NASA 1979); "Appollo-Soyuz Summary Science Report", Vol 11; "Earth's Observations and Photography" (1979); "Green Egypt" in Arabic, (Cairo 1979); "Desert Landforms of Southwest Egypt: A Basis for Comparison with Mars" (NASA, 1981); "Deserts and Arid Lands" Martinus Nijhoff (1984); "The Geology of Egypt", Brill (1984); "Physics and Desertification", Martinus Nijhoff (1986); "Remote Sensing and Resource Exploration", World Scientific (1989); "The Gulf War and the Environment" Gordon and Breech (1994); US Bureau of Mines Certificate of Merit in Ore Reserves and Rock Formation, National Aeronautics and Space Administration, Exceptional Scientific Achievement Medal, (1971); Alumni Achievement Award for Extraordinary Scientific Accomplishments, (University of Missouri, USA, 1972); Certificate of Special Commendation, (Geological Society of America, 1973); Honour Citation for Contributions to World Community AAUG, (1973), Lunar Science Team Award, (1974); Certificate of Merit of World Organization of Aerospace Education, (1979), Arab Republic of Egypt Order of Merit 1st class (1981); Honorary Degree of Doctor of Science, New England College (1989); Outstanding Achievement Award, Egyptian-American Association (1990); Golden Door Award, International Institute of Boston (1991); The American Association for the Advancement of Science Award for Public Understanding of Science and Technology (1992); Arab-American Anti-Discrimination Committee Award For Outstanding Contribution to Science and Space Technology (1995); Egyptian American Professional Society Achievement Award (1995); Favorite Son of Dakahliya Governorate, Egypt (1995). **Sport:** Swimming. **Addr.:** Center for Remote Sensing, 725 Commonwealth Avenue, Boston University, Boston MA 02215, USA.

EL-KETTANI (Idris), Moroccan academic. **Born** on October 10, 1922 in Damascus, Syria. **Married**, 3 children. **Educ.:** Laval University, Quebec, Canada; Mohammad V. University, Rabat, Morocco. Al-Qarawyin University, Fes. Morocco. **Dipl.:** B.Sc. and Ph.D. in Social Sciences. **Ca-**

reer: Director of the Institute of Social Sciences, Rabat, Morocco; Assistant Director General, Ministry of National Education and Director of Islamic and Private Education (1961); Professor, Faculty of Letters, Mohammad V. University, Rabat. **Publ.:** "Islamic Morocco vs Atheism" (1958), Casablanca, "Juvenile Delinquency in Morocco" (1975), Morocco, "The Islamic Movement and the Francofonic Secular Invasion of Morocco" (2000), Morocco. "The Children of Israel in the Era of the Arab Decadence" (1992); "The Gulf War: The End of one Arab Fall" (1992); "From Islamic Califate to Secular Democracy" (under press); "Educational System of Morocco after 25 years of Independence" (1982); "Qur'anic Map of the Human Societies" (1994); "Strategy of Defence for Islamic Security" (1997); "The Islamic Explanation of the Fall of our Arab World (1999) Morocco. Numerous researches and articles in newspapers and journals. **Hobbies:** Islamic and social studies. Founding **Member** of several social, cultural and Islamic societies. **Prof. Addr.:** Faculty of Letters, 3 Avenue Ibn Batouta, P.O.Box 549, Rabat, Morocco.

EL-KHIYARI (Allal, El hachimi), Ph.D., Moroccan scholar. **Born** in Meknes, Morocco in 1934. **Married**, five children. **Educ.:** University of Karaouine, Aalimiya Diploma (1957); Dar al Hadith al Hassaniya (1965-1967), M.A. in Islamic and Contemporary Thought (1975), Doctorate Degree in Islamic Economy (1985). **Career:** Currently President of the Center of Coordination between the National Arab Commissions of the UNESCO, ALECSO, ISESCO; Ministry of Higher Education (Since 1975); Director of the UNESCO and the Arab World Magazine, College of Sharia Magazine, and the Information Bulletin on the Activities of the National Arab Commissions of the UNESCO (Since 1977); Member of the Union of Islamic Universities (since 1969); Head of the Cultural Affairs Department, Ministry of State for Cultural Affairs (1969-72); Member of the Moroccan National Committee for legislative Reform (since 1975); Secretary General of the Scientists Committee (1971-75), Founder of Non-governmental alliance of the Arab Cultural Institutes (1996). **Publ.:** Islam and Contemporary Ideology (1982), Rabbat Sha'ir (theatrical poetry) (1985), Islamic Economy (1988), Investments in light of the Islamic Fikh (in three volumes) (1992). **Decor.:** Medal of Ridha, first class. Member of the Moroccan Writers Union, President of the Cultural Union, Member of the Office of Authors' Rights. **Hobbies:** Scientific Research, poetry and theatre. **Addr.:** P.O.Box: 1597 Hay Salam, Sale, Morocco.

ELALI (Mohyeddin, Abdulhamid), Jordanian administrator. **Born** in Jordan in 1941. **Son** of Abdulhamid Elali **and** Mrs. Khaznah née Assaf. **Married** in 1968 to Husnieh Elali, five children. **Educ.:** Scientific Islamic College; Damascus University. **Career:** Manager of the Accounting Department, Housing Bank, Amman; Manager of the Administration Department in the Housing Bank, Amman. **Hobby:** Reading. **Member:** Sport City. Credit Cards: American Express. **Prof. Addr.:** Housing Bank, Head Office, P.O.Box 7693, Tel. 667126, Amman, Jordan. **Priv. Addr.:** Wadi el Seir, Tel. 819466, Amman, Jordan.

ELAMIN (Elamin Abdelatif), Sudanese diplomat. **Born** on May 30, 1931 in Sudan. **Son** of Abdelatif Elamin **and** Mrs. Fatima Medani. **Married** in 1959 in Sudan to Miss Aisha Abdelrahim, two sons: Housam (1961) and Sami (1968). **Educ.:** Faculty of Agriculture, Cairo University (1957); London School of Economics (1963-64). **Dipl.:** B.Sc. (Agriculture); International Relations Course. **Career:** Social Research Officer, Agricultural Research, Ministry of Agriculture, Sudan (1957-60); Joined the Foreign service as Third Secretary, Consular Department (1960); Chargé d'Affaires, Sudan Embassy in Athens, Greece (1961); Consul General (1st Secretary), Cairo, Egypt (1964-66); Deputy Head of Mission (1st Secretary), New Delhi, India (1966-68); Deputy Head of Mission, Counsellor, Kampala, Uganda (1968-71), London, England (1971- June 1972); Charge d'Affairs, Minister, Moscow, USSR (1972-73); Director, East Europe Department, Head Quarters, Khartoum (1973-74); Director, Minister's Office, Ambassador, Head Quarters, Khartoum (1974-75); Director General, Political Affairs, Khartoum (1975-76); Ambassador to Nigeria, Ghana, Cameroon (1977-78); Ambassador to Sweden, Denmark, Norway, Finland (1978-83); Council of Ministers in charge of manpower development (on secondment) (1984); Director General for Political Affairs, Ministry of Foreign Affairs (1985); Ambassador to Egypt (1985-1992). Has participated in more than 18 world conferences. **Hobbies:** Swimming, fishing, photographing wild life. **Member of:** Maadi Club, Cairo; Sudanese Diplomats Association. **Prof. Addr.:** Ministry of Foreign Affairs, Tel.: 73101, Khartoum, Sudan.

ELAMIN (Mohamed, Abdelrahman Ali), Sudanese Engineer. **Born** in 1944 at Omdurman, Sudan. **Son** of Abdelrahman Ali (deceased) **and** Mrs. née Sokkar Osman M. Kheir. **Married** on June 1977 in Khartoum to Mahfouza Ibrahim, 4 children: Yousra, Omar, Abdelrahman, Ibrahim. **Educ.:** Sudan School Certificate (Port Sudan Sec. School), BSc. (Hon.) in Chemical Engineering -University of Khartoum (1969); MSc. -University of Aston - Birmingham (England) (1970); Ph.D. -University of Wales - Wales, U.K. (1974). **Career:** Lecturer University of Khartoum (1974-78); Senior Technical Consultant, Saudi Industrial Development Fund (1978-91); Assistant Professor, University of Khartoum (1991-92); Director General, Industrial Research Consultancy Center (IRCC), Khartoum (1992- present). **Awards:** The Moulton Gold Medal (1976) from the British Institution of Chemical Engineer of the best research paper of all the publications for that year. **Sports:** Socer, Basket ball, Tennis. **Hobby:** Reading. **Member:** Member of the American Institute of Chemical Engineers. **Prof. Addr.:** P.O.Box 268, Khartoum, Sudan, Tel.: 613753.

ELAMLY (Abdelkader, Mohamad), Egyptian international officer. **Born** on May 2, 1926 in Mansourah City (Lower Egypt). **Married** with children. **Educ.:** Faculty of Sciences, Alexandria University (1943-47); Imperial College of Science and Technology, London, UK (1950-53). **Dipl.:** B.Sc. (physics & mathematics), M.Sc. (meteorology). **Career:** Aviation Forecaster, Meteorological Department (1948-50); Lecturer in Aeronautical Meteorology, Meteorological Department, Faculty of Science, Alexandria University (1953-56); Officer, International Affairs, Meteorological Department, Egypt (1956-64); Technical Officer for Africa, World Meteorological Organisation (WMO), Geneva, Switzerland (1964-67); Representative, Regional Officer for Africa, WMO. **Publ.:** Author of "Meteorology for Aviation". **Prof. Addr.:** WMO, 41 Avenue Guiseppe Motta, Tel.: 022 3-4-64-00, CH-1211, Geneva 20, Switzerland.

ELARABY (Nabil), Egyptian diplomat. **Born** on March 15, 1935, **Married,** 3 children. **Educ.:** Cairo University; New York University Law School. **Career:** Legal Adviser to the Egyptian delegation to the United Nations Middle East Peace Conference, Geneva (1973-75); Director, Legal and Treaties Department of Egyptian Ministry of Foreign Affairs (1976-78); Deputy Permanent Representative to the United Nations in New York (1978-81); Egyptian Ambassador to India (1981-83); Director, Legal and Treaties Department of Egyptian Ministry of Foreign Affairs (1983-87). Since 1966, represented Egypt in various United Nations organs, including the General Assembly, the Security Council, Economic and Social Council, The Commission on Human Rights, the Trade and Development Board of the United Nations Conference on Trade and Development (UNCTAD); and, since 1988, the Conference on Disarmament; Chaired numerous committees and working groups, including the Special Committee on the Charter of the United Nations and on the Strengthening of the Role of the Organization and the United Nations Special Committee on Enhancing the Effectiveness of the Principle of the Non-Use of Force in International Relations; Head the Egyptian delegation to the Taba talks (1986-1989); Agent of the Egyptian Government to the Egypt-Israel Arbitration Tribunal; Permanent Representative of Egypt to the United Nations, New York (1991-1998); Vice President of the G.A. 48th and 52nd Sessions; Member of the International Law Commission (1994-); Member, Judicial Tribunal of the Organization of Arab Oil Producing Countries (OAPEC) (1991-). **Publ.:** several articles (in English) on International law and diplomacy; several articles (in Arabic) on the Middle East peace process. **Addr.:** Cairo, Egypt.

ELASS (Hisham, Dr.), Syrian chemical engineer. **Born** on October 25, 1929, in Jubbata Alzeit, Damascus, Syria. **Son** of Assaad Elass (Landlord) **and** Mrs. nee Hussune Balhawan. **Married** on January 6, 1963 in Damascus, to Afaf Soued, two girls: Rasha (23.5.1959), Roula (08.08.1973). **Educ.:** Secondary School, Damascus; Ecole Nationale Superieure de Chimie de Strasbourg, Strasbourg University, France. **Dipl.:** Licence es-Science; Chemical Engineer; Doctor Engineer. **Career:** Research Engineer, Topsoe Laboratories (Copenhagen 1958-59); Minister of Industry and Energy, (Syria, Oct. 1963- Feb. 1966); Managing Director, Research and Testing Centre (Damascus, Oct. 1966- Jan. 1969); Project Manager UNIDO/UNDP Project (Algiers, Jan. 1969- March 1974); Deputy General Manager, Arab Petroleum Investments Corporation (APICORP, April 1987 to present). **Main Activities:** APICORP was established by the Arab Countries Member of OAPEC; Evaluation of Petroleum and Petrochemical Projects, Promotion of Pan Arab Projects, Trade and Project Finance, Syndicated Loans in the Arab Countries, Investment and Treasury Operations. **Sports:** Tennis, Swimming. **Member of:** the Engineers Association of Syria. **Credit Cards:** Amex, Master Card, Acces. **Prof. Addr.:** Arab Petroleum Investments Corporation (APICORP), P.O.Box 448 Dharan Airport 31932, Tel.: 966-3-8647400, Telex: 870068 APIC SJ, Saudi Arabia, Tel.: 8579500 (Home).

ELBARADEI (Mohamed, M. Dr.), Egyptian Diplomat. **Born** on 17 June 1942. **Married,** 2 children: one daughter and one son. **Education:** Doctorate Degree (J.S.D.) International Law, New York University School of Law, 1974; Master Degree (L.L.M.) International Law, New York University School of Law, 1971; Diploma of Advanced Studies, Administrative Law, Cairo University School of Law, 1964; Licence in Law, Cairo University School of Law 1962. **Languages:** Arabic, English and French. **Career:** *Professional Experience:* More than 30 years of experience with various international organizations as a diplomat, international civil servant, and scholar. Intimately familiar with the activities and processes of international organizations, particularly those within the United Nations System. Extensive experience and wide expertise in the work of the IAEA, including activities in technical cooperation, nuclear verification and nuclear safety; its working methods and management practices; and its political, legal, and financial framework. His positions over the past 30 years include: As of 1 December 1997 - Director General, IAEA, Vienna. 1993-end November 1997 - Assistant Director General for External Relations, IAEA, Vienna. Responsibilities included directing the Agency's Policy Coordinating Office; interacting with Member States and International Organizations on policy issues; and negotiating safeguards agreements with Member States. 1991-1993 Director of External Relations, IAEA, Vienna. 1987 - 1991 Director of the Legal Division and Legal Adviser, IAEA, Vienna. 1984 - 1987 Representative of the Director General of the IAEA to the United Nations, New York. 1980 - 1984 Senior Fellow and Director of International Law and Organizations Programme, U.N. Institute for Training and Research, New York. 1981

- 1987 Adjunct Professor of International Law, New York University School of Law. 1978-1980 Permanent Mission of Egypt to the United Nations, Geneva; Alternate Representative to the Committee on Disarmament. 1974 - 1978 Special Assistant to the Foreign Minister, Ministry of Foreign Affairs, Egypt. 1973 - 1974 Senior Fellow Center for International Studies, New York University. 1967 - 1971 Permanent Mission of Egypt to the United Nations, New York. 1964 - 1967 Department of International Organizations, Ministry of Foreign Affairs, Egypt. *Multilateral Experience:* Participated as his country or the IAEA representative in the following multilateral activities: United Nations General Assembly (Political, Legal, Administrative and Budgetary Committees), (1966-1970, 1975-1977, 1984-1986); Security Council (1967-1971); Committee on disarmament, Chairman of Committee on Effective International Arrangements to Assure Non-nuclear-Weapon States Againts the Use or Threat of Use of Nuclear Weapons (1979-1980); Review conferences of the Treaty on the Non-Proliferation of Nuclear Weapons (1985, 1990, 1995); Agency for the Prohibition of Nuclear Weapons in Latin America (1988); Organization of African Unity/UN Group of Experts to draft the African Nuclear-Weapon-Free-Zone Treaty (1993-1995); United Nations Development Programm (1967-1969); International Labour Organization (1978-1980); World Health Organization (1979-1980); Third United Nations Conference on the Law of the Sea (1977-1979); World Food Conference (1974); Commission on Human Rights (1980); Committee on Definition of Aggression (1967-1970); Conference of the Heads of States and Governments of the Non-Aligned Countries (1964); League of Arab States (1974-1977). *Professional Activities, Associations:* Member of presidential and ministerial delegations as a diplomat, and representative of the IAEA in missions to many countries in Africa, Asia, Europe and the Americas. Has lectured widely on international law and organizations; arms control and non-proliferation and on the peaceful uses of nuclear energy. Has taken part as a panelist in numerous professional and academic meetings and associations, including the Carnegie Endowment for International Peace; International Law Association; The Salzburg Semionar; American Society of International Law; Aspen Institute for Humanistic Studies; Programme for Promoting Nuclear Non-proliferation; U.N. Institute for Disarmament Research; India International Centre; United States United Nations Association. Member of a number of professional associations, including the International Law Association; the American Society of International Law; the Nuclear Law Association. **Publications:** "The New Poor: Land Locked, Shelf Locked and other Geographically Disadvantaged States", New York University Journal of International Law and Politics, in collaboration, (1974); "The Right of Innocent Passage through Straits", doctoral dissertation, New York University School of Law (1974); "The International Law Commission: The Need for a New Direction", in collaboration, UNITAR Publication (1981); "Crowded Agendas, Crowded Rooms - Institutional Arrangements at UNCLOS III: Some Lessons in Global Negotiations", in collaboration, UNITAR Publication (1981); "Model Rules for Disaster Relief Operations" UNITAR Publication (1982); "The Egyptian-Israeli Peace Treaty and Access to the Gulf of Aqaba, A new Legal Regime", American Journal of International Law (1982); "The Codification and Progressive Development of International Law", American Journal of International Law (1982); "The Role of International Atomic Energy Agency Safeguards in the Evolution of the Non-Proliferation Regime: Some Lessons for other Arms Control Measures", International Law of Arms Control and Disarmament, United Nations Publication (1991); "The International Law of Nuclear Energy", Basic Documents, in collaboration, Martinus Nijhoff Publishers (1993); "Verifying Non-Proliferation Pledges: The Evolution and future Direction of the IAEA Safeguards System", Leiden Journal of International Law (1995); "On Compliance with Nuclear Non-Proliferation Obligations", Security Dialogue (1996). **Prof. Addr.:** International Atomic Energy Agency (IAEA), P.O.Box 100, Wagramerstrasse 5, A-1400 Vienna, Austria, Tel.: +43 1 2600 21111, Fax: +43 1 2600 29805. E-mail: M.ElBaradei@iaea.org.

ELDAWI (Abbas, Abdel Galil), Sudanese businessman. **Born** on April 4, 1924 in Atbara, Sudan. **Son** of Abdel Galil Fadlalla Eldawi **and** Mrs. Zarifa Abdelrahim Mahmoud. **Married** in 1950 in Port Sudan to Thouraya Imbabi Said, five sons: Issam (1950), Salah (1951), Tawfig (1961), Mohamed (1964), Tarig (1965) and four daughters: Nourjhan (1954), Narjes (1955), Wafaa (1956) and Salwa (1959). **Educ.:** Primary School (English and Arabic). **Dipl.:** Commercial award. **Career:** Exporter of Sudan produce and raw hides and skins, Importer of agri-machineries, electric generators, automotive parts, confirming house agents, building materials. Owner of two companies, National Products Co. (Est. 1956) and ABC Trading Co. (Est. 1966). **Award:** Chamber of Commerce International and African Award (1986). **Hobby:** Trade Information. **Member:** Automotive Club U.S.A.; Overseas Automotive Council U.S.A. Credit Card: Visa. **Prof. Addr.:** P.O.Box 315, Port Sudan (Red Sea), Tel: 3666, 2012, 3250, Telex: 70038 and 22178 DERMA, 70032 ZADA and 22410 NAPCO, Sudan. **Priv. Addr.:** Transit Area, House, Tel: 5618, Sudan.

ELEHADAN (Saleh Ibn Saad), Saudi civil servant. **Born** in 1949 in Riyadh. **Dipl.:** B.A. in Shari'a (Islamic Law). **Career:** Inspector General, Ministry of Labour and Social Affairs (1966-68); Lecturer, Imam Muhammad Ibn Saud Islamic University (1974-80); Director, Judicial Affairs, Ministry of Justice, since 1980; delivered numerous lectures in universities in Saudi Arabia, Morocco, Tunisia and the U.S.A.; member, Muslim Students Association, Indiana; member of Board, Muhammad Ibn Saud Islamic University; attended the Faculty of Language

Conference, Mallibar, India. **Honours:** A Medal Awarded by Colombia University. **Publ.:** The Jihad in Islam; Criticism of the Principles of Communism; Islamic legal decisions and several research works. **Hobbies:** Travel, reading. **Prof. Addr.:** Ministry of Justice, P.O.Box 5981, Tel.: 405 9536, Riyadh. **Priv. Addr.:** Tel.: 458 4891, Riyadh, Saudi Arabia.

ELEISH (Mohamad Gamaliddine), Egyptian economist. **Born** in 1928 in Cairo, Egypt. **Son** of Gamaliddin Eleish. **Married**, two children. **Educ.:** B.Com., Cairo University, Egypt (1948-51); Ph.D. in Economics, University of Edinburgh, UK (1960-61). **Career:** Head of various units in the Ministry of National Planning, including Head of Input / Output Unit and Head of Housing and Construction Unit, Cairo (1956-61); Assistant Professor and Director of Research, Institute of Management Development, Cairo (1961-62); Economic Affairs Officer, UN Economic Commission for Africa, Addis Ababa, Ethiopia (1962-64); UN African Institute for Economic Development and Planning, Dakar, Senegal; Lecturer in Economics and Chairman of Research Committee (1964-66); Industrial Development Organisation (UNIDO), (1966-68); Acting Chief, Survey Section, UNIDO (1968-69); Chief, Survey Section UNIDO (1969-74); Chief, Special Studies Section; Chief, Developing Economies Section; Chief, Developing Economics Section; Chief of the Intersectoral Issues Branch, Department of International Economic and Social Affairs (IESA), UN, New York (since 1974). Former **President** of the Art Club, UN New York **Publ.:** "The Input / Output Model in a Developing Economy" (1963); "Uses of the Input / Output Model in Development Planning in Under-developed Countries" (1965); "An Introduction to the Input / Output Model" (1962); "Use of the Input / Output Model in Calculating Foreign Exchange Requirements" (1967) and various publications in the field of development and economics. **Sport:** Tennis. **Hobbies:** Painting, music. **Addr.:** Cairo, Egypt.

ELETR (Mohamed Kamal Ahmed), Egyptian agricultural economist and president of Helwan University, Cairo, Egypt. **Born** on July 1, 1933 in Qalyobia, Egypt. **Son** of Ahmed el-Etr (Teacher) **and** Mrs. Hikmat née Khalifa. **Married** in July 1956 in Cairo to Safia Hassouna, 3 children: Tarik (6/12/1957); Amal (10/10/1959); and Amany (20/2/1962). **Educ.:** Banha Primary and Secondary School, Ain Shams University for Undergraduate study and Alexandria University for Postgraduate Studies. **Dipl.:** B.Sc. Horticulture, Ain Shams University, Cairo, Egypt (1953); Diploma Post Graduate Studies of Cotton, Alexandria University, Egypt (1960); M.Sc. Agricultural Economics, Alexandria University, Egypt (1965); Ph.D. Agricultural Economics, Alexandria University, Egypt (1971). **Career:** Teacher and Senior Teacher, Secondary Schools of Agriculture (1955-71); Assistant Professor (1971); Associate Professor (1975); Professor of Agricultural Economics, Helwan University, Egypt (1980); Head of Department of Agriculture Economics, Helwan University (1978-87); Vice-Dean, Faculty of Agriculture, Helwan University (1978-84); Dean, Faculty of Agriculture, Helwan University (1984-87); Vice-President, Helwan University, Alex. Branch, Alexandria (1987-89); Vice President and President of Helwan University (from 1987 - to date); Agricultural Economic Expert, Saudi Agricultural Bank, Riyadh, Saudi Arabia (February - August 1975); Associate Professor of Agricultural Economics Riyadh University (recently named King Saud University); (September 1975 - April 1977), Riyadh Saudi Arabia; Agricultural Economic Expert, Arab Company for livestock development, Arab League, Damascus, Syria, (April 1977 - May 1978). **Fields of Research:** Agricultural Policy, Price Analysis, Cotton Economics, Project Evaluation and Appriasal, Production Economics (specially in Field Crops, livestock and Poultry). **Fields of Editing Textbooks:** Microeconomics, Cooperatives, Cotton Economics, Statistical Methods, Scientific Research Approaches (In Arabic). **Published Papers in English Language:** Demand Logic and statistical Demand Functions for Egyptian Cottons, Egyptian Cotton gazette, Alexandria, (July 1974); el-ETR, K, A-Khalifa, I., Sobhi, and N.G. el-Karim Farm Efficiency and Productivity in Egypt. A literature Review, Economics Supplementary Research Series No.8, University of California, Davis (1983); el-ETR, K & E. el-Yamani & I. Sobhi, and A.K. el-Saied Farm Efficiency and Productivity in Countries with conditions similar to Egypt: A literature Review, Economics supplementary Research Series No.9, ADS-Egypt Project, University of California, Davis (1983); Statistical Estimation of the number of Palms per hectar in Date Cultures, M.K. el-ETR, A.M. el-Prince, A.M. Turjoman, The Second Symposium on Date Palm, (March 1986). Date Palm Research Center, King Faisal University, Kingdom of Saudi Arabia. **Published papers in Arabic Language:** International Demand Functions for Egyptian Extra long Staple Cotton, 8th Symposium for Statistical Research, Cairo University (1972): Determinants of Export Capacity of Egyptian Cotton to Eastern Europe, 1st symposium of cotton, Alexandria (1973); The Impact of International Competition of External Demand for Egyptian Extra long Staple Cotton (with Dr. Mahmoud Sherif, Alexandria University), 1st symposium of Cotton, Alexandria (1973); Saudi Agriculture, The main Economic features of Saudi Agriculture Sector, (with Dr. Thenayan), Dean, Faculty of Agriculture, Riyadh University, 1st Conference of Moslem Agricultural Scientists, Riyadh University, Saudi Arabia (1977); Analysis Study of Farm Machinery and Farm equipments Market in Saudi Arabia, (with Dr. Thenayan and Dr. Rajaa el-Amir, Department of Agri. Econ., Riadh University) Research and Industrial Developing Centre, Ministry of Industry, Saudi Arabia (1977); Economic Utilization of Feed Resources for Meat Production in Egypt (with Dr. Sobhi, Agr. Econ. Dep., Helwan University), 4th International Congress of Statistics, Computer Science and Social Research, Ain Shams University, Cairo

(1979); Possibilities and Impact of Changing Internal Marketing System of Cotton in Egypt, Helwan University Research Magazine (1980); Production Competition, Competitive Situation between Egyptian Cottons and Similar Cottons, Helwan University Research Magazine (1980); Estimation of International Demand Elasticities for Egyptian Extra long Staple Cotton, Helwan University Research Magazine (1980); Economic Impact of Changing Export Prices of Egyptian Cottons on Fluctuations of Egyptian Cotton Exports to important Importing Markets of Western Europe, 1st Congress of Economics of Egyptian Agriculture, Ministry of Agriculture, Egypt (1980); Consuming Pattern of Milk and Milk Products and Estimation of Income Elasticity for Milk in Alexandria governorate (with Dr. Abd el-Naby, Agr. Econ. Dep. Alex. Univ.), 1st Congress of Economics of Egyptian Agriculture, Ministry of Agriculture Egypt, (1980); Economic Impact of Competition between Synthetic Fibers and Cotton on International Economic Sector, (with Dr. Dairy, Ministry of Agriculture), 1st Congress of Economics of Egyptian Agriculture, Ministry of Agriculture, Egypt (1980); Response Functions of Some Major Field Crops in Egyptian Agriculture, (with Dr. I. Sobhi and Others), Research and Studies Magazines, Helwan University (1986); A Study for Relationship Between Price Agricultural Policy and Egyptian Cotton Production, (with Dr. I. Sobhi and others), Research and Studies Magazine, Helwan University (1986); Evaluation of Using Nitrogenous Chemical Fertilizers in Production of Some Field Crops, (with Dr. I. Sobhi and others), Research and Studies Magazine, Helwan Univ. (1986); A Study of Nitrogenous Chemical Fertilizers Sufficiency in the World with Emphasis on Egyptian Agriculture, (with Dr. I. Sobhi and others), Research and Studies Magazine, Helwan Univ. (1986); Economic Efficiency of Cotton ginning industry (with Dr. H. Y. Amaish), Research and Studies Magazine, Helwan University (1987); Prospect of Future Economic Policies in Egyptian Agriculture in the Light of National and International Economic Fluctuations, (with Dr. Samy Afify Hatem), Second Annual Conference of Universities; Universities and Agricultural Development, Supreme Council of Universities, Cairo, Egypt (1991). **Master thesis:** Production and Marketing of Peanut in Egypt and Factors Responsible of Production, Consumption, Prices, Exports and Income Fluctuations, Alexandria University, Egypt (1965). **Ph.D. Dissertation:** Econometric Analysis of International and Regional Demand Functions for Egyptian Cotton, Alexandria Univ. (1970). **Sports:** Walking and Swimming. **Hobby:** Gardening. **Member:** Full membership of Sporting Club in Alexandria, Zamalek and Tawfekeya Clubs in Cairo. **Prof. Addr.:** Helwan University, 96 Ahmed Oraby Str., Mohandessen, Giza, Tel.: 3446441, Cairo, Egypt. **Priv. Addr.:** 90 D. Tersana Bldg., Ahmed Orabi Str., 6th Floor, Giza, Egypt. Tel.: (Cairo) 3447239, (Alex.) 5870368.

ELFADL (ALI Mohamed, Ahmed), Sudanese General Manager, Middle East Insurance Co. (s) Ltd. **Born** in 1950 in Khartoum, Sudan. **Son** of Mohamed Ahmed "Farmer" **and** Mrs. Sittana Elrayah. **Married** in 1978 in Khartoum to Afaf Osman, 5 children: Mohannad, Ayman, Myada, Ebtihal, Mohamed. **Educ.:** El Magal Primary - Korti Secondary - Marawi High Secondary - Khartoum University, Bsc and Master "Insurance" Register For Ph.D. "Insurance". **Dipl.:** B.Sc Business Administration, Faculty of Economics, University of Khartoum; Islamic Economics "Diploma" Faculty of Social Studies, Omdurman Islamic University; C.I.I. "Partone", Advanced Insurance "Diploma" Swiss Insurance Training-Centre (S.I.T.C.), Computer Operation. **Languages:** Fluent Arabic and English. **Career:** General Manager and Underwriter Middle East Insurance Co. (1980-up to now); Deputy General Manager United Insurance co. (1975-1979). **Other Information:** Representative of the Chartered Insurance Institute in Sudan and Responsible for-Examination for Sudan Centre; Lecturer "Insurance Subjects" at: "Ahlia University", "Sudan University of Science & Technology", "Police College", "Elnisr College", "Elnilein University". Treasurer of the Association of Sudanese Insurers and Reinsurers Companies, Member of the Arab Management Society "AMS" (AMERICA). **Social Activities:** Member of high committee of the North highway, President of Tizkar Sport Club-Khartoum North, Head of the Investment Committee - Marawi Province Federation, Head of the Investment Committee - Takafol Khartoum North, Secretary General of Elmagal and Elhigair - Northern Estate-Charity Committee. **Medals:** Three University Medals - Three Certificate of Studies from International Federation in Both football and Athletics. **Sports Practised:** Football - Athletic. **Hobbies:** Football - Reading. **Clubs and Associations:** Khartoum Athletic Federation "Chariman", Tizkar Football Club "President". **Prof. Addr.:** Middle East Insurance Co. (S) Ltd., P.O.Box 3070 Khartoum, Tel.: 722344, 722202, Fax: +249 11 779266 and P.O.Box 3071 Khartoum, Tel.: 781824, Sudan. **Home Tel.:** 315174, Khartoum, Sudan.

ELFATOUN (Inji, Hassan), Egyptian artist. **Born** in 1924 in Cairo, Egypt. **Widow. Educ.:** self-educated. **Career:** painter; has participated in art exhibitions since 1942; had first private exhibition in Cairo, Egypt in 1952, followed by others in Paris, Rome, Berlin, Warsaw, Sofia, Prague, New Delhi and Moscow. Member, Atelier du Cairo, Egypt (1951). **Publ.:** "Eight Million Women with US" (1947), "Egyptian Women" (1949), "al-Salam Wal-Jala" (1951). **Award:** First prize in landscapes, Ministry of Information and Culture (1959). **Addr.:** Hassan Sabri Street, Zamalek, Cairo, Egypt.

ELIAS (Ibrahim), Sudanese economist and politician. **Born** on August 29, 1923 in Omdurman, Sudan. **Married** in 1948 to Alia Elias, three daughters and five sons. **Educ.:** Gordon Memorial College, Khartoum; Queen's University, Belfast, Northern Ireland; Manchester University, England. **Dipl.:** B.Sc., M.Sc., Ph.D. (Economics). **Career:** teacher (1949-56); Trade Officer, Ministry of Commerce, Industry and Supply (1956-62); Assistant Managing Director, Sudan Industrial Bank (1962-65); Assistant Under-Secretary of State, Ministry of Economics (1965-69); General Manager, Gulf Fisheries, Kuwait (1969-70); Managing Director, Blue Nile Brewery, Khartoum; Chairman, Leather and Plastic Industries Corporation (1970-72); Minister of the Treasury (1972-74); former Chairman of the El-Nilein Bank and of Sudan-Kuwait Investment Company; former Director, The Sudanese Investment Bank, Khartoum. **Dipl.:** Author of "Studies in Sudan Economy" (1969). **Hobbies:** Horse breeding, reading and chess. **Priv. Addr.:** Tel.: 54516, Omdurman, Sudan.

ELISSA (Raja, Issa), Jordanian journalist. **Born** 1922 in Jaffa, Palestine. **Son** of Issa El Issa. **Married. Educ.:** B.A. in Political Sciences, American University of Beirut, Lebanon (1942); Diploma in Journalism, University of Columbia, New York, USA (1960). **Career:** Journalist, "Falastin" newspaper, Jaffa (1942-48); Publisher and Editor of "Falastin" in Jerusalem (1951); Publisher and Editor of "Jerusalem Star", Jerusalem (1966); Co-owner of Jordanian Company for Press and Publishing (1967); Editor of "Palestine News" (1967); Deputy Director General, Jordanian Press Organisation, Publishers of "al-Ra'i" and "Jordan Times" from 1977-1987; Founder and Director General, Jordan Distribution Company Ltd.; Secretary General of Jordan Journalists Syndicate (1953-1954); Secretary General of the Arab Distributors Union 1979 1981. **Publ.:** Many articles in Arabic and English in the Jordanian Press. **Hobby:** Reading. **Addr.:** P.O.Box 375, Tel.: 630191, 630192, Telex: 22083 DISTAG JO, Fax: (962-6)635152, Amman, Jordan. E-mail.: jda@go.com.jo.

ELKADIRI (Boubaker), Moroccan politician. **Married. Career:** Active in Nationalist political movement; helped prepare the Proclamation of Independence (1944); imprisoned on political charges (1944-46); Inspector General of the Istiqlal Party; member of the Istiqlal Party Executive Committee re-elected member of the Istiqlal Party Executive Committee at its Congress (1974), presently member of Parliament. **Founder** of Ecole Nahda at Sale for revival of Arabic Education, Co-founder of the Moroccan Association for the Support of the Palestine Struggle, Secretary General of the Beirut based Front for Support of the Palestine Struggle. **Publ.:** Founded monthly review "al-Imane" for Islamic culture and the Association de Jeunesse pour la Renaissance Islamique. **Addr.:** al-Imane, P.O.Box 356, Rue Arkenssous, Rabat, Morocco.

ELKHATIB (Numan), Jordanian Vice President, Prof. of Law. **Born** on September 3, 1954 in Jerusalem, **Son** of Ahmad Elkhatib (deceased) **and** Mrs. Hamdeh Elkhatib. **Married** on August 10, 1984 in Jerusalem, 3 children: Ahmad, Razan, Mohamad. **Educ.:** Mutah School, Private. **Career:** Advocate, Cairo (1980-82); Advocate, Amman (1982-); Assistant Professor in Law (1984-); Associate Professor (1990-); Dean of Students (1990-); Professor of Law, Vice-President (1997-). **Member:** Sports Federation of Chinese University, Sports Federation of Jordanians University, Mutah University Best Faculty Member. **Hobbies:** Sport, Travelling. **Assoc.:** Bar Association, Jordan. **Prof. Addr.:** Mutah University, P.O.Box 7, Mutah al-Karak, Jordan, Tel.: 06-617860. **Priv. Addr.:** Tel.: 06-811894, Jordan.

ELMANDJRA (Mahdi), Moroccan academic. **Born** in 1933 in Rabat, Morocco. **Married,** two children. **Educ.:** B.A. in Chemistry and in Political Science, Cornell University, USA (1954); Ph.D. in Economics, London School of Economics, UK (1957); School of Oriental and African Studies, UK (1954-55); Faculty of Law, University of Paris, France (1960-62). **Career:** Assistant, Faculty of Law, Rabat, Morocco (1957-58); Assistant, Moroccan School of Administration (1957-58); Counsellor, Permanent Mission of Morocco to the UN, New York, USA (1958-59); Director General, Radiodiffusion Television Morocaine (1959-60); Head of African Division, UNESCO (1961-63); Director, Executive Office of the Director General of UNESCO (1963-66); Assistant Director General for Social Sciences and Culture, UNESCO (1966-69); Professor and Researcher, Centre of International Studies, London (1970); Assistant Director General for Pre-Programming UNESCO (1970-74); Special Adviser to the Director General, UNESCO (1974-76); Professor, Faculty of Juridical, Economic and Social Sciences, University of Mohamad V (since 1976). **President**, World Federation of Future Studies, WFSF (1976-80); President, Futuribles International (1982-90); Founding President, Moroccan Association for Human Rights, **member** of Academy of the Kingdom of Morocco, the Club of Rome. SID and of several other Development societies and associations; African Academy of Sciences. **Publ.:** "The Arab League 1945-55" (London 1957); "Nehru and the Modern World" (New Delhi 1967); "The Political Aspects of the North South Dialogue" (Rome 1978); "No Limits to Learning", Report to the Club of Rome (1979); "Maghreb 2000" (1982); "The Future of International Cooperation" (1986); "Maghreb of Francophonie" (1988); Human Rights and Development (1989); Islam and the Future (1990); The First World Cultural War (1991), and other works; Retrospective des Futurs (1991); Nord-Sud: Prelude à l'Ere Post-Coloniale (1992); "La Décolonisation Culturelle: Défi du 21ème Siècle (1996); "Massar Fikr" (1997) "Reglobalization of Deglobalization" (1999). **Medals:** Officier de l'ordre des Arts et des Lettres, France; Men of Achievement Award, Cambridge, Order of the "Rising Sun" (Japan), Medal of the French Academy of Architecture, Medal of Peace of the Albert Einstein International Foundation. **Addr.:** P.O.Box. 53, e.mail: elmandjra@elmandjra.org; web page: //www.elmandjra.org, Rabat, Morocco.

ELMOALLIM (Mohamed), Egyptian publisher. **Born** in 1917 at Kafr Elsheikh, Egypt. **Son** of Ibrahim Almoallim **and** Mrs. Tag Elmoallim. **Married** in 1941 in Cairo, two sons: Ibrahim and Adel. **Educ.:** Cairo University, Faculty of Science, Egypt. **Career:** Teacher (1942-44); Publisher and Printer (1945); Journalist (1944-49); Broadcaster (1949-51); Editor in-Chief of Broadcasting Magazine (1951-52); Expert in Publicity; Publisher since 1959 to date. **Awards:** Many awards and prizes in the Publishing field since 1949. **Hobbies:** Reading, Walking and Swimming, **Member:** Heliopolis Sporting Club, Establishing member of the Publisher's Association in Egypt. **Prof. Addr.:** Dar al-Shorouk, 16 Gawad Husni Str., Tel.: 202-3934578, 202-392333, Fax: (02)3934814, Telex: 93091 SHROCK UN, Cairo, Egypt.

ELNAGHY (Mohamed, Abdel Wahab, Prof.), Egyptian Vice-President, Minia University, Minia, Egypt. **Born** on February 11, 1939 in Zarka, Egypt. **Son** of Abdel Wahab Elnaghy (deceased) **and** Mrs. née S. Elhadidi Abdou. **Married** on August 7, 1962 in Cairo, Egypt to Elezbawy, 2 children: Tarik (July 3, 1963) (Engineer); Khalid (May 1, 1967) (Medical Doctor). **Educ.:** Mansoura Secondary School, Egypt; Ain Shams University, Cairo, Egypt; Kansas State University, Manhattan, Kansas, U.S.A. **Dipl.:** B.Sc. Ain Shams University, Egypt; M.Sc., Ph.D. Kansas State University, U.S.A. **Career:** Professor of Microbiology Assiut University; Head Botany Department, Assiut University; Dean Faculty of Science and Professor of Microbiology, Minia University; presently Vice-President for Student Affairs, Minia University. **Other Information:** Member of High Supreme Council of Egyptian Universities; Member of Egyptian Botanical Society; Member of Permanent Committee for Promotion of Professors and Assistant Professors; Award from Egyptian Scientific Association. **Hobby:** Sports (Football). **Member:** El-Shams Club, Cairo. **Prof. Addr.:** Minia University, Tel.: 086-323544, Cairo, Egypt. **Priv. Addr.:** 8 Sharia Abdel Rahman Ibn Ouf, Tel.: 2475085, Cairo, Egypt.

ELSALAWY (Ahmed Nabil), Egyptian diplomat. **Born** on November 9, 1934 at Zagazig, Sharkia Province, Egypt. **Son** of Abdel Wahab Elsalawy (Member of the Local Council of Sharkia Province, Member of Parliament, Egypt, Farmer Landlord), **and** Mrs. Hekmat nee Hussein Sadek Assem. **Married** on February 14, 1963 in Cairo to Sahar Elehwany, 3 children: Dalia Elsalawy (6/11/64), Dr. Randa (17/10/65), Khaled (2/05/70). **Educ.:** Zagazig Primary and Secondary School, Faculty of Law Ain Shams University, Cairo, Egypt. **Career:** Attache at M.F.A., Cairo (1957); Attache in Sofia (1958-60); Attache in Cairo (1960-61); 3rd Secretary in Mogadishu (1961-63); 2nd Secretary in Addis Abada (1963-65); Ministry of Foreign Affairs, Cairo (1965-67); Legal Division I.A.E.A., Vienna (1967-68); 1st Secretary in Stockholm (1969-74); Counsellor Department, Protocol Department M.F.A., Cairo (1974-76); Counsellor & Minister Counsellor in Bonn (1976-81); Vice-Director of Protocol, Cairo (1981-83); Ambassador to Angola (1983-87); Head of Africa Department, Cairo (1987-89); Ambassador to Indonesia and Papua New Guinea (1989-1992); Ambassador of Egypt to Athens, Greece (1992-). **Awards:** Order of Merit Grade 3, 2, 1, of Egypt; Order of STAR, Sweden; Federal Order of Merits, Germany. **Sports:** Pingpong, Tennis and Chess. **Hobbies:** Reading, Farming. **Member of:** Diplomatic Club M.F.A., Cairo; Gezira Club, Cairo; Shooting Club, Giza; Board African Society, Cairo. **Credit Cards:** American Express and Citibank Visa. **Prof. Addr.:** Embassy of Egypt, 3Vas. Sofias Avenue, Athens, Greece, Tel.: 3640544, 3618612/3, Fax: 3603538. **Priv. Addr.:** 24, Mavromichali Street Filothei, Athens, Greece, Tel.: 6844214. **Cairo Addresse:** 9 El Anab Street, El Mohandessin, Cairo, Egypt. Tel.: 3609432.

ELYAS (Mohamad Atta' Allah Hasan), Saudi businessman. **Born** in 1921 in Mecca, Saudi Arabia. **Educ.:** educated by studying the Holy Quran. **Career:** Founder and Chairman of the Board, Arabic Cars Co., National Economical Co., Taysir Hotels, factories and establishments; one of the first businessmen to establish hotels and factories in the Kingdom of Saudi Arabia. **Hobby:** studying the Holy Quran. **Addr.:** Elyas Square, Shamiah, Tel.: 5742881 (Office) adn Tel.: 5420615 (Home), Mecca, Saudi Arabia.

EMAM (Hani, Shafik), Saudi businessman. **Born** on February 22, 1932 in Mecca, Saudi Arabia. **Son** of Shafik Emam (businessman) **and** Mrs. Kawkab Emam. **Married** to Bouran Kabbani on November 27, 1957 in Saudi Arabia, 2 children: Imam (1968), Enam (1970). **Educ.:** Columbia University, New-York. **Dipl.:** B.S. Economics, M.A. Economics. **Career:** Ministry of Communications, Director of Deputy Minister's Office, Railroad Affairs; Aramco, Economic Department, New-York; Adviser, Saudi Delegation to the UN General Assembly; Deputy Director, Saudi Public relations Bureau, New-York; Coordinator, Public Relations Programme of Ministry of Foreign Affairs; Chairman, Saudi Braun Limited (Petro-Chemical, Refinery, Fertilizers and Power Generation); Chairman, Saudi Concrete Prefab Industries Limited (Civil engineering, flooring system); Chairman, Saudi Ensas Company Limited (Appliance Sevices); Chairman and Managing Director, Saudi Real Estate Development Co. (Property Development); Vice-Chairman, Saudi Marine Transportation Co. Ltd. (Shipping), Vice-Chairman, Arabian T.R. Oil Services Company Ltd. (Manufacture and marketing of Acrolein and Chemicals); President, Saudi Technical Services & Trading (Holding); President and Chief Executive, Saudi International Investment Company; Chairman, Universal Arab Holdings Limited, Cayman Island; Chairman, Arab International Trust U.K. Company Ltd. London. Director, Saudi Security & Technical Services (Company Limited Insurance); Proprietor, National Real Estate Development and Management

(Property Management); ex-Lecturer, King Abdulaziz University, Jeddah (taught petroleum economics) (1973-75); served as special representative of UNICEF to Saudi Arabia, United Arab Emirates and Qatar (1975-76); Director, Arab Carribean Bank Ltd.; Vice-Chairman, Financial and Investment Services for Asia Limited (FISA), Hong Kong; Chairman & Managing Director, National Clay Brick and Building Materials Industries Company Ltd., Riyadh; Vice-Chairman, Tamimi Fouad & Al-Emam Food Company Ltd. (SAFEWAY), Jeddah; Director & Member of Executive of Committee, Delta International Bank, Cairo. **Publ.:** Research: "The Economy Saudi Arabia and the 1956-59 Crisis"; Economic Editor, Daily al-Madina. Jeddah (1965-67). **Sport:** Swimming. **Hobbies:** Remodelling and renovation of old houses; Reading. **Member:** Arab-European Business Council, Geneva; European Management Forum, Switzerland. **Credit Cards:** American Express, Diners Club. **Prof. Addr.:** P.O.Box 1716, Tel.: 6532511 (five lines), Jeddah. **Priv. Addr.:** P.O.Box 1716, Tel.: 6824294, Jeddah, Saudi Arabia.

EMARAH (Muhammad, Muhammad), Moroccan economist. **Born** in 1927 in Azmur, Morocco. **Married**, 1 son, 1 daughter. **Educ.:** Moroccan Management School; Ecole Nationale d'Administration, Paris, France. **Career:** Deputy Mayor of Casablanca (1956-60); Administrative Office Manager, Ministry of Post, Telegraph and Telecommunications (1960-61); First Adviser, Embassy in Paris (1961-65); General Manager, Government Insurance Foundation (1965-82); Deputy Chairman, Moroccan Chamber of Commerce, Casablanca (1977-85); Chairman of Holdinka (for tourism, import export, foodstuffs) (1982-). **Decor.:** Order of Satisfaction, King Hassan of Morocco (1970), Officer of the Legion of Honour, France (1963). **Addr.:** 30 el-Guesh al-Malak Street, Casablanca 01, Morocco.

ENANY (Farida Mohamad Khalil, Miss), Saudi diplomat. **Born** in October 1949, in Mecca, Saudi Arabia. **Dipl.:** B.A. (Sociology), Cairo University; M.A. (Public Relations and Advertising), Cairo University. **Career:** Member of First Arab Conference on specifications and equality production; First Attaché, Arab League; attended 26th, 27th sessions of Arab League Economic Council; attended Arab League Information Officers' Meeting, 1976; sub-editor of Monthly Bulletin of Arab League Specifications Organization. **Hobbies:** Reading, sports, music. **Prof. Addr.:** Medina Road, Residence of Sheikh M. Khalil Enany, Saudi Arabia.

ENANY (Fuad Mohamad Khalil), Saudi businessman. **Born** in 1945 in Mecca, Saudi Arabia. **Dipl.:** M.A. (Political Science). **Career:** Bureau Manager for Under-Secretary of State, Ministry of Agriculture and Water; Acting member of Subsidiary Council of Endowments (Waqfs); member of Symposium on Food and Population Growth, Cairo; attended Major Cities Conference, Milan 1975; Former Vice-President of Jeddah Municipality; owner of Hader Trading Est. **Addr.:** Enany House, Kilo 2, Mecca Road, Jeddah, Saudi Arabia.

ENANY (Hassan Mohamad Khalil), Saudi businessman. **Born** in 1942, in Mecca, Saudi Arabia. **Dipl.:** B.Sc. Economics and Political Science, Cairo University. **Career:** Second Secretary, Saudi Embassy, London (1968-74); owner and Chairman of Enany Group of Companies (Encotrade, Famco, Fasco, al-Manara). **Act.** General Trade, Import, Export, Construction, Contracting and Agencies, Development, Consultancy, Management etc. **Hobbies:** Sport, travel. **Addr.:** P.O.Box 5865, Tel.: 4780038, Telex: 4789773, Telex: 201351, Riyadh, Saudi Arabia.

ENNABLI (Nouriddin), Tunisian agricultural engineer. **Born** in 1940 in Souss, Tunisia. **Married**, four children. **Educ.:** Ecole Nationale Supérieure Agronomique, Rennes, France; Ecole Supérieure d'Hydraulique, Toulouse, France; Diploma in Engineering in Hydraulic Agronomy. **Career:** Assistant, National Institute of Agronomy of Tunisia (1968); Lecturer (1973); Professor, National Institute of Agronomy of Tunisia; Head of Department of Rural Engineering (since 1978); Consultant Engineer, Groupement d'Ingénieurs Conseil GIC and SCET International (1973). **Publ.:** Many articles and papers in professional journals. **Sport:** Swimming. **Hobbies:** Cinema, travelling. **Addr.:** Tunis, Tunisia.

ENNACEUR (Mohammed), Tunisian administrator and politician. **Born** on March 21, 1934 at el-Jem, Tunisia. **Married,** 5 children. **Educ.:** Law, Tunis Institute for Advanced Studies; University of Paris Panthéon Sorbonne. **Dipl.:** Graduated in Law; Ph.D. in Law; Specialisation: Social Law; Subject of Thesis: "The ILO and the development of Social Law in Tunisia and Libya". **Career:** Political Posts: Governor (June 1972 to May 1973); Commissioner General for Employment and Vocational Training (June 1973 to December 1973); Minister of Labour and Social Affairs (January 1974 to December 1977 also from November 1979 to October 1985); Barrister (1977-79); President of the Economic and Social Council (November 1985 to February 1991); Ambassador: Head of the Permanent Mission of Tunisia to the United Nations Office and the International Specialised Agencies at Geneva (August 1991-1996). **Administrative Posts:** Government Administrator at the Ministry of Labour and Social Providence (June 1957 to December 1959); Attaché de Cabinet at the Ministry of Public Health and Social Affairs (December 1959 to February 1961); Chef de Cabinet to the Minister of Public Health and Social Affairs (February 1961 to February 1964); Head of the Labour and Manpower Division, Ministry of Social Affairs (February 1964 to June 1967); "President Directeur Général: of the Vocational Training and Employment Office (July 1967 to June 1972). **Other political responsibilities held by election:** Member of the Central Committee, Rassemblement Constitutionnel Démocratique (1988); Member of the Political Bureau, Destourian Socialist Party (1980 to 1986); Member of the Central Committee, Destourian Socialist Party (1974 to 1978); Mayor of el-Jem (1963 to 1972, 1979 to 1980, 1985 to 1990); Member of the National Assembly (1974 to 1979, 1981 to 1985). **International and Regional Activities: U.N.** UNICEF: Member of the UNICEF Executive Board (1963 to 1964): Member of the UNICEF Programme Evaluation mission to India (1983), ECOSOC: Representative of Tunisia in the Commission for Social Development (1963 to 1966); Chairman of the Commission for Social Development (1966). UNRISD: Member of the Board, United Nations Research Institute for Social Development (Geneva) (1966 to 1972). ECA: Head of the Tunisian delegation, 70th session of the Economic Commission for Africa, Tripoli (1982). **I.L.O.:** Head of the Tunisian delegation to ILO African Regional Conferences and the International Labour Conference (1960 to 1972, 1974 to 1977, 1980 to 1985); President of the World Employment Conference Geneva (June 1976); President of the 71st session of the International Labour Conference, Geneva (1985). **I.B.E.** Head of the Tunisian delegation, International Conference on Education, Geneva (1980); **O.A.U.,** Head of the Tunisian delegation, OAU Ministerial Conferences (February 1980); Head of the Tunisian delegation to the OAU Social Commission (1980 to 1985); **Arab League:** President, Executive Bureau of Arab Ministers of Social Affairs (1980 to 1985); Chairman and rapporteur of the Arab League evaluation mission on drought victims in certain African countries (The Sudan, Somalia, Djibouti, Mauritania) (1985). **Non Aligned Movement:** Chairman, Coordination Bureau of Non Aligned and other developing countries, ILO (1980 to 1985). **Decorations:** National; Grand Cordon of the Order of Independence; Grand Cordon of the Order of the Republic; Gold Labour Medal. Foreign: Grand Cordon of the Order of Léopold (Belgium); Grand Cordon of the Order of Orange Nassau (the Netherlands); Grand Cordon of the Order of the Grand-Duchy of Luxembourg; Senior Officer of the National Order of Merit of France; Senior Officer of the National Order of Côte d'Ivoire; Knight Commander of the British Empire (KBE); Commander of the National Order of Merit of Germany. **Other Activities:** Founding President of the Tunisian Association of Social Law (1985); Founding Director of the Tunisian Social Law Review (biannual); Vice-President of the International Labour Law and Social Security Society; Founding President of the EL Jem International Symphonic Festival since 1986. **Publ.:** The ILO and the Development of Social Law in Tunisia and Libya (Subject of Doctoral Thesis); Euro-Maghreb migration and the EEC'S Mediterranean policy (International Studies Review no.21, 4/86); For a reform of the Economic and Social Council (Tunisian Law Review, special issue, 1985); Labour Law and Employment (Tunisian Social Law Review, 2/87); For a new wage policy (Tunisian Social Law Review, 2/87); Tunisian social policy since independence and its place in development (Labour and Development Review, 10/87); Child Rights: myth or reality? (International Studies Review, 1/90); The Social Audit (Labour and Development Review, no.11, 1988); Dismantling Bureaucracy to stimulate the Economy (Institute for Development Financing - IFID - Review, December 1988); Participation in Tunisia (Tunisia Social Law Review, 1988); For a reform of Sickness insurance (Tunisia Social Law Review, 1989); The Tunisian Code and Human Rights (Tunisian Social Law Review, 1990); The social dimension in the Maghreb: reality and outlook (Tunisian Social Law Review, 1990); The enterprise and the social environment (Publications of the Arab Institute of Directors of Industry, 1990); Maghreb immigrants in Europe and the future of Maghreb-European relations (Lecture given at the International symposium on relations between the countries of the Maghreb and the EEC; organised by R.C.D., 4-5 Novembre 1990, R.C.D. publication); Which Labour Law in Africa? Summary report of the 1st African Labour Law and Social Security Congress, Tunis 1991 (Special issue of the Tunisian Labour Law Review, R.C.D. publication). Labour Law and Globalisation (Publications of Sfax University; The Labour statute in the Society of information (Publication of Gerim-University of Sfax). **Prof. Addr.:** 10 Rue du Mali, 1002 Tunis, Tel.: (216-1)848439, Fax: (216-1) 847943, Tunisia. **Priv. Addr.:** 15 Rue Othman Kaaki, 2026 Sidi Bon Saïol, Tunisia.

ERIANE (Abdallah, al), Egyptian former diplomat. **Born** in 1920 in Egypt. **Educ.:** Faculty of Law (Cairo University) (U.S.A.). **Dipl.:** Bachelor of Law (1942), Master of Arts in Political Sciences (1948), Doctor in Philosophy (1951). **Career:** Professor of International Law, Cairo University (1952-61); Director of the Legal and Treaties Department, Ministry of Foreign Affairs (1961-65); Chairman of the Sixth Committee (Legal) of the General Asembly, United Nations (since September 1965); Head or Member of the Egypt delegations to numerous international meetings, Organizations, Committees and Commissions all over the world (1953, 1955, 1958, 1961 and 1963); Ambassador of Arab Republic of Egypt to France (1970). **Prof. Addr.:** c/o Ministry of Foreign Affairs, Cairo, Egypt.

ESSAFI (Mohamad), Tunisian diplomat. **Born** on May 26, 1930 in Kelibia. **Son** of Boubaker Essaafi **and** Fatma Sfaki. **Married** in 1956 to Miss Edwige Klat, 2 children. **Educ.:** Sadiki College, Tunis and University of Paris. **Career:** Secretary of State of Foreign Affairs, Tunis (1956); Tunisian Embassy (London 1956-57); First Secretary to Tunisian Embassy in Washington (1957-60); Director of American Department, Secretary for Foreign Affairs, Tunis (1960-62); American Department and International Confederation Department (1962-64); Ambassador to United Kingdom (1964-69); Secretary General, Ministry of Foreign Affairs (1969-70); Ambassador to

USSR (1970-74); Ambassador to Federal Republic of Germany (1974-76); to Belgium, Luxenbourg and EEC (1978-79); Perm. Rep. to UN (Jan. Aug. 1980); UN Sec. Gen.'s Special Representative for Humanitarian Affairs in S.E. Asia (1980-81); Chief of Cabinet of UN Sec.Gen (1982); UN Under-Secretary-Gen. and Disaster Relief Co-ordinator (July 1982). **Award:** Commander Order of the Tunisian Republic. **Sports:** Shooting and reading. **Addr.:** UNDRO, Palais des Nations, 1211 Geneva, Switzerland.

ESSEBSI (Begi, Qaid), Tunisian politician. **Born** in 1926 in Tunisia. **Son** of Qaid Essebsi. **Educ.:** Licence in Law, University of Paris, France. **Career:** Played a prominent role in the movement of the independence of Tunisia; Director of Tourism; Director of Police and Security; Minister of Interior (1965-69); elected member of the Central Committee at the Party Congress of Bizerta (1964); joined the Politburo (1965); elected member of the National Assembly (1969); Minister of State in Charge of Defence; Ambassador to France (1970); excluded from Destour Socialist Party (1974), decision repealed by President Bourguiba (1980); Minister of State (1980); Minister of Foreign Affairs (1981-86); Ambassador to the Federal Republic of Germany (1986); re-elected member of Central Committee (1965) and of the Politburo (1981). **Member of:** Neo-Destour Party (1942), one of the leaders of the Destour Students in Paris; Vice President of the Association of Muslim North African Students. **Medals:** Grand Cordon of the Republic; Order of Independence. **Addr.:** Ministry of Foreign Affairs, Tunis, Tunisia.

ESSEBSI (Slahiddin), Tunisian lawyer. **Born** in 1933 in Tunisia. **Married**, one son. **Educ.:** B.A. in Law and Economic Sciences, University of Paris, France; Certificate of Higher Commercial Studies, Ecole des Hautes Etudes Commerciales de Paris. **Career:** Lawyer; Vice President of the Municipal Council of Tunis (1963-72). **President** of the Cultural Commission; member of the National Cultural Committee (1966-72); of the American Society of International Law. **Hobby:** Fishing. **Sports:** Golf, tennis, swimming. **Addr.:** 25 Avenue du 7 Novembre, Tel.: 243930, 256012, Tunis, Tunisia.

EYERS (Patrick), British diplomat. **Born** on September 4, 1933. **Son** of Arthur Eyers (Journalist) **and** Mrs. Nora Carpenter. **Married** on September 5, 1960, 3 children: Simon, Sophie, Sam. **Educ.:** Clifton College; Gonville and Cains, Cambridge; Institut Universitaire de Hautes Etudes Internationales (IUHEI), Geneva. **Dipl.:** B.A. (Honours). **Career:** Royal Artillery (1952-54); Cambrige (1954-57); IUHEI (1958-59); Joined Diplomatic Service August 1959, served at various times in the Foreign and Commonwealth Office and in Dubai (1961-63); Brussels (1964-66); Aden (1969-70); Abidjan (1970-71); Berlin (1971-73); Bonn (1977-81); and as Ambassador at Kinshasa (1985-86); Algiers (1987-89); East Berlin (1990); Ambassador to Amman, Jordan (1991-1993), retied from Her Majesty's Diplomatic Service in 1993. **Awards:** Commander of the Order of St. Michael and St. George (CMG); Lieutenant of the Royal Victorian Order (LVO); Officer of the Order of Leopold I (Belgium). **Sports:** Tennis, Skiing, Sailing. **Hobby:** Music. **Member:** Kandahar Ski Club, Hurlingham Club. **Prof. Addr.:** British Embassy, P.O.Box 87, Tel.: 823100, Amman, Jordan. and Foreign & Commonwealth Office, King Charles Street, London SW1A 2AH 071 270 3000, United Kingdom.

EZZAT (Fawzia Huss, H.H. Princess), Wife of H.R.H. Prince Fawwaz ben Abdulaziz, former Governor of Holy Mecca Province. **Born** in 1936. **Educ.:** diploma in French Studies. **Career:** conducts wide activities in the field of women's charity societies; made a large contribution to the creation and support of women's societies in the Western Province; Chairman of Jeddah Women's Charity Society; founding member of Tihama, publisher of Who's Who in Saudi Arabia; founder of Cairo-Saudi Bank Ltd. **Addr.:** H.R.H. Prince Fawwaz ben Abdulaziz Mansion, Jeddah, Saudi Arabia.

EZZAT (Galal, Amin), Egyptian lawyer. **Born** on January 22, 1929 in Cairo. **Son** of Amin Ezzat **and** Mrs., née Fatma Ismail Fahmy. **Married** to Nadia Abdel Aziz el-Dib, 2 children: Ninive and Sherif. **Educ.:** Helmeya Secondary School (Cairo); Faculty of Law, Cairo University. **Dipl.:** secondary Education Certificate, LL.B. **Career:** Lawyer (1953); Director-General, Chamber of the Film Production Industry, Federation of Egyptian Industries, Cairo (1957); Director-General for Public, Foreign and Industrial Relations; Federation of Egyptian Industries (1975). **Hobbies:** Cinema and reading. **Sports:** Football, basketball, horseriding and swimming. **Member:** National Club; Gezira Sporting Club. **Prof. Addr.:** Federation of Egyptian Industries, 26a, Sherif street, Tel.: 49486 - 49489 - 49488, Cairo. **Priv. Addr.:** 25, Hassan Assem street, Zamalek, Tel.: 809049, Cairo, Egypt.

EZZI (Fakhry Hussein), Saudi civil servant. **Born** in 1936. **Dipl.:** B.Sc. (Economics and Political Science). **Career:** Translator, Customs Department, Director of Administration, Medina Press Organisation; Secretary, Customs Training Centre; Director of Saudi Textile Co. Ltd., Jeddah; also member of Board; attended Second Conference of the International Islamic News Agency General Assembly; Administrative Director of International Islamic News Agency (II-NA). **Publ.:** al-Elaq'at al-Tijariyyah al-Dawliyyah (International Trade Relations); several other books on Saudi Customs Regulations and Uniform Customs Tariffs. **Addr.:** P.O.Box 3623, Jeddah, Saudi Arabia.

EZZI (Wasfi Hussein), Saudi businessman. **Born** in 1931 in Medina, Saudi Arabia. **Dipl.:** B.A. (Accounting), Faculty of Commerce, King Saud University. **Career:**

Worked in Courts of Law, up to 1952; Customs Department, up to 1970; commercial business since 1970; owner of Ezzi Trading Establishment; Chairman of the Board, Saudi Textile Co. Ltd. represented Saudi Arabia in the Arab League as Customs Tariff expert for four years. **Hobby:** Reading. **Prof. Addr.:** P.O.Box 3549, Tel.: 6360710, Jeddah. **Priv. Addr.:** Tel.: 6874032, Jeddah, Saudi Arabia.

F

FABIAN (Kalarickal Pranchu), Indian Diplomat. **Born** on September 23, 1940 at Udayamperoor, Ernakulam District, State of Kerala, India. **Son** of Shri K.J. Francis **and** Mrs. Annamma Francis. **Married** to Usha Fabian 2 children: Son (Amal Fabian, 17) and daughter (Anupa Fabian, 14). **Educ.:** Graduated from Maharaja's College, Ernakulam, wth Bachelor of Science degree (Physics main and Mathematics subsidiary). **Career:** Worked with India Meteorological Department at Kodaikanal and Bombay (1961-1964); Joined Indian Foreign Service in July, 1964; Thirs Secretary in Embassy of India, Tananarive, Madagascar (1965-1969); Second Secretary/First Secretary in Embassy of India, Vienna, Austria (1969 1972). Concurrently, Alternate to the Resident Representative of India to: (i) the International Atomic Energy Agency, Vienna, (ii) the United Nations Industrial Development Organization. Under Secretary/Deputy Secretary, Ministry of External Affairs, New Delhi (1972-1976); First Secretary/ Counsellor in Embassy of India, Tehran, Iran (1976-1979); Deputy High Commissioner, High Commission of India, Colombo, Sri Lanka (1979-1982); Deputy High Commissioner/Acting High Commissioner, High Commission of India, Ottawa, Canada (1982-1985); Ambassador of India to Finland at Embassy of India, Helsinki (1985-1989); Joint Secretary (Gulf Division), Ministry of External Affairs, New Delhi (September 1989-June 1992); Promoted Additional Secretary in June, 1992; Reached Doha, Qatar, on November 17, 1992; presently Ambassador of India to the State of Qatar. **Member:** Delhi Gymkhana Club (New Delhi) and Doha Sheraton Club (Doha, Qatar). **Prof. Addr.:** Embassy of India, P.O.Box 2788, Doha, Qatar, Tel.: 672025.

FADDA (Nasrat, Dr.), Palestinian executive. **Born** in 1924. **Son** of Rashid Fadda. **Married** in 1954. **Educ.:** Biological Sciences, Imperial College of Science, London; American University, B.A. (Hons) Beirut (1945); Royal College of Science, B.Sc., London (1951); Associate Royal College of Science (1951); Imperial College of Science (D.I.C.) (1955); University of London, Ph.D (1955). **Career:** Held various Senior Posts in Agricultural Research, Sudan Government (1955-66); Cotton Research Corporation, Adviser on Cotton Research to the Government of Zambia (1966-67); Project Manager, FAO, Institute of Agricultural Research, Ethiopia (1967-75); Director, Operations Department, Arab Fund for Economic and Social Development, Kuwait (1975-); Director General, International Centre for Agricultural Research in the Dry Areas (ICARDA). up to 1994. **Publ.:** Prolific Author of Articles. **Member:** Royal Overseas League, London; Farmer's Club, London. **Hobbies:** Travel and Sports. **Addr.:** Aleppo, Syria.

FADHIL (Murtada Mohammed), Omani General Manager. **Born** in 1953 in Muttrah (Oman). **Son** of Mohamed Hassan Fadhil-Businessman. **Married** in 1983 to Nasreen Jaffer, 4 children: Amour (1984), Manar (1986), Hayan (1988), Marwa (1992). **Educ.:** University of New Haven U.S.A. - B.Sc. IND Eng. - 1979. **Career:** Managing Director-HTTC Group of Companics (1983-1989); Managing Director - National Aluminium Products Co. (1990-1993); General Manager - Oman Development Bank SAOG - 1990 to Date. **Other Information:** Member of American Association of Engineers. **Sports:** Swimming, Volleyball and Walking. **Prof. Addr.:** Oman Development Bank (SAOG), P.O.Box 309 Muscat P.C. 113, Tel.: 738577, Fax: 740461, Sultanate of Oman.

FADHLI (Abdul Hadi Mirza Mohsen, al), Saudi academic. **Born** in 1935 at al-Ahsa, Saudi Arabia. **Dipl.:** B.A., M.A., Ph.D. **Career:** Associate Professor, Faculty of Arts, King Abdulaziz University; former Chairman of Arabic Language Department, Faculty of Arts, King Abdulaziz University (1978-81); member Literary Society of Iraq; member of Board, Jeddah Literary Club. **Publ.:** many books and research papers on the Arabic language and the Holy Qur'an. **Hobby:** Reading, travel. **Addr.:** Tel.: 6883592 (Home), Jeddah, Saudi Arabia.

FADL (Abdallah Ibn Saleh, al), Saudi diplomat. **Born** in 1925 in Mecca, Saudi Arabia. **Dipl.:** Degree in Shari'a (Islamic Law). **Career:** Official at Royal Cabinet (1946) and Ministry of Foreign Affairs, (1959); Former Ambassador to Bahrain and Libya; member of the Saudi delegation to the UN (1966); Ambassador to Malta; Ambassador to Syria (1990-). **Honours:** King Abdulaziz Order, First Class; King Khalid Order, Excellent degree. **Publ.:** articles in local and foreign newspaper. **Sports:** Swimming, horse-riding. **Addr.:** Jeddah, Saudi Arabia.

FADL (Abdulkader, M., al), Saudi businessman. **Born** in 1932 in Jeddah, Saudi Arabia. **Educ.:** received general education, supplemented by commercial training. **Career:** Chairman, al-Fadl Group; owner and President of Alpha Trading and Shipping Agencies, Economic Development Entreprises and Electronic Maintenance Services Ltd.; partner and Board member of al-Fadl, Bin Laden J and P Corp., B.R.C. al-Fadl (Saudia) Ltd.; Jeddah Cement

Company, al-Jazirah Bank Ltd., Chamber of Commerce and Industry, Jeddah, Trans Arabia (Saudia) Ltd.; Electro-Mechanical Engineering Co. and Rabya Trading and Agriculture. **Hobbies:** studying Arabic literature and history. **Addr.:** P.O.Box 15, Tel.: 6672653 (Office) and Tel.: 6692355 (Home), Jeddah 21411, Saudi Arabia.

FADL (Ali, Mohamad), Sudanese physician. **Born** on April 14, 1932 in Sudan. **Son** of Mohamad Fadl Hamad (Schoolmaster) **and** Mrs. Sittana Idriss Abdallah. **Single. Educ.:** Dueim Intermediate school; Hantoub secondary school; Faculty of Medicine, Khartoum University; University of Edinburgh; University of London. **Dipl.:** M.D. (Khartoum), Dipl. Public Health (Edinburgh), Dip. Nutrition (London), Dip. Tropical Medicine & Hygiene; Ph.D. (London). **Career:** Medical Practitionar (1956-59); Medical Registrar (1959-60); Research Assistant (1961-63); Lecturer, Faculty of Medicine, Khartoum University (1963-71); Head, Department of Preventive Medicine (1971-75); Dean, Faculty of Medicine and Deputy Vice-Chancellor, Khartoum University (1975-77); Vice-Chancellor, University of Khartoum (1977-1981); Minister of Health (1981-85). **Member:** Medical Council of the Republic of Sudan. **Awards:** Gold Medal of Education; Republican Decoration (2nd class). **Sports:** Lawn tennis and swimming. **Assoc.:** Association of Preventive Medicine; Association of Family Planning; Population and Family Planning Organisation; Nutrition Society. **Priv. Addr.:** P.O.Box 2966, Khartoum Tel.: 80282-72224.

FADL (Mohamad, Fathi, al), Egyptian mechanical engineer. **Born** on June 22, 1921 in Mansourah Governorate. **Educ.:** Faculty of Engineering, (Cairo University). **Dipl.:** Bachelor of Science. **Career:** Mechanical Engineer; Managing-Director of the Precision Industries Company; Managing-Director of the Arabian Engineering Corporation; Director of the Misr Tanker Company, of the Kuwait Engineering and Trading Company. **Addr.:** 15, Ismaïl Pasha Street, Garden City, Cairo, Egypt.

FADL (Othman Ibrahim, al), Saudi businessman. **Born** in April 1925, in Medina, Saudi Arabia. **Dipl.:** Secondary School Certificate. **Career:** Managing Director, Suliman and Othman Ibrahim al-Fadl Co.; Chairman, Breton Saudi Arabia Marble Manufacturing Co.; member of Board, al-Madina Publications Establishment. **Addr.:** 6510564, Jeddah 21411 Saudi Arabia.

FADULALLA (Awad, al Karim), Sudanese diplomat. **Born** in 1938 in Omdurman, Khartoum, Sudan. **Married. Educ.:** University of Khartoum, Sudan; Institute of Public Administration. **Dipl.:** B.A. **Career:** 1st Secretary, Embassy to Somalia; 3rd Secretary, Embassy to Italy; Ambassador, Permanent Representative of Sudan, UN, Geneva, Switzerland (1973); Ambassador to France (1990-). **Hobby:** Tennis. **Addr.:** Ministry of Foreign Affairs, Khartoum, Sudan.

FAER (Mohamad Zamel, al), Saudi academic. **Born** in 1943 in Taif, Saudi Arabia. **Dipl.:** Diploma in Chemistry; Ph.D. Heidelberg, Germany. **Career:** Joined University of Petroleum and Minerals, Dhahran, as Chemistry Lecturer (1974); Assistant Professor (1977); Dean, Science Department since 1979; participant, Arab Chemists Association seminars; several international chemistry seminars. **Publ.:** three articles on chemistry research. **Hobbies:** Swimming, chess. **Addr.:** Science Department, KFUPM, P.O.Box 138, Tel.: 8602118 (Office) and Tel.: 8606258 (Home), Dhahran, Saudi Arabia.

FAHHAM (Chaker), Syrian academic. linguist and literarian. **Born** in 1921 in Homs-Syria. **Educ.:** B.A., M.A. and Doctorate, Cairo University. **Career** Professor, Faculty of Letters-Damascus University (1963-91); Minister of Education (Aug.4,1963- Nov. 12,63); Vice Dean, Faculty of Letters (1963-Oct.64); Ambassador to Algeria (Oct. 27,1964-July 8, 68); Rector, Damascus University (July 18, 1968-Nov.20, 1970); Minister of Higher Education (Nov. 21, 1970-Sept. 25, 73); Minister of Education (Sept.26, 1973-Jan. 23,78);Minister of Higher Education (Feb. 1, 1978-Jan. 14, 80); Member of the Arabic Language Academy (Feb. 16, 1971); Vice President, Arabic Language Academy (Dec. 31, 1977-March 30, 93); President, Arabic Language Academy (Apr. 1, 93-to date); General Director, Arabic Encyclopedia (April 1, 1981-Dec. 31, 94). **Member** for Life of: Academy of Iraq (1971); Academy of India (1976); Academy of Jordan (1984); Royal Academy for the Studies of Islamic Culture, Jordan (1988); Academy of Egypt (1996); Academy of the Kingdom of Morocco (1996); Vice-President of the Union of Arabic Language Academies of the Arabic World (1996). And also Member of: Consulting Board of the Palestinian Encyclopedia (1971); Consulting Board of the Institution of Arabic Manuscripts, Cairo (1977); Chief Supervisor of the Magazine of Historic Studies (1980-94); Board of Trustess of the Institute of the History of the Arabic and Islamic Sciences, Frankfurt (1981-to date); Board of Trustees of the Institution of the International Cooperation for the Development of the Arab-Islamic Culture (ALESCO) (1983). He participated in a big number of Committees, Conferences, Councils and Institutions in Syria, the Arab World and abroad concerning literary, linguistic, educational and cultural causes. **Publ.:** Wrote a big number of books essays and studies of literary and linguistic nature. **Award:** the International King Faisal Prize for literature (1988). **Prof. Addr.:** Dr. Chaker Fahham, President, The Arabic Language Academy, P.O.Box 327, Damascus, Syria.

FAHMY (Abdulazim), Egyptian statesman. **Born** in 1921 in Upper Egypt. **Educ.:** Secondary and Higher. **Career:** Minitry of Interior (20 years), Under Secretary of State of the Ministry of Interior (1953-62); Minister of Interior (1964-65); in the diplomatic corps, Egyptian Ambassador to Hungary (1965-68); Ministry of Foreign Affairs (1969). **Addr.:** c/o Ministry of Foreign Affairs, Cairo, Egypt.

FAHMY (Ismail), Egyptian former Minister. **Born** on October 2, 1922 in Cairo. **Educ.:** University of Cairo. **Dipl.:** Licentiate of Law (Faculty of Law). **Career:** Joined the Ministry of Foreign Affairs (1946) in mission in Paris (1947-48); Member of the Egyptian Delegation to the United Nations (1949-57); Permanent Representative to the International Atomic Energy Agency (1957-60); Represented his country to numerous Meetings, Commissions and Conferences in Egypt and abroad (1964-65 and 1966); Elected Vice-Chairman, then Chairman of the First Committee (Political and Security) of the 22nd session of the General Assembly, United Nations (1967), Director of the Department of International Organizations and Conferences, Ministry of Foreign Affairs (1966-69); Minister of Tourism (1970-73); Minister of Foreign Affairs (November 1973-1977). **Addr.:** 22 Saray al-Gezira, Zamalek, Cairo, Egypt.

FAHMY (Mohamad Ali, General), Egyptian armed forces officer. **Born** in 1920 in Cairo, Egypt. **Son** of Ali Fahmy **and** Hanem el-Gabry. **Married** to Nadia Abaza in 1959, three children. **Educ.:** Engineering Faculty of Cairo University; Military Academy, Staff College, Air Defence Academy in Kalinin, U.S.S.R. **Career:** Instructor, Senior Officers' Studies Institute (1952-63); Army Operations Department (1952-58); Commander 2nd Light A/A Regiment (1958); 14th A/A Regiment (1958-59), 64th A/A Regiment (1959-61); Air Defence Chief of Staff (1968-69); Commander in Chief Air Defence Forces (1969-75); C.-in-C. Armed Forces (1975-78); Military Adviser to the President (1978); rank of Major General (1965), In private Business since 1984. **Medals:** Order of Liberation, Memorial Order of Founding of U.A.R., Military Star; Star of Honour (PLO); Yugoslav Start with Gold Belt, First Class; Order of King Abdul Aziz, First Class, and numerous ribbons and medals. **Publ.:** Two books on the Palestinian Campaign, Germany; a Threat to Peace; Germany between East and West; The Fourth Service; The History of the Egyptian Air Defence Force. **Addr.:** Cairo, Egypt.

FAHOUM (Khalid, al), Palestinian politician. **Career:** Member of the Palestine Liberation Organization (PLO) Executive Committee under Ahmed Shukairi (1964-67); joined Central Committee of PLO as an independent Member (1970); became Chairman of the Palestinian National Council (PNC) in July 1971; led a delegation to President Sadat in 1972 to explain certain differences between Egyptian and PLO policy; accompagnied a delegation led by Yasser Arafat to Moscow (1972); elected Head of PLO Central Committee, January 1973, a new body of about 20 Members (a forum for discussion of PLO policy formulated by the Executive Committee) presently living in Damascus. **Addr.:** Damascus, Syria.

FAHOUM (Munzer), Jordanian banker. **Born** on September 13, 1927 in Irbid, Jordan. **Son** of Ibrahim Fahoum (Farmer) **and** Mrs. Bakiza Khoja. **Married** on October 15, 1954 in Nablus to Miss Tarab Masri, 3 children: Ibrahim, Omar, Lubna. **Educ.:** Arab College, Jerusalem; University of Edinburgh. **Dipl.:** Master of Arts (M.A.). **Career:** Senior Industrial Analyst, Aramco (1952-57); Deputy Manager, Arab Bank (1957-63); Manager (1963-74); Regional Manager (1974-77); and since then Assistant General Manager; Vice Chairman, Nigeria Arab Bank, Vice Chairman, South Cement Co.; Board member of: Housing Bank; Chairman Industrial Development Bank of Jordan; Jordan Lime and Silicate Brick Co.; National Community College of Jordan. **Clubs:** World Affairs Council (Jordan); Arab Bankers Association (London). **Sports:** Swimming, walking. **Hobby:** Reading. **Credit Cards:** American Express. **Prof. Addr.:** Arab Bank, Head office, P.O.Box 950545, King Faisal Street, Amman, Tel.: 5660131. **Priv. Addr.:** Zahran Street, 4420 5th Circle, Amman, Tel.: 5672759.

FAIEK (Mohamad, Mohamad), Egyptian politician. **Born** in 1929 in Cairo, Egypt. **Son** of Mohamad Faïek. **Married:** 2 Children. **Educ.:** Secondary and Higher. **Career:** Minister of National Guidance (June 1967); President, Egyptian Delegation to the African Summit (September 1967); Minister of Information (1968-70); Minister of State for Foreign Affairs (1970-71); Elected Member of the People's Assembly (January 1969). **Addr.:** People's Assembly, Cairo, Egypt.

FAISAL (Abdul Aziz Ibn Mohamad, al), Saudi academic. **Born** in 1943 at Awdat Sudair. **Dipl.:** Ph.D. al-Azhar University, Cairo. **Career:** Instructor, Scientific Institutes (1968); Inspector, Scientific Institutes (1972); Assistant Professor, Faculty of Arabic Language, King Saud University; participant member of Arabization effort conference, Rabat, Morocco (1980). **Publ.:** Ibn Kathir Poem, two vol.; Literary Criticism; al-Samma Ibn Abdullah poems; Verification of al-Kashiri; several magazine articles; a number of broadcast speeches and programmes. **Addr.:** P.O.Box 5512, Tel.: 4741336 (Home), Riyadh, Saudi Arabia.

FAISAL (Abdullah Mohammed, al), Saudi Academic. **Born** in 1945G, 1364A.H at Auda Sudhair, Saudi Arabia. **Dipl.:** Ph.D. (Business Administration, Major Accounting and Minor International Marketing), University of Oklahoma-USA (1979); M.A. (Accounting), University of Utah-USA (1973); B.A. (Accounting and Business Administration, College of Administrative Sciences (formerly Faculty of Commerce) (1969) **Career: In Teaching:** Associate Professor, Department of Accounting, (Nov. 1984-Oct. 90); Professor, Department of Accounting, College of Administrative Sciences, King Saud University (Oct 1990-July 94). **In Administration** Director, Research Center, College of Administrative Sciences, King Saud University (Sept. 1981-August. 1982); Deputy Managing Director,

Saudi British Bank, Riyadh (on loan from KSU) (August. 1982- Feb. 1984); Chairman, Department of Accounting, College of Administrative Sciences KSU, Riyadh (May 1989-Apr. 1991) and (June 1985-June 87); Dean College of Administrative Sciences, KSU, (Oct. 1990- July 95); President, KSU, (July 1995- to date). **Member** Editorial Staff, Scientific Journal, College of Administrative Sciences, KSU, Oct. 1981- Augt. 82); Graduate Studies Board (Sept. 1987-Sept.91); Scientific Board, KSU, Riyadh (Sept. 1991-Dec.92); Board of Directors, Finance Accounting and Islamic Banking; Editorial Advisory Board, Asian Review of Accounting Kowloon, Hong Kong;Part-time Consultant for a number of Government Bodies in the Kingdom of Saudi Arabia. **Publication, Research and Scientific Work:** Capital Real Cost-Hordmann Model-Capital Asset Model Vs. Accounting Model, Economics & Management Journal, KSU (Arabic) (1982); Formulating and Selecting Accounting Theory, Economics and Management Journal, KSU (Arabic) (1983); Introduction to Accounting Study (Book), prepared for the Ministry of Education-Riyadh (Arabic) (1983); Finance Accounting in Commercial Banks (Book), KSU-Riyadh (Arabic) (1985); Using Financial Ratios in Classifying Economics Establishments, Accounting and Insurance Journal, Cairo University (Arabic) (1985); The relation between Market Prices of Shares and the Contents of Financial Report of the Saudi Corporation, The Egyptian Journal for Commercial Studies, Faculty of Commerce, Mansura (Vol. XI-Arabic) (1987); Accounting Principles and Foundations (Book-Part I) Approved by the Scientific Board in its 4th Session for the year 1988-89 as a part of Minimum Requirements for the Promotion to Grade of Professors (Arabic); Marketing Cost Analysis by Market Segments is a Feasible Guide for Marketing Decisions, The Scientific Journal for Economic and Commerce, Faculty of Commerce, Ain Shams University (Vol II-English) (1988); Is Zakat Included in the Corporation Expenses or Not A View Point, Public Administration-Riyadh, (Vol. 62-Arabic) (May 1989); Accounting Principles and Foundation (Book-Part II), published by Author, Frazdark Prince Shop-Riyadh, (Arabic) (1990); Towards Intellectual Framework for Finance Accounting in the Non-Interest Banks, Scientific Journal for Economic and Commerce, Ain Shams University, (Vol. II-Arabic) (1989); Study of Health Service Costs Provided by the Ministry of Health in Kingdom of Saudi Arabia - prepared by the Research Center Of Administrative Science College, KSU-Riyadh (Arabic); The Accounting profession in Saudi Arabia International Hand Book of Accounting Education and Certification Process, School of Business, North Carolina Central University (English) (1991); Some Lights on Finance Accounting in Islamic Banks, Field Study, Scientific Research Journal, Faculty of Commerce-Alexandria University, (Vol. 27-Arabic) (1990); A Proposed Criterian for General Interpretation of Finance Statements of Islamic Financial Enterprises and Banks, a paper for Discussion Finance Accounting Society for Islamic Financial Enterprises and Banks, Jeddah (Arabic) (1991); Objectives of Financial Accounting in Islamic Financial Enterprises and Banks in the GCC Countries and the Role of Government, Private and professional Organizations of the Objectives, Concepts and Standards of Finance Accounting in the Field Study. A Seminar on Finance Accounting in the Islamic Accounting Finance Enterprises and Banks, Bahrain (12-13 Dec. 1992) (Arabic); Fianncial Administration in King Abdulaziz Era (1419). **Hobbies:** Travel and Gardening. **Address:** President, King Saud University, Tel. (Home) 966-1- 4530991, Tel. (Office) 966-1- 46770112, Fax: 966-1-4677580, Riyadh 11451, Saudi Arabia.

FAISAL (Chukri, Omar), Syrian university professor. **Born** in 1918 in Damascus. **Son** of Omar Faisal. **Educ.:** Damascus and Cairo Universities. **Dipl.:** Secondary Certificate, Bachelor of Arts (1941-42); Licentiate of Law, Damascus University, Master of Arts, Doctor in Literature (Cairo University). **Career:** Journalist, contributed to the daily "al-Amal al-Qawmy"; Professor at Deraa College, the Arab Institute of Damascus; Proceeded for a mastership in Arts (1946-47); Lecturer in Damascus University (1954-57); Professor Universities of Damascus and Beirut. **Publ.:** Joint author of five books on teaching. **Addr.:** Tel.: 112843, Damascus, Syria.

FAISAL (Muhammad, Abdul Rahman), Sudanese politician. **Born** in 1934 in Omdurman, Sudan. **Married. Educ.:** University of Khartoum, Sudan. **Career:** Worked in the Judiciary (1958-62); International Labour Organization (1962-74); Minister of State for Presidential Affairs (1974-75). **Addr.:** Khartoum, Sudan.

FAITURI (Muhammad, Abdul Salam, al), Libyan official. **Career:** Elected Chairman of the Popular Committee for the Tripoli Governorate (1976); Minister of Social Affairs and Social Security (1976); Secretary for Social Security in the General People's Committee and Social Security (1977). **Addr.:** Tripoli, Libya.

FAKHFAKH (Mokhtar), Tunisian President and General Manager. **Born** on August 10, 1930 at Sfax; Tunisia. **Son** of Ahmed Fakhfakh **and** Mrs. Fattouma née Marakchi. **Married** on April 26, 1957 at Sfax to Samira Karray, 2 children: Hind and Khaled. **Dipl.:** Degree in Law. **Career:** High ranking officer of the Central Bank of Tunisia, Chairman and General Manager, Société Hotelière et Touristique de Tunisie (1961-67); General Manager of Commerce, Ministry of Economy (1967-69); President and General Manager. Banque du Sud (1969-1971). General Manager Banque de Developpement Economique de Tunisie (1971-1978). Président and General Manager, Compagnie Financière et Touristique de Tunisie (1979-80). President and General Manager, Banque Internationale Arabe de Tunisie (since 1980 to present). **Awards:** Great Officer of the order of the Republic. Officer of the order of the 7th of November. **Sport:** Golf. **Member:** Tunis Golf

Club. **Credit Cards:** Mastercard, Visa, American Express. **Prof. Addr.:** Banque internationale Arabe de Tunisie, 70-72, Avenue Habib Bourguiba, Tel.: 340.722 Tunis-Tunisia. **Priv. Addr.:** 44, Rue du 1er Juin, Tunis- Tunisie.

FAKHFAKH (Moncef), Tunisian director general of National Archives. **Born** on May 7, 1947 in Sfax, Tunisia. **Son** of Ali Fakhfakh (Merchant) **and** Mrs. née Emna Bejar. **Married** on March 21, 1976 in Sfax to Amel Fenniche, 2 children: Yassine and Leila. **Educ.:** Faculté des Lettres de Tunis, Ecole des Chartes (Lecteur Libre). **Dipl.:** Masters in History (1970), Doctorate 3rd cycle (archives). **Career:** Teacher in secondary schools (1970-81); Director of studies in Institute of Documentation, Tunis (1982-86); Director general of National Archives since 1986. **Work:** Director general of National Archives; Supervisor of National System for Record Management. **Other Information:** Vice President, International council on Archives; Chaiman of International association of francophone archivists. **Award:** Chevalier de l'Ordre des Arts et de Lettres (France). **Prof. Addr.:** 122, Blvd. 3 Avril 1838, 1030 Tunis, Tel.: (216.1) 260556, Fax: (216.1) 569175 Tunisia. **Priv. Addr.:** 11 rue Médina, Mastoura Nasr II, 2037 Menzah 8, Tunis, Tunisia.

FAKHR (Ahmad, Ismail), Egyptian official. **Born** on April 5, 1931 in Cairo, Egypt. **Married**, 2 sons. **Educ.:** National Defence College; Royal College of Defence Studies, London, UK; American University, Cairo; University of National Defence, Washington, DC, USA. **Dipl.:** M.A. in International Business; Diploma in International Security. **Career:** Procurement Office, Egyptian Embassy in Moscow, USSR (1970-72); Air Defence Officer, General Headquarters of Egyptian Armed Forces (1972-79); Director, National Defence College, Ministry of Defence (1979-81); Representative of Egyptian Armed Forces, International Institute of Strategic Studies, London (1979-83); Director, Nasser Higher Military Academy, Ministry of Defence (1981-82); Assistant to the Minister, Ministry of Defence (1983); Editor-in-Chief of "Egyptian Defence Journal" (1983-); Director, National Centre for Middle East Studies. **Publ.:** "Military Schools of Thought", Ministry of Defence, Cairo (1968), "The Defence of Egypt" (1982). **Decor.:** President's Decoration of Merit (1972); Presidents Decoration of the Republic (1973). **Hobby:** Music. **Member:** International Alumni Council, American University, Cairo. **Prof. Addr.:** Egyptian Defence Journal, al-Ahram Building, al-Galaa Street, Cairo, Egypt and National Centre for Middle East Studies, 1 Kasr el-Nile Str., Bab el-Louk, P.O.Box 18, 11513 Cairo, Egypt. **Priv. Addr.:** 27 Dr. Khalil Abdel Khalek Street, Heliopolis, Cairo, Egypt.

FAKHR EL DIN (Galal, Dr.), Egyptian Political Scientist. **Born** on December 15, 1936 in Cairo, Egypt. **Son** of Zaki Fakhr El Din (landowner) **and** Mrs. Eltifat Hussein El Alfi. **Married**, 2 sons: Karim (1972) and Omar (1984). **Educ.:** Victoria College, University of Texas, St. Mary's University, University of Georgia. **Dipl.:** B.A. in Government; M.A. in Economics; Ph.D. in Political Science. **Career:** Public Relations (1961-63); University Professor (1966-78); Vice President, Petroleum Development Services Corporation (1978-1986); President Farabi College (1987-92); Consultant (1993- to date). **Sports:** Swimming, Horse-back riding. **Hobbies:** Reading, travelling. **Member:** Guezira Sporting Club. **Prof. Addr.:** 80 Mohi El Din Str., Mohandeseen, Tel.: 3602237/38, Fax: 3603310, Cairo, Egypt. **Priv. Addr.:** 4 Finni Street, Dokki, Tel.: 7608401, Cairo, Egypt.

FAKHREDDINE (Mohamad), Sudanese diplomat. **Born** on October 12, 1924. **Son** of Mohamad Abdulbagi **and** Mrs. Souad Abdurahman. **Married**, one daughter: Reem. **Educ.:** School of Arts, Khartoum, Gordon College, University of Durham (England). **Dipl.:** Diploma in English and Arabic languages (School of Arts, Khartoum), Bachelor of Arts, Honours Philosophy and Psychology (University of Durham). **Career:** Teacher at Institute of Education, Bakht ar-Rawda, Sudan (1946-47); Controller, Publications Bureau, Sudan (1954-56); Chief of Protocol and Head of UN Section, Ministry of Foreign Affairs, Sudan (1956); Ambassador to Pakistan and Afghanistan (1960); Ambassador to People's Republic of China (1964); Permanent Representative to the U.N. (1965-70); Ambassador to Canada (1967); Under-Secretary for Foreign Affairs, Sudan (1971); Ambassador to USSR (Oct. 72-74), Ambassador to Ethiopia (1975); Director UN North African Centre of the Economic Commission for Africa. **Addr.:** P.O.Box 316, Tangier, Morocco.

FAKHRO (Abdul Rahman, E.), Bahraini Consultant General Surgeon. **Born** on September 14, 1948 at Muharraq, Bahrain. **Son** of Ebrahim Fakhro (Merchant) **and** Mrs. Aysha Abdul Rahman Fakhro. **Married** on August 1979 in iraq to Sahar Al Kaisi, 3 children: Abdulla, Deena, Mohd. **Educ.:** Bahrain Government and Private School: Manama Secondary School, Al Hedayat Al Khalifa School; Ain Shams University, Cairo; Royal College Education. **Dipl.:** M.B.; B. Ch.; Fellow of Royal College of Surgeon Ed.- FRCS (Ed.). **Career:** Consultant and Specialist General Surgeon till now; also till now: Assistant Undersecretary Pan Arab Medical Union, Member of Royal College of Surgeon and Assistant Professor, Arabian Gulf University; President, Bahrain Medical Society (1984-1987); Chief of Medical Staff (December 1991); Consultant General Surgeon and Specialist Salmaniya Medical Centre and Assistant Professor Arabian Gulf University. **Other Information:** Active member of the International Surgical Association, Active member with the Franco Arabian Cancer Foundation. **Awards:** Medal of Honour Secondary School; President, Bahrain Medical Society for two Periods. **Sports:** Jogging, Ex-Fishing, **Hobby:** Reading. **Member:** Member of the International Surgical Association, Member with the Franco Arabian

Cancer Foundation. **Credit Card:** Visa. **Prof. Addr.:** P.O.Box 22213, Muharraq, Bahrain. **Priv. Addr.:** House No. 308, Road 2505, BI 225, Tel.: Resid.: 322355, Clinic: 274000, Hospital: 255555, Muharraq, Bahrain.

FAKHRO (Ali, Mohamed, Dr., H.E.), Bahraini cardiologist and Ambassador of Bahrain to France, Belgium and Spain. **Born** on June 15, 1932, in Bahrain. **Son** of Mohamed Fakhro **and** Mrs. Fatima Fakhro. **Married**, 5 children: Amal, Nada, Hamed, Samah and Elham. **Educ.:** B.Sc. - American University of Beirut, Lebanon-1954; MD - School of Medicine-AUB-Beirut, Lebanon-1958; Intership -Baylor University Hospital, Dallas, Texas, USA-1958-59; Residency-University Hospital, Alabama, USA-1959-61; Fellowship, 1963-65- (Gastroenterology & Cardiology) in Alabama University, Peter Bent Brigham Hospital and Harvard School of Public Health; American Board of Internal Medicine 1965. **Memberships of Organizations:** 1973-81, 1988-95: President Red Crescent Society; 1976-82: Member of Executive Board of Council of Arab Ministers of Health; 1978-81: Member of Executive Board of World Health Organization; 1980- Present: Trustee member, Board of trustees of Institute for Arab Unity Studies; 1981-95: Member of Board of Trustees of Bahrain Center for Studies & Research; 1982- Present: Trustee member, Board of trustees of Institute of Palestine Studies; 1983-87, 1990-95: Chairman, High Council of Arab Board of Medical Specialities; 1985-93: Chairman, Board of Trustees of Arabian Gulf University, Bahrain; 1986-95: Chairman, Board of Trustees of Bahrain University; 1987-95: Member of the Board of Trustees of Arab Child Development Organization; 1988-95: Member of Arab Thought Forum, Amman, Jordan; 1990-91: Chairman, Board of Directors of Arabic Encyclopedia (Arabia); 1991-95: Member of the Executive Board, UNESCO; 1992- Present: Member of the WHO Expert Advisory Panel of Public Health Administration; 1992- Present: Member of International Advisory Council American University of Beirut; 1994-96: President Elect ICET (International Council for Education of Teachers); 1995- Present: Vice Chairman of Board of trustees of Arab Thought Forum, Amman, Jordan; 1996-98: President ICET; 1997-Present: Member, Consultative Committee for Middle East, World Bank. **Career Background:** 1995- Present: Ambassador of the State of Bahrain to France, Belgium and Spain; 1982-95: Minister of Education of Bahrain; 1971-82: Minister of Health of Bahrain; 1970-71: Head of Health Department, Government of Bahrain; 1966-70: Consultant Cordiologist and Assistant Director of Medical Services, Bahrain Government Hospital, Bahrain; 1961-63: Consultant Internal Medicine Department, Bahrain Government Hospital, Bahrain. **Awards:** 1958: The Alpha Omega Alpha Membership; 1978: The Shousha Foundation Prize and Medal Presented by the World Health Organization; 1982: Gold Medal presented by the American University of Beirut for outstanding services in the field of health; 1993: Silver Medal awarded by UNESCO at the Twenty-Seventh Session of the General Conference of UNESCO held in Paris during Ocotber/November 1993; 1996: Honorary Diploma presented by ICET; 1996: Bahrain's First Class Medal presented by His Highness the Amir of Bahrain. **Publications:** Articles, Lectures, etc... Several articles on Cardiac Care of Coronary Cases in the American Heart Journal, with Dr. B. Lown and Dr. T.R. Harrison; Numerous lectures, interviews and articles in the fields of health, education and cultural issues. **Interests and Hobbies:** Tennis, Reading and Music. **Languages Known:** Arabic, English and French. **Prof. Addr.:** Embassy of Bahrain, 3 bis, Place des Etats-Unis, 75116 Paris-France, Tel.: 01 47 23 48 68, Fax: 01 47 20 55 75.

FAKHROO (Abdallah, Darwish), Qatari trader, contractor and co-owner of companies. **Born** in Qatar. **Son** of Darwish Fakhroo. **Educ.:** Secondary and Higher. **Career:** Owner of Modern Home, Atlas Insurance Co., Darwish Travel Bureau, Qatar Cold Stores, Darwish Automobiles, People's Car Company, Darwish Electric Co. and Arabian Gulf Trading Centre, The Oasis Hotel and Darwish (U.K.) Ltd. **Addr.:** P.O.Box 71, Tel.: 2781 (10 lines), Doha, Qatar.

FAKHROO (Nasser, Ahmad Abidan), Qatari company director. **Born** in Qatar. **Son** of Ahmad Abidan Fakhroo. **Educ.:** Secondary and Higher. **Career:** Founder and President General Manager of the National Cement Company, since 1965. **Addr.:** P.O.Box 1333, Tel.: 21688, Doha, Qatar.

FAKHROO (Qassem, Darwish), Qatari trade contractor and owner of companies. **Born** in Qatar. **Son** of Darwish Fakhroo. **Career:** Owner of Darwish Trading Company; Kassem Darwish Fakhroo and Sons-Mechanical and Electrical Contractors; KDS-Commercial Division; KDS-Transport Division; Gulf Automobile and Trading Co.; Gulf Housing and Contracting Co. Ltd.; Gulf Timber and Joinery Co. Ltd.; Darwish Travel Bureau; Qatar National Travels; Oasis Hotel; Darwish Engineering; Qatar Communications Company; Darwish Engineering (U.A.E.); Darwish Trading Co. (U.A.E.) **Prof. Addr.:** P.O.Box 350 and P.O.Box 92, Tel.: 422781 (10 lines), Telex: 4298 TRADAR DH, Doha, Qatar.

FAKI (Mohamad, Hassan), Saudi man of letters and Poet. **Born** in 1924 in Saudi Arabia. **Married**, children. **Educ.:** Received general education, followed by extensive supplementary reading. **Member:** Jeddah Literary Society. **Publ.:** Author of collected Poems, also contributor to leading newspapers and magazines. **Prof. Addr.:** c/o "al-Madina" newspaper, P.O.Box 807, Jeddah, Saudi Arabia

FAKI (Mohamad, Mohamad Hassan), Saudi diplomat. **Born** on 14 October 1939 in Mecca, Saudi Arabia. **Dipl.:** B.A. (Political Science), American University, Cairo, Egypt (1960); Diploma from Centre of Diplomacy, American University, Washington D.C. (1963); M.A. (International Relations), American University, Washington D.C. (1965). **Career:** Attaché, Ministry of Foreign Affairs, Jeddah (1960), at the Saudi Embassy, Washington D.C., U.S.A. (1963-69), at the Ministry of Foreign Affairs, Jeddah (1969-73); First Secretary, Saudi Embassy, Cairo, Egypt (1973-77); Saudi Ambassador to Nigeria (1977). **Hobbies:** reading, music, swimming. **Addr.:** Ministry of Foreign Affairs, Jeddah, Saudi Arabia.

FAKIEH (Abdul Rahman, Abdul Qadir), Saudi Businessman and poultry breeder. **Born** in 1943 H.' 1925 A.D. in Mecca, Saudi Arabia. **Married** with Children. **Educ.:** General Education. **Career:** Businessman, set up in 1383 H. F.P.F. Establishment and a very important large and modern chain of poultry breeding stations in Saudi Arabia; Founder/Owner of a chain of Al Tazig restaurants for grilled chicken; Member of the Board and Member delegate to Mecca for Construction and Building; Member of Board of Trustees of King Abdulaziz and Men's Establishment for the Care of the talented; President of Holy Mecca Awkaf; President of the Directorate Council for Grain Pressing for Forage Production; President of the Directorate of the Sea Wonders Co.; Member for Collecting contributions for prisoners in Holy Mecca; Member of the Board "Nadwa" newspaper; Member of Benevolent Society in Holy Mecca; Honorary Member at Jeddah Center for Science and Technology; Member of the Benevolent Association to help the Young for marriage;Honorary Board Member of "Al Wihdah al Riadi Club"; Founder and Member of the Board of the Handicapped Children Association in Holy Mecca; Founder and Chairman of the Board of "Fakieh Research and Development Center". **Formerly:** Member of the Board of Mecca Electric Co. in Taef and Holy Mecca; Member of the Board of Public Harbors Establishment; Member of the Board of the National Agricultual Development Co. (NADEC); Founder Member of Mecca Medical Center; Honorary Member of the Benevolent Society in Taef; Member of the Board of Mecca Chamber of Commerce and Industry (1413-1417 H.); Member for Development Services, Committee; Member in the Economic Committee. **Hobbies:** Reading and Travel. **Prof Addr.:** Fakieh Poultry Farms, P.O.Box 6002, Tel.: -2-966 5572225, Mecca, Saudi Arabia.

FAKIEH (Omar Abdulkader Mohammad), Saudi former State Minister. **Born** in 1928 in Mecca, Saudi Arabia. **Educ.:** Boston University (U.S.A.). **Dipl.:** M.A. (Business Administration). **Career:** Head Industrial Section Ministry of Finance (1953-54); Chief of Accounts, Directorate General for Petroleum & Mineral Resources (1954-60); Deputy Minister of Commerce (1960-72); Director General, Saudi Railroad Organization (1972-73). Deputy Minister of Post, Telegraph and Telephone (PTT) (1973-75); President General Auditing Bureau (1975-87). State Minister, Member, Council of Ministers & President General Auditing Bureau (1987-Aug. 1995). **Membership in Professional Organizations:** International Organization of Supreme Audit Institutions (INTOSA); Organization of Supreme Audit Institutions of Arab Countries (ARABOSA); Governing Board of the Organization of Supreme Audit Institutions of Asian Countries (ASOSA); Supreme Council for King Faisal University; Supreme Council for ARAMCO (Saudi Arabia). **Affiliations:** Member American Accounting Association (AAA) USA; Member National Accounting Association (NAA) USA; Member International Internal Auditors USA; Member American Management Association (AMA) USA. **Awards:** King Abdul Aziz Sash (Grade 2). **Hobby:** Reading. **Addr.:** P.O.Box 8612, Jeddah 21492, Kingdom of Saudi Arabia.

FAKIH (Ahmad, Hassan), Arab-British businessman. **Born** in Beirut, Lebanon. **Married**, 3 daughters. **Educ.:** Beirut College. **Dipl.:** Diploma in Business Administration. **Career:** Managing Director and Partner of Middle East Hotel Co., Kuwait (1968-77); Executive Administrator, Pan Gulf Management Co. (1977-85); Property Manager, Messila House Ltd., London, UK (1977-85); Managing Director, Intuition Group. **Priv. Addr.:** Shenley Cottage, Shenley Hill, Radlett, Hertfordshire, United Kingdom.

FALAH (Hassan, Ali), Bahraini Company General Manager. **Born** in 1948 in Muharraq, Bahrain. **Son** of Ali Falah. **Married** in 1975, 2 sons, 2 daughters. **Educ.:** B.A. (Accounting). **Career:** Superintendent of Price Control Office (1971-73), Superintendent of Budget (1973-76); Director of State Budget (1976-1994); Director of Audit (1994-1995) Ministry of Finance and National Economy, Bahrain; General Manager of Bahrain Saudi Aluminium Marketing Co.; Member of the Board of Gulf Petrochemical Industries Co. (GPIC), Bahrain. **Director, Member:** Alumni Club, Bahrain; Marine Club Bahrain; Muharraq Sport Club, Bahrain. **Hobbies:** Reading and sports, Travels. **Addr.:** Bahrain Saudi Aluminium Marketing Co., P.O.Box 20079, Tel: 537726, Fax: 537728 Telex: 9110 BALCO BN, Bahrain.

FAM (Aziz), Egyptian physician. **Born** in 1919 in Fayoum, Egypt. **Married**, 1 Son, 1 daughter. **Educ.:** Faculty of Medicine, University of Cairo, Egypt; Fellow of International College of Surgeons, fellow of American College of Surgeons. **Dipl.:** MB, BCH, MCH in Medicine. **Career:** Demonstrator at Cairo University Hospital (1946-55); Lecturer in Urology, Faculty of Medicine, Cairo University (1955-62), Assistant Professor in Urology (1962-68), Professor or Urology (1968-); owner-director of private clinic or urology and genito-urinary surgery; Member of the Health Committee of the National Democratic Party; Chief of the Council of the Coptic Church, Garden City; Chief and Treasurer of Project of St. Mark Hospital; Chief of Urology Department, Coptic Hospital, Cairo; corresponding Member, American Urology Association (1973-). **Publ.:** various papers and articles on genito urinary surgery in professional journals. **Prof. Addr.:** Ramses Building, Ramses Square, Cairo; Egypt.

FANEK (Fahed, Najeeb), Jordanian consultant, economic and Political Columnist. **Born** in April 13, 1934, in Amman, Jordan. **Son** of Najeeb Fanek (businessman) **and** Mrs., née Helalah Nemri. **Married** on April 13, 1958, Husn, to Miss Maha Fanek, 5 children: Jehad (1959), Ghada (1960), Nadia (1963), Najeeb (1964), Ma'amoun (1968). **Educ.:** High School-Irbed Secondary School, Jordan; College, Ein Shams University, Cairo. **Dipl.:** B.Com. Major Accounting; M.B.A. and Ph.D. in Business Administration from California Coast University. **Career:** Teacher (1951-59); Banking, Arab Bank (1963-66); Public Accounting, Saba & Co. (1966-72); Airline Executive, Vie-President Finance, Alia/The Royal Jordanian Airline (1972-85), Certified Public Accountant and Financial Consultant (since 1985); also daily columnist in Al Rai newspaper as economic and political commentator and analyst, and weekly columnist in Jordan Times. **Publ.:** Author of twelve books in Arabic as follows: Banks and Jordanian Economy (1964); Jordan in the Age of Central Bank (1968); The Agricultural Sector in Jordan (1970); Economic Thought in Jordan (1972); Cooperation Between Syria & Jordan in Civil Aviation (1976); Tourism in Jordan (1978); Profitability of Jordanian Banks (1981); Jordan's economic and Social Development Plans (1982); Jordan's Economy Tomorrow (1983); Economic Challenges (1985); Economic Insights (1986); Press and Responsible Freedom (1997). **Sport:** Swimming. **Hobbies:** Reading, writing, travelling. **Member** of various clubs and associations. **Credit Card:** Visa. **Prof. Addr.:** Fahed Fanek & Co., P.O.Box 950244, Tel.: 5603902, Amman. **Priv. Addr.:** Daheyat al-Hussein, P.O.Box 950244 Tel.: 5931770, Amman 11195, Jordan.

FAQIH (Abdallah, Saleh), Saudi civil servant. **Born** in 1939 in Mecca, Saudi Arabia. **Married,** with children. **Educ.:** Secondary Education. **Dipl.:** Secondary School Certificate. **Career:** attended the 1st Conference of Saudi Men of Letters, King Abdul Aziz University; member of Board of Arab Centre; member of Committee for the Regulation of Graphic Material, Publications and Organisations; former Director of Publications Department, Ministry of Information, Jeddah. **Hobbies:** reading and music. **Priv. Addr.:** Tel.: 51151, Jeddah, Saudi Arabia.

FAQUIH (Osama J.), Saudi statesman. **Born** in 1942 in al-Madina. **Son** of Jaafar. **Married,** 5 children: two Boys, Three Girls. **Educ.:** Riyadh University, Saudi Arabia; University of Arizona, U.S.A. **Dipl.:** Bachelor's degree in Business Administration and Accounting; Master's degree in Business Administration. **Career:** Lecturer at the University of Riyadh (1969-75); Director of Capital Loans Dept. in the Saudi Fund for Development (1975-80); Assistant Deputy Finance Minister of Saudi Arabia for Int'l Dev. Cooperation Affairs, Deputy Finance Minister for Int'l Economic Cooperation since 1983; Chief Executive and Chairman of the Board of the Arab Trade Financing Program; Chairman of the Board of Governors of the OPEC Fund for International Development: Co-Chairman of the Arab Group in the Economic Cooperation Committee for the Arab-European Dialogue; Chairman of the Board of Directors of the Gulf Development Agency in Egypt since 1984; Chairman of the Board of Directors of Saudi Credit Bank (1983-85); Chairman of the Saudi National Committee for Trade Financing since 1987; Chairman of the Board of Directors of the Saudi-Egyptian Company for Industrial Investment since 1988; Chairman of the Governing Council of the Common Fund for Commodities since 1990; Alternate Governor for Saudi Arabia of the Multilateral Investment Guarantee Agency; Director General and Chairman of the Board of the Arab Monetary Fund; Minister of Commerce (since Aug. 1995). **Prof. Addr.:** Ministry of Commerce, P.O.Box 1774, Riyadh 11162, Saudi Arabia.

FARAH (Abdul Aziz), Sudanese bank manager. **Born** in 1931 in Port Sudan. **Married** in 1955, 2 sons, 2 daughters. **Educ.:** Alexandria University, Egypt (B.Sc.); Diploma in Auditing. **Career:** Joined National Bank of Egypt, Sudan (1953-61); Bank of Sudan, Sudan (1962-76); Manager, Arab Bank Ltd., Dubai, UAE (1976-). **Addr.:** P.O.Box 11364, Tel.: 285973, Telex: 46126 A/B ARAB EM, Dubai, UAE.

FARAH (Abdulrahim Abi), Somali politician. **Born** in 1919. **Educ.:** University of Exeter and Balliol College, Oxford. **Career:** Ambassador to Ethiopia (1961-65); Permanent Representative of Somalia to UN (1965-72); UN Commissioner for Technical Co-operation (1972-73); UN Assistant Secretary General and Coordinator Special Economic Assistance Programmes, Under Secretary General for Special Political Questions (1979-86); Under Secretary General for the Department for Special Political Questions, Regional Cooperation, Decolonization and Trusteeship (Jan. 1987-90); Minister of Construction (1991). **Prof. Addr.:** Mogadishu, Somalia.

FARAH (Ali Abdi), Djibouti Deputy at the National Assembly, and Diplomat. **Born** on February 16, 1947 in Djibouti. **Educ.:** High School of Djibouti. **Career:** Teacher (1969-1972). Civil Administrator, Deputy General Secretary of CFA; Diplomatic Attache of the President of the Republic; Head of General Administration and Consular Affairs Department, Ministry of Foreign Affairs; First Counsellor at Embassy of Djibouti in Tunisia; Member of Executive Committee of RPP. Minister of Energy, Mines and Natural Resources (8/6/1995); Elected Deputy at the National Assembly (19/12/1997 - to date). **Prof. Addr.:** National Assembly, P.O.Box 138 Djibouti, Djibouti.

FARAH (Cæsar, E.), Educator, University Professor. **Born** on March 13, 1929 in Portland, Oregon, U.S.A. **Son**

of Salim Khalil Abi Farah (deceased) **and** Mrs. Lawrice Nasrallah Farah. **Married** to Dr. Irmgard Tenkamp, 7 children: Six by a previous marriage: Ronald M. (1955), Christopher E. (1956), Ramsey S. (1957), Laurence J. (1962), Raymond L. (1967), Alexandra D. (1969), Elizabeth (1989). **Educ.:** International College (Beirut), Stanford University, Princeton University. **Dipl.:** B.A. (with distinction 1952) in History and International Relations, M.A. & Ph.D. in Near Eastern and Islamic Studies. **Career:** U.S. Foreign Service (USIS-Delhi) as Public Affairs Assistant (1956-57); USIS-Karachi as Educational Exchange Officer (1957-58); Assistant Professor History, Portland State University and California State, L.A. (1959-64), Indiana University (1964-69), University of Minnesota (1969 to present); Visiting Professor, Harvard University; Cambridge University; Karl Franzens Graz Austria; University of Munich; Professor of Arabic and Islamic Studies and the Modern Middle East; Chairman, Department of South Asian & Middle Eastern Studics (1988-91); Active in community affairs, Organizer & Director Upper Midwest Consertium for Middle East outreach former president local chapter of AAUG, Former president of Stanford Alumni Association of Minnesota, lectures widely and made presentation on radio, television. Also International Lecturer by invitation from European and Middle Eastern Universities. **Publ.:** Nine books and 50 major scholarly articles. **Awards:** Fulbright and others. **Sports:** Swimming, diving, skiing. **Hobbies:** Stamp collecting, reading, travel. **Member:** Calhoun Beach Club, Stanford and Princeton Clubs of Minnesota, Middle East Studies Association of North America, Royal Asiatic Society of Great Britain. **Prof. Addr.:** 839 Social Sciences Tower, University of Minnesota, Tel.: (612)6240580, Mineapolis, Min. 55455, USA. **Priv. Addr.:** 5125 Blake Rd. Edina, MN, 55436, Tel.: (612) 938-2747, U.S.A.

FARAH DIRIR (Saleh Hadji), Djibouti diplomat and scientist. **Born** in 1937 in Djibouti. **Married,** two children. **Educ.:** University of London and Kansas State Teachers' College. **Dipl.:** M.Sc. **Career:** Lecturer in physical sciences and adviser, Ministry of Education and Higher Education, Somalia; Chairman of Sciences and Math. Division, Associate Dean of Academic Affairs, Assistant Dean and Dean of College of Education, National University of Somalia (1964-77); Member, later Chairman, National Science Committee; Chief, Permanent Mission of Djibouti to UN (1977-79); Permanent Representative to UN (1979). **Prof. Addr.:** c/o Ministry of Foreign Affairs, P.O.Box 1863, Djibouti.

FARAH (Fawzi, E.), Lebanese executive. **Born** in 1948 in Lebanon. **Son** of Elias Farah. **Single. Educ.:** California State University; John Hopkins University. **Dipl.:** B.A. (Econ); M.A. (Intl. Econ.) (1975). **Career:** Joined Citibank, New York (1975-76); Manager of the Corporate Financial Department, Industrial Bank of Kuwait (1976-81); Senior Manager, Credit Division, Commercial Bank of Kuwait, Safat, Kuwait (1981-). **Member:** Arab Banker's Association, UK. **Director** of Middle East Research Group. **Publ.:** Articles published by Industrial Bank of Kuwait. **Sports:** Swimming and skiing. **Addr.:** P.O.Box 2861, Tel.: 417785, 417950, Telex: 22004 A/B CBK, Safat, Kuwait.

FARAH (Idriss, Harbi), Djibouti Deputy at the National Assembly. **Born** in 1937 in Dikhil. **Educ.:** Journalism Diploma. **Career:** Director "La Nation newspaper" until 1982. Elected Deputy at the National Assembly (21 May 1982 - to date); Minister of Interior and Decentralization (4 Feb. 1993 - 28 Dec. 1997); Elected 08/01/1998 2nd Vice-President at the National Assembly Office; Member of the National Defence Commission. **Prof. Addr.:** National Assembly, P.O.Box 138 Djibouti, Djibouti.

FARAH (Mohamed, Dini), Djibouti Deputy at the National Assembly. **Born** in 1943 at Tadjourah. **Educ.:** Secondary. **Career:** Director of Civil Prison of Gabode. Member of Central Committee of RPP; Minister of Civil Service and administrative Reform (8 June 1995 - 19 April 1997); Minister of Public Works (19/04/1997); Elected Deputy at the National Assembly (19/12/1997 - to date), became Minister of Justice (18 Dec. 1997). **Prof. Addr.:** National Assembly, P.O.Box 138 Djibouti, Djibouti.

FARAH (Salih), U.A.E. lawyer. **Born** in 1930 in Sudan. **Son** of Farah Abdel Rahman (civil servant) **and** Mrs. Fatima Hamid. **Married** in 1957 in Sudan to Miss Khadija Hassan, 2 children: Zeinab (1958), Ahmed (1960). **Educ.:** University of Khartoum, University of London, Gray's Inn-London. **Dipl.:** Diploma of Civil Law, Khartoum; LL.B., London; Dipl. of Gray's Inn, Barrister-at-Law. **Career:** Senior Legal Counsel of the Sudan Government (1956-67); Chief Justice of Abu Dhabi (1967-73); Adviser of H.H. the President of U.A.E. (1973). **Member:** English Bar, the Sudan Bar, U.A.E. Bar, Member of the University of Khartoum Association, Member of the Convocation of the University of London. **Award:** Order of Merit (Egypt). **Sports:** Horse-riding, walking, cycling. **Hobby:** Travelling. **Credit Card:** American Express. **Prof. Addr.:** P.O.Box 280, Tel.: 41010, Abu Dhabi, U.A.E. and Atbara Str., P.O.Box 1829, Tel.: 78421, 77518, Khartoum, Sudan.

FARAIDY (Abdulatif Abdallah, al), Saudi physician. **Born** in 1947 in Mecca, Saudi Arabia. **Dipl.:** Ph.D. in Pediatrics, West Germany. **Career:** Associate Professor of Pediatrics, Faculty of Medicine and Medical Sciences, King Faisal University; Dean, Students Affairs, King Faisal University, Dammam; member of Faculty of Medicine and Medical Sciences Council; Vice President, King Faisal University. **Publ.:** Accidental Poisoning in Children (Ph.D. thesis); Children, Good Health Check-List; several articles in al-Faisal Medical Journal and al-Jamiah Journal. **Prof. Addr.:** King Faisal University, P.O.Box 1982, Tel.: 03-

8577984, Dammam 31441. **Priv. Addr.:** Tel.: 03-8646704, Dammam, Saudi Arabia.

FARGE (Antoine, Raymond), French bank delegate. **Born** in 1926. **Married** in 1956. **Dipl.:** Ph.D. in Law. **Career:** Joined Société Générale as Deputy Manager; Manager, Société Générale Orléans; Manager, Mantes; Manager, Casablanca; Manager, Tours (1948-66); General Manager, Société Française de Banque et de Dépôt (subsidiary of Société Générale) Belgium (1966-71); General Manager, French Arab Bank for International Investment (subsidiary of Société Générale in Paris) (1971-76); Regional Delegate, Société Générale Bank, Egypt; Councillor, du Commerce Extérieur de la France; Director, Société Générale Bank SAE; Egypt. **Awards:** Officer, Ordre du Mérite National, France; Knight Ordre de la Couronne, Belgium. **Member:** Cercle de l'Union Interalliée Paris. **Hobby:** Golf. **Addr.:** P.O.Box 2620, 9 Talaat Harb Street, Cairo, Egypt.

FARHAN (Abdulqarim), Iraqi army officer and statesman. **Educ.:** Secondary and Staff College of Baghdad and Baghdad College of Law. **Career:** Commander of Battalion, Commander of Acting Brigade (1958-59); Commander of First Division (1963); Minister of Culture and Guidance (1963-65); Secretary General of the Arab Socialist Union of Iraq (1964-65); Member of the Revolutionary Command Council (1964); Minister of Agrarian Reform (1967); Minister of Agriculture (1968). **Awards:** ar-Rafidain Medal (first grade), Jordanian Star (first grade) and Many other military decorations. **Addr.:** al-Mansour, No 91/8, Baghdad, Iraq.

FARHAN (Hamad, al), Senator - Jordan Senate - Upper House of Parliament. **Born** on 17 February 1921 in Nuaimah, Jordan. **Son** of Farhan el-Hamad (Farmer) **and** Mrs. née Rahma el-Ali. **Married** on 9/1/1964 in Amman to Yusra Tilfah, Eight Children: Hania (1965), Maha (1966), Manaf (1967), Yassar (1969), Waleed (1970), Ahmad (1971), Nisreen (1972) and Maissa (1974). **Educ.:** Irbid Secondary School, Jordan; Salt Secondary School, Jordan; American University of Beirut, Beirut; London University, London. **Dipl.:** B.A. (Science), American University of Beirut; Fellowship of London University, London. **Career:** Public Works Department (1941) Jordan; Teacher, Salt Sec. School (1942-43); Director, Irbid Sec. School (1943-45); Inspector of Education (1945); Secretary Cabinet of Ministers (1947); Director of Statistics Dept. (1949); Under-Secretary of Economy (1951); Minister of National Economy (1955); Senator - Jordan Upper House of Parliament (1989); now Chairman and Managing Director of Arab Shipping Co. Ltd., Amman, Jordan. **Decors:** Jordan Nahda Decoration (1948); Spanish Iron Cross (1949); Syrian Istiklal Decoration (1957). **Sports:** Football and tennis. **Hobbies:** Chess and Reading. **Member:** Centre of Arab Unity Studies, Jordan; Arab Organization for Human Rights, Jordan. **Prof. Addr.:** Arab Shipping Co. P.O.Box 757, Tel.: 623135/6/7, Telex: 21225/ 21435 ARSHIP JO, Fax: 962/6/638137, Amman, Jordan. **Priv. Addr.:** Queen Alia Street, No.87, Amman, Jordan.

FARHAN (Ishaq, Ahmad), Jordanian academic. **Born** in 1934 in Ain Karem, Jordan. **Son** of Ahmad Farhan. **Married**, seven children. **Educ.:** B.Sc. American University of Beirut, Lebanon; M.Sc. in Physical Chemistry, AUB; and Ph.D. in Education, Columbia University, USA. **Career:** Head of Teachers Education Department (1964); Head of Curriculum Department (1964-70); Minister of Education and of Islamic Affairs (1970-73); Director General of Royal Scientific Society (1975); President of Jordan University (1976-78); Member of National Consultative Council (1978); Professor of Education, Yarmouk University, Jordan (since 1978). **Member** of: the Islamic Association of Studies and Research, Amman; the Boards of Trustees of Universities, community colleges, scientific associations and many other scientific enterprises. Special expertise in curriculum and textbook development. **Publ.:** Books, research papers and studies published in various journals. **Medals:** Excellent Decoration of Education, Jordan (1974). **Addr.:** P.O.Box 19095, Amman, Jordan.

FARID-MESSIHA (Kamal), Egyptian University Professor. **Born** on January 27, 1926 in Cairo. **Son** of Farid Messiha (Ex-Controller of Rates and Fares, Egyptian State Railways) **and** Mrs. Esther Nasr. **Married** in July 1958, 2 children: Magda and Magdi. **Educ.:** Collège des Frères des Ecoles Chrétiennes; Collège des Pères Jésuites; French Department, Faculty of Arts, University Fouad the First, Cairo (1945-49); Ecole Normale Supérieure (High Teaches College), Saint-Cloud, France (1952-54); Ecole du Louvres, Paris (1952-54); Institut de Langue et Littérature Françaises, Faculty of Arts, University of Paris (1952-56). **Dipl.:** Bachelor of Arts in French Literature and Language (Cairo University, June 1949); Certificat de Fin d'Etudes, Ecole Normale Supérieure (High Teachers College), Saind-Cloud, France (July 1954); Doctor of Philosphy in the French Seventeenth Century, Paris University (First Honour). **Career:** Teacher of French, Khedive Ismaïl School and Aïn Shams School, Cairo (January 1951 - June 1952); Lecturer of French, High Teachers College, Cairo (1956); Lecturer of French Literature, Aïn Shams University; Cairo (1957-64); Associate Professor of French Literature, Aïn Shams University, Cairo (1964-66); Research Associate with the National Centre for Scientific Research in Paris, France (1966); Visiting Associate Professor of the French 17th Century at Washington University, Missouri, U.S.A. (Academic year 1966-67); Visiting Professor of the French 17th Century, University of California, U.S.A. (Academic year 1967-68); Actually Associate Professor at the Department of French Language and Literature, University College for girls, Aïn Shams University, Cairo. **Publ.:** Author of various publications, articles and researches, including: "Antoine de Courtin, 1622-

1685" (Principal Thesis), Nizet Ed. in Collaboration with the National Centre for Scientific Rresearch in Paris; "Classicisme Comparé Lettres et Arts", "Le Cid" and its influence on the Literature; "Marivaux et la Comédie d'Amour"; Translation of Jean Giraudoux's Play "Siegfried" (master-pieces of the Theatre); "L'Impressionnisme en Orient et en Occident"; "la Collaboration de l'Ecole et de la Famille"; "Le Théâtre Classique Arabe". **Dist.:** A Price for the Thesis from France-Egypt Association, Paris (1956). **Hobbies:** Critics of Fine Arts and Classics. **Member** of Heliolido Sporting Club, Heliopolis, Cairo; Aïn Shams Teaching Staff Club, Cairo. **Prof. Addr.:** Asma Fahmy Street, Heliopolis, Tel.: 826565, Cairo. **Priv. Addr.:** 29, al-Aziz-Bellah Street, Zeitoun, Tel.: 860957, Cairo, Egypt.

FARID (Mohamad, Ibrahim), Egyptian banker. **Born** in 1928 in Cairo. **Son** of Late General Ibrahim Farid (Army Officer) **and** late Mrs. Neemat Mansour. **Married** in June 1957 to Mrs. Sawsan Farid, three children. **Educ.:** Faculty of Commerce, Cairo University, Egypt. **Dipl.:** B.Com. **Career:** Managing Director, National Bank of Egypt (1977-80); Chairman, National Societe General, Cairo (1978-80); Deputy Chairman & Managing Director, National Bank for Development, Egypt (1980-88); Chairman & Managing Director, Egypt Arab African Bank, Egypt (Dec. 1988- April 1990); Currently Vice Chairman & Managing Director, Arab African International Bank, Egypt since May 1990. **Hobby:** Reading. **Member:** Heliopolis Sporting Club. **Credit Cards:** American Express, Visa. **Prof. Addr.:** Arab African International Bank, 5 Midan al-Saray al-Koubra, Garden City, P.O.Box 60, Magless El-Chaab (11516), Tel.: 3557517, Cairo, Egypt. **Priv. Addr.:** 57 "A" Osman Ben Affan Str., Tel.: 2903785, Heliopolis, Cairo, Egypt.

FARID (Morris, Nazmi), Egyptian painter. **Born** on April 6, 1917 in Akmim, Egypt. **Married**, 2 sons, 2 daughters. **Educ.:** College of Applied Arts, Cairo. **Dipl.:** B.A. **Career:** Draftsman, Faculty of Archaeology, Cairo University; had 14 private exhibitions (1952-83); private collections in USA, UK, France, Belgium, Sweden, Chile, Federal Republic of Germany, Italy and Jordan. **Prof. Addr.:** 11 Aziz Osman Street, Zamalek, Cairo, Egypt.

FARID (Samir, Muhammad), Egyptian statistician. **Born** in 1942 in Egypt. **Married**, 2 daughters. **Educ.:** Cairo University; Egypt; Leeds University. **Dipl.:** B.Sc. in Statistics, Ph.D. in Demography. **Career:** Lecturer, Institute of Statistics, Cairo University (1963-70); Consultant, Office of Population Censuses and Surveys, London (1970-77); Member, The International Union of the Scientific Study of Population, the International Statistical Institute, The Hague; Demographic Expert, International Statistical Institute, London (1977-). **Publ.:** "The Current Tempo of Fertility in England and Wales, HMSO," London (1974), "Population Growth in Syria," London (1983) in English, "The Demographic Transition in Egypt" in Arabic. **Hobbies:** Swimming, writing, chess. **Prof. Addr.:** 10 Brocas Close, London NW3, United Kingdom.

FARID (Zuhair), Egyptian physician. **Born** on December 25, 1927 in Bani Suef, Egypt. **Married. Educ.:** Cairo University, Egypt; University of Chicago, USA; London University, UK. **Dipl.:** M.B., Ch.B. in Medicine, Diploma in Tropical Medicine. **Career:** Hospital House Office, Ministry of Public Health, Egypt (1952-54); Member of the Staff of US Naval Medical Research Unit No.3 (NAMRU), Cairo (1954-56); Seymor Comen Fellow of Medicine, University of Chicago (1957-59); Member of Staff of NAMRU No.3, Cairo (1959-63); Member, Expert Committee on Brucellosis (1963-); Lecturer, London School of Hygiene and Tropical Medicine, University of London, UK (1963-64); Director of Tropical Medicine Department, NAMRU No.3, Cairo (1964-); Fellow of the British Royal Society of Tropical Medicine and Hygiene; Member, the American Society of Tropical Medicine and Hygiene; Member, the Society of Biological Sciences; visiting lecturer, London School of Hygiene and Tropical Medicine; Consultant, Abbassiyah Fever Hospital, Ministry of Public Health (1967-); Member, the Expert Committee on Nutrition and Parasitic Diseases (1970). **Publ.:** co-author with M. Sabbur, Dar al-Maaref, Cairo, Egypt of "Textbook of Infectious Diseases"; articles on tropical diseases published in professional American and British journals. **Decor.:** Commandatore of Italian Government (1972). **Addr.:** 9 al-Mahad al-Suissri, Zamalek, Cairo, Egypt.

FARIS (Mustafa), Moroccan economist. **Born** on December 17, 1933 in Morocco. **Married. Educ.:** National School of Roads and Bridges, Paris (France). **Dipl.:** B.Sc. (Civil Engineering). **Career:** Civil Engineer, Department of Public Works (1956-61); Director of Supply, National Irrigation Office (1961-65); Director-General, Hydraulic Engineering (1965-69); Secretary of State for Planning attached to Prime Minister's Office (1969-71); Minister of Finance (1971-72); President, Director General, Banque Nationale pour le Développement Economique (1972); Vice-President, International Commission on Large Dams: Governor, International Bank for Reconstruction and Development (IBRD); African Development Bank; President Director General, Banque Nationale pour le Développement Economique (1972-77 and 1981 to 1995); Chairman, Société des Ciments d'Agadir; Director Berliet-Maroc, Sidet-Société Immoblière de Développement Touristique; Minister of Agriculture (1977-80); presently Chairman Banque Marocaine pour le Commerce et l'Industrie S.A. **Addr.:** P.O.Box 407 Rabat, Morocco.

FARISI (Rifaat, Izzet, al), Iraqi Lawyer. **Born** on November 9, 1935. **Son** of Izzet Rifaat al-Farisi (deceased in 1959) **and** Mrs. Fahima al-Naqishli. **Married** on August 23, 1984 to Meead al-Zahawi. **Educ.:** Victoria College,

Alexandria, Egypt (1944-53); Then graduated from College of Law, Baghdad University, Iraq; Has taken a course in insurance from the College of Insurance, London. **Career:** After discharge from Army (conscript) as 2nd Lieutenant in 1962, he joined Baghdad Insurance Co. (later merged with National Insurance Co.); He continued his career with National Insurance Co. as Assistant General Manager; Until retirement on 25.1.1988. Presently working as a lawyer in Baghdad. **Sport:** Swimming. **Member:** Alwiyah Club (Social Club). **Prof. Addr.:** Temporary office address: c/o Mr. Munem Alkhateeb Legal Bureau, Minas bldg., South Gate, Tel.: 7740320, 8889656, Baghdad, Iraq. **Priv. Addr.:** Baghdad, Iraq.

FARNAWANI (Taha, Muhammad, al), Egyptian diplomat. **Born** on October 1, 1929 in Cairo, Egypt. **Married**, 3 children. **Educ.:** University of Switzerland; University of Paris, Paris. **Dipl.:** Ph.D. in Economics, Ph.D. in Cooperation. **Career:** Director of Arab Affairs Bureau, Cabinet of the Republic of Egypt (1964-67); Adviser and Chargé d'Affaires, Embassy in Damascus, Syria (1967-69); Minister Plenipotentiary, Director or Arab League Bureau, Economic Counsellor of the Arab League and Permanent Delegate of Egypt, Arab League Organization (1969-75); Secretary General of the Constituent Committee, Union of Franco-Arab Banks (1969-71); Secretary General and Member of the Board, Franco-Arab Chamber of Economics (1971-75); Member of the Board, Franco-Arab Jurisconsults Association (1971-75); Director of Management Information System, Ministry of Foreign Affairs, Egypt (1975-76); Member of the Board of Namibia Institution, United Nations (1979-80); Ambassador of Egypt to Zambia (1979-80); Zimbabwe (1980-82); Director of Palestinian Affairs, Ministry of Foreign Affairs (1982-). **Publ.:** "Egypt and Maritime Law" (1966), "UNESCO and Israel" (1972), "Franco-Arab Cooperation" (1973), "The Franco-Arab Annual Guide" (1974-75); Edited a bi-monthly magazine "Franco Arab Economic Cooperation" (1971-75). **Decor.:** Order of Merit (1st Class), Egypt in 1970; Ordre National du Merite (Commander), France in 1982. **Medals:** Medal of Merit, Greece (1970), Medal of Independence, Zimbabwe (1983). **Hobbies:** Tennis, swimming, riding, shooting, volleyball. **Member:** Gezira Sporting Club; Heliopolis Club, Egypt; International Club, Paris; Captain and Member, Egypt National Basketball team to Helsinki (1952). **Prof. Addr.:** Ministry of Foreign Affairs, 4 Nile Street, Giza, Egypt. **Priv. Addr.:** 36 Nehru Street, Merryland Garden, Masre al-Jadida, Cairo, Egypt.

FARRA (Muhammed, Hussain, el), Jordan Diplomat. **Born**on April 20, 1927 in Khan Yunes, Palestine, **Son** of Hussain El-Farra and Mrs. née Muftiya Yusuf. **Educ.:** Suffolk University, Boston University and University of Pennsylvania. **Dipl,:** Bachelor of Law (1950); Master's Degree of Law (1951); Doctor of Jurisprudence, G.S.D. (1958). **Career:** Lecturer in the American University (1955-59); Member of the Syrian Delegation to the UN (1952-54); Speaker of the League of Arab States (1955-59); Vice-President of the Arab Students Organization to the USA (1954-55); Member of the Jordan Delegation to the UN General Assembly (10 sessions); Accredited Minister Plenipotentiary of Jordan to the Arab Republic of Egypt (1963); Deputy Permanent Representative of Jordan to the UN (1962-64); Ambassador and Permanent Representative of Jordan to the UN (Nov. 1965- March 1971); President of the Security Council (March 1966); Ambassador to Spain (1971) **Head or Member** of several Delegations to the General Assembly to the UN, New York and to the meetings of the League of Arab States in New York, Lebanon, Geneva and Egypt; Former Assistant Secretary General for Palestine Affairs at the League of Arab States. **Publ.:** Author of a Book "Year of no Decision" published in English and translated to Arabic language. **Dist.:** Recipient Mathewson Prize of Boston University (1951). Represented Jordan in many Arab Foreign Ministers Conferences in various capitals of the Arab States. **Address:** 5 Abdel Qawi Ahmad street, Off el-Urouba, Heliopolis, Cairo, Egypt.

FARRADJ (Fuad, Dimitri), Jordanian businessman. **Born** in 1925 in Nablus, Palestine. **Son** of Dimitri Farradj. **Married**. **Educ.:** B.Sc., Mechanical Engineering, Fuad University, Cairo, Egypt (1948). **Career:** Engineer, Ministry of Public Works (1949-51); Board member, Jordan Cement Factories; Engineer with CAT Co Qatar (1951-52); Assistant Under Secretary (Mechanical and Electrical), Ministry of Public Works (1952-56); Private Consulting Office (1956-57); General Manager, Contracting and Concrete Construction Co. (1957-62); owner and partner, Farradj and Co. (Commercial Bureau), Engineering Services (Contractors) (1962-65); President, Association of Engineers, Minister of Municipalities and Rural Affairs (1965-66); Chairman of Board of Directors, Bureau of Engineering Services, Director, Farradj and Co. **Addr.:** Bureau of Engineering Services, P.O.Box 974, Tel.: 21662, 25616, Telex 21317, FARRAJ JO, Amman, Jordan.

FARRAG (Abdelmegid, M.), Egyptian academic. **Born** on January 5, 1928 in Egypt. **Son** of late Moustafa Farrag (Merchant) **and** late Mrs. Adila M. Abdulla. **Married** in 1950 in Alexandria, Egypt to Ragaa M. Saleh, 3 children: 1 son, Shireen (30.11.1952), 2 daughters: Omayma (21.10.1955), Mayar (23.06.1960). **Educ.:** Cairo University, Egypt (1944-48), Birmingham University, England (1950-52 and 1952-54), London School of Economics, England (1954-57). **Dipl.:** B.Sc. (Econ) (1948); Post Graduate Diploma in Statistics (1950); Post Graduate Commerce Diploma (1951); M.Sc. (1954); Ph.D. (1957). **Career:** University Career (1948- to date); and continuing United Nations Career (1962-68), (1972-73); (1978); (1989-91). **Work:** Teaching; Research, Consulting and Advisory roles to Governments. United Nations, UN Specialised agencies and the World Bank. **Awards:** Highest Order of Science and Arts from the President of the Republic of Egypt,

UAR Population Award from the Year 1995. **Sports:** Walking. **Member:** Sporting Club Cairo, IUSSP (Belgium), ISI (Netherland), CICRED (Paris). **Prof. Addr.:** Professor Emeritus, Faculty of Economics and Pol. Science, Cairo University, Cairo, Egypt. **Priv. Addr.:** 26 Road 213, Digla, Maadi, Tel.: 3532993, Cairo, Egypt.

FARRAG (Nureddin, Dr.), Egyptian Chief Executive and General Manager. **Born** on November 27, 1932 at Damanhour, Egypt. **Son** of Mahmoud Farrag. **Married** to Mrs. Fawkia Ibrahim Shehata, 2 sons: Faris (December 11, 1971), Hossam (May 12, 1974). **Educ.:** LL.B. Faculty of Law, Cairo University (1952); Post-Graduate Diploma, Private Law, Cairo University (1953); Public Law (1954); M.Sc. (Economics), Money and Banking, University College London (1959-60); Ph.D. (Economics), International Economics, London School of Economics (1963-64). **Career:** Assistant Lecturer in Commercial Law, Faculty of Law, Ain Shams University, Cairo (1953-56); Lecturer in Economics, Faculty of Law, Ain Shams University, Cairo (1964-65); Economic Advisor, Oil Affairs, Ministry of Finance and Oil, Kuwait (1965-73); Economic Advisor, Ministry of Oil, Kuwait (1974-75); Chief Executive and General Manager, Arab Petroleum Investments Corporation (APICORP), Saudi Arabia (1976- present); Chairman, Board of Governors, Oxford Institute for Energy Studies, Oxford, U.K. (1988- present); Chairman, ABB Arab Engineered Systems and Control Co. (ABB ARESCON), Bahrain (1986- present); Member, Supervisory Board, Banque Arabe Internationale d'Investissement (BAII), Paris, France (1990- present); Member, Board of Directors, Arabian Industrial Fibers Co. (Ibn Rushd), Saudi Arabia (1995- Present); Member, Board of Directors, Alexandria Carbon Black Co., Egypt (1994- Present). **Member:** American Economic Association; Oxford Energy Policy Club. **Publ.:** Contributed papers on Oil, Finance and Economic Development since late sixties to: OPEC, OAPEC and Oxford Energy Seminars; Arab Energy Conferences; Group of Thirty: Study Group on Oil and the International Monetary and Financial Systems; IHT, IMI, Euromoney and MEED Conferences. **Languages:** Arabic, English and French. **Hobbies:** Reading, Music, Theatre and Light Sport. **Credit Cards:** Amex Gold Card, Visa Gold Card. **Prof. Addr.:** Arab Petroleum Investments Corporation (APICORP), P.O.Box 448, Dhahran Airport 31932, Saudi Arabia, Tel.: 966(3)864-7400, 895-1015, Fax: 966 (3) 898-1883 (Management), Telex: 870068 APIC SJ, Saudi Arabia.

FARRASH (Abdul Malak, Othman), Saudi academic. **Born** in 1934 in Saudi Arabia. **Married,** with children. **Educ.:** Faculty of Arts, Cairo University. **Dipl.:** B.A. (Sociology) (1957). **Career:** Sociology Inspector, Ministry of Education, Saudi Arabia; Assistant Director-General, Youth Welfare Administration (1962); Youth Welfare Consultant, Ministry of Labour and Social Affairs (1964); Deputy-Director, Social Affairs Department, Supreme Planning Council (1964); attended a number of UN General Assembly Meetings (1965, 1967, 1973, 1975) as member of Saudi Arabian Permanent Delegation to UN; attended the Arab League Social Studies Seminar, Committee for Follow-Up of Population Activities in the Arab Countries (a joint UN Demographic Fund/Arab League Committee). **Sports:** Swimming and tennis. **Priv. Addr.:** Technical Cooperation Administration, Riyadh, Saudi Arabia.

FARSY (Fouad Abdul Salam, al), Saudi official. **Born** in 1945 in Jeddah, Saudi Arabia. **Dipl.:** LL.B., M.A. (International Relations), M.A. (American Governments), Ph.D. (Political Science). **Career:** Lecturer, Faculty of Commerce (Political Science Department), King Saud University (1976); Instructor (1976-77); Assistant Deputy Minister for Information, Ministry of Information (1977-79); Deputy Minister for Industry, Ministry of Industry and Electricity; member of the Arabian Society for Arts and Culture in Riyadh; member of the Board of Saudi Industrial Development Fund, Saudi Consulting House, S.A. Organization for Specifications and Measurements, Iron and Steel Co. in Jubail, Kingdom's representative at the Conferences of GOIC; member of the Saudi American Joint Commission, member of the Saudi German Joint Commission; the Kingdom's representative at many international conferences. Presently Minister of Information. **Publ.:** Kingdom of Saudi Arabia: A Case Study in Development, (in English); The Circumstances Which Led to the Creation of NATO, (academic research), regular weekly articles in local newspapers about international events. **Hobbies:** Reading, swimming, walking. **Prof. Addr.:** Ministry of Information, P.O.Box 370, Tel.: (1) 4068888, Riyadh, 11161 Saudi Arabia.

FARSY (Mansour Mohamad Hassan), Saudi M.D. **Born** Mecca, in 1935. **Dipl.:** B.Chem., M.D. **Career:** General Practitioner, King's Hospital, Jeddah; Assistant Director, Ajyad Hospital, Mecca, Director-General, Saddad Hospital; Director-General, Taif Hospital for Chest Diseases; Saudi delegate to conference of chest diseases, England. **Hobbies:** Reading, sport. **Addr.:** Taif Hospital for Chest Diseases, Taif, Saudi Arabia.

FARSY (Mohamad Aly Hassan), Saudi jeweller. **Born** in 1922 in Mecca, Saudi Arabia. **Dipl.:** Diploma of Saudi Islamic Institute (Ilmi), Mecca. **Career:** Has been in the jewellery business since 1942; private jeweller and consultant to H.M. the late King Abdulaziz and H.M. the late King Saud; consultant to public and government agencies in the field of Jewellery; appointed Chief Jeweller in 1959; member of Mecca Chamber of Commerce. **Prof. Addr.:** al-Farsy Jewellery, al-Marwa, Tel.: 5747772, Mecca. **Priv. Addr.:** Tel.: 5427773, Mecca, Saudi Arabia.

FARSY (Mohamad Said Hassan), Saudi official. **Born** in 1934 in Mecca, Saudi Arabia. **Dipl.:** B.Sc. (Architecture and Town Planning), Faculty of Engineering, Alexandria University, Egypt (1961). **Career:** Field Engineer, Town Planning Office of the Western Region, Assistant to the Manager (1962-72); Mayor of Jeddah (1972-80); Lord Mayor of Jeddah since 1980; member, Supreme Hajj Committee, Housing Committee, Makkah Municipal Council; Head of Coordinating Committee for Jeddah Planning; member, Supreme Committee for Water and Sewage in the western Region, Foreign Relations Committee, Arab Towns Organization; Head, Prince Fawaz Project for Cooperative Housing Programme; member, the Annual Meeting for the Grand Cities Mayors, Committee for the Planning Northern Frontiers of Saudi Arabia with Jordan; Head of Committee for Jeddah Housing Distribution Programme. **Honours:** Honorary Doctorates from the University of Korea and Seoul University; grand medals from Jordan, Korea, China, Italy, Tunisia, Indonesia, Britain, Sweden, Argentina and Equador. **Publ.:** participated, organized and completed more than fifty reports concerning the planning of several main towns and cities in the Western Region of Saudi Arabia. **Hobbies:** Collecting antiques, drawings and designs, reading history. **Addr.:** al-Farsi House, al-Hamra District, Tel.: 6672384, Jeddah, Saudi Arabia.

FARSY (Zaky Mohamad Aly), Saudi civil engineer. **Born** in 1946 in Mecca, Saudi Arabia. **Dipl.:** B.Sc., M.Sc. (Civil Engineering), University of California (Berkeley). **Career:** Deputy Director, Town Planning Office, Western Region (1973-76); member of board of South Pacific Property Co. (for the Middle East); founder and Director of Engineering Design Bureau, Jeddah. **Hobbies:** Reading, listening to music. **Addr.:** Farsy Building, Bughdadia, Jeddah, Saudi Arabia.

FASSI (Abbas, al), Moroccan Politician. **Born** in 1940 in Berkane, Morocco. **Married. Educ.:** Mohammed V. University, Rabat. **Dipl.:** Licence in Law. **Career:** joined Istiklal Party (1958); President, General Union of Moroccan Students (1961); Member of the Bar, City of Rabat (1964); Member, National Council of Istiqlal and of its Central Committee (1965); Secretary of Bar of Rabat (1971); Member, Executive Committee of Istiqlal Party (1974); Minister of Housing (1977-80); Minister of Social Affairs and Handicrafts (1981-86); Ambassador of Morocco to the Arab League (1986); Ambassador of Morocco to France until 1994; presently Secretary General of Istiqlal Party. **Addr.:** Istiqlal Party, 4 Charia Ibnou Toumert, Rabat, Morocco.

FASSI-FIHRI (Ahmed), Moroccan administrator. **Born** in 1938 in Oujda, Morocco. **Married**, four children. **Dipl.:** Degree in law, Administrative Studies. **Career:** Head of the Private Secretariat of the Minister of Interior (1956); Head of the Office of the Minister of Minerals and Geology (1958); Attaché to the Office of the Minister of Foreign Affairs (1959); Chargé d'Affaires, Moroccan Embassy in Berne, Switzerland (1960); Governor of the city of Meknes (1963); Head of the Office of the Minister of Sahara and Mauritania (1964); Founder and Director of the School of Library and Information Sciences (ESI) (1974-78); Founder and Director of the Centre National de Documentation (CND), Ministry of Planning (since 1967). **Publ.:** articles in the field of information and Documentation in Arabic and French. **Awards:** Order of Ridha Morocco (1975, 1980); Commander of the Crowns Order, Morocco (1987); Officer of the crowns order, Morocco (1992). **Member** and Founder of the Moroccan Association of Librarians and Information Scientists (AMI); Prior President of the National Association of Information Scientists. Secretary-General of Moroccan Society for Future Studies. **Prof. Addr.:** 3 Lotissement Nezha, Charia Bir Kacem, Tel.: 75-20-50, Rabat, Morocco.

FASSI (Mahdy Abdallah, al), Saudi film director. **Born** in 1944. **Dipl.:** B.Sc. (Directing) Cinema Institute, Cairo. **Career:** Directed several motion pictures and TV serials, including Shu'lah la Tantafi (Inextinguishable Flame), cinema film, al-Qina' (The Mask), TV. **Honours:** winner of First Prize, Cinema Institute; Special Appreciation, Lucarno Festival. **Addr.:** Jeddah TV, Tel.: 6445222, Jeddah, Saudi Arabia.

FATANI (Ebtissam M. Saleh, Mrs.), Saudi academic. **Born** on April 1, 1943, in Mecca, Saudi Arabia. **Dipl.:** M.A. (Social Work). **Career:** English language Teacher, Secondary School; Assistant Headmistress, Dar al-Tarbyah, Riyadh; Headmistress, same; Assistant Supervisor, King Abdulaziz University Director of Administration, girls' College, Umm al-Qura University, Mecca; one of the founders, Feminine Cooperative Society for Handywork; member of Board of Welfare Society, Taif and Umm al-Qura, Makkah; took an active part in the institution of the Nursery and Kindergarten Sections, Umm al-Qura Welfare Society. **Hobbies:** Reading, social work, writing. **Prof. Addr.:** Umm al-Qura University, Girls' Section, Tel.: 5564770, Mecca. **Prof. Addr.:** Tel.: 5431283, Mecca, Saudi Arabia.

FATANI (Hameedah Abdul Rahman, Mrs.), Saudi academic. **Born** in 1939 in Mecca, Saudi Arabia. **Dipl.:** B.A. (Education and Psychology); preparing for High Islamic Studies Diploma. **Career:** teacher (1961); Assistant Headmistress (1963); Headmistress (1970); General Inspector (1971); Director, Summer Courses; Dean, Girls' College of Education, Mecca (since 1975); ex-member, Umm al-Qura Welfare Soociety; supervises cultural weekly meetings in the college; member of Board, Girls' College of Education, Jeddah; coordinator with the Algerian Women's Cultural Delegation to Saudi Arabia, 1977. **Publ.:** several journalistic articles. **Hobbies:** Reading, diction and elocution. **Addr.:** al-Jaza'er Street, al'Utaibah, Tel.: 5434983 (Office) and 5424156 (Home), Mecca, Saudi Arabia.

FATANI (Jamal Abdul Qadir), Saudi academic. **Born** in 1936 in Mecca, Saudi Arabia. **Dipl.:** M.B.B.CH., Ph.D. **Career:** Former Lecturer, Department of Anatomy, Faculty of Medicine, King Saud University, Riyadh; Assistant Professor and later Associate Professor, Department of Anatomy, Faculty of Medicine, King Saud University, Riyadh; Chairman and Head of the Department of Anatomy, Faculty of Medicine, King Saud University, Riyadh; member, King Saud University Council, Vice Dean and later Dean, Faculty of Medicine; member, Association of Anatomy, American University, Beirut; British International Association of Anatomy; member of Constituent Committee, Faculty of Medicine; attended the following International Conferences of Anatomy: Ninth International European Conference of Anatomy, Manchester, Tenth International Conference of Anatomy, Tokyo, International Conference on Anatomy for the Middle East Countries, American University of Beirut, International Conference of Mexico, National Conference of Anatomy, Patha, India, International American Association of Anatomy Congress Argentina, International Symposium on Morphological Sciences, Rio de Janeiro (Brazil). **Publ.:** several papers published in International Journals. **Hobbies:** Travel, sports. **Addr.:** Department of Anatomy, College of Medicine, King Saud University, P.O.Box 2925, Riyadh, Saudi Arabia.

FATANI (Khalid), Saudi Certified Public Accountant. **Born** in 1938, in Makkah, Saudi Arabia. **Dipl.:** B. Com. **Career:** Chief Accountant, Ministry of Finance (1963-1964); Director, Financial Department, Ministry of Agriculture and Water (1964-1969); General Manager, of Dallah Establishment (1969-1970); General Manager, Daghistani and A.Wahab Accountants and Auditors (1970-1972); Senior Partner Coopers & Fatani & Co. (1976-1978); Owner and Director-General Fatani Legal Accountants Firm in Riyadh, Jeddah and Dammam (1972-1981). Fellow of the Middle East Society of Associated Accountants. Partner, Executive President, Saudi Accounting Bureau (1982-1996). Owner, Saudi Accounting Bureau (1996-till Now); Member of Moores Rowland International (1982-till Now); Member of High Committee for Accounts in the Kingdom of Saudi Arabia (1979-1982); Member of Saudi Accounting Association (1989-1992); Member of Professional Ethics Committee (Saudi Organization for Certified Accounts - SOCPA) (1997-till now; Chief Assistant of Professional Ethics Committee (SOCPA); Fellow of Arab Society of Certified Accountants (UK); Member of American Administration Institute; Participate in Several Lectures for Developing Accounting Principles in Saudi Arabia under the Supervision of Riyadh University; Member of Saudi Organization for Certified Public Accountants. **Hobbies:** Reading and Tourism. **Address:** P.O.Box 376 Riyadh 11411, Saudi Arabia.

FATANI (Mohamed Noor Yaseen), Saudi academic/associate professor of civil engineering. **Born** on January 15, 1944 in Mecca, Saudi Arabia. **Educ.:** Bachelor of Science in Agricultural Engineering from California State Polytechnic University, majoring in soil and water area. As an honor student in both high shcool and university, his scholarship was extended for Master of Science in Civil Engineering. He obtained the M.Sc. from the University of Arisona, Tucson, Arizona, USA; Also awarded a scholarship to obtain Ph.D. in Civil Engineering. **Dipl.:** B.Sc. in Agricultural Engineering; M.Sc in Civil Engineering (1973); Ph.D. in Civil Engineering. **Career:** in 1973 appointed Material Engineer, Materials and Laboratory dept., Ministry of Cimmunications, then Assistant Director, and in 1974 Director of the said department, also involved in training all new engineers joining the Ministry. He joined King Abdulaziz University in 1980; Assigned to establish and direct the Scientific Reseach Department in the college of Engineering (1981); Appointed Vice Dean for Research and Academic Affairs (1982); then within eight months elected Dean of the College of Engineering for a three-year term; Elected Chaiman of the Civil Engineering Department in (1989) for a period of two years. He has chaired many committees on the professional, administrative and academic affairs and worked extensively both as a professional engineer and a researcher. He organised the first Saudi Engineering Conference, the largest gathering of engineers in the Kingdom. **Dipl.:** translation of book on Soil Mechanics: Use of Sulphur in Asphaltic Pavement, Sand Bricks. **Prof. Addr.:** Civil Engineering Department, King Abdulaziz University, P.O.Box 9027, Tel.: 6879202, 6879130, 6879404, Telex: 601141 Kauni SJ, Jeddah, Saudi Arabia.

FATANI (Zakariya, Yahya Abdallah), Saudi scientist and civil servant. **Born** in 1938 in Mecca, Saudi Arabia. **Married,** with children. **Educ.:** Secondary and higher. **Dipl.:** B.Sc. (Geology). **Career:** Assistant Director Geological Administration; now Director of Technical Services Administration, Directorate General of Mineral Resources. **Sport:** Swimming. **Hobbies:** Reading and music. **Prof. Addr.:** P.O.Box 345, Tel.: 33133, 33359, Jeddah. **Priv. Addr.:** Tel.: 33820, Jeddah, Saudi Arabia.

FATHI (Sayed, Abdulrahim), Egyptian academic. **Born** on May 5, 1935 in Egypt. **Married** in 1961 in Cairo to Hikmat Ali, 3 children: Hani, Mohamed and Sameh. **Educ.:** Ein Shams University, Cairo; University of Birmingham, England. **Dipl.:** Ph.D. in Psychology and Special Education. **Career:** Ein Shams University, Cairo (1968-70); University of Sanaa, Yemen (1970-77); King Saud University, Saudi Arabia (1977-78); Kuwait University (1978-86); Dean, College of Education, Arabian Gulf University, Bahrain, Teaching - Counseling - Research Consultation in Special Education and Teaching programs for the Handicapped (1986- to present). **Sports:** Running. **Hobby:** Reading. **Prof. Addr.:** Arabian Gulf University, P.O.Box 26671, Tel.: 265211, Manama, Bahrain. **Priv.**

Addr.: Arabian Gulf University Complex, Tel.: 440252, Manama, Bahrain.

FATIH (Mohamad Beshara, al), Sudanese army officer. **Born** in 1932 in al-Obeid, Sudan. **Son** of Beshara al-Fatih. **Educ.:** Military Academy (1950-52); training course in Egypt; Staff course at Camberley, UK. **Career:** Commissioned into Artillery; Private Secretary to President Abboud (1958-64); Staff Appointment at Khartoum (1964-65); Garrison Commander, Yei (1965); joined Instructors' Staff at the Sudanese Staff College; Commandant, Staff College (1970); Adjutant General (1971); appointed Deputy Chief of Staff (1972). **Addr.:** Ministry of Defence, Khartoum, Sudan.

FATTAL (Dia Allah, el), Syrian diplomat. **Born** in 1927. **Married**, two children. **Educ.:** Syrian University, Damascus; School of International Service, American University, Washington, D.C., USA. **Career:** With Legation to Holy See, Rome (1952-57); Second Secretary, Addis Ababa (1958-61), Second, then First Secretary, Washington, D.C. (1962-65); Chargé d'Affaires (1965-67); Counsellor, Mission to UN, New York (1967-72); Ambassador to Holy See, Rome (1975-81); Permanent Representative to UN, Geneva (1981-86), Permanent Representative to UN, New York (1981-). **Addr.:** Ministry of Foreign Affairs, Damascus, Syria.

FAWZI (Ahmad), Jordanian engineer and statesman. **Born** in 1927 in Amman. **Educ.:** Baghdad University. **Dipl.:** of Engineer. **Career:** Joined Ministry of Public Works (1950-53), Assistant Under-Secretary and Under-Secretary (1953-64); Secretary of Amman Municipality (1964-67); Minister of Rural and Municipal Affairs in the Cabinet of Mr. Bahjat at-Talhouni (October 1967- April 1968); Minister of Public Works (April 1968); Minister of State and Minister of Transports (1968-69); Secretary of Amman Municipality (1968-73). **Awards:** Order of al-Kawkab (1st rank), Order of the Istiqlal (1st rank), Order of an-Nahda, Order of Tunisian Republic, etc... **Priv. Addr:** Jabal Amman, Tel.: 41888, Amman, Jordan. **Prof. Addr.:** c/o Municipality of Amman, Amman, Jordan.

FAWZI (Samiha al-Sayyid), Egyptian academic. **Born** in 1951 in Cairo, Egypt. **Married**, 2 daughters. **Educ.:** Cairo University, Egypt. **Dipl.:** M.Sc. in Economics. **Career:** Assistant Lecturer, Faculty of Economics and Political Science, Cairo University (1972), Assistant Professor (1979), Professor (1984-). **Prof. Addr.:** Faculty of Economics and Political Science, Cairo University, Egypt. **Priv. Addr.:** 10H Nile Street, Giza, Egypt.

FAYALA (Mohamad), Tunisian professor. **Born** on August 20, 1927. **Married**, 2 children. **Educ.:** Secondary Studies, Sadiki College (Tunis), Higher Studies, University of Bordeaux (France). **Career:** Schoolmaster; Headmaster (Lycée de Garçons Sousse) (Tunisia); Headmaster and School Inspector. **Member:** Tunisian Association of Mathematical Sciences, Tunisian Commission for the Advancement of the teaching of Mathematics (Unesco), Sporting Association of Sousse (1958), Municipal Counsellor (Sousse 1969). **Publ.:** Author of several books on mathematics. **Award:** Officer, Order of the Republic. **Addr.:** Lycée de Garçons, Sousse, Tunisia.

FAYEZ (Akef, Mithkal, al), Jordanian politician. **Born** in 1924 in Jordan. **Son** of Mithkal al-Fayez. **Educ.:** Aley School (Lebanon). **Career:** President Jordanian Agricultural Association (1945); Chief of Protocol for tribes, Royal Palace (1946); Co-Founder, Jordanian People's Party, Member then President House of the Representatives (1947); Speaker (1962); Minister of Agriculture (1957), of Development (1958), of Defence (1959), of Communications (1960), of Public Works (1961-62); Minister of Communications, Tourism and Antiquities (1967); Minister of Communications (October 1967- December 1968); Vice Prime Minister and Minister of the Interior (1970-76); Minister of State for Prime Ministerial Affairs (1970); Senator (1976). **Awards:** Renaissance Medal, 1st Class; Star of Jordan, 1st Class; Iraqi Rafidain Order, 1st Class; Independence Medal, 2nd Class; Moroccan Military Order, 1st Class. **Addr.:** Amman, Jordan.

FAYEZ (Khaled, Mohamed, Al, Dr.), Saudi. Chief executive officer, Gulf Investment Corporation, Safat, Kuwait. **Born** in 1946 in Saudi Arabia. **Son** of Mohamed al-Fayez. **Married**, 3 daughters and 1 son. **Education:** 1968 B.A. Economics, Whitman College, Walla Walla, Washington State, USA; 1970 M.A. International Relations, Fletcher School of Law & Diplomacy, Tufts University, Medford, Mass., USA; 1971 M.A.L.D. (Master of Arts in Law & Diplomacy), Fletcher School of Law & Diplomacy, Tufts University, Medford, Mass., USA; 1974 ph.D. Economics & International Relations, Fletcher School of Law & Diplomacy, Tufts University, Medford, Mass., USA. **Career History:** 1974-1976 a) Economic Advisor, Ministry of Finance and National Economy, Saudi Arabia; b) Economist and Senior Credit Officer, Saudi Industrial Development Fund, Saudi Arabia. 1976-1983 General Manager, Gulf International Bank B.S.C., Bahrain; 1984 to date Chief Executive Officer, Gulf Investment Corporation, Kuwait. **Board Membership:** Vice Chairman, Gulf International Bank B.S.C., Bahrain; Member of the Board and Member of the Audit Committee, Saudi International Bank, London, UK; Board Member of Riyadh Bank, Riyadh, Saudi Arabia. **Sport:** Swimming. **Hobby:** Reading. **Credit Card:** American Express. **Prof. Addr.:** Gulf Investment Corporation P.O.Box 3402 Safat, 13035 Kuwait, Tel.: 2431911, Kuwait.

FAYEZ (Mohamad Ali, al), Saudi former minister. **Born** in 1937 at Hail. **Dipl.:** B.A. (Law), M.A. (Public Administration). **Career:** Legal Adviser, the Council of Ministers (1960-70); Governor and then Chairman, Board of Directors, the General Organization for Social Insurance; Deputy Minister of Labour and Social Affairs; Minister of Labour and Social Affairs (1983 to Aug. 1995). **Addr.:** Riyadh, Saudi Arabia.

FAYEZ (Mohamad Hamed, H.), Saudi engineer. **Born** in 1943 in Jeddah, Saudi Arabia. **Dipl.:** M.Sc. (Civil Engineering), Swiss Institute of Technology (Zurich). **Career:** project Manager, Projects & Trading Co. (1968-73); member of Board, Saudi Arabian Electricity Corporation; member of Board of Shareholders, National Quarries Co., of Concrete Co. and of Fast Co.; honorary member of Saudi Arabian Union Club; General Manager, FAST Contracting Co. **Hobby:** Reading. **Addr.:** P.O.Box 5180, Jeddah, Saudi Arabia.

FAYEZ (Zuhair, Hamid), Saudi architect. **Born** in 1944 in Jeddah (Saudi Arabia). **Married**, children. **Educ.:** Secondary and University of Colorado (USA). **Dipl.:** B.Sc., M.Sc. (Architecture). **Career:** Architect in American practice, Denver, Colorado (USA); introduced the most up-to-date architectural techniques into Saudi Arabia (one of his achievements is building the air supported stadium, University of Riyadh). **Sport:** Football. **Prof. Addr.:** Zuhair Fayez Office, P.O.Box 5445, Jeddah 21422, Tel. 6547171, Fax: 6543430, Jeddah, Saudi Arabia.

FAYYAD (Khalid, Abdallah, al), Jordanian politician. **Born** in 1927 in Aeir al Ghusoun, Tulkarm, Jordan. **Son** of Abdallah al Fayyad. **Married**, five children. **Educ.:** Diploma in General Agriculture (1946); specialist course of orchards, California Polytechnic, USA (1961). **Career:** Director of Agriculture, Nablus (1967); seconded as Director of Agriculture, Abu Dhabi (1967-68); retired (1973); member of Tulkarm Jordan Chamber of Deputies; appointed by HM King Hussain as member of National Consultative Council (since 1978). **Medals:** Independence Medal, Jordan (1972). **Sport:** Walking. **Hobbies:** Political Science, Agricultural Sciences. **Addr.:** P.O.Box 8212, Tel.: 39811, Amman, Jordan.

FAYYAD (Mohamed Suleiman, Abdel Mohti), Egyptian writer. **Born** on Feb. 7, 1929 in Barhamtouche, Mansura Governorate, Egypt. **Educ.:** Higher Education in Arabic Studies, Azhar University, Egypt (1956); International Teaching Diploma, Azhar University, Egypt (1959). **Career:** Teacher of Arabic in Salt Secondary School, Jordan (1956-1957); Teacher at the Dawadmy Preparatory School, Saudi Arabia (1960-1961); at Dar Al Moallimine in Taef, Saudi Arabia (1961-1962); Secondary Badary School, Assiut Governorate (1962); Preparatory Ras Tine School (1962); Abbassiya Secondary School Moharram Bey, Alexandria, Egypt (1963-1965); Dar Al Moallimine, Giza, Egypt (1965-1978); Secretary at Dar Al Moallimine Library, Giza, Egypt (1978-1979) than Agent (1979-1984) after that, he resigned and dedicated himself to writing. Acting Editor and writer in Egypt for Radios & Televisions (1955-1956); Police (1957-1959); Alchahr (1960); Writer and Editor at Al Joumhouria Newspaper (1960); Assistant Editor "Ibdah" Magazine, Egypt (1983-1985 and 1992-1993); Egyptian Arbitration Committee Member in Stories Writing Competition (1969), at Al Hilal Newspaper in Egypt (1989), He supervised 2 issues of Al Hilal Magazine (1968-1969); Linguistic specialist for Arab Computer Projects for Arabic Programs at the International Society (Sakhr) Kuwait (1988-1989), and IBM (Egypt) (1989); Correspondent, Beirut Literature Magazine in Egypt (1972-1973); in 1954 his stories were published in Magazines at; Al Adab, Aklam, Police, Chahr, Mawkaf al Adabi, Al Arabi, Mountada, Magazine, Al Kateb, Ibdah, Al Hilal, Saout el Kuwait, and broadcasted some at the Radio station, Egypt and BBC, London. **Publ.:** Collection of short stories and novels including: **Short stories:** Atshan ya Sabaya, Egypt (1961), Wa Wa baadouna at Toufane, (Egypt 1968) (Irak 1976), Ahzane Hozairane, Beirut (1969), Al Ouyoune, Beirut (1972), Zaman alsamt waldabab, Beirut (1974), Wafat Amel Matbaha, Egypt (1983), Al Ziïba, Egypt (1989), Zat al Ouyoune asaliah, Egypt (1992). **Short Novels:** Alkarine wa la Ahad (2 novels), Egypt (1982), Alsourah wal zoll wal fallah Alfassih (2 novels), (Irak 1976), (Egypt 1985). Voices: Irak (1972), Egypt (1978), Paris in French (1990), Münich in German, (1992) London in English (1993), New York in English (1993) and a Group of Stories: Volume 1 (1993), Volume 2 and 3 (1994) in Cairo and other publications. **Members:** Writers Union, Journalists Union, Cinematographic Union, etc. **Awards:** Several academic. **Addr.:** The General Egyptian Book Organisation, Corniche el-Nil, Bulaz, Cairo, Egypt.

FAYYAD (Zeid Abdulaziz Zeid, al), Saudi educator. **Born** in 1930 at Rawdat Sudair. **Dipl.:** Graduate, Faculty of Shari'a (Islamic Law), Riyadh. **Career:** Member, Ifta' (Islamic Decisions) board; Instructor, Religious Institute, Faculty of Shari'a, Imam Muhamad Ibn Saud Islamic University, Riyadh; member, Presidency of Jurisdiction; Assistant Director of Libraries, Ministry of Education, General Director of Libraries; member Islamic Jurisprudence Conference, Directors of Education Conference, Riyadh and several information conferences. **Publ.:** several articles in newspapers and magazines; broadcasted speeches; eleven published books and manuscripts. **Hobbies:** Research, reading, writing, collecting newspaper cuttings on various subjects. **Addr.:** P.O.Box 637, Tel.: 4024753 (Home), Riyadh, Saudi Arabia.

FEILAT (Fahmi, Areslan, Abul), Jordanian executive. **Born** on May 11, 1960 in Karak, Jordan. **Son** of Areslan Ahmed Abul Feilat **and** Mrs. Seham Asaad al-Jaabari. **Married** on November 16, 1986 in Kuwait, 1 child, Osama (June 1988). **Educ.:** High School of Karak, Jordan (1966-78); B.Sc. Polytechnic School, Middlesborough, England. **Dipl.:** Advanced level, Coolchester Institute of Higher Education, Coolchester, England. **Career:** Sales Manager

(1975-78); Site Engineer (1982-85); Construction Manager (1985-88); Marketing work for an American company in the Middle East; Manager of Khalifa Bin Khalid Trading and Construction Company Limited (trading section, water drilling section and contracting section) (1988-to present). **Sports:** Swimming, tabble tennis, padminton, snooker. **Hobbies:** Travelling and drawing. **Member:** I.A.P.A. **Prof. Addr.:** P.O.Box 9825, Doha, Tel.: (974)448-565, Qatar. **Priv. Addr.:** P.O.Box 425556 Amman, Tel.: (962-6)602-721, Amman, Jordan.

FEKIH (Mungi), Tunisian politician. **Born** on November 25, 1935 in Kairouan, Tunisia. **Married,** 3 children. **Educ.:** Maîtrise de Langue et Litterature Arabe. **Career:** Governor of Kairouan, Tunisia; Official, Arab Bank, African Economic Development Department, Tunis, Tunisia; Cabinet Chief and Director of the Office, Secretary General of the Arab League (1979-80). **Addr.:** Tunis, Tunisia.

FELLAGUE-ARIOUAT (Mustafa), Algerian international civil servant. **Born** on January 31, 1931 in Blida, Algiers (Algeria). **Married. Educ.:** Training School, Algiers (1951-52); National Centre of Specialised Pedagogy, Beaumont (France, 1945-55); Institute of Biometrics & Vocational Guidance, Faculty of Science, University of Marseilles (1959-61). **Dipl.:** Certificate of Pedagogy (1952). **Career:** Military Service (1956-58); Teacher, Department of Education (1958-59 & 1953-56); Vocational Guidance Adviser, Department of Education, Algeria (1961-63); Head, Training & Recruitment, ESSO Standard, Algeria (1963-64); Personnel officer, World Health Organisation (WHO), Congo (1965-68); Personnel Officer, WMO, Geneva (1968-72); Chief, Personnel Division, WMO, Geneva (Switzerland) (1972 to 1987); Chief, Common Services Division, WMO, Geneva (Switzerland); retired 1991. **Sports:** Bowling, tennis and fishing. **Hobbies:** Bridge, chess and reading. **Addr.:** Algiers, Algeria.

FELLOUSE (Rachid, al), Moroccan academic. **Born** on July 30, 1937. **Married,** 2 children. **Educ.:** Moroccan School of Administration, Higher Studies at the Moroccan School of Administration. **Dipl.:** Primary Diploma, Licence in Law. **Career:** Professor at Regional School of Instructors; Head of the Pedagogy Bureau to the Delegation of the Ministry of National Education, Head of the Pedagogy Organization to the Ministry of National Education, in charge of the Instruction Division. **Member:** Treasurer, Higher Council of Popular Culture, Association of Old Pupils of the Moroccan School of Administration, National Council of the Party of Istiqlal, Secretary-General, Association of Young Arabs. **Publ.:** Author of several plays and novels published in journals and broadcast on the R.T.M. **Addr.:** 4, Rue Marassa, Blvd. Amar Ibn Yassir, Rabat, Morocco.

FENJIRO (Abdeljalil), Moroccan News Agency Executive. **Born** in Rabat, Morocco on August 5, 1938. **Educ.:** graduated from the Institute of Moroccan High Studies, from the International Centre for Higher Education of Journalism (Strasbourg, France, 1965). **Career:** Reporter, Journalist, editor in chief, Director of Information in Maghreb Arabe Presse (Rabat) from 1962 to 1974; Director General of MAP since January 1974; former correspondent to various media bodies such as Newsweek, the Office of French Radio and Television, Associated Press; former editorialist at the Moroccan Television; senior lecturer in the High Institute of Journalism (Rabat). **Decorated** Ouissam Alarch of Knight Order (Morocco), Chevalier d'Ordre National du Merite (France); recipient of the Certificate of consideration and merit delivered by ALESCO-UNESCO Club, (Rabat); decorated by the government of Egypt, 1964, government of Tunisia, 1968, government of Italy, 1991. He is a founding member of the Non-Aligned News Agencies Pool (NANAP), of the International Islamic News Agencies (IINA), of the Federation of Arab News Agencies (FANA), of the Panafrican News Agencies (PANA), of Maghreban News Agencies Pool and of the Alliance of Mediterranean News Agencies (AMAN) of which he is President. **Prof. Addr.:** Maghreb Arabe Presse, Avenue Allal Ben Abdellah, P.O.Box 1049, Rabat 10000, Morocco.

FENJIRO (Abdelkader), Moroccan Hotelier. **Born** on January 7, 1936 in Rabat. **Married** on November 10, 1962 in Rabat to Naget Rachid, 2 children: Nabil (04.8.1966), Kenza (12.12.1972). **Educ.:** Secondary studies, Ecole Hotelière. **Dipl.:** 2 Hostelry degrees, Cooking, Hostelry Administration. **Career:** Probation in France (1954-1956), Director General: Hotel Tour Hassan, Rabat (1958-1963); Hotel Palais Jamaî, Fes (1963-1966); Hotel La Mamounia, Marrakech (1966-1971). **Awards:** Civic French Merit. Arts Sciences and Letters. **Sports:** Tennis, Golf. **Hobbies:** Nature, Plants, Environment, Ecology. **Member:** Rotary Club Koutoubia, Marrakech. Since 1969. founding owner and administrator of the "Roseraie" Hôtel Résidence, Located in the high Atlas Mountains (1000 meters Altitude). One hour drive from Marrakech, the Roseraie is a touristic resort, in an ecological and naturalwise environment. Bungalows, Gastronomy, swimming pools, Tennis, horse stables, spa and health center etc... **Credit Cards:** Visa, Access, Diners. **Professional Adress:** La Roseraie, Val d'Ouirgane, P.O.Box 769, Marrakech, Morocco. **Office in Marrakech:** Hivernage. Rue Harroun Errachid, Immeuble KATY'S R.C. N°2, Tel.: 212 4 43 91 28, Fax: 212 4 43 91 30. **Private Tel.:** 212 4 32 92 64.

FESSILI (Mahmoud, Said, al), Tunisian businessman. **Born** in 1930 in Djerba, Tunisia. **Married,** 5 children. **Educ.:** Business studies. **Career:** Director of various companies (1967-); Company Manager, STPCM (1967-70); Export Consultant, Kléber SA (1967-73); Vice President, Chambre Syndicale du Caoutchouc and UTICA (1975); Chairman and General Manager, STPCM (1974-), Sotromar SA (1980-). **Prof. Addr.:** Rue No.15 La Charguie,

2035 Tunis-Carthage, Tunis, Tunisia. **Priv. Addr.:** P.O.Box 19, 2015 Le Kroni, Tunis, Tunisia.

FEZZANI (Mohamed Ali, Hussein), Libyan bank manager. **Born** in 1938 in Benghazi, Libya. **Son** of Hussein Fezzani. **Married** in 1966, 3 sons, 1 daughter. **Educ.:** Secondary School Certificate. **Career:** Barclays Bank, Benghazi, Libya (1956-60); British Bank of the Middle East, Benghazi, Libya (1960-65); Assistant Manager, Bank of North Africa, Benghazi, Libya (1966-70); Wahda Bank, Benghazi Libya (1970-75); Libyan Arab Foreign Bank, Tripoli, Libya (1975); Assistant General Manager, UBAF Bank Ltd., London, UK (1975-80); Deputy General Manager, UBAF Bank Ltd., London, UK (1980-85); Deputy Chief Executive & General Manager, UBAF Bank Ltd., London (1985-). Director: Arab International Bank, Cairo. **Member:** Anglo-Arab Association; Arab Bankers' Association. **Hobbies:** Reading and Music. **Addr.:** 8-10 Mansion House Place, Tel.: 44/20/7648/7777, Fax: 44/20/7600/3318, Tlx: 22961, London EC4N 8BJ, UK.

FIDO (Abdullahi, Ali), Somali Professor of Psychiatry. **Born** on July 1, 1946 at Mogadishu, Somalia. **Son** of Ali Fido (Businessman) **and** Mrs. Ossobo Fido. **Married** on June 30, 1976 to Pat Fido, 3 children: Mohamed (15.5.1973); Miriam (25.12.1980); Sara (10.9.1986). **Educ.:** Crimean Medical School (USSR), American University of Beirut (Lebanon), Edinburgh University (UK). **Dipl.:** M.D., D.P.M., M.R.C. Psych. **Career:** General Medical Practitioner; Registrar in Psychiatry, Consultant in Psychiatry, Professor of Psychiatry. **Other Information:** Fluent in 5 languages: Somali, Italian, English, Russian, Arabic. **Awards:** Honour degree MB. BS; W.H.O. medal as the best fellow; Best clinical teacher prize. **Sports:** Football, Basketball, Tennis. **Hobbies:** Music, Reading, Dancing. **Member:** The Crockfords Int. Ltd. **Credit Card:** Visa. **Prof. Addr.:** Kuwait University, Faculty of Medicine, P.O.Box 24923 Safat, Tel.: (965)5312300, (965)5330467, Kuwait 13110, Kuwait. **Priv. Addr.:** P.O.Box 24923 Safat, Tel.: 5321837, Kuwait.

FIER (Mohamad Hussein, al), Saudi academic. **Born** in October 1945 in Taif, Saudi Arabia. **Dipl.:** Ph.D. (Economic Geography), U.S.A. **Career:** Headmaster, Tarabah Intermediate School (1968); Assistant Professor, Department of Geography, Faculty of Education (1968-70); Professor, Faculty of Arts and Faculty of Education, King Saud University since 1977; former Supervisor, Social Club, Faculty of Education and current Supervisor, Social Club, Faculty of Arts, King Saud University; member of American Association of Geographers; member of Archaology Society, King Saud University; ex-member of the Muslim Students' Organization in the U.S.A. and Canada. **Hobbies:** Poetry, swimming. **Prof. Addr.:** Faculty of Arts, King Saud University, Tel.: 4810000, Riyadh, Saudi Arabia.

FIGHI (Hadi, Mohamad), Lybian official. **Career:** Former Director and Assistant General Manager, Libyan Arab Foreign Bank, Tripoli, Libya: Director, Banco Arabe Espanol SA, Madrid, Spain; Director, Arab Bank for Investment and Foreign Trade, Abu Dhabi, UAE; Vice Chairman, Banque Arabe Libyenne Mauritanienne Pour le Commerce Extérieur et le Développement, Nouakchott, Mauritania. **Addr.:** Tripoli, Libya.

FIKRY (Mohamad Essam, Aziz), Egyptian physician. **Born** on May 1, 1923 in Cairo. **Son** of Aziz Fikry **and** Mrs., née Jamal Sabri. **Married** on April 30, 1954 to Miss Haifa Azab, 2 daughters: Nadia and Hala. **Educ.:** Alexandria Univesity. **Dipl.:** Bachelor of Medicine (1948), M.D. (1950); Doctor of Medicine (1953). **Career:** Registrar, Medicine Department, Alexandria University (1951-53), Tutor Department of Medicine (1953-60), Assistant Professor (1960), Professor 1967, Chairman Department Int. Medicine Private Practice Medicine, Alexandria since 1958. **Publ.:** Author of studies on gastro-enterology and geriatric medicine, discovery normal values for gastric and pancreatic secretions and intestinal absorption, discovery of low gastric and pancreatic secretions and reduced intestinal absorption in patients with fibrosis of liver due to schistosomiasis; Studies normal functions in the elderly and effect of disease on these functions. **Publisher:** 26 books in internal medicine. **Prof. Addr.:** 22, Chamber of Commerce Place, Alexandria, Egypt.

FILALI (Abdellatif, Dr.), Moroccan former Prime Minister, Minister of Foreign Affairs and Cooperation. **Born** on February 26, 1929. **Dipl.:** Ph.D., University of Paris, France. **Career:** Minister Plenipotentiary (1957), he was appointed Chargé d'Affaires of the Kingdom of Morocco to the United Nations from 1958 to 1959. Chargé d'Affaires of the Kingdom of Morocco in France in 1960 and 1961, he was appointed by His Majesty the King, upon His Majesty's accession to the Throne, Director of the Royal Cabinet and the Royal Protocol from 1961 to 1963. He was later successively designated as Ambassador of His Majesty the King to the Benelux countries in 1964, Ambassador to the Popular Republic of China in February 1965 and Ambassador to Algeria in 1967. In 1968 he was appointed by His Majesty the King, Minister of Higher Education. After serving as Ambassador of His Majesty the King to Spain, he was designated as Minister of Foreign Affairs in September 1974, after which he was appointed anew Ambassador to Spain and, later in April 1978, Permanent Representative of the Kingdom of Morocco to the United Nations in New York. In April 1980, he was appointed Ambassador of His Majesty to London before he was elected Perpetual Secretary of the Academy of the Kingdom of Morocco, a task he was assigned until April 1982. On November 30, 1983, he was appointed Minister of Information. On February 16, 1985, His Majesty the King designated him as Minister of Foreign Affairs and Cooperation, Keeping the portfolio of Information until November, 1985. In August 1992, he was disignated as Minister of State for Foreign Affairs and Cooperation. On May 25, 1994, His Majesty the King assigned to him the task of constituting the government. On June 7, 1994, He, as Prime Minister, introduced the new government to His Majesty the King, while keeping the portfolio of the Foreign Affairs. On January 31, 1995, upon being summoned by His Majesty to lead a new government, he was appointed Prime Minister, Minister of Foreign Affairs and Cooperation; Appointed Minister of State and Minister for Foreign Affairs and Cooperation (March 1998 - April 1999). **Addr.:** Rabat, Morocco.

FILALI (Abdulaziz, al), Moroccan magistrate. **Born** in June 1924. **Educ.:** Lycée Gouraud (Rabat), Lycée Lyautey (Casablanca), Ecole Nationale d'Organisation Economique et Sociale (Paris), Institut des Hautes Etudes (Rabat). **Dipl.:** Doctor of Law. **Career:** Barrister at Law (Casablanca 1951-55); President Court Appeal of Tangier and Court Appeal of Rabat since 1955; President of the Centre Africain de Formation et de Recherche Administratives pour le Développement since 1964; member, Commission of Arabization of Code of Commercial Law; Counciliator and Arbitrator, International Centre of Settlement of Investment Disputes, Washington DC; Arbitrator, Franco-Arab Chamber of Commerce (1976); President of the Arbitrary Council of the Maritime Chamber of Casablanca; Chargé de Mission de Conseiller; Ministry of Habous and Islamic Affairs, **Dist.:** Doctor Honoris Causa of Grenoble University. **Publ.:** "Notes Judiciaires" (in French), "Marriage in Moroccan Law" (in arabic). **Addr.:** Angle Blvd. Alexandre 1er et Blvd. de la Grande Ceinture, Casablanca, Morocco.

FINAISH (Mohamad), Libyan international civil servant. **Born** on March 13, 1936 in Tripoli, Libya. **Married,** with children. **Educ.:** Faculty of Commerce, University of Cairo (1955-67). **Dipl.:** B.Com (1959), M.A. (Economics) (1967), Ph.D. (Economics) (1972). **Career:** Assistant to the Public Relations Manager, Libya Shell, Tripoli (1960-61); Foreign Relations Director, Senusi University, Beida (Libya 1962); Secretary General, Bank of Libya (1963-65); Director, Research Department, Central Bank of Libya (1972-73); Alternate Executive Director, International Monetary Fund (IMF), Washington (1974); Director, UBAF Arab American Bank, New-York (1975). **Addr.:** Tripoli, Libya.

FIRDAWCY (Mohammed, Larbi), Moroccan secretary general of Institute Hassan II of Agro and Vet. Medicine. **Born** on March 13, 1945 in Meknes, Morocco. **Son** of Bennasser Firdawcy (Inspector of Telecommunictions) **and** Mrs. Lekbira. **Married** in 1974 to Maria Bebbati, 3 children: Leila (1976), Omar (1979), Hamza (1985). **Educ.:** Institut National Agronomique (INA) Paris; Faculté des Lettres Sorbonne, Paris; Faculté des Sciences economiques, Université Montpellier. **Dipl.:** Agricultural Engineer; Speciality in Rural Economy; Certificate in Sociology; Doctor in Economical Sciences. **Career:** Professor in rural economy; Director, National School of Agriculture (Meknes); Director of Studies and Secretary General, Institute Hassan II; President of Association of Faculties of Agriculture in Africa (A.F.A.A.). **Work:** Expert in human resources and rural development. **Other Information:** Member National Bureau, Moroccan Economist Association; Member National Bureau, Moroccan Agricultural Engineers Association. **Hobbies:** History, Sociology, Music. **Prof. Addr.:** Institut Agronomique et Veterinaire Hassan II, P.O.Box 6202 Rabat Institute, Tel.: 778468, Telex: 36873, 360.89, Fax: 77.58.38, Rabat, Morocco.

FISHAWY (Saad Samuel, el, Dr.), Egyptian lawyer and financial adviser, residing in the USA. **Born** on February 20, 1924 in Tanta, Egypt. **Married** on September 15, 1960 to Miss Mona Yusuf Milad, 3 sons: Sani, Karim and Paul. **Dipl.:** B.A. (Honours), Law School, University of Cairo, Egypt (1940- June 1944); The Shari'a (Islamic Law) Special Award (1941); M.A. (Honours) in Civil Law and Economics, Law School, Cairo University, Egypt (1949 and 1950); Doctor of Law, University of Chicago Law School, Chicago, USA (June 1959). **Career:** District Attorney for Luxor (1945); Partner, Saba Habashy Law Firm, Cairo (1946-53); Private Law practice, Cairo (1953-57); Attorney, IBRD (World Bank), Washington DC, USA (September 1959- May 1963); General Counsel, Kuwait Fund for Arab Economic Development, Kuwait (May 1963- September 1966); Senior Counsel for the Arab Countries, Legal Department, IBRD, Washington DC, USA (September 1966- November 1974); Adviser, Finance Department, IBRD, Washington DC, USA (December 1974- November 1976); Special Adviser to the President, IBRD, Washington DC, USA (December 1976-95); First Foreign Lawyer accredited by the Court of Appeal of Wahington D.C., (1988); Consultant G. William Miller & Co., Inc. (1987 - to present). Professor of Shari'a (Islamic Law); Columbia Law School (1978-1979 and Georgetown University (1980-to present). **Languages:** Arabic, English, French, **Sports:** Swimming, Tennis. **Hobby:** Chess. **Publ.:** Freedom of Belief (1953). **Addr.:** 4155 North 27th Street, Arlington, Virginia 22207, Tel.: Residence (703) 5251244, U.S.A.

FITOURI (Mohamad), Tunisian lawyer and statesman. **Born** on April 4, 1925 in Kairaouan, Tunisia. **Married,** with two children. **Educ.:** Lycée Carnot, Tunis; Institut des Hautes Etudes, Tunis; Faculty of Law, Paris University. **Dipl.:** LL.B. **Career:** Lawyer (1952); Advocate Court of Cassation (1962); City Councillor, Tunis (1969); elected to National Assembly (November 1969); Minister of Justice (1970-71); Minister of Finance (1971). **Member:** Bar Association, Tunis; United Nations Economic and Social Council. **Addr.:** Tunis, Tunisia.

FOUAD (Fouad Abdulla), Saudi businessman **Born** on

July 6,1951 in Dammam, Saudi Arabia. **Son** of Abdulla Fouad Abdul Aziz Bubshait and Mrs. Maryam Hassan Sater. **Married** in 1976 to Nouriya Mohammad al-Fadhel (Bahraini), Four sons Abdulla Fouad Junior, Fahad Fouad, Mohammad Fouad and Ahmed Fouad. **Educ.:** al-Shamalaya School, Moharraq (Bahrain); al-Hidaya al-Kalifa School, Moharraq (Bahrain); American University in Beirut (Lebanon) **Dipl.:** BB.A (Bachelor of Business Administration) **Career:**President & Senior Executive of Abdulla Fouad Group of Companies, Saudi Arabia since 1975. **Director:** Mantech Co. Ltd; Mantech Computers & Telecommunication Ltd; Abdulla Fouad-Impalloy Ltd. Co. **Member:** National Association of Accountants (membership 1975); Association of Business Management (membership 1976); Young presidents Organization (Membership 1994). **Sport:** Tennis **Hobbies:** Fishing, music, photography. **Credit Card:** American Express, Visa; and Master Card. **Add**: P.O. Box 257, Dammam 31411, Saudi Arabia, Tel.: (03) 8324400, Fax: (03) 8345722, E-Mail info@abdulla-fouad.com.

FOZAN (Ibrahim Fozan, al), Saudi academic. **Born** in 1944 at Buraidah. Ph.D. (Literature & Criticism-Modern). **Career:** Associate Professor Faculty of Arabic language, Muhammad Ibn Saud Islamic University; Dean of Admissions Office (the same university). **Publ.:** Hijaz Literature between Imitation and Renovation, (1981), Cairo; Hijaz, Factors of its Modern Rise (1981), Riyadh; Verification of the Poems of Sheikh Saleh ibn Salman, (1981), Damascus; Hijaz Literature between al-Awwad and al-Qurashi; The Concept of Unity of the Poem in Arabic Literature. **Hobbies:** Research on modern Arab Peninsula Literature. **Addr.:** P.O.Box 15914, Tel.: 4773766, Riyadh, Saudi Arabia. **Priv. Addr.:** Tel.: 4788608, Riyadh, Saudi Arabia.

FRAYAN (Hamad Bin Mohamed, al), Saudi official. **Born** in 1937. **Educ.:** B.A. and M.A. in Islamic Sharia; Ph.D. in Administration and the System of Ruling in Islam. **Career:** Successively Administrative Inspector; Judicial Inspector; Director, Chief Justice's Office for Juridical Affairs; Deputy Director General; Director General of the Ministry of Justice; Assistant Deputy Minister; Presently, Deputy Minister for Administrative and Financial Affairs. Participated in Symposium of Upgrading Judges in the Arab World held in Morocco, sponsored by Council of Arab Ministers of Justice, Arab League, Participated in the conference of Arab Organisation for Social Defence; The Arab League, Cairo. **Member** of al-Gazira Organisation for Press, Printing and Publishing, Partime Lecturer in the Higher Institute of Judiciary. Former Judge (Qadi) in the Committee of the Commercial Disputes Settlement. Former Partime Lecturer in the Institue of Public Administration. **Publ.:** "Preservation of Money and Mind and their Impact in the Reformation of the Society", "The Opinions of Ibn Taimiya in the Administration and Ruling", "The Rudiments of Administrative thought in the Kingdom of Saudi Arabia" and Various essays and researches. Lectures and Broadcast Talks. **Hobbies:** Reading, swimming and shooting. **Prof. Addr.:** Ministry of Justice, P.O.Box 4525, Riyadh 11137, Saudi Arabia.

FREEMAN (Chas. W. Jr.), American diplomat. **Born** on March 2, 1943 in Washington, D.C., U.S.A. **Son** of Charles Wellman Freeman (Engineer/ Businessman) **and** Mrs. Carla Park Freeman (Architect). **Married** in 1962 in Massachusetts, U.S.A. to Patricia Trenery, 4 children: Carla Park Freeman, Charles W. Freeman III, Edward Andrew Freeman (Dec.), Nathaniel Trenery Freeman. Divorced in 1993. **Married** Margaret Van Wagenen Carpenter, Assistant Administrator for Asia and the Near East, Agency for International Development, 1993. **Educ.:** Universidad Nacional Autonoma de Mexico, Yale University; The Harvard Law School; Foreign Service Institute School of Chinese Language and Area Studies. **Dipl.:** B.A., J.D., Certificate in Interpreting (Chinese/ English). **Career:** Vice Consul, Madras, India (1966-68); Taiwan (1969-71); Department of State (1971-74); Visiting Fellow East Asian Legal Research, Harvard University (1974-75); Deputy Director for Taiwan (1975-76); Director, Public Programs (1976-77); Director, Plan's and Management (1977-78); Director, USIA Programs (1978-79); Acting U.S. Coordinator Refugee Programs (1979-); Director, Chinese Affairs Department of State (1979-81); Minister U.S. Embassy Beijing (1981-84); Minister U.S. Embassy Bangkok (1984-86); Principal Deputy Assistant Secretary of State for Africa (1986-89); U.S. Ambassador, Riyadh (1989-92); Assistant Secretary of Defence for Regional Security Affairs (1993-). **Awards:** Superior Honor Awards (1978&83); Presidential Meritorious Service Awards (1984-87-89); Group Distinguished Honor Award (1988); Secretary of Defence Meritorious Service Award (1991); Distinguished Honor Award (1991); Order of King Abdelaziz, First Class (1992). **Sports:** Swimming, sailing, tennis. **Hobbies:** Computers, reading. **Prof. Addr.:** Office of the Secretary of Defence, The Pentagon, Room 4E838, Washington, DC 20301-2400, U.S.A.

FRY (Patrick George, William), Export sales manager and resident Middle East representative, Sterling Cable Company, now stationed in Bahrain. **Born** on 24 Octobr 1929, at Chandlers Ford (UK). **Son** of William Henry Fry (railway executive) **and** Mrs., née Gladys Eva Payne. **Married** to Mary Catherine on 26 September, 1959 at Reading (UK). **Educ.:** Clarks College, Southampton. **Dipl.:** London Chamber of Commerce (Maths, English, Commercial Geography); Higher School Certificate. **Career:** H.Q. Staff, British Railways (1946-51); Pirelli General Cable Works (1951-53); Sterling Cable Company since 1953; Export Sales Manager of the said company (1961-75), appointed Middle East Resident Representative of the said company and stationed in Bahrain since 1975. **Sports:** Golf and Badmington. **Hobbies:** Music and Literature. **Member:** Club Balfour. **Priv. Addr.:** P.O.Box

49, Tel.: 52811, Bahrain. **Prof. Addr.:** P.O.Box 49, Tel.: 54745, Bahrain.

FUAD (Ibrahim Amine), Saudi statesman. **Born** in 1924 in Mecca. **Educ.:** Higher Training Institute of Mecca. **Career:** Inspector of Finance, Secretary and Advisor of the Ministry of Finance, former Minister of State. **Member** and Vice-Chairman of al-Wihda Club. **Addr.:** Mehallet Geuad, Bir Balila, Mecca, Saudi Arabia.

FUAD (Naamat, Ahmad), Egyptian academic. **Born** in 1934 in Cairo, Egypt. **Married**, 3 children. **Educ.:** Cairo University, Egypt. **Dipl.:** M.A. in Literature, Ph.D. in Arabic Literature. **Career:** Professor, Cairo Academy of Arts (1969-); Professor, the International Institute of the Islamic Banks, Cyprus; Professor of Arabic Literature and Comparative Studies, University of Tripoli, Libya (1968-70); Visiting Professor at Marmara University, Turkey, New York University, USA, several Military Institutes, Institute of Diplomatic Studies, Cairo (1980-82); Member of, Human Rights Society, Egyptian Writers' union, Permanent Committee for Historical Monuments, Union of Islamic Banks, Scientific Society for the Preservation of Heritage and Historical Monuments; contributed to several organizations, International Pen Club, Society of Modern Literature and the Folklore Committee at the High Council of Culture; Professor of Arabic Literature and Comparative Studies, Helwan University, Egypt (1979-), Academy of Arts, Egypt (1979-). **Publ.:** "The Character of Egypt", "Nile in Egyptian Literature", "Islamic Facts", "Making Peace". **Addr.:** 1 Shara al-Aziz Othman, Shaqqa 3, Zamalek, Cairo, Egypt.

FUAD (Omar, Ahmad), Egyptian economist. **Born** in 1923 in Egypt. **Son** of Ahmad Fuad. **Career:** Economic Chef de Cabinet to late President Gamal Abdel Nasser; Director of Misr Bank (1954); First President, Misr Foreign Trade Company; member of the National Assembly (1964 and 1969); Chairman of the Assembly's Economic Affairs Committee; Managing Director, Chairman, Misr Bank (1969) elected to the People's Assembly and was Chairman of its National Plan Committee (1971); National Council for Production and Economic Affairs (1974); **Member** of the General Committee of Citizen's War Committees (1970). **Addr.:** Cairo, Egypt.

FUAD (Sultan Abdel Latif), Egyptian banker. **Born** in 1931 in El Minia. **Son** of Abdel Latif Sultan Fuad. **Married** in 1956, 1 son, 1 daughter. **Educ.:** University of Cairo, B.C. (1951), P.G.S. (Econ). I.M.F. Institute, Diploma, Financial Analysis. **Career:** Exchange Control, Central Bank of Egypt (1951-71); Co-ordinator, International Monetary Fund, Yemen (Sanaa) (1971-74); General Manager, Arab International Bank (1974-75); Misr Iran Development Bank (1975); Vice Chairman and Managing Director (1975-80); Chairman, Misr Iran Development Bank, Cairo, Egypt (1980); Member of the Board of: Misr American Consultants Company; Misr Iran Hotels Company; General Authority of Capital Markets; Consultative Committee of the Private Investment Encouragement Fund; Steering Committee of International Executive Service Corps and National Council of Production; Membership of Egypt US Business Council; Arab European Management Forum; International Banker's Association; Society for Advancement of Management of the American Management Association and Egypt Business Association. **Hobbies:** Reading, Tennis and Swimming. **Member:** Heliopolis Sporting Club; Automobile Club; Rotary Club, Cairo. **Addr.:** Cairo, Egypt.

FUHAID (Faisal, Massud, al), Kuwaiti financial consultant. **Born** in 1939 in Kuwait. **Son** of Massud al-Fuhaid (of Ojeman Tribe). **Married** in 1964, 2 sons. **Educ.:** Kuwait and Cairo Universities. **Dipl.:** BBA (1966). **Career:** Private Secretary, Office of H.H. The Crown Prince (1966-70); General Manager, Arab African Bank (1970-73); Founder and Chairman, Financial Consulting Bureau, Kuwait (1973-); Chairman of Arab Television Company, Member of the Board of International Resources and Finance Bank, Nova Park Group and Arab Gulf Oil Magazine. **Publ.:** Arab Oil. **Hobbies:** Swimming and sailing. **Addr.:** P.O.Box 22173, Tel.: 426836, 443575, 443679, Telex: 22083 A/B COLTING, Safat, Kuwait.

FUHAID (Khaled, Massud, al), Kuwaiti statesman. **Born** in Kuwait. **Son** of Massud al-Fuheid. **Educ.:** Secondary and Higher. **Career:** Elected Deputy, Former Minister of National Education (1965); former member, National Assembly; President, Kuwait Teachers' Association. **Addr.:** Kuwait City, Kuwait.

FUHAID (Mohamad Abdallah al-Mut), Saudi diplomat. **Born** in 1924 in Onaizah, Saudi Arabia. **Dipl.:** Diploma of the Saudi Scientific Institute, Mecca. **Career:** Clerk, later Auditor, Riyadh Finance Department (1942); Code Operator, Ministry of Foreign Affairs, Jeddah (1945); Attaché, Ministry of Foreign Affairs (1947); Attaché at the Saudi Embassy in Baghdad, promoted to First Secretary (1950-55); Chargé d'Affaires, Saudi Embassy in Baghdad (1955-57); Director Arab League Department, Ministry of Foreign Affairs (1957-60); First Secretary, Saudi Embassy in Tunisia, then Minister Plenipotentiary at the Saudi Embassy in Sudan (1962-64); Minister Plenipotentiary, Saudi Embassy in Cairo (1965); Saudi Ambassador to Pakistan, Syria and Sultanate of Oman League Meetings (1958-60). **Honours:** King Abdul Aziz Distinguished Decoration; al-Rafidain Order, 2nd Grade, awarded by Iraq Government; Star of Pakistan Medal (Pakistan Government); Distinguished Syrian Decoration awarded by Syrian Government. **Hobby:** Reading. **Priv. Addr.:** Tel.: 6657797, 6658547, Jeddah, Saudi Arabia.

FULAIJ (Abdul Latif, al), Kuwaiti politician. **Born** in 1932 in Kuwait. **Educ.:** Durham University, UK. **Career:**

Assistant Secretary General, Kuwait National Assembly; Chairman, the National Assembly (1976); Businessman (1986-). **Hobbies:** Swimming, fishing, gardening. **Addr.:** Kuwait City, Kuwait.

FULAIJ (Faisal, Saud, al), Kuwaiti banker. **Born** in 1933 in Kuwait. **Son** of Saud al-Fulaij. **Married. Educ.:** Mubarakiyah School; Cairo University, Egypt. **Career:** Kuwait Municipality; Chairman, Kuwait International Finance Co. SAK; former Member of the Board, Deputy President and then Chairman of Kuwait Airways; Director, Kuwait Real Estate Bank KSC, Safat, Kuwait. former Director, Bank of Lebanon and Kuwait, Lebanon. **Addr.:** Kuwait City, Kuwait.

FULAIJ (Khalid, Fulaij Ali, al), Kuwaiti businessman. **Born** in 1931 in Kuwait. **Son** of Fulaij al-Fulaij. **Married** in 1951, 3 sons and 7 daughters. **Career:** Prominent Businessman (General Merchant). **Directorships:** Bank of Bahrain and Kuwait, Bahrain; Bank of Oman, Bahrain and Kuwait, Oman; Bank of Lebanon & Kuwait SAL, Lebanon; National Industries Co., Kuwait and Kuwait Metal Pipes Industries Co., Kuwait; former Chairman, Kuwait Shipbuilding and Repairyard Co.; Deputy Chairman, The Gulf Bank KSC, Safat, Kuwait; former Chairman Kuwait Oil Co. KSC. **Member:** Kuwait Sporting Club, Kuwait. **Hobbies:** Reading and Walking. **Addr.:** P.O.Box 3200, Tel.: 2445366, Telex: 22001, 2783, A/B GULFBANK KT, Safat, Kuwait.

FULAYFIL (Rashid, Ali), Bahraini official. **Born** in 1931 in Muharraq, Bahrain. **Married,** 4 children. **Educ.:** American University of Beirut. **Dipl.:** M.D., B.Sc. in Medical Sciences. **Career:** Consultant, Bahrain Government Hospital (1962-65); Chief of Services, Ténès, Algeria (1966-69); Chief of Services, Hospital Centre of University of Oran, Algeria (1970-72); Instructor, University of Oran Hospital, Algeria (1972-74); Assistant Professor, University Hospital of Oran, Algeria (1974-80); Assistant Under Secretary, Hospital and Training Affairs, Ministry of Health, Bahrain (1980-82); Member, Bahrain Medical Society; Under Secretary, Ministry of Health (1982-93). **Publ.:** co-author of numerous works on medical subjects (in French). **Hobbies:** Poetry, philosophy, gymnastics, tennis. **Member:** Bahrain Achaelogical Society; Member, College Council, College of Medicine & Medical Sciences, Arabian Gulf University; Member, Academic Council, University of Bahrain; Chairman, Board of Education, College of Health Sciences, Ministry of Health, Bahrain; President of National Institute for disabled. **Prof. Addr.:** East Raffaâ, P.O.Box 28312, Raffa, Bahrain.

FULLER (Michael John), Banker. **Born** on July 20, 1934 in U.K. **Son** of Thomas Frederick Fuller and Mrs. Irene Emily. **Married** in 1955 to Maureen Rita Fuller (divorced 1989) in 1990 to Eizabeth Frost, 4 children: Nicholas (6.2.1960), Richard (30.9.1962), Jaqueline/Laura 7.2.1996 (Twins). **Educ.:** Wallington Country Grammar School. **Dipl.:** FCIB (1980). **Career:** National Service, Command RAF (1950-1952); Midland Bank (1948-1990) various branch and head office posts: GP Public Affairs Advr. (1977-1979); Regional Director - Southampton (1979-1981); General Manager, Midland & Wales (1981-1982); General Manager, Business Development (1982-1985) UK Operations Director (1985-1987); Deputy Chief Executive (1987-1989); Chief Executive (1989-1990) UK Banking Sector; General Manager, National Bank of Abu Dhabi (1991-1992); Chief Executive Officer, Al Ahli Commercial Bank (1992-). **Other Information:** Fellow of the Royal Society of Arts, FCIB. **Sport:** Rough Golf. **Hobbies:** Reading, Travelling. **Member:** Raf Club **Credit Cards:** Mastercard/Visa. **Addr.:** Al Ahli Commercial Bank, P.O.Box 5941, Manama, Bahrain, Tel.: (0973) 209101.

FULY (Hanafi, Ahmad, al), Egyptian lawyer. **Born** in 1927 in Cairo, Egypt. **Son** of Ahmad al-Fuly. **Married,** seven children. **Educ.:** LL.B, Cairo University, Cairo, Egypt (1952). **Career:** Assistant Public Prosecutor (1954); Public Prosecuotor (1956); Judge (1962); Legal Adviser, High Dam Committee (1963); Adviser, Ministry of Electricity (1971); Legal Adviser, Ali and Fahad Shobikshi Group of Companies, The Shobokshi Maritime Company, Tihama Advertising and Market Research Company. **Member** of Egyptian Lawyers Union, the International Bar Association, London. **Prof. Addr.:** Ali and Fahad Shobokshi Group of Companies, P.O.Box 5470, Tel.: 6658208/9, Jeddah, Saudi Arabia.

FURAIH (Abdul Rahman, Farhan, al), Kuwaiti administrator. **Born** in 1934. **Married,** 5 children. **Career:** Managing Director of Arab Gulf Co. (1961), al-Zahraa Medical Co. (1975), al-Farih Banking Co. (1980), al-Farih Financial Group (1980), Marine Contracting Co. Ltd. (1985). **Hobbies:** gardening, chess. **Prof. Addr.:** Marine Contracting Co. Ltd., el-Helaly Street, Kuwaiti Building, 13014 Safat, Te;.: 240100, 2432125, Kuwait City, Kuwait. **Priv. Addr.:** el-Nozah, Group 40 House 13, Street 31, Block 3, Safat, Kuwait City, Kuwait.

FURAIH (Ibrahim, Salih, al), Saudi academic. **Born** in 1945 in Riyadh, Saudi Arabia. **Married,** with children. **Educ.:** Faculty of Arts, King Abdul Aziz University. **Dipl.:** B.A. (1969), M.A. (1971). **Career:** Teacher of English language and literature, College of Education, Riyadh; teacher of English, Military College, Riyadh; Newscaster, Radio Riyadh English Service; now Inspector-General of English Language teaching, Ministry of Education. **Member:** Committee for introducing comprehensive schools in Saudi Arabia; Committee for Textbooks, Ministry of Education. **Hobbies:** Swimming and chess. **Prof. Addr.:** Department of Intermediate Education, Ministry of Education, Riyadh, Saudi Arabia.

FURAIH (Othman, Salih, al), Saudi academic. **Born** in

1936 in Onaiza, Saudi Arabia. **Son** of Salih al Furaih. **Married**, three children. **Educ.:** Cairo University; Universiy of Durham, UK; University of Khartoum, Sudan. **Dipl.:** B.A., Arabic Language and Literature (1962); M.A. Arabic Literature (1969); Ph.D., Arabic Literature (1977). **Career:** Faculty of Arts, Riyadh University, Saudi Arabia: Tutor (1962); Lecturer (1969); Instructor (1977); Assistant Professor (since 1978) and Faculty member, Riyadh University. **Medals and Awards:** Social Board Award, Student Affairs, Riyadh University (1979). **Sports:** Tennis, volleyball. **Hobby:** Arabic literature, the Abbasid Period. **Addr.:** Arabic Department, Faculty of Arts, Tel. 4029500, 4811000, Riyadh University, Saudi Arabia.

FURATI (Malik), Tunisian engineer. **Born** on August 28, 1939 in Sfax, Tunisia. **Married. Educ.:** Dipl. Eng., France. **Dipl.:** Licence es Sciences. **Career:** Senior Engineer and Head of the Dam Division (1963-70); Director, Tunisie Cables et Cablerie de Grambatia; Chairman and General Manager, STUCOM, CICEM, TUNICOM. **Addr.:** Rue el-Fouledh, Megrine 2014, Riadh, Tunisia.

FUTAIH (Abdulaziz, al), Yemeni diplomat. **Born** on February 2, 1936 in Kadas (Hugariah). **Educ.:** Aïn Shams University (Cairo); Western Maryland College (Westminster); University of Nevada (Reno); Mackay School of Mines (University of Nevada). **Dipl.:** Bachelor of Science in Geology, Bachelor of Science in Physics, Master of Science. **Career:** Field Geologist, surveyor and environmental Engineer with several firms in Nevada and California (U.S.A.); Joined in the Head Office for Technical Aid to the Yemen, Sana'a (1963-64); Deputy Minister of Public Works and Head of the Department of Mineral Resources (March 1964- May 1964); Member of the High Economic Council (June 1965- October 1965); General Director of Water projects and Head of the Department of Mineral Resources (October to September 1966); Minister of Agriculture (September- December 1966); Permanent Representative of Yemen to the United Nations Organization, New York (February 1967- December 1968); Joined Ministry of Foreign Affairs since 1969. **Addr.:** Sanaa, Republic of Yemen.

FUTTAIM (Majid, Mohamad, al), UAE businessman. **Career:** Prominent Businessman of UAE; Chairman of Middle East Finance International Ltd., Hong Kong; Chairman, Dubai Insurance Co. (S.A.D.); Director, Arab Emirates Investments Ltd., UAE; Director and Chairman, Middle East Bank Ltd., Dubai, UAE; President of "al-Futtaim Group" (Holding); President of Oman National Electronics. **Addr.:** P.O.Box 152, Dubai, UAE and P.O.Box 555, Abu Dhabi, U.A.E.

G

GAAFAR (el-Sayed), Egyptian veterinary parasitologist. **Born** on January 18, 1924 in Tanta. **Son** of Mohamad Hegab Gaafar **and** Mrs., née Bahiya Salama. **Married** on August 30, 1949 to Miss Irma Fileen Bird, 4 children: Joseph-Omar, Wayne-Samir, Daniel-Sharif and Gail-Magda. **Educ.:** Cairo University, Kansas State University, Texas A.&M. University. **Dipl.:** Bachelor of Veterinary Science (1944), Master of Science (1949), Doctor of Philosophy (1950), Doctor of Veterinary Medicine (1955). **Career:** Assistant Parasitologist, Veterinary Pathological Laboratory, Cairo (1944-47); Parasitologist (1950-51); Emigrated to the United States of America (1951), Naturalized (1956); Veterinarian, Rutherford Veterinary Hospital, Dallas (1952-54); Joined the Faculty of Texas A.&M., College Station (1955-58); Associate Profesor (1956-58); Faculty Purdue University, Lafayette, Indiana, since 1958; Professor of Parasitology since 1964. **Publ.:** Author of several publications on effect trace minerals on parasitism, pathogenesis ascarids, pathology of parasitic diseases. **Member** and officer of numerous American and world Associations of veterinary medicine and parasitism. **Prof. Addr.:** Veterinary Pathological Building, Purdue University, Lafayette, Indiana 47906, (U.S.A.). **Priv. Addr.:** 2620, Newman Road, West Lafayette, Indiana 47906, U.S.A.

GAAFAR (Mohamad Ali Bakhit), Sudanese politician. **Born** in Sudan. **Son** of Ali Bakhit Gaafar. **Educ.:** University of Khartoum, Sudan; University of Exeter, UK; University of London, UK, Cambridge University, UK. **Dipl.:** Ph.D. in Political Science. **Career:** Deputy Under Secretary, Ministry of Local Governments, Sudan; Lecturer in Public Administration, University of Khartoum; Minister of Local Government (1971-75); played an important role in the negotiations leading to the Addis Abeba Agreement on Southern Sudan; active in the political development and practical organisation of the Sudanese Socialist Union (SSU); Deputy Secretary General, Sudanese Socialist Union (1974); member of the SSU Political Bureau since its establishment (Party dissoved in 1986); Chief Editor of "al-Sahafa" newspaper (1974). **Leader** of the People's Assembly and Assistant Secretary General of the SSU (1975). **Addr.:** Khartoum, Sudan.

GAAFAR (Youssef, Mazhar), Egyptian businessman. **Born** in 1929 in Cairo, Egypt. **Married,** 2 daughters. **Educ.:** University of Cairo, Egypt. **Dipl.:** LL.B., Diploma of Law. **Career:** Lawyer, Court of Appeal (1951-57); Managing Director and Chief Executive of Estimar Travel; Vice-President, Chamber of Tourism (1972-75); Member of the Board of the International Union of Chambers of Tourism and Union of Chambers of Tourism (1967-69) and (1974-76). **Member:** Gezira Sporting Club; Cairo Automobile Association. **Prof. Addr.:** Estimar Travel, 13 Shara Qatar al-Nile, Cairo, Egypt. **Priv. Addr.:** 4 Shara al-Salih Ayoub, Zamalek, Cairo, Egypt.

GABALLAH (el-Sayyid, Sayyid), Egyptian statesman. **Born** in October 1916 in Cairo (Egypt). **Married,** with children. **Educ.:** Cairo University; Wisconsin University, Madison (USA). **Career:** Lecturer, Cairo University; Head, Agricultural Economics Section; Under-Secretary of State for Planning (1963-71); Minister of Planning (1971-74). **Member:** Central Committee, Arab Socialist Union; United Nations Institute of Economic Development and Planning for Africa. **Prof. Addr.:** The People's Assembly, Cairo, Egypt.

GABANDI (Abdallah, Ahmad, al), Kuwaiti executive. **Born** in 1946 in Kuwait. **Son** of Ahmad Al Gabandi. **Married** in 1974, 1 son. **Educ.:** Detroit Institute of Technology, B.Sc. Mechanical Engineering, USA. **Career:** South Shuaiba Power Station, Kuwait (1971-74); Delegated by Kuwait Foreign Trading, Contracting and Investment Co., Petroleum Pipelines Co. (SUMED), Egypt (1974-75); Chairman, Kuwait Foreign Trading, Contracting and Investment Co., Safat Kuwait (since 1975); former Chairman, Kuwait Real Estate Investment Consortium, Kuwait; Compagnie Internationale de Developpement Minier (CIDEM), Paris, France; former Vice-Chairman and Managing Director, Sudanese Kuwaiti Investment Co., Khartoum, Sudan; Korf Industries Inc., Charlotte, USA; former Vice-Chairman, Arab Iron and Steel Co., Bahrain, Arab Petroleum Pipelines Co. (SUMED), Egypt, Gulf Cement Co., Ras el-Khaimah, UAE and Kuwait Marine. **Member:** Kuwait Engineer's Society. **Hobbies:** Swimming and horse riding. **Addr.:** P.O.Box 5665, Tel.: 2449031, Telex: 22035, 22021 A/B MAADEN, Safat, Kuwait.

GABEL (Amal Hassan, Mrs.), Saudi civil servant. **Born** in 1947, in Jeddah, Saudi Arabia. **Dipl.:** B.A. (Sociology and Psychology). **Career:** Member of founding committees of women's charity societies in the Western Region; supervised the establishment of the Faisalite Charity Society, Jeddah, the "Umul Qura" Charity Society, Mecca, Women's Charity Society in the Western Region; supervised the field work for surveying sections of old Jeddah; contributed to the programme of rehabilitating women prisoners; Social Supervisor, Administration of social Affairs, Western Region, Jeddah. **Publ.:** field research on social welfare for the disabled as a basic variant in development; an applied study on the Saudi society. **Addr.:** Administration of Social Affairs, Jeddah, Saudi Arabia.

GABRIEL (Nabil, Aziz), Egyptian vice-principal of Collège de la Sainte Famille, Cairo. **Son** of Aziz Gabriel (pharmacist) **and** Mrs., née Marcelle Rathle. **Born** on November 25, 1942 in Cairo. **Educ.:** College de la Sainte Famille, Cairo (1947-60); La Baume St. Marie in Provence (France) (1961-63); Maison St. Michel, Toulouse (France) (1963-64); Faculty of Science, Toulouse University (1963-65); Les Fontaines (1965-67); Fourvières (Missions Seminary) (1969-73). **Dipl.:** Egyptian Baccalaureate (sciences) (1960); Degree in philosophy (1967); Bachelor of Theology (1973). **Career:** teacher of religion, Collège de la Sainte Famille (1967-69); ordained to the priesthood (1973); now Principal of Collège de la Sainte Famille, Cairo, Egypt; Secretary General of Catholic School Association. **Publ.:** Coptic Spirituality (1973). **Sport:** Sculling. **Hobbies:** Photography and reading. **Remarks:** Fluent in Arabic, French and English. **Prof. & Priv. Addr.:** Collège de la Sainte Famille, 1 Bustan el-Maksy Street, Faggala, Tel.: 900411, Cairo, Egypt.

GADDAL (Saeed, Ayoub, al), Sudanese businessman. **Born** in 1923 at Singa (Sudan). **Son** of Ayoub al-Gaddal (General Merchant) **and** Mrs., née Nafiesa el-Khalifa. **Married** in 1964 to Insaf Ali Arabad (deceased), married a second time in 1973 to Sakina el-Mamoun, 6 children: Gaddal M., Mahaf Asim M., ALi M., Manal and Maysa. **Educ.:** School of Design; Arts School, University College of Khartoum; Central School of Art and Craft, London. **Dipl.:** University College diploma; Central School of Art diploma; Senior Management Certificate. **Career:** Teacher, elementary and intermediate school (1942-47); teacher, Secondary school (1952-55); Lecturer, School of Fine and Applied Art (1958-64); Principal, College of Fine and Applied Art (1964-71); General Manager, Blue Nile Packing Corporation since 1971; Designed various stamps for the Post and Telegraph Department; also emblems for the Army, Police and Market; took part in designing various national parks. **Member:** National Stamps Committee; National Committee for Arts, Literature and Culture; Association of Artists (Honorary member). **Sport:** Tennis. **Hobbies:** Gardening and music. **Clubs:** Graduates Club; Khartoum Club and Hilal Sports Club. **Prof. Addr.:** P.O.Box 385, Khartoum, Tel.: 80535, Khartoum, Sudan.

GADHI (Ibrahim Gadhi, al), Saudi official. **Born** on 13 November 1934. **Dipl.:** B.A. (Sociology), Faculty of Arts, Cairo University. **Career:** Administrative Manager of Directorate of Education (until 1955); Secretary General of Saudi Cultural Office in Cairo (until 1964); Director of Foreign Missions, Ministry of Education (until 1966); Cultural Attaché to Iran, Turkey, Pakistan (until 1968); Cultural Attaché to Iraq and Kuwait (until 1971); Assistant Director General of Administration, Ministry of Education; Cultural Attaché to Federal Republic of Germany; Cultural Attaché to Lebanon and Syria; Deputy Minister of Information for Administrative Affairs. (1976-1993); on August 20, 1993 Appointed as Shura Council Member. **Addr.:** Shura Council, Tel.: 4821666, P.O.Box 27075, Riyadh 11417, Saudi Arabia.

GAI (Martin Majier), Sudanese barrister, politician. **Born** in 1938 in Sudan. **Married**, seven children. **Educ.:** LL.B., University of Khartoum. **Career:** Legal Assistant in Judiciary (1967); Judge of Second Grade (1969); Judge of First Grade (1972); Province Judge (1976); Deputy Speaker, People's Regional Assembly, Southern Region (1978); Regional Minister, Co-operation, Commerce and Supply (1979); Regional Minister of Coordination and Legal Affairs, Juba (1980). **Medals:** Medal of Neilin, 2nd Class. **Sport:** Tennis. **Hobby:** Gardening. **Addr.:** Tel.: 2694, Juba, Sudan.

GAILANI (Ahmad, Zafar), Iraqi diplomat. **Born** in 1925 in Baghdad, Iraq. **Son** of Zafar Gailani. **Married**, one daughter. **Educ.:** LL.B., Law College, Cairo University, Egypt, (1947). **Career:** Iraqi Bar Association (1948); Ministry of Foreign Affairs, Baghdad (1949); Attaché, Embassy of Iraq, London (1951-54); Vice Consul, Karmanshah, Iran (1954-58); 2nd Secretary, Embassy of Iraq, Egypt (1958-61); Director, Afro-Asian Section, Political Department, Ministry of Foreign Affairs, Iraq (1961-63); Counsul General, New York, USA (1963-67); Acting Chief of Protocol in Presidential Palace (1967-69); Minister-Counsellor, Embassy of Iraq to Spain (1969-71); Ambassador of Iraq to Saudi Arabia (1972-76); Ambassador of Iraq to Pakistan concurrently accredited to Thailand (1976). **Medals:** Afghanistan, Star Decoration, 3rd Grade (1951); Coronation Medal, UK (1952); France, Order of Merit Commodore (1968); Spain Order of Merit (1971). **Addr.:** Ministry of Foreign Affairs, Baghdad, Iraq.

GAIN (Abdalrazag, Abdallah, al), Saudi economist. **Born** in 1941 in Medina, Saudi Arabia. **Married**, 4 children. **Educ.:** King Saud University, Saudi Arabia; Missouri University, USA. **Dipl.:** B.A. in Economics and Political Science, M.Sc. in Economics. **Career:** held various positions in the Ministry of Planning, Saudi Arabia (1960-), Member of several government committees, currently Assistant Deputy Minister. **Hobbies:** travelling, reading. **Prof. Addr.:** P.O.Box 50545, Riyadh 11533, Saudi Arabia.

GAIN (Abdulbar, al), Saudi academic. **Born** in 1937, in Medina, Saudi Arabia. **Dipl.:** M.S. (Meteorology) 1976; Ph.D. (Arid Lands Resources Sciences) 1974. **Career:** Member, National Environmental Protection and Coordination Committee, the Council of Regional Organization for the Protection of the Marine (Gulf) Environment; Vice President, IUCN; IUCN Regional Counsellor; member, IUCN Commission on Environmental Planning, the International Council of Enviromental Law, WHO Inter-Governmental Panel of first GAPP Global Experiment and WMO Technical Commission on Atmospheric Sciences; Vice President, UNEP, (1981-82); Vice-President, Meteorology and Environmental Protection Administration (MEPA); Saudi Arabia's Representative to the Governing Council of UNEP; member, the Commission on Environmental Planning, the National Advisory Board, Fauna of Saudi Arabia, Sigma XI and the Editorial Board of Arid Lands Abstracts'. **Prof. Addr.:** P.O.Box 1358, Tel.: 6718085, 6710448, Jeddah. **Priv. Addr.:** Tel.: 6510187, Jeddah, Saudi Arabia.

GALAL (Mohamad, Nadir), Egyptian artist, film director. **Born** in 1941 in Cairo, Egypt. **Son** of Nadir Galal. **Married**, three children. **Educ.:** B.A. in Commerce; Diploma of Higher Institute of Cinema. **Career:** Research Assistant, Higher Institute of Cinema (1965); Assistant Producer (1970); Producer and Director (1970); Producer and Director (since 1971). **Hobbies:** Cinema, chess, bridge. **Prof. Addr.:** Galal Films Company, Producers and Distributors, 85 Ramses Street, Cairo, Egypt. **Priv. Addr.:** 4 Granada Street, Roxy, Tel.: 866642, Masr al-Gedida, Cairo, Egypt.

GALAL (Mohamed, Noman), Egyptian Diplomat. **Born** on April 10, 1943 at Assiut, Egypt. **Son** of Noman Galal. **Married** in 1970 to Kawther el-Sherif, 2 children: **Educ.:** B.A. Political Science, very good Degree with Honor, Faculty of Economics and Political Science, Cairo University (1965), M.A. Political Science, very good, Cairo University (1974), Ph.D Political Science, with First Honor Degree, Cairo University (May 1980). **Career: Professional Experience:** Joined the Ministry of Foreign Affairs since 1965, working in different Departments: Legal Department - Office of the Under Secretary - Diplomatic Institute - Cabinet of the Deputy Prime Minister and Minister for Foreign Affairs. **Positions and Functions Abroad and at Home:** Administrative Officer (Legal & Treaties Affairs), Legal Department (1965); Attache (Training Course for two years), Diplomatic Institute (1966); Attache (Political Affairs), Information Department (1968-1969); Attache & Third Secretary for Political & Economic Affairs, Embassy in Jordan (1969-1972); Vice Consul (Consular Affairs), Embassy in Kuwait (Apr. 72-Sept.72); Consul (Consular Affairs), Embassy in Abu Dhabi (1972-1973); Second Secretary (Political Affairs of East Asia), Legal Department (1974-1975); Political, Economic, Cultural & Consul Affairs, Embassy in Norway (1975-1979); Lecturer & Research Advisor for newly appointed Diplomats in the Ministry as well as supervision of official Publications (the White papers about the Foreign Policy), Diplomatic Institute in Cairo (1979-1980); First Secretary, Embassy in New Delhi (1980) - Counsellor (Political Affairs) (1981-1985); Counsellor, Cabinet of the Deputy Prime Minister and Minister for Foreign Affairs (June 1985 - July 1987); Minister Plenipotentiary, egyptian Mission to the United Nations, New York (1989-92); Permanent Representative of Egypt to the Arab League, Cairo (1992-95); Ambassador of Egypt to Pakistan, Islamabad (1995-96). **Other Experience: A. Attended Seminars.** Political Science Seminar in Beirut, Lebanon (1974); U.N. Trade Promotion Seminar in Oslo, Norway, (November 1978); U.N. Trade Promotion Seminar in Helsinki, Finland (June 1979); Assumed the Secretariat of the Eighth Meeting of the Directors of Diplomatic Academies and Institutes of International Relations held in Cairo (June 24-26, 1980); South and West Asia in Crisis: Quest for Regional Security at Jawaharlal Nehru University, New Delhi, India (30 Sept. 1 Oct. 1981); West Asia Since Camp David, at Aligarh Muslim University, Aligarh, India (December 17-18, 1981); All India Political Science Association Annual Conference 1984, Jodpur, India; Indo-Egyptian Seminar, New Delhi, (March 1986); Egyptian Political System Seminar, Faculty of Economic and Political Science, Cairo University (April 1986); «Egyptian Foreign Policy», Center for Political Studies, Cairo University (June 1986); Egyptian-Chinese Seminar, Institute of Diplomatic Studies, Cairo (1987). B. **Member of the Egyptian Delegation to:** Conference of the Foreign Ministers of Non-Aligned Countries, New Delhi (Feb. 1981); New Delhi Consultations (Feb. 1982); Meeting of Heads of Science and Technology Agencies of Developing Countries, New Delhi (May 1982); Seventh Non-Aligned Summit Conference, New Delhi (March 1983); World Tourism Organization Conference, New Delhi (October 1983); Non-Aligned Countries Ministerial Meeting at Lunand, Angola (September 1985); Eight Non-Aligned Countries Summit at Harare, Zimbabwe (August-September 1986); The Summit of the Organization of the Islamic Conference at Kuwait (January 1987); Forty-Second Sessions of the U.N. General Assembly, New York (1987). **Publications and Research:** Over 40 Publications in Arabic and English (Some of which have translated to Norwegian), and Half a dozen Books. Tittles Include: A. In Arabic: Cultural Revolution in China, Thesis for Master Degree (not published), Cairo University (1974); Organic Equilibrium in the Political Thought of El-Farabi, in Arabic Issues Magazine, Beirut (May 1975); Norwegian Public Opinion and Middle East Crisis, an article in «Al-Siyasah El-Dawlya», International Politics (April 1976); «Social Democracy in Norway», published by the Egyptian Book Organization, Cairo (1978); «Cultural and Politics in China», published by Al-Ahram Institution (1979); «Socialist Party in Japan», published by Al-Ahram Institution in 'Comparative Studies about Social Democracy', Cairo (1980); Sino-Japanese Relations 1949-72, Thesis for Ph.D. Degree (not published, Cairo University (April 1980); Protocol between Islamic Tradition and Modern Practice, (not published) (1980); The Eight Meeting of the

Directors of Diplomatic Academies and Institutes of International Relations, Al-Siyasah Al Dawlya (October 1980); «Social and Political Development in India», Al-Siyasah Al Dawlya, Cairo (July 1986); «Political and intellectual tendencies in Egypt today», Egyptian History Series No. 4, Egyptian Book Organization, Cairo (1987); «Non-Alignment in a Changing World», the Second One Thousand Book Series, Egyptian Book Organization, Cairo (1987). B. **In Norwegian (Translated from English):** Egyptian Point of View in Middle East Crisis (1977); Place of Jerusalem in Islam, published in Terja Sudbrandson Og Egil Wyller eds., Arabarne og Islam, Universities Forlaget, Oslo (1978). C. **In English:** National University System in Egypt, World Higher Education Communique, Vol. 3 No. 2, (Spring 1981), Institute of International Education, New York, USA, pp. 17-19; Cultural Factor and Political Change in Developing Countries, Philosophy and Social Action, Vol. VIII No. 3, (July-September 1982), New Delhi, pp. 39-44; Egypt's Approach to Middle East Peace, Sino-American Relations, an International Quarterly, Vol. VIII No. 3, (Autumn 1982), Taiwan, pp. 17-25; Egypt's Foreign Policy and Non-Alignment, Punjab Journal of Politics, Vol. VII No. 1, (Jan. -June 1983), pp. 109-120; Egypt and Non-Alignment, Secular Democracy, Annual Number 1983- Non-Alignment Summit Special Issue, New Delhi, pp. 107-111; Al-Azhar, the oldest Islamic University, Secular Democracy, (May 1983), New Delhi, pp. 16-17; Nation Building in Egypt: An Analytical Note, Secular Democracy, Independence Day Special Issue, (1983), Vol. XVI Nos. VII and VIII, New Delhi, pp. 54-56; «Egypt and the Problem of Nation Building», Man and Development, Vol. V No. 4, (Dec. 1983); Statistical Political Analysis for the business of the Seventh Non-Aligned Summit, Philosophy and Social Action, Vol. IX No. 3, New Delhi (July-September 1983); The Arab Mind: An Egyptian Case Study, Man and Development, Vol. VI No. 2, Chandigarh, India (June 1984); «The Arab World: Issues and Challenges», Problems of Non-Alignment, Vol. 2 No. 2 (Jun-August 1984); «Egyptian Foreign Policy: A Preliminary Note on Vision and Action», Man and Development, Vol. VIII No. 2 (June 1986); «Political Thought in Africa», Man and Development, Vol. IX No. 2, Chandigarh, India (June 1987). **Prof. Addr.:** 36 East 67 Street, New York, Tel.: 1212 8796300, N.Y. 10021, U.S.A. and Ministry of Foreign Affairs, Cairo, Egypt.

GALAL (Osman, Mahmoud), Egyptian academic. **Born** on November 9, 1931 in Cairo, Egypt. **Married,** 1 son, 1 daughter. **Educ.:** Cairo University, Egypt; Birmingham University, England. **Dipl.:** M.D., Ph.D. **Career:** Assistant Professor, then Head of Child Health Department, National Research Center; Member, the Academy of Science and Technology, the American Society of Clinical Nutrition and the American Nutrition Association; Director of Nutrition Institute. **Publ.:** published numerous articles on child health and nutrition. **Medal:** Medal for Science and Art, Egypt (1980). **Member:** Gezira Sporting Club. **Prof. Addr.:** 69 Kasr el-Eini Street, Cairo, Egypt. **Priv. Addr.:** 17B Mohamed Mazhar, Zamalek, Cairo, Egypt.

GALALY (Enan), Egyptian chairman, Helnan Hotels. **Born** on January 1, 1947 in Cairo, Egypt. **Son** of Raouf el-Galaly (Jurist, General Manager) **and** Mrs., née Ihsan Mansour. **Single. Educ.:** Elementary and secondary schools, Egypt; School of Commerce, Denmark and Hotel School, Denmark. **Dipl.:** Diplomas in Hotel Administration and Business Administration; Training courses, Hotel Operations. **Career:** Head waiter (1969); Executive Assistant Manager, Hotel Hvide Hus, Aalborg (1970); Director General of Hotel Hvide Hus, Aalborg (1975), then Managing Director, Hvide Hus Hotel Chain (1979); Founder, sole shareholder and chairman of Helnan International A/S Ltd. (1982), a Holding company owning the following subsidiaries: Hotel Phonix Aalborg, Scandinavian Tours Aalborg and Copenhagen, Scandinavian Investment Co., Scandinavian Trading Co., Scandinavian Management Co., managing Hotel Hvide Hus, Aalborg, Shepheard Hotel Cairo and Palestine Hotel Alexandria; Helnan International USA owning Riverside Hotel Tampa, Florida; Consulting Adviser for several hotels and tourism projects in international markets. **Medals:** received several honorary degrees and medals from Universities and Associations. **Sport:** Swimming. **Hobbies:** Travelling. **Member:** Cairo Guezirah Club; Heliopolis Sporting Club. **Prof. Addr.:** Vesterbro 77-DK 9000 Aalborg, Tel.: 98-120011, Aalborg, Denmark.

GALANDER (Maj. Mahmoud), Sudanese journalist. **Born** on September 4, 1947 in Port Sudan. **Son** of Mohamad Galander **and** Mrs., née Amina Sherief. **Married** on June 15, 1978 to Butheina. **Educ.:** Suakim elementary school; Port Sudan intermediate and secondary school; University of Khartoum. **Dipl.:** B.Sc. (Economics); Psychological Warfare Diploma. **Career:** Teacher (1970-71); Officer and journalist since 1971: Managing-Editor of the Military Weekly Newspaper and Monthly Magazine (since 1972-); Editor since 1973. **Awards:** May 25th Medal; Asoumoud Medal; Unity Medal; Vladimir VI Medal. **Sports:** Soccer and tennis. **Hobbies:** Cinema and fiction. **Prof. Addr.:** Army H.Q., P.O.Box 16, Tel.: 70334, 76305, Khartoum. **Priv. Addr.:** Tel.: 54469, Omdurman, Sudan.

GAMALEDIN (Awad, Aly), Egyptian professor. **Born** in Egypt in 1929. **Son** of Aly Gamaledin **and** Mrs. Anissa Abdelfattah. **Married** to Azza Soussa, two children. **Educ.:** Commercial Law. **Dipl.:** Doctorat d'Etat in private law. **Career:** Professor, chief of section of Commercial and Maritime Law. **Addr.:** 48 Giza Street, Giza, Cairo, Egypt.

GAMASSY (Mohamad, Abdulghani, al), Egyptian army officer. **Born** in September 1921 in Egypt. **Son** of Abdulghani al-Gamassy. **Married,** 3 children. **Educ.:** Military College (Cairo), Specialization in the U.S.S.R. and the U.S.A. **Dipl.:** Bachelor of Military Sciences; graduated from Military College. **Career:** Joined the Egyptian Army Service, Promoted General, then Major General Assistant, then Chief of Staff of the Egyptian Armed Forces (December 1973), took part in the Arab War against Israel in 1967 and 1973; Minister of War and Commander-in-Chief of the Armed Forces (Dec. 1974); Deputy Prime-Minister, Minister of War and War Production; Commander in Chief of the Unified Arab Forces (March 1976). **Awards:** Several Arab & Foreign decorations. **Addr.:** Ministry of Defence, Cairo, Egypt.

GAMEH (Abdel Ghani), Egyptian banker and executive. **Born** in 1930 in Cairo, Egypt. **Married** in 1955, two children. **Educ.:** Cairo University, Faculty of Commerce, Cairo. **Dipl.:** B.Com. with "First Grade of Honour" (1953). **Career:** At the National Bank of Egypt (since 1953) in 1986 acting Chairman of same for two years. Ex. Chairman of Credit International d'Egypte and Chairman, Bank of Alexandria, Chairman of Bankers Association of Egypt. former Chairman, Egyptian American Bank. **Hobby:** Reading. **Member** of the Three Sporting Club, Cairo. **Addr.:** Cairo, Egypt.

GAMMAL (Ahmad, Mokhtar, al), Egyptian executive. **Born** in 1933 in Egypt. **Son** of Mokhtar Mohamad Gammal. **Married** in 1969. **Educ.:** Victoria College, Egypt. **Dipl.:** B.A. (1968). **Career:** Joined Merrill Lynch in 1970; Account Executive and Assistant Vice President, Merrill Lynch, Kuwait (1970-80); Manager, Bahrain (1980-81); Manager and Vice President, Merrill Lynch, Dubai, UAE (since 1981). **Member:** Passport Club, Dubai., **Addr.:** P.O.Box 3911, Tel.: 225261, Telex: 45563 A/B MERLE EM, Dubai, UAE.

GAMMOH (Sami, I.), Jordanian executive and economist. **Born** in 1940 in Jordan. **Son** of Ibrahim Gammoh (retired army officer) **and** Mrs. Jamila Gammoh. **Married** in 1954 to Miss J. Sydny, two children. **Educ.:** The American University of Beirut; Syracuse University, Maxwell School, New York. **Dipl.:** B.A. (1962); M.A. (1967) and several training diplomas with World Bank and IMF and United Nations fellowships. **Career:** Economic Counsellor and Jordan Representative to the Arab Economic Unity Council (1968-73); Director of the Special Bureau, Ministry of Foreign Affairs (1979-80); Lecturer University of Jordan, the Economics and Commerce Department (1979-80); Deputy ambassador to the United Nations, Consul General in New York (1974-79); Director General of Budget Department (1980-84); Director, general manager, Middle East Insurance Co. Ltd. (since 1984); Minister of Finance (May 1993- Jan. 1995). **Member** of: the Board of Trustees of Queen Noor Foundation; the Board of several voluntary organisations; Jordan Club, Foreign Affairs Council. **Credit Card:** Visa. **Prof. Addr.:** P.O.Box 1802, Tel.: 605144, Amman, Jordan. **Priv. Addr.:** Tel.: 819334, Amman, Jordan.

GANDOUL (Said, Abdul Aziz, al), Saudi educationalist. **Born** in 1923. **Educ.:** College of Sharia (Islamic Law), Mecca, Saudi Arabia. **Dipl.:** B.A. in Islamic Law. **Career:** Director or Religious Institute, Mecca (1957); Assistant Director General, Department of Education (1965); Director General, High School Education (1966); Member of Supreme Commission for Islamic Indoctrination; Member of the Board of Imam Schools; Assistant Director General of Education; Vice President of Control and Investigation Board. **Publ.:** several books on education and religion. **Hobby:** Reading. **Prof. Addr.:** Riyadh, Saudi Arabia.

GANZOURY (Kamal, Ahmed, el, Dr.), Egyptian politician. **Born** in Cairo in 1933. **Educ.:** Cairo University and Michigan University. **Dipl.:** M.A., Ph.D. **Career:** Governor of Beni Suef and Under Secretary, Ministry of Planning (1975); former consultant for planning and development at UN; former head of National Planning Institute, Ministry of Planning (1982-85); Deputy Prime Minister and Minister Planning and International Co-operation (1985-89); Deputy Prime Minister and Minister of Planning (1990 to Jan. 1996); Prime Minister (Jan. 1996 - October 1999). and former Chairman, National Investment Bank. **Addr.:** Cairo, Egypt.

GARABET (Samir, Noori), Iraqi engineer. **Born** in 1934 in Iraq. **Married,** 2 children. **Educ.:** University of Leeds, England; Institution of Civil Engineers, UK (MICE, Member); Council of Engineering Institutions, UK (Chartered Engineer). **Dipl.:** B.Sc. in Civil Engineering. **Career:** Senior Civil Engineer, Iraq Petroleum Company (1964), Technical Assistant of General Management (1965), Senior Assistant (1970); Chief Engineer of Northern Petroleum Organization (1975); Chief Engineer of Planning, (1978-84), Head of Planning Department, Northern Petroleum Organization (1984-); **Hobbies:** Tennis, badmington, travelling, swimming. **Member:** Iraqi Engineers Society. **Prof. Addr.:** Planning Department, North Oil Company, P.O.Box 1, Kirkuk, Iraq.

GARANG (Enok, Madlingde), Sudanese politician. **Born** on January 1, 1934 in Upper Nile Province, Sudan. **Married,** 4 children. **Educ.:** Manchester College of Science and Technology (printing course), Africa literature Centre, Zambia (Journalism). **Career:** Malakal Printing Press (1959); Manager of the Spearhead Press; Editor of "Light Magazine" and published "The Voice of Southern Sudan" Teacher, Africa literature Centre, Zambia; Co-Founder, Southern Sudan Association, London, Director and Editor of "The Grass Curtain", London (1970-72); External Spokesman, South Sudan Liberation Movement (1970-72); participated in Addis Ababa negotiations on Southern Sudan (1972); Regional Minister for Information and official spokesman of the Transitional Higher Executive Council (1972-73); elected Member of the Regional Assembly for the Bor District (1973); Regional Minister for

Cooperatives and Rural Development (1973-75); Regional Minister of Information, Culture, Youth and Sports (1976). **Medal:** Medal of Two Niles for Peace (1st Class). **Addr:** Bor District, Upper Nile Province, Sudan.

GARGOUR (Nadim), Jordanian businessman. **Born** in 1951, in Jordan. **Son** of Hanna Gargour (Trader). **Married** in New York in 1974 to Patricia McCormick; 2 children, Hanna and Karim. **Educ.:** Collège des Frères, Jordan; Reading University in England, Bradford University, U.S.A. **Dipl.:** B.A. in Economics and Sociology; M.B.A. International Business. **Career:** Managing Director, Hansa Line West Germany (1976-77); T. Gargour et Fils, Amman (1977 to date); also Managing Mercedes Agency, Shipping Department, Trading Department; Aqaba Tourist House Hotel. **Sports:** Squash, swimming. **Hobby:** Music. **Credit Cards:** Visa and Amex. **Prof. Addr.:** P.O.Box 419, Wasfi Tal Street, Amman, Tel.: (6)5524142. **Priv. Addr.:** Sweijieyeh, Amman, Jordan.

GARNAOUI (Habib), Tunisian senior civil servant. **Born** on November 9, 1932 at Sousse (Tunisia). **Son** of Garnaoui Belhassen (tailor) **and** Mrs., née Ben Gadha Hallouma. **Married** to Kenani Zineb on September 13, 1958 at Sousse 4 children: Mondher, Karim, Leila and Hicham. **Educ.:** Lycée of Sousse; Faculty of Science Lyon University (France); Faculty of Science, University of Marseilles, Aix-en-Provence (France); Institute of Living Languages, Nice (France); Faculty of Law and Economics, Tunis University (Tunisia). **Dipl.:** Baccalaureate (Mathematics), B.Sc. (Pure Mathematics), B.Sc. (General Mathematics), B.Sc. (Tax Inspector). **Career:** Tax Inspector (1957-61); Chief Inspector (1961-64); Chief, State Tobacco Corporation (RNTA) (1964-69); Sub-Manager RNTA (1969-74); Manager, Société Tunisienne de Banque; now Chairman, Director-General, Mechanical Workshops of the Sahel since 1974; President, Central Section, Franco-Tunisian Chamber of Commerce and Industry; Managing-Director SAHELMOB Company; Mayor of Sousse Town (1980-85). **Awards:** Knight, Order of the Republic. **Sports:** Swimming, table tennis and football. **Hobbies:** Theater-going, music and travel. **President:** Club Jeune Science of Sousse. **Prof. Addr.:** Municipality of Sousse. **Priv. Addr.:** Khezama, Route Touristique, Sousse, Tunisia.

GASIM (Awn Sharif, al), Sudanese academic. **Born** on October 15, 1933 in Khartoum, Sudan. **Married,** 5 children. **Educ.:** University of Khartoum, Sudan; London University, UK; Edinburgh University, UK. **Dipl.:** B.A., M.A., Ph.D. **Career:** Lecturer, London University (1960-61); Senior Lecturer, Khartoum University (1969); Head of the Translation Department, Khartoum, University (1969); Chief Editor of "Sudanese Studies" published by the Institute of African and Asian Studies, University of Khartoum; Minister of Religious Affairs and Waqfs (1971). **Publ.:** "Primary Readers for the Sudan" In Arabic (1969), "The Diplomacy of the Prophet Muhammad" in Arabic (1970); "Dictionary of Sudanese Colloquial Arabic" (1971), "Aspects of the Cultural Renaissance" (1971), "Basrawi Poetry in the Omayyad Age" (1972), "In the Battle of the Heritage" (1972), "Religion in Everyday Life" (1974), "From the Prophet's Teaching" (1975), "Islamica: Spiritual Heritage and National Renaissance" (1976). **Decor.:** Order of the Constitution (1973); Order of the Two Niles (1975). **Medals:** Gold Medal of Arts, Science and Letters (1975). **Hobbies:** Islamic culture, civilization, walking, reading. **Addr.:** Khartoum, Sudan.

GASM ELSEED (Elamin Dafalla, Prof.), Sudanese Professor Veterinary theriogenology (Now State Minister). **Born** on June 26, 1948 at Elhilalya (Sudan). **Son** of Dafalla Gasm Elseed (deceased) **and** Mrs. Zynab Ahmed Hussein (deceaded). **Married** on June 10, 1979 to Omsalama Kamlir, six children: three girls and three boys: Lubada 1980, Jihad 1982, Ryan 1985 (Girls); Abdelrahman 1988, Mohamed 1992, Moneeb 1996 (Boys). **Educ.:** Elhilalya Elementary (1955-1959), Elhilalya mid-Secondary (1960-1963), Hantoub Secondary (1964-1968), Khartoum University-Veterinary Science (1968-1973). **Dipl.:** Ph. D. Trinity College, Dublin, Ireland (1978-1981), FRVCS, Royal Veterinary College Uppsala, Sweden (1985). **Career:** 1973-1976 - Field Inspector, Veterinary; 1976-1978 - Research Officer Central Veterinary Laboratories, Khartoum; 1978-1981 - Ph.D Research Student, Dublin, Ireland; 1981-1989 - Assistant & Associate Professor University of Khartoum; 1989-1994 on secondment King Faisal University Saudia; 1994-1996 Deputy Governor & Minister of Agriculture, Kassala State; 1996-1998 Deputy Governor & Minister of Agriculture, Gedarif State. **Other Information:** August 1998-March 1999, State Minister, Ministry of Agriculture, Khartoum; March 1999 - to date, State Minister, Managing Director, Sudan Gezira Board. **Hobbies:** Social activities & Reading. **Prof. Addr.:** Sudan Gezira Project, Barakat, Tel.: 00249 516/80061 and 80145, Fax: 00249 11 471715, Khartoum, Sudan. **Priv. Addr.:** Barakat, Tel.: 00249 516/80098, Khartoum, Sudan.

GAWDAT (Gorgi Aziz), Egyptian accountant. **Born** on July 20, 1950 in Cairo, Egypt. **Son** of Gorgi Aziz (deceased) **and** Mrs., née Marguerite Kamel Morkos. **Married** to Miss Ola Naugy on September 2, 1980. **Educ.:** Saint Paul College of the Christian Brothers (1955-64); De la Salle College, then Tewfikiyeh School (1965-68); Faculty of Commerce, Cairo University (1969-73). **Dipl.:** Secondary Education Certificate (1968); B.Com. (1973). **Career:** Joined Egyptair (April- September 1974); Bank Misr Head Office, Cairo (1974- Sept. 1980); now Asst. Chief Accountant, Oman Investment and Finance Co. Ltd. (S.A.O.) at Muscat, Sultanate of Oman, since October 1980. **Sport:** Football. **Hobbies:** Music, reading. **Prof. Addr.:** Oman Investment & Finance Company Ltd. (S.A.O.), P.O.Box 5476 Ruwi, Sultanate of Oman. **Priv. Addr.:** 17 Baysouni Street, T-era'a el-Boulakiyah, Shubra District, Tel.: 940175, Cairo, Egypt.

GAZARIN (Adel Ismail, Dr. Eng.), Egyptian mechanical engineer, industrial consultant. **Born** on March 20, 1926 in Alexandria. **Married**, 2 Boys. **Educ.:** Faculty of Engineering, Alexandria University; High Technical School of Zurich (E.T.H.), Mechanical Department. **Dipl.:** B.Sc. in Mechanical Engineering (June 1946); Doctor Engineer, E.T.H. Zurich, (June 1951); Doctoral Thesis Subject: Design of Blades of Turbo-Machinery. **Further Studies and Training:** Several Months of Training in Different Swiss Firms (Brownboveri-Oerlikon) (Sept. 1951- Janv. 1952); Special Summer Course and Research at the A.I.T. Cambridge USA, Foreign Students Summer Project (May 1953 to Sept.); Special Top Management Course at the National Institute of Management Development A.R.E. (May 1964 to June). **Career:** (Professional and Work Experience:) Lecturer, Faculty of Engineering, Alexandria University (1952-55); Special Assignment for Purchasing of Production Equipment in West Gemany (1955-59); Ministry of Industry (Head of Industrial Control Department for Engineering Industries) (1957-59); Planning Manager, el-Nasr Automotive Manufacturing Co. (1959-62); Technical Manager & Member of the Board, el-Nasr Automotive MFG. Co. (1962-64); Factories General & Member of the Board, el-Nasr Automotive Manufacturing Company (1964-68); Chairman & Managing Director, el-Nasr Automotive Manufacturing Company (1968-83); Chairman of the Engineering Industries Corporation (1983-86); presently, Chairman of Federation of Egyptian Industries, Industrial Consultant. **Other Professional and Business:** Chairman of the Federation of Egyptian Industries; Chairman of Ferrometalco (J.V. Co. for Production of Steel Structures); Board Member of Misr Arab African Bank; Board Member of the "el-Moltaka el-Arabie INV. Co."; Board Member of Egyptian Social Fund; Board Member of Egyptian Business Men Assoc.; Board Member of Egyptian American Business Council; Chairman of the Egyptian Italian Business Council; Member of the Governing Body of the "ILO Geneva"; Board Member in Egyptian Academy of Science; Member of the National Council for Production. **Member:** Member and Past President of International Rotary Club of Cairo; Member of Gezira Sporting Club; Member of Cairo Automotive Club. **Decor.:** 2 Egyptian Decorations of High Merit; 2 Italian Decorations; 1 Yugoslav Decoration; 1 Polish Decoration. **Sports & Hobbies:** Swimming, photography. **Languages:** Arabic, English, German, French. **Prof. Addr.:** Int. Industrial Consultation Office, 46, Syria Str., Mohandessin, Tel.: 3601640, 3480248, Fax: 3482404, Telex: 20916 R.G. UN, Cairo, Egypt. **Priv. Addr.:** 25, Mecca Str., Mohandessin, Cairo, Egypt.

GAZZAR (Abdel Hadi, el), Egyptian painter and professor. **Born** in 1925 in Egypt. **Educ.:** Faculty of Fine Arts, Cairo University; Rome Academy of Fine Arts (Italy). **Career:** Exhibited works at the 28th and 30th Venice Biennali, Brussels International Exhibition (1958); Sao Paulo Bienal (1961), Cairo, Alexandria and Rome; now professor of Painting, Cairo University. **Prof. Addr.:** Faculty of Fine Arts, Cairo University, Egypt.

GAZZAZ (Abbas Ahmad), Saudi M.D. and civil servant. **Born** in 1936 in Mecca, Saudi Arabia. **Dipl.:** B.Chem., M.D. **Career:** General Practitioner, King's Hospital, Jeddah; Assistant Director, same hospital; Director of Jeddah Central Hospital; Assistant Director General of Protective Medicine, Ministry of Health. Member of Middle Eastern Medical Conference, Iran, WHO meeting, Geneva, Gulf States Ministers of Health meetings, Abu Dhabi (1977) and Kuwait (1978). **Hobbies:** Reading, light sports. **Priv. Addr.:** Tel.: 4769076, Riyadh, Saudi Arabia.

GAZZAZ (Hassan Abdul Haye), Saudi businessman, writer and columnist. **Born** in 1918 in Mecca, Saudi Arabia. **Educ.:** Received general literary education. **Career:** typist, General Automobiles Company (1938); employee, Ministry of Finance (1947); Director General of Formation and Publishing Department (1956); founder, Arafat weekly newspaper (1957); founder and editor-in-chief of "al-Bilad" daily newspaper (1958); founder, Arafat Factorics (1968); Board member, Jeddah Electricity Co. (1957-64); Founder, and Director General, Arafat Brick and Pottery Pipe Factories. Visited and represented "al-Bilad" newspaper in the United States of America and European countries by invitation among groups of prominent journalists from the Middle East. **Publ.:** Meshwari Maa Al Kalemah (My Pace with the World) Two books consisting of ten chapters; Also prepared a study about "Information at the time of King Abul Aziz Al-Saud" **Awards:** Received the Golden Key for the City of San Francisco from its Mayor **Addr.:** Jeddah, Saudi Arabia.

GEGHMAN (Yahya Hamoud), Yemeni diplomat. **Born** on September 24, 1934 in Jahanah. **Son** of Hamoud and Mrs. Ezziya Geghman. **Married** in 1971 to Cathya Geghman, two children, one son Laith and one daughter Kindiya. **Educ.:** Law, Political Sciences & Economics, Cairo, Paris, Damascus, Boston & Columbia Universities. **Career:** Teacher of Arabic Language and Literature, Kuwait (1957-59); Director General, Yemen Broadcasting System; Special Adviser, Ministry of Foreign Affairs; Governor, Yemen Bank for Reconstruction & Development; Secretary General, Supreme Council Tribal Affairs (1962-63); Deputy Permanent Reprentative to UN (1963-66); Minister Plenipotentiary Yemen Embassy to U.S.A. (1963-67); Minister of Foreign Affairs (1968-69); Minister of State & Personal Representative of the President (1969); Deputy Prime Minister, Founder & President Supreme Council for Youth's Welfare and Sport (1969-71); Governor IBRD IMF (1969-71); Permanent Representative to UN (1971-73); Ambassador to U.S.A. (1972-74); Minister of Foreign Affairs (1974-75); Deputy Prime Minister for Economic and Foreign Affairs (1975-76); Adviser, Personal Representative to the President (1977-85); Chief of **Bureau** South Yemen Affairs, Chairman Yemen Reunification

Commissions (1980-83); Ambassador to Switzerland, Permanent Representative to UN Vienna & UNIDO (1985-90); Permanent Representative to UN European HQ & Other Organizations, Geneva (1985-); Governor and Executive Director UN Common Fund for Commodities, Amsterdam (1989-); Member of Governing Council UN Compensation Commission (1991); President Diplomatic Committee on Host Country Relations (1991). **Publ.:** Co-authored book on Yemen, published various articles and poems. **Hobbies:** Reading, writing, horseback riding, swimming, chess, music. **Prof. Addr.:** Mission Permanente de la République du Yemen auprès de l'Office de l'ONU à Genève, Chemin du Jonc 19-1216 Cointrin (Genève), Switzerland.

GENAWI (Hamza, Mohammed), Sudanese General Manager Khartoum stock exchange. **Born** on January 1, 1948 in Sudan. **Son** of Mohammed Genawi (Farmer) **and** Mrs. née Fatima Nasralla. **Married** on December 2, 1970 at Khartoum to Maria Elsayed, 4 children: Khalid, Eman, Ali, Esam. **Educ.:** Khartoum Commercial High School, Cairo University, Khartoum Branch. **Dipl.:** Management of Sales & Zakat From Quoran University Omdurman Sudan. **Career:** Sudan Commercial Bank (1967-1979); Faisal Islamic Bank (Sudan) (1979-1982); Al Baraka Bank (Sudan) (1982-1986); Sudanese Saving Bank (D.G. Manager) (1992-1994); Khartoum Stock Exchange (G. Manager) (1994- up to now). **Sports Practised:** Basket Ball. **Hobby:** Reading. **Clubs:** Khartoum (3) Football Club. **Prof. Addr.:** Albaraka Tower, Khartoum, Tel.: 00249-11-782250, Sudan. and Khartoum Stock Exchange, Tel.: 00249-11-782225, Khartoum, Sudan. **Priv. Addr.:** Omdurman Almorada West, Tel.: 00249-11-561090, Sudan.

GERMANOS (Raymond), Lebanese lawyer. **Educ.:** Licence en Droit from the Faculty of Law in Beirut and Damascus (1954); Damascus University, Syria (Finance Economics). **Career:** Lawyer (1955); Secretary to the Board of Directors, Gefinor Group of Companies, Lebanon (1963); Legal and Administrative Departments Manager, Arab Investment Co. SAL (1964); Manager, Gefinor Group; Manager, Gefinor, Paris (1977-); Assistant General Manager, Arab Investment Co. SAL, Beirut (1978); Secretary General, Gefinor Investment Ltd., Geneva, Switzerland; Director of Trade Exchange Co. SAL; société des Immeubles Modernes SAL; Société Nationale pour les Projets Fonciers SAL. **Addr.:** 23 Avenue de la Porte Neuve, Luxembourg.

GERMOUNI (Muhammad), Moroccan academic. **Born** on October 11, 1947 in Morocco. **Married** 2 sons. **Educ.:** Faculté des Sciences Economiques de Rabat et de Grenoble, Institut d'Etudes Politiques de Grenoble (France). **Dipl.:** Ph.D. in Economics, Diplomé de la Section Economique et Financière de l'I.E.P. **Career:** Director, Banque Nationale pour le Développement Economique; Professor in Economics /Faculté des Sciences Economiques, Rabat; Member of the Executive Committee of the International Economic Association / Paris- International Consultant. **Publ.:** several papers and essays published in professional journals. **Hobbies:** Tennis, swimming, gymnastics, music. **Prof. Addr.:** P.O.Box 407, Rabat, Morocco.

GEZAIRY (Hussein Abdul-Razzaq), Saudi physician and politician. **Born** in 1934 in Mecca, Saudi Arabia. **Dipl.:** M.S.B. CG, Cairo University (1957); Diploma in General Surgery, Cairo University (1960); F.R.C.S., London (1965), **Career:** General Practioner, King Saud University (1960); Registrar in both Brompton and Royal Free Hospitals, London, Founding Dean, Faculty of Medicine, King Saud University (1966); Lecturer, Assistant Professor then Associate Professor in General Surgery, Faculty of Medicine, King Saud Univesity; Professor of General Surgery (Leading Cardiac Thoracic Surgery), external examiner, Faculty of Medicine, King Saud University; former Minister of Health; participated in ordinary and special sessions of Health and the Arab Gulf States, WHO Regional Sub-Committee A' annual meetings for Eastern Mediterranean, World Health Assembly Sessions, international confernces for medical education, Saudi medical seminars and conferences, ministerial consultation attended by both the Ministers of Health and the Ministers of High Education (under the auspicies of WHO), Tehran, 1978; member of the Ministerial Region Consultation Committee, WHO; President of the Higher Board, Arab Council for medical specialization, Arab Board; presently director of the World Health Organization (WHO), regional office for the Eastern Mediterranean. **Honours:** King Abdulaziz Order, Second Class, granted by H.M. the late King Khalid Ibn Abdulaziz; Leopold II Medal (the Grand Ornament), granted by His Majesty the King of Belgium; Bright Star Decoration, National Republic of China, November 1981. **Hobbies:** reading, sports, listening to music. **Addr.:** P.O.Box 5583, Riyadh 11432, Saudi Arabia and P.O.Box 1517, Alexandria 21511, Egypt.

GHADBANE (Adel, al), Egyptian writer and poet. **Born** in Aleppo. **Educ.:** Secondary. **Career:** Joined the Egyptian State Railways, Interpreter, the Cairo Mixed Courts; Professor of Arabic Literature, Holy Family College of the Jesuits Fathers in Cairo; Joined Dar al-Maaref Publishing and Printing House in Cairo (cir. 1937); former Head of the Publishing Department and Managing-Director of Dar al-Maaraf; contributed numerous studies and articles to leading Arabic newspapers and periodicals; Much travelled visiting most of Western Europe, the U.S.A. and Latin America, notably Argentine where he received a rousing welcome by the Lebanese and Syrian communities there. **Publ.:** "Naguib al-Haddad", "Min Wah' al-Iskandaria", "Ahmas el-Awal", etc. **Prof. Addr.:** Dar al-Mareef, Corniche Road, Cairo. **Priv. Addr.:** Tagher Bldg., Garden City, Cairo, Egypt.

GHAFARI (Hussain Muhammad, Lt. Col.), Yemeni diplomat. **Born** in 1930 in Yemen Arab Republic. **Married**, 1 son, 3 daughters. **Career:** Manager, Taiz Airport (1967); Military Attaché, Yemen Arab Republic, Embassy to USSR (1972-74); Military Attaché, Yemen Arab Republic Embassy to Iran (1974-76); Minister of Communications (February 1976); Ambassador to Ethiopia (1992-). **Hobbies:** football, table-tennis, reading history. **Addr.:** Ministry of Foreign Affairs, Sanaa, Republic of Yemen.

GHAIB (Mukhlis, Mouloud), Iraqi physician. **Born** on April 10, 1931 in Tiberit, Iraq. **Son** of Mukhlis Mouloud (Former President of the Chamber of Representatives) **and** Mrs. Bidour Rajab ar-Rifaï. **Married** to Nawar Abdulfattah on December 29, 1960, 3 children: Soumaya, Mohamad-Hader and Nadya. **Educ.:** Mamouniya Primary School; Gharbiya Intermediate School; Geneva University Medical College; Liverpool University Tropical Medicine and Hugiene School; Mustansiriya University, College of Law. **Dipl.:** Bachelor in Science and Medicine, Licence in Science and Medicine, Doctor in Medicine, Diploma in Tropical Medicine and Hygiene, Specialist in Public Health, Bachelor of Law. **Career:** Doctor, Private Clinic (1957-60); Doctor in School Health Directorate (1960-62); Director of School Health Services (1962-63); Director General of Medical Services (1963-64); Member of the Iraqi Delegation to the World Health Organization (1964); Director of School Health Services (1964-68); Acting Dean of High Institute of Health Professions; Lecturer at Baghdad University, President and Member of several committees; Head of Iraqi Delegation to Health Education in Kuwait; Representative of Arab League in Arabian Gulf, Cairo; Member of Delegation to Social and Welfare Conference in U.S.A.; Minister of Municipal and Rural Affairs (1968). **Publ.:** Research work and Thesis on the Intervation of Salivary Glands, several research works on School Health, several works on schistosomaiasis (Belharizia Heamatobium and Treatment). **Sports:** Hunting and Boating. **Hobbies:** Lectures and research work. **Member** of al-Mansour Club, Doctors' Association, Iraqi Medical Society, Red Crescent Society, Cancer Society, Cooperative Association of Medical Professions, President of People's Refuge Association. **Priv. Addr.:** al-Mansour, Tel.: 36520, Baghdad, Iraq.

GHAIDAN (Saadoun, Gen.), Iraqi army officer and politician. **Born** in 1930 in Iraq. **Married**, five children. **Educ.:** secondary and Military College. **Career:** Commissioned second Lieutenant (1953); Commander Republic Body-Guard Forces (1968); General commanding Baghdad Forces (1969); member Revolutionary Command Council (since 1968); Minister of the Interior (1970-74); of Communications (1974-78); Deputy Prime Minister (1979-82). **Addr.:** Baghdad, Iraq.

GHAITH (Saeed, Khalfan al), United Arab Emirates politician. **Born** in Dubai, United Arab Emirates. **Career:** Director, Political Dept., Ministry of Foreign Affairs, (1972-73); Minister of State for Information, (1973-77); Minister of State for Cabinet Affairs, 1975 to present. **Addr.:** Ministry of State for Cabinet Affairs, Zayed 1st Street, P.O.Box 899, Abu Dhabi, United Arab Emirates.

GHALEB (Awad, Hejazi), Palestinian financial manager. **Born** in 1943 in al-Ghabsieh. **Son** of Saleh Ghaleb. **Married** in 1973, 3 sons. **Educ.:** Cairo University. **Dipl.:** B.Com. **Career:** Auditor, Aweida Shattara & Co., Beirut (1967); Auditor, Aweida Shattara & Co., UAE (1968); Financial Manager, al-Nasr Group, Dubai, UAE (1969-); Director, al-Nasr Group; al-Nasr Trading Division, Dubai; al-Nasr Engineering Division, Dubai; al-Nasr Trading Division, Abu Dhabi; Crescent Oil Fields Supply, Sharjah and Abu Dhabi; al-Nasr Film Co.; al-Nasr Novelty Stores. **Member:** Dubai Country Club. **Addr.:** P.O.Box 1106 Deira, Tel.: 661625-29, Telex: 45638 A/B ALNASR EM, Dubai, UAE.

GHALEB (Mohamad, Anaam), Yemeni economist. **Born** in 1932. **Married**, 2 children. **Educ.:** Cairo University, Egypt; University of Texas, USA. **Dipl.:** Licence in Law, M.A. in Economics. **Career:** Director of Central Planning Organization; Minister of Economy; Minister of Higher Education; Minister of Information (March/June 1974); Consultant to the Central Planning Organization and Dean of the National Institute of Public Administration. **Publ.:** various works in economics. **Hobbies:** writing poetry and short stories, reading poetry, economics, music, walking. **Prof. Addr.:** P.O.Box 102, Sanaa, Republic of Yemen.

GHALEB (Mourad), Egyptian diplomat. **Born** on April 1, 1922 in Cairo, Egypt. **Married** in 1953 to Shoukreya Ali Mohamad, two children. **Educ.:** Secondary and Military College, Cairo; Cairo University. **Dipl.:** Degree in Medicine (1945). **Career:** Professor of Medical Faculty, Cairo University (1950); Medical Adviser in Egyptian Embassy to USSR (1953); Secretary and Counsellor, Egyptian Embassy to USSR; Director of the President's Office for Political Affairs (1957); Under-Secretary Foreign Affairs, Ministry of Foreign Affairs, Cairo (1959-60); Ambassador to Zaire Republic (1960); Ambassador to USSR (1961-70); Appointed to Arab Socialist Union (ASU) Elections Supervisory Committee (1971); alternate Member of the Central Committee (1971); Minister of State for Foreign Affairs (1971); Minister of Foreign Affairs (1972); Minister of Information (1973); Resident Minister in Tripoli, libya (1973); Special Presidential Envoy to mediate in Kuwait-Iraq border dispute (1973); accompanied late President Sadat to Arab Summit (1973); Ambassador to Libya (1974); Ambassador to Yugoslavia (1974), resigned (1977); now President, Afro-Asian People's Solidarity Organization (AAPSO). **Sports:** Swimming, Tennis. **Hobbies:** Reading, Camping. **Prof. Addr.:** 89 Abdulaziz al-Saud

Street, Manial, Cairo, Egypt. **Priv. Addr.:** 78, an-Nil Street, Abu al-Fetooh Building, Giza, Tel.: 982100, 855454, Cairo, Egypt.

GHALI (Yusuf, Iskandar), Egyptian university professor. **Born** on January 15, 1929 in Cairo. **Son** of Dr. Iskandar Ghali (Barrister) **and** Mrs. Bedour Boctor. **Educ.:** Collège de la Sainte Famille, Cairo, Egypt (1937-47); Faculty of Agriculture, Cairo University (1948-51); University of Minnesota, U.S.A. **Dipl.:** Bachelor of Science (Agriculture 1951); Master of Science (Biochem 1956); Doctor of Philosophy (Biochem 1959). **Career:** Demonstrator at the Faculty of Agriculture Biochemistry Department, Cairo University (1952-61); Lecturer at the Said Faculty, Biochemistry Department (1961-67); Staff member at the University of Minnesota (U.S.A.); Biochemistry Department (1963-64); actually Associate Professor at the Faculty of Agriculture, Biochemistry Department, Cairo University, in mission in Algeria. **Publ.:** Author of "The constitution of Starch Galactose-Codextrin", in collaboration with Dr. M.H. Fisher and Dr. F. Smith (Cereal Chemistry 45, No.5, 421 published in 1968; "The constitution of an Amylopectin-Xylose Codextrin", in collaboration with Dr. F. Smith (J. Chem. Egypt 10, No.3, 267), published in 1967; "Isolation of Starch from Legume Seed" in collaboration with Dr. M. Ghanem, Pakistan J. of Science 19, No.4, 175 published in 1967: "Separation and Chemical Study of Starch from Corn Grains", in collaboration with Dr. Abdulkaher and Dr. A. Fawzi, Pakistan J. of Science 18, No.3, 112 published in 1966: "The Effect of Steeping on the Horny and Floury Varicities of Corn Grains" in collaboration with Dr. Abdulkaher and Dr. A. Fawzi, Alexandria, J. Agricultural Research 16, No 1, 1968: "Chemical Study concerning starch modified with hypochlorate", in collaboration with Dr. Abdulkaher and Dr. A. Fawzi, published in Alexandria in J. of Agricultural Research 16, No.2, 1968; "The Production of Starch and Flour from Sweet Potatoes", in collaboration with Dr. Abdulkaher, published in the Annals of Agricultural Science (Aïn Shams University), 11, No.1, 1959-66; "Oxidation of Polysaccharides eith Lead Tetraacetate" in collaboration with Dr. Abdulakher, Dr. A. Youssef and Dr. A.N. Michalinos J. Chem, Egypt, 6, No.1, 107 (1963); "The constitution of Polysaccharides from Prinkly Pears Plants" (op. ficus indica) in collaboration with Dr. M. Abdulqader and Dr. A. Khalifa (This paper was accepted at the first Arab Chemical Conference held in Cairo in 1966). **Sports:** Swimming and shooting. **Member** of Heliopolis Sporting Club, Cairo, Egypt, Egyptian Chemical Association. **Priv. Addr.:** 5, Ibrahim Lakaki Street, Heliopolis, Tel.: 873349, Cairo, Egypt.

GHALLAB (Abdul Karim), Moroccan academic. **Married,** 3 sons. **Educ.:** Cairo University, Egypt. **Dipl.:** B.A. in Literature. **Career:** Minister Plenipotentiary, Ministry of Foreign Affairs, Morocco (1956-59); Editor in Chief "Risalat al Maghrib", "al-Alam" (1960-); "al-Bayna" and "Afaaq"; Professor of Literature; Former Member of Parliament; Member of the Moroccan Royal Academy, Member of Moroccan Writers Union, Former Secretary General of Moroccan Journalist Union. **Publ.:** numerous books on literary criticism, historical and political studies (1961-79); several novels and short story collections (1965-77). **Decor.:** Order of the Republic, Egypt (1956); Order of Merit, Tunisia (1972). **Hobbies:** Writing, golf. **Prof. Addr.:** 11 Avenue Allal Ben Abdullah, P.O.Box 141, Rabat, Morocco.

GHAMDI (Ali Abdullah Mughram,al-), Saudi Academic. **Born** in 1942 at Baljurashi, Saudi Arabia. **Dipl.:** B.A. (Honours) (Geg. 1966) College of Education, Makkah, Saudi Arabia; Ph.D. (Dunelm) (Geog. 1973) Durham University, England. **Career:** Lecturer, Assistant Professor, Head of Department, Department of Geography, King Abdulaziz University, Jeddah, Saudi Arabia (until 1981); Director General, Islamic Cultural Center London, England (1981-95); Director, King Fahad Academy, England (1996 - to present). **Publ.:** Assarah, Saudi Arabia (Ph.D. Thesis). **Hobbies:** Reading, Photography and Travel **Address:** The King Fahad Academy, Bromyard Avenue, Acton, Tel.: 0208 7430131, Fax: 0208 7497085, London W3 7HD, England.

GHAMDI (Ali Ahmad Ali, al), Saudi academic. **Born** in 1947 at Baljurashi. **Dipl.:** M.A. and Ph.D. (English Language and Literature). **Career:** Associate Professor, Dept. of English, College of Arts, King Saud University; Member, Modern Language Association. **Hobbies:** Reading, research, traveling and political analysis. **Prof. Addr.:** Dept. of English, College of Arts, P.O.Box 2456, Tel.: 4675435, Riyadh 11451, Saudi Arabia.

GHAMDY (Ali G. Ma'adhah, al), Saudi chemical engineer. **Born** in 1945 at Bani Salim Baljurashi. **Dipl.:** Ph.D. (Chemical Engineering) (1978). **Career:** Demonstrator, King Fahd University of Petroleum and Minerals (KFUPM) (1971); Assistant Professor, Chemical Engineering Department, KFUPM (1978-82); Associate Professor, Chemical Engineering Department and Manager, Petroleum and Gas Technology Division, Research Institute, KFUPM (1982-). **Member:** American Institute of Chemical Engineers (AIChE), American Chemical Society (ACS), Tau Beta Pi (Engineering Honor Society), Omega Chi Epsilon (Chemical Engineering Honor Society) and the International Desalination Association (IDA); International Desalination and Environmental Association (1981-85); member of the board, Eastern Petrochemical Company, (SHARQ) Jubail, (1982-86); National Committee on Petrochemicals, and Editorial Board, Arabian Journal for Science and Engineering; participated in several national and international professional conferences and radio and television programmes. **Publ.:** Articles in professional journals, books and report, relating to energy, natural gas processing, polymers and Plastics, petrochemical industry in Saudi Arabia and water desalination; Co-author of a book on polymer degradation. **Award:** Citation of Excellence from UN Environment Program; First OAPEC (Organization of Arab Petroleum Exporting Countries) Scientific Award (1990); Prince Mohammad Ibn Fahd Awards for Best Research Projects (1987-1989). **Hobbies:** reading, travel, photography. **Addr.:** King Fahd University of Petroleum and Minerals, P.O.Box 83, Tel.: 8603888, 8603883, Dhahran, 31261 Saudi Arabia.

GHAMDY (Ali Saeed S., al), Saudi administration general manager; al-Madina Press and Publication Establishment. **Born** in Mount Shada (Ghamid). **Educ.:** Secondary School Education. **Career:** Registrar, Riyadh Court (1957-58); Registrar, State Income, Ministry of Finance (1958-61); Secretary, Compensation Committee, Ministry of Finance (1961-63); Secretary, Under Secretary, Ministry of Finance (1963-64); Manager, Western Province Branch, Ministry of Works and Housing (1964-66); Inspector, Ministry of Transportation (1966-68); General Manager, Financial Affairs, Jeddah Islamic Port (1968-70); General Manager, General Administration, and Member of the Board, al-Madina Press Establishment and Dar al-Elm Printing & Publication Company (1972-91); **Hobbies:** Reading and journalism. **Addr.:** al-Madina Press Est., P.O.Box 807, Tel.: (02)6712100, Fax: (02)6711877, Telex: 605000 EILAN SJ., Jeddah 21421, Saudi Arabia.

GHAMDY (Mohamad Ibn Ibrahim, A., al), Saudi businessman. **Born** in 1925 at Baljurashi, Ghamid. **Career:** Active in the fields of commerce, industry and construction; one of the founders of Tihama for Advertising, Public Relations and Marketing Research; member of Board, Jeddah Refinery Co. (SARCO); sports welfare societies. **Addr.:** al-Buraimy Street Makkah Road, Kilo 4, Tel.: 6875567, 6890516 (Office) and 688-176 (Home), Jeddah, Saudi Arabia.

GHAMMAI (Salim, Humad, al), UAE official. **Born** in 1945 in Sharjah, United Arab Emirates. **Married**, 3 children. **Dipl.:** B.A. in Education. **Career:** Secondary School Teacher, then Headmaster; Director of Technical Department, Ministry of Education; Assistant Under Secretary, Ministry of Education (1978-). **Hobbies:** Reading, tennis, table-tennis, cinema, football, travelling; Former Vice **Chairman** of the Board, UAE Football Association and Sharjah Sports Club. **Prof.Addr.:** P.O.Box 897, Sharjah, United Arab Emirates.

GHAMMAZ (Hamed, Mustafa, el), Egyptian bank manager. **Born** in 1929 in Fariskour, UAR. **Son** of Mustafa el-Ghammaz. **Married** in 1958, 2 sons, 2 daughters. **Educ.:** Cairo University. **Dipl.:** B.Com. (Honours) (1951). **Career:** National Bank of Egypt (1951-77); Assistant Managing Director, Chase National Bank, Cairo (1977-78); former General Manager, Nile Bank, Cairo, Egypt (since 1978). **Addr.:** Cairo, Egypt.

GHANDOUR (Muzzamil, Sulaiman), Sudanese former diplomat. **Born** in 1928. **Educ.:** Fort Leavenworth, USA (Staff Course); Nasser Military Academy, Egypt (Military Course). **Career:** joined regular army; Battalion Commander (1962-63); Commander of the Infantry School Gebeit (1967), promoted to Brigadier (1968); Military Attaché, Embassy to UK (1967); appointed to Ministry of Foreign Affairs with rank of Ambassador; Ambassador to West Germany (1971); non-resident Ambassador to Austria (1972); Adviser to the Presidency on Foreign Economic Cooperation (1974). **Addr.:** Khartoum, Sudan.

GHANDOURAH (Abdulaziz Mohamad), Saudi civil servant. **Born** in 1936 in Mecca, Saudi Arabia. **Dipl.:** B.Sc. (Civil Engineering). **Career:** Director, Road Department, Jeddah (1963-71); Director General, Technical Department for Roads and Seaports; Director General, Mina Development Project since 1975; member of the Royal Commission for Jubail and Yanbu; participant, Conference of Arab Ministers of Housing. **Prof. Addr.:** P.O.Box 6172, Tel.: 6659503, Jeddah. **Priv. Addr.:** Tel.: 8624907, Jeddah, Saudi Arabia.

GHANDOURAH (Sulaiman Mohamad Hussain), Saudi official. **Born** in 1930 in Mecca, Saudi Arabia. **Dipl.:** Diploma (Business Administration), Institute of Public Administration, Cairo; a course in Management, American University, Cairo. **Career:** General Director of Personnel, Ministry of Communications (1956), Administration and Personnel Affairs (1962), Financial Affairs (1961); Adviser to H.E. Minister of Communications for Financial and Administrative Affairs (1965); Director General of Administration of Telegraph and Telephone, Ministry of P.T.T., (1975); Assistant Deputy Minister of P.T.T. (1977) Deputy Minister of Post, Telegraph and Telephone for Financial and Administrative Affairs. **Hobbies:** Reading, travel. **Addr.:** Malaz, Riyadh, Saudi Arabia.

GHANDOUR (Ali I.), Jordanian Citizen, Lebanese **Born** in Beirut on May 28, 1931 **Educ.:** Primary and Secondary education at International College, Beirut; College education in Aircraft Maintenance Engineering at New York University; graduated in (1953). **Career:** Served as Engineer and Aviation Expert for safety and airworthiness at Lebanese Civil Aviation Department (1954-56); Chief Engineer, later V.P. Technical Affairs for Lebanese International Airways (1956-62); Helped organize and start the Jordanian National carrier, Alia-the Royal Jordanian Airline, assuming the function of Managing Director (1963-1974); Chairman and Chief Executive Officer (1974-89); Former Adviser to His Majesty the late King Hussein on Civil Aviation, Civil Air Transport and Tourism (1989-99): President, ARAM Trading and Technology, Beirut and Amman; Chairman, ARAM International Investments,Amman, Jordan; Chairman, Jordan Tourism Investments, Amman, Jordan; Co-Chairman and President, Aviation Pioneers & Consultants SARL; Member of the Board, Lebanon Invest, Beirut; Member of the Board Jet Airways (I) Ltd., Mumbai; Member of OMECA (Organisation Mondiale des Experts-Conseils-Arbitres) for arbitration in the French Courts on aviation matters. Other **Key Positions** and **Directorships** previously and currently held: Member of Board of Trustess, American University of Beirut (March 1979 to present); Member of the Advisory Council, the Center for Contemporary Arab Studies, Geogetown University, Washington D.C. (1979-90); Chairman, Center's Advisory Council, Georgetown University (Nov. 1979-April 90); Member of the Board, University of Jordan, Center for Strategic Studies (1983-89); Member of the Board, World Affairs Council of Jordan (Dec. 1977-May 91); Royal Jordanian Academy of Aeronautics: Founder (1965); Vice President (1965-75); Chairman of the Board of Trustees (1975-89); Arab Wings Amman: Founder; Chairman (1976-89); Royal Jordanian Falcons: Founder (1976); Chairman (1976-89); Flight Safety Foundation, USA: Member of the Board of Governors (1984-95); Member of the Higher National Committee, The Jerash Festival, Amman; Member of the Board Trustees, Royal Society of Fine Arts, Amman; Member of the Board of Trustees, Royal Endowment for Culture and Education, Amman; Member of the Board of Trustees, American Center of Oriental Research; Member of the Board of Trustees, Queen Noor Al-Hussein Foundation; World Aerospace Foundation Organization, Member of the Board of Directors. **Decorations:** Commendatore dell-Ordine Al Merito della Republica Italianna (Nov. 1983); Commandeur, Ordre National du Merite de la Légion d'Honneur, France (March 1985); Tenda Kehormatan, Indonesia (1986); Grand Cordon of the Order of Al Nahda of Jordan (1989); Sitara Quaid-E-Azam (Pakistan); Sitara I of Pakistan; Grand Decoration of Honour in Silver with Sash for Service to the Republic of Austria; National Order of the Cedars, Lebanon; Commander of National Order, Sweden. **Address:** ARAM Trading & Technology Ltd: **in Beirut:** P.O.Box 55606, Tel.: 961-1-865640, Fax: 961-1-798654, Beirut, Lebanon. **in Amman** P.O.Box 960913, Tel.: 962-6-5536738, Fax: 962-2-5537451, Amman 11196, Jordan.

GHANEM (Najeeb, Saeed, Dr.), Yemeni Professor of Pharmacology and former Minister of Health. **Born** in 1954 in Aden, Yemen. **Son** of Saeed Ghanem Saleh (Clerk) and Mrs. née Om-Al Khair-Hassan Fadel. **Married** to I. Abo Taleb in 1962 in Sanaa, 7 children. **Educ.:** Primary School, Aden, Yemen; Intermediate School, Aden, Yemen; Secondary School, Aden, Yemen; Kuwait University, Kuwait; London University College, London, England. **Dipl.:** B.Sc. (Medical Science) Kuwait University; M.Ph. and Ph.D. (Pharmacology) London University. **Medal:** Presidential Medal of Yemen Unity. **Sports:** Football, Swimming, Walking. **Hobbies:** Reading, Writing, Drawing. **Prof. Addr.:** P.O.Box 477, Sanaa. **Priv. Addr.:** Tel.: 967-1-340830.

GHANEM (Shokri), Libyan, Director, Research Division, OPEC Secretariat. **Born** on October 9, 1942. **Son** of Mohammed GHANEM, Merchant **and** Mrs. Zohra EL MAJRESE. **Married** on February 26, 1976 in Tripoli, Libya to Nagat Elhadi Ben Kura, four children: Mohamed, Ghada, Nahla, Aiya. **Educ.:** University of Libya, Benghazi. Fletcher School of Law and Diplomacy. **Dipl.:** 1963 B.A. Economics, University of Libya, 1972 M.A. Economics, Fletcher School of Law and Diplomacy, 1973 M.A.L.D. Law and Diplomacy, 1975 Ph.D. International Economics, Fletcher School of Law & Diplomacy. **Career:** Professor of International Economics, Faculty of Economics, Al-Fateh University, Tripoli (1988-1993); Academic Visitor, School of Oriental and African Studies, University of London (1982-1984); Chief Economist, Arab Development Institute, Tripoli, Libya (1977-1988); held the positions of Director of Marketing, Director of Economic Affairs, Under Secretary and Chief Advisor at the Ministry of Petroleum in Libya from 1968-1977; Deputy Director and Director of Foreign Trade, Ministry of Economy in Libya (1963-1968). **Associations:**Member of Arab Thought Forum; Member of Instituto de Empresa; Member of International Petroleum Exchange. **Prof. Addr.:** OPEC, Obere Donaustrasse 93, 1020, Vienna, Austria, **Priv. Addr.:** Kratochwjlestrasse 12/61, 1220 Vienna, Austria.

GHANIM (Abdallah Mohamad, al), Saudi educator. **Born** in 1936 at Jalajel. **Dipl.:** B.A. Shari'a (Islamic Law). **Career:** Headmaster of Al-Noor Institute (for the blind) (1960-62); Director of special education, Ministry of Education, later Director General; member, International Deaf and President of the Regional Bureau of the Middle East Committee for the Affairs of the Blind (MECFAB); member, International Deaf and Blind Association; member of the International Council for the Aid of the Visually Handicapped; President, Executive Committee of the Regional Bureau for the Affairs of the Blind; Vice President of WCWB and IFB; President (Middle East Region), The International Child Care Association for the Visually Handicapped; member, Board of Consultants, the World Health organization. **Honors:** Medal of Merit, first class awarded by King Hussain of Jordan; Medal of Merit from President of Tunisia, al-Habib Bourguiba; Gold Medal of Honour from the Federation of the German War Blind; other Gold Medals awarded from Arab States. **Hobby:** reading. **Prof. Addr.:** The Regional Bureau of the MECFAB, Tel.: 4032409, Riyadh. **Priv. Addr.:** Tel.: 4763701, Riyadh, Saudi Arabia.

GHANIM (Abdallah, Yusuf, al), Kuwaiti businessman. **Born** in Kuwait. **Son** of Yusuf al-Ghanem. **Married. Educ.:** Mubarakiyah School, Kuwait; Glasgow University, UK. **Career:** Minister of Water and Electricity (1974); Second Deputy President of the Kuwait Chamber of Commerce and Industry (1970-); Former Chairman of Kuwait Insurance Co.; Minister of Education (1990- April 1991); Chairman of Equipment Ltd; Y.I. Alghanim and Partners.

Chairman, United Gulf Bank EC, Manama, Bahrain. (until 1988). **Hobbies:** Swimming and fishing. **Addr.:** Y.I. ALGHANIM and Partners WLL, P.O.Box 435, Safat 13005, Tel.: 2402273, Fax: 2402272, Kuwait.

GHANIM (Ahmed, Kamel), Egyptian artist. **Born** on July 21, 1931 in Cairo, Egypt. **Married,** 2 sons, 1 daughter. **Educ.:** Cairo University, Egypt. **Dipl.:** B.Com. **Career:** Comedian in numerous radio and television programmes and in feature films. **Award:** Critics Association Prize at the International Film Festival, Cairo (1984). **Member:** al-Ahly Club, Zamalek Club, Gezira Sporting Club and Tersana Club. **Addr.:** 125 Shara' Abdel Aziz al-Su'ed, Menila, Cairo, Egypt.

GHANIM (Habib), Tunisian banker. **Career:** Director, Société Tunisienne de Banque, Tunis, Tunisia. Director, Union Tunisienne de Banques S.A., Paris, France. Deputy Chairman, The Arab Libyan Tunisian Bank, Beirut, Lebanon. Director, Société Financier de Gestion (Sofiges), Tunis, Tunisia; UBAF Arab Italian Bank S.P.A.; President and Chief Executive, Arab Banking Corporation, Rome, Italy. **Addr.:** 1, Avenue Habib Thameur, P.O.Box 638, Tel.: 258000, 242833, Telex: 12376-77, Tunis, Tunisia.

GHANIM (Ismail), Egyptian lawyer and statesman. **Born** on May 24, 1924 in Alexandria, Egypt. **Married** in 1951 to Myna Kathleen McGrath (deceased, 1959) and remarried to Martje Schotanus, four children. **Educ.:** Faculty of Law, Alexandria University; Faculty of Law, Paris University; Institute of Comparative Law, New York University (USA). **Career:** Lecturer, Faculty of Law, Paris University; also, Ayn Shams University (1951); Dean, Faculty of Law, Arab University in Beirut (Lebanon) (1962-63); Dean, Faculty of Law, Ayn Shams University (1966-68); Vice-Rector of the said university (1968-70), then rector (1971-74); Permanent delegate to the United Nations Education, Social and Cultural Organisation (UNESCO), Paris (1970-71); Minister of Culture (May-September 1971); Chairman, Council for the Social Sciences (1971); Vice-Premier and Minister of Higher Education and Scientific Research (1974-75). **Publ.:** Author of "Le Droit du Travail" (1962), "La Vente" (1963), "Le Droit Subjectif" (1963), "Les Droits Réels Principaux" (1962), "La Théorie Générale des Obligations" (1966-67). **Member:** Executive Board, Cairo Governorate; Board, Academy of Scientific Research. **Addr.:** Cairo, Egypt.

GHANIM (Kutayba, Yusuf, al), Kuwaiti diplomat and businessman. **Born** on October 12, 1945 in Kuwait. **Married,** three children. **Educ.:** University of California, Berkeley, USA. **Dipl.:** B.A. **Career:** Minister Counsellor Economic Affairs to the Permanent Mission of St. Christopher and Nevis to the United Nations. **Hobby:** Education and its development in the Arab World. **Prof. Addr.:** Mission of St. Christopher and Nevis to the United Nations, 414 East 75th Street, New York, NY 10021, USA.

GHANIM (Mohamad Hafez), Egyptian statesman. **Born** in 1925. **Educ.:** Cairo and Paris Universities. **Career:** Lecturer, Faculty of Law, Alexandria University (1949); Professor of Public International Law and Vice Dean of the Faculty of Law, Aïn Shams University (1960-68); Minister of Tourism (1968-69); Vice President of the Faculty of Laws, Aïn Shams University; Minister of Health (Aug.-Oct. 1969); Minister of National Education (July 1969-72); Secretary General, Arab Socialist Union (1971); Secretary, Economic Affairs, ASU (July 1972); First Secretary, ASU (1973); Secretary-General, Egyptian International Law Association; Deputy Prime-Minister, Minister responsible for Social Development and Services (1976). **Dist.:** State Prize for best publications in field of international Law and Political Science (1969). **Publ.:** Author of "Public International Law" (in arabic) 1964, "International Organization" 1967. **Addr.:** 3, Bergas Street, Garden City, Cairo, Egypt.

GHANNAM (Mohamad, Ahmad, al), Egyptian educationalist. **Born** on January 12, 1928 at Talkha town, Dakahliyah Governorate (Upper Egypt). **Married,** children. **Educ.:** Faculty of Arts, Cairo University (1944-48); Higher Institute of Education, Cairo (Egypt) (1948-50); Faculty of Education, Ayn Shams University, Cairo (1953-55); Columbia University, New York (1956-59). **Dipl.:** Bachelor of Arts, (1948), Master of Arts (Education) 1955, Ph.D. (Education) 1959. **Career:** Social Science Teacher, Secondary School (Egypt), Consultant in Education Planning, Ministry of Higher Education, Cairo; Researcher, Department of Education Research, Ministry of Education, Cairo; Instructor, Ayn Shams University, Cairo (1961); Visiting Professor of Education, Baghdad University (Iraq) (1964-67); Associate Professor of Education, Ayn Shams University, Cairo (1967); Professor of Education Administration, Faculty of Education, Ayn Shams University, Cairo (1972-74); Regional Officer for Education Planning and Administration, UNESCO; Head, Planning Centre Regional Office for Education, Beirut, Lebanon (1974). **Publ.:** "The Teacher in Egyptian School and Society" (1953), "The Future of Higher Education in Iraq" (1967), "Politics in Educational Planning" (1970), "Education in the Arab States viewed from the Marrakesh Conference" (1971), "Methodology in Education" (1972), "Administration Technology" (1972). **Awards:** State Prize in Arts (Egypt) (1972). **Member:** Ayn Shams Professors Association; Association of Graduates of Education Institutes, Cairo. **Spec. Intr.:** Education Planning & Administration, Social and Philosophical Foundations of Education. **Hobbies:** walking and gymnastics. **Priv. Addr.:** Cairo, Egypt.

GHANNAM (Soliman Mohamad, al), Saudi academic. **Born** in 1939 in Riyadh, Saudi Arabia. **Dipl.:** Ph.D. (Modern History of the Near East and the Arab Peninsula). **Career:** Assistant Librarian, Central Planning Organization (1964-66); Assistant Lecturer, Department of History and Civilization, Faculty of Shari'a (Islamic Law), Umm al-Qura University Committee for the Promotion of Scientific Research; Assistant Professor of History, Faculty of Arts, King Abdulaziz University; member of Committee for Coordinating Plans and Programmes of the Department of Archaeology. **Publ.:** Nazarat wa Ara'a fil Tarikh wal Turath (Views and View-points in History and Tradition) a series of articles published in al-Yamamah weekly magazine (1974); al-Tarikhul Hadith lil Jaziratil Arabia (Modern History of the Arab Peninsula). **Hobbies:** Sports, travel. **Priv. Addr.:** Tel.: 6873780, Jeddah, Saudi Arabia.

GHARABALLY (Ahmad, Sayed Hachem, al), Bahraini businessman. **Born** in Bahrain. **Son** of Sayyed Hachem al-Gharabally. **Career:** Chairman, Ahmad Sayed Hashem al-Gharabally Ltd.; General Agent and Distributor for Fiat, Midland Electric Manufacturing Company, Olivetti Company, Siemens (Germany), Innocenty (Italy), Centrolex (Czechoslovakia), Societa Edison (Italy), Alcan S.A. (Switzerland), Chief Agent for Royal Insurance Company; Chairman, Gulf Electrical Engineering SAK, Kuwait. **Addr.:** Dubai, U.A.E.

GHARAYBA (Abdulkarim), Jordanian academic. **Born** in 1933 in North Jordan. **Educ.:** American University of Beirut, University of London. **Dipl.:** Bachelor of Arts, Doctor of Philosophy. **Career:** Professor since 1960, Visiting Professor of History, Syrian University of Damascus, Director, Antiquities Department, Amman, Professor of History, Riyadh University (Saudi Arabia), former Director of the History Department, Jordan University (1966). **Addr.:** University of Jordan, Amman, Jordan.

GHARBI (El Mostafa), Moroccan international officer. **Born** on February 9, 1935, at el-Jadida (Morocco). **Married**, with children. **Educ.:** Faculty of Law, University of Rabat (Morocco, 1954-55); University of Paris (1956-60); Ecole Supérieure des Postes, Téléphones et Télégraphes, Paris (1958-60). **Dipl.:** Bachelor of Law, Post and Telecommunications Diploma. **Career:** Held various positions in the Ministry of Posts, Telegraphs and Telephones, Rabat, Morocco, (1956-65); Director of Postal and Financial Services, Ministry of Posts, Telephone and Telegraph, Rabat, Morocco (1965-71); Counsellor, Universal Postal Union (UPU) Berne (Switzerland) (1971-78); Senior Counsellor, in charge of postal studies since 1978; Assistant Director-General in charge of postal Services, and Studies from 1981; Assistant Director-General in charge of legal and administrative questions from 1990. **Sports:** tennis. **Prof. Addr.:** Universal Postal Union, Tel.: 031/350 31 11, Case Postale CH-3000 Berne 15, Switzerland. **Priv. Addr.:** Merzenacker 29, Tel.: 031 9410046, CH-3006 Berne, Switzerland.

GHARIB (Muhieddine, al, Dr.), Egyptian Politician. **Born** on May 28, 1936 in Cairo. **Married,** 3 sons. **Educ.:** B.Sc., Economics, Cairo University (1957); Ph.D., Economy and Financial Policies (1966). **Career:** Professor (1966), Vice Dean (1986) Faculty of Economics and Political Sciences, University of Cairo; Secretary of Environment Research Council, Scientific Research Academy (1970-72); Projects Manager, Abu Dhabi Fund for Arab Industrial Union (1972-78); Head, Executive Body, General Authority for Investment and Free Zones; Minister of Finance (1996-1999). **Address:** Cairo, Egypt.

GHARIB (Salahuddin Muhammad), Egyptian politician. **Born** in 1926. **Married**, 3 children. **Career:** started working in a textile plant; Head of Personnel, Modern Textiles Company, Alexandria, Egypt; Vice President, Union of Spinning and Weaving Workers (1968); elected to the National Congress of the Arab Socialist Union (ASU); elected to the ASU Central Committee in 1968; Secretary General Federation of Arab Textile Workers on its foundation (1969); Alternate Member of the ASU Organizing Committee (1970); elected President of the Egyptian Federation of Labour and President of the Union of Spinning and Weaving Workers (1971); Member of the provisional Secretariat of the ASU (1971); Assistant Secretary, ASU Central Committee, for Alexandria (1971); ASU Secretary for Labour (1971); Chairman of the Manpower Committee of the People's Assembly, after his election as one of the Deputies for Alexandria; Minister of Manpower (1972); Secretary for Labour in ASU (1973); Minister of Manpower and Works (1974-75). **Addr.:** Cairo, Egypt.

GHARNIT (Abdallah), Moroccan politician. **Born** on June 14, 1929 in Marrakech. **Educ.:** Faculty of Law (Paris). **Dipl.:** LL.B. **Career:** Magistrate, occupied important functions in the administation mainly; interim director of Political Affairs, Ministry of Interior; General Manager, Moroccan Television; Director, Youth & Sport; on mission in the Royal Cabinet High Commissioner, "Entraide Nationale" (1968); Secretary of State to the Prime Minister for National Promotion and Handicrafts (1972); Minister of Social Affairs and Handicrafts (1977-82); elected to Parliament (1977). **Prof. Addr.:** Rabat, Morocco.

GHAROURI (Mohamad, Sayed, al), Egyptian politician. **Born** at Abou Kebeer, Sharkiyeh Governorate, in 1927. **Married** and father of two sons. **Educ.:** Faculty of Sciences, Cairo University; La Sorbonne, Paris, France. **Dipl.:** B.Sc. (chemistry), Ph.D. (Dyestuffs chemistry). **Career:** appointed Manager of el-Nasr Dyestuffs Company, Mahallah el-Kobra; appointed Manager of Misr Rayon Company, Kafr el-Dawaar, Egypt (1973); appointed Manager of Misr Spinning and Weaving Company, Mahallah el-Kobra (1975); Egyptian Minister of Industry (1983-85). **Addr.:** Cairo, Egypt.

GHASSIB (Humam, Bishara), Jordanian academic. **Born** on April 27, 1948 in Amman, Jordan. **Educ.:** University of Manchester, UK.: B.Sc. in Physics (1971); Diploma for Advanced Studies in Science (1972); Ph.D. in Theoretical Physics (1974). **Career:** Postdoctoral Fellow, University of Manchester, U.K. (1974-75); Assistant Professor of Physics, University of Jordan (1975-81); Associate Professor of Physics (1981-86); Professor of Physics (1986-); Visiting Fellow, Cornell University, USA (1983-84); Chairman, Department of Physics, University of Jordan (1986-88); Chairman, Department of Graduate Studies for Engineering, Mathematical and Physical Sciences (1989-90); Dean of Academic Research (1990-1994); Editor-in- Chief, «Dirasat» (a refereed research journal); General Editor, numerous monographs published by the University of Jordan (1990-1994); Editorial Board Member of «The Cultural Journal», Jordan University (1983-); Editor-in-Chief (1989-1999); President, Jordanian History of Science Society (1993-1999). **Member** For many years of the British Institute of Physics, American Physical Society and New York Academy of Sciences; Associate Member, International Centre for Theoretical Physics (1977-90); Arab Thought Forum (2000-); Life Member, Jordan Academy for Arabic, Jordan. **Publ.:** «The Scarlet Notebook»: Reflections of a Passerby. Beirut (1981) in Arabic; «Classical and Modern Physics» Volume One, Amman (1981) in Arabic; «Proceedings of the First International Petra School of Physics», Irbid (1986); «The Concept of Heat in our Arab-Islamic Heritage», Amman (1987) in Arabic; "Sindbad the Physicist and Einstein's Relativity" Amman (2000) in Arabic. Numerous articles in international journals. **Awards:** Fulbright Award, Council for International Exchange for Scholars, Washington DC, USA (1983-84); Life Membership, Jordan Academy of Arabic, Amman (1984-); Abdul Hameed Shoman Prize for Young Arab Scientists in Fundamental Sciences, Amman (1987); Fellow, Third World Academy of Sciences, Trieste, Italy (1988). Al-Hussein Order of Merit for Distinguished Contribution. **Hobbies:** Reading; Writing; Classical Music; History and Philosophy of Science. **Member:** Life Member, Jordan Academy of Arabic, Jordan. **Prof. Addr.:** Department of Physics, Faculty of Science, University of Jordan, Tel.: (00962-6) 5355500; Telex: 21629 UNVJ JO; E-mail: hghassib@nic.net.jo, Fax: (00962-6) 5355511 or 5355522, Amman, Jordan.

GHATHAMI (Abdallah Mohamad, al), Saudi academic. **Born** on 16 February 1946 at Onaizah, Saudi Arabia. **Dipl.:** Ph.D. Exeter University, England. **Career:** Chairman of Communication Department (1979-81); Professor and Chairman of Arabic Language Dept., King Abdulaziz University; Honorary member, Society of Culture and Arts, Taif. **Member:** Literary Club, Jeddah British Society for Middle Eastern Studies (Manchester); attended Contemporary Arabic Literature Conference, London, 1981. **Publ.:** Book: "Fi al-Shi'r al-Hur" (Free Poetry); "al-Nahr al-Zami" (a collection of poems), "al-Khati'a aw al-Takfir" (A structuralist Study of Modern Arabic Poetry) (1985), Jeddah. **Hobbies:** Swimming, reading. **Priv. Addr.:** Tel.: 6883536, Jeddah, Saudi Arabia.

GHATTAS (Stephanos II, H.E.), Egyptian Patriarch of Alexandria and Spiritual leader of the Catholic Coptic community of Egypt. **Born** on January 16, 1920 at Cheikh-Zein-Eddine Near Tahta (Governorate of Sohag) in Upper Egypt. **Educ.:** Primary and Secondary Studies, Jesuits College (Cairo). **Career:** Received his Ecclesiastical Studies of Philosophy and Theology, College «De Propaganda Fide»; Ordained to the Priesthood on Mars 25, 1944 in Rome; Professor of Philosophy and Theology at «Great Seminary» of Tahta and Tanta (1945-1952); Became Lazarist in Paris (1954); then in Beirut, Lebanon (1954-1960); then Treasurer and Superior of Lazarists in Alexandria (1960-1967); Ordained Bishop for Thebes-Luxor (June 9, 1967); Administrator Apostolic of the Catholic Coptic Patriarchate to take the place of S.B. Stephanos 1er Sidarouss (February 24, 1984); Elected Patriarch of Alexandria for the Catholic Copt (June 9, 1986- present). **Addr.:** Catholic Coptic Patriarchate, 34, Ibn Sandar Street, Pont de Koubbeh, P.O.Box 69 Palais de koubbeh, 11712 Palais de koubbeh, Tel.: 2571740, 2599494, Fax: 202/ 4545766, Cairo, Egypt.

GHAZI (Ghazi Said), Syrian lawyer/consultant. **Born** on November 8, 1938 in Damascus, Syria. **Married** in 1962, two children. **Educ.:** Damascus University, Damascus. **Dipl.:** Licence in Law, specialized in Administrative and International Law. **Career:** Private law practice in Damascus, Syria (since 1962); Consultant, Iraq Petroleum Co. (1966-72); Consultant for FAO in Yemen (1984-). **Hobbies:** Horse riding and swimming. **Prof. Addr.:** Bureau of Legal Services, Salhia Street, P.O.Box 4238, Tel.: 229798, Damascus, Syria.

GHAZZAWI (Abbas Faiq), Saudi diplomat. **Born** in 1932 in Mecca, Saudi Arabia. **Career:** Director General of T.V. and Broadcasting; Minister Plenipotentiary at the Saudi Embassy in Rome; Ambassador to Chad; Attorney and Legal Adviser; Ambassador at the Ministry of Foreign Affairs, Head of the Afro-Asian Department; member 3rd Islamic Summit Conference, Makkah; Foreign Ministers Islamic Conference, Makkah; Foreign Ministers Islamic Conferences, Fez, Islamabad and Baghdad; presently Ambassador to the Federal Republic of Germany. **Honours:** King Abdulaziz Order (First Class and Excellent Class). **Publ.:** several articles and short stories published in local newspapers. **Hobbies:** Reading, writing, walking. **Prof. Addr.:** P.O.Box 2335, Tel.: 6654646, Fax: 6659155, Jeddah. **Priv. Addr.:** Tel.: 6659143, Jeddah, Saudi Arabia.

GHEDIRA (Muhsin), Tunisian businessman. **Born** on December 30, 1936 in Tunis, Tunisia. **Married. Educ.:** Ecole d'Application d'Ingénieurs des TP, Paris, France. **Career:** Roads and Bridges Department, Beja District (1962-64); Senior Purchaser (1964-67); Managing Director, SRTGT (1967); Managing Director and Chairman of Société Hotelière Kuriat Palace. **Prof. Addr.:** Avenue de la Gare, 2033 Megrine, Tunis, Tunisia.

GHEITH (Muhammad, Ahmad), Arab-American geologist. **Born** on February 11, 1925 in Egypt. **Married**, 1 son, 1 daughter. **Educ.:** Cairo University, Egypt; University of Minnesota, USA. **Dipl.:** B.Sc., M.S. in Geology, Ph.D. in Geochemistry and Economic Geology. **Career:** Lecturer, Faculty of Science, Ain Shams University, Cairo, Egypt (1952-57); Fellow of the School for Advanced Study, Massachusetts Institute of Technology, USA (1957); Consultant Geologist, Technical Bureau of Mining and Commerce in Egypt and Sudan (1956-57); Assistant, Associate, then Professor of Geology, Boston University, USA (1958-64); Chairman and Professor of Geology, Geology Department, Boston University (1964-95); Visiting Professor, American University in Cairo, Egypt, Kuwait University and other Universities in the Middle East (1973-74); Visiting Professor, Qatar University (1981); UNESCO delegate (1956-78); UNESCO Consultant (1975-76); UNESCO Consultant to the Applied Geology Centre in Saudi Arabia (1976-78); Fellow of the Geological Society of Egypt, Sigma XI, National Association of Geology Teachers, American Crystallographic Association, American Association for the Advancement of Science, New York Academy of Science, American Association of University Professors, American Geophysical Union, International Mineralogical Association, Association of Egyptian-American Scholars, Association of Arab-American University Graduates; Former Vice-President, and President of Boston Geological Society; Professor of Geology, Boston University (1975-1995); Emeritus Prof. Dept. of Earth Sciences, Boston University (1996-); Director of Special External Programmes for the Middle East, Boston University (1980-). **Publ.:** many articles and scientific and technical journals in several countries. **Hobbies:** Ping-pong, hiking, bridge, swimming. **Prof. Addr.:** 21, Winsor Road, Billerica, MA, 01821-3717, USA, Tel.: (508) 6676569.

GHENIMA (Mohamad), Tunisian banker. **Born** on May 15, 1929 at Akouda (Tunisia). **Married** in 1961 to Anissa Smida, three children. **Career:** Joined Destour Socialist Party; Assistant Director-General, National Bank of Tunisia; Governor, Central Bank of Tunisia (1974). **Addr.:** Tunis, Tunisia.

GHERAB (Mohamed, Habib), Tunisian diplomat. **Born** on May 8, 1926 in Tunis, Tunisia. **Son** of Tijani Gherab **and** Mrs. Hanifa Gorgi. **Married** on June 22, 1958 to Fawzia Ladjimi, 3 children: two sons, Habib (1959) and Fawzi (1962), one daughter, Noha (1978). **Educ.:** Graduate of College Sadiki, Tunis; Master of Laws of the Univeristy of Paris, France. **Career:** Lawyer at the Tunis Court of Appeal (1955-); Chargé de Mission to the Minister of the Interior, Tunis (1956-57); Director of the Cabinet of the Minister of the Interior, Tunis (1957-62); Governor, Director-General of the Regional and Communal Administration and Director of the Cabinet of the Minister of the Interior, Tunis (1962-65); Tunisian Ambassador to Spain, Madrid (1965-67); Ambassador Special Counsellor to the Minister for Foreign Affairs, Tunis (1967-69); Assistant Secretary-General, Director of Personnel of the United Nations, New York (1969-79); Under Secretary-General of the United Nations, New York (1979); Secretary-General of the United Nations Conference on New and Renewable Sources of Energy, New York (1979-81); Tunisian Ambassador to the U.S.S.R., Moscow (1981-87); Lawyer, International Consultant, Tunis (1987-); **Member:** Secretary-General of the Neo-Destour Party Federation in France, Paris (1953-55); Elected Member of the Central Committee of the Destour Socialist Party, Bizerta Congress (1964); Member of the Tunisian delegation to the 23rd session of the U.N. General Assembly, New York (1968); Member of the Board of Trustees of Lycée Français de New York (1980-). **Awards:** Grand Cross, Order of Isabel La Catolica, Spain; Grand Officer, Order of the Republic, Tunisia; Grand Officier, Order of the Wissam Alaouite, Morocco; Commander, Order of La Pleiade, French Speaking Parliamentarians Associations. **Addr.:** 24 Avenue de France Tunis 1000, Tunisia.

GHERIB (Mohamed), assumed Name **Hamadi,** Tunisian Diplomat. **Born** on February 18, 1935 in Tunis. **Son** of Abderrahman **and** Mrs. Ouacila. **Married** to Raoudha Gherib, 2 children: Emna Gherib (29 November 1971), Aicha Gherib (11 June 1973). **Educ.:** Secondary: Sadiki College, Tunis; Undergraduate Studies: University of Tunis; Arabic and English Languages: University of Aix en Provence-France; Political Science Graduate: University of Aix en Provence-France. **Dipl.:** Licence Arabic, Licence English, Diploma Political Science. **Career:** United Nations Secretariat; Tunisian Mission to the United Nations, New York; Department of International Cooperation at the Ministry of Foreign Affairs in Tunis; Staff-Assistant to the Minister of Social Affairs, Youth and Sports; Head of Sections at the Department of European and Consular Affairs; Counsellor (Political and Press Affairs), Tunisian Embassy in Paris; Head of West-Europe Section, Ministry of Foreign Affairs; Minister-Counsellor, Deputy Head of Mission, Tunisian Embassy in Washington (1978-1983); Deputy Director, Department of American Affairs, Ministry of Foreign Affairs; Staff-Assistant to the Minsiter of Foreign Affairs; Ambassador of Tunisia to Mauritania (1987-1991); Dean of the Diplomatic Corps in Nouakchott; Ambassador of Tunisia to Indonesia since February 1992, to the Philippines since April 1992, to Brunei Darussalam; to Singapore since May 1992, to Malaysia since May 1993, to Thailand since September 1993, **Awards:** National Decoration - Commander of the Republic. **Sports:** Jogging, Swimming. **Credit Cards:** American Express, **Prof. Addr.:** Embassy of Tunisia, P.O.Box 6435, Tel.: (62-21) 5703432, 5703492, Jakarta 10064, Indonesia. **Priv. Addr.:** Indonesia: JL. Imam Bonjol No. 40-42, Jakarta Pusat, Tel.: (62-21) 3107449, and in Tunis: Rue des Amandes, Immeuble F-3, Appartement F-5, El Manar I, Tel.: (216-1) 883-267, Tunis, Tunisia.

GHEZAL (Ahmad), Tunisian diplomat. **Born** in 1930 in M'Saken, Tunisia. **Married**,2 children. **Educ.:** Sadiki College, Tunis; Institut d'Etudes Politique, Toulouse, France. **Career:** Tunisian Ministry of Foreign Affairs (1958); Tunisian Embassy, Yougoslavia (1959-62); Tunisian Embassy, Belgium and EEC (1962-67); Head of European Division, Ministry of Foreign Affairs (1969-70), Tunisian Embassy, USA (1970-74); Director of Political Affairs, Ministry of Foreign Affairs, Tunis (1974-77); Chef de Cabinet, Ministry of Foreign Affairs (1974-77); Ambassador to Austria and Hungary and Permanent Representative to International Organizations in Vienna (1977); Formerly, Permanent Representative of Tunisia to the United Nations, New York. **Prof. Addr.:** Ministry of Foreign Affairs, Tunis, Tunisia.

GHIRBAN (Hamad Ibn Mohamad, al), Saudi civil servant. **Born** in 1937. **Dipl.:** B.A. (Islamic Law). **Career:** Former Administrative Inspector, Judiciary Inspector General Qadi Bureau Director for Judicial Affairs, Deputy Director General then Director General, Ministy of Justice; Assistant Deputy Minister for Administrative Affairs, Ministry of Justice; member for Jazirah Press Printing and Publishing Organization, Riyadh Literary Club; former member of Social Service Centre, Riyadh; attended Arab Social Defence Organization Conference, Arab League, Cairo Conference on the Message of the Mosque, Muslim World League, Makkah. **Publ.:** The Development of the Judiciary System in Saudi Arabia, Non-Muslim-Paid Tax (Jiziah) in Islam (research works under publication). **Hobbies:** Swimming, shooting, reading. **Addr.:** Ministry of Justice, Riyadh, Saudi Arabia.

GHISSASSI (Abdellatif), Moroccan politician. **Born** on November 16, 1937 at Taza (Morocco). **Married. Educ.:** Lycée Moulay Idriss, Fez (Morocco); Lycée of Oujda; Lycée Lyautey, Casablanca (1956-57); Ecole Nationale des Ponts et Chaussées, Paris (1957-61); National School of Civil Aviation (ENAC); Paris (1961-62). **Career:** Engineer and Head of Air Bases (Morocco) (June 1962- Jan. 1966); Chief Engineer and Chief of Air Bases (Jan-1966 to 1972); Director of Works, International Airport, Rabat (July 1967- May 68); Deputy Secretary General, Ministry of Public Works and Communications (May-Oct. 1968); Secretary General, Ministry of Works and Communications (Oct. 1968- Nov. 1972); Minister of Public Works and Communications (Nov. 1972- April 1974); Minister of Commerce, Industry, Mines and Merchant Shipping (1974); President, Consulting Committee on Maghreb (1975); Minister of Finance (10 Oct. 1977-79); Minister of Agriculture and Agrarian Reform (1979); Elected member of the Parliament since 1977; Chairman and Managing Director, Ste. Maroc Emirats Arabes Unis de Développement (1982); Chairman: Fénie Brossette, Fonderie de Plomb de Zellidja, Hôtel les Almohades de Tanger, Palmariva Club Agadir, Zellidja, Palmariva Club Marrakech; Director: Africa Palace Maroc, Protec S.A., Sanad, S.B.C., S.N.C.E., Etc... **Addr.:** Mohammadia, Morocco.

GHOBASH (Said, Ahmed, al), United Arab Emirates politician. **Born** in Ras al-Khaimah, United Arab Emirates. **Career:** Ambassador to the USA (till 1977); Minister of Planning, United Arab Emirates (1977-83); Deputy Chairman, the Commercial Bank of Dubai Ltd; Minister of Economy and Trade (Oct. 1992-1998). **Addr.:** P.O.Box 2668, Dubai, United Arab Emirates.

GHOFAILY (Ibrahim Fahad, al), Saudi academic. **Born** in 1948 in Jeddah, Saudi Arabia. **Dipl.:** Ph.D. (Public Administration and Comparative Governments). **Career:** Occupied several administrative jobs in Modern Industries Co., Raytheon Co., Robert Matheo Co.; Demonstrator, Faculty of Economics and Administration, King Abdulaziz University; Assistant Professor and Vice-Dean, Faculty of Economics and Administration, King Abdulaziz University; member of American Society of Public Administration, American Institutional Research Association, Institutional Research Conference, 1980. **Publ.:** Manpower Development in Saudi Arabia; Attitudes of Saudi Youth Toward Work and Vocational Education; Summary of The Third Saudi Five Year Development Plan. **Prof. Addr.:** King Abdulaziz University, P.O.Box 1540, Tel.: 6431870, Jeddah. **Priv. Addr.:** 6652393, Jeddah, Saudi Arabia.

GHONEIM (Hassan, Bahjat Ghoneim), Egyptian artist. **Born** in 1948 in Dessouk, Kat al-Sheikh, Egypt. **Married. Dipl.:** B.Com. (1975). **Career:** Member of the Plastic Arts Syndicate (1979-) and most Cairo arts societies; General Secretary, Cairo Atelier for Artists and Writers (1982-); Director of al-Salam Gallery, National Centre for Plastic Arts (1982-). **Publ.:** several general and private art exhibitions in Cairo and Alexandria, Egypt. **Award:** First Prize for Painting, Kafr el-Sheikh Governorate (1965); the Painting Prize, Alexandria, Biennale (1980); First Prize of the Arts Festival (Plastic Art) (1981) and First Prize of the Goethe Institute (1981). **Hobbies:** Music, reading. **Prof. Addr.:** 1 Shara al-Sheikh al-Mersefi, Zamalek, Cairo, Egypt. **Priv. Addr.:** 2 Shara Karim al-Doula, Maydan Talaat Harb, Cairo, Egypt.

GHONEIM (Samir, A.), Saudi academic and executive. **Born** in 1946 in Mecca, Saudi Arabia. **Dipl.:** Ph.D. (Chemistry), Birmingham University, England. **Career:** Assistant Professor (1974), Associate Professor (1977) and later Vice Dean, Faculty of Science (1978), King Abdulaziz University; former Director General, Saudi Public Transport Company (SAPTCO); member the Royal Institute of Chemistry (RIC), England, the International Union for Public Transportation, the American Public Transit Association (APTA) and the American Management Association (AMA); member, Board of Directors, Saudi Automotive Services (SAASCO). **Publ.:** a Ph.D. thesis and several articles on chemistry and transportation. **Prof.**

Addr.: P.O.Box 10667, Tel.: 4648230, Riyadh. **Priv. Addr.:** Tel.: 4653515, Riyadh, Saudi Arabia.

GHORBAL (Abdullatif), Egyptian barrister and magistrate. **Born** in Egypt. **Educ.:** Secondary and Higher. **Dipl.:** Licentiate of Law. **Career:** Barrister, Judge, President of Higher Court of Justice, Former Under-Secretary of State Ministry of Justice, Chairman, Cairo Agricultural Company, Director, Alexandria Flour Milling Company, Orient Bonded Stores. **Member** of Gezira Sporting Club, Alexandria Sporting Club, Alexandria Racing Club. **Summer Residence:** Smouha City, Ramleh, Tel.: 63936, Alexandria, Egypt.

GHORBAL (Ashraf), Egyptian diplomat. **Born** on May 22, 1925 in Alexandria, Egypt. **Married**, 1 daughter. **Educ.:** Cairo University, Egypt; Harvard University. **Dipl.:** B.A., M.A., Ph.D. in Political Science. **Career:** joined the Egyptian Diplomatic service in 1945; served in United Nations, New York and Geneva; held posts at the Egyptian Embassies in Paris, London and Ottawa; Member of the Egyptian delegation to the Franco-Egyptian negotiations following the Suez Canal invasion in November 1956; participated in several international conferences, including the non-Alligned Conference, Belgrade (1961), the Tri-Lateral Conference (Egypt, India, Yugoslavia, New Delhi); Head of Egyptian Interests, Egyptian Embassy in Washington (1968-72); Assistant Adviser, President for National Security Affairs (1972); worked closely on the formulation of Egyptian foreign policy with group of experts, with special reference to the period following the 1973 War; Press Adviser to late President Sadat (1973); participated in Camp David negotiations (1978) (1973-82), retired from diplomatic service (1982). **Prof. Addr.:** c/o Ministry of Foreign Affairs, Cairo, Egypt. **Priv. Addr.:** 2, Shafic Mansour, Zamalek, Cairo, Egypt.

GHORDAN (Said Ali), Saudi businessman. **Born** Ghamid, in 1930. **Educ.:** Received general education. **Career:** Employee at the Ministry of Finance (1946-56); member of Chamber of Commerce and Industry, Eastern Province; member of Board of Dhahran Electric Power Co., Gulf Gases Co., Saudi Arabian Fertilizer Co. (SAFCO), Assir Tourist and Trading Co., Red Sea Development Co.; Cofounder of al-Sharq magazine; owner of Arabian Provision and Services Company, Dammam, attended various Chamber of Commerce Conferences. **Hobbies:** Swimming. **Addr.:** P.O.Box 131, Dammam, Saudi Arabia.

GHOZALI (Sid-Ahmed Ali), Algerian politician. **Born** on March 31, 1937 at Marnia, Algeria. **Educ.:** University of Damascus, Syria; Ecole des Ponts et Chaussées, Paris, France. **Dipl.:** B.A. in Philisophy and B.Sc. in Civil Engineering. **Career:** School Teacher (1962); Director of Energy, Minister of Industry and Energy; Adviser, Ministry of the Economy (1964); Undersecretary of State, Ministry of Public Works (1964-65); Director General, then Chairman, Société Nationale de Transports et de Commercialisation des Hydrocarbures- SONATRACH (1966-86); Head of Daira LARBAA Iraten (1963); Tindouf (1964); Tizi Ouzou (1966); Blida (1967); Wali of Tizi Ouzou (1968); Annaba (1974); Minister of Energy and Petrochemical Industries (1977-79); Minister of Irrigation (1979); Minister of Housing and Construction (1980-84); also Member of the Permanent Secretariat of the FLN (1984-); Minister of Foreign Affairs (Sept. 1989- June 1991); Prime Minister, (June 18, 1991- July 8, 1992). **Sport:** Tennis. **Addr.:** Algiers, Algeria.

GHUNEIM (Abdul Rahman, Khalid, al), Kuwaiti official. **Born** on January 4, 1938 in Kuwait. **Married**, 4 children. **Educ.:** San Jose State College, California, USA. **Dipl.:** B.Sc. in Electrical Engineering. **Career:** Engineer, Ministry of Posts, Telegraphs and Telephones (1962); Deputy Chief Engineer (1964); Fellow of Institute Electrical and Electronic Engineers, USA, Institution of Electrical Engineers, London, UK; Managing Director, Kuwait Electrical Wiring Accessories Co. Kuwait and al-Abraq Trading Company, Kuwait; Chairman, INMARSAT Council (1979-81); represented Kuwait in many international and Arab conferences and meetings; Chairman and Vice President of Kuwait Reinsurance, Arab Insurance Co, Beirut, Kuwait Financial Centre; Director of Kuwait Insurance Co., Bahrain and Kuwait Insurance Co., United Insurance Co., Ras el-Khaima, Bank of Lebanon and Kuwait; Member of Arab Insurance Federation Union; Honorary Owner and Sponsor of the Indian School, Kuwait. Under Secretary, Ministry of Communications (1969-); Plenipotentiary and Head of Delegation, all meetings of INTELSAT (1969-). **Publ.:** "Telecommunications in the State of Kuwait", ITU Journal Telecommunications (1972), "Telecommunications and Development in the Third World, Practices and Prospects", "Erricson Review" (1976) Sweden, "Kuwait's Development in Communications and its Significance to Friendly Countries" (lecture in Tokyo, Japan 25 April 1977), "Arab European Cooperation in Telecommunication Industries" (lecture), "Arab European Cooperation Symposium" (May 1978) in Montreux, Switzerland, "Establishment of Telecommunication Services", "View from a Developing Country" (1979), "Forum 79" (lecture) ITU Geneva, Switzerland. **Hobbies:** football, gardening. **Prof. Addr.:** Ministry of Communications, P.O.Box 27 Safat, Kuwait, Kuwait.

GHUNEIM (Khalifa, Khaled, al), Kuwaiti former diplomat and statesman. **Born** in 1921. **Educ.:** American University of Beirut. **Career:** Deputy Chairman of National Bank of Kuwait, Member of Kuwait Tanker Co., Kuwait Currency Board, Kuwait Development Board, Ambassdor of Kuwait to United Kingdom (1961-62), Minister of Commerce (1963-65). **Addr.:** Kuwait city, Kuwait.

GHUNEIM (Sayyid, Muhammad), Egyptian academic. **Born** on August 10, 1922 in Egypt. **Married**, 3 sons, 1 daughter. **Educ.:** Cairo University, Egypt; Ain Shams University, Cairo; Geneva University, Switzerland. **Dipl.:** B.A., Diploma of Higher Studies in Teaching, in Psychology, M.A. in Mental Health, Ph.D. **Career:** Demonstrator, Faculty of Education, Ain Shams University (1951); Assistant Professor (1959), Associate Professor, Faculty of Arts (1967); Professor of Psychology, Kuwait University (1968-72), Ain Shams University (1973-77); Vice Dean, Faculty of Arts, Ain Shams University (1973-77); Professor of Psychology, Faculty of Education, United Arab Emirates University (1977); Dean of Faculty of Education, United Arab Emirates University (1979-84); Professor of Psychology, Ain Shams University (1984-). **Publ.:** several books on psychology (in Arabic). **Prof. Addr.:** Ain Shams University, Kasr el-Zaafaran, Abbasiya, Cairo, Egypt.

GHUNEIM (Yacoub, Yusuf, al), Kuwaiti politician. **Born** in 1933. **Educ.:** Dar al-Ouloum, Cairo, Egypt. **Career:** Ministry of Guidance and Information; Director of Television (1962-65); Under Secretary, Ministry of Education (1965); Minister of Education (1978-82); Businessman (1982-). **Addr.:** Kuwait City, Kuwait.

GHURAIR (Majed, Ahmad, al), UAE executive. **Born** in Dubai. **Son** of Ahmad al-Ghurair. **Career:** Participated in various management levels in al-Ghurair Family business entreprises; Founder of Emirates National Bank (1978); Chairman and Managing Director, Emirates National Bank, Dubai, UAE (1978). **Addr.:** P.O.Box 1, Deira, Dubai, UAE.

GHURAIR (Saif, Ahmed Majid, Al), UAE banker. **Born** in Dubai. **Son** of Ahmed Majid Al Ghurair. **Career:** Head of the Present diversified Corporate Structure of the Al Ghurair Group; Chairman, National Cement Co. Ltd., Dubai; Chairman, Bank of Oman Ltd., (to change to MASHREQ BANK P.S.C. with effect from October 1, 1993), Dubai, UAE. **Addr.:** P.O.Box 1, Tel.: 693311, Telefax: (04) 691852, Deira, Dubai, UAE.

GHURBAL (Munsif, Muhammad), Tunisian administrator. **Born** on July 30, 1934 in Sfax, Tunisia. **Married,** 3 children. **Educ.:** Ecole Centrale des Arts et Manufactures, Paris, France. **Dipl.:** Dip. Ing. **Career:** Director, Tunisian Electricity and Gas Company (1960-69); Assistant Director General, Tunisian Mining Company (1969-70), Tunisian Cement Company (1970-74), Tunisian Construction Company (1974-79); Vice President, Association of Alumni of the Ecole Centrale des Arts et Manufactures of Tunisia (1975-); Director General, Tunisian Construction Company (1979-). **Prof. Addr.:** 15 Avenue Slimen Ben Slimen, 2092 El Manar 2, Tunis, Tunisia. **Priv. Addr.:** 8 Rue Virgile, 1002 Tunis, Tunisia.

GIBALI (Hussain, Mahmoud, al), Egyptian painter. **Born** on May 18, 1934 in Egypt. **Married,** 1 son. **Educ.:** Instituto Statale d'Arte, Urbino, Italy. **Dipl.:** B.Sc. in Fine Arts, Diploma in Lithography. **Career:** Professor, Alexandria College of Fine Arts, Egypt (1969, 1972 and 1975); Professor at the High Institute of Leonardo da Vinci, Cairo (1969-70); M.A. and Ph.D. thesis supervisor in fine arts; participated in numerous private and public art exhibitions in Italy, Morocco, Netherlands, North America, Yugoslavia, Norway, Qatar and Egypt; Professor and Head of Graphics Department, Cairo College of Fine Arts (1979-); Member of the Supreme Council of Culture, Ministry of Culture (1979-), Administration Committee of the Plastic Arts Syndicate (1979-); President, Egyptian Graphics Society (1979-). **Award:** State Prize of Art, Ministry of Culture (1979) and several other prizes from Italy and Egypt. **Medal:** Medal of Science and Art (1st Class) (1979). **Hobbies:** Swimming, tennis. **Member:** Hunting Club. **Prof. Addr.:** College of Fine Arts, Shara Ismail Muhammad, Zamalek, Cairo, Egypt. **Priv. Addr.:** 9 Shara Ahmad Sucarno, al-Agouza, Madinat al-Awqaf, Giza, Egypt.

GIEN (Abdul Aziz Abdul Aziz, al), Saudi official. **Dipl.:** of Engineering, U.S.A. **Career:** Radio maintenance engineer; air traffic controller; member of Pilgrimage Sub-Committee; member of Board of International Civil Airport Association; attended several conferences of ICAO (International Civil Aviation Organization), International Civil Airport Association; Director, Jeddah International Airport **Sport.:** swimming. **Addr.:** Jeddah International Airport, Jeddah, Saudi Arabia.

GLAOUI (Abdessadeq, al), Moroccan Diplomat. **Born** on December 24, 1924 in Marrakech, Morocco. **Educ.:** Doctorat in Law. **Career:** Président civil Court Marrakech (1944); Prosecutor Heneral High Cherifian Tribunal Rabat (1957); Minister-Counsellor Embassy of Morocco, Washington D.C. (1962); Ambassador to Scandinavian countries (1965), To Federal Republic of Germany (1968), To France (1970), To the U.S.A. (1971); Chargé de mission at the Prime Minister's Cabinet 1973; President of the Supreme Court of Audit (1976). **Addr.:** Supreme Court of Audit, P.O.Box 706, Rabat, Morocco.

GOBAIR (M. Ibn Ibrahim, al), Saudi official. **Born** in 1930 at al-Mugammaa, Saudi Arabia. **Dipl.:** Faculty of Shari'a (Islamic Law) Diploma. **Career:** Former Judge of the Third Court of Appeal, Riyadh; President Supreme Judiciary Board, Ministry of Justice; President, Permanent Committee, Supreme Judiciary Board; President, Supreme Court of Grievances (Diwan al-Mazalem); member of King Faisal Welfare Association; member of Board of Judiciary High Institute, of Supreme Committee for Planning Information Policy and of Supreme Advisory Committee of Social Insurance; member of the Saudi Ulamas delegation to Europe to explain Human Rights according to Islam. **Publ.:** radio and TV religioux talks. **Hobbies:** Reading. **Prof. Addr.:** Diwan al-Mazalem (Supreme Court of Grievances), Tel.: 4023230, Riyadh. **Priv. Addr.:** Tel.: 4763727, Riyadh, Saudi Arabia.

GOFAIL (Abdulmagid), Egyptian engineer, Governor of al-Wadi al-Guadid. **Born** in 1928 in Damanhour. **Married**, 2 daughters. **Educ.:** Alexandria University. **Dipl.:** Bachelor in Engineering (1952). **Career:** Joined the Army Engineers (till 1963), Director General, Supplies land Sector (1960), Member of the Constitutional Assembly, Governor of al-Wadi al-Guadid (New Valley) since May 1968. **Addr.:** al-Guadid Province, Egypt.

GOHAR (Mohamad, Abdulhamid), Egyptian university professor. **Born** in Egypt. **Son** of Abdulhamid Gohar. **Educ.:** Cairo University (Faculty of Medicine) and Edinburgh. **Dipl.:** Doctor of Philosophy (London), Doctor of Hygiene (Cambridge), Diploma in Tropical Medicine (London). **Career:** Professor of Bacteriology, Faculty of Medicine. **Addr.:** 25, al-Boustan Street, Tel.: 26599, Cairo, Egypt.

GOHARGI (Hassan Abdulaziz), Saudi civil servant. **Born** in 1928 in Mecca, Saudi Arabia. **Educ.:** Received secondary school education. **Career:** Held several posts in the Passport Department, the Directorate of Public Security, and the Bureau of the Cabinet of Ministers, Assistant Director for Government General Finance Affairs then Director, Projects and Organization Division; Director of Jeddah Passports Department, Ministry of Interior (1966) and later Central Inspector of Passports, Western Region for six years; Head of the Department of Public Information for four years; Secretary General, Saudi Red Crescent; participant member of the Red Crescent conferences abroad; member of several welfare societies and Makkah Welfare Society. **Publ.:** several articles in local newpapers on social and administrative affairs. **Hobbies:** Writing; reading, music, travel. **Prof. Addr.:** P.O.Box 9427, Tel.: 4352082, Riyadh. **Priv. Addr.:** Tel.: 4657749, Riyadh, Saudi Arabia.

GOHARY (Hassan Abbas Salem, al), Saudi surgeon. **Born** on 1 February 1925 in Mecca, Saudi Arabia. **Dipl.:** M.D., M.B., B.Ch., Cairo University (1953); Royal College of Surgeons, England (1959); Fellow, American College of Surgeons (1974). **Career:** Surgeon, Arabian American Oil Co. (Aramco); Member of Special Petromin Committee for Planning Medical Care Centres for the Industrial Project of al-Jubail and Yanbu; Lecturer, Medical Department, Aramco Hospital; has extensive experience in general and orthopaedic surgery and hospital planning; Ex-Director, Medical Education and Training Department, Arabian American Oil Co. (Aramco). **Hobbies:** Swimming, chess. **Addr.:** Dhahran, Saudi Arabia.

GOMAA (Chaaraoui), Egyptian army officer and statesman. **Born** in Upper Egypt. **Son** of Mohamad Gomaa. **Educ.:** Secondary and Military Academy. **Career:** in Police Corps, Promoted General; Vice Prime Minister and Minister of Interior (1969); Secretary General of the Central Committee of the Arab Socialist Union (September 1969). **Awards:** Several Egyptian and Foreign decorations. **Addr.:** Cairo, Egypt.

GORASHI (Hasan Abdalla, al), Saudi diplomat. **Born** in 1930 in Mecca, Saudi Arabia. **Educ.:** Elementary and secondary school educations, Falah School, Mecca; Scientific Institute Certificate, B.A. Hons. (History), King Saud University. **Career:** Chief News Announcer, Saudi Broadcasting Station; Assistant Director General of Economic Affairs Department; Deputy Director then Director General of Finance Minister's Office (1973); Minister Plenipotentiary and later Ambassador, Ministry of Foreign Affairs; Saudi Ambassador to Khartoum; one of the prominent writers and poets of the Kingdom; Kingdom's representative to many political and literary conferences and festivals both Arab and European countries including: Abi al-Qasim al-Shabi (Tunisian Poet) Festival, Tunisia (1965); al-Akhtal al-Saghier Festival (1969): Amin Nakhla Festival, Lebanon; Saudi Cultural Week, Lebanon (1974); Men of Letters Conference, China (1976); participant member of the Saudi Arabian Literary Week, Gulf States (1980); member of the Arab Language Committee, Cairo; Secretary General of Okaz Festival, Kingdom of Saudi Arabia. **Honours:** Medal of the Republic 2nd Class and a Cultural Medal awarded by the Tunisian Government. **Publ.:** author of 13 collections of verses titled: Basmat Molawanah, Mawakeb al-Zekrayat, Ah Ams al-Dae', Tabakan, Suzan, Alhan Montaherah, Neda' al-Dena, al-Nagham al-Azraq, Bohairat al-Atash, Lan Yadi' al-Ghad, Felestin wa Kebrya' Aol Jarh, Zeham al-Ashwaq, Endama Tahtareq al-Qanadil, Zakharef Fawq Atlal Asr al-Mojoon; a collection of short stories titled; Annat al-Saqyah and another titled Hath Fi al-Zalam; a collection of research articles titled, Shouk Wa Ward; a collection of short articles titled, Ana Wa Alna; books titled Tajribati al-Sherayah; published 10 collections of his verse in two vols, among the Series of Arab Leading Poets, titled, Hassan Abdullah Gorashi Collection. **Addr.:** Jeddah, Saudi Arabia.

GORGI (Abdulaziz), Tunisian artist painter. **Born** on June 2, 1928 in Tunis. **Educ.:** Fine Arts School. **Career:** Contributed since 1949 to several art Exhibitions in Egypt, Tunisia, France, Italy and U.S.A. **Works:** Decorated the Posts Office in Tunis, The Presidency Palace (Akanes), Ulysse Hotel (Djerba), Embassy of Tunisia in Paris. **Dist.:** Prize of Tunis (1966). **Addr.:** Tunis, Tunisia.

GOSAIBI (Abdulaziz Hamad, al), Saudi businessman. **Born** in 1926 in Jubail, Saudi Arabia. **Dipl.:** Secondary School Certificate. **Career:** Civil servant, Jeddah Customs Department; Managing Director and Member of Board of Ahmed Hamad al-Gosaibi and Brothers, Khobar; Industrialist, Agent for several foreign companies; member of Khobar Municipal Council; member of Board of Great Hotel Co., Cairo; Managing Director, Saudi United Insurance Co. Ltd.; member of Board of Dammam Electric

Co., Dammam Chamber of Commerce, Riyadh Hotel, Social Security Authority; member of founding Committee of Saudi-Korean Loading and Unloading Co.; contributed to the establishment of several loading and unloading companies in Dammam; contributed to the establishment of several Saudi charity societies; established the Pepsi-Cola plant in Khobar; member of Arab European World Finance and Insurance Conference, now leading businessman; ship agent, owner of shipping companies, co-owner of the Pepsi-Cola plant, co owner of can manufacturing facility, owner of Gusaibi Hotel, Khobar and Chairman of Saudi American Bank, Riyadh. **Awards:** Honorary Doctorate in International Economics, London University. **Prof. Addr.:** Saudi American Bank, P.O.Box 833 Riyadh 11421 and Prince Talah Street, P.O.Box 106, Tel.: 8642865; Khobar, Saudi Arabia.

GOSAIBI (Fahad, A.R., al), Saudi businessman. **Born** on December 10, 1921 at Alahssa, Saudi Arabia. **Son** of Sheikh Abdulrahman Algosaibi (businessman). **Married** on May 31, 1947, 8 children: 2 sons and 6 daughters: Fayez, Fawaz, Farida, Fadia, Fawzia, Feriyal, Fairouz and Fida. **Educ.:** Bahrain school; Jamia Miliya Islamiya, Delhi; Fellowship School, Bombay; American University of Beirut (Lebanon). **Dipl.:** B.A. **Career:** Started Business in 1940; now Proprietor and Director of Abdulrahman Algosaibi G.T.B., of National Milk Factory, Riyadh, of Saudi Travel and Tourist Agency (STATCO), of Algosaibi Travel Agency, Bahrain; Shareholder (25%) of Riyadh Beverage Company; real estate in Saudi Arabia, the Arabian Gulf and USA. **Sports:** Tennis, Swimming, Shooting, Fishing and horseriding. **Club:** Equestrian club. **Credit Cards:** American Express and Diners cards. **Prof. Addr.:** P.O.Box 215, King Abdul Aziz Street, Tel.: 20815, 20811, 20816, 21215, Riyadh 11411, Saudi Arabia.

GOSAIBI (Khalid, Mohamed, al), Saudi businessman. **Born** in 1934 in Saudi Arabia. **Married. Educ.:** B.A. in Economics, University of Southern California, USA. **Career:** Government Administration (1964); worked with the Water Project Planning Staff in Ministry of Agriculture and Water; Director General of Dammam Port and Saudi Railways (1968-72); Vice Governor, Saudi Arabian Monetary Agency (1980); member of the board of Riyadh Bank, Riyadh, Saudi Arabia and Saudi International Bank, London, U.K.; Chairman, Arab Investment Co. S.A.A., Bahrain. **Addr.:** P.O.Box 9626, Riyadh 11423, Saudi Arabia.

GOUDA (Venice Kamel), Egyptian former Minister of State for Scientific Research. **Born** on October 7, 1934. **Daughter** of Kamel Gouda (Accountant) **and** Mr. née Victoria Attallah. **Widow,** 2 children: Leila (1963), Shereen (1968). **Educ.:** B.Sc., Ain Shams University (1956); M.Sc., Cairo University (1959); Ph.D., Cairo University (1962). **Dipl.:** D.Sc., Ain Shams University 1994) **Career:** Assistant Research Chemist, National Research Centre, Egypt (1956-1960); Assistant Research Chemist, Portland Cement Association, USA (1960-1961); Research Chemist, National Research Centre, Egypt (1962-1966); Research Associate Professor, Clarkson College of Technology, USA (1966-1968); Research Associate Professor, National Research Centre, Egypt (1966-1974); Visiting Scientist, Corrosion Centre, Ohio State University, USA (1974-1975); Chairman of Physical Chemistry Department and Director of Applied Inorganic Chemistry Division, National Research Centre, Egypt (1978-1980); Research Professor, National Research Centre, Egypt (1974-1982); Chairman of the Physical Chemistry Department, National Research Centre, Egypt (1982-1984); Senior Research Scientist and Manager, Corrosion Program, Kuwait Institute for Scientific Research (1984-1990); Director, Applied Inorganic Chemistry Division, National Research Centre, Egypt (1991-1993); Minister of State for Scientific Research (October 1993-July 1997). While holding this position, supervised and shared in putting the National Science and technology Policy and a number of priority technology strategies have been formulated. These include: Genetic Engineering and Biotechnology, Electronics and Informatics, Textiles, Marine Technologies and Pharmaceuticals. Headed the negotiations that led to: 1) The conclusion of many Scientific agreements between Egypt and other countries for raising the capabilities of research centers. 2) Grants and Funds for Research centers and institutions affiliated to the MOSR. 3) Opening many scientific channels with developed countries to exchange scientists and to have junior Egyptian researchers trained abroad. 4) Utilization of the capabilities of distinguished Egyptian Scientists living abroad by working as part-timers in research centers and institutions as emeritus professors or as consultants for the Ministry. 5) Enhancing the scientific and technological cooperation between the scientific sectors in different Ministries for solving national problems, and also with private sector. **Delegations:** Have officially represented Egypt as Head of several official delegations including: In 1994: Germany, USA, Pakistan, Romania. In 1995: Hungary, France, Switzerland, India, Malaysia, Singapore, Pakistan and USA. In 1996: Indonesia, Italy, USA, India. In 1997: Switzerland and Germany. **Other Information:** Professional and Affiliations: The International Corrosion Council, representing Egypt (active member in various committees); National Association of Corrosion Engineers (NACE, USA) - member and the Regional Representative in the Technical Practices committee responsible for editing and preparation of NACE standards; Austrian Corrosion Association (Honorary member); Egyptian Corrosion Society (Founder member and the former secretary general); Chemical Society of Egypt; Society of Graduates of the Faculties of Sciences, Egypt; The Arab Society of Materials Science. Conferences, Scientific Visits and Lectures: Attended all International Corrosion starting from 1975 till present and also attended several annual conferences of the National Association of Corrosion Engineers. Contributed to research activities and/or delivered lectures in several countries including USA (MIT, NSF, NBS, US AID, OSU, NYSUB, UT), England (NPL, UMIST/University of Leeds, City of London Polytechnic, British Council guest scientist), Belgium (CEBELCOR), Iraq, Kuwait, Abu-Dhabi and Bahrain. Research and Experience: Major field is corrosion, corrosion inhibition, and corrosion monitoring. Have special interest and experience in corrosion of steel in concrete, stress corrosion cracking, corrosion fatigue, erosion-corrosion and diagnosis of engineering failures. Supervised several students at the National Research Centre, the Building Research Institute and the Faculty of Science (Ain Shams University) during their studies leading to M.Sc., and Ph.D. degrees. Author and Co-author of 92 publications and two patents. **Medals and Decorations:** Egyptian Academy of Scientific Research and Technology Award for remarkable scientific contribution (Junior Scientists Level) (1974); Presidential First Decoration and Medal of Sciences and Arts (Arab Republic of Egypt) (1976); National Research Centre Award in Recognition of outstanding scientific achievements (Senior Scientists Level), Egypt (1984); Kuwait Foundation for the Advancement of Sciences Award and Honorary Certificate for scientific excellence in applied sciences, field of corrosion (Arab States Level) (1986); National Research Centre Honorary Certificate (1982 and 1989); Scientific Professionals Syndicate Honorary Certificate for Pioneering Chemists (1991); International Fellow Award of the National Association for corrosion Engineers (NACE, International) (1994). **Sports:** Swimming, Tennis and Table Tennis. **Hobbies:** Reading, Music and Gardening. **Member:** Shooting Club. **Credit Card:** Visa Card. **Priv. Addr.:** 15 El-Zahra Street, Dokki, Tel.: 3378793, Mobile: 012/3314560, Cairo Egypt.

GOULED (Ahmad Haji Aden), Somalian diplomat. **Born** on January 1, 1929 in Galcaio, Somalia. **Son** of Haji Aden Gulaid (Former Commercial) **and** Mrs. Halan Mohamad Aptidon. **Married** to Mariam Mohamad Giama (Somalia) on June 1952, 9 children: Aian, Saida, Abdallahi, Aden, Mohamad, Mulky, Ibrahim, Abdurrahman and Abdulaziz. **Educ.:** Secondary School in Mogadiscio and University of Rome (1956-57). **Dipl.:** Gratuated from Mogadiscio School of Political and Public Administration (1956). **Career:** District Commissioner in the Somali Republic (1957-59), Promoted to Regional Governorship (1960-67), Appointed President of the Port Authorities Agency of Somali Republic (1965-67), Somalian Ambassador to Saudi Arabia (1969). **Addr.:** Ministry of Foreign Affairs, Mogadishu, Somalia.

GOULLI (Salheddine, al, Dr.), Tunisian lawyer and statesman. **Born** on June 22, 1919 at Sousse (Tunisia). **Married:** one child. **Educ.:** Sousse College; Faculty of Law, Paris University (France). **Dipl.:** L.L.B., L.L.D. **Career:** In private industry (1947-56); active in Tunisian Politics, Neo-Doustour Party (1947-56); Consul-General, Marseilles (France) (1956-58); Embassy Counsellor, United States of America (1958); Minister (USA) (1959-62); alternate Executive Director, International Bank of Reconstruction and Development (IBRD) (1961-62); Ambassador to Belgium, also accredited to the Netherlands and Luxembourg (1962), also permanent representative to the European Economic Community (EEC); Representative to United Nations (1969); Ambassador to USA (1969-74), also accredited to Mexico (1970-74), and Venezuela (1972-74). **Awards:** Grand Cordon, Order to the Tunisian Republic (1966). **Addr.:** 2 rue des Roses, Lamarsa, Tunisia.

GOUSSOUS (Wadie Hanna), Jordanian journalist. **Born** in 1920 in Karak, Jordan. **Married,**1 son, 1 daughter. **Educ.:** American University of Beirut, Lebanon. **Dipl.:** B.Sc. **Career:** Press Correspondent (1942-58); Assistant Director of Publications (1958-66); Head of Press and Research Department, Hashemite Royal Court (1966). **Addr.:** Amman, Jordan.

GOWHARY (Yousry, Abdel Razik, El, Prof. Dr.), Egyptian Professor of Geography, Head of Geographical Department. **Born** on November 2, 1937, Cairo, Egypt. **Son** of Abdel Razik el-Gowhary (Dr.) **and** Mrs. née Fatma Masri. **Married** in 1960 to Sadia Mohamed Soliman, 4 children: Hatem el-Gowhary (1961), Asnaf (1963), Tamer (1967), Khalid (1971). **Educ.:** Alexandria University, Egypt (B.A.), Reading University England (M.A., Ph.D.). **Dipl.:** B.A., M.A., Ph.D. **Career:** Professor of Geography, Head of Geographical Department. **Prof. Addr.:** Minya University, Tel. 326458, Egypt. **Priv. Addr.:** Alexandria, Tel.: 5704323, Egypt.

GREIS (Jalil, Michel), Egyptian surgeon. **Born** on February 12, 1950 in Cairo, Egypt. **Educ.:** Cairo University Medical School; Fellow, Royal College of Surgeons, Edinburgh, United Kingdom. **Dipl.:** M.D. **Career:** Plastic surgeon (hand and burns) at el-Salam Hospital and Anglo-American Hospital in Cairo, Egypt. **Hobbies:** Horse riding, jogging, classical music. **Member:** Gezira Sporting Club. **Prof. Addr.:** 31 Ministry of Agriculture Street, Cairo, Egypt. **Priv. Addr.:** 17 Hassan Sabri Street, Zamalek, Cairo, Egypt.

GUAL (Peter Gatkuouth), Sudanese politician. **Born** in 1938 in Sudan. **Married** in 1966, six children. **Educ.:** B.Sc. in Economics, University of Khartoum, Sudan. **Career:** Assistant Inspector of Finance, Bank of Sudan (1964); Technical Adviser on Economic Planning to Ministry of Souther Sudan Affairs (1971); Minister of State and General Adviser on Southern Sudan Affairs (1972); Director General, Special Fund for Southern Region (1973); Commissioner, Upper Nile Province (1973); Regional Minister of Finance and Economy (1975); Vice President, High Excecutive Council for Southern Region of Sudan (1976). **Member** of the Political Bureau, Sudanese Socialist Union and Regional Minister of Finance and Economic Planning. **Medals:** Order of Al Nilayn, 1st Class; Order of the

Constitution; Order of National Unity; Order of the Republic, 1st Class. **Sport:** Tennis. **Hobbies:** Hunting, fishing. **Addr.:** Juba, Sudan.

GUBLAN (Yusuf, Muhammad, al), Saudi academic. **Born** in 1949. **Married. Educ.:** Riyadh University, Saudi Arabia. **Dipl.:** B.A. in Education and Psychology, M.A. in Behaviouristic Management. **Career:** Director of English Language Centre, Institute of Public Administration (1983-85), Director General, Training Programmes (1985-). **Publ.:** "Athar al-Tadrib al-Wadhifi Ala al-Ridha Ann al-A'mal" (1981). **Medal:** Medal of Estimation, Riyadh University (1975). **Hobbies:** Writing, reading, poetry, football. **Prof. Addr.:** P.O.Box 205, Riyadh, Saudi Arabia.

GUEBEILY (Mohamad Abdel Maaboud), Egyptian nuclear scientist. **Born** on February 5, 1921 in Cairo, Egypt. **Educ.:** Faculty of Science, Cairo University; Curie Laboratory, Paris (France). **Dipl.:** B.Sc. (chemistry). **Career:** Chemist, Chemical Department, then Demostrator, Faculty of Science, Cairo University (1946-52); Institute of Atomic Energy, Norway (1956); Assistant Professor, Nuclear Chemistry Faculty of Science, Cairo University; Joined the Atomic Energy Establishment, Cairo (1957); Head, Nuclear Chemistry Department (1958); Director, Technical Bureau of Nuclear Power Reactor Project (1963); Director, Egyptian Atomic Energy Establishment (1965); former Chairman, Supreme Committee for Nuclear Power Reactor; former Chairman, Joint Arab Scientific Council for Utilisation of Atomic Energy for Peaceful Purposes. **Member:** Supreme Council for Scientific Research; Scientific Advisory Committee for International Energy Authority. **Addr.:** Cairo, Egypt.

GUEDI (Ahmed, Djama), Djibouti Deputy at the National Assembly. **Born** in 1954 in Djibouti. **Educ.:** B.T.S. level. **Career:** Accounting Agent of Onac. **Member** of LPAI (1975-1979) then RPP (1979- to date), Member of ADEPF. Elected Deputy at the National Assembly (19/12/1997- to date). President of the Finance Commission, General Economy and Planning and Commission Member of National Defence. **Prof. Addr.:** National Assembly, P.O.Box 138 Djibouti, Djibout.

GUELDON (Hassan, Elmi), Djibouti Deputy at the National Assembly. **Born** in 1936 in Djibouti. **Career:** Military in the French Army (1957-1972) (Retired); Chief of Staff of FLCS. Employee of Airport (Air-Djibouti) (1972-1975) - Airport Chief of Security (1972-1982); President of Vegetables and Fruits Syndicate; Secretary General of Retired Military Association; Militant of RPP and President of (Annexe du Quartier 7). Member of Political Bureau; Elected Deputy at the National Assembly (1982-to date); Member of Permanent Commission and of Exchange and Production Commission; Member of Supreme Court of Justice. **Prof. Addr.:** National Assembly, P.O.B-Nox 138 Djibouti, Djibout.

GUELLAL (Charif), Algerian former diplomat. **Born** on August 18, 1932 in Algiers. **Educ.:** University of Paris (La Sorbonne) and in Algeria and England. **Career:** Propagandist for the "National Front of î Liberation" (N.F.L.) at outbreak of Algerian Revolution; Representative of General Union of Algerian Workers (Tunis, 1956); Representative of Algerian Provisional Government in Cairo (1957); Foreign Affairs Adviser to President Ben Bella (1961-63); Ambassador to United States of America (1963-67); Accredited also to Canada and Mexico. **Addr.:** c/o Ministry of Foreign Affairs, Algiers, Algeria.

GUENNEZ (Mahmoud), Algerian official. **Born** in Algeria. **Career:** joined the Resistance during War of Independence (1954); Officer of National Liberation Army (ALN); Deputy Chairman, then Chairman, Amicale des Algériens in Europe, after Independence; Commander in Chief of the Milices Populaires; President of the Defence and Interior Commission, first National Assembly; Minister of War Veterans (1970); Member of the Central Committee of the National Liberation Front Party; Vice President, National People's Assembly (1977). **Prof. Addr.:** Algiers, Algeria.

GUERKALA (Abdallah, Dabaleh), Djibouti Deputy at the National Assembly. **Born** in 1945 at Tadjourah. **Career:** Hospital Director (1990-1996). Democratic Union Afar (1963-1966); Coordination Office with "Parti Mouvement Populaire"; Coordination Assistant General Secretary of PMP and UDA; Member of LPALI and RPP; President of "Comité des Sages"; Elected Deputy at the National Assembly (19/12/1997 - to date); Member of the Permanent Commission, Legislation Commission and General Administration of the Republic. **Pro. Addr.:** National Assembly, P.O.Box 138 Djibouti, Djibouti.

GUESSOUS (Izeddine, Muhammad), Moroccan politician. **Born** on January 1, 1941 in Fes, Morocco. **Married,** 4 daughters. **Educ.:** Institut des Hautes Etudes Politiques, Paris. **Dipl.:** in Business and Political Studies. **Career:** Commercial Director, Office Cherifien des Phosphates, Paris, France (1969-70); Group Financial Director, OCP, Rabat, Morocco (1971-77); Delegated Trustee, Commercial Bank of Morocco (1978); Member of Moroccan Association of Economists; Chairman of the Administrative Council, Institut Supérieur du Commerce et d'Administration des Entreprises; Minister of Tourism (1978); Minister of Industry and Commerce (1979) Minister of Industry, Commerce and Tourism (1981); Minister in charge of relations with the European Economic Community (1985-86); Ambassador to Spain (1991-). **Decor.:** Moroccan Order of the Throne; Grand Officer of the Senegalese Order of Merit; Commander of the British Empire, UK; National Order of Merit, France; Grand Cross of Civil Merit, Spain; Grand Officer of the Order of the Tunisian Republic. **Hobby:** tennis. **Prof. Addr.:** P.O.Box 1362, Avenue Mohamed V, Rabat, Morocco.

GUIGA (Chacha), Tunisia artist painter. **Born** in 1930 in Tunisia. **Educ.:** Fine Arts School, Algiers. **Career:** Artist Painter, Contributed to several Art Exhibitions in Tunisia, Algeria and France (1963). **Works:** "Procession". **Member** of several Art Associations in Tunis. **Addr.:** Tunis, Tunisia.

GUILAIGAH (Abdallah Bin Mohamad al), Saudi statesman. **Born** in 1940 in Buradah, Saudi Arabia. **Son** of Mohamad al Salih Guilaigah. **Educ.:** B.A. in Arabic Language, Riyadh University, Saudi Arabia. **Career:** Demonistrator; Assistant Bureau Director, Ministry of Agriculture and Water; Director, Irrigation and Dams Division; Director General, Project Execution Administration; Director General, Ministry of Agriculture and Water Affairs; Deputy Minister for Water Affairs; Governor of Saline Water Conversion Corp. **Hobby:** Reading. **Addr.:** Saline Water Conversion Corporation, P.O.B. 5968, Riyadh 11432, Saudi Arabia.

GUILLEMIN (Henri), French executive. **Born** on July 4, 1947 in Paris. **Son** of Jean Guillemin (retired) **and** Mrs. Armelle Simon. **Married** on June 25, 1977 to Diane Heidsieck, three children: Laure, Vincent and Marine. **Educ.:** College Saint Joseph, Reims; Faculté des Sciences Economiques Assas (Paris II); Institut d'Etudes Politiques (Section Eco-Fi); **Dipl.:** D.E.S. Sciences Economiques; Master of Business Administration. **Career:** Crédit Lyonnais, Real estate department and special financing dept. (1973-78); Banque Indosuez Singapore International, Corporate Credit Officer (1978-82); Domestic Credit Manager, Jeddah Head Office, Saudi French Bank (1982-84); Deputy Regional Manager, Saudi french Bank, Riyadh (1984-86); General Manager, Banque Indosuez, Bahrain (1986-to present). **Sports:** Golf, tennis. **Hobby:** Reading. **Credit Card:** Visa. **Prof. Addr.:** Banque Indosuez, P.O.Box 5410, Tel.: (973) 257019, Manama, Bahrain. **Priv. Addr.:** Tel.: (973) 232028, Manama, Bahrain.

GUINDI (Amina, El, Dr.), Egyptian Minister of Insurance and Social Affairs. **Born** on September 18, 1942 in Cairo, Egypt. **Daughter** of Hamza Mahmoud el Guindi. **Married** to Mahmoud El Deib, 2 children: Osama and Dina. **Educations:** Ph.D. in Sociology, Alexandria University; M.A. in Social Planning, Helwan University; B.Sc. of Social Work Faculty, Helwan University. **Career:** Secretary General of the National Council for Childhood and Motherhood; Rapporteur of the National Commission for Women; Member of Shura Assembly "Senator" and Deputy of Health, Population and Environment Committee in Shura Assembly; Member of the National Services Council, specialised National Councils; Member of the International Committee for Children's Rights; Vice President of the Executive Committee for the Forum for Africans and Arab Parliamentarians on Population and Development. Presently Minister of Insurance and Social Affairs. **Other Information:** Member of the Board of Directors of the Higher Council for Pre-University Education; Member of the Board of Directors of Radio and Television Union, Head of Child and Woman Programs Committee; Member of the Board of Directors of the Regional Center for Adult Illiteracy; Head Department of Youth Welfare, Helwan University; Teachning Sociology in Helwan University. **Hobby:** Reading, Music. **Prof. Addr.:** 19 El Maraghy Str., El Agouza, Cairo, Egypt, Tel.: 202-337-0039/ 202-337-5467/ 202-337-8573, Fax: 202-337-5390. **Priv. Addr.:** 7 Osman Ibn Affan St. Mohandessen, Egypt.

GUINDI (Fadwa, al), Arab-American academic. **Born** on July 16, 1940 in Cairo, Egypt. **Married,** 1 son, 1 daughter. **Educ.:** University of Texas, Austin, USA; the American University, Cairo, Egypt. **Dipl.:** B.A. in Political Science, Ph.D. in Anthropology. **Career:** Research Assistant, Social Research Centre, American University in Cairo (1960-65); NIMH Fellow (1969-72); Teaching Assistant, Anthropology Department, University of Texas, Austin (1967-69); Assistant Professor of Anthropology, University of California (UCLA) Los Angeles (1972-79), Associate Research Anthropologist, UCLA (1979-81); Visiting Associate Professor of Anthropology, University of Southern California, Los Angeles (1981); Fulbright Senior Research Scholar, Visiting Research Professor at the Middle East Research Centre and the Social Studies Department, Faculty of Arts, Ain Shams University, Cairo (1981-82); Member of, Association Internationale pour l'Etude des Religions, American Association for University Professors, American Research Centre in Egypt, Association of Egyptian-American Scholars, Association of Arab-American University Graduates, Association for Women in Science, Middle East Research in Anthropology, and Association of Academic Women, UCLA; Fellow of American Anthropological Association, Middle East Studies Association, American Association for the Advancement of Science and of Royal Anthropological Institute. **Publ.:** "Life Crisis Rituals Among the Kenuz" (1972), "The Nature of Belief Systems", "Religion in Culture", "The Angels in the Nile", "A Theme in Nubian Ritual" and "A Structural Analysis of Zapotec Ritual", as well as several other books. **Hobbies:** Theatre, music. **Prof. Addr.:** Department of Anthropology, Haines Hall, UCLA, Los Angeles, California 90024, USA.

GUINDY (Hosny), Egyptian Chief Editor - Journalist. **Born** on October 11, 1940. **Son** of Habib Guindy - Lawyer **and** Mrs. née Kawkab Boulos. **Married** on April 25, 1950 to Moushira Abdel Malek, one Girl: Yasmeen (September 28, 1980). **Educ.:** The American University in Cairo. Heliopolis Secondary School, Cairo; Heliopolis Elementary School, Cairo. **Dipl.:** B.A. Psychology (Major) - Journalism (Minor) in 1963, General Certificate of Education - Egyptian High School diploma - 1959. **Career:** Chief Editor, Al-Ahram "Weekly" (1991 - present time); Deputy Chief Editor (Al-Ahram Daily) for Foreign Affairs (1980-1991); Assistant Chief Editor (Al-Ahram Daily) for Foreign Affairs (1975-1980); Foreign Editor (Al-Ahram Daily) (1972-1975); Assistant Foreign Editor (Al-Ahram Daily) (1968-1972); Foreign Desk Reporter (Al-Ahram Daily (1963-1968). **Hobbies:** Reading - Sports. **Clubs and Associations:** (Heliopolis Sporting Club, Cairo), (Member of Society of Bahaa el Din's Friends. **Prof. Addr.:** Al-Ahram Weekly, Al-Galaa Str., Al-Ahram Bldg., Tel.: 5783094, Cairo Egypt. **Priv. Addr.:** 4 Ibn Ayas Str., Manshiet El-Bakry, Tel.: 4522255, Cairo, Egypt.

GURG (Issa, Salih, al), UAE businessman. **Born** in 1925 in Dubai, UAE. **Married,** 2 sons, 3 daughters. **Career:** Director, Union Bank of the Middle East and Vice-Chairman, National Bank of Fujairah; Shareholder and Director of FOSECO MINSEP UAE PVT LTD. **Member** of the Institute of Directors, UK; Local Advisor, British Bank of the Middle East (1948-60); Chairman, Issa Salih al-Gurg Group of Companies (1963-). **Prof. Addr.:** P.O.Box 325, Dubai, United Arab Emirates.

GWAIZ (Abdul Aziz, al), Saudi academic. **Born** in 1941 in Riyadh, Saudi Arabia. **Dipl.:** B.Sc.; Ph.D. (Physical Chemistry). **Career:** Chairman, Chemistry Department, University of Petroleum and Minerals (KFUPM) (1973-75); Dean, Faculty of Science, KFUPM (1975-77); Vice-Rector for Academic Affairs, University of Petroleum and Minerals since (1977); member of COMPLES Solar Energy Society, American Chemical Society, American Physical Society; member of the Board for the Gulf and Arabian Peninsula Studies Journal; member, World Petroleum Congress; Director of Corrosion Research Project. **Publ.:** articles in the areas of Spectroscopy, Lasers and Solar Energy and Research. **Honorary membership:** Phi Lambda Upsilon Honour, Chemical Society. **Hobbies:** Reading, swimming, numismatics. **Prof. Addr.:** King Fahad University of Petroleum and Minerals, Tel.: 8602100, Dhahran. **Priv. Addr.:** Tel.: 8606297 Ext. 6297, Dhahran, Saudi Arabia.

H

HABABI (Abdallah Saleh), Saudi diplomat. **Born** in 1930 in Taif, Saudi Arabia **Dipl.:** B.Com., Cairo University. **Career:** Attaché, Ministry of Foreign Affairs (1952); Third Secretary, Second Secretary, First Secretary, Adviser, Minister Plenipotentiary, Ambassador; Ambassador to Brazil; member of Saudi delegation to UN sessions and Arab League meetings. **Honour:** King Abdulaziz Order of Excellence. **Publ.:** a number of articles. **Hobbies:** reading, tennis, **Addr.:** Ministry of Foreign Affairs, Riyadh, Saudi Arabia.

HABACHE (Georges), Palestinian physician and political leader. **Born** in 1925 in Lydd. **Married**, one daughter. **Educ.:** Secondary in Amman and Higher at the American University of Beirut. **Dipl.:** Doctor of Medicine (1950). **Career:** Physician, Patriot, Political Leader, Founded the "Harakiyines Party" (1948), Led the Palestinian reprisals against Israeli occupation, Founded and Headed the Democratic and Popular Front of Liberation of Palestine (P.F.L.P.) until June 2000. **Addr.:** P.F.L.P. Head Office, P.O.Box 12144, Damascus, Syria.

HABASHI (Wadi), Sudanese academic. **Born** on August 14, 1917 at Merwi, Sudan. **Married**, with children. **Educ.:** Primary and Secondary education locally; Faculty of Agriculture, University of Khartoum (1938-42); University of Oxford (England) (1951-52). **Dipl.:** B.Sc. (Agriculture). **Career:** Worked at the al-Aalyab, Burgaeb and White Nile development schemes; Agricultural inspector for Merwi, Dongla and Halfa areas in the Nothern Province; Adviser to the first Sudanese Minister of Agriculture; Assistant Director for Planning and Development, Department of Agriculture (1952-55); Director, Department of Agriculture (1955-66); Director, of Production, Equatoria Schemes: member of the administrative council Gezira scheme; Chairman, Administrative council of el-Gash Scheme Commission; Head of Advisory commission for Agricultural Research; member of Studies Commission, Faculty of Agriculture, University of Khartoum; resigned from civil service (1966); joined the Food and Agriculture Organisation (FAO) (1966-71); Director, Joint Economic Commission for Africa (ECA) and the UN, Addis Ababa (Ethiopia); Joined the International Bank and the Kuwait Fund of Arab Development (Oct. 1971); Recalled to Khartoum to become Minister of Agriculture (Oct. 1971-73); Minister of Agriculture, Food and Natural Resources (1974); Chairman National Council for Research (1975); President, Organization for African Unity, Scientific Council for Africa (1975). **Addr.:** Khartoum, Sudan.

HABBAL (Adnan Mohamad Adib, al), Saudi physician. **Born** in 1936 in Mecca, Saudi Arabia. **Dipl.:** B.Sc. (Chemistry and Biology), School of Arts and Science, American University of Beirut (1961); M.D., School of Medicine, American University of Beirut (1965); speciality training, Department of Radiology, Medical Centre, American University of Beirut (1967-69); ECFMG Permanent Certificate (1969); Department of Radiology and Nuclear Medicine, Rush-Presbyterian St. Luke's Medical Centre, Chicago, Illinois, U.S.A. (1969-70); staff member, Rush-Presgbyterian St. Luke's Hospital, Chicago (1970-72); Aramco Supervisor Management Course. **Career:** Instructor, Abraham Lincoln School of Medicine, Chicago (1967-70); Adjunct, Rush-Presbyterian St. Luke's Hospital, Chicago; Assistant Professor, Rush-Presbyterian Medical Centre, Chicago (1970-72); Radiologist, Dhahran Health Centre, Aramco; Consultant in Radiology, Aramco's Contract Hospitals, al-Khobar; Chief Radiology Services, Assistant Director Speciality Medical Department Support Service and Director Impatient-Speciality Medical Department, Aramco, Dhahran Executive Medical Director, Aramco. **Member:** Chicago Roentgen Society (1970), American Board of Radiology (1970); corresponding member of American College of Radiology, member of the American College of Surgery; attended Radiology Society of North American Convention; American College of Radiology Convention. **Publications:** several scientific papers. **Hobbies:** Photography, classical literature. **Prof. Addr.:** P.O.Box 2657, ARAMCO, Tel.: 8748391, Dhahran. **Priv. Addr.:** Tel.: 8755274, Dhahran, Saudi Arabia.

HABBAL (Zaki Abdulhamid, al), Iraqi diplomat. **Born** in 1940 in Mosul, Iraq. **Married** to Sallama F. Al Habbal, 4 daughters. **Educ.:** Baccalaureus of Journalism, Baghdad University; Diploma in Persian Language, Kabul University. **Career:** worked in the Press and in the Iraqi News Agency (INA) (1959-72); First Secretary, Ministry of Foreign Affairs (1972-75); First Secretary, London (1975-76); Counsellor, Moscow (1976-79); Counsellor, Kampala (1979-81); Ambassador, Kabul (1982-85); Ambassador, Jakarta, Indonesia (1985- till now). **Member:** Honorary member of Indonesia Committee of "Daghammarskjold World Organization of Press and Diplomatic Cooperation" and many other clubs in Indonesia. **Addr.:** Embassy of Iraq, 38, Jalan Teuku Umar, Tel.: 3904067-9, Fax: 3904066, Telex: 69186 IRAQI IA, Jakarta, Indonesia.

HABIB (Fawzi), Egyptian economist. **Born** on June 14, 1922. **Married. Educ.:** Cairo University, Cairo; Johns Hopkins University, USA; New York University; North Carolina State College, USA; Duke University, USA. **Dipl.:** Diploma in Economics, M.S. in Agricultural Economics, Ph.D. in International Finance and Development. **Career:** Attorney and Taxation Consultant; Legal and Financial Counsellor, Bank Misr, Nile Ginning Co., Ottoman Bank, Barclays Bank, Egypt (1947-53); Representative of French Insurance Co., to British and other European manufacturers of chemicals and agricultural machinery (1944-53); Senior Economist, World Bank, Latin American Department (1956-61); Financial Adviser to the President of Panama (1962-66); Associate Professor, Florida State University in Panama (1962-64); Senior Investment Officer, International Finance Corporation, Washington DC, USA (1966-71); Chief Investment Officer (1971-78); Member of American Economics Association and American Bankers Association; Senior Adviser, International Finance Corporation in charge of problem cases, larger investments and development banks (1977). **Publ.:** "The Pace and Direction of Growth of Agricultural Export Economies" (1958), "Factors Affecting the Foreign Demand for Long Staple Egyptian Cotton" (1956). **Hobbies:** Music, tennis, travelling, international finance. **Prof. Addr.:** International Finance Corporation, 1818 H Street, Washington DC 20433, USA.

HABIB (Fayez, Ibrahim, al, Dr.), Saudi academic. **Born** in 1942 in Cairo, Egypt. **Married,** children. **Educ.:** Riyadh University (Now King Saud University); Indiana University Bloomington, Ind. U.S.A. **Dipl.:** B.Com. (Hons.) (Economics and Political Science) (1964-65); M.A. (Economics) (1968); Ph.D. (Economics) (1973). **Career:** Lecturer and Assistant Professor of Economics: Faculty of Commerce, Military Academy, Centre for Training and Applied Research, Ministry of Labour; Chairman, Marketing and Economics Research Committee, Faculty of Commerce (Oct. 1973- May 1976); Member of Riyadh University Board (Now King Saud University) (Jan. 1976- May 1976); Deputy General Management for Economic and Commercial Affairs of the Arab Organization for Industrialization, Cairo, Egypt (May 1976- Nov. 1977); Chairman of the Board of Directors of the Arab American Vehicles Company "Jeep Vehicles", Cairo, Egypt. A Joint Venture Company between Arab Organization for Industrialization and American Motors Corporation (Nov. 1977- June 1979); Chairman, Liquidation Committee, Arab Organization for Industrialization (1979-); Member of the Applied Medical Sciences Council, King Saud University (1979-80); Chairman, Economics Department, College of Administrative Sciences, King Saud University, Riyadh, Saudi Arabia (1979- Nov. 1986); Member of the Girls Education Center Council, Riyadh University (Now King Saud University), Riyadh, Saudi Arabia (1982-); Member of King Saud University Board, Riyadh, Saudi Arabia (1984-86); Consultant to UNDP Working on Regional Development Planning for Saudi Arabia in collaboration with the Ministry of Municipality and Rural Affairs (1985-); Dean, College of Administrative Sciences, King Saud University (Dec. 1986-); Professor of Economics (July 1990- to present); Chairman, Research Center, College of Administrative Sciences, King Saud University, Riyadh (1986-1992); Chairman, Center of Arabian Gulf Studies (1988-1992); Member of the International Editorial Board, Journal of Economic & International Relations, a Quarterly Journal published by the Asian Research Service, Hong Kong (1988- Present); Member of the Supervisory Committee, Al-Amin Journal, Issued by the General Directorate for Relations and Guidance, Ministry of Interior, Kingdom of Saudi Arabia (1990-1993); Chairman, Editorial Board, Saudi Economic Journal, Saudi Economic Association, Riyadh, Saudi Arabia (1993- Present); Consultant, King Abdulaziz Center for Science and Technology, Riyadh, Saudi Arabia (1994-Present); Member. Scientific Council of King Saud University, Riyadhl Saudi Arabia (1994- Present); Consultant, Consultative Council ("Majless Al-Shuraa"), Kingdom of Saudi Arabia (1995); Member of College of Administrative Sciences Council, King Saud University (1995); Member, Editorial Board, Journal of Diplomatic Studies, Institute of Diplomatic Studies, Riyadh, Saudi Arabia (1995- Present). **Publ.:** Co-author of 3 Marketing and Research Works for the Industrial Development and Research Centre (in Arabic); Co-author of a text book on National Income and Foreign Trade, published in 1976, 1980, 1983 (in Arabic); "Economic Effects of October 6, 1973 War...", "The Oil, The Economic Strength of the Arabs", published in Journal of Faculty of Commerce, Riyadh University, No.4, 75/75, pp. 268-80 (in Arabic); Co-author of a working paper on "Inflation in Saudi Arabia", 1976 (in Arabic) (unpublished); "Process and Procedures of Preparing the Social and Development Plan", a lecture delivered in the short-term training courses on: Managing the National Economy, Economics Department, College of Commerce, Riyadh King Saud University, 1977 (in Arabic); "Strategy of Economic Development", with reference to Saudi Second Development Plan, published in the 7th ed. of the College of Administrative Sciences Journal 1981, (in Arabic); Co-author of a paper on "The Effect of the Agricultural Policy of the European Economic Community on Trade with Saudi Arabia", unpublished, 1980 (in Arabic); "The Meaning and Measurement of Development", published in the College of Commerce Journal, University of Alexandria, 1981 (in Arabic); Co-author of 2 books on Principles of Economics for the Ministry of Education, Saudi Arabia, published by the Ministry, late 1981 (in Arabic); "Economic Development: Theory and Practice in Developing Countries", published by King Saud University, 1983 (in Arabic); "Theories of Development and Growth", published by King Saud University, 1983 (in Arabic); "Toward Measuring the Absorptive Capacity of the Saudi Economy (1390-91) - (1399-1400)" (Co-author), published in Journal of the Gulf and Arabian Peninsula Studies, Vol. IX, No. 36, October 1983 (in Arabic); "Trade Relationship Between Saudi Arabia and Asian Countries: An analytical Study", published in the Proceedings of the 6th International Symposium on Asian Studies, 1984 (Co-author); "Consumption-Income Adjustment Process in Rich Oil Producing Countries: The Case of Saudi Arabia", Economic Analysis and Policy Journal of the Economic Society of Australia and Newzealand, Vol 17 No.1, March 1987, (Co-author); "Inflation in Saudi Arabia (1956-58 and 1975-78)" (in Arabic) presented in a Symposium on Managing Commercial Bank, Community Service Centre, King Saud University, 1983 (Unpublished); "An Analytical Study of the Structure of Saudi Arabian Exports and Imports: (1968-82)" (in Arabic), to be published in 'Egypt Contemporaine' (Egypt), (Co-author); "An Economic Model for Forecasting Saudi Arabian Exports", (in Arabic), to be published in 'Egypt Contemporaine' (Egypt), (Co-author); "An Econometric Study of the Determinants and Behavior of Saudi Arabian Imports", (in Arabic), Journal of Administrative Sciences, King Saud University, Riyadh, Vol 11 (2), 1986, (Co-author); "An Analytical Study of the Balance of Payments of the Members States of the Gulf Cooperation Council: (1970-82)", published in Asian Profile (Hong Kong), Vol. 14, No.1, February 1986, pp.61-72 (Co-author); "The Effect of the Oil Boom on the Saudi Imports Functions: An Econometric Study", (in Arabic), published in Journal of Administrative Sciences, King Saud University, Riyadh, Vol. 12 (1), (1987) (Co-author); "Saudi Trade Relationship with the EEC countries: An Analytical Study (1966-82)", published in the Asian Economic Review, XXVIII, No.2 of August 1985; "Foreign Trade of the GCC countries: Pattern and Direction During the Period (1968-85) an Analytical Study", published in Journal of Public Administration, Institute of Public Administration, Riyadh; "The Effect of the Spatial Distribution of Industries on Regional Disparities in Saudi Arabia: A Case Study of Saudi Industries", published in Journal of the Gulf and Arabian Peninsula Studies, Volume XV, No.58, April 1989; "Principle of Macro Economics", published by Tihama, Riyadh, Saudi Arabia, (1988); "Military Industry: The Arab Project Towards Development Integration among the Arab Countries", The Journal of College of Commerce for Scientific Research, Alexandria University, Egypt, Volume 26, No.1, (1989) (in Arabic); "The Effects of External Economic Factors on a Single Resource-Base Economy: The Case of Saudi Arabia (1982-86)", The Journal of Economics and Law Studies, Faculty of Law, Ein Shams University, Cairo, Egypt, No.32; "Pattern of Growth and Structural Change in the Saudi Economy (1970-85)": An Analytical Study, published in Journal of Economics and International Relations. A Quarterly Journal published by Asian Research Service, Hong Kong, Volume 3, No.3, Autumn 1990; "Basic Needs Approach - The Case of Selective Muslim Countries" - A Study to be published soon. **Member:** Moslem Social Scientists Society (U.S.A.). **Addr.:** King Saud University, College of Administrative Sciences, P.O.Box 2459, Riyadh 11451, Tel.: 4674350, Fax: 4674216, Telex: 401019 KSU SJ, Saudi Arabia.

HABIB (Hassib, Saleh), Iraqi businessman. **Born** on December 12, 1930 in Iraq. **Married,** 3 children. **Educ.:** Baghdad University, Iraq. **Dipl.:** B.Sc. in Engineering. **Career:** Engineer, Water Refinery Corporation, Baghdad (1954-60); Member of Iraqi Engineers Association (1956-), Iraqi Engineers Syndicate (1959-); Owner and Chief Executive of Hassib Saleh Company for Engineering (1960-); Founder and Member, High Board of Arab Contractors, Morocco (1983-); Deputy Chairman of the Union of Iraqi Contractors, Iraq (1984-). **Hobbies:** Table tennis, swimming. **Prof. Addr.:** Hassib Saleh Building, Nidhal Street, Baghdad, Iraq. **Priv. Addr.:** al-Aadhmeiha, Hai al-Shammasiyah 318, Zuqaq 7, No.54, Baghdad, Iraq.

HABIB (Malallah, Ali), Omani diplomat. **Born** on December 10, 1926. **Married,** 1 son, 3 daughters. **Career:** Employee at the Treasury Department (1943-44); Translator at the Department of Foreign Affairs (1945-46); Secretary, Diwan Affairs Department (1946-49); Senior Clerk, Department of Foreign Affairs (1949-52); Chargé d'Affairs, Omani Embassy to New Delhi (1973-74); Ambassador to Cairo (1974-77); Ambassador to Iran (1977-79); Chief of Political Affairs, Ministry of Foreign Affairs, Muscat (1979-81); Ambassador to United Kingdom (1981-82); Under Secretary, Ministry of National Heritage and Culture, Oman; Member, State Consultative Council (Parliament); Director, Minister of Foreign Affairs Office, Muscat (1982-). **Publ.:** "Outline of the History of Oman". **Decor.:** Order of Merit, Egypt; Order of the Republic (Grade 1), Egypt; Humayun (Grade 1), Iran; Knight of the Grand Cross of the Royal Victorian Order, UK. **Award:** Civil Award III, Oman; Distinguished Service Award conferred by the Special Representative to H.M. Sultan of Oman. **Hobbies:** Reading, swimming. **Prof. Addr.:** al-Habib & Co. L.L.C., P.O.Box 2663 Postal Code 112, Ruwi, Oman.

HABIB (Mustafa, Salman), Arab-British lawyer, pharmacist. **Born** in 1935 in Basra, Iraq. **Married. Educ.:** University of Bradford, UK; Lincolns Inn, London, UK. **Dipl.:** B. Pharm, Ph.D., Barrister at Law. **Career:** Pharmacist in General Hospital Practice (1960-68); Researcher, Bradford and Munich Universities (1968-74); Member, Pharmaceutical Society of Great Britain (1972); Fellow, Royal Society of Health (1972); Member, Lincolns Inn (1976); Managing Director of a pharmaceutical Company (1974-79); Associate Member, the Chartered Institute of Arbitrators (1984); Member of the London Court of International Arbitration (1989); Barrister, Temple (1980-). **Publ.:** Work on thin LC published in "Journal of Chrom" (1974-79), "Trade Restraint", Pharmaceutical Journal (1984). **Hobbies:** Reading, walking. **Prof. Addr.:** 10 King's Bench Walk, Temple, London EC4, UK. **Priv. Addr.:** 131 Gloucester Road, London SW7 4TH, UK.

HABIB (Randa), Jordanian journalist. **Born** on January 16, 1952 in Beirut, Lebanon. **Daughter** of Farid Habib (Ambassador) **and** Mrs. Hind née Tamer. **Married** on June 12, 1973 in Amman to Adnan Gharaybeh, two children: son, Saif (12/3/1977), daughter, Yara (9/3/1980). **Educ.:** St. Joseph University Beirut School; French Lycée in Rio de Janeiro (Brazil). **Dipl.:** Sciences Administratives et Politiques. **Career:** Journalist at Lebanese "Le Jour" and Weekly "Ousbou al-Arabi" and "Magazine"; since 1980 in Agence France Presse (A.F.P.); Director of Amman Bureau, since 1987; Correspondent of Radio Monte Carlo (RMC), since February 1988. **Other Information:** Writes for "Politique Internationale". Head of the Foreign Correspondents in Jordan (since 1996). **Sports:** Swimming, Tennis. **Member:** Dunes Club and Royal Automobile Club. **Credit Card:** American Express and Visa Card. **Prof. Addr.:** Agence France Presse, Jebel Amman, 2nd Circle, P.O.Box 3340, Tel.: 4642976, 4644978, Amman, Jordan. **Priv. Addr.:** Tlaa al-Ali, 3, Soam Street, Tel.: 5520005, Amman, Jordan.

HABIB (Rauf), Egyptian lawyer and Trade Mark Agent. **Born** on February 28, 1930, at Beni-Suef, Upper Egypt. **Son of** Dartaous Habib (Head of Department, Egyptian State Railways) **and** Mrs., née Adila Chenouda. **Married** to Annette Ninette Asfar, in Cairo, on November 18, 1978. **Educ.:** Farouk 1 Secondarty School (1942-47); Faculty of Law, Cairo University (1947-51); American University (1970-73). **Dipl.:** LL.B. (1951). **Career:** Training in law practice (1951-53); registration at Court of Appeal, Cairo (1963); registration at Supreme Court (1970); now Barrister at Law specialized in civil and commercial cases; Trade Mark Agent since 1963; Legal Adviser to U.N.H.C.R., Cairo - Y.M.C.A., Cairo; Italian Embassy, Cairo; BBC, Cairo Office, Dr. Thilo Gmbh (Federal Republic of Germany); Armenian Catholic Patriarchate; Episcopal Church, Cairo; GEC-Marconic Electronics Laison Office, Cairo; Nalco Italiano; Wander Scientific Office, Cairo, **Sports:** Tennis, swimming, billiard. **Hobbies:** Reading, fishing, classical music and playing the piano. **Club.:** Gezireh Sporting Club, Cairo, **Prof. Addr.:** 54, Abdel Khalek Sarwat Street, Flat 31, Tel.: 913975, Cairo. **Priv. Addr.:** 3, Kobessi Street, Tel.: 905751, Cairo, Egypt.

HABORY (Ali, Hamoud, al), Yemeni civil servant. **Born** on November 17, 1933 in Sanaa, Republic of Yemen. **Married**, 3 sons, 1 daughter. **Educ.:** Arab Marine Academy, Alexandria, Egypt. **Dipl.:** in Master Marine. **Career:** Chairman of Ports and Marine Affairs Corporation (1963-). **Hobbies:** Handball, volleyball, swimming. **Prof.Addr.:** 26th September Street, Hai el-Tujari, Hodeidah, P.O.Box 3183, Republic of Yemen. **Priv, Addr.:** Villa Captain Ali H. alhabory, Seaside, Hodeidah, Republic of Yemen.

HABTOOR (Khalaf, Ahmed, al), U.A.E. Businessman - Chairman - Al Habtoor Group of Companies. **Born** on November 21, 1949 in Dubai. **Son** of Ahmed Mohammad al Habtoor. **Married,** 6 children: Rashid, Mohammad, Ahmed, Noora, Amna, Mira. **Career:** Chairman, Al Habtoor Group of Companies. Ex Member of the Board of Directors - Director Board Chamber of Commerce. **Awards:** Received the Order of the Cedar of Lebanon-Knights Class. Special Merit Award for his Contribution to his Establishment of Ibn Khaldoon Awards. **Hobby:** Tennis. **Prof. Addr.:** P.O.Box 25444, Dubai, Tel.: 3431111, United Arab Emirates.

HABTOUR (Sultan, Khalifa Sultan, al), U.A.E. businessman, official. **Born** in 1942. **Son** of Khalifa Sultan al-Habtour. **Married** in 1969, 1 son, 1 daughter. **Dipl.:** B.A. in Military Sciences (1967). **Career:** Director, Contracting Company (1968-70);. Owner, Contracting Company (1968-70); Owner, Contracting Company and General Trading (1972-74); Secretary of State, Ministry of Public Works; Under-Secretary, Ministry of Labour (1971 to present). Member of Civil Service Council (1972-76); Member of Municipality Council; Director, Abu Dhabi Electricity Company; former Director, Commercial Bank Ltd., Abu Dhabi, UAE; Vice-Chairman, Federal Commercial Bank, Abu Dhabi, UAE. **Hobbies:** Poetry, Photography, Painting, Literature, Volleyball, Swimming and Hunting. **Addr.:** Ministry of Labour, Abu Dhabi, UAE.

HACEN (Moctar Ould Mohamed, El), Mauritanian Mineral Economist. **Born** on October 30, 1959 at Tidjikja (Mauritania). **Son** of Mahmoud O.M. El Hacen, Retired School Master **and** Mrs. Aicha M.M. Ahmed. **Married** on December 1, 1985 in Tidjikja, to Deija M. El Hadrami, four children: Aicha, Zeinabou, Hasni and Aminstou. **Educ.:** Western Australian School of Mines, Curtin University of Technology, Australia; Institut International Technique de Banque, CNAM, Paris, France; Ecole Normale Supérieure (ENS), Mauritania; University of New Brunswick, Fredericton, Canada. **Dipl.:** Master of Science (M.Sc.), Mineral Economics; Certificate in Banking Economics and Financial Analysis, Professorship in English Literature and Linguistics, Certificate in English Language. **Career:** May 1997 - Now: Deputy Director General, GEMAK, Mauritania; August 1991 - May 1997: Company Secretary and Office Manager, MORAK; January 1987 - August 1991: Company Secretary and Office Manager, SAMIN; October 1981 - January 1987: Company Secretary and Head of Department, SAMIN. **Sports Practised:** Tennis and Jogging. **Hobby:** Reading. **Prof. Addr.:** GEMAK, P.O.Box 5576, Nouakchott, Mauritania, Tel.: +(222) 2 56423, 57498/499, Fax: +(222) 2 56320, e-mail: Gemal0@toptechnology.mr **Priv. Addr.:** P.O.Box 3775, Nouakchott, Mauritania, Tel.: +(222) 2 56721.

HACHEME (Abdou, al), Mauritanian Lawyer. **Born** on January 28, 1941 in Boutilianit (Mauritania), **Son** of Sidi Abdella Al Hacheme **and** Mrs. Makfoula Mohamed Soleim. **Married** in 1984 to Zeheib Abdelvetah, 4 children:

Hacheme (1985), Makfoula (1987), Selmaā (1989), Adnanke (1991). **Education:** Faculté de Droit et Science Economique Rue d'Assas Paris - St. Johns University, New York University, Colombia University - New York. **Dipl.:** Master Degree International Law - USA, P.H.D. in International Relations. **Career:** Chargé d'Affaires a.i. Mauritania Embassy, Washington DC (1964-1966); Consul of Mauritania in Paris (1966-1969); Chargé d'Affaires a.i. Embassy of Mauritania in Washington (1970-1972); From 1973 to 1978 Administrator of United Nations at United Nations Secretariat in New York; In Charge of the Refugees Problems of Lebanon; In Charge of the General Assembly of United Nations; In Charge of the Security Council Affairs at Secretariat in New York. **Awards:** Légion d'honneur Française. **Sports Practised:** Aviation. **Hobby:** Pilot Bimoteur. **Clubs and Associations:** President of "Alliance Française" in Mauritania. **Address:** P.O.Box 527 Nouakchott, Tel.: 222-251919, Fax: 222-252034, Mauritania.

HADARY (Mahmoud el-Sayed, el), Egyptian professor of dentistry. **Born** on September 15, 1925 Alexandria, Egypt. **Son** of Mr. el Sayed M. el-Hadary (contractor) **and** Mrs. Fatma M. née Farghali. **Married** on June 21, 1956 to Miss Nabila Saleh Eid. two daughters: Magda M. el-Hadary and Hanaa M. el-Hadary. **Educ.:** Moharrem Bey Nursery School, Moharrem Bey Elementary School, Abbassia Secondary School, University of Alexandria. **Dipl.:** Diploma of Dental Surgery (Alexandria University), Master of Science (University of Michigan, U.S.A.). **Career:** Clinical Demonstrator (1951); lecturer (1959); Associate professor (1964); Professor of Dentistry (1972); Chairman of Dental Anatomy and Histology Dept. (1972); Chairman of Conservative Dentistry Dept. (1972); Vice Dean of Post Graduate Studies Faculty of Dentistry (1974); Dean faculty of Dentistry (1978); President of University of Alexandria (1980); Senator (1980-86); Also Private practice. **Member of:** Egyptian Dental Academy; President of Public Service and Scientific Association of Dental Students; Rotary East Club; Chairman of Education Committee Economic Association for Businessmen; Vice President (Association for future of Disabled); President of Egyptian American Friendship Association Alexandria; President of Scientific Association for Dental Students. **Medals:** Republic Medal of Science and Art First Grade; Gold Medal of Jeddah City. **Sport:** Swimming. **Hobby:** Birds and Poultry. **Member of:** Sporting Club; Youth Club; Alexandria Club; Rotary Club; Arm Club. **Credit Cards:** American Express. **Prof.Addr.:** University of Alexandria, Dental Faculty Tel. 4831328, Alexandria. **Private Addr.:** Masgaid el-Hadaia Bulkly, Tel. 5871260, Alexandria, Egypt.

HADARY (Osman, al), Sudanese former diplomat. **Born** in 1920. **Married** to Fahima al-Hadari in 1950. **Educ.:** Gordon College (Khartoum), (Khartoum), Khartoum School of Science, University of Alexandria (Faculty of Medicine). **Dipl.:** Cambridge School Certificate, Gordon College, Khartoum, (Khartoum School of Science); M.B.B. Ch. (Doctor of Medicine and Surgery), University of Alexandria. **Career:** Resident at Alexandria Hospitals (1949-50); Private medical practice (1950-56); Sudanese Ambassador to Pakistan (1956-59), to United States of America (1959-64), to Arab Republic of Egypt (1964). **Addr.:** Ministry of Foreign Affairs, Khartoum, Sudan.

HADDAD (Adham K.), Group General Manager. **Born** in 12 September 1938 in Syria. **Son** of Aref Haddad (Merchant and Mrs Shakreyah Haddad. **Married** in 18.9.1979 to Mrs. Souhir née Tayfour, 3 children: Dina (1982), Aliaa (1983) and Aref (1990). **Educ.:** Bachelor of Law, Damascus University (1969); M.A. Fairleigh Dickinson University, New Jersey, USA (1975) in International Studies of International Law; M.A. New York University, USA (1980) in the Political Science of International Relations, **Career:** Assistant Manager, Registry Office Central Administration Department, Sugar and Agricultural Products Industries Corps., Syria (1962-67); Head of Correspondence Office, United Arab Industrial Corporation, Damascus-Syria, Member of the Board of Purchasong Committee (1967-72); Administration Manager, Arabian General Investment Corp., AGICO Dubai, U.A.E.(1981-94); Group General Manager, Khalifa Juma Al-Nabooda Group of Companies, Dubai-U.A.E. (1994-to present). **Hobbies:** Reading and music. **Member:** Union of Arab Jurists; New York University Alumni; Fairleigh Dickson University Alumni. **Prof. Addr.:** P.O.Box 626, Dubai, Tel.: 00971 4 398883, U.A.E. **Private Addr.:** Jumeirah Beach Road, Villa No.9 Tel.: 00971 4 3441737 Dubai, U.A.E.

HADDAD (Ahmad, Ali, al), Yemeni diplomat. **Born** on October 2nd, 1936 at Ibb, Yemen. **Son** of Ali Al-Haddad (Judge) **and** Mrs. Taqya al-Haddad. **Married** on September 24, 1967, 1 child: Bassema (1968). **Educ.:** Khedive Ismail High School, Cairo; Cairo University, Faculty of Law (1958-60); University of Vermont, USA (1961-64). **Dipl.:** B.A., Graduate studies at Colorado University and the New School of Social Research, New-York. **Career:** Director of International Organisation at the Ministry of Foreign Affairs (1964-65); Director General, same Ministry; Under-Secretary, Ministry of Foreign Affairs; Head, Foreign Office in Taiz (1968); Head, Economic and Technical Department (1969); Chargé d'Affaires, Yemen Embassy, Bonn, F.R.G. (1970); Deputy Permanent Representation at the Yemen Mission to the United Nations (1971-74); Head, Political Department, Ministry of Foreign Affairs (1975-76); Ambassador, United Nations Office, Geneva (1977); Ambassador Permanent Representation at the United Nations, New-York (1978-79); Ministry of Foreign Affairs; Ambassador, Kingdom of Belgium and European Economic Communities (1980); accredited to Luxembourg (1983). **Sports:** Tennis, swimming. **Hobbies:** Reading, Photography. **Member:** New York Health and Raquette Club. **Credit Card:** American Express. **Prof. Addr.:** Ministry of Foreign Affairs, Sanaa, Republic of Yemen.

HADDAD (Farid, Sami), Arab-American surgeon of Lebanese origin. **Born** in 1922 in New York, USA. **Married**, 2 sons, 1 daughter. **Educ.:** American University of Beirut; Chicago, New York, USA. **Dipl.:** B.A., M.D., FACS. **Career:** Chief Resident, Presbyterian Hospital in Chicago (1951-53); Special Fellow, Memorial Hospital, New York (1953-54); Urologist, Orient Hospital, Beirut (1954-57), President, Lebanese Urology Association (1957-67); Editor in Chief of the "Lebanese Medical Journal" (1961-68); President of the Lebanese Order of Physicians (1969-70); President of Marjiyoun Hospital, Lebanon (1972-77); Surgeon/Urologist, Obeid Hospital, Riyadh, Saudi Arabia (1977-78), Chief of Staff (1979-81); Vice President, International Society of the History of Medicine (1975-80); Member of the New York Academy of Medicine, the International Society of Urology, the Alpha Omega Alpha, the Athenaeum of Argentina; Chief of Urology, VA Medical Center, Phoenix, Arizona, USA (1981-1991). **Publ.:** over 1052 articles on medical history. Medicine, Surgery and on Urology in professional magazines and journals in English, French and Arabic. **Decor.:** Officer of the National Order of the Cedars; Knight of the National Order of the Cedars; Commander of the National Order of the Cedars. **Medal:** Award Medal of the Egyptian Medical Association. **Hobbies:** Collecting coins and manuscripts. **Prof. Addr.:** 4332 E Piccadilly Road, Phoenix, AZ 85018, USA.

HADDAD (Ghassan, M.R. Prof. Dr.), Syrian Politician and academic. **Born** in 1926 in Syria. **Educ.:** Secondary Education (1944); Military College, Syria (1948); Staff Officers College, Syria; Higher studies in the Soviet Union; Studies in Germany and Poland. **Dipl.:** B.Sc.; M.Sc.; DSC in Planning and Statistics; Professor of Economics. **Career:** Held important military positions until he reached the rank of Staff major General (1963); Elected Member of the Revolutionary Command Council as well as Minister of Planning (1963-66). He was fully devoted thereafter to Scientific research; Studies in Germany and Poland (1965-75); Occupying the posts of Expert of Economy and Chief Expert at the Ministry of planning and professor for Higher studies in Iraq (1975-85); Currently, he is Professor at the Institute of national and Socialist Studies, Al Mustansiriyah University Baghdad, Iraq (1985- present), as from early September 1993 appointed Dean of the Faculty of Arab History and Culture relevant of the "Association of Arab Historians" (a League of Arab States body) in addition to his previous occupations. Elected amid the 5000 Intellectual and Scientific Personalities distinguished about the World by the Cambridge Encyclopeadia. Has lectured in several University and Higher Institutes. **Publ.:** Many publications in both Arabic and French; Has participated in many conferences and Sientific symposia, particularly in those concerned with planning and development in the Third World. **Medals:** Has been awarded many distinguished medals and honours. **Member:** General Federation of Arab Economists; General Federation of Arab Writers; Association of Arab Historians. **Add.:** Institute of National and Socialist Studies, Al-Mustansiriyah University, P.O.Box 6025 Mansour, Tel.: 5412348 (Ins.), 5540854 (Res.), Baghdad, Iraq.

HADDAD (Ghassan, Saad), Jordanian, Bank Manager. **Born** in 1943 in Irbed. **son** of Sa'ad Haddad. **Married** in 1978, 2 daughters and 1 son. **Educ.:** Post Graduate Diploma in Systems analysis and Design. **Career:** Served different Banks in Jordan, Kuwait and UAE for 33 years. Regional Manager-Banque Libanaise pour le Commerce (France), Abu Dhabi, UAE. **Member:** Institute of Bankers; Institute of Data Processing Management Ltd.; Marbia Club, Sharjah, UAE. **Addr.:** P.O.Box 43184, Tel.: 97150-6422450, Fax: 9712-780850 Abu Dhabi, U.A.E.

HADDAD (Jerrier, Abdulmassih), Syrian electrical engineer. **Born** on July 17, 1922 in New-York. **Son** of Abdulmassih Abdo Haddad (Journalist, Founder of "Al-Sayeh") **and** Rashida Shaker. **Married** to Margaret Van Hamlin (deceased); a second time to Carol Jane Mc Cowen on September 7, 1974, 5 Children: Mary Rashida de Garmo, Helen Margaret Abu Shaheen, Suzanne Louise Baktash, Albert John and Alexander Lansdowne. **Educ.:** Cornell University. **Dipl.:** Bachelor of Science in Electrical Engineering. **Career:** Began as a Teaching Assistant, Cornell University (1944-45); with International Business Machines Corporation (1945), Beginning as Laboratory Technician successively various engineering positions Laboratory Manager, Director Advanced machine development, General Manager Special Engineering products division (1945-59), General Manager Advanced systems development division (1959-1961), Vice-President systems design and engineering (1961-63), Director, Engineering, Programming and Technology of Electrical and Electronics Engineers (1963), IBM Vice President (1967-77); Retired in 1981. **Member** of Associations for Computing Machinery, Institute of Electrical and Electronics Engineers, American Association for Advancement of Science, Sigma XI. Tau Beta Pi, Eta Kappa Nu, Holder 13 American patents, plus Foreign Filing. **Addr.:** 162, Macy Road Chilmark Park, Briacliff Manor, Tel. (914) 9417061, New-York 10510 (U.S.A.)

HADDAD (Mustafa, al), Syrian university professor and statesman. **Born** in 1930. **Educ.:** Universities of Damascus and Paris (La Sorbonne). **Dipl.:** Doctor of Literature. **Career:** Teacher in Aleppo (1954); Faculty of science Damascus University (1960); Minister of Education; Assistant Professor Damascus University (1964); Minister of Higher Education in the Cabinet of Dr. Youssef Zouayen (September 1965- October 1966); Vice Chairman of Syrian Delegation to Conference of Arab Ministers of Education, Kuwait (1968); Professor, University of Damascus (1969); Minister of Energy and Mineral Resources (1970-72); former President, University of Damascus. **Addr.:** Damascus, Syria.

HADDAD (Pierre, Naaman), Egyptian cleric. **Born** on October 14, 1923 in Cairo, Egypt. **Son** of Naaman Haddad (merchant) **and** Mrs., née Bahgat Khayat. **Educ.:** College of the Christian Brothers, Cairo (1932-44); St. Anne Seminary, Jerusalem (1945-50). **Dipl.:** B.Com. (1954), Bachelor (Philosophy and Theology) (1950). **Career:** Ordained to the priesthood 2nd July 1950; teacher at Rayek Seminary (Lebanon) (1950-60); Curate of Greek Catholic Cathedral, Manshieh, Alexandria (1960-70); Headmaster, Greek Catholic College, Alexandria (1967-70); of Greek Catholic College, Heliopolis (1970-72); attended refresher courses at St. Paul's Monastery and St Joseph University (Lebanon), now serving St. George's Parish. **Spec.Int.:** Child education. **Sports:** Football, volley-ball and swimming. **Prof. Addr.:** Greek Catholic Patriarchate, 16 Daher street, Tel.: 905790 and 904697, Cairo, Egypt.

HADDAD (Radhia), Tunisian politician. **Born** in 1922 in Tunis, Tunisia. **Married**, 2 sons, 2 daughters. **Educ.:** general. **Career:** Director, Bourguiba Nursery School; President of the National Union of Tunisian Women, resigned on March 8, 1972 following intervention of the Socialist Destour party in the internal affairs of the Union; Deputy in the National Assembly, elected in 1959 (first Tunisian woman Deputy), in 1964 and 1969. Vice President of the Tunisian Holiday Camps (1967), Associate President of the Tunisian Girl Guides (1967); Member, Central Committee of the Socialist Destour Party (1968-71); Member of the National Planning Council (1968-); Director of "El-Marraa" review (1961-72) in Arabic; Vice President, the International Council of Women (1970); Assistant Secretary General, National Union of Arab Women (1971); Businesswoman (1979-). **Addr.:** Bourguiba Avenue, Carthage, Tunisia.

HADDAD (Robert, M.), Arab-American academic. **Born** on October 1, 1930 in New York, USA. **Married,** 1 son, 3 daughters. **Educ.:** University of Pittsburgh, USA, University of Michigan, USA, Harvard University, USA. **Dipl.:** B.Sc., M.A., Ph.D. in History and Middle Eastern Studies. **Career:** History Lecturer at Smith College; Northampton, Massachussetts, USA (1960-65), Assistant Professor of History (1965-68), Associate Professor of History and Religion (1968-73), Professor of History and of Religion; (1973-82); Sophia Smith Professor of History and Professor of Religion (1982-93); Sophia Smith Professor of History and Professor of Religion; Emeritus; President, American University of Beirut (1993-19.12.1996). Chairman, Department of History, Smith College (1973-77); President, Orthodox Theological Society, America (1974-76); Member of the Middle East Studies Association, Eastern Orthodox/Roman Catholic Theological Consultation and the American Historical Association. **Publ.** "Syrian Christians in Muslim Society: an Interpretation", Princeton University Press (1970); "The Ottoman Empire in the Contemporary Middle East", "Aftermath of Empire", Smith College (1975); "On Melkite Passage to the Unia: the Case of Cyril al Za'îm (1672-1720)", **Christians and Jews in the Ottoman Empire**, Holmes and Meier (1982); "Iconoclasts and Mu'tazila: the Politics of Anthropomorphism", **Byzantium and Islam**, Hellenic College Press (1982); "Eastern Orthodoxy and Islam: An Historical Overview", **The Greek Orthodox Theological Review** (1986); "Eastern Christians in Contemporary Arab Society", **The Vatican, Islam and the Middle East**, Syracuse University Press (1987); "Why Not an Islamic State?", **International Area Studies Programs, Occasional Papers**, University of Massachusetts (1989); "The Conversion of Eastern Christians to the Unia", **Conversion and Continuity: Indigenous Communities in Medieval Islamic Lands**, "Pontifical Institute of Medieval Studies in Toronto" (1990); "Constantinople over Antioch, 1516-1724: Patriarchal Politics in the Ottoman Era", **The Journal of Ecclesiastical History** (1990). **Hobby:** Carpentry. **Prof. Addr.:** c/o American University of Beirut, 850 3rd Avenue, 18th Floor, New York, N.Y. 10022-6297, U.S.A.

HADDAD (Soubhi), Syrian diplomat. **Born** on October 25, 1930, in Hama, Syria. **Son** of Mahmoud Haddad (Businessman) **and** Mrs. Shishakli Haddad. **Married** on June 14, 1959 in Cairo to Dalal el-Rayyes Haddad, 4 children: Rana (29 May 1960), Randa (13 September 1962), Majed (10 November 1965), Mousef (2 April 1967). **Educ.:** Primary, Secondary, High Schools at Hama, Syria; 1 Year General Education at Damascus University; 2 Years at Military Aviation College in Alepo; 1 Year at Willington Staff College. **Dipl.:** One Year at Willington Staff College in India. **Career:** Deputy Commander of Military Base in Damascus (from July 1967 until 1969); Military Based Commander (1970-78); Commander in Chief of the Syrian Air Force and Air Defence (1978-87); Ambassador of Syria to Prague, (6 April 1988 to 1993), now retired. **Meddals:** Medal of Honour, Cavalryman Rank, Medal of Bravery, Medal of Merit. **Sports:** Tennis, swimming, walking. **Hobby:** Reading. **Member:** Membership of Baas Party since 1948. **Credit Card:** Eurocard. **Addr.:** Damascus, Syria.

HADDAD (Sulaiman, Ahmad, al), Kuwaiti banker. **Born** in 1930. **Educ.:** Kuwait Aazamieh Secondary School; Cairo University. **Career:** Secretary Education Council of Kuwait; Former Financial Assistant, Ministry of Education; Member of Constituent Assembly; Member of National Assembly (1963-76): Director, Arab African International Bank, Egypt; Chairman, ARTOC Bank Ltd., Int. Resources and Finance Bank; Director, Arab Investment Co. in Kuwait and Asia; Director, Arab Asian Investment Co.; Director Arab International Resources and Finance Bank, Luxembourg; Director, Arab International Trust, Luxembourg; Director, Arab Malaysian Development Bank, Berhad, Malasia. **Addr.:** P.O.Box 23974, Arab Gulf Bldg., al-Sour Str., Safat, Tel.: 421390-4, Kuwait.

HADDADIN (Muwaffaq), Jordanian medic. **Born** in 1942 in Ma'an, Jordan. **Educ.:** University of Wahington, USA; University of Kansa, USA. **Dipl.:** Ph.D in Pharmacology (1972). **Career:** Assistant and Associate Professeur in the College of Medicine at the University of Jordan, Amman (1972-80); Administor of Pharmacy Office, Yarmouk University, Jordan (1980-83); Board Member of Arab Company for Antibiotic Medical Industry in Baghdad, Iraq; Director of Arab Company for Drug Industries and Medical Appliances, Jordan (1983-). **Publ.:** several articles published in scientific journals. **Medals:** Two medals of honour, Yarmouk University, Jordan. **Member:** Jordanian Pharmacist Society. **Hobbies:** Chess, classical music, swimming. **Prof. Addr.:** Arab Company for Drug Industries and Medical Appliances, P.O.Box 925161, Amman, Jordan.

HADDAWY (Abbas Abdallah), Saudi civil servant. **Born** in 1925 in Mecca, Saudi Arabia. **Dipl.:** Diploma of Higher Institute of Physical Education. **Career:** Teacher; Inspector; Assistant Director General of Youth Welfare; International Commissioner, Saudi Arabian Boy Scouts Association; member of Arab Scouts Committee; attended International Boy Scouts conferences in Greece, Mexico, Japan, Morocco, Libya, Algeria, Lebanon; Chairman of Saudi delegation to Arab sporting tournaments held in Morocco, Kuwait, Lebanon, Egypt. **Addr.:** Directorate General of Youth Welfare, Ministry of Education, Tel.: 4043452, Riyad, Saudi Arabia.

HADEED (Omar Mohammed Jaber Hasan), Kuwaiti banker. **Born** in 1952 in Kuwait. **Son** of Mohammed Jaber Hadeed. **Married,** two children: Farouq in (1975) and Nawal (1978). **Educ.:** California State University, San Jose; California State University Sonoma. **Dipl.:** B.Sc. Industrial and Systems Engineering; Master of Business Administration- Finance. **Career:** Treasury Manager, Industrial Bank of Kuwait (1980-87); Acting General Manager, Kuwait Asia Bank E.C., Bahrain (1987-present). **Sports:** Football, tennis, billiard. **Hobby:** Reading. **Member:** Marina Club, Bahrain; Member of Bahrain Bankers Society. **Prof.Addr.:** Kuwait Asia Bank E.C., Box 10401, Tel/522825 (D), 532111 (G), Manama, Bahrain. **Priv.Addr.:** al-Murkh St. 84, House 112, Block 531, Budiya, Bahrain.

HADI (Abdul Hamid, Saif Manih, al), Yemeni official. **Born** in 1946. **Married,** 1 son, 2 daughters. **Educ.:** Police College, Cairo, Egypt; College of Law, Baghdad University, Iraq. **Career:** Police College (1969); Legal Adviser, the Ministry of Local Administration; Director, Office of the Minister of interior; Member of the Development Organization, of the Board of Water and Electricity Corporation; Member of the Consultative Council; Under Secretary, Ministry of Municipalities. **Hobbies:** History, literature. **Prof. Addr.:** al-Idhaa (Broadcasting) Quarter, Sanaa, Republic of Yemen.

HADI (Mahdi, Muṣṭafa, al), Sudanese politician. **Born** in 1932 in Omdurman, Sudan. **Educ.:** Faculty of Arts, University of Khartoum. **Dipl.:** B.A. (1955). **Career:** Personnel Officer (1955-58); attached to the Ministry of Foreign Affairs, (1958-69); Chargé d'Affaires, Sudanese Embassy at Nijamena (Chad) (1963); attached to Sudan's Mission at the UN, New York (USA) (1965-69); Adviser, Sudan Embassy in Moscow (USSR) (1969); Ambassador and Adviser to the President of the Revolution Command Council (1969-71); Head, Preparatory Committee, Sudanese Socialist Union (SSU); Secretary-General, Presidential Affairs (Oct. 1971); Minister of State for Presidential Affairs (1971-Oct. 1973); Commissioner, Khartoum Province (1974); Presently Assistant Secretary General for Social and Cultural Affairs at the League of Arab States. **Addr.:** League of Arab States, Midan al-Tahrir, Cairo, Egypt.

HADI (Mobarak, Adam, al), Sudanese diplomat. **Born** in 1938 in Hilaliya, Sudan. **Married,** 5 children. **Educ.:** University of Khartoum, Sudan; International Institute of Management, Paris, France; Institute of Human Rights, Strassbourg, France. **Dipl.:** B.A. in Literature, Diploma in Management and Degree in Human Rights. **Career:** 3rd Secretary, Sudan Embassy in Jeddah, Saudi Arabia (1961); 2nd Secretary, Press Attaché, Beirut, Lebanon (1964), 1st Secretary, Algeria (1967); Counsellor, Paris (1972); Ambassador to Zaire (1975); Minister Plenipotentiary, Director of Press and Information Department, Ministry of Foreign Affairs, Khartoum, Sudan; Ambassador to Oman (1979-80); presently Ambassador to Zaire. **Hobbies:** Music, playing string instruments, swimming, walking, football, tennis, reading. **Prof. Addr.:** Ministry of Foreign Affairs, Khartoum, Sudan.

HADI (Omar, Ramadan, al), Libyan mechanical engineer and statesman. **Born** on November 11, 1934. **Son** of Ramadan Ahmad al-Hadi **and** Mrs. Camila Sadeq. **Married** on December 16, 1965 in Washington, 3 children: Nader, Mazin and Nadia. **Educ.:** University of Delaware, University of Illinois, Cairo University. **Dipl.:** Master of Engineering (1966), Doctor of Philosophy, Mechanical Engineering (1968), Bachelor of Science (1969). **Career:** Dean Faculty of Engineering, University of Libya (1969), Minister of Communications and Public Works (1969). **Addr.:** P.O.Box 2034, Tel.: 41768, Tripoli, Libya.

HADID (Mohamed Jawad), Palestinian bank manager. **Born** on December 18, 1938 in Tabaria, Palestine. **Son** of Fuad Hadid and Mrs. Fatmeh Hadid. **Married** to Miss Ghada Jassem Hamad, 3 children: Samer, Rami and

Mohamed Jamal. **Educ.:** High School in Damascus (1957), Arts and Languages Branch. Damascus University, Damascus, Syria. **Dipl.:** General Culture Certificate (1958-59); Bachelor of Arts (1959-62); Major in Socialogical, Psychological and Phylosophical Studies. **Career:** Arab Bank Ltd., Damascus (1957-62); Instructor of education and teaching methods, Teachers Training School (1962-63); Social Worker, Social Development Centre, al-Ahsa, Saudi Arabia (1963-64); Joined Oatar national Bank, S.A.Q. (Bank commenced business formally on January, 1, 1965) and worked up his position from November 13, 1964 to June 1, 1978 as Head of Accounts Dept. (Jan. 1965- August 1965), International Auditor (August 1965-1966), Account under probation (1966-67), Account "A Signature" (1967-74), then became Assistant Manager supervising daily operations (1974-75) and then Manager of the Central Office of Qatar National Bank (Nov. 1, 1975- June 1, 1978); Deputy General Manager of Arab Jordan Investment Bank, Jordan (June 1, 1978 to present), his main duties: Acting General Manager, Overall responsibility for AJIB's activities including setting up of the Bank as the first investment/ merchant bank in Jordan and the development of its business and reporting directly to the Chairman and Board of Directors including submitting plans and schemes for development of the Bank's business in all areas. **Board Member** of Association of Banks in Jordan and Chemical Industries Co., Jordan. Member of the pannel formed by the Board of Directors of Association of Banks in Jordan to discuss financial topics publicly through regular lectures; Contributes essays to "Banks in Jordan monthly magazine", occassionally gives interviews to Jordanian T.V. and Broadcasting Station and has been appointed by Union of Arab Banks as a banking arbitrator in the Arab banking community. Special assignments: Prepared the feasibility study relating to the opening of a branch for Qatar National Bank in London, assisted in the establishment of Qatar National Bank's Branches in Qatar; In April and May 1975 completed an "Executive Training program" with Manufacturers Hanover Trust Co., London, also attended in 1977 a special training course in Frankfurt, West Germany in investment banking. **Sport:** Tennis. **Hobbies:** Reading, photography, table tennis and swimming. **Credit Cards:** Golden American Express; Golden Visa. **Prof. Addr.:** Arab Jordan Investment Bank, P.O.Box 8797, Tel.: 664120, Amman, Jordan. **Priv. Addr.:** Shmeisani, near Tyche Hotel, Tel.: 663746, Jordan.

HADIDI (Helmi, el), Egyptian politician. **Born** on October 1925, in Egypt. **Career:** Professor of Bone Diseases, Faculty of Medicine, University of Cairo; Assistant Secretary General Committee for Social Affairs, National Democratic Party; former, member People's Assembly; member, Shoura Council (1984-); Minister of Health (1985-86). **Addr.:** Cairo, Egypt.

HADIDI (Taher, Abdel Razzak, el), Egyptian senior petroleum expert. **Born** in 1923 in Dumiat, Egypt. **Son** of Abdel Razzak el-Hadidi, landlord, **and** Mrs. Hosn Badawi Mahmoud. **Married** in 1949 in Egypt to Miss Mawahed el-Minawi, four children. **Educ.:** Cairo University (1939-44); Princeton University (1945-48); Pennsylvania State University (1953-55). **Dipl.:** B.Sc. in Civil Engineering (1944); B.A. in Geology (1947); M.Sc. in Geological Engineering (1948); Ph.D. in Petroleum Engineering (1955). **Career:** Professor of Petroleum Eng., Cairo University (1956-66); Vice Dean of Engineering, Cairo University (1964-66); Managing Director, Egyptian General Petroleum Corp. (1966-68); Undersecretary of State for Petroleum, Egypt (1968-73); Senior Petroleum Expert, Qatar (since 1973). **Work:** Selection of the High Dam in Egypt; Initiated General Petroleum Company in Egypt; Participated in creating about 1000 Petroleum Engineers as a core for the Petroleum Industry in the Arab World; participated in all Petroleum Arab Conferences under the auspices of the Arab League in the Sixties; participated in the formulation of national oil industry in Qatar including the North Fields Gas Project; participated in the OPEC activities in Seventies. **Medals:** Highest decoration of Industry and Commerce in Egypt; Decoration of the Republic of Egypt. **Member of:** American Association of Petroleum Geologists, Sigma Xi For the advancement of Science Phi Beta Kappa, Lambola Psi Epiloy. **Credit Cards:** American Express. **Prof. Addr.:** P.O.Box 2112, Tel.: 831207, 491430, Doha, Qatar, Arabian Gulf. **Priv. Addr.:** Tel.: 416366, Doha, Qatar, Arabian Gulf.

HADIDI (Tahsin), Egyptian rheumatologist. **Born** on June 23, 1931 in Cairo, Egypt. **Married,** two children. **Educ.:** Cairo University, Egypt; In UK. **Dipl.:** M.B., B.Ch. (1954); Member of the Royal College of Physicians (1963); Fellow (1968); **Career:** Head of Rheumatology, Hospital of Maadi Armed Forces (1964-82); Member of the French Society (since 1966) and West German Society of Rheumatology (since 1982); Professor of Rheumatology, al-Azhar University (1982-). **Publ.:** published medical articles; Member of editorial board "International Rheumatology" Paris (1970-), "Clinical Rheumatology", Rome (1980-); "Medicine International", London (1980-); and "Arthritis and Rheumatism", West Germany (1984-). **Awards:** Order of the Republic (1982); Order of Distinguished Service, Medical Syndicate of Egypt (1980). **Hobby:** Tennis. **Member:** Gezira Sporting Club. **Prof. Addr.:** 4, Rushdi Street, Cairo, Tel.: 749084, Egypt. **Priv. Addr.:** 51, Muhammad Madhar Street, Zamalek, Cairo, Egypt.

HADITHI (Anwar, Abdul Qadir, al), Iraqi politician. **Born** in 1926 in Iraq. **Educ.:** Military College, Baghdad, Iraq. **Career:** held several military posts; took part in the 1958 Revolution and the Baath Revolution (1968); Secretary General of the Revolutionary Command Council (1963), Imprisoned for 3 years after the coup by Abdul Salam Arif (1963); Minister of Social Affairs, Transport, Municipalities and Labour (1968-77); Ambassador, Ministry of Foreign Affairs, then Ambassador to Czechoslovakia; Ambassador to Finland. **Addr.:** Ministry of Foreign Affairs, Baghdad, Iraq.

HADJ (Elie, el), Banker. **Career:** Vice President, Philadelphia National Bank (1974-80); Managing Director, al-Rajhi Company for Islamic Investments Limited, London, UK (1980-88); former Chairman, Studies and Economic Research Sub-Committee, Arab Bankers Association, London, UK. Regional Manager, Arab Bank Limited. London (1988-91); Managing Director, Arab National Bank, Riyadh, Saudi Arabia (1991 to date). **Addr.:** Arab National Bank, P.O.Box 56921, Riyadh 11564, Saudi Arabia.

HADJ TAIEB (Mohamed), Tunisian executive. **Born** in 1941 in Sfax, Tunis. **Married**, 1 son, 2 daughters. **Educ.:** Graduate of High Commercial Studies, Paris (1967) H.E.C., Paris. **Career:** Attaché, State Cabinet Secretary of National Planning & Economy (1967-69); Assistant General Manager, National Office of Fishery (1969-74); Assistant General Manager, Caisse Nationale d'Epargne Logement (1974-1987); President Director General, Office du Thermalisme (1988-1989); Presently President Director General, Pharmacie Centrale de Tunisie; Vice President, Executive Office of the Institut Arabe des Chefs d'Entreprise; Teacher, Ecole Nationale d'Administration. **Awards:** Knight, Ordre de la Republique Tunisienne, Tunis. **Member:** Assistant Secretary General at the General Union of Companies for Savings and on Immovable loans; President of Socialist Party at the C.N.E.L. (1978-80). **Prof. Addr.:** Pharmacie Centrale de Tunisie, 51, Avenue 10 Décembre 1948, 1082 Cité Mahrajane, Tel.: 783011, 789301. 785833. Fax: 784645, Telex: 14424-18824, Tunis, Tunisia.

HADLAQ (Mohammad Abdulrahman, al), Saudi academic. **Born** in 1941 at Shaqra. **Dipl.:** M.Litt, Ph.D., Edinburgh University. **Career:** Assistant Professor, Arabic Language Department, College of Shari'a and Islamic Studies, King Abdulaziz University, Makkah (1978-80); Professor, College of Arts, King Saud University; Vice-Dean of Graduate School at King Saud University (1995-1997), Dean of Graduate School (1997-1998), Dean of College of Arts (1998-). **Addr.:** Department of Arabic Language, College of Arts, King Saud University, P.O.Box 2456, Riyadh 11451, Saudi Arabia.

HADRI (Ikram, Makni, Mrs.), Tunisian Director of Cooperation & Training. **Born** on November 24, 1962 at Sfax, Tunisia. **Daughter** of Houcine Makni (Mechanic) **and** Mrs. Makni, Abdennader. **Married** on November 4, 1989 at Sfax to Mr. Imed Hadri, one boy: Ramzi Makni. **Educ.:** Lycée 25 Juillet-Graduated June 1981; Bachelor degree and Master's degree and Master's degree in Ceramic Engineering and Science, Alfred University, New York State (May 1988). **Dipl.:** Master's degree in Ceramic Engineering and Science. **Career:** Department of Information & Public Relations (1989); Director of Information and Public Relations (1990); Director of Training and Events (1991); Director of Cooperation and Training (Chamber of Commerce and Industry of Sfax) (1992- to date). **Other Information:** Director of Child's Song Festival, Member of Cultural Committee of Sfax. **Sports:** Karate, Volley ball. **Hobby:** Music. **Member:** Cultural Women's Club, Cultural Committee of Sfax. **Addr.:** Tunis, Tunisia.

HAEKAL (Ahmad, Mohammad Hussein), Egyptian lawyer. **Born** on July 3, 1939 in Giza, Egypt. **Married. Educ.:** Cairo University, Egypt. **Dipl.:** LL.B., Postgraduate diploma in Law and International Law. **Career:** Lawyer since 1961; Information Officer, Arab League (1965-81); Member of American Bar Association; Member, Egyptian Society of International Law (1963); First P.C.O. (Professional Conference Organizer) in Egypt, Member of A.I.I.C. Geneva (1978). **Publ.:** edited his fathers Dr. Haykal's unfinished works in the field of Islamic history and Arabic Literature. **Hobbies:** Reading, politics, history, travelling. **Member:** Gezira Sporting Club. **Prof. Addr.:** 18 A Ahmad Hishmet Street, Zamalek, e.mail: haekal@link.com.eg, Fax: (202)3351415, Cairo, Egypt.

HAFFAR (Bishr, Lutfi), Saudi businessman. **Born** in 1936 in Damascus, Syria. **Son** of Lutfi Haffar. **Educ.:** B.A. from American University of Beirut (1958); M.A., Heidelberg University, Germany (1961). **Career:** Businessman in Saudi Arabia (1967-73); member of the Board of Bri Fiber Industries, UK; Fairway Marines, UK; Chairman of the Board of al-Bishr Trading, Riyadh, Saudi Arabia. **Prof. Addr.:** P.O.Box 3497, Tel.: 4784448, Riyadh, Saudi Arabia. **Priv. Addr.:** Tel.: 766533, Riyadh, Saudi Arabia and 59, Ennismore Gardens, Flat 2, London SW7, England.

HAFFAR (Said, Muhammad, al), Syrian academic. **Born** in 1930 in Damascus, Syria. **Married**, 3 children. **Dipl.:** B.Sc. in Natural Sciences, B.A. in Education and Pedagogy; M.Sc. in Environment and Radiobiology, Ph.D. in Industrial Fermentation. **Career:** Member of the International Union for Conservation of Nature and Natural Resources; Professor, Universities of Damascus and Qatar; Professor and Head of Department of Fundamental Sciences, University of Damascus (1960-); Professor of Medical Biology, Faculty of Medicine, University of Damascus (1973-); UNESCO Expert for Environmental Sciences and Environmental Education, University of Qatar (1978-). **Publ.:** several books, articles and lectures; "Man and Environment Problems", University of Qatar (1981), "Geocancerology" (1983). **Prof. Addr.:** P.O.Box 2713, Doha, Qatar; Supreme Council of Sciences, P.O.Box 4762, Damascus, Syria.

HAFIZ (Faisal Abdallah), Saudi academic. **Born** on 17 September 1942 in Medina, Saudi Arabia. **Dipl.:** B.i. (Political Science) Indiana University, M.A. (Political Science, Hons.) Northern Arizona University, Ph.D. (International Relations), University of Nebraska-Lincoln. **Career:** Student-worker, Saudi Arabian Airlines, during intermittent summers; student-worker, Arabian American Oil Company (1951-53); Voluntary teacher for intermittent periods, primary schools, Al-Khobar, was put on the Dean's list and atained the M.A. degree with honours Northern Arizona University; Research Assistant, Departement of Political Science, University of Nebraska (1975-76); was awarded a Regent's Fellowship for Research, University of Nebraska (1976-77); member, the Muslim Students Association; active member, American Political Science Association, (APSA), the Political Science Committee, Faculty of Economics and Administration, King Abdulaziz University and al-Murshid Management Counsulting Services; attended several Political Science conventions. **Publ.:** sone articles in local newspapers; co-author, Political Socialization of Secondary School Students in Jeddah (a research survey accepted for publication by the Centre for Research and Development, Faculty of Economics and Administration, King Abdulaziz University); Changes in Saudi Foreign Policy Behaviour, 1964-75: A Study of the Underlying Factors and Determinants (Ph.D. thesis). co-editor, Who's Who in Saudi Arabia. **Hobbies:** Reading, swimming, bowling, American football. **Prof. Addr.:** King Abdulaziz University, Faculty of Economics and Administration, P.O.Box 9031, Tel.: 6879033 Ext. 1684, Jeddah. **Priv. Addr.:** Tel.: 6713089, Jeddah, Saudi Arabia.

HAFIZ (Fuad, A.), Saudi diplomat. **Born** in 1938 in Medina, Saudi Arabia. **Educ.:** completed his secondary school education in Lebanon. **Career:** Began his career as an employee with the General Directorate for Radio, Press and Publications, Jeddah, Ministry of Information; later joined the Diplomatic Section, Ministry of Foreign Affairs, Jeddah; Chargé d'Affaires, Embassy of the Kingdom of Saudi Arabia, Libya and later Chargé d'Affaires, Addis Ababa, Ethiopia; Consul, Embassy of the Kindgom of Saudi Arabia, Rome, Italy; member of the International Civil Aviation Organization, Rome; presently Deputy Consul-General, U.S.A. **Honour:** Cavalier Medal, the Republic of Italy. **Hobbies:** Reading books on international diplomacy, poetry. **Prof. Addr.:** Ministry of Foreign Affairs, Consular Affairs Department, Tel.: 6690900, Jeddah. **Priv. Addr.:** Tel.: 6716376, Jeddah, Saudi Arabia.

HAFIZ (Hisham Ali), Saudi publisher. **Born** in 1931 in Madina, Saudi Arabia. **Dipl.:** B.A. (Political Science), Cairo University (1955); B.Sc. (Military Science), Cairo Military Academy (1955). **Career:** Officer in Saudi Royal Army (1955-57); Diplomat, Saudi Foreign Ministry (1957-62); Editor-in-Chief, al-Madina daily newspaper (1960-62); Diplomat, Foreign Ministry (1971); member of Saudi permanent delegation to U.N. European headquarters, Geneva; Founder member of Arab Transport Co.; Chairman of Saudi Research and Marketing Co.; Publisher of Asharq al-Awsat, the international daily newspaper of the Arabs, published in London and printed in 8 locations araound the world; Publisher of al Majalla, political weekly news magazine, published in London; Publisher of Sayidaty, weekly social magazine, published in London; Publisher of Arab News, the first English language daily in Saudi Arabia; Publisher of al-Muslimoon, religious weekly newspaper, published in London; Co-owner of al-Madina Printing and Publication Co.; Partner, Saudi Public Projects Co.; attended all U.N. conferences on Aquatic Science, Geneva (1958); all U.N. conference in Geneva (1965-71). **Publ.:** editoral ex-officio writing; a study on Black Muslims in U.S.A. **Hobbies:** Reading and travel. **Addr.:** SRMC Building, Madina Road, P.O.Box 4556, Jeddah 21412, Saudi Arabia.

HAFIZ (Ibrahim), Libyan businessman. **Born** in 1932 in Fezzan, Libya. **Married. Career:** Owner of a large trading and contracting firm; has interests in printing machinery, supplies and building materials. Owner of marble and carpentry factory; has interests in major Libyan travel agency, property owner. **Representative** of Libyan Employers' Groups, ILO. **Addr.:** Ibrahim Tel.: 30149, 34736 and 41080, Tripoli, Libya.

HAFIZ (Mohamad Ali), Saudi publisher. **Born** in 1937 in Medina, Saudi Arabia. **Dipl.:** B.A. (Journalism), Cairo University (1960). **Career:** Assistant Director General of Press, Ministry of Information, (1960); Editor-in Chief, al-Madina newspaper (1961-64); Deputy General Manager of Medina Press Organization; Publisher, Ashraq al-Awsat (Middle East), Arabic International daily newspaper; published in London; co-owner and publisher, daily Arab News, Sayidaty, al-Majalla and al-Muslimoon magazines: owner, al-Medina Printing and Publishing Co.; member of Constituent Board of King Abdulaziz University; attended Arab League Information Conferences (1961). **Publ.:** daily column and editorial writings in al-Madina daily newspaper. **Hobby:** Reading. **Prof. Addr.:** P.O.Box 4556, Tel.: 6534239, Jeddah, Saudi Arabia.

HAFIZ (Omar, Z.A.), Saudi academic. **Born** in 1951 in Medina, Saudi Arabia. **Dipl.:** Ph.D. (Economics). **Career:** Demonstrator (1975-78); Lecturer (1978-81); Assistant Professor, Faculty of Economics and Administration, King Abdulaziz University, Jeddah, since 1981; member, King Abdulaziz University, Jeddah, since 1981; member, King Faisal Welfare Society; Chairman, King Abdulaziz University Cultural Committee for the academic year 1981/82; Deputy Director of International Centre for Research in Islamic Economics. King Abdulaziz University. **Publications:** Public Expenditure of Saudi Arabia, Structure and Growth (M.A. thesis); A Foreign Trade Model for Saudi Arabia: an Econometric Approach (Ph.D. thesis). **Hobby:** Reading, writing. **Prof. Addr.:** Faculty of Economics and Administration, King Abdulaziz University, Tel.: 6879404 Ext. 1480, Jeddah. **Priv. Addr.:** Tel.: 6716357, Jeddah, Saudi Arabia.

HAG (Musa Ismail, al), Sudanese politician. **Born** on March 29, 1942 at Elobeid, Sudan. **Son** of el-Hag Musa (army officer) **and** Mrs., née Fahima Elsaid Bakri. **Educ.:** University of Khartoum; University of Poitiers (France); University of Tours (France). **Dipl.:** LL.B., M.A. (Sociology), Ph.D. (Sociology). **Career:** University of Khartoum (1975); State Minister for Information and Culture (1979-81); member of the Political Bureau S.S.U. (1979-81); member of the executive Bureau of Central leadership S.S.U. (1983); Director, Institute for Political and Strategic Studies (1983). **Awards:** Order of the Republic (1st class). Order of Sciences and Culture granted by President of France. **Hobby:** Reading. **Priv. Addr.:** Tel.: 73416-43232, Khartoum, Sudan.

HAGE (Ali Nasr, al), Sudanese academic. **Born** in 1918 in Sudan. **Educ.:** Gordon Memorial College, American University of Beirut. **Dipl.:** Bachelor of Arts. **Career:** on staff of Gordon Memorial College (1935-47); Vice-Principal Institute of Education, Ruda (1947-51); Assistant Director (Personnel) Ministry of Education (1952-54); Deputy Director (1954-56); Director (1956-58); Vice-Chancellor, Khartoum University (1958-62); Member Board of Directors, Barclays Bank, D.C.O., Khartoum (1962); Associated University of London Institute of Education (1950); Honorary Doctor of Laws, University of Khartoum (1967). **Addr.:** Khartoum, Sudan.

HAGE (Mahgoub, Amine, al), Sudanese army officer and statesman. **Born** in 1920 in Sudan. **Educ.:** Gordon Memorial College (Khartoum) and Staff College (United Kingdom). **Career:** Commissioned (1941); rose to Major-General (1962); Minister of Communications, Agriculture, Irrigation and Hydro-Electric Power (1959-61); Minister of the Interior and Local Government (1961-62); Minister of Commerce, Industry and Supply (1962-64). **Addr.:** Khartoum, Sudan.

HAGI (Mohamad, al, Ibn Ismaïl Ibn Yusuf), Yemeni statesman. **Born** in 1927. **Educ.:** Taiz and Amira School. **Career:** Assistant to his father Qadi (Judge) Ismaïl Ibn Youssef (1942-54); Joined Shariah Court, Taiz (1954-55); Member of Appeals Committee; Joined the Royal Bureau (1958-62); Chief of Legal Affairs, Qadi of Sana'a Province (1962-63); Minister of Justice (1967). **Addr.:** c/o Ministry of Justice, Sanaa, Republic of Yemen.

HAIDAR (Haidar, Mahmoud), Jordanian broadcasting official. **Born** in 1938 in Haifa, Palestine. **Married,** 4 children. **Educ.:** UCLA, USA. **Dipl.:** M.A. in Public Administration. **Career:** Secretary Editor of "al-Jihad" newspaper (1962-63); Announcer and Producer, Jordan Radio (1963-65), Chief Announcer (1965-70), Director of Programming (1970-74); Special Adviser to the Director General, Jordan Television (1974-78); Director of Cultural Programmes (1978-80); Member of Writers' Association (1974-); General Director, Culture and Arts Department (1980-). **Decor.:** Honorary Doctorate, World Academy of Arts and Culture. **Awards:** al-Istiklal Award (1971), al-Kawkab award (1981). **Hobby:** Swimming. **Prof. Addr.:** P.O.Box 6140, Amman, Jordan. **Priv. Addr.:** Dahiat al-Rasheed, Amman, Jordan.

HAIDAR (Mohamad Abdul Rahman, al), Iraqi academic. **Born** in 1945 at Zudair, Iraq. **Dipl.:** Ph.D. (Electrical Engineering). **Career:** Assistant Lecturer, Faculty of Engineering, King Saud University; Assistant Professor, Faculty of Engineering, King Saud University. **Publ.:** six specialized papers. **Hobbies:** Music, reading. **Addr.:** Riyadh, Saudi Arabia.

HAIDAR (Mohamed Haidar), Syrian politician. **Born** in 1931. **Educ.:** Secondary Schools, Lattakia, University of Damascus. **Career:** Teacher in Lattakia, Hama (1951-60); Ministry of Agrarian Reform (1960-63); Director, Alghab Establishment, Hama (1963); Director Agrarian Reform, Damascus, Daraa, Alsuweidaa (1964); Director Legal and Administrative Affairs, Ministry of Agriculture and Agrarian Reform (1965); Governor, Alhasakeh (1966); Teacher, Damascus (1968); member Command Damascus Branch of Baath Arab Socialist Party, Damascus (1968); Temporary Regional Command of Baath Arab Socialist Party (1970), member of both Regional and National Commands of BASP, member of General Command Progressive National Front of Syria and Minister of Agriculture and Agrarian Reform until 1973; First Deputy for Economic Affairs (1973-76); member of National Command of BASP (1980-); member of the National Progressive Front (1980-). Lawyer in Damascus City (1985-1993). **Addr.:** Place al-Marjeh, Al Faihaa Bldg. Center, 6th Floor, P.O.Box 29 and 30, Tel.: 224499, Damascus, Syria.

HAIDAR (Qazem), Iraqi painter. **Born** in 1932 in Baghdad. **Educ.:** Baghdad Fine Arts Institute (1956), then London (1962). **Career:** Professor of Fine Arts in Baghdad. **Works:** Exhibitions in London, Paris, Rome, New York, Beirut (Gallery One and Sursock Museum). **Member** of Baghdad Artists Association. **Addr.:** Baghdad, Iraq.

HAIDER (Sajjad), Pakistani Chartered Accountant. **Born** on December 6, 1935 in Bhopal (Centre India) and belongs to a distinguished family from Murshidabad West Bengal. (The family name is mentioned in the book by Major Walsh on the «distinguished families of Murshidabad» kept at a well known library at Oxford, U.K.). His family migrated to Pakistan in 1952 and he proceeded to United Kingdom in 1953 to study Chartered Accountancy. **Married** on April 5, 1962 in Karachi to Shameen Siddiqi, 3 children: one daughter, Saleha Amina (1963), 2 sons: Shahab Bilal (27.1.64), Ali Quais (26.5.1967). **Career:** Whilst in United Kingdom he was articled to a firm of Chartered Accountants in the city, Murton Gill & Jefferies (now Littlejohn Frazier) and passed, at first attempt, in 1958, the final examination of the Institute of Chartered

Accountants of England and wales. Was admitted as an associate (ACA) member of the Institute in January 1959 and a fellow (FCA) member in 1968. Is also a fellow member of the Institute of Chartered Accountants of Pakistan. Joined A.F. Ferguson & Co. Pakistan in April 1959 and remained with the firm till April 1976 when at the insistence of some prominent families/groups in the United Arab Emirates he formed SAJJAD HAIDER & CO., Chartered Accountants which was one of the first firms of Chartered Accountants to be registered in Dubai. A.F. Ferguson & Co., a price Waterhouse International Firm, was and is the largest firm of Chartered Accountants in Pakistan. He Joined as an Assistant Manager and was admitted to the Partnership in 1966. He was a member of the special committee and the executive committee of the firm. He had a wide range of experience with the firm in audit, management consultancy and taxation and was considered an articulate member of the firm. Upon formation of Sajjad Haider & Co. he was, inter-alia, involved in the formation of Emirates Telecommunications corporation, Middle East Bank, Arab Emirates Investment Bank and of several other industries and commercial companies, and in some of the critical investment and management decisions in respect of most of the aforementioned projects particularly the first three. He has contacts with the Government and with the prominent families in the area. **Sport:** Travelling. **Hobbies:** Reading and Music. **Member:** World Trade Club, Dubai, U.A.E., Sind Club, Karachi, Pakistan. **Credit Cards:** American Express, Diners and Visa. **Prof. Addr.:** Sajjad Haider & Co., Chartered Accountants, 904 Dubai Pearl Building, Jamal Abdul Nasser Square, P.O.Box 3251, Tel.: 222126/7, Fax: (9714) 238881, Dubai, United Arab Emirates. **Priv. Addr.:** Villa No.3, Road 332/6 Jumeirah, Tel.: 446100, Dubai, United Arab Emirates.

HAIKAL (Ahmed Abdel Maksoud, Dr.), Egyptian politician. **Born** in 1922 in Egypt. **Educ.:** Faculty of Dar el-Uloom. **Career:** Dean, Faculty of Dar el-Uloom for six years; Head, Educ. committee of People's Association; member, Supreme Council of Culture; Deputy Rector for Postgraduate Studies, University of Cairo; Cultural Counsellor, Spain (1973); Minister of Culture (1985). **Awards:** State award for Prominence in the Arts (1985); now Member of the Political Bureau of the National Democratic Party. **Addr.:** Cairo, Egypt.

HAIKAL (Fayza, Mohamed Hussein), Egyptian academic. **Born** on April 11, 1938 in Cairo, Egypt. **Widow,** 2 children. **Educ.:** Cairo University, Egypt; Oxford University, UK. **Dipl.:** B.A. in Archaeology, Ph.D. in Egyptology. **Career:** Member of Egyptian Exploration Society (1962-); the American research centre (1991-); the German Archeological Institut (1989-); Vice-President of the International Association of Egyptologists (1991-); Director of the North Sinai Archeological Salvage Project (1992-); Assistant Archeologist, Egyptian Antiquities Documentation (1960-1961); Lecturer, Cairo University (1966-72); Assistant Professor (1972-84), Professor (1984); Professor, American University of Cairo (1984-). **Publ.:** several papers in national and international journals: "Two Hieratic Funerary Papyri of Nesmin" in 2 volumes (1970) and (1972). **Hobbies:** Cinema, Fine Arts, reading. **Member:** Gezira Sporting Club. **Prof. Addr.:** Sociology Department, American University of Cairo, 113 Sharai Kasr El Aini, P.O.Box 2511, Cairo, Egypt. **Priv. Addr.:** 9 Shara al-Jabaliya Street, Flat 309, Zamalek, Cairo, Egypt.

HAIKAL (Kawthar, Mohamed Ali), Egyptian broadcasting official. **Born** on November 5, 1939 in Alexandria, Egypt. **Married,** 2 daughters. **Educ.:** Cairo University, Egypt. **Dipl.:** in Psychology and Sociology. **Career:** Director and Programme Producer, Egyptian Television (1960-74), Science Programme Supervisor (1974-80), General Supervisor of Cultural Programmes (1980-84); Member of the Union of Cinema Employees. **Publ.:** numerous cinema screenplays; "A Bird in the Cage" (series) in 1961; "The Meeting" (short story for television) in 1974. **Decor.:** Egyptian Order of Merit for Literature (1982); Egyptian Order of the Republic for Sciences, Arts and Literature (1982); Order of Merit, Egyptian Filming Union (1983). **Medal:** Gold Medal (1983). **Addr.:** 18 el-Enshirah Street, al-Awkaf City, Agouza, Cairo, Egypt.

HAIKAL (Mohamad, Hassanein), Egyptian journalist. **Born** in 1924 in Cairo, Egypt. **Married,** three sons. **Educ.:** Cairo University. **Career:** Staff reporter, Egyptian Gazette (1943); reporter "Rosal Yussef" weekly (1944); reporter "Akhbar el-Youm" weekly (1958-52); Editor "Akher Saa" illustrated weekly magazine (1953-56); Editor-in-Chief, al-Ahram newspaper (1957-74); Chaiman, al-Ahram Establishment Board (1959-74); member, Central Committee, Arab Socialist Union (1968-74); Minister of National Guidance (April- October 1970); Political Adviser to late President Nasser; and later to President Anwar Sadat; now Writer and free lance journalist. **Publ.:** Author of "Iran Fawka Burkaan", "Asamat al-Mouthaqqafin", "Maza Jara fi Souriya", "Nahnou wa America" (1967), "The Road of Ramadan" Collins, London (1975), "Sphinx and Commissar" (1979), "The Return of the Ayatolla" (1981), "Autumn of Fury" (1983); "Suez Through Egyptian Eyes (1986). **Addr.:** c/o André Deutsch Ltd., 105 Great Russel Street, London, W.C.I., United Kingdom.

HAIKAL (Walid, Hassan), Syrian Chairman/ Managing Director. **Born** on October 8, 1942 in Syria. **Son** of Hassan Haikal **and** Mrs. née Marguerет Tattar. **Married** in 1972 in Beirut to Siham Nouhra, 3 daughters: Elissar, Nadine, May. **Educ.:** University of Damascus (Syria), St. Joseph University (Beirut), University of Cairo (Egypt). **Dipl.:** LLB (University of Damascus), M.A. in Law (St. Joseph University), Penalty Law (University of Cairo). **Career:** Elected as Secretary of the Publicity and Advertising Syndicate in Beirut; Director, Arab Advertising Agency,

Beirut; presently Chairman/Managing Director, Arab Advertising, Dubai. **Work:** Opened Arab Advertising Agency (AAA) in Beirut (1968); in Cairo (1976); in Dubai (1979). **Other Information:** Drafted the Advertising Law in UAE and Sultanate of Oman's Ministry of Information. Member of IAA; Ex Vice-President of IAA UAE Chapter. **Sport:** Swimming. **Hobbies:** Reading, Article Writing, Tennis. **Member:** IAA (N.Y. - London), GCC AA (UAE). **Credit Card:** American Express. **Prof. Addr.:** Arab Advertising Dubai, Muraqqabat Road, Bu Haleeba Plaza Bldg., 5th Floor, Flat 501 & 502, P.O.Box 1269, Tel.: 629456/7/8, Dubai, United Arab Emirates. **Priv. Addr.:** Al Maktoum St., Gulf Air Building, 5th Floor, Flat No. 502, Tel.: 232158, Dubai, United Arab Emirates.

HAIRAT (Taha, Mohammad), Syrian statesman. **Born** in 1936, in Syria. **Son** of Mohamad Hairat **and** Mrs. Hasna née al-Musalmani. **Married** to Miss Hadije Salamat, six children. **Educ.:** Deraa Institute for Teachers, Damascus, Faculty of Law, Damascus. **Career:** Teacher in elementary Schools, Inspector in a secondary school, Principal director of Department of Education, Director of the Social Problems and Labour, Minister of the authorities of local administration. **Member** of the Regional leadership of the Arab Socialist Party BAAS for two electoral mandates; Chief of Department (National partisan Movement); Head of the Department "Agricultural" of the Regional leadership of the Arab Socialist Party BAAS; Head of Department "Education" in the Regional leadership of the ASPB. **Sport:** Swimming. **Hobby:** Reading. **Addr.:** Damascus, Syria.

HAJ (Awad, Ahmad Hassan, al), United Arab Emirates official. **Son** of Hassan al-Haj. **Born** in 1949 in Dubai, United Arab Emirates. **Married,** five children. **Educ.:** B.A. in History, Faculty of Arts, Baghdad University, Iraq (1972). **Career:** 3rd Secretary, Chargé d'Affaires, UAE Embassy to Sudan; Director of Culture and Information, Department of Economics; Deputy Director, Department of Culture and Information, Ministry of Foreign Affairs; seconded to "al-Ittihad" daily newspaper; director of Bureau in Dubai and Northen Emirates (1978-79); Deputy Director General of Administration and Finance, Ministry of Foreign Affairs (1980); Director General, Consular and Foreigners Department (1980). **Sports:** Swimming, table tennis. **Hobby:** Reading. **Prof. Addr.:** Ministry of Foreign Affairs, Department of Consular Affairs and Foreigners, Tel.: 369628, Abu Dhabi, United Arab Emirates.

HAJARAH (Hassan Hamzah), Saudi official. **Born** in 1937 in Mecca, Saudi Arabia, **Dipl.:** Diploma of International Centre of Basic Arab World Education Sirs el-Layan Egypt (1956); B.Sc. (Agriculture), Ein Shams University, Egypt (1961); M.Sc., Arizona University, U.S.A., (1965); Ph.D. (Barren Land in Saudi Arabia), Durham University, U.K. **Career:** Former Director General, Public Land Department, Ministry of Agriculture; Demonstrator, Assistant Professor and Head of Biology Department, Faculty of Sciences, King Abdulaziz University; Chairman, Meteorology and Arid Land Institute, KAU; Interim Mayor, Taif Municipality; organized 1st and 2nd conference of Red Sea and Aden Bay Environmental Studies Programme, supervised by KAU and UNESCO, Jeddah; organized the Conference on Agricultural Development and Arid Land Strategy, Sacramento, California, USA; participated in the International Conference for Combating Desertification, Nairobi, organized by UN (1977); participant member, the First Conference of Biological Sciences of Saudi Biological Society, Riyadh (1977), The First Agricultural Conference of Muslim Scientists, Riyadh (1977), Third Conference of Mineral Wealth, Rabat (1977), 2nd Conference of Saudi Biological Society, Jeddah (1978), Kuwait Regional Conference of Authorized Delegates for Protection and Development of Marine Environment and Coastal Regions, Kuwait (1978). **Publ.:** Possibility of Agricultural Development in the Kingdom of Saudi Arabia, Grazing and Administration in the Kingdom of Saudi Arabia, (translated), Problems of Arid and Semi-Arid Lands in the Kingdom of Saudi Arabia; (accepted for publication); a paper submitted to the First Agricultural Conference of Muslim Scientists, Riyadh (1977), on Water Resources and Population Activities, Red Sea Coastal Plain; another paper submitted to Faculty of Sciences magazine, KAU, Environment Pollution, One of the Problems of the Modern Epoch; articles: Lack of Manpower for Agricultural Development, delivered in a seminar on Agricultural Education, Combatting Desertification in the Kingdom of Saudi Arabia in Iqra magazine, Possibilities of Agricultural Expansion in the Desert of the Kingdom of Saudi Arabia, delivered at the 1st Scientific Seminar about Desert and its Dangers. **Hobby:** Horse riding. **Addr.:** Jeddah Municipality, Saudi Arabia.

HAJERI (Abdul Razzak, Abdul Rahman, al), United Arab Emirates businessman. **Born** on December 1, 1953 in Sharjah, United Arab Emirates. **Married,** 4 children. **Educ.:** Cairo University, Department of Business Management, Egypt. **Dipl.:** B.Sc. in Commerce. **Career:** Businessman, Director in several companies; **Publ.:** several articles on economics. **Hobbies:** swimming, reading, table tennis. **Prof. Addr.:** P.O.Box 578 Sharjah, United Arab Emirates.

HAJERI (Yusuf), Saudi physician. **Born** in 1918 in Saudi Arabia. **Educ.:** University of Cairo. **Dipl.:** Bachelor of Medicine, Bachelor of Surgery. **Career:** Doctor, Mecca Hospital (1943-44); Medical Officer, Ministry of Finance (1944-51); Chief Medical Officer, Jeddah Municipality (1951-56); Director Quarantine Hospital and Maternity Hospital, Jeddah (1956-59); Ministry of Health, Riyadh (1960); Director of Technical Office and Medical Officer, Riyadh Area (1961,62); Ministry of Health (1962-66). **Addr.:** Riyadh, Saudi Arabia.

HAJI (Yusuf, al), Kuwaiti businessman. **Born** in 1921 in Kuwait. **Son** of Jasim al-Haji. **Educ.:** in Kuwait. **Career:** Administrator, Ministry of Health; Minister of Waqfs (Religious Endowments) and Islamic Affairs (February 16, 1978), Businessman (1982-). **Addr.:** Kuwait City, Kuwait.

HAJJAM (Saud Abdulaziz, al), Saudi civil servant. **Born** in 1939, in Medina, Saudi Arabia. **Educ.:** Secondary Studies. **Career:** Teacher; Assistant Inspector; Inspector; Manager, Administration Office of Ein al-Zarka Authority; later Head of Administrative Affairs, Ein al-Zarka Authority; Director, Ein al-Zarka Water Authority; member of the Literature Club, Medina; Chairman of Board of the Government Employees Co-operative Association, Medina; member of the Administrative Council, Medina. **Publ.:** several literary, social and religious articles, **Hobbies:** Reading, travel. **Addr.:** Ein al-Zarka Water Authority, Medina, Saudi Arabia.

HAJJAR (Taj), Jordanian businessman. **Born** on July 10, 1929 in Damascus, Syria. **Married**, 5 children. **Dipl.:** M.A. in Economics and Political Science. **Career:** Managing Director of a company (family business) in Syria for 6 years; President, United Trading Corporation Ltd. (Member of the United Trading Group), Amman, Jordan; President, United Trading Co. Ltd., Jordan. **Hobbies:** Tennis, swimming. **Prof. Addr.:** P.O.Box 1408, Amman, Jordan.

HAKIM (Hamdi, al, Dr.), Egyptian governor, Governorate of Menoufiyeh. **Born** in June 1924 in Fayoum, Egypt. **Educ.:** Faculty of Agriculture, Faculty of Pharmacy, Cairo University. **Dipl.:** B.Sc. (Agronomy) (1944) B.Sc. (Pharmacy) (1948). **Married** with one son (holder of Ph.D. Engineering from Manshester University) and one daughter. **Career:** Proprietor-Manager of his own pharmacy in Fayoum; elected member of the People's Assembly (Parliament) in two consecutive elections up to 1961; appointed director general, Pharmacy Department, Ministry of Health (1967); appointed Under-Secretry of State for Health in 1975; selected as United Nations Adviser for Anti-Narcotics Research; elected president of the Pharmacists Association (1976), Governor, Governorate of Menoufiyeh (1982). **Addr.:** Fayoum, Governorate, Egypt.

HAKIM (Jacques, Yusef), Syrian lawyer, university professor. **Born** in 1931 in Damascus. **Son** of Yusef Hakim (Barrister, former Minister) **and** Mrs., née May Azar. **Educ.:** Mariste Brothers College (Damascus), Faculty of Laws (Syrian University), Beirut Faculty of Laws and Economical Science (St. Joseph University), Lyon University (France), Institute of Economics (University of Colorado) (U.S.A.). **Career:** Lawyer in Damascus (1952), Professor at the Faculties of Laws and Economical Sciences in the Universities of Damascus and Beirut (1958). **Publ.:** Author of "Le donnage de source délictuelle en Droit Musulman" (1964), "Le Vol en Droit Libanais et Comparé" (1960), Lectures on National Income, Social Security, Civil Law, Maritime Law, Criminal Law, Several articles and pamphlets. **Sports:** Tennis, swimming and riding. **Prof. & Priv. Addr.:** Parliament Street, Tel.: 331170, Damascus, Syria.

HAKIM (Maximos V, Salim, H.B. Mgr.), Patriarch of the melkite greek catholic church of Antioch and all the East, of Alexandria and Jerusalem. **Born** «Georges» on 18 May 1908 at Tantah (Egypt). **Son** of Salim Rizkallah Hakim **and** Mrs. née Eugénie Ghazaleh. **Ancestors:** H.B. Maximos II Hakim (Patriarch of the Melkite Greek Catholic Church in 1761). **Educ.:** St. Louis College of Tantah (Egypt), St Famille College of the Jesuits Fathers (Cairo), St. Anne Seminary of the White Fathers in Jerusalem (1922-30). **Dipl.:** Egyptian Baccalaureat (secondary education certificate), M.A. (Theology). **Career:** Ordained to the priesthood on 20 July 1930 in Jerusalem, teacher at the Patriarchal College of Beirut (1930-31), Vice-Principal of Patriarchal College of Cairo (1931-34), Principal of the said college (1934-43), ordained by H.B. the late Cyrille IX Moughabghab (Patriach of the Melkite Greek Catholic Church from 1927 to 1947), archbishop of Acre; Nazareth and all Galilee (13 June 1943-21 November 1967), member of the Melkite Greek Catholic Delegation at the Oecumenic Council of Vatican II (1962-65), raised by the Ain-Traz Saint Synod to the dignity of Patriarch of the Melkite Greek Catholic Church of Antioch and all the East, of Alexandria and Jerusalem since 22 November 1967, Member of the congregation for Oriental churches (Vatican) since 1968, President of the Greek Catholic community Council since June 1969. **Publ.:** Author of «Paroissien Byzantin» (several impressions since 1933), «Pages d'Evangile lues en Galilée» (4 impressions since 1954, translated into English, Dutch, Italian and Spanish), «Vie de Jésus» (1954), founded «Le Lien» in 1936, «ar-Rabita» (1944 Parish Bulletin), Founder of the «Laure du Tabernacle de Dieu», of «Moniales de l'Annonciation» (1958) of several hospitals, churches, schools, orphanages, seminaries, Old People's Homes, clubs, monasteries etc... **Awards:** Officer, Legion of Honour (1965) then Commdr., Legion of Honour in 1966, Grand Croix in 1990. **Dist.:** Honorary Doctorate Notre-Dame University and Other American Universities, Laval University (Canada) and Algiers University (Algeria). **Remark:** fluent in 7 languages. **Winter Residences:** in Syria: Melkite Greek Catholic Patriarchate, Tel.: 433129 and 433131, Bab Sharki, Haret az Zeitoun, Damascus. In Egypt: Cairo, ad-Daher Street, No. 16, Tel.: 5904697, at Alexandria, Jawhar Street, Tel.: 226422. In Lebanon: P.O.Box 50076, Tel.: 413111, Beirut. **Summer Residence:** Ain Traz.

HAKIM (Moh. Riad), Syrian Chairman-General Manager, Commercial Bank of Syria. **Born** on July 9, 1930 in Idlib, Syria. **Son** of Moh. Hilmi Hakim (Medical Doctor) **and** Mrs. née Fatimah Batal. **Married** on January 30, 1959 in Damascus to Rabiha Hilmat Hakim, 2 daughters: Rania Hakim (1960), Medical Doctor; Lana Hakim (1966), Decoration Engineer. **Educ.:** American University of Beirut, Beirut (Lebanon). **Dipl.:** B.A. Economics (1954). **Career:** Joined Arab Bank Ltd. (1959); Arab Orient Bank (1963); Commercial Bank of Syria, 1967, presently Chairman and General Manager. **Sports:** Scouting. **Credit Cards:** Visa - Citibank. **Prof. Addr.:** Commercial Bank of Syria, P.O.Box 933, Tel.: 2214508, Damascus, Syria. **Priv. Addr.:** Assad Village, Dimas, Damascus, Syria.

HAKIM (Muntazar), Saudi academic. **Born** on 12 December 1942 in Medina, Saudi Arabia. **Dipl.:** B.Sc. (Metallurgical Engineering) (1967); M.Sc. (Science) (1971); B.A. (Radio and TV) (1972); M.A. (Educational Administration) (1972); Ph.D. (Educational Administration) (1974). **Career:** Demonstrator, later Lecturer, King Abdulaziz University; Dean of Admission and Registration, King Abdulaziz University; Assistant Professor, Department of Public Administration, Faculty of Eonomics and Administration, King Abdulaziz University; member of Phi Delta Kappa, U.S.A., American Association for Collegiate Registration and Admission (AACRO), King Abdulaziz University Council, King Abdulaziz University Curriculum Committee, Housing Committee and Computer Committee; member of the Board, Prince Fawwaz Cooperative Housing Project. **Publ.:** training programmes for the planning of educational administration in Saudi Arabia. **Hobbies:** Reading, training programmes for the planning of educational administration in Saudi Arabia. **Hobbies:** Reading, travel. **Addr.:** King Abdulaziz University, Tel.: 6879033 Ext. 210, Jeddah. Saudi Arabia.

HAKIM (Rida Talib), Saudi executive. **Born** in 1931 in Medina. **Dipl.:** B.A. (Economics). **Career:** Radio Maintenance Technical Engineer (1953-60); Manager, Operations, Saudia (1963); Manager, Commercial Affairs (1967); General Manager, Commercial Affairs (1970); General Manager, Commercial Affairs (1970); General Manager, External Affairs and Commercial Planning (1970); Executive Vice-President, Arab & International Affairs, Saudia. Saudi Arabia Airlines Corporation; Chairman, Commercial Committee, Arab Air Carriers Organization (AACO); Saudia Representative to International Air Transport Association (IATA) meetings; has attended all IATA conferences on Traffic and its General Assembly and all Arab Air Carriers Organization (AACO) conferences on Air Traffic. **Hobbies:** Reading, sports. **Addr.:** 3rd Floor, Saudia Building, Tel.: 6822209 (Office) and 6651899 (Home), Jeddah, Saudi Arabia.

HAKIMI (Said, Muhammad, al), Yemeni politician. **Born** in Yemen Arab Republic. **Married**, 2 sons, 4 daughters. **Educ.:** general. **Career:** Trade unionist and businessman (1960-62); Commander of the National Guard (1962-63); Member of the President's Office (1963-64); Member of the Secretariat, National Assembly (1964-65); Director, Prime Minister's Office (1967-68); Director General, Hodeida Customs (1968-69); Director, Customs Department (1969-70); Minister of State for Supplies (1971-72); Governor of Taiz (1972-74); Secretary, Political Organization of the Yemeni Union; Deputy Chairman of the follow-up and Rectification Committee; Minister of Supply (1975); Ambassador to Kuwait (1976-90). **Hobbies:** History, reading. **Prof. Addr.:** Ministry of Foreign Affairs, Sanaa, Republic of Yemen.

HAKKI (Mohamad, I.), Egyptian diplomat. **Born** in 1933. **Married**, 2 daughters. **Educ.:** Cairo University, Egypt; Georgetown University, USA; Fellow, American Political Science Association; Fellow, the Centre for International Affairs. **Career:** Press Attaché, Egyptian Embassy, Washington, DC (1957-58); Press Attaché, Egyptian Embassy in Accra, Ghana (1058-59); Head of the American Desk, "al-Ahram" newspaper (1958-66), Foreign Editor (1966-72); Specialist in Public Affairs, IBRD (world Bank) (1973-75); Minister Counsellor for Press and Information, Embassy of Egypt, Washington, DC, USA; Member of the National Press Club, Washington, DC, of the Journalists Association, Cairo, of the Harvard Club, New York, USA. **Medals:** Medal of Merit (1956); Medal of Merit (1st Class) (1975). **Priv. Addr.:** al-Gazira al-Wusta Street, Zamalek, Cairo, Egypt.

HALABI (Ali, Abda, al), Jordanian businessman. **Born** on November 1, 1939. **Married**, six children. **Educ.:** Ankara University, Faculty of Sciences, Turkey (1962), **Career:** General Manager, al-Daman, Saudi Arabia (1962-66); Arabia (1966-67); Operations Manager, al-Koseibi Fishing Co., Saudi Arabia (1967-72); Honorary Consul for Mauritania, Amman (1984-); **Hobbies:** reading, sports, gardening. **Addr.:** Amman, Jordan

HALABI (Mohamed, Ali, el), Syrian politician. **Born** in 1937 in Damascus, Syria. **Educ.:** Teachers Training School and Damascus University. **Career:** Teacher (1954-62); member, Regional Command of Baath Party, Damascus; Mayor of Damascus; member of Arab Federal Assembly; member of People's Council, Speaker (1973-78); Prime Minister (1978-80); President of Arab Parliamentary Union (1974-76). **Addr.:** Damascus, Syria.

HALAWA (Nabil), Egyptian engineer and Governor of Kafr el-Sheikh Governorate. **Born** in 1932, Mit Badr Halawa, Gharbiyeh Governorate. **Educ.:** Faculty of Engineering, Ayn Shams University. **Dipl.:** B.Sc. Electrical Engineering. **Career:** Engineering officer, Egyptian Armed Forces; Chairman, Alexandria Public Transport Authority; Chairman of the Cairo Public Transport Authority; Governor of Kafr el-Sheikh (1983). **Addr.:** Cairo, Egypt.

HALAWANI (Seham Abdul Rahman, Mrs.), Saudi academic. **Born** in 1945. **Dipl.:** B.A. (History), Riyadh University. **Career:** Primary school teacher; clerk in the

Health Unit; Director of Secondary Girls' Institute; Director, Secondary Institute, Mecca. **Member** of Umul-Qura Charitable Society for Women, Mecca. **Addr.:** Secondary Institute, Mecca, Saudi Arabia.

HALBUBI (Ahmad, Yaqub, Yusuf, al), United Arab Emirates official. **Born** in 1948 in Abu Dhabi, United Arab Emirates. **Married**. **Dipl.:** B.A. in Economics. **Career:** Secretary, Permanent Planning Committee (1974); Director of Administrative and Financial Affairs Section, Ministry of Planning (1975). **Hobbies:** Hunting, chess, poetry, history. **Prof. Addr.:** Abu Dhabi, United Arab Emirates.

HALFAWY (Mohamed, el), Egyptian Industrial Chemist. **Born** on March 7, 1920 in Mansourah city, Lower Egypt. **Married**, with children. **Educ.:** Faculty of Science, Cairo University; Imperial College of Science and Technology, London (UK); Massachusetts Institute of Technology (USA). **Dipl.:** Bachelor of Science (B.Sc.), Master of Science (M.Sc.), Ph.D. (London), D.I.C. (London). **Career:** Associate Professor and Lecturer, University of Alexandria; Professor of Chemistry, University of Baghdad (Iraq); Director General, Industrial Planning Administration, Ministry of Industry, Cairo; Director General, Industrialisation Organisation, Ministry of Industry, Cairo; Managing Director, Petrochemical Project, Ministry of Industry, Cairo; Project Manager and Director, Industrial Research Institute (Sudan); Senior Industrial Development Field Adviser, United Nations Industrial Development Organisation (UNIDO), Beirut (Lebanon) (1969-74), Senior Interregional Adviser, Chemical Industries UNIDO, Vienna (1974-81); At Present Private Consultant. **Publ.:** "Introduction to Physical Chemistry", "Manual on Qualitative Analysis", also several articles and papers on electrolytic polishing of metals, electrodepostion, mineral dressing, the fertilizer industry, petrochemical development, industrial research. **Awards:** First Degree Award of Honour for Services to Industry. (Egypt). **Member:** Shooting club, Cairo. **Sports:** Table tennis and walking. **Hobbies:** Classic Music and reading. **Addr.:** Gallmeyergasse 18/4/18 A-1190, Vienna, Austria.

HALIM (Tahia, Muhammad, Ahmad), Egyptian artist. **Born** on September 9, 1919 in Egypt. **Educ.:** Academie Julian, Paris, France. **Career:** Taught art privately in Cairo (1952-60), later in the High Institute of Arts (1963); Member of the Supreme Council of Arts, Egypt; invited to exhibit her work in the United Kingdom in 1951 and 1977, the Italian Biennale in 1954, 1956 and 1970, one Brazilian Biennale in 1954, Sweden (1966), East Germany (1971), Poland (1971), France (1972) and Yoguslovaia (1976); full-time artist (1960-). **Publ.:** Her Work has been bought by the Guggengeim Museum of Modern Art, New York, the National Museum of Warsaw, the National Museum of Stockholm, the Museum of Modern Art in Cairo and Alexandria and several corporations and governmental agencies and private collectors in Egypt and Throughout the world. **Awards:** the Guggengeim Prize (1958); Egyptian Incentive Award in Art (1964). **Medals:** Golden Medal, Salon du Caire; Egyptian Medal of Arts (1st Class). **Member:** Cairo Atelier Club. **Addr.:** 3 Shara Bin el-Nabeh, Apt. 12, Zamalek, Cairo, Egypt.

HALLALI (Abdullah, Hussain, al), Yemeni diplomat. **Born** in 1930 in the Republic of Yemen. **Educ.:** University of Cairo, Egypt. **Dipl.:** B.Sc. in Commerce and Accountancy. **Career:** Director General of Technical Office (later the Central Planning Organization (1968-71); Member of the Consultative Assembly (1971); Secretary General, Yemen Development Organizations (1973-75); Minister of Labour, Social Affairs and Youth (1975); Ambassador to Czechoslovakia (1976). **Addr.:** c/o Ministry of Foreign Affairs, Sanaa, Republic of Yemen.

HAMAD (Abdullatif, Yusuf, al), Kuwait economist. and former Minister **Born** in 1937 in Kuwait. **Son** of Yusuf al-Hamad (Landlord and Merchant). **Married** to Feddah Yusuf al-Qatami in 1965, one child: Rasha. **Educ.:** American University, Cairo (1955-58); Claremont Men's College, California (1958-60); Harvard Graduate School of Arts and Science (1960-62). **Dipl.:** Bachelor of Arts, (International Affairs-Honours) (1960). **Career:** Member of the Kuwait delegation to the United Nations during Kuwait's application for admission to the U.N. membership (1962); Administrative Assistant to the Kuwait Fund for Arab Economic Development (April 1962- November 1962); Acting Director-General to the Kuwait Fund for Arab Economic Development (November 1962- May 1963); Director, Kuwait Investment Co. (1963); Deputy Chairman, Kuwait Investment Co. (1964); Treasurer, The South and Arabian Gulf Society, Educational and Philanthropic (1963-67); Chairman, Middle East International Fund (1969); Director, American Express International Fund (1969); Director, Kuwait Fund for Arab Economic Development (May 1963); Alternate Governor for Kuwait, World Bank (1964-81); Managing Director, Kuwait Investment Co. (1965-74), director (1974-77); Director, Manager, Tunisian Kuwaiti Development Consortium, Tunisia; member, Joint Ministerial Committee Board of Governors, World Bank and IMF (1974); member, Brandt Commission (1976-79); The Assistance Authority for the Gulf and Southern Arabia (1967-81); Executive Director, Arab Fund for Economic and Social Development (1972-81); Chairman, Compagnie Arabe et Internationale d'Investissements, Luxembourg (1973-81); Chairman, National Investment Group, Kuwait (1977-79); Minister of Finance and Planning (1981); Chairman, Kuwait Prefabricated Buildings Co. 1965; Chairman, The United Bank of Kuwait Ltd., London (1966); Trustee, Kuwait Institute for Economic and Social Planning in the Middle East since 1967; Director, The South and Arabian Gulf Society, Educational and Philanthropic since 1967; Chairman, Middle East International Fund (1969); Director of the American Express International Fund (1969); presently,

Director General and Chairman of the Board of Directors of Arab Fund for Economic and Social Development (AFESD). **Prof. Addr.:** P.O.Box 2912, Tel.: 39079 and 32686; Kuwait City, Kuwait and P.O.Box 21923, Safat 13080, Kuwait.

HAMAD (Hamad, Ahmad Abdul-Latif, al), Kuwaiti businessman. **Born** in 1925 in Kuwait. **Son** of Ahmad Hamad. **Married. Career:** Chairman, Commercial Bank of Kuwait SAK, Kuwait; Chairman, Kuwait Drilling Co.; Arab Financial Management Co.; Director, Pearl Holding, Luxembourg; Director, Kuwait French Bank, Paris; Director, Pearl Investment Co., Manama, Bahrain. **Addr.:** P.O.Box 5809, Tel.: 246570, Telex: 9353 A/B LULUAH BN, Manama, Bahrain and P.O.Box 2861, Safat 13029, Kuwait City, Kuwait.

HAMAD (Issa, Ahmad, al), Kuwaiti diplomat. **Born** in 1925 in Kuwait. **Married**, 2 sons, 2 daughters. **Educ.:** Mubarakiyah School, Kuwait. **Career:** Under Secretary and Director of Administration, Ministry of Foreign Affairs; Ambassador, Embassy of Kuwait to Rome and the Vatican; represented Kuwait at several educational conferences; Member of Kuwaiti delegation to the United Nations; Ambassador of Kuwait, Paris, France; Ambassador to Yugoslavia. **Hobbies:** Swimming, fishing, reading. **Prof. Addr.:** Ministry of Foreign Affairs, Kuwait City, Kuwait.

HAMAD (Riad Ahmad Mohamad ben), Saudi businessman. **Born** in 1950, in Jeddah, Saudi Arabia. **Dipl.:** B.A. Business Administration (Marketing.) **Career:** Member of Chamber of Commerce and Industry, Jeddah; owner and Director, Saudi Economic Research Centre; General Manager, Commerce Dept; Ahmed M. ben Hamad Establishments. **Honour:** Black Belt, First Grade, J.K.A. **Hobbies:** Tennis, judo. **Addr.:** P.O.Box 94, Jeddah, Saudi Arabia.

HAMAD (Yacoub, Yusuf, al), Kuwaiti businessman. **Born** in 1928 in Kuwait. **Son** of Yusuf al-Hamad. **Married,** 1 son, 3 daughters. **Educ.:** Mubarakiya School, Kuwait; Cairo University. **Dipl.:** B.Sc. in Commerce. **Career:** Director, National Bank of Kuwait, Safat, Kuwait; President, al-Makhazin al-Baida Company of Kuwait; Director, Hamra Group of Companies; Director, Kuwait Cinema Company; Japanese-Arab Company. **Hobbies:** Reading, swimming and cinema. **Addr.:** P.O.Box 95, Abdullah al-Salem Street, Tel.: 422011, Telex: 22451, Safat, Kuwait.

HAMAD (Yusef, A., al), Saudi official. **Born** in 1932, in Zubair, Saudi Arabia. **Married** in 1966 in Dammam to Miss F.A. al-Jamai, 5 children: Khalid, Eman, Faisal, Manal and Abdalla. **Educ.:** Tri-State University, Angola, Indiana (USA) **Dipl.:** B.Sc. in Electrical Engineering. **Career:** Electrical Engineer; Manager, Electric Dept., S.G.R.R.O; Chief Engineer, S.G.R.R.O.: Deputy General Manager, S.G.R.R.O. (Saudi Government Rail Road Organization); Deputy Minister for Electricity Affairs, Ministry of Industry and Electricity; Chairman, S. Consolidated Elect. Co. E. Region; Chairman, AlJubail Fertilizer Co. **Credit Cards:** American Express, Diners Club. **Prof. Addr.:** P.O.Box 5729, Tel.: 4775229, 4772595, Riyadh, Saudi Arabia.

HAMADA (Anwar), Syrian politician. **Career:** Member, Syrian Socialist Union; Minister of State (1974-76); Minister of Social Affairs and Labour (1976-79); Minister of State (1980). **Addr.:** Damascus, Syria.

HAMADI (Ábdallah, Fadel, al), UAE official. **Born** in 1949 in Dubai, United Arab Emirates. **Dipl.:** Degree in Law and Sharia (Islamic Law). **Career:** Adviser in the Legislative and Judicial Department, Ministry of Justice; Director of Administration and Technical Affairs, Ministry of Justice. **Hobbies:** reading, swimming. **Prof. Addr.:** Ministry of Justice, Islamic Affairs and Awqaf, P.O.Box 2272 Airport Road, Abu Dhabi, United Arab Emirates.

HAMADOU (Ali, Moussa), Djibouti Deputy at the National Assembly. **Born** in 1950 in Obock. **Educ.:** Secondary. **Career:** Head of Department of State Finance (1970-1974); Head of Labour at Rural Engineer Services (1975-1976); Port of Djibouti (Encadrement du docker) (1976-1977); Public Health (1996-1997). Member of RPP (1979-1991); Member of Parliamentary opposition (1991); Member of Central Committee of FRUD (1994). Elected Deputy at the National Assembly (1977-1992) reelected Deputy at the National Assembly (19/12/1997 - to date). Commission Member for the Social Development and Environment Protection. **Prof. Addr.:** National Assembly, P.O.Box 138 Djibouti, Djibouti.

HAMADOU (Barkat, Gourad), Djibouti Prime Minister, and Deputy at the National Assembly. **Born** in 1930 in Dikhil. **Career:** Elected Deputy at the National Assembly (23 Nov. 1958); Minister of Education (9 June 1960 - 3 Dec. 1963); Minister of Public Health Until 5 Nov. 1966; Reelected Deputy at the Chamber of Deputies (17 Nov. 1968 - 17 Nov. 1973); President of Parliamentary Opposition (1975-1977); Senator at French Senate (1965-1977); Deputy at the National Assembly (8 May 1977 - to date); Prime Minister in charge of Port (12 October 1978 - 23 Nov. 1987); first Vice-President of Political Bureau; Prime Minister in charge of Urban Planning and Housing (23 Nov. 1987 - 3 Feb. 1993); Prime Minister (4 February 1993 - to date); **Prof. Addr.:** National Assembly, P.O.Box 138 Djibouti, Djibouti and Prime Minister's Office, Djibouti.

HAMADOU (Gourad, Mohamed), Djibouti Deputy at the National Assembly. **Born** on December 1, 1966. **Career:** Technician at RTD. Member of Central Committee of RPP; Member of Dikhil Youth Associations; Elected Deputy at the National Assembly (18/12/1992 - to date);

Commission Member of National Defence. **Prof. Addr.:** National Assembly, P.O.Box 138 djibouti, Djibouti.

HAMADOU (Ibiro, Ahmed), Djibouti Deputy at the National Assembly. **Born** in 1952 at Hanlé (district Dikhil). **Career:** Nursing. Elected Deputy at the National Assembly (21 May 1982 - to date); Member of RPP; Minister of Labour and Professional formation (17 Oct. 1993 - 16 Oct. 1994); Member of National Defence Commission, **Prof. Addr.:** National Assembly, P.O.Box 138 Djibouti, Djibouti.

HAMADY (Mohamed, Ould), Mauritanian Journalist/ Director-General of "Agence Mauritanienne d'Information" (AMI). **Born** in 1950 at Chinguetti/ Mauritania. **Son** of Ahmed Ould Hamady/ Tradesman **and** Mrs. née Tellava mint Limam Ahmed. **Married** on August 1, 1974 at Nouakchott to Miss Leila, 4 children: Ahmed (22/3/1976), Sidi Ahmed (24/2/1978), Tareck (28/11/1980), Cheikhani (22/3/1987). **Educ.:** Lycee of Nouakchott, Ecole Normale (Nouakchott), Algiers University. **Dipl.:** Baccalaureate, Higher Diploma, Licence. **Career:** Director of Information in Radio Mauritania (1977); Press Consultant at the Presidency of the Republic (1979-); Director of the Written Press at the Ministry of Information (1986); Director of Audio-Visual (1988); Secretary General at the Ministry of Information (1989); director in the Press Office at the Presidency (1990); Director General for the Television of Mauritania (1991); director General of "Agence Mauritanienne d'Information" (AMI) since 1977. **Sports Practised:** Walking. **Associations:** Association des Journalistes Arabes, Ligue Mauritanienne des Droits de l'Homme. **Prof. Addr.:** E-mail: ami@mauritania.mr, Tel.: 253856, Mauritania. **Priv. Addr.:** E-mail: hamady@mauritania.mr, Tel.: 252067. P.O.Box 494 Nouakchott, Mauritania.

HAMAM (Abdel-Hamid), Jordanian musician. Professor of Music. **Born** on September 11, 1943 in Lydda, Palestine. **Married,** 3 children. **Educ.:** Diploma in Composition form Die hochschule fur Musik und Darstellendekunst in Wien (Vienna-Austria); Maitrise in Ethnomusicology (education musicale) from the Sorbonne Paris IV, France; Ph.D. in Composition and Musicology from the University College of Wales (Aberystwyth) Britten. His professors: Otto siegl, Gottfried von Einem, Hanns Jelinek, Alfred Uhl, Edith Weber, Tran Van Khe and Ian Parrott. **Career:** Lecturer at the Music Institute, Amman (1968-1973), Director of the Institute (1973-78). Professor, Fine Arts Department, Yarmouk University, Irbid, Jordan; Chairman (1983-1985) and (1994-95), Assistant Dean (1993-94) and (1996-1997), Vice Dean (1997-1999), Director (1995-1996) college of Architecture and Arts, Al al-Bait University, al-Mafraq, Jordan. **Awards:** Gold Medal of the Arab Song Festival, Damascus, 1977; Chairman or Member in many committees for Musical contests. Recognition letter from Queen Noor for his contribution in Jerash Festival, 1983, Founder Member, Arab Academy of Music, Member of Several National and International Music Societies and Associations. Chairman of the National Team for Musical Education, Ministry of Education, Jordan. Expert for Music Education in Yemen (1992). **Publications:** many articles in classified specialized journals on different subjects concerning Arab music. Book: Mu'âradatu al-'Arûd, a study of Arabian musical metrics, 1991. Book: the Music and its Teaching Methods, 1996. Musical Events and Concerts: prof. Hamam's compositions were performed in Jordan, Egypt, Morocco, Britten, Germany and Austria. His compositions includ works for orchestra, chambre ensembles, sonatas, choires and songs. His style is very much romantic with many modern traits and Arabian musical elements. **Address:** P.O.Box 4678, Yarmouk University, Irbid Jordan. Tel.: Residence: 02/7060050. Office: 7271100, Ex. 2581, Fax: 02/ 7274682, 02/7274725.

HAMAMA (Faten), Egyptian actress. **Born** on 1932 in Egypt. **Married** in the first time to Mr. Salah Zulfiqar, divorced. one child: Nadia. **Married** in the second time to Mr. Omar ach-Sharif (Actor), divorced, one child: Tareq. **Educ.:** Secondary. **Career:** Actress, appeared in several films since 1939, eg. "A Happy Day" (1939), "Le péché" (1964), "Great Love" (1968 with Farid al-Atrache and Youssef Whaby), "Lahzet Daaf" (1971) etc.. **Addr.:** Cairo, Egypt.

HAMAMSY (Ahmad Kamel, al), Egyptian orthopaedic surgeon. **Born** on April 27, 1921 in Damietta, Egypt. **Son** of Mohamad Kamel al-Hamamsy **and** Mrs. Zeinab al-Alaily. **Married** to Miss Laila Shukry on January 16, 1955, 2 children: Sayed Amr and Abdussalam. **Educ.:** La Salle College, Faculty of Medicine, Cairo University. **Dipl.:** Diploma of Surgery, Diploma of Orthopaedics, M.Ch. (Master of Surgery, Orthopaedics). **Career:** House Surgeon (1945); Resident Registrar (1946); Clinical Demonstrator (1948); Lecturer (1950); Assistant Professor (1958); Professor (1966); Professor of Orthopaedic Surgery, Faculty of Medicine, Cairo University and Consultant Orthopaedic Surgeon, Mabarrah Hospital. **Sports:** Tennis, Yachting and swimming. **Hobbies:** Bridge and Chess. **Member:** Gezira Sporting Club, Cairo Yacht Club, Automobile Club, Secretary General, Egyptian Orthopaedic Association. **Prof. Addr.:** 15, Sharif Pasha Street, Tel.: 51527 Cairo, Egypt. **Priv. Addr.:** 20, Hassan Sabry Street, Tel.: 802624, Zamalek, Cairo, Egypt.

HAMAR (Abdul Malik Yousef, al), UAE former bank governor. **Born** in 1935 In Bahrain. **Married,** 2 children. **Educ.:** American University of Beirut, B.A. (1957); University of Bristol, Post Graduate Certificate in Education (organisation & management) (1959); American University of Beirut, M.A. **Career:** Superintendent Ministry of Education, Culture and Planning, Bahrain (1968-70); Undersecretary of Ministry of Education, Abu Dhabi (1971-73); Ambassador at Ministry of Foreign Affairs, Abu

Dhabi, UAE; Managing Director, UAE Currency Board (1978-80); Governor of the UAE Currency Board; former Governor, Central Bank of the UAE, Abu Dhabi, UAE. **Publ.:** "Development of Education in Bahrain" (1940-65) in English; "Bahrain Throughout History", "Bahrain - Abu Dhabi" written for local periodicals in Arabic. **Member:** International Bankers Association; WIFC. **Hobbies:** Reading and Music. **Addr.:** Abu Dhabi, UAE.

HAMARNEH (Michael, Yacub), Jordanian official. **Born** on December 8, 1935 in Jerusalem. **Married** on January 3, 1964 to Miss Khelia, 3 children: Dima, Rania and Omar. **Educ.:** American University of Beirut, AUB, Lebanon; Boston University, USA. **Dipl.:** B.A. **Career:** Teacher (1958-62); Director of Public Relations, Tourism Authority (1962-67); Counsellor, Jordan Tourist Authority, New York, USA (1967-71); Information Director for Jordan, Washington DC, USA (1973-77); Director General, Ministry of Tourism and Antiquities; Undersecretary, Ministry of Information; Board Member of: Royal Jordanian Airlines (ALIA), Restco Hotel Corporation, International Continental Hotel and Jordan Spa Company for Main Hot Springs; Director of Jordan Tourist Authority (1977). **Hobby:** Swimming. **Credit Card:** American Express. **Prof. Addr.:** Ministry of Tourism and Antiquities, P.O.Box 224, Tel.: 42315, Telex: 21741, Amman, Jordan. **Priv. Addr.:** Fifth Circle, Tel.: 42459, Amman, Jordan.

HAMARNEH (Najwa), Jordanian financial manager. **Born** in 1952 in Amman. **Daughter** of Jubran Hamarneh. **Married. Educ.:** Jordan University, B.Sc. (1973); Project Evaluation Training Course, USA. **Career:** Accountant and Co-ordinator, The Royal Scientific Society, (1973-76); Finance Manager, Pension Fund, Amman, Jordan (1976-); Director of: Jordanian Securities Corporation; Jordan Management and Consultancy Co. **Member:** Statistical Cooperative Society. **Hobbies:** Music, reading, travelling. **Sport:** Table tennis. **Addr.:** P.O.Box 3294, Tel.: 816181, 5 lines Telex: 21716 A/B FUND JO, Amman, Jordan.

HAMARNEH (Sami, Khalaf), Jordanian museum curator. **Born** on February 2, 1928 in Mabada. **Son** of Khalab Hamarneh **and** Noura Zumut. **Married** to Miss Nuzha Aijaj, 1 child: Paris. **Educ.:** Syrian University (Damascus), North Dakota State University (U.S.A.) Wisconsin University (U.S.A.) **Dipl.:** Bachelor of Science (1948), Master of Sciences (1956), Doctor in History of Pharmacy and Medicine (1959), Higher studies in History of Medicine, Pharmacy and Chemistry. **Career:** Came to the United States of America (1952); Curator in Charge at U.S. National Museum of Smithsonian Institution since 1959; Visiting Prof.: University of Aleppo, Syria (1979); King AbdulAziz University, Jeddah, Saudi Arabia (1982-83); King Fahd Medical Research Centre President of the American Institute of the History of Pharmacy (1977-81), and Editorial Board of the Journal for the History of Arabic Science, Aleppo, Syria (1977-81). Professor, Yarmouk University and Jordan University (1984-90); Professor, International Islamic Thought and Civilization, Malysia (1993 - May 99); Now retired. **Publ.:** Author of "A Pharmaceutical View of Abulcasis al-Zahrawi in Moorish Spain" (1963), "Bibliography of Medicine and Pharmacy in Medieval Islam" (1964) "Origins of Pharmacy and Therapy in the Near East" (Tokyo, Naito, 1973); The Physician Ibn al-Quff, Cairo, (1974); Pharmacy Museums, Washington D.C. 1981. and many other books and articles. **Awards:** Recipient Star of Jordan Medal (1965) and Kremers National Award, (1966). **Member:** American Association History of Medicine, American Institute History of Pharmacy, Arab History of Pharmacy. **Addr.:** 4631, Massachusetts Avenue, N.W. Washington D.C. 20016 - E-mail: fham@erols.com, Tel.: 1+202 364 1052, Fax: 1+202 364 1052.

HAMAWI (Maamoun, al), Syrian former official. **Born** in Damascus. **Educ.:** University of Berlin. **Dipl.:** Doctor of Political Science from the University of Berlin, Doctor of Philosophy and History. **Career:** Ministry of Foreign affairs (1945-64); Syrian Ambassador to Washington and Bonn; now working on the Publication of an encyclopedia of political terminology. **Publ.:** Author of several books on international law and foreign Affairs eg. "The Policy of Great Britain in Palestine" (Berlin, 1943), "The Political History of the Arab Revolution" (in German, 1944), "Diplomacy" (1947), "Diplomatic Terms" (in English and Arabic, 1949). **Remark:** Fluent Arabic, French, English and German. **Addr.:** Damascus, Syria.

HAMDAN (Abdallah al-Aqeel al-Solaiman, al), Saudi academic. **Born** in 1936 in Mecca, Saudi Arabia. **Dipl.:** B.Sc. (1961); Ph.D. (Geology) (1965). **Career:** Lecturer in Geology, King Saud University (1965-66); Dean, Faculty of Agriculture (1966-71); Assistant Professor, Faculty of Science (1972); Associate Professor (1972); Chairman, Department of Geology (1974-76); Professor of Geology, King Saud University; Geological Consultant to Ministry of Communications; former member of King Saud University Council and Supreme Council of the Universities; member of Muslim Student Society, U.K. and Ireland; attended a conference of British Scientists (1964), a symposium on University Administration, Wisconsin, U.S.A. (1970) and the Fifth International Conference on Sedimentaries, Nice (1975). **Publ.:** Sedimentary Rocks, (1975); three research papers published in the Faculty of Sciene Journal. **Hobbies:** Reading, swimming, walking. **Addr.:** Geology Department, King Saud University, Tel.: 4773816 (Office) and 4778770 (Home), Riyadh, Saudi Arabia.

HAMDAN (Abdul Rahman Abdul Aziz, al), Saudi public servant. **Born** in 1934 in Mecca, Saudi Arabia. **Dipl.:** B.A. (Geography). **Career:** Clerk, Director Public Education Bureau; Secretary, Professional Inspectorate; Director of Bureau, Under-Secretary of State, Ministry of Education; Secretary, Supreme Council for Arts and Science; Director-General, Minister of Education Bureau; former Chairman of Board of al-Hilal Sporting Club, Rivadh; member of Saudi Football Federation; attended Conference of Arab Ministers of Education, Tripoli (Libya), Cairo, Morocco, Baghdad. **Publ.:** Collection of Poems. **Hobbies:** Football, swimming. **Addr.:** Ministry of Education Bureau, Riyadh, Saudi Arabia.

HAMDAN (Ibrahim, Yusuf), Jordanian research scientist. **Born** in Nablus, in 1938. **Son** of Yusuf Hamdan. **Married** in 1976 in Kuwait to Miss Randa Khaizaran, two children. **Educ.:** Ohio State University, Columbus, Ohio; University of Wyoming, Laramie, Wyoming; California State University, California. **Dipl.:** B.Sc. (1969); M.Sc. (1970); Ph.D. (1973); Diploma of Agriculture, Jubaiha Agriculture College, Amman, Jordan (1956). **Career:** Project Leader, Agriculture Dept., KISR, Kuwait (1974-76); Head, Agriculture Dept., KISR, Kuwait (1976-80); Manager, Biotechnology Dept., KISR, Kuwait (1980). **Member** of: Honour Society of Sigma XI; Honour Society of Gamma Sigma Delta, Agriculture; Honour Society of Phi Kappa Phi; International Editorial Advisory Board of Enzyme and Microbial Tech. Journal; International Editorial Board of Biotechnology Letters Journal; UNEP/UNESCO/ICRO Panel on Applied Microbiology and Biotechnology; Editorial Board of the MIRCEN Journal of Applied Microbiology and Biotechnology; Executive Committee of International Organisation for Biotechnology and Bioengineering (IOBB). **Credit Card:** American Express. **Addr.:** Amman, Jordan.

HAMDAN (Mohamad Aqeel al-Soliman, al), Saudi civil servant. **Born** in 1924 in Mecca, Saudi Arabia. **Educ.:** received religious education at the al-Ilmi Institute, Mecca. **Career:** Civil Servant, Ministry of Finance; Secretary to the Deputy Minister of Finance; Director of the Bureau of the Deputy Minister of Communications; Director of the Bureau of the Minister of Communications; Director-General of the Ministry of Communications attended Arab League Conferences on Communications, Cairo. **Hobby:** reading (history and literature). **Addr.:** Riyadh, Saudi Arabia.

HAMDAN (Mohammad, Ahmad), Jordanian academic. **Born** on November 3, 1934. **Married,** 1 son, 1 daughter. **Educ.:** Cairo University, Egypt; Sydney University, Australia. **Dipl.:** B.Sc. in Mathematics; Ph.D. in Statistics. **Career:** Fellow of Sydney University (1960-63); Assistant Professor, Associate Professor and Professor of Mathematics, American University of Beirut, Lebanon (1964-77) and American University at Cairo, Egypt (1977-78); Visiting Professor of Statistics, Virginia Polytechnic Institute and State University, U.S.A. (1969-71) and (1974-75); Professor of Mathematics and Dean of the Faculty of Science, Yarmouk University (1976-77); Dean of Students, Dean of Research and Dean of the Faculty of Science at University of Jordan (1978-82), (1982-84), (1984-86); President of Yarmouk University (1986-89); President of the Hashemite University, Jordan (1992- present); Minister of Education and Higher Education, Jordan (Dec. 89-Dec. 90). Participated in numerous international conferences, Member of the International Statistical Institute, the American Statistical Association, the Third World Academy of Science, the Islamic Academy of Science and the Jordan Academy of Arabic Language. **Publ.:** «Estimation of the correlation Coefficient in contingency tables with possibly non-metrical characters», «Correlation in a bivariate normal distribution with truncation in both variables», «On the structure of the tetrachoric series». **Hobbies:** Tennis, football, reading. **Prof. Addr.:** President of the Hashemite University, University Liaison Office, Ministry of Higher Education, P.O.Box 138, Amman, Jordan, Tel.: 962 684 2700, Fax: 962 684 3864.

HAMDAN (Yusuf Hamdan, al), Saudi executive. **Born** on 14 July 1940 in Riyadh, Saudi Arabia. **Dipl.:** M.B.A., University of Texas, Austin, Texas. **Career:** Technical Affairs Manager at Central Department of Statistics (1966-73); Assistant General Manager of Engineering Projects and Products Co. (EPPCO) (1973-75); Deputy Minister of Commerce, Ministry of Commerce (1975-80); General Manager of Building & Manufacturing (till 1989); Chairman of Saudi United Commercial Bank; Vice Chairman: Arab Solar Energy Co. Ltd.- SHAMSCO; Second Vice President of Chamber of Commerce & Industry Riyadh; Former Director: a) National Industrialization Co. b) GRC (S.A.) Ltd. c) Saudi Finnish Contracting Co. Ltd.- SAFINCO d) Saudi Arabian Standard Organization; Presently, Owner and President of Yousif Al-hamdan Trading Est. (YAHT) and its subsidaries; House of Measurement, Alwaseet National Office, and Al Najat Medical Technology. **Honours:** The Spanish Order del Merito Civil Econienda de Numero (1977); the Taiwan Order of Brilliant Star with Grand Cordon (1978). **Publ.:** several articles in local newspapers and magazines. **Hobbies:** Reading, swimming. **Addr.:** P.O.Box 6838, Tel.: 4770022 (Office) website: www.waseet.com, Riyadh, Saudi Arabia.

HAMDANI (Adnan Hussain, al), Iraqi politician. **Born** in 1940 at Circa, Iraq. **Career:** Director-General, President's Office (August 1970); Member, Board of Administration, National Minerals Company (October 1970); Member, Arab Baath Socialist Party Regional Leadership (January 1974); Secretary-General, Committee of the Follow-Up on Oil Affairs and Implementation of Agreements; Head, Public Relations Bureau, Revolutionary Command Council (RCC) (March 1974); head, Revolutionary Command Council, Vice-Chairman's Office (November 1974); Minister of Planning (May 1976); Member of the RCC (September 1977); Deputy Prime-Minister and Chief of the President's Office (1980). **Addr.:** Baghdad, Iraq.

HAMDANI (Ismail), Algerian statesman. **Born** in 1930 at Bordj Bouareridj, Algeria. **Married. Educ.:** University of Algiers and University of Aix-en-Provence. **Dipl.:** LL.B. (Islamic and French Law). **Career:** Provisional Executive (1962-63); Technical Counsellor, Office of Minister of Information (1963); Counsellor, Algerian Embassy to Belgium, examining future relations between Algeria and EEC (1963-64); Head, Press and Information Service, Ministry of Foreign Affairs, and Technical Counsellor, same Ministry (1964); Director, Juridical and Consular Affairs, Ministry of Foreign Affairs (1964-68); Counsellor, Juridical and Consular Affairs, Presidency (April 68- Oct. 70); Deputy Secretary-General of the Cabinet Oct. 70- April 77; Secretary-General to Government of President Boumediene and President Chadly Ben Djedid (April 77- July 80); Member of the Central Committee of the FLN Since 1979; Counsellor, Presidency (1980-83); Ambassador of Algeria to the Nordic Countries, located in Stockholm (1983-84); Ambassador to Spain (1984-86); Ministry of Foreign Affairs (1986); Ambassador of Algeria to France (July 1988 - July 92); Prime Minister of Algeria (Dec. 98 - Dec. 99). **Addr.:** Algiers, Algeria.

HAMDI (Gamil, Mohamad), Egyptian international civil servant. **Born** on November 16, 1929 in Cairo (Egypt). **Married,** with children. **Educ.:** Institut des Sciences Politiques, Paris (1948-51); Ecole des Hautes Etudes Commerciales, Paris (1951-54). **Dipl.:** LL.B., B.Sc. (Economics), BBA (Bachelor of Business Administration). **Career:** Department Head, Auditor, Textile firm, Cairo (1954-58); Administrative Manager, Textile firm, Cairo (1958-62); Auditor, United Nations Operation in the Congo (ONUC), Leopoldville (1962-64); Administrative Officer, Congo Desk, Bureau of Administration Management and Budget (1964-66); Chief, Budget Section, Bureau of Administration Management and Budget, UN, New York (1967-68); Deputy Resident Representative, United Nations Development Programme (UNDP), Manilla, (Philippines 1968-70); Deputy Resident Representative, UNDP, Ankara (Turkey) (1970-73); Resident Representative, Central African Republic UNDP, Bangui (1973); UNDP, New York (1978); UNDP, Tunis (1979-81). **Prof. Addr.:** United Nations, N.Y. U.S.A.

HAMDI (Monir, K.), Egyptian executive. **Born** in 1944 in Cairo, Egypt. **Son** of Mostafa Kamal Hamdy. **Married** in 1977, 1 son, 2 daughters. **Educ.:** Ain Shams University, B.Com. Cairo (1964); New York University, M.BA., New York (1974); Advanced Professional Certificate in Quantitative Analysis (1977). **Career:** The Nile Company for the Export of Agricultural Crops, Cairo (1964-70); Auditor, (1964); Senior Auditor (1967); Chief Accountant (1969); Credit Analyst, Chemical Bank, New York (1970-74); Loan Examiner, American Express International Banking Corporation, New York (1974-78); Loan Officer, Syndications, UBAF Arab American Bank, New York (1978-81); Alahli Bank of Kuwait, KSC, Kuwait, Manager, Multinational Finance Division, (1981), Senior Manager, Commercial Operations Division (1985), Senior Manager, Credit Division (1986). **Member:** Beta Gamma Sigma, The Honorary Society for Business Graduates, USA; Hunting and Equestrian Club, Kuwait. **Hobbies:** Reading, and Travelling. **Addr.:** P.O.Box 1387 Safat, P.C. 14014, Tel.: 2441147, Telex: 22067, 44431. A/B AHLIFAXA, Safat, Kuwait.

HAMED FAHMI (Noha al-Sayyid), Egyptian academic. **Born** on December 20, 1934 in Cairo, Egypt. **Married,** 1 son. **Educ.:** Cairo University, Ain Shams University, Egypt. **Dipl.:** M.A. in Sociology, Ph.D. in Sociology. **Career:** Research Assistant, National Centre for Social and Criminological Research (1961-67), Researcher (1967-73), Expert (Lecturer) (1973-77), Senior Expert and Assistant Professor (1977-80); Member of the Egyptian MAB and Scope National Committee, UNESCO (1977-); Advisor and Head of the Urbanisation Research Unit (1980-); Consultant, Neighbourhood Urban Services Project (1982-). **Publ.:** Author of numerous chapters, papers and contributions to proceedings on social planning, housing, urbanisation, rural development and technology (in Arabic, English and French). **Addr.:** 2 Maamal el-Sokkar, Garden City, Cairo, Egypt.

HAMED (Mahmoud, Salah El-Din), Former Minister. **Born** in December 9, 1927. **Married:** 2 children. **Educ.:** B. of Commerce, Cairo Universiry (1949); Master's Degree in Economics, Leeds University, UK (1958); Doctorate of Economics, Edinburgh University, UK (1961). **Career:** Professor, Economics of Finance at: Faculty of Commerce Cairo University, Faculty of Economics & political Science, Cairo University, National Planning Institute, National Institute of Management Development (1961-1974); Economist, World Bank-Washington, USA (1965-70): Economic Advisor, Abu Dhabi Fund for Economic Development, UAE (1974-76); Minister of Finance, Egypt (1976-78) Advisor, Central Bank of Egypt (1979-81); Minister of Finance, Egypt (1982-86); Governor, Central Bank of Egypt (1986-93); Economic Advisor, Arab Monetary Fund (1993-Nov.94); Presently, Chairman of the Board of Directors and Managing Director, Misr Iran Development Bank (since 1994). **Other Activities:** Member of Committees formed to develop the financial system and tax laws in the Arab Republic of Egypt; Participated in research concerning the development of Uganda's tax system in collaboration with Edinburgh University, UK; Egypt's Governor at the IMF, African Development Bank. **Publ.:** Writer of many articles as regards the Sales tax in Egypt, Sales Tax in Developing Countries and Financial Policy in Developing Countries. **Address:** Misr Iran Development Bank, Nile Tower 21, Charles degaulle Ave., Giza, P.O.Box 219 Omran 12612, Cairo, Tel.: 5727311, Fax: 5701185, Egypt.

HAMID (Abdul Munim), Iraqi ophthalmic surgeon,

academic. **Born** in 1928 in Mosul, Iraq. **Married**, four children. **Educ.:** M.B., Ch.B., University of Baghdad; DO, RCP, RCS, University of London, UK; Degree in Ophthalmology, University of Baghdad. **Career:** Resident House Surgeon, Basra Hospital (1956-58); Doctor, Ramad Hospital, Baghdad (1963-65); Director and Ophthalmologist, Najaf Hospital (1967-69); Lecturer, Mosul Medical College, University of Mosul (1970-75); Director, Mosul Hospital (1972-76); Professor of Ophthalmology, Mosul Medical College, University of Mosul. **Member** of the Ophthalmological Society of UK. **Hobby:** Reading arabic and Middle Eastern history. **Addr.:** Ophtalmology Section, Department of Surgery, College of Medicine, Tel.: 90570, University of Mosul, Mosul, Iraq.

HAMID (Ibrahim, Mahmoud), Sudanese Agriculturalist. **Born** on January 1, 1956 in Kassala, Sudan. **Son** of Mahmoud, Farmer **and** Mrs. Halima. **Married** in February 1992 in Kassala to Wisal, 4 children: Mahmoud, Mohamed, Modather, Mozamil. **Educ.:** Khartoum University (M. Sc.), Alexandria (B. Sc.), Hambat Institute (Diploma) and, Kassala Higher School. **Career:** Governor Kassala State (August 1997-); Commissioner Senar Province (July 1995 - August 1997); Commissioner Eastern Darfour Province (July 1993 - June 1995); Minister of Agriculture (1981-1992); N.G.O.S., Care International and Finida. **Sports Practised:** Basket & Volley-Ball. **Hobby:** Reading. **Associations:** Sudanese Association of GRIC. **Prof. Addr.:** Kassala, P.O.Box 229, Tel.: 23166, Sudan. **Prof. Addr.:** Kassala, Governor House, Tel.: 22047, Sudan.

HAMID (Izzeddin), Sudanese former minister. **Born** on June 18, 1938 in Omdurman (Sudan). **Son** of Hamid el Hassan **and** Mrs., née Khadija Mohamad el-Bashir. **Married** on Octobre 15, 1966 to Miss Nunno el-Kheir el-Hassan, 3 children: Rihab, Randa and Rwayda. **Educ.:** Elementary and intermediate stages in government schools (Sudan); Secondary education in Khor Taqat (1954-58); Faculty of Arts, Khartoum University (1958-62); Fernand Coq Institute, Brussels (Belgium); Europa Institute, University of Amsterdam. **Dipl.:** B.A. (Economics and History), Dilp. French Language, M.A. **Career:** Teacher of English, Ahlia Secondary School, Omdurman (1962); Joined Sudan Foreign Service (1962); posted to France and Belgium in Junior diplomatic assignments (1965-69); Consellor (External Relations), General Secretariat of the Revolution Command Council (1970-71); posted to Permanent Delegation of the Sudan to United Nations holding respectively, the posts of Counsellor, Minister Plenipotentiary, Deputy Permanent Representative; Ambassador to Belgium, the Netherlands and Head of Mission to the European Economic Community (1975-76); Vice-Chairman, Economic and Financial Committee of the UN General Assembly (29th session); Leader of Sudan delegation to Euro-Arab Dialogue meeting of experts in Rome, and Chairman of Arab Group Committee on Agriculture and Natural Resources (July 1975); Minister of State, Presidency of the Republic (Feb. 1976); Minister of State for Egypt's Affairs, Presidency of the Council of Ministers (1977); Minister of State for Council of Ministers Affairs (17 Aug. 1979); Minister of Industry till 1982. **Awards:** Order of the Republic (2nd class), Officer, National Order of Chad. **Addr.:** Khartoum, Sudan.

HAMID (Mustafa, Yahia), Egyptian orthopaedic surgeon. **Born** on March 24, 1932 in Cairo, Egypt. **Married:** 2 children. **Educ.:** Cairo University, Egypt. **Dipl.:** M.B., B.Ch., Diploma on General Surgery and Orthopaedics. **Career:** Houseman, Kasr el-Aini Hospital (1957-58); Resident, Orthopaedic Surgery, Red Crescent Hospital (1958-61); Lecturer in Orthopaedic Surgery, Algiers University Hospital (1962-67), Assistant Professor of Orthopaedic Surgery (1967-75), Professor (1975-82), Consultant Orthopaedic Surgeon, Almaza Hospital, Egypt (1983-). **Prof. Addr.:** 86 Ahmad Esmat Street, Ain Shams, Cairo, Egypt. **Priv. Addr.:** 70 Mustapha Nahas Street, Madinat Nasr, Cairo, Egypt.

HAMIDY (Abdul Rahman Ibn Saad, al), Saudi academic. **Born** in 1939. **Dipl.:** B.A. (1970); M.A. (1971); Ph.D. (Adult Education), U.S.A. (1975). **Career:** Former employee, Girls' Schools Administration; Assistant Professor, Faculty of Education, King Saud University; member of Adult Education Association of America and several King Saud University Committees; attended second Computer Conference, Riyadh and Education Conference, Kuwait. **Publications:** Motivational Factors Towards Literacy in Riyadh, Saudi Arabia (Ph.D. Thesis, 1975); Adult Educational Duties of the College of Education in the Arab World. **Hobby:** Sports. **Addr.:** Riyadh, Saudi Arabia.

HAMILI (al-Shiba Said Abdul Hadi, al), United Arab Emirates oil expert. **Born** in 1950 in Abu Dhabi, United Arab Emirates. **Son** of Abdul Hadi al Hamili. **Married,** two children. **Educ.:** Experience in oil industry (ten years). **Career:** Deputy Manager of Abu Dhabi Marine Operating Co.; Under Secretary, Ministry of Petroleum and Mineral Resources; United Arab Emirates representative to Organisation of Arab Petroleum Exporting Countries (OAPEC); member of the Board of Directors of the Arab Tanker Company; Member of Tourism Club. **Sport:** Tennis. **Hobby:** Billiards. **Addr.:** Ministry of Petroleum and Mineral Resources, P.O.Box 59, Abu Dhabi, Tel.: 61076, United Arab Emirates.

HAMILI (Sultan Ghanoum, al), UAE politician. **Born** in al-Ain, United Arab Emirates. **Married,** 3 sons. **Educ.:** general; courses in finance. **Career:** Ministry of Municipalities and Agriculture, al-Ain (1970); Assistant Secretary General to Council of Ministers, Abu Dhabi (1971); Member of the United Arab Emirates Federal Assembly since its foundation (1972); Secretary General of the

Executive Council, Abu Dhabi, UAE; Director General of Personal Accounts to HH the Head of State (1972). Retired From Government Service in 1987. Owner and Chairman of Dhafir Group of Companies-General Trading, Construction and Engineering, Automobile, Consumer Electronics, Real Estate & Property Development, Insurance and Sponsorship & Representation. **Hobbies:** Hunting, swimming, water-skiing, reading, history, poetry. **Prof. Addr.:** Chairman, Dhafir Group of Companies, P.O.Box 4330 Abu Dhabi, United Arab Emirates, Tel.: 774670, 774656, Telex: 22385 EM, Fax: (02)776786.

HAMMAD (Burhan), U.A.E. UN Official. **Born** on April 27, 1929 in Nablus, Palestine. **Educ.:** Faculty of Law, Baghdad, Iraq; Yale Law School, New Haven, Connecticut, USA. **Dipl.:** LL.B., LL.M. and JS.D. in International Law. **Career:** Lawyer in Nablus (1953-57); Assistant Director, Arab Information Centre, West Coast Branch, San Fransisco, California, USA (1961-62), Acting Director, Arab Information Centre, Southern Regional Office, Dallas, Texas, USA (1962); Acting Director, Arab Information Center, New York, USA (1963-73); Senior Adviser, Mission of Jordan to the UN (1964-73); Executive Secretary, Group of Arab Delegations to the UN (1963-73); attended sessions of the General Assembly since the 18th Session, preparation of legal briefs, especially on Arab issues, for the use of Arab Delegations; drafting of resolutions on various items before the UN organisms; representing the Arab Group in negotiations with other groups or member states; Member of American Society of International Law and Jordanian Bar Association; Extensive lecturing at collegs, universities, civic groups and churches on matters relevant to the UN and oil concession agreements in the Middle East; United Arab Emirates Representative, Special Political Committee, Six Committee and the Law of the Sea Conference (1973-); Senior Adviser for Legal and Political Affairs, United Arab Emirates Permanent Mission to the UN (1973-). **Publ.:** "The Egyptian-Israeli General Armistice Agreement in Proper Perspective", "Middle Eastern Oil Concessions: Some Legal and Policy Aspects of Relations Between Grantors and Grantees (JSD Thesis)", "The Right of Passage in the Gulf of Aqaba"; numerous legal papers and briefs on items before the various organisms of the UN. **Prof. Addr.:** Mission of the United Arab Emirates to the United Nations, 747 Third Avenue, New York, NY 10017, USA.

HAMMAD (Juma), Jordanian journalist. **Born** in Palestine in 1923. **Married**, seven children. **Educ.:** Secondary. **Career:** Contricuted to "al-Ghad" Magazine (1947); Worked in telegraph department, Palestine Police; self employed (till 1953); Head of Bureau of Islamic Congress, Jerusalem (1954-60); founding partner of "al-Manar" in Jerusalem (1961); Director of "al-Manar" and editor of "al-U'fuq al-Jadid" cultural magazine; Founded "Akhbar al Yaum" newspaper in Amman (1961-62); Editor of "al-Manar" (1962-67); Manager and Editor of "al-Dastour" newspaper (1967-73); member of the Jordanian Senate (1971-74); Secretary General of Arab National Union (1973-74); Partner and General Manager of Jordanian Press Foundation member of the National Consultative Council (since 1978). **Hobbies:** Arabic literature, political analysis. **Prof. Addr.:** al-Ra'i newspaper, P.O.Box 6710, Tel.: 667171, Telex: 21497, Amman, Jordan.

HAMMAD (Mohamad, Abdalla Mohamad, al), Saudi educator. **Born** in 1940 in Riyadh al-Khabra, Saudi Arabia. **Son** of Abdullah Mohamad Al Hammad. **Married**, 3 children (2 boys and 1 girl) **Dipl.:** B.A. (Arabic Language), Imam Mohammed Bin Saud Islamic University, Riyadh (1959); B.A., College of Commerce (now College of Admn. Sciences) King Saud University, Riyadh (1962); M.A. (public Administration, Indiana University, USA (1968); Ph.D. (Government and Administration), Indiana University, USA (1973); Diploma "Education for the Leaders and Educationist in the Arab World", American University of Beirut, Lebanon (1959-60); Diploma "Middle Management", Institute of Public Administration, Riyadh. **Career:** Lecturer and Assistant Professer, Riyadh University (now King Saud University), Riyadh (2 years); Assistant Professor, King Abdulaziz University, Jeddah (2 years) and Adviser to Higher Council of the Universities; Executive Director for Regional Bureau of Middle East Committee for Blinds, Riyadh; Director General of Planning & Programmes (Assistant Deputy Minister) Ministry of Municipalities and Rural Affairs, Riyadh (3 years); Presently: Director General, Arab Urban Development Institute (Affiliate to Arab Towns Organization, Riyadh 5 years). **Act. & Publ.:** Contributor to a number of antholo gies about the Arab City, Islamic Civilization and heritage, one of which is the "Arab City: Its Character and Islamic Cultural Heritage", published in two volumes (volume one contains papers prepared in Arabic, and volume two in English, including thirty other books; contributed many articles in the literary and scientific areas to Saudi and non-Saudi magazines and newspapers; co-editor of the ARAB CITY: The Arab Towns Organization periodical (Kuwait); Editorial Board member of "Mujtama Wa Umran", Periodical (Tunisia). **Hobbies:** Reading, writing and swimming. **Member:** IULA, The Netherlands; International New Towns Association, Netherlands; IASIA, Brussels, Belgium; IIAS, Brussels, Belgium; IFHP, The Hargue, Nederlands, ICMA, Washington D.C.; IFLA, France; MESANA, Tucson, AZ; RIPA, London; SID, Rome, Italy; TCPA, London. **Prof. Addr.:** Arab Urban Development Institute, P.O.Box 6892, Tel.: 4419158, 4419876, 4418100, 4418235, Telex: 203566 AUDI SJ, Riyadh 11452. **Priv. Addr.:** al-Malaz, Tel.: 4789318, Riyadh P.O.Box 3823 Saudi Arabia.

HAMMADI (Saadoun, Dr.), Iraqi Politician. **Born** on June 22, 1930 at Kerbala, Iraq. **Educ.:** American University of Beirut, Lebanon; Wisconsin University, USA. **Dipl.:** Ph.D. in Agriculture; Economics A.U.B. Graduation. **Ca-**

reer: Editor, Al-Jumhuriyah newspaper; Professor of Economics, University of Baghdad (1957); Deputy Head of Economic Research, National Bank of Libya, Tripoli, Libya (1961-62); Minister of Agrarian Reform (1963); Economic Adviser to Presidential Council, Government of Syria (1964); Economic Expert, UN Planning Institute, Syria (1965-68); President, Iraqi National Oil Company (1968); Minister of Oil and Minerals (1968-74); Minister of Foreign Affairs (1974); Minister of State (1983-88); Minister of State for Foreign Affairs (1989); Deputy Prime Minister (1990); Prime Minister (23.3.1991- 14.9.1991) and member of the Revolutionary Command; Member of the Arab Baath Socialist Party and former Chairman of the National Assembly. **Publ.:** Views About Arab Revolution; Towards a Socialist Agrarian Reform. **Addr.:** Baghdad, Iraq.

HAMMOUDA (M. Faruk), Syrian aviation official. **Born** on June 3, 1930. **Married**, 2 daughters. **Educ.:** University of Damscus, Syria; Cairo University, Egypt; in USA and UK. **Dipl.:** B.A., Postgraduate Diploma, Licences of Air Navigation. **Career:** Chief of Operation Section, Directorate General of Civil Aviation, Damascus, Syria (1959), Chief of Licencing and Training Section (1963); Director of Civil Aviation School In Damascus (1966); Chief of Air Traffic Services, Arab Civil Aviation Council (ACAC), Cairo, League of Arab States (1970); Director of Air Navigation of ACAC, Cairo (1978); Director and Counsellor of Air Navigation, ACAC, Rabat, Morocco (1981-). **Publ.:** numerous papers and articles; Chief Editor of "Civil Aviation" magazine, Syria. **Hobbies:** Swimming, chess. **Member:** The Hunting Club, Cairo; the Syrian Gliding Club, Syria. **Prof. Addr.:** Arab Civil Aviation Council, 17 Rue al-Nasr, Rabat, Morocco.

HAMMOUDA (Mona, Tareq, Mrs.), Saudi academic. **Born** in 1949. **Educ.:** Faculty of Arts, King Abdul Aziz University; University of Southern California (USA). **Dipl.:** B.A. (English), M.A. (English) (1975). **Career:** Schoolmistress, Third Intermediate school, Jeddah (1970-74); Assistant Dean, Girls College of Education, Directorate of Women's Education (1974-75); Lecturer in English language and Literature, Girls College of Education. **Publ.:** Author of "Intermediate Girls Schools in Saudi Arabia". **Member:** Arab Students Organisation, University of Southern California. **Hobbies:** Reading and travel. **Addr.:** Girls College of Education, Jeddah, Saudi Arabia.

HAMMOURI (Mohamad, Sadeq, al), Jordanian executive. **Born** in 1938 in Hebron, West Bank, Jordan. **Son** of late Sadeq Shukri al Hammouri **and** Mrs. Ezzeyah Saed al-Hammouri. **Married** in 1963 in Baghdad to Miss Khadeejah al-Sharif, five children. **Educ.:** B.A. in Economy, Faculty of Commerce, University of Cairo, Egypt. **Career:** Insurance, Marine Insurance in Baghdad (1958-60); Business and Transport in Baghdad (1960-63); Banking at Baghdad Bank (1963-66); Business in Cairo (1966-70); Business and International Trade in Kuwait (1970-75); Branch Manager in Afro-Arab Co. for Investment and International Trade in Baghdad (1975-76); Area Manager, Syria, Lebanon and Jordan of Afro Arab Co. for Investment and International Trade (since 1976). **Sports:** Tennis and light sports. **Hobbies:** Music, travel and reading. **Prof. Addr.:** Diab and Midani Bldg., Buhsa, Kahal, P.O.Box 5168, Damascus, Syria. **Priv. Addr.:** Malki Abdul Muneim Riad Street, Tel.: 710042, Damascus, Syria.

HAMMUDI (Saad, Kassim), Iraqi politician. **Born** in 1937 in Baghdad, Iraq. **Career:** Journalist since 1955; Former Chairman of al-Jamahir Press House and Editor of "al-Jumhuriyah"; President of the Press Union; Vice Chairman, International Organization of Journalists (1976); Minister of Information (1977); former Editor in Chief of "al-Thawra" daily newspaper. **Addr.:** Baghdad, Iraq.

HAMRANI (Mohamad, Ali, al), Saudi businessman. **Born** in 1949, in Mecca, Saudi Arabia. **Son** of H.E. Sheikh Ali Mohamad Alhamrani (late) (businessman). **Educ.:** Preparatory, elementary, secondary education in Lebanon; University education in U.K. and U.S.A. **Dipl.:** Bachelor Degree. **Career:** started in 1973 in Alhamrani Enterprises, Founded by late Sheikh Ali Mohamed Alhamrani; Chairman on the Board of the Directors: Alhamrani Enterprises and its branches (1976): Alhamrani Enterprises (Holding Co.), Alhamrani Trading & Import Est., Alhamrani Co. For Industry, Alhamrani Universal Co. Ltd., Jeddah Bowling Centre; President and Managing Director of Siraj H. Zahran & Co. (Nissan Datsun Car Agents); member of the Board of Directors, Chamber of Commerce and Industry, Jeddah; Chairman of the Board of Sahab for Tourism & Aviation; Chairman of the Alhamrani Charity and Education Fund; Member of the Board of: Arabian Aviation Services Co. Ltd.; Saudi Refineries Co.; King Abdulaziz University (Research Center). **Sports:** Flying, scuba diving, fishing, sailing. **Hobby:** reading. **Member:** Jeddah Bowing Centre, Permanent Member of the Committee for the Relief of Afganistani Refugees. **Credit Card:** American Express. **Prof. Addr.:** P.O.Box 5260, Tel.: 21259, 21198, 20566, Jeddah, Saudi Arabia. **Priv. Addr.:** P.O.Box 1229, Tel.: 59976, Jeddah, Saudi Arabia.

HAMROUCHE (Mouloud), Algerian politician. **Born** on January 3, 1943. **Married**, 1 child. **Dipl.:** LL.B., M.A. in Political Science. **Career:** Senior Officer of National Liberation Army (ALN) (1958); Acting Member of FLN Central Committee Fourth Congress; Titular Member of FLN Central Committee Fifth Congress; Director General of Protocol to the Presidency (1979-84); Secretary General of the Government (1984-1988); Prime Minister (September 16, 1989- June 4. 1991). **Addr.:** Algiers, Algeria.

HAMZA (Abdulaziz al-Masri), Sudanese former diplomat. **Born** in 1931 in Sudan. **Son** of Dr. Nasri Hamza

(Deputy Vice-Chancellor Ahfad College). **Married** to Maymoona M.Hamza, one child: Hind. **Educ.:** Khartoum University. **Dipl.:** Diploma in Arts (with Merit, in English). **Career:** Regional Inspector, Ministry of Labour (1953-56), Second Secretary of Embassy, Bonn (West Germany) (1956-59); Member Sudan Mission to United Nations, New York (1959-60); First Secretary of Embassy, Washington D.C. (1960-61); Chargé d'Affaires, Sudan Embassy in Beirut (1961-62); Counsellor of Embassy, Baghdad (Iraq) (1962-63); Chargé d'Affaires, Sudan Embassy (Kuwait) (1963-64); Head of Political Section, Ministry of Foreign Affairs HQ, Khartoum (1956); Ambassador of Sudan to Lebanon, Syria and Jordan with residence in Beirut (1968-71). **Awards:** Order First Class from West Germany and two C.M.G. (Companion of the Order of St. Michel and St. George), awarded by H.M. Queen Elizabeth II. **Sports:** Hockey and swimming. **Addr.:** c/o Ministry of Foreign Affairs, Khartoum, Sudan.

HAMZA (Abdulrazzak, Mohamad), Saudi. **Born** in Mecca on 18 October 1933. **Son** of Mohamad A. Hamza (Teacher, Imam of Mecca 1st Mosque Holy Kaaba) and Mrs. Rogaya. **Married** on June 14, 1957 to Miss Samiha Abual Samh, 3 children: Iman (1958), Hisham (1961) and Ayah (1972). **Qualifications:** Two High Diploma (1958), Masters Degree in Education (1973) U.S.C. **Career:** Schoolteacher, Director of Riyadh University Library (1959-61); Director General of High Education (1962-65); Director of Educational Instrument and Systems Directorate (1966-69); Director General of Investigation and Disciplinary Board (1973-1984). Counsellor at the Ministry of Haj and Endowments (1985-1995). Chairman of the Disciplinary Board of the Members of the Mutawefeen who serve Pilgrims. **Memberships:** Member of the American society of Senior Educators. Member of Okaz Journalism Corporation. Honorary member of al Wihda Sports Club-Mecca. **Sports:** Football. **Hobbies:** Reading, photography, sport, collecting antiquities. **Addr.:** Jeddah, P.O.Box 5599, Jeddah 21432, Tel. 6447743, Saudi Arabia.

HAMZA (Mohamad Abdulmalek), Egyptian engineer, diplomat, director of companies. **Born** in Egypt. **Married** to Miss Enayat Murad. **Educ.:** Secondary and Higher Studies. **Dipl.:** Doctor of Engineering. **Career:** Former Minister Plenipotentiary to Turkey, Director of Companies. **Member:** Gezira Sporting Club, Automobile Club of Egypt, Shooting Club. **Addr.:** 126, Pyramids Road (near Kom al-Akhdar), Cairo, Egypt.

HAMZA (Raouf, Abdul Majid), Egyptian painter. **Born** in 1932 in Cairo, Egypt. **Educt.:** Helwan University, Egypt; Academy of Rome, Italy, Ravennal, Italy. **Dipl.:** Diploma of Fine Arts, Doctorate in Fine Arts. **Career:** Art Director, Egyptian Cinema (1960-72); Cinema and Theatre Costume and Set Designer, Cairon (1960); Professor, Helwan University in Egypt (1960-). **Awards:** First Prize, Egyptian Art Festival (1957); Second Prize, Catania, Sicily (1958); Third Prize, Marquota, Rome (1958); First Prize, Parri, Italy (1959). **Priv. Addr.:** 8 Tahran Street, Dokki, Cairo, Egypt.

HAMZAWI (Abdul Aziz), Tunisian diplomat, retired. **Born** in 1935. **Married** 1 son. **Educ.:** Graduate of the Paris I.E.P. "Sciences PO" (International Relations) and of the Sorbonne's Faculty of letters, France (Modern languages); the Fletcher School of law and Diplomacy, **USA**; International Program of Harvard Business School, **USA. Dipl.:** I.E.P. Diploma, M.A. and Ph.D. in International Relations, **Career:** Director of Studies, National School of Administration (1964-66); Director of Administrative and Consular Affairs, Ministry of Foreign Affairs (1966-69); Ambassador to Canada (1969-73); Minister of State for Foreign Affairs (1973-74); Ambassador to Iran and Pakistan (1975-79); Ambassador to Belgium Luxembourg and the E.E.C. (1980-81); International Consultant (1982-87); Permanent Representative to the U N, Geneva (1987-88); Ambassador to Washington, Mexico and Caracas (1980-90); Ambassador to U.K and Ireland (1991-92). **Addr.:** 58, Rue Hédi Zarrouk, Sidi Bou Saîd, 2026, Tunisia.

HAMZAWI (Ibrahim, Kamal), Syrian former statesman. **Born** in Damascus. **Son** of Kamal Hamzawi **and** Mrs. Aycha Fatma. **Married**, 6 children: Bacel, Hassan, Anis, Abia, Salam and Zafar. **Educ.:** Syrian University. **Dipl.:** LL.B. **Career:** Lawyer, Judge (Court of First Instance), President of the Criminal Court, Judge at the Court of Cassation, Mayor of Damascus, former Minister of Justice. **Sports:** Swimming, tennis and shooting. **Hobbies:** Bridge and reading. **Prof. Addr.:** Law Courts, Tel.: 115223, Damascus, Syria. **Priv. Addr.:** 25, Kortoba Mohgreen, Tel.: 334124, Damascus, Syria.

HAMZEH (Zaid), Jordanian physician and politician. **Born** in 1922 in Salt. **Educ.:** Universities of Cairo and London. **Dipl.:** B.Sc. **Career:** Held many posts in Ministry of Health; Director of Ear, Nose and Throat Hospital (1965); ran private clinic (since 1965); Minister of Health (1985- April 1989). **Addr.:** Amman, Jordan.

HANAFI (Abdulaziz A., Eng.), Saudi Engineer. **Born** in 1946 in Makkah Al-Mukarramah, Saudi Arabia. **Dipl.:** B.Sc. (Civil Engineering) NMSU, USA (1969) and Diploma in Concrete. **Career:** Industrial Study and Development Centre, Head of Industrial Estate in Saudi Arabia (1969-74); Head, Engineering Department, Nada International (1974-75); Owner and Director General, Hanafi Contracts & Trading Corporation; Honorary Consul General of the Republic of Maldives in Saudi Arabia; Director General of Al-Bilad Establishment for Journalism & Publicity; Managing Director of Sugar Cone Factory; President, Charitable Society for Memorizing the HOLY QURAN-Jeddah region; President of Parent Committee Al-Sager School, Vice President Federation of Contractors from Islamic Countries; Vice President, The Patient Committee. **Member** American Society of Civil Engineering and Saudi Al Umran Society Jeddah; Jeddah Chamber of Commerce; Member of Board of Directors Umm Al Qurah Meseum, Makkah; Foundation for Islamic Education Inc.; The Haramain and Al-Masjid AQSA Charitable Organisation; Charitable Organisation of ANTI SMOKING; Member of board of Trustees Darul Ihsan University-Dakka (Bangladesh); Supervisor of Manpower Development Program in International Islamic Relief Organisation. **Decor:** Certification of Appreciation with DISTINCTION from Organisation of Islamic Conference (OIC). **Hobby:** Reading. **Address:** P.O.Box 5995 Jeddah 21432, Saudi Arabia, Tel.: 966 -2-6608411, 966.2.6612151, Fax: 966-2- 6611755, E-Mail: HANAFIAZ@YAHOO.-COM

HANANIA (Daoud, Lt. Gen. (Ret.)), Jordanian cardiac surgeon. **Born** on 24th June, 1934 in Jerusalem. **Son** of Anastas Hanania (Senator and Lawyer) **and** Mrs. Claire Hanania née Nashawati. **Married** on 5th January, 1975, to Nada Yousef Pio, four children: 1 daughter, 3 sons: Mai (1975), Zeid (1976), Marwan (1978) and Imad (1984). **Educ.:** Al-Ummah College, Jerusalem; Collège des Frères, Jerusalem; St. Mary's Hospital Medical School; University of London. **Dipl.:** M.B., B.S. (1957); F.R.C.S. (1961); F.A.C.C. (1977); F.I.C.A. (1979), Hon. FRCSI (1980); Hon. FRCS Edin. (1980); Hon. FRCS Glasgow (1988); F.A.C.S. (1971). **Career:** Internship (1957-58) at Army Base Hospital, Amman. House Sgn. & Surg. Registrar in General Surgery and Casualty, Royal Northern Hospital, London (1959-61); Resident in General and Thoracic Surgery, Army Base Hospital Amman (1959, 1961-64); Attending Sgn. in General & Thoratic Surgery; Army Base Hospital Amman (1965-68); Fellow in Thoracic & Cardiovascular Surgery, Baylor College of Medicine, Houston (1968-69); Chief Department of Surgery, Army Base Hospital Amman (1970-73); Chief Cardiovascular Surgery Dept., King Hussein Medical Center (1973-82); Chief Cardiovascular Surgery Dept. Queen Alia Heart Institute (K.H.M.C. (since 1982). Director, King Hussein Medical Centre (1972-1976); Director, Royal Medical Services (1976-1988); Director, National Medical Institution (1988-1989). Also Director General of National Institute for Curative medicine, Amman 18.10.87); Chief, Cardiovascular Surgery Dept., Queen Alia Heart Institute, K.H.M.C.; King Hussein Medical Centre: Clinical Professor of Surgery, Jordan University of Science and Technology (21.1.87); Director General and Chief Cardiovascular Surgeon, Arab Centre for Heart and Special Surgery; Senator-Jordan Parliament (1989-1997). **Publ.:** Several in local and international Medical Journals. **Medals:** Jordanian Kawkab Medals of the Third, Second and First Orders, (1965-70-77); Jordanian Nahda Medal of the Third Order and First Class, (1968-94); Jordanian Istiqlal Medals of the Second and First Orders; (1969-72); K.B.E. (March 1984): "Légion d'Honneur" (July 1984). **Sports:** Tennis, Swimming, Horse-Back Riding. **Hobby:** Middle East Politics. **Member** of Several Clubs which include the Denton A. Cooley Cardiovascular Surgical Society (since 1975); council member of Association of the Thoracic & Cardiovascular Surgeons of Asia (since 1979). **Credit Cards:** American Express. **Prof. Addr.:** Director General, Arab Centre for Heart and Special Surgery, P.O.Box 3128, Tel: 865199 Amman, 11181 Jordan. **Priv. Addr.:** P.O.Box 2135, Tel.: 841411, Amman, Jordan.

HANANIA (Edward, Ibrahim), Jordanian solar designer. **Born** on May 16, 1937 in Bethlehem. **Son** of Ibrahim Hanania (Lawyer) **and** Mrs. née Mary Zarzar. **Married** on August 13, 1964, four children: Caroline, Iyad, Ziad and Ehab. **Educ.:** Bethlehem High School, State University of Lebanon, Alexander Hamilton Institute. **Dipl.:** Business Administration (B.A.), Modern Management, Executive Skills Diploma. **Career:** Chief Instructor, Business Education UNRWA/U.N. (1964-73); President, Thermo Solar Heating Company (1973-75); Chairman and General Manager, Arab Solar Industries Co. Amman, Jordan; Director General, West Asian Programmes, International University of Science (IUS). **Medals:** The Arch of Europe; The American Gold Star for Technology. **Sports:** Tennis. **Hobby:** Horse Riding. **Credit Cards:** Diner's Club, Visa. **Prof. Addr.:** P.O.Box 2858, Tel.: 962-6-663355, Amman, Jordan. **Priv. Addr.:** Abdoun, Tel.: 962-6-819592, Amman, Jordan.

HANNA (Moneer, Khalaf), Egyptian urologist. **Born** on December 13, 1939 in Elsenbeccaween, Egypt. **Married**, 2 daughters. **Educ.:** Fellow, Royal College of Surgeons, UK. **Dipl.:** Diploma from the American Board of Urology. **Career:** Chief of Pediatric Urology Division and Clinical Professor of Urology, New York University; Chief of Pediatric Urology Division, Long Island Hillside Medical Center; Fellow of the American College of Surgeons and American Academy of Pediatrics; Director of Pediatric Urology, Children's Hospital, New Jersey; Clinical Professor of Surgery, New Jersey University of Medicine (1981-). **Publ.:** 84 papers and chapter in text books. "Operative Urology", USA "Sexual Dysfunction in Childhood and Adolescence", USA (both in English) as well as other publications. **Award:** Grayson Carrol Award, American Urological Association (1976). **Hobbies:** Tennis, boating, music. **Prof. Addr.:** Department of Urology, Suite D-3, New York University, 530 First Avenue, New York, NY 10016, USA. **Priv. Addr.:** Roc Harbour, 2-B Covelane N., North Bergen, New Jersey 07047, U.S.A.

HANNUSH (Basim, Abdulmasih), Syrian international civil servant. **Born** on July 24, 1927 in Kamishli, Syria. **Married**, children. **Educ.:** American University in Beirut (Lebanon) (1947-49); Harvard University (1953-56). **Dipl.:** B.Sc. (Economics) (1952), M.Sc. (Economics), Ph.D. (Economics) (1956). **Career:** Economic Affairs Officer, Middle East Study Section, Department of Economic and

Social Affairs (ESA) UN, New York; Head, Economic Unit, UN Reginal Social Affairs Office, Beirut (1963); Chief, Economic Section, United Nations Economic and Social Office in Beirut (UNESOB) (1963-72); Deputy Director, UNESOB (1972-74); Chief, Economic Research and Planning Division, Economic Commission for West Africa (ECWA), UN. **Sports:** Tennis and swimming. **Hobbies:** Reading and gardening.

HANTUCHE (Mahdi, Saleh), Iraqi Dean of College. **Born** in 1921 in Baghdad. **Married** to Miss Iqbal al-Hussaini. **Educ.:** American University of Beirut, University of California, University of Utah. **Dipl.:** Bachelor of Arts, Master of Science, Doctor of Philosophy. **Career:** Assistant Engineer, Irrigation Department; Special Lecturer, University of Utah (U.S.A.); Principal Hydrologist, New Mexico Institute of Technology, (U.S.A.); Dean, College of Engineering of Baghdad. **Addr.:** Baghdad, Iraq.

HARAKAT (Bennacer), Moroccan businessman. **Born** on April 25, 1918 in Casablanca, Morocco. **Married,** 3 children. **Educ.:** General. **Career:** Joined the Nationalist Movement (Parti National) in 1936 as active militant; Active in the Moroccan Independence Movement (1944-55) as responsible of the organization and coordination of the Nationalist Movement in Casablanca; Official, Ministry of the Interior, acting as Magistrate; Assistant of the Governor in Casablanca Province (1956), Chef de Cercle, Settat (1957-59). Transferred to Khouribage in 1959; Secretary General of Casablanca Province (1960-63); Secretary General of Agadir Province (1963-64); Director of Société Filatis (1964-71), Administrator Director of Société Le Matin-Maroc Soir "Newspapers" Unique Administrator of Somaded SA (1975-83) and Sonir SA (1976-1982), Director of the newspaper al-Mithaq al-Watani (1977-79); Chairman of Moubadala (Since 1987); Unique Administrator of LMS (1980-86); Director General of société Eddar el-Beida (Since 1984). **Hobbies:** jogging, reading. **Addr.:** 20, Rue Ahmad Amine, Casablanca 01, Morocco.

HARASANY (Hamid Mohamad), Saudi M.D. and businessman. **Born** in 1920 in Mecca, Saudi Arabia. **Dipl.:** M.B. B.Ch., Cairo University (1948). **Career:** Chief of Pilgrim Guides (1951-61); Minister of Public Health (1961-62); Physician at a private clinic; former Director General, Mecca Printing and Information Establishment (at present publisher of al-Nadwah daily Newspaper); member, the Arabian Cement Company Ltd., Jeddah; former member, the National Company, the Red Sea Club, the Advisory Committee for Social Security Department and King Abdulaziz University; Vice President of the Philanthropic Society, Makkah. **Publ.:** Story of Diabetes Mellitus (Medical book in Arabic). **Hobbies:** reading about medicine. **Addr.:** Nozha Street, Tel.: 5427610 (Office) and 5421104 (Home), Mecca, Saudi Arabia.

HARAZEEN (Hamad, Hassan), United Arab Emirates businessman. **Born** in 1940 in Palestine. **Son** of Hassan Harazeen. **Married**, two children. **Educ.:** B.Com. in Accountancy; attended courses on financial planning, management, economics in UK and USA. **Career:** Auditor with UK firm (1960-66); Assistant Director of Finance, Qatar Government (1966-71); Assistant Director of Finance, Abu Dhabi Government (1971-73); Director of Budget and Financial Affairs, Abu Dhabi Government (1973-82); member of Abu Dhabi Claims Committee (Arbitration), Abu Dhabi Government General Projects Committee, Higher Commission for Administrative Development, Abu Dhabi Civil Service Council and other committees for planning, finance and industrial projects; Vice Chairman and Managing Director, Union Cement Company, Ras al-Khaima, United Arab Emirates; member of the Board of Directors of National College, Shouaifat School, Abu Dhabi; Managing Director, Management and Financial Consultants (MAFCO) (since 1982). **Medals:** Honorary Citizen of Houston, Texas, USA (1975); selected by Houston, City Council to serve as goodwill ambassador (1975). **Addr.:** P.O.Box 244, Tel.: 335108, 339400, Telex: 23086 GETACO EM, Abu Dhabi, United Arab Emirates.

HARBI (Abdallah Ibn Abdallah Ibn Ebeid al-Zayed, al), Saudi academic. **Born** in 1932 at al-Aflag, Saudi Arabia. **Dipl.:** Ph.D. (Islamic Law). **Career:** Director of General Administration, Islamic University (1961-66), teacher, Riyadh Islamic Institute (1966-70); Lecturer, Faculty of Shari'a, King Saud University (1970-75); Deputy Director, Higher Institute of Jurisprudence (1965); Director of Higher Institute of Islamic Dawa (Islamic call), Imam Muhammad Ibn Saud University; member of Supreme Council of Imam Muhammad Ibn Saud Islamic University; member of International Conference on the Mission of the Mosque. **Honours:** Order of Merit, Republic of Guinea; Medal (officer degree), Republic of Mauritania. **Publ.:** several books on Islamic law and history of Islamic legislation. **Addr.:** P.O.Box 4847, Tel.: 4054448, Riyadh, Saudi Arabia.

HARBI (Abdallah Salih, al), Saudi executive, **Born** in 1942 in Mecca, Saudi Arabia. **Dipl.:** B.Com. (Business Administration), Cairo University. **Career:** Deputy Director, Industrial Development and Research Center. **Hobbies:** Swimming, chess. **Addr.:** Industrial Development and Research Centre, Riyadh, Saudi Arabia.

HARBI (Jamal), Algerian economist. **Born** in 1940 in Algeria. **Married,** 2 children. **Educ.:** in Algeria and Paris, France. **Dipl.:** Diploma in Political Sciences, Ph.D. in Economics. **Career:** Assistant Professor, Faculty of Economic Sciences, Algiers (1969); Assistant Administrator, United Nations World Food Programme, Cairo, Egypt (1969); Adviser, United Nations World Food Programme, Aden, People's Democratic Republic of Yemen (1973);

Regional Administrator, United Nations Development Programme (UNDP), New York, USA (1975); Resident Representative, UNDP, Djibouti (1979-). **Publ.:** articles on economic development published in UNDP News. **Hobbies:** Swimming, travelling, jogging, tennis, music, cinema, theatre. **Prof. Addr.:** UNDP HQ, One United Nations, New York, NY 10017, USA.

HARBI (Mousseddine), Algerian diplomat. **Born** on November 6, 1936. **Married,** 1 child. **Educ.:** University of Grenoble, France. **Dipl.:** Blit. MA in Diplomatic Section. **Career:** Militant in MTLD (1951), in UGEMA and FLN (1956); imprisoned in 1958; First Secretary in Politics, Algerian Permanent Mission, United Nations (1962); Director of African Affairs at the Ministry of Foreign Affairs; Ambassador to Angola Until 1984; Deputy Minister (Cooperation), Ministry of Foreign Affairs. **Prof. Addr.:** c/o Ministry of Foreign Affairs, Algiers, Algeria.

HARIMI (Karim, Ahmad, al), Omani politician. **Born** in 1935 in Muscat, Oman. **Married. Educ.:** short course in post office administration in UK. **Career:** Cable and Wireless, Muscat; Imports and Purchases Department, Ministry of Electricity and Water, Kuwait; Director of Posts, Telegraphs and Telephones, Oman (1970); Director of National Development Council (1973); held several ministerial posts in the Public Works and Development Departments; Minister of Posts, Telegraphs and Telephones (1980-83); Counsellor to HM Sultan Qaboos (1983-). **Addr.:** Ruwi, Muscat, Oman.

HARIRI (Ghazi), Syrian senior research officer. **Born** on 17 July 1937, Dael, Deraa. Syria. **Son** of Majed Hariri (Civil Worker and farmer) **and** Mrs. Falha Hariri. **Married** on 1 August 1959 to Sahar Reich, two children. One daughter, Mirvat (8 June 1960) and one son, Ayas (21 March 1962). **Educ.:** Faculty of Agriculture, University of Alexandria, Egypt; Ruthamsted Experimental Station, University of London, England. **Dipl.:** B.Sc. in Agriculture; (1960) Alexandria, Egypt; Ph.D. in Entomology (1965) London, England. **Career:** Professor, Faculty of Agriculture, University of Aleppo (1965-87); Dean of Agriculture, University of Aleppo (1968-69, 1975-79); Vice President, University of Aleppo (1979-81); Senior Research Officer, International Service for National Agricultural Research, The Hague, Netherlands (since 1983). **Work:** Founder President of the Arab Society for Plant Protection (1979-82). Former **member** of the FAO/UNEP Panel of Experts on Integrated Pest Control (1978-86). **Sports:** Walking and cycling. **Hobbies:** Music (classic and folklore). **Credit Card:** American Express. **Prof. Addr.:** ISNAR, P.O.Box 93375, Tel.: 070-496100, 2509 AJ The Hague, Netherlands. **Priv. Addr.:** P.O.Box 7441, Tel.: 224004, Aleppo, Syria.

HARIRI (Saleh, Jamal, al), Saudi senior civil servant. **Born** in 1917 in Mecca, Saudi Arabia. **Educ.:** al-Azhar University, Cairo, Egypt. **Dipl.:** B.A. (Islamic Legislation). **Career:** Teacher, Government schools, Mecca, subsequently Ta'if; Inspector Presidium of the Judiciary (now Ministry of Justice); Assistant Chief, Ministry of Health headquarters; Director-General of the Inspectorate, Ministry of Health; now Director, Legal Department, Ministry of Health. **Publ.:** Author of "Prince Abdullah al-Faisal and Saudi Missions", "Saudi Army in Palestine". **Prof. Addr.:** Legal Department, Ministry of Health, Riyadh, Saudi Arabia.

HARNAFI (Mimoon), Moroccan bank manager. **Born** in 1931 in Berkane. **Son** of Abdul Rahman Harnafi. **Married. Educ.:** HEC Paris (Economics, Finance, Business Administration, Law); Classical Arabic; British Chamber of Commerce Diploma; United Nations Proficiency of English. **Career:** Held several Government Positions in Morocco (1964-67); Special Assistant to the Executive Secretary of the United Nations Economic Commission for Africa, Addis-Ababa (1967-70); Senior Executive Officer at United Nations Headquarters New York (1970-72); General Manager, Compagnie d'Assurances et de Réassurances "Atlanta", Casablanca (1972-76); Deputy Secretary General, UBAF, Paris and then Manager of Economics and Financial Studies Department (1976-); General Manager, Union de Banques Arabes et Françaises, Seoul, Korea (1981-84); ALUBAF Arab International Bank E.C. **Member:** French Association of Economics; Circle of Chief Ecomnomists of French Banks; Golf Club, Casablanca, Morocco; Club Nautique, Morocco. **Hobbies:** Swimming, Tennis and Water-Skiing. **Addr.:** P.O.Box 1224, Tel.: 778-808881/5, Telex: K26400 A/B UBAFSK, Seoul, Korea.

HAROON (Abdulwahab Rachid, al), Kuwaiti Chairman and Managing Director. **Born** in 1947 at Kuwait. **Married**; children. **Educ.:** Shuwaikh Secondary School, Kuwait University, California State University, University of California, Western Illinois University, University of Wisconsin. **Career:** Member in the Geographical Dept. at Kuwait University (1972-1976); DY. General Manager at Kuwait Transport Company (1976-1977); DY. Chairman & Managing Director at Kuwait Transport Company (1977-1985); Presently DY. Chairman of al Ahlea Circle Cleaning K.S.C.; and Chairman and Managing Director, Kuwait Public Transport Co. S.A.K. **Other Information:** Before the Invasion-Member of the Board of Directors of some Companies and Member of the Board of the Gulf Bank K.S.C. During the Invasion, he has been working as «Head of the Transport Team» in New York and Saudi Arabia Co-ordinating with civil Affairs Forces of the U.S. Army. **Credit Cards:** American Express, Diner's Club. **Prof. Addr.:** Kuwait Public Transport Co., P.O.Box 375, 13004 Safat, Kuwait, Tel.: (965) 2442594. **Priv. Addr.:** Mishref, Block 4, Street 4, House 40, Tel.: (965) 5380599, Kuwait.

HAROUN (Ahmad, Rashed, al), Kuwaiti Director General- Kuwait Chamber of Commerce and Industry. **Born** in 1943 in Kuwait. **Son** of Rashed Al-Haroun **and** Shaikha Hamad Abdulla Al-Hothi. **Married** on February 10, 1974 in Kuwait to Fardous Al-Fozan, four children: Esra, Hamad, Rashed and Faisal. **Educ.:** B.A., - 1973 - Arab Beirut University. **Career:** (1) Secretary of the Finance & Economic Committee at the Kuwait Parliament - 1968-1977 (2) Deputy Dir. general at the Public Institution social Security - 1977-1984 (3) In Trading & Cont'g Business - 1984-1994 (4) Member of the Board of Directors of the National Real Estate Co. - 1981-1983 (5) Member of the Board of Directors at the Kuwait Clearing Co. - 1984 (6) Chairman of the Kuwait Seif Co. - 1983-1984 (7) Member of the Arbitration Authority Committee for the Forward Deals - 1983-1984 (8) Chairman of the Abdulla Al-Salem Co-operative Society - 1985-1987 (9) The Coast Investment & Development Co. - 1987-1993 (10) Member of the Municipal Council - 1993-1994. **Hobby:** Reading. **Associations:** Member in many non-profit societies. **Credit Cards:** Visa and Diner's **Prof. Addr.:** P.O.Box 775 Safat, 13008 Kuwait. Tel.: 2403683/4 (KCCI). **Priv. Addr.:** Dahiyat Abdulla Salem, Block-2, Plot-28, Bldg. 17, Tel.: 2571393, Kuwait.

HAROUN (al-Awad, Haroon), Sudanese mathematician. **Born** in 1930 at Getaina, Sudan. **Son** of el-Awad Haroon **and** Mrs., née Fatima Omar. **Married** in 1957 to Faiza Satti at Getaina, 4 children: Isam, Amina, Awad and Amal. **Educ.:** University College of Khartoum, University of London. **Dipl.:** B.Sc. **Career:** Assistant Inspector, Ministry of Trade (1952); Chairman and Managing Director, Trade and Services Corporation (1973-75); Under-Secretary, Ministry of Commerce and Supply (1969-73); Under-Secretary, Ministry of Finance and National Economy (Department of Trade and Supply) (1969-73); Under-Secretary, Ministry of Finance and National Economy (Department of Trade and Supply) (1975-76); Minister of Commerce and Supply (1976). **Awards:** el-Nilain Medal (1st class). **Hobbies:** Reading, listening to radio, watching football. **Clubs:** Graduate club; Racing club (Steward). **Priv. Addr.:** Mogran, Tel.: 76874, Khartoum, Sudan.

HART (Christopher, C.), Banker. **Born** on January 14, 1948 in Calcutta, India. **Son** of Joseph Hart **and** Mrs. Eleanor L. McNair. **Married** on March 4, 1976 in London to Rachel M. Hart, one daughter, Claire E. Hart. **Educ.:** George Town University, Washington, D.C. (1966-70); University of Michigan, Ann Arbor (1970-71) (1972-73). **Dipl.:** B.S., M.BA. **Career:** US Army (1971-72); Joined Citibank in 1973, International Audit (1973-76), Operations Manager (1977-80) and Credit Manager (1980-83); Bank of America (1983-85) as Marketing and Credit Manager; Branch Manager of Scandinavian Bank in Bahrain (1985-87), International Desk Head, Scandinavian Bank, London and Fin. Inst. Department Head (1988-). **Sport:** Scuba Diving. **Credit Card:** Amex, Visa, Masters. **Prof. Addr.:** 2-6 Cannon St., London EC4M 6XL, Tel.: 236-6090, United Kingdom. **Priv. Addr.:** 17 Pembridge Villas, London W11, Tel.: 229-6166, London, United Kingdom.

HARTHI (Fahad al-Orabi, al), Saudi academic. **Born** in 1945 at al-Murayfia. **Dipl.:** Doctorat d'Etat (Arts and Humanitics), Sorbonne University, Paris. **Career:** Demonstrator, King Saud University (1970-72); Literary Editor, al-Riyadh newspaper, later Director of its Paris Office (1972-80); Assistant Professor, Faculty of Arts, King Saud University; General Manager, Yamama Magazine; member of the Organization d'Universités Partiellement ou Entièrement des Langues Françaises (O.U.P.E.L.F.); Headed Saudi delegation (150 members) to the "Cultural Week" in Algeria (1984); Participated to "Assilla Festival" in Morocco and contributed to a symposium with famous Arab intellects called "Cultural Interaction between the Arabian East and West"; Participated to many academic and informatory symposiums; Member of the Advisory Committee for Arabic Culture, Unesco (The 4th Conference held in Morocco, November 1985); Founder Member of the Arabic Council for infancy and development (Participated in all it's meetings and conferences); Member of the high Committee for the evaluation of the radio and TV Programme Founded in 1985 and headed by the Minister of Information; Member of al-Yamamah Press Est. Board (Publisher of al-Yamamah Weekly, al-Riyadh, and al-Riyadh daily); Prepared the Program for the major Cultural Symposium at "al-Ginadriya Festival" in 1987, He chose the theme and contributed to the Organization, and coordinated the activities; Member of many official information delegation which accompanied the Saudi leaders abroad; Member of the official information delegation to Arabic and Islamic Summits since 1980; Participated in many book exhibitions and Saudi Cultural Weeks Organized abroad (Book-exhibition in Frankfort, Cultural Week in Morocco, Cultural Week in Sweden...). **Honour:** Medal awarded by the Spanish Government. **Publ.:** preparing to translate his Ph.D. dissertation into Arabic and to publish a group of novels; regular contributor to most local newspapers since 1970; published a book in arabic titled "Waktllar - Time for Disgrace" (about the Gulf Crisis), Riyadh (April 1991). **Hobbies:** Reading, writing, travel. **Addr.:** Faculty of Arts, King Saud University, Riyadh, and/or al-Yamama magazine, P.O.Box 6737, Riyadh 11452, Tel.: 4765323 (Office), Fax: 4775162, Telex: 201664 JAREDA SJ and Tel.: 4654340 (Home), Riyadh, Saudi Arabia.

HARTHI (Hussain, Mohsin, al), Saudi businessman. **Born** in 1941 in Taif, Saudi Arabia. **Son** of Mohsin Alharthi **and** Mrs. Sadia Saleh Aldebagh. **Married** on July 16, 1969 to Miss Lala Mohjuddin Nazer, 8 children: Sharaf, Rakan, Wed. **Educ.:** B.C.E., University of Texas (1964). **Career:** Assistant manager, Technical Department, Saudi

Arabia Ministry of Education, Riyadh (1964-65); Deputy Dean, then acting Dean Faculty of Engineering, Riyadh University (1965-68); Chief resident engineer and manager Projects & Trading Co., Riyadh (1968-70); President, NADCO, Riyadh (1970); Director National Quarries Co., SAGE, SAMEC, Okaz Newspaper, Tihama Advt. Co., Dallah Industries. **Member:** International Investment Group. **Addr.:** Riyadh, Saudi Arabia.

HARTHY (Mashoor, Ali, al), Saudi Major-General (Ret.). **Born** in 1923 in Mecca, Saudi Arabia. **Son** of Sharaf Ali bin al-Hussain al-Harthy. **Married** to Jaleela al-Harthy, in Mecca in 1945, 6 children: Nabila, Nayl, Leila, Adel, Muwaffak and Reem. **Educ.:** Military Academy, Tayef, Saudi Arabia; Senior Officers College, Cairo (Egypt). **Dipl.:** Military Diploma. **Career:** Posted to G-3 Unit Riyadh (1967); Commander of Infantry School, Tayef (1952); Commander of Senior Officers College, Riyadh (1957); Military Attaché, Federal Republic of Germany (1961); Military Attaché, Saudi Embassy (UK) (1964). **Awards:** Awarded medal and decorations by Egypt, France, Belgium, England. **Sports:** Tennis and walking. **Hobbies:** Reading and music. **Credit Cards:** American Express. **Prof. Addr.:** al-Harthy Company, P.O.Box 6249, Jeddah, Saudi Arabia.

HARTHY (Mohamad, Sulaiman, al), Omani diplomat. **Born** on March 15, 1928 in Oman. **Married,** 3 children. **Educ.:** Religious studies. **Career:** Ambassador of Oman of Tunisia (1973-77); Ambassador at the Ministry of Foreign Affairs (1978-81). **Hobby:** Swedish Exercises. **Addr.:** Muscat, Oman.

HARZALLAH (Ahmad), Tunisian producer, Cinema ad T.V. **Born** on January 27, 1938 in Monastir. **Educ.:** Centre Experimental de Cinema, Rome (Italy). **Career:** Producer, attached to Satdec (1960-64); Chief of Production and Programmes, Educational TV, Institut de l'enseignement pour Adultes (1966-68); Producer (1968); Especially interested in the theoretical and practical problems of applying audio-visual techniques in education and development; Vice-President, l'Association des Jeunes Cinéastes Tunisiens; Jury, International Amateur Film Festival, Kelibia (Tunisia); Contributor to professional journals; Films include: le Pur Sang Arabe (1963), Gamoudi (1964), al-Fouladh (1966), Sogicot (1966), Vers la Connaissance (1967), Pélerinage à la Mecque (1964), le propos des Nattiers de Nabeul (1964-68), Tazerka. **Award:** Special Prize, Japon Prize (1968). **Addr.:** 8, Rue de Sicile, Sousse, Tunisia.

HASAN (Amin, Mohamad), Jordanian lawyer. **Born** on November 2, 1925 at Arrabeh. **Son** of Mohamad Hasan (deceased) **and** Mrs. Khadra Hasan. **Married** on December 16, 1950 in London, Ericsson, 3 children: Samir (1951), Nabil (1952), Randa (1957). **Educ.:** The Arab College: London University. **Dipl.:** LL.B. (Barrister at Law, 1951). **Career:** Prosecutor General (1952-56); Executive Director for Foreign Aid (1956-58); Assistant Secretary General, Development Board (1960); Deputy Mayor of Amman (1965-78); Presently Lawyer. **Sports:** Indoor sports. **Hobbies:** Chess, reading classics. **Member:** Jordanian Lawyer's Association; Conciliation and Arbitration Center for the Union of Arab Banks. **Credit Card:** American Express. **Prof. Addr.:** P.O.Box 2444, Amman, **Priv. Addr.:** Shmeissani, Tel.: 666888, Jordan.

HASANI (Baqir, Hussain), Iraqi diplomat. **Born** on February 12, 1915, in Baghdad, Iraq. **Single. Educ.:** Columbia University, New York (1936-39); Baghdad University (1947-51). **Dipl.:** B.Sc. (1939) and LL.B. (1951). **Career:** Director of Commerce and Registrar of Companies, Trade Marks and Patents, Ministry of Economy, Baghdad (1947-51); Director General, Contracts and Economic Research, Development Board, Baghdad (1951-54); Director General of Income Tax, Ministry of Finance (1954-55); Director General and Chairman of the Board of Directors, Tobacco Monopoly Administration, Ministry of Economy, Baghdad (1956-59); Ambassador to Austria (1959-63); Chairman, Board of Governors International Atomic Energy Agency (IAEA), Vienna, Austria (1961-62); Special Adviser to the Director general, IAEA (1963-66 and 1970-76); Adviser to Saudi Arabian Mission to IAEA (1978-82); Head of Iraqi Delegation to the General Conference of IAEA and delegate to UNO General Assembly for many years; Delegate to the International Passeport Conference (Geneva), the International Conference on Diplomatic Immunities and Privileges (Vienna) and the World Bank. **Member** of the Board of Directors of Rafidain Bank and the Electricity Board (Baghdad). **Sports:** Swimming and riding. **Hobbies:** Coin and stamp collecting. **Awards:** Rafidain Decoration (Iraq); Grand Golden Decoration with Ribbon (Austria). **Addr.:** Via Civelli 9, Tel.: (0332)228859, 21100 Varese (Italy); and 43 Maidenhead Court Park, Tel.: (0628)38573, Maidenhead, Berkshire, SL6 8HN England.

HASHAR (Khamis, al), Omani banker. **Born** in 1937 in Sultanate of Oman. **Son** of Ali Juma Hashar. **Married** in 1959, 4 sons, 2 daughters. **Educ.:** Educated in Kenya, East Africa. **Career:** Joined British Bank of the Middle East, Kuwait (1960); Dubai and Abu Dhabi (1961-64); al-Ghurair Group of Companies, Abu Dhabi (1968-70); General Director, Oman Enterprises (1970-74); Joint Partnership in Banking, Real Estate, Poultry, Farming, Industrial Activities since 1974; Chairman, Union Bank of Oman, Oman (1981-); Chairman, Oman National Fisheries Co. SAO; Oman Farms Co. LLC; Oman Enterprises. Vice Chairman, Mahajer al-Rawdaha; Managing Director, Gulf Express Co. and Travel and Tourism, Director, Salalah Hotels Co.; Partner in Oman Products Distributing Centre, Dubai; Oman Chamber of Commerce and Industry. **Member:** al-Arouba Sports Club; Capital Area Yacht Club. **Addr.:** P.O.Box 4565, Ruwi, Tel.: 734611-12-13 (Office), 701826 (Residence), Telex: 3434 A/B ETIHAD MB, Muscat, Sultanate of Oman.

HASHIM (Abdallah Hashim), Saudi businessman. **Born** in 1915 in Jeddah, Saudi Arabia. **Career:** Formerly employee at a private office; Government employee for seven years; member of International Oxygen Manufacturers Association, Chamber of Commerce and Industry, Jeddah; introduced the manufacture of industrial and medical gases, ship-building, tin industries; deals in supplies and contracting; President Abdallah Hashim Est. **Honour:** Gold Medal awarded by Ministry of Commerce. **Hobbies:** Fishing, travel. **Addr.:** P.O.Box 44, Zipcode: Jeddah 21411, King Khalid Street, Tel.: 6472200 (5 lines) (Office) and Tel.: 6621500, Jeddah, Saudi Arabia.

HASHIM (Fuad, Dr.), Former Egyptian Minister of Economy. **Born** in 1928, Suez Governorate. **Educ.:** Faculty of Commerce, Cairo University; Manchester University; Leeds University. **Dipl.:** B.Sc. Commerce (1949); M.Sc. (Econ.) 1954; Ph.D. (Econ.) 1956. **Career:** appointed lecturer in Economics, Cairo University; appointed United Nations expert (1966); selected as consultant to the Presidency of the Republic; full professor of economics, Cairo University (April 1970); Minister of Economy from 3 January to 2 September 1982. **Addr.:** Cairo, Egypt.

HASHIM (Hashim Abdu), Saudi Director General and Editor-in-Chief. **Born** in 1938 at Gizan, Saudi Arabia. **Education:** Ph.D. On (Library Science) from Cairo University 1984. **Career:** Employee at customs Dept. Gizan; Editor, Al Madina newspaper, Jeddah; Managing Editor Al-Riyadi magazine (now al-shabab); Managing Editor, Iqra weekly magazine; Deputy Editor-in-Chief, Albilad daily newspaper, Jeddah; Political Commentator, Saudi Radio; Director General and Editor-in-Chief, Okaz daily newspaper, Jeddah since 1981; Member of the Consultative Council (Saudi Parliament); Member of board, Okaz Organization for Press and Publications; Member Donation Committee for Bosnia-Herzegovina and Somalia Makkah Province, Saudi Arabia; lecturer, Library Science and Mass Communication Departments, Facutly of Arts, King Abdulaziz University, Jeddah 1985-1994. **Publ.** Studies on Soccer; Quantitative and Qualitative Trends in Saudi Arabian Periodicals. **Addr.:** Okaz Organization for Press and Publications, P.O.Box: 1508, Jeddah -21441, Tel.: 6724004, 6722630 (Office) and 6711968 (Fax) Jeddah, Saudi Arabia.

HASHIM (Hashim Said, Major General (Rtd.)), Saudi businessman. **Married,** 2 sons, 2 daughters. **Educ.:** Makkah High School; Military School, Taif; trained at Air Services Training, Hamble; Royal Air Force, United Kingdom. **Dipl.:** Licence from British Civil Air Training Board. **Career:** Commander Flying School and Technical Training (1952-58); Director Air Force Operation (1958-63); Attaché to the Embassy USA (1963-66); Commander Royal Saudi Air Force (1966-72), Then developed business: **Chairman:** Trading and Industrial Group (Holding) Ltd. (TIG), TIG-Tesco International Ltd. (TIG-Tesco), TIG-Maintenance Arabia Ltd. (TMAL), Arabian Contracting Company Ltd. (ACC), Saudi Polystyrene Plant (SPP), Aluminium Products Co. Ltd. (ALUPCO), Aluminium Manufacturing Co. Ltd. (ALUMACO), IT IS Fashion (Dubai). **Addr.:** P.O.Box 2500, Jeddah 21451, Tel.: (02) 6531680, Telex: 601110 TIG SJ, Fax: 6519168, Jeddah Saudi Arabia; Hashim Said Hashim Est (HSH Est).

HASHIM (Jawad M.), Iraqi economist and politician. **Born** on February 10, 1938 in Iraq. **Son** of Mahmoud Hashim **and** Mrs. Nasrat nee Baqer. **Married** in 1961 to Salwa al-Rufai, two sons. **Educ.:** London School of Economics and Political Science, University of London, UK. **Dipl.:** Ph.D. **Career:** Professor of Statistics, University of Baghdad (1967); Director General, Centre Statistical Organization (1968); Minister of Planning (1968-71); member Economic Office, Revolutionary Command Council (1971-72); member UN Economic Commission for Western Asia (ECWA) (1975); member Consulative Group on International Economic and Monetary Affairs (Rockefeller Foundation), Economists Association, Iraq, Study Group on Energy and World Economy; Fellow, International Bankers Association. **Publ.:** National Income, Its Methods of Estimation; The Evaluation of Economic Growth in Iraq (1950-70); Development of Iraq's Forein Trade Sector (1950-70); Capital Formation in Iraq (1957-70); as well as eighteen articles and several papers. **Hobbies:** Sport, driving, reading. **Addr.:** Abu Dhabi, United Arab Emirates.

HASHIM (Malik, Mohamad), Egyptian academic. **Born** in 1945 in Cairo, Egypt. **Married,** 2 children. **Educ.:** Michigan University, USA; Cairo University, Egypt. **Dipl.:** M.A. and Ph.D. in Linguistics. **Career:** Instructor at Cairo University (1965-68); Instructor, Princeton University, USA (1969-72); Lecturer, Cairo University (1972-). **Publ.:** Editor of "Flights of Fantasy: Arabic Short Stories", Elias Publishers (1984). **Medal:** Medal of Science, Cairo University (1966). **Hobbies:** Painting, photography, music. **Prof. Addr.:** 22 Taha Hussain Flat 29, Zamalek, Cairo, Egypt.

HASHIM (Mohamad), Egyptian lawyer and statesman. **Born** in Egypt. **Married** to daughter of late Hussain Sirry Pasha. **Educ.:** Faculty of Law (Cairo University). **Dipl.:** Licentiate and Doctor of Law. **Career:** Former Minister of Interior, Former Deputy, General Manager of several companies. **Member:** Automobile Club of Egypt. **Addr.:** 17, Maahad as-Swisry Street, Zamalek, Tel.: 806567, Cairo, Egypt.

HASHIM (Mohamad, Ali), Syrian academic. **Born** in 1936 in Aleppo, Syria. **Son** of Ali Hashim. **Educ.:** M.D., University of Damascus, Syria; Ph.D. Medicine and Endocrinology, Moscow, USSR. **Career:** Deputy Dean, Faculty of Medicine, University of Damascus, Syria; member of Parliament (1970-72); Minister of State (1971-72); Minister of Higher Education (1972-78); Professor, Faculty of Medicine , University of Damascus, Syria (1978). **Addr.:** Faculty of Medicine, University of Damascus, Syria, Barada Street, al-Khuja Bldg., Damascus, Syria.

HASHIM (Zaki), Egyptian Barrister-at-law, Chairman of Companies. **Born** in Cairo. **Married** To Miss Amal Fikry Hashim. **Educ.:** Cairo University and Harvard University. **Dipl.:** Bachelor of Law, Master of Arts, Doctor of Philosophy. **Career:** Barrister-at-Law; Chairman, Finance Committee, Council of public services; Formerly Secretary-General of National Bank of Egypt; Deputy-Counsellor in the State Council and Legal Adviser, League of Arab States. **Publ.:** Author of "The United Nations". **Member** of Gezira Sporting Club, Racing Club of Cairo. **Hobbies:** Tennis and Music. **Addr.:** 23, Qasr an-Nil Street, Tel.: 49343, Cairo, Egypt.

HASHIMI (Abdulhamid, M., al), Syrian academic. **Born** in 1921 in Damascus, Syria. **Dipl.:** Ph.D., B.T. (Psychology). **Career:** Professor and Chairman, Department of Education and Psychology, College of Education, Umm al-Qura University; former member of the University Council, King Abdulaziz University, Jeddah; ex-member of the Board, College of Education, Research and Development Centre Makkah. **Publ.:** Developmental Psychology; Individual Differences; The Arabian Educator: Muhammad, Messenger of Allah. **Hobbies:** Reading, walking. **Addr.:** P.O.Box 8598, Jeddah, Saudi Arabia.

HASHIMI (Alawi, Hashim Hussain, al), Bahraini associate professor. **Born** on September 6, 1946 in Manama, Bahrain. **Son** of Hashim Hussain al-Hashimi (Businessman) **and** Mrs. Husnyya née Salman al-Sharaf. **Married** on January 23, 1969 in Bahrain to Miss Kamilah, 4 children: Wassem (7 Oct. 1979), Samaa (14 March 1981), Saba (3 Nov. 1987) Kameel (20 Nov. 1992). **Educ.:** Manama Secondary School; East London College of Commerce; Arab University of Beirut; University of Cairo; Tunisian University. **Dipl.:** General Secondary Certificate; O.N.D. in Business Studies; B.A. in Arabic literature; M.A. in modern Poetry; Ph.D. in Stylistic Studies. **Career:** Private Business (six separate years); Bahrain Radio (1969-71); Journalist (six separate years); presently Dean of the College of Arts; Lecturer and Associate Professor at Bahrain University. **Work:** Teaching, Researching, composing in Poetry and Criticism. **Publ.:** Published 3 Poetry books and eight books in Criticism of Poetry. **Hobbies:** Travelling and Reading. **Member:** Bahrain writers and literators Association. **Prof. Addr.:** Bahrain University, P.O.Box 32038, Tel.: 449300, Manama, Bahrain. **Priv. Addr.:** 1200 Budayya Rd., Villa Jidhafs 426, Tel.: 591414, Manama Bahrain.

HASHISH (Majdy, Ahmad), Egyptian auditor. **Born** in 1934 in Cairo, Egypt. **Married**, 3 children. **Educ.:** Cairo University, Egypt. **Dipl.:** B.Com.; Postgraduate Diploma in Taxation. **Career:** Certified Public Accountant; Member of the Board of Arab World Company for Trading and Arab Investment for Urbanisation **Member:** Gezira Sporting Club, Hunting Club. **Prof. Addr.:** P.O.Box 2085, Cairo, Egypt. **Priv. Addr.:** 22 Shara Kasr el-Nil, Cairo, Egypt.

HASHWE (Edward, Kamal), Syrian lawyer. **Born** in 1935 in Hama, Syria, **Married**, 3 sons, 1 daughter. **Dipl.:** LL.B. in International Law. **Career:** Lawyer; journalist; Member of Central Committee of Syrian Arab Socialists Party, the former Syrian Lawyers Trade Union and the Union of Arab Writers; Director of Population Census and Legislation, Ministry of Labour, Syria (1960-61). **Publ.:** The Interpretation of "Unified Laws of Labour", "Towards a Progressive Ideology of Working Class", "The Handbook of Arab Laws", "The Exploration of Petrol" (a Study of the Use of Arab Petrol as a Weapon). **Hobbies:** Writing, swimming. **Addr.:** al-Alassi Street, Damascus, Syria.

HASSAN (Abdallah, al), Sudanese diplomat. **Born** in 1925 at Tokar, the Red Sea, Sudan. **Educ.:** Gordon Memorial College. **Dipl.:** BPA (Bachelor of Public Administration) (1949). **Career:** Joined the Ministry of the Interior and worked his way up to District Commissioner (1949-56); Consul-General to Uganda and Kenya; attached to Ministry of Foreign Affairs (Aug. 1958-59); Head, Political Section, Ministry of Foreign Affairs (1959-60); Ambassador to Ghana (Oct. 1960-64); Director, Ministry of Information and Labour (1964); Ambassador to France (1965-67); Ambassador to Ethiopia (1967-69); Under-Secretary of State, Ministry of Foreign Affairs (July 1969- Jan. 1970); Ambassador to the Soviet Union (Jan. 1970- July 1971); Ambassador to the Court of Saint James, London (July 1971- Oct. 1972); Minister of Natural Resources (Oct. 1972- May 1973); Minister of the Interior (May 1973-75). **Member:** Political Bureau, Sudan Socialist Union (SSU); (now dissolved); Secretary, Central Council of Solidarity, Friendship and Peace. **Addr.:** Khartoum, Sudan.

HASSAN (Abdulhamid), Egyptian physician, **Born** in 1941 in Egypt. **Educ.:** University of Cairo, Egypt. **Dipl.:** M.B. in Medicine; M.D. in General Surgery. **Career:** President of the General Union of Students, Egypt (1968-69); Member, General National Conference (1968-71); Cairo Youth Secretary (1971-73); Deputy Youth Minister (1973-79); President of Youth Department, National Council for Youth and Sports; Minister of State for Youth and sports (1979-84); Youth Secretary, National Democratic Party; Member of the Central Committee (1971-); Member of the People's Assembly (1973-); President Supreme Council for Youth and Sport (1973-); Member of Arab Socialist Union (1974-); Governor of

Giza (1984-). **Prof. Addr.:** 10 Mudiriyat al-Tahrir Street, Garden City, Cairo, Egypt.

HASSAN (Abdulrazak, Abdulla), Bahraini banker. **Born** in 1952 in Hidd, Bahrain. **Married. Educ.:** Master of Science in Management from MIT, Boston. **Career:** Chartered Bank (1968-71); Chase Manhattan Bank (1971-77); Assistant General Manager, National Bank of Bahrain BSC, Manama, Bahrain (1977-1993) General Manager, National Bank of Bahrain (1994- to date). **Directorships:** Chairman, Benefit Network Company; Chairman, NBB Guaranteed Fund, Board Member and Executive Committee Member of National Import and Export Company. **Membership** of Professional Organisations: Deposit Protection Committee; Bankers' Society of Bahrain. **Hobby:** Sports. **Addr.:** P.O.Box 106, Manama, Bahrain.

HASSAN (Ahmad, Mohamad, al), Sudanese physician. **Born** in 1930. **Educ.:** University of Khartoum, Sudan; University of Edinburgh, UK, University of London, UK. **Dipl.:** Medical Degrees. **Career:** Doctor (1956-57); Research Assistant, University of Khartoum, Sudan (1958-60), Lecturer in Pathology (1962-63), Senior Lecturer and Head of Department (1965-66), Professor of Pathology (1966-73); Dean, Faculty of Medicine, University of Khartoum (1966-73); Deputy Vice Chancellor (1971); Minister of Higher Education and Scientific Research (1971-72); Chairman of Medical Research Council, National Council for Research. **Prof. Addr.:** Medical Research Council, P.O.Box 2424, Khartoum, Sudan.

HASSAN (Ahmad, Yusuf, al), Syrian professor, Historian of Islamic Science. **Born** on June 25, 1925 in Mshirfi, Palestine. **Son** of Yusuf al-Hassan (Farmer) **and** Mrs. Salha al-Ali. **Married** in 1952 to Miss Leila Khalil, six children: Sameh, Sawsan, Randa, Ayman, Maha, Omar. **Educ.:** Government Arab College, Jerusalem; Cairo University; Imperial College of Science and Technology, London; University College, University of London. **Dipl.:** B.Sc., D.I.C., Ph.D. **Career:** Prof. Faculty of Engineering, Aleppo University (1954-82); Dean, Faculty of Engineering (1964-67); Minister of Petroleum, Electricity and Mineral Resources (1967-70); President, University of Aleppo (1973-79); Director, Inst. for the History of Arabic Science, Aleppo University; Professor University of Toronto (1983-87); Member of the UNESCO'S International Scientific Commission for the multivolume work, Aspects of Islamic Culture, and Chief Editor of History of Science and Technology in Islam. Edited and wrote several books and papers on Islamic Science and technology, including (as co-author) Islamic Technology, an illustrated history, which was translated into several languages. **Awards:** Knight, Légion d'Honneur; Member, International academy for the History of Science (Paris); Member, Iraqi Academy (Baghdad). **Sport:** Walking. **Hobby:** diversified academic and industrial interests. **Member** and Council member in many national and international associations (mostly learned). **Prof. Addr.:** 66 York Rd., Toronto, Ont., Canada M2L 1H6. **Priv. Addr.:** P.O.Box 467, Tel.: 2663818, Aleppo, Syria.

HASSAN (Ahmed, Mohamed), Djibouti Deputy at the National Assembly, and M.D. **Born** in 1945 in Djibouti. **Educ.:** University Studies. **Dipl.:** Doctorate in Medicine, Master in Communal Health. **Career:** Director of Hôpital Peltier. Member of PMP (1963-1967); Spokesman of FLCS in 1977; Member of RPP (1979-1997); Member at the National Assembly (1977-1982) reelected Deputy at the National Assembly (19/12/1997 - to date). President of the Commission for Social Development, Environment Protection and the Commission of Foreign Affairs. **Prof. Addr.:** National Assembly, P.O.Box 138 Djibouti, Djibouti.

HASSAN (Bakr, Ahmad, Dr.), Saudi Academic. **Born** on February 27,1945 in Medina, Saudi Arabia. **Married** 3 children. **Dipl.:** Ph.D; in Mathematics Education (1979), University of Oregon-USA.; B.Sc. and M.Sc. In Mathematics from Arizona State University USA. **Career:** Professor of Mathematics in KFUPM in Dhahran Saudi Arabia; Chairman, Mathematical Sciences Department, KFUPM for more than six years during his chairmaship, the first Ph.D. Program in Mathematics was established in Saudi Arabia; Also established a bilingual preschool in KFUPM where he was the Chairman of the Board for thirteen years; Chosen by the Islamic Educational Scientific & Cultural Organization (ISESCO) in Rabat, Morocco as Chairman of the Expert Committee to develop Mathematics Curriculum for the Muslim Countries at the intermediate and secondary Levels; also selected Member, National Committee, (Ministry of Education) to review the New Mathematics Texts at elementary and intermediate level; Representative, KFUPM in many National and International Committees; Visiting Professor/Scholar in University of Illinois in Champaign, Urbana-USA; Department of Applied Mathematics and Theoretical Physics, University of Cambridge, England and Shell Center for Mathematical Education University of Nottingham, Nottingham-England, During his work at KFUPM, he was the Chairman or Member of many standing or ad-hoc Committees; Moved to Saudi Aramco Oil Company in Dhahran, Saudi Arabia (end 1993), he was initially in charge of the technical training in the area of Computer and communications then worked in the information and technology planning; Currently, Consultant in Information and Technology. He was chosen as a Saudi Aramco Representative in the Long Term Comprehensive Plan for Science & Technology Team sponsored by King Abdulaziz City of Science and Technology (KACST) and in the workshop on the transfer of technology in the Arab World. He is an Active **Member** in the Community: Member of the Saudi Computer Society where he held several positions; was Chairman of the Technical Committee for three Conferences on Computer Technology held in three different years sponsored by the Saudi Computer Society and the Chamber of Commerce and Industry in the Eastern Province; Also Chief Editor of the quarterly publication of the Computer Society named Zagil; Also Member of the Arab Thought Forum and the Gulf Development Forum. **Publ.:** Published several books and articles in the area of mathematics education. **Hobby:** Travelling, Reading and Walking. **Address:** c/o Aramco, P.O.Box 10662, Dhahran 31311, Saudi Arabia. Tel.: 966-3-872-8700 (work), 966-5581-6165 (Mobile), E-Mail: Hassanba@aramco.Com.sa or Hassanba@hotmail.com.

HASSAN (Farkhonda), Egyptian geochemist. **Born** in 1930 in Cairo, Egypt. **Married**, 2 children. **Educ.:** B.Sc. Cairo University (1952); Diploma in Psychology & Education, Ain Shams University (1954); M.Sc. American University in Cairo (1966); Ph.D. University of Pittsburgh, U.S.A. (1970). **Career:** Member of People's Assembly of Egypt (The First House of the Egyptian Parliament, (1979-1984); Vice-Chairman of the Parliamentary Committee on Foreign Relations (1979-1984); Member of Shoura Assembly of Egypt (The Second House of the Egyptian Parliament (1984-1989) and (1992- Present); Chairman of the Standing Parliamentary Committee on: Human Development & Local Administration (1995- Present) Chairman of the Special Parliamentary Committees of the Shoura Assembly on: The Land Use Plan of Egypt (1987), The Nuclear Program of Egypt (1988); Honorary Member of the Inter-Parliamentary Union (1984-Present), and Chairman of the IPU Committee on Science, Education and Environment (1979-1980); Caracas-Venezuela; Chairman of the Sciences & Engineering Department of the American University in Cairo (1975-1980). Member of many official governemental delegations (during the past 20 years) to various parliamentary and UN conferences related to Science, Technology, Development and Environment; Vice Chairman of the Executive Board of the Third World Organization of Women in Sciences (TWOWS) in the Third World Academy of Sciences, Trieste, Italy; Member (co-chair of the steering committee) of the International Policy Action Committee of Women, Environment & Development Organization (WEDO) (New York-USA); Member of the Executive Committee of the International Federation of Advanced Studies (IFIAS), 1991 Toronto, Canada; Chairman of the Gender Science & Development Program (1993-present); Vice-President of the Scientific Association of Arab Women to promote the utilization of Science and Technology in Development and Protection of the Environment; Head of Women Sector of the National Democratic Party, of Egypt. **Publ.:** Co-author of 4 official school textbooks on natural sciences (in Arabic); Author and co-author of numerous papers on geological subjects published in national and international specialized journals, author of "The Planet Earth", Dar el-Maaref (1978); Author of 3 official school textbooks on geology and natural sciences (in English). Prepare and present a Weekly TV program "Science Era" that started in 1962 and continues till present The Science Era Program is concerned with the popularization of the scientific and technological achievements and their environmental impact. **Award:** Holder of the Order of Merit of Arts and Sciences, First Class (1980). **Hobby:** Squash (Egyptian Universities' Champion) (1951). **Prof. Addr.:** Department of Science, American University in Cairo, 113 Sharia Kasr el-Aini P.O.Box 2511, Tel.: 3542966/69, Cairo, Egypt. **Priv. Addr.:** 20 al-Aanaab Street, Mohandessin, Dokki, Giza, Egypt.

HASSAN (Hani, al), Palestinian politician. **Born** in 1937 in Haifa, Palestine. **Educ.:** University of Darmstadt, West Germany. **Dipl.:** graduated in Construction Engineering. **Career:** Helped develop Fatah Organization; European Chief of Fatah (1967); Fatah spokesman in Jordan during the 1970 crisis; Chairman, Palestinian Political Affairs Department of Fatah (1974); Deputy to Salah Khalaf in Jihaz al-Rasd of Fatah; Has directed PLO and Fatah relations with China and led PLO delegations to China; requested Chinese support for the PLO at the UN (1974); Member of the Palestinian Parliament, Central Council of Fatah Movement.

HASSAN IBN TALAL), Former Crown Prince of Jordan. **Born** in 1947 in Amman. **Educ.:** Harrow School, England, Christ Church, Oxford University. Brother of H.M. late Hussein ibn Talal, King of Jordan and heir to the throne. Acting Regent during absence of King Hussein, Ombudsman for National Development (1971 - Jan. 1999); Founder of Royal Scientific Society of Jordan (1970); Honorary General of Jordanian Army. **Publ.:** A Study on Jerusalem (1979); Palestinian Self Determination (1981). **Addr.:** Office of the Prince, The Royal Palace, Amman, Jordan.

HASSAN (Izziddin, Osman), Egyptian gynaecologist. **Born** in 1930 in Egypt. **Married,** 1 son. **Educ.:** Cairo University, Egypt. **Dipl.:** Diploma in General Surgery, M.B., Ch.B. in Obstetrics and Gynaecology. **Career:** Consutlant, Egyptian Ministry of Health (1950-65); Lecturer and Assistant professor, Mansoura Faculty of Medicine (1965-67); Medical Board, Egyptian Family Planning Association (1970-); Committee of Family Planning, Egyptian Minsitry of Health (1969-); Professor and Chairman of Obstetrics and Gynaecology, Mansoura Faculty of Medicine (1974-); Director of Egyptian Fertility Care Society (1978-); Secretary General of Egyptian Society of Gynaecology and Obstetrics (1980-). **Publ.:** "Fertility Care" (1982), "el-Osrah" (1983). **Hobbies:** Horse riding, shooting, yachting, swimming, tennis. **Addr.:** 24 Boustan Street, Cairo, Egypt.

HASSAN (Khalid, al), Palestinian politician. **Born** in 1928 in Haifa, Palestine. **Career:** Active in Islamic Liberation Party; Secretary, Development Directorate, Kuwait; joined Yasser Arafat and other Founding Members of

Fatah and was partly responsible for Fatah relations with Arab Governments; joined Palestine Liberation Organization Committee (1969-73); formerly Head of PLO Executive Committee Political Department; Member of Palestinian Parliament.

HASSAN (Khalid, al-Haj), Jordanian politician. **Born** in 1931 in Amman, Jordan. **Married. Educ.:** University of Louisiana, USA. **Dipl.:** M.A. in Mechanical Engineering and Irrigation. **Career:** held Civil service posts; Director General, Jordanian Electric Power Company (1957); Minister of Agriculture (1957-62); Director General, Jordan Cement Factory (1962-64), (1965-72); Minister of Agriculture (1964-65), (1972-73); Minister of Transport (1974-76); Minister of Labour and Social Affairs (1983-87). Minister of Transport and Communications (1988-89). **Addr.:** Amman, Jordan.

HASSAN (Layla, al, Mrs.), Saudi academic. **Born** in 1935. **Dipl.:** B.Sc. (Chemistry), University of Baghdad (1959); Ph.D. (Physical Chemistry), University of Wales (1957). **Career:** High school teacher of chemistry (1959-65); analytical chemist (Geochemical Analysis) (1965-69); Vice Dean and Associate Professor of Chemistry and Biology Department, Girls' College, Jeddah; member of Girls' College Board of Directors; Fellow of Royal Chemical Society, U.K. **Publications:** Chemisorption and Catalysis on Gamma-irradiated Magnesium Oxide (Ph.D. thesis, March 1977, University of Wales), Absorption and Decomposition of N2O on Y-Irradiated MgO (Journal of the Chemical Society, Faraday Transaction I, 1975, Vol.71). **Hobby:** reading. **Addr.:** c/o M.A. al-Dugaither, Director, Environmental Protection, P.O.Box 1358, Jeddah, Saudi Arabia.

HASSAN (Mahmoud Yousry), Egyptian architect-planner. **Born** on October 1, 1933 in Egypt. **Son** of Mahmoud Hassan (Teacher) **and** Mrs. Arifa Mustafa. **Married** in 1958 in Cairo, Egypt to Ragaa Mahmoud, 3 children: 2 sons, Ahmed (1960), Tarek (1963) and one daughter, Mai (1965). **Educ.:** Beni Suef High School (Egypt); Cairo University, Faculty of Engineering (Egypt); Massachusetts Institute of Technology & Harvard University (U.S.A.). **Dipl.:** B.Sc. (Architecture, Cairo Univ. 1954); DIP. G.S. (City Planning, Cairo Univ., 1957); M.Sc. (City Planning, Cairo Univ. 1961); Ph.D. (City & Regional Planning, M.I.T., 1965). **Career:** Assistant Professor Beirut Arab University and Cairo University (1966-72); Associate Professor (1972-77); Professor of City and Regional Planning, Cairo University (1977- to date); Dean, Faculty of Urban and Regional Planning (1979-1993). Private Professional Practice in the Fields of Architecture, Urban Design and City Planning since 1966 in Egypt, Saudi Arabia, Lybia and Lebanon. **Other Information:** Planning Consultant for a number of Egyptian and International Agencies Including U.N.D., UNDP and UNCRD. **Awards:** National Medal of Arts and Sciences, 1st Degree (1983); International Medal of the Organization of Arab Cities (1990). National Merit Awards for Professional and Scientific Contribution of: Egyptian Syndicate of Engineers (1989 & 1992), Federation of Egyptian Architects (1990), Cairo University (1999). **Hobby:** Photography. **Member:** Maadi and Shooting Clubs, Cairo; EG. Associate of Architects; EG. Associate of Planners. **Prof. Addr.:** Faculty of Urban and Regional Planning, Cairo University, Orman Giza, Tel.: 5700830, Fax: 727288, Giza, Egypt. **Priv. Addr.:** 39 Kasr el Nil Str., Cairo. Tel.: (202)392/4401, Fax: (202)390/2292, Egypt.

HASSAN (Mamoon, Ibrahim), Sudanese executive. **Born** in 1938 in Wadmedani, Sudan. **Son** of Ibrahim Hassan. **Married** in 1968, 4 children. **Educ.:** B.A. (Econ. Hist.); U.N. New York, Course in Multilateral Diplomacy. **Career:** Ministry of Foreign Affairs Khartoum (1975-76); Sudan Ambassador to Belgium, Luxembourg, the Nederlands (1976-77); Diplomat in Multilateral Diplomacy in Pakistan, U.N. (New York), G.D.R., EEC, Belgium, Netherlands, Luxembourg; Sudan Ambassador to Kuwait, Bahrain (1977-78); Director of International Organisation, Khartoum; Director-General, Inter Arab Investment Guarantee Corporation, Safat, Kuwait (1988 to present). **Addr.:** P.O.Box 23568, Tel.: 548346, Telex; 22562 A/B KAFEEL, Safat 13096, Kuwait.

HASSAN (Mohamad, Ahmad), Bahraini executive. **Born** in 1951 in Bahrain. **Married,** 2 sons. **Educ.:** Secondary School, Bahrain. **Career:** British Bank of the Middle East (1969); Citibank (1969-77); Assistant General Manager, Operations, National Bank of Bahrain B.Sc., Manama, Bahrain (1977-). **Member:** Bankers Club. **Hobby:** Sports. **Addr.:** Manama, Bahrain.

HASSAN (Moussa, Ismail), Djibouty Deputy at the National Assembly. **Born** in 1960 in Djibouti. **Career:** Nursing at "Centre de la Santé publique communautaire" in Hayableh; President of Annex Hayableh (RPP); Member of ADEPF. Elected Deputy at the National Assembly (19/12/1997 - to date); Member of Foreign Affairs Commission, Social Development and Environment Protection Commission. **Prof. Addr.:** National Assembly, P.O.Box 138 Djibouti, Djibouti.

HASSAN (Mustafa, Othman), Sudanese politician. **Born** in 1929 in Omdurman, Sudan. **Married,** 6 children. **Educ.:** Secondary in Omdurman; Military College, Staff College Course in India and Artillery course in Egypt. **Dipl.:** Graduated from Military College (1962). **Career:** Joined the Artillery; Lieutenant-Colonel appointed Military Governor of Port Sudan (May 1961); Colonel and Assistant Commander, Artillery Troops, Atbara (March 1965); Transferred to the Republican Palace, As Assistant Commander, Artillery; promoted Brigadier and appointed Deputy Chief of Staff Administration (1969); Major-General (September 1970); retired from the Army; Deputy

Minister of defence (November 1971); Deputy Minister of Transport (October 1972- October 1973); Minister of State for Construction and Public Works (until January 1975); Minister of Construction and Public Works (January 1975- September 1977); Minister of Transport (August 17, 1979-82) **Addr.:** Khartoum, Sudan.

HASSAN (Said, Mohamed), Djibouti Deputy at the National Assembly. **Born** in 1948 at Tadjourah. **Career:** Nursing (Ministry of Public Health); Member of RPP; Elected Deputy at the National Assembly (18/12/1992 - to date); Member of Legislation Commission, General Administration of the Republic and Commission for Social Development and Environment Protection. **Prof. Addr.:** National Assembly, P.O.Box 138 Djibouti, Djibouti.

HASSAN (Salaheddine), Sudanese executive. **Born** in 1929 in Omdurman, Sudan. **Son** of Hassan Abdul Rahman. **Married** in 1957, 2 sons, 3 daughters. **Educ.:** Khartoum University, School of Law (1951); Academic Postgraduate Dip. (1963); L.L.M., London University (1965). **Career:** Joined Sudan Judiciary (1952); Judge of the High Court, Khartoum (1968); President, Khartoum University Council (1969-71); Chief Justice of Qatar, Doha (1972-77); Head of the Legal Department, Arab Monetary Fund, Abu Dhabi, UAE (1978). former President of Khartoum University Council. **Member:** Doha Club; Khalidya Palia Hotel Club. **Hobbies:** Swimming and Tennis. **Addr.:** Khartoum, Sudan.

HASSAN (Subhi, Rashid, al), Jordanian lawyer. **Born** in 1917 in Jordan. **Married**, 4 sons, 1 daughter. **Educ.:** University of Damascus, Syria. **Dipl.:** B.A. in Law. **Career:** Lawyer (1941-46); Judge (1946-59), Chief Judge (1959-62); Director General of Lands and Surveying Department (1962-71); Head of the Military and Civil Retirement Committee (1971-); Legal and Local Adviser, Ministry of Finance (1971-). **Hobbies:** Law, reading, travelling, gymnastics. **Prof. Addr.:** P.O.Box 8895, Jabal al-Hussain al-Sharqiyeh, Amman, Jordan.

HASSANEIN (Sayed, Hanafi), Egyptian university professor. **Born** on October 10, 1932 in Cairo. **Son** of Hanafi Hassanein **and** Mrs., Nabiha Abdallah Hassan. **Married** to Layla Hassanein on April 21, 1966. **Educ.:** Secondary School, Khalil Agha, Cairo University, Aïn Shams University. **Dipl.:** Bachelor of Arts, Master of Arts, Doctor of Philosophy (Arabic Literature), High Diploma in Psychology and Education. **Career:** Professor at Cairo University since 1955; Visiting Professor Bogota Universities "National and laveriana" Colombia, Latin America. **Dist.:** 2 Medals of Academic Studies (1958 and 1962). **Member** of the Club of the Staff of Cairo University. **Sports:** Swimming and Tennis. **Hobbies:** Poetry and music. **Prof. Addr.:** Cairo University, Cairo, Egypt. **Priv. Addr.:** 97, Hussain Street, Madinet-al-Attebba, Dokki, Cairo, Egypt.

HASSAWI (Mubarak Abdul Aziz, Al), Kuwaiti businessman. **Born** in 1925 in Kuwait. **Son** of Abed Al Aziz Al Hassawi. **Married**, 2 sons, 6 daughters. **Educ.:** Secondary School, Kuwait; Special Course in Customs Management, Alexandria, Egypt. **Career:** Head of the Customs Department, Kuwait (1963-78); Member of Parliament for 12 years until it was dissolved. Head of Foreign Affairs Committee; Deputy Chairman of Bank Of Sharjah, Sharjah, Chairman of Kuwaiti Commercial Real Estate Centre, Chairman for the following Hotels and Companies: (Sharjah Carlton Hotel, Sharjah Continental Hotel, Beach Hotel Sharjah, Golden Beach Motel, Sharjah And Kuwait Manufacturing Company, Fawaz Refrigeration And Air Conditioning Company) Sharjeh, UAE, **Member**, Al-Qadisa Club, **Hobbies**, Hunting, Riding and Swimming. **Addr.:** P.O.Box 421, Tel.: 377345, Fax: 359204, Telex No. 68458 HASSAWI, SHARJAH, UAE.

HASSAYEN (Abdallah Soliman, al), Saudi civil servant. **Born** in 1933 at Shaqra, Saudi Arabia. **Dipl.:** B.A. Shari'a (Islamic Law); Higher Diploma, Cairo; M.A. (Public Administration). **Career:** Director of the General Education Service, General Directorate of Broadcasting, Press and Publications (1956-60); Director of Education, Taif (1962-74); Director of Education, Jeddah (1974-77); Director General, Scholarships and International University Relations, Ministry of Higher Education; Member of Jeddah Literary Club; has participated in several conferences on education in Saudi Arabia and abroad. **Publ.:** Afkar Bela Zaman (Thoughts Without Time); Ala el-Darb (On the Road); Ashek el-Zalam (Lover of Dakness); Shaerat el Retha' (Poet of Lamentation). **Prof. Addr.:** Ministry of Higher Education, Tel.: 4644007, Riyadh. **Priv. Addr.:** Tel.: 4780546, Riyadh, Saudi Arabia.

HASSEB (Kheireddine), Iraqi economist. **Born** on August 1, 1929 in Mosul, Iraq. **Married** in 1955, 3 children: one son, two daughters. **Educ.:** Baghdad University, Iraq; London University, U.K.; Cambridge University, England. **Dipl.:** B.A. in Economics and Commerce; M.Sc., Ph.D. **Career:** Civil Service, Ministry of Interior (1947-54); Head of Research and Statistics Department, Iraq Petroleum Company (1959-60); Director General, Iraqi Federation of Industries (1960-63); Lecturer, University of Baghdad (1960-61) and (1961-63); Governor, Central Bank of Iraq (1963-65); Alternate Governor for Iraq, International Bank for Reconstruction and Development (1963-65); Governor for Iraq, International Monetary Fund (1963-65); President, General Organization of Banks (1964-65); Acting President, Economic Organization (1964-65); Member, Board of Directors, Iraq National Oil Co. (1967-68); Associate Professor of Economics, Baghdad University (1965-71); Professor of Economics, Baghdad University (1971-74): Chief of Natural Resources, Science and Technology Division, United Nations Economic Division for Western Asia (1974-80); Director General, Centre for Arab Unity Studies, Lebanon (1978-83); Chief of

Natural Resources, Science and Technology Division, United Nations Economic Commission for Western Asia (1982-); **Publ.:** "The National Income of Iraq 1953-61" (1964); "Workers, Participation in Management in Arab Countries" (1971) (in Arabic); "Sources of Arab Economic Thought in Iraq 1900-71" (1973) (in Arabic); as well as various articles in Arabic and English. **Addr.:** Baghdad, Iraq.

HASSEN (Mulay, al), Mauritanian diplomat. **Born** on August 5, 1936 in Nouakchott, Mauritania. **Married**, children. **Educ.:** University of Dakar (Senegal). **Dipl.:** Bachelor of Laws. **Career:** Director of Protocol, Ministry of Foreign Affairs, Nouakchott (1961-68); Ambassador to Ivory Coast, also accredited to Mali (1968-71); Ambassador to USA, Washington DC (1971-73); Ambassador, Permanent Representative of Mauritania, New York, also accredited to Canada. **Awards:** Decoration from Mauritania and many African and European Countries. **Sports:** Soccer and shooting. **Hobbies:** Motoring and reading. **Prof. Addr.:** Ministry of Foreign Affairs, Nouakchott, Mauritania.

HASSO (Abdul Rahman, Abdullah, al), Iraqi academic. **Born** in 1934 in Mosul, Iraq. **Married**, 3 children. **Educ.:** M.B., Ch.B., Ph.D. in Haematology; Member, ACP. **Career:** Junior Lecturer (1966), Clinical Pathologist (1972); Head of Medical Research Laboratory, College of Medicine, University of Mosul, Iraq (1972); Head of Pathology Department (1976-); Assistant Professor (1976-). **Publ.:** numerous papers and articles in professional medical journals. **Hobby:** Tennis. **Member:** Social Cultural Centre, Medical Syndicate. **Prof. Addr.:** Department of Pathology, College of Medicine, University of Mosul, Iraq.

HASSOUMI (Ali, al), Tunisian Teacher. **Born** on September 4, 1933. **Married**, 1 child. **Educ.:** L'Ecole Franco-Arabe, Rue Sidi, Ali Azouz, Lycée Carnot, l'Ecole Normale Supérieure. **Dipl.:** Baccalaureat, Licentiate History and Geography. **Career:** Teacher, Secondary Schools (Tunis), Director, I.E.A. Economic Journal I.E.A. (African Economic Information). **Addr.:** 116, Blvd. du 20 Mars, Bardo, Tunisia.

HASSOUN (Mohamad Abdallah, al), Saudi executive. **Born** in 1942 in Jeddah, Saudi Arabia. **Dipl.:** B.A. (Economics and Geography), Kansas University, U.S.A., Diploma (Law and Economics of Air Transportation), I.C.A.O. **Career:** Former Director General, Saudi Public Transport, Western Region; Supervisor, Saudia (Saudi Arabian Airlines) Planning and Research Department (1965); Manager, Saudi International Affairs Department (1967); Regional General Manager for Gulf and Far East (1972); Saudia Assistant Vice President, Riyadh (1975); Vice President of Marketing, Saudia (1976); Group Vice President and General Manager, Sales, Abdulatif Jameel Company Ltd. Deputy Director General of Okaz Organization, publisher of "Okaz" (Arabic) and "Saudi Gazette" (English) daily news-papers (1985). **Member of:** Board of Ittihad Sports club, Jeddah (1980); President of the Arab American Student Club, University of Kansas (1964). **Publ.:** several articles on air transport planning and international bilateral air traffic agreements. **Hobbies:** Reading, billiards, volleyball. **Prof. Addr.:** Okaz Organization for Press and Publication, P.O.Box 5941, Tel.: 660-0789, Jeddah 21441 Saudi Arabia. **Priv. Addr.:** P.O.Box 10760, Jeddah 21443, Saudi Arabia.

HATEM (Mohamad Abdulqader), Egyptian politician. **Born** in 1917 in Alexandria, Egypt. **Son** of Abdulqader Hatem. **Married**, 4 children, one son, three daughters. **Educ.:** Cairo University and Military Academy (Egypt); London University (U.K.). **Dipl.:** M.Sc., Ph.D. **Career:** Member, National Assembly (1957); Adviser to the Presidency, subsequently Deputy Minister for Presidential Affairs (1957); Minister of State (1959); Minister of Culture, Guidance and Tourism (1962); Deputy Prime Minister for Cultural Affairs and Guidance (1965); Deputy Prime Minister and Minister for Culture and Information (1971-74); Chairman al-Ahram (1974); Assistant to the President of the Republic and Supervisor-General of Specialized National Councils (1974-); elected Member of People's Assembly for Abdin Constituency (1979); former Member Secretary General, Arab Socialist Union; Head, Egyptian Political Science Society (1957-); Egyptian-Spanish Friendship Association (1966); Egyptian-Japanese Friendship Association (1970); Professor, al-Azhar (1980-81); **Decor:** Honorary doctorates from two French Universities, and Democratic People's Republic of Korea. **Publ.:** Public Opinion, Propaganda "Theories and Experiences", Information and Propaganda, Rommel in Siwa, (in Arabic); Land of the Arabs, The Egyptian Civilization, Life in Ancient Egypt (in English). **Addr.:** 20 Hassan Assem, Zamalek, Cairo, Egypt.

HATOUM (Platon, Assad), Lebanese Doctor. **Born** on December 19, 1935 in Kfarsalwan, Lebanon. **Son** of Assad F. Hatoum **and Mrs. Zaher** Hatoum. **Married** on November 4, 1961 in Beirut to Miss Afaf Abdelbaki, three children: Kamal, Karim an Naji. **Education:** (La Faculté Française de Médecine) - Beirut. **Dipl.:** (M.D.) diplôme de Docteur en médecine (1962). Complementary Studies: Certification Medicine from the Educational Council for Foreign Medical Graduates (1962), Fellow in Physical Medicine and Rehabilitation in New York University School of Medicine (1964-1966), Fellow of the New York University Medical Center (1966-1968), Felllow of the American Board of Physical Medicine and Rehabilitation (1968), Fellow of the American Board of Rheumatology (1968) and (1970), Fellow of the Chinese Academy of the Acupuncture-Beijing (1976). **Career:** Vice-President, International Rehabilitation Medicine Association (1990- to date); Owner and Practicing Rheumatologist (1962- to date), Physical Medicine (1966 - to date), Acupuncturist (1976 - to date) and Manual Medicine doctor (1966 - to date); Resident in Rheumatology at the Veteran's Administration Hospital (1966-1968); Resident in Rehabilitation Medicine in New York University Medical Center (1964-1966); President of Kfarsalwan Municipality (1998- to date). **Works:** Owner and Practicing Doctor of the Institute for Spinal and Rheumatic Diseases, Physical Medicine and Rehabilitation in Beirut, Lebanon (1969- to date) and the Dr. Platon Hatoum's clinic in Riyadh - K.S.A. (1976 - to date). **Member:** Founding Member of the American Rheumatology Association (1986- to date), Lebanese Medical Association (1962 - to date), American Academy of the Physical Medicine and Rehabilitation (1995 - to date), American College of Rheumatology (1969 - to date), International Manual Medicine (1986 - to date), International Society of Acunpuncture (1972 - to date). **Sports Practised:** Walking, and home Exercises. **Hobbies:** Painting and Reading. **Credit Cards:** Golden Visa, American Express. **Prof. Addr.: Lebanon:** P.O.Box 113-6398 Hamra-Beirut-Lebanon, Dar El-Baidaa Bldg., Mme Curie St., Tel.: +(961)1/810887, +(961)1/811331 - Mobile: +(961)3/855088. **Kingdom of Saudi Arabia:** P.O.Box 66188 Riyadh Old Airport Road, Tel.: +(966)1/476-9769, Saudi Arabia.

HATTAR (Michael, Mizyad), Arab-American academic. **Born** on March 17, 1934 in Salt, Jordan. **Married,** 1 son, 1 daughter. **Educ.:** Greenville College, Illinois, USA; Western Washington State University, USA; Junior College, State of California (Standard Teaching Credential Specialization in Secondary Mathematics). **Dipl.:** B.A. and M.Sc. in Mathematics. **Career:** professor of Mathematics, Don Bosco Technical Institute (1962-76); Chairman, Mathematics Department, Junior College, Don Bosco Technical Institute (1968-76); Professor of Mathematics, Mount San Antonio College (1968-); Mathematics Instructor, Secondary Learning Centre Specialist, Ontario High School, Clifornia (1976-). Publisher of "Sawt al-Mughtarib" (Arabic newspaper). **Publ.:** Editorials and articles in "Sawt al-Mughtarib" newspaper; "Linear Algebra and Matrices", National Foundation Series adaption into Arabic (1972). **Awards:** Teacher of the Year Award (1969) and (1970), Don Bosco Technical Institute; Institute for the Advancement of Engineering Award (1969); Teacher of the Year Award, Industrial Education Council of San Gabriel Valley, California (1970), **Hobbies:** Soccer, table tennis. **Member:** Founder of United Arab Community Club, President (1975-76); Founding committee Member, Arab Cultural Centre of Southern California Active Member of the Organization of Arab Students and Arab Community Affairs; Member of the Association of Arab-American University Graduates, Los Angeles Chapter, President (1970-72); Member of US Omen South Bay Chapter, President (1974). **Addr.:** 1247 Dore Street, West Covina, California 91792, USA.

HAWAMDAH (Mahmood, al), Jordanian engineer. **Born** in 1930 in Tafila, Jordan. **Educ.:** B.Sc. in Mining Engineering, UK (1956). **Career:** Engineer at Jordanian Phosphate Company (1956-66); Director of Phosphate Project (1966-71); Vice President, National Resources Authority (1971-74); Minister of Public Works (1974-76); Minister of Transport (1976); General Manager of Dar Al Handasah Consultants (Shair & Partners), Amman, Jordan (1980-83); Minister of Public Health (1984-87). **Addr.:** P.O.Box 5215, Tel.: 666916, Amman, Jordan.

HAWARI (Ahmad, Mahmood), Egyptian journalist. **Born** on April 12, 1921 in Cairo, Egypt. **Married,** children. **Educ.:** Polytechnic College. **Dipl.:** B.Sc. (Engineering). **Career:** Director, Arab Information Centre Press Office, New York (1955-58); Managing Editor, Middle East News Agency, Cairo (1958-65); Director, Magazine Department, National Publishing House (1965-67); Chairman, National Distributing Company (1967); Publishing Manager "al-Qatib el-Araby" Publishing House (1967-69); Adviser, Editing and Publishing Organisation (1969-71); Director-General, Egyptian Book Organisation (1971-72); former Chairman, Middle East News Agency. **Awards:** Gold Cross, Order of King George I of Greece (1960). **Priv. Addr.:** Isis Building, Garden City, Cairo, Egypt.

HAWARI (Mohamad, Abdul Qadir, al), Egyptian businessman. **Born** in 1935 in Cairo, Egypt. **Son** of Abdul Qadir al-Hawari. **Married,** three children. **Educ.:** Commercial studies. **Career:** Member of the Board of Directors of the Arab-Egyptian Bank (1958-60); Chairman, Egyptian Steel and Metal Commercial Company (1960-67); private business (1967-74); member of the Permanent Committee for the Distribution of Building Materials (since 1977); owner of Ezzat al-Hawari Stores, steel wholesalers, metal and timber; President, Egyptian Co for Trade in the Free Zones (1980). International Football **Referee** (elected with 18 other referees for World Cup, Tunisia 1977). **Award:** Certificate of Gratitude, Ministry of Public Works; FIFA Decoration (International Federation of Association Football). **Sports:** Football, tennis, squash. **Hobbies:** Literature, travel. **Addr.:** 76 Tarik al Nil, Tel.: 982291, Giza, Cairo, Egypt.

HAWAS (Hamad Saleh, al), Saudi civil servant. **Born** on 15 September 1940 at al-Ahsa, Saudi Arabia. **Dipl.:** M.A. (Business Administration), (1965). **Career:** Employment Adviser of Aramco (1966-70); General Director of Personnel and Staff, University of Personnel and Staff, University of Petroleum and Minerals (1978-80); Director General of Jubail Port. **Member** of Jubail Welfare Society. **Hobby:** Reading. **Addr.:** Jubail Port Tel.: 3612824 (Office) and 3611948 (Home), Jubail, Saudi Arabia.

HAWATMEH (Nayif), Palestinian politician. **Born** in 1935 in Salt, Jordan. **Educ.:** Zarqa College, Amman, Hussein College, Amman; Cairo University; Egypt; Beirut

Arab University, Lebanon. **Dipl.:** Degrees in Politics and Economics. **Career:** Member of the Arab Nationalist Movement; following Arab-Israel War in 1967 helped found the Popular Front for the Liberation of Palestine (PFLP) led Democratic Front for the Liberation of Palestine (DFLP); helped editing "al-Hurriyah" DFLP paper; General Secretary of DFLP; headed DFLP delegation to Moscow (1975). **Addr.:** Damascus, Syria.

HAWIZ (Tayib, Nazhat M., al), Iraqi economist. **Born** in 1931 in Iraq. **Educ.:** Birmingham University, UK. **Dipl.:** B.A. in Economics. **Career:** Chartered Accountant of a British accounting firm in UK; returned to Iraq to become Professor of Accounting and Adiministration, Baghdad University, Iraq; Member of the Board, National Insurance Company of Iraq, Central Bank of Iraq; Vice Chairman, Iraqi Oil Board; President, Iraqi Economists Association; Director of Finance, Arab Fund for Economic and Social Development, Kuwait (1973). **Addr.:** Baghdad, Iraq.

HAY (Morven Charles), British executive. **Born** in 1947 in Edinburgh. **Son** of William Douglas Hay. **Married** in 1972, 1 son, 1 daugther. **Educ.:** Latymer Upper School, Hammersmith, London, United Kingdom. **Dipl.:** B.Sc. (Maths) (1969); M.B.A. (Finance) (1972). **Career:** Rio Tinto Finance Corp. (1969-71); Western American Bank (1972-75); Crocker National Bank (1975-78); National Commercial Bank (1978-80); Fellow of Royal Statistical Society; Senior Vice President, Arab Banking Corporation, Bahrain, (1980-to present). **Member:** Bahrain Marina Club: Carlton Club, London. **Hobbies:** Politics, Art, Drama and Boating. **Addr.:** P.O.Box 5698, Tel.: 261819, 245301, Telex; 9434/5 A/B ABCBAH, Bahrain.

HAYARI (Adel, al), Jordanian lawyer. **Born** in 1938 in Salt, Jordan. **Married. Educ.:** Baghdad University, Iraq; Cairo University, Egypt. **Dipl.:** LL.B., M.A. in Law, Ph.D. in Law and Finance. **Career:** Lecturer; Member of Jordan Economists Association, of Jordan Civil Lawyers Union; Assistant Secretary General, Arab Economists Union; Lecturer, College of Economics and Commerce, Jordan University (1969-87). **Publ.:** "Tax on National Income", Constitutional Law and "Jordanian Constitutional System". **Addr.:** Amman, Jordan.

HAYARI (Ali, Ahmad, al, General), Jordanian diplomat. **Born** in 1923 in Salt, Jordan. **Married. Educ.:** British Cadet, Jordan Arab Army (1941-42); 2nd Lieutenant (1942-43), Major (1947-48), 1st Lieutenant (1943-45), Captain (1948-55), Colonel (1955-56), Brigadier (1956); General, Chief of Staff (1956); Chief of Staff. Jordanian Armed Forces (1969-70); Minister of Defence (1970); Ambassador to Cairo (1971-72); transferred to Foreign Ministry, Amman after break in diplomatic relations (1972-73); retired in 1973. **Decor.:** Syrian Order of Merit (2nd Class); Egyptian Order of Merit (2nd Class); Commodore of Lebanese Order of the Cedars. **Medals:** Independance Medal (1st Class); Renaissance Medal (2nd Class). **Addr.:** Jabal Amman, P.O.Box 1168, Amman, Jordan.

HAYAT (Habib, Hassan Jowhar), Kuwaiti banker. **Born** in 1934 in Kuwait. **Son** of Hassan Jowhar Hayat. **Married** in 1960, 4 sons, 1 daughter. **Dipl.: B.A. (Business and Economics) in 1957**. **Career:** Ministry of Public Health, Kuwait, former Undersecretary for Administration and Financial Affairs, and formerly Member of Parliament; Chairman of Arab Asian Investment Company, Kuwait; and formerly Member of Board, Arab African International Bank, Cairo; and Bahrain Arab African Bank, Bahrain. Member of Board in Kuwait Airways Corporation (KAC), Kuwait; Chairman, Shaab Cooperative Society, Kuwait; Board Director, al-Ahli Bank of Kuwait; Proprietor of Hayat Trading and Contracting Corporation, Kuwait; al-Hayat Trading Co. W.L.L., Kuwait and Hayat Marble Co., Kuwait; Minister of Communications (June 1990); Minister of Communications and States Minister for Housing Affairs (November 1992). Minister of Public Works and Minister of State for Housing (13 April 1994). **Member:** Equestrian and Hunting Club; Shaab Marina Club. **Hobbies:** Social Affairs and Sports. **Addr.:** P.O.Box 1668 Safat, Kuwait 13017. Tel.: 4835080, 2617538, Fax no. (965) 2626666, Telex: 22916 A/B HABIB, Safat, Kuwait.

HAYDARI (Buland, al), Iraqi poet. **Born** in 1926. **Career:** Was one of the pioneers of the free verse movement in the 1950s which revolutionized Arabic poetry; actually lives and works in London. **Publ.:** has published eight collections of poems since 1946 including "Aghani al-Medina al-Mayyita" (Songs of the Dead City), "Khutwat fil Ghurba" (Steps in Exile), "Khafqat al-Tin" (The Throbbing Clay), also translations of T.S. Eliot and studies of art and literature; "Songs of the Tired Guard", London, UK (1977), collection of poems translated into English. **Addr.:** Baghdad, Iraq.

HAZAIMAH (Rifai), Jordanian administrator. **Born** in 1937 in Irbid, Jordan. **Married**, 1 son, 5 daughters. **Educ.:** Georgetown University, Washington, USA. **Dipl.:** B.A., M.A. in Law, Diploma in Management. **Career:** Public Prosecutor, Police Court (1968); Director of Foreign Affairs Department (1973); Public Relations Director, Department of Public Security (1974); Director General, Civil Affairs Department (1977-84). **Publ.:** Several works on civil affairs and on taxation (in Arabic). **Decor.:** Order of Independance. **Prof. Addr.:** P.O.Box 2740, Amman, Jordan.

HAZIM (Ignace, Mgr.), Syrian ecclesiastic. **Born** in 1921 in Mharde, Syria. **Educ.:** l'Institut Saint Serge, Paris. **Career:** Director of a secondary Theological Institute, Beirut, Lebanon; Rector of Theological Institute, Antioch, and then elected Bishop of Latakia (1966), took up post (1970); Greek Orthodox Patriarch of Antioch and All the Orient (1979-); President, Middle East Ecumenical Council; member Central Committee of Ecumenical Council of Geneva. **Publ.:** La resurection et l'homme d'aujourd'hui; and in Arabic: I Believe, The Telling of your Word Enlightens, The Church in the Middle East (translation of the work by father Corbon); God's Design. **Addr.:** Greek Orthodox Patriarchate, P.O.Box 9, Damascus, Syria.

HAZMI (Fahad Zamil, al), Saudi railways executive. **Born** in 1934 in Medina, Saudi Arabia. **Educ.:** College Studies, special courses in Management at American University at Beirut, Tunisia, Spain; Ashraje College in U.K. and U.S.A. Also attented Executive Administration & Finance symposiums in the Kingdom of Saudi Arabia. **Career:** Director, Personnel Civil Service Bureau; Director of Planning, Organization and Statistics, SRO; Director of Personnel and General Services Dept., SRO.; Assistant Director General for Administration Affairs, SRO. Now at present working as Vice President, Operations, SRO. Member of Board al-Nahda Sporting Club. Participated in Symposium as Officials from Arabian Gulf Ports. **Honour:** Gold Medal of Saudi Railways Authority. **Hobbies:** reading, football. **Address:** Saudi Railways Organization, P.O.Box 36 Dammam 31241, Saudi Arabia, and P.O.Box 92, Dhahran Airport 31411, Saudi Arabia.

HAZMI (Mansour Ibrahim, al), Saudi academic. **Born** in 1935 in Mecca, Saudi Arabia. **Dipl.:** Ph.D. (Modern Arabic Literature), School of Oriental and African Studies, University of London (1966). **Career:** Assistant Professor, Arabic Department, Faculty of Arts, King Saud University (1966); Dean, Faculty of Arts (1973-76); Head, Arabic Department, Faculty of Arts (1977-79); Dean, Girl's Section for University Studies and Professor of Modern Arabic Literature, Faculty of Arts, King Saud University since 1981; Editor-in-Chief, Bulletin of the Faculty of Arts, King Saud University (1970). **Member** of the Editorial Board of Addarah Quarterly Journal (1975); member of the King Faisal International Prize Committee; member of the Arab Universities Union. **Publ.:** Muhammad F. Abdu Hadid, the Novelist; Bibliography of Saudi Writings in Periodicals and Journals, Umm al-Qura; The Art of Fiction in Modern Saudi Literature; Ashwag Wa Hikayat, verse. **Prof. Addr.:** P.O.Box 53910, Riyadh 11593, Saudi Arabia. Tel.: 4632030, Fax: 4633218.

HAZZAH (Ahmad, Soliman), Egyptian bank executive. **Born** in 1928 in Cairo, Egypt. **Son** of Soliman Ahmad Hazzah. **Married** in 1950, 3 children. **Educ.:** Cairo University (1949); New York University (1969); **Dipl.:** Ph.D. in Economics (1972). **Career:** Chairman, Alnasr Co., Cairo (1964-66); Senior Management Science Consultant, Mobil, New York (1967-72); Director Corporate Planning, Chase Manhattan Bank, New York (1972-76); Gulf Division Executive, Chase Manhattan Bank, Bahrain (1980-81); Gulf & Arabian Peninsula Regional Executive, Chase Manhattan Bank, Bahrain (1980); Director, Chase National Bank, Egypt (1977-). **Member:** Rotary Club. **Addr.:** Cairo, Egypt.

HAZZAM (Fahd, S., al), Saudi civil servant. **Born** on 12 November 1942 at Wadi Dawasir. **Dipl.:** Ph.D. (Administration), Arizona State University. **Career:** Director of Administration and Assistant Professor, University of Petroleum and Minerals, Dhahran, since 1975; Director of Manpower Development, Jubail Project; The Royal Commission for Jubail and Yanbu (on loan from UPM 1980); Acting Dean of Business and Technical Affairs. U.P.M.; Board Member and General Manager Al Youm Printing and Publishing. Dammam. **Publ.:** contributes regulary to local and international periodicals **Hobbies:** chess, horse riding, writing poetry. **Addr.:** Riyadh, Saudi Arabia.

HAZZAZY (al-Tayyib Tahir, al), Saudi TV producer. **Born** in 1941 in Mecca, Saudi Arabia. **Dipl.:** B.Com. (Economics and Public Administration). **Career:** Formerly film editor; sound engineer; assistant producer; directed many TV plays; TV Producer, Jeddah TV Service. **Hobbies:** Travel, reading, photography. **Addr.:** TV Service, Ministry of Information Building, Jeddah, Saudi Arabia.

HAZZEH (Bishara), Syrian faculty dean. **Born** in Syria. **Educ.:** Secondary and Higher. **Dipl.:** Doctor in Science. **Career:** Dean of the Faculty of Science, University of Damascus (1964-66); Professor of Botany at the said University (since 1967). **Addr.:** Damascus University, Tel.: 115100, Damascus, Syria.

HEDDA (Ali), Tunisian diplomat. **Born** on October 30, 1930 at Sousse, Tunisia. **Married** in 1958 to Nadra Becheur, one daughter, one son. **Educ.:** Institute of Political Sciences, Paris. **Career:** Attaché, Tunisian Embassy, Washington DC (1956); Ministry of Foreign Affairs, Tunis (1957); Seconded to Secretary of State for Planning and National Economy, Tunis (1958); Minister Plenipotentiary, Tunisian Embassy, Rome (Italy) (1966); Ambassador to Senegal, also accredited to Mali, Mauritania, Guinea, Liberia, Sierra Leone and the Gambia (1970); Director, Institute of Cooperation, Ministry of Foreign Affairs; Director, Office of the Prime Minister (1973); Ambassador to USA (1974). **Awards:** Grand Officer, Order of the Republic (Tunisia); Order of the Republic (Italy). **Prof. Addr.:** c/o Ministry of Foreign Affairs, Tunis, Tunisia.

HEFNY (Anissa, Mahmoud, al), Egyptian academic. **Born** on August 11, 1927 in Berlin, Germany. **Married,** 3 sons. **Educ.:** Cairo University, Egypt: Free University, West Berlin; St. Mary's Hospital, London, UK. **Dipl.:** M.D. in Paediatrics. **Career:** Head of Paediatric Department, Cairo University (1963-); Member of the Egyptian Paediatric Association (1954), Egyptian Medical Association (1955), British Allergy and Clinical Immunology Society (1970) and several other European Professional associations; Professor of Paediatrics, Cairo University (1973-); Allergy and Premature Units and General Paediatrics Unit, Children's Hospital, Cairo University (1978-); Vice President of Egyptian Allergy Society (1983). **Publ.:** Various research papers in general paediatrics and allergy. **Decor.:** Gud Wkon og Gen, Denmar (1962); Silver Star, East Germany (1975). **Hobbies:** table tennis, golf; Egyptian Universities table tennis champion (1950), winner of several gof prizes (1954-80). **Prof. Addr.:** 22 Tala'at Harb Street, Cairo, Egypt. **Priv.Addr.:** 4 el-Saleh Ayoub, Zamalek, Cairo, Egypt.

HEGAZI (Abdel Aziz, Dr.), Egyptian politician. **Born** on January 3, 1924 in Cairo, Egypt. **Educ.:** Faculty of Commerce, Cairo University (1964); Birmingham University (UK). **Dipl.:** P.Phil. **Career:** Dean, Faculty of Commerce, Ayn Shams University, Cairo (1966-68); elected member, National Assembly (1969); Minister of Treasury (1968-73); Deputy Prime Minister; Minister of Finance, Economy and Foreign Trade (1973); Chairman, Production and Economic Affairs Committee (1972); First Deputy Premier (1974-75); presently, Chairman Bank of Commerce and Development. **Addr.:** Cairo, Egypt.

HEGAZI (Ahmad), Egyptian film star. **Born** on June 18, 1945 in Cairo, Egypt. **Educ.:** Faculty of Arts, Cairo University. **Career:** Started at the lowest rung of artistic life in "The Interloper" produced by Noor el-Sherif in 1966; portrayed a press foreign correspondent in "Cairo 1930" produced by Salah Abu Seif; gradually assumed more important parts in such film as "Yogel's complaint", "The Secretive Man" a TV serial produced by Mohamed Nabih until he was discorvered by the famous Italian Producer Roberto Rossillini in 1967 in "Civilisation", two years later he was selected a leading man in a joint Egyptian-Polish production "Seven Brides in Cairo", and the Polish film "Kidnap" under the direction of Fodayewaf Shelestsiky. **Sports:** Swimming and tennis. **Hobbies:** Classical literature and music. **Addr.:** 3 Ahmad Said street, Tel.: 820193, Cairo, Egypt.

HEID (Mohamad Ibrahim, al), Saudi businessman. **Born** in 1932 at Dirayah, Saudi Arabia. **Educ.:** King Abdulaziz's Sons' School, Riyadh. **Career:** Inspector General of the city of Riyadh; Secretary to Prince of Riyadh; Director General of RIO Corporation for Trade and Agencies; Director General of al-Iqbal Saudi Establishment; owner of General contracting; member of Board, Yanbo Cement Co., Okaz Press Establishment; member of Riyadh Welfare Society; major share-holder of several companies; founding member of Board, Tihama for Advertising, Public Relations and Marketing Research. **Honour:** medal from Queen Juliana, Netherlands. **Hobbies:** Travel, reading. **Prof. Addr.:** RIO Corporation for Trade and Agencies, P.O.Box 1544, Tel.: 6710950, Jeddah. **Priv. Addr.:** Tel.: 6826642, Jeddah, Saudi Arabia.

HEIKAL (Nabil, Ismail), Egyptian. **Born** in 1931 in Cairo, Egypt. **Married** to Fatma (Rawia), 2 sons: Ismail, Telecom Engineer, Cairo University and Rehab, Bachelor of Law, Cairo University. **Educ.:** Lausanne Hotel Business School, Switzerland (1948-52) **Languages:** Arabic, English, French. **Career:** Formerly Director, Egyptian Government Tourist Office in N.Y, USA to promote Tourism from the Americas; Chairman & C.E.O. Egyptian Hotels Co.; Chairman, Egyptian Swiss Hotels Co.; Current position: Consultant, Misr Travel; N.H. Consultancy in Hospitality & Tourism. **Other Activities:** Associations (Professional): Member, Luxor Tourism Promotional Board (1965-68); Expert for World Tourism Organization, Establishing Classification of Hotels in the Arab World (1976); Training Expert, Arab Tourism Association (1978-84); Member National Specialized Board-Presidency-Tourism Branch (1985-98); Board Member, Egyptian Hotel Association (1982-86); Board Member, Egyptian Tourism Chambers Union (1990-92). **Membership:** Active Member, Automobile Club of Egypt; Active Member, Shooting Club of Egypt, Board Member (1988-92); Active Member Ferrosseyyah Club (Equastration); Senior Active Member, Rotary Club of Giza; Past District Governor (Rotary District 2450) (1993-94); Past Active member of Sakl Club of Cairo (Amicale des Professionels de Tourisme) (1984-93); Honorary Secretary (1987-92). **Address:** 17 Nawal St., Dokki, Giza 12311, Tel.: 202 7841277, Egypt.

HEJAILAN (Jamil, al, Shaikh), Saudi Statesman. **Born** in 1927 in Buraida, Saudi Arabia. **Married**, 3 sons. **Educ.:** Secondary and Higher. **Dipl.:** B.A. Law, University of Cairo, Egypt. **Career:** Ministry of Foreign Affairs; Third Secretary, Saudi Embassy to Iran (1953); Chargé d'Affaires, Embassy to Pakistan; Director General of Broadcasting, Press and Publication (1960); Ambassador to Kuwait (1961-63); First Minister of Information (March 1963- December 1970); Minister of Health (December 1970 to March 1974); Ambassador to Federal Republic of Germany (1974-76); Ambassador to France (1976); Presently, Secretary-General, Co-Operation Council for the Arab States of the Gulf. **Addr.:** Co-Operation Council for the Arab States of the Gulf. P.O.Box 7153, Riyadh 11462, Saudi Arabia.

HEJAILAN (Mustafa Ibrahim, S., al), Saudi civil servant. **Born** in 1950 in Cairo. **Dipl.:** M.A. (Public Administration). **Career:** Deputy Director of Saudi Arabian Jubail Industrial Project; former member of Foreign Capital Investment Committee; participated in the preparation of Second Five-Year Saudi Development Plan; Vice-President of Red Sea Ports, Ports Authority; Board Director United Saudi Commercial Bank, Riyadh. **Hobby:** Reading. **Addr.:** P.O.Box 5162, Riyadh, Saudi Arabia.

HEJAILAN (Salah Ibrahim, al), Saudi legal adviser. **Born** in 1940 at Buraidah, Saudi Arabia. **Dipl.:** B.A. (Law) (1962); Diploma of Administrative Law (1964), M.A. (International Public Administration) (1968). **Career:** Legal Adviser to the Council of Ministers (1962-73); member of Board of Discipline of the Grievance Board (1963-72); member of the Board of Directors, Ports Authority (1976 to date); Partner and member of the Board of Directors of: Mobil Marine, J.A. Jones Saudi Arabia Ltd., Saudi Finance International Corp. (Geneva), Adriaan Volker Saudi Arabia, Petrola Saudi Arabia and others; member of various government committees for legislation (1968-73); offers legal services to major organizations and companies; founding member of a number of companies in various fields. **Publ.:** a manual on the Saudi Companies Regulations; several legal articles in various publications. **Prof. Addr.:** P.O.Box 1454, Tel.: 4650723, Riyadh. **Priv. Addr.:** Tel.: 476344, Riyadh, Saudi Arabia.

HELAISSI (Abdurrahman, al, Shaikh), Saudi former diplomat. **Born** on July 24, 1922. **Educ.:** Universities of Cairo and London and in Islamic Religious Law. **Career:** Official at Ministry of Foreign Affairs; Secretary in Embassy, London (1947-54); Under-Secretary, Ministry of Agriculture (1954-57); Representative at United Nations and at conferences on Health, Agriculture, Wheat, Sugar and Locusts; Head of Delegation fo FAO (Food and Agriculture Organisation) (1955-61); Ambassador to Sudan (1957-60); Attended Conference of Non-Aligned Nations, Belgrade (1961); Ambassador to Italy and Austria (1961-66), to United Kingdom and Denmark (1966-76). **Publ.:** Author of "Rehabilitation of the Bedouin" (1959). **Addr.:** c/o Olaiya, Division 3, P.O.Box 8062, Riyadh, Saudi Arabia.

HENABLIA (Dhaoui), Tunisian politician. **Born** in 1922 in le Kef, Tunisia. **Married. Educ.:** medicine. **Career:** Active Member of the National Assembly (1959-); Vice Present of the National assembly (1969); Minister of Agriculture and Member of the Political Bureau of the Socialist Destour Party (1971-74); Member, Political Bureau of the Socialist Destour Party (1974-81); Minister of the Interior (1977-79); Minister of Public Health (1979-81). **Addr.:** Tunis, Tunisia.

HENAIDY (Hamid Mohamad), Saudi academic. **Born** in 1948 in Jeddah, Saudi Arabia. **Dipl.:** B.Sc. (Business Administration), M.B.A. (Accounting), Ph.D. (Accounting). **Career:** Assistant Professor, Department of Accounting, King Abdulaziz University; Adviser to Jeddah Municipality on Administration and Financial Affairs; Supervisor of Economics Department, Okaz; member and Representative of American Accounting Association; member of the National Association of Accountants, U.S.A.; member of the Arab Association of Cost Accounting, Cairo; member of the Permanent Committee for King Abdulaziz University Budget Study; KAU Executive Committee; participant member International Conference of Accounting and Auditing, Cairo, Egypt; Annual Convention of the National Association of Accounting, U.S.A.; Government Accounting Development Conference, Institute of Public Administration, Riyadh; participated in several seminars within the Kingdom and abroad and submitted research papers; Adviser to several Government and private organizations. **Publ.:** Managerial Accounting, Tax Accounting, in addition to several articles published in U.S.A. and Saudi Arabia. **Hobbies:** Reading, writing, travel. **Prof. Addr.:** P.O.Box 5605, Tel.: 6876875, Jeddah. **Priv. Addr.:** Tel.: 6829130, Jeddah, Saudi Arabia.

HENEIN (Naguib, Elias), Editor of "Le Progrés Egyptien", Cairo. **Born** on July 26, 1917 in Alexandria, Egypt. **Son** of Elias Henein Bey (former Magistrate) **and** Mrs., née Rosine Iskandar Bassilios. **Educ.:** St Paul College of the Christian Brothers (1925-28); Collège de la Sainte Famille (1928-29); De la Salle College of the Christian Brothers (1929-32); Koronfish College of the Christian Brothers (1933-36); Cairo University, 1st year of Medicine (1937); Faculty of Medicine and Pharmacy, St Joseph University of Beirut (Lebanon) (1940-42). **Dipl.:** Egyptian Baccalaureat (sciences) (1936); B.Sc. (natural sciences) (1942). **Career:** Joined Société Orientale de Publicité (Jan. 1946), as a junior staff reporter on their French Language daily newspaper "Le Progrés Egyptien"; moved to "Le Journal d'Egypte" in September 1946 in charge of the local newsroom, working his way up to sub-editor in 1949 then to deputy editor in 1954; returned to Société Orientale de Publicité (publishers of French, English and Arabic language newspaper) in 1954 where he was assigned to "La Bourse Egyptienne" as Assistant Editor (1954-64); now Editor of "Le Progrés Egyptien" belonging to Société Orientale de Publicité; was one of the team of newspaper editors selected by the Egyptian Government to cover President Sadat's trip to Western Europe in 1976. **Hobby:** Billiard (French and Snooker). **Spec. Int.:** Reading history and economy. **Sport:** Tennis. **Club:** Shooting and Fishing Club, Dokki, Giza, Cairo, Heliopolis Sporting Club. **Priv. Addr.:** 10 Ramses street, Tel.: 96109, Heliopolis. **Prof. Addr.:** "Le Progrés Egyptien" newspaper, 24 Zakharia Ahmed street, Tel.: 49000, Cairo, Egypt.

HENNAWE (Khair, Mahmoud, al), Jordanian businessman. **Born** on April 10, 1938 in Yafa, Palestine. **Married**, 1 son, 5 daughters. **Educ.:** Sussex College for Science and Technology, UK. **Dipl.:** M.Sc. in Economics of Marine Transport. **Career:** Purchasing Department Manager, Qatar (1962-73); General Manager of El Momtaz Transport Co., Kuwait (1974-77); Managing Director and Owner of International Corporation for Marine Transport, Jordan (1977-). **Publ.:** "As You Wish", poem (1982), "Light in the Darkness of the Night", poem (1982), "The Three Mysteries", children's bock (1984). **Hobbies:** Poetry, writing, reading. **Prof. Addr.:** Khalil Ibn al-Walid Street, Amman, Jordan; P.O.Box 513, al-Aqaba, Jordan.

HESHMAOUI (Mustafa), Algerian diplomat. **Born** in 1934 in Algeria. **Married**, 3 sons, 2 daughters. **Educ.:** School of Infantry, Iraq: Frunza Staff College, Moscow, USSR. **Dipl.:** B.A. in History and Geography. **Career:** Officer, Lieutenant, Algerian Liberation Army (1957), Captain (1962), Major (1972), Commander of Unit (1968); Secretary of the Algerian National Liberation Party (1977); Member, Central Committee of the Party (1979); Ambassador Extraordinary to Lebanon (1980-89). **Decor.:** Order of Bravery (1958). **Prof. Addr.:** Ministry of Foreign Affairs, Algiers, Algeria.

HEWEDI (Amine, al), Egyptian army officer, diplomat. **Born** in 1921 in Egypt. **Educ.:** Military and Staff Colleges, Arab Republic of Egypt and General Staff College, Fort Leaven-worth, U.S.A. and Press College Egypt. **Career:** Former Army Officer, Formerly Egypt's Ambassador to Morocco; Ambassador to Iraq (1963-66); Minister of War (1966-68); Elected Member of the People's Assembly, Minister of State in charge of Egyptian Information in 1969. **Publ.:** Author of Speeches in Strategy (1955), Sunk-Tso (1957). **Addr.:** c/o People's Assembly Cairo, Egypt.

HEYINE (Mohamed Saleck Ould), Mauritanian mining engineer. **Born** in 1947, in Akjoujt, Mauritania. **Educ.:** Primary School, Akjoujt; Lycée of Nouakchott; Mining Institute of Moscow. **Dipl.:** Baccalaureat, Master of Science in Mining. **Career:** Blasting Engineer at SNIM (1975-1977); Head of Mining Department (1987-1982); Mining Manager (1983-1985); Managing Director, SNIM Company (1985-). **Sport:** Fishing. **Credit Card:** Diner's Club. **Prof. Addr.:** P.O.Box 42 Nouadhibou, Tel. 45190, Mauritania.

HIBSHI (Hashim Bakor), Saudi academic. **Born** in 1944 in Mecca, Saudi Arabia. **Dipl.:** M.Sc. Mathematics); Ph.D. (Mathematics), University of Arizona (1974). **Career:** Staff member, Department of Mathematics, Faculty of Science, Umm al-Qura University, Mecca; Chairman of Mathematics Department, Faculty of Education, Umm al-Qura University, Mecca. **Hobbies:** football, reading. **Adress:** Umm al-Qura University, Tel.: 5564770, Mecca, Saudi Arabia.

HIBSHI (Mohamad Ali), Saudi academic. **Born** in 1934 in Mecca, Saudi Arabia. **Dipl.:** Ph.D. (Teachers' Training), University of London (1975). **Career:** Secondary School teacher; Cultural Relation Department, Ministry of Education, Assistant Dean, Faculty of Shari'a (Islamic Law), Mecca; Vice President for Higher Education and Research, King Abdulaziz University since 1977; member of Conference on International Education, Geneva; member of ALECSO Conferences. **Publ.:** Tatawur al-Ta'leem Ál'Ali Fil Mamlakatil Arabia al-Saudiah (Development of Higher Education in the Kingdom of Saudi Arabia), Tatawur Idadilnoallimin Fil Mamlakatil Arabiah al-Saudiah (Development of Teachers' Training in the Kingdom of Saudi Arabia). **Hobbies:** Reading, travel. **Addr.:** King Abdulaziz University, P.O.Box 1540, Tel.: 6879033, Jeddah, Saudi Arabia.

HIDAYAT (Salahuddin), Egyptian scientist. **Born** in 1920 in Egypt. **Educ.:** B.Sc. Alexandria University, Egypt. **Career:** Director of the Chemical Research Section of the Armed Forces; member of Free Officers' Movement; Director General, Atomic Energy Organization and Director of the Office of Scientific Research in the Presidency (1960); First Minister of Scientific Research (1961-64); Chairman, Atomic Energy Organisation (1964-67) led the Egyptian Delegation to the UN Conference on the application of Science and Technology (1963) and was elected Vice President of the Conference; Egyptian representative on Advisory Committee for the application of Science and Technology to development; Presidential Adviser on Scientific Research (1967-72); Chairman of the Council of Scientific Research; Council of Ministers of the Confederation of Arab Republics (1971); Director of Scientific and Technical Affairs in Arab League with special responsibilities for atomic energy; President of the Egyptian Scientific Professions Syndicate; President of the Development Consultants' Association; Regional Secretary of the World Federation of Scientific Workers. **Addr.:** Cairo, Egypt.

HIFNAWI (Mustafa, Mitwalli, al), Egyptian engineer. **Born** on February 1, 1923 in Samamoud, Egypt. **Married**, two children. **Educ.:** Alexandria University, Egypt; St. Andrews University, UK. **Dipl.:** B.Sc. in Civil Engineering (1946); Ph.D. (1951). **Career:** Assistant Professor and Lecturer at Ain Shams University, Cairo (1951-59); Scientific and Cultural Adviser to Egyptian Embassy in Austria (1959-60), and in London (1959-66); Vice Chairman, Greater Cairo Planning Commission (1966-73); Chairman, State Organisation for Physical planning (1973-75); Chairman, State Organisation for Housing, Building and Planning Research (1975-78); Minister of Housing, Egyptian Government (1978-80); Member of the Council for Housing and Construction; Head of Rural Development, Academy of Science and Technology; Emeritus professor, Ain Shams University, Cairo (1966-); Chairman of the Board, Misr Abu Dhabi Property Development Company (1983-). **Publ.:** "Housing Finance and Land Policies", Government Publications (1976); "Low-Cost Housing", 4 Volumes, Government Publications (1978); "National Policy for Housing in Egypt" (1978); "Housing Social Survey between 1952 and 1980 in Egypt", Govt. Publications (1983). **Member:** Egyptian Engineer's Syndicate; Egyptian Engineer's Society; Rotary Club; Automobile Club of Egypt) Gezira Sporting Club and Shooting Club. **Medal:** Medal of Merit, 1st Class, Egypt (1975). **Prof. Addr.:** 26 Sherif Street, Immobilia Bldg., Tel.: 758386, 770726, Telex: 93876 MAP-CO Un, Cairo, Egypt. **Priv. Addr.:** Flat 21, 6A Ismail Mohamed Street, Zamalek, Tel.: 403278, 407319, Cairo, Egypt.

HIJAZI (Arafat, Mahmood), Jordanian journalist. **Born** in 1927 in Hebron, Jordan. **Son** of Mahmoud Hijazi. **Married**, six children. **Educ.**: Diploma in Journalism from Egyptian National College. **Career:** Head of section, Jordanian Ministry of Interior (1952-55); Broadcaster and Producer for Jordan Radio (1956-59); Editor of "al-Manar" daily newspaper; Editor of "Akhbar al-Yaum" newspaper; Publisher and Editor of "al-Sabah" newspaper; Publisher and Editor of "Amman al-Massa" weekly; Editor of "al-Destour"; President of Jordanian Press Association (1970-73); President of Professional and Trade Unions Assembly (1970); Lecturer. **Member** of Permanent Office of Union of Arab Journalists (1970), member of Excutive of International Press Association; member of Palestine National Council. **Publ.**: Twenty books, mainly on Palestine (1950-74); translated "The Bulgarian Resistance and Palestine Liberation War" into Russian and Bulgarian. **Hobbies:** Travel, reading (specially military affairs). **Prof. Addr.**: c/o Al Destour newspaper, P.O.Box 591, Tel.: 664153, 669345, Amman, Jordan.

HIJAZI (Ismail), Jordanian statesman. **Born** in 1915 in Hebron, Jordan. **Married**, 12 children. **Educ.**: Secondary and Higher. **Dipl.**: Diploma in Agriculture; Certificate in Education. **Career:** Teacher; Headmaster; Minister of Agriculture in the Cabinet of Mr., Wasfi at-Tall (1965-67); Elected Deputy of Amman (1967); Minister of Reconstruction and Planning in the Cabinet of Mr. Saad Jomaa (1967); Member, Chamber of Deputies (1954-75). **Awards:** Star of Jordan, 1st Class; Order of the Holy Sepulchre. **Publ.**: many political and literary articles in Jordan Press. **Addr.**: Amman, Jordan.

HIJAZI (Narryman Asaad, Miss), University lecturer. **Born** in 1952, in Tripoli, Lebanon. **Dipl.**: B.Sc., Public Health, American University of Beirut, M.S. (Industrial Health), London University. **Career:** Member of King Faisal Society, Commission for Health; Lecturer in Protective Medicine Dept., King Abdulaziz University. **Hobby:** reading. **Addr.**: King Abdulaziz University, Faculty of Medicine, P.O.Box 1540, Jeddah, Saudi Arabia.

HIJAZI (Saad Sliman), Jordanian physician. **Born** in 1938 in Irbid, Jordan. **Married,** 1 son, 4 daughters. **Educ.**: Royal College of Physicians, Dublin, Eire; London University, UK. **Dipl.**: DCH in Child Health, Ph.D. in Child Growth and Nutrition. **Career:** Resident Doctor in Pediatrics, Amman Children's Hospital (1962-64); Fellow in Nutrition, Ann Arbor School of Public Health, USA (1964-65); Consultant in Pediatrics and Head of Nutrition, Asrafieh Hospital and Ministry of Health, Amman (1965-74); Portdoctoral Fellow at the Institute of Child Health, School of Medicine and Consultant at Amman University Hospital (1976-81), Associate Professor and Chairman of Community Medicine Department (1980-83); Member of numerous national and international societies and committees; Dean of Faculty of Medicine and Professor of Nutrition and Child Health, Jordan University of Science and Technology, Jordan (1983-91); Professor of Nutrition Child Health and Vice-President, JUST (1991-). **Publ.**: "Child Growth and Nutrition in Jordan" (Factors and Patterns), Royal Scientific Society Press, Amman (1976), "Mother and Child Health", a textbook for Nursing Students (in Arabic), Amman (1980); author and co-author of numerous contributions on pediatric subjects to "Jordan Medical Journal" and international medical publications in Europe and USA; co-author of several books. **Prof. Addr.**: Jordan University of Science and Technology, P.O.Box 3030, Tel.: 962-2-295111/ 2716, 2717, Fax: 962-2-295123, Telex: 55545 JUST JO. Irbid, Jordan.

HIKMAT (Yanal, Omar), Jordanian politician. **Born** in 1934 in Jordan. **Son** of Omar Hikmat. **Educ.**: B.A., University of California, Los Angeles (UCLA), USA (1956). **Career:** Head of Publications Council (1957); Foreign Ministry (1959-68); Attaché Embassy to Lebanon; Assistant Head of Royal Protocol (1968-70); Head of Royal Protocol (1971); Minister of Tourism and Antiquities (27 April 1989-1993). **Addr.**: Amman, Jordan.

HILAL (Ahmad, Ezzedin), Egyptian Engineer and politician. **Born** in 1924 in Alexandria (Egypt). **Educ.**: Faculty of Engineering, Cairo University; specialisation in petroleum production and refining in the Netherlands and the United Kingdom; Nasser Higher Military Academy (National Defence College). **Dipl.**: B.Sc. (Engineering), B.Sc. (Chemistry), Graduate Staff College. **Career:** Manager, Suez Petroleum Refinery; Director General, Operations Division, the Egyptian Petroleum Authority; Deputy Director General, Egyptian General Petroleum Corporation (EGYPC), Refining and Processing Affairs (1967-71); appointed Chairman of the Board, Egyptian General Petroleum Corporation (1971-73); Minister of Petroleum (1971-73); Minister of Petroleum (1973); Emissary of President Sadat after the War of October 1973; Minister of Petroleum (Sept. 1974- May 1980); Minister of Industry and Mineral Resources (Oct. 1977- May 1980); Deputy Prime Minister for Production and Minister of Petroleum (1980-84). **Addr.**: Cairo, Egypt.

HILAL (Fouad), Syrian executive. **Born** in 1934 in Aleppo, Syria. **Son** of Kamel Hilal **and** Mrs. Olga née Abdulmessih. **Single. Educ.**: American College, Aleppo; Syrian University, Damascus, Syria. **Dipl.**: Licentiate in Law (1957); Specialisation Certificate in Commercial Law. **Career:** Lawyer (since 1957); Managing Director of Syrian Maritime and Transport Agencies, SA (since 1970); Managing Director of Catoni Trading and Transport Company SA (since 1970); Secretary General of the Syrian Chamber of Shipping (1971-79); President of the Syrian Association of Travel Agents, Aleppo. **Author:** (In Arabic): Incentives of International Transit in Syria; Incentive of Tourism in Syria; Aleppo Tourist Guide, 1990, 1992 & 1994 (372 pages). **Member** of the Institute of Directors, London.

Prof. Addr.: P.O.Box 811, Tel.: 2211074, Fax: 2246155, Aleppo, Syria. **Priv. Addr.:** Baghdad Street, Tel.: 2219207, Aleppo, Syria.

HILAL (Karim Tawhid), Egyptian bank manager. **Born** in 1949. **Son** of Tawhid Hilal. **Married** in 1979, 2 sons. **Educ.:** Cairo University. **Dipl.:** B.A. Business Administration. **Career:** Joined Chase Manhattan & Manufacturers Hanover Trust Co., London (1971-72); Arab International Bank, Cairo (1972-73); Arab African International Bank, in various department, the last being Head of International Finance (1973-79); al-Bahrain Arab African Bank (1979-81); General Manager, Arab Asian Bank (1981); former Director, Arab Asian International Ltd. Hong Kong and Anglo Middle East Finance Co, Bahamas. **Publ.:** "Wanted an Arab Bank", Euromoney (April 1977); "Gulf Banking and the Asian Challenge", APS (1982). **Member:** Founding member and Fellow of Arab Bankers Association, London; Gezira Sporting Club, Cairo; Int. Automobile Club. **Hobbies:** Squash, Soccer, Tennis, Photography, Music and Reading. **Addr.:** P.O.Box 5619, Tel.: 233129, Telex: 8583 A/B ABMAL, Manama, Bahrain.

HILALI (Abdurrazzaq, al), Iraqi former bank executive. **Born** in 1916 in Basra. **Educ.:** High Teachers Training College and Law College (Graduate). **Career:** Assistant Chief, Royal Ceremonies; Assistant Master of Rural Teachers Schools (1942); Acting Director of Physical Training Department (1942-46); Superintendent of Social Affairs (1946-47); Former Assistant Director General of Agricultural Bank. **Publ.:** Author of "Social Talks and Views" (1944), "40 Days in London" (1945), "Reflections on Rural Reform" (1950) all in Arabic. **Award:** Order of Astor (3rd. Class) of Afghanistan. **Addr.:** A'shamiya, Haibat Khatoum 3-3-28, Baghdad, Iraq.

HILLAL (Ali, El-, Dean), Egyptian Minister of Youth, Egypt. **Born** on August 20, 1944 at Kalyoubia, Egypt. **Married** on July 21, 1966 to Miss Eglal A. Bahgat, 2 children: Bahaa (Male) (2/6/1968) and Nora (Female) (16/6/1972). **Educ.:** Faculty of Economic and Political Science, Cairo University, Egypt. McGill University, Canada. **Dipl.:** B.Sc. in Political Science 1964, Faculty of Economics and Political Science, Cairo University; MA. In Political Science (1968), McGill University, Canada; Ph.D. in Political Science 1972, McGill University, Canada. **Career:** Minister of Youth, Egypt, (1991-); Dean, Faculty of Economics and Political Science (1994-99); Secretary-General of the Supreme Council of Universities (1994-97); Chairman, Department of Political Science, Cairo University (1992-94); Director, Center of Political Research and Studies, Cairo University (1986-94). **Other Information:** Visiting Professor to the University of California, Los Angeles, Princeton University, Calgary University and the American University in Cairo. **Author** of many publications in Arabic and English. **Medals and Decorations:** Decoration of Arts and Sciences of the First Order in 1979. **Prof. Addr.:** Ministry of Youth, July 26 Str., Sphinx Square, Cairo, Egypt. Tel.: (202) 3461113, (202)3468859, Fax: (202)3469025.

HILMI (Mahdi, Ibrahim), Iraqi university professor. **Born** in December 1931 in Diwania. **Son** of Ibrahim Hilmi **and** Mrs., née Nouriya Khodr al-Khachali. **Married** in 1959 to Miss Fawzia Rachid al-Attar (Dentist), 4 children: Urfane, Rabab, Mustafa and Omar. **Educ.:** Colorado State University, Duke University (U.S.A.). **Dipl.:** Bachelor of Science, Master of Science, Doctor of Philosophy. **Career:** Laboratory Demonstrator (1959-62); Baghdad University, Instructor (1967); then Assistant Professor of Physiology, Mossul College of Medicine since 1971. **Publ.:** Author of several scientific studies. **Sport:** Tennis. **Hobby:** Photography. **Prof. Addr.:** Mossul, Tel.: 2241 (ext. 828), Iraq. **Priv. Addr.:** ad-Dawwasa, Mossul, Iraq.

HILMI (Mustafa Kamal Dr.), Egyptian statesman. **Born** in 1922. **Educ.:** Ain Shams University, Cairo. **Dipl.:** B.Sc., M.Sc. and Ph.D. in Philosophy of Science and Organic Chemistry. **Career:** Professor, Faculty of Engineering, Ain Shams University; Secretary General, High Council of the Universities (1962); Under-Secretary, Ministry of Higher Education; Egyptian Delegate to UNESCO, Paris (1971); Minister of Education (April 1974- May 1980); Minister of State for Education and Scientific Research (1980-85) and Deputy Prime Minister for Services (1983-85); Member in the Political Bureau of the National Democratic Party (since 1986 to present). and Speaker, Majlis Ash-Shoura. **Addr.:** Cairo, Egypt.

HIMD (Riyad, Ahmad Mohamad, bin), Saudi businessman. **Born** in 1953, in Jeddah, Saudi Arabia. **Son** of Ahmad Mohamad Bin Himd. **Educ.:** California University, USA; Georgetown University, Washington DC, USA. **Dipl.:** MBA; M.A. in Political Science. **Career:** Owner and Director of Saudi Economical Center, Jeddah, Saudi Arabia; General Manager, Commercial Department, Ahmed Mohamad Bin Himd Est.; member of Chamber of Commerce and Industry, Jeddah. **Medals:** Black Belt, 3rd Dan. member of JKA. **Sports:** Tennis, Karate, skiing, water skiing. **Addr.:** P.O.Box 5468, Jeddah, 21422, Saudi Arabia.

HIMDY (Fuad, Amin), Saudi businessman. **Born** in 1930 in Mecca, Saudi Arabia. **Son** of Amin Himdy. **Married**, seven children. **Career:** President, al-Imtiaz Trading and Industrial Co., Mecca; former President of Mecca Chamber of Commerce and Industry. **Hobbies:** Reading, poetry. **Prof. Addr.:** P.O.Box 412, Tel.: 5745278, Mecca, Saudi Arabia. and Mecca Chamber of Commerce and Industry, P.O.Box 1086, Mecca, Saudi Arabia. **Priv. Addr.:** Tel.: 5424828, 5732447, Mecca, Saudi Arabia.

HINDAWI (Dhoukan, Salim), Jordanian politician. **Born** on February 18, 1927 in Jordan. **Married**, 2 sons, 1 daughter, **Educ.:** Cairo Univesity, Egypt, also in USA. **Dipl.:** B.A. in Social Studies, MED. **Career:** Teacher (1950-53); Head master (1953-54); Principal of Teachers' Training College (1956-60); Assistant Under Secretary of Education (1961-65); Under Secretary, Minister of Information (1965); Minister of Information, Education and Social Affairs (1965-70); President of the Board of trustees, Community Arab College, President, Arab Community College Company; Ambassador to Kuwait (1970-73); Ambassador to Cairo, Egypt (1977-79); Minister of the State (1986); Minister of Education (1986-87); **Publ.:** "Palestinian Issue", textbook for Jordanian Schools. **Decor.:** Order of the Jordanian Star; Order of Kingdom of Saudi Arabia; Order of the Tunisian Republic; Order of the Egyptian Republic as well as several other decorations from various countries. **Hobby:** chess. **Prof. Addr.:** Community Arab College, P.O.Box 926845 Amman, Jordan. **Priv. Addr.:** P.O.Box 921699, Amman, Jordan.

HINNAWI (Mustafa Chalabi, Mahjoob, al), Egyptian army officer. **Born** in Upper Egypt. **Son** of Mahjoob al-Hinnawi. **Educ.:** Secondary and Military Academy. **Career:** Army Forces, Promoted Colonel then General, Commander-in-Chief Egyptian Army (1968-69). **Addr.:** Egyptian Headquarter, Egyptian Army, Cairo, Egypt.

HISHAM (Awad), Syrian banker. **Born** in 1936 in Deir Ezzor, Syria. **Son** of Zikki Hisham. **Married** in 1977, 4 daughters. **Educ.:** Arabic Baccalaureate. **Career:** 24 years in Banking. **Member** of the Board of Syrian Jordanian Bank; Acting Deputy General Manager and Member of the Board of Directors of Popular Credit Bank, Damascus, Syria. **Hobby:** Reading. **Addr.:** P.O.Box 2841, Tel.: 224636, 459192, Damascus, Syria.

HOKAIL (Abdelaziz Mohamad, al), Saudi executive. **Born** on 16 December 1942 at al-Majma'h. **Dipl.:** B.Sc. (Petroleum Engineering). **Career:** Manager, Oil Production Aramco (1974-78); Senior Vice President, Aramco (Arabian American Oil Company) since 1980; Appointed Member Saudi Aramco Board of Directors (March, 1989); Appointed Executive Vice President, Manufacturing Operations (December 1, 1992); Appointed Chairman of the Board of Directors, Saudi Aramco Shell Refinery Company (SASREF) (August, 1993). **Member:** Society of Petroleum Engineers; member of the Board, Organization of Vocational Training and Technical Education; has attended several conferences related to his career. **Publ.:** several studies and articles. **Addr.:** P.O.Box 1172, Aramco, Tel.: 8755980, Dhahran, Saudi Arabia.

HOMIEDAN (Abdullah, Hamad), Saudi University Professor. **Born** in 1951, Riyadh, Saudi Arabia. **Son** of Hamad A. Homiedan (businessman) **and** Mrs. née Nora S. Qarzai. **Married** in 1976 at Riyadh to Hind S. Jarallah, 4 children: Rana (1978), Majid (1981), Saleh (1985), Hamad (1992). **Educ.:** B.A., King Saud University, Riyadh (1975), English Language teaching, Institute of Riyadh (1976), M.A., Ph.D., University of Kansas, Lawrence (1983). **Career:** Teacher, Institute of Higher Technical Education (1975-1976); Teaching Assistant, English Department KSU (1976-1983); Assistant Professor, Center for European Languages & Translation (CELT) (1983-1990); Director, CELT (1990-1991); Director, Institute of Languages & Translation (1991). **Other Information:** Chairman of ILT, Council; Member of KSU Academic Council (board of Regents); Member of University Supreme Council. **Awards:** Doroth Hagland Award, Dissertation of the year 1983. **Sports:** Table Tennis, Walking. **Hobbies:** Travel, Reading. **Member:** TEFL, TESOL. **Credit Card:** Visa. **Priv. Addr.:** Tel.: 4675127, Fax: 4678803, Saudi Arabia.

HOMOOD (Kamal, al), Jordanian diplomat. **Born** in 1921 in Jordan. **Widower. Educ.:** Aley National College, Lebanon; University of London, UK. **Dipl.:** Diploma in International Relations. **Career:** Officer in the Jordanian Army (1941-50); Military Attaché, Jordan Embassy in London, UK (1946-50); Foreign Ministry (1950-52), Head of Royal Protocol (1952-54); counsellor, Embassy of Jordan in London (1954-56); Charge d'Affaires, Embassy to Iran (1957); Minister Plenipotentiary, Embassy to Chile (1957-61); Ambassador to Iran (1962); Head of Ceremonies Department, Ministry of Foreign Affairs (1960-64); Ambassador to India (1964-68); Ambassador to Iraq (1969-71); Head of Political Department, Ministry of Foreign Affairs (1971-72); Acting Secretary General at the Foreign Ministry (1972); Ambassador to the Arab League (1972-73); Ambassador to USSR (1973-77); Secretary General to the Foreign Ministry (1977-79); Ambassador to China (1979-87); Ambassador at Ministry of Foreign Affairs, Amman (1987-); Retired (1987). **Medal:** numerous medals and decorations. **Prof. Addr.:** P.O.Box 5135, Zehran Post Office, Amman, Jordan.

HOMSI (Naoom, Victor), Syrian chairman of company. **Born** on May 14, 1921 in Paris, France. **Son** of Victor Homsi (Merchant) **and** Mrs., née Nada Hindieh. **Married** in January 1969 to Mrs. Eva Manachi Rabbath. **Educ.:** St. Louis de Gonzague College (Paris), St. Joseph University (Beirut). **Dipl.:** L.L.B. (St. Joseph University). **Career:** Deputy General-Director of the Electricity and Transports Office of Aleppo City, living in Lebanon since 1960, President of the "Recherches et Réalisations Industrielles" S.A.L. (1960). **Member** of the Touring Club. **Addr.:** Beirut, Lebanon.

HORANIEH (George), Syrian executive. **Educ.:** Licence en Droit, Faculty of Law, Damascus University, Syria (1965); Dip. of Advanced Studies in Economics; Faculté de Droit et de Sciences Economiques, Ph.D. Paris. **Career:** Department of Studies and Planning and Chief, Economic Bureau of the Governor, Central Bank of Syria (1970); Chief Economist, Economic Bureau of the President of the Republic of Syria (1973); Minister of State for

Planning Affairs, Syrian Government (1976); Chief Executive, Gefinor Investment Management Co. SAL, London. **Addr.:** 23 Avenue de la Porte Neuve, Luxembourg.

HOSHAN (Ahmed Hamad, Al), Saudi executive. **Born** in 22.11.1933 in Madinah, Saudi Arabia. **Career:** General Manager, Government Employees Cooperative Society, Riyadh; Member of the Board, Riyadh Chamber of Commerce; Founder Member, Saudi Cairo Bank; Editor; in Chief, "Yamamah" Riyadh Newspaper (Arabic); C.E.O., Yamamah Press Establisment Chairman, Hoshanco Group. **Prof. Addr.:** Hoshanco, Head Office, P.O.Box 59 Riyadh 11411, Saùdi Arabia. Tel.: 00966-1-4766800, Fax: 00966 1 4775977, E-Mail: chairman@hoshanPG.com

HOSHAN (Mohamad, H., al), Saudi lawyer. **Born** on April 14, 1929 in Madina, Saudi Arabia. **Married,** 2 sons, 4 daughters. **Educ.:** Cairo University, Faculty of Law, Egypt; University of Poitiers, France; University of Paris, France. **Dipl.:** LL.B., Diploma in Higher Studies, LL.D. **Career:** Director General of Pensions Department, Ministry of Finance and National Economy (1957-61); Legal Adviser, Ministry of Finance and National Economy (1961-70); Senior Officer for Specialized Studies, Legal Department, Organization of Petroleum Exporting Countries (OPEC) (1966-68); Assistant Professor of Law and Chairman of Law Department, University of Riyadh (1970-73); Attorney at Law. **Publ.:** Co-author of "Introduction to the Study of Law: a comparative approach"; Editor of the "Saudi Arabian Legal Encyclopaedia", a commentary on and a compilation of Saudi regulations and laws (in Arabic and English). **Hobbies:** Sifism, biographies, swimming, photography, philosophy. **Prof. Addr.:** P.O.Box 2626, Riyadh, Saudi Arabia and P.O.Box 25888, Riyadh, Saudi Arabia.

HOSNI (Ahmad, Hussein), Egyptian executive. **Born** in 1927 in Tanta, Egypt. **Son** of Hussein Hosni. **Married** in 1961, 1 son, 2 daughters. **Educ.:** Cairo University, B.Com. Accountancy (1949); Manchester University, B.A. Commerce, England. (1954); Chartered Accountant (1958). **Career:** Senior Accountant, Economic Development Organisation; Assistant Manager, General Public Organisation for Engineering; Associate Professor, Professor, Deputy Director and Chairman, National Institute of Management Development; Export Consultant to I.L.O. and UNIDO; Consultant in Industrial Management, Yemen Arab Republic; Managing Director, Finance, Egyptian Poultry Co. Consultant, The Arab Investment Bank, Cairo, Egypt. **Member:** Institute of Chartered Accountants in England and Wales; Egyptian Society for Accountants and Auditors; Heliopolis Sporting Club, Heliopolis, Egypt. **Publ.:** "How to make Budgets more Effective"; "Management Accounting and Operations Research"; "The Game Theory"; "Cost of Capital as a Criterion for Capital Investment". **Hobby:** Swimming. **Addr.:** 126 Nozha Street, Tel.: 875578, Heliopolis, Cairo, Egypt.

HOSNY (Mohamed Wafik), Egyptian, alternate executive director, World Bank, Washington, DC. USA. **Born** in 1934. **Married. Educ.:** Aïn Shams University, Cairo, Egypt. University of London, UK., M.Sc. in Economics. **Career:** Shell Oil Company, Egypt (1954-57); Second Secretary, Embassy of Egypt to Sweden (1957-62); First Secretary, Research Department at the Ministry of Foreign Affairs (1962-64); Study Leave, University of London (1964-67); Head of Economic Section, Department of International Organisation (1968-69); Head, Technical Assistance Section, Department of International Organization, Ministry of Foreign Affairs, Egypt (1969-72); Economic Affairs Minister, Permanent Mission of Egypt to United Nations, New York (1972-76); Director, Department of International Economic Relations, Ministry of Foreign Affairs (1976-79); Ambassador of Egypt to Bucharest, Romania (1979-83); Director, Department of International Economic Relations (1983-86); Former, Alternate Executive Director, World Bank, Washington, DC. USA. **Publ.:** "Oil, Development Cooperation and the International Monetary System"; "Money, Inflation and Economic Development in Egypt"; "The New International Economic Order, Africa: from Cooperation to Economic Integration: The Lagos Plan of Action"; "The Role of Private Initiative in Economic Development: Prospects for African Countries". **Hobbies:** Economic and Diplomatic Matters, Swimming. **Member:** Guizera Sporting Club, Cairo, Egypt; Tennley Sporting Club, Washington, DC. **Addr.:** Cairo, Egypt.

HOSSAYAN (Mohamad, Mutlaq, al), Kuwaiti executive. **Born** in 1948 in Kuwait. **Son** of Multaq al-Hossayan. **Married** in 1974, 2 sons and 2 daughters. **Dipl.:** B.Sc. in Mechanical Engineering (1972). **Career:** Mechanical Engineer, Kuwait National Petroleum Co.; Vice Chairman, SAMIA, Mauritania; Manager, Real Estate, Kuwait Foreign Trading Contracting and Investment Co. KFTCIC, Safat, Kuwait; Chairman: Mubarakiah Poultry, Kuwait; Arab Trading Steel Co., Bahrain; Vice Chairman, SNIM (mining company); Arab Iron and Steel Co.; al-Mutlaq Real Estate Co., Kuwait. **Hobbies:** Swimming and soccer. **Addr.:** P.O.Box 5665, Tel.: 2412535, Telex: 2021, 2035 MAADEN KT, Safat, Kuwait.

HOUHOU (Djamel Eddine), Algerian politician. **Born** on October 23, 1934 in Algeria. **Married,** 3 children. **Educ.:** Secondary and Higher. **Dipl.:** (DES) in Economics. **Career:** Director of French Relations, Ministry of Foreign Affairs (1962-71); Ambassador to Canada (1971-74); Ambassador to Egypt (1974-77); Minister of Youth and Sports (1977-82); Member, Central Committee, FLN (1979); Ambassador Extraordinary and Plenipotentiary to France (1979-84); Minister of Public Health (1984-91). **Addr.:** Algiers, Algeria.

HOUM (Abdelmajid, al), Algerian diplomat. **Born** in 1934. **Married,** 4 children. **Dipl.:** Diploma in Political Science. **Career:** Director of School Instruction, Ministry of Education (1963-65); Protocol Director, President's Council (1966-67); Advisor to President Boumediene, And Secretary General (1973-79); Member of the General Committee FLN (1979); Minister of Tourism (1979-84); Ambassador Plenipotentiary and Extraordinary to Moscow, USSR (1984-1990). **Prof. Addr.:** Ministry of Foreign Affairs, Algiers, Algeria.

HOUMED (Gadito, Hassanle), Djibouti Deputy at the National Assembly, and Businessman. **Born** in 1945 in Dikhil. **Career:** Businessman. Member of Central Committee of RPP; Elected Deputy at the National assembly (18/12/1992 - to date); Member of National Reconciliation; Member of Permanent Commission and Member for Social Development and Environment Protection. **Prof. Addr.:** National Assembly, P.O.Box 138 Djibouti, Djibouti.

HOURIEH (Mohamad, Ali), Syrian academic. **Born** on July 19, 1934 in Lattakia, Syria. **Married,** 2 children. **Educ.:** Imperial College, University of London, UK; American Institute of Chemical Engineering, USA; University of Washington, USA. **Dipl.:** B.Sc., Ph.D. in Chemistry, Diploma in Chemical Engineering. **Career:** Member of American Chemical Society Washington, USA, American Nuclear Society, USA and American Institute of Chemical Engineers; Professor of Chemistry, University of Aleppo (1976-); President, University of Aleppo (1979-). **Publ.:** "Chemistry" (in Arabic) in 1967, "Organic Chemistry" (in Arabic) in 1968, "Analytical Chemistry" (1970), "Modern Methods of Chemical Analysis", "Studies on Photoionization" (1966) in English; several papers on energy. **Member:** the National Geographic Society (USA). **Prof. Addr.:** University of Aleppo, P.O.Box 686, Aleppo, Syria.

HOUSNI (Mohamad), Iraqi artist and sculptor. **Born** in Iraq. **Educ.:** In Iraq and in France. **Dipl.:** Diploma (Paris). **Career:** Artist Sculptor, Professor at the Fine Arts Institute of Baghdad, Contributed to several Arts Exhibitions in Iraq and France. **Member** of Artists Association of Iraq. **Addr.:** Baghdad, Iraq.

HOUT (Shafik, al), Palestinian politician. **Born** in 1932 in Jaffa. **Son** of Ibrahim al-Hout. **Educ.:** American University of Beirut, Lebanon (1953). **Dipl.:** graduated in science; B.A. in Psychology. **Career:** School master in Beirut, then in Kuwait; became one of the staff of "al-Hawadess", a Lebanese leading weekly magazine (1956); Editor of al-Hawadess; appointed Director of PLO Political Office in Beirut (1964); helped forming Abtal al-Auda (Heroes of Return) in 1966, a guerrilla organization later joined to the PDFLP; contributing editor of "al-Muharrir" official magazine. Member of the PLO Executive Committee (resigned in August 1993). **Addr.:** Tunis, Tunisia.

HOUTY (Abdul Rahman, Ibrahim), Kuwaiti former minister. **Born** in 1938 in Kuwait. **Married,** four children. **Educ.:** B.Sc. in Engineering, University of California, Berkeley, USA. **Career:** Ministry of Electricity and Water (1963); Ministry of Information (1964); Chief Engineer and Assistant Under Secretary, Ministry of Information (1965-87); Minister of Public Works (1988-89); President of Kuwait Society of Engineers; represented Kuwait at several conferences on Radio and Television Broadcasting in Canada, Switzerland, Egypt, Iraq, Bahrain, Qatar and Kuwait. **Hobbies:** Touring, sea fishing. **Addr.:** Kuwait City, Kuwait.

HRAYMAL (Issa, Khalfan, al), UAE diplomat. **Born** in 1946 in Sharjah, United Arab Emirates. **Married,** 3 sons. **Dipl.:** B.A. in Geography. **Career:** 3rd Secretary, Foreign Ministry, Abu Dhabi, UAE (1970-71); UAE Consul General in Bombay, India (1973-74); Ambassador to Algeria; Ambassador to Saudi Arabia (1987-). **Hobbies:** Politics, economics, poetry, reading. **Prof. Addr.:** Embassy Of UAE, P.O.Box 94385 Riyadh 11693, Saudi Arabia.

HUBAISHI (Hussein Ali, al), Yemeni politician and lawyer. **Born** on March 4, 1927 in Aden. **Son** of Ali al-Hubaishi. **Married** in 1958 to Margaret (Zahr), 2 children: Tariq and Salwa. **Educ.:** Secondary studies (1949). **Dipl.:** Graduated in International Law; Licence in Law (1955); Diploma in Education Administration. **Career:** Teacher (1948); Principal, Belqis College (1964-68); Deputy Prime Minister for Economic and Foreign Affairs for six months in 1969; Legal Adviser to the Presidential Council and Council of Minister and Head of State Legal Office (1968); Minister of State and Adviser to the Presidency and Council of Minister (March 1979); Legal Adviser and former Minister of State (June 1982). **Member:** Board of Yemen Airlines Corporation; Board of Sanaa University; Board of International School; Board of the Yemen National School; Board of the Centre for Yemeni Studies. **Hobbies:** Education, law, customs (anthropology and sociology), walking, reading, writing. **Addr.:** The Legal Office, Republican Palace, Tel.: 2752, Sanaa, Republic of Yemen.

HUDAITHI (Abdullah, I., al), Saudi businessman. **Born** in 1944 at al-Bekarriah, Qassim, Saudi Arabia. **Dipl.:** B.A. (Commerce) Riyadh University. **Dipl.:** in Public Administration Birmingham university, United Kingdom. **Career:** Founding Member of several companies and corporations; an official of the Ministry of Agriculture and water (1967-75); member of the Board, Manufacturing & Building Co. Ltd. (MABCO), Saudi Continental Insurance Co, Arab National Bank, Arab Solar Energy Co. (SHAMSCO), Arabian Lamah, Makkah Hotel Co. and the Arab and Saudi Tennis Federation, Saudi Hotels & Resort Areas Co., Saudi advanced Industries Co., Middle East Propulsion Center; Vice President Asian Tennis Federation: Chairman, Coaching Committee of Asian Tennis Federation, Central Corporation (CECORP) and the Saudi Vetonit Company (Saveto); **Publ.:** several social and sports articles in the period 1960 to 1970. **Hobbies:** Sport, reading. **Prof. Addr.:** P.O.Box 1549, Riyadh 11441, Tel.: 4778421, Saudi Arabia.

HUGAIL (Abdallah, Mohamad, al), Saudi businessman. **Born** in 1940 in Saudi Arabia. **Son** of Mohamad al-Hugail. **Married**, four children. **Educ.:** Degree in Arabic. **Career:** Assistant to the Secretary of Management, Ministry of Planning; General Manager of Employee Relations, Ministry of Municipalities; General Manager of Ministry of Municipalities; Assistant Deputy Minister of Municipalities; Partner, Trading and Development Partnership, Electrical and Mechanical Supplies, Arab-German Civil Works Co. Ltd., Civil Construction and Contracting, Moroweh Public Relations and Advertising Co., member of the Founding Committee of Saudi Cairo Bank; Chairman, Saudi British Bank, Riyadh. **Publ.:** Articles on literature, politics and social sciences. **Sports:** Swimming, table tennis. **Addr.:** P.O.Box 1327, Tel.: 4039607, 4039871, 4013204, 4013520, Riyadh, Saudi Arabia.

HULABY (Abdul Aziz, S., al), Saudi academic. **Born** in 1941 at Qassim, Saudi Arabia. **Dipl.:** B.A., King Saud University, Ph.D., St. Andrews University, U.K. **Career:** Professor, King Abdulaziz University (1975); Professor, Department of History, King Saud University (1976-78); Vice Dean, Faculty of Arts, King Saud University. **Member:** Society of History and Archaeology; Centre of Scientific Research, Faculty of Arts, member of Council of same Faculty and of the Department of History; attended the symposium on the History of the Arabian Peninsula and the symposium on Information Studies in the Arab World. **Hobbies:** Reading, music, travel. **Addr.:** Faculty of Arts, King Saud University, Tel.: 4811000, Riyadh, Saudi Arabia.

HUMAIDAN (Ali), UAE diplomat. **Born** in 1931. **Married. Educ.:** Baghdad University, Iraq; University of Paris, France. **Dipl.:** Licence in law; Doctorate in Political Science. **Career:** Deputy Representative of Kuwait to UNESCO, Paris, France (1967-69); Professor, Political Science Department, University of Kuwait (1969-70); Legal Adviser for Federal Affairs, Government of Abu Dhabi, UAE (1971-72); Permanent Representative (with rank of Ambassador) of the UAE to the UN, New York (1972-80); UAE Ambassador to Canada (1976-80); Director of the Department of International Organisations, Ministry of Foreign Affairs, U.A.E. (1982-87); Ambassador of U.A.E. to Syria (1987-89), Retired in 1989. **Addr.:** Dr. Ali HUMAIDAN, Advocate and Legal Consultant, P.O.Box 3470, Abu Dhabi, U.A.E.

HUMAIDAN (Humaidan Abdallah, al), Saudi academic. **Born** in 1944 at Qassim, Saudi Arabia. **Dipl.:** B.A. (Islamic Law), Faculty of Shari'a; Ph.D. (Law), St. Andrew's University, U.K. (1973). **Career:** Demonstrator, Faculty of Shari'a (Islamic Law) (1966); Assistant Professor, Umm al-Qura University, Mecca. **Addr.:** Umm al-Qura University, Tel.: 5564770, Mecca, Saudi Arabia.

HUMAIDAN (Ibrahim, Mohamed), Bahraini politician. **Born** in 1939. **Married. Educ.:** Cairo University, Egypt; Rabat University, Morocco. **Career:** private practice as lawyer in Bahrain; Assistant Public Prosecutor, then Public Prosecutor; Legal Adviser, Ministry of Labour and Social Affairs (1972-75); Chairman, Bahrain Telecommunications Co.; Minister of Transport (1975-1995); Minister of State (1995-1996). Presently, President, The Consultive Council. **Prof. Addr.:** P.O.Box 10325, Manama, Bahrain.

HUMAIZI (Yaqub, al), Kuwaiti businessman. **Born** in 1930 in Kuwait. **Married. Educ.:** Cairo University, Egypt; Liverpool University, UK. **Career:** Private enterprise; member of the Constituent Assembly (1962); Chairman, Livestock Transport and Trading Company (1973-82). **Hobbies:** Travel, aquatic sports. **Prof. Addr.:** Livestock Transport and Trading Company, Arabian Gulf Street, P.O.Box 42, Tel.: 873784, Telex: 22336, Kuwait, Kuwait.

HUSNI (Adel, Muhammad), Egyptian businessman. **Born** in 1938 in Alexandria, Egypt. **Married**, 3 children. **Educ.:** Cairo University, Egypt; New York University, USA. **Dipl.:** B.Sc. in Commerce, Ph.D. in Business Management. **Career:** Member of Higher Specialised Councils, Corniche el-Nil, Cairo, Egypt; Owner and Chairman of Sphinx Tours, Alexandria, New York and Los Angeles (1966-). **Member:** Gezira Sporting Club, Heliopolis Sporting Club. **Prof. Addr.:** 2 Behler Street, Kasr el-Nil, Cairo, Egypt. **Priv. Addr.:** 16 Osman Abdel Hafiz Street, Madinat Nasr, Cairo, Egypt.

HUSSAMI (Argan), Syrian executive. **Born** in 1923 in Damascus, Syria. **Son** of Saad al-Dine Houssami. **Married,** in 1959. **Educ.:** Academic; Bachelor's Degree in Law. **Career:** Joined Syrian Lebanese Bank (1947); Bank Official, Central Bank of Syria (1958); Head of the Inspection Dept. and Head of the Banking Control Dept.; Secretary General, Central Bank of Syria, Damascus, Syria (1982-). **Addr:** 29 Ayar Street, P.O.Box 2254, Tel.: 224800-2, Telex: 11007, 119186, 11910-11 A/B MARKAZISYR, Damascus, Syria.

HUSSAMI (Mazhar), Syrian businessman. **Born** in 1918 in Syria. **Educ.:** Licence en Droit, Faculty of Law, Damascus. **Career:** President, Mazhar Houssani & Bros. (1953); Chairman, Middle East Construction Co. SAL (1962); Chairman Trade Exchange Co. SAL (1966). Director, Gefinor Investment Ltd. (1982-); Société de Développment Immobilier SAL (1982-); Société Nationale pour les Projets Fonciers SAL (1982-); Chairman, Middle East Construction Co. SAL; Trade Exchange Co. SAL.; Director, Gefinor Real Estate N.V., Geneva, Switzerland. **Addr.:** 23 Avenue de la Porte Neuve, Luxembourg.

HUSSEIN (Abdillahi), Somali banker. **Born** in 1947 in Hargeisa. **Son** of Haji Hussein Omar. **Married** in 1973, 1 son, 3 daughters. **Educ.:** Banking Diploma. **Career:** Officer Trainee, Grindlays Bank Ltd. Hergeisa, Somalia (1965-66); Head Office, London (1966-68); Hargeisa Covenanted Officer (1968-70); Manager (1970-71); Branch Manager, Banco di Roma, Mogadishu (1971-73); Internal Auditor, Currency Board (Central Bank), Abu Dhabi (1973-78); Manager, Banking Supervision Department, UAE Central Bank, Abu Dhabi, UAE (1978-85). **Member:** Institute of Bankers, London; Institute of Internal Auditors, UK Charter. **Hobbies:** Swimming, music and travel. **Addr.:** Mogadishu, Somalia.

HUSSEIN (Abdirizak, Haji), Somali diplomat. **Born** on December 24, 1924 at Galcaio, Somalia. **Married**, with children. **Educ.:** Self-education. **Career:** Director of Studies, Somali Youth League, Mogadishu (1944-54); Petitioner, UN Trusteeship Council, New York (1955), President, Somali Youth League (1956-57); Somali University Institute, Mogadishu (1957-59); Member, National Assembly (Somalia) (1959-60); Minister of Communications and Public Works (1962-64); Director, Democratic Action Party, Mogadishu (1966-69); Chief, Delegation of Somalia, UN General Assembly (1973-74); Ambassador, Permanent Representative of Somalia (1974). **Prof. Addr.:** Ministry of Foreign Affairs, Mogadishu, Somalia.

HUSSEIN (Abdul Aziz), Kuwaiti statesman. **Born** in 1920 in Kuwait. **Married** in 1948, 2 sons and 1 daughter. **Educ.:** Primary Schooling in Kuwait; Faculty of Letters, Cairo University; Post-Graduate studies in Cairo and London. **Dipl.:** B.A. (Arabic Language and Literature). **Career:** Director, Kuwait Cultural Bureau, Cairo (1945-50); Director-General, Department of Education (Kuwait) (1952-61); Kuwait Representative at UNO (1961); Ambassador of the State of Kuwait to Egypt, also accredited to the Arab League, Cairo (1961-63); Minister of State for Cabinet Affairs (Kuwait) (1963-65); Minister of State for Cabinet Affairs and Chairman of the National Council for Culture, Arts and Letters (1971-85); Adviser to His Highness the Amir of Kuwait since 1985. **Chairman:** Overal Planning of Arab Culture Committee. **Member:** the Board of Trustees, of the Institute of Arabic and Islamic Sciences at the University of Frankfurt; the International Fund for the Promotion of Culture (Unesco). **Publ.:** "Kuwait Society". **Prof. Addr.:** Amiri Diwan, Seif Palace, Kuwait. Tel: 2424282.

HUSSEIN (Abdul Razzak), Kuwaiti businessman. **Born** in 1939 in Kuwait. **Married**, 2 sons. **Educ.:** University of California, Berkeley, USA. **Dipl.:** B.Sc. in Petroleum Engineering. **Career:** Kuwait Oil Company; Assistant Under Secretary, Ministry of Oil; Managing Director and Deputy Chairman, Planning Administration and Finance, Kuwait Petroleum Corporation (1980); Member, Kuwait Institute for Scientific Research, the International Energy Development Corporation, the Arabian Oil Company; Member of the Board, Santa Fe International Corporation; former Deputy Chairman and Managing Director of Kuwait Foreign Petroleum Exploration Company. **Addr.:** Kuwait, Kuwait.

HUSSEIN (Abdulkader Muhammad), Saudi Businessman. **Born** in 1932 in Mecca, Saudi Arabia. **Married** to Mrs. Bahija Kamel Mufti (Wife); having 1 son and 6 daughters. **Educ.:** B.A. (1956); M.A. (1958); M.B.A. (1975). **Career:** Worked for the Ministry of Post and Telecommunications (for 14 years); President, Saudi Center for International Trade & Technical Supplies (I.T.T.S.) (1987-till present); Company General Manager (for about 17 years); Member of the Board of Director of BETA CO.; Governmental Public Relation Manager, Detecon Al-Saudia Co. **Hobbies:** Swimming, Horse-ridding and Football. **Member:** Al-Etihad Club and Al-Wehda Club. **Prof. Addr.:** P.O.Box 15671, Riyadh 11454, Saudi Arabia E-Mail: scitts.sa@zajil.net

HUSSEIN (Ahmad Mahmood, Ould, al), Mauritanian army officer. **Born** in 1938 at Moor, Mauritania. **Son** of el-Hussein Ould Nagi (Cattle Breeder). **Married** To Miss Khadijetou mint Sidi Haiba, 4 children. **Educ.:** Koran school in Boutilimit (1947-53); Boutilimit Teacher Training College (1953-57); Armour and Cavalry School, Saumur (France) (1960-61); Ecole d'Application de Saint Maixent (1964-65); General Staff College (France) (1969-70). **Dipl.:** CEPE (1953), CAP (1957); Graduate Armour and Cavalry school (1961); Graduate General Staff School. **Career:** Assistant teacher (1957-60); Head of Military Section (1961-62); Deputy Military Commander (1962-63); Commander Military Unit (1963-66); Head of Instruction Directorate, National General Staff (1966-68); Deputy Chief of Staff (1970). **Awards:** Knight, Order of National Merit (France); Medal of Honour (Mauritania). **Addr.:** Nouakchott, Mauritania.

HUSSEIN (Aziza, Shukry, Mrs.), Egyptian international civil servant. **Born** on May 30, 1919 at Zifta, Gharbiyah Governorate, Egypt. **Married**, with children. **Educ.:** American University in Cairo (1940-42); Institute for Social and Criminological Research, Cairo (1970). **Dipl.:** B.A. (Social Science) (1942). **Career:** Appointed, UN Commission on Status of Woman since 1962; Member, Ad Hoc Committee on Fertility studies, UN (1966): Member, UN Advisory Mission on Family Planning to Pakistan (1968); Vice President for Middle East and North Africa, International Planned Parenthood (1970); Chairman, Expert Group on the Role of Women in Development, UN (1972); Rapporteur, National Commission on Status of Women, Cairo; Chairman, Cairo Family Planning Association; Vice Chairman, Governing Body, International Planned Parenthood since 1973, Rapporteur, working Group for UN Convention on Elimination of Discrimination Against Women (1974); Member, UN Comission on the Status of Women. **Publ.:** Author of "Role of Egyptian Women in Social Reform" (1954), "Egyptian Children in an Era of Awakening" (1959), "Changing condition of women and its effect on children" (1967), "Status of women in family law in the United Arab Republic" (1964). **Awards:** Kamal Medal (1955); Imitizia award for social service (1972). **Member of:** UN Association; Red Crescent Society; President, Cairo Women's Club; Franklin Book Programme; Romanian-Egyptian Friendship Society; Hoda Sharawy Society; Friend of the Routist Society; International Peace Academy. **Hobbies:** Music and reading. **Sport:** Swimming, yoga. **Prof. Addr.:** UN Commission on the Status of Women, 3 Midan Moustafa Kamel, Tel.: 918857, Cairo, Egypt. **Priv. Addr.:** 10, Ahmed Nessim street, Giza District, Tel.: 842031, Cairo, Egypt.

HUSSEIN (Hamzah, Abbas), Kuwaiti banker. **Born** in 1934 in Kuwait. **Educ.:** American University of Beirut. Attended several postgraduate courses in money and banking (1960-62). **Career:** Government Official (1959); Administrative Assistant, Civil Service Commission (1959-60); Secretary and Currency Officer, Kuwait Currency Board (1963-68); Deputy Governor General, Bank of Kuwait (1968-73); Governor (1973); Chairman, Banking Studies Centre of Kuwait (1970-). **Addr.:** Kuwait City, Kuwait.

HUSSEIN (Hassan), Egyptian executive. **Born** in 1951 in Alexandria, Egypt. **Son** of Mahmood Hussein. **Married** in 1977, 1 daughter. **Educ.:** College de la Salle, Cairo Egypt; Cairo University BBA (1973); Computer Science Certificate (1973); French Literature Certificate. **Career:** Loan Syndication Officer, Arab African International Bank (1974-76); Training in Euro-Market Specialisations, Berliner Handels Gesselschaft Und Frankfurter Bank (BHF-Frankfurt); Senior Assistant Manager, Citibank Lending Officer (1976-79); Citibank Middle East and North Africa Training Centre (1976-77); ARLABANK; Head, Regional Marketing and Syndications Group, Arab Latin American Bank, Bahrain (1979-). **Member:** Arab Bankers' Association, London. **Hobbies:** Football, tennis and judo. **Addr.:** Government Road, P.O.Box 5070, Tel.: 232124, Telex: 9345 A/B ARLABK, Manama, Bahrain.

HUSSEIN (Hussain Abdul Latif), Saudi civil servant. **Born** in 1931 in Mecca, Saudi Arabia. **Educ.:** received general education. **Career:** Has held several government posts including Assistant Director, General Bureau, Ministry of Finance; Director, Department of Financial Representation and Director, Department of Government Property; Director General of Alms and Income Tax Department; member of the Board, Agricultural Bank; member of Foreign Capital Investments Committee; Chairman, Disciplinary Action Board, Ministry of Finance; member of Maccah Welfare Society; has attended several Arab League conferences and several international conferences on taxation. **Prof. Addr.:** 13 Mutanabi Street, Malaz, Tel.: 4044058, Riyadh. **Priv. Addr.:** Tel.: 4778333, Riyadh, Saudi Arabia.

HUSSEIN (Hussain, Mustafa), Egyptian academic. **Born** in 1939. **Married,** 3 children. **Educ.:** Ain Shams University, Cairo; Cairo University, Cairo; International Institute of General Management, Paris, France. **Dipl.:** LL.B., Diploma in Management Law and General Management. **Career:** Assistant Administrator (1962-72); Legal Adviser for Governorate of Aswan (1975); Member of the Board of High Institute for Social Services, Governorate of Aswan (1975); Professor of Management Law at Ennaba University, Algiers (1976-82); Secretary General, National Judiciary Studies Centre (1984-85). **Publ.:** "Management Law" (1976), "Local Management" (1977), "Working Law" (1978). **Hobby:** Tennis. **Member:** National Sports Club, Cairo. **Prof. Addr.:** National Judiciary Studies Centre, al-Abassi Square, Cairo, Egypt. **Priv. Addr.:** 13 al-Dabour al-Frenzawy, Abou el-Ela, Cairo, Egypt.

HUSSEIN (Mansour Ibrahim), Egyptian politician. **Born** in 1923. **Career:** Former school teacher and headmaster in el-Fayoum; Ministry of Planning (1962-67); First Under Secretary, then Deputy Minister of Education (1977-84); member Shoura (Advisory) Council (1981); President Egyptian Teachers' Union; Minister of Education (1985-87). **Publ.:** many books and studies in the field of education. **Addr.:** Cairo, Egypt.

HUSSEIN (Mohamad, Taha), Egyptian academic. **Born** on February 14, 1929 in Cairo, Egypt. **Married,** 1 son, 1 daughter. **Educ.:** Dusseldorf College of Applied Arts, West Germany; Cologne University, West Germany. **Dipl.:** Ph.D. **Career:** Teacher (1954-55); Teacher at the Faculty of Arts, Ministry of Higher Education (1955-57); Visiting Fellow, Cologne University, West Germany (1957-63); Professor at the Faculty of Arts, Ministry of Higher Education (1963-69), Section Head (1969-78); Dean at the Faculty of Arts, Helwan University (12978-81); Member of International Graphics Association (1980); High Council for Culture (1980). **Publ.:** "Influence of Islamic Art on Western Art" (1963), "Catalogue of Ten Egyptian Artis in Essen Museum", West Germany (1970). **Decor.:** Order of Merit for Graphics (1st Class) (1952), Order of Merit for Photography (1st Class) (1982). **Member:** Cairo Shooting Club, Cairo. **Addr.:** 22, 4 Vieny Street, Dokki, Cairo, Egypt.

HUSSEIN (Mustafa, Mahmoud), Egyptian writer. **Born** on December 27, 1921 in Shibeen al-Kuom, Menofiah, Egypt. **Married,** 1 son, 1 daughter. **Educ.:** Cairo Medical College, Egypt. **Dipl.:** M.B. **Career:** practised until 1960; Editor of "Rose al-Yusif" magazine (1954-). **Publ.:** several studies of Islamic literature; numerous novels, short story collections and plays. "Rajol Tahta al-Sefr" Novel (1970). **Award:** State Prize for the Best Novel

(1970). **Addr.:** Masjed Mahmoud, Maidan Gamiat al-Dowal al-Arabiah, al-Mohandiseen, Cairo, Egypt.

HUSSEIN (Raad Bin Zeid, el, H.H. Prince), Lord Chamberlain to His Majesty Late King Hussein of Jordan the' Royal Hashemite Court. **Born** in Berlin in 1936. **Son** of Emir Zeid el-Hussein, one of the four sons of Sherif Hussein bin Ali, of the Hejaz, the father of the Arab Revolt of 1916. **Married,** five children, four sons and a daughter. **Educ.:** Completed his elementary education in Baghdad, and secondary education in Victoria College, Alexandria, Egypt. In 1960 he earned his B.A. Degree with Honours as a Member of Christ's College, Cambridge, UK and in 1963 his M.A., and from 1960 to 1963 he served as Research Assistant at the newly established Middle East Centre, Cambridge University. **Career:** First Chamberlain to the Royal Hashemite Court, Amman, Jordan from 1963 to 1965; He served as Director-General of the Youth Welfare Organization from 1965 to 1974, and at the same time Was President of the Jordan Olympic Committee. He was appointed as the Minister of the Royal Hashemite Court from 1974-75. Since that date he is serving as the Lord Chamberlain to the Royal Hashemite Court. He is also President of the Jordanian Radio Amateur Association, President of the Friendship Society for the Blind, president of the Friends of the Jordan Eye Bank, President of the Jordan Sports Federation for the Disabled, Vice-President of the Jordanian-American Centre for Archaeological Research, and Lately President of the Jordanian-Scandinavian Friendship Society, President of the Jordanian Special Olympics Organization and President of the Society of the Friends and Relatives of the disabled, Board Member of the Arab Council for Child Development, Board Member of the International Fund Sports for the Disabled, President of the Jordanian-Swedish Medical Society, President of the Jordanian-French Medical Association, and President of the Petra National Trust, and General Committee member of Jordanian Olympic Committee, President of the Committee in Charge of the restoration of the tombs of the Companions of the Prophet, Committee member for the execution of the National Museum for Antiquities' Project. **Medals:** Recipient of the Order of Renaissance, 1st Class, Jordan (1966), the Order of the star, 1st Class, Jordan; (1967), and the order of Renaissance with Diamonds, Jordan (Dec. 1992). **Foreign Dec.:** In 1966 KCVO, (Hon) + 1984 GCVO (HON). **Hobbies:** Reading (Cosmology and Seti, topics on Human Endeavour). **Sports:** Golf, Tennis, (Snow Skiing and Wind Surfing) **Prof. Addr.:** Royal Palace, Tel. 637341, Telex: 21332, 21333, RYL PLO JO, Amman Jordan, **Residence:** Tel.: 814567, Amman, Jordan.

HUSSEIN (Saddam, General), President of Iraq. **Born** in 1937 in Takrit, Iraq. **Married** to Miss Tofa, 4 children. **Educ.:** al-Karkh Secondary School, Baghdad, Iraq; al-Qasr al-Aini Secondary School, Cairo; Cairo University, Egypt; al-Mustansariyah University, Baghdad. **Dipl.:** Licentiate of Laws; Master in Military Science (honour grade) with all its rights and privileges, also invested a badge of staff. **Career:** Joined the Baath Party (1956); lived in Syria and Egypt after he had been sentenced to death for attempted execution of General Kassem (1959-63); returned to Iraq (1963); member of 4th Regional Congress and 6th National Congress, Baath Party (1963); Member of Regional Command (1963); Member of the National Baath Congress, Syria (1964); arrested for plotting to overthrow President Abdul Salam Aref (October 1964); Member of Baath National Command (since 1965); Deputy-Secretary, Regional Leadership (1966); Leading role in July 1968 Revolution; Vice-President, Revolutionary Command Council (November 1969); Vice-Chairman, Revolutionary Command Council and Deputy to the President (November 1969); re-elected member, National Leadership (1970); Deputy Secretary-General, Iraqi Baath Party; Chairman, Higher Committee for Northern Affairs; Chairman, Follow-Up Committee; Chairman, Planning Council; Rank of General (January 1976); President of the Republic of Iraq (Summer 1979); elected Secretary-General, Regional Leadership on 16 July 1979; elected Deputy. Secretary, National Leadership on 8 October 1979. **Publ.:** Author of many political and ideological books. **Award:** Order of Rafidain (1st Class) (Civil Kind) on 7 February 1974; Order of Al-Thawra (Revolution). **Addr.:** Presidential Palace, Baghdad, Iraq.

HUSSEINI (Aishah Ahmad, al, Mrs.), Egyptian academic. **Born** in 1946 in Cairo, Egypt. **Dipl.:** M.A. (Educational Administration), U.S.A.; Ph.D. candidate. **Career:** Lecturer, Girls' College, King Abdulaziz University; Supervisor of Girls' College Library; Vice Dean of Girls' Faculty of Economics and Administration; Vice Rector for Administrative Affairs, Girls' College, King Abdulaziz University. **Member:** Association of Women Educationalists (AWA), U.S.A., the Preparatory Committee for the Annual Regional Conference of Women in the Gulf and the Arab Peninsula; member of Board, al-Faisaliyah al-Nessaiyah Welfare Society, Jeddah, Jeddah Private Schools. **Publ.:** History of Education in the Arab World, with particular reference to Saudia Arabia; Women and Administrative Development in Saudi Arabia, presented at the Conference of Women and Development in the 1980's, Kuwait. **Hobbies:** Decoration, handicrafts, travel. **Priv. Addr.:** Tel.: 6832876, Jeddah, Saudi Arabia.

HUSSEINI (Amin, Yunis, al), Jordanian politician. **Born** on December 17 1929 in Jerusalem. **Married,** 2 children. **Educ.:** American University of Beirut, Lebanon; St. Louis, USA. **Dipl.:** B.A. in Economic Sciences, Diploma in Law and Cooperation, M.A. in Administration, **Career:** Cooperative Consultant in Sudan (1951-53); Minister of Foreign Affairs and Social Welfare (1963-65); Secretary General of the Federation of Jordanian Chambers of Commerce and the National Committee of the International Chamber of Commerce; Minister of Transport (1967-70). **Decor.:** Order of the Jordanian Star. **Hobby:** Swimming. **Member:** Royal Automobile Club, al-Hussein Sport City, also member of several Charitable societies. **Prof. Addr.:** Federation of Jordanian Chambers of Commerce, P.O.Box 7029 Amman, Jordan.

HUSSEINI (Faysal), Palestinian politician. **Born** in 1940 in Baghdad. **Educ.:** in Baghdad and Cairo. **Married** 2 sons. **Career:** Palestinian Liberation Organisation Bureau in Jerusalem (1964); Military Academies of Aleppo and Damascus, Syria (1966); Organized a Military Camp for Fedayin in Lebanon (1967); returned to Jerusalem (1967); Imprisoned and house arrested several times by the Israelis; Appointed head of delegation in talks with U.S. Secretary James Baker in 1991 and Head of the Palestinian Advisory Council. **Addr.:** Jerusalem, West Bank Occupied territories.

HUSSEINI (Khairy, al), Egyptian aviation official. **Educ.:** Cairo University. Cairo, Egypt; Institute of Air and Space Law, McGill University, Montreal, Canada. **Dipl.:** B.A. in Law and Economics, M.A. and Ph.D. in Law. **Career:** Legal Member of Egyptian Civil Aviation Authority (1957); Part time Lecturer in Civil Aviation Law, Cairo Institute of Civil Aviation (1967); Director General of International Air Conventions Bureau, Civil Aviation Authority (ICAO) (1970); Instruction, International Organization of Air Transport, al-Azhar University, Cairo, Egypt (1977-78); Vice Chairman of the ICAO Legal Committee (1974-); Representative of Egypt on the ICAO Council (1978-); participated in numerous international conferences under the auspices of ICAO, ACAC and AFCAC. **Publ.:** Numerous books, papers and articles. **Prof. Addr.:** Civil Aviation Authority, 31 26th July Street, Cairo, Egypt. **Priv. Addr.:** 32 Dimashk Street, Madinat al-Muhandiseen, Dokki, Cairo, Egypt.

HUSSEINI (Mohamad Ibrahim, al), Saudi former civil servant. **Born** in 1928. **Dipl.:** B.A. (Economics) (1950). **Career:** Petroleum Statistician (1957); Economic Expert (1959); Director, Economic Division (1962); Director, Economic Department, Organization of Petroleum Exporting Countries (OPEC) (1967-70); Director General of Economic Affairs, Ministry of Petroleum and Mineral Resources; member of Arabian Oil Co. Ltd. (1964-69); attendent Arab Petroleum Conference, UN Conference on Raw Materials and Development, UN Conference on Trade and Development. **Publ.:** some research work on oil trade. **Hobbies:** Reading, music, games. **Addr.:** Ministry of Petroleum, Riyadh, Saudi Arabia.

HUSSEINI (Muhieddine, M., al), Jordanian diplomat. **Born** in 1930 in Bethlehem, Palestine. **Married,** 1 son, 2 daughters. **Educ.:** American University of Beirut, Lebanon; Tulane University, New Orleans, USA. **Dipl.:** B.A. in Economics, M.A. **Career:** Financial and Planning Economist, Jordan Development Board (1960-64); Minister of Communications (1972-74); Ambassador to Kuwait (1975-79), Ambassador to Iran (1979); Ambassador to Morocco (1980-84); Member of Chamber of Deputies (1965-82). **Decor.:** Star of Jordan (1st Class) (1974). **Hobbies:** Arabic poetry, tennis, riding, travelling. **President:** al-Urwa al-Wuthqa Society, Amman (1964-71). **Prof. Addr.:** Ministry of Foreign Affairs, P.O.Box 1577, Amman, Jordan.

HUSSEINY (Mohamed Saeed, Al), U.A.E. executive, former Minister. **Born** in 1932 in Aden, Yemen. **Son** of Saeed Al-Husseiny. **Married** in 1955, 2 sons, 3 daughters. **Dipl.:** B.A. (London) **Career:** Owner and Managing Director of several Companies. Vice-Chairman National Bank of Sharjah, U.A.E. **Addr.:** P.O.Box 486, Sharjah. Tel.: 5336677, Fax: 5331739.

I

IBBINI (Fayez, Said), United Arab Emirates Managing Director. **Born** on July 6, 1954. **Son** of Said Ibbini (Businessman) **and** Mrs. Anisah. **Married** on September 2, 1978 to Janine Nevins, UK, 2 children: Julia Fayez Ibbini (3.12.1980), Zakaria Fayez Ibbini (28.7.1986). **Educ.:** Scientific College, Amman; London Academy, UK; Leeds University, UK. **Dipl.:** B.Sc. Electrical and Electronic Engineering. **Career:** Family Business-Trading (1978-); Computer analyst Programmer, Special Systems Co. (1979-); Computer Consultancy Services, Jordan (1980-); Established Alpha Data in Abu Dhabi in partnership with Hamoodah Group (1981-); Started Alpha Data, Dubai (1987-); Established Office 2000, Abu Dhabi (1989-); Established The Laptop Shop-Both Office 2000 and The Laptop Shop are wholly owned subsidiaries of ALPHA DATA (1991-). **Sports:** Squash, Diving and Cycling. **Hobbies:** Reading and Photography. **Member:** Intercon. **Credit Cards:** Amex and Visa. **Prof. Addr.:** Airport Road, Next to Dubai Islamic Bank, P.O.Box 45384, Abu Dhabi and Alpha Processing Services, P.O.Box 203, Abu Dhabi, United Arab Emirates.

IBN SALAMAH (Ibrahim A., Dr.), President of Arab House for Industrial Consultancy (ADDAR) & Country House for Commercial Services. **Born** in 1938 in Riyadh, Saudi Arabia **Dipl.:** Hon. Dr. of Science, U.K.; B.Sc. (Mathematics), Texas, USA; Two diplomas in Industrial Studies, Holland (1970 and 1971). **Career:** Saudi Vice Chairman & Managing Director of Saudi Basic Industries Corporation (SABIC); Director, Industrial Research Department, Studies and Development Center (a Government Institution providing Industrial Consultancy Services to Government and Private Industries); Director General, Planning and Projet Evaluation, SABIC; Marketing Ltd.; Chairman, SABIC Chairman SABIC Marketing Services Ltd.: Chairman, National Methanol Company (IBN SINA); Chairman, Saudi European Petrochemical Company (IBN ZAHR); Chairman, AL-Jubail Fertilizer (SAMAD); Vice Chairman, Saudi Petrochemical Company (SADAF); Vice Chairman Saudi Yanbu Petrochemical Co. (YANPET); Vice Chairman, Gulf Petrochemical Industries Co., a partnership between SABIC Petrochemical Industries Co of Kuwait and the State of Bahrain. **Publ.:** Some articles on Industrial Development, Technologies and Feasibility studies of certain projects. **Hobbies:** Swimming, Camping and Reading. **Address:** P.O.Box 56565 Riyadh 11564, Saudi Arabia, Tel.: 4643879, Fax 4640941.

IBRAHIM (Abdul Aziz al-Tayib), Sudanese academic. **Born** in 1932 in Khartoum, Sudan. **Married**, 5 sons. **Educ.:** Cairo University, Egypt; University of Khartoum, Sudan; Minnesota, USA. **Dipl.:** B.Sc., M.Sc., M.PH., Ph.D. **Career:** Lecturer at University of Khartoum (1967); Senior Lecturer (1971); FAO Expert as Reader, Makarere University, Uganda (1975-77); FAO Expert, Veterinary Investigation Officer, Hama, Syria (1977-78); Professor, University of Khartoum (1979); Professor and Head of Department, Preventive Medicine and Public Health, Faculty of Veterinary Science, University of Khartoum; Member, WHO Expert Panel of Food Hygiene (1968-75). **Publ.:** numerous scientific articles in journals published in Sudan, Egypt, UK, USA and Kenya. **Hobbies:** Photography, tennis. **Prof. Addr.:** The Sudan Journal of Veterinary Science and Animal Husbandry, P.O.Box 321, Khartoum Sudan.

IBRAHIM (Abdul Kadir), Egyptian former official. **Born** on December 29, 1923 in Cairo, Egypt. **Educ.:** American University in Cairo, Egypt; Chicago University, Chicago, Illinois, USA; Princeton University, Princeton, New Jersey, USA. **Dipl.:** B.A., M.A., Ph.D. **Career:** Research in Management, Labour Problems and Manpower in Egypt, Labour and National Planning Commission Department (1956-55); Research Staff, Industrial Relations Section, Princeton University, Princeton, New Jersey, USA (1955-57); Staff Member, Field Service Department and Labour Management Relations Branch, ILO, Geneva (1957-62); Staff Member, ILO Near and Middle East Field Office, Istanbul, Turkey (1962-65); Senior Member, ILO, Geneva, Management Development Branch (1965-67); Deputy Director, ILO Regional Office for Africa, Addis Ababa, Ethiopia (1967-68); Head, Research and Studies Section, Management Development Branch of ILO, Geneva (1969-73); Director, ILO Area Office, Islamabad, Pakistan (1973). **Publ.:** "Socio-Economic Changes in Egypt" (1952-64) in Arthur M. Ross (ed), translated into Arabic "Some Labour Problems of Industrialization in Egypt" in Annals of the American Academy of Political and Social Science, Philadelphia (1956); "Human Resources for Egyptian Entreprise", New York (1958), "Relations and Economic Development", London (1966), "Training Managers for Development; Methods and Techniques" published by UN Institute for Training and Research in "The Making of the Manager", New York (1974). **Hobbies:** Swimming, skiing, mountain walking, philately, reading. **Addr.:** Cairo, Egypt.

IBRAHIM (Abu el-Qassim Mohamad, Maj.), Sudanese politician. **Born** in 1937 at Omdurman, Sudan. **Educ.:** el-Mourada Elementary school; Omdurman Intermediate school; Khartoum secondary school; Military College of Sudan until 1961. **Career:** Commissioned, (1961); Posted to the Central Command at El Obeid (1962); Four months training in parachuting in Aldershot, England (1962); worked on the training programme to create a Parachute Corps in Sudan (1963); Posted to Southern Command; Instructor, Infantry Training School at Gabeit (1968-69); Became member of the Revolutionary Command Council (1969); Minister of Local Government (Oct. 1969- July 1970); Assistant Prime Minister for the Armed Forces (July-Nov. 1970); Minister of the Interior (Nov. 1970- Oct. 1971); Minster of Health (Oct. 1971- Oct. 1973); Minister of Health and Social Welfare (Oct. 1973-1974); Minister of Agriculture, Food and Natural Resources (1974-76); Commander Khartoum Province (1976-79), and Vice-President (1977-79). Minister of National Assembly Affairs; Minister of Health (Jan. 2000-). **Addr.:** Khartoum, Sudan.

IBRAHIM (Akram, Nashat), Iraqi administrator. **Born** in 1920. **Married,** 2 sons. **Educ.:** Baghdad University, Iraq; Cairo University, Egypt. **Dipl.:** LL.B., Master in Criminal Law, Ph.D. **Career:** Teacher of Law, Iraq Police College (1954-69); General Director of Iraq National Center for Social and Criminal Research (1970-73) and (1977-79); Assistant Managing Director for Social and Intellectual Affairs, Arab League (1974-76); Assistant General Manager, Arab Labour Organization (1980 82); Secretary General, Arab Interior Ministers' Council (1982). **Publ.:** "Criminal Psychology" (1955), "For the Sake of Truth and History" (1962), "Criminal Research Authority" (1960). **Hobbies:** Research, reading. **Addr.:** Baghdad, Iraq.

IBRAHIM (Ali Omar Jabir), Saudi journalist. **Born** in 1940 at Jizan, Saudi Arabia. **Career:** Jounalist, al-Bilad newspaper; Editor al-Usbo'ai Tijari (Commercial Week) weekly magazine; Sub-Editor, al-Madina daily newspaper; former Managing Editor, Okaz daily newspaper. **Publ.:** daily columns, weekly articles, literary pages. **Addr.:** Office, Jeddah Tel.: 27300; Home, Jeddah 52471, Saudi Arabia.

IBRAHIM (Ezzeddin), Egyptian academic, **Born** in 1928 in Cairo Egypt **Educ.:** Cairo University Egypt, University of London, U.K. B.A. Ph.D. **Career:** Formally Professor of Arabic Literature, Riyadh University, Saudi Arabia. Rector of U.A.E University, Visiting Professor to Oxford University, U.K., Michigan Ann Arbor University U.S.A. Was C.E.O. of the Zayed Charitable and Humanitarian Foundation Abu Dhabi. Presently Cultural Advisor to the President of the U.A.E.: Active In Islamic and Cultural Affairs and Inter-religious dialogue: associated with the Islamic Conference Organisation, Jeddah and Trustee of a number of Centres of Learning in U.K. Germany, Pakistan and Kuwait. **Publ.:** Numerous publications on Islamic and Educational Subjects and co-author of some 20 books on Arabic Literature. **Address:** P.O.Box 3360, Abu Dhabi, United Arab Emirates.

IBRAHIM (Hassan), Jordanian former minister. **Born** on January 1, 1928. **Son** of Anis Ibrahim **and** Mrs. Latifah Ahmad. **Married** to Nuha Nahas, on October 18, 1953, children: Rula, Reem, Rand and Luma. **Educ.:** Najah National College, Nablus (1942-46); American University of Beirut, Lebanon (1946-52); New-York University, USA (1957-58). **Dipl.:** B.A. (Political Science and Law); M.A. (History and Public Administration); Diploma (General Administration, from UN) (1958). **Career:** Teacher in Kuwaiti Schools (1952-53); Clerk, Ministry of Economy (1953-54); Chief Clerk, Ministry of Finance (1954-55); Civil Service Commission (1956-59); First Secretary, Minister of Foreign Affairs (1959-61); Adviser, Ministry of Foreign Affairs (1961-63); Minister Plenipotentiary, Jordanian Embassy, Egypt (1965-68); Ambassador, Arab Council of Economic Unity (1968-69); Ambassador, Soviet Union (1969-73); Ambassador, Ministry of Foreign Affairs (1973); Head, Political Department, Ministry of Foreign Affairs (1973); Secretary-General, Ministry of Foreign Affairs (1973-76); Minister of State for Foreign Affairs (February- July 1976); Minister of Reconstruction and Development (July 1976- June 1978); Minister of Reconstruction and Development and Minister of State for Foreign Affairs (June 1978- Dec. 79); Minister of State for Reconstruction and Development (July 1980-82); Minister of Occupied Territories Affairs (1982-84); now Secretary General, Council of Arab Economic Unity. **Addr.:** P.O.Box (1) Mohamed Farid Street, Cairo, Egypt.

IBRAHIM (Hassan), Egyptian politician. **Born** on February 7, 1917 in Alexandria, Egypt. **Educ.:** Military College, Air Force College, Cairo. **Career:** Officer, Flight Officer, Squadron Leader, Wing Commander, Egyptian Air Force (1940-52); Member of the Revolution Supreme Council (1952-56); Chairman, National Production Council and the High Dam Committee (1954-56); Minister of State for the United Arab Republic Presidency Affairs (1954-56); Minister of State for Planning and Chairman of the Planning Committee (1954-56); President, an-Nasr Company for the Manufacture of Pencils and Graphite Products (1957-61); President, Paints and Chemical Industries Company (1957-61); President (1961-62); Member, Arab Republic of Egypt Presidency Supreme Council (1962-64); Vice-President of the Arab Republic of Egypt (1964-66); President, Middle East Finance and Consultation Company, Egyptian Granite Company, Egyptian Catering and Contracting Company (1974); Honorary Member, at-Tahrir Club, Cairo; Honorary President, Union Athletic Club of Alexandria, until 1954; Honorary member of all Egyptian Clubs and all the Athletic Clubs of the Arab Republic of Egypt. **Awards:** The Nile Collar of the Egypt (1956), The Syrian Grand Ribbon of Merit Order (1948), The Libyan Grand Ribbon of the Independence High Standing Order (1952), The Yugoslavic Flag Order of First Grade (1955), Le Grade d'Officier de L'Ordre de la Valeur du Cameroun (1963), Le Grade de Grand Officier de L'Ordre, Officier de Grand Ribbon of Ma'rab Order (1964), The Bulgarian People's Order of First Grade (1965), The Polish Grand Ribbon of "Polonia Restituta" Order (1965), The Grand Ribbon of the Yugoslavic Star Order (1965), The Grand Ribbon of the Lebanese Honorary Order of Merit (1965), The German Democratic Republic Golden Star of Nations Friendship (1965), The Moroccan Merit (1965), The Malaysian Collar of "Defender of State" (1965). **Addr.:** Khartoum Street, No.6, Heliopolis, Cairo, Egypt.

IBRAHIM (Hassan Hamdi, Dr.), Egyptian physician and former university president. **Born** on August 27, 1925 in Cairo. **Son** of Mohmmed Ibrahim **and** Mrs. Zenab nee Kamel. **Educ.:** Cairo University. **Career:** Demonstrator, Cairo University (1951-95); Lecturer (1959-64); Associate Professor of Physiology (1964-70); Professor and Chairman Department of Physiology (1970-71); Dean, Faculty of Medicine (1974-77); Vice-President, Cairo University (1977-79); President Assiut University (1979-80), President, Cairo University (1980). **Publ.:** more than 60 publications on physiology in international journals. **Addr.:** Cairo, Egypt.

IBRAHIM (Ibrahim Ibn Abdulaziz, bin), Saudi official. **Born** in 1926 at Hail, Saudi Arabia. **Career:** Governor of al-Qunfidah Zone, (1951-61); Deputy; Mecca Governorate (1961-69); Consultant, Ministry of Interior (1969-70); Deputy Aseer Governorate (1970-79); President, Welfare Society of al-Bana Area; Governor of al-Baha Zone. **Hobbies:** reading, falconry. **Addr.:** al-Baha Governorate Tel.: 7251812, Saudi Arabia.

IBRAHIM (Izzat Khalil al-Douri), Iraqi politician. See **DOURI (Izzat, Ibrahim Khalil, al).**

IBRAHIM (Mahmoud, Ahmad), Jordanian academic. **Born** on July 13, 1924 in Tulkarm, Palestine. **Married,** 1 son, 6 daughters. **Educ.:** London University, UK. **Dipl.:** M.A. in Arabic and Islamic Studies, Ph.D. in Arabic Literature. **Career:** Assistant Dean, College of Teachers in Libya (1955-58); Assistant Under Secretary, Ministry of Education, Jordan (1965-67); Dean of Postgraduate Studies and Scientific Research, University of Jordan, Amman (1976-78); Arabic Cultural Expert, UNESCO, Paris (1978-80); Dean at Faculty of Arts, University of Jordan (1980-83); Member, Jordanian Academy of Arabic Language (1976-); Honorary Member, Iraqi Academy (1978-); Member of the Society of Islamic Research and Studies, Amman, Jordan (1980-); Professor of Arabic Literature, University of Jordan (1983-). **Publ.:** several books of Islamic studies and historical research; "The Echo of the Crusade in Ibn al-Qaysarani" poetry (1971), "Abu Hayan al-Tawheidi: Science, Language and Human Matters" (1974). **Medal:** Medal of Education, (1st Class), Kingdom of Jordan (1984). **Hobbies:** attenting academic conferences, writing, reading. **Prof. Addr.:** P.O.Box 13268, Jordanian Academy of the Arabic Language, Amman, Jordan; Faculty of Arts, University of Jordan, Jordan.

IBRAHIM (Mohamad Abdel Fattah), Former Egyptian Statesman. **Born** 28 September 1921, Cairo. **Educ.:** Faculty of Commerce, Cairo University. **Dipl.:** B.Sc. (Com). **Career:** Elected Chairman of Accountants Division, Businessmen Association, and Secretary General of the Arab Accountants and Chartered Accountants Association; Director General of Finance of the Engineering Industry Authority; Director General of Production Cooperation Authority; Chairman of Administration Consultancy Institute which is concerned with the economic and technical problems of industrial units; First Secretary, Ministry of Finance; Minister of Finance (1974); appointed Governor of the Central Bank of Egypt (1976); reelected for a second tenure of office as Governor of the Central Bank of Egypt in February 1980; Deputy Prime Minister for Financial and Economic Affairs (January 3 to 2 September 1982). **Assoc.** Fellow of the Accountants and Chartered Accountants Association of Great Britain. **Addr.:** Cairo, Egypt.

IBRAHIM (Mohamad, Fuad), Egyptian economist. **Born** on December 22, 1927 in Cairo, Egypt. **Widower** of late Nabila Said, one son, one daughter. **Educ.:** B.Sc., M.Sc., Ph.D. (Economics 1952), LL.B. (Comparative Law); Diploma of Higher International Studies. **Career:** Professor of Public Finance, Cairo University (1952); Editor-in-Chief Economic Weekly Supplement, al-Ahram Daily newspaper, Cairo; General Manager and Managing Director, al-Ahram daily newspaper (1960-76); President and General Manager, SICEP company (1976); now President, Arab Research and Administration Centre (ARAK), and Government Managing Commissioner, Dar el-Maaref Printing and Publishing House (1977). **Publ.:** Author of a number of books on Public Finances, and contributor to various Encyclopedias. **Hobbies:** Reading, music and gardening. **Priv. Addr.:** 20 Hassan Sabri Street, Tel.: 808833, Cairo, Egypt.

IBRAHIM (Mohamed Nabil, H.E.), Egyptian banker. **Born** on May 25, 1931 in Cairo, Egypt. **Married** in 1958, one son. **Qualifications:** Bachelor of Commerce, Faculty of Commerce, Cairo University, 1952; Diploma, High Studies in Finance and Taxation, Cairo University, 1954; Degree in Finance, California University, U.S.A., 1957; Diploma, High studies in Business Management, Business Management Institute, Cairo University, 1959; Diploma of the Business Management Development Institute (I M E D E), Lausanne University, Switzerland, with the cooperation of Harvard University, 1962, **Current Positions:** Chairman, National Bank of Egypt International Limited-London, London-Dec. 1992; Chairman, Misr Exterior

Bank, Cairo-1982; Board Member, Central Bank of Egypt, Cairo - Prime Minister decree No. 1154 published 24/9/1986; Board Member, British Egyptian Chamber of Commerce, London; Chairman, Bilateral Committee of the Egyptian Spanish Chamber of Commerce, Cairo. **Previous Positions:** Professor, Cairo University, Faculty of Commerce, Cairo, 1964-1974; Secretary General, Union of Arab Banks, 1975-1977; Chairman, Banks Association of Egypt, 1982; Chairman, Banque Misr, 1984; Chairman, National Bank of Egypt, 1987; Member, Consultative Council, 1989-1991; Member, American Chamber of Commerce, Cairo. **Scientific Accomplishments and Researches:** Co-Author: "Practical Aspects of Commercial Banking Policies", - Arabic Language; co-Author: "Scientific and Practical Study, Organization of Syrian Banking" - Arabic Language; Field Studies on Banking Activities in the following countries: Kuwait, Lebanon, Syria, Iraq, Bahrain and Qatar; Planning and Administrative Control; Commercial Banking Policies; Modern Aspects and Means of International Financing. **Leisure Interests:** Golf, Reading, Classic Music. **Clubs Membership:** Guezira Sporting Club, Cairo; Rotary Club, Cairo; Automobile Club, Cairo; Sporting Club, Alexandria. **Decorations and Awards:** The Spanish Gran Cruz De la Orden Del Merito Civil. (November 1987); Commandeur De l'Ordre National Du Merite, France. (June 1989); The First Class Medal Award Of Excellence, Egypt. (December 1989); Nomination as "The Arab Banker For Year 1994" by the Union of Arab Banks. **Prof. Addr.:** Misr Exterior Bank, Cairo Plaza Building, Corniche el Nil, P.O.Box 272 Ataba, Cairo, Egypt. **Priv. Addr.:** 23, El Gabalaya Street, Zamalek, Cairo (Third Floor, Apartment 5), Tel.: 778021, Fax: 762806.

IBRAHIM (Mokhtar, Ibrahim, Dr.), Egyptian Banker. **born** on December 27, 1934. **Married:** 2 sons. Qualifications: Bachelor of Arts Commerce (1955); Bachelor of Arts, Law (1968); Diploma, Banking Management (1962); M.A. Economics (1962); PH.D. Economics (1981); **Career: Presently:** Chairman Al Rowad- FinCorp Securities Brokerage Co., Deputy Chairman- FinCorp Investment holding - Board Member Stock Exchange (Cairo - Alexandria) - Board Member Pyramids International Recreational & Resort Co- Board Member - Al Ahram For touristic Investments Co. **Previous Posts:** 1977 - 1994 Misr Iran. Development Bank (General Manager Board Member); 1958 - 1976 Central Bank of Egypt (Several Position) Director Credit Control, Deputy General Manager Financial Affairs and Deputy General Manager Banking Affairs, 1956 - 1957 Lecturer Faculty of Commerce Ein Shams University. Board Member Tractor & Engineering Co. Chairman, Egyptian Company for Housing, Development and Reconstruction, Board Member - Investment Credit Guarantees Company; Board Member - Misr Tourism Company Board Member Egyptian Company for Electrical Cables: General Assembly Member Holding Company for Land Reclamation. **Memberships Societies and Organizations:** Deputy Chairman - Egyptian Capital Market Association Member, Commerce Syndicate (Accouting Branch: Member, the Egyptian Society for Economics, Statistics, and Legislation; Member, Egyptian Businessmen Association; Member - Society for Advanced Management; Fellow Member - Egyptian Tax Society. **Other Posts** Former - Board Member of the Faculty of Commerce, Zagazig University, Part time Professor - Masters Program, Faculty of Commerce, Ein Shams University, Cairo University ; Alexandria University; Helwan University and Sadat Academy; Consultant for Training Programs regarding the development of banks employees in the Arab World, Egypt as well as the Union of Arab Banks: Former Board Member; price planning Authority Banking Operations Expert before the Legal Committees and Departments: Former Board member - Misr Real Estate and Touristic Investment Company Former board member - Egyptian Company for Agricultural Products; Former Board member - Egyptian Marble and Granit Company: **Research Work Articles & Publications** Related to economic topies in general and Banks and Investment in particular published in several specialized Magazines, daily newspapers in Egypt and Arab Countries Following is a small list of such work - Banks in Egypt (180 pages) El Ahram publications (1988); Banking Finance (312 Pages), Anglo-Egyptian Library-second edition (1988); Investment Banks 400 pages) Anglo-Egyptian Library-second edition (1987); Specialized Banking Activities (250 pages) Central Book Agency (1980); Statistical Application (150 pages), El Nahda Publishing House (1957); participating in Conferences related to investment and finance in Egypt and Abroad with a number of reports and studies **Private Address:** Villa 111 Rabwa Compound - Sheikh Zayed City Giza Tel: 012- 2112452. **Prof. Addr.:** 2 Abdel Moneim Riyad Dokki - Giza Tel.: 7497258-7497263

IBRAHIM (Moulay, Abdallah), Moroccan statesman. **Born** in 1918 in Morocco. **Educ.:** Ben Yusuf University, Marrakesh city and Paris University (Sorbonne). **Dipl.:** LL.B. **Career:** Joined Istiqlal (Independence) party (1944-59); Editor "al-Alem" newspaper and mouthpiece of Istiqlal party (1950-52); imprisoned for political reasons (1952-54); Secretary of State for Information and Tourism, First National Government (1955-56); Minister of Foreign Affairs (December 1958- May 1960); Secretary, Casablanca Chamber of Commerce (1961-62); leader, Union Nationale des Forces Populaires since 1959 to present. **Prof. Addr.:** Union Nationale des Forces Populaires, Casablanca, Morocco.

IBRAHIM (Muhsin), Palestinian politician. **Born** in 1923, **Educ.:** American University of Beirut, Lebanon. **Career:** apointed Member of the Administrative Council, Arab Nationalist Movement (ANM) in 1959; Member of the Lebanese delegation at the Afro-Asian Solidarity Congress in Beirut (1960); Secretary General of the ANM "al-Hurriyah" Newspaper (1963); Which expressed views of the Popular Front for the Liberation of Palestine (PFLP) on the latter's formation, but in 1969 following Ibrahim's accession to the Popular Democratic Front for the Liberation of Palestine (PDFLP), al-Hurriyah became the latter's official newspaper; Head, PDFLP External Affairs Department (1970); Elected Member of Presidium of Arab Front for Palestine (Decembre 1974). **Addr.:** Damascus, Syria.

IBRAHIM (Murtada, Ahmad), Sudanese civil engineer. **Born** on December 17, 1926 in Khartoum. **Son** of Ahmad Mohamad Ibrahim (School Teacher) **and** Mrs. Aisha Mohamad Ahmad Fadi. **Married** to Ingeborg Ibrahim in London in September 1955, 2 children: Sami and Hassan. **Educ.:** Khartoum University (Faculty of Engineering). **Dipl.:** Diploma in Civil Engineering, Khartoum University. **Career:** Assistant Civil Engineer, Ministry of Irrigation and H.E.P.(1951); Deputy Under-Secretary, Ministry of Irrigation and H.E.P. (1968); Co-Manager, Hydro, Met. Survey, Entebbe-Uganda (1967-69); Minister of Irrigation and Power (May 1969). **Sports:** Football and tennis. **Hobby:** Reading (Technical books and stories). **Member** of the Institution of Civil Engineers, London (M.I.C.E.) and Sports Clubs. **Prof. & Priv. Addr.:** P.O.Box 878, Khartoum, Sudan.

IBRAHIM (Rashid Ibrahim, Sultan), U.A.E. administrator. **Born** in 1948. **Married**, 1 daughter. **Educ.:** Baghdad University, Iraq. **Dipl.:** B.A. in English Literature. **Career:** Director, Youth and Sports Office, United Arab Emirates (1972); Director of Personnel Affairs, Government Department, Abu Dhabi (since 1974). **Hobbies:** travel, table-tennis. **Prof. Addr.:** Personnel Affairs Department, Abu Dhabi, United Arab Emirates.

IBRAHIM (Saad, Ahmad), Sudanese academic. **Born** on October 10, 1931 in Khartoum, Sudan. **Married,** 3 sons, 2 daughters. **Educ.:** Kitchener School of Medicine; Guy's Hospital Medical School; Royal College of Physicians, London, UK. **Dipl.:** Ph.D. **Career:** Medical Officer, Ministry of Health (1957-59); Research Assistant at the Faculty of Medicine (1960); Lecturer in Biochemistry, Faculty of Medicine (1964), Senior Lecturer (1968), Professor (1972); WHO Visiting Professor to Aleppo Medical School, Syria (1969-70); Member of Biochemical Society, England (1962) and the International Society on toxicology, Geneva (1970); Director of the Board for Post-Graduate Medical Studies (1976-77); Chairman, Medical Research Council, Sudanese National Council for Research (1977-79); Dean, Faculty of Medicine (1977). **Publ.:** numerous research papers, books, analysis on haemoglobinopathis, inborn errors of metabolism and toxicology of snake and scorpion venoms. **Hobbies:** Reading, hunting, fishing. **Prof. Addr.:** P.O.Box 102, Khartoum, Sudan.

IBRAHIM (Sun'allah), Egyptian writer. **Born** in 1937 in Egypt. **Educ.:** Law. **Career:** Journalist, imprisoned for political activities (1959-64); travelled to Lebanon (1968); East Berlin, and Moscow where he studied film making; returned to Cairo and published many short story collections. **Addr.:** The General Egyptian Book Organisation, 117 Sharia Corniche el-Nil, Cairo, Egypt.

IBRAHIMI (Ahmed, Taleb), Algerian politician. **Born** in 1932 in Setif. **Married,** two children. **Educ.:** Heamatology. **Career:** Publisher of Le Jeune Musulman (1952-54); President, l'Union Generale des Etudiants Musulmans Algeriens (1954-55); imprisoned by French for activities in Front de Liberation Nationale (1957-62); imprisoned for opposition to government of Ahmed Ben Bella (1964-65); Minister of National Education (1965-70); Minister of Information and Culture (1970-77); Minister-Counsellor to the President of the Republic (1977-82); Minister of Foreign Affairs (since 1982- September 1989). **Member:** Executive Council UNESCO (1968-74); Political Bureau, FLN (since 1982 to present), master of conferences on islamic civilization, National School of Administration, corresponding member, Academy of the Arabic Language, Cairo; corresponding member of Arab Academy of Damascus, member of Institute of Islamic Arab Science, Frankfurt; Royal Academy of Jordan for Research into Islamic Civilization. **Publ.:** Lettres de Prison (1966); De la Décolonisation à la Révolution culturelle (1972); **Addr.:** Algiers, Algeria.

IBRAHIMI (Lakhdar), Algerian diplomat. **Born** on January 1, 1934 in Algeria. **Married** in 1964, one daughter and two sons. **Educ.:** University of Algiers; University of Paris. **Dipl.:** LL.B. and B.A. **Career:** Permanent Representative, National Liberation Front (FNL) and later of Provisional Government of Algeria, Southeast Asia (1956-61); General Secretariat, Ministry of External Affairs (1961-63); Ambassador to Egypt, also Permanent Representative to League of Arab States, and Ambassador to Sudan (1963-70); Ambassador to united Kingdom (1971-1979); Member of the Central Committee of the FLN (1979-1983); Assistant Secretary General (with rank of Minister Plenipotentiary) for special Affairs, league of Arab States (1984 to June 1991); Minister of Foreign Affairs, (June 18, 1991- Sept. 1993). Presently United Nations Political Advisor.**Addr.:** Algiers, Algeria.

IDBIES (Ibrahim, Mohamad), Jordanian chief accountant. **Born** in 1942. in Arraba, Jordan. **Son** of Mohamad Idbies (businessman) **and** Mrs. Amina née Nimer. **Married** in 1969 in Kuwait to Miss Aida Dirhalla, three children. **Educ.:** B.Com. from Cairo University, Egypt (1965), attended 11 courses in Financial Management, Financial Analysis, Internal Auditing and Computer. **Career:** Chief Accountant for Messrs. Abdul Hamid Mansour al-Mazidi and subsidiary company (1975-78); Chief Accountant with al-Ahlia Investment Co. KSC Kuwait (since 1983) with following responsibilities: Financial Reports, Cashflow, following Investments and subsidiaries, shares and Real Estates, Contracts with banks, preparing the

Balance sheet; Chief Accounts for Messrs. Mohamad Abdulrahman al-Bahar with following responsibilities: Budgeting, cashflow, sales policy, credit policy assists the General Manager and Departmental Managers with Financial and cost informations to product plans and budgets; Member of the Management Committee (1978-83). **Work:** Supervises 30 accountants. **Sport:** Swimming. **Hobbies:** Drawing, space study. **Member** of Touristic Enterprises, Kuwait. **Credit Cards:** Visa. **Prof. Addr.:** al-Ahlia Investment Co. P.O.Box 22816, Tel.: 2445744, 2445844, 2456827, Safat, Kuwait. **Priv. Addr.:** Tel.: 5631728, Kuwait.

IDD (Zuhair, Ali), Yemeni executive. **Born** in 1932 in Aden. **Married** to Raga Abdurrahman in 1962 in Aden, Five children: Arig, Haret, Abeer, Afra and Samar. **Educ.:** Government Intermediate school; Roman Catholic Highschool. **Career:** Pursur at sea (1949-55), Shipping Accounts (1955-65); General Manager, Halal Shipping Co. (1965-66); Operation Manager, Government Shipping Co., (1966-69); General Manager, National Shipping Co., National Dockyards; Aden Coaster and Stevedoring (1970-73); also Deputy Director General of above companies (1973-80); Chairman of Shipping Board (1971-73); Acting Director General, Deputy Director General and Chairman of the Board of Directors of Yemen Ports Authority (1980-83); Member of Yemen Ports and Shipping Corporation Board (1980-83). **Sports:** Soccer and tennis. **Member:** Tilal Sports Club. **Priv. Addr.:** Plot No.11A, 1st Floor, Section "E", Street No.4, Mirsaba, Crater, Tel.: 51160. Aden, Republic of Yemen. **Prof. Addr.:** c/o Yemen Ports Authority (Port of Aden), Head Office, Steamer Point P.O.Box 1316, Aden Tel.: 22666, 24638, Aden Republic of Yemen.

IDRIS (Abdallah, bin Abdul Aziz), Saudi academic. **Born** in 1930 at Nagd, Saudi Arabia. **Educ.:** Emam Mohamed Ibn Saud Islamic University. **Dipl.:** B.A. in Arabic Language and Islamic Law "Sharia". **Career:** Technical Inspector, Intermediate and secondary Institutions; Inspector and Director, Examination Board, Colleges and Institutions; General Manager, Technical Education, Ministry of Education; Editor, "el-Dawla" Newspaper; General Manager, "el-Dawla" Islamic Magazine; Secretary-General, Higher Council for promotion of Arts and Letters; now General Manager of publication and culture, Emam Islamic University; Saudi representative, Abi Farace al-Hamadani Literary Festival, Damascus, Syria (1963); Saudi Representative. el-Merbid Festival, Basra, Iraq (1974); attended 10th conference of Arab Men of Letters, Algiers, Algeria (1975). **Member:** Higher Council for promotion of Arts and Letters; Supercision Committee editing "al-Darah", quarterly magazine by King Abdul Aziz Research Center; Board administration, "al-Darah" journal; Board administration, "el-Dawa" Islamic Magazine; Head of Club of Arts, Riyadh. **Publ.:** "Contemporary Poets of Nagd" study and critical analysis and Digests, (1960); "On My Yacht" a Divan 1983; "in Order not to Tread Thorns", Critical Essays. **Awards:** granted the Bagde of Honour in Pioneership during the conference of "Saudi Artists" which was held at King Abdul Aziz University (1974); granted the Golden Medal with the Badge of Honour during this conference. **Priv. Addr.:** Tel.: 4761003, Riyadh, Saudi Arabia.

IDRIS (Abdulgader), Saudi businessman. **Born** in 1922. **Career:** Manager of the late King Faisal's Palace Garage; accompanied the (late) King Faisal on several military expeditions; owner, al-Azizi'yya Hotel and Idriss Commercial Center, Taif. **Hobby:** Gardening. **Addr.:** al-Azizi'yya Hotel, Tel.: 7326222, Taif, Saudi Arabia.

IDRIS (Azzam), Sudanese Agricultural Specialist. **Born** on February 2, 1958 in Omdurman-Khartoum/ Sudan. **Son** of Ezzeddine Idris El-Sayed **and** Mrs. née Khogali Younis. **Married** on October 6, 1988 in Medani to Muna Ali, 4 children: Mohammed, Myada, Malaz, Oola. **Educ.:** Ahlia Higher School, University of Alexandria, Faculty of Agriculture - B.Sc. (1981), University of Gezira - M.Sc. (1990) Sudan, University of Khartoum - Ph. D. (1998) Sudan. **Career:** Deputy Manager, Rahad Agricultural Corporation (1998 - to date); Manager of Finance, Investment and Marketing (1996-1998); Executive Manager of Rahad Agricultural Corporation (1992-1996); Crop Protection Specialist of Rahad Agricultural Corporation (1988-1992); Field Supervisor (Manager) (1984-1988); Field Supervisor (Assistant) (1981-1984). Visiting Teacher University of Khartoum (1992- to date). **Sports Practised:** Ping Pong and Swimming. **Member** of Sudanese Environment Protection. **Prof. Addr.:** Rahad Agricultural Corporation, P.O.Box 2523, Khartoum, Sudan, Tel.: 780806. **Priv. Addr.:** Omdurman, Thora House, No. (741) Block No. (5), Tel.: 536687, 535831, Mobile - 12302802, Sudan.

IDRIS (Bahaa Eddin, Mohamad, Dr.), Sudanese former statesman. **Born** in 1935 in Omdurman, Sudan. **Educ.:** primary and secondary education at Omdurman; Faculty of Science, University of Khartoum; Tuberingen University, Federal Republic of Germany. **Dipl.:** B.Sc., Ph.D. (Science) (1959). **Career:** Demonstrator, Faculty of Science, Khartoum University (1955); Lecturer, University of Khartoum (1960); Director, Hydrobiological Research Unit, University of Khartoum (1969-70); Deputy Secretary-General National Council for Research (1970-72); Minister of State for Cabinet Affairs (Oct. 1972- May 1973); Minister for Presidential Affairs (1977). **Addr.:** Khartoum, Sudan.

IDRIS (Hussain), Sudanese official. **Born** in 1924 in Wad Medani, Sudan. **Educ.:** University of Khartoum, Sudan; University of London, Imperial College, UK, University of Nottingham (1963). **Dipl.:** B.Sc. in Botany, Ph.D. in Agricultural Botany. **Career:** Agricultural Officer for Mechanised Crop Production Schemes, near Gedaref

(1950-52); Inspector of Agriculture, Sudan Northern Province (1952-53); Lecturer in Crop Husbandry, University of Khartoum (1953-54); Agronomist and Director of Tozi Research Station in Sudan (1957-60); Deputy Director, Agricultural Research Division, Ministry of Agriculture, Wadi Medani (1963-64); General Director, Sudan Agricultural Research Corporation, Wadi Medani (1964-70); FAO Project Manager, Agricultural Research and Training, People's Democratic Republic of Yemen (1972-73) FAO Regional Consultant on Agricultural Research, Cairo (1971); FAO Project Manager, Agricultural Research and Training, People's Democratic Republic of Yemen (1972-73); Minister of State for Research and Services, Ministry of Agriculture, Food and Natural Resources, Khartoum (1973-77); Co-ordinator, UNDP Project to establish Cotton Development International, New York (1977-79); Director, Special Unit for Technical Co-operation among Developing Countries, UNDP, New York (1979). **Publ.:** author of several research papers on sorghum, maize and cotton and on the organization and administration of agricultural research in the Sudan and the Near East. **Addr.:** Khartoum Sudan.

IDRIS (Jumaa Awadh, Lieutenant Colonel), Libyan military. **Born** in 1938. **Married**, 3 daughters. **Career:** Joined Libyan Army in 1958; attended platoon commanders' course in UK (1968); attended all-arms tactics course, UK (1968); Director of Naval Training (1969); promoted Lieutenant Colonel (1970); Commander of Air Defences (1972); participated in Anglo-Libyan talks (October 1975) as head of Libyan Air Defence Scheme. **Addr.:** Tripoli, Libya.

IDRIS (Kamil, E. Dr.), Director General, World Intellectual Property Organization (WIPO), Secretary General, International Union for the Production of New Varieties of Plants (UPOV). **Educ.:** *Academic Distinctions:* Sudan School Certificate (Distinction), Bachelor of Law (LLB), Khartoum University (Sudan), Bachelor of Arts in Philosophy, Political Science and Economic Theories, Cairo University (Egypt), Diploma, Public Administration, Management Department, Khartoum (Sudan), Master in International Law and International Affairs, Ohio University (USA), Doctorate (PhD) in International Law, Graduate Institute of International Studies, Geneva University (Switzerland), Doctorate Thesis: "Case study on the Treaty Establishing a Preferential Trade Area for Eastern and Southern African States". **Academic Interests: Certificates:** International, Economics, International History and Political Science, International Law of Development, The Law of International Waterways, International Law of Financing and Banking Systems (All from the Graduate Institute of International Studies (Geneva). **Languages:** Arabic, English, French, Spanish (good knowledge). **Career: Principal Positions:** Director General of the World Intellectual Property Organization (WIPO) and Secretary-General of the International Union for the Protection of Plant Varieties (UPOV), (Geneva, since November 1997); Deputy Director General, WIPO (Geneva, 1994-1997); Director, Development Cooperation and External Relations Bureau for Arab Countries (including the supervision of specific activities in Central and Eastern European countries (1990-1992), WIPO (Geneva, 1985-1994); Senior Program Officer, Development Cooperation and External Relations Bureau for Africa, WIPO, (Geneva, 1982-1985); Attorney-at-Law, Advocate and Commissioner for Oaths, Sudan; Professor of International Law; Ambassador, Sudanese Foreign Service; Legal Adviser, Permanent Mission of Sudan to the United Nations Office, Geneva (1979-1982); Coordinator and Spokesman of the African Group and the Group of 77, Geneva (1981-1982). Member, United Nations International Law Commission (ILC) (1992-1996). **Teaching:** Lecturer in Philosophy and Jurisprudence, University of Cairo (1976-1977) Lecturer in Jurisprudence, Ohio University, USA (1978); External Examiner in International Law, Faculty of Law, University of Khartoum (1984); Lecturer in Intellectual Property Law, Faculty of Law, University of Khartoum (1986); Lecturer in several international, regional and national seminars, workshops and symposia; Member, International Association for the Advancement of Teaching and Research in Intellectual Property Law (ATRIP). **Professional Experience:** Part-time Journalist, El-Ayam and El-Sahafa (Sudanese) newspapers (1971-1979); Lecturer, University of Cairo (1976); Assistant Director, Arab Department, Ministry of Foreign Affairs, Khartoum (1977); Assistant Director, Research Department, Ministry of Foreign Affairs, Khartoum (January-June 1978); Deputy Director, Legal Department, Ministry of Foreign Affairs, Khartoum (July-December 1978); Member of Sudan Permanent Mission to the United Nations Office, Geneva (1979-1982); Vice-Consul of Sudan in Switzerland (1979-1982); Legal Adviser of Sudan Permanent Mission to the United Nations Office, Geneva (1979-1982); Senior Program Officer, Development Cooperation and External Relations Bureau for Africa, World Intellectual Property Organization (WIPO) (1982-1985); Director, Development Cooperation and External Relations Bureau for Arab and Central and Eastern European Countries, WIPO (1985-1994); Ambassador, Ministry of Foreign Affairs, Sudan (current status at national level); Deputy Director General, WIPO (1994-1997); Director General, WIPO, since 1997; Secretary-General, International Union for the Protection of Plant Varieties (UPOV), since 1997. **Special:** Member, Advisory Council on Intellectual Property (ACIP), Franklin Pierce Law Center (Concord, New Hampshire, 1999); Member, United Nations International Law Commission (ILC) (1992-1996); Vice-Chairman of the International Law Commission (ILC) as its forty-fifth session (1993); Representative of the ILC in the thirty-fifth session of the Asian-African Legal Consultative Committee; Member, Working Group of the ILC on the drafting of the Statute of the International Criminal Court; Member, Drafting Committee of the ILC; Legal Expert in a number of Ministerial Committees between sudan and other countries; Member of the Legal Experts Committee of the Organization of African Unity (OAU), which formulated several regional conventions; Legal adviser in the Ministerial Councils and the Summit Conferences of the OAU (Khartoum, July 1978) (Monrovia, July 1979); Participant in several meetings and international conferences of WHO, ILO, ITU, WIPO, Red Cross and the Executive Committee of the High Commissioner for Refugees; Member of Special Committees established for fund raising for refugees in Africa; Repporteur of the Third Committee (Marine Scientific Research) of the Summary Ninth session of the Third UN Conference on the law of the Sea (Geneva, 1980); Head of Sudan Delegation to the OAU Preparatory Meeting on the Draft Code of Conduct on Transfer of Technology (Addis Ababa, March 1981); Spokesman of the African Group and the Group of 77 on all issues pertaining to Transfer of Technology, Energy, Restrictive Business Practices and Technical Co-operation among Developing Countries at the twenty-third sessions of the Trade and Development Board (Geneva, February and September 1981); Head of Sudan Delegation and Spokesman of the African Group and Coordinator of the Group of 77 at the fourth session of the UN Conference on the Code of Conduct on Transfer of Technology. (Geneva, March-April 1981); Spokesman of the Group of 77 on Chapter 9 (Applicable Law and Settlement of Disputes) at the UN Conference on the International Code of Conduct on Transfer of Technology (Geneva, March - April 1981); Head of Sudan Delegation and Chairman of the Workshop on Legal Policies on Technology Transfer (Kuwait, September 1981); Chairman of the African Group and the Group of 77 at the first session of the Intergovernmental Group of Experts on Restrictive Business Practices (Geneva, November 1981); Chairman of the Permanent Group of 15 on Transfer and Development of Technology, within the United Nations Conference on Trade and Development (UNCTAD) (Geneva, 1980-1983); Spokesman of the African Group and the Group of 77 at the meeting on the Economic, Commercial and Developmental Aspects of the Industrial Property System (Geneva, February 1982); Coordinator of the African Group and the Group of 77 at the first, second and third sessions of the interim Committee on the International Code of Conduct on Transfer of Technology (Geneva, March, May, September - October 1982); Coordinator of the African Group and the Group of 77 at the Meeting of Governmental Experts, on the Transfer Application and Development of Technology in the Capital Goods and Industrial Machinery Sectors (Geneva, July 1982); Coordinator and Spokesman of the African Group and the Group of 77 at the intergovernmental Group of Experts on the Feasibility of Measuring Human Resource Flaws on Reverse Transfer of Technology (Brain-Drain) (Geneva, August-September 1982); Coordinator of developing countries on the drafting of the resolution concerning the mandate of the Office of the United Nations High Commissioner for Refugees, during the thirty-third session of the Executive Committee of the UNHCR (Geneva, October 1982); Coordinator and spokesman of the African Group and the Group of 77 at the Meeting of governmental Experts on the Transfer, Application and Development of Technology in the Energy Sector (Geneva, October-November 1982); Coordinator and spokesman of the African Group and the Group of 77 at the fourth session of the Committee on transfer of Technology (Geneva, November - December 1982); **Judicial Experience and Professional Membership of Associations:** Member of the United Nations International Law Commission (ILC) (1992-1996); Member and Chairman of several legal experts committees established within the OAU, Professor of Public International Law, University of Khartoum, Sudan; Member of the Sudan Bar Association (Khartoum), Member of the African Jurists Association (Dakar and Paris), Registered Advocate and Commissioner for Oaths in the Republic of Sudan. **Projects and Documents:** Formulated and negociated, on behalf of WIPO, numerous projects relating to development cooperation in the field of intellectual property, organized, on behalf of WIPO, various seminars and workshops and presented several lectures; Drafted various documents on developmental aspects of intellectual property; supervised and managed (on administrative and substantive aspects) projects executed in Africa, Arab Countries, Asia, Latin America, and Central and Eastern European countries. **Conferences, Seminars, Courses and Symposia:** Represented Sudan in numerous international and regional conferences; participated in many seminars, symposia, discussion groups, and addressed graduate students on various international academic disciplines; represented WIPO, in various meetings, seminars and symposia; Represented WIPO on several UNDP Policy and Operations Programmes: Undertook a study tour at the Max Planck Institute (Munich) in the field of teaching of intellectual property law (1986). **Publications:** Euro-Arab Dialogue (June 1977); State Responsibility in intellectual law (September 1977); The Theory of Human Action (September 1977); The Philosophy of "Haddith" and "Sunna" in Islamic law (January 1978); The Docrine of Jurisdiction in International Law (December 1978); American Embassy in Tehran Case (March 1979); the legal Regime of the Nile (December 1980); Issues pertaining to Transfer and Development of Technology in Sudan (May 1981); China and the Powers in 19th Century (May 1981); Legal Dimensions of the Economic Cooperation among Developing Countries (June 1981); The Common Fund for Commodities (June 1981); General Aspects of Transfer of Technology at the National and International Levels (November 1981); Preferential Trading Arrangements among Developing Countries (February 1982); North-South Insurance Relations: The Unequal exchange (December 1984); The Law of Non-Navigational use of International Water Courses; the International Law Commission's draft articles: An overview (November 1995); The Theory of Source and Target in Child Psychology (January 1996); A Better United Nations for the New Millenium (January 2000). **Articles:** A number of Articles on law, economics, jurisprudence and aesthetics published in various newpapers and periodicals. **Decorations:** Awarded the Scholars and Researchers State Gold Medal, Presented by the President of the Republic of Sudan (1983) and presented also by the President of Academy of Scientific Research and Technology of Egypt (1985); Commander, Ordre national du Lion, Senegal (1998); Medal of the Bolshoi Theatre, presented by the Director of the Bolshoi Theatre Russian Federation (1999); Honorary Medal, Presented by the Rector of the Moscow State Institute of International Relations, Russian Federation (1999); Honorary Medal of the Gulf Cooperation Council (GCC), Saudi Arabia (1999); Awarded the Golden Plaque of the Town of Banska Bystrica, presented by the Mayor of Banska Bystrica, Slovakia (1999); Golden Medal of Matej Bell University, presente by the Dean of the University Banska Bystrica, Slovakia (1999). **Honorary Degrees:** 1999 Honorary Professor of Laws, Peking University, China; 1999 Doctor Honoris Causa, The Doctor's Council of the State University of Moldova, Republic of Moldava; 1999 Doctor Honoris Causa, Frnanklin Pierce Law Center (Concord, New Hampshire), U.S.A.; 1999 Doctor Honoris Causa, Fudan University (Shangai) China. **Prof. Addr.:** World Intellectual Property Organization (WIPO), 34, chemin des Colombettes - 1211 Geneva 20 - Switzerland, Tel.: (41-22)338-9111, Facsimile: (41-22)733-5428, e-mail: wipo.-mail@wipo.int.

IDRIS (Mustafa Mohamad Ali), Saudi official. **Born** in Mecca, Saudi Arabia. **Educ.:** General Secondary School Certificate 1948. **Career:** Deputy Director of Budget Department, Ministry of Finance; Administration Director, Cabinet of Ministers; Director-General of Administration, the Royal Cabinet; attended UN courses of Technical Assistance Programme fellowship on public revenue and principles of administration; has been working for the last 13 years under the Royal auspices of H.R.H. Prince Sultan ben Abdulaziz. **Publ.:** a book on applied taxes. **Hobbies:** Reading, swimming. **Addr.:** al-Mallaz, Jareer Street, Riyadh, Saudi Arabia.

IDRIS (Yusuf), Egyptian physician and writer. **Born** in 1927. **Educ.:** Faculty of Medicine, Cairo University. **Dipl.:** Medical Doctor (specialisation in Psychiatry). **Career:** Physician, Politically active since 1951, several times imprisoned; Writer. **Publ.:** Author of "The Republic of Farhat", "The Cotton King", "The Critical Moment", "al-Farafir", "The Hero", "The Sin", "The Vice", etc... **Dist.:** Awarded Hiwar literary prize (1965) (but refused award); Medal of Republic (1966). **Addr.:** 100 Nile Street, Dokki, Cairo, Egypt.

IDRISS (Moussa, Ahmed), Djibouti Deputy at the National Assembly. **Born** in 1933 in Djibouti. **Career:** Member of Central Committee of RPP. Elected Deputy at the Chamber of Deputies (17 Nov. 1963-1968); President of PMP (Parti Mouvement Populaire) (1962-1968); Elected Deputy at the National Assembly (24 April 1987 - to date); President of finance Commission of the 3rd Legislature; Member of finance Commission, General Economy and Planning. **Prof. Addr.:** National Assembly, P.O.Box 138 Djibouti, Djibouti.

ILTIREH (Omar, Farah), Djibouti Deputy at the National Assembly. **Born** in 1923 at Ali-Sabieh. **Career:** Consul General at Diré-Dawa. Member of Chamber of Deputies (1968-1973); Member of Central Committee of RPP; Elected Deputy at the National Assembly (18/12/1992 - to date); Member of Foreign Affairs Commission and National Defence Commission. **Prof. Addr.:** National Assembly, P.O.Box 138 Djibouti, Djibouti.

IMADY (Mohammed A, Dr.), Syrian economist. **Born** on December 1, 1930 0n Damascus, Syria. Son of Mohammed Jawdat Imady, Land Owner and Yusra Hawasly. **married** in 1956 in New York to Mildred Elaine Rippey. 3 Children, Susan (1957), Muna (1962), Omar (1966): **Educ.:** Damascus University (1953), New York University (1958). **Dipl.:** B.A., M.A., Ph.D. in Economics. **Career:** Assistant Secretary General-Ministry of Planning - Syria (1964-67); Deputy Minister of Planning - Syria (1968-71), Minister of Planning - Syria (1972); Minister of Economy and Foreign Trade - Syria (1972-79); President of the Board, general Director of the Arab Fund for Economic & Social Development (1979-85); Professor in the School of Economics and Commerce, Damascus University (1960-1979) (1985-1996); Minister of Economy and Foreign Trade (1986- to present). **Books:** University texbook "Economic Development and Planning" Many articles on Arab Economic Development and Finance. **Member:** Higher Council of Sciences (1965-74) & (1993); Higher Council of Universities (1969-71); President of Arab Economists Association (1971-73); Honorary President of the Economics Society in Syria (1970-72); Chaired the Annual Meeting of the IBRD and IMF in Manila (1976); Chaired several meetings of the Arab Economic and Social Council and the Council of Arab Unity; Headed Syrian Delegations to many countries and to several Arab and International Conferences; Member of the parliament in Syria (1977-81). **Awards:** Founders Day Award, New York, University (1960); several Medals and Decorations from: West Germany; France; Iran; Bulgaria, Indonesia, Guinea, Hungary, Yugoslavia. **Clubs:** Arab Thought Forum **Credit Cards:** American Express. **Prof. Addr:** Minister of Economy and Foreign Trade, Damascus, Syria.

INDARKIRY (Yasin, S.), Saudi official. **Born** in 1936 in Mecca, Saudi Arabia. **Dipl.:** Ph.D. **Career:** Former Director General for Manpower, Ministry of Labour; Director of Regional Labour Office (Central Region); Director General of Vocational Training Department; Director of

Statistics Division, Ministry of Interior; Presently Assistant Deputy Minister, Ministry of Labour and Social Affairs; has represented Saudi Arabia at many conferences, such as the International Labour Conference, Euro-Arab Dialogue and the Organization of the Islamic Conference; Adviser, Advisory Committee, International Institute for Labour Studies, Geneva; Chairman, Board of Directors, Islamic Centre for Technical and Vocational Training and Research, Dacca; member, Working Group, National Centre for Science and Technology, Riyadh; Adviser, Manpower Affairs, Ministry of Interior, Riyadh; member, The American Sociological Association, Washington, D.C. **Publ.:** The New Saudi Society; lectures and broadcast talks. **Hobbies:** Reading, photography. **Prof. Addr.:** Ministry of Labour, Tel.: 4776226, Riyadh. **Priv. Addr.:** Tel.: 4764075, Riyadh, Saudi Arabia.

IRHAYIM (Tarik, al), Iraqi engineer. **Born** in 1937 in Iraq. **Married**, 6 children. **Educ.:** Birmingham University, UK. **Dipl.:** B.Sc. in Petroleum Production Enginnering, Ph.D. in Chemical Engineering. **Career:** Army (1959-61); Assistant Petroleum Engineer, Ministry of Oil (1961-63); Reservoir Engineer, KOC, Kuwait (1966-68); Area Reservoir Engineer, IPC, Kirkuk (1968-70); Project Manager, Under-ground Storage, Northern Oil Company (1980-); Deputy Director Fields (1989); Director Fields (1993-). **Publ.:** "Bulk Volume Measurements" (1964), "Thermal Analogue Studies" (1965), in IP and Chemical Engineering. **Hobbies:** Bridge, classical music, reading. **Prof. Addr.:** North Oil Company, P.O.Box 1, Kirkuk, Iraq.

IRSHEID (Walid, Jamil), Jordanian banker. **Born** in 1936 in Haifa, Palestine. **Married**, 3 children. **Educ.:** University of Damascus, Syria. **Dipl.:** B.A. in Commerce. **Career:** Banker, Arab Bank Ltd. in Latakia, Nablus, Dubai and Amman branches; Arab Bank Regional Management, Bahrain (1956-76); Deputy Manager, Société Générale, Bahrain (1976-). **Hobbies:** Reading, music. **Prof. Addr.:** Société Générale, P.O.Box 5275, Manama, Bahrain.

IRTEIMEH (Nayef), Jordanian (banking computer system analyst and programmer). **Born** on November 13, 1956 in Amman. **Son** of Sa'ud Irteimeh (Landlord) **and** Mrs. Falha Mukhaimer. **Married** to Miss Mariam Irteimeh on 5.6.81 in Amman. **Educ.:** Colchester College, England; Southall College, England; University of Houston, U.S.A. **Dipl.:** HND in Technology; B.Sc. Applied Mathematical Science and Computer Programming. **Career:** Marketing Employee, Tenneco Oil Co. (1980-1981) U.S.A.; Manager of a General Maintenance Co. (1981-1984) U.S.A.; Computer Program, Municipality of Amman (1984-1987) Amman; System Analyst and Programmer, Jordan Cooperative Organization (1987-). **Member:** The National Association of Consumer Protection; Member of a Cooperative Society. **Sports:** Jogging, Walking. **Hobby:** Reading. **Credit Cards:** American Express; Master Card. **Prof. Addr.:** The Cooperative Bank, P.O.Box 330077, Tel. 896195, Amman.

IRYANI (Abdalla, Hassan, al), Yemeni accountant. **Born** in 1941 in Iryan, Yemen. **Son** of Hassan Ahmad Iryani. **Married** in 1961, 1 son, 7 daughters. **Educ.:** Ain Shams University, Cairo. **Dipl.:** B.A. in Accounts (1967). **Career:** Director of Central Accounts and Inspector Auditor of General Administration and Branches, Yemen Bank of Reconstructions and Development; Director, Central Bank of Yemen. Director of a number of local companies, including Yemen Drug Co; Chairman of Yemen's Chartered Accountants. **Member:** Member of General Union of Arab Accountants and Auditors. **Hobbies:** Sports and Reading. **Addr.:** Zubairy Street, P.O.Box 1956, Tel.: (02) 208887, Tlx: 2489 MUGHAD YE, Sanaa, and P.O.Box 11389, Sanaa, Republic of Yemen.

IRYANI (Abdul Karim, al, Dr.), Yemeni politician. **Born** on February 20, 1935 in Iryan, Yemen Arab Republic. **Son** of Qadi Ali al-Iryani. **Married** in February 1969, 2 children: Rasha (1971), Rabab (1975). **Educ.:** University of Texas (USA); University of Georgia (USA); Yale University (USA). **Dipl.:** Ph.D. in Biochemical Genetics. **Career:** Director of Wadi Zeid Agricultural Project (1968-69); Head of Central Planning Organization (1972-74); Minister of Development and Head of Central Planning Organization (1974-January 1977); Minister of Education and President of Sanaa University (August 1976-79); Minister of Agriculture (March- July 1979); Prime Minister (June 1982- Nov. 1983); Chairman of the Supreme Council for the Reconstruction of Areas affected by Earthquakes (Nov. 1983- Nov. 1985); Deputy Prime Minister, Minister of Foreign Affairs and Chairman of the Supreme Council for Petroleum and Mineral Resources (Nov. 1985- May 1990); Minister of Foreign Affairs Republic of Yemen (since May 1990-1993); Minister of Planning and Development (1993-1995); Deputy Prime Minister and Minister of Foreign Affairs (since June 1995) Prime Minister (since Sept. 1999). **Hobbies:** Chess. **Addr.:** Minister's Office, Sanaa, Republic of Yemen.

IRYANI (Mohamad, Abdulla, al), Yemeni diplomat, army commander. **Born** in 1942 in Yemen. **Son** of Abdallah al-Iryani. **Married** in 1963, six children. **Educ.:** Military Academy (1961). **Career:** Appointed to various ranks and positions in the armed forces; Commander of Northern Province (1963-64); Infantry commander; Deputy Chief of Staff; Deputy Defence Minister; Deputy Commander in Chief of the Armed Forces; member of the Politburo; Commander in Chief of the Armed Forces (till 1974); Ambassador Extraordinary and Plenipotentiary to the UK (1974-81); Ambassador to Federal Republic of Germany (1982-1988). **Sports:** Tennis, swimming. **Addr.:** Ministry of Foreign Affairs, Sanaa, Republic of Yemen.

ISHAK (Mustafa, Hassan), Sudanese academic. **Born** in 1927 in Khartoum, Sudan. **Son** of Hassan Ishak. **Married** three children. **Educ.:** B.Sc. (High Honors), St. Andrews University (1952); Ph.D. (Honors) (1958). **Career:**

Professor of Chemistry, University of Khartoum; Dean, Faculty of Science (1962-68); Deputy Vice Chancellor (1967-68); Vice chancellor (1971-74) Consultant to the Minister for Higher Education and Deputy Chairman University Grants Committee (1975-81). On Secondment to the King Saud University as advisor for Postgraduate Studies. **Addr.:** P.O.Box 321, Tel.: 76193, Khartoum, Sudan.

ISHAQ (Yaqub Mohamad), Saudi publisher and editor. **Born** in 1942 in Mecca, Saudi Arabia. **Dipl.:** B.A. (Arabic Language); Higher Diploma in Education and Psychology. **Career:** Teacher of Arabic Language, Shat Secondary School (1969-73); Administrative Controller, Control and Investigation Board (1973-77); Editor-in-Chief Hassan organization for Press and Publication. **Publ.:** daily broadcasted programme for children, Yohka An since 1979; Series; Saudia Children's Book (published by Saudia Airlines) A story for Each Animal (Published by Tihama); My Beloved Home (published by Tihama) Towards A Better Society (published by Dallah/Avco) Bravery and Heroes; Military Culture; Islamic Education (privately published); A Book for a Saudi Child (published by Saudi Arabian Society of Arts and Culture). **Hobbies:** Sports, writing for children. **Prof. Addr.:** P.O.Box 5588, Tel.: 6316916, Jeddah. **Priv. Addr.:** Tel.: 6652875, Jeddah, Saudi Arabia.

ISKANDAR (Azmi, Naguib), Egyptian former diplomat, Director-General of Newspaper Company. **Born** on November 26, 1920 in Cairo. **Son** of Naguib (Bey) Iskandar **and** Mrs. Faika Ishaq Famous. **Educ.:** Preparatory and Secondary (Christian Brothers Schools) (St. Paul and Khoronfish), Faculty of Law, Cairo University. **Dipl.:** Bachelor of Law, Cairo University (1944); Certificate of International Law, The Hague, Holland (1952). **Career:** Barrister (1944-46); in the Diplomatic Service (1946-53); Vice-Consul in Jerusalem (1947-48); Acting Consul General to Greece (1949-52); Member, Egyptian Delegation to United Nations (1952-53); "Chairman and Managing Director" "Le Scribe Egyptien" S.A.E. (Business Equipment Centre). **Awards:** Knight George I, Greece (1956), Knight St. Marc (Greek Pope). **Sports:** Golf and horse riding. **Hobbies:** Reading, travelling and music. **Member** of Automobile Club of Egypt, Active Member of Diplomats Club, Gezira Sporting Club, Cairo, Rotary Club, Egyptian Society of international Law, Egyptian Society of Politic and Legislation. **Priv. Addr.:** 6, Mountazah Street, Zamalek, Tel.: 3418971, Cairo, Egypt.

ISLAM (Samer, M., Saleh), Saudi M.D. and technical adviser. **Born** in 1938, in al-Hasa, Eastern Province Saudi Arabia. **Son** of M. Saleh Islam **and** Mrs., née Maryam Al-Maghlouth. **Married** in 1967 to Miss Samira Kattan, 3 children. **Dipl.:** M.D. Alexandria University; Higher Diploma (Pediatrics), Higher Diploma (Diseases of the Abdomen), Alexandria University; M.M. (Public Hygiene); M.M. (Maternal Health), Harvard University. **Career:** Paediatrician, Jeddah General Hospital; Assistant Director, Planning Programming and Budget Unit (for Planning Affairs); Director of Health Offices Division, Preventive Medicine Department; Director of Health Zones and Hospitals Department, Ministry of Health; Technical Adviser, Office of the Minister of Health; Director of Hospitals and Health Regions, Department of Curative Medicine (1973-75); now Supervisor General of the King Khaled Eye Specialist Hospital in Riyadh. **Act.:** Served on several Ministerial and inter-ministerial committees in Saudi Arabia, the Gulf, Arab and International bodies. **Awards:** Certificate for 15 years of distinguished service given by the Minister of Health. **Publ.:** field research paper on children's natural growth, Alexandria University; field studies on the welfare of children including handicapped children, Harvard University. **Hobbies:** Reading, gardening, sightseeing. **Sports:** Table tennis. **Addr.:** P.O.Box 1956, Riyadh, Saudi Arabia.

ISLAM (Samira, Ibrahim), Saudi professor of pharmacology. **Born** in al-Hafuf, al-Ahsaa, Saudi Arabia. **Daughter** of Late Ibrahim Mustafa Islam (Director General, Ministry of Finance) **and** Mrs. née Saadia Mustafa Fathallah, 3 children: Khaled Darhouse, Kholoud Darhouse, Nagham Darhouse. **Educ.:** English Girls' College, Alexandria (Egypt). **Dipl.:** B.Sc. in Pharmacy and Pharmaceutical Chemistry (1960); Biochemical Analysis (1961); Drug Analysis (1962); Ph.D. in Pharmacology (1970); all from Alexandria University, Egypt. **Career:** All work in King Abdulaziz University, Girls' Section, Saudi Arabia: Lecturer (1971-73); Academic Advisor, Makkah and Jeddah, (1973-75); Head of Science Depts. Faculty of Education, Makkah (1973-75); Asst. Professor (1974); Supervisor of Faculty of Science, Jeddah (1975-78); Associate Professor (1979); Vice Dean Faculty of Medicine and Allied Sciences, Jeddah (1975-80); Dean of Nursing (1978-80); Part time Adviser and Dean of School of Health Sciences for girls of Armed Forces (1981-84). **Work:** Instrumental in Gaining admission for women as full time and regular students to Saudi Universities; The founder and first establisher of first Science Dept. in Girls' Section, Faculty of Education, Makkah (1973); of the Medical and Science Faculties, Girls' Section, Jeddah (1975); the first Nursing Faculty in the Kingdom, Jeddah (1976); the girl's school of Health Sciences for the Armed Forces Hospital, Jeddah (1981); the first Drug Monitoring Service in the Country (1982); Director, Manager, First International Conference for women in Saudi Arabia "The Philosophy of Nursing", Jeddah (1977); Participant in the Ministerial Consultation "Health Service and Manpower Development", Tehran (1978); Consultant for the Ministry of Health for Manpower Development (1979); Organisor and Director of the first workshop in the Kingdom on Medical Education in collaboration with WHO Regional Office (1979); All the time Lecturing Biochemistry Department, then Pharmacology Department. **Awards:** The first Saudi Woman to obtain a University degree, a Ph.D. degree, and to become an Associate Professor in all fields, the first Saudi person to receive a Ph.D. in the field of Pharmacology and Pharmacy; since 1983 till 1993 the only Saudi woman Professor in any field, also the first Saudi Pharmacology Professor (men and women). Published more than 63 articles in the area of speciality in international journals and meetings. **Sports:** Tennis, **Hobby:** Gardening. **Member of:** Women's Welfare Society; Arab Union of Pharmacists; Pharmacology Society; World Health Organisation Regional Advisory Panel on Health Manpower Development; Assoc. for the Study of Medical Education, U.K.; British Pharmacological Society, U.K.; The International Soceity for the Study of Xenobiotics, (U.S.A.). **Prof. Addr.:** Faculty of Medicine and Allied Sciences, King Abdulaziz University, P.O.Box 12653, Jeddah 21483. **Priv. Addr.:** University Street, P.O.Box 449, Jeddah 21411, Saudi Arabia.

ISLAM (Saud Saleh), Saudi Economist, Consultant, Journalist and Businessman. **Born** on 20 September 1948 in Dammam, Saudi Arabia. **Dipl.:** B.Sc. (Economics/ Chemistry) (1972) Salford University; M.Sc. (Economics/ Petrochemicals), UMIST (1974); Ph.D. (Management), Bath University (1981). **Career:** Family Business Partner (1975-78); Financial Editor of Saudi Gazette and Editor in Chief (1979); Board Member, Okaz Press and Publishing 1980; Member - Royal Economic society, American Management Association, Institute of Directors; London, currently Board Member & Director General, Yanbu Cement Co. Ltd.; Also Executive Director, SICO, Board Director, Yanbu Chamber of Commerce & Industry, Board Director General Organisation for Social Insurance (GOSI), Riyadh. Associate, Royal Institute of Chemistry. **Publ.:** Banking in Saudi Arabia, B.Sc. Economics paper (1971); Middle East Petrochemical feasibility study (M.Sc. paper, 1974); Comparative Crossnational Study of British/Saudi Management (Ph.D. 1981). **Hobbies:** Reading, travel, swimming, tennis, golf, **Addr.:** P.O.Box 603, Jeddah 21421, or P.O.Box 40075, Jeddah 21499, Saudi Arabia.

ISMAIL (Abdullah), United Arab Emirates official. **Born** in 1927. **Married. Career:** Formerly Iraqi Secretary for Oil Affairs; former Under Secretary, Ministry of Minerals, United Arab Emirates; Adviser to the Ministry of Petroleum and Mineral Resources, Abu Dhabi, UAE. **Prof. Addr.:** P.O.Box 59, Abu Dhabi, United Arab Emirates.

ISMAIL (Abdulmalek), Yemeni statesman. **Born** on 26 November 1936 in Aden, Republic of Yemen. **Educ.:** Secondary and Higher. **Career:** Editor, "al-Nour" and "Haqiqa" (1961-63); Vice-Chairman, General Union of Petroleum Workers (1961-62); Chairman, petroleum Workers Union (1962-64); Vice-President, Arab Federation of Petroleum Workers (1962-65); Leading member, National Liberationf Front (1963-65); Director, National Front Office, Cairo (1965-66); Member, General Command, National Liberation Front (1966-68); Minister of Labour and Social Welfare in the 1st Government of the Southern Yemen Republic (November 1967- April 1968); Minister of Economy, Commerce and Planning (April 1968-70); Permanent Representation to United Nations (1970-73); Ambassador to Egypt (1973-75); Ambassador to Sudan (1975). Head of Nairobi Mission of Arab league States Organization (March 1983). **Addr.:** Ministry of Foreign Affairs, Sanaa, Republic of Yemen.

ISMAIL (Ahmad, Sultan), Egyptian mechanical engineer. **Born** on April 14, 1923 in Port Said, Suez Canal Zone (Egypt). **Married** in 1957 to Rawhia Riad. **Educ.:** Faculty of Engineering, Cairo University. **Dipl.:** B.Sc. (Engineering). **Career:** worked as shift engineer, maintenance engineer at various power stations (1945-64); member, Executive Board Electrical Projects Corporation (1964), National Defence College (1967); Governor, Menufiyeh Province (1968-71); Minister of Power (1971-1976); Deputy Prime Minister (1976-78). **Awards:** Order of the Egyptian. Republic (1st class). **Hobbies:** Reading and travel. **Priv. Addr.:** 43, Ahmed Abdel Aziz Street, Dokki District, Tel.: 3474422, 3468700, Cairo, Egypt.

ISMAIL (Ali, Abukar, Gen.), Somali army officer. **Born** in 1947 in Burao, in the then British Somaliland. **Married,** with children. **Educ.:** elementary and intermediate school in Sheikh (1947-57); secondary education in Amud (1954-58); Officer's training in England: 2 years at the Royal Military Academy, Sandhurst, 6 months at the Infantry school, Westminster and Hythe (1958-61); attended a Batallion Commanders' course, Mogadishu. **Career:** Somaliland Scouts (1961); Second Grade Commander, Officers' school, Mogadishu (1961-62); Head, Organisation Office, General Command of the Armed Forces (1962-63); Batallion Commander, Chisimaio (1965-67); Commander, Infantry School, Mogadishu (Sept. 1967-70); promoted Colonel and appointed Secretary for Information and National Guidance (March 1970); Vice-President (July 1971), and promoted General; also Secretary-General for Party Affairs (July 1976); discussed with President Kaunda (1973) and with the Nigerian Head of State the liberation of the still-dominated African territories, and the Zambia-Rhodesia conflict; attended the 10th Revolution anniversary celebrations of Congo, Brazzaville; attended in Havana the Cuban PC Congress. **Addr.:** Mogadishu, Somalia.

ISMAIL (Hassan, Mohamad), Egyptian engineer. **Born** in 1917 in Dakhalia, Egypt. **Married,** 1 son, 3 daughters. **Educ.:** Cairo University, Egypt, California Institute of Technology, USA. **Dipl.:** B.Sc. in Civil Engineering, Ph.D. **Career:** Professor of Hydraulics, Cairo University (1956-60), Head Irrigation and Hydraulics Department (1968-69), Dean, Faculty of Engineering (1968-69), Vice President (1969-71), President, (1971-75); Minister of Education and Culture (1978-79); President of the

Academy of Science and Technology (1979-80); Member of the American Society of Civil Engineers and of Egyptian Engineers; President of Pacer Consultants (1980-). **Publ.:** "General Planning of the North West Coast" (1977), "Planning of Egyptian Ports" (1978), "Planning Doumiat Port" (1981), "Planning of American New Town". **Decor.:** Egyptian Order of Merit (1st Class) (1975), Egyptian Order of the Republic (1st Class) (1979). **Award:** Merit Award of the Republic for Sciences (198O). **Hobby:** Swimming. **Member:** Cairo Automobile Club; Cairo Shooting Club. **Prof. Addr.:** 3 Hassan Kamal Street, Dokki, Cairo, Egypt. **Priv. Addr.:** 26 el-Nahde Street, Dokki, Cairo, Egypt.

ISMAIL (Mohamad, A.), Saudi academic. **Born** in 1935 at Ashaiqer. **Dipl.:** M.S., ED.D. **Career:** Officer of Saudi Ministry of Finance; teaching staff member, Riyadh University; member of the Preparatory Committee of the symposium on Psychology and Islam; Supervisor of Art and Culture Society, Faculty of Education, Riyadh University (1976-77); Assistant Professor, Riyadh University. **Hobbies:** Reading, walking. **Addr.:** Faculty of Education, Riyadh University, P.O.Box 258, Riyadh, Saudi Arabia.

ISMAIL (Mohamad, Othman), Egyptian politician, **Born** in 1931 in Assiut, Egypt. **Married. Educ.:** Law. **Career:** practised law in Assiut; Member of the National Assembly, Deputy for Assiut (1964); elected Secretary of the Arab Socialist Union (ASU) in 1968, Governorate Committee for Assiut; elected to Central Committee of ASU; Member, Central Committee's Internal Affairs Committe (1968); reelected to National Assembly (1969); Governor of Aswan (1971); Presidential Adviser for People's Assembly Affairs and Secretary for Organization (1971); Governor of Assiut (1973-84); Businessman in Assiut City (1984-). **Addr.:** c/o Governorate of Assiut, Assiut, Egypt.

ISMAIL (Mohamad, Zakaria), Syrian statesman. **Born** in Syria. **Son** of Zakaria Ismaïl. **Educ.:** University of Damascus, University of Paris (La Sorbonne). **Dipl.:** Doctor in Economy (1952). **Career:** Joined the Ministry of Finance (1952-53); Joined the Ministry of Foreign Affairs, in Missions in Italy and Cyprus (1954-56); Syrian Ambassador to Budapest (1968-71); Assistant, Minister of Foreign Affairs (1971); Deputy, Minister of Foreign Affairs (1972); on secondment to the U.N., Deputy Executive Secretary at ECWA, Economic Commission of Western Asia. Assistant Secretary- General (International Affairs) LEAGUE OF ARAB STATES. **Addr.:** Damascus, Syria.

ISMAIL (Muhammad Hafiz), Egyptian diplomat. **Born** in 1919. **Married. Educ.:** Military Academy, Cairo; Royal Military Academy, Woolwich, UK (1937); Staff College (passed out in first position) (1944). **Career:** Military Attache, Embassy to USA (1951); Director, Office of the Commander in Chief, Abdul Hakim Amer; General (1953-60); Assistant Under Secretary, Ministry of Foreign Affairs (1960-64); Egyptian Delegate to the Geneva Disarmament Conference (1964); Ambassador to UK (1965), to Italy (1967) and to France (1968); Minister of State (1970); Head of the General Intelligence Service (1970); Minister of State for Foreign Affairs (1971); Adviser to the President for National Security Affairs with rank of Deputy Prime Minister (1971); Head of Cabinet and Adviser to the President (1973); Ministry of Foreign Affairs with rank of Ambassador (1974); Ambassador to USSR (1974-77); Ambassador to France (1977), now retired. **Addr.:** Ministry of Foreign Affairs, Cairo, Egypt.

ISMAIL (Mustafa), Iraqi statesman. **Born** in Iraq. **Educ.:** Secondary and Higher. **Career:** Minister of Municipal and Rural Affairs (1962), Minister of Public Works and Housing in the Cabinet of Mr. Abdurrahman al-Bazzaz (1965-66), Minister of Communications and Acting Minister of Municipal and Rural Affairs in the Cabinet of Mr. Nagi Taleb (1966-67). **Addr.:** Baghdad, Iraq.

ISMAIL (Sabri, Dr.), Egyptian executive. **Born** in 1924 in Malawi. **Married. Educ.:** in Egypt; Postgraduate studies in Law in France (1946-50); Doctor of Law. **Career:** Lecturer in Law Faculty, Alexandria University, Egypt; Later Professor of Economics; Secretary-General of the Egyptian Communist Party (1955); Member of the Egyptian Economic Organization (1958); Appointed Economic Adviser to the President (1959); Became a Member of the Arab Socialist Union Secretariat and Editor in Chief "Dar al-Maarifa" publishing house (1966); Director, al-Ahram Economic Research Organization (1968); Director, Egyptian National Planning Institute (1970); Deputy Minister of Planning (1971); retained as Managing Director of National Planning Institute; retained in new Cabinet (1971) with title changed to Minister of State for Planning (1972); Minister of Planning (1974-75); Secretary-General, Scientific Conference of Egyptian Economists; Member, Academic Advisory Board, UN African Institute of Development & Planning, Dakar, Senegal (1971-); Member, Academic Committee, UN African Institute of Development and Planning, Kuwait; Founding Member of the Third World Forum; Deputy Chairman, Council for the Development of Economies and Social Research in Africa; presently Deputy General Manager, Nasser Social Bank, Cairo, Egypt. **Publ.:** "Economie et Structure Economique" (1952); "Lectures in Economics" (1954). "The Organization of Public Sector"; "Confrontation with Israel 1969"; "Political Papers 1972". **Addr.:** Cairo, Egypt.

ISMAIL (Tawfic, Abdo), Egyptian Administrator. **Born** on February 15, 1929 in Egypt. **Married,** 1 son, 1 daughter. **Educ.:** Cairo University, B,A. Business Administration, M.B.A. American University in Cairo **Career:** Army Officer (1949-54); Ministry of Tourism (1955-56); Sales Manager at Misr Petroleum Co. (1957-64) and (1970-71); Commercial Minister, The Egyptian Embassy in Bonn,

West Germany (1966-69); Under Secretary; National Council for Production and Economic Affairs, President's Cabinet (1971-80); Member of the Peoples Assembly (1976), (1984), (1987), (1990) and (1995); Member of the Shoura Council (1980); Minister of Tourism and Civil Aviation (1982-1984), Minister for Peoples Assembly and Shoura Council, Member of the Board of Directors of Dakahlia Commercial Bank (1980-82), President and Managing Director (1990 - Till Now); **Member:** Egyptian National Club, Gezira Sporting Club, Egyptian Automobile Club. **Addr.:** 34 Muhammad Mazhar Street, Zamalek, Cairo, Egypt Tel.: 3411177.

ISSA (Abdulaziz Ibn Ibrahim Ibn Abdulaziz, al), Saudi chief justice. **Born** in 1929 at Shaqra. **Dipl.:** Higher Certificate, Faculty of Shari'a (Islamic Law), Mecca. **Career:** Judge, Taif and Jeddah Courts; Assistant to Chief Justice, Jeddah; Chief Justice, Supreme Shari'a Court, Jeddah; member of Supreme Judicial Council; member of Commercial Disputes Court, Jeddah. **Hobby:** Reading. **Addr.:** Supreme Shari'a Court, Jeddah, Saudi Arabia.

ISSA (Abdulrahman Abdul Latif al-Ali), Saudi Businessman. **Born** in 1940 at al-Ahsa. **Dipl.:** B.A., Business Administration and Economics), Whittier College, California, U.S.A. (1964). **Career:** Liaison officier with the Ministry of Finance and National Economy, (1964-66); ex member of Board of Social Insurance Organization, Chamber of Commerce and Industry, Riyadh; Riyadh Bank Ltd; Riyadh Electric Company and Suburbs. **Shareholder of:** The United Saudi Commercial Bank. **Owner** of Allissa Trading Est. Also part of following companies. ALISSA Trading and Contracting Co. Ltd., CHEMACO Trading and Contracting Ltd., BALSAM Sports Contracting Co. Ltd. **Addr.:** P.O.Box 6097, Jeddah 21442, Saudi Arabia.

ISSA (Ahmad, Babikir)), Sudanese official. **Born** in January 1931 at el-Kamlin, Sudan. **Educ.:** primary and secondary education locally; Faculty of Arts, University of Khartoum; University of Birmingham, England (1957). **Dipl.:** B.Sc. (Economics), B.A. (History), BPA (Bachelor of Public Administration) (1957), LL.B. **Career:** Assistant District Officer, and later Inspector in Darfur Province (1955-60); Secretary General, Nile Waters control Committee, Ministry of the Interior (1960); Director General, Industrial Development Corporation, Carboard and Dry Onion Factories, Kassala; Deputy Director, Industrial Development Corporation, Khartoum; Commissioner for Refugees, Ministry of Interior, Khartoum (1967-70); Secretary General, Council of Ministers (Feb. 1970- Jan. 1975); Commissioner for Gezira Province since Jan. 1975. **Prof. Addr.:** Office of the Commissioner of Gezira province, Wad Medani, Sudan.

ISSA (Ahmad, Bakor, el-Haj), Saudi civil servant. **Born** in 1929 in Saudi Arabia. **Educ.:** Faculty of Engineering, Riyadh University. **Dipl.:** B.Sc. (Engineering). **Career:** Communications Engineer; Director of Technical department for Wire and Wireless Affairs, Ministry of Communications, later Director of the Department of Planning, Budgeting and Training; Co-Director of the training project for Wire, Wireless and Broadcasting Communications; attended Several international conferences in Europe, the Americas and Japan; now Director of Training Institute for Wireless and Broadcasting, Ministry of Telegrams, Post and Telephones, (Riyadh). **Member:** International Electronic and Electric Engineering Society, New York (USA); Board of Training Council. **Sport:** Swimming. **Hobbies:** Reading and travel. **Prof. Addr.:** Ministry of Telegrams, Post and Telephones, Tel.: 23121, Riyadh. **Priv. Addr.:** Tel.: 67201, Riyadh, Saudi Arabia.

ISSA (Fawzi, Sultan, al), Kuwaiti businessman. **Born** in 1944 in Kuwait. **Son** of Sultan al-Issa. **Married. Educ.:** American University in Beirut, Beirut, Lebanon. **Career:** Managing Director of Bank of Kuwait and the Middle East, Deputy Chairman, International Financial Advisers, investment company with British merchant bank connections; Director of Research to the Kuwait Arab Fund for Economic and Social Development; Director, United Bank of Kuwait, Jordan. **Addr.:** International Financial Advisers, P.O.Box 4694, Fisheries Bldg., Tel.: 448171, Kuwait, Arabian Gulf.

ISSA (Husam, Muhammad), Egyptian academic. **Born** on March 23, 1939 in Cairo, Egypt. **Married,** 2 daughters. **Educ.:** University of Paris, France. **Dipl.:** Ph.D. in Law. **Career:** Lecturer, Faculty of Law, Ain Shams University, Cairo (1969-74); United Nations University Senior Programme Officer; Associate Professor, Ain Shams University, Cairo (1976-). **Publ.:** "Capitalisme et Sociétés Anonymes", LGDJ, Paris (1970), "The Multi-National Companies", Arab Organization for Studies and Publications, Beirut (1980). **Hobby:** History. **Addr.:** 2 Mukarar Aljazair Street, Dokki, Cairo, Egypt.

ISSA (Ibrahim, Abdullatif, Ali, al), Saudi businessman. **Born** in 1936 at Alahsa, Eastern Province, Saudi Arabia. **Son** of Ali Alissa. **Career:** Owner of Ibrahim A. Alissa Est. whose activities are: Real Estate Consultants, Commercial Advisors, Bank consultants, Agents, Representatives of companies, commercial agencies. Chairman of Souks Co. Ltd., Partner of: Geerco; Maymoun Travel Agency, Al Khobar: General Food and Households Exports to Saudi Arabia, Washington D.C. (under foundation); Chemaco Trading and Contracting Co.; Balsam Sports Contracting Co. Ltd.; Alissa Trading & Contracting Co. Ltd.; Director, Saudi French Bank, Jeddah. **Prof. Addr.:** Ibrahim A. Alissa, P.O.Box. 1559, Tel.: 8578260, 8578512, Telex: 67022 ALISSA SJ and 670091 Souks Sj, al-Khobar, Saudi Arabia.

ISSA (Ibrahim, Mohamed, al)), Saudi businessman.

Born in 1928 at Shagra. **Educ.:** received general education. **Career:** founding member of Tihama for Advertising, Public Relations and Marketing, Research; member of Board, Okaz daily newspaper, Dar Okaz Printing and Publishing, National Shipping Company of Saudi Arabia (NSCSA), Saudi Hotels and Resort Areas Co., Arab Cement Co. Jeddah and Yanbu Cement Co., Al Bank Al Saudi Al Fransi, Jeddah. **Hobbies:** Reading, travel. **Prof. Addr.:** P.O.Box 1629, Tel.: 6672080, 6672084, 6672092, Jeddah. **Priv. Addr.:** Tel.: 6823431, 6823157, (Car) 2019924, Jeddah, Saudi Arabia.

ISSA (Mohamad, Ali Ahmad), Saudi academic. **Born** in 1939 at Gizan. **Dipl.:** Ph.D. (Science). **Career:** Vice Dean of Students' Affairs, King Saud University (1976), later Dean (1981); Associate Professor of Physics, Faculty of Sciences, King Saud University. **Publ.:** several scientific research papers pertinent to Solid State, accepted for publication by foreign scientific journals. **Prof. Addr.:** College of Science, Physics Department, King Saud University, P.O.Box 2455, Tel.: (01) 4676435, Telex 201019 K.S.U. Riyadh, Saudi Arabia, **Priv. Addr.:** Tel.: (01) 4648624, Riyadh.

ISSA (Mohamad, Mohamad Bin), Moroccan journalist. **Born** in 1937 in Morocco. **Married. Educ.:** Cairo University, Egypt; University of Minnesota, Minneapolis, USA; Rockfeller Foundation (Documentary Films and Communications), New York; Columbia University, New York (Psychology). **Dipl.:** B.A. in Journalism and Communications. **Career:** Head of Programmes, Radio Africa Maghreb, Morocco (1956-59), Director of Youth Centre, Tangiers, Morocco (1959-60); Reporter, Moroccan Radio and Television, Cairo (1960-61); Permanent Mission of Morocco, New York (1964-65); Information Officer, Office of Public Information (OPI), UN New York and Addis Ababa (1965-67); Regional Information Officer for Africa, FAO, Accra (1967-71); Development Support Communications Officer, FAO, Rome (1971-73); Assistant Director, Information Office, FAO (1973-74); Director, Information Division, FAO, Rome (1974). **Publ.:** "Rural Development Support Communication Model", "Grains de Peau", "Tout est dans la Photo" (1973). **Hobbies:** Design, architecture, photo journalism, inter-community communications and rural development. **Prof. Addr.:** Information Division, FAO, Via delle Terme de Caracalla, 00100 Rome, Italy. **Priv. Addr.:** 15 Via Guerrieri, 00100 Rome, Italy.

ISSA (Omar, Saleh), Sudanese engineer. **Born** on August 17, 1937 at Bara, Sudan. **Educ.:** primary and secondary education in Omdurman and Khur Takt; Faculty of Engineering, Khartoum University (1963); further studies in Engineering, USA (1965-66). **Dipl.:** B.Sc. (Engineering), M.Sc. (Engineering). **Career:** Engineer in the Ministry of Labour (1964); Chief Engineer, Bahr el-Ghazal Province (1971); Deputy Minister for Youth and Sports (1976). **Member:** National Assembly; Sudan Socialist Union (SSU); SSU Central Committee for Khartoum Province; SSU Women's Committee; SSU Committee for Economic and Development Affairs. **Addr.:** Khartoum, Sudan.

ISSA (Shaker), Iraqi economist. **Born** in 1940 in Basrah, Iraq. **Son** of Musa Issa (farmer) **and** Mrs. Shaika née Abdulhamid. **Married** in 1971 in Basrah to Miss Najat Nadhum, three children. **Educ.:** Baghdad University, College of Economics and Commerce; Cairo University, Faculty of Economics and Political Sciences; University of London, SOAS. **Dipl.:** B.Sc. in Economics, Baghdad (1962); M.Sc. in Economics, Cairo (1972); Ph.D. in Economics, London (1978). **Career:** Economic Researcher, Ministry of Planning, Economics Department, Baghdad (1968-70); Director of National Accounts Dept., Central Statistical Organisation (1971-74); Lecturer, University of al-Mustansiriya, College of Economics (1972-74); Senior Expert for Research and Statistics in the Central Bank of United Arab Emirates (since 1978). **Sports:** Swimming, bolling. **Hobby:** Fishing. Member of Iraq and U.A.E. Economists Associations. **Prof. Addr.:** P.O.Box 854, Tel.: 368200, 368481, Abu Dhabi, United Arab Emirates.

ISSA (Sulaiman, al), Syrian writer and poet. **Born** in 1922 in Antioch. **Educ.:** Antioch, Damascus and Baghdad. **Dipl.:** Bachelor of Arts. **Career:** Professor at Ma'moun College of Aleppo (1945-65). **Publ.:** Author of several books of Collected Poems, including "Maal Fagr", "Rimal Atcha", "Kassayed Arabiya", "al-Farès al-Dayekh" (1969). **Addr.:** Damascus, Syria.

ISSAWI (Charles Philippe, Elias), Economist. **Born** on March 15, 1916 in Cairo. **Son** of Elias Issawi **and** Mrs., née Alexandra Abouchar. **Married** on July 20, 1946 to Miss Janina M. Haftke. **Educ.:** Magdalen College, Oxford University, L.L.D.h.c. (1989). **Dipl.:** Bachelor of Arts (1937), Master of Arts (1944). **Career:** Ministry of Finance (1937-38); Chief, Research, National Bank of Egypt (1938-43); Professor, American University of Beirut (1943-47); Came to the United States of America (1947); Naturalized (1957); Member, Middle East Unit, Economic Department, U.N.O. (1948-55); Member Faculty, Columbia since 1955; Professor of Economics (1965-75) Director, Near and Middle East Institute (1962-64); Consultant, F.A.O. (1955) and U.N. (1956); Board Editor, Middle East Institute Journal since 1958; Vice-President, Middle East Studies Association (1968); President, Middle East Association (1973); Bayard Dodge Professor of Near Eastern Studies, Princeton University, USA (1974-1986), **Publ.:** Author of "Egypt: an Economic and Social Analysis" (1947), "An Arab Philosophy of History" (1950), "Mushkilat Qawmiya" (1959), "Egypt in Revolution" (1963); co-author of the "Economics of Middle Eastern Oil" (1962); "The Economic History of Middle East, 1800-1914" (1966); "The Economic History of Iran 1800-1914"

(1971); "Issawi's Laws of Social Motion" (1973); "Oil, The Middle East and the World"; "The Economic History of Turkey" (1980); "The Arab Legacy" (1981); "An Economic history of the Middle East and North Africa" (1982); "Modern Arab Thought" (1983). **Member** of several societies and organisations. **Addr.:** Princeton University, Department of Near East Studies, Princeton, New-Jersey, USA.

IZZIDDIN (Ibrahim), Jordanian politician. **Born** in 1934 in Beirut, Lebanon. **Educ.:** American University of Beirut. **Dipl.:** B.A. **Career:** served in Ministry of Communications, Prime Minister's Office, and Press Section of Ministry of Foreign Affairs (1955-58); Deputy Director, Book Publishers, Beirut (1958-65); Director of Foreign Press, Ministry of Information (1965-68); Under Secretary (1971-75); Press Secretary to H.M King Hussein (1968-70); Director Public Relations for Alia (Royal Jordanian Airlines) (1970-71); Ambassador to Switzerland (1975-77); to Federal Republic of Germany (1977-78); to U.K. (1978-83), to U.S.A. (1983-84); Head Administration, Civil Service Commission (1985-89); Minister of State for Prime Ministerial Affairs (27 April 1989- Oct. 1989); Minister of Information (Nov. 1989- Dec. 1990); Minister of State for Prime Ministerial Affairs (Nov. 1991-May 1993). **Decor.:** Order of Istiqlal (Second Class), Cedar of Lebanon. **Addr.:** Amman, Jordan.

IZZIDDIN (Sayyid, Mohamad), Sudanese politician. **Born** in 1934 in Dongola, Sudan. **Educ.:** Teachers Training College; University of London, UK; American University of Beirut, Lebanon (Course in Rural Education). **Dipl.:** Diploma in Education and Psychology. **Career:** Member of the Sudanese delegation to the 20th session of the UN General Assembly and the Arab Prime Ministers' Conference; elected to the Constituent Assembly (1965); Minister of Industry; General Manager of Sudan Insurance and Reinsurance Company; Secretary for Workers' Affairs and Member of the Political Bureau of the Sudan Socialist Union (SSU) (1972-74); Speaker of the People's Assembly (1974-85). **Addr.:** Khartoum, Sudan.

IZZIDIN (Yusuf), Iraqi academic. **Born** in Iraq. **Educ.:** University of Alexandria, Alexandria, Egypt; University of London, UK. **Dipl.:** B.A. in arabic Literature and Language; M.A.; Ph.D. in Philosophy. **Career:** Occupied several government posts for number of Years; Currently Professor of Literature, Faculty of Arts, University of Riyadh, Saudi Arabia; Editor in Chief of al-Kitaab; Member of the editorial staff of al-Jumhuriyah for several years; Editor in Chief of al-Nadwa; Member of the Tunis Academy, Cairo Academy, Iraqi Academy of Science, Academy of Arabic Language, Damascus and Amman; Member of the Indian Academy of Sciences, Society of Comparative Literature, Royal Society of Literature, UK. **Publ.:** Author of "Daoud Pasha and Mameluks in Iraq"; Numerous Works in Arabic and English, criticism and other subjects. **Decor:** several medals and prizes. **Addr.:** Riyadh, Saudi Arabia.

J

JAABARY (Sharif, Abdulkader, al), Jordanian administrator. **Born** in 1924 in al-Khalil, Palestine. **Married**, 3 sons, 4 daughters. **Educ.:** Faculty of Commerce, Cairo University, Egypt. Training course with Midland Bank, United Kingdom. **Dipl.:** in Commerce. **Career:** Assistant Manager, Arab Bank, Cairo (1949-57); Manager, National Commercial Saudi Bank, Cairo (1957-60); Gulf Representative of Arab Bank (1962-70); General Manager and Member of the Board of Directors of Arab National Bank, Riyadh (1985-). **Hobbies:** Swimming, basket ball, football. **Member:** al-Ahly Club, Cairo. **Prof. Addr.:** P.O.Box 56921, Riyadh, Saudi Arabia.

JAAFAR (Ahmad, Mohamad), Kuwaiti Businessman. **Born** on January 12, 1938. **Son** of Mohamad Jaafar. **Married** in 1960 to Eileen, 3 children: Tarik, Mishal, Sara. **Educ.:** Shuwaikh School, Kuwait (1954-57); South Devon Technical College, UK (1957-58). **Career:** Joined Kuwait State Police; Inspector, Kuwait Police; Oil Company (KOC), London Office (1960); Personnel Officer, Payroll Employees Division, KOC (1961); Personnel Department, KOC (1964-70); Superintendent, Payroll Employees Divisions; Staff Superintendent; Acting Manager, Local Relations; Acting Manager, Services, Manager, Personnel and Local Affairs, KOC (1974); Chairman and Managing Director, KOC (1975); In private business since 1981. **President:** al-Shabab Football Club, Kuwait. **Addr.:** Kuwait City, Kuwait.

JAAFAR (Ezzat, Mohammad), Kuwaiti politician and businessman. **Born** on January 12, 1912 in Beirut, Lebanon. **Son** of Mohammad Moustapha Jaafar (Merchant) **and** Mrs. née Bahia Mohammad Badr al-Misri. **Married** on July 18, 1963 in Beirut to Miss Salma Ramez Kronfol, 7 children: Mohammad (1964), Bahia (1965); Layla (1968), Ezzat (1969), Jaber (1971), Zaynab (1972) and Ahmad (1974). **Educ.:** Lycée French of Beirut. **Dipl.:** B.Sc. Business Administration. **Career:** Former Chief of the Cabinet to their late Highnesses, the Rulers of Kuwait (1935-60); Former Owner of Diners Club of Kuwait Branch. Currently Chairman of: The Kuwaiti Danish Dairy Co. W.L.L., Arabian Construction Company, Carnaval Store and Green Gardens Co.; Member of the Board of Libano-Suisse Co., Beirut; Honorary Diplomatic Counsellor of the Kuwait Embassy to Lebanon. **Decor.:** Commander of the French Legion of Honour as well as other decorations from Egypt, Lebanon, Syria, Jordan and Iraq. **Hobbies:** Horse riding, swimming. **Life Member** of the Alumni Club of Beirut. **Credit Cards:** Diners Club; Golden Visa. **Prof. Addr.:** P.O.Box 176, 13002 Safat, Tel.: 2432045, Kuwait, Kuwait. **Priv. Addr.:** al-Sour Street, Villa Ezzat M. Jaafar, No. 39-41 al-Sharq, Tel.: 2432582, Kuwait.

JAAFAR (Khaled, Mohamad), Kuwaiti politician. **Born** on June 12, 1922 in Kuwait. **Son** of Mohamad Mustafa Jaafar. **Educ.:** Mubarakia School. **Career:** School Teacher (1940-43); Chief Cashier at Kuwait Municipality (1943-45); Kuwait Oil Company (1945-61); Lord Chamberlain to Amir of Kuwait (1961-62); Head of Cultural and Press Department, Foreign Affairs (1962); Deputised for Under-Secretary of State in the Minitry of Foreign Affairs (1962-63); Ambassador of Kuwait to the United Kingdom (1963-65), concurrently to France (1965); Ambassador to Lebanon (1965-70); concurrently to Turkey (1970-73); Chairman of Kuwait Investment Board; Chief of Protocol, Ministry of Foreign Affairs (1973-74); Ambassador to USA (1975-80); Minister of Foreign Affairs (1981) Retired. **Addr.:** Kuwait City, Kuwait.

JAAFAR (Moncef), Tunisian diplomat. **Born** in 1936 in Tunis, Tunisia. **Son** of Hedi Jaafar. **Married** in 1964 to Miss Saida Doria, three children. **Educ.:** Faculty of Law, Bordeaux, France; Institute of Political Studies, Bordeaux, France. **Dipl.:** Bachelor of Public Law and Political Science. **Career:** Embassy secretary at the Ministry of Foreign Affairs of Tunisia (1959); Chargé d'Affaires of Embassy of Tunisia at Rabat, Morocco (1961); Director and Chief Editor of newspaper L'ACTION-Tunis (1963-72); Member of Parliament (1969-74); Ambassador to East Germany (1973-80); Ambassador to Hungary, Czechoslovakia with residence in East Berlin (1980); Ambassador-Director of Political Affairs for Asia in the Ministry of Foreign Affairs (1981); Ambassador to Japan, Indonesia, Republic of Korea and Australia with residence in Tokyo (1981-88); Ambassador Director of the Department of Documentation, Research and Planing (1988) - Chairman and General Manager of Tunis Afrique Presse TAP (1989) - Directeur General, Inspecteur General of Ministry for Foreign Affairs (1991-1994); Member of the Central Committee of Destour Socialist Party (1971); Member of the Commission for the Revision of the Constitution of Tunisia. **Publ.:** numerous articles and editorials in the newspaper "L'ACTION"-Tunis (1963-72). **Medals:** Commander of the Order of Friendship between people (East Germany); several other decorations from Iran, Ivory Coast, Hungary. Leading **Member** of "Africa Club", one of the largest sports associations of Tunisia; President of Tunisia & Federal Rep. of Germany Friendship Association. **Credit Cards:** American Express, VISA. **Priv. Addr.:** Panorama El-Menzah - Menzah 9C, Tunis, Tunisia.

JAAFAR (Taha), Egyptian banker. **Born** in 1918 in Cairo, Egypt. **Son** of Mohd. Jaafar. **Married** in 1953. **Dipl.:** LL.B. **Career:** Egyptian Ministry of Economy (1943-62); Banking foundation (1962-63); Office Manager for Foreign Educational Affairs (1963-65); Deputy Chairman, Arab Land Bank (1965-1988). **Publ.:** "Companies Ordinance", Egypt (1958). **Member:** al-Jazirah Club Cairo. **Hobby:** Reading. **Addr.:** Cairo, Egypt.

JABBES (Frej), Tunisian administrator. **Born** in 1922 in Kairouan, Tunisia. **Married. Educ.:** University of Dijon, France. **Dipl.:** in Mathematics. **Career:** Inspector of Schools; Administrator in Ministry of Education; Governor of Medicine, South Tunisia (1969); Secretary of State for Education; Technical Training Department (1960-73); Director General of Office National de l'Huile (1973); Head, Office for Tunisian Workers Abroad (1973); Businessman (1984-). **Prof. Addr.:** Tunisian Chamber of Commerce, rue des Entrepreneurs, Tunis, Tunisia.

JABBOUR (Georges), Syrian statesman. **Born** in 1938 in Safita. **Married:** to pharmacist Maria Anie Chebat, two sons: Jaber and Zaher. **Educ.:** Universities of U.S.A. **Dipl.:** Doctor in Political Science (1964). **Career:** Judge, International civil servant, academic, Joined the Presidency in 1970 as adviser and director of Political Studies; Advisor, Arab Center for strategic Studies, Damascus (since 1998). **Publ.:** "Arabism in Arab Constitutions", "Settler Colloni alism in Southern Africa and Middle East" and: "Al Arab Wa Houkouk el Insan" (Damascus, 1990) in 76 pages, "Al Ounsouriya Al Sahyouniya Walmoujtamah Al Douali" (Damascus, 1991) in 71 pages, "Al Ourouba Wal Islam Fi Aldasatir Al Arabiye" (Aleppo, 1993) in 206 pages, "Nahoua Alam Arabi Lilsiyasa" (Beirut and Damascus, 2nd edition, 1993) in 176 pages, "Al Fikr Al Siyasi Al Maaser fi Souriya" (Beirut and Damascus, 2nd edition, 1993) in 567 pages, "Safita Wa Mouhitouha Fi Alkarn Al Taseh Ashar" (Latakia, 1993) in 41 pages, "Souriya: 1918-1968" (Damascus, 1993) in 145 pages, "Al Ouman Al Moutahida Wal Siyasa Al Doualiyat Wama Yakhousou Al Arab" (Damascus, 1994) in 67 pages, "Risala Ila Kadasat Al Baba" (Beirut, 1995), "Houkouk Al Insan Al Arabi fi Alam Al Yaoum" (Damascus, 1995) in 62 pages; "Hilf Al-Foudoul" (Damascus, 1998 in 119 pages); "Nahou Istratigia Siyasia Arabia" (Damascus, 1999 in 52 pages); "Al-Islam wa Oropa" (Damascus, 2000 in 92 pages). **Addr.:** P.O.Box 9877, Damascus, Syria.

JABER (Mamdouh), Syrian army officer and statesman. **Born** in Syria. **Educ.:** Military Academy. **Career:** Syrian Army General; Minister of Public Works in the Cabinet of Dr. Yusuf Zouayen (March 1965); Minister of Defence (1966); Minister of State for the Presidency (January- March 1966); Minister of Public Works (March 1966-69), of Affairs of Frontline Villages (1969). **Addr.:** Damascus, Syria.

JABER (Mohamed, Saleh), Jordanian economist and financial analyst. **Born** in 1940 in Jerusalem. **Son** of Ibrahim Jaber **and** Mrs. Zahra née Hadad. **Married**, with five children. **Educ.:** Baghdad University, Iraq; Columbia Pacific University, USA, College of Data Processing, USA. **Dipl.:** B.Sc. in Commerce and Economics; M.BA. **Career:** Accountant A.S.H. al-Garabally (1962-64); Senior Auditor of Farid Mansour and Partner FCA (1964-73); Senior Economic Research of Ministry of Commerce and Industry, Kuwait (1975-76); Finance manager of Kuwait Hotels Co. SAK (1976-81); Finance and Administrative Manager "Burhan Kuwaiti Trading and Contracting Co." (1981-82); Financial Adviser of Jordan Kuwaiti Bank (1982); Executive Director of Amman Chamber of Industry (since 1985 to present). **Pub.:** Author of a Leading book in investment in Arabic Language "Investment in Stocks, Bonds and Security Analysis" (1982). **Medals:** "Industrial Shield" (1982). **Priv. Addr.:** Shmeisani 5569 S. Qanouni Road, Amman, Jordan.

JABOUR (Abdullah Sulaiman, al), Saudi academic. **Born** in 1944 at Qassim, Saudi Arabia. **Dipl.:** Ph.D. (Literature), Edinburgh University, U.K. **Career:** Teacher, Yamamah Secondary School, Riyadh (1965-67); Demonstrator, Faculty of Sharia, Mecca (1967-68); Lecturer, Faculty of Sharia (Islamic Law), Umm al-Qura University, Mecca. **Publ.:** some research work on Mecca and Medina poets in the pre-Islamic and Islamic eras, and poetry of war in Mecca and Medina. **Hobby:** Reading. **Prof. Addr.:** Faculty of Sharia, Department of Arabic, Umm al-Qura University, Tel.: 5564770, Mecca, Saudi Arabia.

JABR (Fuad, Mohamad), Jordanian banking executive. **Born** in Nablus, Jordan in 1948. **Son** of Mohamad Jabr **and** Mrs. Enaya Mohamad Saed Jabre. **Married** in 1975 in Kuwait to Miss Randa Anwar Jabre, four children. **Educ.:** University of Jordan, Amman. **Dipl.:** B.Sc. in Commerce and Economics, political studies and public administration. **Career:** Commercial Bank of Kuwait (1970-75); Riyadh Bank, Medina, Saudi Arabia (1975-77); Bank of Bahrain and Kuwait, Kuwait (1977-81); K.F.T.C.I.C., Kuwait (1977); Gulf Financial Center, Kuwait (1981-82); Assistant General Manager, Bahrain Middle East Bank (E.C.), Bahrain (since 1983). **Hobby:** Reading. **Prof. Addr.:** P.O.Box 797, Tel.: 275345, Manama, Bahrain.

JABR (Issamiddin, Shafik), Egyptian banker. **Born** on June 10, 1929 in Egypt. **Married**, 1 daughter. **Dipl.:** B.A. in Commerce. **Career:** Employed at Banque Belgium (1951), Head of Commercial Sector (1958); Assistant Manager, Port Said Bank (1961), Manager Port Said Bank, Muhammad Farid Branch (1968); Manager, Foreign Relations Department, Arab African Bank (1970); Assistant General

Manager, Arab African Bank, Deputy General Manager; Chief General Manager, Arab African International Bank. **Hobbies:** Football, horses. **Addr.:** Abdel Khalik Tharwat Street, P.O.Box 1143, Cairo, Egypt.

JABR (Sami), Egyptian egyptologist. **Born** in Egypt. **Married** to Miss Lorette Guidot. **Educ.:** Bordeaux University, La Sorbonne, Archæological Institute of Liverpool. **Dipl.:** Licentiate and Doctor of Law, Archæologist Diploma. **Career:** Director Egyptology Institute, Professor of Ancient Egyptian History, Director of excavation research of the Cairo University at Heliopolis West, Vice-President of the Egyptian Institute. **Awards:** Knight of the Legion of Honour, Commander the Phoenix Order of Greece. **Addr.:** Heliopolis, Tel.: 861920, Cairo, Egypt.

JABRA (Jabra, Ibrahim), Iraqi writer, poet and painter. **Born** in 1920 in Bethlehem. **Son** of Ibrahim Jabra. **Married** in 1952 to Miss Lamia Barqi el-Askari, 2 children: Sadeer, Yasser. **Educ.:** Secondary and Higher. Cambridge and Harvard Universities. **Dipl.:** B.A. M.A. **Career:** Writer, Journalist, Painter; Lecturer, Rashidiyah College, Jerusalem (1944); Lecturer in English Literature, College of Arts and Sciences, Baghdad (1948-52); Research Fellow, Harvard (1952-54); Senior Staff, Iraq Petroleum Company (IPC), Baghdad (1954-72); Head of Department, Iraq National Oil Company (INOC), Baghdad (1972); Head of Department, Ministry of Oil Baghdad; part-time Lecturer, Baghdad University (1956-64); Visiting lecturer, University of California, Berkeley, USA (January to June 1976). **Publ.:** Author of several studies on Jawad Salim, Muhammad Ghini, Touma al-Khoury, Abdurrahim Mahmoud and Riad ar-Rayess, Author of "The Eighth Crusade", "Contemporary Novel", "A Survey of the Theatre" etc... **Remark:** many of the studies are translated into French, English, German and Italian. **Addr.:** 1518 al-Mansour, Tel.: 514411, Baghdad, Iraq.

JABRIL (Abdul Majeed), Saudi composer, violinist and radio and TV announcer. **Born** in 1939. **Dipl.:** Diploma of Music (Violin), Army School of Music, Taif. **Career:** Member of Saudi Arabian Arts Society; composed a number of oriental musical pieces; attended several music conferences in Algeria, Tunisia, Kuwait, Bahrain and Abu Dhabi. **Hobbies:** Reading, music. **Prof. Addr.:** Music Department, Broadcasting Service, Tel.: 6445222, Jeddah. **Priv. Addr.:** Tel.: 6427217, Jeddah, Saudi Arabia.

JAD (Ali Bakor), Saudi academic. **Born** in 1940 in Medina, Saudi Arabia. **Dipl.:** M.A., Leeds University (1967); Ph.D. (English Literature), Oxford University (1974). **Career:** Demonstrator, Department of English, King Saud University; Assistant Professor, same University; member of the Oxford Society, the Oxford Union, the British Society for Middle East Studies, Faculty of Arts Conference and Research Committee; attended Conference on Modern Arabic Literature, University of London (1973), the Conference on the Message of the University, King Saud University (1974). **Hobbies:** Reading, travel, music, watching TV, cinema and theatre. **Addr.:** Faculty of Arts, King Saud University, Tel.: 4811000, Riyadh, Saudi Arabia.

JADAAN (Fahmi, Rajeh), Jordanian academic. **Born** in 1939 in Ain Ghazal, Jordan. **Married**, 1 son, 1 daughter. **Educ.:** University of Sorbonne, Paris. **Dipl.:** Ph.D. in Islamic Philosophy. **Career:** Head of Philosophy Department, University of Jordan (1976-78); Dean, Faculty of Literature (1979-80), Dean, Department of Scientific Research (1980-81); Member of the Board of Directors of Institut du Monde Arabe (1982-83); Administrator of Islamic Studies Centre, Yarmouk University (1982-83); Head of Philosophy Department, University of Jordan (1983-). **Publ.:** several academic research papers in "Studia Islamica" magazine, Paris, "l'Influence du Stoicisme sur la Pensée Musulmane" Imprimerie Catholique, Beirut, Lebanon, "Foundations of Progress on Islamic Thiners about the Contemporary Arab World" (1981), "Heritage Theory", Lebanon. **Prof. Addr.:** Faculty of Arts, Department of Philosophy, University of Jordan, P.O.Box 13063, Amman, Jordan.

JADIDI (Arsalan), Moroccan statesman. **Born** in 1926 at Jadida. **Educ.:** Secondary in Rabat. **Career:** Teacher (1945-50); Cadre, "Office Chérifien des Phosphates" (OCP) (1950); Secretary General, Khouribga Miners (1950-60); Secretary General, "Union des Phosphates", Secretary General, Mining Resources Federation (1964); Board member, National Social Security Fund (CNSS) (1970); Deputy, Chamber of the Representatives (1970); Minister of Youth, Sports, Labour and Social Affairs (August 1971- April 1974); High Commissioner, National Promotion (April 1974- October 1977); Member of Parliament (1977); Minister of Labour and National Revival (1979-83); Leader, Parti National Démocrate. **Addr.:** 18 rue de Tunis, Rabat, Morocco.

JADO (Ahmad Ismail), Saudi academic. **Born** in 1942. **Dipl.:** B.Sc. (Pharmacy) (1963), Ph.D. (Pharmaceutical Chemistry), U.S.A. (1971). **Career:** Professor Pharmaceutical Chemistry and Chairman of the Department, College of Pharmacy, King Saud University; Consultant and member of Technical Committee for Drug Registration, M.O. Health; Director of Central Laboratory for drug analysis, M.O. Health; Consultant, Forensic Studies, Arab Security Center, Riyadh; Member of Saudi Pharmaceutical Society, American Pharmaceutical Society. **Publ.:** Several papers in medicinal chemisty and Forensic Sciences. **Hobbies:** Travel, Sports. **Business Address:** College of Pharmacy, King Saud University, Riyadh, Saudi Arabia, Tel.: 467-7340.

JAFAR (Hamid), Iraqi executive. **Born** in 1947 in Baghdad, Iraq. **Son** of Dr. Dhiya Jafar (former Cabinet Minister) **and** Mrs., née Melouk Khan. **Married** on October 9, 1975 to Sawsan Badr al-Fahoum, 2 sons Abul-Majid, Badr and one daughter, Razan. **Educ.:** St. Paul's School, London (UK); Churchill College, Cambridge University. **Dipl.:** B.A., M.A. (Honours). **Career:** General Manager, Sharjah Petroleum Company (1970-72); Vice-President, Crescent Petroleum Sharjah (1972-74); President and Chief Executive Officer of the said company since 1974. **Hobbies:** Chess, Philately, Islamic Manuscripts and Art, Shooting. **Member:** Young Presidents' Organization. **Prof. Addr.:** P.O.Box 211, Tel.: 543000, Telex: 68015 CRESPT EM, Fax: 542000, Sharjah, U.A.E.

JAFF (Akram, Hamid, al), Iraqi international civil servant. **Born** on July 14, 1929 in Halabcha, Sulaymanya, Iraq. **Educ.:** Colorado State University (1948-51); University of Kentucky (1951-52); Oregon State University (1955-57). **Dipl.:** B.Sc., M.Sc. (Plant Genetics). **Career:** Director-General, Ministry of Economy (1963-65); Minister of Agriculture (1965-66); Chairman, Tobacco Administration, Bagdad, Iraq (1966-69); Lecturer, Baghdad University (1969); Senior Agricultural Adviser and Country Representative of FAO/UNDP (Food and Agriculture Organisation - United Nations Development Programme) in Somalia (1970-73); now UNDP Officer in Charge of Somalia (1973-80); FAO Representative Egypt (1980); and FAO Rome, Italy (1981-). **Publ.:** Author of "Soil Insects and Control", "Tobacco Industry in Iraq". **Member:** raqi Management Association; Iraqi Petroleum Company; Iraqi Rafidain Bank. **Hobbies:** Reading and music. **Sports:** Walking and swimming. **Prof. Addr.:** FAO, Rome, Italy.

JAFFAR (Nabil, Khalid), Kuwaiti executive. **Born** in 1953 in Kuwait. **Son** of Khalid Jaffar. **Married** in 1979, 1 son. **Educ.:** Brummana High School, Lebanon; U.S.I.U. B.Sc., San Diego, California, USA. **Career:** Controller of USA Investments, Ministry of Finance, Kuwait (1976-81); Director of Foreign Investments, Kuwait Commercial Real Estate Center, Safat, Kuwait (1981-); Director, Kuwait Investment Company (KIC); Gulf International Insurance Company (GIIC); al-Mal Kuwaiti Company; Kuwait Pacific Finance Company. **Hobbies:** Swimming, Coin & Fossil Collecting. **Addr.:** P.O.Box 1368, Tel.: 417821-4, Telex: 22082 A/B HASSAWI KWT, Safat, Kuwait.

JAHNI (Ali Ibn Talal al), Saudi Politician. **Born** in 1945. **Educ.:** B.Sc., Business Administration, USA (1970); M.Sc., Mathematical Economics, USA (1973); Ph.D., Economics, University of California (1977). **Career:** Assistant Analyst to the Director of Budget, Bank of America, Saudi Arabia; Lecturer, Assistant Analyst to the Director of Budget, Bank of America, Saudi Arabia; Lecturer, Princeton University, USA; Assistant Professor, King Fahd University (1978); Dean, Department of Industrial Management King Fahd University (1980); Secretary General, Public Corporation for Military Industries (1986); Economic Researcher, Ministry of Planning; Minister of Posts, Telegraphs and Telephones (1995 - June 1999) **Address:** Riyadh, Saudi Arabia.

JAIDAH (Ali, Mohamad), Qatari economist and oil expert. **Born** in 1941. in Doha, Qatar. **Son** of Mohamad Jaidah. **Educ.:** University of London. **Dipl.:** B.Sc. in Economics (1965); M.Sc. in Petroleum Economics (1966). **Career:** Head of Economics Division, Department of Petroleum Affairs, Ministry of Finance and Petroleum (1966-71); Director of Petroleum Affairs, Ministry of Finance and Petroleum (1971-76); Secretary General of OPEC (1976-78); Managing Director and member of the Board of Directors, Qatar General Petroleum Corp. (1979); Qatar Governor of OPEC (1976); member of the Executive Office of OAPEC (1976); participated in all negotiations related to the oil industry in Qatar including the take over of equity in Qatar Petroleum Corporation and Shell Company of Qatar; participated in establishing the Qatari National Organisation for Oil, the Qatar General Petroleum Corporation and Qatar Petroleum Producing Authority; participated and headed Qatari Delegations to OPEC and OAPEC and other petroleum conferences and meetings on several occasions and in various capacities. **Publ.:** Various papers and addresses on pricing of oil, OPEC and the future of oil supply, the future of world energy as seen by oil producing countries and OPEC and the future energy markets; OPEC policy options. **Medals:** Decoration awarded by the Federal President of Austria. **Addr.:** Doha, Qatar.

JAK (Mohamad Hassan, al, Dr.), Sudanese agricultural expert. **Born** on June 22, 1936. **Son** of Hassan al-Jak (Shendi tribesman). **Married** in 1963 to Minn Nawal Mahmoud Taha, 2 sons: Ammar, Yasir. **Educ.:** in the U.K. **Dipl.:** B.Sc. in Agriculture, University of London (1963); Ph.D. in Agriculture, University of Edinburgh (1966). **Career:** Senior Scholar, University of Khartoum (1961); Lecturer, Department of Animal Production, UK (1966); Senior Lecturer, Department of Animal Production, UK (1973); Secretary, Cooperative Committee, Sudanese Socialist Union, Khartoum (1976); Minister of State for Agriculture, Food and Natural Resources (August 1979); consultant, Arab Organization for Agricultural Development, Khartoum Former **Secretary** of the Sudanese Philosophical Association; Secretary, Scientific Progress; Member, Sudanese Agricultural Association. **Publ.:** several scientific papers in US, German, Sudanese and British journals, **Sport:** Tennis. **Addr.:** c/o Organization for Agricultural Development, P.O.Box 474, Tel.: 78760 (Home Tel.: 611277), Telex: 22554 AOAD SD, Khartoum, Sudan

JAK (Said, Ahmad, Dr.), Sudanese academic and politician. **Born** in 1930 in Khartoum, Sudan. **Married,** with children. **Educ.:** Gordon Memorial College; Faculty of Engineering, Khartoum University, And in the United States of America. **Dipl.:** B.Sc., Ph.D. (Engineering). **Ca-**

reer: joined the Ministry of Public Works, (1954-56); set up Engineering Consulting and Designing Office; lecturer, Civil Engineering, University of Khartoum; worked on water and electricity projects for Shedi and Berber towns; founder and board member, Sudanese Teachers Association; Ministry of Works (1969-70); Minister of Transport and Communications (June 1970- August 1971). **Member:** Sudanese Engineers Society; American Engineers Society. **Prof. Addr.:** Sudanese Engineers Society, Khartoum, Sudan.

JAKKA (Abdullah, Ali Issa), UAE official. **Born** in 1948 in Ras al-Khaimah, United Arab Emirates. **Married,** 2 children. **Educ.:** Kuwait University. **Dipl.:** B.A. **Career:** Department Head, Ministry of Education (1970), Deputy Headmaster (1971); School supervisor (1971); 3rd Secretary, Ministry of Foreign Affairs (1972), 2nd Secretary; Director of Administration and Finance, Ministry of Waqks (Islamic Endowments) and Islamic Affairs (1981), Assistant Under Secretary (1981-). **Hobbies:** Swimming, volleyball, football. **Prof. Addr.:** Ministry of Waqfs and Islamic Affairs, P.O.Box 753, Abu Dhabi, United Arab Emirates.

JALAL (Mahsoun), Saudi economist. **Born** in 1936 in Saudi Arabia. **Son** of Bahjat Jalal. **Educ.:** Cairo University; Rutgers University, USA; University of California, USA. **Dipl.:** Ph.D. (Econ.) **Career:** Professor, Dept. of Economics, Riyadh University (1967-75); Consultant to various Government agencies (1967-75); Vice Chairman, Managing Director, Saudi Fund for Development (1975-79); Member Civil Service Council (1975-); Director, Saudi Basic Industries Corp.; Chairman, Nassau (1979-). Chairman, Saudi Inv. Banking Corp.; OPEC Fund (1979); Saudi Tunisian Dev. Investment Co. (1981); Chairman, Eastern Petrochemical Co.; presently Chairman of National Industrialization Co.; Director, Saudi International Bank, London, U.K. **Publ.:** Principles of Economics; other books and articles on Economic Development and Economic Theory. **Addr.:** P.O.Box 26707, Riyadh, Saudi Arabia.

JALAL (Mohamad, Bin Yusuf), Bahraini businessman. **Born** in 1920 in Bahrain. **Son** of Yusuf Jalal. **Married. Educ.:** In India and Bahrain. **Career:** Civil Servant in Bahrain for a number of years; entered business as joint contractor for construction in Saudi Arabia; established his own building construction company in Bahrain; trading interests in the field of construction include equipment and building materials, mechanical plants, commercial vehicles, oil field supplies and interior design furniture; office supplies and equipment, travel agency and a catering company; numerous joint ventures and associated companies; nominated for Constitutional Assembly (1972-73); former President of Bahrain Chamber of Commerce and Industry; Chairman of Bahrain Company; Chairman of al-Ahli Commercial Bank, Bahrain; Arab Engineering & Contracting Co,; Mohamed Jalal & Sons Co. Ltd. and Board member of several other Bahrain Companies. **Hobby:** Travel. **Prof. Addr.:** Mohamad Jalal and Sons Co. Ltd., P.O.Box 113, Tel.: 55544, Telex 8233, Manama, Bahrain.

JALAL (Saleh, Mohamad), Saudi radio producer. **Born** in 1936. **Educ.:** general education. **Career:** Former employee, Royal Saudi Air Force; member of Saudi Arabian Arts Society; founder member of Saudi Arabian Arts Society in Western Region; a well-known radio announcer of colloquial songs and poetry; Director of Folklore Programmes, Jeddah Broadcasting Service. **Hobbies:** writing songs, plays, colloquial poetry. **Prof. Addr.:** Jeddah Broadcasting Service, Tel.: 6445222, Jeddah. **Priv. Addr.:** Tel.: 6657240, Jeddah, Saudi Arabia.

JALBAN (Mohamad Abdallah), Saudi official. **Born** in 1936, at Abha, Saudi Arabia. **Dipl.:** B.A. (Arts), Riyadh University. **Career:** Administration Inspector, Ministry of Municipalities; Mayor of Jubail; Mayor of al-Khobar; member of Arab Cities Organization. **Hobbies:** Tourism, reading. **Addr.:** al-Khobar Municipality, Eastern Province, Saudi Arabia.

JALLABI (Ebrahim M., al), Bahraini, vice president (credit department) previously al-Bahrain Arab African bank, at present, Bahrain Arab International Bank, Manama, Bahrain. **Born** in 1952 in Bahrain. **Son** of Mohammed Ebrahim al-Jallabi. **Educ.:** Gulf Technical College, Bahrain; Mantrust Training Centre, New York. **Career History:** Citibank OBU, Bahrain; al-Bahrain Arab African Bank (1979); Assistant Manager (1981); Assistant Vice-President for Loans Administration Department (1982); Vice-President, Loans Administration Department (1983); Vice-President, Credit Department (1986). **Language Spoken:** Arabic & English. **Leisure Interests:** Swimming, Bowling. Tennis, Squash. **Clubs:** Bahrain Bankers Club, Bahrain. **Address:** P.O.Box 20488 Manama, Bahrain, Telex: 9380, 9381 ALBB (BAIB) BN, Tel. 230491, Ext: 205

JALLAD (Jaber), Syrian executive. **Born** in 1938 in Damascus, Syria. **Son** of Irfan Jallad. **Married** in 1954, 1 son, 1 daughter. **Dipl.:** B.Sc. (Management). **Career:** Assistant Manager, "Alyat" Syria (Mercedes Benz Agent) (1964-65); Joined Merill Lynch since 1965. New York; Account Executive, Kuwait (1965-69); Account Executive, Kuwait (1969-75); Manager (1975-80); President and Manager, Merrill Lynch, Kuwait and Gulf Area (1980-). **Member:** Gazelle Club, Kuwait; Hunting and Equestrian Club, Kuwait. **Hobby:** Sports. **Addr.:** P.O.Box 4906, Tel.: 420102, Telex: 22149 A/B MERLEAP, Safat, Kuwait.

JALLOW (Raymond), Arab-American economist. **Born** in 1930 in Baghdad, Iraq. **Educ.:** University of Baghdad, Iraq; University of Southern California, USA, University of California, Los Angeles (UCLA) USA. **Dipl.:** B.A., M.A. in Business Administration, Ph.D. in Business

Economics. **Career:** Supervisor of Revenue Department, Iraqi Railways (1947-52); Economist, Research and Planning Department, United California Bank (actually First Interstate Bank), Los Angeles (1959-66), Vice President, Chief Economist (1966-70), Senior Vice President, Chief Economist (1979-81); Chief Economist, First Interstate Bancor (1979-81); Lecturer in Economics and Monetary fields in USA and other countries; Adviser to corporations in USA, Europe, Middle East and the Far East. President, Arab Students Association (1958), President, American Muslim Association, Los Angeles (1959-61), Founder and First President, National Association of Business Economists (Southern California) (1968-70); Chairman, US Organization for Medical and Educational Needs (1972); Board Director of US OMEN, Trust Company the Financial Committee of the Seaver Institute, Board of Regents and California Lutheran College; Member of the Economist Advisory Council, American Bankers Association, Washington, DC (1972-75), Member of the American Management Association and the American Statisticians Association; Advisory Member, California Polytechnic State University; President, Jallow International Ltd., Los Angeles (1981-). **Publ.:** "Asset Management and Long Range Planning for Banks", "Economic and Monetary Forecast", "The Energy Crisis- Its Implications for the USA", "Revolution in International Finance", "Impact of Oil Shortages on Business and Industry". **Hobbies:** Reading, travelling, Middle Eastern Affairs. **Prof. Addr.:** 2530 Park Oak Court, Los Angeles, California 90068, USA.

JALLUD (Abdul Salam Ahmad), Libyan politician. **Born** in 1940 in Tripolitania, Libya. **Married**, one child. **Career:** commissioned with Army (1965); represented Revolutionary Command Council to foreign embassies following 1969 Revolution; Deputy Prime Minister (January 1970); headed Libyan delegation in oil talks leading to revised payments (1971); took over responsibility for National Oil Company (Sept. 1973); on abolition of post of Deputy Prime Minister in August 1971, served as Minister of Economy and Industry and Acting Treasury Minister; Prime-Minister (1972-77); Member of five-man General Secretariat (March 1977). **Addr.:** Tripoli, Libya.

JAMA (Rabile, God), Somali statesman. **Born** in 1942 in Borama (Somalia). **Educ.:** Elementary and intermediate schools in Borama and Amud, Somalia (1950-57); Secondary education in Amud and Sheikh (1957-61); Wesleian University; USA (1961-65); University of Massachusetts, USA (1968-69). **Dipl.:** B.A. (Economics & Statistics) 1965, M.A. (Economics) (1969). **Career:** Joined the Ministry of Planning (1965-68); Director of Planning Section, Ministry of Planning and Coordination (1969-70); Director-General, Ministry of Planning (April 1970- March 1973); Director-General, Ministry of Livestock, Forestry and Ranges (March 1973- Dec. 1974); Secretary of State for Tourism and National Parks (Dec. 1974- Jan. 1976); Adviser to the Supreme Revolutionary Council Economic Committee (Jan-July. 1976). **Prof. Addr.:** Mogadishu, Somalia.

JAMAI (Tayib), Moroccan businessman, journalist. **Born** in 1936 in Fes, Morocco. **Educ.:** Diploma from School of Journalism and Public Relations. **Career:** Representative of Morocco at the World Assembly of Youth, Brussels, Belgium (1964-68); Representative of the Moroccan Office of Exterior Commerce, OCE in Africa (1969-70); Journalist; Director of "A'Maal al-Maghrib". **Hobby:** Reading. **Addr.:** 1 Rond Point Saint Exupéry, Tel.: 273483, 26044, Casablanca, Morocco.

JAMAL (Adel Mahmoud), Saudi banker. **Born** in Mecca, Saudi Arabia. **Educ.:** American University in Cairo, Egypt; George Washington University. **Dipl.:** B.A. in Economics and Political Sciences, M.A. in International Affairs. **Career:** National Commercial Bank, Jeddah (1968-69); Saudi Arabian Ministry of Foreign Affairs and Embassy in Washington (1969-76); Banque Arabe et Internationale d'Investissement, Paris (1977-78); Manager of Saudi International Bank, London (1978-82); Member of Arab Bankers Association, London; Manager of Riyadh Bank, Jeddah (1982-). **Hobbies:** Tennis, music, arts. **Prof. Addr.:** c/o Riyadh Bank, P.O.Box 1047, Jeddah 21431, Saudi Arabia.

JAMAL (Ahmad, Mohamad), Saudi scholar. **Born** in 1925 in Mecca, Saudi Arabia. **Educ.:** received extensive religious schooling at al-Islami Institute, Mecca. **Career:** Member of the presidium of the Judiciary (1940); Supreme Legal Court; Ministry of Interior; member of Shura Council (National Advisory Council) (1955); member of Endowments Council (Waqf), Mecca; Professor of Islamic Culture, King Abdulaziz University, Jeddah; Municipal Council, Cultural Committee of Muslim World League, International Islamic Organizations Union; attended several Islamic conferences in Pakistan, Spain, Yugoslavia and Morocco. **Publ.:** Ala Ma'idatil Quran (At the Banquet of the Qur'an) in four volumes; Muftarayat Ala al-Islam (False Charges Against Islam); Muhadharatun fil Thaqafatil Islamiah (Lectures on Islamic Culture), Isti'mar Wakifah (Colonialism and Struggle), Qadayah Mo'aserah fi Mahkamat al-Fikr al-Islami (Contemporary Cases in the Court of Islamic Thought); Makanek Tohmade (You will be Praised if you Keep in Your Place); al-Jihad Fi al-Islam (Struggle in Islam); Islamic Economics; Insurance Policies. **Hobbies:** Reading. **Addr..:** al-Thaqafa Bookstore, Tel.: 5424118, Mecca, Saudi Arabia.

JAMAL-ELLAIL (Ghazi Abdul Qadir), Saudi civil servant. **Born** in 1930. **Dipl.:** Elementary School Certificate. **Career:** Successively wireless operator, teacher, wireless supervisor, controller of foreign news service; Director of Political Monitoring Department, Ministry of Information. **Honours:** 3 orders of merit awarded as member of Saudi information delegation to Egypt and Lebanon during

Royal visits. **Hobby:** Reading. **Addr.:** Ministry of Information, Jeddah, Saudi Arabia.

JAMAL-ELLAIL (Nawal Mahjoob, Mrs.), Saudi physician. **Born** in 1943. **Dipl.:** Diploma, Obstetrics and Gynæcology, University of Cairo. **Career:** Girl Students' supervisor, Saudi Cultural Bureau Pakistan; General Practitioner, Gynæcology Hospital, Makkah (1970-75); Obstetrician, Gynæologist, in same hospital (1975-77); Supervisor, King Abdulaziz Medical College, Mecca. **Hobbies:** Reading, sports. **Prof. Addr.:** ar-Rusayfah, Mukhattat-Badr, Tel.: 5435203, Mecca. **Priv. Addr.:** Tel.: 5423385, Mecca, Saudi Arabia.

JAMAL (Jasim, Yousif), Qatari diplomat. **Born** in 1940 in Qatar. **Married**, three children. **Educ.:** Northeast Missouri State University, New York University. **Career:** Ministry of Education; Director of Admin instractive Affairs (1958-63); Cultural Adviser, U.S. (1963-68); Director of Cultural Affairs (1968-72); Permanent Representative to UN (1972-84); concurrently accredited as Ambassador to Canada, Brazil and Argentina; Ambassador, Ministry of Foreign Affairs. **Addr.:** Ministry of Foreign Affairs, P.O.Box 250, Doha, Qatar.

JAMAL (Saleh Mohamad), Saudi businessman. **Born** in 1920 in Mecca, Saudi Arabia. **Dipl.:** secondary school education. **Career:** Clerk ar Bait al-Mal (Treasury); Assistant Clerk, Court of Law; Worked as a government employee in various jobs at Bait al-Mal (Treasury), Court of Law (Notarial), Mecca High Court, Second Court of Law for Urgent Affairs; Accountant, al-Bilad newspaper; Editor-in-Chief, Hera' magazine and al-Nadwah newspaper; Manager, (Albilad Alsaudiya) Daily Newspaper; member, the Medical Aid Society, the Constituent Council of King Abdulaziz University, Higher Board (Ministry of Pilgrimage); member, Supreme Council of Umm al-Qura University Mecca Municipal Council, the Executive Council of Mecca Chamber of Commerce and Industry, the Cultural Chamber of Commerce and Industry, the Cultural Club (Mecca); participant member, the Conference of the Union of Chambers of Commerce, Industry and Agriculture for the Arab Countries; member of the Board, Mecca General Projects Co.; Chairman, Makkah Welfare Society; owner, Dar el-Thaqafah Printing Press and al-Thaqafah Bookshop; former President, Chamber of Commerce and Industry and the Municipal Council, Mecca. **Publ.:** Madinat al-Rasool (city of the Prophet); A Guide Book for Pilgrims and several articles in newspapers. **Hobbies:** Reading. **Addr.:** Saudi Arabia.

JAMALI (Abdul Hussain, al), Iraqi diplomat. **Born** in 1929 in Iraq. **Married. Educ.:** Baghdad College of Law, Baghdad; University New York, USA. **Dipl.:** LL.B; M.A. in Political Science. **Career:** Second Secretary, Embassy of Iraq, Lebanon (1958); First Secretary, Embassy of Iraq, Ghana, Syria, Egypt; Head of Arab Affairs Department, Ministry of Foreign Affairs (1967-69); Ambassador (1969-71); Under Secretary, Ministry of Foreign Affairs (1971-79). **Addr.:** Ministry of Foreign Affairs, Baghdad, Iraq.

JAMALI (Assim, Dr.), Omani politician. **Born** in Oman. **Career:** Director of Lands and Municipalities; Minister of Environmental Affairs (May 22, 1979-82); Ministry of Public Works (1986-89). **Addr.:** Muscat, Sultanate of Oman.

JAMEEL (Yousef Abdullatif), Saudi leading businessman. **Born** in 1945. **Educ.:** B.Sc. (Economic), American University of Cairo, Egypt. **Career and business interests:** Vice Chairman-International Investment, Abdul Latif Jameel Group Companies, Importer and sole distributors of Toyota Vehicles, Toshiba, Akai and Phildo electronic home appliances in Saudi Arabia. **Other businesses:** Real Estate and Investments in Saudi Arabia and Overseas, Shipping, Insurance and out door advertising; vehicle distributorship in the U.K. **Address:** Abdul Latif Jameel Company Ltd., P.O.Box 7012, Jeddah 21462, Tel.: 669-1133, Saudi Arabia.

JAMIL (Fuad, al), Iraqi public administrator. **Born** in 1918 in Amarah. **Educ.:** American University of Beirut. **Dipl.:** Bachelor of Arts. **Career:** Director of Broadcasting; Controller of Supply; Inspector specialist (English language) and Director Ministry of Education of non-Government and Foreign Schools; Director Fundamental Education and Literacy Campaign; Ministry of Education. **Addr.:** 21-23, Seif al-Islam Street, Baghdad, Iraq.

JAMIL (Ghalib, Ali), Yemeni diplomat. **Born** in 1937. **Educ.:** in Yemen, Saudi Arabia, Egypt; Wilamette University, Salem, Oregon, USA. **Career:** Director, Foreign Minister's Office; Director General, Foreign Ministry (1966); Deputy Permanent Representative to the UN (1967); Deputy Minister for Foreign Affairs (1973-75); Ambassador to Iraq (1975-79); Ambassador to Morocco (1979-81); Ambassador to France (1983-86); Ambassador to Saudi Arabia (1984-91). **Prof. Addr.:** Embassy of the Republic of Yemen, P.O.Box 94391, Riyadh 11693, Saudi Arabia, c/o Ministry of Foreign Affairs, Sanaa, Republic of Yemen.

JAMIL (Sana'), Egyptian dramatic actress. **Born** in Mallaoui, Upper Egypt. **Educ.:** Bon Pasteur Convent School (Cairo), Institute of Dramatic Art (Cairo). **Dipl.:** Diploma from the said Institute. **Career:** Dramatic Actress, Member of the "Modern Theatre" (1952), Assimilated by the "Egyptian National Theatre" (1954), Student of Zaki Toulaymat and Fatouh Nachaty, bagan her Theatrical career by acting in Molière and Beaumarchais comedies: "Le Malade Imaginaire", "Le Médecin malgré lui", "Les Précieux Ridicules", "Le mariage de Figaro", etc..., then started to act leading dramatic roles, specially Shakespearians "The Merchant of Venice" (1957), "Macbeth"

(1960-61), acted in many motion pictures: "Bidaya wa Nihaya" (1960), "Bilah Doumouh" (1962), "Fagr Yom Gedid" (1962), "al-Moustahyl", "al-Zawga al-Thanya", "al-Baad Yaiche Marratein", "Fidaki Ya Falastine" (1969), a play in Beirut "Carte Blanche" (1969). **Addr.:** Cairo, Egypt.

JAMIL (Taleb), Iraqi lawyer and businessman. **Born** in 1919. **Educ.:** Baghdad College of Law. **Career:** Practice (1941-53); Secretary General of Iraqi Bar; Director General of Legal and Economic Affairs; Director General of Commerce and Economy (1953-59); Returned to Private Practice (1959-64); Under-Secretary of State, Ministry of Economy (1953-59); Returned to Private Practice (1959-64); Under-Secretary of State, Ministry of Economy (January- July 1964); President Insurance Organisation (July-December 1964); Permanent Delegate to Arab Economic Unity Council; League of Arab States (Cairo) with rank of Ambassador (December 1964- August 1968); Chairman, Asia Printing and Publishing Co. **Addr.:** Baghdad, Iraq.

JAMJOOM (Abdullatif Mohamad Salah), Saudi dental surgeon and businessman. **Born** in 1923 in Jeddah, Saudi Arabia. **Dipl.:** D.Sc. Faculty of Dentistry, Cairo University. **Career:** Dental Surgeon at Government Public Hospital, Jeddah; Director of Public Hospital, Jeddah; runs a private pharmaceutical business; member of Board, al-Bilad newspaper; Director Jamjoom Vehicles & Equipment. **Hobby:** Reading. **Prof. Addr.:** P.O.Box 415, Tel.: 6310629, Jeddah. **Priv. Addr.:** Tel.: 6429639, Jeddah, Saudi Arabia.

JAMJOOM (Adnan Mohamad Rashid), Saudi academic. **Born** in 1945 in Jeddah, Saudi Arabia. **Dipl.:** Ph.D. (General Surgery), West Germany. **Career:** Member, Surgery Department, King Faisal Specialized Hospital, Riyadh (1977); Instructor and Specialized Consultant of Surgery, Faculty of Medicine, King Abdulaziz University (1977-79); Associate Professor and Specialized Consultant of Surgery, General Surgery Department, Faculty of Medicine, King Abdulaziz University; Chairman, Prince Fahd Medical Research Centre; has attended and acted as Secretary of the Sixth Medical Assembly, Jeddah (1981). **Publ.:** Management of Advanced Cancer of Head and Neck. **Hobbies:** Reading, fishing. **Prof. Addr.:** Tel.: 6436417, Jeddah, Saudi Arabia.

JAMJOOM (Ahmad, Salah), Saudi businessman and former minister. **Born** in 1925 in Jeddah, Saudi Arabia. **Married**, 5 children. **Educ.:** University of Cairo, Egypt; Training course in International Taxation at Harvard University. **Dipl.:** B.BA. (Bachelor of Business Administration). **Career:** Executive, Arab Bank Ltd. (1950); Assistant Director-General, Revenue Tax Department, subsequently Director-General; Manager, Arabian Cement Co. Ltd. (1957-58); Minister of State and Chairman of the Economic Development Committee (1958-59); Minister of Commerce (1959-60); Chairman, Saudi Arabian Airlines Corporation; Minister of Commerce and Industry (1960-62); Chairman of Jamjoom Vehicles & Equipments; General Manager, Madina Press Organisation, Jeddah Chairman of the Board, Islamic Education Center; Director, Faisal Islamic Bank, Khartoum, Sudan; Chairman, Faisal Islamic Bank, Pakistan. **Member:** Supreme Council, King Abdul Aziz University. **Hobby:** Reading. **Prof. Addr.:** P.O.Box 1247, Tel.: 6877096, Jeddah, Saudi Arabia.

JAMJOOM (Asaad Hassan), Saudi civil servant. **Born** in 1923. **Dipl.:** Diploma of Engineering (Electrical). **Career:** Principal of Trades School, Jeddah (1949); Inspector General of Industrial Education, Ministry of Education (1958); Director General Agriculture and of Water Affairs, Ministry of Agriculture and Water; founding member of Saudi Popular Education Organization; member of Board of Red Sea Club; attended Conference on the Utilization of Atomic Energy in Water Desalination, Medina, FAO Conference, Rome: Ministry of Agriculture and Water delegate to World Exhibition (EXPO), Osaka (1970). **Hobbies:** Swimming, fishing, travel. **Prof. Addr.:** P.O.Box 2548, Tel.: 6876022, Jeddah. **Priv. Addr.:** Tel.: 6423895, Jeddah, Saudi Arabia.

JAMJOOM (Hisham Mohamad Nour Dr.), Saudi businessman. **Born** in 1941. **Dipl.:** B.Com. (Industrial Management); Philo Marketing. **Career:** Legal Department, Ministry of Petroleum and Mineral Resources; Labour Relations Department, Aramco; Deputy General Manager of Jamjoom Building Co.; Manager of Radua Trading Co., member of Board, Chamber of Commerce and Industry, Jeddah; member of American Management Association (AMA); Chairman, Sugar Cone Factory; Chairman, National High Education Limited; has attended several conferences on management and labour regulations. **Publ.:** Industrial Management and Saudi Arabia; Psychology of Management; several articles published in local press. **Prof. Addr.:** P.O.Box 2538, Jeddah 21461, Tel.: 6897808, Saudi Arabia.

JAMJOOM (Isam Mohamad Rasheed), Saudi civil servant. **Born** in 1938 in Jeddah, Saudi Arabia. **Dipl.:** B.Sc. (Electrical Engineering); M.Sc. Engineering, (Desalination). **Career:** Director of Western Region Electricity; Plant Operation Engineer; member of the Mechanical Engineers Association, U.S.A.; Assistant Governor, Desalination Authority. **Hobbies:** Reading, tourism. **Addr.:** Desalination Authority, Jeddah, Saudi Arabia.

JAMJOOM (Mohamad, Abdul Wahid), Saudi economist. **Born** in 1938 in Cairo (Egypt). **Dipl.:** Ph.D. (Economics). **Career:** Accountant, Saudi Arabian Monetary Agency; subsequently, Chief in the said Department; Economic Expert, Director of Research Division, Saudi Arabian Monetary Agency (SAMA); Lecturer in Economics, Banking Institute, SAMA; attended several conferences of

Ministers of Finance, Ministers of Finance Meetings for approval of the Arab Bank agreement for Economic Development in Africa; attended Islamic Bank preparation committee meetings, the meeting of Finance Ministers to approve the Agreement estabishing this Bank, participated in the preparation of the Agreement establishing the Arab Monetary Fund, attended Central Banks Governors and Finance Ministers meetings to approve this agreement, also the Meetings of Governors of Muslim Central Banks, the meetings of Governors of Arab Central Banks, the International Monetary Fund and International Bank for Reconstruction and Development meetings, several conferences of Islamic Foreign Ministers, the Islamic Countries Economic delegates and representatives committees, OPEC meetings, etc.; now Director-General of Economic Research Department, SAMA. **Publ.:** Dissertation "Saudi Arabian Foreign Trade & Balance of Payments". **Prof. Addr.:** Saudi Arabian Monetary Agency, Head Office, P.O.Box 11169. Tel.: 4787400, Riyadh, Saudi Arabia.

JAMJOOM (Muhammad Muhammad Omar), Saudi engineer. **Born** in 1946. **Married**, 1 son, 5 daughters. **Dipl.:** B.Sc., M.Sc. and Ph.D. in Civil Engineering. **Career:** Teaching Assistant, Virginia University (1970-71), (1972-75); Assistant Professor of the College of Engineering, King Abdul Aziz University (1975-76); Dean, College of Engineering, King Abdul Aziz University (1976-82); Dean for the Faculty of Meteorology and Environmental Studies (1982); Secretary General, King Abdul Aziz University (since 1982); **Publ.:** author of several articles on traffic and transportation engineering; translated a book on construction management. **Hobbies:** poetry, journalism, tennis, volleyball, swimming. **Prof. Addr.:** Ministry of Higher Education, King Abdul Aziz University, P.O.Box 1540, Tel.: 6882208, Jeddah, Saudi Arabia.

JAMJOOM (Shihab Mohamad), Saudi academic. **Born** in 1946 in Jeddah, Saudi Arabia. **Dipl.:** B.A. (Theatre Arts, Specializing in Production and Direction of Film and T.V.), University of California, U.S.A.: M.A. (Communication Management), University of Southern California; Ph.D. (Communication Administration and Education); special training in major Hollywood studios and Educational T.V. stations. **Career:** Former Director of Audio-visual Centre and Educational T.V., King Abdulaziz University; one of the first founders of Educational T.V. in Saudi Universities; founder of Educational T.V. in Saudi universities; founder of the largest audio-visual network in Saudi Arabian institutes of higher education; Professor of Communication, King Abdulaziz University; Adviser to the Minister of Information; has attended and participated in Educational T.V. conferences and lectured at several conferences in the fields of communication and open-learning conferences; supervised the preliminary plan for the Open University and the Academy of Communication Arts projects in the Gulf States. **Publ.:** Uses of Media in Higher Education in Saudi Arabia. **Hobbies:** Reading, photography. **Prof. Addr.:** Tel.: 6895693, Jeddah. **Priv. Addr.:** Tel.: 6434172, Jeddah, Saudi Arabia.

JAMJOOM (Yusuf Mohd. Salah), Saudi Businessman. **Born** in 1930 in Jeddah, Saudi Arabia. **Dipl.:** in Business Administration. **Career:** Chairman of the Board of Directors, Hotel Jeddah Trident; President, Jamjoom Medicine Store; Member of the Board, Abdullatif Mohd. Salah Jamjoom & Brothers; Member of the Board, Madina Printing Press. **Hobbies:** Table Tennis Photography. **Prof. Addr.** P.O.Box 935 Jamjoom Building, Al-Ammariya, Tel.: (02) 6422463, 6422563, Fax: 6440964, E-Mail: jamjoomms@yahoo.com., Jeddah 21421, Saudi Arabia.

JAMMAL (Mohamad Amin Ahmad, al), Saudi TV director of production. **Born** in 1922, in Mecca, Saudi Arabia. **Dipl.:** Secondary School Certificate, TV Diploma, U.S.A. **Career:** Radio engineer, Mecca Broadcasting Service (1956); Supervisor of Outdoor Broadcasts, Saudi Broadcasting Service; Supervisor of General Radio Maintenance, Chief Engineer, Jeddah TV Service, later Director of Production and co-ordination; in 1961 he invented a sound repercussion device which he presented to Saudi Broadcasting Service; the device worked well, and he was given a financial prize by H.R.H. (then Crown Prince) Khalid ben Abdulaziz. **Hobbies:** Music, photography. **Addr.:** Jeddah TV Service, Jeddah, Saudi Arabia.

JAN (Mohammed Younis Yaqob, Dr.), Saudi Citizen. **Born** in 1943 in Jeddah (Saudi Arabia). **Dipl.:** MD, Facharzt (Paed), Bonn, Federal Republic of Germany. **Career:** Associate Professor and Consultant Paediatrician; Member of German Paediatric Society, Member of Saudi Paediatric Society, Member of the Arab Board for Medical Specialization and Director of Postgraduate Paediatric Training/Paediatric Department/Faculty of Medicine and Allied Health Science/King Abdulaziz University. **Research and Publ.:** Research in Normal Growth and Laboratory Values Among Saudis Living in the Area of Jeddah. Many Publications in The Field of Specialty. **Addr.:** King Abdulaziz University Hospital, P.O.Box 6615, Jeddah 21452, Saudi Arabia, Tel.: 6952088, **Priv.** Tel/Fax: 6209421.

JANABI (Nawal, Yusif, al), Iraqi academic. **Born** in 1937 in Baghdad, Iraq. **Married**, one daughter. **Educ.:** University of Baghdad, Iraq; George Washington University, USA; Brunel University, London, UK. **Dipl.:** B.Sc. (1960); M.Sc. (1967); Ph.D. (1970). **Career:** Demostrator, University of Baghdad (1960-64); Homograft Department, National Heart Hospital and Cardiothoracic Institute, University of London (1970-75); Assistant Professor, Department of Microbiology, College of Medicine, al-Mustansiriyah University, Iraq; Professor of Microbiology, College of Medicine, al-Mustansiriyah University, Iraq. **Publ.:** Researches and articles in professional journals.

Hobby: Music. **Prof. Addr.:** Department of Microbiology, School of Medicine, al-Mustansiriyah University, P.O.Box 14132, Baghdad, Iraq.

JANAHI (Abdul Latif, Abdul Rahim), Bahraini, Managing Director & Chief Executive Officer. **Born** on December 21, 1939 in Bahrain. **Career:** He is one of the Pioneers in Islamic Bankimg & Islamic Insurance. He Promoted the Idea of Islamic Banking & Islamic Insurance in Bahrain and was behind Establishing many Banks, Financial Institutions mainly in Bahrain and Outside Bahrain. He is the First Bahraini to be appointed as General Manager of Nation's First Insurance Company and the First Bahraini to be appointed as General Manager for a Bank in Bahrain. Before Joining the Bahrain Islamic Bank, He was the General Manager of Bahrain Insurance Co. His Experience in Insurance Stands for 35 years and he is well known as one of the Pioneers in Insurance Sector. He is one of the Founding Shareholders, Member of the Board of Directors and the Executive Committee of Bahrain Islamic Bank, Functioning as Managing Director/ Chief Executive Officer, **since 1979). Other Informations:** He is one of the Founding Shareholders and Chairman of Takaful International, (Formerly Bahrain Islamic Insurance Co.). One of the Founding Shareholders and Deputy Chairman of Islamic Investment Co. Bahrain. Former Deputy Chairman & Chairman of Executive Committee of Islamic Trading Co. former Deputy Chairman & Executive Member of Al Rajhi Islamic Insurance Co. One of the Founding Shareholders, Director and Member of the Executive Committee of Al Baraka Islamic Bank, Arab Islamic Bank, Islamic Insurance & Reinsurance Co. Bahrain. Member of the Board of Directors of Dubai Islamic Bank, Islamic Bank Bangladesh Ltd. Economic Expert for Islamic Doctrine Congregation Board. Regular Contributor Through Media on Islamic Banking, Finance, Insurance and Present Day Islamic Products. **Publ.:** Authored a number of Books on Islamic Banking and Insurance and has over 43 Researches and Papers Presented on many occasions in Ceremonies, University, Etc... **Awards:** Has been Awarded a Prize by His Excellency the Prime Minister of Bahrain. **Prof. Addr.:** Bahrain Islamic Bank, Al Salam Tower, P.O.Box 5240, Manama, Bahrain, Tel.: 535888.

JANAIDY (Abdul Rahman, A., al), Saudi architect. **Born** in 1937 in Mecca, Saudi Arabia. **Dipl.:** B.Sc. (Architecture). **Career:** Assistant Director of Technical Administration Service, Ministry of Finance; Director of Technical Architectural and Consultations Bureau; member of Chamber of Commerce; has designed several public buildings, such as King Abdulaziz Military Museum, Riyadh Central Hospital, Ministry of Planning Building, al-Baha Governorate, etc. **Hobbies:** reading recent architecture studies. **Addr.:** Azeeziyah Building, Apartment 113, Riyadh, Saudi Arabia.

JANDOOL (Said ben Abdul Aziz, al), Saudi academic. **Born** at al-Aflaj, in 1923. **Dipl.:** B.L. (Islamic Law), Faculty of Islamic Law, Mecca. **Career:** Principal of al-Ilmi Saudi Institute, Mecca (1955); Assistant Director-General of Secondary Education (1965); Assistant Director-General of Education (1966); member of Sub-Committee on Education, Supreme Committee on Islamic Orientation, Constituent Committee of Imam Educational Institution; has been entrusted with several educational and cultural missions in various Arab countries. **Publ.:** Books published: al-Tawheed Wal-Tahzeeb (Monotheism and Cultivation), al-Dorar al-Fidhdhiyyah al-Kitabil Tawheed (Notes on the Book of Monotheism by Shaikh Mohamad ben Abdul Wahab); books under publication: Difa'on' Anil Islam (A Defence of Islam), Hatta La Naqa'a Fil Teeh (How to Avoid Going Astray). **Hobby:** Reading. **Addr.:** Riyadh University Quarter, Riyadh, Saudi Arabia.

JAOUHARI (Sidi el-Ghali, al), Moroccan manufacturer and executive. **Born** in 1938 at Taghzout, Morocco. **Son** of Hadj el-Ghali el-Jaouhari (Artisan) **and** Mrs., Born Aziza el-Alami. **Married** to Miss el-Idrissi since 1964, 8 children: Lalla Nadia (1965), Mohamed (1967), Miriam (1968), Samira (1970), Zakaria (1972), Yahia (1976), Lalla Jihane (1980) Lalla Sara. **Educ.:** Religious education at the Coranic School, of a bazar (1965). **Career:** exporter (1970); producer and exporter of Berber carpets since 1972; manufacturer since 1976; Chairman and General Manager, Groupe Berbère Carpet Mocary; the first organizer of the manufacture of standardized Berber carpets; promoter of industrialization of hand-tied carpets. **Honours:** Honorofic member of several handicrafts associations. **Sport:** Footing, tennis, swimming. **Hobbies:** News, reading, music. **Member:** First Vice-President, Municipal Council of the city of Sale; first vice-president, Anpetan (Association des Producteurs Exportateurs); First Vice-President, Association Arts de Taghzout. **Credit Cards:** Carte Blanche Wafabank, Diners Club. **Prof. Addr.:** P.O.Box 292, Tel.: 875.27, Telex: 31934 Rabat, Morocco. **Priv. Addr.:** 22, Avenue de Meknes, Tel.: 235 48, Rabat, Morocco.

JARADAT (Faisal, Muhammad), Jordanian poet. **Born** on February 27, 1955 in al-Sella, al-Hartheia, Jordan. **Married,** 2 children. **Educ.:** In Jerusalem; Beirut University, Lebanon. **Dipl.:** Diploma in Management; B.A. in Literature. **Career:** Official, Qatar Petroleum Organization, Qatar (1986-). **Publ.:** "Engraved on the Wall of Silence", Poetry Record (1984), "Nefehat" (1986). **Prof. Addr.:** Marka al-Shamaliah, P.O.Box 15175, Amman, Jordan.

JARALLAH (Abdallah, Hassan, al), Kuwaiti businessman. **Born** in 1935 in Kuwait. **Son** of Mr. Hassan Jarallah al-Hassan (Merchant) **and** Mrs., née Munira Ahmad al-Rasheed. **Married** in March 1963 in Kuwait to Miss Nawal Khaled Hajii, 4 children: Reem (1963), Rehab (1965), Rana (1970), Hassan (1980). **Educ.:** Mubarakia School,

Cairo University (1954-58). **Dipl.:** Bachelor of Commerce. **Career:** Accountant, Kuwait Commisions Cairo (1.9.1958); Rank of Cultural Attaché in Kuwait Commision (1960); Advisor for Cultural Affairs in Kuwait Commission (1965); Asst. Under-Secretary, Ministry of Education (Adm. & Finance) (1967); Vice-Chairman and Managing Director, Kuwait Egyptian Investment Co., Cairo (1974); Chairman and Managing Director, Warba Insurance Co. (1977); Director, Kuwait Shipping Co. (1967-74); Director, Arab African Bank (1974-77); Director, Arab African Mauritanian Bank, Mauritania (1974-77); Minister of Commerce and Industry (April 1991-1992). **Medals:** Arab Association for Cultural, Scientific & Educational activities; Gamal Abdul Nasser. **Clubs:** Vice-President, Arab Association for Cultural, Scientific and Educational Activities (1964); Chairman of Same (1970-74); Hunting & Equestrian Club, Cairo; Kuwait Graduates Association. **Prof. Addr.:** P.O.Box 24282, Safat, Kuwait City, Kuwait, Tel.: 2445140. **Priv. Addr.:** Dahiyat Abdulla Salem, Jamal al-Din Afghani Street, House No.23, Kuwait.

JARALLAH (Ahmad, Abdelaziz), Kuwaiti journalist. **Born** in 1942 in Kuwait. **Married. Career:** Joined "al-Rai al-Aam" newspaper; founder of "al-Siyasah" newspaper (1968); owner and editor of "al-Siyasah", "Arab Times" and "Arab Yearbook". "Al Hadaf". **Addr.:** Dar al-Siyasah Printing, Publishing and Distributing House, P.O.Box 2270, Safat 13023, Tel.: 4813566, Telex 2332 SIYASA KT, Kuwait.

JARALLAH (Mohamad Ibrahim, al), Saudi academic. **Born** in 1944 at Qassim, Saudi Arabia. **Dipl.:** B.Sc. (Civil Engineering), King Saud University; M.Sc., Stanford University; Ph.D. Michigan University. **Career:** Deputy Director of Teachers Trainning Institute, Ministry of Education (1964-67); Demonstrator, King Saud University (1972-73); Member of the Faculty since 1978; Director General of University Projects, King Saud University since 1980; Minister of Municipal and Rural Affairs (since Aug. 1995). **Member;** American Society for Civil Engineers (ASCE), TRB, AAPT, American Society for Testing Materials (ASTQ); member of the Board, Research Centre, Faculty of Engineering, King Saud University; member, International Conference for Structural Design of Asphalt Pavement; member, Chi Epsilon. **Publ.:** several research papers and a book to be published. **Hobbies:** Travel, swimming, reading. **Prof. Addr.:** P.O.Box 3236, Tel.: 4765158, Riyadh. and Ministry of Municipal & Rural Affairs, Nasseriya Str., Riyadh 11136, Saudi Arabia. **Priv. Addr.:** Tel.: 4572729, Riyadh, Saudi Arabia.

JARARI (Abdullah, al-Abbas, al), Moroccan official. **Born** in 1921 in Rabat, Morocco. **Educ.:** Quarawyin University, Fes, Morocco; American University of Beirut, Lebanon. **Dipl.:** B.A. in Islamic Studies and Moroccan History; Diploma in Education. **Career:** Professor of Education in Morocco; General Inspector of Education in Morocco. **Publ.:** numerous articles and works on education. **Decor.:** Order of the Throne, Morocco. **Medal:** Medal from Libya. **Hobby:** Music (Arabic and Andalusian). **Member:** Moroccan Scientists Federation; The Council of Moroccan Scientists. **Addr.:** 11 Zanqit al-Qadi Ayad, Rabat, Morocco.

JARBOU (Abdulaziz, S., al), Saudi executive. **Born** in 1954 at Hail, Saudi Arabia. **Dipl.:** B.Sc., M.Sc., Ph.D. (Chemical Engineering). **Career:** Demonstrator, University of Petroleum and Minerals (1971-76); Assistant Professor (1976-77); Chemical Engineer (SABIC) (1977-80); Director General Projects Implementation, Saudi Basic Industries Corporation (SABIC) since 1980. **Hobby:** Swimming. **Prof. Addr.:** P.O.Box 5101, Tel.: 4760365, Riyadh, Saudi Arabia.

JARRAR (Abdul-Rahim, Ibrahim), Jordanian international civil servant. **Born** in 1919 at Jineen, West Nablus, Palestine. **Widower,** with children. **Educ.:** Arab College, Jerusalem (1935-38). **Dipl.:** B.A. **Career:** Schoolmaster, Minister of Education (1958-60); Private business (1952-66 & 1960-61); Member of Parliament, Jordan (1961-62 & 1950-58); Governor, Ministry of Interior, Jordan (1966-72); Representative of Jordan, Advisory Commission, United Nations Refugees and Works Agency (UNRWA), (1972); member of the National Consultative Council of Jordan (1982-83). **Member:** Nablus Charitable Organisation; Prisoners' Care Association; Martyrs' Families Relief Association; Jordanian Rehabilitation Association; Cancer-Combat Association. **Sports:** Tennis and swimming. **Addr.:** P.O.Box 950464, Amman, Jordan.

JARRAR (Walid), Jordanian engineer. **Born** in 1932 in Haifa, Palestine. **Married,** 2 sons, 1 daughter. **Educ.:** Baghdad University, Iraq; Ankara University, Turkey. **Dipl.:** Diploma in Civil Engineering, in Road Engineering. **Career:** Engineer, District of Ma'an (1955); Engineer in Charge of Amman-Ma'an desert road (1956); Director of Road, Kuwait Ministry of Public Works (1957-59); Director of Public Works, Amman Municipality (1965); Assistant Secretary, Amman Municipality and Technical Adviser (1966-76); Member of Jordan Engineering Association and Kuwait Engineering Association; Civil Engineer Consultant (1977 To present). **Publ.:** "Kuwait Roads and Modern Methods of Road Planning", Ministry of Works, Kuwait (1959) in Arabic, "The Uses of Asphalt" (1963), "Planning and Construction of Kuwait International Airport - First Stage". **Decor.:** Star of Jordan (3rd Class) (1966). **Medal:** Independence Medal (3rd Class) (1957). **Hobbies:** Travelling, swimming, reading, theatre. **Prof. Addr.:** Amman Municipality; P.O.Box 5018 Amman, Jordan.

JARRAYA (Salah), Tunisian Chairman of Magriplast, Director of the UTIC Group. **Born** on September 5, 1959.

Son of Mohamed Jarraya, farmer (deceased) **and** Mrs. née Habiba Turki. **Married** on December 27, 1981 at Sfax to Faiza Maaloul, 3 children: Yahya, Yosra, Youssef. **Educ.:** Stanford University (California), Ecole Polytechnique (France), Ecole Sainte Geneviève (Versailles, France), Khaznadar High School (Tunis, Tunisia). **Dipl.:** High School «BAC» (June 1978), Engineering (June 1982), MBA (June 1986). **Career:** Financial & Legal VP, Eternit Group (ETEX), France (September 1982-November 1990); Board Executive Director, Owner and Chairman of UTIC: Mr. Chaibi Taoufik, UTIK Group (CHAIBI), Tunisia (November 1990- to present) and also presently Chairman of Magriplast. **Sport:** Golf (Hcp still in the 20's). **Hobby:** Playing cards (for fun not for money). **Member:** Golf Country Club of Carthage. **Prof. Addr.:** Magriplast, P.O.Box 62, Tunis Cedex 1080, Tunisia.

JARWAN (Sayf Ali, al), United Arab Emirates politician and businessman. **Born** in 1938 in Ras al-Khaimah, United Arab Emirates. **Son** of Ali al-Jarwan. **Married** in 1955, 4 sons: Ali, Yusuf, Jamal, Hanan; 3 daughter: Mona, Meriam, Jamila. **Educ.:** General secondary education: courses in management. **Career:** Director-General, Ras al-Khaimah Municipality (1964-73); represented Ras al-Khaimah in the Rulers' Council before the creation of the United Arab Emirates; Member of the committee establishing the UAE; Member, UAE Delegation, UN (1975); Ambassador to Kuwait; Ambassador to Egypt (1977-79); Minister of Labour and Social Affairs, United Arab Emirates (July 1979- Oct. 1986); Minister of Economy and Trade (1986); former Minister of Labour and Social Affairs; co-owner of al-Wihda General Trading and Contracting company Ltd., Sharjah; Founder, Ras al-Khaimah magazine (in Arabic); participated in First, Second and Third Conferences of the Organization of Arab Cities. **Member:** Amman Club, Ras al-Khaimah. **Hobbies:** Football. **Addr.:** Ministry of Labour and Social Affairs, Minister's Office, Abu Dhabi, UAE. **Priv. Addr.:** P.O.Box 11, Ras al-Khaimah, Tel.: 337, United Arab Emirates.

JASSIM (Jawad), Kuwaiti artist painter and sculptor. **Born** in 1943 in Kuwait. **Educ.:** United States of America. **Dipl.:** Bachelor of Arts (in Fine Arts 1967). **Career:** Professor at the Academy of Fine Arts (1967); Attaché at the Ministry of Guidance and Information in charge of the al-Badr Museum; Participated in 20 exhibitions in Iraq and Foreign countries, America and Kuwait. **Remark:** Amongst his Paintings "Boats", "Windward". **Addr.:** Kuwait City, Kuwait.

JASSIM (Muhammad, Abdul Aziz, al), Saudi official. **Born** in 1936 in Riyadh, Saudi Arabia. **Dipl.:** M.A. in Public Adiministration and Supervision. **Career:** Teacher; Inspector, Administrative Director, Assistant Director General, Ministry of Education; General Director of Cultural Affairs, Ministry of Education; Assistant Deputy Minister for Financial and Administration Affairs, Ministry of Petroleum; participated in several educational conferences such as the Education Conference in Geneva, the Scouts Conference in the UK and UNESCO Conferences in Paris; paticipated in establishing the Social Services and Development Centres in Saudi Arabia. **Publ.:** Papers, articles, lectures and radio broadcasts in the radio and local press. **Hobbies:** Reading, collecting books, photography. **Prof. Addr.:** P.O.Box 11541, Riyadh, Saudi Arabia.

JASSIM (Saadun, Mohamad, al), Kuwaiti executive. **Born** in Kuwait in 1933. **Son** of Mohamad Jassim. **Married**, three children. **Educ.:** B.Sc., American University of Cairo, Egypt (1956). **Career:** Assistant for Press Affairs, Kuwait Press and Publications Department; Assistant Under Secretary for Administration and Finance, Ministry of Guidance and Information (1962); Under Secretary, Ministry of Information (1965-84); Businessman (1984-). **Member** of the Society of the Protection of Environment, Chief **Editor** of Kuwait Red Crescent Society Magazine. **Medals:** Commander of the National Order of Cedar, Lebanon (1971); King Abdul Aziz Order, 1st Class, Saudi Arabia. **Sport:** Swimming. **Priv. Addr.:** Tel.: 811905, Kuwait.

JASSIR (Hamad Ibn Mohamad, al), Saudi man of letters. **Born** at al-Burud, Najd. **Dipl.:** degree in Islamic law. **Career:** Teacher; Headmaster of Yanbu school; judge; Director of Education, Jeddah; Dean of the Faculty of Shari'a (Islamic law), Riyadh; owner and founder of al-Yamamah Establishment for Publication, Research and Translation; owner of al-Arab magazine. **Publ.:** several literary and history books; columnist and critic. **Prof. Addr.:** P.O.Box 137, King Faisal Str., Riyadh 11411, Saudi Arabia.

JAWA (Jamal Hassan), Saudi executive. **Born** in 1930 in Mecca, Saudi Arabia. **Dipl.:** B.A. (Accounting), Cairo University (1953). **Career:** Administrative Assistant (1952-53); Secretary, Ministry of Finance (1953-54); Director of Riyadh Branch, Alireza and Company; Vice-President of Arab Drilling Co.; Chairman of Executive Committee, Iron and Steel Plant; Chairman of Executive Committee, Petromin Co. for Tankers; Deputy Chairman of Executive Committee, Petromin for Marketing Co.; Executive Deputy Governor, Petromin; Saudi Representative, OPEC Executive Bureau; Chairman of Board, Arab Petroleum Investments Corp. **Hobbies:** Reading, bridge. **Prof. Addr.:** P.O.Box 448, Dhahran Airport 31932, Saudi Arabia.

JAWAD (Faisal, Hassan), Bahraini Deputy Chairman and Chief Executive Officer of Jawad Group of Companies, Bahrain. **Born** on June 6, 1953 in Bahrain. **Son** of Hassan Mohamed Jawad (Businessman) **and** Khatoon Naser. **Married** on March 1, 1981 in Bahrain to Judith Patricia Jawad, 4 children: Kareem Faisal Jawad, Jameel Faisal Jawad, Jawad Faisal Jawad and Sophie Jawad. **Educ.:** Twickenham College, Twickenham, Middlesex,

England. **Dipl.:** M.B.A. Degree. **Career:** Officer Manager (1975-1977); Manager (1978-1981); Executive Director (1982-1985); Managing Director (1986-1991); Deputy Chairman and Chief Executive Officer of Jawad Group of Companies (1992- to date). **Work:** Entire control of administration and financial direction of the Group as well as policy making decisions. **Other Information:** Executive powers within the Group. **Awards:** Paul Harris Fellow of the Rotary Foundation of Rotary International- Orlando (1986)- Dairy Queen Winner's Circle- Washington DC (1988)- Dairy Queen Top Brass. **Sport:** Lawn Tennis. **Hobbies:** Swimming, Camping, Skiing, Sailing. **Member:** Rotary Club of Sulmaniya, Bahrain (President 1984-1985); Swissair Travel Club, Zurich, Switzerland. **Credit Cards:** Amex, Visa, **Prof. Addr.:** Jawad Cold Stores, «Jawad House», 171 Sh. Issa Avenue, P.O.Box 430, Tel.: (0973) 253032, Fax: 273866, 273605, Telex: 8347 JAWAD BN, Manama, Bahrain. **Addr.:** No. 1 Jawad Garden 1318, Road 1841, Barbar 518 Bahrain, Tel.: (0973) 692564, Manama, Bahrain.

JAWAD (Jawad, Habib), Bahraini Businessman. **born** in 1942 in Bahrain. **Married,** 5 children. **Education:** Chartered Institute of Management Accountants Examinations (1970). **Prof. Activities:** Fellow of the Institute of Financial Consultants; Fellow of the Chartered Institute of Management Accountants among others. **Career:** Bahrain Petroleum Co. (1956-70); Saba and Co. (1970-73); Price Waterhouse (1973-79); established his own company, Jawad Habib & Co. in 1980 which became a member of Coopers & Lybrand in 1990 and Later merged with Price Waterhouse in 1998 to form Price Waterhouse Coopers. **Prof. Addr.:** P.O.Box 787, Manama Bahrain.

JAWHAR (Saud, Obaysan, al), Saudi executive/ Petroleum Engineer. **Born** in 1938 Riyadh. **Married,** 4 sons, 1 daughter. **Educ.:** Kansas University, USA. **Dipl.:** B.Sc. in Petroleum Engineering (1965). **Career:** Project Engineer of Jeddah Refinery, Petromin, later General Production Manager; Member of the Board of Directors of Arab-Saudi Organisation for Specification and Measurement; Deputy Production Manager of Riyadh Refinery, Saudi Arabia. **Hobby:** reading. **Prof. Addr.:** Petromin Riyadh Refinery, P.O.Box 3964, Tel.: 4981523, Telex: 201015, Saudi Arabia.

JAZAIRY (Idriss), Algerian diplomat and international administrator. **Born** on May 29, 1936. **Married,** 4 children. **Educ.:** Master of Arts, Oxford University, U.K.; Ancien élève, Ecole nationale d'administration, Paris, France; Master in Public Administration, Harvard, University, U.S.A. **Career:** (a) at the national level in Algeria: Chief of Economic and Social Department, then Director of International Cooperation at the Ministry of Foreign Affairs (1963-71); Adviser at the Presidency of the Republic (1971-77); Under-Secretary-General, Ministry of Foreign Affairs (1977-79); Ambassador to Belgium, Luxemburg and EEC (1979-82); Ambassador-at-large specializing in international economic affairs, Ministry of Foreign Affairs (1982-84). (b) at the international level: President of the Board of Governors of the African Development Bank (1971-72); Chairman, UN General Assembly Committee of the Whole on the North-South Dialogue (1978-79); President, International Fund for Agricultural Development (IFAD) since 1984. **Prof. Addr.:** Office of the President, IFAD, Via del Serafico 107, Tel.: 54591, Telex: 620330 IFAD, 00142 Rome, Italy.

JAZAIRY (Muhammad), Iraqi journalist. **Born** on June 30, 1939 in Basra, Iraq. **Married,** 2 daughters, 1 son. **Educ.:** self education in literature, economic and political studies, history and social sciences; extensive training in journalism since 1953. **Career:** Journalist, with "al-Jumhuriya" (1972), Chief Editor "al-Jumhuriya" (1972), Chief Editor "al-Jumhuriya"; Editor in Chief of "al-Jumhuriya al-Ousbou'i"; Member and Secretary of General Federation of Arab Writers (1975-); Member of the Arab Journalists Union (1968-) and of the Iraqi Journalists Union (1959-); Member of the International Organization of Journalists as well as member of other cultural associations, committees and societies; Editor in Chief of "Funun" magazine (1980-); Secretary of the Federation of Applied Arts Critics (1982-). **Publ.:** published numerous books in Iraq (in Arabic) as well as several conference magazines. **Hobbies:** Music, literary criticism, gymnastics, travelling. **Addr.:** Hay al-Mathna, Mahalla 618, Street 20, Building 41, Flat 8, Zayuna, Baghdad, Iraq.

JAZI (Dali), Tunisian lawyer. **Born** on December 7, 1942 in Tunisia. **Married,** 2 children. **Educ.:** University of Paris, France. **Dipl.:** Diplomas in Higher Studies in Public Law and in Political Science. **Career:** Attachée in the Office of the Minister of National Education (1968-69) and (1970-71); Assistant Secretary General, Union of Tunisian Youth in charge of foreign relations (1970-71); lawyer in Tunis and Assistant Professor in the Faculty of Law and Political and Economic Science, Tunis; Vice President, Tunisian Union of Young Lawyers; Member of the Tunisian Delegation to the UNESCO General Conference, Paris (1970); Member of the Tunisian Delegation to the 3rd Conference of the Pan-African Youth Movement (1970); visited various foreign countries representing the Tunisian youth movement; Treasurer of the Founding Office, Tunisian League for the Defence of the Rights of Man; Contributor to the "Contact" Tunisian magazine (1973-74), Minister of Public Health (1990-1991); Minister of Higher Education (since Jan. 1995). **Hobbies:** Music, football, tennis. **Addr.:** 14 Rue de Touraine, Cité Jardins, Tunis, Tunisia.

JAZI (Rakan, Inad, al), Jordanian politician. **Born** in 1928 in Jordan. **Married. Educ.:** Royal Military Academy in Sandhurst, UK; Military Staff College, USA; High Military College of Nassir Academy, Egypt. **Career:** Cadet

Officer, Arab Legion of Jordan (1947); Tank Regiment Commander (1962); Armoured Brigade Commander (1965); Second in Command of Armoured Corps (1969); Commander of Infantry Division (1970); Military Attaché, Embassy to UK (1970-71); Military Adviser to HM the King (1972); Director of the Officers' Affairs (1973); Assistant Chief of Staff for Manpower, with rank of Major General (1974); Minister for Prime Minister's Affairs (1974) and (1976). **Decor.:** Star of Jordan (2nd Class). **Medals:** Independence Medal (1st Class), Loyal Service Medal, Chinese Medal. **Addr.:** Shmeissani, Amman, Jordan.

JEFRY (Abdallah Abdul Rahman), Saudi writer and journalist. **Born** in 1939 in Mecca, Saudi Arabia. **Educ.:** Received secondary school education supplemented by extensive reading. **Career:** Supervisor of Publications, Ministry of Information; sub-Editor, Okaz, Madinah Monawarah and al-Bilad daily newspapers; Editor, Okaz daily newspaper; Editor, then Deputy Editor-in-Chief, al-Awsat Sharq daily newspaper and al-Mejalla magazine; former member of al-Bilad daily newspaper. Supervisor of Cultural and Arts Dept. at al-Sharq al-Awsat Newspaper. **Member** of Jeddah Literary Club. **Publ.:** three collections of short stories, Hyatun Ja'ea (Hungry Life), al-Jidar al-A'akhar (The Other Wall), al-Zama' (Thirst) Nubt (heart Beatings); Hewarn fi al-Huzun al Dafié (Dialogue in the Warm Grief); Faqat (Only); Juzun Min Hulum (Part of Dream); and numerous other stories and poems. **Hobbies:** Reading, travel. **Prof. Addr.:** Saudi Research and Marketing Co. Tel.: 6691888, Jeddah.

JEFRY (Safi Aqeel), Saudi physician. **Born** in 1940 in Mecca, Saudi Arabia. **Dipl.:** M.B. (Skin and Venereal Diseases), Ain Shams University, Cairo, Egypt; Vienna University, Austria. **Career:** Physician, specialist in skin and venereal diseases, King's Hospital, Jeddah; Member (for life) of American Medical Association; attended medical conferences on skin and venereal diseases held at Cairo University, Ain Shams University and Alexandria University. **Hobbies:** Travel, sport. **Prof. Addr.:** King's Hospital, Tel.: 6423415, 6422622, Jeddah. **Priv. Addr.:** Tel.: 6420698, Jeddah, Saudi Arabia.

JERAISY (Abdulrahman, Ali, al), Saudi businessman. **Born** in 1931 at Riyadh, Saudi Arabia. **Career:** Chairman of Jeraisy Group of Companies; President of Chamber of Commerce and Industry, Riyadh; former President of Council of Saudi Chambers of Commerce and Industry. Chairman TAIB Bank E.C., Bahrain. **Hobbies:** Reading and farming. **Addr.:** King Fahad Road, P.O.Box 317, Riyadh 11411, Saudi Arabia.

JERASH (Mohamad al-Abdallah, al), Saudi academic. **Born** in 1943. **Dipl.:** B.A. King Saud University (1965); M.A. University of Durham (1969); Ph.D., Manchester University (1972). **Career:** Professor of Geography and former Vice Dean, Faculty of Arts, King Abdulaziz University. **Member:** of the Royal Geographical Society, London; member of the American Geographical Association, New York, Association de Geographes Français, Paris. **Prof. Addr.:** Department of Geography, King Abdulaziz University, P.O.Box 8229, Tel.: 6952612, Jeddah 21482, Saudi Arabia.

JETTOU (Driss), Moroccan Minister of Finance, Trade, Industry & Handicraft. **Born** on 24 May at al Jadidah (Morocco). **Married**, 4 children: **Educ.:** Moroccan High School Diploma; Bachelor on University of Sciences of Rabat (Morocco); Management and Business Administration, Cordwainers Colleges, London. **Career:** Moroccan Minister of Finance, Trade, Industry & Handicraft since August 1997; Minister of Trade, Industry & Handicraft since November 1997 - March 1998. **Medals:** Knight Grade on the Alaouite Wissam, Legion d'Honneur from France & Italy. **Addr.:** Rabat, Morocco.

JIBOURI (Hamid, Alwan, al), Iraqi politician. **Born** in 1930 in Hilla, Iraq. **Educ.:** American University of Beirut, Lebanon. **Career:** Ministry of Finance; Editor of "al-Shaab" newspaper (1963); Director General of Information, Ministry of Culture and Information; Minister of State for Presidential Affairs (1968-69); Minister of Culture and Information (1969-70); Minister of Youth (1970-72); Minister of Culture and Information and President of the Iraqi Youth Organization (1972-74); Minister of State (1974-76); Liaison Minister, Autonomous Region of Kurdistan (1975-75); Head, Office of the Vice Chairman of the Revolutionary Command Council with rank of Minister (1976-77); Minister of State for Foreign Affairs (1977-84); Ambassador of Iraq to Tunis, until August 1993. Resigned. **Addr.:** Now Living in London U.K.

JIBOURI (Hazim, Ahmad, al), Iraqi UN official. **Born** in 1925 in Mosul, Nineveh, Iraq. **Married. Educ.:** Cairo University, Egypt; Utah State University, Logan, USA; North Carolina State University, Raleigh, USA. **Dipl.:** B.Sc., M.Sc., Ph.D. **Career:** Head of the Department of Field Crops, Ministry of Agriculture, Iraq (1957-59); Professor of Plant Genetics, University of Libya (1958-62); Senior Agronomist, FAO, Libya (1958-62), Agronomist, FAO, Italy (1965-57); Regional Plant Production and Protection Officer, FAO, Thailand (1967-74); Chief of Crop Policy and Planning Unit, Plant Production and Protection Division, FAO, Italy (1974-75). **Publ.:** numerous articles and books on agricultural subjects. **Hobbies:** Agronomy, agricultural planning, plant breeding, international agricultural development and research, golf. **Prof. Addr.:** FAO, Via delle Terme di Caracalla, 00100 Rome, Italy.

JIBOURI (Nadhima, Abdul Jabbar, al), Iraqi academic. **Born** in 1937 in Hindiyadh, Iraq. **Married**, 2 sons, 1 daughter. **Educ.:** University of Baghdad, Iraq; Oklahoma

State University, USA, Texas A and M University, USA. **Dipl.:** B.Sc. in Biology, M.Sc. in Zoology, Ph.D. in History and Embryology. **Career:** Laboratory Assistant, Biology Section, College of veterinary Medicine, University of Baghdad, Iraq (1963-66); Graduate Assitant, USA (1966-71); Assistant Professor, Biology Section, College of Veterniary Medicine, University of Baghdad (1971). **Publ.:** several scientific articles (in English) and one paper (in Arabic). **Prof. Addr.:** Biology Section, College of Veterinary Medicine, University of Baghdad, Baghdad, Iraq.

JIBRIL (Ahmad), Palestinian politician. **Born** in 1935 in Ramle. **Career:** Syrian Army; Syrian Chess Champion (1956); left Syrian Army in 1958 and founded the Palestinian Liberation Front (PLF) in Syria (1961); began military operations (1965); following 1967 War, PLF was briefly part of the Popular Front for the Liberation of Palestine (PFLP), later withdrew to become the PFLP-General Command, a non-political organization which did not join the Palestine Liberation Organization (PLO), and its Leader. Member of the Rejection Front. **Addr.:** Damascus, Syria.

JIBURY (Falik, Khidir, al), Arab-American academic. **Born** in 1934. **Married**, 1 son. **Educ.:** University of Baghdad, Iraq; Oregon State University, USA. **Dipl.:** B.Sc., M.Sc., Ph.D.; Registered Professional Engineer, State of California (1976). **Career:** Head, Land Use and Classifications, Ministry of Development, Iraq (1955-56); Assistant Professor, University of Baghdad (1960-61); Irrigationist, University of California (1961-80); Visiting Professor, American University of Beirut, Lebanon (1967-68); Member of California Water Commission (1978-80); Adviser to, The Libyan Ministry of Land Development, The Iraqi Ministry of Agriculture, The Mexican Ministry of Wate Resources and the US National Academy of Sciences, Water Management Board; Member, International Committee of Irrigation and Drainage, Society of Agriculture Engineers, American Society of Agronomy Soil Science, California, Irrigation Society, California Irrigation Insitute, Society of Agronomy and Western Society of Soil Science; Member of the State Water Resources Control Board (1980-). **Publ.:** numerous papers published in technical and scientific journals (in English and Spanish). **Decor.:** Irrigation Engineer Man of the Year (1976). **Hobbies:** Tennis, jogging. **Prof. Addr.:** Fresno, California, USA.

JIDDI (Muhammad, Ali, al), Libyan politician. **Born** in 1937 in Bani Walid, Libya. **Educ.:** University of al-Azhar, Cairo, Egypt. **Dipl.:** Degree in Law. **Career:** Public Prosecutor, Fezzan; Judge, Souk al-Juma'a Court; Secretary for Justice in General People's Committee (1981); Minister of Justice (1969-81); President of the Supreme Court (1981-84). **Addr.:** Tripoli, Libya.

JISHI (Jamil Abdallah, al), Saudi executive. **Born** in 1937 at Tarout. **Dipl.:** B.Sc. (1966); M.Sc. (1967); Ph.D. (1974) (all in Industrial Studies and Development) (1967-75); Saudi Development Fund (1975-76); Royal Commission for Jubail and Yambu (1976-81); Deputy Governor, Electricity Corporation; member of Board, National Gas Company, Saudi Consulting House, Islamic Welfare Society; Director General, the Arab Investment Company, Riyadh, Saudi Arabia. **Prof. Addr.:** Arab Investment Company, P.O.Box 4009, Riyadh 11491, Saudi Arabia.

JISHI (Majid, Jawad, al), Bahraini engineer and Politician. **Born** in 1931. **Son** of Jawad al-Jishi. **Married**, four children: one son and three daughters. **Educ.:** American University of Beirut, Lebanon. **Dipl.:** Degree in Civil Engineering (1955). **Career:** worked as an Engineer with the Public Works Department, Bahrain (1955-57); worked with contracting firms in Qatar as Construction Engnieer (1957-61); as Project Engineer on roadworks, Ministry of Public Works, Kuwait (1961-64); in Private Consultancy, Bahrain (1964-68); Director of Public Works, Abu Dhabi (1968-70); Director of Planning, Ministry of Development & Engineering Services, Bahrain (1970-73); Under Secretary, Ministry of Development & Engineering Services, Bahrain (1973-75); Minister of Works, Power & Water, Bahrain (1975 to-date); Chairman of the Board of Directors Arab Shipbuilding and Repair Yard, Bahrain (1974-78). Member of the Bahrain Supreme Council for Petroleum chaired by H.H. the Prime Minister; Member of the Board of Trustees of the Bahrain Center for Research & Studies chaired by H.H. the Crown Prince; Member of the Bahrain Traffic Supreme Council; Member of the Board of Trustees of Bahrain University; President of the Bahrain Classical Music Society. **Addr.:** Ministry of Works, Power & Water, Minister's Office, P.O.Box 6000, Tel.: 522000, Manama, Bahrain.

JOHANY (Ali Ibn Talal, al), Saudi academic. **Born** in 1945 at Yanbu. **Dipl.:** Ph.D., University of California, U.S.A. **Career:** Economic Research, Ministry of Planning, Riyadh (1972-74); Assistant Professor, Faculty of Industrial Management, KFUPM (1978); Dean, Faculty of Industrial Management, King Fahad University of Petroleum and Minerals, Dhahran (1980); Consultant to many Government departments and Agencies; has Participated in various televised lectures and discussions. Minister of Posts, Telegraphs and Telecommunications (since August 1995-June 1999). **Publ.:** The Myth of the OPEC Cartel Publisher: John Wiley and Sons (1980); Essays in Economics (in Arabic) (publisher: Tihama, 1980). **Hobbies:** Reading, writing. **Priv. Addr.:** Tel.: 8606457, Dhahran, Saudi Arabia.

JOMAIH (Mohammed, Abdullah, al), Saudi businessman. **Born** in 1918 in Saudi Arabia. **Son** of Abdullah al-Jomaih. **Married. Educ.:** Islamic studies and general education. **Career:** Started his business career in 1936 with the establishment of Abdulaziz and Mohamed A. al-Jomaih group of companies; Co-Founder and ex-Chairman of Riyadh Electricity Company; Co-Founder and ex-Managing Director of Yamama Cement Co.; Co-Founder and former Director of Saudi Gas Co., Saudi Standard Organization. Chairman and President of Abdulaziz and M.A. al-Jomaih group of companies; Chairman of al-Jomaih and Shell Lubrication Oil Co., and Saudi Crowncaps Manufacturing Company. **Hobby:** Reading. **Member:** Equestrian Club; The Charitable Association (Gamiyat Albir); Member of General Motors Honorary Club and of the advisory council of the President of General Motors. **Decor.:** Recipient of Decoration and title of Cavaliere from the President of the Republic of Italy; Order of Merit (awarded by the President of the Federal Republic of Germany); Honorary Commander of the Civil Division (awarded by Her Majesty Queen Elizabeth the Second); Peace through Commerce Medallion (awarded by the United States Department of Commerce). **Credit Card:** American Express. **Prof. Addr.:** al-Jomaih Building, P.O.Box 132, Riyadh 11411, Tel.: 4788811 (ten lines), Riyadh, Saudi Arabia.

JORIO (Maati), Moroccan diplomat. **Born** in 1934 in Rabat, Morocco. **Married**, 4 children. **Educ.:** Toulouse University, France. **Dipl.: LL.B., Diploma in Political Sciences. Career:** Administrative Affairs Director at the Ministry of Public Works and Communications (1957-64); Secretary General, Ministry of the Interior (1964-71); Minister of Agriculture and Agrarian Reform (1971-72); Ambassador to Romania (1973-77), Ambassador to USSR (1977-78), to Spain (1978-81), to Libya (1981-82), to Canada (1982-84) and Ambassador to USA (1984-). **Prof. Addr.:** Ministry of Foreign Affairs, Rabat, Morocco and Embassy of the Kingdom of Morocco, 160121 Street NW, Washington DC, USA.

JOSEPH (Pazhunnan Verghese), Indian civil engineer. **Born** on March 15, 1947 in Shornur Kerala, India. **Son** of late P.T. Verghese and Mrs. Mathiri Verghese. **Married** on Janaury 1, 1978 in Pazhanji Kerala, India to Miss P.M. Prema, two children; Sindhumol Joseph (1978) and Noble PJ (1981). **Educ.:** Government High School Pazhanji Kerala, India; Matha College for Agriculture Kunnamkulam Kerala, India. **Dipl.:** in Civil Engineering. **Career:** Worked as NCO in Indian Para Military Force and attended various training courses during service (1968-75); Currently working as Manager of Gulf Estate Agency (since 1985), dealing in real estate. **Medal:** Decorated with three medals (during Liberation of Bangladesh) when he attended in military operation during INDO-PAK War 1971. **Sports:** Football, basketball. **Hobby:** Playing Cards. **Prof. Addr.:** Gulf Estate Agency, P.O.Box 432, Tel.: 427911, 414866, 325434, Doha, Qatar. **Priv. Addr.:** Tel.: 434603, Doha, Qatar.

JOUHARGY (Yousef, Ismail Ghulam), Saudi civil servant. **Born** on December 31, 1929 in Mecca, Saudi Arabia. **Son** of Ismail Ghulam Jouhargy (General Merchant). **Married** in 1953, 9 children: Dr. Waffaa (1954), Hama (1956), Dr. Inaam (1959), Alnooman (1962), Elhaam (1963), Alsamawal (1970), Sereen (1973), Raood (1974), Noor (1978). **Educ.:** Faculty of Commerce, Riyadh University, **Dipl.:** B.Com. (Bachelor of Accountancy and Business Administration). **Career:** Accountant (1948); Inspector (1954); Chief of Budgeting Division (1956); Chief Inspection Board (1957); Director, Budgeting Department (1958-64); General Director, Budgeting Department, Ministry of Defence and Aviation since 1968; Member of several official committees; member of Board of Government Employees Cooperative Society for Supplies, Riyadh; Delegated to Arab Organization for Industrialisation in Egypt, as General Director Account Department (1976-79). **Hobbies:** Poetry, Music, Excursions. **Prof. Addr.:** P.O.Box 197, Tel.: 2310792, Riyadh. 11411 **Priv. Addr.:** Tel.:2319726, 4762460, Riyadh, Saudi Arabia.

JOUKHDAR (Mohamed Saleh), Saudi economist. **Born** in 1932 in Jeddah, Saudi Arabia. **Married** in 1957 to Malik Intabi, three children: one son, two daughters. **Educ.:** University of California and Southern California. **Dipl.:** M.A. **Career:** Economic Adviser to Managing Director of Petroleum and Minerals, Saudi Arabia (1958); Director-General Ministry of Petroleum and Mineral Resources (1961); Director, Arabian Oil Co. (1961-66); Secretary-General of OPEC (1967-68); Deputy Minister of Petroleum and Mineral Resources (1969); Director, PETROMIN (1970-73); Ambassador in Charge of Petroleum and Economic Affairs, Ministry of Foreign Affairs (1973-74); Petroleum Consultant (1974-). **Member** American Society of Economists; Trustee, King Fahad University of Petroleum and Minerals. **Addr.:** Ministry of Petroleum and Mineral Resources, P.O.Box 757, Riyadh 11189, Saudi Arabia.

JOURY (Yacoub), Jordanian international civil servant. **Born** on July 9, 1922 in Jerusalem. **Married**, with children. **Educ.:** Young Men's Christian Association School, Jerusalem (1943-45); Jerusalem Tutorial Classes (1945-47). **Dipl.:** B.A. **Career:** Programme Assistant and Radio Producer, Palestine Broadcasting Service, Jerusalem (1939-48); Chief News Editor and English Commentator, Hashemite Broadcasting Service, Ramallah (Jordan, 1949-53); Press and Information Officer, Tourist Department (Jerusalem, 1953-57); Consul General and Member, Permanent Mission of Jordan, New York (1957-62); Deputy Resident Representative, United Nations Development Programme (UNDP) Mogadisho, Somalia (1962-64); Deputy Resident Representative, UNDP, Dacca, Pakistan (1964-68); Resident Representative, Nepal, UNDP, Director, UN Information Centre, Kathmandou (1968-75); Iraq (1975-79); Jamaica (1979-). **Awards:** British Council of Amman Scholarship (1953); French Government Scholarship (1954). **Addr.:** Amman, Jordan.

JUFFALI (Ahmad), Saudi businessman. **Born** on October 15, 1924 in Saudi Arabia. **Son** of Abdallah Juffali (businessman). **Married** to Suad Juffali, 4 children: Walid, Maha, Tarek and Khalid. **Educ.:** Mecca & London. **Career:** Managing Director, Messrs. E.A. Juffali & Bros (1945); Member Board of Directors; Saudi Electric Co. (1952); Medina Electric Co. (1958); Saudi Cement Co. (1958); Honorary Danish Consul General (1959); Director, Saudi Monetary Agency (1960-68); Chairman, National Insurance Co. S.A. since 1974; Chairman, Petrosery since 1975; Chairman, National Automobile Industry Co. Ltd. since 1975; Chairman, Arabian Metal Industries Ltd. since 1975; Chairman, Fluor Arabia Ltd. since 1976; Chairman, Juffali-Sulzer Saudi Arabia Co. Ltd. since 1976; Arabia Electric Co. Ltd. since 1976; Saudi-Building Systems since 1976; Semco Arabia Ltd. 1976; Beck Arabia 1976; Saudi Steel Products Co. (1978); Saudi Refrigerator Manufacturing Co. (1980); Saudi Ericsson Communications Ltd. (1980). **Member:** Saudi German Cooperation Committee 1976. **Awards:** Knight (1st grade) conferred by Her Majesty the Queen of Denmark. **Sports:** Swimming and walking. **Credit Cards:** American Express; Barblay. **Prof. Addr.:** E.A. Juffali & Bros., P.O.Box 1049, Tel.: 6422222, Jeddah 21431 Saudi Arabia. **Priv. Addr.:** Othman Bin Affan street, Sharafiyeh, Tel.: 6534444, Jeddah, Saudi Arabia.

JUFFALI (Ali, Abdallah, al), Saudi businessman. **Married**, 4 sons, 1 daughter. **Career:** Chairman E.A. Juffali & Bros.; Member of the Board of Directors of Saudi Airlines and Saudi-Electric Company; Chairman of National Electric Power Company, Jeddah and several other companies. **Prof. Addr.:** P.O.Box 1049, Jeddah, Saudi Arabia.

JUINDI (Ahmad, Yusuf, al), Egyptian businessman. **Born** in 1924 in Zifta-Gharbieh, Egypt. **Married**, 2 sons, 2 daughters. **Educ.:** Cairo University, Egypt. **Dipl.:** LL.B. **Career:** Chairman of National Company for Investment, Cairo; Managing Director of Comintor Investment and Trading. **Member:** Gezira Sporting Club, Cairo, Egypt; Hurlingham Club, London, UK. **Addr.:** 11 Seraya el-Ezbekia Street, Manial Shiha, Cairo, Egypt.

JUMA (Abdulla, Mohammed), Bahraini electrical engineer. **Born** in 1946 in Bahrain. **Married**, 3 children. **Educ.:** University of Salford, U.K. **Dipl.:** B.Sc. in Electrical Engineering. **Career:** Distribution Engineer, Electricity Directorate (1970-74); Project Engineer, Electricity Directorate (1974-76); Chief Engineer, Electricity Directorate, (1976-76); Acting Director of Electricity (1976-78); Director of Electricity, Electricity Directorate, Ministry of Works, Power and Water, Bahrain (1978-92); Assistant Under Secretary Electricity, Ministry of Works, Power and Water (1992-95); Minister of Electricity and Water (1995). **Hobbies:** Swimming, Photography. **Prof. Addr.:** Ministry of Electricity & Water, P.O.Box 2, Manama, Bahrain. Tel.: 0973 522000, Fax: 0973 537151.

JUMA (Hassan Ali), Bahraini Managing Director. **Born** in July 1948 in Muharraq, Bahrain, **Educ.:** Fellow of the Chartered Institute of Management Accountants, England. **Career History:** Bahrain Petroleum Company (1964-75); Second Vice President, Chase Manhattan Bank OBU (1975-79); Deputy General Manager, National Bank of Bahrain Bahrain (1981-84), General Manager and Chief Exective Officer (1984-94), Chief Executive Officer (1994-97), Present Position since January 1997). **Directorships:** Board Member of National Bank of Bahrain; Arab Banking Corporation; Arab Financial Services; Bahrain Telecommunications Co.; Bahrain Institute of Banking & Finance; Banco Atlantico. **Address:** P.O.Box 106, Manama, Bahrain.

JUMA (Hussain, Makki, al), Kuwaiti businessman. **Born** in 1929 in Kuwait. **Son** of Makki al-Juma. **Married** in 1964, 1 son, 8 daughters. **Career:** Chairman, Arab Japanese Finance Ltd. (UBAN); Hong Kong and Aluminium Extrusion Ltd., Kuwait; Member of the Board of Directors, Union of Arab and French Banks (UBAF), Paris; UBAF Bank Ltd., London; UBAF Arab American Bank, New York; Artoc Bank and Trust Ltd., Bahamas; Kuwait Chamber of Commerce and Industry; Kuwait Investment Group, Kuwait; Pearl Investment Company, Bahrain; Willco Kuwait Trading, Kuwait, Adviser, Arab Investment for (ASIA) Kuwait; Blanket Industry Co., Kuwait; member of National Assembly (Parliament) (1974-76); Board Director, Kuwait-French Bank, Paris. **Addr.:** P.O.Box 24501, Safat, Kuwait City, Kuwait.

JUMA (Noman), Egyptian academic. **Born** in 1934. **Married**, 2 daughters. **Educ.:** University of Paris, France. **Dipl.:** Ph.D. in Civil Law. **Career:** Deputy to the Attorney General (1956-61); Professor of Civil Law, College of Law, University of Paris (1966-71); Assistant Barrister at French Court of Cassation (1966-71); Head of Civil Law Department and Professor, Cairo University (1971-84); Barrister at Law and International Arbitration (1975-). **Publ.:** "Théorie de Source de l'obligation" (1966), "al-Madkhal Il'illom al-Qanouniah" (1974), "al-Dhahir Ka"masdar Llihaq" (1976), "al-Houkouk al-Ainiah" (1982). **Addr.:** 20 A el-Mansour Mohammed, Zamalek, Cairo, Egypt.

JUMAA (Madhat), Jordanian former diplomat. **Born** on August 19, 1920. **Educ.:** Cairo University. **Career:** Arab League, Cairo (1945-47); First Secretary and Counsellor; Cairo (1947-52); Counsellor and Chargé d'Affaires, London (1952-53); Ambassador to Pakistan (1953-55); Chief of Protocol, Royal Palace, Amman (1956); Under-Secretary for Press and Broadcasting (1956-58); Ambassador to the U.S.A. (1958-59), to Morocco (1959-62), to Federal German Republic (1962-65), to Lebanon (1965-67), to United Kingdom (1967). **Awards:** various decorations. **Addr.:** Amman, Jordan.

JUMAA (Salah, Mohamad), Jordanian statesman and

agricultural expert. **Born** in 1927, in Tafila, Jordan. **Married. Educ.:** Cairo University, Cairo; London University, UK. **Dipl.:** B.Sc. (Agricultural Sciences) (1953); M.Sc. (Agricultural Sciences) (1956). **Career:** Teacher, al-Jabiha Agricultural College (1953-54); Principal, al-Jabiha Agricultural College; Supervisor, Agricultural Studies, Ministry of Agriculture; Head, al-Jabiha Agricultural Research Station (1956-63); Director of Forestry, Ministry of Agriculture (1965-68); Ambassador, FAO in Rome (1968-71); Deputy General Manager, Agricultural Loans Corporation, Ministry of Supply (1972); President, Union of Agricultural Engineers (1966-68 and 1972-76); Minister of Agriculture and Supply (July- November 1976); Minister of Agriculture (November 1976, re-appointed on June 1978-80); presently Regional Representative for the Near East of F.A.O. in Rome. **Awards:** 3rd Class, Independence Medal. **Addr.:** F.A.O., Via delle Terme di Caracalla, 00100, Rome, Italy.

JUMAH (Hassan, Fahmi), Iraqi academic. **Born** on May 15, 1937 in Baghdad, Iraq. **Married**, 3 children. **Educ.:** Baghdad University, Iraq; University of Wisconsin, USA, University of Maine, USA. **Dipl.:** B.Sc., M.Sc., Ph.D. **Career:** Agricultural Engineer, Ministry of Agriculture and Agrarian Reforms, Iraq (1959); Lecturer at the Faculty of Agriculture, Baghdad University (1964-68), Dean of Veterinary Science Faculty, Baghdad University (1968-69); Director General, Agriculture and Natural Resources Department and supervisor for overall Agricultural and Veterinary Faculties in Iraq (1963 70); Dean of Agriculture and Forestry Faculty, Mosul University, Iraq (1973), Professor (1973); Minister of Agriculture and Agrarian Reforms, Iraq (1974-77); Adviser, Ministry of Higher Education and Scientific Research, Iraq (1977-80); Director General of Arab Organisation for Agricultural Development Khartoum, Sudan (1980-). **Publ.:** various reseach papers on agricultural problems, agricultural development and education. **Hobbies:** General readings in history and political sciences, in addition to sports. **Present Addr.:** Director General, Arab Organization for Agricultural Development, P.O.Box 474 Khartoum, Sudan.

JUMAYAN (Mikhael), Jordanian official. **Born** in 1915. **Educ.:** American University in Cairo, Egypt. **Career:** Interpreter (1940-43), Teacher (1943-45); Government Agency Secretary (1945-47); Assistant Chief Accountant (1947-50); Registrar of Patents, Trademarks and Companies (1950-55); Divisional Head Assistant, Civil Service (1955-57), Divisional Head (1957-62); Assistant Under Secretary (1962-65), Under Secretary (1965-68); Antiquities Director (1968-69); Director of the Institute of Public Administration (1970-72); President of A.U.C. Alumni Club (1976-1992); representative of Jordan in AUC Alumni Council; represented Jordan at several Arab and international conferences. **Publ.:** Translation of International Laws of Chess from Arabic into English, "Fundamentals of Supervision" (1964); translated into Arabic "Fundamentals of Public Administration" (1969) as well as papers on public administration "Eastern Cultural Influences on the Western Civilization Through the Crusades". **Prof. Addr.:** P.O.Box 2077, Amman, Jordan.

JUNAID (Mohamad Ahmad, al), Yemeni politician. **Born** in 1934 in Hodeida, Republic of Yemen. **Married** in October 1965, 1 daughter: Jamila. **Educ.:** London University, UK. **Dipl.:** B.Sc. in Engineering. **Career:** Director of Technical Section, Hodeida Public Works Office (1964-65); Deputy Technical Director and member of the Board of the Yemen Petroleum Company (1965); Under-Secretary, Ministry of Public Works (1967); Chairman of the Agricultural Development Board (1968); Minister of Agriculture (1968-71); Minister of Development (1971-72); Minister of the Treasury and Finance (1973); Deputy Prime Minister for Economic and Financial Affairs (1977); Minister of Electricity, Water and Sewerage (1982-84); Governor Central Bank of Yemen, Sanaa and Minister of Finance (since June 1995 - Sept. 1999); Minister for the Civil Service and Administrative Reform. **Hobbies:** Gardening and flower cultivation, music, studying history and development plans of the Arab States. **Addr.:** Sanaa, Republic of Yemen.

JUNDI (Mohamad Mumtaz, Sayed Ahmad), Egyptian university professor. **Born** on October 29, 1922 in Fariskour. **Son** of Sayed Ahmad Jundi. **Married** in December 1960, 2 children: Majdi and Mouhsen. **Educ.:** Cairo University, Ohio State University. **Dipl.:** Bachelor of Science (Agriculture 1946), Master of Science (1950), Doctor in Philosophy (1954). **Career:** Demonstrator (1947), then Lecturer (1955), then Associate Professor (1962), then Professor (since 1970) at the University of Cairo. **Publ.:** Author of numerous books and scientific studies including "Food Technology" (5 volumes), "Agricultural Industries" (2 volumes), "The Healthy Nutrition". **Sports:** Tennis and Walking. **Hobbies:** Reading and Traveling. **Addr.:** Cairo, Egypt.

JUNDI (Sayyid, Awad, al), Egyptian neurosurgeon. **Born** in 1931 in Egypt. **Married**, 2 daughters. **Dipl.:** M.B., B.Ch., Diploma in Surgery, Fellowship of the Royal College of Surgeons (1963). **Career:** Head of Neurosurgery Department at Maady Hospital, Cairo; Fellow, International College of Surgeons; President of Egyptian Society of Neurological Surgeons. **Publ.:** author of various papers on neurosurgery. **Awards:** from the Moroccan and Indonesian Governments. **Member:** Heliopolis Sporting Club, Automobile Club of Egypt and the Alexandria Yachting Club. **Prof. Addr.:** Clinic - 16 Abdel Khalek Sarwat Street, Cairo, Egypt. **Priv. Addr.:** 13 Abdel Kader Hamdy Street, el-Haj el-Khamis, Heliopolis, Cairo, Egypt.

JUNEIDI (Muhammad, Said), Jordanian journalist. **Born** in 1930 in Jordan. **Married**, 2 children. **Educ.:** in Cairo, Egypt as well as two years studies in Finland

(Folklore). **Dipl.:** Diploma in Journalism. **Career:** worked in the Civil Service, Ministry of Foreign Affairs, Ministry of Education (1955-70); Journalist in Lebanon, then in London of leading Arabic magazines. Editor in Chief of "Arab Business Magazine" and "al-Ann". **Publ.:** various novels in Arabic; "Hamsat al-Khreif", "Shams al-Ghouroub al-Jounoun". **Hobby:** Reading. **Member:** Jordan Press Association, British Press Association. **Addr.:** 77 Highlands Heath, Putney Heath, London.

JURUF (Radwan, S., al), Saudi Arabian Academic. **Born** in 1948 in Jordan. **Dipl.:** B.Sc. (Architectural Engineering); M.Sc. and Ph.D. (Civil Engineering). **Career:** Demonstrator, College of Petroleum and Minerals (1973-74); Assistant Professor, Civil Engineering Department, University of Petroleum and Minerals (1978-84) Associate Professor, Civil Engineering Department, King Fahd Universty of Petroleum and Minerals (1984-now). **Publ.:** a Ph.D. dessertation, several research papers in international refereed journals and conferences and two technical dictionaries. **Hobbies:** Sports and Arts. **Prof. Addr.:** P.O.Box 1466 King Fahd University of Petroleum and Minerals, Tel.: 860-2559, Dhahran, Saudi Arabia. **Private Addr.:** Tel.: 860-6418, Dhahran Saudi Arabia. Fax: 860-2870. E-mail: rsjuruf@kfupm.edu.sa and rsjuruf@yahoo.-com.

JUSTINYYAH (Darwish Saddiq, Dr.), Saudi academic. **Born** in 1938, in Makkah, Saudi Arabia. **Educ.:** Ph.D. Economics. **Career:** Assistant Professor, Department of Economics, Faculty of Economics and Administration, King Abdulaziz University, Jeddah, Saudi Arabia. Director, Centre for Research in Islamic Economics, King Abdulaziz University, Jeddah; Economic Consultant, Ministry of Planning, Riyadh. **Hobbies:** Reading. **Addr.:** P.O.Box 16711, Jeddah 21474, Saudi Arabia.

K

KAABI (Muhammad, Rashid, al), Qatari journalist. **Born** in 1956 in Doha, Qatar. **Married,** 3 children. **Educ.:** Central University, Michigan, USA; took courses at the American Institute of Informatics, USA. **Dipl.:** B.A. in Political Journalism. **Career:** Assistant Manager, Press Office of the Prince of Qatar (1977-80); Editor in Chief Of "al-Khalij al-Jadid" magazine; Ministry of Information (1977-82); Press Office Manager to his Royal Highness the Crown Prince and the Defence Minister. **Publ.:** numerous articles in Qatari newspapers. **Prof. Addr.:** P.O.Box 4000, Doha, Qatar.

KABBAA (Abdullah Saud), Saudi Academic. **Born** in 1939 in Buraidah, Saudi Arabia. **Dipl.:** Ph.D., Faculty member, Political Department, King Saud University, Ph.D. earned in 1980 from Southern Illinois University, USA. **Main field:** International Relations with special interest in Strategic Studies and National Security. Besides his work at King Saud University, he was a lecturer at King Abdulaziz Military Academy and at the Institute of Diplomatic Studies, Ministry of Foreign Affairs. He also served as a member of different departmental and university committees and became the chairman of the Research Center at the College of Administrative Sciences for two years. In addition, he worked for the ministries of Commerce, Finance, and Municipal Affairs before joining the political Science Department at King Saud University. He was the main speaker at the convention held in Houston, Texas in 1982 on the occasion of the Saudi National Day which was sponsored by the Saudi Cultural Office and attended by a host of American businessmen. He served on the Strategic Committee during the Iraqi invasion of Kuwait. Member of the American Political Science Association. Attended several Political Science Conventions. **Publ.:** Author of the following books: (1) Saudi Arabia and the UN, (2) Saudi Foreign Policy, (3) World Strategy and Saudi National Security, (4) Saudi-Yemeni Relations. Published several political analyses in Saudi Press. Taught the following courses: (1) Modern Diplomacy, (2) Saudi Foreign Policy, (3) Comtemporary World Problems, (4) Methods of Scientific Research, and (5) International Relations. **Address:** P.O.Box 60810, Riyadh 11555, Saudi Arabia.

KABBAJ (Mohamad), Moroccan former minister. **Educ.:** Polytechnic School of Paris; National School of Engineering of Paris; The Paris School of Economics. **Dipl.:** Engineering, further studies of Econometry. **Career:** Head of Public Works Department in Tetuan (1960-73); Director of Roads at the Ministry of Public Works (1973-80); Member of the Royal Cabinet in charge of the fixed links across Gibraltar (1980); Minister of Equipment and Vocational Training (1981-1993); Minister of Finance & Foreign Investments (Feb. 1995-1997). **Awards:** Ouissam, Order du Trone (rank of Knight). **Addr.:** Rabat, Morocco.

KABBANI (Fadil, Khairy), Saudi official. **Born** in 1916 in Mecca, Saudi Arabia. **Educ.:** Camborne School of Mines, UK; Colorado School of Mines, USA. **Dipl.:** ACSM, D.Sc. in Metal Mining. **Career:** Production and Distribution Section Chief, Office of the Minister of State for Development Projects, Ministry of Finance, Jeddah (1947); Head, Mining Department, Mines and Companies Bureau, Ministry of Finance; Deputy Director General, Petroleum and Mineral Affairs, Ministry of Finance and National Economy (1954-61); Assistant Deputy Minister, Directorate General of Mineral Resources, Ministry of Petroleum and Mineral Resources, Jeddah (1961-63); Deputy Minister Mineral Resources; Associate of Camborne School of Mines; Member of the Board of Directors of, General Organization of Petroleum and Minerals (PETROMIN) (1962-75), the Board of Trustees of College of Petroleum and Minerals (1963-75), the Board of Governors of International Atomic Energy Agency (IAEA), Vienna, Austria (1972-74), Saudi Arabian Permanent Representative, Permanent Mission to IAEA, Vienna; Member of the Constituent Commission of King Abdul Aziz University (1963-70); Member of the Council of King Abdul Aziz University (1967-71); Chairman, Council of Deans, College of Petroleum and Minerals (1970-71); headed Saudi Delegations to the annual 13th to 18th Conferences of the International Atomic Energy Agency, Vienna (1969-74); Headed Saudi Delegation to the international Conference on the Conservation of the Natural Resources, Turkey (1970), 4th International Conference on the Peaceful Uses of Atomic Energy, Geneva, Switzerland (1971), Round Table Conference of the Arab Heads of Geological Surveys, Cairo, Egypt (1971); represented Saudi Arabia at the Solar Energy Conference, France (1974); Alternative Head, Second Arab Conference on Mineral Resources, Jeddah (1974); Member the Management Board, International Geological Cooperation Programme (IGCP) (1973-75). **Publ.:** "Geophysical and Structural Aspects of Central Red Sea Rift Valley". **Hobbies:** colleting mineral crystals, stamps and coins, reading. **Addr.:** al-Kandara Airport Road, P.O.Box 553, Jeddah, Saudi Arabia.

KABLY (Reda Ali), Saudi academic. **Born** in 1937. **Educ.:** Ph.D. (Organic Chemistry). **Career:** Dean of Students, King Saud University; Lecturer, Faculty of Science, King Saud University; Assistant Professor, King Saud University; Fellow of the Chemical Society, U.K.; Dean of Admissions and Registration, King Abdulaziz University, Jeddah. **Publ.:** two papers published in the Journal of the Chemical Society, U.K. **Addr.:** King Abdulaziz University, Tel.: 6879033, Jeddah, Saudi Arabia.

KABODAN (Abdel Hamid), Egyptian banker. **Born** in Damanhour, Egypt on 17.6.24. **Married** to Aziza Fawzi, 2 children. **Educ.:** Alexandria University. **Dipl.:** Bachelor of Law (1948); Diploma of graduate Studies in Economics and Banking. **Career:** General Manager, Bank of Alexandria, Cairo; General Manager, Barclays Bank, Algiers; Member of the Board of Directors: of Central Bank of Egypt; Arab African Internationl Bank, Cairo-Misr-America Intl. Bank, Cairo; Chairman, Development Industrial Bank, Cairo, retired in 1984. **Clubs:** Cairo Gezira Club. **Member: Rotary Club. Credit Cards:** Viza, Bankamerica. **Priv. Addr.:** 7 Bustan el-Saidi Street, Cairo, Tel.: 746048.

KADA (Mohamad), Algerian executive. **Born** in 1941 in Algiers. **Son** of Khalifa Kada. **Married**, 2 sons, 2 daughters. **Educ.:** Secondary School, Algiers, Baccalaureat Mathematics and Technology Avignon, France; Bachelor Engineering, Troy, N.Y. (1965); M.Sc., CIT, Cranfield, UK (1968); Paris University IX, DEA, Management (1975). **Career:** Air Algiers (1965-77); Head of Technical Studies; Technical Director; Adviser to the Management; Consultant, INPED (1978); Organisation and Methods Officer, Islamic Development Bank, Saudi Arabia (since 1978). **Member:** RAES, UK; RPI, Alumini Association; Cranfield Association. **Addr.:** P.O.Box 5925, Tel.: 636 1400, Telex: 401137 A/B ISDB SJ, Jeddah, Saudi Arabia.

KADDOUMI (Farouk, al), (Abulutf), Palestinian Politician. **Born** in 1930, near Nablus, Palestine. **Educ.:** Cairo University, Egypt. **Dipl.:** Graduated in Economics and Political Science. **Career:** Founder member of Fatah; Member of Palestinian Liberation Organization (PLO) Central Committee; responsible for PLO relations with Egypt and Iraq (until 1967); Member, Executive Committee, PLO (since Feb. 1969); Head of the PLO Political Department (July 1974); resigned from the PLO Executive Committee Head of Foreign Relations in January 1973 but rejoined April 1973; Contributed to UN Debate on Palestine (1974); Presently Head of Political Dept. in the PLO Executive Committee. **Addr.:** Tunis, Tunisia.

KADDOUR (Abdul Hafid, Bin Ahmad, Shaikh), Tunisian businessman. **Born** on January 28, 1920 in Le Kef, Tunisia. **Married** 1 son. **Educ.:** al-Khadria Mosque (theological Studies), Le Kef, Tunisia. **Career:** Shaikh of al-Khadria Mosque; farmer; Honorary President, National Syndicate of the Breeders of Thoroughbred Horses in Tunisia. **Decor.:** Order of Tunisia Independance (1960). **Addr.:** Haras d'Abida, Le Kef, Tunisia.

KADDOUR (Mohammed, Ghassan, el), Syrian civil engineer, Chairman of Arab Union of Railways, President Director General of Syrian Railways. **Born** in 1952 in Al-Bab, Syria. **Son** of Ahmed el-Kaddour (Businessman) **and** Mrs., née Hamida el-Chehaby. **Married** in 1979 in Aleppo, Syria to Miss Miryam Koudsi, 3 children: May (1980), Ayman (1984), Kinda (1989). **Educ.:** Maamoun School; Aleppo Primary and Secondary Schools; University of Aleppo (Engineering Faculty). **Dipl.:** Bacchalaureus in engineering (civil engineer). **Career:** Milihouse Corporation; Chairman-Director General of the General Administration of Syrian Railways since 1983; Chairman of the Arab Union of Railways since 1995. **Prof. Addr.:** General Administration of Syrian Railways, P.O.Box 182, Tel.: 213900, 213901, Telex: 331009 CFS SY, Aleppo, Syria. Fax (963 + 21) 228480, (963 + 21) 225697. Telegr. Address: SIKKETHADID - **ALEP Priv. Addr.:** Society of Defence Factory, Aleppo, Syria.

KADDOURI (Fakhri, Yasin), Iraqi economist. **Born** in 1932 in Baghdad, Iraq. **Married**, 3 children. **Educ.:** Faculty of Commerce, University of Baghdad, Iraq; Faculty of Economic Science, State University of Iowa, USA; Faculty of Economic and Social Science, Cologne University, Federal Republic of Germany; International Marketing Institute, Harvard University, USA; United National European Centre, Geneva. **Dipl.:** B.A., M.A., Ph.D. **Career:** Tutor at the Faculty of Commerce, University of Baghdad; Director of Internal Commerce, Ministry of Economy, Baghdad (1965-68); Minister of Economy, Baghdad (1968-71); Head of Economic Affairs, Revolutionary Command Council (1971-78); Governor of Central Bank of Iraq (1976-78); General Secretary, Council of Arab Economic Unity (1978-83); Member of Follow-up Committee for Oil Affairs and Agreements Implementations (1971-78); Member, Council of Regulating Trade (1968-71) (1976-78); Member of Planning Council, Iraq (1971-78); President of Iraqi Economists Association (1973-75) (1977-78); President, Liaison Committee for Professional and Popular Organizations; Economic Counsellor (1983-). **Prof. Addr.:** Baghdad, Iraq.

KADHI (Abdallah, al), Saudi civil servant. **Born** in 1940 in Mecca, Saudi Arabia. **Dipl.:** Ph.D. (Geology), Bristol University, U.K. **Career:** Vice Dean, Faculty of Science, King Saud University (1976-77); Dean (1977-81); Assistant Deputy Minister, Ministry of Education (1982-). **Member of:** several geological societies; Chairman National Science Committee; member Preparatory Committee for the Higher Committee of Education Policy. **Hobbies:** Swimming, walking. **Prof. Addr.:** P.O.Box 4588, Tel.: 4043552, Riyadh. **Priv. Addr.:** Tel.: 4760286, Riyadh, Saudi Arabia.

KADHI (Solaiman), Saudi executive. **Born** on 17 August 1944 in Mecca, Saudi Arabia. **Dipl.:** B.A. (Radio and Television), Texas University. **Career:** Programmes Consultant, Saudi Television Service; Director of Films Department, Saudi Television Service; member of Supreme Executive Committee, Eastern Media Company, the Largest joint venture in the Arab world for television and cinema productions; one of the leading Saudi experts on television and cinema; Director General of Saudi Medina Studios Operations, Cairo; Director General of Arab Media Company for TV Production and Distribution. **Hobbies:** Reading, sports. **Prof. Addr.:** P.O.Box 1438, Tel.: 4544455, 4544463, Riyadh. **Priv. Addr.:** Tel.: 4832645, Riyadh, Saudi Arabia.

KADHIM (Nuri, Muhammad, al), Iraqi diplomat. **Born** in 1928. **Married**, 3 daughters. **Educ.:** University of South California, USA. **Dipl.:** B.A. in Political Science. **Career:** Ministry of Foreign Affairs (1959); 1st Secretary, Embassy to Turkey (1961); Director of International Conferences, UN Department, Ministry of Foreign Affairs (1964); Counsellor, Embassy to UK (1965); Acting Director General of the United Nations Department and of Conferences Ministry of Foreign Affairs (1966); Counsellor, Embassy to Austria (1966); Legal Department, Ministry of Foreign Affairs (1968); Ambassador in the Ministry of Foreign Affairs, Director General, Ministry of Foreign Affairs, Public Relations Department (1972); Lecturer at Kuwait University (1981). **Addr.:** Baghdad, Iraq.

KADI (Hamid M. Roushdy, el, Dr.), Egyptian Emeritus Professor, Atomic Energy Authority. **Born** on January 13, 1930 in Cairo, Egypt. **Son** of Roushdy el-Kadi (Director General) **and** Mrs. Fatma nee Mohamed el-Sokkary. **Married** on June 30, 1955 in Cairo to Miss Sohair Ismail, Three children: Maha (6 Sept. 1956), Mohammad Cherif (14 July 1961), and Nana (14 July 1961). **Educ.:** Ph.D. in Biological Sciences (1957); M.Sc. in Biological Sciences (1954); B.Sc. (Hons.) in Chemistry and Biology (1950). (All degrees honoured by the Faculty of Science, Cairo University, Egypt). **Languages:** Arabic, English, French, German, Danish. **Career:** Demonstrator on Biology, Zoology Department, Faculty of Science, Cairo University (1950-54); Assistant Lecturer on Biology, Zoology Department, Faculty of Science, Cairo University (1955-57); Lecturer on Marine Biology, Institute of Oceanography, Faculty of Science, Cairo University, (1958-60); UNESCO Fellow on Radioisotope Applications in Hydrobiology (1958-60); Director, Institute of Hydrobiology, Suez, Faculty of Science, Cairo University (1960-63); Associate Professor and Vice-Head, Department of Radioisotopes and Applications, Atomic Energy Establishment, Egypt (1963-65); Vice-Head, Department of Radiobiology, Atomic Energy Establishment, Egypt (1965-67); Research Collaborator, Service de Radiologie, Centre d'Etudes Nucleaires, Commissariat a l'Energie Atomique, France (1967-68); Head in Deputy, Department of Radioisotopes and Applications, Atomic Energy Establishment, Egypt (1969-71); Head, Department of Radiobiology, Atomic Energy Establishment, Egypt (1969-73); Professor on Radiation Biology (April 1971); Director, Project: National Centre for Radiation Technology, Atomic Energy Establishment (1972-76); Director, National Centre for Radiation Research and Technology, Atomic Energy Authority (1977-80); Chairman, National Centre for Radiation Research and Technology, Atomic Energy Authority, Egypt (1981-86); Vice-Chairman, Atomic Energy Authority (1986-87); Chairman and President of Directory Board, Atomic Energy Authority (1987-89); Emeritus Professor of Radiation Biology and Member of Consultancy Board, Atomic Energy Authority (1990 to present). **Part-Time Jobs:** Project Manager, UNDP Project No. EGY/73/037 and EGY/011, title: National Centre for Radiation Technology; Member, Director Board, Egypt Atomic Energy Authority; Member, Council of Planning, Atomic Energy Authority, Egypt; Member, Specialized Councils, Academy of Scientific Research and Technology, Egypt; Scientific Advisor, For Science and Technology, National Commission for UNESCO, Ministry of Higher Education, Egypt; Visiting Professor on Radiation Biology and Irradiation Technology at the Universities of Cairo, Ain Shams, al-Azhar, Alexandria, Tanta, Mansoura, and Zagazig, Egypt; Member, Advisory Board to President, Egyptian Academy of Scientific Research and Technology. Principal Investigator, project: Development of Ionizing Radiation Dosimetry Systems and Standards for Applications in Industrial Radiation Processing. National Bureau of Standards Washington D.C. USA/NCRRT Egypt; Member, Editorial Board, Journal of Isotope and Radiation Research, Middle Eastern Regional Radioisotope Centre for Arab Countries, Cairo, Egypt; Member, Editorial Advisory Board, Arab Journal, Nuclear Sciences and Applications, The Egyptian Society of Nuclear Sciences and Applications, Cairo, Egypt; Editor in Chief, Journal of Radiation Sciences and Applications, NCRRT/NIDOC, Egypt. **Consultancy Jobs:** Vice-Chairman of Scientific Session 4.3 Medical Applic., Fourth UN Conf. Peac. Uses Atomic Energy, Geneva (1972); IAEA Consultant, IAEA Consultant Meeting on Radiation Processing, Cairo, October (1977); Chairman of Scientific Session II, IAEA Symposium 22/9 on Food Preservation by Irradiation, Wageningen, Holland, Nov. (1977); IAEA Advisor, FAO/IAEA/WHO Advisory Group Meeting on International Acceptance of Irradiated Food, Wageningen, Holland, November- December (1977); WHO Expert, WHO/FAO/IAEA Expert Committee on Wholesomeness of Irradiated Food, Geneva, October- November (1980); IIAEA Expert to Zambia on Transfer of Radiation Technology, August- September (1983); Member of IAEA Research Coordination Meeting on Radiation Sterilization of Medical Products and Pharmaceutical Preparation in Africa and Middle East, Nairobi, 5-9 November (1984); Chairman, Session I on Radiation Processing, Int. Conf. Appl. Radioisotopes and Radiation in Industrial Development, Bombay, March (1984); Participant and Elected Member of Board of the International Consulative Group on Food Irradiation, IAEA Vienna, 10-11 December (1984); Principal Investigator, IAEA Research Contract No. 3529/RB: Scientific Consultant, IAEA Research Contracts No. 3528/RB, 3528/RI/RB, 2742/RB. **Prof. Addr.:** 3 Ahmad el-Zumor Street, el-Zohur Sector, P.O.Box 29 Masakin Nasr City, Cairo, Tel.: 2617832, 2618246, Telex: 21830 NCRRT UN, Fax: 2619298, Cairo, Egypt. **Priv. Addr.:** 62 Abul Attahia Street, al-Zohur Sector, Nasr City, Cairo, Tel.: 609745, Cairo, Egypt.

KADI (Ismail, Al-), Syrian Diplomat, Ambassador. **Born** on November 1, 1935 at Harem, Syria. **Son** of Mohamad Omar Al-Kadi (Lawyer) **and** Mrs. Alia. **Married** on July 1960 in Aleppo to Mariam Mohamad, 3 children: 2 daughters, wiladah (1962) and Ouruba (1963); 1 son, Firas (1966). **Educ.:** Faculty of Law, Damascus University. **Dipl.:** LLB, Bachelor of Laws. **Career:** Judge at the Court of Appeal in Aleppo (1960); Counsellor at the Court of Appeal; President of the Court of Appeal (1973); Member of the Front of National Progress leadership (1973 till 1990); Ambassador Extraordinary and Plenipotentiary of Syria in Belgrade, Yugoslavia (May 1990- to present). **Credit Cards:** Diner's Club. **Prof. Addr.:** Embassy of the SAR, Mlade Bosne 31, Tel.: 4449985, Belgrade, Yugoslavia. **Priv. Addr.:** Beograd, Milovana Glisica 3, Tel.: 650232, Yugoslavia.

KADI (Munir Ahmad, al), Saudi academic. **Born** in 1945 in Medina, Saudi Arabia. **Dipl.:** B.Com., M.B.A., M.A. (Economics), M.Sc. (Urban Studies), Ph.D. (Urban and Environmental Studies). **Career:** Economic Researcher, Ministry of Planning (1969-75); Lecturer, KFUPM (1975-80); Assistant Professor, King Fahad University of Petroleum and Minerals, Faculty of Environmental Design since 1981. **Publications:** Contemporary Architecture in Saudi Arabia (Book); Contemporary Housing in Saudi Arabia (Book); Mosques in Saudi Arabia - Old and new (Book). Photographic Publications: The expansion of the Madina Holy Mosques; Night views of the Madina Holy Mosques. Our beautiful country: The Kingdom of Saudi Arabia. **Hobby:** Photography. **Prof. Addr.:** KFUPM No. 1798, Tel: (03) 860-6245. Dhahran 31261, Saudi Arabia.

KADI (Omar Abdallah Abdurahim), Saudi civil servant. **Born** in 1940 in Taif, Saudi Arabia. **Dipl.:** B.Sc. (Architecture); M.Sc. (Town Planning). **Career:** Architect (1965); Town Planning Adviser (1971); Assistant Deputy Minister for Town Planning (1975); former Deputy Minister for Town Planning, Ministry of Municipal and Rural Affairs; Secretary-General, Organization of Islamic Capitals and Cities (OICC). **Prof. Addr.:** OICC, Jeddah, Tel.: (2)698-1953, Saudi Arabia. **Priv. Addr.:** Tel.: 4038847, Riyadh, Saudi Arabia.

KADIRI (Abdelhafid), Moroccan politician. **Born** in 1929. **Educ.:** Institut National d'Agronomie (France). **Career:** Director, Mohamed Douiri's Cabinet; Director, Hajj Omar ben Abdeljalil's Cabinet; member, Editing Board of "al-Istiqlal", "Nation"; Director of "L'Opinion"; Under-Secretary of State for Agriculture (1958); Director, Bureau de Recherches et de Participation Minière BRPM; Minister of Youth and Sports (1977-81); Ambassador in Spain (1982-85). Member of Parliament (1977). **Member:** Istiqlal Party. **Addr.:** Avenue Imam Malik, 43, Rabat, Morocco.

KADR (Abdel Mohamad), Sudanese army officer and government civil servant. **Born** in Khartoum, Sudan. **Educ.:** Military Academy until 1952, then training courses in England and the USA. **Career:** Military Attaché; Instructor, Military Information Service, Sudan General Command; Military Commander of the Sudanese Contingent in the Arab-Israeli war (1967); Chief of Staff (1968); Ambassador to Uganda (1972); Commissioner, Kassala Province (1973). **Prof. Addr.:** Kassala Province, Kassala, Sudan.

KAFI (Ali, Hussain), Algerian diplomat. **Born** on October 7, 1928 in Constantine. **Son** of Hussain Kafi (Mufti) **and** Mrs., née Khadiga Hassani. **Married** on July 30, 1958 to Miss Fatima Boubzari, 3 children: Qassem, Hisham and Houssan. **Educ.:** Faculty of Constantine, Higher studies in Tunis. **Dipl.:** Teacher Training Diploma. **Career:** Joined the National Liberation Army, with the rank of Colonel (1954-61); Algerian Ambassador Extraordinary and Minister Plenipotentiary to Lebanon (1963-66), to Syrian Arab Republic (1967). Head of the High Council of State. (July 1992-Jan. 1994). **Sports:** Horseriding and swimming. **Hobby:** Reading. **Addr.:** Algiers, Algeria.

KAFOUD (Mohamed, Abdul Rahim), Qatari Minister of Education and Higher Education. **Born** in 1949 in Qatart. **Son** of Abdul Rahim Ahmed Kafoud "Descesed". **Married** in 1978 in Doha, 6 children: Fatima (1978), Sara (1980), Omar (1982), Ahmed (1984), Maha (1988), Abdul Aziz (1991). **Diplomas:** B.A. in Arabic Language - Al-Azhar University, Grade (V.Good) (1974), Master degree in Modern Literature (Qatari Modern Literature) - Al-Azhar University, Grade (Excellent) (1978), Ph.D. in Modern Criticism (modern Literary Criticism in the Arabian Gulf) Al-Azhar University, with high distinction (Honours) (1981). **Career:** Teaching Assistant, Department of Arabic, Faculty of Education, Qatar University (1975-1978); Assistant Lecturer, Faculty of Humanities, Qatar University (1978-1981); Lecturer, Department of Arabic, Faculty of Humanities, Qatar University (1981-1986); Assistant Professor 29/10/1986, Professor 9/2/1993; Dean of Students Affairs, Qatar University (1988-1991); Dean, Faculty of Humanities, Qatar University (1991-1995); Deputy Director of Qatar University for Research and Community Service (14/10/1995); Minister of Education and Culture, State of Qatar (30/10/1996); Minister of Education and Higher Education (20/1/1998 to date)

(Chairman of the National Council for Culture, Arts and Heritage, 25/11/1998). **Other Information:** Made numerous contributions to authorship, research and studies and participated in many committees, activities, conferences and forums. **Some Select, Publications:** Qatar Modern Literature (2nd ed. 1982), Modern Literary Criticism in the Arabian Gulf (1982), Short Stories in Qatar (1985), Studies in Contemporary Arabic Poetry in the Gulf (1994), The Traditional and the Contemporary, and the Dilemma of Arab Culture (1997). **Prof. Addr.:** Ministry of Education and Higher Education, P.O.Box 80 Doha- Qatar, Tel.: 413717, Doha, Qatar. **Priv. Addr.:** Southern Khalifa City, Doha, Tel. 874374, Qatar.

KAFRAWY (Hasaballah, el), Egyptian politician. **Born** on November 1930. **Educ.:** Alexandria University. **Career:** Director southern region of High Dam electricity lines until 1966; Chairman, Cana General Contracting Co.; Vice-President of executive Organ for reconstruction of Suez Canal region (1974); President (1975); Governor of Damietta (1976); Deputy Minister for Reconstruction; Minister of Reconstruction and Minister of State for Housing and Land Reclamation (Oct. 1978-86); Minister of Development New Communities, Housing and Public Utilities (1986- to Oct. 1993). **Addr.:** Cairo, Egypt.

KAHTANI (Abdul-Mohsen Farraj Saif, al), Saudi academic. **Born** in 1945 in Riyadh, Saudi Arabia. **Son** of Saif al-Kahtani. **Dipl.:** Ph.D. (Literature). **Career:** High School teacher (1971-74); Assistant Principal, High School (1975-76); Assistant Professor, Arabic Department, King Abdulaziz University (1976-82); Vice Dean, Faculty of Arts and Humanities, King Abdulaziz University (1982-1984); Dean of Student Affairs, King Abdulaziz University (since 1974); **Member** Literary Club Jeddah. **Publ.:** "Mansour al-Faqih, His Life and Poetry", 1980. **Sport:** Swimming. **Hobby:** Shooting. **Prof. Addr.:** P.O.Box 4991, Tel.: 6719629, Jeddah. **Priv. Addr.:** Tel.: 6719740 Jeddah, Saudi Arabia.

KAHTANI (Mohamad Said Abdul Rahman, al), Saudi academic. **Born** in Abha in 1939. **Educ.:** Ph.D. (Horticulture), Kansas State University, U.S.A. **Career:** Assistant professor and later Vice Dean, College of Agriculture, King Saud University; Dean, Colleges of Agriculture and Veterinary Medicine, King Faisal University, Dammam; Acting Vice Rector and later Vice Rector, King Faisal University Rector, King Faisal University. **Member:** Saudi Society for Biological Sciences, the Local Council of Dammam Municipality; Board of Directors, al-Hassa Irrigation and Drainage Authority; the Consultant's Organization for Muslim Youth Assembly; the American Society for Horticulture Science, U.S.A., Plant Growth Regulator Working Group, U.S.A., the International Society for Horticultural Science, U.S.A.; the International Institute of Banking and Islamic Economics; Board of Trustees, al-Iman Est.; Board of Directors, Manarat al-Sharqiya; official delegations of Higher Education to France, Spain, Morocco and Mauretania; Head of King Faisal University delegation to Australia and New Zealand. **Honour:** Medal awarded by President of Mauretania. **Publ.:** co-author, Cultivation of Palm Trees and Production of Dates in Islamic and Arabic World; preliminary studies to evaluate different kinds of Palm trees and some of the routes of Citrus from the Morphology side. **Hobby:** Travel. **Prof. Addr.:** King Faisal University, P.O.Box 1982, Tel.: 8576735, Dammam. **Priv. Addr.:** Tel.: 8644712, Dammam, Saudi Arabia.

KAID (Ahmad), Algerian politician. **Born** in 1921 in Algeria. **Career:** Official in Municipality; member of National Liberation Front (FLN) soon after outbreak of War of Independance (1954); member of First National Council of the Revolutionary Army (1956); Assistant to Houari Boumedienne when latter set up Headquarters at Oujda (1958); visited China as member of Oussedik Delegation (1959); served on General Staff of National Liberation Army (ALN) at Ghardimaou, Tunisia (1960); member of FLN Delegations at Evian and Lugrin negotiations; elected Deputy for Tiaret (1962); Minister of Tourism (1963-64); member of National Assembly, Foreign Affairs Committee, elected member of FLN Central Committee at Party Congress (1964); member of Council of the Revolution (1965); Minister of Finance and the National Plan (1965). In charge of the Party (1967-72); former member of Revolutionary Council. **Addr.:** Front de Libération Nationale (FLN), Place Emir Abdel Kader, Algiers, Algeria.

KAIKSOW (Salman, Ahmad), Bahraini businessman. **Born** in 1920 in Bahrain. **Married**, 6 children: Ahmad, Abdallah, Sami, Nabil, Najeeb and Ali. **Educ.:** Primary in Bahrain; Secondary in India, then comprehensive course in Business and Financial Management. **Dipl.:** Matriculation; B.BA. **Career:** Set up in business in 1938, engaged in trading, agency representation and Civil Engineering contracting; branched out into the electromechanical field (1973) and diversified into hotel and catering by establishing the four-star Tylos Hotel; and several other Companies since. **Prof. Addr.:** P.O.Box 80, Tel.: 251584, 243232, 252600, Fax: 973-262631, Manama, Bahrain.

KAILANI (Mohammad Rasul), Jordanian army officer and diplomat. **Born** in (Salt), Jordan. **Son** of Abdul Haleem Kailani. **Educ.:** B.A. in Law and Economics. **Career:** Army Service, Promoted Colonel then General; Former Chief, Information Service till 1968, Ministry of Foreign Affairs since April 1968 with rank of Ambassador, General Director of Public Security (December 1968), Minister of the Interior (August 1969-Feb. 1970), Advisor to H.M. The King for the Public Security Affairs, Chief Information Service (1971-1974) Ranked Lt. General in the Armed forces. Former Jordanian Ambassador to Saudi Arabia (1985-1989); Member of the Upper House of

Parliament (1989-1993); H.M. the late King's Advisor (1993). **Addr.:** P.O.Box 9240, Amman, Jordan.

KAISSI (Abbas), Moroccan administrator and politician. **Born** in 1926 in Fez, Morocco. **Married**, 3 children. **Educ.:** Qarawiyin University, Fez. **Dipl.:** French Baccalaureat; Degrees in Arts and Law. **Career:** Land Registrar (Conservateur Foncier) for ten years; Deputy Secretary-General of the Government (1966); Under-Secretary of State, Ministry of the Interior (1969-71); Director of Legislation, Ministry of Administrative Affairs; Under-Secretary of State for the Interior (government of April 1972); Minister of Administrative Affairs (November 1972); Director of the Royal Cabinet (May 1973); Minister of Justice (April 1974-77); Secretary-General of the Government (October 1977). **Addr.:** Rabat, Morocco.

KAISSI (Ahmad Izzat), Iraqi psychiatrist. **Born** in Baghdad. **Educ.:** Faculty of Medicine of Montpellier, Faculty of Medicine of Paris. **Dipl.:** Medical Doctor, Diploma of Legal Medicine and Psychiatry of Paris **Career:** Formerly, Research fellow Edinburgh University Department of Forensic Medicine (Under the late Professor Sir Sydney Smith); Director of the Medico-Legal Institute, Baghdad since 1933; Professor of Forensic Medicine, Royal College of Medicine and College of Law (Baghdad); President, Medical Professions Association of Iraq (1952-55), Psychiatrist. **Addr.:** Baghdad, Iraq.

KAISSOUNI (Abdel Moneim), Egyptian politician and banker. **Born** 1916. **Married. Educ.:** Cairo University, Cairo; London School of Economics, UK. **Dipl.:** B.Com., B.Sc., Ph.D. (Economics). **Career:** Joined Barclays Bank, London (1942-43); Lecturer and Assistant Professor of Economics, Cairo University (1944-50); Lecturer and Adviser, Council of Ministers for Post-War Affairs (1944-45); Deputy Director-General of Foreign Affairs, Ministry of National Economy (1949-50); Director, Middle East Department, International Monetary Fund (IMF) Washington DC; Chief Technical Reporter in Middle East (1946-50); Joined National Bank of Egypt (1950-54); Deputy Minister of Finance and Economy (1954); Minister of Finance and Economy (Sept. 1954-60); Member, National Assembly (1957); Minister of Economy and Commerce for Egypt in United Arab Republic (UAR) (1958); Minister of Economy, UAR Central Government (1958-62); Minister of Treasury and Planning (1962-64); Chairman of the Board, Economic Organization (1959); Deputy Prime Minister for Economic Affairs and Finance, and Minister of Economy and Foreign Trade (1964-65); President, UN Conference on Trade and Development, Geneva (1964); Deputy Prime Minister for Financial and Economic Affairs (1965-66); Chairman, Arab International Bank (1971); Chairman, Arab Holding, Luxembourg (1972); Chairman, Arab International Company for Hotels and Tourism (1976); member, Higher Economic Council, Egypt (1974); Deputy Prime Minister for Financial and Economic Affairs (November 1976); Minister of Planning (October 1977- May 1980). **Addr.:** 24 Sesostris Street, Heliopolis, Tel.: 835835, Cairo, Egypt.

KAKI (Ahmed, Saleh), Saudi businessman. **Born** in 1924 in Mecca. **Son** of Saleh Moosa Kaki (exchanger). **Married** in 1957, 3 sons: Mohammed, Hisham and Abdulwahab. **Educ.:** Falah School, Mecca; received education in Egyptian universities. **Career:** Leading businessman and founder member of the National Commercial Bank; Partner and Member of Managing Committee of Saudi Arabian Refineries Company and National Commercial Bank; Partner and Member of Managing Committee of Trade Union Insurance Company, Bahrain; President of Ahmed and Mohammed Saleh Kaki dealing in General trading, agencies, contracting, construction, industry, investment, real estate and hotel businesses. **Sport:** Jogging. **Hobby:** Reading. **Credit Cards:** American Express, Diner's Club. **Prof. Addr.:** Kaki Commercial Center, Medina Road, P.O.Box 1224, Tel.: 6602160, Telex: 401503, Jeddah 21431, Saudi Arabia.

KAKISH (Fuad), Jordanian politician. **Born** on October 18, 1922 in Salt, Jordan. **Married. Educ.:** American University of Beirut, Lebanon; Imperial College, University of London, UK. **Dipl.:** B.Sc. in Engineering, Diploma in Civil and Sanitary Engineering. **Career:** held various government technical posts since 1944 in Ministry of Public Works, Municipality of Amman; Ministry of Interior, Development Board, Municipal Loans Fund; Under Secretary, Ministry of Interior for Municipal and Rural Affairs (1970-71); Member, Chamber of Deputies (1973); Minister of the Interior for Municipal and Rural Affairs (1973-74); Member, Foreign and Financial Affairs Committees in the Chamber of Deputies (1973); Engineer, designing and supervising private buildings; Member of the Aqaba Planning Committee, the Administrative Council of the National Resources Authority and the Institutional Committee of Central Electricity Authority, Member and then Vice President, Scientific Research Council; Member of the Anti-Illiteracy Movement, Supply Council, Youth Organization, Council of the Arab National Union (1972-); Senator (1974). **Prof. Addr.:** P.O.Box 5252, Amman, Jordan.

KALLAL (Zuhair), Tunisian academic. **Born** on February 26, 1930 in Tunisia. **Married**, 2 children. **Educ.:** in Dijon, France; University of Paris, France. **Dipl.:** M.D., Ph.D. in Medicine, Graduate in Experimental Medicine, Diploma in Nutrition. **Career:** Resident at Hospital, Seine Bois Paris (1959); Assistant at the Faculty of Medicine, Tunis (1965); Professor of Experimental Medicine, Tunis (1969); Director of Projects of FAO; Co-Researcher in several univerties, Berkeley, Harvard, Columbia and others; Adviser to the Ministry of Public Health; Member of Several international professional societies and associations; Director of National Institute of Nutrition, Tunis

(1968-); Director, Superior School of Sciences for Nutrition (1972); Head of Department and Professor for Experimental Medicine, Faculty of Medicine, Tunis (1977-). **Publ.:** Founding Director of "Cahiers Médicaux de Tunisie" journal (1970); numerous articles in professional journals. **Decor.:** Order of Tunisian Republic; Order of Independence, Tunisia; Chevalier de la Legion d'Honneur, France. **Hobbies:** Medical ecology, protection of the environment, travelling, music. **Prof. Addr.:** Université de Tunis II, 29 rue Asdrubal, Tunis, Tunisia.

KAMAL (Burham, Taher), Jordanian engineer. **Born** in 1916 in Palestine. **Son** of Taher Kamal (Merchant) **and** Mrs. Aziza nee Nabulsi. **Married,** in 1941 to Suad Malas, three children. **Educ.:** Cairo University and Loughborough College, U.K. **Dipl.:** Electrical Engineering Diploma and Mechanical Engineering Diploma. **Career:** Principal of Technical School in Palestine (1939-48); Professor of Engineering, Syrian University, Aleppo (1948-54); Director Technical Education and Principal of Technical School, Jordan (1967); Under Secretary of Ministry of Education, Jordan (1969-70); Minister of Telecommunications, Jordan (1970); Director of: Jordan Tobacco & Cigarette Co. Ltd., Weaving & Textile Co., Housing Bank, Steel Pipe Manufacturing Co., Arab Orphans' Committee, Board of Education, vocational training Corporation. **Medals:** Istiklal Medal Jordan, Kawkab Medal Jordan, al-Jumhouriya, Egypt, al-Istihqaq, Syria. **Sports:** Swimming, walking. **Hobby:** Travelling. **Prof. Addr.:** Jordan Tobacco & Cigarette Co. Ltd., P.O.Box 59, Amman, Jordan. **Priv. Addr.:** Mithqal al-Fayez Street, 3rd Circle, Jebel Amman, Jordan.

KAMAL (Madiha, Sami), Egyptian broadcasting official. **Born** on March 23 1931 in Cairo, Egypt. **Married,** 2 daughters. **Educ.:** Cairo University, Egypt. **Dipl.:** B.A. **Career:** State Information Department (1956-59); Programme Director of women's programmes, variety shows; Presenter of art programmes and Director of Youth programmes, Egyptian State Broadcasting (1960-); Head of Television, Channel One (1982); Member, Light and Hope Charity Organisation (1978-); Head of Television Channel Two (1983-). **Medal:** Medal from Broadcasting and Television Organisation on 15th anniversary of Egyptian Radio. **Member:** Gezira Sporting Club and Automobile Club, Egypt; Honorary Member of National Sporting Club. **Prof. Addr.:** Television Bldg., Corniche el-Nil, Cairo, Egypt. **Priv. Addr.:** 4 Sad el-Aali Street, Dokki, Cairo, Egypt.

KAMAL (Marwan, Rasim), Jordanian chemist and university president. **Born** in 1933. **Son** of Rasim Kamal **and** Mrs. Aminah nee Abu Hadbah. **Married** in 1964 to Maha Hamzeh, four children. **Educ.:** American University of Beirut; Roosevelt University; De Paul University; University of Pittsburgh; University of Minnesota. **Dipl.:** B.Sc., M.Sc., M.BA., Ph.D. **Career:** Professor of Chemistry (since 1973); Dean, University of Jordan (1978-84); Vice President, Yarmouk University (1984-86); Vice President, University of Jordan (1986-87); President, University of Bahrain (since 1987). **Sports:** Tennis, squash, swimming. **Hobbies:** Reading and music. **Member of:** Kiwanis, ACS, AAAS, Sigma XI. **Credit Cards:** American Express, Visa. **Priv. Addr.:** Hassan Ali Compound, Budaiya, Bahrain.

KAMAL (Munir, Mark), Arab-American engineer. **Born** on February 13, 1936 in Beirut, Lebanon. **Married,** 3 children. **Educ.:** Robert College, Istanbul, Turkey; University of Michigan, USA. **Dipl.:** B.S., M.S. and Ph.D. in Mechanical Engineering and Mechanics. **Career:** Project Engineer, AC Spark Plug Division, General Motors Corporation, Flint, Michigan, USA (1956-59); Associate Senior Research Engineer, General Motors Research Laboratory, Warren, Michigan (1966-68); Supervisor and Research Engineer (1968-70); Delegate at the International Safety Conference, Brussels, Belgium (1970); Programme Manager (1970-71), Assistant Department Head (1971-87), Head of Department (1977); Member of Industry Community, University of Michigan College of Engineering, the American Society of Mechanical Engineers; Member of the Country Lane Home Owners Association and the Society of Automotive Engineers. **Prof. Addr.:** General Motors Research Laboratory, Twelve Mille and Mound Roads, Warren, Michigan 48090, USA. **Priv. Addr.:** 1615 Dutton Road, Rochester, Michigan 48063, USA.

KAMAL (Riad, Burhan), Jordanian Civil Engineer. **Born** in December 1943 in Haifa, Palestine. **Son** of Burhan Kamal (Electrical Engineer; Minister of Posts and Telecommunications, Jordanian Cabinet - 1969) **Married** to Ferial El Solh, 3 children: Zaha, Zein and Ghazal. **Educ.:** Raghadan Secondary School, Amman (1954-60); Imperial College of Science and technology, London University, UK. **Dipl.:** B.Bs. Civil Engineering (1965); M.Sc. Structure Engineering (1966); D.I.C. (1966). **Career:** Section Engineer, Tarmac-Shaheen (jordan) (1967-70) Assistant Chief Engineer, Sir Robert McAlpine, UK (1970-73); Founder and Managing Director, Arabtec, UAE (1974 to present); Leading Civil Engineer Contractor in the UAE. **Member:** World Presidents Organization (W.P.O). **Address:** P.O.Box 3399, Dubai, United Arab Emirates.

KAMALI (Shafiq, al), Iraqi poet and statesman. **Born** in 1930 in Iraq. **Career:** Minister of Youth (1970-76); Ambassador Extraordinary Spain (1977-79); Minister of Information (1979-80); Chairman of the Board, Afaq Arabia Publishing House (since 1980). Deputy **Chairman,** Arab Writers Union (since 1975). **Publ.:** Published three collections of poems which relates Arab History to contemporary history and seek new values from the Arab past. **Addr.:** Afaq Arabia, P.O.B. 4032, Tel.: 22011, 22012, Baghdad, Iraq.

KAMEL (Amin, Helmy), Egyptian industrialist and statesman. **Born** in 1918. **Son** of Osman Kamel. **Educ.:** Engineering and Supplementary military studies. **Dipl.:** B.Sc. in engineering. **Career:** Vice Chairman of the General organisation for Industrialisation (1958-64) (and since 1966); Cabinet Minister for light Industries (1964-66); Part time Adviser to the Minister of Industry of the Arab Republic of Libya (1970-72). Director General of the Centre of Industrial Development (a subsidiary of the League of Arab Countries) (1972-76); Technical Adviser of the Executive Board of the Iron and Steel Complex Misurata, Libya (1975-86); Technical Adviser of the Secretariat of Industry of the Libyan Arab People's Socialist Jumahiriyah (1986). **Member of:** the Central Comittee of the Arab Socialist Union (since Sept. 1968). **Addr.:** Cairo, Egypt.

KAMEL (André), Civil Engineer. **Born** on May 15, 1931 in Bikfaya (Lebanon). **Son** of Frédéric Kamel **and** Mrs. née Isabelle Kachami. **Married** on July 3, 1958 to Rolly Achkar, 4 children: Lena (Mrs Samir Tannous), Katia (Mrs Charles Sakr), Nadine (Mrs Georges Khawam) and Pierre-Frédéric. **Educ.:** Jesuit School and Saint Joseph University, Beirut (Lebanon). **Dipl.:** Civil Engineer. **Career:** (with Dumez Group). Director in Tanzania (1952-1954), Kenya (1954-1958), Managing Director in Nigeria, Lebanon and Middle East since 1958. Chairman and Managing Director Dumez International, Paris (1988-1992); General Manager Dumez Board, Paris (1980-1990); Vice-President and General Manager Dumez, Paris (1987-1991). Member of the Executive committee and Adviser to the President Lyonnaise des Eaux-Dumez Group, since 1991, Paris. Chairman and Managing Director DUMEZ-KAMEL INTERNATIONAL (DUKIM) since January 1993. Vice-President BRGM Nigeria, since 1976. Director Numco-Minatome since 1979. **Distinctions/Medals:** Chevalier of the Legion of Honour (France), officer of the Order of Merit (France), Chevalier of the National Lebanese Order of Merit (Arts & Sciences), Commander of the Order of Saint-Gregory (Vatican). **Prof. Addr.:** DUKIM, 128 rue du Faubourg Saint Honoré, 75008 Paris (France), Tel.: 33 (1) 46.95.40.06, Fax: 33 (1) 46.95.45.59, France. and 7 Sir Mobolaji Bank Anthony's Street, Lagos, (Nigeria). **Priv. Addr.:** 11bis, avenue de Ségur, 75007 Paris (France), and 3 Onitola Avenue, Ikoyi, Lagos, (Nigeria).

KAMEL (Hassan Abdallah, Dr.), Saudi physician. **Born** in Mecca in 1937. **Educ.:** M.B. B.Ch., M.D. M.R.C.P. (United Kingdom), D.C.M. (London). **Career:** Lecturer, College of Medicine, King Saud University, Pediatrics Department (1973); Assistant Professor (1975) and Associate Professor (1979), King Saud University; General Manager, Dallah Establishment; member, Supreme Arabian Medical Specialities Society; pediatrics Professors in the Middle East, Saudi National Society for Maternity and child Welfare; member of the Board, Islamic Welfare Society; has attended all International Pediatrics Societies Conferences, held every 4 years since 1966; Dean, College of Medicine, King Saud University; Chairman and Managing Director, al-Baraka Islamic Investment Bank, Bahrain. **Publ.:** prepared and introduced a T.V. series entiled The Happy Family for 3 years; edited various researsh projects in the Saudi Medical Journal. **Priv. Addr.:** Tel.: 4641131, Riyadh, Saudi Arabia.

KAMEL (Ibrahim, Mustafa), Egyptian Businessman residing in Switzerland. **Born** in 1938 in Dakahliya, Egypt, **Married**, 1 son, 3 daughters. **Educ.:** Faculty of Engineering, Ain Shams University, Cairo, Egypt; Ecole National Superieur des Beaux Arts, Paris France; Cairo University, Egypt. **Dipl.:** B.Sc., DPLG and Ph.D. in Architecture. **Career:** architectural work with various firms in Paris, France (1962-66); Executive Vice President, Consultants International, Paris (1966-70); Chairman, and President of Kamel Holdings SA, and Kamel Brothers SA, Switzerland (1973-); Executive Vice president of Islamic Investment Company (1978-83); Executive Vice Chairman of Dar Al-Maal Al-Islami (DMI) Group (1981-83); President Umma Holdings, Ltd, and Chairman Dar Tadine Al Umma Ltd, and Dar Tadine Tanzania Ltd, Geosurvey Holding Ltd, and Capital Intelligence Ltd (1985-89); Chairman and chief executive officer Petroleum Securities Corporation Ltd (1994-); Chairman of the Kenana Misr holding Company (1992-) Politics: Elected as "Independent" member of the Egyptian Peoples Assembly (Parliament 1990-1995) for the Menouf Constituency, Menoufieh Govern orate, member of the Assembly's Committee of Economic Affairs. **Decor.:** Egyptian Medal of Knowledge, Officer of the National Order of the Popular Revolutionary Republic of Guinea. **Hobbies:** Islamic heritage and arts, Islamic applications in economics, finance, and politics. Swimming, chess, squash. **Addr.:** 2 Chemin Paul Seippel Conches, Geneva, Switzerland, and Sirss El Liane, Menoufieh, Egypt.

KAMEL (Mohamad, Ibrahim), Egyptian diplomat. **Born** in 1927 in Cairo. **Son** of Ahmad Ibrahim Kamel (Counsel, Higher Appeal Court). **Educ.:** Faculty of Law, Cairo University (1943-47); **Dipl.:** LL.B. **Career:** appointed Secretary, State Council, **Cairo;** Joined the Ministry of Foreign Affairs (1956); First Secretary, Egyptian Embassy to the Court of Saint-James, London; moved to Mexico city as counsellor to the Egyptian Embassy there; Counsul in Montreal; Counsellor in Ottawa; Press Attaché in the Ministry of Foreign Affairs, Cairo; In the early 1960s was appointed Ambassador to the Congo until the embassy was closed, when he was recalled to Cairo, Ministry of Foreign Affairs; returning to his former post when diplomatic relations were resumed with Zaire (formerly Congo), Ambassador to Sweden, also accredited to Bonn (Federal Republic of Germany) (1972-77); Egyptian Foreign Affairs Minister (1977- May 1980). **Addr.:** Cairo, Egypt.

KAMEL (Omar, A.), Saudi businessman. **Born** in Mecca in 1951. **Educ.:** B.Sc. (Economics and Political Science). **Career:** Assistant General Manager of Dallah; Vice Chairman, Board of Directors, Dallah-Avco Lilmabani, Saemco and Tasco; member, Board of Directors, the Saudi Automotive Service Company and the Saudi Company for Recreation Centres; Vice President, Administrative Affairs, Dallah-Avco. **Hobbies:** Soccer, track and field, bowling, chess. **Prof. Addr.:** P.O.Box 9367, Tel.: 6691024. **Priv. Addr.:** Tel.: 6675712, Jeddah, Saudi Arabia.

KAMEL (Raafat Wassef, Kamel), Egyptian physicist. **Born** on June 10, 1926. **Son** of Kamel Wassef **and** Mrs., née Kawkab Antoun. **Married** on July 20, 1952 to Miss Kamilia Naguib 3 children: Wafa', Oussama and Maged. **Educ.:** Cairo University. **Dipl.:** Bachelor of Science, with honors (1946), Master of Science (1950) Doctor of Philosophy (1954). Doctor of Science 1968. **Career:** Joined the Cairo University since 1946; Assistant Professor of Physics since 1961; Research Fellow (Bristol University, 1958-59); Lorand Eotvos University, Budapest (1965-66); Lecturer, Cairo College of Engineering since 1964. Professor of Solid-States Physics (1968), Chairman Physics Dept. (1975). **Publ.:** Author of studies on mapping of annealing spectra of cadium and silver and cadium- silver alloys, transformation in copper and gold-copper alloys anelastically and by steady creep methods, quenching and microcreep relaxation for values of Em and Ef for vacancies in gold and cobalt. Introduced Internal friction as tool for study of lattice defects in solids, concept of dissociated vacancy. **Awards:** State Prize for Physics research (1963), Egyptian Medal for Science and Arts (1963). **Addr.:** Cairo University, Giza, Egypt.

KAMEL (Saleh, Abdullah), Saudi Businessman. **Born** in Makkah in 1941. **Married. Qualifications:** Bachelor of Commerce (B.Com.) University of Riyad-Saudi Arabia. **Past Career:** Financial Inspector, Ministry of Finance; Financial Representative, Ministry of Finance. **Present Occupation:** President of Dallah Albaraka Group. **Major Companies & Banks:** Dallah Albaraka Holding Company, Jeddah-Saudi Arabia; Dallah Establishment, Jeddah-Saudi Arabia; Dallah Avco Trans Arabia Company, Jeddah-Saudi Arabia; Dallah Industries Company, jeddah-Saudi Arabia; Dallah Industrial Investment Company, Jeddah-Saudi Arabia; Dallah Transport Company, Jeddah-Saudi Arabia; Arab Media Company Company, Riyadh-Saudi Arabia; Fast Contracting Company, Jeddah-Saudi Arabia; Al-Jazeerah Transport Holding Company,, Jeddah-Saudi Arabia; Saudi Irish Dairy Company, Riyadh-Saudi Arabia; Albaraka Investment & Development Company, Riyadh-Saudi Arabia; Albaraka Al-Saudia Export Promotion & Services Co.- Saudi Arabia; Dallah Telecom, Jeddah-Saudi Arabia; Saudi Company For Recreation Centres, Jeddah-Saudi Arabia; Dallah International Holding Company, Cairo-Egypt; Dallah Agric. Invest. & Animal Production Co. (DAIAPCO), Cairo-Egypt; Arabian Real Estate & Tourism Investment Company, Cairo-Egypt; Samaha Egypt for Trading, Cairo-Egypt; Albaraka Company Ltd. for Export Promotion, Khartoum-Sudan; Albaraka Insurance Company Ltd., Khartoum-Sudan; Al-Amin Securities Company, Manama-Bahrain; Al-Tawfeek For Investment Funds, Manama-Bahrain; Beit Ettamouil Saudi Tounsi Re-Insurance Co. (BESTRE) Tunis-Tunis; Islamic International Tunis Fair, Tunis-Tunis; Arab Thai Investment Company, Bangkok-Thailand; South East Asia Holding Company-Singapore; Dallah Albaraka Malaysia Holding Company, Kuala Lumpur-Malaysia; Samaha fisheries, Nouadhibou-Mauritania; New Restaurants of Spain, Bendirom-Spain; Samaha Holdings-Cayman Islands; Samaha Trading U.K. Ltd., London-U.k.; Dallah Albaraka Investment Co. Ltd.-London, U.K.; Albaraka Investment Company, London-U.K.; Albaraka Bancorp, California-U.S.A.; Albaraka Bancorp, Texas-U.S.A.; Albaraka Bancorp, Chicago-U.S.A.; Albaraka Islamic Investment Bank-Bahrain; Albaraka Bank, Khartoum-Sudan; Albaraka Bank Bangladesh Ltd., Dhaka-Bangladcsh; Albaraka Bank, Alma Ata-Kazakhistan; Albaraka Bank-D'jibouti; Albaraka Bank, Durban-South Africa; Albaraka Bank-Nigeria (Under Establishment); Albaraka Turkish Finance House, Istanbul-Turkey; Albaraka Finance House, Bombay-India; Al-Towfeek Albaraka Investment Bank Ltd., Lahore-Pakistan; Banque Albaraka Mauritanienne Islamique, Nouackchott-Mauritania, Banque Albaraka D'Algerie-Algeria; Beit Ettamouil Saudi Tounsi (B.E.S.T.), Tunis-Tunis; Egyptian Saudi Finance Bank, Cairo-Egypt. **Chairman:** Jordan Islamic Bank For Development and Investment, Amman-Jordan; Islamic Banks Portfolio-IDB Jeddah, Saudi Arabia; Islamic Trading Co., Manama, Bahrain; Islamic Arab Insurance Company, Dubai, U.A.E.; Islamic Company for Insurance and Re-Insurance, Manama-Bahrain; Tihama Company For Advertisement, Public Relations & Market Research, Jeddah, Saudi Arabia; Egyptian Saudi Finance Bank, Cairo, Egypt; Alam Al-Roum Real Estate Co., Cairo, Egypt. **Deputy Chairman:** Arab Agricultural Investment Co., Manama-Bahrain. **Board Member:** National Development Bank, Khartoum-Sudan; OKAZ Organization For press & Publications, Jeddah, Saudi Arabia; Makkah Hotels Company, Saudi Arabia; Saudi Hotels & Resorts Company, Saudi Arabia. **Founder:** Faisal Islamic Bank, Cairo-Egypt; Faisal Islamic Bank, Khartoum-Sudan; Saudi Livestock Trade & Transport Co., Saudi Arabia; National Saudi Shipping Co., Saudi Arabia; Saudi Arabian Public Transport Co. (SAPTCO), Saudi Arabia. **Membership in Financial, Educational and Social Organizations:** Board Member of Saleh A. Kamel's Centre For Commercial & Islamic Researches-Al-Azhar University, Cairo, Egypt; Member of Supervisory Committee of Financial Accounting Organization For Islamic Banks And Financial Institutions; Member of the Saudi Accounting Association, Riyadh, Saudi Arabia; Member of the Trustees of the Arabic & Islamic Sciences History Institution-Frankfurt University, Germany; Member of the Saudi Legal Heritage-Riyadh, Saudi Arabia;

Member of the Founders Council of the Islamic Relief Organization; Board Member of the Yemeni Economic Association, Sanaa University, Sanaa, Yemen; Member-Board of Trustees of The Arab Institute For Banking & Financial Studies; Member-Board of Trustees, Intl., Islamic University, Islamabad; Member of High Committee of The Financing Fund of Arab Scout Organization; Member of World Scout Foundation-Paden Powell; Member of the High Committee of World Scout Friendship; Head of Trustees Board-Iqraa Society, London; Member-Board of Trustees, Munazamat Al-Dawa Al-Islamia, Khartoum, Sudan; Member of the Handicapped Children's Charitable Society, Riyadh, Saudi Arabia; Member of the Islamic Organization For Medical Sciences; Honorary Member of Islamic Civilization Research - Royal Academy, Jordan; Honorary Member of the Arab Bankers Association, England; Honorary Member of the Board of Trustees, Omar Bin Al-Khattab Foundation, Los Angeles, CA., U.S.A.; Honorary Member of Saudi Economic Society, Riyadh, Saudi Arabia. **Researches & Other Activities:** Being the President of Dallah Albaraka Group, Sheikh Saleh A. KAMEL pioneered the implementation of Islamic values worldwide in fields of Economics and Banking as an alternative to the contemporary conventional systems. He wrote many papers, researches on Islamic, Economics and Banking as well as he delivered many speeches and lectures in various countries. His written works included but not limited to the following:- Thoughts and inquiries about Zakat - Concept of Trusteeship in money and development of earth - Islamic instruments for increase in demand. He has established the following research centres: Saleh A. Kamel's Centre for Research in Islamic Economics, King Abdul Aziz University, Jeddah, Saudi Arabia; Saleh A. Kamel's Centre for Commercial & Islamic Researches, Al Azhar University, Cairo, Egypt. He has strong relationships with almost all Islamic Research Institutions and Universities worldwilde. He is the author of a book (two volumes) which is: «BAHAI FAITH ALLEGATIONS AND ITS NEGATIONS IN THOUGHT AND DOGMA» **and** «A DIALOGUE BETWEEN A MUSLIM AND A BAHAI». **Hobbies:** Travelling, Reading. **Address: Riyadh:** P.O.Box 1438, Tel.: (01) 4544455, Saudi Arabia. **Jeddah:** P.O.Box 430, Tel.: (02) 6710000, Saudi Arabia.

KAMHAWI (Walid), Jordanian physician. **Born** in 1923 in Nablus, Palestine. **Dipl.:** M.D., Diploma in Gynaecology and Obstetrics. **Career:** General Practitioner and Director of Kamhawi Hospital, Nablus, Palestine (1951-62); Gynaecologist (1962-73); Assistant General Secretary, Arab Medical Federation (1963-73); President of Jordan Medical Council (1963-69); Member, Executive Committee of Palestine Liberation Organisation (1964-65); President of Family Planning Society of Nablus (1965-74); President of Palestine National Fund, Palestine Liberation Organisation (1974-81); Governor of Arab Fund for Economic and Social Development (1975-81). **Publ.:** "Catastrophe and Reconstruction" (in Arabic). "Planned Parenthood" (in Arabic). **Hobbies:** Swimming, reading, travelling. **Addr.:** P.O.Box 950408, Amman, Jordan.

KAMI (Hassan, Mohamad Aly), Egyptian Opera singer. **Born** on October 1940. **Son** of Mohamad Aly Kami (former civil servant) **and** Mrs., née Nosrat el-Sherif. **Married** to Nagwa Alfy Fakhry on 28 August 1958, 1 child: Sherif. **Educ.:** College de la Sainte Famille, Cairo (1948-58); Faculty of Law, Cairo University; National Higher Conservatory; Dante Alleghieri Conservatory, Cairo (1959-64); studied under Professor Achille Brasehi, Rome, 1965. **Dipl.:** Egyptian Baccalaureat (secondary education certificate) (1958); L.L.B. (1964); Higher Musical Studies diploma. **Career:** started musical career at Cairo Opera House (1964) with Lucia De Lamermoor, followed by La Traviata, Madame Butterfly in 1969, La Bohême in 1970; in 1971 visited 8 republics of the USSR where he sang in Mme Butterfly, La Traviata, La Bohême; guest star in Lithuania where he assumed the leading tenor role of Radames in Aida, and was the first Egyptian singer to appear as Radames (1973); sang also in Poland in 1974, notably in Warsaw, Wroclaw, Lublin; participated in 1973 in the international Mme Butterfly competition, in Tokyo (Japan) returning there two years later as guest star on the invitation of the organising committee of the Mme Butterfly international competition, and gave four recitals respectively in Tokyo, Nagasaki, Osaka and Fuykuoka. **Awards:** received the Medal of Merit from the Japanese Premier for his "meritorious" opera performance. **Hobbies:** Reading & travelling. **Sports:** Swimming, horseriding and physical training. **Clubs:** Gezireh Sporting Club. **Prof. Addr.:** Bon Voyage Travel Agency, 16 Adly street, Cairo. **Priv. Addr.:** 49, Sudan street, Medinet el-Mohandessin, Dokki, Tel.: 858507, Cairo, Egypt.

KAMIL (Hassan Ahmad), Egyptian administrator. **Educ.:** Military Academy. **Career:** Artillery Colonel; Chef de Cabinet, General Mohamed Neguib until end of Neguib Presidency; promoted Head of Protocol Department (1964); Ambassador to Greece (1968-73); Grand Chamberlain in the Presidency (1973-74); Director of President's Private Office (1974). **Addr.:** Cairo, Egypt.

KAMMAL (Muhammad, Said Wasfi), Palestinian politician. **Born** in 1938 in Nablus, Palestine. **Educ.:** in Baghdad, Iraq and Alexandria, Egypt. **Career:** joined Arab Nationalist Movement (ANM); left ANM (1966) to join Fatah; President, General Union of Palestine Students; Assistant Director of the PLO, Cairo Office (1973); Deputy to Farouk Kaddoumi in PLO Political Department (1974); PLO delegate to the pre-summit meeting of Arab Foreign Ministers (1974); Member of the Political Staff of the PLO Office in Cairo, Egypt; joined PLO delegation to the UN for General Assembly debate on Palestine. **Addr.:** Tunis, Tunisia.

KANAAN (Abdul Halim), Jordanian executive. **Born** in 1923 in Nablus. **Son** of Rashed Kenaan. **Married** in 1951, 1 son, 3 daughters. **Educ.:** Jerusalem, B.Com. (1945); AIB (London). **Career:** Joined Arab Bank Ltd. since 1949; Alexandria, Egypt (1949-52); Assistant Manager, Tanta, Egypt (1952-59); Manager, Mansoura, Egypt (1959-62); Manager, Benghazi (1962-68); Manager, Arab Bank of North Africa, Benghazi (1968-77); Deputy General Manager, Investment Bank for Trade and Finance L.L.C. Abu Dhabi, UAE (1977-80), now retired. **Member:** Rotary Club. **Addr.:** Amman, Jordan.

KANAAN (Faisal Mohamad), Saudi geologist. **Born** in 1941 in Taïf, Saudi Arabia. **Dipl.:** B.Sc. (1964); M.Sc. (1966), Ph.D. (Geology, Geochemistry). **Career:** Geologist (1966-68); Senior Economic Geologist then Deputy Chief Geologist, same Ministry; Directorate-General of Mineral Resources (1968-74); then Deputy Chief Geologist, same Ministry; member of Geological Society of America (U.S.A.), Society of Economic Geologists (U.S.A.). **Hobbies:** Soccer, track and field, bowling, chess. **Addr.:** P.O.Box 1970, Jeddah, Saudi Arabia.

KANAAN (Shukri), Jordanian bank manager. **Born** in 1930 in Palestine. **Son** of Fayek Kanaan. **Married** in 1959, 1 son, 2 daughters. **Educ.:** Commerce. **Career:** Arab Bank Ltd., Jordan (1951-58); Riyadh Bank, Saudi Arabia (1958-80); Manager (1965-80); Manager, Arab African International Bank, Dubai, UAE (1980); Director, Gulf Riyadh Bank, Bahrain (1980). **Addr.:** Amman, Jordan.

KANAAN (Taher Humdi), Jordanian economist and banker. **Born** in 1935 in Nablus. **Son** of Hamdi Kanaan **and** Mrs. Najia née Rasheed Quttaineh. **Married** in 1960 in Lebanon to Ilham Yahia Kahwaji, three sons: Omar, Oussama and Raed. **Educ.:** Primary and Secondary Schools at al-Najah National College, Nablus; American University of Beirut, Lebanon; Cambridge University, U.K. **Dipl.:** B.A. in Economics (1954-1958); PH.D. in Economics (1958-1963). **Career:** Economics Advisor and Director, Arab Fund for Development, Kuwait (1983-85); Minister of Occupied Territories Affairs (1985-86); Minister of Planning (1986-89); General Manager, Industrial Development Bank (1989-1995); Board of Directors, Arab Society for Economic Research; Board of Trustees Institute of Palestine Studies; Board of Trustees, Center for Arab Unity Studies; Jordan Board of High Education. Minister of Development Affairs (Sep. 1998 - Jan. 2000). **Sports:** Swimming. **Hobbies:** Reading, Computer Systems. **Credit Cards:** American Express, Visa. **Prof. Addr.:** Industrial Development Bank, P.O.Box 1982, Tel.: 642216/19, Amman, Jordan.

KANAWATY (George, Daoud, Dr.), Egyptian UN official. **Born** on September 17, 1930 in Tanta, Egypt. **Son** of Daoud Kanawaty. **Married** in 1962 to Georgette Bookalam. **Educ.:** Alexandria University, Egypt; Illinois University, USA. **Dipl.:** B.Sc. in Chemistry and Geology, Alexandria University, Egypt; M.Sc. in Management and Ph.D. in Business Management, Illinois University, USA. **Career:** Chemist and Head of Labour Management Relations, Misr Beida Dyers (1950-60); ILO expert in production management; served in Cambodia and Cyprus (1963-68); ILO Regional Adviser for Africa in Management Development (1968-69); ILO Project Manager in Tunisia (1969-70); Associate Professor of Management, Director of Master Programme in Management Sciences and member of university Senate: University of Ottawa, Canada; Chief of Management Development Banch, ILO, Geneva, Switzerland (1973-82); Director Training Dept. ILO (1982- 1990); Management and human resources development consultant to the World Bank and other international organisations (1991- Present). **Languages:** Arabic, English, French, some Spanish. **Publ.:** "Cotton Bleaching, Dyeing and Finishing" (in Arabic, 1954); co-author of "Career Planning and Development", "Management Consulting, a guide to the Profession" (Geneva 1976), "Managing and Developing new Forms of Work Organization" (Geneva 1980-81); also Several papers published by ILO and other organizations fellow International Academy of Management. **Member:** of the Board International Institute of Education Planning, Paris and member Adviser Board world Centre, Washington. **Prof. Addr.:** Fax (4122) 3616021, Geneva, Switzerland.

KANAZEH (Najeh), Jordanian auditor. **Born** in 1944 in Nablus. **Son of** Abdulkareem Kanazeh (Kanazeh Tribe). **Married** in 1974, 3 daughters. **Dipl.:** B.A. Business Administration. **Career:** Officer in charge, Arab Bank Ltd. Fujeirah (since 1967); Accountant, NBAD, Ajman; International Auditor, Bank of Abu Dhabi, Dubai, UAE. **Hobbies:** Music and swimming. **Addr.:** P.O.Box 4436, Tel.: 226141, Dubai, UAE.

KANDIEL (Asaad M.), Saudi businessman. **Born** in Jeddah in 1929. **Educ.:** B.Sc. (Commerce), Cairo University. **Career:** General Manager, Sharbatly Cold Storage Co.; Manager of Trading Establishment; Financial Manager and later Vice President of Siraj Zahran and Co.; contractor; shareholder and member of Board of Services, Trading and Contracting Co. **Hobbies:** Swimming, fishing, tourism, photography. **Prof. Addr.:** 77 Ali Ibn Abi Taleb Street, Sharafia, P.O.Box 525, Tel.: 6516202, 6513306, Jeddah. **Priv. Addr.:** Tel.: 6513294, Jeddah, Saudi Arabia.

KANOO (Abdul Latif Jassim, Dr.), Bahraini administrator. **Born** on December 22, 1935 in Bahrain. **Son** of Jassim Kanoo. **Married**, 2 sons: Mohamed and Tariq. **Educ.:** Bahrain Primary and Secondary; Imperial College, London University, U.K.; University of Pittsburgh, U.S.A.; University of Texas, U.S.A. **Dipl.:** D.I.C., Imperial College, London; Master's Degree (in Civil Engineering), University of Pittsburgh; Doctorate (in Civil Engineering), University of Texas; Honorary Doctorate, University of

Anha (Korea). **Career:** Founder and First President, Bahrain Society of Engineers and Reporter General for the Arab Housing Ministers Conferences; former President, and Board Director, Bahrain Historical and Archeological Society; first President, Bahrain Philatelic Society; Ex-Chairman, Bahrain Korean Friendship Society; Ex-Chairman, Bahrain Aluminium Extrusion Company; presently, Deputy Chairman, Housing Bank of Bahrain; Under-Secretary, Ministry of Housing (since 1975- to date) and through his work, involved in a number of important and pioneering projects in Bahrain. He inspired the concept of the Beit al-Qur'an, a universal Islamic Centre dedicated to the Holy Qur'an and an instrument of becoming a unique institution in the Islamic World. Under his present guidance and since the opening of the Beit al-Qur'an in March 1990, this Islamic institution has sponsored a number of important lectures and activities and has held a number of Exhibitions. **Publ.:** Numerous Cultural, scientific and engineering publications, both locally and internationally. Writer for al-Watheeka (The Document), "al-Hidayah", "al-Bahrain publications". He had a weekly column in al'Ayam newspaper under the title "al-Kalima al-Tayyiba" (The Good Word). **Member:** Chartered Engineer; British Institute of Structural Engineers; American Society of Civil Engineering, member of the board, College of Science at the Arabian Gulf University, Bahrain. **Hobby:** Collecting of Islamic Works of Art, Calligraphy, Qur'anic Manuscripts and Islamic Coins. **Awards:** Medal of Bahrain; Highest Award for achievement, State of Bahrain in 1990 and May 1991; Award from Bahrain Society of Engineers in recognition for his exemplary contribution and efforts towards Society. **Addr.:** P.O.Box 45, Manama and Ministry of Housing. P.O.Bx 802, Manama, Bahrain.

KANOO (Abdulaziz, Qassim), Saudi Businessman. **Born** on December 23, 1932 in Manama, Bahrain. **Son** of Haji Qassim Kanoo (Businessman). **Married** on May 6, 1956, to Sarah, 4 children: Ali, Saud, Bader and Nawaf. **Education:** American University of Beirut, Beirut (Lebanon); Millfield School, Somerset (UK). **Career:** Deputy Chairman & Deputy Group Chief Executive Officer of Yusuf Bin Ahmed Kanoo, Chairman of: Saudi Arabian Industrial Trading Est., Baroid (Saudi Arabia) Ltd.; Saudi Arabian Lube Additives Co. Ltd., Al Jazeera Tourism Co., Bahrain; Vice Chairman of Investcorp Bank E.C., Director of: General Organisation of Petroleum & Minerals (PETROMIN), General Organization for Social Insurance (GOSI), Eastern Province Cement Co., Saudi Public Transport Co. Saudi Arabia, Kanoo Terminal Services Ltd., United Arab Shipping Agencies Co. (SA) Ltd. **Sport:** Swimming. **Hobbies:** Gardening, reading and ornithology. **Prof. Addr.:** P.O.Box 37, Dammam 31411, Saudi Arabia, Tel.: 03-8348880, Fax: 03-8345369/8339146, **Priv. Addr.:** same as above. Tel.: 8348880, Fax: 8345369, 8339146.

KANOO (Abdulla Ali), Saudi businessman. **Born** on 25 December, 1927, son of Ali Mohamed Kanoo. **Married** in 1967, 5 children: Ali, Hana, Lamiya, Saphia, and Ahmed. **Educ.:** in Bahrain and American University of Beirut. **Career:** Chairman and Chief Executive Officer of the Yusuf Bin Ahmed Kanoo Group of Companies; Chairman or the Board, National Bank of Bahrain; Member, Advisory Committee, Centre for Maritime Co-operation, London; Member, Advisory Committee (Shipping Agents), King Abdulaziz Port, Dammam, Saudi Arabian; Member, International Insurance Society Inc., Alabama, USA; Member National Committee for Insurance Services, Council of Saudi Chambers of Commerce, Saudi Arabia. **Hobbies:** Reading, travelling. **Prof. Address:** Kanoo Building, Al Khalifa Road, P.O.Box 45, Bahrain. Tel. 224466. Facsimile 229122 also Kanoo Tower P.O.Box 37, King Saud Street, Dammam 31411, Saudi Arabia Tel (3) 8348880 Facsimile (3) 8345369.

KANOO (Ahmad, Ali), Bahraini businessman. **Born** on July 22, 1922 in Manama, Bahrain. **Son of** Ali Mohamad Kanoo. **Married** in 1944, 3 children: Yusuf, Fawzi, Affaf. **Educ.:** in Bahrain and American University of Beirut. **Career:** Chairman of the Group Board of Yusuf Bin Ahmed Kanoo Group of Companies; Chairman of the Board, National Bank of Bahrain; Chairman of the Board, Bahrain Ship Repairing and Engineering Company; Chairman of the Board, Bahrain Hotels Company; Vice Chairman, Investcorp Banking Ltd.; Member, Bahrain Consultative Assembly (1973); Chairman, National Bank of Bahrain B.S.C., Manama. **Sport:** Swimming. **Hobbies:** Reading, Travelling. **Prof. Addr.:** Kanoo Building, al-Khalifa Road, P.O.Box 45, Tel.: 254081, Telex: 8215 KANOO BN, Manama, Bahrain.

KANOO (Yusuf, Ahmed), Bahraini merchant. **Born** in Bahrain. **Son of** Ahmad Kanoo. **Career:** Agent for Travel, Shipping and Insurance, Manufactures' Representatives and General Engineering Workshops. **Addr.:** P.O.Box 45, Tel.: 254081 (9 lines), Manama, Bahrain.

KAOUD (Ghazi, Yusuf Khamis), Palestinian bank manager. **Born** in 1941 in Palestine. **Son of** Yusuf Kaoud. **Married** in 1968, 2 sons, 4 daughters. **Dipl.:** B.Com. **Career:** Ministry of Defence, Gaza (1963-64); Ministry of Finance, Gaza (1964-66); al-Ghurair Group of Companies, Dubai (1966-71); Manager, Bank of Oman Ltd. Ajman (1971-). **Hobbies:** Reading, walking and Watching Television. **Addr.:** P.O.Box 11, Tel.: 422017, 422440, Telex: 69575 A/B OMNAJ, Ajman, UAE.

KARAGHOULI (Saleh, al), Iraqi university professor. **Born** in 1933 in Baghdad. **Son** of Abdulkarim al-Karaghouli (Professor) **and** Mrs. Sadiqa al-Barzanji. **Married** to Christiane Fassat in Paris in 1953, one child: Ziad. **Educ.:** Institute of Fine Arts, Baghdad, Ecole Nationale Supérieure des Beaux Arts, Paris. **Dipl.:** Diploma from the Institute of Fine Arts, Baghdad (1952), Diploma from

L'Ecole Nationale Supérieure des Beaux Arts in Paris (1960). **Career:** professor at the Institute of Fine Arts, Baghdad (1960-67); Professor at the Academy of Fine Arts, University of Baghdad since 1967. **Dist.:** Prizes and medals from Paris. **Remark:** participated in Exhibitions in Paris and in Baghdad, made a statute of ar-Razi, a fountain, two pieces about Palestine, a monument all in Baghdad. **Sports:** Swimming, football and hunting. **Hobbies:** Music and birds collection. **Member of:** Society of Iraqi Artists, Union of Iraqi Artists. **Prof. Addr.:** Academy of Fine Arts, Tel.: 22026 Baghdad, Iraq. **Priv. Addr.:** Karrada Sharqiya, Kherbanda, House No. 7A/7/21, Tel. 97804, Baghdad, Iraq.

KARAH (Bashir Abdel Magid), Libyan banking executive. **Born** in 1948 in Tripoli, Libya. **Son** of Abdulmagid Karah **and** Mrs. Aisha née Nashnoush. **Married** in 1975 in Tripoli, Libya to Miss Amal S. el Ghadamsi, two children. **Educ.:** Central Bank of Libya training center. **Career:** Central Bank of Libya (1967-70); Libyan Arab Foreign Bank, Tripoli (1974-77); Dubai Branch Manager (1979-81) with Arab Bank for Investment and Foreign Trade; Banking Operation Manager, with Arab Bank for Investment and Foreign Trade, Abu Dhabi (1981-84); Sook Branch Manager with Arab Bank for Investment and Foreign Trade (1984-85); Managing Director Banque Arabe Libyenne- Mauritanienne pour le Commerce Extérieur et le Développment, Nouakchott (1986). **Sport:** Football. **Credit Cards:** American Express. **Addr.:** Tripoli, Libya.

KARAM (Georges Toufiq), Egyptian company chairman and board director. **Born** on July 17, 1921, in Alexandria. **Educ.:** Victoria College of Alexandria, Royal Agricultural College of Cirencester, Gloucester (England). **Career:** Chairman and Managing- Director of the Commercial and Estates Co. of Egypt (Ex-S. Karam and Bros.). **Member:** Alexandria Sporting Club, Yacht Club of Egypt, R.A.C. Association (England). **Addr.:** 438, al-Hourriya Avenue, Rushdy Mansions, Haykal Bldg. Rushdy, Ramleh, Tel.: 62049, Alexandria, Egypt.

KARAM (Hussein M.), Kuwaiti executive. **Born** in 1946 in Kuwait. **Son** of Mohamad Karam. **Married** in 1976, 1 son, 3 daughters. **Dipl.:** B.Sc. (Maths, minor Computer Science). **Career:** Technical Support Manager, Ministry of Planning (1971-77) Data Processing Manager Public Institution for Social Security (1977-81); Senior Manager, Data Processing Division, Commercial Bank of Kuwait SAK, Kuwait (since 1981); Board Member of Kuwait Computer Society. **Hobbies:** Fishing and swimming. **Addr.:** P.O.Box 2861, Tel.: 744044, Telex: 22004, Safat, Kuwait.

KARAM (Jihad), Iraqi international civil servant. **Born** on December 2, 1936 in Beirut (Lebanon). **Single. Educ.:** American University in Beirut, Lebanon (1958-69). **Dipl.:** B.A. (Political Science) (1958), M.A. (Political Science) (1961), LL.D. **Career:** Private Law Practice, Beirut (1969-70); Ministry of Foreign Affairs, Baghdad (1970-71); Chief Delegate, Conference of Group of 77, Lima (1971); Vice Chairman, Delegation of Iraq to the Third United Nations Conference on Trade And Development (UNCTAD) Conference, Santiago, Chile (1972); Delegate to Conference of Ministers of Non-Aligned Countries, Guyana (1972); in Algiers, Algeria (1973); Chief Delegate UNCTAD Working Group on Charter of Economic Rights & Duties of States, Mexico (1974), Chairman, Economic and Financial Committee, UN General Assembly (1974) also Ambassador to Brazil (1971-1973). **Hobbies:** International Law, Economic. **Addr.:** Ministry of Foreign Affairs, Baghdad, Iraq.

KARAMI (Mohamad Salih), Saudi academic. **Born** in 1946 in Mecca, Saudi Arabia. **Dipl.:** B.A. (1966); M.A.T. (1970); M.S. (1972); M.Ed. (1972). **Career:** Assistant Lecturer, Teacher American Junior High and High Schools; President, Association for the Better Understanding of Near East Affairs; Chairman of Public Relations and Special Events, Organization of Arab Students in the University of Cincinnati; Lecturer, Department of Geography, Faculty of Education, Umm al-Qura University, Mecca. **Member:** Arab League; President, Student Islamic Association of Cincinnati; of Muslim Student Association of the U.S.A. and Canada, and Association of Arab-American University Graduates; Board of Arab- American Association of Greater Cincinnati, Organization of Arab Students in the U.S.A. and Canada, American Geographical Society, Association of American Geographers, National Geographical Society, National Council of Geographic Education. **Publ.:** writings in local press, four books (under publication). **Hobbies:** Stamps, reading, coins, music, tennis, golf. **Addr.:** Department of Geography, Faculty of Education, Umm al-Qura University, Mecca, Saudi Arabia.

KARAR (Ahmad, Karar), Sudanese politician. **Born** in 1926 in Sudan. **Educ.:** elementary education in Singa; Intermediate education in Rufaa; Secondary education in Omdurman; Faculty of Arts, Khartoum University; University of Nottingham, England (1960); Oxford University, England (1965). **Dipl.:** B.A. (1949), BPA (Bachelor of Public Administration) 1960, B.Sc. (Anthropology) 1965. **Career:** Assistant Executive Officer (1949-51); Executive Officer of North Gedaref Municipal Council (1951-52); Executive Officer of Kassala (1952); Executive Officer of Aroma (1954); Assistant Inspector of Bibor (1954-59); Assistant Lecturer, University of Khartoum (1964-66); Deputy Secretary-General, Council of Ministers (March 1966- June 1968); Secretary-General, Council of Ministers (March 1966- June 1968); Secretary-General, Council of Ministers (June 1968- Nov. 1969); Under-Secretary of State, Ministry of Cooperation and Rural Development (Nov. 1969- Oct. 1971); Commissioner, Blue Nile Province (Oct. 1971-73); Commissioner, Gezira Province (1973- Jan. 1975); Minister of Local popular Government (January 1975- February 1976). **Addr.:** Khartoum, Sudan.

KARARA (Houssam, Mahmoud, Dr.), Egyptian-American engineer. **Born** on September 5, 1928 in Cairo, Egypt. **Son** of Mahmoud Mohamad. **Married** on May 14, 1955 to Albertina Gulietta Panchetti, 2 daughters: Anna-Maria, Mervet. **Educ.:** University of Cairo, Egypt; Swiss Federal Institute of Technology, Zurich. **Dipl.:** B.Sc. (1949), Dr. of Science Technology (1956). **Career:** Engineer, Ministry of Public Works, Egypt; Field Engineer, Idfina dam construction (1949-51); Field Engineer, La Grande Dixence dam construction, La Grande Dixence Company, Sion, Switzerland (1952); Scientific Collaborator, Institute of Photogrammetry, Swiss Federal Institute of Technology, Zurich (1955-56); went the USA (1956), naturalized (1962); Assistant Professor, at Urbana-Champaign (USA) (1956-61); Associate Professor (1961-66); Professor of Civil Engineering since 1966, University of Illinois at Urbana-Champaign; Consultant on Photogrammetric Engineering to industrial and governmental mapping agencies in USA and abroad. **Awards:** Talbert Abrams Award (1959), (1961); Presidential Meritorious Award (1966), (1971), (1972), (1976), (1979); Fairchild Photogrammetric Award (1974); Research Prize, American Society of Civil Engineers (1963). **Member:** American Congress on Surveying and Mapping; American Society of Photogrammetry and Remote Sensing American Society of Civil Engineers; Canadian Institute of Surveying; Belgian British, French, German Societies of Photogrammetry and Remote Sensing; President, Commission V International Society for Photogrammetry (1972-76) **Publ.:** several articles in professional journals. **Prof. Addr.:** Department of Civil Engineering, University of Illinois, Newmark Civil Engineering Lab, 205 N. Mathews Ave., Urbana, IL. 61801, USA.

KAREM (Mahmoud, Dr.), Egyptian statesman, Director, Disarmament and Peaceful uses of Nuclear Energy Dept. MFA, Cairo, Egypt. **Born** in Cairo in 1949. **Educ.:** American University, Cairo and University of South Carolina, USA. **Dipl.:** B.A. in Political Science, Ph.D. in Philosophy (with distinction. **Married** to Miss Yasmina M. Taha, two daughters. **Career:** Member of the bureau of the Prime Minister of the Confederation of Arab Republics (1972-75); Rapporteur of a Presidential Delegation to six African Countries (1973-74); joined Egyptian diplomatic service as Diplomatic Attache and member of the bureau of the Minister of State for Foreign Affairs (1975-77); Third Secretary and later Second Secretary, Permanent Mission of Egypt to the United Nations, New York (1977); Alternate Representative to the First Committee of the General Assembly of the United Nations in New York (1977-81); elected by acclamation as Rapporteur of the Disarmament Commission in New York and further elected by the commission as Chairman of its main working group on the Reduction of Military Budgets (1981); appointed Member of the Cabinet of the Minister for Foreign Affairs in Cairo, 1984); also served as member of Egypt's delegation to the 15th Foreign Ministers Meeting of the Organization of the Islamic Conference in Sanaa, Yemen (1984); also member of Egypt's delegation to the Meeting of the Foreign Ministers of the Non Aligned movement Delhi (1986), Fifth Islamic Summit Conference in Kuwait (1987); Meeting of Ministers of Foreign Affairs of the Mediterranean Members of the Movement of the Non Aligned Countries in Brioni, Yugoslavia (1987); Assistant Professor of Political Science at the American University in Cairo (1986-88); lecturing young career Egyptian and other African Diplomats in training at the Institute for Diplomatic Studies (since 1984); Presently Director, Disarmament and Peaceful uses of Nuclear Energy Dept. MFA, Caïro Egypt. **Medals:** Egyptian Presidential Decoration IV order; USC's Educational Foundation "Fellow of the Foundation" award; membership of the Jonathan Maxcy Club; Gamma Chi Chapter of Pi Sigma Alpha. **Member of:** Egyptian Association of the United Nations, Egyptian Association of International Law, Egyptian- American Friendship Association, the Alexandria Chapter, Governing Council of International Studies Association. **Author of** numerous articles and a book on "The Establishment of a Nuclear Weapon Free Zone in the Middle East: Policy, Problems and prospects" with Greenwood Press, Publisher of Praeges. In 1989 his book was chosen by CHOICE, a monthly review service published by the Association of College and Research Librarian in the United States, as one of the best books in the field of International relations for its "outstanding academic standard". The announcement was published in the May 1989 issue of CHOICE, later on the same work was nominated for the Annual Mershon award of Ohio State University for the best first book in the field of national security studies. Writing a monograph on the National Concept of security of Egypt, published by the United Nations Institute for disarmament Research (UNIDIR). His recent publication include a Chapter on a Middle East Perspective of Regional Approaches to Disarmament published by Dartmouth, U.K., 1993, and a Historical Overview of the patterns of involvement of the U.N. for denuclearizing the M.E., Canada, Aurora Papers, 1993. He also published articles for IEEE SPECTRUM and ASA (Applied Science & Analysis U.S.A.). **Prof. Addr.:** Disarmament Dept. Ministry for Foreign Affairs, Maspero, Cairo, Egypt.

KARIM (Ghada, Hasan), Physician and medical historian. **Born** on 19 November 1939 in Jerusalem, Palestine. **Daughter of** Hasan Karmi (lexicographer) **and** Mrs., née Amina Saleh al-Rifai. **Educ.:** University of Bristol, England; University College, London, St. Antony's College, Oxford. **Dipl.:** M.B. Dh.B. (medical degree), University of Bristol (1964); M.R.C.P. (member of the Royal College of Physicians), London (1967); Ph.D. (History of medicine), University of London (1978). **Career:** Hospital Doctor (1964-72); Wellcome research fellow in history of medicine, the Wellcome Institute for History of Medicine, London; Lecturer, History of Medicine, Aleppo University Medical School, Syria (1978-79); Assistant editor, Journal for the History of Arabic Science; now, Assistant Professor in History of Arabic Science, Yarmouk University, Jordan. **Awards:** Medical Suple Prize for the best student in the final undergraduate year at Bristol University (1963). **Member:** British Medical Association, British Society for Middle Eastern Studies, International Society for the History of Medicine. **Addr.:** Amman, Jordan.

KARIM-LAMRANI (Mohamad), Moroccan former Prime Minister. **Born** on May 1, 1919 at Fez, Morocco. **Career:** Economic Advisor to his Majesty the King; Joined Office Chérifien des Phosphates (OCP) after Independence; Director, OCP (1959-63); President, Compagnie Africaine des Banques; Chairman and Managing Director, Crédit du Maroc (on merger of the Compagnie Africaine des Banques with Crédit Lyonnais Maroc) (March 1966); Director General, OCP (1967); Chargé de Mission, Royal Cabinet (August 1967); Minister of Finance (April 1971); Prime Minister of the caretaker Government (August 1971); formed new Government (April 1972); replaced as Prime Minister by Ahmed Osman (November 1972); President of the World Phosphate Institute (June 1973); President, Maroc Chimie; Director, Banque Marocaine du Commerce Extérieur; Chairman, Crédit du Maroc, Casablanca; Prime-Minister (Nov. 1983 Sept. (1986); Presently, Managing Director, Office Chérifien des Phosphates; and President, Phosphates de Boucraa S.A.; Prime Minister (August 1992-Feb. 1995). **Prof. Addr.:** Casablanca, Morocco.

KARKDAN (Mohamad Saied Salim), Saudi executive. **Born** in 1932 at al-Wajh. **Dipl.:** Diploma of Higher Postal Institute. **Career:** Staff Manager, Government Liaison and Air Mail Affairs (1970); Manager, Government Relations (1971); Manager, Government Affairs (1975); Manager, Government Liaison, Saudia- Saudi Arabian Airlines Corporation; member, Executive Council Meeting of Arab Postal Union (1962); attended Universal Postal Union (UPU Conference), Vienna (1963); Arab Postal Union, Ninth Conference, Cairo (1971); Arab Postal Union Consultative Council Meeting, Beirut (1973); Chairman of Air Mail Committee, Arab Air Transport Union; member of Air Mail Committee, International Air Transport Association; founder, Charity Fund, al-Wajh, Saudi Arabia. **Publ.:** political articles in al-Bilad daily 1974. **Hobbies:** Swimming, fishing, reading. **Addr.:** Saudia Building, Jeddah, Saudi Arabia.

KARKOUTI (Mustapha), Syrian born Journalist-Author. **Born** on October 3, 1943 at Latakia, Syria. **Son** of Ahmad Aref Karkouti (Baker and Carpenter) **and** Mrs. Chafika Khafateh. **Married** on January 1978 in London to Faten Omary, 3 children: Shahla, Ahmad, Talal. **Educ.:** Youssef Azma and Jole Jammal (Syria), Arab University of Beirut and Lebanese University (Lebanon), Hull University. **Dipl.:** BAs., MA. **Career:** Beirut Lycee (1965-1968); Orient Press, Beirut (1968-1973); London Correspondent for Assafir, Beirut (1974-1990); Deputy-Editor, Arab Business Magazine, London (1976-1980); Editor, AB, London (1980-1983); Qatar's News Agency, London Correspondent (1983-93); Editor, Huna London, BBC World Service (1988-93); Director of Public Relations and promotion, MBC TV (1993-95); Head of Evaluation, MBC TV (1995-98); Media Consultant and Journalist (1999 till now). **Publ.:** Translated several Books on Iran, Libya, Europe. **Sports:** Swimming, Walking. **Hobbies:** Chess, Reading, Theatre, Music. **Member:** President, Foreign Press Association, London, Arab Club of Britain; BBC Club, Syrian Arab Association. **Credit Cards:** AE, Access, Visa, Switch. **Prof. Addr.:** BBC British House, Strand, London, Tel.: (71) 257 2818, Fax: 208 932 7068. **Priv. Addr.:** 36 Mulgrave Rd., Ealing, London WS ILE, Tel.: (208) 997 0267. E-mail: mkarkouti@composet.yc.com.

KARMOUL (Akram, Jamil), Jordanian engineer. **Born** on August 13, 1939 in Jordan. **Married**, 4 children. **Educ.:** Strathclyde University, Glasgow, U.K.; Imperial College, London University, U.K. **Dipl.:** M.Sc. in Mining Engineering (1966); Ph.D. in Economic Engineering (1977). **Career:** Exploration and Mining, Natural Resources Authority (1961-1972); Director, Industry and Mining Planning (1972-1979); Director, Science and Technology Department, Ministry of Planning (1979-80); Director General of Industry, Ministry of Industry and Trade, Jordan (1980-1987); General Manager and Board Member of the Industrial, Commercial and Agricultural Production Co. of Jordan at Russaifi; Associate Consultant of the Arab Consulting Centre of Jordan (1988); Director of Industry at Dalla/al-Baraka Group of Companies, Jeddah, Saudi Arabia (1989 and 1990); Chief of Industry and Technology at ESCWA (UN, Economic and Social Commission for Western Asia) (1990-94); Private Consultant and Owner of a Plan for Water Treatment (1994 to present). **Former Board Member of:** Public Mining Company; Arab Mining Company; Syrian Jordanian Industrial Co.; Natural Resources Authority of Jordan; Higher Council of Science and Technology in Jordan (1980); College of Sciences, University of Jordan; Consultation Committee of Energy at the Royal Scientific Society of Jordan; Technical Consultation Committee of the Arab Industrial and Mining Development Organization (AIDMO) in Morocco, and finally Former Board Member of ten industrial companies in Saudi Arabia, Jordan, Morocco, Tunis, Yemen and Egypt. **Publ.:** Various articles and studies on industry, mining and investment. **Patented:** New discovery at the Ministry of Industry and Trade of Jordan in 1988. **Hobbies:** Travelling, reading and swimming. **Prof. Addr.:** P.O.Box 960555, Tel.: (9626) 5157222, Fax: (9626)5155826, Amman, Jordan.

KAROUI (Hamed, Dr.), Tunisian former Prime Minister. **Born** on December 30, 1927 in Sousse. **Married,** four children. **Educ.:** Baccalaureate, Sousse (1946); Medical Studies, Specializing in Pulmonary disorders, France (1946-55). **Career:** Specialized Physician and Head of Department, Sousse Regional Hospital (starting 1957); Member National Assembly (1964, reelected 1981-1989); Deputy Speaker, Chamber of Deputies (1983-86); Mayor of Sousse (1985); Minister of Youth and Sports (1986-87); Director with Cabinet Rank, Destour Socialist Party (1987-88); Minister of Justice (1988-89); Member, Democratic Rally (RCD) (1988-to date) and Political Bureau (1989-to date); Prime Minister (Sept. 1989-1999). **Address:** Tunis, Tunisia.

KAROURI (Muhammad, Othman al-Hussan, al), Sudanese agricultural engineer. **Born** in 1939 in Nuri, Sudan. **Married**, 1 son, 1 daughter. **Educ.:** University of Khartoum, Sudan; Aberdeen University; University of London, Wye College, UK. **Dipl.:** B.Sc. in Agriculture, M.Sc. in Soil Science, Ph.D. in Soil Science. **Career:** Assistant Researcher of Agricultural Research Corporation, Sudan (1961-62); Head of soil Science Section, Hudeiba Rersearch Station, Sudan (1965-70); Head of Soba Agricultural Research Station, Sudan (1974-77); Vice President of Sudanese Soil Science Society; Part-time Lecturer, the Institute of Environmental Studies, University of Khartoum, Sudan; Member of the National Committee for Education, Culture and Science and the Sudanese Society for Protection of the Environment; Director of Agricultural Research Council, National Council for Research, Khartoum (1977-). **Publ.:** numerous scientific papers published in the annual "Reports of Sudan", Agricultural Research Corporation; numerous publications in scientific journals such as "Journal of Agricultural Science" and others. **Hobbies:** conservation of natural resources and protection of the environment swimming, gardening, chess. **Decor.:** Eisenhower Fellow (1977). **Prof. Addr.:** Agricultural Research Council, P.O.Box 6096, Khartoum, Sudan.

KARRAR (Gaafar), Sudanese Director, Gaafar Karrar & partners (Consultants) in Environment & Development. **Educ.:** Secondary & Higher Studies. **Degrees:** Bachelor of Veterinary Science; Dip Tropical Veterinary Medicine; Doctor of Philosophy. **Career:** Director of Research; Under Secretary, Ministry of Animal Resources; First Under Secretary, Ministry of Agriculture; Assistant Secretary General, World Conference on Desertification. **Address:** No 8 Str. No 1 Amarat, P.O.Box 1218, Khartoum, Sudan. Tel.: (249-11) 778358 and 471382, Fax: 782187, E-mail: gaafarkarrar@sudanmail.net.

KASHIF ALGHITA (Bakir, Ahmad), Iraqi engineer. **Born** in 1922 in Iraq. **Married**, 3 children. **Educ.:** American University of Beirut, Lebanon; University of California, Berkeley, USA, Utah State University, USA, also in London. **Dipl.:** B.Sc. in Civil Engineering, M.Sc. in Irrigation, Ph.D. in Irrigation and Drainage Engineering, FICE. **Career:** Engineer, Directorate General of Irrigation, Baghdad (1951) Chief Engineer (1958). Director General of Irrigation (1959); Inspector General of Irrigation, Baghdad (1970; Professor of Irrigation, Drainage and Hydrology, College of Engineering, Baghdad University, Iraq (1971); Consulting Engineer; headed several official Iraqi delegations. **Publ.:** "Hydrology and Its Application" (1982), University of Musul, "Hydrology for Geographers" (1982), University of Baghdad, as well as several other books and researches. **Decor.:** Order of Salvation (1954). **Hobbies:** Arabic and English poetry, walking, reading, chess. **Addr.:** 12/18/601 al-Mansour, Baghdad, Iraq.

KASHIF (Ali, Fahmi, Mahmoud, al), Egyptian agricultural Engineer. **Born** in Benisuif, Egypt. **Married,** 1 son, 1 daughter. **Educ.:** Johns Hopkins University, USA; Cornell University, USA. **Dipl.:** M.Sc. and Ph.D. in Engineering. **Career:** Chief Engineer, High Aswan Dam Authority (1956-58); Director of Technical Assistance Bureau, Ministry of Planning (1958-61); Technical Director and President of REGWA (State-owned company for groundwater research) (1961-65); Director of Groundwater Research and Exploitation, General Desert Development Organisation, Cairo (1965-67); Project Manager in Algiers, Qatar and West Africa, FAO (1967-73); Land Reclamation Consultant at the Ministry of Development and Land Reclamation (1979-81); Member of Egyptian Syndicate of Engineers: Consultant at the Centre for Arab Development Studies and Consultancy (CADSAC) (1981-). **Publ.:** "Hydrogeology of Kharga Oases in Egypt", GDDO (1966) (in English), "Fresh Water Estimates of Rawdetain", Kuwait Ministry of Electricity & Water (1967) in English, "Agricultural Development of Hodna Basin in Central Algeria", Algerian Ministry of Agricultural & FAO (1971) in French, "Groundwater Balance in Qatar", Qatar Ministry of Agriculture & FAO (1973) in English. **Decor.:** Order of Merit, 4th grade (1957). **Hobbies:** Swimming, reading, music. **Member:** Egyptian Italian Association, Gezira Sporting Club. **Addr.:** 5 Dr. Taha Hussein, Zamalek, Cairo, Egypt.

KASHMIRY (Mohamad Abdul Rahman), Saudi auditor. **Born** in 1930 in Medina, Saudi Arabia. **Dipl.:** B.Com. (Accountancy and Administration). **Career:** Formerly with Saudia as manager, Budgeting Administration; then Acting Manager, Finances; Acting Manager, Administrative Affairs; Deputy General Manager; Finance Manager, General Accounts, Assistant General Auditor, Saudia-Saudi Arabian Airlines Corporation. **Hobbies:** Football, table tennis. **Addr.:** P.O.Box 4933, Jeddah, Saudi Arabia.

KASMEERI (Nouri, A.), Saudi engineer. **Born** 1940 in Taif, Saudi Arabia. **Dipl.:** M.Sc.; Ph.D. (Structural Engineering). **Career:** Lecturer, King Saud University (1965), Assistant Professor (1970); also associate of Development and Supplies Co. and Saudi Construction Co. **Hobby:** Reading. **Prof. Addr.:** P.O.Box 664, Tel.: 4811000, Riyadh. **Priv. Addr.:** Tel.: 4760190, Riyadh, Saudi Arabia.

KASRY (Samir, Mohamed Fouad, el), Egyptian bank Chairman and Managing Director. **Born** on November 4, 1934 in Cairo, Egypt. **Son** of Mohamed Fouad el-kasry. Two sons: Mohamed and Ashraf. **Educ.:** Faculty of Commerce, Cairo University. **Dipl.:** B.Com (1955). **Career:** General Manager, Banks Control Department, Central Bank of Egypt (1977); Assistant Sub-Governor, Central Bank of Egypt (1978); Managing Director, Alexandria Kuwait International Bank (1978-84); Sub-Governor, Central Bank of Egypt (1984-85); Vice Chairman and Managing Director (1985-88); Chairman and Managing Director, Bank of Commerce and Development-El-Tegaryoon (Jan. 1989 to present) **Directorships:** Vice Chairman and Board Member of: Alektesadia for Housing and Reconstruction; Misr International Hospital Cairo. **Membership** of professional Organization: Specialized National Councils. **Club.:** Es-Shams. **Hobbies:** Reading, Carpenter Work. **Credit Card:** Visa and Master. **Sports:** Walking **Prof. Addr.:** 13, 26th July Square (Sphinx) Mohandessin, Tel.: (202) 3479070, 3475002, Giza, Egypt **Priv. Addr.:** 5 Mostafa Moktar Helipolis, Tel.: (202) 2422605 and 2422604 Cairo, Egypt.

KASSAB (Adnan Ali), Iraqi administrator. **Born** in 1934 in Iraq. **Educ.:** Higher Institute of Industrial Engineering, Baghdad. **Career:** Resident Engineer, Army Canal Project (1961-63); Director of Administration, Industrial Government Projects (1963-64); later arrested and imprisoned; Director General, Iraqi Ports Administration (1968-71); President, National Oil Company (1971-72); President, State Construction Contracting Company (1972). **Addr.:** State Construction Contracting Company, Insurance Building, Rashid Street, Baghdad, Iraq.

KASSAR (Nagat, Taysir), Egyptian official. **Born** on January 22, 1938 in Cairo. **Married** to Dr. Mohamed Wafik Abou Atlah on 22 January 1960, 2 children, one daughter and one son. **Educ.:** Abbaissiyeh Secondary School (1949-55); Faculty of Law, Ayn Shams University (1956-59); Faculty of Law, Cairo University; American University, Cairo (1976). **Dipl.:** LL.B. (1959), LL.B. International Law (1960); Mass Communications diploma. **Career:** Head, United Nations Section, External Relations Department, The People's Assembly (Parliament), Cairo (1965-69); Legal Researcher, People's Assembly (1960-65); Reference Assistant, United Nations Information Centre, Cairo (Egypt). **Publ.:** Several research studies on international law, for the People's Assembly, including: "The Yugoslav Constitution" (1961), "Jewish Immigration to Palestine" (1962); "The Arab Refugees Problem" (1962), "The Problem of Israeli shipping through the Suez Canal" (1963), "The Arabian Gulf Problem" (1967), etc. **Hobbies:** Research work and reading. **Prof. Addr.:** United Nations Information Centre, 1, Osiris street, Garden City District, Tel.: 20959, Cairo. **Priv. Addr.:** 11 Abdul Rahman el-Barkouki street, Manial District, Tel.: 845837, Cairo, Egypt.

KASSEM (Abdul Rauf, al, Dr.), Syrian politician. **Born** in 1932 in Damascus. **Educ.:** Damascus University, School of Arts, Istambul and Geneva Universities. **Dipl.:** in Architecture. **Career:** Teacher of architecture, School of Fine Arts, Damascus; Dean (1964-70); Head, Architecture Department, School of Civil Engineering, Damascus University (1970-77); Rector (1977-79); concurrently engineer (1964-77); Governor of Damascus (1979-80); elected member Baath Party Regional Command (1979), Central Command of Progressive National Front (1980); Prime Minister (1980-87); member, Higher Council for Town Planning (since 1968); member of National Union or Architects' Permanent Commission on Town Planning (1975) Honorary Professor Geneva University (since 1975). **Addr.:** Damascus, Syria.

KASSEM (Tarek, Jamal), Saudi banker residing in the U.K. **Born** in 1946 in Safad, Palestine. **Married,** 1 son. **Educ.:** City of London Polytechnic, London, UK; **Dipl.:** Degree in Business law and Finance. **Career:** Trainee, Arabian American Oil Company (ARAMCO), Dhahran Saudi Arabia; Management Trainee, Electro Components (Holdings) Ltd., London (1970-1973); Institutional Sales Executives, Vickers da Costa London (1973-74); Chief Executive, Arab Bank investment Company Ltd. (1974-87); Chairman and Managing Director, Quanta Group (Holdings) Ltd. (1987-88). **Other Directorships (1988-1992):** Malvern Property Company PLC; R & G Financial Services Ltd; Walker, Crips, Weddle, Beck Plc; Noel Gay Financial Services Ltd; Quanta Securities Ltd.; Quanta Group (Financial PR) Ltd; Quanta Group (Property Services) Ltd. **Current:** Managing Director, TJK Consultants Limited, London (1992-); Senior Middle East Advisor, Dutsche Bank A.G. London and Global Banking Division (1992-). **Priv. Addr.:** Flat 1, 8 Sydney Street, London, SW3 6PP, United Kingdom.

KASSIM (Habib Ahmad), Bahraini former minister. **Born** 1943. **Educ.:** in Bahrain and Lebanon. **Dipl.:** B.A. Economics, American University of Beirut (1965). **Career:** Teacher, al-Hoora Secondary School, Bahrain (1965-67); Member, Department of Finance; Bahrain Development Office (1967); Director of Commerce and Industry, Ministry of Finance and Economy (1971); Under-Secretary, Ministry of Commerce and Agriculture (September 1975); Minister of Commerce and agriculture (from June 1976 to June 1995). **Addr.:** Manama, Bahrain.

KASWANI (Salim, Yusuf al), Jordanian official. **Born** on September 28, 1938. **Married,** 3 sons, 1 daughter. **Educ.:** Cairo University, Egypt. **Dipl.:** M.A. in Law; Ph.D. **Career:** Area Manager, Ministry of Internal Affairs, later Executive Manager and Assistant Deputy Minister; Legal Consultant to the President of the National Council; Consultant, Legislative Bureau; Chairman of Association for the Reform and Security of the Jordanian Family; Member of Jordanian Lawyer's Association. **Publ.:** "al-Markaz al-Kanouni le Madinat al-Koas" (1977), "Child Rights in Jordanian Legislation" (1979), "Mabade'e al-Kanouni al-Destouri" (1983). **Hobbies:** Travelling, reading, studying. **Prof. Addr.:** P.O.Box 5190, Amman, Jordan.

KATAMI (Abdul Rahman, A.), Saudi official. **Born** in Mecca, Saudi Arabia. **Dipl.:** B.Sc. (Civil Engineering), (1964); Higher Diploma (1970). **Career:** Engineer, Roads and Bridges Projects, Ministry of Communications (1965-68); Director of Maintenance (1970-74); Director General for Construction (1974-81). Assistant Deputy Minister of Communications for Technical Affairs. **Prof. Addr.:** Tel.: 4021575, Riyadh. **Priv. Addr.:** Tel.: 4761386, Riyadh, Saudi Arabia.

KATCHADURIAN (K.J.A.), Banker. **Born** in 1933. **Married**, two children. **Educ.:** Terra Sancta (1948); University of London, Matriculation AA (1951); Pace University, New York, BBA Finance and Accounting (1965); Pace University, New York, MBA, Financial Management (1966). **Career:** Intra Bank, Beirut (1952-56); Bank of America- VP Multinational Corporate (1956-71); Allied Bank International, New York, SVP US and Canada and Special Industries (1971-82); Bahrain Middle East Bank, former General Manager and Chief Executive (1983). **Awards:** Certificate of Achievement, US Army (1959), (1960). **Sports:** Tennis, swimming, soccer. **Member:** American Management Association, New York; American Institute of Banking, New York. **Addr.:** Manama, State of Bahrain.

KATHIRI (Said Bin Mohammed, Samhan, al), Omani journalist and Businessman. **Born** in 1942 in Najd, Southern Region of the Sultanate of Oman. **Married**, 4 children. **Educ.:** General. **Career:** Chief Editor and Owner of Al-Akidah Printing Press and Arabian Establishment for Marketing and General Trading. **Hobbies:** History, literature, geography, politics. **Prof. Addr.:** P.O.Box 900, P.C. 113, Muscat, Sultanate of Oman.

KATIB (Mohamad Nour), Saudi TV executive. **Born** in 1946 in Mecca, Saudi Arabia. **Dipl.:** Diploma (TV Production) Italy. **Career:** has occupied several posts in Saudi Radio and Television Service; introduced some of the best Saudi TV productions; Director of Jeddah Television Station. **Prof. Addr.:** Jeddah Television Station, Ministry of Information, Tel.: 6426332, Jeddah. **Priv. Addr.:** Tel.: 6652572, Jeddah, Saudi Arabia.

KATIB (Saif el-Deen, Abdalla, al), Egyptian academic. **Born** in 1947 in Cairo, Egypt. **Married**, 2 children. **Educ.:** Cairo University, Egypt. **Dipl.:** M.D. in Urology. **Career:** Assistant Lecturer, Cairo University (1972-78); Lecturer (1978-83); Member of the Institute of Urology, London University, UK (1979-80); Assistant Professor, Cairo University (1983-). **Publ.:** several publications in the field of urology. **Hobbies:** Photography, shooting, music. **Prof. Addr.:** el-Katib Hospital, 17 Dr el-Katib Street, Dokki, Cairo, Egypt. **Priv. Addr.:** 22 Marashli Street, P.O.Box 140, Zamalek, Cairo, Egypt.

KATKHOUDA (Louay), Syrian international civil servant. **Born** on February 18, 1929 Aleppo, Syria. **Married** with children. **Educ.:** Federal Institute of Technology, Zurich (1946-51). **Dipl.:** B.Sc. (Chemical Eng.) (1951). **Career:** Military service (1951-53); Chief, Tests and Research Laboratories, Damascus (1953-54); Research Chemist, Industrial Research Institute (1954-58); Chief, Chemical Engineering Division (1958-60); Deputy Director, Department of Technology, Industrial Research Institute, Lebanon (1960-66); Industrial Development Officer (1966-69); Acting Chief, Industrial Institutions Section, United Nations Industrial Development Organisation (UNIDO) (1969-70); Chief, Industrial Institutions Section, UNIDO, Vienna, since 1971. **Publ.:** Author of "Role of Standardisation in Industrial Development" (1954) "Requirements for Industrial Research in Developing Countries" (1969). **Member:** Association of Lebanese Engineers; Association of French Professional Engineers; American Oil Chemists Society. **Sports:** Tennis and swimming. **Hobbies:** Literature and music **Prof. Addr.:** UNIDO, P.O.Box 707, Tel.: 0222 43-50-0, A-1011 Vienna 1, Austria. **Priv. Addr.:** 2, Phourusgasse, Tel.: 0222 57-11-92, A-1011, Vienna, Austria.

KATLABI (Hussain, Yahya, al), Syrian entomologist. **Born** in 1940 in Hama, Syria. **Married**, 1 son, 4 daughters. **Educ.:** University of Alexandria, Egypt. **Dipl.:** B.Sc., M.Sc. in Agriculture (Entomology); Ph. D., Zeuzera Pyrina L. (Cossidae, Lepid) (1987). **Career:** Researcher (1965-71); Chief of Entomological Research Department, Plant Protection Research, Ministry of Agriculture and Agrarian Reform, Syria. **Publ.:** "Hylesinus Olieperda F." in Arabic (1966), "Dacus Olease G. Density" in Arabic (1967), "A Guide to Olive Pests" (1975), "Control of Dasyneura Oleae L." in French (1977), "Life Cycle of Dasyneurs Oleae L." In French (1979), "Parasites on Dasyneura Oleae L." in French (1980), "Plalygaster Sp. indoparasite of Dasnyeura Oleae L." in French (1983) "Monitoring of the flying periods of codling moth adults through the ferman traps" In Arabic (1984); "Endoparasites on the Larva of olive twige midge (Clinodiplosis Oleisuga Trag)" In arabic (1985); "Flying period of t he leopard moth (Zeuzera Pyrina) on olive trees in Syria" In Arabic (1986-87). **Addr.:** 72 Jaber Ibn Hayan Street, No 7, al-Sait Bldg., Shimal al-Koztari, Tijara, Damascus, Syria.

KATTAN (Imad), Jordanian architect/ planner. **Born** on Sept. 3, 1951 in Amman, Jordan. **Son of** Mahmoud

Kamal Kattan (businessman) **and** Mrs. Ilham. **Married** on April 24, 1983 to Leen Halawa, **Divorced** 1986. **Married** on May 25, 1988 to Nawal Abdalla. **Educ.:** Islamic College & Bishop's School, Amman; Wellington College UK; Bath University UK; Liverpool University UK. **Dipl.:** B.Sc. and MCD. **Career:** Senior Architect Planner at CH2M Hill, Portland, Oregon USA (1977-82); Manager Partner at UBMC Amman, Chairman and Managing Director at UDC, Amman, Partner at Akram Abu Hamdan & Partners Office; Lecturer of Architecture of Jordan University Amman. **Sports:** Tennis, Squash and Jogging. **Hobby:** Photography. **Clubs:** Royal Auto Club, Amman. **Credit Cards:** American Express and Visa. **Addr.:** P.O.Box 404, Tel.: 622359, 625053, Fax: 962-6-648043, Amman, Jordan.

KATTAN (Mannaa Khalil, al), Egyptian academic. **Born** in 1925 at al-Manoufiya, Egypt. **Educ.:** Higher Certificate, The Faculty of Islamic Theology (Master of Education). **Career:** Taught in secondary schools, (1951-53); in scientific institutes, (1953-56); Shari'a College and the Arabic Language College of Riyadh, (1956-72); in the Higher Judicial Institute (1966-72); Director, The Higher Judicial Institute and the Higher studies Department, Imam Muhamad Ibn Saud Islamic University; regularly makes oratorical speeches, supervised more than 50 Ph.D. & 100 Masters Degree reserches; gives lectures, participates in symposia, writes articles; preaches in the Mosques, Universities and in the media; member of the Preparatory Committee for the Supreme Committee on Education Policy in the Kingdom; member, the Islamic World Association Conference, the Islamic Conference of Karachi and the Conference of al-Kodse, the Conference of the University Messaga, the World Conference of the Islamic Economy, the Conference of Propagation and Propagators, the (Islamic) Propagation and Propagators, the Islamic Jurisprudence Week, Mohamad Ibn Abdul Wahab Week and other conferences. **Publ.:** various articles on the Explanation of Verse Judgements, Research in the Quranic Sciences, Jurisprudence and Philology in Islam (History and Courses); Three books on Islamic Culture, for Islam. **Hobbies:** Reading, research. **Prof. Addr.:** Imam Muhammad Ibn Saud Islamic University, Tel.: 4054832, Riyadh and P.O.Box 18097, Riyadh 11415, Saudi Arabia. **Priv. Addr.:** Tel.: 4643395, Riyadh, Saudi Arabia.

KATTAN (Mohamad Ali Ahmad), Saudi official. **Born** in 1936 in Mecca, Saudi Arabia. **Dipl.:** Ph.D. (Sociology). **Career:** Assistant Professor, Sociology Department, Faculty of Arts, and Dean, External Students Department, King Abdulaziz University, Jeddah; former Secretary of the Saudi Educational Mission Abroad, Cairo; Assistant to Saudi Permanent Delegate to UNESCO, Paris; Lecturer, Faculty of Arts, King Abdulaziz University; attended several UNESCO conferences; Deputy Mayor of Jeddah. **Publ.:** Social Psychology (book); Social System of Islam (sociology notes). **Hobby:** Reading. **Prof. Addr.:** Municipality of Jeddah, P.O.Box 7687, Tel.: 6672384, Jeddah. **Priv. Addr.:** Tel.: 7615287, Jeddah, Saudi Arabia.

KATTAN (Mohamad Amin Mohamad), Saudi broadcaster. **Born** in 1943 in Mecca, Saudi Arabia. **Dipl.:** Diploma, Trades Schools. **Career:** Successively radio actor, programme introducer, drama student, Higher Institute of Dramatic Arts, Cairo; Announcer, Jeddah Broadcasting Service. **Hobbies:** Music, travel. **Prof. Addr.:** P.O.Box 2085, Tel.: 6445222, Jeddah. **Priv. Addr.:** Tel.: 643 9666, Jeddah, Saudi Arabia.

KAWALIEH (Houssein, Omar), Djibouti Deputy at the National Assembly. **Born** in 1955 in Djibouti. **Educ.:** Manipulator in Radiology (Diplôme d'Etat). **Career:** 1st President of Cultural Association SITTI; Elected Deputy at the National Assembly (19/12/1997 - to date); Secretary-rapporteur of the Foreign Affairs Commission and Member of the Permanent Commission. **Prof. Addr.:** National Assembly, P.O.Box 138 Djibouti, Djibouti.

KAWAR (Fakhri Anis, Najib), Jordanian writer. **Born** in 1945 in Jordan. **Married**, 2 children. **Educ.:** in Beirut, Lebanon. **Dipl.:** Licence in Arabic Literature. **Career:** Journalist of "al-Akhbar" newspaper in Jordan (1978-79); Published short stories in various Arabic magazines as well as television plays and series for children; Journalist at "al-Rai" newspaper (1974-78), (1981-). **Publ.:** children's stage play "Watan al-Assafer" (1983); several short stories collections. **Member:** Arab Writers Association, Damascus, Jordanian Journalists Union and Jordanian Writers Association. **Addr.:** al-Rai newspaper, P.O.Box 6710, Amman, Jordan.

KAWAR (Ghassoub F.), Jordanian Businessman. **Born** on November 28, 1949 in Amman, Jordan. **Son** of Faddoul Kawar (Officer) **and** Mrs. nee Najla Jabbour. **Married** on February 3, 1980 in Amman to Maha Jiryes, 3 children: Faddoul (05/05/1981), Ramez (10/10/1983), Shaden (12/05/1990). **Educ.:** Tawjihi - Bishop's School, Amman; American University of Beirut (AUB) B.Sc. Major Mathematics. **Dipl.:** Diploma in Shipping, London School for Foreign Trade. **Career:** Teacher (Bahrain Government); Assistant Manager Amin Kawar & Sons (1974-77); Manager Aqaba Shipping Company (1979-84); General Manager Amin Kawar & Sons (1984- to date). **Work:** Shipping, Forwarding and Travel Agents. **Sports:** Basket Ball. **Hobbies:** Reading, Swimming and Sports in General. **Member:** Rotary International, Royal Automobile Club. **Credit Cards:** American Express, Diner's Club. **Prof. Addr.:** Amin Kawar & Sons Co., P.O.Box 222, Tel.: 603703, Amman, Jordan. **Priv. Addr.:** P.O.Box 184505, Tel.: 821155, Amman, Jordan.

KAWAR (Kamel, Amin), Jordanian businessman. **Born** in 1925. **Son** of Amin Kawar (pharmacist) **and** Mrs. Mary Kuzma. **Married** to Widad Irani in 1955, four children.

Educ.: Bishops School Amman; School Metalliferous Mining Cornwall UK and University of Arizona, USA. **Dipl.:** B.Sc in Mining Engineering; M.Sc. in Geology. **Career:** Petroleum Engineer ARAMCO, Saudi Arabia (1950-54); Water Well Drilling in Jordan and Syria (1954-57); petroleum Engineering North East Syria (1957-58); Ground Water Exploration (1958-60); Government of Jordan Dept. Head Water, Petroleum and Mineral Exploration (1962-74); private business (since 1974) also partner and Vice Chairman Amin Kawar & Sons (Shipping, Forwarding, Insurance); Member of several Board of Directors, Chairman, Aqaba Shipping Co. (PVT) Ltd. etc. **Sports:** Walking & golf. **Hobby:** Photography. **Credit Cards:** American Express, Visa. **Prof. Addr.:** 24 Abdul Hamid Sharaf Str., Shmeisani, P.O.Box 222, Amman, Jordan. **Priv. Addr.:** Tel.: 674787, 2 Wirwar Str. Radwan, P.O.Box 222, Amman, Jordan.

KAWAR (Tawfiq, Amin), Jordanian Businessman, **Born** on November 4th, 1927. **Qualifications:** LLB University College/London University, Barrister-At-Law (Lincoln's Inn January 1952). **Career:** 1952-1955, Jordan Phosphate Mines Co./Amman. Secretary of the Board of Directors/Mines Manager at Rouseifeh. 1955-1957, Jordan Phosphate Mines Co./Amman, Sales Export Manager. 1957-1965, Amin Kawar & Sons Co./ Amman, Managing Director since 1965, Amin Kawar & Sons Co./Amman, Chairman/ Managing Director and since 1966 Honorary Consul General for Denmark in Jordan. **Ex Board Memberships:** Aqaba Port Corporation; Jordan Phosphate Mines Co. Ltd.; Amman Chamber of Commerce 1974-1986; Jordan Chemical Industries Co. Ltd; Jordan National Shipping Lines Co. Ltd. (The National Line of Jordan) 1977-1986 (also one of the founders) and Vice-Chairman for the last four years; Central Bank of Jordan, 1986-1989; Jordan National Bank, 1992-1996, Aqaba Ports Corporation. **Present Board Memberships - Public Shareholding Companies:** Jordan Investments Co. Ltd. (manufacturers of Amstel Beer and soft drinks); Jordan Wood Industries (JWICO) (Manufacturers of wooden doors, Kitchens, office and bedroom furniture); United Insurance Co./Vice Chairman. **Private Shareholding Companies:** In addition to above, also Chairman/ Managing Director of the following: United RoRo Shipping Agencies; Red Sea Shipping Agency; Manara Shipping Agency; **Others:** ex Shipping Agents Association - Jordan, Chairman, 1974-1996; ICC / National Committee of Jordan, Vice-President. **International Organisation:** Multiport Ship Agencies Network, London (an international club of 92 leading ship agents spread out in 95 countries around the world, founder member), Chairman 1982-1985 & 1995-1996; member of the ICC / Commission on Maritime and Surface Transport, Air Cargo and Air Transport, Paris 1988-Until present; Member of the Board of Directors of ICC/ IMB (International Maritime Bureau/ Commercial Crime Service, London), since 1990 until present. **Societies:** Enrolled in the following Societies: Anglo Jordanian Society, London (Life member); Petra National Trust (life member); Amman Rotary Club (since 1960 and was President in 1972-1973, Rotary District Governor 1996-1997, District 2450 comprising Bahrain, Cyprus, Egypt, Jordan, Lebanon and Sudan and now member) Jordanian Scandinavian Friendship Association, (founder and President); The National Society for the Preservation of the Heritage of Madaba and its Surburbs (founder and ex honorary secretary and now advisor); Member of: Jordanian British Society, Amman; Jordanian Businessmen Association; Jordan-Japan Friendship Association, Amman; Jordanian-Korean Friendship Association, Amman; World Affairs Council; Welfare Association, Geneva; American-Anti Discrimination Committee, Washington, DC; Royal Society for Conservation of Nature, Amman; Es-Salt Development Corporation; Jordan Lebanese Association. **Clubs:** The Orthodox Society Amman (honorary treasurer); Member of: Royal Automobile Club; Dunes Club; French Jordanian Business Club. **Awards:** Decorated by Denmark, Egypt, Sweden, Jordan, and Great Britain as Honorary OBE. **Sports** previously Tennis, Squash and presently walking. **Hobbies:** Reading, Art Collection. **Address:** Amin Kawar & Sons Co., 24 Sharif Abdul Hamid Sharaf St., Shmeisani, P.O.Box 222 Amman 11118 - Jordan. Tel: (962 6) 5603703 -13 lines, Fax: (962 6) 5604664, E-mail: tawfiq@kawar.com.jo; Telex 23111, 21212 Kawar jo. Aqaba port Office: Tel: (962 3) 2014217/8, Fax: (2013618), P.O.Box 22 Aqaba.

KAWARI (Hamad, Abdelaziz, al), Qatari diplomat. **Born** in 1948 in Doha, Qatar. **Son** of Abdelaziz al-Kawari. **Married** to Miss Zeinab al-Badrawi in 1973, three children. **Educ.:** College of Dar al-Ulum, Cairo University and Jesuit University in Beirut. **Dipl.:** B.A. **Career:** Chargé d'Affaires, Beirut (1972-74); Ambassador to Syria (1974-79); to France, also accredited to Spain, Switzerland, Italy and Greece and Permanent Representative to UNESCO (1979-84); Permanent Representative to UN (1984-89); presently Ambassador to U.S.A. **Medals:** Légion d'Honneur and honours from governments of Syria, France, Spain and Italy. **Hobbies:** Sports and reading. **Addr.:** Ministry of Foreign Affairs, Doha, Qatar.

KAWARI (Issa, Ghanem, al), Qatari politician. **Born** on February 20, 1942 in Doha, Qatar. **Son** of Ghanem Jasim al-Kawari. **Married**, 4 children: Talal, Mai, Hameedah and Saud. **Educ.:** American Unisersity of Beirut, AUB, Beirut; University of Exeter, Exeter, England. **Dipl.:** B.A. in Public Administration and Political Studies (1969); Ph.D. in Public Administration and Economics. **Career:** Director of Administration of Shell Co. (1961-65); Shell Co. of Qatar (June 1969- Dec.14, 1970); Director of Deputy Amir's Office, Qatar (Dec.15, 1970- Feb.21, 1972); Director of Amir's Office (Feb.22 1972- July 1989); Minister of Information (April 1972- July 1989); Minister of Diwan Amiri Affairs (since July 1989 to July 1995). **Medals:** King Abdul-Aziz al-Saud Sash (2nd Order), Kingdom of Saudi Arabia (April 29, 1973); Medal of the Republic (1st Order), Arab Republic of Egypt (July 10, 1974); Medal of the "Kwakab" of Jordan (1st class), Hashimite Kingdom of Jordan (July 15, 1974); Highest Order, Medal of the Republic, Republic of Tunis (July 22, 1975); Grand Order "al-Alawi" Medal, Kingdom of Morocco (July 25, 1975); Medal of the Crown (2nd Order), Iran (Nov. 13, 1975); Grand Officier de la Légion d'Honneur, Republic of France (Dec.9, 1975); The Medal of Oman (2nd Order), Sultanate of Oman (Dec.20, 1975); Diagam Tanda Kehormation, Republic of Indonesia (Oct.12, 1977); Order Francisco de Miranda en la Primera Class, Venezeula (May 19, 1979); Kuwait Medal (Sash) (1st Class Order), Kuwait (Feb.15, 1982); Medal of Merit for Distinguished Diplomatic Service, (Guang Hui Medal), Republic of Korea (April 21, 1984); First Class Order of the Sacred Treasure, Japan (April 23, 1984); Knight of the Grand Cross of the Royal Victorian Order (KGCVO); U.K. (Nov. 1985); National Order of Cedar- Grand Sash- (June 22, 1986). **Sports:** Tennis, skiing, water skiing, horse-riding and swimming. **Credit Cards:** American Express; Diner's Club. **Addr.:** In exile in France.

KAWARI (Mohamad, Yusuf), Qatari businessman and Company Director. **Born** in Qatar. **Son** of Yusuf Kawari. **Educ.:** Secondary and Higher. **Career:** Director and Partner "Trading and Building Contracting Company"; Chairman, Mohd. Yusuf al-Kawari & Sons; Mycko Steel. **Addr.:** P.O.Box 323 and P.O.Box 2668, Doha, Qatar.

KAYAL (Alawi, Darweesh, Dr.), Saudi former government minister. **Born** on December 5, 1936 in Jeddah, Saudi Arabia. **Son of** Darweesh Kayyal (civil servant). **Married** in 1964 in Jeddah, 3 children: Amro, Hawazen and Hesham. **Educ.:** American University in Beirut (Lebanon); American University, Washington (USA), University of Colorado, Boulder, Colo. (USA). **Dipl.:** B.BA. (Bachelor of Business Administration), M.A. (Master of Business Administration), Ph.D. (Political Science). **Career:** Lecturer, Riyadh University (1961-63); Director General, Social Insurance (1963-72); Director General of Posts, Telegraph and Telephone (1972-75); Minister of PTT (since 1975 to 1995). **Awards:** Grand Cordon, King Abdulaziz; National Order of Merit; Knight Legion of Honour (France), The order of Diplomatic Merit (South Korea), the order of Star (1st class) (Jordanian), the order of Civil Merit (Spanish), the order of Brilliant Star (Taiwan). **Member:** American Political Science Association. **Attended** numerous international conferences as Head of the Saudi Delegation. **Addr.:** Riyadh. Kingdom of Saudi Arabia.

KAYAL (Rashad Abdallah), Saudi executive. **Born** in 1932 in Jeddah, Saudi Arabia. **Dipl.:** Secondary School Certificate 1957, training courses in Jeddah, Riyadh, Beirut, U.S.A. **Career:** Assistant Supervisor, Accounting Department, PETROMIN (1966); Supervisor, Accounting Department (1967); Manager, Administration and Marketing Administration, Secretary of Board of PETROMIN Lubricating Oil Co.; former member of Constituent Committee, Jeddah Lubricant Oil Refinery Co.; Director Kaynart Company Ltd. **Hobby:** Fishing. **Addr.:** P.O.Box 526, Jeddah 21421, Saudi Arabia.

KAYALI (Fawzi, al), Syrian politician. **Born** in 1923 in Aleppo, Syria. **Career:** Lawyer; Civil Servant at the Ministry of Labour and Social Affairs; Minister of Culture, Tourism and National Guidance (1970-76); former Secretary General of Syrian Arab Socialist Union and Member of Arab Socialist Union (ASU). **Addr.:** Damascus, Syria.

KAYALI (Maher, Said), Jordanian businessman. **Born** in 1948 in Ramleh, Palestine. **Married**, 2 children. **Educ.:** University of Wisconsin, USA. **Dipl.:** MBA. **Career:** Director of Arab Institute for Research and Publishing (AIRP), Beirut, Lebanon (1973-); Director of Third World Centre (1979-); Member of the International Progress Organisation, Vienna, Austria; Deputy Secretary General, Union of Arab Publishers (1984). Director, Al-Faris Publishing and Distributing Co. **Publ.:** "Marxism and Guerilla Welfare" (1973), "Orwell" (1973), "The Non-Jewish Jew" (1973), "What is Hortory" (1986), "Military Dictionary" (1986), all published by AIRP Beirut, Lebanon. **Hobby:** Sports. **Prof. Addr.:** P.O.Box 9157, Amman 11191, Tel. (6)6605432, Jordan.

KAYED (Hassan Ali), Jordanian politician. **Born** in 1918. **Married. Educ.:** American University of Beirut, Lebanon; Cairo University, Egypt. **Dipl.:** Egyptian Baccalaureate, (1940); Licence in law (1948). **Career:** Public Prosecutor, Ministry of Justice, Kerak (1946); Court President of first Instance, Kerak (1953); Attorney General for Amman (1958); Under Secretary, Ministry of Education (1961), Ministry of Justice (1962); President of the Appeals Court (1962); Minister of Education (1963-64); Senator (1963-71); Minister of the Interior (1967-68); President of the Council of Employees (1971-76); Senator (1976-84); Minister of the Interior (1984). **Medal:** Independance Meal (2nd Class). **Hobby:** reading Arabic poetry and prose. **Priv. Addr.:** Jabal Hussein, Tel.: 660833, Amman, Jordan.

KAYED (Mahmoud), Jordanian journalist. **Born** in 1933 in Salt, Jordan. **Married**, 3 children. **Educ.:** Damascus University, Syria. **Dipl.:** Ordinary National Diploma in Jordan, Degree in Law. **Career:** Official at the Ministry of Information; Director General and Member of the Executive Committee, National Union Organisation (1972-74); Director of the Editorial Board of "Al-Rai" newspaper (1974-76); Editor in Chief (1976-88); Member and Deputy Chairman of Arab Information Studies Centre (1980-); Member of the National Consultative Council (1982-84); Chief of the Journalists (1980-81), (1983-84); Member of the Board of Directors of the National Company for

Financial Investment Co. (1984-); Member of the Board of Economics and Commerce, University of Jordan (1985-); Presently, Chairman Jordan Press Foundation. **Hobbies:** Sports, travelling, reading. **Prof. Addr.:** P.O.Box 6710 Amman, Jordan. **Priv. Addr.:** al-Shumaysani, Said Qutub Street, Amman, Jordan.

KAYED (Yasin, Abdul Fattal, al), Jordanian businessman. **Born** in 1931 in Zarqa, Jordan. **Married**, 3 sons, 1 daughter. **Educ.:** Cairo University, Egypt. **Dipl.:** B.A. in Economics. **Career:** Chief of Customs, Authorities of Amman (1969); Head of the Affairs Department, Ministry of Finance, Jordan (1970); Assistant Deputy Minister of Finance (1972); Deputy Minister of Finance, Customs (1982-84); Member of the Administrative Board, Jordanian oil Refinery Co; the Joint Jordanian-Syrian Free Zone Co., the Jordanian Posts Organization and the Jordanian Free Zones organization; Director of General Water Corporation (1984-). **Decor.:** Order of the Jordanian Star (2nd Class). **Prof. Addr.:** General Water Corporation, Amman, Jordan.

KAZ (Abdallah, Ibrahim Abdallah, al), United Arab Emirates executive. **Born** in 1946 in Ras al-Khaimah, United Arab Emirates. **Son** of Ibrahim Abdallah al Kaz. **Married**, two children. **Educ.:** B.A. in Commerce (Accounting) (1971). **Career:** Financial Director, Electricity Authority, Ras al-Khaimah; Deputy Financial Director, Ministry of Finance and Industry. **Member** of Amman Sports Club. **Sport:** Football. **Addr.:** Ministry of Finance and Industry, P.O.Box 433, Abu Dhabi, United Arab Emirates.

KAZEM (Muhamad, Ibrahim), Egyptian academic. **Born** on December 26, 1928 in Cairo, Egypt. **Married**, 1 son, 2 daughters. **Educ.:** College of Education, Ain Shams University, Cairo, Egypt; Graduate School, University of Kansas, USA. **Dipl.:** B.Sc., MED, Ph.D. **Career:** Teacher in Egyptian Schools and in Aleppo Teachers' College, Syria (1950-54); First President of International Educators Organization (1956); Cultural Attaché of Egypt to the Philippines (1959-60); Assistant Professor of Education, Ain Shams University, Cairo (1957-63); Associate Professor (1963-70); Founding Dean, College of Education, al-Azhar University, Cairo; Head of Department and Professor of Department of Foundations of Education (1970-); Founding Dean, Faculty of Education, Doha, Qatar (1973-77); Chairman of the Fund Raising Committee for the Istanbul World Conference of the World Council for Curriculum and Instruction (1976); First President, University of Qatar, Doha (1977); Chairman of the Council for Higher Education, Arab Bureau of Education for the Gulf States, Saudi Arabia (1980-81); Member of the Founding Committee, Arab Gulf University, Bahrain (1980-81); Member of the Board of the Institute for the History of Arab Islamic Sciences, West Germany (1981-83); Member of the Philosophy of Education Society, USA; Chairman of the Finance Committee, World Council for Curriculum and Instruction, USA (1982-). **Publ.:** "Educational Planning in Egypt", International Institute of Educational Planning, Paris (1972) in English, "Educational Needs of Children in Egypt", National Centre for Social Research, Cairo (1973) in Arabic and several other books on education as well as articles published in magazines and journals. **Decor.:** Decorations from Philippines. **Addr.:** Cairo, Egypt.

KAZEMI (Abdul Latif, al), Kuwaiti businessman. **Born** in 1927 in Kuwait. **Son** of Abdul Hussain al-Kazemi (businessman). **Married** 3rd time to Thurya (1988), seven children: Zainab, Diya, Ibtisam, Hani, Alaam, Tariq and Mohamed Ali. **Educ.:** Kuwait University. **Career:** Member of Parliament until 1975; Chairman of Finance and Economic Committee; General Secretary of Inter-Parliamentary Union Committee; Chairman, Foreign Affairs Committee and Rapporteur (1965-72); Managing Director, United Arab Shipping, Trading and Contracting Services and Gulf Trading & Maritime Est.; has extensive business interests; Chairman Abdul Latif al-Kazemi, al-Kazemi International Commercial Group. **Credit Cards:** American Express, Diner's Club, Visa, Master Card; Berkley. **Addr.:** United Arab Shipping, Trading & Contracting Services WLL. P.O.Box 403, 13005 Safat, Kuwait, Tel.: 2463150-1-2-3, Fax: 2423714, Telex: 22105 or 22722 UNITED KT. and 46525 GULFEST KT., Kuwait. **Priv. Addr.:** Keifan, Kuwait.

KAZEMI (Abdul Muttaleb, al), Kuwaiti politician. **Born** in 1936 in Kuwait. **Married** in 1969, two children. **Educ.:** Cairo University, Boulder University, Colorado, U.S.A. **Dipl.:** M.A. Econ. **Career:** Director General State Budget Department, Ministry of Finance and Oil (1961-71); member of the National Assembly (1971); Former Chairman National Assembly Financial and Economic Committee; Director, Arabian Oil Company until 1967, Managing Director Kuwait International Investment Co. (1973-75); Minister of Oil (1975-78); representative to many conferences including Afro-Asian Conference for Economical Co-operation, Businessman since 1982. **Addr.:** c/o P.O.Box 403, Safat, Kuwait City, Kuwait.

KAZEMI (Zaid Abdul Hussain, Hassan, al), Kuwait businessman. **Born** in 1916. **Educ.:** General. **Career:** worked for "Abdul Muhsin Ali Kharafi and Muhammad Almatrook" (1933); established his own business in partnership with Abdul Rahman al-Bisher in 1943; Elected Member of Parliament (1963-71); Member of Planning Board Council (1972-77); Member of Committee for the Revision of the Constitution (1980). **Addr.:** P.O.Box 30 Safat 13001, Kuwait City, Kuwait.

KCHOUK (Hatem), Tunisian executive. **Born** in 1948 in Le Bardo, Tunisia. **Son** of Nejib Kchouk. **Married** in 1978, to Aida Jenatel, 3 children: 2 sons and 1 daughter.

Educ.: Business School, Business Law Institute, Harvard Business School, PMD (1979). **Career:** North Western Mutual Life Insurance Co., Milwaukee Wisconsin, USA (1970-); Joined Credit Commercial de France since 1971; 1971-1982: C.C.F Senior Vice President, Head of Middle East Near East Africa Dept.; 1979-82: Managing Director CCF Cofiges SA (Geneve), Member of the Board CCF MO (France); 1982-90: Founder - Chairman, CEO, Arab Tunisian Bank (Tunis); 1986-90: Founrder - Chairman, CEO Arab Financial Consultants (Tunis); 1988-90: Member of Economic and Social Council of Tunisia, Member of the Board of ENS Carte Ins. Co.; 1986- to day: Vice President of Esperance Sportium de Tunis; 1990-94: E.V.P., CCF (Paris); 1994- to day: Managing Director of Franlington Maghreb S.A.; Member of the Board: COFIB SA. Tunis; 1994-97: CCF Paris, Adviser for the Creation of Banque d'Affaires de Tunisie. **Addr.:** 6, Rue Alain Chartier, Tel.: 01 56080076, 75015 Paris, France.

KECHOUD (Mohamed), Algerian Minister for Relations with Parliament. **Born** on august 22, 1938 at Constantine. **Son** of Amar Kechoud - Trader **and** Mrs. née Aldjia Chenouf. **Married** in 1963 in Constantine to Djeghri Nabi, 6 children: Rekia, Noufel, Mouna, Oukeil, Asma, Haïfa. **Educ.:** Education School Constantine/ IBN Badis Institute Constantine/ University of Algiers/ University of Constantine/ Institute of Law-Algiers. **Dipl.:** Degree in Arab Literature/ Degree in Law/ Higher Degree in Administrative Law (Master). **Career:** President of Regional Council (Mayor)/ Director of Centers for the Martyrs' Children/ Inspector - Ministry for Moudjahidine (M.F.M.)/ Deputy Director for Social Affairs (M.F.M.)/ Regional Director/ Central Director for Social Affairs (M.F.M.)/ Central Director for Grants and Allocations/ Secretary-General (M.F.M.)/ Central Director for Grants and Allocations/ Secretary-General (M.FM.)/ Member of the National Council for Transition (Parliament)/ Joined the National Liberation Army in the End of 1955/ Sentenced to Death/ Escaped from the Jail-Constantine. **Medals:** Medal of Member of the National Liberation Army. **Sports Practised:** Football-Player in a National football Team. **Hobbies:** Reading/ Listening to Music. **Clubs:** President of a Football Club/ Previously. **Prof. Addr.:** Palais du Gouvernement (Office of the Prime Minister, Algiers, Algeria.

KEFI (Abdelrrazak Jilani), Tunisian politician. **Born** in 1938 in Kairouan, Tunisia. **Married**, 2 daughters. **Dipl.:** M.Sc. in Physical Sciences; Diploma in Chemical Engineering (Atomic Industries). **Career:** Chef de Cabinet, Ministry of Education (1980-81); Joint Secretary General, General Union of Tunisian Students (1961-63); Managing Director of Radiodiffusion Télévision Tunisienne (1981-82); Advisor to the Prime Minister (1982-83); Minister of Information (1983-86). **Decor.:** Spanish Order of Civil Merit (1983) Grand Officer of the French National Order of Merit (1983); Spanish Order of Civil Merit (1983); Grand Officer of the Order of the Republic, Tunisia (1984); Grand Officer of the Tunisian Order of Independence (1985). **Hobby:** Sports. **Priv. Addr.:** Rue Kaab Ibn Malek el-Menzah V, Tunis, Tunisia.

KEICHE (Sulaiman, al), Syrian politician. **Born** in Syria. **Educ.:** Secondary and Higher. **Career:** Minister of Information, Minister of Culture and National Guidance in the Cabinet of Dr. Youssef Zouayen (September 1965-October 1966), Minister of National Education (1966-68). **Addr.:** Damascus, Syria.

KEILANI (Musa, al, Dr.), Jordanian diplomat. **Married**, 2 sons and 1 daughter. **Educ.:** Baghdad University, Iraq; Cairo University, Egypt; University of Rome, Italy (Publicity and Information Course). **Dipl.:** B.A. in Literature, Ph.D. **Career:** Director General, Jordan News Agency (1971-73); Ambassador to Bahrain (1973-75); Director of Information (Ambassador Rank), Ministry of Foreign Affairs, Amman. Director of Press and Publications (1985-88); Editor-in-Chief Ad-Dustour Daily Newspaper (1990-1993). **Publ.:** "Israel, the years of Oppression", "Political Persuasion and Islam" (1985), "Fundamentalist Movements in Jordan" 1989). Weekly articles in Jordanian Newspapers. **Medals:** Independence Medal of Jordan (1st Class); Kawkab Medal, Jordan. **Prof. Addr.:** P.O.Box 926864, Amman, Jordan.

KELLOU (Mohamad, Massoud), Algerian diplomat. **Born** on March 17, 1931 in Mansoura (Setif). **Son** of Arezki Kellou. **Married** in 1965 to Anyssa Abdelkader, 3 daughters. **Educ.:** Faculty of Law, Universities of Algiers and Montpellier. **Dipl.:** Licentiate in Law (1954), Diploma of Advanced Studies (1955). **Career:** Lawyer in Algiers; Vice-President of Algerian Moslem Students Union (U.G.E.M.A.) in charge of Foreign Affairs; Member of F.L.N. (National Liberation Front); Representative in United Kingdom (1957-61); Chief of Provisional Government of Algeria, Diplomatic Mission to Pakistan (1961-62); Director, African, Asian and South American Affairs, Ministry of Foreign Affairs, Republic of Algeria (1962-63); Ambassador to United Kingdom (1963-64), to Czechoslovakia (1964-70), concurrently to Hungary (1965) and Poland (1966), to Argentine, Chili, Uruguay and Bolivia (1970) Embassy at Algeria 8, Pascoe Avenue-Belgravia, Harare, Zimbabwe; Ambassador to People's Republic of China (1975-77); Elected Member of Parliament for Setif in Algeria (1977); Chairman of the Foreign Affairs Committee of the People's National Assembly (March 1977-July 1979); Ambassador to Bonn, Federal Republic of Germany (1979-82), Ambassador to the Republic of Zimbabwe, Harare, (1982-84), Minister Plenipotentiary in the Ministry of Foreign Affairs in Algiers. **Priv. Addr.:** 40, Boulevard des Martyrs, Algiers, Algeria.

KERDOUDI-KOLALI (Abdeslam, Habib), Moroccan neurosurgeon. **Born** on 26 February 1931 at Fez, Morocco.

Son of Habib Kerdoudi-Kolali (retired) **and** Hajja Fattouma Tazi. **Married** in Casablanca to Françoise Bastide, 3 children: Nadia, Leila, Myriam Nora. **Educ.:** Faculty of Medicine of Paris. **Dipl.:** M.D. specialised in Neurosurgery. **Career:** Surgeon of Hospitals; Head Physician, Casablanca Sector; Head, Neurosurgery Service, Hospital Averroes, Casablanca. **Publ.:** Numerous publications. **Sports:** Football, tennis, swimming. **Member:** C.C.C. Casablanca; Yacht Club Mahamadia. **Prof. Addr.:** 54 Blvd. Omar Idrissi, Tel.: 267942, 278034, 267300, 272001, Casablanca, Morocco.

KERSTEN (Jean Hendrik Jr.), Manager of Maritime Agency, Honorary Consul of the Netherlands in Casablanca. **Born** in the Netherlands. **Son** of Jean Hendrik Kersten (maritime agent) **and** Mrs., née Adrian. **Married** in 1957 to M.H. de Ponthaud. **Educ.:** Secondary School. **Career:** Reserve officer of the Dutch Naval Force, Probationer with Nievelt-Goudrian and Co. (Rotterdam), Seconded to Nantes (France), then to Casablanca (Morocco), Deputy-Director of the subsidiary Eurofrican Cargoes in Casablanca, President of the Dutch-Moroccan Chamber of Commerce (1958), Honorary Consul of the Netherlands in Casablanca since 1957. **Prof. Addr.:** 7 Aristide-Birand Street, Casablanca, Morocco.

KETTANI (Hamza, al), Moroccan academic. **Born** in 1940 in Morocco. **Married,** 3 children. **Educ.:** University of Damascus, Syria; University of Paris, France. **Dipl.:** B.Sc. in Physics and Chemistry; Ph.D. in Mineral Chemistry and Physics. **Career:** Research Engineer, BRPM Mineral Treatment Laboratories (1962-68); Teacher of Chemistry, Lycée Mohammed V, Rabat (1964-65); Teacher of Mineral and Organic Chemistry, Ecole Normale Superieure (1964-66); Director of the Office of the Minister of Higher Education (1968-); Lecturer, Mohammadia Engineering School, Mohammad V University (1969-); Chairman of Minerology Department, Mohammad V University (1970-); Head of Department of Mineral Engineering, Mohammadia Engineering School (1970-75); Visiting Professor, Laval University, Quebec, Canada (1970); Visiting Professor, University of California, Berkeley, USA (1972); Member of the National Association of Mining Engineers; Member of the National Union of Moroccan Engineers, the Technical Committees for the Preparation of the Five Year Plan, the Moroccan Geology Association and Member of the Rabat Council; Member, French Association Doctors of Science; Director of Mohammadia Engineering School, Mohammed V University (1975-); WHO Consultant for Training of Sanitary Engineering Staff (1977-); Minister of Posts and Telecommunications (Feb. 1995-Aug.A 1997). **Publ.:** numerous papers published in professional magazines and journals. **Hobby:** Swimming. **Prof. Addr.:** Mohammadia Engineering School, P.O.Box 765, Agdal, Rabat, Morocco and Ministers Office, Ave. Moulay Hassan, Rabat, Morrocco.

KHABBAZ (Abdallah, M.), United Arab Emirates executive. **Born** in 1943 in Amman, Jordan. **Son** of Major Morris Khabbaz (Assistant to Chief of Army Staff) **and** Mrs. Narjes Sirhan. **Married** in 1968 in Toronto, Canada to Mary Ann Resurreccion, two daughters. **Educ.:** American University of Beirut. **Dipl.:** B.A. **Career:** Commercial Manager for Middle East of Sabena - Belgian World Airlines (till 1979); General Manager, Pakistan for Gulf Air (1979-80); joined the private company of the chairman of Gulf Air, His Excellency Ali Bin Khalfan al-Dhahry, Ali & Sons Company as Managing Director; Also Chairman of Publication Committee & Managing Editor of "Business Administration" Magazine; AUB Correspondent of "al-Masorif" (the Banks) Magazines. **Sports:** Swimming and walking. **Hobbies:** Reading Management/ Financial Books and other related novels, travel. **Member of:** SIND Club, Karachi; The Country Club, Abu Dhabi. **Credit Cards:** AMEX, VISA, Euro Card. **Prof. Addr.:** Ali & Sons Co. Bldg., Zayed II Street, P.O.Box 915, Tel. (09712) 723900, Telex: 23900 ABKA, Telegraph: ABKACORP, Abu Dhabi, UAE.

KHADDAM (Abdulhalim), Syrian politician and vice president of Syrian Arab Republic. **Born** in 1932, in Banyas, Tartous, Syria. **Educ.:** Damascus University. **Dipl.:** Bachelor of Law **Career:** Lawyer; Governor of Damascus (1964); Minister of Economy and Foreign Trade (1969); Vice-Prime Minister and Minister of Foreign Affairs (1970-84); represented his country as an observer at the Lebanese Reconciliation Conference held in Geneva (31.10.83- 4.11.83) and in Lausanne (12- 26.3.84). **Member** of the Leadership Baath Party; presently, Vice-President of Syria. **Addr.:** Minister's Office, Damascus, Syria.

KHADDURI (Mubarak, Salih, al), Omani politician. **Born** in 1942 in Oman. **Educ.:** University of Baghdad, Iraq; University of Glasgow, UK, University of London, UK. **Dipl.:** M.B., Ch.B., Diploma in Tropical Medicine and Hygiene. **Career:** Consultant (internal medicine and paediatrics), Ruwi Hospital, Omani Ministry of Health; Minister of Health (1974). **Prof. Addr.:** Muscat, Oman.

KHADEM (Hassan, Saad), Egyptian chemist. **Born** on March 24, 1923 in Cairo. **Son** of Saad Khadem **and** Mrs., née Ni'mat Zulfiqar. **Married** on September 5, 1952 to Miss Nadia Said, 2 children: Samiha and Saad. **Educ.:** Cairo University, Alexandria University, Imperial College of London, University of Zurich (Switzerland). **Dipl.:** Bachelor of Science with honors (1946), Doctor of Science, Technology E.T.H. (1949), Doctor of Philosophy (1952), Doctor of Science (1964), Doctor of Science (1967). **Career:** Joined the Faculty of Science, Alexandria University since 1952, Professor of Organic Chemistry since 1964, Fulbright Scholar Ohio State University (1963-64). **Publ.:** Author of studies and researches on synthesis of heterocyclic compounds from sugars, leading to discovery of two new reactions of Sugar osazones.

Awards: National Scientific Award and Medal (1963). **Member** of America, British, Swiss and Egyptian Chemists societies. **Prof. Addr.:** Alexandria University, Alexandria. **Priv. Addr.:** 19, Maarouf ar-Rassafi street, Ramla, Alexandria, Egypt.

KHADEM (Shamseddine, al), Iraqi former general manager Rafidain Bank. **Born** in 1928. **Educ.:** Graduate, College of Commerce and Economics, Baghdad. **Career:** Central Bank of Iraq (six years), Ambassador, Ministry of Foreign Affairs, General Manager Rafidain Bank of Baghdad (1963). **Office:** Baghdad, Iraq.

KHADER (Bishara), Palestinian writer. **Born** in 1944 in Zababdeh, Palestine. **Educ.:** University of Louvain, Belgium; Johns Hopkins University; Bologna Centre, Italy. **Dipl.:** B.A. in Political Sciences, Diploma in International Relations, Ph.D. in Political, Social and Economic Sciences. **Career:** Director, Arab Research Centre, University of Louvain (1973-). **Publ.:** "Anatomie de Sionisme et d'Israêl", Algiers (1974) French and Spanish translations, "Textes de la Révolution Palestinienne", Paris (1975), co-author with Naim Khader, French and Italian translations, "Histoire de la Palestine", Tunis (1976-79), 3 vols., "Dialogue Euro-Arabe et Crise Energetique", University of Louvain Arab Research Centre (1976), co-author with Naim Khader, "Transfers Technologiques", UCL (1980), "Le Monde Arabe et Développement Economique", Paris (1981), "Coopération Euro-Arabe: diagnostic et prospective", CERMAC-UCL (1984). **Hobbies:** Piano, chess, tennis. **Prof. Addr.:** CERMAC, 3 Place Montesquieu, SHI 1348 Louvain-la-Neuve, Belgium.

KHADER (Mohamad), Tunisian pedagogical adviser. **Born** on 1st August 1929. **Married**, 6 children. **Career:** Teacher, Lycée de Bizerte, (1952), Pedagogical Adviser (1962), Deputy Mayor, Bizerte (1957-60), Municipal Counsellor (1960-63), First Vice-President, Municipality of Bizerte (1966-69), Municipal Counselor (1969). **Publ.:** Author of various articles in Tunisian Journals and reviews. **Addr.:** 39, Rue de Tunis 39, Bizerte, Tunisia.

KHADER (Sudgi), Jordanian professor of soil science, Dean of Research and dean of faculty of agriculture. **Born** on November 20, 1937 at Deir el-Ghusun, Tulkarm, Jordan. **Son** of Rafieg Khader **and** Mrs. née Nasrah Qedan. **Married** on June 29, 1975 in Tulkarm to Wisam Breik, 2 children: Rawand (29.7.1976), Iyas (6.11.1980). **Educ.:** Deir el-Ghusun School (1951); al-Fadiliyyah School - Tulkarm (1953); Kadoorie-Agricultural School - Tulkarm (1956); University of Hohenheim-Stuttgart-Hohenheim. **Career:** Assistant Professor, University of Hohenheim (Nov. 1966 - Jan. 1971); Associate Professor, University of Libya, Tripoli (Jan. 1971 - Oct. 1974); Professor of Soil Science, University of Jordan, Amman (Oct. 1974 - till now); Chairman of Soil Department (1975-80); Associate Dean (1980-84); Dean of Research (1989-90); Dean-Faculty of Agriculture, Amman (1990-92); Professor of Soil Science, Department of Soil and Irrigation, Amman. **Other Information:** He got Fulbright Scholarship at University of Hawaii (1984-85); and D.A.A.D. Germany scholarship for June-September 74, 78, 83, 86, 89, 90 at Universities in Germany. **Sports:** Swimming. **Hobby:** Photography. **Member:** German Soil Science Association, International Soil Science Association, Arab Biology Union. **Credit Card:** Visa. **Prof. Addr.:** University of Jordan, Faculty of Agriculture, Tel.: 5355000-2517, Amman, Jordan. **Priv. Addr.:** Rasheed Subburb, Tel.: 5167185, Amman, Jordan.

KHADIR (Abdullah Hassan, al), Sudanese diplomat. **Born** in 1925 in Sudan. **Married**, 2 sons. **Educ.:** Faculty of Arts, Gordon College, Khartoum. **Dipl.:** Diploma in Arts and Degree in Public Administration. **Career:** Ministry of the Interior (1949-56); District Commissioner; 1st Secretary, Ministry of Foreign Affairs (1956); Consul General to Uganda and Kenya; Head of Political Section, Ministry of Foreign Affairs (1958); Ambassador to Ghana (1960-64); Director, Ministry of Information and Labour; Ambassador to France (1965-69); Under Secretary, Ministry of Foreign Affairs (1969); Served on Sudanese delegation to UN and the Organization of African Unity; Ambassador to the Court of St. James, London, UK (1971-72); Ambassador to USSR (1972); Minister of Natural Resources (1972-73); Minister of the Interior (1973-75); visited Libya and USSR in 1974; Secretary General to the Presidency (1975). **Addr.:** Khartoum, Sudan.

KHADRAWY (Mohsen, el, Prof. Dr.), Egyptian academic. **Born** on August 1, 1935 in Cairo, Egypt. **Son** of Mohammed el-Khadrawy. **Married** on May 1963 in Cairo, Egypt to Prof. Dr. Widad Gad, 2 children: one daughter, Mme Nedaa, Mohsen (August 1965), one son, Gehad Mohsen (July 1970). **Educ.:** High School, The Faculty of Fine Arts, Cairo; The High Institute of Art Education, Cairo. **Dipl.:** M.S., Ph.D. of Art. **Career:** General Director of Art Museums, Cairo (1957-1985); Museologist, Restorator, Art Critic, Artist (Painter); presently Dean, Faculty of Fine Arts, Minia University, Egypt. **Other Information:** I.I.C. London, I.C.O.M. Paris. **Hobbies:** All sorts of Art. **Member:** Zamalek Club. **Prof. Addr.:** Faculty of Fine Arts, Minia University, Tel.: 086323085, Minia, Egypt. **Priv. Addr.:** 53, Str. Groud Gamal, Agouza, Giza, Tel.: Home 3473265, Workshop: 3742595, Cairo, Egypt.

KHAFAGY (Mohamed, Abdel Moneim), Egyptian poet and professor. **Born** in 1915 in Egypt. **Son** of Abdel Moneim Khafagy **and** Mrs. Shouk Khafagy. **Married** in 1943, one son. **Educ.:** Azhar University. **Dipl.:** Licentiate of Literature and Doctorate of Literature. **Career:** Teacher of Arabic language and Arabic Literature in the Azhar University (1948); Dean of the Faculty (1974-78); Chairman of al-Hadara Magazine (1986). **Publ.:** Published about 500 books on literature, poetry, history and islamic writings. **Decor.:** First class medal of Science and Arts given by President Mubarak. **Hobbies:** Reading, writing, music. **Prof. Addr.:** P.O.Box 46 Mohamed Farid Post Office, Cairo, Egypt.

KHAFAJI (Abbas, Nasser Hussin, al), Iraqi university professor. **Born** in 1930 in Baghdad. **Son** of Nasser Hussain al-Khafaji **and** Mrs., née Abbasia Tohma. **Married** on August 1965 to Miss Soumayya Faeq Hassan, 4 children: Nada, Zaid, No'm and Maha. **Educ.:** Universities of Arizona, Colorado, Virginia and Texas. **Dipl.:** Bachelor of Science in Civil Engineering (1953), Master of Science in Irrigation and Drainage Engineering (1956), Master of Science in Structural Engineering (1963), Master of Science in Soil and Foundation (1964), Doctor in Irrigation and Applied Hydraulics (1961). **Career:** Instructor, Universiy of Baghdad (1956-59), Assistant Professor, Virgin Polytechnic Institute, U.S.A. (1961-64) and University of Baghdad (1964-65), Assistant Professor and Dean of Engineering College, Mosul University (1965-70), Associate Professor (1970-72) then Professor of Civil Engineering, University of Mosul since August 1972. **Publ.:** Author of numerous studies and papers printed in U.S.A., Iraq and Poland. **Member** of several Honour and Professional societies. **Hobby:** Reading. **Priv. Addr.:** al-Majmou'a ath-Thaqafia, Tel.: 4231/51, Mosul, Iraq.

KHAFAJY (Hassan Ali), Saudi academic. **Born** in 1938, in Mecca, Saudi Arabia. **Dipl.:** Ph.D. (Urban Sociology). **Career:** Vice Dean (1966), Dean, Faculty of Education, Mecca (1966-72); Associate Professor, Sociology Department, Faculty of Arts, King Abdulaziz University. **Member:** King Abdulaziz University Council (1972-74); Higher Council of Faculties (1966-72); Alternate Chairman, member of Joint Council of the Faculties of Shari'a (Islamic Law) and Education, Mecca (1972); member of Constituent Board, King Abdulaziz University (1966-71). **Publ.:** Dirasat Fi Ilmil Ijtima (Studies in Sociology) (1972-73), al-Taghayyor al-Ijtimaie Wal Mujtama al-Mutahaddir (Social Change and Urban Community) (1972-84), Tareekhul Tafkeer al-Ijtima'ie (History of Social Thought) (1976); articles; radio talks and programmes. **Hobbies:** Reading, travel. **Addr.:** Jeddah, Saudi Arabia.

KHAIR (Marwan, Mahmoud), Jordanian official. **Born** in 1939 in Amman, Jordan. **Married**, 2 children. **Educ.:** Michigan State University, USA; Florida State University, USA. **Dipl.:** M.A. and Ph.D. in Mass Communications. **Career:** Chief News Editor, Amman Radio and Jordan TV (1963-72); Founder and Head of Informational communication and Development Department, Jordan TV (1974-75); Head of News Department (1980-81); Head of Planning and Research Department (1981); Head of Programming Department (1981-84); Assistant Professor of Yarmouk University (1984); Director, Ministry of Youth (1986-). **Publ.:** "Proceedings of the Sixty Asian-Pacific Cultural Scholars Convention" Taipei (1982) and Rabat (1983) in Arabic; articles in "Journal of Speech Communication" (1978). **Hobbies:** Sports, reading. **Addr.:** Jabal al-Hussain, P.O.Box 921004, Amman, Jordan.

KHAIRAT (Taha), Syrian diplomat, politician. **Born** in Deraa, Syria. **Educ.:** M.A. in Law. **Career:** Member of the Baath Regional Command (1971); member of the Arab Socialist Baath Party Command in Syria (1971); Minister of Local Administration (1975); Ambassador to Sofia, Bulgaria (1982). **Addr.:** Ministry of Foreign Affairs, Damascus, Syria.

KHAIRI (Ishaq, Najati, al), Jordanian dentist. **Born** in 1947 in Ramla, Jordan. **Married**, 3 sons. **Dipl.:** B.DS. in Dentistry, Ph.D. in Orthodontics. **Career:** Dental Surgeon (1970); Orthodontist, Ministry of Health (1977), Jordanian Medical Center (1980); Member of the Board of Jordanian Dentists Association. **Publ.:** "Vacam in Orthodontic Treatment of Children". **Addr.:** P.O.Box 926816, Amman, Jordan.

KHAJAH (Fareed, al), Bahraini trader. **Born** in Bahrain. **Son** of Mohamad Saleh (merchant) **and** Mooza Jassim al-Khajah. **Married** to Raja Yusuf Lori. **Career:** Director of al-Khajah Group of Companies. **Clubs:** Marina Club. **Credit Cards:** American Express, London No. 1 Club. **Addr.:** North Industrial Area, Sitra, Tel.: 730611, 731138, 731139, 730811, Bahrain.

KHALAF (Essam A.), Bahraini Civil Engineer **Title:** Director of Roads. **Born** in 1956 in Bahrain. **Son of Abdulla Khalaf (deceased) and** Mrs. Naziha Al-Meer (deceased). **Married** on February 10, 1987 in Bahrain to Dr. Samira Al-Matrook, 2 children: Ali (1992), Razan (1995). **Educ.:** American University of Beirut, University of Texas at Austin, Virginia Polytechnic Institute of State University, University of Bahrain. **Dipl.:** B.Sc. Civil Eng. (Aug. 1978), M.Sc. Civil Eng. (Transportation Planning) Aug. 1981, Diploma-Advance Management. **Career:** Trainee Road Engineer (1978-1980); Road Engineer (1981-1986); Senior Traffic Engineer (1986-1989); Manager Traffic Engineer & Planning (1989-1992); Director of Roads (Jan. 1992- Now). **Medals:** His Highness the Amir of Bahrain Medal for Academic Executive (1981); University of Bahrain Dean's Prize (1985); General Committee of Traffic Safety Decoration (Certificate); Bahrain Society of Engineers Decoration (Certificate). **Sport:** General Fitness. **Hobby:** Reading. **Credit Cards:** American Express, Visa. **Prof. Addr.:** P.O.Box 5, Roads Directorate, Manama, Bahrain, Tel.: (0973) 534477. **Priv. Addr.:** P.O.Box 12112, Manama, Bahrain, Tel.: (0973) 721801.

KHALAF (Hussain), Egyptian lawyer and statesman. **Born** in Egypt. **Educ.:** Cairo and Paris Universities. **Dipl.:** Licentiate and Doctorate in Law. **Career:** Lecturer in Law, Cairo University (until 1958 and 1961-64); Minister (1958-61); Minister of Foreign Cultural Relations (1964-65);

Leader of Arab Republic of Egypt Delegation to United Nations (Geneva, 1965); Ambassador to Iraq (1966-68). **Addr.:** c/o Ministry of Foreign Affairs, Cairo, Egypt.

KHALAF (Khadem), Iraqi diplomat. **Born** in 1922 in Najaf. **Educ.:** American University of Beirut, Higher International Studies Institute of Paris. **Dipl.:** Bachelor of Arts (Economics, 1943). **Career:** Ministry of Foreign Affairs, Permanent Mission of Iraq to the United Nations (1948); Represented his country at several organization, conferences, committees; Director General of the United Nations Department in the Ministry of Foreign Affairs (1962-64); Under Secretary of the Ministry of Foreign Affairs (1964-66); Permanent Representative of Iraq at the United Nations (1966-67); Head of Iraqi Delegation to International Conference on Human Rights (1968); Ambassador to United Kingdom (1968). **Addr.:** Ministry of Foreign Affairs, Baghdad, Iraq.

KHALAF (Khaled Yusuf, al), Saudi civil servant. **Born** in 1944 at Hail, Saudi Arabia. **Dipl.:** Ph.D. (Thermochemistry) USA. **Career:** Assistant Professor, University of Petroleum and Minerals (1974); Head, Chemistry Department 1975; Director Oil Testing Center (1976); Director General Saudi Arabian Standards Organization (1977). Chairman, Food Safety Permanent Committee. **Member:** American Chemical Society, International Housing Association; Board, SASO; Higher Committee, Environment Protection Agency (EPA). **Publ.:** Scientific papers in international chemical periodicals in addition to articles published in local magazines and newspapers. **Hobbies:** Swimming, tennis, football, Reading. **Prof. Addr.:** P.O.Box 7481, Tel.: 4520035, Riyadh 11461, Kingdom of Saudi Arabia.

KHALBOUS (Ali), Tunisian businessman and president director general. **Born** on May 23, 1941 in Nabeul, Tunisia. **Son** of Sadok Khalbous (decesased) **and** Mrs. Habiba née Bouhanek. **Married** on December 20, 1969 in Tunis to Mounira Said, two children: Slim (02/01/1971), Sonia (10/05/1974). **Educ.:** Institut des Hautes Etudes Commerciales. **Dipl.:** Diplôme des Hautes Etudes Commerciales. **Career:** Assistant General Manager, Société Tunisienne d'acconage et de Manutention; Counsellor, Société Nationale de cellulose; President Director General at "Transtours"; presently President Director General, "S.N.T.R.I" - Société Nationale de Transport Interurbain. Several times Vice-President at the Municipalities of Tunis and Ariana. **Award:** Officer of the Order of Tunisian Republic. **Member:** President de l'Association des Diplomés en Hautes Etudes Commerciales; President, Tunisian Rotary Club. **Prof. Addr.:** "S.N.T.R.I", Société Nationale de Transport Interurbain, Rue No. 8007, Avenue Mohamed V, P.O.Box 40, Zone Montplaisir 1002 Tunis Belvédère, Tel.: 781.005, 784.433, Telex: SNTRI 13335 TN, Tunis, Tunisia. **Priv. Addr.:** 82, Rue Abderrazak Chraibi, Tel.: 244.199, Tunis, Tunisia.

KHALED (Ahmed), Tunisian politician and author (writer).. **Born** in 1936 in Sousse, Tunisia. **Married. Educ.:** University of Paris, France. **Dipl.:** M.A. **Career:** Chargé de Mission to the Prime Ministry (1970); Major of Sousse (1975-80); Former Central Committee Member of Destourien Socialist Party; Former Member of Fondation Nationale de l'Etablissement de Textes, des Etudes et de la Traduction; former Council Member of the Organisation of Arab Towns (OVA); Former International council Member of Federation Mondiale des villes Jumelées (FMVJ); Head of the Cabinet, Ministry of Cultural Affairs and General Inspector of National Education (1981-89); Secretary of State for Education (1989-90); Minister of Culture and Information (1991). Ambassador of Tunisia (Rabat, Morocco) (1991-92); Ambassador of Tunisia (Moscow) (1992-96). **Priv. Addr.:** 1 Rue Tahar Ben Achour, Hamman-Lif, Tunisia.

KHALED (Faisal, al), Kuwaiti politician. **Born** in 1944 in Kuwait. **Son** of Abdul Razzak Khaled. **Married** in 1973, 3 sons, 1 daughter. **Dipl.:** B.A. (Econ.) **Career:** Civil Service Commission, Kuwait (1971-72); Economist, Kuwait Fund for Arab Economic Development (1972-74); Director of Operations (1974-78); Deputy Director General (1978-81); Director General, Kuwait Fund for Economic Development, Kuwait (1981); Member of the Board, Central Bank of Kuwait; Governor, OPEC Fund for International Development, Representing Kuwait; Deputy Governor IFAD, Kuwait; Governor, Arab Fund, Kuwait; Minister of Commerce and Industry (1988- April 1991). **Hobby:** Swimming. **Addr.:** Kuwait City, Kuwait.

KHALED (Hag Abdalla, al), Sudanese bank manager. **Born** in 1937 in Omdurman. **Son** of Khaled Khalid. **Married** in 1962, 1 son. **Educ.:** Sudan and U.K. Banking and Management Courses. **Career:** Barclays Bank (1957-69); Bank of Khartoum (1969-77); Deputy General Manager Faisal Islamic Bank, Khartoum Branch, Sudan (since 1977). **Addr.:** P.O.Box 2415, Tel.: 75590, Telex: 519 A/B BANK ISLAMI, Khartoum, Sudan.

KHALED HASSAN (Abbas, Major General), Sudanese politician. **Born** in 1936 in Sudan. **Married**, three children. **Educ.:** Graduated from Military College (1958); Courses in UK (1959 and 1961). **Career:** Commisioned into the Armoured Corps (1958); Played a leading part in the 25 May 1959 Revolution; Deputy Commander in Chief and Chief of Staff with rank of Brigadier (1969); Major General (1970); First Vice President (1969); became one of the inaugural members of the Political Bureau of the Sudan Socialist Union (SSU) (1972); appointed to Central Committee of the SSU (1974), (Party now banned). **Addr.:** P.O.Box 1850, Khartoum, Sudan.

KHALED (Mansour), Sudanese diplomat and lawyer. **Born** in 1931 in Omdurman, Sudan. **Son** of Khalid Mohamed **and** Sara née Sawi. **Educ.:** University of Khartoum,

Sudan; University of Pennsylvania, USA; University of Algiers, Algeria; University of Paris, France. **Dipl.:** LL.B (1957); LL.M (1960); Diploma of Higher Studies (1963); LL.D (Doctorat d'Etat in International law) (1965); **Career:** Attorney in Khartoum (1957-59); Legal Officer, UN Secretariat, New York (1962-63); Assistant Resident Representative, UNDP, Algeria (1964-65); Bureau of Relations with Member States at UNESCO Paris (1965-69); Visiting Professor of International Law, University of Colorado (1968); Minister of Youth and Social Affairs (1969-71); Special Consultant and Personal Representative of the UNESCO Director General for UNRWA Fund Raising Mission (1970); Chairman, Delegation of the Democratic Republic of Sudan to the XXV session of the UN General Assembly (1970); Chairman of the Delegation of the Democratic Republic of the Sudan to the XXVI, XXVII, XXVII, XXIX sessions and the Sixth Special Session of the UN General Assembly 1971, 1972, 1973 and 1974; Permanent Representative of the Democratic Republic of the Sudan to the UN (1971); President of the UN Security Council (1972); Minister of Foreign Affairs (1971-75); Chairman of the OAU Ministerial Committee on the impact of oil prices on Africa and Afro-Arab economic cooperation (1973-75); Minister of Education (1975-77); Member of the Political Bureau of the Central Committee of the Sudanese Socialist Union (1974-78); Assistant to the President for Foreign Affairs and Coordination (1967); Fellow, Woodrow Wilson Center, Smithsonian Institution in Washington, D.C. (1979-89); Special Consultant and Personal Representative of the Executive Director of UNEP, UN (1982); Visiting Professor on Development Studies at the University of Khartoum, Sudan (1982); Consultant on Finance and Investment (1980-); Consultant on International Affairs, UN, Switzerland (1982-); **Publ.:** "Private Laws in Sudan" (1970), "The Nile Basin, Present and Future" (1971), "Solution of the Southern Problem and its African Implications" (1972), "A Dialogue with the Sudanese Intellectuals", "The Decision-Making Process in Foreign Policy" (1973) and "The Sudan Experiment with Unity" (1973. **Addr.:** P.O.Box 3029, Khartoum, Sudan.

KHALED (Mohsen), Egyptian Banker. **Born** in 1944 in Egypt. **Married**, two children. **Educ.:** Graduate School of Business, Long Island University, New York, USA. **Career:** The Chase Manhattan Bank, New York, (1971-82); as Team Leader in Systems and Data Processing Group (1971-75); 2nd Vice President, Credit and Marketing, Institutional Banking, Western U.S. (1975-79); Vice President in charge of the Saudi Arabian Division (1979-82); United Gulf Bank Bahrain (since 1982), as Head of Credit and Marketing (1982-85) and Chief Operating Officer (1985-1994) Chief General Manager International based in London supervising the Int'l branches and subsidiaries of AAIB. (1994 to present) Chief General Manager, Arab African International Bank Head Office based in Cairo. **Sports:** Tennis, horse riding, skiing. **Prof. Addr.:** Arab African International Bank, P.O.Box 60, Magless El-Shaab, (11516) Cairo, Egypt.

KHALED (Rasheed, Osman), Sudanese economist. **Born** in 1930 in Omdurman, Sudan. **Son** of Osman Khalid. **Married** in 1959, 1 daughter, 2 sons. **Educ.:** University of Khartoum, Sudan; University of Saskatchewan, Canada. **Dipl.:** B.A. Honours (Econ.); M.A. (Econ.) **Career:** Inspector of Finance, Ministry of Finance, Khartoum (1954-56); Economist, UN Economics Affairs Department (1956-61); UN Budget Adviser, Government of Somalia (1961-62); UN Adviser, Institute of National Planning, Cairo (1962-64); Economist, International Monetary Fund (1965-69); Fiscal Adviser, Ministry of Finance, Indonesia (1969-71); IMF, Fiscal Affairs Dept. Chief of Budget Division (1971-75); Adviser at Assistant Director's level, IMF, USA (1976-). **Publ.:** "Fiscal Policy, Development Planning and Annual Budgeting 1969"; "Control and Management of Central Government Finances in the United Kingdom 1970". **Hobbies:** Tennis, Arabic and English Literature, History and Philosophy. **Addr.:** 3201 Kent Street, Tel.: (301) 9465736, Kensington, Maryland 20795, USA.

KHALED (Sulaiman, Humud al-Zaid, al), Kuwaiti official. **Born** in 1934 in Kuwait. **Son** of Humud al-Zaid al-Khaled. **Married**. **Educ.:** Ahmadiah School, Kuwait; Mubarakiyah School, Kuwait; Cairo University, Egypt. **Career:** Ministry of Customs and Ports (1962); Under-Secretary, Ministry of Customs and Ports (1973); Minister of Communications (1975) and reappointed (1978); represented Kuwait at several International Customs and Ports conference. **Addr.:** Kuwait city, Kuwait.

KHALEDI (Adnan Mohamad Tahir, al), Saudi academic. **Born** in 1943. **Dipl.:** M.A. (English). **Career:** Teacher of English, Inspector-General of English, member of the Professional Board, Secondary School Education Bureau; member, Association to Teachers of English as a Second Language, U.S.A., International Education Union, Switzerland; Acting Director-General, Saudi Arabian International Schools; attended Conferences on Teaching Foreign Languages in the Arab Countries, Damascus, Conference on Translation in the Arab Countries, Kuwait, Conference on Teaching English as a Second Language, U.S.A. **Publ.:** Developing Teaching Techniques of English in the Arab Countries, English Laboratory Notes for Secondary Schools (with others). **Addr.:** Ministry of Education, Riyadh, Saudi Arabia.

KHALEDI (Walid), Palestinian academic. **Born** in Jerusalem, Palestine. **Married**, 3 children. **Educ.:** Oxford University, UK. **Dipl.:** B.A., B.Lit. **Career:** Research Member of Arab Office (1946); Lecturer, Department of Oriental Studies, Oxford University (1952-56); resigned over UK role in Tripartite Invasion of Egypt (1956); Assistant Professor, Political Studies Department, American University of Beirut, Lebanon (1956-65); Editor of "Arab Political Documents and Chronology of Arab Politics" (1963-66); Research Associate, Near Eastern Studies Department, Princeton University, USA (1960-61); Adviser to Iraq Delegation to UN General Assembly in special session following Middle East June War (1967); Founder and Member of the Board of Trustees, Institute of Palestine Studies, Beirut (1963); Professor, Political Studies Department, American University of Beirut (1965). **Publ.:** Editor of "From Heaven to Conquest", "Readings on Zionism and the Palestine Problem until 1948" Beirut (1971), as well as articles in Encyclopaedia of Islam, Cassell's Encyclopaedia of World Literature and Encyclopaedia Britannica. **Priv. Addr.:** Mme Curie Street Beirut, Lebanon.

KHALFALLAH (Khalfallah al-Rashid Mohamad Ahmad), Sudanese judge. **Born** in 1930 in Merowe District, Sudan. **Son** of Mohamad Khalfallah. **Married,** six children. **Educ.:** Law Diploma, University of Khartoum, Sudan; Law Degree and Diploma in International Law, University of Cambridge, UK; LLM, University of London, UK. **Career:** Legal Assistant in the Corps of Judges (1960); Legal Adviser, Ministry of Justice (1962); Attorney General (1967); Chief Justice of Judiciary (1972); elected President of the Permanent Legal Committee of the Arab League; member of the Sudanese Society for International Relations and International Law; member of the Egyptian Society of Economics, Legislation and Statistics. **Publ.:** "Law and the Citizen", Ministry of Information, Sudan (1967); articles in the local newspaper. **Medals:** Order of the Two Niles (1975); Order of King Abdul Aziz, 3rd Class (1971); Jumhuriya Order, 1st Class. **Sports:** Tennis, swimming. **Addr.:** P.O.Box 763, Khartoum, Sudan.

KHALFAN (Maqbool, Habib Jaffar), Qatari banking executive. **Born** in Doha, Qatar in 1955. **Son** of Habib Jaffar Khalfan. **Educ.:** B.Com., Cairo University, Egypt. **Career:** Chartered Bank Ltd. (1968-70); United Bank Ltd. (1970-79); Doha Bank Ltd. (Commercial Manager) (1979-84); Asst. General Manager (1984-86); Deputy General Manager (1986-87); General Manager (since 1988). **Member of:** Doha Club; Businessmen's Club. **Prof. Addr.:** Doha Bank Ltd., P.O.Box 3818, Doha/Qatar. **Priv. Addr.:** Tel.: 671184, al-Hilal Area, Doha, Qatar.

KHALID (Abdulrazzak, Al), Kuwaiti President - Kuwait Chamber of Commerce and Industry. **Born** on March 1, 1930. **Son** of Khalid Zaid AL-Khalid (businessman) **and** Mrs. née Haya M. Al-Zibn. **Married** in 1960 to Nawar H. Al-Naqeeb, 4 children: Harith, Khalid, Maysa and Sulafa. **Educ.:** B.A., Commerce & Economics, Cairo University, Egypt 1953. **Career:** (General Trading); Vice Chairman of the Independent Petroleum Group; Chairman of the Kuwait National Committee of I.C.C.; Vice President of Arab-British Chamber of Commerce and Industry; Board Member of Kuwait Foundation for the Advancement of Sciences; Vice Chairman & Board Member of the National Bank of Kuwait; Board Member of the Kuwait Oil Tanker Co.; currently, President of Kuwait Chamber of Commerce & Industry. **Other Information:** Member of the First Parliament of the State of Kuwait, Chairman of Kuwait Economic Society. **Sport:** Swimming. **Hobby:** Reading. **Credit Cards:** American Express, Diners, Visa & Master. **Prof. Addr.:** P.O.Box 775, 13008 Safat, Kuwait, Tel.: 00965- 2440580/2433899, Fax: 2404110/2440127. **Priv. Addr.:** 00965-5611744, Kuwait.

KHALIFA (Abdullah Bin Khalid, al, Shaikh), Bahraini minister of justice and islamic affairs. **Born** in 1922. **Son** of Shaikh Khalid al-Khalifa. **Married,** 10 children: 4 sons, 6 daughters. **Career:** Judge, Junior Courts; Member, Court of Appeal; President, Rifaa Municipality (until 1967); President, Manama Municipality (1967); Head, Department of Municipalities and Agriculture; Member, State Council (1970); Minister of Municipalities and Agriculture (1971); Minister of Justice and Islamic Affairs (since September 1975 to present). **Addr.:** Ministry of Justice and Islamic Affairs, Minister's Office, P.O.Box 450, Tel.: 531222, Manama, Bahrain.

KHALIFA (Abdullah Bin Salman Bin Khalid, al, Brig. Gen. Shaikh), Bahraini army commander. **Born** in 1945 in Muharraq, Bahrain. **Educ.:** Diploma in Military Science, Royal Military Academy, Sandhurst, UK; pilot training; various special courses; passed Staff College Course, UK. **Career:** Platoon Commander; Training Company Commander; Infantry Company Commander; Battalion second in command; Battalion Commander; former Chief of Staff, Bahrain Defence Force. **Sports:** Golf and general sports. **Hobby:** Fishing. **Addr.:** Ministry of Defence, P.O.Box 245, West Rifaa, Tel.: 665599, Telex: 8429 BN, Bahrain.

KHALIFA (Abdulrahman, al-Mahdi), Jordanian politician, lawyer. **Born** in 1918 in Salt, Jordan. **Son** of al Mahdi Khalifa. **Married,** eight children. **Educ.:** University of Damascus. **Dipl.:** B.A. in Law. **Career:** Assistant Attorney General; Chief Judge, Court of First Instance, Jordan, Amman; Head of Income Tax Department; Secretary General of Amman Municipality; Minister of Finance for several times; Head of the Royal Cabinet; Minister of the Royal Court; Chief Auditor; Head of Department of Civil Service; Member of the Chamber of Deputies for several times; Member of the Senate; Lawyer. **Medals:** Order of the Renaissance, Jordan; Order of Independence, Jordan; Order of Rafidain, Iraq; decorations from Lebanon, Syria, Greece, France and Britian. **Sports:** Walking. **Hobbies:** Legal and financial affairs. **Prof. Addr.:** P.O.Box 2316, Tel.: 42461, 665086, Amman, Jordan.

KHALIFA (Abdulrahman Bin Mohamed, al, Shaikh), Bahraini official. **Born** in Bahrain in 1942. **Son** of late Shaikh Mohamed al-Khalifa. **Educ.:** Faculty of Law, Cairo

University. **Career:** Judge in the Minor, Middle and Criminal Court; President of High Civil Court; Deputy of High Civil Court; appointed as judge (1960); Chairman Delmon Gulf Construction; former Chairman of Bahrain Islamic Bank; Vice President of Alms Fund Directorate; Vice President of Pilgrimage Directorate; Editor of al-Hidaya Islamic Magazine; Under-Secretary at the Ministry of Justice and Islamic Affairs. **Sports:** Tennis, sport excercist, swimming. **Hobby:** Reading. **Member** of Bahrain Graduates Club. **Credit Cards:** American Express. **Prof. Addr.:** Ministry of Justice, P.O.Box 450, Manama, Bahrain and P.O.Box 5786, Manama, Bahrain.

KHALIFA (Ahmad, Mohamad), Egyptian international civil servant. **Born** on October 1, 1923 in Alexandria, Egypt. **Married,** children. **Educ.:** Faculty of Law, Cairo University. **Dipl.:** LL.B., B.A. (Criminal Science), Ph.D. (Sociology of Law). **Career:** Assistant District Attorney, Egypt; Lecturer, Faculty of Law, University of Baghdad (Iraq); District Attorney, Egypt; President, African Conference of Social Affairs Ministers (1967); Minister of Social Affairs, Egypt; Chairman, Social Science Council, Academy of Science, Cairo (Egypt); Member of Presidential Advisory Council for Social Affairs, Cairo (Egypt); Chairman and Professor Center for Social and Criminological Research, Cairo (Egypt); Chairman, UN Committee for Crime Prevention & Control; Representative of Egypt, UN Commission for Social Development; Chairman, UN Sub-Commission on Prevention of Discrimination and Protection of Minorities. **Publ.:** "The General Theory of Incrimination" (1959), "Introduction to the Study of Criminal Behaviour" (1962), "Socialism and Social Methods of Scientific Research" (1963), "Social Planning in Egypt" (1970), "A view for a View" (1985). **Award:** Academy of Science (Egypt), State Award of Highest Merit in Social Sciences (1984). **Sports:** Golf and swimming. **Prof. Addr.:** Director, UNESCO Regional Arab Centre for Social Science Research and Documentation, Zamalek P.O. Tel. (2)3470019, Cairo. **Priv. Addr.:** 18 Hassan Assem Street, Zamalek, Tel.: (2)3401372, Cairo, Egypt.

KHALIFA (Daij Bin Khalifa, al, Shaikh), Bahraini official. **Born** in 1938 in Bahrain. **Son** of Khalifa al-Khalifa. **Married. Educ.:** Nautical College, UK. **Career:** Port Manager, Minaa Sulman (1966); Director General, Customs and Ports (1970); Assistant Under Secretary, Ministry of Finance and National Economy, Customs and Ports Affairs; Chairman of the Arab ship Building Repair Yard. **Addr.:** Ministry of Finance and National Economy, Customs and Ports Directorate, P.O.Box 15, Tel.: 243533, Telex: 8642 BN, Manama, Bahrain.

KHALIFA (Hamad, Bin Issa, Shaikh, al), Ruler of the State of Bahrain. **Born** on January 28, 1950, in Bahrain. **Son** of HH Shaikh Issa Bin Sulman al-Khalifa. **Married,** 2 sons: Sulman and Abdulla. **Educ.:** Secondary in Bahrain; Sandhurst and Mons, UK; Fort Leavenworth, Kansas, USA. **Career:** Commander, Bahrain National Guard (1969-71); Member, State Administrative Council (1970-71); Minister of Defence (1971-88); has represented Bahrain at Regional and International Conferences. **President,** Bahrain Scientific Society. Succeeded as Amir of Bahrain on the death of his father (March 1999). **Sports:** Tennis, football, golf, riding, swimming. **Addr.:** The Royal Palace, Manama, Bahrain.

KHALIFA (Khaled bin Abdallah, al, Shaikh), Bahraini minister. **Born** in 1922. **Married,** 1 son. **Career:** Judge of Junior Courts; Member of Court of Appeal; President, Rifaa Municipality until 1967. President, Manama Municipality (1967); Head, New Department of Municipalities and Agriculture & Member of the State Council (1970); Minister, Municipalities and Agriculture (1971-74); Minister, Justice and Islamic Affairs; Acting Minister of Commerce and Agriculture (1975-76); Chairman, The Housing Bank, Manama, Bahrain; Minister of Housing (since August 1975 to present). **Addr.:** Diplomatic Area, P.O.Box 802, Tel.: 232300, Telex: 8599, Manama, Bahrain.

KHALIFA (Khalifa Bin Sulman, al, Shaikh), Bahraini Prime Minister. **Born** in 1936. **Married,** three children. **Educ.:** Private in Bahrain and in London. **Career:** Appointed first President of the Education Council (1957-60); appointed Head of Finance (1960-66); Chairman, Administrative Council (1966-70); Co-Ordinate of Foreign Aid and Technical Assistance; Chairman, Committee for the Register of Commerce; Chairman, Joint Committee for Economic and Financial Studies; President, State Council (January 1970-73); Prime Minister (1973- to date); re-appointed in 1978 Head of the Supreme Defence Council; Chairman, Bahrain Monetary Agency and other official Organisations. **Awards:** "Khalifite Medallion" the highest order of Merit, granted by the Amir (19.12.79). **Hobbies:** Reading, travelling and motoring. **Addr.:** Office of the Prime Minister, P.O.Box 1000, Tel.: 262266, Manama, Bahrain.

KHALIFA (Khatim, Sir, al), Sudanese politician. **Born** on January 1, 1919 in Dueim, Sudan. **Married** to Zahra el-Fadil, 4 children. **Educ.:** Gordon Memorial College; Gordon Memorial College Teaching Section, Khartoum (1937); Exeter College Oxford University (1944-46). **Career:** Teacher at Bakht Errida Training Institute 1938-44); Province Education inspector at Juba responsible for introducing Arabic in the Southern Sudan education system (1950-57); Assistant Director of Education for the Southern Province (1957-60); participated in coordinating the academic systems between the Northern and the Southern regions of Sudan; As he was in the South, the Ministry of Education took over the supervision of the Southern schools from the missionaries; Principal Technical Institute, Khartoum (1960-64); Deputy Under-Secretary, Ministry of Education (1964); Prime Minister (Oct. 1964- June

1965); Principal, Technical Institute, Khartoum; Ambassador to Italy (1966- March 1968); Ambassador to the Court of Saint James, London (March 1968-69); Adviser to the Minister of Higher Education and Scientific Research (Oct. 1972- May 1973); Minister of Education and Higher Education (May 1973- June 1975). **Addr.:** Khartoum, Sudan.

KHALIFA (Laroussi), Algerian engineer, statesman and diplomat. **Born** in 1923 in Algiers. **Educ.:** National Agriculture Institute of Maison Carrée (Algiers) and University of Paris. **Dipl.:** of Engineering. **Career:** Professor at National School of Horticulture of Paris (1954), Member of National Liberation Army, F.L.N. (National Liberation Front) (1954-64), Minister of Industry and Power (1962-62), Algerian Ambassador to United Kingdom (1964). **Publ.:** Author of "Le Manuel du Militant Algérien" (1962). **Addr.:** Algiers, Algeria.

KHALIFA (Mohamad, Atiyattulah, al), Bahraini administrator. **Born** in 1953 in Manama, Bahrain. **Married**, 1 son. **Educ.:** Combined Honours degree; Postgraduate course in business management. **Dipl.:** Degree in Computer Science. **Career:** Head, Central Statistics Organisation, Bahrain (1982); Director, Bahrain National Oil Co. **Hobbies:** Tennis, swimming. **Prof. Addr.:** P.O.Box 5835, Manama, Bahrain.

KHALIFA (Mohamad, Bin Khalifa Bin Hamad, al, Shaikh), Bahraini politician. **Born** in 1937. **Son** of Shaikh Khalifa Bin Hamed Bin Issa al-Khalifa. **Married** in 1959, 4 children: Fawaz, Tallal, Lamia and Amani. **Educ.:** Degree from Royal Military Academy, Sandhurst, UK. **Career:** Police Inspector, Public Security Department (1959); Director, Immigration and Passports (1966); Deputy Director-General, Public Security Department (1970); Deputy Director-General, Public Security Department (1970); Minister of the Interior since 1973 to present. **Sports:** Tennis, Basket-Ball. **Addr.:** Ministry of the Interior, Minister's Office, P.O.Box 13, Tel.: 254021, Manama, Bahrain.

KHALIFA (Mohamad Bin Mubarak Bin Hamad, al, Shaikh), Bahraini politician. **Born** in 1935. **Son** of Shaikh Mubarak Bin Hamad al-Khalifa **and** Mrs., daughter of Abdallah Bin Jabr al-Dosari and sister of the Head of the Amiri Court, Yusuf Rahma al Dosari. **Married**, with children. **Educ.:** in Bahrain; American University of Beirut, Lebanon; Oxford University, UK. **Dipl.:** Modern History, and Diploma in International Law, University of London. **Career:** After his studies, returned to Bahrain (1961); Listener and Candidate for the Bench, Bahrain Courts; Director of Information (1962); Head, Political Bureau (1968); which became Department of Foreign Affairs (1969); appointed State Council (1970); Minister of Foreign Affairs since 1971 to present. **Prof. Addr.:** Ministry of Foreign Affairs, Minister's Office, P.O.Box 547, Tel.: 258200, Manama, Bahrain.

KHALIFA (Mohamad Bin Sulman, al, Shaikh), Bahraini administrator, judge. **Born** in 1940 in Bahrain. **Son** of Sulman al-Khalifa. **Married. Career:** President of the Education Council and President of Harbour Advisory Board (1960); Chief of Police and Public Security in succession to the late Shaikh Khalifa Bin Mohamad (1961); Judge of the Appeal Court (1966); resigned (1967). **Addr.:** Ministry of Justice, P.O.Box 450, Tel.: 253339, Manama, Bahrain.

KHALIFA (Mohamad, Dawud, al), Sudanese agricultural expert and politician. **Born** in 1924 in Khartoum, Sudan. **Son** of Dawud al-Khalifa. **Married**, four children. **Educ.:** B.Sc. in Agriculture, Faculty of Agriculture, University of Khartoum (1943-48). **Career:** Ministry of Agriculture (1948-59); Manager of Habasha Pump Scheme (1948-49); Inspector of Agriculture, Agriculture Development of Kosti District (1949-51); management Supervision of the Gash Delta Scheme for producing cotton and sorghum under flood irrigation (1951-53); Senior Inspector of Agriculture (1953-55); Chief of Agriculture Education (1966-69); Deputy Managing Director and member of the Board of Directors for the Agriculture Bank of Sudan; member of National Assembly and Minister of local Government (1968-69); Director of Agricultural Consultant Services Sudan Ltd. (1970-72); Senior Agriculture Advisor, Country Representative of FAO in Iraq (1972). **Publ.:** "Tobacco, A Possible Cash Crop in the Future Development of Sudan"; "The Philosophical Society of the Sudan". Founding **member** of the College Council, University College for Women, Sudan. **Sport:** Horse riding. **Hobby:** Reading. **Addr.:** P.O.Box 1500, Khartoum, Sudan.

KHALIFA (Mohammed Elamin), Sudanese Minister for Cabinet Affairs. **Born** on January 1, 1949 in El Nuhud, Western State. **Son** of Mohammed Younis Khalifa, Farmer **and** Mrs. née Halima Osman Khareef. **Married** in 1949 to Fatma Elamin ElRayah, 4 children: Mohammed El Hassan (June 1977), Fadwa (December 1980), Ahmed (March 1982), Hajir (August 1984). **Educ.:** Military College, African University. **Dipl.:** Military Science, D'awa and Islamic Studies, Electronic Warfare. Diploma in Military Science, Sudan Military College (1973), Diploma in signals Georgia U.S.A. (1980), Diploma in Electronic Warfare, Egypt (1989) (Institute), Diploma in D'awa and Islamic Studies (International Africa University), Master of Military Science, Sudan Command and Staff College. **Career:** Member of the Revolutionary Command Council (1989), Speaker of the Parliament of Sudan (1992-1998); Presently Minister for Cabinet Affairs. **Medals:** Medal of Accomplishment (Political Accomplishment). **Sports Practised:** Foot Ball, Chess. **Hobbies:** Reading, Writing, Hunting. **Clubs and Associations:** Culture Association Club. **Prof. Addr.:** Council of Ministers, Tel.: 778861, Khartoum, Sudan. **Home Tel.:** 330925. Sudan.

KHALIFA (Mohsen, Amin), Egyptian diplomat. **Born**

on June 2, 1934 in Beni Suef, Egypt. **Son** of Amin Khalifa (Lawyer, Member of Wafd Party, Representive in Parliament for Beni Suef) **and** Mrs. Methal nee Ramzi Ahmed el-Kamal. **Married** on October 20, 1968 in Cairo to Sanaa Abdel Meguid, 2 sons: Amin (18/1/1971), Aymen (7/12/1972); **Educ.:** Amiri Primary School (1946); Prince Farouk Secondary School (1951); Faculty of Law, Cairo University, February 1957. **Dipl.:** Bachelor of Law (1957). **Career:** Lawyer (1954-60), Joined Diplomatic Corps (1960) and served in the following countries: Chile (1962-65); Bolivia (1965-66); North Yemen (1969-71); Iraq (1971-73); Bulgaria (1975-76); Yugoslavia (1976-79); Tanzania (1981-85); Benin (1988-); Ambassador Extraordinary and Plenipotentiary fo A.R. of Egypt to Republic of Benin (DIPLOMAT); Dean a.i. of the Diplomatic Corps in Benin. Member in African Society in Egypt. Two Researches Entitled "Petroleum of Iraq" were commended by the Arab League and the Egyptian Ministry of Foreign Affairs; Involved in Environmental Projects in Egypt. **Decor.:** Egyptian Republican Decoration (Gomhoria) (1983); National Decoration of Benin, Degree of a Knight (Commandor) (1991). **Sports:** Tennis, swimming, horse riding, golf, squash and jogging. **Hobbies:** Reading history, politics and theology; traditional music, poetry and theatre. **Member:** Egyptian Syno-of Lawyers; Tahrir Diplomatic Club; Shams Club; Tanzania Yacht Club, Heliopolis Sporting Club. **Prof. Addr.:** Embassy of Egypt, P.O.Box 1215, Tel.: 300842, Cotonou, Benin. **Priv. Addr.:** 34 el-Shaheed Abdel Moniem Ismaeel Street, Almaza, Heliopolis, Tel.: 2901172, Cairo, Egypt.

KHALIFA (Rashid, Bin Khalifa, al, Sheikh), Bahraini official. **Born** in 1952 in Bahrain. **Son** of Khalifa Bin Hamad al-Khalifa. **Married**, 4 children: Noor, Khalifa, Hessa, Mohammed. **Educ.:** University of Hastings. **Dipl.:** High Diploma in Art and Design. **Career:** Director of Tourism and Archaeology (1984); Assistant Under Secretary for Tourism and Archaeology, Ministry of Information (1988-); **Other Information:** Chairman of Bahrain Art Society; Chairman of Tourism Projects Company. **Sports:** Walking. **Hobby:** Painting. **Member:** Bahrain Art Society. **Credit Cards:** AMEX - Diner's Club. **Prof. Addr.:** P.O.Box 29229, Tel.: 211024, Manama, Bahrain, and Ministry of Information, Tourism and Archaeology, P.O.Box 26613, Manama, Bahrain.

KHALIFA (Taher, Sulaiman), Syrian engineer. **Born** in 1924 in Damascus. **Son** of Sulaiman Khalifa. **Educ.:** Belgium: **Dipl.:** Agronomist Engineer, Doctor in Agronomy. **Career:** Ministry of Agriculture, Director of Education Section in the said Ministry (1956). **Hobby:** Reading. **Addr.:** Midan Square, Damascus, Syria.

KHALIL (Ahmed, T.), Egyptian diplomat. **Born** in 1925 in Cairo. **Married**, one son. **Career:** with Ministry of Foreign Affairs (since 1948), posts in London and Rome (since 1962), served Permanent Mission to UN, New York (1962-66); Head Department of International Organisations (1969-72); Head of Egypt's Interest Section, Washington D.C. (1972-74); Ambassador to Finland (1974-78); to Belgium, Luxembourg and EEC (1979-83); Under Secretary, Ministry of Foreign Affairs (1978-79), Permanent Representative to UN (1983); Fellow, Center for International Affairs, Harvard University (1967-68). **Addr.:** c/o Ministry of Foreign Affairs, Cairo, Egypt.

KHALIL (Fakhruddin), Syrian executive. **Born** in 1933 in Safita, Syria. **Son** of Khalil Khalil. **Married** in 1953, 4 sons, 1 daughter. **Educ.:** The American University of Beirut. **Dipl.:** B.A. (Econ.) 1956; M.A. (Econ.) 1958. **Career:** Research Assistant, American University of Beirut, Economic Research Institute (1956-58); Bank Manager and Regional Manager, Banque du Caire, Syria and Banque de l'Unité Arabe, Syria (1959-66); Chairman, General Manager, Commercial Bank of Syria, Damascus (1967-71); Director, Union de Banques Arabes et Française (UBAF) (1970-71); General Representative, UBAF, Beirut (1972-75); Director, Senior Executive Vice President, UBAF Arab American Bank, New York, USA (1976); Founding President and Director-Arab Bankers Association of North America. **Member:** Alumni Association of North America, Inc.; Member, Board of Advisors, College of Business Administration, St. John's University, New York; Honorary Member, Omicron Delta Epsilon, St. John's University Chapter; Garden City Country Club; The Board Room. **Hobbies:** Tennis and swimming. **Addr.:** Residence: 115 John Street, Garden City, Tel.: (516)742-359, New York, NY 11530, USA.

KHALIL (Khairy, Aziz), Egyptian journalist. **Born** in 1937 in Egypt. **Son** of Aziz Khalil. **Married**, two children. **Educ.:** B.A. in History, Cairo University, Cairo, Egypt. **Career:** Expert on Third World Affairs; Consultant, al-Ahram Center for Political and Strategic Studies, Arab Affairs Section and Sino-Soviet Affairs Section; political writer; translator for Agence France Press, Middle East News Agency, Cairo. **Publ.:** "People's War and People's Army"; "The Algerian Experiment in Development and Modernisation"; "Revolution and Social Change"; "The Tunisian Experiment in Development"; translated several works into Arabic including, Allende: "The Lessons of Failure"; "Guevara: Is he the Trotsky of Cuban Revolution?", "Herbert Marcuse: Is he the Lenin of the Sexual Revolution?"; military history, drama, poetry. **Addr.:** 15 Abdu al-Hamouli Street, Abbassiya, Cairo, Egypt.

KHALIL (Mahmoud Salahiddin, Yusuf), Egyptian businessman. **Born** in 1949 in Giza, Egypt. **Married**, 2 children. **Educ.:** Cairo University, Egypt; ICL Computer Programming Course. **Dipl.:** B.Com. **Career:** Assistant Auditor, State Auditing Department (1969-73); Auditor of Y. Salaheddine and M. Salaheddin, Public Accountants (1973), Senior Auditor (1974-78). **Member** of the National Association of Accountants, Egyptian United Nations Associations and the American Chamber of Commerce; Partner of Y. And M. Salaheddine (1978-). **Hobbies:** Bridge, photography, squash. **Member:** Egyptian Shooting Club, Gezira Sporting Club. **Prof. Addr.:** 27 Talaat Harb Street, Cairo, Egypt. **Priv. Addr.:** 4 el-Saleh Ayoub Street, Zamalek, Cairo, Egypt.

KHALIL (Mirghani Sulaiman, Brigadier), Sudanese diplomat, former army officer. **Born** in 1933 in Omdurman, Sudan. **Son** of Sulaiman Khalil. **Married**, four children. **Educ.:** Military College, Sudan (1953-55); Signals Course, UK (1957); Diploma, Military Science, Staff College, Jordan (1969). **Career:** Officer in the Armed Forces; commissioned in the Signals Corps at al-Obaid; served in Khartoum (1961); Second in Command of the Signals School (1962-65); Military Attaché, Sudanese Embassy in Kenya (1965-68); promoted Lieutenant Colonel and assigned to the HQ of the Sudan Armed Forces (1968); Leader of the Eastern Command, Sudan (1970-72); Head of Technical Committee for the Organisation of the Armed Forces of the South (1972); Sudan Armed Forces Director of Military Intelligence (1972-75); Ambassador to Kuwait, Lebanon and Kenya (1975-80); Ambassador to Ethiopia (1980). **Medals:** Medal of Independence; Order of Long and Excellent Service; and several other medals. **Sport:** Polo. **Addr.:** Ministry of Foreign Affairs, Khartoum, Sudan.

KHALIL (Mohamad, Ahmad), Egyptian banker. **Born** in 1932 in Kaloubeya, Egypt. **Married**, 1 son, 3 daughters. **Educ.:** Cairo University, Egypt; National Institute for Higher Management, Cairo. **Dipl.:** B.Com., Diploma in Higher Management. **Educ.:** held several positions in Misr Bank since 1953; currently General Manager of Misr Bank, Zamalek Branch, Cairo. **Member:** Gezira Sporting Club. **Prof. Addr.:** 10 el-Kamel Muhammad Street, Zamalek, Cairo, Egypt. **Priv. Addr.:** 4 Abdou Badran Street, Manial, Cairo, Egypt.

KHALIL (Mohamad, Ibrahim), Sudanese politician. **Born** in Sudan. **Son** of Ibrahim Khalil. **Career:** Former Police Commissioner, Minister of Local Government (February- June 1965), Ministry of Foreign Affairs (June 1965). **Member:** al-Umma Party. **Addr.:** c/o Ministry of Foreign Affairs, Khartoum, Sudan.

KHALIL (Mohamad, Kamaleddine), Egyptian diplomat. **Born** in Egypt. **Son** of Kamaleddine Khalil. **Educ.:** Secondary and Higher. **Career:** Lecturer in International Public Law (1941-56); Director of Research Department, Ministry of Foreign Affairs; Chargé d'Affaires, then Ambassador to United Kingdom (1960-61); Director, North American Department, Ministry of Foreign Affairs (1961-64); Egyptian Ambassador to Jordan (1964-66), to Sudan (1966-71); Under-Secretary of State for Foreign Affairs (1971-74); Ambassador to Belgium, and to EEC (1974). **Publ.:** Author of "The Arab States and the Arab League" (2 volumes), 1962. **Addr.:** Ministry of Foreign Affairs, Cairo, Egypt.

KHALIL (Mostafa, Dr.), Egyptian engineer, politician and banker. **Born** in 1920. **Educ.:** University of Cairo, Illinois University, USA. **Dipl.:** M.Sc., D.Phil. **Career:** Served in Egyptian State Railways (1941-47, 1951-52); training with Chicago-Milwaukee Railways (U.S.A., 1947); lecturer in Railways and Highway Engineering, Ain Shams University, Cairo (1952); Technical Consultant to Transport Committee, Permanent Council for National Production (1955); Minister of Communications and Transport (1956-64), of Industry, Mineral Resources and Electricity (1965-66); Deputy Prime Minister (1964-65); resigned from Cabinet (1966); Head of Broadcasting Corporation (1970); Secretary General, Central Committee Arab Socialist Union (1970-76); Prime Minister (1978-80); also Minister of Foreign Affairs (1979-80); member of the Political Bureau, National Democratic Party (since May 1980 to present); Chairman Arab International Bank, Cairo (since 1980 to present). **Addr.:** Arab International Bank, 18 Abdel Khalek Sarwat Street, P.O.Box 1563, Cairo, Egypt.

KHALIL (Muhammad Khalil, Dr), Former Jordanian Lawer and International Judge. **Born** 14 December, 1925, Tayibah, Palestine. **Married** 2 sons, 2 daughters. **Educ.:** Palestine Intermediate, Arab College, Jerusalem (1945); Palestine Government scholar to U.K (1945-49); LL.B. (Hon.), Liverpool University (1948); completed 1st year LL.M., University College, London University (1949); Barrister-at-law, Middle Temple, London (1949); LL.D. International Law, Leyden University, Holland (1952). **Career:** Secretary General, Libyan Royal Court, Benghazi/Tripoli (1952-54); Legal Adviser to H.M. King Idriss Sanussi, Libya (1954-55); Assistant Professor of International Law, A.U.B. Beirut, Lebanon (1956-59); Advocate, Amman, Jordan (1959-61); Legal Adviser to: Shell Co. of Qatar (1961-63); Board of Directors, Iraq Natural Oil Co., Baghdad (1964-65); SONATRACH, Algiers (1965-71); Ministry of Electricity and Water, Kuwait (1972); Managing Director, Pan Arab Consultants for Petroleum, Economy and Industry Development, Beirut (1973-77); Consultant, OAPEC Kuwait (1975-77); Legal Adviser, Board of Directors QPPA (1977-82) (Doha) then Qatar General Petroleun Corporation, Doha (1982-86) Legal Expert, Minister's Office, Ministry of Finance and Petroleum, Doha (1982-86); Judge, OAPEC Judicial Tribunal, Kuwait (1981-87). **Publ.:** "The Arab States and the Arab League: A Documentary Record", 2 vols., 1741 pp., in English, Beirut (1962) then reprinted London (1987-90); "The General Agreement of Participation: A Legal, Economic and Financial Assesment", in English (Ed.), Beirut (1973); "Towards an Optimal Production and Investment Strategy of the Arab Petroleum Exporting Countries in the Light of Altern. Energy Sources through the Year 1985" in English (Ed.), Beirut (1974); **Honours:** Vice-President.

"International Freindship League", Liverpool (1946-47); Honorary President of the "First pan Arab Students' Congress in Europe" Leyden, April 1950; Founding Member of the Shaybani Society of International Law, Germany (1954); Member, select Committee of the Abdulhamid Shoman Foundation's Award of Excellency for Distinguished Young Arab Scholars" Amman (1992); Member, Board of Trustees, Applied Science University, Amman (1993-97). **Languages:** Arabic, English, French and Dutch. **Hobbies:** Reading, Photography, Sports "watching", Music and Travel. **Address:** P.O.Box 11-5631, Beirut, Lebanon or/and P.O.Box 140978, El-Biader, Amman 11814, Jordan.

KHALIL (Nabil Bin), Tunisian journalist. **Born** on August 30, 1930 in Tunis, Tunisia. **Married. Educ.:** Journalism Training Centre, Paris. **Dipl.:** Licence in Law. **Career:** Head of Tunis-Afrique Press (TAP) Office in Algiers (1962-63); Head of TAP Office in Paris (1963-68); Assistant Editor in Chief of TAP Agency (1968), Editor in Chief of the television review on Radio Television Tunisienne (1968-70); Director of Information, Radio Television Tunisienne (1970-71), Director of Foreign Relations (1971-72), Editor in Chief of "Le Temps" French daily newspaper; Director of Ben Express Publishing Company (1972-75). **Publ.:** co-author of "Sadiki et les Sadikiens" and "La Tunisie en Marche". **Decor.:** Officer of the National Order of the Republic of the Ivory Coast (1965); Knight of the Order of Merit of the FDR (West Germany) (1968); Knight of the Order of Merit of Grand Duchy of Luxembourg (1969). **Hobby:** Tennis. **Addr.:** 129 Avenue Bourguiba, Carthage, Tunis, Tunisia.

KHALIL (Najih, Muhammad), Iraqi academic. **Born** in 1935 in Iraq. **Educ.:** University of Wales, UK; Oklahoma State University, USA. **Dipl.:** M.A. and Ph.D. in Civil Engineering. **Career:** Under Secretary, Ministry of Municipal and Rural Affairs; Under Secretary at the Ministry of Public Works and Housing (1974); Chairman of the Engineers' Union (1969); Minister of Industry and Minerals (1977-80); Professor at the University of Baghdad, Iraq (1980-). **Addr.:** Baghdad, Iraq.

KHALIL (Osman), Egyptian lawyer, former faculty dean, counsellor of Kuwaiti State. **Born** in Egypt. **Educ.:** Secondary and Higher. **Dipl.:** Doctor of Law (Public and Private Law), Cairo University and Paris University. **Career:** Lawyer, Dean of Faculty of Law (Ain Shams University); Professor of Constitutional Law at the said University; Counsellor of Kuwait State. **Publ.:** Contributed to the Draft Constitution of Kuwait, Barrister in Cairo and Kuwait. **Addr.:** Kuwait and Cairo, Egypt.

KHALILI (Saud bin Ali, al, Shaikh), Omani businessman. **Son** of Ali al-Khalili (Bin Ruwaha Tribe). **Educ.:** Religious education at Nizawa, Oman by his uncle (former Imam of Oman, Mohamad bin Abdullah al-Khalili). **Career:** Minister of Education (1970); Head, Omani Goodwill Mission touring Arab World (1971); Ambassador to Egypt and Arab League (1972-74); Ambassador to Kuwait (1974-77); Private business (1977-). Director, the Oman Bank for Agriculture and Fisheries S.A.O.; Chairman, Oman National Electric Co. S.A.O. **Addr.:** P.O.Box 4393, Tel.: 701761, Telex: 3046, Ruwi, Oman.

KHALIS (Abdul Latif), Moroccan official. **Born** in 1935 in Rabat, Morocco. **Married. Educ.:** studies in Rabat, Morocco. **Career:** Government Administration (1967); Education Department; Head of Service, Dducational Broadcasting Division; Head, Cultural Division of the Educational Department; Cabinet Chief, Ministry of Higher Education; Ministry of Posts, Telegraphs and Telephones (PTT); Ministry of Sports and Youth Affairs; Cabinet Chief, Ministry of Labour, Social Affairs, Sports and Youth Affairs; Director General, Radiodiffusion Télévision Marocaine (1978). **Addr.:** Rabat, Morocco.

KHALIS (Salah Abdul Rahman), Iraqi academic. **Born** in 1925 in Basrah, Iraq. **Married,** 2 children. **Educ.:** Higher Institute for Teachers, Baghdad; University of Paris, France. **Dipl.:** Licence in Arabic Language, Ph.D. in Literature. **Career:** Lecturer at the College of Arts, Baghdad University (1953-58); Director General of Education (1958-61); Professor, Moscow University (1961-67); Chief Editor of "al-Thaqafa" monthly Magazine. **Prof. Addr.:** al-Thaqafa Journal, al-Tahrir Square, Baghdad, Iraq.

KHALISI (Yassin, Mahmoud), Iraqi businessman. **Born** in Baghdad, Iraq. **Educ.:** Yale University, USA. **Dipl.:** M.Sc. in Philosophy, Ph.D. in Archaelogy. **Career:** Archaelogist, General Archaelogy Directorate, Baghdad (1964-69); Member of, the National Society for American Arab, the American society for Arabic Language Teachers, the Arab American Chamber of Commerce, the American Chamber of Commerce andthe Middle East Studies Society in North Africa; Researcher and Lecturer, University of California, USA (1975-); President of Arabico Company Ltd. (1978-). **Publ.:** "Bit-Kispim in Mesopotamian Architecture", XII, Italy (1976), "Tell al-Fakhar", "Assur 1/6", Malibu, USA (1977), "The Court of Palms", a Functional Interpretation of the Mari Palace, Undena Publications, Malibu, USA (1978). **Hobbies:** Reading, jogging, tennis, writing, football. **Prof. Addr.:** Arabico Inc., 864 South Robertson Blvd., Suite 105, Los Angeles, CA 90035, USA.

KHALLAF (Hamid M.), Saudi geologist. **Born** in 1941 at Yanbu. **Dipl.:** B.Sc., M.Sc. (Geology). **Career:** Geologist, General Directorate of Minerals Resources; attended Second Arab Conference for Mineral Resources, Jeddah (1974). **Publ.:** research papers on degree sheet of Jeddah, Afif Area; North Western Hejaz Area. **Hobbies:** Reading, travel. **Prof. Addr.:** General Directorate of Mineral Resources, Tel.: 6310355, Jeddah. **Priv. Addr.:** Tel.: 6653520, Jeddah, Saudi Arabia.

KHAMIS (Abdallah Ibn Mohamad, bin), Saudi leading man of letters. **Born** in 1920 at al-Malaga, near al-Dera'iya, Saudi Arabia. **Dipl.:** B.A. (Islamic Law and Arabic Language), Mecca (1945). **Career:** Director, al-Ihsa Scientific Institute; Director of Islamic Law and Arabic Language Faculties, Riyadh; Director General, Presidency of Judges; Deputy Minister, Ministry of Communications; President, Governor, Riyadh Governorate; Chairman, Dera'iya Multi-purpose Welfare Committee; member, the Charitable Fund Society, Riyadh; member, Umm al-Qura Calendar Committee; member of the Higher Information Committee; Adviser, Ministry of Information; Vice President, Peoples Committee for Collecting Donations for the Palestine Issue; member of the Board, al-Jazeerah Organization for Press and Publications; member of the editorial staff of al-Arabia magazine; al-Darah magazine; member of the Committee for Denominating Districts and Squares of Riyadh city; the Iraqi Scientific Association, Iraq, Arabic Language Association, Cairo, the Monumental Council for al-Deray'iya. **Honours:** Order of Merit for Culture, Tunisia; the Gold Medal for Pioneers awarded by King Abdulaziz Univesity; Band of Honour and Sash of Recognition awarded by Fatah Organization of Palestine; a medal from the President of France. **Publ.:** Books: A Month in Damascus; The Folk Literature; Rashid al-Khalawi; Passage Between al-Yamama and al-Hijaz; The Wonders (3 vols.); On the Hillocks of Yamama (Poetry); al-Yamama Geographical Dictionary (2 vols.); Our Country and Oil; Out of Pleasant Evening Chats; in addition to other books in the process of being published; numerous articles. **Hobbies:** Travel, hunting, reading, folk literature of Arabian Peninsula. **Addr.:** al-Malaz, Jareer Street, P.O.Box 1798, Tel.: 4788510, Riyadh. **Priv. Addr.:** Tel.: 4645603, Riyadh, Saudi Arabia.

KHAMIS (Abdul Rahman Mohamad, al), Saudi executive. **Born** in 1947, at al-Attar, Sidair. **Dipl.:** M.Sc. (Engineering Management). **Career:** Engineer (1974); Director of Engineering Department (1976); Assistant Director General, Real Estate Development Fund; Deputy Governor for Administration and Finance, Saline Water Conversion Corporation. **Addr.:** Saline Water Conversion Corporation, P.O.Box 5968, Tel.: 4760023, Riyadh, Saudi Arabia.

KHAMIS (Abdul Razzak, al), Kuwaiti official. **Born** in 1930. **Married. Educ.:** in Kuwait. **Career:** Administrative and Financial Affairs, Ministry of the Interior, Kuwait (1948); Permanent Under Secretary at the Ministry of Defense (1974-86), retired. **Addr.:** Kuwait City, Kuwait.

KHAMIS (Mohamad Hamoud), Yemeni politician. **Born** in 1940 in Wadi Bani Hushaigh, republic of Yemen. **Son** of Hamoud Nasser Khamis. **Married** in 1964, 7 children: 6 sons: Samir (1966), Amin (1967); Khalid (1968); Sadiq (1970), Yusri (1974), Ibrahim (1976) and 1 daughter: Bushra (1971). **Educ.:** Secondary School, graduate of Police College. **Career:** Assistant Director-General, Police and staff of the Police College; Deputy Director-General of Public Security (1966-68); Director General of Security (1968-70); Director of the Department of General Administration, National Security (1971); Director, National Security (1972); Director of the Central Office, National Security (1975-79); Minister of the Interior (1979-82); **Hobbies:** Romantic and detective novels. **Addr:** Sanaa, Republic of Yemen.

KHAMMACHE (Amer), Jordanian politician. **Born** in 1924, in Salt, Jordan. **Married. Educ.:** Arab British College (Middle East) (1944); British Military Institutes in the Middle East and UK (1944-49); Royal Air Force Academy, UK (1949); American Military Staff College in Leavenworth, USA (1958). **Career:** Jordan Army (1941); Commander of Artillery Corps (1957-62); Director of Organization and Planning at Jordan Army Headquarters (1963-64); Chief of Staff at Jordan Army Headquarters, with rank of Major General (1965-67); Chief of General Staff, Jordan Army, with rank of Lieutenant General (1967-69); Minister of Defence (1969); Minister of Defence and Transport (1969); Minister of the Royal Court (1972-73); Political Adviser to HM the King (1973-74); Senator (1974-84). **Decor.** Independance Medals, 1st Class, 2nd Class, 4th Class; Renaissance Medal, 3rd Class; Star of Jordan, 3rd Class; Medal of Loyal Service: Libyan Medal, French Medal. **Addr.:** Tel.: 37341, Shmaisani, Amman, Jordan.

KHAMRI (Abdullah, al), Yemeni politician. **Born** in 1930 in Aden, Republic of Yemen. **Career:** joined National Liberation Front (NLF) in 1964; Director of NLF, Cairo; Member of NLF Executive Committee (1968); Member, Ideological and Cultural Affairs Department, NLF Executive; Minister of State for the Council of Ministers and Minister of Information (1973-75); Personal representative of the Chairman of the Presidential Coucil; visited USSR for study (1976); Minister of State for Cabinet Affairs (1980-82); Member of the Political Bureau, Yemen Socialist Party (1980-1991). **Addr.:** Aden, Republic of Yemen.

KHAN (Imran R.), Pakistani banker. **Born** on October 7, 1950 in Lahore, Pakistan. **Son** of A. Rashid Khan (Army Officer) and Mrs. Maimoona Rashid Khan. **Married** on January 23, 1973 in Karachi to Miss Shahida Khan, 2 children: Anouk Khan (daughter) (1/12/74), Nayef Khan (son) (13/9/77). **Educ.:** Karachi Grammar School; University of Karachi. **Dipl.:** Graduate (B.A. Economics). **Career:** worked for American Express Bank since June 1968; (In Karachi till Oct. 1984), from Nov. 1984 seconded to Egyptian American Bank, Cairo (an Affiliate of Amex). **Sports:** Tennis, Golf. **Hobby:** Reading. **Member:** Sind club,

Karachi; Gezira Sporting, Cairo. **Credit Cards:** Amex, Visa, Mastercharge. **Prof. Addr.:** Egyptian American Bank, 6 Hassan Sabri Street, Zamalek, P.O.Box 1825, Cairo 11511, Tel.: 63415411, Egypt. **Prof. Addr.:** 11, Ebn Zanki Street, Zamalek, Tel.: 63400997, Cairo, Egypt.

KHAN (Mahmoud, Abdul Latif), Saudi composer of lyrics. **Born** in 1936 in Mecca, Saudi Arabia. **Educ.:** received general education suplemented by extensive musical education and practice. **Career:** in business for 25 years; has taken part in several musical performances in Cairo (Egypt), Abu Dhabi (United Arab Emirates), Kuwait Bahrain, Iran, Algeria and Tunis; now senior Civil Servant, Department of Music, Ministry of Information. **Sports:** Football and cycling. **Hobby:** Music. **Prof. Addr.:** Department of Music, Ministry of Information, Tel.: 26222 Jeddah. **Priv. Addr.:** Tel.: 21039, Jeddah, Saudi Arabia.

KHANACHET (Samer, Subhi), Kuwaiti executive. **Born** in 1951 in Paris, France. **Son** of Subhi Khanachet. **Married** in 1977, 1 sons. **Educ.:** M.I.T., B.Sc. (Chemical Engineering) (1973); B.Sc. (Management) (1973); Harvard, M.B.A. (1975). **Career:** Executive Vice President, Sharjah Group Co., Kuwait. **Addr.:** P.O.Box 24328, Tel.: 444147-9 Telex: 22781 A/B SHARGRO KT, Safat, Kuwait.

KHARAFI (Jasim, Mohamed, al), Kuwaiti Businessman, Statesman. **Born** 08th. Dec. 1940 in Kuwait. **Married. Educ.:** Victoria College, Alexandria, Egypt. **Career:** Chairman, Mohamed Abdulmohsin Al Kharafi & Sons W.L.L. (private enterprise); Member National Assembly (1975-1980-1985). Former Minister of Finance and Economy (1985-1990). **Sport:** Swimming. **Hobby:** Fishing: **Addr.:** Mohamed Abdulmohsin Al Kharafi & Sons W.L.L., P.O.Box 886 Safat, 13009 Kuwait. Tel.: 4813622, Fax. 4813339, Tlx. 22071 & 23569 Kharafi Kwt.

KHARAFI (Mohamad Abdul Mohsin, al), Kuwaiti businessman. **Born** in 1919. **Married. Educ.:** in Kuwait. **Career:** Established Kharafi Industries Establishment, a leading Contracting firm; Vice President of the Board, of Directors of Kuwait Chamber of Commerce (1986); Founder Member (in 1952) and Vice Chairman (1965) of National Bank of Kuwait; Director, Kuwait Oil Tanker Company; Kuwait Cinema Company; Elected to National Assembly (1967); Vice Chairman: FRAB Bank (France), FRAB Bank International (Paris) Chairman FRAB Bank (Middle East) E.C., Bahrain; Director FRAB Holdings SA, Luxembourg (1982-); Director, of Rifbank Beirut; Chairman, National Bank of Kuwait S.A.K., Safat, Kuwait (1980-). **Addr.:** Abdullah al-Salem Street, Tel.: 422011, Telex; 2451, 2043 KT, P.O.Box 95, 13001 Safat, Kuwait and P.O.Box 886, 13009 Safat, Kuwait.

KHARRAT (Edwar, al), Egyptian writer. **Born** in 1926 in Alexandria, Egypt. **Educ.:** Alexandria University, Egypt. **Dipl.:** LLB. **Career:** Assistant Secretary General, Afro-Asian People's Solidarity Organisation, Cairo, Egypt; writer of short stories and literary critic; Won several prizes; Associate Senior Member of St. Anthony's College, Oxford University, UK (1979); Lectured at, School of Oriental and African Studies, University of London, England; Editor of "The Lotus", "The Afro Asian Writings" (quarterly of the Afro-Asian writers Association); Assisted in the editing of "Gallery 68". **Publ.:** translations of several works into Arabic; two collections of short stories, several novels. and five books of literary criticism. **Prof. Addr.:** 45 Ahmad Hishmat Street, Zamalek, Cairo, Egypt.

KHASAWNA (Ali Mahmoud), Jordanian Economist. **Born** on July 10, 1929 in Ni'aimeh, Irbid, Jordan. **Married** in July 1959, 2 daughters and 2 sons. **Educ.:** in Lebanon, U.S.A. and England. **Dipl.:** B.A. Economics, American University of Beirut, Lebanon (1953); M.A. Economics, George Washington University, Washington (1955); Special training for six months in the International Bank for Reconstruction and Development, Washington (1958); M. Phil, Economics, London University; Ph.D. Economics, London University. **Career:** Teaching Economics as part-time job with the Teachers College in Amman, Jordan (1953); teaching Economics as part-time job with the Army Police College of Jordan (1956-57); Manager of Supplies Department, Manager of Trade & Supplies Department, Manager of Research & Economic Studies Department, Manager of Industries Department with Jordan Ministry of Economy; Manager, Arab Bank, Khartoum, Sudan (1959-60); General Manager, Kuwait Oil Tanker Company (since 15 October 1960) and as Managing Director (July 1967- December 1975); Vice-Chairman, Jordan Shipping Co.; Member of the Board of Directors of Aqaba Port; Member of the Board of Directors of the Arab Federation for the Chemical Fertilizers based in Kuwait (1975); General Manager, Arab Potash Company, Amman (December 1975- March 1977) and Chairman & Managing Director, same company (March 1977-78); Teaching the Economics of Petroleum, Jordan University (1977-78). **Work:** Member of Board of Directors of Jordan Central Electrical Company as a representative of Jordan Government; Member of Board of Directors of Olive Oil Refinery as a representative of Jordan Government; Member of Economic Development Committee, Jordan Government; Secretary of Economic Development Committee; Member of Industries Loans Committee, Jordan Government; Preparing, broadcasting and publishing the Price Bulletin on behalf of the Ministry of Economy, Jordan Government; Member of Jordan Government Delegation in the negotiation with the World Bank Representatives for reviewing the World Bank's Draft Report on the Jordan Economy which has later been published by the Bank in the book form; Member of Jordan Economic Delegation in the negotiations between the Government of both Jordan and Syria, held in Damascus in 1956, which ended with an agreement for the unification of the Economy of both countries (the Agreement was not implemented for certain political circumstances); Representative for Jordan Government on the Arab League Economic Experts Committee which met in Lebanon in 1956 and concluded with an agreement project for the unity of the economy of all the Arab League Member Countries; Representative for Jordan Government on the Joint Committee of Economists (Iraq and Jordan Governments) which was responsible for all the arrangements and studies of unifying the economy of both countries as a result of their confederation (1958); Member of the Jordan Government Committee which has translated from English to Arabic the report of the World Bank of the Economy of Jordan (1954); Member of the Committee which had done the formulation of the Law of the Development Board of Jordan; Member of the Committee which had done the formulation of the Amalgamation of the Jordan Agricultural Credit Institutions; Expert of the Refugees Individual Economic Projects financed by the United Nations; Attended Arab Oil Conference: Cairo, Baghdad, Algeria and Dubai; attended World Seatrade Conference in London (1974). **Member:** Executive Committee, International Association of the Independent Tanker Owners; Executive Committee, Steam Ship mutual underwriting Association Ltd., London; Naltic Exchange, London; Institute of Directors, London; Middle East Section. Chamber of Commerce, London; Institute of Marine Engineers, London; Executive Committee, Kuwait Shipping Association. **Priv. Addr.:** Tel.: 65204, 66933, Amman, Jordan.

KHASAWNIH (Sami), Jordanian University Professor. **Born** in 1939 in Irbid, Jordan. **Son** of Abdullah Khasawnih (farmer) **and** Mrs. Aneesah Khasawnih. **Married** in 1986 at Jeddah, Saudi Arabia to Sana' Malbi, 4 children: Diala (1975), Alma (1978), Abdullah (1987), Abdul-Hameed (1990). **Educ.:** State University of New York at Plattsbourgh, State University of New York at Albany. **Dipl.:** B.Sc., M. Sc., Ed.D. **Career:** Instructor, Teacher Training College; Member, University Faculty, College of Education, University of Jordan; Vice-Dean, Department Chairman; Dean, Faculty of Educational Sciences, University of Jordan; UNESCO Consultant; ALECSO Consultant; Visiting Professor- Member of several Universities. **Member:** Phi Delta, Kappa - Jordan's Writers' Society. **Prof. Addr.:** University of Jordan, Tel.: 843555/3450, Amman, Jordan. **Priv. Addr.:** P.O.Box 13064, Tel.: 844200, Amman, Jordan.

KHASH (Mohamad Najib, al), Syrian agriculturalist. **Born** in 1927, in Massyaf, Syria. **Son** of Najib al-Khash. **Married**, three children. **Educ.:** B.Sc. in Botany, Zoology and Chemistry, London University (1956), M.Sc. and Ph.D. in Plant Pathology University of Arizona, USA (1965-69). **Career:** Researcher, Plant Pathology Laboratory, Ministry of Agriculture (1963-64); Director of Agricultural Scientific Research, Ministry of Agriculture (1970-71); General Director the Arab Center for the Study of Arid Zones and Dry lands (since 1971 to present). **Member** of the Board of Trustees of the International Food Policy Research Institute. **Addr.:** The Arab Center for the Study of Arid Zones and Dry Lands, P.O.Box 2440, Damascus, Syria.

KHASHO (Yusif, Saad), Jordanian musician. **Born** in 1927 in Jerusalem. **Married**, 1 daughter. **Educ.:** Academia Gentium Pro Pace. **Dip.:** Degree in Law, Piano, Composition and Orchestra Conducting and Music. **Career:** Lands Department, Palestine (1945-47); Music Teacher in Jerusalem (1947-48); Organist, Basilica of Holy Sepulchre, Jerusalem (1942-48); Orchestra Leader in Syria and Lebanon (1949-55); Choir Master, orchestra conductor and music orchestrator, Sydney, Australia (1955-66); Director, Jordanian Conservatorium of Music (1966-68); Musical Adviser in Libya (1969-72); Director of Musical Studies Centre, CSM, Rome, Italy (1972-). **Publ.:** 12 Symphonies including "Jerusalem Symphony" (1968), "Hussein's Jordan No. 2" (1968), as well as Melodies from Jordan and several other records. **Decor.:** Order of Independence (3rd Class) (1966); Order of the Jordanian Kawkab (3rd Class) (1968). **Hobbies:** Music, arts, reading. **Addr.:** Amman, Jordan.

KHASHOKJY (Sadaqa Hasan), Saudi official. **Born** in 1928 in Medina, Saudi Arabia. **Dipl.:** Baccalaureate; Diploma: Journalism, Law Studies (Damascus University). **Career:** Director, Passport Department, Medina; member of Welfare Society, City of Medina Endowments Council; Board member, Medina Water and Drainage Department, Medina Governorate Administrative Council, Municipal Council; Mayor of Medina; participant, Organization of Arab Cities, Organization of Islamic Capitals, Organization of Large Cities, Italy. **Publ.:** "al-Medina al-Monawarah: The First Municipality in Islam". **Hobbies:** Reading, soccer. **Prof. Addr.:** al-Medina Municipality, Tel.: 8231160, Medina. **Priv. Addr.:** Tel.: 8222254, Medina, Saudi Arabia.

KHATEEB (Mohammad Shahhat, H.), Saudi Professor of Comparative and International Education. **Born** in 1954 in Al Madinah Al-Munawwara, Saudi Arabia. **Son** of Shahhat Khateeb (Social Security Off.) **and** Mrs. née Aydah Sadaka (Headmaster of Elementary School). **Married** on Shaban 27, 1983 in Jeddah to Haiyfa Idriss, 4 children: Faisal (1984), Daniah (1987), Reem (1989) and Abdulaziz (1992). **Educ.:** Saad Bin Moaaz Elementary Shcool in Madinah, Al Farooq Preparatory School in Madinah, OHOD Secondary School in Madinah, King Abdulaziz University in Makkah for B.A., UCLA for Master, and USC for PH.D. **Dipl.:** B.A. (1976) in Education and Psychology (King Abdulaziz University), M.A. (1981) in Sociology of Education (UCLA Los Angeles), PH.D. (1985) in Comp. and Inrena. ED (U.S.C. Los Angeles). **Career:** 1977: Teacher at Madinah Institute for Teacher Education; 1977-1978: Deputy Principal of Madinah Institute for T.E.; 1978: T.A. at King Saud University in Riyadh; 1985: Assistant Professor; 1989:

Associate Professor; 1994: Prof. Full.; 1993: Director of the Center of Educational Research; 1995: Dean of the College of ED., King Saud University, Riyadh. Recently, the General Director of King Faisal Schools, Riyadh, Saudi Arabia. **Other Information:** President of the Saudi Association of Education and Psychology. **Decors:** Price Winner of Education by the Arab Bureau of Education for the Gulf States. **Sport:** Basket-Ball. **Hobbies:** Writing Research "40 Articles and 16 Books Now". **Associations:** Egyptian Society for Comparative Education. **Prof. Addr.:** P.O.Box 44558, Riyadh 11614 Tel.: 4887330 or 4827257, Fax: 4821521, Saudi Arabia E-Mail. dgkFs@KFF.com. **Priv. Addr.:** Tel.: 01/468 3662, 04/824 3700, Mobile Phone: 412100.

KHATIB (Abdul Karim, al), Moroccan politician. **Born** in 1921 in al-Jedida, Morocco. **Married**, 1 son, 5 daughters. **Dipl.:** M.D., Surgeon. **Career:** participated in the Moroccan Resistance and the Formation of Arab Maghreb Resistance Army; Founding Member of the Popular Movement (1957); Founder and Leader of the Popular Constitutional Democratic Movement (after the split in the Movement); Minister of Employment and Social Affairs (1961); Minister of Health (1962); presided over the first Moroccan Parliament (1963-65); State Minister (1977); Lecturer at Universite Mohammed V. **Hobbies:** Carpet collection, horse riding, philatelist. **Prof. Addr.:** c/o Medical Syndicate, Rabat, Morocco.

KHATIB (Abdulilah, al-), Jordanian Politician. **Born** on March 31, 1953 in Salt. **Married,** three children **Educ.:** B.A., Political Science, PANTEIOS, Athens, Greece; M.A., International Communications, American University, USA; M.A., Social Change and Development, John's Hopkins University, USA. **Career:** Official, Embassy of Jordan to Athens (1976-81); Attaché, Department of International Organizations, Ministry of Foreign Affairs; Member, Delegation of Jordan to UN general Assembly (1982); Second Secretary, Embassy of Jordan to USA (1984-88); Director, Special Bureau, Ministry of Foreign Affairs (1988-93); Assistant General for Investments, Middle East Insurance Co. (1993-94); General Manager, Aldammam for Investments (1994-95); General Manager, Jordan Cement Factories Co. (1996-98) Minister of Tourism (1995-96); Minister of Foreign Affairs (1998-to date). **Address:** Ministry of Foreign Affairs, P.O.Box 35217, Amman, Jordan.

KHATIB (Ahmed, al), Syrian politician. **Born** in Suwaydaa, Syria in 1933. **Son** of Hassan al-Khatib **and** Hindiya al-Farra. **Married** to Souraya al-Khatib in 1959, three children. **Career:** formerly, Head, Syrian Teachers Association; member, Presidential Council (1965-68); Acting President of Syria (1970- Jan. 71); Chairman, People's Council (Feb.- Dec. 1971); President, Fed. Ministerial Council Federation of Arab Republics (1972-75); member, Ba'ath Party, elected to Leadership Committee (May 1971). **Hobby:** Shooting. **Addr.:** c/o Syrian Ba'ath Party, Damascus, Syria.

KHATIB (Farouk S.), Saudi academic. **Born** in 1948 in Mecca, Saudi Arabia. **Dipl.:** Ph.D. (Economics). **Career:** Demonstrator (1972) and later Lecturer (1975) King Abdulaziz University; member, the Econometric Society, U.S.A. and the International Economic Islamic Conference; General Consultant, Tihama for Advertising, Public Relations and Marketing Research; Associate Professor, Faculty of Economics and Administration, King Abdulaziz University. **Honour:** a medal for outstanding achievement in education, 1972. **Publ.:** some articles on the Demand for Housing in Saudi Arabia. **Prof. Addr.:** King Abdulaziz University, Faculty of Economics and Administration, P.O.Box 9031, Tel.: 6444444, Jeddah. **Priv. Addr.:** Tel.: 6918344, Jeddah, Saudi Arabia.

KHATIB (Fuad Abdulhameed, al), Saudi diplomat. **Born** in 1925 in Mecca, Saudi Arabi. **Dipl.:** B.A. in Economics and Political Science. **Career:** Served as a member of the Diplomatic Corp in the following countries: Pakistan, Iraq, U.S.A., Nigeria, Turkey and Bangladesh; Acting Ambassador in Turkey (March 1976 to June 1976); Ambassador to Bangladesh, also held the position of Ambassador Extraordinary of Saudi Arabia to Nepal and Bangladesh; member of the Saudi delegation to several conferences of the U.N. and the Organization of Islamic Conference; led several Saudi Arabian delegations to more than 13 African countries; Director, Department of Islamic Affairs, Ministry of Foreign Affairs, Jeddah; member, the Arab Peace Committee to Yemen, the Committee of the Organization of Islamic Conference for the cause Philippine Muslims and Okaz Press Establishment, Jeddah. **Publ.:** Towards a perfect Living System (booklet); a widerange of lectures (in Arabic and English) on topics relating to Politics and Islam delivered at Various National and international conferences and seminars. **Hobbies:** Reading, participation in religious and social activities. **Prof. Addr.:** Ministry of Foreign Affairs, Riyadh, Saudi Arabia.

KHATIB (Hisham), Jordanian politician. **Born** on January 5, 1936 in Acre. **Son** of Mohamed Khatib and Mrs., née Fahima Tabari. **Married** to Maha Khatib, 3 children: Mohammad, Lein and Issam. **Educ.:** University of Ain Shams, Egypt; University of London, UK. **Dipl.:** B.Sc. in Engineering (1959); B.Sc. in Economics (1967); Ph.D. in Electrical Engineering (1974). **Career:** Chief Engineer, Jerudalem District Electrical Co. (1955-74); Deputy Director General, Jordan Electricity Authority (1974-76); Senior Energy Engineer, Arab Fund, Kuwait (1976-80); Director General, Jordan Electricity Authority (JEA) (1980-84); Minister of Energy and Mineral Resources, Jordan (1984-89) Minister of Planning (1993-95). **Decor.:** Decorated in Jordan, Spain, Vatican, Austria, Italy and Indonesia. **Sport:** Jogging. **Hobby:** Antiques of the Holy

Land. **Member:** F.IEE; F.IEEE; Jordan Engineering Association; Jordan Fine Arts Association. **Credit Cards.:** Visa, American Express, Access. **Priv. Addr.:** P.O.Box 925387, Tel.: 5621532, Amman, Jordan.

KHATIB (Ismail, Muhamad al-Arabi, al), Moroccan academic. **Born** in 1942 in Tetuan, Morocco. **Married,** 2 daughters. **Educ.:** Dar al-Hadith al Husniya, Rabat, Morocco. **Dipl.:** B.A. in Islamic Studies and Higher Studies. **Career:** Teacher, Moroccan Schools (1969); Professor, Faculty of Islamic Law, University of Quarawyin, Fes, Morocco (1973), Professor of Islamic Thought, College of Islamic Studies, Tetuan (1975-); Supervisor of "Rasa'il al-Nour" Journal and Director of "al-Nour" Journal. **Hobbies:** Jogging, walking, Moroccan Andalusian heritage. **Member:** Moroccan Scientists Federation. **Prof. Addr.:** Beirut Street, 112 Tetwan, P.O.Box 4060, Tetwan, Morocco.

KHATIB (Mahmoud, Ibrahim, al), Egyptian businessman. **Born** in 1954 in Cairo, Egypt. **Married,** 1 daughter. **Educ.:** Faculty of Commerce, Cairo University, Egypt. **Career:** Captain of the Egyptian National Football Team (1971-); Member, International Arab Team (1982-83); Head of a sports company; Captain of the International Egyptian Team (1973). **Decor.:** 6 times Best Egyptian Football player. **Award:** Golden Ball Award, French Football Magazine (1983). **Prof. Addr.:** 4 el-Mathaf el-Zerate, Giza, Dokki, Egypt. **Priv. Addr.:** 10 Ahmed Sabri Street, Zamalek, Cairo, Egypt.

KHATIB (Mohamad, al), Jordanian journalist and politician. **Born** in Ramth, Jordan, in 1930. **Educ.:** Cairo University. **Dipl.:** B.A. **Career:** Director of Middle East News Agency, Cairo (until 1964); Founder of Jordanian News Agency, Petra; former Director of Press and Publications, Director Radio Jordan, Plenipotentiary Minister at Ministry of Foreign Affairs and Government of Ma'an, Karak and Balqa Governments; Minister of Information and Minister of Culture, Tourism and Antiquities (1985-89). **Addr.:** Amman, Jordan.

KHATIB (Mohamad, Fathallah), Egyptian academic and politician. **Born** on January 1, 1927 in Gharbieh Governorate (Egypt). **Married** in 1960 to Amira Mohamad Khadr, three daughters. **Educ.:** Faculty of Commerce, Cairo University and University of Edinburgh, Scotland. **Career:** Director of Research, United Nations Section, Arab States Delegation Office, New York (1958-61); lecturer in Political Science, University of Cairo (Egypt); Reader in Political Science (1961-67); Professor of Comparative Government (1967-71); Dean, Faculty of Economics and Political Science (1968-71); Minister of Social Affairs, Cairo (May- September 1971); Adviser to the President of the Republic on Home Economy and Social Affairs (1971-72); Secretary-General, Arab Socialist Union, Cairo Governorate (1971-72); Minister of State and Chairman, Council of Foreign Affairs, Arab Republic of Egypt (December 1971). **Publ.:** author of "Power Politics in the United Nations" (1962), "Local Government in the Arab Republic of Egypt" (1964), "Introduction to Political Science" (1969). **Hobbies:** Reading and music. **Prof. Addr.:** Faculty of Economics and Political Science, Cairo University, Cairo. **Priv. Addr.:** 11 Ibn Zinky street, Zamalek District, Cairo, Egypt.

KHATIB (Mohamad, Khedr), Saudi academic. **Born** on June 1937 in Medina, Saudi Arabia. **Dipl.:** Ph.D. **Career:** Demonstrator (1965); Chairman of Physics Department (1980); Assistant Professor, Department of Physics, Faculty of Science, King Saud University. **Member:** American Society for Physics. **Publ.:** Principles of Electronics. **Prof. Addr.:** Physics Department, Faculty of Science, King Saud University, Tel.: 4829012 Ext. 293, Riyadh. **Priv. Addr.:** Tel.: 4711000, Ext. 2415, Riyadh, Saudi Arabia.

KHATIB (Omar, Ismail, al), Jordanian academic. **Born** in 1931 in Ain Karm, Jerusalem. **Son** of Ismail al-Khatib. **Married,** seven children. **Educ.:** Syracuse University, USA; Ohio State University, USA. **Dipl.:** B.A. in Social Sciences (1956); M.A. in Television and Radio and Ph.D. in Public Communications Media. **Career:** Head of Production Department, Jordan Broadcasting Station (1959-61); General Supervisor of Programmes, Jordanian Broadcasting Station (1963-64); seconded by Jordanian Government as television and radio consultant, Saudi Arabia (1964-67); Assistant General Manager, Jordanian TV Corporation; Director of Abu Dhabi Radio and Television; Director of Arab League Offices, Dallas, Texas, USA (1973); Professor of Information, Jordan University (1973-75); Consultant to the United Arab Emirates (UAE), Ministry of Culture and Information for Television Affairs and Deputy General Manager of UAE Television; Professor of Mass Communications, University of Riyadh, Saudi Arabia (since 1980). Member of Information Committee in Arab Studies Department and various academic associations in the information field. **Sports:** Swimming, squach. **Hobby:** Reading. **Addr.:** University of Riyadh, P.O.B. 2454, Riyadh, Saudi Arabia.

KHATIB (Walid, Hashem), Jordanian businessman. **Born** in 1938. **Son** of Hashem Abdulsalam Khatib **and** Mrs. Wadad née Eid Khatib. **Married** in 1962 in Jerusalem, to Fadwa Khalil Triki, four children. **Educ.:** Kinsington University of USA. **Dipl.:** Master of Arts "Business Administrations". **Career:** Manager, West German company; Manager, Arab Advertising Agency. **Medals:** Amman Chamber of Industry Shield; GEA West German Co. Golden Model. **Sports:** Swimming, jogging. **Hobbies:** Reading, travelling, driving. **Member** of Lions Club. **Credit Cards:** Visa Card. **Prof. Addr.:** P.O.Box 7434, Tel.: 665273, Amman, Jordan. **Priv. Addr.:** Um-Othayna, Tel.: 815540, Amman, Jordan.

KHATIB (Yassir, Abdul-Hameed, al), Saudi academic. **Born** in Taif in 1946. **Educ.:** Diploma in Islamic Studies; Diploma in Demography; M.B.A. **Career:** Former advisory expert, Arab League Industrial Development Centre; member of UN Demographic Centre, Cairo; Lecturer, Faculty of Economics and Administration, King Abdulaziz University. **Publ.:** research paper on the development of elementary education and its future progress in Saudi Arabia, submitted to UN Demographic Centre. **Hobbies:** Football, reading. **Addr.:** Khalid Ibn el-Waleed, Medina Road, Khatib Building, Flat 15, Tel.: 6879033, Jeddah, Saudi Arabia.

KHATIBI (Abdul Kibir), Moroccan writer. **Born** in 1938 in al-Jadida, Morocco. **Career:** Director, Institute of Sociology, Rabat, Morocco (1966-70); Professor, Faculty of Arts, Mohammed V. University, Rabat; attached to the University Center of Scientific Research; Editor in Chief of "the Social and Economic Bulletin of Morocco" **Publ.:** "Le Lutteur de Classe à la Manière Taoiste" poetry, "La Manier Taouée" novel (1971), "La Blessure de Mon Propre" (1974), "Vomito Blanco" Essays (1974). **Hobbies:** Philosophy, literature, history. **Addr.:** Rabat, Morocco.

KHATRAWI (Mohamad, al-Eid, al), Saudi academic. **Born** in 1935 in Medina city, Saudi Arabia. **Educ.:** King Abdul Aziz University, Jeddah, Saudi Arabia. **Dipl.:** B.A. (Islamic Law), M.A. (Literature and Criticism). **Career:** Teacher in religious institutes; Lecturer, Faculty of Islamic Law; Secondary school teacher; Vice-Principal of secondary school; attended the first conference of Saudi Men of Letters (1974); Principal of Qiba secondary school. **Publ.:** author of "Guide to Worship", "Glories of Riyadh", "Pre-Islamic War Poetry". **Sport:** Basketball. **Hobbies:** Reading and music. **Addr.:** Qiba Secondary school, Medina, Saudi Arabia.

KHATTAB (Ezzat Abdul Majid), Saudi academic. **Born** in 1939. **Educ.:** Ph.D. (English Literature). **Career:** Assistant Lecturer, Lecturer in English, Chairman of the Department of English, King Saud University; Dean, Faculty of Arts, King Saud University. **Addr.:** Faculty of Arts, King Saud University, Riyadh, Saudi Arabia.

KHATTAB (Mahmoud, Chit), Iraqi army officer and writer. **Born** in Iraq. **Son** of Chit Khattab. **Educ.:** Secondary and Military Academy. **Career:** In the Army, General; Former Minister; Writer; Member of the Arab Academy in Baghdad. **Publ.:** Author of several works including "Road to Victory". **Addr.:** c/o Arab Academy, Baghdad, Iraq.

KHATTABI (Larbi), Moroccan politician. **Born** in 1929 in Tetouan, Morocco. **Married**, three children. **Educ.:** Literary studies in France and Spain; Studies in International Organisation, School for International Studies, Geneva, Switzerland. **Career:** Inspector of Education in Tetouan; Senior Civil Servant, Ministry of Posts and Telecommunications and Ministry of Foreign Affairs; Permanent Moroccan Delegate to the UN in Geneva, and later in Vienna, Austria (1968); Minister of Employment and Social Services (1974); President, Governing Body of International Labour Organisation ILO (1977); Minister of Information (1980); Keeper of the Royal Library (since 1980). **Publ.:** various articles in Arab press. **Addr.:** Royal Library, Royal Palace, Rabat, Morocco.

KHATTECH (Hichem), Tunisian General Manager. **Born** on March 1948 in Tunis, Tunisia. **Son** of Chedly Khattech (Doctor) **and** Mrs. Essia Lakhoua. **Married** in April 1990 in Tunis to Rim Chaubane, 3 children: Mehdi (1980) in Tunis to Rim Chaubane, 3 children: Mehdi (1988), Chedly (1991), Nour (1993). **Educ.:** Ecole des Mines, Paris (France), Institut Français du Petrole. **Dipl.:** General Engineer. **Career:** ETAP (Tunisian National Oil Co.) 1978-1982); Paktank Tunisia (1983-1987); Maghrib Oil S.A. (1987-) and Presently its General Manager. **Sports:** Tennis, Swimming. **Hobby:** Yachting. **Prof. Addr.:** Maghrib Oil, P.O.Box 85, 2048 Ariana, Tel.: 717576, 718185, Tunis. Tunisia. **Priv. Addr.:** Lasoukka, Choutrana 2, Tel.: 764607, Tunis, Tunisia.

KHAYAL (Abdul Malik A., al), Saudi academic. **Born** in 1941 at al-Majmaah, Saudi Arabia. **Dipl.:** Ph.D. (Geology). **Career:** Assistant Professor of Geology Department; Vice Dean of Faculty of Science, King Saud University; Dean, Faculty of Science, same University. **Member:** Advisory Council; American Society of Geology and of American Society of Petroleum Geologist; King Saud University Supreme Council and the Faculty Council. **Act.:** participated in developing the Faculty of Science, King Saud University; attended the conference on the Mission of the University. **Publ.:** reports on the Mineral Resources of the South-Western, Eastern, Central and Western regions on Saudi Arabia. **Hobbies:** Swimming, reading. **Prof. Addr.:** Faculty of Science, King Saud University, Tel.: 4761155, Riyadh. **Priv. Addr.:** Tel.: 4762122, Riyadh, Saudi Arabia.

KHAYAL (Fahd Alabdallah, al), Saudi official. **Born** in 1931 in Riyadh, Saudi Arabia. **Dipl.:** M.Sc. (Economics). **Career:** Governor, OPEC (1963); Assistant Deputy Minister for Technical Affairs, Ministry of Petroleum and Mineral Resources (1971); Deputy Minister for Technical Affairs and Companies, Ministry of Petroleum and Mineral Resources (1973); Chairman, Executive Committee, Getty Oil Company, Saudi/ Kuwait Joint Committee; member of Saudi delegations to several AOPEC conferences. **Priv. Addr.:** Tel.: 8325474, Dhahran, Saudi Arabia.

KHAYAT (Abdallah Omar), Saudi major businessman. **Born** in 1937 in Mecca, Saudi Arabia. **Educ.:** received general education. **Career:** Owner and Director General of Sahar Trading Est., Sahar Printing Press (Jeddah Industrial Zone), Sahar Printing Press (Yambu), Sahar Carpets House, Sahar Pharmacy, Sahar Sports Travel Agency (Manarah Marckets), Jeddah; established a modern $ 20 million computer - programmed press in Industrial Zone, Jeddah; member of Jeddah Chamber of Commerce and Industry; former General Manager of Mecca Bureau of al-Bilad daily, Editor-in-chief of Okaz Daily, Managing Editor of Okaz daily, participated in press coverage of most of late King Faisal's State visits to Arab, African and Western countries. **Member:** of the First Conference of Arab Journalists, Cairo (1966), 2nd Conference of Arab Journalists, Kuwait (1967); **Publ.:** Wamadat Qalam (Flashes of the pen) and Mukhtarat al-Khayyat (in 10 vols.) (Selections by Khayat). **Hobbies:** Travel, sports. **Prof. Addr.:** Tel.: 6316249, 6314405, Jeddah, Saudi Arabia.

KHAYAT (Abdeiah Ismail Abdul Rahman, Mrs.), Saudi academic. **Born** in Mecca in 1947. **Educ.:** B.B.A. (Business Administration), preliminary studies leading to M.A. postgraduate diploma in Journalism, Diploma (Administration and Educational Planning), King Adulaziz University (1979), M.A. (Administration and Educational Planning); Umm al-Qura University (1981). **Career:** Director of Girls' Secondary School, Jeddah; former teacher at the 20th School Mecca; Supervisor, Deputy Director of the 13th School, Jeddah; Director of Fourth Girls' Intermediate School, Jeddah; Assistant Director, Guidance Division, Western Province, General Directorate of Girls' Education, Jeddah and Editor, Women's Affairs, al-Bilad daily newspaper. **Member:** of Faisaliyah Women's Society. **Publ.:** press interviews with the wives of the Presidents of Egypt and Tunisia; a field study for B.A. degree entitled Purchasing Decisions in the Saudi Family. **Hobby:** Reading. **Prof. Addr.:** Zagzoug and Matbouli Building, Flat 8, Baghdadiyah, Tel.: 6514672, Jeddah. **Priv. Addr.:** Tel.: 6432033, 6429689, Jeddah, Saudi Arabia.

KHAYAT (Abdul Muhsin Abdul Kareem, al), Saudi civil servant. **Born** in 1939 at Hail, Saudi Arabia. **Dipl.:** M.B.A. (Business Administration). **Career:** Teacher, Supervisor, Budget Researcher and Director, Vocational Training Centres Department; Director, Riyadh Vocational Training Centre, Ministry of Labour and Social Affairs; attended several conferences on training, Arab League Training Course for Manpower, Training and Planning Officials, Cairo; Director General, Department of Finance and Administration, General Organization of Technical Education and Vocational Training. **Publ.:** two books on vocational training and on-the-job training and upgrading. **Hobbies:** Travel, teaching, reading. **Prof. Addr.:** General Organisation of Technical Education and Vocational Training, P.O.Box 7814, Tel.: 4786981, Riyadh. **Priv. Addr.:** Tel.: 2310223, 2310184, Riyadh, Saudi Arabia.

KHAYAT (Talal, M. Nuri, al), Iraqi academic. **Born** in 1935 in Mosul, Iraq. **Married,** 2 sons, 2 daughters. **Educ.:** University of Baghdad, Iraq; University of London, UK. **Dipl.:** M.B., Ch.B., M.Sc. in Biochemistry. **Career:** Lecturer, University of Mosul (1964); Assistant Professor (1972); Head, Biochemistry Department (1979); Associate Professor of Biochemistry. **Publ.:** "Serum Proteins in Diabetics" (1971), "Iraq" (in English), "Amilhar and Metabolism of Metals", West Germany, "Thyroglobulin Biosynthesis in Various Diseases", West Germany (1979). **Hobbies:** Travelling, swimming, music, writing, chess. **Prof. Addr.:** Medical Biochemistry Department, Mosul College of Medicine, Mosul, Iraq.

KHAYAT (The Bey John Victor), Arab-American businessman. **Born** in 1934 in Haifa, Palestine. **Married,** 2 sons. **Educ.:** Prior Park College, Bath, UK; Christchurch College, Oxford University, UK; Lincoln's Inn, UK; Harvard Business School, USA. **Dipl.:** M.A. Oxon. Barrister at law, PMD. **Career:** General Manager of Eckes International, Germany (1968); Managing Director of Felli Pizzinini SRL, Italy (1969); Middle East Representative of a banking Group in Germany (1974-); **Decor.:** Order of Independence, Jordan. **Hobbies:** Yachting, riding, shooting, skiing, excavations, arts and music, egyptology. **Addr.:** 20 Eaton Place, London SW1, United Kingdom.

KHAYATA (Abdul Wahab, Dr.), Syrian banker, former minister. **Born** on February 24, 1924 in Aleppo, Syria. **Son** of Ismail Khayata (deceased) **and** Mrs. Fatma Othman, née Hammami (deceased). **Married** to Miss Fathia Debbas in 1955 and to Miss Lamya Zakri in 1983, four children: Dr. Sahar Khayata, Dr. Mazen Khayata, Miss Rana Khayata and Talal Khayata. **Educ.:** Law School, Ecole Française de Droit, Lebanon (1946-49); London School of Economics (1949-51); University of Louvain, Belgium (1949-53). **Dipl.:** Doctorate in Finance (1953). **Career:** Deputy Governor and other functions at the Central Bank of Syria, Damascus (1953-63); Professor/Lecturer of Economics and Financial Analysis: University of Damascus, Syria (1956-68); Undersecretary, Ministry of Planning, Syria (1963-68); Minister of Planning, Syria (1965); Advisor in Finance, United Nations, Beirut, Lebanon (1969-71) (1973-74); Deputy Director for Europe and Middle East, UNDP, New York (1971-73); General Manager, Frab Bank International, Paris, France (1974-78); President and Deputy Chairman, Central Bank of Oman (December 7, 1987 till January 5, 1990); President, Central Bank of Oman, (January 6, 1990 till June 8, 1991); Advisor to the Deputy Chairman, Central Bank of Oman (June 9, 1991 till October 11, 1993). **Publ.:** Author of many books and publications, such as: "Principal of Economics" (500 pages), 1st Edition (1958), "Balance Sheet Analysis" (3 editions, the latest in 1967), "Planning Technology" (Lecture notes given at Damascus University 1966-68) and "Financial Planning" (Lecture notes delivered at the Kuwait Institute for Economic and Social Planning in the Middle East - 195 pages in English, 1970, 1971). Published many Articles: "Some Monetary Aspects of Arab Financial Surpluses" a paper submitted to the conference held in Kuwait from April 30- May 2, 1974 by the Kuwait Chamber of Commerce and Industry - in Arabic, "The Impact of Middle East Funds on the Euromarket" a paper prepared for the Financial Times Conference - Middle East in World Finance - held in Beirut in Sept. 1974 - in English, "La Cooperation Franco Arabe et l'Economie Mondiale - Aspect Monetaire - presented to the Colloque Franco Arabe" on the theme "Les Pays Producteurs de Matières Premières et les pays Industrialisés" in Casablanca - Nov. 1974 in French, "The Need for New Institutions in the context of Arab European Financial Cooperation", a paper presented to the Arab European Business Cooperation Symposium held in Montreux, Switzerland on 25 Oct. 1976, "Development of Banking Activity in the Sultanate within the framework of a growing Economy" - in French and Arabic, a paper presented to the Meeting of the Franco Arab Chamber of Commerce on the occasion of Omany Day on March 24, 1981 in Paris, "Role of the Arab Monetary Cooperation in Strengthening the position of the balances of Payments in Arab Countries", a paper presented during the Seminar on the Prospects of International Monetary Developments and Arab Monetary Cooperation in the 1980s organised by the Central Bank of Jordan in cooperation with the Arab Monetary Fund and the Arab Thought Forum held in Amman in Nov. 1983 and "The Future of Investments in the Gulf", a paper presented at the Symposium on U.S. - Arab Banking and Investment organised by the American Arab Affairs council and the U.S. - Arab Chamber of Commerce Inc. held in New York during Sept. 20 and 21, 1984. **Member:** Ras al-Hamra Recreation Centre, Sultanate of Oman; Pool and Racquet Club, Muscat Intercontinental Hotel; Arab Economic Association, Syria; Auditors Society, Syria; Union of Arab Banks, Beirut; Arab Bankers Association, London; Arab Thought Forum, Amman, Jordan. **Awards:** The Order of Oman Award (Third Class) from his Majesty Sultan Qaboos Bin Said during the celebration of 14th National Day of Oman (1984). **Sports:** Chess, swimming, tennis. **Addr.:** P.O.Box 373, madinat Qaboos, Postal Code: 115, Sultanate of Oman, Tel.: 600744, Fax: (968) 698195. **Address in Syria:** Aleppo: P.O.Box 8242, Aleppo, Syria. Damascus: P.O.Box 9396, New Mezza, Damascus, Syria.

KHAYATT (Shaker, Albert), Investment banker. **Born** on December 5, 1935 in Alexandria, Egypt. **Son** of Albert George Khayatt (landowner and Member of Parliament) **and** Mrs., née Winnifred Shaker Khayatt. **Married** on February 4, 1963 in Cambridge, Mass., USA; to Miss Edith L. Yuengling, 4 children: Samiha Christine (1965), Djenan Wyn-Alma (1966), Shaker Albert Jr. (1969), Shafika Marga (1973). **Educ.:** in Alexandria, Egypt: Ramleh Primary School, Ramleh Secondary School, College St. Marc, Alexandria University; in the USA Massachusetts Institute of Technology, Harvard Graduate School of Business Administration. **Dipl.:** B.Sc., Alexandria University; S.M., Massachusetts Institute of Technology (Graduate School); M.B.A., Harvard Graduate School of Business Administration. **Career:** Sr. Assoc., H.N. Whitney, Goadby & Co., N.Y.C. (1966-69); Executive V.P., Laidlaw- Coggeshall Inc., N.Y.C. (1974-76); Exec. V.P., Laidlaw Adams & Peck., N.Y.C. (1976-78); President, Equipco-Khayatt Inc. (1979 to date); President, Khayatt and Company, Inc., N.Y.C. (1979 to date). **Work:** Private placements, mergers, acquisitions, investments, consulting, financing; Director of: Mitchell Energy & Development Corp. (Houston, TX, USA), (Director) American Capital Management. **Sports:** Horsemanship, sailing. **Hobby:** Photography. **Member:** Harvard, DTA (all in N.Y.C.); Edgartown (Mass.) Yacht Club; Pottsville Country Club (PA). **Credit Cards:** American Express, Diners Club, Visa, Master Charge. **Prof. Addr.:** 50 Broad Street, Tel.: (212)7973030, New York, N.Y. 10004, USA. **Priv. Addr.:** 137 Doubling Rd., Tel.: (203)869-2970, Greenwich, CT 06830, USA.

KHAYER (Yahya M.Z. al), Syrian academic. **Born** in 1940 in Dair Zor, Syria. **Married**, 4 daughters. **Educ.:** Damascus University, Damascus, Syria; Glasgow University, UK. **Dipl.:** B.Sc. and Ph.D. in Civil Engineering. **Career:** Demonstrator, Damascus University (1970); Lecturer, Damascus University (1979); Professor, Damascus University (1990); former Minister of Euphrates Dam. **Hobbies:** Arabic Literature and poetry. **Prof. Addr.:** Damascus University, Civil Engineering Faculty, Damascus, Syria.

KHAYRAT (Alai'ddin Muhammad), Egyptian diplomat. **Born** in 1928. **Married,** 2 sons, 1 daughter. **Educ.:** Cairo University, Egypt and Dijon University, France. **Dipl.:** LL.B., Graduate Diploma in General Law. **Career:** Third Secretary, Egyptian Embassy in Belgium (1957-60); 2nd Secretary, Egyptian Delegation to the United Nations, New York, USA (1960-63); 1st Secretary, Egyptian Embassy in Iraq (1966-69); Consultant and Deputy Minister of UN, Geneva, Switzerland (1972-76); Ambassador to the Netherlands (1979-83). **Decor.:** Nassau Holland Order (1st Class) (1983). **Member:** Rowing Club. **Prof. Addr.:** Ministry of Foreign Affairs, 3 el-Nile Street, Cairo, Egypt.

KHAYYAT (Ahmed, Taha), Saudi industrialist. **Born** in 1945 in Mecca, Saudi Arabia. **Dipl.:** (Architecture and Technical Specialization in Construction Technology). **Career:** Director, Permits Department, Jeddah Municipality (1972); Owner, el-Khayyat Red Bricks Manufacturing, el-Khayyat Ready Mix Concrete Co., and el-Khayyat Commercial Center. **Addr.:** el-Khayyat Red Bricks Manufacturing, P.O.Box 3300, Tel.: 6514385, Jeddah 21471, Saudi Arabia.

KHAZEN (Farid, F., al), Lebanese engineer. **Born** in 1943 in Lebanon. **Son** of Fuad F. al-Khazen (Civil Engineer) **and** Mrs., née Mary Boulos. **Married** in 1973 to Kay White, London (UK). **Educ.:** International College, Beirut (Lebanon); American University in Beirut. **Dipl.:** B.Sc. (Civil Engineering). **Career:** Site Engineer with Arenco,

Bahrain (1964-68); Construction Manager, Arenco, Bahrain (1968-73); General Manager, Arenco, Bahrain since 1973; Partner and Board member of: Arenco, Box 823, Bahrain; Gulf Painting Co. Bahrain; Arab Engineering and Contracting Company, Sharjah; Roots Engineering & Contracting Company, Dubai; Arenco Services, Beirut (Lebanon). **Prof. Addr.:** P.O.Box 823, Tel.: 714192-713220, Bahrain. **Priv. Addr.:** 37 Clarance Terrace, Regents Park, London N.W.1, UK.

KHAZRAJI (Majid, Mohamad, al), United Arab Emirates official. **Born** in 1943 in Dubai, United Arab Emirates. **Son** of Mohamad al-Khazraji. **Married,** three children. **Educ.:** Licence in Law, College of Islamic Sharia, al-Azhar University, Cairo, Egypt. **Career:** Adviser, Legal Advisory and Legislation Department, Ministry of Justice, Director, Social Planning Department, Ministry of Planning; Acting President, State Audit Institution, United Arab Emirates. **Sports:** Swimming, long distance walking. **Hobby:** Reading Arabic poetry. **Addr.:** State Audit Institution, P.O.Box 3320, Tel.: 23900, Abu Dhabi and Tel.: 664040, Dubai, United Arab Emirates.

KHEDERY (Muwaffaq, al-), Iraqi businessman. **Born** in 1934 in Baghdad, Iraq. **Married,** 2 sons and 1 daughter. **Educ.:** University of Denver, Colorado, USA. **Dipl.:** B.Sc. in Industrial Management. **Career:** Member of the Board of Directors of the Baghdad Chamber of Commerce (1960-65); Economic Adviser and Marketing Consultant; President of Soltroia, S.A. (Portugal Land Development). **Hobbies:** Golf, tennis, swimming, skiing, waterskiing. **Addr.:** SOLTROIA S.A., Av. Eng. Duarte Pacheco, Empreendimento Amoreiras, Torre 2, 7 Andar, Sala 1, 1000 Lisboa, Portugal. Tel.: (01) 3871023/63, 3871174, 3874296. Fax: (01) 3883235. Telex: 66246 STROIA P.

KHEIR (Ahmad, Mohamad), Sudanese former statesman. **Born** in Sudan. **Educ.:** Gordon Memorial College and Khartoum School of Law. **Career:** Advocate (1944), Member of the Sudan Delegation which negotiated Sudan's future (1946), Formely Vice-President and President of National Committee for the Constitution, Minister of Foreign Affairs (1958-64) and Mineral Resources (1962-64). **Publ.:** Author of "The Struggle of a Generation" (in Arabic), "Calamities of the British in the Sudan" (in English), "Sudan Appeals to U.N.O.". **Addr.:** c/o Ministry of Foreign Affairs, Khartoum, Sudan.

KHEIR (Yahya, Muhammad, al), Sudanese academic. **Born** in 1938 in Khartoum, Sudan. **Married,** 1 son, 2 daughters. **Educ.:** Pharmacy. **Career:** Pharmacist (1962-70); Lecturer at the University of Khartoum, Sudan (1970-74), Associate Professor (1974), Dean, Faculty of Pharmacy, University of Khartoum, Sudan. **Prof. Addr.:** Faculty of Pharmacy, University of Khartoum, P.O.Box 1996, Khartoum, Sudan.

KHELEF (Abdelaziz), Algerian economist. **Born** in 1943. **Married,** 2 children. **Dipl.:** DES in Economics. **Career:** Economic Service Manager of Somelgaz (1968); Director General of Industrial Planning and Development (1972-77); Secretary General, Ministry of Light Industry (1977-79); President of Finances and Resources Sub-Commission, FLN Central Committee Economic Affairs Commission (1979-80); Minister of Commerce (1980-86); Minister of Finance (1987- Sept. 1989); Secretary of State for Maghreb Affairs (Sept. 1989- June 1991); formerly Secretary General at the Presidency of the Republic. **Addr.:** Algiers, Algeria.

KHELEF (Yehia), Algerian economist. **Born** on December 8, 1929 at Beni-Mellal, Morocco. **Married,** with children. **Educ.:** Faculty of Law, University of Paris. **Dipl.:** LLB. (1953). **Career:** Director, Caisse Fédérale de Crédit Agricole, Morroco (1958-62); Secretary General, Caisse Nationale de Crédit Agricole, Morocco (1962); Deputy Director, Caisse Algérienne de Développement pour le Financement des Entreprises (1963); Adviser to the Ministry of Finance, Algeria (1970-72); Executive Director, International Bank for Reconstruction & Development (IBRD) Washington, USA since 1972. **Member:** National Council of Credit. **Sports:** Swimming and tennis. **Hobbies:** Reading and music. **Prof. Addr.:** International Bank of Reconstruction & Development, 1818 High Street NW, Tel.: 202 393-6360, Washington DC 20433, USA.

KHELIL (Ismail), Tunisian politician. **Born** in 1932 in Gafsa, Tunisia. **Married,** 1 daughter. **Educ.:** Faculty of Law and Institute of Political Science, University of Grenoble, France. **Dipl.:** LLB, LLM. **Career:** Secretariat of State for Foreign Affairs, United States Division, Tunis, Tunisia (1957); Secretary, Tunisian Embassy in Rome and Representative of Tunisia with FAO (1957-60); Counsellor and Minister Plenipotentiary, Tunisian Embassy in Washington, D.C. (1960-64); Alternate Executive Director of World Bank (for Tunisia and seven other countries) (1962-64); Ambassador Director for International Cooperation, Ministry of Foreign Affairs, Tunis (1964-67); elected Mayor of Gafsa (1966-69); Ambassador to London, UK (1969-72); Ambassador to Belgium, Luxembourg and Representative of Tunisia to the EEC (1972-78); Director General for International Cooperation, Ministry of Foreign Affairs, Tunis (1978-79); President and Director General of Tunis Air, Tunis (1979-80); Executive Director of World Bank (1980-84); participated in many sessions of the UN and represented Tunisia at several meetings of the Organisation for African Unity and the Arab League; led the Arab Delegation to the Euro-Arab Dialogue (1977); Minister of Planning (1983-87); Governor of the Central Bank (1988-89). **Decor.:** Commander of the Order of the Republic, Tunisia. Various decorations from Morocco, Italy, Spain, Finland, Iran, Norway, Ivory Coast, Federal Republic of Germany, Romania, Luxembourg and Belgium; Officer of the Order of Tunisian Independence. **Addr.:** Tunis, Tunisia.

KHEREIJI (Abdul Karim Abdul Aziz, el), Saudi businessman. **Born** in 1936 in Medina, Saudi Arabia. **Dipl.:** B.A. (Economics). **Career:** Runs his own business. Founder Member of: Al-Youm Press Organization, National Shipping Company of Saudi Arabia, Saudi Edible Vegetable Oil Co., Dhahran International Exhibition Centre, Prince Recreation Centre, Half-Moon Bay, King Fahad Park, Dammam. Chairman of: Arabian Cigna Insurance Co., International Insurance Co.; Deputy Chairman of: Eastern Province Chamber of Commerce and Industry (3 sessions); Owner of: Elkhereiji Trading & Electronics-Electronics Division, Elkhereiji Trading & Electronics - Machinery Division, Elkhereiji Cold Stores, Medical Diagnostic & Treatment Centre, Jubail Plastic Factory. **Hobby:** Reading. **Address:** Elkhereiji Trading & Electronics, P.O.Box 25 Dammam 31411, Tel.: (03) 8322555, 8324441, 8324442, Fax: 8346206, Saudi Arabia.

KHEREIJI (Mansur M., al), Saudi official. **Born** in 1933 in Medina, Saudi Arabia. **Dipl.:** B.A., M.A. (English Literature). **Career:** Inspector, English Language, Ministry of Education (1958); Instructor, King Saud University (1959-60); Lecturer, King Saud University (1962); Assistant Professor, King Saud University (1968-69); member, Officers and National Guard Club; attended various conferences in an official capacity during the reign of the late King Faisal; Deputy Chief of Royal Protocol. **Honours:** medals from several countries. **Publ.:** literary articles and stories in local papers. **Prof. Addr.:** Tel.: 4658444, Riyadh. **Priv. Addr.:** Tel.: 4039400, Riyadh, Saudi Arabia.

KHERROUBI (Mohamad, Cherif), Algerian politician. **Born** in 1934 in Algeria. **Married**, five children. **Educ.:** University of Baghdad. **Dipl.:** B.Lit. **Career:** Teacher (1964-67); Deputy National Commissioner for FLN (1968); National Secretary, General Union of Algerian Workers (UGTA 1969-73); Wali of Tizi Ouzou (1974-79); member, Central Committee FLN (1979); Minister of Education and Basic Teaching (1979-84); Minister of National Education (1984-85); Minister of Justice (1986-Sept. 1989). **Addr.:** Algiers, Algeria.

KHIDR (Abdulfattah), Saudi academic. **Born** in 1941 in Egypt. **Married** two sons. **Educ.:** LL.B., Ain Shams University, Egypt (1967); LL.M., Cairo University, Egypt (1970); LL.B., Cairo University (1975). **Career:** Research Assistant, National Research Center, Cairo, Egypt (1974); Expert, Institute of Public Administration, Riyadh (1972-75); Assistant Professor, Forensic Law, Institute of Public Administration, Riyadh (1976-79); Associate Professor, Institute of Public Administration, Riyadh (1980). **Publ.:** Studies on forensic science. **Sports:** Running. **Hobby:** Music. **Priv. Addre.:** Tel.: 4647058, Riyadh, Saudi Arabia.

KHIRBASH (Mohammed, Khalfan), U.A.E. Minister of State for Finance and Industry. **Born** on October 16, 1956 in Dubai. **Son** of Khalfan Bin Khirbash. **Married,** 7 children: Hind (1981), Asma (1983), Alia (1985), Mai (1989), Fatima (1992), Abdulla (1994), Abdulrahman (1994). **Educ.:** B.A. -Boston University: 1979, M.a.- Boston University: 1982, Ph.D. -Exter University: 1991, Visiting Researcher - Harvard University: 1994. **Career:** Chairman of Emirates Industrial Bank, Vice Chairman of Emirates General Petroleum Corporation, Emmar Properties Company (PJSC), Tabreed (PJSC) and Member of Board of Directors of Gulf Investment Corporation. Governor for the United Arab Emirates at the International Monetary Fund and World Bank, Alternate Governor of the Arab Fund for Economic and Social Development, Kuwait, Islamic Development bank, Saudi Arabia, Opec Fund, Chairman of Dubai Islamic Bank. Presently Minister of State for Finance and Industry. **Awards:** Prize of H.H Sheikh Rashid for Academic Excellence - 1991. **Sports Practised:** Swimming. **Credit Cards:** American Express. **Prof. Addr.:** Minsitry of Finance & Industry (U.A.E.), P.O.Box 1565 Dubai, Tel.: 00971 (4) 3939333, 02-723261, Dubai, U.A.E. **Priv. Addr.:** Dubai Al Jumeira, No. 4, Tel.: 00971 (4) 3944444, United Arab Emirates.

KHLAT (Theodore Jules), Egyptian merchant. **Born** in 1927 in Paris. **Son** of Jules Khlat **and** Mrs., née Madeleine Abouchanab. **Educ.:** Victoria College (Alexandria), Selwyn College (Cambridge). **Dipl.:** Master of Arts. **Career:** Director, Egyptian Bonded Warehouses, Egyptian Petroleum Storage Company, New Egyptian Company, Gharbiah Land Company, Filature Nationale d'Egypte. **Member** of Alexandria Sporting Club. **Addr.:** 34, Souria Rushdi Street, Ramleh, Tel.: 61353, Alexandria, Egypt.

KHLEF (Mustafa, Muhammad Bin), Moroccan academic. **Born** on October 20, 1942 in Fes, Morocco. **Married**, 2 children. **Dipl.:** Ph.D. in Statistics. **Career:** Member, International Institute for Statistics (1975-); Principal, National Institute of Statistics (1977-). **Publ.:** "al-Ehtimalat wa al-Ehsaa" (1975), "Tamarin fi al-Ehtimalat" (1984). **Prof. Addr.:** P.O.Box 6217, Rabat, Morocco.

KHLEFAWI (Abdel Rahman, Gen.), Syrian army officer. **Born** in Damascus, in 1927. **Married**, four children. **Educ.:** Schools in Damascus; entered Military College and graduated a Lieutenant (1950), promoted to Major General (1971); attended courses abroad, especially in France and the U.S.S.R. **Career:** Served in Syrian Arab Army; Government Deraa, Chairman of Municipality and Chief of its Police; later Governor of Hama; Representative of Syria, Joint Arab Command, Cairo (1965-67); Chief of Martial Court; Chief, Dept. of Officers' Affairs (1968-70); Minister of the Interior, Deputy Martial Judge (1970-71); member, House of People (1971); Prime Minister (1971-72, 1976-78); member Progressive National Front; elected as member in Regional Leadership of Socialist Arab

Ba'ath Party and Chief of Economic and Financial Bureau. **Addr.:** Damascus, Syria.

KHLEIFAT (Awad, Mohamad), Jordanian former Minister of the Interior. **Born** in Jordan in 1945. **Son** of Mohamad Khleifat. **Married,** four children. **Educ.:** Jordan University; London University. **Dipl.:** B.A. in History; D.Lit. in History. **Career:** Teacher, Jordan University (1967-73); Assistant Professor (1973-78); Associate Professor (1978-83); Professor (since 1983); Deputy, Jordan University (1979-80); Head of the History Dept. (1982-84); Editor Jordan University Studies Magazine (1982) Ministry of Culture and Youth, (27 April 1989- Sept. 1989); Minister of the Interior (1996). **Publ.:** the Abadia Movement, The Kingdom of the Arabie Rabi'a in the Valley of the Nile, Educational and Social Institutions. **Member** of the Jordanian Writers Union. **Hobbies:** Reading, travel. **Addr.:** P.O.B. 13265, Amman, Jordan. and Ministry of the Interior, P.O.Box 100, Amman, Jordan.

KHODAIR (Mohamad Abdallah Abdul Rahman, al), Saudi academic. **Born** in 1935 in Shaqra. **Dipl.:** M. Phil. (Microbiology). **Career:** Official, Arab Bank; Assistant Lecturer, Faculty of Science, Riyadh University; Lecturer of Microbiology, Riyadh University; member of Saudi Biological Society. **Hobbies:** travel, ancient monuments. **Address:** P.O.Box 4738, Riyadh, Saudi Arabia.

KHOCALI (Ali), Sudanese University Professor. **Born** in 1930 in Omdurman. **Son** of Khogali Ismaïl **and** Mrs., née Rugiya Ali Ahmad. **Married** in 1962 to Miss Firial Darwiche Haidari, 3 children: Saeb, Khaled and Hicham. **Educ.:** St. Andrews and Oxford University. **Dipl.:** Doctor in Medicine (1961), D.K.S.M. (1954). **Career:** Physician (1954-56); Assistant Professor (1956-58); then Full Professor, University of Khartoum (1967-71); Dean, Faculty of Medicine and Assistant Rector, University of Khartoum since 1971. **Publ.:** Author of numerous scientific studies. **Sports:** Tennis and Swimming. **Hobbies:** Reading and Music. **Prof. Addr.:** P.O.Box 102, Tel.: 72224, Khartoum, Sudan.

KHOGALI (Mohamad), Sudanese businessman. **Born** in 1921 in Sudan. **Son** of Khogali el-Sheikh **and** Mrs. Sakma Ahmad Abdul Gasim. **Married** in 1956 in Sudan to Miss Bahga Mahgoub, three children. **Educ.:** University of Khartoum, University of Cambridge, UK. **Dipl.:** B.A., M.A. from University of Cambridge. **Career:** Educational Service (1946-56); Economics Section, Ministry of Foreign Affairs (1956-58); Under Secretary at the Ministry of Commerce and Industry (1958-66); Minister of Agriculture (1966-67); various business affairs (since 1967). **Credit Card:** Visa, Barclay. **Prof. Addr.:** P.O.B. 1887, Tel.: 81531, Khartoum, Sudan. **Priv. Addr.:** St. 25, New Extention, Tel.: 41998, Khartoum, Sudan.

KHOJAH (Abdallah Sharar), Saudi official. **Born** in 1922. **Dipl.:** B.A. (Islamic Law). **Career:** Former teacher; Director of Chambers of Commerce; Director, Saudi Regional Anti-Israel Boycott Office; Legal Adviser; Attended Arab League Council Meetings, Conference of Arab Ministers of Finance and Economy, Anti-Israel Boycott Conferences. **Address:** Ministry of Commerce, P.O.Box 1774, Riyadh, Saudi Arabia.

KHOJAH (Abdul Aziz M.), Saudi Official. **Born** in 1942 in Mecca, Saudi Arabia. **Dipl.:** Ph.D. (Chemistry), Birmingham University, U.K. **Career:** Instructor, Faculty of Education, Mecca (1970); Dean, Faculty of Education and Director of King Abdulaziz University, Mecca (1972); Chairman, Executive Council of Islamic Countries Broadcasting Stations, Executive Council of Islamic Press Agency, Saudi Arabian Permanent Delegation, the Governmental Council for the Improvement of Communication, UNESCO; member, Conference of Information Ministers of the Arabian Gulf States, Conference of the Arab Information Ministers; Deputy minister for Information Affairs, Ministry of Information since 1976. **Honour:** Shield of Merit from King Abdulaziz University, Mecca. **Publications:** several works of research in Chemistry and two collections of Arabic poems. **Hobbies:** reading, poetry. **Address:** Ministry of Information, Tel.: 4013104, Riyadh, Saudi Arabia.

KHOJAH (Akram, Major General), Saudi former airforce commander. **Born** in 1930 in Saudi Arabia. **Married. Educ.:** Joined Military School in Taif (1947); obtained Licence with British Civil Air Training Mission; trained at AST Hamble and with Royal Air Force, UK; Air Attaché, Embassy to UK (1966-69); returned to Saudi Arabia as Base Commander, Taif; appointed Base Commander, Dhahran (1969), Vice Commander of Saudi Air Force Dhahran (1969), Vice Commander of Saudi Air Force (1973). **Addr.:** Ministry of Defence, Riyadh, Saudi Arabia.

KHOJAH (Tala't Mohamad), Saudi Academic. **Born** in 1943 in Mecca, Saudi Arabia. **Dipl.:** Ph.D. (Botany). **Career:** Assistant Lecturer then Lecturer, Faculty of Science, King Saud University; Assistant Professor of Science, King Saud University. **Member:** Saudi Biological Society; Arab Biologists' Conference First and Second Conferences of Biological Issues of Saudi Arabia. **Publications:** several specialized research papers. **Hobbies:** walking, tabletennis. **Address:** Botany Department, Faculty of Science, King Saud University, Tel.: 4350514, Riyadh, Saudi Arabia.

KHOLY (Hussein, A., al), Arab American academic. **Born** in 1933 in Mansura, Egypt. **Married,** three children. **Educ.:** Cairo University; Hungarian Academy of Sciences; Eotvos Lorand University. **Dipl.:** B.Sc., Kandidat (Russian Equivalent of Ph.D.), Dr. of Nat. Sc. **Career:** Demonstrator, Faculty of Sciences, Cairo University (1957-58); Lecturer, Faculty of Sciences, Cairo University (1961-63); Lecturer, University of Khartoum, Sudan (1963-64); Visiting Scientist, Experimental Institute of Lighet Metals, Italy (1964); Assistant Professor of Mathematics and Science (1964-65); Assistant Professor and Chairman, Department of Mathematics and Physics (1968-72); Professor and Chairman, Department of Mathematics and Physics (since 1973); Professor and Head of the Physics Unit, American University of Cairo, Egypt; Consultant to the Egyptian Government, the Libyan Government; Consultant to several American national and multinational companies, schools and laboratories. **Publ.:** many books in English, German, Dutch and papers published since 1961. **Hobbies:** Reading. **Sports:** Swimming. **Addr.:** 4 Pitney Drive, Mendham, New Jersey 07945, U.S.A.

KHOLY (Ussama, Amin, al), Egyptian university professor. **Born** on 9 October 1923 in Cairo. **Son** of Mr. Amin el-Kholy (University professor) **and** Mrs., née Nagiyya Ibrahim. **Married** on June 1964 in Cairo to Nahed Habib, 2 children: Amani and Amin. **Educ.:** Cairo University, London University, M.I.T. **Dipl.:** B. Eng. (Hons), D.I.C., Ph.D. **Career:** Lecturer (1951-58); Associate Professor (1958-65); Professor since 1965; Director, Scientific Computation Centre, Cairo University (1967-70); Counsellor, Egyptian Embassy, Moscow (1970-75); Assistant Director General Arab Educational, Cultural and Scientific Organisation (ALECSO) (1977-80). **Hobby:** Music. **Member:** Meadi, Shooting Clubs. **Prof. Addr.:** Timco, 1, Amrika el-Latiniya, Garden City, Tel.: 986030, Cairo. **Priv. Addr.:** 13, Street No. 265, New Meadi, Tel.: 37325, Cairo, Egypt.

KHOMAIS (Bakr Abbas), Saudi diplomat. **Born** in 1930 in Jeddah, Saudi Arabia. **Dipl.:** M.A. (Public administration), Syracuse University, U.S.A. **Career:** Employee, Ministry of Finance; Assistant Director of Economic Affairs, Ministry of Finance; Secretary General for Technical Assistance, Supreme Planning Board; Director, Agency for Technical Cooperation, Council of Ministers; Minister Plenipotentiary; Ambassador, Ministry of Foreign Affairs; Ambassador to Indonesia; presently Ambassador to Venezuela. **Member:** Board of Directors of several national and foreign companies; has attended several economic, cultural, political and social conferences and seminars around the world. **Honour:** Bintang Mahaputra, Medal awarded by the Indonesian Republic. **Publications:** The International Bank for Reconstruction and Development and its Role in Assisting Underdeveloped Countries; Improvement of Public Administration and Fundamentals of Budget Application. **Hobby:** swimming. **Prof. Addr.:** Ministry of Foreign Affairs, Tel.: 6690900, Jeddah. **Priv. Addr.:** Tel.: 6654211, Jeddah, Saudi Arabia.

KHOMAIS (Yusuf Abdallah, al), Saudi academic. **Born** in 1949 at Buraidah, Saudi Arabia. **Dipl.:** B.Sc. (Mathematics), King Saud University, M.Sc. and Ph.D. (Mathematics), Reading University, U.K. **Career:** Demonstrator, Mathematics Department, Faculty of Science, King Saud University; Lecturer, Mathematics Department, same Faculty. **Address:** Faculty of Science, King Saud University, Riyadh, Saudi Arabia.

KHOQAIR (Isam, Mohamad), Saudi dental surgeon, also dramatist and columnist. **Born** on September 11, 1927 in Mecca (Saudi Arabia). **Educ.:** Faculty of Dentistry, Cairo University. **Dipl.:** M.D. **Career:** Director of the Mecca Health Unit; Assistant Director for Health Affairs Medina (Saudi Arabia); Director of the Central Hospital, Medina; Director of the School Health Unit in Jeddah; attended the Jerusalem Medical conference in 1961; the Baghdad Medical conference in 1969 and the Cairo Medical conference (1974-75). **Publ.:** Author of "When the Night is Quit" (a play), "Spring comes late" (collection of one-act plays). **Hobby:** cartoon drawing. **Prof. Addr.:** P.O.Box 1272, Tel.: 24585 Jeddah. **Priv. Addr.:** Tel.: 21246, Jeddah, Saudi Arabia.

KHOQAIR (Jamil Abdul Rahman), Saudi businessman. **Born** in 1922. **Dipl.:** Ph.D. Hons. (Economics), London University. **Career:** Owner and Director-General, Jamil Khoqair Est. for Contruction and General Trade. Contracting, General Trading, Tourism, Drug Stores, Jewelleries, Earth Studies, Shipping); ex-member of Board, Riyadh Bank; Chairman of Blue Sea Shipping Co. Ltd.; Chairman of SAMROCO; Chairman of SAMINCO. **Hobbies:** reading, travel. **Address:** P.O.Box 642, Riyadh, Saudi Arabia.

KHORSHED (Ahmed, Mahmoud Hafez, Dr.), Egyptian Professor of Food Technology, Director of Food Technology Research Institute. **Born** on December 12, 1941. **Son** of Mahmoud Khorshed. **Married** in Egypt 1968 to Galina Khorshed, 3 children: Galina Khorshed (1968); Gamal Ahmed Khorshed (27.6.1971); Mona Ahmed Khorshed (10.2.1973). **Educ.:** Faculty of Agriculture, Cairo University. **Dipl.:** BSc. in food science (1962, Egypt); M.Sc. in food technology (1966, Egypt); P.H.D. in food technology (1972, USSR). **Experience:** Teacher Assistant, Food Tech. Dept., Faculty of Agriculture, University of Assiut (1962-66); Food Tech., Dept. (1964-66); Ph.D. 1972 (1968-72); Maize Lab Manager, Department of Bread and Pastry Research, ARC. (1973-86); Director of Bread and Pastry Research Department ARC. (1986-88); Director of Central Lab. For Food Tech. Res. (1988-91); Director of Food Technology Research Institute (1992- present). **Publ.:** has more than 50 published scientific articles within the fields of Nutrition. Special Foods, Food Processing, Milling, Backing and Food Fortification. Book (in Arabic) titled Smokeless Bakeries. **Major Achievement:** Preparation of Special foods for patients and children; Designing baking ovens for different uses at home and in the villages; Nutritional Education; Studies on baking and pastry improvers; Economical milling of cereals; Development of Egyptian villages and reclaimed areas; Management of Scientific conferences; Using TV, News & Radio in Spreading good nutritional habits and using the scientific approach in food preparation; Training people for better bread and pastry procedures; Modifying nutrition and baking courses in agricultural high schools; Inventions in food industry (3); He supervised number of M.Sc. and Ph.D. theses in the areas of Food Nutrition and Technology; He lectured number of Food. Nutrition and Food Science and Technology courses, both undergraduate and graduate, in the Egyptian Universities. In addition, he presented seminars in the above-mentioned areas to the interested people from the army and industry; He presented Scientific Papers, in several Local and foreign conferences. Conducting some projects: He is the principle investigator of the following projects that belong to the National Agricultural Research Project (NARP). Improvement of Balady bread production; Preparation and production of well-digested infant food from cereals and legumes; Functional properties of plant protein and possible modification use in industry; Improvement Women efficiency in Food Production (FAO); He also is of the principle investigator in: a- Improving Quality of Hard Wheat Project. b- P.I. In the Project of Balady Bread. c- P.I. of soybean utilization. d- Food Consumption Monitoring System Project. **Membership in Egyptian and International Agencies:** Egyptian Association of Food Science; American Association of Cereal Chemists AACC; International Cereal Chemists ICC; Permanent Committee for School Nutrition Program; Egyptian Standardization Association of Food; Association of Medicine and Law; Health and Development Organization; Egyptian Society of Nutrition; Egyptian association for nutrition. **Prof. Addr.:** Agricultural Research Center, Food Technology Research Institute, 9 El Gamaa Str., Giza, Egypt, Tel.: 624669, Fax: 624669. **Priv. Addr.:** El-Alfi Str., 21 apt. 14 Azbakia, Cairo, Egypt, Tel.: 3831930.

KHOSHAIM (Bakr Hamza), Saudi academic. **Born** 1941 in Medina, Saudi Arabia. **Dipl.:** B.Sc. 1968 (Mechanical Engineering) King Saud University; M. Eng. (1972) and Ph.D. (1975) in Mechanical Engineering, University of Liverpool, UK **Career:** Solar Program Director (Associate Professor), King Abdulaziz City for Science & Technology; attended various International and national conferences; especially interested in solar and other renewable energy research technologies, design engineering, refrigeration and airconditioning. **Publications:** Over 40 technical papers in international journals of repute. **Hobbies:** chess, travel. **Address:** MRI/SOLERAS, P.O.Box 5927, Riyadh 11432, Kingdom of Saudi Arabia.

KHOSHAIM (Reda Hassan), Saudi businessman. **Born** in 1938, in Medina, Saudi Arabia. **Dipl.:** Ph.D. (Business Administration) 1975. **Career:** Economist, PETROMIN (1963-65); Assistant Manager, Directorate of Zakar (Poor Tax) and Income Tax, Eastern Province; lecturer in Economics and Business Administration, King Abdulaziz University; member of Dammam Chamber of commerce and Industry, Islamic Society, U.S.A; owner and General Manager of Khusheim Stores for Industrial Equipement; established the Khusheim factory for Hydraulic presses in Damman; member of several international economic conventions; attended Chartered Accountants' Conferences, Arizona, Michigan, Texas, U.S.A. **Honour:** Merit Membership of the Accounting Society, Arizona, U.S.A. **Hobies:** chess, table tennis. **Address:** P.O.Box 119, Dammam, Saudi Arabia.

KHOUADJA (Brahim), Tunisian engineer. **Born** in 1927 in Tunisia. **Married,** four children. **Dipl.:** Licence in Mathematics, Diploma in Telecommunication Engineering (1954). **Career:** Principal Engineer, General Engineer, Chief Engineer, Director of Telecommunications Department (1966); Director General of Telecommunications (1971); Secretary of State for PTT (1979), Ministry of Transports and Communications (1983); Minister of Communications (1985- April 1989). **Decor.:** Citations dans l'Ordre de la Republique, de l'Indépendance et du 7 Novembre. Tunis. **Addr.:** 14 Rue Didon, Tunis, Tunisia.

KHOURI (Nicola, Najib), Arab American physicist. **Born** in Beirut Lebanon in 1933. **Son** of Najib Khouri. **Married,** two children. **Educ.:** American University of Beirut; Princeton University. **Dipl.:** B.A., Ph.D. **Career:** Assistant Professor, AUB (1957-58); member, Institute of Advanced Study, Princeton University, USA (1959-60 and 1962-63); Associate Professor, AUB (1961-62); Visiting Associate Professor, University of Columbia, USA (1963-64); Consultant, Brookhaven National Laboratory (1963-73); Associate Professor Rockefeller University, USA (since 1968); **Publ:** articles in professional journals. **Trustee,** American University of Beirut; Brearley School, New York City, USA. Fellow American Physicists' Society. **Prof. Addr.:** Rockefeller University, New York City, New York NY 10021. **Priv. Addr.:** 4715 Iselin Avenue Riverdale, New York NY 10471, USA.

KHOURI (Said, Tawfik), Lebanese executive. **Born** in 1923. **Married,** 3 sons, 2 daughters. **Educ.:** St. Lukes School, Haifa; American University of Beirut. **Career:** Managing Director and President, Consolidated Contractors Co; Chairman, Kuwait Industrial Refinery; Director, Banque d'Investissement et de Financement, Lebanon; Chairman, Investment Bank for Trade and finance, Sharjah, UAE. **Addr.:** al-Durouba Street, P.O.Box 1885, Tel.: 355391-2, Telex: 68083 A/B INVEST EM, Sharjah, UAE.

KHOURI (Zuhair, Saleh), Jordanian Chairman & General Manager, The Housing Bank, Amman-Jordan, since 1973. **Born** in 1926 in Karak, Jordan. **Son** of Saleh Khouri. **Married** to Leen Khouri, 3 children. **Educ.:** Studies in Karak, Jordan (1932-42) and in Salt, Jordan (1942-44); London School of Economics (1951-52) (1955-56); American University, Washington (1960-61). **Career:** Clerk for Steel Bros. & Co. (1944-45), Accountant, Import and Export Section (1954-61), then Head Section of Currency Control Dept. (1961-61); Assistant Secretary Currency Board (1961-64); Head of Dept. of the Central Bank of Jordan (1964-68); Executive Director, Central Bank of Jordan (1968-73); General Manager and Chairman of the Board of Directors, The Housing Bank, Amman (1973-). **Memberships:** Chairman of The Board -Association of Banks in Jordan; Chairman of The Board -Jordan Holiday Hotels Company - Amman, Jordan; Vice-Chairman -Jordan International Bank - London; Vice-Chairman of Tunis International Bank, Tunis; Vice-Chairman -Industrial Estates Corporation, Jordan; Member of The Board of Directors -Central Bank of Jordan; Member of The Board of Directors, Industrial Development Bank, Jordan; Jordan Representative To Union of Arab Banks; Member of The Board of Trustees, Arab Institute For Banking Studies; Member of The Board of Directors -Municipality of Greater Amman; Member of The Board of Trustees, HRH The Regent's Award. **Awards:** Medal of Independence -First Order; Medal of Independence -Second Order; Al Kawkab Medal -Second Order; Al Kawkab Medal - Third Order. **Prof. & Priv. Addr.:** The Housing Bank, P.O.Box 7693, Tel.: 667126, Amman, Jordan.

KHOWEITER (Abdul Aziz Abdallah, al, Dr.), Saudi minister. **Born** in 1927 at Onaizah, Saudi Arabia. **Dipl.:** Ph.D. (History). **Career:** Vice Rector of King Saud University; Head of the Directorate of Suprevision and Follow-up; Minister of Health; Minister of Education (1975 to Aug. 1995). Presently Minister of State. **Member:** Chivalry Club, Charity Society; President of Arab-Saudi Scouts Society, Supreme Council of Arts and Literature; member of Supreme Council of Education, Higher Council of Universities, Committee for Administrative Reform, and Council of Pensions Fund; attended Conference of International University, International Conference of Public Health, Conference of Public Health, Conference of ALESCO. **Honours:** King Abdulaziz Order of Merit, Second Class; Republican Order, Democratic Republic of Sudan, First Class. **Publications:** Fi Turuk al Bahth (Methodes of Research); ed. Tarikj Shafi Ibn Ali (History of Shafi Ibn Ali). **Hobby:** reading. **Address:** Riyadh, Saudi Arabia.

KHOWEITER (Hamad, al), Saudi diplomat. **Born** on 26 December 1929 at Unaizah, Saudi Arabia. **Dipl.:** B.A. (Language and Literature). **Career:** Member of the Executive Board of UNESCO, Paris; Permanent Delegatd of the Kingdom of Saudi Arabia to UNESCO; member of the International Committee of L'Olivier Symbole, Paris; travelled widely all over Europe, Asia, and Africa. **Prof. Addr.:** Permanent Delegation of the Kindgom of Saudi Arabia to UNESCO, 1 rue Miollis, Tel.: 5775656, Ext. 5378, 75015 Paris, France, **Priv. Addr.:** P.O.Box 2145, Riyadh, Saudi Arabia.

KHOZAI (Mohamad, A., al), Bahraini statesman. **Born** on May 17, 1940 in Manama, Bahrain. **Married** to Dr. Bahiya J. Aljishi, one son, Firas (1975). **Educ.:** Public Primary and Secondary School in Bahrain; Matriculation, Cairo, Egypt (1961) Faculty of Arts, University of Cairo, Egypt (1966); School of English, Leads University, U.K.; London, U.K. Course on the Administration of the Arts, Polytechnic of Central London, London, U.K. (1972); School of Oriental and African Studies, University of London, London, U.K. (1978). **Dipl.:** B.A., M.A. (English Literature); Ph.D. (Arabic Drama). **Career:** Teacher in the Primary Stage with the Department of Education, Bahrain (1958-60); Teacher in the Secondary Stage with the Department of Educationa, Bahrain (1966-68); Lecturer at the Men's Teacher Training College, Bahrain (1969-71); Superintendent of Culture and Arts, Ministry of Labour and Social Affairs, Bahrain (1971-75); Director of the Directorate of Culture and Arts, Ministry of Information, Bahrain (1978-86); Director of the Directorate of Publications, Ministry of Information, Bahrain (1986-). **Publ.:** Early Arabic Drama (1984); The Islands of Bahrain (Translator) (1985); The Heroes of Marlowe's Major Plays (Dissertation); "BAHRAIN" entry in "World Theatre Encyclopedia" to be published by UNESCO' "A Miscellany of Middle Eastern Articles" (Contributor) (1988); Translated a number of Short Stories in the Local Press; Published a number of Studies and Essays on Literary Criticism in the local Press and periodicals; Attended a number of International and Regional conferences dealing with topics related to both professional and personal interests; Editor of "Dilmun", Journal of the Bahrain Historical and Archaeological Society. **Member of:** Middle East Studies Association of North America; British Society of Middle Eastern Studies; Bahrain Historical and Archaeological Society; President of Bahrain Chess Federation; President of Zone 11 of FIDE, (International Chess Federation). **Hobbies:** Drama, history, translation, chess, bowling, tennis, travels. Languages: Arabic, English, French. **Addr.:** Ministry of Information, Directorate of Publications, P.O.Box 253, Tel.: 689077, Telex: 8399 INFORM BN, Fax: 685114, Manama, Bahrain.

KHUDAYRI (Tariq, Shamel Al-), Iraqi engineer. **Born** in 1929 in Iraq. **Son** of Shamel Khudairi. **Married. Educ.:** American University of Beirut, Oklahoma State University, USA, Michigan State University, USA, **Dipl.:** M.Sc. in Chemical Engineering; Ph.D. in Chemical Engineering. **Career:** Tutor, Oklahoma College for Agriculture and Mechanics (1955-57); Assistant Researcher, Michigan State University USA (1957-60); Professor and Head of Engineering Dept. Chemical and Assistant Dean of the Engineering Faculty, Baghdad University (1960-68); Technical advisor and member of the Board, Vegetable Oil Extracting Company, Baghdad (1960-66); Director and Consultant Engineer, Industrial Consultancy Office, Baghdad (1966-73); Senior Consultant in Industrial Affairs, Arab Countries Industrial Development Organisation, Cairo (1970-73); Ex-pert, Regional advisor and Arab Countries Programme Director, United Nations Industrial

Development Organisation, (since 1973). Free Lance Consultant on Industrial Development (since 1993). Member, American Institute of Chemical Engineers (since 1964); member of the Board, Syndicate of Iraqi Engineers. Editor member, Muhandes magazine (1961-1967) and consultative committee member of Energy Communication Magazine, USA (since 1977). **Publ.:** Oil and Arab Cooperation; Iraq Manufacturing Strategy Through the Sixties; Petrochemical Industries in the World; General outlooks on Arab Petrochemical Industry; Intergration of Arab Petrochemical Industry with Oil Refining; Manufacturing Industries in the Arab Region and Alternative Projects for Integration; Manufacturing Industries in Iraq, Status and Prospects for Restructuring; Series of Articles on Socio-Political Status in the Arab World. **Sports:** Swimming, hunting, tennis. **Hobbies:** Reading, arabic music, classical music. **Prof. & Priv. Addr.:** Villa Norfolk, Estrada de Charneca, Charneca, 2750 Cascais, Portugal.

KHULAIFY (Saleh Abdallah, al), Saudi Public Servant. **Born** in 1924 at al-Bakriya, Saudi Arabia. **Educ.:** received general education supplemented by technical training in telecommunications. **Career:** Several technical and administrative posts; Chairman of Administrative Council, Chairman of Promotional Committee, Chairman of Committee of Delegations and Overtime Hours, Chairman of Committee on Tenders; Director-General of Telegraph and Telephone Department, Central Region; attended conferences on telecommunications. **Address:** Riyadh, Saudi Arabia.

KHUMAYIS (Abdallah, bin Mohamad bin), Saudi man of letters. **Born** in 1921 in Diriyyah (Saudi Arabia). **Educ.:** Faculty of Sharia (Islamic Law), Mecca; Faculty of Arabic Language, Mecca. **Dipl.:** B.A. (Law), B.A. (Arabic Language and Literature). **Career:** Principal of "al-Ilmi" Religious Institute, al-Hassa (1956); Director, Faculty of Sharia (Islamic Law) (1958); Director-General, Presidium, of the Judiciary (1959); Under-Secretary of State, Ministry of Communications (1963); Director, Riyadh Water Department; attended several literary conferences abroad and Saudi Men of Letters Conference, King Abdul Aziz University; now Secretary-General Okaz Literary Festival; President of Riyadh Literary club. **Member**; Board of "Jazirah" Press Organisation; Board of Charity, Riyadh; Popular Committee for the Welfare of Palestinian Fighters and Martyrs; Editorial Board, King Abdul Aziz Archives Magazine "Darah". **Publ.:** Author of "A Month in Damascus", "Folklore Literature in the Arabian Peninsula", "Figurative Expressions", "Collected Poems". **Awards:** Literary Vanguard Order of Merit; Medal, King Abdul Aziz University; Order of Merit for Literature (Tunisia). **Hobbies:** Touring the Arabian Peninsula and reading. **Prof. Addr.:** 3, Jareer street, Malazz, Riyadh, Saudi Arabia.

KHUSHAIBI (Hassan, Ahmed, al), Libyan executive. **Born** on June 2nd, 1941 in Tajuraa, Tripoli, Libya. **Son** of Ahmed al-Khushaibi (Farmer) **and** Mrs. Zainab al-Abani. **Married** on October 3, 1968 to Hamida M. Nasif, 7 children: Amal, Ahlam, Siham, Ahmed, Usama, Hisham and Narjis. **Educ.:** The University of Texas at Austin, U.S.A. **Dipl.:** BBA, MPA + Certificate indicating gratuation in the Honours Program. **Career:** 10 years related to computing and 18 years related to accounting and reporting (gave two courses, design of accounting informations systems and use of computers in accounting). **Sports:** Swimming and running. **Member:** Beta Alpha Psi, Beta Gamma Sigma; also Member for life in the Accounting Fraternity and Management Fraternity. **Prof. Addr.:** Wahda Bank, Nssir Street, P.O.Box 452, Benghazi, Libya and Wahda Bank, Megarief St. Tripoli, Libya. **Priv. Addr.:** Oggab, Tajuraa, Tel.: 690061, Tripoli, Libya.

KHUSHNAW (Anwar, Ibrahim Salih), Iraqi official. **Born** in 1930 in Iraq. **Married**, five children. **Educ.** LL.B. **Career:** Assistant Director, State Organisation for Food Industries, Baghdad; Director General, National Tobacco State Company (since 1974); Chairman, Arbil Chamber of Commerce. **Sport:** Walking. **Hobby:** Reading. **Addr.:** National Tobacco State Company, Baghdad, Iraq.

KILANI (Fuad, Zeid), Jordanian international officer. **Born** on August 10, 1931 at Nablus (Jordan). **Married**, with children. **Educ.:** Faculty of Medicine, Cairo Universiy (1949-56). **Member:** Royal College of Physicians; Baylor University, Texas (1965-66), M. Hospital Administration; Methodist Hospital, Texas (1969); Fellowship in Cardiology. **Dipl.:** M.B. (1956), B.G.H. (1966). **Career:** Chief, Medical Department, Army Base Hospital (1966-70); Commanding Officer, Army Base Hospital (1970-73); Member, Executive Board, World Health Organisation (WHO), Ministry of Health, Amman (Jordan). **Publ.:** "Hypermetabolic Microcondiral Diseases" (1972). **Awards:** Decoration of Independence, First and Second Grade; Star of Jordan, 1st class. **Sports:** swimming and shooting. **Hobbies:** reading and chess. **Prof. Addr.:** Ministry of Health, Tel.: 39181 Amman, Jordan. **Priv. Addr.:** Tel.: 365525, Amman, Jordan.

KILANI (Haitham, al), Syrian diplomat. **Born** on August 6, 1926 in Damascus. **Married. Educ.:** in Damascus, Syria; in Paris, France and in Leipzig, East Germany. **Dipl.:** Diplomas from the Syrian Military Academy, Damascus (1947), from the Staff Air Force Academy in Paris, France (1953), from the Air War Superior Academy in Paris (1956) and from the University of Leipzig, Germany (1969-72). **Career:** Officer at the Syrian Air Force (1948-61); Chief of Syrian Air Staff (1958); Ambassador to Algeria (1962); Ministerial Counsellor at the Ministry of Foreign Affairs (1962-64); Director of the Economic Department (1963-64); Ambsassador to Morocco (1965); General Inspector at the Ministry of Foreign Affairs (1966-67), then Secretary General (1968-69); Ambassador to East Germany (1969-72), to Canada and Mexico (1972); Ambassador, Permanent Representative to UN, New York, USA (1972-83); Chief Editor of :Arab Affairs: published by the League of Arab States, Cairo (1984-). **Publ.:** "The Strategic and Military Importance of the United Arab Republic" (1958), "When Israel Attacks" (1964), "The Strategic Position of the Arab World" (1966), "The Arab Military Strategy" (an historic study) (1968) "The Israeli Military Doctrine" (Vol.1- 1970, Vol.2- 1989), "The Military Struggle for Arab Unity" (1973) and "Military Strategies of Arab-Israeli Wars" (1991), "The Military Balance Between Arabs and Israel" (1993). **Prof. Addr.:** League of Arab States, Midan al-Tahrir, Cairo, Egypt.

KILANI (Zeid, Mohamad), Jordanian aeronautical engineer. **Born** in 1944. **Son** of Mohamed Kilani. **Married**, four children. **Educ.:** Cairo University; Beirut Arab University. **Dipl.:** B.Sc. and L.L.B. **Career:** Flight Safety Director, Jordan Civil Aviation Authority (1966-73); Executive Vice President, Royal Jordanian Airlines (1973- to date); owner of Khadra Company (since 1976); member of the Board, Jordanian Water and Sewage Projects Company (since 1981); member of Jordan Association of Engineers (since 1966); member of the Advisory Committee of Electronic Department, Royal Scientific Society (since 1983); Member of the Advisory Committee Chamber of Industry-Jordan (1993). **Member of:** the International Society Club of Jordan. **Sport:** Swimming. **Prof. Addr.:** The Royal Jordanian Airlines, P.O.B. 302, Amman, Jordan. **Priv. Addr.:** P.O.B. 1043, Amman, Jordan.

KIM (Sang-Bae), South Korean executive. **Born** in 1939 in Seoul, Korea. **Son** of Hyum-Kee Kim. **Married** in 1970, 1 son, 1 daughter. **Educ.:** College of Commerce, Seoul National University; Graduate School of Business Administration of University of Wisconsin, Wisconsin, USA. **Dipl.:** B.A. in Economics (1963). **Career:** Joined Korea Exchange Bank since 1968; Promoted to Assistant Manager (1970-71); Tokyo Branch (1971-74); Manager, (1975-79); Deputy General Manager, Korea Exchange Bank, Regional Headquarters for Middle East and Africa, Bahrain (1979-); Director, Cairo Far East Bank S.A.E. **Hobbies:** Golf and Swimming. **Addr.:** Yateem Centre, P.O.Box 5767, Tel.: 258282, 254333, 255418, Telex: 8846 A/B KGXBK BN, Manama, Bahrain.

KINDI (Adnan AbdulHamid, al), Iraqi official. **Born** in Iraq in 1925. **Son** of AbdulHamid al Kindi. **Educ.:** University of Manchester. **Career:** Oil Planning and Construction Administration; President of the State Organisation for Industrial Design and Construction; Iraq representative for Industrial Affairs, Moscow (1979-84). Counsellor, Ministry of Industry (since 1984). **Addr.:** State Organisation for Industrial Design and Construction, P.O.B. 5614, Baghdad, Iraq.

KINDI (Mohamad Khalifa, al), United Arab Emirates politician. **Born** in 1931 in Abu Dhabi, UAE. **Career:** Director of Customs and Ports; then Minister of Education, Abu Dhabi; Member, Government Planning Council; United Arab Emirates Minister of Planning and Head of Department of Planning in Abu Dhabi Executive Council; United Arab Emirates Minister of Public Works and Housing (since January 1977 to 1990): Chairman of National petroleum Construction Co. Ltd. (NPCC); Director, Abu Dhabi National Oil Co. **Work:** visited UK in 1973 as a guest of the British Council in his capacity of Minister of Education. **Addr.:** P.O.Box 2058, Abu Dhabi, U.A.E.

KIRRESH (Maher, Khamis), Jordanian banker. **Born** in 1930 in Jerusalem. **Son** of Khamis Kirresh. **Married** in 1963, 3 sons, 2 daughters. **Educ.:** Institute of Bankers, London. **Career:** British Bank of the Middle East, Amman (1954-61); British Bank of the Middle East, Benghazi (1962-66); Wahda Bank, Benghazi (1967-76); Arab Bank Amman (1976-79); Manager, Jordan Islamic Bank, Amman (1979-). **Member:** Association of Banks in Jordan; Dealers' Club. **Hobby:** Reading, **Addr.:** Amman, Jordan.

KIRSHY (Abbas Muhammed, al), Yemeni economist. **Born** in 1943 in Taiz, Yemen. **Son** of Muhammed Abdo Kirshy. **Married**, 6 children. **Educ.:** American University of Beirut, Lebanon; University of Rhode Island, USA. **Dipl.:** B.A. in Economics and Political Science; M.A. in the Economies of Development. **Career:** Assistant Director of the Companies Department in the Ministry of Economy (1969-70); Vice Chairman of Yemen Drug Company (1970-71); Director, Industrial Department Technical Office of the Supreme Council of Planning (1971); Adviser of Yemen Mission to the United Nations, New York, USA (1973-74); Director of the Prime Minister's Office for Economic Affairs (1974-75); Deputy Permanent Representative, Yemen Mission to the United Nations in Geneva, Switzerland (1975-76); Chairman of the Industrial Bank of Yemen (since 1976); Member of the Board of International Bank of Yemen (1979-) and of Yemen Investments Company (1983-); **Hobby:** hunting. Founder **Member** of Yemen Economic Society (1985-). **Credit Cards:** 3744- 022393- 31008. **Prof. Addr.:** Industrial Bank of Yemen, Zubairy Street, P.O.Box 323, Tel.: 207381, 207379, 207384, Telex: 2580 INDBNK YE, Sanaa, Republic of Yemen.

KITTANI (Ismat), Iraqi international civil servant. **Born** on April 5, 1929 in Amadiyah (Iraq). **Married**, with children. **Educ.:** Knox College, Galesburg (USA). **Dipl.:** B.A. (Political Science and English) 1951. **Career:** High School Teacher, Iraq (1951); joined Ministry of Foreign Affairs, Baghdad (Iraq, 1952-56); seconded to Permanent Mission of Iraq, New York (1957-60); Permanent Representative of Iraq, Geneva (1961-64); Chief, Specialised Agency and Accounting Affairs, UN (1964); Secretary, Economic & Social Council (ECOSOC), UN (1965-66);

Director, Executive Office of the Secretary General, UN (1967-69); Deputy Assistant Secretary General, IAAC (1969-70); Assistant Secretary General, IAAC (1971-73); Assistant Secretary General, Executive Assistant to the Secretary General, UN, New York (1973). **Addr.:** Baghdad, Iraq.

KLIBI (Chedli), Former secretary general of the league of Arab states. **Born** on September 6, 1925 in Tunis. **Son** of Hassouna Klibi (Civil Servant) **and** Mrs., née Habiba Bannani. **Married** on March 15, 1956 to Miss Kalthoum Lasram, 3 children: Monia, Leila, Mahdi. **Educ.:** College Sadiki, Tunis; The Sorbonne, Paris. **Dipl.:** "Agregation" in Arabic Literature (Sorbonne-Paris). **Career:** Journalist and Professor (1951-57); Director General of the Tunisian Radio and Television (1958-61); Secretary of State for Information and Cultural Affairs, Tunis (1961-64); Mayor of Carthage (since 1963); Secretary of State for Cultural Affairs (November 1964); Minister of Culture and Information (1971-73); Director of Depart. Staff of the President of the Republic of Tunisia (1974-76); Minister of Cultural Affairs (1976-78); Minister of Information (September 1978); Secretary General, League of Arab States (June 1979- Sept. 1990). **Publ.:** "The Arabs and the Palestinian Question"; "Islam and Modernity"; "Culture: a civilizational Challenge"; various essays and articles. **Member:** Central Committee of the Destour Socialist Party (P.S.D.) (since 1964); Elected Member of the Political Bureau of P.S.D. (January 1968) **Awards:** Grand Cordon, Order of Independence; Grand Cordon, Order of the Republic; various foreign decorations. **Addr.:** Tunis, Tunisia.

KLIBI (Ridha), Tunisian diplomat. **Born** in Tunisia in 1927. **Married. Educ.:** M.A. **Career:** Director, Chamber of Commerce, Tunis (1955-56); Ambassador to Sweden, Denmark Finland and Norway (1960-67); to Senegal, Mauritania, Guinea, Mali, Sierra Leone, Gambia and Liberia (1967-69); to Switzerland and Austria (1969-70); Director of Consular Affairs, Ministry of Foreign Affairs (1970-73); Ambassador to China and Vietnam (1973-76); to Morocco (1976-78); to Czechoslovakia (1978-80); Director of Ptlitical Affairs Europe and USA, Ministry of Foreign Affairs (1980-82); Ambassador to Yugoslavia (1982). **Prof. Addr.:** Ministry of Foreign Affairs, Tunis, Tunisia.

KOCHIN (Abdi, Mahmoud), Djibouti Deputy at the National Assembly. **Born** in 1949 in Djibouti. **Career:** Secretary at the Accidents Services of "Société L.Savon & Ries" (30/04/1966- 27/02/1972); Accountant Secretary at the Purchasing Service of CDMB (Heron) (21/12/1972 - 31/12/1992). Elected Deputy at the National Assembly (18 December 1998 - to date). Central Committee Member RPP. Vice-President of the Finance Commission, Economy and Planning and Member of the Permanent Commission. Secretary-rapporteur of the Supreme Court of Justice. **Prof. Addr.:** National Assembly, P.O.Box 138 Djibouti, Djibouti.

KODMANI (Nazem), Syrian international civil servant. **Born** on November 5, 1927 in Damascus (Syria). **Married**, with children. **Educ.:** Faculty of Law, University of Syria (1946-49); Faculty of Law, St. Joseph University, Beirut (Lebanon); Faculty of Law, University of Paris. **Dipl.:** LL.B., LL.D., Ph.D. (Political Science) 1964. **Career:** Attorney (1950-56); Various diplomatic posts in France, South Africa, Guinea, Libya, Tunisia, Egypt (1956-68); Ministry of Foreign Affairs, Damascus; Programme & Research Division, Triad Corporation, Beirut (1968-71); Head, External Relations and Public Information Office, Inter-Governmental Maritime Consultative Organisation, London since 1971; Senior Liaison Officer in Charge with the U.N. System, UNESCO (1977-86). **Prof. Addr.:** 7 Place de Fontenoy, Tel.: 4568.10.00, 75007 Paris. **Priv. Addr.:** 4 Ave. Allert de Mun Tel.: 4723 6835, 75116 Paris.

KOMSANY (Kamel, Abdallah, Taha), Saudi public servant. **Born** in 1952 in Jeddah, Saudi Arabia. **Son** of Abdallah Taha Komsany. **Educ.:** Architecture. **Dipl.:** B.Sc. M.Sc. in Architecture, prep. Ph.D. in Architecture and Planning, Durham University. **Career:** Mayor of Al Sharfia Municipality; Director of Symposiums and Lectures; International Associate of the Royal Town Planning Institute; member of the Arab Urban Development Institute. **Publ.:** "A New Theory of Architecture". **Hobbies:** Photography. **Sports:** Football, tennis. **Addr.:** P.O.Box 4103, Telex: 402391 LANA SJ, Jeddah, 21491, Saudi Arabia.

KOOLI (Mongi), Tunisian politician. **Born** on March 15, 1930 in Ksar-Hellal, Tunisia. **Married**, 3 children. **Educ.:** After the primary school studies in his mother town, was educated at "Collège Sadiki" (Tunis) where he passed the "Baccalaureat"; Faculté de Droit, University of Paris, France. **Dipl.:** Licence in Public Law and Political Science. **Career:** Secretary-General, Union Générale des Etudiants Tunisiens (UGET) (1959); Assistant Director of Socialist Destour Party (1960-64); Governor of Jendouba (1964); Governor of Bizerta (1967-69); Director-General of National Security (1969-70); Ambassador to Spain (1970-74); Secretary of State for Foreign Affairs (1974-76); Mayor of Ksar Hella since May 1975; Minister of Public Health (1976-80); Lawyer at the Supreme Court of Appeal (1978-80); Minister delegate responsible for Prime Minister's Office and Director Socialist Destour Party and Head of Political Bureau (1980-84). **Awards:** Grand Cordon Order of Tunisian Independence; Grand Cordon, Order of the Tunisian Republic; various foreign decorations. **Addr.:** Tunis, Tunisia.

KORAYEM (Badr Ahmad), Saudi journalist. **Born** in Yambu al-Bahr in 1939. **Educ.:** B.A. (Sociology), King Abdulaziz University. **Career:** Director of General Programmes, Jeddah Broadcasting Station (1976); Director General of Broadcasting Station (1980); owner of Construction and Trading Establishment; one of the leading Radio and Television personalities in Saudi Arabia in the past decade; Deputy Editor-in-Chief, Okaz Newspaper. **Honours:** decoration awarded by many countries. **Publications:** Social Development in Saudi Arabian Society: Applications on Social Development Centres, History of Saudi Broadcasting (a book). **Hobby:** reading. **Prof. Addr.:** Okaz Newspaper, P.O.Box 9218, Tel.: 6710738, Jeddah. **Priv. Addr.:** Tel.: 6512183, Jeddah, Saudi Arabia.

KORAYEM (Muhammad Samir, Salim), Egyptian economist. **Born** on October 6, 1930 in Beni Suef, Egypt. **Married**, two children. **Educ.:** Cairo University, Egypt; International Banking School, Prague, Czechoslovakia; American University of Cairo, Egypt. **Dipl.:** B.A. in Accounting and Public Finance (1952); Diplomas in Taxation and Public Finance (1954), in Planning and Finance (1963); Professional Diploma in Management and M.A. in Business Management (1975). **Career:** Tax Officer (1952); Head of Economic Cooperation with European Countries (1965); Deputy Director General of the International Finance Department at the Ministry of Economy and Economic Cooperation (1975); Under Secretary of State for International Finance; Minister of Finance (1977); Fellow of Economic Development Institute, Washington D.C., USA; Part-time researcher of the Economic Department of Arab League; part-time Lecturer in Business Management at the American University in Cairo, Egypt. **Prof. Addr.:** 8 Adly Street, Tel.: 916214, Cairo, Egypt.

KORDI (Khalil Abdulfattah), Saudi academic. **Born** in 1947 in Medina, Saudi Arabia. **Dipl.:** B.Sc. (Commerce); M.Sc. and Ph.D. (Accounting). **Career:** Demonstrator, Department of Accounting, King Saud University (1966-71); Assistant Professor and Chairman, Accounting Department, King Saud University. **Member:** National Association of Accountants, American Accounting Association. **Publications:** writes occasionally in Saudi newspapers and specialised magazines. **Hobby:** chess. **Prof. Addr.:** King Saud University, Faculty of Administrative Science, P.O.Box 2459, Tel.: 4358411, Riyadh. **Priv. Addr.:** Tel.: 4811000, Riyadh, Saudi Arabia.

KORDI (Mahmoud Taher), Saudi Physician. **Born** in Mecca in 1929. **Educ.:** M.D. (Medicine Surgery), Cairo University; Ph.D. (Physiology), London University. **Career:** Lecturer, Physiology Department, King Saud University (1973-75) Assistant Professor (1975-81); Chairman, Cultural Committee, Faculty of Medicine; Director, Research Centre; Associate Professor King Saud University (1981-). **Member:** World Conference of Physiology Science. **Publications:** informative articles in Saudi newspapers, research in international specialized magazines, Saudi T.V. programmes. **Hobbies:** reading, sports. **Prof. Addr.:** Faculty of Medicine, King Saud University, P.O.Box 2925, Tel.: 4782020, Riyadh. **Priv. Addr.:** Tel.: 4811000 Ext. 2155, Riyadh, Saudi Arabia.

KORSHY (Muna, Ahmad), Egyptian businesswoman. **Born** in 1942. **Married. Educ.:** B.A. in English Literature, Cairo University. **Career:** Conference Organizer, AFRASEC (1967); Head of Industrial Information Center, Algerian Chamber of Commerce (1970); Director, Egyptian Business Services (since 1973). Member of the Gezira Sporting Club, Automobile Club. **Prof. Addr.:** 13A Marashly Street, Flat 1A, Zamalek, Cairo, Egypt. **Priv. Addr.:** 3 Ahmed Pasha Street, Garden City Cairo, Egypt.

KOSHAK (Abdulkadir Hamzah), Saudi official. **Born** in Makkah in 1939. **Educ.:** B.Sc. (Architectural Engineering); M.Sc. (L.A.E.P.). **Career:** Engineer, Ministry of Interior, Jeddah (1962); Director of Technical Office, Ministry of Interior, Riyadh, (1964); Director of Central Administration for Engineering Services, Municipalities Administration, Ministry of Interior, Riyadh (1968); General Director for Engineering Affairs, Riyadh (1970); Former Mayor of Holy Capital, Makkah (1977); Owner, Bureau of Architecture and Engineering Consultant office. Assistant Deputy Minister for Technical Affairs, Ministry of Municipalities (1980); **Honorary member:** al-Wehda Social and Cultural Club, Makkah; General-Secretary, Islamic Cities Organization; member of the Board, Islamic Research Centre, Istanbul; member, Islamic Assembly Organization. **Publications:** Mobile Homes Districts. (M.Sc. Thesis). **Hobbies:** reading about engineering and vocational sciences. **Prof. Addr.:** P.O.Box 1210, Tel.: 5368968, Mecca. **Priv. Addr.:** Tel.: 5369241, Mecca, Saudi Arabia.

KOSHAK (Yahya, Hamza), Saudi civil engineer. **Born** on November 21, 1942 in Mecca, Saudi Arabia. **Son** of Hamza Ahmad Sultan Koshak **and** Mrs. Hafieza Hasan Sudqi. **Married** on December 14, 1968 in Mecca to Mariem Husain al-Sowaigh, 6 children: Khalid, Amal, Hannan, Mona, Ahmad and Mohamad. **Educ.:** Engineer College, Ain Shams University. Cairo (1963-65); Eng. College, Riyadh University (1966-67); Washington University, USA (1970). **Dipl.:** B.Sc. (Civil Eng.), Riyadh University, Eng. College (1966-67); M.Sc. (Civil Eng.), Washington University, USA (1970). **Career:** Held official post as Civil Engineer at the Ministry of Interior Agency for Municipal Affairs; Deputy Mayor of Mecca for technical affairs; an Associate with the British firm Watson Consulting Engineers; held the post of Director General of Water and Sewage Departments, the Western region (for four years); now running his own architecture and engineering office and is Saudi Partner in Dar al-Handasa Company. **Publications:** a paper on the dual method of water networks, a paper on Zam Zam Water, a research on Ain Zubaida (Zubaida Water Well) and old water conduits in Mecca. **Hobbies:** painting, photography. **Prof. Addr.:** P.O.Box 3507, Tel.: 6655562, 6694005, Jeddah. **Priv. Addr.:** Tel.: 6655539, Jeddah, Saudi Arabia.

KOSHMAN (Muhammad Nassim), Kuwaiti economist. **Born** on October 25, 1935 in Lebanon. **Married**, 3 sons. **Educ.:** University of Grenoble, France. **Dipl.:** Degree in law and economics. **Career:** Attorney at the Court of Appeals, Dakar, Senegal (1959-61); Head of Permanent Mission to the UN in New York, USA and Chargé d'Affaires of Mauritania in Washington D.C. (1961-64); Executive Director of the International Development Association, the International Finance Corporation, the World Bank and Principal Resident Representative of Mauritania to the World Bank Group with rank of Ambassador (1963-74); Special Adviser to the President of the World Bank for liaison with OPEC Members (1974-76); Ambassador of Mauritania to USA, Brazil and Mexico (1976-78); Investment Consultant in Washington D.C. (1978/80); Adviser to the Kuwait Fund for Arab Economic Development. **Hobbies:** reading, swimming, music, chess, writing. **Awards:** Senegal Grand Officer of the National Order (1969); Commander of the Order of Merit, Central African Republic (1970); Grand Officer of the Order of Merit, Chad (1970); Commander of the National Orders of Ivory Coast (1970), of Congo (1970), of Upper Volta (1971) and of Benin (1972); Order of San Carlos, Columbia Grand Cross (1973); Commander of the Order of National Merit, Mauritania (1976) and various other awards. **Prof. Addr.:** Kuwait Fund for Arab Economic Development, P.O.Box 2921, Tel.: 439075, Kuwait, Kuwait.

KOTAITE (Abdullatif), Syrian statesman. **Born** in 1932 in Damascus. **Educ.:** Mechanical Industry at Alexandria University. **Career:** Former Director General of the Union of Textiles Industries (April 1st, 1968-October 1968); Minister of Industry in the Cabinet of General Hafez al-Assad (1970). **Remark** Has a perfect knowledge of Arabic, English, German and Italian. **Addr.:** Damascus, Syria.

KRIM (Fateh), Algerian Professor of University. **Born** on October 22, 1954 in Setif, Algeria. **Son** of Salah Krim (Professor) **and** Mrs. née Fatima Bourba. **Married** on August 2, 1991 in Setif to Salima Saifi. **Educ.:** Université Claude Bernard, Lyon, France; Université Grenoble, Ecole Centrale (France). **Dipl.:** Engineering, Doctorate. **Career:** Professor, Université Grenoble (1980-1983); Design Engineer, Cit AlCatel, Paris (1983-1986); Professor, University Setif, Algeria (1986-1993); Vice-Rector, Research and Post Graduation. **Awards:** Honor Diploma of Engineer (France). **Sports:** Jogging, Swimming. **Hobby:** Computer. **Member:** Swimming Club. **Prof. Addr.:** University of Setif, Electrical Institute, Tel.: (05) 910080, 19000 Setif, Algeria. **Priv. Addr.:** Cité du 8 Mai 45, BTG1 No. 535, 19000 Setif, Algeria.

KRONFLI (Sami, Joseph), Sudanese executive. **Born** on September 29, 1961 in Khartoum, Sudan. **Son** of Joseph Kronfli (Chemist) **and** Mrs. Suad Bonduki. **Married** on December 22, 1988 in Khartoum to Miss Jessica Kabbabe. **Educ.:** Comboni College, Khartoum; Faculty of Economics and Social Studies; University of Khartoum. **Dipl.:** B.Sc. (Business Administration). **Career:** Store Keeper (1979-80); Accountant (1981-82); Deputy Administration Manager (1983-84); Managing Director, Khartoum Commercial Agency (1985-todate), Pharmaceutical importers and distributors, sole agents for Ciba, Merck Sharp & Dohme, Bristol Myers, Syntex, etc. importing and distributing to all parts of the Sudan, pharmaceuticals, parapharmaceuticals, medical equipment and cosmetics and supplying all Government tenders. **Sports:** Tennis, Swimming, squash. **Hobbies:** Reading, Travelling. **Member:** Pharmaceutical Importers Association. **Credit Card:** American Express; Visa Card: Master Card. **Prof. Addr.:** P.O.Box 646 Khartoum, Tel.: 80197, 70847, 72072, Sudan. **Priv. Addr.:** same, Tel.: 41779, Sudan.

KTARI (Mohamed, Hedi), Tunisian President of Sfax University. **Born** on February 13, 1939 in Sfax, Tunisia. **Son** of Mahmoud Ktari (Businessman) **and** Mrs. Fatouma Mellouli. **Married** on November 25, 1985 in Sfax to Fathia Fakhfakh, 5 children: Mahmoud Riadh (17.07.1968); Leila (27.01.1973); Emna (8.02.1987); Nadia (20.03.1988); Myriam (26.08.1989). **Educ.:** Faculté des Sciences Mathématiques, Physique et Naturelles de Tunis; Faculté des Sciences de Paris; Institut National Agronomique de Paris; Faculté des Sciences et Techniques de Montpellier. **Dipl.:** Licence es Sciences Naturelles; Advanced Studies in Entomology; Advanced Studies in Embryology; Forest and Agricultural Entomology; State Doctorate Biological Sciences. **Career:** Demonstrator (1961-1963); Assistant (1965-1967); Chief of the Works (1968-1971); Lecturer (1971-1975); Professor (since 1975); 1st President and Founder of the Tunisian Association of Sea Sciences; 1st President and Founder of the Maghrébine Association of Sea Sciences. **Other Information:** Director of Animal Biology Unit (1972-1976); Director of Natural Sciences Department (1978-1980); President of Sfax University (since 1987). **Awards:** Laureate of Presidential Prize (1963); Officer, Order of the Republic (1990); Commander, Order of Educative Merit. **Sport:** Swimming. **Hobby:** Environment Activity. **Member:** Société des Sciences Naturelles. **Prof. Addr.:** Route de l'Aeroport Km1, Tel.: (04) 240.678, (04) 244.423, 3029 Sfax, Tunisia.

KUAIBA (Muftah Mohamed), Libyan official. **Career:** Governor of Misurata; Minister of Municipalities (Nov. 1974-76); Minister for Youth Affairs (Oct. 1976-77); Secretary for Youth, General People's Committee (1977-1988); currently Secretary of General People's Committee for Marine Wealth. **Addr.:** Office of the Secretary, Tripoli, Libya.

KUDSI (Fawwaz, Nazem), Former U.A.E. Diplomat. **Born** on September 29, 1941 in Aleppo, Syria. 3 Sons. **Educ.:** University of Aleppo, Syria. **Diplo.:** LL.B. **Career:** practiced law in Syria (1969); Acting Director of the Center of Documentation and Research, Amiri Court in

Abu Dhabi (1970); Head, Protocol Department, Ministry of Foreign Affairs (1972-82); Ambassador, Ministry of Foreign Affairs (1982-87); Senior Partner and Lawyer, Kudsi Law Firm, Abu Dhabi (1987-present) **Medals:** Decorated with medals by King Hussein of Jordan, King Khaled of Saudi Arabia, French President, Italian President, Tunisian President and President of Mauritania. **Hobbies:** Tennis, horse riding, skiing, swimming, and legal, political and historical thought. **Prof. Addr.:** P.O.Box 46010, Tel.: 6336500, Abu Dhabi, United Arab Emirates.

KUFTARO (Ahmad Muhammed Amin, His Eminence, Shaikh), Grand mufti of Syria, head of the supreme council of fatwa, head of religious scholars. **Born** in Damascus in 1915, Syria. **Son** of Muhammad Amin Kuftaro (A grand Scholar). **Educ.:** Private studies under the tutorship of the elite jurisprudents and scholars of Islam in Damascus. **Dipl.:** Several discretionary and honorary Doctorates in the teaching of the principles of the religion and calling for Islam, granted to his Eminence by several state universities in several Islamic states. **Career:** After his father's death, his Eminence Ahmad Kuftaro took the role of preaching and calling for the spiritual values. He still gives Islamic lectures in various places especially in Abun Noor Mosque, where thousands of male and female Muslims attend his lectures. Teacher of Islam in Dar el-Fatwa in Quneitra (1948); moved to Dar el-Fatwa in Damascus (1950); Mufti of Damascus (1951); First Mufti of Damascus and member of the Supreme Council of Fatwa. The Founder of al-Ansar Society and the Islamic Institutes for Call and Guidance in Damascus (1958); elected Grand Mufti of Syria and Head of the Supreme Council of Fatwa as well as the Supreme Council of Wakf (1964); elected as a member of the Central Council of the Afro-Asian Islamic Organisation, Bandung Indonesia. **Islamic Activities:** One of the founders of the League of Scholars. Member of the Syrian delegation to the Islam-Christian Conference held in Lebanon (1954); visited many European countries wherein he met many Orientalists and other eminent persons who were concerned in the Islamic Studies; Also visited most of the Islamic Centres there; attented the 5th session of the Islamic World Conference, in Baghdad (1962); delivered a speech in al-Aksa Mosque in Jerusalem (1964); received an invitation from the universities of Indiana-Michigan and Ohio Associations where he delivered more than fifty lectures about Islam and the problems of the age as well as the Palestinian Question; represented Syria in the meetings of the Central Council of the Afro-Asian Islamic Organisation in Jakarta-Indonesia; accepted an invitation from the Chairman of the Religious Department in Minor Asia where he met many of the Soviet officials (1969); As a result of his contacts many mosques were really reconstructed and reopened; He also contributed in opening the Supreme Islamic Institute in Tashkand; was at the head of a delegation to the common meeting of the International Islamic Conference, held in Jakarta-Indonesia (1970); Established the great Islamic Foundation known as AbuNnurIslamic Foundation (seven floors) (1971); visited Algeria, Iran and India giving lectures in Islamic Conferences there (1972-74); accepted an invitation from the Vice President of East Germany where he met many officials and made discussions with a delegation representing the Faculty of Theology in Berlin University. An official statement was issued later in which both sides confirmed the Oneness of God and that Jesus and Muhammad (peace be on them) where the Messengers of God (1980); delivered a lecture in the Academy of Science in Moscow, its topic was "Islam and peace" (1981); represented the Muslim Side in the Inter-Religious Conference in Moscow (1982); represented the Syrian Scholars in the International Conference for Peace, held in Prague, Czechoslovakia (1983); was on the head of a delegation to attend the "Round Table Conference for Peace" in Moscow (1984); accepted an invitation to lecture in the universities of Rome, Milan and the Vatican, he also visited his Holiness the Pope in the Vatican and met some officials there (1985); participated in the "Islamic Conference" held in Pako city in the Soviet Union (1986); visited Poland and East Germany to lecture in the Scientific Centres about: "Islam and Peace", "Islam and the Modern Problems", also visited the Vatican and held a summit meeting with his Holiness the Pope (1987); visited Bulgaria wherein he participated in the celebration for opening "Sophia Mosque" and for establishing the new "Imam Institute" (1988); accepted invitations to Visit U.S.A., Turkey and the Soviet Union where he delivered lectures in the Conferences, Universities and Islamic Centres (1989); elected, Chairman of the Religions side in the "Global Forum on Environment and Development for Survival" held in Moscow between (15-19 Jan. 1990); accepted an invitation to visit the Muslims in Japan and China where he met the Leaders of the Islamic Centres and Organisations and gave speeches before thousands of Muslims (1991); then he went to Korea to attend the "Global Forum of Spiritual and Parliamentary Leaders on Human Survival" (May 1991); gave lectures about the "Views of Islam in Solving the Problems of the Modern Age"; Two Weeks later he attended an "Islamic-Christian Conference" in Istanbul, heading the Islamic side in the Inter-religious dialogue (Oct. 1991). **Awards:** Sitarat Pakistan Medal, Medal of Justice. **Sports:** Daily walking, Swimming. **Prof. Addr.:** Abu Nour Islamic Foundation, P.O.Box 4656, Damascus, Syria.

KUHAIMY (Ahmad, al, Shaikh), Saudi diplomat. **Born** in 1925 in Damascus, Syria. **Married**, five children. **Educ.:** B.A. in Economics and Political Science. **Career:** political Attaché, Saudi Embassy to Iraq (1947); 3rd Secretary, 2nd Secretary, 1st Secretary, Counsellor, Minister Delegate, Ambassador to Jordan; Ambassador to Iraq (1981); Ambassador in Lebanon. **Medals:** King Abdul Aziz Medal; Star of Jordan, 1st Class. **Sports:** Swimming, riding. **Hobbies:** Reading arabic literature, hunting. **Prof. Addr.:** c/o Ministry of Foreign Affairs, Nasseriya Street, Riyadh, Saudi Arabia.

KULAIB (Ali, Ghanim), Yemeni engineer. **Born** in 1924 in Aden, Yemen. **Married,** five children. **Son** of Ghanim Kulaib. **Educ.:** B.Sc. in Engineering, St. Andrews University, Scotland (1955); member of the Institute of Civil Engineers (1961). **Career:** Teacher in Aden (1949-52); Engineer, George Wimpy, U.K. (1955-58); Engineer, Senior R.E. and State Engineer, Aden (1958-62); Director of Public Works and Permanent Secretary, Ministry of Communications, South Yemen (1962-68); Chairman, Little Aden Township (1968-69); Senior Resident Engineer, Mecca Project for Watson Saudi Arabia (1969-79); Associate Partner (1976); Manager for Saudi City Project in Jeddah, Saudi Amoudi Group (since 1980). **Sports:** Tennis, table tennis. **Hobbies:** Chess, travel. Tel.: 6530186, Jeddah, Saudi Arabia.

KURKI (Khalid, Abdalaziz, al), Jordanian writer and academic. **Born** in Jordan in 1946. **Married,** four children. **Educ.:** University of Jordan and Cambridge University. **Dipl.:** M.A. (1977), Ph.D. (1980). **Career:** Teacher (1969-74); Assistant Editor "University Studies" Magazine (1974-77); Vice Dean, Faculty of Letters, University of Jordan (1983-84); Professor; Chairman, Jordanian Writers' Union (since 1985). Member, Office of the Arab Union for Literature (1984). **Pub.:** "Taha Hussein", "The Arab and Islam"; "Fiction in Jordan". **Hobbies:** Travel, reading, writing. **Addr.:** Faculty of Letters, University of Jordan, Amman, Jordan.

KURNAS (Salim Sultan), Saudi academic. **Born:** Hail, in 1937. **Dipl.:** B.Sc. (1966); M.Sc. (1971). **Career:** Computer Draftsman, Arabian American Oil Company (Aramco) (1948-64); Secretary Faculty of Education, Riyadh University (1966-72); now Assistant Lecturer, Faculty of Education, Riyadh University. **Member:** National Association of Science Teachers in the U.S.A. (1971-72). Science Teachers Association in Britain (1967-68). **Scholarships:** from Aramco (1959, 1962), Ministry of Education (1964-66), UNESCO (1967-68, 1969, 1972), University of Riyadh (1972 to date). **Honours:** Second Place in University Trophy in Debating, at University of Wisconsin - Milwaukee (1966). **Sports:** Football, tennis, swimming. **Hobby:** Chess. **Priv. Addr.:** Tel.: 36692, 21925, Riyadh, Saudi Arabia.

KURSH (Muhammad Ahmad), Egyptian executive. **Born** on May 14, 1940 in Assiout, Egypt. **Married,** Two children. **Educ.:** Cairo University. Faculty of Commerce, Egypt. **Dipl.:** B.Com. (1964); diploma in Finance (1970). **Career:** Deputy 1976-79); Secretary General, International Relations and National Security Committee, Senate (1980-); Senator (1980-); Chairman of Gico Trade Company; Owner of Gi Fleur Essential Oils & Cosmetics Factory, Fayoum; Owner of Kurshi Candy Factory, Egypt. **Member:** Shooting Culb; Automobile Club of Egypt; Gezira Sporting Club. **Prof. Addr.:** 53, Zahraa Street, Tel.: 490902, Mohandiseen, Egypt. **Priv. Addr.:** 11 Rashdan Street, Dokki, Tel.: 986461, Cairo, Egypt.

KURSHUMI (Abdallah, Hussain Ahmad, al), Yemeni statesman. **Born** in 1932 in Sana'a, Yemen. **Son** of Hussain bin Ahmad al-Kurshumi (landowner) **and** Mrs. née Masaidah al-Kurshumi. **Married** in 1960 to Lufiyah Barakat, 2 children: Khalid and Omari. **Educ.:** Primary and Secondary in Sana'a; Faculty of Engineering, Ayn Shams Univesity, Cairo (Egypt). **Dipl.:** B.Sc. (Engineering) (1959). **Career:** Engineer (1959-62); appointed Minister of Public Works in the first Republican Government (28 Sept. 1962-31 Oct. 1962); retains his post in the 2nd Government (31 Oct. 1962- 27 April 1963); Minister of Communications (23 Apr. 1963- 10 Feb. 1964); returns to the Ministry of Public Works as Consulting Engineer (1965-67); Minister of Transport (3 Apt. 1969- 8 July 1969); Prime Minister (1969- Feb. 1970); Chairman, Yemen Bank of reconstruction and Development (1971), also Chief of the Bridges and Roads Division, Ministry of Public Works (1973-74); Minister of Works (January 1975); Minister of Public Works and transport until May 1990; Minister of Reconstruction (May 1990 to June 1995). **Addr.:** Sanaa, Republic of Yemen.

KUTUBI (Orfan, Kader, al), Syrian economist and consultant. **Born** in 1923 in Syria. **Son** of Kader al-Kutubi. **Married,** three children. **Dipl.:** Ph.D. in economics. **Career:** Assistant Professor, then Professor, then Head of Department of Economics, Damascus University; Professor of Economics, Lebanese University, Arab University in Lebanon and Cairo University. Also Director, Damascus Civil Airport; General Director of Civil Aviation, Syria; Deputy Director, then Director, Maritime Transport in Syria; Vice Minister of the Economy and Foreign Trade; Vice President of Economic Board, presently, independent Economic Consultant. **Author** of five books. **Addr.:** Principality of Monaco.

KUWAIZ (Abdullah, el, Dr.), Saudi economist. **Born** on August 21, 1939 in Dawudmi, Saudi Arabia. **Son** of Ibrahim Abdullah el-Kuwaiz **and** Mrs. Sarah Mohamed al-Husaini. **Married** on April 14, 1959 in Riyadh to Norah I. el-Kuwaiz, two sons and two daughters: Taha (1961), Haifa (1962), Samra (1964), and Mohammed (1976). **Educ.:** King Saud University, Riyadh; Pacific Lutheran University, USA; St.Louis University, USA. **Dipl.:** B.A. (Economics and Political Science); M.A. (Economics); M.B.A.; Ph.D. (Economics). **Career:** Member of the Board and Member of the Executive Committee, Gulf International Bank, Bahrain (Nov. 1977-); Member of the Governing Board of Oxford Energy Institute (1982-); Chairman of Arab Monetary Fund, Abu Dhabi, U.A.E.

(April 1987-89); Deputy Minister, Ministry of Finance and National Economy, Riyadh, Saudi Arabia (March 1988-Aug. 1995); Associate Secretary General for Economic Affairs, Gulf, Cooperation Council for the Arab States of the Gulf, Riyadh, Saudi Arabia (1981-1996); General Manager, Gulf International Bank. **Sports:** Running and Swimming. **Hobby:** Reading. **Credit Card:** American Express, Diner's. **Prof. Addr.:** Gulf International Bank, 3 Palace Ave., Manama 317, Al-Dowali Bldg., P.O.Box 1017, Manama, Bahrain. **Priv. Addr.:** P.O.Box 10866, Riyadh 11443, Saudi Arabia.

KWEIDER (Mohamed, Rateb), Syrian executive. **Born** in 1954 in Damascus, Syria. **Son** of Fauzi Kweider (Tradesman) **and** Mrs. née Fatimeh Hamwi. **Married** in 1982 in Damascus to Miss Chirin Hourieh, one son: Bassel (1983). **Educ.:** Ibn Athil Secondary School, Damascus; Faculty of Economy, Damascus University, Damascus. **Dipl.:** Degrees in Economics, Trade and Accounting. **Career:** joined the General Organization for Trade and Distribution (G.O.T.A.), Damascus in 1976 and was employed in the Commission Department; Manager of the Syrian Duty Free Shops (1981); Assistant General Manager (1987); Currently Chairman/ General Manager, General Organization for Trade and Distribution (1988-) dealing in import-export, agencies, barter and duty free shops. **Decor.:** Several letters of appreciation and congratulations from the Council of Ministers and H.E. Minister of Economy and Foreign Trade, Syria. **Sport:** Swimming. **Hobby:** Music. **Prof. Addr.:** The General Organization for Trade and Distribution, "GOTA", P.O.Box 15, Damascus, Syria. Tel.: 2210396 - 2210397 - 2210949. Fax: 2219232. **Priv. Addr.:** Baghdad Avenue, Tel.: 456767, Damascus, Syria.

L

LABIB (Abdel Rahman), Egyptian politician. **Born** in 1924. **Dipl.:** B.Sc., civil Engineering (1945). **Career:** Ministry of Housing Public Utilities, (Chairman of Housing & Development organization 1973-1976); Chairman of General Authority for Building & Housing Cooperatives (1976-1984); Minister of Housing & Public Utilities (1985-1986); Now Senior Advisor & Consultant: Ministry of Reconstruction & New Communities & Housing & Public Utilities. **Addr.:** 10 Bayomi Nassar Str., Heliopolis, Cairo, Egypt.

LADGHAM (Salah), Tunisian diplomat. **Born** in 1927 in Tunisia. **Married. Career:** Chargé d'Affaires, Embassy to Spain (1960-62); Ambassador to Czechoslovakia (1962-66); Ambassador to Netherlands (1966-70); Director of Political Affairs, Ministry of Foreign Affairs (1970-74); Ambassador to Turkey (1974). **Addr.:** c/o Ministry of Foreign Affairs, Tunis, Tunisia.

LADJIMI (Bechir Mahmoud), Tunisian businessman. **Born** on May 9, 1940 in Tunis, Tunisia. **Married,** 1 son, 1 daughter. **Educ.:** University of Milan, Italy. **Dipl.:** Laurea in Engineering. **Career:** Director and General Manager of Société Tunisienne d'Industrie Automobile (1967); Chairman and General Manager of ISOFRIGO SA; Vice President, Syndicat de la Mécanique et de la Fonderie, Syndicat des Constructeurs Automobile; Chairman and General Manager of COTREL (1981-). **Prof. Addr.:** Zone Industrielle la Charguia, Rue 14, Carthage, Tunis, Tunisia.

LADRISSI (Muhammad, Bin Issa Ifrata), Moroccan engineer. **Born** in 1940 in Casablanca, Morocco. **Married,** 2 children. **Educ.:** National Hydrographical School, France. **Dipl.:** Degree in Marine Engineering. **Career:** Officer at the High Institute for Marine Studies (1958-61); Engineering Official, Moroccan Marine Co. (1961-65), Chief Engineer (1965-68); Moroccan Representative and Consultant of Germanischer Lloyd; Member of the High Institute for Marine Studies and of the Completion Council for Experience; Assistant Director of the Board of Marine Arbitration in Morocco; Fleet Manager, Moroccan Marine Co. (1973-). **Prof. Addr.:** Moroccan Marine Company, 7 al-Mokawama Street, Casablanca, Morocc. **Priv. Addr.:** Villa Samia, Street 4, Longchamps Cil, Casablanca, Morocco.

LAGU (Joseph, Major-General), Sudanese army officer. **Born** on November 21, 1931 in Sudan. **Married,** 6 children. **Educ.:** Rumbeck Secondary School; Military Academy, Omdurman (Sudan). **Career:** served in the Sudan Armed Forces (1960-63); joined South Sudan Liberation Movement (SSLM) 1963; leader (SSLM) 1969; signed peace agreement with the Government (March 1972); appointed General, Sudanese Army (1972); Commander-in-Chief, Sudanese Armed Forces, Southern Command (1974); President, Higher Executive Council, Regional Government. (1979-85); formerly Permanent Representative United Nations. **Publ.:** Author of "The Anya-Nya, What we fight for" (1972). **Awards:** Order of the Two Niles (1972). **Addr.:** Ministry of Foreign Affairs, Khartoum, Sudan.

LAHBABI (Driss), Moroccan Physician. **Born** on 12 December 1932 in Fes, Morocco. **Son** of Ahmad Lahbabi (trader) **and** Mrs., née Khaddouj Slaoui. **Married** on 29 March 1966 in Paris, to Miss Michelle Verborne, 2 children: Malic and Maya. **Dipl.:** M.D. **Career:** Gyneacologist; Chief Physician, Maternity Service, Hopital el-Farabi; Assistant, Maternité Rabat; Physician, Sid Soufi Maternity, Casablanca. **Sport:** Swimming. **Hobby:** Reading. **Member:** Sun Club, Casablanca. **Prof. Addr.:** 160, Mustafa El Maani St., Tel.: 272704, Casablanca. **Priv. Addr.:** Erraha 3, St. 2 No.8, P.O.Box 12560, Casablanca 01, Morocco.

LAHBABI (Hassan), Moroccan M.D. Surgeon. **Born** on 27 December 1927 in Fes, Morocco. **Son** of Mohamad Lahbabi (Trader) **and** Mrs., Omkeltoum Benkirane. **Married** on 25 May 1958 to Miss Farida el-Alami, 4 children: Karim, Majid, Ali, Mehdi. **Educ.:** College Moulay Idriss, Fes; Faculty of Medicine, Paris, France. **Dipl.:** M.D., Diploma d'Etat; Laureate from the Faculty of Medicine, Paris. **Career:** Intern (1953-56); Resident Surgeon (1956-58); Chief Surgeon (1958-75); Physician Director General, Polyclinique de la Securité Sociale, Casablanca. **Works:** "Kystes Hydatiques au Maroc", "Ulcéro Gastro-duodenaux en milieu morocain", "Aspecto particuliers des affections gynécologiques au Maroc", "Les goitres au Maroc", **Member:** President, Société Morocaine de Chirurgie (1960-72); member, Société Internationale de Chirurgie, Vice-President, Société Morocaine des Sciences Medicales (1972). **Sport:** Swimming. **Hobbies:** Movies, Traveling. **Addr.:** 16, Blvd. du Lido, Casablanca, Morocco.

LAHBABI (Mohamad, Aziz), Moroccan dean of faculty. **Born** on December 25, 1922 in Fès (Morocco). **Married,** one son. **Educ.:** National School of Oriental Languages (Paris), La Sorbonne, Caen University (Faculty of Letters and Faculty of Science). **Dipl.:** Diploma from National School of Oriental Languages (Paris), Licenciate of Philosophy, La Sorbonne, Caen University, Diploma of Higher Studies, Doctor of Letters (State Doctorate), La Sorbonne. **Career:** National Centre of the Scientific Research, Paris (1953-58), Member of cultural missions and congresses to Europe, China, Middle East, Near East, U.S.S.R., U.S.A., India, Central Asia, Africa, Canada, Japan; Professor of Philosophy at the Faculty of Science and Humanitarian Science, Muhammad V University, Rabat (December 1958); Honorary Professor at the Instituto Superior di Scienze Umani (Urbino); Dean, Faculty of Letters and Humanitarian Science, Muhammad V University (December 1961); became Honorary Dean of same Faculty (February 1, 1969); also Professor of philosophy at the Universitites of Algiers, Algeria and Muhammad V, Morocco; Correspondent Member of the Academy of the Arabic Language, Cairo; Member of the Mediterranean Academy, Italy; Member of the Academy of the Kingdom of Morocco; Member of Academie des Sciences d'Outre-Mer, Paris; Member Académie Internationale de la Philosophie de l'Art, Bern, Switzerland; Director and Founder of "La Maison de la Pensée", Rabat. Elected "Prince de la Nouvelle", title given at the "Hôtel de Ville", Paris, by Presidents L.S. Senghor and Jacques Chirac. **Publ.:** Manager and founder of the Arabic Review "Afâq" (Horizons); Director of the "Etudes Philosophiques et Littéraires" review; Author of: **in French:** "Songs of Hope" (poems), "Misères et Lumières" (poems) 5 editions, (Paris and Casablanca), "De l'Etre à la Personne" (3 editions), Paris, Algiers and Rabat, "Du clos à l'ouvert" (20 subjects on National Culture anb Human Civilization) 4 editions in Algiers and Paris, "Liberté ou Libération?" (3 editions, France and Morocco), "Le Personnalisme Musulman" (3 editions, Paris), "Florillège poétique arabe et berbère" (Paris), "Ma voix à la recherche de sa voie" (poems) (2 editions, Paris and Casablanca), "Ibn-Khaldûn" (5 editions, Paris and Rabat), "Les déracinés" (Scénario), "L'ère de la détraumatisation" (Beirut), "Espoir Vagabond" (Novel), 4 editions (Paris and Rabat), "Douleurs Rythmées" (Arab and Berber divine poems), "Fath au rendez-vous de l'espérance et l'Algérie au rendez-vous de la résurrection" Volume I, "Poésie à plusieurs voix" (Volume II) (Algiers), "al-Muïm" dictionary of philosophy and human sciences, English, French, Arabic, (Casablanca), "Le monde de demain" (Casablanca and Sherbroke, Canada), "Ivre d'Innocence", poems (Paris), "Adil", poems (Casablanca), "Espérance, malgré la mort", poems (Paris and Rabat), "Morsure sur le fer" short story, (Paris and Rabat), "Oeuvre poétique" one Volume. "La crise des valeurs" (Paris and Rabat), "La rose se meurt", poems (Paris and Rabat). **In Arabic:** "Mufakkirû-al-Islam" (Rabat), "Bu's wa diyyâ" poems (Beirut), "al-Add alâ el-Hadîd" 2 editions (Tunis), Mina-al-Kaïn ilâ-Achakhc" 3 editions (Cairo), "Achakhçânya al-islamia" 2 editions (Cairo), "Réflexions sur le langage, le bavardage et la langue", essay (Tripoli-Tunis), "Jil addamâ" novel, 4 editions (Beirut-Rabat), "Min-al-huryât ila -taharrur" 3 editions (Cairo), "Min-el-Moghaliq ila-el-munfatih" 2 editions (Cairo), "Vocabulaire philosophique", french-Arabic, 2 editions (Rabat), "Waraqât fi elfalsafât el-islamya" (Casablanca), "Yatim tehta assifr" (Casablanca), "Exir-el-hayât" Novel sciences fiction, 2 editions, (Cairo and Casablanca), "Ibn Khaldûn" 2 editions (Beirut), Some of the Works edited have been translated in about thirty Languages (Albanian, German, English, Chinese, Spanish, Mongol, Russian, Turkish, etc...), several Works have been accepted as courses in Universities, and many thesis have been retained such as, Eliana de leva, "Il personnalismo filsofie specifica del Musulmani" (University of Palermo, 1967), Fadel Sidarouss "Les fondements de l'Anthropologie philosophique de Mohamed Aziz Lahbabi" (St. Joseph University, Beirut, 1971), Marcello Aldo Giannasi "Il ensiero di Mohamed Aziz Lahbabi" (University of Milan, 1968), Claudia Gnecco "La produzione litteraria di Lahbabi" (Rome), Kamîd el-Hadj "Le personnalisme réaliste de Lahhabi" (Aix-en-Provence, France), **other studies** on M.A. Lahbabi by Richard Mc. Carthy (Oxford), "The Thirsty Generation an Islamic Response", by Sighrid Hunke "Mouhamed Aziz Lahbabi Philosopher, Poet and Patriot" (Bonn), by P. Monenteau and B. Jourdan "Labhabi, Homme de dialogue", "Lahbabi, l'Homme et l'oeuvre" (in French, English, Swedish, Italian, Spanish, German and Arabic (3 volumes), etc... **other Works** of Lahbabi under print, "Les Cahiers demainistes", "La crise des modèles" (in French and Arabic), "Pour une nouvelle catégoriale", "La modernité: Attitude Islamique", Faces et préfaces", oeuvre poétique (Volume II), "L'élixir de la vie" (French translation). **Award:** Throne Wissam. **Dist.:** Laureate of the International Prize "Bravo" (London-Paris, 1955), First Literary Prize of Morocco (1959). **Member:** Pen Club, "Société des Gens de Lettres", Director Committee of the International Society of Philosophy, President of the "Rives Méditerranéennes Club", of the philosophic Society of Morocco. **Addr.:** Nadwa 78, Rue Tolaytila (el-Andalousse), Tél.: (07) 412-56, P.O.Box 25 Temara, Morocco.

LAHHAM (Duraid), Syrian former faculty lecturer, actor. **Born** in 1934 in Damascus. **Married** to Miss Hala Bitar (Damascus University Graduate), 3 children: Sear, Abir and Dina. **Educ.:** Secondary and Higher (Damascus University). **Dipl.:** Bachelor of Science in Chemistry; Degree of Higher Psychology and Pedagogy. **Career:** Faculty Lecturer, University of Damascus (1955-60); On the Stage since 1960; Comedian at the Syrian Broadcasting Corporation, the Syrian and Lebanese TV. **Publ.:** Author of several comedies, Portrayed in many comical film productions, including "The Pearls Necklace" (1965), "Dream Castle" (1966), "Love Affair in Istanbul" (1967), "as-Saalik" (1968), "Khayyat as-Sayyidate" (1969) and many others. **President** of the Syrian Association of Artists (1967). **Hobby:** Music (accordeonist). **Addr.:** Syrian Broadcasting Corporation, Omayya Square, Damascus, Syria.

LAHLOU (Abdallah), Moroccan agriculturalist. **Born** in 1943 in Fes, Morocco. **Married**, three children. **Educ.:** Agronomical Engineering, National Institute of Agronomy, Paris, France Rural Engineering of Waters and Forests, Paris. **Career:** Director of the Office of Agricultural Valuation of Ouarzazte (1969-72); Director General, National Society of Agricultural Development, SODEA, (1972-77); Vice President of the Franco Arab Chamber of Commerce. **Sports:** Walking, jogging, cycling. **Prof. Addr.:** Office de Commercialization et d'Exportation, P.O.B. 259, Casablanca, Tel.: 366249, Morocco.

LAKHANI (Arif), Pakistani bank manager. **Born** in 1945 in India. **Son** of Abdul Kader Lakhani. **Married** in 1975, 1 son, 2 daughters. **Dipl.:** M.B.A. (1974). **Career:** Manager, Habib Bank Ltd., Pakistan (1963-69); General Manager, Habib Cooperative Bank, Karachi (1970-74); Manager, Bank of Credit & Commerce International, Oman (1974-75); Vice President, Habib Bank A.G. Zurich, Dubai, UAE (1975-). **Member:** Institute of Bankers, Pakistan; al-Nasr; The Sheraton; **Hobbies:** Swimming and Music. **Addr.:** P.O.Box 3306, Tel.: 229985, Telex: 45716 A/B SWBANK EM, Deira, Dubai, UAE.

LAKHDAR GHAZAL (Ahmad), Moroccan academic and Correspondent for the Syrian Academy **Born** on 30.10.1917 in Fés, Morocco. **Son** of Lakhdar Mohamad (Professor) and Mrs. Fatima Bent Abderrahman Layachi. **Married** in 1950 to Miss Reine Laurence Louise Chaignaud. 4 children: Faouzi (1951), Nousia (1952), Taoufiq (1954) and Mazia (1961). **Educ.:** Collège Moulay Driss de Fés, Lycée mixte de Fés, Lycée Gouraud (Rabat), Faculté de Lettres de Paris. **Dipl.:** 1st and 2nd Baccalaureates; Certificate of Arabic Philology and Practical Arabic Studies (1939); Certificate of Arabic Literature (1941); Certificate of Classical Literature (1947); Diploma of Higher Studies (Paris 1948); Aggregation of Arabic (Paris 1950). **Career:** Professor in the Collège Bérbère d'Azrou (1939); Lecturer and Professor at the University of Algiers (1950-52); Professor at the Direction de l'Instruction Publique du Maroc (1952-56); In the Ministry of National Education as: Founder, organiser and Director of the Department for Basic Education and Fight against Illiterasy (1956); General Secretary of the Mohammed V University of Rabat (1959-1969); Founder and Director of the Institut d'Etudes et de Recherches pour l'Arabisation (IERA) (1961); Founder and Technical Counselor of Bureau Permanent de Coordination de l'Arabisation dans le Monde Arabe (1961); Director of Cabinet then General Secretary in the State Ministry in the Cultural Affairs (1968-71); Back to IERA as Director (1972); Member of the Conseil International de la Langue Française (1972); Elected as Vice-President of the Conseil International de la Langue Française (1992); Designated as Representative of Morocco in the Réseau International de Néologie et de Terminologie (RINT) (1992) **Publ.:** "Perfectionnement des Caractères d'Imprimerie, écriture arabe" (1964), "Système de Composition Arabe Standard" (1976); Introduction of Arabic in Information Systems (informatique); Technical Solutions to Arabic Writing Problems (1994); and many other publications. **Awards:** Wissam du Trône avec la Mention de Commandeur; Chevalier de l'Ordre National du Mérite. **Sports:** Table tennis, swimming, outdor walks. **Prof.Addr.:** Académie du Royaume, B.P. 5062, Morocco. **Priv.Addr.:** 8 Rue Oulad Bouziri, Tel.: 75-70-80, Rabat, Morocco.

LALLA AICHA (H.R.H. Princess), Moroccan diplomat. **Born** in Morocco. **Eldest daughter** of King Mohamad V (Former Ruler of Morocco). **Educ.:** Secondary and Higher. **Career:** Moroccan Ambassador to United Kingdom (1965), to Italy; returned to Rabat. **Award:** Grand Cordon of the Order of the Throne. **Addr.:** The Royal Palace, Rabat, Morocco.

LALLA FATIMA ZOHRA (H.R.H. Princess), President of the National Union of the Moroccan women. **Born** on June 13, 1927 in Morocco. **Daughter of** King Abdulaziz Alaoui **and** Queen Yasmine Alaoui. **Married** to Hassan Ben Mahdi Alaoui in 1949 at Tetouan, one child; Oum Koulthoum. **Educ.:** General Education at Tangiers. **Career:** President of the National Union of the Moroccan Woman (U.N.F.M.), Rabat. **Prof. & Priv. Addr.:** 3, Afghani Street, Rabat, Morocco.

LAMRHILI (Ahmad, Mohamad), Moroccan academic. **Born** in 1945 in Fes, Morocco. **Son** of Mohamad Lamrhili. **Married. Educ.:** Diploma, Institute of International Relations Studies, Paris, France; Diploma, Practical School for Higher Studies, Paris; B.A. and Ph.D. in Sociology, Paris. **Career:** Head of Project, Ministry of Information, Rabat (1973-75); Director, Center of the Formation of journalists, Rabat (1974-75); Assistant Professor, Faculty of Arts, Fes (1975-79); Director of the planning of the City of Fes (1975-79); Researcher, Institute of Studies and Research for Arabisation, Rabat (since 1979); Director of "al-Asaas" review. **Member of:** the World Federation of Twin Towns, the Town planning Collective of United Cities. **Publ.:** Many articles and papers published in journals and magazines. **Hobby:** Cinema. **Addr.:** al-Hurriya Street, Hayy al-Salaam, P.O.Box 543, Tel.: 87279, Tabriquat, Sale, Morocco.

LANGHADE (Jacques), French academic. **Born** on January 22, 1935 in Beirut, Lebanon. **Son** of Eraste Langhade (Director of ESIB, Beirut) **and** Mrs. Christine Mihiere. **Married** in 1968 in Paris to Thérèse Roisin, 3 children: Gaëtan, Solveig, Dimitri. **Educ.:** Sorbonne (Paris). **Dipl.:** Doctorat d'Etat -ès- Lettres - Agregation. **Career:** Professor, Université Michel de Montaigne, Bordeaux 3 (1979-90) and (1996-99); Director, Institut Français de Damas (1990-96); Director, Centre de Documentation de la Source in Rabat. **Other Information:** Member correspondent of the Academie Arabe de Damas. **Prof. Addr.:** La Source, P.O.Box 4412, Rabat, Morocco, Tel.: 07 726652, Fax: 07 205114. **Priv. Addr.:** 24, Avenue du Chellah, P.O.Box 4412, Rabat, Morocco, Tel.: 07 207720.

LANJAWY (Ali Nasir), Saudi executive. **Born** in 1945 in Jeddah, Saudi Arabia **Educ.:** General Certificate of Education (Arts). **Career:** Typist (1965-69); Supervisor of Administrative Services, Saudia (1969-70), Administrative Director of Clerical Services (1970-73); General Director, Administrative Services, Saudia; attended the TWA Value Analysis programme in Cairo, and the Modern Administration programme in Beirut and Saudi Arabia. **Hobbies:** reading, swimming. **Address:** Saudia, P.O.Box 167, Jeddah, Saudi Arabia.

LAOUANI (Othman), Tunisian diplomat. **Born** in 1938 in Kairouan, Tunisia. **Dipl.:** Diploma in Political and Touristic Studies, Doctorate in Public Law, Auditor of International Law Academie of La Haye. **Career:** Secretary to the Tunisian Ambassador in Paris; Advisor to the Tunisian Embassies in Stockholm, Copenhagen, Helsinki, Oslo, Bonn, Cairo and Khartoum, Ambassador to Zaire, Ruwanda, Burundi and Angola; Attaché and Deputy Director of the Office of the Ministry of Foreign Affairs (1978-80); Ambassador to Turkey (1983-); Director of Union of Arab Maghreb in the Ministry of Foreign Affairs (1988-1990); Director of International Conferences in the Ministry of Foreign Affairs (1991-1992); Director of Consular Conventions in the Ministry of Foreign Affairs (1993); Member of Tunisian delegation in the 47 General Assembly Sessions of U.N. (1992). **Decorations**: Officier de l'Ordre de la Republique Tunisienne; Commandeur de l'Ordre de l'Etoile Polaire du Royaume de Suède; Commandeur de l'Ordre du Mérite de la Republique Arabe d'Egypte. **Prof. Addr.:** Foreign Ministry, Tunis, Tunisia.

LARAKI (Abdellatif), Moroccan banker, executive. **Born** in 1934 in Fès, Morocco. **Married,** 5 children: Fatiha (22.11.1955), Samia (02.06.1959), Dounia (03.04.1964), Amine (10.11.1986), Ghalia (06.09.1990). **Educ.:** Higher Education: Institut de Sciences Politiques de Grenoble; Secondary Education: College Moulay Driss - Lycée Lyautey; Primary Education: Institut Ben Abdellah. **Dipl.:** Licence ès Sciences Economiques, Grenoble; Baccalauréat at Lycée Champolion in Grenoble. **Career:** Head of Research and Documentation then personel, Banque Marocaine pour le Commerce Extérieur (October 1959-January 1961); Regional Manager, Banque Populaire de Casablanca (February 1961- January 1966); Deputy General Manager, Banque Centrale Populaire (January 1966-July 1974); General Manager, Banque Centrale Populaire, 101, Bd. Zerktouni - Casablanca 01 (July 1974- July 1985); Deputy President of Credit Populaire du Maroc (CPM), and Chairman Managing Director of Banque Centrale Populaire (since July 1985-). President for first and second session of Conseil National de la Jeunesse et de l'Avenir (CNJA); Vice-President of Confédération Internationale du Crédit Populaire (CICP) (September 1985- October 1988), presently President of CICP. Chairman of the Board of: Banque Chaabi du Maroc in France; Arab Bank Maroc; Maroc Assistance; Société de Développement et d'Investissement de la Ville de Fès et de sa Région (Sed Fes); Société Essalaf Chaabi. Member of the Board of many National Companies: Bank al-Maghrib; Comité de Crédit et du Marché Financier; Groupement Professionnel des Banques du Maroc; Bank al-Amal; Crédit Immobilier et Hotelier (CIH.); Consortium Moroco-Koweitien de Développement; Sofac Credit; Maghrebail; Société Nationale d'Investissement; Société Nationale des Autoroutes; Société Palm Bay; Maghreb Arab Trading Company (MARTCO); Institut Hautes Etudes de Management (HEM), and International Companies: Union des Banques Arabes; Arab Financial Services Company; Moroccan American Foundation; Club des Dirigeants des Banques d'Afrique Francophone; World Assembly of Small & Medium Enterprises (WASME); President, Banque Populaire Maroco-Centrafricaine; Director, Banque Populaire Maroco-Guinéenne. **Awards:** Officier de l'Ordre du Trône, Elected African Banker for the Year 1985. **Hobbies:** Tennis, Bridge, Water Skiing, Hunting. **Member:** Fondation Pasteur, SOS Village d'Enfants. **Addr.:** Villa "quiétude", Rue 9, No.3 - Longchamp - Casablanca, Tel.: 36.30.67, Morocco, and Crédit Populaire du Maroc, 101 Boulevard Zerktouni, P.O.Box 10622, Tel.: 22.25.33, 27.62.81, Telex: BANCEPO 21.723, Fax: 20.19.32, Casablanca 20170, Morocco.

LARAKI (Ahmad), Moroccan politician. **Born** on October 15, 1931 in Casablanca (Morocco). **Married** to Badia Sebti, 3 children: Amina, Ali and Leila. **Educ.:** Faculty of Law, University of Paris. **Career:** Joined the Ministry of Foreign Affairs (1956-57); Permanent Representative to United Nations (1957-59); Ambassador to Spain (1962-65); to Switzerland (1965-66); to USA and concurrently accredited to Mexico, Canada and Venezuela (1966-67); Minister of Foreign Affairs (1967-69); Prime Minister (1969-71); in charge of medical affairs (1971-74); Minister of State in charge of Foreign Affairs (1974); Appointed on March 14, 1998 Secretary of State for Environment. **Addr.:** Rabat, Morocco.

LARAKI (Azzedine, Dr.), Moroccan former prime minister. **Born** in 1929 in Fez. **Married** in 1959 in Rabat, to Khadija Bennani, 3 children: Karim, Younes, el-Ghali. **Educ.:** Primary and secondary in Fez, Faculty of Medicine (Paris). **Dipl.:** M.D. (1957) (specialized in pneumology); Agrégation (1967), **Career:** Former Intern, Hospitals in Morocco; Former Assistant Chief Medic., Oujdah Province; Director, Cabinet of Ministry of National Education (1958); Director, Cabinet of Ministry of Health (1959); Head, Avicenne Hospital (1960); Titular Professor (1972); Minister of Education and Cadre Training since October

10, 1977, and re-appointed (March 27, 1979- Nov. 83-85); Prime Minister (1986-1992); Secretary General, Organisation de la Conférence Islamique since January 1st, 1997. **Publ.:** Author of several scientific and litterary publications. **Awards:** Knight, Ouissam du Trône: Ouissam of King Abdel-aziz (2nd Class); Order du Palme Académique. **Sport:** Horseriding and walking. **Member:** of several national and international scientific organizations; Union Moroccan Authors; Académie du Royaume du Maroc; Istiqlal Party since 1942: Executive Committee, Istiqlal Party. **Priv. Addr.:** 82, Blvd. Beni Znassen, Tel.: 514-51, Souissi, Rabat, Morocco.

LARI (Adnan Mohamad), Saudi executive. **Born** in 1941. **Dipl.:** M.Sc. (Geology), USA. **Career:** Director-General of al-Aroussa furniture factory and stores; former Director of Expedition Affairs and Technical Adviser on Expeditions, Directorate-General of Mineral Resources, Ministry of Petroleum and Mineral Wealth; Geologist, Department of Rocks and Minerals, Directorate-General of Mineral Resources; Saudi representative at the Fifth Mineral Wealth Conference, Pakistan, and the Minerals Conference, London. **Address:** The Directorate-General of Mineral Resources, Tel.: 33133 Riyadh. Also in Jeddah, Saudi Arabia.

LARI (Ridah, Mohamad), Saudi journalist. **Born** on November 1, 1938 in Jeddah, Saudi Arabia. **Son** of Mohamed Larry (Employee) **and** Mrs., née Aisha Hassan Abdulwasi. **Married** to Miss Zohour Abdulkarim Habib, 2 children: Ahmed (1966) and Mohamed (1970). **Educ.:** Victoria College, Cairo; Cairo University; Faculty of Economic and Political Science. **Dipl.:** B.S. Political Science. **Career:** Diplomatic Attaché; 3rd Secretary, 2nd Secretary, Ministry of Foreign Affairs; Editor in chief, Okaz Daily Newspaper; Presently Editor in Chief of Saudi Gazette daily English newspaper. **Work:** Major political commentator; several articles and columns, author of a book "The Western Desert (Past, Now and Future)"; Interviewed a number of Heads of State (Arabs and others). **Awards:** Cavalier Ensignia, Government of Spain; al-Merito Civil, Government of Spain; Award from Government of Senegal; al-Galal al-Sharifa, Government of Morocco. **Sport:** Football. **Hobby:** Reading and travelling. **Prof. Addr.:** P.O.Box 5576 Jeddah 21432 Saudi Arabia **Priv. Addr.:** P.O.Box 8896 Jeddah, 21492, Saudi Arabia.

LAROUI (Abdallah, Mohamad, Dr.), Moroccan university professor. **Born** on November 7, 1933 in Azemmour (Morocco). **Son** of Mohamad Laroui (Trader) **and** Mrs. Rakia Abdulqabir, one child: Issam. **Educ.:** Lycée Moulay Youssef (Rabat), La Sorbonne and Institute of Political Studies (Paris). **Career:** Counsellor of Foreign Affairs, Rabat (January 1960- December 1963); visiting Professor of North African History, UCLA, California (1967-70); Professor of History, Rabat University since 1964. Member of the Academy of the Kingdom of Morocco; Recipient of Premi International de Catalunuya 2000. **Publ.:** Author of "The Contemporary Arab Ideology" (Paris 1967), Translated into Italian (Milan 1969), Translated into Arabic (Beirut 1970); "The History of the Maghrib", translated into English (Princeton University Press, 1977); "The Crisis of the Arab Intellectual" (Paris 1974), translated into English (University of California Press, 1976); "The Concept of Ideology" (Beirut 1980). "The Concept of History" (Beirut 1992) "The Concept of Reason" (Beirut 1996); "Islam and History" (Paris 1999). **Prof. Addr.:** Faculty of Letters, University of Rabat, Rabat. **Priv. Addr.:** 6 Rue Muhammad Rounda Souissi, Tel.: 07 758004, Rabat, Morocco.

LAROUI (Rkia, Mrs.), Moroccan academic. **Born** on February 22, 1956. **Daughter** of Ahmed Laroui (Official at P.T.T.) **and** Mrs. née Kenza Chouiter. **Educ.:** Laval University, Quebec, Canada; University of Sherbrook, Sherbrook, Canada; Mohammed V University, Rabat, Morocco. **Dipl.:** Ph.D. in Educational Sciences, Masters in Sociolinguistic, D.E.A., Licence ès-Arts, Diploma from the Ecole Normale Supérieure. **Career:** Assistant of Research and Education. Faculty of Educational Sciences, Quebec (1984-87); Assistant Professor, Responsible of Formation Cycle, Rabat (1981-84); Lecturer, E.N.S. of Meknes (1987-88); Lecturer, Faculty of Arts Hassan II Ben Msik (1988-91); Visiting Professor, Paris V, 1989; Professor, Faculty of Arts, University Hassan II Ben Msik, (1991-); presently, Senior Lecturer at the University, Head of the French Department. **Awards:** Medal from the University of Sherbrook, Honour Medal from Minister of Education of Quebec. **Hobbies:** Travelling, reading. **Member:** Chairman of the Cultural Commission, Doukkalas Association, International Pedagogy Association. **Prof. Addr.:** Faculté des Lettres Ben Msik, Université Hassan II, P.O.Box 7951 sidi Othmane, Tel.: 705098, Casablanca, Morocco. **Priv. Addr.:** Rue 30 No.97 el-Farah, Casa, Tel.: 815153, Morocco.

LASKY (Ahmad), Moroccan civil engineer and politician. **Born** on April 30, 1932. **Married,** 3 children. **Educ.:** Casablanca High School, Ecole Spéciale des Travaux Publics (Special Public Works School), Ecole Nationale des Ponts et Chaussées (National School of Roads and Bridges, Paris). **Dipl.:** of engineering. **Career:** Public Works Engineer (Casablanca, 1956); Chief Engineer Agadir Region (1959); Chief Engineer Casablanca Region (1960-62); Director of the Casablanca Harbour (1962-65); Minister of Public Works and Communications (1965-67); President Director General, Royal Air Maroc (Civil Aviation Co.) (1967-77); Minister of Agriculture and Agrarian Reform (August 1970); Deputy for one of the Casablanca constituencies in parliamentary elections (August 1970); Minister of Secondary, Technical and Higher Education (April 1971-72); Deputy for Parliament since 1977; First Vice President of Parliament (1977-83); President of Foreign Affairs and Defence Parliamentary

Commission (1984-92). 1983- Present President of CAUB. 1993- Present, Member of Consultative Council for the Human Rights. **Publ.:** Technical articles. **Hobbies:** Football and Swimming. **Awards:** Officer Order of the Throne (Morocco); Order Georges I (Greece); Commander, Order of Istiqlal (Tunisia); Egyptian Order; Iranian Order. **Addr.:** Commune Urbaine de Sidi Bel Yout, Casablanca, Morocco.

LASRAM (Abdelaziz), Tunisian politician. **Born** on March 25, 1928 in Tunis; Tunisia. **Married**, 3 children. **Educ.:** Lycée Carnot, Tunis; University of Paris, France; Ecole Nationale d'Administration, France. **Dipl.:** Licence in Law. **Career:** Administrator, Tunisian Government (1957); Joined Ministry of Foreign Affairs (1958); Head, Planning Department (1959); Counsellor, Embassy to USSR (1960-61); Under-Secretary for Commerce Division with the Secretariat of State for Planning and Finance (1965-70); promoted to Ambassador's rank (April 1970); Director, International Co-operation, Ministry of Foreign Affairs; Secretary-General, Ministry of Foreign Affairs (1971-72); President, Director-General of Tunisian National Bank (1972-74); Minister of National Economy (1974). **President:** Club Africain, Sporting Association. **Addr.:** Tunis, Tunisia.

LATRECHE (Abdulhamid, Lieutenant-Colonnel), Algerian military expert. **Born** in 1931 in Algeria. **Educ.:** Military School, Saint-Maizent, France; training course in USSR. **Career:** 2nd Lieutenant, French Army; joined National Liberation Army (ALN); member of military staff office; Commander of Oran military sector with rank of Major (1964); Director of Ecole des Blindés, Batna (1966); Director of Military Aviation (1968); Secretary General, Ministry of National Defence (1971); Ambassador to Czechoslovakia (1984-). **Addr.:** Ministry of Foreign Affairs, Algiers, Algeria and Algerian Embassy, Korejska 16, 125 21 Prague, Czechoslovakia.

LAWZI (Ahmad Abdel Karim), Jordanian politician. **Born** in 1925 at Jubeiha near Amman, Jordan. **Married. Educ.:** Secondary school in Jordan; Teachers Training College, Baghdad, Iraq. **Dipl.:** B.A. in Literature (1950). **Career:** Teacher (1950-53); Assistant to chief of Royal Protocol (1953-56); Chief of Royal Protocol (1956-61); Head of Ceremonies, Ministry of Foreign Affairs (1957); Member, Chamber of Deputies (1961-62, 1962-63); Assistant to Chief of Royal Court (1963-64); Ministry of State for Prime Minister's Affairs (1964-65); Senator (1965); Minister of Interior for Municipal and Rural Affairs (1967); Senator (1967); Minister of Finance (1970-71); Member of Board of Trustees of Jordanian University; Prime Minister and Minister of Defence (1971, 1972-73); Senator (1973-78); President of the National Consultative Council (1978-79); chief of Royal Court (1979-85); President of the Senate (1984). **Decor.:** Star of Jordan, 1st Class; Order of Independence, 2nd Class; Order of Renaissance, 2nd Class. **Addr.:** Jabal Amman, Tel.: 41278, Amman, Jordan.

LAWZI (Salim, Abdelkarim), Jordanian administrator. **Born** in 1941 in Jubaiha, Jordan. **Son** of Abdelkarim Lawzi. **Married**, three children. **Educ.:** Diploma in Agriculture, Syria (1962); B.Sc. in Agruculture (Forestry), Mosul, Iraq (1970); M.Sc. in Forestry Science and Management, USA (1974); Ph.D. in Development of Natural Resources and Exploitation of Soil, Colorado University, USA (1976). **Career:** Inspector (1962-64); Head of Department (1965-67); Head of Department of Nurseries and Soil Preservation (1970-73); Lecturer, University of Jordan, College of Agriculture (1976-80); Deputy Minister of Agriculture (1980-81); currently Director, Agricultural Credit Corporation, Jordan. Member of the Jordanian Society, Royal Society for the Protection of the Environment, Amman. **Sports:** Tennis, squash and walking. **Priv. Addr.:** Jubaiha, P.O.B. 10, Tel.: 843030, 842100, Amman, Jordan.

LAYAS (Mohamed), Libyan banker. **Born** on December 10, 1943 in Derna, Libya. **Son** of Hussein Layas **and** Mrs. Ghazzala Layas. **Married**, four children. **Dipl.:** B.A. (Business Administration and Accounting). **Career:** Ministry of Foreign Affairs (1966); Mission of Libya to the United Nations (1969-72); Currently Deputy Chairman of Libyan Arab Foreign Bank. **Prof. Addr.:** Dat el-Imad Complex, P.O.Box 2542, Tower No.2, Tel.: 42428, 41429, Tripoli, Libya.

LAYOUNI (Abdelwahab), Tunisian President Director General Socomena and T.T.C. **Born** on May 15, 1941 in Tunis. **Son** of Mahmoud Layouni (tradesman) **and** Mrs. née Bathta Chaabane. **Married** on July 21, 1972 to Afifa Mnif, 2 children: Ines (21 October 1973), Slim (24 December 1979). **Educ.:** Lycée Alaoui; Ecole Navale (France); Higher War Naval Academy (U.S.A.); Institute of Defence (Tunisia). **Dipl.:** Diploma Ecole Navale de Brest, (France), Diploma Higher War Naval Academy (U.S.A.), Diploma, Institute of National Defence (Tunisia). **Career:** Officer, Naval Ships and Naval Base; Director, Lighthouses and Beacons; Chief, National Marine Operations; Director, Naval Academy; Deputy Chief Marine Operations; Deputy Chief of Staff of the Navy; Presently, President Director General, Socomena and T.T.C. **Other Information:** Expert at I.A.L.A., Expert Marine Representative at O.N.I. (1980-1983); Member C.N.E., ... **Awards:** Military Medal; Order of the Republic. **Sport:** Football. **Hobby:** Sport. **Member:** Tunisian Stadium (Tunisia). **Prof. Addr.:** Rue Hamadi Gharbi, Tel.: 350077, Tunisia and Socomena, P.O.Box 10, Menzel Bourguiba 7050, Tunisia. **Priv. Addr.:** 67 C Manar I, Tunisia.

LEADER (Malcolm Ashley), Australian diplomat. **Born** on April 3, 1945 in Perth Western Australia. **Son** of Albert Kylie Leader (Soldier) **and** Mrs. Clarice May née

Truscott. **Married** on April 22, 1967 in Perth, Australia to Faye Ellen Daniell, three children; Michael, Jennifer, Andrew. **Educ.:** John Curtin Senior High School, Fremantle, Western Australia; University of Western Australia. **Dipl.:** B.A. (Hons) (1968); Ph.D. (French Studies) (1974); **Career:** Senior Tutor in French Studies, University of Western Australia (1969-70); Joined Department of Foreign Affairs, Canberra (1971); Third Secretary, later Second Secretary, Australian Embassy, Paris (1972-74); Department of Foreign Affairs, Canberra (1975-77); First Secretary, Australian High Commission, Port Moresby (1977-79); Australian Consul-General, Noumea (1980-82); Department of Foreign Affairs and Trade, Canberra (1983-87); Minister, Australian Embassy, Paris (1987-91); Minister, Permanent Delegate, Australian Delegation to UNESCO (11 Feb. 1991-); Australian Ambassador to Saudi Arabia, Presentation of Credentials (POC): 6 October 1991; Concurrently Australian Ambassador to: Republic of Yemen - POC: 19 October 1991; State of Qatar - POC: 11 November 1991; **Sports:** Squash, tennis. **Prof. Addr.:** Australian Embassy, P.O.Box 94400, Riyadh 11693, Saudi Arabia.

LECLERCQ (Patrick, Henry), French ambassador in Egypt. **Born** in France in 1938. **Son** of Henry Leclerq **and** Mrs. Françoise née Gallant. **Married** in 1981 in France, three children. **Educ.:** Institut d'Etudes Politiques, Ecole Nationale d'Administration (E.N.A.). **Dipl.:** of Institut d'Etudes Politiques E.N.A. **Career:** Ministry of Foreign Affairs (1966); Second Secretary in Madrid (1967-71); Second Councellor in the French Permanent Mision at the U.N., New York (1971-76); Assistant Director at the Minister's Cabinet (1976-78); Diplomatic Consellor of the President of the Republic, Mr. Giscard d'Estaing (1979-81); Consul General in Montreal (1982-85); Ambassador in Amman (1985-89); Director for North Africa and Middle East in Ministry of foreign Affairs (1989-91); Ambassador in Cairo (from 1991). **Medals:** Chevalier de la Legion d'Honneur, Officier de l'Ordre National du Merite, various foreign decorations. **Credit Cards:** American Express, Visa. **Prof. Addr.:** French Embassy, 29 Guiza Avenue, Guiza, Cairo, Egypt.

LEHETA (Adel, Mohamad Aly), Egyptian executive. **Born** on 29 Octobre 1931 in Port Said, Egypt. **Son** of Mohamad Ali Leheta. **Married** on 1 January 1960 to Kesmat Abdel Ghaffar Abdel Alim, 3 children: Nehal (1961), Cherine (1962), Mohamad (1968). **Educ.:** Secondary School; Faculty of Commerce, Ain Chams University. **Dipl.:** Bachelor of Commerce; High Level Cotton Diploma. **Career:** General Financial Manager and Member of Board of Directors of Eastern Cotton Company; Chairman of Cotton Arbitration & Testing Organization; Chairman, Alexandria Commercial Co. (exporting raw cotton). **Sport:** Football, Basket Ball, Swimming. **Member:** Alexandria Sporting Club; Chief Alexandria Zone Basket Ball (for 8 years); Chairman, Smouha Club (8 Years); Yacht Club of Egypt; Commerce Club; Shooting Club; Rotary. **Credit Cards:** Visa Card, American Express. **Prof. Addr.:** 1, Dr. Ahmed Abdel Salam St., Tel.: 80020, Alexandria. **Priv. Addr.:** 5, Ebn Kassem St., Rouchdy, Tel.: 842000, Alexandria, Egypt.

LEMEILEN (Abdulaziz Mohamad, al), Saudi academic. **Born** in 1940. **Educ.:** M.A. (History and Civilization). **Career:** Secondary School teacher; Head of Department, Directorate of Education, Riyadh; Head of Department, Public Statistics Authority; (Ph.D. candidate) former Vice Dean, Faculty of Social Science, Islamic University of Imam Muhammad Ibn Saud. **Publication:** Influence of Environment on Administration in Saudi Arabia. **Address:** Riyadh, Saudi Arabia.

LIASSINE (Mohamad), Algerian engineer **Born** in 1934 in Dellys, Algeria. **Educ.:** Ecole Polytechnique, Paris, France. **Career:** Engineer, Roads Department; Director of Industrialization, Ministry of Industry (1963); Director, Industrial Production, Office Algérian de l'Action Commerciale (OFALAC); National Managing Director, National Steel Corporation (1964); General Manager, Bureau D'Etudes et de Réalisations Industrielles (BERI); Member, Advisory Council for Hydrocarbons, Mines and Energy (November 1967); Minister of Heavy Industry (April 1977 - March 79), re-appointed (8 March 1979-82). **Addr.:** Algiers, Algeria.

LIMHAISEN (Mohamad, Abdul Rahman), Saudi bank executive. **Born** in 1949 in al-Zulfi, Saudi Arabia. **Son** of Abdul Rahman Limhaisen. **Married** in 1977, 1 daughter. **Educ.:** Chemical Engineering, Washington State University, B.Sc. USA (1973); B.Sc. (Chemistry) (1974); Northwest Missouri State University, M.B.A., USA (1976); Banking Certificate from Chase Manhattan Bank; admitted to Ph.D. programme with University of Nebraska. **Career:** Chase Manhattan Bank (1976-79); Training Courses in Credit Analysis (1976-77); Controllership-Financial Management (1978-79); successively Senior Analyst, Loan Officer, Project Manager and Controller General, Saudi Industrial Development Fund (SIDF), Riyadh, (1980-83); Deputy General Manager and corporate Secretary, United Saudi Commercial Bank, Riyadh, (1983 to date). **Publ.:** Academic papers dealing with Management issues plus Masters thesis on Saudi Arabian Economy. **Member:** American Management Association; Menniger Foundation, Smithsonian Foundation; Riyadh Athletic Club. **Hobbies:** Sports, Squash, swimming, travelling, fishing, reading and classical music. **Addr.:** P.O.Box 25895, Tel.: (01) 4784200, Telex: 405461, Riyadh, Saudi Arabia.

LINDERS (Albert, Frederikus), English teacher, College de la Sainte Famille, Cairo. **Born** on April 12, 1935 at Beuningen (Netherlands). **Son** of Henri W. Linders **and** Mrs., née Antoinette M. Sluiter. **Educ.:** Primary, preparatory, secondary (technical) in the Netherlands. **Dipl.:** B.A. (philosophy) in the Netherlands; M.A. in France (1971); M.Sc. (linguistics) from Georgetown University (USA) (1973); Oriental studies (Arabic) (Lebanon), 5 guest scholarships from the Swedish Institute. **Career:** Ordained to the Priesthood in the Society of Jesus (1970); now in charge of English at College de la Sainte Famille, Cairo (Egypt). **Sports:** Swimming, **Spec.Int.:** Yoga. **Prof. & Priv. Addr.:** College de la Sainte Famille, P.O.Box 73-Faggalah, Cairo, Egypt. Tel.: 900411.

LINJAWY (Osman Abdallah), Saudi Engineer. **Born** on March 1943 in Jeddah, Saudi Arabia. **Dipl.:** B.Sc. (Electrical Engineering), London University. **Career:** Electrical Engineer, Saline Water Conversion Office (1968-71); Electrical Engineer, Watson S.A. (1971-73); Associate, Watson S.A., (1973-74); Partner, Linjawi Trade Limited, Arabian Chemical Terminals; Managing Director and authorized member of Board, Industrial Services Company Limited; Chairman, Delta Group Limited, Saudi Chemical Industries Company Limited, Arabian Chemical Trading; Director, Arabian Homes. **Hobbies:** Swimming, football. **Address:** Linjawi Centre, P.O.Box 11232, Jeddah - 21453, Saudi Arabia.

LOGALI (Hilary Paul), Sudanese politician. **Born** in 1931 in Juba, Sudan. **Educ.:** Rumbek Secondary School; Khartoum College of Cairo University; University courses in Baghdad (Iraq), and in UK and USA. **Career:** Inspector, Ministry of Finance; Secretary-General, Southern Front (July 1965); Minister of Co-operation and Labour (May 1967- May 1968); Sales Manager, Bata Shoe Company (May 1970); Commissioner for Equatoria Province (with rank of Minister) (1971-72); Member, Political Bureau of the Sudan Socialist Union (SSU) and of the Transitional Higher Executive Council in Southern Sudan (1972); elected to the People's Regional Assembly for the Juba Constituency (December 1973); Speaker of the People's Regional Assembly (1975-1978); former Chairman, University of Juba. **Addr.:** P.O.Box 185, Juba, Sudan.

LOITA (Habib, Mohamed), Djibouti Deputy at the National Assembly. **Born** in 1942 in Dikhil. **Career:** Elected Deputy at the National Assembly (8 May 1977 - to Date); Minister of National Defence (1978-1985); Member of Permanent Commission and National Defence Commission; Member of Supreme Court of Justice (8/01/1988). **Prof. Addr.:** National Assembly, P.O.Box 138 Djibouti, Djibouti.

LOZA (Sarah, Fahim), Egyptian academic. **Born** in 1938 in Assiut, Egypt. **Married,** 1 son, 1 daughter. **Educ.:** Institute of Social Sciences, Netherlands; Alberta University, Canada. **Dipl.:** M.S. in Social Sciences, Ph.D. in Sociology. **Career:** Lecturer at Alberta University, Canada (1972-73); Assistant Professor at Windsor University, Canada (1973-75); Consultant, Institute of National Planning (1975-76); Consultant, Population and Family Planning Board (1976-81); Member of the Union of Social Scientists, Egypt (1972-); Member of the American Sociological Association (1973-); Member of the International Union for the Scientific Study of Populations (1979-); President and Sociocultural Research Consultant, Social Planning, Analysis and Administration Consultants (SPAAC) (1981-). **Publ.:** "Egyptian Population Studies: An Annotated Bibliography", 3 vols, Population & Family Planning Board (1979) and (1983), "Social Science Research for Population Policy Design: Case Study of Egypt", IUSSP (1982). **Member:** Gezira Sporting Club, Egypt. **Prof. Addr.:** 18 Shagaret el-Dor Street, Zamalek, Cairo, Egypt. **Priv. Addr.:** 18-B Marashly Street, Zamalek, Cairo, Egypt.

LUAL LUAL (Akuey Lawrence), Sudanese politician, poet. **Born** Bahr al Ghazal, Southern Sudan. **Educ.:** Faculty of Arts, Khartoum University, Khartoum, Sudan; **Career:** Elected to Constituent Assembly, (1968); several teaching posts (1969-71); seconded to Resettlement Commission (1973); elected to Regional Assembly (1973-77); Regional Minister of High Executive Council, Minister of Education, (1975-78); elected member of Regional Assembly (1978); Minister of High Executive Council Affairs, (1979-1985). **Prof. Addr.:** Juba, Sudan.

LUQMAN (Ali Muhammad Ali), Yemeni businessman. **Born** on August 6, 1918 in Aden. **Married,** 4 sons, 1 daughter. **Educ.:** American University in Cairo, Egypt. **Dipl.:** B.A. **Career:** Managing Editor of "Fatat al-Jezirah" (Arabic daily newspaper) (1940-62); Editor in Chief of "al-Qalam al-Adani" (Arabic weekly newspaper) (1953-63) and of "al-Akhbar: (Arabic daily newspaper) (1963-67); Assistant Director of Rashid Trading Corporation, Taiz, Yemen. **Publ.:** poetry in Arabic "al-Watar al-Maghmour", "Ashjan fil Lail", "al-Warrad" and several others in English; poetic dramas in Arabic, "Pygmalion", "al-Dhil al-Manshood", "Qais wa Leila", "Samra al-Arab" and "al-Adail al-Mafqood". **Hobbies:** Journalism, literature (mainly poetry). **Member** of poetry clubs, press clubs and literary associations. **Prof. Addr.:** P.O.Box 4960, Tel.: 2908, Taiz, Republic of Yemen.

LUTFI (Aly), Egyptian economist and politician. **Born** on October 6, 1935, Cairo, Egypt. **Son** of Mahmoud Lutfy. **Married** in 1966 to Miss Eglal Mabrouk, one son. **Educ.:** Aïn Shams and Lauzane Universities. **Dipl.:** Ph.D. **Career:** Faculty of Commerce, Aïn Shams University (1957); Professor and Chairman, Department of Economics (June 1980-); Professor High Institute of Cooperative and Administration Studies; Part-time Professor, Institute of Arab Research and Studies, Cairo; Member of the Board of Directors, Bank of Alexandria (1977-78), Bank of Commerce and Development, Cairo (1981-); Member Legislative, Political Science and Economic Association (1977), Delta Sugar Co. (1978), Bank of Commerce and Development (June 1980-); Minister of Finance (1978-80);

Prime Minister (1985-86); Speaker of the Shoura Council (November 1986); **Awards:** Ideal Professor Award, Egyptian University (1974); Gold Mercury International Award (1979). **Publ.:** Economic Evolution; Economic Development; Economic Planning; Studies of Mathematical Economics and Econometrics; Financing Problems in Developing Countries; Industrialization Problems in Under-Developed Countries; many research papers in economics. **Hobbies:** Tennis, reading, travel. **Addr.:** 29 Ahmed Heshmat Street, Zamalek, Cairo, Egypt.

LUTFI (Sharif), Egyptian economist. **Born** in 1932 in Egypt. **Married**, 2 children. **Educ.:** Alexandria University, Egypt; Postgraduate work in Budapest, Hungary; Harvard University, USA. **Dipl.:** B.A. (Econ.); Ph.D. **Career:** Joined Egyptian Diplomatic Service in 1960; Head of Research, Egyptian National Bank; transferred to Egyptian Ministry of Economy; First Under-Secretary of the Ministry (1972); Financial Expert, Oman National Development Council, IBRD, Oman (1974); Adviser to H.M. the Sultan of Oman and Secretary of Oman General Development Council; Director Oman Petroleum Development. **Prof. Addr.:** c/o Petroleum Development Oman, P.O.Box 81, Muscat, Sultanate of Oman.

M

MAAIUF (Faruk, Abdullah, al), Iraqi official. **Born** in 1938 in Umara, Iraq. **Married**, 5 children. **Educ.:** Baghdad University, Iraq; Mustansirya University, Basrah, Iraq. **Dipl.:** B.Sc. in Mechanical Engineering, B.Sc. in Commerce and Economics. **Career:** Engineer, Electricity Administration for Southern Iraq, Basrah, Iraq; Director of Electricity Administration for Southern Iraq (1969); General Director of General Company for Fertilizers, Basrah, Iraq (1972); Secretary General of the Arab Union for the Producers of Chemical Fertilizers, Kuwait (1979); Director General, Ministry of Industry (1980). **Publ.:** articles in the "Bulletin of Union and the Bulletin of OAPEC on Management Industry and Marketing". **Hobbies:** Arabic poetry, reading. **Addr.:** Baghdad, Iraq.

MAAMAR (Mukhtar), Tunisian engineer. **Born** in 1938 in Bizerte, Tunisia. **Married**, 2 sons, 2 daughters. **Educ.:** Aeronautical Engineering and Mechanics. **Career:** Technical Manager of SOMETAL, Casablanca (1972-77); President of Amical des Industriels de Bizerte et Aragon, Spain; Founder and President of Aero-Club de Bizerte; Manager of SOTUBO (Société Tunisienne de Boulonnerie) - MATUBO, Tunis (1977-). **Decor.:** Chavelier of the Order of the Republic (National Defence). **Member:** Lions Club of Bizerte. Tunisia. **Prof. Addr.:** 168 Avenue Habib Bourguiba, Bizerte, Tunis, Tunisia.

MAAMDOURI (Mahmoud), Tunisian diplomat. **Born** in 1925 in Nabeul, Tunisia. **Married,** 3 children. **Educ.:** Sadiki College, Tunis; Sorbonne, University of Paris. **Dipl.:** Graduated in Mathematics, Sorbonne, University of Paris. **Career:** Teacher in Paris and Tunis; elected to the Tunisian National Assembly (1959); Ambassador to Yugoslavia, Greece, Romania, Bulgaria, Hungary (1964-69); Ambassador to Sweden, Norway, Finland, Iceland (1969-73); Ambassador to Federal Republic of Germany (1973-74); Secretary of State, Prime Minister's Office, responsible of Information (1974). **Publ.:** Author of works on the theory of Destourian Socialism. **Addr.:** c/o Ministry of Foreign Affairs, Tunis, Tunisia.

MAAMOUN (Saad), Egyptian policitian. **Born** on 14 May 1922 in Cairo, Egypt. **Educ.:** Military Academy (1940); Staff College (1952), studied tactics and strategy in Moscow, Nasser Higher Military College, Cairo, Egypt. **Career:** Lecturer in tanks and armour, Staff College, Cairo (1955); appointed tanks brigade commander; director of the Arab Expeditionary forces in North Yemen; Chief of armed forces operations; assistant to Chief of Staff; commander of the 2nd army corps (Jan. 1 1973); took part in the October 1973 war agaisnt Israel, and led his troops across the Suez Canal; appointed Governor of Marsa Matrouh, then Governor of Menoufiyeh, then Cairo Governor (14 May 1977); promoted to General (25 September 1982); appointed Minister of Local Government (1983-84); **Awards:** 23 decorations and medals, including the Star of Military Honour, and the Republic Medal. **Addr.:** Cairo, Egypt.

MAAMOURI (Muhammad), Tunisian academic. **Born** in 1941 in Nabeul, Tunisia. **Married**, 2 children. **Educ.:** Faculty of Letters, University of Paris, France; Cornell University, USA. **Dipl.:** M.A., Ph.D. **Career:** Assistant, Department of English, University of Tunis (1967-69); Senior Assistant (1969-76), Lecturer (1976-84); Director, English Department, Institut Bourguiba des Langues Vivantes (1968-74); Director of International Institute of Linguistics, Tunis (summer schools) (1976-79); and (1985); Director of the English Department, Institut Bourguiba des Langues Vivants (1974-); Council Member of the International Centre for Research in Fundamental and Applied Linguistics (1980-); Senior Vice Chairman, Arab Committee, Association des Universités partiellement ou entièrement de Langue Française (1982-); Professor of Linguistics, University of Tunis (1984-). **Publ.:** several articles in national and international Arab and linguistics journals; Co-author of "l'Arabe fundamental", CERES (1927), "Tunisian Arabic": a Beginner's Course (1972), "Votre Guide d'Arabe Tunisien", Tunis (1973); General Editor of Language and Linguistics Series, "Paper on English for Special Purposes", "The Hammamet Conference" (1975), "Terminologie Franco-Arabe" Tunis (1980), Language and Linguistics Series "Language in Tunisia" (1983). **Decor.:** Chevalier, Ordre des Palmes Académiques, France (1977), Commander of the Order of the British Empire, UK (1980). **Prof. Addr.:** 47 Avenue de la Liberté, 1002 Tunis, Belvedere, Tunisia.

MAANI (Walid, Al), Jordanian, Neuro Surgeon. **Born** in 1946 in Karak, Jordan. **Son** of Salem Saqr, Educator **and** Mrs. Zahra Maani. **Married** in 1973 in Amman to Miss Maisoun Armouti, 4 children: Tarek (1975), Noor (1977), Tamara (1983), Khaled (1988). **Educ.:** Al Hussein College, Amman-Jordan; Alexandria School of Medicine, Egypt. **Dipl.:** MBBCH (1969), Diploma of General Surgery (1971), FRCS (Edinburgh) 1975. **Career:** Assistant Prof. of Neurosurgery (1978-1983); Associate Prof. of Neurosurgery (1983-1987); Professor of Neurosurgery

(1987- now); Dean of Graduate Studies (1992-1994); Dean of Research (1994); Vice President, University of Jordan (1994-98); President, University of Jordan (1998- now). **Other Information:** Member Governing Council of International Brain Research Org.; General Secretary of EAC-IBRO. **Sport:** Walking. **Hobbies:** Stamp Collecting, Photography. **Member of:** EAC, JMA, CNS, SBNS, IBRO. **Prof. Addr.:** University of Jordan, Amman, Jordan, Tel.: 5355000. **Priv. Addr.:** P.O.Box 950390, Amman 111-95, Jordan.

MAANINOU (Mohamad, Saddik), Moroccan journalist. **Born** in 1944 in Tangier, Morocco. **Son** of Saddik Maaninou. **Married:** three children. **Educ.:** Licenciate in Law. **Career:** Head of the News Department, Moroccan Television (1974); Chief Editor, Moroccan Television (1975); Official Commentator, Moroccan Television (1976); Director of "Le Combat" newspaper (1963-65); covered the October War (1973); attended Arab Development Conference in Algiers and many international conferences. **Medals:** Green March Medal. **Addr.:** La Pépinière, Sale, Tel.: 32010, 80285.

MAAOUI (Muhammad, Muncef), Tunisian businessman. **Born** in 1934 in Tunis, Tunisia. **Married. Dipl.:** M.Sc. in Business studies, Ph.D. in Economics. **Career:** Director of Tunisian Society of Banks, Tunis; Director of International Union of Banks, Tunis; Managing Director of Tunisian Society of Banks, Paris; Chairman of the Tunisian Federation of Insurance Companies; Member of the Board of several private, public, national and international companies; Member of the Board of the World Federation of Finance and Development Institutions and the Republic of Niger Development Bank; Chairman of the Organisation des Assurances Africaines; Member of the Board of the Association of Africa Finance and Development Institutions (1980-); Chairman and Managing Director of Maghrébia insurance and Reinsurance Company (1981-). **Prof. Addr.:** Maghrébia SA, 1A Rue de Grèce, 1000 Tunis, Tunisia.

MAARUF (Taha, Muhyiddin), Iraqi Politician. **Born** in 1924 in Suleimaniyah. **Son** of Muhyiddin and Fatma Maaruf. **Educ.:** College of Law, Baghdad, Iraq. **Career:** joined the Ministry of Foreign Affairs; Embassy to Egypt (1960); Ministry of Foreign Affairs (1964); Minister, Embassy to United Kingdom (1968); Minister of State (1968-70); Minister of Works and Housing; Ambassador, Ministry of Foreign Affairs (1970); Ambassador to Italy (1970-74), non-resident Ambassador to Albania (1971), non-resident Ambassador to Malta (1972); led the Iraqi delegation to Sudan (1974) and to North and South Yemen and Somalia (1977); Vice President of the Republic (1974-March 1991). Member, of the Revolutionary command council. **Addr.:** Baghdad, Iraq.

MABRO (Robert, Emile), Arab-British academic. **Born** in 1934 in Alexandria, Egypt, CBE. **Married**, 2 daughters. **Educ.:** Alexandria University, Egypt; University of London, UK, Oxford University, UK. **Dipl.:** B.Sc. in Engineering, M.Sc. in Economics, M.A. **Career:** Civil Engineer in Egypt (1956-62); Leon Fellow, University of London, UK (1966); Lecturer at the School of Oriental and African studies, University of London (1967-69); Senior Research Officer, Economics of the Middle East, Oxford University, UK (1969-). Director, Oxford Institute for Energy Studies (1983-); Fellow, St. Antony's College, Oxford University (1971-); Director of the Oxford Energy Seminar (1979-); Consultant on Oil Problems and Economics to ILO, OPEC, UNIDO, IBRD. **Publ.:** "The Egyptian Economy (1952-72)", Clarendon Press, Oxford (1974) Arabic Edition, Cairo (1976), "The Industrialization of Egypt (1939-73)", co-author with Samir Radwan, Clarendon Press (1976); as well as articles in academic journals. **Member:** The Royal Economic Society; **Founding Member** and Honorary Secretary of Oxford Energy Policy Club. **Prof. Addr.:** St. Antony's College, Oxford University, Oxford, United Kingdom.

MABROUK (Ezzedin, al, Dr.), Libyan lawyer and former minister. **Born** in December 1932 in Tripoli (Libya). **Married** on Sept. 18, 1967 to Ilham in Tripoli, 4 children: Nadir, Fatoma, Hani and Darin. **Educ.:** Primary and Secondary schools at Tripoli; Faculty of Law, Cairo University; London University. **Dipl.:** LL.B., LL.M. **Career:** Legal adviser to a petroleum company, Tripoli; Public prosecutor, Tripoli; Judge summary court, Tripoli; President, Tripoli court; Counsellor, Supreme Appeal Court (1956); Libya's representative, Legal Department, Organisation of Petroleum Exporting countries (OPEC), then Senior Legal adviser (1964-66); Minister of Petroleum, Libya (1970-76); led the Libyan delegation to OPEC's 21st conference in Brazil (1970); visited Yugoslavia (1973) to explain that his country's policy is to link the transactions of selling oil to friendly countries, to agricultural and other projects in Yugoslavia; went to Ecuador as leader of the Libyan delegation to OPEC's 40th conference in 1974; also flew to Kinshasa for talks on the energy crisis (1974). In the same year he went to Cairo (Egypt) to attend an OPEC meeting whose agenda included the establishment of investment companies, and a Fund to assist Arab countries affected by the rise of oil prices. In 1976, he discussed with the Japanese authorities in Tokyo cooperation berween the two countries, in various fields, particularly oil and prospecting; Secretary for Petroleum, General People's Committee (1977-81). **Prof. Addr.:** c/o P.O.Box 256, Tel.: 37078, Tripoli, Libya.

MABROUK (Hedi), Tunisian diplomat. **Born** in 1921 in Tunisia. Married. **Educ.:** University of Algiers, Algeria. **Career:** entered Public administration in 1939; Governor of Sbeitla (1956-58); Governor of Gafsa (1958-60), Governor of Le Kef (1960-62); President, the Tunisian State Shipping Company (1962-66); Director General and President of International Harvester Company, Tunis; General Commissioner of Textiles and concurrently President of the National Federation of Exporters (1967); Director of Central Administration, Ministry of National Economy (1973); Ambassador to France (1973-85); Minister of Foreign Affairs (1986-87). **Addr.:** Tunis, Tunisia.

MABROUK (Saleh Abdel, Lt-Col.), Sudanese politician **Born** in 1936 in Kadugli (Sudan). **Married**, with 2 children. **Educ.:** elementary and intermediate schools in Omdurman (Sudan); Khor Tagat secondary school; Sudan Military College (1957-59). **Career:** posted to Signal Corps (1959) and served with the Sudanese contingent in Egypt at the Suez Canal front; in charge of communications (1969); Secretary General, Revolutionary Command Council (1970); Minister of Youth, Sports and Social Affairs (1972-73); Minister of State for Presidential Affairs (May 1973-74); Minister of Egyptian Affairs (1974-76). **Addr.:** Khartoum, Sudan.

MADADHA (Khaled), Jordan Ambassador. **Born** on October, 1937 in Salt/Jordan. **Married**, twin children (boy & girl) born in 1983. **Present Occupation:** Ambassador to the Kingdom of Belgium (13.1.1994)-); Head of the mission to the European Union (17.5.1994-); Ambassador to the Kingdom of the Netherlands (31.8.1994-); Ambassador ot the Grand-Duchy of Luxemburg (3.2.1995-). **Previous Experience:** Ambassador to the Federal Republic of Germany, Sweden, Denmark and Norway (1990-1993); Ambassador to Japan, Republic of Korea and the Philippines (1985-1990); Director of Political Department at Foreign Ministry, Amman (1984-1985); Ambassador to Greece (1979-1984); Director of Prime Minister's Office in Jordan (1977-1979); Director a.i. of Political Department at Foreign Ministry, Amman (1976-1977); Diplomat at Embassy of Jordan in Cairo (1972-1976); Diplomat at Political Department at Foreign Ministry, Amman (1971-1972); Diplomat at Embassy of Jordan in Syria (1965-1971); Diplomat at Foreign Ministry in Amman (1964-1965); Joined Foreign Ministry, April 1964. **Education:** M.A. Degree in Economics at American University of Beirut (February 1964), B.A. in Economics at A.U.B. (June 1960). **International Conferences and Meetings:** Member of Jordan Delegation to U.N. General Assembly Sessions (1977, 1978 and 1984); Member of Jordan Delegation to all Euro-Arab Dialogue Meetings in Cairo, Abu-Dhabi, Tunisia and Luxembourg (1974-1976). **Decorations:** The Greek Decoration of the Grand Cross of the Rank of Honour (1984); The Jordanian Decoration of Independence of the First Rank (1988); The Japanese Decoration of the Grand Cordon of the Order of the Rising Sun (1990); The Korean Republic Decoration of the Order of Diplomatic Service Merit (1990); The German Grand Cross of the Order of Merit (1993); The Dutch Grand Cross in the Order of Orange Nassau (1994). **Hobbies and Sports:** Reading, swimming, jogging; Cultural activities (theatre, plays, movies, concerts, etc.). **Addr.:** Jordan Embassy, Av.F. Roosevelt 104-1050 Brussels, Belgium, Tel.: (02) 6407755.

MADANAT (Nabih, Ayed), Jordanian banker. **Born** in 1931 in Karak, Jordan. **Married**, 2 children. **Educ.:** in Jordan. **Career:** joined the British Bank of the Middle East in 1950; transferred to Tripoli, Libya to assist in the opening of a new branch (1952); British Bank of the Middle East Headquarters, London (1970); Branch Manager (1980); Member of the Anglo-Jordanian Society, the Arab Bankers Association and the Arab Club of Britain. **Hobbies:** chess, backgammon, cards. **Addr.:** 195 Brompton Road, London SW3 ILZ, United Kingdom.

MADANI (Bouraoui), Tunisian urban architect. **Born** on January 22, 1940. **Married** in 1962, 2 children. **Career:** Principal Engineer, President Director General, State Society, Tunisian Society of Engineers and Technicians. **Member** of Socialist Party, Lions Club **Addr.:** 47, Avenue Farhat Hached, Tunis, Tunisia.

MADANI (Ezzeddine), Tunisian official. **Born** in 1938 in Tunis, Tunisia. **Married**, 1 daughter. **Educ.:** University of Tunis, Tunisia; College de France. **Dipl.:** B.A., Diploma in Arabic Language and Literature, Anthropology and Sociology. **Career:** Cultural Editor of "al-Amal" Arabic Journal (1971-73); Director of the International Festival, Hammamat, Tunisia (1978); Director, Cultural Affairs of the City of Tunis (1980-); Cultural Editor of "al-Amal" (1981-). **Publ.:** several short story collections and numerous plays. **Addr.:** 18 Rue des Abricotiers, Le Bardo, Tunis, Tunisia.

MADANI (Farid, Omar), Sudanese executive. **Born** in 1944 in Khartoum, Sudan. **Son** of Omar Medani. **Married** in 1973, 2 sons. **Educ.:** University of Khartoum, B.Sc. Economics (1969); Iran Center for Management M.B.A. (1974). **Career:** Joined the Ministry of Finance and National Economy in 1969; Financial Officer (1969-74); Senior Officer (1974); Assistant Under Secretary and Director of Minister's Office (1975-77); Head of Economic Research Section, Emirates and Sudan Investment Company (1977-78); Director, Emirates Khartoum Investment Co. Ltd. Director and Company Secretary, Emirates and Sudan Investment Company, Khartoum (1978-). **Publ.:** "Workers and Work in Islam"; "Economics in I lam" and prolific articles in Sudanese press. **Member:** Mei ıber of the Executive Committee of Sudanese Economists Society; Volleyball Club. **Hobby:** Reading. **Addr.:** P.O.Box 7026, Telex: 22524 EMCU, Khartoum, Sudan.

MADANI (Ghazi Bin Obaid Dr.), Saudi academic. **Born** in 1936 in Medina, Saudi Arabia. **Dipl.:** B.A. (Business Administration), Cairo University; M.B.A., Ph.D. (Business/Finance) Arizona University, USA (1972). **Career:** Supervisor, Organization, Later Director, Coordination and Control Department, Petromin (1964-65);

Demonstrator, Faculty of Economics and Administration, KAU; Lecturer (1973); Assistant Professor (1975); Vice Dean, Faculty of Economics and Administration (1974-78); Associate Professor (1979); Dean, Faculty of Economics and Administration (1978-81); Associate Professor, Department of Business Administration, Faculty of Economics and Administration and Vice Rector for Administration Affairs, King Abdulaziz University (1982-85); Member of the Board, KAU (1.3.1986 - 25.9.1993); participated in the establishment of the Center of Research on Islamic Economy in 1979 and appointed its President since 18.1.1988; Dean since 1979. **Member** of Board, al-Madina for Press and Publishing, Dar al-Ilm Company, National Methanol Company, SABIC. **Member:** Associate of American Schools of Business Administration. **Publication:** several articles and research papers. **Hobbies:** chess, table tennis. **Prof. Addr.:** King Abdulaziz University, P.O.Box 1540, Tel.: 6952011, Jeddah. 21441. **Priv. Addr.:** Tel.: 6400724, Jeddah, Saudi Arabia.

MADANI (Hamza Ali S., al), Saudi Academic. **Born** in 1942 in Jeddah, Saudi Arabia. **Dipl.:** Ph.D. (Commercial Law), France. **Career:** Legal adviser to Ministry of Planning, the Chamber of Commerce and Industry; part-time Professor, Institute of Diplomatic Studies; Assistant Professor, Faculty of Economics and Administration, King Abdulaziz University, Jeddah. **Publications:** Commercial Societies in Islamic Law and French Law, Comparative Study (Ph.D. Thesis). **Hobby:** reading. **Prof. Addr.:** P.O.Box 1448, Tel.: 6869033 Ext. 1401, Jeddah. **Priv. Addr.:** Tel.: 6718892, Jeddah, Saudi Arabia.

MADANI (Iyad Amin), Saudi Businessman, **Born** on 26th April 1945 in Makkah, Saudi Arabia. **Degree:** B.Sc. (Production Management). **Career:** Appointed Minister of Haj (Pilgrimage) and a member of the Council of Minister, Saudi Arabia, in June 1999; Member of Majlis Al-Shoura (Consultative Council for two years (1997-1999); Member of the Consultative Assembly of the Gulf Cooperation Council for one year; Director General of Fikra-Media & Marketing Consultants from 1993; From 1981-1993 Worked as a Director General of Okaz Organization for press and Publication: Editor-in-Chief (1976-1980) of English daily. "Saudi Gazette"; From 1970-1976 Satff manager and later District Manager of Saudia, Saudi Arabian Airlines. **Membership:** member of the Board of Trustees of the Gulf Arab University in Bahrain; Member of the Committee for the development of International trade, Saudi Chambers of Commerce; Member of Gulf Development Group; Member of the Board of Trustees of "King Abdul Aziz & His Companions" Association for the Talented; Member of the Saudi National Educational Council; Member of the Board of Madina Philanthropic Society: Board member of SISCO (Saudi Industrial Services Co.), SIDC (Saudi Industrial Development Company), SBM (Saudi Building Materials) and Saudi French Bank, **Honour:** Best Employee Award 1975, Saudia. **Publications:** Numerous and regular contributions to local and Arab periodicals and newspapers. **Hobbies:** Hiking, chess ans Swimming. **Office/Private Address:** P.O.Box 8004, Jeddah, Zip Code -21482, Saudi Arabia.

MADANI (Sayed, Mustafa, al), Sudanese diplomat. **Born** in August 1931 in Umdurman. **Son** of Mustafa al-Madani **and** Mrs., née Zainab Nour. **Married** in 1959 to Miss Aida Gamal Ahmad, 3 children: Amgad, Ahmad and Amal. **Educ.:** Cambridge University (England). **Dipl.:** Bachelor of Arts, Master of Arts. **Career:** Ministry of Finance (1956); Ministry of Foreign Affairs (1958); Member of the First Delegation of Sudan to the United Nations (1956); Sudanese Consul General in Syria (1958-60); Attached to the Sudanese Embassies to Egypt (1960), to England (1961), to Lebanon (1963-66); Ambassador to Lebanon (1966-69); Ambassador to the Federal Republic of Germany (1970-73). **Award:** Medal Order of the Republic (Egypt). **Prof. Addr.:** c/o Ministry of Foreign Affairs Khartoum, Sudan.

MADANI (Yusuf, al), Saudi exchange manager. **Born** in 1944 in Jeddah, Saudi Arabia. **Son** of Mohammad Madani. **Married** in 1976, 2 sons, 1 daughter. **Educ.:** Faculty of Commerce (1971). **Career:** Joined Riyad Bank since 1971. Manager, Foreign Exchange, Riyad Bank, Jeddah, Saudi Arabia. **Member:** Arab Bankers' Association; International Dealers' Association; International Bond Dealers' Association. **Hobbies:** Basketball and ping-pong. **Addr.:** P.O.Box 1047, Tel.: 6430175, Telex: 400619 A/B RYADEX SJ, Jeddah, Saudi Arabia.

MADCOTT (Toby, Dr.), Former sudanese government minister. **Born** in 1939 at Tonj District, Bahr el-Ghazal Province (Sudan). **Married**, with children. **Educ.:** primary education locally; secondary education at Ahfad School in Omdurman; Facultly of Medicine, Charles University, Prague (Czechoslovakia). **Dipl.:** M.D. **Career:** Joined the Ministry of Health (1967); elected member of the Constituent Assembly; appointed member of the Twenty-Five Man Committee for the Sudanese Socialist Union (SSU); appointed Minister of State (Aug. 1971); Commissioner (with Ministerial rank) of Bahr el-Ghazal Province; Minister of Culture and Information, Southern Regional Government (1973- July 1975). **Addr.:** Khartoum, Sudan.

MADDAH (Talal), Saudi leading singer and musician. **Born** in 1936. **Educ.:** recieved general education. **Career:** Famous as top Saudi singer all over the Arab world; his singing gave Saudi folk songs a pan-Arab reputation. **Address:** c/o Saudi Arts and Cultural Society, Tel.: 6712328, Jeddah, Saudi Arabia.

MADFA (Hamad, Abdul Rahman, al), United Arab Emirates Politician. **Born** on October 1, 1949. **Educ.:** Received Education in Kuwait, Johns Hopkins University (U.S.A), South Eastern University Washington D.C. **Dipl.:**

B.A. (English) Kuwait, M.Sc. (Political Science) U.S.A., Proficiency of Foreign language (English), Honorary Ph.D. from South Eastern University Washington D.C. **Career:** English Language Teacher, Sharjah (1971-1972); Member of the Permanent mission to the UN. New York (1972-1974); Chargé d'Affaires and Head of the mission of U.A.E. Embassy in Washington (1974-1975), Ambassador to Iraq (1975-1977); Ambassador to Washington and Mexico (1977-1979); Minister of Health (1.7.1979); Minister of Education (1991-1997). **Prof. Addr.:** Ministry of Health, P.O.Box 848, Abu Dhabi, United Arab Emirates.

MADFAI (Husham Hassan Fahmi, al), Iraqi civil engineer. **Born** in 1928 in Baghdad, Iraq. **Son** of Hassan F. al-Madfai (Officer-Gov. Official) **and** Mrs. Wajiha née Shaick Noori. **Married** in 1953 in Baghdad, Madhloom, 2 children: Ghada, Architect (1954); Kumait, Consulting Engineer (1958). **Educ.:** Central High School Baghdad (1946). **Dipl.:** Graduate of University of Baghdad, Engineering College (1950); Diploma in Civil Engineering (1950). **Career:** Goverment Engineering Designer (1950-59); Chief Housing Construction Department MOH (1959-64); Consulting Engineer (Dar al-Imara Partner) (1964-80); Technical Deputy Mayor of Baghdad (1980-86); Consulting Engineer (1986-); **Work:** Feasibility Studies of Projects Civil Engineering Projects; Design & Supervision Consulting Engineers; Expert in Housing Policies; Expert in Major Projects Planning, Design and Management. **Sports:** Football, tennis, swimming. **Hobbies:** Painting, photography and archeology. **Prof. Addr.:** 302/14/22, Maghrib Street, Tel.: 4225021/22, Baghdad, Iraq. **Priv. Addr.:** 609/6/4, Mansur, Tel.: 5414634, Baghdad, Iraq.

MADFAI (Kahtan Hassan Fahmi, al, Dr.), Iraqi architect. **Born** in 1927 in Baghdad, Iraq. **Son** of Hassan F. al-Madfai (Officer-Gov. Official) **and** Mrs. Wajiha née Shaick Noori. **Married** in 1957 in Athens to Miss Lili Vorres, one child: Linya (Architect). **Educ.:** Central High School, Baghdad; University of South Wales, U.K. **Dipl.:** B. in Architecture (1952); Ph.D. in Philosophy of Architecture (1986). **Career:** Senior Partner (Dar al-Imara) Baghdad; Governor Official and Consulting Architect (1952-63); University Teacher and Architect Consultant (1963-75); Consulting Architect (1975-). **Work:** Architecture and Planning; Major Projects Planning, Desing and Management; Chairman and Member of many International and National Architecture Competition Committees. **Sports:** Swimming, walking. **Hobbies:** Poetry, painting, philosophical studies. **Member:** Architecture Club, Baghdad; Union and Society of Engineers, Baghdad. **Prof. Addr.:** Athens, Greece and 302/14/22, Tel.: 4225021/22, Baghdad, Iraq. **Priv. Addr.:** 11 Aristoxenov, Pangrati Athens, Tel.: 7217189, Athens, Greece, and Tel.: 4220680, Baghdad, Iraq.

MADKOUR (Mohamad, Abdel-Khalek), Egyptian senior research scientist. **Born** on 8 January 1948, in Cairo (Egypt). **Son** of Dr. Ibrahim Bayoumi Madkour (President, Academy of Arabic Language) **and** Mrs. Bahia Madkour. **Married** on 15 February 1970 to Miss Afkar M. el-Kharadly, 2 children: Mahynour (1971) and Monya (1977). **Educ.:** College de la Sainte Famille (Egyp); B.Sc. Statistics, Faculty of Economics and Political Sciences (1969), Cairo University. M.Sc. Information Sciences, Ecole des Hautes Etudes en Sciences Economiques et Sociales (E.H.E.S.S.), Sorbonne, France (1975); Ph.D. Information Sciences, Ecole des Hautes Etudes en Sciences Economiques et Sociale, (E.H.E.S.S.), Sorbonne, France (1978). **Career:** IDCAS Staff Member (1969-June 1980); Electronic Data Processing (E.D.P.) Manager (1972-80), Co-ordinator of IDCAS Activities in the North African Region (1969-72); Consultant to the Arab Regional Centre for Research & Documentation in Social Sciences (ARCSS), attached to UNESCO since 1977; Director, Management Information System Division, Phoenix Corporation, in charge of all information EDP system design since 1978; National Project Manager, Scientific Technical Information Project (STI) part of an Applied Science & Technology Program under a Project Grant Agreement between U.S. Agency for International Development and the Egyptian Academy of Science and Technology since May 1980; Senior Research Scientist, Georgia Institute of Technology, Atlanta, Georgia, (1980-82); Director, Organization and Microfilming Centre, al-Ahram. **Member:** Gezira Sporting Club, American Express, Diner's Club. **Sports:** Soccer, Handball and Tennis. **Hobbies:** Bridge and Billiards. **Prof. Addr.:** Organization & Microfilming Centre, al-Galaa Street, Tel.: 745551, Cairo. **Priv. Addr.:** 8 Nile Street, Giza, Tel.: 896175, Giza, Egypt.

MADOUH (Mohamad, Mahmoud), Kuwaiti businessman, **Born** in Kuwait in 1938. **Son** of Mahmoud Madouh. **Married,** three children. **Career:** Deputy Chairman of the Kuwait Shipping Co.; Deputy Chairman of the United Arab Shipping-Company; Assistant Under Secretary for Industrial Affairs, Ministry of Commerce and Industry; wide business interests. **Addr.:** Kuwait City, Kuwait.

MAGBOOL (Gadi M., Dr.), Saudi Academic. **Born** on March 2, 1948 in Sabya, Saudi Arabia. **Son** of Mohammad Magbool (Government Service) **and** Mrs. Aisha. **Married** in 1981 to Sawsan Al-Muallemi, 2 children: Adil (1982), Ola (1984). **Educ.:** Medical School, Vienna, Austria; German Board in Pediatrics, University of Dusseldorf, Germany. **Career:** Vice-Dean for Academic affairs (1986-87); Chairman, Department of Pediatrics (1988-89); Dean, College of Medicine and Medical Sciences, KFU (1990-92); Vice-President, King Faisal University (1992 to date) and Consultant of Pediatrics. **Sports:** Tennis and Swimming. **Member:** Member, Al-Itifaq Club, Dammam, Member of Handicapped Association in Eastern Province, Executive Director of Saudi Diabetes and Endocrine Association in Eastern Province, Chairman of the Arab

Board Diabetes A. **Prof. Addr.:** King Faisal University, P.O.Box 1982, Dammam 31441, Tel.: (03) 8577984, (03) 8572814 HIFAX, Telex: 870020 Faisal SJ, Saudi Arabia.

MAGDI (Ibrahim), Egyptian physician, surgeon, university professor. **Born** in Egypt. **Educ.:** Cairo University, Royal College of Surgeons (London). **Dipl.:** Doctor in Medicine, Specialization in Surgery, Fellow of the Royal College of Surgeons. **Career:** Physician and Surgeon; Professor of Gyneacology and Medicine, Cairo University. **Member:** Automobile Club of Egypt, Gezira Sporting Club. **Addr.:** Boulos Hanna Street, Dokki, Tel.: 806066, Cairo, Egypt.

MAGDUB (Taha, Muhammad al, Gen.), Egyptian army officer. **Born** in 1926 in Port Said. **Married**, 3 daughters. **Educ.:** Egyptian High Military Academy. **Dipl.:** B.Sc. and M.Sc. in Military Science. **Career:** Chief Liaison Officer, Egyptian Army and Assistant Head of Operations during October 1973 War; participated in all negotiations with representatives of the Israely Army at Kilometre 101 and Geneva; signed the second Israeli-Egyptian Disengagement Agreement (1975); Member of the Egyptian Delegation at the Egyptian-Israeli negotiations in Cairo (1975-79); Ambassador, Ministry of Foreign Affairs (1979-80); Ambassador to Poland (1980-84); Assistant Minister of Foreign Affairs (1984). **Publ.:** "Zionist Militarism", Part one (1970), Part Two (1971); "The Ramadan War (October 1973)" (1974). **Decor.:** Order of Merit, President of Egypt (1979). **Medals:** Several military Medals and ribbons, Medal of the Egyptian Republic (1974). **Hobbies:** writing, reading. **Member:** Egyptian Hunting Club. **Prof. Addr.:** Ministry of Foreign Affairs, Cairo, Egypt. **Priv. Addr.:** 12 Koroom Street, Apt. 4, Mohandiseen, Dokki, Giza, Egypt.

MAGHOUR (Kamal, Hassan), Libyan politician. **Educ.:** Cairo University. **Career:** Legal Adviser to the oil industry in Libya (1970); has represented Libya at the International Court of Justice, The Hague; Ambassador to UN (1972-76); to France (1976-78); to People's Republic of China (1978-81); Head Petroleum Secretariat (1982-84). **Addr.:** Tripoli, Libya.

MAGHRABI (Mahmoud Abid), Saudi Executive. **Born** in Jeddah, in 1944. **Dipl.:** B.A. (Accountancy and Economics). **Career:** Secretary, Financial Manager, Deputy Manager, General Manager, Arab Club, USA (1966-69); Staff Manager, Materials, Saudia; Staff Manager, Materials and Equipment (1973); Acting Manager, Cost Accounting, Saudia; Manager of Aircraft Maintenance Accounts and Fixed Assets, Corporate Controller (1979), Financial Advisor to Executive Vice President - Finance, Saudia, (1981); Now, General Manager - Corporate Budgets, Saudi Arabian Airlines Corporation. **Hobbies:** Reading, writing. **Prof. Addr.:** Saudia, P.O.620, CC: 660, Jeddah, Tel: 686-2090, Saudi Arabia.

MAGHRABI (Mahmoud Sulaiman), Libyan politician. **Born** in 1935. **Educ.:** Secondary and Higher, Georges Washington University. **Dipl.:** Doctorate of Laws. **Career:** Teacher in Colleges of Arabian Gulf Emirates; settled in Libya and obtained Libyan nationality in 1962; Consultant to Esso Standard Co.; Prominent Member of Federation of Workers Unions (unrecognized by the Monarchy); one of the founders of Petroleum Workers Union; sentenced to 4 years jail for political and private reasons in connection with his Libyan Nationality; Prime Minister of the first Cabinet after the fall of the Monarchy and proclamation of the Republic, on September 1, 1969, Resigned on January 15, 1970; prominent role in talks with operating oil companies (1970); permanent Representative to U.N. (January 1971- January 1973); Ambassador to U.K. (May 1973-December 1976). **Publ.:** Author of many booklets on the attitude of the Libyan Government regarding the Israeli-Arab war in June 1967. **Addr.:** Tripoli, Libya.

MAGHRABI (Mohamad Abdul Wahib), Saudi civil servant. **Born** in 1923 in Jeddah, Saudi Arabia. **Educ.:** received general education. **Career:** Former clerk in charge of files, Ministry of Finance; Secretary Customs Division, Chief of Correspondence Division, Customs Directorate; Assistant to Director-General of Customs; former member of Customs Committee, General Directorate of Customs; Secretary-General of Western province Customs Administration; Chairman of Customs Committee of First Instance, Western Province. **Hobbies:** reading, travel. **Address:** Western Province Customs, Secretariat, Jeddah, Tel.: 6432421. **Priv. Addr.:** Tel.: 6652086, Jeddah, Saudi Arabia.

MAGHRABY (Salahiddin, al), Arab-American academic. **Born** in 1927 in Fayoum, Egypt. **Married**, 3 daughters. **Educ.:** Cairo University, Egypt; Ohio State University, USA, Cornell University, USA. **Dipl.:** B.Sc. in Mechanical Engineering. M.Sc. and Ph.D. in Industrial Engineering. **Career:** Tutor in the School of Engineering, Cairo, Egypt (1949); Engineer, Foreign Inspection Office of Egyptian State Railways in London, Budapest and Brussels (1949-54); Research Assistant, Cornell University, Ithaca, NY, USA (1955-58); Research Leader, Western Electric Company, Research Centre at Princeton, New Jersey, USA (1958-62); Associate Professor of Yale University, New Haven, Conn., USA (1962-67); University Professor, Operational Research and Industrial Engineering (1967); Director, Graduate Programme in Operational Research, North Carolina State University (1967-76). **Publ.:** "The Design of Production Systems" (1966), "The Theory of Activity Network" (1976), "Handbook of Operations Research" (1976) as well as several chapters and articles in lecture series. **Hobbies:** science fiction, history, design and operation of integrated and distribution systems, tennis, swimming. **Addr.:** 124 Perquimans Drive, Raleigh, North Carolina 27609, USA.

MAGHRIB (Yusuf Mohamad Saleh), Saudi academic. **Born** in 1943 in Mecca, Saudi Arabia. **Dipl.:** Ph.D. (Physiology of Plants). **Career:** Former Demonstrator, Faculty of Science, King Abdulaziz University; Lecturer, Faculty of Science, King Abdulaziz University. **Publications:** research papers on economic and desert plants appropriate to Saudi Arabia's climate. **Hobbies:** sport, philately, coin collecting. **Prof. Addr.:** Department of Biology, Faculty of Science, King Abdulaziz University, Tel.: 6879033, Jeddah. **Priv. Addr.:** Tel.: 6427037, Jeddah, Saudi Arabia.

MAGSABI (Omar Ahmad, al), Libyan politician. **Born** in Libya. **Career:** Senior Official, Ministry of Education; Member, Faculty of Agriculture, Tripoli university; Minister of State for Nutrition and Marine Wealth (1977-79); Secretary for Light Industries, General People's Committee (1979-82). **Addr.:** Tripoli, Libya.

MAHAFZAH (Ali Mufleh), Jordanian academic. **Born** on March 15, 1938. **Married**, four children. **Dipl.:** Doctorat Troisième Cycle, in Islamic Studies/History (1971), Paris III (Sorbonne Nouvelle); Doctorat d'Etat in Arts and Humanities (1980) Paris I (Sorbonne Pantheom). **Career:** Diplomat (1962-71), Prof. at Jordan University/ Amman (1971-81), Assistant Dean, Faculty of Arts, Jordan University (1976-78), Dean of Public College and Vice President, Mu'tah University, al-Karak/Jordan (1981-84), President, Mu'tah University (1984-89), President, Yarmouk University, Irbid/Jordan (1989-1993 President), Prof. at Jordan University (1994- present). **Publ.:** Jordanian-British Relations (1921-57), Contemporary History of Jordan, The Emirate (1921-46), Arab Intellectual Trends in the Renaissance Period (1798-1914), German-Palestinian Relations (1841-1945), Attitudes of France, Germany and Italy towards Arab Unity (1918-45), Intellectual Movement in Palestine and Transjordan (1775-1925), Political Thought in Palestine (1918-48), Political Thought in Jordan (1916-46), 2 vols.; co-author of a number of titles. **Awards:** Jordanian Independence Medal/Fourth Order (1964), Iron Cross/Third Order (1965) from Federal Republic of Germany, Legion of Honor of the Chevalier Order (1971), from the French Government, The Academic Palm Medal (1988), Jordanian Education Medal of the Highest Order (1992), State Prize of Merit for Social Sciences (1992), from the French Government. Membership of **Associations and Committees:** Member of a number of academic and educational associations, councils and committees on the national, regional and international levels. **Prof. Addr.:** Jordan University, Amman/Jordan, Tel.: (06) 843555, Fax: 962-6-832318.

MAHALLAWI (Mohamad Nagy, al), Egyptian professor of medicine, formerly president of Ain Shams university. **Born** on May 6, 1917 in Cairo. **Son** of Mohamad el-Mahallawi (Professor, Azhar University) **and** Mrs. Rokaia Nasr el-Adli. **Married** to Mrs. Efimed El Kady in April 1947 in Cairo, 4 children: Nagwa (1948), Mohamad Nabegh (1949), Nagla (1951), Mohamad Nasser (1952). **Educ.:** Faculty of Medicine, Cairo University. **Dipl.:** M.B., B.Ch (Cairo-1940); M.D. (Medicine) (1946). **Career:** Lecturer in Medicine, Cairo University (1947); Ass. Professor, Ain Shams University (1951); Professor of Medicine (1959); Dean of Faculty of Medicine (1969); President of Ain Shams University (1974); Chairman, Board of Center for Research and Development in Science Education; Chairman of Board of Middle East Research Center; President, Egyptian Society of Nephrology; Member of Supreme Council of Universities; Member of the Committee of the National Prizes (Egyptian Academy of Science and Technology); Member of the National Committee of UNESCO; Member of the Committee for Science and Technology (National Committee of UNESCO); Member of Committee for the Sector of Medical Education; Member of Board of Egyptian Medical Association; Member of the Association of the Medical Schools of Africa (Individual membership), **Member:** "Institut d'Egypte". **Publ.:** Twenty one published papers on Nephrology, General Medicine and Medical Education. **Awards:** el-Estehkak Medal, al-Gomohoriya Medal. **Hobby:** Reading, Music. **Member:** el-Saed Club, Heliopolis Club. **Prof. Addr.:** 32, el-Falaki Street, Tel.: 24287, Cairo. **Priv. Addr.:** 17 Wali al Aid Street, Koba Garden, Tel.: 823166, Cairo, Egypt.

MAHASNEH (Adel, Mohamad), Jordanian academic. **Born** in 1945 in Kofor Khal, Jordan. **Son** of Mohamad Mahasneh (retired airforce officer) **and** Mrs. Shera Mahasneh. **Married** in 1984 in Amman to Miss Raja Mahasneh, Five children. **Educ.:** el-Fateh Secondary School, Amman; University of Jordan, Amman; University of Heriot-Watt (Edinburgh), UK. **Dipl.:** B.Sc., Post Graduate Diploma in Industrial Microbiology (1974). M.Sc. Microbiology (1975). Ph.D. Microbiology (1977). **Career:** Assistant Professor of Microbiology (1978-83); Associate Professor of Microbiology (since 1983); Assistant Dean of the Faculty of Sciences in the University of Jordan (since 1983); Professor of Microbiology 1987; Chairman of the Biological Sciences Department, University of Jordan (1986-89); Dean of the Faculty of Science (1993-); Member of the University Council for 1985 and (1989-90). **Publ.:** Author of 70 Scientific Articles published in European, American and Arab Scientific Journals. **Award:** Distinction Award of research in the University of Jordan (1986). **Sports:** Hill walking, Ground tennis. **Hobby:** Horseriding. **Member of:** ASM (USA); SGM (UK); JBS, RSCN (Jordan). **Credit Card:** Visa. **Prof. Addr.:** Dept. Biol. Science, University of Jordan, Tel.: 843555, ext. 2622 or 2304, Amman, Jordan. **Priv. Addr.:** al-Jubaha, Amman.

MAHASNEH (Ali, Mohamad), (assumed name Abu Omar), Jordanian translator-writer. **Born** in 1943 in Kufr Khal, Jordan. **Son** of Mohamad Mahasneh (retired military officer) **and** Mrs. Shira Ali Mahasneh. **Married** in 1976 in Amman to Miss Khawla Kayyali, five children.

Educ.: al-Fateh Highschool, Amman; Teacher Training Center, Jordan; Business Eng. Training, UK; Damascus University, Syria. **Dipl.:** B.A. in Geography. **Career:** Technical writing/ translation (1968); Literary writing/ translation (1972); also worked as teacher, Petrol Refining Account./med. detailman, Translator/ writer. **Publ.:** Literary works, poems, short stories, essays published in various Arabic periodicals in Kuwait, Libya, Saudi Arabia and UAE (since 1974). **Awards:** Man of the Year 1985, King Khaled International Airport, Riyadh. **Sport:** Swimming. **Hobbies:** Billiard, antique collection. **Prof. Addr.:** K.K.I.A., P.O.Box 22531, Tel.: 2211455, Riyadh 11416, Saudi Arabia. **Priv. Addr.:** Tel.: 2203772, Riyadh 11416, Saudi Arabia.

MAHASSINI (Marwan, al), Syrian physician. **Born** in Syria. **Educ.:** Secondary and Higher. **Dipl.:** Doctor in Medicine. **Career:** Physician, Professor at the Faculty of Medicine of Damascus Univesity; Member of the Arab Academy of Damascus. **Addr.:** Damascus University, Damascus, Syria.

MAHAYNI (Mazhar, Hassan, al), Syrian surgeon, **Born** in 1918 in Damascus. **Son** of Hassan al-Mahayni. **Educ.:** Damascus Faculty of Medicine. **Dipl.:** Doctor in Medicine, **Career:** Surgeon, professor of Surgery at the Faculty of Medicine, Surgeon in Mahaini Hospital. **Publ.:** Author of "Surgical Diseases". **Award:** Gold Medal of the Syrian Merit. **Addr.:** c/o Faculty of Medicine, Damascus, Syria.

MAHAYNI (Thabit, Ghalib), Syrian academic, businessman. **Born** in 1932 in Damascus, Syria. **Son** of Ghalib Mahayni. **Married**, three children. **Educ.:** B.A. in Economics, Boston University, Mass., USA. **Career:** Assistant Director General, Damascus Chamber of Commerce (1958); member of the Board of Directors of the Bank of Arab Unity (1960); member of the Council of Damascus Municipality (1960); Lecturer, College of Business Administration, Damascus University (1961); General Director, Damascus Chamber of Commerce (1972); member of the People's Council (1977). **Sports:** Tennis, swimming. **Hobbies:** Music and Poetry. **Prof. Addr.:** P.O.B. 218, Tel.: 111339, Damascus, Syria.

MAHBOUB (Abdallah Abdul Karim), Saudi academic. **Born** in 1939 in Riyadh, Saudi Arabia. **Dipl.:** M.A. (General Linguistics). **Career:** Former Demonstrator, English Department, Faculty of Arts, King Saud University; Lecturer, in the Said department. **Publication:** Some aspects of the Najdi Dialect Grammar, a research work submitted to the University of Leeds, U.K. **Prof. Addr.:** P.O.Box 333, Tel.: 4811000, Riyadh. **Priv. Addr.:** Tel.: 4356178, Riyadh, Saudi Arabia.

MAHDI (Abdallah Omar), Saudi Director-General of Civil Aviation. **Born** in 1935 in Mecca, Saudi Arabia. **Dipl.:** High School Certificate supplemented by specialized courses in air traffic service, radar technique, flight safety and investigation of flight incidents, at the University of Southern California. **Career:** Chief, Air Traffic Control (1958); Director, Air Traffic Services (1964); member of International Civil Aviation Organisation (ICAO), Montreal, Canada; Permanent member of Board of Saudia-Saudi Arabian Airlines Corporation; attended several ICAO Conferences in Montreal and other European and Arab cities, chaired some ICAO Conferences and some regional ICAO Conferences. **Honour:** Shining Star Medal, Republic of China. **Hobbies:** reading, golf. **Address:** Civil Aviation Department, Jeddah, Saudi Arabia.

MAHDI (Abdul Wahab Rauf), Iraqi academic. **Born** in 1938 in Hindiyah, Iraq. **Married**, 3 children. **Educ.:** University of Baghdad, Iraq; Oklahoma State University, USA, Texas A. & M University, USA. **Dipl.:** B.V.M., M.Sc. and Ph.D. in Animal Physiology. **Career:** Reserve Army Officer (1962-64); Demonstrator, Physiology Department, College of Veterinary Medicine, Baghdad University (1964-66); Graduate Assistant in USA (1966-71); Faculty Member of College of Veterinary Medicine, Baghdad University (1971-); Head of Physiology Department (1974-). **Publ.:** P.Sc. and Ph.D. thesis in English; various scientific articles (in English and Arabic) in Professional Journals. **Hobbies:** chess, cycling, fishing. **Prof. Addr.:** Physiology, Pharmacology and Biochemistry Department, College of Veterinary Medicine, University of Baghdad, Baghdad, Iraq.

MAHDI (Ahmad Abdurrahman, al), Sudanese politician. **Born** in 1933 in Sudan. **Educ.:** Victoria College (Alexandria) and New College (Oxford). **Career:** Private Secretary to late Imam Abdurrahman al-Mahdi, Leader of Ansar movement; Manager Director "Dairat al-Mahdi" comprising Aba Island and White Nile Agricultural Schemes, Estate Co., Khartoum; various political and social appointments; Minister of the Interior (1965-67); former Minister of Information Social Affairs, and Minister of Defence. **Addr.:** Khartoum, Sudan.

MAHDI (Kamis Amer), Saudi academic. **Born** in Jeddah in 1945. **Educ.:** B.Sc. (Physics) (1970); B.Sc. (Mathematics) (1969), University of Texas, Austin; M.Sc. (Nuclear Engineering), University of London (1974). **Career:** Head, Rector, Physics Section, Mineral Resources Directorate, Jeddah. **Member:** Associate member of British Institute of Physics; member of Institution of Nuclear Engineers: attended Fourth International Conference on the Peaceful Uses of Atomic Energy, also some IAEA Annual Conferences and Agency Board of Governors meetings. **Address:** P.O.Box 345, Tel.: 6310355, Jeddah, Saudi Arabia.

MAHDI (Mohsin, Sayyid), Iraqi educator. **Born** on June 21, 1926 in Karbala. **Son** of Sayyid Mahdi **and**

Mrs., née Fatima Hassan. **Married** on May 31, 1959 to Miss Cynthia M. Risner, 2 daughters; Fatima and Nadia. **Educ.:** American University of Beirut, universities of Chicago, Paris and Freiburg. **Dipl.:** Bachelor of Business Administration (1947), Doctor of Philosophy (1954). **Career:** Instructor, Law College, University of Baghdad (1955-57); Came to the United States of America (1957); Assistant Professor of Arabic, University of Chicago (1957-62); Associate Professor since 1962; Professor of Arabic and Islamic Studies since 1965; J.R. Jewett Professor of Arabic and Director of Center for Middle Eastern Studies, Harvard University since 1969; Vis. Professor, University of Freiburg (Germany) 1961 and 1965. **Publ.:** Author of "Ibn Khaldoun's Philosophy of History" (1957), "Die Geistigen and Sozialen Wandlungen in Nahen Osten" (1961), "al-Farabi's Philosophy of Platon and Aristotle" (1962), Co-editor "Medieval Political Philosophy, A sourcebook" (1963). **Member of:** several cultural Associations. **Remark:** Fluent in Arabic, French and German. **Addr.:** 1737 Cambridge St., Cambridge, Mass. 02138, USA.

MAHDI (Sadeq, al), Sudanese politician. **Born** in 1936 in Sudan. **Son** of the late Saddiq al-Mahdi and great-grandson of Imam Abdurrahaman al-Mahdi. **Educ.:** Combony College (Khartoum), and St. John's College (Oxford). **Career:** Member, House of Representatives; Prime Minister (1966-67); Leader, al-Omma Mahdist Party (1961- to present); deported to Egypt following Ansar Uprising (1970); returned in 1972; left Sudan again in 1974 and returned in 1977; Prime Minister in (1986-June 1989) detained by the new Revolutionary Government and released in August 1995. **Publ.:** Author of "Problems of the South Sudan". **Addr.:** Khartoum, Sudan.

MAHDI (Salah, El), Tunisian musician, artist. **Born** on February 9, 1925 in Tunis, in a family of artists. As his father was a music teacher whose home served as a meeting place for some of the best Tunisian and Foreign musicians, Salah El Mahdi had been exposed very early to the different types of Arab music and rythms, which he performed on litle instruments, half-lute, half-violin, he had made himself. **Educ.:** Along with his secondary school studies, he attended a course of oriental music taugh by the Syrian musicologist Aly Derwish and the Tunisian Khemaïs Ternane at the Rashidia Institute. Moreover, owing to the Italian musician Bonura, he was given exposure to western music. Having become one of the best flutists in the Arab World, Salah El Mahdi performed on the Radio, then in public throughout his secondary school education, and during his university studies at the department of letters (Zituna University), at the Faculty of law, and at the Institute of Administration in Tunis. Some years later, he got his Doctorat degree in musicology at Poitiers University in France. **Career:** At the Age of 18, Salah El Mahdi became teacher of Music at the Rashidia Institute, and in 1949 he was appointed director of the later institute. Being also composer, he was given access to the French Association of Writers, Composers and Publishers (Société des Auteurs, Compositeurs et Editions de Musique - S.A.C.E.M.) in Paris, and ultimately became one of its permanent members. Soon after the foundation of its Tunisian equivalent association, he was made Honoris Causa member of the S.A.C.E.M. In 1951 he passed the competitive examination of Tunisian Magistrature was appointed judge at the Law Courts of Tunis - As a result of this, he had to reduce, temporarily, his artistic activity and to restrict himself to composing under the pseudonym of "ZIRYAB", the Andalousian musician, and to writing musical criticism in newspapers like ESSABAH, ESSARIH and EL AMAL. He wrote plays for the Radio and on the stage, he performed many roles with the troup of El-Kawakab Association of Tunis, of which he later became President. After Tunisian Independence, he was called upon to direct the department of Fine Arts at the Ministry of Education. Thus, he took part in the setting up of the National Academy of Music, Dance and Dramatic Art, and organized the teaching of artistic subjects in high schools. In 1961, he was at the head of the Direction of Music and Fold Art at the Ministry of Culture, after which he was appointed President of the National Cultural Committee and fulfilled this function along with the Presidency of the National Committee of Music until he retired. In 1962, he founded the National Troup of Popular Arts. In 1969, he set up the Tunisian Symphonic Orchestra under the tutorship of the Ministry of Culture and set up also the National Society for the Preservation of Coran, and the National School of Coranic Intoned Psalms. On the international level, he took part in many congresses organized by various UNESCO institutions or by the National Organizations of many countries, namely the French CNRS and the American Society of Musical Education. **Salah El Mahdi has also been member of the following:** The Executive Committee of the Islamic Organization of History, Culture and Art, which has its headquarters in Istambul (Turkey); The High Committee of Islamic Civilisation whose headquarters are in Istambul (Turkey); The Executive Committee of the International Counsel of Music which has its headquarters at UNESCO. **He's also been Vice-President of the Following:** The committee Director of the International Society of Musical Education; The International Institute of Music, Dance and Dramatic Art, by audio-visual devices; The International Institute Counsel of Folk Music. **He is at Present:** Founding Member of the International Institute of Comparative Music in Berlin; President of the World Organization of Folk Arts and Traditions, which relates to UNESCO and has its headquarters in Vienna (Austria). **Publ.:** Author of more than 700 compositions including classical and folk songs as well as instrumental music, both oriental and western. Among his compositions are 4 nubas, several muwashahs, bashrafs, a few symphonic poems, some chamber music and various other musical pieces to be performed on the piano, the flute, the violin and the harp. His symphonic works had been performed both at Moscow's and Leningrad's festival. Mr. Salah El Mahdi is indebted for his collecting and compilation of the Tunisian musical heritage and his publication of it in a set of small volumes. Arab music owes to him a vast literature: he is indeed the author of many musical, historical and literary works on the subject. These have been published in Arabic and French, and sometimes translated in to other languages. Medals: Order of the Republic, Second Class, Tunisia; Order of Labour; Order of Culture, First Class; Grand Prix de la Ville de Tunis. Prize of Appreciation from the City of Tunis (1985) and the League of Arab States (1999) from the Arab Music Section. **Addr.:** Club ZIRIAB. Dr. Salah El Mahdi, 71 Bis, Rue de Palestine - Tunis, Tel.: - Fax: 00 216 793 278.

MAHER (Abdel Munim Maher, Ali), Egyptian businessman. **Born** in 1922 in Alexandria, Egypt. **Married,** 2 sons. **Educ.:** London University, UK. **Dipl.:** M.Sc. and Ph.D. **Career:** Consultant to the FAO, UN (1956-60); Consultant to the Ministry of Agriculture (1960-70); Professor and Head of Plant Protection Section, Assiout University; General Secretary of Zoological Society and Egyptian Association for Conservation. Chairman of the Board of Directors of Aradis Co. (1982-); Private Consultant (1982-). **Publ.:** "The Economical Insects" (1970), "Insecticides for Agriculture" (1978), "Rodents and the Way to kill them in Kuwait" (1980). **Decor.:** Egyptian Order of Merit for Agriculture and Science (1983), Egyptian Order of Merit for Arts and Sciences (1st Grade), Egyptian Order of Merit (4th 3rd & 2nd Grade). **Hobbies:** travelling, swimming, sports. **Prof. Addr.:** P.O.Box 318, Dokki, Giza, Egypt.

MAHER EL SAYED (Aly), Egyptian diplomat, **Born** on January 4, 1939 in Cairo, Egypt. **Married** in 1972 in Teheran to Sherry el-Mahdi, 2 children: Shirine (1975), Sherif (1979). **Educ.:** Lycée Français d'Heliopolis, Cairo; College de la Sainte Famille, Cairo; Faculty of Law, Cairo University, I.I.A.P., Paris. **Dipl.:** LL.B. **Career:** Joined Diplomatic Service (1962); Served in Egyptian Embassies in London, Teheran, Canberra, Paris; Director of Cabinet of Dr. Boutros Boutros Ghali, Minister of State for Foreign Affairs (1983); Appointed Ambassador to Tunisia (1987-); Permanent Representative to the Arab League (1988) Director of Cabinet of Mr. Amro Moussa, Minister of Foreign affairs (1992-92); Ambassador to France (since 1993). **Prof. Addr.:** Egyptian Embassy, Tel.: 0153678830, Paris, France.

MAHER (Mustafa), Egyptian engineer, Director of Companies. **Born** in Egypt. **Married** Miss Neemat Maher. **Educ.:** Cairo University and London University. **Dipl.:** Bachelor of Science, Member of Institute of Electrical Engineers. **Career:** Former Under Secretary for Commerce and Industry, Companies' Director. **Member:** Gezira Sporting Club. **Addr.:** 1, Kamel Muhammad, Zamalek, Tel.: 800237, Cairo. **Summer Residence:** 423, Army Road, Laurens Station, Ramleh, Tel.: 63298, Alexandria, Egypt.

MAHERZI (Mohamad, al), Tunisian Diplomat. **Born** on September 3, 1934 in Tunis (Tunisia). **Married** in 1958 to Saida el-Ghariany, four daughters. **Educ.:** Sadiki College, Tunis (1947-55); National Press Institute, University of Tunis (1955-57). **Career:** Joined United Nations European Office, Geneva (1963); attended several courses organised by UN in Geneva, Addis Ababa, Rome, Alexandria and New York; staff correspondent "al-Amal" newspaper (1959-62); Director, Televised current affairs programmes, Tunis (1965-70); Deputy Director, UN Information Centre, Tunis (1962-65); Press Director, Ministry of Foreign Affairs (1970-72); member. Neo-Destour Political Party; Counsellor, Tunisian Embassy, London (1972). **Awards:** Bizerte Medal; Knight, Order of the Tunisian Republic. **Sports:** Soccer and motoring. **Hobbies:** reading and music. **Addr.:** Ministry of Foreign Affairs, Tunis, Tunisia.

MAHFOUZ (Khalid Ibn Salim, bin), Saudi businessman. **Career:** Chairman and General Manager of National Commercial Bank, Jeddah; leading businessman; owner and Chairman of Board of several companies and agencies for foreign companies; founding member and member of Board of Saudi Bank, Paris; shareholder, Tihama for Advertising, Public Relations and Marketing Research; Director, Saudi International Bank, London, U.K. **Address:** National Commercial Bank, King Abdulaziz Street, P.O.Box 3555, Tel. 6446644, Telex: 405571/2/3, Cable BANK SAUDI, Jeddah, Saudi Arabia.

MAHFOUZ (Mahfouz, bin Salim, bin, Shaikh), Saudi executive. **Son** of Salim bin Mahfouz (Saiar Tribe). **Career:** Private entrepreneur; Partner, Saudi International Group Ltd.; Saudi Touristic Development Co. Ltd.; Carte Blanche Co. Ltd.; Saudi International Development Co. Ltd.; Saudi Electronic and Microwave Co. Ltd.; Senior Director, National Commercial Bank, Saudi Arabia. Chairman, United Saudi Lebanese Bank, Beirut, Lebanon. **Addr.:** P.O.Box 5580, Tel.: 350030, 351030, Telex: 21234, Beirut, Lebanon and National Commercial Bank, P.O.Box 3555, Tel. 6446644, Telex: 405571/2/3, Cable: BANK SAUDI, Jeddah, Saudi Arabia.

MAHFOUZ (Naguib), Egyptian writer. **Born** in 1911 in Egypt. **Educ.:** University of Cairo, **Dipl.:** Philosophy. **Career:** Writer, Director of Department, Ministry of Education; contributor to al-Ahram daily; member of Board of Dar al-Maaref Publishing House and Internationally well Known. **Publ.:** Author of several books in Arabic, eg. "Play of Destiny" (1939), "Radobis" (1943), "Struggle of Tayiba" (1944), "Nes Cairo" (1945), "Kham al-Khalili" (1946), "Zuqaq al-Madak" (1947), "Bin al-Kasrein" (Trilogy), "Welad Haretna", "al-Less was Kilab", "Qasr al-Shok" (1967), "al-Terka" (1968), "Sous l'Omrelle" (1969). **Awards:** State Prize; Order of Independence; Order of the Republic; received Nobel Prize for Arabic Literature in 1988. **Addr.:** 172 Nile Street, Agouza, Cairo, Egypt.

MAHFOUZ (Said ben Saleh, bin), Saudi leading businessman. **Born** Hadramout, in 1931. **Educ.:** Received general education. **Career:** Accountant, National Commercial Bank, Jeddah; Manager, National Commercial Bank, Jeddah and Mecca branches; Deputy Governor of same Bank; founder and shareholder of several General Trading, Industry and Contracting Companies; member of Board, Mecca Printing and Information Establishment, Red Sea Development Co., SAFCO and Saudi-Egyptian Co. **Hobbies:** reading, travel. **Address:** P.O.Box 1077, Jeddah, Saudi Arabia.

MAHI-BAHİ (Abdelhamid), Algerian former Minister of Justice. **Born** on August 15, 1940 in Oran, Algeria. **Son** of Kaddour Mahi-Bahi (deceased) **and** Mrs. née Kheïra Attia. **Married** in 1985 in Oran to Fatima Zarat, 3 children: Ghazlène, Nadym, Selmane. **Educ.:** University of Oran. **Dipl.:** Bachelor of Law. **Career:** Magistrate, President of Tribunal (1967-1987); President of Court of Justice (1987-1992); Minister of Justice (1992-April 1994). **Other Information:** Former Moujahed; officer of the National Liberation Army; War invalid. **Award:** Medal of the National Liberation Army. **Sports:** Horse-Riding, Piloting. **Hobbies:** Painting, Chess Amateur. **Addr.:** 14 Avenue Mokhtar, Oran, Algeria.

MAHIEDDIN (Mohamad, N.), Algerian lawyer. **Born** in 1944 in Oran, Algeria. **Educ.:** University of Algiers, Algeria. **Dipl.:** LL.B in Public Law, Diploma in Higher Studies in Public Law. **Career:** Head of Department of Law (1972-73); Director of the Institute of Law and Administrative Sciences of Oran University (1977-1980); Director of "Centre de Recherche et d'Information Documentaire en Sciences Sociales et Humaines" of Oran University (1985-1993); Member du Comité Consultatif International de "Maghreb Review" (Londres U.K.) (since 1987); Member of the "Association Internationale des droits de la Famille"; Professor of the Institute of Law and Administrative Sciences of Oran University; Visiting Professor, University of Lyon III (France) Member, Comité Scientifique des "Cahiers des Droits Maghrébiens" (Casablanca-Morocco); member, Comité de rédaction de la revue "Confluences" (Oran-Algeria); Member, Conseil de la Revue "Insaniyat" (Centre de Recherche en Anthropologie Sociale et Culturelle-CRASC, Oran). Author of Several articles on Muslim Law in the European Magazines and on History of Political Thoughts. **Addr.:** P.O.Box 1171, Oran el-Menouar, Algeria, 1 rue Audebert, Oran, Algeria.

MAHIUT (Rabah), Algerian journalist. **Born** in 1936 in Algeria. **Educ.:** Faculty of Law, Algiers University (1971). **Career:** Journalist with National Liberation Front (FLN) in France; editor on "al-Shaab" (later "Le Peuple" and then "el-Moudjahid") (1962-64); Information and Guidance Department of FLN Headquarters, Algiers (1964-66); "el-Moudjahid" (1967-68); producer-reporter on Radio-Télévision Algiers (1968-71); Staff reporter on "Révolution Africaine" (1971-72); Press Attaché, Central Administration (1972). **Publ.:** "Le Pétrole Algérien" (1974), Algiers. **Addr.:** Algiers, Algeria.

MAHJOUB (Bechir, Mohamad), Tunisian academic. **Born** in 1935 in Mahdia, Tunisia. **Son** of Mohamad Mahjoub. **Married**, three children. **Educ.:** University of Paris. **Dipl.:** Ph.D. in mathematics. **Career:** Mathematics lecturer, University of Tunis (1963-66); Course Head in Mathematics, University of Paris (1966-67); Associate Lecturer, CNAM, Paris (1967-70); Senior Lecturer, University of Tunis (1970-74); Professor (since 1974); Director of Studies, ENS, Tunis (1971-73); Founder and Director ENSET, Tunis (1973-75); Founder and Dean, Faculty of Science and Technology, Monastir (1975-77); General Director of higher education in Tunis (1977-88); Delegate of Tunisia at UNESCO (1988-92); Professor, University of Qatar (since 1992). President, Tunisian Association for Mathematical Sciences (1971-78); Honorary President (since 1978); life member, Fondation Nationale pour la traduction, l'établissement des textes et les études Beit el-Hikma (since 1983). **Medals:** Officer of the Order of the Republic, Tunisia; Officer of the Legion D'Honneur, France; Officer of the Order of Merit, France. **Prof. Addr.:** 1, Rue de Beja, 1030 Tunis, Tunisia. **Priv. Addr.:** 9 Rue des Narcisses, 1004 el-Menzah, Tunisia.

MAHJOUB (Kamil), Sudanese politician. **Born** in 1930 in Sudan. **Career:** Headmaster of Dongola Private School (1955-56); Ministry of cooperation and Rural Development following the May 1969 Revolution; Member, Political Bureau of the Sudanese Socialist Union (SSU) (1972); Head of the SSU Guidance and Development Committee; SSU Secretary for Rural Development (1974); Member of People's Assembly (1974). **Prof. Addr.:** P.O.Box 1850, Khartoum, Sudan.

MAHJOUB (Makkawi, Babiker), Sudanese politician. **Born** in 1919 in Khartoum, Sudan. **Son** of Babiker Mahgub. **Married. Educ.:** University of Khartoum, University of Leicester and University of London. **Career:** Foreign Service after Independence; Ambassador to Saudi Arabia and Kuwait; Adviser on the newly established Qatar Foreign Service (1970); Under Secretary, Ministry of Foreign Affairs, Sudan (1971); returned to Qatar on secondment; Secretary for External Relations in the sudanese Socialist Union (1974); member of the People's Assembly; Minister of Foreign Affairs (1975-77). **Addr.:** Khartoum, Sudan.

MAHJOUB (Mohamad), Iraqi politician. **Born** in 1938 at Samarra, Iraq. **Dipl.:** B.Sc. in Political Science. **Career:**

Teacher (six years); Member, Revolutionary Command Council Bureau (1968); Governor General of Diyala, Basra and Wasit (1969); Member of Baath Party Regional Command (January 1974); Chairman, Cultural Affairs Bureau; Revolutionary Command Council (RCC), Cultural Affairs Bureau; Member, Higher Committee for Northern Affairs; Minister of Education (November 1974); Member, RCC (September 1977); Minister of Education (16 June 1980-82). **Addr.:** Baghdad, Iraq.

MAHJOUB (Osman), Sudanese journalist and politician. **Born** in Sudan. **Educ.:** Secondary and Higher. **Career:** Journalist, Editor of "al-Ayyam" (daily 1953), Minister of Information in the Cabinet of Mr. Boubakr Awadallah (May 1969). **Addr.:** P.O.Box 363, Khartoum, Sudan.

MAHJOUBI (Mherdan), Moroccan politician. **Born** in Oulmes, Morocco in 1924. **Married. Educ.:** Military Academy, Meknes. **Career:** Captain in the French Army (1951-53); Commander of Oulmes (1951-53); Governor of Rabat after Independence; Founder and Secretary General of the Movement Populaire; Member of the National Council of the Resistance and of the Liberation Army; Minister of Defence (1961); elected Representative of Rabat at the Chamber of Counsellors (1963); Minister of Agriculture (1964); Minister of Defence (1966-67); elected Deputy for Khemissat (1970); Minister of State for Posts and Telecommunications (1977). **Publ.:** Poems publisher of al-Massira magazine. Held exhibitions of his work in Morocco, Algiers, Paris, Geneva and London. **Hobbies:** Painting and writing. **Addr.:** Rabat, Morocco.

MAHMAH (Mostepha, el), Moroccan journalist. **Born** in 1943 in Asilah, Morocco. **Son** of Abdeslam el-Mahmah (Trader) **and** Mrs. Fatima. **Educ.:** University Mohamad V, Rabat. **Dipl.:** Doctorate (3rd century); B.A. in Sociology. **Career:** Sociology; Editor in Chief, Revue al-Irchad. **Pub.:** "La Société d'Asilah et le Théâtre" (1975); "La Femme Marocaine et le Souffisme au 17ème siècle" (1975); "L'histoire du théâtre enfantine au Maroc" (1986); Asilah "Etude Historique et social"; Liaison du détroit de Gibraltar"; plus several social articles published in Moroccan and Arab magazines and newspapers. **Member:** Union of Moroccan Writers, Association of Moroccan Sociologists; ex-General Secretary of Moroccan Journalists's Association, Spanish language. **Sport:** Football. **Hobbies:** Writing and reading. **Prof. Addr.:** B.P. 4044, Hassan, Tel.: 632-10, Rabat, Morocco.

MAHMOUD (A.K. al-Nouri), Bank manager. **Educ.:** Kuwait University (1971). **Career:** Assistant General Manager, The Bank of Kuwait & the Middle East KSC (1971-78); Chairman and Managing Director, Kuwait Insulating Material Manufacturing Co. (1977-80); former, Managing Director, United Gulf Bank, Manama, Bahrain. **Addr.:** P.O.Box 5964, Tel.: 233789, Telex: 9556 BN, Manama, Bahrain.

MAHMOUD (Ali Hasan), Bahraini Businessman. **Born** in Bahrain on 21 March 1948. **Son** of late Hasan Mahmood (businessman). **Bachelor. Dipl.:** Started Secondary education in U.K.; Degree in Business Management, Higher Diploma in Business Management and Marketing (1972). **Career:** Joined family business in 1972 and worked in various departments until becoming the General Manager. **Work:** Administration of the entire group of companies and finance control. Languages: Arabic, English, French, some German and Italian. **Member:** Bahrain Chamber of Commerce and Industry. **Hobbies:** Boating, swimming, athletics. **Credit Cards:** American Express, Diner's Club. **Prof. Addr.:** P.O.Box 302, Tel.: 254303, Manama, Bahrain. **Priv. Addr.:** Tel.: 250567, Manama, Bahrain.

MAHMOUD (Fatima Abdel, Dr.), Sudanese former minister. **Born** in Khartoum (Sudan). **Married**, with Children. **Educ.:** Faculty of Medicine. **Dipl.:** M.D. (Public and Children Health); Diploma in Public Health Administration. **Career:** Deputy Minister for Youth, Sports and Social Affairs; Deputy Minister for Social Welfare; Member of the People's Assembly; of Sudanese Socialist Union (SSU) Central Commission; of SSU Youth Secretariat; of SSU Women Secretariat; Assistant Secretary General, Sudanese Council for Peace, Solidarity and Friendship; President, Mother and Child Committee, Khartoum Province; President of the Commission on the Status of Women. **Publ.:** "The Sudanese Women and the Land of Struggles", "Socio-Economic Status of Sudanese Women", "The Sudanese Women Through the Philosophy of President Gaafar Numeiri". **Hobbies:** Music and Writing. **Addr.:** Khartoum, Sudan.

MAHMOUD (Galal Eddine), Egyptian engineer. **Born** on December 19, 1927 in Cairo (Egypt). **Married** in 1977 to Shatilia Samia in Cairo. **Educ.:** Collège de la Sainte Famille, Heliopolis and Cairo (Egypt); Lycée Saint Louis, Paris; Faculty of Engineering, Cairo University. **Career:** Founder and General Manager, United National Engineering & Trading Company; Chairman, Board of Directors, The Flourescent & Electrical Industries; Board Delegate, Universal Piling Company. **Awards:** Paul Harris Fellow. **Clubs:** Rotary Club, Heliopolis, Cairo & Rotary International. **Prof. Addr.:** 1 Borsa el-Guedida street, Kasr el-Nil District, Tel.: 56865- 50485- 971265- 961983- 966596- 965217- 841761, Cairo. **Priv. Addr.:** 6, el-Nile street, Giza District and 2, Amosis street, Heliopolis, Tel.: 841761 & 965217, Cairo, Egypt.

MAHMOUD (Khalil, Othman), Sudanese businessman. **Born** in 1930 in Sudan. **Son** of Othman Mahmoud. **Educ.:** Veterinary Science in Egypt. **Career:** Sudanese Ministry of Animal Resources; financial and investment adviser, Kuwait; founder of leading "Gul" firm; owner of textile, glass, pharmaceutical and other factories in Sudan. **Addr.:** Gulf International (Sudan), P.O.Box 2316, Khartoum, Sudan.

MAHMOUD (Mahmoud Mohamed), Egyptian former Minister of Economy and Foreign Trade. **Born** on March 31, 1930. **Married,** has a son and a daughter. **Academic Degrees:** Bachelor of Commerce 1951, Cairo University; High Diploma in Taxes 1954, Cairo University. **Former recent Position:** Minister of Economy and Foreign Trade (14/10/1993). **Previous Positions:** 4/9/1951 Joined Bank Misr, Worked with different departments; 16/6/1965 appointed manager of Bank Misr, Benghazi Branch, Libya; 18/11/1967 Seconded to El Nahda El Arabia Bank, Libya; 13/3/1971 Returned back to Bank Misr, Cairo Branch; 1/7/1977 Seconded to Misr International Bank as Director and General Manager; 16/4/1983 resigned from Bank Misr; January 1984 Appointed Deputy Chairman and Managing Director, Misr International Bank; January 1986 Appointed Chairman, and Managing Director, Misr International Bank; 5/12/1987 Appointed Chairman, Bank Misr until 30/3/1990 when reached retirement age, besides being Chairman, Managing Director of Misr International Bank. **Other Information:** 1985 Appointed member in the Board of Directors and Member of the Executive Committee of Arab Italian Bank (UBAE) Rome, Italy; 1988 Appointed member of the Board of Directors of the Money Market Authority; 1989-1990 Chairman of the Banks' Association of Egypt; 24/6/1992 Appointed member of the shoura Council. Presently, Chairman, Export Development Bank of Egypt. **Special Honors:** 1987 Received the Decoration of Merit, First Class. **Prof. Addr.:** Export Development Bank of Egypt, Evergreen Bldg., 10 Sharia Talaat Harb, Cairo, Egypt.

MAHMOUD (Mohamad, Hamid), Egyptian politician. **Born** in 1926 in Egypt. **Son** of Hamid Mahmoud. **Married,** two children. **Educ.:** Law. **Career:** Elected to National Assembly (1957); Secretary of the National Assembly (1960): Legal Adviser to Shaikh Abdullah al Sabah of Kuwait, Arab Socialist Union, and secretary to same for Buheira (1971); Assistant for Lower Egypt Affairs to Sayed Ahmed Marei; Governor of Giza (1973-74); Minister of State fo Local Government and Popular Organisations (1974); Minister of State for Local Government, Youth, Popular and Political Organisations (1976). **Addr.:** Cairo, Egypt.

MAHMOUD (Mohamad, Saleh), Iraqi physician and politician. **Born** in Iraq. **Son** of Saleh Mahmoud. **Educ.:** Secondary and Higher. **Dipl.:** Doctor of Medicine. **Career:** Physician, and former Minister of Health. **Addr.:** Haibat Khatoun, 21-13, Baghdad, Iraq.

MAHMOUD (Muhammad Ihab, Ibrahim), Egyptian economist. **Born** in 1934. **Married** two sons. **Educ.:** Ain Shams University, Cairo; African Planning Institute, Dakar, Senegal. **Dipl.:** B.A. (in Commerce); diploma in Economic Planning Development. **Career:** in the Ministry of Finance, Egypt (1962); Budget Administration Director, United Arab Emirates Ministry of Finance and Industry, Abu Dhabi. **Member:** al-Ahli Club; Gezira Club; al-Shams Club, Cairo. **Hobbies:** Tennis, swimming. **Prof. Addr.:** P.O.Box 3126, Tel.: 43838, Abu Dhabi, United Arab Emirates.

MAHMOUD (Talaat), Egyptian engineer, former faculty dean, managing director. **Born** in Egypt. **Educ.:** Secondary and Cairo University. **Dipl.:** Doctor of Engineering. **Career:** Managing Director Misr Concrete Development Company; Former Dean Faculty of Engineering, Aïn Shams University. **Addr.:** 35, Ahmad Hishmat Street, Zamalek, Tel.: 806677, Cairo, Egypt.

MAHROOS (Ali, Ebrahim, al), Bahraini current Minister and former diplomat. **Born** in 1942 in Manama, Bahrain. **Son** of Ibrahim al-Mahroos. **Married:,** Four children. **Educ.:** B.Comm Damascus University, Syria; M.A. in Political Science, Lebanese University Lebanon. **Career:** Ministry of Education (1965-68); 3rd Secretary, Ministry of Foreign Affairs (1968-70); 1st Secretary, Director of the Office of the Minister of Foreign Affairs (1970-72); Director of Administrative and Financial Department, Ministry of Foreign Affairs (1972-74); Bahrain's Ambassador to Lebanon (1974-76); Bahrain's Ambassador to UK and Denmark (1976-80); Director of Political Department, Ministry of Foreign Affairs (1980-91); Member of the Board of Directors, Bahrain Petroleum Company (Bapco) (1980-91); Bahrain's Ambassador to France, stationed in Paris and accredited to Belgium and Spain, and Permanent Representative of the State of Bahrain to U.N.E.S.-C.O. (1991-1995); Secretary-General of the Council of Ministers in the Ministry of Cabinet Affairs and Information, State of Bahrain (1995-99); Minister of Works and Agriculture (1999 to date). **Prof. Addr.:** Ministry of Works and Agriculture, P.O.Box 5, Manama, Bahrain.

MAHRUG (Smail), Algerian economist. **Born** in 1926 in Algeria. **Married. Educ.:** University of Paris. **Career:** Director of the National Committee for Technical Planning, Algeria (1962); Technical Counsellor for Economic Affairs at the Presidency; Director General of Finance under the President (1964); member of the Board of Société Nationale de Recherche et d'Exploitation des Pétroles en Algérie; Minister of Finance (1970-76); Chairman, Group of 24, International Monetary Fund (1974); Chairman, Union Méditérranéenne de Banques, Paris (1977-83). **Addr.:** Algiers, Algeria.

MAHSAS (Ahmad, Ali), Algerian politician. **Born** in 1925 in Algeria. **Son** of Ali Mahsas. **Career:** Joined National Liberation Movement (1947); Minister of Agriculture and Agrarian Reform in September 1964; Member of Political Bureau of F.L.N. (Front de Libération Nationale) (1964), Member of the Revolutionary Command Council (July 1965-66), Member of the O.C.R.A. (1966). **Addr.:** Algiers, Algeria.

MAHSHIE (George, T.), Arab American lawyer. **Born** in Syracuse, New York 1926. **Educ.:** Syracuse University. **Dipl.:** B.A. in Liberal Arts College; L.B. Syracuse University Law College. **Career:** Practiced law in New York State Courts, Federal Courts, United States Supreme Court and various governmental agencies. President Mahshie Realty; Former Member of the Board of Directors of the National Association of Arab Americans; former Vice President and Member of the Board of Trustees of the United Holy Fund; former Member of the Board of Trustees of the Antiochian Orthodox Christian Archdiocese of New York and all North America. **Priv. Addr.:** 313 Wedgewood Terrace, Dewitt, New York 13214, USA. **Prof. Addr.:** 731 James st., Syracuse New York 13203 USA.

MAIMANEE (Abdullatif, A. al), Saudi civil servant and leading columnist. **Born** in 1939 in Jeddah, Kingdom of Saudi Arabia. **Dipl.:** B.A. (Political Science), Cairo University, M.A. (International Economy), American University, Washington D.C. **Editor-in-Chief:** English Daily "Saudi Gazette". **Career:** Attaché, Ministry of Foreign Affairs, Saudi Embassy, Tokyo, Japan; Third Secretary, Saudi Embassy, Washington D.C., U.S.A.; member of Saudi Economic Joint Committee; attended seventh UN special session; member of fourth UN Trade and Development Conference Counsellor: Permanent Mission of Saudi Arabia to U.N. European Office, Geneva, Switzerland; Minister Plenipotentiary and Director General Economic Department, Ministry of Foreign Affairs, Riyadh, K.S.A.; Ambassador Extraordinary and Plenipotentiary of the Kingdom of Saudi Arabia to the People's Republic of Bangladeh on November 12, 1984 and Dean of the Diplomatic Corps in October 1989; Appointed Ambassador of Saudi Arabia to the Islamic Republic of Iran. **Publications:** Arab Oil In World Politics (M.A. thesis); Who pulls sun (Novel) contributes regularly to Okaz daily newspaper; has a weekly column in the same paper. **Hobbies:** reading, tourism, Fishing and Music. **Prof. Addr.:** Ministry of Foreign Affairs, Jeddah, Saudi Arabia.

MAJALI (Abdel Salam, Attalah, Dr.), Prime Minister and Minister of Defence. **Born** in 1925 in Karak, Jordan. **Son** of Attalah Majali **and** Mrs. Khadijah Surouji. **Married** on February 18, 1956 to Joan Mary Lachlan, London (UK), 3 children: Samer, Susan, Shadi Ramsey. **Educ.:** Karak Primary School; Salth Secondary School; Faculty of Medicine, Damascus University. **Dipl.:** M.D., Diploma of Laryngology and Otology; Honorary Doctorate, Hacettepe University, Ankara (Turkey); Fellow of the American College of Surgeons since 1961. **Career:** Medical Officer, Jordanian Armed Forces (1948-50); Commanding Officer and ENT Consultant, Base Hospital, Jordanian Armed Forces, Amman (1953-59); Director, Royal Medical Services (1960-69); Minister of Health (1971); President, University of Jordan, Amman (1971-76); Professor, Faculty of Medicine, University of Jordan (since 1973); Minister of Education and Minister of State for Prime Ministry Affairs (1976-79); President, University of Jordan (1980); Prime Minister (May 1993-Jan. 1995); reappointed Prime Minister and Minister of Defence (March 1997-). **Awards:** Medal of Jordan Independence; Jordan Star; Medal, St. John of Jerusalem; Medal of Long Loyal Services, Royal Military Forces; Distinctive Medal of Education. **Member:** Jordan Medical Association; Military Surgeons of America (Associate Member); Member, National Guidance Council (1980); Vice-Chairman, Board of Trustees, University of Jordan; Member, Royal Commission, Mu'ta University; Member, University Council, U.N. University (Tokyo) since 1977; Chairman of the Board, Jordanian World Affairs Council since 1980; Expert Advisory Panel on Health Manpower Development, WHO. **Priv. Addr.:** P.O.Box 913, Tel.: 812341, Amman, Jordan.

MAJALI (Abdulwahab, al), Jordanian politician. **Born** in Jordan. **Educ.:** Secondary and Higher. **Career:** Politician; Deputy; Minister of Interior and Minister of State for Prime Minister (1965-66); Elected Deputy for Amman (1967); Minister of Finance and Minister of State in the Cabinet of Mr. Saad Joumaa (April 1967- December 1968). **Addr.:** Amman, Jordan.

MAJALI (Habès, al), Jordanian army officer. **Born** in 1914 in Karak, Jordan. **Educ.:** Secondary and Military Academy. **Career:** Army Service, Promoted General then Marshal, Former Commander in Chief of the Jordanian Armed Forces (1965-67); Minister of Defence (October 1967-68); Senator (1967); Chief Master of Ceremonies to HM King Hussain of Jordan; Commander-in-Chief of the Jordanian Armed Forces and General Military Governor (Sept. 1970); Minister of the Royal Court (1976). **Awards:** Renaissance Medal, 1st Class; Independence Medal; Iraq Rafidain Medal; Syrian Medal of Merit; other Foreign and Arab decorations. **Addr.:** Shmaissani, Tel.: 67475, Amman, Jordan.

MAJALI (Nasouh, Salem), Jordanian former minister. **Born** in 1942 in Irbid, Jordan. **Son** of Salem Majali. **Married,** four children. **Educ.:** Lebanese University, Beirut, Lebanon. **Dipl.:** B.A. in English Literature. **Career:** Instructor, Royal Military Academy (1965-73); Director General, Jordan News Agency (1973-77); Jordan Hashimite Broadcasting Agency (1977-85); Radio and Television Corp. (1986); Chairman of Al Shab daily newspaper (1984-85); Minister of Information (27 April 1989- Oct. 1989). **Medals:** Medal of Independence, first order. **Sport:** Tennis. **Hobbies:** Reading, Music. **Addr.:** Amman, Jordan.

MAJALI (Rakan, Mohamad), Jordanian politician. **Born** in 1943 in Jordan. **Son** of Mohamad Majali. **Married,** four children. **Educ.:** Damascus University. **Dipl.:** LL.B. **Career:** Director, Editorial Board, al-Raie newspaper (1971-74); Editor in Chief, Akhbar Newspaper (1974-81); Chief of Jordanian Journalists (1977-81); Deputy Chairman, Union of Arab Journalists (since 1978); presently President, Jordan Press Association, and Editor al-Akhbar, ar-Rai and Jordan Times Newspapers. **Hobbies:** Reading. **Addr.:** P.O.Box 6788, Hai al-Madena el-Riyadhia, Amman, Jordan.

MAKARI (Samir, Raid), Egyptian economist. **Born** in 1942 in Assuit, Egypt. **Son** of Raid Makar. **Married,** two children. **Educ.:** Strathelyde University, UK; Leicester University. **Dipl.:** M.Sc. in Economics, Ph.D. in Economics. **Career:** Assistant Professor, Helwan University (since 1984); Assistant Professor, American University of Cairo AUC (since 1984). **Publ.:** The Stock Exchange; Economic Theory. **Prof. Addr.:** 9 Sebaueh el-Masry Street, Nas City, Cairo, Egypt. **Priv. Addr.:** 10 el-Kamel Mohamed, Zamalek, Cairo, Egypt.

MAKDAMI (Hussein, Abdallah, al), Yemeni politician. **Born** in Beni al-Harith, Yemen in 1927. **Son** of Abdallah Makdami. **Married,** five children. **Educ.:** Teachers' Institute. **Career:** Director of Hodeida Hospital (1953-61); Deputy Minister of Health (1963-65); Minister of Education (1975-80); former Secretary General of the Supreme Committee for Financial and Administrative Correction. **Medals:** Order of the Republic of Egypt. **Hobbies:** Hunting, farming, reading literature and Yemen poetry. **Addr.:** Sanaa, Republic of Yemen.

MAKDISI (Faiz), Syrian financial manager. **Born** in 1948 in Syria. **Son** of Ghattas Makdisi. **Married** in 1977, 1 son. **Dipl.:** Ph.D.; M.B.A. (Finance). **Career:** Technical Adviser, Abu Dhabi Fund (1977-81); Senior Project Manager, Abu Dhabi Fund, Dubai (1982-). **Member:** Syrian Order of Engineers; al-Nasr. **Hobby:** Bridge. **Addr.:** P.O.Box 3501, Tel.: 473320, Telex: 47878 A/B SHUAA EM, Dubai, UAE.

MAKDISI (George), Arab-American academic. **Born** in 1920 in Detroit, Michigan, USA. **Married,** six children. **Educ.:** University of Michigan; Georgetown University, Washington DC; Princeton University, Sorbonne, University of Paris. **Dipl.:** B.A., B.Sc., Docteur ès-Lettres, M.A. **Career:** Assistant Professor of Near Eastern Studies, University of Michigan (1957-59); then Associate Professor; Lecturer in Semitic Languages, Harvard University (1959-61); Associate Professor of Arabic, (1961-63), and Professor (1963-73); Harvard University; Chaire d'Etat, College de France, Paris; Professor of Arabic and Islamic Studies, University of Pennsylvania, USA (since 1973); Visiting Professor, University of Paris, Sorbonne (1978-79); Directeur d'Etudes, Ecole Pratique des Hautes Etudes, Paris (1981-82); Director, Center for the Study of Byzantium, Islam and the Latin West, University of Pennsylvania (since 1979); Chairman of the Department of Oriental Studies, University of Pennsylvania (1975-78). **Publ.:** The Rise of Colleges (1981); The Rise of Humanism (1989), and Many books and numerous articles in Professional Journals. **Sports:** Walking, hiking. **Hobbies:** gardening, cooking, classical music, reading, museums. **Prof. Addr.:** 841 Oriental Studies Dept. Williams Hall, University of Pennsylvania, USA.

MAKHLOUF (Mahmoud Hassanain), Egyptian attorney and legal adviser. **Born** in Tanta. **Married** to Miss Wadad A. as-Sidfy. **Educ.:** Faculty of Law (Cairo University). **Dipl.:** LL.B. **Career:** Formely Prosecuting Advocate, State Legal Development and Assistant Director, Government Taxes, Attorney and Legal Adviser, Sahara Petroleum Co. in Egypt, Colorado Petroleum Corporation in Tunis, Libya, Middle East and Arabian Gulf, General American Oil Co. in Egypt, Geophysical Service International in Middle East. **Member:** Gezira Sporting Club, National Sporting Club. **Addr.:** 3, al-Aziz Osmane Street, Zamalek, Tel.: 800160, Cairo, Egypt.

MAKKAWI (Amal Abbas, al), Egyptian broadcasting official. **Born** in 1932 in Egypt. **Son** of Abbas Makkawi. **Married,** three children. **Educ.:** Cairo University, Egypt. **Dipl.:** LL.B.; M.A. (Information in Radio and Television). **Career:** General Manager of Cultural Programmes, Egyptian television, then Head of Channel One; board member, High Council of Universities, Union of Women University Graduates and the Simplification of Sciences Organisation of Cairo University. **Publ.:** Cultural Broadcasting in the Arab World; Adult Education as Part of the Educational System in Developing Countries. **Medals:** Minia University Order of Merit; Ministry of Information Merit Award. **Member** of Yacht Club, Cairo Shooting Club, Riding Club. **Sports:** Swimming, squash. **Addr.:** 19 Ahmad Arabi Street, al-Mohandiseen, Cairo, Egypt.

MAKKAWI (Makkawi, Awad, al), Sudanese lawyer. **Son** of Awad Makkawi. **Born** in 1944 in Omdurman, Khartoum, Sudan. **Educ.:** University of Khartoum, Sudan. **Dipl.:** LL.B. **Career:** Member of the Board, Sudanese Council for Friendship, Solidarity and Peace; Secretary General, UN Association of Sudan; Solicitor and Barrister, Sudan; Programme Assistant UNDP, Sudan; member, Executive Committee, World Federation of United Nations Association, Sudan; member of Advancement of Science Society, Sudan, Sudan Law Society Preparatory Committee. **Publ.:** The Role of Law in the Control of the Human Environment (1972); Economic and Social Problems and Environmental Issue (1973). **Sports:** Tennis, table tennis. **Hobbies:** Law, development, international affairs. **Addr.:** WFUNA, P.O.Box 913, el-Gamaa Ave., Khartoum, Sudan.

MAKKI (Ahmad Abd Nabi), Omani minister. **Born** on December 17, 1939 in Muscat, Oman. **Married** in 1970 to Piedad Macki, 2 children: Dina (1971) and Sami (1974). **Educ.:** High Institute, Cairo (Egypt) (1961-65); Faculty of Commerce, Cairo University. **Dipl.:** B.Com., B.Sc. (Economics). **Career:** Director of Offices, Prime Minister and

Minister of Foreign Affairs (1970-71); First Permanent Representative of Oman to U.N. (1971-72); Under-Secretary, Minister of Foreign Affairs (1972-73); Permanent Representative to U.N. (1973-75); Ambassador to U.S.A. (1973-75); Ambassador to U.S.A. (1973-77); Non-Resident Ambassador to Canada (1974-77), to Argentina (1975-77); Ambassador to France (October 1977); non-Resident Ambassador to Belgium (November 1978), to Spain (December 1978), to Portugal (April 1980); Permanent Delegate to UNESCO (November 1977); Head of Mission to EEC (March 1980); Under Secretary of Commerce and Industry (1982); Minister for Civil Service (1996); Presently Minister of National Economy. **Awards:** Medal of Merit, 2nd Class (Egypt). **Hobby:** Reading. **Addr.:** P.O.Box 506, Muscat 113, Oman.

MAKKI (Hassan Mohamad, Dr.), Yemeni Politician. **Born** on December 22, 1933 in Hodeida, Yemen Arab Republic. **Married. Educ.:** University of Rome, Italy (1953-56); University of Bologna, Italy (1960). **Dipl.:** Doctorate in Economics (1960). **Career:** Adviser, Ministry of Economy (1960-62); Deputy-Minister of Economy; Chairman, Yemen Bank for Reconstruction and Development, Sanaa; Minister of Economy (1963-64); Minister of Communications (1965); Minister of Foreign Affairs (1964, 1966), (1967-68); Ambassador to Italy (1968-70); Ambassador to the Federal Republic of Germany (1970-72); Deputy Prime-Minister for Economic and Financial Affairs (1972-74); Prime-Minister (February-June 1974); Deputy Prime Minister for Economic and Financial Affairs (June-October 1974); Permanent Representative to the UN with Rank of Ambassador, New-York, USA (1974-75); President of the Sanaa University (December 1975-76); Ambassador to Italy (1976-79); Minister of Foreign Affairs (1979-80); Deputy Prime Minister for Economic Affairs (1980-84); Deputy Prime Minister (since 1986- May 1990); first Deputy Prime Minister of the Republic of Yemen (May 1990 to 1994). **Member:** National Council for Peace and Solidarity, Sanaa, YAR. **Addr.:** Sanaa, Yemen Arab Republic.

MAKKI (Hatem, al), Tunisian artist painter. **Born** in 1918 in Djakarta (Indonesia). **Educ.:** Secondary and Higher. **Career:** Artist Painter, Contributed to several Art Exhibitions in France (1947-48), U.S.A., China, Tunisia, Italy, Sweden, England, Denmark, Egypt, Japan and Holland. **Works:** "Tableau de Famille" (Family Gathering). **Addr.:** Tunis, Tunisia.

MAKKI (Mohamad Ali Hussein), Saudi Civil Servant. **Born** in 1931 in Mecca, Saudi Arabia. **Dipl.:** B.A. (Agriculture). **Career:** Director of Al Kharji Agricultural School; Director of Kharj Agricultural Department; Agricultural Guidance Department; Adviser to Ministry of Agriculture and Water; member of Board of Industrial Development and Research Centre, Saudi Standardization Organization; Director General, Secretarial Department, Ministry of Agriculture and Water; attended several FAO conferences abroad. **Address:** Ministry of Agriculture and Water, Tel.: 4012777, Riyadh, Saudi Arabia.

MAKKI (Munir), Omani Ambassador in France. **Born** on March 28, 1954 in Muscat, Oman. **Son** of Abdulnabi Makki (Businessman) **and** Mrs. née Khadija Al Jamali. **Married** on April 14, 1982 to Miss Amal Al Asfoor, 5 children: Ali, Amaal, Fatima, Mohammed, Faris. **Educ.:** Saidiya Primary School in Muscat, Canford School in Wimborne (U.K.), American University of Washington, New York University (U.S.A.), Université de Paris Sorbonne. **Dipl.:** Licence ès Political Sciences, Master of Arts in International Relations, Higher Studies on Contemporary History. **Career:** 2nd Secretary, Ministry of Foreign Affairs (1977); Permanent Delegation of Oman to the United Nations, New York (1979); 1st Secretary (1980), at the Ministgry of Foreign Affairs (1983); Counsellor Embassy, Chargé d'Affaires in Austria and Permanent Representative of Oman at the United Nations Organization in Vienna (1984-87); Minister Plenipotentiary (1987); Ambassador in France (since 1987); Ambassador in Belgium, Spain and Portugal at the European Community, Tchad, Senegal and Ivory Coast (since 1988). **Awards:** Numan order (Oman), Commander, Legion of Honour (France). **Hobbies:** Reading, Travelling. **Sports Practiced:** Tennis, Swimming. **Prof. Addr.:** Embassy of Sultanate of Oman, 50 Av. d'Iéna, 75116 Paris, France. **Priv. Addr.:** 1 Av. du Marechal Maunoury, 75016 Paris, France.

MAKKIYAH (Mohamed Saleh Aziz), Iraqi architect. **Born** in Baghdad in 1917. **Married,** two children. **Educ.:** Liverpool School of Architecture, UK, Cambridge University. **Dipl.:** Ph.D. **Career:** Founder and Principal, Baghdad School of Architecture (1959-71); principal in private practice todate with own offices set up in Baghdad, Bahrain, Muscat, London, Doha, UAE. Several memberships of societies at institutes in the UK, Baghdad, Athens and USA. **Notable projects:** Planning of the Historic City of Muscat; Ministry of Finance Muscat; Majlis and Office of HE the HEIR Apparent, Bahrain, Sheikh Mohamed Ben Mubarak Bldg., Bahrain etc. **Medals:** Various architectural competition awards, including Kuwait State Mosque First Prize, Retail Market Dubai, First Prize. **Addr.:** 26 Westbourne Grove, London W2, UK.

MAKKIYAH (Taher, Darwish), Jordanian executive. **Born** in 1949 in Jerusalem, Palestine. **Son** of Darwish Makkiyah. **Single. Educ.:** St. Georges School, Jerusalem, High School Diploma (1967); Birzeit College, West Bank Associated Degree (1969); American University of Beirut, B.B.A. (1972); Tulane University, New Orleans, Louisiana, M.B.A. (1974). **Career:** Trainee Manager, Manufacturers Hanover Trust Company (1974). Credit Officer (Assistant Secretary) 1976; Vice President and Branch Manager, Manufacturers Hanover Trust, Bahrain (1979-85). **Member:** Council Member and Treasurer of the

Bahrain Bankers Society. **Hobby:** Sports. **Addr.:** P.O.Box 5471, Tel.: 254375, 254353, Telex: 8556 A/B MHTBN, Manama, Bahrain.

MAKOSHI (Abdallah A., al), Saudi academic. **Born** on 15 March 1944 at Qassim, Saudi Arabia. **Dipl.:** B.A. (Mathematics); M.A. (Mathematics); Ph.D. (Curiculum and Methods of Teaching Mathematics). **Career:** Lecturer, Faculty of Education, King Saud University (1973-74); member of the National Society for the Development of the Committee for the Study and Analysis of Mathematics Books for Elementary and Secondary Schools, Ministry of Education; Assistant Professor and Chairman, Curriculum and Instruction Department, Faculty of Education, King Saud University. **Member:** the National Council of Teachers of Mathematics, U.S.A. (NCTM), Phi Delta Kappa, American Educational Research Association. **Publications:** Methods of teaching Mathematics (in two volumes) and a book on Arithmetic and Algebra. **Prof. Addr.:** P.O.Box 3330, Tel.: 4024700 Ext. 227, Riyadh. **Priv. Addr.:** Tel.: 4811000 Ext. 2051, Riyadh, Saudi Arabia.

MAKTOUM (Ahmad Bin Rashid Bin Said, al, Shaikh), United Arab Emirates former Defence Minister. **Born** in 1950. **Fourth Son of** Shaikh Rashid bin Said al-Maktoum, Ruler of Dubai. **Educ.:** Military in the UK, Mons Officer Cadet Training College (September 1972). **Career:** Colonel in Chief, Dubai Defence Force; former Minister of Defence, Dubai; Chairman, Emirates Airlines. **Sports:** Hunting, Motoring and Shooting. **Addr.:** Emirates Airlines, P.O.Box 686, Dubai, United Arab Emirates.

MAKTOUM (Hamdan Bin Rashid, al, Shaikh), United Arab Emirates Politician. **Born** in 1945. **Second son of** Shaikh Rashid al-Maktoum. **Career:** Deputy Prime Minister, United Arab Emirates (December 1971- December 1973); President, Dubai Municipal Council and Governing Board of Rashid Port, Dubai (1973); Chairman, Dubai Aluminium Co., Dubai; UAE Representative at IMF, OPEC and to Arab States; Chairman, United Arab Emirates Currency Board, Abu Dhabi (1973-80); Governor, Islamic Development Bank, Jeddah; United Arab Emirates Minister of Finance and Industry (1973-). **Hobbies:** Hunting. **Addr.:** Ministry of Finance, P.O.Box 433, Abu Dhabi, United Arab Emirates.

MAKTOUM (Hasher Maktoum Juma'a, al, Shaikh), United Arab Emirates official. **Born** on September 14, 1945 in Dubai. **Son** of Maktoum Juma'a al-Maktoum (deceased) **and** Sheikha Sa'eed al-Maktoum. **Married** in 1972 in Dubai to Ameena Humaid Matar al-Tayer, Five children: Maryam (July 26, 1973), Maktoum (March 12, 1977), Maitha (July 2, 1980), Wafa (August 4, 1982), Saeed (August 4, 1982). **Educ.:** UAE School, Training Courses in BBC TV, Times of London, Central Office of Information as Government Press Officer, Diploma in Marketing & Promotion. **Career:** Director of Dubai Information at Dubai Municpality; Editor-in-Chief of Akhbar Dubai (Dubai News); UAE Ambassador to Iran (1973 to 1976); Director of Dubai Information Department (1979 till now); Director General & Editor-in-Chief (Incharge) al-Bayan Newspaper (1980 till now); President and Owner Al Ahmadia Contracting and Trading. **Sports:** Tennis, table tennis, martial arts, jogging, and swimming. **Hobbies:** Tennis and reading. **Member:** President, UAE Tennis Association, Dubai; President, World Trade Club, Dubai; President, UAE Chivalry Union, Dubai. **Prof. Addr.:** P.O.Box 1695, Tel.: 370255, Dubai, United Arab Emirates, and al-Bayan Press, Printing & Publishing Est., P.O.Box 2710 and P.O.Box 2596, Dubai, United Arab Emirates.

MAKTOUM (Maktoum Bin Rashid, al, Shaikh), Ruler of Dubai and Vice-President and prime-minister of the United Arab Emirates. **Born** in 1940. **First son of** HH Shaikh Rashid al-Maktoum. **Married** in 1971. **Career:** Deputy Ruler of Dubai and Ruler of Dubai as from October 1990 and Vice-President and Prime-Minister of the United Arab Emirates. **Addr.:** Minister's Office, P.O.Box 831, Abu Dhabi, United Arab Emirates.

MAKTOUM (Mohamad Bin Hasher, al, Shaikh), United Arab Emirates judge. **Born** in 1925. **Son** of Hasher al-Maktoum. **Career:** Superviser of the Law Courts for several years; Chairman of the Law Courts, Dubai, **Addr.:** The Law Courts P.O.B. 4700, Tel.: 224935, Dubai, United Arab Emirates.

MAKTOUM (Mohamad Bin Rashid Bin Said, al, Shaikh), United Arab Emirates politican. **Born** in 1946. **Third son of** Shaikh Rashid al-Maktoum. **Educ.:** Mons Officer Cadet Training College, UK. **Career:** Director of Police and Public Security, Dubai; United Arab Emirates Minister of Defence. (since 1986 to date). **Hobbies:** Flying Hunting. **Addr.:** Ministry of Defence, Minister's Office, P.O.Box 2838, Dubai, United Arab Emirates.

MALAIKA (Jamil), Iraqi engineer, professor and faculty dean. **Born** in 1921 in Baghdad. **Educ.:** American University of Beirut, University of California, State University of Iowa (U.S.A). **Dipl.:** Bachelor of Arts, B.Sc. (in Engineering Honours), Master of Science in Irrigation, Doctor of Philosophy. **Career:** Professor and Head, Civil Engineering; Department, College of Engineering; Member of American Society of Civil Engineers, Member of International Association of Hydraulic Research, Member of American Society for the Promotion of Scientific Research. **Member of:** the Alumni Club, Iraqi-American Club. **Hobbies:** Tennis and swimming. **Addr.:** P.O.Box 171, Baghdad, Iraq.

MALAIKA (Nazik, al), Iraqi poet. **Born** in 1923 in Baghdad, Iraq. **Educ.:** Arabic Literature, Teachers' Training College, Baghdad. **Career:** Pioneer of modern Arabic poetry; Lecturer, Mosul University, Iraq. **Publ.:** "Ashiqat al-Layl" (1947); "Shazaya wa Ramad" (1949); "Qararat al-Mawja" (1957); also Literature studies and works of criticism in which she defines the nature of the new form adopted in contemporary poetry. **Prof. Addr.:** University of Mosul, Mosul, Iraq.

MALAIKA (Siraj Saleh), Saudi professor of surgery. **Born** in Mecca in 1930. **Educ.:** M.D., F.A.C.S., American Board of Surgery (General Surgery). **Career:** Consultant Surgeon, King Saud University Hospital; Professor of Surgery, Faculty of Medicine, King Saud University. **Member:** Fellow of American College of Surgeons (FACS) and fellow of Association of Surgeons of Great Britain and Ireland; attended the Conference on Cancer, Copengahen, 1968, World Health Organization (WHO) Conference, Boston, U.S.A., 1969, several conferences of the American College of Surgeons and the International College of Surgeons. **Honour:** Order of Merit granted by the late Shah of Iran. **Publications:** Books: al-Is'afat al-Awwali'yah (First Aid), al-Tamreedh al-Fanni Fi Ghorfat al-Amaliyyat (Professional Nursing in the Operating Room), Human Echinococcosis in Saudi Arabia (1981); Volvulus of the Stomach (1982); Experience and Results of the Surgical Treatment for Duodenal Ulcer Disease in Saudi Arabia; Common Bile Duct Infection, Cholangitis and their Relationship to Postoperative Complications; Cryohaemorrhoidectomy; proceedings of the 5th Saudi Medical Meeting (1980); Traumatic External Pancreatic Fistula, Saudi Medical Journal (1980). **Hobby:** swimming. **Address:** P.O.Box 2925, Riyadh, Saudi Arabia.

MALAK (Mohamad Ali), Saudi Academic. **Born** in 1941 at Hail, Saudi Arabia, **Dipl.:** Ph.D.; Ed.D. (in Mathematics Education). **Career:** Elementary School teacher (1954-55); School District employee (1955-62); secondary school teacher (1969-70); teaching staff member, King Saud University (1976-81); member of the Faculty of Education and Assistant Dean, Admission and Registration, King Saud University. **Member:** National Council of Teachers of Mathematics, U.S.A.; Committee for the Evaluation of Mathematics Curriculum, Ministry of Education. **Publications:** various articles and research papers (in Arabic). **Address:** Admission and Registration, King Saud University, Tel.: 4811000 Ext. 2111, Riyadh, Saudi Arabia.

MALAMI (Yahya Abdallah, al), Saudi official, **Born** 1929. **Dipl.:** M.A. (Police Administration). **Career:** Police Officer in Abha; Chief of Police in Qangharah: Chief of Police in Yanbu; District-Chief, Mecca; Director of the Riyadh Police Administration; Head of Criminal Investigations, Riyadh; Director of the Security Service Cultural Office, of the Traffic Administration, of the Police Emergency Service, of the Services Administration, of the Criminal Offences Department; now-General Director of the Prisons General Administration; attended International Association of Police Organizations Conference (Vienna 1956), International Traffic Conference (Paris, 1965), International Traffic Conference (Morocco, 1968); UN Traffic Regulations Conference (1968), International Conference on Road Accidents (Kyoto 1969); International Conference for Road Safety (Paris 1971), International Conference of Policies Chiefs (1974), International Conference for combating Narcotics (Toronto 1974), Sixth Regional Conference for Combating Narcotics (Riyadh 1974), Arab League Treatment of Offenders Preparatory Conference (1973), Arab Chiefs of Police Conferences (1974, 1975); Fifth UN Conference on the Treatment of Convicts (Toronto 1975). **Publ.:** Security and Society, Security and Planning (forthcoming), Road Manners (forthcoming). **Sport:** Swimming. **Hobby:** Reading. **Prof. Addr.:** Almalz, Tel.: 27248 Riyadh. **Priv. Addr.:** Tel.: 62904, Riyadh, Saudi Arabia.

MALHAS (Abdul Rahim, Dr.), Jordanian Surgeon. **Born** on June 28, 1937. **Son** of Qasim Malhas (Surgeon) **and** Mrs. Suad Jude. **Married** in 1977 in Amman to Rosa Madi, 2 children: Shadeer (1978), Haneen (1980). **Educ.:** American University of Beirut. **Dipl.:** BSc. (1959); M.D. (1963). **Career:** Surgeon; Minister of Health, Jordan (1993-1994). **Other Information:** Taekown-Do Black Belt Dan 1 Certificate of Computer programming in Basic. **Hobbies:** Sports, reading, computers. **Prof. Addr.:** Malhas Hospital, P.O.Box 984, Tel.: 636140, Amman, Jordan. **Priv. Addr.:** P.O.Box 20, Tel.: 817589, Amman, Jordan.

MALHIS (Ramez, M.), Jordanian chemical engineer. **Born** in Jordan in 1925. **Son** of Masoud Malhis **and** Mrs. Bahiyah Bishawi. **Married** to Aida Shaker in 1960, five children. **Educ.:** Louisiana State University, Baton rouge, Louisiana, U.S.A. **Dipl.:** B.Sc. in Chemical Engineering (1957). **Career:** Palestine Government employee (1945-48); Aramco Oil Accounts (1949-52); Cities Service Oil Co., USA Refinery Engineer (1957-60); Jordan Petroleum Co. Refinery Management (1960). Also Board member in following Jordanian Companies: Jordan Petroleum Refinery Co.; Intermediate Petrochemical Industries Co.; Jordan Polymers Co.; Union Explosivos Rio Tinto - Middle East Co. Member of the following honour societies: Tau Beta pi (Engineering); Phi Lambda Upsilon (Chemistry); Phi Mu Epsilon (Mathematics); Phi Kappa Phi (Honorary Scholastic). **Sport:** Swimming. **Hobby:** Reading. **Credit Cards:** American Express. **Prof. Addr.:** P.O.Box 176, Zerka, Jordan. **Priv. Addr.:** Refinery Residence, Zerka, Tel. 630716, Jordan.

MALHOOQ (Abdallah Ibn Abdul Rahman, al), Saudi diplomat. **Born** in Riyadh in 1927. **Educ.:** B.A. Faculty of Dar el-Oloum Cairo, Egypt. **Career:** General Superintendent, Aramco Schools (1945); Director of Administration, Dhahran Emirate (1947); Chief, Press and Publicity Bureau, Saudi Arabian Royal Embassy, Beirut (1955); Director, Oriental Department, Ministry of Foreign Affairs

(1959); Director, Arab Department, (1960); Counsellor, Saudi Embassy, Beirut (1961); Minister Plenipotentiary (1966); Ambassador to Sudan (1968); Ambassador to Algeria (1980); Presently Ambassador to the Hellenic Republic, Greece; former Chairman of al-Khott Company for Printing, Publishing and Translation; former Editor-in-Chief of Akhbar al-Dhahran (Dhahran News) newspaper (1952-54), former member of Lebanese Political Science Society; attended several Arab League meetings including those of the Committee on the Amendment of the Charter of the Arab League (1960-61); the Arab Foreign Ministers Conference, Baghdad (1961) the Arab Information Permanent Committee Meetings, Shtura (1962) UNESCO Meeting, Beirut (1964), the Saudi Heads of Diplomatic Missions Meetings, Jeddah (1973) and the Algerian festivities marking the 20th anniversary of Algeria's Independence (1974); member, the Saudi delegation of the Arab Summit conference (Saudi Arabia, Egypt, Syria and Algeria) in Algeria (1974) the Islamic Thought Congress Meeting, Algiers (1974), the Islamic International Conference, London (1976) and the Saudi Heads of Diplomatic Missions of Europe Meeting, Geneva (1981). **Honours:** Commander of Order of Cedar of Lebanon; Order of Two Niles (Sudan); King Abdulaziz Order First Class; King Abdulaziz Order, Distinguish Class. **Publications:** Books: Ilmu al-Ijtima (Sociology), al-Nahdhatu al-Adabiyyah Fi Najd; several articles on development in Saudi Arabia published in some Arab and Foreign newspapers and magazines. **Hobbies:** reading, swimming. walking. **Address:** Ministry of Foreign Affairs, Jeddah, Saudi Arabia.

MALIBARI (Salem, Ahmad), Saudi university Professor. **Born** on February 12, 1940 in Mecca. **Son** of Ahmad Malibari **and** Mrs., née Fatima Basri. **Married** in 1967 to Miss Najat Nather. **Educ.:** Universities of Riyadh and London. **Dipl.:** Bachelor of Science (Chemistry), Doctor of Science. **Career:** Assistant (1964), Professor (1967) then Dean of the Faculty of Science King Saud University; Secretary General, King Saud University; Associate Member of the Royal British Institute, King Saud University; Managing Director, Dallah Industries; President and owner of modi Establishment; has Attended several conferences. **Publ.:** al-Tahleel al-Kayfi (Qualitative Analysis), al-Kimya al-Ammah (General Chemistry) two books); research papers published in scientific journals. **Hobbies:** reading travel. **Prof. Addr.:** P.O.Box 41646 or 6752, Riyadh, Saudi Arabia.

MALIK (Ahmad Abdalla, al), Saudi civil servant. **Born** on 28 December 1936 at al-Russ, Saudi Arabia. **Educ.:** Riyadh University; Indiana University, USA. **Dipl.:** Bachelor of Economics (1964); M.A. (1966); Ph.D. (Economics) (1970). **Career:** Operations Officer, Communications Corps School; Communications Officer, Arab League Security Forces; Director of Provisions Department, Communications Corps; Director of Contracting Department, Maintenance Corps; Director of Department of Foreign Contracting, Ministry of Defence and Aviation since 1973; Saudi representative in negotiations with oil companies held at the OPEC headquarters in Vienna (1971-72); attended International Monetary Fund Conference (1971), OPEC meetings (1971-72); Director General, Saudi Arabian Monetary Agency; Member, Committee for Liquidation of the Arab Organization for Military Industrialization; Member, Board of Directors, Arab Organization for Military Industrialization (1975-79); Member, Committee, Strategy for the Third Development Plan of Saudi Arabia since 1980; Chairman, Arab Investment Co. S.A.A., Riyadh; Director, Saudi Fund for Development, Riyadh; Director, Saudi International Bank, London, U.K. **Publ.:** "Monetary Sources of Inflation in Saudi Arabia" (co-author of this article published by the Federal Reserve Bank of San Francisco, 1979). **Member:** Board of Saudi Credit Bank and Arab Organization for Military Industrialization. **Awards:** Decorations from Republic of Korea, Republic of China (Taiwan), Saudi Arabia, France and Egypt. **Hobbies:** Swimming, Tennis, Horse-riding. **Prof. Addr.:** P.O.Box 4009, Riyadh. 11491 Saudi Arabia.

MALIK (Khalid, Hamad, al), Saudi journalist. **Born** in al-Rass in 1944. **Educ.:** Secondary School Certificate. **Career:** Occupied various jobs in Ministry of Commerce and Board of Grivances; Editor of al-Yamamah magazine; joined al-Jazirah daily as News Editor; Managing Editor, member of Board of al-Jazirah Press, Printing and Publishing Organization; former Editor-in-Chief of al-Jazirah daily newspaper; Attended Arab Conference of Information Studies on Population, Development and Reconstruction. **Publications:** Editorials and other press writings exofficio. **Address:** al-Jazirah Organization, P.O.Box 354, Tel.: 4021022, Riyadh, Saudi Arabia.

MALIK (Razouk, H, Dr.), Legally known as Raymond H. MALIK, Arab American Scientist, Economist, Corporate Executive, Inventor, Professor, Author. **Born** on February 4, 1933 in Lebanon. **Son** of Hanna Z. Malik (Businessman) (deceased) **and** Clarice R. Malik (Founder of educational institutions) (deceased). Single. **Educ.:** Renaissance School, Schweifat, Lebanon; St. Louis, Teheran, Iran; La Sorbonne, Paris; Valparaiso, Indiana; Simpson College, Indianola, Iowa; S.I.U., Carbondale, ILL. **Dipl.:** B.A. in Business Administrn. (1950); B.S. in Bus. Administrn. and Economics (1951); M.S. (1956); Ph.D. in Electronics and Econs. (1959); Sc.D.; Multy Lingual; **Career:** Supr. of stores UKCC, Teheran, Iran (1940-44); Supr. Aramco, Beirut, Lebanon (1952-54); Member Grad. Faculty Advisor, ILL. State University (1954-59); Professor Head, World Trade Program, YMCA College, Chicago U.S.A. (1966-74); President, Malik International Enterprises Ltd. Chicago U.S.A. (1959-); Advisor U.S. Congl. Advisor Bd. (1982-); **Author:** The Guide to Youth, Health and longevity (1980); Do you really need Glasses (1988). **Inventor**, Selectric typing elements and mechanism (1959),

Pioneer developer interplanetary communications system (1961), heater-humidifier-dehumidifier (1963), Ednl. math toy (1965), circle of sound concept of sound propogation (1967), introduced modular concept in color TV (1973), Gamma ray breast cancer detector (1976), Auto-ignition instant hot water heater (1981), water filter, purifier and softener (1984), No Doze Warner (1985), indoor-outdoor barbeque grill (1985), Massager with Infra-red Heat (1986). Designed and introduced telephone shoulder rest with adjustable mechanism (1962); Electronic Telephone (the trim Line) 1964; Modular Telephone (1975). **Honors:** Fulbright Scholar (1948-50); Methodist Church Scholar (1950-51); So. Illinois University Fellow (1954-59); Notable American Award (1978); Wisdom Hall of Fame (1987), Austrian Legion of Honor. **Member:** American Management Association; American Econo. Association; American Marketing Association; Import Club U.S.; International Bus. Council, IEEE; International Platform Association; Pres. 's Assn., AAAS; National Assn. Self-employed, Imperial Austrian Legion of Honor; International Students Assn., Phi Beta Kappa, Sigma Xi, Delta Rho, Beta Gamma Sigma, Alpha Phi Omega; Deacon, Memb. Pastor-congl. Community, Youth and Young Adult Ednl. Community; St. George Orthodox Church, Cicaro, ILL.: Fundraiser March of Dimes, St. Jude Hosp.; American Cancer Society; American Heart Fund and numerous others. **Sports:** Tennis, baseball, football, running. **Hobbies:** Reading Sports, handyman, building electronic and mechanical equipment. **Credit Cards:** American Express; Citicorp; Diners; Chevy Chase and many others. Visa and Master Card. **Prof. Addr.:** P.O.Box 3194, Chicago, Illinois 60654-0194, 312-334-6785.26.5. U.S.A. **Priv. Addr.:** Chicago, Illinois 60654-0194.26.5. U.S.A.

MALIK (Reda, Ahmad), Algerian politician. **Born** on December 12, 1931 in Betna. **Son** of Ahmad Malik (Lawyer) **and** Mrs., née Z. Ladijouze. **Married** in January 1963 to Miss Rafida Chériet, 2 children: Ahmad and Amina-Aïcha. **Educ.:** College of Bougie, Lycée Bugeaud (Algiers), Faculty of Letters (Algiers University), Faculty of Letters (University of Paris). **Career:** Member, Committee General, General Union of the Algerian Students; Director of the "al-Moujahed" newspaper, Tunis (1957-61); Speaker and Member of the Delegation of the "Front de Libération Nationale" (National Liberation Front) to Evian Meetings (May 1961- March 1962); Algerian Ambassador to Belgrad (1963-65), to Paris (1965-70); Ambassador to USSR (1970-77); Minister of Information and Culture (1977-79), Member Central Committee, FLN (1979); Ambassador to U.S.A. (1979-82); Ambassador to U.K. (1982-85); former Member of the High Council of State, and Prime Minister (September 1993-April 1994). Leader Alliance Nationale Republicaine. **Addr.:** 2 Rue Ahmed Bey, Algiers, Algeria.

MALIK (Saleh Abdallah), Saudi official. **Born** in al-Rass, Gassiem in 1940. **Educ.:** Ph.D. (Sociology), University of Michigan, 1973. **Career:** Professor, Sociology Department, King Saud University (1973-74); General Secretary, Imam Muhammad Ibn Saud Islamic University (1975); Deputy Minister for Municipal and Rural Affairs (1976); member of the Board, Electricity Corporation and Desalination Corporation. **Member:** of the Preparatory Committee for Education Policy, the Higher Committee for the Development of Riyadh City, the Higher Executive Committee for the Development of the Diplomatic Quarter, Riyadh, the Committee for the development of Fiza, Gizan and Kasr el-Hokm areas in Riyadh and the Higher Committee for Children's Welfare. **Hobbies:** reading, swimming, travel. **Priv. Addr.:** Tel.: 4763296, Riyadh, Saudi Arabia.

MALKI (Abdul Hamid), Tunisian official, judge. **Born** in 1925 in Tunis, Tunisia. **Married**, four children. **Educ.:** Law Studies, Paris, France. **Career:** Judge in Tunis (1961-64); Vice President of the Court of First Instance, Tunis (1964); President of the Chamber of Commerce (1965-75); Governor of Gabès (1973); Governor of Tunis (1973); Minister of Justice (1984). **Addr.:** Tunis, Tunisia.

MALKI (Mohamad Hassan Alawi, al), Saudi intellectual and scholar. **Career:** Ex-Professor, Umm al-Qura University, Mecca; official authorized to perform marriage contracts; part-time member, Muslim World League; ex-member of the committee of judges in the international contest for memorization of the Qur'an; attended several conferences nationally and abroad. Runs a private scientific and intellectual religious school at the Holy Mosque in Mecca, **Publications:** numerous books on Islamic ethics, jurisdition, heritage and history. **Prof. Addr.:** Omar Bin Abdulaziz Street, Mecca. **Priv. Addr.:** Tel.: 5436266, Mecca, Saudi Arabia.

MALKI (Shebib, Lazim, al), Iraqi politician. **Born** in Baghdad in 1936. **Married**, six children. **Educ.:** Baghdad University. **Dipl.:** B.Sc. in Law; diploma in International Law. **Career:** Governor of Karbala (1968-72); Governor of Nineveh (1972-73); Deputy Minister, Ministry of Agriculture (1973-75); Chairman-Iraqi Lawyers' Union (1975); Secretary General, Arab Jurists Union (since 1975) and of the Permanent Committee for Human Rights and Political Freedom in the Arab World (1979); Deputy Chairman, International Lawyers' Union (1976); member of the Consultative Committee, International Organisation of Anti Racial Discrimination (1979); Minister of Justice (March 1991 to present). **Publ.:** "The Law as a Tool for Arab World"; "The Unified Arab Parliament". **Hobbies:** Reading, riding, hunting. member of Iraqi Hunting Club. **Prof. Addr.:** al-Mansour, P.O.Box 6026, Baghdad, Iraq and Ministry of Justice, Baghdad, Iraq.

MALLAKH (Kamal, al), Egyptian artist, archæologist. **Born** on 26 October 1924 in Assiut, Egypt. **Educ.:** Cairo University and Military Engineering College. **Dipl.:** B.A.

Architecture, Master of Arts. **Career:** Antiquity Department of Egyptian Government (1944), Director of Giza Area and Lower Egypt (1945); worked as illustrator and art critic: "al-Ahram" (1945); "Akhbar al-Yawm" (1950); art and archæology commentator, Egyptian Broadcasting Service (1950); Held oneman exhibitions two paintings in Cairo Museum of Modern Art; member of the Higher Council for the Arts and Literature; member of Higher Council of Antiquities; Chairman of the Egyptian Association of Writers and Critics. **Publ.:** Author of books on art, archæology and the discovery of solar boats. **Award:** Medal of Merit for Arts and Literature, Gold Medal Cedar (Lebanon). **Prof. Addr.:** al-Ahram newspaper, Gala' Street, Cairo, Egypt. **Priv. Addr.:** 173, Twenty Sixth of July Street, Zamalek, Cairo, Egypt.

MALOUM (Zeine, Ould), Mauritanian economist. **Born** in 1930 at Tidjikja (Middle Mauritania). **Son** of Mohamad Abdallahi (businessman). **Married** to Miss Oumalkelthoum Diallo, 7 children. **Educ.:** Primary school at Tidjikja and the Koran school at Kiffa (1942-46); De Rosse College (1946-50); National School of Insurance, France (1961-62); Institute of Economic Development & Planning, Dakar (Senegal, 1968). **Dipl.:** B.Sc. (Economics). **Career:** Secretary to the Treasury (1950-57); Deputy Special agent and head of Secretariat (1957); founded Mauritanian Insurance Control Service (1962); Civil Administrator (1964-66); Director of communications (1966-67); Director of Cabinet, Ministry of the Interior, then Secretary General of the said ministry (1967-68); Governor of the VIth Region (1970) and Director General of the Mauritanian Development Bank (1971). **Member:** Parti du Peuple Mauritanien, and former member of Entente Mauritanienne (now banned). **Addr.:** Nouakchott, Mauritania.

MAMOOTIL (George), Indian banker. **Born** in 1926 in Kerala, India. **Son** of Cherian Mamootil **and** Mrs. Aliamma Cherian Mamootil. **Married** in 1952 to Miss Sara George, three children. **Educ.:** Syndenham College of Commerce, Bombay. **Career:** Joined Citibank NA, Bombay (1947); Sub Accountant (1962); Pro Manager (1964); Accountant (1966); Assistant Manager (1968); Overseas Assignment (1970); Manager Dubai Branch (1972); Designated International Officer (1973); Manager Beirut Branch (1974); Program Manager Middle East, Assistant Comptroller (1975-78); Assistant Comptroller Middle East, Africa (1978-81); Assistant Vice President Samba, Riyadh (1981-83); Retired from Citibank (1983); Joined as Senior Vice President, Controller of Bahrain International Bank (since 1983 to present). **Medals:** Recipient of "Citibank Foundation Award for World Tour" (1964). **Hobby:** Bridge. **Prof. Addr.:** P.O.B. 5016, Tel.: 274545, Manama, Bahrain. **Priv. Addr.:** House No. 423, Road No. 3614, Block 336 Tel.: 712866, Adliya.

MANA (Abdulla, Saleh al), Qatari former minister. **Born** in 1946. **Son** of Saleh Alhamad al-Mana. **Married:** two sons, Khalid and Hamad, one daughter, Khoulod. **Educ.:** Arab University of Beirut. **Dipl.:** B.A. in Economics and Administration. **Career:** Ambassador to U.S.A. (1972-79); Ambassador to Belgium (1979-83); Ambassador to Saudi Arabia (1985-89); presently Minister of Communication and Transport (July 1989-1996). **Hobbies:** Swimming, Tennis. **Member:** Doha Club. **Priv. Addr.:** Tel.: 424832, Doha, Qatar.

MANAA (Abdallah Soliman), Saudi journalist. **Born** in 1938 in Jeddah, Saudi Arabia. **Dipl.:** B.D.S. (Dental Surgery) Alexandria University; Ph.D. **Career:** Assistant Director, Jeddah Central Hospital; Director, Health Affairs Department, Taif; Executive Editor, al-Bilad daily newspaper; Editor-in-Chief; Iqra'a weekly magazine. **Member:** Jeddah Literary Club; former Vice President of Union Club, Jeddah; member, Constituent Committee, al-Bilad Press Organization: has attended several Arab and Islamic Dental Conferences. **Publications:** Lamasat (Touches); Anees al-Haya'ra (Companion of the Lost); al-Taraf al-A'Khar (The Other End) in addition to some short stories and articles. **Prof. Addr.:** Iqra'a weekly magazine, al-Bilad Publishing Organization, P.O.Box 3029, Tel.: 6429187, Jeddah, Saudi Arabia.

MANAA (Ibrahim M. Abdallah), Saudi academic. **Born** on 12 December 1946, in Jeddah, Saudi Arabia. **Dipl.:** B.Sc. (Chemistry) 1972; M.A. (Instructional Systems Technology) 1973. **Career:** Specialist, Instructional Systems Technology; Director of Educational TV; Director of Educational Materials; Director of Teachers' Trainning Institute; Dean, Teachers' Junior College, Mecca; member of Mecca Cultural Club; member of National Audio-visual Association, U.S.A.; National Association of Educational Technology and Communications; member of Higher Council of Teachers' Junior Colleges. **Publication:** Instructional Systems Technology (under publication). **Address:** Teachers' Junior College, P.O.Box 2064, Mecca, Saudi Arabia.

MANDIL (Salah, Hussein), Sudanese Computer Scientist and UN senior official. **Born** on September 8, 1941 in Omdurman (Sudan). **Married**, with Children. **Educ.:** Queen's University, Belfast (UK), B.Sc. (Electronic Engineering) (1965), M.Sc. (Electronics (1966), Ph.D. (Computer Science) (1971). **Career:** Lecturer, University of Khartoum (1966-67); Deputy Manager, Computer Centre, University of Khartoum (Sudan, 1967-68); Leader, Information Systems Technology, International Business Machines Ltd. IBM Scientific Centre, UK (1971-73); Consultant, Public Administration Division, UN New York (1971); Information Scientist, Headquarters Programme Committee Secretariat, World Health Organisation, (WHO) Geneva (Switzerland) (1974-76); Manager Information Systems Programme, WHO, Geneva; Director, Division of Information Systems Support, WHO,

Geneva (1977-91); Director-Adviser on Informatics & Telematics, WHO, Geneva (1991-). **Publ.:** Author of numerous articles on Macro Processing, micro Computing, Information Systems; and their uses in the United Nations and in member states; and the relevance and uses of informatics and telematics in medical & health care, nationally and internationally. **Member:** numerous international societies and associations of computing, telecommunications, information systems, informatics, telematics including Tele Medicine, And, member of editorial boards of a few international journals on health informatics & telematics. **Hobbies:** Photography and travel. **Sports:** Soccer, swimming and tennis. **Prof. Addr.:** Director, AOI, WHO, 20 avenue Appia, Tel.: 44.22 791 2426, CH-1211, Geneva 27 (Switzerland). **Priv. Addr.:** CH-1297 Founex, Switzerland.

MANDILY (Fatma Abdalla, Mrs.), (al-Sharifa), Saudi academic. **Born** in Mecca. **Dipl.:** M.A. (English Literature). **Career:** Demonstrator, English Department, Faculty of Arts, Riyadh University. **Member:** Board, Women's Revival Association, Riyadh; Jezira Girls Club. **Publ.:** Contributes regularly to local papers and Saudi Radio; M.A. thesis on the influence of Arabic poetry on Tennyson. **Hobby:** reading. **Prof. Addr.:** P.O.Box 2121, Riyadh, Saudi Arabia.

MANDURAH (Ruqayah Abdul Latif, Mrs.), Saudi academic. **Born** in 1949 in Mecca, Saudi Arabia. **Dipl.:** M.A. (Curricula and Methodology). **Career:** Elementary schoolmistress; clerk; Assistant Headmistress of an elementary school; Lecturer and Director of Women Students' Affairs, Umm al-Qura University, Mecca. **Member:** Umm al-Qura Welfare Society. **Publications:** contributes regurlarly to local magazines and newspaper. **Prof. Addr.:** Women's Section, Umm al-Qura University, Tel.: 5564770, Mecca. **Priv. Addr.:** Tel.: 5421569, Mecca, Saudi Arabia.

MANEI (Abdallah Ibn Soliman Ibn Mohamad, al), Saudi judge. **Born** in 1929 at Shaqra. **Dipl.:** B.A. and M.A. Shari'a (Islamic Law). **Career:** Served as a teacher in primary Schools (1949-51); in scientific institutions (1954-56); Inspector, Ministry of Education (1957-58); member, Legal Opinion Society (1958-77); Vice President, the Presidency of Legal Opinion, Propagation and Guidance; Judge, Mecca Court of Cassation; participant member, Supreme Board of Omniscientists; member, Supreme Council of Endowments, Al Daawa' Journalism Est.; participated in the Supreme Conference of Cassation and Appeal Judges, Australia; founder and Chairman of Bawarid tribe Welfare Society in Shaqr'a. **Publications:** Paper Currency; Ramadan Islamic Decisions; Hajj (Pilgrimage) Islamic Decisions; Spotlight on Socialism. **Hobby:** research on Islamic Studies (Shari'a). **Prof. Addr.:** Cassation Court, Azizyah, Tel.: 556-1767, Mecca. **Priv. Addr.:** Tel.: 558-6254, Mecca, Saudi Arabia.

MANEI (Mohamad ben Sulaiman, al), Saudi diplomat. **Born** in 1934, in Shaqraa'. **Dipl.:** B.A. (Islamic Legislation). **Career:** Schoolteacher; Inspector of Islamic Education; General Inspector of Primary Education; Assistant Head of Primary Education; headed several boards of examinations at the Ministry of Education; supervised the printing of school textbooks for the Ministry of Education for two years; former Cultural Attaché, Saudi Embassy in Oman. **Hobby:** reading Arabic poetry and literature. **Address:** Ministry of Foreign Affairs, Riyadh, Saudi Arabia.

MANNAI (Ahmed, Abdulla), Qatari businessman. **Born** on 25 October 1931 in Bahrain. **Son** of late Abdulla Al-Mannai **and** Mrs. Essa Al-Mannai. **Married** to Amina Mannai, seven children: Khalid, Haya, Muna, Abdulla, Dina, Leena and Walid. **Education:** General Education. **Career:** After General education, entered business at a young age, established Mannai Trading Company in 1950. Today The Mannai Group has widely diverse number of activities covering not only trading but engineering, construction, computer, oil-field, offshore, agricultural services, telecommunication and air travel; **Chairman:** Mannai Corporation (Q.S.C.) and Subsidiary Companies. **Director:** Qatar Insurance Co. SAQ, Investcorp Bank E.C., Gulf Publishing and Printing Organization. **Award:** "Commandeur de la Legion d'Honneur" by the French Government, in April 1986 and "Gulf Businessman of the Year-1989". **Sports:** Skiing and Jogging. **Hobby:** Reading. **Member:** Middle East Association, London. **Address:** Mannai Corporation (Q.S.C.), P.O.Box 76, Doha, Qatar, Tel.: 412555, Fax: 411982, Telex: 4208 Mannai DH, E-Mail: mancorp@qatar.net.qa.

MANNAI (Salem Abdulla, al), Bahraini engineer. **Born** in Qalali, Bahrain on 15.5.39. **Son** of Abdulla Isa al-Mannai (Merchant) and Hessa. **Married** to Mrs. Munira al-Jalahma on 26.11.70. 3 children. **Educ.:** American University of Beirut, University of Florida, U.S.A., World University, Tucson, Arizona, U.S.A. **Dipl.:** B.E., M.E. and Ph.D. in Engineering. **Career:** Senior Partner and Director of Mannai Engineering Co. Ltd., P.O.Box 849, Manama, Bahrain; Sole owner, Mannai Trading Center, Manama, Bahrain. **Medals:** Golden Medal presented by His Highness, the Amir of Bahrain (1969). **Sports:** Table Tennis, Badminton. **Hobbies:** Walking, reading, swimming. **Clubs:** Marina Club. **Prof. Addr.:** P.O.Box 849, Manama, Bahrain, Tel.: 213726. **Priv. Addr.:** No. 1527, Road 2733, Adliah, Manama 327, Bahrain, Tel.: 714470.

MANNIE (Mohamad Abdallah, al), Saudi academic. **Born** in 1943 at Qasab, Saudi Arabia. **Dipl.:** Ph.D. (Education Administration). **Career:** Lecturer, Faculty of Education, King Saud University (1972); Assistant Professor, same faculty since 1976; Chairman of Education Department since 1979; Vice Dean, College of Education since 1982; Vice Dean of Graduate Studies since 1993. **Member:**

British Education Administration Society; member of Commonwealth Conference on Education Administration. **Hobby:** reading, Computer. **Prof. Addr.:** Faculty of Education, King Saud University, Tel.: 4674461. Riyadh. **Priv. Addr.:** Tel.: 4828650, Riyadh, Saudi Arabia.

MANOUKIAN (Ardag, H.E. Mgr.), Archbishop of the armenian community in Iran. **Born** in 1931 in Beirut. **Educ.:** Beirut and Antelias Seminary, and at Lyon (France). **Career:** Ordained to the Priesthood (1951) and then Archimandrite (1953); Consecrate Bishop in Antelias (1956); Armenian Catholicossat of Cilicie (Antelias, 1956-60); Editor "Hassk" review; elected Prelate of the Armenian diocese of Teheran and Archbishop of the Armenian Community, same town, since 1960. **Publ.:** Author of 20 books in Armenian. **Awards:** Order of Hamayoun III of Iran (1968). **Residence:** The Armenian Orthodox Archbishopric of Teheran, Avenue Ostad Najatollahi, No. 311, 15988 Teheran, Iran.

MANQOUR (Nasser Hamad, al), Saudi diplomat. **Born** in 1927 in Riyadh, Saudi Arabia. **Dipl.:** B.A. (Literature), Cairo University, (1952). **Career:** Attaché, Ministry of Foreign Affairs (1952), Director of Education in Najd Region (1954); Assistant Director General of Education (1955); Director General, Education (1956); Director General of Ministry of Education (1975); Rector of Riyadh University (1958); Minister of State for Cabinet Affairs Minister of Labour and Social Affairs (1959); Ambassador to Japan, Republic of China and Republic of Korea (1964); Ambassador to Sweden, Denmark and Norway (1968); Ambassador Extraordinary and Plenipotentiary of Saudi Arabia to the United Kingdom and to Ireland (1980) and 1982 respectively. **Member:** Supreme Council of Manuscripts; Board, al-Yamamah Press Organization; Chairman of Board, Riyadh Electricity Company (1962); Head of Saudi delegation to General Education Conference, Geneva (1958). **Honours:** King Abdulaziz Order (Second Class); Gran Crus, Orden del Merito Civil, Spain; Grand Cordon of the Order of Brilliant Star, Republic of China; Grand Cross of the Victorian Order, United Kingdom. **Publications:** articles in al-Yamamah magazine (1953), Riyadh daily newspaper (1962), al-Madina daily newspaper (1962). **Address:** Ministry of Foreign Affairs, Riyadh, Saudi Arabia.

MANQOUSH (Mohamad Ahmad, al), Libyan official. **Born** in 1937 in Benghazi, Libya. **Career:** Chairman, Libyan Airlines; former Member, Supreme Consultation Technical Committee and Head, National Construction Corporation; Minister of Housing and Utilities (1971-77); Secretary for Housing, General People's Committee (March 1977-79); formerly Secretary-General of Great Man-Made River Authority in Tripoli. **Addr.:** Tripoli, Libya.

MANSOUR (Abdel Hamid), Syrian international civil servant. **Born** on 18 March, 1922 in Hama (Syria). **Married**, with children. **Educ.:** University of Toulouse, France (1947-51), (1949-52) and (1952-55). **Dipl.:** B.Sc (Agronomy) (1950), B.Sc. (Natural Science) (1955), Ph.D. (Agroeconology). **Career:** Director, Agrarian High School, Damascus, Syria (1955-56); Chief, Ecology Department, Ministry of Agriculture and Agrarian Reform (1956-58); Director General of Agriculture, Ministry of Agriculture, Damascus (1958-61); Adviser to President, United Arab Republic (1961); Director, Department of Agriculture and Planning (1961); Dean, Faculty of Agriculture, University of Aleppo, Syria (1961-63); Director of Programming, Ministry of Planning, Damascus, Syria (1964); Professor of Mediterranean and Tropical Agronomy, University of Toulouse, (France, 1964-71); Senior Agricultural Adviser and Country Representative, Food and Agriculture Organisation and United Nations Development Programme (FAO /UNDP), Algiers (Algeria). **Publ.:** Author of "Contributions à l'Amélioration des Conditions de Greffage", "Sur l'Intérêt du Bouturage sous Brouillard dans la Génétique du Cotonnier", "Essai sur l'Aptitude du Bouturage de Certains Arabes Fruitiers Méditerranées", "Problèmes Pastoraux et Humanis Dans les Zones Arides du Moyen Orient", "Contributions à l'étude Bioclimatologique de la Syrie" (1964). **Member:** Society of Natural History, France; Association of Agrarian Engineers, France; Inter-Arab Centre for Research and Study in the Arid Zones, Damascus; Boule-Rêvée club, Toulouse, France. **Sports:** Soccer, horseriding, swimming and bowling. **Hobbies:** Herborizing and music. **Priv. Addr.:** 67, chemin Mohamed Gacem, el-Mouradia, Tel.: 60-65-51, Algiers, Algeria.

MANSOUR (Ahmad, Abdallah, al), United Arab Emirates statesman. **Born** in 1943 in Abu Dhabi, United Arab Emirates. **Son** of Abdallah al Mansour. **Married**, three children. **Educ.:** Commercial studies, Cairo, Egypt (1960-61). **Career:** Secretary of Documents and Research Office, Amiri Court, Abu Dhabi (1969); Deputy Director of Labour and Social Affairs Department, Abu Dhabi (1971); Under Secretary, United Arab Emirates, Ministry of Planning (since 1972). **Sport:** Swimming. **Hobby:** Poetry. **Addr.:** Ministry of Planning, P.O.B. 904, Tel.: 362271, Telex: 22920, Abu Dhabi, United Arab Emirates.

MANSOUR (al-Fatih, Ahmad, al), Sudanese journalist. **Born** in 1923 in Abyad, Sudan. **Son** of Ahmad al-Mansour. **Married**, six children. **Educ.:** Diploma of the Institute of Science; Special Studies in Journalism, Egypt. **Career:** Owner of Kardofan Press Organisation; member of the Boards of the Cooperative Bank of Sudan, Sudan Press House; Kardofan Transport Co., former Editor in Chief of "Kordofan" newspaper. **Medals:** Order of Science, Sudan (1974); Order of Merit, Egypt (1964). **Prof. Addr.:** The Kardofan Press and Trading House, P.O.Box 49, Tel.: 2284, 2210, Obeid, Sudan.

MANSOUR (al-Motaz), Egyptian bank manager. **Born**

on September 21, 1940 in Dakahlia, Egypt. **Son** of Ahmad Mohamad Mansour. **Married** in 1965, 2 daughters. **Educ.:** English School, Cairo; London School of Economics. **Dipl.:** B.Sc. (Econ.) 1962; M.Sc. (Econ.) 1964; Post Graduate (Ph.D) studies 1964-1967. **Career:** Graduate Tutor; London School of Economics (1965); lecturer, Regent Polytechnic, London (1965-66); Graduate Tutor, University college, London (1966); Economist, UNCTAD, Geneva (1966-1970); International Trade and Finance Unit, ECWA (UN) (1970-74); Chief Division, Arab Fund, Kuwait (1974-77); Manager, Projects Department of Misr Iran Development Bank (1978-81); General Manager, Misr Iran Development Bank (1981-83); General Manager and Board Member, Misr Iran Development Bank (1983-85); Managing Director, Misr Iran Development Bank (since Oct.1985); Chairman, el-Gezirah Hotels and Tourism Company; **Member**, Egyptian Businessman's Association; Bank's Association of Egypt; Arab Banker's Association; American Chamber of commerce; Ex-Board Member, General Authority for Investment & Free Zones; Ex-Board Member, Private Investment Encouragement Fund; Member, Assembly, Maritime Transportation Holding Company. Member, Specialized national Council; Member, National Democratic Party (Financial & Economic Affairs Committee). **Hobbies:** Fine Arts, Music, Reading, Tennis, Sailing. **Member:** el-Guezirah Sporting Club; Cairo Yacht Club. **Addr.:** Misr Iran Development Bank, Nile Tower-21 Giza Street, P.O.Box 219 Orman 12612, Tel. 5727311, Telex: 22407, 20474, Fax: 5701185, Cairo, Egypt.

MANSOUR (Anis, Mohamed), Egyptian writer. **Born** in 1924 in Egypt. **Son** of Mohamed Mansour. **Educ.:** Cairo University. **Dipl.:** B.A. in Philosophy. **Career:** Chairman of the Board "el-Geel" Magazine; Editor in Chief "Akher Sa'a" magazine (1970-76); Editor in Chief and Chairman of the Board of: "Dar al-Maaref October" (1976) and of "Wadi al-Nil" (1984); Member of Consultative Assembly, the Supreme Council for Journalism, the High Council of Arts now Editor in Chief, "Mayo" Organ of the National democratic Party. **Publ.:** "Around the World in 200 Days" (1960); "In the Salon of al-Akad" (1983); "The Eternal 100 Personalities" (1980); "In Politics" (4 Vols), (1983). **Medals:** Honorary State Prize for Travel Literature (1982); State Prize of High Esteem (1982); Indian Honorary State Prize for Positive Constructive Thought (1982). **Member** Positive Constructive Thought (1982). **Member of:** Gezira Sporting Club. **Hobbies:** Reading and tennis. **Addr.:** Sharia el-Galaa, Cairo, Egypt.

MANSOUR (Ibrahim, Moneim), Sudanese politician. **Born** in 1933 at en-Nahud (Sudan). **Married**, with children. **Educ.:** Primary education locally: ed-Dueim Intermediate school; Hantoub secondary school; Faculty of Commerce, Alexandria University (Egypt). **Dipl.:** B.Com. **Career:** Joined Government service and was attached to the Ministry of Commerce; worked with the Agricultural Bank became Deputy Director, Khartoum Textile Company; Member, Board of Directors, Sudan Textile Company; General Manager, Gulf International Corporation in Khartoum (1964); Minister of Economy and Trade (Oct. 1971- Oct. 1972); Minister of National Economy (Oct. 1972- May 1973); Minister of Finance and National Economy (May 1973- Jan. 1975); Minister of Finance and Economic Planning concluded an agreement with the Government of India for the exchange of long-staple cotton against Indian Jute, Machinery and chemicals (1972); led the Sudanese delegation to China where he signed a trade agreement. **Prof. Addr.:** P.O.Box 2316, Khartoum, Sudan.

MANSOUR (Jamaleddin, Mohamad), Egyptian diplomat. **Born** in 1923 in Cairo, Egypt. **Son** of Mohamad Jamaleddin. **Married,** two daughters. **Educ.:** B.A. in Political Economics, Cairo University, Egypt; B.A. in Military Sciences, Military College, Egypt (1944), **Career:** Member of the Free Officers Group (1952); joined Ministry of Foreign Affairs (1953); Consul General in Marseille (1954-56); First Secretary and Chargé d'Affaires, Brussels (1956-57); Consul General in Trieste, Italy (1957-61); Chargé d'Affaires, Paris (1963-64); Ambassador to Federal Republic of Germany (1964-65); Head of Western Europe Department, Ministry of Foreign Affairs, Egypt, (1965-69); Ambassador to Thailand (1969-71); Ambassador to Zaire (1971-73); Ambassador to Cyprus (1973-75); Deputy Minister of Foreign Affairs (1975-77); Ambassador and Head of the Relationship Office, Syria (1977-78); Ambassador to Yugoslavia (1978-81), retired. **Medals:** Order of Merit 2nd Class, Egypt (1971); Order of Knighthood, Italy (1966); Order of the Cross, Sweden (1966); Order of the White Elephant 1st Class, Thailand (1972). **Hobbies:** Hunting, fishing, reading literature, poetry, politics and economy. **Addr.:** 1 Zaim Ghandi Street, Garden City, Cairo, Egypt.

MANSOUR (Mohamed, el), Moroccan professor of history. **Born** on February 23, 1948 at Province of Chefchaouen, Morocco. **Son** of Mukhtar el-Mansour **and** Mrs. née Tama Benchra. **Married** in 1971 in Morocco to Fatima Harrak, 2 children: Safouane (1976), Fadil (1981). **Educ.:** American University of Beirut, Université de Paris VIII, University of London (SOAS). **Dipl.:** B.A. in History, Master in History, Ph.D. History (SOAS). **Career:** Lecturer (1982-86); Full Professor (since 1986); Chairman of the Department of History at Mohammed V University, Rabat; **Publ.:** "Morocco in the Reign of Mawlay Sulayman", Menas Press, 1990. **Other Information:** Visiting Professor at Princeton University (Spring 1992); MESA visiting Scholar for 1991. **Sports:** Tennis. **Member:** Association Marocaine pour la Recherche Historique. **Prof. Addr.:** Department of History, Faculty of Letters, Rabat, Morocco. **Priv. Addr.:** 811, rue Cadis, Secteur 3, Hay Salam, Tel.: (7)78-64-78, Sale, Morocco.

MANSOUR (Sabri Muhammad), Egyptian artist. **Born** on March 27, 1943 in Bakhati, Egypt. **Married**, one daughter. **Educ.:** Cairo Academy of Fine Arts, Egypt; San Fernando Royal Academy of Fine Arts, Madrid, Spain. **Dipl.:** B.Sc. (in Photography) (1964); M.Sc. (1972); Professorship in Drawing. **Career:** Assistant Lecturer in the Academy of Fine Arts, Cairo (1964-72), Lecturer (1972-79), then Assistant Professor (1979-84) and now Professor (since 1984); **Member** of the Plastic Arts Committee, Supreme Council of Culture (1980-82), then Secretary (1983-84); Board Member of the Union of Plastic Artists (1983-84). Has participated in national and international art exhibitions in Cairo, Alexandria (Egypt) and Madrid (Spain). **Member:** Gezira Club, Eghpt. **Hobby:** jogging. **Prof. Addr.:** College of Fine Arts, Mansour Mohammad Street, Zamalek, Cairo, Egypt; 23B Ismail Mohammad Street, Tel.: 817321, 417321, Zamalek, Cairo, Egypt.

MANSOUR (Saleh Abdul Aziz, al), Saudi academic. **Born** in 1935 in Buraidah. **Dipl.:** B.A. (Shari'a) (1959); M.A. the Higher Institute of Justice (1966); Ph.D. (Islamic Law and Civil Law), Faculty of Shari'a, al-Azhar University, Cairo (1976). **Career:** Teacher, Scientific Institute of Imam Muhammad Ibn Saud University; member of the teaching staff and later Dean, Faculty of Shari'a, King Saud University; Dean, Faculty of Sharia (Islamic Law) and Religious Principles, Imam Muhammad Ibn Saud Islamic University, Gasseim; Supervisor, Faculty of Arabic and Social Sciences, Gassiem. an occasional lecturer in mosques and broadcasting stations. **Member:** Buraidah Welfare Society; attended the Conference for Combating Drug Addiction and Alcoholism, Baghdad, (1976). **Publications:** Islamic View of Smoking; Islam and Alcoholism, twice reprinted; Islamic Jurisprudence and Ibn Taymiah, two vols. **Hobbies:** reading about Islamic Jurisprudence. **Prof. Addr.:** Faculty of Shari'a and Religious Principles, Buraidah, Tel.: 3231788, Gasseim. **Priv. Addr.:** Tel.: 3233803, Gasseim, Saudi Arabia.

MANSOUR (Sami), Egyptian journalist. **Born** in 1935 in Cairo, Egypt. **Educ.:** B.A. in Political Science, Cairo University, Egypt (1958); M.A. in Political Science (1962) and Ph.D. in Political Science (1965) from Cairo University, Egypt. **Career:** Political Commentator "al-Ahram" newspaper (1958-69); Editor "al-Ahram" Central Desk (1969-76); Head, International Relations Unit, al-Ahram Center for Political and Strategic Studies (since 1976). **Publ.:** "Confronting Israel" (1963); "Nigeria: The Straying Giant" (1965); "Masks of American Imperialism" (1968); "The Collapse of the Revolution in the Third World" (1969); "Militarism and Industry"; "Hiroshima and the Atomic Bomb". **Addr.:** 48 Mohamad Farid Street, Cairo, Egypt.

MANSOUR (Sanaa, Ali), Egyptian broadcaster. **Married. Educ.:** University of Cairo, Egypt. **Dipl.:** B.A. in Journalism (1962). **Career:** Broadcaster for the Middle East Broadcasting Corporation (1964-68); Senior Brodcaster, Radio Monte Carlo (1972-78); Director of Entertainment Programmes (since 1987). **Member:** Gezira Sporting Club, Egypt. **Hobby:** silk drawing. **Addr.:** 13, Ibrahim Naguib Street, Garden City, Tel.: 20197, Cairo, Egypt.

MANSOURI (Abdul Rahman Amin), Saudi official. **Born** in 1934 in Mecca, Saudi Arabia. **Dipl.:** completed his primary and secondary education in Mecca, B.A. (Law), M.A. (Public Law). **Career:** Began Career in 1955; became the Consul General of Saudi Arabia in New York and then Chargé d'Affaires in Paris; attended most of the Arab and Islamic conferences and sessions of the U.N. General Assembly and Arab League; accompanied His Majesty the late King Khalid and H.R.H. Crown Prince Fahad (presently King Fahad) on most of their state visits to various Arab, Islamic and Foreign countries; practiced Law (1966-74); participated in negotiating and drafting of border treaties between Saudi Arabia and other countries; represented the Saudi Arabian Government on legal assignments concerning military and defence matters; member of the Kingdom's Supreme Information Council since 1981; appointed Deputy Minister for Political Affairs in 1977; selected as a Judge in the OAPEC Judicial Council and was elected as president of the Tribunal in 1982. **Honours:** Honorary Doctorate, Republic of Korea; Orders of Merit from several Arab, Islamic and European countries. **Hobby:** reading. **Address:** Ministry of Foreign Affairs, P.O.Box 495, Tel.: 6690900, Jeddah, Saudi Arabia.

MANSOURI (Abdul Wahab Hassan), Saudi engineer. **Born** in 1942 at Taif, Saudi Arabia. **Dipl.:** Ph.D. **Career:** Lecturer, Vice Dean, Faculty of Engineering, King Saud University; Secretary, Faculty Council (1972-74); Assistant Professor Civil Engineering Department, Faculty of Engineering, King Saud University. **Member** of National Society for the Improvement of Mathematics, Muslim Student Association of the U.S.A. and Canada, American Institute of Reinforced Concrete, American Association of Civil Engineering; attended Conference of Engineers, Shiraz, Iran, Conference on Mechanical Applications in Engineering, Boulder, Colorado; participated in the evaluation of consultancy work for King Saud University and King Abdulaziz University and King Abdulaziz University buildings; participated in design work for Dharan Airport Hotel. **Publications:** research work on the properties and advantages of local wood in comparison with imported wood; the oretical studies on water tanks; some research articles in the scientific journal of the Faculty of Engineering, King Saud University. **Hobbies:** reading, swimming, football. **Address:** P.O.Box 800, Tel.: 4811000, Riyadh, Saudi Arabia.

MANSOURI (Abid Rashid, Salmin, al), U.A.E. executive. **Born** in 1920 in Abu Dhabi. **Married**, Six sons.

Career: Director of Abu Dhabi National Company for Building Materials; Member of al-Ain Minicipal Council; Chairman of al-Mazroui and Partners; Owner of Rasco Company. **Hobbies:** hunting, falconry, Islamic thought and culture. **Prof. Addr.:** P.O.Box 2443, Tel.: 823834, Abu Dhabi, U.A.E. and P.O.Box 1229, al-Ain, United Arab Emirates.

MANSOURI (Ben Ali), Moroccan former minister. **Born** on May 3, 1944 in Nador. **Dipl.:** Ecole Supérieure de Commerce (France) (1966); Spanish Chamber of Commerce (Paris) (1967). **Career:** appointed at the "Office Chérifien des Phosphates"; on mission at the State Secretariat for National Promotion and Handicrafts; Director, Ministry of Agriculture and Agrarian Reform; Chief of Cabinet, Ministry of Co-operation and Cadre Training; Assistant Director, Chief of the Civil Services Division; Deputy and President of the Provincial Assembly of Nador; Minister of Tourism (1977-79); Minister of Administrative Affairs (1979-81); Minister of Transport (1981-83); Member of parliament and Deputy of Nador (1983-). **Addr.:** Rabat, Morocco.

MANSOURI (Darwish, Mohamad Ali, al), United Arab Emirates administrator. **Born** in 1948, in Abu Dhabi. **Son** of Mohamed Ali al-Mansouri. **Married**, three children. **Career:** Editor of al-Ittihad newspaper, Director of General Administration, Ministry of Foreign Affairs; Director Consulate and Passports Department, Ministry of Foreign Affairs. **Sports:** Swimming. **Hobbies:** Fishing and hunting. **Addr.:** Ministry of Foreign Affairs, P.O.Box 1, Abu Dhabi, United Arab Emirates.

MANSOURI (Hamad Hamid Zaiban, al), United Arab Emirates official. **Son** of Zaiban al-Mansouri. **Born** in 1941. **Married**, nine children. **Career:** Representative of the Ruler of Abu Dhabi in India (1971); United Arab Emirates Consul General in Bombay, India; Office of Complaints and Suggestions, former Minister of State for Prime Ministerial Affairs. **Sports:** Diving. **Hobbies:** Hunting, fishing, reading books on industrial technology. **Addr.:** Abu Dhabi, United Arab Emirates.

MANSOURI (Hussein Ibrahim, al), Saudi former minister. **Born** in 1932, in Mecca, Saudi Arabia. **Dipl.:** graduated from al-Falah School, Mecca. **Career:** Began with the Ministry of PTT; held several gorvernment posts in the Departments of Telegraph, Post, Telephone, Railroad, Ports and Roads; Director General Ministry of Communications (1960); Deputy Minister, Ministry of Communications (1964-75); Minister of Communications (since 1976 to Aug. 1995). **Honours:** several Orders of Merit and Medals. **Hobby:** reading. **Address:** Riyadh, Saudi Arabia.

MANSOURI (Tareq, Ahmad), Saudi civil engineer. **Born** on December 5, 1947 in Mecca, Saudi Arabia. **Married. Educ.:** Colorado State University, USA. **Dipl.:** Ph.D. in Civil Engineering (1980). **Career:** Assistant Professor at the University of Petroleum and Minerals (1980-80); Principal Civil Engineer of Bechtel Corporation (1982-83); Special Projects Manager, International Airports Projects (1983); **Publ.:** co-author of two articles on liquifaction in soil mechanics (1981) (1983). **Member:** American Society of Civil Engineers. **Hobbies:** Sport, reading, photography. **Prof. Addr.:** International Airports Projects, P.O.Box 6326, No.1011 Manager Housing, Tel.: 6853311, Telex: 401933 IAPJED SJ, Jeddah, Saudi Arabia.

MANZER (Bruce Monroe), American Librarian. **Born** on April 8, 1936 at Ballston Spa, New York U.S.A. **son** of James William Manzer **and** Mrs. Lottle Fitzgerald. **Educ.:** Union College (Schenectady, N.Y.); University of Michigan; University of Chicago. **Dipl.:** B.S. (Chemistry); A.M. (library science); Ph.D. (library science). **Career:** Acquisitions librarian & reference assistant, Battelle Memorial Institute, Columbus, Ohio (1960-64); Librarian, Inorganic Chemicals Division, The Glidden Co., Baltimore, Maryland (1964-66); Assistant Librarian, Technical Processing, The University of California Lawrence Livermore Laboratory, Livermore, California (1966-67); Editor, «Chemical Abstracts Service Source Index», Chemical Abstracts Service, Columbus, Ohio (1967-70); Science Librarian & Associate Professor, Illinois State University, Normal, Illinois (1974-81); University Librarian & Associate Professor, University College of Bahrain, Bahrain (1981-83); Visiting Associate Professor, Graduate School of Library and Information Science, University of Illinois at Champaign-Urbana (1983-84); Chief, Science & Technology Division, New York Public Library, New York City (1984-86); Chief Medical Librarian, College of Health Sciences, Ministry of Health, Bahrain (1986 to present) **Concurrent teaching experience:** Visiting Lecturer, School of Librarianship, University of Washington, Seattle, Washington (summer 1973); Visiting Assistant Professor, Graduate School of Librarianship, University of Denver (summer 1977); Fulbright Professor, Dept. of Librarianship & Information Science, Cairo University, Cairo, Egypt (1978-79). **Publ.:** Author: «The Abstract Journal», 1790-1920; «Origin, Development, and Diffusion», Metuchan, Scarecrow Press, 1977; «Saratoga Country Bibliography», Saratoga Springs, Southern Adirondack County Library System, 1982; «Medicine, Nursing & Allied Health Sciences in Bahrain: an Annotated Bibliography», Bahrain, College of Health Sciences, 1987. Editor: «Chemical Abstracts Service Source Index», Washington, American Chemical Society, 1969; «New Technical Books» (1984-86), New York, New York Public Library. Donor of the Manzer Collection of Local History to the Ballston Spa Public Library, Ballston Spa, New York (more than 1,000 volumes). **Honors:** Beta Phi Mu (Library Science Honorary); Commendation for Service to the Government of Egypt, U.S. - Egypt Bi-National Commission for Educational and Cultural Exchange, 1979; Fulbright teaching grant, Cairo University (1978-79). **Membership:** Fulbright Alumni Association. **Community Service:** Board of Managers of the Al-Rajah School (Amerian Mission School) (1994-), (Chairman, 1994-1996). **Hobbies:** Music, book collecting. **Credit Cards:** American Express. **Prof. Addr.:** Ministry of Health, P.O.Box 12, Bahrain, Tel.: 255555. **Priv. Addr.:** House 342, Road 116, Block 1001, Jasra, Bahrain, Tel.: 611659.

MAOUI (Abdul Aziz), Algerian diplomat. **Born** in 1929 in Algeria. **Married. Educ.:** University of Algeria. **Dipl.:** Licence en Droit. **Career:** Secretary General, Ministry of Foreign Affairs (1964); Minister of Tourism (1965-77); Ambassador to USA (1977-80). **Addr.:** Ministry of Foreign Affairs, 6 Rue Ibn Batram al Mouradia, Algiers, Algeria.

MAQBUL (Taj al-Sirr Ahmad, General), Sudanese former army commander. **Born** in 1933 in Talvdi, Sudan. **Married,** six children. **Educ.:** Cambridge University; Sudanese Military College; Indian Staff College. **Dipl.:** B.A. and Certificates from Staff Colleges. **Career:** Captain (1958); Major (1961); Lieutenant Colonel (1969); Brigadier (1970); General (1974); Chairman and General Manager, State Corporation for Cinema. **Medals:** Order of the May Revolution. **President** of the Union of the Graduates of Ahfad Schools. **Addr.:** P.O.Box 2705, Khartoum, Sudan.

MARAKCHI (Mohamad), Moroccan businessman. **Born** in Fes Morocco. **Married,** Five children. **Educ.:** B.Sc. **Career:** Member of several Moroccan economic organisation; Director General, Maghreb Industries SA; Director and Partner CAPLAM, Kleber Colombe; Director General, Industries Marocaines Modernes, Procter and Gamble: Director, SODIPI, Camping Gaz International. **Sport:** Golf. **Addr.:** Maghreb Industries, 35 Avenue Khalid Ibnou Loualid, P.O.Box 2516, Tel.: 350296, 250597, Ain Sebaa, Casablanca, Morocco.

MARAQA (Jawad, Muhammad), Jordanian mass media expert. **Born** in 1938 in al-Khalil, Palestine. **Married,** 2 sons, 1 daughter. **Educ.:** Damascus University, Syria; Teacher's College, Amman, Jordan. **Dipl.:** BA in Philosophy and Social Studies. **Career:** Teacher; Head of Administration and Office Manager to the Minister of Information; Managing Editor of Jordan News Agency Programme Manager of Jordan Television; Programme Manager of Qatar Television, later General Manager of QTV.; Assistant General Manager, Ministry of Information; Production Centre Manager, Jordan Television; General Manager of Jordan News Agency; Chairman & General Manager of the Jordan company for T.V., Radio & Cinema Production (since June 5, 1986-). **Prof. Addr.:** Jordan company for T.V., Radio & Cinema Production Ltd., P.O.Box 950571/620149, Tel.: 773902, 773906, Telex: 23572 JPTV JO, Fax: 962-6-746055, Amman, Jordan.

MARAQA (Muhammad, Isaac Abdul Haye), Jordanian administrator. **Born** in 1934 in al-Khalil, Palestine. **Married,** 5 children. **Educ.:** Royal college of Surgeons, UK, American College of Surgeons, USA. **Career:** General Surgeon, Royal Medical Service (1964); Head, Surgery Department, el-Hossein Medical City (1973-76); Manager of el-Hossein Medical City (1976-78); Consultant Brain Surgeon, Jordan clinic (1978); Member of National Advisory Council (1980-84); Member of the Board of Islamic Hospital (1982-); Member of the Board of the Islamic Cultural Centre (1984-). **Decor.:** Order of Independence (1st Class), Jordan (1974). **Hobby:** reading. **Prof. Addr.:** P.O.Box 17065, Amman, Jordan.

MARAR (Toufiq, Salim), Jordanian civil engineer. **Born** on November 14, 1913 in Madaba (Jordan). **Son** of Salim Marar **and** Mrs. Azizeh Marar. **Married** to Laure Aziz Salem in July 1947, 5 children: Souheil, Eva, Ousama, Hanan and Amjad. **Educ.:** College of the Christian Brothers (1922-30); The High Engineering School (Beirut). **Dipl.:** Bachelor of Science in Civil Engineering (1939). **Career:** Civil Engineer, Public Works Ministry, Jordan; Promoted to District Engineer, Northern District (3 years); Transferred as District Engineer, Balga District; then Chief Engineer in the Technical Department; Promoted to Assistant Under-secretary of State for Public Works; Under-Secretary of State for Public Works and Director of Civil Aviation; Delegated to represent Jordan in the Technical Committee for the rehabilitation of the Hedjaz Railway (April 1947); Founder and President of the Society of Engineers and Architects, Jordan (1948) and the Order of Engineers and Architects (1958); Founder of T. Marar, Trading Business for building materials (1958); Formed with two other partners the General Equipment Company (a Contracting firm for Civil Engineering Works which executed Road Dams Irrigation Contracts in Jordan). **Awards:** Knighthood of St. Sylvester by Pope Pius XII (1953) and the Silver Medal of the Order of the Holy Sepulchre. **Member:** Board of Trustees of Cheshire Homes, President of the Amman Lion Club (2 years), Chairman (2 years), Deputy District Governor (one year), Chairman of the Extension Programme (one year), Has many activities and Contributions in Philantropic Societies: St. Vincent de Paul, The Humanitarian Society, Jordan Red Crescent, etc... **Remark:** Planned and supervised the execution of more than fifty schools, colleges, churches, convents and hospitals. **Addr.:** P.O.Box 1569, Amman, Jordan.

MARAYATI (Boutros, Mgr.), Syrian archbishop of Armenian Catholic Diocese. **Born** on February 26, 1948 in Aleppo, Syria. **Son** of Bahjat Marayati (Accountancy) **and** Mrs. Victoria Sabeh. **Educ.:** "Frères Maristes" College of Aleppo; Patriarchal Seminary of Bzommar (Lebanon); Gregoriana University of Rome (Italy); University of Aleppo (Syria). **Dipl.:** Master of Philosophy; Master of Divinity; Bachelor of Armenian Religious Science; Bachelor of Arabic Literature. **Career:** Member of Middle East

Bible Federation (1989); Member of Middle East Council of Churches (1990); Member of Catholic Assembly of Syria (1990); Member of Armenian Catholic Permanent Synod (1991); President of Catholic Catechism Society in Aleppo (1990). **Prof. Addr.:** Rue Tillel, 121, P.O.Box 97, Tel.: 218955, Aleppo, Syria. **Priv. Addr.:** Rue Tillel, 121, Tel.: 213946, Aleppo, Syria.

MARDI (al-Tayib, al, Colonel), Sudanese official. **Born** in 1927 in Sudan. **Married. Educ.:** took courses in USA, UK and Pakistan; Military College. **Career:** retired from army in 1957; recalled to service in 1959; Military Attaché, Embassy to USA and Embassy to UK; retired in 1969; Presidential Secretariat (1972); Member of the Commission for Returnees; Member of the First People's Assembly, Chairman of its National Defence Committee; Commissioner of Darfur (1973) and Northern Darfur when province was divided (1974). **Addr.:** Northern Darfur, Sudan.

MARDI (Mahmoud, al), Bahraini journalist. **Born** in 1928 in Bahrain. **Married** in 1960 to Miss Ahmadi, four children: Mawahib, Ra'ed, Rula and Mo'anis. **Educ.:** Bahrain secondary school. **Dipl.:** Matriculation. **Career:** Commercial assistant, British Bank (1948-54); Manager, Banque du Caire (1954-62); Founded, Arabian Printing and Publishing House, Bahrain; Editor, "al-Adwa" weekly; "Akhbar al-Khalij", daily; Gulf Daily News (English); General Manager, Gulf Industrial Investment Co. **Sports:** Table tennis and badmington **Hobby:** Fishing. **Member:** Bapco club; al-Ahli club. **Credit Card:** American Espress. **Prof. Addr.:** P.O.Box 250, Manama, Bahrain. **Priv. Addr.:** Samaniya, Tel.: 52878, Bahrain.

MAREI (Ahmad), Egyptian radiologist. **Born** in Egypt. **Educ.:** Secondary and Higher, Edinburgh University. **Dipl.:** Bachelor of Medicine, Specialisation in Radiology. **Career:** Radiologist; Professor of Radiology, Faculty of Medicine (Cairo University). **Member:** Gezira Sporting Club. **Addr.:** 26, al-Gazira al-Wousta Street, Zamalek, Tel.: 805467, Cairo, Egypt.

MAREI (Hassan), Egyptian engineer and statesman. **Born** in Egypt. **Educ.:** Secondary and Higher. **Dipl.:** of Engineering. **Career:** Engineer, Former Deputy Under-Secretary for Education, Professor, Faculty of Engineering. Former Minister of Commerce and Industry. **Addr.:** 15, Abu-Bakr as-Saddiq Street, Heliopolis, Tel.: 62608, Cairo, Egypt.

MARGHALANY (Yousuf Abdul Mannan), Saudi academic. **Born** in 1941. **Educ.:** Ph.D. **Career:** Assistant Professor; Head, Department of Chemistry, Faculty of Education, Umm al-Qura University, Mecca. **Publication:** Practical Chemistry, a textbook for first year secondary school. **Hobbies:** sports, reading. **Prof. Addr.:** Faculty of Education, Umm al-Qura University, Tel.: 5564770, Mecca. **Priv. Addr.:** Tel.: 5431434, Mecca, Saudi Arabia.

MARHOUN (Muhamad Ali, al, Dr.), Saudi academic. **Born** on August 8, 1950 at Qatif. **Dipl.:** B.S. and M.S. degrees in General Engineering and Mathematics from King Fahd University of Petroleum and Minerals (KFUPM), Saudi Arabia; Ph.D. degree in Petroleum Engineering from Oklahoma University, Norman, Oklahoma, United States. **Career:** Professor of Petroleum Engineering, King Fahd University of Petroleum and Minerals, Dhahran, Saudi Arabia; former Chairman of Petroleum Engineering Department at KFUPM; Has interest in Petroleum Fluids Properties and Reservoir Simulation. **Publ.:** published numerous research and technical papers. **Member of:** Society of Petroleum Engineers of AIME and Petroleum Society of CIM. **Address:** King Fahd University of Petroleum and Minerals, P.O.Box 198, Dhahran 31261, Saudi Arabia, Tel.: 8602536, Telex 801060 KFUPM SJ, Fax: 966-3-8604447.

MARIA (Francis), Management consultant, lecturer, executive, educator, community leader (local, national and international). **Born** on January 1, 1913 at Lowell, Massachusetts, U.S.A. **Son** of John Maria (Proprietor, Grocery Store-born in Saidnaya, Syria) **and** Mrs. Mary Saba Maria - (born in Saidnaya, Syria). **Unmarried. Educ.:** Cross Street School, Bartlett Junior High, and Lowell High School (Public Schools in Lowell, Mass). Boston Un. College of liberal Arts (A.B.); Boston Un. Graduate School (M.A.); B.U. and Harvard Graduate Schools Extension Program (Ph.D.). **Dipl.:** Lowell High School (1931 and 1932); A.B. cum Honnore, Boston Un. Liberal Arts (1936); Phi Beta Kappa (1936) national scholarship honor fraternity; Boston University Graduate School (1937); Phi Delta Kappa (1973) national educational honor society; Prof. Augustus Howe Buck Scholar and Graduate Fellow, B.U.'s Highly coveted scholarship and fellowship; Doctor of Humane Letters, Honorary Degree, 1995 Commencement, University of New Hampshire. **Career:** Education; teacher, athletic coach, and administrator (1937-43), high School and College; Military service: World War II. U.S. Marine Air Corps (1943-46); Executive in Industry, including Vice President for Industrial and Public Relations, Merrimack Manufacturing Company, large textile industry, Lowell, Massachusetts (1946-56). Government service (1960 to present), has served at different intervals as Member, U.S. Delegation to Eleventh General Assembly of UNESCO, Paris; Special Assistant to the Governor of Massachusetts (1961-63); Staff Aid and Consultant to the Governor of Massachusetts (1965-67) and Deputy Commissioner, Dept. of Banking and Insurance (1967-75). Management Consultant and Lecturer, Frank Maria and Associates, Boston, Mass. and Warner, New Hampshire (1957 to present).Consultant to the Secretary General of the World Muslim League, Dr. Abdulla Omar Nasseef, on American Ecumenical Affairs and on Justice and Peace Issues (1984-1985). **Act.:** Active leader in Church, ecumenical, charitable, cultural, social service, educational and civic organizations, especially in Arab-American Affairs on regional, national and international levels. Among the many organizations that he has been active with are the following: Arab and American Peoples Association, Sharjah, U.A.E. and New York City, U.S.A., (1980-1986); National Association of Arab Americans (1972-present); Chairman, Dept. of Near East and Arab Refuge Affairs (1968-1982) and Ecumenical Committee (1982-present) Antiochian Orthodox Christian Archdiocese of North American; World Council of Churches' 6th Assembly in Vancouver, British Columbia, Canada, July 22- August 11, 1983, U.S.A. Delegate with the Greek Orthodox Church of Antioch and All the East, Damascus, Syria; the National Council of Churches in the U.S.A.: Member of the Governing Board, the Executive Committee, the Inter-Faith (Christian-Jewish-Islamic) Committee, the Minority Caucus, and the Middle East Committee of the Division of Overseas Ministries (1970-present); Chairman, Coordination Committee of Arab American Christian and Islamic Organizations in New England (1970-present); Presiding Officer, First International Convention of Arabic speaking emigrants in Syria and Lebanon in 1950; President, Syrian and Lebanese American Federation (1949-51); Initiating Chairman, First Meeting of Arab American Leaders with a President of the United States (President Harry Truman, Octobre 2, 1951); National Chairman, Arab American Republican Committee; etc. Medals and Decorations: Boston University Distinguished Public Service Award, 1957; Syrian and Lebanese American Federation's Outstanding Achievement Award (1960); New York Salaam Club's Man-of-the-Year Award (1969); Nicholas G.Beram Veterans' Association Distinguished Public Service Award (1970); Citation on UNESCO Diplomatic Service, President Dwight D. Eisenhower (January 1961); Citation on Service to the Governor and the Government of the Commonwealth of Massachusetts, Governor John A. Volpe (December 1962); ACTION-English-Arabic Newspaper, Man of the Year Award (1970); Cleveland Federation of Lebanon-Syrian American Clubs, First Annual Distinguished Service Award (August 1973); American Near East Refugee Relief, Inc., Meritorious Service Award (September 1973); Antonian Silver Medal of Merit, Antiochian Orthodox Christian Archdiocese of North America (June 1974); "Ecumencial Committee's First Peace with Justice Award, 1991, and the Antonian Gold Medal, October 31 1993"; American Arabic Association's Distinguished Public Service Award, June 1981; National Association of Arab American's First Distinguished Service Award, May 1, 1982; National Palestine Human Rights Campaign, Human Rights Award, Octobre 14, 1982, etc. The American Arab Anti-Discrimination Committee's Arab Heritage Award, September 6, 1985; "Lifetime Achievement Award for Justice and Peace, April 1992"; The American Arab Chamber of Commerce's Robert P. Zahka Community Service Award, October 15 1986; National Council of Churches in the USA's Citation for Leadership in Christian/Islamic Rels. May 1987; "Honorary Member and Participant in the History of the Mills, Lowell Industrial National Park, Lowell, Massachusett6s, 1989 and 1993"; **Sports:** Basketball (playing, coaching and refereeing; has one of the best coaching records in the USA). **Hobby:** Writing, Lecturing, Theatre, Radio and T.V. production and guest appearances, Gardening, Community activities. **Member:** AMARA (American Arabic Association), Founder and past president; National Association of Arab Americans, founding charter member, Board of Directors, Executive Committee, Chairman of Key Committees (Political Action and Government Liaison, Planning and Resolutions, Public Relations, and Ecumenical Affairs) and Vice President; Arab and American People's Association, Chairman of American Committee; Standing Conference of Middle Eastern Religious Leaders (Consultant-1976); Antiochian Orthodox Christian Archdiocese of North American, Ecumenical Committee and Consultant on Middle Eastern Affairs, 1968-present; Co-ordinating Committee of Arab American Religious and Civic Organizations in New England (1971-present) Chairman; World Council of Churches, American Delegate from the Church of Antioch; National Council of Churches in the USA, Executive Committee (1979), Governing Board, 1970, Middle East Committee (1970); Arab Heritage Committee, National Republican Party, Chairman (1968-80); North American Debut and Tour of Lebanon's renowned singer "Fayrouz" and Lebanon's Folkloric Troupe (September and October 1972), Community Affairs Director; Project Loving Care for Arab Children in Palestine and in Lebanon (1969-present), Co-Developer and Co-promoter; American-Arab Anti-Discrimination Committee, (1980 to present) Founding charter member and national council member; American Friends of the Middle East (now AMID-East), a founder and national council member, 1951; Co-ordinating Committee of Church-related and other Voluntary Agencies engaged in refuge relief and other humanitarian activities in the Middle East (1969-1973), Iniating Chairman; "A Plea for Justice for people of the Holy Land" National Cathedral, Washington, D.C., (January 27, 1971), Program Chairman; etc. **Media Citations:** In numerous articles on his volunteer service to the Arab American community, to the just Arab cause, Christian-Islamic relations, and to justice and peace in the Middle East, the American press has refered to him as "Mr. Arab American" and the Arab American press has hailed him as "The Arab American of the Century", **Philanthropy:** To continue his volunteer work for Justice and Peace in the Middle East through humanitarian, charitable, education and ecumenical activity, with public relations and political activity, the following have been established: The Francis Maria Foundation for Justice and Peace Headquartered in Warner, NH; Antiochian Orthodox Christian Archdiocese Francis Maria Fund for Justice and Peace, Englewood, NJ; The Yale Maria Endowed Fund at the University of NH, Durham, in honor of Friend and Author Prof. William E. Yale; The

Francis Maria Classroom in the School of Management Building, Boston University, Boston, MA; Dr. Frank Maria Conference Room and Book-shelf at Pillsbury Free Library, Warner, NH; The Maria Fund for Ecumenical and Interfaith Activity at the United Church of Warner; The Dr. Maria fund at New England College in Henniker, NH, and Arundel, West Sussex, England; The Frank Maria distinguished Lecture Series at St. Anselm College, Manchester, NH; The Maria Bookshelf at Magdalen College in Warner, NH; Cumberland College, Williamsburg, KY; Scholarships at the University of Beirut in Lebanon (AUB) and through American Near East Refugee Aid (ANERA); Near east Catholic Welfare; UNICEF, American-Arab Organizations; Native American Charities; area Churches and Charities; Habitat for Humanity and others. **Recent Honors:** Honorary "Doctor of Humane Letters" by the University of New Hampshire, Durham, NH in 1995: The National Council of Churches in the USA established the Maria Fund for Justice and Peace in the Middle East in 1999. **Prof. Addr.:** P.O.Box 46, Warner, NH, USA 03278. **Priv. Addr.:** 71 Old Pumpkin Hill Road, Warner, NH, Tel.: (603)456-3454, USA.

MARINI (Abu Bakr, al), Moroccan journalist. **Born** in 1939 in Sale, Morocco. **Married**, two daughters. **Educ.:** Degrees in Education and Law (1969); M.A. in Higher Studies, Dar al-Hadith al-Hassaniya. **Career:** Head of Conferences and Editor in Chamber of Deputies (1972); Private Secretary to the Minister of Education (1973); founder and Editor of "al-Fanoun" arts magazine of the Ministry of State for Educational Affairs; Editor of "al-Atfal" (The Children) Magazine. **Publ.:** Poetry, "Freedom Spoke to Me" in Arabic (1970); "The Holy Struggle"; "Legend about the Octobre War" (1973); "Umm Khaltoun-20th Century Miracle"; four anthologies, ten plays, three collections of stories, a collection of proverbs entitled "Zanabeq Wa Ashwak". **Medals:** The Green March (1975). Member of the Scientists Association. **Hobbies:** Chess, rowing, educational issues. **Addr.:** 14 Zanqat al Marini, Bad Ibsayen, Sale, Morocco.

MARNOCH (Iain Archibald), British executive. **Born** in 1940 in Scotland. **Son** of Duncan Marnoch. **Married** in 1966, 1 son, 1 daughter. **Educ.:** Strathallan School, Scotland; University of Michigan, USA; University of Strathclyde, Scotland. **Dipl.:** M.I.B. (1962). **Career:** The Chartered Bank in London, Middle East and Manila (1962-72); Vice President, Chase Manhattan Bank, New York, Chicago and Bahrain (1972-80); Assistant General Manager, Dubai Bank Ltd., Dubai (1981-83); General Manager, Bank of Oman, Bahrain and Kuwait S.A.O., (B.O.B.K.) (1984 to present). **Member:** Institute of Directors; RAC Club, England. **Hobbies:** Waterskiing and Gliding. **Addr.:** Bank of Oman, Bahrain and Kuwait S.A.O.G., P.O.Box 1708, Ruwi 112, Tel.: 703687, Telex: 3290 OBK ON, Telefax: 705607 Sultanate of Oman.

MARRI (Jaber, Abdulhadi, al, Dr.), Qatari executive. **Born** in 1952 in Qatar. **Son** of Mr. Abdulhadi al-Marri (Head of a Sect). **Married** in Doha, Qatar. **Educ.:** Tulsa University, USA; West Virginia State University, USA. **Dipl.:** B.Sc. Petroleum Engineering (1977), M.S. Petroleum Engineering (1980) and Ph.D. Petroleum Engineering (1983). **Career:** Acting Manager, Petroleum Engineering Department (1984); Deputy Managing Director, Qatar General Petroleum corporation (1986); Acting General Manager, North Field Development Project (1987); Managing Director, Qatar General Petroleum Corporation (1988-); Board Director, Qatar National Bank, Qatar; **Member:** Society of Petroleum Engineers; AMA International. **Credit Card:** American Express; Diner's Club; Visa. **Prof. Addr.:** QGPC, P.O.Box 3212, West Bay, Tel.: 491491, Doha-Qatar. **Priv. Addr.:** P.O.Box 3212, Tel.: 882511, Doha, Qatar.

MARROW (Anwar, S.), Iraqi banker. **Born** on August 1, 1921 in Baghdad. **Educ.:** College of Law (Baghdad). **Married** to Miss Violette E. Sarafa. **Career:** Director, Loans and Investments, Central Bank of Iraq. **Member:** Alwiyah Club, Baghdad Club. **Addr.:** 74-37, Battawiyenn, Meshah, Baghdad, Iraq.

MARSAGHAWI (Hassan, Sadiq, al), Egyptian academic, judge. **Born** in 1923 in Zaqazig, Egypt. **Son** of Sadiq al-Marsaghawi. **Married**, two children. **Educ.:** Ph.D. in law, Cairo University (1954). **Career:** Deputy Procesutor General; Judge; Lecturer, College of law, Alexandria University, Egypt; Professor, College of law, Alexandria University (since 1965); Lawyer at the Court of Appeal. **Publ.:** Many books on the implementation and interpretation of different aspects of law. **Hobbies:** Reading, Walking. **Addr.:** 13 Kamil Gailani Street, Babsharqi, Tel.: 33155, Alexandria, Egypt.

MARSH (Ian Kelvin), British executive. **Born** in 1953 in London, UK. **Son** of Harry Marsh. **Married** in 1978, 1 daughter. **Educ.:** Grammar School; King's College, London; Associate Institute of Bankers Studies (1978). **Career:** Joined American Express International Banking Co. since 1972; Head Cashier, Keflavic Iceland (1972-73); Branch Manager, Harrogate, U.K. (1973-74); Branch Manager, Morocco (1974-75); District Manager, Greece (1975-76); Management Trainee, Greece (1976-78); Assistant Treasurer, Greece; Assistant Vice President, American Express International Banking Co., Dubai (1981-86). **Member:** Institute of Bankers: Morgan Sports Car Club; Hash House Hariers Passport Businessmans Club. **Hobbies:** Running, Tennis, Squash, Windsurfing, Swimming and Photography. **Addr.:** P.O.Box 3304, Tel.: 223236, Telex: 46245, 45810 A/B AMEHBK EM, Dubai, UAE.

MARSOT (Afaf Lutfi al-Sayyid), Egyptian academic. **Born** in 1933 in Cairo, Egypt. **Married**, 2 daughters. **Educ.:** Oxford University, Oxford, UK; Stanford University,

USA; American University in Cairo, Egypt. **Dipl.:** D.Phil. in Oriental Studies, M.A. in Political Science, B.A. in Sociology. **Career:** Professor of Near East History, University of California, Los Angeles, California, USA; Acting Director of Near East Centre, University of California, Los Angeles (1966-67); Member of the American Research Centre in Egypt; Member, American Historical Association; Member and Former President, The Middle East Studies Association (1977); Member and Former President of The American Research Centre in Egypt (1990-93); Editor of The International Journal of Middle East Studies (1979-1984). **Publ.:** "Egypt and Cromer" (1967), "Egypt Liberal Experiment" (1976); "Egypt in the reign of Muhammad Ali" (1983); "A short History of Egypt" (1985). Over 25 articles. **Prof. Addr.:** Department of History, University of California, Los Angeles, California 90024, USA.

MARTO (Michel, Issa, Dr.), Jordanian banker. **Born** on August 21, 1940 Son of late Issa Marto (Businessman) and late Mrs. Wardeh Marto. **Married** on Sept. 25, 1970 in Beirut, Lebanon to Lucy Peridakis, three children: Ilene, Issa and Iman. **Educ.:** Middle East University, Ankara, Turkey; University of Southern California, Los Angelos, California, USA; Stanford University, Palo Alto, California, USA. **Dipl.:** B.Sc. (1962); M.A. (1968); Ph.D. (1970). **Career:** Economist, Central Bank of Jordan (1963-70); Director, Royal Scientific Society (1971-74); Economic Adviser to HRH Crown Prince Hassan (1974-75); Economist, the World Bank, Washington, D.C. (1975-77); Deputy General Manager, Jordan Fertilizer Industry (1977-79); Deputy General Manager Bank of Jordan (1979-87) and Managing Director of Bank of Jordan (1987-89); Deputy Governor, Central Bank of Jordan (1989); Minister of Finance (since Sept. 1998). **Publ.:** Published books: "A Systems Analysis of Farm-to-Market Food Losses in the Area of Bogota, Colombia" University of California (1968); "A money Sypply Model for Jordan, 1970, Ph.D. Dissertation, University of Southern California, (published by Central Bank of Jordan)". Published articles: "Money Supply Determination-Theory and Approaches" Ekonomska Analiza (Yugoslavia), "Housing in the Jordan Valley" RSS (June 1972); "Role of Agriculture and irrigation in the Economic Development of Jordan" Presented: Jordan Development Conference, (Nov. 1972), Amman, Jordan; "An Econometric Money Supply Model for Jordan 1951-72", RSS, (1974); "Food and Population in the Middle East: Tendencies and Problems" (Nov.1974) reprinted by the Institute of Middle Eastern and North African Affairs in 1976; "Current Macroeconomic Trends and Prospects in the Middle East" (Seminar) "Interest Rate Deregulation: Remarks for Possibilities in Jordan" (May 1988); "Arab Capital Flight and External Debt" (Jan. 1987); "Financial and Economic Challenges facing Middle East after the Gulf War" presented in Istanbul (June 1991). **Award:** Order of the Star of Jordan, decorated by H.M. King Hussain (1975). **Member:** Royal Automobile Club; Jordan British Society; Jordan Greek Society. **Credit Card:** American Express. **Prof. Addr.:** Ministry of finance, Amman, Jordan. **Priv. Addr.:** P.O.Box 2927, Tel.: 816745 Amman, Jordan.

MARWAN (Mohamad, Ashraf), Egyptian businessman. **Born** in 1944 in Cairo, Egypt. **Married.** two children. **Educ.:** B.Sc., M.Sc. and Ph.D. in Chemistry, Cairo University, Egypt. **Career:** Presidential Staff (1967); Assistant of Information Secretariat (1968); Secretary for Information to the President (1971); Presidential Secretary for Foreign Relations (1974); Chairman of Arab Organisation for Industrialisation (1975); chairman, MESTIMO Investment Co. **Addr.:** Cairo, Egypt.

MARZOOQ (Abdus-Sabour), Saudi academic. **Born** in 1925 in Cairo, Egypt. **Dipl.:** Ph.D. (Modern Arabic Literature), Cairo University. **Career:** Former Professor, Arabic Literature, Umm al-Qura University; Director General, Rabetat al-Alam al-Islami (Muslim World League). **Publications:** several books on society, Quranic studies, literature and other topics; various articles in local newspapers. **Hobby:** reading. **Address:** Muslim World League, Mecca, Saudi Arabia.

MARZOOQ (Ahdi, F., al), Kuwaiti executive. **Son** of Fahd al-Marzouq. **Married** to Nadia al-Haroun, 1 child: Sattam. **Educ.:** Faculty of Commerce, Ayn Shams University, Cairo (Egypt). **Dipl.:** B.Com. (Accountancy) (May 1969). **Career:** Financial Director, Kuwait Airways Corporation; Chairman, Kuwait Publishing House. **Sports:** Soccer and swimming. **Prof. Addr.:** Souq al-Kuwait Building, 6th floor, P.O.Box 23915, Safat, Kuwait. **Priv. Addr.:** Abdullah as-Salem District, Block No. 4, Tel.: 544626, Kuwait.

MARZOOQ (Jasim Khalid), Kuwaiti politician. **Born** in 1933 in Kuwait. **Son** of Khalid al-Dawud Marzuq. **Married. Educ.:** Mubarakuyah School, Kuwait; Cairo University, Egypt. **Career:** Deputy Head of Kuwait Municipality; Head of Kuwait Municipality; Minister of Education (1970- February 1978); Chairman of the Board of Kuwait University; Director-General of Arab Union of Municipalities; Minister of Education (February 16, 1978-82); Minister of Commerce and Industry (May 1982). **Addr.:** Kuwait City, Kuwait.

MARZOOQ (Salim, Khalid, al), Kuwaiti politician. **Born** in 1940. **Married. Dipl.:** Degree in Engineering. **Career:** Ministry of Public Works (1970); established contracting business; has joint venture with Consultants, Mott Hay and Anderson (UK) on road building projects; entered National Assembly in 1971; re-elected in 1975 for constituency of Qibla; interests in oil affairs. **Prof. Addr.:** The National Assembly, Kuwait, Kuwait.

MARZOOQI (Hassan, Abdul Rahman, al), UAE administrator. **Born** in 1937 in Ajman, UAE. **Married,** 5 sons, 3 daughters. **Educ.:** general. **Career:** private business; Administration Section, Ministry of Education, Qatar (1963); Director of Fahd Bin Ali al-Thani Office, Qatar (1962); Director, Administrative and Financial Affairs, Ministry of Youth, Abu Dhabi (1972-). **Hobby:** reading. **Member:** Emirates Club. **Prof. Addr.:** Supreme Council of Youth and Sports, Director of General Secretary Office in Abu Dhabi, P.O.Box 539 Abu Dhabi, United Arab Emirates.

MARZOOQI (Yusuf, Ahmad, al), Saudi executive. **Born** in 1939 in Jeddah (Saudi Arabia). **Educ.:** Faculty of Commerce, Ayn Shams University, Cairo (Egypt). **Dipl.:** B. Com. **Career:** joined the Saudi Arabian Airlines Corporation (Saudia); Chief, Charters and Pilgrims' Flights Accounts Division, Saudia; then Chief of External Sales Audit Division; Chief, Freight and Mail Division; Supervisor of Payment Accounts, Staff Manager of Paymcnt Accounts; Manager, Expenses Administration of Saudia; Asst. Corp. Controller-Disbursement (Saudia); corporate Treasurer (Saudia). **Member:** National Sporting club; al-Rabie Sporting club, Jeddah. **Sports:** Football, Basketball and volleyball. **Hobbies:** reading and photography. **Prof. Addr.:** Saudi Arabian Airlines Corporation, P.O.Box 620, CC 670, Jeddah, Saudi Arabia.

MASANNAT (Youssef M., Prof. Dr.), Jordanian Professor of Geotechnical Engineering, University of Jordan. **Born** on April 29, 1944. **Son** of Matri Suleiman Masannat (deceased) (trade) **and** Mrs. Mary Yousef Sawalha (Masannat). **Married** on July 29, 1973 in Amman to Juliette M. Tadros, 4 children: Yara (December 18, 1974); Mais (March 21, 1977); Faris (November 13,1979); and Sami (September 26, 1981). **Educ.:** Catholic School (1950-1960); Al-Hussein College, Amman (1960-1962); Ain Shams University, Egypt (1962-1966); University of Arizona, Tucson, Arizona (1969-1973). **Dipl.:** B.Sc. Applied Geology (1966); M.Sc. Geological Engineering (1971); Ph.D. Geological Engineering (1973). **Career:** Geotechnical Consultant, Ministry of Public Works and Housing, Jordan (1989-97); and Ministry of Water and Irrigation (1994- till now Head of Department of Civil Engineering, University of Jordan (1990-1991); Dean of Faculty of Engineering, University of Mu'tah (1991-1992); Vice-President University of Mu'tah (1990-1993); Head of Technical Committee, Karameh Dam, Jordan (1993); presently Professor of Geotechnical Engineering, University of Jordan. **Awards:** Second Prize, Cultural Contest, Egypt (1965); Superior Academic Achievement Award, Arizona (1970); First prize, American Institute of Mining Engineers, Arizona Students Chapter (1971). **Sport:** Tennis. **Hobbies:** Trips, Reading and Writing scientific and ec6onomic articles. **Member:** Association of Jordanian Engineers, Orthodox Club, Council for the Accreditation of Higher Education Institutions; Association for Graduates of American Institutes and Universitites. **Prof. Addr.: Faculty of Engineering, University of Jordan, Tel.: 5355000/2738, Amman, Jordan. Priv. Addr.:** Engineer's Housing Project, **Shmeisani**, Building A, Apartment 5, Tel.: 5666942, **Amman**, Jordan.

MASARWA (Tariq, Saleem), Jordanian journalist. **Born** in 1936 in Madaba, Jordan. **Married,** 2 sons. **Educ.:** in West Germany. **Dipl.:** Diploma in Information Studies. **Career:** Head of Political Department, Ministry of Information; Chief of Planning Department, Jordanian Television; Press Attachée, Jordan Embassy in West Germany; Information Advisor, Qatar Government; former Managing Director of "Destour" newspaper; Chief Editor and Member of the Board of "Dar al-Sha'ab Publishing Company"; Director General and Member of the Board of Television Production Company. **Hobby:** reading. **Prof. Addr.:** Dar al-Sha'ab, P.O.Box 3037, Amman, Jordan. **Priv. Addr.:** al-Kamaliya, Suwaylih, Amman, Jordan.

MASHAT (Mahmoud Ahmad), Saudi executive. **Born** in 1945. **Dipl.:** M.A. (Hospital Administration). **Career:** Former accountant, Saudi Arabian Monetary Agency (SAMA); Training Executive, Banking Institute, SAMA; Economic Researcher, SAMA; Assistant Director, Kings Hospital, Jeddah. **Publ.:** Economic currency survey, a contribution to SAMA Report (1970-71). **Prof. Addr.:** Saudi Arabian Monetary Agency, Airport Street, Tel.: 29238, Jeddah, Saudi Arabia.

MASHAT (Mohamad, Sadiq, al), Iraqi diplomat. **Born** in 1930 in Iraq. **Son** of Sadiq al-Mashat. **Married. Educ.:** in Iraq and USA. **Career:** Secretary of State, Ministry of Education; Ambassador, Ministry of Foreign Affairs; Ambassador, Embassy of Iraq, Paris, France (1969-70); President, Mosul University (1970); Minister of Higher Education and Scientific Research (1977-78); Ambassador, Embassy of Iraq, Vienna, Austria (1978-81); Ministry of Foreign Affairs, Baghdad, Iraq (1981-84); Ambassador to France (1984-87); Ambassador to UK. (1987). **Addr.:** Ministry of Foreign Affairs, Baghdad, Iraq.

MASHHADY (Mahmoud Issa), Saudi businessman. **Born** in 1935 in Medina, Saudi Arabia. **Dipl.:** B.A. (Philosophy), Cairo University, 1961; postgraduate, Michigan State University. **Career:** Senior staff member, Aramco (1962-67); Director, Public Relations Department, Petromin (1967-74); owner and Director General of International Trading Bureau, Overseas Catering Establishment, Arabian Public Relations Agency and al-Mashhady Labour Expatriation Bureau; member of the Chamber of Commerce and Industry. **Honour:** a decoration awarded by H.M. King Hassan II of Morocco. **Publications:** Ibtisam, a novel published in Cairo, (1960); Love is not Enough, a collection of short stories, published in Mecca (1972, reprinted in 1980). **Prof. Addr.:** al-Hammad Bldg., Main Ulaya Road, P.O.Box 1249, Tel.: 4659932, Riyadh. **Priv. Addr.:** Tel.: 4655092, Riyadh, Saudi Arabia.

MASHHOUR (Mashhour, Ahmad), Egyptian executive. **Born** in 1918. **Married. Educ.:** Fouad I University (Degree in Engineering), Cairo, Egypt; Staff College, UK; Fort belvoir, USA. **Career:** Joined Ministry of Transport (1941); Army engineer (1942); Lecturer, Egyptian Academy of War (1948-52); Staff Officer, Egyptian Corps of Engineers; Director of Transit, Suez Canal Authority (1956); Director, Timsah Shipbuilding Company, Ismailia; Deputy Chairman, Suez Canal Authority (1964); Promoted to Chairman (1965); Reelected as Arab Socialist Union Secretary for Ismailia (1968) and elected to the Central Committee of the Arab Socialist Union (1968); **Addr.:** 6 Lazoghli Street, Garden City, Cairo, Egypt.

MASHTA (Tuham, Lieutenant Colonel), Tunisian airforce officer. **Born** in 1935 in Tunisia. **Married. Educ.:** Ecole de l'Air, Salon, France (1957); studies in USA (1968-69); course in France (1971-73). **Career:** Flying Instructor; Commander First Air Unit (1965-68); nominated Commanding Officer of the Tunisian Air Forces (1971); Acting Chief of Staff of the Tunisian Air Force (1974). **Addr.:** Ministry of National Defence, Tunis, Tunisia.

MASKATI (Hussain Mahdi, al), Bahraini businessman. **Born** in 1925 in Bahrain. **Son** of Mahdi al-Maskati **and** Mrs. Madinah née al-Mukhariq. **Married** in 1950 in Bahrain to Layla Arrayed, 6 children: Dr. Nabeel, Adel, Nada, Khalid, Dr. Maha, Shatha. **Educ.:** Bahrain Government Educational Intitutions. **Career:** Established a Small Trading Firm (1945); Started Paper Conversion Plant (1958); Started Polythene Extrusion Plant (1978); Started Injection Moulding Plant (1988); Managing Director, Maskati Bros. & Co.; Chief Executive, Maskati Commercial Services W.L.L.; Managing Director, Tylos Paper Factory Co. **Sports:** Swimming. **Hobby:** Reading. **Member:** al-Orooba Club, Bahrain. **Credit Cards:** American Express, Visa. **Prof. Addr.:** Maskati Bros. & Co., P.O.Box 24, Tel.: 72.99.11, Telex: 8621 PAPER BN, Fax: (973) 72.54.54, Manama, Bahrain. **Priv. Addr.:** Tel.: 590303, Bahrain.

MASKATI (Khalid, al), Bahraini Businessman. **Born** on January 23, 1959 at Manama, Bahrain. **Son** of Hussain Al Maskati (Businessman) and Mrs. Layla Al Arrayyed. **Education:** American University of Beirut, Texas tech University, B.A. in Business Administration, Industrial Sciences. **Career:** Sales Manager, Maskati Bros. & Co. (1980-1985); General Manager, Maskati Bros. & Co. and Managing Director of Maskati Commercial Services (1986-1989). Onwards 1990 to present: Managing Director of Maskati Bros. Group of Companies.; Director, Maskati Commercial Services; Director, Gulf Trading & Development Co.; Director, American Mission Hospital,; Executive Member, Shura Consultative Council (1997 to present),; Member of Prime Minister Awards Committee (1998),; Executive Director of the board, Chamber of Commerce and Industry, Bahrain. Director, MCS Plastics, (U.K) Ltd **Member:** Rotary Club of Sulmaniya, Manama, Bahrain. **Address:** Maskati Bros. & Co., P.O.Box 24, **Tel.:** (973) 729911, Manama, Bahrain. **Private Address:** P.O.Box 3031, Manama, Bahrain.

MASMOUDI (Mohamad, Abdul Rahman, al), Tunisian administrator. **Born** in 1934 in Sfax, Tunisia. **Married,** 3 children. **Educ.:** Sorbonne, Paris, France. **Dipl.:** B.A. **Career:** Official at the National Museum (1958-61); Director of Publishing, National Company for Publishing (1961-63); History and Geography Teacher and Senior Researcher, Art and Heritage Museum, Sfax (1963-65); Supervisor and Research, National Art and Heritage Centre (1965-73); Researcher and Director General of Arab House of Book Company (1965-76); Member of the International Council of Museums; Founder of Publishing Company (1976), Founder of the National Department for Traditional Industries, Qatar; Chief Executive and Managing Director in Traditional Industries (1977); Chairman of International Artifex Society, Paris (1984-). **Publ.:** "Tunisia" (1968), "Sfax City" (1979), "Creation in the Traditional Industries" (1980). **Member:** The Tunisian Writers' Union. **Priv. Addr.:** Sidi Faraj, Sakra Kalam 15, Tunisia.

MASMOUDI (Mohamad, Mohamad), Tunisian statesman and diplomat. **Born** on May 29, 1925 in Mahdia. **Son** of Mohamad Masmoudi **and** Mrs., née Anna Bennour. **Married** on December 20, 1965 to Miss Alya Boulakbeche, 6 children: Habib, Laila, Mouëz, Mohamad, Azza and Amine. **Educ.:** Sadiki School (Tunis), Lycée Carnot (France), University of Paris. **Dipl.:** Licentiate in Literature. **Career:** journalist; Contributed to "as-Sabah", "al-Houriah", "L'Action", "Afrique-Action"; Minister of State (1954), of Economy (1955), of State (1956); Tunisian Ambassador to France and Yugoslavia (1957); Minister of Information (1958); Elected Deputy (1959); Ambassador to France (1965-69); Minister of Foreign Affairs (1970-74). Exiled. Returned to tunisia in December 1977. **Publ.:** Author of "La Tunisie et la France". **Awards:** Decorated by the Governments of Mauritania, Ivory Coast and Senegal. **Hobby:** Antiquities. **Addr.:** La Manouba, Tunisia.

MASMOUDI (Mustapha), Tunisian civil servant. **Born** on May 23, 1937 in Sfax (Tunisia). **Son** of Abdessalem ben Ali Masmoudi (Merchant) and Mrs. Khadija Khaprat. **Married** to Najet Bin Rashid Fendri, 3 daughters; Haifa, Ahlem, Najla. **Educ.:** Primary and Secondary education in Sfax. Higher education in Tunis. **Dipl.:** PhD in Political science, University Paris II, France; Doctorate of Graduate Studies in Information Sciences, University Paris II; B.A. in Law (droit) University of Paris. **Career:** Director of the State Information Department (June 1970); Chairman and General Manager of "Afrique Press" news agency (February 1974); Secretary of State for Information

(1974-78); Ambassador of Tunisia to UNESCO (1978-82); Education Cultural Counselor to the Prime Minister (1982-86); Director of "l'ACTION" daily Newspaper (1986-87); Acting Executive Director of the Destourian Socialist Party (PSD) (1987); Member of Parliament (1986-94) and Chairman of Information Committee; presently General Manager of the Institute MASSMEDIA; Founder & President of l'Association Tunisienne de la Communication (ATUCOM); Professor of Communication, National Administration High Institute (ENA) (since 1990). **Publ.:** Author of "L'Economie de l'Information en Tunisie" (1975); "Le Nouvel Ordre de l'Information" (1985), "Voie libre pour monde multiple" (1985); L'Afrique face à l'autoroute de l'information" (1995). **Awards:** Officer, Independence Order and officer of the Republic of Tunisia, also various decorations from Egypt, Iran, Norway, Belgium, Luxemburg. **Sports:** Swimming and golf. **Hobbies:** Chess, reading and theatricals. **Member:** La Soukr a Golf Club, Tunis. **Professional Address:** Galaxie 2000 Tour A - 7ème étage - rue d'Irak, Tunis 1002, Tunisia.

MASON (Patrick, John), UK bank manager. **Born** on July 16, 1936 in United kingdom. **Married,** 3 daughters. **Educ.:** Prior Park College, Bath, Somerset, UK. **Dipl.:** Associate Member Chartered Institute of Bankers, London. **Career:** Lloyds Bank Ltd. (1953-61); Grindlays Bank Ltd. (1961-71); Gulf Bank KSC Kuwait (1971-73); UBAF Bank Ltd., London (1973-83); ALUBAF Arab International Bank, Bahrain (since 1983). and Managing Director of ALUBAF International Bank, Tunis. **Sport:** Swimming. **Hobbies:** Theatre and music. Associate Member of the British Institute of Management. **Prof. Addr.:** Alubaf Arab International Bank E.C., P.O.Box 11529, UGB Tower, Diplomatic Area, Tel: 531212, Manama, Bahrain.

MASOUD (Abdul Aziz Abdallah, al), Saudi university lecturer. **Born** in 1941. **Dipl.:** M.A. (Comparative Education). **Career:** Teacher of Arabic, Red Sea Intermediate School, Jeddah (1965-66); Deputy Director, al-Farouq Intermediate School, Jeddah (1966-67); Demonstrator, College of Education, Riyadh University (1967-73); attended the Conference on The Role of The University, Riyadh University. **Address:** College of Education, Riyadh University, Riyadh, Saudi Arabia.

MASOUD (Farid), Egyptian ophtalmic surgeon. **Born** in Egypt. **Educ.:** Secondary and Higher. **Dipl.:** Doctor in Medicine, Specialization in Ophtalmic Surgery. **Career:** Ophtalmic Surgeon; Egyptian Representative, International Association for Research in Ophtalmology and Allied Sciences; Member of Editorial Board of Egypt, Experta Medica; former Director of Research School, Medical Services; Health Controller, South Cairo Zone, Egyptian Ministry of Education. **Member:** Gezira Sporting Club, Racing Club of Cairo. **Addr.:** 29, Emad ad-Dine Street, Tel.: 5919869, Cairo, Egypt.

MASOUD (Mohamad, Ibrahim, Sheikh), Saudi former minister of state. **Born** in January 1919 in Jeddah, Saudi Arabia. **Son** of Ibrahim M. Masoud (Businessman) and Mrs. Fatima Masoud. **Married** in 1949 in Jeddah to Miss Faygam B. Saleh, 5 children: Amal (1950); Ghassan (1951); Zuhair (1952); Ibrahim (1954); Rihab (1959). **Educ.:** Falah Secondary School, Jeddah; Aley Universal College, Lebanon. **Dipl.:** Secondary Certificate, Jeddah; B.S.S., Universal College, Lebanon. **Career:** Teacher, Falah School, Jeddah (1936-37); cipher editor, Department of Minerals and Public Works Ministry of Finance (1941), Head, Provisions Department, Ministry of Finance (1943-48); Minister Plenipotentiary (Grade A) and Inspector of Diplomatic and Consular Corps, Ministry of Foreign Affairs (1958-59); Minister Plenipotentiary, Saudi Embassy, Baghdad (1959-61); Ambassador (1961-68); Deputy Foreign Minister (1968-75); Minister of State and member of Cabinet (1975-Aug. 1995). **Member:** founding Board and Deputy Director General and General Supervisor of al-Bilad daily newspaper; founding Board of Red Sea Club, Saudi Danish Dairy Co., Saudi Arabian Drug Stores; Saudi delegation headed by H.R.H. Prince Abdullah al-Faisal to U.K. and U.S.A. (1952); Saudi delegation headed by the late King Saud to U.S.A. and North Africa (1957); Head of Saudi delegation to Senegal (1961); personal representative of H.M. The King to the meeting of personal representatives of Arab Kings and heads of state, Cairo (1966); Head of joint Saudi-Kuwaiti delegation to the Gulf Emirates in the negotiations for establishing the United Arab Emirates (1970); Head of Saudi delegation to conference of Islamic Solidarity Charter, Jeddah (1971); Saudi Representative on official visits to the Emirates, Bahrain, Qatar (1971); member of official Saudi delegations on official visits by H.R.H. Prince Fahad Ibn Abdulaziz (presently King Fahad) to Cairo, Tunis (1972) and U.K. (1973) Libya (1973), U.S.A. and U.K. (1974); member of Saudi delegation to Conference of Arab Ministers of Foreign Affairs, Finance and Petroleum, Algiers (1975); member of Saudi delegation OPEC summit conference, Algeria (1975); Head of Saudi delegation, Conference of Arab Foreign Ministers, Cairo (1975); Deputy Head of Saudi delegation, Islamic Foreign Ministers Conference, Jeddah, 1975; Saudi Representative to the joint Saudi, Syrian, Lebanese Pease discussions in Lausane, Switzerland; Member of Saudi Delegation Headed by Crown Prince Abdullah Bin Abdulaziz to Spain, U.K., U.S.A; seconded as Arab adviser to American Embassy, Jeddah; involved in electrical and cement companies. **Honours:** Orders of Merit from the Governments of Spain, Egypt, Lebanon, Mauritania, Senegal, Republic of China, U.S.A., Tunisia. **Publications:** articles in local press. **Hobby:** swimming. **Address:** Hayil Str., Al-Hamra, Fax: 6606507, Jeddah; P.O.Box 5666, Jeddah, Saudi Arabia.

MASOUD (Rahman, Mohamad, al), United Arab Emirates businessman. **Born** in 1939 in Abu Dhabi, UAE. **Son** of Mohamad al-Masoud. **Married,** seven children. **Educ.:**

General. **Career:** Chairman, Abu Dhabi Maritime & Mercantile International; Chairman, Mohamad Bin Masoud and Sons and Subsidaries; Director, al-Ain Ahlia Insurance Co.; member of the Federal National Council. President, Abu Dhabi Chamber of Commerce and Industry. **Sport:** Swimming. **Hobby:** Hunting. **Prof. Addr.:** Mohamad Bin Masoud and Sons, P.O.Box 322, Tel.: 822000, Telex: 22249, Abu Dhabi, United Arab Emirates.

MASOUD (Salahiddin Abu-Saif), Egyptian artist. **Born** in 1915 in Cairo, Egypt. **Married,** 3 sons, 1 daughter. **Dipl.:** Diploma in Accountancy. **Career:** Head of Montage Section, Misr Studios (1939-47); Cinema Director of thirty eight feature films (1945-); Head of the Board of Directors of Cinema Production Company (1963-65); Professor of High Institute for Cinema and Academy of Arts (1959-79); Dean of Dialogue Institute (1963-66); Member, Cinema Committee, High Council of Culture (1959-); Member of the Board of Directors of Cinema Financial Projects (1984-). **Publ.:** "The Cinema is Art" (1982), "The Art of Dialogue" (1983). **Decor.:** Egyptian Order of the Republic for Art and Literature (1963), Jules Verne Order, Nantes, France (1980). **Hobbies:** reading, music. **Member:** Cairo Rotary Club, Gezira Sporting Club. **Prof. Addr.:** 252 El Sudan Street, al-Mohandiseen, Cairo, Egypt.

MASOUD (Zuhair Mohamad), Saudi official. **Born** on 27 April 1952 in Jeddah, Saudi Arabia. **Dipl.:** B.Sc. (Economics), University of Southern California; M.Sc. (Economics), University of Southern California. **Career:** Active member of the International Students' Offices at University of Southern California; Director, Manpower Development Department, The Royal Commission for Jubail and Yanbu industrial zones. **Address:** The Royal Commission for Jubail and Yanbu, General Administration of Yanbu Project, Jeddah, Saudi Arabia.

MASRI (Abdallah Hassan), Saudi official. **Born** on 15 September 1947 in Mecca, Saudi Arabia. **Dipl.:** Ph.D. (Anthropology). **Career:** Director General, Antiquities and Museums Department since 1973; Lecturer, King Saud University since 1978; Editor-in-Chief, Atlal, the Saudi Arabian Archæological Journal; Assistant Deputy Minister of Education for Cultural Affairs. **Member:** the Saudi Historical and Archæological Society, Technology Transfer Group Ltd. (Scientific Organization), High Council for Antiquities, High Council for Haj and Endowments, General Committee for UNESCO Conference, ALECSO Conference (UNESCO Arabia), Permanent Committee of Director Generals of Antiquities in Arab Countries. **Publications:** Prehistory in North East Arabia, 1974. (Field Publications). **Hobbies:** fishing, swimming, classical music. **Prof. Addr.:** General Department of Antiquities and Museums, P.O.Box 3734, Tel.: 4351686, Riyadh. **Priv. Addr.:** Tel.: 4646893, Riyadh, Saudi Arabia.

MASRI (Ahmad Fathi, al), Syrian diplomat. **Born** in 1932 in Damascus, Syria. **Son** of Fathi al-Masri. **Married,** two daughters. **Educ.:** B.A. in Law, Diploma in Public Law, Damascus University (1954). **Career:** Attorney (1954-57); Financial Inspector (1957-58); United Arab Republic (UAR) Diplomatic Service (1958); UAR Embassy to Iraq (1960-62); Syrian Chargé d'Affaires, Embassy to Cyprus (1966-67); member of the Syrian Permanent Mission to the United Nations (1969-75); Syrian Representative to the 11th Session of the Governing Council of the UN Development Program; Syrian Representative to the 1st Session of the Ad Hoc Committee on International Terrorism (1973); Syrian Representative to the First Session of the Third UN Conference on the Law of the Sea; member of the UN visiting Mission to Gilbert and Ellice Island (1974); Chairman of the Subcommittee of the Social Committee with regard to the Implementation of the Declaration of Granting of Independence to Colonial Countries and Peoples (1975); Syrian Representative to the First Session of the Board of Governors of the UN Special Funds; Representative in the Preparatory Committee for the Special Session of the General Assembly devoted to the Development and the International Organisation of Legal Affairs; Ministry of Foreign Affairs (1975-78); Chargé d'Affaires, Syrian Embassy, Santiago, Chile (1978); Permanent Representative, Mission to the United Nations (Geneva). **Hobbies:** Music, literature and photography. **Addr.:** Ministry of Foreign Affairs, Damascus, Syria.

MASRI (Awni, Fuad, al), Jordanian politician. **Born** in 1936 in Nablus. **Married,** 2 daughters, 2 sons. **Educ.:** American University of Beirut, Lebanon (1950-59); Purdue University, USA. (1960-61). **Dipl.:** B.Sc. and M.Sc. in Civil Engineering. **Career:** Chairman of the Board of Jordan Dead Sea Industries since 1998; Deputy Chairman of the Board of Jordan National Electrical Company since 1996; Member of the Board of Trustees of Hashimya University and Member of the Royal Commission of the University since 1993; started profession as Construction Engineer, (1959-60); Director of Materials, Study and Design Department, Ministry of Communications, Saudi Arabia (1963-67); Project Manager, military base of Benladen Organization, Jordan (1967-68); Director and Partner of Arabtech Consulting Engineers (1968-80); renamed Arab Bureau Engineers and Consultants-Jordan since 1980; Deputy President of Jordan Engineers Association (1974-76) and President (1980-81); Minister of Public Works (1980-83) and Minister of Planning (1989-90); Member of Jordan consultancy Council (1980-83); Member of Royal Committee for Administrative Development (1984-85); chairman of the Board of Directors of Arab Potash company (1984-85); and Member of the Board (1993-95); Member of the Board of Directors of Phosphate company (1984-85); International law Institute (I.L.I.) Staff member (1985-88); chairman of Arab consultancy Board, Pan Arab Federation of Engineers (1989-); Arbitration in construction disputes (1970-); **Member** of

the executive Committee of Arab Arbitration chamber in **Engineering** and Construction contracts (1988-). **Publ.:** **"Effects** of Different Compaction Methods on Clay Characteristics" (1961) in English as well as several papers in professional journals and Engineering Conferences and Seminars. **Decor.:** Istiqlal Order (1963); Order of Jordanian Star Al-Nahda 1st grade (1981). **Medal:** Cwanghwa Medal, South Korea (1981). **Hobbies:** bridge, reading, swimming. **Member:** Jordan Automobile Club and Road Society. **Prof. Addr.:** P.O.Box 2038, Amman, 11181 Jordan.

MASRI (Mohamad, Qahtan Rafiq, al), Jordanian banker. **Born** in 1938 in Nablus, Palestine. **Married,** 4 children. **Dipl.:** Diploma in Commercial Studies. **Career:** Clerk at Arab Bank Ltd., Amman, Jordan (1956), Arab Bank Ltd., Nablus (1957), Arab Bank Ltd., Aden (1958-59), Arab Bank, Amman (1960); Head of Department, Arab Bank Ltd., Nablus (1960-64); Assistant Accountant, Qatar National Bank, Doha, Qatar (1964), Accountant (1960), Assistant Manager (1976), Manager (1979); Manager of the Main Office and Assistant General Manager of Qatar National Bank, Doha, Qatar (1980). **Hobbies:** tennis, swimming. **Prof. Addr.:** Amman, Jordan.

MASRI (Munib, Rashid, al), Jordanian businessman. **Born** in 1936 in Nablus, Palestine. **Son** of Rashid al-Masri. **Married,** six children. **Educ.:** B.A. and M.A. in Geology. **Career:** Assistant General Manager of Phillips Petroleum Company, Jordan (1959); General Manager, Phillips Petroleum Company (1961); General Manager, Phillips Petroleum Company, Algeria (1963); General Manager and Vice President, Phillips Petroleum Company (Middle East) (1965); Minister of Public Works (1970-71); formed Engineering and Development Group (Holding Company) (1971); Underwriting member of Lloyd's (1974); member of the Board of Directors of Arab Bank Ltd. since 1974; Director, Arab Development Co., Jordan. **Sports:** Basketball, jogging, swimming. **Addr.:** P.O.Box 6147, Amman, Jordan.

MASRI (Salah, Ahmad, al), Yemeni politician. **Born** in 1919 in Sanaa, Yemen. **Married,** 3 sons, 2 daughters. **Educ.:** theological studies in Yemen. **Career:** Private Secretary to Imam Ahmad (1948); Governor of Otmah (1954); Ambassador, Yemen Embassy to Sudan (1955-62); Shaikh of Anss Tribe (1959); Minister of Defence (1962-67); represented the Royalists at conferences with the Republicans held in Saudi Arabia and Sudan; formerly Minister of State for Presidential Affairs (1971). **Hobby:** journalism. **Prof. Addr.:** P.O.Box 1239, Sanaa, Republic of Yemen.

MASRI (Sarwat, Alexander, al), Egyptian pharmacist. **Born** on July 4, 1928 in Tanta, Sohag Governorate. **Son** of Alexander al-Masry (Landowner) **and** Mrs. Badia Kauzmann. **Married** to Therese Aboujaoudé in July 1958, 2 children: Sharif and Hisham. **Educ.:** Sainte-Famille College, Cairo (1938-50); Faculty of Pharmacy, St. Joseph University, Beirut (1951-57); **Dipl.:** Secondary Education Certificate (1950); Bachelor of Sciences (Chem. + Pharm.) (1957). **Career:** Resident dispensing chemist at Hotel Dieu Hospital in Beirut, Lebanon (1955-57); Assistant Pharmacist (1958), now Proprietor of Sarwat Pharmacy, Abdulkhaleq Sarwat Street, Cairo (Egypt). **Dist.:** Biochemistry Medal (for meritorious research work). **Sports:** Football, Basket-ball and Swimming. **Member:** ach-Shams Club, Heliopolis (Cairo). **Remark:** Special interest in Scientific research. **Prof. Addr.:** 36, Abdulkhaleq Sarwat Street, Tel.: 51317, Cairo. **Priv. Addr.:** 6, Hassan Moussa al-Aqad Street, Heliopolis, Tel.: 64826, Cairo, Egypt.

MASRI (Taher Nashat), Jordanian politician. **Born** on March 5, 1942 in Nablus. **Son** of Nashat Masri (deceased) **and** Mrs. H. Solh. **Married** on January 1, 1968 in Amman, to Miss Samar Bitar, 2 children: Nashat (1971); Nadine (1975). **Educ.:** North Texas State University, Denton, Texas; al-Najah National College, Nablus; Aleppo College, Aleppo, Syria. **Dipl.:** B.B.A. **Career:** Central Bank of Jordan (1965-73); Member of Parliament (1973-74); Minister of State for occupied Territories Affairs (1973-74); Ambassador to Spain (1975-78); Ambassador to France and Permanent Delegate to UNESCO (1978-83); Ambassador to Britain (1983); Minister of Foreign Affairs (January 1984- January 1989); Deputy Prime Minister for Economic Affairs (April 1989 - Aug. 1989); Member of Parliament (November 1989-93) and (Nov. 1993-97); Minister of Foreign Affairs (Jan.-June 1991); Prime Minister & Minister of Defence (June 1991- Nov. 91); Chairman of Foreign relations Committee in the Parliament (89-90., 92-93). Member of Upper House Parliament (1998-). **Awards:** Grand Cordon of the Jewelled of Al-Nahda; Al-Nahda 1st Degree; Al Kawkab, 1st Degree; Isabela La Catolica; El Merito Civil; Grand Officier De Legion d'Honneur; Commander Legion d'Honneur; Grand Officier De L'Ordre National De Merite; Grand British Empire GBE; Order of Merit of the FED. Rep. of Germany; Grand Cross, 1st Class; The Knight of Grand Cross of the Order of the REP. of Italy; Grand Cordon de L'Ordre National De Cedre; Grand Decoration of Honour in Gold with Sash for Services to the Republic of Austria; Order of Diplomatic Service Merit Gwanghawa Medal. **Address:** P.O.Box 5550, Amman 11183, Fax: 962-6-4642226 Tel.: Office 4642227. Res. 5920600, E-mail: t.N.masri@index.com.jo.

MASSADEH (Salem), Jordanian Politician. **Born** in 1930 in Irbid, Jordan. **Educ.:** Damascus University, Syria. **Dipl.:** Degree in Law. **Career:** Teacher (1949-50); Audit Department (1955-58); Judge (1958-70); Ministry of the Interior (1970); Governor; Under Secretary (1971); Minister of Justice (1974-76); Chairman of the Board, Jordan-Kuwait Bank (1977-79); Minister of Finance (1977-79) and (1979-84); Director, Jordan Securities Corp., Amman

(1984-); Deputy Prime Minister and Minister of the Interior (April 1989- Dec. 1990). **Addr.:** P.O.Box 926691, Amman, Jordan.

MASSARI (Mohamad al-Arbi, al), Moroccan journalist. **Born** in 1936 in Tetuan, Morocco. **Son** of Ahmed Massari. **Married**, three children. **Educ.:** Diploma from the Institute of Broadcasting, Cairo (1959). **Career:** Producer on Moroccan Radio; Secretary of Department of Production (1958-64); Editor of "AL-ALAM" newspaper (since 1964); Chief Editor; Director (since 1982); member of the National Council and Central Committee of the Istiqlal Party (since 1965); member of the executive committee of the Istiqlal Party (since 1978); Secretary General of Moroccan Writer's Union (1964, 1969 and 1972); Assistant Secretary of the Moroccan Association for Support of the Palestinian Struggle; Assistant Secretary General of the Arab Journalists Union. Member of the Cultural and Scientifique council of the University "Almotamid", Asilah, Morocco; Deputy in the Parliament in 1984; Ambassador of Morocco in Brasilia (since Oct. 1, 1985 until July 31, 1991); Secretary General of the (SNPM) Moroccan Syndicate of Journalists. Editor of Shu-un Magribia (Moroccan Affairs) Review sp. foreign pol. since Oct. 1995. **Publ.:** "The Arabe Battle Against Zionism and Imperialism" (1967); "With Fatah in Ghor" Rabat (1969); "Discussion About the Arabs" Rabat, (1973); "Morocco-Spain, The Last Confrontation" Rabat (1974); "The Land Problem in Our Political Struggle since Independence" Rabat (1980). "Good Morning, democracy" TETUAN, (1985); "The Islam in the American-Arabic Literature" (1990); "Mundos Marooquinos" (1991) in Portuguese; "The Moroccan Information: from Carence to Competence" (1992). **Prof. Addr.:** al-Alam News Paper, P.O.Box 141, Rabat, Morocco. **Priv. Addr.:** 20, ALOCASIA (RIAD), Rabat, Morocco.

MATAR (Ali, Mohamed), Bahrainin Physician and Educator. **Born** on August 8, 1946. **Married. Educ.: B.Sc.**, American University of Beiut, Lebanon (1970); **M.D.**, A.U.B. (includes a year of mixed internship) **(1974)**; E.C.F.M.G., A.U.B. (1974); F.L Ex (State of Missouri), Jefferson City (1976); Residency Training program Certification (Psychiatry), Washington University Hospitals, St. Louis Missouri (a three-year program) (1977); Fellowship (Psychiatry), Washington University Hospitals, St. Louis-Missouri (1978); M.P.H. the Johns Hopkins University, School of Hygiene and Public Health, Baltimore, Maryland (1981); Diplomate in Professional Psychoterapy, The Board of International Academy of Behaviral Medicine, Counseling and psychoterapy, Inc. **(1988) Professional Experience:** Internship, A.U.B. (June 15, 1973-June 14,1974); Residency Training (Psychiatry), St. Louis-Missouri (July 1, 1974-June 30,1977); Fellowship (Psychiatry), Washington University Hospitals, St. Louis Missouri (served as a staff psychiatrist teaching medical students and residents in psychiatry as well as providing service) (July 1, 1977- June 30, 1978); Consultant psychiatrist, Psychiatric Hospital, Ministry of Health, Bahrain (served in several ministry committees) (July 16, 1978-Present); Consultant Psychiatrist, Military Hospital, Bahrain Defence Force (Jan. 1979-Aug.31, 1990); Manager, Office of Professional Standards & Systems Analysis, Ministry of Health, Bahrain (served in several ministry committees) (Oct.1981-March 1986); Adjunct Assistant Professor, Faculty of Health Sciences, A.U.B. (Oct. 1981- July 1987); Chairman, Psychiatric Hospital, Ministry of Health, Bahrain (July 1983-June 1987); Curriculum Committee (End of Program Objectives), College of Medicine Sciences, Arabian Gulf University, Bahrain (Oct. 1983-Feb. 1984) served in several academic committees: Curriculum, Assessment, Community Health Strand and Joint Committee (MOH/AGU): co-Chairman (1987-88) and (1990-91): (1985-Sept. 1995); Assistant Professor, College of Medicine and Medical Sciences, Arabian Gulf University, Bahrain (Jan.1987- June 87) Associate Professor, College of Medicine and Medical Sciences, Arabian Gulf University, Bahrain (July 1, 1987-Oct. 31, 1995); Acting Dean and Chairman, College Council, College of Medicine and Medical Sciences, Arabian Gulf University, Bahrain (May 2, 1987-March 26, 1988); Member, College Council, College of Medicine and Medical Sciences, Arabian Gulf University, Bahrain (1989-Sept. 30, 1995); Chairman, Division of Community Health & Human Behavior, College of Medicine & Medical Sciences, Arabian Gulf University, Bahrain (Nov. 1, 1990-Sept.30, 1995); Consultant Psychiatrist, Military Hospital, Bahrain Defence Force (Feb. 1991-Present); Member, Consultative Council (Shura), Government State of Bahrain (Jan. 16, 1993-Present); Member, Foreign Relations Committee, Shura Council (Jan.16, 1993-Sept. 30, 1996); First Deputy Chairman, Shura Council (Oct. 1, 1996-Oct. 5, 1999); Member, Board of Directors, International Council on Alcohol and Addictions (I.C.A.A) (Aug. 1999-Present); Member, Services Committee, Shura Council (Oct.5, 1999-Present). **Professional Memberships:** Bahrain Medical Society (B.M.S) since 1978: Vice president (1978-79), President (1987-94) American Public Health Association (since 1981); Bahrain Sports Medicine Association (since 1984), Member Executive Committe (1984-90); Amiri Academy of Medical Specialist (since 1984), Member-Executive Committee (1986-89); Advisory Council, International Academy of Professional Counseling & psychotherapy (since 1984); Editor, Bahrain Medical Bulletin (1986-88) European Association of Science Editors (1986-88); American Academy of Clinical Psychiatrists (since 1986; Member National Committee for the Evaluation of Scientific Credentials and Chairman, Subcommittee for the Evalutation of Medical Credentials (1987-94); Founder Member, Bahrain Cancer Society (since 1989); Chief Editor, Journal of the Bahrain Medical Society (1989-94); Member of the Advisory Committee for Science & Technology, Bahrain Center for Studies and Research (since 1990); Member, Arab Board of Medical

Specialties (Psychiatry) and Chairman, Scientific Council (Psychiatry), The Arab Board of Medical Specialties (since Oct. 1997); Honorary President, Bahrain Association for Mentally Retarded (since 1992); President, 8th Pan Arab Congress of Psychiatry (Feb. 9-11, 1999); President, Arab Federation of Psychiatrists (since Feb. 1999). **Committee Membership (Ministry of Health):** Licensing Committee (1982-84); Family Practice Residency Program Committe and Coordinator of Community Medicine (1981-85); Steering Committee (M.O.H./A.U.B.) (1981-83); Office of Plan and Program (Minister's Office) (1983-84); Primary Health Care Committee (1982-86); Cadre Committee (Ad Hoc) (1982-84); Health Census Monograph Project (Bahrain Coordinator): a joint program between the Ministry of Health and the University of Southern California (1982-85); Quality Assurance Committee (1982-83); Medical Board (S.M.C.) (1983-87); Committee Chairman, M.O.H/A.G.U Joint Committee (1986-88) (1990-91); Represented M.O.H. (1982-68) in: Secretariat General of Health for Arab Countries in the Gulf; Gulf Health Planning Committee; Gulf Health Education Committee; Gulf Health Joint TV Program (SALAMATAK). **Publ.:** Psychiatric Diagonosis and Prediction of Drug and Alcohol Dependence (1982); Psychiatric Diagnostic Criteria in Bahrain (1982); Familial Trends of Nocturnal Eneuresis in Bahrain (1983); Drugs and Dependence (1983); Drug Abuse (1985); Iatrogenic Drug Dependence (1986); Health in Bahrain (1985); The Phenomenon of Drug Abuse in Bahrain (1985); Health Implications of Migration to Bahrain (1987); Early Recognition and Prevention of Attempted Suicide in Primary Health Care (1987); Zuclopenthixol Acetate in Viscoleo. A New Drug Formulation: An Open Study of Zuclopenthixol Acetate in Vascoleo in Patients with Acute psychosis including Mania and Exacerbation of Chronic psychoses (1987); Antecedents of Depression in Primary Health Care in Bahrain (1987); Diagnostic Criteria in Psychiatry: A Comparative Study between Medical record, ICD-9 and DSM-IIi Diagnoses in Bahrain (1989); Youth and Narcotics (1989); Clopixol-Acuphase: A New generation of Antipsychotic Drugs An Open Clinical Trial (1990); Recent Stressful Life Events Among Bahrain Adolescents with Adjustment Disorder (1993); Secrets of the Psyche (1995); Overdose Among Bahraini Adolescents and Young Adults: Psychosocial Correlates (1997); Drugs Dependence (1999). **Address:** P.O.Box 33787, Isa Town, Bahrain.

MATAR (Muhammad, Hamid), Sudanese Diplomat. **Born** in 1931 in Masudiya, Sudan. **Married**, 8 children. **Educ.:** Cairo University, Egypt; also in Geneva and New York. **Dipl.:** LL.B, International Relations and Int'l Law. **Career:** Lawyer (1985); Third Secretary, Ministry of Foreign Affairs, Khartoum, Sudan (1959), Second Secretary (1962), First Secretary (1965); Counsellor (1968); Minister Plenipotentiary (1974); Ambassador (1977); Ambassador to the Democratic People's Republic of Korea and the People's Republic of China. **Hobbies:** sports, theatre, cinema. **Addr.:** Ministry of Foreign Affairs, Khartoum, Sudan.

MATBOULI (Mahmood Mohamad Ali), Saudi businessman. **Born** in 1924 in Jeddah, Saudi Arabia. **Educ.:** Secondary School Certificate. **Career:** Employee, Local Establishment, and later Chief Accountant; member, Board of Directors, several Banks in Bahrain; Founder, Partner, and General Manager, Zagzoog and Matbouli Company. **Hobbies:** sight seeing, swimming. **Prof. Addr.:** P.O.Box 556, Tel.: 6519217, Jeddah. **Priv. Addr.: Tel.:** 6654057, Jeddah, Saudi Arabia.

MATBOULY (Fathi, Ahmad, al), Egyptian Economist. **Born** in 1923. **Married**, 1 son, 2 daughters. **Educ.:** Cairo University, Egypt; Insurance Fellowship, Edinburgh University, UK. **Dipl.:** B.Com. and M.Com. in Accountancy. **Career:** Chairman of Shbir el-Kom Spinning and Weaving Co. (1974); Minister of Commerce (1974-76); Owner of Sakara Poultry Farm. **Member:** Gezira Sporting Club. **Prof. Addr.:** 2 el-Kamel Mahmoud, Zamalek, Cairo, Egypt.

MATOUK (Amal, Bishara), Egyptian painter. **Born** in 1936 in Cairo, Egypt. **Educ.:** Accademia de Belle Arti, Rome, Italy. **Career:** Professional Decorator and Antique Dealer; has held and took part in several exhibitions. **Awards:** UNESCO Prize (1st Class) (1956), Via Marguta, First Prize (1958), San Vito Romano, First Prize, Accitreta, First Prize (1960). **Member:** Automobile Club, Gezira Sporting Club. **Prof. Addr.:** 6 Salah el-Din, Zamalek, Cairo, Egypt. **Priv. Addr.:** 20 Mansour Muhammad Street, Zamalek, Cairo, Egypt.

MATROOD (Abdullah, Salman, al), Saudi businessman. **Born** in 1933 in Sayhat, Saudi Arabia. **Son** of Salman Ahmed al-Matrood and **Married** in 1954 in Sayhat, Saudi Arabia to al-Saadha, six sons, five daughters. **Educ.:** Higher Elementary School, Dammam, Saudi Arabia and Partly in U.S.A. **Dipl.:** Business and Management. **Career:** Established laundry and Dry Cleaning Services (industrial type) (1945); Established Dairy & Ice Cream Factory (1968); Established Western and Eastern Baked goods Sweet Goods and Confectionery Factory (1974); Established Dairy Farm with 1000 Milking Cows (1979), which has expanded to 3000 Heads to date. **Founder** of Sayhat Society for Social Services (1962), Home for the Aged and paralized and is the Chairman of this institution which supports medical care and financial aid for the needy; **Medal:** King Khalid Abdul Aziz Medal for the best industry in Eastern Province (1975). **Sport:**Football (in early days). **Hobby:** To Serve the needy and countrymen without forgetting other Nationals. **Credit Card:** American Express; Gold Card. **Addr.:** P.O.Box 97, Alkhobar 31952, Tel: (03) 856 0000, Telex: 897022 MATRUD SJ, Saudi Arabia. **Priv. Addr.:** P.O.Box 97, Tel.: 856 1091, Saudi Arabia.

MATROUDI (Mohamad Ibrahim, al), Saudi academic. **Born** in 1944. **Educ.:** Ph.D. in Literature and Criticism. **Career:** Various administrative jobs (1966-80); Director General, Faculty and Personnel Affairs, King Saud University; Assistant Professor, Faculty of Arts, King Saud University (1980-). **Publications:** Several articles. **Hobbies:** reading, writing, swimming. **Prof. Addr.:** Department of Faculty and Personnel Affairs, King Saud University, Tel.: 4768506, Riyadh. **Priv. Addr.:** Tel.: 4481976, Riyadh, Saudi Arabia.

MATTAR (Ahmed Khalifa), Saudi executive. **Born** in 1936 in Turaif, Hassa, Saudi Arabia. **Educ.:** High School, Columbia University, New York. **Dipl.:** High School, Executive Program in Business Administration, Business Management. **Career:** Joined Saudia Training in 1959; First Officer DC-3, CV-340 and Skymaster in 1961; Captain DC-3 (1963); Captain Boeing 720B/707 (1965); Captain DC-9 (1966); Instructor Pilot (1969); Supervisor Flight Training (1971); Captain L1011 and Instructor Pilot (1975); General Manager Flying (1976); Vice President Flight Operations (1977); Deputy Director General Operations (1978); Director General (1980 to date); Qualified for Command of Boeing 747 (1981). **Prof. Addr.:** Saudi Arabian Airlines, P.O.Box 620, Jeddah 21231, Tel.: 686-2203, Saudi Arabia.

MATTAR (Philip), Historian, Publisher, Teacher. **Born** on January 21, 1944 at Haifa, Palestine. **Son** of Sulayman Mattar (deceased) **and** Mrs. née Minerva Nucho. **Married** in 1971 to Evelyn in Atlanta, Ga., one child: Christina (27 years). **Educ.:** Columbia University. **Dipl.:** Ph.D. **Career:** Executive Director, Institute for Palestine Studies, Washington, D.C. (1984- present); Associate Editor, «Journal of Palestine Studies» (1985- present); Adjunct Professor of History, Georgetown University (1990, 1991, 1994). **Publ.:** «The Mufti of Jerusalem», Columbia University Press (1992); «Encyclopeadia of the Modern Middle East», Co-Editor, Macmillan Publishing Co., 1996; "Encyclopedia of the Palestinians", Editor Facts on File, Inc. (2000). Articles in «Middle East Journal» (Foreign Policy), Middle Eastern Studies. **Awards:** Fullbright Fellow (1978). **Sports:** Jogging, Squash. **Hobbies:** Chess, Reading, Travel. **Member:** Middle East Studies Association. **Prof. Addr.:** 3501 M. St. N.W. Washington D.C. 20007, Tel.: (202) 342, 3990, Ext. 12, Fax: (202) 342-3927; and Columbia University, Middle East Institute, International Affairs Building, 420 West 118th Street, New York, N.Y. 10027, U.S.A. E-mail: pjmattar@ad.com.

MAZIAD (Hamad, al), Saudi official. **Born** in Majma'ah. **Educ.:** B.A. (Law), Cairo University, 1963; M.A. (Comparative Law), Southern Methodist University, Dallas, Texas, U.S.A. **Career:** Secretary of Legal Affairs, Royal Cabinet (1964); Legal Adviser, Vice Chairman, Supreme Committee of Labour Disputes, Ministry of Labour and Social Affairs (1966-68); Legal Adviser, Ministry of the Interior (1971-73); Director General of Border Affairs and Chairman of the Disciplinary Committee, Ministry of Interior. **Member of:** Supreme Committee of Adult Education and Eradication of Illiteracy and several local committees in Ministry of the Interior and Passport and Nationality Department; member of Permanent Joint Saudi-Kuwait Committee; attended following conferences: Conference on Social Reference, Arab League, Cairo, Arab League, UN Conference on the Law of the Sea, Caracas and Geneva, Conference for the Amendment of Anti-Narcotics Convention, Geneva. **Publications:** articles in local press on administrative and international law. **Hobbies:** reading, sport. **Address:** Ministry of Interior, Riyadh, Saudi Arabia.

MAZIDI (Faisal, Mansour, al), Kuwaiti consultant. **Born** on November 29, 1933 in Kuwait. **Son** of Mansour al-Mazidi. **Married** in 1960 to Miss Ayesha al-Masri, 2 children: Wael and Hala. **Educ.:** Mubarakiya School, Kuwait; University of Keele, England. **Dipl.:** Bachelor of Arts in Economics. **Career:** Dept. Finance & Economy (1959); Director, State Chlorine & Salt Bd; Director; Kuwait Oil Co. Ltd. (1960-73); Economic Assistant, Ministry of Finance & Economy (1960); Chairman, Econ. & Intl. Comm. (1961); Director, Kuwait Fund Econ. Dev., Arab Countries (1962); Member, Kuwait University Higher Council (1962-64); Chairman and Managing Director, Kuwait Chemical Fertilizer Co. (1964-71); Chairman, Government Oil Concession Comm. (1963-65); Government Refinery Comm. (1964-66); Director, Petrochemical Ind. Co. (1963-71); Director, Kuwait United Fisheries (1971-74); President of Kuwait Associated Consultants (1971 to date). **Credit Card:** American Express. **Prof. Addr.:** P.O.Box 5443, Tel.: 429384, 417744, Safat, Kuwait. **Priv. Addr.:** Khaldiya, Street No. 47. Area No. 6, Tel.: 810370, 815829, Kuwait.

MAZOUNI (Muhammad, Halim), Algerian academic. **Born** on March 10, 1937 in Algeria. **Married,** 4 children. **Educ.:** Institut d'Administration des Entreprises, Paris, France; London Business School, UK. **Dipl.:** Ph.D. in Applied Mathematics. **Career:** Officer in the National Liberation Army; Associate Professor at General Mechanics and Mechanics of Vibrations, University of Paris-Sud, France (1964-68); Project Head, Arzew Petroleum Refinery (1970-73); Director of the Industrial Zone of Arzew (1971-73); Vice President in charge of Petro Chemistry, GNL and Refining, SONATRACH; Member of the Central Committee of the FLN Party (1979); Vice Minister responsible for electrical, mechanical and electronics industry (1984). **Publ.:** "Development of Downstream Industries", OAPEC Seminar, Oslo (1978), in French as well as other researches and papers published in professional magazines and journals. **Hobbies:** walking, gymnastics, jogging, music. **Addr.:** Arzew, Algeria.

MAZROEI (Rashid), UAE businessman. **Born** in 1940

in Ajman, UAE. **Son** of Humaid Mazroei. **Married** in 1965, 6 sons. **Dipl.: B.A. Economics (1960). Career:** Director, Bahri & Mazroei Group of Companies; Owner, Gulf Wings Travel Agencies; Dealer, Stock and Exchange. Board Member of Abu Dhabi commercial Bank, Abu Dhabi, U.A.E.; Board Member, Dubai Chamber of Commerce & Industry; Board Member, Ajman Heavy Industries. **Hobby:** Snooker, Waterskiing, Golf. **Addr.:** P.O.Box 1247, Deira, Tel: 691610, Fax 664627, Dubai U.A.E.

MAZROIE (Obaid Bin Humaid Ali Al), U.A.E. national and prominent businessman. **Born** in 1934 at Ajman, **Son** of Humaid Ali Al Mazroie. **Married** in 1954, father of 2 sons and 2 daughters. **Career** beginning his impressive career as the Commercial Manager of National Bank of Dubai, a responsibility he successfully carried for 13 years, he topped his banking career by becoming the Founder Member of the Board Representatives of Emirates Commercial Bank, now better known as Abu Dhabi Commercial Bank in 1975, he ventured into new area close to his heart- The Arabic Newspaper "AL FAJR". As the Founder and Chief Editor of Al Fajr he realized the need for modernization, expansion and diversification which has led the group into totally deverse fields, which besides giving it an influential list of contracts has also increased its equity in the market. **Currently,** Chairman of Dar Al Fajr Group of Companies, Partner in Gulf Electronics and Chairman of Reliance Real Estate. **Address:** P.O.Box 505, Abu Dhabi, United Arab Emirates, Tel.: 02-4488300, Fax: 02-4488436, E-mail fajrnews@emirates,net.ae

MAZROUI (Saleh Abdulrahman, al), Saudi civil servant. **Born** in 1934 in Riyadh, Saudi Arabia. **Educ.:** graduate of School of Shari'a (Islamic Law), Imam Muhammad Ibn Saud Islamic University. **Career:** Director of Personnel and Finance Department (1961-66) Islamic University, Medina; Director of Public Claims Department, Ministry of Interior, Riyadh (1966); Director General of Inspection Department, Ministry of Interior; Director General of General Administration, Ministry of Interior; Muslim Affairs fact-finding tours of most South American countries (1978); Muslim Youths International Symposium of North American Muslim Students Federation (1979); participant in Islamic Society Conference in India (1981); Deputy, Investigation and Disciplinary Board. **Member** of delegation for settlement of the problem of Afghani Freedom Fighters. **Hobbies:** reading world news and political reviews. **Prof. Addr.:** Investigation and Disciplinary Board, Airport Street, Tel.: 4011348, Riyadh. **Priv. Addr.:** Tel.: 4352867, Riyadh, Saudi Arabia.

MAZRUI (Abdallah, Humaid Ali), UAE official. **Born** in 1943 in Ajman, United Arab Emirates. **Married,** 5 children. **Educ.:** Baghdad University, Iraq. **Dipl.:** B.A. in Economics and Political Science. **Career:** Deputy Director, Development Office in Trucial States Rulers' Council; Director, Development Officer of the Rulers' Council; Under Secretary, Ministry of Communications (1972); Under Secretary, Ministry of Foreign Affairs, with rank of Ambassador (1974-77); Minister of Labour and Social Affairs (1977-79); Counsellor at Presidential Court (1980-83); Minister of Justice (1983-1989), at present a member of Board of Directors, al-Ittihad Press & Publishing Corporation, Abu Dhabi. **Hobby:** general reading. **Prof. Addr.:** New Medical Centre, P.O.Box 46222, Tel.: 332255, Telex: 22970 NEWMED EM, Fax: (971-2) 320878, Abu Dhabi, United Arab Emirates.

MAZRUI (Abdallah, M.), U.A.E. banker. **Born** on April 10, 1952 in Abu Dhabi. **Educ.:** B.A. Political Science and Economics. **Career:** Representing the Government of Abu Dhabi on the Board of Directors of National Bank of Abu Dhabi and also Managing Director of the Bank; Director on the Board of: Gulf International Bank, Bahrain; UBAN-Arab Japanese Finance Ltd., Hong Kong; Jashammal National Co. (UAE); The Arab Investment Company, Riyadh, Saudi Arabia. **Member:** Industrial Project Committee (Government of Abu Dhabi); Board of Directors of the Arab Bankers' Association, London; Vice Chairman of Social Educational Club, Abu Dhabi. **Hobby:** Reading. **Prof. Addr.:** National Bank of Abu Dhabi, P.O.Box 4, Tel.: 335262, Abu Dhabi, United Arab Emirates.

MAZZAWI (Adel), Jordanian engineer. **Born** on April 7, 1945. **Son** of Elia Mazzawi **and** Mrs., née Marcelle Mazzawi. **Married** to Dina Bakhit on March 22, 1978, 1 child: Elia. **Educ.:** De la salle Secondary School, Cairo (Egypt); Faculty of Engineering, Ayn Shams University. **Career:** set up his own business: Mazzawi Trading Company. **Prof. & Priv. Addr.:** P.O.Box 9151, Tel.: 67731, Amman, Jordan.

MAZZAWI (Musa), Arab-British academic residing in the United Kingdom. **Born** in 1925 in Haifa, Palestine. **Married,** 1 son, 2 daughters . **Educ.:** London University, UK; Gray's Inn, London. **Dipl.:.** LL.B, Ph.D., Barrister. **Career:** Court of Justice, Haifa, Palestine (1943); various teaching and journalistic posts (1950); Holborn College of Law (subsequently the polytechnic of Central London and the University of Westminster) (1961-90); Active on mass media in J.K. and international in defence of the Palestinian point of view. **Publ.:** various radio and television programmes on the Arab-Israel conflict. Ph.D. thesis on Rhodesia's Unilateral Declaration of Independence in International Law and English Law (London) School of Economic, the University of London; Palestine and the Law-Guidelines for the Resolution of the Arab-Israel Conflict, published by Garnet Publishing Limited, Reading, Berkshire RG1 4QS, UK (a comprehensive and authoritative study on the legal aspects of the conflict), U.K. **Priv. Addr.:** obtainable by telephoning Fan number 0044 01189 332897.

MAZZIANE (Mohamad), Moroccan statesman. **Born** in Morocco. **Educ.:** Military Academy. **Career:** Army Service; Promoted Brigadier General; Minister of Defence (August 1965), Minister in charge of the Coordination of the Armed Forces (F.A.R.) (October 1967). **Addr.:** Ministry of Defence, Rabat, Morocco.

MBAZAA (Fuad), Tunisian politician. **Born** on June 16, 1933 in Tunis, Tunisia. **Married. Educ.:** Sadiki College, Tunis; Sorbonne, University of Paris, France. **Dipl.:** Licence in Law and Economics, Sorbonne. **Career:** Active in Student Neo-Destour Party; served in Secretariat of State for Health; Director of Youth and Sports (1964); Director of National Security (1965); Director of Youth and Sports (1967); Governor-Mayor of Tunis (1969); Minister of Youth and Sports (1973-80); Minister of Information and Culture (April 1980- December 1980); Minister of Culture (December 1980); Vice-President of la Marsa Municipal Council; Presently, president of the National Assembly. **Awards:** Commander, Tunisian Order of Independence. **Addr.:** The National Assembly, Tunis, Tunisia.

MEDANI (Mustafa), Sudanese diplomat. **Born** in 1931 in Omdurman, Sudan. **Married**, 5 children. **Educ.:** Cambridge University, UK. **Dipl.:** B.A. and M.A. in Economics. **Career:** Ministry of Foreign Affairs (1956); Member of first Sudani Delegation to the UN (1956); Consul General, Sudanese Embassy in Damascus, Syria (1958-60); Chargé d'Affaires, Beirut, Lebanon (1963-65); Ambassador to Czechoslovakia (1969-71); Acting Under Secretary, Ministry of Foreign Affairs, Khartoum, Sudan (1971-72); Ambassador to Ethiopia (1972-74), to the UN, New York (1974-78), to West Germany, Bonn (1978). **Decor.:** Order of the Republic of Egypt (1960), Order of the Lebanese Cedar, Lebanon (1969), Order of the Republic of West Germany (1978). **Prof. Addr.:** Ministry of Foreign Affairs, Khartoum, Sudan.

MEGALLI (Nabila), Egyptian journalist. **Born** in 1938 in Egypt. **Educ.:** Cairo University, Egypt. **Career:** Journalist, "Middle East Economist" magazine (1958); staff of Middle East News Agency (1963); Staff of Middle East Features Service (1964); DPA (West German news agency) (since 1968); correspondent for "Daily Telegraph" (since 1968); correspondent for "Newsweek" (since 1973) and "Petroleum Intelligence Weekly" (since 1961). **Member** of the Egyptian and Arab Journalists Unions; First Secretary of Foreign Association Correspondents. **Sport:** Walking. **Hobbies:** Reading literature, history. **Prof. Addr.:** 139 al-Tahrir Square, Tel.: 744327, Dokki, Cairo, Egypt.

MEHAIRY (Munir, Mohamad, al), Egyptian professor of medicine, Ayn Shams university, Cairo. **Born** on 5 April 1925 at Damanhour (Egypt). **Son** of Amin el-Mehairy **and** Mrs., Nemat el-Hedeiny. **Married** to Samia Mohamad Fouad on 13 Sept 1946, 3 children: Emad, Hazem and Fatma. **Educ.:** English School, Menouf Preparatory School, Shibeen el-Kom Secondary School, Faculty of Medicine, Cairo University (1937-43). **Dipl.:** M.B.B.CH., Cairo (1943), M.D., Cairo (1946), M.R.C.P. London (1948), Ph.D. London (1949), F.R.C.P. London (1972). **Career:** Lecturer in clinical medicine, Ayn Shams University, Cairo; Assistant Professor in clinical medicine, Ain Shams University, Cairo (1953); Professor of medicine since 1962. Chairman and director of Medical Dept. Ain Shams University (1977-81); President of Egyptian Society of Allergy & Clinical Immunology; At present, Emeritus Prof. Internal Medicine, Ain Shams University; Member at Large of the International Ass. of Allergology; president of North African Chapter of Interasma (1974-80). **Publ.:** produced more than 80 papers on medical subjects between 1948 and 1975. **International Activities:** official visit to Indonesia in 1955 to report on health conditions; attended the meeting of the European Society of Hæmatology, Denmark (1957); the International Congress of Blood Diseases, Tokyo, Japan (1960) also the international congress of blood diseases in Rome, Italy (1958); the International Congress of Allergology, New York, USA, 1961; the meeting of the European Society of Allergology, Basle, Switzerland (1962); the International Congress of Allergology in Madrid, Spain, in 1964; the Pan Arab Medical Congress, Tunisia, 1965; the International Congress of Allergology, Montreal, Canada, 1967. W.H.O. visit to various medical centres and universities in USA, 1967 (New York, Pennsylvania, California & Michigan). International Congress of Allergy (1970 in Florence, Italy) International Congress of Allergy (1973 Tokyo, Japan.) Attended International Congress of Allergology, Buenos Aires (1976), International Congress of Allergy & Clinical Immunology (1982, London, U.K.) **Member:** Fellow of the Royal College of Physicians (1972); Fellow of the Royal Society of Medicine, London. **Awards:** Medal of Egyptian Associations for Scientific Research 1966. Badge of Honour for Sciences and Arts (1980), Order of Merit and Medal of the Republic of Egypt (1982). **Hobbies:** Photography. **Sports:** Swimming. **Clubs:** Heliopolis Sporting Club, Cairo; Ain Shams University Staff Club, Cairo. **Prof. Addr.:** 8, al-Goumhouriya street, Cairo. **Priv. Addr.:** Villa 9, Dr. Halim Abu Seif street, Heliopolis, Cairo, Egypt.

MEHDI (Mohammad, T., Dr.), Iraqi writer, author and lecturer residing in USA. **Born** in 1928 in Karbala, Iraq. **Married** in 1953 in Berkeley, California, USA, 3 daughters, Anisa (1956), Janan (1958), and Laila (1959). **Educ.:** High School of Commerce, Baghdad, Iraq; University of California (Berkeley), USA. **Dipl.:** B.A. (1953), M.A. (1954), Ph.D. (1961). **Career:** Teaching Assistant, Political Science Department, University of California (Berkeley) (1958-60); Advisor to Arab delegations at the United Nations, New York (1961-62); President of American-Arab Relations Committee (1963-); Executive Secretary of Arab Anti-Defamation League (1971); Secretary General, Arab people to American People (1980); Secretary General, National Council on Islamic Affairs (1983-); AP to AP TV Producer (1984-); Editor, Action Weekly Newspaper (1969-71); Publisher, Islam in America (1987-). **Publ.:** Author of articles and books; published "A Nation of Lions... Chained" (1962) "Constitutionalism Western and Middle Eastern" (1963), "Peace in the Middle East" (1967) "Kennedy and Sirhan... Why?" (1968), "Palestine and the Bible" (1972), "Peace in Palestine" (1974) "Terrorism: Why America is the Target!" (1988); has translated several books into Arabic. **Other Information:** Has met with most Arab Kings, Presidents and Heads of States; Appeared on almost all major American radio and TV networks, discussing Arab issues and American policies toward the Middle East, Islam and the future of American in the Third World. Since 1993, Dr. Mehdi has embarked on a project of decorating America during December with the Crescent and Star, secular symbol of the Muslim people, as the country is decorated with Christmas trees and the Hanukkah Menorahs. Despite difficulties and opposition from several quarters, he has succeeded (by 1998) with 25 institutions, including The Chase Manhattan Bank, Citibank, JFK International Airport, Ney York Public Library, Grand Central Station, Federal District Court in Manhattan, The Empire State Building, World Trade Center, Nassua County Courthouse, Brooklyn Borough Hall amongst other places. The displaying of the National Crescent and Star in the White House's Ellipse within 100 feet from the Executive Mansion on December 19, 1997 was an historic occasions. **Award:** Book of the Year Award from Friends of the Book in Beirut (1963) for his book "A Nation of Lions... Chained". **Sport:** Watching American football (on television). **Hobbies:** Walking, reciting Arabic Poetry, flirt with life. **Member:** American Civil Liberties Union; American Legal and Philosophical Society. **Credit Cards:** Visa; United Airlines; Diners Club, etc. **Prof. Addr.:** P.O.Box 416, New York, N.Y. 10017, Tel.: (212) 972-9460, U.S.A.

MEHELMY (Abdel Magid, al), Egyptian exchange dealer. **Born** in 1949 in Cairo, Egypt. **Son** of Mahmood el-Mehelmy. **Married** in 1976, 1 daughter. **Educ.:** Cairo University. **Dipl.:** B.Com. (1972). **Career:** The Chase National Bank SAE, Egypt (1974-76); Assistant Manager, Operation/ Treasury, Citibank NA, Muscat Branch, Oman (1976-77); Deposit Dealer, Banque Arabe et Internationale d'Investissement, Paris (1977-80); Foreign Exchange and Money Market Dealer, BAII (Middle East) EC, Bahrain (1980-). **Member:** Foreign Exchange International Association (A.C.I.); Inter-Arab Cambist Association; Bahrain Forex Association. **Addr.:** al-Arooba Street, al-Arooba Building, Flat 25, P.O.Box 3361, Tel.: 357654, 355249, Telex: 68220 A/B SOPADF EM, Sharjah, UAE.

MEHRI (Abdalhamid), Algerian diplomat. **Born** on April 3, 1926. **Married**, 3 children. **Educ.:** University of Zitouna, Tunisia. **Dipl.:** in Arabic literary studies. **Career:** Active in the Algerian Popular Party (1951-53); Representative of FLN in Syria, Lebanon and Jordan; Director of North African Affairs, GPRA, Cairo (1958); Minister of Social and Cultural Affairs, GPRA (1960); Headmaster of Bouzareah Secondary School (1964-70); Secretary General, Ministry of Primary and Secondary Education (1970-77); Minister of Culture and Education (1979-80); Chairman of Information Committee in charge of Culture and Information; Ambassador to France (1984-85); Ambassador to Morocco (1986-Oct. 88); Head secretariat Permanent Committee FLN (since Oct. 1988). **Prof. Addr.:** Front de Libération Nationale, Blvd. Zirout Yousuf. Algiers, Algeria.

MEHRI (Hassan, al), Bahraini Education Adviser. **Born** on November 12, 1935. **Son** of Ibrahim al-Mehri (Seaman). **Married** on June 29, 1967, 3 children: Hamssa (1968), Nasreen (1972), Ali (1979). **Educ.:** Delhi University; University of Wales, U.K.; Reading University; Oxford University, U.K. **Dipl.:** Post graduate Diploma in Teaching English as a foreign language; Post graduate Diploma in Educational Administration; Fellowship in Education. **Career:** School-teacher (1951-58); Assistant Headmaster of Secondary School (1961-63); Assistant Headmaster of Secondary School (1965-67); Headmaster of Secondary School (1967-69); Headmaster of Secondary School (1969-72); Assistant Director of General Education (1972-75); Director of General Education (since 1975); currently Education Adviser. **Work:** Unpublished dissertation on teaching English grammar to Arab Students. **Medal:** from Ministry of Social Affairs, Bahrain, for services in the Social Field. **Hobbies:** Fishing, Volley ball. **Member:** Alumni Club, Bapco Club. **Credit Cards:** Access, Visa. **Prof. Addr.:** Ministry of Education, P.O.Box 70, Tel.: 37377, Bahrain. **Priv. Addr.:** 1045 West Reffa, Tel.: 665250, Bahrain.

MEHRIK (Yusuf, Ibrahim, al), Libyan academic. **Born** in 1937 in Marsa Matrouh, Egypt. **Married**, 5 children. **Dipl.:** B.Sc. and Ph.D. in Analytical Chemistry and Chromotography. **Career:** Dean of the Faculty of Science, Tripoli (1970-76); General Director of Petroleum Research Centre (1976-78); Director of Environmental Programme, NASR (1978-1986); Director General of Technical Centre (1986-92); Senior Advisor for Environmental Research in National Academy for Scientific Research (1992-99); Chairman, Environment Public Authority (1999-). **Hobbies:** swimming, reading, football, water skiing, bridge. **Prof. Addr.:** P.O.Box 3545, Tripoli, Libya.

MEKKAWAY (Fawzy), Egyptian professor of history. **Born** on April 13, 1939 in Egypt. **Son** of Abdel Razek Mekkaway and Mrs. Zeinab Abdallah. **Married** on December 12, 1963 to Nagwa Yousif, 4 children: Amany, Iman, Inaas, Amira. **Educ.:** Belkas Primery School; Belkas Secondary School; Dakhilia Governorate, Egypt; Faculty of Arts (History Department) Alexandria University, Egypt. **Dipl.:** Diploma in Ancient African History; Institute of African Studies, Cairo University, Egypt; M.Sc. Ph.D.; Greco-Roman era Institute of African Studies, Cairo University. **Career:** Assistant Lecturer - Lecturer, Cairo University; Assistant Professor of History (1982), Tanta University (1984-); Vice Dean, Faculty of Arts, Tanta University, then Dean; becoming Professor in the same Faculty in 1986; Professor of History, Faculty of Girls, King Abdelaziz University, Jeddah, since 1990 till now. **Addr.:** 262 Str., New Maadi, Tel.: 3520425, Cairo, Egypt.

MEKKI (Ismail, el-Misbah), Sudanese economist. **Born** on January 1, 1929 in Obeid (Sudan). **Married**, with children. **Educ.:** Faculty of Commerce, University of Cairo (1949-53); Michigan State University (1962-64). **Dipl.:** B. Com. (1953), M.A. (Economics) (1964). **Career:** Permanent Secretary, Ministry of Finance & Economy, Khartoum, Sudan (1968-71); Budget Adviser, International Monetary Fund (IMF), Yemen (1971); Alternative Executive Director, International Bank of Reconstruction and Development (IBRD) Washington, since 1972; General Manager, Dayo Industrial Co., Sudan; Director, Sudan Development Corporation. **Awards:** Youssef Nahas Prize, University of Cairo (1953). **Prof. Addr.:** IBRD 1818 H Street NW, Tel.: 202393-6360, Washington DC 20433 (USA). and P.O.Box 710, 69 Africa Road, Tel.: 79536, 79540, Khartoum, Sudan.

MEKOUAR (Muhammad), Moroccan Aviation Official. **Born** in 1937 in Fes, Morocco. **Married**, 1 son, 4 daughters. **Educ.:** Ecole Nationale de l'Aviation Civile, Paris, France. **Dipl.:** Diploma in Civil Aviation Engineering. **Career:** Head of Civil Aeronautics Service, Ministry of Public Works (1961-65); Director of Aviation, Ministry of Transport (1965-81), Managing Director, Aviation Administration (1984-84); Chairman of Maghreb Committee for Aerial Transport (1966-68); Chairman of General Assembly of the Council for Civil Aviation in the Arab States (1977-78); Chairman of Royal Air Maroc (1984- to present); Chairman of Organisation of Arab Aerial Transporters (1985-). **Decor.:** Knight of the Royal Order of the Throne, Morocco (1969). **Hobbies:** walking, tennis. **Prof. Addr.:** Royal Air Maroc, Casa Anfa Airport, Casablanca, Morocco.

MEKOUAR (Tahar, Ahmad), Moroccan former diplomat. **Born** on December 2, 1923 in Fès. **Son** of Hajj Ahmad Mekouar B.H.T. **and** Mrs. Fatima Benjelloun. **Married** to Aïcha Benjelloun on October 15, 1949, 5 children: Aziz, Jalil, Rochdi, Mourad and Lotfi. **Educ.:** Lycée Mixte of Fès, Lycée Lyautey at Casablanca, Paris University. **Dipl.:** Political Science, History. **Career:** Chief of Protocol (September 5, 1956); Chargé d'Affaires of the Moroccan Embassy in Rome (September 6, 1956-April 27, 1957); Permanent Delegate of Morocco to the F.A.O., Consul of Morocco in Lisbon (April 27, 1957- August 8, 1958); Chargé d'Affaires at the Moroccan Legation of Lisbon (September 9, 1958- February 1, 1960); Chargé d'Affaires at the Moroccan Embassy of Lisbon (February 1, 1960- December 12, 1961); Director of the General Administration of the Ministry of Foreign Affairs (December 27, 1961- June 30, 1962); Chargé d'Affaires of Morocco in Potugal (June 30, 1962), Chief of Diplomatic Mission (1962-72); Director of Protocol (1972-75); Chairman of various enterprises (since 1975). **Awards:** Decorated by H.M. the King of Morocco (March 1967). **Sports:** Golf, Tennis and swimming. **Member** of the Estoril Golf Club, Royal Golf Dar Salam-Rabat, Morocco; Diner's Club. **Prof. Addr.:** Avenue Marqueis de Tomar No. 7, 2nd Lisboa, Tel.: 533722, Portugal. **Priv. Addr.:** 150 Bd. Rahal El Meskini, Tel.: 314491, 311278, Casablanca, Morocco.

MELKANI (Ahmad Fawzi, Mohamad, al), Syrian judge. **Born** in 1922 in Syria. **Son** of Mohamad al-Melkani. **Educ.:** Arab Law Institute of Damascus. **Dipl.:** Secondary Certificate, LL.B. **Career:** on the Bench, Judge in Deir ez-Zor first instance Court, Conciliation at Salh Ain al-Arab, then at Nebk, Court President, Counsel at the Court of Appeal. **Addr.:** Damascus, Syria.

MELLAKH (Larbi), Tunisian politician. **Born** in 1929 in the Governorate of Bizerta, Tunisia. **Married,** 5 children. **Educ.:** Faculté de Médecine, Marseilles, France (Pharmacy Section). **Career:** Deputy for Bizerta in the National Assembly (1969); Member of the Central Committee of the Socialist Destour Party (1973); Secretary of State to the Minister of Supply (1973). **Decor.:** Officer of the Order of Tunisian Independence. **Addr.:** Tunis, Tunisia.

MEMMI (Albert), Tunisian Professor and Writer. **Born** on December 15, 1920 in Tunis, Tunisia. **Son** of François Memmi (Saddler) **and** Mrs. née Marguerite Sarfati. **Married** on December 24, 1946 in Paris to Miss Germaine Dubach, 3 children: Daniel (8 May 1951), Dominique (18 September 1953) and Nicolas (5 September 1961). **Educ.:** Lycée Carnot, Tunis; University of Algiers, Algeria; University of Paris, France. **Dipl.:** Lic. Philosophy; B.A. (ès lettres-Sociology); P.C.B. Biology; Doctorate in Sociology (1970); Career: Professor, Lycée Carnot de Tunis (1953); Director of Centre de Psycho-Pédagogie de Tunis (1953-57); Research Attaché, C.N.R.S., Paris 1957); Lecturer, Ecole Pratique des Hautes Etudes (1958); Professor responsible for Cultural teaching at the School of "Higher Commercial Studies" (1958); Master of Conferences (1970); Professor (Chaire de Sociology de la Culture), University of Paris-X (1970); Director, Unité d'enseignement et de recherche (U.E.R.) for Social Sciences (1975); Professor Honorary at CESA; Director of Anthropology Laboratories (CEDRES). **publ.:** Author of "La Statue de Sel" (1953); "Agar" (1955); "Portrait du Colonisé" (1957); "Portrait d'un Juif" (1962); "Les Français et le Racisme" (1963); "Anthologie des Ecrivains

Maghrébins" (1965); "La Libération du Juif" (1967); "l'Homme Dominé" (1968); "Le Scorpion" (1969); "Juifs et Arabes" (1974); "LaTerre Intérieure" (1976); "Le Desert" (1977); "La Dépendance" (1979); "Le Racisme" (1982); "Les Ecrivains Francophones du Maghreb" (1984); "Ce que je crois" (1984); "Poême" (1985); "Essai sur l'Ecriture Colorée" (1986). Le Pharaon; Le Buveur et l'Amoureux. **Awards:** Knight of the Legion of Honour; Officer of Academic Palmes; Officer of Arts and Letters; Commander of "Nichan Iftikhar"; Officer of Order of the Tunisian Republic; prize Carthage, Tunis (1953); Prize Fenelon, Paris (1954); Prize Simba of Literature, Rome (1978). Prix de l'Union Rationaliste (1997); Grand Prix Litéraire du Maghreb (1998); Prix tunisie-France (1999). **Sport:** Swimming. **Hobby:** Literature. **Member:** Academy of Overseas Sciences (1975); Vice-President of French Pen-Club (1976-79); Syndic of Syndicate of French Language Writers (1981); Vice-president of the Federation of French Speaking Writers (1984); Member of the Committee Patronage of the House of Writers, Member, Conseil de l'Institut sur le Moyen-Orient de l'Université de Princeton. Etc... **Adr.:** 5, Rue Saint-Merri, Tel. (16-1) 42.78.02.63, 42.78.84.79, 75004 Paris, France.

MENTOURI (Muhammad Salah), Algerian politician. **Born** on April 9, 1940. **Married,** 3 children. **Dipl.:** LL.B., DES (in Economics). **Career:** Member of FLN Civil Organization, Constantine, later in tunisia (1956-60); Member of the General Union of Islamic Students in Algiers (UGEMA) (1960-62); Assistant Director for Coordination and Animation at the Ministry of Works and Social Affairs; Director General, for Social Security at the Ministry of Health; Secretary General, Secretary of State, then Minister of Professional Training (1981-84); Deputy Minister of Sport (1984). **Addr.:** Algiers, Algeria.

MERAD (Rouchdi), Algerian Attorney at Law. **Born** on August 26, 1939 in Annaba. **Son** of Abderrahman Merad, Jurist (Legal Cabinet) **and** Mrs. née Fatima Zohra Said Cherif. **Married** with Feriel Bey-Laggoun on August 4, 1973 in Algiers, Algeria, 3 children: Nail (1.5.74 Algiers), Sihem (18.1.78 Algiers), Reda (18.1.85) Algiers. **Dipl.:** Diploma from Université de Lausanne (HEC) 1963 Switzerland, Diploma from Ecole Nationale des Impôts (Paris) 1965, D.E.S. from Université de Nice (France) 1974. Doctorat d'Etat et these d'aggregation (Université de Nice, France) 1976. **Career:** From 1965 to 1985 Sonatrach (Compagnie Pétrolière d'Etat) Financial Director and Advisor of Chairman General Manager. Government representative during nationalisation American Petroleum Companies in 1967 and French Petroleum Companies in 1971. Since 1985 Attorney at Law, Algiers, Algeria. **Sports:** Swimming, Tennis, Skiing **Credit Card:** Visa. **Prof. Addr.:** 12, rue de la Liberté, 16001, Algiers, Algeria, Tel.: 213.2.73.45.00 & 73.49.00, Fax: 73.81.00.

MERAIKHI (Mohammed, Eid, Al-), UAE executive. **Born** in 1952 in Abu Dhabi. **Son** of Eid Al-Meraikhi. **Married** in 1979, 3 sons, 2 Daughters. **Educ.:** New York University, Bachelor of Economics & Political Sciences (1976). **Career:** Chairman, U.A.E. Central Bank; Board Member, Supreme Petroleum Council, Abu Dhabi; Director, Projects, Abu Dhabi Investment Authority, **Addr.:** P.O.Box 3600, Tel.: 324617, Telex: 22674 ADIA EM, Abu Dhabi, UAE.

MERCADER (Pedro), Spanish economist. **Born** on February 7, 1938 in Gerona, Spain. **Son** of Jose Mercader (Industrial Engineer and Businessman) **and** Mrs. Justa née Canabal. **Married** on November 8, 1981 to Miss Beatriz Mendieta in La Paz, Bolivia, 3 children: Sebastian, Rodrigo, Andrea. **Educ.:** Harvard University - MPA in Government; New York University - M.A. in Ibero-American Affairs; University of Barcelona - Licenciate in Economic Sciences; North Carolina State University - Agricultural Economics; Real Colegio de Alfonso XII - Madrid, High Schooldegree. **Dipl.:** Master in Public Administration - Harvard University, Cambridge-M.A.-USA; Master of Arts - New York University; Licenciado in Economic Sciences - University of Barcelona. **Career:** United Nations Resident Coordinator + UNDP Resident Representative + WFP Representative + UNFPA Representative in Cairo, Egypt from July 1990. Before same positions in Lima, Peru (1986-1990), in Montevideo, Uruguay (1983-86). Prior to that: UNDP Deputy Resident Representative in Bolivia (1980-83), Colombia (1974-76) and Assistant Resident Representative in Colombia (1968-71) and Mexico (1966-67); Senior UNDP Adviser to the World Tourism Organization, Madrid, Spain 1980; Senior Officer, United Nations Volunteer, Geneva-Switzerland, 1979. **Work:** Development Assistance. **Awards:** Orden the Isabel La Catolica of Spain, Medal of the City of la Paz-Bolivia. **Sports:** Horse riding and Jogging. **Hobby:** History. **Member:** Colegio de Economistas de Barcelona and Madrid, Spain. **Credit Cards:** American Express, Visa. **Prof. Addr.:** 1191 Corniche El Nil (Boulac), P.O.Box 982, Tel.: (202) 768517, Fax: (202) 779145, Cairo, Egypt. **Priv. Addr.:** 35 Road 17 (Maadi), Tel.: (202) 3504056, Cairo, Egypt.

MERHEJ (Michel), Syrian businessman. **Born** in 1942 in Hama, Syria. **Married,** 4 children. **Career:** Businessman. **Decor.:** Cavalière Officiale, Italy (1978). **Award:** Award of Peter and Paul (1st Class), Patriarch of Antioch and the Orient (1983). **Hobby:** Human affairs. **Addr.:** Le Roccabella, 24 Avenue Princesse Grace, MC 98000, Monaco.

MERZBAN (Mohamad, Abdallah), Egyptian economist and former statesman. **Born** in January 1918 in Fayoum (Egypt). **Educ.:** Cairo University; Harvard University, Cambridge, Massachusetts (USA). **Dipl.:** B.A., M.A. **Career:** Lecturer, Faculty of Commerce, Cairo University until 1956; Secretary-General, Ministry of Industry (1956-60); Chairman, al-Nar Organisation (1960-61); Chairman, Spinning and Weaving Organisation (1961-

66); **Minister** of Supply and Home Trade (1968-70); Minister of Economy and Foreign Trade (1970-73); also, Acting Minister of Supply and Domestic Trade (1971-73); Deputy Prime-Minister (1972-73); former Chairman, Bank of Credit and Commerce (Misr) S.A.E., Cairo **Publ.:** Author of "Financial Management", "Mathematics of Marketing". **Priv. Addr.:** 44 Mohamed Mazhar St., Tel.: 800741, Zamalek, Cairo, Egypt.

MESHAL (Ahmad Abdallah, al), Saudi civil servant. **Born** in Riyadh in 1943. **Dipl.:** M.A. (Public Administration). **Career:** Former Secretary, Riyadh University; Assistant Director, Foreign Personnel Department, Ministry of Education; Director-General, Personnel Department, Ministry of Education. Director General of Towns Council in the Ministry of Municipal & Rural Affairs. Assistant Director Manager of planning in the same ministry. **Member:** Islamic Organization in the U.S.A. and Canada. **Awards:** Honorary Badge from the University of South California. **Publ.:** several papers on public administration and planning; Director, Unesco Office, Qatar. **Prof. Addr.:** P.O.Box 10218, Tel.: 4765534, Riyadh. **Priv. Addr.:** Tel.: 4654322, Riyadh, Saudi Arabia and UNESCO Office-Doha, P.O.Box 3945, Doha, Qatar.

MESHAL (Ibrahim Abdulrahman, al), Saudi academic. **Born** in 1946 at al-Kharj. **Dipl.:** Ph.D. **Career:** Demonstrator, Faculty of Pharmacy, King Saud University (1972-73); Assistant Professor (1979); Vice Dean, Faculty of Pharmacy, King Saud University. **Publications:** research work; participated in editing a book, "Appropriate Use of Medicines". **Hobbies:** chess, reading, writing. **Prof. Addr.:** Faculty of Pharmacy, King Saud University, Tel.: 4764161, Riyadh. **Priv. Addr.:** Tel.: 4811000 Ext. 2326, Riyadh, Saudi Arabia.

MESHAL (Mohamad, Said Khalil, al), Qatari industrialist. **Born** in 1933 in Palestine. **Son** of Khalil al-Meshal. **Educ.:** B.Sc. in Petroleum Engineering, Cairo University, Egypt (1957). **Career:** Head of Reservoir Engineering Division and later Petroleum Technical Department, Ministry of Petroleum and Mining, Saudi Arabia; Head of Petroleum Department, Ministry of Finance and Petroleum, Qatar (1972); Chairman, Qatar Fertilizer Company (1969); Director General, Industrial Development Technical Center (1972); Director, Qatar General Petroleum Corporation (1974); Chairman, Qatar Steel Company (1977); and various others. Played major role in reorganising Petroleum Industry in Qatar, establishing the Qatar General Petroleum Corporation, nationalisation of Oil Industry in Qatar, organising industrial joint ventures with foreign firms in Umm Said Industrial Estate, south of Doha; played a leading role in industrial and infra-structural activities in Qatar and in organising industrial planning and activities. **Addr.:** Doha, Qatar.

MESHARAFA (Hussain, Abbas), Egyptian diplomat. **Born** in 1934 in Damanhur, Egypt. **Married,** 2 **children. Educ.:** Cairo University, Egypt; College of Defence, Cairo. **Dipl.:** B.A. in Literature. **Career:** Attaché and Third Secretary, Embassy in Madrid, Spain (1958-62); First Secretary, Embassy in Singapore (1966-70); Counsellor, Organisation for African Unity (1972-75); Represented Egypt in the O.A.U. Fact Finding mission on Djibouti (1976); International Conference on Desarmement; International Conference on non Proliferation Treaty. Counsellor and Minister Plenipotentiary, Egyptian Delegation to the United Nations (1978-81); Minister Plenipotentiary, Head of the Egyptian Mission to Tunisia (1983-84); Member of the United Nations Association, Cairo (1982-); Ambassador to Sudan (1985-87). and Ireland (1989- to present). **Medal:** Medal of the Egyptian Republic (3rd Class) (1980), (2nd Class) (1981). **Decor:** "el-Nilien I" from the Republic of Sudan. **Hobbies:** reading, squash, chess. **Addr.:** 11 Shareh al-Themar, Apt. 9, Mohandiseen, Dokki, Giza, Egypt.

MESHARI (Abdulaziz Ali, al), Saudi professor. **Born** in Hail, **Educ.:** M.B., DTM & H, DRCOG, L.M., MRCOG., FRCOG. **Career:** Lecturer, Obstetrics & Gynaecology, Faculty of Medicine, King Saud University; has been an adviser to the Ministry of Health, Security Forces Hospital, and National Guard Hospital, Riyadh former Dean of the Applied Medical Sciences and chairman of the Obstetrics & Gynaecology Department, King Saud University (1980-Date), and Official representative of the Faculty of Medicine in the Arab Board for Medical Specializations on Obstetrics and Gynaecology; has attended several conferences on Obstetrics and Gynaecology throughout the world. **Publications:** 30 papers on Obstetrics and Gynaecology. **Prof. Addr.:** Department of Obstetrics & Gynaecology (36), King Khalid Hospital, Faculty of Medicine, King Saud University, P.O.Box 7805, Riyadh 11472, Saudi Arabia.

MESHARI (Abdulrahman, al), Saudi physician. **Born** in 1939 at al-Hassa. **Educ.:** M.D. (Gynæcology and Obstetrics). **Member:** Royal College of Gynæcologists and Obstetricians, London; attended 29th British Conference on Gynæcology and Obstetrics. **Address:** Riyadh, Saudi Arabia.

MESHARI (Hassan, Ibn Meshary Ibn Ibrahim, al), Saudi businessman. **Born** in 1930 at al-Hassa (Hofuf). **Educ.:** B.Com., Cairo, Egypt (1953); M.A. (Industrial Management), U.S.A., 1960. **Career:** Director General of al-Yamama Cement Co., Riyadh (1960-61); Deputy Minister, Ministry of Finance and National Economy (1961-64); Chairman of Board, King Faisal Settlement Project Authority, al-Hassa, Public Organization for Saline Water Desalination; member of Board of Riyadh Schools, al-Yamamah Press Establishment; Former Minister of Agriculture and Water; Chairman of Board, Saudi Company for Hotels and Tourist Resorts; Charter member of Na-

tional Arabian Horseriding Club; Chairman of several Saudi delegations to FAO Conferences, Rome, Arab League Food Organization Conferences, World Food Conference, Royal Botanical Agricultural Exhibition, U.K. **Honours:** King Abdulaziz Order for meritorious government service, granted by His late Majesty King Faisal; Order of Merit awarded by President of the Republic of Liberia. **Hobby:** reading. **Address:** P.O.Box 209 and P.O.Box 5500, Riyadh, Saudi Arabia.

MESSAADIA (Muhammad, Cherif), Algerian politician. **Born** in 1924. **Married**, 5 children. **Educ.:** Zitouna University, Tunisia. **Career:** Deputy in the constituent Assembly, National Popular Assembly (1962); Member of General Committee (1964); Member, FLN Orientation Commission (1965), Manager, FLN Orientation and Information Department (1968); Coordinator, FLN Central Apparatus (1973), President, FLN Orientation and Information Committee (1977-79); Minister of Moudjahine (1979-80); Member of the Political Bureau (1981-Oct. 1988); Head of the Secretariat, FLN Central Committee (1980-Oct. 1988). **Prof. Addr.:** c/o Algerian National Liberation Party, Blvd. Zirout Yousuf, Algiers, Algeria.

MESSAOUDENE (Said Ait), Algerian politician. **Born** in 1933. **Career:** Major, Air Force, Officers Flying School, Salon, France (1955); Fighter Pilot; joined National Liberation Army (ALN) and led Algerian military missions to China, Iraq and USSR during Independence war; attended course, Aeronautical Division, Moscow Military Academy; following Independence, appointed Air Force Commander, responsible for its reorganization; Counsellor, Aviation Affairs in Presidency; Director-General, Air Algérie (January 1968); Minister of Posts and Telecommunications (Dec. 1972- April 1977); Minister of Public Health (April 1977- March 1979); Ministry of Light Industry (1979-84). **Addr.:** Algiers, Algeria.

MESTIRI (Ahmad), Tunisian politician. **Born** in 1928 in Masra. **Married** in 1956, to Souad Chemik, 4 children. Tahar, Hatem, Moncef and Asma. **Educ.:** Secondary in Tunis; Licence in Law, Faculty of Law, Paris. **Career:** Secretary of State for Justice (1956-58); Secretary of State for Finance and Commerce (1958-60); Member of Central Committee of Neo-Destour Party (1962-64), of Destour Socialist Party (1964-68 and since 1970); Ambassador to U.S.S.R., to Egypt (1958-62), to Algeria (1962-66); Minister of National Defence (1966-68); Minister of the Interior (1970-71); expelled from Socialist Destour Party (1972); expelled from National Assembly (1973); regarded as Head of the group of "Liberals", asking for the liberalization of the political regime and former leader of the MDS Political Party (after resigning as its Secretary General in Sept. 1989); Lawyer in Tunis. **Awards:** Grand Cordon, Order of Tunisian Independence; Grand Cordon, Order of Tunisian Republic; various foreign decorations. **Addr.:** 6, Rue D'Annaba, Tel.: 248084, Tunis, Tunisia.

MESTIRI (Mahmoud), Tunisian diplomat. **Born** on December 25, 1929. **Educ.:** Institute of Political Studies, University of Lyon (France). **Dipl.:** B.A., LL.B. **Career:** Served on several Tunisian delegations to United Nations; Alternate representative to UN (1958-60); Head Tunisian special diplomatic mission to Congo (Leopoldville) (now Zaire) 1960; Assistant to personal representative of UN Secretary-General for Foreign Affairs, Tunis (1965-67); Permanent representative to UN (1967-69); Chairman, UN special commission on the situation with regard to implementation of Declaration on the granting of independence to colonial countries and peoples (1968-69); Ambassador to Belgium (September 1969), to Luxemburg (October 1969), to European Community (November 1969); Ambassador to Federal Republic of Germany (1971-72); Ambassador to Soviet Union, also accredited to Poland (December 1973-75); Ambassador to the U.N. (1976-80); Secretary of State for Foreign Affairs (1982-86); Permanent Representative U.N. (1986-87); Foreign Minister (November 1987) and he represented Tunisia in the Arab Summit of Amman (November 8, 1987); Ambassador to Egypt (1988-1990); presently special representative of the Secretary-General of U.N. for Afghanistan. **Addr.:** Ministry of Foreign Affairs, Tunis, Tunisia.

MESTIRI (Said, Mohamed, Tahar), Tunisian surgeon. **Born** in 1919 in Tunis, Tunisia. **Son** of Tahar Mestiri. **Married**, five children. **Educ.:** Faculty of Medicine, Algiers, Agregation chirurgie generale, Paris, advanced courses in Paris and USA. **Career:** Intern in Algerian and Tunisian Hospitals (1945-51); Assistant Surgeon in hospitals in Tunis (1951-56); Principal Surgeon at the Habib Thameur Hospital and at the Ernest Conseil Hospital (1957-64 and since 1967); Professor of the Tunis Faculty of Medicine; President of the Tunisian Surgery Association; President of the Tunisian Medical Science Society; foreign member of the French Academy of Surgery; member of the Lyon Society of Surgery; former Vice President of the Council of the Tunisian Order of Medicine; participated as Surgeon and Head of the Tunisian Medical Team in Suez during Six Day War (June 1967) and the October War in Damascus, Syria (1973). **Medals:** Commander of Nichan Iftikhar; Bizerta Commemorative Medal; Officer of the Order of the Tunisian Republic; Chevalier of the Order of Tunisian Independence; Commander of the Order of the Tunisian Republic. **Hobbies:** Swimming, bridge; Hispano-Moorish architecture; Tunisian ceramics. **Prof. Addr.:** Ernest Conseil Hospital, Tunis, Tunisia. **Priv. Addr.:** 2070 Route de Gammarth, La Marsa, Tunisia.

METALTA (Ahmad, Ammar), Algerian academic **Born** in 1932 in Wilaya de Skikda, Algeria. **Son** of Ammar Metalta. **Educ.:** Moscow University. **Dipl.:** Ph.D. in Law. **Career:** Secretary General, Union of Algerian Jurists (since 1974), Assistant Secretary General, Union of Arab Jurists (since 1975); President, Management and Juridical

Committee, National Popular Assembly, and Representative in the National Popular Assembly; Counsellor, National Scientific Research Center, Algeria (1977-82). **Publ.:** "Algerian Justice Under the Turkish Rule". **Medals:** National Liberation Army Medal. **Hobby:** Tourism. **Prof. Addr.:** 2 Nahj Rabih Boo Rabi'a, al-Abyar, Algeria. **Priv. Addr.:** Bt. D. Cage 2, Appt 22, el-Biar 16030, Ben Aknoun, Algeria.

METAWEH (Ibrahim Esmat), Egyptian educationist. **Born** in 1923 in Cairo, Egypt. **Son** of Mohamed Metaweh. **Widow,** four children. **Educ.:** Cairo University; B.Sc. (1944); Diploma in Ed., Cairo (1946); M.A. and Ph.D. in Education, University of Minnesota, USA (1952-1954). **Career:** UNESCO Expert, Tripoli, Libya (1955-57); Exchange Mission, USSR (1961-62); Director of Educational Planning, Ministry of Higher Education, Cairo (1962-65); Dean, College of Education, Minia, Assiut, Tanta, Shebin al-Khoum, Kafr al-Shaikh. **Publ.:** Numerous books on rural educational planning, audio visual aids, fundamentals of education, practice teaching and Environmental Education. **Addr.:** Professor, Faculty of Education, Tanta University, Tanta, Egypt.

METWALLI (Suleiman), Egyptian Politician. **Born** in 1927 in Menoufia. **Educ.:** B.S, Civil Engineering, Cairo University (1949); Post-graduate studies in the USA (1954). **Career:** Engineer, Ministry of Irrigation (1949); Officer, Corps of Engineers (1950-54); Member, Technical Directorate, National Council of Production (1954-56); Head, Technical Office, Ninistry of Communications (1956-60); Director General, Organization for National Domestic Transport (1961-66); Chairman, Roads and Bridges Authority (1967-76); Governor of Beni Suef (1976-77); Governor of Menoufia (1977-78); elected to People's Assembly (1979-to date); Minister for Cabinet Affairs (1978-80); Minister of Transport, Communications and Maritime Transport (1980-93); Minister of Transport and Telecommunications (Oct. 1993-Oct.1999). **Address:** Cairo, Egypt.

MEZGHANI (Ridha, Ahmad), Tunisian politician. **Born** in Sfax, Tunisia, in 1946. **Son** of Ahmad Mezghani. **Married,** two children. **Educ.:** In Tunis and Paris. **Dipl.:** LL.B., M.Sc., Doctor of Law. **Career:** Magistrate and Attache to the Cabinet, Ministry of Justice; Teacher of Law, ENA and University of Tunis (1977-81); Teacher of Law, Institute of Public Administration, Riyadh, Saudi Arabia (1981-84); Head of the Cabinet, Ministry of Justice (1985). **Publ.:** "l'Interpretation judiciaire en droit civil IPA (Riyadh)", also several articles on jurisprudential subjects published in Tunisia and France. Member of Club Kiwanis, Tunis. **Priv. Addr.:** Cite Hana Nour 4 Menzah VII, 1004, Tunis, Tunisia.

MEZIANE (Abdulmajid), Algerian politician. **Born** in 1926. **Educ.:** Ph.D. in Philosophy. **Career:** Head of Cabinet to President Ben Bella; General Secretary, Ministry of Internal Affairs (1965); Professor at Algiers and Oran Universities; Vice Dean, University of Algiers (1981); Minister of Culture (1982); Minister of Culture and Tourism (1984-86); Presently, President of the High Islamic Council. **Addr.:** Algiers, Algeria.

MHAIDI (Kadhim, Abdulhamid, al), Iraqi lawyer. **Born** on February 12, 1922 in Baghdad. **Son** of Abdulhamid al-Mhaidi **and** Mrs. Shafika. **Married** to Badria M. Jasim on January 10, 1949, 5 children: Khafra, Mottan, Thaair, Areeg and Duraid. **Educ.:** Elementary and Secondary School, Law College. **Dipl.:** Licentiate in Law. **Career:** Director-General of Baghdad Chamber of Commerce (1963); Director-General of Exhibitions and Trade Fairs (1963); Director-General of Euphrates Cement Company (1964); Director-General of Baghdad Bank (1965); Minister of Economy (1965); Chairman of the Board of the State Organisation of Trade (1966); Minister of Economy (1966-67); Economic Adviser for Baghdad Chamber of Commerce (1967-68); Secretary-General of the Federation of Iraqi Chambers of Commerce. (1969); **Hobby:** Reading. **Addr.:** Baghdad, Iraq.

MHENNI (Hedi), Tunisian Politician. **Born** on December 24, 1942 in Sayada. **Married,** two children. **Educ.:** Medical Sciences Studies. **Career:** Assistant, University of Tunis, Faculty of Medicine (1976); Lecturer (1980); Professor, Pediatrics (1987); Rector, University of Medicine and Sciences (1992); Chairman, National Office for Population and Family Planning; Vice Minister, Public Health (1990); Vice Minister, Technology and Scientific Research (1991); Minister of Public Health (1992-to date). **Address:** Ministry of Public Health, Bad Saadoun, 1006 Tunis, Tunisia.

MICHEL (Antoine), Djibouti Deputy at the National Assembly. **Born** in 1950 at Diré-Dawa. **Educ.:** Secondary. **Career:** Office Employee, Tanslator, Assistant Manager, Head of Sales Department- Public Relations at Marill establishment; Member of RPP; Elected Deputy at the National Assembly (19/12/1997- to date); Commission Vice-President for Social Development and Environment Protection and Member of the Permanent Commission. **Prof. Addr.:** National Assembly, P.O.Box 138 Djibouti, Djibouti.

MIDANI (Ahmad, Toufiq, al), Syrian physician. **Born** in 1917 in Damascus. **Educ.:** Universities of Philadelphia, New York and London. **Dipl.:** Doctor in Medicine, specialisation in internal diseases and general hygiene. **Career:** Physician in the Ministry of Public Health, Chief of Inspectorate-General in the said Ministry; Private Practice. **Publ.:** Thesis on Public Health in Great Britain. **Award:** Medal of Syrian Merit. **Addr.:** Damascus, Syria.

MIDANI (Zuhair, al), Syrian lawyer. **Born** in 1923 in

Damascus, Syria. **Education:** Arab Institute of Law, Damascus, Syria. **Career:** Private law practice; Deputy for Damascus, Unification Council with Egypt (1961); Lawyer, Syria (1968, 1975); Secretary General, Arab Lawyers Union. **Addr.:** c/o Arab Lawyers Union, 13 Shari Ittihad al-Muhamiin al Arab, Garden City, Cairo, Egypt.

MIDHI (Mahmoud, Said), Yemeni politician. **Career:** Representative of Ministry of Economy (1968); member of the First Governorate Command (1969); Permanent Secretary to the Ministry of Commerce, Economy and Planning; former Governor of the Bank of Yemen; elected to Central Committee (1975); Acting Minister of Commerce and Provisions (1975); Minister of Finance (1986-87). **Addr.:** Aden, Republic of Yemen.

MIELCIOIU (Ion), Romanian diplomat. **Born** on September 21, 1934 in Dragasani Vilcea, Romania. **Son** of Ilie Mielcioiu (Farmer) **and** Mrs. Maria née Ionita. **Married** on November 9, 1958 in Dragasani Vilcea to Miss Elena Mielcioiu, one child: Minodora (1965). **Educ.:** Elementary School Dragasani, High School Craiova, Sofia State University-Bulgaria. **Dipl.:** Graduation Diploma in History and Philosophy Issued in 1958 from History and Phylosophy Faculty of the Sofia State University-Bulgaria. **Career:** Diplomatic Attache, 3rd and 2nd Secretary of Romanian Embassy in Sofia, Bulgaria (1959 to 1965); Deputy Director, Romanian Ministry of Foreign Affairs (1966 to 1968); Political Counsellor of Romanian Embassy in Warsaw, Poland (1969 to 1974); Deputy Director, Romanian Ministry of Foreign Affairs (1975-1977); Minister Counsellor of Romanian Embassy in Moscow, USSR (1978 to 1986); Director, Romanian Ministry of Foreign Affairs (1987 to 1990); Ambassador of Romania in Damascus, from April 1990 to date. **Work:** Studies of Various International Issues Published in Romania. **Sports:** Swimming; tennis; volley-ball. **Prof. Addr.:** Embassy of Romania, 8 Ibrahim Hanano, P.O.Box 4454, Tel.: 3327570/71/72, Damascus, Syria.

MIGUIL (Hassan, Farah), Djibouti Deputy at the National Assembly, and Official. **Born** in 1954 in Djibouti. **Career:** Senior Official, Port of Djibouti. General Secretary of LPAI (1975-1979); Quarter 4-6; President of "Annexe 4-6" of RPP (1979-1996). Appointed Minister of Justice (27/03/1996) and Became Minister of Public Works, Urbanism and Housing (28/12/1997); Deputy at the National Assembly. **Prof. Addr.:** National Assembly, P.O.Box 138 Djibouti, Djibouti.

MIKHAIL (Antoun Scandar, Dr.), Egyptian banker. **Born** on August 8, 1938 in Cairo. **Married** on November 3, 1968 in Cairo, 2 children: Rami Antoun Scandar (27.02.1970), Robert Antoun Scandar (12.10.1972). **Educ.:** Primary and Secondary Studies: Collèges des Frères des Ecoles Chrétiennes, Cairo, Egypt; Faculty of Commerce, Cairo University: Bachelor of Commerce, Faculté de Droit de Paris. **Dipl.:** Doctorat en Economie et Administration des Entreprises. **Career:** Since 1955 till now, Egyptian Banking System: Crédit d'Orient S.A.E.; Banque du Caire; Misr International Bank; Banque Paribas, Cairo Branch. **Other Information:** F.E.S.A.A. (Fellow of the Egyptian Society of Accountants and Auditors; F.E.S.T. (Fellow of the Egyptian Society of Taxation); M.I.F.A. (Member of the International Fiscal Association); F.A.B.A. (Fellow of the Arab Banking Association). **Awards:** Egyptian Government Banking Award on January 1, 1992, on the "Bankers Day"; Economic and Financial Award on May 5, 1993 from the President of France (Officier de l'Ordre National du Mérite). **Hobby:** Reading. **Member:** Heliopolis Sporting Club, Medinet Nasr Sporting Club. **Prof. Addr.:** 6 A, Ghandi Street, Garden City, Cairo, P.O.Box 71, Magless El Shaab (Cairo), Tel.: 3555081, Cairo, Egypt. **Priv. Addr.:** 17, El Maahad El Ishtiraky Street, Roxy, Tel.: 2570883, Cairo, Egypt.

MIKOU (Abdelali), Moroccan certified accountant. **Born** on 22 July 1942 in Fes, Morocco. **Son** of late Mohamad Mikou **and** Mrs., Saida Lazraq. **Married** on 31 August 1968 in Fes, to Miss Bahia Tazzi Riffi, 3 children: Syham, Mohamad Jalil, Othman. **Educ.:** Faculté de Droit et de Sciences Economiques, Université de Paris; Institut d'Etudes Statistiques de Paris; Institut d'Etudes de Développement Economique et Social "I.E.D.E.S". **Dipl.:** Baccalaureat (Sciences Exp.); Master (Economic Sciences). **Career:** Officer, Credit Dept., Banque Nationale de Développement Economique (BNDE) (1965-67); Certified Accountant and adviser since 1968. **Works:** Studies on various investment codes in Morocco; several sectorial studies on long-term loans. **Sport:** Swimming. **Hobbies:** Reading, and Movies. **Member:** Past-President, Rotary Club of Casablanca Nord Mohamedia. **Credit Card:** Diner's Club. **Prof. Addr.:** 28 Place Mohammed, Tel.: 223019, 271804, Casablanca 01. **Priv. Addr.:** 27 Avenue Masset, Tel.: 360807, Casablanca 01, Morocco.

MILED (Habib), Tunisian businessman. **Born** in Menzel Bouzella, Tunisia in 1947. **Educ.:** Economics. **Career:** Financial Director of the SOGITEX Group (1970-80); Chairman and Managing Director, Pantaloisia SA (1981-83); Chairman and Managing Director VTL, Sotuves, and Somoves companies (1983-). **Prof. Addr.:** 1 Rue J.J. Rousseau, 1002 Tunis, Tel.: 286593, 281742, Tunisia. **Priv. Addr.:** 27 Avenue Monji Slim, 1004 Meuzah V, Tunis, Tunisia.

MILI (Ali, Fredje), Tunisian official. **Born** in 1943 in Monastir, Tunisia. **Married**, three children. **Educ.:** University of Paris, France. **Dipl.:** Ph.D. in Psychology. **Career:** Consultant of UNESCO in Syria (1971); Researcher for the Canadian Agency of International Development and Consultant for the Research Center of International Development, (1973-74); Visiting Professor, University of Constantine, Algeria (1973-75); Senio Psychologist, Head of Services par interim and Professor, Universities of Monkton, New Brunswick and of Quebec, Rimouski, Canada (1976-78); Senior Psychologist and Clinical Coordinator of the Admission Unit, Institute Philippe Pinel de Montreal, Canada and Doctoral Supervisor, Quebec University, Montreal (1979-80); Head of Project, Ministry of Social Affairs, Tunis, Tunisia and Chief Administrator, l'Office des Travailleurs Etrangers a la Formation Professionnelle et a l'Emploi, Tunis (1981-82); Expert and Head of Services, Arab Organisation for Social Defence (1982); representative of Tunisia to the United Nations (Geneva) (1985). **Member** of the Canadian Society of Psychology. **Hobbies:** Travelling, skiing, golf, archaeology. **Addr.:** Tunis, Tunisia.

MILI (Mohamad), Tunisian engineer. **Born** on December 4, 1917 at Djemmal (Tunisia). **Married**, 5 children. **Educ.:** Ecole Normale supérieure of Saint-Cloud (France); Ecole Nationale Supérieure des Télécommunications, (France), Graduate Engineer (1946). **Dipl.:** B.Sc., M.Sc. (Electrical Engineering). **Career:** Joined the Tunisian P.T.T. Administration (1948); promoted to the rank of Chief Engineer, and later took up duty as Director-General of Telecommunication, Ministry of Posts, Telephone and Telegraph, Tunis, in which capacity he directed the modernisation and renewal of the Tunisian telephone network, in particular by the introduction of the automatic crossbartype system. Before becoming an elected official at ITU, he had, since 1956, led the Tunisian delegation at nearly all major conferences of ITU: Plenipotentiary Conferences (1959 and 1965), Plenary Assemblies of the CCITT (1958, 1960 & 1964). He also took part in the work of several study groups, among them, CCITT Study Groups XI (Telephone Switching and Signalling), XIII (Automatic and semi-automatic telephone networks), and Special B (worldwide automatice telephone network) and CCIR Study Groups IV (space systems and radioastronomy) and IX (radio-relay systems). He has taken an active part in the work of the World Plan Committee which is responsible for the planning of the world telecommunication network. In 1961 he was elected vice-chairman of the Plan committee for Africa and became its chairman in 1964. From 1960 to 1965 he represented Tunisia on the ITU Administrative Council and chaired the XIXth session in 1964. On 4 November 1965 he was elected in Montreux, Switzerland, by the Plenipotentiary Conference of the International Telecommunication Union where he held the rank of Deputy Secretary-General, ITU (1965-67); Secretary-General, ITU, (1967-82). **Awards:** Officer, Order of Independence (Tunisia); Commander, Order of the Tunisian Republic; Order of Vasa (Sweden); Grand Cross, Order of Duerte, Sanchezy Mella with silver star (Dominican Republic); Honour of Merit Medal (Paraguay); Commander, Order of Leopold (Belgium); Officer, Légion d'Honneur (France); Grand Star, Order of Merit of Telecommunication (Gran Placa de la gorden del Merito de Telecommunication (Spain); "Philipp Reis" Medal, awarded by the Ministry of Posts and Telecommunications of the Federal Republic of Germany. **Hobby: Reading. Addr.:** 5, Route de mon Idée, 1266 Thonex, Tel.: (22) 487919 Geneva, Switzerland.

MILIANI (Rajaa Mahmoud Mohamad), Saudi academic. **Born** in 1946 in Mecca. **Educ.:** Ph.D. (Medical Bacteriology), (1976) London University. **Career:** Post-Doctoral Research fellow, Westminister Medical School, London University (1976-77); Lecturer, Faculty of Medicine and Allied Sciences, King Abdulaziz University, (1977-79); Assistant Professor, Vice Dean, Faculty of Science, Girls' College, King Abdulaziz University (1979-). **Member:** the Pathological Society of Great Britain and Ireland, the American Society for Microbiology, the Saudi Biological Society, the Association of Clinical Pathologists, attended several conferences in U.S.A., U.K., Italy, Sweden, Saudi Arabia, the 5th Saudi Medical Meeting, Riyadh, 1980; presented papers at the Skin Microbiology Club, London, 1975. **Publications:** Proceedings of the 6th Arab Science Congress, Damascus (1969); various articles and abstracts in the Journal of Medical Microbiology (1976 and 1978), the Journal of Clinical Pathology (1976) **Hobbies:** music, swimming, riding, research. **Prof. Addr.:** P.O.Box 5607, Tel.: 6879033 Ext. 1460, Jeddah.

MILLS (Grenville, Peter), British executive. **Born** in 1946 in London. **Married** in 1974, 1 son, 2 daughters. **Educ.:** Roosevelt University, Chicago. **Dipl.:** B.A. Maths. (1967). **Career:** Test Centre, IBM, London (1967-68); Assistant Manager, Barclays Bank, London (1968-78); Data Centre Manager, Iran Air, Tehran (1978-79); Data Processing Manager, Union Bank of the Middle East, Dubai (1979-). Joint Founder and Chairman of UAE Computer Society. **Publ.:** Articles in Computer technical press. **Addr.:** Dubai, UAE.

MINYAWI (Nagib, Fahmy, al), Egyptian physician. **Born** on June 2, 1944 in Cairo. **Son** of Aziz Fahmy (Barrister) and Mrs. Cecile Assabgui. **Educ.:** Sainte-Famille College (1949-62), Faculty of Medicine, Cairo University (1962-68). **Dipl.:** Secondary Education Certificate (1962), Bachelor of Medicine and Bachelor of Chemistry (1968). **Career:** House Officer, Qasr al-Aini Hospital (1968-69); acted as interpreter (Arabic-French) at the Arab Medical Congress on bilharsiozis held in Cairo in the premises of the League of Arab States; now has own practice. **Publ.:** Author of "A house Officer Report" (1969) and contributed articles to various magazines, notably "What is cancer" published by "Images" an illustrated French-Language weekly. **Dist.:** A three-year scholarship. **Sports:** Football, basketball and swimming. **Remark:** Has special interest in science, medicine and Sociology. **Prof. Addr.:** 2, Rawda Street, Rawda, Tel.: 843121, Cairo, Egypt.

MIQDADI (Wael, Darwish, al), Iraqi executive. **Born**

in 1929 in Haifa. **Son** of Darwish el-Miqdadi. **Married in 1960,** 1 son, 1 daughter. **Educ.:** Boston University; University of Pennsylvania. **Dipl.:** B.A.; M.B.A. **Career:** Controller, Arab Bank, Baghdad; Deputy General Manager, Kuwait Automotive Imports Co., Kuwait. Managing Director, Kuwait Oil Tanker Co. Ltd., London UK. Managing Director, Sharjah Investments Co. Ltd., London, UK. **Member:** Les Ambassadeurs. **Hobbies:** Swimming, Tennis and Reading. **Addr.:** Baghdad, Iraq.

MIRA (Siraj A., Dr.), Saudi physician. **Born** in 1950 in Mecca. **Educ.:** M.B. B.S. (Lon); MRCS, LRCP (ENG); FRCP. **Career:** Associate Professor, Dean Department of Medicine, Faculty of Medicine, King Abdulaziz University and Consultant Physician, King Abdulaziz University Hospital. **Member:** Royal College of Surgeons and fellow Royal College of Physicians, England. **Hobbies:** classical Arabic music. **Prof. Addr.:** Faculty of Medicine, King Abdulaziz University, Tel.: 6952035, Jeddah. **Priv. Addr.:** Tel.: 6534134, Jeddah, Saudi Arabia.

MIRGHANI (Abdulkarim, Mohamad), Sudanese former diplomat. **Born** on January 1, 1924 in Omdurman (Sudan). **Son** of Mohamad Mirghani (merchant) **and** Mrs. Sakena Sorkati. **Married** to Um al-Hassan an-Nour, in March 1946, six children: Kamal, Aisha, Samia, Mirghani, Hind and Sarrah. **Educ.:** Gordon Memorial College; Faculty of Arts, University of Khartoum; School of Administration, Faculty of Economics, University of Bristol; course of Social Science; University of Utrecht, Holland. **Dipl.:** Certificate of the Faculty of Arts, Khartoum University; Special Bachelor of Arts (Honours), in Economics and Government Diploma in Social Science from University of Utrecht. **Career:** Schoolmaster, National Secondary School (January 1948); Counsellor and Chargé d'Affaires, Sudan Embassy, London (July 1956); Head of Political Section, Ministry of Foreign Affairs, Khartoum (October 1956); Deputy permanent representative U.N. (August 1957); Sudan Ambassador to India, Japan and Ceylan (November 1960); Minister of Commerce, Supply, Industry and Cooperation; Ambassador to Italy, Austria and Albania (July 1965); Ambassador to Greece and Cyprus (June 1966); Ambassador to Egypt and Morocco (August 1968); former Minister of Planning. **Sports:** Basket Ball **and** weightlifting. **Hobby:** Gardening. **Priv. Addr.:** Wad URU Station, Tel.: 50884, Omdurman, Sudan.

MIRGHANI (Mohamad), Sudanese former statesman. **Born** in Abri, Southern Sudan. **Career:** Served in the Sudan Police; Diplomatic Service after Independence; Counsellor, Sudanese Embassy, London; Ambassador to Kenya (1966); Acting Under-Secretary, Ministry of Foreign Affairs; then posted to Cairo; Under-Secretary, Ministry of Foreign Affairs; former Minister of State for Foreign Affairs. **Addr.:** Khartoum, Sudan.

MIRGHANI (Mohamad, al), Sudanese journalist. **Born** in 1932 in Sudan. **Educ.:** Khartoum and University of Besançon (France). **Dipl.:** Bachelor of Arts. **Career:** Foreign News Editor, Al Ayam Press House (1949-58); Manager Regional News Agency and Reuters, Khartoum (1957). **Works:** Sudan Correspondent for Reuters and Daily and Sunday Telegraph, contributor to B.B.C. Programmes. **Addr.:** Regional News Agency, P.O.Box 972, Khartoum, Sudan.

MIRGHANI (Osman, al), Sudanese religious leader. **Born** in Sudan. **Educ.:** Secondary and Higher. **Career:** Religious Head of the Khatmiya Sect in the Sudan after the death of Sir Ali al-Mirghani (1949-1968), Religious Leader of the Union Democratic Party. **Addr.:** Khartoum, Sudan.

MIRZA (Abdulhannan), Pakistani banker. **Born** in 1937 in Pakistan. **Son** of Mirza Abdul Rasheed **and** Begum Zohra Fatima. **Married** in 1966 to Zeenat Mirza, four children. **Educ.:** Pashawar University, Pakistan. **Dipl.:** Bachelor's degree in Economics; diploma from the Institute of Bankers in Pakistan. **Career:** Joined Habib Bank Ltd. in Pakistan as Officer and worked at various branches on different assignments (till 1965); Manager of various branches within Pakistan (1966-70); Handled various controlling assignments at Head Office, Karachi and field jobs (1971-79); reached the rank of Vice President (1979-80); posted as Area Chief Mombasa, Kenya (till 1982); Senior Controlling Jobs at Head Office, Karachi (1982-84); Senior Vice President (1982) General Manager, Bahrain Region comprising of 8 offices in Bahrain, North Yemen, Beirut, Iran and Egypt... "Elevated as Executive Vice President (1988)- Cum- General Manager". **Work:** During 28 years delivered many lectures on various subject on Banking in Pakistan and remained the Honorary Treasurer of the Kenya Institute of Bankers Mombasa Center. **Awards:** was elected as the Associate Member and became diplomated Associate of the Institute of Bankers in Pakistan. **Sports:** Hokey and cricket. **Member** of the Marina Club, Bahrain. **Credit Card:** American Express. **Prof. Addr.:** P.O.Box 566, Manama Center, Manama, Bahrain. **Priv. Addr.:** 13/4 Assalmiah Oasis, Saar Road, Bahrain.

MISHARI (Ahmad Hamad Abdul Muhsin, al), Kuwaiti aviation official. **Born** in 1949 in Kuwait. **Son** of Hamad Abdul Muhsin al-Mishari. **Married,** three children. **Educ.:** B.Sc. in Economic and Political Sciences, Kuwait. **Career:** Commercial Research Officer, Kuwait Airways (1971); Sales Superintendent (1972); Assistant and Deputy Commercial Director (1974), Commercial Director (1975); General Manager, member of the Board of Directors, Chairman, Managing Director (since 1981). **Addr.:** House No.16, Area 9, Reyad Street Shamia, P.O.Box 394, Safat, 13004, Kuwait, Arabian Gulf.

MISKAL (Mahmoud Nadim), Syrian Chairman - General Manager, Commercial Bank of Syria. **Born** on 1938 **in**

Damascus, Syria. **Son** of Ibrahim and Mrs Hadieh Al Mufachi. **Married** on 12th Sept. 1965 in Damascus to **Fafah** Kutoubi, 4 children: Moubin 1965), Medical Engineer; Ghoussoun Miskal (1970), French Literature; Mulham Miskal (1972), Technologist; Ibrahim Miskal (1978), a student at the University of Electronic Engineer. **Educ.:** Damascus University, Damascus, Syria. **Dipl.:** B.A. Business (1967), Banking System Diploma Damascus University. **Career:** Joined Syrian Maritime Co., Commercial Bank of Syria (since 1965), Presently Chairman and general Manager. **Address:** Commercial Bank of Syria, P.O.Box: 933, Tel.: 2214508 Damascus-Syria. **Priv. Addr.:** Afif, Abdel Haq Building - Damascus - Syria, Tel.: 3331652.

MISTIKAWI (Mohamad, Naguib, al), Egyptian journalist. **Born** in 1918 in Egypt. **Son** of Naguib al Mistikawi. **Married**, five children. **Educ.:** Licence in Law, Cairo University, Egypt (1939). **Career:** Chief Editor, Sports Section, "al-Ahram" newspaper (1953). **Member** of the Olympic Committee, Sports Committee, High Council of Youth and Sports Committee, President of the Wrestling Federation; former Egyptian champion of 100 meters running; former 1st Division football player. **Publ.:** Books on sports art and literature. **Medals:** Order of the Republic, 3rd Class; Order of Merit, 3rd Class; Sports Medal, 1st class. **Hobbies:** Shooting, riding, travelling, reading, music, literature. **Addr.:** Sharia 257, Tel.: 35586, Maadi, Cairo, Egypt.

MITABIQANI (Mohamad Hamid, al), Saudi civil servant. **Born** at al-Kark in 1930. **Dipl.:** Ph.D. (Civil Engineering). **Career:** Former engineer, Ministry of Communications; Assistant Secretary-General for Technical Affairs, Supreme Planning Council; Director of Industrial Education; attended following conferences: UNESCO General Conference, Conference on Technical Education in the Developing Countries (Berlin), Conference of Arab Ministers of Education (Rabat, Morocco), Conference of Gulf States' Ministers of Education; actively participated in the working out of cooperation agreements in the field of technical education with the Governments of Federal Republic of Germany, France and Japan; now Director-General of Technical Education, Ministry of Education. **Member:** Industrial Development and Research Center, Saudi Arabian Standardization Organization, Supreme Committee for Personnel Training. **Publ.:** The Role of Technical Education in Manpower Training, Philosophy of Technical and Vocational Education in the Arab Countries. **Hobby:** Music. **Prof. Addr.:** P.O.Box 1491, Riyadh. Saudi Arabia.

MITRIK (Omar ben Abdul Aziz , al), Saudi civil servant. **Born** in 1931 at Shagra, Saudi Arabia. **Dipl.:** Ph.D. (Islamic Studies). **Career:** Former teacher; member of Judiciary Presidency, Board of Appeal, Religious Board, Judiciary Board; Assistant Under-Secretary of State, Ministry of Justice; Lecturer, the Higher Judiciary Insitute; Chairman of several Muslim World League Delegations to many Islamic countries; Under-Secretary of State for Judicial Affairs, Ministry of Justice. **Publications:** Usury and Banking Transactions in the Light of Islamic Law, Lectures in Islamic Jurisprudence. **Address:** Ministry of Justice, Riyadh, Saudi Arabia.

MITWALLI (Abdul-Hamid, Hosni), Egyptian engineer. **Born** in Dakahlia, Egypt in 1921. **Son** of el Issawi Mitawlli. **Married** in 1951 in Egypt to Laila AbdulRahman, four children. **Educ.:** Cairo University; the Johns Hopkins University. **Dipl.:** B.Sc. in Electrical Engineering; M.Sc. in Civil Engineering. **Career:** Engineer at the Ministry of Public Works, Cairo (1944-53); Director General for Planning of Industry and Electrical Energy at the National Planning Commission (1956-57); Technical Secretary and Asst. Secretary General of the National Production Council, Cairo (1953-57); Secretary General of Economic Development Organization, Cairo (1957-60); President of Regwa, Cairo (1960-62); Deputy Director for Planning (1962-66); Advisor to the Ministry of Public Works of Libya for Electrical Activities (1970-71); President, Egyptian Electricity Corp., Cairo (1966-71); Technical Consultant at the Ministry of State at the Ministry of Planning (1974-75); Vice President of the Middle East Contracting Co. in Riyadh, Saudi Arabia (1976-80); CADSAC, Cairo (1980-85); Chairman of the Advisory Committee and of the Board of Directors of the Research and Studies Fund at the Ministry of Development (1985-86); Chairman and Managing Director of Egyptian German Electrical Manufacturing Co. EGEMAC (since 1986). **Member** of the Supreme Council of Energy in Egypt; of the Board of Directors of Electrical Systems Co.; of the Rotary Club of Giza; the Egyptian Shooting Club; The Syndicate of Engineers. **Medals:** Order of Merit: el-Goumhouria First Grade from the President of Egypt. **Addr.:** EGEMAC, Kablat Street, Mattaria Cairo, P.O.Box 2634, Cairo, Egypt.

MITWALLI (Sami), Egyptian journalist. **Born** in 1936 in Sharqiyah Governorate, Egypt. **Married**, three children. **Educ.:** B.A. in journalism (1958). **Career:** Editor, Journalist, "al-Ahram" newspaper; editor in Investigations Department, "al-Ahram"; Head of the Political and Popular Organisations Department, "al-Ahram". (1982-84); Assistant Editor in Chief and Head of News Section (1984-). **Member of:** al-Shams Club. **Hobbies:** Social Sciences, natural sciences, economics. **Prof. Addr.:** al-Ahram Newspapers, al-Galaa Street, Cairo, Egypt.

MOAJIL (Abdallah Hamad, al), Saudi economist. **Born** in 1946 in Jubail. **Educ.:** B.Sc. (Economics and Math.), Ph.D. (Mathematics). **Career:** Professor of Mathematics and Chairman of Mathematics Department, University of Petroleum and Minerals (UPM); Secretary General, Gulf Organization for Industrial Consulting

(GOIC). **Publications:** co-author of Precalculus, Basic Mathematics; several research articles in scientific journals. **Address:** Gulf Organization for Industrial Consulting, P.O.Box 5114, Tel.: 831720, 831234 Ext. 466, Doha, Qatar.

MOALLA (Mansour), Tunisian economist. **Born** on May 1, 1930 in Sfax. **Married,** 4 children. **Educ.:** Secondary Studies, College of Sfax, Higher Studies University of Paris, France, Institute of Political Studies, National School of Administration (1954-56). **Dipl.:** Licensed in Law (1951), Licensed in Letters (1953), L.L.D. (1954). **Career:** Inspector of Finances, General Inspectorate of Finances (1956); entered Tunisian Administration (1957); Technical Adviser, Ministry of Finances, prepared the way for the Central Bank of Tunisia (1958); First Director-General, Central Bank; represented Tunisian Secretary of State for Finances in Franco-Tunisian Negotiation (1959); Representative of Tunisia to the F.M.I. (1961); President Director-General, National Society of Investment; Director of Central Administration: helped establish Council of State and Court of Accounts, helped create African Bank of Development (1962-63); first Vice-President, (1964); Director, National School of Administration (1963); Under-Secretary of State for Industry and Commerce (1967); Director of Central Administration of the Presidency; Head, State Secretariat of Posts, Telegraphs and Telephones (1969); Secretary of State, the Minister of Communications (PTT) (1969-70); Minister of Planning (June 1970-74); Member, Central Committee, Political Bureau, Destour Socialist Party; Minister of Planning and Finance (1980-84); Director, International Arab Bank (1981-86), Tunisia. **Member:** Secretary-General, Paris Section, U.G.E.T. (1953); President, Executive Bureau (1955). **Awards:** Commander of the Order of the Republic and Officer of the Order of Independence. Grand Cordon of the Order of Tunisian Republic. **Priv. Addr.:** 3 Rue Mendès-France, Carthage, Tunisia.

MOAMAR (Abdul Rahman, al), Saudi journalist **Born** in 1938 in Sedous. **Educ.:** Secondary School education. **Career:** Former employee, Cabinet of Ministers; Editor-in-Chief, al-Jazeerah newspaper; Chief Correspondent, Saudi News Agency; Secretary-General, Chamber of Commerce Taif; Manager of Thaqif Publishing House. **Member:** History and Archæology Society, King Saud University; al-Jazeerah Organization for Press and Publication, and Hanifah Printing Press Co. **Hobbies:** reading, travel, attending cultural symposia. **Address:** P.O.Box 18002, Tel.: 4765422, Riyadh, Saudi Arabia.

MOAYED (Nabeel, al), Bahraini Businessman. **Born** on November 5, 1951, Bahrain. **Son** of Moayed Ahmed Al Moayed (businessman) **and** Mrs. Saleema Khalil Al Moayed. **Married** on November 11, 1977 at U.K. to Madeleine Al Moayed, 5 children: Ahmed (13.8.78), Nawaf (22.1.80), Bader (25.4.83), Ghazi (24.12.85), Maryam (24.12.85). **Educ.:** Al Fadhel Preparatory School (1957-1961), Manama Boys Primary School (1961-1963), Al Hoora Intermediate School (1963-1965), Manama Boys Secondary School (1965-1968), American University of Beirut (1968-1972). **Dipl.:** Bachelor of Science (Biochemistry). **Career:** Managing Director of Al Moayyed Group (from 1972- Present); Managing Director of Business International (XEROX) from 1985- Present. **Work:** Managing Director/Own Business. **Sports:** Running, Tennis. **Hobbies:** Running, Tennis. **Credit Cards:** Visa, Access, Mastercard. **Prof. Addr.:** Al Moayed House, 205 Shaikh Salman Hwy, P.O.Box 933, Tel.: 277277, Manama 358, Bahrain. **Priv. Addr.:** No. 8 Nabeel Garden, 203 Shaikh Salman Hwy, Manama 358, Bahrain.

MOAYYED (Sabbah, al), Bahraini finance manager. **Born** in 1923, **Son** of Khalil al-Moayyed. **Married** in 1981. **Educ.:** American University of Beirut, Lebanon. **Dipl.:** B.Sc. Business Administration. **Career:** Citibank, N.A. (1975-81); Project Finance Manager, United Gulf Bank, Manama, Bahrain (1981-). **Member:** Banker's Club; Gulf Hotel **Hobbies:** Tennis and Swimming. **Addr.:** Chamber of Commerce Building, 2nd Floor, P.O.Box 5964, Tel.: 233789, 231838, Telex: 9556-7 9355, Manama, Bahrain.

MOAYYED (Yusuf, Khalil, al), Bahraini businessman. **Born** in 1921 in Manama, Bahrain. **Married** in 1943 to Aisha Almoayyed, 2 sons: Farouk and Fareed, 4 daughters: Layla, Salwa, Mona and Amal. **Career:** Established business in 1939. Chairman of Y.K. Almoayyed and Sons W.L.L. Deputy Chairman of the National Bank of Bahrain. **Credit Card:** Visa, Barclays. **Prof. Addr.:** P.O.Box 143, Tel.: 259606, Telex: 8270 MOAYED BN, Fax: 0973-254130, Manama Bahrain. **Priv. Addr.:** 337 Budaiya Road, Tel.: 253437, 210289, Manama 354, Manama, Bahrain.

MOAZ (Mohamad Fauzy, Gen.), Egyptian governor, Alexandria governorate. **Born** 1928, Manshiyet el-Soltan, Menoufiyeh. **Educ.:** Police Force Academy. **Dipl.:** Police Force Diploma (1949). **Married** with two sons and one daughter. **Career:** Joined the Alexandria Police Force where he worked his way up until 1956; appointed on the staff of the Public Security and promoted to the post of Inspector, State Public Security in 1971, a post which he held until 1977; appointed deputy to the Director of State Security, Northern Zone, in August 1977; appointed Director of Alexandria Security (1978) then obtained the grade of assistant to the Ministry of the Interior. **Address:** Alexandria Governorate, Egypt.

MOBTY (Abdallah Said, al), Saudi businessman. **Born** on 10 October 1951 in Khamis Mushate. **Dipl.:** B.Sc. (Civil Engineering). **Career:** Has held different positions in Almobty Establishment, now President of same. Vice Chairman of Board, Chamber of Commerce and Industry, Abha. **Member** of Board, Saudi Limousine, Central Region. **Prof. Addr.:** P.O.Box 325, Tel.: 2238015, Telex: 906622 MOBTI SJ, Fax: (7) 2230648, Khamis Mushate.

Priv. Addr.: Tel.: 2237031, Khamis Mushate, Saudi Arabia.

MOHAMAD (Abdelhafiz), Jordanian journalist. **Born** in 1928 in Haifa, Palestine. **Married. Career:** Secretary of the Arab Merchants Association, Haifa (1947); member of the Arab Finance House, Haifa (1947-48); Secretary of the Council of Emigrants, Nablus (1948-51); Editor, "al-Jazira" newspaper, Amman (1951-53); Correspondent of Arab News Agency (1953-59); Arab League Representative, Jordan (1959-71); Correspondent, "al-Usbu al-Arabi" (1959-82); Owner and Chief Editor, "Akhbar al-Usbou" (1959 to present). **Publ.:** "The River that United the Arabs" (1964). "The Road to the Holy Land" (1967); "The Struggle of a Great Man" (1968); "The Massacre-Sabra and Shatila" (1982); Deputy **Director** of "Jordan Journalism Association" **Addr.:** P.O.Box 605, Tel.: 677881, 624485, Amman, Jordan.

MOHAMAD (Abdul Hamid Hassan, Dr.), Egyptian governor, Giza governorate. **Born** 16 October 1943 at Sayeda Zeinab, Cairo. **Educ.:** primary, secondary and Cairo University. **Dipl.:** LL.B.; M.B., Ph.D. (Laws). **Career:** elected president of the Undergraduates Union, Cairo University (1968); elected president of the Republic Students Federation (1968); elected member of the People's Assembly (Parliament) representing Sayeda Zeinab constituency, Cairo (1971); appointed deputy Minister of State for Youth (October 1973); appointed chief of the Higher Youth and Sports Council (1974); Minister of State for Youth and Sports (February (1979); head of the Youth Council; now Governor, Giza Governorate since May 1982. **Address:** Giza Governorate, Egypt.

MOHAMAD (Ahmad, Mahmoud), Bahraini executive. **Born** in 1941 in Bahrain. **Married**, 5 children. **Educ.:** Secondary School. **Career:** Director, Bahrain Light Industries; Secretary to the Board of National Bank of Bahrain. **Member:** Bahrain Sport Club; Bankers Club. **Hobbies:** Fishing and Camping. **Addr.:** P.O.Box 954, Mamama, Bahrain.

MOHAMAD (al-Bushra A. Hamid), Sudanese lawyer. **Born** in 1952 in Dongola, Sudan. **Married. Educ.:** University of Khartoum, Sudan. **Dipl.:** LL.B.; Bar Examination Certificate. **Career:** Assistant Labour Inspector, Labour Department in Sudan (1976); Second Class Magistrate, Sudan (1976-77); Resident Manager of the Technical Consultation Bureau, Sudanese Consultancy Company, Sanaa; Partner of Adham and Abu al-Riish and Co. (Sudanese Bar Association (1977); Advocate and Commissioner for Oaths (since 1977). **Hobbies:** basket ball, swimming. **Prof. Addr.:** P.O.Box 2237, Tel.: 74178, **Telex:** 2201, Sanaa, Republic of Yemen, and P.O.Box 2272, Tel.: 81489, 79279, Khartoum, Sudan.

MOHAMAD (Ali, Musa), Sudanese civil servant. **Born** in 1930 in Berber (Sudan). **Married** in 1962 to Asma Mohamad Ali, 3 children: Haydar, Hafiz and Hatim. **Educ.:** Wadi Seidna Secondary school; Khartoum University. **Dipl.:** B.A. (Education). **Career:** Intermediate schoolmaster, subsequently headmaster, and Province Education Officer, Deputy Director, Adult Education, Ministry of Education. **Member:** African Adult Education Association. **Dist.:** Attended and represented Sudan in conferences and seminars on education in Europe and Arab states. **Hobby:** Reading **Prof. Addr.:** P.O.Box 2588, **Tel.:** 70482 Khartoum, Sudan. **Priv. Addr.:** Tel.: 44490, Khartoum, Sudan.

MOHAMAD (Ali, Nassir), Yemeni former president. **Born** on December 31, 1939, Eastern District, Governorate of Abyan, People's Democratic Republic of Yemen. **Educ.:** Teachers Training College (1959); military training at Egyptian Commando School (1965); training course with military engineers (1965). **Career:** Teacher, before Independence; Military commander of the Central Front (1964); Governor of Lahej (1968); Minister of Local Governments (1968); Minister of Education (1974-75); Prime Minister and Minister of Defence (1978-85); chairman of the Presidium of the Supreme People's council and Secretary General of the yemen Socialist Party: elected by first General Congress of the Yemeni Party (1978-86) living in exile following Coup in January 1986.

MOHAMAD (Fakhreddine), Sudanese former diplomat. **Born** in 1924 in Sudan. **Educ.:** Gordon Memorial College, University of Durham (England). **Dipl.:** Graduate School of Arts (1946), Bachelor of Arts in Philosophy and Psychology. **Career:** Member of the Sudanese Delegation to the UN National Assembly (1956), to Accra Conference of African States (1957); Chief of Protocol and Head of the United Nations Section, Ministry of Foreign Affairs (1956-57); Counsellor at the Sudanese Embassy in London (1958-60); Ambassador to Pakistan and Afghanistan (1960-64), to China (1964-65); Permanent Representative at the United Nations Organization (September 1966); Elected Chairman of the Fourth Committee of the 21st session of the General Assembly (1966). **Addr.:** Khartoum, Sudan.

MOHAMAD FAMIL (Abdallah), Djibouti politician. **Born** in 1936 in Obock, Djibouti. **Educ.:** Institute of Political Studies, Paris. **Career:** Member of Union Démocratique Afar (1965-66); former Secretary-General of the Government; President Council of the Government (July 1967- May 1977); Minister of Planning and Development (May - June 1977); Minister of Foreign Affairs (July 1977 - Febr. 1987); Prime Minister and Minister of Defence (Febr. - Sept. 1987); Chairman, Special Commission of Afars (Jan. 1978). **Address:** Djibouti, Republic of Djibouti.

MOHAMAD (Gamal el-Din Attia), Egyptian lawyer. **Born** in 1928 in Egypt. **Son** of Attia Mohamad (civil servant) **and** Mrs. Fatma née Ibrahim. **Married** to Miss Erika Zwirner, four children. **Educ.:** Cairo University, Geneva University. **Dipl.:** Licentiate in Law (1948); Diplomes de hautes etudes en Droit Musulman (1950); PhD in Law (1959). **Career:** Lawyer (in Egypt and Kuwait) (since 1951); Secretary General of Encyclopædia of Islamic Law, Kuwait (1969-70); Managing Director of Islamic Banking System, Luxembourg (1978-84); Legal Advisor, Luxembourg. Editor in Chief of: The Contemporary Muslim (al-Muslim al-Muasir) (since 1974). **Promoter** of Islamic Banks in Dubai, Kuwait, Sudan, Qatar and Denmark. **Member** of Arab Bankers Association, London. **Credit Cards:** Visa, Eurocard. **Addr.:** Cairo, Egypt.

MOHAMAD (Hamza Abdul Aziz), Egyptian businessman. **Born** in Egypt in 1932. **Dipl.:** Secondary School Certificate and two years as commerce undergraduate. **Career:** Police Officer, rose to rank of Colonel then retired; Director, Traffic Department, Prosecutor-General, Inspection; now Businessman, owner, Dia Trade and Industry Corporation, Jeddah. **Hobby:** TV, dramatic and film acting. **Prof. Addr.:** Tel.: 22529, Jeddah, Saudi Arabia.

MOHAMAD (Jassem), Iraqi army officer, former diplomat. **Born** in 1918 in Iraq. **Educ.:** Iraqi Military College, Iraqi Staff College, British Staff College of Camberley (England). **Career:** Artillery Officer (1938); Director of Military Training, Ministry of Defence (1958); Director of Military Operations and Assistant Chief of Staff (1958-59); Commandant Iraqi Staff College (1959-64); Ambassador of Iraq to Jordan (1964-67), to Algeria (1967-69). **Award:** Order of ar-Rafidain. **Addr.:** Baghdad, Iraq.

MOHAMAD (Mohamad, Yusuf), Sudanese lawyer. **Born in** 1929 in Berber, Sudan. **Son** of Yusuf Mohamad Abubakr (merchant) **and** Mrs. Bint Wahab Babiker. **Married in** 1957 in Khartoum to Miss Fayza Babiker, six children. **Educ.:** Diploma in civil law from Khartoum University. **Career:** District judge (1955); Lawyer (since 1957); Member of parliament (1965) representing University Graduates; Member of the Board of Faisal Islamic Bank (1977-85); Member of Parliament (1986) representing University Graduates; Elected Speaker of the Sudan Parliament (1988-1989). Member of the Board of Islamic Insurance Company (Sudan); Chairman of Prevention of Road Traffic Accidents Committee. **Prof. Addr.:** P.O.B. 1185, Khartoum, Sudan, Tel.: (Office) 776333, 780333, 780334, Fax: 781902, (Residence) 464733.

MOHAMAD (Mohsen), Egyptian journalist. **Born** on January 1, 1928 in Alexandria (Egypt). **Married** to Miss Hend Abu al-Saud, TV newscaster 2 children. **Educ.:** Abbas Secondary School, Alexandria (1940-45); Faculty of Arts (English Section), Alexandria University (1952-54); Higher Institute of Social Sciences, Alexandria University (1956-59). **Dipl.:** B.A. (1954), M.A. (Social Sciences) (1957). **Career:** Staff reporter for al-Zamane (now discontinued) and the "Journal d'Egypt" newspaper (1947-52); Head of al-Akhbar newspaper Alexandria Office (1952-56); Chief correspondent of the Middle East News Agency (1956-59); Managing-Editor of al-Goumhouriyah newspaper, Cairo (1959-65); deputy editor of al-Akhbar newspaper (1965); presently President, Dar al-Goumhouriya (which publishes several daily newspapers and periodicals); travelled to most Arab, African and European countries on journalistic assignments. **Publ.:** Collected short stories (1967); Received Press Award. **Member:** Arab Socialist Union, Egypt; Press Correspondents Association, Cairo. **Hobbies:** Reading, radio and TV. **Prof. Addr.:** 24 Zakaria Ahmed Str., Cairo Egypt.

MOHAMAD (Mousto), Syrian executive. **Born** in 1924 in Lattakia, Syria. **Son** of Ibrahim Mohamad. **Married** in 1960, 1 son, 3 daughters. **Dipl.:** B.A. in Law; Diploma in Administrative Law (1956). **Career:** Counsellor in Law at the Ministry of Defence; Counsellor in Administration and Finance at the "Centre des Recherches Scientifiques" at the Ministry of Defence; Administrative Director, Meteorological Establishment; Member of the Board of Directors of Popular Credit Bank and of The Commercial Bank of Syria. Director, Administrative Department, Popular Credit Bank, Damascus, Syria. **Member:** Organisation Committees of the Syrian Government. **Hobbies:** Reading and Bridge. **Addr.:** P.O.Box 2841, Tel.: 333389, Damascus, Syria.

MOHAMAD (Najwa, Ibrahim), Egyptian broadcaster/actress. **Born** on April 28, 1949. **Married**, two sons. **Dipl.:** B.A. (Sociology) (1979). **Career:** Television broadcaster (1964); Cinema actress (1969); Executive Member of the Egyptian Musicians Union (1974-84); **Member:** of Egyptian Actor's Union. **Publ.:** "When Love Went Away" (short story) (1981). **Awards:** Order of Merit (1st class), Egypt (1972); Order of Merit (2nd class), (1982). **Member:** Gezira Sporting Club; al-Ahly Club, **Hobbies:** tennis, running. **Addr.:** 4A Ahmad Mazhar Street, Zamalek, Tel.: 407986, Cairo, Egypt.

MOHAMAD SALAH (Ahmad, Ould), Mauritanian politician. **Born** in 1925 in Chingetti (Northern Mauritania). **Son** of Mohamad Salah Ould Mohamad (cattle-breeder). **Married** to Lemate mint Khyar, 7 children. **Educ.:** Médersa (Koran school) in Atar; French and Arabic Studies; Institut des Hautes Etudes Françaises d'Outre-Mer, Paris (1958-60). **Dipl.:** Brevet d'Etudes Franco-Arabes. **Career:** Cabinet Director, Ministry of the Interior (1958); Director, Central subdivision of Nouadhibou (1960); Commandant, Cercle de Tangent (1960); Minister of Justice and Interior (1962); Secretary, Political Bureau, Parti du Peuple Mauritanien (PPM) (1966); Secretary for Political, Legal and Administrative Studies of PPL, and President of the Supreme Court (1971-Aug 1975); Minister of State for National Sovereignty (August 1975); Visited on official duty: Liberia, Senegal, France, Guinea, Mali in 1962;

Algeria, Ethiopia, Germany, Egypt in 1964; Kuwait, Jordan, Syria, Algeria in 1965; Morocco in 1969, Libya in 1970. **Awards:** Commander, Legion of Honour (France) (1962); Commander, National Egyptian Order; Commander, National Cameroonian Order; Commander, National Guinean Order. **Member:** Parti du Peuple Mauritanien (PPM.), and of the Political Bureau of PPM., since 1961; Party was suspended in 1978 following a military Coup. **Prof. Addr.:** In exile, Paris, France.

MOHAMAD (Y. Yacob), Bahraini executive. **Born** in 1943 in Bahrain. **Married**, 2 children. **Educ.:** Ealing college of Art, Business Administration, UK. **Career:** Bahrain Petroleum Co. Ltd. (1966-70); Citibank (1970-78); Director, Bahrain Car Parks Co., Deputy General Manager, National Bank of Bahrain BSC. Manama (1978-). **Member:** Bahrain Bankers Club. **Hobby:** Swimming. **Addr.:** National Bank of Bahrain, P.O.Box 106, Manama, Bahrain.

MOHAMAD (Zahida, Ibrahim), Iraqi administrator. **Born** in 1926 in Baghdad, Iraq. **Son** of Ibrahim Mohamad. **Educ.:** LL.B. (1948); Victoria School of Libraries, Melbourne, Australia (1954); Library Studies, Rutgers University, New Brunswick, New York, USA (1958-59); six months Training Programme, Princeton University Library, New York (1959); Librarian Training Programme in Copenhagen, Denmark (1967). **Career:** Director, College of Education Library, University of Baghdad (1950-58); Librarian, Central Library, University of Baghdad (1959-63); Director, Archives Department, Central Library, University of Baghdad (1964-75); Director General, Central Library, University of Baghdad (since 1975). **Publ.:** Books on Library science and many researches and studies. **Addr.:** Central Library, University of Baghdad, P.O.Box 12 Wazyria, Baghdad, Iraq.

MOHAMED (Abdi, Ibrahim), Djibouti Deputy at the National Assembly. **Born** in 1945 in Djibouti. **Educ.:** Baccalaureate Level. **Career:** Teacher (1961-1977) Director of "Imprimerie Nationale" (1978-1988); Director of Public Relations at the Information General Secretariat (1988-1997). Militant of PMP, LPA, LPAI and RPP (Adherent Member) President of "Annexe du Quartier 3" (RPP). Elected Deputy at the Nationa Assembly (19/12/1977 - to date), Elected Secretary at the National Assembly Office (8/01/1988- to date). Commission Member for the Social Development, Environment Protection, finance Commission, General Economy and Planning; Member of the Supreme Court of Justice. **Prof. Addr.:** National Assembly, P.O.Box 138 Djibouti, Djibouti.

MOHAMED (Chehem, Ahmed), Djibouti Deputy at the National Assembly. **Born** in 1951 at Day (Tadjourah). **Career:** Head of Document Section at ONED (1 March 1987 - 31 Dec. 1997); Member of MPL, FDLD and FRUD. Elected Deputy at the National Assembly (19/12/1997 - to date); Member of Permanent Commission and Exchange and Production Commission. **Prof. Addr.:** National Assembly, P.O.Box 138 Djibouti, Djibouti.

MOHAMED (Fahmi, Ahmed), Djibouti Deputy at the National Assembly. **Born** on January 22, 1947 in Djibouti. **Career:** Deputy at the National Assembly (21 May 1982-to date); Minister of Industry (1981-1986); Elected First Deputy-Speaker at the National Assembly (30.12.1992); Member of Foreign Affairs Commission and Commission Member of Finance, General Economy and Planning. **Prof. Addr.:** National Assembly, P.O.Box 138 Djibouti, Djibouti.

MOHAMED (Houmed, Daoud), Djibouti Deputy at the National Assembly. **Born** in 1959 at Obock. **Career:** Employee to EDD. Committee Member RPP annex Obock. Elected Deputy at the National Assembly; Member of National Defence Commission, Finance Commission, General Economy and Planning; Member of Supreme Court of Justice. **Prof. Addr.:** National Assembly, P.O.Box 138 Djibouti, Djibouti.

MOHAMED (Ismail Hassan,), Egyptian Governor, Central Bank of Egypt. **Born** on July 2, 1936. **Son** of Hassan Mohamed **and** Mrs. Fatma Ashour. **Married** on September 3, 1966 to Fatma Mostafa, Three children: Yasser, Ahmed, Mostafa. **Career:** Adviser to IMF in Yemen (1975-1978); General Manager Banks Control Dept., Central Bank of Egypt (1980); Vice-Chairman of the Capital Market Authority (1980-1983); Commissioner Islamic Int. Dev. Bank (1986); Chairman Misr American Int. Bank (1988-1993); Chairman Bank of Alexandria, Egypt (1991-1993); Governor Central Bank of Egypt (1994-). **Prof. Addr.:** 31 Kasr El-Nil Street, Cairo, Egypt, Tel.: 3926211/108. **Priv. Addr.:** 38 Abd El-Aziz Fahmy, Tel.: 2446868, Egypt.

MOHAMED (Mohamed, Abdoulkader), Djibouti Deputy at the National Assembly. **Born** in 1951 at Katoumbati (Dikhil). **Educ.:** University Studies. **Career:** Director of ONAC (March 1996 - December 1997); Member of MPL, FDLD, FDLD, of Political Bureau and of FRUD. Elected Deputy at the National Assembly (19/12/1997 - to date); Member of the Permanent Commission, Legislation Commission and General Administration of the Republic; Member of Supreme Court of Justice. **Prof. Addr.:** National Assembly, P.O.Box 138 Djibouti, Djibouti.

MOHAMED (Mohamed, Ali), Djibouti Deputy at the National Assembly. **Born** on April 29, 1952 in Djibouti. **Educ.:** University Studies. **Career:** Official at the Ministry of Trade; Elected Deputy at the National Assembly (21 May 1982 - to date); General Secretary of Executive Committee of RPP; Appointed Minister of Trade, National Economy and Minister of Finance and National Economy (4/02/1993), became Minister of Labour and

Vocational Training (28/12/1997). **Prof. Addr.:** National Assembly, P.O.Box 138 Djibouti, Djibouti.

MOHAMED (Mohamed, Dileita), Djibouti Deputy at the National Assembly. **Educ.:** Terminal Level, Journalism and International Relations Studies. **Career:** Journalist, Chief Editor "La Nation" newspaper. Elected Deputy at the National Assembly (19/12/1997 - to date); Vice-President of the Permanent Commission and Member of Finance Commission, General Economy and Planning. **Prof. Addr.:** National Assembly, P.O.Box 138 Djibouti, Djibouti.

MOHAMED (Mohamed, Kamil), Djibouty Deputy at the National Assembly. **Born** in 1947. **Career:** Head Officer of Arta. Elected Deputy at the National Assembly (18/12/1992 - to date); Member of Central Committee of RPP; Commission Member of Legislation, General Administration of the Republic and of Exchange and Production Commission; Member of Supreme Court of Justice. **Prof. Addr.:** National Assembly; P.O.Box 138 Djbouti, Djibouti.

MOHAMEDOU (Ould Mohamed Mahmoud), Mauritanian diplomat. **Born** in 1944, in ATAR (Mauritania). **Son** of Mohamed Mahmoud Mohamedou (Businessman) **and** Mrs. el-Eza mint Ahmed Wall. **Married** on August 19, 1963 in Atar to Miss Fatimetou mint Cheiguer, 3 children: Kemal, Mohamed-Mahmoud and el-Iza. **Education:** 1964-1976 Superior (Social Sciences) in the U.S.A. (1964), in France (1966-1967), in Tunisia (1974-1976), and in Germany; 1957-1961 Secondary in the Lycee of Rosso; 1953-1957 Qoranic and Primary in Atar. **Career:** October 1994 Ambassador to the Federal Republic of Germany; December 1995 Ambassador to Austria, Finland, Norway, Denmark, Sweden and the ONUDI (residence in Bonn); October 1992 Elected Vice-President of the Preparatory Committee of the 50th Anniversary of the Organization of the United Nations; January 1989 to September 1994 Permanent Representative to the United Nations, Ambassador to Cuba, Ambassador to Canada (residence in New York); Permanent Representative to the World Tourism Organization; June 1984 to December 1988 Ambassador to the Kingdom of Spain, - Vice-Dean of the Group of African States, - Vice-Dean of the Arab Group; August 1980 to June 1984 Ambassador to Algeria, - Dean of the Group of African States, - Vice-Dean of the Arab Group; January 1980 August 1980 Ambassador to Equatorial Africa: Nigeria, Cameroun, Congo and Gabon (residence in Libreville); June 1979 Minister and Chief of Cabinet of the Head of the Government (left this position at own demand in January 1980); March 1979 June 1979 Minister of Youth, Sports, Craft Industry and Tourism; 1976-1979 Permanent Representative of the Islamic Republic of Mauritania to the UNESCO and its Executive Board; 1974-1976 Delegate to the Permanent Consultative Committee of the Maghreb (PCCM). First Counsellor of the Embassy of Mauritania in Tunisia; 1972-1973 Chairman of the African Preparatory Committee of the First Pan-African festival of the Youth and of the International Preparatory Committee of the 10th world youth festival (residence in Tunis); 1970-1973 Elected Deputy Secretary-General of the Pan-African Youth Movement (PYM) in charge of the organization and of the administration (residence in Algiers); January 1974 Entered the mauritanian Ministry of Foreign Affairs; 1967-1970 Inspector of Youth and of Sports, Chief of the National Service of Youth and of Popular Education, Director of International Vacation and Lumber Camps; 1964-1970 Member of the National Bureau of the Mauritanian Youth Association (AJM), Member of the Union of the National Education and Scouts Movement of which he has been Honorary President since 1979. **Summary of Professional Activities:** Mr. Ould Mohamed Mahmoud has done several trainings in the fields of Public Relations, International Relations and Methodology of Management. He has represented the Islamic Republic of Mauritania and the Pan-African Youth Movement at numerous International Conferences in Asia, Africa, America and Europe. He has been, in particular, delegate to the Summits and Conferences of the Economic Community of West African States (ECOWAS), the Organization of African Unitey (OUA), the League of Arab States, the Organization of the Islamic Conference (OIC), the Non-Aligned Movement Countries (NAM), the Union of the Arab Magreb (UMA), the Organization of the United Nations, as well as the inception of gatherings such as the First International Leadership Training Course for Youth (USA, 1966), the First Cultural Festival of the OAU (Alger 1969), the First African Arts Festival (Dakar 1970), the First World Youth Assembly (New York 1970), the First World Assembly for Peace in Vietman (Paris 1972), the First Conference on the African Path of Socialism (Tunis 1975), the First Economic Summit of the OAU (Lagos 1979), the First Pan-African Youth Festival of which he has presided the preparation and setting in Tunis in 1973, the First World Summit on Children (New York 1991), the First World Conference on Human Rights (Vienna 1993), the First Colloquium on the Democratic Process in Africa (Montreal 1993), the First World Conference of the United Nations on Sustainable Development (Barbados 1994), the First UN-Conference on Climate Change (Berlin 1995) and the First World Summit on Social Development (Copenhague 1995). Mr. Ould Mohamed Mahmoud has participated, as head of delegation of the Islamic Republic of Mauritania or of the NGO MPJ, in several international events such as the 10th World Festival of the Democratic Youth (Berlin 1973), the 10th Summit of the OAU (Addis Abeba 1973), the 10th Assembly of the World Council of the Peace (Moscow 1973), and as deputy head of delegation to the 10th Summit of the Non Aligned Countries Movement (Jakarta 1992). He also participated, as honorary delegate, in the annual congress in New York and in Washington, of the National Convention of the African-American Institute (AAI) and of the National Convention of the Arab-American Anti-Discrimination Committee (ADC). Mr. Ould Mohamed Mahmoud has seated, from 1976 to 1978, in the Committee of Convention and Recommendations of the UNESCO and in the Committee of Drafting and Negociations (DNG) of its 19th General Conference. He represented Mauritania from 1989 to 1994 at the UN Special Committee for Peacekeeping and was, from 1993 to 1994, Vice-Dean of the Office, of the UN Conference about Fish Stocks. He has headed several delegations during negociation missions, participated, as Vice-President of the Mauritanian Delegation, to numerous sessions of the General Assembly of the UNESCO and of the United Nations, presided several times the Group of African States and of the League of Arab States, and has taken on the presidency, during the year 1992, of the Group of Ambassadors of the Arab Maghreb Union in New York. **Decorations:** Medal of Merit of the First Pan-African Festival of the Youth (Tunis, July 1973) and Medal of Merit of the Second Festival (Tripoli 1983); Medal of the Xth Festival of the FMJD (Berlin 1973); Commander of the mauritanian Order of the National Merit Istiqaq Al Watani Al Mauritani (Nouakchott, 1979); Commander of the Order of the Equatorial Star (Highest Distinction of the State of Gabon (Libreville, 1980); Honorary professor of the Society of International Studies (SEI) (Madrid 1985); Great cross of the civil Order of the Kingdom of Spain-Madrid 1989; Merit "Diplomatic Corps" of Canada (Ottawa 1993). **Sports:** Running, Chess Game. **Hobby:** Reading. **Credit Cards:** Visa, American Express Gold. **Prof. Addr.:** 211 E. 43rd Street, 20th floor, New York, N.Y.U.S.A. **Priv. Addr.:** 9E. 77th Street, New York, Tel.: (212) 986.79.63, N.Y., U.S.A.

MOHAMMAD BIN TALAL (H.R.H Prince), Jordanian prince, brother and personal representative of Late HM King Hussain of Jordan. **Born** in 1940, second son of late king Talal. **Married,** to H.R.H. Princess Taghrid, 2 sons. **Educ.:** Bishops School, Amman; Islamic College, Amman; Bryanston School, United Kingdom; Ecole Beau Soleil, Villar, Switzerland; cadet at Iraqi Military Academy (1957). **Career:** President of the Tribal Shaikhs Council (1971), resigned (1973); Personal Representative of HM King Hussain (1974); Head of High Committee for Tourism; Four Star General in Royal Jordanian Armed Forces. **Awards:** Order of HM King Abdul Aziz al-Saud, Saudi Arabia; al-Kiladeh al-Hashimi, Jordan; Order of Merit, France; Royal Victorian Order, UK; Order of Mohammad, Morocco; Order of the Brilliant Star, China. **Hobbies:** shooting, riding, hunting, chess. Honorary President of Jordanian Chess Federation and Jordanian Shooting Federation. **Addr.:** Royal Palace, Amman, Jordan.

MOHAMOUD (Abdulkadir, Mohamed), Somali executive. **Born** in 1942 in Galkayo. **Son** of late Mohamed Mohamoud (Chief of the Legal Dept., Government of Somali Democratic Republic), **and** Mrs., née Bayden Hashi Abdulle. **Married** in 1978 in Balad to Miss Ebla Mohamed Abdulle, 6 children: Abdul-fattah (1978), Suad (1980), Sagal (1983), Samira (1985), Samiya (1987) and Mohamed (1988). **Educ.:** University of Mannheim, West Germany; Harvard Institute of International Development. **Dipl.:** MBA; Diploma in Public Enterprise Policy and Management. **Career:** Chief Store Keeper (1969-70); Chief Accountant (1970-72); Commercial Manager (1972-76); General Manager of SOMALTEX (1977-todate) **Medal.:** Copper Medal (for his good work on the 10th Anniversary of the Revolution of Somali Democratic Republic). **Sport:** Indoor games. **Hobbies:** Reading, Social Service. **Prof. Addr.:** Somaltex S.P.A., P.O.Box 28 Mogadishu, Tel.: 22769, Telex: 3729 SOMALTEX, Somalia. **Priv. Addr.:** Tel.: 20702, Mogadishu, Somalia.

MOHANDIS (Abdul Majeed), Saudi certified accountant. **Born** in 1937 in Jeddah, Saudi Arabia. **Dipl.:** B.Com. (Accountancy), Cairo University (1961). **Career:** Various accounting jobs (1951-55); Accountant, Cement Co. (1961-62); Saba Co. (Audit Firm) (1962-70). **Member:** American Accounting Association, Literary and Cultural Club, Jeddah, al-Ittihad Sports Club, Jeddah; participant, K.M.G. (International Audit Firm) annual conference; owner of a certified accounting office. **Hobbies:** reading, table tennis. **Prof. Addr.:** Nashar Commercial Centre, 12th floor, Tel.: 6432805, 6434665, Jeddah, Saudi Arabia. **Priv. Addr.:** Tel.: 6882214, 6876985, Jeddah, Saudi Arabia.

MOHANNADI (Hamad, Rashid, al), Qatari, General Manager - QAPCO - Doha. **Born** in 1958. **Married. Education:** 1975-1980: Bachelor of Engineering Applied Engineering Science - Industrial, Portland State University - U.S.A. **Career: Positions:** Till Present: 1997 - Vice Chairman Qatar Vinyle Company (Q.V.C.) - Doha; 1996 - Board Director Qatar General Petroleum Corporation (QGPC) - Doha; 1993 - Board Member Ras Laffan Liquefied Natural Gas Co. Ltd., Doha; 1992 - General Manager & Board member Qatar Petrochemical Company Ltd. (Qapco), Doha. 1991-1992: Deputy General Manager and Expansion Team Leader Qatar Petrochemical Company, Doha; 1981-1991: National Oil Distribution Company (NODCO), Doha as following: Acting Operation Manager, Head of Refinery no. 2 (Operations department), Head of Export & Oil Movement (Operations Dept.), Engineer in charge of export/import & distribution facilities project, Process Engineer - Operations Dept., Shift Supervisor - Operations Dept., Trainee Engineer. **Hobbies:** Reading, Swimming, Fishing, Camping. **Prof. Addr.:** QAPCO, Tel.: +974 770521 or 323805, Fax: +974 771346 or 324700, Doha, Qatar.

MOHSEN (Mohamad, Said Abdallah), Yemeni politician. **Born** in 1947, at al-Hujriyah, North Yemen. **Son** of Said Abdallah Mohsin. **Married** 2 sons: Khaldoun **and** Wadhad. **Career:** Head of the Criminal Investigation Department (1969); Head, Revolutionnary Security Department (1970); Member Central Committee of the National

Front Political Organization (1972); Minister of State Security (1974); member of the Political Bureau, of the Yemen Socialist Party. **Hobbies:** Literature, sports (especially watching football). **President** of the Executive Committee of the Higher Sports Council in the First Governorate. **Addr.:** Aden, Republic of Yemen.

MOHSEN (Sayed Mohsen Ali, al, Shaikh), Saudi businessman. **Born** in Jeddah, in 1935. **Educ.:** Secondary School. **Career:** Major dealer in men's and ladies' fashion wear; owner of Mohsen Department Stores. **Address:** P.O.Box 3498, Jeddah, Saudi Arabia.

MOJADDIDY (Muhamad Moussa, al), Saudi engineer. **Born** in 1921 in Kabul, Afghanistan. **Dipl.:** Diploma in Applied Engineering, Cairo; Diploma, American University in Washington, 1952. **Career:** Director of Radio Engineering Department, Mecca Broadcasting Station; Director, same department, Riyadh Broadcasting Station Director of Training Institute for Wireless and Radio Communications, Riyadh. **Member:** American Geographic Society. **Honour:** Tunisian Medal of Merit. **Publications:** How to Record Sound; Sound Effects. **Hobbies:** travel, fencing, reading. **Prof. Addr.:** P.O.Box 910, Tel.: 4027982, Riyadh. **Priv. Addr.:** Tel.: 4919794, Riyadh, 11421, Saudi Arabia.

MOJALLID (Mohamad Jameel Mohamad), Saudi director of special programmes, Jeddah broadcasting service. **Born** 1941. **Dipl.:** B.E. (Geography), Faculty of Education, Mecca. **Career:** Employee, Shura Council (1960-63); member of Broadcasting Stations Conference, Riyadh, Conference of Foreign Ministers of Islamic States. **Hobbies:** reading, sport, travel, **Address:** Jeddah Broadcasting Station, Jeddah, Saudi Arabia.

MOKADDEM (Sadeq), Tunisian former statesman. **Born** in 1914. **Educ.:** Lycée Carnot, Tunis; Faculty of Science, Montpellier and Faculty of Medicine. **Career:** Physician in Tunis; Member of Neo-Destour Party since 1934; Secretary of State for Justice (1954-55), for Public Health (1955); Deputy, Constituent Assembly (1956-59); Ambassador to Arab Republic of Egypt (1956-57); Ambassador to France (1962-64); Speaker National Assembly (1964-80) retired. **Awards:** Grand Cordon of Independence, Order of the Tunisian Republic, several Foreign Decorations. **Addr.:** Tunis, Tunisia.

MOKADDEM (Youssef), Tunisian diplomat. **Born** on October 27, 1949 in Tunis. **Son** of Sadek Mokaddem (Politician) **and** Mrs. Wassila Mokaddem. **Married** on August 1, 1973 in Tunis to Miss Najiba Benaissa, two children: Ines (24.2.1975), Mohamed Wassim (11.7.1978). **Educ.:** University of Tunis and Ecole Nationale d'Administration of Tunis. **Dipl.:** Licence in Public Law, Diplome de L'Ena, Capacité d'Avocat. **Career:** Diplomat since 1972. Appointed to the Tunisian Embassy in Ankara, Turkey (1975-1977); and to the Permanent Mission of Tunisia to the United Nations Office in Geneva (1977-1982) and (1987-1990); Ambassador of the Republic of Tunisia to the Sultanate of Oman, Somalia and Djibouti with residence in Muscat (September 1990-1993); Director for African Affairs, Ministry of Foreign Affairs (1993-95); since September 1995 Ambassador of Tunisia to Egypt and Permanent Representative of Tunisia to the League of Arab States in Cairo. **Awards:** Officer of the Order of the Tunisian Republic. **Sports:** Swimming. **Hobbies:** Reading and Playing Cards. **Credit Card:** Visa. **Prof. Addr.:** Tunisian Embassy, 26 rue Al-Guazirah, Zamalek, 11211 Cairo, Egypt. E-mail: Tunisym@gega.net.

MOKBIL (Saeed, Taleb), Yemeni Diplomat. **Born** in 1951 at Lahej, Yemen. **Son** of Taleb Mokbil (died) **and** Mrs. Mlook Hassan. **Married** to Faiza Abdulmageed, 2 children: Sahar, Abdulmageed. **Languages:** Arabic, English, Russian. **Educ.:** Master in international relations, obtained from college of International Law and international relations, Kiev University; Diploma Journalism obtained from international institute of journalism, Berlin. **Career:** presently, Minister Plenipotentiary, Permanent Mission of the Republic of Yemen to the United Nations and Other International Organizations in Geneva. **Work Experiences; Conferences and Sessions:** Press Department, Ministry of Education (1969-1972); Third Secretary, press dep. Ministry of Foreign Affairs (1973-1974); Second Secretary in Yemen Embassy to Somalia (1974-1975); Sent by the Ministry of Foreign Affairs to the Kiev University for specialisation in the field of international relations (1976-1982); Deputy Director Department of International Organizations and Conferences, Ministry of Foreign Affairs (1982-1986); Counsellor, Chargé d'affaires Yemen Embassy to the Republic of Ethiopia (1986-1988); Counsellor, Permanent Mission of the Republic of Yemen to the United Nations and other International Organiszations in Geneva and Vienna (1988-1990); Minister Plenipotentiary, Permanent Mission of the Republic of Yemen to the United Nations and other International Organizations in Geneva (1990-). Member of Yemeni Delegation to the Ministerial and the seventh conference of head of state or Government of New Delhi 1983 Non-Aligned Countries; Member of Yemeni Delegation to the Ministerial and fifth Conferences of head of state of the Organization of Islamic Conference Casa-Blanca, Maroc 1984; Member of Yemeni Delegation to the Foreign Ministerial Conference of the Organization of Islamic Conference Fas, Maroc 1985; Member of Yemeni Delegation to the United Nations General Assembly, Forty Third Session (Third Committee) New York 1988; Head of delegation to the conference on the treaty to control the transboundary movement of hazardous wastes, Basel, Switzerland, 1989; Head of delegation to the general conference of UNIDO, Vienna, 1989; Member of the Observer Yemeni delegation to the economic and social council (ECOSOC) summer sessions, Geneva, 1989, 1990. 1992, 1993; Member of

Yemeni delegation to the International Labour Organization general conference, 46,47 sessions, Geneva, 1989, 1990; Member of the Yemeni delegation to the World Health Assembly, 42-43-45, sessions, Geneva, 1989, 1990, 1992; Member of the Observer delegation to the sessions of the executive committee of UNHCR, Geneva, 1989, 1990. 1991, 1992; Member of Yemeni Delegation to the Fourth review conference on the non proliferation treaty, Geneva, 1990; Member of Yemeni delegation to the eleventh World Meteorological Congress, Geneva, 1991; Member of Yemeni observer delegation to the United Nations commission on Human-Rights, 45-46-47-48-49 Sessions, Geneva, 1989, 1990, 1991, 1992, 1993; Member of Yemeni delegation to the preparatory committees meetings on the World conference of Human-Rights; Participated as an observer in different meetings of the committee sessions on Human-Rights as a committee against torture. Human-Rights committee, Committee of Elimination of Racial Discrimination, and Committee on Civil and Political Rights; Head of Yemeni delegation to the Forty-First Session of the Committee on the Elimination of Racial Discrimination for Consideration the reports of Yemen, Geneva August 1992. **Sports:** Swimming, Walking. **Hobby:** Reading. **Prof. Addr.:** Permanent Mission of the Republic of Yemen, 19 Chemin du Jonc, 1216 Cointrin, Geneva, Switzerland, Tel.: 41/22/7985333. **Priv. Addr.:** 3 Contra-Social, 1203 Geneva, Switzerland, Tel.: 41/22/3402452.

MOKHTAR (Ahmad Mohamad Abbas, Prof., Dr.), Saudi surgeon and professor. **Born** in 1944 in Jeddah. **Educ.:** M.B. (Medicine and Surgery), Ph.D (History of Arab Medicine), Specialization (General Surgery). **Career:** Full Professor since 1993; Professor of General Surgery, Faculty of Medicine, King Abdulaziz University (1977); Consultant and Specialist, General Surgery, University Hospital, KAU; Professor and Consultant, General Surgery, Faculty of Medecine, KAU, Jeddah; has attended several medical conferences. Since 1990 Vice Dean for Clinical Affairs Until now; and From 25 July 1993, K.A.U.; Chairman of Surgical Department K.A.U.H., Jeddah, K.S.A. **Publ.:** al-Razy's Critism of Galinos, Non-Pulmonary Consumption in the Kingdom of Saudi Arabia, Comparison between Rupture Diseases in Saudi Arabia and in West Europe, The Development of Medicine, Teaching Methods and other research topics. Author of a medical, surgical Book titled "Studies about medicine and Surgery of the STOMACH", published in Beirut in 1999 (Al-Maarifa House) -1st edition. **Prof. Addr.:** Faculty of Medicine, King Abdulaziz University Hospital, P.O.Box 6615, Jeddah 21452. **Priv. Addr.:** Tel.: 6209839, Jeddah, Saudi Arabia.

MOKRIN (Zamil A.R., Al), Saudi Engineer. **Born** in 1947 in Riyadh. **Educ.:** B.A. (Architectural Engineering), M.S. and, Ph.D. (Civil Engineering - Structures). **Career:** Asst. Professor, Civil Engineering (1978-80), Chairman, Architectural Engineering (1980-81), Dean, College of Environmental Design (1981-87) at KFUPM, Dhahran. Promoted as Associate Professor in 1987. Area Manager and Consultant to Abalkhail Consulting Engineers (1979-81). Served as Juror, Member on various Committees on Environmental Problems, University bids, Schools, Ministries and Academic Programmes in Saudi Arabia as well as other GCC countries. Renowned Scholar, Professional Manager, Team Leader, Juror and Consultant to national as well as International Organizations. Gave many national and international seminars **Publ.:** Wrote and co-authored numerous publications on structural designs, urbanization & pollution, unfied building code, characteristics of sands in Saudi Arabia. As Project Manager for UGIC, Bahrain, has written a most comprehensive feasibility study for Ferro Alloys project, the first of its kind in the Middle East. **Hobbies:** Light sports, reading, travelling. Presently, General Manager of Gulf Ferro Alloy Co., Alkhobar. **Addr.:** P.O.Box 30250 Alkhobar: 31952. Office Tel.: 857 4557. Fax: 8571547. Residence Telephone: 8606254.

MOLLA (Abdul Majid), Paediatrician. **Born** on January 7, 1941 at Dhaka, Bangladesh. **Son** of late Tamijuddin Molla **and** Mrs. Alimunnessa. **Married** on March 31, 1967 at Dhaka, to Ayesha Molla, 3 children: Miss Nasreen Molla (28.11.1968), Fahmida Molla (9.11.1971), Abusayem Molla (18.10.1976). **Educ.:** University Dhaka (1957-1963), Catholic University of Leuven, Belgium (1968-1975). **Dipl.:** M.B., B.S., (DAc), D.C.H. (Ireland), Ph.D. (Belgium), FRCP (Edin). **Career:** Tutor in Queens University, Belfast (1975-1978); Fellow in Catholic University, Leuven, Belgium (1968-1975); Scientist in CDDR,B (International Centre for Diarrhocal Disease Research, Bangladesh) (1978-1986); Professor and Chairman, Department of Paediatrics, Aga Khan University, Karachi, Pakistan (1986-1992); Professor of Paediatrics, Kuwait University (Oct. 1992- till now). **Other Information:** Medical Scientist. Research Career for 27 Years. Discovered Cereal based Oral Rehydration for Diarrhocal Disease in Children. Published 145 Research papers in International Journal. **Award:** Greatest distinction in Ph.D. (Gold Medal) University of Leuven in 1975. **Sport:** Swimming. **Hobby:** Gardening. **Member:** European Society of Pead. Gastro-Enterology and Nutrition, Asian Society Paediatric Research. **Prof. Addr.:** Department of Paediatrics, Faculty of Medicine, Kuwait University, Tel.: 5319486, Kuwait City, Kuwait. **Priv. Addr.:** House No. 9, Road No. 15, Sector 1, UTTARA, Model Town, Dhaka, Bangladesh.

MOMENA (Fuad Mohamad), Saudi academic. **Born** in 1947 in Mecca. **Educ.:** B.A. (Honours) (Archæology), 1972; M.A. (Honours) (Archæology). **Career:** Lecturer, Department of History, Faculty of Arts and Humanities, King Abdulaziz University. **Member:** American Archæological excavation expedition to Petra, Jordan (1973);

Archæological Institute of America working on Ph.D. thesis in archæology. **Publication:** an article on Ancient Trade Routes of the Arabian Peninsula in Antiquity. **Hobbies:** travel, reading, table tennis, collecting antiques. **Address:** Department of History, Faculty of Arts and Humanities, King Abdulaziz University, Tel.: 6879033, Jeddah, Saudi Arabia.

MOMENA (Solaiman Mohamad), Saudi civil servant. **Born** in 1931. **Dipl.:** B.Com. (Economics and Statistics) (1953). **Career:** Former Deputy Director of Economic Research and Statistics Department, SAMA; attended conferences of International Trade and Development, Geneva (1964); contributed to SAMA First Annual Report (1961), and Statistical Bulletin (1960); now Director of Banking Training Centre, Saudi Arabian Monetary Agency (SAMA), Jeddah. **Member:** Training Board, International Monetary Fund (IMF), Washington. **Sports:** Swimming. **Hobby:** Reading. **Prof. Addr.:** P.O.Box 1815. Jeddah, Saudi Arabia.

MONAIE (Abdallah, Ahmad, al), Saudi publisher. **Born** in 1926 in Mecca. **Educ.:** M.A. (Arabic Language). **Career:** Former Director of Youth Welfare; owner of Asir Printing Press in Abha City; Publisher, Editor-in-Chief of Sports and Youth Magazine. **Member:** Board, al-Madina Newspaper, Jeddah. **Address:** Asir Printing Press, P.O.Box 188, Tel.: 2246005, Abha, Saudi Arabia.

MONEIM (Mohamad Abdul), Egyptian journalist. **Born** on 10 December 1937 in Cairo. **Son** of Mr. Mohamad Abdul Rahman (teacher) **and** Mrs., née Ehsan el-Kaddi. **Married** on 2 July 1964 in Cairo to Miss Zeinab Fawzy, 3 children: Ehab (1965), Ashraf (1966), Tamer (1976). **Educ.:** Military School, Cairo; Faculty of Arts, English Department, Cairo University. **Dipl.:** B.Sc. Degree (Military School, 1960), B.A. Degree (Cairo University, 1967). **Career:** Armed Forces officer (1960-68); Journalist (since 1968), Sub-editor of al-Ahram Newspaper and editor of Military Affairs. **Medicals:** October War Medal (Egypt); Medal of Good Merit (North Korea). **Sports:** Swimming and Jogging. **Hobby:** Billiards. **Member:** National Club. **Prof. Addr.:** al-Ahram Newspaper, al-Galaa Street, Cairo, Egypt. **Prof. Addr.:** 7 Ibn Marawan Street, Dokki, Cairo, Tel.: 755500, Egypt.

MONSHI (Mahmoud A. Saleemuddin), Saudi academic. **Born** in 1949, in Makkah, Saudi Arabia. **Dipl.:** Ph.D. (Chemistry). **Career:** Demonstrator in Chemistry (1972); Associate Professor, Chemistry Department, College of Science, King Saud University. **Address:** Chemistry Department, College of Science, King Saud University, P.O.Box 2455, Riyadh 11451, Saudi Arabia.

MORIWAKI (Akira), Japanese banker. **Born** on March 17, 1948 in Japan. **Married** on November 6, 1976. **Educ.:** Osaka University. **Dipl.:** Bachelor in Law. **Career:** Joined Bot (April 1972); secondment to Miti (1976-78); Assistant Vice-President, Bot New York Agency (1978-82; Assistant Manager, Nagoya Office (1982-87); Assistant Manager, Corporate Banking Division (1987-91); presently Chief Representative in Abu Dhabi, Bank of Tokyo, Ltd. **Prof. Addr.:** The Bank of Tokyo Ltd., Abdulla Bin Solayem Bldg., 9th Floor, P.O.Box 2174, Tel.: 339622, Telex: 23500 TOHBK EM, Fax: 331410, Abu Dhabi, United Arab Emirates.

MORSI (Salah E.), Egyptian academic. **Born** on January 27, 1940 in Alexandria, Egypt. **Son** of late M. el-Sayed Morsi (Administrative Director) and late Mrs. Hanem A. Morsi. **Married** in 1968 in Alexandria to Shadia Medawara, 3 children: Reem, Rania, Karim. **Educ.:** Faculty of Science, Alexandria University; Chemical Engineering Department, Imperial College of Science and Technology, London University. **Dipl.:** B.Sc. (Alexandria) Chemistry; Diploma of Imperial College (DIC) Chemical Engineering; Ph.D. (London) Chemical Thechnology. **Career:** Academic Teaching and Research, R&D, in Industry; Consulting for Industry of Insurance in Materials, Fire and Explosions; Educational Development and reform specially in relation to intergration with the Society and Productive Sects. Alexandria University Professor of Materials Chemistry; Founding Dean, Institute of Graduate Studies and Research, Alexandria University; Secretary General, Supreme Council of Egyptian Universities. **Other Information:** Member of Governing Board of Academy of Scientific Research and Technology; National Council of Education; Advisor, People's Assembly (Education and Research). **Awards:** Chartered Chemist (C. chem) and Fellow of the Royal Society of Chemistry (FRSC) London, U.K.; Medal of Honor, Alexandria University Board. **Sports:** Walking. **Hobbies:** Gardening, Reading. **Member:** Various Clubs in Egypt. **Prof. Addr.:** Suprem Council of Universities, Cairo University Campus, Giza, Tel.: 02-732727, 02-738583, Cairo, Egypt. **Priv. Addr.:** 10, Tieba Str., Mohandessin, Tel.: 02-3486562, Cairo, Egypt.

MORTAGUA (Mohamad, Abdulhamid), Egyptian army officer and surgeon. **Born** in Egypt. **Son** of Abdulhamid Mortagua. **Educ.:** Faculty of Medicine (Cairo University). **Dipl.:** Doctor in Medicine, Specialization in Surgery **Career:** Army General; Surgeon, Director General, Armed Forces Hospital. **Addr.:** Maadi, near Cairo, Egypt.

MORTY (Ali, Abdel Moneïm, al), Egyptian academic and ophthalmic Surgeon. **Born** in 1945 in Cairo, Egypt. **Son** of Abdel Moneïm al-Morty. **Married,** two children. **Educ.:** Cairo University. **Dipl.:** Ph.D. in Ophthalmology. **Career:** Tutor in Ophthalmology, Cairo University (1971-76); Assistant Professor (1980-85). Member of the Egyptian Medical Association (since 1970); Egyptian Ophthalmological Society, American Academy of Ophthalmology (since 1982). **Publ.:** "Vitreous Surgery"; "Retinal Surgery".

Medals: Two Awards from Cairo University. **Addr.:** 30 Shagaret el-Dor, Zamalek, Cairo, Egypt.

MOSHRIF (Mohamad A., Dr.), Saudi geologist. **Born** on July 10, 1943 in Medina, Saudi Arabia. **Son** of Abdul-Ghani Othman Moshrif (Judge). **Married** on June 14, 1972 to Miss Saniya Hamza Zahid, 5 children: one son and four daughters. **Educ.:** Primary, Intermediate and Secondary Schools in Medina, Saudi Arabia; University of Puget Sound, Tacoma, Washington, USA; University of Wales, Swansea, UK. **Dipl.** B.Sc. in Geology from University of Puget Sound, USA (1970); Ph.D. in Geology (1974), Sedimentology, University of Wales (1976). **Career:** Held the following appointments: Professor in Sedimentology. Demonstrator (1971-72), Lecturer (1976-78), Assistant Professor (1978-80), Associate Professor (1980), Professor (1990), Chairman of Geology Department, College of Science King Saud University, Riyadh, Saudi Arabia (1988-90). Member of College of Science Board, The Research Centre Board, Library Committee and Co-editor of the Journal of King Saud University (Sciences); Chairman of Working Group of Earth Sciences; Consultant at the Directorate of Scientific Research, City of King Abdulaziz for Science and Technology (Previous name SANCST); Consultant at Ministry of Planning. **Publ.:** Author of several scientific papers and monographs and abstracts; attended and speaker at several Scientific International Conferences and Congresses; Editor of Four text books, "Principles of Sedimentology" in Arabic for use by Arab States Universities and :Illustrated Dictionary of Sedimentological Terms" Arabic-English, English-Arabic; "Application in General Geology"; "Principles of Earth Science-Physical Geology". Gained Kuwait Foundation for the Advancement of Sciences's Award (1988) on his book "Principles of Sedimentology" (in Arabic) as the best Scientific Arabic written text book; Reviewer of Several Scientific papers published in local and international journals; presently writing his book "Geologic Encyclopedia" in Arabic. **Member** of AAPG; Society of Economic Paleontologists and Mineralogists; International Association of Sedimentologists; Geotimes. **Sports:** Swimming, Jogging, Tennis and Physical Fitness Exercises. **Hobbies:** General reading, Sedimentology. **Prof. Addr.:** Geology Department, College of Science, King Saud University, P.O.Box 2455, Riyadh 11451, Saudi Arabia.

MOSLEH (Samir, Abdul Rahman), Egyptian lawyer, resident in UAE. **Born** in Egypt in 1936. **Son** of Abdul Rahman Mosleh. **Married,** two children. **Educ.:** Law Degree; Higher Studies Diploma in International Law. **Career:** Director of Technical Assistant Office, Egyptian Presidential Cabinet (1963); Director of the Office of the Egyptian Presidential Cabinet; Director of the Egyptian Vice President's Office (1966-68); Director of Legal Affairs, Egyptian National Defence Council (1970); Legal Adviser to the United Arab Emirates Council of Ministers (1972-80); Legal Adviser to ADIA. **Medals:** Winner of long-distance swimming world championship medal. **Addr.:** P.O.Box 3600, Abu Dhabi, United Arab Emirates.

MOSTAFA (Mohamed Khaled), Egyptian consultant engineer (utilities and environment). **Born** on March 24, 1937 in Cairo, Egypt. **Son** of Abdel Wahed Mostafa (Lawyer). **Married** on July 20, 1969 in Cairo, Egypt, one son, Ahmed Khaled (Construction Engineering Department, American University), Cairo (Champion of Horse Riding). **Educ.:** Helwan Primary and Secondary Schools, Faculty of Engineering, Cairo University, Egypt. **Dipl.:** Water Works Engineering, Tokyo, Japan (1975), Sewage Works Engineering, Manchester, UK (1983). **Career:** Vice-Chairman, Greater Cairo Water Supply Authority (1980-82); Chairman, el-Co. for Utilities and Erection (1984-87); Chairman, National Organization for Potable Water and Sanitary Drainage (1987-90); Chairman, el-Nasr Co. for Utilities and Erection (1990- to date); Member of Board, Building and Housing General Organization (1989- to date); President, Misr Consultants (Utilities and Environment); **Other Informations:** Member of: Egyptian Syndicate Engineers, Egyptian Association Engineers, Egyptian Water and Sewage Association, JWWA, AWWA, Housing and Utilities Sector in Research and Technical Academy. **Awards:** The Golden Engineers Medal (1986), Culture Medal (1991). **Sports:** Tennis, table tennis, volley ball. **Hobbies:** Snooker and billiard. **Member:** Shooting, Horse Riding and Aviation Clubs. **Prof. Addr.:** 49 Sarwat Str., Tel.: 3925251, Cairo, Egypt. **Priv. Addr.:** 11 A/Aly Alrobi Str., Tel.: 2585486, Roxi, Egypt.

MOUALLIMI (Abdallah, Yahia, al), Saudi businessman. **Born** in 1952 in Saudi Arabia. **Son** of Yahia al-Mouallimi. **Married,** two children. **Educ.:** B.Sc. Chemical Engineering, Oregon State University, USA (1973). **Career:** Chemical Engineer, Riyadh Oil Refinery (1973-75); Assistant General Manager of Production, Riyadh Oil Refinery (1975-77); General Manager, Aluminium Products Co. Ltd., Dammam, Saudi Arabia (since 1977). **Addr.:** Aluminium Products Co. Ltd. (ALUPCO), P.O.Box 2080, Tel.: 8328489, Dammam, Saudi Arabia.

MOUASHER (Anis), Jordanian businessman. **Born** in 1932 in Sult (Jordan). **Son** of Mansour Mouasher (merchant) **and** Mrs., née Hana Zakka. **Married** to Louly Hanania on April 11, 1966, 3 children: Reem and Maher (twins), and Samer. **Educ.:** Sult Secondary School; American University in Beirut (Lebanon). **Career:** Minister of Finance and Transport (1971-72); Minister of Finance (1972); Businessman, Chairman of the Board of the following companies: Mouasher Cousins Co.; Prefabricated Structures Manufacturing Company; Sabco Engineering Company; Aladdin Industries, Jordan Arab Drug & Trading Company, Building Products Company; Member of the Jordan Consultancy Council; Vice-President, Royal Endowment for Culture and Education; President, Royal Society for the Conservation of Nature. **Awards:** al-Nahda

Medal. **Sports:** Fishing and swimming. **Prof. Addr.:** Mouasher Cousins Co., P.O.Box 1387, Tel.: 24907, Amman. **Priv. Addr.:** P.O.Box 1387, Tel.: 30119, Jabal Amman, Jordan.

MOUASHER (Rajai, S), Jordanian businessman. **Born** in 1944 in Amman, Jordan. **Married. Educ.:** B.Sc. in Chemistry, American University of Beirut, Lebanon; M.Sc. in Marketing, Northwestern University, Illinois, USA; Ph.D. in Marketing, University of Illinois. **Career:** Instructor in Marketing, Northern Illinois University; Assistant Professor, Marketing, Northern Illinois University (1970-71); Assistant for special projects, Royal Scientific Society; Manager, Project Operations Status, Information System, Royal Scientific Society; Chairman of the Board of Directors of Jordan National Bank; Minister of Industry and Trade (1974-76); businessman (since 1975); Board Director, Jordan International Bank PLC, London, UK. **Medals:** Order of the Jordanian Star, 1st class, Jordan; Order of the Sacred Treasure, First Class, Japan; Das Grosse Goldene Ehrenzeichen am Bande fur Verdienste, Austria. **Addr.:** Jordan General Business Company, P.O.Box 2851, Amman, Jordan.

MOUCHILI (Nji Mfouayo), Camerooni diplomat. **Born** in 1938 in Camroon (Foumban). **Son** of Nsangou Mama Nji Mfouayo **and** Mrs. Pasma née Mounsouyoum. **Married** to Miss Kantouma Chintouo. **Educ.:** National School of Administration and Magistrature. **Dipl.:** Diploma in Administration and Magistrature. **Career:** Director of General Administration at the Ministry of Foreign Affairs; Counsellor of Cameroon Embassy in Saudi Arabia; Chargé d'Affaires Ambassador of Cameroon in Egypt and Turkey. **Award:** Officer of the Order of Merit. **Prof. Addr.:** Embassy of Cameroon, 15, al-Israa Str., Mohandessine, P.O.Box 2061, Cairo, Egypt. **Priv. Addr.:** 52, Abdel Moneim Riyadh Str., Mohandessine, Tel.: 3460490, Cairo, Egypt.

MOUDARRI (Nicolas, Soubhi), Syrian executive. **Born** in Damascus, Syria on 25.12.32. **Married** to Rita Victoria Moudarri on 8.7.83. One daughter. **Educ.:** College Lazariste, Damascus. **Dipl.:** B.A. **Career:** Sales Manager, Air India in Damascus, Bahrain, Beirut (1964-66); Manager: al-Ganim Travel Agency, Kuwait (1965-67); UK and Scandinavia, Kuwait Airways, London (1967-70); General Manager: Omei'r Bin Yousuf, Abu Dhabi (1970-74); Europe/ America GULFAIR, London (1974-81); Commercial General Manager, Gulf Air Bahrain (1981-). **Sports:** Swimming, walking, yoga. **Hobbies:** Reading, Music and touring. **Member:** Institute of Marketing, British Institute of Management. **Credit Cards:** American Express, Access, Visa. **Addr.:** Gulfair, P.O.Box 138, Tel.: 247525/6. Bahrain.

MOUHOUMED (Ahmed, Abdillahi), Djibouti Deputy at the National Assembly. **Born** on August 30, 1955 in Djibouti. **Educ.:** Diploma from "Centre Internationale de la Formation de la Profession Bancaire de Paris" (Level DES) (Cadre Superieure de Banque). Manager at BCIMR (entrance date, 19/10/1973). **Member** of LPAI, Member of FRUD since its legalisation (Member of Political Bureau). Elected Deputy at the National Assembly (19/12/1997 - to date). Rapporteur of Finance Commission, General Economy and Planning and Commission Member of the National Defence. **Prof. Addr.:** National Assembly, P.O.Box 138 Djibouti, Djibouti.

MOUKAYED (Assad, Major General), Syrian administrator, businessman. **Born** in Syria. **Educ.:** RAF Technical College, Henlow, UK; Institute of Higher Air War Studies, Cairo. **Career:** Chairman of Syrian Arab Airlines (1965-68 and 72-76); Director of Armed Forces Procurement, Syrian Ministry of Defence (1970-80); Vice President of TAG Group, Paris (since 1980). **Medals:** Syrian Medal for Merit., Syrian Medal for Devotion. **Hobbies:** Travelling, reading, swimming. **Priv. Addr.:** 65 Ave. Foch 75116 Paris, France.

MOUKNASS (Hamdi Ould), Mauritanian statesman. **Born** in 1935 in Nouadhibou (North Western Mauritania). **Son** of Sheikh Ould Mouknass (tribal chief). **Married** to Fatimettou mint Khairatt (Lawyer), 2 children. **Educ.:** Koran school at Boutilimit; Michelet College, Nice (France, 1960); Faculty of Law and Economics, Paris (1960-66). **Dipl.:** LL.B., LL.D. (Doctorate in Laws). **Career:** Director Cabinet of the Minister of Civil Service, Labour and Social Affairs (1967); Legal counsel to the Presidency of the Republic since 1966; High Commisioner for Youth, Sports and Social Affairs (1966-67); Minister of Youth, Information and Cultural Affairs (Jan-July 1968); Minister of Foreign Affairs (June 1968 - July 1978); Minister of State for Foreign Affairs (1975); visited Algiers to discuss matters of mutual interest with his Algerian counterpart (1972); attended the Non-Aligned Conference in Georgetown, Guyana (1973); visited Spain, Abu Dhabi, Lebanon, Somalia and Saudi Arabia in 1974; attended the OAU Ministerial Council in Tanzania (1975). Presently, Minister Counsellor to the Presidency. **Address:** c/o Office of the President, P.O.Box 184, Nouakchott, Mauritania.

MOULINE (Larbi), Moroccan Mining Engineer. **Born** on November, 10, 1934. **Married**, 3 children. **Educ.:** Higher National School of Mines, Saint Etienne, France. **Career:** Engineer, Office of Phosphate Research (1959), Director of Administrative Affairs (1965), Directeur des Travaux et Marches (1967), Technical Director (1970). **Member** of the Lions Club. **Award:** Chevalier de l'Ordre du Trone. **Addr.:** Villa "Mouline", Pinede, Souissi, Rabat, Morocco.

MOUNAYER (H.E. Mgr. Eustache Joseph), Syrian Archbishop. **Born** in 1925 in Qatana (Damascus). **Educ.:** Charfé High Seminary (Harissa), University of Roma. **Dipl.:** Doctorate in Theology and Laws. **Career:** Ordained

Priest (1949), Sacred Archbishop (1971), Assistant of H.B. the Syrian Catholic Patriarch since 1971. Archbishop of Damascus (Syrian Rite) (since 1978). **Addr.:** Archevêché Syrien Catholique, P.O.Box 2129, Damascus, Syria.

MOUNTASSER (Muhammed Salah Eddine), Egyptian journalist. **Born** on August 6, 1933 in Cairo, Egypt. **Son** of Hussein Mountasser (Tradesman). **Married** since 1963 - **Widower** since 1991. **Educ.:** Damietta Elementary School; Tawfikia Secondary School; Faculty of Law, Ain Shams University. **Dipl.:** L.L.B, Ain Shams University (1956). **Career:** Before Graduation he was Journalist at "Akher Saa", Weekly Magazine (1953); Joined work at "al-Ahram", daily newspaper (1958) as Chief of Reportage Department; then Assistant Editor; Newspaper Manager (since 1979 till 1985); Chairman and Editor in Chief (since 1985); presently Chairman of Board of Directors "Dar al-Maaref" Publishing House and Editor in Chief of "October" Weekly Magazine. **Other Information:** After 1967 war in the Middle East, shifted his efforts to the topic of Oil. Was the First Journalist in Egypt to be Specialized in "Oil"; Amongst his most famous Columns an: "An Advice, no more"; "Just a Point of View", "Mere Politics". **Award:** Medal of "Free Kuwait" (October 1991). **Sports:** Walking. **Member:** Cairo Rotary Club, Guizera Club. **Credit Card:** American Express. **Prof. Addr.:** October Weekly Magazine, 1119 Cornish al-Nil, Tel.: 740222, 756939, Cairo, Egypt. **Priv. Addr.:** 143, Tahrir Street, Tel.: 3494494, Dokki, Giza, Egypt.

MOURAD (Farouk Abdul Rahman), Saudi educator. **Born** in 1936 in Mecca, Saudi Arabia. **Dipl.:** Ph.D. **Career:** Director General Centre of Training and Applied Research in Social Development (1970-73); Director General. Centre of Crime Prevention Research, Ministry of Interior (1973-80); President, Arab Security Studies and Training Centre, Riyadh; attended many conferences relating to security and crime prevention. **Address:** Ministry of Interior, Tel.: 4033104, 4766395, Riyadh, Saudi Arabia.

MOURAD (Mahmoud Sidky), Egyptian executive. **Born** in 1918 in Benha, Egypt. **Son** of Rifaat Mourad (Chief Engineer) **and** Mrs. Mounira Sidky. **Married** in 1943 in Cairo to Miss Tawhida Ahmed Kamel, two sons, four daughters: Salwa, Mervat, Aly, Mounira, Mohsen and Rawya. **Educ.:** Faculty of Commerce, Cairo University, Cairo, Egypt; Higher Studies in Finance and Taxes, Alexandria University, Egypt. **Dipl.:** B.A. (Commerce); Fellowship of Economic Development Institute, The World Bank, Washington, USA. **Career:** General Secretary, Ministry of Municipal and Rural Affairs (1955-57); Under Secretary, Ministry of Supply (1958-61); Chairman of the General Organization for Foreign Trade (1965-67); Under-Secretary, Ministry of Commerce and Foreign Trade (1967-69); Deputy Minister, Ministry of Economy (1970-71); Advisor to the U.A.E. Ministry of Economy and Trade, Advisor to the U.A.E. Development Bank (1971-78); Guest of the American, Eisenhower Committee, U.S.A.; Lecturer to the Higher Studies Sect on, Faculty of Commerce, Cairo University; former Chairman and Managing Director of Delta International Bank (1978). **Publ.:** The Monetary Budget in cooperation with Dr. Fuad Mursi; Economic Development in the UAE and a series of information booklets to the Ministry of Information and Tourism, Abu Dhabi. **Decor.:** "Grand Officier" from Samli (1960); "Order of Merit" from Egypt (1950). **Sports:** Swimming, tennis. **Member:** Heliopolis Club; al-Shams Club; Yacht Club. **Prof. Addr.:** c/o Delta International Bank, 1113 Cornish el-Nil, P.O.Box 1159, Tel.: 753494, 753484, Cairo, Egypy.

MOURAD (Mohamad Helmi), Egyptian Academic. **Born** in 1920 in Egypt. **Educ.:** Secondary and Higher. **Dipl.:** Doctorate. **Career:** Vice-Chairman, Cairo University; Rector of Aïn Shams University (September 1967); Minister of Education in the Cabinet of late President Abdul Nasser (March 1968- July 1969). **Publ.:** Author of several books and lectures. **Addr.:** Cairo, Egypt.

MOURAD (Mohamad, Mutaz), Syrian banker. **Born** in 1941 in Damascus, Syria. **Son** of Mutaz Mourad. **Married,** two children. **Educ.:** B.A. in Accounting, Cleary College, School of Banking University of Michigan, USA; School of Bank Administration, University of Wisconsin, USA; M.A., Stonier Graduate School of Banking, Rutgers University, USA; M.A. in Business Administration, University of Miami, USA; Executive Management Program, Harvard University, USA. **Career:** Comptroller, National Bank and Trust Co., Michigan, USA (1967-73); District Comptroller, Corporate Finance Officer, Sun Bank Florida, Inc. (1973-76); Executive Vice President, Sun Bank of Miami (1976-81); Senior Vice President and Deputy General Manager, al-Bahrain Arab African Bank (1981-1987). Member of Michigan Bankers Association, Committee member of Strategic Planning. **Publ.:** Articles in banking publications and frequent speaker in seminars on banking issues. **Sport:** Raquet ball. **Hobbies:** Music, reading. **Addr.:** Manama, Bahrain.

MOURAD (Mustafa Kamil), Egyptian politician. **Born** in 1926. **Married. Educ.:** Military Academy, Cairo (1948). **Dipl.:** B.Com. (1954); M.A. in Politicial Science (1957). **Career:** Artillery Officer, Palestine War (1948); participated in 23 July 1952 Revolution; Member many times of the National Assemblies and People's Assemblies; Chairman of the Eastern cotton Company; elected temporary Deputy Speaker :(1971) and following the ensuing general elections: Chairman of the Assembly's Economic Committee, National Council for Production and Economic Affairs (1974); took over responsibility for Cotton Industry (1975); Leader of the Liberal Socialist Party (1984 to present); Chairman of the Board, al-Ahrar Newspaper published by the Liberal Socialist Party. **Prof. Addr.:** 19

al-Gamhouria Street, Cairo, Egypt. **Priv. Addr.:** 34 Muhammad Madhar Street, Cairo, Egypt.

MOURAD (Omar, Ahmad), Egyptian executive. **Born** in 1948 in Cairo, Egypt. **Son** of Ahmad Mourad. **Married** in 1970, 1 son. **Educ.:** Cairo University. **Dipl.:** B.Com. (1969). **Career:** Reserved Officers Corps, Military Service (1970-75); Manager, Citibank, Cairo, Egypt (1975-79); Manager-Banking Group Head, Citibank, Alexandria, Egypt (1979-80); Assistant General Manager al-Bahrain Arab African Bank (ALBAAB), Bahrain (1981-). **Member:** Gezira Sporting Club; Authomobile Club; Marina Club; Delmon Club. **Hobbies:** Tennis, Squash, Golf Football and Reading. **Addr.:** P.O.Box 20488, Tel.: 230491, Telex: 9380 A/B ALBAAN BN, Manama, Bahrain.

MOUSA (Abdallah, Ali, Hindi), Kuwaiti executive. **Born** on 20 November, 1945 in Haifa. **Son** of Ali Hindi Mousa **and** Mrs. née Sada Mahmoud Makluf. **Married** on December 9, 1971 in Kuwait to Itaf Abdou Ismail el-Ashy, five children; Samer (27-10-1971), Reem (14-2-1974), Rana (14-4-1975), Zaher (24-10-1977) and Moh'd (24-4-1985). **Educ.:** Cairo University, Egypt. **Dipl.:** B.Sc. in Commerce, Major: Accounting and Management. **Career:** Auditor, Nawar Company, Kuwait (1971-73), General Manager, Dar al-Watan, Kuwait (1973-). **Sport:** English Football. **Hobbies:** Writing Articles, Reading interesting books/magazines/newspapers etc... **Member:** Kuwait Sea Club, Kuwait Journalist Association. **Credit Cards:** American Card (Green and Golden), Master Card. **Prof. Addr.:** P.O.Box 1142 Safat, 13012 State of Kuwait Tel.: 4840450, Telex: 22565 ALWATAN. **Priv. Addr.:** Area 1, Blk 6, St. 9, House 20, Surra, State of Kuwait, Tel.: 2560316, 2560336.

MOUSA (Amr), Egyptian government minister, **Born** in 1936. **Educ.:** Cairo University. **Dipl.:** LL.B. (1957). **Career:** Ministry of Foreign Affairs since 1958; Ambassador of Egypt to Switzerland; Ambassador of Egypt to India (1982-86); Ministry of Foreign Affairs, head International Organisations Department (1986-89); Permanent Chief Representative of Egypt to the United Nations (1989-91); Minister of Foreign Affairs (since 20.5.1991). Head of the Egyptian delegation on the Middle East Peace Conference held in Madrid on 30 October 1991. **Prof. Addr.:** Ministry of Foreign Affairs, Cairo, Egypt.

MOUSA (Ismail, al-Haj), Sudanese journalist. **Born** in 1944, in al-Obeid, Sudan. **Son** of al-Haj Mousa. **Educ.:** LL.B, Faculty of Law, University of Khartoum, Sudan; M.A. in Sociology, University of Poitiers, France; Ph.D. in Sociology, University of Tours, France. **Career:** Dean of Students, University of Khartoum (1975); Minister of State for Culture and Information (1976); Secretary, Committee of Culture and Information, Sudanese Socialist Union (1978); Editor in Chief, "al-Ayyam" daily (1978); Minister of Culture and Information (1979); member of the Political Bureau of the Sudanese Socialist Union (1980) (Party banned in 1989). **Publ.:** "The Intellectual and His Role" and other works. **Medals:** Order of the Republic, 1st Class, Democratic Republic od Sudan (1979). **Sport:** Squash. **Hobby:** Reading. **Addr.:** Khartoum, Sudan.

MOUSA (Jaber Salem), Saudi academic. **Born** in 1945 in Abha, Saudi Arabia. **Dipl.:** Ph.D. (Pharmacology) (1976). **Career:** Teaching Assistant (1967-69); Lecturer (1976-78), Assistant Professor (1978-81) and Associate Professor, Faculty of Pharmacy, King Saud University; Vice Dean, Faculty of Pharmacy (1978-80); Chairman, Pharmacology Department, Faculty of Pharmacy (1980-81); Associate Professor. of Pharmacology, Vice Dean, Faculty of Graduate Studies, King Saud University, (1981); attended several conferences and symposia in his field of interest. **Publications:** several research papers on medical and poisonous plants of Saudi Arabia. **Priv. Addr.:** Tel.: 4811000, Ext. 2375, Riyadh, Saudi Arabia.

MOUSA (Jassem Mohamad Othman, al), Kuwaiti executive. **Born** in 1947 in Kuwait. **Son** of Mohamad Othman al-Mousa. **Married** in 1971, 3 sons, **Educ.:** Kuwait public schools; Cairo University, Egypt. **Dipl.:** B.A. Commerce (Accountancy). **Career:** Manager, Gulf Bank, Kuwait (1969-74); Joined Financial Centre since 1974; succesively Manager; Deputy General Manager; General Manager and Vice-Chairman, Kuwait Financial Centre, Safat Kuwait, Director, Korea Kuwait Banking Corp. Kuwait; Jordan Gulf bank, Jordan; Petra Capital Corp. New York, USA and United Insurance Company, UAE; Minister of Public Works (1990- April 1991). **Member:** Forex Club, Kuwait; Kuwait Auditor Society; International Bankers Association, Washington DC **Addr.:** P.O.Box 2344, Tel.: 412131, Telex: 2477 A/B MARKAZA, Safat Kuwait.

MOUSA (Mohamad Ali Hussein), Saudi civil servant. **Born** in Mecca, in 1934. **Dipl.:** received primary and general technical education. **Career:** Wireless technician; Supervisor of the telephone system of Ministry of Internal Affairs; Supervisor, Monitoring Service, Broadcasting Station; Director-General of Financial and Administrative Affairs, Ministry of Information Branch of Western Province; Director of Cement Company Co-operative Society; Assistant Editor of al-Madina daily newspaper; Director of Asir Housing project; Manager of Department of Publications, Mecca; Deputy Director-General of Ministry of Information; attended First Social Leaders Conference, Riyadh (1971); now Manager of Ragab and Silsila Co. **Member:** Board of Asian Announcers, Kuala Lumpur, Malaya (1962). **Publ.:** Articles in leading Saudi newspapers; TV and radio talks; Lectures and Forums. **Prof. & Priv. Addr.:** Rajab & Silsila Co., P.O.Box 203, Jeddah, Saudi Arabia.

MOUSA (Omar, el-Hag), Sudanese military. **Born** on

June 16, 1924 in el-Kawa, Gezire Scheme (Sudan). **Married** children. **Educ.:** Gezira elementary school; Intermediate school, Port Sudan (1935-39); Gordon Memorial College (1939-42); Military Academy, Khartoum (1942-44); 18-month training course in telecommunications at Catterick Camp, Yorkshire, (England, 1948-49); Attended a Company Commanders' course in Sudan (1953); Staff College course (1964). **Career:** Commissioned (1944); was posted to the Fourth Motor Batallion with the British VIIIth Army in the desert war in Egypt (1939-45); posted to Asmara, Eritrea (1945-47); posted to Western Command and trained as a cavalry officer at Nyala (1947); joined the Signal Corps Headquarters; Khartoum (1949-53); served as secretary to the Defence Minister (1956); Promoted captain (1957); Commander of the Sudan Signal Corps with the rank of colonel (1959); promoted Brigadier (Jan. 1965) and Director, Armed Forces Administration; Commander, Northern Command at Shendi (Jan. 1966); Temporary Commander, Southern Command (1966); Commander, Northern and Southern Command (July 1966- May 1977); Minister of Defence (June-Oct. 1969); Minister of National Guidance (Oct. 1969- Oct. 1971); Minister of Information and Culture (Oct. 1971- Jan. 1975); has acted on several occasions as Foreign Minister, Assistant to the Secretary General of the Sudan Socialist Union (SSU) (Party now banned). **Addr.:** Khartoum, Sudan.

MOUSA (Suleiman), Jordaninan writer and historian. **Born** in Rafeed (Irbid Dist.) in 1920. **Married. Education:** Diploma in accountancy. **Career:** Teacher; Iraq Petroleum Co. (1946-50); Jordan Broadcasting (1957-58); Press Dept. (1958-65); Ministry of Informantion (1965-77); Ministry of Culture (1978-84); Editor, "Risalat al-Urdun" and "Afkar"; Cultural Adviser; Municipality of Greater Amman (1985-88); Cultural adviser. **publ:** Professional writer, more than 30 books published, including: History of Jordan in the 20th Century (2 Volumes); Hussein Bin Ali; The Arab National Movement (Al-Harakat al-Arabieh 1908-1924); Jordan in the 1948 War; Luminaries from Jordan (A'lam min al-Urdun - 2 Volumes); Lawrence and the Arabs, an Arab View, Published in Arabic 1962, in English (3 prints - An Arab writes about Lawrence of Arabia) 1988; CAMEOS: Jordan & Arab Nationalism (1997); Awraq min Dafter al-'Ayam (Leaves from a Book life - 2000). Writer in Arabic and English. **Decoration and Awards:** Independance Medal (1971); Award of Abdullah Ibn Al-Hussein for Islamic Civilisation Research (1988); State Merit Award for Culture (1990). **Address:** P.O.box 960364, Amman, Jordan.

MOUSAWI (Faisal Radhi, al), Bahraini Minister of Health. **Born** on April 6, 1944 in Bahrain. **Son** of Radhi Al Mousawi (late), Teacher. **Married** to Mrs. Layla Abdul Rahman, 4 children: Ahmed, Mariam, Nada, May. **Qualifications:** M.B.Ch.B., University of Cairo, Egypt (1966); F.R.C.S., Ireland, February 1975; F.R.C.S., Edinburgh, May 1975. **Present Post:** Minister of Health. **POSTS HELD:** Consultant Orthopaedic Surgeon, Salmaniya Medical Centre; Chairman, Department of Surgery, Salmaniya Medical Centre; Chairman, Department of Orthopaedic Surgery, Salmaniya Medical Centre; Assistant Undersecretary for Medical Services, Ministry of Health; Assistant Professor, College of Medicine & Medical Sciences, Arabian Gulf University. **PROFESSIONAL SOCIETIES:** Fellow-British Orthopaedic Association; President-Gulf Orthopaedic Association; Member-Amiri Academy for Medical Specialties; Member-Editorial Board, Bahrain Medical Bulletin; Member-European Society for Sport Medicine, Knee Surgery and Arthroscopy (EUSSKA). Member-World Orthopaedic Concern. **EXPERIENCE:** Rotary intern: Cairo University Hospital, for one year. House Officer: Department of Surgery, Government Hospital, Bahrain for six months. Sr. House Officer: Department of Surgery, Government Hospital, Bahrain, for one year. Accident & Orthopaedic Surgery Central Middlesex Hospital, London, UK, for nine months. Orthopaedic Surgery St. Helier Hospital, Carshalton Surrey, UK, for six months. General Surgery Nelson Hospital, London, UK. for six months. St. Bartholomew's Hospital, West Smithfield, London, UK, for six months. Registrar: Orthopaedic Surgery Whittington Hospital, London, UK, for one year; General and Traumatic Surgery Wexford County Hospital, Ireland, for eighteen months; Orthopaedic Surgery Whittington Hospital, London, UK, for one year. Consultant: Locum Whittington Hospital, London, UK, for six months (October 1983 to March 1984: Study leave from Ministry of Health); Othopaedic Surgery Salmaniya Medical Centre, Bahrain, since August 1976. Chairman: Department of Surgery, Salmaniya Medical Centre, Bahrain, April 1982-March 1984. Chief of Medical Staff: Salmaniya Medical Centre, June 1982-August 1982. Chairman: Department of Orthopaedic Surgery, Salmaniya Medical Centre, Bahrain. Assistant Undersecretary: Ministry of Health, Bahrain, August 1982-June 1995. MINISTER OF HEALTH: June 1995 to date. **ACADEMIC APPOINTMENTS:** Assistant Professor, Arabian Gulf University, College of Medicine & Medical Sciences. **ARAB BOARD PROGRAM:** Member, Scientific Council, Arab Board for Surgery (1979 to date); Member and Vice Chairman, Training Committee, Arab Board for Surgery (1981 to 1988); Chairman, Arab Board Committee for Sub-specialties in Surgery, Arab, Board for Orthopaedic Surgery (1990 to date); Chairman, Training Committee, Arab Board for Orthopaedic Surgery (1988 to date); Member, High Council for Arab Board Medical Specialties (1983-1987). **ARAB BOARD IN BAHRAIN:** CHAIRMAN, National Arab Board Committee & Coordinator, Arab Board Program in Surgery; Examiner, Ministry of Health Qualification Examination (1982 to date). **ROYAL COLLEGE OF SURGEONS, IRELAND:** Examiner, Part A Fellowship Examination (1992-1993); Examiner, Part B Fellowship Examination (1993 to date). **COMMITTEES:** CHAIRMAN, Manpower Development Committees;

CHAIRMAN, Credential Committee, Salmaniya Medical Centre; Member, Joint Committee, College of Medicine, Arabian Gulf University and Ministry of Health; Member, Affiliation Committee with A.U.B. for Family Physician Training Program; VICE CHAIRMAN, Bahrain Sport Medicine Association; Member, Board of Education, College of Health Sciences; PRESIDENT, Bahrain Medical Society (1977-1978); CHAIRMAN, Medical Seminar Committee (1977-1980); CHAIRMAN, National Disaster Committee (1977-1982). **COLLEGE OF MEDICINE COMMITTEES:** Member (1986-1988) year 4-5 Curriculum Committee; Chairman (1984) Hospital, Health Centers Coordination Committee; Member (1984-1985) Academic & Scientific Committee; Member (1985-1986) Arabian Gulf University; Member (1991) Phase II Curriculum Committee. **TEACHING EXPERIENCE:** 1972-1976 Clinical Teaching to medical students while Registrar at St. Bartholomew's and Whittington Hospitals; Also, Training Residents at these hopitals and while working at Wexford Hospital in Ireland. 1978-1982 Clinical teaching to medical students for King Faisal Medical School, Al-Khobar, Saudi Arabia. 1984 to date Assistant Professor, Arabian Gulf University, Teaching students on hospital rotation. Tutor: Year 4-5; Muscolo Skeletal System Coordinator Problem Coordinator: a) Fracture Humerus, b) Osteoarthritis of the knee, c) Gout. Problem Review: 1) CDH, 2) Rheumatoid hand, 3) Poliomyelitis, 4) Multiple Trauma. Professional Skills Teacher. Resource Person. Examiner: Clinical rotation and Final year Examination in Surgery. **WORKSHOPS:** TUTOR, Course in A.O. Internal Fixation of Fractures in Collaboration with A.O. International. Sultanate of Oman, 1985. TUTOR-Technique Demonstration: First A.O. course in Internal Fixation of Fractures. Scientific Background and Clinical Application-Kuwait Institute for Medical Specialties in Collaboration with A.O. International, Kuwait, 1987. TUTOR-Course Coordinator: A.O. Course in Internal Fixation Technique, Bahrain, 1989. TUTOR, A.O. Course, DAVOS, Switzerland, 1992. **PAPERS PRESENTED IN SCIENTIFIC MEETINGS:** "Multiple Trauma Management". Seminar of Surgical Trauma, Bahrain, 1978. "Back Injuries in Sports". Seminar on Sport Trauma, Bahrain, 1979. "Management of Open Fractures Following Road Traffic Accidents". First U.A.E. Orthopaedic Conference, Dubai, 1981. "Fracture Management in Bahrain, A.O. technique". Oman Trauma Conference, Sultanate of Oman, 1985. "High Tibial Osteotomy". Knee Surgery Symposium, Bahrain, 1986. "Paraoteal Osteosarcoma". Bahrain Medicare Conference. Bahrain, 1987. "Cervical Spine Injuries-Surgical Management". First Overseas Conference of the Royal College of Surgeons, Ireland, Bahrain, 1988. "Arab Board in Aorthopaedic Surgery". First GCC Orthopaedic Association Conference, Bahrain, 1992. "Total Hip Replacement in Sickle Cell Disease". First GCC Orthopaedic Association Conference, Bahrain, 1992. "Early experience with PCA Total Knee Replacement". GCC Orthopaedic Association Conference, Sultanate of Oman, 1993. **PUBLICATIONS:** "Sport Injuries of the Lumbar Region". Bahrain Medical Bulletin, December 1982. "Performance in Bahrain Licensing Examination by Graduates from two Types of Curricula". Hamdy H., **Al-Mousawi F.**, Lammers, Ameen S. and Abdul Wahab A. Academic Medicine, 1991. "Comparison of Performance of Graduates of Innovative Curriculum with Traditional Curricula in Bahrain Licensing Examination". Hamdy H., **Al-Mousawi F.**, Lammers, Ameen S., and Abdul Wahab. A. Bahrain Medical Bulletin. "Prous Coated Anatomic (PCA) Total Knee Replacement - Early Experience in Bahrain". Ierodoconu M., **Al-Mousawi F.**, Al-Aradi A., and Wong J. Bahrain Medical Bulletin, 15,98: 101, 1993. "Ipsilateral Epicondylar and Supracondylar Fracture Elbow in a Child". Ierodonoconu M., **Al-Mousawi F.**, Wong J., and Aradi A. Acta Orthopaedic Helenica. Accepted for publication in May, 1994. **Sports:** Tennis. **Hobby:** Reading. **Addr.:** Ministry of Health, P.O.Box 12, Manama, State of Bahrain, Tel.: 252605, Fax: 252569, Telex: 8511 Health BN.

MOUSSAOUI (Ahmed), Moroccan Minister of Youth and Sports. **Born** on February 4, 1951 at Nador, Morocco. **Married** 3 children. **Dipl.:** Bac Science Ex with mention (1969); Engineering Diploma from "Ecole Nationale d'Agriculture" (1973); Lauréat du Cycle Supérieur de Gestion from "ISCAE"; Attestation of Training in Transport Organisation at "ACTIM" Paris (1983). **Career:** Head of Economic Studies Department and Statistical Surveys at the Ministry of Agriculture; Head of Transport Division at the Ministry of Transport, Chief of Cabinet at the Ministry of Transport; Deputy Director General of the RAPC (Presently ODEP); In charge of Studies at the Ministry of Labour and Social Affairs; **Presently** Minister of Youth and Sports. **Studies and Publications:** Participation in the realisation of several studies and surveys in the Agricultural domain; Participation in the realisation of several studies in the domain of Transport; Teacher at some Institutions and Higher Education Schools. **Associated Activities and Politics:** Member of Political Bureau of M.N.P.; Vice-President of Engineers Association; Member of the Board of "Mohamed V. Foundation". **Languages:** Arabic, French and Spanish. **Prof. Addr.:** Ministry of Youth and Sports, Ave. Ibn Sina, Agdal, Rabat, Morocco.

MOWASWES (Sami A., Dr.), Kuwaiti banker. **Born** on October 30, 1955 in Kuwait. **Son** of Ali J. Mowaswes (Insurance, retired) **and** Mrs. Hiam M. née Doh. **Married** on December 27, 1982 in Jordan to Miss Rania M. Annab, one Child, Farah (10/11/1988). **Educ.:** United States International University, Kennedy Western. **Dipl.:** MBA, Ph.D. (Business Administration). **Career:** Credit Administrator, The First National Bank of Chicago; Credit & Marketing Manager, Banque de Djibouti et Moyen-Orient; Assistant Manager, United Arab Bank (Affiliated to Société Générale); Manager Main Branch, National Bank of Sharjah; Senior Manager Credit, National Bank of Sharjah. **Sports:** Tennis and swimming. **Hobby:** Reading. **Member:** Sports and Social Clubs. **Credit Cards:** American Express, Golden American Express, Visa. **Prof. Addr.:** National Bank of Sharjah, P.O.Box 4, Tel.: (9716) 355581, Sharjah, United Arab Emirates. **Priv. Addr.:** P.O.Box 15758, Tel.: (9714) 668558, Dubai, United Arab Emirates.

MOWSILY (Sami Ahmad), Saudi civil servant. **Born** in 1948 in Taif, Saudi Arabia. **Dipl.:** B.Sc. (Civil Engineering) 1973, M.Sc. (Environmental Engineering), Stanford University, U.S.A. 1972. **Career:** Head, Follow-up Department, Ministry of Planning; Sector Head in charge of Planning Municipality Housing and Water Sectors; Deputy Director-General, Yanbu Industrial Complex, the Royal Commission for the Development of Jubail and Yanbu. Industrial Zones. member of Saudi Arabia /U.S. Joint Co-operation Committee. **Hobbies:** soccer, American football, tennis, classical music. **Address:** Jeddah, Saudi Arabia.

MOWSILY (Soliman Ahmad), Saudi executive. **Born** in 1946 in Mecca, Saudi Arabia. **Dipl.:** B.Sc. (1969), M.Sc. (1972), Ph.D. (1974). **Career:** Former Director of Research and Training, General Organization for Saline Water Desalination; Research Assistant (1970); Teaching Assistant (1971); Research Supevisor (1973); Director of Research, Research and Development Corporation, Jeddah (1974); Director and owner, Soliman Ahmed Mowsily Establishment for Trade and Contracting. **Member:** Committee of Research on Environmental Protection and Desalination. **Publications:** Analysis of Psychoactive Drugs, Water Pollution. **Hobbies:** tennis, reading. **Prof. Addr.:** Jeddah. **Priv. Addr.:** Tel.: 6600203, Jeddah, Saudi Arabia.

MTANIOS (Habib), Syrian academic and former minister. **Born** on January 17, 1939 in Idaideh/Safita, Syria. **Son** of Habib Youssef (Curate) **and** Mrs. Sarah Youssef. **Married** on 17 October 1964 in Lattakia to Miss Nadia Makhoul, Two children: Fakher Habib, Hala Habib. **Educ.:** Idaideh Elementary and Preparatory School; Kafroum Saadeh and Saint Abda (Lebanon); Secondary Schools in Tartous and Safita; B.A. in Economics, Damascus University; M.A., and Ph.D., Leningrad University (Saint Petersburg). **Dipl.:** B.A., M.A. and Ph.D. in Economics. **Career:** Assistant Professor, Damascus University (1971-76); Associate Professor, Damascus University (1977-82), Professor (1982 till now); Vice Dean of Economic Faculty (1972-74), Vice Dean (1981-85); Head of Economic Department (1985-86); Dean of Faculty of Economics (1986-87); Minister of Petroleum and Mineral Resources until June 1992. **Other Information:** Member in Third World Economists' Association; Participation in a number of International Economic Symposiums; A Number of published researches and articles; Writing and translation of a number of Books. Languages: Arabic, French, English and Russian. **Hobbies:** Reading and hunting. **Member:** in the Syrian Teacher's Syndicate. **Priv. Addr.:** Zablatani, Kassaa, Tel.: 423097, Damascus, Syria.

MUALLA (Jamil, Abdel Wahed), Agricultural engineer, former syrian international civil servant. **Born** in 1919 at Antioch, Alexandretta (Syria). **Married**, children. **Educ.:** Faculty of Agriculture, Aïn Shams University, Cairo (1946-50); State Agriculture University, Wageningen (Netherlands); Post Graduate Training; Agricultural Extension & Research (France). **Dipl.:** B.Sc. (Agronomy) (1950). **Career:** Inspector of Agricultural Education. Damascus (1950-52); Director of Agriculture, Ministry of Agriculture, Damascus (1958-64); Agricultural Adviser, Food and Agriculture Organisation (FAO), Congo (1964-66); Agriculture Planning Adviser, FAO, Somalia (1966-68); Senior Agricultural Adviser and Country Representative, Somalia, FAO /UNDP (United Nations Development Programme) (1968-79); Senior Agricultural Adviser and Country Representative, Jordan (1970-71); Consultant Agricultural Engineer: owns Private office. **Publ.:** Author of "Principles of Horticulture", "Economic Insects of Syria", "Agricultural Sciences Textbook"', "Fruit Trees in Syria". **Member:** Agricultural Engineers Union, Damascus. **Hobbies:** Music, reading and photography. **Prof. Addr.:** P.O.Box 5150, Tel.: 115773, Damascus, Syria. **Priv. Addr.:** Tel.: 718832, Damascus, Syria.

MUALLA (Mohamad, Said, al), United Arab Emirates politician, executive. **Born** in 1925. **Son** of Said al-Mulla. **Career:** Director of National Bank of Dubai; Director of the Dubai Electricity company; former chairman Arab Emirates Investment Bank Ltd. Dubai. Minister of communications (1977-1996); and several business interests. **Addr.:** P.O.Box 5503, Dubai, United Arab Emirates.

MUALLA (Rashid bin Ahmad, al, H.H. Shaikh), Ruler of Umm al-Quwain, UAE. **Born** in 1930. **Career:** Chairman, Umm al-Quwain Municipality (1967); constituted the Emirate's first municipal council (1975); Appointed Deputy Ruler of Umm al-Quwain, succeeded as Ruler after his Father's death on February 1981. **Address:** Rulers' Palace, Umm al-Quwain, United Arab Emirates.

MUALLA (Saud Bin Rashid, al), United Arab emirates administrator. **Born** in 1952. **Educ.:** Oxford University, Foreign Diplomatic Course, U.K. **Career:** President of Amiri Court, Umm al Quwain; Chairman of Umm al-Qawain Asbestos and Cement Industries. Co. and Chairman, The National Bank of Umm al-Qawain Ltd. **Addr.:** Amiri Court, P.O.Box 225, Umm al-Quwain, United Arab Emirates.

MUALLA (Sultan Bin Ahmad, al, Shaikh), United Arab Emirates politician. **Born** in 1935. **Second son of** Shaikh Ahmad al-Mualla, former Ruler of Umm al-Qawain. **Career:** Dealt with Umm al-Qawain's dispute with Sharjah over oil resources; Union Minister of Health (1971-73); Minister of Economy and Trade, United Arab

Emirates (1973-82); Chairman, Petroleum and Mineral Affairs Department, Umm al-Qawain. **Addr.:** P.O.Box 9, Umm al-Quwain, U.A.E.

MUAMMAR (Abdallah Ibn Abdulaziz Ibn, Dr.), Saudi Politician. **Born** in 1950. **Educ.:** B.A., Economics, International American University, California, USA (1976); M.B.A., Administration, Development and Organization, International American University, California, USA (1978); M.A., Social Sciences, University of California, Irvine (1981); Ph.D., Social Sciences, University of California, Irvine (1983). **Career:** Director, Department of Research and Studies, General Secretariat of Labor Force (1983); Consultant Office of the Minister of Agriculture (1988); Deputy Minister of Agriculture and Water (1988); Minister of Agriculture and Water (1995-to date). **Address:** Ministry of Agriculture and Water, Airport Road, Riyadh 1195, Saudi Arabia.

MUBARAK (Abdul Aziz Mubarak Latif, al), United Arab Emirates official. **Born** in 1933 in Abu Dhabi. **Son** of Latif al-Mubarak. **Married,** five children. **Dipl.:** B.A. in Business and Finance. **Career:** Assistant Under Secretary of Finance and Financial Administration, Ministry of Education, UAE. **Hobbies:** Gardening, football, Arabic Literature. **Addr.:** P.O.Box 3072, Abu Dhabi, United Arab Emirates.

MUBARAK (Ahmad I.), Saudi engineer. **Born** in 1939 in Jubail. **Educ.:** B.Sc. (Engineering). **Career:** Engineer, Engineering Consulting Department, Arabian American Oil Company (Aramco); Director of Construction Department Royal Commission, Jubail; Director General Jubail Project. **Member:** Board of Directors, the Saudi Consulting House. **Prof. Addr.:** Jubail Industrial City, Tel.: 3414500, Jubail. **Priv. Addr.:** Tel.: 3415326, Jubail, Saudi Arabia.

MUBARAK (Mohamed Hosny), President of the Arab Republic of Egypt. **Born** on May 4, 1928 in the village of Kafr El-Mousselha, Menufia Governorate, Egypt. **Social Status:** Married and Father of two sons. **Educ.:** Joined the Military Academy (November 1, 1947), Graduated (February 1, 1949); Joined the Air Academy (February. 1, 1949), Graduated (March 13, 1950). **Posts:** Occupied various posts in the Air Force; Lectured at the Air Academy From February 1952 to January 1959; Squadron Commander of an IL 28 Formation and Later Brigade Commander of TU 16; Commanding officer of several air bases; Director of the Air Academy (November 2, 1967); Air Force Chief of Staff (June 22, 1969); Air Force, Commander in Chief and Deputy Defence Minister (April 24, 1972); Promoted to Air Marshal (October 1973); Vice-President (April 16, 1975); Elected as Deputy Chairman of the National Democratic Party (August 14, 1978); Elected as President of the Arab Republic of Egypt, October 1981. **Addr.:** Presidency of the Republic, President's Office, Cairo, Egypt.

MUBARAK (Musa, al), Sudanese statesman. **Born** in 1932 at Abu Si'id, Omdurman (Sudan). **Married,** three son. **Educ.:** University of Khartoum; University of London **Dipl.:** B.A., M.A. **Career:** School teacher; lecturer, University of Khartoum, elected Member of Parliament, National Unionist Party (1965-68); Democratic Unionist Party (1968-69); Minister of Industry and Mineral Resources (1969-70); Manager and Editor, "al-Ayyam printing and Publishing House" (1970-71); Minister of Labour (August- October 1971); Minister of State of Cabinet Affairs (1971-72); Minister for the Treasury (Apr.-Oct. 1972). **Prof. Addr.:** P.O.Box. 1701, Khartoum, Sudan.

MUBARAK (Rashid Ibn Abdulaziz, al), Saudi academic. **Born** in 1934 at al-Ahsa, Saudi Arabia. **Dipl.:** Ph.D. **Career:** Former employee, Ministry of Finance; Administrative Director of a Court Law; Director of Chemical Laboratories, Ministry of Agriculture; Assistant Professor, Chemistry, King Saud University, Riyadh. Former member: Higher Council of King Faisal University; member of the Board, National Science and Technology Center; member, Higher Education Certificates Evaluation Committee. **Publications:** articles, lectures and books. **Prof. Addr.:** Faculty of Science, King Saud University, Riyadh. **Priv. Addr.:** Tel.: 4784673, Riyadh, Saudi Arabia.

MUDARIS (Abdul Karim, Al), Iraqi diplomat. **Born** in 11/9/32 in Basra, Iraq. **Married,** children. **Educ.:** University of Baghdad, Higher Institute for Arab Studies & Research, Cairo. **Dipl.:** M.A. in Economics. **Career:** Various posts in Arab League headquarters, Cairo (1955-59); Seconded to Kuwait Ministry of Justice (1960-65); Economic Counsellor, Arab League Office, UK (1969); Head of the Arab League Mission, UK (1973-74); founding member, Secretary-General & Chief Executive, Arab-British Chamber of Commerce, UK (since 1975); Co-ordination & liaison Officer, Joint Arab-Foreign Chambers of Commerce; member of the board of the Arab-Belgium-Luxembourg Chamber of Commerce, Brussels Arab-Portuguese Chamber of Commerce, Lisbon, Arab-Irish Chamber of Commerce, Dublin and the Arab-British Centre, London. **Publ.:** Studies and research papers. **Hobbies:** Music, literature, poetry, swimming. **Addr.:** Arab-British Chamber of Commerce, 6 Belgrave Square, London SW1X 8PH.

MUDARRIS (Abdulaziz M.S.), Saudi Physician. **Born** in 1930 in Medina, Saudi Arabia. **Dipl.:** M.B.B.CH. Diploma of Pediatrics. **Career:** Specialist in children's diseases, King Faisal Hospital, Taif (1956); District Manager of Taif Area (1960); Deputy Minister of Health (1960); owns a special out-patient clinic; Chairman, Board of Directors, Red Crescent Society; President Red Crescent Society since 1963. **Member:** Executive Committee of Arab Red Crescent Societies, Finance Commission of the League of Red Cross Societies, International Committee of Blood Transfusion. **Prof. Addr.:** Red Crescent

Society, Tel.: 4352081, Riyadh. **Priv. Addr.:** Tel.: 4763374, Riyadh, Saudi Arabia.

MUDARRIS (Assaad), Syrian painter. **Born** in Aleppo. **Career:** Painter, contributed to several art exhibitions since 1963 in Aleppo, Tartousse and Beirut. Former Professor, Faculty of Architecture, Aleppo University. **Awards:** Several distinguished medals. **Addr.:** Aleppo, Syria.

MUDAWI (al-Bakir Yusuf), Sudanese banker. **Born** in 1933 in Sudan. **Son** of Yusuf Mudawi. **Married. Educ.:** University of Khartoum, Sudan; University of Oxford, England. **Dipl.:** B.A. in Economics and Higher diploma in Economics. **Career:** Ministry of Finance, Khartoum, Sudan (1955); Bank of Sudan (1960); Assistant General Manager, Deputy Governor, Bank of Sudan (1971-73); Expert IMF (1973-76); Expert Arab Monetary Fund (AMF) (1977-79); General Manager, Faisal Islamic Bank, Khartoum Sudan (1979-90) Chairman New Flour Mill Factories Co. Ltd. ATBARA, Sudan (since 1989); Board Member, Balsam Co. Board of Directors (since 1990); Deputy Chairman, International Association of Islamic Banks (I.A.I.B.) (since 1991); Director and Chairman Board Executive Committee, Faisal Islamic Bank (since January 1991). **Board Member in the following Institutions:** Dar al-Maal al-Islami (DMI Geneve) since 1984; Islamic Development Co. (Sudan) since 1984; Faisal Islamic Bank of Egypt, Cairo, since January 1991. **Address:** Faisal Islamic Bank, (Sudan), P.O.Box 10143, Tel.: 81848, 81920, 73717, Khartoum, Sudan.

MUDBIL (Abdulaziz Hamal, al), Saudi engineer. **Born** on May 5, 1942 in Dharma, Saudi Arabia. **Married,** 3 children. **Educ.:** University of Paget Sound, USA. **Dipl.:** B.Sc. (Geology) (1986). **Career:** Field Geologist at the Ministry of Agriculture and Water, Saudi Arabia (1969-74), Director of Drilling Dept. (1975-77), Director of Riyadh Water Supply (1977-79), Director of Projects Dept. (1979-81) and Deputy Agricultural Bank, Saudi Arabian Company and National Agricultural Development Company. **Prof. Addr.:** P.O.Box 755, Tel.: 4037879, Riyadh, Saudi Arabia.

MUDHAFFAR (Ismail Ali), Bahraini businessman. **Born** on October 9, 1942. **Married,** five children. **Educ.:** Associate Cost and Management Account, United Kingdom. **Career:** Chief Accountant at the Ministry of Health (1973); Director of Finance and Personnel Affair, Ministry of Health (1975); Board Member of Bahrain Aluminium Extrusion Company; Director of Finance and Administration of Arab Iron Steel Company. **Hobbies:** table tennis, billiards, reading, chess, travel, cards. **Prof. Addr.:** P.O.Box 50177, Manama, Tel.: 673311, Manama, Bahrain.

MUFADDA (Mohamad Abdul Rahman, al), Saudi academic. **Born** in 1937 at Oshaygir. **Dipl.:** B.A., M.A., Ph.D.) Arabic Language). **Career:** Teacher, Riyadh Scientific Institute (1958-62); Assistant Professor, Faculty of Arabic Language, King Saud University (1962-66); Associate Professor (1967-68); Associate Professor, Faculty of Arabic Language, King Saud University. **Member:** King Faisal Prize Committee, the Literary Club and the Saudi Society for Culture and Arts. **Publications:** a revision of Taaliq al-Fawayed Ala Tas'heel Alfawayed; several magazine articles. **Hobbies:** reading, writing. **Addr.:** Riyadh, Saudi Arabia.

MUFARREJ (Mufarrej Ibrahim, al), Kuwaiti electrical Eng. **Born** in 1943 in Kuwait. **Son** of Ibrahim al-Mufarrej (Merchant) **and** Sara al-Hajri. **Married** to Badria al-Rumaih in 1973, 3 children. **Educ.:** Illinois Institute of Technology. Chicago. **Dipl.:** B.S. Electrical Engineering. **Career:** Superintendent Control Center, Ministry of Electricity & Water (1969-76); Chairman and Managing Director, Electrical Project Company (1977); Chairman, Kuwait Asbestos & Plastic Industries, Chairman and Managing Director of National Industries Company (1978 to present); Member of the Board of Directors, the Industrial Bank of Kuwait. **Member:** Engineering Association. **Hobby:** Reading and Squash. **Credit Cards:** American Express, Diner's Club, Visa. **Priv. Addr.:** House No.3, Area-2, Str. 23, Tel.: 3544442, al-Nuzha, Kuwait.

MUFFARIJ (Abdallah, Ibrahim, al), Kuwaiti statesman. **Born** in 1937. **Educ.:** Kuwait and Egypt. **Dipl.:** Degree in Islamic Affairs, Cairo University (1959). **Career:** Assistant Under-Secretary, Social and Cultural Affairs, Ministry of Education (1973-75); Minister of Justice, Waqfs and Islamic Affairs (Feb. 1975- September 1976); Minister of Justice (February 16, 1978). **Addr.:** Kuwait City, Kuwait.

MUFTI (Ezzat Kamel), Saudi civil servant. **Born** in 1936 in Medina, Saudi Arabia. **Son** of Kamel Mufti (deceased) **and** Mrs. Zuhriya Mochieddin al-Shaqoun. **Married** in 1962 in Jeddah to Maqboula Mohd. Momina, 4 children: Hala (1965), Mahla (1968), Khaled (1973) and Kholoud (1979). **Dipl.:** B.A. (Public Administration), King Abdul Aziz University, Jeddah. **Career:** Director, Foreign Information Department Branch, Ministry of Information, Jeddah and Editor "News from Saudi Arabia". **Medals:** From Tunisian Prime Minister and Taiwanese Minister of Finance. **Sport:** Swimming. **Hobby:** Reading. **Member:** Jeddah Literary Club; Jeddah Committee for Eradicating Illiteracy. **Prof. Addr.:** Ministry of Information, Foreign Information Department, Jeddah, Saudi Arabia.

MUFTI (Fouad Sadik), Saudi diplomat. **Born** on December 31, 1938 in Medina, Saudi Arabia. **Dipl.:** B.A. Political Science. **Career:** Started Working for the Foreign Service in November 1960, and subsquently posted to Saudi Arabian Embassies in Lebanon, Republic of Mali, Switzerland, Republic of Cameroun and the Republic of

France; Appointed Saudi Arabian Ambassador to the Federal Republic of Nigeria in October 1982; Saudi Ambassador to the Republic of India in April 1985 Presently, Ambassador to the Republic of Lebanon. **Honours:** Legion d'Honneur awarded by the Republic of Cameroun and the Republic of France. **Publications:** Writes often for Saudi and Foreign newspapers and magazines on Politics and Economics and author of several romantic novels in Arabic. **Hobbies:** Literature and Music. **Addr.:** Home-100, Avenue President Kennedy, Paris, France. **Present Addr.:** Royal Embassy of Saudi Arabia, Beirut, Lebanon.

MUFTI (Khalid, Siraj), Saudi economist. **Born** in 1946 in Makkah. **Son** of Siraj Omer Mufti. **Married** in 1972, 3 sons. **Educ.:** Central Missouri State University. **Dipl.:** B.A. Economics (1973). M.Sc (1979). **Career:** SAMA (1973); Economic Research (1973); Petroleum Economics Department (1979); Director, Vice Governor's Office (1980); Senior Economist, Director General's Office, Foreign Department, Riyadh, Saudi Arabia. **Member:** Equestrian Club. **Hobbies:** Swimming, Football and Volleyball. **Addr.:** P.O.Box 7040, Tel. 4787400, Telex: 200350 A/B SAMA Sj, Riyadh, Saudi Arabia.

MUFTI (Mohamad Mohamad), Saudi official. **Born** in 1943 in Mecca, Saudi Arabia. **Dipl.:** B.A. (Economics). **Career:** Accountant, Central Planning Organization, later Treasurer, then Assistant Director General of Administration, Central Planning Organization, which in 1975 became the Ministry of Planning; Assistant Deputy at Ministry of Planning for Administrative and Financial Affairs. **Hobby:** Sport. **Prof. Addr.:** Ministry of Planning, Tel.: 4013292, Riyadh. **Priv. Addr.:** Tel.: 4762613, Riyadh, Saudi Arabia.

MUFTY (Ali Abdel Moneim, al), Egyptian ophtalmolgist. **Born** on September 27, 1945 in Cairo, Egypt. **Married**, two children, **Educ.:** Cairo University, Egypt. **Dipl.:** Ph.D. in Ophtalmogy. **Career:** Tutor in Ophtalmology at Cairo University (1971-76), then Assistant Professor (1980-85); Member of the Egyptian Ophtalmological Society (since 197?), of the Egyptian Medical Association (since 1970) and of the American Academy of Ophtalmogy (since 1982). **Publ.:** "Vitreous Surgey" (1982), "Retinal Surgery" (1984). **Awards:** two awards from Cairo University (1968). **Addr.:** 30 Shargaret el Dor, Zamalek, Tel.: 407253, 709714, Cairo, Egypt.

MUHIEDDINE (Abdurrazzaq), Iraqi politician. **Born** in Iraq. **Educ.:** Secondary and Higher. **Dipl.:** Doctorate. **Career:** Minister of Unity Affairs (1965-66); General Secretary of the Political Committee created between Iraq and the Arab Republic of Egypt Minister of State (1967-68); **Addr.:** Baghdad, Iraq.

MUHIEDDINE (Ahmad Fuad, Dr.), Egyptian statesman. **Born** on February 16, 1926. **Married**, 2 children. **Dipl.:** Bachelor of Medicine & Surgery (1949); Diploma of Radiology (1952); M.D. in Diagnostic Radiology (1958); Graduate of the National Institute for Management Development (1961); Studies in Law and Political Economy, Faculty of Law (1951-53, 1957-58). **Career:** Member of the Students' Union at the Faculty of Medicine (1943-49); Vice-President of the Students' Union at the Faculty of Medicine (1945-49); Secretary of the Students' General Executive Committee (1946); House Officer at Kasr el-Eini Faculty of Medicine (1950); Resident at Kasr el-Eini Faculty of Medicine (1951-52); Clinical Demonstrator and Tutor at Kasr el-Eini Faculty of Medicine (1952-53); Office Director of Public Health Minister (1953-54); Head, Radiology Department, Ministry of Public Health (1956-57); Secretary General, Doctors Syndicate and Secretary General of Medical Professions Union (1956-65); Head, Executive Bureau for Protection against Ionizing radiations (1962-63); Assistant Professor, Kasr el-Eini Faculty of Medicine (1964-68); Head, Parliamentary Group of Menoufia Governorate (1964-68); Secretary of the Socialist Union of Kalyoubia Governorate (1965-68); Governor of el-Shrarkia (1968-71); Governor of Alexandria (1971-72); Governor of el-Guiza (1972-73); Minister of State for Local Government and Popular Organizations (1973-74); Resident Minister in Libya (1974); Head of the High Council of Youth and Sports (1974); Minister of Health (1974-76); Minister of the People's Assembly's Affairs (1976-78); Member of the Politbureau of the National Democratic Party (1979); attended Interparliamentary Union Conferences (15 times); Elected Chairman of Non-Self Government countries and Ethnic Questions in the Interparliamentary Union (5 times); Elected Honorary Member of the Interparliamentary Union; Member of the National Assembly and the People's Assembly (5 terms): Chairman of the Health Affairs Committee (1960), Chairman of the Arab Affairs Committee (1965), Chairman of the Foreign Relations Committee (1978); Prime Minister and Minister al-Azhar (1981-84). **Publ.:** Researches and studies published in political and different Scientific Spheres. **Addr.:** The People's Assembly, Cairo, Arab Republic of Egypt.

MUHIEDDINE (Khaled), Egyptian politician. **Born** in 1922 in Egypt. **Educ.:** University of Cairo. **Dipl.:** Bachelor of Arts (Economics). **Career:** Officer in the Army; Journalist; Elected Deputy; Director of "al-Massa", then "al-Akhba'" then "Akhbar al-Yawm"; General Secretary, National Council for Peace (Cairo); Leader of several Egyptian delegations all over the world; Chairman, Assembly Commission Public services; elected to the People's Assembly (Oct. 1976); Leader, National Progressive Unionist Party. **Award:** Lenin Peace Prize (1970). **Addr.:** National Progressive Unionist Party, 1 Sharia Karim ed Dawlah, Cairo, Egypt. **Priv. Addr.:** 6 Gezira Street, Zamalek, Cairo, Egypt.

MUHIEDDINE (Offat, Mahmoud), Egyptian physician. **Born** in Cairo, Egypt in 1922. **Son** of Mahmoud Muhieddine. **Married**, three children. **Educ.:** Cairo University. **Dipl.:** M.D. in Haematology. **Career:** Tutor, Cairo University (1957); Assistant Professor (1960); Professor of Haematology (1970); Professor of Clinical Pathology. Member of the Egyptian Paediatric Association, Chairman of the Egyptian Association of Haematology. **Member** of Gezira Sporting Club, Royal Automobile Club. **Addr.:** 10 Falaki Square, Badrawi Bldg., Cairo, Egypt.

MUHIEDDINE (Zakaria, Abdulmagid), Egyptian army officer, former deputy president of Egypt. **Born** on May 7, 1918 in Kafr Shoukr, Dakahlieh Province. **Son** of Abdulmagid Muhieddine. **Educ.:** Military College and Staff College (1937). **Career:** Army Officer, Formerly Lecturer Military College and Staff College, promoted Lieutenant Colonel; Member, Command Council of Revolution (1952); Minister of the Interior and Director General of General Intelligence Service (1954-58); Deputy President of Egypt (1960-68); Prime Minister (1965-66); Retired 1969. **Awards:** Liberation Medal, Muhammad Ali Gold Medal, Palestine Medal. **Member:** Army officers Club, Gezira Sporting Club, president Rowing Federation. **Addr.:** 52 al-Thawra Street, Dokki, Cairo, Egypt and 68, Khalifa al-Maamoun Street, Manchiet al-Bakri, Cairo, Egypt.

MUHTADY (Farid Jalal, al), Saudi professor of pharmacy. **Born** in 1939. **Educ.:** Ph.D., London University. **Career:** Lecturer in Phytochemistry (1969-74); Vice dean, Faculty of Pharmacy (1971-73); Head of Pharmacology Department, Faculty of Pharmacy, King Saud University. **Member:** Council of King Saud University; attended Conference on the Message of the University, Riyadh, Fifth Conference of Pharmacology, Dublin, Conference of the British Society of Pharmacists, London. **Publications:** research articles on the medical plants of Saudi Arabia published in local and foreign journals. **Hobbies:** research, reading. **Address:** Faculty of Pharmacy, King Saud University, Tel.: 4765829, Riyad, Saudi Arabia.

MUJAHID (Abdulaziz Mohamad, al), Saudi academic. **Born** in 1951 in Riyadh, Saudi Arabia. **Dipl.:** B.Sc., M.Sc., Ph.D. (Mechanical Engineering). **Career:** Demonstrator, Faculty of Engineering, King Saud University (1974-75); Assistant Professor, Faculty of Engineering, King Saud University. **Member:** International Solar Energy Society, American Society of Mechanical Engineers. **Publications:** four technical papers. **Hobbies:** sports, travel. **Prof. Addr.:** Department of Mechanical Engineering, Faculty of Engineering, King Saud University, P.O.Box 800, Tel.: 4351311, Riyadh. **Priv. Addr.:** Tel.: 4811000, Ext. 2491, Saudi Arabia.

MUKHTAR (Ali Mohamad Abbas), Saudi official. **Born** in 1931 in Mecca, Saudi Arabia. **Dipl.:** Diploma (General Administration), American College, Beirut. **Career:** Secretary General, Directorate of Petroleum and Minerals; Director of Immigration' Jeddah; Director General of Office of the Minister of Hajj; Deputy Minister of Hajj and Endowments; founded Haram Benevolent Fund, Mecca; Assistant Secretary General of the Higher International Council of Mosques, Muslim World League. **Member:** of Mecca Welfare Society; attended several conferences in Egypt and Beirut pertinent to Tourism; other conferences in various Islamic countries in South East Asia, Europe and Africa, for the propagation of Islam; adviser to Mecca Cultural Club. **Publications:** The Mosque Strategy in Islam; Pilgrim's Guide. **Hobbies:** Swimming, reading, travel. **Prof. Addr.:** Muslim World League, Tel.: 5423845, Mecca. **Priv. Addr.:** Tel.: 5743573, Mecca, Saudi Arabia.

MUKHTAR (Fuad Muhammad), Saudi civil servant. **Born** in 1936. **Educ.:** University of Surrey. UK: attented Chartered Accountancy Training course with Whinney Murray & Co. Chartered Accounts, London, UK. **Dipl.:** B.Com. (Accountancy). **Career:** Manager, Revenues Audit Administration of Saudi Arabian Airlines (SAUDIA); Chief of the Individual Companies Department at the Ministry of Commerce Branch, Jeddah; Chairman of the Board for the Settlement of Commercial Disputes; Assistant Director for Industry; Director of Home Trade Department of the Ministry of Commerce; Director and Board Member of Jeddah Industrial Estate, Jeddah. **Hobbies:** reading, travel, listenning to music. **Prof. Addr.:** Jeddah Industrial Estate, Tel.: 34929, Jeddah, Saudi Arabia.

MUKHTAR (Muhammad Gamaliddin), Egyptian archaeologist. **Born** on July 14, 1918 in Alexandria. **Educ.:** Cairo University, Cairo; Iowa State Teachers College; Ain Shams University, Cairo. **Dipl.:** M.A. in Archaeology; Diploma in Education; Ph.D. in Archaeology. **Career:** Assistant Lecturer at the Institute of Education in Alexandria (1914); Lecturer of the Teachers Institute, Cairo (1950); Assistant Professor at the Faculty of Education, Cairo (1956); Head of Scientific Section, Centre of Documentation, Cairo (1957); Director General, Egyptian Department of Antiquities (1967); Under Secretary of State for Antiquities (1968); President, Egyptian Organization of Antiquities (1972); Vice President of International Council of Monuments and Sites, Paris (since 1974); Professor of History and Archaeology, Helwan University (1977); Professor of Archaeology, Faculty of Arts, Riyadh University (1978-); Honorary President of the International Society of Egyptology; Honorary Member of the German, Czechoslovakian and Austrian Archaelogical Societies; Honorary Member of the American Centre of Research, Cairo; Vice President and Member of the Scientific Committee for Drafing the General History of Africa, UNESCO; Member of the Permanent Committee of Archaeological Department, Ministry of Culture. **Dipl.:** numerous books and articles (in Arabic, English and

French); Director of the "Encyclopedia of Egyptian Civilization", Cairo, Volume I (1974), Volume II (1976); Director of Second Volume of "History of Africa", UNESCO (1980) (Arabic, English and French). **Awards:** Honorary Doctor, University of Montpellier, France (1972); Officier of the Legion of Honour. France; Commander of the Legion of Hounour; decorations from Universities and cultural organizations as well as several decorations and medals from Germany, Italy, Poland, Austria and Columbia. **Addr.:** 16 el-Sahab Street, Pyramids Road, Tel.: 852525, Cairo, Egypt; 22 Murad Street, Giza, Tel.: 853535, Cairo, Egypt.

MUKHTAR (Mustapha, Ahmad), Egyptian diplomat. **Born** on March 3, 1919 in Kamaran Island (Red Sea). **Son** of Ahmad Moukhtar **and** Mrs., née Rafiya Sarmad. **Married** to Miss Nihayat Sarmad on June 11, 1946, 4 children; Imam, Amina, Amani, Mohamad. **Dipl.:** Secondary Certificate, Alexandria, Lycée Français (1938); Philosophy (1940), Bachelor of Military Science, Cairo Military Academy (1942). **Career:** Commander Egyptian Army (1942), promoted to Colonel (1960), served Alamein, Suez (1942), Palestine (1948); Military Attaché Czechoslovakia and Yugoslavia (1955-59); Assigned Presidential Office (1960-62); Joined Ministry of Foreign Affairs (1962); Consul General in San Francisco (1962-67); Ambassador to Rumania (1968-69); Ambassador to Hungary (1970-73); Ambassador to Sweden (1973). **Awards:** Order of the Republic (1st class), Egypt; Order of the Nile, Egypt; Order of Merit (1st class), Egypt; Star of the Yugoslav Army; Order of the Hungarian People. **Sports:** Swimming and athletics **Addr.:** Ministry of Foreign Affairs, Cairo. Egypt.

MUKHTAR (Ridha Mohamad Abbas), Saudi diplomat. **Born** in 1937 in Jeddah, Saudi Arabia. **Educ.:** secondary school certificate. **Career:** Employee at the Foreign Ministry 1956, then served in Royal Saudi Arabian Embassies in Ankara, Paris and Teheran; Chargé d'Affaires, Royal Saudi Arabian Embassy, Nouakchott, Mauritania; Chargé d'Affaires, Saudi Embassy, Canada. **Hobbies:** music, sport. **Address:** Ministry of Foreign Affairs, Jeddah, Saudi Arabia.

MULHIM (Mohamad Abdellatif, al), Saudi politician. **Born** in 1937 in Hofuf. **Educ.:** LL.B. (Law), Cairo University (1962); LL.M., Yale Law School. Yale University U.S.A. (1966); J.S.D. Yale Law School (1970); Ph.D. **Career:** Assistant Professor of Law, King Saud University; Dean, Faculty of Administrative Sciences (formerly Faculty of Commerce), King Saud University (1974-75); Minister of State and Member of the Council of Ministers, (1975). **Member:** of various Ministerial committees; former member of Saudia, the Arab Organization Industry; Board of Directors, the Arab Organization of Industry; the council of the Civil Service. **Honours:** King Abdulaziz Order of Merit-Second Class. **Hobbies:** reading. listening to the radio. **Prof. Addr.:** P.O.Box 1800, Riyadh. **Priv. Addr.:** Tel.: 4761577, Riyadh, Saudi Arabia.

MULLA (Badr, Abdallah), Kuwaiti director of companies, honorary consul of Norway in Kuwait. **Born** on September 20, 1937 in Kuwait. **Son** of Abdallah Mulla Saleh (Secretary of State and Company Director). **Educ.:** Victoria College of Alexandria (Egypt). **Career:** Secretary of State of Kuwait (1955-61); Chairman of the following companies: Bader al-Mulla and Bros, Saleh Jamal and Co., Kuwait Commercial Agency, Director of Kuwait Limestone Co., Kuwait Pipe Co., Kuwait Insurance Co., Americana; One of the Board members of: Gazelle Club, Kuwait (wholly owned); Annabel's London (Partly owned), Representative of: Chrysler Corporation, B.M.C., Export Sales Ltd., U.S. Royal Philco Corporation, G.E.C., National Cash Register, PYE Ltd., Chriscraft Boats, Middle East Air-lines, K.L.M., Iraqi Airways, Shipping Lines, Concordia Line, Compagnie Maritime Belge S.A., Everett Star Line., **Dist.:** Key to the City of Detroit. **Sports:** Water Skiing and Horse Riding. **Prof. Addr.:** as-Sour Street, Kuwait, Tel.: 23231. **Priv. Addr.:** Omar Ben al-Khattab Street, Tel.: 32402, Kuwait.

MULLA HUSSAIN (Nazar Abdel Rahman), Kuwaiti marine biologist. **Born** in 1947. **Married**, two children. **Educ.:** Western Michigan University, USA. **Dipl.:** B.Sc. (in Biology and chemistry) (1970). **Career:** Member ofthe Board of United Fisheries of Kuwait (1972-); Board Member of Agricultural Projects Company (1984-); Chairman of the Board of Directors of Bibiyan Fisheries Co. (1985-); Deputy General of Kuwait Institute for Scientific Research (1982-); **Publ.:** author and co-author of papers and several articles on marine biological subjects. **Member:** World Mariculture Society; Marine Biological Association of the UK; American Fisheries Society. **Hobby:** gardning. **Prof. Addr.:** P.O.Box 24885, Safat, Tel.: 834378, Telex: 22299 KISR KT, Kuwait, Kuwait. **Priv. Addr.:** House 19, Street 3, Tel.: 5384714, Kuwait, Kuwait.

MULLANE (Terence John), Hon. Consul-General of Morocco in Australia. **Born** on January 28, 1950 in Sydney, Australia. **Son** of Arthur **and** Shirley. **Married** to Gae, 3 children: Rhett, Grant and Rosie. **Educ.:** Marist Brothers College-Eastwood, NSW, Australia. **Career:** Appointed Consul-General of Morocco to Australia and Pacific States in 1980, Paqua New Guinea, Tonga and Vanuatu. Appointed Regional Delegate, Australasia/Pacific of O.N.M.T. in 1986. Elected President, Australian Arab Chamber of Commerce and Industry Inc in 1995. **Sports:** Swimming, Surf Life Saving, diving. **Hobbies:** Reading in Arab and African history and geography. **Memberships:** Australian Arab Chamber of Commerce, North Curl Curl SLSC. **Decorations:** Officer Al-Wassim Alaoui. **Prof. Addr.:** Consulate-General of the Kingdom of Morocco, 11 West Street, North Sydney, NSW, 2060, Tel.: 9957 6717, Australia.

MUMMAR (Abdallah Ibn Abdulaziz Ibn Dr.), Saudi Politician. **Born** in 1950. **Educ.:** B.A., Economics, International American University, California, USA (1976); M.B.A., fornia, USA (1978); M.A., Social Sciences, University of California, Irvine (1981); Department of Research and Studies, General Secretariat of Labor Force (1983); Consultant Office of the Minister of Agriculture (1988); Deputy Minister of Agriculture and Water (1988); Minister of Agriculture and Water (1995-to date). **Address:** Ministry of Agriculture and Water, Airport Road, Riyadh 1195, Saudi Arabia.

MUMNI (Hassan Ahmad, al), Jordanian politician. **Born** on November 11, 1937 in Jordan. **Married,** seven children. **Educ.:** University of Baghdad, Iraq. **Dipl.:** B.A. (in Law). **Career:** Clains Officer in Kuwait; Income Tax Officer (1962-65); Director of Judicial Affairs at the Ministry of Interior (1965-70); Provincial Governor, Minister of Interior (1970-77); Mayor of Irbid (1977-79); Member, National Consultative Council (1980); Minister of Municipal Rural Affairs and the Environment (1980-85). **Publ.:** several works on municipal affairs and local government (in Arabic). **Award:** Order of the Jordanian Star (1981). **Prof. Addr.:** P.O.Box 1799, Tel.: 8785655, Amman, Jordan.

MUNAIS (Abdullatif Abdulkarim, al), Kuwaiti businessman. **Career:** Proprietor of Abdullatif Abdul Karim Munaies and Munaies Trading & Contracting Est.; both Companies working as direct importers and commission agents in foodstuffs items. **Credit Cards:** Visacard of the Commercial Bank of Kuwait SAK. **Prof. Addr.:** P.O.Box 2446 and P.O.Box 44058, Tel.: 432902, 432085 and 416327, Safat, Kuwait. **Priv. Addr.:** Tel.: 514194, Safat, Kuwait.

MUNAIS (Sami, Ahmad Abdelaziz, al), Kuwaiti journalist. **Born** in 1933 in Kuwait. **Son** of Abdelaziz al-Munais. **Career:** Member of Department of Public Health (1958-63); Chief Editor, "al-Talia" weekly (since 1963); member of National Assembly (1963-65) and (1971-75); elected Secretary of Assembly; elected President of Kuwait Journalists Association (1972). **Addr.:** al-Talia, P.O.B. 1082, Mubarak al Kabir Street, Kuwait.

MUNAJED (Abdul-Hamid, al), Syrian former minister of State. **Born** in 1931 in Homs, Syria. **Son** of Mahmoud al-Munajed (Trader) **and** Mrs., née Fawzieh Tanoura. **Married** in 1956 in Homs to Miss Hind Sharafedine, 5 children: Maha, Mohamad Fawaz, Amal, Eman and Mohamad Kusai. **Educ.:** Khaled Ibn al-Walid Secondary School; Homs Damascus University, syria; Sorbonne University, Paris. **Dipl.:** Secondary Cert. (Scientific); Bachelor of Natural Sciences; Education diploma; Doctorate in Paleontology. **Career:** Teacher; Inspector; Minister of State for Environmental Affairs, Syria until March 2000. **Medals:** Awarded several medals in the fields of Biological and Chemicals Sciences. **Sport:** Football. **Hobby:** Reading. **Member:** Teachers' Association. **Priv. Addr.:** Homs, Tel.: 25927, Syria.

MUNJIM (Ali, Abdallah, al), Saudi businessman. **Born** in 1943 in Saudi Arabia. **Son** of Abdallah al-Munjim. **Married,** five children. **Educ.:** General. **Career:** Deputy Director, Abdallah Ali al-Munjim Stores; Director General, Abdallah Ali al-Munjim Fridges and Stores, Riyadh Company for Trade and Refrigeration, Barida Company for Trade and Refrigeration. Member of the Board of the Chamber of Commerce and Industry, Riyadh. **Addr.:** P.O.Box 1544, Tel.: 4766126, 4767127, Riyadh, Saudi Arabia.

MUNSHI (Zaki M.N.), Saudi executive. **Born** in 1941 in Mecca. **Educ.:** Ph.D. **Career:** Director of National Research Laboratory. **Member** of ASP, BGRG, RSS, AAG, SPSE and IBG. **Publications:** in land form classification, land evaluation, Geomorphology, Arid land. **Hobbies:** football, table tennis, chess. **Prof. Addr.:** National Centre for Science and Technology, P.O.Box 6086, Tel.: 4779370, 4788000 Ext. 408, Riyadh. **Priv. Addr.:** Tel.: 4645082, Riyadh, Saudi Arabia.

MUNTASSER (Issam Hussain), Egyptian economist. **Born** on May 1st, 1935 in Egypt. **Married,** two children. **Educ.:** Ain Shams University, Cairo University, Egypt; Princeton University. **Dipl.:** B.A. (Law) and diploma in Economic (1957); M.A. (1964); diploma in Demography (1965); Ph.Dd. in Economics (1972). **Career:** Ministry of Foreign Affairs, Cairo, Egypt (1956-62), (1967-69); Egypty Price Planning Agency (1973); Head of Analysis Division, Projection and Long Term Planing, Ministry of Planning, Cairo (1974-76); Under Secretary of State, Plan Construction Unity Council (1978-79); Professor of Economics, American University of Cairo, Cairo (1979-80); Director of UN African Institute of Economic Development and Planing (IDEP), Dakar, Senegal. **Publ.:** numerous research papers and books (in Arabic and English). **Awards:** State Merit Prize for Economics, Egypt (1981). **Hobbies:** Photography, tennis. **Prof. Addr.:** IDEP, P.O.Box 3186, Dakar, Senegal. **Priv. Addr.:** 22 Taha Hussain Street, Apt. 29, Tel.: 407333, Zamalek, Cairo, Egypt.

MUNTASSER (Omar, Mustafa), Libyan politician. **Born** in 1939 in Misurata (Libya). **Son** of Mustafa Muntasser **and** Mrs., née Aisha Taher. **Married** on Oct. 1963 to Sabria el-Jiamal, in Misurata (Libya), 6 children: Ghada, Tayeb, Maysam, Rasha, Hitaf and Mustafa. **Educ.:** Victoria College, Alexandria, (Egypt, 1949-57); American University in Beirut, Lebanon (1958-60 & 1966-67). **Dipl.:** B.B.A. **Career:** Joined Mobil Oil, Libya (1960-67); Engineering Transportation and Materials Analyst; Director of Economic Department, Ministry of Petroleum (1969-70); Deputy Director General, National Oil Corporation (1970-71); Under-Secretary, Ministry of Petroleum

(1971-74); Chairman Oasis Oil Company of Libya; Chairman and Managing Director, National Oil Corporation, Tripoli, (Libya) (Oct. 1975- Feb. 1979); Secretary of Heavy Industries; (Feb. 1979- Feb. 86); Secretary-General of the General People's Committee; (Feb. 1987- Oct. 1990). Chairman, Board of Governors, Organisation of Oil Exporting Countries (OPEC); Secretary General of the GPC for Economic Planning (1990-1993); Currently Secretary General of the GPC for Foreign Liaison and International Cooperation (Nov. 1992-). **Sport:** Swimming. **Hobby:** Gardening. **Priv. Addr.:** Hadba Khadra, Tel.: 904775, Tripoli, Libya.

MURAD (Murad Ali), Bahraini banker. **Born** in 1954 in Manama, Bahrain. **Married**, two sons. **Educ.:** Institute of Cost and Management, UK. **Dipl.:** General Certificate of Education. **Career:** Citibank (1972-76); National Bank of Bahrain (1977-79); Board Member of Arab Asian Bank; Council Member of Bankers Society of Bahrain; General Manager of Saudi National Commercial Bank, Bahrain (1979); Presently, General Manager, Bank of Bahrain and Kuwait. **Hobbies:** jogging, soccer. **Member:** Arab Bankers Associations, London, UK. **Addr.:** P.O.Box 597, Manama, Bahrain.

MURAYWED (Hassan), Syrian politician. **Born** in 1927 in Kuneitra, Syria. **Educ.:** Secondary and Higher. **Dipl.:** B.A., American University of Beirut, Ph.D. Political Economy, University of Wisconsin, Madison, USA. **Career:** Ministry of Foreign Affairs, Minister of Foreign Affairs (1964-65), Member of the Council of Ministers (1965), Professor, University of Damascus; Member, Executive Board, UNESCO (1974). **Member:** Commissions of Education and Foreign Affairs, Syrian National Council; Syrian Delegation to UN General Assembly. **Publ.:** Articles and studies on comparative international relations, national and universal culture and political economy. **Addr.:** Damascus, Syria.

MURSHID (Ali al-Murshid ben Mohamad, al), Saudi academic. **Born** in 1947 in Buraidah, Saudi Arabia. **Dipl.:** B.LI. (Islamic Law) (1970); M.LI. (Comparative Jurisprudence), al-Azhar University, Cairo, Egypt (1974). **Career:** Secretary, Private Cabinet, Board of Grievances, Riyadh (1966-67); teacher, Ministry of Education (1968-70); attended Conference of the Middle East Committee for the Affairs of the Blind, Riyadh (1972); now Director of Al Nour School for the Blind, Medina. **Member:** Islamic Orientation Committee, Administrative Board for Private Education; Head, Charity Fund, al-Nour School, Medina. **Publications:** three books on Islamis Jurisprudence, including The Crime of Highway Robbery and its Penalty According to Islam, Prescribed and Unprescribed Penalties in Islam. **Hobbies:** Reading, excursions, writing, public service in the field of Islamic Orientation. **Prof. Addr.:** P.O.Box. 1438, Medina, Saudi Arabia.

MURSHID (Reda Abdul Ilah), Saudi politician. **Born** in 1933 in Medina. **Educ.:** B.A. (Business Administration); M.A. (Public Administration), University of Southern California, U.S.A. **Career:** Administrative Assistant to H.E. Minister of Finance and National Economy; Director of Personnel and Senior Administrative Analysts, Central Department for Organization and Administration; Director General of Economic Studies; Assistant Deputy Minister for Pilgrims Affairs, Ministry of Pilgrimage and Endowments. **Member:** the Muslim Association, Los Angeles, California, the Constituent Committee of Saudi Transport Co., and the General Assembly of Arab Tourism Federation; has attended several meetings of formal committees within the Kingdom and abroad; chaired the Saudi delegation to the International Tourism Conference in Spain (1979) and the Philippines (1980); member, Board of Editors, Islamic Consolidation magazine published by the Ministry of Pilgrimage and Endowments. **Honours:** Traveller's Certificate, awarded by Arkansas State Governor, 1975. **Publications:** reports and research articles on finance, commerce, pilgrimage and endowments. **Hobbies:** reading, tourism. **Prof. Addr.:** Ministry of Pilgrimage and Endowments, Riyadh, or P.O.Box. 7585, Tel.: 4010904, Riyadh. **Priv. Addr.:** Tel.: 4788553, Riyadh, Saudi Arabia.

MURSHID (Samir Asad), Saudi academic. **Born** in 1948 in Medina. **Educ.:** B.A. (Political Science); M.P.A., Ph.D. (Government). **Career:** Lecturer, Department of Public Administration, King Abdulaziz University (1974); Assistant Professor, Department of Public Administration, Faculty of Economics and Administration and Vice Dean, Deanship of External Studies, King Abdulaziz University. **Member:** the American Society for Public Administration, the International Institute of Administrative Sciences, the Council of the Faculty of Economics and Administration, KAU and the professional staff, al-Murshid Management Service. **Publications:** Ways to Foil the Oil Cartel: A response, OPEC Bulletin, April 1979; An Evaluation of the Academic Programme at the Faculty of Economics and Administration, a joint research work to be completed in early 1983; OPEC: Its Role as Residual Oil Supplier (Ph.D. thesis). **Hobbies:** reading, swimming, tennis. **Prof. Addr.:** Faculty of Economics and Administration, King Abdulaziz University, Tel.: 6879202, Jeddah. **Priv. Addr.:** Tel.: 6314096, Jeddah, Saudi Arabia.

MURSHID (Talal Asad), Saudi academic. **Born** in 1946 in Medina. **Educ.:** Ph.D. in Public Administration. **Career:** Control and Investigation Board, Minister's office (1971-73); Demonstrator, Lecturer and then Assistant Professor, Faculty of Economics and Administration, King Abdulaziz University, since 1973; founder and Managing Director of al-Murshid Management Services. **Member:** American Society for Public Administration, American Society for Political Science, Pi Sigma Alpha Sigma; Chairman of the Board of Directors, al-Murshid Management Services; has attended various conferences and meetings of societies and organizations, related to career. **Publications:** several research papers. **Prof. Addr.:** P.O.Box. 2908, Tel.: 6603236, Jeddah. **Priv. Addr.:** Tel.: 6886366, Jeddah, Saudi Arabia.

MURSI (al-Sayyid Abdulwahab), Egyptian painter. **Born** in 1931 in Cairo, Egypt. **Son** of Abdulwahab Mursi. **Married**, two children. **Educ.:** B.A., Fine Arts, Cairo University, Egypt (1957); Diploma, Arts Institute for Teachers (1958). **Career:** Painter, General Supervisor of Exhibitions, General Organisation of Arts and Literature; Minister of Education (1977); member of Fine Arts Graduates Association; several exhibitions in European and Arab Countries, including Museum of Modern Art, Cairo, Museum of Alexandria, Museum of Barcelona, The Goethe Institute, Cairo; Exhibitions in Paris and Frankfurt (1981). **Medals:** Many prizes including Second Prize from Biennale Exhibition at Alexandria (1970); Biennale Exhibition at Barcelona, Spain (1971); Biennale Exhibitions in Paris and Madrid. **Hobbies:** Creative art. **Addr.:** 7 Sharia Dr. Mustafa al-Nagdi, al-Sirkh Quarter, Shubra, Tel.: 640905, Cairo, Egypt.

MURSI (Fuad, Kamel), Egyptian international civil servant. **Born** on December 16, 1924, Minya (Egypt). **Married** with children. **Educ.:** Military Academy College, Cairo, Pilot Officer; Faculty of Law, Cairo University; McGill University, Montreal (Canada); Yale University (USA). **Dipl.:** LL.B., LL.M. (Air Law). **Career:** Controller, Civil Aviation Department (1947-50); Chief, Area Control Centre, Civil Aviation Department (Egypt, 1950-53); Scholarship studies USA and Canada (1953-55); Director, Air Transport, Civil Aviation Department (1955-62); Assistant Director General, Civil Aviation Department (1963-65); Deputy Director General, Civil Aviation Department (1965-68); Director General Aeronautics, Civil Aviation Authority (Egypt, 1968-71); Adviser to the Minister of Civil Aviation, Egypt (1971-73); Representative of Egypt, International Civil Aviation Organization (ICAO) Council (Canada). (1974-82). **Priv. Addr.:** 3, el-Misaha Street, Dokki District, Tel.: 848879, Cairo, Egypt.

MURSI (Ibrahim, Guider), Libyan, Director General of Arab Labour Organization. **Born** on July 27, 1947 in Benghazi, Libyan Jamaheria. **Son** of Guider Mursi - Businessman. **and** Mrs. née Jazia Khalil. **Married** on August 27, 1970 in Benghazi to Souad El Manqoush, four children: Guider, Nermeen, Sameh, Noha. **Educ.:** Bachelor of Social Studies, University of Benghazi, Master of Social and Administration Management - University of Cairo A.R.E. **Dipl.:** High National Diploma of Management - University of Granfield College, U.K. **Career:** Minister of Youth and Sports in Libya (1980-1984); Minister of Social Insurance in Libya (1984-1991); Minister of Manpower in Libya (1991-1999). **Other Information:** President of the Arab Family Organization based Tunisia; Vice President of World Family Organization - Based Paris. **Sports Practised:** Jogging, Tennis, Football.**Hobby:** Reading. **Clubs:** El Gezira Club, Cairo - El Ahly Club/ Benghazi. **Credit Cards:** Visa Master - American Diners. **Prof. Addr.:** 7 Messaha Square, El Dokkie, P.O.Box 814 Cairo, Tel.: 3362724, Cairo, Egypt. **Priv. Addr.:** 44 Syria Str., El Mohandesseen, Tel.: 3387866, Cairo, Egypt.

MURSI (Mohamad Khairi), Egyptian university professor. **Born** in 1917 in Alexandria, Egypt. **Son** of Hage Mohamad Mursi **and** Mrs., née Nabawya Darwiche. **Married** in 1941 to Miss Azima Ahmad Ibrahim, 4 children: Amal, Bahar, Laila and Mohamad. **Educ.:** Universities of Cairo and London. **Dipl.:** Bachelor of Arts, Doctor in Philosophy (Psychology). **Career:** Professor, Aïn Shams University since 1952; Dean of Faculty of Arts, Aïn Shams University; Professor, Riyadh University **Publ.:** Author of several studies and books. **Awards:** Merit Medal (First Class). **Sport:** Travelling. **Hobby:** Reading. **Prof. Addr.:** Riyadh University, Tel. 22233, Riyadh, Saudi Arabia. **Priv. Addr.:** Cairo, Egypt.

MUSALLAM (Ali Abdul Rahman, al), Saudi civil servant. **Born** at Qassim in 1935. **Dipl.:** M.A.(Political Science). **Career:** Assistant Principal, al-Ilmi Religious Institute, al-Ahsa; Secretary, Secondary Education Department, Ministry of Education, later Assistant Director, Personnel Department; Director, Organization Division, Ministry of Agriculture; Director-General of Organization; Planning and Budgeting Department, Ministry of Agriculture; attended several general conferences of Food and Agriculture Organisation (FAO), Rome (1969-75), Conference on the International Convention for the Disposal of Waste into the Sea (London), Conference on Human Nutrition (Paris), Conference of the International Agricultural Development Funds (Geneva), World Food Conference (Rome) and all FAO Regional Conferences; Director-General of Administration, Ministry of Agriculture and Water. **Sports:** Bowling. **Prof. Addr.:** P.O.Box 3560, Tel.: Riyadh, Saudi Arabia.

MUSALLAM (Sulaiman Hamad, al), Egyptian academic. **Born** in 1944 in Cairo, Egypt. **Dipl.:** Ph.D. **Career:** Head of Physics Department, Umm al-Qura University Mecca, Saudi Arabia (1975); Vice Dean, Faculty of Education, Umm al-Qura University (1976); Assistant Professor, Physics Department, Faculty of Applied Sciences and Engineering, Umm al-Qura University, Mecca. **Member:** Mecca Cultural Club; attended several Scientific Conferences. **Hobbies:** sports, swimming, reading. **Prof. Addr.:** Physics Department, Faculty of Applied Sciences and Engineering, Umm al-Qura University, Tel. 5564770/ 556540 Ext. 210, Mecca. **Priv. Addr.:** Tel. 5562137, Mecca, Saudi Arabia.

MUSAWI (Gazi, Radhi, al), Bahraini bank executive. **Born** in 1945 in Bahrain. **Married**, two sons. **Educ.:** Baghdad University, Iraq; Bangalore University. **Dipl.:** B.A. in Commerce (1967); M.A. in Economics (1971), **Career:** Teacher at the Kuwait (1971). Manager of Branches (1978); Deputy General Manager, Offshore Unit of Bank of Bahrain and Kuwait (1980-1990); **Hobbies:** reading, chess. **Addr.:** Manama, Bahrain.

MUSAWI (Muhsin, Jassim, al), Iraqi academic. **Born** July 1st, 1944 in Nasr, Iraq. **Married,** 4 children. **Educ.:** Dalhousie University, Canada. **Dipl.:** M.A. (1975); Ph.D. (1978). **Career:** Professor at Baghdad University (1978-83); Member of the Oriental Institue of Chicago, USA (1976-78); Chairman of the Mass Communications Department of Baghdad University (1980-83); Secretary General of Iraqi Union of Writers (1983-); President of Iraqi Critics Association (1983-); Editor-in-chief of AFAQ ARABIYA and Chairman of the Board of Cultural Affairs Directorate (1983-); **Publ.:** "The Revolutionary Theme in the Arabic Novel", (in Arabic) Baghdad (1973); "Scheherazade in England" (in English), USA (1981); "Modernism in the Iraqi Short Story", Beirut (1984); "The Age of the Novel", Baghdad (1985). **Award:** Venezuelan Award for the Arts (1986). **Member:** Journalist's Association (since 1968). **Prof. Addr.:** Afaq Arabiya, P.O.Box 4032, Tel.: 5372865, 4169549, Baghdad, Iraq.

MUSAWI (Salman, Radhi, al), Bahraini executive. **Born** in 1951 in Manama, Bahrain. **Son** of Radhi al-Musawi. **Married,** 2 sons 1 daughter. **Educ.:** University of Bahgdad, Iraq. **Dipl.:** B. Com. (1972). **Career:** External Auditor-Fakhroo Est. Public Accountant; Chief Accountant, Bahrain Monetary agency; Budget and Financial Controller, Ministry of Labour and Social Affairs; Deputy Manager, Manufacturers Hanover Trust Co.; Senior Vice President, United Gulf Bank. **Member:** Bahrain Accounting Society; Alumni Club; Bankers' Club; Uroba Club; al-Ahli Club. **Address:** P.O.Box 5964, Tel.: 233789, Telex 8556/7 A/B UGB ADM, Manama Bahrain.

MUSNAD (Abdulaziz Abdul Rahman, al), Saudi adviser. **Born** in 1938. **Dipl.:** B.A. (Islamic Law); Diploma (English Language). **Career:** General Secretary, Riyadh Welfare Society; General Director of several religious institutes and educational colleges; General Director, Riyadh Electric Company; an occasional lecturer at national universities and schools; an official delegate to several foreign countries; gave religious and social talks on Saudi Radio; presents a weekly social and religious programme on Saudi T.V.; Adviser, Ministry of Higher Education. **Member:** al-Jazirah for Press, Printing and Publishing and al-Gassiem Literary Club. **Publications:** al-Zawaj wal Muhour (Marriage and Dowries); al-Andalus: Tariekh wa Ebrah (Andalusia: History and a Lesson); al-Nahj al-Muhammady (The Muhammadan Path); Ghetha'a al-Rouh (Soul Nourishment); al-Elm al-Mafqoud Fi al-Mawaruth al-Islamiyyah (The Lost Science in Islamic Heritage). **Hobbies:** shooting, swimming, horse riding. **Prof. Addr.:** P.O.Box 17640, Tel. 4033064, Riyadh. **Priv. Addr.:** Tel. 4764773, Riyadh, Saudi Arabia.

MUSTAFA (Adnan, Prof. Dr.), Syrian Academic. **Born** on July 5, 1934 in Syria. **Married,** 4 children. **Educ.:** Ph.D. (Southampton University, England, U.K.- Nuclear Magnetism), CPhs., MInstP., MEPS, MAPS, MAAS, MAN, Professor of Physics, Head of Nuclear Magnetism and Energy Group (NEG)- Damascus University, Syria and Chairman of the Committee on «The Arab Academy of Sciences - ARAS». **Career:** 1969 Lecturer in Physics, Damascus University, Syria; 1970 Visiting Professor, The AUB, Beirut, Lebanon; 1971 Member of The Syrian Atomic Energy Committee, Syria; 1972 Consultant, The Ministry of Industry, Syria; 1973 Member of «The Uppsala Quantum Chemistry Group», Uppsala University, Sweden; 1974 Reader in Physics, Damascus University, Syria; 1974 Minister for Petroleum and Mineral Resources, Syria; 1977 Head of Physics Department, Damascus University, Syria; 1978 Professor of Physics, Damascus University, Syria; 1978 Visiting Professor to «The Science Policy Research Unit - SPRU», Sussex University, Brighton, England, U.K.; 1979 Visiting Professor to «The Cryogenics Institute», Southampton University, England, U.K.; 1979 Assistant Secretary General of OAPEC, Kuwait; 1983 Founder and Head of Nuclear Magnetism and Energy Group, NEG, Damascus University, Syria; 1985 Visiting Professor to «The International Centre for Theoretical Physics - ICTP», Trieste, Italy, 1986 Visiting Professor and Senior Fellow to «The Cryogenics Institute», Southampton University, England, U.K.; 1987 Referee to «The Energy Research Group - ERG», International Development Research Centre - IDRC, Ottawa, Canada; 1988 Chairman of the Committee on «The Arab Academy of Sciences, ARAS»; in 1991 Elected man of the year in the field of Energy R & D by «The International Biographical Centre, Cambridge, England, U.K.; in 1992 Elected man of the year in the field of Energy R & D by «The American Biographical Centre, Raleigh, North Carolina, USA. Since 1974, increasing involvment with energy R & D, Developmental Science and promotion of science in both developing and Arab Worlds. The start of NEG at Damascus University has activated the real collaboration of Syrian inter-university postgraduate research in physics since the late eighties. **Publ.:** «The Slide Ruler»; Dar al-Ma'aarif, Cairo, Egypt; «Experiments in Modern Physics», Damascus University; «Physics for Universities»; «Principles of Energy», Beirut; «Arab Nuclear Power»; «A new Survival Factor», Beirut, and several other articles and research papers published in various scientist and professional journals. **Addr.:** The Arab Academy of Sciences, The Founding Committee, P.O.Box 7726, Damascus, Syria, Telex: 411080 KALAI SY, Fax: 963 11 418 274.

MUSTAFA (Ahmad Farid), Egyptian academic. **Born** on 24 April 1939 in Alexandria, Egypt. **Dipl.:** B.Sc., M.A. and Ph.D. (Architecture). **Career:** Job Captain, Forrest

Coile and Associates, Washington, D.C.; Associate Professor, College of Engineering, Architecture Department, King Saud University; Dean, Faculty of Architecture and Planning, King Faisal University, Dammam. **Member:** Egyptian Society of Engineers. **Publications:** The Possibility of Applying the Values and Principles of the Islamic Arab Town to Contemporary Urban Planning (a book); The University Buildings in Baden-Wurttemberg, West Germany (a paper); New Jarudiyah, Development of a Prototype Low Rise/ High Density Residential Plan for Saudi Arabian Towns (a book); Ahmed Farid Moustapha, Architectural Works (1968-78). **Hobbies:** gymnastics, swimming. **Address:** P.O.Box 2397, Tel.: 8578206, 8577000, Dammam, Saudi Arabia.

MUSTAFA (Ali), Egyptian TV and film star. **Born** on April 21, 1932 in Cairo, Egypt. **Educ.:** Aboukeer Teacher's Training College, Alexandria, Lower Egypt (1954-59); started active life as teacher of mathematics at Sohag Secondary School, Sohag Governorate, Upper Egypt; transferred to Cairo in 1965, now full time TV and film star since 1966; portrayed various characters in more than 20 films, inclucing "Open Door", "Something in My Life", "Night-time Devis", "A Story from Back Home", "Tomorrow We Shall Love", "Diary of a Provincial Public Prosecutor" adapted to the screen from the novel of the same title by Tewfick el-Hakim, Egypt's leading novelist, art critic and essayist, "My Son", "Rabee's Father" etc... **Sports:** Swimming and tennis. **Hobbies:** Reading and music. **Prof. Addr.:** State TV Service, TV Building, Maspero District, Corniche Road, Cairo, Egypt.

MUSTAFA (Chaker, Ahmad), Syrian writer, **Born** in 1921 in Damascus. **Son** of Ahmad Mustafa. **Educ.:** Universities of Damascus and Cairo. **Dipl.:** B.A. **Career:** Ministry of Education (Damascus, Hauran), Librarian at the University of Damascus (1954). **Publ.:** Author of More than 25 books eg. "Hadarat at Tin", "Bainiwa Bainak", "Fi Rikab al-Shaitan", "al-Shi'r wan Nass", "Ma' Goghrafiat al-Bilad al-Arabia", "Maa' Baad az Zoumala", "Fil Tarikh al-Abbassi". **Addr.:** Cha'lan, Tel.: 114289, Damascus, Syria.

MUSTAFA (Farouk, Yusuf), Sudanese bank executive. **Born** in 1938 in Khartoum. **Son** of Yusuf Mustafa. **Married** in 1965, 3 sons 1 daughter. **Educ.:** Khartoum University, Sudan. Diploma in Planning, Dakar. **Dipl.:** B.Sc. (Hons, Econ.) (1964); M.Sc. (Econ.) (1973). **Career:** Banking Development. Commercial Banking Activities since 1964. Director, Institute of Banking. currently Deputy Chairman, Industrial Bank of Sudan, Khartoum, Sudan. **Publ.:** "Vale of Development Banks; Gouilema for Industrial Financing, Market Structure and Economic Performances". **Member:** Lions Club of Khartoum. **Addr.:** P.O.Box 1722, Tel.: 71208, Telex: 22456 UMIT SD, Khartoum, Sudan.

MUSTAFA (Hassan, Mahmoud), Egyptian surgeon. **Born** in 1930 in Egypt. **Son** of Mahmoud Mostafa Aly **and** Mrs. Tafida Mohamed Aly. **Married** in 1956 in Cairo to Nayera Hassan el-Chichini, three daughters. **Educ.:** Faculty of Medicine, Cairo University. **Dipl.:** ENT, General surgery, Doctor Degree of Ear, Nose and Throat. **Career:** Professor of Ear, Nose and Throat, Tanta Faculty of Medicine; Dean of Tanta Faculty of Medicine; Vice President of Tanta University. **Sport:** Tennis. **Hobby:** Touring tennis. **Member of:** Gezira Sporting Club, Twfikia tennis Club; Shooting Club, Authmobile Club. **Credit Cards:** (Golden Visa) VISA **Prof. Addr.:** 26 July Street No.26, Cairo. **Priv. Addr.:** P.O.Box 181, Orman, Cairo, Egypt 12612.

MUSTAFA (Hussein, Mahmoud), Egyptian international civil servant. **Born** on June 16, 1924 at Benha (Lower Egypt). **Married** in 1953, with Samia el-Serafi, 3 children: Khadiga, Mahmoud, Hassan. **Educ.:** Faculty of Engineering, Cairo Universtiy. **Dipl.:** B.Sc. (Engineering). **Career:** Plant Engineer, Helwan Portland Cement Company (Egypt, 1948-51); Plant Chief Engineer, Iraq Portland Cement Company (Iraq, 1952); Technical Manager, Helwan Portland Cement Company (1953-57); General Manager and Member of the Board of Directors of Alexandria Portland Cement Company (1957-63); Member of the Board of Directors of Cement Sales Bureau, Cairo (1960-63); Joined the World Bank Group with the International Finance Corporation (IFC) as cement and building materials expert in 1963; Current position Technical Manager, Engineering Department of IFC; Member: Egyptian Engineers Union. **Member:** Alexandria Sporting Club; Kenwood Country Club, Washington D.C. **Sports:** Fishing, sailing and tennis. **Hobbies:** Reading and classical music. **Prof. Addr.:** International Finance Corporation, 1818 HSt. NW, Tel.: 202-477-1234, Washington D.C. 20433 (USA). **Priv. Addr.:** 7213 Marbury Court, Tel.: (301) 320-3956, Bethesda, MD, 20034 (USA).

MUSTAFA (Izzidin, Ibrahim), U.A.E. educationist. **Born** in 1928 in Cairo, Egypt. **Educ.:** University of Cairo, Egypt; University of London, UK. **Dipl.:** B.A. and diploma of Education; Ph.D. **Career:** Qatar Education Service; Riyadh College of Education, Saudi Arabia; Vice Chancellor of the United Arab Emirates University; Chairman of Islamic Solidarity Fund, Saudi Arabia; Cultural Adviser to the United Arab Emirates President (1971). **Publ.:** "an-Nawasis Forty Hadith", "Hadith Qudsi". **Awards:** Honorary Doctorate of Economics, University of Malaysia. **Addr.:** The Presidential Courts, P.O.Box 3360, Abu Dhabi, United Arab Emirates.

MUSTAFA (Mohamed E.), Egyptian/American University professor and management & accounting consultant. **Born** on November 25, 1934 in Cairo, Egypt. **Son** of Eid Mustafa Mohamed (retired Businessman) **and** Mrs. Zahra Hassan. **Married** in August 1964 in the U.S.A. to Margaret Heiss, 2 sons: Shereef (1967) and Tamir (1972).

Education: Ph.D., University of Illinois, Urbana, Illinois (1965), Major: Accounting, Minors: Management and Finance; M.S., University of Illinois, Urbana, Illinois (1961), Major: Accounting; B.Comm., University of Cairo (Honors), Cairo, Egypt (1956), Major: Accounting. **Academic Experience:** Vice-Chancellor (President), United Arab Emirates University, United Arab Emirates, 1990 to 1992 (Approximately 10,000 students and 900 faculty members in eight colleges and six research centers); Dean, School of Business Administration, California State University, Long Beach (CSULB), (1981-88) (7,000 undergraduate and graduate business majors and 200 full time and part time faculty members); Chair, Department of Accountancy, CSULB, (1975-78 and 1979-80) (2,000 majors and 30 full time faculty positions); Member and Chair, several departmental, school, and university committees, CSULB (1969-90); Director, CSULB International Business Program (1971-72); Full Professor, Dept. of Accountancy, CSULB (1972- present); Associate Professor, Dept. of Accountancy, CSULB (1969-72); Associate Professor, National Institute of Management Development (NIMD), Cairo, Egypt (1965-67); Assistant Professor, American University in Cairo, Graduate Management Program (1965-67 part-time), (1967-69 full-time), on leave from NIMD; Lecturer, University of Southern California, Pepperdine University, Ain Shams University (1968-75 part-time). **Professional Experience:** Consultant to the Egyptian Institute of Accountants and Auditors: Developed the first plan continuing education programs for the accounting profession in Egypt (December 1988); Designed and offered the first continuing education training program on Applying International Accounting Standards in Egypt (May 1989). On the Expert list of the UN International Labor Office (ILO), 1976 to present. Services rendered: An institutional assessment and a development of a strategic plan for The Turkish Institute for Industrial Management, Turkey (1988); An assessment of management development needs for the industrial sectors in the Gulf States (Kuwait, United Arab Emirates, and Bahrain) (1983); Edited and reviewed several research studies for the ILO research department in the area of management development and planning and controlling technology transfers. On the expert list of the World Bank, 1992 to present. Preparing a training strategy for the development of Russian accountants and auditors in a market economy. The assignment was part of an overall World Bank project on: «Russia: Preparation of Training Project» (May 1993). On the expert list of the U.N. Industrial Development Organization, authored a study on Management Accounting for the Implementation of Industrial Projects in Developing Nations (April 1972). Consultant to the Academy for Educational Development, Washington, D.C. Developed the accounting program for the new Department of Accounting, College of Management Science and Planning, King Faisal University (1985). Member of an International Committee made up of six members from the U.S., U.K., and Saudi Arabia that developed the officially adopted Saudi Accounting and Auditing Standards (1982-85). Management and Financial Consultant and Executive Development Trainer for TEAM, a major Management Consulting firm in the Middle East (1975-81). Organizations served: Major construction companies in the Persian Gulf, ministries of the interior, education, defence and finance, Saudi Arabia, the Saudi Railroad organization, Saudi Airlines, Kuwait Airways Corporation, SHUAIBA Authority, Kuwait, and many business concerns and government agencies in other countries in the Middle East. Consultant to South West Regional Laboratory for Educational Research and Development (SWRL), Los Alamitos, California (1977-83). Participated in proposal writing and in consulting missions overseas in the field of education, curriculum development, and training. Management and Financial Consultant and Executive Development Trainer for OFIS (A Management Consulting firm in the U.S.) (1975-81). Faculty Resident, Ernst & Whinney, Spring 1978. The audit division in the Los Angeles office and the Professional Development Div. in the national office in Cleveland. Executive Development Trainer, National Institute of Management Development, Cairo, Egypt (1965-67); Designed directed and taught executive development programs to senior executives in Egypt, Jordan, Syria, Iraq, and Sudan; Consultant to Egyptian corporations (Arab Maritime Company, Mehalla Textile Company) on accounting information systems; Directed a team of 35 researchers (14 researchers, and 21 controllers of major Egyptian corporations) studying financial and accounting problems in the Egyptian economy; Consultant for: Pyramid Brewery Company, Egypt (1967-69), Nasr Company for the Production of Coke and Allied Chemicals, Cairo, Egypt (1969); Taught management development programs for Oil refinery corporations in Suez, and the General Organization for Building Materials and Ceramics, Cairo, Egypt (1967-69). Auditor, University of Illinois, Audit Division (half-time) (1962-64). Participated in auditing University trust funds, Payroll, hospital, theatre, etc...; Auditor, Sherif, Hegazy and Company, Cairo, Egypt (1956-58) (part time). Staff accountant at influential public accounting firm. Participated in auditing banks, manufacturing and trading companies, and was in charge of complete audit assignments. Cost Accountant, General Company for Mineral Wealth, Inc., Cairo, Egypt (1956-58). Head of Cost Accounting Dept., designed and supervised installation of cost accounting system for mining and manufacturing activities. **Research:** Research in Progress: The role of accounting and auditing in the conversion to a market economy in Russia. **Books:** Reform of University Education in the United Arab Emirates, UAE University Press (1992). **Publications and Papers:** A Faculty Development Plan for the Arab Universities, «Higher Education Policy» Vol. 5, No. 4 (1992). Environmental Dimensions of the Gulf: Policy, Institutional, And Educational Perspectives. Proceedings of the «Work-shop on the environmental dimensions of the Gulf» sponsored by the «United Arab Emirates University and the World Bank» (April

1992). Management of Technology Transfer: Planning and controlling the implementation process. Commissioned by the United Nations International Labor Office (January 1990). Recent Trends in Managerial Accounting Education and Training in the U.S. Proceedings of the Third International Conference on Managerial Accounting sponsored by the Egyptian Institute for Accountants and Auditors, Cairo, Egypt (June 1988) pp. 1-14. Framework for the Role of Accounting in the Economic Development of Saudi Arabia. Recent Accounting and Economic Developments in the Middle East, Center for International Education and Research in Accounting, University of Illinois (March 1985), pp. 197-211. Quantitative Methods for Financial Decision Making: The State of-the-art in developing nations: The case of Egypt. Proceedings of the Association of Egyptian-American Scholars conference, Cairo, Egypt (December 1982) (co-authored). Problems and Challenges in Management Development in the Arab Gulf States. Management Review, International Edition (September 1982). Also published in commerce Review, Bahrain Chamber of Commerce and Industry, Issues No. 205 & 206 (April and May 1984). Business and Higher Education. Current Business Perspectives (Spring 1982). Accounting Data for Export Pricing in Developing Nations. Journal of International Business Studies (Spring 1978). The Nature of the Demand for Accounting Doctorates in California: (1976-1980). California CPA Quarterly (June 1978). The Nature of the Demand for Doctorates in accounting. The Accounting Review (October 1975). Problems in Installing Standard Cost Systems. The Journal of the Arab Manager (April 1969). Accounting for Intra-Company Transfer Pricing: A Managerial Approach. Review of Accountancy, Management and Insurance, Faculty of Commerce, Cairo University, Cairo, Egypt (March 1969). Development of the Auto Industry in the U.A.R. «Al Ahram Al Iktissadi», Cairo, Egypt (March 1969). **Case Studies:** The Pharmaceutical Industry. A case study dealing with management information systems and the export decision in developing nations. The Intercollegiate Case Clearing House, Harvard University. Pricing for Export: The Cement Industry. A case study dealing with management accounting in developing nations. The Intercollegiate Case Clearing House, Harvard University. Chucko's Bakery. A case study dealing with management accounting in developing nations. The Intercollegiate Case Clearing House, Harvard University. **Book Reviews:** Principles of Accounting by Reynolds, Sanders and Slevin for the Dryden Press (1982). Principles of Accounting (3 volumes) by Fred Skousen, Harold O. Langenderfer and W. Steve Albrecht for Worth Publishers, Inc. (1979). Management Accounting: A decision emphasis by De Coster and Shafer for Wiley-Hamilton Publishing Company (1977). Accounting for Management Planning and Decision Making by Professors Korn and Boyd for Wiley-Hamilton (1977). Accounting for Management Control by Charles Horngren for Prentice-Hall, Inc. (1976). Financial Accounting by John Tracey for Wiley-Hamilton (1976). Financial Accounting by Bierman and Drebin for McMillan (1970). The Role of Accounting in Economic Development for Al Ahram Al Iktissadi (1969). **Unpublished Material:** The Nature of the National Demand for Accounting Doctorates: (1976-1980). CSULB Bureau of Business Research and Services Occasional Paper (1978). (R) evolution in the Introductory Accounting Course. CSULB Bureau of Business Research and Services Occasional Paper 13 (1977). The Accounting Profession and the Developing of Accounting Principles. CSULB Bureau of Business Research and Services Occasional Paper 11 (1976). Management Accounting for the Implementation of Industrial Projects in Developing Nations. A research study prepared for the United Nations Industrial Development Organization (April 1972). Report on Faculty Seminar in Accounting Education. A mimoegraph for California Certified Public Accountants' Foundation for Education and Research (1970). **Panels, Symposiums, Presentations and Speeches:** A Strategic Approach to Training Russian Managers to Function in a Market Economy, Presented at the «Third International Conference on The restructuring of the Russian Economy» held at The Palace of Congress, the Kremlin, Moscow (May 1993). Requirements for Training Russian Accountants and Auditors for the Market Economy. Presented to the section on finance and accounting at the «Third International Conference on The Restructuring of the Russian Economy», Moscow (May 1993). Environmental Dimensions of the Gulf: Policy, Institutional and Educational Perspectives. Conceived, organized, and chaired the «Workshop on the environmental dimensions of the Gulf» sponsored by the «United Arab Emirates University and the World Bank», Al-Ain, UAE (April 1992). A Plan for Faculty Development in Arab Universities. A key-note presentation at the Plenary Session at the International Conference on «The Creation of an all-Arab Inter-university Network on Faculty Development», sponsored by the United Nations Educational Scientific and Educational Organization, Alexandria, Egypt (Oct. 1991). The Role of Higher Education in a Period of Adjustment. A Regional Perspective. An International Conference on Human resource Development in a Period of Adjustment, sponsored by the U.A.E. Institute of Administrative Development, Dubai, United Arab Emirates (Nov. 1991). Accounting and Third World Debt Crisis. Presented at the School of Accountancy, University of Central Florida, Orlando, Florida (July 1989). Recent Trends in Managerial Accounting Education and Training in the U.S. Presented at the Third International Conference on Managerial Accounting sponsored by the Egyptian Institute for Accountants and Auditors, Cairo, Egypt (June 1988). Developments in the Business and Accounting Education at CSULB. Main speaker, technical meeting of the National Association of Accountants, Long Beach chapter (January 1988). CSULB: The Seventh Largest Business School in the U.S. Long Beach Civic Pride Committee, Long Beach Rotary Club (December 1987).

Panelist on The Changing Role of the CSU and the Professional Environment. California State University, Long Beach Third Academic Senate Retreat (October 1987). Chair of a Plenary session on U.S. -ASFAN Business Relations. Conference on U.S. -ASFAN Relations, California State University, Long Beach (May 1987). Moderator of a session on Management/Devolopment Issues. Conference on Hunger, Population and International Development, California State University, Long Beach (October 1986). The Information Society: Its impact on higher education. IBM Corporation College and University Executive Conference, Palm Springs, California (May 1986). Information Technology: Strategy for changes in higher education. IBM Corporation, (May 1986). Information Technology: Strategy for changes in higher education. IBM Corporation, Focus '86 Public Sector Industry Marketing Forum, Washington, D.C. (Feb. 1986). Information Systems for College and University Executives. IBM Corporation, Customer Executive Program, Poughkeepsie, New York (November 1985). Application Transfer Team Study: A case study in the California State University System. IBM Los Angeles Marketing Conference, Los Angeles, California (May 1985). Session Leader and presenter at the Symposium on Cooperation Among Management Development Institutions, International Labor Office, Geneva, Switzerland (May 1985). Management Development and Its Impact on Trade Opportunities in the Arab World. Inter-mountain Conference on Trade Opportunities in the Arab World, Salt Lake City, Utah (October 1983). Invited participant by the German Government (DAAD) to Germany Today as one of 27 members of American professional schools and graduate research universities, as well as leading representatives of public life, Bonn, West Germany (June- July 1983). New Developments in Computing Machinery and Their Impact on Curriculum, Faculty and Administrative Operations. The American Assembly of Collegiate Schools of Business (AACSB) Annual Meeting, Kansas City, MO (April 1983). Accounting Developments in the Arab World. The National Association of Accountants, Orange County Chapter (November 1982). Business and Higher Education: Partners in progress for the resurgent city of Long Beach. Third Annual Business Symposium, School of Business Administration, CSULB (April 1982). Director of Egypt Today. Symposium at CSULB, part of the American International Symposia sponsored by the Middle East Institute, the Smithsonian Resident Associate Program, and Meridian House International (March-April 1981). Referee and Discussant on three papers on Accounting Education. American Accounting Association Western Regional Conference, Fresno, California (May 1981). The Accounting Profession and Accounting Education in the United States. Faculty and graduate students of the College of Commerce, Cairo University, Cairo, Egypt (January 1981). Quantitative Methods for Financial Decisions: The state-of-the-art in industry and academia. The Association of Egyptian-American Scholars Conference, Cairo, Egypt (December 1980). Economic Development in the Middle East. The International Business Association of the Long Beach Area Chamber of Commerce (October 1980). Panelist, Professional Development Program fro Community College Instructors of Accounting. The Department of Accountancy, California State University, Los Angeles (April 1980). Invited participant, Symposium for Accounting Educators. Ernst & Whinney, Vail, Colorado (July 1979). The Adequacy of the State Universities' Accounting Curricula for the Professional Practice of Accountancy. Student-Practitioner Conference sponsored by the California Society of Certified Public Accountants (November 1978). The Role of Student Organizations in the Professionalization of Accounting Education. Western Regional Meeting of the American Accounting Association, California State University, Los Angeles (May 1978). Moderator and Discussant of Plenary Session on The Institutional Framework of the Accounting Profession. The American Accounting Association's Annual Meeting, Portland, Oregon (August 1977). Invited participant to Trueblood Seminar for Professors. Touche Ross Foundation, Chicago, Illinois (February 1981 and April 1977). The Nature of the Demand for Doctorates in Accounting: (1976-80). American Accounting Association's Western Regional Meeting, San Jose State University (May 1977). Management Information Systems for Export Pricing in Developing Nations with Particular Emphasis on Egypt. Academy of International Business Conferences in Alexandria, Egypt (December 1976). Invited participant to Ernst & Ernst's Symposium for Educators on SEC Reporting. Cleveland, Ohio (April 1975). The Need for Professional Accounting Education. Long Beach-Orange County Chapter of the California Society of Certified Public Accountants (September 1975). The Pharmaceutical Industry. A case study presented at the Intercollegiate case Clearing House Workshop, University of Washington (October 1974). The Nature of the Demand for Doctorates in Accounting. American Accounting Association's Western Regional meeting, California State University, Sacramento (May 1974). The Accounting Profession and the Development of Accounting Principales. American Accounting Association's Western Regional Conference, California State University, Fullerton (May 1973). Pricing for Export: The cement industry. A case study presented at the Intercollegiate Case Clearing House Workshop, the University of Missouri, St. Louis (October 1972). (R)evolution in the Introductory Accounting Course. American Accounting Association's Western Regional Conference, California State University, Hayward, California (May 1972). Chucko's Bakery. A case study presented at the Intercollegiate Case Clearing House Workshop, Brigham Young University. Management Problems in Developing Countries. Kiwanis Club of Long Beach (January 1971). **Academic and Professional Organizations, Services:** American Assembly of Collegiate Schools of Business (AACSB). Activities included membership in: National Accounting Accreditation committee

(1986-89); National Accounting Accreditation Visitation Teams (1986-89); Board of Directors of the Western Region (1986-88). California State Society of CPAS, Foundation for Education and Research, Member of the Committee on Accounting Education (1983-88). International Management Development Organization (INTERMAN), sponsored by the U.N. International Labor Organization, Geneva, Switzerland (1985-88). International Cooperative Agreements with the following University of Jordan (1986); American University in Cairo (1987); Institut International du Commerce, (Paris 1986). American Accounting Association: Activities included: National Advisory Committee to the Director of Education (1979-80); National Committee on Accounting Educators Awards (1978-1979); National Nomination Committee of the Administrators of Accounting Programs (1978-79); National Committee on Publications of the Administrators of Accounting Programs (1977-78). Association of Egyptian-American Scholars, National Vice-President (1984-86). International Association of Students in economics and Business (AIESEC), Advisory Board member (1981-88). Beta Alpha Psi. Activities included: Founder and Advisor, Gamma Omega Chapter (CSULB) (1972-76); National Committee on Chapter Activities of the National Council (1976-77); Initiated and implemented Gamma Omega Chapter involvement in the IRS Volunteer Income Tax Assistant program (VITA) (1972); Initiated, implemented and moderated first Western Regional Annual Conference for Beta Alpha Psi Chapters in Southern California (Feb. 1975). **Community Service:** Elected member of the Board of Directors, Southern California International Business Association (1983-90), Elected member of the Port Ambassadors, Port of Long Beach (1986-90); Appointed member of the Long Beach-Pohang, Korea Sister City Committee (1986-90). Elected member of the Board of Directors, Southland Communications, a publicity held company (1987-88) and a member of the Board of Advisors (1988-90); Elected member of the Board of Directors, Long Beach Area Chamber of Commerce (1984-87) and Orange County Chamber of Commerce (1983-87); Member of the Board of Advisors, the Center for International Commerce, Long Beach Unified School Dist. (1981-85); Member of the Board of Advisors, Center for Economic Education, CSULB (1982-84). **Awards and Honors:** 1977 Faculty Excellence Award in the State of California, presented by the California State Society of CPAS & the California CPA Foundation for Education and Research; Richard S. Claire National Award, presented by Arthur Andersen & Company Foundation (1975); Outstanding Faculty Vice-President, Beta Alpha Psi National Council Award (1975); Gamma Omega Chapter of Beta Alpha Psi Faculty Award (1971, 1973, 1974, 1975, 1976 and 1977); Men of Achievement, Tenth Edition, International Biographical Centre, Cambridge, England (1983); The International Who's Who of the Arab World, London, England, annually since the first edition in 1981; Who's Who in the Arab World, Beirut, Lebanon, annually since 1980-81 edition. **Professional Organizations, Member:** Phi Kappa Phi; Beta Gamma Sigma; Beta Alpha Psi; National Association of Accountants (1963-1983) **References:** An International as well as a national reference list are available upon request. **Executive Summary:** He is a tenured Professor of Accounting at California State University, Long Beach (CSULB). He is the Former Vice-Chancellor (President) of the United Arab Emirates University. At CSULB he was Dean of the College of Business Administration and prior to that he was a chair of the Department of Accountancy. Dr. Mustafa's record in management development is recognized in the U.S. and abroad. In the last two decades, he conducted many assignments for major organizations on capacity building, strategic management, accounting, and management. Chief among them are: **World Bank:** As part of a World Bank project for management training in Russia in 1993, He was responsible for advising a group of twelve Russian experts in the fields of accounting, auditing, and financial managers in formulating a strategy to enable the accounting profession to meet the needs of a market-oriented economy. The Strategy proposed a multi-dimensional action plan aiming at training of trainers, development of Curricula at the universities and generating relevant training resources. It also addressed the needs of specific target groups: chief accountants, financial managers, auditors and accounting technicians. **United Arab Emirates University:** As Vice-Chancellor of the United Arab Emirates University, UAE. He was responsible for eight colleges and six research centers involving about 10,000 students and 900 faculty members. He prepared a strategic plan for the reform of university education in the UAE. The Plan examined the role of university education in serving the UAE, investigated the imperatives for educational reforms, portrayed images of the university in the year 2000, spelled out the strategic management planning process necessary for the realization of these images, and outlined an operational plan for implementing reforms. **Technology Transfer in Developing Nations:** In 1990 He conducted a practical study for the International Labor Office entitled «Management of Technology Transfer: Planning and Controlling the Implementation Process in Developing Nations». Realizing that the ability of developing nations to effectively implement new technology is tied to their ability to effectively manage that technology, He focused on providing a framework for the implementation of technology transfer, identifying critical stages in managing the process, and dealing with the major factors that influence its success. According to the International Labor Office, the study is in high demand. **California State University at Long Beach:** He served as Dean of the College of Business Administration at CSULB from 1981 to 1988. At the time of his appointment, the College was the fifth largest business school in the nation with an enrollment of over 7000 business majors and 200 full time and part time faculty and staff. As Dean, He lead the College in its quest for excellence in teaching, research, and service. His management strategy was to initiate a change in direction, foster a new philosophy, and help establish higher norms. To implement this strategy, he focused on attracting and keeping quality faculty, attracting and maintaining an optimum enrollment of quality students, developing uniqueness in the College's programs, involving the business community in the building process, developing multiple levels of support, increasing internal flexibility, minimizing self-imposed constraints, and building the College's infrastructure for the efficient operation of its academic and administrative functions. In this quest, He conducted several strategic planning processes. Major among them was integrating information technology in the acedemic as well as the administrative functions. The process moved the College from an institution void of information technology to a leading institution in integrating information technology in business education. **The Egyptian Institute of Accountants and Auditors:** In 1988 the Board of Directors of the Egyptian Institute of Accountants and Auditors asked Him to develop a strategy for continuing education for the accounting profession in Egypt. He assessed the training needs, developed a training plan, identified programs contents, and specified implementation requirements. He initiated the implementation process in 1989. **The Turkish Institute of Industrial Management:** In 1988 the International Labor Office asked Him to assess the effectiveness of the Turkish Institute of Industrial Management. The resulting report proposed a management strategy for the Institute to build its managerial capacity, including a mission statement, goals, organizational structure, alternative operational strategies, and an implementation plan. **TEAM:** From 1977-82, as a senior executive development trainer for TEAM, a leading Arab center for management development, He designed, developed, and offered training programs for top level executives to major institutions in the Middle East. **International Labor Office:** Since 1976, He has edited several research studies in management development for the International Labor Office. Thorough field trips, he also assessed management development needs for the industrial sectors in Kuwait, UAE, and Bahrain. **United Nations Industrial Development Organization:** In 1972, as an expert to the United Nations Industrial Development Organization, He authored a study on Management Accounting for the Implementation of Industrial Projects in Developing Nations. **Sports:** Jogging and Swimming. **Prof. Addr.:** Accounting Department, California State University, Long Beach (CSULB), California 90840, U.S.A. **Priv. Addr.:** 9782 Avenida Monterey Cypress, CA 90630, Home Phone: 714-826-1991, Facsimile: 714-826-5268, U.S.A.

MUSTAFA (Mukhtar, Ahmad, Dr.), Sudanese academic. **Born** on January 1, 1940 in Omdurman (Sudan). **Married** in 1971 to Afaf Mwafi Abdel Fatah, one daughter, one son. **Educ.:** Wadi Seidna Secondary School (1955-59); Faculty of Agriculture, University of Khartoum (1959-64); University of Aberdeen, Scotland (1964-66); University of California, Riverside USA (1966-69). **Dipl.:** B.Sc., M.Sc., Ph.D. (agriculture). **Career:** Senior Scholar, Faculty of Agriculture, University of Khartoum (1964-69); lecturer in the said faculty (1969-74); Senior lecturer, School of Agriculture, University of Zambia since October 6, 1974. **Member:** Sudan Society of Agriculture; International Soil Science Society. **Hobbies:** soccer, snooker and travel. **Prof. Addr.:** School of Agriculture, University of Zambia, P.O.Box 2379, Lusaka, **Priv. Addr.:** 48 Chelston South End Properties, Lusaka, Zambia.

MUSTAFA (Niazi), Egyptian director and producer. **Born** in Egypt. **Educ.:** Secondary and Higher. **Career:** Directed and Produced the following pictures: "Salama fi Kheir", "ad Doctor", "Masna'al Zawgat", "Si Omar", "Wadi al-Nougoum", "Ibnaty", "Rabha", "Hababa", "Hassan wa Hassan", "Albani Adam", "Rawia" etc... **Priv. Addr.:** 12, Kora Ben Sherrik Street, Tel.: 96753, Cairo, Egypt.

MUSTAJEL (Sadaka Y.), Saudi professor. **Educ.:** Ph.D. in International Relations. **Career:** Assistant Professor, Political Science Department, Faculty of Economics and Administration, King Abdulaziz University, Jeddah. **Publication:** Nuclear Capabilities of the Arabs and Israel (a book). **Hobbies:** reading, writing, paintings, chess, football. **Prof. Addr.:** P.O.Box 3738, Mecca. **Priv. Addr.:** Tel.: 6725755, Jeddah, Saudi Arabia.

MUTABAGANI (Hamed), Saudi Physician. **Born** in Madina in 1935. **Dipl.:** M.D. (Medicine) (1961-1962); **PH.D.** (General Surgery) (1966-1967); PH.D. (Urology 1969. **Career:** Physician, Ministry of Education (1962); Cultural Counsellor, Saudi Embassy, Rome (1965); Surgeon, Ministry of Education; Professor of Pathological Surgery Rome University; established a new modern private hospital (80 beds); now Director General, Jeddah and Madina National Hospitals. **Publications:** 42 research papers in surgery and medicine published on medical journals. **Awards:** Cavalier, Medal of Honour awarded by President of Italy. **Sport:** Fishing. **Hobby:** Photography. **Prof. Address:** P.O.Box 7692 - Jeddah 21472 - Saudi Arabia.

MUTAHAR (Mohamad, Bin Mohamad, al), Yemeni academic. **Born** in 1950 in Sana'a, Yemen. **Son** of Mohamad al-Muttahar. **Married**, three children. **Educ.:** B.A. in Philosophy and Sociology, University of Libya (1972); M.A. in Educational Management, Indiana University, USA. **Career:** Director General of Planning, Ministry of Education (1972-73); member of the Higher Committee of Educational Development Project (1973-74); Associate Director, Educational Development Project (1974-76); Vice Rector, Sana'a University (1976). **Sport:** Tennis. **Hobbies:** Literature, philosophy, sociology. **Addr.:** University of Sana'a, P.O.B. 1247, Sana'a, Yemen Arab Republic.

MUTAWA (Faisal, Ali, Al), Kuwait Executive. **Born** in 1945 in Kuwait. **Son** of Ali Abdulwahab Al Mutawa. **Married** in 1970, 5 children: Two sons and Three Daughters. **Education:** American University of Beirut. **Diplom:** B.A. **Career:** Board Member of the Kuwait Chamber of Commerce and Industry; V.P. and Managing Director of Ali Abdulwahab, Sons and Co. **Hobbies:** Swimming, Fishing, Tennis, Reading. **Address:** P.O.Box 159, Safat. 13002-Kuwait, Tel.: 2446750, 2424138/9, Fax: 2429968.

MUTAWA' (Faisal, Saleh, al), Kuwaiti diplomat. **Born** in 1927 in Kuwait. **Son** of Saleh al-Mutawa' **Married**, 5 children. **Educ.:** Secondary and Higher **Dipl.:** B.A. (History), University of Cairo. **Career:** Ministry of Education; Under-Secretary, Ministry of Education; Ambassador to USSR; Ambassador to Algeria; Ambassador to France, Head of Ceremonies Department, Ministry of Foreign Affairs. **Sport:** Swimming. **Hobbies:** Reading, sports. **Addr.:** Ministry of Foreign Affairs, P.O.Box 3, Safat, Tel.: 2425141, Kuwait City, Kuwait.

MUTAWAKEL (Yahia Mohamad, al), Yemeni diplomat. **Born** on May 28, 1942 in Shahara, Yemen. **Son** of Mohamad A. Almutawakel (Government Employee) **and** Mrs. Shams Almutawakel. **Married** on July 17, 1966 in Sanaa to Amatalghaffar Almansour, 3 children: Bushra (1969), Mohamad (1971), Ali (1976). **Educ.:** Sanaa Secondary School (1958), Military Academy (Paratrooper) (1960), Military Academy (Heavy Artillery) (1961). **Dipl.:** Officers Infantry Academy of Moscow (1965). **Career:** Director of the Office of the Commander-in-Chief and Prime Minister (1968); Deputy Commander-in-Chief of the Armed Forces (1969); Elected Member of the Consultative Assembly (Parliament) (1970); Appointed Ambassador E. & P. to Egypt and Libya (1971); Member of the Command Council and Minister of Interior (July 1974); Participated in the September 62 Revolution as Artillery Commander; took part in the battles defending the Republic (1962); Participated in the November movement as member of the Defense Council (1967); Played important role in the normalization of Yemeni-Saudi relations (1970); Ambassador E. & P. of the Yemen Arab Republic to the United States of America, Canada and Mexico (1976). **Awards:** Military High Medals. **Sports:** Tennis, bowling, hunting, swimming, **Hobbies: Reading, gun collecting. Member:** European Health Spas, Gas light Club, Pisces Club. **Credit Cards:** Visa, American Express, Master Charge, Central Charge. **Prof. Addr.:** Ministry of Foreign Affairs, Sanaa, Republic of Yemen.

MUTAWAKKIL (Muhammad Abdul Malik Abdul Karim, al), Yemeni academic. **Born** in 1942. **Married,** 5 children. **Educ.:** Cairo University, Journalism Department, Egypt. **Dipl.:** B.A. in Literature. **Career:** First Secretary, Embassy to Egypt (1963); Director General of Press at the Ministry opf Information (1967); Head of Tourist Department (1970); Minister of Supply (1976); Member of the National Committee for Culture and Cooperation; Member of the Higher Committee for Rectification and **Board** Member of Sanaa University. **Hobbies:** reading, walking, gardening, theatre, interest in the development of administrative Sanaa, Republic of Yemen.

MUTAWI' (Hamed Hassan), Saudi editor in chief. **Born** in 1947 in Mecca, Saudi Arabia **Dipl.:** Baccalaureate, Diploma of Business Administration and Economics (Saudi Organization for Popular Education). **Career:** Head of Treasury and Accounting Department, al-Bilad daily newspaper; Manager of Administration, al-Nadwah daily newspaper; Editor-in-Chief, al-Nadwah daily newspaper. **Member** of the Municipal Council, Mecca; member of the Board, Mecca Establishemnt for Publishing and Information. **Publications:** a biography of King Faisal, numerous articles. **Hobby:** reading. **Prof. Addr.:** al-Zahraa Str., Jarwal Sheikh Sayed Halabi Bldg., Mecca, Saudi Arabia.

MUTI (Mohamad Saleh Abdallah), Yemeni politician. **Born** on June 16, 1944, in Aden. **Son** of Saleh Abdallah Muti. **Married. Educ.:** Higher Education at the Technical Institute, Aden. **Career:** active politically and in armed struggle, National Liberation Front; Member, General Command (1968); Member, Executive Committee (1969-70); Minister of the Interior (June 1969-73); Minister of Foreign Affairs (1973), re-appointed in (1979). **Former member:** Political Bureau of the National Liberation Front. **Hobbies:** watching football. **Addr.:** Aden, Republic of Yemen.

MUTLAQ (Abdul Mohsen, al), Saudi leading businessman. **Born** in 1928 at Sudair. **Career:** Chairman of the al-Mutlaq Brothers Group which owns chains of showrooms for furniture in several cities in the Kingdom (Dammam, al-Khobar, Jeddah, Riyadh, Mecca, al-Madina, Abha), Chairman of Heden International (Saudi Arabia) Ltd. and several other Companies. **Member:** Chamber of Commerce and Industry, Dammam; Board of Directors of Saudi British Bank. **Address:** P.O.Box 153, Tel.: 8644360, al-Khobar, Saudi Arabia.

MUTLAQ (Ayda, Mustafa), Jordanian academic. **Born** on November 12, 1942 in Irbid, Jordan. **Married**, 4 children. **Educ.:** Beirut University, Lebanon; Yarmouk University; St. Joseph's University. **Dipl.:** B.A. in Social Studies (1963); M.A. in Psychology (1980); Ph.D. in Psychology (1984). **Career:** Secondary School Teacher (1963-66); Headmistress (1966-77); Dean of High College (1978-82); Executive Council Member of Jordan Women's Union in the Governorate of Irbid; Member of the National Consulative Council (1983-84); Member of the National Advisory Council at the Ministry of Information (1984-85); Member of the Board of Directors of A'mar Irbid, Municipal Council (1983-); Member of the Promotion Council, Ministry of Planning (1986-); Founder Member of Jordan Women's Union. **Awards:** Education Award (1st Class),

Jordan (1984). **Prof. Addr.:** P.O.Box 1658, Tel.: 271022, Irbid, Jordan.

MZAH (Ridha), Tunisian businessman. **Born** in 1945 in Hammam-Lif, Tunisia. **Married**, 2 sons, 1 daughter. **Educ.:** Lycée Technique Hôtelier, Strasbourg, France; Ecole Hôtelière de Bizerte, Tunisia. **Career:** Manager of Sahara Palace Hotel (1969-73); General Manager of Hotel Africa Meridien, Tunis (1978-); Chairman and Managing Director of Société Immobilière et Touristique de Tunisie (SITT) (1981-). Member of the Board of Tunisian Federation of Hoteliers; General Manager of the Africa Sidi Bou Said Lodge (1984-). **Prof. Addr.:** Hotel Africa Meridien, 50 Avenue Habib Bourguiba, Tel.: 347.477, Telex: 15.536/1.4035, Fax: 1.347.432, Tunis, Tunisia.

MZALI (Mohamad), Former tunisian prime minister. **Born** on December 23, 1925 in Monastir, Tunisia. **Son** of Chaabane Mzali **and** Mrs., née Aicha Ghedira. **Married** in 1950 to Fethia Mokhtar, 6 children: Mokhtar, Habib, Houda, Hatem, Rafik and Sarra. **Educ.:** Sadiki School, Tunis; University of Paris, Sorbonne, Paris. **Dipl.:** Baccalaureat, Philosophy (1947); Graduated in Philosophy (1950), Post-graduated in High Literary studies (1954), University of Paris. **Career:** Teacher, La Zitouna University and in Sadiki School (1950-56); Principal private secretary, Ministry of National Education (1956-58); Director-General, Youth and Sport Department (1959-64); Director-General of the Tunisian Radio and Television (1964-68); Minister of National Defence (1968-69); Minister of Youth Sport and National Education (1969-70); Deputy in the Tunisian National Assembly (1970-71); Minister of Public Health (1973-76); Minister of National Education (1976-80); Prime Minister (1980-July 1986). **Activities:** Member of the Central Committee and the Political Bureau of the Destourian Socialist Party (1954-July 1986); Deputy in the National Assembly: elected in 1958, re-elected in 1964-69-74 and 1979; elected town-Councillor of the City of Tunis (1960), and re-elected in 1963; First Vice President of the Municipality of Tunis, and Chairman of "Culture, Youth and Sport Committee" (1960-63); Chairman of Sports Committee (1963-66); President of the Municipality of l'Ariana (mayor 1969-72); President of the Tunisian Olympic Committee (1962-1986); Member of the International Olympic Committee (1965-present); Chairman of the Organizing Committee for Tunis Mediterranean Games (September 1967); IOC Vice-President (1976-1980); Member of "L'Académie des Sports" (France, May 1978); President of the International Committee of the mediterranean Games (Split 1979); Honorary member of the International Committee to Fight Against Violence in Sport; Founder and Editor of the literary review al-Fikr (1955-1986); Head of 1st Tunisian delegation to the General Conference of the Bureau of Education (Geneva-July 1956); Vice-President of the Tunisian delegation, the Head of the delegation to the General Conference of UNESCO (New Delhi, Oct. 1956); Member of the Tubisian delegation to 3rd Arabic Writers' Congress (Cairo, 1957); Head of the Tunisian Delegation to 4th Arabic Writers' Congress (Kuwait, 1958); Head of the Tunisian delegation to the UNESCO Conference on "Sport, Culture, and Work" (Helsinki, 1959); Founder and President of the Union of Tunisian Writers (1970-1980); Corresponding Member of the Arabic Academy in Cairo (1975); Member of the Board of Directors of the International Fair-Play Committee. **Publ.:** in Arabic: On Democracy (1955); History of North Africa-Volume I (translation) (1968); Collected Editorials in "el-Fikr" (1969); French Colonists and the Tunisian Youth Movement (translation) (1972); Attitudes (1973); Studies (1974); Points of view (1975); History of North Africa-Volume II (translated from Ch. A. Julien, French book into Arabic, assisted by B.B. Slama) (1979); Education and the Olympic Movement (published in 4 languages) (1979); Thinkings (1979); "Open Letter" to Habib Bourguiba (in french 1987) (in arabic 1988); "The Parole of Action" (published in 4 languages) (1984), Arabic, French, Italian and Chinese; "Tunisia, What Future" in french, Paris (1991). **Awards:** Grand Ribbon, Order of the Tunisian Independence; Grand Ribbon, Order of the Tunisian Republic; Tunisian "Sportsman Merit" medal; several foreign decorations. **Member:** of the Arabic Academies (Amman, Damascus, Baghdad, Cairo). **Hobbies:** Racing, reading and Olympic sport. **Addr.:** Paris 16, France.

N

NAAMA (Abdulla Hussain), Qatari businessman. **Born** on October 1, 1915 in Doha, Qatar. **Son** of Hussain Naama (deceased). **Married**, 7 children: Youssif, Farouk, Khalid, Naima, Ghada, Mai and Khalifa. **Career:** Umm Said Customs Manager (1949-1955); Established own business i.e. Arabian Library (1953) and Arabian Printing Press (1955) which were the first in Qatar. Chairman & Managing Director of: al-Orouba Press and Publishing House, Arabian Establishment for Commerce, Arabian Trading Company, al-Shark Publicity and Service Agency. **Work:** Chief Editor and Proprietor of al-Arab Daily Newspaper since 1972; Chief Editor and Proprietor of al-Orouba Weekly Magazine since 1970. **Other Information:** Chairman of Qatar Insurance Company from 1964 to 1986; Member of the Board of Directors of Qatar Cinema and Distribution Company. **Awards:** National Order of Merit, French Republic (Dec. 1975); Order of Merit, Second Class, Egypt (July 1974); Order of Merit, First Class, Jordan (July 1974); Order of Allawi, Knight Class (July 1975); Order of Merit - Gulf Cooperation Council (Dec. 1989). **Hobbies:** Stamp and Coins Collection. **Member:** Association for Promotion of International circulation of the Press (DISTRIPRESS); Member of Arab Distributors Union. **Credit Cards:** AM/EXP. Diners Club, Visa, Access Mastercard, Eurocard Etc. **Prof. Addr.:** P.O.Box 52, 633, 2499, 460 Doha, Tel.: 423179, 423278, 425588, Qatar. **Priv. Addr.:** Tel.: 671411, Qatar.

NAAMA (Khalid, Abdullah), Qatari journalist. **Career:** Owner and Editor in Chief. "al-Arab" daily; Writes day-today reports on Qatari scene, Has wide interests in textile retail industry; **Prof. Addr.:** Dar al-Uruba, P.O.Box 3464, Doha, Qatar.

NAAMA (Mustafa Rajab, al), Iraqi academic. **Born** in 1923 in Basra, Iraq. **Married**, 3 daughters. **Educ.:** College of Medicine, University of Baghdad, Iraq. Royal College of Physicians, England (MRCP, FRCP). **Dipl.:** M.B., Ch.B., Degree in Internal Medicine. **Career:** Junior Physician (1950-53); Residency Program, USA (1953-57); Senior Physician, Cardiologist (1964-); Lecturer, Head of Department of Medicine, University of Basra (1968-73); Dean, College of Medicine, University of Basra (1971-78); Member of the Arab Board for medical Specializations; Assistant Professor of Medicine and Consultant, Teaching Hospital, Basra (1974-). **Publ.:** numerous papers and researches (in English) in professional journals. **Hobbies:** ancient history, anthropology, medical literature, fishing. **Prof. Addr.:** College of Medicine, University of Basra, P.O.Box 114 Basra, Iraq.

NAAMA (Naama, Youssef), Iraqi former diplomat. **Born** in 1924 in Iraq. **Son** of Yusuf Naama. **Educ.:** Baghdad University. **Dipl.:** Bachelor of Laws. **Career:** Lawyer, joined the Ministry of Foreign Affairs (1963); Chargé d'Affaires in Belgium (1963-64); served in Baghdad (1964-68); Ambassador to West Germany (1967); General Secretary, Ministry of Foreign Affairs (1968-72); Ambassador to France (1972). **Addr.:** Ministry of Foreign Affairs, Bagdad, Iraq.

NAAMAN (Abdulmagid), Egyptian journalist. **Born** in 1915 in Egypt. **Educ.:** Licenciate in Law. **Career:** Signals Staff Officer; Assistant Director, Radar and Signals Department, Egyptian Air Force (1965); Secretary general, Aswan Governorate; Editor in Chief, Sports Section, "Akhbar al-Yaum" newspaper, Cairo, Egypt. **President:** Sports Journalists Association, Egypt (1970), African Sports Journalists Association, Egypt (1974), Vice President, International Sports Journalists Association (1974). **Publ.:** "Football: Training and Tactics" (1968). **Medals:** Sports Decoration 1st class, Egypt (1975); Nile Decoration 5th Class, Egypt (1950). **Member** of National Sports Club, Cairo; Aviation Sports Club, Gezira Sporting Club. **Sports:** Table tennis, football, athletics. **Addr.:** 111 al-Hegaz Street, Tel.: 869727, Heliopolis, Cairo, Egypt.

NAAMAN (Ahmad, Abdulmagid Sallam), Egyptian physician and university professor. **Born** in Alexandria. **Son** of Abdulmagid Sallam Naaman. **Educ.:** University of Cairo (Faculty of Medicine). **Dipl.:** Doctor in Medicine (1941); specialisation in Gynecology and Obstetrics. **Career:** Physician, Professor of Gynecology and Obstetrics at the University of Cairo. **Prof. Addr.:** University of Cairo, Egypt. **Priv. Addr.:** 144, Fosha Zirinia, Tel.: 61150, Alexandria, Egypt.

NAAMAN (Antoine), Egyptian university professor. **Born** on June 30, 1920 in Port-Saïd. **Son** of Yusuf Naaman. **Married** to Miss Natal, 5 children. **Educ.:** University of Cairo, E.N.S. of Saint-Cloud (France), University of Paris (La Sorbonne). **Dipl.:** Licence ès-Lettres (1942), Higher Diploma in Journalism (1948), Master of Arts (1951), Diploma from the E.N.S. of Saint-Cloud (1951), Doctor in Philosophy (1951), Doctorat d'Etat ès-Lettres (La Sorbonne, 1962). **Career:** Professor, secondary schools, Egypt (1942-49); Professor, Heliopolis University

(1952-54); Head of the French Section at the said university (1954-58); Assistant- Professor at the said university (1962-65); Head of the French Department at the said university (1964-65); Professor and Director of the Modern Languages Department, Ghana University (1965-66); Assistant Professor, then Professor, University of Sherbrooke since 1966; Chairman and General Manager; "Editions Cosmos" since 1969; Director, founder, "Centre d'Etude des littératures d'Expression Française (CELEF)", Faculty of Arts, University of Sherbrooke (1969-74); Founded "Editions Naaman" (Publishing House, 1973), and "Ecriture Française dans le Monde", revue, la Tribune des Francophones (1979). **Publ.:** Author of numerous studies, books and booklets in Arabic, French and English, including, "Les débuts de Gustave Flaubert et sa technique de la description" (1962), "Les Lettres d'Egypte de Gustave Flaubert, d'après les manuscrits autographes" (1965), "Mateo Falcone de Mérimée" (1967), "Guide Bibliographique des Thèses Littéraires Canadiennes de 1921-1976" (1978), etc., 28 Thesis published, 14 under preparation. **Member:** Société d'Histoire Littéraire de la France; American Council on the Teaching of Foreign Languages; Les Amis de Flaubert (Rouen); L'Association Canadienne de Littérature Comparée; L'Association des Professeurs de Français des Universités Canadiennes; L'Association Canadienne- Française pour l'Avancement des Sciences; L'Association Internationale des Docteurs (Lettres) de l'Université de Paris et des autres Universités de France; The Association of Arab-American University Graduates, Inc.; Le PEN International; etc... **Prof. Addr.:** Sherbrooke, Québec, Canada J1H 5K5.

NAAMAN (Ismail, Saïd), Former yemeni diplomat. **Born** in 1941 in Aden. **Son** of Saïd Naaman. **Educ.:** Aden Schools, Dickinson College (Pennsylvania), North-Eastern University (Massachusetts, U.S.A.). **Dipl.:** Certificate of Education, B.Sc. Chemistry and Political Sciences, Master of Science. **Career:** Teacher in Aden (1967); Secretary, Aden Electricity Corporation (August 1967- May 1968); First Permanent Representative of the People Democratic Republic of Yemen to the United Nations Organisation (1968-70); Manager, National Company for Home Trade (1970); **Addr.:** Khalifa Street, al-Mansoura, Aden, Republic of Yemen.

NAAMY (Hashim Said Ali, al), Saudi judge. **Born** in 1920, at Okazy Village (suburb of Abha), Saudi Arabia. **Educ.:** General education, jurisprudence, history and arts. **Career:** School teacher, Abha Primary School (1945); Judge, Mihail Court,Rijal Al Maa Court (1947); Judge, First Urgency Court, Abha. **Member:** Abha Literary Club, Abha Holy Qur'an Committee. **Publications:** five books on history, monuments and literature and one under preparation, Geolgraphical Dictionary of the Southern Region; articles in local newspapers and magazines. **Prof. Addr.:** Abha Urgency Court, Tel.: 2246420, Abha. **Priv. Addr.:** Tel.: 2246316, Abha, Saudi Arabia.

NABAA (Nazir), Syrian artist painter. **Born in Aleppo. Educ.:** Secondary and Higher. **Career:** Artist Painter, contributed to several Art Exhibitions in Syria and the Arab Countries. **Publ.:** Author of several works including the Illustrations of Walid Ikhlassi book "al-Farès ad Dayegh" (1969). **Addr.:** Aleppo, Syria.

NABI (Balkacem), Algerian politician. **Career:** Director, Energy and Oil, Ministry of Industry and Energy (until 1966); President, Director-General, Société Nationale de Recherches et d'Exploitation des Pétroles en Algérie (SN Repal) (1966-70); Wali, Tlemcen (1970-76); Adviser, President's Office (1975-79), Minister of Energy and Petrochemicals (March 1979- Sept. 1989). **Addr.:** Algiers, Algeria.

NABI (Mohamad), Algerian administrator. **Born** in 1934. **Married,** 3 children. **Career:** Associate Director of Professional Training, Ministry of Employment and Social Affairs (1963); Director of Employment (1970); Director of the Presidency (1973); Deputy, Bab el-Oued Region (1977); Vice President later President of Economic Commission of the National Popular Assembly APN; Secretary of State for Vocational Training (1980); Minister of Labour and Vocational Training (1984-85); Minister of Labour and Social Affairs. (1986-Sept. 1989). **Prof. Addr.:** Algiers, Algeria.

NABI (Shamshad), Pakistani executive. **Born** in 1941 in Pakistan. **Son** of Dilshad Nabi. **Married** in 1971, 1 son, 1 daughter. **Educ.:** England and Wales Institute, Chartered Accountant. **Dipl.:** F.C.A. (1966). **Career:** Joined National Investment Trust, Karachi, Pakistan (1967-1980); Head Investments, Islamic Development Bank (1980); Acting Treasurer, Islamic Development Bank, Jeddah, Saudi Arabia (1981-). **Member:** Institute of Chartered Accountants, England and Wales; Economic Development Institute of the World Bank; Karachi Boat Club; Karachi Golf Club. **Hobbies:** Golf, Travelling and Reading. **Addr.:** P.O.Box 5925, Tel.: 6362086, 6363281 (Ext. 525), Telex: 401137, 401407 A/B ISDB SJ & BISLAM SJ, Jeddah, Saudi Arabia.

NABIH (Yusuf, Ayyad), Egyptian economist. **Born** in 1924 in Egypt. **Married,** 1 son. **Educ.:** Cairo University, Egypt. **Dipl.:** M.A. in Cost Accounting, B.Com. in Advanced Accounting. **Career:** Senior Partner of Yusuf Nabih and Company (1951-); Member of the US-Egypt Business Council; Representative of Richard Dans and Company (Bankers); Fellow of Egyptian Society of Accountants and Auditors; Consultant of Siemens AG. **Member:** Gezira Sporting Club. **Prof. Addr.:** 1125 Corniche el-Nil, Cairo, Egypt. **Priv. Addr.:** 22 Kasr el-Nil Street, Cairo, Egypt.

NABRI (Malik, Amin), Sudanese former official. **Born** in 1923 in Singa, Sudan. **Married,** 4 sons, 5 daughters.

Educ.: Gordon Memorial College, Khartoum, Sudan; Sudan Police College, Khartoum. **Career:** held various posts in Legal Department (1943-50); Police College (1951-52), Police Inspector (1953), Chief Inspector of Police (1956), Superintendent of Police (1960); Vice Consul, Embassy of Sudan, Kampala, Uganda (1964-67); Consul General, Fort Lamy, Chad (1967-68); Commandent of Police (1969-71), Assistant Commissioner of Police (1972-75); Under Secretary, Ministry of the Interior (1976); Governor of Northern Province (1977-84). **Decor.:** Order of Outstanding Officer, Republic of Chad. **Medal:** Republic of Sudan Medal. **Hobbies:** reading, national and international current affairs, modern and classical poetry. **Addr.:** Dongola, Sudan.

NABULSI (Hamdallah, Farid), Jordanian engineer. **Born** in 1927 in Salt, Jordan. **Son** of Farid Nabulsi **and** Mrs. Raiefeh Nabulsi. **Married** in 1957 in Amman to Miss Yusra Tamimi, five children. **Educ.:** Cairo University, Egypt (1954); Training Course in Material Engineering, USA (1963). **Career:** Director, Public Works Project, Ministry of Works (1954-63); Director of Materials, Ministry of Works (1963-65); Director of Construction, Ministry of Works (1965-71); Director-General, Housing Organisation (1971-84). Ministry of Municipal and Rural Affairs and Environment (1984-85); Partner in Jordan Engineering Counselling Center (1985). **Awards:** Independence Medal 3rd Class; Star of Jordan, 3rd Class; Star of Jordan, 2nd Class. **Member** of: Jordanian Engineers Ass., Concrete Ass., Roads Ass., American Society of Civil Engineers (ASCE). **Addr.:** Amman, Jordan.

NABULSI (Mohamad, Saïd), Jordanian banker. **Born** in November 1928. **Son** of Hamdi Nabulsi **and** Mrs., née Fatima Nabulsi. **Married** to Naila Nabulsi in September 1957 in Damascus (Syria), 3 children: Hamdi, Samar and Rasha. **Educ.:** University of Damascus (1948-52); Georgetown University, Washington DC (1954-56), (1959-60); University of California, Berkeley (1958-59). **Dipl.:** LL.B., M.A., Ph.D. (Economics). **Career:** Central Bank of Syria (1952-68); Central Bank of Jordan (1968-71); lecturer, University of Amman (Jordan) (1968-73); Minister of National Economy (1972-73); Governor, Central Bank of Jordan (1973 to 1985; Under Secretary General, United Nations (1985-1989); Governor, Central Bank of Jordan (1989-1996). **Publ.:** Studies in Banking Administration; Problems of Monetary Integration in Developing Countries (1964). **Awards:** al-Qawqab Medal (2nd class). **Club:** Automobile club. **Priv. Addr.:** Shmeisani. Tel.: 664827, Jordan.

NABULSI (Omar), Jordanian lawyer and politician. **Born** on April 1, 1936 in Nablus. **Son** of Hajj Nimr Nabulsi **and** Mrs. Safia Ali. **Married** in 1966 to Miss Haifa Hatough, two sons. **Educ.:** Cairo, Ain Shams University; London University. **Dipl.:** LL.B. **Career:** Legal Adviser, Sasco Petroleum Co., Libya (1959-61); Legal and Political Attaché, League of Arab States (1961-69); Assistant Director, Royal Court of Jordan (1969-70); Minister of National Economy (1970-72); Ambassador at the Foreign Ministry, Amman (1972); Ambassador to the U.K. (and concurrently to the Netherlands and Portugal) (1972-73); Minister of Agriculture (June- Nov. 1973) of National Economy (1973-75); Legal and Economic Adviser to Arab Fund for Economic and Social Development (1975-77); Lawyer and Consultant in Corporate and Business Legal Affairs (1977-80); private law practice (1980-); Member National Consultative Council of Jordan. **Award:** Order of al-Kawkab, Jordan (First Class). **Hobbies:** Reading, cricket, squash, music, theatre. **Addr.:** P.O.Box 35116, Amman, Jordan.

NABULSI (Shakir, Faek, al), Jordanian writer. **Born** in 1940 in Salt, Jordan. **Married**, 5 children. **Educ.:** Ain Shams University, Cairo. **Dipl.:** B.A. in English Literature. **Career:** Assistant Director of Abdellatif Jamil Co. (1968-84); General Manager, advertising Department, Tihama Co. (1986). **Publ.:** "Saudi Arabia Tomorrow", Tihama (1985), "The Distance between the Sword and the Neck" (1986), "The Open Ends" (1984), "The Light and the Toy" (1986); also translated several books. **Hobbies:** swimming, running, reading. **Priv. Addr.:** P.O.Box 8596, Jeddah, Saudi Arabia.

NADEEM (Mahmoud Ibn Ahmad Khalil Ibn Mahmoud), Saudi airline executive. **Born** in 1942 in Medina, Saudi Arabia. **Dipl.:** B.Sc. (Mechanical Engineering), M.S. (Engineering Design and Economics). **Career:** Supervisor, Refrigeration Equipments Maintenance Department, Saudia (1970); Director, Utility Maintenance Deparment, Saudia; Worked for twelve years with the Saudi Boys Scouts Society. **Honour:** A Medal for record achievement of work on the job, Saudia. **Publications:** M.A. thesis on the broad guidelines for the selection of aeroplanes for Saudia. **Hobbies:** gardening, space science, repair and development of home appliances. **Prof. Addr.:** Saudi Arabian Airlines, Housing Services Department, No. 570, P.O.Box 620, Tel.: 6827161, Jeddah. **Priv. Addr.:** Tel.: 6512010, Jeddah, Saudi Arabia.

NADER (Mohamad, Jabir), Saudi lawyer. **Born** in 1930 in Medina, Saudi Arabia. **Married**, 2 sons. **Educ.:** Cairo University, Egypt. **Dipl.:** LL.B. **Career:** Attaché, Saudi Arabian Embassy in Kabul (1955-59); Counsellor, Saudi Embassy in Bonn (1960-62), in Baghdad (1968-69); Minister Plenipotentiary, Washington, D.C. (1970-71); Director, The Saudi Arabian Public Relations programme, USA (1970-71); Minister Plenipotentiary, Sana'a (1972-73); established and headed the Research and Legal Department, Ministry of Foreign Affairs; represented Saudi Arabia in the Legal Committee at the UN (1967); practiced law since 1971; established "M. Jabir Nader" Law Firm in 1977; Chairman of Bahra Development Co. Ltd., Jeddah, Saudi Arabia. **Publ.:** "Conciliation and Arbitration in Saudi Arabia", Saudi Chambers of Industry and Commerce (1985). **Hobbies:** music, poetry, reading, swimming, photography. **Prof. Addr.:** 19 Abu Zinada Street, Mushrefah, P.O.Box 3595, Jeddah, Saudi Arabia.

NADI (Mohamad, Abdulmaqsoud), Egyptian nuclear physicist. **Born** on January 27, 1918 in Samanud. **Son** of Abdulmaqsoud an-Nadi **and** Mrs., née U. Seif. **Married** on April 2, 1942 to Miss Samira Labib, 4 children: Adel, Nabil, Nadia and Nazih. **Educ.:** Cairo University, London University. **Dipl.:** Bachelor of Science in Physics with 1st Class honors (1940), Master of Science (1945), Doctor of Philosophy (1948), Doctor in Science (1968). **Career:** Joined the Faculty of Science, Cairo University since 1940, Professor of Nuclear Physics since 1961; Head Physics Department, Egypt Atomic Energy Establishment (1961-70); Research Associate, Yale (1959-60); Dean, Faculty of Science (1972). Vice President of Mansoura University (1973-78); Prof. of Physics, Faculty of Science, Cairo University (since 1978). **Publ.:** Author of research and numerous publications on theory of low-energy nuclear reactions especially those in which two or more nucleus are stripped from projectile by target nucleus. High Energy nuclear physics (Anomalous mean free path for Ultra relativistic particles). **Awards:** Egypt State prize (1960 and 1966). **Member:** Physicists Society (London), American Institute of Physics (U.S.A.). **Prof. Addr.:** Cairo University. **Priv. Addr.:** 50, Dokki Street, Giza, Cairo, Egypt.

NAFEA (Mohammed A., al), Saudi businessman. **Born** on September 1, 1961 in Hofuf, al-Hassa, Saudi Arabia. **Son** of Mr. Abdulmohsen A. al-Nafea (Businessman) **and** Mrs. Nura al-Nafea. **Married** in 1984 in Hofuf, two chidren: Nura and Adil. **Dipl.:** B.A., Diploma in Business Management. **Career:** Managing Director of Abdulmohsen A. al-Nafea Trading Est., Hofuf, Saudi Arabia. **Sport:** Football. **Hobbies:** Stamps collecting, newspaper reading. **Credit Card:** Visa Card. **Prof. Addr.:** Abdulmohsen A. al-Nafea Trading Est., P.O.Box 11 Hofuf al-Hassa-31982 (KSA), Tel.: 03-5875644, 5821470, Telex: 861285 NAFEA, Saudi Arabia. **Priv. Addr.:** as above, Tel.: 5801694.

NAFIE (Abdallah, al), Saudi academic. **Born** in 1937 in Medina, Saudi Arabia. **Dipl.:** Ph.D. (Psychology). **Career:** Assistant Professor, later Professor and Vice-Rector, Riyadh University; Dean, Faculty of Education, Riyadh University; Secretary-General for Teaching and Information Affairs, same university; President, Harby Establishment for Educational and Information Projects; Educational Consultant to several Universities in Planning and Administration; member of Board, International Islamic Schools; member of International Conference for Applied Psychology; member of American High Education Society and of the International Association of Universities Unions. **Publication:** General Psychology. **Hobbies:** swimming, reading, walking. **Address:** P.O.Box 5750, Riyadh, Saudi Arabia.

NAFIE (Ibrahim, Abdel Fattah), Egyptian journalist. **Born** on January 11, 1934 in Suez, Egypt. **Married**, on August 7, 1958 in Cairo to Miss Ola Barakat, two boys: Ahmed Ibrahim Nafie (Nov.14, 1961), Omar Ibrahim Nafie (April 3, 1963). **Educ.:** Primary and Secondary Schools in Suez. **Dipl.:** B.A. Faculty of Law, Ain Shams University, Cairo, Egypt (1956). **Career:** Reporter, Reuter News Agency (1956-57); Editor, Egyptian Broadcasting (1957-58); Economic Editor, Gomhouriya Newspaper (1958-62); Economic Editor, Assistant to Editor-in-Chief & Head of Economic Section: al-Ahram Newspaper (1962-71); Liaison Officer for Middle East Affairs-Foreign Relations Department, The World Bank, Washington (1971-73); Editor-in-Chief; al-Ahram Newspaper (1979-); Chairman of the Board (1984-), also Chairman al-Ahram Investment Co. & al-Ahram Overseas Ltd. **Other Positions:** President Egyptian Press Syndicate (1985-89); Member, Higher Press Council (1981-); Vice President, International Press Conference (1986); Member, National Democratic Party; Member, al-Shourah Council (1991-). President, Arab Press Union (1997-). **Publ.:** Translator and Author of Several Books. **Other Information:** He has visited most of the Capitals of the World and attended most of the economic and political International Conferences; He made several interviews with world leaders. **Awards:** Cultural Shiled from Emirate of al-Shariqah (1986); Memorial Zaki Tolaymat Medal from the Higher Institute of Theatric Arts, Cairo (1986); Order of Merit from the 1st Degree Egypt (1988); Liberation of Kuwait Medal, Cairo (1991). The international Public Opinion Award (1994). **Sports:** Swimming, Jogging. **Hobbies:** Reading, Music, Sports. **Member:** Gezira Sporting Club, Shooting Club, National Club, Egyptian Automobile and Touring Club, Cairo Capital Club. **Addr.:** al-Ahram Establishment, Galaa Str. Tel.: 5786200/300, Fax: 5786126, Cairo, Egypt.

NAFISI (Abdul Wahab, Yusuf, al), Kuwaiti politician. **Born** in 1935 in Kuwait. **Married. Educ.:** Mubarakiyah School, Kuwait; Cairo University, Egypt. **Career:** Auditor-General's Office, representative member, Kuwait Communications Company; Minister of Commerce (1975-78); Minister of Commerce and Industry (February 18, 1978-82). Businessman since **Addr.:** P.O.Box 1568, Kuwait City, Kuwait.

NAFISI (Ghazi, Fahad, al), Kuwaiti businessman. **Born** on 1 September 1941 in Kuwait. **Son** of Fahad al-Nafisi (businessman) **and** Mrs. Nura al-Nafisi. **Married** in 1950 in Kuwait to Muna al-Nafisi, 4 children: Nura, Abdul Aziz, Khaled, Haya. **Educ.:** Victoria College, Maadi-Cairo, Egypt; Cornwall Technical College Cornwall, England; School of Aeronautical Engineering, London, England. **Dipl.:** Diploma in Aeronautical Engineering. **Career:** Operations Manager, Kuwait Aviation Fueling Company (K.S.C.) (1968); General Manager, Kuwait Aviation Fueling Company (K.S.C.) (1969); Chairman, Kuwait Aviation

Fueling Company (K.S.C.) (1970-1976); Member of Board of Directors, Kuwait National Petroleum Company (S.A.K.) (1970-1976); Chairman and Managing Director, Salhia Real Estate Company (S.A.L.) (1974-to date). **Sports:** Hunting and swimming. **Hobby:** Reading. **Member:** Hunting & Equestrian Club, Kuwait; Imperial Falcon Club, Switzerland; Cercle St. Germain des Près, Paris. **Credit Cards:** American Express, Diners Club, Visa Card, Euro Card, Golden Card. **Prof. Addr.:** P.O.Box 23413 Safat, Kuwait, Tel.: 421260. **Priv. Addr.:** al-Dahia, Block 1, House 53, Nist al-Yusuf St., Tel.: 2513818, Kuwait.

NAGGAR (Abdel Moneim, al), Egyptian former diplomat. **Born** on July 7, 1920 in Alexandria (Egypt). **Married** to B. Ahmad el-Naggar, two daughters, one son. **Educ.:** Military academy, Cairo; Staff Academy, Cairo; Faculty of Law, Cairo University; Institute of Higher Studies, University of Paris. **Career:** Egyptian army service (1938-57); Military attaché, Egyptian Embassy in Paris (1953-54); Madrid Embassy (1955-57); Head, East European Department, Ministry of Foreign Affairs, Cairo (1958); Consul-General in Bombay (1959-62), Hong-Kong (1962); Ambassador to Greece (1963); to France (1964-68); Head, Western Culture and Technical Departments, Ministry of Foreign Affairs (1968-71); Ambassador to Iraq (1972-1979). **Sports:** Tennis and shooting. **Prof. Addr.:** c/o Ministry of Foreign Affairs, Cairo, Egypt.

NAGGAR (Ahmad Abdul Aziz, al), Egyptian executive. **Born** in 1932 in Gharbia. **Son** of Mohamad Abdul Aziz el-Naggar. **Married** in 1957, 1 son, 1 daughter. **Educ.:** B.C.M.C. (1952) Cairo University; M.C (1954) Cairo University; PH.D.C., Cologne, West Germany (1959). **Career:** Professor for Post Graduate Studies, Universities of Ain Shams and Cairo (1962-67); Professor of Economics, Umdurman University, Sudan (1967-69); Director, Local Saving Project; Economic Studies, King Abdul Aziz Unviversity (1969-71); General Manager, Ministry of Finance; General Manager, Ministry of Economy; Under-Secretary, Ministry of Social Insurance; Visiting Professor, Kolon University; Vice Chairman, International Institute of Saving and Credit; Director, Economic Department, Islamic Secretariat, Jeddah, Saudi Arabia; Principal, International Institute of Islamic Banking and Economics; Secretary General, International Association of Islamic Banks, Cairo, Egypt. **Work:** He has enriched Islamic Economy with his landmark writings on the intricacies and practical application of economics. **Publ.:** "The Islamic Revival"; "Interest Free Banks"; "An Introduction to the Islamic Economic Theory"; "100 Questions and 100 Answers on Islamic Banks"; "Islam has Another Path"; "Arab Community in the Course of Change" (Trans.); "Strategy of Development in Developing Countries"; "Towards a New Theory of Islamic Economy". **Member:** el-Shams Sporting, Club; Heliopolis Sporting Club; Mina House Club. **Hobby:** Golf. **Prof. Addr.:** P.O.Box 2838, Cairo, Egypt. **Addr.:** 47, Orouba Street, Tel.: 669494, Telex: 94338 A/B IAIB UN, Heliopolis, Cairo, Egypt.

NAGGAR (Said, al), Egyptian former international officer. **Born** on January 21, 1920 at Delingat, Behera Governorate (Egypt). **Married**, with children. **Educ.:** Faculty of Law, Cairo University; University of London. **Dipl.:** LL.B. 1942, M.Sc. (Economics) 1948, Ph.D. (Economics) 1951. **Career:** Lecturer in law, Cairo University; Professor of Economics, Cairo University; Deputy Director of Research, United Nations Conference on Trade and Development (UNCTAD), Geneva (Switzerland); Director, United Nations Economic and Social Office (UNESOB), Beirut (Lebanon) (1971-74); Director, Office of the Secretary General, UNCTAD, Geneva (Switzerland) (1974). **Publ.:** Author of "Principles of Economics" (1958), "Theory of International Trade" (1961), "History of Economic Doctrines" (1973), "Industrialisation and Income" (1953). **Sports:** tennis, mountain hiking and cross country skiing. **Prof. Addr.:** Cairo, Egypt.

NAGUIB (Hassan, Ehsan), Egyptian consulting engineer, project manager and co-ordinator. **Born** on November 18, 1925 in Cairo (Egypt). **Married** to Basmi Ibrahim Seihair in 1958, one son and one daughter. **Educ.:** College de la Sainte Famille, Cairo (1932-1943); Faculty of Engineering, Cairo University (1943-48). **Dipl.:** B.Sc. (Mechanical Engineering), M.Sc. (High Pressure Steam Turbines). **Career:** Technical Office Manager and Peak Lead Shift Engineer, Electric Division, Rural Department, Provincial Water Projects, Cairo Electricity and Gaz Administration (1948-49); Inspecting Engineer, Cairo-North Power Plant (1949-51); Senior Erection Engineer and Director of Works, Cairo-North and Cairo-South Power Plants (1951-54); founder (1/3 rd capital) and co-managing director, United National Engineering and Trading Company (UNECTCO) (1953 to date); founder (1/3 rd capital) and co-managing director, United National Palm Fibres Industry Company (1957-67); Board Director and 10% shareholder, al-Nahda Trading Company (1958-61); founder and 20% shareholder, The Arab Fluorescent and Electrical Industries (1961-71); Mechanical Agent, Benghazi Sewage and Rainwater Drainage System, Howard Humphreys & Sons Consulting Engineers (1971-73); Mechanical Agent, Tripoli Central Hospital, Uniconsult, Cotthborg (Sweden), Consulting Engineers (1973-75). **Latest activities:** Shipyard and dry docks in Alexandria; Nile shipyard at Embaba, Cairo; Extension of Port Said Harbour; Grain silos in Cairo and Alexandria; supply and erection of transformer, switch and pumping stations; electrification of Middle East; Floating pumping stations at Aswan; supply and erection of two main transformers at Edfou, Suez municipality transformer station. Damietta and Faraskour switch stations, travelling cranes of various capacities, eight transformer stations for army factory, seven transformer stations in Lower Egypt; carried out the mechanical piling foundations of: Damanhour public hospital, the Medicine Analysis and Control Building, Kafr el-Sheikh Law Courts, Giza Cinema city, Alexandria Rice Stores, etc. **Prof. Addr.:** 1, el-Borsa el-Guedida street, Tel.: 54462-979052, Cairo. **Priv. Addr.:** 2, el-Kamel Mohamed street, Zamalek District, Tel.: 810150-807703, Cairo, Egypt.

NAGUIB (Mohamad Aziz, Naguib), Egyptian bank executive. **Educ.:** Ein Shams University, Egypt. **Dipl.:** B. Com. (1956). **Career:** Auditor, Bank Misr, Cairo (1956-61); Egyptian Trade Representative, India, Pakistan and Srilanka (1961-68). Manager, Alahli Bank of Kuwait, Kuwait (1968-78); Director and General Manager, Alexandria Kuwait International Bank, Cairo (1979-86). **Member:** Bankers' Club Association Cairo, Egypt; Shooting Club, Dokki, Cairo, Egypt; Vidu Club, Giza, Cairo, Egypt. **Addr.:** 110 Kasr el-Eini Street, P.O.Box 1004, Cairo, Egypt.

NAGUIB (Mohamad, Ibrahim), Egyptian biologist. **Born** on January 24, 1926 in Cairo. **Son** of Ibrahim Nagib **and** Mrs., née Zeinab Saïd. **Married** on July 18, 1957 to Miss Nawal Abounnaga, 2 children: Manal and Ihab. **Educ.:** University of Cairo. **Dipl.:** Bachelor of Science (1946), Master of Science (1949), Doctor of Philosophy (1952), Doctor in Science (1968). **Career:** Faculty of Science, Cairo University since 1946; Assistant Professor since 1962; Director, Botany Department, University of Libya (1957-61); Executive Director, Department of Scientific Relation, Egyptians Scientific Council (1962-63); Staff Middle East Regional Radioisotope Centre, Cairo (1963-64); Member of several Egyptian and international associations and societies. **Publ.:** Author of studies on effect of some organic compounds on metabolic Pathways on higher plants and fungi paticularly carbohydrate, nitrogen and phosphorus metabolism with reference to role of various nutritive conditions on respiration in relation to sugar absorption and Keto acid production particularly in fungi. **Awards:** Egyptian State Prize for Scientific research in biology, Republic Star (3rd Class, 1965). **Addr.:** Merryland Building, Heliopolis, Cairo, Egypt.

NAHAISI (Mohamad Hassan), Libyan executive. **Born** in 1941 in Libya. **Married** in 1960, 3 sons, 6 daughters. **Career:** Joined Barclays Bank DCO, Tripoli (1957-69); became Vice Chairman and General Manager (1974); Chairman and General Manager, Jamahiriya Bank, Tripoli, Libya (1980-1986). **Addr.:** Tripoli, Libya.

NAHAL (Ibrahim, Ayoub), Syrian university professor. **Born** in April 1933 in Lattakia. **Son** of Ayoub Nahal (Librarian) **and** Mrs., née Mehjeh Bitar. **Married** in Aleppo on July 1, 1966 to Miss Dolly Tabet, 3 children: Roula, Ayoub and Rami. **Educ.:** Ecole Nationale Supérieure d'Agronomie (Grignon), Ecole Nationale des Eaux et Forêts (Nancy), Universities of Montpellier and Wageningen (Netherlands). **Dipl.:** Engineer in Agronomy, Civil Engineer in Water and Forestry, Doctor in Agronomy, Engineer Doctorate in Plant Ecology. **Career:** Chief of the Forest Research Department, (1956-58); Professor (1962-72) then Chief of the Department of Plant Production (1973-76) Aleppo University; Editor in Chief, Research Journal of Aleppo University; Senior Regional Adviser on Ecology and Management of Arid and Semiarid Zones (UNEP); Consultant, UNEP, UNESCO, FAO. **Member** of the Académie d'Agriculture de France; Member, Supreme Council of Science (Syria); Fellow, Explorers Club, New-York; Fellow, International Biographical Association, Cambridge **Member of:** Académie Universelle, Lausanne; Technical Advisory Committee to the CGIAR. **Publ.:** 15 books (Arabic), 5 books (French), 2 books (English), 120 Scientific and Technical Papers on Ecology, Forestry and soil conservation (Arabic, French, English). **Sports:** Tennis, Volley Ball and Swimming. **Prof. Addr.:** Faculty of Agriculture, Tel.: 236140, Aleppo University. **Priv. Addr.:** New Chaba, 3 As Sanoubar Avenue, P.O.Box 5008, Aleppo, Syria, Tel.: 2662392.

NAHAS (Gabriel Georges, Bechara), Lebanese physiologist and pharmacologist. **Born** on March 4, 1920 in Alexandria. **Son** of Bechara Nahas **and** Mrs., née Gabrielle Wolf **Married** on February 13, 1954 to Miss Marylin Cashman, 3 children: Michèle, Anthony and Christiane. **Educ.:** Universities of Toulouse, Minnesota and Rochester. **Dipl.:** Bachelor of Arts (1937), Doctor of Medecine (1944), Master of Science (1949), Doctor of Philosophy (1953). **Career:** Came to the United States of America (1947), Naturalized (1962); the Rockfeller Foundation Fellow University of Rochester (1947-48); Fellow Mayo Clinic (1949-50); Research Fellow, University or Minnesota (1950-53); Chief, Laboratoire de l'Hôpital de Marie Lannelongue of Paris (1953-55); Assistant Professor of Physiology, Minnesota University (1955-57); Chief Respiratory Section, Walter Reed Army Institute Research (1957-59); Lecturer Georges Washington University (1957-59); Associate Professor of Anesthesiology, Columbia College of Physicians and Surgeons (1959-62); Professor anesthesiology (1962-92); Research Professor of Anesthesiology New York University Medical Center (1992-); Fulbright Scholar (1966); adj. Professor, Institute Anesthesia, University of Paris (1969-72); Director, Research, INSERM (1972); Program Chairman, Editor Procs. International Postgrad. Course in Anesthesia, Paris (1969-75); Cons; French Ministry Health (1970); UN Division Narcotic Drugs, Geneva (1971-72); Member of Scientific societies all over the world. **Publ.:** Author 700 publications, twelve monographs and three books on medical instrumentation, acid base regulation, Plasma subsitutes, pharmacology of Cannabis and cocaine Drug dependence, epidemiology and prevention. **Awards:** Medal of Freedom (with gold Palm, 1945); Croix de Guerre (3 Palms). Legion of Honour (France); Order of the British Empire; Order of Orange Nassau (Netherlands). Honor medal of the Centennial of the Statue of Liberty. **Prof. Addr.:** New York University, 550, First Avenue, New York

City, N.Y. 10016 and also Institut de Toxicologie, INSERM, 200 Rue Faubourg St. Denis, Paris 10e, France. **Priv. Addr.:** 40E 74, 256 Blvd. St. Germain, Paris 75007, France.

NAHAS (Salim, Jeryes, al), Jordanian writer. **Born** in 1940 in Jordan. **Married,** 1 son, 3 daughters. **Educ.:** Ain Shams University, Cairo, Egypt. **Dipl.:** B.A. in English Literature. **Career:** Editor of "Jordan Times" newspaper "al-Akhbar" newspaper, and "al-Ra'ay" newspaper; Member: Jordanian Writers' Union. **Publ.:** "You Madba" stories (1979), "The Vote" play (1981), "King of the Years" (1983). **Decor.:** Merit Order of Arar, (1982), Jordanian Writers' Union. **Award:** Merit Award for Fiction (1977). **Hobby:** reading. **Addr.:** Jabal Amman, 17 Circle, P.O.Box 9966, Amman, Jordan.

NAHAWI (Noreddin, Salah), Jordanian/French banker. **Born** in 1949 in Damascus, Syria. **Son** of Salah Nahawi (deceased) **and** Mrs. Nazmieh Qadourah. **Married** in 1985 in Abu Dhabi (U.A.E.) to Miss Manal Kayyali, two sons, Hani (1978) and Sami (1991). **Educ.:** Colby College in Walerville, Maine, USA; School for International Training at Brattleboro, Vermont, USA. **Dipl.:** Master of International Administration. **Career:** Jordan National Bank, (1974); Banque PARIBAS, Paris (1975), Oman (1975-78), London (1978-81), Abu Dhabi (1981-85), Paris (1985-87) and Bahrain (1987-89); Bank Dhofar al-Omani al-Fransi, Oman (since 1990). **Sports:** Squash, Tennis. **Hobby:** Reading. **Member** and Founder of Arab Bankers Association. **Credit Cards:** American Express; Visa. **Prof. Addr.:** Bank Dhofar al-Omani al-Fransi, P.O.Box 4507 Ruwi, Muscat, Tel.: (968) 798314, Oman. **Priv. Addr.:** Tel.: (968) 563845, Muscat, Oman.

NAHAYAN (Ahmed Bin Saif, al, H.E. Dr. Shaikh), UAE President and Chief Executive of Gulf Air. **Born** in 1966 at United Arab Emirates. **Son** of H.E. Shaikh Saif Al Nahayan. **Educ.:** Cairo University - University of South California - University of the United Arab Emirates Commercial Pilot Licence. **Career:** Under Secretary, Dept. of Civil Aviation, UAE 1991-Present; Captain, Gulf Air, Present; Chairman, Bahrain Hotels Company 1997- Present. **Hobbies:** Sports (Chairman of UAE Volleyball Association). **Prof. Addr.:** Gulf Air Company G.S.C., P.O.Box 138, Bahrain, Tel.: +973 338888 - 338889. Fax: +973 335568.

NAHAYAN (Hamdan Bin Mohamad, al, Shaikh), United Arab Emirates politician. **Born** in 1930. **Eldest Son of** Shaikh Mohamad Bin Khalifa al-Nahayan. **Career:** Represented Ruler of Abu Dhabi on Das Island (1957-66); Minister of Public Works (June 1971); United Arab Emirates Minister of Public Works and Head of the Department of Works in Abu Dhabi Executive Council (December 1973- January 1977); Deputy Prime Minister (January 1977-1989); **Addr.:** P.O.Box 2934, Abu Dhabi, U.A.E.

NAHAYAN (Khalifa Bin Zayed, al, Shaikh), UAE politician. **Born** in 1947 in al-Ain, UAE. **Son of** the Ruler of Abu Dhabi, H.E. Shaikh Zaid Bin Sultan al-Nahayan. **Career:** Chairman, Abu Dhabi Executive Council; Head, Abu Dhabi Defence Department; Abu Dhabi Finance Department; Supreme Commander, Abu Dhabi Defence Force; Appointed Rulers' Representative in Eastern Province (1966); formally designated Crown Prince and Chairman of the Defence Dept. (1969); Deputy Prime Minister of the United Arab Emirates (1977); presently Chairman, Abu Dhabi Investment Authority. Chairman, Abu Dhabi Fund for Arab Economic Development, Abu Dhabi, UAE; Chairman, Supreme Petroleum Council, Abu Dhabi, U.A.E. **Addr.:** Tourist Club Area, Said Ghobash Building, P.O.Box 814, Tel.: 822865, Telex: 2287 A/B FUND EM, Abu Dhabi, UAE.

NAHAYAN (Mubarak Bin Mohamad, al, Shaikh), United Arab Emirates politician. **Born** in 1935. **Second Son of** Shaikh Mohamad Bin Khalifah al-Nahayan. **Career:** Deputy Chief of Police (1961); Commander of Police and Minister of the Interior for Abu Dhabi (June 1971) and for the United Arab Emirates (December 1971) appointed to Abu Dhabi Executive Council (December 1973); United Arab Emirates Minister of Interior (1971). **Addr.:** P.O.Box 2629, Tel.: 325400, Abu Dhabi, U.A.E.

NAHAYAN (Sultan Bin Zaid al, Shaikh), UAE army commander. Second **Son** of the President of the United Arab Emirates and Ruler of Abu Dhabi; **Born** in 1953. **Married. Educ.:** in Abu Dhabi, UAE and in Cambridge, UK. **Career:** Lieutenant, Armed Forces of Abu Dhabi (1973), Assistant Chief of Staff (1977), Commander in Chief, United Arab Emirates Armed Forces (1978); Representative of UAE in Military Conferences; presently Deputy Prime Minister. **Prof. Addr.:** Office of the Deputy Prime Minister, P.O.Box 280, Abu Dhabi, United Arab Emirates.

NAHAYAN (Suroor Bin Mohamad Bin Khalifa, al, Shaikh), Executive. **Born** in 1950 in al-Ain, Abu Dhabi. **Single. Educ.:** Local School; Course in English Language, UK. **Career:** Chamberlain of the Presidential Court; Chairman, Water and Electricity Department, Government of Abu Dhabi; former Chairman, Abu Dhabi National Oil Company; Vice Chairman, Abu Dhabi Fund for Arab Economic Development, Abu Dhabi, UAE; former Chairman, Central Bank of the U.A.E. **Member:** Abu Dhabi Investment Authority Board; Abu Dhabi Executive Council. **Hobbies:** Reading, Equestrian, Badminton, Swimming and Bowling. **Addr.:** P.O.Box 280, Abu Dhabi, UAE.

NAHAYAN (Tahnoun Bin Mohamad, al, Shaikh), UAE executive. **Career:** Representative of Ruler in Eastern Region and former Chairman, Abu Dhabi National Oil Company; former Chairman, Abu Dhabi Co. for Onshore Oil Operations; former Chairman, Abu Dhabi Drilling Chemicals and Products Ltd.; former Chairman, Abu Dhabi Gaz Industries Co. **Addr.:** Shaikh Khalifa Street, al-Muhairi Building. Tel.: 330822, 342093, Telex: 22455, 22373, 23024, Abu Dhabi, UAE.

NAHAYAN (Zayed Bin Sultan, al, H.H. Shaikh), Head of state of the United Arab Emirates and ruler of Abu Dhabi. **Born** in 1916. **Career:** Governor of Eastern Province of Abu Dhabi, living in al-Ain (until 1966); Ruler of Abu Dhabi (since August 1966); Head of State (President) of the United Arab Emirates (UAE) since December 1971, and Ruler of Abu Dhabi since 1966. **Works:** presided over the development of Abu Dhabi; involved in all major decisions taken by Abu Dhabi and the UAE Governments. **Awards:** Knight Commander, Memorable Order of the Garter, UK. **Hobbies:** Hunting and Falconry. **Addr.:** Ruler's Palace, Abu Dhabi, United Arab Emitates.

NAHI (Ghaleb), Iraqi artist painter. **Born** in Iraq. **Educ.:** Fine Arts Institute of Baghdad (1957-58). **Dipl.:** Specialisation in Italy (1959-64), Diploma from Rome Institute of Fine Arts. **Career:** Artist Painter; Contributed to several Arts Exhibitions in Iraq, Belgium, India, Italy; Professor at the Fine Arts Institute of Baghdad since 1964. **Dist.:** Prizes from Italy. **Addr.:** Baghdad, Iraq.

NAIF (Wijdan Ali Bin, H.R.H Princess), Jordanian art historian. See under **Ali (HRH Princess Wijdan)**.

NAIM (Abdallah Abdulaziz), Saudi businessman. **Born** in 1929 at Onaizah, Saudi Arabia. **Dipl.:** B.A. Cairo University. **Career:** Headmaster of a secondary school, Ministry of Education, Director General of Cultural Affairs (1958-60) Ministry of Education; former Deputy Minister of Labour of Social Security; presently Owner of General Construction Company. **Member** of Equestrian Club, Riyadh. **Addr.:** P.O.Box 25138, Riyadh, Saudi Arabia.

NAIM (Abdallah al-Ali, al), Saudi Official. **Born** Unaizah, Qassim, in 12 January 1932; **Dipl.:** B.A. Hons. (History). **Career:** Primary school teacher; secondary school teacher; Director of Teachers' Institute; Director-General of Education, Riyadh; Director-General of the Administration, Riyadh University; Director-General of Riyadh Gas and Industrialization Co.; authorized member of Board, same company; member of Board, Real Estate Development Fund; member of the Higher Commission for Transferring Embassies to Riyadh; Mayor of City of Riyadh. **Honour:** Medal (class of Commander), France. **Address:** Mayor's Mansion, City of Riyadh, Tel.: 23054, Riyadh, Saudi Arabia.

NAIM (Mohamad Salih), Saudi consultant. **Born** in 1950 at Onizah, Saudi Arabia, **Dipl.:** M. Architecture (U. Wash./USA). **Career:** lecturer, College of Architecture & Planning, King Saud University (1978); Consultant, TURATH Engineering Consultants. **Prof. Addr.:** P.O.Box 50422, Tel.: 4026648, Riyadh, 11523. **Priv. Addr.:** 4654350, Riyadh, Saudi Arabia.

NAIMI (Taha Tayih, al), Iraqi administrator and professor of control engineering. **Born** in 1942 in Iraq. **Married**, 4 sons and 1 daughter. **Educ. and Dipl.:** B.Sc. and A.C.G.I., Imperial College of Science and Technology, University of London, United Kingdom; M.Sc. and Ph.D, Electrical Engineering (Control), University College of North Wales, University of Wales, United Kingdom. **Career:** Lecturer, College of Engineering, University of Baghdad (1969-71); Head, Electrical engineering Department, College of Engineering, University of Baghdad (1971-73); Dean, College of Engineering Technology, University of Baghdad (1973-75); President, University of Technology (1975-81); held several posts in the iraq Engineers Society including its President (1969-78); Member of the Administrative Board of the Iraqi Teachers Union (1973-74); Member of the Council of the Association of Arab Universities (1975-); Member of the Administrative Board of the International Association of Universities (1980-); Member of the Council of the Ministry of Higher Education and Scientific Research (1975-); Secretary General of the Federation of Arab Scientific Research Councils; Member of the Scientific Committee of the Scientific Research council in Iraq (1981-87); Chairman of the Higher Committee for preparing and supervising the establishment of the University of Technology (1974-81); Head of the working team in charge of the preparation of the consultative educational study for al-Rashid University and Salahuddin University; Chairman of the National Commission for the International Association of Automatic Control based at the Iraqi Engineers Society; Honorary Member of the Indian Administrative Society; studed university and higher educational system in the Arab Republic of Egypt for the academic year 1972-73 at the request of Unesco; was the first to introduce continuing education for engineers in Iraq; President, University of Baghdad (1982-). **Publ.:** "A Course in Automatic Control" (1972), "Contemporary Technology" (1976), 2 books in "Engineering Curricula" (one 1988, the other being printed), 2 books in "Automatic Control" (under preparation), 49 specialized and general papers, also number of original papers in continuing education. **Hobbies:** swimming, gardening, reading. **Prof. Addr.:** University of Baghdad, Jadiriya, P.O.Box 10092, Baghdad, Iraq, also P.O.Box 13027, Baghdad, Iraq.

NAIT BELKACEM (Mouloud, Kassim), Algerian politician. **Born** in Bidjaia, Algeria. **Educ.:** Cairo University, Egypt; Sorbonne, Paris, France; Bonn University, Federal Republic of Germany. **Dipl.:** Degree in Philosophy. **Career:** First Deputy representative of provisional Government in Federal Republic of Germany and Sweden; Director of Political Affairs, Ministry of Foreign Affairs;

Counsellor for Diplomatic and Political Affairs at the Presidency (1966); Minister for Comprehensive Education and Religious Affairs (1970); Minister of State for Religious Affairs (1979); Counsellor, Presidency Office for Cultural and Political Affairs; represented Algeria in many cultural and political conferences; Member of the National Liberation Party (FLN) (1983-). **Publ.:** Author of five books and numerous articles. **Decor.:** Decoration of the National Liberation Front, Algeria. **Award:** National Merit Award of the Algerian State. **Hobbies:** literature, history, classical music. **Prof. Addr.:** FLN Party, Algiers, Algeria.

NAJAFI (Hassan, al), Iraqi former bank governor. **Born** in 1926 in Mosul. **Son** of Tawfiq Najafi. **Married,** 2 sons, 4 daughters. **Educ.:** University of Baghdad, Iraq. **Dipl.:** B.A. (1951). **Career:** Director General, Issue Department and Chief of Foreign Exchange Department, Ministry of Finance, Under-Secretary for Budget Affairs, Central Bank of Iraq; Governor, AMF (Arab Monetary Fund), Iraq; Chairman, Iraqi Economists' Society; Member of the Board, GIB (Gulf International Bank). Deputy Governor, Islamic Bank for Development, Bahrain; Governor, Central Bank of Iraq, Iraq (1981-84). **Publ.:** Applications of Documentary Credits; Incoterms; Dictionary of Economics; Foreign Exchange in Jurisdiction and Operation; Dictionary of Banking and Commercial Idioms; Shekel. **Addr.:** Baghdad, Iraq.

NAJI (Talal), Palestinian politician. **Career:** Member of Military Head Quarter and Central Committee of the Popular Front for the Liberation of Palestine General Command (PFLP-GC) as well as one of the Principal Leaders of the group; Elected to Palestine Liberation Organization (PLO) Executive Committee as first PFLP-GC Member in 1974; Head of PLO Education Department (1977). **Addr.:** Damascus, Syria.

NAJIOULLAH (Bouchaib, Muhammad), Moroccan engineer. **Born** in 1938 in Khouribga, Morocco. **Married,** 6 children. **Dipl.:** Diploma in Engineering and in Political Sciences. **Career:** Office Cherifien des Phosphates (1967-77); General Manager of Auto Hall SA (1977-). **Prof. Addr.:** 44 Avenue Lalla Yacout, Casablanca, Morocco. **Priv. Addr.:** 5 Alée des Marronniers, Casablanca, Morocco.

NAJJAR (Elias, Saïd), Syrian former deputy. **Born** in 1922 in Diarbakir. **Son** of Najjar. **Educ.:** Secondary and Higher. **Dipl.:** Specialization in Agriculture (Algiers and Rome Institutes). **Career:** Businessman, Elected Deputy for Kamishli (1947 and 1954). **Publ.:** Author of several articles on agriculture. **Hobby:** Music. **Addr.:** Abou Remmaneh, Tel.: 110572, Damascus, Syria.

NAJJAR (Fauzi M.), Arab-American academic. **Born** on December 19, 1920 in Lebanon. **Married,** 2 sons. **Educ.:** American University of Beirut, Lebanon; University of Chicago, USA. **Dipl.:** B.A., M.A. and Ph.D. in Political Science. **Career:** Instructor at the American University of Beirut (1954-55); Instructor at the American University of Beirut (1954-55); Instructor at the University of Chicago, USA (1955-58), Assistant Professor (1958-61), Associate Professor (1961-66); Professor Emeritus at Michigan State University, East Lancing, Michigan, USA (1961-66) (1966-). **Publ.:** Edited and published al-Farabi manuscripts: Al-Siyasa al-Madaniyaa (The Political Regime), Imprimerie Catholique-Beirut (1964); Fusul Muntaza'ah (Philosophical Aphorisms, Imprimerie Catholique-Beirut (1971); Al-Jam' Bayna Ra'yai al-Hakimayn: Aflatun al-Ilahi wa Aristotalis (1(Harmonie entre les Opinions de Platon et d'Aristote), Institut Français de Damas-Damascus (1999); numerous articles in cultural and political journals and magazines. More recently, a number of articles on Islamic Fundamentalism and the Intellectuals. **Hobbies:** Middle East and Islamic Studies, walking, swimming. **Member:** Middle East Institute, the Middle East Studies Association of North American, Arab-American University Graduates Association and the American Oriental Society. **Prof. Addr.:** 1249 Marigold Ave. e-mail: Najjar@pilot.msu.edu. East Lancing, Michigan 48824, USA.

NAJJAR (Rauf, Salim, Monsignor), Jordanian ecclesiastic. **Born** in 1932 in Haifa, Palestine. **Dipl.:** Ph.D. in International and Canon Law. **Career:** President of the Ecclesiastic Tribunal (1962-); Editor in Chief and Director of "Voice of the Holy Land" monthly review (1968-); Assistant of the Roman Catholic Bishop in Amman; Chancellor of the Apostolic Nunciature in Jordan (1993); Director General of al-Wassifiya Vocational Centre (1968-); Canon of Holy Sepulchre (1970); President of Bethlehem University (1988); Counsellor of International Federation of Catholic Universities; President of the Jordan Academy of Music (1994). Director, Christian Media Center in Jordan since November 1999. **Decor.:** Commander of the Ordre International de l'Etoile de la Paix, Commander of the Order of St. John of Jerusalem, Order of Independence of Jordan (1973); Commander of the Italian Republic (1985); Honorary Prelate of H.H. Pope John Paul II since 1991. **Hobbies:** music, sport, law. **Addr.:** P.O.Box 5634, Amman, Jordan.

NAJJAR (Saeed Mohamad Noor), Saudi executive. **Born** in 1941 in Mecca, Saudi Arabia. **Dipl.:** B.Sc. (Mechanical Engineering), King Saud University (1970) M.Sc. (Desalination Engineering), Glasgow, England. **Career:** SWCC trainee at Jeddah Desalination and Power Plant (1970-75); first Saudi Plant Superintendent of the SWCC Plants in the Western Region (1975-77); Technical Adviser to SWCC (1977-79); Director of Research, Western Region; Director General, Department of Research and Technical Affairs, Saline Water Conversion Corporation (SWCC), Riyadh; attended several conferences on desalination and related fields. **Prof. Addr.:** Saline Water Conversion Corporation. P.O.Box 5968, Tel.: 4774053, Riyadh, Saudi Arabia.

NAJJAR (Zainab, Muhammad Tawfiq, al), Egyptian businesswoman. **Born** in 1926 in Cairo, Egypt. **Married**, 2 daughters. **Educ.:** American University in Cairo, Egypt. **Dipl.:** B.A. in Economics and M.A. in Management. **Career:** Teacher at AUC (1968-74); Managing Director and Partner of Modern Management Methods Company (1973-); Director and Partner of Newtrend Company Ltd. and Wellcon Company Ltd.; Member of Egyptian Business Association (1975-); Member of US Business Council (1975-). **Medal:** Medal for Social Work, Ministry of Social Affairs (1978). **Member:** Automobile Club International Alumni Council, Gezira Sporting Club. **Prof. Addr.:** 6 el-Gezira el-Wousta Street, P.O.Box 2015, Zamalek, Cairo, Egypt. **Priv. Addr.:** 8 Bahgat Ali Street, Zamalek, Cairo, Egypt.

NAKI (Mohammed Ali, al), Kuwaiti, Chairman, Arabian Light Metals KSC. **Born** on April 6, 1941. **Son** of Ali al Naki **and** Mrs. Muhtaram Hussain Mirza. **Married** on April 6, 1966 in Sweden to Tuula Inga L'll Laine, one Child: Nadiyah (06/01/1967). **Educ.:** Commissioned Military Academy/ Royal School of Military Engineering - 1965, Industrial Course at Institute Social Studies 1968, Holland second in command 1965-1968, Kuwait Army Engineers. **Dipl.:** Military Engineers - Industrial Institute Studies. **Career:** Second in Command KAE (1965-68); Member of State KMC (1967 to 1968). October 1968 Private Sector Industrualist Kuwait Aluminium Fabrication, Extrusion Architectural - Arabian Light Metals; Participated in forming Companies diversified activities in several Industries in the Gulf Countries. **Association Membership** GOIC Doha Qatar, Member, Aluminium Technical Organized first Arabal 983 Followed 2 Yearly (Cairo/ Dubai/ Bahrain Committee, Life Member World Wild Life Fund Switzerland, Arab Federation for Engineering Industries (AFEI). Symposiums & Seminars Local/ International Conferences/ Seminars: Delivered Speeches on Subjects Management/ Human Resources/ Industrial Development. **Decor:** President's Medal, Lion of Republic of Finland. **Prof. Addr.:** Arabian Light Metals KSC, Tel.: 00965 3985210, 00965 3984925, Kuwait City, Kuwait. **Priv. Addr.:** 00965 5631136, 00965 5657070, Kuwait.

NAKIB (Ahmad Abdul Wahab, al), Kuwaiti Businessman. **Born** on 30 July 1933 in Kuwait. **Educ.:** Adam State College, Colorado (USA). **Career:** First Secretary, Kuwait Embassy, London (1962-63); Counsellor, first Permanent Mission of Kuwait to the UN (1963-66); Consul-General, Nairobi, Kenya (1966-67); Ambassador to Pakistan (1967-70); Ambassador to U.K. (1971-75) also accredited to Denmark, Norway and Sweden (1971-75); Chairman and Managing Director, Kuwait Projects Co. (1975-1986) and Shareholder Pearl Investment Co. Bahrain. **Addr.:** Kuwait City, Kuwait.

NAQI (Abdulrahim H.), Bahraini Deputy Secretary General, Bahrain Chamber of Commerce and Industry. **Born** in 1956 at Muharraq, Bahrain. **Son** of H. Naqi and Mrs. née A. Abdulla. **Married** on March 4, 1982 in Bahrain to S. Aldurazi, 3 children: Fawaz (1983), Reem (1985), Fahad (1989). **Educ.:** Al Hadia School, Bahrain (1973); B.A. degree (in Economics), Baghdad University (1979). **Dipl.:** Commercial Diploma, Al Hadia School, Bahrain (1973). **Work:** Deputy Secretary General, Bahrain Chamber of Commerce and Industry. **Credit Card:** Amex. **Prof. Addr.:** Bahrain Chamber of Commerce and Industry, P.O.Box 248, Tel.: (0973) 229555/227306, Fax: 0973-212937, Manama, Bahrain.

NAQSHABANDI (Abdul Aziz Abdul Haqq, al), Saudi businessman. **Born** in 1933 in Medina, Saudi Arabia. **Dipl.:** M.A. (Public Administration). **Career:** Former Director of Personnel Division, Army Staff Office (1958); Director of Budgeting and Contracts Administration, Ammunitions and Provision Corps, Ministry of Defence and Aviation; President al-Fahad International Est. **Sport:** swimming. **Address:** P.O.Box 3467, Jeddah 21471, Saudi Arabia.

NAQSHABANDI (Mohamad A.), Saudi architect. **Born** in 1943 in Medina, Saudi Arabia. **Dipl.:** B.Sc. and M.Sc. (Architectural Engineering). **Career:** Runs his own business; Muhammad Naqshabandi Architects and Consulting Engineers and Industrial Development and Construction Establishment (Industrial and General Contracting); former Director, Central Region Engineering Department, Ministry of Interior. **Publications:** Analysis of Skew Plates with Free Edges on Elastic Winkler Foundation. **Hobbies:** music, chess. **Address:** Riyadh, Saudi Arabia.

NASEEF (Abdallah Mohamad Saeed), Saudi civil servant. **Born** in 1930. **Educ.:** received general secondary school education. **Career:** Accounts clerk, Saudia (1947); Freight Agent (1951); Manager, Freight Department (1956); Supervisor Commercial Affairs (1966); Manager, Charters Department (1962); Staff Manager, Commercial Affairs (1968); Assistant Manager, Freight Services (1970); Manager, Freight Promotion (1971-74); now Manager of Governmental Commercial Freight Sales, Saudia-Saudi Arabian Airlines. Former **Member**, International Association of Travel Agents (IATA) (1974-80); actually Manager-Special Affairs, Saudi Arabian Airlines, Jeddah. **Sports:** Football, table tennis. **Hobby:** Reading. **Addr.:** Jeddah. Saudi Arabia.

NASEEF (Abdallah, Omar, Dr.), Saudi executive. **Born** in 1939 in Jeddah, Saudi Arabia. **Married**, 2 sons, 2 daughters. **Educ.:** University of Leeds, UK. **Dipl.:** Ph.D (Geology). **Career:** Demonstrator, Riyadh University. Saudi Arabia (1964); Graduate Studies (UK) (1965-71); Lecturer, Riyadh University (1971-73); King Abdul Aziz university, Jeddah (1973-). Assistant Professor and Head of Geology Department (1973); Secretary General (1974-

76); Associate Professor in Geology (1977-); Vice President (1976-80); President (by Royal Decree) (1980-); Appointed Honorary Member, Royal Academy of Morocco; President, Board of Trustees, East West University, Chicago, USA; Chairman, Board of Governors, Caribbean Educational Institute, Jamaica; Secretary General, International Commission on Muslim Minorities, UK: Member, International Commission for Prevention of Alcoholism, USA; Member, Board of Advisors of Islamic Foundation, leicester, UK; Member, Board of Trustees, Dar al-Islam New Mexico, USA; Member, Advisory Body of Islamic Arts Foundation, UK; Member International Advisory Board of Institute of Policy Studies, Islamic, Pakistan. Member Board of Governors, Faisal Islamic Bank, Khartoum, Sudan; Islamic Bank, Cairo, Egypt. Appointed Deputy Speaker, Shura Council on 20.8.93. **Publ.:** "Emergence of Islamic Solidarity, the Role of Saudi Arabia", London (1976). **Member:** International Association of University Presidents, Korea; International Planning committee of International Association of Islamic Banks, Jeddah; Geological Society UK; Geological Society of America, USA. **Addr.:** King Abdul Aziz University, P.O.Box 1540, Tel.: 6879033, 6879202, 6879404, 6879130, Telex: 401141 A/B KAUNI, Jeddah, Saudi Arabia also P.O.Box 537, Mecca al-Mukarramah, mecca, Saudi Arabia.

NASEEF (Fatima Omar Mohammad), Saudi Associate Professor, Department of Islamic Studies, King Abdulaziz University, Jeddah, Saudi Arabia. **Born** in 1944 in Jeddah, Saudi Arabia. **Married,** 6 children. **Educ.:** B.A. in History, Riyadh University (1390H); B.A. In Sharia (Islamic Law), Umm Al-Qura University (Makkah) (1395H); M.A. in the "Kitab and Sunnah", Umm Al Qura University (Makkah) (1400H); Ph.D. in the "Kitab and Sunnah" Faculty of Sharia, Umm Al-Qurah University (Makkah) (1403H). **Career:** Dean, Girls Section, King Abdulaziz University (1396-1404); Lecturer (10.2.1401); Head of the Department of Islamic Studies (1402-1405); Assistant Professor (promoted on 6.11.1403); Associate Professor (1419) **Academic Work:** Teaching for 19 Years in the University; Discussion of many dissertations/thesis and other academic papers. **Contribution for the University:.** Establishing the Department of Islamic Studies; Promoting Higher Studies in the University beginning with the faculty of Science; Establishing the Faculty of Home Economics; Establishing a nursery Unit for the Children of Female Employees/Staff and Students; Setting up a Cafeteria for Employees/Staff; Realising Financial and Personnel Independance in the Girls' Section; Taking part of the Preparation and Fulfillment of the five-year Development plan for K.A.U. in Jeddah. **Training Courses:** Participation in the drug-combat course held in the university for 3 years; Participation in many courses for Teachers of the Girls' General presidency; Participation in courses held for training Teachers at Quran Schools, WAMY and IIRO; Public service activities through charity societies. **Conferences and Seminars:** The Conference/Syposium on the Medical Sciences and their Curriculae (1397H); Conference on Home Economics and its Curriculum; Conferences held in the (1970s) on Islamic Probagation/Call.; Tours to Islamic Centers for teaching (Tafseer and Fiqh) for Women in the U.S.A. and Canada in the 1980s. **Activities and Committees:** Head of the Islamic Education Committee at the University; Head of the Islamic Education Committee, IIRO's Womens's section; member of the Board of Quran Schools, Advisor at Quran Society. **Published Research:** M.A. Dissertation (Commanding Virtue and Prohibiting Vice: their impact on the reformation of Societies); Ph.D. Theses on Women's Rights and Duties in the Kitab and Sunnah, in Arabic, English, French, Urdu and Bangali Languages; A paper on the "Concept of Competence in Marriage"; A paper on the "Muslim Character in the Light of Kitab and Sunnah" A paper on "AIDS: An Islamic Perspective"; A paper on "Women's natural discharges: Their purity and impurity!". **Address:** Department of Islamic Studies, King Abdul Aziz University, P.O.Box 3, Jeddah 31411, Saudi Arabia.

NASEEF (Hassan Yusuf), Saudi dermatologist. **Born** on 7 November 1921 in Jeddah, Saudi Arabia. **Dipl.:** M.B.C.C.H.B., Cairo, D.C.M.T., London; Diploma Dermatology, London. **Career:** Director of Mecca Health Services (1952-54); Minister of Health (1960-62); owner of private clinic; former member of Literary Club, Jeddah; has attended several health conferences locally and abroad. **Publications:** Family Doctor; A Student Memoir, Tasali (Folk Poetry). **Hobbies:** reading, writing poetry. **Prof. Addr.:** P.O.Box 5502, Tel.: 6428158, Jeddah. **Priv. Addr.:** Tel.: 6656175, Jeddah, Saudi Arabia.

NASER (Samira, Hafiz Khairi), Egyptian artist. **Born** in 1934 in Cairo, Egypt. **Married,** 3 daughters. **Educ.:** Academy of Fine Arts, Department of Photography, Cairo, Egypt. **Career:** held several private exhibitions in Egypt (1969-84) and in Iraq, Denmark and Spain; Member of Fine Art Society, Founder member of the Plastic Arts Syndicate. **Hobbies:** plastic arts, theatre, travelling, reading. **Member:** Hunting Club, Gezira Sporting Club. **Addr.:** 21 Nabil al-Waqqad Street, Dokki, Cairo, Egypt.

NASHAR (Mahmoud M.), Saudi businessman. **Born** on 15 September 1942 in Jeddah, Saudi Arabia. **Educ.:** secondary school education. **Career:** President Nashar Trading Co; Chairman, Flames Health Club Ltd. UKK (1984-); Deputy Chairman, Jeddah Welfare Society (1984-). **Member:** Chamber of Commerce and Industry, Jeddah, Arab British Chamber of Commerce, London. **Hobbies:** swimming, yachting, flying. **Prof. Addr.:** P.O.Box 6697, Tel.: 6692875, Jeddah. **Priv. Addr.:** Tel.: 6515862, Jeddah, Saudi Arabia.

NASHASHIBI (Hikmat, Sharif), Palestinian executive, **Born** in 1943 in Palestine, son of Sharif Nashashibi. **Mar-**

ried, 2 sons and 1 daughter. **Educ.:** American University of Beirut. **Dipl.:** B.B.A. (1966). **Career:** Head of Foreign Trade Department, Kuwait Chamber of Commerce & Industry (1966-68); Investment Manager, Arab Fund for Economic & Social Development (1972-76); Held several positions of General Manager, Kuwait International Investment Company (KIIC) (1976-81); Vice Chairman, Jordan Securities Corporation- Amman; Adviser, KIIC; Consultant, UNCTAD; The Board of Governors of Arab Central Banks and the Arab League; Chief Executive, al-Mal Group, London- U.K. (1981-85); Vice Chairman of Moseley, Hallgarten (1986-89); Estabrook & Weeden, New York; and Chairman of the Arab Bankers Association- London presently, Senior Advisor Investment Banking, at Arab Banking Corporation, Bahrain. **Publ.:** Extensive works is English and Arabic on the subject of OPEC Investments; Three Arabic books on "Developing Arab Capital Markets" and "Investing Arab Financial Surpluses"; English book "Arab Development Through Cooperation & Financial Markets". **Address:** Arab Banking Corporation, P.O.Box 5698, Manama, Bahrain.

NASHASHIBI (Nassiriddin), Jordanian journalist. **Born** in 1924 in Palestine. **Educ.:** American University of Beirut (AUB), Beirut, Lebanon. **Career:** Arab Office, Jerusalem (1945-47); Chief Chamberlain, Amman, Jordan (1951); Director General, Hashemite Broadcasting (1952); Editor "Akhbar al-Yaum" Cairo, Egypt; Chief Editor, "al-Gumhuriyah", Cairo (1959-65); Representative of the Arab League (1965-67); Diplomatic Editor of "al-Ahram", Cairo; Freelance writer and journalist in Europe and the Middle East. **Publ.:** "Steps in Britain" (1948); "What Happened in the Middle East" (1958); "Political Short Stories" (1959); "Return Ticket to Palestine" (1960); "Some Sand" (1962); "An Arab in China" (1964); "Roving Ambassador" (1970); "The Ink is very Black" (1976) and 44 other publications. **Medals:** Order of the Jordanian Star Order of Independence. **Addr.:** 55 Avenue de Champel, Geneva, Switzerland and 26 Lowndes Street, London and P.O.Box 1897, Jerusalem.

NASHER (Abdul Aziz Abdul Wali), Yemeni former Member of Political Bureau and Secretary of Central Committee, Aden. **Born** on May 26, 1945. **Son** of Abdul Wali Nasher. **Married**, 2 children: Husam (1971), Nashuan (1976). **Career:** Former Member of Political Bureau and Secretary of Central Committee of Y.S.P. **Sport:** Swimming. **Hobby:** Reading. **Member:** Goldmor Club. **Priv. Addr.:** Crater, P.O.Box 818, Aden, Republic of Yemen.

NASIB (Yahya Mohammed), Omani businessman. **Born** on September 3, 1941 in Muscat, Oman. **Son** of Mohammed Nasib (Landlord) **and** Mrs. Amna née Ali Moosa. **Married** on November 10, 1968, 3 children: Naseeb (9.3.1970), Natasha (18.7.1971), Nashia (16.8.1977). **Educ.:** St. Lawrence School; St. Patrick College Karachi; Islamia College Karachi. **Degree:** B.A. (Economics). **Career:** Started Yahya Enterprises (1970), and Oman Partner 51% with Costain of U.K.. Real Estate. Defence Supplier. Chairman: International Clothing Industries Supplying American Market; Snowhite Laundry & Drycleaners multioutlet Laundry, Muscat Chemicals; Member Board of Governors Central Bank of Oman; Founder Member Bank of Oman, Bahrain and Kuwait; President Oman British Friendship Association. **Other Information:** International Businessman Controlling Owner 3 hotels in France and Canada, Farm in Britain, Property in Britain and United States, Race Horses in France and Britain. **Award:** Awarded the Prestigious Order of Oman by His Majesty Sultan Qaboos bin Said for excellence. **Sports:** Skiing, Tennis. **Hobbies:** Shooting, Bridge, Horse Racing. **Credit Cards:** American Express, Diners, Visa. **Prof. Addr.:** P.O.Box 286, Postal Code 113, Muscat, Sultanate of Oman. **Priv. Addr.:** Tel.: 560001, Oman.

NASIR (Essam, Abdelaziz), Egyptian businessman. **Born** in 1931 in Cairo, Egypt. **Married,** 2 daughters. **Educ.:** Cairo University, Egypt; Technical University of West Berlin. **Dipl.:** B.Sc. in Electrical Engineering, Diploma and Doctor of Engineering. **Career:** Electrical Engineer for Siemens AG, West Germany (1958-63); Assistant Professor, California University, USA (1961); Professor at Iowa University, USA (1963-70), at The American University of Beirut, Lebanon (1971-73), at the American University in Cairo (1975-76); Electrical Engineer, Engineering Design and Consultancy Centre (1977-80); Fellow of the Institute of Electrical and Electronics Engineers (1964-) and Power Engineering Society (1964-); Director General of Electrical Consultancy Centre (1980-). **Publ.:** "Fundamentals of Gaseous Ionization and Plasma Electronics", New York (1971), "EVH Transmission Line Corona Effects", New York (1972) as well as numerous conference papers and journal articles; Patentee of a Contamination resistant Insulator USA (1970) and of Lightning Arrestors and Method of Using the Same, USA (1969). **Addr.:** 22 Jazirat al-Arab Street, Mohandiseen, P.O.Box 181, Dokki, Cairo, Egypt.

NASIR (Faisal, Abdullatif, Al), Bahraini Vice Dean, Students Affairs and Premedical, College of Medicine and Medical Sciences, Arabian Gulf University. **Born** on June 20, 1955 in Manama, Bahrain, **Son** of Abdullatif Al Nasir (businessman). **Married** in 1984 in Bahrain, 4 children: Khalid, Suleiman, Mahmood, Alaa. **Educ.:** Primary School, Ministry of Education, Bahrain; Private primary school, Egypt; High Secondary School, Bahrain; College of Medicine, Ain Shams University, Egypt; Family Physician Residency Program, University of Beirut, Lebanon; PhD Program, University of Glasgow, Scotland; Training Program, Royal College of General Practitioners, U.K.; Irish College of General Practitioner, Ireland. **Career:** First Bahraini Doctor to obtain high degree in Family Medicine (PhD, MRCGP, MICGP, FRCGP); Organize and Coordinate Family Medicine Examination for Family Medicine Speciality, Arab Board for medical specialities Syria. Leader in dissemination of Family Medicine concept in the Gulf Area. **Awards:** Ministry of Education (1985), Ministry of Education (1987), Research Award (1st prize) BMS (1987), Research Award (2nd prize) BMS (1989); Fellow of the Royal College of General Practitioners, U.K. (1998); **Sport:** Swimming. **Hobbies:** Chess, Stamp Collecting. **Prof. Addr.:** College of Medicine, Arabian Gulf University, P.O.Box 26671 Manama, Bahrain, Tel.: 239707, e-mail: Faisal@mail.agu. edu.bh.

NASIR (Hanna, Musa), Jordanian academic. **Born** in 1936 in Jaffa, Palestine. **Married**, 4 children. **Educ.:** American University of Beirut, Lebanon; Purdue University, USA. **Dipl.:** M.Sc., Ph.D. in Nuclear Physics. **Career:** established "Birzeit University", the first Arab University in Palestine; President of Birzeit University; deported in November 1974 to Lebanon by Israel on charge of supporting the Palestine Liberation Organization; Elected Member of the Executive Committee of PLO (1981-84). **Publ.:** various articles on physics in scientific journals. **Hobbies:** swimming, chess, human rights of the Palestinians under occupation and higher education of the Palestinians. **Addr.:** P.O.Box 9942, Amman, Jordan.

NASIR (Sari), Jordanian academic. **Born** in Jerusalem, Palestine. **Married. Educ.:** University of Illinois, USA. **Dipl.:** B.A., M.A. and Ph.D. in Sociology. **Career:** Assistant Professor at State University of New York (1962-65); Professor, University of Jordan; Professor of Sociology, University of Jordan (1965-). **Publ.:** "The Arab Image in American Popular Culture", "The Arab Image in Britain", "A Study of Arabs in British and American Films", "The Arabs and the English" (1976), 2nd edition (1979). **Member:** The American Sociologists Association. **Prof. Addr.:** University of Jordan, Amman, Jordan.

NASIRI (Obeid bin Seif, al-), UAE Politician. **Born** in 1952. **Educ.:** B.Sc., Economics, Baghdad University (1976). **Career:** Deputy Chairman, UAE Bankers Association; Board Member, National Bank of Abu Dhabi; Director, Commodities Department, Abu Dhabi Investment Authority; Member, National Consultative Council; Minister of Petroleum and Mineral Resources (March 1997-to date). **Address:** Ministry of Petroleum and Mineral Resources, P.O.Box 59, Abu Dhabi, United Arab Emirates.

NASIRI (Rafa), Iraqi artist. **Born** in 1940 in Iraq. **Married. Educ.:** Fine Arts Institute, Baghdad, Iraq; Graphic Arts, Central Academy of Fine Arts, China; studied graphic arts in Lisbon with Gulbenkian Foundation Scholarship. **Career:** Appointed to Institute of Fine Arts in 1964; exhibited at Czech Cultural Centre, Baghdad, International Graphic Art Exhibition, Leipzig (1965), Iraqi Art Exhibition, Berlin (1966), Galeria Gravura, Lisbon, Autumn Salon, Estoril, First International Triennale, India (1968), Baghdad, Beirut, Liege (1969), Third International Biennale of Graphic Art, Cracow, Poland, Exhibition of Iraqi Posters, Baghdad (1970), Four Iraqi Artists Exhibition, National Gallery of Modern Art, Baghdad, Three Iraqi Arts Exhibition, Gallery One, Beirut, First International Biennale of Graphic Art, Norway, Exhibition of Arab Art, Cyprus, Fourth International Poster Biennale, poland (1972), Six Iraqi and Syrian Artists Exhibition, National Gallery of Modern Art, Baghdad and Arab Cultural Centre, Damascus, Fourth International Biennale of drawing, Rijeka, Yugoslavia, Fifth International Poster Biennale, Poland; issued manifesto "The New Vision" in 1969 with a group of Iraqi artists. **Award:** Honour Prize, International Summer Academy, Salzburg, Austria. **Hobbies:** music, reading. **Addr.:** 17/78 Qadissiya, Baghdad, Iraq.

NASR (Abdulrahman, Salman), Sudanese diplomat, administrator. **Born** in 1932 in al-Khandak, Sudan. **Son** of Salman Nasr. **Married**, Five children. **Educ.:** University of Khartoum, Sudan (1956); Birmingham University, UK (1963). Diploma in Public Administration. **Career:** Administrator in several Sudanese directorates; member of the Management Union; Governor of Southern Darfur Province; Governor of Red Sea Province (1977-80); Ambassador to Egypt (1981); attended First Agricultural Conference, Governors Conference, Administration Officers Conference, Administrative Planning Conference in Darfur and the Red Sea and other Political and social care conferences. **Medals:** Order of the Two Niles, 1st Class, Sudan; Order of the Son of Sudan, Sudan. **Sport:** Swimming. **Hobbies: Reading and chess. Addr.:** Ministry of Foreign Affairs, Khartoum, Sudan.

NASR (Anis, Naguib), Egyptian physician. **Born** on November 13, 1951 in Cairo. **Educ.:** College of the Christian Brothers, Heliopolis (1956-66); College de la Salle of the Christian Brothers, Cairo (1966-1970); Faculty of Medicine, Cairo University, Kasr El Ayni (1970-76). **Dipl.:** MBBCH (December 1975). **Career:** General Practitioner, Government Hospital. **Sports:** football and swimming. **Hobby:** Bridge. **Prof. Addr.:** Malawy General Hospital, Tel.: 872302, Miniyeh, Egypt. **Priv. Addr.:** 13, Abbassiyeene Street, Heliopolis, Tel.: 872302, Cairo, Egypt.

NASR (Mohamad Saad, Ahmad Mohamad), Egyptian physicist. **Born** on May 31, 1934 in Assyut. **Son** of Ahmad Mohamad Nasr **and** Mrs., née Fahima. **Married** on October 8, 1959 to Miss Ikbal Bashandi, 2 children: Oussama and Iman. **Educ.:** Cairo University, Uppsala University (Sweden). **Dipl.:** Bachelor of Science in Physics with Honors (1956), Master of Science (1959), Licentiate Fil-Lic (1961), Doctor of Philosophy (1962). **Career:** Demonstrator, Atomic Energy Establishment, Head Spectroscopy group (1956); Nuclear Physicist, Assyut University, Middle Eastern Regional-Radio Isotope Centre for Arab Countries in co-operation with the International Atomic Energy

Agency (Vienna); Expert Nuclear Physics College Advanced Technology, Libya (1966). **Publ.:** Author of several researches on nuclear beta and gamma ray spectroscopy, internal conversion coefficients measurement of gamma radiations, discoveries in nuclear properties and structure. **Member:** Mathematics and Physics Society (Cairo). **Prof. Addr.:** Nuclear Physics Department of Atomic Energy Establishment, Cairo. **Priv. Addr.:** 16, Shaikh Ali Mahmoud Street, Cairo, Egypt.

NASRALLAH (Fida, Miss), Deputy Director, Centre for Lebanese Studies. **Born** on August 29, 1960 in Accra, Ghana. **Daughter** of Bahige Nasrallah (businessman) **and** Mrs. Giselle Nasrallah, Nasrallah. **Educ.:** London School of Economics, London; The School of Translators and Interpreters, Geneva, Switzerland; The University of Dayton, OHIO-USA; American University of Beirut. **Dipl.:** PHD International Relations, London School of Economics; M.Sc. International Relations, London School of Economics; B.A. Political Science, University of Dayton, OHIO. **Career:** 1997- to present: Voter Education and Elections Advisor. Missions Included: Gaza; Yemen; Bosnia; Mali; Yugoslavia; Uganda; Cambodia; Liberia. Indonesia; Tanzania 1990-1997: Deputy Director, Centre for Lebanese Studies, Oxford; 1989-1990: Lecturer in International Relations, London School of Economics. **Other Information:** Member of: The Royal Institute of International Affairs; Royal United Services Institute; Middle East Studies Association of North America; British Society for Middle East Studies. **Decors:** Graduated with Honours - PHI Beta Kappa. **Sports:** Tennis; Table Tennis; Badminton. **Hobbies:** Wine Tasting; Cooking; Theatre; Reading; Swimming. **Credit Cards:** Visa, Master Card. **Prof. Addr.:** 59 Observatory Street, Oxford OX2 6EP, Tel.: (01865) 558465. **Priv. Addr.:** 46 Hormead Rd., London W9 3NQ, Tel.: 020 8960 0995.

NASRI (Hani Yahya Khalil), Saudi academic. **Born** in 1946. **Educ.:** Ph.D. (Islamic Social Philosophy). **Career:** Faculty member and Chairman, Sociology Department, King Abdulaziz University. **Member:** Presidential Club for Distinguished Graduate Students, Fordham University, New York; member, Board of Editors, the Journal of the Faculty of Arts and Humanities. **Publications:** three books and various research articles in academic journals and magazines. **Hobby:** horse riding. **Addr.:** Jeddah, Saudi Arabia.

NASSER (Abdallah Abdul Qadir), Saudi university lecturer. **Born** in 1950, in Mecca, Saudi Arabia. **Dipl.:** B.A. (Economics and Business Administration), U.S.A. (1974); M.A. (Business Administration) (1976). **Career:** Lecturer, King Abdulaziz University. **Hobbies:** sport, travel. **Adress:** Shamiyya Street, Mecca, Saudi Arabia.

NASSER (Hayat, Mohamed), Jordanian bank executive. **Born** on May 3, 1960 in Jericho. **Daughter** of Mohamed Nasser (Trader) **and** Mrs. Zahra. **Educ.:** Jordan University. **Career:** Jordan Co-operative Bank, Amman. **Prof. Addr.:** Jordan Co-operative Bank, 1343, Tel. 665171-4, Telex: JO 21835, Amman, Jordan. **Priv. Addr.:** P.O.Box 8172, Tel. 674524, Amman, Jordan.

NASSER (Mohamad), Moroccan engineer. **Born** on March 22, 1944 at Azrou. **Educ.:** Secondary in Meknes, superior studies in Paris. **Dipl.:** of Engineer from "Ecole Nationale des Sciences Géographiques de Paris". **Career:** Former General Secretary, Irrigation Office (ONMR); General Manager, Topographical Works and Real Estate Conservation; Assistant General Secretary, Ministry of Agriculture & Agrarian Reform (1968); Inspector General, Moroccan Agricultural Cooperations (SCAM & CMA) (1969); Vice-President, Meknes Provincial Council; Minister of Transport (October 10, 1977- Nov. 81). **Decor:** Knight, Order of the Throne (1966). **Addr.:** Rabat, Morocco.

NASSER (Mohamad), Iraqi educationalist and former diplomat. **Born** in 1914 in Iraq. **Educ.:** Teacher Training College (Baghdad), American University of Beirut and Columbia University (U.S.A.). **Dipl.:** Bachelor of Science, Master of Arts, Doctor of Education. **Career:** Schoolteacher (1934-41); Professor of Education and Dean of College of Education at Baghdad University (1941-63); Cultural Attaché and Permanent Representative of Iraq in the Arab League (1945-48); Cultural Attaché in Washington (1948-54); Alternate Delegate at the United Nations (Fifth General Assembly); President Teachers Union of Iraq (1963-64); Member Council University of Baghdad (1963-64); Minister of Education (1964); Ambassador of Iraq to U.S.S.R. (1965-66); Minister of Culture and National Orientation (1966); Professor of Educational Administration and former chairman, College of Education, Kuwait University (1967-77). **Publ.:** Include many School books in Arabic, "Arabic Readings" (2 volumes), 1940, "Civil Education" (1940), "Guide to Higher Education in the U.S.A." (1958) "Readings in Educational Thought". (Vol. 1, 1973); "Arabic-Islamic Educational Thought" (1977). **Addr.:** 46/95 University Community, Baghdad, Iraq.

NASSER (Mohamad, an), Tunisian official. **Born** on March 21, 1934 in ad-Djem (Tunisia). **Educ.:** Secondary and Higher. **Dipl.:** L.L.B., studied employment systems in several countries of Europe. **Career:** Joined the Ministry of Labour and Social Security (1957); Promoted Administrator (1959-60); Chief of the Cabinet of the Ministry of Public Health and Social Affairs (1961-74); Head of the Department of Labour, Vocational Training and Employment; Ministry of Youth and Sports (1965-66); Director-General of the National Institute of Vocational Training (1966); Tunisian Representative the International Labour Conference, at the Executive Board of the United Nations Children's Fund (1964); Member (1962-65) then Chairman of the seventeenth session of the Social Commission of the United Nations Organization (April 1966). **Addr.:** Tunis, Tunisia.

NASSER (Sharif, Ghazi Rakan), Jordanian aviation official. **Born** in 1939 in Cairo, Egypt, **Educ.:** trained as a pilot in the United Kingdom. **Career:** Officer, Jordanian Air Force; Director General of Civil Aviation (1971-72), (1974-82); Managing Director of Arab Wings Co. Ltd. (1982-to present). **Hobby:** Sports. **Prof. Addr.:** P.O.Box 341018, Amman, Jordan.

NATTO (Ibrahim Abbas), Saudi professor. **Born** in 1945 in Mecca. **Educ.:** B.A. (Government) (1968); M.A. (Public Administration) (1970); Ph.D. (Public Education Administration), University of Texas (1973). **Career:** Educational Expert, Ministry of Education, Saudi Arabia (1973-74); Director. Data & Research Documentation Centre, Ministry of Education (1974-76); Dean of Student Affairs, University of Petroleum and Minerals, Dhahran, Saudi Arabia (1977-78); Associate Professor, Faculty of Industrial Management/ Director of Preparatory Programmes, University of Petroleum and Minerals (1979-82); Visiting Scholar, University of Texas at Austin, USA (1982-83); Visiting Professor, Bahrain University Bollege (1983-85); Ast. Vice President, Training & Development, Gulf International Bank, Bahrain, Arabian Gulf; Associate Professor, University of Bahrain. **Member:** Association of Manarat Shargia Schools; University School Board, Dhahran; World Council of Curriculum and Instruction, U.S.A.; First World Conference on Muslim Education, Mecca; Chairman of Philanthropic Fund, Dhahran; Pi Sigma Alpha, Phi Delta Kappa, Phi Kappa Phi. **Publications:** Management: Basic Concepts (Wiley); Educational Ideas (Tihama); **Educational Administration in Bahrain** (Al-Hilaal). and papers and articles published in Saudi Arabia and abroad. **Hobbies:** Photography, Foreign Languages, Chess, Jogging, Poetry Writing. **Prof. Addr.:** University of Bahrain, P.O.Box 32038 Isa Town, Manama, Bahrain. Fax 449636; E-Mail: NATTO (a) cc. uob. ac.bh.

NAUIM (Abdallah al-Ali, al), Saudi official. **Born** in 1932 at Onaizah, Saudi Arabia. **Dipl.:** B.A. Hons. in History. **Career:** Teacher, Primary School, Onaizah (1950); Secondary School (1954); Deputy Headmaster of Secondary Schools in Onaizah, and Jeddah (1955); Director of Teachers' Institute, Riyadh (1957); General Director of Education, Najd Province (1961); Assistant Secretary General, King Saud University (1965); Cultural Attaché for Postgraduate Studies at the Royal Saudi Embassy, London (1970); Director General of National Gas and Industrialization Co. (1974); Mayor of Riyadh since 1976; Founder and Director of Illiteracy Prevention Centre, Onaizah (1952-53); founding member and Secretary of the Cultural Club, Onaizah (1953-55); member and General Secretary of the Supment and Evolution of the City of Riyadh; member, Supreme Committee for the Diplomatic Zone project, Riyadh, Qasr el-Hokm Project; member of the Board, Riyadh Water Supply and Drainage Authority, Saudi Arabian Boy Scouts Society, Riyadh, Saudi Red Crescent Society; Vice President and Managing Director, National Gas and Industrial Co.; member of the Permanent Board, Arab Cities Organization; member of the Board, Muslim Cities Organization, Arab Cities Development Fund; member of the Permanent Board, World Major Cities Organization; member and Vice President of Arab Urban Development Institute; member and Treadurer of Equestrian Club, Riyadh; Founder and President of the Board of Saleh Cultural Centre in Onaizah. **Honours:** numerous Medals awarded by Onaizah. **Honours:** numerous Medals awarded by Jordan, Indonesia, France, Spain, Venezuela, Sultanate of Oman and South Korea. **Publications:** various articles in local newspapers; delivered several lectures at King Saud University. **Prof. Addr.:** The Office of the Mayor, Tel.: 4040512, Riyadh. **Priv. Addr.:** Tel.: 4776360, Riyadh, Saudi Arabia.

NAZER (Abdul Fattah, Dr.), Saudi businessman. **Born** on March 31, 1945 in Jeddah, Saudi Arabia. **Son** of Mohiddin Mohammad Omar Nazer (deceased) **and** Mrs, Zakeia Ahmed H. Nazer. **Married** in 1974 in Jeddah to Miss Iman Ahmed Turki, 5 children: Tai, Seba, Tamara, Mohiddin and Mohammad. **Educ.:** Riyadh University, Riyadh, Saudi Arabia; University of Birmingham, England. **Dipl.:** B.Sc and M.A. (Chemistry); Ph.D (Chemistry). **Career:** Instructor, then Assistant professor, Riyadh University (1965-77); Controller General, Dallah Avco Trans Arabia Co. (DATAC) (1977-78), then Director General (1978-84); Director General, Larsen and Nielsen Saudi Arabia Ltd. (LANSA) (1981-85), Chairman of the Board (1981-88); Vice Chairman, Arabian Aircraft Services Co. (ARABASCO) (1981-); Vice Chairman of DOWTY-ARABASCO Ltd. (1984-); Vice President for Investment, Dallah Group Holding Co. (1984-); Pres./Chairman of the Board, Ittihad Sports Club (1985-87), re-elected (1988); Chairman of the Board, Tihama al-Mona International (1988-); **Member** of the Board of Directors of: Saudi Public Transport Co., Tihama Advertising, General Public Relations and Marketing Co., National Operation and Industrial Services Co., National Environmental Preservation Co., Dallah Human Resources Development Co., Aircraft Accessories Components Co. and Saudi company for Recreation Center. **Medal.:** Cum Laude, King's Cup Champion. **Sports:** Soccer, tennis, squash, golf, athletics, motor racing and horse racing. **Hobbies:** Arts, book reading, cinema, gardening, travel and theatre. **Member:** Saudi Football Federation; Ittihad Sports club; Dinners Club; The White Elephant Club, etc. **Credit Cards:** Amex Card; Visa/Barclay Card; Access/Master Card. **Prof. Addr.:** Dallah Group Holding Co., P.O.Box 430, Jeddah 21411, Tel.: 6710000, Jeddah, Saudi Arabia. **Priv. Addr.:** Cornish, al-Hamra, Jeddah, Saudi Arabia.

NAZER (Ali Gamal, al), Egyptian politician. **Born** on

January 22, 1930 in Aswan, Egypt. **Son** of Mohamad A. al-Nazer. **Married** in November 1966, 2 children: Hatem and Rasha. **Educ.:** Cairo University, Cairo; University of Pittsburgh, Pennsylvania, USA. **Dipl.:** B.A. in Commerce (1950); M.S. (1958). **Career:** Assistant Division Chief, Ministry of Economy (1961); Division Chief, Ministry of Economy (1966); Deputy Director-General, Ministry of Economy (1970); Director-General, Ministry of Economy (1975); Minister of Tourism and Civil Aviation (May 1980-May 1982). **Awards:** Commdr., Order du Mérite, Germany (1976); Grand Chevalier, Italy (1976). **Sports:** Swimming, Tennis. **Member:** Automobile Club, Heliopolis Sporting Club. **Prof. Addr.:** Cairo, Egypt.

NAZER (Fuad), Saudi statesman. **Career:** Former Ambassador to Belgium and Egypt; has served in Saudi foreign service in London and Madrid; Presently Saudi Ambassador to Argentina. **Address:** Ministry of Foreign Affairs, Riyadh, Saudi Arabia.

NAZER (Hisham M.), Saudi former minister. **Born** on 31 August 1932. **Dipl.:** B.A., Honours (International Relations), University of California, U.S.A., 1957; M.A. (Political Science), University of California. **Career:** Joined the Directorate General of Oil and Mineral Affairs (now the Ministry of Petroleum and Mineral Resources) as Adviser (1958) Director General, Ministry of Petroleum and Mineral Resources; also held administrative and technical positions before this appointment; first Governor to represent Saudi Arabia on the Board of Governors of OPEC (1961); Deputy Minister of Petroleum and Mineral Resources (1962-68); President, Central Planning Organization (with a ministerial grade) (1968-75); Minister of State and member of the Council of Ministers (in addition to the Post of President of the CPO) (1971-75); Minister of Planning, since October 1975 to 1990 as well as Minister of Petroleum and Mineral Resources (since 1986-Aug. 1995) and Vice Chairman, Royal Commission for Jubail and Yanbu (November 1975); Chairman, Saudi Arabian Marketing and Refinning Co., Riyadh; Saudi Arabian Oil Company. **Member:** the Higher Committee for Administrative Reforms, the Supreme Council for Petroleum and Minerals, the Higher Council for Universities, the Committee for Mineral Affairs; Board of Directors of the Public Investment Fund; the Supreme Council, King Abdulaziz University, University of Petroleum and Minerals, Muhammad Ibn Saud Islamic University; Chancellor's Associate, Life member, UCLA, U.S.A. **Honours:** King Abdulaziz Sash; National Cedar Medal (Grand Sash Grade), Lebanon; Order of Civil Merit (Gran Cruz), Spain; Order of Diplomatic Service Merit, Republic of Korea; Order of African Redemption (Knight-Great Bant), Republic of Liberia; Republic Medal of First Grade, Egypt, Republic Medal of First Grade, Democratic Republic of Sudan; Sash of Leopold II, Belgium; Sash and Star of Lama, First Grade, Republic of China; Humayun Medal of First Grade, Iran; National Order of Merit, France; First Class Order of the Sacred Treasure of Japan; Gold Medal of Industrial Service, Republic of Korean; Knight Grand Cross of the Royal Order of the Polar Star, Sweden. **Publications:** several petroleum studies in the local and international press, including: Petroleum Price in the Middle East, Towards a Better Understanding of our Petroleum Life, Law of Hydro-carbons in Venezuela, Petroleum in Venezuela, Patriotism and the Responsibility of the Citizen, Power in International Relations, Wealth and the Nation Past and Future and New Trends in Petroleum Policy. **Address:** Riyadh, Saudi Arabia.

NAZER (Ibrahim Omar), Saudi professor. **Born** in 1944 in Jeddah, Saudi Arabia. **Dipl.:** Ph.D. (Physiology). **Career:** Assistant Lecturer, Faculty of Science, Riyadh University (1965-67); Lecturer, (1973-75); Assistant Professor (1975-78); member of Board, Saudi Biological Society (1975-77). **Hobbies:** sport, soccer, billiards. **Address:** Riyadh, Saudi Arabia.

NAZER (Ismail), Saudi lawyer and legal adviser **Born** in 1927. **Educ.:** graduated from King's College, London. **Dipl.:** LL.B. (1950). **Career:** Practising lawyer since 1952; Government Relations officer and Attorney Arabian American Oil Co (1952-62); **Member:** of Inner Temple Bar, London; Lecturer on legal subjets; legal representative of several international companies and banks; member of World Peace Through Law Society; member of International Law Society; member of several charity societies; member of Board, Arab Development Company. **Publications:** newspaper articles. **Hobbies:** reading, lecturing. **Address:** P.O.Box 154, Khobar, Saudi Arabia, 31952.

NAZER (Mansour Othman), Saudi academic. **Born** in Jeddah in 1947. **Educ.:** Ph.D. **Career:** Chairman, Mechanical Engineering Department, University of Petroleum and Minerals, Dhahran. **Member** American Society for Mechanical Engineers, International Society for Solar Energy **Publications:** Transient Performance of a Flat Plate Solar Energy Collector Model, the University of Michigan, Mechanical Engineering Department (Report 1975); Thermal Performance of Building and Two Flat Plate Collector System, Colorado State University (Ph.D. thesis, December 1978); Prediction of the Thermal Performance of Two Flat Plate Collectors under Saudi Arabia Meteorological Conditions, SOLTECH Conference, Bahrain (April 1978) Solar Power Station for a Village in Saudi Arabia, United Nations University seminar on Solar Technology in Rural Settings, Atlanta, Georgia (June 1979); Photovoltaic Concentrator Power Station for a Village in Saudi Arabia, 1980 Photovoltaic Solar Energy Conference, Cannes, France (October 1980); under publication: Comparison of Hot and Cold Storage Systems; Analysis of a Rankin Cycle Air Conditioning Systems. **Prof. Addr.:** UPM, Tel.: 8602540, Dhahran. **Priv. Addr.:** Tel.: 8606279, Dhahran, Saudi Arabia.

NAZER (Naji Mohiddin), Saudi businessman. **Born** in 1943 in Jeddah, Saudi Arabia. **Dipl.:** Ph.D. (Geology) 1973. **Career:** Lecturer. (1973-75) then Assistant Professor, Faculty of Science, King Saud University; Vice Dean for Libraries, King Saud University (1977); Assistant Director General Dallah-Avco for Logistics and Director General, Trans Arabia Supply Company (TASCO); Vice-President Dallah Albarakah Group; Chairman of the Board Dallah Agriculture, Saudi Arabia, Chairman Misr Arab Poultry, Egypt; Member of the Board Albarakah INV. Co., London, Iqra Charity London, Islamic Jordan Bank, Jordan. **Hobbies:** sports, reading. **Address:** P.O.Box 430, Tel.: 6710000, Jeddah, Saudi Arabia.

NAZIR (Osman, Abdulla, el), Sudanese, Managing Director - Kenana Sugar Company. **Born** in 1937 in Medani, Sudan. **Son** of Abdulla El Nazir. **Married** in 1971 in Khartoum to Huda Yousif Ahmed, 5 children: Haytham, Waleed, Yousif, Ahmed, Hala. **Educ.:** University of Delhi B.Sc., M.Sc (Economics), University of Glasgow. **Career:** Managing Director - Kenana Sugar Company (1981-); State Minister for Finance - Ministry of Finance (1979-1981); Under Secretary - Minister of Finance (1975-1979); Deputy Under Secretary - Minister of Finance (1970-1975); Senior Officer - Minister of Finance (1965-1970). **Sports Practised:** Swimming - Football. **Hobbies:** Reading - Art - Decoration. **Prof. Addr.:** Kenana Sugar Company Limited, P.O.Box 2632 Khartoum, Tel.: 0024911 472171, Sudan. **Priv. Addr.:** El Safa - Khartoum, Tel.: 0024911 271921, Sudan.

NAZZAL (Tawfiq), Palestinian executive. **Born** in Jerusalem on 10.3.22. **Son** of Anton Nazzal (Hotel Owner) **and** Djamileh Shamali. **Married** to Marcella Mangini on 18.6.50. 3 sons, Anton (1955), Mario (1957), Roberto (1964). **Educ.:** Secondary and University. **Dipl.:** B.Sc. (in Washington D.C.). **Career:** Chairman, Tawfiq & Nabih Nazzal. **Sports:** Tennis. **Hobby:** Bridge. **Member:** International Hotel Association; Jordan Hotel Association; Rotary Club; President Founder of SKAL CLUB in Jordan; Director Y.M.C.A. **Credit Cards:** American Express, Visa. **Prof. Addr.:** Jordan Int. Co. Building, 3rd Circle, Amman, P.O.Box 10, Tel.: 42350. **Priv. Addr.:** 3rd Circle, Jabal Amman, P.O.Box 10, Amman, Tel.: 4436.

NEDHAMEDDIN (Arfan, Abdul Kader), Syrian journalist. **Born** in 1941 in Damascus, Syria. **Married**, 3 children. **Educ.:** Lebanon University, Beirut. **Dipl.:** M.A. in Economics and Political Science. **Career:** Editorial Secretary of "al-Hayat" newspaper, Beirut (1966), Managing Editor (1969), Editor in Chief (1970-76); Managing Director of "Asharq al-Awsat" newspaper (1978-80), Deputy Editor in Chief (1980-83); Member of the International Press Centre and the National Union of Journalists, UK; Editor in Chief of "Asharq al-Awsat" newspaper (1983-). **Publ.:** "Jerusalem, Belief and Struggle" (1971), "Lebanon - Where To?" (1976), "Hearbeats Between Black and White" (1985). **Hobby:** reading. **Prof. Addr.:** Arab Press House, 182-84 High Holborn, London WCI, United Kingdom. **Priv. Addr.:** 12 Browning Close, Randolph Avenue, Maida Vale, London W9, United Kingdom.

NEKROUF (Younes), Moroccan former official. **Born** in 1916 in Morocco. **Educ.:** Institut des Hautes Etudes Marocaines, Rabat and Universities of Bordeaux and Algiers. **Dipl.:** B.A. **Career:** Government Interpreter (1935-39); School Teacher and Inspector of Schools (1939-55); Director of Cabinet of Minister of Education (1955-57); Cultural Counsellor at Moroccan Embassy in Paris and Permanent Delegate to Unesco (1957-59); Director Cultural Affairs and Technical Assistance, Ministry of Foreign Affairs (1959-61); Counsellor, Minister Plenipotentiary, Embassy to France (1961-64); Ambassador to Senegal, Gambia, Guinea, Liberia (1965-67); Ambassador to Yugoslavia (1967-68); Director of Political Affairs, Ministry of Foreign Affairs (1968-71); Ambassador to India (1971-74); Delegate to UN General Assembly (1965, 1968-71); Moroccan Representative at Various International Conferences. **Publ.:** Author of "Méthode Active d'Arabe" (2 volumes) 1958, various essays and articles of Portuguese colonisation. **Awards:** Officer of the Legion of Honour, Academic Palms (France); Commander, Arts et Lettres (France); Officer, Ouissame Alaouite (Morocco); Officer of the Order of the Throne (Morocco), Grand Officer, National Order of Yugoslavia; Order of Tudor Vladimirescu of Romania; Knight of the Grand Cross, Order of Merit (Italy); Grand Officer, Order of Merit (Senegal). **Addr.:** Rabat, Morocco.

NEMATALLA (Anis G., Dr.), Egyptian Diplomat. **Born** on June 30, 1937 in Egypt. **Son** of Guerguis Nematalla (Engineer) **and** Mrs. Julia Nematalla. **Married** on May 1, 1976 in Cairo, Egypt to Mrs. Magda Rizkalla Lotfy Nematalla, 2 children: Mr. Anda Nematalla & Mr. Nayer Nematalla. **Educ.:** University of Cairo, Egypt; Prague University, Czechoslovakia; Academy of International Law, Mexico City. **Dipl.:** Bachelor Degree in Laws, M.A. International Economic and Political Relations, Ph.D. in International Law. **Career:** Attache, M.F.A., Egypt (1959-1962); Third Secretary Embassy of Egypt, India (1962-1966); Second Secretary, Office of Official Spokesman of the Government of Egypt, Cairo (1967-1968); First Secretary Embassy of Egypt, Czechoslovakia (1970-1974); Counsellor, Embassy of Egypt, Burundi (1976-1980); Counsellor M.F.A., Cairo (1980-1982); Minister Plenipotentiary & Deputy Chief of Mission, Embassy of Egypt, Tokyo, Japan (1982-1986); Protocol Department M.F.A., Cairo (1986-1990); Ambassador of Egypt, Mexico (1990-). **Work:** Professor of «Protocol», Egyptian Diplomatic Institute; Lecturer in Protocol, Administrative Training Center, M.F.A., Cairo; Diplomatic Institute of Somalia; Consultative Council of Egypt; Policy Academy for Strategic Studies; Professor of «Political, Diplomatic and Economic Terminology» and of «Translation from English to

Arabic», Faculty of Mass-Media, Cairo University. **Awards:** Bearer of the Order of the Republic, Arab Republic of Egypt (1982); Order of the Sacred Treasure of Japan (1986); Order of Right, Culture and Peace of Mexico (1991); Bearer of the Order of Academy of Science: Invention Engineering and Research, of Mexico (1992). **Sport:** Tennis. **Hobbies:** Reading, Music. **Member:** Maadi Club, Cairo; University Club, Mexico, and Lebanese Club, Mexico. **Credit Cards:** Banamex, Visa, International Arab Bank. **Prof. Addr.:** Alejandro Dumas 131, Polanco, Mexico, D.F., C.P. 11560, Tel.: 282-12-94. **Priv. Addr.:** Ahuehueies sur 641, Bosques de Las Lomas Mexico D.F., C.P. 11700, Tel.: 596-48-05.

NEMMICHE (Bekhti, Djelloul), Algerian politician. **Born** in 1921. **Married**, 2 children. **Career:** Officer of National Liberation Army (ALN); Director of International Studies at the Ministry of National Defence; African Division Director at the Ministry of Foreign Affairs (1965-66); Ambassador to Guinea (1966-70); Secretary General, Ministry of Public Health (1970-79); Deputy President of Social Affairs Commission at the National Popular Assembly (1977); ALN Member, FLN Central Committee (1979); Ambassador to Mauritania (1979-80); Minister of Moujahidine (1980-1983); Chairman of the National Merit Council (1984). **Prof. Addr.:** Algiers, Algeria.

NESSIM (Magdy, Adib), Egyptian interior designer and decorator. **Born** on June 3, 1948 in Cairo (Egypt). **Married** to Josephine Anne Cassidy in 1976, 1 child: a daughter. **Educ.:** English School, Heliopolis, Cairo; Ayn Shams University, Faculty of Engineering, Department of Architecture; University of Oslo, Urban and Regional Planning. **Dipl.:** B.Sc. (Architectural Engineering) (1971); Certificate of Achievement (Oslo University) (1971). **Career:** Manager, Nessim Brick and Tile Factory (July-Dec. 1971); Head, Interior Design Department, Ghabbour Brothers and Co. (Jan-Sep. 1972); Appointed architect by the Municipality of Aalborg (Denmark) (Oct.-Feb. 1973); set up own consulting office (1973); formed the Engineering Consultants Group (1974), Director of that Group since 1975. **Member:** S.O.S. Children's Village, a benevolent foundation for destitute children. **Sports:** Horseriding, swimming and fishing. **Prof. Addr.:** 13, Antikhana street, Tel.: 97346, Cairo. **Priv. Addr.:** 55, Misr Helwan Road, Maadi, Cairo, Egypt.

NIAZI (Mohamad, Aly), Egyptian international civil servant. **Born** on December 1, 1926 in Alexandria (Egypt). **Married**, with children. **Educ.:** Institute of Chartered Accountants in England and Wales (UK) (1947-53). **Dipl.:** FCA (1953). **Career:** Senior Auditor, Hewat, Bridson and Newby, Cairo (1953-56); Senior Partner, Niazi and Co. (Egypt) (1956-63); Auditor, UN, New York (1964-67); Chief, Administrative Management Section, United Nations Industrial Development Organisation (UNIDO) Vienna (Austria) (1967-73); Deputy Director; Accounts Divisions, Office of Financial Service, UN, New York. since 1973. Now retired. **Clubs:** Alexandria Sporting club and Alexandria Yacht club. **Sports:** Tennis, skiing and swimming. **Priv. Addr.:** Tarrytown, NY 10591, USA.

NIJMEH (Elias, H.E. Mgr.), Syrian archbishop. **Born** in 1920 in Aleppo. **Educ.:** Ste. Anne Seminary (Jerusalem), University of Rome. **Dipl.:** Doctor in Philosophy and Theology. **Career:** Ordained Priest (1944); Secretary, Patriarch Maximos IV Saïgh (1962-65); Professor, St. Esprit University; Sacred Assistant Archbishop, of Patriarch Maximos V Hakim since 1972; Archbishop of Tripoli, Lebanon (1995), retired. **Award:** Lebanese medal (1958). **Addr.:** St. Sauveur Couvent, Jounieh, Lebanon.

NIL (Zakaria, Mustafa), Egyptian journalist. **Born** in 1924 in Dakahliya, Egypt. **Son** of Mustafa Nil. **Married**, five children. **Educ.:** Diploma in Arabic language. **Career:** Journalist (since 1950); Head of Arabic Affairs Department, "al-Ahram" daily newspaper; covered the Iraqi Revolution (1958), the Libyan Revolution (1969) and the Yemen Revolution (1962); also, covered most of the Arab summit conferences. **Publ.:** "Focus of Danger in the Arab Gulf" (1971), and other books. **Medals:** Order of the Tunisian Republic (1971). **Member** of the Hunting Club. **Sports:** Swimming. **Hobbies:** Travel, classical literature, historical novels. **Addr.:** Cairo, Egypt.

NI'MAH (Dr. Hassan, Ali Hussain, Al), Qatari Ambassador to the United Nations. **Born** on February in 1940. **Son** of Ali Hussain Al-Ni'mah. **Educ.:** Cambridge University, London, 1975 Ph.D., Al-Dawha Secondary School/ Ministry of Education, Doha. **Dipl.:** Ph.D. **Career:** Ambassador, Ministry of Foreign Affairs, Doha-Qatar (1975); Ambassador-Embassy of Qatar, New Delhi, India (1976-1989); Ambassador and Permanent Reprensentative to the U.N. New York (1990- untill now). **Hobby:** Poetry Art. **Credit Card:** American Express. **Prof. Addr.:** Qatar Mission to U.N., 747 Third Ave., 22nd Floor, N.Y. 10017, Tel.: 212 486 9335. **Priv. Addr.:** 43 East 70th Street, New York, N.Y. 10021.

NIMATALLAH (Yusuf, Abdul Wahib), Saudi economist. **Born** in 1936. **Educ.:** American University of Beirut; University of Massachusetts. **Career:** Banque de l'Indochine (1952-57); Teaching Assistant (Economics), University of Massachusetts (1963-65); Professor, Monetary and International Economics, University of Riyadh (1965-73); Adviser, Minister of Finance on Money and Banking, Oil Finance and Planning (1967-73); Adviser, Sultan of Oman on Oil, Finance, Central Bank of Oman (1975-78); Alternate Executive Director, IMF (1979-81); Executive Director, IMF (1981), USA. **Addr.:** Riyadh, Saudi Arabia.

NIMIR (Ibrahim Mohamad, Ali), Sudanese banker. **Born** in 1923 in Khartoum (Sudan). **Married**, 6 children. **Educ.:** Gordon Memorial College (1945); University of

Wales (Great Britain); training at the Bank of England, Barclays Bank, D.C.O., London; Midland Bank Ltd., London; Crédit Lyonnais, Paris (France). **Dipl.:** B.A. (Honours) Economy; Dipl. of Arts; B.Sc. **Career:** Inspector of Revenues, Ministry of Finance and Economics (1955-57); Senior Inspector, Exchange Control, Ministry of Finance and Economics (1957-60); Manager, Exchange Control, Bank of Sudan (1960); Assistant General Manager, Bank of Sudan (1961); General Manager, Bank of Sudan (1963); Deputy Governor, Bank of Sudan (1964-67); Co-Managing Director and Vice-Chairman, el-Nilein Bank (1967-70); Chairman and Managing Director, el-Nilein Bank (1970-73); Governor, Bank of Sudan (1973-Feb. 1980); Chairman and Managing Director, National Bank of Sudan (1980). **Member:** Previously Ministerial Council for National Economy; Board of Directors, Sudan Development Corporation (up to Feb. 1980); University Councils, University of Khartoum and Omdurman Islamic University; Alternate Governor for Sudan, Internationl Monetary Fund (IMF) and AMF (Arab Monetary Fund), Abu Dhabi (up to 1980); Board of Directors, Cotton Public Corporation (up to Feb. 1980); European Bank (up to Feb. 1980). **Addr.:** Khartoum, Sudan.

NIMR (Rifaat, Sidqi, al), Jordanian banker. **Born** in 1918 in Nablus, Palestine. **Married,** 3 children. **Educ.:** Cairo University, Egypt. **Dipl.:** B.A. in Commercial Studies. **Career:** Manager of Arab Bank (1947-57); Area Manager of Bank of Riyadh in Saudi Arabia (1957-59); Area Manager of Cairo Bank, Saudi Arabia (1959-62); Area Manager of Saudi National Commercial Bank, Lebanon and Syria (1962-1964); Chairman and Director of Arab Federate Bank, Lebanon (1964-1971); Chairman and Director of Banque Beyrouth pour le Commerce (Commercial Bank of Beirut-BBC), Lebanon (1972-); Chairman of Beirut Building Co. (1979-1986). **Prof. Addr.:** Makdessi Street, Hamra Area, P.O.Box 110216, Beirut, Lebanon. Tel.: (01) 867459, 347981, 342020, Fax: (01) 865073, Telex: 22932/44839 BBC, 21457 Becoba.

NISF (Humud, Yusuf, al), Kuwaiti businessman, statesman. **Born** in 1918 in Kuwait. **Son** of Yusuf al-Nisf. **Married,** eight children. **Career:** Family business; member of the Municipal Council (1960-62); member of Parliament (1963-76); Minister of Public Health (1965); Manager of family business; Minister of Public Works (1971, 1975, 1976). **Addr.:** Mohamed Bin Youssef al-Nisf & Partners, P.O.Box 871 Safat, Kuwait.

NISF (Muhammad, Yusuf, al), Kuwaiti politician. **Born** in 1915. **Educ.:** general. **Career:** Director of the Public Works Department in the 1950s; Member of Joint Council of Shaikh and Merchants set up to draft electoral regulations of the Constituent Assembly (1961), Member of the Constituent Assembly (1961); Minister of Social Affairs (1962-63); Member of the Board of Chamber of Commerce; Director of Kuwait Pipe Company and Kuwait Fund for Arab Economic Development; Former Chairman of al-Ahliya Insurance Company. **Prof. Addr.:** al-Ahliya Insurance Company SAK, P.O.Box 1602, Kuwait, Kuwait.

NIXON (Patrick, Michael), British diplomat. **Born** in Reading, England in 1944. **Son** of John Nixon, Consultant Ophthalmologist **and** Mrs. Hilary Nixon. **Married** in 1968 to Elizabeth Carlton, four sons. **Educ.:** Magdalene College, Cambridge. **Dipl.:** M.A. **Career:** Joined the Foreign Office (1965); Middle East Centre for Arab Studies in Lebanon (1966); Third Secretary, British Embassy, Cairo (1968); Second Secretary (commercial), British Embassy, Lima (1970); Second and later First Secretary FCO (1973); Head of Chancery, British Embassy, Tripoli, Libya (1977); Executive Director, British Information Services, New York (1980); Assistant, later Head, Near East and North Africa Department, FCO (1983-87); Ambassador to Qatar (1987-90); Counsellor, FCO (1990-93); High Commissioner to Zambia (1994-97); Director, FCO (1997-98); Ambassador to the United Arab Emirates (since November 1998). **Medals:** OBE (1984); CMG (1989). **Prof. Addr.:** c/o Foreign and Commonwealth Office, London SWI, United Kingdom.

NOORUDDIN (Nooruddin, Abdalla), Bahraini banker. **Born** in Bahrain in 1945. **Son** of Abdalla Nooruddin. **Married** to Faika Bastaki, 3 Children: Nabeel, Ameera and Abdalla. **Educ.:** Hendon Polytechnic. **Dipl.:** Institute of Cost & Management Accountants. **Career:** Manager-Operations, Chase, Bahrain (1971-76); Deputy General Manager, National Bank of Bahrain (1976-79); General Manager & Chief Executive, National Bank of Bahrain (1980-83); General Manager and Chief Executive of Arab Insurance Group (since 1986) Director of Bahrain Telecommunications Company, Bahrain; Director of Arla Bank International, Bahrain, Director of National Bank of Bahrain. **Sports:** Swimming, Tennis. **Credit Cards:** Visa. **Addr.:** P.O.Box 26992, Manama, Bahrain, Tel.: 231110.

NOSSEIR (Mohamed, Mahmoud), Egyptian Businessman. **Born** in 1937 in Egypt. **Married,** 2 children. **Educ.:** Cairo University, Egypt. **Dipl.:** B.Sc. in Electronic and Communication Engineering. **Career:** Field Engineer, Systems Engineer and Senior Sales Engineer, IBM (Egypt & Arab Countries) (1960-64); Pioneered installation of the first four Computer systems in Egypt; Middle East Engineer and Marketing Consultant to several European companies, London, UK (1965-68); Founder & Managing Director Al Ahram management and Computer Centre (1967-72); Oil trading & Supplier of Crude Oil to several independent refineries, Athens (1972-84); as of (1973), his oil business expanded to a full trading firm, dealing in Oil & Oil products operating out of London (Medoil International); ALKAN CO. (Established 1975); Mr. Nosseir retains overall supervision of the independent management of the Nine Sister companies of which he is the main shareholder & Chairman: ALKAN ESTABLISHMENT, GIZA SYSTEMS ENGINEERING, EGYPTIAN INTERNATIONAL MOTORS, EGYPTIAN INTERNATIONAL SERVICE ENGINEERING, EIM INVESTMENT CO. Ltd. FREE ZONE, EGYPTIAN COMPUTER SYSTEMS, ALKAN BUGSHAN INVESTMENTS, ALKAN-PHARMA, ALKAN AGRO. The group has partnerships & business relations with over 20 US & Multinational Corporations among them, ELI LILLY, IBM, PEPSI COLA, ROCKWELL INTERNATIONAL, DIGITAL EQUIPMENT, ITUCHO CORPORATION, HUGUES AIRCRAFT CO., RENAULT, KOMATSU, YAMAHA, ATLAS COPCO, RJR, NABISCO & RAYTHEON AIRCRAFT (BEECH CRAFT). **Member:** EGYPTIAN BUSINESS ASSOCIATION, AMERICAN CHAMBER OF COMMERCE, SYNDICATE of EGYPTIAN ENGINEERS, THE PRINCE OF WALES BUSINESS LEADERS FORUM. **Prof. Addr.:** 2 Mesaha Square, Dokki-Giza, Egypt. **Priv. Addr.:** P.O.Box 1913, Cairo 11511, Egypt.

NOUH (Adnan Saddiq), Saudi executive. **Born** in 1945. **Dipl.:** B.Sc. (Telecommunication), University of Alexandria 1966; M.Sc. (Solid State Electronics), Carnegie Mellon University 1973. **Career:** Instructor, College of Engineering, University of Riyadh (1966-68); Assistant Professor, System Engineering, College of Engineering; assisted in establishing Analogue Computer Laboratory; Consultant to General Organization for Social Insurance (1973-76); Managing Director of Computer Center, Faculty of Engineering, Riyadh University; responsible for the Information System of Saudi Arabia, Presidency of Youth Welfare, Directing the creation of the information system for Saudi Credit Bank in Riyadh. **Publications:** A system Design for Arabic Characters Recognition by Digital Computer, The 2nd Conference for Pure and Applied Science, ASRS, Manchester, U.K. 1976; A Colour TV Digital Pattern Generator, First Congress of International Technology, Pittsburgh, U.S.A. 1976; An Integral Tunable Active B.P. Filter, IZZZ International Symposium on Circuits and Systems, Phoenix, U.S.A. 1977; A Proposed Experimental Laboratory for Picture Processing by Digital Laboratory for Picture Processing by Digital Computer, The 13th International Conference for Statistics, Computer Science and Social Research, Cairo, Egypt 1977; Some Problems in Digitalization of CTV Signals for the Proposed Arab Satellite, EUROCON 77, Venice, Italy 1977. **Sports:** soccer, swimming. **Address:** P.O.Box 800, Riyadh, Saudi Arabia.

NOUH (Ahmad Ahmad), Egyptian politician. **Born** on December 4, 1921. **Educ.:** Alexandria University and Air Academy, Egypt. **Dipl.:** Engineer. **Career:** Lieutenant-General, Pilot Engineer, General Headquarters Armed Forces; Technical General Manager, Misrair; General Secretary, Ministry of War; Assistant Minister, Ministry of War; Minister of State for Civil Aviation (1971-72); Minister of Civil Aviation (1972-74); Minister of Tourism (1973-74); Minister of Supply and Home Trade (May 1980-1982). **Addr.:** Cairo, Egypt.

NOUIRA (Chekib, Hedi), Tunisian economist. **Born** in 1950 in Tunis. **Son** of Hedi Nouira (former Prime Minister) **and** Mrs., Hamida née Assia. **Married** in 1975 in Carthage to Miss Neyla Jilani, two children. **Educ.:** Lycée Carnot, Tunis; George Washington University, Washington DC, USA; University of Sorbonne Panthéon, Paris. **Dipl.:** B.A. in Economics, M.A. in Economics, Banking and Finance. **Career:** Chase Manhattan Bank Training Program (1974); Conseiller, Economic Development Bank of Tunisia (1976); General Manager, Union Tunisienne de Banques, Paris (1979); Former General Manager and Member of the Board of Directors of Economic Development Bank of Tunisia and various other banks and companies. **Publ.:** Various studies and conferences on Project Financing, Banking in Developping Countries. **Medals:** Commander Order of the Republic of Tunisia. **Sports:** Tennis, water skiing. **Hobbies:** Sailing, fishing, music. **Priv. Addr.:** Sidi Bou Said, Tel.: 340811, Tunisia.

NOUIRA (Habib), Tunisian diplomat. **Born** in 1925 in Monastir, Tunisia. **Married**, 3 children. **Educ.:** University of Zitouna, Tunis and Cairo, Egypt. **Career:** Worked for the Maghreb Arab Bank, Cairo (1952); after Independence joined the Tunisian Foreign Service; Embassy to Libya (1956-57); Embassy to Morocco (1957-59); Embassy to Egypt (1962-64); Embassy to Iraq (1964-65); Seconded to the Ministry of Foreign Affairs Services (1965-66); Ambassador to Libya (1966-67); Ministry of Foreign Affairs, Tunis; Ambassador to Kuwait (1969-73); Ambassador to Iraq (Nov. 1973); Ambassador to Syria (May 1974). **Addr.:** Ministry of Foreign Affairs, Tunis, Tunisia.

NOUR (Mohamad, Abdellatif), Egyptian banker. **Born** in 1953 in Cairo. **Son** of Abdellatif Nour (businessman) **and** Mrs., née Pacenthe Aref. **Married** in 1978 in Cairo to Miss Mona Istanbouli, two daughter. **Educ.:** Faculty of Commerce, Cairo University. **Dipl.:** Accounting. **Career:** In banking (since 1978). General Manager of the Chase National Bank (Egypt) SAE and responsible for all credit and operation activities in the bank branches in Delta. Presently General Manager, Hong Kong Egyptian Bank, Cairo. **Sports:** Football and tennis. **Member:** of Gezira Sporting Club, Cairo; International Club, London. **Credit Cards:** American Express, Access Card. **Prof. Addr.:** 3 Abul Feda Street, Abul Feda Bldg., P.O.Box 126 D, Zamalek, Cairo. **Priv. Addr.:** 3, Road 203, Maadi, Tel.: 3521485, Cairo, Egypt.

NOUR (Mohamed, Abdalla), Sudanese international civil servant. **Born** on June 2, 1925 in Omdurman (Sudan). **Married**, With 4 children. **Educ.:** Bsc. (Hon.) University of London (1948-51); Rothamsted Experimental Station, (1954-56); Ph.D. (Plant Pathology) London University.

Career: Head, Department of Crop Protection (1957); Dean, Faculty of Agriculture, University of Khartoum (1957-69); Deputy Vice Chancellor, University of Khartoum (1962-64); Minister of Agriculture and Forestry, Khartoum (1969-70); Assistant Director General and Regional Representative for Near East, Food and Agriculture Organisation (FAO), Cairo, Egypt (1970-78); Deputy Director General, International Center for Agricultural Research in the Dry Areas (ICARDA), Lebanon (1978-81). Director General of ICARDA (1981-87); Director Regional Bureau for Arab States and Europe (1987-1991); Executive Director, Centre for Environment and Development Arab Region and Europe-CEDARE (1992- to date). **Awarded:** The Republican Order of Egypt (First Class) (1978); the Order of the Nile (Sudan) First Class (1979); Silver Jubilee, Award from the University of Khartoum (1981); Recipient Honorary Degree of Doctor of Science from the University of Khartoum (1983); the cedar Medal of Lebanon (1991). **Member:** Association of Applied Biologists (UK); Philosophical Society, Khartoum. **Present Addr.:** CEDARE, P.O.Box 52 Orman, Giza Egypt, Fax: 5703242, Syria.

NOUR (Tariq Mahmoud, Abdal-Fattah), Egyptian businessman. **Born** in 1945 in Cairo, Egypt. **Married,** 1 son. **Educ.:** Cairo University, Egypt. **Dipl.:** B.Sc. in Business Management. **Career:** Computer Programmer of "al-Ahram" newspaper (1970-76); Member of the Panel of Egyptian Businessmen and of the American Chamber of Commerce; General Director of Americana Advertising Company (1976-). **Hobby:** music. **Member:** Gezira Sporting Club. **Prof. Addr.:** Americana Advertising, 32 Radwan Bin al-Tabib, Tel.: 730855, 732879, Telex: 94388 NOUR UN, Giza, Cairo, Egypt. **Priv. Addr.:** 22 Shara Omar bin al-Khattab, Mohandiseen, Cairo, Egypt.

NOURALLAH (Nourallah), Syrian statesman and former chairman of central bank. **Born** in Syria. **Educ.:** Diploma in Banking. **Career:** Ministry of Finance, Director, then Chairman, then Governor of Central Bank of Syria, Director General, Ministry of Foreign Affairs, Minister of Finance (May 1969). **Addr.:** Damascus, Syria.

NOURANI (Abdelmalek), Algerian former minister. **Born** in 1941. **Married,** 3 children. **Dipl.:** LL.B., Titular of DEA for fittings. **Career:** Member of FLN Civil Organization (1957-59); Officer at the National Liberation Army (1960-62); Presidency Administrator; General Director, Algerian Finance on Regional Equipment; Director General of the President's Office (1981-84); Deputy Minister of Regional Equipment (1984-85); Minister of Housing, Town Planning and Construction (1986-88). **Prof. Addr.:** Algiers, Algeria.

NOURI (Abdulmaleq), Iraqi writer. **Born** in 1921. **Educ.:** in Iraq, Lebanon and France. **Dipl.:** LL.B. **Career:** Writer, Journalist. **Publ.:** Author of "Fattouma" (1948), "Roussul al-Insaniya", "Nachid al-Ard" (1954), "Khashab wa Moukhma" (1967), Translated several articles. **Note:** many of his books were translated into French, English and Russian. **Dist.:** 1 st Prize (1948). **Addr.:** Baghdad, Iraq.

NOURI (Anwar, Abdallah, al), Kuwaiti politician. **Born** in 1941 in Kuwait. **Son** of Abdallah al-Nouri. **Married** in 1965, 1 son, 3 daughters. **Educ.:** University of Wales. **Dipl.:** B.Sc. **Career:** Teacher; Cultural Attaché, Kuwait Foreign Ministry; Secretary General, Kuwait University, former Chairman and Managing Director, The Industrial Bank of Kuwait, Safat, Kuwait. Minister of Education (1988-1989). **Addr.:** Kuwait City, Kuwait.

NOURI (Mahmoud, Abdul Khalik, al), Kuwaiti banker. **Born** in 1949 in Kuwait. **Married,** 1 son, 3 daughters. **Dipl.:** B.A. in Commerce. **Career:** General Manager of Bank of Kuwait and the Middle East; presently Managing Director of United Gulf Bank; Bahrain; Chairman of Kuwait Insulating Material. **Prof. Addr.:** P.O.Box 26487, Safat, Kuwait, Kuwait.

NOWAIS (Hussain Jassem, al), U.A.E businessman. **Born** in 1954 in Abu Dhabi. **Married. Dipl.:** B.Com. in Management and Economics, USA. **Career:** Director of Arinfi Ltd. and Gulf Arab Investment Company; President of Emirates Holdings; Director of Emirates Industrial Bank. **Hobby:** tennis. **Prof. Addr.:** Emirates Industrial Bank, P.O.Box 2272, Abu Dhabi, United Arab Emirates.

NOWAIS (Nasir, Muhammad Ali), UAE official. **Born** in 1945 in Abu Dhabi. **Married,** 3 children. **Educ.:** School of Journalism, Cairo University, Egypt. **Dipl.:** B.A. **Career:** Technical Director of the Ministry of Information (1969); Head of Broadcasting (1969-70); Head of press and Public Relations (1970-73); Head of Television and Broadcasting (1973-76); Under Secretary of the Ministry of Information and Culture (1976-78); Chairman, Abu Dhabi Gulf Hotel; Chairman of Abu Dhabi Sheraton Hotel and Abu Dhabi National Hotels Company; Vice-Chairman, Arab Insurance Group, Bahrain. General Manager of Abu Dhabi Fund for Arab Economic Development (1978). **Prof. Addr.:** Abu Dhabi Sheraton Hotel, P.O.Box 640, Abu Dhabi, United Arab Emirates.

NOWILATY (Rashad M.), Saudi diplomat. **Born** in Mecca in 1929, **Educ.:** B.A. (Honours) (Political Sciences), Faculty of Commerce, Cairo University. **Career:** Diplomatic attaché, Ministry of Foreign Affairs; served as Third and later Second Secretary in the Royal Embassy of Saudi Arabia in Bonn; First Secretary, Adviser, then Minister Plenipotentiary, Saudi Embassy, Beirut, Lebanon; Assistant Deputy Minister, Ministry of Foreign Affairs; Saudi Ambassador to Holland, Senegal, Gambia and Niger; Adviser to Saudi Arabian delegations to the First and Second Arab Summit Conferences; Alternate Delegate to Saudi Arabia to UN General Assembly; Deputy Head of

Saudi delegations to the first three annual conference of the Islamic Foreign Ministers; charged with the preparation of the charter of the conference of Islamic Foreign Ministers, the Islamic International Agreement establishing the International Islamic News Agency; Head of the Saudi Mission charged with negotiating and signing an agreement with Egypt for the settlement of Saudi Arabian private funds previously nationalized by Egypt; member, Saudi Delegations to several Arab League Council and Arab Defence Council Sessions, Cairo, Beirut, Kuwait; member of Saudi delegations on State visits to numerous Arab, European and African countries; member of Saudi delegation to Iran's festivities commemorating the 2,500th Anniversary of the founding of the Persian Empire, the Algerian festivities marking the 10th Anniversary of Algeria's independence. **Honours:** King Abdulaziz Order, Excellent Grade, Lebanese Order of Cedar, Grosses Verdienstkreuz, First Class (Federal Republic of Germany). **Prof. Addr.:** Ministry of Foreign Affairs, Jeddah, Saudi Arabia.

NSOUR (Ali), Jordanian electrical engineer. **Born** on 10.3.1930 at el-Salt, Jordan. **Son** of Yusuf (Farmer) **and** Fadieh Ensour. **Married** to Ne'mat Ensour, 3 children: Nancy (1968), Yusuf (1970), Suzan (1973). **Educ.:** Zerqa Public Primary School; el-Salt Public Secondary School; Battersea Plytechnic Queen Mary College, London University, London. **Dipl.:** B.Sc. Engineering. **Career:** Director, Ministry of Industry and Trade (1959-68); Director General, Jordan Electricity Authority (1968-79); Trade and Industry Minister (1979-80); Managing Director, Jordan Phosphate Mining Co. (1980-1983); Managing Director, Jordan Management & Consultancy Corp. (1983). **Member:** Association of Engineers, Jordan; Institute of Electrical Engineers, U.K.; Institute of Electrical & Electronic Engineers, U.S.A. **Board Member:** of the Board of Directors of Jordan Management & Consultancy Co.; Jordan Phosphate & Mining Co.; Jordan Spinning & Weaving Co.; Jordan Yarmouk Insurance Co.; Director General, Arab Potash Co. Ltd. **Sports:** Tennis, Swimming, Squash. **Hobby:** Reading. **Clubs:** Royal Automobile Club, Sport City Club, Orthodox Club. **Prof. Addr.:** P.O.Box 1470, Amman. **Priv. Addr.:** Abu Qurah Hill, Salth Road, Sport City District, Tel.: 666780, Amman, Jordan.

NUAIMI (Ali Ibn Ibrahim al-), Saudi Politician. **Born in** 1935. **Educ.:** B.Sc. Geology, Lehigh University, USA; M.Sc., Geology Stanford University, USA. **Career:** Aramco (1947); Supervisor, Production Manager, Abqaiq (1969); Assistant Director then Director of Production, Northern Province (1972-75); Vice President, Production Affairs (1975); Vice President, Petroleum Affairs (1978); Member, Board of Directors (1980); Executive vice President, Oil and Gas Affairs (1981); President, Saudi Aramco (1983); Minister of Oil and Mineral Resources (1995-to date) **Address:** Ministry of Oil and Mineral Resources, P.O.Box 757, Airport Road, Riyadh 11189, Saudi Arabia.

NUAIMI (Humaid Bin Rashid, al, Shaikh), United Arab Emirates. **Born** in 1931, Second son of the late Ruler of Ajman, Shaikh Rashid al-Nuaimi. **Married. Career:** Ruler of Ajman since 1981. **Addr.:** al Amir, P.O.Box 1, Tel.: 422122, Ajman, United Arab Emirates.

NUBAN (Said, Abdul Khair, al), Yemeni politician. **Career:** Permanent Secretary at the Ministry of Education (1973-75); Minister of Education (1975); Member of the Presidium of the People's Supreme Council of the Former People's Democratic Republic of Yemen (1986- May 1990). **Prof. Addr.:** Aden, Republic of Yemen.

NUMEIRY (Gaafar Mohamad), Former president of the democratic republic of Sudan. **Born** in 1930. **Educ.:** el-Hijra Elementary School, Omdurman; Wadi Madani Government School, Gezira; Hantoub Secondary School, Gezira; Military College; various courses in Egypt, Federal Republic of Germany and USA. **Dipl.:** Graduated as 2nd Lieutenant from Military College. **Career:** Assigned to Western Command; joined the first batch of officers to establish the Northern Command at Shendi (1957); Southern Command, Juba (1959); with the Free Officers Group played a leading role in the October Revolution of 1964; after its setback transfered to Western Command, El Fasher, subsequently to Eastern Command, Gedaref; Officer in Command of troops at Torit, Southern Command; transferred to Infantry School at Gebeit as 2nd Commanding Officer and Senior Lecture, Then Officer in Command until the May Socialist Revolution, 1969, when he became Chairman of the Revolutionary Command Council; C-In-C of the Armed Forces and Minister of Defence; elected by plebiscite first President of the Republic, 1971; concluded the Addis Abeba Accord with Southern Sudan leaders ending the 17 year-old civil war in the South on the basis of Southern Region Autonomy, Feb. 1972; unanimously elected President of the Sudanese Socialist Union by the First National General Congress, 1974; elected Chairman of OAU for 1978-79; promoted to Field Marshal, May 1979. deposed on 6 April 1985. Now living in exile in Egypt. **Decorations:** Insignia of Honour; Grand Cordon of Honour; Order of the Revolution; Order of Loyal Son of Sudan; Order of Bravery (1st class); Long Meritorius Service Medal (1st class); Independence Medal; Duty Medal (1st class); Medal of Persistence. **Addr.:** Khartoum, Sudan.

NUQUL (Elia, Costandi), Jordanian businessman. **Born** in 1928 in Ramlih, Palestine. **Married**, four children. **Career:** Accountant (1949-51); Assistant manager (1951-52); in 1952 established own Company, Nuqul Brothers, General Manager and Senior Partner; General Manager, Arab Foam Factory Company; General Manager, Nuqul Engineering and Contracting Company; General Manager, Electra Company; Vice Chairman of Middle East Insurance Company. Member of the Board of Directors of Jordan Paper and Cardboard Factories company Ltd.

Member: of the Board of Trustees of the National Orthodox School, Amman; Eisenhower Fellow (1964). **Sport:** Swimming. **Hobby:** Reading. **Addr.:** 2nd Circle, Tel.: 44251, 44767, Jabal Amman, Amman, Jordan.

NUR (Abdul Mohsen, Abou, al), Egyptian military. **Born** on August 4, 1918 in Egypt. **Educ.:** Military Academy. **Career:** fought in Palestine war (1948-49); took part in the Revolution of July 26, 1952, Cairo, which overthrew King Faruk of Egypt; served as military attaché, Egyptian embassies in Sudan, Syria, Lebanon; Deputy Commander of the First Army (1958-62); Governor of Suez City; Minister of State for Agrarian Reform and Land Reclamation (1963-64); Deputy Prime Minister for Agriculture and Irrigation (1964-68); Deputy Secretary-General, Arab Socialist Union (1967-70); Secretary-General, Arab Socialist Union (1970-71). **Addr.:** Cairo, Egypt.

NUR ELMI (Hussein), Somali statesman. **Born** on April 1, 1926 at Obbia (Somalia). **Educ.:** In Mogadishu and Italy. **Career:** Deputy Secretary-General, Territorial Council of Somalia (1954-58); Regional Governor of Hiran (1950-60); of Mogadishu; of Benadir (1960-62); Consul-General, East Africa (1962-63); Ambassador to Tanzania (1963-65); Ambassador to Belgium, also accredited to the Netherlands and Luxembourg, and Permanent Representative of Somalia to the European Economic Community (1965-68); Ambassador-at-large (1969-70); Alternate Permanent Representative to United Nations (1970-72). **Prof. Addr.:** Ministry of Foreign Affairs, Mogadishu, Somalia.

NURUL ALAM (Shah Sufi Mohammad, His Eminency), Bangladeshi Religious and Spiritual leader is the World Peace Envoy and Founder Director General, Dayemi Complex Bangladesh and its permanent representative to the United Nations. He is also the President, World Spiritual Assembly, N.Y., USA and Secretary General, International Organization for World Peace, Disarmament, Development and Human Rights, N.Y., USA. **Born** on February 28, 1953 at Mirsarai, Chittagong, Bangladesh. **Son** of late Muhammad Sirajul Islam. **Married** to Shahzadi Syeda Rokeya Begum (the only daughter of His Holiness Shah Sufi Syed Dayemullah (R.A.) **Educ.:** 3 honourary Ph.D. Degrees have been confered on him by the World Spiritual Assembly and its International forum held in New York City in July 1989. These are (1) Dr. of Comparative Religion (2) Dr. of Divinity and (3) Dr. of Philosophy in Spirituality. **Career:** His Holiness Nurul Alam received spiritual training from his father-in-law and in his place he is now carrying out the supervising duties of four Sufi Orders of the seven hundred years old Islamic Sufi dynasty. He is also rendenring social-welfare, humanitarian and voluntary services initiated by H.H. Mahisawar (R.A.), one of the direct descendants of the Holy Prophet of Islam (Peace be upon him) as early as seven hundred years ago in this country for the downtrodden people. H.H. M.N.Alam serving the cause of neglected humanity, looks after more than a hundred educational institutions-Hiqh Schools, Colleges, Vocational training centres. Madrashas (Religious School), Mosque as well as fifteen orphanages housing several hundred parentless children in Bangladesh. He is the Managing Director of Dayemi Pharmaceutical Laboratory, (Unani), Joint Motwalli of Sufi Nurullah WAQF Estate since 1987. Co-founder of Dayemi Complex Bangladesh represented at the United Nations and in the North America and 100 Religious, Social, Humanitarian and Educational projects in Bangladesh. Since 1982 H.H. Mohammad Nurul Alam has been acting as the permanent representative of the Dayemi Complex Bangladesh to the United Nations in New York, Vienna and Geneva and five Regional Economic Commission offices in Thailand, Ethiopia, Switzerland, Iraq and Chile. Under H.H.M.N.Alam's leadership the Dayemi Complex acquired consultative status with the Economic and Social Council (ECOSOC) of the United Nations as well as Associate Status with the Department of Public Information and UNICEF of the United Nations. Also the Dayemi Complex Bangladesh, While working towards Peace in the Middle East since 1982, has been given Associate Status with the Palestinian Rights Division of the United Nations, New York. H.H.M.N. Alam coordinated many International conferences in support of the United Nations in Dhaka, Bangladeh specially in 1985. 1986 and 1995: He also visited the Holy Al-Aqsa Mosque in Jerusalem and risked his life to negotiate peace between the Palestine and Israeli authorities. His Hollines Hazrat Shah Sufi Sayed Dayemullah (R), the Master of four Sufi Orders, trained H.H.M.N. alam in Spiritual and religious practices for fifteen years. During his pilgrimage to Mecca in 1987 he designated His Holiness M.N. Alam as the official Chief Khalifa (representative) of the Dayera Sharif, a Sufi Institution and Dynasty originally established by the Holy Prophet Mohammad (SM) and followed by his worthy followers. H.H.M.N. Alam organized yearly seminars on behalf of the Dayemi Complex Bangladeh to confer religious and peace awards to distinguished personalities for their outstanding contributions in various fields of humanitarian, social and religious services. In the service of world peace, H.H. has undertaken research project on the subjects of peace, progress, welfare and justice. This study includes an analysis of the prophecy of the emergence of the "Great Imam Mahedi (SM)". The research indicates, he will bring universal peace and a lasting enlightenment for humanity in about the year 2002. H.H.M.N. Alam has travelled extensively in the interest of world peace, visited more than 145 countries and attended over 700 conferences, seminars, congresses around the world, dedicating himself to the cause of peace. **Associations:** His Holiness is the Founder National Chairman of Bangladesh Youth Hostel Association. He is also an executive member of International Association for Religious Freedom, South Asia and President IARF Bangladesh Chapter. H.H. has been the only representative of the Muslim world attending World Peace Congress organized by IARF on behalf of Dayemi Complex Bangladesh since 1982. He is associated with national and international organizations rendering valuable services for the welfare of the common people. **Awards:** Recipient of the 20th Century Award for Achievement given by the International Biographical Centre, Cambridge, U.K. for oustanding contribution towards Peace through Millennium Prophecy. Awarded International Diploma of Honour by American Biographical Institute, North California, USA. He has been designated life time Deputy Governor of the American Biographical Institute in 1995 and has also been awarded "WHO'S WHO OF THE YEAR 1995" by the American Biographical Institute. H.H. is the recipient of International Order of Ambassadors Award 1995 given by American Biographical Institute, North Carolina. He is also a recipient of The Order of International Fellowship given by International Biographical Centre, Cambridge, U.K. He has been declared the Man of the Year 1995 by the Voice of the World's Citizen, New York, U.S.A. for his outstanding contribution towards World Peace, International Security and Human Rights through Millennium Prophecy. H.H. has been nominated for induction into the Five Thousand Personalities of the World Hall of Fame for his outstanding contribution in the field of Millennium Prophecy. He has devoted his life to world peace was nominated as a candidate for the Nobel Peace Prize for the year 1993 by the International Organization for World Peace, Disarmament, Development and Human Rights, N.Y., U.S.A. (Voice of the World's Citizen Special Supplementary, Dhaka August, 1995). And again he has been nominated for the Nobel Peace Prize for the year 1996 as per recommendation of the World Spiritual Assembly, N.Y., U.S.A. **Addr.:** P.O.Box 605, New York, NY 10163. **U.N. Office Addr.:** 211 East 43rd St., Suite 908, New York, NY 10017, Tel.: 646-242-4101, Fax: 609-487-6745, E-mail: whrsc786@aol.com. **Bangladesh Addr.:** 42/2 Azimpur Dayora Sharif Dhaka-1205, Bangladesh, Tel.Fax: 966-3963.

NUSEIBEH (Hazem), Jordanian statesman. **Born** in 1922 in Jordan. **Married**, children. **Educ.:** Rawda College, Jerusalem; Victoria College, Alexandria; American University of Beirut Lebanon; Law School, Jerusalem; Woodrow Wilson School of Public and International Affairs. **Dipl.:** Ph.D. in Political Studies, Princeton University, USA (1945). **Career:** Deputy Chairman of Development Board (1958-60); Under-Secretary, Ministry of National Economy (1959-60); Secretary-General of Development Board (1961-62); Minister of Foreign Affairs (1962-63); Minister of Foreign Affairs (1965); Minister of State for Prime Ministerial Affairs and Minister of Reconstruction (1967-69); Jordan Ambassador to Cairo (1969- February 1971), to Ankara (1971-73), to Italy (1973-75); also accredited to Austria and Switzerland; Ambassador to UN (1976-1985); Minister of State for Prime Ministerial Affairs (1985). **Addr.:** Amman, Jordan.

NUSEIF (Ali, al), Yemeni bank manager. **Born in 1946** in Sana'a. **Son** of Ali al-Nuseif. **Married** in 1971, 3 sons, 1 daughter. **Educ.:** Damascus University. **Dipl.:** B.A. (1971). **Career:** General Manager, Financial Analysis Department, Ministry of Economy (1971-72); General Manager, Government Accounts Department, Budget Finance and Ministry of Finance (1972-74); Chairman, Accounts Organisation for Auditing and Accounts (1974-79); General Manager, Central Bank of Yemen (1979 to present). **Addr.:** P.O.Box 59, Tel.: 259351, Telex: 2280 A/B MARKAZI, Sanaa, Yemen Arab Republic.

NUSEYBEH (Azmi, Izzat), Palestinian civil engineer. **Born** in 1924 in Jerusalem. **Son** of Izzat H. Nuseybeh (merchant) **and** Mrs., née Lama'a al-Alami. **Married** on October 4, 1952 in Aleppo, Syria to busayna Jabri, five children: Lamia, Izzat, Lina, Alaa and Mona. **Educ.:** Rashidiya Secondary School, Jerusalem; American University of Beirut, Lebanon. **Dipl.:** B.A. in Engineering (1944); B.Sc. in Civil Engineering (1946). **Career:** Civil Engineer, syrian Ministry of Defence (1947-53); Deputy Director of Engineering Services, Municipality of Latakia (Syria) (1953-55); Deputy Director of Engineering Services, Syrian Army, Damascus (1955-58); General Manager of Almana Engineering and Contracting, Doha, Qatar (1958-) and chairman/General Manager of Associated Engineer and Contractors Company, Beirut (1963-). **Sports:** Swimming, Brisk Walking. **Member:** Sailing Association, Doha. **Credit Card:** American Express. **Prof. Addr.:** P.O.Box 1909, Tel.: 328390, Doha, Qatar. **Priv. Addr.:** Sirage Street 42, Tel.: 662195, Qatar.

NUSSEIBEH (Zaki, Anwar), United Arab Emirates official. **Born** 1946 in Jerusalem. **Son** of Anwar Nusseibeh. **Married**, 3 Children. **Education:** Rugby School, Warwickshire, UK; MA Honours in Economics, Cambridge University, U.K. **Career:** Head of Research, Ministry of Information, Abu Dhabi (1968-70); Director of Information & Editor in Chief of Emirates News, Ministry of Information, Abu Dhabi (1970-74); Adviser to President of UAE and principal interpreter (since 1974). **Languages:** Arabic, English, French, Italian, Spanish, German & Russian. **Pub.:** various translations (Arabic Poetry) and articles in periodicals. **Decorations:** Commander of the Victorian Order (CVO), U.K.; Commandeer of the Order of Merit, Italy. Officer of the Order of Merit, France. Officer of the Order of Palmes Academiques, France. Officer of the Order of Merit, Spain. Order of Independence, Jordan. **Sports:** Swimming, skiing. **Hobbies:** Classical Music (Opera), languages, reading, Theatre, poetry, and travel. **Address:** Presidential Court, P.O.B. 280, Abu Dhabi, UAE. Tel.: 9712 651887 Fax: 9712 447367 E-mail: zakin@emirates.net.ae.

NUSSEIR (Sweilem), Jordanian lawyer. **Born** in 1941 in Irbid, Jordan. **Son** of Ali Ahmad Nusseir. **Married in** 1970, 1 son, 4 daughters. **Educ.:** Licence in Law. **Career:**

Assistant Manager, Sha'ban Contracting Co., Amman; Social Inspector, Saudi Arabia (1966-73); Lawyer, Irbid, Jordan (1974-78); Amman (1978-). Legal Counsellor, Amman Financial Market, Amman (1978-). **Member:** National College for Engineering and Administration Science; Orthodox Club. **Addr.:** P.O.Box 8802, Tel.: 63172, 37200, Telex: 21711 A/B SUKMAL, Amman, Jordan.

NUWAISER (Mohamad, al), Saudi official. **Educ.:** Received general education supplemented by extensive training in politics, diplomatic ceremonial and protocol. **Career:** Member of the Crown Prince's Cabinet, then that of the late King Faisal; when King Faisal acceded to the throne he was appointed Chief of the Private Royal Office; Chief of the Private Office of HM King Fahad. **Hobby:** reading. **Address:** The Royal Cabinet, Riyadh, Saudi Arabia.

NUWAISER (Saud ben Saleh, al), Saudi civil servant. **Born** at al-Joaf in 1934. **Educ.:** Received general education; a training course at the Public Administration Institute, Cairo, Egypt. **Career:** Soldier; clerk; treasurer; Accountant; Chief Accountant; assists in formulating projects in Sakaka al-Joaf, construction of market places, public parks, roads and other development projects, now Assistant to the Director of al-Joaf Municipality. **Hobby:** Reading. **Prof. Addr.:** Sakaka, al-Joaf Municipality, Saudi Arabia.

NUWAYHID (Hikmat, Suleiman), Lebanese executive. **Born** in 1946 in Beirut, Lebanon. **Son** of Suleiman Nuwayhid. **Married** in 1973, 1 son, 2 daughters. **Educ.:** The American University of Beirut, Associate of Arts, Beirut (1964); The American University, Washington D.C. (1969); **Dipl.:** B.B.A.; M.B.A. **Career:** Training, The Bank of Beirut & the Arab Countries (1966-67); Assistant Manager, The First National Bank of Chicago (Lebanon) S.A.L. (1969-76); Manager, The Industrial Bank of Kuwait K.S.C. (1976-81); Executive Manager, The Industrial Bank of Kuwait K.S.C. (1981); General Manager Arab Investment Co., Bahrain. **Member:** Arab Bankers Association, London; International Cambist Association; Interarab Cambist Association; Forex Club, Kuwait. **Publ.:** Conducted seminars on the Investment and Protection of OAPEC Surplus; The State of Liquidity in the Kuwaiti Dinar Market and other topics. **Hobbies:** Reading, writing and swimming. **Addr.:** Arab Investment Co., P.O.Box 5559, Manama, Bahrain.

O

OBAID (Abdul-Hamid, al), Kuwaiti executive. **Born** in 1932 in Kuwait. **Son** of Abdul Razzak Obaid. **Married** in 1971, 2 sons, 2 daughters. **Dipl.:** B.A. (Econ.); Banking Diploma. **Career:** Director, al-Ahli Auditors; Director, Faisal Islamic Bank, Sudan; Director, Kuwait Finance House, Kuwait; Islamic Northern Bank, Khartoum, Sudan. **Member:** Commercial Cooperative Society; Auditors Co-operative Society. **Addr.:** P.O.Box 5689, Tel.: 461218, Kuwait.

OBAID (Fikri, Makram), Egyptian politician. **Born** in 1916. **Educ.:** University of Cairo Law School. **Dipl.:** M.A. **Career:** Law School Representative on Higher Committee, Cairo University Student Union (1932); joined private law firm (1937-50); Lawyer, Court of Cassation, and own law practice (since 1950); Secretary General Heliopolis Branch, Liberation Rally (1953); member national congress, National Union (1956); appointed to People's Assembly (1976); joined Socialist Liberal Party (1976); then Vice Chairman; appointed Secretary General at Foundation of National Democratic Party; Deputy Prime Minister in charge of People's Assembly Affairs (1978-83); also of Consultative Council Affairs (1980-83); member People's Assembly (1979-84), now member of the Political Bureau of the National Democratic Party. **Addr.:** Cairo, Egypt.

OBAID (Ibrahim Ahmad), Saudi civil servant. **Born** on 17 January 1939 at Asir, Saudi Arabia. **Dipl.:** Ph.D. (International Politics), Indiana University, U.S.A. **Career:** Commissioned 2nd Lieutnant, Saudi Army; Instructor, Saudi Command and Staff College, Adviser and Chairman of the Board, PETROMIN; attended all OPEC ministrial meetings; Director General, Office of the Minister of Petroleum and Mineral Resources; First Chairman of the Board Arab Satellite Communications Organisation; Deputy Minister, Minister of Posts, Telephone and Telegraph, Riyadh. **Member:** International Institute for Strategic Studies. **Honours:** Grand Cordon of the Order of Brilliant Star, Taiwan Republic. **Publications:** numerous articles in specialized magazines and Middle East journals; several articles in local newspapers; Daily OKAZ, Jeddah and al-Jazirah, Riyadh. **Hobby:** reading, **Sports:** swimming, boxing. **Prof. Addr.:** P.O.Box 10878, Tel.: 4012310, 4014686, Riyadh. **Priv. Addr.:** Tel.: 4060006, 4648235, Riyadh, Saudi Arabia.

OBAID (Ismail Abdul-Waheb A.), Saudi official. **Born** in 1930. **Dipl.:** B.A. (Economics). **Career:** Assistant Director, then Director, Boys' Teaching Board, Medina; Director, Girls' Teaching Board; Director, Social Affairs Board, Medina. **Hobbies:** reading, sports. **Address:** Social Affairs Board, Medina, Saudi Arabia.

OBAID (Mohamad Abdul Fattah), Egyptian academic. **Born** in 1938 in Cairo, Egypt. **Dipl.:** Ph.D. (Nuclear Engineering). **Career:** Assistant Professor (1966-72); Associate Professor (1972-79) and later full Professor and ex-Chairman, Electrical Engineering Department, Faculty of Engineering, King Saud University. **Member:** American Nuclear Society (ANS), IEEE and Sigma XI; Consultant King Abdul Aziz City for Science and Technology. **Publications:** several research papers on Nuclear and Electrical Engineering. **Hobby:** swimming. **Prof. Addr.:** Department of Electrical Engineering, Faculty of Engineering, King Saud University, P.O.Box 800, Tel.: 4676799, Riyadh. **Priv. Addr.:** Tel.: 4643095, Riyadh, Saudi Arabia.

OBAID (Rida M. Said), Saudi academic. **Born** in 1936 in Medina, Saudi Arabia. **Dipl.:** B.Sc. (Science). Cairo University (1958); Ph.D. (Physical Chemistry) Birmingham University (1963). England. **Career:** Professor of Physical Chemistry, Faculty of Science, King Saud University; Assistant Lecturer, Faculty of Science, King Saud University (1958); Lecturer, same Faculty (1962); Dean, same Faculty (1962-73); Executive Director and Chairman of the Board of National Centre for Science and Technology, Riyadh; President of King Abdulaziz University, Jeddah (since 1983); member of the Board, al-Yamamah Press, Riyadh; member of Saudi American Labour Committee. **Act.:** Representative of King Saud University to the International Conference of University Presidents held in Seoul, South Korea (1968); Guest of Ford Foundation to visit 32 American Universities (1969); Representative of King Saud University to The International Conference of University Presidents held in Montreal, Canada (1970). **Prof. Addr.:** King Abdul-Aziz University, P.O.Box 1540, Jeddah 21441, Saudi Arabia, Riyadh. **Priv. Addr.:** Tel.: 4767050, Riyadh, Saudi Arabia.

OBAID (Said Fekri Makram), Egyptian administrator. **Born** in Cairo in 1947. **Married**, one daughter. **Educ.:** Cairo University, Egypt, London University. **Dipl.:** B.Sc., M.Sc, Ph.D. **Career:** Production Director, Allied Arab Company for Minerals Industry (1976/78); General Director (since 1979); member of the Institute of Mechanical

Engineers. **Medals:** Bloy Prize. **Member** of Gezira Sporting Club; St. James Club. **Prof. Addr.:** 17 Qasr al-Nile Street. Cairo, Egypt. **Priv. Addr.:** 22 Wade al-Nile Street, Mohandiseen, Cairo, Egypt.

OBAID (Soliman Mohamad), Saudi director of islamic call service. **Born** in 1940. **Educ.:** Secondary School Certificate (Religious Education); B.A. (Geography). **Career:** Clerk, Public Notary Department, Mecca (1956); Radio Announcer (1963/71); Director of Nida al-Islam (The Call of Islam) and the Holy Koran Radio, Jeddah (1972); member of Saudi Arabian Delegation of the Conference of the Islamic States Broadcasting Services (1975); attended the meetings of Saudi Intellectuals with European Jurists and Legislators (1974); Director of Islamic Call Service, Saudi Broadcasting Service, Jeddah. **Address:** Jeddah Broadcasting Service, P.O.Box 570 Jeddah, Saudi Arabi.

OBAID (Taher Ahmad M.), Saudi official. **Born** in 1935. **Dipl.:** B.A. (Economics). **Career:** Economic analyst, Ministry of Finance and National Economy; Director, Minister's Office for Technical Affairs, Ministry of Agriculture and Water; Director-General, Minister's Bureau: Deputy Minister of Agriculture and Water; member of Bord of Trustees, International Dry Territories Research Center; attended Food and Agriculture Organization (FAO) International Conference, International Food conference, Red Sea Ecology Conference, King Abdulaziz University. **Honours:** Orders of Merit from Nigeria and Belgium. **Address:** Ministry of Agriculture and water, Riyadh, Saudi Arabia.

OBAID (Taleb Mohamad Said), Saudi academic. **Born** in 1936 in Medina, Saudi Arabia. **Dipl.:** Ph.D. (Geology). **Career:** Registrar and Assistant Lecturer, Faculty of Science; Dean, Faculty of Engineering; Chairman, Geology Department, King Saud University; Associate Professor of Geology, King Saud University; member of Geological Society, London. **Hobbies:** reading, sports. **Prof. Addr.:** Geology Department, King Saud University, Riyadh. **Priv. Addr.:** Tel.: 4811000, Riyadh, Saudi Arabia.

OBAIDAN (Abdullah, Abdal Aziz, al), Kuwaiti businessman. **Born** in 1938 in Kuwait. **Married,** 3 children. **Dipl.:** B.Sc. in Mechanical Engineering. **Career:** held managerial positions in the cement manufacturing business Kuwait (1968-84); Member of the Board of Directors of Prefabricated Buildings Company, White Cement Co. and Kuwait Cement Company. Chairman of the Board of Directors of Overland Transport Co. (1984-). **Member:** Engineering Association of Kuwait. **Prof. Addr.:** P.O.Box 24611, Safat, Kuwait, Kuwait and P.O.Box 5132, Safat 13052, Kuwait City, Kuwait.

OBAIDAT (Ahmad, Abdul Majid), Jordanian politician. **Born** in 1938 in Hurth, Irbid, Jordan. **Married,** 5 children. **Educ.:** Salahiya School and Baghdad University, Iraq. **Dipl.:** B.A. in Law. **Career:** Teacher, Ministry of Education (1957); Customs Officer (1961); First Lieutenant, General Security Service (1962-64); Assistant Director of Intelligence Service (1964-74); Director of Intelligence Services with rank of General (1974-82); Minister of Interior (1982/84); Prime Minister (1984-85); Member of Senate (1985-). **Medal:** Independence Medal (4th Class) (1965). Renaissance Medal (3rd Class) (1971) and (2nd Class) (1973). **Addr.:** Shmeisani, Amman, Jordan.

OBAIDAT (Jamal, Mohamad), Jordanian administrator. **Born** in 1939 in Irbid, Jordan. **Married,** 4 children. **Educ.:** Damascus University, Syria, also studies in the Netherlands, UK and USA. **Dipl.:** LL.B. **Career:** Cooperation Manager of Jordanian Cooperation Organization (1986); Member of the Arab Union Cooperatives; Member of the Representative Council, Jordanian Cooperation Organisation (1986-). **Hobbies:** sports, travelling, reading. **Prof. Addr.:** P.O.Box 1658, Irbid, Jordan.

OBAIDAT (Khalid, Abdullah), Jordanian diplomat. **Born** on December 6, 1937 in Ajloun, Jordan. **Married,** 3 children. **Educ.** Cairo University, Egypt; Sorbonne University, France. **Dipl.:** B.A. in Political Science, M.A., Ph.D. **Career:** Ministry of Foreign Affairs (1962), 3rd Secretary (1963), 2nd Secretary (1967), 1st Secretary (1971), Counselor (1975); Minister Plenipotentiary (1978); Ambassador (1980); Lecturer at Jordanian University. **Hobbies:** Squash, jogging, swimming. **Addr.:** 6 Dhahyat al-Hussein, Amman, Jordan.

OBAIDI (Abdul Ati, al), Libyan politician. **Born** on October 15, 1939. **Son** of Ibrahim al-Obaidi (Farmer) **and** Mrs. Rabha al-Obaidi. **Married. Educ.:** Libyan University (Faculty of Commerce), Manchester University (Faculty of Technology). **Dipl.:** Bachelor of Arts in Commerce, Libyan University; Master of Science, Manchester University. **Career:** Lecturer, Libyan University (1967-70); Acting Minister of Foreign Affairs (1970); Minister of Labour (1970-77), of Civil Service (1974-77); Chairman, General Popular Committee (1977-79); Secretary-General, General People's Congress (1979-80); Secretary, Bureau for External Relations (1980-84). **Decor:** from Tunisia, Malaysia and the Philippines. **Sports:** Football and Table-tennis. **Hobbies:** Travelling and music. **Priv. Addr.:** Scabli, Sidi Hussain, P.O.Box 2256, Tel.: 3475, Benghazi, Libya.

OBAIDI (Mahdi M, al), Iraqi official. **Born** in 1928 in Baghdad, Iraq. **Married** to Miss Afifa F. Hussain, four children. **Educ.:** University of California (Berkeley). **Career:** Served in Iraqi Ministries of Economy and Trade (1954-83); Director General of Foreign Economic Relations (1969-72); Deputy Minister for Foreign Trade (1972-83); Secretary General Council of Arab Economic Unity.

Amman, Jordan until 1987. **Decor.:** Honorary Medal of Italian Government (1964). **Publ.:** Lectures in Agricultural Co-operation (1961). **Hobbies:** Travel, reading. **Addr.:** 35/ 5/1 Marifa District, Saydia, Dora, Baghdad, Iraq.

OBAIDLI (Ahmad), UAE official. **Born** in 1926 in Bahrain. **Career:** Public Relations Officer for British Petroleum, Bahrain (1966); Secretary to Shaikh Zaid and Head of the Palace office; Minister, United Arab Emirates Embassy in London, United Kingdom; Chairman, al-Obaidli Group of Companies. **Prof. Addr.:** P.O.Box 157, Doha, Qatar.

ODEH (Hanna, Dr.), Jordanian economist. **Born** in 1932 near Ramallah, Palestine. **Educ.:** University of the Hague, Diploma in Economic Planning, Netherlands (1957); Rotterdam University. **Dipl.:** B.A., Mathematical Economics (1959); M.A. (1961); Ph.D. (1963). **Career:** Statistician for UNRWA, Beirut (1953-55); Research Assistant, University of the Hague, Netherlands (1957-58); Lecturer, University of the Hague (1961-63); Joined Jordan Development Board, later National Planning Council (1963); Secretary General (1968-74); Director General, Jordan's Social and Economic Planning (1974-). Director, Jordanian Pension Fund, Jordan; Director, (Representative of National Planning Council), Industrial Development Bank, Amman; Minister of Finance (1985-88). **Addr.:** Zahran Street, P.O.Box 1982, Tel.: 42216, Telex: 21349 A/B IDB JO, Jabal Amman, Amman, Jordan.

ODEH (Mohamad, Dawud), (Abu Dawud), palestinian politician. **Born** in 1937 in Selwan, near Jerusalem, Palestine. **Educ.:** University of Jordan. **Dipl.:** Degree in Law. **Career:** Teacher in Jordan and Saudi Arabia; employed with Kuwait Justice Ministry; returned to Jordan in 1968 and became fulltime Member of Fatah ; Set up Fatah Central Observation Department in Amman (1968); Second in Command of the Palestinian Militia in Jordan (1970); Member of the Revolutionary Council (1970); paid official visit with Sabri al-Banna to North Korea (1972); arrested on sabotage charges in Amman (1973) and sentenced to death; sentence commuted to life imprisonment and later released under general amnesty for Palestinian Guerrilas (1973). **Addr.:** Amman, Jordan.

ODUHO (Joseph), Sudanese statesman. **Born** in 1928 at Lobira, Torit District (Sudan). **Married**, Children. **Educ.:** Okaru Intermediate School; St. A Loysius Senior Secondary School; Nyapea (Uganda); Rumbeck Secondary School; Institute of Education, Bakht-er-Rudia. **Dipl.:** B.A. (Education). **Career:** Teacher (1952-59); headmaster, Palotaka Intermediate School (1960); imprisoned during revolt of Equatorial Corps (September 1955); released (January 1956); Member of Parliament (March-November 1968); went into exile (1968); founder-president, Sudan African National Union (SANU) (1962-63); political adviser (1968-71); imprisoned in Uganda (1963-64); Member for Housing and Public Utilities, Higher Executive Council (April 1972- August 1973); Regional Minister of Education (August 1973- December 1973); Regional Minister of Public Works and Utilities (Dec. 1973-75). **Publ.:** Author of "Problem of Southern Sudan" (1963). **Member:** Political Bureau, Sudanese Socialist Union since 1972, Party dissolved following Military Coup in 1989. Elected to the Regional Assembly for Torit North and East (Dec. 1973). **Prof. Addr.:** Torit, Sudan.

OGAILY (Solaiman Mohamad, al), Saudi academic. **Born** in 1946 in Thanab. **Dipl.:** Ph.D. (Zoology). **Career:** Assistant Lecturer, later Lecturer in Zoology, Department of Zoology, Faculty of Science, Riyadh University. **Hobbies:** table tennis, reading. **Address:** Faculty of Science, Riyadh University, Riyadh, Saudi Arabia.

OJJEH (Akram, Subhi), Saudi businessman. **Born** in 1918 in Damascus, Syria, **Married**, 5 children. **Educ.:** College of Lazarists Fathers, Damascus, Syria; Faculty of Letters, Paris, France. **Dipl.:** Teacher's Diploma. **Career:** Dealer in import export business between France and the Middle East (1946); Founder of Les Deux Mondes in France, Saudi Arabia and Egypt (1947); Publisher of "Le Monde Arabe", Paris (1950); Purchased SS France in 1977 then sold it to a Norwegian corporation in 1979; President and General Manager of Techniques d'Avant Garde (TAG) (1974 to present). **Decor.:** Commander of Legion d'Honneur; Commander of the Order of Leopold II; Officer of Nassau Orange. **Hobbies:** sports, swimming, collecting antique rugs and masterpiece paintings. **Prof. Addr.:** 6 Rue Leo-Delibes, 75116 Paris, France and P.O.Box 2814, Riyadh 21441, Saudi Arabia.

OKASHA (Sarwat), Egyptian art historian. **Born** on February 18, 1921 in Cairo, Egypt. **Son** of General Mahmoud Okasha **and** Mrs., Sania Talaat. **Married** in 1942 in Cairo to Islah Lotfy, 2 children: Dr. Mahmoud Okasha (assistant Prof. Medical School, Yale University, Con. USA) and Mrs. Nora el-Labban. **Educ.:** Military College, Cairo; Staff College, Cairo; Faculty of Arts, University of Cairo; University of Paris. **Dipl.:** M.A. Lit., Faculty of Arts, Cairo University (1951); Docteur ès Lettres, University of Paris (1960). **Career:** Cavalry Officer till 1953; Military Attaché, Bern and Paris (1953-56); Ambassador to Rome (1957-58); Minister of Culture (2 terms 1958-62 and 1966-70); Member of Executive Board, UNESCO (1962-70); retired from political life, elected to a visiting professorship at the Collège de France (1973). **Work:** In addition to promoting every branch of arts during his terms in office he masterminded the multinational campaign conducted in co-operation with UNESCO for saving from destruction the archeological legacy of Nubia which included the Temples of Abu Simbel and Philae. **Publ.:** History of Arts (twenty volumes); has written two substantial volumes: a study of 99 miniatures illustrating a 13th century manuscript of the Assemblies (Maqamat) of el-Hariri and a study of 60 miniatures in a 15th century manuscript of the Persian School, which represent the Prophet Mohammad's Journey by Night to Jerusalem and thence his Ascension to the seventh Heaven (Miraj Nameh); produced Arabic Translation of works on a wide range of subjects, of Ovid's "Metamorphoses" and "Ars Amatoria"; translated also all the English works of Gibran Khalil Gibran, which were reprinted for a ninth edition; "The Muslim Painter and the Divine" (published by Rainbird Publ. Gp., London). **Awards:** received honours from many countries among them: Légion d'Honneur (France); Arts et Lettres (France); Silver Medal (UNESCO); Golden Medal (UNESCO); elected to a corresponding Fellowship of the British Academy (1975); Invited to the Vice-Chairmanship of the International Committee for the Safeguarding of Venice. Offered honorary degree of Doctor of Humane Letters by the American University in Cairo (1995). **Hobby:** Classical Music. **Addr.:** Villa 34, Road 14, Maadi, Tel.: 3505075, Cairo, Egypt.

OKLA (Saleh Mohamad), Saudi academic. **Born** in 1941 in Onaizah, **Educ.:** B.Sc., M.Sc. and Ph.D. **Career:** Former employee of Arabian Oil Company (1968-72); member of teaching staff, King Saud University (1976); Assistant Professor and Dean of Admissions and Registration, Associate Professor (1985), Professor of Geology (1995), King Saud University. **Member:** of American Association of Petroleum Geologists. **Prof. Addr.:** King Saud University, P.O.Box 2455, Tel.: 4676202, Riyadh. **Priv. Addr.:** Tel.: 4770032, Riyadh, Saudi Arabia.

OLALI (Mohamad Mustafa), Egyptian barrister, former faculty dean. **Born** in Egypt. **Educ.:** Secondary and Higher. **Dipl.:** Doctor of Laws. **Career:** Barrister at the Supreme Court of Appeal, Director of National Bank of Egypt, former Dean Faculty of Laws. **Award:** Officer of the Legion of Honour. **Addr.:** 4, Ibn Mansour Street, Manchiet at-Tayarane, Tel.: 860164, Heliopolis, Egypt.

OLAYAN (Suliman, Saleh), founder and Chairman of the Olayan Group. **Born** on November 5, 1918 in Onaiza, Saudi Arabia. **Son** of Saleh Olayan and Heya Al Ghanem. **Married** to the former Mary Perdikis. He has 4 children: Khaled, Hayat, Hutham and Lubna. **Educ.:** in Bahrain. **Career:** After completing his schooling in Bahrain, Mr. Olayan went to work for the Bahrain Petroleum Company (BAPCO). In 1937, he joined the Arabian American Oil Company (Aramco), rising to the position of government liaison officer. He left Aramco in 1947 to establish his own business, the General Contracting Company, the first of many successful ventures. Today the Olayan Group is extensively engaged in distribution, manufacturing, services and investment its principal activities reflect its strong ties to the economic and social development of Saudi Arabia. The Group comprises more than 40 business and financial enterprises in the Middle East and throughout the world. The principal companies of the Olayan Group are: Olayan Investments Company Establishment, Competrol Establishment, Crescent Holding GmbH, Olayan Financing Company, Olayan Saudi Holding Company, Olayan Europe Limited, Olayan America Corporation, Olayan Development Corporation Ltd. Olayan Saudi Investment Company and Olayan Real Estate Company. Mr. Olayan was the founding Chairman of the Saudi British Bank in Riyadh. He was Director of Mobil Corp. (1980-83), Riyad Bank (1963-78), Saudi Arabian Airlines (1965-81) and the Saudi Spanish Bank (1979-84). Served as Chairman of the Riyadh Chamber of Commerce and Industry (1981-89) and as Chairman of the Chamber of Commerce and Industry for all of Saudi Arabia (1984-1987); Member of the International Council of J.P. Morgan and Co. Inc., New York (1979-90); International Councillor and Member of the Advisory Board of the Center for Strategic and International Studies, Washington, D.C. (1977-1995); Member of the International Advisory Board of the American International Group. (1982-99) Mr. Olayan is presently a Board Member of the Institute for International Economics and a Board Member of the Saudi British Bank. He is a Senior Member and International Counsellor Emeritus of the Conference Board. He has been a Member and participant at the International Industrial Conferences in San Francisco since their inception in 1965. He is an Alumnus Member, Rockfeller University Council, New York and member, International Advisory Council, SRI International, Menlo Park, California and Member, International Council of INSEAD, Fontainebleau, France; His past affiliations include Trustee of the American University of Beirut; Lecturer in Residence at Indiana University; lecturer at the John F. Kennedy School of Government, Harvard University; and Member of the Royal Institute of International Affairs, London; Board of CS First Boston, Inc. (1988-1995); He is a Member of the Supreme Council, Saudi Arabian Oil Company (Saudi Aramco). **Publ.:** Papers and articles on the topics of banking, investment, energy and international affairs and has participated in conferences and seminars as a keynote speaker and lecturer on said topics. **Awards:** Great Cross of the Order of Merit (1984) awarded by His Majesty King Juan Carlos of Spain; Honorary Knight Commander of the Civil Division of the Most Excellent Order of the British Empire (KBE), appointed by Her Majesty Queen Elizabeth II (November 1987); Royal Order of the Polar Star, Commander First Class, awarded by His Majesty King Carl XVI of Sweden (1988). **Club Memberships:** Bohemian Club, San Francisco; the Equestrian Club, Riyadh; the Knickerbocker Club, New York; The New York Athletic Club, New York; Pacific-Union Club, San Francisco; and the Royal Automobile Club, London. **Business Address:** The Olayan Group, P.O.Box 8772, Riyadh 11492, Tel.: (966-1) 477-8740, Saudi Arabia.

OMAIR (Ali Mohamad, al), Saudi businessman. **Born** in Fazan in 1936. **Career:** Public Notary, Acting Chief Clerk of a Law Court; Secretary, Under-Secretary of State, later Director, Information and Publicity Office, Ministry of Communications; Managing Editor of al-Jazirah Daily Newspaper; Editor of al-Bilad Newspaper; Secretary of Board of Directors, al-Bilad Press Organization; member of Literary Club, Jeddah; attended First Conference of Saudi Men of Letters; at present running his own business. **Publications:** some articles in local publications. **Address:** P.O.Box 6340, Tel.: 6711000, Jeddah, Saudi Arabia.

OMAR (Abdul Ghafoor Mohamad, Ben), Saudi official. **Born** in Medina, in 1946. **Educ.:** diploma in teacher's training. **Career:** Clerk at al-Zahid Co., Jeddah; employee at Muslim World League; Cashier and Accountant, Mecca Establishment for Printing and Information; Headmaster, al-Elmiah al-Kubra; member of several charity organizations and has played an active part in collecting donations for Tahfeezul Koran Society (Recitation of Koran), Mecca; Director of Chamber of Commerce and Industry, Mecca. **Hobbies:** reading, especially religious and history books. **Address:** Chamber of Commerce and Industry, Mecca; P.O.Box 1086, Mecca, Saudi Arabia.

OMAR (Amin), Egyptian governor. **Born** in 1918. **Educ.:** Secondary and Police Academy. **Career:** Professor, Military Academy; President Egyptian Delegation to Saudi Arabia (1956-58); Director of several companies; Governor of Aswan since May 1968. **Award:** Merit Medal (1st Class, Egypt), Secretary General, Arab Socialist Union Aswan (1956). **Addr.:** Aswan, Egypt.

OMAR (Farouk), Iraqi academic. **Born** on June 6, 1938 in Mosul (Iraq). **Married** to Layla Naja (Lecturer in English Literature at Baghdad University), three daughters and a son: Hala, Nada, Hanan and Harith. **Educ.:** University of Baghdad; University of London. **Dipl.:** B.A. (Honours) in History (1959), Ph.D. (Islamic History) (1967). **Career:** Assistant Professor in the Department of History, College of Arts, Baghdad (1967-74); appointed in December 1974 Director of the Social and Literary Department, Ministry of Higher Education and Scientific Research; appointed Ambassador in 1975, Ministry of Foreign Affairs, Baghdad; Professor of Abbasid History and Islamic civilisation at the College of Arts, Baghdad since 1976; in 1977-78, Research Associate at the University of Lancaster and lecturer on Arab history and Arabic Language at the Intitute of Arabic and Islamic Studies, Lonsdale College, University of Lancaster (UK). Professor of Islamic History. College of Arts, University of UAE, al-Ain, Abu Dhabi (1980-83). **Publ.:** Author of "The Abbasid Caliphate 750-786 A.C." (published in 1969), "Studies in the History of the early Abbasids" (1969), "Harun al-Rashid" (published in the Encyclopeadia of Islam), "The Barmacides" (Published in the Encyclopeadia Britannica), "The nature of the Abbasid Da'wa" (Beirut 1970); History of the Gulf in the Islamic period (Beirut 1982); Islamic Hystory and 20th C. thought, Baghdad (1985). **Awards:** Fellow of the Royal Asiatic Society of the U.K.; The Middle East Studies Association of North America. **Member:** London Convocation; Union of Arab Historians; Iraqi Historical Society; Union of Iraqi Authors and Writers. **Prof. Addr.:** Department of History, College of Arts, University of Baghdad, Iraq.

OMAR (Miftah al-Usta, Dr.), Libyan politician and physician. **Born** in 1935. **Son** of al-Usta Omar (Poet). **Educ.:** in Egypt and the U.K. **Dipl.:** M.D., Pediatrics, Cairo University; Post-graduate course, University of Sheffield, UK. **Career:** Director of Government Hospital, Beida; Minister of Health (1969), and re-appointed, Secretary for Health, General People's Committee (1977-81); Secretary of Interior (January 1981), Secretary-General of the "General People's Congress" (until 1989). **Addr.:** Secretariat, General People's Congress, Tripoli, Libya.

OMAR (Mohamad), Libyan executive. **Born** in 1940 in Tripoli, Libya. **Married** in 1926, 3 sons. 2 daughters. **Educ.:** Case Western Reserve University, USA. **Dipl.:** M.Sc. (Econ.) (1969). **Career:** Joined Central Bank of Libya since 1962; Economist, Central Bank of Libya (1962-74); Deputy Director, Research Division (1974-78); Director of Research and Statistics Division, Central Bank of Libya, Tripoli, Libya (1978-). **Member:** Libyan Arab Economist's Association. **Hobby:** Reading. **Addr.:** P.O.Box 1103, Tripoli, Libya.

OMAR (Mohamad, Abdul Gadir), Sudanese army officer. **Born** in 1929 on Omdurman, Sudan. **Married,** 5 children. **Educ.:** Military Academy. **Career:** Military Attache, Embassy to Ethiopia (1963-66); Commander of the Sudanese troops in the united Arab Republic (1967-68); Commander of the Southern Command (1969-70); Member of the Preparatory Committee to prepare Regional Autonomy Document (1971-72); Chief of Staff, Sudanese Armed Forces (1971-72); Ambassador to Uganda (1972-73); Commissioner of Kassala Province (1973; attended Organization of African Unity Defence Commission Conferences and Arab League Defence Ministers Conferences. **Hobbies:** photography, hunting. **Addr.:** Kassala Province Headquarters, Kassala, Sudan.

OMAR (Mohammed Zayyan , Dr.), Saudi Academic. **Born** in 1941, in Medina, Saudi Arabia. **Educ.:** B.A. History, Riyadh University (1963); M.A. History, University of Arizona (1968); Diploma of Graduate Studies, M.E Center, University of Utah; Ph.D. University of Utah (1970). **Languages:** Arabic (Mother Tongue), fluent English. **Career:** Lecturer from 1970; Dean, Faculty of Arts & Humanities (1971-77); Assistant Professor from 1972 Associate professor from 1976; Professor from 1980; **Present Position:** Professor of History, King Abdul Aziz University, Jeddah; Diplomatic History of Saudi Arabia, Modern

Middle East History; Historical Research Methods; **Academic Activities:** Establishment of Faculty of Arts & Humanities with all its present Departments; Preparation, execution and supervision of the first conference for Saudi men of Letters (1974); Teaching as a visiting Scholar at Vilanova University PA (1985); Teaching at King Abdul Aziz University (1970-99) **Publ.:** "Scientific Research Methods and Techniques" (1982); "Historical Studies" (1976); "U.S. in the Middle East: 1800-1950 and the Arab-Israeli Conflict" in English; "South West Asia in the International Politics"; "Kings Faisal's History, a survey in Historical Criticism"; "Saudi international Relations 1902-1992"; "King Abdul Aziz's Foreign Policy 1902-1953"; a number of papers and articles published in several periodicals and news papers. **Attended Conferences:** World Conference for regional executive chairmen of WACL (World Anti-Communism League) U.S.A. (1977); Tenth Conference for WACL and 13th World Conference for APACL (Asian People Anti Communism League)- Taipie (1978); Europe Islamic Council for future world economy conference-London (1978); First World Islamic Education Conference-Makkah; Fifth Conference for Muslim Community-India (1975); Muslim Social Scientists- U.S.A. (1977); Muslim Student's Association Conference-U.K. (1976); First World Conference on Islamic Education-Makkah; The Role of the University in the Society-Riyadh; First Conference on the Role of the Teacher in Education-Makkah; Iran, Pakistan, Afghanistan in the International Policy-U.S.A., Vilanova University (1985); The Arabs in the next decade- U.S.A., George Town University (1985); International Conference of Saudi History Riyadh (1979); International Conference on Saudi History-Riyadh (1999). **Awards:** Royal Honorary Award, First class with Gold Medal; was awarded the Fullbright Scholarship as a visiting scholar at Princeton University, Princeton-U.S.A. (1995). **Hobbies:** Swimming and Reading. **Address:** P.O.Box 5464, Jeddah 21422, Tel.: 661-1935, 665-9320, Mobile 055320116, Fax: 6732410, Saudi Arabia.

OMAR (Saleh Abdul Aziz, al), Saudi civil servant. **Born** in 1943. **Educ.:** Ph.D. in Economics. **Career:** Director General of Research and Consultancy, Public Administration Institute; Director of General Administration, same institute; Director of Administration, Ministry of Finance and National Economy; Assistant Deputy Minister of Finance and National Economy for Budget Affairs, same institute. Chairman, Governing Board, OPEC Fund for International Development. **Member:** Arab Alumni Society; Economists' Society in the South West U.S.A.; Board, University of Petroleum; Minerals Sewerage and Drainage Department, Riyadh and Arab Co. for Drug and Medical Instruments. **Publication:** Assimilation Power of Saudi Economy and Development Policy (a research study). **Prof. Addr.:** OPEC fund for International Development, P.O.Box 995, 1011 Vienna, Tel.: (1)515640, Fax: (1)5139238, Austria.

OMAR (Siraj), Saudi composer. **Born** in 1945 in Jeddah, Saudi Arabia. **Educ.:** Obtained Secondary School Certificate. **Career:** Began his Career as an employee with the Saudi Arabian Airlines (Saudia) (1960-69). **Member:** Board of Directors, the Arab Society for Culture and Arts, and Head of its subsidiary society in the Western Province in Saudi Arabia; member, the Society of Composers, Paris. **Honours:** Gold Medallion for composing the Saudi Arabian National Anthem. **Prof. Addr.:** The Society for Culture and Arts, P.O.Box 941, Tel.: 642606, Jeddah. **Priv. Addr.:** Tel.: 6533634, 6517255, Jeddah, Saudi Arabia.

OMAR (Walid, al), Iraqi businessman. **Born** in 1942 in Basra, Iraq. **Married**, 3 children. **Educ.:** Imperial College of Technology and Science, London University, UK. **Dipl.:** B.Sc. (Hons), M.Sc. in Thermal Power and Process Engineering, DIC. **Career:** joined teaching staff of University of Basra, Iraq. Teaching Engineering and Marketing; established Omar Engineering Company, a substantial business enterprise with more than five hundred employees dealing in contracting and trading; moved to Beirut, Lebanon to develop his business on inter-Arab basis in 1970; after the outbreak of war in Lebanon he moved his business to London (1975); he plays a leading role in the development of inter-Arab and international business activities and commerce, developing new business opportunities and industries. **Hobbies:** chess, reading, travelling, skiing. **Prof. Addr.:** 39 St. Mary Abbot's Terrace, London W14 8NX, United Kingdom.

OMAR (Yahia), Omani businessman. **Born** in 1931 in Tripoli, Libya. **Married**, three children. **Career:** Libyan Police Service (1954); Manager, Esso Oil Company, Libya (1955); Private enterprise (1958-69); resident in Switzerland (1969); Political and Economic Adviser to HM Sultan Qaboos (1971); former Chairman, Arab International Bank, Cairo, Egypt; Director, Artoc Bank, Bahamas; director and shareholder of several companies. **Addr.:** Muscat, Sultanate of Oman.

OMARI (Abdallah Abdul Rahman, al), Saudi official. **Born** in 1941 at Bani Omar. **Dipl.:** B.A. (Business Administration) U.S.A. **Career:** Began career at the University as Director of the Dean's Office (1974); Director of the Rector's Office, (1977); General Director of Administrative Affairs, King Fahad University of Petroleum and Minerals. **Hobbies:** reading, swimming. **Prof. Addr.:** King Fahad University of Petroleum and Minerals, Tel.: 8603302, 9603300, Dhahran, Saudi Arabia.

OMARI (Farouq, Sunaallah), Iraqi university professor. **Born** in 1937 in Mosul. **Son** of Sunaallah Umari **and** Mrs. née Amihane Hage Rachid Beik. **Married in 1973 to** Miss Hana'Izzeddine Moukhtar. **Educ.:** Baghdad **University**, specialisation in the U.S.A. **Dipl.:** Doctorate in **Geology**. **Career:** Head, Geology Department, Faculty of

Science, Mosul University (1970-72); Dean of the said faculty since 1972. **Sports:** Tennis and Football. **Hobby:** Reading. **Priv. Addr.:** Mahallat an-Nasr, Tel.: 813360, Mosul, Iraq.

OMARI (Mahmud, Ali, al), Jordanian executive. **Born** in 1945 in Irbid, Jordan. **Son** of Ali al-Omari. **Married**, two children. **Educ.:** B.A. in Economics and Commerce, Jordan (1969). **Career:** Auditor, Ministry of Finance, Amman, Jordan (1970); Assistant to the Head of Advance Section (1972); Head of Audit Section, Amman Finance Department, Jordan (1974); Finance Department of Abu Dhabi, on secondment (1975); Principal Finance Officer, Finance Department of Abu Dhabi (1978); Budget Controller, Abu Dhabi (since 1981). **Sport:** Table tennis. **Hobbies:** Chess and travelling. **Prof. Addr.:** Finance Department, P.O.Box 246, Tel.: 366800, Ext, 241, Abu Dhabi, United Arab Emirates. **Priv. Addr.:** Tel.: 829736, Abu Dhabi, United Arab Emirates.

OMARI (Mohamad Eyad), Syrian executive. **Born** in 1936 in Damascus, Syrian. **Son** of Samih Omari. **Married** in 1969. **Educ.:** University of London (L.S.E.). **Dipl.:** M.Sc. (Econ.) (1961). **Career:** Joined Commercial Bank of Syria, Damascus (1962-71); UBAF, Paris (1971-72); UBAF Bank, London (1972-74); Deputy General Manager, European Arab Bank, Brussels (1974-). **Addr.:** 19H Avenue des Arts-Bte 2, Tel.: (02) 2194230, Telex: 26413, 23884 A/ B EURAB B, B-1040 Brussels, Belgium.

OMARI (Mumtaz, al), Iraqi Lawyer. **Born** in Iraq. **Educ.:** Secondary Law College of Baghdad, Syrian University of Damascus. **Dipl.:** Bachelor of Law, Damascus University. **Career:** Lawyer, former Director General, Ministry of the Interior. **Addr.:** Baghdad, Iraq.

OMARI (Nather, Akram, al), Iraqi former diplomat. **Born** on December 15, 1917 in Mosul (Iraq). **Son** of Akram al-Umari **and** Mrs., née Nazimah al-Umari. **Married in** 1946 to Miss May al-Umari, 3 children: Akram, Nawfal and Rayah. **Educ.:** Language College in Baghdad, Cambridge University, **Dipl.:** Higher Commercial Studies and Economics from Cambridge and Liverpool Universities, International Law and Public Law from Columbia University. **Career:** Economic Department of the Ministry of Foreign Affairs in Iraq (1945); Vice-Consul in Beirut (1945), in New York (1946); joined the Iraqi Delegation at UNO, represented Iraq on the Economic and Financial Committee of UNO's General Assembly (1947-49); attached to the Iraqi Embassy in Washington (1949); delegated to the Secretariat of UNO (1951); then to the Department of Technical Assistance for Developing Nations; assigned to the Iraqi Embassy in Beirut (1952); member of the Permanent Iraqi Delegation to UNO; led the Iraqi Delegation to the International Labour Congress in Geneva Counsellor to the Iraqi Embassy in New Delhi (1958); Minister Plenipotentiary and Chargé d'Affaires in London (1959-61); Elected President of the **Afro-Asiatic** Bloc at the World Labour Congress in Geneva **(1962)**; Ambassador Extraordinary and Plenipotentiary to **Lebanon** (1964); to France (July 1967); **Member:** Royal Automobile Club (London). **Sport:** Swimming. **Hobbies:** Oil Painting and Photography. **Award:** Grand Cordon Order of the Cedar (1967). **Addr.:** Baghdad, Iraq.

OMARI (Tarik, Nassib, al), Iraqi engineer. **Born** in 1934 in Damascus, Syria. **Married,** 4 daughters. **Dipl.:** B.Sc. in Electrical Engineering. **Career:** Engineer at Iraq Petroleum Co. Karkouk (1960-69); Engineer at National Petroleum Co., Baghdad, Iraq (1969-71); Senior Engineer, Basra (1971-74); Chairman of the Board of Directors of Iraqi Tanker Co. (1974-79); Member of the Board of Iraqi Petrol Tanker Co (1972-74) and Arab Shipping Co., Bahrain (1974-75); Vice President, United Arab Marine Co. Kuwait (1982). **Publ.:** "The Marine Transport Industry and the Development of Iraqi Tankers" (1978), "The Iraqi Petrol Tanker Company" (1979), "services and Engineering in Petroleum Equipment and Projects" (1982). **Hobbies:** music, reading, swimming. **Addr.:** Baghdad, Iraq.

OMAYA (Mohamed, Ali), Yemeni banker, and former minister. **Born** in Aden in 1942. **Son** of Ali Mohamed Omaya **and** Mrs. Su'ood Abdo Hussein. **Married** in 1972, five children. **Educ.:** Attended banking courses in Baghdad, al-Rafidain Bank; in Paris at UBAF, at London at UBAF. **Career:** Joined the Chartered bank, Aden (1961-69); Deputy General Manager of National Bank of Yemen (1969-71); Minister of Labour and Social Welfare (1971-74); General Manager of National Bank of Yemen (1974-82); Deputy Minister of Foreign Affairs (till 1986); General Manager of National Bank of Yemen and member of the Board of Directors for the Banking System (1986). **Decorations:** Liberation War Medal and sports medal. **Sport:** Swimming. **Hobby:** Reading. **Member** of Tilal Sports Club. **Prof. Addr.:** P.O.Box 5, Tel. 52481/2, Telex: AD 2224/ 2274/ 2308, Crater, Aden, Republic of Yemen. **Priv. Addr.:** Section "C" Street No.4 Sh. Abdulla **Street**, Crater Aden, Republic of Yemen.

OMAYRA (Hassan, Abdul Rahim), Egyptian judge. **Born** in 1936 in Egypt. **Educ.:** Cairo University, Egypt. **Dipl.:** LL.B. **Career:** Judge at the Cairo Court of Cassation (1984-). **Hobbies:** Walking, reading, tennis. **Member:** the Sun Club. **Prof. Addr.:** Court of Cassation, Cairo, Egypt. **Priv. Addr.:** 15 Shaikh Ali Mahmoud Street, Masr al-Jadida, Cairo, Egypt.

OMER (al-Fadil al-Obeid), Sudanese academic. **Born** in 1944 in Sudan; **Married.** 4 daughters. **Educ.:** University of Manchester, UK; University of Khartoum, Sudan. **Dipl.:** Diploma in Bacteriology; PhD in Medicine. **Career:** Physician at the Ministry of Health, Sudan (1969-73); Assistant Lecturer, Khartoum University (1973-76), Lecturer

(1976-82), Associate Professor (1982-83); Associate Professor of Umm al-Qura University, Saudi Arabia (1983-); Member of British Society for General Microbiology, American Society of Sexually Transmitted Diseases, Sudan Society for Infertility and the British Medical Society for the Study of Veneral Diseases. **Publ.:** numerous research papers published in national and international medical journals. **Hobby:** football. **Member:** SOS Children's Village Society and Marrikh Sport Club, Sudan. **Prof. Addr.:** Department of Medical Sciences, Umm al-Qura University, P.O.Box 3711, Mecca, Saudi Arabia.

OMRAN (Abdallah, Hamid), UAE official. **Born** in 1947 in Sharjah, UAE. **Married. Dipl.:** B.A. in Commerce. **Career:** Director of Administrative and Financial Affairs, Ministry of Justice; Director of Technical Department, Ministry of Justice, Dubai (1977-). **Hobbies:** fishing, swimming. **Member:** Abu Dhabi Club. **Prof. Addr.:** Ministry of Justice, Islamic Affairs and Awqaf, P.O.Box 3907, Dubai, United Arab Emirates.

OMRAN (Abdulrahman Ibn Hassan, al), Saudi diplomat. **Born** in 1925 in Riyadh, Saudi Arabia. **Educ.:** received general education and specialized in Arabic Literature. **Career:** Joined Government service in 1940, Bureau of H.R.H. Prince Faisal Ibn Abdulaziz then Deputy to H.M. King Abdulaziz, later Second Assistant to the Chief of the Bureau (1940-50); served as Private Secretary to H.R.H. Prince Sultan Ibn Abdulaziz, at that time Prince of Riyadh, then Minister of Agriculture and later Minister of Communications; Director General, Roads Department (1960-61); in 1961 he was transferred to the Ministry of Foreign Affairs and was appointed Director of the Arab League Department; became Saudi Consul General to Thailand (1963) and Ambassador (1966-75); Saudi Ambassador to Tunisia (1975-80), now retired. **Member:** al-Ahli Sport Club, Jeddah; has attended several Ministry of Foreign Affairs Conferences, Conferences of the Economic Committee for Asia and the Far East. **Honours:** several awards and decorations from Egypt, Syria, Lebanon, Iraq, Jordan and Thailand; King Abdulaziz Order, Excellent Class; the Cedar of Lebanon; the White Elephant, Thailand. **Hobbies:** reading, swimming, walking. **Priv. Addr.:** Tel.: 6604741, Jeddah, Saudi Arabia.

OMRAN (Adnan), Syrian diplomat. **Born** on 9 August 1934 in Syria. **Educ.:** University of Damascuș; Moscos, USSR; and Columbia University, USA. **Career:** Ministry of Foreign Affairs (1962-63); Member, Permanent Mission to UN (1963-66); First Secretary, Syrian Embassy, Moscow (1966-68); Consul-General, Embassy in Berlin, G.D.P. (1968-70); Director, Int. Org. and Conf. Dept., Ministry of Foreign Affairs (1970-71); Palestine Dept. (1971-72); Special Bureau Dept. (1972-74); concurrently member Del. to UN (1970-73). Ambassador to UK and Sweden (1974-80); Asst. Secretary-General for International Affairs, League of Arab States (Oct. 1980-96); Deputy Minister for Foreign Affairs (1996-98); **Minister of** Information (2000-). **Addr.:** Ministry of Information, **Fax:** (11)6617665, Tel.: (11)6619396, Damascus, Syria.

ONSI (Mahmoud Bahir), Egyptian banker. **Born** on December 14, 1916 in Helwan, Egypt. **Married:** two children, one son, one daughter. **Educ.:** Faculty of Commerce, Cairo University. **Dipl.:** B.Com. in Business and Industrial Administration (1940). **Career:** Universal Maritime Company, Suez Canal, Ismailia, Egypt (1941-46); Belgium and International Bank, Egypt (1946-60); Director General, Belgium and International Bank, Egypt (1960-62); member of the Board of Directors and General Manager of National Bank of Egypt (1962-66); Secretary-General, African Development Bank, Abidjan (1966-68); National Bank of Egypt, Cairo (1968-69); Founder and Secretary General, French-Arab Chamber of Commerce, Paris, France (1969-72), Deputy Chairman and Managing Director, Arab African International Bank, Cairo, Egypt (1972); Chairman, Arab African Bank, Nouakchott, Mauritania; Deputy Chairman, African Arab Company for foreign Trade and Development (AFARCO), Nouakchott, Mauritania; member of the Board, Compagnie Financière et Touristique (tourism and hotel development), Tunisia; member of the International Bankers Association, Washington D.C., U.S.A.; member, International Public Relations Association, U.S.A.; member, European Center of Public Relations, Brussels, Belgium, now retired. **Decor:** Officer of the National Order of Merit, France (1977). **Hobbies:** Fencing, riding, golf, music. **Member:** Egyptian Automobile and Touring Club of Egypt, Cairo (1968); Rotary Club; Gazira Sporting Club; Vice-President and Founder of the Arab Public Relations Society, Cairo, Egypt; Founder and Honorary Treasurer of the Association, Egyptian-French Friendship. **Priv. Addr.:** 2 Midan Kasr al-Doubara, Garden City, Cairo, Egypt.

ORABI (Mohamed, Zaki, el), Egyptian banker. **Born** on May 2, 1927 in Cairo, Egypt. **Married,** 2 sons: Aly and Alaa. **Educ.:** Faculty of Law, Cairo University. **Dipl.:** LL.B. **Career:** Formerly Managing Director of el-Nahda Bank, Libya and Director of the Board of Oman Arab African Bank and Amfeco Investment Co., Vice Chairman of Misr Bank, Misr International Bank and Misr Romanian Bank; Managing Director of National Investment Bank; Chairman of Cairo Bank and Cairo Paris Bank; **Currently,** Chairman of National Bank for Development, Cairo. **Prof. Addr.:** 5 el-Borsa el-Gedida Street, P.O.Box 647, Tel.: (2)3563505, Cairo, Egypt. **Priv. Addr.:** Tanta Street No.1, Agouza, Giza, Egypt.

ORAINAN (Hamad Mohamad), Saudi academic. **Educ.:** Ph.D. (St. Andrews University, U.K.). **Career:** Associate Professor of History and Dean, Faculty of Arts and Humanities, King Abdulaziz University, Jeddah. **Publications:** Ibn Khaldun as Historian of Mecca, New Readings of Some Important Events in the Period of the Umayyad. **Priv. Addr.:** Tel.: 7876145, Jeddah, Saudi Arabia.

ORAT ADOR (Peter), Sudanese former minister and former customs officer. **Born** on January 1, 1940 in Thwolong Upper Nile Province. **Son** of Ador Kur Ador (Tribal chief) **and** Mrs., née Aney Jubek Ageng. **Married** on January 2, 1972 to Miss Malakal Luigina Nyabwomyo Alems, 5 children: Anges (1973), Elisabeth (1978), Teresa (1980), Mary (1982), Emmanuel (1984) and Ilyator (dead). **Educ.:** Lul Primary School (1948-51); Intermediate School (1952-57); Rumbek Secondary School (1948-61); University of Khartoum (1962-68). **Dipl.:** B.A. (Hons). **Career:** Teacher in Comboni College for one year (1967); Customs Officer, Assistant inspector (1968-70); Excise Officer, Asst. Inspector (1970-71); Asst. inspector Customs (1971-72); Superintendent of Customs JUBA (1972-73); Attended advance course for customs works in Helsinki, Finland (1974); Controller of Customs Southern Region (1974-76); seconded to the South as Director for Taxation (1976-78); Asst. Director General of Customs Southern Region (1978-80); Director of Customs, Port Sudan (1981-86); Director General of Customs, Port Sudan (1986-89); Represented SUDAN in the Permanent Technical Committee for the Customs Cooperation Council in Brussels (1987-89); Minister of Relief and Refugee Affairs, Khartoum, Sudan (1992). **Hobby:** Reading books. **Member:** Customs Club; Tennis Club. **Priv. Addr.:** House No.2, Block 10, Tel.: 74353, Khartoum, Sudan.

ORGANJI (Rushdi Ahmad), Saudi academic. **Born** in Makkah 1940, Saudi Arabia. **Dipl.:** Ph.D. (Botany), 1972 from Reading Uni., U.K. **Career:** Lecturer, Assistant Prof., and Associate Pro., at Bioloty Dept., Faculty of Education, King Abdelaziz Univ., Makkah Site. Professor of Plant Physiological Ecology from 1989 at Bioloty Dept., Faculty of Applied Science Umm-Al Qura Univ., Makkah. Vice-Dean of Student Affairs (1974). Head of Biology Dept. (1975). Dean of Student Affairs (1976). Dean of Faculty of Education (1976-1980). Head of Biology Dept. (1988-1991). Member of Scientific Council (1989-1992). Head of Research Unit, of Plant Ecology (1980 till now). Supervisor of Higher degree Studies, Faculty of Applied Science 1997. **Publications:** texbook: Some Medicinal and Aromatic Plants of Saudi Arabia. 20 papers in plant Ecology. **Invention:** An instrument for germinating Seeds under the Same pressure, humidity, temperature and light; an instrument for injecting oil with chemicals, Such. as fertilizers, at different depths. **Hobbies:** Reading world literature, history and trourism. **Address:** Faculty of Applied Science, Biology Dept., Umm Al Qura University, Tel.: 5503560 Ext. 6038. Home Tel.: 5566673, P.O.Box 7490, Makkah, Saudi Arabia.

ORRI (Mohamad A.R.), Saudi businessman. **Born** in 1930. **Career:** Owns and runs a fleet of 21 cargo ships on liner trade; agent for Bureau Veritas and Panama Bureau Classification Societies; agents for P and I Clubs and several worldwide shipping companies; Owner and Chairman of Board of Orri Group of Companies. **Prof. Addr.:** Orri Navigation, Lines, Orri Building, P.O.Box 737, Jeddah, Saudi Arabia.

ORSAN (Ali, Okla), Syrian writer. **Born** in 1940 in Syria. **Son** of Okla Orsan. **Married**, four children. **Educ.:** Diploma, High Institute of Dramatic Arts, Cairo, Egypt (1963); Diploma in Drama, France. **Career:** Deputy Director of the National Theatre, Damascus (1966); Secretary of the Artists Syndicate (1968); Director General of Theatres and Music (1969-74); Leader of the Artist Syndicate (1970); member of the Executive Office of the Arab Writers Union (1973-75); Deputy Chairman, Arab Writers Union (1975-77); Assistant to the Minister of Culture and Information (1976); Chairman of Arab Writers Union (since 1977); Deputy Secretary General, General Union of Arab Writers (1979-81); Secretary General, General Union of Arab Writers (since 1981); Deputy Secretary General, Union of African and Asian Writers (1981); Director of the Following Magazines: "al-Kaatib al-Arabi", "al-Mawqif al-Adabi", "al-Turath al-Arabi" and "al-Adaab". **Publ.:** Plays and other works. **Medals:** Medal of Culture, Tunisia (1976); Silver Star, German Democratic Republic (1983). **Hobbies:** Music, literature, drama and theatre. **Prof. Addr.:** P.O.Box 3230 or 11124, Tel.: 618568, Damascus, Syria. **Priv. Addr.:** Tel.: 720271, Damascus, Syria.

OSAILAN (Abdallah Abd el-Raheem), Saudi academic. **Born** in 1944 in Medina, Saudi Arabia. **Dipl.:** Ph.D. (Arabic Literature). **Career:** Teacher, Secondary Scientific Institute; Demonstrator, Faculty of Arabic Language, Imam Muhammad Ibn Saud Islamic University; Assistant Professor, Vice Dean and later Dean of Library Affairs of same institute. **Member:** Imam Muhammad Ibn Saud Islamic University Council and Scientific Research Council. **Publications:** The Investigation of Abi Tamam's Enthusiasm; Abi Tamam's Enthusiasm of the book al-Ijtihad (Diligence); The News of Abi Hafse, Omar Ibn Abdul Aziz; al-Abbas Ibn Marwas al-Silmy al-Shaby, the Poet. **Address:** Imam Muhammad Ibn Saud Islamic University, P.O.Box 5701, Tel.: 4042909, Riyadh, Saudi Arabia.

OSAIMI (Ayed E.), Saudi engineer. **Born** on 28 December 1942 in Taif, Saudi Arabia. **Dipl.:** B.Sc., M.Sc., Ph.D. (Civil Engineering). **Career:** Instructor, University of Petroleum and Minerals (1973-76); Research Assistant, Stanford University (1974-77); Professor of Civil Engineering, University of Petroleum and Minerals (1977-78); member of the American Society of Civil Engineers; Engineering Consultant to the Royal Commission (1977-79); Principal and Vice President of Dar al-Riyadh Consultants. **Honours:** Awards of the Engineering Council of

Sacramento valley and of the American Society for Testing and Materials. **Publications:** several scientific papers, articles and reports relating to geotechnical and civil engineering. **Hobbies:** drawing, painting. **Prof. Addr.:** P.O.Box 5461, Tel.: 8942964, 8944642, 8420670, Dammam, Saudi Arabia.

OSMAN (Abbas, Babiker), Sudanese executive. **Born** in 1941 in Khartoum, Sudan. **Son** of Babiker Osman. **Married** in 1978, 2 daughters. **Educ.:** School of Commerce. Khartoum; Institute for Banking Studies, Khartoum. **Career:** Sudan Commercial Bank, Khartoum (1962-75); Assistant Manager, National Bank of Abu Dhabi, Ras al-Khaimah (1975-). **Member:** Sudanese Association, Ras al-Khaimah, UAE; Sudanese Club. **Hobby:** Football. **Addr.:** P.O.Box 350, Tel.: 28653, 21753, Telex: 99194 A/B MASRAF EM, Ras al-Khaimah, UAE.

OSMAN (Abdillahi Said), Somali Diplomat. **Born** in 1939. **Married,** three children. **Educ.:** Hull, London and Cambridge Universities. **Career:** Secretary and Legal Counsellor, Prime Minister's Office (1964-65); Co-Chairman Consultative Commission for Legislation and Director of Legal Department, Ministry of Justice (1965-68); Director General, Ministry of Justice, Religious Affairs and Labour (1968-71); Judge of Arbitration Court of EEC and the Afro-Malagasy states (1971); General State Attorney and Senior Legal Adviser to President of Somalia (1971-76); Permanent Representative to United Nations Office (1976-84); President Plenipotentiary Conference on Territorial Asylum (1977); Chairman Charter Review Committee Meeting of OAU (1980); Permanent Representative to UNIDO (1981-84); President 27th session of Trade and Development Board of UNCTAL (1983); Chairman, Group of 77 at 6th UNCTAD session (1983); Permanent Representative to United Nations (UN) (1984). **Address:** Mogadishu, Somalia.

OSMAN (Ahmad), Moroccan statesman. **Born** on January 3, 1930 at Oujda, Morocco. **Widower,** H.R.H. Princess Lalla Nezha (late sister of HM King Hassan II). **Educ.:** in Morocco and University of Bordeaux, France. **Dipl.:** LL.B. (1951), Diploma of Higher Studies in Public and Civil Law. **Career:** Joined Royal Cabinet, Legal Affairs, following HM King Mohammed's return from exile; joined Ministry of Foreign Affairs (1957); Head of the European Division (1959); Head of the American Division; Leading Member of Moroccan delegations to UN General Assembly, Conference on Law of the Sea, Arab League Meetings; Secretary General, Ministry of National Defence (1959); Ambassador to the Federal Republic of Germany (July 1961-62); Under-Secretary of State for Industry and Mines, Ministry of Commerce (till November 1963); led Moroccan delegation, Khartoum meeting of African Finance Ministers (July 1963); President, Compagnie Marocaine de Navigation (COMANAV) (May 1963); Ambassador to USA and Canada (April 1967); Minister of Administrative Affairs (October 1970); Prime Minister (November 1972), also Minister of Defence (March 1973); Prime Minister (1974) and (October 1977); Presently President of the Party "Rassemblement National des Indépendants" and former President of the Chamber of Deputies. **Hobby:** Bridge. **Addr.:** c/o Majlis an Nuwab, Rabat, Morocco.

OSMAN (Ahmad, Mahmoud), Egyptian university professor. **Born** on March 8, 1937 in Cairo (Egypt). **Married** to Soheir Abdel Wahab in February 1961, one daughter and two sons. **Educ.:** Victoria College, Cairo (1943-54); Faculty of Medicine, Cairo University (1954-60); Brooks Hospital Cambridge (UK) (1970-71). **Dipl.:** M.B. Ch.B, Cairo University (1960); DMRE (diploma of medical radiology), Cairo University (1964); M.D. Doctor of Medicine, Radiodiagnosis (1968); expert in Gastro-Intestinal radiology. **Career:** Registrar, Cairo Islamic Hospital (1963-64); Head, X-Ray Department, Student University Hospital (1964-68); Registrar Addensbrooks Hospital, Cambridge (UK) (1970-71); now Head, X-Ray Department, Cancer Institute, Cairo University. **Hobbies:** Tennis and Arts. **Prof. Addr.:** 42, Talaat Harb street, Tel.: 44450, Cairo. **Priv. Addr.:** 17 Brazil street, Zamalek District, Tel.: 802802, Cairo, Egypt.

OSMAN (Ali, Issa), Jordanian international civil servant. **Born** in 1920 at Beit Safafa (Jerusalem). **Married,** children. **Educ.:** American University in Cairo (1943-47); Syracuse University, New York (USA) (1947-49); University of Chicago (USA) (1949-54). **Dipl.:** B.A. (1947), M.A. (Western and Islamic Thought) (1954). **Career:** Deputy Director, Regional Centre for Training in Community Development, Arab States, UNESCO (1957-64); Head, Education Research Section, Department of Education UNRWA/UNESCO (1964-71); Representative, Gulf Area, UNICEF (1971-74); Senior Regional Programme Officer, East Mediterranean Regional Office, UNICEF, Beirut (Lebanon) (1974); Senior Advisor in Social Development, The Arab Fund, Kuwait (1977-79); UN Senior Advisor in Social Planning, Ministry of Planning, Kuwait (1979-82). **Publ.:** Author of "The Concept of Man in Islam" (1961). "Community Development in the Arab World" (1962). **Prof. Addr.:** P.O.Box 113-6209, Beirut.

OSMAN (Assaïd Mohamad), Libyan statesman. **Born** in 1922. **Career:** Head of Religions Court (1945); Organized Libyan-Nationalist Activity in Fezzan (1947); Imprisoned by French Authorities (1948-50); Member of the Constituent Assembly (1950); Minister of Health (1951); Deputy to Constituent Assembly (1958); Minister for Economic Affairs (1960); Prime Minister (1960-March 1963); Deputy (1964); Private business since 1964. **Addr.:** Gebara Street 6, Tripoli, Libya.

OSMAN (el-Sayed Mohamad), Egyptian international

civil servant. **Born** on April 3, 1926 at Kafr Hifna, Sharqiyah Governorate (Egypt). **Married,** with children. **Educ.:** Faculty of Arts, Cairo University (1942-46); Institute of Education, Cairo University (1946-48); University of Exeter (UK) (1950-52). **Dipl.:** B.A. (English); Diploma in Education and Psychology; Higher Diploma in English Language and Literature. **Career:** Teacher of English, Secondary schools, Ministry of Education, Cairo (1948-56); Research and Documentation Specialist, Documentation Centre for Education, Ministry of Education, Cairo (1956-57); Programme specialist, Department of Education, UNESCO (1958-69); Senior Reviser and Chief, Arabic Translation Section, UNESCO, Paris (1970-1981). Editor, Unesco Courier, Arabic Edition (1982-April 1986). Retired since. **Publ.:** Translator of "Educational Psychology" (1955), "The Mature Mind" (1957), "The Mind Alive" (1960), "Child Development" (1963). **Priv. Addr.:** 78, Avenue de Suffren, 75015 Paris, France, Tel.: 47343579.

OSMAN (Khalid, Osman, al), Kuwaiti executive. **Born** in 1950 in Kuwait. **Son** of Osman al-Osman. **Married** in 1980, 1 son. **Educ.:** Kuwait University. **Career:** Secretary, Board of Directors, Pearl Investment Company, Manama, **Addr.:** P.O.Box 5809, Tel.: 246570, Telex: 9353 A/B LULUAH BN, Manama, Bahrain.

OSMAN (Khalil, Dr.), Sudanese businessman. **Born** in 1930 in Dueim (Sudan). **Son** of Osman Mahmoud (deceased) **and** Mrs., née el-Toma Hassan Abu Hussein. **Married** in 1956 to Safia Humoudi in Dueim (Sudan), 6 children: Kamala, Hind, Mohamad, Amal, Khalid and Tariq. **Educ.:** Hantoub secondary school (Sudan); Cairo University. **Dipl.:** B.Sc. (veterinary science). **Career:** Veterinary officer, Ministry of Animal Resources (Sudan) (1956-57); Businessman in Kuwait (1957); Owner and shareholder, Textiles Industry, chemicals, glassware, matches, fisheries, aviation, hotels, packaging, pharmaceuticals; holder of equity in Lhorno Co. **Sports:** Sailing, swimming and flying. **Hobby:** Reading. **Credit Cards:** American Express, Diners, Barclaycard. **Prof. Addr.:** Kuwait Tel.: 448310, London, Tel.: 4999948, Sudan Tel.: 34166. **Priv. Addr.:** Windoser 03-4475701, (UK); Tel.: 75428, Sudan.

OSMAN (Mohamad Khair, Dr.), Sudanese educationist and administrator. **Born** in 1928 in Gedaref, Sudan. **Married. Educ:** Bakht el-Ruda; University of Khartoum; Institute of Education, London University. **Dipl.:** Ph.D. in Educational Planning, University of California, USA. **Career:** Teacher in Primary Schools; Assistant Under-Secretary, Curriculum and Books Division, Ministry of Education; Director, Management Research and Productivity Centre, (till october 1972); Minister of Instruction and Education (Oct. 1972-May 1973); Minister of State for Higher Education (1973-Jan. 1975); Ambassador, Ministry of Foreign Affairs. **Hobby:** Travelling. **Addr.:** Ministry of Foreign Affairs, Khartoum, Sudan.

OSMAN (Mohamad, Mohamad), Egyptian engineer. **Born** in 1939 in Cairo, Egypt. **Married,** 3 daughters. **Educ.:** Cairo University, Egypt; London University, United Kingdom. **Dipl.:** B.Sc. and Ph.D. in Chemical Engineering. **Career:** Chief Departmental Engineer, el-Nasr Company for Chemical Pharmaceuticals, Cairo (1960-62); Demonstrator, Chemical Department, Faculty of Engineering, Cairo University (1962-64); Lecturer (1968-73); Associate Professor (1974-78); Member of Petroleum Research and Mineral Committee, Egyptian Academy of Scientific Research and Technology (1974); Member of the Society of Petroleum Engineers, Metallurgical and Petroleum Engineers and American Institute of Mining (1977); Member of Egyptian Business Council (1982); Professor, Chemical Department, Faculty of Engineering, Cairo University (1974); Member of the Board of Directors of Egyptian Engineering Society (1977-80) and (1983); general Manager and Owner of Industrial and Petroleum Engineering Counsultants (IPEC) (1982); **Hobbies:** tennis, swimming. **Member:** Shooting Club, Gezira Sporting Club. **Prof. Addr.:** 12 el-Nil Street, Giza, Cairo, Egypt. **Priv. Addr.:** 47 Giza Street, Apt. 19, Giza, Cairo, Egypt.

OSMAN (Osama Abdul Rahman), Saudi academic. **Born** in 1942 in Medina, Saudi Arabia. **Dipl.:** M.A., University of Minnesota, Ph.D., America University, Washing ton, D.C. **Career:** Former Head, Department of Business Administration; Vice Dean and later Dean, Faculty of Commerce, King Saud University. **Member:** Arab Administrative Science Organization Conferences on Administrative Aspects of Planning, conference on Public Organization; worked as part-time consultant to Ministry of Finance and the General Personnel Bureau. **Publications:** papers published in academic journals and delivered at conferences. **Prof. Addr.:** Faculty of Commerce, King Saud University, Tel.: 4811000, Riyadh. **Priv. Addr.:** Tel.: 4022989, Riyad, Saudi Arabia.

OSMAN (Osman, Ahmad), Egyptian civil engineer. **Born** in 1927 in Ismailia, Egypt. **Son** of Ahmad Osman. **Married** to Samia Wahbi, 5 children: Mahmoud, Ibrahim, Ahmad, Mohamad and Hadia. **Educ.:** Cairo University. **Dipl.:** B.Sc. (Engineering), Cairo University (1940). **Career:** Private Engineer; founder, Arab Contractors Co. (1949); Chairman, Board of Arab Contractors Co.; Minister of Reconstruction and Housing (1974-76); Member, National Assembly representing Ismailia Governorate (1976). **Sports:** Swimming, fishing. **Hobbies:** Theatre, cinema, reading. **Awards:** First Class Medal of the Arab Republic of Egypt; Russian Hero of Labour Medal. **Prof. Addr.:** The Arab Contractors Co., 34 Adly Street, Cairo. **Priv. Addr.:** Alouba Street, al-Ahram, Tel.: 851616, Cairo, Egypt.

OSMAN (Talat), Arab American banking executive. **Born** in 1936 in Palestine. **Son** of Mohamad Osman. **Married** in 1957, 3 sons, 1 daughter. **Educ.:** Northwestern University, USA. **Career:** Director, American Institute of Banking; Director, Junior Chamber of Commerce; Chairman, Islamic Cultural Centre of Greater Chicago; Northbrook, Illinois; President, Arab American Executives Club; Mid America Arab Chamber of Commerce, Chicago. Vice President and Division Administrator, Harris Trust & Savings Bank, Chicago, Illinois; Director, Arab Finance Corporation, Jordan; Arab Finance Corp. S.A.L., Beirut; Arab Finance Management Company, Luxembourg; Arab Finance Income Fund, Luxembourg; Arab Finance Services S.A., Paris; General Manager, Saudi Arab Finance Corp., Luxembourg. Deputy General Manager, al-Saudi Banque, Paris, France; President, Dearborn Financial, Inc., Chicago, Illinois and Milwaukee, Wisconsin; Director of The Marine Corporation, Milwaukee; Chairman of Dansk International Designs, Ltd., Mt. Kisco, New York; President of Arab Bankers Association of North America. **Publ.:** "Technique of Foreign Exchange Trading"; Several articles on the International Monetary System. **Member:** French American Chamber of Commerce. **Hobbies:** Tennis, racquetball and reading. **Address:** Milwaukee, Wisconsin 53202. U.S.A.

OSMANA (Amin), Egyptian Academic. **Born** in Egypt. **Educ.:** Cairo University and La Sorbonne Faculty (Paris). **Dipl.:** Licentiate and Doctor of Philosophy. **Career:** Professor of Philosophy, Faculty of Arts, Cairo University. **Publ.:** Author of "Descartes", "Stoical Philosophy of Muhammad Abdo", "Philosophical Doctrines", "The Essential Traits of French Humour", "In Defence of Science", "Classification of Sciences", etc... **Addr.:** 22, Muhammad Saïd Street, Cairo, Egypt.

OSMANI (Khaled), Syrian financial manager. **Born** in 1931 in Damascus, Syria. **Son** of Ragheb Osmani. **Married** in 1961, 2 sons, 1 daughter. **Dipl.:** B.Sc. (Law); Diplomas in Finance and Economy. **Career:** Head of Section, Administrative Department, Public Petroleum Est.; Manager, Operation Department, Syrian Marine Est., Damascus; Deputy General Manager, Real Estate Bank, Damascus; Deputy General Manager, Syrian Economic Establishment, Damascus; Manager, Administrative and Financial Department, Syrian-Jordanian Bank, Amman, Jordan. **Addr.:** P.O.Box 926636, Tel.: 61138, 61139, Telex: 22102 A/B SYJOBK JO, Amman, Jordan.

OTAIBA (Khalaf, al), United Arab Emirates businessman. **Born** in 1941 in Abu Dhabi, United Arab Emirates. **Career:** Presently Chairman, Abu Dhabi National Tanker Company; Chairman, Abu Dhabi National Insurance Company; Director, Abu Dhabi National Oil Co. **Addr.:** P.O.B. 839, Tel.: 343171, Telex: 22340 EM, Abu Dhabi, United Arab Emirates.

OTAIBA (Maneh, Said, al, Dr.), United Arab Emirates economist and politician. **Born** on May 15, 1946. **Son** of Said al-Otaiba. **Married. Educ.:** Baghdad University, Iraq; Cairo University, Egypt. **Dipl.:** B.Sc. Economics (1969); M.Sc. Economics (1974); Doctoral Thesis (1976). **Career:** Head, Petroleum Department, Abu Dhabi (1969); **Minister** of Petroleum and Industry United Arab Emirates (1972-1973), of Petroleum and Mineral Resources (since 1973 to 1990); member, Abu Dhabi Planning Board; former President, Department of Petroleum, Minerals and Industry; former Chairman of Board, Abu Dhabi Gas Liquifaction Company; Director, Abu Dhabi National Oil Co.; President - OPEC (1979), OAPEC (1980), **Sports:** Swimming, hunting, riding. **Hobbies:** Reading and writing poetry. **Publ.:** The Abu Dhabi Planning Board; The Economy of Abu Dhabi; Organization of the Petroleum - Exporting Countries, Petroleum and the Economy of the United Arab Emirates. **Addr.:** Abu Dhabi, United Arab Emirates.

OTAIBA (Said Bin Ahmad, al), United Arab Emirates businessman. **Born** in 1919 in Abu Dhabi. **Son** of Ahmad al Otaiba. **Married. Career:** Chairman/ Owner of several private Companies; former President of Abu Dhabi Chamber of Commerce and Industry. **Hobby:** Hunting. **Addr.:** P.O.B. 467, Tel.: 341289, 341548, 322548, Abu Dhabi, United Arab Emirates.

OTAIBI (Awad ben Sahwo, al), Saudi businessman. **Born** Almouyah, in 1939. **Dipl.:** B.A. (Education). **Career:** Director of Defina Mayor's office; Schoolmaster, Almouyah School; Director of Taif High School, Taif; owner and Director of Najd Trade Establishment; member of Taif Co-operative Society; member of Board, Tarabah Electrical Co.; member of Board, Qassim Cement Co., Buraidah. **Hobbies:** Reading, tourism, charity work. **Address:** Najd Establishment, Airport Street, Taif, Saudi Arabia.

OTAIBI (Ghazi Sahl, al), Saudi academic. **Born** in 1954 in Mecca. **Educ.:** M.Sc. (Architecture), M.I.T. **Career:** Demonstrator, College of Architecture and Planning, King Faisal University (1977); Vice Dean for Administrative Affairs and Lecturer, Faculty of Architecture and Planning, in same institute. **Publications:** research on Urban Dwelling Environment in Rapidly Growing Cities, Mecca. **Prof. Addr.:** King Faisal University, P.O.Box 1982, Tel.: 8578206, Dammam, **Priv. Addr.:** Tel.: 8649144, Dammam, Saudi Arabia.

OTEIFI (Gamal, al, Dr.), Egyptian lawyer and politician. **Born** on March 9, 1925 in Souhag, Egypt. **Son** of Ahmad Salama al-Oteifi. **Married** in 1953 to Ikba Abou Zekri, 3 daughters: Nemat, Amina, Laila. **Educ.:** Cairo University. **Dipl.:** B.Sc. in Law (1944); Ph.D. in Law (1964). **Career:** District Attorney (1945-53); Attorney (1953-62); Legal Adviser and Member of the Board of

Directors, al-Ahram Organisation (1962-); Member, People's Assembly; Chairman, Legislative Committee, People's Assembly (since 1971); Deputy Speaker, People's Assembly (1972-76); Chairman, Egyptian Society for Economics, Statistics and Legislation, re-elected to the People's Assembly (October 1976 for five years); Minister of Information and Culture (1976-77). **Publ.:** several books and weekly articles in al-Ahram Newspaper. **Awards:** Egyptian Medal of Science and Arts, 1st Class (1972). **Addr.:** 20 Soraya el-Gezira Street, Tel.: 802346, Zamalek, Cairo, Egypt.

OTHMAN (Abdu, Ali), Yemeni politician. **Born** in Yemen. **Educ.:** University of Cairo, Egypt; University of Ohio, USA. **Dipl.:** M.A. in Sociology. **Career:** Administrator in Ministry of Labour and Social Affairs; drafted trade union legislations in 1960; Lecturer in Sociology, Sanaa University (1973); Minister of Municipal Affairs (1974); returned to Sana'a University (1975). **Prof. Addr.:** Sanaa University; P.O.Box 1247, Sanaa, Republic of Yemen.

OTHMAN (Abdul Wahab), Sudanese economist. **Born** in 1936 in Sudan. **Married**, 5 children. **Educ.:** University of Khartoum, Sudan; Charles University, Czechoslovakia. **Dipl.:** B.A., M.Sc. and Ph.D. in Economics. **Career:** Budget Department, Ministry of Finance and National Economy, Khartoum (1961); Purchase and Supplies Director, Ministry of Finance and National Economy (1972); Director of Sudan Government Purchase Office in London (1973); Director General of the Budget (1975); Deputy Minister of Finance (1978); Chairman of Sudan-Kuwait Investment Company; Member of the Board of Public Electricity and Water Corporation, Sudan Airways, Cotton Public Corporation and others. **Addr.:** Khartoum, Sudan.

OUAZZANI (Maitre Thami, al), Moroccan diplomat. **Born** in 1927 in Fes, Morocco. **Married**, 4 children. **Educ.:** University of paris, France. **Dipl.:** Degree in Philosophy and Law. **Career:** called to the Bar, Casablanca (1951); Minister of Industry and Mining (1956); Active in nationalist circles; joined the Union Nationale des Forces Populaires (1959); Ambassador to Yugoslavia and Greece (1961); Secretary General of the Casablanca Group of African States (1962); Director of Bureau des Recherches et Participation Manieres (1963); Minister of Labour and Social Affairs (1963); Minister for Public Services (1964); Ambassador to Algeria (1965); Minister of Tourism (1968); Minister in the Royal Cabinet (1968); Secretary General of Parti Democratique Constitutionnel (1979); Ambassador to Tunisia (1969); Ambassador to London, UK (1971-74); President of DIAC Company, Morocco (1974 to present); Secretary General of Parti Democratique Constitutionnel (1982); presently, Secretary General, Parti Démocratique pour l'Indépendance. **Decor.:** Grand Cordon Alouite as well as Yugoslav and Tunisian Decorations. **Addr.:** 33 rue Soldat Jouvancial, Casablanca, Morocco.

OUAZZANI TOUHAMI (Tayeb), Moroccan engineer. **Born** in 1944 in Fes, Morocco. **Married**, 3 daughters. **Educ.:** ESIEA, Paris, University of Paris, France. **Dipl.:** Diploma of Engineering, Ph.D. **Career:** Head of the Materials Service, Office Cherifien des Phosphates, Khouribga (1973-79); Managing Director of Modulec SA. **Prof. Addr.:** P.O.Box 146, Sale, Morocco, Telefax: 843929. **Priv. Addr.:** 61 Rue Oukaïmeden, Agdal, Rabat, Tel.: 670704.

OUFARA (Saadia), Moroccan professor (physiology animal). **Born** on January 16, 1951. **Daughter** of Ahmed Oufara **and** Mrs. Zahra Nait el-Kadi. **Married** in 1979 to Omar Oufara, 2 children. **Educ.:** University Hassan II - Mohammedia, Faculty of Science and Techniques (Mohammedia). **Dipl.:** Doctorat d'Etat ès-Sciences. **Career:** Assistant Faculty of Sciences, Rabat (1976-80); Assistant Professor (1980-87); Lecturer then Professor (1987-91); presently Professor (Physiology Animal and Cellular Biology). **Publ.:** "Précis de Biology Cellullaire (1996). **Prof. Addr.:** University Hassan II - Mohammedia, Faculty of Sciences and Techniques, P.O.Box 146 Mohammedia-Morocco. **Priv. Addr.:** Tel.: 212 (03) 326179, Fax: (03) 315353.

OULD-KHALIFA (Muhammad, Larbi), Algerian diplomat. **Born** in 1938. **Married**, 4 children. **Dipl.:** B.Sc. in Social Science, DSC. **Career:** Professor of Social Sciences Institute, University of Algiers (1971); Project Head, Ministry of Higher Education and Scientific Research; Counsellor for FLN Central Apparatus (1979-80); Secretary of State for Secondary and Technical Education (1982-84); Ambassador to the People's Republic of Yemen (1984-1986). **Prof. Addr.:** Ministry of Foreign Affairs, Algiers, Algeria.

OUNISSI (Zhor), Algerian politician. **Born** in 1936. **Dipl.:** B.A. in literature and Philosophy, DEA in Sociology. **Career:** Teacher, Editor in Chief of el-Djazaira; Deputy of National Popular Assembly (1977); Secretary of State for Social Affairs (1982); Minister of Social Affairs (1984-85). **Addr.:** Algiers, Algeria.

OUSSEDIK (Omar), Algerian diplomat. **Born** in January 1922. **Career:** Member of the Algerian People's Party in 1945; Major in the National Liberation Army (1954-58); Secretary of State (1958-60); F.L.N. Representative in Guinea (1960-61); Ambassador to Bulgaria (1963-65), to U.S.S.R. (1965-69); Ambassador, Ministry of Foreign Affairs (1970-74); Ambassador to India (1974-80). **Addr.:** Ministry of Foreign Affairs, Algiers, Algeria.

OUSSEIMI (Khaled), Lebanese executive. **Born** in 1928 in Damascus, Syria. **Educ.:** The School of Law, St. Joseph University, Beirut. **Dipl.:** Economic Studies. **Career:** Founder and Chairman of GEFINOR Group of Companies in several Countries mainly dealing in Real Estate and Finance. **Addr.:** 23 Avenue de la Porte Neuve, Luxembourg.

OUZEGAN (Omar), Algerian journalist and statesman. **Born** in Algeria. **Career:** Minister of Agricultural and Agrarian Reform (1962-63); Minister of State (1963-64); Journalist, Editor of "La Révolution Africaine" (1968); Minister of Tourism (December 1964- July 1965). **Publ.:** Author of "Le Meilleur Combat" (1962), "al-Jihad al-Afdhal" (1963). **Addr.:** Algiers, Algeria.

OWAIDHA (Rashed Bin), UAE businessman. **Born** in 1938 in Abu Dhabi, UAE. **Son** of Bin Rashid Oweidhah. **Married** in 1958, 3 sons, **Educ.:** Law studies with Islamic Judge Shaikh Badr. **Career:** Judge's Assistant (1956-57); Private commerce (1957); Founder-Member, Municipal Council (1967); Founder-Member, Abu Dhabi Chamber of Commerce; Member, Abu Dhabi National Consultative Council (1970); Editor-in-Chief, al-Wahda (1973-); Member, The Federal National Assembly (1971-). Member, National Planning Council (1975-); Director, Abu Dhabi Bank; Managing Director, Rashid Bin Oweidha Organization; Chairman, First Gulf Bank, Ajman, UAE; Director, al-Ain Ahlia Insurance Co. **Awards:** From Libya, Algeria, Morocco, Tunisia, Mauritania, Tunisia, Egypt, Somalia, Syria, Iraq and Saudi Arabia. **Member:** al-Jazira Cultural and Sporting Club. **Hobbies:** Reading, History, Classical Poetry, Swimming, Hunting and Chess. **Addr.:** P.O.Box 414, Tel.: 423450, Telex: 69510, 69565 A/B FIGULF, Ajman, UAE.

OWAIDI (Abdallah Shalabi), Saudi chemist and executive. **Dipl.:** B.Sc, in Chemistry, U.S.A. 1969. **Career:** Chemist, Jeddah Oil Refinery (1969-71); Assistant Chief Chemist, Jeddah Oil Refinery (1972-73); Assistant Technical Manager, Petrolube (1974); Technical Manager (1975-78); General Manager, Production Petrolube (1978); Member of the Board of Directors, Petromin Lubricating Oil Refining Co (Luberef); **Publications:** Participation and Presentations in conferences and technical seminars on oil. **Hobbies:** reading, light games. **Prof. Addr.:** Petrolube, P.O.Box 1432, Jeddah 21431, Tel.: 6366404, Saudi Arabia.

OWAIS (Sultan Ali, al), U.A.E. businessman. **Born** in 1935. **Married. Career:** Business interests in Dubai; Abu Dhabi Planning Board (1969); Chairman, National Bank of Dubai, U.A.E.; Director, Arab Emirates Investment Bank Ltd., Dubai U.A.E. **Addr.:** P.O.Box 5503, 303 New Shaikh Rashid Building, Tel.: 222191-3, Telex: 46080 A/B AREMIN EM, Dubai, UAE.

OWEISS (Ibrahim, Mohamad), Egyptian economist, educator, author and an international economic advisor residing in the United States. **Born** on September 25, 1931 in Beheira, Egypt. **Son** of the late Mohamed Zaki Oweiss. **Married** in 1975 to Céline Marie-Joseph Lesuisse. They have one daughter «Yasmeen» and one son «Kareem». **Educ.:** B. Com. in Economics; M.A. in Economics; Ph.D. in Economics Education (1953-55); military service as Lieutenant, Egyptian Armed Forces (1955-58); Economist and Director, Project Evaluation, Egyptian Ministry of Industry, Cairo (1958-60): Lecturer of Economics, University of Minnesota (1961-67), Professor of Economics, Georgetown University since 1967; Director of the Institute of Arab Development, Center for Contemporary Arab Studies at Georgetown University (1975-77); while on leave from Georgetown University, he was appointed First Under Secretary of State for Economic Affairs in Cairo and held the position of the Chief of the Egyptian Economic Mission to the United States with rank of Ambassador (1977-79). As an international economic advisor, he worked for several governments and multinational corporations among which were the governments of Egypt, Panama, Qatar and The Sultanate of Oman as well as for Occidental Oil Company, Deak Perera, Mitsui and Mawarid corporations. He had also served on the board of Dasi Inc. In addition, he held several volunteering positions such as the President of the Arab-American Club in Minnesota (1962-63) and that of The Egyptian-American Cultural Association in Washington, D.C. (1974-75). He was the Chairman of the Board of Faith & Hope USA (1975-77) as well as that of The Howard and Georgeanna Jones Institute for Reproductive Medicine at Eastern Virginia Medical School in Norfolk (1983-1990) after which he was voted as an Honorary Chairperson for life. He was elected for two terms as the President of the Association of the Egyptian American Scholars from 1984 to 1988. In 1975, he was a founding member of the Center for Contemporary Arab Studies at Georgetown University and serves as a life-time member of its Executive Committee. He was also a board member of The Global Economic Action Institute and People-to-People International of which the President of the United States was the Honorary Chairman. He was the Chairman of the Arab-American Business and Professional Association in the USA (1990-93). For a brief time in 1983, he was an advisor to former President Jimmy Carter and was one of the Professors of President Bill Clinton. **Publ.:** he authored over fifty scholarly publications among which are: **The Political Economy of Contemporary Egypt, Petrodollar Surpluses, Arab Civilization, The Israeli Economy: A War Economy, Egypt's Underground Economy,** and in a pioneering research on oil revenues he presented at an international conference at Arden House in New York in 1973, he coined the term «Petrodollars». **Awards:** in addition to other national and international awards, President Mohamed Anwar Sadat awarded him in 1979 with Egypt's Order of Merit, First Class. Her Majesty The Queen of the United Kingdom sanctioned his admission to the Order of St. John as from June 3, 1993. **Sports:** Swimming, tennis. **Addr.:** 4017 Glenridge Street, Kensington, MD 20895-3708 USA, Tel.: (301) 933-7667. Fax: ((301) 933-2211.

OZALP (Mohamad), Egyptian banker. **Born** in 1948 in Cairo, Egypt. **Married**, 2 sons. **Educ.:** Whittier College, California, USA. **Dipl.:** B.A. in Economics and Business Administration. **Career:** Sales Representative of Hilton Hotels (1971-72); Assistant Ofice Manager of McDermott (Cairo) Inc. (1972-74); Administrative Assistant of McDermott (Cairo) Inc. (1974-75), Administrative Manager (1975-76); Operations Manager of Misr International Bank (1976-82), Assistant General Manager (1982-84); Member of the Board of Allweiler-Fard Pump Co. (1981-87); General Manager of Misr International Bank (1984-87). **Member:** Cairo Automobile Club, Gezira Sporting Club. **Prof. Addr.:** 14 Alfy Street, Cairo, Egypt. **Priv. Addr.:** 3 el-Fardos Street, Zamalek, Cairo, Egypt.

P

PACHACHI (Adnan), Iraqi executive. **Born** on May 14, 1923 in Baghdad, Iraq. **Son** of Muzrahim Pachachi. **Married** in 1946, 3 daughters. **Educ.:** in USA. **Dipl.:** B.A., Political Science (1943); Ph.D. (1949). **Career:** Joined Iraqi Foreign Service (1944); Served in Washington, USA and Egypt; Director General, Ministry of Foreign Affairs (1958-59); Iraqi Ambassador and Permanent Delegate to the UN (1959-65); Iraqi Minister of State for Foreign Affairs (1965-66); Minister of State, Government of Abu Dhabi (1974); Personal Representative of the President of UAE; Director, Abu Dhabi Fund for Economic Development; Director, Abu Dhabi National Oil Co. **Awards:** from Iraq, Egypt and Morocco. **Hobbies:** Classical Music, Swimming, Tennis and Walking. **Addr.:** al-Manhal Palace, P.O.Box 280, Abu Dhabi, U.A.E.

PACHACHI (Talal, Nadim al), Iraqi diplomat. **Born** in 1937 in Baghdad, Iraq. **Married**, 1 son. **Educ.:** London School of Economics, London; Trinity College, Cambridge University, Cambridge, UK. **Dipl.:** B.A. and M.A. in Economics. **Career** Third Secretary, Economics Department, Ministry of Foreign Affairs, Baghdad, Iraq (1963-66); Second Secretary, Permanent Mission of Iraq to the UN, Geneva (1966-69); Second Secretary, Embassy of Iraq in Belgium (1966-71); Director, Trade Relations Department, Ministry of Foreign Affairs (1971-73); Counsellor, Permanent Mission of Iraq, UN, Geneva (1973-75); UN Permanent Mission of Iraq (1975-81); Ministry of Foreign Affairs (1981-84); Lecturer at Kuwait University, Kuwait. **Hobbies:** economic development, international relations, tennis, swimming. **Addr.:** Iraq, Baghdad.

PARTOW (Farouk, Abduljalil), Iraqi international civil servant. **Born** on July 17, 1927 in Basrah (Iraq). **Married**, children. **Educ.:** Faculty of Medicine, University of Lausanne (Switzerland) (1945-52); London School of Hygiene and Tropical Medicine (1961-62); Royal College of Physicians and Surgeons, London (1966). **Dipl.:** M.D. (1952), Degree of Public Health, (1962) Degree of Child Health (1966). **Career:** Director, International Health Department, Ministry of Public Health, Baghdad (1958-60); Director, Baghdad Health Department, Ministry of Public Health (1960-63); Pediatrician, Ministry of Public Health, Baghdad (1968-69); Regional Adviser, World Health Organisation, Eastern Mediterranean Office, Alexandria (Egypt) (1969-72); WHO Representative to Yemen, Sana'a (1972-75); at the WHO Regional Office for the Eastern Mediterranean in Alexandria, Egypt as Public Health Administrator (1975-78). Director, Division of Disease Prevention and Control (1978-82) and as Director of Programme Management (1982-83); Assistant Director General, WHO Headquarters, Geneva. Switzerland (1983-1988), retired in 1988. Presently Free Lance Public Health Consultant (Health Management and Organization). Worked with various missions to Arab countries, for WHO and the World Bank. **Sports:** Golf **Hobbies:** Reading. **Addr.:** 71 Rue Saint Jean, Geneva 1201, Switzerland.

PASSI (Vinod), Indian bank executive. **Born** in 1951 in Amritsar, India. **Son** of Sh.A.L. Passi (Hindi Tribe). **Single. Dipl.:** B.Com. (1969); Chartered Accountancy (1972). **Career:** Officer, Commercial Bank, India (1972-77); Branch Manager (1976-77); Accounts Officer, Manufacturing Company (1977-78); Loans and Advances Manager, Commercial Bank (1978-80); Chief Accountant, Bahrain Investment Company (1980); Accounts Manager, Bahrain Investment Company B.S.C., Bahrain (1981-). **Member:** Member, The Institute of Chartered Accounts, India. **Hobby:** Social welfare. **Addr.:** Government Road, Sheikh Mubarak Building, 5th Floor, Suite 506-77, P.O.Box 5808, Tel.: 250053, 230042, 252108, 252199, Telex: 8937 A/B INVEST BN, Manama, Bahrain.

PEDERSEN (Richard, F., Dr.), Seventh and former president of the american university in Cairo (Egypt). **Born** in 1925 in Miami, Arizona. **Married** to Nelda Newell Napier of Detroit, Michigan, in 1953, 3 children: Paige (1956), Jonathan (1958), and Kendra (1963). **Educ.:** College of the Pacific (USA); B.A. (1946); Stanford University (USA); M.A. (1947); Harvard University (USA). Ph.D. (1950). **Career:** Served UN affairs in the State Department (1950-53); The US Mission to the UN in Various capacities (1953-68); including Deputy United States Representative in the UN Security Council with the rank of ambassador (1967-68); Counsellor and principal Foreign policy adviser to the Secretary of State (1969-73); U.S. Ambassador to Hungary (1973-75); Senior Vice-President of the United States Trust Co. (1975-78); President of the American University in Cairo since February 1978 to 1991. **Memberships and Community Service** American Society of International Law, American Foreign Service Association, UN Association of the US, Royal Institute of International Affairs, Middle East Institute, Physicians for Peace. **Awarded** the Order of the Sacred Treasure by the Emperor of Japan, 1988.

PELLETREAU (Robert H.), American diplomat. **Born**

on July 9, 1935, U.S.A. (New York). **Married** in December 1966 to Miss Pamela Day, three children: Katherine (1967), Erica (1969), Elizabeth (1973). **Educ.:** Yale University and Harvard Law School. **Dipl.:** B.A.- Political Science (1957), LL.B. (1961). **Career:** Entered U.S. Foreign Service (1962); Service in Morocco, Mauritania, Lebanon, Jordan, Algeria, Syria; Ambassador to Bahrain (1979-80); Ambassador to Tunisia (1987-91); Ambassador to Egypt (1991-1993) now in Washington D.C., U.S.A. **Work:** Conducted U.S. dialogue with the Palestine Liberation Organization (1988-90). **Other Information:** Member, Council on Foreign Relations, Middle East Institute, American Foreign Service Association. **Addr.:** Washington D.C., U.S.A.

PENDSE (Shashikani, Vishu), Indian bank executive. **Born** in 1942 in Kasara, Mahavashiva State, India. **Son** of Vishnu Pendse. **Married** in 1970, 2 sons. **Educ.:** University of Bombay, India; Institute of Chartered Accountants of India, India. **Dipl.:** B.Com. (1963); Chartered Accountancy (1967). **Career:** Internal Auditor, Central Bank of India (1968-69); Auditor, Price Waterhouse Peat & Co., Bombay (1969-70); Joined Bank of Baroda since 1970; Manager, Bank of Baroda, Ras al-Khaimah, UAE. **Member:** Indian Association, Ras al- Khaimah. **Hobbies:** Reading, Gardening and Sports. **Addr.:** P.O.Box 5294, Tel.: 29293, Ras el-Khaimah, UAE.

PERRY (Brian, Stanley), Irish Bank executive. **Born** in 1944 in Dublin, Ireland. **Son** of Stanley Perry. **Married** in 1968. **Educ.:** Kingston Grammar School; Trinity College, Dublin; **Dipl.:** in Law (1967). **Career:** Bank of Ireland (1962-68); Bank of Nova Scotia, Dublin (1968-71); Bank of Nova Scotia Trust Co., London (1971-72); Bank of Nova Scotia, Dublin (1972-78); Bank of Nova Scotia, London (1978-81); Manager, The Bank of Nova Scotia, Cairo, Egypt (1981-). **Member:** Institute of Certified Accountants; Chartered Institute of Secretaries; Institute of Banker, Dublin and London; Mena House Golf Club. **Hobbies:** Music, Golf, Reading and Swimming. **Addr.:** 93 Abdel Aziz el-Seoud Street, Manial, Tel.: 843178, Telex: 92187 A/B BNSC UN, Cairo, Egypt.

PESHDARI (Babekr, Mahmoud, al), Iraqi politician. **Born** in 1937 in Sulaimaniyah, Iraq. **Educ.:** University of Baghdad, Iraq. **Dipl.:** LL.B. **Career:** Governor of Sulaimaniyah (1974); Chairman of the Legislative Council, Kurdish Autonomous Area (1974-76); Member of the National Progressive Party; Minister of Labour and Social Affairs (1976). **Publ.:** Editor of "al-Amel wal Tanmia", paper on non-alignment, "al-Estegaba al-Hadaria Ila Tahdiat al-Takhalouf" (1981). **Decor.:** Order of the Republic of Mali. **Hobbies:** horse riding, hunting. **Addr.:** Baghdad, Iraq.

PETROS VII, His Beatitude, Pope & Patriarch of Alexandria and all Africa. **Born** on September 3, 1949 at Sichari, Cyprus. **Educ.:** Apostle Varnavas Seminary, Nicosia, Cyprus; Averof High School of Alexandria, Egypt; University of Athens, Theological School, Athens, Greece; University of Dublin, Ireland. **Dipl.:** Diploma in Theology, Diploma in Missiology. **Languages:** Greek, English, French & Arabic. **Career:** Ordained as Deacon, 8/69, Holy Monastery of Macheras, Cyprus; Ordained as Priest, 15/8/78, Holy Monastery of Penteli, Greece; Received Rank of Archimandrite, 6/12/78, Cathedral of St. Nicholas, Cairo, Egypt; Ordained Bishop of Babylon, 7/83, Holy Monastery of Macheras, Cyprus; Elected Metropolitan of Accra & West Africa, 14/6/90; Appointed Exarch of Irinoupolis & East Africa (Kenya - Uganda), 10/91; Named Metropolitan of Cameroon, 11/94; Elected Pope & Patriarch of Alexandria & All Africa, 21/2/97. Participated in interdenominational & inter-Orthodox meetings. **Awards:** Received number of medals & Decorations from various Churches & Institutions & Governments. **Office and Home Address:** Greek Orthodox Patriarchate of Alexandria & All Africa, P.O.Box 2006, Alexandria, Egypt. Tel.: 203-4868595, Fax. 203-4835684, e-mail: goptalex@techmina.com.

PHARAON (Gaith, Rashad), Saudi businessman. **Born** on 7 September 1940 in Riyadh, Saudi Arabia. **Son** of HE Dr. Rashad Pharaon (Personal Adviser to HH King Khaled **and** Mrs., née Reema Kaliazi. **Married,** 3 children; Liana, Laith and Deema. **Dipl.:** B.Sc. (1962); Ph.D. (Oil Engineering) (1963); M.B.A. (Business Administration) (1965). **Career:** Chairman of Board of 17 local and international corporations; his companies in Saudi Arabia and abroad deal extensively in finance, insurance, engineering and professional business management; contributes to development of large-scale industrial ventures both in Saudi Arabia and abroad; Chairman of Board and Director-General of Saudi Research and Development Corporation; one of the Founders and member of Board of Tihama. **Member:** American Arab Association. **Award:** Commandatore of the Italian Republic; King Abdulaziz Award. **Hobby:** world-wide travel. **Prof. Addr.:** Gaith Pharaon Residence, Ruwais, Jeddah, and Kaki Bldg., P.O.Box 6277, Airport Road, Tel.: 6432888, Jeddah, Saudi Arabia.

PHARAON (Hattan, Rashad), Saudi businessman. **Born** in 1953 in Paris, France. **Son** of Rashad Pharaon. **Educ.:** B.Sc., MBA in Business Administration, San Diego, California. **Career:** General Manager of National Bunkering Co. Ltd. (1977) and later Managing Director of National Bunkering Co. Ltd. (1979); Managing Director, Arabian Investments Co. Ltd., International Trade and Development Co., Ltd. **Sports:** Swimming, water skiing. **Hobby:** Economics. **Addr.:** P.O.Box 6471, Tel.: 6675792, 6674628, Jeddah, Saudi Arabia.

PHARAON (Mazin, Rashad), Saudi businessman, architect. **Born** in 1939 in Riyadh, Saudi Arabia. **Son** of Rashad Pharaon. **Married. Educ.:** Architecture diploma from West Germany. **Career:** Shipowner, businessman, contractor; specialised in shipment of crude oil products contracts; Chairman Maphar Company Ltd., National Bunkering Company Ltd. **Addr.:** P.O.B. 730 and P.O.Box 1301, Jeddah, Saudi Arabia.

PRATT (Leighton), American Associate Professor of English Literature and Head of Dept. of English & Modern European Languages, University of Qatar. **Born** on May 27, 1933 at U.S.A. **Son** of Leighton Pratt (deceased) **and** Mrs. Rose Moore Pratt (deceased). **Married** to Dr. Anna Pratt. **Educ.:** University of Geneva, Switzerland; Trinity College, Dublin (Ireland). **Dipl.:** B.A., M.A., Ph.D. **Career:** Makerere University, Kampala, Uganda (1968-73); Jagiellonian University, Krakow, Poland (1973-79); University of Washington, Seattle, Wa, U.S.A. (1979); Birzeit University, Palestine (1980-86); Associate Professor of English Literature and Head of Dept. of English & Modern European Languages, University of Qatar (1987- present). **Hobby:** Fishing. **Prof. Addr.:** Qatar University, P.O.Box 2713, Tel.: 892560, Doha, Qatar. **Priv. Addr.:** Tel.: 831077, Doha, Qatar.

Q

QAATAMI (Jasim Abdul Aziz, al), Kuwaiti businessman. **Born** in 1927. **Educ.:** studied in Kuwait and Cairo, Egypt. **Career:** Police training in Egypt and United Kingdom. Director of Kuwait Metropolitan Police; resigned (1956) Manager of Kuwait Cinema Company (1956-59); Business manager for Yusuf al-Ghanim (1959-61); Under Secretary at the Ministry of Foreign Affairs (1961-62); Member of National Assembly (1963-65) and (1975); resigned (1975); now has various business interests. **Addr.:** Kuwait, Kuwait.

QABAZARD (Mohamad, Hussain), Kuwaiti businessman, industrialist. **Born** in 1920 in Kuwait. **Son** of Hussain Qabazard. **Married**, six children. **Career:** Director General of Ports Department (1953-61); Ministry of Finance and Industry, Oil Affairs (1961-62); led official goodwill visit to far East (1961); member of Kuwait National Assembly (1963-67); served on several parliamentary delegations; business and property interests; member of the Board of Aminoil, developed an important business dealing in marine equipment. **Hobby:** Cinephotography. **Addr.:** Parts International Co. WLL, P.O.B. 671, Safat, Kuwait.

QABBANI (Bouran Khayri) (Hani Emam, Mrs.), Saudi civil servant. **Born** in Taif in 1931. **Dipl.:** B.A. (Social Work), Beirut University College (1955); Higher Graduate Studies in Social Work, School of Social Work, Columbia University, New York (1955-56). **Career:** Social Affairs Officer, Department of Economics and Social Affairs, UN Headquarters, New York (1958-65); Engaged in pioneering work towards establishing university education for women in Saudi Arabia, former director of Women's Section, King Abdulaziz University. **Member:** Executive Board, Women's Welfare Association, Jeddah; Board of Trustees of el-Alanan School, Jeddah; Alumni Association, Beirut. **Publ.:** contributed to UN documents in the field of mother and child welfare and training in social work. Has visited 22 countries in Asia, Africa, Europe, North and South America, **Hobbies:** Gardening, cooking. **Prof. Addr.:** P.O.Box 1716, Tel.: 26274, Jeddah. **Priv. Addr.:** Tel.: 51248, Jeddah, Saudi Arabia.

QABBANI (Fadil, Kheiry), Saudi scientist. **Born** in 1916 in Mecca (Saudi Arabia). **Educ.:** Camborne School of Metaliferous Mining, England (1938-41); Colorado School of Mines, USA (1951-54). **Dipl.:** A.C.S.M., D.Sc. (Metal Mining) (1954) Ph.D. (Mining). **Career:** Assistant surveyor (1935-37); Mine surveyor and chief sampler, Saudi Arabian Mining Syndicate Ltd, Mahad Dahab Mine (1941-47); Chief of Production and Distribution Section, Office of the Minister of State for Development Projects, Ministry of Finance, Jeddah (1947); Deputy Director-General of Petroleum and Mineral Affairs, Ministry of Finance and National Economy (1954-61); Assistant Deputy Minister, Ministry of Petroleum and Mineral Resources Jeddah (1961-63); Chairman, National Geological Committee, Centre for Applied Geology (1970-71); former Saudi Arabian Representative at the Permanent Mission of the International Atomic Energy Agency (IAEA), Vienna. **Member:** Board of Trustees, University of Petroleum and Minerals (1963-75); Managing Board of International Geological Co-relation Programme (1973-75); Council of King Abdul Aziz University. **Attended:** Regional seminar on cartography, Tehran, Iran (1956); Conference on world map, Bonn (1962); International Geological conference, Vienna (1963); UN Regional ore-dressing conference USA (1965); Conference on the structure and evolution of the Red Sea, Royal Society, London (1969); International conference on the conservation of natural resources, Turkey (1970); Solar energy conference, France (October 1974). **Publ.:** author of "Geophysical and structural aspects of the central Red Sea rift valley". **Hobbies:** collecting mineral crystals, coins and stamps, and reading. **Priv. Addr.:** al-Kandara, airport road, P.O.Box 553, Jeddah, Saudi Arabia.

QABBANI (Sahl Khayri, al), Saudi businessman. **Born** in 1929. **Dipl.:** B.Sc. (Engineering). **Career:** Owner and manager, Plastics and Brick Plant, Jeddah; Conducts his own business New Products Industries mainly in building materials and plastics manufacturing; former member of Arabian Cement Co. **Hobbies:** reading, sports. **Address:** New Products Industries, P.O.Box 460, Jeddah 21441, Saudi Arabia.

QABOOS (Qaboos Bin Taymour Bin Said, H.M. Sultan), Sultan of Oman. **Born** on November 18, 1940. **Son** of Sultan Said Bin Taymour. **Married** on March 23, 1976. **Educ.:** Private in UK; Royal Military Academy Sandhurst, UK. **Career:** Officer, Cameronians (Scottish Rifles) (British Infantry Regiment) for six months); returned to Oman; after his father's abdication became Sultan of Oman (1970), carried out a progressive program of Social and Political reform, raising the standard of living of his people and strengthening the country's armed forces also Prime

Minister, Minister of Foreign Affairs, Minister of Finance and Minister of Defence. **Sports:** Horseriding. **Hobbies:** Classical Music, Military History. **Addr.:** Palace of the Sultan, Muscat, Oman.

QABTAN (Khedhr Daoud), Jordanian official. **Born** in 1939. **Married**, 2 children. **Educ.:** Damascus University, Syria; University of Wales, UK. **Dipl.:** LL.B., M.A. in Economics. **Career:** Lawyer in private practive (1963-76); Director of Eshrak Cooperative (1966-76); Legal Adviser, Ministry of Social Development (1980-); Organizing Manager of the Office of the Handicapped (1982-85); Director, Management and Organization Section, International Rehabilitation Organization (1981-). **Hobbies:** reading, writing, poetry, chess. **Prof. Addr.:** P.O.Box 7739, Amman, Jordan.

QADDAMA (Ahmad, Mohamad Badawi), Syrian former journalist. **Born** in 1918 in Syria. **Son** of Mohamad Badawi Qaddama. **Educ.:** Greek-Orthodox College, College of the Christian Brothers in Damascus. **Career:** Journalist since 1931; Founded the daily "as-Sarkha"; Professor (1933); Resumed Journalism (1934); Editor "al-Ayyam" daily (1946); Editor, "an Nidal" daily. **Publ.:** Author of "The Statesman's text book of East and West", "Arab spirit", "Pages of our History", "Arab heroes", "World Heroes of Independence", etc... **Addr.:** Damascus, Syria.

QADHAT (Adel, Ahmad, al), Jordanian administrator. **Born** in 1939. **Married**, 4 children. **Educ.:** Cairo University, Egypt; University of South California, USA. **Dipl.:** B.Com. in Office Management, M.A. in General Management. **Career:** Manager of a Customs Office (1973-75); Assistant Manager, Amman Customs Office (1975-82); Representative of Jordanian Government on the Board of Directors, Industrial Free Zone Areas, Syria (1982-); General Manager of Jordan Customs Offices (1982-). **Prof. Addr.:** P.O.Box 926132, Amman, Jordan.

QADHAT (Salman, Muhammad, al), Jordanian politician. **Born** in 1919 in Jordan. **Married. Educ.:** University of Syria, Syria. **Dipl.:** Licence in Law. **Career:** Ministry of Interior Official (1942-43); Officer in Jordanian Army (1947); Member of Chamber of Deputies (1950-51); District Officer for Ajloun and other areas (1951-55); Assistant Governor of Nablus (1955-56); successively Governor of Ma'an, Jerusalem and Kerak (1956-66); Member, Chamber of Deputies (1963-66) and (1967-74); Currently Head of Legal Committee and Member of Foreign Affairs Committee, National Consultative Council; Member of Chamber of Deputies (1984). **Medal:** Independence Medal (2nd Class). **Hobbies:** travelling, reading. **Addr.:** Jabal Hussein, P.O.Box 6593, Amman, Jordan.

QADI (Abdallah Fadlallah), Saudi civil servant. **Born** in 1939. **Dipl.:** university education in the field of sociology. **Career:** Sub-Editor of the Radio Magazine (1963-65); Assistant Director of Public Relations, Press Department, Ministry of Information, (1965); Acting Head of the Press in Jeddah; Director of Public Relations Department of the Press, Ministry of Information, Jeddah; International Relations Expert, Office of the Deputy Minister of Information for Information Affairs, Jeddah; Director, Press and Foreign Information, Ministry of Information, Jeddah; member of several committees related to the Ministry of Information; member of the Saudi Press delegation to Amman, Jordan; represented the Saudi Ministry of Information in the Casablanca Fair (1970), the Islamic Ministers of Foreign Affairs Conference in Pakistan and the Cairo International Fair (1974). **Prof. Addr.:** Jeddah Branch Press and Foreign Information, Tel.: 6446201, Jeddah. **Priv. Addr.:** Tel.: 6518732, Jeddah, Saudi Arabia.

QADI (Abdul Kadir, al), Qatari official financial. **Born** in 1934 in Palestine. **Married. Career:** Director, The Housing Bank, Amman, Jordan; Director, Gulf International Bank BSC, Manama, Bahrain; Director, Intra Investment Co. S.A.L., Beirut; Representative, Minister of Finance & Petroleum, Qatar; Member, Governing Board, Qatar; The OPEC Fund for International Development, Vienna, Austria; Presently Director, Qatar National Bank S.A.Q., Doha, Qatar, and Chairman, Gulf and Occidental Investment Co. S.A., Geneva, Switzerland and Chairman and General Manager of Arab Jordan Investment Bank, Amman, Jordan, and Director, Jordan International Bank PLC, London, U.K. **Addr.:** P.O.Box 1002, Tel.: 413511, Telex: 4636 A/B QBKGM DH, Doha, Qatar and P.O.Box 8797, Amman, Jordan.

QADI (Abdul Rahman Ibrahim, al), Saudi diplomat. **Born** in 1931 at Onaizah, Saudi Arabia. **Dipl.:** LL.B., Cairo University, Egypt (1955). **Career:** Rose from first diplomatic rank up to the rank of Ambassador, assuming various posts including Consul-General, New York (1968-70); Delegate to UN four times, Attaché and third Secretary, Saudi Embassy, Cairo; attended all Arab Summit Conferences (1960-67), Arab Foreign Ministers Meetings from 1973, Conferences of Non-Aligned Countries (1960-67); member of delegation accompanying H.M. the late King Khalid during his visits to Egypt, Syria and Jordan (1970); also member of delegation accompanying H.R.H. Crown Prince Fahad (presently King Fahad) to Algeria, Kuwait, Iraq; former Saudi Ambassador to Bahrain. **Honours:** orders from Lebanon and Egypt. **Hobbies:** football, music, poetry. **Address:** Riyadh, Saudi Arabia.

QADI (Hamad Abdallah, al), Saudi journalist. **Born** in 1950. **Dipl.:** M.A. (Literature and Criticism). **Career:** Public Relations specialist; Work Inspector; Director of Public Relations; Deputy Editor-in-Chief, al-Majallah al-Arabiah (Magazine published in Riyadh) and Literary Editor, al-

Jazeerah; founder member of Riyadh Literary Club; a regular contributor to press, radio and television; member of several literary and Islamic conferences. **Publications:** Nassib Ibn Rabah: His life and Poetry; supervisor of the weekly literary page and daily columnist of al-Jazeerah daily newspaper. **Address:** P.O.Box 40104, Tel.: 4351804, 4021022, Riyadh, Saudi Arabia.

QADIRI (Abu Bakr, al), Moroccan journalist. **Born** 1914 in Sale, Morocco. **Married,** 9 children. **Educ.:** in Morocco. **Career:** Journalist; Director of "al-Risaala" weekly paper; Director of "al-Iman" monthly magazine; Member, Moroccan Scientists Federation, Moroccan Writers Union and Moroccan Royal Academy; Member of the Executive Council of the Islamic World Conference; Secretary General of the Moroccan Society for the Support of the Palestinian cause; Assistant Secretary General of the Moroccan Society for the Support of the Palestinian cause; Assistant Secretary General of the African Islamic Conference. **Publ.:** articles in Moroccan papers and magazines as well as several books. **Awards:** Medal of the Royal Moroccan Academy; Order of the Throne, Morocco. **Member:** Andalusia Music Society. **Hobbies:** Andalusian music, walking. **Prof. Addr.:** Zankit Aknassous, P.O.Box 356, Tel.: 81757, 81325, Rabat, Morocco. **Priv. Addr.:** al-Massira al-Khadra Blvd., Bettana, Sale, Morocco.

QADOUMI (Ghazi, R.), Jordanian businessman. **Born** on March 31, 1948 in Jordan. **Son** of Rouhi Qadoumi (Businessman) **and** Mrs. Fathia Qadoumi. **Married** in 1975 in Amman to Maram Mallhas, three children: Zaid, Lubna and Luma. **Educ.:** university of Missouri, Columbia. **Dipl.:** B.S.; M.Sc. **Career:** 50% owner and Director of Qadoumi Agricultural Company; 50% owner and Managing Director of National Feed Manufacturing Company; Owner and Director of Ghazi Qadoumi Trading Establishment. **Sports:** Horse riding, skiing and tennis. **Hobbies:** Horses, hunting. **Credit Card:** American Express; Visa Card. **Prof. Addr.:** Ghazi Qadoumi Trading Establishment, P.O.Box 20748, Tel.: 962.6.673750, Amman, Jordan. **Priv. Addr.:** P.O.Box 20748, Tel.: 962.6.817064, Amman, Jordan.

QADOUMI (Hisham), Arab engineer. **Born** in 1942 in Jerusalem. **Educ.:** Business studies and Economics in USA. **Career:** Brown and Root Inc., Houston, Texas; Projects in USA, Western Europe and the Middle East; Civil Engineer, Kuwait; former Engineering Adviser to HH the Amir of Qatar. **Addr.:** Engineering and Technical Office, P.O.Box. 3, Doha, Qatar.

QADUS (Mohamad Ahmad Abdel Hamid), Saudi businessman. **Born** in 1930. **Educ.:** General. **Career:** Successively Lieutenant; Arabic Typist clerk, King's Private Cabinet; Auditor, Chief, Audit Division; Assistant Director, General Board of Control Bureau, Jeddah; actively participates in contracting operations; established a furniture manufacturing factory; now businessman, proprietor of Awg Trading and Contracting Corporation; Jeddah. **Awards:** First Prize Winner in al-Bilad Saudi daily newspaper competition (1973). **Sport:** Football. **Hobbies:** Reading, music, learning languages. **Prof. Addr.:** Commercial and Residential Centre 809, P.O.Box 5112, Tel.: 32000 Extension 334, Jeddah. **Priv. Addr.:** Tel.: 51481, Jeddah, Saudi Arabia.

QAISI (Nuri, Hamudi, al), Iraqi academic. **Born** in 1932 in Baghdad, Iraq, **Married,** 5 children. **Educ.:** Baghdad University, Iraq; Faculty of Literature, Cairo University, Egypt. **Dipl.:** B.Sc., M.A. and Ph.D. in Arabic Language and Literature. **Career:** Lecturer at the Faculty of Arabic Language, Baghdad University; Head, Faculty of Arabic Language, Baghdad University (1974-75); Dean, College of Arts, Baghdad University (1975-78); Member of Iraqi Academy of Science (1979); President, Iraqi Academy of Science; Member, Jordanian Academy of Science; Representative of Iraq at the Consultative Committee of the Arab Institute of Manuscripts, Arab League; Member, Consultative Council, Khartoum Institute for Teaching Arabic Language to non-Arabic speakers; Professor of Ancient Literature, College of Arts, Baghdad University; President of the Institute of Arabic Research and Studies, Arab League Education, Culture and Science Organization. Winner of Saddam's International Prize for Arts-Dean of the College of Arts (1986-). **Publ.:** numerous researches and books published in Iraqi and Arab scientific journals. **Hobbies:** literature and criticism, travelling. **Prof. Addr.:** Baghdad University, P.O.Box 12, College of Arts, Baghdad, Iraq.

QAISI (Riyadh, Mahmoud Sami, al), Iraqi diplomat and lawyer. **Born** in 1939 in Baghdad, Iraq. **Son** of Mahmoud Qaysi. **Married,** three children. **Educ.:** Universities of Baghdad and London. **Dipl.:** LL.M., Ph.D. **Career:** Lecturer, Universities of Baghdad and Mustansiriyah (1966-70); Vice-Dean, College of Law and Politics, University of Baghdad (1969); joined Ministry of Foreign Affairs (1970); First Secretary, later Counsellor, Permanent Mission of Iraq to UN (1970-75); representative at the General Assembly (1970-74), Chairman, Iraqi delegation to Common Bureau of Coordination (1976); member, International Law Commission (1981); Permanent Representative to UN (1982); Ambassador in Ministry of Foreign Affairs (1976); Director General, Legal Department (1979-82); Director General Foreign Services Institution (1979-80). **Publ.:** various legal works. **Addr.:** Ministry of Foreign Affairs, Baghdad, Iraq.

QALAAWI (Muhamad Fahmy, al), Egyptian lawyer. **Born** on August 26, 1917 in Egypt. **Educ.:** Faculty of Law, Cairo University. **Career:** Lawyer at the Supreme Court of Appeal; Former Vice-President, Banca Commerciale Italiana per l'Egitto. **Member:** Rotary Club, Fencing Club of Egypt. **Hobby:** Fencing. **Addr.:** 9, Maspero Street, Cairo,

Tel.: 57932. **Summer Residence:** 73, Glymenopoulo Street, Zizinia, Ramleh, Tel.: 64595, Alexandria, Egypt.

QANDIL (Abdulhamid), Egyptian company manager. **Born** on October 20, 1919 in Menoufieh Province. **Educ.:** Egyptian Government School and Specialised study in Electronics and Mechanical Accounting (London). **Career:** Manager for Egypt of the British Tabulating Machine Co. Ltd. **Member:** National Sporting Club. **Addr.:** 3, Ahmad Moukhtar Hegazi, Rodah, Tel.: 22399, Cairo, Egypt.

QANNOUT (Abdulghani), Syrian statesman. **Born** in 1925 in Hama. **Educ.:** Military School of Damascus. **Dipl.:** Graduated, Military School. **Career:** Army, promoted Colonel; Syrian Regional Minister of Labour and Social Affairs in the Central Cabinet of the United Arab Republic (October 1958- December 1959), at the time of the merger between Egypt and Syria; resigned with the Baathists group Haurani-Bitar (1959); Minister of Public Works and Hydraulic resources in the cabinet of General Hafez al-Assad (November 1970); re-appointed (Sept. 1974-76). **Addr.:** Damascus, Syria.

QAQISHI (Hani, Salem), Jordanian executive. **Born** in 1946 in Salt, Jordan. **Son** of Salem Qaqishi. **Married** in 1979. **Educ.:** City University, London. **Dipl.:** B.A. (1973); M.Sc. (1974). **Career:** Vandervell Products (1972-73); Central Bank of Jordan (1973-79); Arab Jordan Investment Bank, Amman (1979-80); Deputy General Manager, Jordan Securities Corp., Amman (1980-86). **Member:** British Institute of Management; Jordan Economist Association; F.X Dealers' Club; Hussein Sport City; Orthodox Club. **Hobbies:** Reading and Swimming. **Addr.:** Amman, Jordan.

QARAAN (Muhammad Awda, al), Jordanian judge. **Born** in 1916 in Jordan. **Married**, 2 sons, 3 daughters. **Educ.:** Damascus University, Syria. **Dipl.:** LL.B. **Career:** Assistant Attorney General, Ministry of Justice (1940-42); Judge (1942-46); Deputy Minister of the Customs Department at the Ministry of Finance (1951-62); General Manager of Agriculture Credit Foundation (1962-80); Lawyer in private practice; Member of Notable Council (1980-). **Decor.:** Jordan Order of Renaissance (2nd Class) (1960); Jordan Order of Liberation (1st Class) (1961), Syrian Order of Merit. **Prof. Addr.:** The Notable Council, Amman, Jordan.

QARAGULI (Wahbi, Abdul Razzaq Fattah, al), Iraqi diplomat. **Born** in 1929 in Baghdad, Iraq. **Married**, 3 children. **Educ.:** College of Commerce and Economics, University of Baghdad, Iraq; also studies in Switzerland. **Dipl.:** B.A. in Economics, Ph.D. in Political Economy. **Career:** Deputy Permanent Representative of the United Nations in Geneva, Switerland (1964-68); Counsellor, Iraqi Embassy in Algiers, Algeria (1968); Counsellor, Iraqi Embassy in Peking (1970); Minister Plenipotentiary, Iraqi Embassy in Beirut, Lebanon (1972-76); Deputy General Director, Economics Department, Ministry of Foreign Affairs, Baghdad (1977); Ambassador to Indonesia; non-resident Ambassador to Australia, New Zealand, Singapore, Papua New Guinea (1977); Chief of Protocol, Presidential Palace, Baghdad (1978); Ambassador to Malaysia, non-resident Ambassador to Philippines (1980); Ambassador to London, UK (1982-85); Ambassador to Austria (1985-88); now Ambassador to Yugoslavia. **Prof. Addr.:** Ministry of Foreign Affairs, Baghdad, Iraq.

QARAWI (Abdallah Hamad), Saudi official. **Born** in 1933 at Onaizah, Saudi Arabia. **Dipl.:** B.A. Alexandria University. **Career:** Director, Ministry of Labour (1962); Director of Vocational Training Centres (1967); Director General, al-Yamanah Press Organization since 1969; Assistant Director General, King Saud University (1971); Director General, Ministry of Industry (1976); Assistant Deputy Minister (1978); Deputy Minister of Industry; presently General Manager, al-Yamamah Press Establishment, member of the Board, al-Yamamah Press Organization, al-Jazeerah Press, Printing and Publishing Organization and General Organization for Social Insurance. **Publications:** several articles in Saudi newspapers. **Hobbies:** Travel, reading. **Address:** P.O.Box. 851, Riyadh, Saudi Arabia.

QARI (Abdulaziz Ibn Abdul-Fattah), Saudi academic. **Born** in 1945 in Mecca, Saudi Arabia. **Dipl.:** Ph.D. (Jurisprudence), Faculty of Shari'a, University of al-Azhar, Cairo. **Career:** Secondary school teacher; Lecturer, Faculty of the Qur'an and Islamic Studies, Medina Islamic University; Secretary of the Islamic University magazine; Dean and Assistant Professor, Faculty of the Quran and Islamic Studies, Medina Islamic University. **Publications:** two books of instructions on the rules governing the recital of the Qur'an; An Explanation of al-Qadi Literature: A Study and Inquiry (Ph.D. thesis). **Hobbies:** reciting the Qur'an and related literature, composing poetry, Arabic lithography. **Address:** P.O.Box 208, Medina, Saudi Arabia.

QARMALLI (Hassan, Bahaeddin), Saudi physician. **Born** in 1933. **Educ.:** London University, UK. **Dipl.:** M.B., Tropical Medicine and Hygiene. **Career:** General practioner; Director of Airport Quaratine; Director of King's Hospital, Jeddah; Director of Health Affairs, Taif; Director of Quarantine Department; Former Member of the Committee on Health Education and Training, Jeddah; Fellow of the Royal Society of Tropical Medicine, London, UK. attented several WHO courses in Geneva (in 1968, 1969, 1971 and 1972); currently Director of Health Affairs, Jeddah. **Prof. Addr.:** "Health Services for Mecca Pilgrims" (a thesis). **Hobbies:** photography, reading. **Prof. Addr.:** Health Affairs Directorate, Madaries Street, Baghdadia, Jeddah, Saudi Arabia.

QASABI, (Yusuf Othman, al), Saudi executive. **Born** in 1946 at al-Qasab, Najd. **Dipl.:** B.Sc. (Civil Engineering), University of Texas. **Career:** Held several posts at KARA Establishment, now Assistant Director-General. **Hobbies:** sports, reading. **Address:** KARA Establishment, P.O.Box 1359, Makkah, Saudi Arabia.

QASAH (Arif Mohamad Saleem), Saudi physician. **Born** in 1919, in Hamah, Syria. **Career:** Former director, Kandara Hospital, Assistant Director of Health Affairs, Jeddah; poet and literary critic. **Publications:** two collections of Arabic poetry. **Hobby:** literature. **Address:** Health Affairs Directorate, Jeddah, Saudi Arabia.

QASIM (Qasim, Mohamed), Jordanian banker. **Born** in 1944 in Jenin, Palestine. **Son** of Mohamed Qasim Yousuf and Fatema. **Married** in 1970 in Jordan to Rebhieh Qasim, 4 Children: Reham (1973), Ibrahim (1981), Jawad (1982), and Husam (1985). **Educ.:** Cairo University (B. Commerce-1967). **Career:** Manager of Arab Bank Ltd. (1967-74); Vice President of First National Bank of Chicago (1974-83); General Manager of Qatar Islamic Bank, Doha (1984-1989); General Manager and CEO of Al-Ahli Commercial Bank, Bahrain (1989-92); Executive Vice President and Controller General of Faisal Islamic Bank, Bahrain (1992-93); General Manager of Middle East Investment Bank, Jordan (1993-94). **Presently,** General Manager of Qatar International Islamic Bank since July 94. **Address:** P.O.Box 664, Doha - Qatar. **Award:** Order of Merit, First National Bank of Chicago (1981). **Hobbies:** Reading & Music. **Addr.:** P.O.Box 664, Doha, Qatar.

QASIMI (Abdul Aziz Bin Humaid, al, Shaikh), United Arab Emirates politician. **Born** in Ras al-Khaimah, United Arab Emirates. **Career:** Minister of State for Supreme Council Affairs (since 1977 to 1991); Director, Ras al-Khaimah Broadcasting Station; and Chairman, Ras al-Khaimah Information and Culture Department, Ras al-Khaimah. Director of the Emiri Diwan in Ras Al Khaimah for Federal Affairs. **Addr:** P.O.Box. 141, Ras Al Khaimah, United Arab Emirates.

QASIMI (Fahim bin Sultan al, Sheikh), UAE Politician. **Born** in 1948. **Educ.:** B.A., Law, Cairo University (1974); Master's Degree, International Politics, John's Hopkins University, USA (1977). **Career:** UAE Permanent Representative to the United Nations, Geneva (1977-80); New York (1980-84); Director, Legal Department, Ministry of Foreign Affairs (1984-92); Secretary General, Gulf Cooperation Council (1993-96); Minister of Economy and Commerce (March 1997 - to date). **Address:** Ministry of Economy and Commerce, P.O.Box 901, Abu Dhabi, United Arab Emirates.

QASIMI (Faisal Bin Sultan, al, Shaikh), UAE businessman. **Born** in 1940. Third **Son** of Shaikh Sultan Bin Salim, Former Ruler of Ras al-Khaimah. **Married. Career:** joined Trucial Oman Scouts (1954); Mons Officer Cadet School, UK; Jordanian Forces; Member of Staff of the Crown Prince of Abu Dhabi (1970); Under Secretary, Ministry of Defence (1971); Chief of Staff, Abu Dhabi Defence Forces (1973); Chairman of GIBCA Group of Companies as well Chairman of United Arab Bank, Abu Dhabi. **Prof. Addr.:** P.O.Box 2570, Abu Dhabi, United Arab Emirates.

QASIMI (Khalid Bin Humaid, al), United Arab Emirates diplomat, politician. **Born** in 1940 in Umm al-Qawain, United Arab Emirates. **Son** of Humaid al-Qasimi. **Married**, one daughter. **Career:** United Arab Emirates Minister of Electricity and Water (1977); UAE Ambassador to Algeria (1977); Director, Ras al-Khaimah maritime and Mercantile International. **Addr.:** Ras Al Khaimah, U.A.E.

QASIMI (Khalid Bin Saqr, al, Shaikh), UAE politician. Eldest **Son**, Heir and Deputy of the Ruler of Ras al-Khaimah, Shaikh Saqr Bin Muhammad al Qasimi. **Born** in 1940. **Married**, 2 sons. **Educ.:** studied in Ras al-Khaimah UAE, Cairo, Egypt and London, UK. **Dipl.:** Degree in Public Administration. **Career:** Director of United Arab Bank (1975 to present). has set up a number of administrations in the Emirate of Ras al khaimah; supervised the implementation of a number of development and construction schemes; acts as official emissary of his father the Ruler; Chairman of Ras al-Khaimah Oilfields supply Centre and National Bank of Ras al-Khaimah; Director, GIBCA Group of Companies. **Prof. Addr.:** P.O.Box 200 Ras al-Khaimah, United Arab Emirates; United Arab Bank, P.O.Box 3562, Abu Dhabi, United Arab Emirates.

QASIMI (Khalid Bin Sultan, al, Shaikh), United Arab Emirates businessman and administrator. **Born** in 1931. **Married. Educ.:** worked in Saudi Arabia, mainly for Press and radio (1953-60); Businessman in Dubai and in Sharjah; Former Director of Ports, Sharjah. **Addr.:** Sharjah, United Arab Emirates.

QASIMI (Saqr Bin Muhammad, al, Sheikh), Ruler of Ras Al Khaimah, United Arab Emirates. **Born** in 1920. **Married**. with eight sons and seven daughters. **Career:** Ruler of the Emirate of Ras Al Khamaih since 1948 following Sheikh Sultan Bin Salem; joined the United Arab Emirates on February 10, 1972 and he is now a member of the Supreme Council. **Work:** Has done much to spread security in all parts of the Emirate and devoted all his energy to develop the civil, agricultural and industrial projects in Ras Al Khaimah. During his rule, he was able to transfer completely the Emirate of Ras Al Khaimah to a higher degree of progress. Visited many countries in Asia, Europe, America and Africa. **Address:** Ruler's Palace, P.O.Box 1 Ras Al Khaimah, United Arab Emirates, Tel.: 07-222222, Fax: 07-227633.

QASIMI (Sultan Bin Saqr, al, Shaikh), UAE politician. Second **Son** of the Ruler of Ras al-Khaimah, Shaikh Saqr Bin Muhammad. **Born** in 1944. **Married. Educ.:** in the United Arab Emirates; Training course at Mons Military Academy, UK, Junior Staff Course, Warminster, UK. **Career:** served in the Trucial Oman Scouts (1970); Commander, Ras al-Khaimah Mobile Force (1974), colonel (1975); Commander of al-Yarmuk Brigade; Director of United Arab Bank (1983 to present); Chairman, Ras al-Khaimah National Insurance Co.; Chairman Ras al-Khaimah Rock Co. **Prof. Addr.:** United Arab Bank, P.O.Box 881, Sharjah, United Arab Emirates.

QASSAB (Khalid, Abdulaziz, al), Iraqi surgeon. **Born** in 1924 in Baghdad, Iraq. **Son** of Abdulaziz al-Qassab (exminister, President of the Chamber of Deputies). **Married** in 1966 in Baghdad to Miss Hanan AbdulJabbar al-Rawi, three children. **Educ.:** College of Medicine, Baghdad. **Dipl.:** M.B., Ch.B., Medicine (1946); F.R.C.S. (Fellow Royal College of Surgeons of England). **Career:** Resident Surgical Department Teaching Hospital (1947); Assistant Professor, Medical College, Baghdad (1955); Professor of Surgery (1970); Chairman, Surgical Department (1977-80); Consultant Surgeon to Private Hospitals; **Publ.:** About fifty contributions to Medical Journals and conferences about: Cancer of skin, oral cavity, breast, head and neck, etc. **Act.:** Known painter of Landscapes and town sceneries, exhibited in Iraq, Europe, North America, Asia and the Arab Countries. **Medals:** Red Crescent Silver medal. **Sports:** Tennis, swimming. **Hobbies:** Painting, history of architecture, photography, music. **Founder** and President of Iraqi Cancer Society (1962); Founder of Iraqi Society of Plastic Arts (1966). **Prof. Addr.:** P.O.Box 6193, Baghdad, Iraq.

QASSEM (Abdul Aziz Ali, al), Saudi academic. **Born** in 1930 at Onaizah, Saudi Arabia. **Dipl.:** Ph.D (Law). **Career:** Primary School teacher (1950-57); Deputy Director of a Department, Ministry of Education (1957-59); Assistant Lecturer, (1967-69), Lecturer, Faculty of Commerce (1974); Assistant Professor, Department of Law, Faculty of Commerce, King Saud University. **Member:** Muslim Social Scientists Association of the U.S.A. and Canada; attended Muslim Social Scientists Conferences, Indiana (1975), Philadelphia, (1976). **Publications:** Nizamu'l Dhara'ib Fi'l Islam, Wamada Tatbeequhu F'il Mamlakati'l Arabia Al Saudiah (The System of Taxation in Islam and its Adaptability in Saudi Arabia). **Hobby:** reading. **Address:** Faculty of Commerce, King Saud University, Tel.: 481 1000, Riyadh, Saudi Arabia.

QASSEM (Ahmad A.), Saudi academic. **Born** in 1943 in Abo Arish. **Dipl.:** B.Sc., Ph.D. (Insect Endocrinology). **Carrer:** Head of Zoology Department, Faculty of Science, King Saud University; Vice-Dean of Faculty of Science and Associate professor. **Member:** South Eastern Society of Parasitologists and the International Society of Endocrinology, U.S.A. **Publications:** Work papers on: Endocrinology and Parasites in Saudi Arabia, Endocrinology and Stain Technique. **Address:** Department of Zoology, Faculty of Science, King Saud University, Riyadh, Saudi Arabia.

QASSEM (Awn al-Sharif, Dr.), Sudanese academic. **Born** on October 15, 1933 at Halfa yat al Moolook (Sudan). **Married,** children. **Educ.:** Faculty of Arts, Khartoum University; University of London (UK); University of Edinburgh (Scotland). **Dipl.:** B.A., M.A., Ph.D. (Arabic Language and Literature). **Career:** Lecturer, School of Oriental and African Studies, University of London (1959-61); Lecturer, Faculty of Arts, Arabic Department, Khartoum University (1961-64); Senior lecturer (1969), then Director of translation Section (1969-70) in the said university; Minister of Wakfs (charitable endowments and Religious Affairs, Khartoum (1973); Head, Council for Religious Affairs (1980). **Addr.:** Khartoum, Sudan.

QASSEM (Marwan, Sudqi), Jordanian politician. **Born** on May 12, 1938. **Son** of Sudqi Qassem (former Governor, former Mayor of Amman, former Member Upper House of Parliament). **Married** to Joyce Qassem in 1960, 2 children: Layth and Tamara. **Educ.:** Eastern Michigan University. Columbia University, Georgetown University. **Dipl.:** Bachelor of Arts, Master of Arts (International Relation), Columbia University. **Career:** Assistant chief of Protocol, Foreign Ministry (1962), Jordan Consul General in New York (1964); Member of Jordan Delegation, United Nations (1964-66); Acting Director of Protocol (1966-67); Secretary Jordan Embassy, Washington D.C. (1968-72); Secretary to Crown Prince Hassan (1972-75); Director General Royal Hashemite Court (1975-76); Minister of State (1976); Minister of Supply (1977-79); Minister of State for Foreign Affairs (1979-80); Minister Foreign Affairs (1980-83); Chief of Royal Court (1984 April 1989); Deputy Prime Minister and Minister of Foreign Affairs (since 27 April 1989-1 January 1991); Chief of Royal Court (Jan. 1995-Feb. 1996). **Award:** Commander National Order of Cedar (Lebanon). **Prof. Addr.:** The Royal Court, Amman, Jordan.

QASSEM (Mohamad Abdulaziz, al), Saudi civil servant. **Born** on September 16, 1936, in Riyadh, Saudi Arabia. **Dipl.:** M.A. (Public Administration and Supervision) U.S.A. **Career:** Teacher, Inspector, Administrative Director, Assistant Director-General, Director-General of Cultural Affairs, Ministry of Education; Ex Head of the Administrative Board of the Hamadah Agriculture cooperative Society (Washm Region); took part in establishing the Social Services and Development Centres in Saudi Arabia (1960-1961); participated in several educational conferences e.g. thee UNESCO Conferences in Paris, the Education conference in Geneva, the Scouts Conference in The U.K. **Member:** Ex Administrative Board of the Saudi Scouts Society; Now Assistant Deputy Minister for Finance and Administrative Affairs, Ministry of Petroleum and Mineral Resources, Riyadh. **Publ.:** Articles, papers, lectures and radio broadcasts in the local press and radio. **Hobbies:** Reading, Collecting books. **Prof. Addr.:** P.O.Box 27425 Riyadh, 11417, Saudi Arabia.

QASSEM (Mohamad Yahya), Saudi academic. **Born** in 1946. **Educ.:** Ph.D. (Plant Pathology). **Career:** Assistant Professor of Plant Pathology, Department of Botany, Faculty of Science, King Saud University; member of Saudi Biological Society, member. British Mycology Society, Dutch Potatoes Research Society, British Plant Pathology Society. **Hobbies:** travel, Photography, reading. **Address:** Botany Department, Faculty of Science, King Saud University, Tel.: 478374, Riyadh, Saudi Arabia.

QASSEM (Osman, al), Sudanese academic and statesman. **Born** in 1930 in Omdurman (Sudan). **Married,** with five children. **Educ.:** University of Khartoum; also in the United States and the United Kingdom. **Dipl.:** B.Sc. (agriculture). **Career:** Teacher, agricultural Institute of Shambat (1959-63); Assistant Under-Secretary of State, Ministry of Agriculture, Khartoum (1967); Sudanese representative at the United Nations (1967); Minister of Cooperatives and Rural Development (1969-72). **Addr.:** Khartoum, Sudan.

QASSEM (Wajeeh), Jordanian Dean of Engineering. **Born** in 1948 in Raba-Jenin, Jordan. **Son** of Fayez Awwad (Farmer) **and** Mrs. née Rafiqa Mohammad Younis. **Married** in 1977 in Jordan to Miss Sahar, 3 children: Doha (1980), Ayman (1986), Bashir (1987). **Educ.:** University of Baghdad, Ain-Shams University, Michigan State University, University of Toledo. **Dipl.:** B.Sc Physics (1972); M.Sc Exp. Physics (1975); Dual M.Sc Engineering Mechanics & Physics (1983); Ph.D Mech. Engineering (1987). **Career:** A/Dean of Engineering (June 95- Still); Vice-Dean of Engineering (Oct. 93-June 1995); Associate Professor, Faculty of Eng., Yarmouk University (1994- Still); Assistant Professor, Faculty of Eng., Yarmouk University (1989-1994); Biomedical Eng. Site Manager, Orbit Summit Health Ltd., Saudi Arabia (1988-1989); 1/4 Instructor, Dept. of Mech. Eng., University of Toledo, U.S.A. (1985-1987). **Sport:** Football. **Hobbies:** Games, Travel. **Member** in American Society of Mechanical Engineers, American Academy of Mechanics, Society of Engineering Science, WHO'S WHO IN THE WORLD, 1997. **Prof. Addr.:** Yarmouk University, Tel.: 966-2-271100, Ext. 2611, Irbid, Jordan. **Priv. Addr.:** 966-2-271100, Ext. 3566, Jordan.

QASSEMI (Abdul Aziz, bin Mohamad, Shaikh al), United Arab Emirates Businessman and Administrator. **Born** in 1938 in Sharjah (UAE). **Son of** Shaikh Mohamad Saqr Sultan Al Qassemi. **Brother of** H.H. Shaikh Sultan bin Mohamad Al Qassemi, Ruler of Sharjah. **Married** with children. **Education:** with private tutor in Sharjah, English and Military trained. **Career:** Started in Saudi Arabia and Qatar, joined the Trucial Oman Scouts in 1960, commissioned after attending Mons Military Academy, UK (1963), Wali of Khorfakkan province (1968). Also held positions such as Advisor to the Ruler of Ras Al Khaimah, Commander of the Sharjah National Guards, President of the UAE Chambers of Commerce and Industry, Chairman of the Board, Union of UAE Chambers of Commerce, President of Sharjah Chamber of Commerce & Industry. **Awards:** Wissam Al Rafidian (Iraq); Wissam Military Service (UAE). **Hobbies:** Sailing, Hunting, Fishing, writing Poetry. **Club:** Honorary member of various country clubs. Entered the field of Business in the early seventies. **Now,** Chairman of National Investment Company (W.L.L.) Group of Companies and Director of a number of joint stock companies, Crown prince and Deputy Ruler of Sharjah and Special Advisor to H.H. Shaikh Zayed bin Sultan Al Nahyan, President, United Arab Emirates. **Address:** P.O.Box. 17, Sharjah, UAE, Tel.: 355121 Fax: 544495.

QASSEMI (Ahmad Bin Sultan, al, Shaikh), United Arab Emirates statesman. **Born** in Sharjah, United Arab Emirates. **Career:** Minister of Justice; Minister of State (1977-1986); Minister of State Without portfolio (1986 to 1991); former Chairman, National Bank of Sharjah, Sharjah, UAE, Chairman, Gulf International, Dubai, and General Manager, General Enterprises Co., Sharjah. **Addr.:** P.O.Box 1150, Sharjah, United Arab Emirates.

QASSEMI (Khalid bin Abdul Aziz Shaikh al), United Arab Emirates, Businessman and Polo player. **Born** in 1968 in Sharjah (UAE). **Son of** Shaikh Abdul Aziz bin Mohamad Al Qassemi, Crown Prince and Deputy Ruler of Sharjah, **Nephew of** H.H. Shaikh Sultan bin Mohamad Al Qassemi, Ruler of Sharjah. **Married** with a son. **Education:** Formal schooling in Sharjah, English & Business studies in USA and finance and banking training in the UAE. **Career:** Took over as CEO of the family business enterprise (NIC Group of companies), in 1988 and is spearheading major expansion and diversification of the Group. **Hobbies:** Scuba Diving, Hunting, Breeding Arabian Horses, Endurance riding, and is one of the most promising UAE National Polo players, having won several competitions in the UAE and abroad. **Club:** Member of various country clubs, Deputy Chairman of the Higher Polo Committee of the UAE Equestrian & Racing Federation. **Now** Deputy Chairman of National Investment Company (W.L.L.) Group of Companies. **Address:** P.O.Box 17, Sharjah, UAE. Tel.: 355121 Fax: 544495.

QASSEMI (Mohamad Bin Salem, Bin Sultan, al, Shaikh), United Arab Emirates politician. **Born** in 1933, **Married. Educ.:** in Sharjah. **Career:** Went to Saudi Arabia

(1954); worked for Saudi Railways (1955-60); United Arab Emirates Minister for Public Works (1972-73); United Arab Emirates Minister of labour till January 1977; formerly Director of petroleum and Mineral Affairs, Sharjah; President, Sharjah Chamber of Commerce and Industry. **Addr.:** Sharjah, U.A.E.

QASSEMI (Saud bin Khaled, al, Sheikh), UAE businessman. **Born** in Sharjah, UAE. **Married. Career:** Director, National Bank of Fujairah, Fujairah, UAE; Director, First Gulf Bank, Ajman, UAE Director, Sharjah Group Company, Sharjah, UAE; Director, Investment Bank for Trade and Finance L.L.C, Sharjah, UAE, Chairman of al-Saud Ltd. Co., Sharjah, UAE, Chairman, Sharjah Port Authority. **Addr.:** al-Arouba Street, P.O.Box 1885, Tel.: 355391-2, Telex: 68083, 68218 A/B INVESTEM, Sharjah, UAE and P.O.Box 510, Sharjah, UAE.

QASSEMI (Sultan Bin Mohamad, Al, Dr., Shaikh), Ruler of Sharjah, United Arab Emirates. **Born** on July 6, 1939. **Married**, 6 children: 2 sons and 4 daughters. **Educ.:** Cairo University, Exeter University. **Dipl.:** B.Sc. (Agriculture) (1971), Ph.D. (1985). **Career:** Head of Dewan al-Amiri, Sharjah (1971); Minister of Education, U.A.E. (1971); Ruler of Sharjah and Member of Supreme Council of United Arab Emirates, 1972 to date. **Creative Works (Books):** The Myth of Arab Piracy in the Gulf; The Division of the Omani Empire; The British occupation of Aden. **Membership of Associations:** Chairman, Permanent Arab/African Symposium, Arab Family Organization. **Honours:** Hon. Fellowship, Institute of african Asian Studies, Khartoum University, Sudan; Hon. Degree, Faisal Abad University, PAK. **Membership of Professional Societies:** Arab Historian's Union. **Hobby:** Reading. **Addr.:** Government of Sharjah, P.O.Box 1, Sharjah, United Arab Emirates.

QASSIMI (Mohamad Abdallah, al), Saudi consultant and associate professor of medicine. **Born** in 1946 in Cairo, Egypt. **Dipl.:** L.R.C.P., M.R.C.S., F.R.C.P., United Kingdom. **Career:** Consultant (1977); Vice Dean, Faculty of Medicine, King Adbulaziz Univerisity, Jeddah (1979); Medical Editor of Sayidaty weekly Consultant, Associate Professor of Medicine, King Abdulaziz University (1981-). **Member:** Royal Society of Medicine, London, Editing Board King Adbulaziz University Medical Journal. **Publications:** four books on family health, Aids, Primary health Care and diabetes, jeddah (1984-1988); and "Middle Eastern Clinical Medicine" Chapman & Hall, London, 1995; several scientific papers and numerous articles in Ashraq al-Awsat daily and Sayidaty newspapers. **Hobbies:** cycling, swimming. **Prof. Addr.:** Faculty of Medicine P.O.Box 6615, King Abdulaziz University, Tel.: (6952088), Jeddah, Saudi Arabia.

QATAMIN (Mardi, Abdullah), Jordanian administrator. **Born** in 1930 in Jordan. **Married,** 7 children. **Educ.:** Cairo University, Egypt, also studied in Beirut, Lebanon. **Dipl.:** B.A. in Geography, Diploma in Educational Planning. **Career:** Teacher (1955-58); Head of Personnel Department, Kuwait (1961-66); Sociology Teacher in Jordan (1966-69); Head of Compulsory Education Section, Ministry of Education, Jordan (1970-71); Member of the Board of Directors of Arab Ports Union, the Free Zones Corporation, the Phosphate Company and the Arab Association for Marine Transport; Member of the National Consultative Council (1980-82); General Manager of Akaba Railways Corporation (1985-1991). **Decor.:** Order of Independence, Jordan (1974), al-Masira al-Khara'a, Morocco (1975), Order of the Republic, Egypt (1985). **Hobby:** reading. **Addr.:** P.O.Box 470, al-Gabiha, Amman, Jordan.

QATTINIS (Julien), Syrian painter and decorator. **Born** in 1934 in Damascus. **Educ.:** Study trips in Arab Countries and Europe. **Dipl.:** Painting Academy of "Fine Arts Rome" specialisation in Decoration. **Career:** Since 1945, exhibitions: Lazarists- Damascus (1945); Cultural Arab Centre, Damascus 1st Prize (1947); "Spring and Autumn Salon" Damasçus (1959); Gallery "Art Moderne", Damascus (1961); 13th International Exhibition of "Margutta" Rome; "Arciss 31" Munich; the International Exhibition of "Gubio", Italy (1962); 7th and 8th Exhibitions of "Gentes Arts" Palace of Arts Exhibitions, Rome 2nd Prize (1962-63); Exhibition Arab painters, in Italy at the "Felluca" Gallery Rome (1963); Represented Syria with other Syrian painters at the 32nd International Art Festival of Venice (1964); Exhibition Gallery "Palace of Art Exhibition", Rome (1964); "Espace" Gallery Damascus (1964), Retrospective of 1945-65; "Espace" Gallery Damascus and at the French Cultural Centre of Amman (Jordan) (1965); Syrian Painters Exhibition at Sursock Museum Beirut and "National Spring Salon" Aleppo (1966). **Awards:** Gold Medal (1962), 7th Exhibition of "Gentes Arts" Rome, Bronze Medal (1963), "Felluca" Gallery, Rome. **Addr.:** Damascus, Syria.

QAUD (Abdul Mejid, al), Libyan politician. **Born** in 1943 at Ghariar, Libya. **Married. Educ.:** University of Libya, Benghazi; University of Stirling. UK. **Dipl.:** Degree in Engineering; Diploma in Town Planning. **Career:** Chief Engineer, Tripoli Municipality (1969); Mayor of Tripoli (1971); Minister of State for Agricultural Development (November 1972); leading role in Green Revolution; Secretary for Land Reclamation and Development, General People's Committee (March 1977-79); Secretary for Liaison, General People's Committee (1979-81); Secretary for Atomic Energy January (1981-1985); Secretary for Agricultural Reform & Construction (1989); Secretary Agricultural Reforms and Land Reclamation (1990-Nov. 1993); Secretary General of People's Committee (July 1995). **Addr.:** Tripoli, Libya.

QAZIM (Mohamad, Ibrahim), Egyptian academic.

Born in 1928 in Cairo, Egypt. **Son** of Mohamad F. Qazim **and** Mrs., Khadija A. née Abou Hadid. **Married** in 1961 in Cairo to Miss Safaa Yusuf al-Aasar, three children. **Educ.:** Ain Shams University, Cairo; Kansas University, USA. **Dipl.:** B.Sc. in Science and Education (1950); Master of Education (1955); Ph.D. (1957). **Career:** Teacher in secondary schools in Egypt and Syria (1950-54); Assistant professor, Ain Shams University, Cairo (1957-63); Cultural Attaché to the Philippines of the Government of Egypt in Manila (1959-60); Associate professor, Ain Shams University, Cairo (1963-70); First Dean of Education, al-Azhar University, Cairo (since 1970); First Dean, Faculties of Education, Doha, State of Qatar (1973-77); First President, University of Qatar, Doha (1977). **Work:** President and Chairman of the Board of Directors of Center for Research on the Muslim Contribution to Civilisation, California, USA (since 1983); Member of the the Founding Committee and Board of Trustees of Arabian Gulf University, Manama, Bahrain (since 1981); Director, International Council on Education for Teaching, Washington DC, USA (1982-88); Member of the Board of: Regents Raja Suliman Cultural Foundation, Manila (since 1983), Regents Organisation for the Development of Arab Culture (ALECSO), Tunis (since 1983), Administration of Institute of Spain and the Arab World and of the Arab-European University Institute, Carmona, Spain (since 1985); member of the Council of Higher Education for the Gulf States, Riyadh, Saudi Arabia (since 1980); member of the Founding Committee of Institute for the History of Arab-Islamic Sciences, University of Frankfurt, West Germany (since 1981). **Publ.:** Author of three books: "Punishment in Schools" (Arabic) (1959), "Development in Student Values- Follow-Up Study in Five Years" (Arabic) (1962), "2 Trends in Mass Education" (Arabic) (1962); Co-author of five books on education. **Medals and Awards:** Doctor of Humanities (honoris causa) from Islamic University of the Philippines (1983); Plaque of Appreciation, Mindanao State University, The Philippines (1978); Plaques of Appreciation from Ortanez University, the Philippines (1978) and from Islamic University of Philippines (1983); Honorary Citizen of the Marawi City, The Philippines. **Member:** of Phi Delta Kappa, USA: Philosophy of Education Society, USA; World Council for Curriculum and Instruction, USA; International Council on Education for Teaching, USA; Egyptian Academy for Scientific Culture, Egypt; Ain Shams Club, Cairo; Alexandria Sporting Club, Alexandria; Heliopolis Sporting Club, Cairo; Doha Club, Doha, Qatar. **Permanent Priv. Addr.:** Osman Ahmed Osman Apartment Bldg., No.2, Apt. 61, Maryland, Roxy, Cairo, Tel.: 878037, Egypt.

QAZIMI (Zaid, al), Kuwaiti businessman, statesman. **Born** in 1916 in Kuwait. **Son** of Abdul Hussain Hasan al-Qazimi **and** Mrs. Alzelzelah. **Married** in 1943 in Kuwait to Miss al-Bahbahani, eight children. **Career:** Started business in Iran and Basrah (in partnership); started own business with abdulRahman AlBisher (1943) (as agents of Mercedes-Benz in Kuwait, etc.); elected member of Parliament (1963-71); Joined Planning Board Council (1972-77); selected a member of the Committee to revise the Constitution (1980). **Sports:** Walking, tennis. **Hobby:** Reading. Member of Hunting and Equestrian Club. **Credit Cards:** American Express, Diner's Club, Visa Card. **Prof. Addr.:** P.O.Box 47, Tel.: 2411660, 2430055, Safat 13001, Kuwait. **Priv. Addr.:** Aldasma area, Balkis St. patt 2, Home 5, Tel.: 2515777, 2515888, Kuwait.

QAZNA (Mohamad Farjallah), Saudi physician. **Born** on 12 December 1930, in Mecca, Saudi Arabia. **Dipl.:** B.Chem., M.Chem., M.D., F.R.C.S. **Career:** Surgeon, Ministry of Health (1959-74); Research Fellow and Instructor, Washington University (1957-77); Assistant Professor of Surgery, King Abdulaziz University; Fellow, Egyptian Medical Society; Fellow, British Medical Association; member of American Islamic Medical Society. **Publication:** several medical research papers. **Hobbies:** tennis, table tennis. **Address:** Faculty of Medicine, King Abdulaziz University, Jeddah, Saudi Arabia.

QAZZAZ (Ayad, al), Iraqi Professor. **Born** on August 23, 1941. **Son** of Sayyidi Ali al-Qazzaz (died in 1957) **and** Mrs. Sharifa al-Qazzaz (died in 1982) **Divorced**, one child (1964). **Educ.:** University of Baghdad (1958-62); University of California, Berkeley. **Dipl.:** B.A. (1962), M.A. (1966), Ph.D. (1970). **Career:** Assistant Professor (1969-73); Associate Professor (1947-80); Full Professor 1980. **Publ.:** published four books and over fifty articles in Arabic and English in the U.S., Europe and Arab World Journals. **Decor.:** Iraqi Government Grant; University of California, Berkeley Grant; California State University, Sacramento, Grant. **Member:** A.A.U.G., A.S.A, MESA, World Affairs Council, Comstock Club. **Sport:** Tennis, Walking. **Credit Cards:** Visa, Master Charge. **Prof. Addr.:** Dept. of Sociology, California State University, Sacramento, California 95819, Tel.: 916-944-8378, U.S.A. **Priv. Addr.:** 3501 Dutchway, Carmichael, California 95608, Tel.: 916-944-8378, U.S.A.

QEREM (Kamal), General Manager of Qatar Flour Mills Co. **Born** on February 5, 1949 at Badia, Palestine. **Son** of Mustafa Qerem - Mosque Imam **and** Mrs. née Hind Taha. **Married** on October 15, 1978 in Kuwait to Siham Safi, 2 children: Khalid and Ziad. **Educ.:** Bedia Secondary School - Palestine, Ibn Khaldoon Secondary School - Damascus, Damascus University, College of Management & Accountancy - London. **Dipl.:** BSc in Commerce - Damascus University, Diploma - College of Management & Accountancy - London, Associate Member - the Association of Certified Public Accountants. **Career:** July 99 - Now General Manager of Qatar Flour Mills Co. Qatar; Dec. 95 - June 99 Finance Manager of Qatar Flour Mills - Qatar; June 91 - Dec. 95 General Manager of AL-QEREM Consultation Centre - Amman; Jan. 86 - Aug. 90

Finance Manager of Kuwait Interests for Financial Investments Co. - Kuwait; Sept. 84 - Dec. 85 Budget & Cost Controller of Kuwait Building Industries - Kuwait. **Other Information:** Other financial positions from 1974-1984 in Kuwait. **Awards:** 1st Winner in a public Competition for a research thesis on "The problem of divorce in Kuwaiti Society". **Sports Practised:** Table Tennis. **Hobbies:** Computer & Internet. **Club:** Doha Sheraton Club. **Credit Cards:** VISA from Qatar Commercial Bank. **Prof. Addr.:** Qatar Flour Mills Co. P.O.Box 1444, Tel.: 415011 (0), Doha, Qatar. **Priv. Addr.:** Bin Mahmoud Area, Doha, Tel.: 352237 (R), Qatar.

QOSAIMY (Mohamad Dakkayl, al), Saudi assistant mayor, Dammam. **Born** in 1933 at Sinan, Saudi Arabia. **Dipl.:** Diploma in Social Sciences. **Career:** Manager, Social Development; Manager, Social Service Centre, Unaizah; Editor, al-Khalij (Gulf) magazine; Assistant Mayor of Damman. **Hobbies:** reading, sport. **Address:** Dammam Municipality, Dammam, Eastern Province, Saudi Arabia.

QOSTY (Abdul Ghani Mohamad), Saudi editor. **Born** in 1927 in Mecca, Saudi Arabia. **Educ.:** Secondary School Certificate. **Career:** Accountant, Mecca Governorate Secretariat, Mecca; Proof reader, Editor, al-Bilad al-Saudiah newspaper, Macca; Editor, al-Bilad daily; former Staff member, Okaz Organization. **Publications:** Ahzanu Galb (Sorrows of Heart, collection of poems); hundreds of poems and articles published in al-Bilad. **Hobbies:** reading, music. **Prof. Addr.:** al-Bilad Press and Publishing Organization, P.O.Box 6340, Tel.: 6719280, Jeddah, Saudi Arabia.

QUASIMI (Fahim bin Sultan al, Sheikh), UAE Politician. **Born** in 1948. **Educ.:** B.A., Law, Cairo University (1974); Master's Degree, International Politics, John's Hopkins University, USA (1977). **Career:** UAE Permanent Representative to the United Nations, Geneva (1977-80); New York (1980-84); Director, Legal Department, Ministry of Foreign Affairs (1984-92); Secretary General, Gulf Cooperation Council (1993-96); Minister of Economy and Commerce (March 1997-to date) **Address:** Ministyr of Economy and Commerce, P.O.Box 901, Abu Dhabi,ÉUniter Arab Emirates.

QUBBAH (Taysir), Palestinian politician. **Born** in 1938. **Educ.:** studied politics at Cairo University, Egypt; Chairman, General Union of Palestinian Students. **Career:** arrested by the Israelis for alleged subversive activities in the Occupied Territories; after 3 years in prison was deported to Jordan (1971); Representative of Popular Front for the Liberation of Palestine (PFLP) on the Palestinian Liberation Organisation (PLO) Executive Committee (1971-72); compaigned in Lebanese refugee camps on behalf of the Rejection Front (1974); led PFLP Delegation to China in his capacity as Head of the PFLP Foreign Affairs Department (1974). **Addr.:** Damascus, Syria.

QUDAH (Mahmoud Ali, Dr.), Jordanian Professor of English. **Born** on February 1, 1958 in Jordan. **Son** of Ali Qudah (retired) **and** Mrs. Hamdeh Qudah. **Married** in 1990 in Amman to Maysoun Zoubi, 2 children: Nour (1991), Farah (1993). **Educ.:** Ph.D., Michigan State University-USA; M.A. Leeds University-England; B.A. Yarmouk University-Jordan. **Dipl.:** Diploma, Edinburgh University-Scotland; Diploma, Oxford University-England; Diploma Leeds University-England. **Career:** 1996- present: Professor of English; 1994-1996: Dean of Arts, Mu'tha University-Jordan; 1993-1994: Chairman English Dept. & Humanities, Zaytooneh University; 1990-1992: Chairman, English Dept. Mu'tha University; 1987-1990: Assistant Professor. **Medals:** Medal of Distinction from Yarmouk University; A Scholarship from the British Council; Scholarship from government of Jordan & Mu'tha University; Various grants to attend international seminars & Conventions. **Sports:** Athletics & Swimming. **Hobbies:** Reading & Travel. **Clubs:** American Alumni, British Graduate Alumni. **Credit Cards:** American Express & Visa. **Prof. Addr.:** English Dept. Mu'tha University, Kerak-Jordan, Tel.: 962-6-617860. **Priv. Addr.:** P.O.Box 7753, Amman 11118, Jordan, Tel.: 962-697582.

QUNTAR (Aahed S.), Jordanian aviation official. **Born** in 1944 in Amman, Jordan. **Educ.:** Syrian University, Syria; Harvard University, USA. **Dipl.:** Blitt, Diploma in Public Administration; various specialist qualifications in civil aviation. **Career:** Vice President of Air Transport and Tourism Trade Union (1971), President (1972); Member, Executive Committee of Trade Union Federation (1972); Assistant Secretary General for Education and Culture in Trade Union Federation (1973); Secretary General Jordan Trade Union Federation (1974); Manager of Amman Airport, ALIA Royal Jordanian Airlines (1974-77); Station Manager, Heathrow Airport, ALIA Royal Jordanian Airlines (1977-80); Area Mangre, ALIA Royal Jordanian Airlines, Cyprus (1980-82); Assistant Vice President of Cargo Handling, ALIA Royal Jordanian Airlines Amman Airport (1982-); Member of the Higher Committee for Advanced Training of the Workers' Education Board, Organisation for the Promotion of Internal Tourism; President of Workers' Clinic Board; represented Jordan Trade Union Federation in international conferences. President General Manager, Royal Wings Co. Ltd. **Publ.:** Editor of "Sawt Ummal al-Urdan" as well as articles in Jordanian papers; "The Internal Organisation of the Jordanian Labor Movement" (in English), Harvard, USA (1973). **Hobbies:** reading, table tennis, travelling. **Prof. Addr.:** P.O.Box 1065, Amman, Jordan and P.O.Box 314018, Amman, Jordan.

QUOTAH (Mohamad M.N.), Saudi academic. **Born** on

26 July 1943 in Mecca, Saudi Arabia. **Dipl.:** B.Sc. (Civil Engineering), M.A. (Mathematics), M.Sc. and Ph.D. (Operations Research). **Career:** Associate Professor and Vice Director, Research and Development Centre, (1984-85); Faculty of Economics and Administration, King Abdulaziz University (since 1979); Planning and Research Consultant and Training to various firms. **Member:** Operations Research Graduates Assembly, Case Western Reserve University, U.S.A.; American Operations Research Association, Management Information Systems Association, U.S.A.; Higher Studies Committee, Faculty of Economics and Administration, KAU; Data Processing Centre Committee, KAU; Board of Editors and Editor-in-Chief, Economics and Administration Magazine (1982 to present); has attended several conferences on Operations Research, Administration Development and Management Information Systems. **Publications:** Computer Principles, (in print), Management Quantitative Analysis; Business Computer Applications; various articles in the Economics and Administration Magazine; various translations of books and articles to Arabic, i.e. "Mankind at the Turning Point". **Address:** Faculty of Economics and Administration, King Abdulaziz University, P.O.Box 1540, Jeddah, Saudi Arabia.

QURAISHI (Abdul Aziz, al), Saudi official. **Born** in 1930 at Hail, Saudi Arabia. **Dipl.:** M.B.A., F.I.B.A., University of Southern California, U.S.A. **Career:** General Manager, State Railways (1961-68); President, General Personnel Bureau (1968-74); Minister of State (1971-74); Governor for Saudi Arabia, International Monetary Fund, Arab Monetary Fund since 1974; Alternate Governor for Saudi Arabia, Islamic Development Bank; Chairman, Saudi International Bank, London, U.K. **Member:** Board of Directors, Supreme Council for Petroleum and Mineral Resources, General Petroleum and Mineral Organization, Public Investment Fund, Pension Fund; Group of Thirty Managing Director, Ali Zaid al-Quraishi & Bros.; Former Chairman, National Company for Cooperative Insurance, Riyadh; Chairman, Al-Alamiya Insurance Co. Ltd. **Honours:** King Abdulaziz Medal, 2nd class; Order of Brilliant Star Grand Cordon, Republic of China; Order of Diplomatic Service Merit and Gwan Chwa Medal, Republic of Korea; King Leopold Medal, Commander Class, Belgium. **Prof. Addr.:** Al-Alamiya Insurance Co. Ltd, P.O.Box 2374, Jeddah 21451, Saudi Arabia.

QURESHI (Qamarul Haq), Pakistani bank executive. **Born** on December 10, 1937 in Bahwalpur, Pakistan. **Son** of Fazel Haq Qureishi (Doctor) and late Mrs. née Zubaida Khatoon. **Married** on October 22, 1965 in Multan to Naz Parveen, four children. **Educ:** Haily College of Commerce, Punjab University, Lahore, Pakistan. **Dipl.:** DAIBP (Institute of Bankers in Pakistan). **Career:** Served as Manager for 11 years and Zonal Head for 5 years with United Bank Limited in Pakistan, Before his first overseas posting as Country Manager, UBL, Doha in 1981; Transferred to Abu Dhabi (UAE) as General Manager in 1983; Designated to Director and General Manager of Commercial Bank of Oman Ltd. (SAO), Muscat, Sultanate of Oman, a Joint venture of United Bank Limited, with local investors (since Nov. 1986); In recognition to his services, elevated as Senior Executive and Vice President UBL (Pakistan) in 1988. Attended seminars on various subjects of banking organized by Financial Institutions in UAE and London. **Sports:** Cricket, football. **Hobby:** Reading professional, historical and general knowlege books. **Medal:** Awarded Gold Medal by United Bank Limited on completion of his 25 years service. **Credit Card:** American Express. **Prof. Addr.:** P.O.Box 4696 Ruwi, Tel.: 793220-21, Muscat. Sultanate of Oman. **Priv. Addr.:** 15/C Winsir Park, Inchhra, Tel.: 419651, Lahore, Pakistan.

QUTHAMY (Sarah Bassous, al, Mrs.), Saudi journalist. **Born** in 1952 in Mecca, Saudi Arabia. **Dipl.:** Secondary School Certificate. **Career:** Journalist; Editor of Women's page at Okaz Daily newspaper; administrative official at Women's College, King Abdulaziz University. Member of Jeddah Women's Charity Society. **Address:** Jeddah, Saudi Arabia.

QUTUB (Abdul Aziz M.S.), Saudi academic. **Born** in 1950 in Mecca, Saudi Arabia. **Dipl.:** B.Sc., Ph.D. (Physics). **Career:** Demonstrator, King Abdulaziz University (1973-74); Vice Chairman, Physics Department (1980); Chairman (1980-82); Physics Department, Umm Al Qura University; Assistant Professor Physics Department in Said University. **Member:** Institute of Physics, Association of Muslim Scientists and Engineers; Council, Faculty of Education, Umm al-Qura University. **Prof. Addr.:** al-Aziziah, Tel.: 5564770 Ext. 219, Mecca. **Priv. Addr.:** Tel.: 5562738, Mecca, Saudi Arabia.

QUTUB (Ahmad Hassan), Saudi civil servant. **Born** in 1944 in Mecca, Saudi Arabia. **Dipl.:** B.Sc. 1970. **Career:** former Director of the Standards and Metrology Department, Ministry of Commerce and Industry (1970-72); Director General, Saudi Arabian Standards Organization (SASO); member of the Executive Bureau of the Arab Organization for Standards and Metrology (ASMO) of the Arab League; Saudi Arabia's delegate to the General Committee of ASMO; member of the Development Committee (DEVCO) of the International organization for Standardization (ISO), of the American Dairy Science Association (ADSA), of the Oklahoma State Alumni Association; participated in the committees concerned with the formulation of SASO administrative and financial regulations and its organizational structure, some committees concerned with revising the financial and administrative regulations of ASMO, and the preparatory committee for the first Arab Standards Conference. **Publications:** Standardization as Related to Building Materials, with an Analytical Assessment of Standardization in Saudi Arabia; A Guide for the Preparation of Saudi Standards;

A Guide for the Drafting and Editing of Saudi Standards; Standardization. **Hobbies:** reading, photography, music. **Priv. Addr.:** Tel.: 4029975, Riyadh, Saudi Arabia.

QUTUB (Dawud, Yacub), Jordanian executive. **Born** in 1932 in Hebron. **Son** of Yacub Qutub. **Married** in 1959, 5 sons. **Dipl.:** M.A. **Career:** Ministry of Foreign Affairs Jordan, Consul General in Baghdad, Iraq (1959-62); Executive Secretary, Ministry of Finance, Kuwait (1962-65); Kuwait Shipping Company (1965-78); Administration Manager, Kuwait Shipping Co. (1965-70); Deputy General Manager (1970-78); al-Ghanim and al-Qutub Shipping Co. (1978-); Group General Manager (1978-81); Managing Director (1981-1990). Director, Arab Jordan Investment Bank, Jordan. **Hobbies:** Sports and classical music. **Addr.:** Amman, Jordan.

R

RAAFAT (Hani, Mohamad Nessim), Egyptian Safety Specialist. **Born** in 1945, Cairo, Egypt. **Educ.:** Ain Shams University, Cairo; Kuwait University and Aston University, U.K. **Dipl.:** BSc., MSc., Ph.D., CEng., FIMechE, FIOSH, RSP. **Career:** Lecturer Institute of Technology, Kuwait; Assistant Director, Health and Safety Unit, Aston University, UK., Safety Consultant to ILO and Several National and Multi-national Organisations. **Publ.:** Over 40 Scientific Publications on risk assessment and risk management including 4 Books. **Hobbies:** Swimming, reading and snooker. **Prof. Addr.:** Health and Safety Unit, Mech. and Elec. Eng. Dept., Aston University, Birmingham B4 7ET, U.K.

RAAFAT (Mohamad Fuad), Egyptian civil servant. **Born** in September 1960 in Cairo. **Educ.:** Higher School of Commerce. **Career:** Deputy General Manager (commercial section) Misrair, S.A.E. (now Egyptair), former Egyptian Representative at the International Air Transport Association in the Middle East. **Member:** of Gezira Sporting Club. **Addr.:** 8, Fawzi al-Moteï, Tel.: 62686, Cairo, Egypt.

RAAFAT (Sherif Hassan, Waheed), Egyptian executive. **Born** in 1946 in Alexandria, Egypt. **Son** of Waheed Raafat. **Married** in 1972, 1 daughter. **Educ.:** University of Cairo; McGill University, Montreal. **Dipl.:** B.Sc. Chemical Engineering (1970); M.B.A. (1973). **Career:** Management Consultant, Peat, Marwick & Partners, Canada (1973-74); Investment Banker, Kidder, Peabody International Ltd. (1974-77); Manager, Corporate Finance, Abu Dhabi Investment Co. (1977-79); Executive Director, Kidder, Peabody International Ltd., London (1980-). **Member:** Arab Bankers Association; **Hobbies:** Reading, tennis, swimming and Squash. **Addr.:** 39 Church Vale, Tel.: 883.2175, London N2, UK.

RABAH (Sadok), Tunisian Politician. **Born** on July 9, 1948 in Metouia. **Married.** three children. **Educ.:** Baccalaureate in Mathematics, Engineers' School, Versailles, France (1967-69); Degree in Engineering, Ecole Polytechnique, Paris (1971); Degree in Engineering Statistics and Economics, Ecole Nationale de la Statistique de l'Administration Economique. Paris (1973); Director of Studies, National Engineers' School of Tunis (1973-74); In charge of Studies and Financing, Tunisian Electricity and Gas Co. (1975-80); President Director General, Sea-Gas Studies Co. (1981); Director of Hydrocarbons Exploration and Production, Ministry of Economy (1983); Director General of Energy, Ministry of Economy (1984-87); Director General, Tunisian Oil Company (1987-88); Minister of Energy and Mines (1988-89); Minister of Communications (1989-91); Minister of National Economy (1991-Jan. 1995); Minister of Social Affairs (Jan. 1995- June 1996): Minister of Transportation (June 1996-Oct.1997); Minister of Agriculture (Oct. 1997-to date). **Address:** Ministry of Agriculture, 30 rue Alain Savary, 1002 Tunis, Tunisia.

RABBAT (Joseph), Chartered accountant and general manager of comptoir egyptien de représentations, Alexandria dist. **Born** on August 25, 1921 at Tantah city (Lower Egypt). **Married** to Miss Behna Claudine in 1949, 5 children: four daughters and one son. **Educ.:** St. Louis College, Tantah city (primary and secondary education); Faculty of Commerce, Cairo University; Higher French Studies. **Dipl.:** B. Com. (1958); Institute of Bankers (1959); Diploma from Alliance Française, Paris (1957); Graduated from National Institute of Top Management, Cairo. **Career:** Accountant, National Bank of Egypt. Aswan Branch (1956-57); Tantah Branch (1957-58); Mousky District Branch (1958-59); Soliman Pasha Branch (1959-61); Manager, Luxor Branch, National Bank of Egypt (1961-63); Port Said Branch (1963-65); Toussoum street Branch, Alexandria (1965-71); Helwan suburb Branch (1973); Director, Savings Certificates Division, National Bank of Egypt-Head office, Cairo (1973); now Chartered accountant and General Manager of Comptoir Egyptien de Représentations, Alexandria. **Dist.:** Advisor to Greek Catholic church, Ibrahimiyeh District, Alexandria and Patriarcial councillor, President of Greek Catholic Benevolent Society, Alexandria. **Hobbies:** Reading and swimming. **Prof. Addr.:** Comptoir Egyptien de Représentations, Tel.: 5866380- 2, Miss May Street, San Stefano, Alexandria. **Priv. Addr.:** 16, Sidi Gaber Street, Sporting District, Tel.: 841403, Alexandria, Egypt.

RABBAT (Wagdi, Yusuf), Egyptian executive. **Born** in 1946 in Tanta, Egypt. **Son** of Youssef Rabbat. **Educ.:** Cairo University; American University, Cairo. **Dipl.:** B.Sc. (1968); M.Sc. (1974). **Career:** Assistant Teacher, American University of Cairo (1970-74); Seismologist, Geophysical International Co. Inc. Cairo (1974-76); Citibank, Cairo (1975-79); Manager, Citicorp Investment Bank Ltd., London (Since 1979). Vice President, covering the Middle East Region out of London. **Publ.:** Various papers based on M.Sc. thesis on "Optical Centers in Lead Alkaline Glass". **Member:** Heliopolis Sporting Club, Cairo;

RAC, London. **Hobbies:** Swimming and Chess. **Addr.:** 335 Strand, Tel.: 438Æ1205, Telex: 299831, London WC2R 1LS, UK.

RABBAT (Walid B.), Syrian Businessman. **Born** in 1933 in Damascus, Syria. **Married** three children and four grand children. **Educ.:** B.Sc. in Petroleum Engineering. **Career:** Director, Tank Farms and pipeline at Syrian Petroleum Co. (1961-73); Chairman and General Director of SADCOP (1974-75); Chairman and General Director, Walid Rabbat & Co; (1977-now); Manager, SGS Redwood Services Syria (1978-now). **Publ.:** "Petroleum Products losses" (1962); "Petroleum Tanks Calibration" (1970). **Sports:** Swimming and Table Tennis. **Hobbies:** bridge and Reading. **Prof.Addr.:** P.O.Box 4398 Damascus, Syria. Tel.: 961 11 223 7570 Fax: 963 11 222 8565, E-mail petroco@net.sy. **Priv.Addr.:** Malki-A.M. Riad Street, Ghabra & Hammami Bldg., 1st floor, Tel.: 963 11 3738565, Damascus, Syria.

RABIA (Ali, Qassim), Bahraini Businessman. **Born** in 1937 in Muharaq, State of Bahrain. **Son** of Qassim Mohammed Rabia (fisherman) **and** Mrs. Hissa Al-Banky. **Married** first to: Haya Rabia, four children: Thaer, Hurriya, Nassir and Ghada; second to: Khayria Rabia, three children: Rose, Sonya and Jassim. **Educ.:** Bahrain Secondary School; Bapco School; Balham & Tooting College, U.K. **Career:** Trainee Teacher in Bapco; Employee in the Co-operative Compensation Society; General Manager, Car and General Insurance Company; Member in the first Parliament in Bahrain; General Manager, The Vehicles Insurance Fund. **Other Info:** Advocate of Democracy and Human Rights. **Member:** Toastmasters Club. **Hobbies:** Reading and Writing articles about Democracy & Human Rights. **Sports:** Football. **Credit Card:** Visa Card. **Priv. Addr.:** House No. 27, Road No. 201, Muharaq - 202, Tel.: 325273, Bahrain.

RABIAH (Abdul Aziz Ibn Abdul Rahman Ibn Ali, al), Saudi academic. **Born** in 1942 at Heraimla, Central Region, Saudi Arabia. **Dipl.:** Ph.D. (Principles of Islamic Law). **Career:** Teacher in Religious Institutes; Head of Editorial Section, High Institute of Justice; Teacher, Faculty of Arabic Language; Associate Professor, Imam Muhamad Ibn Saud Islamic University, Faculty of Sharia (Islamic Law), the Conference for Combating Crime, held by the Ministry of Interior and the Conference for Celebrating the End of the 14th Higra Century. **Publications:** radio and T.V. programmes, lectures and debates: several books: Suar min Samahat al-Islam; Adillat al tashri'e al-Mukhtalaf fi al-ihtijaj biha; al-Sabab Ind al-Ussoulien; Qadiy'at al-Ulloohiyah wal Nubow'ah ind al-Muslimeen; a regular contributer to al-Daw'ah al-Shari'yah, al-Bohooth al-Ilmiyah, al-Haras al-Watani and al-Jundi al-Muslim, magazines. **Hobbies:** reading, research, writing, current affairs. **Prof. Addr.:** Faculty of Shari'a (Islamic Law), Tel.: 4039386, Riyadh. **Priv. Addr.:** Tel.: 4350883, 4352279, Riyadh, Saudi Arabia.

RABIAH (Othman, Abdul Aziz, al), Saudi official. **Born** in 1940 in al-Mujamma'ah, Saudi Arabia. **Married,** 3 sons, 1 daughter. **Educ.:** University of Heidelberg, West Germany. **Dipl.:** M.B. **Career:** General Practitioner, Central Hospital of Riyadh (1971-79), Health Affairs Director, Qaseem Administration of Health Affairs (1979-82); Director of Medical Licences, Ministry of Health, Riyadh (1982-83), Director of Medical Supply (1983-84); Under Secretary of Planning and Research, Ministry of Health (1984-). **Prof. Addr.:** P.O.Box 4512, Riyadh 11412, Saudi Arabia.

RABIE (Abdul Aziz Mohamad Ali, al), Saudi civil servant. **Born** in 1926. **Dipl.:** B.A. (Arts and Education). **Career:** Teacher, Inspector; Chairman of Board of Co-operative Society for Government Employees, Al Ansor Sporting Club, Medina Literary Club; Chief of Regional Scouts Bureau; General Supervisor of Boy Scout Camps in the Service of Pilgrims; member of Okaz Literary Festival Preparatory Committee; attended the First Conference of Saudi Men of Letters, King Abdulaziz University, the Fifth Seminar Conference on Social Studies (Amman, Jordan), Arab Teachers Conference (Alexandria, Egypt), Conference of the Arab Ministers of Education and Planning (Libya), UNESCO Conference (Paris, 1974), Okaz Festivals Preparatory Conference (Riyadh), 12th Arab Scout Conference (Tunis); now Director, Education Directorate, Medina. **Publ.:** Virtuous Behaviour in the Light of Islam, detailed commentary on collection of Peotry "A Man and His Destiny"; several articles. **Awards:** Medal of a Pioneer of Letters, awarded by King Abdulaziz University, Jeddah. **Sports:** Mountain climbing. **Prof. Addr.:** Medina, Saudi Arabia.

RACHID (Ibrahim), Egyptian lawyer and director of companies. **Married** to Miss Khadiga Ismaïl Pasha Sidqi. **Educ.:** Faculty of Law, Cairo University. **Dipl.:** Bachelor of Law. **Career:** Formerly Senator; Director of companies. **Member:** Sulaiman Pasha Club, Touring Club of Egypt. **Addr.:** 17, Maahad as-Swissry Street, Zamalek, Tel.: 805000, Cairo. **Summer Residence:** 443, Army Road Palace Station, Ramleh, Tel.: 61094, Alexandria, Egypt.

RACHID (Mohamad Kamel, al), Egyptian former magistrate. **Born** in Egypt. **Educ.:** Secondary and Higher. **Dipl.:** Bachelor of Law. **Career:** Former Counsellor Appeal Court. **Member:** Egyptian Society of International Law, Muslem Charity Society, Lawyer's Association. **Addr.:** 7, al-Messaha Square, Orman. Giza, Tel.: 806730, Cairo, Egypt.

RADAIDA (Khalid, Mohamad), Jordanian administrator. **Born** in 1940 in Jordan. **Married,** 6 sons, 1 daughter. **Educ.:** Damascus University, Syria. **Dipl.:** Blitt, Diplomas in Education, Management and Planning, UNESCO. **Career:** Teacher (1961-65); Head of Planning and Teacher, Ministry of Education (1966-74); General Manager, Social

Affairs Department, Ministry of Work and Social Affairs (1976-80); Vice Dean of General Management Institute; Member of University Council; Deputy Manager of Administrative Office (1980-). **Publ.:** "International Geography" (1965), "Arab Geography", "Making and Executing Educational Plans in Jordan" (1973). **Hobbies:** travelling, reading. **Prof. Addr.:** P.O.Box 6470, Amman, Jordan.

RADAIN (Abdulaziz Abdul Malik), Saudi academic. **Born** in 1945 at Taif, Saudi Arabia. **Dipl.:** Ph.D. (Geochemistry), Diploma (Undermining Mapping). **Career:** Geologist, Ministry of Petroleum and Mineral Resources (1968-73); Lecturer, King Abdulaziz University (1973-75); Assistant Professor since 1978; Vice-Dean, Faculty of Earth Science; and Supervisor, University Campus Administration, King Abdulaziz University; Associate Professor (1984); Dean, Faculty of Earth Sciences; has attended many international conferences pertinent to formation of granitic rocks. **Publications:** scientific articles. **Hobbies:** squash, sports. **Addr.Prof.:** Faculty of Earth Science, King Abdulaziz University, P.O.Box 1744, Jeddah 21441, Tel.: 6877904, Saudi Arabia. **Priv. Addr.:** Tel.: 6952095, Jeddah, Saudi Arabia.

RADDADY (Mohamad M., al), Saudi academic. **Born** in 1938 in Medina, Saudi Arabia. **Dipl.:** Ph.D. (Economics). **Career:** Teacher, commercial intermediate schools (1962-65); Assistant Professor, Department of Economics, Faculty of Economics and Administration, King Abdulaziz University (1978); Chairman, Department of Economics; Assistant Professor and Dean, Deanship of External Studies, King Abdulaziz University; Chartered Consultant; Certified Economic Consultant; fellow of the Arab Academy for Banking and Financial Sciences. **Member:** Royal Economic Society, Atlantic Economic Society; attends the conferences of these societies; member, Islamic Economic conference. **Publication:** Investment Rationalization, published by the Centre for Research and Development, King Abdulaziz University. **Recent Publications:** A Guide to GATT and World Trade Organization, Trade in Services, Globalization of Political Economy. **Other Publications:** Maritime Economics. International Financial Markets. **Prof. Addr.:** Dr. Al-Raddady Economic Strategy Consultants, Global Trade & International Financial Markets, P.O.Box 9031 Jeddah 21413, Tel.: 6522866, Fax 6522855, Saudi Arabia.

RADHI (Abdallah, al), United Arab Emirates businessman. **Born** in 1943 in Bahrain. **Married,** two children. **Educ.:** B.A. in Accounting, Cairo University, Egypt. **Career:** Economic Research in Bahrain Chamber of Commerce and Editor of its magazine (1970-71); Deputy Director General, Abu Dhabi Chamber of Commerce and Industry (1972); owner of al-Radhi Trading Company; owner of al-Khalij Publishing and Printing House. **Addr.:** P.O.B. 2375, Abu Dhabi, United Arab Emirates.

RADHI (Abdelouahed), Moroccan Politician. **Born** in 1935 at Sale, Morocco, **Educ.:** Higher Education, Sorbonne, Paris. **Career:** Professor, Faculty of Letters, University Mohamed V; Appointed Head of Philosophy Department, then Searcher Professor at Institut Universitaire de recherche scientifique. Former Member of Administrative Commission of Union Nationale des Etudes Marocaines, Former Secretary of Syndicat National de L'enseignement Supérieur and former Member of National Administrative Commission of Union Nationale des Forces Populaires (UNFD). Elected Member of Central Committee of Union Socialiste des Forces Populaires (USEP) in 1975. Elected Deputy of Sidi Slimane in 1963 presided the Public Service Commission on agrarian reform; reelected in 1977. in 1983 appointed Minister in charge of Cooperation of Mohamed Karim Lamrani Cabinet, Appointed by King Hassan II as Secretary General of Union Arab Africaine in September 1984. In June 1993 elected Deputy at the Parliament; in October 1993 Elected Vice President of the Chamber of Representatives and in 1997 reelected Deputy district of Sidi Yahya-Koidja and Elected Speaker of Parliament. **Medals:** Medal of Throne (Knight Honour) (11 July 1993). **Addr.:** Chamber of Representatives, Rabat, Morocco.

RADI (Essam Radi Abdel Hamid, H.E.), Egyptian engineer and politician. **Born** on September 7, 1925 in Dakahlia, Egypt. **Married,** two sons. **Educ.:** Cairo University, Egypt; Studies in Military Civil Engineering (1951-52). **Dipl.:** B.Sc. in Civil Engineering (June 1951); Diploma in Irrigation & Hydraulics (1966). **Career:** Engineer, Ministry of Irrigation (1951); Engineer, Corp. of Engineers, Ministry of Defence (1951-52); Engineer in Dakahlia Governorate, Ministry of Irrigation (1953-57); Engineer, Egyptian Irrigation Inspectorate, Sudan (1957-60); Sub-Director of Work, Basin Irrigation Projects in Upper Egypt (1960-61); Sub-Director of Work, Qualibia & Ismailia Governorates (1961-63); Senior Engineer, Fayoum Governorate (1963-64); Director of Work & Deputy Inspector, Hydrology Depart., Nile Control Inspectorate (1964-72); Deputy chairman, Water Resources Development Organization in Lybia (1972-76); Director General, Delta Barrage, Irrigation Directorate (1976-79); Under Secretary of State for Projects and Horizontal Expansion (1979-80); Governor for Damietta Governorate (May 1980- July 1984); Former, **Minister** of Public Works and Water Resources. **Important Fields of Work:** Planning, Design and Execution of Irrigation Network & Irrigation Structures; Water Control and Distribution; Operation & Maintenance of irrigation Network & Structures; Studies & Researches for Nile Water Control & Nile Water Development; Upper Nile Projects Studies; Surface & Undergound Hydrology Studies; Irrigation & Drainage Projects for Basin Irrigation Conversion and Horizontal Expansion; Design and Execution of Dams. **Membership of Organizations:** Member of Egyptian Engineering syndicate; Member of Egyptian Society of Irrigation Engineers; Chairman, Steering Committee for High Aswan Dam; Chairman Egyptian comittee for Water Resources, Irrigation & Drainage, Hydrology and Dams, Consultant Engineer, Engineering syndicate; Participated in Many Studies and researches in the fields of Water Resources Development, Upper Nile Projects, Nile Control, Dams and Horizontal Expansion Projects; Participated in many national Conferences; Participated in Seminars & Conferences abroad, in Italy, Lybia and Sudan. **Addr.:** Cairo, Egypt.

RADWA (Abdul Halim Abdul Rahim), Saudi academic. **Born** in 1939 in Mecca, Saudi Arabia. **Dipl.:** B.A. (Art), Rome. **Career:** Teacher of drawing (Art Education); Director of Fine Arts Centre, Jeddah; Chairman, Saudi Arabian Art and Cultural Society; artistic activities locally and abroad; member of the Board, the Saudi Arabian Society; Chairman, Arab Artists Society, Madrid; member, International Arbitration Committee, Spain. **Awards:** 37 material and ideal prizes; First Prize in contest between Italian and Foreign artist, 1963; Second Prize, Spanish Pinali, Lake Polzina Context, Italy. **Hobbies:** drawing, sports, travel. **Prof. Addr.:** Saudi Arabian Society, P.O.Box 941, Tel.: 6675417, Jeddah. **Priv. Addr.:** Tel.: 6821642, Jeddah, Saudi Arabia.

RADWAN (Abdel Aziz, Mohamad), Egyptian businessman. **Born** in 1941 in Egypt. **Educ.:** Oxford University, UK; London University, UK. **Dipl.:** M.A. in Politics, Philosophy and Economics, M.Sc. in Economics. **Career:** Director of Sceptre Resources (1976-), Scarboro Resources (1978-); Consultant of Scimitar Oil SA (1980-). **Hobbies:** classical music, horse racing, hunting. **Member:** Gezira Sporting Club, Automobile Club. **Prof. Addr.:** 149 Old Park Lane, London WI, UK.

RADWAN (Abdel Hamid), Egyptian politician. **Born** in 1941 in Suhag, Upper Egypt. **Educ.:** Faculty of Law. **Career:** Member, People's Assembly (since 1971); headed Parliamentary Group for Suhag (since 1974); former Assistant Secretary General, National Democratic Party; Minister of State for Culture (1981); Minister of People's Assembly and Shoura Council Affairs (1985). **Addr.:** Majlis al-Sha'ab, Cairo, Egypt.

RADWAN (Abdul Wahab, Mohamad, al), UAE broadcasting official. **Born** in 1952 in Sharjah, United Arab Emirates. **Married**, two sons, 4 daughters. **Educ.:** Cairo University, Egypt. **Dipl.:** B.A. in Broadcasting. **Career:** Head of Internal Information Department, Ministry of Information (1977), Manager of Conferences and Public Relations (1979), Manager of Cultural Department (1981); Member of UAE Delegation to UNESCO (1983); Executive Member for Cultural Affairs, UAE Writers Union (1984); Head of Theatre Development Committee (1988); Director General UAE Radio Broadcasting Abu Dhabi (1988- till now). **Hobby:** Reading. **Prof. Addr.:** Emirates Broadcasting Corporation, Radio Station of the UAE, P.O.Box 63, Tel.: 451111, Abu Dhabi, United Arab Emirates.

RADWAN (Ibrahim, Hussain), Egyptian judge. **Born** in 1923 in Dokki, Cairo, Egypt. **Married**, 2 children. **Educ.:** Cairo University, Egypt. **Dipl.:** LL.B. **Career:** Prosecutor and Judge (1953-); Vice President of Cairo Court of Cassation. **Member:** Shams Sporting Club. **Addr.:** 108 Abdel Aziz Fahmy Street, Heliopolis, Cairo, Egypt.

RADWAN (Samir, Mohamad), Egyptian economist. **Born** in 1942 in Egypt. **Married**, 1 son, 1 daughter. **Educ.:** Cairo University, Egypt; University of London, UK. **Dipl.:** B.Sc. in Economics, M.Sc. in Economic Development, Ph.D. in Economics. **Career:** Assistant Lecturer, Faculty of Economics, Cairo University (1963-65); Research Officer at the Institute of National Planning, Cairo and the Aswan National Planning Project, Aswan and Cairo (1963-64); Consultant, ILO, Exploratory Employment Policy Mission to Pakistan (1975); Consultant, ILO Mission to Iran (1974-75); Research Officer, Oxford University, Institute of Economics and Statistics and Senior Associate Member of St. Antony's College, Oxford (1972-76); Senior Economist, International Labour Organisation, Geneva (1976-). **Publ.:** "Capital Formation in Egyptian Industry and Agriculture 1882-1967" (1974), "The Industrialisation of Egypt" (1976) co-author with Robert Mabro, "Egypt and an Open-Door Foreign Investment Policy" (1975), "Agrarian Systems and Rural Development in the Third World" co-editor (1979), "The Anatomy of Rural Poverty" co-author (1977) in English (1985), "Agrarian Reform and Rural Poverty in Egypt" (1977), "Employment Opportunities and Equity in Egypt: a Labour Market Approach" co-author (1982), "Agrarian Policies and Rural Poverty in Africa", co-editor (1983), as well as various articles in international journals. **Hobbies:** history, rowing, Arabic literature. **Addr.:** 31A Chemin des Mollies, 1293 Bellevue, Geneva, Switzerland.

RADWAN (Yusuf Ibrahim, Sheikh), Saudi bank executive. **Born** in 1936 in Jeddah, Saudi Arabia. **Dipl.:** Secondary School Certificate, Egypt; Diploma in Commerce, Diploma in Shipping, London School of Foreign Trade, London. **Career:** Bank Officer, Saudi American Bank, Jeddah (1960-75); General Manager, Saudi American Bank, Jeddah (1975-80); former President Independent Insurance Co. and Saudi Arabia Ltd., Jeddah; former Chairman, Saudi British Bank, Riyadh. **Hobby:** sport. **Address:** Jeddah, Saudi Arabia.

RAFAIAH (Yassine), Syrian writer and poet. **Born** in Syria. **Married** in 1964 to Miss Amal Jarrah (Poet and Writer), 2 children: Bassam and Lina. **Educ.:** Secondary and Higher. **Career:** Poet and Writer. **Publ.:** Author of several poems and articles. **Addr.:** Damascus, Syria.

RAFEI (Abdurrahman, al), Egyptian lawyer and statesman. **Born** in Egypt. **Educ.:** Secondary and Higher Studies. **Dipl.:** Bachelor of Laws. **Career:** Lawyer at the Appeal Court, Former President, Former Minister, Former Senator. **Addr.:** 5, Amine ar-Rafeï Street, Dokki, Tel.: 806246, Cairo, Egypt.

RAHAIMI (Mohamad Asad), Saudi executive. **Born** in 1943 at Yanbu, Saudi Arabia. **Dipl.:** M.Sc. (Geology). **Career:** Manager, Geology Department, Petromin; Assistant General Manager, Oil and Gas Division; General Manager, Oil and Gas Division, Petromin; member of the Board, Yanbu Oil Refinery; Vice Chairman of the Board, Saudi- Bahraini- Kuwaiti Refinery for Heavy Oil, Bahrain. **Hobbies:** reading, tennis, swimming. **Prof. Addr.:** Petromin, P.O.Box 67, Dhahran Airport. Tel.: 8649212, Dhahran. **Priv. Addr.:** Tel.: 8948905, Dhahran, Saudi Arabia.

RAHAL (Abdullatif), Algerian statesman. **Born** in 1922 in Algiers. **Educ.:** Teacher's Training College (Bouzarea), University of Bordeaux (France). **Career:** Teacher of Mathematics, Marnia, Mostoganem; successively teacher, Vice-Principal, then supervisor at Lycée d'Arzrou, Morocco (1954-62); Director of Cabinet of Minister of General Affairs (June-August 1962); Director of Cabinet of President Ahmad Ben Bella (September 1962- January 1963); Ambassador of France (1963); Secretary General, Foreign Office (July 1965- March 1971); Permanent Representative of Algeria to the United Nations (March 1971- June 1977), Minister of Higher Education and Scientific Research (April 1977- March 1979); Ambassador, Permanent Delegate to UNESCO (since September 1979). **Member** of the Executive Board of UNESCO. **Addr.:** Algerian Delegation, 1 Rue Miollis, Tel.: 577.16.10, 75015 Paris, France.

RAHALI (Rahal, Dr.), Moroccan physician. **Born** on 29 December 1934 at Bekrit. **Son** of Maulay Ahmad (man of letters) **and** Ariba Lache. **Married** on 29 December 1961 to Miss Ferre, 1 daughter: Sonia (9.11.63). **Educ.:** Secondary in Meknes; superior at Faculty of Medicine (Bordeaux). **Dipl.:** M.D. (1962), specialisation surgey. **Career:** Chief Medical Officer of Health and Surgery, Provincial Hospital and Medical Centre, Meknes; Former President, Meknes Municipal Council; President, Communal Council Ain Leuh; member, Provincial Council of Meknes; President, Moroccan Red Crescent Committee in Meknes; Minister of Health (1977-83). **Dec.:** Knight, Order of the Throne; Comm., Palmes Académiques; Officer, Mérite National Français; OMS Medal. **Prof. Addr.:** 22, Place Dr. Guignet, Tel.: 20262, Meknes. **Priv. Addr.:** 3 Rue Sultan Molud Abdellah, Tel.: 21533, Meknes, Morocco.

RAHALI (Sidi, Muhammad), Moroccan engineer. **Born** in 1924 in Casablanca. **Married**, 3 sons, 3 daughters. **Educ.:** Professional School of Casablanca, Morocco; Technical School of Berliet, France. **Career:** Constructor and builder of coach bodies since 1942; Director Import and General Manager of Carrosserie Rahali, Mecanical Assemblage Factory; Former Vice President of the Municipality Council of the City of Casablanca; former vice President of the Chamber of Commerce and Industry of Casablanca. **Decor.:** Chevalier de l'Ordre du Trone du Maroc (1968). **Hobby:** boxing. **President:** Moroccan Union of Professional Boxing. **Addr.:** Route des Zenatas, Côtière 111 Km. 11200, Ain Sebaa, 21600, Morocco.

RAHAMA (Mubarak, Othman), Sudanese diplomat. **Born** in 1929 in Omdurman, Sudan. **Married. Educ.:** Warminster, UK (Company Command Course); Camberley Staff College. **Career:** Joined Armed Forces; Commissioned in Camel Corps (1952), Major (1958), Director of Military Training (1969), Military Attaché, Embassy of Sudan to USSR, Poland, German Democratic Republic, Hungary and Bulgaria (1968-69); Commanding Officer of Southern Command for the Southerm Region (1970); Resident Ambassador to Nigeria, non-resident Ambassador to Ghana and Cameroon (1971-76); Resident Ambassador to Peking, non-resident Ambassador to Democratic People's Republic of Korea (1976). **Prof. Addr.:** Ministry of Foreign Affairs, Khartoum, Sudan.

RAHMAH (Ahmad Mirza, al), United Arab Emirates executive. **Born** in 1946 in Dubai, United Arab Emirates. **Son** of Mizra al-Rahmah. **Married**, one daughter. **Educ.:** B.Sc. in Economics and Political Science, Baghdad University, Iraq (1969). **Career:** Deputy Director of Housing and Purchasing Department (1971); Director of Minerals Department, Ministry of Petroleum (1972); Director of the Minister's Office, Ministry of Petroleum and Mineral Resources (1974). **Sports:** Swimming, football. **Hobbies:** Classical poetry, hunting. **Addr.:** Ministry of Petroleum and Mineral Resources, P.O.B. 59, Tel.: 361133, Telex: 22544 MPMR EM, Abu Dhabi, United Arab Emirates.

RAI (Pierre, H.E. Mgr.), Syrian patriarchal assistant. **Born** in 1922 in Aleppo. **Educ.:** St. Sauveur Monastery, Sainte Anne Seminary (Jerusalem), University of Rome (Italy). **Dipl.:** Doctorate in Ecclesiastical Laws. **Career:** Professor, Sainte Anne Seminary: Secretary of late Maximos IV (Patriarch); Superior of the Basilian Congregation (1965-68); Sacred Archbishop, Partriarchal Assistant (September 13, 1968). **Winter Resid.:** Melkite Greek-Catholic Patriarchate in Damascus, P.O.Box 22249, Bab Sharqi, Tel.: 223136 and 223129, Syria. **In Cairo** Daher Street. **In Alexandria** Jawhar Street, Tel.: 26422. **Summer Resid.:** Aïn Traz, Via Rechmaya, Tel.: 551583, Lebanon.

RAINI (Ahmad Saleh, al), Yemeni politician. **Born** in 1928 in Amran, Yemen Arab Republic. **Son** of Saleh Hassan al-Raini. **Married**, 9 children: Mohamad (1951), Ahmad (1952), Anisa (1956), Samir (1958), Abdul Fattah (1959), Najla (1961), Jamal (1963), Ibtisam (1966) and Arwa (1968). **Educ.:** Sanaa Secondary School (1946).

Dipl.: Graduate of Broadcasting Institute, Cairo (1960-61); Institute of Administration, Sanaa (1968). **Career:** Teacher (1946); Principal, Zubaid Schools (1947); Secretary, Ministry of Communications. (1949-62); Radio Broadcaster; Director-General, Political Affairs; Controller-General of Programmes (1949-62); Director-General of Broadcasting (1966); Director-General of Communications (1967); Director General of Broadcasting (1968); Head, Broadcasting Service (1968); Under-Secretary, Ministry of Information (1974); Deputy Minister of Information (with rank of Minister) (1975-79); Minister of social Affairs, Labour and Youth (March 1979-84); appointed Minister of State for Council Ministers Affairs (1986-90). **Awards:** Order to Taqdir (Esteem) from President Nasser, Egypt (1963); Medal of the Republic 4th Class. **Hobbies:** Classical and Modern Arabic literature. **Addr.:** Sanaa, Republic of Yemen.

RAJAB (Abdulaziz Abdallah), Saudi businessman. **Born** in 1926 in Jeddah, Saudi Arabia. **Dipl.:** Technical Diploma, special courses in Business Administration in Europe and U.S.A. **Career:** Leading businessman; President, Rajab and Silsilah Establishments. **Hobbies:** reading, sports, **Prof. Addr.:** Palestine Road, P.O.Box 203, Tel.: 6435404, Jeddah; and Tel.: 4785525, Riyadh. **Priv. Addr.:** Tel.: 6655239, Jeddah; Tel.: 402793, Riyadh, Saudi Arabia.

RAJAB (Abdulhafidh Salem), Omani politician. **Born** in 1937 in Dhofar, Oman. **Son** of Salim Rajab. **Educ.:** Mechanical Engineering in Kiev University, USSR. **Career:** Lecturer in Engineering, Kuwait Technical College; Director Government Workshop and Technical Trades School, Oman (1971); Minister of Economy, Oman (1971); Minister of Commercial and Social Affairs and Labour, Oman (1972); Acting Minister of Economy (1972); Minister of Communications and Public Works, Oman (1973); Minister of Agriculture and Fisheries (1979-1986). **Addr.:** Muscat, Oman.

RAJAB (Mohamad, Zaruk), Libyan politician. **Born** in 1940 in Benghazi, Libya. **Educ.:** University of Libya, Benghazi. **Dipl.:** B.Sc. in Economics, qualified as Chartered Accountant in UK. **Career:** Lecturer in Accountancy and Dean of the Accounting Department, University of Libya; Assistant Professor of Accountancy (1969); Head of the Audit Division; Minister of the Treasury (1972-77); Secretary for the Treasury, General People's Committee (1977); Secretary of the GPC for the Union of the Arab Maghreb (until Nov. 1992). **Prof. Addr.:** Tripoli, Libya.

RAJEL (Ishac, Ould), Mauritanian Minister of Mines and Industry. **Born** on February 12, 1941 in Boutilimit. **Diplomas:** Chief Mining Engineer. **Career:** 1969-75: Director of Mines and Geology; 1975-77: Minister of Mines and Industry; 1977-80: Director General Wharf (Harbour); 1980-83: Director General of Mauritanian Company for oil product Trading: 1984-86: Secretary General of Ministry of Mines and Industry: 1986-89: Director General of Arab Company for Mining in Inchiri; 1989-98: Director General of Mauritanian Office Geological Research. Presently Minister of Mines and Industry. **Sports Practised:** Tennis. **Associations:** Chairman of Tennis Association. **Prof. Addr.:** Tel.: 222 253083, Mauritania, and Ministry of Mines and Industry, P.O.Box 387 Nouakchott, Mauritania, **Priv. addr.:** P.O.Box 199 Nouakchott, Tel.: 222 291940, Mauritania.

RAJHI (Hamad Nasser, al), Saudi engineer. **Born** in 1948 in Mecca, Saudi Arabia. **Dipl.:** B.Sc., M.Sc. (Civil Engineering), University of California, U.S.A. **Career:** President, al-Rajehi Consulting Engineers; Member, American Society of Civil Engineers, Water Supply Improvement Association, Tan Beta Pi, U.S.A.; attended several conferences in the United States and other countries on water supply, resources and desalination. **Publications:** an article, Capacity Expansion of Desalination Plants and Storage Tanks, Water Resources Bulletin. **Hobbies:** reading, swimming, travel. **Address:** P.O.Box 7669, Tel.: 4644252, 4644494, 4649629, 46513457, Riyadh, 11472, Saudi Arabia.

RAJHI (Nasser Hamad, al), Saudi official. **Born** in 1923 at Onaizah, Saudi Arabia. **Educ.:** received general education. **Career:** Superintendent of Telecommunications Office, Council of Ministers; Deputy Chief, Council of Ministers Bureau; Chief of HRH the Crown Prince's Bureau (1964); Participant member of several Welfare and Islamic societies and organizations. **Honours:** a number of decorations awarded by foreign governments on official visits. **Hobbies:** reading, swimming. **Priv. Addr.:** Tel.: 4761124, Riyadh, Saudi Arabia.

RAJHI (Saleh Abdulaziz, al, Sheikh), Saudi banker and leading businessman. **Born** in 1929. **Educ.:** received general education. **Career:** Runs his own business of banking, general trade, contracting and real estate; member of Board of Riyadh Electricity Co., Riyadh Cement Co., Dammam Electricity Co., Gypsum Co., Saudi Cement Co., Eastern Province; member of Board, Riyadh Printing Co., Southern Cement Co.; Chairman, al-Rajhi Banking and Investment Co. **Address:** P.O.Box 28, Riyadh 11411, Saudi Arabia.

RAKBAN (Abdallah al-Ali, al), Saudi academic. **Born** in 1942 at al-Majmaa, Saudi Arabia. **Dipl.:** Ph.D. (Comparative Jurisprudence). Teacher, Religious Institutes (1965-71); Teacher, Faculty of Shari'a (Islamic Law); Assistant Professor and later Associate Professor, Imam Muhammad Ibn Saud Islamic University, Riyadh; Imam and Speaker, Nasiri'yyah Mosque, Riyadh; Associate Professor, Faculty of Shari'a, Imam Muhammad Ibn Saud Islamie University, Riyadh, **Publications:** several books and research projects on jurisprudence and Shari'a (Islamic Law). **Hobby:** reading. **Prof. Addr.:** Faculty of Shari'a,

Imam Muhammad Ibn Saud Islamic University, Tel.: 4021906, Riyadh. **Priv. Addr.:** Tel.: 4839386, Riyadh, Saudi Arabia.

RAMADAN (Abdulazim), Egyptian academic, historian. **Born** in 1925 in Giza, Egypt. **Married**, three children. **Educ.:** B.A. in Literature, Cairo University, Egypt; M.A. in Modern History; Short courses and Seminars in Management and Public Relations, Institute of Management, Cairo. **Career:** Assistant Professor of Modern History, University of Constantine, Algeria (1973); Professor of Modern History, Minufiya University (1978); Head of History Department, College of Education, Minufiya University (1981). **Publ.:** "The Development of the National Movement in Egypt" 3 volumes (1968, 1973) Cairo; "The Egyptian Army in Politics" (1977), Cairo; "The Struggle of Classes in Egypt" (1978), Cairo; "The Struggle Between the Wafd (Party) and the Throne" (1979); "The Revolutionary Thought in Egypt before the 23 July Revolution" (1981), Cairo; "The Egyptian-Israeli Confrontation in the Red Sea" (1981), Cairo; many articles in "al-Jumhuriya" daily newspaper, Cairo, in "Rose al-Yusif" publications and "al-Arab" London. Member of the Society of History, the Egyptian Writers Club, founding member of the National Progressive Unionist Party. **Hobby:** classical music. **Sport:** Walking. **Addr.:** 12 Nakhla al-Muti'i Street, Apt. 4, Heliopolis, Cairo, Egypt.

RAMADAN (Taha, Yassin), Iraqi politician. **Born** in 1938 in Mosul, Iraq. **Educ.:** Military College, Baghdad, Iraq. **Career:** Member, Revolutionary command Council (1969); Chairman of the Trade Council Organization; Commander in Chief of the Popular Army (1970); chairman of the Revolutionary Command Council, Arab Affairs Bureau; Minister of Industry and Minerals (1970); Acting Minister of Economy (1971); Acting Ministerof Planning (1974-76); Minister of Housing and Construction (1976-79); Member of the Revolutionary command Council; and member in the Regional Command, Arab Baath Socialist Party. First Deputy Prime Minister (1979-91); Vice-President (March 1991-); Deputy Prime Minister (since May 1994). **Prof. Addr.:** Karradat Mariam, Baghdad, Iraq.

RAMADANI (Ahmad Siraj), Saudi academic. **Born** in 1949 in Mekkah, Saudi Arabia. **Dipl.:** Ph.D. **Career:** Chairman, Department of Biology (1980-82), Faculty of Science, Umm al-Qura University; member, Society for General Microbiology, London, the Saudi Philatelic Society. Saudi Biological Society, American Society for Microbiology and British Mycological Society. **Hobbies:** Philately, photography, gardening. **Prof. Addr.:** Biology Department, Faculty of Science, Umm al-Qura University, Tel.: 5574644, Ext. 220, Mekkah. **Priv. Addr.:** Tel.: 5360137, Mekkah, Saudi Arabia.

RAMADY (Mohamad, al), Saudi bank executive. **Born** in 1949. **Married. Educ.:** The English School, General Cetificates of Education, Nicosia, Cyprus (1968); University of Leicester; University of Glasgow, Post-graduate Diploma in Economic Development (1973); **Dipl.:** B.A. (Econ) (1972); Ph.D. (1979). **Career:** Tutor in Economics, University of Leicester, UK (1973-78); Treasury Dealer, Citibank, Jeddah (1978-80); Head of Government Financial Institutions, Saudi American Bank, Riyadh, Saudi Arabia (1980-82); Public Sector Head (since 1982) Saudi American Bank. **Publ.:** "The Role of Turkey in Greek and Turkish Cypriot Communal Relations"; Essays on the Cyprus Conflict, New York (1976). **Member:** The Equestrian Club, Riyadh. **Addr.:** Airport Road, Adil Khashoggi Building, P.O.Box 833, Tel.: 4774770, Telex: 200195 A/B SAMBA SJ. Riyadh, Saudi Arabia.

RAMBA (Lubari), Sudanese politician. **Born** in 1936 in Yei District, Sudan. **Educ.:** American University in Beirut, Lebanon. **Career:** Teacher (1962-69); Sales Manager of Mitchell-Cotts Co. (1969-72); Regionl Director of Education (1972-73); First Speaker of the Peoples Regional Assembly, Juba (1973-75); Minister of Public Services and Administrative Reform, Southern Sudan High Executive Council (1975-78); General Manager of Ugandan Refugees Project and Returnees Affairs, Juba (1980). **Prof. Addr.:** The High Council of the Southern Region, Juba, Sudan.

RAMBO (Abdul Wahab Jalal), Saudi oculist. **Born** in 1939 in Mecca, Saudi Arabia. **Dipl.:** M.B. H.CH. (Surgery of the Eye). **Career:** Former General Practitioner; medical specialist; Chief, Medical Services, Saudi Red Crescent; provided voluntary service under the International Red Crescent in Syria; attended some Arab League conferences on sports medicine, Red Crescent conferences in Turkey and Riyadh. **Hobbies:** reading, hunting, research. **Address:** Jeddah, Saudi Arabia.

RAMYI (Ahmad, Dr.), Moroccan physician. **Born** in 1939 in Casablanca, Morocco. **Educ.:** Secondary in Casablanca; Faculty of Medicine of Montpellier (France). **Dipl.:** M.D., Doctorate in Surgery (1959). **Career:** Surgeon, Marrakech Hospital (1963-67); Assistant, Faculty of Medicine of Rabat (1969); Chief Medic, Agadir Province (1972), Minister of Public Health (April 25, 1974- March 14, 1975); Ambassador to Iraq (April 1975- December 1976); Minister of Religious Endowments and Islamic Affairs (October 10, 1977- Dec. 1983); Ambassador to Saudi Arabia (1984 to present); Member of Parliament (1977). **Dec.:** Officer, Order of the Throne. **Prof. Addr.:** Ministry of foreign Affairs, Rabat, Morocco.

RAQABANI (Said Mohamed, al), UAE politician. **Born** in Fujairah, United Arab Emirates. **Career:** Former Member of the United Arab Emirates Federal Council; Minister of Agriculture and Fisheries (1977-to present). **Prof. Addr.:** Ministry of Agriculture and Fisheries,

P.O.Box 213 Abu Dhabi, UAE, and P.O.Box 1509, Dubai, UAE.

RASHDAN (Mohamad, Salim), Jordanian academic. **Born** in 1921 in Salt, Jordan. **Married,** 3 sons, 3 daughters. **Educ.:** American University of Beirut, Lebanon. **Dipl.:** M.A. in Literature and Semitic Languages, Diploma in Administration. **Career:** Lecturer in higher educational institutions in Iraq (1949-50); Lecturer in Teachers College, Damascus, Syria (1951-53); Ministry of Education, Jordan, Supervisor; Head of Department; Editor of "Risalat al-Muallim" magazine (1973-76); Lecturer, Jordanian University (1963-); Inspector of Texts, Jordanian Television (1975-). **Publ.:** numerous translations and books published in Jordan, Syria and Lebanon (in Arabic). **Decor.:** Order of Education, Jordan; Order of Garuda, Indonesia, decoration from Qatar. **Hobbies:** table tennis, travelling, swimming. **Member:** Jordanian Writers Society, City Sporting Club. **Prof. Addr.:** P.O.Box 1755, Amman, Jordan.

RASHED (Fahed Mohammed, Al, Dr.), Kuwaiti Chairman, Arab African International Bank. **Born** on 7 March 1946 in Kuwait. **Educ.:** Claremont Graduate School, California- U.S.A., Faculty of Commerce, Ein Shams University 1968. **Dipl.:** P.H.D. Business Administration (Finance) 1976. **Career:** 1968-1976 Teaching Assistant, Business Administration, Kuwait University; 1976-1978 Assistant Professor of Business Administration, Kuwait University; 1977-1980 Deputy Director General for Investments, Public Institute for Social Security, Kuwait; 1980-1982 Dean, College of Commerce, Economics and Political Science, Kuwait University, Kuwait; 1983-1991 Managing Director, Kuwait Investment Authority (K.I.A.); Nov. 1992 (present) Chairman of Arab African International Bank, Cairo. **Participation:** 1981 Founder: Kuwait Computer Company (Listed on Kuwait Stock Exchange since 1987); 1982 to date Member of the Board, Kuwait Foundation for the Advancement of Science; 1983-1984 Member, Committee for Revitalization of the Kuwait Economy, Chairman, Sub-Committee of Banking and Finance; 1985-1987 Member, High Committee for Modernization of Government Org., Chairman, Manpower Development Sub-Committee; 1986-1991 Member, Civil Service Commission (Ministerial Committee); 1986-1988 Chairman, Steering Committee for Study of Future Strategy of the Kuwaiti Economy; 1986 to date Chairman, Compagnie d'Investissement dans les Technologies Avancées (C I T A); 1992 (present) Member of the Board, Environmental Investment Company, London; 1994 (present) Member of the Board, Union De Banques Arabes et Françaises, Paris; 1995 (present) Member of the Board, Kuwait Computer Company, Kuwait. **Hobbies:** Sports - Music - Theatre - Arts. **Prof.Addr.:** Arab African International Bank, P.O.Box 60, Magless El-Shaab (11516), Cairo, Egypt.

RASHEED (Abdallah Abdul Rahman, al), Saudi educator. **Born** in 1926 at Gassiem, Saudi Arabia. **Dipl.:** M.A. (Comparative Jurisprudence). **Career:** Former teacher (1949); Director of Administration, the Grand Court of Riyadh (1958); Director General, Girls Education (1960); Vice President of Girls' Education; member of Illiteracy Elimination Board; has attended several meetings and conferences on Education. **Hobbies:** reading, travel. **Prof. Addr.:** The General Presidency for Girls' Education, Tel.: 4020036, Riyadh. **Priv. Addr.:** Tel.: 4768050, Riyadh, Saudi Arabia.

RASHEED (Abdul-Rahman Othman), Syrian engineer. **Born** in 1943 in Damascus, Syria. **Dipl.:** Ph.D. (Petroleum Engineering). **Career:** Petroleum Engineer, Petromin (1972-73); Petroleum Engineer, Aramco (1973-75); Chairman of Petroleum Engineering Department, King Fahad University of Petroleum and Minerals. **Hobby:** reading. **Address:** King Fahad University of Petroleum and Minerals, No.357, Tel.: 8603100 Ext. 566, Dhahran, Saudi Arabia.

RASHEED (Ali, al), Saudi civil servant. **Born** in 1929 at Wadi al-Dawasir. **Dipl.:** B.Sc. (Agriculture and Statistics). **Career:** Agricultural Unit Director; Director of Agricultural Statistics; Director of Agricultural Statistics and Economy; Director General of Public Statistics Department; member, Board of Social Insurance Organization and the Central Committee for the First Population Census; Chairman, the Executive Committee of Population Census; Saudi Arabian delegate to the Technical Committee of Arab League; member of International Statistical Institute, Association of Statisticians (U.S.A.); attended the Agricultural Conference (1963), FAO Conferences, Rome (1963), the Conferences on Agricultural Statistics, Amman, Baghdad, Cairo, Beirut and several seminars on statistics, Beirut and Kuwait. **Publications:** studies dealing with the status and problems of desert areas and ways and means of presenting them statistically. **Hobbies:** farming, travel, computers. **Addr.:** Riyadh, Saudi Arabia.

RASHEED (Khalafalla, al), Sudanese court judge. **Born** on February 15, 1930 at Magashi village, Merowe District, Northern Province (Sudan). **Son** of el-Rasheed Mohamad Ahmad (deceased) **and** Mrs., née Bakheita Ali el-O'ni. **Married** in June 1959 to Miss Zahra Ahmad Kheir in Khartoum, six children: Sarah, Muna, Omer, Hind, el-Rasheed and Samia. **Educ.:** Hantoub secondary school; University College Khartoum; University College, London, Cambridge University. **Dipl.:** LL.B. (1955); International Law (Cambridge) (1964); LL.M. (London) (1966). **Career:** Assistant (1955); District Judge, Second Grade (1956); Advocate (1956); Recalled to the Judiciary (1957); District Judge, First Grade (1960); Advocate - General (1967); President Supreme Court (1972) (title changed in 1976 to Chief Justice); Retired on pension (october 1982); Was visiting professor of Law, University of Khartoum, Led the prosecution panel at the trial of the notorious

Mercenary Steiner; sometime part-time lecturer in law, Islamic University of Omdurman, and Faculty of Law, Cairo University (Khartoum Branch); Participated in the codification of the laws of Sudan and helped revise the Code of Criminal Procedure and the Penal Code; Appointed Chairman of the Committee for the revision of laws in Sudan so as to conform to the Sharia Islamiya (May 1977). **Was Member:** Sudanese International Boundary Commission; Board of the Faculty of Law, University of Khartoum; British Institute of International Law; American Juridical Society. Was a member, International Law Commission (1982-1986); Was a member of the Arab Investment Tribunal, A Member of the International Court of Arbitration, Now retired on pension. **Awards:** el-Gomhoriya Order (1st class); el-Nilein Order (1st class); King Abdul Aziz Order (3rd class). **Clubs:** Cambridge Graduate Association; Egyptian Economic, Legislative and Statistics Committee Pres. **Addr.:** P.O.Box 1120 Tel.: 81526 No.59 Block 10 Riyadh Extension Khartoum, Sudan.

RASHEED (Mohamad Ahmad), Saudi educator. **Born** in 1943 at al-Majmaa, Saudi Arabia. **Dipl.:** B.A. (Arabic Language and Literature), Faculty of Arabic Language, Riyadh (1964); M.A. (Education), Indiana University; Ph.D. (Education), University of Oklahoma (1972). **Career:** Teacher, Religious Institutes, Riyadh (1964-65); demonstrator, Faculty of Shari'a and Islamic Studies, Mecca (1965-66) Instructor, Faculty of Education, King Saud University (1972-74); Assistant Professor (1974-79); Assistant Dean (1975-76); Dean (1976-79); Chairman, the Educational Research Centre Council; Supervisor, Diploma and Training Sessions (1972-76); Chairman, Executive Committee for the Curricula of the Training Sessions; Director of recruitment for new faculty (1976-79); Director General, the Arab Bureau of Education for the Gulf States; Associate Professor, Faculty of Education, King Saud University since 1979. **Member:** the Consultative Board of the Ministry of Higher Education; reporter for the Committee on the Equivalence of University-level Certificates; the Committee for Examinations and Interviews for Government Employees; the Administrative Council for Riyadh Schools, King Saud University Council the Supreme Council of King Saud University; Secretary for the National Society for Teaching Arabie Language, Ministry of Education; the Consultative Committee for Educational Research, ALECSO; founding member of the Union of Arab Educators; the governing board of International Institute for Educational Planning, Paris; the Trust, Union of Arab Educators; American Association for Higher Education, American Educational Research Association, Association for Supervision and Curriculum Development, American Association of School Administrators, World Council for Curriculum and Instruction, Life member of International Council on Education for Teaching, Executive Board member of International Council on Education for Teaching. First Conference on the Preparation of Teachers, KAU, Makkah (1974) the Saudi delegation to the Brussels Exhibition of Teaching Materials; has attended numerous national, regional and international symposia and conferences on Education; Minister of Education (since Aug. 1995). **Publications:** participated in compiling texts for the educational curriculum of the Teachers' Training Institutes, Ministry of Education; prepared several research papers individually and in collaboration with others, some of which were delivered in symposia and conferences in Saudi Arabia and abroad. **Hobbies:** reading. **Prof. Addr.:** Arab Bureau of Education for Gulf States, P.O.Box 3908, Tel.: 4780163, Riyadh. and Ministry of Education, P.O.Box 3734, Riyadh 11481, Saudi Arabia. **Priv. Addr.:** Tel.: 403934, Riyadh, Saudi Arabia.

RASHEED (Mohamad Saad, al), Saudi educator. **Born** in 1940 at al-Sha'ara. **Dipl.:** B.A. (Islamic Law and Arabic Language); Diplomas in English Law, Private International Law, Comparative Law (London); Ph.D. (Law), Durham University, England, 1973. **Career:** Teacher of Arabic, Al Yamama Secondary School, Riyadh; demonstrator; Lecturer, Faculty of Shari'a (Islamic Law); Head of Judicial Department, Faculty of Shari'a (Islamic Law), Umm al-Qura University; permanent member, Graduate Society, Durham University; International Delinquent Magistracy attended following conferences: International Conference of Youth Magistrates, Anti-Narcotics, International Conference, Bangkok, 1975. **Publications:** Procedure to Bring a Criminal Action in Saudi Arabia, a research paper submitted to the Islamic Jurisprudence week, Tunis (1974); Narcotics, Crime and Punishment in Saudi Arabia; Narcotics as Viewed by Islamic Law, an address to International anti-Narcotic Conference, Bangkok (1975); Constitutional System of Government and Administration in Saudi Arabia; System of Government and Administration in Saudi Arabia; System of Government and Administration in Islam; The Judicial System in Saudi Arabia. **Hobbies:** reading, travel, sports. **Address:** Faculty of Law, Umm al-Qura University, Mecca, Saudi Arabia.

RASHID (Abdallah Dakhil, al), Kuwaiti engineer, businessman. **Born** in 1933 in Kuwait. **Son** of Dakhil al-Rashid. **Married**, two children. **Educ.:** B.Sc. in Mechanical Engineering. **Career:** Mechanical Engineer, Ministry of Electricity and Water (1964); Deputy Director, Salt Chlorine Plant, Ministry of Electricity and Water (1965); Assistant Under Secretary, Ministry of Electricity and Water (1966); Director General, National Housing Authority (1974); Vice Chairman, Refrigeration Industry and Cold Storage Company. Member of Kuwait Engineers Society and Kasma Sports Club. **Addr.:** P.O.B. 22261, Tel.: 412111, Telex: 22684, RICSCO KT, Safat, Kuwait.

RASHID (Nadir, Lieutenant General), Jordanian businessman. **Born** in 1929 in Salt, Jordan. **Career:** Joined the

Army (1950); Director, General Intelligence (1970-73); Ambassador to Morocco (1973); Former President of the Board of Directors, Jordan Phosphate Mines (1977-87); Senator in the Upper House of the Jordanian Parliament (1989- now); Minister of the Interior (March 1997 - Aug. 1998); presently private business. **Addr.:** Lion Trading Co., P.O.Box 6583, Amman, Tel.: 4893102-3, Jordan.

RASHID (Nasir Ibn Ibrahim, al), Saudi engineer. **Born** in 1939 in Medina, Saudi Arabia. **Dipl.:** B.Sc. (Civil Engineering) (1965); Ph.D. (Civil Engineering) (1970). **Career:** Dean for Technical and Administrative Affairs (1970-72); Dean, Faculty of Engineering, University of Petroleum and Minerals (1972-74); owner of Rashid Engineering, Riyadh; member of the University of Petroleum and Minerals Council (1982); member of the Board of Contractors Classification Committee and Real Estate Development Fund; member of Al Khobar Municipality Council and the American Association of Civil Engineers (AACE); attended several conferences on traffic engineering in the U.S.A; Director, al-Saudi Bank, France. **Publications:** works on new methods of weighing motor vehicles. **Hobbies:** reading, walking, travel. **Prof. Addr.:** P.O.Box 4354, Tel.: 4641188, Riyadh. **Priv. Addr.:** Tel.: 4647716, Riyadh, Saudi Arabia.

RASHID (Nasir Saad, al), Saudi academic. **Born** in 1940 at al-Shara'. **Dipl.:** B.A., Ph.D. **Career:** Teacher, Teachers Institute, Riyadh (1963); Demonstrator, Faculty of Shari'a (Islamic Law), Mecca (1965-66); Chairman of the Arabic Language Department (1975); Professor and Chairman of the Centre for Academic Studies and Revival of Islamic Heritage, Umm al-Qura University; participant member, several conferences and seminars; member of King Faisal International Prize Committee (Arabic Literature). **Hobbies:** reading, writing, hunting, sports. **Prof. Addr.:** Centre for Academic studies and Revival of Islamic Heritage, Umm al-Qura University, Tel.: 5564770, Mecca. **Priv. Addr.:** Tel.: 5565497, Mecca, Saudi Arabia.

RASHID (Rashid Abdulaziz, al), Kuwaiti politician. **Born** in 1933 in Kuwait. **Son** of Abdulaziz al-Rashid. **Married. Educ.:** American University of Beirut, Lebanon. **Career:** Assistant Technical Director, Public Works Department (1959-61); Assistant Secretary, Government Secretariat (1961); Director, Political Department, Ministry of Foreign Affairs (1961-63); Permanent Representative of Kuwait at UN (1963-67); Under Secretary, Ministry of Foreign Affairs (1967-1983); Minister of State for Cabinet Affairs (1984-89). **Addr.:** Kuwait City, Kuwait.

RASHID (Sa'ad Abdul Aziz, al, Prof. Dr.), Saudi, academic and Deputy Minister. **Born** in 1945. **Dipl.:** B.A. (History); Ph.D. (Leeds) (Islamic Archaeology of Arabia and the neighbouring countries). **Career:** Professor in Islamic Archeology, College of Arts, King Saud University, Riyadh; Assistant Deputy Minister and Director General of the Department of Antiquities and Museums, Ministry of Education, Kingdom of Saudi Arabia (From 1996). Secretary, Society of Archaeological Studies, King Saud University; Field Director, Archaeological Excavation in the ancient Islamic site of al-Rabadhah (a well known Islamic city in Arabia situated 300 km. East of Medina Located on the main pilgrim route known as Darb Zubaydah); **Assignments:** Vice-Dean, College of Arts (1979-81); Dean of the Library Affairs, King Saud University (1986-92); Chairman of the Department of Library and Information Science (1989-90); Chairman of the Department of Archaeology and Museology (1994-96); Member of the Saudi Delegation, Member of the Deans Board of the Saudi University Libraries (1986-92), etc. **Presently,** Deputy Minister of Antiquities and Museums. **Seminars and Symposia:** Participated in Seminars in Arabian Studies, in England, Scotland, Germany, Riyadh, Syria, Kuwait, etc.; **Guest lectures** delivered at the London University (1989); King Fahad Academy, London (1989); etc.; **Editorial:** Editorial Board Member for the Journal: **Arabian Archaeology and Epigraphy** published by Munksgaad, Denmark (1990-holding); Contributed to the Encyclopaedia of Islam (New ed. Brill), **Encyclopaedia of Middle East Archaeology** (New York); member, Saudi Arabian Amateur Athletic Federation, Riyadh, since 1978. **Publications:** several articles in Arabic and English in various magazines and journals in English and Arabic, locally and abroad, **Books-entitled: Darb Zubaydah;** The Pilgrim Road from Kuta to Makkah, 1st edition, Riyadh, 1980, the same book in Arabic published in 1993 with additional material (both historical and archaeological). "Ruwawa", Al Madina al Munawwara," Riyadh 1993; and "Kitabat Islamia min Makkah al Mukarama", Riyadh 1995. **Hobbies:** reading, sports. **Address:** Ministry of Education, P.O.Box 3734, Riyadh 11481, Tel. direct. 404 0617- Switch: 402 9500, Ext. 1043-1397, Fax: 404 1391, Saudi Arabia.

RASHID (Yusuf O.), Saudi academic. **Born** in 1941 at Hail, Saudi Arabia. **Dipl.:** Ph.D. (Civil Engineering). **Career:** Dean, Faculty of Engineering, King Fahad University of Petroleum and Minerals. **Address:** Faculty of Engineering, King Fahad University of Petroleum and Minerals, Tel.: 8603100, Dhahran, Saudi Arabia.

RASHOUDY (Ali Ibrahim, al), Saudi official. **Born** in 1939 in Buraidah, Saudi Arabia. **Dipl.:** B.Sc. (Economics and Political Science). **Career:** Teacher; accountant; Director of Labour and Social Affairs, Qassim; Deputy Governor of Qassim; Director of Immigration and Naturalization, Eastern Province; President of Dammam Municipality; Director-General Municipal and Rural Affairs, Eastern Region; member of Board, Water and Sewerage Authority, Eastern Province; member of Arab Cities Conference. **Hobbies:** reading, sport. **Address:** Municipal and Rural Affairs Department, Dammam, Saudi Arabia.

RASHOUDY (Hamad Ibrahim Ali, al), Saudi civil

servant. **Born** in 1939. **Dipl.:** LL.B., P.P.A. **Career:** Successively accounts clerk, Assistant Chief, Transfers Division, Assistant Manager, Legal Division, National Bank; Assistant Director, later Director of Registration Department, Institute of Public Administration; Director of Documentation Centre; administration and organization specialist; Assistant Director General of Customs; Director General of Customs; member of Board of Saudi Arabian Railways Corporation; member of delegations to Conferences of General Director of Customs, Customs Co-operation Council, Brussels, Paris, Buenos Aires. **Hobbies:** reading, travel, swimming. **Prof. Addr.:** Customs Department, P.O.Box 3483, Tel.: 4022515, Riyadh, Saudi Arabia.

RATEB (Aisha), Professor and head of the international law department, faculty of law, Cairo university. **Born** on February 22, 1928. **Married** in 1953 (but now separated). **Educ.:** Faculty of Law, Cairo University (1945-49); Post Graduate studies, Faculty of Law, Paris University (1953-55). **Career:** Appointed Minister of Social Affairs (1971-76); Minister of Social Affairs and Social Insurance (1971-77); resumed teaching in 1977; Ambassador to Denmark and West Germany from (1979-1984) and is now Professor of International Law and Department Head, Faculty of Law, Cairo University. **Honours:** Knight, Legion of Honour (France); Order of Merit (1st class) (Egypt); Order of Merit (Tunisia). **Publ.:** Author of Various textbooks and studies including "Diplomatic and Consular Organisations" (1961); "The Revolution of 26 July 1952" (1964); "International Organisations" (1965); "International Relations" (1966); "Arab International Relations" (1968); "Modern Concept of Neutrality" (1968) etc. **Hobbies:** Reading and research work. **Prof. Addr.:** Faculty of Law, Cairo University, Cairo **Priv. Addr.:** 6, Ibn Malek street, Giza District, Tel.: 3610431, 3610457, Cairo, Egypt.

RATEB (Gamil), Egyptian artist, actor. **Born** in 1926 in Alexandria, Egypt. **Married. Career:** Performed in French plays "Othello", "Hamlet", "Twelfth Night", "Le Malentendu", "Les Parachutistes", "Danse de Mort", "Le Roi Clos"; French films; "Les Jeunes Loups"; British Films "Lawrence of Arabia", "Trapeze"; performed in Various Egyptian films; acted in US, French, Egyptian television programs. **Addr.:** 59 Boulevard Hugo, Neuilly, France and 17 Maahad Swisry, Zamalek, Cairo, Egypt.

RAWABDEH (Abdur-Rauf), Jordanian pharmacist and politician. **Born** on February 18, 1939 at Sarih-Irbid (Jordan). **Son** of Salem Rawabdeh (former merchant) **and** Mrs., née Yomma Ayed. **Married** to Fendieh Rawabdeh on June 27, 1959 at Sarih-Irbid, 11 children. **Educ.:** Irbid Secondary School; American University in Beirut (Lebanon). **Dipl.:** B.Sc. (Pharmacology) with Distinction (1962). Second Year Law, University of Jordan (1982-83). **Career:** Pharmacy Inspector (1962-64); Chief, Pharmacy Section, Ministry of Health (1964-68); Director of Pharmacy and Supplies Department (1968-75); Director of Administration and Service, Yarmouk University (April-June 1976); Minister of Communications (July 13, 1976); Minister of Communications and Minister of Health (1977-78); Member of Jordan National Consultative Assembly; (1978-83); Health (June 1978-Dec. 79), Chairman, Jordan Phosphate Mines Co. (1982-85); Vice Chairman, Jordan Fertilizer Industry Co. (1982-85); Mayor of Amman (Since 1983); Minister of Public Works and Housing (Nov. 1989- Dec. 1990); Deputy Prime Minister and Minister of Education (Jan. 1995- Feb. 1996). **Member:** Jordan Olympic Committee, Chairman. Jordan Football Association, President Sarih Club. **Medals:** Jordan Kawkab Decoration first class (1976); Order of Grand Officer, Italian Republic (1983); Order of Merit, German Federal Republic (1984). **Sport:** swimming. Pharmacists Association. **Priv. Addr.:** University street, P.O.Box 19222, Tel.: 661984, Amman, Jordan.

RAYA (Joseph, H.E. Mgr.), Lebanese archbishop. **Born** in 1917 in Zahlé. **Educ.:** Seminary of Sainte Anne, Jerusalem. **Career:** Ordained to the Priesthood (1941); Head of the Greek Catholic Church in Birmingham (1950-67); Sacred Archbishop of St. John of Acre, Haifa and Nazareth since September 13, 1968. **Publ.:** Author of "The Gospel" translation of "Les Evangiles" (1966). **Resid:** Greek Catholic Archbishopric, Nazareth, Palestine.

RAYALEH (Abdourahman, Hassan), Djibouti Deputy at the National Assembly. **Born** in 1937 in Djibouti. **Educ.:** Licence ès Lettres in Education. **Career:** Professor at C.E.S de Boulaos and Ecole Normale. Technical Consultant at the Minister of National Education. **Member** of "Parti Mouvement Populaire" (1961-1963), Member of RPP. Elected Deputy at the National Assembly (19/12/1997- to date). Vice-President of the Foreign Affairs Commission and Member of the Legislation Commission and General Administration of the Republic. **Prof. Addr.:** National Assembly, P.O.Box 138 Djibouti, Djibouti.

RAYALEH (Meraneh, Boudine), Djibouti Deputy at the National Assembly. **Born** in 1953 in Djibouti. **Career:** Director of the Restauration of Sheraton Hotel. Militant of LPAI, Member of RPP. Elected Deputy at the National Assembly (19/12/1997 - to date); Member of Finance Commission, General Economy, Planning and of Exchange and Production Commission; Member of Supreme Court of Justice. **Prof. Addr.:** National Assembly, P.O.Box 138 Djibouti, Djibouti.

RAYES (Ghazi, al), Kuwaiti diplomat. **Born** on August 23, 1935 in Kuwait. **Married**, 4 children. **Educ.:** Cairo University. **Dipl.:** B.A. in Sociology. **Career:** Third Secretary, Ministry of Foreign Affairs, Kuwait; Kuwaiti Embassy to Washington (1965); Kuwaiti Embassy to Beirut (1965-67); Chairman of the International Affairs Department, Ministry of Foreign Affairs, Kuwait (1967-70); Counsellor, Kuwaiti Embassy to Beirut (1970-73); Ambassador to Bahrain (1974-80); Ambassador to London, UK (1980).

Prof. Addr.: Ministry of Foreign Affairs, Kuwait City, Kuwait.

RAYES (Riad, Najib, al), Syrian journalist, residing in London, UK. **Born** on October 28, 1937 in Damascus, Syria. **Married**, 1 son, 1 daughter. **Educ.:** University of London, UK; Cambridge Technical College and School of Arts. **Dipl.:** B.Sc. in Economics. **Career:** Editor of the "Arab Review", the only Arab Journal published in English in Britain at the time, while still at Cambridge (1958), Foreign Desk of "al-Anwar" newspaper (1961); Co-Fonder of "al-Muharrir" weekly, remained its editor until its publication as a daily newspaper (1962-63); Thomson Fellowship in Journalism and returned to UK to work for the "Sunday Times" (1964), then "Western Mail"; Reporter to "an-Nahar" on the British Political and Literary scene. Foreign Editor and Columnist on International and Arab Affairs, al-Hayat (1964); first Arab to report on Vietnam (1966); toured South-Est Asia reporting on situation in Thailand, Laos, Cambodia, India, Pakistan, Hong Kong, Macao, Taiwan and Singapore; Foreign Correspondent of "an-Nahar" covering the Yemen Civil War, the War of Independence, Aden and South Arabia (1966-68), Iraqi Coup d'Etat (1968), Soviet Invasion of Czechoslovakia (1968-69), Eastern Europe (1969-70), the Greek Colonels Coup (1967), the Somali Dispute (1968), Ulster (1969); attended all the meetings that led to the creation of the United Arab Emirates and the Independence of Qatar and Bahrain; Special Consultant to UNICEF on mission to the Arabian Peninsula (1971); Edited "an-Nahar Arab Report" (1970-76); Managing Director of al-Nahar Press Services, a subsidiary of an-Nahr newspaper; Chairman of Riad el-Rayyes and Associates Ltd. (Information Consultants) (1976-); Editor in Chief of al-Manaar, Arabic weekly (1977-); Columnist in al-Mustakbal, Arab weekly news magazine published in Paris (1979-) writing mostly on Gulf Affairs. **Publ.:** "The Crucial Period" (1965), "Land of Small Dragons - a Journey to Vietnam" (1966), "Death of Others", a collection of poems in Arabic (1972), "The Stuggle for Oil and Oases" (1973), "Dhofar - the Story of the Military Struggle in the Gulf" (1978). **Hobbies:** Literary criticism, poetry. **Prof. Addr.:** 4 Pont Street; London SWIX 93L, UK. **Priv. Addr.:** 4A Moore Park Road, London SW6, United Kingdom.

RAYES (Sabah, Mohammed Amin, al), Kuwaiti consulting engineer-architect. **Born** on March 29, 1939 in Kuwait. **Son** of late Mohammed Amin al-Rayes **and** Mrs. Fatma Isa. **Married** in 1969, in Kuwait, to Sabrieh Ali Abdul Raheem, four children, Kays (1970); Haneed (1971); Dina (1976); Hamad (1981). **Educ.:** B.Sc. in Civil Engineering with minor in Architecture and Metallurgy, Indiana Institute of Technology, Fort Wayne, Indiana, U.S.A. (1965). **Career:** Civil Engineer, Ministry of Public Works, Kuwait (1965-68); Technical Consulting, Aid Program for Developing Countries, Ministry of Foreign Affairs, Kuwait (1968-73); Executive Secretary and Member of Board, Kuwait Society of Engineers (1967-73); Founder, Senior Partner, Managing Director of Pan Arab Counsulting Engineers, kuwait (1968 to date); Chairman, Education Committe, Union of Arab Engineers (1967-84); Member of Board of Trustees-College of Engineering, Kuwait University (1977-83); Member at large of the Steering Group Council on Tall Buildings and Urban Habitat, Lehigh University, Pennsylvania U.S.A.; Director, Kuwait National Industries Co. (1973-76); Director, Gulf Real Estate Development Co. (1976-80); Director, United Gulf Bank, Bahrain (1981-86); Director, Arab Life Insurance company, Jordan (1981-87); Chairman, Gulf Investments Co., Bahrain (1979-86); Chairman, Kuwait Precious Metals Co., Kuwait (1982-86); Deputy Chairman, Tunis International Bank, Tunis (1982-85); Vice-Chairman, Kuwait Department Stores, Kuwait (1983 to date). **Social Activities:** Chairman Safety Society for prevention of Road Accidents, Kuwait (1982 to date); Member of the Higher Traffic Council, Ministry of Interior, Kuwait (1985 to date); Arbitrator in various cases of technical disputes; Expert witness in many Public and closed hearings; Consultant to a number of Community Groups; Represented Kuwait Internationally in many Professional Conferences. **Awards:** Honorary Doctorate degree in civil Engineering, Indiana Institute of Technology (May 1984); Honorary Citizen of the City of fort Wayne, Indiana, U.S.A. **Member:** Hunting and Equestrian Club. **Hobbies:** Water Sports, Horseriding, Collecting antiques and paintings. **Prof. Addr.:** P.O.Box 2105, Safat 13022, Tel.: 2451895-9, Kuwait. **Priv. Addr.:** Dahiyat abdullah Salem, Str. 42, Block 4, Hse 5, Kuwait.

RAYSUNI (Mohamad al-Khadir, al), Moroccan broadcasting official. **Born** in 1930 in Tetouan, Morocco. **Married**, 4 children. **Educ.:** Institute of Religion, Qarawiyin University, Fes, Morocco. **Dipl.:** Diploma in Television (Spain). **Career:** Tetouan radio station (1952); joined National Radio Station in Rabat after Independence (1957); Producer of "The People's radio Magazine", broadcast twice weekly; Head of Department, Arabic Programme Section, Moroccan Radio and Television. **Publ.:** translated many novels into Spanish; published articles in "al-Nahar" newspaper in Tetouan as well as collections of short stories. **Hobby:** walking. **Addr.:** Zarqat al-Murg, Building No.15, Rabat, Morocco.

RAZA (S. Hashim), Indian banker. **Born** in 1930 in India. **Son** of Mohamad Aqil Ansari **and** Mrs., née Aalia Khatoon. **Married** in 1951 in Ghazipur, India to Mrs. Nazera Khatoon, two children. **Educ.:** Lucknow University, India. **Dipl.:** Master of Commerce, diploma of Institute of Bankers in Pakistan. Undergone foreign exchange training at Deutch Bank in West Germany. **Career:** Probationary Officer (1952-59); Senior Grade II Officer (1960-61); Senior Grade I Officer (1962-73); Executive Vice President (1974-76); Senior Executive Vice President (since 1976); Member Executive Board (since 1982); Deputy

General Manager, Middle East Bank Ltd., Dubai. **Hobby:** Islamic studies. **Prof. Addr.:** Muslim Commercial Bank Ltd., Head Office, Adamjee House, I.I. Chundrigar Road, Tel.: 236528, Karachi, Pakistan. **Priv. Addr.:** D/108, Block 5, Federal "B" Area, Tel.: 680238, Karachi, Pakistan.

RAZZAZ (Mostafa, El, Dr.), Egyptian Dean, Dokki College of Education in Special Subjects: Art, Music and Media. Professor of Design, Faculty of Art Education, Cairo University. **Born** in 1942 in al-Dakhlia, Egypt. **Married**, 2 daughters. **Educ.:** Dokki College, Cairo University. **Dipl.:** Doctor of Philosophy degree from the State University of New York a Buffalo, U.S.A. Master and Bachelor degrees from the Faculty of Art Education, Cairo, Egypt. He has done post graduate studies in arts and crafts, Olso University, Norway. **Career:** Since his first private exhibition at the Akhnaton Exhibition Hall in Cairo (1966), Dr. Razzaz has forty-five private shows in Egypt, Holland, Italy, Tunisia, Norway, Sweden, Denmark and U.S.A. He has contributed to thirty-four group shows in Egypt, Latin America, Italy, Canada, Germany, Algeria, Kenya, China, Hungary, Bahrain, Cuba, Brazil, Iraq, Tunisia, Russia, Morocco, Jordan and India. His work is represented in many private and public collections including the Modern Art Museum in Cairo, the Museum of Ohio University, USA, The National Museum of Titograd, Yugoslavia, The National Museum of Oman, Jordan, and the Presidential House in Cairo. He is chairman of the Visual Art Committee of the Supreme Council of Culture and the Egyptian Folk Art Society. He has public and environmental art projects in Cairo and Giza, Egypt. Known as a pronounced Scholar in the fields of art, art education and culture of Egypt, he has published numerous research papers and participated as a lecturer in numerous conferences and symposiums throughout Denmark, Egypt, Japan, India, Morocco, Norway, Sweden and Turkey. Chairman and Jury member for various art committees in national, regional and international art events, symposiums and workshops. Dean, Dokki College of Education in Special Subjects: Art, Music and Media; Professor of Design, Faculty of Art Education, Cairo, Egypt. **Publ.:** Published books with Buffalo Talk Press, Buffalo, New York (1978), Art Curriculum (student and teachers), Cairo (1981-1994), Art Articulation, Cairo (1993) and Mohamed Mahmoud Khalil "The Man and the Museum" (French and Arabic), Cairo 1995. **Prof. Addr.:** Dokki College of Education, 56, Tahrir Street, Dokki, Cairo, Egypt. **Priv. Addr.:** 2 Mohamed Farid Wagdy Street, Manial, Cairo, Egypt.

RERHAYE (Abdelkamel), Moroccan politician. **Born** on January 20, 1941 in Rabat. **Dipl.:** LL.B. **Career:** In the Administration since 1959; Under Secretary of State at the Ministry of Tourism (1971); Secretary of State at the Ministry of Finance (1974); Minister of Commerce and Industry (1977); Minister of Finance (1979); Member of Parliament since 1977. **Prof. Addr.:** Parliament, Rabat, Morocco.

REWASHED (Abdul Rahman S., al), Saudi consultant. **Born** in 1927 in Riyadh, Saudi Arabia. **Dipl.:** B.A. Shari'a (Islamic Law), B.A. (Arabic Language), Diploma (Education). **Career:** Teacher (1956-1960); Institute Director (1961-1962); Assistant Director, Primary Education, Ministry of Education (1963-1965); Director, School Books Department, Ministry of Education (1966-1970); Assistant Director, Civil Rights (1980). **Member:** al-Riyadh Literary Club, and al-Riyadh Printing Press Company; former Editor-in-Chief, al-Da'wa al-Islamiya; Editor-in-Chief, al-Shible Magazine for children. **Hobbies:** reading, writing. **Publications:** several educational books. **Prof. Addr.:** P.O.Box 21291, Tel.: 4352856, Riyadh. **Priv. Addr.:** Tel.: 4356150, Riyadh, Saudi Arabia.

RIAD (Kamal), Egyptian international civil servant. **Born** on June 24, 1922 in Mahalla-el-Kobra (Egypt). **Married**, with children. **Educ.:** Cairo University (1941-46); University of Michigan (USA) (1953-54); Technical High School, Delft (Netherlands) (1945); D.Sc. (Technical Science) (1961). **Career:** Various engineering positions with Ministry of Public Works, Egypt, and private industry since 1946; Ex Chief of Natural Resources Section, Economic Commission for Africa (ECA); Chief of Environmental Coordination Unit, ECWA, Ethiopia. **Member:** Egyptian Engineering Association; International Association for Hydraulic Research. **Sports:** Swimming and golf. **Hobbies:** Philately and photography. **Addr.:** Cairo, Egypt.

RIAHI (Lamine), Tunisian administrator. **Born** in 1940 in Lar Marsa, Tunisia. **Educ.:** Ecole Polytechnique de Lausanne, Switzerland. **Dipl.:** Dip ing. **Career:** Director of National Transport Society; Managing Director and Chairman of Société du Métro Leger de Tunis (1982-); Administrator, National Inter-Urban Transport Society and National Urban Transport Society; Adviser to the Minicipal Council, La Marsa (1985-). **Prof. Addr.:** 6 Rue Khartoum, Tunis, Tunisia. **Priv. Addr.:** 18 Rue Brigaradier, La Marsa, Tunis, Tunisia.

RIAL (Cleto, Hassan), Sudanese statesman. **Born** in 1935 in Sudan. **Son** of Hassan Rial. **Educ.:** Xavier University, Ohio (USA); University of Notre Dame, Indiana, USA; Institute of Social Studies, The Hague, Netherlands; Royal Institute of Public Administration, UK. **Career:** Executive Officer, Ministry of Local Government (1958-59); teacher, Comboui College, Khartoum (1959-60); Finance Inspector, Ministry of Finance and Economy (1962-63); Lecturer, Institute of Public Administration (1963-72); Secretary General, Higher Executive Council of Southern Region (1972). **Publ.:** "Methods and Techniques of Community Development Programs" (1966). **Medals:** Order of the Two Niles. **Addr.:** P.O.B. 17, Juba, Sudan.

RIDA (Abdallah Mohamad), Saudi official. **Born** in 1939 in Jeddah, Saudi Arabia. **Dipl.:** B.A., M.A. (Economics). **Career:** Senior official, PETROMIN; businessman, member of the Reda family of leading businessmen; Senior official in Foreign Ministry for Economic Affairs. **Honours:** several orders of merit from Arab, Islamic and European countries. **Hobby:** reading. **Address:** Ministry of Foreign Affairs, Jeddah, Saudi Arabia.

RIDA (Ismail, Tawfic), Egyptian engineer. **Born** in 1930 in Egypt. **Married**, 1 son, 2 daughters. **Educ.:** Cairo University, Egypt; Swiss Federal Institute of Technology, Zürich, Switzerland. **Dipl.:** B.Sc. and D.Sc. in Engineering. **Career:** Consultant, Planning and Construction Office (1961-); Member of the Swiss Engineers Association, Switzerland (1960-64); Planning and Housing Expert (1972-75); Partner, Planning and Construction Consultancy Centre (1975); Member of Egypt Engineers Syndicate (1953); Vice Chairman, Housing and Development Company (1980-). **Publ.:** "Centre of Cairo City" (1961), "Planning of Motier Province" (1972), "Housing Problems in Newly Constructed Areas" (1984). **Member:** Automobile Club, Hunting Club, Gezira Sporting Club. **Prof. Addr.:** 26 July Street, No.10, Cairo, Egypt. **Priv. Addr.:** 4 el-Saleh Ayoub Street, Zamalek, Cairo, Egypt.

RIDA (Ismat), Syrian painter and graphic artist. **Born** in 1938 in Damascus. **Educ.:** Freie Akademie, Manhein (Germany). **Dipl.:** Painting and specialization in Graphic Art under Master-Painter Paul Berger Bergnier (1964). **Career:** Participated in many Syrian National Exhibitions; First personal exhibitions in Damascus at the "Symposium" of Higher Institutes (1958); Study trip to Germany, where he formed a group of young painters under the name of "Kontrast" Mannhein (1960); Personal Exhibition at the "Imm" Theatre, Mannheim; trip to Berlin for personal research on artistry, pictures and graphics; in Syria since 1966 for a series of Art Exhibitions. **Addr.:** Damascus, Syria.

RIFAAT (Kamaleddine, Mahmoud), Egyptian statesman and diplomat. **Born** in 1921 in Egypt. **Son** of Mahmoud Rifaat. **Educ.:** Secondary and Higher, Cairo, Military Academy. **Dipl.:** Bachelor of Science. **Career:** Served in Armed Forces (1942-45); member, National Assembly (1957); Deputy Minister for Presidential Affairs (1958); Minister of Labour (1961-62); Member, Presidency Council (1962-64); Deputy Prime Minister for Scientific Affairs (1964-66); Minister of Labour in June 1967; Member, Central Committee of the Arab Socialist Union (1968); Ambassador of the Arab Republic of Egypt to United Kingdom (1971-73); Minister of State (1974). **Awards:** Order of the Republic, military Star and Decorations from Morocco, Cameroon, Tunisia, Yugoslavia. **Publ.:** "Strategy", "The Social Experiment", "The Third World and the Socialist Solution", "National Liberation", **Addr.:** Cairo, Egypt.

RIFAAT (Mohamad, Ali), Egyptian economist and businessman. **Born** in Egypt. **Educ.:** Secondary and Higher. **Dipl.:** Doctorate. **Career:** Egyptian Delegate to several Meetings of the International Labour Office (Geneva); Former Board Chairman, the Federation of Egyptian Industries; Former Honorary Adviser to thr Middle East Agency and Allied Publications; Ministry of Information; Secretary General of the Afro-Asian Organization for cooperation. **Addr.:** Cairo Chamber of Commerce Building, P.O.Box 507, Midan al-Falaki, Cairo, Egypt.

RIFAI (Abdulhakim, al), Egyptian former bank deputy governor, honorary faculty professor. **Born** in Egypt. **Educ.:** Faculty of Law. **Dipl.:** LL.B. **Career:** Former Chairman "Mortgage Credit Bank" of Egypt; Under-Secretary of State, Ministry of Finance; Deputy Governor, National Bank of Egypt; Honorary Professor, Faculty of Law (Cairo). **Addr.:** 4, Ahmad Nassim Street, Giza, Tel.: 897527, Cairo, Egypt.

RIFAI (Abdulmoneim, al), Jordanian politician. **Born** in 1917 in Jordan. **Educ.:** American University of Beirut. **Career:** Assistant Chief of Royal Court (1941-42); Consul-General in Cairo, Lebanon and Syria (1943-44); Delegate to Treaty Conference with Great Britain (1946); Under-Secretary of Foreign Affairs (1974); Observer at United Nations (1949); Minister to Iran and Pakistan (1949); Ambassador to United States and Permanent Representatives at united Nations (1953-57), to Lebanon (1957), in Great Britain (1958); Chief of National Guidance (1959); Permanent Representative at United Nations (1959-62); Ambassador to Egypt (1962-66); Minister of State for Foreign Affairs (Octobre 7, 1967- April 25, 1968); Ministry of Foreign Affairs (April 26, 1968- March 24, 1969); Prime Minister (March 1969); Vice Prime Minister and Minister of Foreign Affairs (August 1969- June 1970); headed Jordan delegation to explain United Arab Kingdom project to Kuwait and Syria (1972); led Jordanian delegation to Non-Aligned Nations Conference, Algeria (Sept. 1973); at Middle East Peace Conference in Geneva (Dec. 1973); Ambassador to the Arab League, Cairo; Personal Represelntive to HM King Hussein (June-Dec. 1973); Ambassador to Egypt (Oct.-Dec. 1973); Special Adviser to HM King Hussein for National Affairs (Dec. 1973- Nov. 1974); Senator (1974). **Awards:** Numerous decorations. **Addr.:** jabal Webdeh, Tel.: 21026, Amman, Jordan.

RIFAI (Diyaeddin Taleb, al), Jordanian lawyer. **Born** in 1925 in Safad, Jordan. **Married**, 3 sons. **Educ.:** Queen Elizabeth Institute, Oxford University, UK. **Dipl.:** Licence in Law, Diploma in Public Administration. **Career:** Secretary of Political Department, League of Arab States (1947-50); Private Secretary to late King Abdullah (1950-51); First Secretary, Embassy to Spain (1951); First Secretary, Embassy to Italy (1953-56); Counsellor, Embassy to Iran (1956-57); Charge d'Affaires, Embassy to Saudi Arabia (1958-59); Charge d'Affaires, Embassy to Turkey (1959); Assistant Under Secretary, Ministry of National Economy (1959-62); Legal Adviser to the Civil Service Commission and Audit Bureau (1962-66); Lawyer; Editor of a local newspaper (1966-68); General Director of Broadcasting of the Hashemite Kingdom of Jordan (1968-70); Information Expert to the League of Arab States (1970-71); Representative of the League of Arab States in Nigeria, Cameroon, Ivory Coast (1974-76); Under Secretary, Ministry of Culture and Information (1974-76); Lawyer (1976-). Permanent Adviser to the Arab Union of Broadcasting. **Publ.:** "The Protocol" (1960), "Bag of Memories" (1980). **Decor.:** Order of the Jordanian Star, Order of Independence, Jordan. Order of Merit, Morocco; Order of Merit, Egypt, Order of the Holy Tomb, Vatican. **Hobbies:** table tennis, chess, swimming. **Member:** Jordan Writers Society. **Addr.:** P.O.Box 9663, Amman, Jordan.

RIFAI (Hani, Hussain, al), Jordanian judge. **Born** in 1927 in Dair Abu Said, Jordan. **Educ.:** University of Baghdad, Faculty of Law, Iraq. **Dipl.:** LLB (1951). **Career:** Lawyer (1952); Chief of Clerks of Attorney General Department, Amman; Public Prosecutor, Irbid (1953); Magistrate, Tafila, Jordan (1953); Public Prosecutor, Salt (1954); First Public Prosecutor in Nablus, West Bank (1955-58); Member of the First Instance Court and Magistrate (1959-63); Member of the Appeal Court, Jerusalem (1965); Judge on secondment, Kuwait (1965-71); President of First Instance Court, Salt (1971), Vice President of Appeal Court, Amman (1973), General Inspector of Courts, Amman (1975); Judge in the Administrative Trubunal of the Arab League (1978); Judge in Jordanian Supreme and Cassation Court of Justice)1980); Representative of Jordan in the Legal Permanent Committee of the Arab League and in the Asian-African Legal Consulative Committee; Vice Minister of Justice (1976). **Addr.:** Jabal Hussain, Tel.: 614606, Amman, Jordan.

RIFAI (Hisham), Syrian international civil servant. **Born** on August 11, 1930 in Aleppo (Syria). **Son** of Omar Bessim Rifai (Army Officer). **Married** on June 1, 1968. **Educ.:** Faculty of Law, Syrian University, Damascus; Columbia University. New York (1956-59). **Dipl.:** LL.B. (1959); Ph.D.; Candidate (Public Law and Government). **Career:** Political Affairs Oficer, Department of Trusteeship; United Nations Observer, Cameroon (1959-60); Assistant Secretary, Trusteeship Council Mission to Trust Territories (1956-64); Secretary Subcommittee on Aden, Special Committee on Decolonisation (1964-69); Chief, Studies and Publications Section, Department of Trusteeship; Chief, Council of Namibia Section, Department of Trusteeship; Chief, Political Studies and Advisory Services Section, UN; Principal Officer, Security Council, UN. **Member:** of many U.N. Missions to trust Territories in Africa, the Pacific and Middle East; missions of security Council to solve disputes in Africa. **Hobby:** Music (Violin). **Priv. Addr.:** 319 E 50 Street, New York, NY 10022, USA.

RIFAI (Ihsan, al), Syrian physician. **Born** in 1919 in Aleppo. **Educ.:** French Faculty of Medicine in Beirut. **Dipl.:** Doctor of Medicine, specialization in Paris hospitals. **Career:** Physician; Former Assistant Professor, Faculty of Medicine in Paris; President of the Anti-Tuberculosis Association; Director of the Nursing School in Aleppo; Secretary-General of the Anti-Tuberculosis Commission. **Correspondent** to the French Anti-Tuberculosis Associations. **Addr.:** Aleppo, Syria.

RIFAI (Khalid, al), Jordanian mechanical engineer. **Born** on December 6, 1937 in Ammam (Jordan). **Son** of Samir al-Rifai (Statesman) **and** Mrs., née Alia Shuckry. **Married** to Miss Amira al-Khalil on September 19, 1964 in Amman, 2 sons: Samir and Mohammed. **Educ.:** Victoria College, Alexandria (Egypt); Loughborough University (UK). **Dipl.:** D.L.C. Mechanical Engineering. **Career:** Works Manager, Jordan Cement Factories (1961-68); Contractor (1968); now Partner and Managing-Director, COMEDAT (contracting Co.). **Awards:** Order of Independence (Jordan). **Hobbies:** Radio and music. **Credit Card:** American Express. **Prof. Addr.:** P.O.Box 2146, Amman, Jordan.

RIFAI (Mohamad Mounib, Abdallah Jawdat, al), Syrian statesman. **Born** in 1928 in Damascus. **Son** of Abdallah Jawdat al-Rifaï **and** Mrs. Fayzé Sabban. **Married** to Miss Najah Rabbat in 1955, 4 children; Marwan, Salam, Nasser and Salma. **Educ.:** Tajheez Secondary School, Damascus (1940-47); Syrian University, Damascus, Faculty of Law (1947-50); Homs Military School (1953). **Dipl.:** Bachelor of Law (1950), Homs Military School Diploma (1953). **Career:** Assigned to Military Court (1954-60); Director of the Vice-President of the United Arab Republic Bureau at the time of the merger between Egypt and Syria (1961); Security Service (1961-63); Ambassador of Syria to Yugoslavia (1965-67); Director of Arab Affairs Office, Damascus: Permanent Representative of Arab League for Mediation in Yemen (1973); Syrian Ambassador in United Arab Emirates (1973-76). **Sports:** Tennis and swimming. **Member:** The International Law committee in Arab League, al-Oroua Club, al-Oussra Club and ar-Roudwan Club **Medals:** ten Merit Decorations. **Prof. Addr.:** al-Jallae Street, Tel.: 39976, Damascus. **Priv. Addr.:** al-Koussour Street, Tel.: 448181, Damascus, Syria.

RIFAI (Naïm, al), Syrian faculty dean. **Born** in Syria. **Married** to Miss Riad, 4 children: Chadia, Rafiq, Randa and Rania. **Educ.:** Secondary and Higher. **Dipl.:** Professor in Education. **Career:** Educationalist, Dean of Faculty of Education at the Syrian University of Damascus. **Publ.:** Author of several Educational Books, published in 1959, 1960, 1961, 1964, 1966, 1967 and 1968. **Addr.:** University of Damascus, Tel.: 115100, Damascus, Syria.

RIFAI (Najmuddine), Syrian diplomat and international civil servant. **Born** on September 21, 1925 in Aleppo. **Single. Educ.:** American University in Beirut (Lebanon) (1947-48); Columbia University, New York. **Dipl.:** B.A.

(1947); M.A. (Political Science) (1948); Ph.D. (international relations) (1960). **Career:** joined the Permanent Mission of Syria (1954); Acting Director, Department of International Organisations, Ministry of Foreign Affairs, Damascus (1958-59); Counsellor, Permanent Mission of the United Arab Republic, New York (1959-61); Syrian Ambassador, Representative of Syrian Arab Republic on Committee of Seventeen (Decolonization) (1961-63), was elected Commissioner for Plebiscite in western Samoa (1961); Committee of Twenty Four (1961-63); Director, Deputy to Under-Secretary General Department of Political Affairs Trusteeship and Decolonization, UN (1965-85); Assistant Secretary-General, UN (1985). **Publ.:** "International Political Problems of Syria" (1948), "Evolution of Libya Towards Unity and Independence" (1960). **Addr.:** Damascus, Syria.

RIFAI (Rashid Mohamed Said, al), Iraqi engineer, politician and diplomat. **Born** on May 1, 1929 in Mussayeb, Iraq. **Son** of Mohamed Said al-Rifai (Inspector) **and** Mrs. Fatima Amin née al-Mamoury. **Married** on May 9, 1975 in Iraq to Miss Nabiha al-Timimi, 4 children: Rabab, Said, Faris and Mazin. **Educ.:** American University of Beirut-International College (1950); University of Bristol, U.K. (1954); Purdue University, U.S.A. (1964); Rice University, U.S.A. (1967). **Dipl.:** Intermediate Certificate (First Class) (1950); in Electrical Engineering: B.Sc. (1954), M.S.E. (1964), Ph.D. (1967). **Career:** Assistant Engineer and then Excecutive Engineer, Directorate General of the Post, Telegraph and Telephone, Iraq (1954-62), with two years training (1957-59) with the British Post Office, G.E.C. and other British companies on a Federation of British Industries scholarship' Chief Engineer, Public Company for Electrical Equipment and Appliances, Baghdad, Iraq, (3/68- 7/68); Minister of State for Presidential Affairs, (18 July 1968); Minister of Oil and Minerals (31 July 1968); Minister of State (31 December 1969); Minister of Planning (1 March 1971); Minister of Communication (28 May 1972); Minister of Public Works and Housing, (11 November 1974); Ambassador (10 May 1976); Ambassador Extraordinary and Plenipotentiary to Belgium (15 December 1976); also accredited to the Grand Duche of Luxembourg and the European Communities; Ambasador Extraordinary and Plenipotentiary to the People's Republic of China (10 October 1983); Ambassador Extraordinary and Plenipotentiary to Japan (22 October 1986- 31 July 1993). **Hobbies:** Music, Reading. **Member:** Chartered Engineer and Member of the Institution of Electrical Engineers, U.K.; Member of the Iraqi Engineers Union; Member of the Society of Iraqi Engineers. **Prof. Addr.:** Ministry of Foreign Affirs, Baghdad, Iraq; **Priv. Addr.:** No. 26, Hay Al-Adl, Mahalla 645, Zuqaq 2, Karkh, Baghdad, Tel.: 5539018, Iraq.

RIFAI (Yusuf, Hashem, al), Kuwaiti statesman. **Born** in 1930. **Educ.:** Shuwaikh Secondary School, Kuwait. **Career:** Director, Travel and Residence Department (1961-63); Member of National Assembly (1963-75); Minister of Posts, Telegraphs and Telephones (1964); Minister of State for Cabinet Affairs (November 1964); President of Municipal Council (1966-70); Businessman (1978-). **Addr.:** P.O.Box 420, Kuwait.

RIFAI (Zaid, Samir, al), Jordanian politician and diplomat. **Born** on November 27, 1936 in Ammam (Jordan). **Son** of late Samir ar-Rifaï (Prime Minister) and Mrs. Alia Shukry. **Married** to Miss Mouna Talhouni on September 18, 1965, one child: Samir. **Educ.:** Victoria College, Cairo; Harvard University, Columbia University. **Dipl.:** Bachelor of Arts (Political Science), Master of Arts (International Law and Relations). **Career:** Diplomatic Service (1957); Jordan Embassy in Cairo (1957), in Beirut (1958); Secretary, Jordan Delegation to United Nations; Head of International Affairs Department, Foreign Ministry (1959-62); 1st Secretary, Embassy to UK (1962-64); Assistant Chief of Royal Protocol (1964); Head of Royal Protocol (1964); Head of the Political Dept., Ministry of Foreign Affairs (1964-65); Delegate, General Assembly sessions (1958-65); Assistant Chief, Royal Court (1966); Head of Royal Protocol (1966-67); Head of Royal Protocol and Private Secretary to HM King Hussein (1967); Deputy Chief, Royal Court (1969); Jordanian Ambassador to the UK (1970-71); Political Adviser to HM King Hussein (March 1972- May 1973); Prime Minister, Minister of Defence and Minister of Foreign Affairs (Nov. 1974-76); Prime Minister and Minister of Defence (1985-April 1989), Senator and Speaker since Nov. 1993. **Awards:** Decorations from Jordan, Lebanon, Ethiopia, Morocco, Libya, Pakistan. **Sports:** Tennis, water skiing and cricket. **Hobbies:** Reading and chess. **Priv. Addr.:** Jabal Ammam, Amman, Jordan.

RIHANI (Suliman, T., Dr.), Jordanian Professor and Dean. **Born** on November 4, 1942 in Al Huson, Jordan. **Son** of Tumeh S. Rihani **and** Mrs. Tamam S. Rihani. **Married** in 1973 to Miss Reen J. Rihani, 3 children: Lara (1976), Rafeef (1979), Shadi (1982). **Educ.:** Michigan University (USA) MA. and Ph.D., University of Jordan B.A. **Dipl.:** Ph.D - M.A. (Counseling Psychology), B.A. (Education and Psychology). **Career:** University Teaching (1972- now); Director-Counseling Center (1978-1984); Chairman-Dept. of Psychology (1984-1985 and 1987-1989); Vice-Dean, Faculty of Graduate Studies (1991-1995); Dean, Faculty of Educational Sciences (1995-1999). Other Information: Recipient of Fulbright Exchange grant (1985-1986). **Medal:** University of Jordan's Silver Jubilee Medal. **Hobby:** Reading. **Member:** President-Jordanian Psychological Association. **Prof. Addr.:** Faculty of Educational Sciences, University of Jordan, Amman, Jordan, Tel.: 5355000, Ext. 4041. **Priv. Addr.:** same, Tel.: 5153888, Amman, Jordan.

RIKAISHY (Ahmad, Bin Nassir, el), Omani economist. **Born** in 1945 in Zanzibar. **Son** of Nassir el Kindy. **Married** two children. **Educ.:** American University in Cairo (1965-

69); University of Colorado, USA (1971-73); University of Cambridge, England (1973-74). **Dipl.:** B.A. Economics; M.A. Development Economic; diploma in Development Economics Cambridge University. **Career:** Director for Planning (1975-79); Director General for Planning (since 1979); working at the Development Council, Oman. **Sport:** Swimming. **Hobbies:** Reading, traveling. **Member:** of American Econimic Association, American Association for the advancement of Science, Arab-European Society. **Prof. Addr.:** P.O.B. 881, Tel.: 698828, Muscat, Oman. **Priv. Addr.:** P.O.Box 971, Tel.: 575213, Muscat, Oman.

RIMAWI (Fahad Nimr, al), Jordanian journalist. **Born** in 1942 in Palestine. **Married**, 2 sons, 4 daughters. **Educ.:** Cairo University, Egypt. **Dipl.:** B.A. in Journalism. **Career:** Editor of "Difa" newspaper (1965-67); Editor in Chief, Jordan News Agency (1968-70); Secretary of the Board of Editors of "Afkar" magazine (1970-73); Director, Investigation Department of "al-Raie" newspaper (1975-76); Writer, "al-Destour" newspaper (1978-81); Political Writer, Al Raie newspaper (1981-85); Correspondent for "al-Bayan" magazine, United Arab Emirates; Correspondent, "al-Talie'ah" magazine, Paris (1982-). **Publ.:** "Mawaweel Fi al-Layl al-Taweel", short stories in Arabic (1982). **Prof. Addr.:** P.O.Box 926856, Amman, Jordan.

RING (Bona, Malwal), Sudanese journalist, politician. **Born** in 1935 in Sudan. **Son** of Malwal Ring. **Educ.:** Studied journalism in the USA (1962-63). **Career:** Ministry of Information (1958); Information Officer in Wau; joined editorial staff of the "Sudan Daily" (1961); elected Secretary General of the Southern Front (1964); elected to the Constituent Assembly (1968); Editor of the southern newspaper "Vigilant" (until 1969); Deputy Minister of Information and Culture (1972); Minister of State (1973); Minister of Information and Culture (1976); member of the Board of "al-Sahafa" (1974). **Addr.:** Khartoum, Sudan.

RIZK (George Kamel), Egyptian-British businessman. **Born** in 1927 in Cairo, Egypt. **Married**, 3 children. **Dipl.:** B.Sc. in Economics. **Career:** British Bank of the Near East (1950-56); Exporter in Egypt (1956-62), Consultant and Freelance Financial Broker operating from Geneva (1962-69); Chairman of George Rizk International Finance Limited, London (1973-) and George Rizk International Finance Inc., (1985-). **Addr.:** London. United Kingdom.

ROBLEH (Doualeh, Mohamed), Djibouti Deputy at the National Assembly, and Chartered Accountant. **Dipl.:** Higher Studies, Diploma in Finance and Accountancy, 1st Year of Accountant Survey at "Institut Superieur de Gestion de Tunis". **Career:** Member of RPP, Elected Deputy at the National Assembly (19/12/1997 - to date); Secretary-rapporteur of the Permanent Commission and Commission Member of Finance, General Economy and Planning; Member of Supreme Court of Justice. **Prof. Addr.:** National Assembly, P.O.Box 138 Djibouti, Djibouti.

ROFAEL (Nazmy), Egyptian director, pharmaceutical research and control laboratories, Cairo. **Born** on May 6, 1927 in Tantah city, (Lower Egypt). **Married** to Miss Mona Saad in 1959, 2 children: one son and one daughter. **Educ.:** Tantah Secondary School (1943); Faculty of Pharmacy, Cairo University. **Dipl.:** B.Sc. (Pharmacy) (1947), M.Sc. (Pharmacy) (1968), Ph.D. (1971). **Career:** Deputy Director, Drugs Research and Control Centre (1963-76); represented Egypt in FAO/WHO Codex-Alimantarius Commission, and in Arab and International Pharmaceutical Conferences; now Director, Pharmaceutical Research and Control Laboratories since 1976. **Member:** World Health Organisation Advisory Panel, International Pharmacopoeia (1976). **Publ.:** Board Secretary, Journal of Drugs and Research (published three times a year by the National Organisation for Drug Control and Research, Cairo); also author of several research papers published in specialised journals. **Hobbies:** Photography and chess. **Prof. Addr.:** Pharmaceutical Control and Research Laboratories, 6, Abou Hazem street, Pyramids District, P.O.Box 29, Tel.: 809975, 855582, Cairo. **Priv. Addr.:** 6, Sarayah el-Kobra Square, Garden City District, Tel.: 20630, Cairo, Egypt.

ROMAHI (Seif Ahmad al Wady, al), United Arab Emirates statesman. **Born** in 1938 in Muzeira'a, Palestine. **Son** of Ahmad al-Hajj Abdul Nabi (Mayor). **Married** to Zaka Al-Masri, 1 boy, Yazann (1976) and 2 girls, Liane (1979) and Elana (1982). **Educ.:** The School of Economics & Political Science, Beirut; Lebanese State University; City of Lodon College (presently City of London University College); Southern Illinois University; University of Birmingham, UK; Sophia University, Japan. **Dipl.:** Diploma in Public Law (1957); B.A. in Political Science and Economics (1960); 1st Class Certificate in International Law (1961); M.A. in Government Studies (1967); Ph.D. in Educational Foundations Admin. & Supervision (1969); Ph.D. in Political Science (1980); Professor Rank (1980); Ph.D. (Hon.Doc.) in International Diplomacy (1985). **Career:** Area Educational Superintendent, Dukhan area, Qatar (1960-64); Instructor, Southern Illinois University (1965-69); Associate Professor, M.E. Studies at S.I.U. (1972-73); Associate Professor, promoted in 1980 to Professor, Sophia University, Japan; Professor in Diplomacy and International Law, U.A.E. (1980-83; 1986-91); Professor; Middle East and Islamic Civilisation, International University of Japan (1983-86); Planner and Founder of the 1st private University in Jordan (A.S.U.) (1980-90), Planner, the Jordan University for Women and Zaitouneh University; Vice-Pres., Board of Trustees, Applied Science University, Jordan (1990-93); Administrative Counsellor, the Cabinet of the Prime Ministers of Jordan (1968-72); Vice President, the Emiri Court, Abu Dhabi (1968-73); Representative (rank of Ambassador), the League of Arab

States on furlough from Abu Dhabi Government (1970-72); Planner, co-Founder of UAE Embassies in Tripoli, Libya, in Tokyo, Japan, in Seoul, Korea and Peijing, China; Minister Plenipotentiary, Ministry of Foreign Affairs, U.A.E. (1973-1991); Diplomatic Envoy, representing U.A.E., Jordan and or the League of Arab States to Leaders of some Arab and non-Arab Heads of States (1968-92); Co-founder of the National Bank of Abu Dhabi in Tokyo (1982-86); Planner & Initiator, the foundation of the Arab Bank Representation Office in Tokyo (1985-86); General Manager/Founder of the Arab Int'l Co. for Investment & Educ. (A.I.C.I.E.) (1988-1991), Chairman, A.I.C.I.E. (1990-to present); Vice-President and Professor in Diplomacy and International Law, Applied Science University, Amman, Jordan (1990-to present). **Member:** Life Member, Academy of Islamic Research, Lecknow, India (1972), The Middle East Studies Association in the USA & Canada (1973), Japanese Academy of Middle Eastern Studies (1976), and Japanese Association for Middle Eastern Studies (JAMES) (1979); Fellow, the British Society for Middle Eastern Studies (1977), Life Member, Middle East Institute, Washington (1977), Liaison Office, the Japanese Arab Relations Study Committee (1978). **Publ.:** "The Organisation of the Govt. of Jordan's Administration & Hierarchy" (1968); "Abu Dhabi Public Service Code of 1969" (1972); "Economics & Political Evolution in the Arabian Gulf States (N.Y.1973); "UAE Challenges the Desert to Bloom" (Tokyo, 1982); "The Palestine Question and International Law (Tokyo, 1979); "Theory of State and International Law in Classical Islam" (Tokyo; 1985); "Studies in International Law & Diplomatic Practice, with Introduction to Islamic Law" (Tokyo, 1980); "Arab Customs & Manners" (Tokyo, 1984), "Diplomatic Manners, Etiquette and Protocol" (in Arabic, 1990); "Diplomacy, and the Foreign Service" (in Arabic, 1990). Published Research Papers as: "Tribalism in Eastern Arabia" (1977), "Palestinian Inalienable Rights Under International Law" (1979), "Energy in Japanese - Arab Gulf Relations: A Path for Solidarity and Cooperation" (1979), "OAPEC, UAE & Foreign Aid" (1979), "Sources of Islamic Law of Nations" (1981), "Arabian Gulf Society: Impact of Oil Industry" (1985), "Diplomacy in Islam" (1989); Lectured at universities, UN Seminars and cultural symposia. **Honors:** Decorated by his Majesty King Hussein with Award of Honour, (The Order of Independence) (1969); Recipient (Student of the Year), Southern Illinois University (1965), (Dean's List of Honour) at S.I.U. (1965-70), (British Council Scholar) Selected by the British Council (1966-67), (International Ambassador) S.I.U., nominated in 1982, (Man of the Year), nominated by the American Biographical Institute (1990). **Hobbies:** Calligraphy, painting, poetry, listening to music, travel, reading and research. **Addr.:** In UAE: P.O.Box 8222, Abu Dhabi. In Japan: P.O.Box 128, Akasaka, UAE Emb., Tokyo, Japan. In England: P.O.Box 40, Kensington, London. In Jordan, P.O.Box 35087, Tel.: (962-6) 837-181, 684-121, Fax: (962-6) 828-328, 832-899, Amman, Jordan.

ROSS (Christopher W.S.), American diplomat. **Born** on March 3, 1943 in Quito, Ecuador. **Son** of Claude G. Ross (diplomat) **and** Mrs. Antigone Peterson Ross. **Married** on November 30, 1968 in Staunton, Virginia, U.S.A. to Carol Canning Ross, one child, Anthony Gordon Ross (December 21, 1971); divorced. **Educ.:** American Community School, Beirut, Lebanon (1954-60); Princeton University, Princeton, New Jersey (1960-63), (1964-65); Middle East Centre for Arab Studies, Chemlan, Lebanon (1963-64); Johns Hopkins University School of Advanced International Studies, Washington, D.C. (1965-69). **Dipl.:** B.A. in Oriental Studies, Princeton University (1965); M.A. in International Relations, Johns Hopkins School of Advanced International Studies (1967). **Career:** Editorial Assistant, Middle East Journal (1965-68); Arabic Language Instructor, Columbia University (1966); Arabic Language Instructor, Princeton University (1967); public affairs trainee, U.S. Information Agency, Washington, D.C. (1968-69); junior officer trainee, U.S. Information Service, Tripoli, Libya (1969-70); Director, American Cultural Center, Fez, Morocco (1970-73); Press Attache, American Embassy, Beirut, Lebanon (1973-76); Public Affairs Officer, U.S. Information Service, Algiers, Algeria (1976-79); Deputy Chief of Mission and Chargé d'Affaires, American Embassy, Algiers, Algeria (1979-81); Public Affairs Adviser, Bureau of Near Eastern and South Asian Affairs, Department of State, Washington, D.C. (1981-82); Special Assistant to the Presidential Emissaries to Lebanon and the Middle East (1982-84); Director of Regional Affairs, Brueau of Near Eastern and South Asian Affairs, Department of State (1984-85); Executive Assistant to the Under Secretary of State for Political Affairs (1985-88); American Ambassador to Algeria (1988-91); American Ambassador to Syria (1991-1998). Coordinator for Counterterrorism, Department of State (1998); Executive Director, Search for Common Ground in the Middle East (1999- present). **Languages:** English, Arabic, French, Greek. **Awards:** Superior Honor Award, U.S. Information Agency, 1976 and 1983; Superior Honor Award, Department of State 1988; Presidential Meritorious Service Award, 1983, 1985, 1989, 1993; Distinguished Honor Award, Department of State, 1997. **Hobby:** classic cars. **Member:** Council on Foreign Relations (New York), American Foreign Service Association, Association for Diplomatic Studies and Training, Middle East Institute, Middle East Studies Association of North America, Royal Society for Asian Affairs, American Institute of Meghrib Studies, Princeton Club of Washington, D.C. **Addr.:** 1601 Connecticut Avenue, N.W., Suite 200, Washington, D.C. 20009-1035, U.S.A.

ROSTAMANI (Abdallah, Hassan, al), UAE national businessman. **Born** in 1931 in Dubai, United Arab Emirates. **Son** of Hassan al-Rostamani. **Married** in 1965, 2 sons, 4 daughters. **Educ.:** Secondary School. **Career:** Chairman of al-Rostamani Group of Companies, established three decades ago and operating throughout the

U.A.E., engaged in diversified business activities which includes automobile and automotive products, tyres, lubricants, refrigeration products, travel, tours and foreign exchange, construction and contracting, aviation, insurance, banking, real estate, active participation in the development projects of the Country and also Overseas investments. Also Chairman of Aero Gulf Services; Deputy Chairman, Dubai Insurance Company, Dubai; Director, National Bank of Umm al-Quwain Ltd. **Member:** Dubai Municipality; Dubai Chamber of Commerce and Industry, and Dubai World Trade Club. **Hobbies:** Reading, Photography, Art Collection, Music and Cultural Activities. **Address:** al-Rostamani Group of Companies, P.O.Box 261, Dubai, United Arab Emirates, Tel.: 283166, 238998, 226222, Telex: 45484 MARWAN EM, Fax: (04) 231450.

ROSTAMANI (Abdul Rahman Hassan, al), UAE official. **Born** in 1943 in Dubai, United Arab Emirates. **Educ.:** Cairo University, Egypt. **Dipl.:** Degree in Social Studies. **Career:** Third Secretary, Ministry of Foreign Affairs (1972); Director of Information, United Arab Emirates Government (1972); Director of Personnel Department (1972); Under Secretary and Director of Personnel, Civil Service Commission (1976-). **Hobbies:** Poetry, music, literature, travel, sports, swimming, water-skiing. **Prof. Addr.:** Civil Service Commission, P.O.Box 899, Abu Dhabi, United Arab Emirates.

ROUIGHI (Mohamad), Algerian politician. **Born** in 1942. **Dipl.:** Ph.D. in Agronomy. **Career:** Member, Central Committee, FLN (1979-); President, Subcommission for Agriculture and Hydraulics, FLN (1979); Secretary of State for Forestry (1980); Minister of Hydraulics, the Environment and Forestry (1984-87); Minister of Agriculture (1988-89). **Addr.:** Algiers, Algeria.

ROUIS (Bachir), Algerian politician. **Born** in 1940. **Career:** Director General, Ministry of Agriculture (1969-77); Deputy, National Popular Assembly (1977); Secretary to the Wilaya of Blida; Minister of Post and Telecommunications (1982-84); Deputy and Member, Political Bureau (1984-88); Minister of Information (1984-88). **Addr.:** c/o FLN, Blvd. Zirout Yousouf, Algiers, Algeria.

ROUISI (Moncer, Dr.), Tunisian Politician. **Born** on Septembre 3, 1940 in Degache, Tozeur Governate. **Married,** one child. **Educ.:** Baccalaureate, Mathematics (1960), Studies Mathematics and Physics, Toulouse (1961); B.A., Sociology, Toulouse University (1964); Diploma (1966); Superior Diploma, Demography Department, University of Paris (1969); Ph.D., Sociology, Sorbonne, Paris, **Career:** Head, Demography Department, University of Tunis (1969-73); Visiting Researcher, Harvard University (1975-76); President, National Commision for Scientific Research (1978-79); Expert to the UN, Damascus (1979-80) and Rabat (1980-83); Professor, Faculty of Social Sciences, University of Tunis (1984-88); Member, Democratic Constitutional Rally (RCD) (1988-to date); Adviser to the President and Manger of 1989 presidential campaign (1989-90); Minister of Social Affairs (1991-92); Minister of Vocational Training and Employment (1992-to date). **Address:** Ministry of Vocational Training and Employment, 10 Boulevard Ouled Haffouz, 1005, Tunis, Tunisia.

ROUQI (Mutlag al-Diyabi, al), Saudi civil servant. **Born** in 1927 in Amman, Jordan. **Educ.:** General **Career:** Succesively announcer; Director, Varieties Section; Director, Sautu'l Islam (Voice of Islam) Broadcasting Service; Supervisor, Musical Section; has been working in the broadcasting field for 23 years; now Programme Adviser, Jeddah Broadcasting Service. **Awards:** "Bravery" Order of Merit, Jordanian Army. **Member:** The Literary Club. **Hobby:** Reading. **Prof. Addr.:** Jeddah Broadcasting Station, Ministry of Information Building, Jeddah, Saudi Arabia.

ROUSHDI (Abdul-Munim Negib), Egyptian banker. **Born** in 1926 in Cairo, Egypt. **Married,** 2 children. **Educ.:** Cairo University, Egypt; George Washington University (graduate studies). **Dipl.:** B.A. in Economics. **Career:** Controller of Banks, Central Bank of Egypt (1967); International Monetary Fund Adviser to Bank of Yemen, Aden (1970); Deputy Chairman and Managing Director, Investment Authority, Cairo (1975); Chairman of National Bank of Egypt (1977-); formerly Deputy chairman and Managing Director, Arab African International Bank, cairo. **Publ.:** various articles and pamphlets on economics, finance and banking. **Decor.:** Officer of the Legion d'Honneur, France (1979). **Hobbies:** walking. music. **Prof. Addr.:** P.O.Box 60, Garden City, Cairo, Egypt.

ROUSHDI (Abdulhamid), Egyptian technical consultant. **Born** on February 26, 1918 in Cairo. **Educ.:** Faculty of Agriculture, Cairo University. **Dipl.:** Bachelor of Science in Agriculture. **Career:** Technical Consultant C.M. Salvago and Co., Standard Food Products and Egyptian Bottling, S.A.E. **Member:** Gazira Sporting Club, Cairo Yachting Club, Alexandria Sporting Club. **Hobbies:** Tennis, swimming and squash. **Addr.:** 11, Gabalaya Street, Zamalek, Tel.: 807575, Cairo, Egypt.

ROUSHDI (Jamaleddin Sayid), Egyptian pharmacist. **Born** in 1927 in Cairo, Egypt. **Married,** 2 daughters. **Educ.:** Cairo University, Egypt. **Dipl.:** B.Sc. in Pharmacy, Diploma in Industrial Pharmacy. **Career:** Civilian Pharmacist (1952-54); Officer (Pharmacist), of Egyptian Armed Forces (1954-77); Director of the Scientific Office (1977-82); Consultant of PIACT/PATH Cairo (1982-84). **Member:** Automobile Club, al-Ahly Club, Yacht Club, Officers Club. **Prof. Addr.:** Rushdi Pharmacy, Tariq al-Qaser, Khalf al-Tirsanah al-Bahriah, Ard al-Jamiah, Ombabah, Cairo, Egypt.

ROUSHDI (Mustafa, Sayid), Egyptian businessman. **Born** in 1932 in Cairo, Egypt. **Married**, 2 children. **Educ.:** Faculty of Commerce, Cairo University, Egypt. **Career:** Chief of Cabinet to the Permanent Under Secretary of State, Ministry of Economy (1953-60); Controller of Exports, Export Promotion Organisation (1961-67); General Manager of Foreign Relations, Foreign Trade Organization (1967-71); Chairman of el-Nour Import and Export Company (1972-74); Chairman of Medi Trade Company Chairman of el-Wadi Export Company (1974-); Chairman of Medi Trade Company (1980-); Member of the Board of Anglo-Egyptian Chamber of Commerce (1980-), of Foreign Trade Organisation (1984-); Member of Egyptian/US Business Council (1984-); Member of Egyptian Businessmen's Council; Member of Export Committee, Cairo Chamber of Commerce (1984-). **Hobbies:** shooting, yachting. **Addr.:** 7 el-Aziz Othman Flat 9, Zamalek, Cairo, Egypt; 9 Talaat Harb Street, Cairo, Egypt.

ROUSHDI (Subhi, Khalil), Egyptian businessman. **Born** in 1929 in Egypt. **Married**, 2 children. **Educ.:** Faculty of Law, Cairo University. **Career:** Shareholder and President of Hapi Tourist Company (1962-); Board Director of Misr-Immobilière, Swiss Company with Arab interests, formed to establish and develop residential city in Egypt and owning concession for Mokattam City, Cairo (1975-); Chief Executive and shareholder of Elsara SA, Geneva, Switzerland, company with substantial investments in Egypt especially Ismailia Transport Company (1975-); Chairman and Partner of Giza System Engineering, Egypt which acts as agent for digital computer equipment and similar companies and in software and hardware computer business (1975-); Shareholder and Chairman of Overseas Bank and Trust, Cayman Island; Member of the Board of International Music Society; Chairman of Allied Arab Bank, London, UK (1977); Shareholder and Member of the Board of Bank Für Handel and Effekten, Zurich (1977-). **Hobbies:** swimming, reading, tennis. **Addr.:** Rostam Street, Garden City, Cairo, Egypt.

RQOBAH (Homoud Abdulla, al), Kuwaiti former Minister. **Born** on July 18, 1951 in Kuwait. **Married** on June 15, 1986 in Kuwait to Miss Lamiya Bu-Hannad, one son, Abdulla. **Educ.:** Worcester Polytechnic Institute, U.S.A.; University of Salford, England. **Dipl.:** B.Sc in Chemical Engineering (1974); M.Sc. (1977); Ph.D. (1981). **Career:** Assistant Dean, College of Engineering. and Petroleum, Kuwait University (1982-84); Dean, College of Engineering. & Petroleum, Kuwait University (1984-86); Director General, Kuwait Institute for Scientific Research, Kuwait (1986-88); Minister of Electricity and Water, Kuwait (1988-91); Minister of Oil & Chairman of Kuwait Petroleum Corporation (April 1991- Oct. 1992). **Hobbies:** Hicking, Hunting. **Credit Cards:** American Express, Diner's Club. **Priv. Addr.:** Mushred, Block-6, Lot-263, Rd. 2. Str. 7, Villa 24, Tel.: 4399977, Kuwait.

RSHEIDAT (Najib, Awad), Jordanian lawyer. **Born** on April 19, 1922 at Irbid, Jordan. **Son** of Awad Rsheidat (Farmer) **and** Mrs., née Mariam Dalkamouni. **Married** on May 6, 1950, at Irbid, to Miss Hind Said Elkhatib, 6 children: Fawaz (1951), Fayez (1953), Fawzi (1955), Mazin (1956), Khalid (1960) and Reem (1961). **Educ.:** Secondary School, Salt, Jordan; University of Damascus, Law College, Damascus. **Dipl.:** Law degree. **Career:** Advocate (Octobre 1943- May 1947); Judge (1947-12.10.1962); Member of Parliament (12 Octobre 1962- 20 April 1963); Advocate (until July 1969); during this period: President of the Bar Association (4 years); Governor of Amman (19 July 1969- 19 January 1970); Minister of Interior (20 April 1970- 27 June 1970); Minister of Communications (27 June 1970- 15 September 1970); Advocate (1970-79); Minister of Justice (19 December 1979-July 1980); Private Law Offices (1981-). **Hobbies:** Chess and reading. **Prof. Addr.:** King Hussein Street, British Bank Bldg., Tel.: 3727, Amman. **Priv. Addr.:** Shmeisani, Dastour Paper quarter, Tel.: 63438, P.O.Box 1587, Amman, Jordan.

RUBAIE' (Muhammad Abdul-Rahman, Al-, Dr,), Saudi Professor. **Born** in 1947.**Son** of Abdul-Rahman Hamad Al-Rubaie' **and** Shaikha Naser Al-Sahhood. **Married** in 1970 to Nora Ibrahim Al-Méqerin, 7 children: Hesham, Adel, Riyadh, Hani, Abdul-Rahman, Shaikha, Ruqaiah. **Educ.:** B.A. from Faculty of Arabic, Al-Imam Muhammad Ibn Saud Islamic University (Riyadh); M.A. and Ph.D. from Faculty of Arabic Al-Azhar University in Cairo. **Career:** Teacher in Makkah Scientific Institute (1968); Teacher in Riyadh Scientific Institute (1969). Director of Higher Studies and Missions in Al-Imam University (1975); Dean of Scientific Research (1985); Editor of Al-Imam University Journal (1989); Deputy of Al-Imam Muhammad Ibn Saud Islamic University for Higher studies and Scientific Research, and President of the Scientific Council (1995). **Sport:** Walking. **Prof. Addr.:** Deputy of Al-Imam University, Riyadh 11432 (P.O.Box 5701), Tel.: 4650392, 2586888, Fax 2590008.

RUBAISHI (Ali Ibrahim, al), Saudi Businessman. **Born** in 1938 in Buraidah, Saudi Arabia. **Dipl.:** B.A. (Accounting and Business Administration), King Saud University (1963). **Career:** Worked in the Arabian Bank, National Bank, Saudi Arabian Monetary Agency (1953-62); Director, Budget Accounts Department, Petromin (1962); Has also held the following positions in Petromin: Assistant Supervisor of Accounts Department, Secretary, Accounts Department and General Manager, Coordination and Control Department; Deputy Governor, Coordination and Control, Petromin (1977-89); Chairman, Management Committee of Yanbu Domestic Refinery; Chairman of the Board, The Arabian Marine Petroleum Construction Co.; Petromin representative at many official meetings and conferences; Presently Owner and Charmain of al-Rubaishi Trading Services Office, and Saudi Plant for Reconditioned Drums Co. **Hobby:** Sports. **Addr.:** al-Rubaishi Trading Services Office, P.O.Box 20715, Riyadh 11465, Saudi Arabia.

RUMAIHI (Mohamad, Ghanem, al), Kuwaiti academic. **Born** in 1942 in Bahrain. **Educ.:** Durham University, UK. **Dipl.:** Ph.D. in Social Sciences. **Career:** Vice-Dean, Faculty of Letters, Kuwait University (1974-76), Head of Sociology Department (1974-78), Professor of Sociology (1977-82), Education Programme Council Member, High Studies Faculty (1980-82); Board Member of "al-Khaliz and the Arab Island Studies", university journal (1981); Editor in-Chief of "al-Arabi" magazine, Ministry of Information (1982-). **Publ.:** "Petrol and Social Change in the Arab Gulf" (1975), "Problems of Political and Social Change in Bahrain since the First World War" (1976), "Petrol and International Relations" (1982). **Prof. Addr.:** al-Arabi Magazine, P.O.Box 748, Safat, 13008, Kuwait, Kuwait.

RUMI (Khalfan, Mohamad, al), United Arab Emirates statesman. **Born** in 1945 in Sharjah, United Arab Emirates. **Son** of Mohamad al-Rumi. **Married**, three children. **Educ.:** B.A. in Education, College of Education, Baghdad, Iraq; University of Southampton, UK. **Career:** Deputy Director of Education (1970-72); Secretary of State, Ministry of Education (1972-77); Minister of Health (1977); Minister of Labour and Social Affairs (since 1983 to Oct. 1992); Minister of Information and Culture (Oct. 1992-March 1996); member of the Constituent Committee; participated in many Arab and international conferences; Vice Chairman, National Bank of Sharjah; Chairman, Al-Ittihad Press, Publishing and Distribution Corp.., **Hobbies:** Poetry, History, sociology, reading. **Addr.:** P.O.Box 791, Abu Dhabi, United Arab Emirates.

RUWAIDAR (Ahmad, Said), Egyptian economist. **Born** in 1915 in Egypt. **Married**, three children. **Educ.:** Ph.D. in Economics. **Career:** Lecturer in Economics, Ain Shams University, Cairo, Egypt (1955); Assistant Professor, and Professor of Economics (1958); Director General, Ministry of Economy (1963); Under Secretary, Ministry of Economy (1973-75); Adviser, Ministry of Economy (1977); Fellow of the Economic Development Institute, Washington DC, USA; member of the Egyptian Committee for Economics and Statistics. **Publ.:** "Economic Planning" (1958); "Economics Development" (1964); "Financial and Monetary Policy" (1974); "Economic Development" (1977). **Addr.:** 15 Mahmoud Sidqy al-Mohandis Street, Tel.: 814479, Agouza, Cairo, Egypt.

S

SAAB (Abdulaziz Ahmad), Saudi businessman. **Born** in 1928 in Mecca, Saudi Arabia. **Educ.:** Secondary school education. **Career:** Editorial Secretary, al-Bilad newspaper, Mecca (1952-55); Director General, Israel Boycott Office (1955-56), Jeddah; Director General, Administration Affairs, Ministry of Commerce (1956-58); General Manager, Madina Electric Company Ltd. (1958-69); Chairman, al-Rida Commercial and Contracting Enterprise, Saudi Ascon for Construction and Saudi-Eta for Electro-mechanical Works (a joint venture); Chairman, Chamber of Commerce and Industry, Medina; Honorary member, Dar al-Mal al-Islami Corporation; Secretary General, Medina Welfare Society; Vice Chairman, the Society for teaching the Qur'an; member, the Relief Society for Poor Prisoners, Medina; member, Board of Directors, Saudi Chambers Council, Riyadh, Yanbu Cement Factory; founding member, al-Medina Corporation for Journalism. **Honour:** Arz, Lebanese National Order. **Hobbies:** general reading, travel. **Prof. Addr.:** P.O.Box 1269 and P.O.Box 2818, Tel.: 8229688, Medina. **Priv. Addr.:** Tel.: 8228335, Medina, Saudi Arabia.

SAAD (Ali, Rashid, al), Saudi statistician. **Born** in 1929 in Saudi Arabia. **Son** of Rashid al-Saad. **Married**, five children. **Educ.:** B.Sc. in Agriculture, Cairo University (1953); American University, Cairo (1958); postgraduate studies in the Institute of Research and Statistical Studies (1959); UN Fellowship to study Statistics, UK (1965). **Career:** Director of Statistics, Ministry of Agriculture, Saudi Arabia (1959-64); Director General, Central Department of Statistics, Ministry of Finance and National Economy, Saudi Arabia (since 1965); Leader of Government delegation to several international economic and statistical conferences (since 1964). Member of the International Statistical Institute, The Hague; the International Association of Survey Statisticians, The Hague, the American Statistical Association, Washington. **Publ.:** "Statistical Development in Saudi Arabia" (1966); "The Multi-Purpose Survey of Saudi Arabia" (1976); "Comparison of Male Occupation Specific Labour Force With Life Tables of Saudi Arabia" (1977); "Foreign Trade", and other statistical publications of the Department of Statistics. **Sport:** Swimming. **Hobbies:** Chess, travel. **Prof. Addr.:** Central Department of Statistics, P.O.B. 3735, Riyadh, Tel.: 4013778, Saudi Arabia. **Priv. Addr.:** Tel.: 4014127, Riyadh, Saudi Arabia.

SAAD (Chawqi), Sudanese university professor. **Born** in Sudan. **Educ.:** Secondary and Universities of London and Cairo. **Dipl.:** Bachelor of Science, Master of Science. **Career:** Professor, Senior Lecturer in Civil Engineering, Faculty of Engineering, University of Khartoum. **Addr.:** University of Khartoum, P.O.Box 321, Tel.: 72277, Khartoum, Sudan.

SAAD (Faisal Abdallah, al), Saudi academic. **Born** in 1944 in Taif, Saudi Arabia. **Dipl.:** B.Sc., M.Sc., Ph.D. **Career:** Lecturer, Plant Production Department, Faculty of Agriculture, King Saud University (1972) Assistant Professor (1974); Chairman, Department of Plant Production; Associate Professor, Faculty of Agriculture, King Saud University since 1980; member, Saudi Society for Biological Sciences; attented Conference on Scientific Equipment, Beirut, Conference on Research Co-ordination in Saudi Arabia, Industrial Development and Research Centre, Plant Physiology Conference; has participated in conducting an extension service and feasibility studies. **Publications:** several scientific papers, two books under publication on Plant Science. **Prof. Addr.:** Faculty of Agriculture, King Saud University, Tel.: 435Æ1655, Riyadh **Priv. Addr.:** Tel.: 646.9445, Riyadh, Saudi Arabia.

SAAD (Othman Mohamad, al), Saudi educator. **Born** in 1939 in Damascus, Syria. **Dipl.:** M.A. (Education and Hygiene Recreation). **Career:** Secretary General, the Saudi Arabian Olympic Committee, the Saudi Arabian Football Federation, the Arab Sports Confederation and the Arab Football Federation; executive committee member, the Asian Games Federation; technical committee member, the Football Federation and the F.I.F.A.; attended several International Olympic Committee conferences and the International Football Federation conferences. **Hobbies:** reading, drawing, music. **Prof. Addr.:** P.O.Box 2129, Tel.: 403.3628, 405.4006, Riyadh and P.O.Box 62997, Riyadh, Saudi Arabia. **Priv. Addr.:** Tel.: 4420141, 4420931, Riyadh, Saudi Arabia.

SAADAWI (Nawal, el), Egyptian physician, writer **Born** in Egypt. **Married**, two children. **Educ.:** al-Quasser al-Aini; Columbia University. **Dipl.:** B.Sc. in Medicine; M.Sc. in General Health. **Career:** Doctor, al-Quasser al-Aini Hospitals; Ministry of Health (1955-65); Director of Educational Health Management, Ministry of Health (1966-72); Editor in Chief, "Health" Magazine (1970-73); Consultant (Middle East and Africa) to the UN (1978-80). **Member** of Egyptian Writers' Union, Egyptian Union for Doctors,

Association for Arab Women's Solidarity. **Publ.:** "al-Mara Wa al-Ser'a al-Nafsi"; "al-Mara Wa al-Jins"; "al-Ontha Heah al Asle"; etc. **Medals:** Nobel Prize from the Higher Council for Arts and Literature (1974); Prize of Franco-Arab Friendship, Paris (1982). **Priv. Addr.:** 25 Murad Street, Giza, Egypt.

SAADEDDIN (Ibrahim, Dr.), Egyptian economist and planning expert. **Born** on May 25, 1925 in Sharqiyah, Egypt. **Married** in 1951 to Alia Hassan Hossni Shaker, 3 children: Hossam, Ziad and Mona. **Educ.:** B.Com., Cairo University, Egypt (1945); M.Sc. in Management, University of Illinois, USA (1952); Ph.D. in Business Administration, University of Illinois, USA (1955). **Career:** Lecturer in Cairo University (1955-59); Expert on Organization, Central Ministry of Education (1959-60); Expert, Ministry of Planning (1960-61); Professor and Secretary-General, National Institute of Planning, Cairo (1961-62); Professor and Member of Board, National Institute of Management Development (1962-64); Vice-Chairman, Central Auditing Authority (1947-71); Member of Arab Socialist Union Secretariat (1965-68); Chief Technical Adviser, United Nations Development Programme, Arab Institute of Planning, Kuwait. **Sport:** Walking. **Publ.:** Author of "Principles of Marketing" (Arabic) (1957); "Administrative Policies in Different Social Systems" (Arabic) (1970); several articles in specialised journals. **Prof. Addr.:** Planning Institute, P.O.Box 5834, Tel.: 432897, Kuwait. **Priv. Addr.:** 43, Giza Street, Apt. 73, Giza, Cairo, Egypt.

SAADI (Hani Jameel, al), Saudi civil servant. **Born** in 1948. **Educ.:** Secondary School Certificate. **Career:** Director Shipping Division. Raytheon (1969); Sales Agent Saudi Arabian Airlines; Inspector-General, Auditor's Office; now Supervisor of Free Tickets Office, Saudia-Saudi Arabian Airlines. **Member:** Saudi Arts Society. **Hobbies:** Acting, music. **Prof. Addr.:** Saudia Building, 9th Floor, P.O.Box 622, Jeddah, Saudi Arabia.

SAADI (Majed), Syrian executive. **Born** in 1933 in Damascus, Syria. **Son** of Tawfik Saadi. **Married** in 1963, 1 son, 2 daughters. **Educ.:** Secondary School; Accountancy. **Career:** Assistant General Manager, Real Estate Bank, Damascus, Syria. **Hobbies:** Sports, Reading and Travelling. **Addr.:** P.O.Box 2337, Tel.: 118602-3, Telex: 19171 A/ B REBANK SY, Damascus, Syria.

SAADI (Miazi, Mounir), Egyptian businessman. **Born** on August 18, 1950 in Cairo (Egypt). **Son** of Mounir Saadi **and** Mrs., née Kadria. **Married** to Nagia Mahmoud Sioufi in 1970, 1 daughter: Nada. **Educ.:** French Lycée of Mansourah (Egypt) until 1950; French Lycée, Cairo; College of the Christian Brothers, Daher, Cairo (1951-59). **Dipl.:** Egyptian Baccalaureat, 1959; B.Sc. (Textile Engineering) from the Higher Textiles School of Tournai, Belgium (1963). **Career:** Technical Director at Société Cifran-Sotta - Preen Pail - Mayenne (France) (1963-64); Assistant to General Manager at Société Anonyme des Fibres Nouvelles, Rueil-Malmaison (France) (1964); one of the founders of Société Libanaise de l'Industrie et du Commerce, Beirut (Lebanon); founder and partner, Middle East Garment Co., Beirut (Lebanon) (1964-72); technical and commercial adviser to a number of French and Italian firms exporting to EEC, Canada, Japan and USA (1972-73); Technical adviser to Twiltex Co., Cairo (1973-75); partner and adviser, BASTEX, Cairo. **Sports:** rowing, swimming, and fishing. **Member:** Gezireh Sporting club, Cairo. **Prof. Addr.:** 30, July 26th street, Cairo, Egypt. **Priv. Addr.:** 143, Tahrir Street-Dokki, Cairo, Egypt.

SAADI (Mohamad Ali, al), Iraqi academic, resident in USA. **Born** in 1933 in Baghdad, Iraq. **Son** of Ali Saadi. **Educ.:** Universities of Montana, Massachusetts, Amherst, USA. **Dipl:** B.A. in Political Science and Economics; M.A. and Ph.D. in Political Science. **Career:** Associate Professor, University of Wisconsin (1965-69); Associate Professor, California State Polytechnic University, Assistant Chairman, then Chairman, Department of Political Science. **Publ.:** various papers on the Middle East conflict deliverd at US and international professional conferences. **Hobbies:** classical music; jazz, Arabic music, sailing, swimming, tennis, skiing, literature. **President** of Southern California Chapter, Association of Arab American University Graduates (1975-76). **Prof. Addr.:** California State Polytechnic University, Pomona, California 91767, USA.

SAADI (Mohamad Ali Amin, al), Saudi official. **Born** in 1935 in Ghazza. **Dipl.:** B.S. (Agriculture Economics). **Career:** Head of Agricultural Unit, Jizan; Director, Deputy Minister's Office, Ministry of Agriculture and Water; General Manager, Department of Agricultural Research and Development; Assistant Deputy Minister for Agriculture, Ministry of Agriculture and Water; member, American Agricultural Economists Society, the International Economists Society for Development, Statistics Science Society; member of the Board, Saudi Arabian Agricultural Bank; member of the Board, Grain Silos and Flour Mills General Organization; member of the Board, Saudi Fund for Development. **Address:** Saudi Fund for Development, P.O.Box 1887, Riyadh, Saudi Arabia.

SAADI (Moussa), Moroccan engineer-geologist. **Born** on December 13, 1937 in Oujda. **Educ.:** Secondary in Oujda; Higher at "Ecole Nationale Supérieure de Géologie Appliquée et de Prospection Minière", Nancy; Faculty of Grenoble. **Dipl.:** Engineer-Geologist, B.S. **Career:** Deputy Head of Service, Studies of Mining Deposits (1962-65). Head of Service, Ibid (1966-69); Head of Division of Geology (1970-74); Secretary of State for Trade, Mining Industry and Merchant Marine (1974-77); Minister of Energy and Mines (1977-84); Minister of Tourism (1985-89). Member of the Parliament (1977). **Publ.:** several reports on Geology, Mining research and old mining activities in Morocco published in Morocco and abroad. **Award:** Ouissam Alaouite (Ordre Rida) (1967), Prix Scientifique du Maroc (1970). **Member:** Deputy Secretary-General, National Association of Mining Engineers of Morocco (1967-69); Secretary General, Ibid (1970). **Vice-President** of International Association of Geology. **Addr.:** Rabat, Morocco.

SAADI (Selim), Algerian politician. **Born** in Algeria. **Married**, three children. **Career:** Director of Transport, Ministry of Defence (1963-67); Chief of an Armoured Division (1967-70); Combat Director in the Army (1970-72); Commander of Third Military region with rank of Lieutenant Colonel; member, Central Committee, FLN (since 1979); Minister of Agriculture and, Agrarian Reform (1979-84); Minister of Heavy Industry (1984-85); Minister of the Interior (Sept. 1993-1994); Vice-President-Coordinator of "Alliance Nationale Républicaine" since 1995; Minister of Water Resources, December 1999 - to date. **Addr.:** 3 Rue du Caire, Boite Postale 86 - Kouba, Algiers, Algeria.

SAADIDDIN (Mursi, Abdulhamid), Egyptian writer. **Born** in 1921 in Egypt. **Son** of Abdulhamid Saadiddin. **Married**, one son. **Career:** Ministry of Foreign Affairs; Egyptian Embassy in London as Head of the Students' Office, Assistant Cultural Attaché, Cultural Attaché; Deputy Director of Fine Arts Council, Cairo (1956); Censor of foreign books and publications; Assistant Secretary General and Public Relations Officer for the Afro Asian People's Solidarity Conference (subsequently Organisation) (1958); Cultural Attaché, Embassy to East Germany (1969-72); Controller General, Egyptian Higher Council for the Arts (1973); Director General, Ministry of Information and Culture (1975-78); Chairman of the State Information Service (1977-79); Editor in Chief, Cairo today. **Secretary** of Egyptian Poets, Essayists and Novelists (PEN) Club and Egyptian Writers Union; Chief Censor of English language publications. **Addr.:** 4 Ibn Iyass Street, Cairo, Egypt.

SAATI (Mohamad Amin), Saudi journalist. **Born** in 1945 in Jeddah, Saudi Arabia. **Dipl.:** Ph.D. **Career:** Cashier and Chief Storekeeper, Jeddah Seaport Authority; Managing Editor, Okaz daily newspaper; Head, Cultural Committee, King Abdulaziz University; member, Okaz Organization for Press and Publication; Secretary-General and member of Board, Alahli Sporting Club, Jeddah; member American Society for Public Administration (ASPA). **Publications:** several books on sport, History of Sport in Saudi Arabia, Olympic Games, World Cup and the Saudi Cup, Arabs and Sports. **Hobbies:** football, basketball, baseball. **Address:** al-Faisalia, P.O.Box 4101, Jeddah, Saudi Arabia.

SAATI (Zeiny Jamal, al), Saudi academic. **Born** in 1944 in Mecca, Saudi Arabia. **Dipl.:** Ph.D. **Career:** Lecturer, University of Petroleum and Minerals (1975); Assistant Professor, University of Petroleum and Minerals. **Address:** University of Petroleum and Minerals, P.O.Box 1785, Tel.: 8603630, Dhahran. **Priv. Addr.:** Tel.: 8606585, Dhahran, Saudi Arabia.

SAATY (Hassan, Abdulaziz, al), Egyptian academic. **Born** on Sep. 30, 1916 in Calioub (Suburb of Cairo). **Son** of Abdulaziz as-Saati (Watchmaker) **and** Mrs. Hanin Saleem. **Married** to Fawzeya Diab on January 4, 1943 in London, 2 children: Ezzat (B.Com.) and Samya. **Educ.:** Calioub Primary School (Calioub), Khedive Ismail Secondary School (Cairo), Cairo University (Cairo), Higher Institute of Education (Cairo), University of London. London School of Economics. Bachelor of Arts (1938), Diploma of Education (1939), Diploma in Social Science (1941), Diploma in Mental Health (1942), Doctor of Philosophy in Sociology (1946). **Career:** Lecturer in Social Science, Higher Institute of Social Work, Ministry of Higher Education (1946); Lecturer in Sociology, Faculty of Arts, Alexandria University (1949); Assistant Professor of Sociology, Faculty of Arts, Alexandria University (1953); Professor of Sociology, Faculty of Arts, Aïn Shams University, Cairo (1960); Vice-Dean, Faculty of Arts, Aïn Shams University, Cairo (1962-64); Dean, Faculty of Arts, Aïn Shams University, Cairo (1961-64); Chairman Department of Psychology and Sociology, same Faculty (1967-68); Chairman, Department of Philosophy and Sociology. Dean, Faculty of Arts, Beirut Arab University (1968-1973). **Publ.:** Author of books: "Sociology of Crime", "Sociology of Law", "Studies in the Science of Population", "Industrialisation and Urbanisation", "Khaldunian Sociology" (all in Arabic), Conducted major researches on Prostitution in Cairo, Industrialisation in Alexandria (published in English); Social Survey of Bab ash-Shaeriya District in Cairo (all published); participated in Regional and International Conferences and published papers in their proceedings. **Sports:** Table-tennis and walking. **Hobbies:** Playwriting and music. **Member:** L'Institut d'Egypte, Academy of Islamic Research "EL-AZHER", National Specialized Councils. **Awards:** Medal of the Republic 1977, State Prize of Merit in Social Sciences 1992, King Faysal International Prize in Sociology 1993, Medal of Sciences and Arts (1st Grade) 1995. **Addr.:** 59, el-Thawrah Street, Heliopolis, Cairo, Egypt.

SABA (Fauzi, Fuad, Dr.), Certified public accountant. **Born** on October 2, 1931 in Jerusalem. **Son** of Fuad S. Saba (Certified Accountant) **and** Mrs., née Mohiba K. Maalouf. **Married** to Wendy Sonnenberg, 4 children; Marwan, Emma-Kate, Nadia, Tarek. **Educ.:** St. George's School, Jerusalem; American University of Beirut, Lebanon; Northeastern University, Boston; George Washington University, Washington DC. **Dipl.:** B.B.A. (1925); M.B.A. (Business Administration); D.B.A. **Career:** Partner, Saba & Co., Certified Public Accountant; Partner, Arthur Andersen, Saba & Co. (1957-70); Certified Public

Accountant specializing in petroleum industry, industry accounting and financial problems; International Taxation consultant; Member of American Institute of Certified Public Accountants; Founder and Past-President of MESAA (Middle East Society of Associated Accountants) Member of Board, Third Atlantic Ltd., Senior Partner, Deloitte Touche Saba & Co. (Middle East). **Member:** Ethics Committee, International Federation of Accountants. **Credit Cards:** Amex, Barclaycard, etc. **Prof. and Priv. Addr:** P.O.Box 1131, Tel.: 857-4041, al-Khobar 31952, Saudi Arabia and P.O.Box 9235, Dubai, U.A.E.

SABAA (Hassouna, Mahmoud), Egyptian surgeon. **Born** in Cairo, Egypt in 1926. **Son** of Mahmoud Saba'a. **Married**, two children. **Educ.:** Cairo University. **Dipl.:** B.Ch. **Career:** Head of Surgery Department, Port Said General Hospital (1954-59); Head of Surgery Department, Giza Chest Hospital (1960-63); Director, College of Heart Surgery, Cairo (since 1964). Executive member of Egyptian Heart Surgery Society; member of Royal Society of Medicine, UK; Fellow, Royal College of Surgeons, UK. **Member** of Cairo Shooting Club; of Cairo Automobile Club. **Prof. Addr.:** 52 Abdel Khalek Sarwat Street, Cairo, Egypt. **Priv. Addr.:** el-Nasr Bldg., Nile Street, Giza, Egypt.

SABAH (Ali, al-Khalifa, al-Athbi, al, Shaikh), Kuwaiti economist, statesman. **Born** in 1945 in Kuwait. **Son** of Khalifa al-Sabah. **Educ.:** B.A. in Economics, University of California, Berkeley, USA (1968); M.A. in Economics, School of Oriental and African Studies, University of London, UK. **Career:** Ministry of Finance and Oil (1968); Assistant Under Secretary for Economic Affairs (1972); Under Secretary, Ministry of Finance (1975); negotiator for Kuwait in 1975 negotiations with British Petroleum and Gulf Oil leading to Kuwait nationalisation of Kuwait Oil Company; Minister of Oil (1978-89); Minister of Finance (1990-April 1991); Kuwait's representative on the OPEC Board of Governors (1974-76); Chairman of OPEC Board for the year 1975; Chairman of Gulf International Bank, member of Board of the Central Bank of Kuwait, the Arabian Oil Company; former Chairman, Kuwait Petroleum Corp; Chairman and Managing Director, Kuwait Real Estate Bank KSC. **Addr.:** P.O.Box 22822, Safat 13089, Kuwait City, Kuwait.

SABAH (Ali, Jarrah, al, Shaikh), Kuwaiti economist. **Born** in 1950 in Kuwait. **Son** of Jarrah al Sabah. **Married**, three children. **Educ.:** Economic and Political Science, Kuwait University (1972). **Career:** Second Secretary, Economic Department, Ministry of Foreign Affairs (1972); Counsellor, Kuwait Embassy to Tehran, Iran (1973); Investments Department, Ministry of Finance (1975); Director of Local and Arab Investments Department, Ministry of Finance (1975); Director Arab Banking Corporation, Bahrain; Bahrain Kuwait Insurance Company, Bahrain; Kuwait Reinsurance Co., Kuwait; Chairman, Egyptian Kuwaiti Real Estate Development Co, Egypt. **Sports:** Football. **Addr.:** Kuwait, City, Kuwait.

SABAH (Badria, al, Shaikha), Kuwaiti businesswoman. **Born** in 1920. **Career:** Prominent businesswoman in Kuwait, started business in the late 1960s; Chairman, United Trading Group. **Addr.:** United Trading Group, Abdullah Mubarak Street, P.O.Box 1208 Safat 13013, Telex: 22212 UNTROUP KT, Tel.: 2420115, Safat, Kuwait.

SABAH (Hamad, Ibrahim, al), United Arab Emirates administrator. **Born** in 1934 in Abu Dhabi, United Arab Emirates. **Son** of Ibrahim al Sabah. **Married**, two children. **Educ.:** Degree in Law, Cairo University, Egypt (1958). **Career:** Director General of the Abu Dhabi Chamber of Commerce and Industry (1968-71); Director of Customs (1971-72); Director General of Customs Department, Abu Dhabi (1976). **Sport:** Swimming. **Hobby:** Chess. **Addr.:** Abu Dhabi, United Arab Emirates.

SABAH (Jaber, Abdallah, Jaber, al, Shaikh), Kuwaiti former governor. **Born** 1920 in Kuwait. **Eldest Son** of Abdallah Jaber as-Sabah. **Married**, 1 son. **Educ.:** Victoria College, Alexandria; Law studies in the U.K. (1951-52). **Career:** Deputy to his father in the Courts (later Justice) Department (1952-62); Governor of Ahmadi and the Neutral Zone (January 1962); Minister of Labour and Social Affairs (1990- April 1991); former Provincial Governor of Kuwait. **Hobbies:** Natural History (owned a private zoo), sea-fishing, gardening. **Addr.:** Kuwait City, Kuwait.

SABAH (Jaber al-Ahmad al-Jaber, al, H.H. Shaikh), Ruler of Kuwait. **Born** in 1926 in Kuwait. **Son** of H.H. Shaikh Ahmad al-Jaber al-Sabah (late Ruler of Kuwait). **Married. Educ.:** al-Mubarakiyaah School, Kuwait and by private tutors. **Career:** Public Security Department; special responsibility for Kuwait Oil Company area (1950-56); Representative of HH the Ruler, KOC and Aminoil (1956-59); President, Finance Department and Housing Department with budgetary control over all public departments; Civil Commission and General Oil Affairs Office (1959-62); Ministry of Finance and Economy (1962-63); Minister of Finance and Industry (1963-65); Prime Minister (1965- December 1977); Heir Apparent (1966); Ruler of Kuwait since December 1977. **Addr.:** Ruler's Palace, Kuwait.

SABAH (Jaber al-Ali Salem, al, Shaikh), Kuwaiti former minister. **Born** in 1927. **Educ.:** Private in Kuwait. **Career:** Minister of Public Works (1962-63); Minister of Electricity and Water (1963-64); Minister of Guidance and Information (1964-71); Minister of Guidance and Information and Deputy Prime Minister (1975-77); Deputy Prime Minister and Minister of Information (February 16, 1977-1978). **Addr.:** Kuwait City, Kuwait.

SABAH (Jabir al-Athbi, al, Shaikh), Kuwaiti aviation

officer. **Born** in Egypt in 1935. **Married**, six children. **Educ.:** Oxford University. UK. **Career:** Assistant Under Secretary for Logistics and Procurement in Ministry of Defence (1964-74); Director General, Civil Aviation (since 1974 to present); Director Kuwait Airways Corporation. **Addr.:** Directorate of Civil Aviation, P.O.Box 17, Safat 13001, Kuwait.

SABAH (Mishaal al-Ahmad al-Jaber, al, Shaikh), Kuwaiti official. **Born** in 1938. **Educ.:** Metropolitan Police College, Hendon, UK. **Career:** Head of Security Services (1968); extensive business interests. **Hobby:** Hunting. **Addr.:** P.O.Box 9309, Ahmadi, Kuwait.

SABAH (Mubarak, al-Abdallah al-Jaber, al, Shaikh), Kuwaiti former army officer. **Born** in 1934 in Kuwait. **Son** of al-Abdallah al-Jaber al-Sabah. **Married** to Shaikha Anisa, al-Sabah, 7 children. **Educ.:** in Kuwait; Millfield School, UK; Sandhurst Military Academy. **Career:** Colonel, Public Security Force (1957-59); Deputy Commander-in-Chief (1959-61); Chief of Staff, Kuwait Armed Forces (1961). **Addr.:** Kuwait City, Kuwait.

SABAH (Nasser Mohammed al Ahmed al), Kuwait, Politician. **Born** in 1941. **Educ.:** Completed High School, UK; B.A., Social and Commercial Sciences, Geneva University, Switzerland. **Career:** Third Secretary (1964-65) then Ambassador of Kuwait to UK (1965-66); Permanent Representative to UN, Geneva (1966-68); Ambassador to Iran (1968-78); Undersecretary, Ministry of Information (1979-81); Head, Planning Commission for Oil Information for the Gulf States (1981-85); Minister of Information (1985-88); Minister of Social Affairs (1988-90); Minister of States for Foreign Affairs (1990-91); Minister of Emiri Affairs (Sept. 1991- to date). **Address:** Court of the Emir, P.O.Box 799, Safat 13008, Kuwait.

SABAH (Nasser, Sabah al-Ahmad, al, Shaikh), Kuwaiti businessman. **Born** in 1947 in Kuwait. **Son** of Sabah al-Ahmad al-Sabah. **Married. Career:** Prominent in family business and investments; Founder of Dar al-Athar al-Islamiyyah (The al-Sabah Collection of Islamic Art). **Addr.:** P.O.Box 3389, Tel.: 2448310, Kuwait.

SABAH (Nawaf, al-Ahmad, al-Jaber, al, Shaikh), Kuwaiti former minister. **Born** in Kuwait. **Son** of Ahmad Jaber al-Sabah. **Career:** Governor of the Province of al-Hawali; Minister of the Interior. (1982-1987); Minister of Defence (1988-91); Minister of Labour and Social Affairs (April 1991- 1992). **Prof. Addr.:** Kuwait City, Kuwait.

SABAH (Saad al-Abdallah al-Salem, al, Shaikh), Kuwaiti heir apparent and prime minister. **Born** in 1924. **Son** of former Ruler by an African wife. **Married** to the daughter of late Shaikh Fahad al-Salem. **Educ.:** Private in Kuwait. **Career:** Police Department (1945-53); trained at Metropolitan police College Hendon, UK (1953-54); Deputy Head of Kuwait Metropolitan Police (1954-59); Deputy President, Police and Public Security Department (1959-61); Minister of the Interior (1962-64); Minister of Interior and Defence (1964-78); Head of Ministerial Committee on Labour Problems (1975); Leading government spokesman in National Assembly (until August 1976); Crown Prince and Prime Minister (since 1978 to present); Appointed as Military Governor of Kuwait on 26/2/1991. **Addr.:** Prime Minister's Office, Safat, Kuwait City, Kuwait.

SABAH (Sabah al-Ahmad al-Jaber, al, Shaikh), Kuwaiti politician. **Born** in 1929. **Son** of late Shaikh Ahmad al-Jaber al-Sabah. **Married**, with children. **Educ.:** in Kuwait. **Career:** Member, Higher Executive Committee (1954-56); President, Social Affairs Department, of Printing and Publishing Department (1956-62); Minister of Guidance and Information (1962); Minister of Foreign Affairs (1963); Acting Minister of Finance and Oil (December 1965-67); Acting Minister of Information (1971-75); Deputy Prime Minister, Minister of Foreign Affairs, Acting Minister of the Interior (1978- April 1991); First Deputy Prime Minister and Minister of Foreign Affairs (October 1992 to present); Owner of Gulf Fisheries Company (now United Fisheries of Kuwait); extensive business activities in Kuwait and abroad. **Hobby:** Boating. **Addr.:** Ministry of Foreign Affairs, Kuwait City, Kuwait.

SABAH (Salem, Abdulaziz, al, Shaikh), Kuwaiti economist and Banker. **Born** on November 1, 1951. **Academic Qualifications:** Bachelor of Arts in Economics, 1977 the American University of Beirut, Lebanon. **Present Positions: Since October 1st. 1986,** Governor and Chairman of Board of Directors, Central Bank of Kuwait; Chairman of Board of Directors, Institute of Banking Studies; Member of Board of Directors, Kuwait Investment Authority; Alternate Governor of the State of Kuwait International Monetary Fund; Alternate Governor of the State of Kuwait Arab Monetary Fund. **Since May 17, 1987,** Member of Higher Planning Council. **Since July 11, 1993,** Member of Higher Petroleum Council. **Since April 30, 1994,** Member of Higher Committee for Economic Development and Reform; President of Subcommittee Emanating from Higher Committee for Economic Development and Reform. **Previous Positions:** Deputy Governor, Central Bank of Kuwait (9/2/1986 - 30/9/1986); Executive Director, Banking Supervision and Monetary Policy, Central Bank of Kuwait (15/7/1985 - 8/2/1986); Manager, Banking Supervision Department, Central Bank of Kuwait (8/8/1984 - 14/7/1985); Head, Inspection Section and Deputy Manager, Banking Supervision Department, Central Bank of Kuwait (17/3/1984 - 7/8/1984); Head, Investment and Studies Sections and Deputy Manager, Foreign Operations Department, Central Bank of Kuwait (18/2/1980 - 16/3/1984); Head, Studies Section, Foreign Operations Department, Central Bank of Kuwait (29/5/1978 - 17/2/1980); Economic Analyst, Studies Section, Foreign Operations Department, Central Bank of Kuwait (1/10/1977 - 28/5/

1978). **Hobby:** Reading. **Addr.:** Central Bank of Kuwait, P.O.Box 526 Safat, Kuwait 13006, Tel.: (965) 2436711, 2443384, Fax: 2464887, Telex: 22101/44879/44880, Kuwait.

SABAH (Salem al-Sabah al-Salem, al, Shaikh), Kuwaiti former minister. **Born** on June 18, 1937 in Kuwait. **Son** of the late Ruler HH Sabah al-Salem al-Sabah. **Educ.:** Sharqiyah School, Kuwait; Shuwaikh Secondary School; Kuwait; Oxford University, U.K. **Dipl.:** Law. **Career:** Joined Foreign Service (1962); Head, Political Department, Ministry of Foreign Affairs (1964); Kuwaiti delegate at various Middle Eastern and African conferences, including Arab Summit Conference (Casablanca, October 1965); Ambassador to UK (1965-70); Ambassador to USA and Canada (1970-75); Minister of Social Affairs and Labour (1975-78); Minister of Defence (1978-87); Minister of the Interior (1988- April 1991); Deputy Prime Minister and Minister of Foreign Affairs (April 1991-Oct. 1992); Deputy Prime Minister and Minister of Defence (1993-). **Sports:** Riding and swimming. **President:** Salmiyah Sports Club **Addr.:** Kuwait City, Kuwait.

SABAH (Salih al-Mohamad, al, Major General Shaikh), Kuwaiti army officer. **Born** in 1931 in Kuwait. Member of the Ruling Family of the State of Kuwait. **Married. Career:** Joined military service (1953); trained at Carlisle and Mons, UK (1955); attached to tanks regiment in the British Army in Britain and West Germany; led Kuwaiti Forces in Arab-Israeli War on Egyptian Front (1967); Deputy Chief of the General Staff (1965), Major General (1974). **Addr.:** P.O.B. 998, Tel.: 517731, Kuwait.

SABAH (Saud Nasser Al, Shaikh), Kuwaiti Minister of Oil, Chairman, Kuwait Petroleum Corporation since March 22nd, 2000. **Born** on October 3rd, 1944 in Kuwait. **Married** in 1962 to Shaikha Awatif Sabah al-Salem Al-Sabah, 3 sons: Fawaz (Nov. 9, 1962), Nawaf (July 4, 1971), Sabah (June 5, 1982), 2 daughters: Marahib (Nov.2, 1965), Nayirah (July 29, 1975). **Educ.:** Barrister-at-Law, Gray's Inn London, England (1968). **Career:** Joined the Ministry of Foreign Affairs, Legal Department (1969); Representative of Kuwait to the Conference on the Law of Treaties (1969); Representative of Kuwait to the Seabed Committee of the United Nations (1969-73); elected Vice-Chairman of the Committee, Vice-Chairman of the Delegation of Kuwait to the Conference on the Law of the sea (1974-75); elected Vice-Chairman of the Conference; President, Inter Maritime Consultative Organization (IMCO) General Assembly Session (1979-80); Ambassador to the Court of St. James, Great Britain (1975-80); Concurrently, non resident Ambassador to Norway, Sweden and Denmark (1975-80); Ambassador to the United States of America (1981-92); Concurrently non resident Ambassador to Canada and Venezuela (1981-92); Minister of Information, Kuwait (1992-98). **Address:** Kuwait Petroleum Corporation, P.O.Box 26565 Safat 13126, Kuwait.

SABAT (Khalil, Yusuf, Dr.), Professor emeritus, faculty of mass communication, Cairo university **Born** on 3 June 1919 in Cairo (Egypt). **Son** of Yusuf Sabat (chartered accountant) **and** Mrs., née Heneinah Boutros Beheit. **Married** to Dolly Charles Zananiri in Cairo (1964). **Educ.:** Greek Catholic Patriarchal College (1925-38); Faculty of Arts, Cairo University (1938-42). **Dipll:** B.A. (French Lit.) (1942), M.A. (Journalism) 1946), M.A. (Education) (1947), Ph.D. (Journalism) (1954). **Career:** Lecturer in journalism at the Institute of Journalism (1950-54); Assistant Professor, Department of Journalism, Faculty of Arts, Cairo University (1954-63); Associate Professor, Department of Journalism, Faculty of Arts, Cairo University (1963-72); Professor, Department of Journalism in the said faculty (1972), also seconded to the University of Baghdad, Department of Journalism; Vice-Dean Faculty of Mass Communication, Cairo University; now Professor Emeritus in the same faculty. member of the High Press Counsel, Expert in the National Center of Researches, Member of National Council. **Publ.:** in Arabic: "History of Printing in the Arab East" (1st Ed. 1958- 2nd Ed. 1966); "Press Media" (1st Ed. 1959- 6th Ed. 1991); "Advertising" (1969) 2nd Ed. 1987; "Freedom of the Press in Egypt" (1973); Mass Media, Origins and Developments, 1rst Ed. 1976, 5th Ed. 1987. also numerous research works in the field of mass communication. Translated from French into Arabic Jean-Paul Sartre "Les Mots" 1st. Ed. (1965), Second Ed. (1993), "Sartre-a self-portrait" (1967). **Award:** Press Union Award. Chevalier, Order National du Mérite (France): Order of the Republic (Egypt). **Member:** Journalism Graduates Association Cairo (Egypt). Gezireh Sporting Club, Cairo (Egypt). **Hobbies:** Stamp collecting, classical music and reading. **Prof. Addr:** Faculty of Mass Communication, Cairo University, Tel.: 5726290, 5729878. **Priv. Addr.:** 33 Abdel Khalekh Sarwat Street, Tel.: 3928690, Cairo, Egypt.

SABBAB (Ahmad Abdallah, al), Saudi academic. **Born** in 1942 at al-Ahsa, Saudi Arabia. **Dipl.:** B.S. (Cum Laude) (1966); M.B.A., New York University (1969); Ph.D. (Management, Marketing and Economics), New York University (1973). **Career:** Supervisor, Arabian American Oil Company (Aramco), Dhahran (1966-67); Research Assistant, Management and Marketing Department, New York University (1969-71); part time consultant Urban Assistance Corporation, Graduate School of Business, New York University (1968-73); taught Micre-Economics at William Paterson College, New Jersey (1972-73); taught Micro-Economics at William Paterson College, New Jersey (1972-73); Associate Professor of Economics, King Abdulaziz University. **Act.:** attended Executive Management Programme, American University of Beirut (1974); represented King Abdulaziz University at the International Symposium on Octobre 1973 War, Cairo University (Octobre 1973); participated in the First Arabic Conference on Administrative Training (Tunisia, 1967); member of Supreme Council of King Abdulaziz University; Chairman of the Management Department and Director of Research and Development Centre at King Abdulaziz University; Chairman of First Committee in charge of Planning and Training Activities in the Kingdom of Saudi Arabia. **Address:** Abdulaziz University Compound, Tel.: 687.9033 Ext. 1250, Jeddah, Saudi Arabia.

SABBAGH (Abdul Ghani Mahmoud), Saudi businessman. **Born** in 1948 in Mecca, Saudi Arabia. **Dipl.:** B.A. (Mass Communication) U.S.A., 1974. **Career:** Owner and General Manager, Projects Co., Azhar Trading and Development Co.; General Manager, Shubra Hotel, al-Haram Hotel, Makkah, Taif: member of Board of Sabbagh and Murad Trading Co. **Hobbies:** reading, travel. **Prof. Addr.:** P.O.Box 4521, Tel.: 6532759, Jeddah. **Priv. Addr.:** Tel.: 6432444, Jaddah, Saudi Arabia.

SABBAGH (Bachir), Jordanian academic. **Born** in 1918 in Amman. **Educ.:** American University of Beirut. **Dipl.:** B.Sc. (1942). **Career:** Teacher at Irbid (1943); Headmaster at Irbid (1944), Salt (1946); Acting Islamic Chief Justice and Minister of Social Affairs (1961); Minister of Education (July 1964-65) and (1968-69); Acting Islamic Chief Justice and Minister of Education (1962-64); Deputy-Chairman, Board of Directors of Shereish College (1964-73); Director, Islamic Sciences College (1947-73); Retired in 1973. **Awards:** al-Kawkab Medal (1st and 3rd grades), Egyptian Republic Medal (4th grade). **Addr.:** P.O.Box 385, Tel.: 41331, Amman, Jordan.

SABBAGH (Faisal, al), Syrian physician and neurologist. **Born** in 1919 in Damascus. **Educ.:** Damascus Faculty of Medicine, Universities of Paris and Columbia. **Dipl.:** Doctor in Medicine, Diploma of neurology from the said universities. **Career:** Assistant Professor of neurology in Hospitals, Paris; Assistant of neurology, Neurology Institute of New York; Assistant Professor in the Faculty of Medicine (Damascus University). **Addr.:** Damascus, Syria.

SABBAGH (Hashim Mohamad Ali, al), Jordanian accountant. **Born** in 1942 in Irbid, Jordan. **Son** of Ali al-Sabbagh. **Married**, five children. **Educ.:** Arisona University. **Dipl.:** Ph.D. in Accountancy depl., Faculty of Economics and Science. Jordan University (1971-73); Chairman and General Manager, Amman Financial Market (since 1977); Director, Jordan Fertilizer Industry Co. Ltd. **Publ.:** "Incentive Schemes to Accelerate Development of the Capital Market"; "The Situation in Jordan"; "The Mechanics and Operation of an Islamic Financial Market". **Addr.:** P.O.Box 8802, Amman, Jordan.

SABBAGH (Hussein Rashid, al), Bahraini diplomat. **Born** in 1938. **Married**, three children. **Educ.:** University of Cairo, Egypt. **Dipl.:** B.A. **Career:** Lecturer, University of Cairo (1963-68); joined Ministry of Information, Bahrain (1968); Superintendent of News and Culture Affairs (1970-75); joined Ministry of Foreign Affairs (1975); First Secretary, Embassy in U.K. (1975-76); Chargé d'affaires, Lebanon (1976-79); Counsellor (1979); Ambassador to Iran (1979-82); former Permanent Representative to UN (1982). **Addr.:** Manama, Bahrain.

SABBAGH (Jaafar Abdul Rahman), Saudi educator. **Born** in 1939 in Taif, Saudi Arabia. **Dipl.:** B.Sc., M.Sc. (Engineering), Ph.D. (Engineering), U.S.A. **Career:** Assistant Lecturer, Faculty of Engineering, King Saud University (1963); Assistant Professor (1969-73), Vice Dean (1971-72) and later Dean, Faculty of Engineering, (1971-75); Vice Rector, Umm al-Qura University (1976-79); Professor of Mechanical Engineering and Director of the School of Mechanical and Aeronautical Engineering King Abdulaziz University, Jeddah; Engineering Consultant for a number of establishments and universities; member, the American Scientists Society, the Mediterranean Society for Solar Energy and the International Solar Energy Society; Board member of SANCT and SOLERAS Programme (SANCSTDOE). **Publications:** 21 research papers, co-author of a book on solar energy. **Prof. Addr.:** P.O.Box 9027, Tel.: 687.9033 Ext. 1584, Jeddah. **Priv. Addr.:** Tel.: 6879439, Jeddah, Saudi Arabia.

SABBAGH (Mohamad), Moroccan writer and poet. **Born** in 1927 in Tatouan. **Educ.:** Secondary at Tatouan, Higher in Madrid (Spain). **Career:** Writer, Poet, Journalist. **Publ.:** Author of several books, including "al-Abir al-Multaheb", "Challal al-Assouad", "al-Louhas al-Jarih", "Shajarat an Nar", "Athar al-Qamar" (translated into foreign languages). **Addr.:** Tatouan, Morocco.

SABBAGH (Nemeh, Elias), British, Managing Director and Chief Executive Officer. **Born** in 1951 in Lebanon. **Son** of Elias Sabbagh. **Married** in 1988, 2 children. **Educ.:** Austin College, Texas; L'Institut d'Etudes Politiques, Université de Paris; Johns Hopkins University; University of Chicago; Standord University (September 1990). **Dipl.:** B.A. (Hons) (1972); M.A. (1974); M.B.A. (1976). **Career:** I.B.R.D. (World Bank) Washington D.C., Research Analyst (1973-74); International Banking Department, First National Bank of Chicago (1974-75); Banking and Finance Department, The Industrial Bank of Kuwait, Safat Kuwait (1976-1979); General Manager, National Bank of Kuwait (1979-1998); Managing Director and Chief Executive Officer, Arab National Bank, Riyadh-Saudi Arabia (1998-present). **Publ.:** "Kuwait-Looking for Loans Abroad", "Kuwaiti Banks Wake Up"; Euromoney (1977); "Integration VS Corporation in the Arab World: An Appraisal" published by the Industrial Bank of Kuwait in the Journal of Industry and Finance. (1981); "Revival of Kuwaiti Dinar Bond Market" The Banker (1982); "The Global Challenge for Arab Banks" Euromoney (1984). **Hobbies:** Tennis, swimming and reading. **Addr.:** Arab National Bank, P.O.Box 56921, Riyadh, Tel.: 9661-402-9000, Fax: 9661-403-0052, Saudi Arabia.

SABBAK (Omar Ali), Saudi academic. **Born** in 1947 in Mecca, Saudi Arabia. **Dipl.:** Ph.D. **Career:** Assistant Professor, Chemistry Department, Faculty of Science, King Abdulaziz University (1978-79); Vice Dean, Faculty of Meteorology and Environmental Studies (1979-81); Professor, Department of Environmental Studies, King Abdulaziz University. **Member:** American Chemistry Association; has attended various conferences in U.S.A. **Publications:** research on the quality of Air in the Holy Places. **Address:** Jeddah, Saudi Arabia.

SABBAN (Mohamad, Serour, al, Shaikh), Saudi businessman. **Born** in Saudi Arabia. **Educ.:** Secondary and Higher. **Career:** Minister of Finance and National Economy; ex-Director of Pilgrimage, Agriculture and Broadcasting; Director, Arab Bank Ltd., The Arab Printing and Publicity Co., Arab Export Co., The Arab Saving and Economic Co.; Supreme Leader of the League of the Moslem World; Vice-Chairman of the Football Association. **Awards:** Order of the Cedar (Lebanon). **Addr.:** Riyadh, Saudi Arabia.

SABBOUR (Sameh Saadiddin), Egyptian banker. **Born** in 1934 in Cairo, Egypt, **Son** of Sa'adiddin Sabbour. **Married,** two children. **Educ.:** Cairo University, American University of Cairo. **Dipl.:** B.Com., B.A., M.A. **Career:** Assistant Manager, International Division, Arab African International Bank, Cairo (1974); Deputy Manager, Arab African Bank in Mauritania (1974-76); Area Manager, European Arab Bank Ltd. Obu Bahrain (1978-79); Deputy General Manager, European Arab Bank (Middle East), Bahrain (1979). **Member**, Certified Public Accountants, Egypt (since 1958); member, Bankers Society of Bahrain (since 1979). **Sports:** Tennis, Squash, Swimming, Jogging. **Hobbies:** Aerobics, reading, music, snorkelling, **Addr.:** P.O.Box 5888, Manama, Bahrain.

SABEH (Samir), Syrian bank director. **Born** in 1938 in Damascus, Syria. **Son** of Michel Sabeh. **Married** in 1970, 2 sons, 2 daughters. **Educ.:** Bachelor in Law. **Career:** President, Committee of one of the City Districts in Damascus, Syria. Director, Secretarial and Control Departments, Popular Credit Bank, Damascus, Syria. **Member:** Municipal Council of the City of Damascus, Syria. **Hobbies;** Reading, Chess and Philately. **Addr.:** P.O.Box 2841, Tel.: 440 274, Damascus, Syria.

SABI (Ahmad, Nimr), Jordanian international civil servant. **Born** on August 19, 1919 at Qalqilya, West Bank (Jordan). **Married**, children. **Educ.:** American University in Beirut (Lebanon) (1936-40). **Dipl.:** LL.B. (1940). **Career:** Secondary school teacher, Department of Education and Terrasanta College (Palestine) (1941-46); Information Officer, Arab Office (Palestine) (1946-48); Director General, Tourist Department (Jordan) (1952-57); Chief, Translation/interpretation service (Libya) (1958-65); Assistant, Resident Representative, United Nations Development Programme, UNDP (Nigeria) (1966-70); Deputy Resident Representative, UNDP (Syria) (1970-73); Deputy Resident Representative UNDP (Libya). **Member:** Alumni Association, American University, Beirut. **Club:** Sand Club of Tripoli (Libya). **Sports:** Tennis and swimming. **Prof. Addr.:** UNDP, P.O.Box 358, 69/71, Tel.: 30856, Turkiya street, Tripoli. **Priv. Addr.:** 45 Amat al-Azuz street, Tel.: 71130, Tripoli, Libya.

SABIR (Mohieddine, Dr.), Sudanese academic and statesman. **Born** in 1919 at Dalgo (Sudan). **Married**, children. **Educ.:** Faculty of Arts, University of Cairo; University of Bordeaux (France); University of Paris (Sorbonne). **Career:** Director, Ministry of Social Affairs (1954); Lecturer in Anthropology, Cairo University in Khartoum (1956-59); Editor "el-Istiqlal" and "Sot el-Sudan" daily newspapers; Managing Editor, "al-Zamam" daily newspaper; joined United Nations Educational, Scientific and Cultural Organisation (UNESCO) as expert and head of the Social Sciences Department (1959-68); elected to Constituent Assembly (1968); Minister of Education (1969-72) Director; Arab Literary and Adult Education Organization (ARLO) (1973-75); Director-General, Arab League Educational, Cultural and Scientific Organization (ALECSO) (1975); Permanent-member, Afro-Asian Writer's Association. **Publ.:** Author of "Cultural Change and Commity Development" (1962), "Researches in Community Development Programmes" (1963), "Local Government and Community Development progrannes" (1963), "Nomad and Nomadism Concepts and Approaches" (1966), "Adult Education in the Sudan" (1970); "Studies on Issues Related to Development and Adult Education" (1975); co-author "Adult Education as Science" (1975); as well as numerous studies. **Award:** Order of the Republic, Egypt (1970); Loyal son of the Sudan Order (1971); National Order, Chad (1972). **Addr.:** Khartoum, Sudan.

SABOUNI (Mourhaf), Syrian General Secretary of Arab Union of Railways. **Born in** 1934 in Aleppo, Syrian. **Son** of Ata Sabouni and Mrs née Nadima Munkari. **Married** on 15 May 1965 to Miss Bazigha, 4 children: Luma, Talal, Rana, Moutaz. **Educ.:** Maamoun School, Polytechnic University in Warsovia **Dipl.:** Magister Engineer Mechnical. **Career:** Deputy General Director of Syrian Railways since 1970, General Secretary of Arab Union of Railways since 1983, **prof.Addr.:** P.O.Box 6599, Aleppo, Syria, Tel.: 2667270, 2665611. Fax: 2686000 **Home Addr.:** Engineers Association, Tel.: 5711197, 5714197, Aleppo, Syria.

SABRI (Adnan, Ayub), Iraqi politician, **Born** in Baghdad, Iraq in 1925, **Son** of Ayub Sabri. **Educ.:** Baghdad Military College. **Career:** Assistant Military Attaché. Embassy to U.S.A. (1963), Staff Colonel (1968); Secretary General to the Presidency of the Republic; Minister of State (1968); Acting Minister of Communications. Minister of Communications (1970); Minister of Youth Affairs

(1972); Minister of Transport (1974-76). **Addr.:** Baghdad, Iraq.

SABRI (Ayoub M.), Saudi banker **Born** in 1925 in Medina, Saudi Arabia. **Dipl.:** B.Sc. (Commerce), Cairo University. **Career:** Director General, Zakat, (Alms) and Income Tax Department, Maccah; Assistant Deputy Minister of Finance; former Chairman of the Board, Saudi Credit Bank, Ministry of Finance. **Member:** Law School Alumni Association, Harvard University; ex-member, Ministry of Endowments Fund; Head of the Saudi delegation to the Arab League Economic Council. **Publications:** Comparative Study of Islamic Alms and Modern Tax Systems, published by Harvard University, several articles on economics in local newspapers and magazines. **Prof. Addr.:** Ministry of Finance, Riyadh. **Priv. Addr.:** Tel.: 4760057, Riyadh, Saudi Arabia.

SABRI (Ismail Baligh), Egyptian businessman. **Born** on November 17, 1918 in Cairo, Egypt. **Married**, one daughter. **Educ.:** Faculty of Agriculture, Cairo University. **Dipl.:** B.Sc. Agriculture Science (1939). **Career:** Member, Board of Directors, Kom OMBO Agriculture Co. (1957-61); Managing Director, The General Co. For Land Reclamation (1957-61); President, Société des Sucreries et Distillerie d'Egypte (1966-78); Managing Director, Delta Sugar Co. (1981-87); President, National Co. For Maize Products (1981-87); **Currently:** President, Société Egypto-Française Pour les Industries Agro-Alimentaires (VITRAC); President, Agro Industrial Consultants Egypt (AICE); Director, Nile Bank; President, Agriculture Export Co. (AGREX), Member: Chairman, Egypto-French Businessmen Comittee; President Chamber of Food Industries. **Decor:** Order of Merit (Officer Class), Camerоons (1977); Order of Merit (Officer Class), France (1980); Egyptian Order of the Republic for Sciences and Arts (1982). Ordre National de la Légion d'Honneur (Officer), France (1989). **Member:** Maadi Sporting Club, Gezira Sporting Club. **Hobbies:** Fishing, tennis, swimming. **Addr.:** 29 Yathreb Street, Mohandissine, P.O.Box 200 Dokki, Cairo, Egypt, Tlx 21382 AICEE UN, Fax: (202) 713095.

SABRI (Magdy Sabry), Egyptian diplomat. **Born** in Egypt in 1931. **Son** of Sabry Sabry. **Married**, three children. **Educ.:** Cairo University, **Dipl.:** LL.B. **Career:** Ambassador to Sri Lanka, Saudi Arabia, Greece, Romania, West Germany, UK and Malaysia. **Hobby:** Squash. **Addr.:** 18 Huda Sha'rawi, Abdeen, Cairo, Egypt.

SABRI (Musa), Egyptian journalist. **Born** in 1924, in Egypt. **Educ.:** University of Cairo (1943). **Career:** Joined "Akhbar al-Yaum" (1950); Editor in Chief, "al-Gumhuriya" newspaper (1961-63); Editor in Chief, "Akhbar al-Yaum" (1963-68); Chairman of the Board of Directors and Editor in Chief of Akhbar al-Yaum Publishing House (1969). **Publ.:** Documentation of the 1973 October War, numerous articles, several novels and other books. **Addr.:** Akhbar al-Yaum Publishing House, 6 Sahafa Street, Cairo, Egypt.

SABRI (Osman), Egyptian magistrate. **Born** in Egypt. **Married** to Miss Acychine Kani Zade. **Educ.:** Faculty of Law (University of Paris). **Dipl.:** Bachelor of Law. **Career:** Lawyer, Judge, 1st Instance, Counsellor, Vice President of the Supreme Court of Appeal. **Member:** Alexandria Sporting Club. **Addr.:** 23, Sabri Pasha Street, San Stefano Station, Ramleh, Alexandria, Egypt.

SADDIQ (Shamseddine), Egyptian landowner, architect-engineer. **Born** in Cairo. **Educ.:** Faculty of Building (London). **Dipl.:** of Architect-Engineer. **Career:** Landowner; Architect-Engineer; Business Associations, Federation of Egyptian Industries, Engineers' Association, National Association of Professional Engineers (France), Chamber of Contractors Public and Private Works. **Member:** Shooting and Fishing Club. **Addr.:** 1, Ibn Sina Street, Giza, Tel.: 894594 (Office), 5, Qasr an-Nil Street, Abou Gerga and Aba al-Wakf, Minieh, Tel.: 9, Aba al-Wakf, Egypt.

SADEK (Adel), Egyptian TV and film producer. **Born** on April 25, 1934 in Cairo (Egypt). **Educ.:** Government Secondary School, Zamalek, Cairo; Southern California University (USA). **Dipl.:** B.Sc. **Career:** Assistant to Ramses Nagudib, Veteran Egyptian Film producer; joined the State TV Service in 1960 as Chief of the children's Programme; seconded to Kuwait State in 1963, serving there for one year; now Controller General of all TV production. **Works:** "Bahiya", and TV serials, namely "The Black Cat", "Sabiha", "The Detour", "The Temple", "Heart of Glass", "The Third Man". **Sports:** Shooting and swimming. **Hobbies:** Reading and art collection. **Prof. Addr.:** State TV Service, TV Building, Maspero District, Corniche Road, Cairo, Egypt. **Priv. Addr.:** 26 Garden City, Tel.: 49500, Cairo, Egypt.

SADEK (Amal, Ahmed M.), Egyptian academic. **Born** in 1937 in Giza, Egypt. **Daughter** of Ahmed Sadek. **Married**, two children. **Educ.:** London University. **Dipl.:** B.A.: in Music; Ph.D. in Psychology. **Career:** Lecturer of Psychology, Higher Institute of Music Education (1968); Associate Professor of Psychology (1973); Professor and Head of Department of Psychology and Educational Psychology (1977); College of Art Education, Professor and Head of Department of Psychology; Deputy Dean, College of Education, Helwan University (since 1982). **Publ.:** "Methods of Teaching Music"; "Educational Psychology"; etc. **Medals:** Certificate of Distinction, Egypt. **Hobbies:** Music, travel, sewing, knitting. **Addr.:** 6 Dr. Mohamad Hegab Street, Flat 15, al-Nuzha, Heliopolis, Cairo, Egypt.

SADEK (Hassan, Sadek), Egyptian artist sculptor. **Born** on February 13, 1924 in Cairo, Egypt. **Son** of Sadek Sadek. **Married**, one daughter. **Educ.:** Diploma in Sculpture, Academy of Fine Arts, Cairo; Ph.D. in Ceramics, Prague, Czechoslovakia. **Career:** Cultural Attaché and Councillor, Egyptian Embassy, Berlin, Germany (1969-73); Dean, Academy of Fine Arts, Menia University, Menia, Egypt (1976); Professor and Head of Department of Sculpture, Helwan University (1976-79); member of the Permanent Committee for Professors and Assistant Professors, Supreme Council of Universities (since 1977); Member of several embellishment Committees for Helwan, Cairo, Giza, and Ministry of Culture; Art Consultant to the Helwan University magazine. **Works:** Participated in several exhibitions in Egypt, Europe and U.S.A. **Awards:** Several Local distinctions among which First Class Award from Egypt's President in 1985. **Hobbies:** Classical music, Photography. **Member of:** Sculptors Society. **Addr.:** 17 Brazil Street, Zamalek District, Cairo, Egypt.

SADEK (Hatem), Regional manager, Arab Bank PLC/ Egypt area management. **Born** on January 19, 1943 in Cairo, Egypt. **Son** of Ali Sadek (late) **and** Mrs. Hekmat née Madkour. **Married** in 1964 in Cairo to Dr. Hoda Gamal Abdel Nasser, 2 children: Hala (1/1/1967), Gamal (21/2/1971). **Educ.:** Collège de la Sainte Famille; Faculty of Economics and Political Science, Cairo University. **Dipl.:** B.A. in Economics and Political Science (1964). **Career:** United Arab Republic Presidency- Bureau of the Personal Representative of the Late President Gamal Abdel Nasser (1964-67); Bureau of the U.A.R. President's for Secretary for Information (1967-68); Manager al-Ahram Research Center for Palestinian and Zionist Studies (1968-70); Director of al-Ahram Research Center for Strategic Studies (1970-74); Arab League Bureau of the Secretary General (1974-76); Regional Manager, Arab Bank PLC, Egypt Area Management (1976- to date). **Publ.:** Author of "A Study of Israel's Political Strategy" published by Dar el-Maaref (1968). **Sports:** Water ski, Tennis. **Hobbies:** Reading, Tennis and water ski. **Member:** Gezira Sporting Club and Heliopolis Sporting Club. **Credit Card:** American Express Card. **Prof. Addr.:** 50, Gezirat El Arab St., El Mohandessin, Cairo, Egypt, P.O.Box 68, Tel.: 3029062/61. **Priv. Addr.:** 6 Ibn Katheer St., Giza, Cairo, Egypt.

SADEK (Ibrahim, Hassan), Egyptian-American industrial engineer. **Born** in 1938 in Cairo, Egypt. **Son** of Hassan Sadek. **Married. Educ.:** Cairo University; University of Texas in Austin. **Dipl.:** B.Sc. and M.S. in Mechanical Engineering. **Career:** Consultant, Industrial Studies and Development Center, Riyadh, (1968-70); Assistant Project Manager, Brown and Root Inc., Houston (1966-72); Assistant Vice President of Tractor Inc.; Assistant Chief Engineer, Beuhtel Power Corp. (1974-75); Founder and President, Simpex Engineered Products & Services, Cairo (since 1982); Founder and President, Egyptian Manufacturing and Contracting Co. (Panelex), Cairo (since 1983). **Member of** Engineering Syndicate, Cairo; board member of Chaine de Rotisseurs, Cairo. **Prof. Addr.:** 100 el-Nil Street, Giza, Egypt.

SADEK (Medhat, Abdel Hamid, Dr.), Egyptian executive. **Born** in 1935 in Cairo, Egypt. **Son** of Dr. Abdel Hamid Sadek. **Married** in 1960, 2 sons, 1 daughter. **Educ.:** Cairo University, LL.D. (1955); Alexandria University, Diploma of Economics and Public Finance (1964); Cairo University, Diploma of Public Law (1965); Alexandria University, Ph.D. Economics (1975). **Career:** Banking Career in Egypt since 1955, ultimately as Manager, Banque du Caire, Dubai; General Manager, General Enterprises Co. Dubai (1976-80); Representative, Wardley Middle East Ltd., Bahrain (1980-83). General Manager and Chief Executive, Arab Financial Services Co. (1983-). **Publ.:** "The Banking System in the Planned Economy"; "The Keynesian Analysis". **Member:** Gezira Sporting Club, Cairo. **Addr.:** Arab Financial Services Co., P.O.Box 2152, Manama, Bahrain.

SADEK (Mohamad, Ahmad), Egyptian army officer. **Born** in Egypt. **Married,** 2 sons. **Educ.:** Graduated from Egyptian Military Academy (1938); Frunza Military Academy (USSR). **Career:** Officer in the army, participated to the Palestine campaign (1948), the Suez campaign (1956) as commander of an Infantry regiment; Military attaché at the Egyptian Embassy at Bonn (1962), Back to Egypt (1964); Appointed Director of courses at the Egyptian Military Academy (1965-67); Director of the Information service (Intelligence Department) of the Army (June 1967); Appointed chief of staff in September 1969; Director of Military Intelligence (1966-69); General secretary of the Pan-Arab Organization for the military affairs (September 1969); Lieutenant-General (1970); Minister of War (1971); Deputy Prime-Minister and Minister of War and War Production (1972-73). **Awards:** Egyptian and foreign. **Prof. Addr.:** HQ, Army Forces, Cairo, Egypt.

SADEK (Mustafa, al), Egyptian former under-secretary of state, director of companies. **Born** in Egypt. **Married** to Miss Nahed Asaad. **Educ.:** Faculty of Law (Cairo University). **Dipl.:** Bachelor of Law. **Career:** Former Under-Secretary of State, Ministry of Commerce; Egyptian Minister Plenipotentiary in Rome; Stockbroker, Director of companies. **Awards:** Commander British Empire, Grand Officer Order of the Belgium Court. **Member:** Gezira Sporting Club, Yacht Club of Egypt. **Addr.:** 91, Aboubakr as-Saddiq Street, Heliopolis, Tel.: 60342, Cairo. **Summer Residence:** 204, Army Road, Ramleh, Tel.: 60682, Alexandria, Egypt.

SADEK (Yehia, al), Egyptian company director. **Born** on September 15, 1926 in London. **Married** to Miss Naziha Chahine. **Educ.:** Faculty of Commerce, Cairo University. **Dipl.:** Bachelor of Commerce and Political Science. **Career:** Director General of the "Egyptian Foreign Trade Research and Travel Organization" (E.F.T.R.O.). **Member:** Heliopolis Sporting Club. **Hobbies:** Squash-Racket and Swimming. **Addr.:** 36, Yehia Pasha Ibrahim

Street; Zamalek, Cairo. **Summer Residence:** 204, Army Road, Alexandria, Egypt.

SADHAN (Abdul Rahman M., al), Saudi civil servant. **Born** in 1942 at Abha, Saudi Arabia. **Dipl.:** B.Sc., M.A. (Public Administration). **Career:** Instructor, Director of Research and Consultation at the Institute of Public Administration, Riyadh; Secretary of the Supreme Committee for Administrative Reform (1972-75); Secretary General, Civil Service Council; attended several specialized meetings and conferences locally and abroad. **Publications:** articles in local press, especially al-Yamamah magazine, and al-Jazirah daily newspaper. **Hobbies:** music, reading, theatre. **Prof. Addr.:** Civil Service Council, P.O.Box 9195, Tel.: 4058023, Riyadh. **Priv. Addr.:** Tel.: 4487622, Riyadh, Saudi Arabia.

SADR (Nagib, Hamad, al), Egyptian diplomat. **Born** in 1925. **Married. Educ.:** Degree in Law (1938). **Career:** transferred from Army to Ministry of Foreign Affairs (1956); Counsellor, Embassy to Belgium (1957); Minister (1958); Ambassador to Guinea (1959); Ambassador to Cameroons (1960); Director, African Department, Ministry of Foreign Affairs (1964); attended meetings of Organization of African Unity (1964-68); Ambassador to Algeria (1968-74); Under-Secretary, Ministry of Foreign Affairs (March 1974), responsible for African and Press Affairs. **Addr.:** Ministry of Foreign Affairs, Cairo, Egypt.

SADR (Zakariya, Ahmad, al), United Arab Emirates executive. **Born** in 1912 in Minia, Egypt. **Son** of Ahmad al-Sadr. **Married,** two sons. **Educ.:** B.Sc. in Marine Sciences. **Career:** Officer in Egyptian Navy (1933-44); first Arab Suez Canal Pilot (1945-52); Head of Shipping and Traffic and member of the Board, Suez Canal Authority; former Director of Zaid Port, United Arab Emirates. **Attended** International Conference Against Pollution of the Seas, London, UK (1962) and the Conference for Estimating Cargo Tonnage, London, UK (1969); established compensation fund for the damage of marine pollution, Brussels, Belgium (1971); first Vice Chairman of the International Conference on the Transport of Atomic Materials, Brussels (1971). Member of International Ports Organisation, Tokyo, Japan. **Medals:** Order of Merit, 1st class, Egypt (1966). **Sport:** Swimming. **Addr.:** Abu Dhabi, United Arab Emirates.

SAED (Saif, Said), United Arab Emirates diplomat. **Born** in 1945 in Sharjah, United Arab Emirates. **Son** of Said Saed. **Married. Educ.:** B.A. in History and Education, Kuwait University; diplomatic course in Abu Dhabi, UAE (1972). **Career:** 3rd Secretary, UAE Ministry of Foreign Affairs (1972-73); 2nd Secretary, UAE Ministry of Foreign Affairs (1973-74); 1st Secretary, UAE Ministry of Foreign Affairs (1974-75); Cultural Counsellor, UAE Embassy, Cairo, Egypt (1975); UAE Ambassador to Yemen Arab Republic (1975-84). Attended 35th session of UN General Assembly (1980). **Hobbies:** Arabic literature, history, poetry, cinema, television. **Sport:** Riding. **Addr.:** Ministry of Foreign Affairs, Abu Dhabi, U.A.E.

SAFADAR (Yusuf Mohamad), Saudi certified public accountant. **Born** in 1940 in Mecca, Saudi Arabia. **Dipl.:** Bachelor of Commerce (Accountancy and Administration). **Career:** Manager of Tariff and Aviation Affairs, Saudi Arabian Airlines; Manager of Income Tax Division, Zakat and Income Tax Department; member of Board, al-Ahli Sports Club; Director of Finance, Dallah AVCO Trans Arabian Company, DATAC; has attended several Air Transport Association conferences. **Hobbies:** reading, sports. **Addr. Prof.:** P.O.Box 1438, Riyadh, Saudi Arabia.

SAFADI (Ahmad Issam, al), Saudi educator. **Born** in 1938 in Medina, Saudi Arabia. **Dipl.:** Ph.D. (Education), 1975. **Career:** Science Teacher, Science Inspector; Head of Mathematics and Science Department, Assistant Director of Research and Curriculum, member of Curriculum Sub-Committee, National Higher Committee on Education; Senior Lecturer, King Saud University; Director, Education Technology Centre, King Saud University; Education Planning Expert; attended modern mathematics conference, education planning conference, integrated science conference, conference on philosophy. **Publications:** science textbooks for primary and intermediate schools, chemistry textbooks for secondary schools; some articles. **Hobby:** swimming. **Prof. Addr.:** College of Education, King Saud University, Tel.: 4811000, 4024962, Riyadh, Saudi Arabia.

SAFADI (Hassan), Syrian financial manager. **Born** in 1928 in Damascus. **Son** of Ahmad Safadi. **Married** in 1956, 2 sons, 1 daughter. **Educ.:** Accountancy. **Career:** Managing Director of Financial Affairs, Real Estate Bank, Damascus, Syria. **Hobbies:** Sports and Travelling. **Addr.:** P.O.Box 2337, Tel.: 19171 A/B REBANK SY, Damascus, Syria.

SAFADI (Hisham, J.), Syrian banker. **Born** in 1931 in Damascus, Syria. **Son** of Jamil A. Safadi **and** Mrs., née Shahira I. Malki. **Married** in 1963 in Damascus. **Educ.:** American University of Beirut. **Dipl.:** BBA. **Career:** Income Tax Officer Amman, Jordan, (1953-54); Administrative Assistant to General Manager, Central Government Laboratories, Amman (1954-58); various posts at Central Bank of Jordan last of which was Executive Manager of Foreign Relations Dept. (1964-80); Deputy General Manager, Jordan Fertilizer Industry Company, Amman (1980-82) General Manager, Syrian Jordanian Bank, Amman (since 1982 to present), Board Director Jordan International Bank PLC, London, U.K., Director, Institute of Banking, Amman (1978-82). **Medal:** al-Kawkab al-Urduni (Jordan). **Sport:** Swimming. **Hobby:** Photography. **Credit Card:** American Express. **Prof. Addr.:** P.O.Box 926636, Tel.: 661130, Amman, Jordan. **Priv.**

Addr.: Cairo Street Tel.: 817056, Abdoun, Amman, Jordan.

SAFADI (Housam), Syrian Engineer. **Born** on april 21, 1948 in Damascus, Syria. **Son** of Haider Safadi - Employee **and** Mrs. née Hayat Seibie - Teacher. **Married:** in Damascus in 1953 to Sahar Hamzawi, 3 children: Hani, Sami, Hassan. **Educ.:** Damascus High School, University of Damascus, Kiev Technical Institute-Ukrania. **Dipl.:** Civil Engineer **Career:** Chief Engineer in MHU; Director of Planing in Damascus; Main Engineer of City Planning Local Goverment. **Other Information: Minister of Housing and Utilities** in Syria since 1992. **Hobby:** Swimming. **Prof. Addr.:** Damascus-Ministry of Housing, Fax: 2217570, e-mail: mhu@net.sy, Damascus, P.O.Box 7526, Tel.: 5120197, Syria.

SAFAR (Mahmoud Mohamad), Saudi Minister. **Born** in 17 September 1939 in Mecca, Saudi Arabia. **Dipl.:** B.Sc. and M.Sc. (Civil Engineering); Ph.D. (Civil Engineering with emphasis on Soil Mechanics and Foundation Engineering). **Career:** Member, Faculty of Engineering, King Saud University (1972-76); Dean, Student Affairs, King Saud University (1974-76); Under Secretary, Ministry of Higher Education (1977-84); Secretary General, The Higher Council of Universities; has been engaged in various consulting activities in his field of specialization; Vice President, Im'an Welfare Society, Riyadh; member, the American Society of Engineers, the Founding Committee of the Arab Gulf University, the Advisor Committee for the United Nations University, the Council of Teachers of the East and West University and the University Council of the different Saudi universities; member, Board of Directors, the Supreme Council of Information, the Supreme Council for Sciences, Arts and Literature, and the Higher Education Board of the Arab Gulf States; has attended, participated and chaired various Arab-Islamic and Scientific conferences nationally and abroad; appointed Minister of Pilgrimage (July 11, 1993-) reappointed in August 1995. **Honour:** Order of Merit, the National Republic of China. **Publications:** two books: Development is a Case and Civilization is a Challenge. **Hobbies:** swimming, reading, travel. **Address:** Ministry of Pilgrimage, Riyadh, Saudi Arabia.

SAFFAR (Salman, Mohamad, al), Bahraini diplomat. **Born** on June 21, 1931 in Manama (Bahrain). **Educ.:** University of Baghdad (Iraq) (1954-58); University of Paris (1961-70). **Dipl.:** B.A., Ph.D. **Career:** Officer in charge of Political Affairs, Ministry of Foreign Affairs, Manama (1970-71); Permanent Representative of Bahrain, New York (1971-1981), Ambassador of Bahrain in France (1983). **Sports:** swimming and fishing. **Hobby:** reading. **Prof. Addr.:** Ministry of Foreign Affairs, Manama, Bahrain.

SAFI (Alawi Taha, al), Saudi journalist. **Born** in 1942 at Jizan, Saudi Arabia. **Dipl.:** B.A. (Law), Beirut Arab University, Lebanon. **Career:** Supervisor, Social Specialist, Ministry of Social Affairs and Labour; Assistant Editor and Supervisor of Literary Subjects, al-Bilad newspaper; Assistant Editor and Senior Writer for the supplementary cultural edition, al-Yamama Magazine; Assistant Editor, al-Jazira newspaper; Presently, Editor-in-Chief, al-Faisal Magazine; General Manager, al-Faisal Cultural House. **Honorary member:** Jeddah Literary Club; member, Riyadh Literary Club; the Islamic Press Conference; Assembly of King Faisal International Foundation. Member, National Geographic Society. **Publications:** a book in the form of a collection of short stories; various literary studies, social essays and articles of literary criticism; "Looking Arts From Within", "The Literary Man and His Situation Towards Historical and Strifing Incidents" (a lecture); "International Literature and the Internationality of Literature". **Hobbies:** Reading, travel. **Prof. Addr.:** al-Faisal Magazine, P.O.Box 3, Riyadh, 11411, Kingdom of Saudi Arabia, Tel.: 4653027, 46523026, Telex No. 402600 DRFATH S-J. **Priv. Addr.:** Tel.: 4642210, Riyadh, Saudi Arabia.

SAFRAOUI (Ramadhane), Tunisian businessman. **Born** in 1937 in Djerba, Tunisia. **Married,** four children. **Educ.:** University of Tunis; University of Paris. **Dipl.:** LL.B., Ph.D. **Career:** Tax inspector, ministry of Finance (1956-64); Representative in Tunis, Assurances Groupe de Paris (1965-73); Joint General Director, now Chairman and General Director Compagnie Mediterraneenne d'Assurances et Reassurances (COMAR), Tunis (since 1973); treasurer, vice-president, Tunisian Federation of Insurance Companies (since 1980); founder member, Institut Arabe des Chefs d'Entreprises (since 1984). **Medals:** Chevalier of the Order of the Tunisian Republic. **Addr.:** COMAR, 26 Avenue Habib Bourguiba, Tunis, Tunisia.

SAFWAT (Mahmoud, Abbas), Egyptian lawyer, company director. **Born** on February 13, 1919 in Cairo. **Son** of Abbas Safwat. **Married** in 1947 to Miss Zakiyeh Safwat, one daughter: Niamet. **Educ.:** Course in Business Administration, Institute of Administration, Egypt; Law Degree, Fuad I University, Cairo; Diploma in Political Science and Economics. **Career:** in Mixed Courts (Shebeen al-Kom, 1941-44); Taxation Officer in the Ministry of Finance (1944-47); Advocate before Court of Appeal (1947-61); Director of: "Cairo Weaving Factories Co." (1956-58); Secretary-General, Arab Real Estate Bank (1947); General Manager same bank (1956); Chairman same bank (1967); General Manager, UAE Development Bank (1978); Legal Advisor to financial institutions. **Publ.:** Treaties in Egyptian Company Law (1959). **Hobbies:** Excursions and Reading. **Member:** of Shooting Club, Egyptian National Club. **Addr.:** Cairo, Egypt.

SAGAR (Abdul Aziz, Hamad, al), Kuwaiti statesman and businessman. **Born** in 1913 in Kuwait. **Educ.:** Saint

Mary College, Bombay, India. **Career:** Member of the Municipality Board and of Development Board (1952-55); President of the Kuwait Chamber of Commerce and Industry (1959-present); Chairman of the National Bank of Kuwait S.A.K. 1959-65); Member, Constituent Assembly (1962-63); Minister of Public Health (1963); Chairman, Kuwait Oil Tanker Co. S.A.K. (1961-79); Speaker, First Parliament (1963-65); President, Kuwait Red Crescent Society (1965-1995); Vice-President, Arab-French Chamber of Commerce (1972-present) British Arab Chamber of Commerce (1980-present) and Austro-Arab Chamber of Commerce (1988-present); **Languages spoken:** Arabic (mother tongue), Urdu and English. **Addr.:** P.O.Box 244, Tel.: 2432980, Kuwait and Kuwait Chamber of Commerce and Industry, P.O.Box 775, Safat 13008, Kuwait. Tel.: 2417285.

SAGAR (Hamad, Abdalla, al), Kuwaiti businessman. **Born** in 1934 in Kuwait. **Son** of Abdalla al-Sager. **Married. Career:** Chairman, Kuwait Shipbuilding & Repairyard Company; Director, Kuwait Real Estate Bank; al-Ahlia Insurance Co.; Director, Pearl Investment Co., Bahrain; Director, A.H. al-Sayar & Bros., Kuwait. **Addr.:** P.O.Box 5809, Tel.: 246570, Telex: 9353 A/B LULUAH BN, Manama, Bahrain.

SAGAR (Wael, Jasem, al), Kuwaiti businessman. **Career:** Director, Kuwait Asia Bank EC, Manama, Bahrain; Director, Arab Bankers Association, London; Director, Kuwait International Investment Company SAK, Safat, Kuwait. Director, Kuwait Projects Co. **Addr.:** al-Salhia Commercial Complex, Fahad al-Salem Street, Block 1, 5th floor, P.O.Box 22792, Tel.: 420762, 438273-9, Telex: 22325, 222997 A/B INVEST IT, 2545 KIIC KT, Safat, Kuwait.

SAGR (Abdulaziz N., al), Saudi civil servant. **Born** in 1946 at al-Bear. **Dipl.:** M.Sc., Ph.D. (Computer Science). **Career:** Systems analyst, Petromin Marketing (1970-72); Manager, Systems and Operations, Data Processing Centre, University of Petroleum and Minerals, Dhahran (1972-74); Chairman, Department of Systems Engineering and Computer Sciences, UPM, Dhahran (1979-81); Director General, National Information Centre, Ministry of Interior, since 1981. **Member:** Association of Computing Machinery (ACM), Institute of Electrical and Electronic Engineers (IEEE), Computer Honorary Society and Microprocessor Club; member of the Board, al-Khaleej Computer and Electronic Systems Co. and the Saudi National Computer Conference. **Prof. Addr.:** Ministry of Interior, National Information Centre. Tel.: 4770515, Riyadh, Saudi Arabia.

SAHADEV (Babu), Indian executive. **Born** in 1955 in Perintalmanna, Kerala, India. **Son** of K.V.R. Unni Nair Sahadev (Hindu Tribe). **Married** in 1981. **Educ.:** University of Baroda, India. **Dipl.:** B.Sc. (1974). **Career:** Citibank N.A., Dubai (1975-76); Chief Dealer, American Express Bank Ltd., Dubai, UAE (1976-). **Member:** Forex Association; Indian Sports Club, Dubai. **Hobbies:** Reading, Badmington and table Tennis. **Addr.:** P.O.Box 3304, Tel.: 226296-8, Telex: 47675 A/B AMEXFX, Dubai, UAE.

SAHBANI (Tayeb), Tunisian diplomat. **Born** in 1925 in Tunis, Tunisia. **Married**, 3 children: 2 daughters and 1 son. **Educ.:** Sadiki College, Tunis; Ecole des Langues Orientales, Faculté de Lettres Sorbonne, Paris. **Career:** Arabic Teacher, secondary schools, and in the Institute of High Studies, Tunis; President, Neo-Destour Federation of Tunis (1954-56); Elected Member, National Council of the Neo-Destour (1955); Member, Constituent Assembly (1956); Ambassador to Morocco (1956); Ambassador to Egypt (1957); Secretary General, Foreign Ministry (October 1958); Personal Representative of the U.N., Secretary General at Brussels, dealing with the Congo (1961); leading negotiator for Tunisian Authorities over the Bizerta question (1961-62); Head of Cabinet to President Bourguiba (November 1964); Ambassador to Lybia (1968-69); Ambassador to Yugoslavia, Bulgaria and Romania (Feb. 1973); Secretary General in the Ministry of Foreign Affairs, Tunis- Tunisia (1978); Permanent Representative of Tunisia in the Arab League (1981); State Secretary in the Ministry of Foreign Affairs (1986); Permanent Secretary in the "Rassemblement Constitutionnel Democratique, Responsable for International Relations" (1988); Secretary General in the Socialist and Democratic Interafrican (1991). **Addr.:** Ministry of Foreign Affairs, Tunis, Tunisia, and Interafrican Socialiste et Démocratique, 6, Rue el-Waquidi, 1004 el-Menzeh IV, Tunis, Tunisia.

SAHNOUN (Mohamed), Algerian former political advisor to the president of Algeria. **Born** on April 8, 1931 in Algeria. **Son** of Osman Sahnoun (Teacher) **and** Mrs. Yettou née Tabti. **Educ.:** Sorbonne - New York Universities. **Dipl.:** B.A. - M.A. **Career:** Director Ministry of Foreign Affairs (1962-64); Deputy Secretary General OUA (1964-73); Deputy Secretary General Arab League (1973-74); Ambassador to Federal Republic of Germany (1975-79); Ambassador to France (1979-82); Ambassador to UN. New York (1982-84); Ambassador to U.S. (1984-88); Ambassador to Morocco (1989-90); Advisor to the President of Algeria (1990-91). **Priv. Addr.:** 32, Rue Chenoua Hydra, Algiers, Algeria.

SAID (Abdulaziz Abdul Rahman, al), Saudi academic. **Born** in 1938, at Jalajel, Sudair. **Dipl.:** Ph.D. **Career:** Director of Administration, Riyadh High Court (rank of Judge) (1965); Head of Riyadh Religious Institute (1966); Lecturer, Faculty of Shari'a, (Islamic Law), Riyadh (1972); Dean, Faculty of Shari'a, Riyadh (1974); Vice Rector, Imam Muhammad Ibn Saud Islamic University. **Member:** Council and Higher Council, Imam Muhammad Ibn Saud Islamic University; attended several conferences. **Publications:** Ibn Qudamah Wa Atharoh al-Osouleyah (Ibn Qudamah Principal Works); published research work. **Hobbies:** reading, scientific research. **Address:** Imam Muhammad Ibn Saud Islamic University, Tel.: 4042748, Riyadh. **Priv. Addr.:** Tel.: 4573676, Riyadh, Saudi Arabia.

SAID (Abdulsamad Mutahar), Yemeni executive. **Born** in 1924 in al-Hogariah. **Son** of Mutahar Said (Alaruk Tribe). **Career:** al-Mutahar Co., North Yemen; member, Yemen Bank for Reconstruction and Development, Sanaa, Yemen. Chairman al-Mutahar Motor & Engineering Co.; Yemen Contractors Ltd. **Member:** Sanaa Chamber of Commerce. **Addr.:** P.O.Box 522, Tel.: 207018, 207020, Telex: 2242 A/B AMECO, Sanaa, Yemen Arab Republic.

SAID (Ahmad, Abdu), Yemeni politician. **Born** in 1930 in Yemen. **Son** of Abdu Saïd. **Married. Educ.:** Universities of Cornell and Chicago, USA. **Career:** Minister of Finance (1967-69 and 1971-72); Minister of Development (1973-74); Minister of Communications (1974); Minister for Services, later Minister without Portfolio in administration of Abdul Aziz Abdul Ghani (1975); elected member of the Arab delegation to UNESCO (1987). Founded private preparatory school in Taez. **Addr.:** Taiz, Republic of Yemen.

SAID (Ahmad, Mohamed), Egyptian judge. **Born** on June 12, 1929 in Cairo, Egypt. **Married:** five children, one son, four daughters. **Educ.:** Cairo University, Egypt. **Dipl.:** LL.B. (1948). **Career:** Deputy Attorney, Ministry of Justice (1948-63); Chief Justice (1963-71); Counsellor (1971-80); Chief Justice of Appeal Court (1980-). **Member:** Heliopolis Club. **Addr.:** al-Masri Street, Masr al-Jadida, Cairo, Egypt.

SAID (Amina, al), Egyptian editor, journalist, writer. **Born** in 1914 in Egypt. **Married** to Mr. Zein al-Abidine (Doctor), 3 children (one Engineer and two Faculty Professors). **Educ.:** Secondary and Higher. **Career:** Contributed to "Dar al-Hilal" and "al-Mousawar", Editor of the Monthly "Hawa" and "Elle"; member, Higher Council, Dar al-Hilal Publishing House; one of Egypt's leading journalist and television personalities; represented Egypt at several international conferences; member, Higher Censorship Council; member, Higher Press Council (formed in 1975). **Publ.:** Author of "The Great Goal", "Faces in Shadow" and many others. **Addr.:** Dar al-Hilal, Cairo, Egypt.

SAID (Bashir, Mohamad), Sudanese, journalist. **Born** on December 21, 1921 in Umdurman. **Son** of Mohamad Saïd al-Hage Abdallah (Merchant) **and** Mrs. Zeinab al-Mahdi. **Married** to Buthaina Mahmoud on August 18, 1948, 7 children: Salaheddine, Samia, Samira, Hind, Mohamad, Mahmoud and Ilham. **Educ.:** School of Arts, University of Khartoum; British Council Scholar, Journalism, Britain (1949-50); Practical training in the Office of the London Times; Daily Express, Reuters and Oxford Mail. **Dipl.:** School of Arts Diploma. **Career:** Took up journalismm as reporter (1945), joined Publications Bureau of Ministry of Education (1947); Founded al-Ayam Press Co. Ltd. (1954); Member of the Council of University of Khartoum (1958-61); Joined Office of Public Information, UN Secretariat (1961-63); again member of the Council of University of Khartoum (1967-69); Member of the Board of Directors of Sudan Commercial Bank; Member of Sudan Delegation to United Nations (1956); now Managing Director, al-Ayam Press Co. Ltd., al-Ayam Printing Co. Ltd.; al-Ayam Stationery Co. Ltd. **Awards:** Knighthood (Government of Ethiopia), Sudan Distinguished Medal and Friendship Medal (Bulgaria). **Hobby:** Collection of paintings. **President** of Sudan Press Association. **Prof. Addr.:** P.O.Box 363, Tel.: 33326. Khartoum, Sudan. **Priv. Addr.:** Street No.7, New Extension of Khartoum, Tel.: 42500, Sudan.

SAID (Burham, Hassan), Egyptian administrator. **Born** in 1925 in Egypt. **Son** of Hassan Saïd. **Married,** two children. **Educ.:** Cairo University. **Dipl.:** LL.B. **Career:** Private practice (1947-48); Government lawyer, Ministry of Justice (1948); Office Manager, Minister of Culture (1952); Consultant to the Council of State (1953-69); Manager, Company Interests Department, Ministry of Commerce (1954-59); Legal Adviser, Ministry of Tourism (1972-73); Under Secretary (1973-83); **Medals:** Egyptian Order of Merit (First Class) (1981). **Member of:** Cairo Automobile Club; Gezira Sports Club. **Hobbies:** Reading, sports. **Addr.:** 4 al-Salah Ayoub, Zamalek, Cairo, Egypt.

SAID (Elmahdy, Elmahdy), Egyptian international civil servant. **Born** on December 18, 1921 at Elmahalla, Gharbiyah Governorate (Egypt). **Married,** children. **Educ.:** College of Agriculture, Cairo University (1938-42); Institute of Statistics, Cairo University (1950-51); North Carolina State College (USA) (1952-53). **Dipl.:** B.Sc. (Agriculture) 1942, B.Sc. (Statistics) 1944, M.Sc (Statistics) 1952, Ph.D. (Statistics) 1955. **Career:** Statistical Officer, Ministry of Agriculture (1943-47); Chief, Agricultural Census Branch, Ministry of Agriculture, Cairo (1948-51); Deputy Director, Statistics Division, Ministry of Agriculture (1952-56); Statistical Expert, Food and Agriculture Organisation (FAO); Nicaragua, el-Salvador and Guatemala (1956-59); Assistant to Director, Statistics Division, FAO, Rome (Italy) (1959-63); Regional Statistician, Regional Office for Near East, FAO, Cairo, since 1963. **Publ.:** Author of "A Manual on the Design and Analysis of Experiments" (1956), "Definition of Agricultural Labour Force" (1960), "Statistics of Food and Nutrition" (1961). **Awards:** Phi Kappa Phi, Sigma Xi, Gamma Sigma Delte, Hom. Tarheel North Carolina. **Member:** International Statistical Institute; American Statistical Association; Vice President, Egyptian Statistical Society; Egyptian Society on Population Studies. **Club:** Rotary club, Cairo. **Sports:** Cricket and tennis. **Hobbies:** Music and billiards. **Prof.**

Addr.: FAO, 110 Kasr el-Ayni street, Tel.: 23090, Cairo. **Priv. Addr.:** 10 Road 12, Maadi, Tel.: 34172, Cairo, Egypt.

SAID (Fuad), Egyptian films producer. **Born** in 1935 in Cairo. **Married** in 1968 to Miss Henny (Viennese). **Educ.:** Secondary in Egypt, specialization at the University of Southern California (1953). **Dipl.:** Diploma in Cinematography. **Career:** Cinematographer for TV films (1957); President of the Cinemobile Systems (1970); Worked assistant-cameraman in his uncle's movie Pyramid studio (Cairo) Joseph Aziz; Cameraman on the I Spy television show (1964); Discovered the Cinemobile System (1964); Founded "Fouad Said Productions" (1968). **Award:** Academy Award for technical excellence. **Addr.:** Cairo, Egypt.

SAID (Giuma, Said), Libyan executive. **Born** in 1924 in Zwara, Libya. **Son** of Said Said. **Married** in 1950, 2 sons, 5 daughters. **Educ.:** Italian Arab High School, Tripoli, Libya. **Career:** Administration and Senior Tax Officer, British Administration (1948-52); Head of Administration, Ministry of Public Works, Government of Libya (1953-55); Director, Issue Department, Bank of Libya, Exchange Control Department and Banking Department (1956-77); Member of the Board, Farah Maghred Co., Casablanca, Representing The Libyan Arab Foreign Investment Co. Deputy Director General, Inter-Arab Investment Guarantee Corporation (IAIGC), Safat, Kuwait (1978). **Member:** Centre of Reconciliation and Arbitration, Union of Arab Banks. **Hobbies:** History and Antiquities. **Addr.:** Tripoli, Libya.

SAID (Hamid, Mohamad), Iraqi senior civil servant. **Born** on July 14, 1937 at Dehuk (Iraq). **Married** in 1965 to Ursula Said, in Germany, three children: Dler, Shler and Sherko. **Educ.:** Secondary school; College of Agriculture, Baghdad; University of Freiburg (Germany). **Dipl.:** B.Sc. (agriculture); **Career:** University lecturer; Assistant Dean, College of Agriculture; Director-General of National Forestry; Director General, Iraqi Broadcasting and Television Est. **Sport:** swimming. **Prof. Addr.:** Salihiya, Karkh, Baghdad, Iraq. **Priv. Addr.:** Auari House No. 1250/3/3, Tel.: 60484, Baghdad, Iraq.

SAID (Hashim), Tunisian electronic engineer. **Born** in Tunis in 1947. **Educ.:** Mechanical and electronical engineering. **Career:** Head of Systems Planning Service, STEG (1971-78); Chairman and General Manager, Entreprise Tunisienne d'Electricite (ETEL) and Tunisia Electro-Technique (TET) (since 1978); Director, Cherguia Service Consent (CSC); Forensic expert at the law courts. **Prof. Addr.:** 47 Rue 8601, Zone Industrielle Cherguia, 2035 Tunis Carthage, Tunisia. **Priv. Addr.:** 13 Avenue Farchat Hached, Sidi Rezig. Tunis, Tunisia.

SAID (Hassan, bin Saad, bin), Saudi academic and civil servant. **Born** in 1941 in Riyadh city (Saudi Arabia). **Educ.:** German and American Universities. **Dipl.:** M.A. (Political Science and Economics) Federal Republic of Germany; M.A. (International Relations) USA. **Career:** Adviser on information matters (1970); Director of Publication Board, Ministry of Information; held the posts of Director-General of the Press, Director-General of Broadcasting, and Director-General of the Saudi Press Agency, Ministry of Information; attended the Gulf States Information Exchange Conference, the Gulf States Television Transmission Co-Ordination Conference, the International Islamic News Agency Conference, and the European Law and Legislation Conference; now Assistant Director-General of Saudi Television and Director of Budget and Planning, Ministry of Information. **Hobby:** Gardening. **Prof. Addr.:** Saudi Television, Yarmuk street, al-Badi'a, Tel.: 25512-193, Riyadh. **Priv. Addr.:** Tel.: 53183, Riyadh, Saudi Arabia.

SAID (Kamil, Mohamad), Sudanese official. **Born** in Sudan in 1931. **Son** of Mohamad Said. **Married,** three children. **Educ.:** Khartoum University; Oxford University. **Career:** Governor of the Northern Province; member of the Commission for Reorganization of Sudanese Provinces; member of the Electoral Commissions for the National Assembly; Head of the Electoral Commissions for the National Executive Councils and Local National Councils; member of the Administrative Officers' Union; attended conference on Administrative Development and its Effect on Growth in Developing Countries, Tangiers, Morocco. **Medals:** Order of the Republic, 2nd Class. **Hobbies:** reading, painting and sculpture. **Addr.:** Administrative Headquarters, Northern Province, Dongola, Sudan.

SAID (Mazzouzi Mohamad), Algerian statesman. **Born** in Algiers. **Educ.:** Secondary and Higher. **Career:** Member of the F.L.N. (National Liberation Front); Former Minister of State in Algerian Provisional Government (Tunis, then Algiers); Member of Political Bureau in Charge of Education and Public Health (July 1962- September 1962); Minister for Former Combatants and War Victims (1962-63); Second Vice-President (1963-65); Member of Revolutionary Command Council (1965); Member, Political Bureau FLN (1982); Minister of Labour and Social Affairs (March 1968-80). **Addr.:** FLN, Place Emir Abdelkader, Algiers, Algeria.

SAID (Mohamad Farhi, Ali, Brigadier), Iraqi army officer, diplomat. **Born** in 1927 in Baghdad, Iraq. **Son** of Ali Sa'id. **Married,** four children. **Career:** Commissioned (1951); Military Attaché, Embassy to Jordan (1963-64); Commanding Officer of the 19th Armoured Brigade (1968); member of the Military Bureau of the Arab Baath Socialist Party; Commander of the 2nd Mountain Infantry Division ; Commander of the 3rd Division. **Addr.:** Ministry of Defence, Baghdad, Iraq.

SAID (Mohamad, Hilmi), Egyptian former diplomat.

Born in Egypt in 1925. Son of Hilmi Said. Married, three sons. Educ.: Cairo University. Dipl.: B.A. Career: Third Secretary, Ministry of Foreign Affairs; Egyptian Embassy in Moscow; First Secretary, Embassy of Egypt, Amman, Jordan; Counsellor and Minister Plenipotentiary, Egyptian Embassy Moscow (1971); Ambassador of Egypt to Aden, Yemen (1976); Ambassador of Egypt to Dar es Salaam, Tanzania (1979-82); Director of Arab League Department (1982-85); retired. Decor.: Order of merit 4th Class; Order of the Republic 3rd Class; 2nd Class; Order of the Jordanian Star. Hobbies: Classical music, literature, theatre. Addr.: 17 Mohamad Kamil Mursi Street, Dokki, Cairo, Egypt.

SAID (Mohamed, Helmi Tawfik, al), Egyptian banker. **Born** in 1945 in Cairo, Egypt. **Son** of Tawfik al-Saïd. **Married**, two children. **Educ.:** Ain Shams University. **Dipl.:** B.A. and M.A. in Law and Economics. **Career:** Police Officer (1965-77); Bank Manager, Bank of Credit and Commerce (since 1978); member, International Organisation for Civil Defence, Geneva, Switzerland; General secretary, House Building Corporation, Cairo. **Hobbies:** Shooting, riding. **Addr.:** P.O.Box 4009, al-Haye al-Sabee, Madinet Nasr, Cairo, Egypt.

SAID (Omar, Aden), Djibouti Deputy at the National Assembly. **Born** in 1961 at Dorra (Tadjourah). **Career:** Mayor at Dorra (1976-1991); Head of Administration of Dorra (30/10/1991 - 19/12/1997); Militant of "Mouvement Populaire pour la Libération"; Active Member of RPP; Elected Deputy at the National Assembly (19/12/1997 to date); Member of Permanent Commission and Legislation Commission and General Administration of the Republic. **Prof. Addr.:** National Assembly, P.O.Box 138 Djibouti, Djibouti.

SAID (Qaboos Bin Taymour Bin, H.M. Sultan), Sultan of Oman. See **Qaboos (HM Sultan Qaboos Bin Taymour Bin Said)**

SAID (Rafik), Tunisian academic and diplomat. **Born** on March 16, 1930 in Tunis (Tunisia). **Married** on May 19, 1951. to Charra Mariem, one daughter and one son **Educ.:** Lycée Carnot, Tunis (1942-51); Universities of Paris, Grenoble, Lyon (France); University of London. **Dipl.:** M.A. (French language and literature), B.A. (Education), Ph.D. (International Relations). **Career:** Professor (1957-58); Chargé de mission, Minister of Education (1958-60); Director, Bourguiba Institute of Languages, University of Tunis (1960-62); Director, House of Culture Tunis (1962-66); Director, Cultural Activities (1967-68); First Vice-President, World Organisation of Intellectual Property (1970-71); President, Executive Committee, International Union, for Protection of Literary and Artistic Works (1971-72); Secretary General, Association Internationale de Solidarite Francophone (1972-75); Permanent Delegate of Tunisia to United Nations Educational, Scientific and Cultural Organisation (UNESCO) (1969-1975); Directeur du Cabinet, Minister of Public Health (1975) Directeur du cabinet, Minister of National Education (1976-1980) Ambassador of Tunisia to Canada (1980-86). **Publ.:** Author of "Les Changements Politiques et Sociaux en Tunisie Depuis l'Indépendance" (Georgetown University, USA 1964); "La Politique Culturelle au Brésil" (in collaboration with Pierre Moinot and André Battaini, UNESCO 1969); "La Politique Culturelle en Tunisie" (UNESCO, 1970). **Hobby:** Reading. **Addr.:** 12. Rue Mikhaïl Nouaïma el-Omrane, 1005 Tunis - Tunisia.

SAID (Rushdi, Farag), Egyptian geologist, politician. **Born** in 1920 in Egypt. **Son** of Farag Said. **Married**, two children. **Career:** member of the Egyptian Committee on the Denuclearisation of the Mediterranean (1964); member of the National Assembly; member of Secretariat General of the Arab Socialist Union; Deputy Chairman of Assembly's Foreign Relations and National Defence Committee in the People's Assembly; elected to Inter-Parliamentary Union Executive Council; served on the People's Assembly Committee of Enquiry into the Copt-Muslim disturbances; Egyptian observer at the opening of the European Security Conference in Helsinki; Chairman of the General Egyptian authority for Geological Surveys and Mining Projects. **Addr.:** General Egyptian Authority for Geological Surveys and Mining Projects, Cairo, Egypt.

SAID (Sayyid Fahad Bin Mahmoud, al), Omani politician. **Born** in 1944. Member of the Royal Family. **Married. Educ.:** Saidiyyah School, Muscat and Government secondary school, Bahrain. **Dipl.:** Degree in Commerce, University of Cairo, Egypt; Diploma in Diplomatic Studies, Paris; Academy of Arts in the Hague, Netherlands. **Career:** Appointed Director, Ministry of Foreign Affairs (1971); Minister of State (November 1971); Minister of Information and Culture (December 1972); Deputy Premier for Legal Affairs (March 1980-97); Deputy Prime Minister for the Council of Ministers (1998 to present). **Addr.:** Muscat, Sultanate of Oman.

SAID (Sayyid Faisal Bin Ali, al), Omani politician and diplomat. **Born** in 1928. Member of the Royal Family. **Educ.:** Saidiyyah School, Muscat. **Career:** Teacher; Department of External Affairs (1955); left Oman (1964) and lived abroad until 1970; Director of Education (October 1970); active in founding several new schools; Minister of Economy (March-July 1971); Chargé d'Affaires, Ministry of Foreign Affairs (January 1972); Omani Permanent Representative to the UN; Ambassador to USA (1973); Minister of Education (December 1973-76); Minister of National Heritage (1976); Minister of Culture and National Heritage (1979 to present). **Addr.:** Ministry of National Heritage and Culture, P.O.Box 668, Muscat, Sultanate of Oman.

SAID (Sayyid Shabib bin Taimur, al, H.H.), Omani

diplomat. **Born** on August 22, 1943 in Muscat, Oman. **Son** of His Majesty Sayyid Taimur bin Faisal al-Said **and** Mrs. née Sayyida Nafisa Bundukji. **Married** in 1966 to Gerda Verena, three children: Tarik, Tania and Taimur. **Educ.:** Grammar School, Karachi, Pakistan; Princeton College, London, U.K.; Aero and Auto Engineering College, Chelsea, U.K.; Queen Elizabeth College, Oxford, U.K. **Dipl.:** Senior Cambridge; Matriculation; Diploma in Foreign Service. **Career:** Accountant in London, practising for certified accountancy with Hugil, Tingle and Comber, U.K. (1968-70); Acting Director in the Directorate General of Foreign Affairs and Assistant to the Prime Minister (1970-71); Charge d'Affaires, Court of St. james, United Kingdom to set up the Embassy of Oman in London (1971-early 1973); Charge d'Affaires, Washington DC, U.S.A. to set up the embassy of Oman in Washington (1973-late 1974); Posted to the Islamic Republic of Pakistan, Islamabad as First Ambassador of Oman to Pakistan, to set up Embassy (1974-75); Appointed as the First Ambassador of the Sultanate of Oman, to the Kingdom of Morocco (1975-80); Minister of State and Personal Envoy to his Majesty, Sultan Qaboos bin Said (1981-83); Appointed Minister of Environment, to set up the new Ministry. This appointed made His Highness the first Minister of Environment in the Arab World. Also appointed as Assistant to the chairman, of the Council for the Conservation of Environment and protection against pollution, the Chairman being His Majesty Sultan Qaboos bin Said (1984-86); Appointed Minister of Environment and Water Resources and Deputy Chairman of the newly structured Council of Conversation of Environment and Water Resources (1986-89); Minister of Environment (March 1989-90); Chairman, Tawoos LIC and Subsidiary Companies. **President** of the Oman Equestrian Federation (1984-todate); Presently appointed to the following: Permanent councils and committees, which are also incorporated into the duties and permanent councils and committee, which are also incorporated into the duties and functions of his Highness: Council of Development: Committee for planning the development and environment of the southern region. Committee for the protection and contravention of the laws pertaining to conversation of the environment. Supreme Committee for town planning. Non-Permanent Committees: Ministerial committee for the establishment of the national authority for specifications, measurements and amalgamation of the government laboratories. Ministerial committee for water resources and waste water projects in the Sultanate. Ministerial committee for the study of droughts. Ministerial committee for studies on the southern region environment, water resources, tourism, coastal management and fisheries. **Decor.:** Order of Oman's Renaissance (First Class), decorated by his Majesty Sultan Qaboos bin Said (16 Nov. 1985); Order of the Alwai, decorated by His Majesty Sultan Qaboos bin Said (19 Nov. 1976); Order of Sultan Qaboos (First Class), decorated by His Majesty King Hassan-II, Kingdom of Morocco (4 Nov. 1980); Order of the Nile, decorated by his Excellency Hosni Mubarak, President of Egypt (16 Feb. 1982). **Sports:** Skiing, show jumping, tennis. **Hobbies:** Shooting, collecting art objects. **Prof. Addr.:** P.O.Box 323, Tel.: 696464, Muscat, Oman. **Priv. Addr.:** P.O.Box 22 Muscat, Tel.: 620244, Oman.

SAID (Sayyid Thuwainy Bin Shihab, al), Omani statesman. **Born** in 1924. **Educ.:** Baghdad and Bahrain. **Career:** Teaching profession; Master in Saidiyyah School, Muscat; worked in Sultan's Office (1948-55); worked in office of his father Sayyed Shabib (1956); succeeded him as Governor of Muscat (1970); Personal Advisor to HM The Sultan (October 1970); Member of the council of Ministers and Personal Representative Of HM the Sultan (1985 to present). **Addr.:** P.O.Box 616, Muscat, Sultanate of Oman.

SAIDANE (Ezzedine), Tunisian Deputy General Manager. **Born** on October 10, 1950 at Ksar Hellal, Tunisia. **Son** of Salem Saidane (retired) **and** Mrs. Mahbouba née Chaieb (retired). **Married** on July 17, 1976 in Tunisia to Safia Mahmoud, 5 children: Raya, Amel, Ibtissam, Hiba and Nour. **Educ.:** University of Tunis; University of Minnesota, U.S.A.; Oregon State University, U.S.A. **Dipl.:** Master's Degree of Science, Graduate Studies Licence ès Sciences Economiques University of Tunis, Diploma of Ecole Nationale d'Administration, Tunis. **Career:** Principal Engineer for Planning and Economic Studies; Tunisian Ministry of Agriculture. **Work:** Deputy General Manager, Banque Internationale Arabe de Tunisie, Tunis. Chief Executive Officer, Arab Banking Corporation, Tunis. **Sports:** Tennis. **Hobby:** Music. **Member:** of the BOARD of Directors - SICAV Tresor (Mutual Fund); SICAV Prosperity (Mutual Fund); Chairman and Member of the Board of Arab Banking Corporation, Algeria. Member Forex Club of Tunisia. **Prof. Addr.:** Arab Banking Corporation A.B.C. Building, 2045 Les Berges du Lac, Tunis. **Priv. Addr.:** 88, Avenue Tahar Ben Ammar el-Menzah, 9, - El Manar 1013 - Tunis, Tunisia.

SAIDI (Sharaf al-Deen Saleh, al), Yemeni Ambassador. **Born** in 1944 at IBB Yemen. **Son** of Saleh Nasher al-Saidi (deceased) **and** Mrs. Fatema M. al Ghaithi. **Married** in 1973 to Mrs. Samira N., 6 children: 3 boys and 3 girls: Wessam (1976), Abeer (1977), Lamees (1980), Waleed (1985), Hala'a (1990), Mohamed (1998). **Educ.:** G.C.E. 1963 Egypt, B.S.C 1969 czechoslovakia BRAJO. Field of International Relation. **Dipl.:** Training Course for one Year, Oxford University (1973-1974), External Relations Field; MD New York University (1975-1979); Seminar for Three Months in the Inter-Visitor Program (USA, Washington) (15 May - 15 August 1981). **Career:** Attache Ministry of Foreign Affairs, Sanaa - Yemen (1970); Member of Yemen Delegation to United Nations New York (1975-1979); Chief Protocol Department (1979-1988); Ass. Dep. Minister Sanaa (1984-1900), and (1990-1994); AD. Joint, Yemen Embassy to Poland (1994-1995); Ambassador of Yemen to State of Qatar (1995-1996). **Decor.;** Medal of Republic Second Class (1985) Sanaa, Republic of Yemen. **Prof. Addr.:** Chief North and South America Department Ministry of Foreign Affairs, Sanaa - Yemen, Tel.: 280357 Sanaa. **Priv. Addr.:** Assakania City - Hadda Area - St. No. 3, Tel.: 416183/418735, Sanaa, Republic of Yemen.

SAIEDAN (Abdullah, Mansour), Jordanian writer. **Born** in 1942, in Haifa, Palestine. **Son** of Mansour Saiedan. **Married,** seven children. **Educ.:** Jordan University and from Netherlands. **Dipl.:** B.A. in Arabic Literature also TV and Cinema Directing. **Career:** Inspector, Ministry of Education, Saudi Arabia (1962-66); Director and Broadcaster, Jordan Television (1974-81); Head, Printing Department, Jordan University (1981); Editor, "as-Sabah" newspaper. **Publ.:** "Tomorrow is my Travel" poems; "Palestinian Hearts", poems. "Sha Men al-Ghadab". **Member** of Jordanian Writers' Union. **Hobbies:** Reading, travelling. **Addr.:** as-Sabah Newspaper, P.O.Box 2396, Amman, Jordan.

SAIF (A. Jaleel), Saudi civil servant. **Born** on 4 April 1942 in Tarout Island (Eastern Province), Saudi Arabia. **Dipl.:** B.Sc., M.Sc. and Ph.D. (Traffic Safety Education and Administration). **Career:** Director, Technical Traffic Department, Riyadh; Assistant Director General, Highway Patrol Project; General Supervisor for Driving Education Project in Saudi Arabia; Director General, Organization and Programmes Department, Ministry of Interior; Director General, Foreign Manpower Department, Ministry of Interior, Riyadh. **Member:** International Road Federation, (Switzerland), Road Federation (Switzerland), the National Safety Council (U.S.A.), the American National Association for Safe Driving Education (USA) and the National Safety Council (U.K.); has received several certificates of achievement from various educational institutes in the U.S.A. **Publications:** Comparative Studies of Traffic Rules and Regulations in the Kingdom; Car Driving Technique and Skill; Modern Ways of Conducting Traffic Administration. **Address:** P.O.Box 3743, Tel.: 4026884, Riyadh. **Priv. Addr.:** Tel.: 4654452, Riyadh, Saudi Arabia.

SAIF (Abdullah Saif, al), Saudi engineer. **Born** in 1943 at al-Shoara. **Dipl.:** B.Sc. (Petroleum Engineering). **Career:** Petroleum Engineer, Aramco; Manager, Southern Province Production Department, Aramco. **Hobby:** reading. **Address:** c/o Aramco, P.O.Box 225, Abqaiq oil fields, Saudi Arabia.

SAIF (Khaled Abdulrahman, al), Saudi educator, **Born** in 1940 at Hail, Saudi Arabia. **Dipl.:** Ph.D. (Business Administration Education). **Career:** Teacher, Ministry of Education (1960); Auditor (1962); Secretary (1965); Inspector, Commercial Education (1966); Director, Commercial Education (1968); Dean of Students and Educational Affairs, King Faisal University (1975); Secretary General, K.F.U. 1978); Vice Rector for Academic Affairs, King Faisal University since 1979; Professor-Managerial Psychology, principles of management and statistics, King Saud University (1984); President, Al Saif Management and Economic consultants and Al Saif Research and Education Consultant, since 1990; Conducted studies in Business and Traffic Safety. **Member:** World Organization for Commercial Education, American National Organization for Commercial Education, World American Organization for Administration and Organisation for Higher Studies and Research. Delta Epsilon. **Publications:** the Study of Technical Abilities in the Administrative Sciences and the Preparation of Computerized Data Needed by Instructors Preparing for the Study of Computerized Administrative Data. **Hobbies:** reading, swimming, walking. **Prof. Addr.:** King Faisal University, P.O.Box 400, Tel.: 5826465, al-Ahsa. **Priv. Addr.:** Tel.: 5829721, al-Ahsa, Saudi Arabia.

SAIF (Khaled, bin Musaed, al), Saudi businessman. **Born** on June 5, 1953 in Riyadh (Saudi Arabia). **Son** of Musaed Ben el-Seif (businessman). **Married Educ.:** Riyadh Elementary school; International College, Beirut (Lebanon); **Dipl.:** B.Sc. (Civil Engineering). **Career:** General Manager, Musaed Seif el-Seif Establishment, Beirut Office (1975); Founder, Khaled Ben el-Seif Establishment, Riyadh, Saudi Arabia (1977); Founder, al-Seif Engineering and Contracting, Riyadh, Saudi Arabia (1977); Founder, al-Seif Establishment for Industry, Riyadh (1978); Board Chairman, al-Seif Group of Companies; of Musaed al-Seif & Sons Co. Ltd.; of Mechanical Systems, Ltd.; of Wieacker Saudi Arabia, Ltd. **Sports:** swimming, tennis, table tennis and horsebackriding. **Hobbies:** reading (literature and poetry). **Credit Card:** American Express. **Prof. Addr.:** P.O.Box 2774, Telex: 201156 el-Seif SJ, Cable ELSEIFCO, Riyadh (Saudi Arabia). **Priv. Addr.:** Washem street, Tel.: 4044780, Riyadh 11461, Saudi Arabia.

SAIF (Khalifa Mohammed, Hassan), United Arab Emirates Managing Director & Chief Executive. **Born** in 1952 at Al Ain (U.A.E.). **Son** of Mohammed Hassan SAIF. **Married** in 1980 in Abu Dhabi to Mrs. Saleha Abdulla Al Shamsi, six children: Ahmed (1981), Mohamed (1983), Hassan (1985), Ali (1986), Rawdha (1989), Hessa (1999). **Educ.:** LEEDS - A.C.C.A. C.H., Portmouth Polytechnic - H.N.D. **Career:** Managing Director and Chief Executive Officer, Abu Dhabi Commercial Bank (since 1992 to date). Managing Director - International Petroleum Investment Co. (Oct. 1984 to 31.12.1991); Deputy Managing Director - Abu Dhabi Investment Authority (Sep. 1980 to Oct. 1984); Accountant - Abu Dhabi Marine Operating Co. (Sept. 1978 to Sept. 1980); **Credit Cards:** Mastercard, Diner's Club. **Prof. Addr.:** Abu Dhabi Commercial Bank, P.O.Box 939, Abu Dhabi, Tel.: (02) 696 2222, United Arab Emirates. **Priv. Addr.:** P.O.Box 939 Abu Dhabi, United Arab Emirates.

SAIF (Mohamad, Yusuf), Kuwaiti bank executive. **Born** in 1940 in Kuwait. **Son** of Yusuf al-Saif. **Married** in 1967, 4 daughters. **Dipl.:** B.Com. **Career:** Staff Manager, Gulf Bank (1974-76); Manager, Gulf Bank K.S.C., Safat, Kuwait (1981-). **Member:** Kuwait Sea Club; Hunting Equestrian Club, Kuwait. **Hobby:** Painting. **Addr.:** P.O.Box 3200, Tel.: 445425, Telex: 2001, 22783 A/B GULF BK, Safat, Kuwait.

SAIGH (Nassir, al), Saudi business administration professor. **Born** on October 10, 1942 in Riyadh, Saudi Arabia. **Son** on Mohammad al-Saigh **and** Noura al-Saigh. **Married** on July 15, 1989 in Amman to Azza Hammad. **Educ.:** Indiana Univesity-Bloomington; University of Kentucky-Lexington; King Saud University, Riyadh, Saudi Arabia. **Dipl.:** B.A. (Commerce-1969), King Saud University; MBA (1974), Indiana University; DBA (1979), University of Kentucky. **Career:** Professor, Business Administration Department, King Saud University (1979-present); Head of Business Administration Department, King Saud University (1980-83); Director General, Arab Administrative Development Organization (1983-91). **Awards:** Listed in Who's Who in the World, Marquis Who's Who, Men of achievement. **Hobbies:** Reading and Research. **Member:** International Institute of Administrative Sciences. **Credit Cards:** American Express/ Visa. **Prof. Addr.:** P.O.Box 2459, Tel.: 966-1-467-4066, Riyadh, Saudi Arabia. **Priv. Addr.:** P.O.Box 17159, Tel.: 962-6-687327, Amman, Jordan.

SAIM AL DAHR (Sami Bakor), Saudi legal counsellor. **Born** in 1945 in Jeddah, Saudi Arabia. **Dipl.:** of Law. **Career:** Member of the Legal Board of Saudi Arabian Airlines (Saudia). **Hobby:** reading. **Prof. Addr.:** Law Office, P.O.Box 3058 Tel.: 644806, 6448054, Telex: 403558, SJ LEGAL, Jeddah, 21471. **Priv. Addr.:** Tel. 6673619, Jeddah, Saudi Arabia.

SAJA (Fahad Mohamad, al), Saudi civil servant. **Born** in 1939 in Dhurma, Saudi Arabia. **Dipl.:** B.Sc. (Chemistry). **Career:** Director, Quality Control Laboratory, Dammam; Director, General Directorate for the Protection of Consumers, Ministry of Commerce; member of Board of Saudi Arabian Standardization Association; member of British Chemical Society. **Prof. Addr.:** Ministry of Commerce, Tel.: 4014684, Riyadh. **Priv. Addr.:** Tel.: 4764173, Riyadh, Saudi Arabia.

SAKAKINI (Wadad), Syrian writer. **Born** in Syria. **Married** to M. Zaki al-Mahassini. **Educ.:** Secondary and Higher. **Career:** Writer and Novelist, Professor in Damascus and Beirut, now living in Cairo. **Publ.:** Author of several literary Studies, including "Karam Milhem Karam", "Maraya an Nass", "as-Sitar al-Marfou", "Noufouss Tatakallam", "al-Hob al-Mouharram", "Arw Bint al-Khoutoub", "al-Achika al-Moutasawifa", "Chahiraat minal Chark wal Gharb", "Kassem Amine", "Neqat alal Hourouf". **Addr.:** Cairo, Egypt.

SAKER (Ahmad, Dr.), Syrian diplomat. **Born** on December 9, 1936 in Syria (Jableh city). **Son** of Mahmoud Saker (landlord) **and** Mrs. Hasna Saker. **Married** on February 3, 1960 to Layla Hassan Saker, four children: Lina, Firas, Homam, Manaf. **Educ.:** Doctor's degree in political economy (1975). **Career:** Diplomat in Czechoslovakia, Iran, India, Turkey and USSR. (1966-75); Minister Plenipotentiary in the Syrian Ministry of Foreign Affairs in Damascus and at the same time lecturer of political economy in Damascus High Planning Institute (1976-79); Minister Plenipotentiary in the Permanent Mission of Syria to the United Nations Office in Geneva (1980-85); Presided many syrian delegations to many Conferences in UNCTAD, WIPO and Centre for Human Rights. Elected a lot of times as spokesman for the Group of 77 in Geneva on different subjects. Elected several times as a president of different Committees and Groups during his mission in Geneva; Director of America's Division at the Ministry of Foreign Affairs in Damascus (1985-88); Ambassador Plenipotentiary and Extraordinary of Syria to Poland (March 25, 1988). Completed his mission to Warsaw on November 15, 1993). **Publ.:** Innumerable articles in newspapers and magazines on economic, political affairs and human rights. **Languages:** Arabic, English, French and some Russian. **Sports exercised before:** Football, tennis. **Hobbies:** Reading, painting. **Prof. Addr.:** Ministry of Foreign Affairs, Damascus, Syria.

SAKET (Bassam, Khalil), Jordanian economist. **Born** on January 21, 1944, **Married**, 3 children. **Educ.:** Baghdad University, Iraq, (1962-1966); Oxford University, Jesus College, post graduate diploma in Economics (1968-1970); IMF Washington D.C., USA, diploma in Financial Analysis (1973); Keele University, Ph.D. in Economics (1973-1976). **Career:** Analyst and Economic Researcher Central Bank of Jordan (1966-1970); Senior Economist, Head of the Domestic Economy and Development (1970-1973); Economic Advisor to HRH the Crown Prince, Royal Court (1978-1984); Director of the Economic Dept. of the Royal Scientific Society and Member of the Executive Committee (1976-1984); Managing Director, Government Investment Corporation (1984-1986); Secretary General of the Royal Hashemite Court (1986-1989); Minister of Agriculture (1989); Chairman of the Board, the Jordan Cement Factories, (1990-1992); Minister of Industry and Trade, (1993); Chairman of the Board, the Jordan Cement Factories, (1994-). **Publ.:** Author and co-author of various books on economics and economic development in the Arab World and Jordan in particular. Award: decoration from His Majesty King Hussein, the president of Italy and the president of Austria. **Member:** International Development Society, Washington D.C; The Foreign Affairs Council, Amman; The Arab Youth Forum, Amman; Jordanian Economists Society, Amman; Board member of the Queen Noor Foundation; Board of Trustees of the Amman National University; Board of directors of the Amman Baccalaureate School; Commissioner of the Jordanian - American Commission for Educational Exchange (Fulbright); Chairman of the Board, the Jordan Trade Association. **Hobbies:** Squash, basket ball, music and swimming. **Prof. Addr.:** P.O.Box 109 Amman - Jordan, Tel. Res. 671925 Fax. 693818 - Tel. Off. 729901 - 729953 Fax: 729921 and Jordan Cement Factories Co. Ltd., P.O.Box 610 Amman - Jordan.

SAKIJHA (Ibrahim, Ali), Jordanian journalist. **Born** in 1926 in Jaffa, Palestine. **Son** of Ali Sakijha. **Married**, three children. **Educ.:** Palestine Matriculation. **Career:** Editor, "al-Falastin" newspaper; Jaffa, Palestine (1944-48); Editor, "al-Masri" newspaper, Cairo, Egypt (1948-49); Assistant Editor, "al-Jazira" and "al-Nasr" dailies, Amman (1949-50); Assistant Editor "al-Falastin" newspaper, Jerusalem (1950-67); Manager and Editor of "al-Destour", Amman (1967-75); General Manager and Editor of "al-Shaab" Amman; Vice Chairman of the Board of Dar al Shaab Company for Printing, Publishing and Distribution; President of Jordanian Press Association; Adviser to Jordanian Television (1969-71); Editor, "Sawt al-Shaab" (since 1983). Member of the Secretaries' Council, International Arab Information Center, Cairo; member of the Permanent Bureau of the Arab Press Foundation. **Medals:** Medal of His Holiness the Pope (1964). **Hobby:** Writing short stories and articles. **Addr.:** al-Shaab Newspaper, P.O.B. 925155, Tel.: 661234, 667101, Amman, Jordan.

SAKKA (Jawad Omar, al), Saudi executive. **Born** in 1933 at Beir Saba'a, Palestine. **Dipl.:** B.A. (Law), M.A. (Comparative Jurisprudence), New York University. **Career:** Assistant Attorney General, Gaza Strip; Legal Adviser, Ministry of Petroleum and Mineral Resources, Saudi Arabia; member, Foreign Capital Investment Committee; Director General, Legal Affairs, Ministry of Petroleum and Mineral Resources; member of the Board, Arabian Oil Company Ltd.; attended some of the Arab Petroleum Conferences, most of the conferences of the Organization of Petroleum Exporting Countries (OPEC) and most of the Council of Ministers meetings of the Organization of Arab Petroleum Exporting Countries (OAPEC); participated in the Symposium on Private Investment Abroad, Dallas, Texas, 1967; attended the International Peace Through law, 1965 and Iran Management Development Programme, 1969. **Honour:** al-Alawy Order of Merit, 3rd Grade, awarded by King Hassan II of Morocco. **Hobbies:** reading, swimming, music. **Address:** Ministry of Petroleum and Mineral Resources, P.O.Box 757, Tel.: (1)478-7977, Riyadh. **Priv. Addr.:** Tel.: 4760357, Riyadh, Saudi Arabia.

SAKKAB (Emile, Sam'an), Palestinian businessman. **Born** in 1925 in Jerusalem. **Son** of Sam'an Yousuf Sakkab **and** Mrs., née Latifa Theodor Baramki. **Married** in 1956 to Henriette I. Atalla in Jerusalem, five children: Simon, Mary, Ibrahim, Randa and Lina. **Educ.:** St George College. **Dipl.:** Matriculation (1943). **Career:** In business since 1943, Chairman of Sakkab Trading Establishment, Amman since 1976. **Member:** Orthodox club. **Prof. & Priv. Addr.:** P.O.Box 9295, Cable: Sakkab, Tel.: 9626611260, Fax: 9626611261, and 24261, Amman, Jordan.

SAKR (Issa), Kuwaiti artist painter and sculptor. **Born** in 1940 in Kuwait. **Educ.:** Obtained a scholarship for the free painting (1960), Academy of Fine Arts, Cairo. **Dipl.:** From the said Academy. **Career:** Artist painter and sculptor, participate to 31 exhibitions in Kuwait and foreign countries. **Remark:** mongst his sculptures "Le martyr de l'amour", "Le misérable", "La femme au tambour" and amongst his paints "L'araignée", "Le portrait hideux", "Dans l'impasse", "Kaiss et Leila", etc... **Addr.:** Kuwait City, Kuwait.

SAKR (Sakr, Ahmed), Egyptian President of Menoufia University. **Born** on February 26, 1940 at Quesna, Menoufia. **Son** of Ahmed Sakr. **Married** on August 26, 1966 to Dr. Sohair Abdel Aziz, 3 sons: Yasser (8.3.1968), Sameh (7.3.1970), Hany (6.5.1978). **Educ.:** Cairo University (Egypt), University of Michigan and Michigan State University (U.S.A.). **Career:** Research Assistant, Institute of National Planning (1962-1964); Expert, Institute of National Planning (1970-1973); Expert and Assistant Professor Faculty of Commerce, Kuwait University (1973-1977); Senior Expert and Professor, Institute of National Planning (1977-1982); Head, Economics Department and Vice-Dean, Faculty of Commerce, Menoufia University (1982-1987); Vice-President, Menoufia University (Jan. 87-31 Aug. 1993); President (14 August 1993- to present). **Sports:** Light Sports Specially Walking. **Hobby:** Reading. **Prof. Addr.:** Menoufia University, Shebin el Kome, Egypt. **Priv. Addr.:** 179, El Hegaz St., Heliopolis, Cairo, Egypt, Tel.: (02) 777620 (Office), (02) 2452344 (Home).

SALAH (Abdallah), Jordanian statesman and diplomat. **Born** in 1922 in Jordan. **Educ.:** Bishop Gobat's School (Jerusalem), American University (Beirut). **Dipl.:** Bachelor of Law. **Career:** Field Education Officer, United Nations Relief and Works Agency (Unrwa), Jordan (1952-62); Ambassador to Kuwait (1962-63), to India (1963-64), to France (1964); Minister of Foreign Affairs (1964 and 1967); Minister of Transport in the Cabinet of Mr. Saad Jomaa (1967); Ambassador of Jordan to Belgium and France (May 1967); Minister of Foreign Affairs in the Cabinet of Mr. Wasfi at-Tall (October 28, 1970- 13 August 1972); Ambassador to the U.S.A. (June 1973- April 1980); Ambassador to Switzerland (May 1980- February 1983); Ambassador, Permanent Representative to the United Nations in New York (February 1983-1991); Member of the Upper House of Parliament (Feb. 1991- present). **Awards:** Several decorations. **Addr.:** P.O.Box 950409, Amman 11195, Jordan.

SALAH (Adnan Kamel), Saudi political columnist and businessman. **Born** at al-Wahat, Saudi Arabia. **Educ.:** Secondary School Certificate. **Career:** Teacher (1957-64); General Manager of Mecca Advertising Agency (1967-75); owner and chairman of Sahara Express Tourist and Travel Agency; member of International Advertising Association (IAA), New York, International Chain of Industrial and Technical Advertising (ICITA), New York; attended International Advertising and Public Relations Conference, Portugal (1970), International Conference on Industrial and Technical Advertising, Teheran (1973). **Hobbies:** reading, swimming. **Prof. Addr.:** P.O.Box 6489, Tel.: 6447709, Jeddah. **Priv. Addr.:** Tel.: 631755, Jeddah, Saudi Arabia.

SALAH (Butros Alphonse), Jordanian administrator. **Born** in 1927 in Nablus, Jordan. **Married**, two children. **Educ.:** Law Studies, Jerusalem (1945-48); Administration, UK (1957). **Career:** Teacher, Terrasanta College, Jerusalem (1945-47); Teacher, Gaza College (1946-47); Teacher, de Lasalle College, Jerusalem (1947-49); Employee, Arab Insurance Company, Jerusalem and Beirut (1948-49); employee at Aramco, Dhahran, Saudi Arabia (1950-51); Assistant Director, CAT Company, Beirut (1952-54); General Commercial Director, CAT Southern Gulf Company, Bahrain (1954-60); Director General SINCO Company, Amman (1960-62); Partner and Director, Jordan Traders Co. (1962-63); Administrative Director and Public Relations Director ALIA Airlines (1963-65); Director General, Jordanian General Relations Company (1965-67); Director of Public Relations, Ministry of Information (1967-69); Information Attaché; Jordanian Embassy, London UK (1969-70); Director of Press and Public Relations Department, Ministry of Information; Acting Director of Press and Publications Department; Director General Jordanian News Agency (1972-73); Director of Public Relations, Ministry of Culture and Information (1973-76); Adviser, Ministry of Culture and Information (1976); Under Secretary, Ministry of Information (1978-84); Legal Advisor to Government Institutions. member of the World Affairs Council, of the National Higher Committee of the Jerash Festival. **Medal:** Order of the Jordanian Star (1972). **Addr.:** P.O.Box 1714, Amman, Jordan.

SALAH (Hassen), Tunisian President of Afrika Maritime Group. **Born** on August 26, 1950 at Mahdia/Tunisia. **Son** of Ahmed Salah (Agriculturist) **and** Mrs. Hadda Amara (Salah). **Educ.:** He Studied in Tunisia and Germany. **Dipl.:** in Shipping/Marketing/Management. **Career:** Shipping Adviser for North Africa in Italy (1972-74); Shipping Adviser for North Africa in Germany, also for Arabian Shipping Companies (1975- untill now). **Other Information:** Speaking 6 Languages (German, English, Italian, French, Spanish, Arabic). Creator of the First Private Shipping Line between France and Tunisia/Most Modern Organisation in Tunisia. Shipping, Farwarding/ Land Transport Warehousing/Travel Agency. **Sports:** Football, Tennis. **Hobby:** Yachting. **Members:** in Germany/Spain, Member of several Clubs. **Credit Cards:** Amex, Diners, Visa, Master, etc... **Prof. Addr.:** AFRIMAR, 5 Rue Champlain, P.O.Box 716 Tunis 1001, Tunisia. Tel.: 345856. **Priv. Addr.:** Marsa, Rue de la Liberté, Tel.: 743551, Tunis, Tunisia.

SALAHDINE (Mohamed), Moroccan professor of economics. **Born** on March 18, 1947. **Son** of Abdelkebir Filali Salahdine (employee insurance company) **and** Mrs. née Zhor Figuigui. **Married** in 1981 in Morocco to Atika Sermouh, 2 children: Widad (February 19, 1981), Talal (November 27, 1982). **Educ.:** Lycée Moulay Ismaïl (1961-67); University Mohamed V Faculty of Law (1967-72); University of Paris (1973-81). **Dipl.:** Economics Licence (1972); Diploma of Sociology, Paris (1979); Ph.D. University of Economics, Paris X (1981). **Career:** Socio economist - Expert in Economy of Development. **Work:** "Attaché Direction" Mutuelle Agricole Marocaine, Rabat (1972-74); Permanent Director of Center Socio Cultural. Le Relais Paris (1976-80); Director of Economics Department, University of Fez (1981-89); Project Manager Catholic Relief Services (1989-93). **Publ.:** 4 Books and Several Studies on Women & Development, Author of on informal sector & Poverty in Morocco for World Bank, USAID, ILO, and Moroccan Ministries. **Award:** Honor Citizen of Mauritania. **Sports:** Football. **Hobby:** Music. **Member:** Association Culture et Développement, Association Marocaine de solidarité et de développement. **Prof. Addr.:** Faculty of Law, Fez, P.O.Box 2139, Tel.: 2125641305, Morocco, and Catholic Relief Services, P.O.Box 98, Rabat, Morocco. **Priv. Addr.:** 47, Ave. de France Agdal, Tel.: 2127778755, Rabat, Morocco.

SALAHUDDIN (Ahmad Mushfiq), Pakistani bank manager. **Born** in 1947 in Gujrat, India. **Son** of Salahuddin. **Married** in 1979, 1 daughter. **Educ.:** University of Punjab, Lahore. **Dipl.:** B.A.; LL.B. **Career:** Habib Bank Ltd. (1973); Forex Training, Foreign Exchange Branch, Habib Bank Ltd. (1974); Joined Habib Bank AG Zurich (FEX Side) (1977); Appointed Officer in Charge (1980); Deputy Manager, Habib Bank AG Zurich, Dubai, UAE (1981). **Hobbies:** Cricket, Tennis, Hockey and Football. **Addr.:** P.O.Box 3306, Tel.: 220008, Telex: 45716 A/B SWBANK EM, Deira Dubai, UAE.

SALAHUDDIN (Mohamad), Saudi journalist, publisher, advertiser. **Born** in 1934 in Saudi Arabia. **Married** to Miss Safiah J. Bajunaid, three children. **Educ.:** Michigan University, Ann Arbor, USA. **Dipl.:** B.A. in Near Eastern Studies; M.A. in Political Science. **Career:** Sub editor, al-Nadwa Daily, Makkah (1959-63); Manager, Libraries Department, Ministry of Pligrimage and Endowment, Saudi Arabia, Makkah (1963-64); Executive Editor, al-Madina Newspaper, Jeddah (1964-73); Publisher and Editor of Saudi Review, Jeddah; Chairman of: Saudi Publishing and Distributing House, Jeddah, Islamic Press Agency

Ltd., Makkah Advertising and Publicity Ltd., Yathrib Communications Ltd.; Publisher of: Arabia-The Islamic World Review, Islamic World Defence, Islamic World Medical Journal, Islamic Finance, al-Amwal. **Member of:** International Public Relations Association (IPRA); International Advertising Association (IAA). **Prof. Addr.:** P.O.B. 4288, Tel.: 644-6308, 643-2841, Telex: 402687 FONOON SJ, Jeddah Saudi Arabia 21491. Also, in UK: Crown House, Crown Lane, East Burnham, NrSlough, Bucks SL2 3SG. Telex: 847031 ARABIA, Tel.: Farnham Common (02814) 5177. **Priv. Addr.:** Tel.: 687-4415, Jeddah 21491, Saudi Arabia.

SALAMA (Anis Mustafa), Egyptian businessman. **Born** on December 29, 1926 in Cairo, Egypt. **Married:** three children, two sons, one daughter. **Educ.:** Diploma in Hotel Management, Ecole Hotelière de Lausanne, Switzerland (1949). **Career:** Secretary General, el-Fayoum Real Estate, Egypt (1951-54); General Manager, Auberge el-Fayoum, Egypt (1951-54); Hotel Splendid, Switzerland (1954-55); Gezira Palace, Egypt (1955-58); Owner and Manager, Consultant and Representative Office, Egypt (1970-); General Delegate, ACCOR Group (1975-); Member of the Board of Directors, Arab Company for Hotel and Touristic Investment (1978-); Chairman, Egyptian Hotel Association; Expert, National Council for Production, Presidency of the Republic; and other memberships through the domain of tourism. **Hobbies:** Reading, swimming, golf. **Member:** Gezira Sporting Club, Alexandria Club, Automobile Club. **Address:** 28 Tala't Harb Street, Cairo, Egypt.

SALAMA (Jamal Yusuf), Saudi academic. **Born** in 1946 in Medina. **Dipl.:** Ph.D. (Chemistry) (1972). **Career:** Demonstrator, Physics Department; then Lecturer, Faculty of Science, Riyadh University; member of Faculty of Science Council, Committee on Technicians' Training, Faculty of Science; Fellow of Royal Chemical Society, London; attended Conference on the Teaching of Chemistry (Spain), Society of Physics Conference (Damascus); now Assistant Professor of Chemistry, Faculty of Science, Riyadh University. **Sports:** Tennis, football. **Hobby:** Music. **Prof. Addr.:** Chemistry Department, Faculty of Science, Riyadh University, Riyadh. Saudi Arabia.

SALAME (Joseph, Mgr.), Lebanese former bishop of Aleppo. **Born** on December 24, 1914 in Antelias (Lebanon). **Educ.:** Secondary, Theology and Law at the Univesity of St. Joseph (Beirut). **Career:** Ordained to the Priesthood (March 10, 1940); General Vicar for the Diocese of Cyprus (1940-66); Dean of the Theological League of Lebanon; Judge for 7 years in the Patriarchal Higher Court (Clerical Personal Status Tribunal); Sacred Bishop of Aleppo in April 1967. **Addr.:** Harissa, Lebanon.

SALAMI (Ali, Ahmad, Nasir), Yemeni diplomat. **Born** in 1933 in Yemen. **Career:** Active in politics and former member of the National Liberation Front with Qahtan al-Shaabi; fostered union between Front for the Liberation of South Yemen (FLOSY) and NLF 1966; following Independence 1967 worked in Ministry of Education; Ambassador to Libya; member and Secretary general of the Presidency Committee of the People's Supreme Council (1980-1986). **Addr.:** Aden, Republic of Yemen.

SALEH (Abdalla, Essa, al), Kuwaiti engineer. **Born** in 1937 (Kuwait). **Son** of Essa al-Saleh (Contractor) **and** Mrs., née Dalal Abdullatif. **Married** on October 1968 (Kuwait) to Miss F. Abduljaber, 2 children. **Educ.:** University of Pacific, Stockton, California (U.S.A.). **Dipl.:** Bachelor Degree of Science, in Electrical Engineering. **Career:** 3 years service in Ministry of Electricity and Water and Ministry of Public Works; in Government of Kuwait (3 Years), member of Board of Directors in Kuwait National Petroleum Co. and Kuwait Spanish Petroleum Co.; same time Managing-Director of Kuwait Metal Pipe Industries. **Hobby:** Photography. **Prof. Addr.:** P.O.Box 519, Safat, Tel.: 428744, Kuwait, **Priv. Addr.:** Tel.: 519736, Kuwait.

SALEH (AbdulJawad), Palestinian politician. **Born** in 1932 in Ramallah. **Married**, four children. **Educ.:** American University in Cairo. **Career:** Teacher in Libya; returned to West Bank and established his own contracting business; elected mayor of al Bireh (1967) and returned with large majority in municipal elections; deported to Jordan by the Israelis (1973); member of the Palestinian Liberation Organisation (PLO), member of Palestine National Front (PNF); Deputy Head of the Occupied Homeland Department (1974); in charge of the Executive Office for Home Affairs. **Addr.:** Tunis, Tunisia.

SALEH (Abu Bakr Othman Mohamad), Sudanese politician. **Born** in 1930 in Wadi Halfa, Sudan. **Son** of Othman Mohamad Saleh. **Married** in 1960 to Miss Hamida Gaafr, 3 children: Imam, Osama, Khalid. **Educ.:** Faculty of Arts, Khartoum University, Sudan. **Dipl.:** B.A. **Career:** Teacher, Secondary School Tonj and Khor Taqat (1955); 3rd Secretary, Ministry of Foreign Affairs (1956); 2nd Secretary, Political Section, Ministry of Foreign Affairs (1958); Secretary, Ministry of Foreign Affairs (1963); Counsellor, Ministry of Foreign Affairs (1964); Minister Plenipotentiary, Ministry of Foreign Affairs (1965); Ambassador to Algeria (1966); Secretary-General of the Presidency (Ministerial Rank) (1972); Ambassador to Yugoslavia (1973); Ambassador to France, Switzerland and Holy See (1974); Minister for Cabinet Affairs, in Prime Minister's office (1979). **Awards:** Star Decoration (Romania). **Publ.:** several articles in Arab and Sudanese press; co-editor of Socialist Magazine. **Hobbies:** Music, reading and chess. **Addr.:** Khartoum, Sudan.

SALEH (Ali Abdullah, Gen.), President of the Republic of Yemen. **Born** in 1942. **Career:** Participated in 1974 coup; Security Chief, Taiz Province (till 1978); member

Provisional Presidential Council, Deputy Commander in Chief of Armed Forces (June - July 1978); President of Yemen Arab Republic and Commander in Chief of Armed Forces (July 1978); reelected for a third term of five Years in office (18 July 1988); Elected President of the unified Republic of Yemen on 24 May, 1990. **Addr.:** Office of the President, Sanaa, Republic of Yemen.

SALEH (at-Tayyeb), Sudanese writer. **Born** in 1929 in Sudan. **Educ.:** Khartoum University; Exeter University, U.K. **Career:** Writer in charge of Drama Department, BBC, Arabic Section (12 years); Technical Adviser, Sudan Broadcasting Service, Khartoum; Director of Information, Qatar. **Publ.:** Author of "Irs al-Zein", "The Season of Migration to the North". **Addr.:** Khartoum, Sudan.

SALEH (Bashir, Mohamad), Sudanese businessman. **Born** in Sudan. **Son** of Mohamad Saleh. **Educ.:** Gordon Memorial College, Kitchener School of Medecine. **Dipl.:** Doctor in Medicine. **Career:** Associate of the English Association of Accountants and Auditors; Associate of the Institute of Commerce of Birmingham; Managing Partner, Sudan Commercial Company; Associate Manager Dairat al-Mahdi. **Addr.:** P.O.Box 1103, Tel.: 3418 Khartoum, Sudan.

SALEH (Dawood, al), Kuwaiti businessman. **Born** in 1928 in Kuwait. **Son** of Musaad Saleh. **Married** in 1960, 3 sons, 1 daughter. **Dipl.:** B.A. (1952). **Career:** Chairman of family business. Vice President, Musaad al-Saleh Real Estate Ltd., Kuwait; Vice President, Union Bank of Oman, Muscat, Oman; Managing Director, Gulf Bank, Safat, Kuwait; Director, Construction Materials Industries, Muscat. **Member:** Several Local Clubs. **Hobbies:** Reading and Walking. **Addr.:** P.O.Box 1092 Safat, Kuwait.

SALEH (Faiqa Saeed, al, Miss), Bahraini senior information specialist. **Born** on October 25, 1954 in Manama, Bahrain. **Daughter** of Saeed al-Saleh (deceased) **and** Mrs. Khadija Mahroos. (deceased) **Educ.:** University of Baghdad; University of London Institute of Education; University College London; University of London, University College; University of Bahrain. **Dipl.:** B.A. degree in Arts in English Language and Literature (1976); Diploma in Education; Major in Comparative Education and Education in Developing Countries (1983); Diploma in Library and Information Studies (1989); M.A. degree in Arts in Library and Information Studies, Major: Information Systems and Automation (1991) Diploma in Advanced Management (1993). **Career:** Documentalist and Translator (January 1977 - May 1979); Supervisor of Studies and Research (June 1979 - Sep. 1986); Senior Information Specialist (All the above are at the Educational Documentation Section, Ministry of Education) (Oct. 1986-); **Publ.:** Studies and Research: Education Objectives in some countries: a comparative study (1980); Educational innovation in Bahrain: 1978-80 (1981); Directory of postgraduate degress obtained by Bahraini citizens from 1964-84 (1984); Educations in Bahrain: Development and innovations (1985); Secondary education in Bahrain in view of the student-teacher ratio and the factor affecting this ratio (1985) (co-author); Survey on higher academic qualifications abilities for the State of Bahrain (1988) (co-author). Papers and Reports on the development of education in Bahrain presented to the International Conferences of Education 36th, 37th, 38th, 39th and 40th sessions; Educational Research in Bahrain: a report presented to the fourth meeting of the Deans of Education Colleges and Educational Research Officers (Abu-Dhabi, April 1985); Periodicals in Libraries; Abstracting and abstracts (Both the above were lecture papers presented to the school librarians training course in Bahrain (1987); Translated articles on cooperative learning (1991). Series: Education in the world series- No.1-47 (1979-87); a series published six times a year, abstracting and translating the national reports on education all over the world. Thesis: Planning for library automation at the Educational Documentation Section in Bahrain (M.A. 1990); Directory of Ministry of Education's Systems and legislations; Educational Theses Abstracts Vol I (1992) Vol II (1996); Effective Schools research: Practice and Promise (translated in 1992); Directory of Conferences and Seminars Proceedings: 1974-1989. 5 Volumes (1994); Request for proposal for an integrated library system for the Central and Muharraq Public libraries (1995). **Lectures and Training: Introducing Computers in Libraries:** (Two lectures presented to the Public Librarians in Bahrain within an organized course by the Directorate of Public Libraries, Ministry of Education, in March and May 1991). **Educational Information Resources:** (A Lecture presented to the Master degrees students at the University of Bahrain-College of Education-Research Methodology course - in April 1993. Several papers have been presented). **Training Course on Computerized Documentation Using Micro CDS/ISIS Software Package. Bahrain 14-28 November 1994.** (The training course has been organized by the Ministry of Education in Bahrain with the assistance of the UNESCO/IBE. Miss Faiqa Al-Saleh was the coordinator of the course. She wrote all the papers in Arabic as well as lecturing and gave the practical sessions with the cooperation of Mrs. Jeannine Thomas in charge of Software applications and Training at the IBE. Since 1992-Miss Faiqa Al-Saleh is in charge of training one or two of the Learning Resources Diploma's Students of the University of Bahrain at the Educational Documentation Section, Ministry of Education as part of their requirements - Practicum Course -. **Others (Information Bulletins) - Editor and supervisor -** Educational Indicative Abstracts; Educational Periodicals Index; Accessions List. Ministry of education Legislations Index; Specialized Bibliographic Lists; Educational Information (Periodical). **Hobbies:** Music, cooking. **Member:** British Library Association, Bahrain Library Association (Secretary). **Credit**

Cards: Master Card and Visa. **Permanent Address:** Educational Documentation Section, Ministry of Education, P.O.Box 43, Tel.: 710599 or 710381, Fax: 710376, Manama, Bahrain. **Priv. Addr.:** P.O.Box 534, Tel.: 400106, Manama, Bahrain.

SALEH (Fawzi Musaad, al), Kuwaiti executive. **Born** in 1935. **Educ.:** in the USA. **Career:** al-Saleh Musaad & Sons (Contractors and Civil Engineers); Chairman, Kuwait Metal Pipes Industries Company; Member of the Board of several investment and shareholding companies; Chairman, Agriculture Development Co.; Deputy Chairman, Real Estate Company, Kuwait. Managing Director and Vice Chairman, Sharjah Group Company, Safat, Kuwait. Chairman, Sharjah Group Trust, Curacao, Netherlands. **Addr.:** 8 Handelskade, Curacao, Netherlands Antilles and P.O.Box 1092 Safat, Kuwait.

SALEH (Galabawi, Muhammad), Sudanese UN official. **Born** on January 1st, 1932 in Northern Province, Sudan. **Married. Educ.:** University of Khartoum, Sudan; New York University, USA; UN Fellowship for studies in USA, United Kingdom and Egypt (1961-62); UN Fellowship for sutdies in Africa and Europe (1964-66); **Dipl.:** B.A. In Economics; Diploma in Public Law and Administration (1952-57); MPA (1961-57). **Career:** held various posts with municipal councils in Sudan (1956-60); Executive Officer, Abu Hagar Rural Council, Blue Nile Province, Sudan (1960-61); Head of Local Government Section of the Institute of Public Administration, Sudan (1960-65); Director of the Institute of Public Administration, Khartoum (1965-70); Chief, Local Government Section of UN Public Administration Division (1970-73); Chief, Personnel Administration and Training Section of UN Division of Public Administration and Finance (1973-77); Dean, Sudanese Public Service; Under Secretary at the Ministry of Public Service and Administrative Reforms, Khartoum (1977-78); Director General of African Training and Research Centre in Adminitration for Development in Tangiers, Morocco (1978-80); Member of African Association of Public Administration and Management, Dar es Salaam, Tanzania and of Middle East Institute, Washington D.C. USA; Director General of the Institute of Public Adminitration, Riyadh (1981). **Publ.:** numerous books in fields of organisational studies, administration and development. **Hobbies:** African tribal folklore, photography. **Addr.:** Khartoum, Sudan.

SALEH (Hani, Abdul Rahman), Jordanian academic. **Born** on April 14, 1937 in al-Lid. **Married,** 4 sons. **Educ.:** Cairo University, Egypt; Tennessee University, USA. **Dipl.:** B.A. in Literature; M.A. and Ph.D. in Education Sciences (1964-66); **Career:** Lecturer at Jordan University, Amman (1966), Associate professor (1970), then Professor (1975); Dean, College of Education, Jordan University (1980); **Publ.:** "The Philosophy of Education" (1967) (in Arabic); "Towards an Islamic Formulation of curriculum Development"; "Curriculum Management" (1980) (1981) as well as other works. **Member:** Jordanian Society of al-Kitab. **Hobbies:** reading, swimming, walking. **Addr.:** Jordan University, College of Education, Tel.: 843555, Amman, Jordan.

SALEH (Ibrahim, Mahmoud), Egyptian cameraman. **Born** on May 5, 1935 in Cairo (Egypt). **Educ.:** Faculty of Arts, Cairo University; Berlin Cinema Institute, Federal Republic of Germany. **Dipl.:** B.A. **Career:** Cameraman at State Television. **Works:** "Palace of Desire" (1967), "Just a Girl", "Furnished Flat", "The Pickpocket", "Beautiful Aziza" (1968), "Forbidden Love" (1969), "Lovers Lane" (1970), "A Boy, a Girl and the Devil" (1971), "Merciless", "The Night's Lion", "Three Brothers", "Athens by Night" produced for the West German TV; awarded 1st prize in Munich amounting to 12,000 DM. **Sports:** Cycling and motoring. **Hobbies:** Music and stamp collecting. **Prof. Addr.:** State TV Service, TV Building, Maspero District, Corniche Road; also 100 Kasr el-Nil street, Tel.: 21486. **Priv. Addr.:** 7 el-Khalifa el-Maamoun, Heliopolis, Tel.: 86356, Cairo, Egypt.

SALEH (Maqbool, Hameed Mohammed, al), Omani businessman. **Born** on July 28, 1945 in Muscat, Oman. **Son** of Hameed al-Saleh (Businessman). **Married** in Muscat to Miss Masooma Salman Faidhallah, 5 children: Ammar (1971), Eihab (1975), Ghadeer (1978), Rami (1981) and Hadeel (1985). **Educ.:** in Muscat, Oman; Sultan Oman's Armed Forces. **Career:** Under Secretary in the Ministry of Diwan Affairs and Ministry of Social Affairs and Labour; Deputy Chairman of Commercial Bank of Oman Ltd; Chairman of Oman Holdings International Co. LLC. Douglas - OHI LLC, Hydromatic Construction Co. LLC, Wattayah Motors LLC. OHI (Europe) Ltd.; OHI (France) S.A.R.L. and Oman United Exchange Co. LLC. **Sport:** Squash. **Hobbies:** Squash, hockey, music. **Credit Cards:** American Express; Midland Gold-mastercard. **Prof. Addr.:** Oman Holdings International Co. LLC, P.O.Box 889, Muscat, Postal Code 113, Sultanate of Oman, Tel.: 702666, Telex: 3398 Ammar ON, Fax: 703862. **Priv. Addr.:** Tel.: 560573, Muscat, Sultanate of Oman.

SALEH (Mohamad, Musaad, al), Kuwaiti journalist, lawyer. **Born** in 1933, Kuwait. **Married. Educ.:** Cairo University, Egypt. **Career:** Lawyer; Chairman, "al-Hadaf" weekly magazine, journalist "al-Watan" daily newspaper; formerly President of the Kuwait Journalists Association and of Kuwait Lawyers Association. **Hobby:** Reading, press and parliamentary affairs. **Addr.:** Al Hadaf, P.O.B. 2270, Safat, Kuwait.

SALEH (Mohamad, Uthman), Saudi official **Born** in 1936 in Saudi Arabia. **Dipl.:** Ph.D., Cambridge University, England. **Career:** Lecturer, King Saud University, Director General, Ministry of Interior; Deputy Secretary, Control and Investigation Board. **Prof. Addr.:** Control and Investigation Board, Tel.: 4010824, Riyadh. **Priv. Addr.:** Tel.: 4022487, Riyadh, Saudi Arabia.

SALEH (Nassir Abdullah, Al), Saudi academic. **Born** in 1942 A.D., 1462 A.H. in Al-Madinah, Saudi Arabia. **Married,** 4 boys and 2 girls. **Educational History:** Secondary, Scientific Institute, 1959. B.A., King Saud University, Riyadh, 1964, Major: Geography. M.A., Arizona University, Tucson, Arizona, U.S.A., 1970, Geography. Ph.D., Durham University, Durham, England, 1976. **Ph.D. Thesis:** The Emergence of Saudi Arabian Administrative Areas: A study in Political Geography. **Academic Ranks:** Assistant Instructor, Faculty of Education, 1965-1970. Lecturer, Faculty of Education, 1971-1975. Assistant Professor, Faculty of Education, 1976-1980. Associate Professor, Faculty of Social Sciences, 1980-1984. Professor, Faculty of Social Science, 1985- Present. **Academic/Administrative Occupations:** Deputy Dean, Faculty of Education, 1976-1977. Dean, Deanship of Admission/ Registration, 1977-1980. Director General, Girls Campus, 1977-1980. Under Secretary-General, Organisation of Islamic Capitals, 1980-1984. Head, Geography Department, 1985-1988. General Supervisor, Hajj Research Centre, 1988-1990. Dean, Faculty of Social Sciences, 1990-1995. Dean, Institute of Scientific Research, 1995- Present. Member and Secretary of Academic Promotion Committee, 1981-1984. Member and Secretary, Academic Council, 1984-1993. Member, King Abdul Aziz University Council, 1977-1980. Member, King Abdul Aziz University High Council, 1977-1980. Member, Umm al-Qura University Council, 1981-1983, 1990- Present. Member, Umm al-Qura University High Council, 1990-1995. Member, Saudi Geographical Society, 1980- Present. Member, Administrative Council of the Saudi Geographical Society, 1988-1990. Member, Institute of British Geographers, 1980-1986. Member of many academic and administrative special purpose committees within King Abdul Aziz University and Umm al-Qura University; Supervisor of many Ph.D. and M.A. Theses; Referee for many academic promotion candidates; Principal referee for the publication of many books, research projects, articles, papers etc. **Selected Publications:** * Quantitative Geography. * Population Geography of Saudi Arabia. * Some Aspects of Educational Geography of Makkah province. * Geographic Aspects of Traditional Architecture of Saudi Arabia. * Capital Cities: A Study in Political Geography. * Traffic Accidents in Makkah: Spacial and Temporal Patterns. * Political Geography of Saudi Arabia. * The Religious Function of Makkah and its Effect on its Urban Structure and Patterns. * Urban and Regional Planning in Saudi Arabia. * The Status of Geography in Saudi Arabia; * Provincial and District Delimitation in Saudi Arabia. * The Importance of Quantitative Methods in Discovering Regional Variations in Saudi Arabia. * Traffic Accidents in Makkah in 1413 A.H. with Emphasis on Locational Patterns. * Boys Elementary Schools in Makkah: Distribution Patterns. * Sites and Locations in the Holy Quran. **Hobbies:** reading, travel. **Address:** Umm Al-Qura University, P.O.Box 715, Makkah, Saudi Arabia.

SALEH (Othman Ibn Nasser, Ibn), Saudi journalist. **Born** in 1915 at al-Majma'ah, Saudi Arabia. **Educ.:** school education and also self-taught in a private school in 1935; worked at the first Government school at Majma'ah, (1937); worked at the Anjal Institute (now the Capital Model Institute) for 27 years, Director General of the Institute until 1970; Editor-in-Chief, Islamic Research Magazine (1975); founding member and member of the Board, al-Jazeerah news-paper; member, Holy Quran Memorization Society, the Saudi Arabian Red Crescent Society and Supreme Council of Endowments; Chairman, Regional Council of Endowdments, Riyadh; has **participated** in several conferences representing the Saudi Arabian Red Crescent Society, The Muslim World League and other regional and international symposia and conferences. **Honours:** A medal from the late King Faisal; Order of Merit, Lebanon (granted by former President of Lebanon, Camille Chamoun). **Publications:** articles and editorials in various magazines and news-papers. **Hobby:** travel. **Prof. Addr.:** al-Khazan Street, P.O.Box 2810, Tel.: 402-2324, Riyadh. **Priv. Addr.:** Tel.: 4054905, Riyadh, Saudi Arabia.

SALEH (Saleh, Muhammad), Sudanese Agricultural Engineer. **Born** in Sudan. **Career:** Government service, Municipal Engineer (1942); Agricultural Engineer (1943-45); Chief Surveyor (1954-51); Field Inspector of Sudan Gezira Board (1951-55); Group Inspector (1955-56); Assistant General Manager (1956-62), then General Manager (1962-64); former Managing Director of Sudan Agricultural Bank (1965). **Prof. Addr.:** Khartoum, Sudan.

SALEH (Zaki Abdul Rahman, al), Saudi executive. **Born** in 1937 at Buraidah, Saudi Arabia. **Educ.:** secondary school certificate. **Career:** Joined Saudia in February 1952; successively held the positions of Controller Flight Operations, Chief Controller, Assistant Manager Flight Operations, Manager Security, General Manager, Security since 1977. **Activities:** attended a number of ICAO and IATA meetings and seminars and was twice elected member on Security Advisor Committee of IATA, responsible for developing ways to protect the airline industry from sabotage, hijacking and embezzlement, etc; was first Saudi to obtain Flight Dispatcher Licence from FAA, New York; later Flight Operations Officer Licence of Civil Aviation from Pakistan; has taken various professional courses; awarded diploma in Aviation Security and Safety by the FAA Oklahoma, U.S.A. **Prof. Addr.:** Saudia Head Office, P.O.Box 620, Tel.: 6862336, 6315269, Jeddah. **Priv. Addr.:** Tel.: 6313716, Jeddah, Saudi Arabia.

SALEM (Abdulmoneim, Abdulaziz), Egyptian engineer. **Born** on May 25, 1943 in Cairo (Egypt). **Son** of Abdulaziz Salem **and** Mrs., née Nabawiya Messalam.

Educ.: Sidq al-wafa Primary School (1945-48), Fouad I Secondary School (1949-53); Cairo (Egypt). **Dipl.:** Secondary Certificate (1953), Cairo (Egypt). **Career:** Junior Clerk (1954) at the Egyptian Engineering and Automotive Supply Agencies (Cairo); worked his way up to Senior Executive in charge of Government Tenders and market promotion. **Hobby:** Photography and mechanical do-it-yourself. **Prof. Addr.:** The Egyptian Engineering and Automotive Supply Agencies, 18, Nagib ar-Rihani Street, Tel.: 913277, Cairo. **Priv. Addr.:** Nasr City, Building No.8, Apt. 207, Cairo, Egypt.

SALEM (Ahmad), Egyptian statesman. **Born** in 1920 in Alexandria, Egypt. **Educ.:** University of Alexandria. **Dipl.:** Diploma in Civilization and philology, in Tourist Studies. **Career:** Professor of French, University of Alexandria; Cultural Attache, Egyptian Embassy in Switzerland; Co Chairman, Misr Travel and Shipping, Cairo; Tourist Counsellor, Egyptian Embassy in France; Director of the Arab League Office in Paris; Ambassador of Egypt to China (1984). **Member** of the Board of Association Mondiale pour la Formation Professionelle touristique. **Hobbies:** Music, painting, reading, tennis. **Addr.:** Ministry of Foreign Affairs, Cairo, Egypt.

SALEM (Georges), Syrian writer. **Born** in 1933 in Aleppo. **Educ.:** Damascus University. **Dipl.:** Master of Arts (1956). **Career:** Professor, Secretary then Director of the Cultural Institute of Aleppo (1959-63). **Member** of the Arabian Writers Association (1970). **Publ.:** Author of ten studies and novels and more than 15 translations Mauriac Saint-Exupéry, Camus). **Addr.:** Aleppo, Syria.

SALEM (Hadaha, Sultan, al), Kuwaiti journalist. **Born** in 1936. **Daughter** of Sultan al-Salem **and** Mrs., née Aïsha Mohamad. **Married** in 1953, 5 children: Nawaf, Talal, Abdurrahman, Nawal and Salem. **Educ.:** Sharquiah Secondary School. **Career:** Teacher (1950-56); Journalist; Editor of "al-Majaliss". **Publ.:** Author of "al-Maqassed", "Nissa' fil Quraan" and "Awraq Musafira". **Hobbies:** Literature, history reading, poetry and politics. **Prof. Addr.:** al-Majaliss, P.O.Box 5605, Tel.: 4841178, Kuwait. **Priv. Addr.:** al-Khalidiya, St. 48, 810091, Kuwait City, Kuwait.

SALEM (Hassan, Air Commodore), Egyptian civil servant. **Born** on July 23, 1928 in Alexandria (Lower Egypt). **Married**, children. **Educ.:** Flying Academy, Cairo; Management Course, Ireland. **Career:** Egyptian Air Force (1952-71); Military and Civil Accident Investigator, Egyptian Force and Civil Services (1958-74); General Manager of Operations, Board of Executives, Egyptair (1973-74); Adviser to the Chairman of Egyptair; **Sports:** swimming and motoring. **Priv. Addr.:** Gezira Wosta, Zamalek District, Cairo, Egypt.

SALEM (Hussain), Egyptian businessman. **Born** in 1933 in Cairo, Egypt. **Married**, two children. **Educ.:** B.Sc in Commerce, Cairo University, Egypt. **Career:** Director Economic Research in the Spinning Support Fund, Cairo, Egypt; Director Of General Administration of Spinning and Textiles, Arab Foreign Trading Company, Cairo, Egypt; Director General of the Egyptian Products Commercial Center, Baghdad, Iraq; Director General and member of the Board of Directors of the Arab Foreign Trading Company; Director General of the United Arab Emirates (UAE) Trading Company. Member of the Tourism Club, of the Sporting Club and Automobile Club, Cairo, Egypt. **Sports:** Swimming, squash, cycling. **Addr.:** United Arab Emirates Trading Company, P.O.Box 4171, Tel.: 43830, Abu Dhabi, United Arab Emirates.

SALEM (Khalil, Dr.), Jordanian educator and banker. **Born** in 1921 at Husn. **Dipl.:** B.A., First Class Honours, American University of Beirut (1941); Diploma of Education, University of London (1950); Doctorate in Educational Administration, Columbia University (1960). **Career:** Teacher in Secondary Schools (1941-49); Inspector of Education (1950-56); Director of Cultural Affairs (1956-59); Assistant Under-Secretary of Education (1960-62); Minister of Social Welfare and Minister of State for Prime Ministry Affairs (1962); Minister of National Economy and Minister of State for Prime Ministry Affairs (1962-63); Governor of the Central Bank of Jordan (1963-73); President of the National Planning Council (1973-74); Ambassador to France and Permanent Delegate to Unesco (1975-78); Ambassador to Belgium and EEC (non-resident) (1975-78); General Manager, Arab Finance Corporation (Jordan 1979-present). **Act.:** Member of the Jordanian National Commission for Unesco (1951-62); Member of the Jordanian Scientific Association (1956-60); Member of the Board of the Arab Scientific Union (1957-59); Member of the Kappa Delta PI (Columbia chapter) (1959); Member of the Council of Scientific Research (1965-74); Member of the Board of Trustees of the University of Jordan (1963-76); Member of the Jordan Development Board (later National Planning Council) (1963-74); President of the Authority of Tourism and Antiquity (1962-63); Chairman of the Cooperative Union (1965-68); Member of the International Consultative Committee for Literacy (1967-70); Member of the Economic Security Committee (1967-73); Deputy Chairman of Alia Airlines (1971-74); Deputy Chairman of the Royal Scientific Society (1970-73); Chairman of the Public Insurance Corporation (1971-73); Chairman of the Institute of Banking Studies (1971-73); Associate Member of the Committee of Twenty (IMF) (1972-73); Associate Member of the Development Committee (IBRD) (1974); Chairman of the National Committee for Population (1973-74); Chairman of the Committee for Environment (1973-74); Governor of IMF or IBRD (1963-74); Member of the Advisory Council for Budget (1963-74); Member of the Executive Board of Unesco (1976-80); Member of the Consultative National Council & Chairman of its Financial and Administrative Commission (1978-present); Member of the Supreme Council of Education (1979-82); Vice-Chairman of the Board of AFC (Jordan) (1979-present); Member of the Royal Commission for Moutah University (1980-present); Member of the Council of Higher Education (1982-present); Secretary-General of Arab Thought Forum (1981-present); President of "Administrative Consultants" (1983); President of Brokers Association (1983); Member of three public Shareholding Companies (1983); Chairman of ar-Rai Newspaper. Represented Jordan, and participated in many national, regional and international conferences and seminar; had the honour of accompanying H.M. King Hussein, and H.R.H. The Crown Prince in many state visits in different countries; led Jordanian delegations to discuss, with other countries' representatives, matters of development, aid and financing. **Publ.:** Author and/or co-author of 15 textbooks in mathematics; collaborated in the translation of a publication on Multiple Class Teaching; wrote and published a large number of articles, lectures and broadcasts in mathematics; popular science, education, administration, economics and banking, Jordan planning and development; lectured in the University of Jordan on "Money and Banking" (1966-68). **Awards:** Several decorations from Arab and foreign states as well as following Jordanian Decorations: al-Nahdah, Third Order (1956); al-Istiqlal, Second Order (1958); al-Kokab, First Order (1962); al-Nahdah, First Order (1974). **Prof. Addr.:** Arab Finance Corp. (Jordan), P.O.Box 35104, Tel.: 666198, Tlx.: 21875 JO, Amman, Jordan.

SALEM (Mamdouh Mohamad), Egyptian police officer, administrator and politician. **Born** in 1918 in Alexandria. **Educ.:** received Education in Egypt; Metropolitan Police College (UK). **Career:** Police Commander, Alexandria (1964-67); Governor of Assiut (1967); Governor of Gharbiya (1970); Governor of Alexandria (1970-71); Minister of the Interior (1971); Member of the Arab Socialist Union Central Committee (1971); Deputy Prime Minister, and Minister of the Interior (1972-75); Deputy Military Governor General (1973); Prime Minister (1975-77); Prime Minister and Minister of the Interior (1977); Adviser to President Mubarak of Egypt. **Addr.:** Mamar Bahlar, Kasr al-Nil, Cairo, Egypt.

SALEM (Mohamad, Mamdooh, Mohamad), Egyptian judge **Born** in 1927 in Port Said, Egypt. **Married**, three children. **Educ.:** LL.B. from Cairo University, Egypt. **Career:** Judge, Justice and Director General of Managing Illegal Gain; Deputy President, Court of Cassation; member of the Board, Educational Co operation Society of Cleopatra Schools. **Member** of Heliopolis Club. **Hobbies:** Tennis, walking. **Addr.:** Villa 28, Rasheid Street, Masre al-Gadeeda, Cairo, Egypt.

SALEM (Mohamad, Nabil, Ahmad), Egyptian surgeon. **Born** in Giza, Egypt. **Married**, one daughter. **Son** of Ahmad Salem. **Educ.:** M.S. in Physical Medicine and Rehabilitation; Diplomas in General Surgery and Orthopaedic Surgery. **Career:** Chief, Post Medical and Rehabilitation Department, Agouza Hospital and Police Hospital, Cairo; Head of Post Medical and Rehabilitation, Egyptian Armed Forces; Secretary, Egyptian Society of Orthotics and Prosthetics. **Member:** American College of Sports Medicine; Vice President African Handball Federation, member, Egyptian Handball Federation. **Addr.:** Clinic: 1 Gawad Hosni Street, Abddai, Cairo, Egypt. **Priv. Addr.:** 13 Ibrahim Naguib Street, Garden City, Cairo, Egypt.

SALEM (Mohamad, Omeish), Libyan economist. **Born** on March 5, 1932 at Derna (Libya). **Married** on August 22, 1963 to Samira Elyagizi, one daughter, five sons. **Educ.:** El Nur Primary school, Derna (Libya) (1943-47); Benghazi Secondary school (1947-51); Helwan Secondary school, Cairo (Egypt) (1951-52); Ayn Shams University, Cairo, (1952-56); Cairo University (1954-56); American University, Washington D.C. (USA) (1969-70). **Career:** Issue Department, National Bank of Libya (1956); Assistant Director of Trade; representative of Minister of Economy to Petroleum Commission, Ministry of National Economy (1957); Commercial Attaché, Embassy of Libya, Washington D.C. (1960-62); Director, Trade and Economic Affairs, Ministry of Economy (1962-64); Director-General, Department of Statistics and Census (1964-68); Assistant Under-Secretary of State for Economic Affairs, Ministry of Economy (1968-70); attended in-service Training Programme for African Economists, United Nations Headquarters, New York (1968); Governor, District of Jabal Akhdar (1970-72); Libya's representative, Board of Trade and Development, United Nations Conference on Trade and Development (UNCTAD), Geneva, (1972); Ambassador, Ministry of Foreign Affairs (1972); Rapporteur, Sub-Committee on Banking, Credit and Foreign Exchange (1972-73); Director, Industrial Development Institution; vice-president, African Development Bank, Abidjan, (1973). **Member:** Higher Committee for Arts and Literature; Libyan Intellectual Society; General Economic Committee. **Sports:** Swimming and jogging. **Hobbies:** Reading and music. **Addr.:** Tripoli, Libya.

SALEM (Mubarak, Khalfan), Omani Bank Manager. **Born** in 1943 in Oman. **Son** of Khalfan Salem. **Married** in 1968, 2 sons 5 daughters. **Educ.:** Commercial Studies, AMB Banking (1977). **Career:** Banking since 1966. Manager, Main Branch and Branches Coordinators, Union Bank of Oman, Ruwi, Oman. **Hobby:** Reading. **Addr.:** P.O.Box 4222 and 4565, Tel.: 734611-2-3, Telex: 3434 A/B ETIHADBANK MB, Ruwi, Oman.

SALEM (Salim, A.K.), Iraqi international officer. **Born** on August 29, 1925 in Mosul (Iraq). **Married, children. Educ.:** American University in Beirut (Lebanon) **(1945-**48); University of Cincinnati (USA) (1949-51); **University of Southern California, Los Angeles. CA, USA (1952-58).**

Dipl.: B.A. (Political Sciences) (1948), Ph.D. (Political Sciences) (1958). **Career:** Diplomacy, Ministry of Foreign Affairs, Baghdad (Iraq); Director, Ministry of Information, Baghdad (Iraq); Director, Office of Public Information (OPI) UN, Beirut (Lebanon); Director, UNIC, Beirut, UN; Director, UNIC, Nairobi (Kenya) - Established by him; now Director, UNIC New Delhi, India. **Prof. Addr.:** UNIC, UN, New Delhi, India.

SALEM (Sami, Ali), Egyptian businessman. **Born** in 1937 in Cairo, Egypt. **Son** of Ali Salim. **Married**, Three children **Educ.:** B.A. in Commerce; Management and Industrial Studies. **Career:** Manager, Chemical Industries Company (1960-69); Commercial and Technical Consultant, T. Maneklal Company, India (1960-69); Swastic Textile Trading and Manufacturing Company, Bombay, India (1960-69); owner, Middle East Chemical Manufacturing Company; Area Manager, ARTOS Company, West Germany; Local Area Agent; Crossroll Company, Halifax, UK. **Sport:** Water skiing. **Hobbies:** Hunting, music. **Addr.:** Cairo, Egypt.

SALHI (Abderrahim), Moroccan director general. **Born** on January 24, 1936 in Casablanca, Morocco. **Son** of Mehdi Salhi and Mrs. Fatima née Larbi. **Married** in to R'kia Alaoui, 2 children: Rachid (22 October 1964), Ali (28 July 1966). **Educ.:** Secondary: College, Musulman, Lycée Lyautey, Casablanca; Ecoles Supérieures de Commerce Française, Ecole Supérieure de Commerce de Bordeaux, University of Paris. **Dipl.:** Diploma from Ecole Supérieure de Commerce de Bordeaux (1961); Licence en Droit from University of Paris; Doctorat d'Etat in Economical Sciences, Grenoble (1968). **Career:** Inspector, Bank of Morocco (1961-1965) then Director; Charge de Mission to the Prime Minister (1972). **Work:** After being administrator in several organisms public and semi-public, appointed by H.M. King Hassan II, Director General of Regie des Tabacs in February 1975. **Decor:** Awarded Knight Order of the Throne. **Sports:** Tennis, Swimming, Horse riding. **Member:** of the Moroccan Economists Association. **Prof. Addr.:** Régie des Tabacs, Moulay Idris 1er Blvd., Tel.: 28.97.14, 28.41.09, Telex : 21.090, Casablanca, Morocco.

SALIBA (Jacob), Arab-American businessman. **Born** on June 10, 1913 at East Broughton, Quebec, Canada. **Son** of Said Saliba. **Married** on May 31, 1942 to Miss Adla Mudarri, 3 children: John, Thomas and Barbara. **Educ.:** Boston University, USA. **Dipl.:** B.S. (1941). **Career:** Senior Supervising Engineer, Thompson & Lichtner Co., Boston (1944-49); President, Kingston Dress Co., Cornish, Maine (1948-61); Executive Vice-President, member of Executive Committee, Cortland Corp. Inc., New York City (1954-59); Director, Executive Vice-President, Sawyer-Tower Inc., Boston (1955-56); President, same firm (1956-59); Director (1955-60); Vice President, Farrington Manufacturing Co., Executive Vice-President, Farrington Packaging Corp., Farrington Instruments Corp. (1959-61); President, Northeast Industries Inc. (1961); President, Fanny Farmer Candy Shops (1965-66); W.F. Schrafft & Sons Corp. (1967-68); President, Frozen Foods Division, W.R. Grace & Co. (1966-68); President, Katy Industries Inc. (1965-present); Director, Missouri-Kansas-Texas Railroad. A.M. Castle & Dic Co. R.E. Bush Universal Inc.; Midland Insurance Co., Spl. Cons. Air Meterial Command, USAF Dayton, Ohio (1942-43); consignment to Chief Air Staff, USAF (1952-54); Company Chairman Airforce Spare Study Group (1953). **Member:** Museum of Science Corporation Massachusetts General Hospital, Naval Architects and Marine Engineers Methodist Clubs; Union League Sky, New York City, Algonquin, Boston; Bridgeton Highlands Country, Bridgeton, Maine. **Prof. Addr.:** Katy Industries, Inc., 4368 Prudential Tower, **Tel.:** 6172664100, Boston, MA 02199.

SALL (Abdul Aziz), Mauritanian statesman. **Born** in 1924 at M'Bout (Middle Mauritania). **Son** of Zakaria Sall (male nurse). **Married** to Sy Tokosselle (midwife). **Educ.:** Primary school at Rosso (1935-38); Regional school at Boghé (1938-41); **Career:** Forwarding Clerk, Mauritanian Government (1945-47); Accountant in the General Treasury of AOF (1948-58); Chief Accountant Higher Council AOF (Afrique Occidentale Française), Dakar, Senegal (1960-61); First Counsellor, Mauritanian Embassy to Washington USA (1961); Director, Cabinet of the President of the Republic of Mauritania (1961-68); Minister of the Interior (1968-71); Secretary, Organisation for National Movements and for Information (1971-Aug 1975); Minister of State for National Guidance (1975-June 1976); Delegate to Monrovia Conference (1960); Delegate to OAU (Organisation of African Unity) Conference, Accra, Ghana (1965); to OAU Conference in Egypt (1966); to OAU Conference in Kinshasa (Zaire) (1967). **Member:** Parti du Peuple Mauritanian (PPM), (now dissolved). **Awards:** Officer, National Merit Order (Mauritania); Commander, Order of the Pioneers (Liberia) (1960); Officer, Cameroonian Merit (1963); Officer, Upper Volta Merit (1964); Officer, Order of Merit (France) (1967); Commander, Order of Merit (Egypt) (1967). **Hobbies:** Reading and music. **Addr.:** Nouackchott, Mauritania.

SALLAL (Abdallah), Yemeni army officer and politician. **Born** in 1915 in Sana'a. **Married**, 4 children: Ali (Former Ambassador to U.S.S.R.), Hachem, Gamal and Amer. **Educ.:** In Iraq (1936-38). **Career:** Returned from Iraq to Yemen (1938); Imprisoned (1939); Army Service since 1940; Imprisoned for Political Reasons (1948-55); Governor of Hodeida (1959-61); Imprisoned (1961-62) for political reasons; Chief of Staff to the Imam of Yemen (1962); President of the Revolutionary Council, Prime Minister (1962-64); Minister of Foreign Affairs (1963-64); President of the Security Council (1964-67); Abdicated (November 7, 1967). **Addr.:** Cairo, Egypt.

SALLAM (Ismail, A.), Egyptian Minister of Health and Population. **Born** on July 12, 1941 in Monofia, Egypt. **Son** of A. Sallam. **Married** on May 15, 1979 to Wafia B. Etiba, 3 sons: Tamer, Karim and Hisham. **Education:** Bachelor of Medicine and Surgery with honors 1964, Ain Shams University. **Dipl.:** Diploma in advanced surgery (distinction), Ain Shams University 1966, E.C.F.M.G. 1970, FRCS England 1970, LRCR/MRCS (London) 1970, Ph.D. Glasgow University 1973, Honorary FRCSR 1996. **Career:** Minister of Health and Population since 1996; Member of Consultative Assembly (1989). Prof. of Cardiovascular Surgery, Ain Shams University. Chairman for Department of Cardiovascular Surgery, Ain Shams University (1990). Chairman of Health Committee for National Democratic Party (1986-1994). Chairman for Health, Environmental and Population Committee for Consultative Assembly (1985). Council Member, Faculty of Medicine, Suez Canal University. Vice President (Egyptian Society of Cardiology). Chairman, Supreme Health Council (1989). **Other Information:** Established and artificial heart pump for the support of failing heart. Published over 200 articles. Initiated family medicine, womens health centers and clubs and has a leadership of health sector reform in Egypt Distant Learning and Telemedicine. **Prof. Addr.:** 3, Magles El Shaab Street, Cairo, Egypt, Tel.: 3541507, Fax: 3553966, 3559422, E.Mail: islam@idsc. gov.eg **Priv. Addr.:** 2, Al-Nadi Street, Roxy Square, Heliopolis, Cairo, Egypt.

SALLAM (Mohamed Abdulaziz), Yemeni diplomat. **Born** in 1933 in Taiz. **Son** of Abdulaziz Mohamed Sallem **and** Hend Abdulla Ali. **Married** to Maryam Ahmed al-Awami in 1960, three children. **Educ.:** Secondary in Helwan, Egypt; Stockbridge School, Mass. and Temple University, Philadelphia, Pa., U.S.A. **Career:** Engaged in private sector (1960-61); Instructor, Belguis College (1961-62); Director General Ministry of Public Health (1962-63); Minister and Charge d'affaires, Embassy in Baghdad (1963-64); Deputy Minister of Foreign Affairs (1964-65); Chairman Board, Yemen Drug Co. (1965-66); Minister of Foreign Affairs (1966-67); Director General, Office of the Prime Minister (1970-71); Ambassador in London (1973-75); Ambassador, Deputy Permanent Representative to UN (1975-76); Permanent Representative (1976-78, 1982-85); Chief of Cabinet for Technical Affairs in Office of the Prime Minister (1978-82); leader of delegations to various international conferences including UN General Assembly 1965, Fifth Emergency Special Session, Fourth Summit Conference of Arab League 1967. **Hobbies:** Chess, music. **Addr.:** Sanaa, Republic of Yemen.

SALLOUM (Ahmed, Mohamed, al), Saudi, Engineer/ Administrator. **Born** in 1942 in Makkah, Saudi Arabia. **Married** to Mrs. Soaad Mohamed Al-Thamimi, 6 children. **Educ.:** M.S. in Civil Engineering (with distinction) University of Pittsburgh, USA 1973. **Languages:** English, Italian and (Native) Arabic. **Professional Experience:** Associate Instructor, College of Engineering, Riyadh University, Riyadh, Saudi Arabia (1974); Chief Materials Engineer, Haj Project, Ministry of Communications, Riyadh, Saudi Arabia (1975); Assistant Director, Ministry of Foreign Affairs, and Diplomatic Quarters Project, Riyadh, Saudi Arabia (1976); Deputy Director, Ministry of Foreign Affairs and Diplomatic Quarters Project, Riyadh, Saudi Arabia (1979); Director General, Construction, Operations and Maintenance, Riyadh Development Authority, Riyadh, Saudi Arabia (1984); Instructor (Part Time) "Construction Management" and "Local Administration", Institute of Public Administration, Riyadh, Saudi Arabia (1984); Adviser (15th Civil Service Grade) to Riyadh Municipality and Riyadh Development Authority, Riyadh, Saudi Arabia since 1984; Deputy Mayor of Riyadh for Construction and Projects & Adviser to Riyadh Development Authority, Riyadh, Saudi Arabia (1990-1995); Director General, Arab Urban Development Institute, Riyadh, Saudi Arabia (June 1995-). **Seminars and other Events Attended:** "Project Evaluation" Seminar Held by the Institute of Public Administration and World Bank, Riyadh, Saudi Arabia (1975), "Project Management" Seminar in Houston, Texas, USA (1978), Participated in many conferences and Symposiums of Municipal Operation/ Organization. **Credit Cards:** American Express. **Prof. Addr.:** Arab Urban Development Institute, Tel.: 4802777, 4802555, Fax: 4802666, P.O.Boix 6892, Riyadh 11452, Saudi Arabia. E-mail: info@aud-ins.org. **Home Tel.:** 4705499, Saudi Arabia.

SALLOUM (Hamad Ibrahim Mohamad, al), Saudi civil servant. **Born** in 1939 in Dhurma. **Dipl.:** B.A. (1960), M.S. (1970), Ph.D. (1974). **Career:** Teacher, later Principal, Intermediate school (1960-61); Director of teachers' training institute (1961-64); Principal of secondary school (1965-69); visiting Professor, Faculty of Education, King Saud University; Director of Education, Riyadh Zone. Assistant Minister Deputy, Ministry of Education (1981-86); Saudi Arabian Educational Attaché, Saudi Arabian Education Mission-USA (1987-96); Director General, Institute of Public Administration (1996-99). **Member:** National Association of Modern Mathematics; Chairman of Central Province Sub-Committee for Adult Education and Literary Advancement; member of Services Committee; Head of Preparatory Committee for Higher Committee for Administration Reform, Saudi Arabia; Member of Central Committee for Training, Saudi Arabia, Member and Vice-Chairman of Board of Directors, Institute of Public Administration, Saudi Arabia. Attended number of Conferences on Education UNESCO General Conference, 1968. **Hobbies:** travel, reading, sport. **Prof. Addr.:** P.O.Box 1922, Riyadh 11441, Tel.: 4761717. **Priv. Addr.:** Tel.: 4826068, Riyadh, Saudi Arabia.

SALLOUM (Nasser Mohamad, al), Saudi official. **Born** on 4 November 1936 in Medina, Saudi Arabia. **Dipl.:** B.Sc., M.Sc., Ph.D. (Civil Engineering). **Career:** Began his career with the Ministry of Communications as a resident

Engineer (1965), later became Head of Study Department (1965-68); Assistant Director General of Technical Administration (1968-70); Director General of Projects (1974-75) and then Assistant Deputy Minister for Technical Affairs (1975-76); Deputy Minister of Communications (1976); Minister of Transport (since Aug. 1995). **Member:** American Society of Civil Engineers (ASCE); Board of Directors, the Saudi Arabian Railways Authority and the International Road Federation. **Hobbies:** reading, travel. **Prof. Addr.:** Ministry of Transport, Riyadh, Saudi Arabia.

SALMAN (Fadhil, Hassan), Iraqi diplomat. **Born** on March 12, 1923 in Iraq. **Son** of Hassan Salman (former Officer in the Iraqi Army). **Married** in 1962, one daughter. **Educ.:** Law College, Baghdad, University of Paris. **Dipl.:** Licence in law of the Law College, Baghdad (1944), State Doctorate in Law, University of Paris (1955). **Career:** Lecturer, Faculty of Law and Faculty of Commerce, University of Baghdad (1955-59); Joined the Foreign Service (August 1959); Appointed Counsellor at the Iraqi Embassy in Teheran and Chargé d'Affaires until the end of 1963; Appointed Counsellor at the Iraqi Embassy in Teheran and Chargé d'Affaires until the end of 1963; Appointed Permanent Representative of Iraq to the European Office of the UNO in Geneva (February 1964-June 1966); Appointed Director General of the Political Department, Ministry of Foreign Affairs (1967); Appointed Plenipotentiary Minister and Chargé d'Affaires of the Iraqi Embassy in Paris (October 1967); Appointed Ambassador of Iraq to Indonesia (1968). **Publ.:** Author of "L'Instruction préparatoire et la Liberté individuelle" (Thesis for doctorate to the University of Paris, 1955), "L'Action Publique" (Lectures in Arabic for the students of the Law College, Baghdad), "International Relations" (Lectures in Arabic for the students of the Faculty of Economics and Commerce, Baghdad). **Prof. Addr.:** Ministry of Foreign Affairs Baghdad, Iraq. **Priv. Addr.:** Adamya, Haybat and Khaloon No. 17A/9/25, Tel.: 27626, Baghdad, Iraq.

SALMAN (Mohammad), Syrian former minister of information. **Born** in 1940 in Lattakia, Syria. **Son** of Hasan Salman **and** Mrs. Najla Ali. **Married** in 1969 in Lattakia to Suheila Dawoud, "an Arabic Literature Teacher", Four children: Reem Mohammad Salman (1971), Suzi Mohammad Salman (1973), Rana Mohammad Salman (1975), Najla Mohammad Salman (1977); **Educ.:** Saqre Qureish Elementary School, Secondary School for Male Students in Lattakia, The Lebanese University, Damascus University, Institute of Orientalism, The Soviet Science Academy. **Dipl.:** B.A. in Law, Ph.D. in Economics. **Career:** Baath Arab Socialist Party Damascus University Branch assistant-deputy Secretary (1972-1980); Governor of Raqqa (from June 1980 to November 1987), Member of the Central Committee of the Baath Arab Socialist Party (from 1980 to date); Minister of Information (from 1987 March 2000). Member Baath Arab Socialist Party. **Priv. Addr.:** Autostrade al-Mezze, opposite Aljala city, Damascus, Syria.

SALMAN (Mohammad, Mahmoud), Egyptian surgeon, ophthalmologist. **Born** in 1934 in Cairo, Egypt. **Son** of Mahmoud Salman. **Married**, two sons. **Educ.:** Ph.D. in Ophthalmic Medicine and Surgery; B.Ch. in General Surgery. **Career:** Assistant professor of Ophthalmology, Cairo University then Professor. **Member of:** Gezira Club, Shooting Club; Yacht Club. **Priv. Addr.:** 13 Ahmad Abdel Aziz Street, Aguza, Cairo, Egypt. **Prof. Addr.:** Department of Ophtalmology, Faculty of Medicine, Cairo University; Clinic: 16 Sherif Pasha Street, Cairo, Egypt.

SALMAN (R. Moosawi, al), Bahraini bank executive. **Educ.:** Baghdad University (1972). **Career:** Accountant and Financial Controller, Bahrain Monetary Agency; Ministry of Labour and Social Affairs. Deputy Manager, Manufacturers Hanover Trust Company (1976-81); Assistant Vice President and Manager of Administration- Designate, United Gulf Bank, Manama, Bahrain. **Addr.:** Manama, Bahrain.

SALMAN (Saeed, Abdullah, Dr.), United Arab Emirates former Minister and presently President of Ajman University College of Science and Technology. **Born** in 1945 at Ras Al-Khaimah. **Son** of Abdullah Boumhair (late) **and** Mrs. Moza Saeed. **Married** to, 1. Moza Abdullah Boumhair, 2. Aicha Ahmad Izz Khaleel, 8 children: Khaled Saeed Abdullah (1970), Osamah (1972), Ahmad (1974), Maha (1977), Thamer (1977), Iman (1980), Mohammad (1980), Abdullah (1984). **Dipl.:** P.H.D. in Technical Education Systems, Paris University, 1986. **Career:** Judge Assistant at Ras Al-Khaimah high court; Secretary General of Abu-Dhabi consultant council before federation; Minister of housing and town planning in the first federal government following independence in 1971; Minister of Agriculture and Fishery; First Ambassador representing U.A.E. in Paris and to the European Common Market; Minister of Education and Youth Affairs; and president of the University of the U.A.E.; UNESCO executive council member on two successive sessions between 1980-1985; A businessman after leaving the Ministry until 1988; Established Ajman University College of Science and Technology in 1988, and now its President. **Credit Cards:** American Express & Diner's Club. **Prof. Addr.:** Ajman University College, P.O.Box 346, Tel.: 06-425255, Ajman, United Arab Emirates. **Priv. Addr.:** Tel.: 06-425111, Ajman, U.A.E.

SALMAN (Said, Abdallah), United Arab Emirates statesman. **Born** in 1945 in Ras al-Khaimah, United Arab Emirates. **Son** of Abdallah Salman. **Educ.:** B.A. al-Azhar University, Cairo; DEA, Faculty of Law, Sorbonne, Paris; Doctorat d'Etat, Sorbonne, Paris. **Career:** Minister of Housing, later Minister of Housing and Public Works (1973-77); Ambassador of UAE to Paris (1977-79); Minister of Education and Youth, Abu Dhabi (1979-83); Director, Central Bank, Abu Dhabi (1984); Member of the Executive Board of UNESCO. **Addr.:** Abu Dhabi, United Arab Emirates.

SALMAWY (Mohamad), Egyptian writer and journalist. **Born** in 1945 in Cairo, Egypt. **Married,** two children. **Educ.:** B.A. in English Literature, Cairo University, Egypt; M.A. in Mass Communications, American University in Cairo, Egypt; Diplomas in Drama and Modern English Literature, Oxford and Birmingham Universities. **Career:** Lecturer, Cairo University (1966-70); Freelance editor and radio announcer, Radio Cairo (1963-75); Editor, Foreign Desk, "al-Ahram" newspaper, Cairo (1970-77); Expert, Board of al-Ahram Center for Political and Strategic Studies (1977-79); Foreign Editor, "al-Ahram" newspaper, Cairo (1979-1987); Under-secretary of State for Culture (1988-1989); Managing Editor, al-Ahram Weekly (1990-); Owner of Aleph Publishing House (1983-). **Member** of Egyptian Press Syndicate, Cairo; the Union of Arab Journalists, Alumni of Salzburg Seminary in American Studies, Salzburg, Gezira Sporting Club, Maadi Sporting and yacht Club, the Old Victorian Association, London. Imprisoned for political activity (1977). **Publ.:** "The Foreign Editor" (1976); "Origins of British Socialism" (1978); "Come Back Tomorrow & Other Plays" (1983); "Murderer at Large" (1985); "Concerto for the Nay & Other Stories" (1988); "Salome" (1989); "Two Down the Drain" (1990); "The Flower and the Chain" (1991) etc... **Sports:** Riding, swimming. **Hobbies:** Music, reading, Antiques. **Addr.:** 9 Road 216, Tel.: 3522531, Maadi, Cairo, Egypt.

SALTI (Amer), Jordanian banker. **Born** on 22.12.39 in Amman, Jordan, **Son** of Omer Salti and Lutfieh Khadra. **Married** to Rebecca Buchanan in 1965, 2 children. **Educ.:** Brigham Young University, University of Utah, U.L.C.A., Berkeley University and Sorbonne. **Dipl.:** B.A., M.P.A., Ph.D., Doctorat de Troisième Cycle. **Career:** Instructor at Brigham Young University (1966-68); Assistant General Manager, Arab Development Society (1973-74); Assistant Manager, City Bank in Beirut and Amman (1975-78); Assistant General Manager (Finance), Arab Jordan Investment Bank (1979-to present); Deputy Chairman, Livestock & Poultry Co. (1980-present); **Member:** Board member of: Industrial Development Bank (1981), Arab International Insurance Co. (1982-present), Intermediate Petrochenicals Industries (1980-present). **Sports:** Tennis. **Clubs:** Rotary, Royal Automobile Club, Amman, P.O.B. 8797, Tel.: 668629. **Priv. Addr.:** Shemeisani, Amman, Tel.: 668852.

SALTI (Sami), Jordanian businessman. **Born** in 1926 in Jerusalem. **Married,** three children. **Educ.:** B.A. in Business Administration. **Career:** Managing Director of J. Salti & Sons Company (steel suppliers) (since 1950); Honorary Consul General for Austria in Jordan (1965). **Medal:** Crox d'Officier from the President of the Austrian Republic (1972). **Sports:** Tennis, swimming. **Addr.:** P.O.B. 832, Tel.: 25495, Amman, Jordan.

SAMATER (Mohamed, Ali, Lt. Gen.), Somali former vice-president and prime minister, **Born** in 1931 in chisimaio, Somalia, **Married,** children. **Educ.:** Elementary education at Chisimaio, Intermediate school in Mogadishu (1949); Training course with the artillery of the Somali Security Forces (Nov. 1950); Intermediate school in Magadishu (1950-52); Officer's training course with the Somali Security Forces (1952-54); Military Academy, Rome (Italy) (1954-56). **Career:** Commandant Somali Police (1956), Maj-Adjutant (1958-65); Commandant, National Army (1967); Major General (1973); Vice President, Supreme Revolutionary Council, Secretary of State for Defence (1971-76); Commander in chief, Armed Forces (1971-78); Former Vice President Political Bureau, Somali Socialist Revolutionary Party; Minister of Defence (1976-81, 1982-); Chairman Defence and Security Committee, Supreme Council of the Revolution (1980-82); Vice President of Council (1981-82); reappointed Vice-President and Prime Minister (1986-90). **Addr.:** Somalia.

SAMI (Amin), Egyptian diplomat. **Born** in Egyptian Ministry of Foreign Affairs; Ambassador to Morocco; Ambassador to Mali (1963-64); Ambassador to Poland; Ambassador to Netherlands (1976-80). **Addr.:** Ministry of Foreign Affairs, Cairo, Egypt.

SAMI (Sherif Mahmoud Murad), Egyptian businessman. **Born** on October 18, 1932 in Cairo, Egypt. **Married,** two sons. **Educ.:** Cairo University. **Dipl.:** B.Sc. in Military Science (1953); B.Sc. in Commerce and Business Management (1971). **Career:** Egyptian Armed Forces Officer (1953-57); Republican Guard (1957-61); The President's Private Secretariat (1961-71); Businessman, Managing Director, and Chief Executive of Several Companies. **Member:** Gezira Sporting Club, Equestrian Club, Yacht Club. **Hobbies:** Tennis, riding. **Addr.:** Sharikat Feror II Tawkelat al-Tegariah, 48 Gizah Street, Emaret Borg al-Orman, Appartment 83, P.O.Box 1585, Gizah, Egypt.

SAMIR (Faisal, al), Iraqi statesman. **Born** in 1922 in Iraq. **Educ.:** King Faisal II High School, Universities of Baghdad and Cairo. **Dipl.:** Bachelor of Arts, Master of Arts, Doctor of Philosophy. **Career:** Teacher (1947); Later Lecturer Baghdad University (1950); Director General of Education (1958); Minister of National Guidance (1959-61); Minister Plenipotentiary and Ambassador of Iraq to Indonesia (1961-63); **Publ.:** Author of "Sawt at-Tarikh". (1947), "Tawrat al Zinj" (1954), various translations. **Addr.:** Ministry of Foreign Affairs, Baghdad, Iraq.

SAMKARI (Sami Yousuf), Saudi senior civil executive. **Born** in 1945 in Jeddah. **Educ.:** California State College, USA. **Dipl.:** M.A. (Economics and Business Administration). **Career:** Bonafide executive in **Saudi Arabian Air-**

lines Corporation having served as: Supervisor Banking and Foreign Exchange (1970), Staff Manager, Banking and Foreign Exchange (1971), Manager Cash Operations (1972), Corporate Treasurer (1975), Vice President Finance (1979), Financial Advisor (1983) and currently General Manager, Corp, Budgets (1985- to date). **Member:** Southern California University Alumni Congress, Los Angeles, California. Attended exofficio several Aviation Conferences, training and courses. **Sports:** Hunting, swimming. **Hobby:** Photography. **Priv. Addr.:** Alkhaldiyah, Behind Mini Market, Tel.: 6829315, Jeddah, Saudi Arabia.

SAMMAN (Abdul Mohsin M.), Saudi diplomat, **Born** in 1917 in Medina, Saudi Arabia. **Educ.:** Received religious elementary education, the Higher Certificate of Religious Sciences, Medina, Certificate of Arts and Crafts, Faculty of Atbarah, Sudan. **Career:** Minerals analyst, Mahd al-Zahab mine, al-Meraigib mine (Yambu), Um al-Quryat mine (al-Wajh), (1940-49); left the office of mines and companies and joined the Ministry of Foreign Affairs in 1949; has held several positions at the Ministry of Foreign Affairs, later Ambassador. **Member:** several internal committees at the Ministry. **Honours:** Spanish Order awarded by General Franco of Spain; King Abdulaziz Order, Excellent Grade. **Hobby:** football. **Prof. Addr.:** Tel.: 6690900, Jeddah. **Priv. Addr.:** Tel.: 8324659, 8239900, Dhahran, Saudi Arabia.

SAMMAN (Adnan, Taha), Saudi businessman. **Born** in 1939. **Educ.:** Secondary School Certificate. **Career:** Director, Administration and Financial Affairs, Organization for Saline Water Desalination (1973); Director General, Administration and Financial Affairs (1974-75); Assistant for Administrative and Financial Affairs to H.R.H. the Governor General, Organization for Saline Water Desalination; attended International Conference on Saline Water Desalination, several FAO conferences, Conference on the Use of Atomic Energy for Peaceful Purposes; founder of al-Samman Establishment. **Hobby:** swimming. **Prof. Addr.:** P.O.Box 1874, Tel.: 651.5251, 651.5392, Jeddah. **Priv. Addr.:** Tel.: 6600883, Jeddah, Saudi Arabia.

SAMMAN (Ali, al), Egyptian journalist. **Born** in Egypt. **Educ.:** Cairo and Paris University. **Dipl.:** Doctor of Political Science, University of Paris. **Career:** Journalist, "al-Ahram" newspaper correspondent in Paris. **Addr.:** al-Ahram, al-Gal' Street, Cairo, Egypt.

SAMMAN (Ghada, Wagih, al), Syrian writer. **Born** in Syria. **Daughter** of Wagih al-Samman (University Professor and Dean). **Married** in 1970 to Bashir Daouk (physician), one child. **Educ.:** American University of Beirut, London University. **Dipl.:** Bachelor of Arts, Doctor of Philosophy. **Career:** writer, journalist. **Publ.:** Author of 10 books, including "Mon destin, tes yeux", "Pas de Port de Beyrouth", "Les départs des vieux ports" (1973), to "al-Hawadess" (Beirut) "La Chute au Sommet" (1967). **Hobby:** Reading. **Addr.:** Beirut, Lebanon.

SAMMAN (Nabil, Abdullatif), Jordanian bank executive. **Born** on 10 August 1939, Jerusalem. **Son** of Abdullatif Samman (textile engineer) **and** Mrs., née Nimat Rehime. **Married** to Najah Kamal on 1.3.69 in Qatar, 3 children. **Educ.:** St. Georges School in Jerusalem. (GCE) plus several banking diplomas. **Career:** Clerk in different Departments (1960-64); Head of different Departments (1964-72); Assistant Manager (1972-75); Branch Manager (1975-78); Manager Commercial Banking Dept. (1978); presently Assistant General Manager, Arab Jordan Investment Bank, Amman. **Medals:** Two **Sports:** Football, Basketball, Swimming, Cross Country. **Hobbies:** Taperecording, Photography, Music. **Clubs:** Crown Soorts Complex. **Prof. Addr.:** P.O.B. 8797, Shmeisani, Amman Tel.: 5681448. **Priv. Addr.:** Jabal Amman, 6th Circle.

SAMMAN (Nizar Hassan), Saudi official. **Born in** 1941 in Medina. **Dipl.:** Ph.D. (Political Science), M.A. (Administration), M.A.T. (Education, Teaching Social Sciences). **Career:** Former statistical expert and adviser, Central Statistical Department; Organization Adviser and expert and later Deputy Director, Central Department of Organization and Management; Director General, Central Department for Government purchases, Ministry of Finance and National Economy; Director General, Organization and Programmes, Ministry of Interior; Assistant Deputy Minister for Organization and Programmes, Ministry of Interior, Riyadh. **Member:** Saudi delegation to the Executive Council of the Arab League's Organization of Administration Sciences, the American Political Science Association and the American Society for Public Administration. **Publications:** research articles on Political Science, Local Government, Public Administration, Economics, Statics and Planning. **Hobbies:** reading, swimming. **Prof. Addr.:** Ministry of Interior, Tel.: 402.6884, 401.1944 Ext. 281, Riyadh. **Priv. Addr.:** Tel.: 476.3942, 478.6081, Riyadh, Saudi Arabia.

SAMMAN (Qadi Ali, bin Ali, al), Yemeni former government minister. **Born** in 1925 in Bir al-Azad, North Yemen. **Married**, children. **Educ.:** locally. **Career:** Appointed Zaydit Qadi (Judge) and Minister of Justice (September 1969- February 1971); following the ministerial reshuffle of 17 April 1972 he was elected Governor of Ibb Province in the southern-most district of Yemen; Recalled to the Ministry of Justice in June 1974, he was placed at the head of the Higher Law Council, Sana'a; Minister of Wakfs and Guidance (March 1979-to May 1990). **Addr.:** Sanaa, Republic of Yemen.

SAMMAN (Yasser Shahir, al), Saudi civil servant. **Born** in 1935 in Damascus, Syria. **Dipl.:** B.A. (Political Science). **Career:** Diplomatic Attaché; Third Secretary, Saudi Arabian Embassy, Jordan; Treasurer, Diplomatic Club, Amman, Jordan. **Sports:** Swimming, tennis. **Hobby:**

Chess. **Prof. Addr.:** Foreign Ministry, Jeddah. **Priv. Addr.:** Sarraj Villas, Palestine Street, Medina Road, Jeddah, Saudi Arabia.

SAMRA (Khairi, Ahmad), Egyptian neurosurgeon. **Born** in 1938 in Cairo, Egypt. **Son** of Ahmad Samra. **Married**, three children. **Educ.:** Cairo University. **Dipl.:** Diploma in Surgery, of Neurology and Psychiatry; Masters Degree in Surgery. **Career:** Lecturer in Neurosurgery, Cairo University (1962-65); Fellowship in Psychosurgery, Maryland, USA (965); Fellowship in Neurosurgery, Hartford, USA (1966); Fellowship in Neurosurgery, St. Barnabas Hospital, New York, USA (1966-69); Associate Professor of Neurosurgery, Cairo University (1970-76); Professor of Neurosurgery (since 1976). **Member:** American Congress of Neurosurgeons, American Society of Cryosurgery; American Geriatric Society; Egyptian Society of Neurosurgery; Middle East Society of Neurosurgery. **Publ.:** Author of numerous scientific papers published in Egyptian and international journals. Member of Gezira Sporting Club. **Hobbies:** Football, tennis. **Prof. Addr.:** 16 Sherif Street, Cairo, Egypt. **Priv. Addr.:** 8 el-Mansour Mohamed, Zamalek, Cairo, Egypt.

SAMRA (Mahmoud Dawood), Jordanian academic. **Born** in 1924 in Palestine. **Married**, one son, two daughters. **Educ.:** Faculty of Arts, Cairo University; School of Oriental and African Studies, University of London (UK). **Dipl.:** B.A. in Arabic Studies (1950); Ph.D. (1958). **Career:** Deputy Editor in chief, al-Arabi magazine (1958-64); Associate Professor of Literary Criticism, Arabic Department, University of Jordan; Professor of Literary Criticism (1966-); Dean, Faculty of Arts, University of Jordan (1968-73); Vice-President, University of Jordan (1973-) now President; Vice-President of Jordan Academy of Arabic; Vice-President of the Royal Society of Fine Arts, Jordan; President of the Association of Jordanian Writers; member of Iraqi Academy of Science. **Publ.:** Essays in Literary Criticism, Beirut (1959); Contemporary Writers, Beirut (1961); Western Travellers in the Levant, Beirut (1967); The Young Writers, Amman (1970), The Angry Young Writers, Beirut (1973); On Literary Criticism, (in arabic), Beirut (1974); translated several Books from English into Arabic; several articles and papers in English and Arabic; published mainly in al-Arabi, Middle East Forum. **Awards:** Prize, University of London (1958); Order of Independence, 1st Class, Jordan (1973). **Addr.:** University of Jordan, P.O.Box 1682, Amman, Jordan.

SAMRA (Moheb, Mohamad, el), Egyptian diplomat. **Born** in 1927 in Egypt. **Son** of Mohamad al-Samra. **Married**, two sons. **Educ.:** Cairo University. **Dipl.:** LL.B.; B.Sc. **Career:** Counsel, Jerusalem (1956-58); Counsel General, Mogadishu, Somalia and Hargisa (1958-63); Head of Egyptian Embassy Branch Benghazi Libya (1964-65); Consul General Geneva (1965-67); Counsellor Embassy in Bern (1967-68); Consul General in London (1971-74); Minister Plenipotentiary, Embassy in Vatican (1974-75); Ambassador to Singapore (1979-83); Ambassador to Tunis Feb. 1985 till 12th March 1987, date of retirement. **Decor.:** Several army medals; Medal of the Republic (Fourth Class), (First Class). **Member** of Gezira Sporting Club; **Hobbies:** Riding, swimming, golf. **Addr.:** 11 al-Higaz St., Mohandiseen, Tel.: 3480412, 3480914, Cairo, Egypt.

SANABANI (Abdallah, Mohamad, al), Yemeni former central bank governor. **Born** in 1935 in Yemen. **Son** of Mohamad al-Sanabani. **Married** in 1962, 3 sons, 2 daughters. **Dipl.:** B.A. **Career:** Vice-Chairman, Deputy Governor, Central Bank (1971). Governor, Central Bank of Yemen, Yemen (1978-90). **Addr.:** Sanaa, Republic of Yemen.

SANE (Yousef, Hamad, al), Kuwaiti banker. **Born** in 1952 in Kuwait. **Married** in 1983, 2 daughters. **Educ.:** California Lutheran College. **Dipl.:** M.B.A. **Career:** Assistant in the Faculty of Commerce, Kuwait University. Financial Assistant, Assistant Manager, Manager, Corporate Finance Dept., Executive Manager, Banking & Finance Dept., former General Manager, Chairman and Managing Director, The Industrial Bank of Kuwait, Safat, Kuwait. **Addr.:** Kuwait City, Kuwait.

SANOUSSI (Badriddine), Moroccan diplomat. **Born** in 1933 in Fes, Morocco. **Married**, children. **Educ.:** Licentiate in law, University of Bordeaux, France; Licenciate ès Letters, Mohamad V University, Rabat, Morocco; Diploma of the Center of Business Preparation, Paris, France. **Career:** Counsellor of the High Cherifian Tribunal (1956-57); Chargé de Mission, Ministry of State and of Public Function (1957); Chargé de Mission, Ministry of National Defence (1957); General Secretary, Tobacco Management (1958-63); Director of the Royal Cabinet (1963-64); Under Secretary of State for Commerce, Industry, Mines and Merchant Marine (1964-65); Under Secretary for Administrative Affairs (1965-66); Minister of Posts and Telecommunications (1966-70); Deputy for Benslimane, House of Representatives (1970); Minister of Youth, Sports and Social Affairs (1970-71); Ambassador to USA (1971-74); Ambassador to Iran (1974-76); Ambassador to UK (1977-80). **Medals:** Officer of Ouissame Alouite, and many foreign decorations. **Addr.:** Rabat, Morocco.

SANOUSSI (Mohamad, Nasir, al), Kuwaiti official. **Born** in 1938 in Kuwait. **Son** of Nasir al-Sanoussi. **Married**, three children. **Educ.:** B.A. in Mass Communications, USA; Diploma in Broadcasting, USA; Institute of Drama, Cairo, Egypt; Training Courses with ITN and BBC, London, UK (1962). **Career:** Director of Kuwait Television (1972); Assistant Under Secretary for Television Affairs and Cinema (since 1973); Chairman of the Board of Directors of Modern Networks Company; member of the Board of Baalbeck Studio, Lebanon; Chairman of the Board of Arab Company for International Production;

member of the Board of the Gulf States Organisation for Programme Production; Chairman of Gulf Festival for Television Production and Kuwait Cine Club. **Hobbies:** Television and cinema productions. **Addr.:** P.O.Box 25795, Tel.: 431712, 419584, Kuwait TV, Kuwait City, Kuwait.

SAQQAF (Mohamed, Hashim, al), Jordanian economist. **Born** in Jordan. **Son** of Hashim Saqqaf. **Married**, children. **Educ.:** B.A. in Accountancy; M.A. in Economics and Marketing. **Career:** Company Controller, Ministry of Economy, then Manager of Economic Co-operation; then Jordanian Representative in the Arabic Union for Economy; Deputy Minister of Industry and Commerce; Vice Chairman, Board of Directors, Jordanian Phosphate Co., Chairman of the Board of Directors of Syrian Jordanian Industrial Co. **Medals:** Order of the Renaissance, Jordan; Order of Independence, Jordan. **Addr.:** P.O.Box 30 or P.O.Box 925411, Amman, Jordan.

SARHAN (Ahmad, Zeid), Kuwaiti statesman. **Born** in Kuwait. **Son** of Zeid Sarhan. **Educ.:** Secondary and Higher. **Career:** President of the National Assembly of Kuwait (1967 until dissolved in 1986). **Addr.:** Kuwait City, Kuwait.

SARHAN (Khalid, Mohamed), Jordanian bank manager. **Born** in 1942 in Shwaida. **Son** of Mohamad Sarhan. **Married** in 1970, 1 son, 3 daughters. **Educ.:** Cairo University. **Dipl.:** B.Sc. (Econ.). **Career:** Ministry of Kuwait (1965-67); Arab Bank Ltd. (1967-70); Manager, Bank of Oman Ltd., Fujairah, UAE (1970-to present). **Member:** Hilton Club. **Hobbies:** Reading and swimming. **Addr.:** P.O.Box 270, Tel.: 22754, Telex: 89078 A/B OMANFJEM, Fujairah, UAE.

SARHAN (Mansour, Mohamed), Bahraini Director of Public Librairies. **Born** January 1, 1945. **Son** of Mohamed Sarhan (Merchant) **and** Mrs. née Sakina Ismail. **Married** on August 22, 1971 to Zahra Dashti, 3 children: Nazha (1973), May (1977), Mohammed (1982). **Educ.:** Beirut Arab University (Lebanon-1972), Bombay University (India-1980), Leeds Polytechnic (UK - 1985). **Dipl.:** B.A. (History) Beirut Arab University (1972), B.A. (Library Science) Bombay University (1980), MA (Librarianship) Leeds Polytechnic (1985). **Career:** Bahrain Ministry of Education, English Teacher (1963-1973); Librarian of Manama Public Library, Bahrain (1973-1975); Chief of Public Libraries - Bahrain (1975-1989); Director of Public Libraries - Bahrain (1989). **Work:** 7 articles and papers on librairies in Bahrain. **Publications:** Author of three books in Arabic. The Book and the Libraries (1983) Bahrain National Bibliography (1992) Cultural Movement in Bahrain 1940-1990 (1993). **Hobbies:** Reading and listening to Music. **Credit Cards:** American Express and Visa. **Prof. Addr.:** Ministry of Education, P.O.Box 43, Tel.: 231105, Manama, Bahrain. **Priv. Addr.:** 50 Road 4301/ Nuwidrat 643/ Bahrain/ 700214.

SARKI (Ahmed, Rushdi, Mohamed, Yusif), Egyptian administrator. **Born** in 1933 in Cairo, Egypt. **Son** of Mohamad Yusif Sarki. **Married**, two children. **Educ.:** University of Vienna. **Dipl.:** B.A. in Tourism. **Career:** Several posts as Hotel Manager in al-Ain Hilton, United Arab Emirates; Addis Ababa Hilton, Hilton Nile Cruises, Egypt; currently Resident Manager Nile Hilton, Cairo. **Member of the:** International Hotel Association; Gezira Sporting Club. **Hobbies:** Golf, shooting. **Addr.:** Nile Hilton, Liberation Square, Cairo, Egypt.

SARKIS (Nicolas), Oil economist. **Born** on December 28, 1935 at Yabroud (Syria). **Son** of Ata SARKIS **and** Mrs. Mountaha KASSIS. **Married** on October 28, 1967 to Claude MOUSSALLI, three children: Ziad (1968), Walid (1969) and Jihad (1971). **Educ.:** Frères Maristes, Jounieh, Lebanon, French University (Beirut), Paris University (Paris). **Dipl.:** Doctorat in Economics - Paris. **Career:** Director of the ARAB PETROLEUM RESEARCH CENTER (1966-2000); Director of ARAB OIL & GAS MAGAZINE, published in English, Arabic and French (1966-2000); Oil consultant (1965-2000). **Publ.:** Author of various books on the Arab oil industry. **Credit Cards:** Amex, Visa. **Prof. Addr.:** Arab Petroleum Research Center (APRC), 7, Avenue Ingres, 7516 Paris, Tel.: 33(0)1 45243310, Fax: 33(0)1 45201685, E-mail: aprc@arab-oil-gas.com Web site: www.arab-oil-gas.com. **Priv. Addr.:** 28 Rue de Franqueville, 75116 Paris, Tel.: (33(0)1/45030282, Paris, France.

SARKIS (Paul, Antoine), Egyptian cleric. **Born** on September 18, 1933 in Cairo. **Son** of Antoine Sarkis (pharmaceutical agent) **and** Mrs., née Victoria Ouanes. **Educ.:** College de la Sainte Famille, Cairo (Egypt) (1940-51); Bikfaya Noviciate (Lebanon) (1951-52); Laval Juniorate (France) (1953-54); scolasticate (philosophy), Chantilly (France) (1954-57); University of Paris (Sorbonne) (1954-57); St. Joseph University of Beirut (Lebanon) (1961-63); Aïn Shams University, Cairo (Egypt) (1965-66); University of Chicago (USA) (1971-72). **Dipl.:** Egyptian Baccalaureate (secondary education cetificate) (June 1951); Licentiate in Arabic (1957); Teacher's Training Certificate (November 1966). **Career:** Ordained to the priesthood (Society of Jesus) (September 1964); Invigilator and teacher at College de La Sainte Famille (1957-61); Vice-Principal (1965-70) and (1972-73), Rector (1973-79); Vice-Principal (1979-81). Spiritual Director and Teacher at St mary's Seminary (WAU, Bahr el-Ghazal, SUDAN). Regional Superior of the Jesuits in Egypt (1984-86). Provincial Superior, near East Province, Society of Jesus (1986-95); Director CARITAS-EGYPT (1995). **Prof. & Priv. Addr.:** College de la Sainte Famille, Tel.: 5900411 and 5900892, Cairo, Egypt.

SARTAWI (Sufian, Ibrahim), Jordanian banker. **Born** in 1930 in Sarta/Nablus, Jordan. **Son** of Ibrahim Sartawi. **Married**, five children. **Educ.:** University of Cairo, Egypt.

Dipl.: B.A. in Commerce. **Career:** Chairman of the Board, Jordan Kuwait Bank; member of the Board of the Arab International Hotels Co., Ifa Banque. **Prof. Addr.:** Jordan Kuwait Bank, P.O.Box 9776, Tel.: 663530, Amman, Jordan. **Priv. Addr.:** Tel.: 827405, Amman, Jordan.

SARY (Ahmad M.), Yemeni executive. **Born** in South Yemen in 1947. **Dipl.:** B.Sc. **Career:** Programmer-Analyst (1972); Manager of External Computer Services, Saudi Arabia (1975); Manager of Academic Computer Services (1976); Director, Data Processing Centre; founding member of the Board of the Royal Saudi Computer Society; has organized four national computer conferences. **Publication:** First Steps in Automation. **Hobbies:** squash, reading. **Address:** Data Processing Centre, King Fahad University of Petroleum and Minerals, Dhahran, Saudi Arabia.

SASSI (M. AbdulHamid), Tunisian engineer. **Born** in 1934 in Gabes, Tunisia. **Educ.:** L'Ecole des Ponts et Chaussées, Paris. **Dipl.:** Civil Engineering. **Career:** Chief Engineer of Le Kef; Chief Engineer of Sousse; Chief Engineer, Ministry of Public Works in charge of major projects; Chairman and Managing Director of the major Projects Organisation (1965-71); Secretary of State at the Ministry of Public Works and Housing (1971-73); Secretary of State to the Minister of Supply; Minister of Transport and Communications (1976). **Decor.:** Grand Officer of the Tunisian Order of Independence. **Addr.:** Tunis, Tunisia.

SASSI (Omar al-Tayyeb, al), Saudi academic. **Born** in 1939 in Mecca, Saudi Arabia. **Dipl.:** M.A. (1969); Ph.D. (German and Comparative Literature) (1972). **Career:** Taught Arabic Language in Germany; attended First Conference of Saudi Men of Letters, Mecca 1974; XXIX Internationaler Feriekursus für Germanisten der Universität Münser, West Germany; Vice-Dean, Faculty of Arts and Assistant Professor, King Abdulaziz University, Mecca. **Publications:** The Influence of the One Thousand and One Nights Tales on the German Romantic novel (M.A. dissertation); Popular sayings in Mecca: a comparative study with German and other Arab saying (Ph.D. thesis), Short History of Arabic Studies in Europe 1976, Studies in Arabic Literature 1978. **Hobbies:** travel, reading. **Address:** al-Rajhi Buildings, Block 4, Appt. 77, Mecca Road, Jeddah, Saudi Arabia.

SATI (Iklil), Jordanian businessman, former diplomat. **Born** in 1926 in Damascus, Syria. **Career:** Private Secretary to King Abdallah (1949); Ministry of Foreign Affairs (1950-61); Deputy Head of Royal Protocol (1961-63); Head of Royal Protocol (1964-66); Ambassador to Spain (1967-70); Secretary General to Ministry of Foreign Affairs (1970-72); businessman since retirement from Ministry of Foreign Affairs. **Hobby:** Shooting. **Addr.:** P.O.Box 5139, Amman, Jordan.

SAUD (Abdallah al-Faisal, Ibn Abdulaziz, al, H.R.H. Prince), Poet and businessman. **Born** in Riyadh, in 1923. The **eldest son** of late King Faisal. **Educ.:** received **general** court education supplemented by private tutoring and extensive reading. **Career:** one of the major **poets** in contemporary Arabic literature; Assistant and Special Adviser, during his father's term of service as Viceroy of Hijaz province; assumed the post of Minister of the Interior for some time; left government service to devote his efforts to a wide complex of commercial and business ventures; Owner and Chairman of Board of several companies and agencies, foremost among which are General Motors Agency, Saudi Shipment Co.; Qassim Cement Co.; SAPPCO; Sony Electronics etc; Founder of King Faisal's International Charity Society. **Publications:** Mahroum: Min Wahye el-Hiram (Deprived of Joy; poems inspired by deprivation) a collection of poetry which has occupied an important place in modern Arabic literature. **Hobbies:** reading, poetry, writing. **Address:** Prince Abdullah al-Faisal's Palace, P.O.Box 5, Jeddah, Saudi Arabia.

SAUD (Abdallah Ibn Abdulaziz, al, H.R.H. Prince), Crown prince. **Born** in 1924. **Son** of the founder of the Kindgom, the late Abdulaziz. **Educ.:** received a court education in religion, chivalry and politics. He was **tutored** at school and in the Royal Court by great Ulemas (Scholars of Islam), and supplemented his education **by vast** reading in all fields. **Career:** when the late King Faisal succeeded to the throne, became President of the National Guard, a most important sector of the Saudi Armed Forces; Second Deputy Prime Minister (1975-82); has made several state visits to the U.S.A., and European, Arab and African countries; during 1977 paid several state visits to various countries, notably Spain, the U.K. and France, the purpose of these visits was to establish stronger ties between these countries and the Kingdom of Saudi Arabia; towards the end of 1977 he paid an important visit to the U.S.A. with the aim of developing and consolidating the Saudi National Guard; after the death of King Khalid, and the coronation of King Fahd, he became Crown Prince, First Deputy Prime Minister and Commander of the National Guard (June 1982-to present). **Address:** Council of Minister, Riyadh, Saudi Arabia.

SAUD (Abdallah Ibn Musa'id Ibn Abdulrahman, al, H.R.H. Prince), Saudi leading businessman. **Born** in 1945 in Riyadh, Saudi Arabia. **Dipl.:** M.A. (Economics). **Career:** Member of Board of Directors of First Arabian Investment Co., Luxembourg, Saudi Arabian Investment Co. Ltd., Jeddah, Edward Bates and Sons Ltd., London; Chairman of Board of Saudi Carrier Co., Riyadh; member of Board of Saudi Prefab Co., Riyadh; member of Constituent Committee, South Cement Plant, Jizan. **Hobbies:** reading, swimming. **Address:** P.O.Box 580, Riyadh, Saudi Arabia.

SAUD (Abdul Karim), Syrian diplomat. **Born in 1930**

in (Djebleh) Lattakia, Syria. **Married**, three children. **Educ.:** Licence in Law (1953); Licence in Literature (1967) Damascus University; Ph.D. in French Literature (1972), France. **Career:** First Counsellor, Ministry of Planning (1971-76); Lecturer of French Literature, Damascus University (1972-75); Lecturer of Political Economy, Damascus University; Minister Counsellor, Embassy of Syria, Cairo, Egypt (1977); Plenipotentiary Minister Head of the Diplomatic Mission of Syria to China (1978-81); Permanent Delegate of Syria to UNESCO-Paris (1988-91). **Hobbies:** Economy, literature, poetry. **Addr.:** Ministry of Foreign Affairs, Damascus, Syria and 1, Rue Miollis, UNESCO, Paris 75015, France 8/13 Syrian Delegation.

SAUD (Abdul Rahman, Ibn Abdulaziz, al, H.R.H. Prince), Major businessman and former deputy minister of defence. **Born** in 1931. **Son** of late King Abdulaziz, founder of the Kingdom. **Educ.:** Received high school education in Saudi Arabia; military cadet, California Military High School, California, U.S.A., B.BA. (Economics and Business Administration), University of California, U.S.A. **Career:** Founder of the National Gypsum Co.; private business; established modern farms in various provinces of Saudi Arabia; founder of Printing, Publication and Press Organisation, Jeddah; founder of al-Khat Printing, Publication and Translation, Dammam; founding member of Riyadh and Jeddah Electric Power Companies, Electric Co., Eastern Province, Saudi Gas Co. and a number of cement plants in Saudi Arabia; visited most Arab and European countries, U.S.A. and Brazil; Former Deputy Minister of Defence and Civil Aviation (1988). **Address:** Prince Abdul Rahman ben Abdulaziz Mansion, Riyadh, Saudi Arabia.

SAUD (Ahmad, Ibn Abdulaziz, al, H.R.H. Prince), Former Deputy Minister of the Interior. **Born** in Riyadh, in 1941. **Son** of late King Abdulaziz, founder of the Kingdom. **Educ.:** B.Sc. (Political Science). **Career:** Private business; Deputy Governor of Mecca; member of the Governorate Supreme Hajj (Pilgrimage) Committee and of Western Province Planning Committee; Chairman, Board of National Gypsum Company; Vice-President, Supreme Hajj Committee; chairs several other government committees; active member of the Supreme Committee for Western Province Planning and Social Development; former Deputy Minister of the Interior. **Hobby:** Desert travel, hunting and sports. **Honours:** several Orders of Merit from Kings and Presidents of Arab and Islamic countries. **Priv. Addr.:** H.R.H. Prince Ahmed Mansion, Jeddah, Saudi Arabia.

SAUD (Badr Ibn Abdul-Muhsen, Ibn Abdulaziz, al, H.R.H. Prince), President of the saudi arts society. **Born** Riyadh, in 1953. **Dipl.:** B.A. **Career:** Has devoted his efforts since his graduation to the promotion of Saudi Arts particularly poetry, music, painting and folk singing; founded for this purpose the Saudi Arts Society, the first Saudi Organization responsible for the promotion of Saudi Arts within and outside Saudi Arabia; a major and acknowledged poet, several of whose compositions have been put to music and sung by major Saudi folk-singers. **Hobbies:** reading, music. **Address:** Jeddah, Saudi Arabia.

SAUD (Badr Ibn Abdulaziz, al, H.R.H. Prince), Deputy president of the national guard. **Son** of the late King Abdulaziz, founder of the Kingdom. **Educ.:** Received courtly as well as regular education in religion, politics and diplomacy. **Career:** occupied several posts, the most recent of which was Minister of Communications before he assumed his responsibilities as Vice-President of the National Guard. **Address:** Presidency of the National Guard, Riyadh, Saudi Arabia.

SAUD (Bandar Ibn Abdallah Ibn Abdulrahman, al, H.R.H. Prince), Saudi Arabia. **Dipl.:** B.A. (Political Science). **Career:** Director General Ministry of Interior; President, Arab and Saudi Arabian Cycling Association; Assistant Deputy Minister of Interior for Provincial Affairs. **Publications:** several articles in local newspapers. **Prof. Addr.:** Ministry of Interior, P.O.Box 2833, Tel.: (1)401-1111, Riyadh. **Priv. Addr.:** Tel.: 405-8537, Riyadh, Saudi Arabia.

SAUD (Bandar Ibn Abdulaziz, al, H.R.H. Prince), Saudi leading businessman. **Born** in Riyadh in 1921. **Son** of late King Abdulaziz. **Educ.:** Received Court education in Islamic religion, modern science and chivalry. **Career:** Businessman Holder of the following distinguished decorations: Order of the Republic First Grade, Order of the Nile (Egypt), Iraqi Kingdom Order. **Address:** P.O.Box 5977, al-Bedie'ah Riyadh, Saudi Arabia.

SAUD (Bandar Ibn Faisal, al, H.R.H. Prince), Saudi prince. **Born** in 1943. **Son** of late King Faisal. **Educ.:** in USA; RAF Bracknell, UK (Staff Course). **Career:** Captain, Royal Saudi Air Force; lightning Pilot; Head, Royal Saudi Air Force negotiation teams. **Addr.:** Ministry of Defence and Aviation, Riyadh, Saudi Arabia.

SAUD (Bandar Ibn Khalid, Ibn Abdulaziz, al, H.R.H. Prince), Saudi businessman. **Born** in 1935. **Son** of His Majesty King Khalid. **Career:** owner and chairman of the Board of al-Bandar International Corporation Ltd. for construction and real estate, engaged in building 3.000 Residential units in the southern area of Jizan. **Prof. Addr.:** al-Bandar International Corporation, P.O.Box 2048, Jeddah. **Priv. Addr.:** Prince Bandar Ben Khalid's Palace, Riyadh, Saudi Arabia.

SAUD (Bandar Ibn Sultan Ibn Abdulaziz, al, H.R.H. Prince), Saudi diplomat. **Born** on March 2, 1949 **in Taif,** Saudi Arabia. **Son** of H.R.H. Prince Sultan Ibn **Abdulaziz** al-Saud. **Married** to H.R.H. Princess Haifa bint **Faisal Ibn**

Abdulaziz al-Saud, 5 children: 2 sons, 3 daughters. **Educ.:** R.A.F. College, Cranwell, U.S.A.F. **Career:** Advanced Program and Johns Hopkins University; fighter pilot, Royal Saudi Air Force (1969-82); in charge of Special Saudi Arabian Mission to U.S.A. for purchase of defence equipment (1981); Defence and Military Attaché, Saudi Arabian Military Mission to U.S.A. (1982-83); Ambassador to U.S.A. (1983-). **Hobbies:** Flying, reading. **Addr.:** Embassy of Saudi Arabia, 601 New Hampshire Ave. N.W., Washington, D.C. 20037, U.S.A.

SAUD (Fahad, Ibn Abdulaziz, al, H.M. King), Born 1923. **Educ.: Son** of the the late King Abdulaziz, founder of the Kingdom of Saudi Arabia, received a court education in religion, chivalry and politics. **Career:** Towards the end of his father's reign, Prince Fahad became First Minister of Education when the then Directorate of Education became a Ministry; During that time, he presided over several Saudi delegations to the Arab League, Morocco and Lebanon; Minister of the Interior; Second Deputy Prime Minister and Minister of the Interior until the death of his brother, the late King Faisal in 1975; represented Saudi Arabia as Chairman of Saudi delegations to several Arab and international conferences; visited a large number of world capitals where he conducted political talks aiming at strengthening Saudi relations with several countries of the world on the basis of mutual interest and respect; During the reign of the late King Faisal, became Chairman of more than one supreme council; e.g. the Supreme Council of National Security, the Supreme Council of Educationl Policy, the Supreme Council of Saudi Universities, the Supreme Council of Oil Affairs, the Supreme Council of Youth Welfare and the Supreme Committee of Pilgrimage. He was awarded an Honorary Doctorate from King Abdulaziz University in 1975; Among the major political achievements of H.R.H.. Prince Fahad during 1977 was the State visit he paid to the U.S.A. as spokesman for all Arabs on the Middle East crisis; During that visit Prince Fahad held talks with President Carter on the nature of peace in the Middle East, the Palestinian problem and the right of Palestinians to a homeland. As a result of these talks President Carter admitted, for the first time, that the Palestinians have a right to establish a homeland. Later, Prince Fahad paid a State visit to Spain where he held important talks with King Juan Carlos. In their joint communiqué, the Spanish King and the Saudi crown Prince confirmed their desire to work for the establishment of a new international monetary system based on justice and equality leading to further co-operation between industrialized and developing countries; crowned King of Saudi Arabia and Prime Minister after the death on June 13, 1982 of late King Khalid. **Addr.:** Royal Palace, Riyadh, Saudi Arabia.

SAUD (Fahd Bin Sultan Bin Abdulaziz, al, H.R.H. Prince), Saudi governor of Tabuk Province. **Born** 1950. **Dipl.:** B.A., history, King Saud University, Riyadh (1970). **Career:** Present Governor of Tabuk Province; Honorary Chairman of King Abdul Aziz Benevolent Society, Tabuk; Honorary Chairman of Tabuk Agricultural Development Company; Honorary Chairman of Saudi Pharmaceutical Society. **Hobbies:** Reading, Hunting. **Address:** Governor of Tabuk Province, Kingdom of Saudi Arabia.

SAUD (Faisal Ibn Bander Ibn Abdulaziz, al, H.R.H. Prince), Saudi Prince. **Born** in 1943 in Riyadh, Saudi Arabia. **Dipl.:** B.A., King Saud University, 1969. **Career:** Director of Organization and Administration Department, Ministry of Defence and Aviation (1973); Training Supervisor, Ministry of Post, Telephones and Telegram (1974); Deputy Governor, Asir Province (1978); Vice Governor of Asir since 1981; presently Governor of Qasim. **Prof. Addr.:** Qasim Governorate, Qasim, Saudi Arabia.

SAUD (Fawaz Ibn Abdulaziz, al, H.R.H. Prince), Former governor of Holy Mecca Province. **Son of** the late King Abdulaziz, founder of the Kingdom. **Born** Taïf, 1934, **Educ.:** Received Court education, supplemented by extensive reading and private tutoring at the hands of grand Ulemas. **Career:** Occupied for some time the post of Governor of Riyadh; sponsor of Prince Fawaz Housing Project for Limited Income Citizens in Jeddah; as Governor of Holy Mecca Province H.R.H. Prince Fawaz is ultimately responsible for the organization and supervision of the annual Hajj (Pilgrimage) season, a great **Islamic** event in which over 2 million Muslims from all over the world gather yearly in Holy Mecca to perform pilgrimage. **Honours:** Order of Cedar of Lebanon; Spanish and other decorations; several orders of merit from Arab, Islamic and Western countries. **Hobbies:** swimming, horseriding. **Address:** Jeddah, Saudi Arabia.

SAUD (Hathloul Ibn Abdulaziz, al, H.R.H. Prince), Saudi leading businessman. **Born** in Riyadh, in 1941. **Son** of Late King Abdulaziz. **Career:** Leading businessman; Vice President of Najd Corporation. **Hobbies:** sport, hunting. **Address:** al-Hajj Wal Auqaf Street, Shomal al-Muraba, Riyadh, Saudi Arabia.

SAUD (Khaled al-Abdallah al-Faisal, Ibn Abdulaziz, al, H.R.H. Prince), Saudi leading businessman and former official. **Born** in 1942 in Taïf, Saudi Arabia. **Grand son** of late King Faisal. **Educ.:** B.Sc. (Political Science), Taïf, 1942 Cambridge University **Career:** Former official, Saudi Monetary Fund; Director-General, of Arab Trade, Navigation and Aviation Corporation; one of the founders of cement industry in Saudi Arabia; Chairman, IMIANTIT Industrial Ltd. **Hobbies:** reading, travel. **Address:** IMIANTIT Arab Saudi Co. Ltd., Riyadh, Jeddah and Damman, Saudi Arabia.

SAUD (Khaled al-Faisal, Ibn Abdulaziz, al, H.R.H. Prince), Saudi official. **Born** in 1940 in Mecca, Saudi Arabia. **Son** of His late Majesty King Faisal. Governor of the Southern Province of Assir. **Educ.:** B.A. (Political Economy), Oxford University, England. **Career:** Director-General, Youth Welfare Department (1967-71); established al-Faisal Press Establishment, publisher of the monthly cultural magazine al-Faisal; member of Board of Trustees, King Faisal International Charity Association; Chairman of Board, Assir Press Establishment; Presently Governor of the Southern Province of Assir. **Address:** Abha, Assir Province, Saudi Arabia.

SAUD (Majid Ibn Abdulaziz, al, H.R.H. Prince), Saudi minister, governor of Holy Mecca. **Son** of the late King Abdulaziz, founder of the Kingdom. **Born** in 19 October 1938. **Educ.:** Received regular schooling in Riyadh as well as a court education at his father's palace in politics, economics and public administration; since boyhood, he has shown a deep interest in Arab and foreign cultures and in learning foreign languages, especially English and French; his extensive reading in social history and cultural fields enabled him to have an excellent command of various aspects of Arab and European cultures; visited most Arab and western countries; Minister of Municipal and Rural Affairs (1975-1986); Governor of Mecca (with Ministerial Rank) (1975-to date); **Honours:** several Orders of Merit (First Class) from various countries. **Hobby:** falconry. **Address:** Mecca Governorate, Mecca, Saudi Arabia.

SAUD (Mishal Ibn Abdul Aziz, al, H.R.H. Prince), Saudi prince - one of the eldest son of late King Abdul Aziz, brother of his Majesty King Fahad Bin Abdul Aziz, the present King of Saudi Arabia. **Career:** Former Minister of Defence (1951); Former Governor of Makkah Province and now Chairman of the Board of Yanbo Cement Co. and one of the biggest saudi Businessmen, specially real estate and investment. **Address:** P.O.Box 7152, Riyadh 11462, K.S.A., Tel.: Office: 4828233, Res.: 4812078, Fax: 4826770, Telex: 407642 MISHAL SJ, Saudi Arabia.

SAUD (Mishal Ibn Mohamad Ibn Saud Ibn Abdulaziz, al, H.R.H. Prince), Saudi businessman. **Born** on 24 August 1936. **Dipl.:** B.A. **Career:** Runs his own business of general trade, manufacturing and agencies for interior decoration and furniture; Chairman of Board, Mish'al Ibn Mohamed Ibn Saud Establishment; Chairman, Saudi Orient Maritime Co. Ltd.; Vice Chairman of Board, Al Mashoura Establishment; member of Several welfare societies. **Address:** H.R.H. Prince Mohamad Ibn Saud's Mansion, al-Nasseriyah, Tel.: 402 3723 (Office) and 4023712 (Home), Riyadh. Saudi Arabia.

SAUD (Mohamad, Faisal, al, H.R.H. Prince), Saudi arabian executive. **Born** in 1937. **Son** of late King Faisal. **Married. Educ.:** Menlo University, Business Administration (1963). **Career:** Low Level Officer, Saudi Arabian Monetary Agency (1964); One of the Founders of Islamic Development Bank, Jeddah (1976); Owner, Iceberg Transport International Ltd; Islamic Investment Co. (1977); Head, Dar al-Maal al-Islami, Geneva, Switzerland; Chairman, Massraf Faisal al-Islami Bank and Trust Bahamas Ltd., Bahamas; and Chairman, Dar al-Maal al-Islami Trust, Bahamas. **Address:** Dar al-Maal al-Islami, P.O.Box 42, 84 Avenue Louis-Corsai, Geneva, Switzerland.

SAUD (Mohamad Ibn Saud, Ibn Abdulaziz, al, H.R.H. Prince), Saudi official. **Born** on 21 March 1934, in Riyadh, March 1934, in Riyadh, Saudi Arabia. **Educ.:** Secondary School Certificate; received private tutoring. **Career:** Chief Chamberlain of late King Saud ben Abdulaziz; Chief, Royal Cabinet; ex-Minister of Defence and Aviation; member of Board and of constituent Boards of several companies; participated in the foundation of Jeddah Refinery and several factories in Jeddah and Riyadh; attended the conference of Ministers of Defence, Cairo and several other international and regional conferences in company of the late King Saud; member of several Charity Societies and Sports Clubs; presently Governor of Baha Province. **Honours:** several Orders and Medals from all Arab and African countries and some European countries. **Hobbies:** drawing, swimming, hunting and horse-riding. **Address:** Governorate of Baha, Saudi Arabia.

SAUD (Muqren Ibn Abdulaziz, al, H.R.H. Prince), Saudi official. **Born** on 15 September 1945 in Riyadh, Saudi Arabia. **Son** of the Late King Abdulaziz. **Dipl.:** B.Sc. (Aviation Sciences), M.A. (Military Sciences). **Career:** Has served as a pilot since 1968; became Flying Instructor (1973); Commanding Officer, 7th Air Squadron, Royal Saudi Air Force (1975); Deputy Director of Operations and Planning, Royal Saudi Air Force (1977); Presently Governor of Hail region; Chairman of the Board, Hail Welfare Society; Honorary Chairman of the Board, Hail Agricultural Development Company. **Honours:** King Abdulaziz Sash, Order of Merit, Egyptian Military Air Force. **Hobbies:** reading books and scientific magazines, music, hawk hunting. **Address:** Hail Province Governorate, Hail, Saudi Arabia.

SAUD (Muteb Ibn Abdulaziz, al, H.R.H. Prince), Saudi minister. **Born** in 1931. **Son** of late King Abdulaziz, founder of the Saudi Kingdom. **Educ.:** received a regular and court education supplemented by private tutoring in various fields of knowledge and extensive reading in economics, politics and culture. **Career:** Deputy Minister of Defence and Aviation; Governor of the Province of Holy Mecca; visited Arab and European countries, and U.S.A.; presently **Minister** of Housing and Public works. **Honours:** various Orders of Merit from Arab and European countries. **Hobbies:** falconry, reading. **Address:** Ministry of Housing and Public Works, P.O.Box 56095, Riyadh, 11554, Saudi Arabia.

SAUD (Nasser Ibn Abdulaziz, al, H.R.H. Prince), Saudi prince. **Born** in 1919 in Riyadh, Saudi Arabia. **Son** of the late King Abdulaziz. **Career:** first Prince to assume the post of Governor of Riyadh after annexing Hejaz to the Kingdom. **Address:** Prince Nasser's Palace, Riyadh, Saudi Arabia.

SAUD (Nawaf, Ibn Abdulaziz, al, H.R.H. Prince), Saudi prince. **Born** in 1933 in Riyadh, Saudi Arabia. **Son** of late King Abdulaziz. **Educ.:** studied in the U.S.A. for a short period. **Career:** During the reign of his late brother, King Saud, assumed the post of Chief of the Royal Cabinet; also served under the late King Faisal as Chief of the Royal Cabinet and Special Adviser to the King. **Address:** Prince Nawaf Mansion, P.O.Box 2833, Riyadh, 11134, Saudi Arabia.

SAUD (Nayef, Ibn Abdulaziz, al, H.R.H. Prince), Saudi minister. **Born** in 1933. **Son** of late King Abdulaziz, founder of the Saudi Kingdom. **Educ.:** besides regular schooling and private tutoring at the hands of great Ulemas (Scholars of Islam), received a thorough training in politics, diplomacy and security affairs. **Career:** Governor of Riyadh, Capital of the Kingdom of Saudi Arabia; Governor of the Holy City of Medina; Deputy Minister of the Interior; Minister of State for Internal Affairs; has made several state visits to the Gulf States and Emirates to conduct talks on the security of the region; member of several official Saudi delegations headed by the late King Faisal and Crown Prince Fahad ben Abdulaziz; Minister of the Interior (1975-to present). **Honours:** Supreme Orders from various Gulf and Arab States. **Hobby:** falconry. **Address:** Ministry of the Interior, Riyadh, Saudi Arabia.

SAUD (Salman Ibn Abdulaziz, al, H.R.H. Prince), Saudi minister **Born** in 1936. **Son** of late King Abdulaziz, founder of the Saudi Kingdom. **Educ.:** Received a court education at the hands of great Ulemas (scholars of Islam) supplemented by private tutoring in various fields of knowledge. **Career:** As Governor of Riyadh, (with Ministerial Rank); shares in many affairs of government, attends summit conferences held in the capital and takes part in political talks with foreign Heads of State besides his work in running the local affairs of the Saudi Capital; Chairman of several charity projects and societies; Chairman of the Supreme Committee for planning the City of Riyadh. **Hobbies:** reading, falconry. **Address:** Riyadh Governorate, Riyadh, Saudi Arabia.

SAUD (Sattam Bin Abdulaziz Bin Abdul Rahman, al, H.R.H. Prince), Saudi prince. **Born** on January 21, 1941 in Riyadh, Kingdom of Saudi Arabia. **Educ.:** San Diego University, California, U.S.A. **Dipl.:** B.A. and Honorary Ph.D. from the University of San Diego, California, U.S.A. **Career:** Deputy Governor of Riyadh Region and then Vice Governor of Riyadh Region; Vice Chairman of Riyadh Benevolent Society, Vice Chairman of Riyadh Development Authority, Vice Chairman of Riyadh Water and Sewage Authority; Chairman of the Committee of Private Rights. **Address:** Governorship of Riyadh Region, P.O.Box 1261, Riyadh 11431, Kingdom of Saudi Arabia.

SAUD (Saud Ibn Abdul Mohsen, Ibn Abdulaziz, al, H.R.H. Prince), Saudi official. **Born** in 1947. **Educ.:** B.A. (Business Administration). **Career:** Director, Health Housing and Environment Sectors Department, Central Planning Organization; Director of Co-ordination and Follow-up, Ministry of Health; participated in the establishment of the first company for electric cables; attended the Conference on Health and Environment, Harvard and Johns Hopkins Universities, U.S.A.; Deputy Governor, Holy Mecca Province. **Hobbies:** Horse-riding, falconry. **Address:** Mecca Province Governorate, Jeddah, Saudi Arabia.

SAUD (Saud Ibn Fahad, Ibn Abdulaziz, al, H.R.H. Prince), Saudi businessman **Born** on 8 October 1950. **Dipl.:** B.Sc. (Economics), California, U.S.A. **Career:** conducts wide business activities and patronizes several companies; his personal and professional contributions to the national economy are invaluable; founding member of the board of the Faisal Islamic Bank in Egypt; and founding member of the Board of several industrial institutions, notably the insecticides factory and the tyres factory; chairman of Board, Tihama for Advertising Public Relations and Marketing Research, co-publisher of "Who's Who in Saudi Arabia". **Hobby:** sports. **Address:** P.O.Box 4397, Riyadh, Saudi Arabia.

SAUD (Saud Ibn Faisal, Ibn Abdulaziz, al, H.R.H. Prince), Saudi minister. **Born** in Riyadh, Saudi Arabia. **Son** of late King Faisal. **Dipl.:** B.A. (Economics), Princeton University, U.S.A. **Career:** Former Deputy Minister of Petroleum and Mineral Wealth; founder member of the King Faisal International Charity Society; Minister of Foreign Affairs (since 1975-to date); headed the delegation of the Kingdom of Saudi Arabia to the 1976 Session of the UN General Assembly; he acted as Special Envoy of late King Khalid in several diplomatic and political missions; participated actively in pan-Arab efforts to end the civil war in Lebanon; member of Saudi Delegation to Arab restricted summit, Riyadh 1976 and full-scale Arab summit, Cairo, October 1976; member of Saudi delegation accompanying His Majesty late King Khalid on his state visits to Cairo, Pakistan, Syria, the Sudan, France and Belgium. **Hobby:** reading. **Address:** Ministry of Foreign Affairs, Riyadh, Saudi Arabia.

SAUD (Sultan Ibn Abdulaziz, al, H.R.H. Prince), Saudi Minister. **Born** in (1928). **Son** of late King Abdulaziz, founder of the Kingdom. **Educ.:** Received a regular and court education in religion, modern culture and diplomacy; has been tutored at the hands of great Ulamas (Religious Scholars) at his father's palace; His education was supplemented by extensive reading in all fields of knowledge as well as visits to various countries of the world. **Career:** Governor of Riyadh (1947), Minister of Àgriculture (1954); Minister of Transportation (1955); member of most Saudi delegations headed by the late King Faisal to Arab and Islamic Summit Conferences, state visits and UN General Assembly sessions; Vice President of the Supreme Committee for Education Policy; Minister of Defence and Aviation and Inspector General (1963); Chairman of the Board of Saudia Airlines (1963); Chairman of the Board of the General enterprise of Military Industries; Chairman of the Council of Manpower (1980), Second Deputy Prime Minister and Minister of Defence & Aviation and Inspector General in (1982 to date); and Chairman of The Supreme Council for Islamic affairs (1994). **Honours** Orders of Merit (First Class) from various Western and Arab countries; **Address** Ministry of Defence and Aviation, Riyadh, Saudi Arabia.

SAUD (Talal Ibn Abdulaziz, H.R.H. Prince), Saudi politician and international official. **Born** in 1934. **Son** of late King Abdulaziz ibn Saud. **Educ.:** Prince's School, Royal Palace, Riyadh. **Career:** positions held in his early 20's include responsibility for the Royal Palaces, minister of Communications; former Minister of Economy and Finance; former Ambassador to France; founder of Riyadh's first girls' school, first private hospital and Mecca's first college for boys; passport cancelled in 1962; exile in Egypt; returned to Saudi Arabia (1964); Chairman, Consolidated Contractors Co. WLL, Saudi Arabia; now Special Envoy, UNICEF and President Arab Gulf Programme for UN Development Organisations "AGFUND". **Hobbies:** history, amateur radio, swimming. **Prof. Addr.:** P.O.Box 18371, Riyadh 11415, Saudi Arabia. **Addr.:** 11 Ave. Montaigne, 75008 Paris, France.

SAUD (Turki Ibn Abdulaziz, al, H.R.H. Prince), Saudi prince. **Born** in 1932 in Riyadh, Saudi Arabia. **Career:** Founder and President, Arab Student Aid International (ASAI); former Deputy Minister of Defence and Aviation; Presently Chairman, Arabian Cement Co. Ltd., Jeddah. **Hobbies:** reading, hunting. **Prof. Addr.:** Arabian Cement Co. Ltd., P.O.Box 275, Jeddah, Saudi Arabia.

SAWA (Tajuldin Mohamad ben Ali), Saudi senior civil servant. **Born** in 1947 in Mecca. **Dipl.:** B.Sc., Faculty of Education, Mecca (1970); M.A. (Education), Mibugare State University (1973). **Career:** Teacher of Mathematics in Secondary School (1970-71); educational researcher (1973); member of National Committee for Developing Mathematics; attended several educational conferences; now Director, Research Division, Ministry of Education. **Publ.:** mathematics teaching methods for elementary schools, some school mathematics textbooks for blind students. **Hobbies:** Photography, reading. **Prof. Addr.:** Ministry of Education, Riyadh, Saudi Arabia.

SAWAF (Abdulaziz, al), Syrian chairman of companies. **Born** on June 15, 1923 in Damascus. **Married** to Miss Juhaina as-Sawwaf. **Educ.:** American University of Beirut; Harvard Business School. **Dipl.:** Bachelor of Arts, Master of Business Administration. **Career:** Division Manager, Esso Standard (Near East); Chairman of the Board, Trans Orient and Transit Corporation; Director of Banks. **Member:** Rotary Club, Orient Club, Arab Club. **Addr.:** Damascus, Syria.

SAWAF (Fayeq Bakor, al), Saudi academic. **Born** in 1930 in Mecca, Saudi Arabia. **Dipl.:** Ph.D. (Modern History). **Career:** Employee in General Board of Accountancy, Ministry of Finance (1947); Vice Principal of Umara Model School, Taif (1951); Inspector, Ministry of Education (1957); Lecturer in Modern History. Department of History, Faculty of Shari'a (Islamic Law), Umm al-Qura University. **Member:** Chamber of Commerce, Mecca, 1957, 1959; attended some UNESCO conferences. **Hobby:** reading. **Address:** Mecca, Saudi Arabia.

SAWAF (Mohamad Mahmoud, al), Saudi adviser. **Born** in 1915. **Dipl.:** LL.M. (Islamic Law), al-Azhar University, Cairo. **Career:** Teacher of Arabic and Islamic Religion, Primary Schools; Lecturer, Faculty of Shari'a, Baghdad; Inspector of Mosques, Endowments General Directorate; Professor, Faculty of Shari'a, Mecca; Adviser to the Ministry of Education. **Member:** Constituent Congress of Muslim World League; Executive Bureau of Muslim World Congress, Karachi; Permanent Bureau, General Congress, Karachi; Permanent Bureau, General Congress on the Palestine Question, Amman, Jordan; Supreme Advisory Council, Islamic University, Medina; worked for 5 years as special envoy of the late H.M. King Faisal. **Honour:** Knight of the Most Excellent Order of Merit, awarded by Head of the Government of Comoro Islands. **Publications:** Nida' ul-Islam (The Call of Islam); Swatu'l Islam (The Voice of Islam); al-Muslimoon Wa al-Falak (Muslims and Astronomy), al-Mukhatatat al-Isti'mariyyah, Li Mukafahat al-Islam (Anti-Islamic Imperialist Schemes); Ma'rakatu'l Islam Aw Waqai'una Fi Filistine Bayna al-Amsi Wa Yawn (The Battle of Islam, or the Incidents of Palestine Yesterday and Today); Ta'leemu'l Salah (Praye teaching); al-Siyam Fi'l Islam (Fasting in Islam); Zawjati Nabiyyi'l Tahirat (The Prophet's Immacullate Wives); Rihlati Ila al-Diyari Islamiyyah: Afriqqia al-Muslimah (My Journeys into Islamic Countries; Muslim Africa). **Address:** P.O.Box 894, Tel.: 5420023 (Home). Mecca, Saudi Arabia.

SAWAHRI (Khalil, Hussein, al), Jordanian writer. **Born** in 1940 in Jerusalem. **Son** of Hussein Sawahri. **Married,** five children. **Educ.:** Damascus University. **Dipl.:** B.A. in Philosophy and Sociology. **Career:** General Manager, Dar al-Karmel Publishing & Distributing. **Member** of Jordanian Writers Union, Member of Palestinian Writers Union & Member of Lotus Prize Jury. **Publ.:** "al-Bachoura Cafe House"; "Period of Occupation"; "al-Anka'a and the

Land", "Night visitor", etc. **Decorations:** Palestinian Short Story Award & Irani Short Story Award Jordan. **Addr.:** Dar al-Karmel Publishing and Distributing, P.O.B. 17067, Tel.: 605580, Amman, Jordan.

SAWAMURA (Shozaburo), Japanese executive. **Born** in 1933 in Tokyo, Japan. **Son** of Hatsuichi Sawamura. **Married** in 1966, 1 son, 2 daughters. **Educ.:** Tokyo University of Foreign Studies. **Dipl.:** B.A. (1957). **Career:** Joined Mitsui Bank since 1957 in Tokyo, New York, Hong Kong and Singapore; Chief Representative for the Middle East, Mitsui Bank Ltd., Manama, Bahrain. **Member:** Japanese Society for Bahrain. **Addr.:** P.O.Box 26859, Tel.: 253805, Telex: 9427 A/B MITGIN BN, Manama, Bahrain.

SAWI (Abdel Moneim, al), Egyptian journalist. **Born** in 1918, Cairo. **Educ.:** Faculty of Arts, Cairo University. **Dipl.:** B.A. **Career:** War correspondent for "al-Misry" assigned to the Western Desert to cover the battle of "al-Alamein" which ended with the crushing defeat of Rommel's panzers at the hands of Gen. Montgomery; in 1952 joined "al-Tahrir" (Liberation) daily newspaper, the officiel mouthpiece of the Revolutionary Command Council led by the late President Abdel Nasser; appointed director-general of the Middle East News Agency (M.E.N.) the first state-owned press agency; appointed Under-Secretary of State, Ministry of Culture; acted as Egyptian Government representtive with UNESCO during the international campaign to salvage the historic vestiges of Nubia prior to the building of the Aswan High Dam; elected President of the Press Association (1973), re-elected to the same post in 1975; former Board Chairman of "Dar al-Tahrir" the state-owned publishing house; member of the People's Assembly (Parliament). **Publ.:** more than 25 literary novels some of which were adapted for TV film productions. **Addr.:** Cairo, Egypt.

SAWI (Amir, al), Sudanese diplomat. **Born** in 1921. **Educ.:** University of Bristol, UK. **Dipl.:** In Public Administration. **Career:** Assistant Representative of Sudan in Cairo, Egypt (1953); District Commissioner in Kosti (1956); Assistant Under Secretary, Ministry of Foreign Affairs (1956-57); Deputy Under Secretary, Ministry of the Interior (1960); Permanent Under Secretary (1965-70); Under Secretary, Ministry of Public Services and Administrative Reform (1971); Doyen of the Sudan Civil Service; Ambassador to UK (1976). **Addr.:** Ministry of Foreign Affairs, Khartoum, Sudan.

SAWI (Tawfic, al), Egyptian bank executive. **Born** in 1948 in Cairo. **Son** of Hassan el-Sawi. **Married** in 1973, 1 son, 1 daughter. **Educ.:** Cairo University; American University of Cairo. **Dipl.:** B.A. Business Administration (1972); M.B.A. (Econ.) (1974). **Career:** Citibank N.A. Cairo (1975-80); Citibank N.A. Houston Texas (1980-81); Citibank N.A. New York (1981); Senior Vice President, Arab Asian Bank, Manama, Bahrain (1981-). **Member:** Arab Bankers Association; al-Maadi Sporting Club; Marina Club. **Hobbies:** Tennis, Squash and Photography. **Addr.:** P.O.Box 5619, Tel.: 233129, Telex: 8583 A/B ABMAL, Manama, Bahrain.

SAYAD (Jalal Mustafa, al), Saudi academic. **Born** in 1936 in Egypt. **Dipl.:** B.Sc. (1959); M.Sc. (1964); Ph.D. (1966). **Career:** Lecturer (1966-69); Assistant Professor (1969-74); Professor of Statistics, King Abdulaziz University, Jeddah since 1974. **Member:** Royal Statistical Society, International Statictical Institute, Bernoulli Society of probability and Mathematical Statistics and International Association of Statistical Computation. **Publications:** 15 research papers on statistics published in international journals. **Hobbies:** tennis. **Address:** Jeddah, Saudi Arabia.

SAYAH (Mohamad, Melki), Tunisian former statesman. **Born** on December 31, 1933 in Bomhjer. (Tunisia). **Son** of Melki Sayah (Agriculturist) **and** Mrs. Chelbia Bouzid. **Married:** to Miss Lilia Ennouvri on December 4, 1959, 3 children: Chelbia, Ziad and Shiraz. **Educ.:** Sadiki College, Sfan College, University of Tunis. **Dipl.:** Bachelor of Arts. **Career:** General-Secretary of the General Union of Tunisian Students (1960-62); Assistant-Director of the Neo-Destour and Director of "L'Action" newspaper (September 1962- October 1964), Director of the Destour Socialist Party (October 1964- December 1969), Secretary general of State for Information (1969-70); Permanent Representative of Tunisia to UN. Specialized agencies Geneva (1970-71); Minister of Public Works and Housing (1971-73); Director of Socialist Destour Party (1973); Minister of Youth and Sports (1973); Minister Delegate to the Prime Minister; Deputy Prime Minister for Planning (May 1976-80); Minister of Equipment and Housing (April 1980- Dec. 80); Minister of Equipment (1980-82); Minister of Supply (1983-85); Minister of Equipment and Housing (1985-87); Minister of State for Education, Teaching and Scientific Research (1987-88). **Addr.:** Tunis, Tunisia.

SAYAR (Ali, Abdallah), Bahraini journalist. **Born** in 1926 in Bahrain. **Son** of Abdallah Sayar. **Married. Educ.:** Bahrain Technical School and Cairo Technical School. **Career:** Worked in Saudi Arabia and Kuwait; co-operated in Bahrain Founder and editor-in-Chief of "AL-QAFILAH" Newspaper and later "al-Watan". Member of the Higher Executive Committee (1956); worked in Kuwait Ministry of Social Affairs and Labour (1956); worked for commercial firms in Bahrain (1957-69); founder and Editor in Chief, "Sada al-Usbu" weekly newspaper (1969-to present); member of the Constituent Council (1973). **Addr.:** P.O.Box 549, Manama, Bahrain.

SAYARI (Hamad Saud, al), Saudi civil servant. **Born** in 1941 in Dhurma. **Dipl.:** M.A. (Economics), University of Maryland, U.S.A. (1971). **Career:** Instructor of Economics, Institute of Public Administration; Secretary General,

Public Investment Fund; Director General Industrial Development Fund; Chairman of the Board, Saudi Industrial Development Fund; Vice Governor then Governor, Saudi Arabian Monetary Agency. **Prof. Addr.:** P.O.Box 2992, Tel. 463.3000, Riyadh, Saudi Arabia.

SAYARI (Sulaiman Abdulaziz), Saudi public servant. **Born** in 1940 in Riyadh, Saudi Arabia. **Dipl.:** B.Com. (Business Administration). **Career:** Deputy Head of Education Administration; Assistant Director of Boys Education; delegated to the Girls Education Administration as Assistant Director; member of the Boys Education Board, Riyadh; member of the Supreme Founding Committee, Riyadh; Head of the Boys Education Board, Riyadh. **Hobbies:** reading, swimming. **Address:** Riyadh, Saudi Arabia.

SAYED AHMAD (Mohamad, al), Egyptian journalist, writer. **Born** in 1928 in Cairo, Egypt. **Married,** two children. **Educ.:** Electronic Engineering Diploma, Cairo University, Egypt (1956); Licence in Law, Ain Shams University, Cairo (1957). **Career:** Imprisoned for leftist activities at university (1950-52); imprisoned for political activities (1959-64); Director, left wing Publishing House al-Dimukratiya al-Gadida; Editorial Writer for "al-Akhbar" (1965-68); "al-Ahram" (1968); writer, "al-Ahram"; writer of political studies; member of the Legislation and Economic Society, Cairo. **Publ.:** "On the Eisenhower Doctrine" (1957); "Economic World Crisis" (1958); "Study on Egyptian Socialism" (1964); "After the Guns Fall Silent" (1975). **Member** of Cairo Sporting Club. **Addr.:** 22 Ibn Zanki Street, Zamalek, Tel.: 755500 Cairo, Egypt.

SAYED (Gaballah, al), Egyptian former statesman. **Born** in 1917 in Egypt. **Educ.:** Secondary and Higher. **Dipl.:** Doctorate. **Career:** Professor of University; Under Secretary of Ministry of Planning (1963-68); Minister of Planning (1968-73). **Addr.:** Cairo, Egypt.

SAYED (Gamal, el), Egyptian electronics engineer and politician. **Born** in 1918. **Educ.:** Military Academy, Faculty of Engineering, in U.K. and Czechoslovakia and Staff College of Supreme Miligary Academy. **Dipl.:** Ph.D. **Career:** Played prominent role in Octover 1973 War; former member Board Arab Industrialization Organization; Assistant to Minister of State for Military Production (1982). **Addr.:** Ministry of Military Production, 5 Sharia Ismail Abaza, Kasr el-Eini, Cairo, Egypt.

SAYED HASSAN (Muwaffaq, al), Syrian economist. **Born** in 1929 in Damascus, Syria. **Married,** three children. **Educ.:** University of Damascus; University of Paris, Sorbonne. **Dipl.:** B.A. in Law; Diploma of Higher Studies in Economic Sciences; Ph.D. in Economic Sciences. **Career:** Lecturer, Damascus University (1978-83); Assistant Professor (1983-88); Professor (1988- to date); Vice President for Academic Affairs, Damascus University; Chairman of the Editorial Board, Damascus University Journal; Chairman of the University Council for Academic Affairs, Damascus University. **Publ.:** Economic Analysis (in Arabic); "Contemporary Economic Problems", a university textbook; The Payment Balance and the Current Conditions of our Monetary Economics; Visions of Possible Economic Policies, Damascus University Journal. **Hobbies:** Economic, studies, literature, swimming. **Addr.:** University of Damascus, Damascus, Syria.

SAYED (Hussain, Mohamad, al), Saudi lawyer. **Born** in 1919. **Son** of Mohamad al Sayyid. **Married,** four children. **Educ.:** LL.B. Alexandria University, Egypt; postgraduate Diploma, Economics and Public Law, Alexandria University; M.A. and Ph.D. in Taxation, Alexandria University. **Career:** Inspector of Income Tax (1961); University Teacher, Riyadh University (1961-63); Dean of Faculty of Commerce, Riyadh University (1963-70); Legal Adviser for the Rector (1970-73); Deputy Dean of Admission and Registration (1973-76); Legal Consultant for Saudi Basic Industries Corporation SABIC (1976-78); Partner, Shawwaf and al-Sayyid Law Office. **Publ.:** "Taxation Accounting in thc Kingdom" textbook (1970); several articles in Saudi Newspapers, magazines, Riyadh University publications and foreign professional journals in Arabic and English. **Addr.:** Shawwaf and al-Sayed Law Office, P.O.Box 2700, Tel.: 4785145, 4782510, Riyadh, Saudi Arabia.

SAYED (Ibrahim Ahmad, al), Saudi civil servant. **Born** in 1940 in Abha, Saudi Arabia. **Dipl.:** B.A. (English Language and Literature and Library Science). **Career:** Chief Librarian, Faculty of Arts, King Saud University; Head of Periodicals Department, Central Library, King Saud University; Chief Librarian, Central Library, King Saud University; Chief Librarian, Faculty of Education, Abha; Director General of Tourism Development Department. **Member:** the Literary Socicty at Abha; Board, Abha Public Library; American Librarians Association conferences. **Publications:** some articles specialized library sciences periodicals. **Prof. Addr.:** P.O.Box 354, Tel.: 2246133, Abha. **Dipl.:** Tel.: 2245251, Abha, Saudi Arabia.

SAYED (Mamoun, Mohd, al), Sudanese executive. **Born** in 1937 in Mahasi. **Son** of Mohd. el-Sayed Hamad. **Married** in 1973, 1 son, 2 daughters. **Educ.:** University of Khartoum, Sudan. **Dipl.:** LL.B. (1960). **Career:** Judge (1960-69); Legal Counsel, Attorney General's Office (1969-70); Legal Adviser and Company Secretary, State Trading Corporation (1970-74); Legal Adviser, Sudan Development Corporation (1975-82). Deputy Chairman and Managing Director, Sudan Development Corporation (1976-82). Director, Sudan Rural Development Company; Sudan Rural Development Promotion Company; Sudan Eagle Cement Co.; Kenana Sugar Company; Cotton Textiles Mills Company. **Addr.:** Khartoum, Sudan.

SAYED (Mohamad, Lutfi, al), Egyptian academic. **Born** in 1932 in Alexandria, Egypt. **Son** of Lutfi al Sayed. **Married**, four children. **Educ.:** University of Alexandria; University of Michgan. **Dipl.:** M.Sc., Ph.D. **Career:** Electrical Engineer (1953-61); Associate, Clarkson College, Potsdam, NY (1967-68); Professor, Cairo Institute of Technology, Helwan; Dean, Faculty of Engineering and Technology, Helwan (1977-79); Vice president, University of Helwan, Cairo (since 1979). **Hobby:** Swimming. **Addr.:** 7 Mudiriyet al-Tahrir. Street, Garden City, Cairo, Egypt. **Priv. Addr.:** 10 Street No.256, Maadi, Cairo, Egypt.

SAYED (Mustafa, al, Dr.), Former egyptian minister of economy and foreign trade. **Born** in 1938. **Educ.:** Faculty of Law, Ayn Shams University, Cairo; Leeds University (UK). **Dipl.:** LL.B. (1954); Ph.D. (Economics and International Commerce) from Leeds University. **Career:** assigned to the Cabinet of the Attorney General (1954-1956); Professor of law, Faculty of Law, Cairo Univesity; Secretary General, Faculty of Political Economics, Cairo University; Member of the People's Assembly (Parliament), Cairo; Elected chairman of the economic commission, National Democratic Party; Minister of Economy and Foreign Trade until 1 September 1982, following Cabinet reshuffle. **Addr.:** Cairo, Egypt.

SAYED (Mustafa, Amr, el), Egyptian American chemist. **Born** on May 8, 1933 in Zifta. **Son** of Arm el-Sayed and Mrs., Zakia Ahmad. **Married** on March 13, 1957 to Miss Janice Jones, 5 children: Leyla, Tarick, James, Dorria and Ivan. **Educ.:** Aïn Shams University, Florida State University. **Dipl.:** Bachelor of Sciences (1953), Doctor of Philosophy (1959). **Career:** Came to the United States (1954), Naturalized (1965); Research Associate, Florida State University (1958-59), Harvard (1959-60); California Technical Institute, Pasadena (1960-61); Ass. Professor, University of California, Los Angeles (1961-64); Associate Professor of Chemistry (1964-67); Professor of Chemistry since 1967; Consultant, North American Aviation Minute Man Programme (1965-66), Electro-Optics (1962-65), Member of a number of National Research council committees (1980-), Editor; Journal of Physical Chemistry (1980-); International Journal of Physical Chemistry (1983-). **Publ.:** Author of over 250 papers on mechanisms of molecular origin of phosphorescence, mechanism of energy transfer processes, spectra and structure of molecular crystals, vacuum ultraviolet spectroscopy and photoionization processes, laser spectroscopy Picosecond laser. Studies of Photobiological systems, Laser multiphoton ionization, dissociation mass spectrometry. **Member:** of several associations. **Award:** Distinguished Teaching Award, University of California (1964); Fresenius National Award (1967); McCoy Research Award (1969); Alfred P. Sloane, Guggenheim Fellowship (1965). Fairchild Fellow, California Institute of Technology (1981); Elected to the U.S. National Academy of Sciences (1980). **Priv. Addr.:** 3325 Colbert Avenue, Los Angeles, California, CA 90066, USA.

SAYEGH (Anis), Palestinian writer. **Born** in 1931 in Tiberias, Palestine. **Married. Educ.:** AUB, Beirut; University of Cambridge. **Dipl.:** Ph.D. in History. **Career:** Director of the palestine research Center (1966-76); injured in letter bomb attack (1972); Director of the Palestine Programme at the Arab Center for Higher Studies in Cairo; Editor in Chief, Counsellor "The Palestinian Encyclopaedia" (1982). **Publ.:** "The Sectarian Lebanon"; "The Arab Concept in Egypt"; "The Hashiemet and the Palestinian Problem"; "Palestine and the Arab Nationalism", etc. Supervised several theses in Cairo, University, Ain Shams University, Cairo; American University in Beirut. **Addr.:** Amman, Jordan.

SAYEGH (Salim Wahban, Bishop), Jordanian ecclesiastic. **Born** in 1935 in Jordan. **Son** of Wahban Sayigh. **Educ.:** B.A. in Philosophy and Theology; Ph.D. in Law, Latheral University, Rome. **Career:** President of the Latin Patriarchal Court in Jerusalem (1967-79); Rector of the Latin Patriarchal Seminary (1976-81); Bishop and Vicar General of the Latin Patriarchate in Jordan (since 1982). **Publ.:** "Le Statu Quo des Lieux-Saints", (1971); "The Christian Family's Guidebook". **Medals:** Commander of the Equestrian Order of the Holy Sepulchre of Jerusalem. **Hobbies:** table tennis, volley ball, chess, history, ecclesiastical law. **Addr.:** Latin Vicariate, P.O.B. 1317, Amman, Jordan.

SAYEGH (Yusuf A.), Palestinian economist. **Born** in 1916 in Syria. **Educ.:** American University of Beirut; Johns Hopkins University. **Dipl.:** M.A., Ph.D. **Career:** Assistant Economics Professor, American University of Beirut (1953-57); Associate Professor, and Director, Economic Research Institute (1957-62); Professor (1963-74); Economic Adviser, Planning Board of Kuwait (1964-65, and 1973-77); Adviser, Organisation of Arab Petroleum Exporting Countries (1973-77); Chairman, Planning Board, National Fund of Palestine Liberation Organisation (PLO) (1971-74); Adviser, Arab Fund for Economic and Social Development, Kuwait (1976). **Publ.:** "Bread with Dignity: Socio-Economic Content of Arab Nationalism" (1961); "Entrepreneurs of Lebanon" (1962); "Economics and Economists in the Arab World" (1964); "The Israeli Economy" (1966); "The Strategy of Action for the Liberation of Palestine" (1968); "The Economies of the Arab World: Development since 1945" (1978); "The Determinants of Arab Economic Development" (1978); "The Arab Economy: Past Performance and Future Prospects" (1982); "Arab Oil Policy in the 1970s: Opportunity and Responsibility"; Also co-Author "A Second Look at the Lebanese Economy" (1966); "Country Study"; "The Economics of the Arab World". **Addr.:** Amman, Jordan.

SAYEH (Hamid Abdullatif, al), Egyptian banker, economist. **Born** in 1921 in Egypt. **Son** of Abdullatif al-Sayih.

Educ.: B.A. in Commerce, Cairo University, Egypt; M.A. in Commerce, University of Denver, USA; Ph.D. in Finance and Economics, University of Kentucky, USA. **Career:** Director of the National Bank of Egypt, Cairo; Lecturer, Cairo University; various senior government posts (since 1954); Assistant Under Secretary and later Under Secretary, Ministry of Economy (1960); participated in talks with International Bank for Reconstruction and Development (IBRD) for the Aswan High Dam and later in financial negotiations with France and UK; Egyptian Deputy Director of IBRD; Under Secretary of International Economy, Ministry of Economy and Foreign trade; Chairman and Governor of the National Bank (1971); Minister of Economy and Economic Co-operation (1976-80); member of the Suez-Mediterranean Pipeline Finance Committee; Director of the Arab International Bank; Economic and Financial Adviser and member of the National Production Council; presently, Chairman, Hongkong Egyptian Bank, Cairo, **Prof. Addr.:** P.O.Box 126 D, Zamalek, Cairo, Egypt.

SAYER (Musaid Badir Mohamad Nasir, al), Kuwaiti businessman. **Born** in 1947 in Kuwait. **Son** of Mohamad Nasir al-Sayer. **Married** four children. **Educ.:** B.A. in Business Administration, Kuwait University. **Career:** Owner and Director, Mohamad Nasir al-Sayer and Sons Est.; President, Musaid Badir al-Sayer Est.; member of the boards of several major companies. **Member:** of the Hunting and Equestrian Club, Kuwait and the Tourist and Entertainment Club, Kuwait. **Addr.:** Musaid Badir al-Sayer Est., P.O.B. 21666, Tel.: 410697, 418721, 418682, Safat, Kuwait.

SAYER (Sayer Bader Al-), Kuwaiti Aeronautical Engineer A successful Kuwaiti Businessman. **Born** in 1951 in Kuwait. **Career:** Director of the Al-Sayer Group of Companies -Kuwait & Dubai; Member of the Board for ACFIT, Europhinex Management Company S.A. Luxembourg, Capital Trust S.A., The International Investor -KCC, Kuwait Computer Company - KSC. **Sports:** Scuba diving & water skiing. **Hobbies:** Chess, Contact. **Addr.:** P.O.Box 485, 13005 Safat, Kuwait, Tel.: (965) 481 6181/3, Fax: (965) 484 8610.

SAYRAFY (Adnan Abdul Ghani), Saudi academic. **Born** in 1945 in Saudi Arabia. **Dipl.:** M.A. (Physical Education). **Career:** Teacher at the Teacher's Training Institute; Demonstrator at the Faculty of Education, Umm al-Qura University. **Hobbies:** football, reading, photography. **Address:** Physical Training Department, Faculty of Education, Umm al-Qura University, Mecca, Saudi Arabia.

SBIHI (Abdul Hadi), Moroccan diplomat, agronomist. **Born in** 1925 in Sale, Morocco. **Married. Career:** Head of the **Private Office** of the Minister of National Economy; **Inspector, Ministry** of Agriculture; Governor of the Province of Casablanca (1961); Minister Plenipotentiary and Permanent Delegate of Morocco to FAO (1961); Ambassador to the Ivory Coast (1965-67); Ambassador to USSR (1967-70); Head of the Office de Commercialisation et d'Exportation (OCE), (1970); Minister of Agriculture and Agrarian Reform (1971); Ambassador to Norway, Sweden and Denmark (1973). **Addr.:** Ministry of Foreign Affairs, Rabat, Morocco.

SCHELHOTH (George, H.E. Mgr.), Syrian archbishop. **Born** in 1920 in Aleppo, Syria. **Educ.:** Jerusalem Seminary; Charfé Seminary (Lebanon). **Career:** Ordained to the Priesthood (1945); Secretary, Archbishop of Aleppo; Director, St. Joseph School (Aleppo); Priest in Gerablos then in Aleppo (St. Ephrem Church); Founder of the Y.C.W. in Syria and many other movements; Founder of the Secular Institute of Jesus the Worker; Sacred Syrian Catholic Archbishop of Damascus (8 September 1971). **Publ.:** Author of many books in Arabic. **Addr.:** Foyer Jésus Ouvrier-Ouartier al-Chahba, Aleppo- Syria.

SCHLINGENSIEPEN (Georg Hermann, Dr.), German diplomat. **Born** on February 8, 1928 in Bonn. **Son** of Hermann Schlingensiepen (Professor of Theology) **and** Mrs. Eva nér Michaelis. **Married** on March 22, 1957, 4 children: Irene, Karl Hermann, Georg Ferdinand, Reimar. **Educ.:** Universities of Bonn, Oxford, Göttingen, Berlin. **Dipl.:** Doctor of History, Exams for the Diplomatic Service. **Career:** Diplomat since 1957 in Moscow, Athens and other places; Ambassador in Damascus (1987-1993). **Awards:** Orders from Peru, Greece and Germany. **Sports:** Horse Riding, Table Tennis. **Hobby:** Piano. **Member:** Horse clubs in Lima and Damascus. **Prof. Addr.:** German Embassy, Damascus, Syria.

SCHUSTER (Wolfgang, Dr.), Austrian executive. **Born** on October 17, 1951 in Vienna, Austria. **Son** of Josef Schuster (Headmaster) **and** Mrs. née Gertrude Spielvogel. **Married** on April 1, 1986 to Miss Fiona Griessler, one son, Dominik (1987), one daughter, Veronika (1991). **Educ.:** University of Economics and Business Administration, Vienna, (1971-79). **Dipl.:** Ph.D in Business (Thesis on second economic development plan in Saudi Arabia); Research Scholarship, University of Riyadh (1979). **Career:** Manager, Austrian Airlines, Beirut (1981-83); Manager, Congress and Incentive Dept., Austrian Airlines, Vienna (1984-86); Manager, Austrian Airlines, Jeddah, Saudi Arabia (1987-); **Sports:** Skiing, scuba-diving. **Hobbies:** Travelling, Islamic Numismatics. **Member:** Skal Club; Chaine des Rottisseurs. **Credit Cards:** Diners, Airplus. **Prof. Addr.:** Austrian Airlines, Alamoudi Center, Medina Raod, P.O.Box 8021, Tel.: 6602356, 6655611, 6651454, Jeddah 21482, Saudi Arabia. **Priv. Addr.:** P.O.Box 3886, Jeddah 21481, Saudi Arabia.

SEBALEY (Fahad Ebaid Mohamad, al), Saudi academic. **Born** in 1945 in Renaih. **Dipl.:** Ph.D. (Islamic

History). **Career:** Instructor (1969); Director, Teachers' Preparatory Institute (1970-76); Vice-Dean, Faculty of Shari'a and Arabic Language, Abha. **Member:** Abha Literary Club; Secretary, Abha General Library Council; Southern Welfare Society. **Prof. Addr.:** Abha, Faculty of Shari'a and Arabic Language, Tel.: 2244143, Abha. **Priv. Addr.:** Tel.: 2246184, Abha, Saudi Arabia.

SEBIA (Khalaf Ahmad Ashour, al), Saudi businessman. **Born** in 1922 in Yanbu, Saudi Arabia. **Educ.:** secondary school education, Diplomas from Institute of Administration, United Nations and Institute of Administration, Egypt. **Career:** Accountant, Yanbu Municipality (1949-50); Accountant, Zakat and Taxation (1950-56); Controller, Ministry of Finance; Tax Inspector, Tax Department, Riyadh; Chief of Collection Division, Tax Department, Assistant Director later Director, Tax Department, Riyadh; Director of the Tax Department for the West Coast, Jeddah; Businessman, General trading and contracting Agencies; significant participant in social activities, Yanbu. **Former President:** Radwa Sports Club, Yanbu, now member of Club. **Publications:** many articles in local newspapers, preparing to publish a book containing these articles. **Hobbies:** reading, fishing, writing. **Prof. Addr.:** P.O.Box 6265, Tel.: 6532856, Jeddah. **Priv. Addr.:** Tel.: 6693701, Jeddah, Saudi Arabia.

SEBTI (Zine el-Abidine), Moroccan diplomat, economist. **Born** in 1935 in Fes, Morocco. **Married,** three children. **Educ.:** Economics, Christ Church College, Oxford University, UK; Diploma of Foreign Service Studies; Postgraduate Studies in Economic Development, United Nations Institute for Training and Research UNITAR, New York, USA. **Career:** Counsellor, Office of the Secretary of State for Foreign Affairs (1964-67); Minister-Counsellor, Moroccan Embassy in Madrid, Spain (1967-71); Chef de Cabinet, Ministry of Foreign Affairs, Rabat (1971-72); Minister Plenipotentiary and Director of Economic Affairs and of Co-operation, Ministry of Foreign Affairs (1971-77); Ambassador of Morocco to Belgium, Luxembourg and the EEC (1977-85); non resident Ambassador of Morocco to Ireland (1982-85); representative of Morocco at various international conferences. (since October 85) Ambassador-Director of Europeen and American Affairs, Ministry of Foreign Affairs and Cooperation, Rabat, and General Director of International Cooperation, (since 1 August) Ambassador of Morocco to Italy, Malte and Permanent Representative to FAO IFAD and WEP in Rome and non Resident Ambassador to Albania. Elected President of the Board of Directors of "Centre Islamique Culturel d'Italie". **Publ.:** "The Effects of International Trade on the Economic Progess of Underdeveloped Countries", and several other essays and papers published in professional journals and magazines. **Medals:** Order of al-Ridha, Morocco; Order of Throne, Morocco, Grand Cordon Belge et Grand Cordon du Grand Duché du Luxembourg Grand Croix de l'ordre de Malte "Promerito Melitensi", Grand Cordon de la République Italienne and Medals of Spain, Denmark, Libya. **Sport:** Tennis. **Hobbies:** Hunting, painting, photography. **Addr.:** Embassy of Morocco, Italy, Rome and Ministry of Foreign Affairs, Rabat, Morocco.

SEDRANI (Saleh Hamad Ali, al), Saudi academic. **Born** in 1946 at Haffer al-Baktin. **Dipl.:** B.Sc., Ph.D. (Biochemistry). **Career:** Employee at General Presidency of Faculties and Academic Institute (1966-70); Demonstrator, King Saud University (1974-75); Faculty member since 1979; Leader of Social Committee, Faculty of Medicine, King Saud University (1979-80); Assistant Professor, Faculty of Science, King Saud University. **Member:** Saudi Biological Society; Faculty of Science Council; attended several conferences on Calc. Tissues and Vitamin D. **Publications:** articles on biochemistry; a book under preparation. **Hobbies:** reading, research. **Prof. Addr.:** Faculty of Science, King Saud University, P.O.Box 2455, Riyadh. **Priv. Addr.:** Tel.: 4811000 Ext. 2462, Riyadh, Saudi Arabia.

SEFROUI (Abdeslam Ameur Ben Lahcen, General), Moroccan army commander, diplomat. **Born** in 1923 in Sefrou, Morocco. **Married,** three children. **Educ.:** Meknes Military Academy (1934). **Career:** Served in Morocco and Indochina; Captain (1955); Governor of Agadir Province after Independence; Staff Officer in African High Command (1956); accompanied Crown Prince to Cairo (1959); Major (1965); Commander of 11th Battalion at Casablanca City (1965-67); Colonel (1965); Commander of the Light Security Brigade (1968); Commander of Meknes Military Academy (1968); Commander of Royal Guard (1971); General (1971); Commander of the Moroccan Expeditionary Contingent in Syria (1973); Commander of the Moroccan Infantry Forces and the Royal Guard (1975-78); Ambassador of Morocco to Holland (1978-80). **Addr.:** Ministry of Foreign Affairs, Rabat, Morocco.

SEHAIMI (Mansour, A., al), Saudi oil expert. **Born** in 1942 in Makkah, Saudi Arabia. **Married,** five children. **Educ.:** University of Texas, USA. **Dipl.:** B.Sc. in Petroleum Engineering. **Career:** Petroleum Engineering, Ministry of Oil and Mineral Resources; Drilling and Production Engineer; Construction Engineer, Jeddah Oil Refinery; Shift Supervisor (1967-71); Chief Process Engineer (1971-74); Technical Services Manager (1974-76); General Manager of Production (1976-78); Assistant to the Chairman and member of the Board of Directors (1978). **Hobbies:** Table tennis, swimming. **Addr.:** Jeddah, Saudi Arabia.

SEHILI (Mahmoud), Tunisian artist painter, **Born** on July 27, 1931 in Tunis. **Married** on April 11, 1959 in Paris with Gabriele Buth, 3 children: Thouraya (1959), Lilia (1961), Raouf (1969). **Educ.:** Finer Arts School (Tunis); "Ecole des Beaux-Arts" (Paris). **Dipl.:** Diplôme Supérieur des Arts Plastiques. **Career:** 8 years in Paris: Teacher, "Institut Technologique d'Art, d'Architecture et d'Urbanisme", Tunis; Director, Art Gallery in Tunis "Irtissem", Tunis, since 1977. **Awards:** Several 1st Prizes and a Golden medal at an exposition at "Cagnes sur Mer", France; 1st Prize of the Town of Tunis in 1963. **Sports:** Fishing. **Hobbies:** Music, Playing the luth, Composition of Arabic music. **Prof. Addr.:** Sidi Bou Saïd, Tel.: 272619, Tunisia. **Priv. Addr.:** 4, Rue Victor Hugo, Tel.: 275621, Carthage, Tunisia.

SEJINI (Amin Salih), Saudi executive. **Born** in 1942, in Mecca, Saudi Arabia. **Dipl.:** Public Administration and Science Diploma. **Career:** Former Manager of Steffens und Noelle; Manager of J.V. AEG-Telefunken & Thomson Houston; Assistant Branch Manager, Kanoo, Riyadh; Exeuctive Director of the Board, Yusuf Ben Ahmed Kanoo Est. **Hobby:** reading. **Address:** Yusuf Ben Ahmed Kanoo Establishment, Airport Street, Riyadh, Saudi Arabia.

SEJINI (Hussein, Abdullah), Saudi administrator. **Born** in 1938 in Makkah, Saudi Arabia. **Son** of Abdullah Sejini. **Married**, three children. **Educ.:** University of Southern California. **Dipl.:** M.A. in Economics. **Career:** Director, Planning Department, Central Planning Organization (1964-76); Assistant Deputy Minister for Sectoral Planning, Ministry of Planning (1976-82); Deputy Minister of Planning (1982). Chairman of the Board, National Industrial Gaz Co., Board Member of the Economic Offset Committee, and member of Saudi-American, Saudi-German and Saudi-Egyptian Joint Economic Commissions, Haj Planning Committee, Higher Committee for Riyadh Development, environmental, Protection Coordination Committee, and others. **Hobbies:** Swimming, reading, tennis, and yoga. **Addr.:** P.O.Box 358 Riyadh 11182, Saudi Arabia; Tel.: 4011444, 4011333; Telex: 404660 DEPLAN SJ, Fax: 4010385.

SEJINI (Omar Abdallah), Saudi official. **Born** in 1939 in Mecca, Saudi Arabia. **Son** of Abdallah Sejini. **Married**, 3 children: 2 sons and 1 daughter. **Dipl.:** M.A. (Public Administration). **Career:** Executive Director, Islamic Development Bank and representative of Saudi Arabia at the Bank; Director General, Banks Control Department, Saudi Arabian Monetary Agency, Riyadh; Controller of Arab Banks Union; member of Board of Saudi Credit Banks, United Bank, Dammam, Bank Melli Iran, Jeddah; member of Founding Committee; International Gulf Bank, Bahrain; has greatly contributed to the execution of Saudi banking policy; has contributed in developing banking services all over Saudi Arabia; attended Arab-European seminar, Switzerland, Arab Banking Seminar, Beirut; Director, Islamic Development Bank, Jeddah. **Address:** Saudi Arabian Monetary Agency, P.O.Box 2992, Riyadh, Saudi Arabia.

SEJINI (Saud A.), Saudi physician. **Born** in 1940 in Mecca, Saudi Arabia. **Dipl.:** M.R.C. Path., D.C.P. M.B.B. Ch. **Career:** Honorary Registrar, Middlesex Hospital United Kingdom (1971-73); Senior Registrar, United Bristol Hospital, United Kingdom (1973-76); Vice Dean, Faculty of Medicine, King Abdulaziz University (1977); Associate professor, Department of Haematology, Faculty of Medicine, King Abdulaziz University; Founder, King Fahad Medical Research Center and Post-Graduate School of Medicine (1979); participated in the organization of the 3rd Saudi Medical Meeting (1978). **Publications:** Lymphocyte Response to Blood Transfusion in Man: A Comparison of Different Preparations of Blood. **Prof. Addr.:** Department of Haematology, Faculty of Medicine, King Abdulaziz University, P.O.Box: 6615, Tel.: 6896207, Jeddah. **Priv. Addr.:** Tel.: 6829085, Jeddah, Saudi Arabia.

SEKFALI (Zine Eddine), Algerian administrator. **Born** in 1938. **Married**, two children. **Educ.:** University of Algiers. **Dipl.:** LL.B.; Master of Law. **Career:** General Attorney at Annabo; Director, Ministry of Justice; Advocate General in High Court; General Director, Ministry of Internal Affairs, then General secretary; General secretary to the Prime Minister (1980-84); Deputy Minister of Tourism (1984). **Addr.:** Algiers, Algeria.

SEKLA (Kamal, Yusuf), Egyptian Canadian physician. **Born** in 1930 in Cairo. **Son** of Me. Yusuf S. Sekla (lawyer, former Inspector-General, Ministry of Finance) **and** Mrs. Marie Sekla. **Educ.:** Sainte Famille College Cairo (1935-45), Faculty of Medicine, Cairo University (1945-52), Institute of Medical Pathology and Endocrinology, Rome (1954-55). **Career:** Intern, Resident and later, Assistant-director of the Medical and Laboratory Departments at the French Hospital, Cairo; Awarded a scholarship for Foreign Medical Research; Assistant at the Institute of Medical Pathology (University of Rome); Medical Officer of the Barclay's Bank, Lycée Français and St. Joseph School, Cairo; Consultant-Physician to the Victoria Hospital, Cairo; now established in Montreal Quebec Province, Canada. **Publ.:** Author of "Oral Antidiabetics" (Médecine d'Egypte, March 1960) and several French poems. **Sports:** Tennis and golf. **Hobbies:** Literature (French, English, Italian and Arabic), History, Geography, Paleontology and Natural Sciences, painting, drawing, photography and music. **Priv. Addr.:** Montreal, Q.P., Canada.

SELMI (Saida Bin Abid), Tunisian geologist. **Born** in 1946 in Tunis. **Son** of Bin Abid. **Married**, two children. **Educ.:** University of Strasbourg, France. **Dipl.:** B.Sc., M.Sc. in Geography, Ph.D. in Geomorphology. **Career:** Head of Laboratory, Assistant; Head of Geomorphological Laboratory; Head of the Department of Geomorphology, Ministry of Agriculture. **Hobbies:** Reading, travelling. **Addr.:** 11 Rue 12 Mai 64, Cité 25 Juillet, Ariana, Tunis, Tunisia.

SENANY (Musaad Muhammad, al), Saudi former

Minister. **Born** in 1948 in Onaizah, Saudi Arabia. **Married**, 3 children. **Educ.:** King Saud University, Riyadh; University of Arizona, USA. **Educ.:** B.A. in Accounting and Business Administration (1970); M.A. in Accounting and Management (1974). **Career:** Financial Department General Organization for social Insurance, Riyadh (1974-81); Director General of Finance and Administration (1977-78), Deputy Governor (1978-83), and now Vice Chairman of the Board of Directors (since 1983); Member of the Board of Directors of Saudi Ceramic Company (1977-83); Yanbu Cement Company (1977-81) and Saudi Investment Bank (1978-81); former, Minister of Labour and Social Affairs. **Member:** Equestrian Club, Riyadh. **Hobbies:** reading, swimming. **Prof. Addr.:** Old Airport Road, P.O.Box 2963, Tel.: 4777735, Telex: 2011143 GOSI SJ, Riyadh 11461, Saudi Arabia.

SERAJ (Amin Abdallah), Saudi physician and administrator. **Born** in 1936 in Mecca, Saudi Arabia. **Educ.:** Royal college of surgeons, Edinburgh. **Dipl.:** M.D. Fellowship. **Career:** Owner of a private clinic (1961-67) and (1970-72); ENT Specialist, Jeddah Public Hospital (1961-67); Glasgow (1968-70); ENT Consultant, Jeddah Public Hospital (1970-72); Teacher and Vice-Dean, Faculty of Medicine, King Saud University (1972-74); Assistant Professor (1974-78) and Dean, Faculty of Dental Medicine (1975-81); Director General, Saudi health Care Co. (on secondment) (1982-84); Head, Department of E.N.T., College of Medicine, King Saud University (1986-87); General Director, Dallah Hospital (on secondment- organizing and commissioning a 220 beds private hospital (1987-89); Associate Professor and Consultant, Department of E.N.T., College of Medicine, King Saud University (since 1977). Member of several academic and social committees within the King Saud University; Royal College of Surgeons, U.K.; British Medical Society; University Counil and the Higher Council of King Saud University; Editorial Board, King Abdul Aziz Medical Journal; International Who's Who of Intellectuals, U.K.; Consultant to several government organizations regarding planning and administrative decisioss; attended several conferences and symposiums such as the First Medical symposium, the Fifth Saudi Medical Conference, the First Symposium of Dental Medicine. **Honour:** Honorary citizen, Houston, Texas, U.S.A. **Publ.:** Book regarding Clinical Otolaryngology, ENT diseases for Students and G.P's and several articles on E.N.T. deseases. **Hobbies:** Reading, swimming, listening to music. **Prof. Addr.:** Faculty of Medicine, Department of E.N.T. King Abdul Aziz University Hospital, P.O.Box 245, Riyadh 11411, Saudi Arabia. **Priv. Addr.:** P.O.Box 4997, Riyadh 11412, Tel.: 4545747, Riyadh, Saudi Arabia.

SFAR (Rachid), Tunisian politician. **Born** on September 11, 1933 in Mandia, Tunisia. **Educ.:** Lycée des Garçons, Sfax; Institut des Hautes Etudes, Tunis; Ecole Nationale des Impôts, Paris. **Career:** Inspector of Taxes (1960); Director General, Régie Nationale des Tabacs et Allumettes (1965); Director of Taxation, Ministry of Finance (1969); Secretary General, Ministry of Education (1971-73); Ministry of Finance (1973-77); Minister of Mines and Energy (1977-78); Minister of Defence (1978-80); Minister of Health (1980-83); Minister of National Economy (1983-86); Minister of Finance and Economy (April-July 1986); Prime Minister (1986-88); Permanent Representative of Tunisia, The European Community (1991-); Deputy to National Assembly (1979-); Member, General Committee and Politburo, Party Socialist Destourien (1979-). Socialist Destourien (1979-); **Awards:** Grand Cordon, Order of the Independence; Grand Officer, Order of the Republic. **Addr.:** 278 Ave. de Tervuren, 1150 Brussels, Belgium.

SHAAFY (Mohamad Said Munshit), Saudi university professor. **Born** in 1937 in Abha, Saudi Arabia. **Dipl.:** Ph.D. (History of Saudi Arabia). **Career:** Secretary-General of King Abdulaziz Archives Institution (Darat almalik Abdulaziz); Assistant Professor of Saudi History, Riyadh University; Chairman of Department of Information, Riyadh University since 1976. **Publications:** research papers on the history of Saudi Arabia. **Address:** P.O.Box 3312, Riyadh, Saudi Arabia.

SHAALAN (Abdel Karim Mohamad), Egyptian surgeon. **Born** in 1933 in Sharkieh, Egypt. **Son** of Mohamad Sha'alan. **Married**, four children. **Educ.:** Diploma, American Board of Surgery; Fellow, American College of Surgeons; Fellow international College of Surgeons. **Career:** Head of Surgery, Doctors Hospital, Detroit, USA (1963-82); Chief of Staff (1975-82); Surgeon at four hospitals, Michigan USA; Medical Director, Assalam International Hospital, Maadi, cairo, Egypt; member, Roy D McClure Surgical Society; Board of Directors, Assalam International Hospital, Cairo. **Member** of Gezira Sporting Club. **Addr.:** 143 Tahrir Street, dokki, Cairo, Egypt.

SHAALAN (Abdulaziz Ibn Abdul Rahman Ibn Mohamad), Saudi academic. **Born** in 1937 in Shaqra', al-Washm. **Dipl.:** Higher Degree, Faculty of Arabic Language, Riyadh. **Career:** Teacher, secondary education, Religious Institutes (1963-67); Director, Shaqra' Religious Institute (1967-70); Assistant Professor, Vice Chairman, Eloquence and Criticism Department, Faculty of Arabic Language, Imam Muhammad Ibn Saud Islamic University; member of the Board, University Council and Faculty Council; participated in some conferences and symposia, including the Directors of Religious Institutes conference, Curriculum Committee. **Publications:** two research papers on Al Soura (Image) in Pagan (pre-Islamic) Verse and Eloquence Science, Proceeds and Development; has participated in three series on Eloquence and the Holy Quran Miracle for Riyadh Broadcasting Station. **Prof. Addr.:** Faculty of Arabic Language, Imam Muhammad Ibn Saud Islamic University, Tel.: 402 3566, Riyadh. **Priv. Addr.:** Tel.: 402 4939, Riyadh, Saudi Arabia.

SHAAR (Mohamad, Sayid, al), Sudanese administrator. **Born** in 1924 in Sudan. **Son** of Sayid al-Shaar. **Married,** three children. **Educ.:** University of Khartoum, Sudan; Institute of Social Studies, The Hague, Holland. **Dipl.:** B.Sc.; Master of Public Administration. **Career:** Former Commissioner. **Decor.:** Order of the Republic, 2nd Class. **Hobbies:** reading, tennis, **Addr.:** Dweim, Sudan.

SHAASHA (Jawdat, Rouhi), Jordanian businessman. **Born** in 1918 in Ghaza, Palestine. **Son** of Rouhi Salim Shaasha. **Married,** 3 sons, 2 daughters. **Career:** Prominent Jordanian entrepreneur and businessman. chairman, Jordan Insurance Co.; Jordan Finance and Credit Corporation; Director, Housing Bank, Jordan; Jordan Petroleum Refinery Co.; Jordan Cement Factories Co.; former Chairman, Cairo-Amman Bank, Amman, Jordan. **Member:** Rotary Club, Amman, Jordan. King Hussein Club; Royal Automobile Club; Hussein Youth City Club. **Hobby:** Reading. **Addr.:** P.O.Box 420, Tel.: 23884, Telex: 1312 A/B SHASHA JO, Amman, Jordan.

SHAATH (Nabil), Palestinian politician. **Born** in 1938 in Galilee, Palestine. **Educ.:** Doctorate from the Wharton school, USA. **Career:** taught economics at American University of Beirut. Member of the Advisory Council, Fatah Central Committee; Head of Fatah Advisory Council; former Director of Palestine Liberation Organisation Planning Center. **Addr.:** Tunis, Tunisia.

SHABAN (Hickmet, Ali), Iraqi engineer and industrialist. **Born** in 1931 in Baghdad, Iraq. **Son** of Ali Shaban (Businessman) **and** Mrs. Theba Sadia. **Married** on December 21, 1959 in Baghdad to Widad M. Abdul-Hussein, three sons, one daughter: Basil, Mohammad, Zainab And Ali. **Educ.:** University of Washington, Seattle, U.S.A. **Dipl.:** B.Sc. (Mechanical engineering) (1954). **Career:** Engineer, Ministry of Development (1954-1959); Head of 5th Technical Division, Ministry of Works and Housing (1959-62); Managing Director of Al Saffar Weaving and Spinning, company privately owned; consulting engineer; Member of Board of Directors of Iraqi Federation of Industry and of Iraqi Jute Company (1963); Vice President, Iraqi Federation of Industry; Member of Board of Directors, Industrial Bank; Vice President, International Chamber of Commerce (Iraqi Branch); Managing Director, al-Saffar Company; Member of Board of Directors, Iraqi specifications and standards (1964-68); Managing Director and President, United Industry Company and consulting engineer (1969-72); Managing Director, National Engineering Company (1972-86); Managing Director and Co-Owner, Alnish Heat Exchange Manufacturing Co.; Managing Director and Co-Owner, National Electrical Industry Co. Ltd. (1987-to date). **Work:** Consulting work (390 projects); Contracting work (35 projects). **Award:** Presidential Decree for distinguished services in industry (1988). **Sport:** Tennis. **Hobbies:** Reading, travel. **Member:** Alwiyah Club, Baghdad; Who's Who Britain; Who's Who U.S.A. **Prof. Addr.:** P.O.Box 3053, 83A/1 Bustan Kubba, Tel.: 7186092, Baghdad, Iraq.

SHABOU (Omar), Tunisian journalist. **Born** in 1947 in Tunis, Tunisia. **Married. Educ.:** University of Tunis, Tunisia. **Dipl.:** Degree in Journalism. **Career:** Editor in Chief of Socialist Destour Party organ L'ACTION (1971); Executive Assistant to the Director of the Socialist Destour Party; Director of "Dialogue" Magazine. **Medals:** Officer of the Order of the Tunisian Republic. **Hobbies:** Football, chess. **Addr.:** 102 Rue du Pacha, Tunis, Tunisia.

SHADI (Ali Ahmad, al), Saudi businessman. **Born** in 1948. **Dipl.:** Commercial Studies Diploma. **Career:** Editing Manager of Riyadh Chamber of Commerce Gazette; Director of Bureau of Information and Publication, Ministry of Finance; Assistant Manager of Administration, Arab Investment Co., Riyadh; member of Dar-el-Watan Publication and Information Establishment; member of Board, United Corporation for Paper Products and Printing. **Hobbies:** reading, sport. **Address:** Dar-el-Watan Publication and Information Establishment, Riyadh, Saudi Arabia.

SHADI (Mohamad, Fuad), Egyptian administrator. **Born** in Cairo, Egypt in 1925. **Married,** two children. **Educ.:** Cairo University. **Dipl.:** LL.B., M.A. in Sociology. **Career:** Staff, Ministry of Foreign affairs (1950-70); Manager of public Relations, Hilton International (1970-80); Managing Director, Ismailiya Hotel (since 1980). **Member** of Ma'adi Club; Automobile Club. **Addr.:** 35 el-Nadi Street, Maadi, Cairo, egypt. **Priv. Addr.:** 20 Shehab Street, Apartment 20, Mohandiseen, Cairo, Egypt.

SHADI (Mohamad Ibn Ahmad, al), Saudi businessman. **Born** in 1938 in Riyadh, Saudi Arabia. **Educ.:** Received general education. **Career:** Editor-in-Chief of al-Yamamah magazine (1966-79); Chairman of the Board, Society for Culture and Arts. **Member:** al-Yamamah, Organization for Press and Publishing, al-Watan for Publishing; International Press Club, London. **Publications:** articles in local newspapers, 3 books. **Hobbies: reading,** sports. **Address:** P.O.Box 3310, Tel.: 4644659, 4772300, Riyadh, Saudi Arabia.

SHAER (Ali Hassan, al), Saudi former minister. **Born** in 1927 in Medina, Saudi Arabia. **Educ.:** learnt the Holy Qur'an at the age of ten, obtained a secondary school certificate from the Missions Preparatory School in Mecca; B.A. (Military Sciences), the Military Academy (1949); B.A. (Literature), History Department, King Saud University. **Career:** Chief Instructor, the Military School, Taif; Director, Topography Division, Military Operations Department; Commander, Medina Military School for four years; Commander, King Abdulaziz Military Academy for seven years; Military Attache, Pakistan, for four years; Ambassador to Lebanon (1975-83); **Minister of Informa-**

tion (since 1983-to Aug. 1995). **Honours:** King Abdulaziz Medal, first class, several other distinctions by Saudi Arabia, Pakistan, Jordan and Lebanon. **Address:** Riyadh, Saudi Arabia.

SHAFEI (Hussain, Mahmoud, al), Egyptian politician. **Born** on February 8, 1918 in Tanta, Egypt. **Son** of Mahmoud al-Shafeï (Senior Irrigation Official). **Married** in 1948 to Magda Gabr, 3 children: 2 sons, 1 daughter. **Educ.:** Military Academy (Cairo). **Career:** 2nd Lieutenant (1938); Palestine war (1948); Promoted Colonel, Graduate Staff College (1953); Appointed Officer in charge Cavalry Corps; Minister of War and Navy (1954); Minister of Social Affairs (1954-58); Minister of Labour and Social Affairs (1958-61); Minister of Social Affairs and Wakfs Presidency Department (1961-62); Member of Presidency Council (1962-64); Deputy Prime Minister and Minister of Wakfs (1967); then Vice-President of Egypt (Oct. 1970-April 1975). President Egyptian delegation to OAU Summit Conferences (1973-74). **Hobbies:** Riding, tennis, swimming, drawing. **Addr.:** 6 Sharai Wizaret, el-Ziraa Dokki, Giza, Egypt.

SHAFEI (Mohamad Zaki, al, Dr.), Egyptian lawyer, faculty dean. **Born** in 1922. **Educ.:** law Faculty, Cairo University; Princeton University, USA. **Dipl.:** Doctorate of Law (1942); M.A., Economics (1947); Ph.D. Political Economics (1950). **Career:** Lawyer, Professor of Commerce, Law Faculty (Cairo, University); First Dean, Faculty of Economics and Political Science, Cairo University (1960); Member, Supervising Committee for Arab Socialist Union (ASU) Elections (1968); Alternate member, ASU Central Committee; Member, ASU Economic Sub-Committee; appointed, National Council for Production and Economic Affairs (Feb. 1974); Assistant Secretary-General, Arab League; Minister of Economy and Economic Co-operation (April 1975- Feb. 1977). **Addr.:** Cairo, Egypt.

SHAFEI (Tharwat), Egyptian administrator. **Born** in 1931 in Cairo, Egypt. **Married**, one son and one daughter. **Educ.:** Cairo University. **Dipl.:** B.A. in Literature. **Career:** Several posts, including Presidency in Egyptian Television Network Channel Two; former Director General (1984). **Decor.:** Chevalier d'Ordre Nationale de Grande Merite. **Addr.:** 6 Street of el Brazil, Zamalek, Corniche el-Nile, Cairo, Egypt.

SHAFIQ (Dorai, Ahmad), Egyptian journalist. **Born** in 1919 in Egypt. **Daughter** of Ahmad Shafiq. **Married** to Dr. Noureddine Ragaï. **Educ.:** University of Paris. **Career:** Journalist, Editor of "The New Woman" (1944, Published in Separate French and English Editions), "Bentan-Nil" (Published in Arabic), "Katkout and Doria Shafiq Magazine" (Arabic), Organized Bent an-Nil Union (Feminist Movement) 1948. **Publ.:** Author of "Good Adventure", "Sultan in Bondage", "Lost Love", "Art for Art's Sake in Ancient Egypt", All in French. **Addr.:** 6, Salaheddine Street, Zamalek, Cairo, Egypt.

SHAFIQ (Mohamad, Nuri), Jordanian educationalist. **Born** in 1927 in Tafilah, Jordan. **Son** of Nuri Shafiq. **Married**, five children. **Educ.:** B.A. Cairo University, Egypt (1950); M.A. Teachers College, Columbia University, New York (1954); Teachers College, Columbia University, New York (1964). **Career:** Teacher (1950-53); Instructor, Amman Teachers College, Jordan (1954-59); Editor of "Risalat al-Mu'allim" (1956-59); Administrator, Ministry of Education (1959-61); Under Secretary, Ministry of Education (1963-67); Administrative Adviser to the Prime Ministry of Education (1963-67); Administrative Adviser to the Prime Minister (1967-68); Civil Service Commissioner and Chairman of the Board of Directors of Jordan Institute of Public Administration (1968-70); Vice Chairman of Jordan Development Board (1970-71); President of the National Planning Council (1971-73); Minister of Finance (1973); General Manager, General Construction Co. Ltd. (1973-74); Director General, Royal Scientific Society (1974-75); Management Consultant to the Prime Minister (1975-78); President and Director General, Arab Consulting Association (1976-78); Civil Service Commissioner (1978-79); Minister of Education (1978-79); Minister of Education (1979-80); Education Consultant, Arab College (1981-82); Secretary General, Council of Higher Education (1982-85); President of U.A.E. University (1985); member of the Board of Trustees of Jordan University (since 1977); founder and member of the Board of Trustees of the Arab College (since 1975); Deputy Mayor of the City of Amman (since 1980); member of the Arab Thought Forum (since 1981). **Publ.:** many articles and research papers published in Jordan and the Arab world. **Addr.:** P.O.Box. 2003, Tel.: 21033, Amman, Jordan.

SHAH (Rajnikant C.), Engineer/ Managing Director. **Born** on June 23, 1950 at Amreli, India. **Son** of Chandulal K. Shah (Business) **and** Mrs. Savita C. Shah. **Married** to Aruna R. Shah, 2 children: (son) Poorav R. (18/06/1975), (Daughter) Julie R. (27.07.1980). **Educ.:** SHRI J.N.V. Vidyalaya, Surendranagar (1966); Shri M.P. Shah Science College, Surendranagar (1967); Lukhdhirji engineering College, Morvi-Gujarat (1972). **Dipl.:** Bachelor of Engineering (1972). **Career:** 1972-74 M/S K.B. Mehta Engineers, Gujarat, Iffco Fertilizers Plant at Kalol, India (Site Engineer); 1974-75 M/S Gherzi Eastern Ltd., Bombay, Spinning Mills in U.P. State, India (Resident Engineer); 1975-77 M/S Eastern Contracting Co. Ltd, Sharjah, Civil Engineering & Construction in the U.A.E. (Planning Engineer). **Other Information:** 1977 Onwards - Managing Director of New Age Co. LLC. Dubai - Sharjah - Abu Dhabi. To look after Overall Management of the Company Engaged in Trading & Engineering Employing over 50 Employees. **Awards:** Awarded T.M. Sanghvi Gold Medal for Standing First at Final Engineering Degree at

Saurashtra University, Gujarat-India in 1972, Commemorative Medal of Honour Awarded by American Biographical Institute INC (ABI) North Carolina, USA in 1990. **Sports Practised:** Swimming. **Hobbies:** Writing, Philanthrophy, Psychology, Nature Cure, Touring American Society of Civil Engineers, ASCE, New York - USA. **Associations:** National Fire Protection Association (NEPA) Boston-USA, Institute of Engineers - India, International Parliament for Safety & Peace - Holland. **Prof. Addr.:** New Age Company LLC, P.O.Box 4396, Dubai-UAE, Tel.: 2664000. **Priv. Addr.:** B-205 on Srinath Krupa, Subhash Road, Kandivli (West) Mumbai 400 067 - India, Tel.: 807 4093.

SHAH (Sayed Tahir El-Hashemi), Advisor and author. **Born** on Nov. 16, 1966. **Education:** Bryanston School; United States International University at campuses in London, Nairobi & San Diego. **Career:** Research Director to Institute for Cultural Research, London & to The Institute for the Study of Human Knowledge, San Francisco. Headed various international research projects. Lectured on cultural systems, inter-cultural issues & on research findings (at I.C.R., I.S.H.K. etc.). Advisor to The Institute for Health Sciences, London & to Kraettli Business Consultants, Zurich. Project co-ordinator & logistician at Afghan Relief Charity at North West Frontier Province, Pakistan. Led field research in numerous countries, including Madhya Pradesh, India, Rwanda, & Kivu region, Zaire. Consultant to several international organisations in the U.S.A., Europe, & the Middle East. **Publications:** (books) Middle East Bedside Book, Journey Through Namibia, Cultural Research, Spectrum Guide to Jordan, Beyond the Devil's Teeth; Sorcerer's Apprentice; (monographs) Secret Societies of Sierra Leone, Ainu: Ancient People of Japan, Macumba: Developing Faith of Brazil, Kafiristan: Land of Light, Gonds of Central India, Moriscoes & the Demise of the Arab Empire in Spain, Private International Law: Law In Search of Law. Authored numerous articles, published in international journals, magazines & newspapers on Middle Eastern & Arab society, psychology, human thought, travel, Islamic art, etiquette & anthropology. Trail of Feathers. **Interests:** phonetics, archaeology & travel. Associations: Royal Overseas League, Royal Geographic Society; Royal African Society; Institute of Directors; Royal Society for Asian Affairs; Anglo-Peruvian Society; PEN, Royal Society for Literature; Royal Anthropological Society; Institute for cultural Research; Institute for the Study of Human Knowledge. Address: P.O.Box 2227, London NW2 3BP, U.K., Tel.: 44-20-7377-9463, E-mail: shahtahir@hotmail.com.

SHAHAT (Mahmoud, Abdul Hamid, al), Egyptian academic. **Born** in 1930 in Egypt. **Son** of Abdulhamid al-Shahat. **Married**, one daughter. **Educ.:** Cairo University and University in USA. **Dipl.:** B.Sc., M.Sc. and Ph.D. in Agricultural Economics. **Career:** Assistant Professor; Associate professor; Professor Head of Agricultural Economic Department; Vice Dean; Chairman of the Permanent Promotional Committee for Associate Professors of the Egyptian Universities; member of the Permanent Promotional Professors Committee of Egyptian Universities; **Chairman of the Permanent Promotional** Committee for Professors of the Egyptian Universities; Visiting Professor, Warsaw University, Poland (1978); External Examiner, Ife University, Nigeria (1978-79); **Visiting** Professor, Kiel University, Germany; Visiting Professor, Kassel University, Germany; Taught at Libya University; taught at Liberia University, West Africa; taught at Lemoge University, France; Member of the Agricultural Economics Society, Egypt. **Publ.:** Many research papers on agricultural reform and development in Egypt. **Hobbies:** Music, travelling, swimming, croquet. **Member** of the Political economy, Statistics and Legislation Society member of the Heliopolis Sporting Club. **Prof. Addr.:** Faculty of Agriculture, Minya University, Egypt. **Priv. Addr.:** 14 Alseil Street, roxy, Heliopolis, Egypt.

SHAHBANDAR (Mustafa), Syrian executive. **Born** in 1938 in Damascus, Syria. **Son** of Basheer Shahbandar. **Married** in 1964, 1 son, 3 daughters. **Dipl.:** B.A. Commerce; Banking High Diploma; National Accounts Diploma. **Career:** Misr Bank, Syria (1959); Head of Accounts, Misr Bank (1961-67); Popular Credit Bank, Syria (1967-80); Assistant Manager, Popular Credit Bank, Syria (1967-70); Manager, Popular Credit Bank, Syria (1970-80); Manager, Accounts and Foreign Relations Department, Syrian Jordanian Bank, Amman, Jordan (1980-). **Member:** American Economic Association. **Addr.:** King Hussein Street, al-Abdali P.O.Box. 926636, Tel.: 61138, Telex: 2102 A/B SYJOBK JO, Amman, Jordan.

SHAHBANDAR (Salah Abdulrahman), Egyptian academic, surgeon. **Born** in 1924, in Egypt. **Son** of Abdulrahman Shahbandar. **Married**, two children. **Educ.:** Cairo University; Memorial Sloan-Kettering Institute, NY. **Dipl.:** M.B., B.Ch.; M.D.; Cancer Surgery, Memorial Sloan-Kettering Inst. **Career:** Surgery Resident, Cairo University, Egypt; Demonstrator, Cairo University; Lecturer, Assistant Professor; Professor of Surgery, Cairo University; Vice Dean, National Cancer Institute, Egypt; Dean, National Cancer Institute; member of the Board of the Massachusetts Institute of Technology, Cairo University Programme; researcher for National Cancer Institute at the South West Oncology Group, USA. **Decor.:** Order of the Republic, Egypt. **Addr.:** 73 Abdel Aziz Second Street, al-Manial, Egypt.

SHAHID (Leila), Palestinian Politician. **Career:** PLO Representative to Ireland; PLO Representative to Holland and Denmark (1991-93); and PLO Director of Information bureau in LA HAYE (1991-93); and since August 24, 1993 PLO General Representative to France. **Addr.:** Délégation Générale de Palestine, Paris, France.

SHAHIDI (Ibrahim, al-Ouazzani, al), Moroccan producer. **Born** in 1929 in Fes, Morocco. **Son** of al-Ouazzani al-Shahidi. **Married**, four children. **Educ.:** Moroccan Institute of Higher Studies; Paris Drama School; Sarah Bernhardt Theatre; Simon Institute of Drama; National Conservatoire of Dramatic Art (1949-55). **Career:** Teacher of Arabic (1948-49); Head of Amateur Theatrical Department, Youth and Sports (1958); Producer on Moroccan Radio (1959-62); Head of Drama Department, Moroccan Radio (1963-72); Head of Programmes and Production Department, Radio and Television (since 1972). **Publ.:** Articles and studies on theatre in various newspapers and magazines. **Script-Writer:** Films: Amina. Kadâou Allah (Juridiction divine). Houbboune wa Wafâe (Amour et fidélité). **Medal:** Wissam al-Ridha, 1st Class (1972). **Member:** President of Moroccan Authors' Association. **Hobbies:** Riding and chess. **Sport:** Swimming. **Prof. Addr.:** 12 Ave. de France, Rabat-Aghdal, Tel.: 62009, Morocco. **Priv. Addr.:** Tel.: 72938.

SHAHIN (Farouk Mohammad), Egyptian, academic. **Born** on January 1st, 1941 in Cairo. **Married**, 2 daughters. **Educ.:** Higher Institute of Public Health, Alexandria University; cairo University, Egypt; Mondon School of Hygienne and Tropical Medicine, UK; **Dipl.:** diploma of Nutrition (1967); diploma of International Medicine (1968); M.Sc. in Nutrition (1970) and Ph.D. in Nutrition (1973). **Career:** Founder of the Egyptian Physiological Association and of the Egyptian Nutrition Association; Deputy Dean of Nutrition Institute. **Member:** Cairo shooting Club; Gezira Sporting Club. **Prof. Addr.:** Nutrition Institute, 16A Kasr el-Aini Street, Tel.: 847476, Cairo, Egypt. **Priv. Addr.:** 10, Nile Street; Tel.: 725803, Giza Egypt.

SHAHIN (Ibrahim, Majid), Kuwaiti architect. **Born** in Kuwait in 1948. **Educ.:** Washington State University; University of Pennsylvania; Technical University in Prague. **Dipl.:** B.A., M.A., Ph.D. all in architecture. **Career:** member of the Board, Kuwait National Housing Authority; Head of Urban Design Section, Kuwait Municipality, Assistant Director, National Housing Authority, Director General (since 1976); Secretary of the Supreme Council of Housing; member and Vice Chairman of the Credit & Loan Bank; Minister of State for Municipal Affairs (April 1991- Oct. 1992). **Hobbies:** Oil Painting, tennis, antiques books. **Addr.:** P.O.B. 23385, Safat, Kuwait.

SHAHIN (Sulaiman, Majid), Kuwaiti diplomat. **Born** in 1937 in Kuwait. **Son** of Majid Shahin. **Married. Educ.:** Cairo University, Egypt. **Career:** Ministry of Foreign Affairs; member of the Kuwaiti delegation to the UN, New York; Head of Department, Office of the Under Secretary, Ministry of Foreign Affairs; Ambassador to Bahrain (1971-73); Ambassador to the United Arab Emirates (1973-75); Ambassador to Egypt (1975). **Addr.:** c/o Ministry of Foreign affairs, P.O.Box 3, Sour Street, Kuwait.

SHAIBANI (Mohamad, Bin Abdul Rahman, al), Saudi official. **Born** in 1920 in Medina, Saudi Arabia. **Career:** Ministry of Finance in Dammam; Head of the Office of the Governor of the Eastern province; Ministry of Information in Jeddah; Deputy Minister of Information, Broadcasting and Television. **Addr.:** Riyadh, Saudi Arabia.

SHAIHLY (Abdul Kareem, al), Iraqi official. **Born** on July 6, 1937 in Baghdad (Iraq). **Educ.:** New York Institute of Technology (1973); University of Baghdad (1974). **Dipl.:** B.Sc., M.D. **Career:** Arab League Information Officer, Cairo (Egypt, 1960-63); Ambassador to Lebanon (1963-68); Iraqi delegate to Arab League Council, Cairo (1967-71); Appointed member of the Iraqi Revolutionary Command Council (1968-72); Led Iraqi delegation to UN General Assemly (1968-71); Minister of Foreign Affairs (1968-72); Iraqi delegate to UN General Assembly, New York (1972-74); former Iraqi Ambassador and Permanent Representative of Iraq, New York (1975). **Prof. Addr.:** Ministry of Foreign Affairs, Baghdad, Iraq.

SHAIKH (Abdulaziz A. al), Saudi academic. **Born** in 1943 in Riyadh, Saudi Arabia. **Dipl.:** 1965 Bachelor of Arts University or Riyadh, 1970 Master of Arts Michigan State University, 1977 Ph.D. University of Wisconsin Madison, Wisconsin. **Career:** 1966-1967 Graduate Assistant, Geography Department, Univ. of Riyadh, 1979-1980 Director of the College of Arts Research Center, 1980-1983 Editor, Risalt Al Jamiah News paper, 1980-1983 Chairman, Masscomunication Department, 1982-1988 Dean, College of Arts, King Saud University, 1998-Present, Chairman of the Geography Department, King Saud Univ. 1997-Present, Chairman of the Board, saudi Geographical Society, 1995-Present, Chairman of the Riyadh Atlas Committee, 1990-Present, Chairman of the Riyadh District Atlas Committee, 1986-1987, Member of the Advisory Board, Journal of Arabic Studies, Kuwait, 1980-1981, Member of the Board, Journal of Humanities, Kuwait 1995-1997, Member of the Editorial Board, King Saud Univ. Jo., Arts, attended several conference within the Arab World, U.S.A and Australia. **Publications:** several articles in Arabic and English, two books. **Hobbies:** travel, reading. **Address:** Geog.Dep., College of Arts, King Saud Univ., P.O.Box 2456, Riyadh 11451, Tel: 4675365 (Office) and 4703547 (Home), Riyadh, Saudi Arabia, E-mail: aashaikh@ksu.edu.sa.

SHAIKH (Hassan, Ali, al), United Arab Emirates official. **Born** in 1940 in Ras al-Khaimeh, UAE. **Son** of Ali al-Shaikh. **Married**, seven children. **Career:** Deputy Director of Labour, United Arab Emirates Ministry of Labour; Head of Visa Section, Ministry of Labour and Social Affairs. **Member** of Abu Dhabi Club. **Addr.:** Abu Dhabi - United Arab Emirates.

SHAIKHLY (Abdul Qadir Jassim, al), Iraqi academic, veterinary scientist. **Born** in 1940 in Baghdad, Iraq. **Son** of

Jassim al-Shaikhly. **Married** four children, three sons and a girl. **Educ.:** BVMS, College of Veterinary Medicine, University of Baghdad (1965); Ph.D., University of Bristol, UK (1972). **Career:** Veterinary Inspector, Veterinary Services of the Iraqi Army (1965-67); Instructor in Veterinary Anatomy, University of Baghdad (1964-68); Lecturer in Anatomy, College of Veterinary Medicine, University of Baghdad (1972-77); Assistant Professor of Anatomy; Professor of Veterinary Anatomy; Head of the Department of Veterinary Anatomy and Histology. **Member:** The Iraqi Veterinary Medical Society, the World Association of Veterinary Anatomists. **Prof. Addr.:** College of Veterinary Medicine, al-Ameria, Baghdad, Iraq. **Priv. Addr.:** al-Ameria, House No. 28/41/630 Baghdad, Iraq.

SHAIKHLY (Salah, al), Iraqi economist, UN official. **Born** in 1939, in Baghdad, Iraq. **Married:** two children, **Educ.:** University of Manchester. **Dipl.:** B.Sc., M.Sc., Ph.D. in Economics and Resource Forecasting. **Career:** Senior Research Officer, London School of Economics (1966-67); Senior Lecturer, Baghdad University and Adviser to the Planning Board for Social and Educational Planning (1967-68); Dean of the College of Business Administration, Baghdad University (1968-69); member of the Board of Directors, Management Development Center, Baghdad (1968-71); Chairman of Iraq National Computer Committee; Member of the Board of Directors, Central Bank of Iraq, acting Director, Management Development Center; President, Central Statistics Org., Baghdad (1968-76); Acting Governor, Central Bank of Iraq (1976); President and Chairman of the Board of Directors, Iraqi Fund for External Development; Assistant Administrator and Regional Director for Arab States, UN Development Program, New York (1978-84;; Director NEIO Research Center, Oxford (1984-). **Publ.:** "Manpower Planning: A Five Year Forecast". **Hobbies:** tennis, photography, gardening. **Addr.:** NEIO Research Center, 20 St. John St., Oxford, UK.

SHAIR (Jamal, Abdul, al), Jordanian physician. **Born** in 1928 in Salt, Jordan. **Son** of Abdul al-Shair. **Married,** four children. **Educ.:** American University of Beirut; Dublin University, Ireland. **Dipl.:** B.A., M.D. Fellow of the Royal College of Surgeons. **Career:** Assistant Surgeon (1957-58); gynaecologist and obstetrician, Amman (since 1960); member of the National Consultative Council of Jordan (since 1978); Minister of Municipalities and Environment (1979-80); member of the board of the Ahli Hospital. **Publ.:** numerous articles, in journals and magazines in Jordan. **Hobbies:** Political Studies. **Addr.:** Ahli Hospital, P.O.Box 1596, Amman, Jordan.

SHAIR (Wahib, Abdo), Jordanian businessman, accountant. **Born** in 1939 in Salt, Jordan. **Married** in 1965, one son. **Educ.:** B.Sc. in Economics, University of London (1960); Fellow of the Institute of Chartered Accountants. **Career:** Lecturer at the American University of Beirut (1964-66); Senior Partner of Shair and Co. (since 1965). **Member:** of the Board of Trustees of the Amman Baccalaureate School since 1987, Founder President of the Jordanian Association of Certified Public Accountants (1988-90) (JACPA); Member of the Royal Commission for drafting the National Charter, 1990. Managing Director of the Amman Financial Market (The Stock Exchange) (1996-97); Chairman and Managing Director, Jordan Gulf Insurance Co. (1997- till now). **Address:** P.O.Box 1911 Postal Code 11118, Tel.: 5620001, 4612334, Amman, Jordan.

SHAKAA (Riyadh, al), Jordanian lawyer and politician. **Born** in 1941 in Nablus, Jordan. **Educ.:** University of Cairo. **Dipl.:** B.A. **Career:** Lawyer and member Jordanian Bar Association; member Lower House of Parliament for Nablus (1985); Minister of Justice (1985-88). **Addr.:** Amman, Jordan.

SHAKAR (Karim, Ebrahim, al), Bahraini diplomat. **Born** on 23 December 1945 in Bahrain. **Son** of Ebrahim al-Shakar. **Married,** three daughters. **Educ.:** Primary and Secondary in Bahrain Schools; Delhi University (1970). **Dipl.:** B.A. (Political Science). **Career:** Attache, Ministry of Foreign Affairs, State of Bahrain (1970); Training at the Second Diplomatic Course of the Ministry of Foreign Affairs of Kuwait (Jan-March 1971); Third Secretary, Ministry of Foreign Affairs (August 1971); Second Secretary (June 1972; First Secretary (August (1974); Senior First Secretary (January 1978); Counsellor (October 1981); Member of the Permanent Mission of the State of Bahrain to the United Nations at Headquarters (1972-76); Chief of the Section of Foreign Affairs and International Organization, Ministry of Foreign Affairs (Jan. 1977- Aug. 1982); Member of Bahrain Delegation of the General Assembly (27, 28, 29, 30, 33, 34, 35 and 36th Sessions); Member of Bahrain Delegation to the General Assembly Sixth and Seventh special Sessions and the Ninth special Emergency Session; Member of Bahrain Delegation at several Sessions of ECOSOC, UNDP and UNCTAD; Member of Bahrain Delegation at several Sessions of UN Human Rights Commission; Member of Bahrain Delegation to the third U.N. Conference of the law of the Sea, 2nd, 4th and 5th Sessions; Participated in several Meetings of the General Committee of Euro-Arab Dialogue; Participated at several Ministerial Conferences of Arab League, Islamic Conference Organization and Non-Aligned &Third World Countries (Group 77); Headed Bahrain Delegation to the Sixth United Nations Conferences on Trade & Development, Belgrade (1983), and Seventh Session of UNCTAD, Geneva (1987); Headed Bahrain Delegation to the Second Conferences to Combat Racism and Racial Discrimination (August 1983); Participated in Several Sessions, Meetings and conferences of the U.N. Specialized Agencies and Other International Organizations in Geneva; (ILO-WHO-ITC-ICRC-WIPO-GATT etc..); participated in several Sessions, Meetings and Confetences of the United Nations and other International Organizations and Specialized Agencies in Vienna; Represented Bahrain at ILO Governing Body (1982-84); Ambassador Extraordinary and Plenipotentiary, Permanent Representative of Bahrain to the U.N. Office in Geneva and other International Organizations in Switzertland (since September 1982 until 31 July 1987); Consul General of Bahrain to Switzerland (since October 1982 until 31 July 1987); Ambassador Extraordinary and Plenipotentiary (non-resisent to the Federal Republic of Germany (since 4 May 1984 until 31 July 1987); Ambassador Permanent Representative of the State of Bahrain to the United Nations Office and UNICO, Vienna, Austria (since 21 May 1984 until 31 July 1987). (non-resident); Ambassador Extraordinaire and Plenipotentiary (non-resident) to Austria (since 14 June until 31 July 1987); Chairman of the Special Committee on Preferences of UNCTAD, 14th Session held on 26 May 1986); Ambassador, Permanent Representative to UNIDO (as Specialized Agency) (since 8 July 1986 until 31 July 1987; Permanent Representative of the State of Bahrain to the United Nations (August 1987-1988); presently Ambassador to U.K. **Prof. Addr.:** Embassy of Bahrain, 98 Gloucester Road, London SW74AU, United Kingdom.

SHAKER (Abdul Magid), Tunisian diplomat. **Born** Sfax, Tunisia. **Married**, three children. **Career:** President of the General Union of Tunisian Students in France; Lawyer; Councel for the defence of Algerian Leader, Mohamad Ben Bella; Administrative Director of the Neo Destour Political Bureau; Secretary of State for Agriculture (1962); Secretary of State for Information; Ambassador to Algeria (1966-70); Ambassador to Yugoslavia (1970-72); Ambassador to Sweden, Norway, Finland and Iceland (1973); Ambassador to Spain (1982). **Addr.:** Ministry of Foreign Affairs, Tunis, Tunisia.

SHAKER (Amir, Mustafa), Egyptian businessman, politician. **Born** in 1923 in Cairo, Egypt. **Son** of Mustafa Shaker. **Married**, two daughters. **Educ.:** Staff College; London University. **Dipl.:** M.Sc. in Engineering. **Career:** Army Signal Corps (1942-52); Office Manager to President Nasser, Revolutionary Command Council (1952-61); Editor in Chief "al-Gumhuria" newspaper. "al-Akhbar" newspaper (1956); Ambassador to Venezuela; Ambassador to Belgium and Luxembourg (1963-66); Minister of Tourism (1967-68). **Publ.:** "The Truth about Communism", "This is Zionism", "Social Integrity", "Turkey and the Arab World", "The British Empire in the Middle Way". **Medals:** Egyptian Order of the Republic (First Class); Order of Lebanon; Order of King Leopold, Belgium; Egyptian Military Star. **Member:** Gezira Sporting Club, Automobile Club, Cairo Shooting Club. **Hobbies:** tennis, swimming, reading, travel. **Addr.:** 6 Ibn el-Mabih Street, Zamalek, Cairo, Egypt.

SHAKER (Azza Fuad, Mrs.), Saudi broadcaster. **Born** in 1941 in Mecca, Saudi Arabia. **Dipl.:** Diploma of Education, Rome University. **Career:** Educator and radio announcer; Director of a school, General Directorate of Girls' Education; Inspector of women's social institutions, Ministry of Labour and Social Affairs; the first female voice to broadcast from Saudi Arabian Radio; writes and produces women's radio programmes as well as cultural and religious programmes; owner, Indo-Arab Air Service; member of the Board of Nahada Women's Welfare Society, Riyadh; edits the first monthly women's bulletin in Saudi Arabia, published by this Society. **Publications:** Ashri'atul layl, (Sails of the Night), a collection of poems. **Address:** P.O.Box 9259, Tel.: 6828854 (Home), Jeddah, Saudi Arabia.

SHAKER (Farid Amin Mohamad), Saudi Academic. **Born** in 1943 in Jeddah, Saudi Arabia. **Dipl.:** B.A. (Architecture), M.A. (Urban Design). **Career:** Lecturer in Architecture, King Saud University; G.T.A. in Architecture Ohio State University, US; Has a consultant firm for practicing architecture, planning, urban design and construction supervision; ex-member of supreme Hajj Planning and Co-ordination Committee; architectural consultant to King Saud University, Saudi Real Estate Company, Saudi Development Fund, Government of Dubai and the United Arab Emirates. **Publication:** co-author of Architectural Patterns in the Central Region of Saudi Arabia. **Hobbies:** reading, travel. **Address:** P.O.Box 4627, Tel.: 4647147, Riyadh, Saudi Arabia.

SHAKER (Fatin Amin, Mrs.), Saudi former editor-in-chief "Sayyidati' Magazine". **Born** on 3 September 1941. **Dipl.:** Ph.D. (Sociology). **Career:** Assistant Professor of Sociology, King Abdulaziz University; Supervisor of Women's Activities, Community Development Programme, Jeddah; prepared and introduced the first women's radio programme in Saudi Arabia (1961-65); Assistant Professor of Sociology, St. Joseph's College, U.S.A. (1970-71); former Editor-in-Chief, "Sayyidati' Magazine". **Member:** American Sociological Association, U.S.A., Faisaliyah Women's Association, Jeddah; attended conference on Education for Mankind, Chicago, U.S.A., Training Workshop for Social Workers, Morocco; was active during the 1960s in various social programmes. **Publications:** The Status of Women in Islam and their Changing Role in Saudi Arabia (M.A. thesis); Modernization of the Developing Nations (Ph.D. dissertation). **Address:** c/o Mr. Amin Shaker, P.O.Box 675, Jeddah, Saudi Arabia.

SHAKER (Field Marshal Sharif Zaid Bin), Jordanian army commander and former Prime Minister. **Born** in 1934 in Amman, Jordan; **Son** of Amir Shaker who came to Jordan with HM late King Abdullah. **Married**, 2 children. **Educ.:** Victoria College, alexandria, Egypt; Sandhurst Military academy, United Kingdom; Long Armour Course in USA; Staff College in Leavenworth, USA.

Career: Companion of HM King Hussain (1955-57); Assistant Military Attaché, Embassy of Jordan to UK (1957-58); Commander, 1st Infantry Regiment (1963), Lieutenant Colonel, Commander of Armoured Brigade (1964); Commander of Royal Armoured Corps; Brigadier Commander of 3rd Armoured Division; Major General (1970); Assistant Chief of Staff for Operations (1970); Chief of Staff (1972), Lieutenant General (1974); Commander in Chief, Jordan Armed Forces (1976-89); Prime Minister and Miniter of Defence (April 1989- Dec.89); Chief of the Royal Court (Dec. 1989- Nov. 1991); Prime Minister and Minister of Defence (Nov. 1991- May 1992); Chief of the Royal Court (June 1992-Jan.1995); Prime Minister and Minister of Defence (Jan.1995-Feb.1996). **Decor.:** Order of the Star of Jordan (1st Class); numerous decorations from Arab and other countries. **Medal:** Renaissance Medal (1st Class). **Addr.:** Amman, Jordan.

SHAKER (Ghassan, I., H.E. Sheikh), Saudi Arabian National, Personal Advisor to His Majesty the Sultan of Oman, Businessman, Banker, Industrialist and Diplomat. **Born** on June 20, 1937 in Jeddah, Saudi Arabia. **Divorced**, five children: Three sons and two daughters. **Educ.:** Victoria College, Alexandria, Egypt (1944-56); St. John's College, Cambridge University (1956-59). **Languages:** Arabic, English, Turkish, (French). **Career (International):** Founder, Director and Shareholder: Banorient, Geneva, Switzerland (Banking); Founder, Director and Shareholder: Banorabe Holding S.A., Luxembourg (Banking); Founder, Director and Shareholder: Holding du Liban et d'Outre Mer S.A., Luxembourg (Banking); Founder, Director and Shareholder: Banorabe S.A., Paris, London, Dubai, Sharjah, Oman (Banking); Director and Shareholder: Banque du Liban et d'Outre Mer, S.A.L., Lebanon (Banking); Founder, Director and Shareholder: Arab Eastern Insurance Co., Bahrain (Insurance & Brokerage); Founder, Director and Shareholder: Ankara Enternasyonal Otelcilik A.S., Turkey (Ankara Hilton Hotel); Founder, Director and Shareholder: Izmir Enternasyonal Otelcilik A.S., Turkey (Izmir Hilton Hotel); Founder, Director ad Shareholder: Mersin Enternasyonal Otelcilik A.S., Turkey (Mersin Hilton Hotel); Director and Shareholder: Transmediterranean, S.A.L., Lebanon, Jordan, U.A.E., (Consumer Products Representation and Distribution); Founder, Director and Shareholder: Izmir Hilton Golf and Country Club, Turkey (Golf Club and Country Development); Founder, Director and Shareholder: Gulf Conversion Co. Ltd., Ajman, U.A.E. (Tobacco Products Manufacturing). **Career (Saudi Arabia):** Chairman and Shareholder: Ibrahim Shaker Company, Saudi Arabia (Electrical Appliances Representation and Distribution); Chairman and Shareholder: Saudi Trading and Distribution Company, Saudi Arabia (Cigarettes Representation and Distribution); Chairman and Shareholder: Saudi Specialist Construction Company, Saudi Arabia (Electrical and Mechanical Contracting); Chairman and Shareholder: Hussein Aoueini and Company, Saudi Arabia (Insurance and Brokerages Agencies); Chairman and Shareholder: Saudi Trading and Distribution establishment, Saudi Arabia (Consumer Products Distribution, Storage and Warehousing); Founder, Director and Shareholder: A.S.E.A. Brown Boveri, Saudi Arabia; Founder, Director and Shareholder: Arabian Electrical Industries Ltd., Saudi Arabia. **Awards:** Grand Officier de la Légion d'Honneur-France; Cavalieri di Gran Croce-Italy; Grand Order of the Republic-Egypt; Grand Order of the Renaissance-Jordan; Grand Order of the Sultanate-Oman; Grand Order of Yak Homayon-Iran; Grand Order of the Star-Jordan; Grand Order of Renaissance-Oman; Grand Order of Civil Merit-Spain; Grand Order of the Republic-Tunis. **Member** of the Board of Regents-Georgetown University, Washington, D.C.; Special Advisor and Honorary Ambassador-UNESCO, Paris. **Addr.:** P.O.Box 156, Riyadh, Saudi Arabia, Tel.: 4020520, and P.O.Box 50, Jeddah, Saudi Arabia, Tel.: 6435011, and Flat 11, 17 Grosvenor Square, London WIX 9LD, England.

SHAKER MAHMOUD (Saadoun), Iraqi politician. **Born** in 1939 in Baghdad, Iraq. **Educ.:** Graduated College of Law and Politics, Baghdad University (1975). **Career:** Director-General of Intelligence (1972); Member, Iraqi Baath Party Regional Command (10 January 1977); Minister of State without Portfolio (23 January 1977- September 1977) Minister of Interior (1980-87); Member of the Revolutionary Command Council (1977-90). **Addr.:** Baghdad, Iraq.

SHAKHASHIR (Radi, Shukri), Palestinian pharmaceutical chemist. **Born** in 1922 in Jerusalem. **Son** of Shukri Shakhashir. **Married** in 1945, six children. **Educ.:** American University of Beirut. **Career:** Pharmacy owner and wholesale drugstore (1960); deputy chairman of Arab Pharmaceutical manufacturing company (1964). **Hobby:** Reading. **Member:** A.U.B. Alumni club, Amman. **Addr.:** Amman, Jordan.

SHALHOOB (Ghazi Saleh Bin), Saudi businessman. **Born** in 1941 in Jeddah, Saudi Arabia. **Dipl.:** Diploma of Commerce. **Career:** Former officer, Saudia-Saudi Arabian Airlines; member of Chamber of Commerce, Jeddah; Proprietor and Manager, Shalhoob Aluminium Factory. **Hobbies:** reading, football. **Address:** Khalid ben al-Walid Street, Sharafia, P.O.Box 5303, Jeddah, Saudi Arabia.

SHALI (Khusruw, Ghani), Iraqi academic. **Born** in 1938 in Sulaimaniya, Iraq. **Son** of Ghani Shali. **Married**, two chlidren. **Educ.:** University of Baghdad; University of Edinburg. **Dipl.:** B.Sc.; M.Sc.; Ph.D. in Agriculture. **Career:** Dean of Students, University of Sulaimaniya (1974-76); Head of Soil Department, College of Agriculture, University of Sulaimaniya (1976-77); then General Registrar; Dean of College of Agriculture then assistant Professor and President of the University (1976-82). **Member** of the British society of Soil Science, of the International Society of Soil Science. **Publ.:** Articles in the University Journal ZANCO. **Hobby:** travel. **Addr.:** Baghdad, Iraq.

SHALLAH (Rateb, Dr.), Syrian businessman. **Born** in 1932. **Son** of Badreddin Shallah (businessman) **and** Mrs., née Isaaf Masri. **Married** in 1961 to Miss Salma Attar, four children. **Educ.:** Bootham School, York, UK, Hull University, Hull, UK; the University of Oxford, UK; University of California, Berkeley. **Dipl.:** B.A., MBA, Ph.D. **Career:** President and Manager of B.C. Challah Corp. (since 1962); Chairman and Manager of R. Shallah, Beirut (since 1962); Lecturer at Damascus University (1958-68); Lecturer at the American University of Beirut (1965-67); Chairman of Syrian Chambers of Commerce since 1992; CHAIRMAN of Damascus Chamber of Commerce since 1992. Works mainly in family establishment which is a wide ranging holding company. **Member** of Cosmos and the Hermits. **Medal:** Gold Medal From Czechoslovakia (1983). **Sports:** Lawn tennis and squash. **Credit Card:** American Express. **Prof. Addr.:** P.O.B. 150, Tel.: 4414005-4414000, 3718005-3710005, Damascus, Syria.

SHALLAL (Ahmed, Shakir), Iraqi diplomat. **Born** in Baghdad in 1926. **Son** of Shakir Shallal. **Married:** four children. **Educ.:** Fuad University, Cairo; Cairo University. **Dipl.:** M.A., Ph.D. **Career:** Professor, Baghdad Universiy (1950-58, 1961-63); Cultural Attaché, Embassy of Iraq. Rabat, Morocco (1958-61); Under Secretary, Ministry of Information, Baghdad, Iraq (1963-66); Director with the title of Ambassador, Arab League Information Center, Washington DC. Now retired. **Publ.:** "Alkhayyam"; "Asroh Wa Robaiyyatoh"; "Aqlam" magazine. Members of al-Mansour Club, Union of Men of Letters. **Addr.:** 6220 Lakeview Drive, Falls Church, VA 22041, USA.

SHAMAA (Abdel Rahman, Dr.), Egyptian diplomat. **Born** on April 21, 1933 in Mahmoudia-Behaira, Egypt. **Son** of Abdel Lateef Shamaa **and** Mrs. Dawlat Shinhab. **Married** to Aida Megahed in April 1963 in Cairo, 3 children: Khaled, Hala, Amal. **Educ.:** Abbasia secondary school, Alexandria (1952); Faculty of Law, Alexandria University (1956); Rome University; Cairo University. **Dipl.:** Diploma in Public Law, Cairo University (1956); Diploma in Administration, (1960); Doctorate in Philosophy of Law from Rome University (1969). **Career:** Third secretary, Ministry of Foreign Affairs, Embassies of Egypt in: Rome, Damascus, Kinshasa, Brazzaville, Brussels; former Ambassador of Egypt in Republic of Yemen. **Other Information:** one of the most wellknown personalities in Egypt since 1988. **Awards:** Cavalieri-Italy (1970); L'Ordre de la Couronne de Grand Officier, Belgium (1989). **Sports:** Swimming. **Hobby:** Arts. **Member:** Zamalek Club, Cairo. **Prof. and Priv. Addr.:** 12 Midan el Misaha, Dokki, Cairo, Egypt. Tele.: 719623.

SHAMAIMARI (Muhammad al-Salah al-Hammad, al, Major-Gen.), Saudi army officer. **Born** in 1920. **Educ.:** Military School, Taïf. **Career:** Commissioned (1943); former Commander of the 11th Brigade in Jordan; Deputy Chief of Staff (1965-71); Chief of Staff (1971); First Chief of General Staff (1973-1996). **Addr.:** Ministry of Defence, Airport Road, Riyadh, Saudi Arabia.

SHAMI (Abdul Hamid Mohamad Yahya, al), Saudi civil servant. **Born** in 1948 in Mecca. **Dipl.:** B.A. (History). **Career:** Director of Telecommunication Centre, Mecca; Supervisor, Jeddah Postal Institute; attended Fourth Postal Conference (Jeddah 1975), Constituent Council Arab Higher Postal Institute Council (Cairo 1975); now Director of Administrative Communication Centre, Western Region Postal Administration. **Prof. Addr.:** Western Region Postal Administration, Jeddah, Saudi Arabia.

SHAMI (Ahmad, al), Yemeni diplomat. **Born** in Yemen. **Career:** Royalist Foreign Minister (1964-70); member of Republican Council (1970-71); Ambassador to UK (1971-73); Ambassador to France (1973-75). **Addr.:** c/o Ministry of Foreign Affairs; Sanaa, Republic of Yemen.

SHAMI (Faruq Yahya), Saudi businessman. **Born** in 1941 in Jeddah, Saudi Arabia. **Dipl.:** M.A. (Marketing Psychology). **Career:** Administrative Secretary, Saudi Embassy, Vienna, Austria (1968-69); representative of Swiss Watch Factories for Saudi Arabia and Gulf States (1970-75); General Manager, International Markets Agency. **Member:** International Centre for Watch and Jewellery Factories, Lausanne; member/ representative, Jewellery Organization, West Germany; member of Alexander Marketing Institute, U.S.A.; member of Board, Louis Roselle Co., Candino Co.; attended Universal Postal Union Conference, Vienna, 1964, International Conference, Vienna, 1964, International Conference on Watch Trade, Montreaux, Switzerland. **Publication:** Watch Trade in Saudi Arabia and the Arab Gulf, a book published under the auspices of the Union of Swiss Watch Factories. **Hobbies:** tennis, cricket, swimming, football. **Address:** Yahyashami Building, King Abdulaziz Street, Bab Sharif, Tel.: 6429960 (Office) and 6431231 (Home), Jeddah, Saudi Arabia.

SHAMI (Hassan), Moroccan engineer **Born** in Fès, Morocco in 1938. **Educ.:** Engineering, Ecole Nationale des Ponts et Chaussées, Paris. **Career:** Director of Public Works in Meknes., Director of the Development of Casablanca Port; Director of the Port of Casablanca; Director of Hydraulics; Minister of Public Works and Communications; Director General of the Office de Commercialisation et d'Exportation (1971); Chairman of Societe Marocaine de Navigation Atlas. **Addr.:** 81 Avenue Houmane El Fetouaki, Casablanca, Morocco.

SHAMIKH (Mohamad A., al), Saudi academic. **Born** in 1933 at Onaizah. **Dipl.:** Ph.D. **Career:** Professor, **Arabic** Language Department, King Saud University; Former

employee at the Directorate of Secondary Education, **Ministry** of Education, Riyadh; member, King Faisal Prize Committee for Arabic Literature; has attended several international conferences; member, the Arabic Language Sciences Committee, Ministry of Education. **Publications:** al-Ta'lim Fi Makkah Wa al-Medina), al-Nathr al-Adabi Fi al-Mamlakah al-Arabia al-Saudia, (Prose in the Kingdom of Saudi Arabia), Nasha't al-Sahafa Fi al-Mamlakah al-Arabia al-Saudia, (Development of the Press in the Kingdom of Saudi Arabia), The Quarter Writer (in English). **Prof. Addr.:** P.O.Box 2013, Riyadh. **Priv. Addr.:** Tel.: 4789140, Riyadh, Saudi Arabia.

SHAMIYA (Shafick), Egyptian film producer. **Born** on 27 September 1934 in Cairo (Egypt). **Educ.:** Collège de la Sainte Famille, Cairo; Faculty of Arts, Cairo University; Institut de Hautes Etudes Cinématographiques, Paris (France); **Dipl.:** B.A. Film Production Diploma. **Career:** Documentaries "Silver Nile" (1965), "Kasr el-Ayni" (1966); TV featurettes: "Without Words" (1966), "People are battering Antar" (1967) adapted to the screen from the novel of the same title by Ihsan Abdul Kouddous, a well-known Egyptian novelist and journalist contributing mainly to al-Ahram Arabic-language newspaper, "al-Ahrar" (The Freemen), adapted from the Egyptian novelist Yussef Idriss; full feature films: "A Question of Honour", "Woman's Springtime" adapted from the novel of the same name by Naguib Mahfouz. **Sports:** Football, tennis and swimming. **Hobbies:** reading and classical music. **Prof. Addr.:** State TV Service, TV Building, Maspero District, Corniche Road, Cairo, Egypt. **Priv. Addr.:** el-Goumhouriya street, Tel.: 903216, Cairo, Egypt.

SHAMMA (Khalil, al), Iraqi academic. **Born** in 1935 in Najaf, Iraq. **Son** of Mohammed Hassan al-Shamma' (Businessman) and Mrs. Zahra al-Shamma'. **Married** in 1963 in Baghdad to Adiba Hummadi, four children, 3 daughters: Saher, Hiyam, Najwa and one son: Hussain. **Educ.:** Ghazi Elementary School, Najaf; Najaf Intermediate School; Najaf Secondary School; American University of Beirut, B.B.A.; American University of Beirut, M.B.A.; University of California, Berkeley California, U.S.A., Ph.D.; World University, Arizona, U.S.A., Ph.D. **Dipl.:** Bachelor of Business Administration (1952); Master of Business Administration (1959); Ph.D. Business Administration (1962); Ph.D., Business Management (1987). **Career:** Assistant, College of Commerce, University of Baghdad (1963); Chief, Statistics and Research Department, Central Bank of Iraq (1964-65); Economic Advisor, State Economic Organization (1965-66); Director, Economic and Administrative Research Center, University of Baghdad (1967-1968); Chairman, Department of Business Administration, University of Baghdad (1968-69); Dean, College of Administration and Economics, University of Baghdad (1969-70); Chairman, State Reorganization Committee, Revolution Command Council (1970-77); presently University Teaching, Consultations. **Publ.:** Author of many books in Business Adiminstrations, with emphasis on Finance, Banking and Organization; Many published articles in Arabic and English; Member of Base Board of Directors of National Insurance Company and Central Bank of Iraq. **Awards:** Appreciation for Public Service by Mr. President of the Republic (two times) and many other appreciations. **Hobby:** Islamic and Modern History. **Member:** Accountants and Auditor's Association of Iraq; Association of Iraq Economists; Teachers Association of Iraq. **Prof. Addr.:** College of Administration and Economics, University of Baghdad, Tel.: 4220071, Baghdad, Iraq. **Priv. Addr.:** House 84, Street 11, Zone 506, Mustansiriyah Quarter, Tel.: 4166921, Baghdad, Iraq.

SHAMMAS (Said, Yacoub), Former kuwaiti diplomat, now businessman. **Born** on July 27, 1927 in Kuwait. **Son** of Yacoub Shammas. **Educ.:** Mobarakiya School (Kuwait); College of Commerce (Bristol); London School of Economics, University of Oxford. **Career:** Manager, Municipality Department, Kuwait (1954-55); Administrator Assistant, Civil Service Committee (1955-57); Deputy Director General (1958-60); Consul General and Chargé d'Affaires of the Kuwaiti Mission to the United Nations Organization (1962-63); Ambassador to U.S.S.R. (1964-67); Concurrently to Poland, Czechoslovakia, Hungary and Rumania (1965-67), to France (1967-70), Chef de Protocole, Ministry of Foreign Affairs, Kuwait (1971-72); Ambassador to Kenya (1972-73); Retired from Government service to chair his group of companies: Saeed & Daulat; Saeed & Ghoryafi; Saeed & Samir Bookstore; Safitrac Limited (1973-present). **Addr.:** P.O.Box 5445, Safat, Kuwait.

SHAMS (Ibrahim M.S.), Saudi banker. **Born** in 1931 in Jeddah, Saudi Arabia. **Married**, 4 children: **Educ.:** Secondary School (Matric). **Career:** Bank Indochine (1951-62); Head of Accounts, Riyadh Bank Head Office (1962-65); Inspector, Riyadh Bank (1965-67); General Controller, Riyadh Bank Head Office (1967-69); Manager, Jeddah Branch, Riyadh Bank (1969-71); Assistant General Manager, Riyadh Bank (1971-73); Deputy General Manager, Riyadh Bank (1973-79); General Manager, Riyadh Bank, Riyadh, (from 20.12.1979 uptill now). **Directorships:** Member, Board of Directors for Jeddah Oil Refinery Co. since 1969; Chairman, Board of Directors, Gulf Riyadh Bank, Bahrain since 1978; Chairman, Board of Directors, Saudi Travellers Cheque Co. since 1983; Member of Banking Committee (SAMA) since 1987; Member, Board of Directors, Saudi Cable Co. Ltd. (1988); Member, Board of Directors, Saudi Airlines since 1988. **Membership of Professional Organisations:** Union of Arab Banks; Arab Bankers Association; Islamic Banks International Association. **Sport:** Swimming. **Hobby:** Reading. **Credit Cards:** Amex, Visa, Master Access. **Prof. Addr.:** Riyadh Bank, Head Office, P.O.Box 22621, Riyadh 11416, Tel.: 4013030, Telex: 407490 RYDX SJ., Fax: 4040090, Saudi Arabia.

SHAMSA (Mohamad, Sadiq, Bakir), Iraqi academic. **Born** in 1943 in Najaf, Iraq. **Son** of Bakir Shamsa. **Married**, three children. **Educ.:** B.Sc. in Economics; M.A. in Social and Economic Sciences; Ph.D. in Accounting. **Career:** Head of Management Development, University of Baghdad (1977); Deputy Dean of Faculty of Management and Economics, University of Baghdad (1977-78); Dean of Faculty of Management, Salahuddin University (since 1978); member of the Board of the Syndicate of Accountants (1978); Deputy Chairman of Iraqi Economists Association, Sulaimaniya; Professor, Baghdad University (since 1982). **Publ.:** co-author of "Specialized Accounting"; "Tax Accounting", etc. **Addr.:** Baghdad University, Jadiriya, Baghdad, Iraq.

SHAMSI (Abdul Aziz, Nasser, Rahma, Al), U.A.E. Diplomat, Ambassador of United Arab Emirates in France. **Born** in 1956 at Ajman (United Arab Emirates). **Son** of Nasser Al Shamsi (Businessman). **Married** in 1982 to Miss Hissa Al Otaiba, Doctor in Computing, 4 children: Saud, Abdallah, Fatima, Alyazia. **Educ.:** Cairo University. **Dipl.:** Licence in Business Management. **Career:** 3rd Secretary of Political Affairs at Central Administration (1980) then in Belgium (1982); 2nd Secretary, Tunisia (1984); Permanent Mission at the European Office, United Nations, Geneva (Switzerland) (1985-1989); Director, United Arab Emirates Delegation (1988-1989); Sub-Manager at Arab World Department, Central Administration (1990-1991); Ambassador to Brazil (1991-1993), to Argentina and Chili (1993-1995) to France (since 1995); Permanent delegate at UNESCO (since 1995). **Sports Practised:** Tennis. **Prof. Addr.:** Embassy of U.A.E., 3 rue de Lota, 75116 Paris, France. **Priv. Addr.:** 20 Av. Charles Floquet, 75007 Paris, France.

SHAMTE (Haroub, Mohamad), UAE bank manager. **Born** in 1945 in Zanzibar, Ras al-Khaimah. **Son** of Mohamad Shamte. **Married** in 1978, 2 sons. **Educ.:** Technical College; University Degree, Zanzibar. **Career:** Joined British Bank of the Middle East since 1965. Currently, Manager, British Bank of the Middle East, Ras al-Khaimah, UAE. **Member:** Oman Sports Club. **Hobbies:** Reading and Sports. **Addr.:** P.O.Box 9, Tel.: 28214, 22488 (Office), 28570 (Residence), Ras al-Khaimah, UAE.

SHANDIRLI (Abdulkadir), Algerian former official. **Born** in 1915 in Algiers, Algeria. **Married**, two children. **Educ.:** School of Political Science, Algiers and University of Paris. **Career:** served in French Army in Algeria, later in France and Germany; edited newspaper for French troops in France and Germany; Editor of French newspaper in Shanghai; Head of Public Rèlations at UNESCO, Paris; Representative, National Liberation Front, UN, USA, during War of Independence; first Permanent Representative of Algeria at the UN; Director General of Political, Economic and Cultural Affairs, Ministry of Foreign Affairs; Director of National Oil Company SONATRACH, and Head of Special organisation set up by the UN Special Fund on the planning of the Algerian chemical industry; chairman of the National Liquid Methane Corp. (1969-75); former Director, Arab Fund for Economic and Social Development (1975). **Addr.:** Algiers, Algeria.

SHANFARI (Said bin Ahmed, al), Omani former minister and businessman. **Born** in 1939 in Salalah, Sultanate of Oman. **Educ.:** in Dhofar and Saudi Arabia. **Career:** Worked from 1954 to 1960 for an Arab Oil Company in the Gulf area; Directed several businesses in Salalah and Muscat. **Ministerial Posts:** His Majesty Sultan Qaboos bin Saeed al-Moazam appointed H.E. Said bin Ahmed al Shanfari in November 1974 Minister of Agriculture, Fisheries and Minerals. After a cabinet reshuffle on 22.5.1979 H.E. Minister Shanfari was given the portfolio of the Ministry of Petroleum and Minerals. **Ministerial Councils:** Deputy Chairman of the Gas Council; Member of the Development Council; Member of the Financial Affairs Council; Member of the Council for Conservation of Environment; Member of the Planning Committee for Development and Environment of the Dhofar Governate; Member of the Education and Vocational Training Council. **Hobbies:** Swimming, horse riding, travelling and reading. **Address:** Muscat, Sultanate of Oman.

SHANSHAL (AbdulJabbar Khalil, General), Iraqi army officer. **Born** in 1920 in Mosul, Iraq. **Son** of Khalil Shanshal. **Married. Career:** Chief of Staff of 3rd Division (1963); Chief of Staff, (1963); Commander of Staff College (1964); Commander of 4th Division, Mosul and Commander of Mosul Garrison (1966); Deputy Chief of General Staff (1970); Minister of State for Military Affairs (1982-1988); Minister of Defence (1988-91); Minister of State for Military Affairs (1991 to present). **Addr.:** Ministry of Defence, Baghdad, Iraq.

SHANTI (Ahmed Mahmoud Salman, al), Saudi Professor. **Born** on March 2, 1932 in Jaffa, Palestine (Now Saudi Arabian). **Son** of late Mahmoud Salman Al Shanti (Farmer) **and** Mrs. née Mariam Abdel Rahman Oweida. **Married** in 1959 in Saudi Arabia to Fadwa Zarour, 6 children: Amal Eman, Mahmoud, Basem, Hanan, Yasser. **Educ.:** Ein Shams University (Cairo) B.Sc.; Cairo University (Cairo) M.Sc.; Imperial College (London) Ph.D. and DIC. **Dipl.:** Diploma of Imperial College, London. **Career:** Geologist in Ministry of Petroleum and Mineral Resources and Head of Geology Department (1957-1974); **Dean,** Institute of Applied Geology and Faculty of Earth Sciences, King Abdul Aziz University, Jeddah (1974-1979); Professor of Geology, Economic Geology, King Abdul Aziz University, Jeddah (1979- present). **Sports:** Swimming, Jogging. **Hobby:** Reading. **Member:** Local Clubs. **Credit Card:** American Express. **Prof. Addr.:** P.O.Box 1744, Tel.: 695 2318, Jeddah, Saudi Arabia. **Priv. Addr.:** 172 -sh. Khalid Bin Al Walid, Ash-Sharafiah, Jeddah, Saudi Arabia.

SHAQWARA (Yahya, Ali), Jordanian economist. **Born** on August 8, 1938 in Nablus, Jordan. **Married,** two sons. **Educ.:** University of Nuremburg, West Germany (1969-72); **Dipl.:** Ph.D. in Economics and Social Sciences. **Career:** Head of Research Section at the Ministry of Culture and Information, Jordan (1973); Head of Research Section in Royal Scientific Society, Jordan (1975); Manager for Consultancy for Talal Abu Ghazalah International, Jordan (1978); Lecturer at Jordan University, Amman; General Manager of Shaqwara Consultancy Bureau, Jordan (1980-). **Publ.:** "The Role of Mass Communication System in National Development of Jordan" (1973) (in German); "The Impact of Investment Law on Industry and Tourism in Jordan" (1976) (in Arabic); "The Role of Journalism in National Development in Jordan" (1977) (in Arabic and German). **Hobbies:** Tennis, swimming, Arabic and German poetry, **Addr.:** P.O.Box 7214, Tel.: 56026, Jordan.

SHARABI (Burhan, S.), Jordanian Executive. **Born** in Nablus on April 3, 1934. **Son** of Shukri Sharabi **and** Mrs. née, Nohad Hajawi. **Married** in 1966 in Jordan to **Fayza Sharabi,** two daughters: **Rania** (1967) and **Rawan** (1970). **Educ.:** Alsalaheya School, Nablus; Alexandria University, Egypt; Colorado State University, U.S.A. **Dipl.:** B.Sc.; Masters. **Career:** (1960) Teacher in the Ministry of Education. (1962-1992) Deputy Director General/Agricultural Credit Corporation. (1992-1994)Consultant with IFAD in San'a/Yemen. **Currently:** Retired. **Sports:** Jogging, Swimming. **Hobbies:** Sports, Reading. **Member:** King Hussain Club, Hussein Youth Club. **Credit Card:** American Express. **Address:** P.O.Box 1874 Amman, Jordan, Tel.: 5524725 & 5538912.

SHARABI (Nazim, Bishara), Jordanian banker. **Born** in 1916 in Nablus, Jordan. **Son** of Bishara Sharabi. **Married,** four children. **Educ.:** B.A. in Political Science, American University of Beirut, Lebanon (1937); M.A. in Political Science AUB (1941); Diploma in Social Studies, Birmingham University, UK. **Career:** Lecturer, AUB (1938-41); Probation Officer, Palestine (1942-48); Assistant Field Director, League of Red Cross Societies, East Jordan (1948-49); Controller of Imports and Exports, Jordan (1949-51); Under Secretary, Ministry of Social Welfare, Jordan (1951-54); Senior Manager, Arab Bank Ltd., Head office, Amman, Jordan (1954-63); Minister of Finance and Minister of National Economy (1963-64); Assistant General Manager, Arab Bank Ltd., Head Office, Amman (1965-68); Minister of National Economy (1968-69); Assistant General Manager, Arab Bank Ltd., Amman (1969-80); Banking Consultant since 1980. **Medal:** Order of the Jordanian Star, 1st Class. **Sport:** Tennis. **Hobby:** Reading. **Priv. Addr.:** Tel.: 41567, Amman, Jordan.

SHARAF (Abdulaziz Mohamad), Egyptian journalist. **Born in** 1940 in Dakahliya, Egypt. **Son** of Mohamad Sharaf. **Married. Educ.:** College of Arts, Cairo University, Egypt (1968); M.A. in Journalism (1971); **Ph.D. in** Mass Communications, Cairo University (1975). **Career:** Journalist (1968); Teacher, Cairo University (1972-75); Professor of Information and Mass Communications, al-Azhar University (1976); Literary Editor "al-Ahram" newspaper. Member of the Egyptian Writers Association; member of the Egyptian Journalists Association. **Publ.:** "Lutfi al-Sayyid"; "Philosopher of the Nation" (1963); "Resistance in Contemporary Algerian Literature" (1971); "Creative Vision" (1971); "Mass Media and the Language of Civilization" (1979); "The Art of Editing for Mass Media" (1980) and several other publications. **Medals:** 1st Prize, Egyptian Journalists Association (1966); 1st Prize, Arabic Language Academy (1970); 2nd Prize, Arab League Economic, Cultural and Social Organisation ALECSO (1973). **Prof. Addr.:** al-Ahram Newspaper, al-Galaa Street, Tel.: 7550, Cairo, Egypt. **Priv. Addr.:** 17 Digla Street, Madinat al-Muhandisin, Cairo, Egypt.

SHARAF (Kamal, AbdulKarim), Syrian former minister. **Born** in 1944 in al-Suweida, Syria. **Son** of Abdulkarim Sharaf. **Married,** three children. **Educ.:** Ph.D. in Economics. **Career:** Minister of Planning (1981-85); Assistant Professor, Damascus University (since 1975); Minister of Higher Education (1985); Chairman of the Economics Society, Syria Deputy Secretary General, Arab Economics Union, member of the High Chamber of Science (since 1981). **Publ.:** "Economic Resources", "Economic Theories". **Addr.:** Damascus, Syria.

SHARAF (Laila, A), Jordanian administrator. **Born** in 1940 in Beirut, Lebanon. **Married,** two sons. **Educ.:** American University of Beirut. **Dipl.:** B.A. and M.A. in Literature. **Career:** Senator, Jordan Senate (Upper House of Parliament); Chairperson, Board of Trustees Philadelphia University, Jordan; Member, Board of Trustees American university of Beirut; Member, Board of Trustees Arab organization for Human Rights; Vice president, The Royal Society for the Conservation of Nature; Vice Chairperson Higher Committee for the Jerash Festival for Culture and Arts; Member, World Affairs Council, Jordan; member, Board of Trustees, Arab Thought Forum; Former Minister of Information, Jordan **Addr.:** P.O.Box 94, Jubeiha, Jordan.

SHARAF (Sharif Fawaz), Jordanian former minister. **Born** in 1938 in Amman, Jordan. **Educ.:** American University of Beirut. **Career:** Ministry of Foreign Affairs (1961-62); Prime Minister's Office (1962-63); Jordanian Mission, UN (1963-65); Ministry of Foreign Affairs (1965-66); Youth Care Organization (1966); Director-General, Jordan Youth and Sports Organization (1974-76); Minister of Culture and Youth (November 1976), re-appointed (1978-80). **Addr.:** Amman, Jordan.

SHARAFEDDIN (Abdallah, Mustafa), Libyan academic. **Born** in 1924 in Tripoli, Libya. **Son** of Mustafa

Sharafeddin. **Married**, four children. **Educ.:** B.A. in Laws and Economics, Cairo University, Egypt. **Career:** Head of Naturalization and Consular Affairs Department, Ministry of Foreign Affairs (1956-57); Editor in Chief, "el-Ayyam" newspaper; Dean of the Libyan Bar Association (1968-78); Editor in Chief "el-Muhami" magazine; Lawyer; founder member of the legislative council for the State of Tripolitania; Permanent Office of the Arab Lawyers' Union, Permanent Office of the Arab Jurist Union, Permanent Committee for Human Rights in the Arab World; Head of the International Organization for Eliminating All Forms of Racial Discrimination; Chairman of the Committee for the Right to Work in the Islamic Sharia in the Seminar of Human Rights in Islam, (1980). **Addr.:** Tripoli, Libya.

SHARAIHA (Wadie J.), Jordanian economist. **Born** on August 15, 1939, in Jordan. **Married,** two children. **Educ.:** Baghdad University, Iraq; Charles University; Harvard University, USA; Maison University, USA. **Dipl.:** B.A. in Law (1961); M.Sc. in Economic Development (1963); Ph.D. in Economic Planning and Development (1965); Courses in Marketing and Management (1969). **Career:** Senior Economist for Jordan Development Planning Council (1965-67); Associate Professor of Economics Department at the University of Jordan (1969); Professor of the Economic Development and planning at University of Jordan (1971); Head of Economics and Statistics Department (1971-75); Director of Development and Planning (1974-76); University Planning Adviser, University of Kuwait (1976-78); Member of the Academy Advisory Board of Georgetown University, Washington D.C. (1981); Member of the jordan Economic Society, the Steering Committee for Industrial Development of Jordan; Member of the Board of Directors of King Hussain Fund for Research and Member of the Board of Trustees of National College, Amman; Distinguished Member of the International Advisory Board of the Association for Anthropological Diplomacy, Williamsburg, USA: Dean, Faculty of Economics and Commerce Professor of Economic Development and Planning at the University of Jordan (1979). **Publ.:** "Economic Development in Jordan" published by the Higher Institute for Arab Studies (1967); "Economic Growth and Population Policy in Jordan, ECWA" (1971); "Arab Common Market: Economic Analysis" (1972); "Economic Development in Jordan" (1976); "Gulf Economic Integration", Kuwait Chamber of Commerce (1977); "The Role of Budge in Economic Planning", Rabat (1980) and several others. **Prof. Addr.:** University of Jordan, Faculty of Economics and Commerce, P.O.Box 5201, Tel.: 843555, Amman, Jordan.

SHARARI (Hesham, Fayez, al), Jordanian politician, agricultural engineer. **Born** in 1939 in Ma'an, Jordan. **Son** of Fayez al Sharari. **Married**, two sons, one daughter. **Educ.:** B.Sc. and M.Sc. in Agricultural Engineering. **Career:** Director and Supervisor, Ministry of Agriculture; Mayor of Ma'an; Deputy Director, Public Railway Services, Ministry of Communications; member of the National Consultative Council, Ministry of Youth (1984). **Member** of the Agricultural Cooperative Organisation, Queen Alia Fund and various Agricultural Societies. **Medals:** Medal of Municipality Councils, Ministry of Municipalities, Jordan; Medal of the Silver Jubilee, Ministry of Interior, Jordan. **Priv. Addr.:** Ma'an Jordan.

SHARAWI (Walid, Mohamad), Saudi senior executive. **Born** on December 13, 1942 in Jeddah (Saudi Arabia). **Son** of Mohamad Said Sharawi (merchant) **and** Mrs. Khatoun Sour. **Married** to Samia H. Naim on January 1, 1974; 3 children: Gaith, Zaina, Ulla. **Educ.:** Dar al-Thakafa Secondary School, Damascus (Syria); Damascus University. **Dipl.:** B.Com. also attended the following courses: "Techniques of Modern Management", "Management by Objectives", "Pan Arab Action Learning Programme", "Management Grid". **Career:** Auditor, Saba & Co., Jeddah (1966-67); Personnel Officer, Zahid Tractors Co.(May-Aug 1967); Senior Auditor, Raytheon Service Co., Jeddah (Aug.1967- Mar. 1969); Joined Saudia Airlines, as assistant to General Manager for accounting since 1969; now working as Manager, Catering Services at KALA. **Hobbies:** reading, music, journalism and arts. **Prof. Addr.:** Saudia Catering, Tel.:4864861 Telex SITA Code "JEDHFSV", Commercial: 403138 SV CATR SJ, Home Tel. No.: 582 1900, 682 1932, P.O.Box 2231, Jeddah 21451, Saudi Arabia.

SHARA' (Farouk, Al-), Syrian Minister of Foreign Affairs. **Born** in Dara'a in 1938. **Married,** 2 children. **Academic Studies:** B.A. in English Literature - University of Damascus (1953); International Law - London University (1972). **Positions Held:** He held several major posts in the Syrian Arab Airlines as: Office Manager at Dubai (U.A.E.); Regional Manager in London; Commercial Director and Member of the Board of Directors in Damascus. Ambassador of the Syrian Arab Republic in Italy (1976-1980); Minister of State for Foreign Affairs (1980-1984); Appointed Minister of Foreign Affairs (11 March 1984-). Represented Syria in several Arab, Islamic and International Conferences, and acted as Special envoy of H.E. Late President Hafez ASSAD to several leaders of Arab and Foreign Countries. During his tenure as Minister of State for Foreign Affairs he acted as Minister of Justice and several times as Minister of Information. **Addr.:** Ministry of Foreign Affairs, Damascus, Syria.

SHARBAN (Ali Abdulaziz, al-, Dr.), UAE Politician, **Born** in 1950. **Educ.:** B.A., English, University of Baghdad (1976); M.A., Linguistics, American University, Washington (1983); Ph.D., Linguistics, University of Essex, UK (1988). **Career:** Lecturer, Research Director, Dean of Basic Education Program then Deputy Vice Chancellor for Planning Affairs, Emirates University (1988-98); Assistant Undersecretary for Finance and Administrative Affairs, Ministry of Public Works and Housing (1976-

80); **Minister of Education and Youth** (March 1997-to date). **Address:** Ministry of Education, P.O.Box 295, Abu Dhabi, United Arab Emirates.

SHARBATLY (Abdulaziz Abdallah), Saudi businessman. **Born** in 1950, Jeddah, Saudi Arabia. **Dipl.:** B.A. (Business Administration). **Career:** General merchant; Managing Director of Development Establishment for Trade & Contracting, Jeddah, Sharbatly Trade Bridge Co., London, England. **Hobbies:** horseriding, reading. **Address:** P.O.Box 6493, Jeddah 21442, Saudi Arabia.

SHARBATLY (Ibrahim Hassan Abbas al-Sayed), Saudi businessman. **Born** in 1952 in Jeddah, Saudi Arabia. **Dipl.:** Higher Diploma in Commerce and Economics. **Career:** General Superintendent, Sharbatly Corporation (1965); General Manager, Ibrahim Sharbatly Organization; Vice-president, Arabian Automobile co.; General Manager, Commercial Office, H.E. Alsayed Hassan Sharbatly's Corporation; Owner Saudi Arab Marketing Corp.; shareholder in several Saudi and Arab firms. **Hobbies:** reading, swimming. **Address:** P.O.Box 5968, Jeddah 21432, Saudi Arabia.

SHARBATLY (Kamal Abdallah), Saudi businessman. **Born** in 1952 in Jeddah, Saudi Arabia. **Dipl.:** B.A. (Commerce), Beirut University. **Career:** Founder, Chairman and Managing Director, Sharbatly Establishment for Trade and Development; general merchant importer and distributor of fresh, chilled and frozen foodstuffs; owner and operator of a cold storage unit; a major supplier of foodstuffs to government agencies and several other private agencies; owner of a precast concrete construction plant. **Hobbies:** fishing, yachting. **Prof. Addr.:** P.O.Box 293, Tel.: 6470149, Jeddah, Saudi Arabia.

SHARBATLY (Saud Hassan), Saudi businessman. **Born** in 1954 in Jeddah, Saudi Arabia. **Educ.:** awarded an honorary B.A. degree from Cambridge. **Career:** Deputy General Manager of Arab Auto Company and al-Tawhid Establishment, Managing Director of Ohoud Establishment for Trade and Contracting, Sultan Establishment for International Trade and the Saudi Centre for Provisions and Imports; owner of Ohoud International Tourism; General Manager of his father's (H.E. al-Sayyid Hassan Abbas Sharbatly) business enterprises (1976-79); member, Ittehad Club; active in economic, cultural, social and benevolent services. **Hobbies:** poetry, reading, sports. **Prof. Addr.:** P.O.Box 5939 and P.O.Box 6673, Sharbatly Building, 4h floor, Apt. 61, Qabel Street, Tel.: 6477553, 6479669, Jeddah. **Priv. Addr.:** Tel.: 6673151, Jeddah, Saudi Arabia.

SHARBATLY (Abdul Rahman Hassan), Saudi leading businessman. **Born** in 1943. **Dipl.:** G.C.E., Victoria College, Cairo Egypt. **Carrer: Primary Business Interests:** Owner, Arabian International Corporation: a diversified business concern involved in commercial activities, hotels and real estate development projects; **Chairman:** Golden Pyramids Plaza Company, Egypt (Building Company for tourist complex); Saudi Arabian Marketing Corporation, Saudi Arabia (Dealers of Porsche, Audi & VW cars); Al Nahla Trading & Contracting Company, Saudi Arabia (Investment Company dealing in real estate, shares, etc); **Other Directorships:** Riyadh Bank, Saudi Arabia; Saudi Arabian Refinery Company, Saudi Arabia; Beirut Riyadh Bank, Lebanon; Saudi Company for Hardware, Saudi Arabia; Marketing Services & Commercial Projects Company, Saudi Arabia; JGC Saudi Arabia Limited, Saudi Arabia; Al Watany Bank, Egypt; **Currently:** Member, Consultative Council, Principality of Makkah.

SHAREKH (Mohamad, al), Kuwaiti businessman. **Born** in 1942 in Kuwait. **Married. Educ.:** Cairo University, Egypt; Williams College, Williamstown, Massachusetts, USA. **Dipl.:** B.Sc. Economics (1965); M.A. in Development Economics. **Career:** Kuwait Customs (1958); Posts, Telegraphs and Telephones Department (1959-65); Deputy-Director, Kuwait Fund of Arab Economic Development (1965-73); Partner and Manager, Electronics International Ltd., Kuwait (1970-73); Member of the Committee, Industrial Projects, Prime Minister's Office, Kuwait (1972); Executive Director, IBRD (World Bank), Washington DC, USA (1973-74); Chairman, al-Alamiah Co. (1977 to present). **Member:** Kuwait Economists Society; Federation of Arab Economists. **Hobby:** Chess. **Addr.:** P.O.Box 23781, Safat, Kuwait City, Kuwait.

SHARI (Saduk, al), Jordanian politician, army officer. **Born** in 1923 in Huwara, Irbid, Jordan. **Married. Educ.:** Senior Commanders' Certificate, British Staff College Certificate. **Career:** Officer cadet; 2nd Lieutenant; platoon commander and training officer (1942-43); Staff Captain, Mechanised Brigade; Staff Captain, 1st Infantry Division; Brigade Major, 3rd Infantry Brigade; Commanding Officer (1953); Commander, National Guards (1954); Chief of Staff, Arab Jordanian Army (1957); Deputy Commander in Chief of the Arab Hashemite Union Army (1958); Chief of Staff, Arab Jordanian Army, retired (1959); Director General of the Passports Department; District Governor, Irbid District (1972); Minister of Supply; Minister of State for Foreign Affairs (1974-76); member of the Arab National Union Council. **Decor.:** Independence Medal, 4th Class; Renaissance Medal, 3rd Class; Star of Jordan, 2nd Class; Independence Medal, 1st Class; Operational Medal for World War II; Operational Medal for Palestine; Egyptian Military Medal of Merit, 1st Class; Syrian Military Medal of Merit, 1st Class; British War Star Medal; Chinese High Star Medal, 1st Class. **Addr.:** Tha'a al-Ali, Amman, Jordan.

SHARIE (Abdallah al-Nafie, al), Saudi academic. **Born** in 13 July 1937 in Medina, Saudi Arabia. **Dipl.:** Ph.D. **Career:** Dean, Faculty of Education (1970-72); Secretary

General, King Saud University (1972-73); Vice Rector (1973-76); Chairman, Harbi Information and Educational Projects (1976-78); Professor of Psychology, King Saud University. **Founding member** and member of the Board, Iman Charity Society; member, International Islamic Schools Federation; former member of the Board, King Saud University Council, the Higher Council of the Universities and the Scientific Council; Adviser to the Arab Gulf University; former member of the Board, Public Administration Institute; attended several international and regional conferences on education and psychology. **Publications:** several articles and research topics on different psychological subjects. **Hobbies:** swimming, walking. reading. **Prof. Addr.:** P.O.Box. 10344, Tel.: 4024700, Riyadh. **Priv. Addr.:** Tel.: 4656993, Riyadh, Saudi Arabia.

SHARIEF (Farooq A.M.), Saudi academic. **Born** in 1948 in Mecca, Saudi Arabia. **Dipl.:** B.Sc. (Geology and Chemistry); M.Sc. and Ph.D. (Geology). **Career:** Instructor and Lecturer, Department of Geology, King Saud University; Assistant Professor. Faculty of Geology, King Saud University; active member, American Association of Petroleum Geologists; member, International Association of Sedimentologists, Working Party on Natural Resources, and Saudi Arabian National Centre for Science and Technology. **Publications:** Geological Bibliography of the Arabian Gulf, various articles on the Geology of the Middle East. **Hobbies:** sports, reading, travel. **Prof. Addr.:** Department of Geology, King Saud University, Tel.: 4789020, Riyadh. **Priv. Addr.:** Tel.: 4785373, Riyadh, Saudi Arabia.

SHARIF (Abdul Sattar Tahir), Iraqi politician. **Born** in 1933 in Kirkuk, Iraq. **Son** of Tahir Sharif. **Career:** member of the Kurdish Democratic Party; Secretary Third Branch of KDP, Secretary General, (1973); Minister of Housing (1974); Minister of Municipalities (1974-76); Minister of Transport (1976); presently Committee's Secretary General, Kurdish Revolutionary Party. **Addr.:** Baghdad, Iraq.

SHARIF (Abubakr, Ali, al), Libyan politician. **Born** in 1940 in Benghazi, Libya. **Educ.:** Cairo. **Dipl.:** Economic Studies (1964-66). **Career:** trading business in Misurata; Director, General Organization for Industrialization; Head, General Planning Authority; Minister of Economy (1972-77); Secretary for Economy, General People's Committee (March 1977-1982). **Addr.:** Tripoli, Libya.

SHARIF (Fuad), Egyptian administrator. **Born** in 1926 in Egypt. **Married**, four children. **Educ.:** Ph.D. in Business Administration, University of Chicago, USA; one year post doctoral research, Harvard Business School, USA. **Career:** Founder, National Institute of Management Development, Cairo (1961); UN Office, New York, wrote about management problems (1967); assisted in the reorganization of UN internal administration; one of 23 interregional advisers; Minister of State for Cabinet Affairs and Administrative Development (1976-1980). **Addr.: Cairo**, Egypt.

SHARIF (Kamel, Ismail), Jordanian politician. **Born** in 1926 at Gaza, Palestine. **Married. Educ.:** Arabic Literature, Journalism, French Literature. **Career:** Officer, Palestine Liberation Army Commander, Palestine War (rank of Major) (1947); Commander, Fedayeen Operations, Suez Canal Zone (1951); Assistant Secretary-General, Islamic Congress (1954); Jordanian Ambassador to several Asian and African countries; Ambassador, Ministry of Foreign Affairs (1961); Ambassador to Nigeria (1961); Ambassador to Bonn, West Germany (1967); Ambassador to Nationalist China and Japan (1969-71); Ambassador to Pakistan (1971-73); non-resident Jordanian Ambassador to Malaysia (1972-73); Senator (1973-74); Minister of Waqfs, Islamic Affairs and Holy Places since July 1976-1984); General Manager al-Dustour (constitution) daily newspaper (1987); Secretary General Islamic International Council for D'awa (appeal) and relief (1987); Senator (1989). **Awards:** Golden Order for Bravery, Egypt; Star of Palestine Medal; Order of Jordanian Star Medal and Medal of Independence (First degree). **Member:** Islamic League of Mecca. **Priv. Addr.:** P.O.Box. 591 Tel.: 661957, Amman, Jordan.

SHARIF (Mohamad Ahmad, al), Libyan politician. **Educ.:** in the USA. **Career:** Dean Faculty of Education, University of Libya, Tripoli; Minister of Education (July 1972-1977); Chairman, Islamic-Christian Dialogue, Tripoli (January 1976); Secretary for Education, General People's Committee (March 1977-81). **Addr.:** Tripoli, Libya.

SHARIF (Mohamad, Sami Abdelmajid), Egyptian businessman. **Born** in 1925 in Egypt. **Son** of Abdelmajid Sharif. **Married**, three sons. **Educ.:** Alexandria University. **Dipl.:** LL.B.; Graduate Diploma in General Law, Politics and Economics. **Career:** Board member, Spinning and Weaving Industries; member of the Egyptian Chamber of Commerce; member of the Egyptian Industries Union. **Member** of Alexandria Shooting Club, Alexandria Sporting Club; Alexandria Social Club. **Addr.:** 445 Camal Mahmoudia Street, Nouzha, Alexandria, Egypt.

SHARIF (Mohammad, Omar, Al-), Syrian former Governor, Central Bank of Syria. **Born** on May 1, 1930 at Ariha, Syria. **Son** of Mohammad Omar **and** Mrs. **Khadija. Married** to Najat Shukri, 3 children: Omar, Wael, **Azzah. Educ.:** University of Damascus. **Dipl.:** B.A. in Law. **Career:** Assistant Director, Department Customs Syrian Arab Republic, Damascus (1963-64), Director, Department Customs (1964-74); Minister of Finance (1975-1977); Assistant Secretary General, Arab Economic Unity Council, The Arab League, Cairo (1977-79), Amman, Jordan (1979-87); Governor, Central Bank of Syria, (Damascus 1987); Governor, World Bank for Construction, and Development, Washington (1987); Member, Syrian Arab

Republic Higher Council, for Planning, Finance and Development, Damascus (1974). **Priv. Addr.:** P.O.Box 33074, Damascus, Syria.

SHARIF (Nabil, M., el), Chief Editor-AD-Dustour Newspaper - Jordan. **Born** on October 20, 1952 in Arish, Egypt. **Son** of M. El-Sharif (ex-minister of Information) **and** Mrs. H. El-Sharif. **Married** in 1982 in Amman to Manal Abu-Eisheh, 5 children: Shada, Farah, Joud, Tareq, Hashem. **Educ.:** Kuwait University - Kuwait (B.A.), (M.A. PHD) Indiana University - USA. **Dipl.:** Daves' School of English - London. **Career:** 1984-1989 Assistant Professor, Yarmouk University; 1989-1993 Assistant Professor Jordan University; 1993 - Present Editor-in-Chief Ad-Dustour Newspaper. **Other Information:** Media expert on Arab Press. **Medals:** Jordanian Writers Association medal. **Sports Practised:** Jogging. **Hobby:** Reading. **Clubs and Associations:** World Editors forum and International Press Institute. **Credit Cards:** Visa. **Prof. Addr.:** Tel.: 962 6 5697059, Amman, Jordan, **Priv. Addr.:** Tel.: 962 6 5152515, Amman Jordan.

SHARIF (Omar, ach), Borrowed name for **CHALHOUB (Michel),** egyptian screen actor. **Born** on 10 April 1932 in Cairo, Egypt. **Married** Miss Faten Hamama (Actress), one child: Tareq. Divorced. **Educ.:** College of the Christian Brothers, Victoria College (Alexandria). **Career:** Screen, Radio and Stage Actor. **Works:** Starred in Motion Pictures, including "Doctor Zhivago", "The Night of the Generals", "The Fall of the Roman Empire", "The Yellow Rolls-Royce", "Funny Girl" (Hollywood 1967), "Mc Kenna's Golg" (Hollywood 1968), "Mayerling" (with Ava Gardner, Hollywood 1968), "Che" (Guevara), "Rudolph Valentino" (1968), "Christopher Colombus" (1968) "The Tamarind Seed", "Juggernaut", "Funny Lady", "Ace Up my sleeve", "Crime and Passion", "Ashanti", "Bloodline". **Dist.:** Several Prizes (Cannes). **Publ.:** "The Eternal Male" (autobiography 1978). **Hobby:** Bridge (International Champion). **Addr.:** c/o William Moriss Agency (UK) Ltd., 147 Wardour Street, London, W.1., England.

SHARIF (Rashid Ibn Rajih Mohamad, al), Saudi academic. **Born** in 1944. **Dipl.:** B.A. (Islamic Law); Ph.D., Cambridge University, U.K. **Career:** Demonstrator, Lecturer, Faculty of Shari'a and Islamic Studies, Makkah; Dean of Faculty of Shari'a and Islamic Studies, Umm al-Qura University, Mecca; Rector, Umm al-Qura University. **Member:** Orientation Committee for Hajj, Umm al-Qura University Council, the Supreme Council of the Universities and Mecca Literary Club; Nozabah Electric Company; attended the Tenth Conference on Islamic Thought, Algiers, the Conference on the Message of the Mosque, Mecca, the Conference on the Message of the University and Teachers' Training Conference, Mecca. **Publications:** collection of poems Islamic and Literary Studies (under publication); a series in Alloghatu al-Khalidah (Immortal Language) programme. **Hobbies:** reading, swimming, sports. **Address:** Umm al-Qura University, **Tel.:** 5564770, Mecca, Saudi Arabia.

SHARIF (Safwat, al), Egyptian minister of information. **Born** in 1933, Cairo. **Educ.:** Military Academy; Institute of Strategic Studies. **Career:** Joined the Presidency of the Republic (1957-1974); Director General, local information, State Information Department (1975); Director of foreign information service, State Information Department; member of the Arab Information Committee (1975); Secretary, Ministry of Information (December 1977); chairman of the Information Authority (October 1978); member of the Media Committee (August 1979); member of the constituent committee, National Democratic Party; Chief, Council of TV and Radio Trustees (June 1980); Minister of Information since 3 January 1982-to present. **Address:** Ministry of Information, Cairo, Egypt.

SHARIF (Salem, Mohamad, Dr.), Somali politician. **Born** in 1935, Hudur District, Bakol Region (Somalia). **Married**, children. **Educ.:** Columbus Institute, Genoa, Italy until 1956. **Dipl.:** Teacher's Diploma, LL.B. **Career:** Teacher at the Laws and Economics Institute, Hamar, Somalia, (1956-58); Economic and Commercial Adviser, Somali Embassy in Cairo (1962-65); Director, Ministry of Commerce and Industry (Feb.-June 1966); Director, Ministry of Health and Labour (June 1967- May 1969); President, National University (May 1970-Feb. 1974); Secretary of State for Higher Education (1974-July 1976). **Member:** Central Committee, Somali Socialist Revolutionary Party (SSRP). **Addr.:** Mogadishu, Somalia.

SHARKAS (Ahmad, Hikmat), Jordanian academic. **Born** in 1939 in Jordan. **Educ.:** Alexandria University; New York state University; Hartford University. **Dipl.:** B.Sc.; M.Sc.; Ph.D. **Career:** Assistant Librarian, Jordan University; Research Fellowship, Hartford Fellowship (1970-76); General Manager, National Libraries and Archives (since 1976). **Publ.:** numerous articles in Arabic and English language magazines. **Hobby:** Reading. **Addr.:** P.O.Box 6070, Amman, Jordan.

SHARMA (S.L., Dr.), Indian executive. **Born** in 1920 in India. **Married** in 1948, 3 sons, 1 daughter. **Educ.:** in India. **Dipl.:** Bachelors Degree (1941); Masters in Business (1943); Ph.D. (1950). **Career:** Teaching Finance, Management, Industrial Problems and Government Policy (1958); Director, Small Scale Industries, Promotion and Development Organisation, Government of India; Director, Training and Research Indian Institute of Foreign Trade (1964); Expert Consultant, Industries Studies and Development Centre, Riyadh, Saudi Arabia (1965); short UNIDO assignment with the Government of Qatar (1968); UN Expert Consultant (1969-76); Industrial Planning Project Formulation and Evaluation of the Arab Planning Institute, Kuwait; Project Adviser, Kuwait Foreign Trading

Contracting and Investment Co. (KFTCIC), Safat, Kuwait (1976-); Chairman of SLS & Sons, Dubai. **Member:** Institute of Chartered Secretaries, London. **Publ.:** Over 40 articles and papers on subjects like inflation, Import Substitution, foreign trade, capital accumulation, etc. **Hobbies:** Reading, tennis, horse-riding, and swimming. **Addr.:** P.O.Box 5665, Tel.: 447827, 632530, Telex: 2021, 2035 A/B MAADEN KT, Safat, Kuwait. and P.O.Box 1769, Dubai, U.A.E.

SHARQAWI (Abdulrahman, al), Egyptian writer. **Born** in 1920 in Egypt. **Career:** lawyer, civil servant, ournalist; Chairman of the Board of "Rose el-Yousef" (1977); Chairman of the Higher Council of Literature and the Arts (1977); Secretary General of Afro-Asian Solidarity; member of the National Specialized Councils. **Publ.:** al-Shawar'a al-Khalfaya; Ma'sat Jamila; al-Fata Mahran. **Addr.:** 17 al-Mathaf al-Zieraie, Dokki, Cairo, Egypt.

SHARQI (Hamad Bin Saif, al), United Arab Emirates statesman. **Born** in 1936 in Fujairah, United Arab Emirates. **Son** of Saif al-Sharqi. **Career:** Governor of Fujaira; United Arab Emirates Minister of State (1971-73); Deputy Ruler and Chairman of Municipal Council, Fujairah (since 1973). **Addr.:** Amiri Court, P.O.Box 1, Government House, Tel.: 22313, Telex: 89000 SHARQI EM, Fujairah, United Arab Emirates.

SHARQI (H.H. Shaikh Hamad Bin Mohamad, al), Ruler of Fujairah, United Arab Emirates. **Born** in 1949. **Educ.:** Police Administration in UK (1967-69); Mons Military Academy, UK (1970). **Career:** member of the Supreme Council of the United Arab Emirates (UAE); first ruler of a member state in the United Arab Emirates to be appointed by a decree of the Supreme Council of the Union; United Arab Emirates Minister of Agriculture and Fisheries (1971-74); Ruler of Fujairah (since 1974). **Addr.:** P.O.Box 1, Tel.: 22443, Telex: 8900 SHARQI EM, Fujairah, United Arab Emirates.

SHASH (Mohamad, M., al), Syrian businessman **Born** on December 22, 1931 in Damascus (Syria). **Son** of Mustafa al-Shash (businessman) and Mrs., née Yusra al-Tawashi. **Married** on February 12, 1955 in Damascus to Hayfa al-Shash, four children: Nada, Nuha, Tahani, Rana. **Educ.:** Faculty of Commerce, Cairo University; Wharton School, Pennsylvania University (USA); International Institute of Management Sciences, Delft (Holland). **Dipl.:** B.Com. with First honours degree (Major Business Administration) (1953); M.B.A. (Finance and Banking) (1958); B.Sc. (Industrial Management and Costing) (1960). **Career:** Director, al-Futtaim Group of Companies, Dubai (1975-76); Economic Adviser, syrian Arab Republic Government (1968-75); Auditor and financial adviser in Damascus (1966-68); Director, Syrian State Import and Export Corporation (Simex) (1964-66); also Board member, Syrian Arab Airlines; General Manager, Syrian Arab Airlines (1962-64); Manager, Performance Evaluation Dept., Syrian Economic Organisation (1961-62); Head, Industrial Costing Dept., Ministry of Industry, Damascus (1959-61); Assistant Manager of the Banks' Control Dept., in the Central Bank of Syria (1958-59); Lecturer of Business Administration in: Damascus University (1958-73); In Amman University (1968-73). Now member of Board of Directors, al-Futtaim Group of Companies, and Managing Director of al-Futtaim Real Estate Development and Investment Company. **Publ.:** author of "Sales Management of Industrial Enterprises", "Introduction to Business Administration Study", "The Organization and Management of Central Bank of Syria", "Industrial Organization and Production Management", "Finance Management and Analysis", and many other articles and papers in the field of Management, Administration and Economics. **Sports:** Jogging and table tennis. **Hobbies:** Reading and touring. **Prof. Addr.:** P.O.Box 152, Tel.: 226660-224101/9, Dubai; **Priv. Addr.:** Tel.: 221656, Dubai, United Arab Emirates.

SHATA (Bakri, Salih), Saudi official. **Born** in 1936 in Mecca, Saudi Arabia. **Son** of Salih Shata. **Educ.:** M.A. Public Administration. **Career:** General Commissioner of Saudi Arabian Pavilion, Expo, Osaka, Japan; Administrative Assistant to Under Secretary of State, Ministry of Commerce; member of various Government Committees on Government Schools Nutrition, Government Purchases and Warehouses; attended several Conferences of General Agreement on Tariffs and Trade (GATT) and UNIDO; Director General of Central Administration For Government Purchases, Ministry of Finance and National Economy. **Sports:** Swimming, bowling. **Addr.:** Government Purchasing Dept., Ministry of Finance and National Economy, P.O.Box. 3483, Tel.: 401.3334, Telex: 201626, Riyadh, Saudi Arabia.

SHATHLY (el-Shathly Mohamad, al), Egyptian geologist. **Born** in 1923 in Egypt. **Son** of Mohamad el-Shathly. **Married**, one son. **Educ.:** Cairo University; University of London. **Dipl.:** B.Sc.; DIC; Ph.D. **Career:** Director, Mineral Research Central Laboratories, cairo; Senior Scientific Officer, International Atomic Energy Agency, Vienna, Austria (1959-61); Deputy Chairman, Atomic Energy Est., Cairo (1962-77); President, Nuclear Raw Materials Corp., Cairo; member of the board, Research and Groundwater Company (1975-80); member of the committee, International Comparative Geological Programme; member of the board, Aswan Marble and Granite Company (since 1980). **Publ.:** Ocean Basins and Margins; Resource Sensing from Space - Prospects for Developing Countries; Fuel and Heavy Water Availability. **Medals:** Medal of Science and Art (First Class), Order of Merit (First Class). **Member** of Cairo Yacht Club. **Addr.:** P.O.Box 11571, Mokattam Post, Street 14, Mokattam City, Cairo, Egypt.

SHATIT (Ghassan), Jordanian executive. **Born** in 1938

in Naour, Jordan. **Son** of Eid Shatit. **Married** in 1967, 3 daughters. **Dipl.:** B.A. (Econ.). **Career:** Arab Bank Ltd. (1966-71); Private Business (1971-74); Head of Banking Dept., Housing Bank, Amman (1974-). **Member:** National Orthodox Club, Amman. **Addr.:** Amman, Jordan.

SHATLI (Mohamad Nagui, Dr.), Egyptian politician. **Born** in 1939 at Menoufiyeh city. **Married,** two sons and one daughter. **Educ.:** Faculty of Agriculture, Cairo University; University of Louisiana, USA. **Dipl.:** Bachelor of Agronomy (Cairo University); Ph.D. (Agriculture) from Louisiana State University. **Career:** Lecturer in agronomy, Faculty of Agriculture, Asiyut University; Full Prof. Faculty of Agriculture, Mennoufiyeh University; appointed Deputy Director of Mennoufiyeh University; appointed Secretary of the National Democratic Party for Mennoufiyeh Governorate; appointed Governor of Kafr el-Sheikh Governorate (21 st September 1981); Minister of Supply (1983-86). **Address:** Cairo, Egypt.

SHATTI (Ibrahim, al), Kuwaiti official. **Born** in Kuwait in 1930. **Married. Educ.:** M.A. in Geology, Durham University. **Career:** Director of Research, Ministry of Social Affairs and Labour; Assistant Under Secretary, Ministry of Foreign Affairs; Chairman of Kuwait Petrochemical Industries Company; Director of HH The Emir's Office (since 1967). **Publ.:** Editor of a history textbook. **Addr.:** Amiri Diwan, P.O.B. 799, Safat, Kuwait.

SHATTI (Mohamad, Abdelkarim, al), Kuwaiti administrator. **Born** in Kuwait in 1952. **Son** of Abdelkarim Shatti. **Married,** three children. **Educ.:** Cairo University; Pittsburgh University, Pennsylvania. **Dipl.:** B.A. and M.A. in Library Science. **Career:** Deputy Chief, Library Division, Ministry of Education (1981-82); Director General, Information Center, General secretariat of the Gulf Cooperation Council (since 1982); member of the American Libraries Society (1978-80). **Hobbies:** reading, swimming. **Addr.:** P.O.Box 17280, al-Kadidia, Kuwait. General Secretariat of the Arab Gulf States Cooperation Council, P.O.Box 7153, Riyadh, Saudi Arabia.

SHAWAF (Abdul Muin), Saudi businessman. **Born** in 1939. **Married,** three sons. **Educ.:** M.A. in Political History. **Career:** Administrative Manager; Civil Engineering Consultant, Riyadh, Saudi Arabia; Director General, al-Rajhi Development Co. Ltd., Contracting and Trading. **Member** of Riyadh University Society. **Sports:** Table tennis, swimming. **Addr.:** al-Rajhi Development Co. Ltd., P.O.Box. 4301, Tel.: 4765116, 4760576, Riyadh, Saudi Arabia.

SHAWAF (Najdad, Abdurrazzaq, al), Iraqi former diplomat. **Born** on March 23, 1915 in Baghdad. **Son** of Abdurrazzaq al-Shawaf (C.S.) **and** Mrs. Fatima Lemaan **Rassim. Married** to Charlotte Souad al-Shawaf, on **November 9, 1944, Berlin,** 3 children: Nabil, Bassil and Muna. **Educ.:** Primary and Secondary School (Baghdad), The National College of Aley, Lebanon (Freshman), The Royal Military College of Baghdad, University of Berlin. **Dipl.:** Bachelor of Arts, Diploma of the Military College, Diploma in Philosophy and Political Science. **Career:** Second Lieutenant of Cavalry (1937-40), First Lieutenant (1941-46); Free lance journalist (1946-52); Member of the United Nations Mission in Libya, Unesco (1953-60); Assistant D.G., Ministry of Oil, Baghdad (1961-62); Minister Plenipotentiary at the Ministry of Foreign Affairs, Baghdad (1963); Minister and Chargé d'Affaires of Iraq to the Federation of Nigeria (1964); Ambassador of Iraq to the Federation of Nigeria and the Republic of Ghana (1966-68); Ambassador of Iraq to the Syrian Arab Republic (1968-69); Ambassador at the Ministry of Foreign Affairs, Baghdad (1969), now retired. **Sports:** Riding, polo, tennis, swimming, reading and Chess game. **Prof. Addr.:** Karradet, Tel.: 31633, Meriam 86/1, Baghdad, Iraq.

SHAWAF (Tarek, M.A., Dr.), a leading Saudi Engineer and businessman. **Born** in 1933 in Saudi Arabia. Mr. Shawaf was **one of the first students from Saudi Arabia** to be sent to the United States to study engineering. He **graduated** from Worcester Polytechnic Institute **(WPI)** the third oldest U.S. engineering educational institution in 1952. **Founded Saudconsult** in 1965 and is considered a pioneering professional in the field of engineering consultancy in Saudi Arabia. Mr. Shawaf is the founder and chairman of one of the oldest and largest engineering consulting firms in the Kingdom, Saudi Consulting Services (Saudconsult). **Addr.:** P.O.Box 2341, Riyadh 11451, Tel.: 966-1-4659975, Fax: 966-1-4647540, Telex: 401231 Shawaf SJ.

SHAWAN (Aziz, al), Egyptian conductor and composer. **Born** on May 6, 1916 in Cairo. **Son** of Aziz Ibrahim al-Shawan **and** Mrs., née Farida Mikhail. **Educ.:** College of the Christian Brothers; Moscow Conservatoire. **Dipl.:** Bachelor of Commerce. **Career:** began to learn the violin at the age of nine under the guidance of Joseph Aubervon, a student of Kubelick; awarded a scholarship to the Berlin Conservatoire but failed to attend due to his father's objections to a musical career; due to accidental paralysis of his small finger which crushed all hopes of his being a virtuos violinist, he turned to theory, harmony, the piano, and later on, composition and orchestration. One turning point in Shawan's career was reached when he entered into correspondence with the well known Russian composer A.I. Khatchadurian to whom he sent his manuscript scores for advice and guidance. Many of Khatchadurian's letters carry extremely encouraging remarks about the originality of style, its genuine character, and the eloquent rendering of oriental inspiration. In 1967 Khatchadurian extended an invitation to Shawan to attend the Tchaikowsky Conservatoire in the composition class supervised by Khatchadurian himself. **Works:** author of "Fantasy for Orchestra" (1945), "First Symphony" (1946), "Ouverture for ANTAR, an opera" (1947-48), "Symphonic poem" (1950), Symphonic pictures: "Abu Simbel" for chorus and orchestra, Meditation for violin and piano, 3 Arabesques for piano solo, Third Symphony "Expulsion of the Hyksos", etc... **Awards:** 1st Prize for Composition (1964), Ministry of Culture; Order of Science and Fine Arts (1st class). **Sports:** swimming and walking. **Hobbies:** Reading and Egyptology. **Prof. & Priv. Addr.:** 11 al-Qubbah street, Heliopolis, Tel.: 869314, Cairo, Egypt.

SHAWI (Hisham, Ibrahim, al), Iraqi academic and former diplomat. **Born** on 16 March, 1931 in Baghdad, Iraq. **Son** of Major General Ibrahim al Shawi. **Married,** two children. **Educ.:** B.A. (with distinction) in Political Science, American University of Beirut, Lebanon (1952); M.Litt. in International Relations, St. Anthony's College, Oxford University, Oxford, UK (1956). **Career:** Assistant Instructor, Instructor, Ass. Professor, Head of Department of Politics, Universities of Baghdad and al-Mustansyria (1958-70); Dean, College of Law and Politics, al-Mustansyria University (1970-72); Ambassador, Ministry of Foreign Affairs (1972); Permanent Representative of Iraq, UN Office, Geneva (1972); Minister of Higher Education and Scientific Research (1972-74); Minister of State (1974-75); Minister of State for Foreign Affairs (1975-76); Ambassador, Ministry of Foreign Affairs (1976-77); Permanent Representative of Iraq, UN, New York, USA (1977); Head of the Diwan of the Presidency of the Republic of Iraq (1977-78); Ambassador, Ministry of Foreign Affairs (1978); Ambassador to the Court of St. James, London (1978-82); Ambassador to Austria (1982-85), Ambassador to Canada (Sept. 1985- Aug. 1993), Non-resident Ambassador of Iraq to Jamaica, (July 1986- Aug. 1993), Non-resident Ambassador of Iraq to Grenada, (November 1987- Aug. 1993), Chairman of the Iraqi Atomic Energy Commission (1972-74), Governor for Iraq on the Board of Governors of the International Atomic Energy Agency (1974-76). **First President** of the Iraqi Political Science Association. **First President** of Iraqi UN Association, Representative of Iraq, Commission of Human Rights, member of the UN Subcommission on Prevention of Racial Discrimination and Protection of Minorities (1972-74). Resigned in August 1993. **Publ.:** "The Art of Negotiation", "An Introduction in Political Science" (1967), "From the Essence of the Matter" (1966); "The Wilsonian Conception of International Life" (a thesis). **Addr.:** Now Living in London, United Kingdom.

SHAWI (Khalid, al), Iraqi economist, oil official. **Born** in 1930 in Baghdad, Iraq. **Married,** three children. **Educ.:** Baghdad University; University of Michigan; Institut de Cape d'Aie, France. **Dipl.:** LL.B., LL.M., SJD. **Career:** Commercial Attaché (First Secretary), Embassy of Iraq to London; General Manager, Commercial Bank of Iraq; deputy Director, Iraqi National Oil Company; Director, State Organisation for Insurance (1964-65); Deputy Minister of Economy (1965); Minister of Industry and Acting Minister of Finance (1966-67); Dean, Faculty of Law and of Political Science, Mustansiriya University (1968); Professor and Head of Department of Law, Garyunis University, Libya; Counsellor and Director of Legal Affairs, Organisation of Arab Petroleum exporting Countries (since 1978). **Publ.:** "The Role of the Corporate Entity in International Law"; "Commercial Companies (Iraqi Law)"; "The Commercial Documents"; "Theory of Taxation and the Libyan Tax Legislation"; "The Campaign of Jewish Settlement in Barqa", etc. **Member** of the Iraqi and the International Law Syndicate; the Society of Comparative Insurance; Mansour Club. **Hobbies:** music, swimming, walking, reading biographies; contemporary history and political thought. **Addr.:** Baghdad, Iraq.

SHAWI (Mundhir, al), Iraqi educationist, statesman. **Born** in 1928 in Baghdad, Iraq. **Educ.:** LL.B., College of Law, Baghdad, Iraq (1951); Doctorat d'Université, Political Science, Toulouse, France (1961). **Career:** Professor of Constitutional Law and Jurisprudence, College of Law, Baghdad University, Baghdad, Iraq (1961-74); Head of Law Department, College of Law and Politics, Baghdad University, Iraq (1969-73); Minister of Justice (1974); member of the National Assembly (1980). **Member** of Iraqi Scientific Academy (since 1980). **Publ.:** Several books and articles on constitutional law and jurisprudence; papers on legal reforms. **Addr.:** Baghdad, Iraq.

SHAWI (Nazar Nadhif, al), Iraqi academic. **Born** in 1928 in Baghdad, Iraq. **Son** of Nadhif al-Shawi. **Married,** four children. **Educ.:** Michigan University; George Washington University. **Dipl.:** B.Sc. and Ph.D. **Career:** University of Baghdad: Lecturer, Assistant Professor; Professor; Deputy Dean; Head of Microbiology Department, (1956-65). Director, Central Institute for Microbiology; Technical and Administrative Superintendent of Iraqi Institutes (1969); President of the University of Mosul (1969); President of University of Basra (1970); Consultant, Ministry of Higher Education and Scientific Research Organisation (1977); Secretary General, Federation of Arab Scientific Research Councils (since 1977); member of the Council of medical and Social Research (1967); Higher Education Planning Committee (1972); Council of Higher Education and Scientific Research in Iraq (1976); General Health Committee, WHO (1970) and several other committees. **Addr.:** Federation of Arab Scientific Research Councils, P.O.B. 13027, Baghdad, Iraq.

SHAWLY (Abdul Aziz Abdallah), Saudi engineer. **Born** in 1941 in Mecca, Saudi Arabia. **Dipl.:** M.Sc. (Electronic Engineering). **Career:** Successively clerk, physicist, electronics engineer; Atomic Energy Equipment Maintenance Engineer member of Technical Committee, Prince Fawwaz Project of Co-operative Housing; has attended some International Atomic Energy Agency Conferences. **Address:** Directorate General of Mineral Resources, Tel. 6310355, Jeddah, Saudi Arabia.

SHAWQI (Farid, Mohamad Abdo), Egyptian actor. **Born** in July 1925 in Egypt. **Son** of Mohamad Abdo Shawqi. **Married** a third time Miss Hoda Sultan, 3 daughters: Mona, Nahed and Maha, Divorced. **Educ.:** Secondary and Dramatics. **Career:** State Domain (Cairo), then turned to the stage and screen starring in more than 180 motion pictures, including "Summer Holidays", "Three Thieves", now with National Theatre Company (Shakespeare's repertoire). **Addr.:** Cairo, Egypt.

SHAWQI (Mohamad, Tawfik), Egyptian oil official. **Born** in 1931 in Alexandria, Egypt. **Son** of Tawfik Shawki. **Married**, three daughters. **Educ.:** Petroleum Engineering, Cairo University, Egypt. **Career:** joined the Oil Wells Co. (1947); Director of Fields; Director of Operations, General Oil Co. (1958-66); Chairman of the Board of Suez Gulf Petroleum Co. (1966-77); Expert, General Petroleum Organisation (1977); Chairman of the Board of Balaum Petroleum Co. (1977-83); Director of Counsultancy Office (since 1984). **Medals:** Order of the Republic, 3rd Class. **Member** of the Automobile Club and al Gezira Club. **Hobbies:** swimming, tennis. **Addr.:** 155 Mohamad Farid Street, Cairo, Egypt.

SHAYBA (Ali, al), Yemeni senior army officer. **Born** in North Yemen. **Married**, children. **Educ.:** Elementary and secondary locally; received military training in the Soviet Union. **Career:** Commissioned Colonel in the North Yemeni Air Force, but was demoted on 13 June 1964 following the Coup d'Etat; rehabilitated in 1965 he was appointed member of the Revolutionary Command Council, Chief of land operations, and Instructor at the Military Academy. On 13 October 1977, he was commissioned by the Head of State to chair the special committee investigating the circumstances of the murder of late President al-Hamdi. On 19 October 1977 he visited a number of Arab countries to discuss his country's policy within the Arab Nation. On his return to Sana'a on 26th October 1977 he was appointed Chief of Staff of the North Yemeni Armed Forces. **Addr.:** Sanaa, Republic of Yemen.

SHAZLI (Abdulmoneim, al), Egyptian army officer. **Born** in Egypt. **Educ.:** Secondary and Military Academy. **Dipl.:** Former student of the Military Academy of Egypt, of the Egyptian Staff College. **Career:** Suez Campaign (1956); the Arab-Israeli war of June 1967; General of division. **Awards:** Egyptian and foreign, Commander National Order of Cedar (October 1969). **President** of Heliopolis Club. **Prof. Addr.:** Sporting Club of Heliopolis, Cairo suburb, Egypt.

SHAZLI (K., Abdussalam Mohamad, al), Egyptian nutritionist. **Born** on January 14, 1923 in Tantah. **Son** of Abdussalam Mohamad al-Shazli **and** Mrs., née Nazli Rustom. **Married** on April 24, 1950 to Miss Nazli Ali al-Dorri, 2 children: Muhieddine and Aley El Din. **Educ.:** Cairo and Edinburgh Universities, Roweet Research Institute, Aberdeen. **Dipl.:** Diplomas from the said universities and institute. B.Sc. (hons) Edinburg University, Ph.D. Aberdeen University. **Career:** Demonstrator, Faculty of Agriculture, Alexandria University (1943-51); Lecturer (1951-58); Assistant Professor (1958-65); Professor since 1965; Joined the Universities of Ohio and California (1958, 1959, 1963, 1964), **Publ.:** Author of numerous studies on protein degradation in rumen, discovery of branched chain volatile fatty acids as break down products of rumen fermentation, stickland type reaction was discovered and separation of S-amino valeric acid, method for estimation of diamino pimelic acid in rumen microorganisms and estimation of net growth, starch inhibition of cellulose digestion, role of urea in its relief. Ex member of Biochemical Society, Britain, Member of Egyptian Society of animal production. **Prof. Addr.:** University of Alexandria, Alexandria. **Priv. Addr.:** 27, El Geish Street, Alexandria, Egypt.

SHAZLI (Kamal Mohamed, al), Egyptian Politician. **Born** on February 16, 1934, in Monoufia. **Married,** four children. **Educ.:** B.A. Law, Cairo University (1957). **Career:** Assistant Secretary General, Socialist Union (1974); Member, National Assembly for al-Bagour (1969 and 1971); Member, People's Assembly (1979); Organizing Secretary General, National Democratic Party (1981); Minister of State People's Assembly and Shura Council Affairs (1993-to date). **Address:** Office of the Prime Minister, Sharia Magles al-Shaab, Cairo, Egypt.

SHAZLI (Saad, Mohamad el-Husseiny, al, Gen.), Egyptian army officer. **Born** on April 1, 1922 in Cairo (Egypt). **Married** on December 12, 1943 to Zinat Mohamed Metwally, three daughters. **Educ.:** Primary school, Basyoun village (1928-33); Khediv Ismail Secondary School, Cairo (1933-38); Faculty of Science, Cairo University (Oct.1938- January 1939); Military College (1939-43); Administrative Course (1947); Junior Officer's Command Course (1950); Staff College, Cairo (1951-52); Fort Benning Infantry School (USA, 1953); Cairo University (1952-54); Command and leadership course (Soviet Union, 1958-59). **Career:** Office of the Guards (1943-48); Platoon Commander, 1st Arab-Israeli War (1948); Paratroop Commander (1956-58); Chief of Staff, Paratroop Brigade (1960); Commander, Egyptian United Nations Contingent in Congo (1960-61); Military attaché, Egyptian Embassy, London (1961-63); Brigade Commander, Yemen civil war (1965-66); Commander, Shazly Group, Egyptian Israeli War (1967); Commander, special forces (1967-69); Commander Red Sea District (1970-71); Chief of Staff, Egyptian Armed Forces (May-December 1973); Ambassador, Egyptian Embassy, London (December 1973-75); Ambassador to Portugal (1975-78); founded Egyptian National Front (March 1980), Secretary-General (1980); Founder and Chief Editor, al-Gabha Magazine (August 1980). **Awards:** Officer, Order of the Republic (Egypt); Military Star; Military Medal of Courage (Egypt);

United Nations Congo Medal; decorations from Korea, Syria, Yemen West Germany and Palestine Liberation Organisation. **Sports:** air gliding, shooting, fencing and golf. **Hobby:** chess. **Publ.:** "How an Infantry Division can cross a water barrier" (1973), "Fonética Arabe Com Letras Portuguesas" (1978), "Kuranunn Karim" (1978), "Memoires of the 73 War" (1979), "The Crossing of the Suez" (1980), "The Arab-Israeli Conflicts in the Past and in the Future" (1982), "Four Years in the Diplomatic Service" (1983), "Arab Military Option" (1984). **Addr.:** Algiers, Algeria.

SHEBANI (Omar), Libyan academic, educationalist. **Born** in 1930 in Libya. **Educ.:** Ain Shams University; Boston University and George Washington University. **Career:** Assistant Director, Teachers College, University of Libya, Benghazi (1965); Director of Youth Department (1968); Professor, University of Libya (1970). **Addr.:** University of Libya, Benghazi, Libya.

SHEHAB (Ibrahim, Khalil), Egyptian academic, educationalist. **Born** in 1923 in Sohag, Egypt. **Son** of Khalil Shehab. **Married,** three children. **Educ.:** Cairo University; Columbia University. **Dipl.:** B.A.; M.A. and Ph.D. **Career:** Assistant Professor of Curriculum, Teachers College, Cairo (1958-63); Professor of Curriculum, Faculty of Education, Ain Shams University (1963-68); Professor of Curriculum, Faculty of Education, Tripoli, Libya; Professor and Head of Department of Curriculum, Faculty of Education, Ain Shams University (1972-75); UNESCO Expert, educational Research Center, Baghdad (1975-76); Professor of Curriculum, Faculty of Arts, Education and psychology, Mustansiriyah University, Baghdad (1976-78); UNESCO Expert in Curriculum and Evaluation and Head of the Department of Curriculum, University College of Arts, Science and Education, Bahrain (since 1978). **Publ.:** numbrous articles on education and teaching. **Hobbies:** Music, drama, travel, swimming, backgammon, cards, reading, walking. **Addr.:** University College of Arts, Science and Education, P.O.B. 1082, Manama, Bahrain. **Priv. Addr.:** 68 al-Zahraa Street, Apt. 4, Dokki, Giza, Egypt.

SHEHAB (Moufid, Mahmoud), Egyptian Minister of Higher Education and Scientific Reaearch, Egypt. **Born** on January 1, 1936 in Alexandria, Arab Republic of Egypt. **Son** of Mahmoud Shehab. Educator in the Egyptian Ministry of Education. **Married** to Dr. Hoda Magdy El-Sayed, one Child: Hany. **Educ.:** Primary and Secondary Education at the French Lycée, Alexandria (1943-1952), Faculty of law, Alexandria University (1952-1956). **Dipl.:** Post-Graduate Diploma in Law, Faculty of Law, Alexandria University; Scholarship from Cairo University for a Ph. D. in Law (Doctorat d'Etat) From the Sorbonne, Paris (1957-1963). **Career:** Lecturer in Public International Law, Cairo University; Assistant Professor in Public International Law, Faculty of Law, Cairo University, up till 1971; Teaching Assistant, thereafter lecturer, the International Faculty for Comparative Law, France (1961-1963); **Teaching Assistant,** Faculty of Law, Alexandria University (1957); Acting Head of the International Law Department, Faculty of Law, Cairo University (1973); Professor of Public International Law, Faculty of Law, Cairo University (1976); President of Cairo University from 1/9/1993 till 7/7/1997; Presently Minister of Higher Education and Scientific Research. **Other Information:** Member of the Egyptian Shura Assembly and Head of the Arab and Foreign Affairs and National Security Committee. **Chairman** of the Board of Directors of the Human rights Supporters Society since 1994. **Awards:** 1991: Order of the Glorious (First of September), 1995: La Legion d'honneur Order, 1996: Order of Merit. **Sports Practised:** Walking. **Hobby:** Reading - Music. **Prof. Addr.:** 4 Ibrahim Naguib st., Garden city, Cairo, Egypt, Tel.: 202-3552155, **Prif. Addr.:** 24 El-Iskandar ElAkbar St., Heliopolis, Cairo, Egypt, Tel.: 202-2905850.

SHEHABI (Ali, Saleh, al), Bahrain businessman. **Born** in 1948 in duraz, Bahrain. **Son** of Saleh al-Shehabi (Mechant) **and** Mrs. Taqeyya A. Shaheed. **Married in 1963** in Bahrain to Badreya Abdulla, five sons, one daughter: Hussain (1968), Roqayya (1970), Shehab (1976), Saleh (1978), Jaffar (1984) and Hassan (1985). **Educ.: Bahrain** Secondary School; willesden College of Technonoly; Somerset University. **Dipl.:** Auto Eng.,; B.Sc. (civil); MBA (Business Admin.); D.Sc. **Career:** Supervisor Auto Workshop, Bapco (1971); Teacher at Secondary Technical School (1973); General Contractor since 1968 (Shehabi Trading & Contracting). **Founder** of Federation of Arab Contractors. **Hobbies:** Reading, travellling, voluntary work, human assistance. **Prof. Addr.:** Shehabi Trading & Contracting, P.O.Box 5136, Tel.: 274811, Manama, Bahrain. Also - P.O.Box 846, Sayhat 31972, Saudi Arabia.

SHEHABI (Hikmat, Lieut. Gen.), Syrian army officer. **Born** in 1931 in Syria. **Married. Educ.:** in Syria, USA, USSR. **Career:** Armed forces; Chief of Staff of the Syrian Armed Forces (since 1974). **Addr.:** GHQ, Chief of Staff Office, The Armed Forces, Damascus, Syria.

SHEHABI (Mahmoud), Bahraini, bank executive. **Born** 1955. **Son** of Hajjeh Akbar Shehabi. **Married,** 2 children. **Educ.:** Commercial Diploma (1973); Advanced Accounting with GTC, Bahrain; 9 month in-house credit training with Chemical Bank New York. **Career:** Bank of Bahrain and Kuwait, Bahrain (1973-76); Chemical Bank, Bahrain - Financial Controller (1980-82), Operations Manager (1982-83), Corporate Marketing Officer (1984-). **Publ.:** Articles in Akhbar al-Khaleej, **Member:** Bahrain Historical and Archaelogical Society; Bahrain Bankers' Club. **Hobby:** Reading. **Addr.:** P.O.Box 5492. Telex 8562 A/B CHEMBK, Tel.: 252619, Manama, Bahrain.

SHEHABI (Samir Sobhi), Saudi diplomat. **Born in** 1925 in Jerusalem. **Dipl.:** B.A. American University, **Cairo;**

legal Studies, Yale University and Cambridge University. **Career:** Chargé d'Affaires, Rome (1959-61); Ambassador to Turkey (1964-73); Ambassador to Somalia (1973-74); Ambassador to the U.N. (1979); Ambassador to Pakistan (1980); attended many U.N. and Islamic Organization Conferences; Ambassador, Permanent Representative of Saudi Arabia to United Nations (1983). **Honours:** King Abdulaziz Order, Excellent Class, Sitara Pakistan Decoration. **Hobbies:** photography, sports. **Address:** 405 Lexington Avenue, 56th floor, New York, N.Y. 10017, U.S.A.

SHEHADI (Nadim), Lebanese economist. **Born** on February 11, 1956 in Beirut, Lebanon. **Son** of Fawzi Shehade (Engineer) **and** Mrs. Nadia née Dagher. **Married** in December 1986 in London to Claude Chahine, Two children: Lama (1989), Marwan (1990). **Educ.:** American University of Beirut, University of Kent at Canterbury, University of Leicester, University of Nottingham, The London School of Economics. **Dipl.:** B.A., M.A. **Career:** UNDP Beirut (1981); Director, Centre for Lebanese Studies, Oxford (1986- to date); Publisher Ithaca Press, London (1988-90). **Other Information:** Member of Council, British Society for Middle Eastern Studies. **Sports:** Cycling, Swimming, Jogging. **Hobbies:** Antiquarian Books and Maps, Pre-Cinema Optical Toys. **Member:** British Society for Middle Eastern Studies, Middle East Studies Association, Magic Lantern Society of Great Britain, Etc. **Prof. Addr.:** Centre for Lebanese Studies, 59 Observatory St., Oxford OX2 6EP, Tel.: (0865) 58465, U.K. **Priv. Addr.:** 13 Acfold Rd., London SW6 2AJ, U.K.

SHEHRI (Mohammad, Al, Dr.), Saudi Professor of Surgery. **Born** on March 11, 1959 in Taif, Saudi Arabia. **Son** of Yahia Al-Shehri **and** Mrs. Fatima Ali. **Married** in 1978 in Al-Namas to Miss Sara Al-Shehri, 7 children: Asma, Samya, Yahya, Khalid, Iman, Maimarah, Shahd. **Educ.:** College of Medicine, King Abdul Aziz University; University of Ottawa, Canada. **Dipl.:** FRCSC, FACS. **Career:** Asst. Prof. & Consultant General Surgeon, KSU, Abha College of Med. & Asir Central Hospital-1990; Dean, College of Medicine, King Saud University, Abha (1992-1999); Associate Professor of Surgery-1999; Vice President, King Khalid University for Graduate Studies and Research. **Awards:** Award of excellency for cultural & Social activities for Saudi Student Clubs in North America, 1989. Awards of the Teacher of the Year from the Students of the College of Med. Abha, 1990/1991. **Hobby:** Reading. **Prof. Addr.:** King Khalid University, P.O.Box 418, Tel.: 966-7-2290813, Saudi Arabia.

SHEIBAN (Abdullah Bin Ali Bin), United Arab Emirates businessman. **Born** in 1932 in Abu Dhabi, United Arab Emirates. **Son** of Ali Bin Sheiban. **Married,** five sons. **Career:** Worked for 20 years in Abu Dhabi Government and later United Arab Emirates Government; Under Secretary, Ministry of Social Affairs; member of the Board of Directors of UAE Trading Company; President of the Board of Administration of the International School of Shoueifat, Abu Dhabi. **Sports:** Swimming, skiing. **Prof. Addr.:** P.O.B. 462, Abu Dhabi, United Arab Emirates. **Priv. Addr.:** Tel.: 361462, Abu Dhabi.

SHEIBANI (Talaat, al), Iraqi former statesman. **Born** in 1917 in Iraq. **Educ.:** College of Law (Baghdad), Cairo University (Egypt), Indiana University (U.S.A.). **Dipl.:** Doctor of Philosophy. **Career:** Lawyer (1941-43); Teacher, College of Commerce and Economics of Baghdad (1951-53); Director Economic Bureau, Ministry of Development (1954); Director General Federation of Industries (1957-58); Minister of Planning (1959-63); Acting Minister of Oil (1959-60). **Publ.:** Author of "Influencing Powers on Constitution" (1954), "The Reality of Agricultural Property in Iraq" (1958). **Addr.:** al-Khansa Street, Nagib Pasha, Baghdad, Iraq.

SHEIKH (Abdallah M., al, Dr.), Saudi academic. **Born** in 1943 in Mecca, Saudi Arabia. **Dipl.:** B.Sc., Ph.D. (Botany). **Career:** Demonstrator, Faculty of Science, King Saud University (1967); Lecturer (1973); Assistant Professor (1975); Chairman of Botany Department (1978-80); Associate Professor, Faculty of Science, King Saud University since 1980. **Member:** Saudi Arabian Biological Society, British Ecological Society; former member of the Board, Faculty of Science Council, Saudi Biological Society; Presently Minister of Justice. **Publications:** Research and books on Plant Ecology, Botany, Biology, Agriculture; broadcasted scientific agricultural programmes and a documentary film about the Ecomoly of Sarawat Mountain. **Hobbies:** Scientific excursions, travel, photography. **Prof. Addr.:** Department of Botany, Faculty of Science, King Saud University, Tel.: 4785447/93, 4786210 Ext 231 or 210, Riyadh and Ministry of Justice. **Priv. Addr.:** Tel.: 4811000 Ext. 2667, Riyadh, Saudi Arabia.

SHEIKH (Abdel Wahab, Mohamad Saleh, H.E.), Saudi executive. **Born** in 1919 in Jeddah, Saudi Arabia. **Son** of Mohamad Saleh Shaikh (al-Shaikh Tribe). **Married,** 3 sons, 2 daughters. **Educ.:** al-Falah School, Jeddah; Bennett College, London. **Career:** Teacher & Secretary, al-Falah School, Jeddah (1935-39); Translator, Secretary, Treasurer and Accountant, Aramco (1939-48); Financial Adviser, Assistant Manager, Banque de l'Indochine et du Suez (1948-57); Vice Governor, Saudi Arabian Monetary Agency (1957-62); Minister of Commerce and Industry (1962); Executive Director, Islamic Development Bank, Jeddah; Director, Riyadh Bank, Jeddah, Saudi Arabia. **Hobbies:** Football, Basketball and Reading. **Addr.:** P.O.Box 1047, Tel.: 6432416-18, Telex: 401006, 401232. A/B RYADEX, Jeddah, Saudi Arabia.

SHEIKH (Abdul Malek Ibn Abdallah Ibn Ibrahim, al), Saudi educator and journalist. **Born in 1933 in Riyadh,** Saudi Arabia. **Dipl.:** B.A. Islamic **Law (Shari'a). Career:**

Teacher, Religious Institute, Ahsa (1959) and Riyadh (1961); Educational Supervisor, Ministry of Education (1961); Director, Teachers Preparatory Section, Examination Department, Ministry of Education (1962); Assistant Director General, Secondary Education (1966); Cultural Attaché, Austria (1967) Yemen (1972) and Tunis (1974); General Secretary, al-Darah Magazine. **Member:** Board of Directors, al-Darah Magazine. **Publication:** Judicial System in Islam (a thesis). **Hobbies:** reading, television viewing. **Address:** al-Darah Magazine, P.O.Box 2945, Riyadh, Saudi Arabia.

SHEIKH (Abdulaziz Ibn Mohamad Ibn Ibrahim, al), Saudi notary. **Born** in 1919 in Riyadh, Saudi Arabia. **Dipl.:** graduated in Islamic Classical Studies. **Career:** Public notary; research worker; Saudi Library Director (1948); principal of Riyadh Scientific Institute, (1955); Deputy Grand Qadi (Judge), (1959); Vice-Chairman, Faculties and Scientific Institute (1967); President of Imam Muhammad Ibn Saud Islamic University; menber of Higher Committee on Education Policy, Supreme Council for the promotion of Science, Arts and letters; permanent member, Major Social Scientists, USA; Chairman, Advocation of Good Deeds Board. **Publications:** Awdah al-Masalek Li Ma'refat Ahkam al-Manadek (The Clearest Paths of Know Ritual's Decision of Ritual); Alamr Bi Alma'rouf Bayn al-Madi Wa al-Hader, Matbo-atoh Wa Tahikikat (Advocate of Good Deeds, Past and Present Publications and Investigation); articles and lectures in the Muslim World league Journal and in some scientific academic periodicals. **Hobbies:** travelling and gardening. **Address:** el-Thalathin Street, Olaya, Tel.: 435 7180 (Office), and 465 8421, 475 8418, 465 8419 (Home), Riyadh, Saudi Arabia.

SHEIKH (Abdulrahman Ibn Abdulaziz, al, Dr.), Saudi former minister. **Born** on 2 June 1942 in Mecca, Saudi Arabia. **Dipl.:** B.Sc., and Ph.D. (Agricultural Economics). **Career:** Began his career in 1971 as an Assistant Professor and later became Dean, Faculty of Agriculture, King Saud University (1972-74) part-time consultant, the Industrial Research and Development Centre, Riyadh (1972-74); Vice Rector, king Faisal University, (1974-75); member of the Board and managing Director, the Agricultural Credit Bank, Riyadh (1972-75); Chairman, Board of Directors, Saline Water Conversion Corporation, Riyadh, the Saudi Fisheries Company and the National Agricultural Development Company; Grain Silos and Flour Mills Organization; member, the Board of Trustees of four Saudi Arabian universities and the Supreme Council of the universities; present Minister of Agriculture and Water until Aug. 1995. **Publications:** Agriculture and Economic Development with Special Emphasis on Strategy for Saudi Arabian Economic Development (Ph.D. thesis); some research papers in his field of specialization. **Address:** Riyadh, Saudi Arabia.

SHEIKH (Abid, Mohamad Saleh), Saudi Arabian statesman. **Born** on January 1, 1919 in Jeddah. **Son** of Mohamad Saleh Shaikh (Merchant) **and** Mrs. Rugaya Mohamad Siraj. **Married** to Amneh Asfahani in 1938, 5 children: Nawal (Mrs. Hassan Ashran), Thuraya (Mrs. Humoud Badr), Issam, Samir and Oussama. **Educ.:** al-Falah School (Jeddah), Bennett College (London). **Dipl.:** High School Certificate (with honours), Diploma of Advanced Studies in Commerce and Finance. **Career:** Teacher and Secretary, Treasurer and Accountant (consecutively) with Aramco (1939-48); Treasurer, Head of Bills Department, Finance Adviser and Assistant Manager of Banque de l'Indochine (1948-57); Controller General, of Foreign Exchange, Deputy Minister, Saudi Arabia Government (1957); Vice Governor for Saudi Arabia Monetary Agency (Central Bank); Minister of Commerce and Industry (1962). **Sports:** Football and Basketball. **Hobby:** Reading. **Member** of the Red Sea Club. **Priv. Addr.:** Malaz Quarter, Riyadh, Saudi Arabia.

SHEIKH (Amjad), Pakistani, bank executive. **Born** in 1954 in Kasur **Son** of M. Aslam Sheikh. **Single. Educ.:** commerce graduate **Career:** D.A.I.B. United Bank Ltd. Dammam Saudi Arabien (1970-81) Accountant Middle East Bank Ltd. Dubai-UAE. Administrative Director-Banque de Djibouti et du Moyen Orient-Djibouti. **Member:** Institute of Bankers in Pakistan. **Hobbies:** studies, sports and travelling. **Address:** B.P. 2471 Djibouti telex: 5943 Tel.: 351190, 351130.

SHEIKH (Esam Abid Mohamad Salih), Saudi educational attaché **Born** in 1948 in Jeddah, Saudi Arabia. **Dipl.:** Ph.D. (Marine Biology). **Career:** Assistant Professor, Faculty of Oceanography, King Abdulaziz University, Jeddah; Educational Attaché, the Saudi Arabian Educational Mission, Canada. **Member:** Board of Trustees, East West University; attended a meeting in his field of interest composed of experts from countries bordering the Red Sea. **Publications:** in the process of publishing a work entitled, Phytoplankton Ecology and Production of the Red Sea off Jeddah, Saudi Arabia. **Hobbies:** Racquet ball, swimming, fishing, reading. **Address;** King Abdulaziz University, Jeddah, Saudi Arabia.

SHEIKH (Fazal-ur-Rahman Amir Bakhsh), Saudi national, Consultant physician. **Born** in 1928 in Rangoo, Pakistan. **Degree.:** M.B.B.S. (1951): M.R.C.P., Edinburgh (1959): F.R.C.P., Edinburgh (1979). **Career:** House Physician and Clinical Teacher-Mayo Hospital and King Edward Medical College, Lahore (1951-57): Various hospitals in England and Scotland (1958-59): Assistant Professor of Medicine, Pakistan (1960-61): Physician to late King Khalid Bin Abdul Aziz (1964-1982); Member of British Medical Association: Fellow, Royal Society of Medicine, London: Fellow, Royal, College of Physicians, Edinburgh: Fellow, American College of Cardiology, USA, Adviser to The Royal Court-with **rank of a minister**

(1982-1995), retired but retained as consultant Physician to The Royal Court to date. Patron, Pakistani International School, Riyadh, Taif. Member of Board of Trustees for Al Shafa Trust Eye Hospitals, Pakistan. Appointed Visting Professor of Al Shifa' Institute of Ophtalmology, Rawalpindi, Pakistan (Honorary) (Nov. 1997). **Welfare Activities:** Young Muslims Association, Kenya, Pakistani Community Schools in the Kingdom. **Honours:** King Abdul Aziz Medal and Distinquish Service Medals from Pakistan (Hilal-Imtaiz), France, Belgium, U.K. (Knighthood), Germany, Iran, Jordan, Egypt, Spain, Qatar and Bahrain. **Hobby:** reading. **Prof. Addr.:** Tel.: 4415509. Riyadh. **Priv. Addr.:** P.O.Box 2658 Riyadh, 11461 Saudi Arabia. Tel.: 4826574, Riyadh, Saudi Arabia.

SHEIKH (Hassan ben Abdallah ben Hassan, al), Saudi official. **Born** in 1924 at Medina. **Dipl.:** B.A. (Arabic Language and Islamic Studies); Faculty of Islamic Law (Sharia), Mecca. **Career:** Member of the Judiciary Presidum, Western Region (1956-60); Vice-President of the Judiciary (1960-62); Vice-President of the Judiciary (1960-62); Minister of Education (1962); Minister of Education and Health (1962); Chairman of National UNESCO Committee (1962), Supreme Council for the Promotion of Science, Letters and Arts (1962), Saudi Boy Scouts Society (1962); Vice-Chairman of Supreme Committee on Education Policy (1964), Supreme Council of Universities; Chairman of Supreme Committee on Antilliteracy and Adult Education; President of Supreme Council for Antiquities (1972), Supreme Council of King Abdulaziz's Archives (Daratu al-Malik Abdulaziz) (1971); Chairman of Supreme Committee for Islamic Orientation; President of International Symposium of Muslim Youth; Honorary Consultant to International Universities Council; Attended Ministers of Education Conference (Baghdad), International Conference on Anti-illiteracy, (Teheran), Ministers of Education and Planning Conference (Libya), Conference of the Ministers of Higher Education and Scientific Research (Baghdad), several conferences in Saudi Arabia. **Publ.:** Author of Dawrona Fil Kifah (Our Rate in Struggle); Khawatir Juziyyah (Fragmentary Memories); Karamatul Fardi Fil Islam (Individual Prestige in Islam), published in both English and Arabic; al-Mar'ah; Maza Fa'al Biha al Islam (Woman; What has Islam offered Her?); regular contributions to the press. **Awards:** King Abdulaziz Order of Merit; Datu Order of Merit (Republic of Philippines); Honorary Ph.D. degree (Education), Mindanao State University, Philippines (1975); Honorary Ph.D. Degree, Soochow University, Republic of China (1975). **Hobbies:** reading, writing. **Prof. Addr.:** Minister's Bureau, Ministry of Higher Education, Riyadh, Saudi Arabia.

SHEIKH (Ibrahim Ibn Mohamad Ibn Ibrahim, al), Saudi former minister. **Born** in 1929 in Riyadh, Saudi Arabia. **Dipl.:** B.A., Faculty of Shari'a, Imam Muhammad Ibn Saud University, Riyadh (1956). **Career:** Deputy of the Grand "Mufti" of Saudi Arabia; Minister of Justice (1975-89). **Hobbies:** reading, taking walks. **Address:** Riyadh, Saudi Arabia.

SHEIKH (Mohamad Ibn Abdulaziz Ibn Abdallah Ibn Hassan, al), Saudi academic. **Born** in 1946 in Taif, Saudi Arabia. **Dipl.:** Ph.D. in Civil Engineering (specializing in Transport Engineering). **Career:** Assistant Professor, Civil Engineering Department, King Saud University (1975); Director General of Riyadh Diplomatic Quarter and the Minstry of foreign Affairs Staff Housing Projects, (1976); Dean, Faculty of Engineering, King Saud University; member American Society of Civil Engineers, Transport Research Association the Higher Commission for the Development of the City of Riyadh and the Higher Committee for the Development of Qasr al-Hukum (Governance Palace) in Riyadh; Minister of Municipal and Rural Affairs until Aug. 1995; Minister of State (since Aug. 1995). **Address:** Riyadh, Saudi Arabia.

SHEIKH (Saleh ben Abdelaziz ben Mohamed ben Ibrahim, al,H.E.), Saudi Minister. **Born** in 1378 H. in Riyadh, Saudi Arabia. **Educ.:** Secondary Education, Riyadh, Saudi Arabia. **Dipl.:** Licence from Islamic University of Imam Mohamed Ibn Saud, Faculty of Fundamentals of Religion then Academic to same University until 1416. **Career:** Has religious and Instructive texts and Lectures, 800 in number; Appointed by H.M. the King, Deputy Minister for Islamic affairs, Awkaf (Religious Endowments), Call and Guidance (1416 H.) then Minister of Islamic Affairs, Awkaf (Religious Endowments), Call and Guidance (1420 H.); General Supervisor to H.M. King Fahd Complex for Printing in Medina; President of Higher Awkaf Council (Religious Endowments); President of Call and Guidance Council; President of High Council for Benevolent Associations to the Holy Koran; General Supervisor for the management of Mosques and Antiquity Projects; President of Trustees for World Symposia for Islam Youths; President of Executive Council for Awkaf (Religious Endowments) Minister and Islamic Affairs; Member of International Islamic Council for Summons and Rescue in Cairo. Participated in Symposiums and conferences having different subjects inside the Kingdom, in America, Europe, Africa and Others. Participated and Reporting of Several Scientific Works: Supervision and revision of Encyclopaedia "Al Hadith Acharif" (6 books); He has also numerous article and reports in the different Education of Islamic Law, some printed. **Prof. Addr.:** Ministry of Islamic Affairs, Awkaf (Religious Endowments), Call and Guidance, Riyadh, Saudi Arabia.

SHELAL (Ait), Algerian diplomat. **Born** in 1929 in Messaoud, Algeria. **Married**, three children. **Educ.:** University of Paris, France. **Dipl.:** Doctorate. **Career:** President of General Union of Muslim Algerian Students; Ambassador to Italy (1967-71); Ambassador to Belgium (1971); also accredited to Netherlands and Luxembourg;

Secretary General, Non Aligned Conference, Algiers (1973); Delegate, North-South Dialogue, Paris (1975-76). **Addr.:** Ministry of Foreign Affairs, Algiers, Algeria.

SHENAIBER (Abdul Aziz Abdulah, al), Saudi official. **Born** in 1936. **Dipl.:** B.Sc. (Petroleum Enginering). **Career:** Petroleum Engineer 1965); Technical Adviser, Minister's Bureau, Ministry of Petroleum (1967); Director, Development Division (1968); Director, Minister's Bureau (1971); Director General, Ministry of Petroleum (1971-75); Deputy Minister for Administration and Financial Affairs, Ministry of Petroleum and Mineral Resources (1975 to date). **Member:** the Board of Trustees, University of Petroleum and Minerals (1975-86); member of the Board, Public Organization for Sea Water Desalination (1975-86); Vice President, World Petroleum Conference (1975-79); has attended international conferences on Energy, World Petroleum Conference, Arab Petroleum Conference and the Atomic Energy Conference. **Prof. Addr.:** Ministry of Petroleum and Mineral Resources, P.O.Box 247, Riyadh 11191, Tel.: 4761899, Riyadh. **Priv. Addr.:** Tel.: 4775861, Riyadh, Saudi Arabia.

SHENDY (Wagih), Egyptian politician. **Born** in 1936 in Cairo, Egypt. **Son** of Waheed M. Shendy. **Married** in 1964, 1 son, 1 daughter. **Educ.:** Heliopolis University, Cairo; Georgetown University, Washington DC, USA, Masters in International Trade Law. **Dipl.:** B.Com. (1957); LL.B.; Ph.D. (International Finance) (1964). **Career:** Commercial Attache, Egyptian Embassy, Washington DC, USA; Egyptian Representative, FAO, Trade Committee; Assistant Professor, Howard University, Washington DC, USA; Permanent Representative, International Economy Organization, Washington DC, USA; Vice Chairman, International Cotton Advisory Committee; Chairman, Finance & Information Committees, International Cotton Advisory Committee; Acting Commercial Counsellor, Washington DC, USA; Associate Professor, American University, Egypt; Professor, King Abdul Aziz University, Jeddah, Saudi Arabia; Professor and Chairman, Economics Department, Mansourah University, Egypt; Under-Secretary of State, Ministry of Economy and Economic Cooperation; Director, Arab Investment Bank, Egypt. Permanent Egypt's Representative, International Bank of Reconstruction and Development, International Monetary Fund and other UN Agencies; Egyptian Minister of Investment and International Cooperation (1982-84); **Publ.:** International Trade Organizations, Cairo (1971); International Payments and International Currency Crisis Cairo (1974); Twenty-two articles dealing in International Finance, International Trade, International Finance, International Trade, International Payments and Petroleum Economics. **Member:** International Rotary. **Hobbies:** Reading, Music and Sports. **Addr.:** Corniche al-Nil, P.O.Box 1147, Tel.: 753301-2, Telex: 93792 A/B INVBK, Cairo, Egypt.

SHENOUDA (Hilmy, Said), Egyptian executive. **Born** in 1925 in Khartoum, Sudan. **Son** of Shenouda. **Married** in 1961, 2 sons, 1 daughter. **Educ.:** Cairo University, Egypt. **Dipl.:** B.Com.; High Cert. of Taxation. **Career:** Joined The National Bank of Egypt since 1943. Held different key posts in the Bank; General Manager, Main Branch, Cairo. General Manager, Documentary Credits and Executive General Manager, The National Bank of Egypt, Cairo (1982). Director, Société Générale, Cairo. **Member:** Gezira Sporting Club; Rowing Sporting Club. **Hobbies:** Music and tennis. **Addr.:** 8, Samir Zaki Street, Zamalek, Tel.: 801213, Telex: 92238 A/B NBE CRO UN, Cairo, Egypt.

SHERBINI (Emadeddine, Abbas, al), Egyptian engineer. **Born** on October 20, 1921 in Zagazig, Sharquieh Governorate (Egypt). **Son** of Abbas al-Sherbini (Barrister) **and** Mrs., Nagiya Zeitoun. **Married** to Suraya Khalafawy in 1949, 3 children: Sara, Ezzeddine and Omar. **Educ.:** Toufiquieh Secondary School (1937-42), Faculty of Engineering, Cairo University, Faculty of Law, Cairo University (2 years). **Dipl.:** Secondary Education Certificate (1942), Bachelor of Science (Engineering), Machines and Engines (1949). **Career:** Engineer at the Egyptian State Railways (1949-51); Engineer at the Railways Production Office (1951-60); Head of the Railways Production Office (1960); promoted Deputy-Director of the Diesel Maintenance Shop (1960-62); Director General of the Planning and Production Office (1962-65); Director General of the Technical Research Department at the Ministry of Transport. **Sport:** Shooting (in 1954 he was selected to lead the Shooting Team representing Egypt at the Olympic Games). **Member:** of Cairo Shooting Club and Head of the Shooting Department. **Remark:** He Travelled extensively throughout the world, visiting in his official capacity the U.S.A., Japan, Honolulu, the U.K., the Continent (all the countries of Eastern and Western Europe). **Prof. Addr.:** Ministry of Transport, Qasr al-Aini Street, Tel.: 26838, Cairo, Egypt. **Priv. Addr.:** 52, Abdulkhaleq Sarwat Street, Tel.: 930909, Cairo, Egypt.

SHERBINI (Ibrahim, Khalil, al), Egyptian judge. **Born** in 1923 in al-Mansoura, Egypt. **Son** of Khalil Sherbini. **Married**, three children. **Educ.:** Cairo University. **Dipl.:** LL.B., M.A. **Career:** National Court Judge (1951-55); High Court Adviser (1955-75); General President, National Assembly (since 1975); Chairman, Advisory Committee Council (since 1980); Consultant, High Committee of Supervision. **Publ.:** "Clearance of Superintendences"; "Explaining the General Foundation of Law and Public Sector Workers Under the Superintendency". **Member** of Cairo Shooting Club and Cairo Automobile Club. **Addr.:** 20 Omar Ibn el-Khattab Street, Dokki, Cairo, Egypt.

SHERBINY (Mahmoud Gharib, Disouky, el), Egyptian academic, engineer. **Born** in 1946 in Sharkiyah, Egypt. **Married. Educ.:** Cairo University; University of Salford, UK. **Dipl.:** M.Sc. and Ph.D. in Mechanical Engineering. **Career:** Research Assistant, Technical University of Denmark; **Teaching Assistant**, Faculty of Engineering, Cairo University; Research Associate; University of Salford, UK (1973); Research Fellow, Loughborough University of Technology, UK (1975); Assistant Professor (1976); Associate Professor (1980); Professor of Machine Design, Cairo University (1985); Chairman of the **Egyptian Society** of Tribology since (1987); Chairman of Cairo University center of Tribology (1991). Vice Dean for Student affairs (1994) Dean Faculty of Engineering (1995). **Decorations:** the Egyptian State Prize of Engineering Science (1980); the First Class Science Decoration of Egypt (1980); MI-MechE; C.Eng. **Addr.:** Department of Mechanical Design, Faculty of Engineering, Cairo University, Giza, Cairo.

SHERIF (Osama Mahmoud, el), Jordanian publisher; chief editor: the star weekly and Arabia.on.Line (www.arabia.com). **Born** in 1960 in Jerusalem. **Son** of Mahmoud el-Sherif. **Married** on April 20, 1984 to Gada Yasser Amro, 2 children: Rawan (1985), Omar (1987). **Educ.:** Islamic College, Amman; New England College, England; University of Missouri, U.S.A. **Dipl.:** B.A. Journalism (Publishing). **Career:** Editor the Jerusalem Star (1984); Chief Editor, The Jerusalem Star (1986); Editor ad-Dustour daily (1988); Publisher and Chief Editor The Star (1990-); Publisher al-Ghad al-Iktissadi (1990); President Media Services International (Info-Media) (1988); Consultant for ASharq Arabic daily, Doha, Qatar; Middle East Correspondent and Editor the World Paper, Boston. **Other Information:** Columnist in a number of local, Arab and International papers. **Sports:** Travel, professional photography, swimming, trekking and horesback-riding. **Hobbies:** Photography, travel, fiction writing. **Member:** Jordan Press Association, Royal Automobile Club, Royal Society for the Conservation of Nature. **Credit Card:** Visa. **Prof. Addr.:** The Star, P.O.Box 9313, Tel.: 4648-298, Amman, Jordan.

SHERLALA (Kassem Mohamad), Libyan former official. **Born** in 1936 in the Socialist People's Libyan Arab Jamahiriya. **Educ.:** Libya. **Dipl.:** Graduated from Cairo University (1960); Post-Graduate Degree, American University, Washington, USA (1962). **Career:** Joined Central Bank of Libya, then known as National Bank of Libya (1959); appointed Director, Economic and Research Division, Central Bank of Libya (1968); Governor, Central Bank of Libya (1969-70); **Addr.:** Tripoli, Libya.

SHEROOQI (Salem), Bahraini banker and businessman. **Born** in 1931 in Bahrain. **Son** of Abdalla Senan Sherooqi. **Married**, 4 sons, 2 daughters. **Dipl.:** Management Diploma, Belgium. **Career:** Director, Bank of Bahrain & Kuwait, B.Sc., Manama, Bahrain; Director, Bank Oman Bahrain & Kuwait; Bahrain Investment Co.; Marine Safety & Technical Services; al-Amar Est.; Arabian Printing & Publishing House, Bahrain. **Member:** Six Continents Club; Marina Club. **Hobby:** Reading. **Addr.:** Government Road, P.O.Box 597, Telex: 8919 BAKUBK, Manama, Bahrain.

SHIBEIKA (Izzeddine Makki), Sudanese diplomat. **Born** in 1928 in Sudan. **Married** in 1958 to Miss Louyja Hassan, 2 children. **Educ.:** Khartoum University and London Schools. **Dipl.:** Bachelor of Arts, Diploma of Public Administration. **Career:** District Officer (1952-53), District Commissioner, Kermak (1953-54) and Akobo (1955-56); First Secretary, Ministry of Foreign Affairs (June 1956); in Mission to Baghdad (1956-58); Consul General to Uganda and Kenya (1958-60); Counsellor, United Nations (1961); Minister acting Under-Secretary Ministry of Foreign Affairs (1961-64); Ambassador to Somalia (1964). **Publ.:** Author of various papers and lectures on the history and economy of the Sudan. **Member:** Rotary Club of Baghdad and Mogadishu. **Prof. Addr.:** c/o Ministry of Foreign Affairs, Khartoum, Sudan.

SHIBEL (Abdul Rahman Saleh), Saudi civil servant. **Born** in 1936. **Dipl.:** B.A. (Islamic Law). **Career:** former school-teacher; member of Charity Fund; Medina, Literary Society, Medina; Administrative Inspector, Ministry of Education; member of First Conference of Saudi Men of Letters, Mecca 1973. **Publications:** Da'wat al Sheikh Mohamad Abdul Wahab (The Influence of Sheikh M. Abdul Wahab on Modern Islamic Thought). **Address:** Department of Education, Medina, Saudi Arabia.

SHIBEL (Mohamad al-Solaiman, al), Saudi poet and educator. **Born** in 1931 at Onaizah. **Dipl.:** Higher Diploma (Islamic Law and Arabic Language), Faculty of Shari'a, Mecca. **Career:** Teacher and later Principal, intermediate school; Deputy Director, secondary school; Director, King Abdulaziz Secondary School, Mecca. **Member:** the Board, Mecca Organization for Printing and Information; contributed to Saudi literary movement. **Prof. Addr.:** King Abdulaziz Secondary School, Mecca. **Priv. Addr.: Addr.:** Tel.: 5436007, Mecca, Saudi Arabia.

SHIBRY (Mohamad Sad, al), Saudi civil servant. **Born** in 1943 at al-Nammas. **Dipl.:** B.A. (Arabic Literature). **Career:** Former Assistant Director of Telegraphs, Posts and Telephones. Dammam; later Chief of Administrative Division, Telecommunication Agency; Ministry of Posts, Telegraphs and Telephones; Director of Planning; Training and Budgeting, Directorate General of Telegraphs; delegated to function as Director of Central Province; now Director (by delegation) Western Province Postal Department. **Hobby:** reading Arabic literature. **Prof. Addr.:** Postal Administration, Western Province, Tel.: 32685, Jeddah, Saudi Arabia.

SHIDDI (Ali Ibn Ahmad, al), Saudi publisher and writer. **Born** in 1946 in Riyadh, Saudi Arabia. **Son** of Ahmad al Shiddi. **Educ.:** General. **Career:** Editor in Chief of Tigarat-at-Riyadh Magazine (1968-71); Manager of Information Bureau in the Ministry of Finance (1971-

75); writer and editor in al-Jazira Newspaper (1976-83); President of Dar al-Watan for Publishing and Information; President of International Catering and Trading Establishment; Director f Administration of The Arab Investment Company; Board member of Alrajhi Banking and Investment Corporation; Board member of Saudi Hotel Services Company. **Hobbies:** Reading, sports. **Addr.:** P.O.B. 3310, Tel.: 01-4653313, 4644659, Riyadh, Saudi Arabia.

SHIHAB-ELDIN (Adnan), Kuwaiti scientist and nuclear engineer. **Born** in 1943; **Married,** three children. **Educ.:** B.Bs. in Electrical Engineering; M.Sc. in Nuclear Engineering; Ph.D. in Nuclear Engineering, University of California, Berkeley, USA. **Career:** currently the Director of the Division for Africa, and East Asia and the Pacific, Department of Technical Cooperation, at the International Atomic Energy Agency (IAEA) in Vienna, Austria. Prior to joining the IAEA, from December 1991 to February 1999, he served as Director of the UNESCO Regional Office for Science and Technology and as the UNESCO Representative in Egypt, Sudan, and Yemen. Dr. Shihab-Eldin has taught and directed research at a number of universities and research centers in Kuwait, Switzerland, and the United States. In Kuwait, he served as Vice Rector for Academic Affairs at Kuwait University from 1976 to 1980 and was the Director General of the Kuwait Institute for Scientific Research (KISR) from 1976 to 1986. Dr. Shihab-Eldin is a member of many national, regional, and international professional societies; he has also served as a member of the Board of Directors of more than 30 companies, foundations, as well as advisory committees. He has published more than 100 scientific papers, articles and reports, and co-authored 5 books in the areas of Nuclear Physics and Chemistry, Nuclear Engineering, Energy Systems and Environmental Policy, Management and Development of Science & Technology in Developing Countries, and other related fields **Addr:** International Atomic Energy Agency, Wagramer Strass 5, P.O.Box 200, A-1400 Vienna, Austria.

SHIHADEH (Musa, Abdel-Aziz), Jordanian Executive. **Born** in 1941 in Beir Ma'een. **Son** of Abdel-Aziz Shihadeh. **Married** in 1969, one son and 3 daughters. **Educ.:** Beirut Arab University. **Dipl.:** B.Com. (Accountancy); M.B.A., (USA) University of San Francisco. **Career:** Arab Bank Ltd., Amman (1961-66); Jordan National Bank, Amman (1966-80); Deputy General Manager Jordan Islamic Bank, Amman (1980-82). General Manager, Jordan Islamic Bank, Amman (since 1982), Vice-Chairman since 1995; **Publ.:** How to Audit a Bank, Monograph, published by Arab Banks Union. **Hobby:** Reading **Addr.:** P.O.Box 926225, Tel.: 5677377, Telex: 21125, 23993, Fax: 5666326, A/B ISLAMLIJO, Amman, Jordan. E-mail: Musa@islamicbank.com.jo.

SHIHAIL (Abdulaziz Mohamad, al), Saudi executive. **Born** in 1943 in Mecca, Saudi Arabia. **Dipl.:** B.Sc. (Management), M.Sc. (Public Administration). **Career:** Partner and Executive Manager, Saudi Butane Factory (1973-74); Partner and President, United Saudi Co. for Development and Contracting (1974); Director General, al-Sari Establishment for Contracting & Trade. **Honorary member:** al-Hilal Sports Club; member, Board of Saudi Butane Factory. **Hobbies:** reading, photography, hunting. **Prof. Addr.:** al-Sari Establishment, Airport Road, Tel.: 4762594, Riyadh. **Priv. Addr.:** Tel.: 4022433, Riyadh, Saudi Arabia.

SHIHAIL (Faisal Mohamad Abdul Aziz, al), Saudi official. **Born** in 1935. **Dipl.:** M.A. (Public Administration). **Career:** Director-General and Member of Board, al-Jezirah Press Organization (1966-69); Member of Board of Arab League Arab Maritime Transport Academy; Vice-Chairman of Inter-Governmental Maritime Consultant Organization (1971-73); Saudi Chief Delegate to Conference on the Law of the Sea, Caracas (1973); member of Maritime Safety Conference, Conference on Freight Line, London; Lecturer Riyadh University; working on Ph.D. dissertation on Economics of Maritime Transport, University of Paris. **Member:** Saudi Olympic Committee; Vice-Chairman of Saudi Football Federation, al-Hilal Sporting Club; Constituent member of Riyadh Private Schools. **Publ.:** books under publication on Public Administration, Planning and Control. **Sport:** Swimming. **Hobbies:** Chess, reading. **Prof. Addr.:** Ministry of Communications, Roads and Posts Affairs, Tel.: 23108, Riyadh. **Priv. Addr.:** Tel.: 62521, Riyadh, Saudi Arabia.

SHIHATA (Ibrahim), Egyptian executive **Born** in 1937 in Damietta, Egypt. **Married,** 3 children. **Educ.:** Cairo University, LLB. (1957); **Dipl.** in Public Law (1958); Dipl. in Private Law (1959); Harvard University, SJ.D. (1964). **Career:** Conseil d'Etat, Cairo (1957-60); Member, technical Bureau of U.A.R. President in Damascus (1959-60); Associate Professor, International Law, Ain-Shams (1964-66; 1970-72); Legal Adviser, Kuwait Fund for Arab Economic Development (1966-70; 1972-76); Director-General, the OPEC Fund for International Development, Vienna, Austria (1976-83); Executive Board member, International fund for Agricultural Development, Rome (1977-1983); Vice President and General Counsel, World Bank, then Senior Vice President, World Bank (1983-98); Secretary-General, International Centre for Settlement of Investment Disputes (ICSID) (1983-) Chairman, International Development Law Institute (Rome), (1983-) Honorary Chairman, Egyptian Center for Economic Studies (Cairo) (1999-); Board Member, Oxford Energy Club; Oxford; Board Member, International Fertiliser Development Center, Alabama (1979-84); Trustee, Centre of Research on the New International Economic Order, Oxford; Member, North-South Round Table. Founding Member, Institute of Transnational Arbitration (Houston) and WHO Association (London); Member, International Council for Commercial Arbitration (1998-). **Publ.:** "The Power of the International Court to Determine its own

Jurisdiction" (English, 1965); "International Air and Space Law" (Arabic, 1966); "International Joint Ventures" (Arabic 1969); "Treatment of Foreign Investment in Egypt" (Arabic, 1972); "secure and Recognized Boundaries" (Arabic, 1974): "The Arab Oil Embargo" in English, Arabic & Spanish (1975); "International Guarantees for Private Foreign Investments" (English, 1972); "the Other Face of OPEC" in English, French and Spanish (1982); MIGA and Foreign Investment (English and Chinese 1988); The European Bank for Reconstruction and Development (1990); Legal Treatment of Foreign Investment (English, 1993); The World Bank in a Changing World, vol. II (1995); vol.III (forthcoming January 2000); Complementary Reform (English, (1997) and Russian (1998)); The World Bank Inspection Panel in Practice (2nd ed., 1999); Toward Comprehensive Reform (Arabic, 1993); My Will for My Country (Arabic, 2nd. ed.1999). Other books and published essays on various subjects related to development and international law subjects. **Addr:** 4501 W St., NW, Washington DC 20007.

SHIHATA (Shirine Hamza, Mrs.), Egyptian broadcaster **Born** in 1946 in Cairo, Egypt. **Dipl.:** B.A. (History). **Career:** Announcer, Jeddah Broadcasting; has made a significant contribution to Broascasting and the Press; one of the female pioneers in the field of Broasdasting in Saudi Arabia. **Publications:** edited, to My Daughter Shirine, a collection of letters written by the late Hamza Shehata to his daughter. **Hobbies:** reading, writing, playing the piano and organ. **Prof. Addr.:** P.O.Box 7425, Tel.: 6533487, Jeddah. **Priv. Addr.:** Tel.: 6657651, Jeddah, Saudi Arabia.

SHINAWY (Ahmad A.), Saudi executive. **Born** in 1939 in Mecca, Saudi Arabia. **Dipl.:** Ph.D. (Business Administration). **Career:** Director of Planning, Budget and Statistics, Ministry of Commerce; Director General, Grain Silos and Flour Mills Organization; member of Board, Riyadh Schools; member of Board, Grain Silos and Flour Organization; part-time lecturer, Institute of Public Administration. **Publications:** The Role of Accounting and Accountants in the Developing Economy of Saudi Arabia; articles in accounting periodicals. **Hobby:** reading. **Prof. Addr.:** P.O.Box 3402, Tel.: 4768944, Riyadh. **Priv. Addr.:** Tel.: 4020260, Riyadh, Saudi Arabia.

SHIQDAR (Hashim Noor), Saudi civil servant. **Born** in 1925 in Mecca, Saudi Arabia. **Dipl.:** B.Sc. (Geology). **Career:** Geologist; Director, Geological Department, Directorate General of Mineral Resources; Director, Chemical Laboratory; Director, Technical Affairs Department; Director of Projects, Directorate General of Mineral Resources, Jeddah. **Member:** Saudi Arabian permanent delegation to Board of Radioactive Isotopes Centre for the Arab States, Cairo; attended Conference on Maps for Southeast Asian Countries, Bangkok, General Conference of the International Atomic Energy Agency, Vienna, Second Conference on Mineral Resources in the Arab Countries, Jeddah. **Publication:** co-author of Geology textbook for Secondary School (2nd Class). **Prof. Addr.:** General Directorate of Mineral Resources, Tel.: 6310355, Jeddah. **Priv. Addr.:** Tel.: 6654073, Jeddah, Saudi Arabia.

SHIRAWI (Khalid, Abdulla, al), U.A.E. Businessman. **Born** on September 22, 1961 in Dubai, UAE. **Son** of Abdulla Shirawi **and** Mrs. Zubaida. **Married** in 1992 in Dubai/ Hessa, four children: Hamdah, Abdulla, Aysha, Mohammad. **Educ.:** Boston University - MS/MIS, University of Southern California - BS/BA. **Career:** General Manager, Modern Plastic Industry - 10/1987; Executive Director, Arabian Oasis Food Co. LLC-01/1989; Executive Director, Pastalini Food Processing Industries LLC-02/1995. **Prof. Addr.:** Arabian Oasis Food Co. LLC., P.O.Box 6323, Dubai, U.A.E., Tel.: 00971-4-2852465, Fax: 00971-4-2856976. **Home** Tel.: 00971-4-3496633.

SHIRAWI (Yousuf, Ahmed), Bahraini Politician. **Born** on October 10, 1927 at Muharraq, Bahrain. **Married** to May Al Arrayyed, 6 children. **Educ.:** Primary and Junior High School, Bahrain; Senior Secondary (Prep) I.C., Bahrain; BA American University of Beirut, lebanon (1950); Higher Education, Glasgow, UK, 1953-55 (ARTC). **Career:** Teacher, Hostel Warden, Headmaster of Bahrain Secondary School (1950-53); Higher Education, UK (1953-55); Assistant Director of Education, Directorate of Education (1955-57); Secretary to the Administration Council Assistant to the Secretary of the Government (1956-70); Director of Oil Affairs, Finance Directorate (1963-70); Director of Development Bureau, Finance Directorate (1967-70); Head of Department, Department of Development & Engineering Services (1970-71); Minister of Development & Engineering Services (1971-75); Acting Minister of State for Cabinet Affairs (1982-92); Minister of Development & Industry (1975-1996). **Other Appointments Held:** Chairman, Bahrain Petroleum Company BSC (c); Chairman, Aluminium Bahrain BSC (c); Chairman, Bahrain National Oil Company; Board Member, Gulf Air; Chairman, Executive Committee, Gulf Air; President, Bahrain Chess Association; Vice-Chairman, Bahrain Centre for Studies and Research; Member of the Board of Trustees, Bahrain University; Member of the Board of Trustees, Centre for Global Energy Studies; Emeritus Trustee, American University of Beirut; Member, OAPEC Ministerial Council; Member, International Strategic Studies Centre, Washington. **Addr.:** Manama, Bahrain.

SHISHEKLY (Saifuddin al-Hussain al-Ali, al), Syrian physician. **Born** in 1921. **Dipl.:** M.B.B.Ch. **Career:** Lieutenant Doctor, Syrian Army (1949); physician, Jizan (1951); physician, Mecca (1954); Assistant Director, Health Affairs, Eastern Province (1955); Director, Central Hospital, Riyadh (1956); Chief, Health Department, Riyadh City Secretariat (1957); Director, Military Health Department,

Saudi Arabian Army (1962); Director General, Independent Hospital Department (1964); Director General of Health Affairs, Eastern Province (1955); Director, Central Hospital, Riyadh (1956); Chief, Health Department, Riyadh City Secretariat (1957); Director, Military Health Department, Saudi Arabian Army (1962); Director General, Independent Hospital Department (1964); Director General of Health Affairs, Eastern Province. **Member:** Emergency Medical Commission on the Combat of Commercial Fraud, Ministry of Social Affairs; Charter member, American Association of Military Surgeons; attended the Conferences on Military Medicine in Venezuela and the United States and the World Health Organization Conference. **Hobbies:** sports, farming, poetry. **Address.:** Ministry of Health Branch, Dammam, Saudi Arabia.

SHISHTAWY (Saied, al), Egyptian expert agronomist and international officer. **Born** on March 12, 1929 at Tantah city, Gharbiyah Governorate (Lower Egypt). **Educ.:** Faculty of Agriculture, Cairo University; Ohio State University, Columbus (USA). **Dipl.:** B.Sc. (Agriculture) (1961), Ph.D. (Agricultural economy) (1963). **Career:** Chief, Scientific and Technical Documentation Section, National Research Centre, Cairo (1955-60); Researcher, Ohio State Univrsity, Columbus (1963-64); Assistant Professor, Bluefield State College USA (1963-64); Adviser, Government Agricultural Institute of National Planning, Egypt; Professor of Agricultural Economy, University of Cairo (1964-65); Rural Institutions Officer, Food and Agriculture Organisation (FAO) Iraq and Tanzania (1965-69); Deputy Chief and Officer, Near East and North Africa Bureau FAO, (1970-73); Chief, Regional Bureau for the Near East & North Africa, Development Department, (FAO) Rome (Italy) since 1974. **Publ.:** author of "Effect of Membership Relations on Patronage in a Farmer Cooperative" (1961), "Statistical Analysis of the Interrelationships of Major Factors reported by 51 Ohio Agricultural Cooperative Managers" (1963), "Survey and Plan for Irrigation Development in the Pangani and Wami River Basins" (1968), "Study of Selected Agricultural Reform Programmes" (1970). **Awards:** Alpha Kappa Delta; Gamma Sigma Delta. **Member:** Kiwanis International Club. **Sports:** golf and swimming. **Hobbies:** reading and music. **Prof. Addr.:** Food and Agriculture Organisation, Via Delle Terme di Caracalla, Tel.: 579700100, Rome (Italy). **Priv. Addr.:** Via Alessandro Magno, Isola 5, Villino 4, Tel.: 06-609.11.55, Rome, Italy.

SHO'ALA (Abdulnabi Abdulla Al), Bahraini businessman. **Educ.:** University of Bombay (India). **Degree:** B.A. (Politics & Public Administration). **Career:** Ministry of Foreign Affairs, Bahrain (1973). **Founded:** Gulf Markets International Bahrain (1977); Chairman, Gulf Hill & Knowlton (1985); Director, Middle East Research & Consultancy (MERAC); Chairman, Telegulf Directory Publications WLL; Chairman, Al Fanar Travels WLL; Chairman Gulf Translations WLL; Chairman, Aptech Information Systems, (Middle East) WLL; **Chairman,** Grafix Arabia WLL; Vice-President of Bahrain Chamber of Commerce & Industry; Member of the Shura Council, State of Bahrain and its Executive Committee. **Member:** Institute of Public Relations (UK). **Sports:** Swimming and Horse Riding. **Prof. Addr.:** Bahrain Tower, 1st Floor, Government Avenue, P.O.Box 1557, Manama, Bahrain, Tel.: 213600/213800, Fax: 213700.

SHOBOKSHI (Abdul Majeed A.), Saudi leading journalist, **Born** in 1927 in Jeddah, Saudi Arabia. **Dipl.:** al-Falah Secondary School Certificate. **Career:** Former Officer, Jeddah Police Department; Director of Haj Department; Director, Foreigners Control Office; Director, Passports Department; Director, Jeddah Police Department; presently Editor-in-Chief, al-Bilad daily newspaper. **Member:** Constituent board, King Abdulaziz University; General Committee of King Faisal Welfare Society; Jeddah Welfare Fund; Board, al-Bilad Press Organization; Chairman of the Kingdom's delegation to the 1st and 2nd Conference of Arab Journalists. **Honours:** two Orders of Merit from Tunisia and Morocco. **Hobby:** reading. **Address:** al-Bilad Newspaper, P.O.Box 6340, Tel.: (2) 671.1000, Jeddah, 21442, Saudi Arabia.

SHOBOKSHI (Ali Hussein), Saudi leading businessman. **Born** in 1940 in Jeddah, Saudi Arabic. **Dipl.:** Educated Ein Shams University, Cairo; B.Sc. (Business Administration). **Career:** Chairman, Ali and Fahd Shobokshi Group; Chairman of Board of Arab Investment Co.; President, Orient International Agencies; Chairman and Managing Director, Okaz for Printing and Publishing Company; founder and authorized member of board of Tihama for Advertising, Public Relations and Marketing Research, General Associated Contracting, Electric Works and Maintenance Corporation; Chairman, Shobak Co. for Catering; founder, Saudi International Consulting Centre; Chairman, Shobokshi Agencies; Chairman, Shobokshi Maritime Co.; partner in a number of Corporations in Saudi Arabia and Overseas; has made substantial contributions to the development of Saudi National Economy. **Hobby:** cricket. **Address:** Ali and Fahd Shobokshi Group, P.O.Box 5470, Jeddah 21422, Saudi Arabia.

SHOBOKSHI (Fahad Hussein), Saudi leading businessman. **Born** in 1939 in Jeddah, Saudi Arabia. **Educ.:** Educated in U.S.A.; B.A. (Commerce and Business Administration). **Career:** Member of Board of Red Sea Insurance Co.; one of the founders of Tihama Co.; Co-Chairman of Board, General Associated Contracting (G.A.C.), Electrical Works and Maintenance Corporation; authorized member of Board, Saudi Advertising Co.; member of Board, Saudi Hotels Co., Riyadh, Okaz Distribution Co., Faisal Islamic-Egyptian Bank, Egypt, International Investment Group, U.S.A., Oriental Production and Distribution Co., Sharjah, U.A.E.; has made substantial contributions to Saudi national economy. **Honour:**

Honorary Consul of Sri Lanka. **Hobbies:** reading, travel, swimming. **Address:** Ali and Fahad Shobokshy Group, P.O.Box 5470, Jeddah 21422, Saudi Arabia.

SHOBOKSHI (Ossama A.), Saudi academic. **Born** on 21 October 1942 in Jeddah, Saudi Arabia. **Dipl.:** M.B., B.Sc., M.D., C.C.S.T., Ph.D. **Career:** Lecturer, Faculty of Medicine, King Abdulaziz University (1975-77); Assistant Professor (1977-80) Hospital Supervisor; Associate Professor, and Vice Dean for Hospital Affairs, Faculty of Medicine, King Abdulaziz University; Minister of Health (since Aug. 1995). **Publications:** Several articles about medicine published in al-Bilad newspaper, in addition to other scientific papers. **Hobbies:** navigation, aviation, antiquities. **Address:** Faculty of Medicine, King Abdulaziz University, Tel.: 6871193/9, Jeddah, Saudi Arabia and Ministry of Health.

SHOCAIR (Amin, Khalil), Jordanian businessman, pharmacist. **Born** in 1925 in Amman, Jordan. **Son** of Khalil Shocair. **Married. Educ.:** Certificate of Services, College of Medicine, Syrian University, Damascus (1944); Degree in Pharmacy, School of Pharmacy, College of Medicine, Damascus University, Damascus (1948). **Career:** Elected President, First Council of the Jordanian Pharmaceutical Association upon establishment (1957-59); President of same association (1977-81); member of the Executive Council of Arab Pharmacists Union, APU (1979-81); Chairman of the Board of Directors of the Arab Pharmaceutical Manufacturing Co. Ltd., Salt; Jerusalem Insurance Co. Ltd., Amman; Afro-Arab Techni Chemicals Ltd., Lagos, Nigeria; owner and manager of al Hayat Pharmacy, Amman, the Arab Drug Store, Amman; organiser of the first professional seminar "Pharmacy Profession on the Verge of the 21st Century" February 1980. Member of the National Executive Council. **Publ.:** Many articles, lectures and speeches on cultural, political and scientific subjects. **Medals:** Gold Medal of APU, 1st Class. **Addr.:** P.O.Box 42, Salt, Jordan.

SHOCAIR (Mahmoud Abd Alayyan), Jordanian writer. **Born** in 1941 in Jerusalem. **Son** of Abd Alayyan Shocair. **Married,** five children. **Career:** Worked for "al-Jihad" and "al-Quds"; contributed to "al-Fajr" and "al-Sha'ab". **Publ.:** Short story collections, "Khubz al-Akharin"; short story collection "al-Turab"; Children's novel "al-Arous al-Makhtouf"; several television series and articles on cultural affairs in various Arabic magazines. Member of Jordanian Short Story Writers' Association. **Sports:** Table tennis. **Hobby:** classical music. **Addr.:** P.O.Box. 2793, Jordanian Writers' Association, Amman, Jordan.

SHOIB (Mohamad, Othman), Egyptian international civil servant. **Born** on August 22, 1921 in Cairo (Egypt). **Married,** children. **Educ.:** Faculty of Medicine, Alexandria & Cairo Universities (1938-46); Harvard University (USA, 1947-48); Columbia University (USA, 1949-50); John Hopkins University (1966). **Dipl.:** M.B., B.Ch., MPH, DPH. **Career:** Senior Lecturer in Preventive Medicine, Faculty to Medicine, Cairo University (1950-54); Head, Department of Preventive Medicine, Cairo University (1956-58); Head, Department of Occupational Health, Institute of Public Health, Alexandria University (1956-59); Director, International Health Division, Ministry of Public Health, Cairo (1959-60); Chief Medical Officer, Social & Occupational Health, World Health Organisation (WHO) Geneva (1960-64); Director of Health Service, Regional Office of Eastern Mediterranean, WHO since 1964. **Publ.:** Author of "Principles of Public Health" (1954), "Epidemiology of Communicable Diseases" (1958). **Awards:** Order of the Republic (Egypt). **Member:** Egyptian Medical Association; American Public Health Association; American Academy of Occupational Medicine; Argentine Association for Industrial Medicine; Finnish Association for Industrial Medicine. **Clubs:** Egyptian Automobile Club, Smouha District, Alexandria; Smouha Sporting Club; Syrian Arab Club; Alexandria Sporting Club. **Sports:** swimming and golf. **Hobbies:** Photography and reading. **Prof. Addr.:** WHO, Ahmed Hamid Badawy Street, P.O.Box 1517, Alexandria, Tel.: 30090, Egypt.

SHOMALI (Ahmad Abdulaziz), United Arab Emirates official, educationalist. **Born** in 1945 in Bahrain. **Son** of Abdulaziz Shomali. **Married,** five children. **Educ.:** B.A., Baghdad University. **Career:** Administrative Affairs Supervisor, Ministry of Education; Head of Educational Planning Section, Ministry of Education. **Hobbies:** Travel, fishing. **Addr.:** Ministry of Education, P.O.Box 295, Abu Dhabi, United Arab Emirates.

SHOMAN (Abdel Hamid), Jordanian banker/businessman. **Born** in 1947 in Jerusalem. **Son** of Abdel Majeed Shoman. **Married** in 1976, 1 son, 2 daughters. **Dipl.:** B.B.A. (AUB). **Career:** Joined Arab Bank Ltd., (since 1972); Regional Manager, Arab Bank Ltd., Manama, Bahrain (1972-76); Assistant General Manager, Arab Bank Ltd., Amman, Jordan (1976-) Member, Board of Directors of: Arab Bank Ltd.; Oman Arab Bank; Arab Tunisian Bank; Arab Computing Company, Arab Australia Ltd., Member, Board of Trustees of: Abdel Hamid Shoman Foundation. **Member:** Royal Automoble Club, Jordan. **Hobby:** Reading. **Addr.:** P.O.Box 950545, Tel.: 660115- 660131, Telex: 23091 A/B ARABNK JO, Amman, Jordan.

SHOMAN (Abdul Majeed), Jordanian banker. **Born** on June 15, 1912 in Beit Hanina, Palestine. **Son** of Abdul Hameed Shoman (Banker) **and** Mrs. Zahwa. **Married** in 1946 in Jerusalem to Naila Hilmi, 2 children: Mohammad Abdul Hameed (1948), Ahmad (1950). **Educ.:** School Education obtained in Palestine and U.S.A., New York University. **Dipl.:** B.Sc. and M.A. in Economics. **Career:** Banker (1936- to present); Assistant General Manager, Arab Bank (1936-46); Manager, Arab Bank (1946-49);

Deputy Chairman, Arab Bank (1949-74); Chairman General Manager, Arab Bank (1974- to present). **Decor.:** al-Nahda Decoration, First Independence Decoration, Second Independence Decoration. **Sports:** Walking. **Hobby:** Reading. **Prof. Addr.:** Arab Bank PLC, P.O.Box 950545, Tel.: 664104, Amman, Jordan. **Priv. Addr.:** Tel.: 641146, Amman, Jordan.

SHOMAN (Issa), Jordanian bank manager. **Born** in 1934 in Jerusalem. **Son** of Salim Shoman. **Married** in 1968, 2 sons, 1 daughter. **Educ.:** American University of Beirut. **Dipl.:** B.A. **Career:** Senior Manager, Arab Bank Ltd., Dubai, UAE. **Member:** I.A.P.A.; Country Club; Passport Club. **Hobby:** Tennis. **Addr.:** P.O.Box 11364, Tel.: 227012, **Prof. Addr.:** 46126 A/B ARABEM, Dubai, UAE.

SHOMAN (Khalid, A.H.), Jordanian banker. **Born** in 1931 in New York, U.S.A. **Married**, with 2 children. **Educ.:** St. George's School, Jerusalem; Victoria College, Alexandria, Egypt. **Dipl.:** B.A. and M.A. in Economics, Jesus College, Cambridge University. **Career:** Manager, Arab Bank Ltd. (1956-57); Assistant General Manager (1957-74); Deputy Chairman and Deputy General manager: Arab Bank Ltd., (1974-96); Deputy Chairman and President (1996- date). **Directorships: 1-Chairman:** Arab Bank Australia Ltd., Sydney; Arab Tunisian Bank, Tunis; Arab Holding Company B.V.; Islamic International Arab Bank; Arab Investment Bank SAL; Arab Financial & Consultancy. **2-Deputy Chairman:** Arab Bank Plc, Jordan; Oman Arab Bank; Arab Bank (Austria) AG, Vienna; Arab Bank Investment Co., London; Arab Bank AG, Frankfurt, Germany; Abdul Hamid Shoman Foundation; Arab Real Estate Company for Administration & Investment Ltd., Arab National Leasing Company; Arab Finance & Holding Co.; Arabian Computing Investment Co.; Arab Bank Holding International N.V.; Finance Accountancy Mohassaba; Arab Computing Company, Jordan; **3-Director:** Arab National Bank, Saudi Arabia; Arab Bank (Switzerland) LTD, Switzerland; Central Bank of Jordan. **Hobbies:** Squash, racing, scubadiving, flying and reading. Member of Royal Automobile Club, Hussein Sport Club. Credit Cards: American express and Diner's Club. **Prof. Addr.:** Arab Bank Ltd., Head Office, P.O.Box 950545, Res. tel. 664105, Amman, Jordan. **Priv. Addr.:** Jabal Amman, Tel. 642256, Amman, Jordan.

SHORAFA AL HAMMADI (Ali Mohamed), United Arab Emirates Official. **Born** in 1944 in Sharjah (UAE). **Educ.:** Bachelor of Military Science from Cairo Military Academy (1966), later attended a six months military course in U.K. **Career:** Worked for one year in B.P. (1961); Chief of Personnel Dept., Kuwait State Office in Dubai (1962); Director of Civil Service Commission, Government of Abu Dhabi (1966-1967); Deputy Director of Protocol, Govt. of Abu Dhabi (1968); UAE Ambassador to Sudan, 1972 to 1973; Director of Presidential Court - 1973 till todate. **Highlights of activities:** Supervised the Work of the Committee that organized the UAE Federation; Participated in the Committee that defines the various UAE institutions particularly the relations between local and Federal Government; Supervised the preparation of the local Ministerial System, as well as the evaluation and setting up of the Administrative System of the Abu Dhabi Government; Represented the Abu Dhabi Government at the Youth Technical Committee Conference, held in Algeria in 26th January, 1970. **Addr.:** United Eastern Company, P.O.Box 7615, Abu Dhabi, United Arab Emirates.

SHORFI (Abdallah), Moroccan diplomat, statesman. **Born** in 1927 in Fes, Morocco. **Married. Career:** Royal Cabinet on Declaration of Independence (1956); Counsellor, Embassy to Spain; Chargé d'Affaires, Embassy to France; Consul General, New York; member of the Permanent Delegation to the United Nations; Director of the European Department, Ministry of Foreign Affairs; Ambassador to West Germany; returned to the Ministry of Foreign Affairs; Secretary General (1961); Under Secretary of State (1964); Ambassador to Spain (1967-69); Ambassador to USSR (1970-73); Ambassador to the Court of St. James, London, UK (1973-76). **Addr.:** Ministry of Foreign Affairs, Rabat, Morocco.

SHOURBAJI (Mohamad, Mounir Tarek), Jordanian executive. **Born** in 1943 in Cairo, Egypt. **Son** of Mounir Shourbaji. **Married** in 1972, 1 son, 1 daughter. **Educ.:** H.N.D. (Business Studies). **Career:** Arab Bank Ltd, Beirut; Midland Bank Ltd, London; S and S Shourbaji, Beirut; Director of Merrill Lynch Pierce Fenner and Smith Ltd, Futures Department, London (1970-). **Hobby:** Sports. **Addr.:** International House, World Trade Centre, 1 St. Katharine's Way, London E1 9UN, U.K. Tel.: 01-481-9800, Telex: 8951228 A/B: MERMEG.

SHOWWAF (Saied, Ali ash-), Saudi academic. **Born** on August 21, 1948 in Qatif, Saudi arabia. **Married**, 2 children. **Educ.:** American University, Washington DC; State University of New York, Albany. **Dipl.:** Master in Public Administration, as well as Doctorate. **Career:** Director, English Language Canter at the Institute of Public Administration; Director of Studies, Higher Committee for Administrative Reform; Member of the American Society of Public Administration and Academy of Management; Editor, Public Administration Journal; Director General, Programme Design and Development, Institute of Public Administration (1985-). **Publ.:** "Administrative Linkages between Planning and Organizational Implementation" (1985); "Administrative Reality of Telecommunication and Water Services" (1986), Organization Effectiveness Variables Measure (1989). **Hobbies:** Reading, writing, music swimming, travelling and camping. **Prof. Addr.:** P.O.Box 205, Riyadh 11141, Saudi Arabia.

SHRYDEH (Borhan, Najib), Jordanian businessman.

Born in 1939 in Jordan. **Son** of Najib Shrydeh. **Married**, five children. **Educ.:** B.Sc. in Mathematics and Physics; M.A. in Business Administration; Ph.D. in Management Science. **Career:** Research Mathematician, Allen Bradley Co., Milwaukee, USA (960-61); Operation Research Analyst, US Steel South Works, Chicago (1961-64); Project Manager, Computer Systems, Interlake Steel Cor., Chicago (1965-68); Co-operative Manager, Computer Systems and Programming, Admiral Corporation, Chicago (1968-70); Manager, Store Merchandising Systems, Montgomery Ward, US (1970-74); Manager, Economic Data Bank, Royal Scientific Society, Amman (1975-76); Director General Jordan Department of Statistics (since 1979). **Publ.:** Several articles on demography; Economic Data Bank Development in a Developing Nation. **Hobbies:** Theatre, music, painting, bridge, chess, golf. **Addr.:** Department of Statistics, P.O.B. 2015, Amman, Jordan.

SHUABI (Salih Muslih Qasim Majdul, Major), Yemeni politician. **Born** in 1940. **Career:** Participated in armed struggle in Shaibi and Dathina areas in association with Ali Ahmed Nasr al-Bishi; Commander of the 22nd Brigade since its formation in June 1970; member of the Political Bureau; member of the People's Supreme Council; Minister of Defence (1982-85); Minister of the Interior (1986). **Addr.:** Aden, Republic of Yemen.

SHUAIB (Faysal, Abdussalam), Kuwaiti businessman. **Born** in 1934 in Kuwait. **Son** of Abdussalam Shuaib. **Married. Educ.:** B.A. in Politics, University of Nottingham, UK. **Career:** Ministry of Foreign Affairs, Kuwait; 2nd Secretary, Kuwaiti Embassy to UK (1963-65); Ministry of Commerce (1965-66); business enterpreneur (since 1966); Director, Mohamad A. Shuaib and Brothers Abdus Salam Shuaib and Sons, Faisal A. Shuaib, Public Relations and Advertising; Kuwait Delegate to GATT in Geneva (1964-66); represented Kuwait at the first UNCTAD, Geneva (1964). **Sport:** Swimming. **Hobbies:** Theater, music, cinema, fishing, antiques, cooking. **Addr.:** P.O.B. 115, Safat, 13002, Kuwait.

SHUAIB (Hamid, Abdussalam), Kuwaiti architect, town Planner. **Born** in 1932 in Kuwait. **Son** of Abdussalam Shuaib and Mrs. Sabika Abdulla Ishaq. **Married** in 1959 in United Kingdom to Linda Moulding, four children: Suzan, Thia, Derek, and keith. **Educ.:** Oxford School of Architecture, UK; University of Liverpool, UK. **Dipl.:** Diploma in Architecture (1958); Diploma in Civic Design (1964). **Career:** Since his graduation and till 1960, worked in the field of architecture with the London County Council Housing Department and in other consulting offices in London. Assistant Architect, Ministry of Public Works, Kuwait (April 1960- June 1962); Planner, Planning Department, Kuwait Municipality (1965-72); Chief Architect, Kuwait Municipality: (July 1972- Sept. 1984); Partner and Managing Director, Pan Arab Consulting Engineers (PACE) (established in 1968 with his partner Eng. Sabah al-Rayes), Which is one of the Largest engineering offices in Kuwait providing all engineering and architectural services. Represented Kuwait in several Regional and International Conferences, as the United Nations Environment programme (UNEP) Governing Council held between 1976 and 1984, the United Nations Commission on Human Settlements (Habitat) in Helsinki (1983) and the preparatory and Ministerial Meetings for the regional organization for the protection of the Marine Environment. **Founder**, Member and former President (1965-70); of the Kuwait society of Engineers; Founder, Kuwait Environment Protection Society of Which he is the President since 1982; Former President, Arab Union Federation; Member, Bahrain Society of Engineers; Member, Royal Institute of British Architects (RIBA) since 1960 and Member of the Royal Town Planning Institute since 1978; Member of the Higher Council for Housing and Chairman of the Planning Committee; Founding Member of the Kuwaiti Society of the Handicapped and kuwait Heart Foundation; Founder Member of the Kuwaiti Science Club. **Sports:** Horseback riding, tennis, sailing. **Hobby:** Music. **Member:** Equestrian Club; Ramada Assalam. **Credit Cards:** Diner's Club; Westminster; Visa. **Prof. Addr.:** P.O.Box 1031 Safat, Tel.: 2669600, 13011 Kuwait, Kuwait. **Priv. Addr.:** P.O.Box 115 Safat, Tel.: 2548888, 13002 Kuwait, Kuwait.

SHUAIB (Muhammad, Abdul Salam, al), Kuwaiti businessman. **Born** in 1924 in Kuwait. **Married**, 5 children. **Educ.:** received education in Kuwait. **Career:** Teacher; Businessman; Member of the Board of Directors of the Kuwait Chamber of Commerce and Industry; Director of Abdul Salam Shuaib's sons Trading Company Ltd; Managing Director of Muhammad A. Shuaib and Brothers. Trading Company Ltd; Member of the Board of Directors of the Port Authority (since 1979). **Hobbies:** Swimming, fishing, sports. **Prof. Addr.:** P.O.Box 115, Safat, Kuwait, Kuwait.

SHUAIR (Gamal, Mohamad), Egyptian diplomat. **Born** in al Zagazig, Egypt in 1925. **Son** of Mohamad Shuair. **Married**, three children. **Educ.:** B.A. in Military Science (1946). **Career:** Assistant Military Attache, Ministry of Defence in Egypt (1955-58); Consul General, Embassy in UK (1968-70); Ambassador to Libya (1970-73); Under Secretary, Union of Arab Republics, Ministry of Foreign Affairs, Cairo (1974-75); Ambassador to el-Salvador, Nicaragua and Costa Rica (1977-81); Assistant Minister of Foreign Affairs for Cultural Relations (1982-85). **Medals:** Mohamad Ali Golden Ribbon, Medal of Palestine, Ministry of Defence, Egypt; Medal of the Golden Knight, paraguay; Order of the Republic of Egypt (Second Class), Order of merit (First Class), Grand Order of San Salvador. Member of the Diplomatic Club; Officers' Club, Heliopolis Club. **Prof. Addr.:** Ministry of Foreign Affairs, 4 Shara' al-Nile, Gizah, Cairo, Egypt. **Priv. Addr.:** 44 Nehru St., Heliopolis, Cairo, Egypt.

SHUBAILY (Abdulrahman Abdulaziz, al), Saudi former diplomat. **Born** in 1930 at Onaizah, Saudi Arabia. **Career:** Began his career with the late King Abdulaziz Royal Cabinet (1946-51); joined the Diplomatic Corps at the Ministry of Foreign Affairs (1951); member of the Diplomatic Corps, Royal Embassy of the Kingdom of Saudi Arabia, Syria (1953-55), Lebanon (1955-58) and Cairo (1959-62); Consul General of the Kingdom of Saudi Arabia to Palestine, Jerusalem (1963-67); appointed Minister Plenipotentiary, Beirut (1967-72). **Honours:** National Decoration of Cedar-Commander rank - the Republic of Lebanon; King Abdulaziz Decoration - Excellent rank. **Publications:** a booklet titled "al-Ru'iya wa al-Tahawwol" (vision and transformation) - republished in the form of article serie (in Arabic) by al-Majallah Magazine (1982); his Jerusalem memoirs were published in series of articles in al-Muslimoon Magazine (1982); a regular political contributor to Asharq al-Awsat newspaper. **Address:** P.O.Box 3814, Jeddah, Saudi Arabia.

SHUBEILAT (Laith, Farhan), Jordanian politician, engineer. **Born** in Amman, Jordan in 1942. **Son** of Farhan Shubeilat. **Married**, nine children. **Educ.:** B.Sc. in Civil Engineering, American University of Beirut; M.Sc. in Structural Engineering, George Washington University, Washington DC, USA. **Career:** General Manager, al-Wafa Engineering Contracting Company (1969-75); President, Laith Shubeilat Engineering Bureau (1976-79); Shubailat Badran Kailani Architectural Consultancy Engineering (President) (since 1980); Jordanian Engineers Association. President of Omar Ibn al-Khattab Zakat Society. **Prof. Addr.:** P.O.Box 182571, Imam Ali Street, Amman, Jordan. **Priv. Addr.:** Marj al-Hammam, Alia Housing Estate, Amman, Jordan.

SHUGDAR (Ibrahim Y.), Saudi academic. **Born** in 1948 in Mecca, Saudi Arabia. **Dipl.:** Ph.D. (Chemical Engineering). **Career:** Chemical Engineer, Ministry of Petroleum and Mineral Resources, (1973-74); Assistant Professor and Vice Dean, Faculty of Engineering, King Abdulaziz University, Jeddah. former President, Students Association, University of Petroleum and Minerals, Dhahran; former President, the General Committee for Social Activity, King Abdulaziz University; attended several international conferences relating to his field of interest. **Publication:** Production of Raw Petrochemicals from Natural Gas. **Hobby:** soccer. **Prof. Addr.:** King Abdulaziz University, Faculty of Engineering, P.O.Box 9027, Tel. 6890068, Jeddah.

SHUKRALLAH (Ibrahim), Egyptian, former official. **Born** on February 1, 1923 in Alexandria (Egypt). **Married** to Jeannette Tadros on January 7, 1950, 3 children: Hani, Alaa and Hala. **Educ.:** Cairo University, American University of Cairo, Bonn University, the Higher Institute of Arabic Studies (Cairo). **Dipl.:** Bachelor of Arts, Honours, English Literature (1944), Bachelor of Arts, Honours, Psychology (1952), Diploma in German Literature (1953), Master of Arts, Arabic Studies, of the Higher Institute of Arabic Studies (Cairo). **Career:** Local news editor, The Egyptian Mail (1941-42); Foreign News Editor, al-Assas Daily newspaper in Cairo (1942-43); Editor-in-Chief The Tripoli Times (1943-45); Assistant Director of Information at the Arab League (1946-65); Director of the Arab League Information Center in Ottawa (1965-71); Acting Chief of Mission, UN (1970); Director of Information, Arab League (1971-73); Chief Representative of League of Arab States Mission in India and South East Asia (1974). **Publ.:** Images from the Arab World (1943); Non-Alignment; Hope and Fulfilment (1961); The Show Trial of Adolf Eichman (1962). **Priv. Addr.:** 5 Khan Yunis Street, Engineers Quarter, Tel. 81677, Cairo, Egypt.

SHUKRI (Adel, Mohamad), Egyptian economist. **Born** in 1931 in Cairo, Egypt. **Son** of Mohamad Shukri. **Married**, three children. **Educ.:** Ph.D. in Economics, Cairo University, Egypt; Ph.D. in Political Science, Berlin University. **Career:** Attaché in Egyptian Embassy to Germany; Secretary in Egyptian Embassy, Czechoslovakia; Director of Research Department, Maritime Transport; Assistant Lecturer in Economics and Political Science, University of Khartoum, Sudan; Expert in UN Technical Aid program, Economic Adviser to United Arab Emirates Government; Founder and President of Euro-Arab Consultant and Implementation Group (ECOJECT). **Publ.:** Articles on economics and politics; "South East Asia Treaty Organisation", Cairo (1958); "Nazism Between Ideology and Practice", Cairo (1964). **Sport:** Tennis. **Hobbies:** Poetry, Music, billiards, chess. **Priv. Addr.:** 18 Aly Ibn Aby Taleb St., Mohandissin, P.O.Box 55, Orman, Giza, Cairo, Egypt.

SHUKRI (Ahmad al-Siba'i), Moroccan lawyer. **Born** in 1938 in sidi Qassim, Morocco. **Married**, 3 children. **Dipl.:** Licence in Law; Diploma in Higher Studies in Law; **Ph.D.** in Law. **Career:** Assistant Professor of the Faculty of Law (1962); Lecturing Professor (1969); Professor (since 1971); Head of Mission at the Royal Cabinet; Professor of Law at Dar al-Hadith al-Husniya, Rabat, at Hassan II University, Casablanca and Muhammad V University, Rabat; Member of the Academic Council of the Faculty of Law, of the Moroccan Lawyers Federation; Member of the Editorial Board of "Law" Moroccan Magazine, Politics and Economics, published by the Faculty of Law. **Publ.:** numerous articles in Moroccan paprs and magazines; several books on Moroccan law (in Arabic). **Member:** Tennis Club. **Hobbies:** tennis, football, reading literature and history. **Addr.:** Zarhun Street, Zankit Bark al-Leil, Villa Shukri Suisse, Rabat, Morocco.

SHUKRI (Ahmad Ibrahim), Saudi academic. **Born** in 1932. **Dipl.:** B.A. Cairo University (1959); M.A., Ph.D. (Educational Planning), London University (1965, 1972). **Career:** Former Inspector, Ministry of Education, King Abdulaziz University, Mecca; now Supervisor of Training

Courses, King Abdulaziz University, Mecca Branch. **Hobbies:** Reading, travel. **Addr.:** Mecca, Saudi Arabia.

SHUKRI (Ibrahim), Egyptian politician. **Born** in 22 September 1916. **Career:** Joined "Young Egypt" (Misr al-Fatat') party (1935); shot in Cairo strike (1935); managed family estate, Sharbeen; Secretary-General, Misr al-Fatat (1946); elected Vice-President, then President, Socialist Party (formerly Misr al-Fatat) (1947-53); member for Kahaliya, People's Assembly (1949-52); imprisoned for opposing the monarch (1952); released after Revolution (1952), returned to estate; joined Arab Socialist Union on its formation (1962); elected to Executive Committee (1964); re-elected member for Kahaliya (1964-68); President, Farmers' Union and Secretary Professional Association (1965-68); Governor, Wadi A-Gadeed (1968-76); elected to People's Assembly (1976); Minister of Agriculture and Agrarian Reform (Feb.77- May 78); Minister of Land Agrarian Reform (Feb.77-May 78); Minister of Land Improvement (May-Oct. 1978); Chairman, New Socialist Labour Party and Man; Editor, al-Sha'b (party newspaper) (Oct. 1978-); Leader of the Opposition, People's Assembly (since 1979). **Addr.:** 12 Sharia Awali El Ahd, Cairo, Egypt.

SHUKRI (Ibrahim, Mohamad), Egyptian academic, physician. **Born** in 1944 in Cairo, Egypt. **Son** of Mohamad Shukri. **Married**, two children. **Educ.:** Ph.D. in Pediatrics, Cairo University, Egypt. **Career:** Professor of Pediatrics, Cairo University, Egypt. **Publ.:** "Me, My Child and the Doctor". **Addr.:** 13 Yusuf al-Gundi Street, Bab al-Loq, Cairo, Egypt.

SHUKRI (Maher, Ganj, Dr.), Jordanian executive. **Born** in 1947 in Amman, Jordan. **Son** of Ganj Shukri. **Married** in 1976, 2 sons, 1 daughter. **Educ.:** American University, Cairo B.A. Eco. and Political Science (1969); Institut International d'Administration Publique (Economie et Finance). **Diplome;** University of Paris 1 Sorbonne - Pantheon; Ph.D. (Econ.) (1976). **Career:** Jordan Centre for Industrial Development (1969-71); Central Bank of Jordan since 1971; Forex, Investment Officer, Central Bank of Jordan (1971-76); Assistant, Head of Foreign Relations Department (1976-77); Assistant Controller, Foreign Relations Department (1977-78); Head of Foreign Relations Department, Central Bank of Jordan, Amman (1978-82). Managing Director, Finance & Credit Corporation (1982-85). Deputy Governor, Central Bank of Jordan (1985-89); Managing Director, Amman Bank for Investments; Chairman, Jordan Spinning & Weaving Co., Jordan Marketing Corporation, Nayzak Tool & Die Manufacturing Co. **Publ.:** "Applied Studies in Foreign Banking Operations" (1981). **Hobbies:** Chess, swimming and tennis. **Addr.:** P.O.Box 925802, Tel. 691757, Telex: 23199 AM Bank Jo, Amman, Jordan.

SHUKRI (Mohamad, Aziz), Syrian academic, lawyer. **Born** in Damascus, Syria in 1937. **Son** of Subhi Shukri. **Married. Educ.:** Licence in Law, Damascus University (1959); LLM University of Virginia (1961); Doctor of the Science of Law, Columbia University (1964). **Career:** Associate Judge at the Council of State; Lecturer of International Law, Damascus University (1964-70); Assistant Professor of International Law, University of Kuwait (1970-75); Professor of International Law (1975-77); Assistant Dean for Academic Affairs, University of Kuwait (1976-77); Professor of International Law and Organization, Damascus University (since 1980); Chairman of the Department of International Law (1984-85 and 1987- to present). **Publications:** numerous books and articles in English and Arabic, including the Concept of "Self Determination in the United Nations" (1965), "Introduction to Public International Law" (1980), "International Terrorism, A Legal Critique" (1991); "The International Dimensions of the Palestinian Question" (1991). **Hobbies:** Music and Poetry. **Address:** P.O.Box 10418, Damascus, Syria.

SHUKRI (Sabih, Mahmoud), Iraqi executive. **Born** in 1928 in Baghdad, Iraq. **Son** of Mahmoud Shukri. **Married** in 1969. **Educ.:** University of Baghdad; University of London. **Dipl.:** B.Sc. (Com.); B.Sc. (Econ.). **Career:** Joined Rafidain Bank since 1958: General Manager, Rafidin Bank, Baghdad (1958-63); Manager, London (1963-65); Regional Manager, Jordan (1965-72); Arab Bank, London (1972-77); Managing Director and Chief Executive, Arab Bank Ltd., London, UK (1977-83); Chairman, Arab-British Chamber of Commerce; International Who's Who of the Arab World; Sanctuary Investment; President, al-Mubarakah Finance. **Member:** International Music Society; London Philharmonic Orchestra Society; Les Ambassadeurs; Hurlingham Club; Overseas Banker's Club; Royal Automobile Club; Shooting and Horseriding. **Addr.:** 2, South Audley Street, Tel. 01-4938885, London W1Y 5DQ, UK.

SHUKRI (Shaker Mahmoud), Iraqi former army officer and diplomat. **Born** in 1917. **Educ.:** Secondary and Military Academy. **Career:** Served in Iraqi Forces, promoted Major General (1965); Assistant Chief of General Staff (1958); Ambassador to Spain (1963-66), to United Kingdom (1966); Minister of Defence (April 1966-July 1968). **Awards:** Grand Cross of Isabella the Catholic (1966), Order of Rafidain Class I. **Addr.:** Baghdad, Iraq.

SHUKRI (Yahya Farid), Saudi businessman. **Born** in 1946 at Abha, Saudi Arabia. **Dipl.:** B.Sc. (Mining Engineering). **Career:** Engineer, Ministry of Petroleum and Mineral Resources (1968-70); Engineer, E and Eter Co. for Tunnel Construction, Abha. **Hobbies:** painting, mechanical engineering. **Prof. Addr.:** P.O.Box 305, Tel.: 2245592, Abha. **Priv. Addr.:** Tel.: 2246173, Abha, Saudi Arabia.

SHUMMO (Ali Mohamad), Sudanese administrator. **Born** in 1932 in Khartoum, Sudan. **Son** of Mohamad Shummo. **Married**, five children. **Educ.:** B.A. in Islamic

Law and Jurisprudence; M.A. in Psychology and Pedagogy; Postgraduate Studies in Co-operative Law; M.Sc. **Career:** Director General, Sudan then Under Secretary of Television; Deputy Under Secretary, Ministry of Information and Culture, Sudan; Adviser to the Minister of Information and Culture, Abu Dhabi; Minister of State for Youth and Sports (1977-78); member of the Board of Trustees of International Broadcasting Institute; member of International Advisory Committee for Libraries, Documentation and Archives; former President of Arab States Broadcasting Union, also Chairman of Programme Committee; member of the NAB, USA; former member of the Administrative Council of the International Radio and Television Organisation and President of the Jury for Developing World. **Publ.:** Has contributed to different organisations with articles and designs for projects. **Medals:** medals from Emperor Haile Selassie of Ethiopia; President Lubke of the Federal Republic of Germany. Prize, International Television Festival. **Addr.:** Khartoum, Sudan.

SHUWAIMAN (Abdul Kareem Mohamad, al), Saudi senior civil servant. **Born** in 1945 at Unaizah. **Dipl.:** Higher Diploma in Law, Institute of Public Administration, Riyadh (1973). **Career:** Legal Adviser, Customs Department, Customs Secretariat, Jeddah (1974); member of Customs Committee, Customs Secretariat, Jeddah; now Director, Jeddah International Airport Customs Department. **Hobby:** reading. **Prof. Addr.:** Quarayyat Close to al-Ahtigyha School, Jeddah, Saudi Arabia.

SIBAI (Nouhad), Syrian executive. **Born** in 1920 in Syria. **Educ.:** University, Syria Licence en Droit; University of Paris, France, Diploma of advanced studies (Commercial Law); University of Geneva, Switzerland. **Dipl.:** Ph.D. **Career:** Professor, Damascus University, Syria (1949); Legal Adviser and Director, Société d'Assurances Syrienne, Syria (1953); Dean, Facutly of Commerce and Chair Professor of Maritime Law, Damascus University, Syria (1961); Minister of National Economy, Syria (1962); Managing Director, Gefinor Finance S.A., Switzerland (1967); Director, Gefinor Investment Management SAL; Gefinor Finance; Gefinor Bank Ltd; Arab Investment Co., Director, Gefinor Investment Ltd., Geneva, Switzerland. **Publ.:** in the fields of Commercial Maritime and Air Laws, as well as Insurance and Banking activities. **Addr.:** 23 Avenue de la Porte Neuve, Luxembourg.

SIBAI (Saad al-Himaidi, al), Saudi academic. **Born** in 1939. **Educ.:** Secondary School Certificate. **Career:** Teacher, Ministry of Education (1961-67); Superintendent of Education, General Directorate of Girls' Education, Riyadh (1967-74); Chief Personnel Section, Department of Girls' Education, Jeddah; now Chief, Education Section, Deputy-Director, Department of Girls' Education, Jeddah. **Hobby:** Reading. **Prof. Addr.:** Ministry of Education, Department of Girls' Education, Jeddah, Saudi Arabia.

SIBAI (Zohair Ahmad, al), Saudi academic. **Born** in 1939 in Mecca. **Dipl.:** M.B.B.Ch., Cairo (1963); D.T.M., Germany (1969); M.P.H., U.S.A. (1966); D.F.H., John Hopkins University. U.S.A. (1969). **Career:** Director, Planning, Budgeting and Programming Division, Ministry of Health (1969-73); member of American Public Health Association, Royal Society of Medicine (London), Committee on the Evaluation of the Problems of Youth in Saudi Arabia; has been preparing and presenting weekly TV Programme and daily radio programme on health education for 5 years; now Assistant Professor of Public Health and Community Medicine, Faculty of Medicine, Riyadh University. **Publ.:** Author of Public Health in Arab Community (in Arabic). **Awards:** First Prize for best article (physiology of Memory) given by Saudi Arabian Broadcasting Service. **Sport:** Swimming. **Hobby:** Chess. **Prof. Addr.:** Faculty of Medicine, Riyadh University, Riyadh, Saudi Arabia.

SIDDIQI (Ehsan, Rab), Pakistani executive. **Born** in 1931 in Saharanpur. **Son** of Viqar Ali Siddiqi. **Married** in 1967. **Dipl.:** B.A. (Econ.); D.A. I.B.P. (1953). **Career:** Lloyds Bank Ltd. (1948); National Bank of Pakistan, Pakistan (1951); National Bank of Pakistan, Hong Kong (1967-72); Paris (1976-79); Senior Vice President and Manager, National Bank of Pakistan, Bahrain (1979-). **Member:** Association of Institute of Bankers, Pakistan; Pakistan Arts Council. **Hobbies:** Chess, reading, and travelling. **Addr.:** P.O.Box 775, Tel. 244185, Telex: 9222 A/B NAT PAK BN, Manama, Bahrain.

SIDDIQI (Vakil Ahmad), Pakistani bank executive. **Born** in 1940 in Nehtaur, India. **Son** of Shabbir Ahmad Siddiqi. **Married** in 1969, 1 son, 4 daughters. **Educ.:** Karachi University. **Dipl.:** M.A. (Econ.); D.A.I.B.P. **Career:** Probationary Officer, Central Bank of Pakistan (1962-63); Muslim Commercial Bank Ltd., Karachi (1963-67); Credit Division, National Bank of Pakistan, Karachi (19657-77); Senior Officer, Bank of Oman Ltd., Dubai (1977-78); Bank of Oman, Main Brach, Ras Al Khaimah (1978-81); Manager, Bank of Oman, Ras al-Khaimah, UAE (1981-). **Hobby:** Reading. **Addr.:** P.O.Box 700, Tel. 21178, 31275, Telex: 99219 A/B OMAN EM, Ras al-Khaimah, UAE.

SIDI BABA (Ahmad, Ould), Mauritanian politician. **Born** in 1940 in Atar (North Western Mauritania). **Married** Miss Fatimedou, 2 children. **Educ.:** Primary school in Atar (1947-52); Lycée Faidherbe, Saint Louis, Senegal. **Dipl.:** B.A. (Higher Education), M.A. (Pedagogy), UNESCO Certificate (Educational Planning). **Career:** Director General of Education in Mauritania (1966-67); Director, School of National Administration (1968-71); Minister of Culture & Information (1971-Aug. 1975) Minister of Construction (1975-Aug. 1976); Minister of State for Human Resources and Islamic Affairs (1976-78); visited several countries on official missions, including

France, Morocco, Ivory Coast, Senegal, Spain, Guinea, Mali; held talks with the Libyan Prime Minister, Abdessalam Jalloud, Tripoli (1974). **Member:** Presently, Chairman, Rally for Democracy and National Unity; Minister Counsellor to the presidency. **Address:** Office of the President, P.O.Box 184, Nouakchott, Mauritania.

SIDI BABA (Ould Dey), Moroccan diplomat and former minister. **Born** in 1921 at Atar (Western Region of Mauritania). **Educ.:** Secondary and Higher. **Married,** 2 children. **Career:** joined the Ministry of Foreign Affairs as counsellor (1958); Head, African Division, Ministry of Foreign Affairs, Rabat (1959-61); Ambassador to Guinea (1961); Deputy Permanent Representative to United Nations, Washington D.C. (1962-64); Served on UNO Security Council (1963-64); Commissioned by UN Secretary General to study the problems of Apartheid in South Africa (1964): Head of UN Security Council's special study commission sent to Cambodia and Vietnam (1964); Permanent representative to UNO (1965-67); Appointed vice president, UN Council of Trade at the UN Conference on Trade and Development (UNCTAD) 1965; Minister in the Royal Cabinet (March 1965- May 1971), Ambassador to Saudi Arabia (May 1971- June 1972); Moving ambassador to supervise the OAU Summit, and was made responsible for implementing Moroccan policy on OAU issues during King Hassan's OAU presidency June (1972-73); Minister of National Education, Rabat (May 1973- April 1974), Minister of Wakfs and Islamic Affairs (1974-77); elected Speaker of Parliament (Oct. 1977); Member, National Defence Council (March 1979). **Awards:** Commander, Alawite Throne; Grand Order of Merit, Niger; Officer, Order of Independence (Libya); Commander of Merit (Syria). **Prof. Addr.:** Parliament Bldg., Rabat, Morocco.

SIDKI (Atef), Egyptian politician. **Born** in 1930 in Egypt. **Educ.:** Law School and Sorbonne, Paris. **Career:** Professor of General Finance, Cairo University (1958-73); Cultural Attaché, Egyptian Embassy, Paris (1973-80); President Government Advisory Council Commission for Economic and Financial Affairs (1980-85); President Government Audit Office (1985-86); Minister of International Cooperation (1987- May 1991); Prime Minister (May 1991 to Jan. 1996). President, Société Egyptienne d'Economie Politique, de Statistique et de Législation. **Address:** 16 Ramses Avenue, P.O.Box 732, Cairo, Egypt.

SIDKI (Aziz), Egyptian politician. **Born** in 1920 in Cairo, Egypt. **Educ.:** Cairo University, University of Oregon and Harvard University. **Dipl.:** B.Eng., M.A., Ph.D. **Career:** taught Cairo University; Technical Counsellor to the President (1953); Ministry for Industry (1956-63); Deputy Prime Minister and Minister for Industry and Mineral Wealth (1964-65); Minister for Industry, Petroleum and Mineral Wealth (1968-71); Deputy Prime Minister (1971-72); Prime Minister (1972-73); Acting General Secretary, Arab Socialist Union (1971-73); Personal Assistant to President Sadat (1973-75); has participated in various international conferences on industrial affairs. **Addr.:** 17 Switzerland Institute Street. Zamalek, Cairo, Egypt.

SIDKI (Izziddin), Egyptian academic, dental surgeon. **Born** in 1914 in Alexandria, Egypt. **Married,** five children. **Educ.:** BDS, University of Cairo, Egypt; Higher Dental Diploma in Oral Surgery. **Career:** Professor of Operative Dentistry and Endodontics, Dental School, University of Cairo; Chairman, Operative, Endodontics, Crown and Bridge Department; Dean, Faculty of Dentistry; President, Supreme Board of Dental Education; President, Egyptian Dental Syndicate, President, Board of Dental Examiners. **Member** of Egyptian Dental Association. **Publ.:** Editor in Chief of Egyptian Dental Journal. **Addr.:** 5, Midan Falaky, Cairo, Egypt.

SIENY (Hussein Sulaiman Omar, al), Saudi faculty lecturer. **Born** in 1930 in China. **Dipl.:** M.A. (Islamic Jurisprudence) 1975. **Career:** Primary School teacher (1951-59); Intermediate School teacher (1969); Lecturer, Faculty of Sharia, Mecca. **Address:** Faculty of Sharia, Mecca, Saudi Arabia.

SIENY (Mahmoud Ismail), Saudi academic. **Born on** 3 March 1942 in Medina, Saudi Arabia. **Dipl.:** Ph.D. **Career:** Assistant Director, Islamic Centre, Washington, D.C. (1969-73); Deputy Chairman, English Department, Faculty of Education, King Saud University (1974-75); founder and Director, Arabic Language Institute, King Saud University (1975-81); Associate Professor of Applied Linguistics, English Department, Faculty of Education, King Saud University. **Member:** the Association of Teachers of English for Speakers of Other Languages (TESOL), U.S.A., the American Council of Teachers of Foreign Languages (ACTFL), U.S.A., and the American Association of Applied Linguistics; member of Board, SYSTEM (International Journal of Education Technology and Language Learning Systems), United Kingdom. **Publications:** author of 2 books; co-author of 5 books; co-editor of 2 books. **Hobby:** photography. **Prof. Addr.:** King Saud University, Faculty of Education, English Department, Riyadh. **Priv. Addr.:** Tel.: 4656108, Riyadh, Saudi Arabia.

SIJELMASSI (Mohamad), Moroccan diplomat. **Born** in 1932 in Fes, Morocco. **Married. Educ.:** Law studies at Universities of Bordeaux, France and Rabat, Morocco. **Career:** Chef de Cabinet, Ministry of Labour (1956); admitted to the Magistrature (1957); Chargé de Mission in Cabinet of Prime Minister (1956); Chargé de Mission, Royal Cabinet (1966); Under Secretary of State, Royal Cabinet, (1967); Under Secretary of State in Ministry of Foreign Affairs (1967); represented Morocco at Organisation of African Unity, Foreign Ministers Conference, Addis Ababa (1970); Minister in the Royal Cabinet (1970);

Ambassador to Algeria (1971); Ambassador to USSR (1973-77); Ambassador to Norway, Denmark and Sweden (1977-1981). **Addr.:** Ministry of Foreign Affairs, Rabat, Morocco.

SIKSIK (Dawud, Sulaiman), United Arab Emirates official. **Born** in 1944. **Son** of Sulaiman Siksik. **Married,** two children. **Educ.:** al-Hussein College, Amman, Jordan; UN Vocational Center, Jerusalem. **Career:** Private Secretary to HH Ruler of Abu Dhabi (1967-72); Private Secretary to HH the President of the United Arab Emirates (1972-74); Minister Plenipotentiary attached to Presidential Palace as Director of Administration and Finance. **Medals:** Order of Independence, Jordan; Rafidain Order, Iraq. **Sports:** Swimming, water skiing, tennis. **Hobbies:** Reading, theatre. **Addr.:** Manhal Palace, Abu Dhabi, United Arab Emirates.

SILAY (Silay, Mohamed), Djibouti Deputy at the National Assembly. **Born** in 1954 at Mabla (Obock). **Career:** Employee of Port Office (1976-1977); Employee to the Directorate of the Security and Service Documents (Presidency) (1978-18/12/1997); Elected Deputy at the National Assembly (19/12/1997); Member of Foreign Affairs Commission, Legislation and General Administration of the Republic Commission. **Prof. Addr.:** National Assembly, P.O.Box 138 Djibouti, Djibouti.

SILSILAH (Abdallah), Saudi businessman. **Born** in 1941 in Mecca, Saudi Arabia. **Educ.:** attained a secondary school certificate and was privately tutored in some special courses in Business Administration. **Career:** Vice President, Rajab and Silsilah; Member of the Board of Directors of several companies associated with Rajab and Silsilah; member, Board of Directors, Jeddah Chamber of Commerce and Industry; one of the founders of the Saudi American Bank. **Hobbies:** Reading, sports, travel. **Prof. Addr.:** P.O.Box 203, Tel.: 6715606, 6715907, Jeddah. **Priv. Addr.:** Tel.: 6653557, Jeddah, Saudi Arabia.

SIMAIKA (Samir, Mahfouz), Egyptian Consultant Obstetrician & Gynaecologist to the Coptic & Salam Hospitals & the Hayat Medical Centre. **Born** on February 27, 1936 in Cairo (Egypt). **Son** of Youssef Simaika **and** Samira Mahfouz. **Married** to Yolande Cassab on July 2, 1967 in Cairo, 2 children: Youssef and Marianne. **Educ.:** Gezireh Preparatory School (1942-46); English School, Heliopolis (1946-53); Kasr El Ayni Faculty of Medicine (1953-59). **Dipl.:** M.B., B.Ch. (Honours), Cairo University; Diploma Surgery, Diploma Obstetrics & Gynaecology. **Career:** Consultant Obstetrician and Gynaecologist to the Coptic and Salam Hospitals and the Hayat Medical Centre. **Member:** then Fellow: Royal College of Obstetricians & Gynaecologists; Fellow International College of Surgeons. **Publ.:** Leucorrhea in Egyptian Females, Rare Functioning Ovarian Tumors. **Award:** Madden Gold Medal in Clinical Surgery. **Sport:** Squash & Walking. **Hobbies:** Reading, Stamp Collecting & Egyptology. **Club:** Gezireh Sporting Club & Automobile Club. **Prof. Addr.:** 80 Gomhoriya St., Cairo. **Priv. Addr.:** 39 Farid St., Heliopolis, Cairo, **Egypt.**

SIMAIRI (Abdul Mahain Salma Abdul Rahman, al), Saudi bureau director for His Royal Highness the governor of holy Mecca district. **Born** in 1942 in Mecca. **Dipl.:** B.Com. (Business Administration). **Career:** Deputy Governor of Yanbu (1966-67); Administrative Investigator, Holy Mecca Governorate (1967-68); Assistant Director, His Royal Highness Governor of Holy Mecca's Bureau (1968-70); member of Board, Prince Fawwaz Project of Co-Operative Housing, Jeddah. **Awards:** Commander, Order of Cedar of Lebanon (1972). **Sports:** swimming, fishing. **Hobbies:** Reading, travel. **Prof. Addr.:** His Royal Highness Governor of Mecca Bureau, Mecca Road, Kilo 2, Jeddah, Saudi Arabia.

SIMAIRI (Latifa, al, Miss), Saudi academic. **Born** in 1951 in Riyadh, Saudi Arabia. **Dipl.:** M.A. (Curricula and Methodology). **Career:** Primary Schoolmistress; Deputy Director of an intermediate school; Deputy Director of a secondary school; Lecturer, Curricula Department, Faculty of Education, Women's Section, Umm al-Qura University, Mecca. member of Umm al-Qura Welfare Society. **Hobby:** Reading. **Address:** Women's Faculty of Education, Umm al-Qura University, Mecca. **Priv. Addr.:** Tel.: 5564770, Mecca, Saudi Arabia.

SIMBAWA (Amin Mohamad Ibrahim), Saudi businessman. **Born** in 1946 in Mecca, Saudi Arabia. **Dipl.:** M.A. (Industrial Management) (1970). **Career:** Lecturer in industrial management, the Royal Technical Institute, Riyadh (1971) and the Higher Technical Institute, Riyadh (1972); Director, Commercial Education (1973-75); Director General, Makkah Textile Mill (1976-78); Executive Manager, KARA Industrial Estate, on the Jeddah-Taif Non-Muslim Road, which includes various factories; Assistant General Manager, KARA Establishment, Jeddah; Member of the Saudi Arabian Delegation to West Germany, 1974. **Hobbies:** Reading, sports. **Prof. Addr.:** P.O.Box. 533, Jeddah. **Priv. Addr.:** Tel.: 6714607, Jeddah, Saudi Arabia.

SINDI (Abdallah Mohamad), Saudi academic. **Born** in 1944 in Jeddah, Saudi Arabia. **Dipl.:** B.A. (International Relations); M.A. (Political Science); Ph.D. (International Relations). **Career:** Director, Scholarships Department, King Abdulaziz University (1971-72); Director of Translation Department, Faculty of Economics and Administration, Research and Development Centre, KAU; Professor of Political Science, KAU; Assistant Professor, Faculty of Economics and Administration, King Abdulaziz University; participant member, King Faisal Conference, California, USA (1978); member, the International Institute of Public Administration. **Publications:** King Faisal and Pan-Islamism, a chapter in King Faisal and the Development of

Saudi Arabia, edited by Willard Beling, Croom Helm, London 1980. **Hobbies:** reading, travel, sports. **Address:** P.O.Box. 5675, Jeddah, Saudi Arabia.

SINDI (Abdul Aziz Mohamad), Saudi engineer. **Born** in 1946. **Dipl.:** B.Sc. (Civil Engineering). **Career:** Assistant Quantities Engineer, Makkah Sewage Co. (1968-70); Project Charge of asphalt laying, Makkah Governorate Secretariat (1971); Chief, Engineering Department (1973); Director, Technical Department (1974); Director of Engineering Department (1975); Mayor Assistant, Makkah Municipality, (1975), member of Higher Pilgrimage Technical Sub-Committee, Technical Board of Real Estate Development Fund, Arab Town Planning Organization, Board of Governorate Secretariat; Arab Cities Organization Conference. General Manager of Engineer Abdul Aziz Sindi's Office since 1978. **Hobby:** Reading. From among his books are (THIS IS THE ISLAM) + (SUMMARYOF SUBJECT FOR PILGRIMAGE AND (UMRAH) + (BOOKLET ON ENGINEERING SYSTEMS)) **Prof. Addr.:** Mecca, al-Mansour Street, Office of Engineer Abdul Aziz Mohammad Sindi, P.O.Box 2190, Holy Makkah, Saudi Arabia. Fax: 0096625361075, E-mail: Sindi_Consult@hotmail.com.

SINDI (Ali Abdulrassul), Saudi businessman. **Born** in 1933 in Mecca, Saudi Arabia. **Son** of Abdulrassul Sindi. **Married**, four children. **Career:** Administrative Section of Civil Aviation Department; Assistant Director General of Civil Aviation (1953-68); Chairman, Express Contracting and Trading (since 1968); Chairman, Saudi International Aeradio Ltd. **Sport:** Tennis. **Addr.:** P.O.Box. 2951, Tel.: 6654585, Telex: 401082 SINDICO SJ, Jeddah, Saudi Arabia and P.O.Box 15357, Riyadh 11444, Saudi Arabia.

SINDI (Kamil A.), Saudi official. **Born** on 3 January 1932. **Educ.:** High School. **Career:** Deputy Director-General, Civil Aviation Department, Jeddah 1956; Director General, Civil Aviation Directorate, Jeddah 1961; Director-General, Saudi Arabian Airlines 1967; President, Arab Air Carriers Organization (AACO) 1971; member of the Executive Committee of IATA since 1974; Assistant Minister of Defense and Civil Aviation for Civil Aviation of the Government of Saudi Arabia (with rank of Minister) from 1979 unitl his retirement for health reasons in 1983. Reporting directly to him during this period were: President of Civil Aviation, Director-General of Saudi Arabian Airlines, Directorate of International Airport Projects, Directorate of Meteorology and Environmental Projection. Played an active part in establishing the Saudi Civil Aviation Department, later Saudia Airlines; set-up Marine and Meteorological Observation Centers and Telecommunication Sections; started the first Technical Training Institute in the Arab world for air-traffic controllers, radio operators, meteorological observers and radio maintenance technicians; participated in the creation of an Air Cadet Training Center; participated in numerous Civil Aviation Conferences, and was elected Vice-Chairman of an ICAO Conference in Montreal; under his leadship, Saudia concluded the purchase of four Boeing jets in 1962 thus becoming the first airline in the Middle East to fly the big jets, member of Wings Club New York, USA Publication: various articles in aviation magazine. **Honour:** Knight of the Order of Orange. **Hobby:** Reading. **Address:** P.O.Box 1327 Jeddah 21431, Saudi Arabia.

SINDI (Mohamad Bakor), Saudi executive. **Born** in 1943 in Makkah. **Educ.:** Received general education in Makkah. **Dipl.:** Diploma of Metrology; Technical Training (1964); Diploma of English (Advance Level), Saudia (1967); Senior Management Course, Beirut, Lebanon (1972); Associate of Arts Degree, Fulerton College, Fulerton, California (1978); Bachelor of Arts Degree in Accounting, California State University, Fulerton, California (1980); Master Degree in Business Administration, California State University, Fulerton, California (1982). **Career:** Disbursement Secretary (1968-69); Saudia; Supervisor, General Ledger (1969-70) Saudia; Staff Manager-Ledger (1970-75) Saudia; Acting Manager-General Accounting (1975-76); Saudia; Asst. Corp. Controller-Credit Operations (1983-89); Saudia; Corporate Controller-Corporate Accounting (1989 to date) Saudia. **Member:** Arab American Association of Orange County Honorary Society at Fulerton College, California. **Awards:** International Understanding Award, CSUF (1980); Semifinalist Distinguished Men at Fulerton College (1978). **Interest:** Editor and columnist for al-Bilad Daily Saudi News Paper; Translator for Saudi Television, Jeddah; Translating news from Arabic to English and Vice-Versa. **Hobby:** Literature and programming in Computer. **Addr.:** Finance Division, Corporate Accounting Department, Cost Center 620, P.O.Box 620, Jeddah 21231, Saudi Arabia.

SINDI (Suliman, Bakur), Saudi academic. **Born** in 1944 in Taif, Saudi Arabia. **Son** of Bakur Sindi. **Educ.:** B.Sc. (Police Science) (1969); M.Sc. (Police Administration) (1972); Ph.D. (Traffic Safety Education) (1975, all from Michigan State University). **Career:** Curriculum Specialist and Consultant Ministry of Education, Saudi Arabia; Director of Centre for Statistical Data and Educational Documentation, Ministry of Education, Saudi Arabia; Director General for Development of Higher Education, Ministry of Higher Education, Saudi Arabia; Educational Attache and Head of the Saudi Arabian Educational Mission in Canada (since 1984). **Publ.:** Driving Schools in Saudi Arabia: Symposium at College of Education, King Saud University (1984); Comparison between the Police System in Saudi Arabia and the Police in USA (Thesis for Master's Degree); A rational and Comprehensive Traffic Safety Education Program for Saudi Arabia (Thesis for Ph.D. Degree); "Cost Analysis Per Student" at Ministry of Education, Saudi Arabia (1978); "Strategies in Educational Planning and Curriculum Development"; "Developing and Organising Curriculum in

Saudi Arabia" (1977); translated "The Research Evidence of the Effects of Grades" by G.B. Jackson (1975); presented a report "Statistics on Educational Development in Saudi Arabia" in a Conference in Egypt (1978); various additional articles written in national and international educational journals and periodicals. **Member of:** World Council for Educational Curriculum Development; Arab Chiefs of Police Association; Saudi Arabian National Committee for Traffic Safety. **Hobbies:** Reading, writing. **Sports:** Swimming. **Addr.:** Saudi Arabian Educational Mission, 99 Banks Street, Suite 1144, Otawa, Ontario K1P 6B9, Canada.

SINDI (Zuhair Farid), Saudi official. **Born** in 1953 in Medina, Saudi Arabia. **Dipl.:** M.Sc. (Civil Engineering). **Career:** Assistant Deputy Director for Management, Operations and Maintenance, International Airports Projects; Executive Director, King Abdulaziz International Airport, Jeddah. **Member:** International Airports Operating Council; American Society of Civil Engineers (ASCE); first Airport Director of an International Airport of his size in the Kingdom of Saudi Arabia; participated in the preparation, supervision and implementation of plans for management, operation and maintenance of KAIA. **Hobbies:** Sports, reading. **Prof. Addr.:** King Abdulaziz Internatinal Airport Tel.: 6854212, Jeddah. **Priv. Addr.:** Tel.: 6854161, Jeddah, Saudi Arabia.

SINGH (Bawa Gurnam), Indian businessman. **Born** on July 9, 1931 in Chakwal. **Son** of Bawa Hari Singh (Businessman) **and** Mrs. née Harnam Kaur Maini. **Married** on September 25, 1955 in New Delhi to Jagmohan Kaur Bawa, two daughters: Inni and Rita and two sons: Bawa Harvinder and Goldie Bawa. **Educ.:** Indian School, Zahidan (Iran); D.A.V. College, Dehra Dun, India; Kennedy Western University, California. **Dipl.:** MBA; (now writing Ph.D.). **Career:** Joined his father's business in 1948 in Kuwait; Established Globe Commercial Co. in Kuwait (1964); Currently, one of the partners of Globe Commercial Co. and looking after Company's business in the United Arab Emirates dealing in management, finance, banking, sales and imports. **Other Info.:** A keen sportsman and started cricket in Kuwait, took interest and played almost all sports, presently a keen Golfer Playing to handicap of 13. **Honorary** Chairman of Indian School in Kuwait and of Kuwait Sports, Kuwait; Honorary Chairman of Kuwait Hawks Cricket Club. **Sports:** Hockey, cricket, golf. **Hobbies:** Sports, reading, social activities. **Member:** Ahmadi Golf Club, Ahmadi, Kuwait; Hunting and Equestrian Club, Kuwait; Indian Arts Club, Kuwait; Indian Club, Abu Dhabi; Delhi Golf Club, Delhi, India. **Credit Card:** American Express. **Prof. Addr.:** Globe Commercial Co., P.O.Box 3435, Tel.: 333649, 341696, Fax: 352527, Abu Dhabi, U.A.E. **Priv. Addr.:** Globe Commercial Co. W.L.L., P.O.Box 4580 Safat, 13046 Safat, Tel.: 4834383, 4831728, Telex: 22515 GLOBECO, Fax: 4831907, Kuwait, Kuwait.

SIRAGE (Abdulhamid, Abdallah), Jordanian former diplomat. **Born** in 1918 in Mecca. **Son** of Abdallah Sirage. **Educ.:** American University of Beirut. **Dipl.:** Bachelor of Science. **Career:** Attached to the Ministry of Foreign Affairs; Counsellor and Chargé d'Affaires at the Embassy of Jordan to Lebanon 1955-57). **Awards:** al-Kawkab Medal (Jordan), Commander Order of the Cedar (Lebanon). **Addr.:** Amman, Jordan.

SIRAGEDDINE (Abdulhamid), Egyptian agronomist, former deputy. **Born** in Egypt. **Educ.:** Secondary and Higher Studies. **Career:** Agronomist, director of companies, former deputy. **Member:** Gazira Sporting Club, National Sporting Club, Autmobile Club of Egypt, Faroussia Club. **Addr.:** 10, Ahmad Pasha Street. Garden City, **Tel.:** 21903, Cairo, Egypt.

SIRAGEDDINE (Anis), Egyptian engineer-architect. **Born** in Cairo. **Married** to Miss Leila Ali Ibrahim. **Career:** Former Director General Cairo Roads and Ways Administration; Deputy Director-General, Cairo Municipal Corporation. **Addr.:** Ibn Malek Street, Arous an-Nil Building. Giza, Cairo, Egypt.

SIRAGEDDINE (Jamil), Egyptian landowner. **Born** in Egypt. **Educ.:** Secondary and Higher. **Career:** Director of Companies; former Vice-President of the Chamber of Deputies, Landowner. **Member** of Alexandria Sporting Club. **Addr.:** 4, Ahmad Kamel Street, Pyramids Road, Tel.: 895578, 897191, Cairo, Egypt.

SIRAGEDDINE (Yassine), Egyptian barrister, director of companies. **Born** in Egypt. **Educ.:** Secondary and Higher. **Dipl.:** Bachelor of Laws. **Career:** Barrister; Director of Companies; former Deputy; Proprietor and Publisher "al-Nidaa" Magazine. **Member:** Automobile Club of Egypt, National Sporting Club. **Addr.:** al-Giza Street, Giza, **Tel.:** 894767, Cairo, Egypt.

SIRAJ (Ahmad A.), Saudi official. **Born** on 5 February 1933 in Mecca, Saudi Arabia. **Dipl.:** B.A. (Law), Cairo University; Diploma (Military Studies), Cairo. **Career:** Assistant Legal Adviser with the rank of First Lieutenant and later Captain, Ministry of Defence (1954 and 1956 respectively); First Attaché, Ministry of Foreign Affairs (1957); Third Secretary, Royal Saudi Arabian Embassy (1960); Second Secretary, Saudi Arabian Embassy, Cairo (1964); First Secretary, Ministry of Foreign Affairs (1966); Director, Eastern Department (Political Affairs for Asia and Africa) (1972); Minister, Plenipotentiary, Executive Secretariat, Ministry of Foreign Affairs (1981); attended the following conferences: the 20th session of the U.N. General Assembly, 3rd Arab Summit Confernce, Alexandria, nonalignment Summit Conference, Cairo, 1st Islamic Conference, Jeddah, the Islamic Summit Conference, Makkah, 2nd Summit Conference of the Gulf Corporation Council (GCC), Riyadh and several other GCC and Islamic **Summit** Conferences. **Publications:** some articles in local **newspapers**; wrote some manuscripts for Radio talks. **Hobbies:** swimming, tennis. **Prof. Addr.:** Ministry of Foreign Affairs, Tel.: 6690900, Jeddah. **Priv. Addr.:** Tel.: 6651659, Jeddah, Saudi Arabia.

SIRAJ (Ahmad Abdul Rahman), Saudi meteorologist. **Career:** Director of Forecasts Department, General Directorate of Meteorology; Has 20 years' experience in the field of meteorology and weather forecasts. **Honour:** Medal from Korean Airforce. **Address:** General Directorate of Meteorology, Riyadh, Saudi Arabia.

SIRRY (Gazbia Hassan), Egyptian Artist painter, academic. **Born** in 1925 in Cairo, Egypt. **Married. Educ.:** Diploma of Painting, High Institute of Fine Arts, Cairo; Diploma of Art Education; Post Graduate qualification, Slade College, London University and studies in Paris and Rome. **Career:** Lecturer in Painting, Art Education Institute, Cairo; Assistant Professor and Professor of Painting, Art Education College, Helwan University, Cairo (1965-81); member, Syndicate of Plastic Arts, Cairo, Societe des Amis d'Art, Cairo, Egyptian Society of Graphic Arts; Fine Arts Committee, Supreme Council of Culture, Cairo; 62 oneman exhibitions in Egypt, Arab Countries Africa, Europe, North America (1953-2000); 32 group exhibitions Egypt, Arab Countries Europe, Americas and Asia, (1950-2000); 19 international (1952-2000); paintings requisitioned by museums in Cairo, Alexandria, Menya, Egypt, Evansville, Washington (USA); Peking, Tunis, Paris, Vernon (France) and private collections. Los Angeles, San Francisco. **Medals:** Order of Sciences and Arts (first degree). Honorary Prize Bienale Venise (1956); State Prize (1970) and others. **Publ.:** "Gazbia Sirry" published by Ministry of Information (1984) and American University Cairo (1998) and others including Encyclopedia de la Peinture Roberts (1976) and Petit Larousse (1979). **Hobbies:** reading, travelling, swimming, fishing. **Addr.:** 31 al-Gezira al Wosta Street, Zamalek, 11211 Cairo.

SISI (Abdul Kader, Abdul Rahman, al), Egyptian banker. **Born** in 1934 in Cairo, Egypt. **Son** of Abdul Rahman Sisi. **Married** in 1960, 1 son, 3 daughters. **Educ.:** University of Aïn Shams, Egypt. **Dipl.:** B.A. Commerce (1958); **Career:** Kuwait Investment Company, KSC (1962-67); Joined Alahli Bank of Kuwait since 1967. Deputy Chairman, Arab International Finance Co., Luxembourg; Managing Director, "Kuwmiss" Inc. USA; General Manager, Alahli Bank of Kuwait KSC, Safat, Kuwait; former, Vice-Chairman, First Arabian Corp. S.A., Luxembourg. **Member:** Arab Bankers Association; The General Committee of Egyptian Expatriates; The Sea Club, Kuwait; al-Jazeerah Club, Cairo; al-Shams, Cairo. **Hobbies:** Swimming, reading, football and tennis. **Addr.:** Cairo, Egypt.

SKALLI (Ali), Moroccan diplomat. **Born** in 1927 in Fes, Morocco. **Married**, four children. **Educ.:** B.A. in Law and Political Sciences, University of Paris, France. **Career:** Société Métallurgique, Luxembourg (1954-56); **Counsellor**, Moroccan Embassy to France (1956); Ministry of Foreign Affairs, Morocco, Head of Consular Affairs, Head of Social Affairs, Head of International Organizations, Head of European Affairs; Minister Plenipotentiary and Chargé d'Affaires, Moroccan Embassy in Paris, France; Ambassador to Federal Republic of Germany (1970); Secretary General, Ministry of Foreign Affairs (1971-74); Ambassador, Permanent Representative to the UN, and the international organisations in Geneva and Austria (1974). **Addr.:** c/o Ministry of Foreign Affairs, Rabat, Morocco.

SKHIRI (Neji), Tunisian banker. **Born** on February 15, 1934 Monastir. **Son** of Ahmed Ben Hamida Skhiri (Landowner) and Mrs., née Khadouja Kacem. **Married in 1962** in Monastir to Miss Nebiha Slimane, 4 children: Wajdi (1963), Rym (1967), Hella (1972) and Azza (1976). **Educ.:** Lycée Technique of Tunis; Lycée de Garçons, Sousse; University of Institute of Higher Studies, Tunis; Centre de Formation Bancaire de Paris, France. **Dipl.:** diploma in Banking. **Career:** Joined the Banque de France in order to constitute the 1st team of the Central Bank of Tunisia (1957-58); Held top management positions in several Banks in Tunisia: The Central Bank Bank of Tunisia (1959-80); Deputy General Manager, then Chairman General Manager, Banque du Sud, Tunisia (1980-84); Chairman General Manager, Société Tunisienne de Banque Tunisie (1984-87); Chairman General Manager, Union Internationale de Banques, Tunisia (1987-89); Maghreb Arab Bank (1989-91); Banque Tuniso-Qatarie d'Investissement (1991-95); Chairman, NSK Finances (1995- date). President of town Council of Monastir: President of Chambre Tuniso-Italienne; Vice President then President of Union of Arab Banks. **Decor.:** Officer of the Order of the Republic; Khight of the Order of Independance. **Sports:** Swimming, footing. **Prof. Addr.:** Union Internationale de Banques, 65, Avenue du 7 Novembre, P.O.Box 224, Tel.: 340763, Tunis, Tunisia. **Priv. Addr.:** 3, Rue Hamidi, el-Menzah, I-1004, Tel.: 751584, Fax: 232363 Tunis, Tunisia.

SLAWI (Idriss), Moroccan statesman. **Born** in 1926 in Fez, Morocco, **Educ.:** University of Grenoble, France. **Career:** Joined the family firm; attached to Staff of Governor of Casablanca (1955); Asst. Director Chief of Regional Security, Casablanca (1956); Under-Secretary of State for the Interior (May-Dec. 1958); Minister of Industry, Commerce and Mines (May 1960-June 1961); Secretary-General, Casablanca Group Liaison Office, Bamako, Mali (1961-62); Director of Royal Cabinet; Minister of Public Works (October 1962- January 1963); Minister of Finance (January 1963- August 1964); Minister of National Economy and Agriculture (November 1963- August 1964); Governor, Banque du Maroc (Central Bank of Morocco) (1964-67); Minister of Justice (1968-69); Director General, Royal Cabinet (1969-71); Permanent Representative at UN, Geneva (1974); Representative to International Court of Justice in Western Sahara Case (June-July 1975); Counsellor to HM King Hassan (since Oct. 1977); Chairman, General Manager, Société Nationale d'Investissement (1978-80). **Addr.:** Rabat, Morocco.

SLIM (Taieb), Tunisian former statesman **Born** in 1914 in Tunisia. **Educ.:** Tunis Lycée; University of Paris. **Career:** Member of Destour Socialist Party; detained (1941-43); Head, Tunisian Office, Cairo (1949); Established Tunisian offices (New Delhi, Diakarta, Karachi); Head, Foreign Affairs, Presidency of the Council of Ministers (1955-57); Ambassador to United Kingdom (1956-62); Permanent Representative to United Nations (1962-67); Secretary of State, Personal Representative of the President (1967-70); Ambassador to Morocco (1970-71); Minister of State (1971-72); Ambassador, Permanent Representative to UN, Geneva (1973-74); Ambassador to Canada (1974-76); Minister of State (1976-77); Permanent Representative of Tunisia to the UN (1981). **Member:** Political Bureau Neo-Doustour Party (1971-74); Maghreb Bureau, Cairo. **Addr.:** Tunis, Tunisia.

SLIMANI (Othman), Moroccan economist. **Born** in 1941 in Fes, Morocco. **Married,**three children. **Educ.:** Degrees in Law and Economic Sciences. **Career:** Inspecteur des Finances; Secretary General, in Ministry of Finance Department; assignments abroad, particularly with the IMF in Washington, Secretary of State for Economic Affairs in Prime Minister's Office (1977); President-Director General, Credit Immobilier et Hotelier (since 1980). **Addr.:** 187 Avenue Hassan II Casablanca, Morocco.

SMAIL (Muhammad Bin), Tunisian printer. **Born** on June 5, 1927 in Jerba, Tunisia. **Married,** 2 son. **Educ.:** Faculty of Law, Grenoble University, France. **Career:** Editor in Chief of "L'Action" newspaper and other journals (1955-63); Head of the Minister of Information Office and General Director of Tourism (1959-60); Director General of Radio Television Tunisienne (RTT) (1969-70); Founder and Director of Ceres Productions (offset printing and publishing) (1978-). **Addr.:** 6 Rue Alain Savery, Tunis, Tunisia.

SMAILA (Milad, Abdulsalam), Libyan politician. **Career:** Under Secretary, Ministry of Planning; Minister of State for Cabinet Affairs (1976-77); Secretary for General People's Committee Affairs, General People's Committee (1977). **Addr.:** Tripoli, Libya.

SNOUSSI (Ahmad), Moroccan statesman. **Born** in Morocco. **Educ.:** Secondary and Higher. **Career:** Minister of Information in the Cabinet of Mr. Mohamad Benhima (July 1967); Minister of Information in the cabinet of Dr. Ahmad Laraki (1969); Ambassador to Nigeria (1965-67); Ambassador to Cameroon; Ambassador to Tunisia (1971-73); Ambassador to Algeria (1973-75); **Ambassador** to Mauritania (1978-January 1980). 1981-1990 businessman: President Cement Group Lafarge. President Cement Group CINOVCA. President of National Association of Cement producers. President of National association of High Sea fishing companies. Permanent representative of Morocco to the United Nations (Oct. 1991-); President of the Security Council (Feb. 1993). **Addr.:** 3, Rue de la Victoire, Rabat, Morocco and Permanent Mission of Morocco to the United Nations, 767 Third Avenue, 30th Floor, New York, N.Y. 10017, U.S.A.

SOBAIHI (Mohamad Ahmad, al), Saudi official. **Born** in 1941 in Mecca, Saudi Arabia. **Dipl.:** Ph.D. **Career:** Held various government posts at the Ministry of Telegraph Post and Telephone (1955-57); Ministry of Defence (1958-62); Ministry of Information, 1962 - to present, Program Consultant and Director, Second Channel, Saudi Television, Ministry of Information; **Publication:** Usage of Television for Fulfillment of Social Needs. **Hobbies:** reading, sports, swimming. **Address:** Ministry of Information Riyadh, Saudi Arabia.

SOBHI (Ibrahim Mohamad, al), Saudi academic. **Born** in 1940 in Medina, Saudi Arabia. **Dipl.:** B.A., King Saud Univrsity. **Career:** Editor, Examination Department, Directorate of Boys' Education, Medina; Personnel Manager, Girls' Education Administration, Medina; Liaison Officer, Directorate General of Girls' Colleges; General Director, Girls' Colleges, Western Region; member, Manshiah District Municipal Council, Medina. **Publications:** Research: Decision Making, Administrative Leadership, Administrative Planning. **Hobby:** reading. **Prof. Addr.:** P.O.Box. 2410 and 9498, Tel.: 6513408, Jeddah. **Priv. Addr.:** Tel.: 6894944, Jeddah, Saudi Arabia.

SOBHI (Mohamad, Ibrahim), Egyptian director general of the international bureau of the universal postal union. **Born** on March 28, 1925 in Alexandria, Egypt. **Son** of Ibrahim Sobhi (General) **and** Mrs., née Zenab Affiffi. **Married** in 1950 to Miss Laila Ahmad, 3 children: Nagwa, Ahmad and Hesham. **Educ.:** Cairo University, Egypt. **Dipl.:** B.A in Engineering (1949). **Career:** Construction of roads and airports in the Engineer Corps, Egypt (1950); Technical Secretary on the Communications Commission, Permanent Council for Development and National Production, Egypt (1954); One-year fellowship studying transport and communications services in the U.S.A., Vanderbilt University, Nashville/Tenn. (1955-56); Technical Director in the Office of the Minister of Communications for Posts, Railways and Coordination between means of transport and communications, Egypt (1956-61); Attended the UPU Congress, Ottawa, Canada (1957); Attended the UPU Consultative Committee for Postal Studies (CCPS) session, Brussels, Belgium (1958); Director-General of the Sea Transport Authority, while **remaining** member of the Technical Committees of the Postal Organization, Egypt (1961-64); Under-Secretary of State for Communications and member of Board of the Postal Organization, Egypt (1964-68); Chairman of the Board, Postal Organization of Egypt, and Secretary General of the African Postal Union in Cairo (1968-74); Attended, as Head of the Egyptian delegation, the UPU Tokyo and Lausanne Congresses, and the sessions of the CCPS set up by the former Congress (1969-74); Director of the Executive Bureau in charge of Egyptian projects in Africa, including construction of the "Hôtel de l'Amitié", Bamako (Mali), and a number of roads (1963-74); Director-General of the International Bureau of the Universal Postal Union, Berne (Switzerland) (1975-present); Assumed the task of Secretary-General of the 18th UPU Congress in Rio de Janeiro (Brazil, September/October 1979) where he was reelected as Director General of the International Bureau of the UPU for a second five years, term. **Awards:** Order of Merit, 1st Class, Egypt (1974); Holder of the "Heinrich von Stephan" Medal, Federal Republic of Germany (1979); Order of Postal Merit "Gran Placa" Spain (1979). **Hobbies:** Philately, Music, Croquet. **Member:** Heliopolis Sporting Club, Officers Sporting Club, Philatelic Society of Egypt. **Credit Card:** American Express. **Addr.:** Woltpoststrasse 4, 3000 Berne 15, Tel.: 432211, Switzerland.

SOLAIM (Soliman Abdul Aziz, al), Saudi former minister. **Born** in 1941. **Dipl.:** B.Com., Cairo University; M.A. (International Relations), University of Southern California; Ph.D. (International Relations), John Hopkins University 1970. **Career:** Director, Department of Foreign Relations and Conferences, Ministry of Labour; Assistant Director-General of General Organization of Social Insurance; Professor of Political Science, Riyadh University (1972-74); Deputy Minister of Commerce and Industry for Trade and Provisions (1974-75); Minister of Commerce (since 1975-to Aug. 1995); Minister of Finance and National Economy (Aug. 1995-1996). Chairman of Board, Saudi Arabian Specifications and Standardization Organization, Wheat Silos and Flour Mills Organization; attended several economic conferences in Saudi Arabia and abroad. **Address:** Riyadh, Saudi Arabia.

SOLIMAN (Mohamed, Ibrahim), Egyptian Professor, Faculty of Engineering, Ain Shams University, Cairo Egypt and Minister of Housing, Utilities and Urban Communities. **Born** on June 6, 1946, Cairo, Egypt. **Married,** 3 children: **Educ.:** Ain Shams University, Cairo, Egypt, McGill University, Montreal, Canada. **Dipl.:** 1969: B.Sc., Ain Shams University, Cairo, Egypt - Civil Engineering Department, Structural eng. Division (Honor Degree); 1970-1972: M. Eng., Ain Shams University, Cairo, Egypt (Civil Engineering Department). 1973-1975: M. Eng., McGill University, Montreal, Canada (Civil Engineering Department); 1975-1979: Ph.D., McGill University, Montreal, Canada (Civil Engineering Department). **Languages:** English, Arabic. **Career: Activities:** Minister of Housing, Utilities and Urban Communities; the **International** Association for Major Metropolises, "METROPOLIS"; Professor, Civil Engineering Department, Ain Shams University, University, Cairo, Egypt; Member of the Egyptian Society of Civil Engineers Board of Directors; Secretary General of the Canadian Society for Civil Engineers in Egypt; Member of the Canadian - Egyptian Friendship Society; President of McGill University Alumni in Egypt; Consultant Engineer. **Experiences:** 1970-1973: Research Assistant, Civil Engineering Department, Ain Shams University, Cairo, Egypt. 1973-1979: Research Assistant, Civil Engineering Department, McGill University, Montreal, Canada. 1979-1984; Lecturer, Ain Shams University, Civil Eng. Dept. Structural Division: Consulting Engineer. 1984-1989: Assistant Professor, Ain Shams University, Cairo, (Consulting Engineer). 1989 - to date: Prof., Ain shams University, Cairo, Egypt. 1969 - to date: Accomplished more than 150 researches, in the different Structural Engineering fields; Published in the international scientific periodicals and magazines and presented in the local and international scientific conferences. 1979-1993: Managing a private consulting engineering office; (design & supervision of engineering projects in the fields: Town Planning, Housing complexes, Touristic villages, Bridges, Factories, Rehabilitation and restoration of a lot of important projects. 1993-1996: Minister of State for New Urban Communities; **1996 - to date: Minister of Housing, Utilities and Urban communities. Clubs and Associations:** Vice Chairman & Member of the Board of Directors of 'METROPOLIS", Secretary General of Canadian Engineers Society in Middle East, Member of the Egyptian Civil Engineers Society Board of Directors. **Prof. Addr.:** 1, Ismail Abaza St., Kasr El Aini, Cairo, Tel.: +20(2)7921403/5, Egypt.

SOLIMAN (Yehia, Dr.), Egyptian physician. **Born** in 1932 in Cairo, Egypt. **Married,** two children. **Educ.:** M.B., B.Ch., M.D., LMSSA, London; Tropical diseases, London University. **Career:** Medical Officer, Hilton Hotels International, Unilever, Liquid Air Factory and insurance companies (1959-66); Medical Registrar, National Heart Hospital, London (1966-67); Medical Registrar, Harefield Hospital, UK and watford General Hospital. Medical Officer and private practitioner, London (since 1968). **Hobbies:** Golf, cricket, squash, football. Member of Harlingham Club, London. **Addr.:** 21 Wimpole Street, London W1, UK.

SONBOL (Said), Egyptian senior columnist al-akhbar newspaper. **Born** on April 21, 1929. **Son** of Ibrahim Rifaat (Lawyer) **and** Mrs. Aida née Zaklama. **Married** on July 31, 1971 in Cairo to Fadia Ebeid, five children, 4 daughters: Hanan (4.2.1973), Noha (21.2.1974), Reem (27.1.1976), Aida (19.3.1977) and one son, Sobhi (5.8.1980). **Educ.:** Cairo Primary School, Assiut Secondary School, Faculty of Science, Cairo University. **Dipl.:** B.Sc. (1949). **Other Informations:** Covered several important International

Events, Carried Interviews with several Heads of States, the latest with President Bush of U.S.A. (March 1991). **Career:** Reporter, el-Masry Newspaper (1950-52); Reporter al-Akhbar Newspaper (1952-56); Senior Reporter, Middle East News Agency (1956-57); Economic Editor, al-Akhbar (1957-1961); Deputy Chief Editor, Akhbar el-Youm (1961-65) then Managing Editor (1965-85); Editor in Chief al-Akhbar (1985-91); Chairman of the Board of Directors Akhbar al-Youm Publishing House (1989-91); Member of Board of Press Syndicate; Member of High Council for TV and Broadcasting; Deputy Chairman of Supreme Press Council. **Awards:** Order of Merit (First Class) by the President of Egypt (May 1991); Distinguished Award by U.N.F.P.A. for best coverage of Population Issues. **Sports:** Fishing, Tennis. **Hobbies:** Music, Reading, Photography. **Member:** Automobile Club, Rotary Club, Sporting Club. **Credit Cards:** AMX, Visa, Euro Card. **Prof. Addr.:** Akhbar el-Youm, 6 al-Sahafa Str., Tel.: 756333, Cairo, Egypt. **Priv. Addr.:** 46, Nehru Str., Heliopolis, Tel.: 2580778, Cairo, Egypt.

SORAYA (Ahmad Mohamad Abdulaziz, al), Saudi academic. **Born** in 1943 in Rawda-Sidair. **Dipl.:** B.Sc., Riyadh University; Ph.D., Edinburgh University. **Career:** Associate Professor, College of Science, King Saud University (1968-71); Lecturer (1976-78); Assistant Professor, Department of Physics, King Saud University since 1978; member, American Physics Society, Energy Utilization Group of Saudi Arabian National Council of Science and Technology (SANCST); Chairman, Department of Physics, College of Science, King Saud University; member of Council, College of Science, King Saud University; co-Chairman, International Symposium on Application and Technology of Ionizing Radiation. **Publications:** Nine research papers and one book in the field of nuclear and radiation physics. **Prof. Addr.:** Department of Physics, College of Science, King Saud University, P.O.Box 2455, Riyadh, Saudi Arabia.

SORKHOU (Masoud), Kuwaiti financial manager and public accountant. **Born** in 1948 in Kuwait. **Son** of Ebrahim Sorkhou. **Married** in 1978, 1 daughter. **Dipl.:** Certified Accountant. **Career:** Assistant Auditor, Whinney Murry & Co., England (1975-76); Head of Budget Division, Kuwait Oil Company, Kuwait (1976-78); Financial Manager, Bank of Kuwait and the Middle East, Safat, Kuwait (1980-82). Assistant General Manager, Treasury, Computer and Financial Controls (1982-85). Fellow of Chartered Association of Certified Accountants in England and Wales. **Hobby:** Sports. **Addr.:** P.O.Box 3385, Tel.: 2462958, 2414328, Safat, Kuwait.

SOROUR (Ahmed, Fathi), Egyptian politician. **Born** in 1933 in Egypt. **Career:** Joined Ministry of Education in 1986, later Dean, Faculty of Law, Cairo University, Vice-President at said University, Lawyer at the Court of Cassation, author of many references of criminal law, Vice-President of the International association of penal law, Cultural Counsellor at Egyptian Embassy in Paris (1965-1967); Representative of the Arab League in Unesco (1972-1978); Vice-President of the Executive Board (1989-1993), got the prize of the state merit of social sciences; Member, National Democratic Party; President, People's Assembly (1990- to date). **Addr.:** People's Assembly. Cairo, Egypt.

SOROUR (Ihab, Zaki), Egyptian diplomat. **Born** in 1935 in Cairo, Egypt. **Son** of Zaki Sorour. **Married**, three children. **Educ.:** Bain Military Science; B.A. in Commerce; M.A. in Arts and Political Science; Ph.D. in Political Science; Diploma in Foreign Trade Planning, UN Geneva. **Career:** President of African Affairs Bureau (1953-67); Director, Economic Research Department, Ministry of Economy and Foreign Trade (1968-71); Commercial Counsellor, Tokyo, Japan (1972-74); Political Counsellor for Ministry of Foreign Affairs, Cairo; member of Egyptian Delegation to United Nations, New York (1975) Charge d'Affaires of Egypt to New Zealand; Ambassador of Egypt to New Zealand (1976); participated in various official Egyptian delegations since 1970. **Medals:** Order of the Revolution; Order of the Republic. **Hobbies:** tennis, squash, hunting, swimming, travel, chess, backgammon. **Member** of Economic and Legislative Association, Cairo; International Law Association, Cairo; African Assembly, Cairo; International Trade Center, Geneva; World Trade Center, New York and the Foreign Correspondents Club, Tokyo. **Addr.:** Ministry of Foreign Affairs, Cairo, Egypt.

SOUDAH (Claude, Anton), Arab American banker, international financial manager. **Born** in Jerusalem in 1937. **Son** of Anton Soudah. **Married**, three children. **Educ.:** B.A., College of Business Administration, Seattle, University of Washington; American Institute of Banking, Seattle Chapter; School for International Banking, University of Colorado; Pacific Coast Graduate School, University of Washington. **Career:** Management Trainee, International Division, Seattle-First National Bank, Seattle, Washinton (1966-67); Assistant Vice President, International Division (1967-71); Vice President and Manager, Seattle Office, International Division (1972-74); Vice President and Manager, Americas Region, International Division, Washington (1974-79); Vice President and General Manager, Europe Region, International Division, London (since 1979). **Member** of Overseas Bankers Club; member of Arab Bankers Association, London, member of Woolnoth Society. **Hobbies:** reading, writing, stamp collecting, travel, backgammon, soccer. **Addr.:** 28 Hanover House, St. John's Wood High Street, London NW 8 7DY, U.K.

SOUDANI (Ferid), Tunisian diplomat. **Born** on September 14, 1930 in Tunis (Tunisia). **Married** on February 28, 1964 to Khedija Louadi. **Educ.:** Sadiki College, Tunis; Faculty of Law, University of Paris. **Dipl.:** LL.B. **Career:** Director, "al-Ama" newspaper (1957-60); Minister, Tunisian Embassy, Rabat (Morocco, 1966-67); President Director-General, Tunis Afrique Presse news agency (1967-71); Secretary-General, Union of African Information Agencies (1961-71); Ambassador to Ivory Coast (October 1974), also accredited to Niger since December 1974, and to Ghana (January 1975), to the Republic of Benin (1975). **Addr.:** Ministry of Foreign Affairs, Tunis, Tunisia.

SOUELEM (Nadir, Mohamed), Egyptian academic, plastic Surgeon. **Born** in 1926, in Cairo, Egypt. **Son** of Mohamed Souelem. **Educ.:** M.B., B.Ch., FRCS, London. **Career:** lecturer in General Surgery, Ain Shams Univesity, Cairo; Plastic Surgeon, East Grinstead, UK; Assistant Professor of Plastic Surgery; Professor of Plastic Surgery, Head of the Burns and Facio Maxillary Department, and of Plastic Surgery Department. Ain Shams University. **Publ.:** many research papers an plastic Surgery. **Medals:** Order of the Republic. **Member** of the International Association for sports Medicine, the Medical committee, the African Football Confederation; President of the Egyptian Association for Plastic Surgery. **Hobbies:** tennis, swimming, music. **Prof. Addr.:** 26 Adly Street, Cairo, Egypt. **Priv. Addr.:** Shafik Mansour Street, Zamalek, Cairo.

SOUFI (Mahmood, Al), Bahraini General Manager - Bahrain Aluminium extrusion Company (BALEXCO). **Born** on February 10, 1953 (Manama - Bahrain). **Married** in 1983 to Parwana Mohammed Haji Nasimi, 3 children: Mohammed (19/8/1985), Ahmed (09/08/1989), Hesham (10/08/1995). **Educ.:** Manama Secondary Technical School, Derby College of Further Education (UK), Nottingham Polytechnic (UK), Derby College of Art & Technology (UK), Gulf College (Bahrain). **Dipl.:** 1976-1977 Diploma in Mechanical & Production Engineering-Management from Nottingham Polytechnic, 1972-1976 - Higher National Diploma (HND) in Mechanical Engineering - Ordinary National Certificate in Mechanical Engineering from Derby College of Art & Technology, 1971-1972 Certificate (General Course) in Mechanical Engineering from Derby College of Further Education, 1970-1971 General Engineering Certificate from Gulf College, 1966-1970 Diploma from Manama Secondary Technical School. **Career:** 1991- Present General Manager Bahrain Aluminium Extrusion Company (BALEXCO) (22000mt Aluminium Extrusion Integrated Company); 1987-1991 General Manager; 1986-1987 Acting General Manager; 1984-1986 Sales Manager; 1982-1984 Regional Sales Manager; 1978-1979 Regional Sales Manager-Bahrain Saudi Aluminium Marketing (Marketing from Alba of Primary and Atomised Aluminium from Alba-Turnover US$500 million: 1978-1979 Engineer Aluminium Bahrain (ALBA) (smelter with a capacity of 5000,000TPA). **Other Information:** A Member of Bahrain Society of Engineers. **Other Training & Seminars:** (Period 1980-1999). **A. Regional** General Management Short Courses: - Changes a Principle Centered Leadership, - Computer Courses, - International Risk and Protection techniques, - Times Management, - Management for Young Executives, - Fundamentals of Finance and Accounting, - Privatisation in the Middle East. **B. International** - Tom Peters Seminar, - KAIZEN Conference, - The Chartered Institutes of Marketing (UK. (one month), - Strategies Marketing Course, - IMD Geneva - Switzerland (one month), - Managing Corporate Resources. **International Conference (Period 1985-1999)** +World Economic Forum, Davos, Switzerland, +Metal Bulletin Alluminium Conferences. 6th Aluminium Extruder Technology, + Aluminium Extruders Council USA, +Metal Bulletin Aluminium Conferences, +6th Aluminium Extruder Technology (Aluminium Extruder Council USA. **Industrial Training:** 1971-1975 + Aluminium Bahrain - Alba 3 months seminar every year apprentice, 1976 +2 months with AITON, UK. Production of piping for high and Low pressure conditions, 1981 + Four months with Kaiser Aluminium, West Virginia, USA, + Reynolds Can Manufacturing North/ Carolina, USA, + Century Extrusion Company Scotland, U.K. **Sports Practised:** Squash, Tennis, Jogging, Swimming. **Hobbies:** Reading, Writting, Fishing, Art Collector. **Clubs and Assiociations:** Member of Bahrain Society of Engineers. **Credit Cards:** Visa Card. **Prof. Addr.:** BALEXCO, P.O.Box 1053, Manama, Bahrain. **Priv. Addr.:** Villa No., 153, Road No. 61, Block 360, Manama, Bahrain.

SOUMARE (Diaramouna), Mauritanian politician. **Born** in 1931 in Ajarsaracolé (Southern Mauritania). **Son** of Adama Soumaré (Farmer). **Married** to Nany Sy, 8 children. **Educ.:** Ecole Nationale des Douanes, France (1966-67). **Career:** Director of Commerce (1969); Minister of Commerce and Transport (1970); Minister of Finance (1971); Minister of Finance & Commerce since August 1975; Minister of Social and Rural Development (1976). **Member:** Parti du Peuple Mauritanian (PPM) (Party suspended in 1978). **Prof. Addr.:** Nouakchott, Mauritania.

SOURANI (Jamil, al), Palestinian politician. **Born** in Jerusalem in 1923. **Career:** Lawyer in Gaza and Chairman of the Palestinian Lawyers' Association (1959); member of the Legal Committee of the Palestine National Union; member of Palestine Liberation Organisation Executive Committee (1966); led PLO delegation to North and South Yemen (1968); Palestinian Visiting representative to North Korea and East Berlin (1969), PLO Delegation to the Arab Foreign Ministers' Conference in Cairo. Visited London (1974) with request to British Government to support the Palestinian cause at the UN General Assembly; presently Secretary General of the Palestinian National Council; and Secretary and Head of the Administrative affairs Dept. of the Executive Committee since 1987. **Addr.:** Tunis, Tunisia.

SOURIAL (Samuel Habib, Rev. Dr.), Egyptian ecclesiastic. **Born** on February 28, 1928 at el-Wasta Beni Suef, Egypt. **Son** of Habib Sourial (Civil Engineer) **and Mrs.** Mounira Yani née Saleh. **Married** on December 15, 1955 in Cairo to Fawzia Fahim Ayad, 2 children: Rozana (July 23, 1957), Rafik (September 25, 1959). **Educ.**: Social Sciences from the American University (1952), in Journalism from Syracuse University, Syracuse, N.Y., U.S.A. (1955), At the San Francisco Theological Seminary, San Anselmo, California, U.S.A. D. Min 1982. **Dipl.**: B.D. from the Cairo Evangelical Theological Seminary Cairo, Egypt, M.A. In Journalism from Syracuse University Syracuse, N.Y. U.S.A. (1955), D.D From Muskingum College, New Concord, Ohio, U.S.A. (on May 9th 1982). **Career:** Director General: of the Coptic Evangelical Organization for Social Services (since 1950); President: The Protestant Churches of Egypt (since 1980). **Honorary Degrees:** Honorary of Doctors in Law St. Xavier University, Antigonish, Nova Scotia, Canada on December 4, 1994; Honorary Doctors Degree (Doctors Degree in Peace making) from Westminister College, Pennsylvania, USA on January 4, 1995. **Hobby:** Reading. **Credit Card:** American Express. **Prof. Addr.**: P.O.Box 1304, Tel.: 5903952, Fax: 5904995, Cairo, Egypt. **Priv. Addr.**: Tel. 2454062, Cairo, Egypt.

SOUSS (Ibrahim), Palestinian former official, novelist and poet. **Born** in 1943 in Jerusalem. **Educ.**: Institut d'Etudes Politiques, Paris; Fondation Nationale des Sciences Politiques, Paris; Ecole Normale de Musique; Royal College of Music, London. **Career:** President of the General Union of Palestine Students, Paris (1971-72); PLO Permanent Observer to UNESCO, Paris (1975-80); Director of PLO Liaison and Information Bureau in France (1978-1988, Ambassador of Palestine in Senegal (1983-85); Delegate General of Palestine in France (1989-1993). Appointed Regional Assistant General Director for Arab Affairs in the International Labour Organisation (1998-). **Hobbies:** painting. reading, tennis, piano, musical composition. **Addr.**: John Kennedy Street, Mimosa Bldg., P.O.Box 11-4088, Tel.: 01-371576, Beirut, Lebanon.

SOUSSA (Ahmad), Iraqi director general of surveys. **Born** in 1920 in al-Hillah. **Educ.**: American University of Beirut, Colorado College, Georges Washington University, John Hopkins University. **Dipl.**: Bachelor of Science, Master of Arts, Doctor of Philosophy. **Career:** Director General Iraqi Surveys. **Publ.**: "The Capitalatory Regime of Turkey, Its History, Origin and Nature", "Iraqi Irrigation Handbook", "Irrigation in Iraq, Its History and Development", "The Hindiyah Barrage, Its History Design and Function". **Member:** of Phi Betta Kappa, Iraqi Academy, Iraqi Engineering Society, Iraqi Pen Club. **Awards:** Wedell Place Prize 1928 by the George Washington University. **Addr.**: Adhamiya. Nagib Pasha 30-3-27, Baghdad, Iraq.

SOUSSA (Antoine, Michel), Jordanian businessman. **Born** in 1928 in Haifa, Palestine. **Married:** four children. **Education:** University of Haifa, preparatory medicine (1947). **Profession:** Expert in the cigarette industry and Expert in industrial printing Gravure and Offset. **History of Positions:** Assistant Manufacturing Superintendent in Eastern Tobacco Co. in Cairo (1948-1952). Vice-President, Managing Director and Founder of Jordan Printing & Packaging Co. Ltd. Member of the Board Of Directors Of Jordan Tobacco and Cigarette Co. Ltd. until 1995. Assistant General Manager Jordan Tobacco & Cigarette Co. Ltd. (1961-1981). Member of the Board Of Directors and Treasurer of Amman Chamber of Industry (1961-1982). Member of the Board Of Directors of Jordan Social Security (1978-1984). Former Vice-President of Jordan Kraft Center. Representative of Jordan employers at the seminar of the International Labour Organisation, Beirut (1961); Employer Representative ILO 68th and 69th Conference in Geneva; Delegate of the Amman Chamber of Industry to the Tripartite Committee for amendment of the Jordan Labour Law (1960), (1967), (1970) and (1980/81). **Social Activities:** Treasurer of YMCA, Amman. President of the Greek Catholic Benevolent Society (1986-1992). **Awards:** Best Sportsman of the year in Jordan (1952). Winner of several sports medals Haifa, Cairo and Amman, member of the Royal Automobile Club/Amman, King Hussein Club/Amman. **Decoration:** "CROSS OF JERUSALEM" Decorated by His Beatitude Maximos The V. **Address: Business:** P.O.Box 6868, Amman 11118 Jordan. **Home:** P.O.Box 2888, Amman, Jordan.

SOWAINE (Ali Sulaiman), Saudi administrator. **Born** in 1950 in Saudi Arabia. **Married**, three children. **Educ.**: B.A. and M.A. in Library Science. **Career:** Head of Technical Processing, IPA Library (1979-83); Director, Central Library of IPA (since 1984); Consultant for Saudi Arabian Government Libraries. **Publ.**: "Library Use Made by Government Employees"; several articles in Arabic in field of Library Science. **Hobbies:** reading, research, traveling, camping. **Addr.**: P.O.Box 205, Riyadh, Saudi Arabia.

SOWAYGH (Ibrahim Abdul Karim, al), Saudi academic. **Born** in 1937 in Medina. **Dipl.**: B.Pharm (1964); Ph.D., (Microbiology) (1971). **Career:** Research scholar (1965-71); Professor in Microbiology, Dean College of Pharmacy, King Saud University (1975-78), Dean College of Allied Medical Sciences, King Saud University (1979-81); Established Health Consultancy House (1984). **Advisor** to the Minister of health and also Incharge of **Medical** Supplies, Medical and Pharmaceutical Licensing, **Laboratories** and Blood Banks Departments (1986-91). **Fellow:** The Royal Society of Medicine, UK and **Member: The** British Society for General Microbiology; the American Society for Microbiology. **Publ.**: Research on infectious diseases and health education in Saudi Arabia, several books of translations. **Hobby:** Reading. **Prof. Addr.**: P.O.Box 50003, Riyadh 11523, Saudi Arabia. (Tel.: 009661-477-6292, Fax: 009661-478-4714).

STINO (Kamal, Ramzi), Egyptian statesman. **Born** in Egypt. **Son** of Ramzi Stino. **Educ.**: Secondary and Higher. **Dipl.**: Doctor in Agriculture. **Career:** Former Professor at the Faculty of Agriculture; Former Minister of Supplies (1959, 1962, 1963); Deputy Prime Minister for Supply and Home Trade (1964); Member of General Secretariat Arab Socialist Union 1966; Director-General Arab Organization for Agricultural Development. **Addr.:** 27, Rifaï Street, Giza, Tel.: 807214, Cairo, Egypt and Arab Organization for Agricultural Development, 4 el-Gamaa Street, P.O.Box 474, Khartoum. Sudan.

SUBAIE (Abdulaziz, Abdallah. Turki, al), Qatari administrator. **Born** in 1946, in Doha, Qatar. **Son** of Turki al-Subaie. **Married**, five children. **Educ.:** B.A., Cairo University. **Career:** Manager of Cultural Affairs, Ministry of Education (1971-72); Manager of Arts Affairs (1975-77); Deputy Director (1975-78), Deputy (since 1979). Member of High Council of Education; former Editor in Chief "Altarbia" magazine, member of Advisory Council of Under Secretaries of the Arab Gulf in Bahrain (1985). **Publ.:** "Contemporary Educational Affairs". **Hobbies:** reading. Swimming. **Addr.:** P.O.Box 3737, Doha, Qatar.

SUBAIT (Abdul Rahman S., al), Saudi academic. **Born** in 1945, in Mecca, Saudi Arabia. **Dipl.:** Ph.D. (Education). **Career:** Teacher, Teachers' Training Institute (1969); Demonstrator, Riyadh University (1970); Staff Member and Vice-Dean, Faculty of Education; Associate Professor of Psychology, Riyadh University; member of Association for Humanistic Psychology (U.S.A.); member of Board, Students' Fund, Riyadh University; member of Preparatory Committee of Arab Faculties of Education Seminar; member of Preparatory Committee for Islamic Psychology Seminar. **Publications:** Elementary School Teachers in Saudi Arabia (a paper); Psychological Preparation of Elementary School Teachers (Ph.D. thesis). **Address:** Faculty of Education, Riyadh University, Riyadh, Saudi Arabia.

SUBHI (Mahmoud, Mohamed, Abdulsalam, Shaikh), Libyan academic, islamic scholar. **Born** in 1924 in Tripoli, Libya. **Career:** elected to Chamber of deputies (1956); Dean of Faculty of Islamic Studies, University of Libya (1969); named member of Benghazi Constitution Committee of Arab Socialist Union (1971); member of Libyan delegation to Islamic Conference, Tripoli, Head of Islamic Call Society, has accompanied President Kaddafi at his first visit to Europe. **Addr.:** al-Fateh University, Faculty of Islamic Studies, P.O.Box 13040, Tripoli, Libya.

SUCCAR (Abdul Latif), Syrian diplomat. **Born** on December 27, 1925, in Damascus, Syria. **Married. Educ.:** American University of Beirut, Lebanon; New York University, USA. **Dipl.:** B.A. in History and Political Science (1943-47); M.A. in Government (1949-53); **Career:** Secretary of the Syrian Permanent Mission to UN, New York (1948); Political Affairs Officer, UN, New York (1951-61); Consultant for Syrian Foreign Ministry (1956-61); Deputy Civilian Officer, UN Operation in the Congo (1961-63), Chief of Foreign Aid Section (1962-63); Acting Director of the Bureau of Economic Coordination, Zaire (1963); Deputy Resident representative, Somalia (1965-68); Resident Representative of the United Nations Development program, Yemen (1968-71); Regional Representative for Saudi Arabia and the Gulf Area (1971). **Hobbies:** Swimming, travel, reading, international relations, international trade, business finance and international economic development. **Prof. Addr.:** United Nations Development Program, al-Washem Street, P.O.Box 558, Tel.: 63153, 22564, Riyadh, Saudi Arabia.

SUCCARI (Owais, R.), Arab-American academic. **Born** in 1939 in Damascus, Syria. **Educ.:** B.A. and Ph.D. in Business. **Career:** Ministry of Planning, Damascus, Syrian (1961-64); Professor of Management, Louvarium University, Kinshasa, Zaire, (1968-71); Associate Professor, Management Department DePaul University, Chicago (since 1972); Executive Director Mid America-Arab Chamber of Commerce, Chicago (since 1974); **member** of the Academy of Management, the Academy of International Business, Chicago Association of Commerce and Industry, Chicago Council or Foreign Relations. European International Business Association. **Publ.:** "International Petroleum Market: Policy Confrontation Between the Common Market and the Arab Countries". **Hobbies:** reading, music, sailing. Swimming. **Addr.:** Mid America-Arab Chamber of Commerce, 135 S. LaSalle Street, Suite 2050, Chicago, I11. 60603, USA.

SUDAIRY (Abdallah Abdulaziz, al), Saudi businessman and Diplomat. **Born** in 1929 in Mecca, Saudi Arabia. **Career:** Prince of Qurayyat Area and Inspector General, Northwestern Borders of Saudi Arabia (1954-1963); Deputy Minister for Municipal and Rural Affairs, Ministry of Interior (1963); Chairman, Board of Directors, al-Ghat Cooperative Society; Vice Chairman, Board of Directors, al-Sudairy Charitable Foundation; Director, Saudi American Bank; Chairman, Board of Directors, al-Jazirah Establishment for Printing, Press and Publication, Arab Farmers Corporation, Tarfa Company and al-Arniyyah Company Ltd.; President, Dousar Enterprise for Development and Investment; presently Ambassador to Kuwait. **Prof. Addr.:** al-Badi'a, P.O.Box. 2347, Tel.: 4357987, Riyadh and Embassy of Saudi Arabia, P.O.Box 20498, 13026 Safat, Kuwait City, Kuwait. **Priv. Addr.:** Tel.: 4352388, Riyadh, Saudi Arabia.

SUDAIRY (Abdelmuhsin Mohamad, al), Saudi official. **Born** in 1937 in Riyadh, Saudi Arabia. **Dipl.:** B.A. (Agronomy), Colorado University, M.A. (Agronomy), Arizona University. **Career:** Various assignments at the Ministry of Agriculture and Water (1962-72); Saudi Ambassador to FAO, Rome (1972); Chairman of the Preparatory Committee for the establishment of IFAD (1975); Chairman of the Executive Board of IFAD; former President of the International Fund for Agricultural Development of the

United Nations (IFAD) (1977-1980); has participated in numerous conferences on development, agriculture and nutrition. **Publications:** Numerous articles in world newspapers and magazines. **Hobbies:** Reading, swimming, walking. **Address:** Jeddah, Saudi Arabia.

SUDAIRY (Abdulrahman Ahmad Mohamad, al), Saudi Official. **Born** in 1918 at al-Ghat. **Educ.:** Received general Education. **Career:** Chairman, Board of Directors, al-Jouf Cooperative Committee, al-Jouf Medical Care Committee and al-Jouf Employees' club; Chairman, Board of Directors, al-Sudairy Charity Society of al-Ghat; member, Board of Directors, the Islamic Welfare Society; has established a public library and a kindergarten in Jouf. **Hobbies:** Farming, taking walks. **Prof. Addr.:** Sakaka, Tel.: 6421801, Jouf. **Priv. Addr.:** Tel.: 6421940, Jouf, Sudariyya, Saudi Arabia.

SUDAIRY (Faisal Abdulrahman, al), Saudi businessman. **Born** in 1945 in al-Jouf, Saudi Arabia. **Son** of Abdulrahman al-Sudairy. **Married**, six children. **Educ.:** B.Sc. and M.Sc. in Economics. **Career:** Under Secretary, Ministry of the Interior; Director of Saudi Affairs, British Aircraft Ltd. Riyadh, Saudi Arabia; Founder and Director, al-Jouf Association; Chairman, Oreib Group of Companies, member of Board of Directors of Arab Agricultural Co. **Publ.:** "The Kingdom of Saudi Arabia and its Economic Progress" (1977). **Hobbies:** reading. riding, squash. **Addr.:** P.O.Box 3790, Riyadh, Saudi Arabia.

SUDAIRY (Prince Sultan Abdul Rahman, al), Saudi official. **Born** in 1947 at Sakaka. **Dipl.:** M.A. **Career:** Chief of the Bureau of al-Jouf Governorate (1971); Deputy Chairman, Community Cooperative of al-Jouf; Deputy Chairman, Community Health and Care of al-Jouf; Chairman of Committee of City Planning; Deputy Governor of al-Jouf since 1975 presently Governor. **Hobby:** Falconry. **Prof. Addr.:** Governorate of al-Jouf, Sakaka, Tel.: 6241805, al-Jouf. **Priv. Addr.:** Tel.: 6241914, Sakaka, al-Jouf, Saudi Arabia.

SUDAIRY (Saad el-Nasser, al), Saudi official. **Born** in 1935 at el-Ghat. **Dipl.:** B.A. (Law). **Career:** Governor of el-Ghat 1962-67; Chairman of Uhud Sporting Club, Deputy President of Charity Fund, Medina; member of the Supreme Committee of Pilgrimage; Deputy Governor of Medina. **Hobby:** Sport, swimming, reading especially law books. **Address:** Governorate of Medina, Saudi Arabia.

SUDAIRY (Salman Ibn Turkey Ibn Nasser, al), Saudi civil servant. **Born** on 20 May 1954 in Riyadh, Saudi Arabia. **Dipl.:** B.A. and M.A. (Architecture), M.A. (Urban Planning), Ph.D. Project Management. **Career:** Director of Housing, Ministry of Interior (1979-82); General Director, Directorate of Projects, Ministry of Interior, Riyadh (1982-1984); Professor, College of Architecture & Planning, King Saud University, Riyadh (from 1986). **Publ.:** Landscape Architecture in Saudi Arabia; Community Development in Saudi Arabia; Large Scale Construction Project Management, Design, and executive. **Addr.:** P.O.Box: 9546, Riyadh, Saudi Arabia.

SUDAIRY (Sultan Ibn Abdulaziz Ibn Ahmad, al), Saudi official. **Born** in 1935 at al-Grayyat. **Dipl.:** B.Sc. (Economics and Business Administration). **Career:** Inspector of Western Borders and Emir (Governor) of al-Grayyat Province; Chairman, Board of Directors, al-Garyyat Cooperative Society; Chairman, Administrative Council for al-Grayyat Province; Chairman, al-Grayyat Welfare Society; participates in various social activities. **Address:** al-Grayyat Province. Tel.: 1703, Saudi Arabia.

SUDAIRY (Turki ben Khalid, al), Saudi former minister of state. **Born** in 1936 in Abha, Saudi Arabia. **Dipl.:** B.A. (Political Science). **Career:** Head of International Commercial Relations, Ministry of Commerce (1962); Assistant Director of Statistics, Ministry of Finance (1964); General Secretary, Central Organization Management (1966); Vice-President, Public Personnel Bureau (1971); Chairman, Board of Directors, Riyadh Private Schools; President of Civil Service Bureau; former Minister of State. **Sports:** Swimming, tennis. **Address:** Riyadh, Saudi Arabia.

SUDAIS (Abdallah Abdulaziz, al), Saudi religious educator. **Born** in 1951 at Qassim, Saudi Arabia. **Dipl.:** B.A. (Islamic Law), King Saud University. **Career:** Teacher (1972-74); Director of Mecca Religious Institute (Ilmi), attended Conference of the Directors of Religious Institutes, Riyadh (1976). **Publications:** Modern Quranic Studies; several articles in local publications. **Prof. Addr.:** al-Ilmi Institute, Tel. 5422021, Mecca. **Priv. Addr.:** Tel. 5426362, Mecca, Saudi Arabia.

SUDAIS (Mohamad Sulaiman, al), Saudi academic. **Born** in 1943 at al-Bukairiyah, Qassim, Saudi Arabia. **Dipl.:** Ph.D. **Career:** Teacher, intermediate schools (1967-68); Graduate assistant, King Abdul-Aziz University, Mecca (1968-69); Assistant Professor, KAU (1976-79); Deputy Head of Arabic Language Dept., Faculty of Education, King Saud University (1979-81); Assistant Professor and Head of Arabic Language Dept., King Saud University; Associate Professor (1985); Professor (1995); Participated in revising the Arabic edition of Saudi Arabian Third and Fourth Development Plan. Member of the editorial board of ad-Darah, a Saud quarterly magazine. **Publications:** 1.A **Selection of Current Najdi Arabic Proverbs**, (A Critical and Comparative Study), Arabic-English, Libraire de Liban Publishers, Beirut, 1993. 2. Translated the first section of Alois Musil's the **Manners and Customs of the Rwala Bedouins**, the translation into Arabic was publiched by KSU in Riyadh, 1994. 3. **Hada'iq al-'Adab** by Abu Muhammad Ubeid Allah b. **Muhammad** al-'Abhari, edit. by M.S. al-Sudais. Published by the editor

1995, and many articles and papers in Local and Arab Periodical. **Priv. Addr.:** Riyadh, Dept. of Arabic, College of Arts, KSU, P.O.Box 2456, Riyadh 11451, Tel.: 4569065.

SUGAIR (Hamad Abdallah, al), Saudi M.D. and official. **Born** in 1932. **Dipl.:** B.Chem., M.D. (Chest Diseases and T.b.). **Career:** General Practitioner, then Specialist, Riyadh Central Hospital; Director of Chest Diseases Department, Ministry of Health; Deputy Minister of Health for Health Affairs; President of Saudi Red Crescent Society; now member of AlShora Council (Counsultative Council); **Act.:** participated in several WHO conferences; attended Arab Ministers of Health conferences, participated in several Red Crescent Red Cross Federation conferences. **Hobbies:** Swimming, travel, reading. **Prof. Addr.:** P.O.Box 3024, Red Crescent Society, Tel.: 4420164, Riyadh, 11471. **Priv. Addr.:** Tel.: 4766005, Fax: 4778685, Riyadh, Saudi Arabia.

SUHAIL (Faisal Mohamad, al), Saudi official. **Born** in 1935 in Riyadh, Saudi Arabia. **Dipl.:** B.Sc. (Economics); M.A. (Business Administration). **Career:** Director-General of Ports Authority; Assistant Deputy Minister of Communications for Roads and Ports; Director-General of Railways Authority and Damman Port; member of Board, al-Jazirah Press and Publication Establishment; member of al-Hilal Sports Club; member of Saudi Olympic Union; member of Board, Railways Authority, Ports Authority, Dammam Municipal Council, AMCO International, Arab Academy for Sea Transpor; presently President of Saudi Railways Authority. **Publication:** Administration, Planning and Organization. **Honours:** Orders of Merit from South Korea and the Republic of China (Taiwan). **Address:** Saudi Arabian Railways Authority, P.O.Box 36, Dammam, Saudi Arabia.

SUHEIMAT (Ali, Mohamad), Jordanian politician. **Born** in 1936 in Karak, Jordan. **Married**, four children. **Educ.:** B.Sc. in Civil Engineering. **Career:** Engineer, Government, of Jordan (1960-64); Engineer with private Contractors (1964-68); member of Jordan Development Board (1968-71); Under Secretery, Ministry of Transport (1971-73, 76-79); Minister of State for Prime Ministerial Affairs (1979); Deputy Prime Minister and Minister of Transport (1991-1992). **Medals:** Order of the Jordanian Star, Award from Austria. **Addr.:** P.O.Box 7403, Amman, Jordan.

SUIDAN (Jad), Lebanese bank executive. **Born** in 1947 in Beirut, Lebanon. **Son** of Anis Suidan. **Married** in 1979. **Educ.:** American University of Beirut. **Dipl.:** B.B.A. **Career:** Whinney Murray & Co., London & Middle East (1969-77); Financial Controller, The Arab Investment Co., Riyadh (1977-80); Deputy Director General, The Arab Investment Co. S.A., Saudi Arabia (1980-). **Member:** Arab Banker' Association, London; Chartered Accountants in England and Wales. **Hobbies:** Swimming, tennis and travelling. **Addr.:** P.O.Box 4009, Tel.: 482-3444, Telex: 201011, 201236 A/B ARBVST SJ, TAIC SJ, Riyadh, Saudi Arabia.

SUKI (Wadi, Najib), Arab American physician, academic. **Born** in 1934 in Khartoum, Sudan. **Married. Educ.:** B.Sc. and MD. **Career:** Fellow in Experimental Medicine, Southwestern Medical School, University of Texas (1959-61); Associate Professor of Medicine, Baylor College of Medicine then Professor (Since 1971): Chief of Renal Section, Methodist Hospital, Consultant in Nephrology, Capilford Hall, USAF Medical Center, Fellow of the American College of Physicians, member of the International Society of Nephrology, American Society of Nephrology, American Physiological Society etc. President of Southern Society for Clinical Investigation (1978-79); Associate of the European Dialysis and Transplantation Association, member of: the Alpha Omega Alpha, the editorial Board of "the Kidney", "Kidney International", "Journal of Clinical Investigation", "Nephron". Associate Editor of "American Journal of Nephrology". Chairman of the Medical Adivsory Council, Kidney Foundation, Houston and Greater Gulf Coast (1969-71); Chairman, National Medical Advisory Council, National Kidney Foundation; member of the Executive Committee, Council or Kidney in Cardiovascular Disease, American Heart Association (1971-75); member of the Scientific Advisory Board (1977-78); President of the Scientific Advisory Board, National Kidney Foundation (1979-80); President, American Society of Nephrology (1997-98). **Publ.:** Contributor to several Professional Journals. **Prof. Addr.:** 6550 Fannin St., Houston, TX 77030 USA.

SUKKAR (Yousef, Y.), Jordanian Businessman. **Born** in 1944 in Sa'lt, Jordan. **Son** of Yacoub Sukkar and Mrs. Lulu Said Abujaber. **Married** in 1973 in Amman, Jordan to Nuha Najib Bakhit, 2 children: Son Yacoub and Daughter Tamara. **Education:** American University of Beirut, Lebanon; B.A Economics, Institute of Social Studies; The Hague, Netherlands, M.A. **Career:** Head of External Economy and Statistics, Research Division, Central Bank of Jordan; General Manager of Philips - Jordan; Managing Director of Transmed Shareholding; Chairman and Managing Director of Mideast International Trading Shareholding Co., Amman-Jordan; Managing Director of Safaripak Shareholding, Jeddah-Saudi Arabia; Managing Director of Alahlia Commercial Centers Public Shareholding, Amman-Jordan. **Member of:** International Business Association; AUB Alumni Club; Royal Automobile Club; Rotary Philadelphia. **Credit Cards:** Master Card Gold, Amex Gold. **Prof. Addr.:** P.O.Box 2431, Amman 11181, Jordan, Tel.: 684606/684435. Priv. Addr.: Jabal Amman, 154 Zahran Street, Amman, Jordan.

SUKKARY (Ali Hassan), Saudi academic. **Born** in 1933 in Mecca. **Educ.:** Faculty of Education, Mecca (1959). **Career:** Successively: teacher; Assistant Principal of Intermediate School; Principal of Commercial School;

Director of Manpower and Imported Labour Department, Western Region; now Principal of al-Falah Intermediate and Secondary School, Jeddah. **Member:** Honorary member of National Sporting Club. **Publ.:** Articles on manpower training. **Prof. Addr.:** al-Falah School, Bab Maccah, Tel. 29950, Jeddah. **Priv. Addr.:** Tel. 33398, Jeddah, Saudi Arabia.

SULAIMAN (Fahad Abdul Rahman, Al-), saudi businessman, **Born** in Jeddah, Saudi Arabia. **Dipl.:** B.Sc. Political Science and Business Administration, Western Michigan University, USA; Post-Graduate work on International Law and Economics, Oxford University. **Career:** Board Member, Director, General Partner and co-Owner, Ana' am al-jazira Trading Co. Ltd., Riyadh; Partner and co-Owner in Semiramis Hotel Company. Cairo President and Owner, Al-Baha Trading Corporation, Jeddah. **Hobbies:** Photography and Diving. **Address:** P.O.Box 1271, Jeddah 21431, Tel 6606452, Fax: 6604615, Saudi Arabia.

SULAYEM (Sultan, Ahmed, Bin), UAE Chairman of Jebel Ali Free Zone Authority, Managing Director - Dubai Ports. **Born** in 1955 in Dubai. **Son** of Ahmed Bin Sulayem, Former Minister. **Married,** 7 children. **Educ.:** Educated in Dubai and the USA, he received a Bachelors degree in Economics from Temple University, Philadephia, in 1981. **Career:** Returning home to manage the family business in residential and commercial real estate, he was appointed Assistant Director for Jebel Ali Port Affairs by H.H. Sheikh Mohammad Bin Rashid Al Maktoum. In addition, Sultan Bin Sulayem has occupied the position of Chairman of Jebel Ali Free Zone since it was established in 1985. Dubai Ports Authority was created by the merger of Port Rashid and Jebel Ali Port in May 1991 and Sultan Bin Sulayem was appointed Chairman and Managing Director, in addition to his duties as Chairman of the Free Zone. The merger of the two organisations streamlined operations and administration and the combined marketing drive resulted in a considerable increase in shipping. By the end of 1998, DPA had achieved a record throughput of 2.8 million TEU's. At the same time, the number of international companies which have set up operations in the free Zone is now around 1500 companies from over 88 countries. Mr. Bin Sulayem is a member of several international organisations, among which is the Young President's Organisation. In recognition of his unstinting efforts and achievements, Mr. Bin Sulayem was named Chief Executive of the Year 1991 at the annual Gulf Business Awards. He also won the Al Majalla Business Personality of the Year 1992. On 12 March 1993 he was elected by the World Economic Forum as one of the Global Leaders for Tomorrow in their January/ February 1993 issue of the magazine "World Link". He is a regular participant at the international "Think Tank", the World Economic Forum held annually in Davos, Switzerland. **Awards:** CEO of the Year 1991 - Gulf Business Award, Business Personality of the Year 1992 - Al Majalla, 1993 he was elected by the World Economic forum on the Global Leaders for Tomorrow. **Sports Practised:** Sea Sport (Diving). **Credit Cards:** Amex, Visa. **Prof. Addr.:** P.O.Box 17000, Dubai Ports Authority, Tel.: +971-4-815000, Dubai, UAE. **Priv. Addr.:** P.O.Box 1714, Dubai, UAE.

SULAYTY (Hamad, Ali, Al), Ph.D., Bahraini Civil Servant. **Born** on January 1, 1944. **Married,** 5 children. **Present Professional Status:** 1982 - date Undersecretary of The Ministry of Education, and Acting; 1981 - date Actg. Sec. General, Bahrain Center for Research and Studies. **Academic Degrees:** 1966 Bachelor in Education and Psychology/Baghdad University, Iraq; 1970 Master in Management and Educational Planning/American University of Beirut/Lebanon; 1980 Ph.D./Indiana University/ U.S.A. **Career Back Ground:** 1975-1982 Asst. Undersecretary for Planning and Curricula/Ministry of Education; 1972-1975 Director for Planning Educational Information/ Ministry of Education; 1971-1972 Chief Specialist for Planning Educational Information Ministry of Education; 1970-1971 Specialist for Planning Educational Information Ministry of Education; 1967-1969 Lecturer for Education and Psychology/Bahrain; 1958-1960 Teacher in Elementary Education/Bahrain; 1960-1962 Journalist in a Weekly Magazine/Bahrain; Assisted the Bahrain Center for Research and Studies in a Supervisory. **Memberships of Organizations:** Member in Board of Planning and Coordination/State of Bahrain (1971-1975); Member in Board of Arab League Executive for Education and Culture and Science (1972-1978); Member in Board Trustees of Bahrain Center for Research and Studies (1981-); Member in Executive Council for Arab Bureau; Member in Board of Education in Gulf University; Member in Board Trustees of Bahrain Bayan School (1986-); Advisor for Educational Magazine Issue Kuwait University; Head of National Committee for Evaluation & Qualification/ State of Bahrain (1985-); Supreme Council for Technical Training (Bahrain, 1995-). **Interests & Hobbies:** Fishing and Tennis. **Languages Known:** Arabic and English. **Address:** Ministry of Education, P.O.Box 43, Manama, State of Bahrain.

SULEIMAN (Abdallah Ghati, al), Saudi former civil servant. **Born** in 1921 at Hail, Saudi Arabia. **Educ.:** Received his secondary education at al-Ma'ahad al-Elmi. **Career:** Director, Private Affairs, Office of the Viceroy of Hejaz; Director, Confidential Affairs Office, Ministry of Interior; Director General, Minister's office, Ministry of Interior; Director General, al-Mujahedeen General Directorate; now retired. **Member:** al-Jabaleen Literary Club; various other literary activities. **Publication:** A Book of Poems, in process of publication. **Hobby:** literature. **Address:** Tel. 4770468, Riyadh, Saudi Arabia.

SULEIMAN (Abdul Aziz Abdallah, al, Sheikh), Saudi leading businessman. **Born** in 1934 in Mecca. **Educ.:** Secondary school in Egypt, Lafayette University, U.S.A., and technical financial training at Chase Manhattan Bank, New York. **Career:** Deputy Ministry of Petroleum and Monetary Affairs (1951-53); Vice-Chairman, Saudi Arabian Monetary Agency (SAMA) (1953-55); Chairman of Board of Directors; Saudi Hotel Co., Arabian Cement Co. Ltd. (Jeddah), Rolaco Trading and Contracting, Siraj Zahran Co., Suleimaniyah Real Estate, Saudi Light Industry (SLIC), Saudi Capital Corporation (Saudicorp), Zahran Contracting Co., Saudi Arabian Bandag Co., (Jeddah), Cement Product Industry Co. and al-Jezira Bank; founder of Saudi Maritime Navigation Co.; member of Board of SOFIMO (Société Financière pour le Moyen-Orient, Beirut), FRAB-Bank (Paris), FRAB-Holding (Luxembourg), Boonton Holding Co. (New Jersey, U.S.A.), Saudi National Electric Co. (Jeddah), Saudi Refinery Co. (Jeddah); founder and Chairman of Board of al-Hamadany Society for Chivalry and Preservation of Arab Legacy. **Awards:** Lebanese Order of Merit. **Sports:** Horse-riding. **Hobbies:** Reading, music. **Prof. Addr.:** Bank al-Jezira, P.O.Box 6277, Jeddah 21442, Saudi Arabia.

SULEIMAN (Abdul Ghani Hamza), Saudi academic. **Born** in 1940 in Mecca, Saudi Arabia. **Dipl.:** Ph.D. **Career:** Deputy Dean of College of Pharmacy (1967-69); Dean of College of Pharmacy (1969-75); Professor and Faculty Member, Chemistry Department, Faculty of Science, King Abdulaziz University, member, the National Scientific Society, the National Chemical Society; attended some Gulf Ministers of Agriculture Conferences; participated in FAO conferences and chemical conferences; Consultant to the Ministry of Agriculture. **Publications:** Five academic books, 16 scientific papers and Ph.D. thesis. **Hobbies:** reading, music, football. **Prof. Addr:** Chemistry Department, Faculty of Science, King Abdulaziz University, Tel.: 6879589 Ext. 1422, Jeddah. **Priv. Addr.:** Tel. 6712280, Jeddah, Saudi Arabia.

SULEIMAN (Abdul Mohsen Abdul Rahman, al), Saudi businessman. **Born** in 1946 in Jeddah, Saudi Arabia. **Dipl.:** B.Sc. (Electrical and Industrial Engineering) (1971); M.A. (Honours) Audio-Visual Media. **Career:** Owner and President, Best Trading Corporation; Jeddah; Media Specialist, Western Michigan University, U.S.A.; member of Industrial Management Society. **Publication:** An audio-visual presentation on Saudi Arabia at Western Michigan University Library in Kalamazoo, Michigan. **Hobbies:** Photography, deep-sea fishing. **Prof. Addr.:** P.O.Box 1271, Tel. 6533384, 6530461, Jeddah. **Priv. Addr.:** Tel. 6711566, Jeddah, Saudi Arabia.

SULEIMAN (Ahmad al-Abdallah, al), Saudi businessman. **Born** in 1938, in Mecca. **Dipl.:** B.Com. (International Commerce). **Career:** Director of the Office of Shaykh Abdallah al-Sulaiman (1960-68); Deputy-Head of Siraj Zahran and Partners (1961-63); **member** of firm of Abdallah al Sulaiman; member of the Boards of al-Bilad firm, the Arab Cement Co. Ltd., and Tihama; owns al-Sawari Merchants and Agents firm and Ahmad Abdallah al Sulaiman General Trading Co.; has shares in the Saudi Arabian Bandag. Co. and the Arab Cement Co. Ltd; General Manager of Siraj Hamid Zahran and Partners Co. **Prof. Addr.:** Abdallah Suleiman & Sons, P.O.Box 2337, Jeddah, Saudi Arabia.

SULEIMAN (Badr el-Din, Mohamad Ahmad), Sudanese Politician. **Born** on March 13, 1933 in the White Nile Province, Sudan. **Son** of Mohamad Ahmad Suleiman. **Married** in 1967 to Dr. Saud al-Tojani al-Minakhy, 4 children: Amru (1968), Rawiya (1969), Reem (1972), Sara (1974). **Educ.:** University of Khartoum, Sudan. **Dipl.:** Degree in Law. **Career:** Administrative Officer, local government (1960); Lawyer (1960-68); Director, private industrial sector (1968-72); member, Political Bureau of the Sudanese Socialist Union (SSU) and of the First National Assembly (July 1972); Member of the second National Assembly (until January 1975); Assistant Secretary-General of the SSU (February 1976); Minister of Industry (Jan. 1975-77); Chairman, al-Ayyam Printing and Publishing Company (February 1974); Minister of Finance and Economy (August 17, 1979-1982). Presently, Minister of Education. **Member:** Political Bureau, Sudanese Socialist Union. **Awards:** Order of the Republic, 1st Class; Order of Kuwait, 1st Class. **Sports:** Football, tennis. **President,** Omdurman Graduates Club. **Addr.:** Ministry of Education, P.O.Box 2184 Khartoum, Sudan.

SULEIMAN (Fahad al-Abdallah, al), Saudi businessman. **Born** in 1939 in Mecca, Saudi Arabia. **Dipl.:** B.A. (Economics). **Career:** Delegated member, Abdulaziz al-Abdullah al-Suleiman Company and Semiramis Hotel Company; Agent, Jeddah Freight Companies and several agricultural companies; agent for sale and distribution of Airplanes; agent for international consultants and experts on fisheries and agriculture, general contracting, decor and electric equipments; owner, Kandar press and Shamsan Pharmacy; owner, Fahad al-Abdallah al Suleiman Est. for Trade and Contracting; Manager, Siraj Hamid Zahran Co. and General Manager, Kandarah Palace Hotel, Jeddah Palace Hotel and affiliated hotels. **Hobby:** fishing. **Prof. Addr.:** P.O.Box 2337, Jeddah, Saudi Arabia.

SULEIMAN (Ghassan Abdul Rahman, al), Saudi businessman. **Born** in 1954 in Jeddah. Saudi Arabia. **Dipl.:** B.Sc. (Business Administration), Notre Dame University, U.S.A. **Career:** Co-owner and Director, Best Trading Corporation; Director General and owner, Avis Rent-A-Car, Saudi Arabia. Director, owner: Arabian Medical Supply Co.; Director of Arabian Consumer Co./master-card, Saudi Arabia. **Hobbies:** Reading, sports. **Addr.:** P.O.Box 1271, Tel.: 6533384, Jeddah. Saudi Arabia.

SULEIMAN (Jameel Ahmad Mohamad Abdu), Saudi diplomat. **Born** in 1930 in Mecca. **Dipl.:** Teachers' Trainning College; M.A. (Arabic Language and Literature, Education and Psychology). **Career:** former Secondary School teacher; Inspector, Assistant Inspector-General; Director, Primary Education and Anti-Illiteracy Department ; Director, Teachers' Training Institutes; Director-General, Educational Planning; Director, Statistics and Research Unit; member of Editorial Board, Educational Publications Magazine (Majallatu al-Nashr al-Tarbbawiyyah), Committee on the Equivalence of Scientific Qualifications; attended First Conference on Teachers' Training, King Abdulaziz University; Conference on the Function of the University in Society; Conference on the Function of the University. Riyadh University; Cultural Attaché, Royal Saudi Arabian Embassy in Mauritania. **Publ.:** Author of School books for boys and girls, on Arabic language for primary, preparatory and secondaary schools; books on Islamic education; research papers on teacher training. **Hobbies:** Reading. Gardening. **Prof. Addr.:** Permanent: Ministry of Education, Riyadh, Saudi Arabia.

SULEIMAN (Magdi Ahmad), Egyptian governor of south Sinai governorate. **Born** on 1st April 1930 at Demsas, Dakahliyeh Governorate, Egypt. **Married** one daughter and two sons. **Educ.:** Military Academy. **Career:** worked his way up in the Armed Forces to Commander of the Xth Division, Air Defence which participated in the October 1973 war with Israel; appointed Chief of Staff, Air Defence; appointed Governor of South Sinai Governorate in March 1983. **Address:** South Sinai Governorate, Egypt.

SULEIMAN (Michael, Wadie), Arab-American university professor. **Born** in Tiberias, Palestine on February 26, 1934. **Son** of Wadie M. Suleiman (deceased) **and** Mrs., née Jameeleh K. Ailabouni (deceased). **Married** on August 31, 1963 to Penelope Ann Powers in Marion, Ohio (USA), 2 children: Suad Michelle (1971) and Gibran Michael (1973). **Educ.:** Bradley University, Peoria, Illinois; University of Wisconsin, Madison, Wisconsin. **Dipl.:** B.A., Bradley University (1960); M.S., University of Wisconsin (1962); Ph.D., University of Wisconsin (1965). **Career:** Assistant Professor, Political Science,Kansas State University (1965-68); Associate Professor, Political Science, Kansas State University (1968-72); Professor, Political Science, Kansas State University (1972-90); University Distinguished Professor (1990- present); Head, Department of Political Science, Kansas State University (1975-82). **Act.:** Mid-America State Universities Association (MASUA) Honor Lecturer; National Endowment for the Humanities (NEH) Grant; Smithsonian Institution Grant; American Institute of Maghribi (North Africa) Studies (AIMS); Council for International Exchange of Scholars Fellowship (1984); Faculty Research Abroad (Fulbright-Hays) Fellowship (1980, 1983-84, 1993); American Philosophical Society Traveling Fellowship (1974); American Research Center in Egypt Fellowship (1972-73); Ford Faculty Research Fellowship (1969-70); Research Associate, University of Denver-Social Science Foundation (summer 1978); University of Wisconsin Vilas Traveling Fellowship (1963-64). **Publ.:** of more than 50 articles and books, on political science and politics. **Awards:** Distinguished Graduate Faculty Member Award, Kansas State University; University Distinguished Professor, Kansas State University. Contemporary Authors; International Who's Who of the Arab World; International Scholars Directory; Who's Who in the Midwest; American Men and Women of Science. Dictionary of International Biography; International Who's Who of Intellectuals; International Authors and Writers Who's Who; **Member:** Middle East Studies Association, Chairman, Committee on Pre-Collegiate Education (1975-79); Member, Board of Directors (1980-82); American Political Science Association; Association of Arab-American University Graduates (AAUG) Board of Directors (1970-72); Member of Advisory Board (1976), President (1977), Executive Committee (1978); Midwest Political Science Association; The Middle East Institute. Board of Directors American Institute of Maghribi Studies; Editorial Board: **Internatinal Journal of Middle East Studies, Arab Studies Quarterly, Journal of Arab Affairs;** Editor of Westview Press Series on "State, Culture and Society in Arab North Africa" (1989-); Member, Governance Board, American Ethnic Studies Program, Kansas State University (1987-89); Editorial Board, **Arab Journal of International Studies** (Arabic, Wash., D.C. (1987-88); Editorial Board, **Maghreb Review** London (1988-); and Editorial Advisory Board, **The News Circle** (1989); Press and television interviews and commentaries for National Public Radio (NPR), Public Broadcasting Service (PBS), C-Sapn, CNN, and **Washington Post**. **Sport:** Table tennis. **Hobbies:** Chess and theatre. **Credit Cards:** American Express, Visa. **Prof. Addr.:** Department of Political Science, Kansas State University, Tel.: (785) 532-6842, Manhattan, KS 66506. **Priv. Addr.:** 427 Wickham Road, Tel.: (785) 539-2127, Manhattan, KS 66502, USA.

SULEIMAN (Mohamad Sedqi), Egyptian politician. **Born** in 1919 in Egypt. **Married**, 4 children. **Educ.:** Cairo University (Polytechnic Faculty), Military Academy. **Dipl.:** of Engineering for Polytechnic Faculty (Cairo). **Career:** Engineer in the Egyptian Army with the rank of Colonel, in Charge of the Public Sector Organization after the Nationalization of the Suez Canal and the subsequent international uproar over the waterway; Minister of the Aswan High Dam in the Cabinet of Mr. Zakaria Muhieddine until September 1966; Prime Minister (September 9, 1966-June 1967); Vice Prime Minister and Minister of Industry Hydraulic Affairs, Electricity and High Dam in June 1967; Member, Central Committee of the Arab Socialist Union (1968). **President** of the Egyptian-Soviet Friendship Association. **Addr.:** Cairo, Egypt.

SULEIMAN (Mustafa, Dawud), Egyptian financial official. **Born** on March 17, 1929 in Cairo. **Married**, 5 children. **Dipl.:** B.Sc. in Commerce and Finance (1955);

Diploma in Cost Accountancy (1960). **Career:** Finance Manager (1974); General Manager of Egyptian Real Property Company for Land Reclamation; Contracting and Commercial business; part time chartered Accountant. **Hobbies:** interst in international trade reated to building and construction equipment. **Member:** Commerce Club; the Egyptian Accountants Association. **Addr.:** 2, Dr. Abdul Hamid Said Street, Cairo, Egypt.

SULEIMANI (Saleh H, al), Ph.D.; Assistant professor and vice dean, dental department, faculty of medicine, king Saud university; saudi physician. **Born** in 1940 in Mecca, Saudi Arabia. **Dipl.:** Diploma (Medicine and Surgery), (1970); Ph.D. (General Surgery) (1977) and Doctorate of Medicine, Bonn (1977). **Career:** Assistant Professor and Vice Dean, Dental Department, Faculty of Medicine, King Saud University. **Publications:** Appendicitis: Diagnosis, Operation and Fatality, (Ph.D. thesis), Hydatid Cyst, Treatment of Piles. **Hobbies:** Reading, music. **Prof. Addr.:** Faculty of Medicine, King Saud University, Riyadh. **Priv. Addr.:** Tel. 4775784, Riyadh, Saudi Arabia.

SULTAN (Ahmed Ismail), Egyptian engineer. **Born** on April 14, 1923 in Port Said, Egypt. **Married. Educ.:** Faculty of Engineering, Cairo University, Egypt (1945); management of electricity generating Station, UK and France; National Defence College (1967). **Career:** Shift Engineer, Maintenance and Project Engineer, various power stations (1945-64); Director and member of the Executive Board, Electrical Projects Corporation (1964-68); Governor of Minufiya (1968-71); Minister of Power (1971-76); Deputy Prime Minister for Production and Minister of Power and Energy (1976-78); Consultant Engineer since October 1981 to date. **Decor.:** Order of the Republic 1st Class. **Addr.:** 2 Okasha Street, Dokki, Cairo, Egypt.

SULTAN (Ahmed Mustafa Hussein), Egyptian businessman. **Born** in 1943 in Dumyat, Egypt. **Married:** two sons. **Educ.:** Ain Shams University, Cairo, Egypt. **Dipl.:** B.Sc. in Commerce; M.Sc. in Business Management. **Career:** Member, Arab British Chamber of Commerce; Co Founder of the Egyptian British Chamber of Commerce; Chairman and Managing Director, Flarmagate Ltd. for Import Export, London. **Hobby:** reading. **Addr.:** Flarmagate, Kinsington High Street, 9 Cumberland House, London, UK.

SULTAN (Amin Kassim Mohamed), Yemeni businessman. **Born** on March 4, 1928. **Married,** six children, three sons and three daughters. **Educ.:** Diploma in Commerce, London Chamber of Commerce (1949). **Career:** Commerce (1948), established al-Kawthar Factory, textile and tyre Factories; co-Founder of the First National Bank; Merchant and Commercial Adviser; President of the Yemen chamber of Commerce for 6 Years; Member of the Board of Directors of the Central Bank; Owner of Amin Kassim Sultan and partners; representative of several Companies. **Hobbies:** reading, hockey, football, swimming. **Addr.:** P.O.Box 4888, Taiz, Republic of Yemen.

SULTAN (Fawzi), Kuwaiti executive. **Born** in 1944 in Kuwait. **Son** of Hamad Sultan. **Married** in 1974, 1 son, 1 daughter. **Educ.:** American University of Beirut, Bachelor of Arts (1966); Yale University, USA. **Dipl.:** M.A. (1970). **Career:** Kuwait Fund for Arab Economic Development (1966-67); Managing Director, Bank of Kuwait and the Middle East (1971-81); Director, United Bank of Kuwait and Ifabanque S.A., Paris. Chairman, International Financial Advisers KSC, Safat, Kuwait (1981-). **Member:** Kuwait Economist Society. **Hobbies:** Jogging, swimming and fishing. **Addr.:** P.O.Box 4694, Tel. 448170-1-2, Telex: 22385 A/B IFA KT, Safat, Kuwait.

SULTAN (Fuad, Abdellatif), Egyptian former minister of tourism and civil aviation. **Born** on January 26, 1931 in Egypt. **Married,** 2 children: Ahmed, (Civil Engineer, Ein Shams University); Yasmine, (B.C.- Ein Shams University). **Educ.:** B.C. Cairo University, International Monetary Fund Institute (Financial Analysis and Policy) (1951-68). **Dipl.:** Post Graduate Studies in Economics (1954 and 1959), Cairo University. **Career:** Chairman and CEO of ALAhly for Development & Investment (ADI), (1995); Minister of Tourism and Civil Aviation (Sept. 1985-1993); Chairman of Misr Iran Development Bank (1980-85); Vice Chairman of Misr Iran Development Bank (1975-80); Acting General Manager of the Arab International Bank, Cairo (1974-75); Advisor, the International Monetary Fund, assigned to Yemen Arab Republic to set up a Central Bank in Sanaa (1971-74); The Central Exchange Control Administration at the National and Central Banks of Egypt (1951-71). **Member** of the National Council for Production and Economic Affairs and the Arab Bankers Association, London; Ex-Chairman of the Egyptian Section at the Egypt - U.S. Business Council and of the Investment Committee; Egyptian Banks Association and Board Member of: Egyptian Businessman Association; Investors Union in Egypt; German-Arab Chamber of Commerce. **Sports:** Rowing, Swimming and Tennis. **Hobby:** Reading. **Clubs:** Cairo Rotary, Heliopolis Sporting Club, Automobile Club. **Bus. Addr.:** ADI, 1191 Cornish El Nil, World Trade Center, 10th Floor, Cairo, Tel.: 00202 5780790/2, Fax: 00202 5780793, Cairo, Egypt.

SULTAN (Ghazi Hashim), Saudi official. **Born** in 1936 in Jeddah, Saudi Arabia. **Dipl.:** B.Sc. (Geology and Chemistry), Cairo University; M.Sc. (Geology), University of Texas, U.S.A. **Career:** Assistant Director of Aerial Photography (1958) Accountant; Assistant Mineralogist; Economic Geologist; Director General, Mineral Resources (1966); Assitant Deputy Minister for Mineral Resources (1974); Deputy Minister for Mineral Resources since 1975. **Member:** Board of Directors, Jeddah Refinery, Petromin, University of Petroleum and Minerals. **Hobbies: Reading,**

sports, music. **Prof. Addr.:** Office of the Deputy Minister of Mineral Resources, P.O.Box 345, Tel. 6310466, Jeddah. **Priv. Addr.:** Tel. 6874802, Jeddah, Saudi Arabia.

SULTAN (Hisham Essa, al), Kuwaiti executive. **Born** in 1940 in Kuwait. **Son** of Essa al-Sultan (Geniaat Tribe). **Married** in 1965, 2 sons, 1 daughter. **Dipl.:** B.S. (Mathematics); B.S. (Chemical Engineering). **Career:** D.P. Supervisor, Planning Ministry (1965-67); Process Engineer, Kuwait National Petroleum Co. (1967-72); Petrochemical Industries Co. (1972-76); Assistant Operations General Manager, Gulf Bank, Kuwait (1976-). **Addr.:** P.O.Box 3200, Tel. 445366, Telex: 2001 A/B GULFBANK, Kuwait.

SULTAN (Ibrahim Mohamad, al), Saudi senior civil servant. **Born** in 1930. **Career:** Employee, Finance Department, Riyadh; Director-General (grade "A"), the Royal Office; Attaché, Saudi Arabian Royal Embassy, Morocco, Bureau Director for Minister of Foreign Affairs; Counsellor, later Minister Plenipotentiary, later Ambassador, Foreign Ministry; attended Arab Foreign Ministers Conference (Baghdad 1960), Arab Joint Defence Council Meetings (Cairo 1960), Conference of the Non-Aligned Countries (Belgrade 1960), Arab League Council Session (Casablanca 1958), UN General Assemby 21st Session, First and Third Conferences of the Islamic States Foreign Ministers (Jeddah 1970-71); now Under-Secretary of State for Administrative and Financial Affairs, Foreign Ministry. **Awards:** Senior Officer Order, Lebanon; Sultan Qadarat, Philippines; decoration from Iran; Key to the City of Sydney, awarded upon and official visit; Shining Star awarded by the President of the Republic of China. **Sports:** Swimming, walking, **Hobby:** Reading. **Prof. Addr.:** Ministry of Foreign Affairs, Jeddah, Saudi Arabia.

SULTAN (Mahmoud Abdullah), Saudi executive. **Born** on 15 December 1933 in Medina, Saudi Arabia. **Dipl.:** Diploma in Business Administration and various management courses. **Career:** Warehouse Keeper, Lead Operator, Head Operator, Supervisor, Assistant Superintendent, Manager, General Manager, Jeddah Oil Refinery Co., former Chairman and Executive Managing Director, Petromin Lubricating Oil Co. **Member:** Security Commission of the Petromin Industrial Zone, Jeddah; 9th International Oil Conference, Japan. **Honours:** Service Awards: 5 years, Saudi Arabian Mining Syndicate; 10 years, Aramco and 15 years, Petromin. **Hobbies:** Reading, table tennis. **Priv. Addr.:** Tel. 6605534, Jeddah, Saudi Arabia.

SUMAIE (Abdallah, al), Kuwaiti businessman. **Born** in 1950 in Kuwait. **Son** of Nasser al-Sumaie (Merchant). **Educ.:** Graduate, Senior High School (1970); University of Kuwait, Law (1974). **Career:** Chairman, al-Sumaie Dair Beauty Co.; Chairman, The Arab Cooperation Trading & Cont. Co.; President, National Commercial Enterprises; President, Abdullah Al Sumaie Est. **Work:** Leading authorities, prominent business executives, making executive decisions to cover the grading of case problems and management. **Member:** Kuwait Sport Club. **Prof. Addr.:** P.O.Box 8474, Tel.: 2522285, 2521285, 2542314 Telex 22836 (Oilland). Salmia, Kuwait.

SUNBUL (Salim), Saudi diplomat. **Born** in 1928. **Educ.:** B.A. in Political Science, Faculty of Commerce, Cairo University, Egypt (1953). **Career:** Attaché, Foreign Ministry (1953); 3rd Secretary, Saudi Embassy, UK (1955); Assistant Director of Protocol (1956); Acting Chargé d'Affaires, Saudi Embassy, France; Chargé d'Affaires, Saudi Legation, Cyprus (1960); Head of Department of Protocol, Foreign Ministry. **Medals:** Several Orders of Merit from Arab Countries. **Addr.:** Jeddah, Saudi Arabia.

SUNNA (Sami, Jaddallah), Jordanian agricultural engineer. **Born** on January 31, 1931 in Jordan. **Married. Educ.:** Ecole Nationale d'Agriculture de Grignon, France (1949-53); Iowa State University, USA (1957-58); Unversity of Montpellier, France (1960-63). **Dipl.:** Diploma in Agricultural Engineering; Ph.D. in Plant Ecology. **Career:** Principal for Rabba Agricultural School, Jordan (1953-55); Assistant Director of the Agronomy Division at the Ministry of Agriculture (1955-63); Chief of the Agricultural Planning Section of Jordan Development Board (1963-66); Director of Agricultural Marketing Department, Jordan (1966-68); Assistant Director of Agricultural Research and Extension Department at the Ministry of Agriculture, Jordan; Adviser for World Food Programme, Egypt (1968-72); senior Adviser of World Food Programme/UNDP, Algeria (1972-75); Director General of Jordan Valley Authority (1975-76); Deputy Director General of Agricultural Credit Corporation (1976-80) and then Director General (1980-). **Addr.:** Amman, Jordan.

SUQAIR (Saleh Abdallah, al), Saudi diplomat. **Born** in 1925 in Buraidah, Qaseem. **Dipl.:** B.A. (Law); M.A. (Political Science). **Career:** Third Secretary, Counsellor, Minister Plenipotentiary, Ambassador; Director of Department of Islamic Affairs Ministry; of Foreign Ministers Conferences, UN General Assembly Sessions; member of several UN and Arab League Committees; formerly Chairman of the Islamic Solidarity Fund, Organization of the Islamic Conference, former Saudi Ambassador to India. **Publ.:** Political Parties in Arab Countries; an M.A. dissertation (under publication). **Award:** King Abdulaziz Order of Merit (First Grade), Order of Cedar of Lebanon, Order of the Sultanate of Oman. **Sport:** Swimming. **Hobby:** Reading. **Prof. Addr.:** Ministry of Foreign Affairs, Jeddah, Saudi Arabia.

SURAISRY (Jobarah Eid), Saudi academic. **Born** in 1949 at Yanbu. **Dipl.:** B.A. (Economics/ Political Science), M.A., Ph.D. (Economics). **Career:** Assistant Professor, Department of Economics, Faculty of Administrative Sciences, King Saud University. **Member:** the Board, the Research Centre of the Faculty of Administrative Sciences, King Saud University. **Hobbies:** reading, sports. **Prof. Addr.:** Faculty of Administrative Sciences, King Saud University, Tel.: 4811000 Ext. 2434, Riyadh, Saudi Arabia.

SUWEIDI (Ahmad Khalifa, al), United Arab Emirates politician. **Born** in 1937 in Abu Dhabi. **Son** of Khalifa Bin Mohamad al-Suweidi. **Married** in 1957, 6 children: Mohamad, Nasser, Hamad, Mawza, Muna, Khawla. **Educ.:** Cairo University, Cairo. **Dipl.:** B.A. in Economics and Political Science. **Career:** Assistant, Minister of Finance, Abu Dhabi (1957); Director of the Ruler Court, Abu Dhabi (1958); Head of the Ruler Court, Abu Dhabi (1970); Minister of State for Ruler's Affairs, Abu Dhabi (1971); United Arab Emirates Minister of Foreign Affairs (1971-1975); Member, Abu Dhabi Executive Council; Chairman of the Board, Abu Dhabi National Bank; Deputy President of the Investment Council, Deputy President of the Currency Council; Vice-Chairman, Central Bank of the U.A.E; Director Abu Dhabi National Oil Co. **Sports:** Golf, Water-skiing, billiards, tennis, swimming, fishing. **Hobbies:** Arabic Literature, poetry, history. **Addr.:** Abu Dhabi, United Arab Emirates.

SUWEIDI (Mohamad Habroush, al), United Arab Emirates official. **Born** in 1946. **Educ.:** Baghdad University, Iraq; Qatar and two years in UK. **Career:** Deputy Director, Amiri Court (1969); Minister of State for Financial and Industrial Affairs (1971). Director, Abu Dhabi Fund for Arab Economic Development, Abu Dhabi, UAE; Chairman National Drilling Co.; presently Chairman, National Bank of Abu Dhabi; former President Abu Dhabi National Oil Co. **Addr.:** P.O.Box 4, Abu Dhabi, UAE.

SUWEIDI (Mosbah, Mohamad, al), United Arab Emirates official. **Born** in 1950, Sharjah, United Arab Emirates. **Son** of Mohamad al-Suweidi. **Married**, one son. **Educ.:** Diploma in Commerce, Kuwait (1970); Diploma, International Institute of General Commerce, Cairo, Egypt (1972). **Career:** Chief Accountant, Sharjah Electricity Company (1970); Accountant, Ministry of Finance; Head of Salaries Department, Ministry of Finance; Deputy Director of Financial and Administrative Affairs, Ministry of Islamic Affairs and Waqfs (1975); Deputy Chairman of Wahda Company for General Contracting and Trading, Sharjah, United Arab Emirates. **Sports:** Football, swimming. **Hobbies:** Short story writing, travel. **Prof. Addr.:** al-Wahda General Contracting and Trading Company, Sharjah, Tel.: 24286, United Arab Emirates. **Priv. Addr.:** Tel.: 44354, Abu Dhabi, United Arab Emirates.

SWAILEM (Abdul Mohsen, al, Shaikh), Saudi executive. **Born** in 1927 in Riyadh, Saudi Arabia. **Educ.:** High School. **Career:** Member Riyadh Chamber of Commerce and Industry; Board Member, Riyadh Water Supply and Drainage Service; Director, Riyadh Bank Ltd., Riyadh. **Hobby:** Reading. **Addr.:** King Abdel Aziz Street, P.O.Box 1047, Tel.: 64312, Telex: 400619 A/B RYADEX SJ, Jeddah, Saudi Arabia.

SWAYEH (Omar), Libyan executive. **Born** in 1948 in Djanzur, Libya. **Son** of Ahmad Swayeh (Seaah Tribe). **Married** in 1979, 1 daughter. **Educ.:** University of Tripoli, Libya. **Dipl.:** B.A. (1974). **Career:** Assistant Manager, Libyan Arab Foreign Bank, Tripoli, Libya; Manager, Banque Arabe Libyenne Togolaise du Commerce Extérieur, Lome, Togo. **Addr.:** P.O.Box 9874, Tel.: 212829, 212830, Telex: 5301 A/B BALTEX, Lome, Togo.

SWEDAN (Daw, A.), Libyan, Assistant Secretary General League of Arab States. **Born** on February 17, 1938. **Son** of Ali S. Swedan **and** Mrs. Reem Sulieman. **Married** in December 1962 to Mrs. Aysha Delawi, 6 children: Osama (1963), Hussien (1964), Salah (1966), Laila (1971), Reema (1972), Faisal (1978). **Educ.:** University of Libya (1962), Howard University, Washington D.D. (1966). **Dipl.:** B.A. (Sociology & Anthropology) (1963). M.A. (International Relations, African Affairs). **Languages:** Arabic, English, Italian, Russian. **Career:** General Director of Afro-Asian Department Ministry of Foreign Affairs, Libya (1970); Deputy Representative of Libya to U.N. (1973-1975); Ambassador of Libya to U.S.S.R (1976-1981); Secretary General of Ministry of Foreign Affairs of Libya (1982-1988); Ambassador to U.S.S.R (1988-1989); Assistant Secretary General of the League of Arab States since 1989. **Other Information:** Lecturer of Modern History University of Libya (1967-1969). **Hobbies:** Photography, Travel. **Prof. Addr.:** League of Arab States, P.O.Box 11642, Tel.: 002/02/5796401, Cairo, Egypt.

T

TABARI (Hisham, R.), Jordanian engineer. **Born** on September 15, 1934 at Jaffa (Palestine). **Son** of Dr. Rashid Tabari (M.D.) **and** Mrs., née Maleeha Murad. **Married** in February 1965 to Miss Aida Faruki in Kuwait, three children: Ranya, Ahmad and Dalya. **Educ.:** International College, Beirut (Lebanon) (4 years); Roosevelt University, Chicago, Illinois (USA); Illinois University, Urabana, I11. (USA). **Dipl.:** B.Sc. (Mathematics), B.Sc. (Engineering). **Career:** Civil Engineer, Government of Kuwait (1960-62); Partner in Contracting Co. (Kuwait) (1962-65); Partner in Ranya Trading Co. since 1965. **Sports:** Table tennis and swimming. **Hobbies:** Reading, collecting brass and art objects. **Club.:** Marbella club; Moose club. **Credit Card:** American Express. **Prof. Addr.:** P.O.Box. 433, Tel.: 357347, Sharjah, U.A.E.

TABARI (Marwan), Palestinian businessman. **Born** in 1933 in Jerusalem. **Son** of Rachid Tabari (M.D.) **and** Mrs., née Maliha Tabari. **Married** on 25 June 1963, to Badrieh, 5 **children**: Suha, Hiba, Ruba, Shada and Rachid. **Educ.:** al-Umma school, Jerusalem; Victoria College, Alexandria (Egypt); American University of Beirut, Roosevelt College, Chicago (U.S.A.). **Dipl.:** B.Sc. (Biology). **Career:** Manager, Equipment Ltd. (Kuwait (1966-68); In Abu Dhabi Managing Director & Partner of Al Ittihad Drug Stores & Ranya Trading Co. (from 1968). **Sport:** soccer. Squash, tennis, swimming. **Credit Card:** American Express. **Prof. Addr.:** P.O.Box 602, Tel.: 211600, Abu Dhabi, U.A.E.

TABBAH (Fuad Ezzat), Jordanian businessman. **Born** in 1915 in Damascus, Syria. **Son** of Fuad Tabbah. **Married,** three children. **Educ.:** Degree in Law. **Career:** Chairman and General Manager, Ezzat F. Tabbah and Sons Company;Honorary Consul General of Chad Republic, Jordan. **Medal:** Order of the Jordanian Star, 3rd Class; Awarded of the Jordanian al-Kawkab Medal of the "Third Order". **Addr.:** P.O.Box. 229 Tel.: 671509, Telex: 1703 FOUAD JO Amman, Jordan.

TABBAH (Tawfik), Jordanian businessman. **Born** in 1921. **Married** four children. **Career:** Founder and President of Royal Jordanian Airlines (ALIA) (1964); founder and member of the Board of Directors, Central Bank of Jordan, Amman; Vice Chairman, Amman Chamber of Commerce; Chairman, United Trading Co. Ltd.; Trans-orient Co.; Tawfic Automobile & Equipment Co. **Medals:** Independence Medals, 2nd and 3rd Class, Jordan. **Sports:** Swimming, riding. **Hobby:** Flying. **Addr.:** United Trading Company Ltd., P.O.Box. 1408, Tel.: 36385, Amman, Jordan.

TABIE (Ahmad Ali), Saudi academic. **Born** in 1940, Al Bahah. **Dipl.:** B.A. (Geography). **Career:** Primary School teacher (1955-64); joined Faculty of Education (1964-68), intermediate school teacher (1968-71); sent to the U.S.A. for an Administration Course (1971-73); now Educational Inspector, Ministry of Education. **Member** and Sports Trainer, Bani Dhabrian Sporting Club, Bahah Region; member of Educational Inspectorate, Bahah Education Administration; former member, Muslim Students, U.S.A. **Hobby:** Reading. **Prof. Addr.:** c/o Ahmad Mansour's Shop, Baha Market Place, Baha, Saudi Arabia.

TADLAOUI (Mohammed,), Moroccan engineer. **Born** in 1939 in Meknes, Morocco. **Married,** 2 sons & 1 daughter. **Educ.:** University of London, UK; Imperial college, UK; Institution of Civil Engineers UK. **Dipl.:** B.Sc. in Civil Engineering, DIC, MICE. **Career:** Research Engineer, UK (1963); Project Engineer U.K. (1966); Consulting Engineer, Morocco (1973); Founder, President and General Director of SOCOPLAN, Consulting Engineering Firm (1975); Co-Founder and member of the Moroccan Association of consulting Engineers of Morocco (AMCI), (1976); General secretary of the regional Association GRANDE ISMAILIA, RABAT Section (1994). Member of the Lions Club. **Hobbies:** swimming, tennis, history Arabic literature. **Fluent Languages:** Arabic, English, and French. **Priv. Addr.:** Residence Al Mansour, Zankat Moulay Slimane, Rabat, Morocco.

TADMORI (Ahmed Jalal, al), Syrian academic and journalist. **Born** in 1940 in Damascus (Syria). **Son** of Mohammed Adeeb Al-Tadmori (businessman) **and Mrs.,** née Swad al Sha'alan. **Married** on June 21, 1973 to Hind Toubaji two sons Khalid, Nasser & two daughters Khulood and Nada. **Educ.:** As'ad Abdullah Secondary school, Damascus; University of Baghdad; Faculty of Arts, Cairo University. **Dipl.:** M.A. and M.D.: The Arab History Institute of high Studies, Baghdad 1990. Ph.D.: Georgian University, Oriental Studies Institute, and Georgian Science Academy 1997. **Career:** Journalist, (1961 onwards) Political observer (1961-65), writer and author for many books & researches, Baghdad; Manager of Broadcasting Programme (1963-65), Baghdad; Political observer in Arab voice, Cairo (1965-1967), Director of Information & Tourism Dep. and **Editor of Ras Al-Khaimah Magazine**

(1969-1986), Director of Documentaries and studies Center in Emiri Court Ras Al-Khaimah (1986-1996). Now Adviser for Emiri Court Chief (from March 1996). **Member** of Union Arab Historian, and member of Arab Union Journalists. **Prof. Addr.:** P.O.Box 565, Tel.: 9717-2227212, 2362218, Mob.: 97150-6474454, Fax: 9717-2227127 Ras Al-Khaimah, U.A.E.

TAHA (Abdel-Rahman al-Tayeb, Dr.), Sudanese Manager, Islamic Corporation for the Insurance of Investment & Export Credit. **Born** on January 10, 1941 at Kosti/ Sudan. **Son** of Al-Tayeb Ali Taha. **Married** to Amal El-Tigani Ali, 3 children: Ayman (7/2/1974), Rabah (8/10/ 1977), Lubna (11/12/1982). **Educ.:** Ph.D. in Business Administration, University of California, Los Angeles, 1970. MBA (Master of Business Administration) University of California, Berkeley, 1966. BS (Business Administration) University of California, Berkeley, 1965. **Career:** 1994-Present, The Manager, Islamic Corporation for the Insurance of Investment & Export Credit. - 1992-1994, Director, Trade Finance Department & Acting Director, Trade Information & Service Department, Arab Trade Financing Program, Abu Dhabi, U.A.E. - 1992-1993, Director, Technical Department, Arab Trade Financing Program. - 1990-1992, Managing Director, Mawrid International Trade and Investment Services Co., Ltd., London, U.K. - 1988-1990, Director of Operations, Inter-Arab Investment Guarantee Corporation, Kuwait. - 1984-1988, Director of Research, Inter-Arab Investment Guarantee Corporation. - 1978-1984, Economist and Senior Economist, the World Bank, Washington D.C., U.S.A. - 1975-1978, Director General, Higher Education Finance Commission, Khartoum, Sudan. - 1970-1975, Assistant & Associate Professor, Department of Business Administration, University of Khartoum, Sudan. **Credit Card:** AMX. **Prof. Addr.:** Jeddah 21454, P.O.Box 15722 K.S.A., Tel.: (9662) 6374061, Saudi Arabia. **Priv. Addr.:** Jeddah, Al-Nahdah Dist., Tel.: (9662) 6220178, Saudi Arabia.

TAHA (Elzubeir, Beshir), Sudanese Physiological Psychology and Minister of Higher Education. **Born** on December 24, 1945 at Wadmedawi, Khartoum Sudan. **Son** of Nasr Beshir Taha - Farmer **and** Mrs. Fatima Siddig. **Married** in 1974 to Aziza Sharief, 7 children: Tamadur, Afraa, Abdalla, Allaa, Musab, Mohamed, Huda. **Educ.:** University of Khartoum (1972) (BA) - University of Birmingham (MA) U.K. - University of Sussex, 1978 (MSc) - University of Sheffield, 1982 (Ph.D.). **Career:** Professor of Psychology. Faculty of Arts. U.K. (1993); Associate Professor University of U.A.E. (1988-1993); Associate Professor, Department Psychology, University of Khartoum (1986-1988); Part Time Lecturer, Faculty of Medicine, Gezira University; Part Time Lecturer, High Institute of Music & Drama (1982-1985); Deputy-Vice Chancellor, University of Khartoum (1994-1998); Vice-Chancellor, University of Khartoum (1998); **Minister of Higher Education** & Scientific Research (1999-). **Other Information:** Chairman & Supervision of Committees (Laws, status & Regulations of Sudanese Police Academy (1999); Post Graduate Diploma & Medicine Psychology, University of Khartoum; Post Graduate Diploma & Main Clinical Psychology. **Decorations:** He has been Granted some Decorations from Educational Institution & Non-Governmental Organisations. **Sports Practised:** Swimming - Running. **Hobby:** Reading. **Prof. Addr,:** Ministry of Higher Education & Scientific Research, P.O.Box 2081, Tel.: 779312, Khartoum. Sudan.

TAHA HUSSAIN (Munis), Egyptian former UN official. **Born** in 1921. **Married**, 1 daughter. **Educ.:** Cairo University, Egypt; Agrégation de Lettres, University of Paris, France. **Dipl.:** Degree in Literature, Doctorate Lettres. **Career:** Professor of French Language and Literature, Cairo University (1951-61); senior UNESCO Official (1962-1984); former Head of International Diffusion of Culture, UNESCO, Paris. **Publ.:** "L'Islam dans la littérature romantique en France", Cairo (1962) as well as numerous articles in Egyptian journals. **Hobbies:** comparative literature, the plastic arts, music, theatre, swimming. **Addr.:** 42, Rue Poussin -75016, Paris, France.

TAHA (Mohamad, Fathi), Egyptian international civil servant. **Born** on January 15, 1915 at Cairo (Egypt). **Married**, children. **Educ.:** Faculty of Science, University of Cairo (1939-43); Imperial College of Science and Technology, University of London (1937-38). **Dipl.:** B.Sc. (Physics), DIC (Meteorology) (1938). **Career:** Lecturer, Faculty of Science, Cairo University (1942-44); Vice President, World Meteological Organisation (WMO) Regional Commission for Africa (1947); Second Vice President, Executive Committee WMO (1959-63); Member, Outer Space Exploration Committee, Academy of Science, Cairo (1967); Chairman, National Committee on Geodesy and Geophysics, Academy of Science, Cairo (1967); President, Permanent Meteorological Committee, League of Arab States, Cairo (1971); Chairman, Board of Directors, Egyptian Meteorological Authority (1971); President and member, Executive Committee, WMO; Under-Secretary of State (Egypt). **Member:** Union of Scientific Workers. **Publ.:** Author of "Climates in the Near East", "Climate and Meteorology North of the Tropic of Cancer" (1960). **Awards:** Order of Merit (Egypt). **Prof. Addr.:** Koubry el-Qubbah, Tel.: 863-304, Cairo, Egypt. **Priv. Addr.:** Elkhalifa Elmaamoun street, Tel.: 862-020, Cairo, Egypt.

TAHA (S.A.), Egyptian academic. **Born** in 1947 in Suez, Egypt. **Dipl.:** B.Sc., M.Sc. and Ph.D. (Pharmacology). **Career:** Teacher (1974); Assistant Professor, King Saud University (1976); Head, Department of Pharmacology, King Saud University since 1981; **Member:** Clinical Pharmacology Society, Britain. **Publications:** Several articles in his field of interest. **Address:** King Saud University, Faculty of Pharmaciology, Tel.: 4774649 (Office), and

4011267 (Home), Riyadh, Saudi Arabia.

TAHER (Abdulhady Hassan), Saudi Official. **Born** in 1931 at the Madina, Saudi Arabia. **Married,** 2 sons and 1 daughter. **Educ.:** University of Cairo, Egypt; Aïn Shams University, Cairo, Egypt; University of California, Berkeley, USA. **Dipl.:** Ph.D., University of California, **Career:** Joined Saudi Arabian Government service in 1955; Director-General, Ministry of Petroleum and Mineral Resources (1961); Governor, The General Petroleum and Minerals Organizations (Petromin) (1962); Minister of State and Governor of Petromin (1978). **Act.:** Chairman and Managing Director, Jeddah Oil Refinery Company; Head of the Saudi Delegation, Conference on International Economic Cooperation (CIEC) (Paris 1976-77); Member, Board of Directors, Arabian American Oil Company (ARAMCO) and member of its Executive Committee; Honorary Member of the American Society of Petroleum Engineers and the American Management Association Geo Club; Part-time lecturer, University of Riyadh, Petroleum Economics (early 1960s). **Publ.:** "Income Determination n the International Petroleum Industry" (Paragamon Press, Oxford-1966); "Development and Petroleum Strategies in Saudi Arabia" (1970); Papers on Economic and Petroleum Affairs delivered at several local and international conferences. **Addr.:** Jeddah, Saudi Arabia.

TAHER (Adel), Former egyptian minister of tourism. **Born** in 1923 in Cairo, Egypt. **Son** of Ibrahim Taher. **Educ.:** Graduate, Military Academy (1946). Diploma from International Recreation Service (1956). Studies of the functioning of the UN at UN Headquarters, N.Y. (1960). **Career:** ADC to the Minister of War (1946-1954); Direcotr, Cabinet of the Minister of Municipal Affairs (1955); Secretary, Higher Council of Youth (1956); member of the Executive Committee, International Sports and Physical Education Council (September 1962); promoted Assistant Secretary, Ministry of Youth (1964); Secretary, Ministry of Tourism and Youth (1965-80); Deputy director, Arab Tourism Federation (July 1974); First Secretary, Ministry of Tourism (January 1976); Chairman, Board of Directors, Egyptian Tourism Promotion Authority (1981); Minister of Tourism (3 January- 2 Sept. 1982); Tourism, Sports and Recreation Consultant at Delta Internationl Council of Sports Science and Physical Education for Africa and the Middle East (since 1962). **Member:** of the Executive Board of the world Leisure Recreation Association (Since 1954), of American Society of Travel Agencies, of Latin American Confederation of Tourist Organisation. Vice President of the International Council of Sports for Africa and the Middle East (since 1962). **Publ.:** Many, some of which: "Youth its Past, Present and Future" (1964): "Tourism Youth" (1971); "Health Tourism" (1973); "Sport and Tourism" (1983). **Award:** UNESCO Philip Noel Baker award (scientific research). Egyptian Republic of the first degree for Sports. "Golden Helm" for competence and dedication to develop Tourism. **Address:** Cairo, Egypt.

TAHER (Mirza, Ali Murad), UAE executive. **Born** in 1947 in al-Maaridh, Ras al-Khaimah, UAE. **Son** of Ali Murad Taher. **Married:** in 1976, 1 son, 1 daughter. **Career:** Commercial Manager, National Bank of Ras al-Khaimah, UAE (1978). **Addr.:** P.O.Box. 5300, Tel.: 21127, **Telex:** 46757, Ras al-Khaimah, UAE.

TAHER (Mohamad Omar), Saudi academic. **Born** in 1941 in Mecca, Saudi Arabia. **Dipl.:** B.Sc., Ph.D. (Zoology). **Career:** Lecturer, Zoology Department, Faculty of Science, Riyadh University; Assistant Professor, same faculty. (1975); Chairman, Department of Zoology, Faculty of Science, Riyadh University; member of Board, Saudi Biological Society; attended several scientific conferences. **Hobbies:** Travel, sport. **Address:** Zoology Department, Faculty of Science, Riyadh University, Riyadh, Saudi Arabia.

TAHER (Samir), Egyptian steel company executive. **Born** on February 7, 1923 in Cairo. **Married** in 1955, 2 daughters. **Educ.:** Cairo and Glasgow Universities. **Dipl.:** Bachelor of Science, in Chemistry and Geology (1944), Doctor of Philosophy (1949). **Career:** Joined the Egyptian Laboratories (1944-50); Lecturer in Metallurgy, Aïn Shams University (1950-55); Works Manager, Egyptian Iron and Steel Company (1955-61); Director, Technical Manager (1961). **Member** of several societies, organizations and companies. **Publ.:** Research in field, Pioneer in Developing first integrated iron and steel works in Egypt. **Award:** Order of the Egyptian Merit. **Prof. Addr.:** 19, Gabalaya Street, Zamalek, Cairo. **Priv. Addr.:** Egyptian Iron and Steel Company, Helwan, near Cairo, Egypt.

TAHER (Thabet, Abdul Rauf, al), Jordanian businessman. **Born** in 1928 in Nablus, Palestine. **Son** of Abdul Rauf al-Taher. **Married,** one son. **Educ.:** Netherlands University, Harvard University, USA. **Dipl.:** M.A. in Public Administration; Diploma in Marketing; Diploma in Industrial Management. **Career:** Head of Division, Civil Service Commission; Administrative Assistant, Secretary of the Board of Directors, General Manager, Jordan Phosphate Mines Company Ltd.; Director General, Arab Mining Company; Member of the board of Directors of Jordan Phosphate Company, Jordan Fertilizer Company; Vice Chairman, Arab Potash Company, Jordan; Director, Jordan Fertilizer Industry Co. Ltd.; member of the Amman Chamber of Industry, Amman, Jordan; Vice President, World Phosphate Institute (1974); Minister of Energy and Mineral Resources (Nov. 1989- Dec. 1992). Chairman, National Petroleum Co. (1997-99); Chairman, Petra Drilling Co. (since Jan. 2000-); Deputy Chairman, Jordanian Businessmen Association (since 1997-); Secretary General, Federation of Arab Businessmen (since 1997-). **Addr.:**

P.O.Box. 830155, Tel.: 5931807, Fax: 59831166 JO, Amman, Jordan.

TAHRI (Izzeddine, al), Egyptian former air force officer. **Born** on August 4, 1918 in Mansourah Province. **Married** to Miss Nazli Sharif Sabry. **Educ.:** Military Academy. **Career:** formerly, Squadron Leader, Egyptian Air Force, Landowner. **Award:** Star of Palestine. **Member:** Gezira Sporting Club, Automobile Club of Egypt. **Hobbies:** Golf, tenis, squash, swimming. **Addr.:** 25, Qasr al-Aali Street, Garden City, Tel.: 22422, Cairo, Egypt.

TAI (Muhibiddin, al), Iraqi engineer. **Educ.:** trained as a Civil Engineer. **Career:** Head of Society of Civil Engineers, Iraq (for 4 years); Under Secretary, Ministry of Works and Housing (1968); Head of the Central Follow-up and Inspection Committee, Ministry of Planning (1972); Under Secretary, Ministry of Interior (1980-83); Engineer (1983-). **Addr.:** Baghdad, Iraq.

TAIBA (Abdul Kader Khalil), Saudi academic. **Born** in 31 December 1940 in Mecca, Saudi Arabia. **Dipl.:** B.A., M.A. (Educational Administration), Chapman College, California, 1969. **Career:** Secretary, Board of Trustees, King Fahad University of Petroleum and Minerals (KFUPM), Dhahran; Director, Rector's Office, KFUPM; Assistant Director for Academic and Administrative Affairs Centre of Applied Geology, Graduate Institut, KFUPM; Director of Students Affairs, KFUPM; Supervisor, Admission and Registrations, King Abdulaziz University, Mecca Branch (presently known as Umm al-Qura University); Educational Consultant, Umm al-Qura University; Lecturer, Faculty of Education, Umm al-Qura University; member, Registrars' Association, U.S.A., participated in a Registrars' Association, U.S.A., participated in a Registrars' Conference, U.S.A., **Hobbies:** Reading, swimming. **Address:** P.O.Box 3711, Tel.: 5562521 (office), and 5432521 (home), Mecca, Saudi Arabia.

TAIBA (Mahmoud), Saudi official. **Born** in 1936. **Married. Educ.:** studied Electrical engineering in USA. **Career:** entered Arabian American Oil Company "Aramco"; then studied electrical engineering in USA under Aramco auspices; on return, was appointed to Ministry of Commerce; Director General, Industrial Research and Development Centre (1967); Chairman, Saudi Fertilizer Co. (SAFCO). **Prof. Addr.:** The Saudi National Oil Company, Dhahran, Saudi Arabia.

TAIBA (Mustafa), Saudi Arabian director general of curative medicine. **Born** in 1925 in Mecca, Saudi Arabia. **Son** of Abdullah Taiba **and** Mrs., Fatima Sabban. **Married** to Anna Mansouri, 6 children: Mehrez, Sawsan, Mohamad, Dena, Ghada and Reima. **Educ.:** Falah School in Mecca; Special Section, same school, of learning of Koran by heart; Madrasat Tahder el-Biathat, Mecca; Medical College, Cairo University; Royal College of Surgeons, London. **Dipl.:** M.D.; Higher Studies, Royal College of Surgeons, London. **Career:** Surgeon, Aramco, 4 years; Director and Surgeon of King Saud Hospital, Jeddah; Surgeon and Director of Tabouk Military Hospital; Assistant Director General of Medical Services, Ministry of Defence; Director General, Jeddah Health Area; Director of Medical Centre of SAUDIA; Director General of Curative Medicine, Ministry of Health, for the last 14 years; Headed or member of many delegations to Medical conferences, symposia or meetings. **Sports:** Tennis, Billiards. **Hobby:** Reading and Gardening. **Member:** el-Frosia Club in Riyadh. **Prof. Addr.:** Ministry of Health, Riyadh. **Priv. Addr.:** Malaz, Tel.: 4044414 or 4040476, Riyadh, Saudi Arabia.

TAIMA (Fuad, Khazal), Arab-American businessman. **Born** in 1935 in Baghdad, Iraq. **Married,** 1 son, 4 daughters. **Educ.:** Baghdad College, Iraq; Wharton School, University of Pennsylvania, USA. **Dipl.:** B.Sc. in Business, M.A. in Business Administration. **Career:** Economic Consultant to Arab World UN Mission (1960-68); President of Averroes Incorporation (1971-); Vice President of AAUG, Washington, DC (1970-72); Co-Founder of National Association of Arab Americans (1972); Co-Founder of Northern Virginia Export Import Association (1974); Co-Founder of Mid Atlantic US Arab Chambers of Commerce (1975); President of Taima and Associates Incorporation (1971-); Regional Vice President of US Arab Chamber of Commerce (1976-). **Hobbies:** Socio-economic philisophies, literature, tennis, swimming, cycling. **Member:** Les Ambassadeurs Club, London and the Middle East Institute. **Addr.:** Averroes Incorporation, 6825 Redmond Drive, Drawer T. Mclean, Virginia, USA.

TAJEDDINE (Abdeslam), Moroccan executive. **Born** in Casablanca, Morocco. **Son** of late Chouaib Tajeddine **and** late Mrs. Halima Tajeddine. **Married** on August 19, 1967 in Casablanca to Miss Zoubir Habiba, three children: Hynd (1970), Nadia (1972) and Noriman (1975). **Educ.:** Ecole Industrielle, Casablanca; Oklahoma State University "OSU" ,USA; Istituto Direzionale Idrocarburi, Milano, Italy; Faculté des Sciences Juridiques, Econom. et Sociales, Université de Rabat, Maroc. Institut Supérieur de Commerce et d'Administration des Entreprises "Iscae", Casablanca. **Dipl.:** B.S. in Mechanical Engineering; M.S. in Petroleum Eng; Diplome du Cycle Supérieur de Gestion; Diplome CPAE et diplomes Cedes (Faculté de Rabat); Diplome de l'Institut d'Etudes Internationales et des Pays en Voie de Développement (Université de Toulouse). **Career:** In Petroleum Refinery: Maintenance Engineer (1962-67); Maintenance-Security and Develop. Engineer (1967-70); Technical Manager, (SAMIR) (1971-74); General Manager of Seblima (Bituminous refinery) (1974-84); July 1984-to present Attaché of General Director of SAMIR Refinery; President of

Maintenance sub-committee related to the committee of the Oil Industry of Maghreb "C.M.I.P." (February 1989- February 1992); President of Maintenance and Process sub-committee related to the committee of Oil Industry of Maghreb "C.M.I.P." (since February 1992); Permanent Secretary of the Committee of the Oil Industry of Maghreb "C.M.I.P." (since July 1990). (Since October 1992), President of the Group of representatives of Moroccan Firms attending te Mediterranean Meeting of Industry, held annually in Marseilles-France and sponsored by the Chamber of Commerce and Industry Marseilles-Province (C.C.I.M.P.). **Publ.:** "La Siderurgie en Suède" - "Conditions Préalables à la Réussite d'Une Action de Formation de Cadres Moyens dans les Entreprises Marocaines - Etude de Cas". "Le Rôle du BEPI dans l'Industrialisation du Maroc". **Member:** Laureat de la Fondation des Bourses Zallidja (Paris-1955); Member du Conseil Prefectoral de Casablanca (1976-82) -Member et Rapporteur du Budget du Conseil Municipal de Mohammedia (1976-82). **Medal:** Wissam Errida (Sa Majesté Hassan II) (1969); Chevalier de la République d'Italie (1969). **Sports:** Tennis, golf and swimming. **Hobbies:** Golf, reading, painting. **Member:** Lion's Club International Association; as well as different social and cultural associations. **Credit Card:** Diner's Club. **Prof. Addr.:** SAMIR, P.O.Box 89, Mohammedia, Tel.: 212 (3) 327480/92, Morocco. **Priv. Addr.:** Villa Adil Ave., Yacoub el-Mansour, Tel.: 212 (3) 31 03 35, Mohammedia, Morocco.

TAJER (Mohamad, Mahdi al), UAE diplomat. **Born** in 1931 in Bahrain. **Married**, 6 children. **Educ.:** Preston Grammar School, Lancashire, UK. **Career:** Director of Port and Customs, Dubai (1955-63); Director of H.H. the Ruler of Dubai's Affairs and Director of Petroleum Affairs Department, Dubai (1963-); Director of National Bank of Dubai Ltd. (1963-); Chairman of Dubai Petroleum Company (1963), Director of Dubai Petroleum Company (1963); Chairman of Dubai National Air Travel Company (1966); Director of Qatar-Dubai Currency Board (1965-73); Chairman of South Eastern Dubai Drilling Company (1968-); United Arab Emirates Ambassador Extraordinary and Plenipotentiary to Court of St. James, London (1972-1982); Ambassador of United Arab Emirates to the Court of St. James (1983-86); Vice Chairman of the World of Islam Festival (1976); Chairman of the Board of the Arab-British Chamber of Commerce, London, UK; Director of United Arab Emirates Currency Board (1973-); Director of Dubai Dry Dock Company (1973-); Adviser to the Ruler of Dubai; Director of Allied Arab Bank Ltd., London (1977-); **Decor.:** Honorary Citizen of the State of Texas, USA (1963). **Hobby:** Patron of arts and culture. **Prof. Addr.:** P.O.Box 207, Dubai, U.A.E.

TAKAWI (Abdullah Mohammed, al), UAE diplomat. **Born** in 1948 in Ras al-Khaimah, UAE. **Married**, 4 sons, 2 daughters. **Educ.:** Exeter, UK. **Dipl.:** OND in Business Management and Diploma Modern Management and He graduated from pacific Western University California, U.S.A. in Political Science. **Career:** Secretary of the Department of Education (1970); Arab Planning Institute, Kuwait (1974); Officer, British Bank of the Middle East; Manager of Administration and Finance to the Higher Supreme Council Affairs, Ministry of Foreign Affairs; Third Secretary (1976); Member of UAE Delegation to 31st Session of UN General Assembly, Second Secretary (1977), First Secretary (1978); Head of the Mission, Embassy of UAE, Dacca, Bangladesh (1979-1982); Counsellor (1981); Counsellor in U.A.E. Embassy in Kuwait (1982-1987). He attended a training Program on diplomacy of Negotiations (1984). He also worked as Minister Plen. Embassy of United Arab Emirates in Cairo (1988-1994); He also worked as Chargé d'Affaires, Embassy of UAE in Philippines and Brazil (1996-98); He also worked as Chargé d'Affaires, Embassy of UAE in Sri Lanka (1999); At Present, he has been appointed as Consul General, Consulate General of UAE, Mumbai in February 2000. **Hobbies:** reading, travelling. **Prof. Addr.:** Ministry of Foreign Affairs, P.O.Box 1, Abu Dhabi, U.A.E.

TAKLA (Laila, I.), Egyptian politician. **Married**, two children. **Educ.:** Cairo University, Egypt; University of Southern California, USA; New York University, USA. **Dipl.:** LL.B.; Diploma in Social Studies; M.A.; Ph.D. **Career:** Lecturer in Administration, New York University, USA: Lecturer, Higher Institute of Administration, Cairo University, Cairo, Egypt; Chairman, Foreign Affairs Committee, People's Assembly; member of the Central Commitee of the Arab Socialist Union (1971); member of the National Specialised Councils (1972); Public Administration Expert, Arab League (1969); Representative of Egypt, UN General Assembly (1973); Vice President, International Parliamentary Union (1977); Chairman of the Committee on Education; President of the Finnish-Egyptian Society (1976); Chairman, National Committee on Environmental Law; Chairman, UN Experts Group on the Advancement of Women (1976). **Publ.:** "Public Administration; Principles and Dynamics" 2 Volumes, 1968, 1971, 1976; "The Six Hour War: An Analysis of the Arab-Israeli Octobre War" (1973); "The Ombudsman: A Comparative Study" (1971). **Sports:** Swimming, tennis. **Hobbies:** Sculpture, folk arts. **Addr.:** People's Assembly, Cairo, Egypt.

TAKY (Ziad, Dr.), Lebanese executive. **Born** in 1941. **Son** of Abdul Hamid Taky. **Married** 1966, 2 sons, **Dipl.:** Ph.D. (Economics) (1970); M.B.A. (1966). **Career:** Assistant Professor, American University of Beirut, Lebanon (1971-72); Associate Professor, Haigazian College (1973-76); Manager and Chief Economist, The Industrial Bank of Kuwait (1971-79); Assistant General Manager and Chief Economist National Bank of Kuwait, Safat, Kuwait (since 1979). **Publ.:** Author of several Articles in Economic Financial Magazines. **Member:** Economic Honorary (Omicron Delta Epsilon); Hunting and Equestian Club, Kuwait. **Sports:** Tennis, bowling, swimming. **Hobby:** Reading. **Addr.:** Abdulla al-Salem Street, P.O.Box 95, 13001-SAFAT - Kuwait, Tel.: 2463803, Telex: 44836 A/B NATBNK KT. Fax: 2463804.

TAL (Ahmad, Yusuf, al), Jordanian official. **Born** in 1930 in Irbid, Jordan. **Married**, 5 children. **Educ.:** American University of Beirut, Lebanon; Sind University, Pakistan. **Dipl.:** M.Sc. in Educational Administration, Ph.D. in Education. **Career:** Teacher, Irbid Secondary School (1957-62); District Governor, Ministry of Interior (1962-64); Director of Education, Ministry of Education (1968-74); Cultural Counsellor, Jordan Embassy in Islamabad, Pakistan (1974-80); Director of Community College, Ministry of Education (1980-85); Adviser to the Minister of Education (1985); Secretary General of the Ministry of Higher Education (1985); Member, National Society for the Study of Education in USA (1974-); Member of the Council of Higher Education, Jordan (1985-). **Publ.:** "Education in Jordan" in Arabic and English, "Higher Education in Jordan", Ministry of Higher Education (1986). **Medal:** Independence Medal from H.M. King Hussein of Jordan (1973). **Hobby:** tennis. **Member:** Hussein's Sports City. **Prof. Addr.:** Ministry of Higher Education, Wadi Saqra, Amman, Jordan.

TAL (Hajim Khalaf, al), Jordanian official. **Born** in 1920 in Irbid, Jordan. **Married. Educ.:** American University of Beirut, Lebanon; Karachi University, Pakistan. **Dipl.:** B.A. in History and Politics, M.A. **Career:** Minister Plenipotentiary, Foreign Ministry (1947-62); Under Secretary, Ministry of Interior (1962-67); Private business (1967-71); Assistant Secretary General of Tribal Shaikhs Council (1971-72); Inspector General, Ministry of Finance (1972); Director General, Municipal and Village Loan Fund (1972-80); Director General of the Orphans Institute (1980-83). **Medal:** Renaissance Medal (2nd Class). **Decor.:** Star of Jordan (2nd Class). **Addr.:** Sweilih, Amman, Jordan.

TAL (Hisham Falih, al), Jordanian lawyer. **Born** in 1946 in Irbid, Jordan. **Educ.:** Damascus University, Syria. **Dipl.:** LL.B. **Career:** Lawyer (1966-); Member of the National Consultative Council (1982-84); Minister of Justice (from Jan. 1995-Feb. 1996); Minister of State for Prime Minister's Affairs (1996). **Hobby:** reading. **Addr.:** Amman, Jordan.

TAL (Mraiwid, al), Jordanian diplomat. **Born** in 1928 in Irbid, Jordan. **Married**, two children. **Educ.:** London School of Economics, UK (1955-57); University of Pittsburgh, USA (1961). **Career:** Joined UN and worked as Economic Consultant in Saudi Arabia, Lebanon and Morocco and at Headquarters in New York; Counsellor at Ministry of Foreign Affairs (1962-67); Counsellor, Embassies to West Germany and Tunisia (1967-69); Head of UN Department at the Ministry of Foreign Affairs (1969-70); Chief of Royal Protocol (1970); Secretary General to the Royal Diwan and Private Secretary to the King (1970-72); Economic Adviser to HRH Prince Hassan (1972-74). **Addr.:** The Royal Court, Amman, Jordan.

TAL (Mulhem Wahbi, Yousif, El-), Jordanian Lawyer. **Born** in Irbid, Jordan in 1937. **Married**, no children. **Educ.:** High School, Irbid Highschool; Law Degree, Cairo University. **Dipl.:** LL.B., International Institute of Sirs El-Lian, Egypt. **Career:** Established "Al-Rakeeb", Weekly Political Newspaper in 1962 (banned in 1964 by the jordanian Government); Chief Editor, News Section, Press Departmetn; Established and Headed the Political Department at the Ministry of Information; Assistant Deputy, Ministry of Information; Director General, Jordanian News Agency; Director General, Jordanian News Corporation; Chief Editor, Al-Rai' (daily newspaper); Ambassador, Ministry of Foreign Affairs; Joined the Jordanian Bar Association to practice law (up until now); Secretary General, Jordanian Constitutional Front; Committee Chief for Coordination, Jordanian National Opposition Parties; Chief Spokesman, Jordanian Opposition Party; Chief, Jordanian National Committee for supporting Lebanon. **Decor.:** Jordanian Independance Medal. **Hobbies:** Reading, Music, Stamp collecting. **Address:** P.O.Box 5522 Zahran Post Office, Amman, Jordan.

TAL (Saad, al), Jordanian university professor and former minister. **Born** in 1934 in Irbid, Jordan. **Married. Dipl.:** Jordanian General Secondary School Certificate (1951); Egyptian General Secondary School Cerificate (1953), B.A. Mathematics and Education (1957); M.A. Education (1960); Doctorate in Philosophy (1963). **Career:** Teacher, Primary School (1951-52); Teacher, Secondary School, Irbid (1953-58); Teacher, Hawara Teachers' College (1958-65); Cultural Counsellor, Jordanian Embassy to Lebanon (1965-69); Assistant Professor, Jordan University (1969-72); Professor of Education and Dean of the College of Education, Jordan University (1972); Minister of Education (1980); Director and General Manager, Jordan Petroleum Refinery Co. **Publ.:** Author of articles on teaching methods, and translation of educational textbooks. **Priv. Addr.:** P.O.Box 1079, Tel.: 630151, Amman, Jordan.

TAL (Safwan, Khalaf, al), Jordanian academic. **Born** in 1938 in Irbid, Jordan. **Married**, three children. **Educ.:** B.A. in Archaeology; M.A. in Archaeology and Byzantine and Islamic Arts; Ph.D. in Islamic Art and Architecture. **Career:** Inspector of Antiquities, Department of Antiquities, Jordan (1968-74); Instructor, Jordan University (1974-80); Head of Department of

Antiquities, Jordan University (1975-79); Assistant Director of Jordan University and Director of Cultural and Public Affairs (1976-81); Associate Professor (1981); Head of Department of Antiquities, Jordan University (1975-79); Assistant Director of Jordan University and Director of Cultural and Public Affairs (1976-81); Assistant Secretary General, Federation of Arab Universities, Riyadh, Saudi Arabia (since 1982). **Publ.:** "Development of Arabic Script in the First Hijri Century" in Arabic; "Development of Coins in Jordan", in Arabic. **Addr.:** P.O.B. 2873, Riyadh, Saudi Arabia.

TAL (Sohair Salti, al), Jordanian journalist. **Born** in 1952 in Irbid, Jordan. **Married**, 1 daughter. **Dipl.:** B.Com. in Accountancy. **Career:** Journalist; Member of the Board of Directors of Jordan Women's Union (1979-80); Member of Jordan Journalists' Union, Women University Graduates' Club and Jordan Writers' Union. **Publ.:** short story collection (1982), "Stories in Women's Problems in Jordan" (1985). **Hobbies:** reading, sports, travelling, cars. **Addr.:** P.O.Box 950573, Amman, Jordan.

TALAAT (Ahmed, Samih), Egyptian lawyer and politician. **Born** in 1920 in Cairo, Egypt. **Son** of Abd el-Wahab Pacha Talaat **and** Hamida Hilmy. **Married** to Nazly el-Chourbagy in 1955, two children. **Educ.:** Elsaideyha Secondary School, Faculty of Law. **Dipl.:** M.L. **Career:** Assistant Prosecutor (1942-51); Judge (1951-58); Deputy of Court (1958-59); Chief of Court (1959-63); Counsellor at Appeal Court (1963-67); General Lawyer (1967-69); expelled from office (1969); reinstated as counsellor for Court of Cassation (Supreme Court) (1972); Supreme Counsel, Union Supreme Court, United Arab Emirates (1973-76); Minister of Justice, Egypt (1976-78); resigned (1978); member Shoura Association (1980); lawyer and Law consultant (since 1978). **Decorations:** Kuwait Badge of Honour (First Class) (1977). **Hobbies:** rowing, reading, farming. **Addr.:** 321 el-Ahram Street, Guiza, Cairo, Egypt.

TALAAT (Mahmoud), Egyptian former dean of faculty, governor. **Born** in Egypt. **Educ.:** Faculty of Engineering. **Career:** Engineer, Former Managing Director, Misr Concrete Development Co.; Former Dean of Faculty of Engineering, Aïn Shams University; Governor of Damietta Province. **Addr.:** Damietta Province, Cairo, Egypt.

TALAWY (Farouk, al, Dr.), Egytian former governor of New Valley governorate. **Born** in 1940 at Bakariya Tetla, Minyeh, Egypt. **Married** and father of four sons. **Educ.:** Faculty of Agriculture, Minyeh University, and advanced agriculture studies in France. **Dipl.:** B.Sc. (Agriculture), M.Sc. (Agriculture), Ph.D. (Agriculture). **Career:** Lecturer at the Faculty of Agriculture, Minyeh University; appointed Secretary of the National Democratic Party, Minyeh (9 November 1980); Governor of the New Valley Governorate (1983). **Address:** New Valley Governorate, Egypt.

TALEB (Bashir), Iraqi army officer and diplomat. **Born** in Iraq. **Educ.:** Secondary and Military Academy. **Career:** in the Iraqi Armed Forces; promoted Colonel; Commander of the Republican Guard; promoted General (1967); Ambassador of Iraq to Jordan (1968-69). **Addr.:** Baghdad, Iraq.

TALEB (Bassam), Syrian journalist. **Born** in 1945, in Damascus. **Married**, one son. **Educ.:** B.A. in Philosophy and Sociology. **Career:** Editor of "Diyaruna Wal Aalam" a magazine financed by the Ministry of Finance and Petroleum in Qatar (since 1976). **Publ.:** A novel in Arabic. **Hobby:** Reading. **Addr.:** P.O.Box 3534, Doha, Qatar.

TALEB (Choaïb), Algerian diplomat. **Born** in Tlemcen. **Married** to Miss Leila, 2 daughters: Lamia and Amal. **Educ.:** Paris Faculty of Medicine, Lausanne Faculty of Political Science. **Dipl.:** Bachelor of Political Science. **Career:** One of the founders of the Revolutionary Organization UGEMA (Union Générale des Etudiants 1955); Arrested for political reasons 4 times (1955-58); Returned to Algeria (1962); Joined Ministry of Foreign Affairs; Delegate to France (1963-67); Algerian Ambassador to Lebanon (1967). **Prof. Addr.:** Ministry of Foreign Affairs, Algiers, Algeria.

TALHI (Jadallah Azzuz, al), Libyan former secretary of the people's committee. **Dipl.:** Degree in Civil Engineering, University of Liege. **Career:** Mines Department, Ministry of Industry and Minerals, Minister of Industry and Minerals (16 July 1972-77); Secretary, Industry and Minerals, General People's Committee (March 1977-1979). Secretary of the General People's Committee (1979-1987) Secretary of the People's Committee of the People's Bureau for Foreign Liason (1988-89); Secretary of the GPC for Strategic Industries (1992); Secretary for the Great Man-made River Project (1994-). **Addr.:** Office of the Secretary. Tripoli, Libya.

TALHOUNI (Adnan), Jordanian diplomat. **Born** in 1947 in Irbid, Jordan. **Married**, 3 children. **Educ.:** American University of Beirut, Lebanon; Columbia University, USA; Middle East Institute, Columbia University. **Dipl.:** B.A. in Political Science, M.A. in International Affairs, Certificate in Middle East Studies. **Career:** Assistant Secretary General, Assistant Chief of Protocol, Royal Hashemite Court, Amman, Jordan (1973-85); Ambassador to Switzerland and Austria (1985-90); Director of European Section, Ministry of Foreign Affairs, Jordan, (1990-91); Ambassador to Morocco (1991-93); Director of the Office of Her Majesty Queen Noor, Amman, Jordan; Presently Ambassador to France. **Decor.:** decorations from Spain, France, Austria, Italy, West Germany, Egypt and **the**

United Kingdom. **Prof. Addr.:** Embassy of Jordan, Paris, France.

TALLAB (Ra'fat Hashim), Saudi senior civil servant. **Born** in 1938. **Dipl.:** B.Com. (Accountancy and Business Administration); several courses in sales, reservation, traffic, freight, administration. **Career:** Clerk (1956); Deputy Director of Land Department, Jeddah Municipality (1958); Director of Technical Department (1960); Freight Agent, Saudia-Saudi Arabian Airlines (1964); Deputy Manager, Freight Administration (1966); Accounting Auditor; attended several Conferences, including Arab Air Carriers Organisation-Beirut; Association of Islamic Countries Airlines, MEOCA (Middle East Operating Carriers Association); Saudia's Chief Accredited Representative to IATA Tariff Conferences, Chairman of Yield Improvement Committee for Saudi Arabia, Secretary of the Board of Airlines Representatives (BAR) for Saudi Arabia; Member of IATA Passengers & Steering Group + Member of IATA Interline Proration Advisory Committee; now General Manager, Industry IATA Affairs Department, Saudi Arabian Airlines. **Hobbies:** Reading, writing. **Priv. Addr.:** Tel.: 6726362, Jeddah, Saudi Arabia.

TAMARZISTE (Muhammad Bechir), Tunisian economist. **Born** in 1957 in Kairouan, Tunisia. **Educ.:** Institut Supérieur de Commerce, Paris, France, also studied in Tunis, Tunisia. **Career:** Development Bank (1982-83); General Manager of Compagnie Tunisienne des Lampes (CTC) (1983-). **Prof. Addr.:** Km 2, Route de Sousse, Sidi Fathallah 2023 Tunis, Tunisia.

TAMEEM (Mohsin Mohammed, Al, Dr.), Saudi professor. **Born** in 1950 at Wadi ed-Dawasir. **Dipl.:** M.B., B.Sc., F.R.C.S. **Career:** Professor and Consultant, General Surgery, Faculty of Medicine, King Saud University; Executive Director, Academic Affairs Dept., Saudi National Guard Health Affairs. **Sports:** swimming. **Prof. Addr.:** Faculty of Medicine, King Saud University, Riyadh. Saudi Arabia. **Priv. Addr.:** P.O.Box 2925, Riyadh 11461, Tel.: 467-1575.

TAMER (Farouk Mohamad Said), Saudi businessman. **Born** in 1932, Jeddah. **Dipl.:** Bachelor of Pharmacy. **Career:** Chairman of Farouk, Maamoun Tamer & Co.; Major dealer in: Pharmaceutical, Medical Supplies and Equipment, Toiletteries, Cosmetics, Food Stuff and Consuler Products. **Hobbies:** Photography, reading, sailing, travel. **Prof. Addr.:** P.O.Box 180, Jeddah 21411, Saudi Arabia, Tel.: (Office) 6435600, (Home) 6694325, Jeddah, Saudi Arabia.

TAMER (Maamoun Mohamad Said), Saudi businessman. **Born** in 1934, in Jeddah. **Dipl.:** B. Com.; **Career:** Owner, President of Farouk, Maamoun Tamer & Co. Major dealer in pharmaceuticals, Medical Equipment and Supplies and Consumer Products. **Sports:** Horseriding, swimming. **Hobbies:** Photography, reading. **Addr.:** Farouk, Maamoun Tamer & Co., Tamer Building, Wadi Huraymelaa' Street, al-Ammariyah District, P.O.Box 180, Jeddah 21411, Tel.: 6435600, Fax: 6439839, Telex: 601215 TAMER SJ., Saudi Arabia.

TAMIMI (Adnan Amin), Iraqi former UN official. **Born** in 1919 in Nablus. **Married. Educ.:** American University of Beirut, Lebanon; Birmingham University, UK; Columbia University, USA. **Dipl.:** B.A., M.S. **Career:** Deputy Resident Representative, UN Development Programme (UNDP), Egypt; Senior Programme Officer, United Nations Industrial Development Organization (UNIDO), Vienna, Austria; Assistant Chief, Technical Assistant Unit, Economic Commision for Asia and the Far East, UN, Bangkok, Thailand; Programme Officer, Technical Assistant, Administration, UN, New York; Social Affairs Officer, Department of Economic and Social Affairs (ESA), UN; Social Affairs Officer, United Nations Economic and Social Office in Beirut (UNESOB), Beirut; Senior Programme Management Officer, Section for Africa, UNIDO, Austria; Retired in 1983. **Hobbies:** swimming, sports, tennis. **Addr.:** Baghdad, Iraq.

TAMIMI (Amer, Zeyab Bader, al), Kuwaiti executive. **Born** in 1944 in Kuwait. **Son** of Zeyab Bader Tamimi. **Married** in 1970, 2 sons, 2 daughters. **Educ.:** Clarkson College, New York; US Census Bureau. **Dipl.:** B.Sc. (Economics) (1968); Diploma in Statistics (1973). **Career:** Statistical Controller, Central Statistics Office Planning Board, Kuwait (1968-75); Deputy Manager, Kuwait Real Estate Investment Consortium (1975-80); Managing Director, Farah-Maghreb, Casablanca, Morocco (1980-). **Addr.:** 46 Avenue des F.A.R., Tel.: 313096, Casablanca 01, Morocco.

TAMIMI (Hamdi A.), Arab-American academic. **Born** in 1924 in Hebron, Palestine. **Married**, 5 children. **Educ.:** Sterling College, USA, University of Colorado, School of Medicine, Denver, Colorado, USA. **Dipl.:** B.Sc., M.Sc. and Ph.D. **Career:** Fellow in Microbiology, Columbia School of Medine; Instructor at School of Nursing, Colorado General Hospital (1955-57); Research Associate and acting Chairman, Microbiology Department, School of Dentistry, WEashington University, ST. Louis, USA (1957-59); Professor and Chairman, Microbiology Department, school of Dentistry, University of Pacific, San Francisco, USA (1960-); Lecturer, University of California, Berkeley, USA (1961-76); Lecturer on Human Diseases, College of Marin, Kentfield, California, USA (1968-79); Consultant, Mary's Help Hospital, Daly City, California, USA (1968-73); Chairman, Faculty Appointments and Promotions Committee, University of the Pacific (1964-66); Lecturer on Human Diseases, Merck Chemical Company, San Francisco, USA (1969) and Veteran Administration Hospital, San Francisco, USA (1175-78);

Committee Member on Professional Education and Admission, American Dental Association, Chicago, Illinois, USA (1970-73); President of Islamic Center of San Francisco Inc., San Francisco California, USA (1968-73); Member of the American Association of Dental Schools, Chicago, Illinois (1972-77); Member of the American Society of Microbiology, American Association of University Professors, New York Academy of Sciences, International Association of Dental Research and several other associations and societies. **Publ.:** numerous articles in professional journals. **Priv. Addr.:** 113 Yolo Street, Corte Madera, CA 94925, USA.

TAMMAR (Abdul Wahab, al), Kuwaiti executive. **Born** in 1926. **Career:** Former Chairman, Sudanese-Kuwaiti Investment Company, Sudan; Chairman, Arab Banking Corporation; Chairman, Arab Insurance Group BSC, Bahrain; Vice Chairman, Banco Arabe Espanol, Spain; Chairman, Arab Latin American Bank, Peru; Chairman, Kuwait Foreign Trading, Contracting and Investment Co. SAK and its offshore, the Afro-Arab Company for Investment and Trade. **Addr.:** Kuwait City, Kuwait.

TARAMAN (Khalil Shawki), Arab-American academic. **Born** in 1939 in Cairo, Egypt. **Married**, 2 sons. **Educ.:** Ain Shams University, Egypt; University of Wisconsin, USA; Texas Technical University, USA. **Dipl.:** B.Sc., M.Sc. in Mechanical Engineering, Ph.D. **Career:** Instruction at Ain Shams University, Cairo, Egypt (1964-67); Instruction at the University of Wisconsin, USA (1967-69); Research Fellow, Texas Technical University (1969-70); Assistant Professor, University of Detroit (1970-73); Associate Professor (1973-76); Director of Manufacturing Engineering, University of Detroit; Professor and Chairman of Mechanical Engineering Department, University of Detroit (1977-); Consultant to Ford Motors, General Electric, US Arabian Development and Bendix; supervised research at Chrysler and Carboloy Systems of General Electric; Member of the American Institute of Industrial Engineers, Westinghouse and General Motors, American Society of Engineering Education, the American Society of Mechanical Engineers and Numerical Control Society; International Directory, Society of Manufacturing Engineers; Chairman of the Founder Chapter, Society of Manufacturing Engineers; Member of the Egyptian American Scholars' Association and of the International Education Committee; Vice Chairman of the International Machining Technology Division; Chairman of the Material Removal Council; Member of Alpha Pi Mu Honor Society of Industrial Engineers and the Pi Tau Sigma Honor Society of Mechanical engineers; Member of the International Honor Awards Committee. **Publ.:** "Computer Aided Design/Computer Aided Manufacturing" (1980), SME Books as well as numerous articles and reviews in engineering and technical journals. **Medal:** Medal of Science, the Best Instruction and Outstanding Educator of America. **Hobbies:** classical music, tennis, travelling. **Prof. Addr.:** Department of Mechanical Engineering, University of Detroit, Detroit, Michigan 48221, USA.

TARAWNAH (Ahmad, Mahmud, al), Jordanian politician. **Born** in 1920 in Karak, Jordan. **Son** of Mahmud al-Tarawnah. **Married**, three children. **Educ.:** B.A. in Law, University of Damascus, Syria. **Career:** Judge (1942-50); member of the Chamber of Deputies (1950-60); President of the Chamber of Deputies; member of the Regency Council; Minister of Agriculture and Commerce (1950); Minister of Communications and Public Works (1954); Minister of Education (1957); Minister of Finance (1958); Minister of Defence (1959); Minister of Justice (1960); Chief of the Royal Court; President of the East Ghor Canal Authority (1963); Chief of the Civil Service Commission (1965); Deputy Prime Minister and Minister of the Interior (1972-73); President of the National Consultative Council; Senator. **Publ.:** Numerous articles published in journals and magazines. **Medals:** Order of Independence, Jordan; Order of the Jordanian Star, Jordan; Order of Renaissance, Jordan; Higher Order of Renaissance, Jordan; Order of Education, Jordan; Order of the Tunisian Republic; Order of Al Alawi, Morocc; several other decorations from various countries. **Sports:** riding, walking, gymnastics. **Hobbies:** Chess, backgammon, reading Arabic and English poetry, history and religion. **Addr.:** P.O.Box 2453, Tel.: 21512, 41719, Amman, Jordan.

TARAWNAH (Naji, Hussain), Jordanian judge. **Born** in 1930. **Married. Educ.:** Damascus University, Syria. **Dipl.:** B.A. in Law. **Career:** Judge at the Ministry of Justice (1955-72); President of the Income Tax Board of Appeal (1972-74); Minister of Justice (1974-76). **Addr.:** Jabal Amman, Amman, Jordan.

TARAZI (Fuad, Philip), Iraqi lawyer and journalist. **Born** in 1926 in Basra. **Son** of Philip Tarazi. **Educ.:** College of Law. **Dipl.:** Bachelor of Law. **Career:** Lawyer and Journalist. **Publ.:** Author of "Marxism". **Member:** Lawyer's Club, Teachers Club. **Hobbies:** Swimming and Tennis. **Addr.:** Boustan al-Khass, Baghdad, Iraq.

TARBAGHIA (Mansour, Saleh), Libyan businessman. **Born** in 1940 in Benghazi, Libya. **Son** of Saleh H. Tarbaghia **and** Mrs. Kadige M. **Married** to Badria Omar, 9 children. **Educ.:** Benghazi Higher School (Business and Management School). **Dipl.:** received Higher Diploma. **Career:** Chairman of Tarbaghia & Bros.; Chairman of AL TAAWAN GENERAL SERVICE COMPANY; Manager of Customs Clearance Office; Member of Libyan Chamber of Commerce; Member of Libyan Businessmen Society; Member of Libyan Trade Union. **Sport:** Football. **Prof. Addr.:** Tarbaghia & Bros. Company, P.O.Box 21, Benghazi, Libya.

TARBAGHIA (Nabil M.), Libyan businessman. **Born**

on June 20, 1967 in Benghazi, Libya. **Son** of Mansour Tarbaghia **and** Mrs. Badria née Omar. **Educ.:** Department of Computer Sciences, Faculty of Sciences, Garyounis University. **Dipl.:** B.Sc. (Computer Science). **Memberships:** Member of American Institute of Management Sciences (U.S.A.). Member, International Energy Science; Member, Libyan Trade Union. **Career:** Chairman of AL-ASSER AL HADEATH COMPANY for manufacturing Computers; Accounts manager of Tarbaghia Company; Director of AL TAAWAN GENERAL SERVICE CO. **Sports:** Football, Swimming. **Address:** P.O.Box 21, Benghazi, Libya.

TARBAGHIA (Tarek M.), Libyan mechanical engineer. **Born** on June 6, 1966 in Benghazi, Libya. **Son** of Mansour Tarbaghia **and** Mrs. Badria née Omar. **Educ.:** Benghazi Higher Secondary School, Faculty of Engineering; Garyounis University, B.Sc. (Eng.). **Dipl.:** Diploma in Mechanical Engineering (Honours), Master Degree in Mechanical Engineering, M.Sc. (Mech.). **Career:** Chairman of Corrosion Society; Chairman of AL-TAAWAN Consultant Office. **Memberships:** Member of American Institute of Management Sciences (U.S.A.); Member of Network Center (U.K.); Member of Libyan Enineering Union; Member of Materials Society; Member of Hydrogen Society; Member of Solar Society; Member of Plant Institute; Member of Mechanical Engineers Institute; Member of Production Institute; Associate Member of Royal Aeronautical Society (U.K.); Member of Bayan Society for Science; Member of British Academy of Management; Member of World Network; Member of World Renewable Energy; Member of Libyan Ultrasonic Society; Member of Libyan Engineering society; Founder Member of Environment Society; Member of Engineering Journal; Chairman of Corrosion Society; Chairman of First International Conference for Environment and Development. **Publications:** Four Papers in Mechanical Engineering (Design Cad and Cam); Two Papers in Project Management; One Paper in Solar Energy; One Paper in the Field of Finite Element Method; One Paper in the Field of Materials Engineering. **Books:** Co-author of a Book Title "Strength of Materials Laboratory", Co-author of "Industrial Management and Operation Research (under press). Published 38 papers in Engineering field in International conferences held in Libya, Egypt, Morocco, England, Ireland, China, Italy, Denmark, Germany, Pakistan, Belgium, U.S.A., Swotzerland, Sudan, Singapore, Korea. **Honours:** Annual Award of Distinguished from Academic Research Institute (1990); Prize of Technical Education (1992); Prize of Bayan Society for Science (1993). **Career:** General Manager of Tarbaghia Company; Director of All-Taawan General Service Company; Deputy Chairman of al-Asser al-Hadeath Company for Manufacturing Computers. **Sports:** Golf, Basket Ball, Billiard. **Member:** of Football Club, Member of Basket Ball Club, Member of Golf Club. **Hobbies:** Classical music, collecting antique pens, and antique paintings. **Address:** P.O.Box 21, Benghazi, Libya.

TARIQI (Abdallah), Saudi oil executive. **Born** in 1919. **Son** of Houmoud **and** Lolwa Tariki. **Married** first time Eleanor Nicholas (1948), second time Maha Jumblatt (1969), two children. **Educ.:** Universities of Cairo and Texas. **Career:** worked as trainee with Texaco Inc. in W. Texas and California (1945-49); Director, Oil Supervision Office, Eastern Province, Saudi Arabia (under Ministry of Finance 1949-55); Director General of Oil and Mineral Affairs (Saudi Arabia 1955-60); Minister of Oil and Mineral Resources (1960) Director Arabian American Oil Co. (1959-62); Leader Saudi Arabian delegation at Arab Oil Congresses (1959, 1960); Independent Petroleum Consultant (since 1962); Chairman Arab Petroleum Consultants; co founder of OPEC; **Publisher** of monthly petroleum magazine Naft el-Arab; adviser to Algerian, Libyan, Emirates and Kuwait governments on oil matters. **Hobbies:** breeding Arab horses. **Addr.:** KAC Building, floor 10, Apt. 3, al-Sharie al-Hilali, Kuwait, P.O.Box 22699 Safat, Kuwait.

TARKAIT (Salah, Abdul Wahab, al), Kuwaiti administrator. **Born** in 1951. **Married,** 2 children. **Dipl.:** B.Sc. in Industrial Engineering, M.A. in Business Administration. **Career:** Project Manager and Deputy Director, National Industries Company (1969-79); Chairman of the Board of Directors of Kuwaiti Plastics and Concrete Manufacturer (1978-80); Member of the Board of Directors of Electronic Calculator Co. (1983-); Chairman of the Board of Directors of a Mining and Industrial Company in the United Arab Emirates (1985-); Director, National Industries Company (1985-). **Prof. Addr.:** National Industries Company, P.O.Box 3314 Safat, Kuwait, Kuwait.

TARQAN (Abdall Mohamad Said), Jordanian (banking-computer system analyst). **Born** on July 27, 1964. **Son** of Mohamad Said (Landlord) **and** Mrs. Rashd Habjoka-F. **Educ.:** Islamic High School, University of Jordan. **Career:** System Computer Analyst and Programmer from 1986 to 1991; Chief of Computer Section in J.C.O. Bank; **Member,** The National Association for Consumer Protection. **Sports:** Swimming. **Member:** al-Jel Club, al-Ahle Club. **Prof. Addr.:** The Co-operative Bank, P.O.Box 1343, Tel. 665171-4, Telex: JO 21835, Amman, Jordan. **Priv. Addr.:** Tel. 667762, Amman, Jordan.

TARRAF (Noureddine), Egyptian physician and former statesman. **Born** in Egypt. **Educ.:** Secondary and Faculty of Medicine. **Dipl.:** Doctor of Medicine. **Career:** Former President Executive Council of Egyptian Region of United Arab Republic (1958-60) during the merger between Egypt and Syria; Minister of Health (1961-62); member Presidency Council (1962); Deputy Prime Minister and Minister of Justice, Labour and Youth Affairs (1964-66). **Addr.:** Cairo, Egypt.

TARYAM (Abdullah, Omran, Dr.), UAE politician. **Born** in 1945 in Sharjah, United Arab Emirates. **Married,**

2 sons, 1 daughter. **Educ.:** Cairo University, Egypt. **Dipl.:** B.A. in Literature and History. **Career:** Director of Education, Sharjah Government (1968-71); Editor of "al-Khalij" newspaper Minister of Justice in first United Arab Emirates Government (1971-72); Minister of Education (1972-77); Minister of Education (1977); Minister of Justice (1996). **Decor.:** Orders from Tunisia and Morocco. **Hobbies:** poetry, literature, basket-ball, volley-ball, tennis. **Prof. Addr.:** Ministry of Justice, Sharjah, United Arab Emirates.

TASHKANDI (Abbas Saleh), Saudi academic. **Born** in 1945 in Mecca. **Educ.:** Cairo. **Dipl.:** B.L.S. (1965); M.L.S. (1969) and Ph.D. (Arabic Manuscripts), Pittsburgh University (1974). **Career:** Assistant Librarian, King Abdulaziz University (1966-68); participated in establishing King Abdulaziz University Library and a specialized Library for Saudia-Saudi Arabian Airlines Corporation; Assistant Professor and Dean of Library Affairs (1974-84); Now Professor and Secretary General of the Scientific Council of King Abdulaziz University, and Dean of Library Affairs (1995-). **Member:** ALA, Beta Phi Mu, IFLA, in U.S.A. **Publ.:** The Scientific Role of Libraries. **Sport:** Swimming. **Hobbies:** Chess, drawing. **Prof. Addr.:** King Abdulaziz University, P.O.Box 1540, Jeddah.

TASHKANDY (Abdul Jalil A.), Saudi faculty professor. **Born** in 1942 in Kabul, Afghanistan. **Dipl.:** Ph.D. (Library and Information Sciences). **Career:** Library Technician (1968-70); Head of Arabic Section (1970-72); Demonstrator, KAU (1973); Lecturer (1977); Assistant Professor, Faculty of Arts and Humanities, King Abdulaziz University, Jeddah; member, American Library Association and Federation International Documentation; attended the 2nd Conference of Arab Bibliography, 1977; participant member of the Conference on the Information Networks, Pittsburgh, 1979 and the American Library Association, 1980; participated in establishing several libraries. **Publications:** Ph.D. Thesis Bibliographical Contral of Saudi Arabia, 1977; writes occasionally in al-Bilad and Okaz daily newspapers and the magazine of the Faculty of Arts and Humanities, KAU. **Hobbies:** reading, swimming, travelling. **Address:** Faculty of Arts and Humanities, KAU, Tel.: 6879130 and 6879202 (Office) and 687-5046 (Home), Jeddah, Saudi Arabia, Jeddah and Okaz Organization for Press and Publication, P.O.Box 1508, Jeddah 21441, Saudi Arabia.

TASHKANDY (Abdulaziz Mohamad Issa), Saudi eye surgeon. **Born** in 1926, Mecca. **Educ.:** in Cairo. **Dipl.:** M.B., C.H.B. (1958 Cairo), D.O.M.S. (Alexandria 1964); U.K. post-graduate studies for F.R.C.S., Birmingham; U.K. post-graduate studies for M.S.; D.O.M.S. Barraquer Institute, Spain. **Career:** Eye Surgeon and Director of the Eye Hospital in Jeddah (1960), Mecca (1960), Riyadh (1970); Medical Officer, Cairo University Hospital, Moorfields Eye Hospital and others in the U.K.; owns private clinics in Saudi Arabia; external examiner in the Riyadh Faculty of Medicine; **Member** of Egyptian Medical Association (1958), Egyptian Ophtalmic Committee (1958), Oxford Ophtalmic Congress (1966); appointed by the Ministry of Health to supervise and improve eye services in Saudi Hospitals, undertaking research into operations by unqualified doctors for trichiasis and cataract in some rural districts; Eye Surgeon and Chief, Eye Department, Riyadh Central Hospital. **Member:** the Barraquer Institute (1975). **Publ.:** Several scientific articles and lectures; radio and television interviews; a book on eye diseases. **Sport:** Swimming. **Hobbies:** Reading, gardening. **Prof. Addr.:** P.O.Box 15042, Tel.: 453 1900, Riyadh. **Priv. Addr.: Tel.:** 4658321, 4658461, Riyadh, Saudi Arabia.

TASHKANDY (Ahmad Mohamad), Saudi executive. **Born** in 1929 in Mecca, Saudi Arabia. **Dipl.:** B.Sc. (Commerce), Cairo University, (1958) **Career:** Director-General of Jeddah Chamber of Commerce and Industry (1959-62); Economic Consultant, Ministry of Petroleum and Mineral Wealth, Riyadh (1963-69); Chairman of Board, al-Arra Electric Co.; Director-General of the Administration, General Electrical Establishment; member of several OPEC Conferences; member of conferences of Arab League Economic Council. **Publications:** Aramco and Oil Concessions; The OPEC: the Right Path for Oil Solidarity. **Honour:** Spanish Order of Merit (Class of Knight). **Addr.:** General Electrical Establishment, Riyadh, Saudi Arabia.

TASHKANDY (Farhat Khourshid), Saudi Consultant. **Born** in 1950 at Taif, Saudi Arabia, **Dipl.:** M. Architecture (MIT, USA). **Career:** Lecturer, College of Architecture & Planning, King Saud University (1979); Consultant, **Al-Naim Architects Engineers and Planning Consultants. Prof. Addr.:** P.O.Box 27360, Riyadh 11417, **Tel.:** 4731143. **Priv. Addr.:** 4932834, Riyadh, Saudi Arabia.

TASHKANDY (Mohamad Ali), Saudi professor. **Born** in 1939 in Taif, Saudi Arabia. **Dipl.:** Ph.D. (Civil Engineering) **Career:** Assistant Professor, Faculty of Engineering, Riyadh University. **Publications:** research papers on construction works and reinforced concrete. **Hobbies:** Reading, sport. **Address:** P.O.Box 800, Riyadh, Saudi Arabia.

TASSAN (Ibrahim, Abdulrahman, al), Saudi official. **Born** in 1937 in Mecca, Saudi Arabia. **Dipl.:** M.A. (Public Administration). **Career:** Department Head, Ministry of Finance (1959), Director of Deputy Minister's Office (1960), General Inspector (1969); Deputy Minister for Administration, Ministry of Finance; member of Board, Agricultural Bank, Hotel and Recreation Resorts Company, African Development Bank. **Hobbies:** Reading, travel. **Address:** P.O.Box 131, 4023160 (Office) and 4769951 (Home), Riyadh, Saudi Arabia.

TATAWY (Nawal, Abdel-Moneim, el, Dr.), Egyptian former Minister of Economy and Foreign Trade, (Jan. 2, 1996 -July 8, 1997). **Born** on September 14, 1942 in Cairo. **Daughter** of Dr. Abdel-Monem el-Tatawy (Radiologist) **and** Mrs. H. Zayed. **Married** to Mohamed Kassem (Economist financial analyst), two sons: Hisha and Sherif. **Educ.:** American College for Girls, Cairo, Egypt; American University in Cairo, Egypt; University of Wisconsin, Madison, Wisconsin, U.S.A. **Dipl.:** High School and College Diploma; B.A. in Economics and Political Science; M.A. and Ph.D. in Economics. **Career:** National Bank of Egypt, Cairo (1970-71); United Nations, New York (1973-74); World Bank, Washington, D.C. (1975-79); General Manager, Investment Sector, Arab Investment Bank, Cairo (1979-to date responsible for all medium and long-term lending, appraising and setting up projects, equity participations, companies follow-up. Participated in numerous conferences and seminars and publications in Egypt and abroad in the Fields of economics, business, management and finance. **Sports:** Tennis, Walking. **Hobbies:** Reading, Listening to music. **Member:** Shooting Club, Dokki, Giza. **Prof. Addr.:** Arab Investment Bank, 1113 Cornish el-Nil Street, P.O.Box 1147, Tel.: 753116, Cairo, Egypt. **Priv. Addr.:** 16, Square 26 of July, Agouza, Giza, Egypt.

TAWASHI (Rashad, Kamel, al), Arab-Canadian professor of industrial pharmacy. **Born** on September 26, 1933 in Giza, Egypt. **Son** of late Kamel Hassan Tawashi **and** Mrs. Zeinab Tawashi. **Married** on November 16, 1961 to Miss Eitedal el-Simillawi, 4 children: Maha (1962), Manal (1963), Ahmad (1967) and Mona (1969).**Educ.:** University of Alexandria, Egypt; University of Basel, Switzerland. **Dipl.:** B.Sc. Pharmacy, University of Alexandria (1955); Ph.D. Pharmacy technology, University of Basel (1960). **Career:** Research Scientist, Ciba AG, Basel (1961); Lecturer of Industrial Pharmacy. University of Alexandria (1961-65); Research Associate, University of Michigan (1965-67); Assistant Professor (1967), Associate Professor (1970), Full Professor (1975), University of Montreal, Canada; Visiting Professor, University of Montpellier France (1973); Visiting Scientist at the Federal Institute of Technology, Zurich (1971); member of different scientific and professional Associations; Chairman, Montreal Pharmaceutical Discussions Group; participated in the establishment of the 1st School of Pharmacy in Libya (1975). President, Association of Faculties of Pharmacy of Canada (1984). **Awards:** Visiting Scientist award from the Medical Research Council of Canada; listed in Who is Who in the East American Men and Women of Science; Who is Who in Education. **Member:** AAAS, New York Academy of Science. **Prof. Addr.:** Faculty of Pharmacy, University of Montreal, Tel.: 3436455, Montreal, Quebec. **Priv. Addr.:** 66 Hyde Park Beaconsfield, Quebec, Tel.: 6951210, Canada.

TAWATI (Ahmad M.), Saudi academic. **Born** on 20 October 1939 in Mecca, Saudi Arabia. **Dipl.:** Ph.D. (Political Science). **Career:** head of the Department of Industrial Statistics, Ministry of Commerce and Industry (1962-65); Director of Administration, King Abdulaziz University (1972-74); Secretary General of Master Plan, King Abdulaziz University (1976-79); Assistant Professor, 1976; Associate Professor and Assistant Dean for Graduate Studies and Scientific Researches, Faculty of Economics and Administration K.A.U. Head of Equestrian Club, K A U; **Member:** American Society for Public Administration, American Political Science Association; has attended many conferences on political science and public administration. **Publications:** Several research papers on public administration published in the Journal of Economics and Administration, Faculty of Economics and Administration, King Abdulaziz University. **Address:** P.O.Box. 9031, King Abdulaziz University, Tel.: 6952139 (Office) and 6205841, Mobile: 55691044 Jeddah, Saudi Arabia.

TAWFIK (Abdel Fattah, Zakaria), Egyptian executive. **Born** in 1920 in Egypt. **Educ.:** Cairo University, Egypt. **Career:** Bank Misr; Commercial Attaché, Brussels, Madrid (1948-57); Director General, Exchange Control Office (1961); Under-Secretary for Cotton Affairs, Ministry of Economy (1961-65); Chairman, Cotton Organization (1965-75); Minister of Commerce and Supply (1975-78); President, Afro-Asian Organisation for Economic Cooperation (1972); Member, Economic Researches Council, Academy of Scientific Research. former Chairman, Suez Canal Bank, Cairo, Egypt. **Awards:** From Italy, Belgium, France, Greece and Spain. **Addr.:** Cairo, Egypt.

TAWFIK (Ahmad, Talaat), Egyptian politician. **Born** in 1921 in Tantah city (Egypt). **Educ.:** Faculty of Engineering, Cairo University; studied Aeronautics in USA. **Dipl.:** B.Sc. (Engineering) (1942), B.Sc. (Aeronautics); **Career:** Director, Cairo International Airport; Board Chairman, Messrs. EGYCO (a Contracting and Engineering firm); General Manager, Engineering and Industrial Projects Company; General Manager, General Contracting Organisation; seconded to Libya in January 1977 where he served as Director, Executive Reconstruction Department, Tripoli; Minister of Housing, Cairo (1978). **Prof. Addr.:** Cairo, Egypt.

TAWFIK (Farouk M. Omar), Saudi civil servant. **Born** in 1943 in Mecca, Saudi Arabia. **Dipl.:** M.A. (History). **Career:** Secretary, Ministry of Foreign Affairs (1972-73); First Secretary, Saudi Embassy, London (1973). participates in the activities of the London Islamic Centre. **Publications:** Several articles in various press media. **Hobbies:** Reading, writing, chess. **Address:** Embassy of Saudi Arabia, London, U.K.

TAWFIK (Mohamad Omar, Sheikh), Saudi man of

letters and intellectual. **Educ.:** Graduated from Dar el-Ulum al-Sharia (School of Islamic Sciences), Medina. **Career:** Teacher at Dar el-Aytam (Orphan School), Medina; civil servant, Directorate of Telegrams and Post; civil servant, Omul Qura Official Bulletin; Official, Office of the Attorney General; retired from civil service at his request; private business; chosen by the Late King Faisal as Minister of Communications, in King Khaled's First Cabinet, was reappointed for the same portfolio; contributed through extensive writings to the development of Saudi cultural life. **Publ.:** articles, radio talks, active participation in literary and cultural papers and magazines. **Hobbies:** Reading, writing. **Prof. Addr.:** P.O.Box. 6063, Jeddah.

TAWFIK (Mustafa, Mohamad), Egyptian diplomat. **Born** in 1924 in Cairo, Egypt. **Married**, 2 children. **Educ.:** Madrid University, Spain. **Dipl.:** B.Sc. in Military Science, B.A. in Political Science. **Career:** Adviser Embassies in Spain (1961-64), Libya (1964-67); Ambassador to North Korea (1969-71), to Kenya (1971-74), to East Germany (1975-77) and to Argentina (1980-). **Decor.:** Order of Merit (1st Class), Egypt (1977). **Medal:** Medal of the Republic (2nd Class) (1968), Medal of Merit, Knight Order, Argentina (1984). **Hobbies:** swimming, tennis, golf. **Member:** Diplomatic Club, Cairo Automobile Club and Gezira Sporting Club. **Addr.:** 4 Yahia Ibrahim Street, Apt. 6, Zamalek, Cairo, Egypt.

TAWFIK (Nizar Ibrahim), Saudi official. **Born** on 10 October 1944 in Taif, Saudi Arabia. **Dipl.:** Ph.D. (Organic Chemistry). **Career:** Instructor, King Abdulaziz University (1970); Vice Dean, Faculty of Education (1970-72); Dean, Faculty of Science (1972-78); Dean, Faculty of Meteorology and Environmental Studies, king Abdulaziz University, (1981-82); Director General, National Metreorological and Environmental Centre (MEPA) (1978-88); Vice President, Metreology and Environmental Protection Administration (MEPA), Ministry of Defence and Aviation since 1988. **Publications:** Textbooks; Practical chemistry, Organic Chemistry; Fifteen published papers. **Hobbies:** Reading, Photography. **Address:** P.O.Box: 11760, Jeddah 21463, Saudi Arabia, Tel.: 6519868 (office) and 6209743 (Home).

TAWFIK (Ruhiyah, Mohamad Tawfiq), Egyptian artist. **Born** in 1927. **Married**, 1 daughter. **Educ.:** Faculty of Fine Arts, Cairo University, Egypt; Prague Academy of Fine Arts, Czekoslovakia. **Dipl.:** Ph.D. in Fine Arts. **Career:** Sculptor and Head of Department of Ceramics, Agricultural Museum (1955-65); Director, Mohammad Mahmoud Khalil Museum, Ministry of Culture (1967-69); Consultant, Technical Office of the Minister of Culture (1981-). **Hobby:** classical music. **Member:** Sculptor's Association, Fine Arts Federation, Gezira Sporting Club. **Addr.:** Manzil 17, Shareh al-Brazil, Zamalek, Cairo, Egypt.

TAWFIK (Taher), Iraqi politician. **Born** in 1934, Andar Governorate, Iraq. **Dipl.:** Graduate College of Engineering, Baghdad University (1967). **Career:** Personal Secretary to President of Republic (1969-72); Member, Iraq Baath Party Regional Command (1977); Minister of State without portfolio (23 January 1977); Member, Revolutionary Command Council (September 1977); relieved of his post as Minister of State; Minister of Industry and Minerals (1980). **Addr.:** Baghdad, Iraq.

TAWFIK (Tawfik Ibrahim), Saudi businessman. **Born** in 1919. **Dipl.:** M.B.A. (Business Administration); courses in marketing and administration. **Career:** Director, Exhibitions Department, Ministry of Commerce; Director, Industrial Estates Department; Acting Director-General of Industry; Director of Industrial Information, Industrial Development and Research Centre; attended some UNICO conferences (United Nations Industrial Development Organization); Director-General of Supply, Ministry of Commerce, Riyadh; Director, Saudi Fisheries Co. **Sports:** Watching football. **Hobby:** Travel. **Addr.:** Riyadh, Saudi Arabia.

TAWIL (Bahgat, Ahmad, al), Egyptian diplomat. **Born** on November 23, 1917 in Alexandria (Egypt). **Educ.:** Faculty of Commerce, Cairo University (1935-39); Faculty of Sciences, Cairo University (1942-44); Columbia University, New York (1950-52). **Dipl.:** Bachelor of Commerce (1939); M.A. (statistics) (1944); Ph. D. (Econ. & Statistics) (1952). **Career:** Instructor (1940-46); visiting lecturer, School of Social Work, Cairo (1952-57); Special Assistant and counsel, Egyptian Embassy to US (1953-55); Director-General, Department of Statistics and Census, Cairo (1957-61); Director, Regional Statistical Training Centre (1961-62); Head, Statistics & Demography Division, Economic Commission for Africa (ECA), Addis Ababa (1962-65); Representative of UN Secretary General, East Pakistan (1971); Acting Director, OTC, ESA, UN (1972-73); Director, Office of the Assistant Secretary General for Special Political Questions, UNO, New York, (1974). **Member:** Egyptian Statistical Society; National Club of Commerce, Cairo. **Clubs:** Maadi Sporting Club, Cairo. **Addr.:** Cairo, Egypt.

TAWIL (Ibrahim, Abdul Fattah, al), Egyptian legal advisor, lawyer. **Born** in 1925 in Alexandria, Egypt. **Son** of Abdul Fattah al-Tawil. **Married**, two sons. **Educ.:** B.A., Law, Alexandria University (1946). **Career:** Lawyer (1946); Arab African International Bank (AAIB) Legal Department (1970); Assistant General Manager, Arab African International Bank (1975); Legal Adviser and Secretary General of the Board AAIB (since 1979). Member of the Egyptian Bar Association, Egyptian Automobile Club, Algezira Sport Club. **Hobbies:** Reading, tourism. **Addr.:** 44 Abdul Khalek Tharwat Street, Tel.: 916710,

920390, Telex: ARBFR 92071, ARBFRO 363, Cairo, Egypt.

TAYA (Maawiya Ould Sid Ahmed, Col.), President of Mauritania. **Career:** served in Saharan War (1976-78); Chief of Military Operations, then Commander garrison at Bir Mogkrein; Minister of Defence (1978-79); Commander national gendarmerie (1979-80); Minister in charge of Permanent Secr. Military Committee for National Recovery (1979-81); Army Chief of Staff (1980-81); (1984); President of Mauritania (since 1984- to date). **Addr.:** Office of the President, Présidence de la République, B.P. 184, Nouackchott, Mauritania.

TAYARA (Mohamad, Ghassan), Syrian engineer, politician. **Born** in 1938 in Syria. **Son** of Ghassan Tayara. **Married,** one son. **Educ.:** Diploma in Engineering, Moscow, USSR; Ph.D. in Technology. **Career:** Director of Center of Technical Training and Center of Development and Production, Damascus, Syria (1974-80); President of the Syndicate of Syrian Engineers (since 1980); member of the parliament (since 1980). **Publ.:** Articles and papers on production and development published in professional journals and magazines. **Sport:** Swimming. **Addr.:** P.O.Box 2336, Sahat Yusif al-Azma, Bina Dar, Tel.: 113540, 114916, Telex: 411962, Damascus, Syria.

TAYARD (Carol, Youssef), Lebanese architectural engineer. **Born** on March 3, 1936 in Bsous, Lebanon. **Son** of Youssef A. Tayard (Engineer-Contractor) and Mrs. Bertha F. Khalaf. **Married** on February 11, 1960 in Beirut to Miss Leila Dr. Youssef Hitti, 3 children: Bettina, Paola and Youssef. **Education:** American University of Beirut. **Dipl.:** B.S. in Architectural Engineering (1961); Complementary Studies "Construction Technology and Management" in coop. with University of Manchester, England and the British Building Research Station, London. **Career:** Ministry of Public Works, Architectural Department Security and Customs bldgs., Lebanon (1961-75); Owner and President of "Y.A.T.S. Co." Engineering Contracting and Trading, Lebanon (1965 to date); Managing Director, Aafak - Y.A.T.S. J.V., Engineering & Construction Division, Saudi Arabia (1978-80); President, Y.A.T.S. Co. Consulting, Contracting & Landscaping, Saudi Arabia (1981 to date) sponsored by Alafak Corp.: Carol Tayard and Associates: Architects, Interior Design and landscaping (1985 to date) Saudi Arabia, Lebanon and Greece; Founder, "Unpredictable architecture" (1993). **Works:** Architectural Designs: Palaces, Villas, Tourist Resorts, Municipal & Public Buildings (Turnkey); Civil Construction: Bridges, Compounds, Villas, Marinas, Municipal & Private; Interior Design and Landscaping, Municipal and Private (Turnkey). **Registration:** Class a Architect, Consultant, registered under No. 66 at Ministry of public works, Lebanon (1987); Architect, Consultant, Town Plannning Department Abu-Dhabi UAE (1976-92); Architect Consultant registered under No.19 at Ministry of Planning, Iraq (1977); Consultant in J.V. with Levantis, Athens, Greece (1982-85). **Branch Offices:** Y.A.T.S. Co. offshore, Limasol, Cyprus (since 1983); Y.A.T.S. Co. Itageno Projetti, Napoli, Italy (1972-76); Y.A.T.S. Co. Palpanis J.V., Athens, Greece (since 1974); Y.A.T.S. Engineering, Contracting and Trading, Beirut, Lebanon (since 1965), Saudi Arabia (since 1985), Carol Tayard and Associates, Lebanon (since 1975); "SARAB Art Gallery" Jeddah, Saudi Arabia (1978-80); "Atelier Carol Tayard" Zouk Mkayel Lebanon (since 1985); Y.A.T.S. C&G Computer and Graphic Arts, Lebanon (since 1996). **Sports:** Swimming, Tennis, Water sports, Body Buildings and Shooting, **Hobbies:** Antiques Collector, Painter and Arabic Poet Writer. **Member:** Lions Club, Beirut-Lebanon; Union of Architects and Engineers; A.U.B. President Club. **Credit Cards:** Golden Visa, American Express. **Adress:** Lebanon: Y.A.T.S. Carol Y. Tayard and Associates (Hamra - Naccash - Zouk Mkayel), P.O.Box 146 Zouk Mkayel, Lebanon, Tel.: 961 9 210821/2; Tel./Fax: 961 4 523119; Mobile: 961 3 341981, 961 3 309179; e-mail: caroltayard@lynx.net.lb and candg@inco,com.lb Saudi Arabia: Y.A.T.S. Carol Tayard and Associates, P.O.Box 2195, Jeddah 21451, Mobile 961 3 341981 Greece: Y.A.T.S. & Palpanis, 13 Peston Str., Gr-11362 Athens Tel.: 30 1 8251111, Fax: 30 1 8821324 Cyprus: Y.A.T.S.-Offshore, Limasol, Tel.: 357 5 321819.

TAYER (Ahmad, Humaid, al), United Arab Emirates statesman. **Born** in 1950 in United Arab Emirates. **Son** of Hamid al-Tayer. **Married. Educ.:** B.A. in Economics, Faculty of Economics and Political Science, Cairo University, Egypt (1973). **Career:** Director, Economic Department, Ministry of Finance and Industry (1973-74); Director General, Ministry of Finance and Industry (1974-78); Vice Chairman of Arab Investment and Foreign Trade Bank; Board of Amman Insurance Company; Alternate Governor of United Arab Emirates at International Monetary Fund and World Bank, Islamic Development Bank; Assistant Under Secretary, Ministry of Finance and Industry (1978-1986); Minister of State for Finance and Industry (1986-1996); Minister of Communication (1996- present); Chairman of Emirates International Bank; Chairman of Commercial Bank of Dubai Ltd. **Sport:** Football. **Hobbies:** Literature, science, economics. **Addr.:** Ministry of Communications, P.O.Box 900, Abu Dhabi, United Arab Emirates.

TAYIB (Abdallah, al), Sudanese writer and corresponding member of Academy of the Arabic Language. **Born** in 1921 in Damer West (Sudan). **Educ.:** Gordon University (Sudan); Higher Teacher's Training College (Sudan); School of Oriental and African Studies, London University. **Dipl.:** Teacher's Diploma (1942), Doctorate of Oriental Studies, London University Ph. D., London University (1949). **Career:** English Teacher, Bakht al-Redha Teacher Training Institute; joined Department of Arabic, University of Khartoum; Head, Faculty of Arabic, Ahmads

Bello University, Zaria, Nigeria (1964); Professor of Arabic, University of Khartoum, Then Dean of the Faculty of Arts (1966); Vice-Chancellor, University of Khartoum (July 1974); Professor Emeritus, University of Khartoum; Maître de Conference, Arabic Department, University of Mohamad Ben Abdallah, Fes, Morocco. **Member:** Linguistic Academy, Cairo; Committee to review structure of Khartoum University (1974). **Publ.:** Author of various publications, including "Guide to Arabic Versification", "Friend of the Nile", "Key to Four Poems by Zir-Remma", "Modern tendencies in Prose - writing", "The Volcanoes", "The Changing Customs of Riverain Sudan", "Abbas Mahmoud al-Akkad, The Poet", "Night and the Stars", "The Nature of Arabic Verse". **Addr.:** P.O.Box 1996, Khartoum, Sudan.

TAYIB (Abdul Malik, al), Yemeni diplomat. **Born** in 1935 in al-Nadra, Yemen. **Educ.:** in Sanaa. **Career:** Minister of Education (1968-69); candidate for the three members Republican Council (May 1972); Head of Council of Ministers, Action Committee (1972-73); Ambassador to Libya (1973-74); Minister for Local Government in the Administration of Muhsin al-Aini (1974-75); and of Abdulaziz Abdul Ghani; Ambassador to Libya (1976); Ambassador to Moroccol Presently Ambassador to Pakistan. **Addr.:** P.O.B. 400, Sanaa, Yemen Arab Republic.

TAYIB (Ibrahim, al-Tayib, al), Sudanese medical doctor and businessman. **Born** on April 18, 1937 at el-Duiem, White Nile Province (Sudan). **Son** of Ibrahim al-Tayib al-Salam (businessman) **and** Mrs., née Nimma Sulman el-Subai. **Married** in October 1975 to Miss Huda Mohamad Gaffar, one daughter: Raasha. **Educ.:** Elementary and Intermediate schools, Port Sudan; Ahfad secondary school, Omdurman; Warsaw Medical Academy (Poland). **Dipl.:** M.D. specialisation Child Health (Pediatrics). **Career:** Served as general practitioner between 1965-70 in Khartoum, Khartoum North, Omdurman and Port Sudan clinical hospitals; Senior medical inspector, Southern Division, Red Sea Province; Deputy Consultant to the Governor of the Red Sea Province for medical affairs; in business from 1970 as Chairman, Ibrahim Eltayeb al-Salam and Sons (Est. 1930), real estate owners, traders, agents, consultants; holders of 50% equity, Red Sea Tannery Co. Ltd. (joint venture with Sudan Ministry of Industry); Director, Dauss International Co. (USA/Saudi Arabia/Sudan); Director/Partner, Dauss International Co. (Sudan/Saudi Arabia). **Sports:** Swimming and basket-ball. **Hobbies:** Reading and music. **Clubs:** Khartoum Sailing club; Port Sudan International club. **Credit Cards:** American Express. **Prof. Addr.:** Elsheikh Mustafa Building, Gamhouriya street, Suite No.62, P.O.Box 1282, Tel.76780, 78660, Khartoum. **Priv. Addr.:** Port Sudan, P.O.Box 626, Tel.4858, Sudan.

TAYIB (Jameel M.S.), Saudi geologist. **Born** in 1943 in Mecca, Saudi Arabia. **Dipl.:** B.Sc., M.Sc. (Applied Geology). **Career:** Assistant to the Chief Geologist, Senior Geologist, General Directorate of Mineral Resources; member of Stratigraphis Committee of Geology, U.S.A., Arab Mineral Resources Conference, Morocco 1977, International Geological Conference, Cairo 1978. **Publications:** Technical Report of Jeddah-Mecca, Geological Report of al-Wajh, Technical Report of Taif. **Hobbies:** Sport, reading. **Address:** P.O.Box 345, Tel. 6310355, Jeddah, Saudi Arabia.

TAYIB (Mohamad Said), Saudi publisher. **Born** in 1939. **Dipl.:** B.A. (Economics and Political Science). **Career:** Assistant Director of the Department of Emigration and Passports, Mecca; Head of the Department of Practical Studies, Al Thaghr Model Schools, Jeddah; Director General of the Office of Pilgrimage and Endowments; Founding member, President and member of the Board Tihama for Advertising, Public Relations and Marketing Research; Founding member and Chairman of Intermarkets Saudi Arabia International Co. for Advertising Services; Delegated member of Tihama Distribution Co.; participated actively in the establishment of the University in Jeddah, later to become King Abdulaziz University; travelled extensively throughout the western world, Japan, and the Middle East; was an occasional columnist in local news papers. **Hobbies:** Reading, writing, swimming. **Prof. Addr.:** Tihama for Advertising, Public Relations and Marketing Research, P.O.Box 5455, Tel. 644-4444. 21422, Jeddah. **Priv. Addr.:** Tel. 671-7726, Jeddah, Saudi Arabia.

TAYIB (Nezhet), Iraqi economist. **Born** in 1929 in Baghdad, Iraq. **Son** of Mohamad Tayib. **Married** in 1967, 1 son, 1 daughter. **Educ.:** University of Birmingham, England; Institute of Chartered Accountants in England and Wales. **Dipl.:** B.Com.; Chartered Accountant. **Career:** Professor, University of Baghdad, Iraq (1956-63); Chartered Accountant in Baghdad, Basrah and Mosul, Iraq (1956-66); Chairman and General Manager, Bank of Kuwait and The Arab World S.A.L., Beirut, Lebanon (1966-73); Director of Finance, Arab Fund for Economic and Social Development, Kuwait (1973-). Managing Director, Multinational Finance Co. Ltd., Luxembourg. **Member:** Institute of Chartered Accountants in England and Wales. **Hobby:** Swimming. **Addr.:** Luxembourg.

TAYIB (Noory T., al), Saudi faculty professor. **Born** in 1945 in Taif, Saudi Arabia. **Dipl.:** B.Sc. and Ph.D. **Career:** Demonstrator, Faculty of Science, King Saud University (1970-72), Lecturer (1976-78); Assistant Professor (1978-80); Chairman, Social Committee, Faculty of Science, (1977-79); member, Faculty of Science Council; member, Saudi Arabian Biological Society, the British Experimental Animal Society and the Royal Society of Animals, U.K. **Publications:** research work on Saudi animals. **Hobbies:** Reading, travel. **Address:**

Zoology Department, Faculty of Science, King Saud University, Tel.4787823 (Office) and 4811000 Ext. 2663 (Home), Riyadh, Saudi Arabia.

TAYIB (Sulaiman Saleh), Saudi M.D. **Born** in 1934 in Mecca. **Dipl.:** M.D. **Career:** Practitioner, Department of Surgery, Department of Obstetrics and Gynaecology, University of Cologne (West Germany), Department of Abdominal Disease, Deputy-Director. Quarantine Department and King Hospital; member of Doctors Syndicate, West Germany; former member, Islamic Society, Cologne (West Germany); Director of Clinics; Chairman, Nutrition Committee, the King's Hospital, Jeddah; Director, Quarantine Department and Assistant Director, King Hospital. **Sport:** Swimming. **Prof. Addr.:** King's Hospital, Tel.: 6422266, Jeddah, Saudi Arabia.

TAYMUR (Emad al-Deen), Egyptian businessman. **Born** in 1944. **Married**, 2 daughters. **Educ.:** Faculty of Commerce, Egypt. **Dipl.:** B.A. in Business Administration. **Career:** Sales Representative, Dar el-Maarif (1965-66); Public Relations Manager, Arab Research and Advertisement Centre (1966-67); Deputy General Manager of el-Ahram Management and Computer Centre (1967-74); General Manager of Alkan Trading Co. (1974-82); Managing Director and Partner of Alkantrac (1982); Member of the Board of Valley Investment Co. (1977-); Member of the Board of el-Sharkia National Contracting Co. (1982-). **Hobbies:** swimming, tennis. **Member:** Gezira Sporting Club. **Prof. Addr.:** 5 Haroun Street, Dokki, Giza, Cairo, Egypt. **Priv. Addr.:** 22 Taha Hussein, Zamalek, Cairo, Egypt.

TAYYAR (Adnan, Mohamad, al), Iraqi executive. **Born** in 1930 in Baghdad, Iraq. **Son** of Mohamad al-Tayyar. **Married** in 1957, 5 daughters, **Dipl.:** B.Sc. (Law). **Career:** Banking; Held Managerial positions (1951-66); Vice Chairman, African International Bank, Manama Bahrain; former Chairman and President, Rafidain Bank, Baghdad, Iraq (1980). **Member:** Hunting Club; Alwiya Club, Baghdad, Iraq. **Hobbies:** Swimming and sports. **Addr.:** Baghdad, Iraq.

TAZI (Abdelhaq), Moroccan politician. **Born** in 1932 in Fez, Morocco. **Educ.:** National Agricultural College. **Dipl.:** Agricultural Engineer. **Career:** Agricultural engineer, Meknes; Senior Official, Ministry of Agriculture; joined Istiqlal (1944) and was active in Paris (1957-58); Member, National Council and Executive Committee of the Istiqlal; Secretary of State for Cadre Training since Octobre 1977 and re-appointed on March 27, 1979; Secretary of State for Foreign Affairs (1983); Presently General Manager, AFRICERAME – Cerame Afrique Industries. **Addr.:** Africerame, Cerame Afrique Industries Route 110 (par Chefchaouni), Ain Ain Sebaâ 2100, Morocco.

TAZI (Abdurrahman, Hamad, al), Moroccan diplomat. **Born** on December 21, 1929 in Marrackech. **Son** of Hamad at-Tazi **and** Mrs., née Rahma Berrada. **Married** on September 16, 1962 to Miss Ghita Sebti, one child: Hicham. **Educ.:** University of Lille (1953). **Career:** Industrial Engineer (1949-53); Director of Industrial Production, Ministry of Commerce and Industry (1956); Economic Counsellor of Moroccan Embassy, Bonn (1957-58); First Counsellor, Permanent Moroccan Mission to United Nations (1961); Moroccan Representative at Economic Commission of United Nations (1961); Director-General of Economic Affairs, Ministry of Foreign Affairs in Rabat, (1962); Executive Director for Afghanistan, Ghana, Indonesia, Laos, Libya, Malaya, Morocco, Tunisia, International Bank of Reconstruction and Development (World Bank) (1962-72); former President of the Moroccan National Committee of the International Chamber of Commerce, Casablanca. **Sports:** Skiing, tennis and squash. **Addr.:** Casablanca, Morocco.

TAZI (Ahmed), Moroccan senior servant (director general) and former minister. **Born** on November 8, 1928 at Taza, Morocco. **Son** of Haj Jilali Tazi and Rkia Bent Haj Abdelkader. **Married** on September 15, 1959 in Taza to Miss Badia Lahsaini, 3 children: Dalila, Chakib and Fawzi. **Educ.:** Moulay Youssef College of Rabat, Morocco; Lycée Saint-Louis, France; Higher Electricity School (Supelec), Paris, France. **Dipl.:** B.Sc (Electrical Engineeering) (1952). **Career:** Head of Cabinet, Ministry of Public Works (1959-61); Director General, Water and Electricity Distribution Corporation, Casablanca, Morocco (1961-64); Minister of Public Works and Communications (April 25, 1974- October 4, 1977); Chairman and Director General of National Office of Electricity (1964). **Decor.:** Officer, Ouissam Alaouit; Commander, Order of the Throne (Morocco); Grand Commander, Order of Merit of the Italian Republic; Ouissam al-Massira; Chevalier de la légion d'honneur de la Republique Française. **Priv. Addr.:** 52, Rue Jean Jaures, Casablanca, Morocco.

TAZI (Anas), Moroccan Executive. **Born** on February 18, 1945 at Fès. **Son** of Abdallah Tazi **and** Mrs. Ghita Lebbar. **Married** to Mrs. Fatiha Lebbar, 3 children: Salma (16.08.71); Omar (26.05.74); Kenza (04.08.82). **Dipl.:** Baccalaureat (1963); Licence ès Economic Sciences (1966). **Career:** Banking formation at Crédit Lyonnais France (1966-1968); Branch Manager, Crédit du Maroc (1969-1974); Commercial Manager at the Société Chérifienne des Pétroles SCP (1974-1975), Commercial and Financial Manager (1975-1980); Financial and Participations Manager (1981-1990); Deputy General Manager for Finance and Information (Since 1990); Deputy General Manager for Finance and Juridical Operations (Since 1994). **Other Information:** Professor at the «Institut Technique de Banques» (I.T.B.) in Casablanca. **Sports:** Golf, Tennis. **Prof. Addr.:** S.C.P. Hay Ryad Secteur 10, Rabat, Tel.: (7) 71.03.07 to 18. **Priv. Addr.:** 191, rue Bni Yakhlef, Lot Ambassador, Route des Zaërs, Rabat, Morocco.

TEDDER (Gerald Leon), British executive. **Born** in 1931 in London, U.K. **Son** of Cecil L. Tedder. **Married** in 1961, 2 sons, 1 daughter. **Educ.:** Oxford University. **Dipl.:** M.A. (1957). **Career:** Dutch/Shell Group (1958-68); Brandts/Grindlay S.A. (1967-71); C.W. Capital Ltd. (1972-75); Managing Director, B.A.I.I. (Middle East) E.C. (1976-82); Chairman, Bankers Society of Bahrain (1978-82); currently Chairman, B.A.I.I. (UK) Ltd. **Member:** Carlton and Garrick Clubs. **Hobbies:** Sailing, painting, reading and history. **Addr.:** B.A.I.I. (UK) Ltd., Swan Gardens, 10 Piccadilly, London W1, U.K.

TEISSIER (Henri-Antoine-Marie), Archbishop of Algiers. **Born** on July 21, 1929 in Lyon, France. **Son** of Henri Teissier **and** Mrs. Marie Claire Richard. **Educ.:** Collège des Jésuites (Montpellier), Lycée Français (Rabat), University of Rabat (Morocco), of Paris-Sorbonne (France), of Cairo (Egypt), of Algiers (Algeria). **Dipl.:** Licences ès lettres classiques, Licence in Philosopy, Licence in Theology, Licence ès lettres arabes, diplômé d'Arabe de l'Ecole Nationale des Langues Orientales. **Career:** Vicar in Algiers, Belcourt 1958-62; Director of Charity and movements of the diocese of Algiers (1962-66); Director of Centre d'Etudes diocesiens in Algiers (1966-72); Bishop of Oran (1973-81); Archbishop of Algiers (1981-). **Publ.:** Three books: "Eglise en Islam", Paris Centurion (1984); "La Mission de l'Eglise", Paris, DESCLÉE (1985); "Histoire des Chrétiens d'Afrique du Nord", Paris (1986). **Other Information:** President Bishops' Conference of North Africa (1981-); **Prof. Addr.:** Archbishopric of Algiers, 13 rue Khelifa Boukhalfa, Tel.: 63.42.44, Algiers, Algeria. **Priv. Addr.:** 22 Chemin d'Hydra, el-Biar, Tel.: 78.47.47, Algiers, Algeria.

TERAIQY (Abdulaziz), Saudi civil servant. **Born** in 1938 at Zelfi (Najd), Saudi Arabia. **Dipl.:** B.A. (Business Administration). **Career:** Director, Technical Assistants Institute; Assistant Director of Programmes and Planning, Ministry of Municipal and Rural Affairs; attented the Technical Training Conference; delegate from the Ministry of Municipal and Rural Affairs to the economic and cultural commission with the United Kingdom, France and Finland; President of Dammam Municipality. **Hobby:** History. **Address:** Dammam Municipality, Dammam, Saudi Arabia.

TERMANINI (Radwan), Syrian executive. **Born** in 1945 in Syria. **Married** in 1968, 2 sons. **Dipl.:** D.E.S. (Econ.) **Career:** Project Economist, Marcona Corp., USA; Marketing Director, Kaiser Engineers, USA; Projects Manager, Abu Dhabi Investment Authority, UAE; Chairman, Arab Leasing Co., Bahrain; Director, Arab Leasing Holdings, Luxembourg; General Manager, Arabian General Investment Corporation, Dubai, UAE (1982-). **Member:** American Economics Association; Institute of Directors. **Hobbies:** Tennis and jogging. **Addr.:** P.O.Box 3501, Tel.: 474734, Telex: 47878 A/B SHUAA, Dubai, UAE.

TERZI (Shaikh Kamel), Tunisian religious leader. **Born** in Tunisia. **Educ.:** Theology. **Career:** Director of the Religious Affairs and Wakfs (Ministry of Charitable Endowments and Council of Ministers), Member Executive Bureau of Islamic Congress (1967). **Addr.:** Tunis, Tunisia.

TERZI (Zuhdi, Labib), Palestinian diplomat. **Born** in 1924 in Jerusalem, Palestine. **Married**, 2 children. **Dipl.:** Degree in Law. **Career:** Civilian Service, British Army, World War II; Active Journalist in Palestinian nationalist movement; Representative of Palestine Liberation Organization (PLO), Brasil (1964); Representative of PLO, Office of the League of Arab States, Argentina; Head of the League of Arab States Office, Spain; PLO Delegation, UN, New York (1974-75); Permanent Observer of PLO, UN (1975-1991). **Decor.:** Knight of the Order of the Holy Sepulchre, Patriarch of Jerusalem (1966). **Addr.:** Tunis, Tunisia.

TEVAL (Shehadeh), Jordanian bank executive. **Born** in 1922 in Madaba, Jordan. **Son** of Salameh Teval. **Married. Educ.:** Terra Sancta College, Jerusalem. **Career:** Director, Housing Bank, Jordan; Director, Arab Jordan Investment Bank, Jordan (1981). **Hobbies:** Motor Sport, Art and Antiques Collection. **Addr.:** Police College Street, P.O.Box 7693, Tel.: 67126-9, Telex: 21693 A/B ISKAN JO, Amman, Jordan.

THABET (Adel, Ahmed), Egyptian scientist. **Born** in 1924 in Cairo, Egypt. **Married. Educ.:** Cairo University, Egypt. **Dipl.:** B.Sc. (Hons) in Geology, M.A. in Journalism. **Career:** Geologist, Geological Survey Centre of Egypt, Cairo (1145-49); Director, Scientific and Technical Information and Documentation (1949-57); Technical Bureau, National Research Centre (1957-62); Scientific Divisions, Science Council (1962-64); Scientific Relations, Ministry of Scientific Relations (1964-71); Director General of Scientific Relations, Scientific Research Centre (1971-76); Under Secretary of State, Ministry of Scientific Research, Cairo (1176-84); Regional Adviser in Science and Technology, UN Economic Commission for Western Asia, Beirut, Lebanon (1981); Member of the Egyptian Syndicate of Scientific Workers (1951-); UNESCO International Committee on Bibliography (1954-58); Member of the Board of International Science Policy Council (1976-); Adviser in Science and Technology, ALECSO, Tunisia (1984). **Publ.:** Two books about Science and Technology (in Arabic) as well as numerous scientific papers published in international and foreign books and journals. **Decor.:** Order of Merit, Czechoslovakia (1970). **Hobbies:** travelling, swimming, reading. **Member:** Gezira Sporting Club. **Priv. Addr.:** 31 al-Gazeira al-Wosta Street, Zamalek, Cairo, Egypt.

THABET (Rashed, Mohamed), Yemeni former state minister. **Born** on September 1944 in Aden. **Son** of Mohamed Thabet (Engineer) **and** Mrs. Fatema née Hasson. **Married** to Miss. Fatoom A. Lattiff. **Educ.:** primary and Secondary Education, University Degree in Social Sciences. **Career:** chief Editor of al-Hariss Magazine and Director General of Radio and Television (since January 1972- June 1973); Minister of Information (June 1973- April 1975); State Minister for Ministerial Affairs (since April 1975- October 1975); Ambassador in Cairo (since November 1975-1977); Minister of Information (since December 1977- October 1980); Minister of Culture (1980-86); State Minister for Yemen Unity Affairs (1986-89); **Decorations:** Medal of 22nd June, Medal of Faithful. **Sports:** Swimming. **Addr.:** Aden. Republic of Yemen.

THAKAFI (Yusuf Ali, al), Saudi professor. **Born** in 1948 in Taif, Saudi Arabia. **Dipl.:** Ph.D. (History). **Career:** Teacher, Ministry of Education since 1972; Demonstrator, King Abdulaziz University, Jeddah; Assistant Professor, Umm al-Qura University; member, Middle East Studies of North America Association, British Society for Middle East Studies, American Historical Association. **Honour:** Medal, awarded by H.M. King Fahad, for excellence in University Studies. **Publications:** Akhnaton; al-Mosleh al-Dini; Political Relations between Egypt and the Ottoman Empire during the 1st quarter of the 16th Century. **Hobby:** Reading. **Address:** Umm al-Qura University, Faculty of Shari'a, History Department, Tel.: 5566477 (Office) and 5589417 (Home), Mecca, Saudi Arabia.

THANAYAN (Abdallah Sheikh, al), Saudi technician and businessman. **Born** in 1941 in Medina (Saudi Arabia). **Son** of al-Thanayan al-Subaie **and** Mrs., née al-Hajja. **Married** in Jeddah in 1976. **Educ.:** Medina Secondary School. **Career:** Laboratory technician, Ministry of Communications up to 1972; Proprietor and General Manager of al-Thanayan Co. **Sports:** Football and swimming. **Hobbies:** Reading and TV. **Credit Card:** American Express. **Prof. Addr.:** P.O.Box 2007, Jeddah, Saudi Arabia.

THANAYAN (Abdallah Thanayan, al), Saudi academic. **Born** in 1944 in Onaizah, Saudi Arabia. **Dipl.:** B.Sc. (Economics), 1966; M.Sc. and Ph.D. (Agricultural Economics), 1970. **Career:** Research Assistant, Texas University (1969-70); Lecturer and later Chairman, Department of Agricultural Economy; Vice Dean, Faculty of Agriculture, King Saud University; Economic Adviser to the Ministry of Finance and several other organizations; Managing Director, Arab Livestock Development Co., under the auspices of the Union of Arab League Economic Council; member of the Board, the Arab Sudanese Co. for Animal Production, the Arab Company for Animal Production, Ras Al Khaimah, the Arab Company for Poultry Production, Fujairah and the Saudi Arabian Company for Poultry Production; member of Subsidy Committee, Ministry of Finance; member of Technical Committee, Ministry of Petroleum. **Publications:** Several studies and research projects on the evaluation of agricultural and animal projects; various scientific articles on agricultural economics. **Address:** Jeddah, Saudi Arabia.

THANAYAN (Abdulaziz, al), Saudi civil servant. **Born** in 1938. **Dipl.:** B.A. (Sociology), Cairo University. **Career:** official, Ministry of Labour and Social Affairs; Mayor of Riyadh; Under-Secretary of Foreign Affairs for Administrative and Financial Affairs; Deputy Minister of Foreign Affairs for Administrative and Financial Affairs; attended as Mayor of Riyadh several local and international conferences on town planning and construction; attended as Deputy Foreign Minister several conferences; Chairman of Saudi delegation to 8th Conference of Islamic Foreign Ministers, Tripoli, Libya (1977); Chairman of Saudi delegation to Arab-African Dialogue Conference, Niger (1978). **Honours:** several Orders of Merit from Arab, Islamic and European countries. **Hobby:** reading. **Address:** Ministry of Foreign Affairs, Jeddah.

THANAYAN (Muayyad Abdallah, al), Saudi legal adviser. **Born** in 1928 in Baghdad. **Dipl.:** Bachelor of Law; Doctor of Law, (Honoris Causa) from International University Foundation, U.S.A. **Career:** Lawyer (1961-73); joined the Ministry of Commerce at Dammam as legal Adviser (1973-77); Lawyer and Legal Adviser (since 1977); Member of the Chamber of Commerce and Industry in Dammam; Deputy Director General of the International Biographical Center in U.K. **Member** of the Historical Association in U.K., the Transport Trust in U.K., the Military Book Society in U.K., of the History Guild in U.K., the Military Guild in U.K., the National Geographic Society in U.S.A. **Hobbies:** Philately, numismatics. **Addr.:** P.O.Box 2566 Dammam, Saudi Arabia.

THANI (Abdul Aziz Bin Khalifa, al, Shaikh), Qatari politician and former minister of finance and petroleum. **Born** on December 12, 1948 in Doha, Qatar. **Son** of HH Shaikh Khalifa Bin Hamad al-Thani, Ruler of Qatar. **Educ.:** in Qatar and the USA. **Dipl.:** B.A. (Political Science and Economics) (1972); M.A. (1974) from Northern Indiana University, USA. **Career:** Deputy Minister of Finance and Petroleum (December 1972); President, Qatar Monetary Agency (1972); Chairman, Qatar National Petroleum Company (1973); Chairman of the State of Qatar Investment Board; Governor for Qatar to the International Monetary Fund and World Bank for Reconstruction and Development (since 1972); Chairman of the Board of Directors of Qatar National Bank (since 1972) and AK Group of Companies, Qatar. Represented Qatar in many international and regional conferences; formerly Minister of Finance and petroleum. **Addr.:** AK Group Contracting, P.O.Box 1991, Doha, Qatar.

THANI (Ahmad Bin Saif, al, Shaikh), Qatari politician. **Born** in 1946 in Qatar. **Son** of Saif al-Thani. **Married. Educ.:** Diploma in Public Administration, London (1971). **Career:** Ambassador to the Court of Saint James, London (1971-77); presently Minister of Justice and Minister of State for Foreign Affairs until 1991; Minister of Justice (1991-1995); Minister of State (July 1995-). **Addr.:** Minister's Office, Doha, Qatar.

THANI (Bin Harib Bin Issa), United Arab Emirates politician and businessman. **Born** in 1946 in Ajman, UAE. **Educ.:** Cairo University, Egypt. **Dipl.:** Diploma in Administration and Social Affairs. **Career:** UAE Minister without Portfolio; United Arab Emirates Minister of Islamic Affairs and Waqfs (Religious Endowments) (1973-77); Minister of Electricity and Water, Dubai (1977); Businessman (1982-). **Addr.:** Dubai, United Arab Emirates.

THANI (Hamad Bin Jassim Bin Jaber, H.E. Shaikh), Qatari Minister and Businessman. **Born** in 1959. **Married,** 10 children: five sons and five daughters. **Career:** H.E. Shaikh Hamad bin Jassim bin Jaber Al-Thani was named Minister of Foreign Affairs on September 1, 1992, his most recent appointment in a professional career which has been devoted exclusively to public service for the State of Qatar. Under the leadership of the Emir, His Highness Shaikh Hamad bin Khalifa Al-Thani, Shaikh Hamad has been the principal architect of Qatar's new foreign policy. As Foreign Minister, he worked to expand Qatar's ties with countries outside the Araba World and increased the number of states with which Qatar has formal diplomatic relations. This new era has witnessed a remarkable expansion of Qatar's bilateral ties with leading nations of Asia, Africa and Europe. In recent years, Qatar has also dramatically strengthened its political, economic and security ties with the United States. Shaikh Hamad has actively participated in the Middle East peace process, and as a member of the cabinet, has played a key role in helping to develop new policies, including plans for municipal elections, lifting press censorship, and drafting a new constitution. Shaikh Hamad is also Chairman of the High Ministerial Committee for Economic Affairs. Shaikh Hamad began his government career in 1989, as Director of the Office of the Minister of Municipal Affairs. In July, 1989, he became the first minister of the newly combined Minister of Municipal Affairs and Agriculture. Shaikh Hamad has served in a number of other positions, including: Acting Minister of Electricity and Water, Chairman of the Board of Directors of Qatar Electricity and Water Company, President of the Central Municipal Council, and Director of the Emir's Special Project Office. He also served on the Board of Directors of Qatar General Petroleum Corporation, and was a member of the Higher Planning Council. **Hobbies:** Reading, hunting, falconing and skiing. **Addr.:** Ministry of Foreign Affairs, P.O.Box 250, Doha, Qatar.

THANI (Hamad Bin Khalifa, al, H.H. the Amir Shaikh), Amir of State of Qatar, and Minister of Defence. **Born** in 1949. **Eldest Son** of HH Shaikh Khalifa Bin Hamad al-Thani, former Ruler of Qatar. **Married,** 3 children. **Educ.:** in Qatar and Royal Military College, Sandhurst, UK (July 1971). **Career:** Appointed Commander-in-Chief, Qatar Security Forces on February 22, 1972; leading part in modernization of Qatar Armed Forces; Heir Apparent (1977); Heir apparent, Minister of Defence (1977-1989); reappointed Minister of Defence (July 1989-1995); Amir of State of Qatar, and Minister of Defence (July 1995-). **Addr.:** Diwan Amiri, Doha, Qatar.

THANI (Khalifa Bin Hamad, al, H.H. Shaikh), Former Amir of State of Qatar and former prime minister. **Born** in 1932 in Rayyan. **Married,** five children: Shaikh Hamad, Shaikh Abdul Aziz, Shaikh Abdullah, Shaikh Mohammad, Shaikh Jassem. **Career:** Amir of the State of Qatar since 22nd February 1972 until July 1995; Deputy Amir and Heir Apparent (1960-1972); Prime Minister (2 April 1970); Minister of Finance (5 November 1960); Minister of Finance and Petroleum (29 May 1970 - 10 December 1972); Minister of Foreign Affairs (3 September 1971 - 23 February 1972); President-designate of the Provisional Confederation of the Arab Gulf States (7 July 1968). During his early career His Highness occupied other several posts including: Minister of Education, Head of Security in the First Oil Project, Head of Civil Courts, Chairman of Investment Board, Chairman of the Board of the Qatar and Dubai Monetary Agency. **Medals and Decorations:** Qiladat al-Jumhuriah (Collar of the Republic), Egypt (5 June 1971); Qiladat ash-Sharaf (Collar of Honor), Sudan (29 April 1972); Qiladat Badr al-Kubra (Grand Collar of Badr), Saudi Arabia (1st May 1973); Qiladat an-Neel al-Uzma (Grand Collar of the Nile), Egypt (24 August 1973); Wisam Mauritania (Order of Mauritania), Mauritania (May 1974); Qiladat al-Hussain Bin Ali (Collar of al-Hussain Bin Ali), Jordan (18 July 1974); Wisam al-Istiqlal (Order of Independence), Tunisia (22 July 1975); al-Wisam al-Muhammadi (Grand Muhammadi Order), Maghreb (24 July 1975); Grand Sash (Legion d'Honneur), France (27 October 1975); Qiladat Pehlawi (Legion d'Honneur), Iran (13 November 1975); National Order of the Lion, Senegal (20 November 1975); Qiladat Oman al-Kubra (Grand Collar of Oman), Oman (20 December 1975); Collar of Simon De Bolivar, Venezuela (21 April 1977); Medal of the Republic of Indonesia, Indonesia (12 October 1977); Knight Grand Cross of the Order of St. Michael and St. George (GCMG), United Kingdom, (21 February 1979); Isabella Medal, Spain (3 November 1980); Qiladat Mubarak al-Kabeer (Collar of the Great Mubarak), Kuwait (15 February 1982); Grand Order of Pakistan, (16 April 1984); Grand Moging Hua Medal, Korea (21 April 1984); Wisam Zahrat al-Kuraiztalum, Japan (23 April 1984); Knight Grand Cross of the Order of the Bath (GCB), United Kingdom (12 November 1985); Sash of Merit, Rank Extraordinaire, Lebanon (22

June 1986); Knight Grand Cross, Italy (15 January 1992). **Address:** In Exile.

THANI (Nasir Bin Khalid, al, Shaikh), Qatari businessman and former minister. **Born** in 1915. **Married. Career:** businessman in Doha; interests in several national public shareholding companies. Head of Israel Boycott Regional office in Qatar; Minister of Economy and Commerce (1970-83). **Addr.:** P.O.Box 82, Tel.: (Priv) 324442, 325842, Doha, Qatar.

THANI (Rashed, Awaida, al, Shaikh), Qatari administrator. **Born** in 1953 in Qatar. **Married. Educ.:** Michigan University, USA. **Dipl.:** B.Sc. in Economics. **Career:** Economist, Petroleum Affairs Department, Ministry of Finance and Petroleum (1977); Deputy Managing Director of Qatar General Petroleum Corporation (1979); Chairman of the Technical Committee, Qatar Liquified Natural Gas Project-LNG North Field (1980); Chairman of the Board of Directors of the Arab Maritime Petroleum Transport Company (1984- to present); Member of the Board of Directors of Qatargas Corporation (1984); Managing Director of Qatar General Petroleum Corporation (1985-89); Editor in Chief of Ad Dawri Weekly Sports Magazine. **Hobbies:** reading, swimming. **Prof. Addr.:** P.O.Box 310, Doha, Qatar.

THANI (Suhaim Bin Hamad, al, Shaikh), Qatari former minister and businessman. **Born** in 1940. **Brother** of H.H. Shaikh Khalifa Bin Hamad al-Thani, Ruler of Qatar. **Career:** Minister of Foreign Affairs (1972); presently businessman. **Addr.:** Doha, Qatar.

THARIANI (Ahmad Hussain), Pakistani executive. **Born** in 1933 in Bombay India. **Son** of Roshan Ali Thariani. **Married** in 1963, 1 son, 2 daughters. **Dipl.:** LCC ACCTTS, England. **Career:** Joined Habib Bank Ltd., Karachi since 1949; Deputy Manager (1958); Manager (1960); Area Chief (1969); Assistant Vice President, Habib Bank Ltd., England (1972); Transferred to Colombo (Sri Lanka) (1977); Promoted Senior Vice President, Habib Bank AG Zurich, Sharjah (1980); Executive Vice President, Habib Bank Ltd., Sharjah, UAE (1981-). **Member:** International Beach Club, Sharjah; Lions Club, Karachi; Rotary Member, Colombo. **Hobby:** Music. **Addr.:** P.O.Box 1166, Tel.: 3512268, Telex: 68061 A/B SHABIB EM, Sharjah, UAE.

THEWAYB (Muhammad, Ahmad, al), Jordanian politician. **Born** in 1941 in Bethlehem, Palestine. **Married,** 6 children. **Educ.:** University of Jordan, Jordan. **Dipl.:** B.A. in History and Diploma in Management. **Career:** served as a Teacher and Official for 23 years in the Ministry of Education; Member of the Chamber of Representatives, Jordan. **Hobby:** reading. **Priv. Addr.:** P.O.Box 184365, Amman, Jordan.

THOR (Ali, Lutfi, al), Yemeni politician. **Born** on September 18, 1940. **Son** of Lutfi al-Thor. **Married** in 1966 to Nouriya, 4 children: Raja (1968), Yahya (1970), Mona (1971), Hana (1972). **Educ.:** College of Commerce, Cairo University (1964); training course on Development, USA (1965); B.Sc. (1968). **Career:** Member of the Higher Economic Committee (1964-65); Government Representative and member of the Board in the Yemeni Company (1965-66); Member, Board of the Yemeni Bank for Reconstruction and Development (YBRD); Manager of the Sanaa Branch (1966-67); deputy chairman, Yemeni Bank for Reconstruction and Development (1967-68); Chairman of the Yemeni Bank (1968); Deputy, President of the Yemen National Assembly; Chairman of the Assembly's Economic Committee (1968-69); Minister of Finance (1969-70); Chairman of YBRD (1970-73); Minister of Economy (1973-74 and 1974-76); Executive member of the Board of the Yemeni Bank (1966-76); Minister of Development and Chairman of the Central Planning Organization (1976). **Sport:** Swimming. **Hobbies:** Poetry, fiction, **Addr.:** Sanaa, Republic of Yemen.

THUKAIR (Fawzi, Ahmed, al), Saudi Academic. **Born** in 1953 in Basrah, Iraq. **Son** of Ahmad al-Thukair. **Dipl.:** Ph.D. (Mathematics). **Career:** Demonstrator, King Faisal University (1975); Assistant Professor, King Faisal University (1981); Associate Professor, King Saud University. **Member of:** The American Mathematical Society, The Mathematical Association of America. **Publ.:** Number Fields with Equal L-Series on Zeta Functions, in addition to numerous research articles in International mathematics journals. Also Author and translator of many text books in Mathematics. **Hobbies:** reading. **Addr.:** P.O.Box 25384, Riyadh 11466, Saudi Arabia, Tel.: 4676516, 4676511.

THUWAINI (Abdul Muhsin Faisal), Kuwaiti businessman. **Born** in 1930. **Married. Career:** Contractor; member of the Board of Directors of Kuwait Chamber of Commerce and Industry; Chamber of Kuwait Contractor Unions; Chairman, the Arab European Financial Management Co. S.A.K.; Ahmadiah Contracting & Trading Co. WLL; and member of the board of several shareholding companies. **Addr.:** P.O.B. 446, Safat, Kuwait and P.O.Box 24100, 13101 Safat, Kuwait.

THUWAINI (Abdullatif Faisal, al, Major General), Kuwaiti administrator. **Born** in 1927 in Kuwait. **Married,** nine children. **Career:** Attended Interpol conferences on Crime Prevention and Offenders Treatment, local conferences for police commanders. Founding **Member:** of the Hunting and Riding Club; Director, Arab European Financial Management Co. S.A.K.; member of the Administrative Board and Manager of the Hunting and Riding Club. Manager of a horse racing club. Founding member of al-Ahly Sports Club (now the Kuwait Club) and of Teachers Club. Counsellor at the Ruler's Palace (1981-).

Addr.: Ministry of the Interior, P.O.B. 11, Tel.: 4816111, Safat, Kuwait.

TIBAH (Abdul Qadir Mohamad Khalil), Saudi academic. **Born** in 1940. **Dipl.:** M.A. (Educational Administration) California, U.S.A. (1969). **Career:** Administrative Director, University of Oil and Minerals; Secretary of the Administrative Council of the University of Oil and Minerals; Director of the Rector's Office, University of Oil and Minerals; Director of Students Affairs, University of Oils and Minerals; participated in the U.S.A. Registrars Conference; now Lecturer, Faculty of Education, King Abdulaziz University (Mecca) and in charge of the Credit Hours System and the Registration Department. **Member:** The Registrars Association, U.S.A. **Sports:** Swimming, riding. **Hobby:** Reading. **Addr.:** Mecca, Saudi Arabia.

TIBAH (Abdul Rahman Mohamad Khalil), Saudi academic. **Born** in 1930 in Mecca. **Dipl.:** M.A. (Education and Administration) (1967, 1973). **Career:** Teacher; Assistant Director of the Foreign Scholarships Department; Assistant-Director of Personnel; Director of the Foreign Scholarships Department; Assistant-Director of Higher Education; General-Director of Higher Education; Director of Organisation and Administration; Lecturer at Teachers' Training College, Mecca; Lecturer at King Abdulaziz University; member of the Board of Prince Fawaz Cooperative Building Society; participated in King Abdulaziz Teachers Training Conference, and the Ministers of Education Conference; attended the fourth UNESCO session; now Director of the General Administration of King Abdulaziz University. **Hobby:** Reading. **Prof. Addr.:** Tel.: 6832876, Jeddah, Saudi Arabia.

TIBAH (Mustafa Abdallah), Saudi physician. **Born** in 1926. **Dipl.:** B.M., B.Ch. **Career:** Surgeon, Aramco (1957-60); Director and Surgeon, King's Hospital, Jeddah (1960-62); Director and Surgeon, Tobuk Military Hospital (1962-63); Assistant Director of Medical Service, Ministry of Defence (1963-64); Director, Jeddah Quarantine; former member of Board, Saudi Red Crescent; now Director-General of Curative Medicine, Ministry of Health. **Hobbies:** reading, contemplation. **Prof. Addr.:** Ministry of Health, Tel.: 4024867 (Office) and 4355950 (Home), Riyadh, Saudi Arabia.

TIBBU (Mohamad Ali), Libyan politician. **Born** in 1930 in Fezzan, Libya. **Career:** Lecturer, Faculty of Agriculture, University of Libya; Assistant Director General, Agricultural Bank, Sebha; Minister of Agriculture and Agrarian Reform (1970-77); Secretary for Agriculture and Agrarian Reform, General People's Committee (1977-79); **Addr.:** Tripoli, Libya.

TIGANI (Mohamad Tom), Sudanese politician. **Born** in Sudan. **Career:** Ministry of Education; Dean at the Higher Teachers Training Institute; Under Secretary; Chairman of the Board, Management Development and Production Centre (1973); Secretary for Youth Affairs and Sports, Sudanese Socialist Union (SSU) (1974-75); Minister of State for General Education (1975-76). **Addr.:** Khartoum, Sudan.

TILLISI (Khalifa, Mohamad), Libyan academic. **Born** in 1930 in Tripoli, Libya. **Married,** 2 sons, 4 daughters. **Career:** Assistant Secretary General, House of Representatives (1960), Secretary General (1962-64); Minister of Culture and Information (1964-67); Ambassador (1968-70); President of Arab Book House (1974-); Secretary General of Libyan Writers' Union (1976-80); Secretary General of the Publishers Union (1982). **Publ.:** "al-Shaby and Gobran" (1957), "Rafik Sha'aer al-Watan" (1964); also poems in Arabic as well as an Italian-Arabic dictionary. Arab Poetry Antologia (7 volumes); ANNAFIS (Arab Dictionary); Lorca Complete Poetry Works (Translation); Tagore Poetry Works (Translation); Author of many books concerning Libyan history. **Decor.:** Italian Merit of the Mediterranean, Tunisian Order of Cultural Merit (1975). Alfatah Libyan Decoration for the Pioneers in Litterature Field; Alfatah Libyan Reward for the Arts and Literature; tunisian (Magreb Cultural Reward); **Member:** Libyan Academy; Honorary, Giordan Academy; Tunisian Academy; Doctor of Honoris Causa, Instituto Orientale (Napoli, Italy). **Prof. Addr.:** P.O.Box 4800, Tripoli, Libya.

TILMISANY (Abdul Karim), Saudi academic. **Born** in 1944. **Dipl.:** B.Pharm. (1976); Ph.D. (Pharmacology) (1976). **Career:** Demonstrator, Faculty of Pharmacology, Riyadh University (1967-69); member of Medicinal Plant Research Society; member of British Biochemical Society; Assistant Professor, Faculty of Pharmacology, Riyadh University. **Publications:** two papers on drugs and pharmacology. **Hobbies:** squash, soccer. **Address:** Riyadh, Saudi Arabia.

TLASS (Lieutenant General Mustafa), Syrian Army Officer and Statesman. **Born** in Al-Rastan City in the Governorate of Homs on 11.5.1932. **Married** in 1958 to Miss Lamia al-Jabiri, 4 children: Nahed, Firas, Manaf, Saria. He is a grand father to "Akram Al-Ujeh" Nahed's son; to "Yara", "Mira", and "Lara". Firas's children; to "Mustafa" and "Lamya", Mounaf's Children. **Résumé of Functional Activities:** Received his elementary education in Homs. In 1948, he was awarded the preparatory Schooling Certificate in Khaled Ibn Al-Waleed Secondary School in Homs. He was also awarded the Secondary Schooling Certificate (Baccalaureate) - Literary Section in 1951 in Abdul Hamid Al-Zahrawi Secondary School. Joined the teaching profession between 1950-1952 and served as sports instructor and as scoutmaster in Al-Qraya School in Al-Suwayda Governorate of "Jabal Al-Arab". Joined the Military College on 1.11.1952, then was transfered to the

Air Force-Air Force College from 1.2.1953 to 16.6.1953 when he was turned to the Armour College to be graduated as a second Lieutenant in Armour Troops on 1.11.1954. Followed an Engineer Section Commander training course in the year 1955. He also followed a course in "The Combat of Armour Subunits, According to the Eastern Military Doctrine". In the fall of 1959, he was selected as the best well-informed officer to represent the Syrian Army in a contest-seminar with the Egyptian Army. Nominated to work in the Southern Region UAR (Egypt) on 26.12.1959 for his political activity and for being the party member in charge of Adnan Al-Malki Camps - Qatana -, and served on the Egyptian front "Sinai", then was transfered to Caire where he followed a training course to be qualified as tank battalion commander. Participated in Al-Baath Arab Socialist party underground military organization and was in the leading military committee. He stayed in Cairo till 28.9.1961, The date of the Secession from the United Arab Republic because of the conspiracy of the adversaries of the union which began in February 1958. Appointed after his return from Egypt, in the First Training Centre, and he was transfered early 1962 to the Ministry of Supply where he worked as inspector. On 31.3.1962, he took part in the "Free Officers" movement in Homs, then in Aleppo, as a consequence the next day he was apprehended and sent to prison with his colleagues. On March 8, 1963 the Revolution took place, as an aftermath he was restored to service in the Armed Forces, then appointed commander of a tank battalion in the Fifth Armoured Brigade and Chairman of the National security court in the Central Military region. on 1.4.1965, he was elected member of the Military Bureau and on 1.9.1965 member of the National Revolutionary Council. On 1965-1966, he followed a "Commanding and Staff" training course in the Commanding and Staff College and Received a High mark "Very Good". On 20.12.1965, under the instruction of Minister of Defence and the Sanction of the Party Regional Leadership, of which he was member, he dismissed the pro-right wing officers in Party - Amin Al-Hafez Group -, then The National Leadership, as a countermeasure took over succeeding the Regional Leadership and forming a new Cabinet from which Supporters of the previous regime were kept away. He was put under the disposal of the National Leadership in Damascus. Participated in Planning and executing 23 February 1966 Movement when he was a Lieutenant colonel, and appointed as Commander of Central Region and the Fifth Armoured Brigade. On 3.11.1966, he was elected chief of the Military Emergency Court. Assigned to Command General Command Reserve During the third Arab-Israeli war "June 1967" Which was not Commited to battle because of the Cease-fire on the three fronts. Promoted exceptionally to Major General on 14.2.1968, and appointed as First Deputy Minister of Defence, this is in addition to his post as Chief of the General Staff of the Army and Armed Forces. Followed a "Higher Commanding and Staff" Training course in 1969-1970 and achieved on "Excellent" mark. He was the right - hand man to General Hafez Al-Assad, when the great leader launched the Rectification Movement on 16.11.1970, that day marked the beginning of Syria's National esteem. Appointed Minister of Defence on 25.3.1972, a post he holds ever since in the successive cabinets formed in the Government on the next day to his holding office as Defence minister, he was appointed First Deputy Commander - In-Chief of the Army and Armed Forces. On 20.8.1973, he was appointed Deputy Chief of the Higher Military Council of the Syrian-Egyptian Army and Armed Forces, the Council assigned to plan for October Liberation war in 1973. On 6.10.1973, he fought in the glorious October war and was deputy to the heroic leader Hafez Al-Assad who fulfilled then a national victory. On 5.2.1977, he was appointed member of the Syrian-Egyptian United Political Leadership. On 1.1.1978, he was promoted to Lieutenant General. On 3.6.1982, he Carried out the instructions of the commander - In-Chief Hafez Al-Assad Confronting the Israeli army which invaded Lebanon and preventing its expansionist goals; the mission was successfully accomplished. Nominated First Deputy Prime Minister and Minister of Defence on 11.3.1984, 8.4.1985, 1.11.1987 and on 29.6.1992, in addition to his post as Deputy Commander - In-Chief. Since March 1963 Revolution, he stands By Comrade General Secretary of Al-Baath Party, President of the Republic General Hafez Al-Assad in confronting all the Crises the Country went through which were depicted from without or emerged from within and he was always his right-hand assistant in confounding their subversive goals, and the aims of the planners and executors of conspiracies. **Résumé of Cultural Activities:** Lieutenant General Moustafa Tlass is considered one of the most prominent pioneers of culture in the Arab World and one of the most knowledgeable and highly-productive writers. He is a member of the Union of Arab Writers, the author of forty one books on military, literary, political, historical, and botanic issues. Some of these books are translated into French, Russian, German, English, Spanish, Portuguese, Italian, and Hebrew. In February 1972, he obtained Diploma of the Military Academy of General Staff, Named after K.E. Vorshelov (U.S.S.R). From the above-mentioned Academy he also obtained, on 20.5.1980, Doctorate Degree in Military Science. On 13.4.1990, he obtained the Doctorate Degree in Historical Science from the Institute of Military history in Moscow. On 24.11.1991, he was unanimously elected an active member in the Arabic Language Academy of Damascus. On May 26, 1992, he was awarded honorary Doctorate Degree from Humanitarian Academy of the Soviet Armed Forces. On 22.9.1992, he was elected a Foreigner active member of the Academy (Academician) in the Natural Sciences Academy of the Russian Federation. On 14.9.1993 He was awarded a degree master of science in engineering from the military academy for armoured troops. On 6.9.1994, he was granted the title of Honorary professor in Military Science from the General Staff Academy of the Russian Federation. And he was elected on 3.12.1994 a genuine member of the Military Sciences Academy of the Russian Federation. On 1986 Obtained International Great Prize of the Foreign poetry from Cultural Institute of Solenzara. He has been selected for permanent documentation in five Hundred leaders of influence of the American Biographical Institute (1995). Having Realized the importance of books, together with the Arms, he founded a publishing house in 1983 "Dar Tlass for Research, Translation, and Publishing", (The income of the House is dedicated for martyrs' children in Syrian Arab Republic) which had the main aim of confronting the Zionist ideology and enhancing the National Arab Thinking under the banner of progress and love of Homeland. So far more than seven-hundred books have been published by the House and in various fields of knowledge; thus stimulating Arab Cultural thought from within encouraging it to cope with the procession of civilization, "Dar Tlass" made an agreement also with the French "Larousse" establishment to issue "Al-Imad Dictionary" of Literature, Science, Arts, and Media. **Résumé of Party Activities:** Joined Al-Baath Socialist Party in its early days on 28.5.1947. In 1951 he became an active member in the Party and was appointed Secretary of Al-Rastan Section. On 8.8.1965, he was elected member of the Party Regional Leadership, re'elected in late September 1968 and during the Fourth Exceptional Conference of the Party held in March 1969. When the Regional and National Leadership of the party met on 13.5.1969, he was elected member of the party politbureau. On 6.2.1971, he was elected member of the People's Assembly. In April 1975, he was elected member of the Regional Leadership, after holding the Sixth Regional Conference. On 8.1.1977, he was appointed head of the Armed Forces Party Committee. In January 1980, he was elected member in the party Central Committee, and in the Regional Leadership In January 1985, he was re'elected member of the Central Committee, and of the Regional Leadership. **Practices the following hobbies:** reading, writing, photography, tennis, swimming, and walking. He is a vegetarian and never eats meat unless as a courtesy. **Printed Works:** The Scientific and Technological Progress and the Development of the Armed Forces (1980); A Selection of the Prophet's Sayings (1984); The Message of Islam, the Arab Prophet (1984); The Algerian Revolution (1984); The Great Arab Revolution (1984); The Patron of Jerusalem Bishop Caputchi (1984); Kamal Adwan Operation (1984); The Atlantic Knight Ukba Ibn Nafii (1984); Algerian Knight Emir Abdul Kader (1984); Guerrilla Warfare (1984); Assault (1984); Israeli Invasion of Lebanon (1985); Sabra and Shatella Massacre (1985); Zenobia, Queen of Palmyra (1985); Sword of God Khalid Ibn Al-Waleed (1985); Al-Assad said This (1985); Combat Intelligence (1985); The Everlasting Achievement of the Soviet People (1986); Dictionary of Arab Names (1986); A Poet and a poem 2 Vols. (1986); The Arab-Israeli war (1986); New American Strategy (1987); Matzo of Zion (1987); Horizons of Israeli Strategy (1987); Lenin (1987); Damask Rose (1987); Garlic and Long Age (1987); Steadfastness Front in Camp David (1987); Soviet Art of War from Kutuzov to Joukov (1988); Hymns (1988); Armed Struggle Against Zionist Challenge (1989); Palestinian Revolution (1989); Medical-Botanic Dictionary (1989); Pillow of Insomnia (1989); A Reply to Satan (1990); Mirror of My Life (1990); Folk Medical Herbs (1990); Fortress of "Crac des Chevaliers" (1990); Confidence of Violet (1991); Wolf in World Poetry (1991); Joys of Human Thought (1991) **Sidenotes:** Holds Thirty-nine Syrian, Arab and Foreign orders and medals. **List of Orders:** Lieutenant General Moustafa Abdul-Kader Tlass was granted the following orders: **Syrian Orders:** Order of the Anniversary of the Establishment of United Arab Republic; Order of Victory Token; Order for Loyalty of the Third Degree; Order for Loyalty of the Second Degree (Replacement); Medal of the Army's Day; Order of March 8, 1963; Order of the Syrian Arab Army; Order for Combat Training of the First Degree; Syrian Order for Merit of the Second Degree; Order for Loyalty of the Excellent Degree (Replacement); Order for Long Service and Ideal Instance; Syrian Order for Merit of the First Degree (Replacement); Order of the 25th Anniversary of the Syrian Arab Army Establishment; Order of Military Honour of Knight Degree; Order of the 6th October 1973; Order of Courage of the First Degree; Syrian Order for Merit of the Excellent Degree (Replacement); Order of Peace in Lebanon; Order of the Protection of March 8th Revolution; Order of the 25th Anniversary of March 8th Revolution; Order of the 50th Anniversary of the Syrian Arab Army Establishment. **Arab Orders:** He was allowed to accept and hold the following orders: Order of Moroccan Military Merit of the Excellent Degree (Ribbon); Order of the Anniversary of Palestinian Liberation Army Estabishment, from Palestinian Liberation Organization; Order of Honour Star, from the Executive Committee of Palestinian Liberation Organization; Order of the two Niles of the First Degree from the Sudan Republic President; Order of Honour Star, from the Egyptian Arab Republic President; Order of Lebanon Cedar of Higher Officer Degree. **Foreign Orders:** He was allowed to accept and hold the following orders and medals: Medal of the 20th Anniversary of the Great National war Victory (1941-1945), from the Soviet Government; Medal of the 40th Anniversary of the Great National war of the Soviet Union; Soviet Order for Strengthing of Combat Concord; Soviet Order for Friendship Between Nations; Order of Senegali Merit of Higher Officer Degree; Order of the Republic Flag of the First Degree from Democratic Republic of Korea; Order of Service Struggle of Gold Order Degree of German Democratic Republic; Order of French Merit of the First Degree; Order of 30th Anniversary of Cuban Army Establishment; Order of Education and Defence of the First Degree of Czechoslovakia Republic; Great Silver Order, the Highest Order for distinguished Service in the Republic of Austria; Honourary Order of General Staff Academy of the Armed Forces in Russian

Federation Republic. **Addr.:** Ministry of Defence, Minister's Office, Damascus, Syria.

TLEMSANI SLIMANI (Othmane), Moroccan economist. **Born** on October 13, 1941 in Fes, Morocco. **Married,** 1 child. **Dipl.:** degrees in Law and Economic Sciences. **Career:** Teacher of Political Economy at the Moroccan School of Administration; Finance Inspector; Secretary General, Ministry of Finance Department; several assignments abroad specially with the imf in Washington; secretary of State for Economic Affairs in Prime Minister's office (1977); Director General of Credit Immobilier Hotelier (1979-). **Prof. Addr.:** 187, Hassan II Avenue, Casablanca 01, Morocco.

TLILI (Ahmad), Tunisian trade unionist and statesman. **Born** in Tunisia. **Educ.:** Secondary and Higher. **Career:** Member of Bureau and Former Secretary-General of Tunisian Workers General Union; First Vice-President of Bureau of National Assembly since 1959; Member of Political Bureau of Destour Socialist Party (November 1964). **Addr.:** Tunisian Workers General Union, Muhammad Ali Square, Tunis, Tunisia.

TOBBAL (Lakhdar Bin), Algerian politician. **Born** in 1923 in Constantine, Algeria. **Career:** Member of Coordination and Action Centre (1951); Undertook command of Wilaya II (1956); Minister of Interior in First Provisionl Government, nominated Member of Triumvirate (1960); Minister of State in Provisional Government inaugurated (1960); Visited China and USSR with Ferhat Abbas (1960); participated in negotiations leading to Evian Agreement (1962); Chairman of Board, National Steel-Manufacturing Company (SNS). **Prof. Addr.:** SNS, 5 Rue Abou Moussa, Algiers, Algeria.

TOBIA (Maguid), Egyptian writer. **Born** in 1938 in Egypt. **Dipl.:** B.Sc. in Mathematics, Diploma in Script Writing and M.A. in Film Production. **Career:** Official at the Higher Council of Arts and Literature (1969-78); Author of several film scripts and scenarios; Official and freelance writer at the Ministry of Culture. Member of the Egyptian Writers' Union, Society of Egyptian Film Critics, Chamber of Cinema Industry, Supreme Council of Culture and Story Committee. **Publ.:** several short story collections and novels, including "The Music Kiosk, Hanan". **Award:** Winner of Short story Club Award (1964), First Prize from Egyptian Cinema Institute for film scenarios and State Encouragement Prize for the Best Novel. **Hobbies:** reading, travelling, literature, cinema. **Addr.:** 15 al-Liwaa Abdul Aziz Ali, Heliopolis, Cairo, Egypt.

TOHME (Georges, Joseph), Syrian diplomat. **Born** on March 1, 1921 in Damascus. **Son** of Joseph Tohmé and Mrs., née Wadia Chamiyé. **Married** to Miss Rose Zuraq on June 7, 1947, 3 children: Ramez, Hala and Maged. **Educ.:** Syrian University (Damascus), American University (U.S.A.). **Dipl.:** Bachelor of Arts (1942), Master of Arts (1944), Doctor of Philosophy (1951). **Career:** Joined Syrian Ministry of Foreign Affairs (1941); Attaché Syrian Embassy to London (1945-46); also Alternate Delegate to Unesco, Attaché Syrian Embassy in Washington (1947-52); also delegate to Foreign Operations Administrations; Alernate Government International Monetary Fund (1950); Director United Nations and Treaties Department of Foreign Affairs Ministry (1952-54); Assistant Professor of Philospphy and Assistant to the Dean of Arts and Science Faculty, American University of Beirut (1954-56); Alternate Delegate Executive Board Unesco (1954-57); Director Research Department of Foreign Affairs Ministry (1956-57); also Delegate to the United Nations General Assembly; Represented Syria on the United Nations Trusteeship Council (1958); Consul General of Arab Republic of Egypt in New York City (1961-63); Consul General of Syrian Arab Republic in New York City (1963); Deputy Permanent Representative at the United Nations (1961-69); Minister of National Economy in the Syrian Arab Republic (1963-64); Lecturer and Professor of Philosophy at the Syrian University of Damascus (1963-64); Syrian Delegate to the Executive Council for Agriculture Organization (1967); Elected Chairman of the Fourth Committee (Trusteeship and Non-Self-Governing Territories) of the 22nd session of the General Assembly of the United Nations (September 1967- September 1968); Ambassador and Permanent Representative to the UN (1965-72); Adviser to Organization of Arab Petroleum Exporting Countries (OAPEC). **Publ.:** Author of numerous works, in English and Arabic, e.g. "Islam" (1957), "The Climax of Phisolophical Conflict in Islam" (1953), "The Constitution and Electoral Laws in Syria, where Islam and Christianity Meet" (1960), "The Dynamics of Neutrelism in the Arab World: A Symposium" (1964), "Arab Emigrants in the United States" (1965). **Awards:** Order Syrian Merit, Commander Order St. Paul and St. Peter (Greek Orthodox Patriarch of Damascus). **Remark:** Fluent Arabic, French, English and German. **Addr.:** OAPEC, P.O.Box 20501, Tel.: 420051, Kuwait.

TOLBA (Mostafa, Kamal, Dr.), Egyptian international civil servant, under secretary general, executive director of the U.N. environment programme. **Born** on December 8, 1922 at Gharbia, Egypt. **Son** of Kamal Tolba and Mrs. Shafika Abu Samra. **Married** to Saneya Zaki Labib, no children. **Education:** Cairo University; London University. **Dipl.:** B.Sc. Special Degree in Botany with first Class Honours, Faculty of Science, Cairo Unviersity; D.I.C. (Diploma of the Imperial college), London; Ph.D. Plant Pathology, London University, Fellow of Imperial College. **Career:** Lecturer (1949); Assistant professor (1958); Assistant Secretary-General, National Science Council of Egypt (1959); Secretary-General, National Science Council of Egypt (1961); Professor of Microbiology, National Research Centre (1965); Under Secretary of State for Higher Education

(1965-71); Professor, Chair of Microbiology, Cairo University (1968); Minister of Youth (1971); Visiting Professor, Cairo University (1971-73); President, Egyptian Academy pf Scientific Research and Technology; Deputy Executive Director, United Nations Environment Programme (1973-75); Executive Director, United Nations Environment, Programme (1976-present). **Work:** More than 200 official and public statements addresses and lectures, some 95 articles in technical magazines on plant diseases and four books on environmental policy. **Awards:** State Prize of Egypt in Biology (1959); Decorations from twelve contries including Spain, Hungary, Jordan, Poland, Morocco, Egypt and U.S.A. Honorary Degrees of Doctor of Science from Moscow University, from the State Faculty of Agriculture, Gembloux, from Hanyang University, Seoul, Korea, from Kenyatta University, Kenya and Honorary Professorship from Beijing, china in recognition of services to the world in the field of Environment. Elected fellow of the Imperial College, London. **Hobby:** Reading. **Credit Cards:** American Express and Master. **Professional Address:** UNEP, P.O.Box 30552, Tel: 230800, Nairobi, Kenya. **Private Address:** 46 Mosaddak Street, Dokki, Giza, Cairo, Egypt.

TOM (Ali, al), Sudanese economist. **Born** in 1931 in Khartoum, Sudan. **Married. Educ.:** University of Khartoum, Sudan (1951-56); Oxford University, UK; National Planning Institute, Egypt. **Dipl.:** Diplomas in Agricultural Science and Economics, Certificate in Agricultural Planning. **Career:** Inspector of Provincial Agriculture, Sudan (1956-58); Senior Agricultural Planning Economist, Ministry of Agricultural Planning, Sudan (1959-63); Agricultural Planning Economist, FAO (1963-65); Regional Land Tenure and Settlement Officer for Africa, FAO, Addis Ababa, Ethiopia (1956-68); Investment Economist, FAO, Rome, Italy (1968-69); Minister of Agrarian Reform and Production, Sudan (1969-70); Minister of Agricultura in Sudan (1970-71); Director, FAO Agricultural Division, Economic Commision for Africa (ECA), UN, Addis Ababa (1971); Member of International Association of Agricultural Economists, African Association for Advancement of Agricultural Science, Arab Association of Agricultural Engineering, Sudan Philosphical Society, International Development Association and Sudan Agricultural Society. **Publ.:** numerous books on agricultural reform and development. **Hobbies:** swimming, music, photography, numismatics, table tennis, basketball. **Member:** Ethiopian Creative Arts Centre. **Prof. Addr.:** ECA, UN, P.O.Box 3001, Addis Ababa, Ethiopia.

TOMBOURA (Joseph James), Sudanese politician. **Born** in 1929 in Wau. **Educ.:** University of Khartoum, Faculty of Engineering, specialisation in the United State of America. **Dipl.:** B.Sc. (Engineering), M.Sc. **Career:** Joined the Southern Front (an extreme wing of the Sudan African National Union formed in 1958); Elected to the National Constituent Assembly (May 1968); Served as Minister of Public Works, Communicatins and Transport (1978-80) under the regional presidency of Lt.-Gen. Lagu; Elected by President Numeiry as secretary for the regional Sudanese Socialist Union (the country's sole legal party) now dissolved; Elected to the third Regional People's Assembly in June 1980 and to the fourth Assembly in May 1982, as a representative for Western Equatoria. **Address:** Khartoum, Sudan.

TOUKAN (Ala Uddin, Dr.), Jordanian Physician. **Born** in 1947 in Jerusalem, Palestine. **Son** of Baha Uddin Toukan (diplomat) **and** Mrs. née Hanan Hashem. **Married** to Randa Ala Uddin Toukan, 3 children: Alia, Hanan, Oraib. **Educ.:** University of London, UK; University of Western Ontario, Canada; Boston University, U.S.A. **Dipl.:** M.B., B.S. (London), American Board Internal Medicine, American Board Gastroenterology, Fellow of the Cannadian College of Physicians of Canada, Fellow of American College of Physicians. **Career:** Clinical Research Associate, Boston University (1975-1977); Assistant Professor of Medicine, Jordan University (1978-); Chief, GI and Liver Section, Jordan University Hospital (1978-); Fulbright Scholar, Atlanta USA (1985); Professor of Medicine, Jordan University (1989-); Chairman, Department of Medicine, Jordan University (1990-); Dean, Faculty of Medicine, Jordan University (1991-). **Sport:** Swimming. **Hobbies:** Gardening, Music, Reading. **Prof. Addr.:** University of Jordan, Tel.: 845845, Amman, Jordan. **Priv. Addr.:** P.O.Box 5192, Tel.: 821816, Amman, Jordan.

TOUKAN (Fadwa), Jordanian writer. **Born** in Jordan. **Educ.:** Secondary and Higher. **Career:** Writer, novelist, poet. **Publ.:** Author of several books, e.g. "Seule avec les jours", "Je l'ai trouvée", "Donnez-nous de l'amour", "Face à la porte close" (Dar al-Adab Edition, Beirut). **Addr.:** Amman, Jordan.

TOUKAN (Fawaz, Ahmad), Jordanian academic. **Born** in 1940 in Jerusalem. **Married,** 1 son, 3 daughters. **Educ.:** Yale University, USA. **Dipl.:** M.A. in Arabic and Semitic Studies, Ph.D. **Career:** Tutor at Jordan University (1968-74); Assistant Professor (1974-); Founder Member of the Jordanian Writers' Union (1974-). **Publ.:** "Mahmoud Darwish": Selected Peoms, translated into English (1973), "The Lake" (1978), "The Puzzled" (1979), "The Merchant and the Sparrow" (1985). **Award:** State Prize for Poetry, Kingdom of Jordan (1978), Prize for Best Poet, Arab Organization for Education, Culture and Sciences (1979). **Hobbies:** music, producing documentary films, squash. Deputy Chairman of Jordan Squash Union (1981-). **Addr.:** Dhahiat Iskan al-Jamia al-Ordoniah, P.O.Box 13052, Amman, Jordan.

TOUKAN (Mohamad, Abdul Rahman), Jordanian executive. **Born** in 1918 in Salt, Jordan. **Educ.:** Secondary School, Salt (1937); Damascus University, Syria. **Dipl.:**

Licence in Law (1941). **Career:** Teacher, Ministry of Education (1937-40); Judge and Prosecutor, Ministry of Justice (1942-48); Ministry of Foreign Affairs (1948-49); President, Court of First Instance; Member, the Appeals Court, Amman (1950-51); Assistant Secretary, Amman Municipality (1953-55); Minister of State, Prime Ministerial Affairs (1966); Minister of Transport (1966); General Manager, Bank al-Ahli (1966-71); Deputy Governor, Central Bank (1971-73); Deputy Governor, Central Bank (1971-73); Mayor of Amman (1973). **Awards:** Star of Jordan; Order of King Abdul Aziz (2nd Class). **Addr.:** Amman, Jordan.

TOUQ (Muhieddeen Sh.), Jordanian Director-United Nations. **Born** in 1944 in Amman, Jordan. **Son** of Shaban Touq (deceased) **and** Mrs. Khireieh (deceased). **Married** in 1977 in Amman to Miss Hiba Nabulsi, 2 children: Toleen (1979), Yanal (1982). **Educ.:** Jordan University (1962-66), Ball State University-USA (1968-69), Purdue University-USA (1969-72). **Dipl.:** B.A. Psychology (1966) Jordan University, M.A. Educ. Psychology (1969) Ball State University, Ph.D. Educ. Psychology (1972) Purdue University. **Career:** Minister of Administrative Development (1994-95); Deputy Director of Educ. UNRWA/UNESCO (1992-1994); President of Philadelphia University (1991-1992); Dean of the College of Educ. - UAE University (1984-1990); Dean of Students-Jordan University (1982-1984); Professor of Psychology (1973-1990). **Other Information:** Author of Six Books, Author & Co-Author of More than Fifty Research papers, Attended More than Fifty National, Regional & Inter Conferences. Head of Jordan Basketball Federation (1991-1993), Member of the National Olympic Committee (1994-). **Sports:** Basketball, Handball. **Hobbies:** Sports, Reading, Gardening. **Member of:** APA, AERA, NAGTC, ICET, WCCI, JEA, JPS. **Credit Cards:** AMEX, Visa. **Prof. Addr.:** P.O.Box 484, Amman, Jordan, Tel.: 671121. **Priv. Addr.:** P.O.Box 13223, Amman 11942, Jordan, Tel.: 842004.

TOURI (Abdelaziz), Moroccan Director of Patrimony. **Born** in 1949 at Azrou, Morocco. **Son** of Said Touri (Tradesman) **and** Mrs. Khaddouj Bent Driss. **Married** in 1988 in Azrou to Badia Aourarh, 1 daughter, Tilila. **Educ.:** Faculty of Letters, University - Mohamed V, Rabat, Morocco; Sorbonne, Paris IV, France. **Dipl.:** State Doctorate es-Lettres. Speciality: Islamic Art and Archeology. **Career:** Professor of History and Geography (1973-1976); Assistant Director, Institut National des Sciences de l'Archéologie et du Patrimoine (INSAB-Rabat) (1986-1988); Director of Patrimony at the Ministry of Cultural Affairs (1988-). **Other Information:** Director of the Archeological Mission Maroco-Française des Jbala-Ghomara (North of Morocco) since 1984-1985; Président-Fondateur du Comité Marocain de l'ICOM. **Awards:** Knight «des Lettres et des Arts (France). **Sport:** Jogging. **Hobbies:** Travelling, Reading. **Member:** Société Marocaine d'Archéologie et du Patrimoine. **Prof. Addr.:** 17, rue Michlifen, Rabat, Tel.: 671381. **Priv. Addr.:** 333, Av. Hassan II, Diour Jamaa, Rabat, Morocco.

TOURI (Rashid), Algerian academic. **Born** in 1928. **Educ.:** Faculty of Science, Algiers University, Algeria; Sorbonne, University of Paris, France. **Dipl.:** Degree in Mathematics, Agregation in Mathematics. **Career:** Teacher in Algiers teaching in secondary Schools; Lecturer in mathematics at the Faculty of Science, Algiers University; Dean of the Faculty of Science, Algiers University (1964); Rector of Algiers University (1970). **Prof. Addr.:** University of Algiers, Faculty of Science, 2 Rue Didouche Mourad, Algiers, Algeria.

TOUTOUNJI (Lucien, Sami), Egyptian executive. **Born** in 1936 in Cairo, Egypt. **Son** of Sami Toutounji. **Married** in 1961, 1 son. **Educ.:** Cairo University, Egypt; University of Geneva, Switzerland. **Dipl.:** B.A. (Business Administration); M.B.A. **Career:** Export Department, Sudan Import and Export Company, Cairo (1954-57); International Finance Corporation, Washington DC, USA (1965-74); Manager, Export Dept., Sudan Import and Export Co. (1965-74); Senior Executive Manager, Industrial Bank of Kuwait KSC, Kuwait (1974-86); Chairman and Managing Director, Pyramids Paper Mills SAE (since 1986). **Addr.:** P.O.Box. 103, Mohandessin, Giza, Egypt.

TOWAGRY (Ali, Ibn Mohammed Ibn Abdullah,), Saudi academic. **Born** in 1932 at Buraidah, Saudi Arabia. **Education: Dipl.:** M.A. Educational Administration, Kansas University U.S.A., 1970. Ph.D. Educational Administration, Arkansas University. A member of the Arkansas Alumni Association. A fellow of the International Institute for Educational Planning, Paris. **Career:** Director General of the Arab Bureau of Education for the Gulf States (ABEGS) since 1988; A member of the Board of Trustees for the Arab Gulf University since 1988; Editor-in-Chief of Risalat Al Khaleej Al Arabi (An Educational and Cultural Periodical); General Supervisor of "Arab Gulf Journal of Scientific Research"; An Observer of UNESCO's General Conference and the International Conference on Education since 1988; A participant in ALECSO's and ISESCO's General Conferences; Presentation of a speech on Activities and Positions of the ABEGS for each Conference; General Supervisor of The Project for Developing and Unifying Educational Curricula in the member states; General Supervisor of the ABEGS' publication program (286 titles published up till now); Head of the Committee of Co-ordinating and developing institutions for the preparation of Teachers of Special Education; Attended most of the national, regional and international meetings on Education held during the last decade. **Publications:** Two research papers given at the above conferences; a paper on Organization Analysis and Proposed Reoganization of the Ministry of Education, K.S.A. **Hobby:** Reading. **Address:** Arab Bureau of Education for the Gulf States, P.O.Box 3908, Riyadh 11481, Saudi Arabia, Tel.: 4774627, 4789889/

4774644, Fax: 4783165, Telex: 401441 Tarbia SJ. (Home Tel. No.:) 4784917.

TRABOULSI (Antoun, Badi), Syrian barrister. **Born** in 1919 in Homs. **Son** of Badi' Traboulsi. **Educ.:** Damascus and Beirut. **Dipl.:** Bachelor of Law at the Damascus Faculty of Law. **Career:** Lawyer at the Municipal Treasury and Representative of the Homs Bar Association Homs. **Addr.:** Boustan Oiwane, Tel.: 405, Homs, Syria.

TRABOULSI (Hassan), Syrian banker. **Born** in Damascus, Syria on 1954. **Son** of Dr. Izzat Traboulsi (former Minister of Finance) **and** Mrs. Souad Traboulsi. **Married. Educ.:** University of Wisconsin, USA. **Dipl.:** B.B.A. **Career:** Manager at Arab Finance Cor. Paris-Beirut (1977); Investments Advisor at the Central Bank of UAE, Abu Dhabi (1980); Representative of Citicorp; Investment Bank for the Middle East (1982). **Sport:** Squash. **Credit Cards:** All. **Addr.:** Manama, Bahrain.

TRABOULSI (Ibrahim Yusuf), Saudi academic. **Born** in 1946, in Jeddah, Saudi Arabia. **Dipl.:** Ph.D. (Bacteriology), University College of North Wales, U.K. **Career:** Demonstrator, Faculty of Agriculture, King Saud University Instructor, Assiatant Professor; Associate Professor of Microbiology and Chairman, Department of Plant Protection, Full Professor of Microbiology and Plant Pathology, King Saud University; member, Biological Society of Saudi Arabia, Association of Applied Biologists, U.K., Federation of British Plant Pathologists, U.K., American Phytopathological Society; participated in fourteen national and international scientific conferences and meetings. **Publications:** Practical Microbiology, Three Books for applied Biology (for Secondary Schools in the Kingdom of Saudi Arabia); Principal investigator for two major Projects on Agricultural Problems on National Scale; participant in several specialized programmes on Riyadh Radio and TV. **Hobbies:** Reading, swimming. **Address:** Faculty of Agriculture, King Saud University, Tel.: 4678426 (Office) and 4686155 Ext. 2625 (Home), Riyadh, Saudi Arabia.

TRABZOUNI (Muhieddin Rashad), Saudi academic. **Born** in 1938, Cairo, Egypt. **Dipl.:** Ph.D. (Accountancy). **Career:** Inspector, General Control Board, Cost Accountant, PETROMIN; member of Conference on Islamic Economics (1975), several M.N. Conferences; now Lecturer, King Abdulaziz University, Jeddah. **Sports:** Swimming. **Hobby:** Reading. **Addr.:** Jeddah, Saudi Arabia.

TRIKI (Mahmud), Tunisian journalist. **Born** in 1936 in Tunisia. **Married**, two children. **Educ.:** Licentiate in Law and Economics, Paris, France. **Career:** Head of Department, Tunisian Agricultural Bank (1965); Editor in Chief, Socialist Destour Party organ "l'Action" (1967); Director of the Tunisian Party Company (1969); Prime Minister's Office (1970); Director of the Political Affairs in the Prime Minister's Office (1972); Chairman and Managing Director of Tunis-Afrique-Press (TAP); President of the Union of Arab Press Agencies; Coordinator of the Press Agencies of the Non Aligned Countries. **Medals:** Officer of the Order of the Tunisian Republic (1972); Chevalier of the Order of Tunisian Independence (1976); Grand Officer of the Egyptian Order of Merit (1972). **Sport:** Football. **Hobbies:** Sociology, theatre, poetry, hunting, archaeology. **Addr.:** 25 Ave. Habib Bourguiba, Tel.: 249000, Tunis, Tunisia.

TUHAMI (Abdul Rahman), Moroccan physician, and former minister. **Married. Educ.:** M.D., Faculty of Medicine, Toulouse, France; specialist training in Neurology, France. **Career:** Averroes Hospital, Casablanca, Morocco; in charge of hospitals al Youssefiyya, Essaouira and Demi-Mellal; Chief Physician, Averroes Hospital, Casablanca (1971); Minister of Public Health in Lamrani Government (1972); Private Physician to HM the King (since 1974); Minister of Public Health (1975-77). **Addr.:** Rabat, Morocco.

TUHAMI (Hassan), Egyptian statesman. **Born in 1924** in Egypt. **Career:** President of the Islamic Conference (1959); Ambassador to Austria (1961); Chief Observer on the Egyptian Delegation to the International Atomic Energy Agency; member of the Cabinet (1968); Secretary General of the Cabinet (1969); Director General of the Arab Socialist Union (ASU) (1969); Minister of State (1970); Presidential Adviser (1970); Secretary General, Islamic Conference (1971). **Addr.:** Cairo, Egypt.

TUHAMI (Mohamad Sharif), Sudanese geologist. **Born** in 1934. **Married**, 4 children. **Educ.:** Punjab University, India: University of Arizona, USA; University of London, UK. **Dipl.:** B.Sc., M.Sc. and Ph.D. in Geology. **Career:** Geologist, Sudanese Geology and Mining Corporation (1958-66); Director of Water Corporation (1966-69); Adviser to a number of Foreign Companies (1969-78); Member of the Central Committee of the Sudanese Socialist Union; Minister of Energy and Mining (1978-85). Presently, Minister of Irrigation and Water Resources. **Decor.:** Order of the Two Niles (al-Nilayn) (1st Class), Sudan. **Hobby:** tennis. **Addr.:** Ministry of Irrigation and Water Resources, P.O.Box 878 Khartoum, Sudan.

TUMA (Elias, H.), Professor of Economics, Emeritus, (1994-) Tuma's Foothill Trees, owner and operator, (1992-). **Born** in Palestine. **Son** of Father Hanna Tuma and Bahji Khalil Kaloush. **Married** in 1959, three children. **Educ.:** University of Redlands, California, B.A. Cum Laude, Sociology, (1957); University of California Berkeley, California, Ph.D., Economics, (1962). **Career:** Probation officer for Arab Juveniles (1950-55) Israel; Assistant Professor of Economics University of Saskatchewan, Saskatoon, Sask, Canada (1963-65); Assistant Professor, Associate Professor, and Professor of Economics, University of California, Davis, California, (1965-1994); Professor, American University of Cairo and Director of Education Abroad Program of the University of California in Egypt, (1981-83). **Pub.:** Nine books and over 80 journal articles and research reports, including. "Twenty-Six Centuries of Agrarian Reform" Univ. of California Press, 1965, "Economic History and the Social Sciences, Problems of Methodology", Univ. of California Press, 1971; "Peacemaking and the Immoral War. Arabs and Jews in the Middle East" Harper and Row, 1972; "The Economic Case for Palestine", with Haim Darin-Drabkin, Croom-Helm, 1978; "Economic and Political Change in the Middle East", Pacific Books, 1987; "Cultural Diversity and Economic Education", with Barry Haworth, Pacific Books 1993, "The Persistence of Economic Discrimination has been published a monthly, Another Viewpoint for ten years. Comparative Study", Pacific Books, 1995. **Hobbies:** Wood carving, swimming gardening, photography. **Member:** American Economic Association Middle East Economic Association. **Prof. Addr.:** Department of Economics, University of California, Davis, California 95616-8578. e-mail: tuma@vfr.net; web site: http://www.econ.ucdavis.edu/ faculty/ tuma/ avpindex.html.

TUNI (Sayed Mohamad), Egyptian academic. **Born** in 1926 in Bani Swaif, Egypt. **Married. Dipl.:** Ph.D. in Animam Husbandry, Anima and Poultry Nutrition. **Career:** Teacher at al-Azhar University (1950); Teacher, Minia Agricultural Secondary School (1951); Deputy Principal, Aswan Agricultural School; Associate Professor at the High Institute of Agriculture, Minia (1956); Associate Professor, College of Agriculture, Minia (1967); Professor, Minia Agriculture College (1973); Professor and Head of Animal Husbandry Department, Minia Agricultural College (1973-). **Publ.:** numerous essays published in various academic journals. **Prof. Addr.:** College of Agriculture, University of Minia, Egypt.

TUNISSI (Abdallah B.), Saudi leading businessman. **Born** on 14 January 1945 in Mecca, Saudi Arabia. **Dipl.:** B.A. (Economics), University of London. **Career:** President, Toonsi Development and Contracting Company; member of the Board of Directors, Makkah Chamber of Commerce; founding member of the Saudi Cairo Bank, Makkah Philanthropic Society and Makkah Welfare Society; Fellow of the Royal Society of Arts, U.K. **Publications:** co-author of The Arab World. **Hobbies:** Reading, travel. **Address:** P.O.Box 262, Tel. 6872319 and 6871957 (Office), and 6890741 (Home), Jeddah, Saudi Arabia.

TUNISSI (Abdul Rahman Salih al-Fedal, al), Saudi academic. **Born** at Medina in 1934. **Dipl.:** B.A. (Sociology). **Career:** Inspector of Social Education; social expert-adviser, Ministry of Education; Director of External Relations, Ministry of Education; Director of Physical Education and Activities, Ministry of Education; Director-General of Youth Affairs, Ministry of Education; Secretary of the Saudi Scouts Society; member of the Saudi Red Crescent Society; member of Supreme Council of King Abdulaziz University, Supreme Council for Youth Welfare; member of the Tributory Committee for Haj Pilgrimage; contributed in developing physical and artistic education grammars in Saudi Schools; helped in laying down the administrative system for the Ministry of Labour and Social Affairs; participated in the meeting of the International Education Bureau (Geneva), Illiteracy Conference (Teheran), Arab Ministers of Education Conference (Kuwait), Social Development Conference (Beirut); now Director-General of al-Thagr Model Schools. **Honour:** Arab Scouts Necklace. **Sport:** Swimming. **Hobby:** Photography. **Prof. Addr.:** al-Thagr Model School, Mecca Road, Tel. 6896624 (Office) and 6878151 (Home), Jeddah, Saudi Arabia.

TUNISSI (Mohamad al-Taib, al), Saudi retired general and presently businessman. **Born** in 1926 in Medina, Saudi Arabia. **Dipl.:** Diploma, Higher Studies Institute, Medina; took courses in Administration Affairs Management and Leadership and Military Affairs. **Career:** Office Manager, Artillary and Military Troops; Assistant Chief of Logistics; Director of Ordinance Corps; General Manager, Military Factories and Armed Forces Public Affairs; Assistant Chief of the Unifed Arabian Command, Cairo; Chief of Military Operations; General Director of Public Security; Ambassador, Ministry of Foreign Affairs; Director General of Dallah-Avco Joint Venture Co.; owner of Tunisif Trading, Industry, Contracting Establishment; honorary member, al-Ahli Club; member, al-Itihad Club, Jeddah Hunting Club, Cairo, Okaz Establishment, Jeddah, Welfare Society, Riyadh; Chairman of Tunisi Establishment, Omega Co., al-Majd Printing, Arabian Co. for Animal Production and Saudi Tile Factory; member of Gulf Co., Estate Development, al-Shams Pyramid Hotels, Saudi Sea Transport and Saudi Cars Mack and Tata; life membership of the Conference of the Islamic Institute for Defence and Technology, London. **Honours:** King Abdulaziz Decoration; Palestine Star; Orders of Merit from Syria and Egypt; the Moroccan Military Decoration, the Lebanese National Cedar Decoration, the Iranian Crown Decoration. **Publ.:** Military Management. **Hobbies:** Reading, travel. **Address:** P.O.Box 6030, Tel. 6650851 (Office) and 6604751 (Home), Jeddah, Saudi Arabia. Jeddah.

TURABI (Hassan Abdallah), Sudanese politician. **Born** in 1932 in Kassab, Sudan. **Son** of Abdullah Turabi (former Judge). **Married** in 1961 to the Sister of Sudanese leader Sadek Mahdi, six children: Saddik (Agronomist), Asma, Issam, Salma, Mohd Omar, Oussama. **Educ.:** in Sudan, London, and Paris. **Dipl.:** Graduated, Faculty of Law, University of Khartoum, Sudan (1958); Higher degrees, London University, UK (1961); Paris University, France (1964). **Career:** Joined the Islamic Brotherhood (1954-); Lecturer in Law, University of Khartoum; Dean of the Law Faculty, University of Khartoum (1964); resigned to become Secretary General of the Islamic Charter Front; graduate member, Constituent Assembly (1965); imprisoned twice; Attorney-General, Cabinet (17 August 1979); in 1992 visited Egypt, U.S.A., Canada; in April 1996-2000 president of the National Assembly. **Addr.:** Khartoum, Sudan.

TURAIFI (Nasser Ibn Aqeel, al), Saudi academic. **Born** in 1948 in Hail, Saudi Arabia, **Dipl.:** M.A. (Jurisdiction), Ph.D. **Career:** Teacher, Hail Religious Institute (1970-71); Riyadh Religious Institute (1971-73); Instructor, Faculty of Arabic Language, King Saud University (1973-74); Lecturer (1974-75); Vice Dean, Faculty of Arabic Language and Social Sciences (1975-77); teachers at the Faculty of Shari'a (Islamic Law), Faculty of Osoul el-Din (Religious Rules), Faculty of Internal Security Forces, Riyadh; former Secretary of the Council of the Faculty of Arabic and Social Studies, King Saud University; Assistant Secretary to the Islamic Jurisprudence Conference, Riyadh, 1976; representative of the Board for Scientific Research, Decisions, Advocation and Guidance to the Islamic Education Conference, Kenya, 1977 and the Conference of the Prophet's Narration Experts, Kashmir, India, 1978. **Prof. Addr.:** P.O.Box 15439, Riyadh. **Priv. Addr.:** Tel. 4654508, Riyadh, Saudi Arabia.

TURK (Mohamed Abdel Moneim Ibrahim), Egyptian banker. **Born** on June 14, 1930 in Rashid, Egypt. **Son** of Ibrahim Hassan Turk **and** Mrs. N.S. Zidan. **Married** in 1956 to Neima Youssef Zidan, two sons: Ibrahim (1957) and Hassan (1960). **Educ.:** Alexandria Secondary School (1949); Alexandria University, Faculty of Commerce (1953) and Faculty of law (1959); Central Bank Institution and Management Institution. **Dipl.:** in Banking (1966), in Economics (1970) and in Management. **Career:** Loan Officer, Development Industrial Bank (1954); Manager, Industrial Bank, Alexandria (1962); Manager, Bank of Alexandria (1970); Director, Development Industrial Bank, Alexandria Branch (1976); General Manager and Member of the Board of Development Industrial Bank (since 1984). President, Democratic Unionist Party. **Sports:** Tennis, French Billiard. **Hobby:** Tennis. **Member:** Alexandria Sporting Club. **Prof. Addr.** Development Industrial Bank, 110 Galaa Street, Cairo, Egypt. **Priv. Addr.:** 33 Delta St. Sporting, Alexandria, Egypt.

TURKI (Abdallah Ibn Abdulmohsen, al), Saudi Minister. **Born** in 1939 in Riyadh, Saudi Arabia. **Dipl.:** Ph.D. (Jurisprudence). **Career:** Secondary school teacher: Director of an institute; Professional Inspector; teaching staff member, Faculty of Shari's (Islamic Law); Dean, Faculty of Arabic Language; Vice-Rector and laer Rector, Imam Muhammad Ibn Saud Islamic University; member, King Faisal Philanthropic Organization, the Middle East Research Centre, Surabaya, Indonesia and the Organization of Islamic Da'wa, Khartoum; member of the Council, the Islamic University, Medina, King Saud University; the Supreme Council of Information and the Universities' Supreme Council; Appointed Minister of Islamic Affairs Endowments, Call and Guidance (July 11, 1993-). **Publications:** Onsoul Mazhab al-Imam Ahmad Ibn Hanbal (Rules of the Creed of Imam Ahmad Ibn Hanbal), Asbab Ikhtilaf al-Fuqaha' (Reasons for Creed Differences), anaqeb al-Imam Ahmad Ibn Hanbal (Good Traits of Imam Ahmad Ibn Hanbal), editor. **Address:** Riyadh, Saudi Arabia.

TURKI (Abdul Aziz Abdallah, al), Saudi Official. **Born** on August 12, 1936 in Jeddah, Saudi Arabia. **Married,** 2 children. **Educ.:** B.A. (Business Administration), Cairo University, 1964. **Career:** Secretary General, Organization of Arab Petroleum Exporting Countries (OAPEC), since 1 March 1990; Deputy Minister, Ministry of Petroleum and Mineral Resources, Saudi Arabia, since 1975- seconded to OAPEC as of 1 March 1990; Secretary General, the Supreme Advisory Council for Petroleum and Mineral Affairs, Saudi Arabia (1975-90); Saudi Arabia's Governor to OPEC (1975-90); Member, the Board of Directors of the Saudi Ports Authority (1987-1989); Chairman, Pemref (Petromin-Mobil Yanbu Refinery Company Ltd.), (1982-89); Member, the Board of Directors of the Arabian Oil Company Ltd. (1980-89); Member, ARAMCO'S Board of Directors (1980-89); Member, the Petromin Board of Directors (1975-89); Chairman, the Board of Directors of Arab Maritime Petroleum Transport Company (AMPTC), Kuwait (1981-87); a. Assistant Secretary General, OAPEC (1970-75), b. Acting Secretary General, OAPEC (1 March- 21 September, 1973); Director of General Affairs, Directorate of Mineral Resources, Saudi Arabia (1968-70); Director, Office of the Minister of Petroleum and Mineral Resources, Saudi Arabia (1966-68); ARAMCO, Saudi Arabia (1954-66); American Embassy, Jeddah (1953-1954); Banque de l'indochine, Saudi Arabia (1949-52). **Sports:** Tennis, Swimming. **Addr.:** Organization of Arab Petroleum Exporting Countries (OAPEC), P.O.Box 20501, Safat 13066, Kuwait, Tel.: 5340713, Fax: 5340694.

TURKI (Abdul Aziz Rashid, al), Saudi academic. **Born** in 1942, in Medina, Saudi Arabia. **Dipl.:** M.B.A. (Personnel Administration). **Career:** Teacher (1969-70); Supervisor of Scholarships Department, King Abdulaziz University (1973-74); Personnel Manager (1974-77); former Director General of Administration, King Abdulaziz University (1977). **Hobbies:** Reading, sports. **Addr.:** Mecca, Saudi Arabia.

TURKI (Abdul Rahman Ali, Al-), Saudi Arabian Businessman. **Born** in 1931. **Educ.:** Faculty of Commerce. **Dipl.:** B.B.A. (Bachelor of Business Administration). **Career:** Chairman & Chief Executive Officer of A.A. TURKI Group of Companies, Saudi Arabia; Board Member of the Council of Saudi Chamber of Commerce; Major shareholder and Board Member of several Saudi and International Companies. **Act.:** Manufacturing, servicing, trading and representing major activities in: Electro-Mechanical, Petrochemical, Instrumentation, Controls, Industrial, Electrical and Construction Materials. Food Products. Packing and Forwarding, Travels, Insurance. Hospitals & universities Catering and General Services. Printing. Cars Agency. Civil Works Constructions, Industrial Installations, HVAC, Water Proofing, Soil Engineering. Industrial Maintenance. Ship Chandling, Ports & Marine Operations. Electric Panel Boards Manufacturing. Construction Materials Manufacturing. **Address: Saudi Address:** P.O.Box 718, Dammam 31421, Saudi Arabia, Tel.: 966-3-8335588, 8332339, Fax: 966-3-8339881, Telex: 801067 Turki SJ. **International Addresses: Europe:** ATCO Development Ltd., 42, Albermarle Street, London, W1X 3FE, Tel.: 44-71-4913664, Fax: 44-71-6291120, Telex: 298836 Turki G. **U.S.A.:** ATCO Development Inc., 11777, Katy Freeway, Suite 175, Houston, Texas 77079, Tel.: 1-713-8701500, Fax: 1-713 8701545, Telex; 203188 Atco UR.

TURKI (Ali Mohamad al-Ali), Saudi judge. **Born** in Qassim in 1944. **Dipl.:** B.A. (Islamic Jurisprudence). **Career:** Accountant; Inspector, Director Administrative Department, Ministry of Commerce and Industry; Judge, Ras el-Khaimah Court of Law, Ras el-Khaimah Emirate, U.A.E.; member of Supreme Court of Appeal, Ras el-Khaimah Emirate, U.A.E.; member, Legal Advisory Board (Fatwa). **Publ.:** M.A. dissertation on leave and wages according to Islamic Law. **Addr.:** Riyadh, Saudi Arabia.

TURKI (Fawaz), Palestinian writer. **Born** in 1940 near Haifa, Palestine. **Educ.:** Bourmouth College, Hampshire, United Kingdom. **Career:** Teacher in Australia and Europe; employed with Victoria Education Department, Australia; travelled widely in India; currently lives in Paris as a teacher and writer. **Publ.:** "The Disinherited: Journal of a Palestinian Exile", New York and London (1972), **Addr.:** Paris, France.

TURKI (Hilmi Qasim), Saudi senior civil servant. **Born** on 27 November 1944 in Jeddah, Saudi Arabia. **Dipl.:** Ph.D. (Industrial Economics). **Career:** Demonstrator, Faculty of Economics, University of Freibourg, Switzerland (1971); Assistant Professor of Economics (1972); General Manager, Planning and Research, Saudia; Adviser to the General Director of the Royal Commission for Yanbu Project (1978); Adviser to Swiss Credit Bank (Credit Suisse) 1980; attended the International Aviation Conference, Beirut, and the International Association of Travel Agents (IATA) conference on Cost Accounting; member of various international associations. **Publications:** Economic Significance of Oil Production for Industrialization of Saudi Arabia (Ph.D. Thesis); several research articles in German and French, including a dissertation on the Importance of Economic Development presented to the University of Freibourg. **Hobbies:** Reading, swimming, travel. **Address:** al-Harthy Building, P.O.Box 5856, **Tel.:** 6670272 (Office) and 6650472 (Home), Jeddah, **Saudi** Arabia.

TURKI (Ibrahim), Tunisian diplomat. **Born** on November 13, 1930. **Married**, 3 children. **Career:** Teacher of Arabic until 1956; Secretary of State for Foreign Affairs (1956-59); Head, Department of Economic Affairs (1959); attended economics crash course; joined United Nations General Secretariat (1959-60); Joined Ministry of Foreign Affairs (1961); Minister Plenipotentiary (1962); Consul-General, Paris (1962-65); Minister, Tunisian Embassy to Algeria (1965-67); Director, Political Affairs, Ministry of Foreign Affairs (1967-70); Ambassador to the Netherlands (1970-73); Ambassador to UK (1974-76); Secretary of State to the Minister of Foreign Affairs (1977). **Awards:** Commander, Order of the Tunisian Republic; Grand Cordon, Dutch Order of Nassau; various other foreign decorations. **Addr.:** Ministry of Foreign Affairs, Tunis Tunisia.

TURKI (Ibrahim, Al, Dr.), Saudi Professor and Businessman. **Born** on February 1956 in Jeddah, Saudi Arabia. **Son** of Abdulaziz Al-Turki, Businessman **and** Mrs. Née Fatima Al-Zoghaibi. **Married** on July 1977 in Saudi Arabia, 8 children: Osamah, Abdulaziz, Anas, Abdullah, Atikah, Nora, Minairah, Raneem. **Educ.:** Washington State University, Colorado State University, King Saud University, The Economic Institute. **Dipl.:** Ph.D, MS, B.Sc. **Career:** Board Member, The National Agricultural Development Co. (1995-97); Deputy Chairman, Gazan Agricultural Development Co.; General Manager: Saudi Livestock Transport and Trading Co. (1993-1995); Dean: College of Management Sciences and Planning (1987-1993). **Sports:** Walking, Swimming, Table Tennis. **Hobbies:** Reading... **Associations:** American Management Association. **Credit Cards:** American Express, Visa, Master Card. **Prof. Addr.:** P.O.Box 90859, Riyadh, Saudi Arabia, Tel.: 966 1 492 0368, 966 1 419 0197.

TURKI (Kamaluddin, Zaki, al), Egyptian diplomat. **Born** in 1920 in Egypt. **Son** of Zaki al-Turki. **Married. Career:** Served in the Egyptian Air Force (1958); **Ministry** of Foreign Affairs; Counsellor, Embassy to Libya (1964); Consul General, Marseilles (1964-66); Ambassador to Congo-Brazzaville (1966-70); Ambassador to Denmark (1970-73); Head of East European Department, Ministry of Foreign Affairs (1973-74); Head of West European Department (1974). **Addr.:** Ministry of Foreign Affairs, Cairo, Egypt.

TURKI (Mansoor, I., al), Saudi economist. **Born** in Saudi Arabia on 11/11/42. **Son** of Ibrahim al-Turki, (businessman). **Educ.:** King Saud University, Riyadh; Colorado State University, USA; **Dipl.:** B.Sc., M.S., Ph.D., (Honorary Doctor of Laws) from several universities. **Career:** Assistant Instructor (1963), Assistant Professor (1971), Vice Dean (1972-74) Department of Economics, King Saud University; Economic Advisor, Ministry of Finance and National Economy (1973-74); Coordinator, Saudi Arabian-United States Joint Commission on Economic Cooperation (1974-81); Deputy Minister of Finance and National Economy for Economic Affairs (1974-79); President, King Saud University and Chairman of the University Board (1979 to date). **Medals and Decorations:** Grand Officer de l'Ordre de Leopold (Belgium); Order of Diplomatic Service Merit (Republic of Korea); al-Merito Civil (Spain); Grand Officer of the First Order (Maruritania); The Grand Cordon of the Order of the Brilliant Star of the Republic of China (Taiwan); The Grand Cordon of the Order of the Brilliant Cloud of the Republic of China (Taiwan). **Addr.:** P.O.Box 2454, Tel.: 467-000, Riyadh, Saudi Arabia.

TURKI (Mohamad Turki, al), Saudi M.D. and university rector. **Born** in 1939 at al-Bakeriah (al-Rassim). **Dipl.:** B.A., M.D. (with Honours); M.R.C.P. **Career:** Lecturer; Assistant Professor, College of Medicine and Medical Sciences, Riyadh University; Dean, College of Medicine and Medical Sciences, King Faisal University, Dammam; Vice Rector, King Faisal University, Dammam. **Publications:** Several studies published in scientific journals. **Address:** King Faisal University, P.O.Box 4908, Tel.: 8577984, 8577000, Dammam, Saudi Arabia.

TURKI (Yusuf Ibrahim al-Sulaiman, al), Saudi academic. **Born** in Jeddah in 1940. **Dipl.:** B.Sc. (1962); Ph.D. (Chemistry) (1972). **Career:** Chemist, Aramco (1962); demonstrator; Lecturer, Faculty of Science (1972); attended British Chemical Society annual meetings (1968-71), Conference on Science and Technology (CASTARAB) as liaison officer; laid down regulations for explosives in Saudi Arabia; now Assistant Professor, Faculty of Science, Riyadh University since 1975. **Member:** British Chemical Society, American Chemical Association. **Publ.:** 6 research papers published in scientific journals. **Sports:** Fishing, volley-ball. **Hobby:** Reading. **Prof. Addr.:** P.O.Box 1538, Riyadh, Saudi Arabia.

TURKI (Zouheir), Tunisian artist painter. **Born** on November 19, 1924 in Tunis. **Educ.:** Fine Arts School (Stockholm). **Career:** Artist Painter, Professor at Sadki College; Contributed to several Art Exhibitions in Tunisia, Italy, France, Czechoslovakia and Sweden. **Works:** "Le Masseur du Bain Maure". **Dist.:** Prize of the International Art Exhibition of Tunis. **Addr.:** Tunis, Tunisia.

TWAIJRI (Abdul Aziz Ibn Abdul Mohsin ben Mohamad, al), Saudi civil servant. **Born** in 1915 at al-Majma'h. **Educ.:** General education, supplemented by extensive reading. **Career:** Financial Director, Sudair and al-Zulf Zone (1933); Director of Finance, al-Magma'a Administration Affairs, National Guard (1961-77); **member** of National Security Council; member, Personnel Council, al-Yamamah Press Organization; Assistant Vice-President, The National Guards since 1975. **Hobbies: Reading,** swimming, walking. **Publ.:** several articles; A dialogue between Abi al-Ala' and al-Motanabi. **Prof. Addr.:** The National Guards Headquarters, Olaya, Tel.: 491 8500 (Office), and 4646303 (Home), Riyadh, Saudi Arabia.

TWAIJRI (Abdulaziz Ibn Ali, al), Saudi official. **Born** in 1944 at Buraidah, Saudi Arabia. **Dipl.:** M.A. (Public Administration), University of Southern California. **Career:** Institute of Public Administration, Assistant Director General of Customs; Deputy Head of National Guard for Finance and Administration since 1981; participant, Customs Cooperation Council meetings, Brussels, Arab League meetings. **Publications:** several articles published in National Guard's magazine; research in accountancy at the Institute of Public Administration. **Hobbies:** Reading, research. **Address:** National Guard Headquarters, Tel.: 491 8724 (Office) and 476 8872 (Home), Riyadh, Saudi Arabia. **Telephone:** Office 491-8724; Home 476-8872, Riyadh.

TWAIJRY (Abdul Aziz ben Saleh ben Sulaiman al-Fahd), Saudi senior civil servant. **Born** in 1935. **Dipl.:** B.L.; M.L. (Islamic Law), Higher Judiciary Institute, working toward a Ph.D. degree. **Career:** Teacher, al-Tamma Secondary School, Riyadh; Administrative Inspector, Ministry of Education; Professional Inspector; made studies on delinquents and their treatment from the point of view of Islamic Law; road accidents, reasons, consequences and recommendation for treatment, working on Ph.D. degree; now Juridical Investigator, Ministry of Justice. **Hobbies:** Reading, writing. **Prof. Addr.:** Ministry of Justice, Tel.: 405-5339 (Office) and 476-4382 (Home), Riyadh, Saudi Arabia.

TWAIJRY (Ahmad, Saleh, al), Saudi economist. **Born** on December 20, 1942 in Riyadh, Saudi Arabia. **Son** of Saleh Saab al-Twaijry (Trader) **and** Mrs., Najdya Hamoud al-Mutlaq. **Married** to Farida Abdella al-Twigry, 3 children: Shaden (1973); Nora (1976); Salman (1979). **Dipl.:** B.A. Economics, Cairo University (1962); M.A. Economics, Michigan State University (1969); Higher Diploma in Economic Development, Institute of Social Studies, The Hague, Holland (1971). **Career:** Private Financial Analyst (1962-66); Economic Researcher, Petromin Org. (1966-69); Director of Industrial Research, Industrial Studies & Development Co. (1970-72); Part-time Instructor of Economics, Institute of Public Administration (1972-73); Director General of Industry (1972-76); Deputy Ministry of Industry (1976-79); Vice-Chairman of Saudi Consulting House (Government Organization) since 1979. **Awards:** Golden Decoration from President of Republic of China, Taiwan (1978); Minister of Industry Rewarding Certificate (1979). **Sports:** Horseriding, football, table tennis. **Hobbies:** reading (literature, economics, history books). **Mem-**

ber: Jockey Club of Riyadh. **Credit Cards:** American Express, Diner's Club. **Priv. Addr.:** Olya, Tel.: 4642327, al-Wasel Street, Saudi Arabia.

TWAIJRY (Yusuf, Saleh, al), Saudi executive. **Born** in 15 June 1940 in Cairo, Egypt. **Dipl.:** M.P.A., University of Southern California. **Career:** Researcher, Institute of Public Administration, Riyadh (1966-69); Programmes Director (1969-72); Deputy Director General (1972-75); member of Board, Chamber of Commerce and Industry, Riyadh (1979-81); General Manager, Saudi Ceramic Co. since 1975. **Sports:** Horseriding, swimming. **Address:** P.O.Box. 3893, Tel.: 4791820 (Office) and 576-5739 (Home) Riyadh, Saudi Arabia.

U

UQBI (Ahmad H., al), Saudi academic. **Born** in 1938 in Medina, Saudi Arabia. **Dipl.:** Ph.D. (Modern History). **Career:** Director of Lands and Legal Cases Administration and General Inspection Department, Municipality Directorate; Director of Personnel and Administration, Saudi Agricultural Credit Bank; Honorary member, Jeddah Literary Club; Adviser (Part-time) to Ministry of Foreign Affairs and Professor of Saudi Studies, Diplomatic Sciences Institute. **Publ.:** Ph.D. thesis, Anglo-French Rivalry in the Arabian Peninsula in 19th Century; King Abdulaziz and President Roosevelt Meet; The Turks and their Relations with Muslim States and the Ottoman Empire; The Struggle Between the Ottoman and Habsburg Empires. **Hobbies:** Reading, research works and travel. **Addr.:** Tel.: 6805491 (Home), Jeddah, Saudi Arabia.

URAISH (Mahmud, Abdallah), Yemeni politician. **Born** in 1943 in Rada, North Yemen. **Career:** Entered oil industry with British Petroleum; active in trade union politic and was Secretary of the Caltex Branch of the General Union of Petroleum Workers; Acting General Secretary of Petroleum Workers' Union (1965); Finance Minister (1967); Adviser to the President on Planning Affairs with rank of Minister (1969); Acting Finance Minister (1969); Deputy Prime Minister for Financial and Economic Affairs (1969); Minister of Finance (1971-74); Ambassador to German Democratic Republic, and non resident Ambassador to Czechoslovakia, Poland and Hungary, former member of the Central Committee, former member of the People's Supreme Council. **Addr.:** Ministry of Foreign Affairs, Sanaa, Republic of Yemen.

USAMA (Malluhi), Syrian executive. **Born** in 1943 in Damascus, Syria. **Son** of Abdul Illah Usama. **Married** in 1978, 1 son. **Educ.:** American University of Beirut, Lebanon. **Dipl.:** B.A. (Public Administration) (1967); B.B.A. (Business Administration) (1980). **Career:** Teacher, Chouf National College, Lebanon (1968); Public Auditor, Talal Abou Ghazaleh (1974); Financial Controls Dept., Commercial Bank of Kuwait (1975); Assistant Manager Banking, Arab European Financial Management Co. (1980); Marketing Manager, United Gulf Bank, Bahrain (1982-). **Hobbies:** Painting and Music. **Addr.:** P.O.Box 5964, Tel.: 233789, Telex: 9556-57. BN, Manama, Bahrain.

USH (Muhammad Abul Faraj, al), Syrian academic. **Born** in 1916 in Damascus, Syria. **Married**, 2 sons, 5 daughters. **Educ.:** University of Damascus, Syria; University of Saint Joseph, Beirut; Seminar Training on Sasanian, Arab Sasanian and Islamic Coins, American Numismatic Society, New York, USA. **Dipl.:** Licence in History, Diploma in Education, Doctorate in History (Arabic Literature). **Career:** Director of Education in Deir Zor, Syria (1950-51); Professor of History, Damascus (1951-53); Curator of Islamic Art Section, National Museum of Damascus, Syria (1953-55); Chief Curator, National Museum of Damascus (1955-65); Director of the Historical Documents (Archives), Damascus (1965-67); Chief Curator of the National Museum, Damascus (1968-74); Profesor of History and Archaeology, University of Qatar (1974). Reporter for Numismatic Literature, Islamic Art Publications. **Publ.:** several books and researches on Islamic Art, numismatics, epegraphy and archaeology published in Arabic, English and French. **Hobbies:** Travelling, swimming, numismatics, Islamic arts and history. **Addr.:** Muhajireen, Shamsiyyah, 5th Jeddah, 73 Damascus, Syria.

UWAIDH (Ahmad, Abdallah), Yemeni businessman. **Born** in 1947 in Hadramaut, Yemen. **Married**, one son. **Educ.:** B.A. in Commerce, University of Damascus, Syria. **Career:** Accountant, Internal Trading Co., Mukalla (1971-72); Director of Finance and Administration, Directorate of Trade; Deputy Director General for Finance and Administration, Internal Trading Co. (1974-79); Director General (since 1979). **Sports:** Swimming, table tennis. **Hobbies:** Arts, Arabic literature. **Addr.:** Internal Trading Co., Sanaa, Republic of Yemen.

V

VAN STEENBERGS (Ignace), Belgian diplomat. **Born** in 1933 in Gent (Belgium). **Married:** 3 children. **Dipl.:** Ph.D. Law, M.A. Ec. **Career:** Consul General Houston, Texas (1972-78); and Munchen (1980-81); Brussels Foreign ministry Director African Affairs (1981-83) and Western Hemisphere (1988-91); Ambassador to Kuwait (1991-). **Awards:** Com. K, Com. O.C. (g.D.Lux). **Prof. Addr.:** Belgian Embassy, P.O.Box 3280, Safat 13032, Tel.: 5722014/15, Kuwait.

VASSILIADES (Lambros, Prodromos), Egyptian painter. **Born** in 1944 in Cairo, Egypt. **Educ.:** High Institute of Arts "Leonardo da Vinci", Italy. **Dipl.:** Diplomas of Architecture, Advertising, Painting and Decoration. **Career:** Art Director, Radar Advertising Agency (1970-67); Professor at the High Institute of Arts "Leonardo da Vinci", Italy (1965-73); Scholarships in Rome (1975-77); Scholarship, the Academy of Florence, Italy; Scholarship, International Institute for Theatre Research, Venice (1976-78). **Hobbies:** books, films, antiques. **Addr.:** 9 Ahmed Sabry Street, Zamalek, Cairo, Egypt; Komninon 8 Panorama, Salonika, Greece.

VERDUGA (Claude), Moroccan urban architect. **Born** on May 4, 1928. **Educ.:** Diploma, l'Ecole Nationale Supérieure des Beaux Arts (Paris), Institut d'Urbanisme (Paris). **Career:** Head, Central Office of Studies, Morocco (1957-59); Consultant Urbanist for the reconstruction of Agadir. **Member:** of Executive Committee, International Union of Architects. **Publ.:** Enquete Urbaine de Tanger, Les Centres Urbains de Tanger, Les Centres Urbains de la Vallée du Ziz. **Honours:** 1st Prize School of Engineers, Rabat (1959); 3rd Prize, gardenat Hambourg (1963); 1st Prize, Plastic Sanitary Ware (Paris, 1964). **Addr.:** 12, Zankat Ibn Aïcha, Rabat, Morocco.

VO TOAN (Claude), Moroccan artist-painter. **Born** on April 28, 1929. **Educ.:** Academie de la Grande Chaumière, Montparnasse, Paris (France); The Julian Academy, Ecole du Louvre. **Married** to the Architect Cong Vo Toan. **Career:** Exhibitions at: Rabat, Morocco (1962-69), Galerie Vendome (1970), Paris (France). **Addr.:** 13, Avenue de Vesoul, Rabat, Morocco.

VO TOAN (Cong), Moroccan Architect. **Born** on March 5, 1924. **Educ.:** School of Fine Arts (1948-54), Paris, France, D.P.L.G., Architectural Association School of London (1954). **Married** to the artist Claude Vo Toan, 2 children. **Career:** Architect, the Republic of Vietnam for the International Exposition and Fairs (1957-61); Architect, King Hassan II of Morocco for the building of the Mausoleum of the King's Father, Muhammad V (1961-72). **Member:** Society of diploma Architects for the Government (Paris), Study, Group for the Coordination of Underground Urbanism, order of Architects of Paris and Morocco. **Publ.:** Garages-Parkings (1960), Memorandum of the International Architectural Competition for the Cenral London Mosque (1969) and several articles in architectural magazines. **Honours:** Prize Achille Leclerc; Prize Arfridson; Prize Paul Bigot, Institut of France (1956-58); First Prize, Diploma of Architecture (Paris 1954); Gold Medal of Higher Studies of Architecture (1958); 3rd Prize, International Architecture Competition for the Central London Mosque (1969). **Addr.:** 13, Avenue de Vesoul, Rabat, Morocco.

VOLES (Ivan), Czechoslavak diplomat. **Born on** May 8, 1945 in Vizovice. **Son** of Jaromir Voles (Official) **and** Mrs. Jenovefa Dobrovolna. **Married**, on April 25, 1970 in Jablonec N.N. to Hana Pechova, 1 child: Petr (1974). **Educ.:** Secondary Economic School, Jablonec N.N. (1951-63), High School of Economics, Prague (1963-64), Institute of Foreign Relations, Moscow (1964-69). **Career:** Ministry of Foreign Affairs of Czechoslovakia (1969); 3rd Secretary, Czechoslovak Embassy in Baghdad (1972-77); 1st Secretary, MFA (1977-80); Ambassador, Aden (1980-83); Deputy Director of Arab Department, MFA (1984); Director of Arab Department, MFA (1984-88); Director of Arab and African Departments, MFA (1988-89); Ambassador, Cairo (1990-); **Award:** Order of Friendship, PDRY. **Sports:** Tennis. **Hobbies:** Islamic and Arab History, Architecture. **Member:** National Geographic Association, USA. **Credit Card:** Amex. **Prof. Addr.:** Czechoslovak Embassy, 4, Dokki Street, Tel.: 3485531, Giza, Egypt.

W

WABERI (Ahmed Guirreh), Djibouti Deputy at the National Assembly, and Minister of National Education. **Born** in 1947 at Grand-Bara (Dikhil District). **Career:** Tax Inspector in the Direct Contributions, Head of Section of Tax of Profits. Member and General Secretary of LPA, LPAI and RPP. Minister of National Education since 4 February 1993. Member of the Executive Committee in charge of elections of RPP, Elected Deputy at the National Assembly. **Prof. Addr.:** National Assembly, P.O.Box 138. Djibouti, Djibouti and Ministry of National Education, Djibouti.

WABERI (Mohamed, Aden), Djibouti Deputy at the National Assembly. **Born** in 1957 at Ali-Sabieh. **Educ.:** University Studies. **Career:** Senior Official of BDMO. Member of Central Committee of RPP; President of ADEPF; Member of International Federation and of Family Planning of the Arab World. Elected Deputy at the National Assembly (18/12/1992 - to date); Member of Permanent Commission and the Commission for Social Development and Environment Protection. **Prof. Addr.:** National Assembly, P.O.Box 138 Djibout, Djibouti.

WADUD (Mohamad, al), Yemeni physician. **Born** in 1930 near Taiz, Yemen Arab Republic. **Educ.:** University of Prague, Czechoslovakia. **Dipl.:** M.D. **Career:** practicioner at Taiz Hospital (1965-66); Minister of Health (1968-69); Director of Health for Taiz (1969-74); Minister of Health (1974-75). **Addr.:** Sanaa, Republic of Yemen.

WAFA (Jamil, Amine), Bahraini executive **Born** on April 30, 1932 in Jerusalem. **son** of Amin Wafa (Real Estate, Deceased) and Mrs Nafisah (Deceased). **Married** on July 4, 1961 in Jordan to Miss Haya Mounla of North Lebanon three children: Lina (1962), Ramzi (1967) and Sami (1970) and a grandfather of three **Educ.:** Amriya College, Jaffa: American University, Cairo; British Transport College, Woking, England; Standford University Palo Alto, California, **Dipl.:** Business Administration. **Career:** Commenced employment with BOAC airline (now British Airways) for almost 25 years. In 1974 established a partnership Company under the name of "UNITAG", Director of Bahrain Airport Services; Chairman and Chief Executive of World Travel Service; Chairman of Arab Exchange Company; Chairman and Chief Executive of Sunshine tours. **Founder Member** of the National Council Tourism, Bahrain; founder Member of the Bahrain Marina Club, Founder member of the International Advertising Association (IAA) Bahrain Chapter Bahrain Founder Member and First President of the SKAL Club, Bahrain. **Decor:** Awarded the "Croix du Commandre Oeuvre Humanitaire" France (1965); Awarded the "Order of the Cedar" by the President of the Republic of Lebanon (1971); Awarded the "National order of Merit" by the President of the French Republic (1978). **Sports:** Tennis, Cross Country Walking (winter season) and Golf **Hobbies:** Music, (light production) **Bus. Addr:** P.O.Box 830, Manama, Bahrain Tel: (973) 226246, Fax: (973) 224648, E-mail unitag@batelco.com.bh Bahrain priv. **Addr.:** P.O.Box 231 Manama Bahrain.

WAGHLANI (Solaima Mohamad), Tunisian economist. **Born** in 1939 in Djerba, Tunisia. **Married,** 3 daughters. **Educ.:** University of Paris, France; Montreal University, Canada. **Dipl.:** B.Sc. in Economics, Diploma in Commercial Studies. **Career:** Director of National Bank for Development of Tourism (1978-82); Vice President for Africa, Islamic Financial House, Geneva, Switzerland (1982-83); Director General of ANIGA Business and Finance Corporation, Geneva (1983-). **Member:** Geneva Lions' Club, Switzerland. Founder Member of Association de Sauvegarde de l'Ile de Jerba. **Addr.:** 50 Chemin de la Chevillarde, 1208 Geneva, Switzerland.

WAGIE (Mohammed, al-Bashir, al), Sudanese agro-industrialist. **Born** in Sudan in 1929. **Son** of al-Bashir al-Wagie **and** Mrs. Hannan Ali. **Married** in 1962 to Nafisa al-Wagie in Wad Medani, five children. **Educ.:** University of Khartoum, Faculty of Science; University of Nottingam, Faculty of Agriculture; Technical University, West Berlin, Sugar Industry. **Dipl.:** B.Sc. in Agriculture, Crop Production (1959); Diploma in Sugar Technology (1970). **Career:** Field Officer at the Ministry of Agriculture; Research Officer at the Ministry of Agriculture; Director Sugar Corp, at Gunied Sugar Factory and Newalfa Sugar Factory at the Ministry of Trade and Industry (1971-77); Managing Director Kenana Sugar Company (1977-81); Minister of Industry and Chairman K.S.C. (1981-84). Managing Director, Whie Nile Sugar Company Ltd., (1997- to now). **Work:** Worldwide travelling mainly related with development in Sudan also well associated with Arab Funds - World Bank. **Medals:** Production Medal (1970); Distinction Order (1980); Nile Order (1982). **Sports:** Tennis, swimming. **Hobbies:** Reading, music. **Prof. Addr.:** Agrotech, Khartoum, P.O.Box 650, Sudan.

WAHAIBI (Abdallah ben Nasser ben Mohamad, al),

Saudi academic. **Born** in 1930. **Dipl.:** Ph.D. (History). **Career:** clerk at a Law Court; Director-General of Primary Education; Director-General of Education; Secretary-General, Riyadh University; member of Board of Saudi Credit Bank, Al Faisal Settlement Project, al-Yamam Press Organization, Riyad University Council; former member of Riyadh University Higher Council; Adviser to Arab League Educational, Scientific and Cultural Organization (ALESCO); attended several educational and academic conferences, now Assistant Professor of History, Riyadh University. **Publ.:** Articles in English and Arabic on education and history. **Sport:** Swimming. **Hobby:** Travel. **Prof. Addr.:** P.O.Box 3002, Riyadh, Saudi Arabia.

WAHAIBI (Mohamad H., al), Saudi faculty professor. **Born** in 1941 at Thadig. **Dipl.:** Ph.D. **Career:** Demonstrator, Botany Department, 1972; Assistant Professor, Botany Department, Faculty of Science, King Saud University since 1979; member, Saudi Biological Society, American Society of Plant Physiologists, Sigma XI. **Publication:** "Respiration". **Hobbies:** Research, reading, writing. **Address:** Botany Department, Faculty of Science, King Saud University, Tel. Office 478-1374; Home 481-1000 Ext. 2639, Riyadh, Saudi Arabia.

WAHBA (Magdi, Mourad), Emeritus professor, english department, faculty of arts, Cairo university since 1949. **Born** on 19 October 1925 in Alexandria (Egypt). **Son** of Mourad Wahba (High-Court Judge) **and** Mrs., née Victoria Ibrahim. **Married** to Josephine Salkind on 13 July 1955 in London, 3 children: Mourad, Youssef and Sadek. **Educ.:** The English School, Cairo; Faculty of Law, Cairo University; Faculty of Law, Paris University; Exeter College, Oxford. **Dipl.:** LL.B. (Cairo and Paris); diploma of International Law, Paris; M.A., B.Lit.; D.Phil. (Oxon). **Career:** appointed lecturer in the English Department, Faculty of Arts, Cairo University in 1949. **Publ.:** "Dictionary of Literary Terms" (English/Arabic/French); "La Politique Culturelle en Egypte" (UNESCO). **Translations:** "The Dreams of Sheherazade" by Taha Hussein, "Ibrahim the Writer" by al-Mazini; collaboration with Ahmed Kamel Moursi "Dictionary of the Cinema"; editor of "Cairo Studies in English"; author of "Readings in Literature and Politics" and "Dryden and Dramatic Poetry". **Awards:** Officer, Legion of Honour (France); Ordenom Jugoslovenske Zastave Sa Zalatnim - Vencem. Commendatore dell' Ordine al-merito della Republica Italiana. **Member:** Shura Council (Senate) Arabic Academy, Cairo. **Prof. Addr.:** Faculty of Arts, Cairo University, Giza, Cairo. **Priv. Addr.:** 4A Ibn Zanki St., Tel. 803369, Cairo, Egypt.

WAHBI (Mohamad), Egyptian diplomat, writer. **Born** in 1934 in Cairo, Egypt. **Married. Educ.:** B.A. English Literature, Cairo University, Egypt (1955); M.A. in Political Science, New Delhi University, India (1964). **Career:** Arab League Office, New Delhi (1965-70); Acting Chief Representative, Arab League Office, New Delhi (1970-72); Director, Information and Planning, Arab League Office, Cairo (1972-74); Acting Director, Arab League Office, London (1976-79); Elizabeth Collard Gant (for research and publications), for the improvement of the Arab-European relations (1979); Consulting Editor, "Middle East Economic Digest" (1979-80); Press Attaché, Egypt, Embassy to Federal Republic of Germany (1980); talks and lectures on Arab affairs in Britain, India and other European countries; Editor of "al-Arab" New Delhi (1965-72); State Information Service, Cairo; Press Councellor in Washington (1987). **Member:** of the Strategic Studies Institute, London. **Publ.:** Articles published in "Rose al-Yousef"; "National Herald", "Patriot Arab Socialism" New Delhi (1966); "Arab Quest for Peace" New Delhi (1971); co-author "West Asian Crisis" (1967); "Meerut" (1968). **Sports:** Squash, swimming. **Hobbies:** Violin, literature, theatre. **Addr.:** Ministry of Foreign Affairs, Cairo, Egypt.

WAHDAN (Samir, Sayed, Dr.), Egyptian financial adviser. **Born** in 1930 in Cairo, Egypt. **Son** of Sayed Ali Wahdan. **Married** in 1958, 2 daughters. **Educ.:** Ph.D. Financial Management U.S.A.; Master of Commerce-Cairo University; B.Com. -Cairo University. **Career:** Thirty six years in Finance Oil and Investment fields-on function, consultation, Top management and Executive level for financial, Investment and Oil Companies. **Consultation:** Finance, and project promotion Consultant for the following Companies; Egyptian Saudi, Investment Company; Joint Arab Investment Corporation; Malaco Alimar; Aviation Consulting Center; Consultant to a number of Projects during formation and Construction period. **Organization and Finance: Iraq Republic:** Eldora-Elwind-Elkayara Eltagi Refineries; Solphar Plant Karkok; Suez Oil Company; Deminez Company; Meridive; Feasibility Studies & Finance during Career, Member of Board of Directors for the following companies; periods are overlaping and consecutive. Egypt Alexandria Refinery; Western Desert Petroleum Co.; Boskalis Westminster Construction Company; Nile Shoe Company; Joint Arab Building Material Co.; Arab Sunley Construction Company; Egypt Financial Investment Co.; Aviation Consulting Services (President). **U.A.E.:** Abu Dhabi Marine Operating Co.; Abu Dhabi Petroleum Co.; Zadco-Offshore Oil Company; Ummeldakh Development Company; Abu Dhabi Dredging Company; Abu Dhabi National Drilling Co. **Pakistan:** PAC Arab Refinery; PAC Arab Fertilizer. **Executive Role:** Finance Manager for: Abu Dhabi National Oil Co.; Alexandria Refinery; Western Desert Petroleum Co.; General Petroleum Organization; Compagnie Orientale de Petrole; National Oil Company. **Publ.:** "Responsibility Centres for Refinery Accounting"; "Standard Cost for Petroleum Industry"; "Product Cost Systems for Petroleum Products"; "Accounting Procedures for Operating Companies". **Member:** Gezira Sporting Club, Cairo. **Prof. Addr.:** P.O.Box 120 Orman, Tel.:

729076, Giza, Egypt. **Priv. Addr.:** 107 Abdel Aziz al-Saud, Manial, Tel.: 841711, Cairo, Egypt.

WAIS (Ahmed Aouled), Djibouti Deputy at the National Assembly. **Born** in 1947 in Djibouti. **Career:** Assistant Head Department of Domains. **Member** of the Central Committee of RPP. Elected Deputy at the National Assembly (18/12/1992 - to date); Member of the Permanent Commission, Legislation Commission and General Administration of the Republic; Member of the Supreme Court of Justice. **Prof. Addr.:** National Assembly, P.O.Box 138 Djibouti, Djibouti.

WAIS (Elmi, Obsieh), Djibouti Deputy at the National Assembly. **Born** in 1942 at Ali-Sabieh. **Educ.:** Secondary. **Career:** Director of OPT; Member of PMP, LPAI and RPP (Ali-Sabieh); Elected Deputy at the National Assembly (19/12/1997 - to date); Appointed Minister of Interior and Decentralization (28/12/1997). **Prof. Addr.:** National Assembly, P.O.Box 138 Djibouti, Djibouti.

WAJIH (Mohamad Khadim, al), Yemeni politician. **Born** in 1940 in Zabid, Yemen Arab Republic. **Educ.:** in Aden (1948-60) in the U.K. (1960-65). **Dipl.:** B.Sc. Economics, University of London, UK (1962-65). **Career:** Entered National Assembly and was appointed Director-General of the Yemen Petroleum Company (1971); Director-General, Bajil Cement Factory (1971-75); Minister of Agriculture (January 1975-79); Minister of Education (March 1979); Minister of finance (1986); Minister of Communications and Telecommunications (1988); Minister for Civil Service in the new Republic of Yemen (May 1991 to June 1995); Minister of Petroleum and Minerals Resources (1996 to date). **Addr.:** Sanaa, Republic of Yemen.

WAKED (Maher, A.), Jordanian Commissioner - Jordan Securities Commission. **Born** on JUly 3, 1941. **Son** of A. Waked (Ex Minister of Justice & Senator, Jordan) **and** Mrs. née Lutfieh Fareez. **Married** on August 29, 1972, 4 children: Nada, Abed, Layan, Adie, **Educ.:** Various Universities in the U.S.A. **Dipl.:** B.Co - MBA (Accounting) - MPA (Public Finance) - PHD - Public Finance - Other Professional Designates. **Career:** Ex Department Head of Central Bank of Jordan's, Ex Assistant General Manager - Bank of Jordan, Commissioner-Jordan SEC **Other Information:** Various Other Assignments in Advisory Capacities in Jordan And Abroad. **Hobbies:** Reading, Tours, Photography, Writing. **Clubs:** Many. **Prof. Addr.:** P.O.Box 8802, Tel.: 60717, Amman 11121, Jordan.

WAKIL (Abdulwahid, al), Egyptian businessman, architect. **Born** in 1943 in Giza, Egypt. **Educ.:** B.Sc., Faculty of Engineering; Ain Shams University, Cairo, Egypt. **Career:** Lecturer, Department of Architecture, Ain Shams University (1965); worked with Professor Hassan Faghy for Ministry of Culture and Ministry of Tourism on various projects and research (1970); began to work privately designing palaces and private residences in indigenous style, developing traditional style in building industry. **Publ.:** Article on "Modern Concepts of Arab Architecture", "Arab News" Jeddah (1976); "Construire Comme Nos Aieux", Safa, Beirut (1972). **Hobbies:** Music, sailing. **Addr.:** 27 Mohamad Kamel Morsi, Tel. 705564, Dokki, Cairo, Egypt.

WAKIL (Mohamad, al), Arab-American academic. **Born** in 1921 in Alexandria, Egypt. **Divorced**, 1 son, 1 daughter. **Educ.:** University of Cairo, Egypt; University of Wisconsin, Madison, USA. **Dipl.:** B.Sc, M.Sc. and Ph.D. **Career:** Lecturer at University of Alexandria, Alexandria, Egypt (1950-52); Research Associate, University of Wisconsin, USA (1954-55); Assistant Professor, University of Minnesota, USA (1954-55); Associate Professor, University of Wisconsin (1957-61); Professor of Mechanical and Nuclear Engineering (1961); Member of American Nuclear Society, American Society for Mechanical Engineers, Combustion Institute and American Society for Engineering Education. **Publ.:** "Nuclear Power Engineering" (1962), "Nuclear Energy Conversion" (1971), Japanese translation (1975), "Nuclear Heat Transport" (1971), Japanese translation (1972), also contributed articles to professional journals. **Award:** Meritorious Paper Award, American Society of Mechanical Engineers (1952), Award for Excellence in Instruction of Engineers, American Society of Mechanical Engineers (1952), Benjamin Smith Reynolds Award, University of Wisconsin, USA (1970), Distinguished Teaching Award, Nuclear Engineering Division, American Society of Engineers (1971), Arthur Holly Compton Award, American Nuclear Society (1979); Fullbright Scholar (1966) (1978). **Member:** Sigma Xi, Pi Tau Sigma and Tau Beta Pi. **Addr.:** 1010 Edgehill Drive, Madison, Wisconsin WI 53705, USA.

WAKIL (Rahim, al), Iraqi sculptor. **Born** on June 30, 1936. **Married** in 1965 to Greta Leyland, 2 children: Ziad and Lina. **Educ.:** Diploma, Fine Arts Institute, Baghdad (1954-59); National Diploma of Design in Sculpture and Design, Chelsea College of Arts, London, UK (1960-65). **Career:** Teacher of Art in High Secondary School, Baghdad (1959-60); Head, Sculpture Department and Art Adviser, Iraqi Museum, Baghdad (1965-71); Lecturer, Fine Arts Institute, Baghdad (1971). **Member:** Iraqi Artists Union; International Association of Art; Baghdad Group. **Hobbies:** Display, illumination, preservation of antiquities displayed, interior decoration. **Addr.:** Fine Arts Institute, Mansour, Baghdad, Iraq.

WAKIL (Saleh, Jawad), Arab American biochemist. **Born** on August 16, 1927 in Karbala'. **Son** of Jawad Wakil **and** Mrs., née Millouk Atrakchi. **Married** on September '15, 1952 to Miss Fawzia Bahraini, 4 children: Sonia, Aida, Adel and Yusuf. **Educ.:** American University of Beirut, University of Washington. **Dipl.:** Bachelor of Science

(1948), Doctor of Philosophy (Biochemistry, 1952). **Career:** went to the U.S.A. (1948); naturalized (1964); joined the University of Washington (1949-52); Assistant Professor, Institute for Enzyme Research, Wisconsim University (1952-59); Faculty Department, Biochemistry Duki, Durham, N.C. since 1959; Professor since 1965. **Publ.:** Author of several publications on discovery of mechanism of fatty acid biosynthesis, isolation of biotin enzymes, Malonyl Co. A, Acyl carried protein and elucidating control of fatty acid biosynthesis. **Member** of several International organizations, of Sigma Xi, Phi. Lambda Epsilon. **Priv. Addr.:** 2527 Sevier Street, Durham, N.C. 27705, U.S.A.

WAL (Michael), Sudanese politician. **Born** in Upper Nile Province, Sudan. **Educ.:** studied in New York, USA. **Dipl.:** B.A., M.Sc. **Career:** Member of the Sudan African National Union in the 1960s; participated in the Addis Ababa negotiations (1972); Regional Minister for Cabinet Affairs (1972-73); stood unsuccessfully for the Regional Assembly Elections in the Intellectuals Constituency (1973); Chairman of the Regional Development Corporation (1973). **Prof. Addr.:** c/o Regional People's Assembly, Juba, Sudan.

WALI (Ibrahim, al), Iraqi diplomat. **Born** in 1930 in Baghdad, Iraq. **Married,** three children. **Career:** Entered Ministry of Foreign Affairs; 2nd Secretary, Geneva, Switzerland (1959); Embassy to Yugoslavia (1962); Embassy to Yemen Arab Republic (1964); Embassy to Stockholm; Chief of Protocol at Republican Palace (1966); Embassy to Yugoslavia (1966); Embassy to Kuwait (1970); Ambassador to France (1972); Director General of Ministry of Foreign Affairs Political Department (1974). **Addr.:** Baghdad, Iraq.

WALLY (Youssuf, Amin, Dr.), Egyptian deputy prime minister and minister of agriculture and land reclamation. **Born** in 1931, Cairo. **Educ.:** Faculty of Agriculture, Cairo University; Higher Studies Including Ph.D. Cairo University. **Dipl.:** B.Sc. (Horticulture) and Ph.D. **Career:** Joined the Faculty of Agriculture, Cairo University, as Demonstrator; Seconded to Ain Shams University Where he was full Professor of Horticulture; Appointed as Technical Consultant in Ministry of Agriculture (1971-1981), in Charge of the International Cooperation; General Secretary of the National Democratic Party; President of World Food Council; Deputy Prime Minister and Minister of Agriculture and Land Reclamation (1989 to present). **Addr.:** Ministry of Agriculture, Dokki-Giza, Cairo, Egypt.

WANNOUS (Mounir), Syrian arab league official. **Born** in 1934 in Tripoli, Lebanon. **Educ.:** studied in Damascus, Syria and France. **Dipl.:** Diploma in civil engineering. **Career:** Deputy Minister for Technical Affairs, Ministry of Municipal and Rural Affairs (1964-70); Minister of Euphrates Dam (1970-74); private practice, consultancy and contracting office (1974-80); Director General, The Standing Conference on Housing and Town Planning, League of Arab States, Tunis (1980-83). **Prof. Addr.:** P.O.Box 4731, Damascus, Syria.

WAQQAD (Ilham Ibrahim M., Miss), Saudi university lecturer. **Born** in 1953 in Mecca, Saudi Arabia. **Dipl.:** M.A. (Psychology). **Career:** Member of Umul Qura Women's Charity Society; Lecturer in Psychology and Supervisor of Admissions, King Abdulaziz University. **Hobby:** Reading. **Address:** Jiyyad Street, Mecca; Women's Section, Mecca Branch, King Abdulaziz University, Mecca, Saudi Arabia.

WARBERI (Ahmed Guirreh), Djibouti Deputy at the National Assembly, and Minister of National Education. **Born** in 1947 at Grand-Bara (Dikhil District). **Career:** Tax Inspector in the Direct Contributions, Head of Section of Tax of Profits. Member and General Secretary of LPA, LPAI and RPP. Minister of National Education since 4 February 1993. Member of the Executive Committee in charge of elections of RPP, Elected Deputy at the National Assembly. **Prof. Addr.:** National Assembly, P.O.Box 138, Djibouti, Djibouti, and Ministry of National Education, Djibouti.

WARRAD (Faek), Palestinian politician. **Born** in 1920 in Tilfit, near to Nablus, Jordan. **Career:** Member of Communist Party in late 1930s; Active in West Bank politics after 1948; Manager of "al-Jabha", the National Bloc newspaper in the election campaign of September 1954, elected to Jordanian Parliament as Member for Ramallah (1956); Leader of the Ansar, newly formed commando group (Partisans) in 1970; Member of the Palestine National Council (1971); Accompanied Yassir Arafat on visit to Moscow (1974). **Addr.:** Tunis, Tunisia.

WARZAZI (Halima, Embarek), Moroccan official. **Born** on April 17, 1933 in Casablanca. **Educ.:** in Casablanca, Madrid and Cairo. **Dipl.:** Licence ès Lettres (Juin 1957). **Career:** Official at the Ministry of Foreign Affairs (November 1957); Cultural Attaché in Washington (August 1959 - Sept. 1961); Attaché in the Cabinet of the Minister of Health and Chief of the Division of Social Welfare (September 1962 - October 1963); Attaché to the Cabinet of the Minister of Foreign Affairs and Minister Plenipotentiary (1964); President of the Commission of Cultural and humanitarian problems at the 21st Session of the General Assembly of the U.N. (September 1966); Member of the National Council for National Promotion (February 1968); Member of the Moroccan Delegation at the International Conference on Human Rights in Teheran (May 1968); Representative of Morocco in the Commission on the Condition of Women for 3 years (May 1968); Member of the Moroccan Delegation at the 24th Session of the Human Rights Commission (February 1969); Member of the Moroccan delegation at the 8th Conference of the O.U.A. Summit (June 1971); Member of the Moroccan delegation at the 9th Conference of the

O.U.A. (June 1972); Member of the Moroccan delegation at the General Assembly of the United Nations (1959-60 and 1964-1993); Member of the Sub-Commission for the protection of minorities and discriminatory measures (April 1973); Special Rapporteur to the Sub-Commission on the exploitation of Clandestine and illicit workers; Member ofthe Committee for elimination of racial discrimination (Jan. 1974-78); Member of the Commission on International Public Service (1974-80); Member of the Honour Committee of the Federation of twin Cities; Member of the Executive Committee and the Executive Board of the International Institute on Human Rights (René Cassin); Member of the Sub-Commission for the Protection of minorities (1978-83); President of the Moroccan delegation at the World Conference against racism (Geneva-1978); Rapporteur to the Sub-Commission (1980); President of the Sub-Commission for the Protection of minorities (1983); President and Rapporteur of the Working Group of the General Assembly Commission on the rights of non-Citizens (1982-86); President and Rapporteur of the Working Group of the Sub-Commission on traditional practices affecting the health of women and children (1985-86); and as an Expert of the Sub-Commission (1988-91); Director of International Organizations at the Ministry of Foreign Affairs (Jan. 1989); Member of the Academic Commission on Human Rights of the Institute of International Human Rights (Sept. 1991); President of the Preparatory Committee of the World Conference on Human Rights (1991-1993); President of the Main Committee of the World Conference on Human Rights (Vienna) (June 1993); Ambassador at the Ministry of Foreign Affairs and Cooperation (1993-). **Addr.:** Ministry of Foreign Affairs and Cooperation, Rabat, Morocco.

WASSIF (Kamal M, Dr.), Egyptian academic. **Born** on January 18, 1916 in Cairo (Egypt). **Educ.:** Tawfikiyeh Secondary School (1926-33); Faculty of Science, Cairo University (1934-1937). **Dipl.:** B.Sc. (Honours), M.Sc., Ph.D. (Zoology). **Career:** Lecturer, Faculty of Science, Cairo University (1947-52); Assistant Professor of Zoology, Ayn Shams University, Cairo (1952-58); Professor of Zoology, Ayn Shams University, since 1958; Head, Zoology Department, Ayn Shams University, (1958-1976); Professor Emeritus, since 1976. Editor, Bulletin of the Zoological Society of Egypt since (1970-83). **Hobby:** travelling. **Prof. Addr.:** Zoological Department, Faculty of Science, Ayn Shams University, Abbasiyeh, Cairo 11566, Tel.: 821633-821096-821031. **Priv. Addr.:** 19 Omar bin Khattab street, Heliopolis, Cairo, Egypt.

WAZIR (Mohammed Abdul Koddos, al), Yemeni diplomat. **Born** in 1933 in Sanaa, Republic of Yemen. **Educ.:** Completed the general secondary education in Egypt; Studied political science and economics in the American University of Beirut. **Married**, Four children. **Career:** Chargé d'Affaires to Rome and non-resident Chargé d'Affaires to Belgrade (1959); Promoted to Minister-Plenipotentiary (1960); Served in the Political Field (1962-70); Ambassador to Beirut (July 1970 - March 1973); Ambassador Extraordinary and Plenipotentiary to Rome (July 1973 - June 1974); Minister of Agriculture (June 1974 - January 1975); Ambassador Extraordinary and Plenipotentiary to the Hashemite Kingdom of Jordan (January 1975); Non-resident Ambassador Extraordinary and Pleniportentiary to Lebanon, Turkey and Pakistan (February 1975); Ambassador Extraordinary and Plenipotentiary to the Federal Republic of Germany (October 1978); Non-resident Ambassador Extraordinary and Plenipotentiary to: Switzerland, Republic of Austria, The Netherlands, Kindgom of Belgium, Duchy of Luxembourg; Permanent Representative to the European Community in Brussels; Ambassador Extraordinary and Plenipotentiary to the Islamic Republic of Pakistan (1981); Non-resident Ambassador Extraordinary and Plenipotentiary to the People's Republic of Bangladesh (7 April, 1984); Non-resident Ambassador Extraordinary and Plenipotentiary to the Democratic Socialist Republic of Sri Lanka (5 May, 1984); Non-resident Ambassador Extraordinary and Plenipotentiary to the Sultanate of Brunei Darussalam (5 December, 1985); Non-resident Ambassador Extrordinary and Plenipotentiary to Malaysia (7 April, 1986); Non-resident Ambassador Extraordinary and Plenipotentiary to the Republic of Indonesia (8 May, 1986); Ambassador Extraordinary and Plenipotentiary to Japan (September 1986); Non-resident Ambassador Extraordinary and Plenipotentiary to Republic of Korea (8 July, 1987); Non-resident Ambassador Extraordinary and Plenipotentiary to Singapore (4 August, 1987); Non-resident Ambassador Extraordinary and Plenipotentiary to Philippines (20 August, 1987); Non-resident Ambassador Extraordinary and Plenipotentiary to Australia (23 November, 1987); presently Ambassador of Yemen to Tokyo, Japan. **Prof. Addr.:** Ministry of Foreign Affairs, Sanaa, Republic of Yemen, and Embassy of the Republic of Yemen, Kowa Bldg., No.38, Room 807, 12-14 Nishi, Azabu 4-chome, Minato-ku, Tokyo 106, Japan.

WAZNA (Mohamad Farajallah), Saudi professor. **Born** in 1930 in Mecca, Saudi Arabia. **Dipl.:** M.B., B.Ch. (Alexandria), D.S. (Alexandria), F.R.C.S., (Edinburgh), F.R.C.S., (London), E.C.F.M.G. (U.S.A.), L.R.C.P., (London), M.R.C.S. (London), M.D. (U.S.A.). **Career:** House Officer, Alexandria University Hospital (1958-59); Senior Surgical Consultant, Ministry of Health (1960-77); Surgical Specialist, Longon University Hospitals (1964-67); Surgical Consultant (1974); Research Fellow, State University of New York and Washington University (1975-77); Assistant Professor of Surgery, KAU Hospital (1978); Associate Professor of Surgery, King Abdulaziz University (1979); Professor of Surgery, King Abdulaziz University (1983), member, Egyptian Medical Association, British Medical Association, American Medical Association, the Islamic Medical Association of North America and the Arab Medical Speciality Board Council. **Publ.:** a number of articles in medical journals, and papers presented at conferences, on various aspects of digestion and obesity. **Address:** Home 6877772, Jeddah, Saudi Arabia **and** 8929 Wilshire Blvd. suite 120 Berverly Hills, Ca. 90211 USA.

WEDYANI (Sulaiman, al), Saudi academic. **Born** in **1948. Dipl.:** B.A. (English and Education); M.A. (English as a Second Language) 1973. **Career:** Teacher of English, Mecca Secondary School (1970); Teaching Assistant, College of Education, Mecca (1971); Lecturer, College of Education, Mecca (1971); Lecturer, College of Education, Mecca. **Publications:** Papers on predictable errors and mistakes made by Saudi students in secondary schools. **Hobbies:** reading. playing football. **Address:** c/o Omar Ben Jabal, Beer Tawa Jarwal, Mecca, Saudi Arabia.

WIEU (Andrew, W. Riang), Sudanese politician, administrator. **Born** in 1928 in Malakal District, Sudan. **Educ.:** School of Public Administration, Khartoum University College, Khartoum, Sudan (1954); graduate studies, Wheaton College, Illinois, USA (1976-77); M.A. International Development and Human Needs, The American University, School of International Service, Washington D.C., USA. **Career:** Various administrative and judicial posts; Local Government Inspector (1956-64); Minister of Agriculture (1965); member of the Constituent Assembly (1968-69); Land Inspector, Southern Region (1970-72); member of National People's Assembly, Deputy Speaker (1972-73); Minister, Department of Inter-Departmental Coordination (1973-75); Minister, Presidential Administrative and Financial Affairs (1975-76); various committees and commissions, Ministry of Southern Affairs Advisory Committee, Public Service Administrative Reform Committee, Southern Sudan Relief and Resettlement Commission, Sudan Socialist Union Central Committee. **Medals:** The Order of the Two Niles, 2nd Class, Sudan (1972); Order of the Republic, 2nd Class, Sudan (1975); Order of Merit, Great Officer, Senegal (1975); Order of Marib, Yemen Arab Republic (1976). **Addr.:** P.O.Box. 533, Khartoum, Sudan.

WISHAHI (Hussein, Ali), Saudi electrical engineer. **Born** in 1934, **Son** of Ali Wishahi (Merchant) **and** Mrs. Thonaya Wishahi. **Married** in 1963 to Hanan Kilani, 4 children: Randa, Khalid, Sana, Huda. **Educ.:** Illinois University, Urbana, Illinois, USA (1954-59). **Dipl.:** B.Sc. Electrical Engineering. **Career:** Head, Planning Department, Riyadh Electric Co.; Manager Electrical Construction Department, Dammam Electric Co.; Owner and founder of Electrical Engineering Office (since 1974). **Sports:** Swimming, shooting. **Hobbies:** Reading and travel. **Prof. Addr.:** P.O.Box. 1599, Rail Street, Tel.: 4013427, Riyadh. **Priv. Addr.:** Khazzan Street, Riyadh, Saudi Arabia.

WISSA (Zikry, Philippe), Head, fine arts department, Collège de la Sainte Famille, Cairo (Egypt). **Born** on March 17, 1927 in Asiyut city, Asiyut Governorate (Upper Egypt). **Married** to Mahassen Ibrahim in July 1956, 2 children: one daughter and one son. **Educ.:** Asiyut Primary; Asiyut secondary school; Faculty of Fine Arts, Cairo University. **Dipl.:** B.A. (Fine Arts) (July 1953); Research diploma (1954); B.A. (Pedagogy) (October 1963). **Career:** Fine Arts Teacher in Government School, Western Cairo Zone; now Head, Fine Arts Department, Collège de la Sainte Famille, since 1957. **Exhibitions:** Participated in Arts exhibitions in 1953 (Alexandria Biennale), Atelier Exhibition, Cairo (1959); Students Exhibitions, yearly from 1959 to 1977. **Works:** Several statues and other arts production including the stained glass windows of a number of Coptic churches in Cairo, Heliopolis and the Abu Sefein Cathedral. **Awards:** First Prize (sculpture) Talaat Harb also Shawky First prize. **Sports:** Swimming and tennis. **Hobbies:** Arts, Reading. **Prof. Address:** Fine Arts Department, Collège de la Sainte Famille, 1 el-Maksy street, Tel.: 900411-900892, Cairo. **Priv. Addr.:** 9 Abdelhamid Abou Heif St., Heliopolis, Cairo, Egypt.

WOHAIBI (Khalfan bin Nasser, al), Omani former Minister. **Born** in 1940 in Muscat. **Educ.:** In Qatar. **Career:** Qatari Department of Health (1956-62); Trade Relations Manager, Petroleum Development Oman (1962-72); Minister of Social Affairs & Labour (1972-79), Acting Minister of Education (1972-73); Chairman of State Consultative Council (1979-81); Minister of Electricity & Water (1981-90). Chairman, Oman Arab Bank SAO (1989); Minister of Water Resources (1990-91); Chairman, National Bank of Oman SAOG (1993-). **Addr.:** P.O.Box 2285 Ruwi, Postal Code 112, Muscat, Sultanate of Oman.

WOL WOL (Lawrence), Sudanese politician. **Born** in 1936 in Sudan. **Educ.:** University of Khartoum, Sudan; Fribourg University, Switzerland; Bordeaux University, France. **Career:** Secretary of the Anyanya Movement delegation at the Addis Ababa negotiations (1971-72); Minister of State for Planing (1972); Member of the Political Bureau of the Sudanese Socialist Union (SSU) (1972); elected to the Regional Assembly (1973); Minister of Planning (1973); Head of the Regional Ministry of Commerce, Industry and Supply (1973). **Addr.:** Juba, Sudan.

Y

YACOUB (George), Iraqi international civil servant. **Born** on December 27, 1923 In Erbil (Iraq). **Married**, 4 children. **Educ.:** Faculty of Law, University of Baghdad (1944-48); Yale University (USA, 1953-54); University of Michigan, Ann Arbor (1954-55). **Dipl.:** LL.B. **Career:** Journalist and private law practice, Baghdad (1948-53); Editor and Broadcaster, Beirut, London (1955-59); Public Information Division UNICEF, New York (1959-62); Press and Publications Division, Office of Public Information (OPI), New York (1962-65); Director, United Nations Information Centre (UNIC), Khartoum (1965-68); Director, UNIC, Karachi, Islamabad (1968-72); Press & Publications Division, OPI, New York (1973-74); Chief, Policy and Programme Section, Information Centre Service, OPI, New York (1973-74); Chief, Information Support Section, External Relations Division, OPI, UN, New York (1974); Director of Information - spokesman, United Nations Force in Cyprus (UNFICYP), Nicosia (1974-81); Principal Officer, UN Radio and Visual services, New York (1981). **Addr.:** Baghdad, Iraq.

YACOUB (Magdi), Egyptian surgeon. **Born** in 1936 in Egypt. **Married**, 3 children. **Educ.:** Cairo Medical School, Cairo University, Egypt. **Career:** Cairo University Medical School Hospital, London, England; National Heart Hospital where he worked under Mr. Donald Ross, pioneer heart transplant surgeon, London; Assistant Professor, Chicago Medical School where he studied the techniques of Professor Norman Shumway of California, Chicago, USA; Hearfield Hospital where he formed a team for heart transplant surgery, Middlesex, England (1969-). **Publ.:** numerous papers and articles in the field of heart transplant surgery and cardiovascular disease. **Prof. Addr.:** 24 Upper Wimpole Street, London WIM 7TA, England.

YACOUBIAN (Philip), Egyptian industrialist, chemical engineer. **Born** on December 10, 1918 in Cairo. **Married** to Miss Mary Lawson Pirie. **Educ.:** Jesuits College, Glasgow University. **Dipl.:** Bachelor of Science (Hons). **Career:** Industrialist, Chemical Engineer, Managing Director of "Yacoubian Brothers", "Hakim and Co.". Life **member** Dyers and Colorists Society, Bradford (England). **Addr.:** 4, Ahmad Hishmat, Zamalek, Tel.: 806133, Cairo, Egypt.

YAFI (Abdulkarim, al), Syrian academic. **Born** in 1919 in Homs, Syria. **Married:** 2 children. **Educ.:** Secondary and Higher. **Dipl.:** Bachelor of Arts; Bachelor of Sciences; Ph.D. **Career:** Professor of Philosophy and Social Sciences, Damascus University. **Member:** International Union of Scientific Study of Population; Arab Academy of Scientific Study of Population; Arab Academy of Syria. **Addr.:** 77 Abdel Moneim Street, Malky, Damascus, Syria.

YAFI (Mohamad Selim, al), Syrian diplomat. **Born** on December 21, 1920. **Educ.:** Maristes Frères School, Damascus. **Dipl.:** LL.B., Damascus University, Syria. **Career:** Ministry of Supply (1943-45); Ministry of Foreign Affairs (1945); Attaché Embassy to Egypt (1945); Attaché, Embassy to Turkey (1946); Counsul, Mersin, Turkey (1949); Chargé d'Affaires, Embassy to Saudi Arabia (1952); Ministry of Foreign Affairs (1954); Director-General, Arab Palestinian Organization; Delegate to Consultative Committee UN Relief and Works Agency (UNRWA) (1954); Chargé d'Affaires, Embassy to Switzerland (1956); Assistant Secretary-General, Ministry of Social and Labour Affairs (1958-62); Director-General, Palestinian Refugees Organization (1958-62); Member, Higher Council of Radio and Television, United Arab Republic (1959-62); Counsellor for Palestinian Affairs, Ministry of Foreign Affairs (1962); Director of Arab Affairs; Director of Administrative and Cultural Affairs, Ministry of Foreign Affairs (1962); Lecturer, Faculty of Commerce, Damascus University (1962-64); Minister, Embassy to France (1964-65); Minister, then Chargé d'Affaires, then Ambassador to Belgium (1966-68); Director of European Affairs, Ministry of Foreign Affairs (1968); Assistant Secretary-General for Political Affairs (1969); Assistant Minister of Foreign Affairs (1970); Assistant Secretary-General of the Arab League (1970); President of Conciliation Committees of Jordan (1970), Oman (1971); Yemen (1972-73). **Publ.:** A study of the Palestinian Question and its Evolution (1961). **Addr.:** Damascus, Syria.

YAGHI (Abdulrahman, Abdulwahab), Jordanian academic, linguistic expert. **Born** in 1924 in Palestine. **Son** of Abdulwahab Yaghi. **Married**, four children. **Educ.:** B.A., M.A., Ph.D. in Arabic Literature (1950-60). **Career:** International Expert with UNESCO for Arabic Language (1962-64); Full Professor of Modern Arabic Literature, Faculty of Arts, University of Jordan, Amman (since 1964); President of Jordanian Society of Writers (1979); member of the Jordanian Committee of the World Peace Council. **Publ.:** Thirty books published in Beirut, Cairo, Amman. "The Soldier who Dreamt of White Lilies" (translated into English); articles on Arabic Literature published in the "Yearbook of Encyclopaedia Britannica" (1975-76); seven books translated from English into Arabic. **Sports:**

Swimming, tennis. **Hobbies:** Modern Arabic literature. **Addr.:** Faculty of Arts, University of Jordan, Amman, Jordan.

YAGHI (Hashim, Abdulwahab)), Jordanian academic. **Born** in 1921 in Palestine. **Son** of Abdulwahab Yaghi. **Married**, three children. **Educ.:** B.A., M.A. and Ph.D. in Arabic Literature, Cairo University (1951-60). **Career:** lecturer, University of Libya (1960-61); Lecturer, King Abdul Aziz University, Saudi Arabia (1961-62); Lecturer, Associate Professor, Full Professor, Jordan University (since 1962); taught at Kuwait University (1975-77); Dean of Scientific Research and Higher Studies, Jordan University (1978-80). **Publ.:** "The Outlook of the Modern Lebanese Society" (1964); "Our Culture in Fifty Years"; "Criticism in Modern Literature"; "Schools of Modern Criticism" and other books on literature. **Hobbies:** Music, poetry. **Sports:** Walking. **Prof. Addr.:** Faculty of Arts, Jordan University, Tel.: 843555, Amman, Jordan. **Priv. Addr.:** Tel.: 37025, Amman, Jordan.

YAGHMOUR (Mohamad Ahmad ben Mohamad Kazem), Saudi civil servant. **Born** in Jeddah, in 1950. **Dipl.:** B.Com. (Business Administration). **Career:** Demonstrator, Faculty of Economics and Administration. **Sport:** Swimming. **Hobbies:** Reading, chess. **Prof. Addr.:** P.O.Box 47, Tel.: 6436946, Jeddah. **Priv. Addr.:** Tel.: 6871296, Jeddah, Saudi Arabia.

YAHYA (Abdul Rahman Ibrahim, al), Saudi faculty lecturer. **Born** in 1949 in Taif, Saudi Arabia. **Dipl.:** M.A. (Education). **Career:** High school teacher (1972); Demonstrator of Education (1972-73); Supervisor of Social activities, Faculty of Education, Riyadh University; Lecturer, Faculty of Education, Riyadh University. **Address:** Riyadh, Saudi Arabia.

YAHYA (Ahmad Hamad, al), Saudi senior civil servant. **Born** at al-Majma'ah K.S.A. in 1942. **Dipl.:** M.A. (Industrial Relations). **Career:** Bank Employee (1956-68); Director of Administrative Affairs, Technical Education Department, Ministry of Education, Riyadh; Head of Employment Department, Ministry of Labour and Social Affairs (1971-73); attended UN Industrial Development Conference for West Asia (Beirut, 1975), Director-General, Main Labour Office, Western Region (1973-81); former Deputy Minister for Labour Affairs, Ministry of Labour and Social Affairs; appointed by H.M. the King as a Member of the Saudi SHURAH Council (1994-98); Ambassador to Kuwait (since 1999-). **Continuous Member:** of Saudi Delegation to ILO Conference, Geneva (1976-92), Saudi Delegation to Arab Labour Conference (1976-93). **Publ.:** Research articles on industrial relations; articles on national manpower development; "Saudisation and Labour Trends in K.S.A." (1998); "People Economy and Labour in the Arab Peninsula in the 19th century" (1999); "Labour and Manpower Development during a century in K.S.A" (2000). **Hobbies:** Reading and Swimming. **Prof. Addr.:** P.O.Box 333, Riyadh 11342; Saudi Arabia.

YAHYA (Ali, M.), Saudi academic. **Born** on 25 January 1942 in Jeddah, Saudi Arabia. **Dipl.:** B.A., M.A., Ph.D. (International Relations). **Career:** Lecturer, Faculty of Economics and Public Administration, King Abdulaziz University (1975-76); Assistant Professor, Part-time, Ministry of Foreign Affairs Diplomatic Institute (1982); Assistant Professor and former Chairman, Political Science Department, Faculty of Economics and Administration, King Abdulaziz University; member, Faculty of Economics and Public Administration Council, King Abdulaziz University, the Political Science Committee and Pi Sigma Alpha (National Political Science Honor Society). **Publication:** Power of Small State: Egypt and the Soviet Union, 1952-1972 (Ph.D. Thesis). **Address:** Political Science Department, Faculty of Economics and Administration, King Abdulaziz University, P.O.Box 9031, Tel.: 6879033, Ext. 1436/6892376, Jeddah, Saudi Arabia.

YAHYA (Anis, Hassan), Yemeni politician. **Born** in 1935 in Aden. **Career:** held various teaching posts; actively involved in the Independence Movement; elected to Political Bureau of National Front Party in 1975; Minister of Economy and Industry (1971-73); Minister of Communications (1973-75); Member of the People's Supreme Council; Vice Chairman of Presidium of Yemen's Council for Peace and Solidarity (1976); Secretary at the Central Committee of Economic Affairs Department (1976-79); Minister of Fishery Resources (1979-82); Deputy Prime Minister (1982-1984); **Prof. Addr.:** Aden, Republic of Yemen.

YAHYA (Mahmoud Yahia Abdulla, al), Kuwaiti scientist. **Born** on 7.2.1944 in Kuwait. **Son** of late Yahya al-Yahya **and** Mrs. Kmasha al-Yousef. **Married** to Miss Aisha Shehab on 8.8.1971 in Kuwait, 7 children: Loai (11.5.1974), Ahmad (25.11.1975), Omar (29.12.1978), Asma (28.4.1980), Yahya (30.8.1981), Kmasha (21.8.1983) and Dana (17.8.1984). **Educ.:** University of Washington (U.S.A.); University of Kuwait. **Dipl.:** B.Sc. in Chemistry, M.Sc. **Career:** Chemist, Kuwait National Petroleum Co. (1969-74); Chief Chemist (1974-76); Assistant Manager Corporate Economics (1976-78); Corporate Planning Manager (1978-87); Board Member (1980-87); Executive Member of the American Management Association (1980); Board Member of Heavy Oil Conversion Co. (1981) and KAFCO (1984); Deputy Managing Director of Planning (1982-87); Executive Assistant to Managing Director-Training Affairs Kuwait Petroleum Corporation (1987-). **Publ.:** "Symposium on Science and Technology for Development in Kuwait", Kuwait Institute for Scientific Research (1981). **Sports:** Walking and Gardening. **Hobbies:** Reading and Watching Cultural TV. Programs. **Member:** Kuwait Graduate Society. **Credit**

Cards: Diner's Club. **Prof. Addr.:** Kuwait Petroleum Corporation, P.O.Box 26565 Safat Pin Code 13126, Tel, 2423099, Telex: 44875, Safat, Kuwait. **Priv. Addr.:** House No. (8), Street 14, Area 5, Tel. 5383129, Mishrif, Kuwait.

YAHYA (Mohamad, Abdul Rahman, al, Dr.), Kuwaiti bank executive. **Born** in 1947 in Kuwait. **Educ.:** B.A. (Economics and Political Science), Austin College Texas, U.S.A.; Ph.D. (International Business Administration), University of Beverly Hills, U.S.A. **Career:** Assistant Professor of Linguistics, University of Texas, U.S.A. (1968-69); Community Services Superior, Arabian Oil Company, Kuwait (1969-71); Since 1971 with Commercial Bank of Kuwait; Between 1971 and 1979 worked in various Capacities. Became Deputy General Manager in September 1979; Promoted as General Manager in January 1982; Chief General Manager, since August 1985 to present. **Other Information:** Director of Bank of bahrain and Kuwait and Director of Bank of Oman, Bahrain & Kuwait. **Prof. Addr.:** c/o Commercial Bank of Kuwait, P.O.Box 2861, Tel.: 2411001, 13029, Safat, Kuwait.

YAHYAWI (Mohamad, Salah), Algerian statesman. **Born** in 1932 in Algeria. **Son** of Salah Yahyawi. **Career:** Member of the Algerian Revolutionary Council (1965); Former Commander of the 3rd Military Region; Director of the "Interarms Academy"; Commandant, Cherchell Military Academy (1965-77); Executive Secretary, FLN (Nov. 1977). **Addr.:** FLN, Place Emir Abdel Kader, Algiers, Algeria.

YAKER (Layachi), Algerian economist, **Born** in 1930 in Algeria. **Married**, 3 children. **Educ.:** University studies in Law and Economics (Algiers and Paris); School of Advanced studies, Sorbonne; **Career:** Chartered accountant; National Secretary Algerian Youth Committee Founding Member; Executive Committee Member, World Assembly of Youth (1952-54 and 1956-58); Vice President Algerian National Students Union (UGEMA) Paris (1955-56); Political Secretary, Ministry of Foreign Affairs, Provisional Government of the Algerian Republic, Cairo (1960-61), National Liberation Front and Provisional Government representative to India and South Asia (1961-62); Minister Plenipotentiary, Director International Cooperation, Ministry of Foreign Affairs (1962-69); Minister of Commerce (1969-77); Member of Parliament (Algiers), Vice President of the National and Popular Assembly (1977-79); Member of the Central Committee of the Party (National Liberation Front); Ambassador to the Soviet Union (1979-82); Ambassador to the United States (1983); Has taken part in a large number of international conferences: Arabe League, OAU, ECA, Non aligned, World Bank and IMF, United Nations,...; President, International Ocean Institute; Member of the Brandt Commission of North-South Issues. **Addr.:** Ministry of Foreign Affairs, Algiers, Algeria.

YAMANI (Ahmad), Abu Mahir, Palestinian politician. **Born** in 1925. **Career:** One of the original supporters of George Habash in the Arab Nationalist Movement; Led the Palestinian section which formed Abtal al-Awda (Heroes of the Return) (1966); was one of the founders of the Popular Front for the Liberation of Palestine (PFLP) (1967); Secretary General of the Palestine Workers' Federation in mid 1960s; Head of PFLP, Tripoli, Libya (1969); commanded PFLP with Wadih Haddad (1970) in Jordan during the temporary absence of George Habbash; elected to the Executive Committee of the Palestinian Liberation Organization (PLO) as representative of the PFLP (1973); led delegation from PLO to Peking to request Chinese support (1973); Head of PFLP during illness of George Habbash (1973); left PLO Executive Committee when the PFLP withdrew from the PLO (1973); accompanied Yasser Arafat on visit to Moscow (1973); Head of PLO Popular Organization (1974), **Addr.:** Damascus, Syria.

YAMANI (Ahmad Zaki), Former saudi government minister. **Born** in Mecca in 1930. **Dipl.:** BLL, Cairo University (1951); M.A. Comparative Law, New-York University, USA (1956). **Career:** Private Legal Adviser; Legal Adviser to Oil Department, Tax Department, Ministry of Finance (1956-58); legal adviser to Council of Minister (1958-60); Minister of State (1962); Minister of Petroleum and Mineral Resources since 1962; Member, Council of Ministers (1960); Director, Arabian American Oil Company (Aramco) (1962); Chairman of Board of Directors, General Petroleum and Minerals Organization (1963-1986); Chairman of Board of Directors, Saudi Arabian Fertilizer Co. since 1966; Secretary-General, Organization of Arab Petroleum Exporting Countries (1968-69); Chairman, Saudi Arabian-Sudanese Joint Commission for Exploration of the Red Sea Resources (1974); President, the Supreme Consultative Council for Petroleum and Mineral Affairs (1975-1986); member of several international law associations. **Hon. Degrees:** Hon. Ph.D., degree, Nihon University (Japan 1969); Hon. Ph.D., Osmania University (India 1975). **Publ.:** Author of Islamic Law and Contemporary Issues (in English and Arabic). **Hobbies:** Sightseeing, music, astrology. **Priv. Addr.:** Geneva, Switzerland.

YAMANI (Hashem Ibn Abdallah Ibn Hashem al-, Dr.), Saudi Politician. **Educ.:** Ph.D., Physics, Harvard University (1974). **Career:** Professor, Physics Department, King Fahd University of Petroleum and Minerals; Chairman, Physics Department; Vice President, King Abdulaziz City for Science and Technology; Director, Department of Energy and Resources, Research Institute, King Fahd University of Petroleum and Minerals; Minister of Industry and Electricity (1995-to date). **Address:** Ministry of Industry and Electricity, Omar bin al-Khattab Street, P.O.Box 5729, Riyadh, Saudi Arabia.

YAMANI (Mohamad Abdu), Saudi Academic. **Born** in 1939 in Mecca, Saudi Arabia. **Dipl.:** B.Sc. (Geology),

Faculty of Science; King Saud University; Ph.D. (Geology), Cornell University, U.S.A. **Career:** Lecturer, Faculty of Science, King Saud University, later Dean of Faculty of Science; Deputy Minister of Education for Technical Affairs, Ministry of Education; Rector, King Abdulaziz University; during his term of service as Rector he established the university as one of the major academic centres in the Middle East; he was responsible for expanding the University to include the two new Faculties of Engineering and Medical Sciences; his activities in the field of information have been numerous, and far-reaching; he has represented Saudi Arabia in several academic and Islamic conferences all over the world; Board Director al-Baraka Islamic Investment Bank, Bahrain. **Publications:** al-Mua'adalah al-Harijah (The Critical Equation), Qissat al-Yad al-Sufla (Story of the Lower Hand), al-Atbaq al-Ta'erah (Flying Saucers), Fatat Min Ha'il (A Girl from Ha'il), al-Insan Wa Ghazw al-Fadha'a (Man and Invasion Of Outer Space). **Hobby:** Reading, **Address:** Riyadh, Saudi Arabia.

YAQUB (Adel, Mohamad), Arab-American academic. **Born** in 1928 in Nablus, Jordan. **Married**, 2 children. **Educ.:** University of California, Berkeley, USA. **Dipl.:** B.A., M.A., Ph.D. **Career:** Instructor at Purdue University, West Lafayett, Indiana, USA (1955-57); Assistant Professor (1957-60); Associate Professor of Mathematics, University of California, Santa Barbara, USA (1960-67); Member of the American Mathematics Society, Mathematics Association of America and of Sigma Xi, Pi Mu Epsilon; Professor of Mathematics, University of California, Santa Barbara, USA (1967-). **Publ.:** "Introduction to Linear and Abstract Algebra" (1971), also contributed research articles in professional journals. **Addr.:** 602 Litchfield Lane, Santa Barbara, CA 93109, USA.

YARED (Michel, Youssef), Deputy regional manager, Air France. **Born** in Beirut. **Son** of Youssef Yared. **Educ.:** Secondary and Higher. **Career:** Representative of Messageries Maritimes in Egypt (1952-58), Air France Deputy Regional Manager in Cairo (1958). **Publ.:** Contributed a number of articles on civil aviation. **Sports:** Football and Basket-Ball. **Member** of Gazira Sporting Club (Cairo). **Prof. Addr.:** Air France, Talaat Harb Square, Tel.: 71848, Cairo, Egypt. **Priv. Addr.:** 9, Maahad Swissi Street, Zamalek, Tel.: 812050 Cairo, Egypt.

YASEEN (Bader Bazie, al), Kuwaiti auditor. **Born** in 1938 in Kuwait. **Married Educ.:** Mubarakiyah School, Kuwait; Cairo University, Egypt; accountancy studies. **Career:** Assistant Under Secretary, Ministry of Finance, Ministry of Commerce; Head of the Kuwait Investment Office, London (1965); Founder and Head of Kuwait Auditing Office. **Addr.:** Kuwait Auditing Office, Bader al-Bazie & Co., P.O.Box 2115, 13022 Safat, Kuwait.

YASSA (Ramzi, Nagui), Egyptian musician. **Born** in 1948 in Cairo, Egypt. **Married,** 1 son. 1 daughter. **Educ.:** Cairo Higher Institute of Music (Conservatoire). Fellow, Trinity College of Music London (FTCL); Assistatura Stagerovka, Moscow Conservatoire; Ecole Normale de Musique, Paris. **Dipl.:** Licence de Concert. **Career:** International concert pianist, performing throughout Europe, Russia, Japan, USA and the Middle East in venue such as the Kennedy Center, The Barbican, Théatre des Champs Elysées, Tivoli, Musikverein etc.; Director, Cairo Opera House (1998); Special Advisor for Music, Egyptian Minister of Culture (1999). **Publ.:** Recorded numerous Cds of Works by Tchaikovsky, Chopin, Beethoven, Prokofiev, Liszt.. **Decor.:** Certificate of Honour at the Tchaikowsky International Competition in Moscow (1975). **Award:** Grand Prix Winner of the Santander International Piano Competition. **Addr.:** 14 Rue St. Cecile, Paris 75009, France.

YASSIN (Anas, Yusuf), Saudi diplomat. **Born** in 1934 in Taif, Saudi Arabia. **Son** of Yusuf Yassin. **Married,** two children. **Educ.:** Victoria College, Alexandria, Egypt (1944-52); University of California, California, USA (1954-56); Honorary Doctorate, University of Osmania, Hyderabad, India. **Career:** Director, National Gibson Company, Riyadh, Saudi Arabia (1958-59); Chairman, Arab Trading Company (1959-61); Founder, al-Nasr Traidng Office, Jeddah (1962); Foreign Ministry (1963); Member Saudi Arabian Delegation to 19th General Assembly of United Nations with rank of Ambassador (1964); Foreign Ministry, Jeddah, Saudi Arabia; Delegate, 21st General Assembly of United Nations; Ambassador to India (1968). **Addr.:** Ministry of Foreign Affairs, P.O.B. 495, Tel.: 6421917, Telex: 401104 KHARIJI SJ., Jeddah, Saudi Arabia.

YASSIN (Aziz, Ahmed, Prof.), Egyptian academic. **Born** on August 13, 1918 in Cairo (Egypt). **Married** in 1951, to Moonira Eleanor Hartmann, two daughters, one son. **Educ.:** Abbasiyah Secondary School; Faculty of Science, Cairo University; Imperial College of Science and Technology, University of London. **Dipl.:** B.Sc., DIC, Ph.D. (Engineering). **Career:** Joined Ministry of Housing and Public Utilities (1939); Promoted Under-Secretary of State (1957); Director-General and Vice-Chairman, Building Research Centre (1954-59); Chairman and President, Tourah Portland Cement Company Board member, Helwan Portland Cement Company, and Sudan Portland Cement Company; Chairman, Egyptian Cement Companies Marketing Board (1959-63); Chairman and President, Egyptian General Organisation for Housing and Public Contracting companies (1963-65); Minister of Tourism and Archaeology (1965-67); Minister of Housing and Construction (1966-68); Board member, Aswan High Dam Authority (1966-68); External Professor in Soil Mechanics, Cairo University (1951-81); External Professor of Civil Engineering, Ayn Shams University; member, Council of Building Research and Technology, Egyptian Academy of Science and Technology (1972-89); Chairman of Society of Civil Engineers since 1991; Chairman of Society of Egyptian Engineers since 1993; Former Secretary General of Union of Arab Engineers. **Publ.:** Author of "Studies on the Bearing Capacity of Piles" (1951), "Bearing Capacity of Deep Foundations in Clay Soils", "Testing Sand Dry Samples with Tri-Axial Apparatus" (1953), "The Industry of building Materials in Egypt" (1957). **Awards:** Commander's Cross with Star, Order of Resurrection (Poland); Order of the Banner of the Hungarian Republic; Order of the Republic (Egypt) 1st class. **Spec. Intr.:** Reading (especially economics, law). **Prof. Addr.:** 34 Talaat Harb Street, P.O.Box 2540, Tel.: 755797, Fax: 761929, Cairo (Egypt). **Priv. Addr.:** 4 Waheeb Doss Street, Tel.: 3500519, Maadi, Cairo, Egypt.

YASSIN (Kateb), Algerian novelist, poet and dramatist. **Born** in 1929 in Constantine. **Educ.:** Secondary and Higher. **Career:** Novelist, poet and playwright (in French Language). **Publ.:** Author of "Soliloques" (1946), "Le Cadavre Encerclé" (1962), "Nedjma" (1956), "Le Cercle de Représailles" (a play, 1959). **Priv. Addr.:** Paris, France.

YASSIN (Mohamad, Osman), Sudanese former diplomat. **Born** in 1915 in Sudan. **Educ.:** Gordon College and London School of Economics. **Dipl.:** Bachelor of Science, Economics, London School of Economics, UK. **Career:** Joined Political Service (1945); Liaison Officer in Ethiopia (1952-53); Governor Upper Province (1954-55); Permanent Under-Secretary for Foreign Affairs since 1956; Member of Sudanese Delegation to United Nations (1956); Delegate to Independent African States Conference, Monrovia (1959); to Accra Conference on Positive Action for Peace and Security in Africa (1960); to Independent African States Conference, Leopoldville (1960); Special Adviser to United Nations on training of Diplomat (1961-62); Special Envoy to Ethiopia and Somalia on border dispute: member African Unity Organisation Commission for Conciliation and Arbitration between Algeria and Morocco; Organizer, First African Finance Ministers Conference, Khartoum (1963); Grading Structure and Salaries Committee of Zambia (1966); joined UN Office of Technical Co-Operation (1966); Resident Representative, UN Development Programme (UNDP), Jordan (1970-75); Chairman, Board of Directors, Sudan Commercial Bank (1975-1986); Honorary member, Institute of Differing civilizations, Brussels. **Publ.:** Author of "The Sudan Civil Service" (1954), "Analysis of the Economic Situation in the Sudan" (1958), "Problems of Transfer of Power the Administration Aspect" (1961), "Germany and Africa" (1962). **Awards:** Knight Grand Cordon of Human Order of Redemption, Liberia; Grand Officer, Order of Menelik II; Republican Order, Arab Republic of Egypt; Star of Yugoslavia; First Order of Jordanian Independence. **Priv. Addr.:** P.O.Box 2201, Khartoum, Sudan.

YASSIN (Sayed), Egyptian academic, writer. **Born** in 1933 in Alexandria, Egypt. **Married,** three children. **Educ.:** Licence in Law, Alexandria University, Egypt (1957); M.Sc. in Criminilogy, Institute of Criminology. **Career:** Research Assistant, National Institute of Criminology. **Career:** Research Assistant, National Institute of Criminology (1957); Researcher, National Institute of Criminology (1960); Expert, National Institute for Social and Criminal Research (Head of Criminal Behaviour Unit) (1967); Director of the Political and Stategic Studies Center, Cairo (since 1975); part time Lecturer, College of Information, Cairo University; Lecturer, Institute of Research and Arabic Studies, Cairo; Professor of Sociology (seconded); American University in Cairo. **Publ.:** "Foundations of Social Research", Cairo; "Studies in Criminal Behaviour and Treatment of Criminals", Cairo; "Social Analysis of Literature", Cairo "Contemporary Criminal Policy", Cairo; "The Arabic Personality Between Israeli and the Arabic Understanding" Cairo. **Sport:** Tennis. **Addr.:** Cairo, Egypt.

YASSIN (Sayed, Mohamad), Egyptian, former director general of the technical and project department of "al-Ahram" newspaper. **Born** on June 23, 1916 in Cairo. **Son** of Mohamad Yassin. **Married,** 3 children: Hala, Mohamad and Assem. **Educ.:** American University of Beirut. **Dipl.:** Bachelor of Arts. **Career:** General Manager, Yassine Glassware (1936-54); Director and General Manager, Cairo Bus Company (1954-56); Managing Director of "Société Générale pour les Produits Céramiques et Porcelaines" (1954-58); Managing Director, Cairo Office for Agencies and Supplies (1958-61); former Director General of the Technical and Project Department of "al-Ahram" Newspaper. **Member:** Gezira Sporting Club. **Prof. Addr.:** al-Ahram, al-Gala'a Street, Tel.: 70770, Cairo, Egypt. **Priv. Addr.:** 7A, Hassan Sabry Street, Zamalek, Cairo, Egypt.

YASSIN (Sufian, Ibrahim), Jordanian executive. **Born** in 1930 in Sartah. **Son** of Ibrahim Yassin. **Married** in 1959, 2 sons, 3 daughters. **Dipl.:** B.Com. **Career:** Controller of Companies; Chairman, Arab Paper Converting & Trading Co., Amman; Director, Institute of Banking Studies. Director, Hotels Company; Board Member, Intermediate University College. Deputy Chairman and General Manager, Jordan Kuwait Bank, Amman. **Member:** National Association for the Mentally Handicapped; Arab Bankers Association, London. **Addr.:** P.O.Box 9776, Tel.: 61165, 62922, Telex: 21994 A/B ARKUBK JO, Amman, Jordan.

YASSINE (Soufian A.F.), Saudi businessman. **Born** on June 15, 1951 in Damascus Syria. **Son** of Abdul Fattah Yassine (Diplomat) **and** Mrs. Zahra Kassem Yassine. **Married** to Mirs. Samia, 4 children: Ramzi, Omar, Areeb, Ablah. **Education:** Brummana High School (Lebanon); American University in Beirut, New England College. **Diploma:** High School Certificate, B.A. in Management and Finance (1977); **Career:** General Manager till 1987, Vice President from 1.1.1989. **Awards:** The British Society of Commerce, The Arab Management Society. **Sports:** Swimming and Tennis. **Hobbies:** Photography, Antiques

Collection. **Member:** British Institute of Management, American Management Association Intl., International Management Consultants, **Credit Cards:** Visa and Master Card. **Professional Address:** P.O.Box 6, Riyadh 11411, Tel.: 966-1-4629664, Saudi Arabia. **Private Address:** P.O.Box 41233, Riyadh 11521, Tel.: 966-1-4034994, Saudi Arabia.

YATEEM (Hussain Ali), Bahraini merchant. **Born** in 1914 in Manama. **Son** of Ali Yateem (Manufacturer's Representative). **Married** in 1934, 5 children: Ali, Mohamed, Mary, Salwa, Shahrazad. **Educ.:** Privately, American Mission School of Bahrain; Brighton Hove and Sussex Grammar School (England). **Career:** Proprietor of "A.M. Yateem Bros.", Manufacturer's Representative, Sole Agent and Distributor for "Carrier", involved in first oil concession in Bahrain (1932); established first water distillation and ice plant (1938); opened plants for industrial gas; agent of Carrier, Brown Boveri, Cutler-Hammer, Landis & Gyr. Du Pont, Nalco Chemicals etc.; Chairman, A.M. Yateem Bros.; Founder Member of Gulf Aviation Company; former President, Bahrain Chamber of Commerce and Bahrain Red Crescent Society. **Sport:** Swimming, **Hobbies:** Walking. Yachting, Gardening. **Addr.** P.O.Box. 60, Tel.: 253444, 253450, Manama, Bahrain.

YATEEM (Shahrazad, Hussain), Bahraini businesswoman, art expert. **Born** in 1951 in Manama, Bahrain. **Educ.:** Studied Fine Arts, Beirut College for Women, Lebanon; Paris University and Sorbonne, Paris, France. **Career:** Opened art gallery in Bahrain (1973); second gallery (1979). Vice President of Bahrain Historical and Archaelogical Society (since 1974). **Sports:** Tennis, swimming and yoga. **Addr.** P.O.Box 60, Manama, Bahrain.

YAZBEK (Qassem), Syrian athlete. **Born** in 1940 in Damascus. **Career:** Athlete since 1960; Champion of the Syrian Arab Republic for all categories (1961); visited Kuwait (1962-64); has been classified 3rd in world championship (1965); World champion in 1966 (Juniors) retired (1967-68); champion of the Arab World for all categories (Cairo 1968); classified 2nd in the international championship of London (1968) and of Belgrade (1967); Sports and athletic club in Damascus. **Addr.** Damascus, Syria.

YAZGHI (Mohamad Driss, al), Moroccan Minister. **Born** in 1935 in Fes, Morocco. **Son** of Driss al-Yazghi. **Married,** two sons. **Educ.:** B.A. in Law. **Career:** Head of Services, Equipment Budget, Ministry of Finance (1960); Lawyer (1964); member of the Central Committee of the National Union of Popular Forces, USFP (1975); Director of "al-Muharrir" daily paper (1975); Director of "Liberation" weekly paper in French; member of Parliament; member of the Central Committee of the Moroccan Society for the Support of the Palestinian Cause; member of the National Syndicate of the Press; member of the Arab Writers Union. Minister of Territorial Administration, Environment, Urban Planning and Housing. (since March 14, 1998-). **Publ.:** Articles in newspapers and magazines. **Sports:** Jogging, swimming. **Hobbies:** Poetry, painting. **Addr.** 5, Ibn Tufail Street, Les Oranges, Rabat, Morocco.

YAZID (Mohamad), Algerian diplomat. **Born** in 1923 in Blida, Algeria. **Married,** three children. **Career:** Active member of Algerian People's Party; President of North African Student's Association in France, in charge of Federation in France for Movement for the Triumph of Democratic Liberties (MTDL); imprisoned by French for political activities (1948-50); member, Revolutionary Committee for Unity and Action and National Liberation Front (FLN), Cairo (1954); Represented FLN at UN (1956); Minister of Information in Provisional Government (1958-62); played leading role in Provisional Government's acceptance of Evian Agreements; has led many missions abroad; President of Afro Asian People's solidarity Organisation, Algiers (1964); re-elected to National Assembly (1964); President of National Assembly Foreign Affairs Commission; Ambassador to Lebanon (1971). **Addr.** Ministry of Foreign Affairs, Algiers, Algeria.

YOUAKIM (Saba, H.E. Mgr.), Lebanese Archbishop of Syria, Arab Republic of Egypt and Lebanon. **Born** on June 2, 1914 in Wardieh (South of Lebanon). **Educ.:** St. Sauveur Seminary (1927-33); Angelicum, Rome (1934-38). **Dipl.:** Graduate in Philosophy and Theology from Rome. **Career:** Ordained to the Priesthood in the Salvatorian Monks Order in Rome (November 30, 1939); Professor (1940-53), then Superior of St. Sauveur Seminary (2 times); Assistant to the Salvatorian Sisters (1951-53); Parish Priest at Zahleh (1953-54); Elected General Superior of his Order (1956-62), Reelected General Superior (1962-68), Sacred Archbishop and Patriarchal Counsellor since September 28, 1968. **Winter Residence:** Greek Catholic Melchite Diocese, Bab Sharki, Tel.: 23129 and 23136, Damascus, Syria; ad-Daher Street, Tel.: 44790, Cairo and Jawhar Street, Alexandria, Tel.: 26422, Egypt.

YOUNES (Gabir Abu Bakr, Brig.), Libyan army officer. **Born** on November 1942 in Zelaa, Libya. **Educ.:** Military College, Tripoli; English Language Centre, Tripoli. **Career:** Promoted Lieutenant (August 1967); participated in coup of September 1969 which overthrew King Idris (q.v.); Member, Revolution Command Council (1969-77); General Secretariat of General People's Congress (1977-78); Commander in Chief of Armed Forces. **Addr.:** General Headquarters of the Armed Forces, Tripoli, Libya.

YOUSEF (Ibrahim M.), Egyptian-Canadian academic.

Born in 1940 in Egypt. **Married** 2 daughters. **Educ.:** Ain Shams University, Cairo, Egypt; University College of Wales, England; University of Edinburgh, Scotland. **Dipl.:** B.Sc., M.Sc., and Ph.D. **Career:** Research Associate, Michigan State University, Michigan, U.S.A. (1967-69); Research Associate, Banting and Best Department of Medical Research, University of Toronto, Canada, (1969-70); Research Associate, Pathology Department, University of Toronto, Canada (1970-72); Assistant Professor, Pathology Department, University of Toronto, Canada (1972-78); Associate Professor, Department of Paediatric, University of Montreal, Canada (1978-83), Professor, Department of Paediatric, University of Montreal, Canada, (1983-88), Professor (tenured), Department of Pharmacology, University of Montreal, Canada (1988-now). Director of the Liver Research Unit Ste-Justine Hospital Research Centre (1978-now). Visiting Associate Professor, Harvard Medical School, Boston, U.S.A. (1983); Chairman, Department of Biochemistry and Clinical Biochemistry; Faculty of Medicine, King Saud University, Abha, Saudi Arabia (1984-85). Member of the International Association for the Study of the Liver; International Association for Clinical Biochemistry; American Association for the Study of Liver Diseases; Founding member of the Canadian Academy of Clinical Biochemistry; Member of the Canadian Association of Clinical Biochemistry, Member of the Canadian Association of the Study of Liver Diseases; The Canadian Association of Gastroenterology; the Canadian Association of Toxicology and the Quebec Association of Clinical Biochemistry. Scholar of the Canadian Liver Foundation (1972-78); **Publ.:** More than 200 papers in books and scientific journals on Liver diseases. **Interest:** International cooperation in the field of liver diseases and research. **Prof. Addr.:** Department of Pharmacology, University of Montreal, C.P.6128, Succ. A. Montreal, Quebec, Canada, H3C 3J7.

YOUSEF (Saleh M. Al), Kuwaiti Chairman & Managing Director. **Born** on May 11, 1950 in Kuwait. **Son** of Mohammad S. Al Yousef **and** Mrs. née Hamda Al Nasser. **Married** on November 27, 1980 in Kuwait to Miss Fatemah H. Al Saqabi, 4 children: Hamda (6.6.82), Mohammad (23.8.84), Humoud (15.11.85), Hanan (5.12.88). **Educ.:** Kuwait University, Faculty of Commerce, Economics & Political Sciences (1973-74); Institute of Banking Studies, Kuwait (1974-75). **Dipl.:** B.Com. (Accounting), diploma in Banking Studies, certificate as External Auditors Category (A). **Training** at the Economics Institute, University of Colorado, USA (1976), at University of Arizona, USA, Intensive English training program (1976), at the Board of Governors of the Federal Reserve System, Washington, DC, Bank Examination School, Banking Studies (1976), at Chemical Bank, New York (1978), at the Central Bank of Egypt (1979). **Career:** Financial Analyst, The Central Bank of Kuwait (1974-87); Deputy Manager, Banking Supervision Dept. and Head of Inspection Section, The Central Bank of Kuwait (1978-84); Executive Manager, Follow-up Dept., The Industrial Bank of Kuwait (IBK) (1.4.84 - 20.4.85), Deputy General Manager, Operations Dept. (21.4.85 - 13.1.87), General Manager (IBK) (14.1.87 - 16.7.88); Chairman and Managing Director of The Industrial Bank of Kuwait (IBK) (17.7.1988 to present). **Board Memberships:** Director, The United Bank of Kuwait PLC, United Kingdom (1988); Board Member, Institute of Banking Studies, Kuwait (1988); Board Trustee, Kuwait Institute for Scientific Research, Kuwait (1988); Member, Industrial Development Committee, Ministry of Commerce & Industry, Kuwait (1988); Board Member, Arab Banking Corporation, Bahrain (1989); Chairman of the Supervisory Board, ABC Daus Frankfurt (1992); Board Member (Gulf Invest-Kuwait (1997). **Previous** Board Memberships: The Industrial Bank of Kuwait (1980-83), The Gulf Bank (1986-88), Security Group Co. (1985-87), Kuwait Insulating Materials Mfg. Co. (1984-87), Banque Tunisio-Koweitienne de Developpement, Tunisia (1984-91). **Member:** Kuwaiti Accountants and Auditors Association; Kuwaiti Graduates Association. **Addr.:** P.O.Box 3146 Safat, 13032 Kuwait, Kuwait City, Tel.: 246-2003/7 **Priv. Addr.:** Dahiat Abdullah, House No.25, Kuwait

YOUSSOUF (Mohamed, Adoyta), Djbouti Deputy at the National Assembly. **Born** in 1944 at Obock. **Career:** Accountant at ONED (Sept. 1966 - Dec. 1977). Vice-President then General Secretary of MPL (1975-1979); General Secretary of FDLD (1979-1991); President then Vice-President of FRUD (1991-1993). Elected Deputy at the National Assembly (19/12/1997 - to date); Member of Foreign Affairs Commission and Production Commission. **Prof. Addr.:** National Assembly, P.O.Box 138 Djibouti, Djibouti.

YOUSSOUF (Mohamed, Ahmed), Djibouti Deputy at the National Assembly. **Born** in 1957 at Obock. **Career:** Principal Consultant in Education. Militant of LPAI; Executive Member of FRUD; Member of Association Committee for the Stability and Wide-Wake for Youths. Elected Deputy at the National Assembly (19.12.1997 - to date); Member of the Foreign Affairs Commission; Treasurer Secretary at the National Assembly. **Prof. Addr.:** National Assembly, P.O.Box 138 Djibouti, Djibouti.

YUNIS (Adil, Assad), Arab-American academic. **Born** in 1930. **Married**, 3 children. **Educ.:** American University of Beirut, Lebanon. **Dipl.:** M.D. **Career:** Intern and Assistant Resident, American University Hospital, Beirut (1954-56); Resident, Barnes Hospital, St. Louis, USA (1956-57); practiced medicine, specialising in haematology in Miami, Florida, USA (1964-); Assistant Professor of Medicine, Washington University, USA (1963-64); Director of Haematology Research and Assistant Professor of Medicine, University of Miami (1946-65); Director, Division of Haematology (1965-); Assistant Professor of Medicine (1965-68); Professor of Biochemistry and Medicine and Director of the Howard Hughes Laboratories for Haematology Research (1968); Leukemia Scholar (1961-66); Member of the American Society of Hematology, American Society of Biological Chemists, the Association of American Physicians and the American Society of Clinical Investigation; Chief of Haematology Department, Jackson Memorial Hospital in Miami, Florida (1965-); **Award:** Research Career Development Award, USPHS. **Priv. Addr.:** Florida, U.S.A.

YUSUF (Abdallah, Yaqub), United Arab Emirates statesman. **Born** in 1949 in Ummal Qaiwan, United Arab Emirates. **Educ.:** B.A. in Arabic, History Department, al-Azhar University, Cairo, Egypt. **Career:** Director of Internal Trade, Ministry of Economy and Commerce (1974). **Sport:** Swimming. **Hobbies:** History of civilizations, hunting, travelling. **Addr.:** P.O.Box 3397, Abu Dhabi, United Arab Emirates.

YUSUF (Dafallah al-Haj), Sudanese former minister. **Born** on June 6, 1934 in Omdurman, Sudan. **Son** of al-Haj Yusuf Medani (businessman) **and** Mrs., née el-Shool Khalil. **Married** on May 3, 1962 to el-Shafa el-Tayeb, five children: Mohamad, Omaymama, Soma, Nasrine and Sarah. **Educ.:** Khor Togab Secondary school; Ashford Secondary school; Faculty of Law, Khartoum University, London University. **Dipl.:** LL.B. (1958). **Career:** Member of Sudan Judiciary; Advocate; General Manager of Nigerian Corporation; Managing-Director Gulf International, Sudan, comprising sixteen companies engaged in industry, services, insurance, trade; Minister of Education; Chairman of National Council for Higher Education; chairman, Sudanese National Commission for Education, Culture and Science; Chairman of the General Conference of Arab League Organization for Science, Education and Culture. **Awards:** Order of the Constitution (Sudan); Order of the Two Niles (Sudan); Order of Oman (Sultanate of Oman); Commander, Legion of Honour (France). **Sport:** Golf. **Hobbies:** reading and writing poetry. **Member:** African Association of Public Administration and Business Management, and formerly of the Executive Board of Unesco. **Addr.:** Khartoum, Sudan.

YUSUF (Mohamad), Egyptian educator and statesman. **Born** in 1917 in Tantah. **Educ.:** Tantah Primary School, Abbassia Secondary School, Teacher Training College. **Career:** Secondary School Teacher; General Director of Personnel, Ministry of Education; Director of Recrutment and Training, Civil Service Bureau; Director General of Secondary Education; Minister of Education, Assistant Under-Secretary of State, Ministry of Education (1957); again Minister of Education (1961). **Addr.:** Cairo, Egypt.

YUSUF (Mohamad, Saleh, al), Saudi academic. **Born** in 1944 at Beishah. **Dipl.:** B.Sc (Biology), M.Sc. (Biology), Ph.D. (Zoology). **Career:** Associate professor in zoology at King Saud University; Member of Saudi Biological Society, Member of American society of parasitologists, Member Academy of zoology of India. **Hobbies:** Light sports. **Address:** Department of zoology, Faculty of Science, King Saud University, Riyadh, Saudi Arabia.

YUSUF (Mohamad, Zayed Mohamad), Saudi senior civil servant. **Born** in Taif, in 1952. **Dipl.:** B.A. (Psychology), Diploma of Curriculum. **Career:** Former Director of Curriculum and Programmes, Medical Service, Ministry of Defence; Chief of Training, Inspection and Missions Division, Medical Service, Ministry of Defence and Aviation, Riyadh. **Sports:** Table tennis, swimming, excursions. **Prof. Addr.:** P.O.Box 40, Taif, Saudi Arabia.

YUSUF (Suha, Sharif), Iraqi businesswoman. **Born** in 1950 in Baghdad, Iraq. **Educ.:** American University of Beirut, Lebanon; Printmaking Department, Royal College of Art, London; Inchbold School of Design, London, UK. **Dipl.:** B.A. in Fine Arts, M.A. in Print, Diploma in Interior Design. **Career:** numerous exhibitions (since 1965); Founder of the Tredex Interior Design which expanded later to form Sayde Interiors Limited (1983-); Director of Sayde (UK) Interiors Limited (1983-). Member of Society of Industrial Artists and Designers and Society of Iraqi Artists. **Hobbies:** riding, judo, yoga. **Prof. Addr.:** Sayde Interiors, 18B Charles Street, London W1, UK. **Priv. Addr.:** 23/5/27 Hariri Street, Baghdad, Iraq.

YUSUF (Yusuf, Shahid), Iraqi accountant. **Born** in 1950 in Baghdad, Iraq. **Son** of Shahid Yusuf. **Married** in 1978, 1 son. **Dipl.:** B.Sc.; ACCA. (UK). **Career:** Credit Department, Citibank, Jeddah and Yemen; Account Executive, Merrill Lynch, Dubai, UAE. **Member:** Association of Certified Accountants. **Hobbies:** Flying and swimming. **Addr.:** P.O.Box 3911, Tel.: 225261, Telex: 45563 A/B 45563 MERLE, Dubai, UAE.

YUSUFI (Muhsin, Muhamad Abdullah, al), Yemeni politician. **Born** in 1939 in Marib, Yemen Arab Republic. **Married**, 2 sons, 1 daughter. **Educ.:** Police College. **Career:** Lieutenant, Police Force; Chief, Sana'a Security Department (1968); Chief, Taiz Security Department (1971); Minister of the Interior (1975-78); Member of the Republican Group, People's Legislative Council of the Yemen Arab Republic; Governor of Taiz (1978). **Hobby:** reading. **Addr.:** Taiz, Republic of Yemen.

Z

ZAANOUNI (Mustafa), Tunisian economist and businessman. **Born** on December 19, 1928 in Sousse, Tunisia. **Married**, 3 children. **Educ.:** in Paris. **Dipl.:** LL.B., Paris; Diploma, Doctorat d'Etat en Economie, Politique et Sciences Economiques, Paris; Diplôme de l'Ecole National d'Administration, Paris. **Career:** Head of Department, Secretariat of State for Planning (1956-58); Head of Economic Affairs Department, Secretariat of State for Agriculture (1959-64); Supervisor, FAO Special Funds Projects (1964-66); Expert in Agricultural Economics, FAO-IBRD (World Bank) co-operation programme (1966-69); Secretary of State to the Minister of Agriculture (1970-71); Secretary of State to the Minister of Planning (1971); Minister Delegate to the Prime Minister in charge of Planning (1975-80); Lecturer, Higher Law School, Higher Agricultural School and Co-operative School, Tunis (1957-64); Businessman since 1985. **Awards:** Grand Officer, Order of Tunisian Independence; Grand Officer, Order of the Tunisian Republic. **Addr.:** Tunis, Tunisia.

ZABARAH (Abdulmalik, Ali), Yemeni businessman. **Born** in Sanaa, Republic of Yemen. **Son** of Ali Zabarah **and** Mrs. Amt al-Malik. **Married** in Sanaa to Ishak, Najwa Abdulmalik, four children: Nora, Saif, Sara and Sami. **Educ.:** Harvard University, USA, OPM Degree DC University, USA; B.S. in Computer Science; Diploma from Police Academy, Sana'a. **Career:** Police Officer (1964-69); System Analyst with NCR (1975-77); Founder and Managing Director of Yemen Computer Company Limited, Sanaa, Yemen (1977-to date); Honorary Consul of Canada, Sanaa, Yemen (1990-to date). Founder/ Owner and Managing Director, AZ Com Ltd., Sanaa (1992- to date). **Prof. Addr.:** Yemen Computer Company Limited, P.O.Box 340, Tel.: 208811/2/3/4, Telex: 2406 YCC YE, Fax: 967-1-209523, Sanaa, Republic of Yemen. E-mail: yccnet@y.net.ye. **Priv. Addr.:** House No.7, Str. 20A, Off Hadda Road, Tel.: 009671 416000, Fax: 009671 414335, Sanaa, Yemen.

ZABIDI (Rashad Ali), Saudi civil servant. **Born** in 1928 in Mecca, Saudi Arabia. **Dipl.:** Mecca, Saudi Arabia. **Dipl.:** Diploma, Institute of Telecommunications, Cairo, Egypt. **Career:** Telephone technician; Telephone Director of Mecca Zone, Director of Technical Office and Projects; Director of Telephones, Telex and Telegraphs, Mecca Zone; Director-General of Automatic Telephones, Mecca Zone; member of Mecca Municipal Council; member of Mutawefeen (Pilgrims' Guides) Organization. **Hobbies:** Reading, sport. **Address:** Azizia Street, Mecca, Saudi Arabia.

ZABIDI (Saud Abdul Aziz), Saudi academic. **Born** in Mecca, in 1945. **Dipl.:** Ph.D. (Sociology). **Career:** General Supervisor of Saudi Student Affairs, Saudi Cultural Bureau (Cairo, Egypt) until 1973; Supervisor of Public Relations, King Abdulaziz University; Supervisor, Department of Public Service (Evening Courses), Faculty of Arts, King Abdulaziz University; now Assistant Professor of Sociology, King Abdulaziz University. **Publ.:** Notes on Thought, Life and Art (published Cairo 1975); Discourses in Modern Issues, The Star Will Never Fall (a novel). **Hobbies:** Literature, music. **Prof. Addr.:** P.O.Box 4676, Jeddah, Saudi Arabia.

ZAFAR (Jamil Ahmad), Saudi Academic. **Born** in 1932 in Mecca, Saudi Arabia. **Dipl.:** M.A. (Arabic Grammar); Ph.D. (Arabic Language). **Career:** Secondary school teacher; School Principal; Bureau Manager for the Director of Education, Mecca; Lecturer, Arabic Department, Faculty of Shari'a, Umm al-Qura University (1970); Assistant Professor, Faculty of Arabic Language, Umm al-Qura University, Mecca; member of the Committee for the Study of Arabic Language Status, Muslim World League; attended the Conference for the Study of Arabic Language Status in the Arab and Islamic countries, Muslim World League, 1973. **Publications:** Ph.D. thesis, Arabic Language; The Verb, Parsing and Formation; Linguistic and Literary Studies of the Holy Quran; prepares and broadcasts several programmes on the Holy Quran, Fi Moheit al-Quran (within Quran circle), al-Nahw al-Qurani (Grammar of Quran), al-Maktabah al-Qura'niah (Quran Library). **Hobbies:** Reading, sports. **Address:** Umm al-Qura University, Faculty of Arabic Language, Tel.: 5423370, Mecca, Saudi Arabia.

ZAFER (Mohamad Ismail), Saudi academic. **Born** in 1934. **Dipl.:** Ph.D. (Education), Michigan State University, East Lansing, U.S.A. **Career:** Educational Supervisor, Elementary Education, Riyadh District; Assistant Dean of Academic Supervision for Secondary Education, Ministry of Education; Educational Adviser, Ministry of Education; Lecturer, King Abdulaziz University, Makkah Branch; Organizer of the First Conference of Teacher-Education in Saudi Arabia; member, the Message of University Conference, Riyadh and other national and international conferences; Vice Dean, Faculty of Education, Umm al-Qura University, 1977; Founder Dean of the Faculty of Education for boys and girls, King Abdulaziz

University, Medina (1979); Associate Professor and Chairman, Department of Islamic Education and Curriculum, Faculty of Education, King Abdulaziz University, Medina Branch; started graduate studies programme at the Faculty of Education leading to Masters and Ph.D. degrees with effect from 1981-82; established the University College and the College of Planning and Technology as Constituent Colleges of King Abdulaziz University, Medina Branch; member, Academic Council, King Abdulaziz University, Jeddah. **Hobbies:** Reading, sports. **Address:** Faculty of Education, King Abdulaziz University, P.O.Box 334, Medina, Saudi Arabia.

ZAGHA (Hisham, Daoud), Jordanian engineer. **Born** in Amman, Jordan on 20.5.43. **Son** of Daoud Zagha (Retired Civil Servant) **and** Mrs. Bahija Zagha. **Married** in 1951 to Miss Elizabeth Conroy, Three Children; Lana (1973), Zeid (1978), Ashraf (1981). **Educ.:** Civil Engineering and Urban Design, Alexandria University, Egypt (1967); State University of New York at Buffalo USA (1970); Project Planning Center, University of Bradford, England (1972); State University of New York at Buffalo USA (1976). **Dipl.:** B.S., Advanced Course in Cost-Benefit Analysis for Infrastructure Projects, Ph.D. **Career:** Municipality of Amman: Design Engineer (1967-68)l Head of Engineering Studies Division (1970-71); Head of Municipal Projects, Projects FollowUp Dept., National Planning Council, Amman (1971-74); Head of Roads, Tourism and Regional Development Div., National Planning Council, Amman (1976-79); Part-time Lecturer at the University of Jordan, School of Engineering (1977-80); Director, Social Projects Department, National Planning Council, Amman (1979-80); Director General, Urban Development Dept. (1980-present). **Member:** Jordan Engineering Association: International Society of City and Regional Planners. Engineering Education Committee (1978-80), Engineering Degrees Evaluation Committee (1982-84); Board of Directors, Hotel Training Institute (1979-80); Board of Directors, Cities and Villages Development Bank, Amman (1979-80); **Publ.:** "Squatter Upgrading: A new Approach to Urban Development Scheme for Jordan"; Development and Application of a Land Use Design Model; "Cratering in Soil", "Stability of Frames". **Sports:** Tennis and cycling. **Clubs:** Royal Automobile Club. **Credit Cards:** American Express, Visa. **Prof. Addr.:** Urban Development Dept., P.O.B. 950504, Amman, Jordan.

ZAHAR (Abdul-Rahman), Egyptian former international civil servant. **Born** on August 22, 1916 in Cairo (Egypt). **Married**, with children. **Educ.:** Faculty of Agriculture, Cairo University (1935-38); University of Edinburgh (1945-48); london School of Hygiene and Tropical Medicine (1965-66). **Dipl.:** B.S. (Agriculture) (1938), Ph.D. (1948), **Career:** Biology teacher, School of Agriculture, Egypt (1938-42); Demonstrator, Entomology, Faculty of Agriculture, Cairo University (1942-44); Entomologist, Insect Control Section, Ministry of Health, Cairo (1949-52); Entomologist, Malaria Control Project, World Health Organisation (WHO) Saudi Arabia (1952-55); Team Leader, Malaria Control Project, Saudi Arabia (1956-58); Senior Adviser, Regional Malaria Eradication Training Centre, Cairo (1959-62); Entomologist, WHO Regional Office, Africa Brazzaville, Congo (1962-65); Regional Entomologist, Regional Office Eastern Mediterranean, WHO, Alexandria (1966-70); Entomologist, Divisions of Malaria and other Parasitic Diseases, Vector Biology and Control WHO, Geneva (Switzerland) (1970). **Publ.:** Author of "The Ecology Distribution of Black Flies in South East Scotland" (1951), "Review of Status of Anapheline Resistance to Residual Insecticides in the Eastern Mediterranean Region" (1959), "Review of the Ecology of Malaria Vectors in the Eastern Mediterranean Region"; Studies on Leishmaniasis Vectors/Reservoirs and their control, Vector Bionomics in the Epidemiology & Control of Malaria Parts I & II. Co-author of "Insect Pests and their methods of control" Cairo (1952), "An Attempt to group freshwater species of the Anopheles Gambia Complex by some Morphological Larval & Adult Charaters" (1970), "The Practical implications of resistance of Malaria vectors to insecticides". (Retired Sep. 1977). **Member:** Shooting Club, Cairo & Alexandria; Alexandria Sporting Club. **Sports:** Tennis, rowing, fishing. **Addr.:** Geneva, Switzerland.

ZAHEER (Anjum), Pakistani bank manager. **Born** in 1944 in Merrut, India. **Son** of Hasan Siddiqui Zaheer. **Married** in 1969, 2 sons. **Educ.:** Agra University, India. **Dipl.:** B.Sc. **Career:** Joined United Bank Ltd., Since 1963; Assiatant Manager, United Bank Ltd., Bahrain (1970-73); Manager, Sharjah, UAE (1973-78); Manager, Dubai, UAE (1978-80); Manager, New York, USA (1980-81); Manager, United Bank Ltd., Dubai, UAE (1981-). **Member:** Hyatt Regency Club, Dubai. **Hobbies:** Swimming and Tennis and Tennis. **Addr.:** P.O.Box 1000, Deira, Tel.: 22253, Telex: 45433 A/B UNITE EM, Dubai, UAE.

ZAHID (Abdul Majid), Saudi businessman. **Born** in 1927 in Jeddah, Saudi Arabia. **Married**, 4 children. **Educ.:** Stanford Business School, USA (Graduate studies). **Dipl.:** Degree in Mechanical Engineering. **Career:** President and Chief Executive Officer of Arabian Motors & Engineering Company Ltd; Ameco Leasing, Ameco Travel, and Trans Arabian Technical Services Co. Ltd. **Member of the Board of:** Saudi Bulkhandling, National Pipe Company, Saudi American Bank. Founding member of Saudi Cairo Bank and United Gulf Bank. Consultant to several leading US and European corporations. Descendant of the well-known merchant family al-Zahid. **Hobbies:** tennis, shooting, camping, swimming. **Addr.:** P.O.Box 166, Dammam 31411, Saudi Arabia, Tel.: (966-3) 826-2411, Fax: (966-3) 827-3491.

ZAHID (Aziz Dia, Ibn), Saudi leading writer. **Born** on 22 January 1914 in Medina, Saudi Arabia. **Career:** Held various posts at the Ministry of Defence and the General Security: Director General for Investigation, Passports and Citizenship (1954); owner of Artivon Establishment for Radio, T.V. and Cinema. **Member:** of the Supreme Council for Science; Arts and Literature; founder member of Jeddah Literary Club; has contributed significant works for radio and television; has been writing for Saudi Press, he is known as a political commentator. **Publications:** nine books and fifteen more under publication. **Hobbies:** photography, music. **Address:** al-Musaideya, opposite Jeddah Secondary School, Tel.: 6652164 (office), 6675164, (Home), Jeddah, Saudi Arabia.

ZAHID (Ebrahim, Mahmoud), Saudi businessman. **Born** in 1920 in Jeddah. **Son** of Mahmoud Zahid (Merchant). **Educ.:** al-Falah School in Jeddah and English School in Bombay (India). **Dipl.:** Master of Arts in Arabic and Matriculation in English. **Career:** Partner of M.M. Zahid and Bros., in Saudi Arabia, and Mideast Auto and Trading Company in Beirut, Distributors for General Motors, Caterpillar, R.C.A., Agents for T.W.A., American Export Line and Hellenic Line. **Member:** Alumni Club, Arrow Club and National Club. (Beirut) and Redsea Club (Jeddah). **Sports:** Swimming and Swedish Exercises. **Hobbies:** Participating in Charity Associations. **Prof. Addr.:** P.O.Box 102, Tel.: 6422177, Jeddah. **Priv. Addr.:** Nuzla Tel.: 6420053, Jeddah, Saudi Arabia.

ZAHID (Kasim Abdul Wahab), Saudi senior civil servant, **Born** in Jeddah, in 1945. **Educ.:** Preparatory and Public Schools in U.K. (1957-64). **Dipl.:** B.A. (Economics and Political Science), U.S.A. (1969); M.A. (International Relations) (1970); M.A.L.D. (International Relations) (1972). **Career:** Now Partner and Director, Zahid Enterprises Co. Ltd., and Asstt. General Manager-System Customer Relations, Saudia-Saudi Arabian Airlines; Represented Saudia in the WACRA (Worldwide Airline Customer Relations Association) Annual Conferences since 1975 at various locations around the world. Elected Member of the WACRA Executive Committee for 1981-82 and Chairman, Baggage Committee, Chairman of Workshops. Selected Workshop Leader in 1980 and 1983. Re-elected as a Member of the WACRA Executive Committee in Singapore for 1984-85. Elected President in Buenos Aires in 1984 Annual Conference. Presided over the WACRA Annual Conference held in Nice in 1985. President Emeritus of WACRA for 1986. Represented Saudia in Air Transport Association of America (ATA)'s "Freight Claims Prevention Seminar" at various locations around the world. Represented Saudia in "Joint ATC/IATA/RAA (Regional Airlines Association) Baggage Tracing and Claims Seminar" in 1986. **Honour:** Dean's List of Undergraduate. **Sports:** Swimming and Squash. **Hobbies:** Reading classical and modern literature; classical music. **Prof. Addr.:** Post Office Box 620, Tel. 686-2426, 631-1635, Jeddah-21231, Saudi Arabia. **Priv.Addr.:** Post Office Box 352, Tel. 631-0969, Jeddah-21411, Saudi Arabia.

ZAHID (Mohamad Wasil Ahmad), Iraqi academic. **Born** in 1924 in Mosul, Iraq. **Married**, 1 son, 3 daughters. **Educ.:** Columbia University, USA; michigan University, USA. **Dipl.:** M.Sc. and Ph.D. in Mathematics. **Career:** Head of Mathematics Department, Baghdad University (1963-68); Dean, Faculty of Sciences, Baghdad University Iraq (1965-69); Professor of Mathematics, Kuwait University (1969); Dean, Faculty of Sciences, Kuwait University (1977-82); Member of the American Association of Mathematicians (1950-); Consultant, Kuwait Corporation for Scientific Progress (1978-). **Publ.:** Several text books on geometry and mathematics (1970-76). **Hobbies:** chess, sports, reading, swimming. **Prof. Addr.:** P.O.Box 6773, Hawaly, Kuwait.

ZAHID (Yusuf, Mahmoud), Saudi Arabian businessman. **Born** in 1920 in Jeddah. **Son** of Mahmoud Zahid (Merchant). **Educ.:** al-Falah School in Jeddah and English School in Bombay (India). **Dipl.:** Master of Arts in Arabic and Matriculation in English. **Career:** Owner, Zahid Tractor and Heavy Machinery Company; Former Head of the family firm M.M. Zahid and Bros., in Saudi Arabia; and Mideast Auto and Trading Company in Beirut, Distributors for General Motors, Caterpillar, R.C.A., Agents for T.W.A., American Export Line and Hellenic Line. **Sport:** Swimming. **Member:** Redsea Club (Jeddah). **Prof. Addr.:** P.O.Box 8928, Jeddah, Saudi Arabia.

ZAHIDA (Ibrahim, Mohamad), Iraqi former administrator. **Born** in 1926 in Baghdad, Iraq. **Son** of Ibrahim Mohamad. **Educ.:** LL.B. (1948); Victoria School of Libraries, Melbourne, Australia (1954); Library Studies, Rutgers University, New Brunswick, New York, USA (1958-59); six months Training Programme, Princeton University Library, New York (1959); Librarian Training Programme in Copenhagen, Denmark)1967). **Career:** Director, College of Education Library, University of Baghdad (1950-58); Librarian, Central Library, University of Baghdad (1959-63); Director, Archives Department, Central Library, University of Baghdad)1964-75); Director General, Central Library, University of Baghdad (since 1975). Retired in 1984, **Publ.:** Books on library science and many researches and studies. **Addr.:** Central Library, University of Baghdad, P.O.Box 12 Wazyria, Baghdad, Iraq.

ZAHIDI ALAOUI (Moulay Zine), Moroccan President Director General of Crédit Immobilier & Hôtelier (C.I.H.). **Born** in 1935 in Marrakech, Morocco. **Educ.:** Baccalaureat (Math.) (1956); High Schools in Toulouse; Ecole Nationale Supérieure des Industries Agricoles et Alimentaires **Dipl.:** Engineer (1962). **Career:** Research Engineer, COSUMAR (Compagnie Sucrerie Marocaine), then Head of Different Dept, COSUMAR, Director-General, Sucrerie des Doukkala (1969-1973); Directorate Generale, COSUMAR (1973); Delegate Member of the Board. "Sucrerie des Zemamra" (1977); Director General, COSUMAR (1980). Nominated Minister by His Majesty the King and he has occupied successively the following Portfolios: November 1983 Minister of Labour and National Promotion; April 1985 Minister attached to the Prime Minister's Office in charge of Economic Affairs; October 1988 Minister of Privatization; August 1992 Minister of Commerce, Industry and Privatization. **President** Director General of Credit Immobilier & Hôtelier (C.I.H.) since 1st January 1994 to date. **Addr.:** C.I.H., 187 Av. Hassan II, Casablanca, Morocco, Tel.: 203250, 278065, 203247, Telex: 23869 S.A.

ZAHRA (Lalla Fatima, H.H. Princess), Moroccan princess. **Born** in Morocco. **Daughter of** late Sultan Abdulaziz (Uncle of Hassan II, King of Morocco). **Married** Prince Moulay Ben al-Mahdi (former Diplomat and Governor of the Central Bank of Morocco). **Educ.:** Privately. **Career:** President of the National Union of Moroccan Women (U.N.F.M.). **Resid.:** Rabat, Morocco.

ZAHRAN (Fuad Mustafa), M.D. Saudi academic. **Born** in Jeddah in 1940. **Dipl.:** B.Med., B.Chem., Cairo University (1965), F.R.C.S. (Ear, Nose and Throat). **Career:** Lecturer of Ear, Nose and Throat, Faculty of Medicine, Riyadh University; member of World Society for Ear, Nose and Throat, King Abdulaziz University Council, Faculty of Medicine Council; attended the International Conference of Ear, Nose and Throat (London 1975); participate in the establishment of the Faculty of Medicine and Medical Sciences, King Abdulaziz University; former Vice-Dean then Dean Faculty of Medicine and Medical Sciences, King Abdulaziz University. **Publ.:** Author of Clinical Ear, Nose and Throat (a short textbook). **Hobby:** Travel. **Addr.:** Jeddah, Saudi Arabia.

ZAHRAN (Hamdia, M., Prof. Dr.), Egyptian vice president for postgraduate studies & research (Helwan University). **Born** on December 6, 1933 in Egypt. **Daughter** of Mahmoud Zahran (Educational Manager) **and** Mrs. née Safa Aid. **Married** in 1957 to Abdel Magid Mansour, 3 children: Ebrahim (23.9.1958), Emam (1.1.1961), Amro (11.3.1961). **Educ.:** Cairo University, Faculty of Law; Sania Secondary School, Cairo: Sania Primary School, Cairo. **Publ.:** Ph.D. in Economics and Public Finance (1970), Cairo University, Faculty of Law (Specialised in Under developed Countries, Planning and Finance in the third world); Diploma: Political Economics-Faculty of Law, Cairo University (1962); Diploma: Applied Economics: Faculty of Law, Cairo University (1963); Master in Economics, Cairo University (1964). **Career:** Assistant Professor of Economics (1975); Professor of Economics (1979); Chairman of Foreign Trade Department Faculty of Commerce (1979-87); Chairman of Economic Department: Faculty of Commerce (1980-87); Vice Dean for graduate studies and research: Faculty of Commerce and Management, Helwan University (1984-87); Vice President for Graduate Studies and Research, Helwan University (1987-). **Work:** Professor of Economics in Helwan University; Senator in Egyptian Shorra Council; Member of Supreme Council of Universities. **Employment Record:** Professor and Chairman of Economic Department of Faculty of Economics and Public Administration, King Abdul Aziz University, Saudi Arabia (1971-77); Chairman and Supervisor for Master Degree Department: Islamic Institution (Cairo 1977-89); Lectural for Master Department Arabic Studies Institution (Cairo 1988-89); Professor Lecturer in Administrative leaders programmes at the central authority for organisation and Management (Cairo 86); Professor Lecturer in Nile Centres programmes for information (Cairo 1985); Visiting professor (Kiel University) West Germany from (1982-85); Professor Supervisor on Economical Researches at the Central Administration for following execution of the plan and administration evaluating for sectors at the central Organization for accounts from (1982-83); Consultant Central authority for accounts from (1982-85); **Memberships in Authorities:** Economical Committee member in Technological Scientific Research Academy (Council of Researches Technological Adminsitrative Sciences); Member of Scientific centre for scientific culture, Cairo; Member of the Specialised National Councils, Cairo; Member of Housing Committee and special studies of Building Researches - General Authority for Planning, Building, Housing Researches (The Authority of the new Societies); Member of ecnomical committee in the Democratic Party; Supervisor on economical Researchers at the central authority for accounts (central administration for following the plan execution and performance evaluation for economic sectors); Member of Economical committee in Commercial Association, Cairo; Member of the Egyptian Committee for Political economics, statistics, legislation-Cairo; Member Cultural races committee Higher Council for youth and sports-Ministry of Youth; Member of Committees and symposiums Arabic Economical Unity Council; Member of economics committee and general finance: the higher council for culture-Cairo (79-80-81); Member of cultural symposium for youths-Giza Governate; Member of the Egyptian delegation for Arabic Unity Studies Centre Conference (Tunis 1983); Economic Conference for Arab Economists Baghdad 1985, (9th Conference); Egyptian Economics Management Conference and its future attitudes (1986); Second annual work meeting around production: (Cairo 1987); Member of General Sector and administrate conference and Peace Challenges-Faculty of Commerce-Helwan University (1980); Member of Housing Symposium-The Ministry of Reclamation (1983); Supervisor member on economical researches at the central administration for following plan execution and the evaluating of administration to the economical sectors in the central Authority for accounts (1982-85); Member of the Permanent Scientific Committee for Professors Promotion-economics sector, general finance and planning-Azhar University; Member of the Permanent Scientific Committee, public finance and planning (Economics and Political Sciences Faculty-Cairo University). **Scientific**

Supervision: Supervision on Ph.D. and Master missions in economics, public finance and planning-Faculty of Commerce and Business administration. Helwan University-Faculty of Home Economics-Islamic Studies Institution - Participation in Supervision on missions. The Faculty of Economics and Political Sciences - Faculty of Law - Cairo University - Faculty of Commerce - Ain Shams University. **Books and Papers Published:** Financing economic development in under-developed countries with applied study for the Egyptian economic plan P.HD. Research (1970); The primary elements in economical theory (1975); Introduction in Economic Planning and economic development (1969); Problems of economic development in the states which are developing with a study for the plan in Egypt (1970); Studies in Money and Banking & International Trade; Studies in Kynesian Analysis and Macro-economics; Economic Planning, theory and applying (1975); Economic development: Theory and Analysis (1978); Economic Theory (Principles and Analysis) (1979); The World Money crisis and a study for economics of the petroleum under developed, exporting countries (1978); Problems of Foreign Trade with a study for the under developed countries (1978); Foreign Trade in Egypt-development politics... problems (1980); Planning of Trade in Egypt (1986); Organizing of foreign trade in Egypt (1988); Planning for development in Egypt through 50 Years (1988); Egyptian Economy its crisis and Problems (1989). **Published Studies and Researches:** Economic Domination and its effects on the structure of international trade (1978); Structural inflation and reflected inflation in the underdeveloped countries (1979); Debts and burdens and repaying in the poor countries (1980); Foreign and import substitution (1981); Structural development for the Egyptian Economy under the open-door policy (1985); Taxes and inflation in Egypt (1986); Standard numbers for prices in Egypt and Economic stability (1984); Sources of financing Economic development in Egypt (English) (1979); Oil prices: strategy and promotion of using Arab Oil (1979); Arab Oil... Production... Prices World Marketing (1980); Subsidy policy and the Economic problem in Egypt (Scientific research Academy research) (1983); A study on subsidy introduced by Helwan University to the High Committee for subsidy-Cairo University (1985); Planning Trade in Egypt and the problems of balance of payment under the economic open-door policy (1988); Changes in Banking system in Saudi Arabia (1979); Foreign Trade attitudes in Saudia: under economic planning system (1979); Foreign Trade policies in Egypt in twenty years (1962-82) Cairo (1983); A research on Egypt Foreign Trade in 1974-84 (Technological scientific research Academy research) (1986); The strategy of Economic development in Egypt (Planning of the Primaries) (1987). **Awards:** Encouraging state prize in Economics and Public Finance (1981) Cairo; Awarded Badge of honour for science and Arts. **Hobbies:** Reading, Music, Travel. **Member:** National Club, Egyptian Society for Economic Statistics and Legislation, Business Club. **Prof. Addr.:** 96 Ahmed Oraby St., El Mohandseen, Giza, Tel.: 3444056/58, Cairo, Egypt. **Priv. Addr.:** 27 el-Maraghy St., Agouza, Tel.: 3499002, Cairo, Egypt.

ZAHRAN (Mohsen, Moharram), Egyptian architect. **Born** in 1935 in Cairo, Egypt. **Married**, 2 children. **Educ.:** Ain Shams University, Cairo; MIT, USA; Princeton University, USA: B.Sc., M.Sc. in Urban Design, Master of Fine Arts in Architecture, Ph.D. in Environmental Planning, TAU Beta PI. **Career:** Architect, Government Design Bureau, Cairo (1965-66); Assistant Professor of Architecture, Alexandria University (1966); Associate Professor of Architecture, Alexandria University (1972); Professor of Architecture (1977); United Nations Consultant and Expert, ECWA, Beirut (1975-80); UNESCO, Paris (1976-77); UNEP, Nairobi (1976-77); UNCHS, Nairobi (1976-77); UNCHBP, New York (1975-78); Dean, Faculty of Architecture, Beirut Arab University, Lebanon (1978-82), Chairman, Alexandria Planning Commission, Consultant to the Governor of Alexandria (1982-), Member High Council of Culture (1990-92), Chairman, Housing Planning Committee, Alexandria City Council (1988-92), Executive Director of General Organization of Alexandria Library (GOAL) (1989-). **Publ.:** Books, Articles and Papers on architecture, urban design, Environmental Planning, housing and urban planning (in English and Arabic). **Decorations and Medal:** -Educational Medal, Egypt (1959), Alexandria University Appreciation Award, Egypt (1977), TAU Beta PI Medal (1962), Alexandria University Merit Award, Egypt's Medal of Distinction of the First Order (1985), **Hobbies:** Hiking, tennis. **Prof. Addr.:** Alexandria University, Shatby, Alexandria, Egypt. **Priv. Addr.:** 23, Roushdy street, Roushdy, Alexandria, Egypt.

ZAHRI (Abo Torab, al), Saudi religious and linguistic consultant. **Born** in 1925 in East Ahmed Pur, Pakistan. **Dipl.:** M.A. (linguistics and Islamic Sciences). **Career:** Teacher, Arabic language, Secondary school; Technical Editor, Research Department, Ministry of Information; Teacher, religion and linguistics, Makkah Mosque; Head, Technical Editors' Department, al-Bilad Newspaper; Religious and Linguistics Supervisor, Ministry of Information; member, first Saudi conference for men of letters. **Publications:** Shawahid ul-Qur'an, al-Sara'ya, Siyar ul-Saha'ba, Kabwat ul-Yara'a, al-Afa'wiq, al-Mustadrak, al-Awa'bid wal-Asma'a and Qaid al-Say'd. **Address:** Ministry of Information, Tel.: 6476222 (Office) and 6654239 (Home), Jeddah, Saudi Arabia.

ZAID (Abdallah Mohamad, al), Saudi academic. **Born** in 1943. **Dipl.:** M.A., Indiana University (1969); Ph.D., Oklahoma University (1972). **Career:** Secondary School Teacher; Lecturer; Assistant Professor; Supervisor, Education Training Centre, College of Education; member of King Abdulaziz University Council; Vice-president of Mecca Literary Club; attended didacta Conference on Educational Aids (Brussels 1974), Directors of Education

Conference (1974), Conference on the Strategy of Arab Education (Ministry of Education 1975); Head, Saudi Delegation to UNESCO Annual Conference on Education; Head, Department of Education, Faculty of Education, King Abdulaziz University; now Director General of Education, Western Province; Representative of Saudi Arabia to the Arab Organization for Literacy Campaign and Adult Education, Baghdad; selected as the First Secretary to the First World conference on Muslim Education. **Publ.:** Teachers reaction to the profession, research work in collaboration with others submitted to the First Teachers' Conference; A Model with a Difference (book in Arabic and English); various articles published in weekly magazines and daily newspapers. **Prof. Addr.:** Directorate General, Ministry of Education, Jeddah, Saudi Arabia.

ZAID (Abdul Mohsin ben Sulaiman, al), Saudi former ambassador. **Born** in Hail in 1916. **Educ.:** Received general education. **Career:** Diplomatic attaché, Saudi Consulate-General, Syria and Lebanon; assumed various diplomatic posts up to the rank of Ambassador; Ambassador to the Syrian Arab Republic; Ambassador to Qatar; **Awards:** Orders from Saudi Arabia, Syria, Senegal, Tunisia. **Prof. Addr.:** Ministy of Foreign Affairs, Jeddah, Saudi Arabia.

ZAID (Abdulaziz Mohamad, al), Saudi academic. **Born** in 1945. **Dipl.:** B.A. Shari'a (Islamic Law), 1966; Diploma in British Law, London Central College, 1972; Ph.D. (Law), University of London, 1978; a course in American Law organized by Harvard University, 1977. **Career:** Teacher, Thaqif Secondary School, Taif (1964); Supervisor of National Culture, Taif Education Directorate (1963); Director of Youth Welfare, Taif (1965-69); Director General of Education, Asir Province; Head of Inspectors, Directorate of Education, Taif (1970-72); Assistant Professor, Dept. of Qada' (Jurisdiction) and Dean of Libraries Affairs, Umm al-Qura University; founding member of Taif Cultural Club. **Publications:** al-Mihrab al-Mahjour (The Deserted Chancel), collection of verse; the Sun Song; Girah al-Layl (Night Wounds), Manuscript; articles and poems in local newspapers. **Address:** Faculty of Shari'a (History Department), University of Umm al-Qura. Tel.: Home 732.2369, Makkah, Saudi Arabia.

ZAID (Ibrahim al-Abdallah, al), Saudi senior civil servant. **Born** in 1937, at Shagra, Saudi Arabia. **Dipl.:** M.A. (Public Administration). **Career:** former Grade "A" Export; Director-General, Preparatory Programmes Department, Institute of Public Administration; member of Board of Saudi Ceramic Factory, Yanbu Cement Plant. **Prof. Addr.:** P.O.Box. 1283, Tel.: 25822, Riyadh. **Priv. Addr.:** Tel.: 36226, Riyadh, Saudi Arabia.

ZAIDAN (Ahmad Mohamad), Saudi businessman. **Born** in 1951 in Mecca, Saudi Arabia. **Dipl.:** Graduate of Radio Technical Centre, 1932; Diploma in Meteorology from R.A.R. in Iraq, 1944; Diploma of G.P.O. Telecommunication Course, England 1951. **Career:** Radio Operator (1932); Director of Royal Mobile Radio Section, (1933); Director of Jeddah Radio Station (1936); Headmaster of Telecommunication Technical School, (1937); Director of Posts Telephone and Telegraphs in Hassa (1938); Director of Posts, Telephone and Telegraphs in Khobar (Dhahran) (1939); Director of Meteorological Service (1944); Deputy Director of Radio Service (1946); Director of Radio Monitoring Service, (1951); Technical Director in H.R.H. the Viceroy's Office (1954); Inspector General, Posts Telegraphs and Telecommunications, (1955); Director General of Posts, Telegraphs and Telecommunications, (1957); Technical Adviser on Automatic Telephone Network, (1960); Deputy Minister of Communications (PTT), (1961-73); Chairman of the Board, Beta Company (Abdul Aziz Zaidan and Partners); represented Saudi Arabia in all plenipotentiary conferences of the International Telecommunication Union as Head of the delegation; between 0956-73 participated in drafting the following International Telecommunications Union as Head of the delegation; between 1956-73 participated in drafting the following International Telecommunications Conventions: Geneva, (1959), Montreaux (1965) and Malaga-Torremolinos (1973); served as member of the Administrative Council of the ITU (1966-76); Chairman, the Arab Postal Union conference (1957) and Arab Telecommunication Union Conference (1966); Chairman of the Council (1967) and Chairman of the Plan Committee for Asia and Oceania, (1968-80); Holder of Diploma of Honour of the ITU (1961-72); Chairman, Electrical & Electric Contracting Co. **Hobby:** HAM Radio Call Sign ZHIHZ. **Address:** P.O.Box 4602, Jeddah 21412, Saudi Arabia.

ZAIDAN (Faisal, A.), Saudi civil servant. **Born** in 1938 in Mecca, Saudi Arabia. **Dipl.:** B.Sc. (Electrical Communications). **Career:** Maintenance Engineer, P.T.T. (1962); General Manager of Projects (1969-72); Assistant Deputy Minister, P.T.T. Riyadh (1972-76); General Manager of Bureau of Engineering and Electronics Consultants (previous Private Office); Deputy Minister of Posts, Telegraphs and Telecommunications for Telephone Affairs; Chairman of Board of Governors, Arab Satellite Communications Organizations; member of Board of Governors, INTELSAT; member of Arab Communications Union. **Hobbies:** Photography. **Address:** Ministry of Posts, Telegraphs and Telecommunications, Riyadh; P.O.Box. 10987, Tel.: 4042404, Riyadh, Saudi Arabia.

ZAIDAN (Faisal Mohamad Hussein), Saudi diplomat. **Born** in 1940 in Mecca, Saudi Arabia. **Dipl.:** M.A. and Ph. D. (Political Science). **Career:** Assistant Professor, Faculty of Economics and Administration, King Abdulaziz University; Assistant Manager, Training Administration, Saudia-Saudi Arabian Airlines; Aircraft Truck Driver, U.S.A.; Director of Public Relations, King Abdulaziz University;

Vice Dean, Admissions and Registration, King Abdulaziz University; Diplomat, Ministry of Foreign Affairs; member American University Registrars' Association; attended conference on Training and Development. **Hobbies:** fishing, travel, bowling, volleyball, carpentry. **Address:** Muhammad Hussein Zaidan, Tel.: (2)6820070 (Home), Jeddah, Saudi Arabia.

ZAIDAN (George, C.), Egyptian international civil servant. **Born** on February 11, 1939 in Cairo (Egypt). **Married. Educ.:** University of Cairo (1955-59); London School of Economics (1959-63); Harvard University (1963-67). **Dipl.:** B.Sc. (Economics) (1963), Ph.D. (Economics, 1967), L.L.B. (1969). **Career:** Various Positions; International Bank for Reconstruction and Development, Washington, (IBRD) D.C. Chief, Operations Division, Population & Nutrition Projects Department (1970-74); Chief, Country Program Review Division, Program and Budgeting Dept. (1975-78); Chief, Industrial Development and Finance Division, Projects Dept., Europe Middle East and North Africa Region (1978-85); Assistant Director in charge of industrial, financial and technical assistance activities in the Europe, Middle East and North Africa Region. **Publ.:** Author of "Benefits and Costs of Family Planning Programmes" (1971), "Population Growth and Economic Development" (1969), "Benefits & Costs of Prevented Births"; co-author of "The Population Work of the World Bank" (1968). **Sports:** Squash and table tennis. **Hobbies:** Bridge and Reading. **Prof. Addr.:** Director's Office, EMENA Project. Department, IBRD 1818 H St, NW, Tel.: (202) 473-2709/10, Washington DC 20433, USA. **Priv. Addr.:** 7007 Longwood Drive, Bethesda, Mayland 20817, Tel.: (301) 469-7081.

ZAIDAN (Ziyad), Saudi senior civil servant. **Born** in Makkah, on August 1, 1947. **Dipl.:** B.A., University of Detroit (1972); M.A. (Hons.), University of Detroit. **Career:** Designer and architect, Wakely-Kushner Architects and Engineers (1968-75); Architect, Eggers & Higgins (1967-68); member of Board, Prince Fawwaz Project for Co-operative Housing; attended United Nations Habitat Conference, Teheran (1975); now Chairman of IDEA International Group and Managing Director IDEA Center; his IDEA Center won two design competitions for the Ministry of Municipal Affairs. **Awards:** Graduated Magna Cum Laude. **Sport:** Horse Riding, swimming, tennis. **Prof. Addr.:** P.O.Box. 1875, Tel.: 6519550, Fax: 6512026, e-mail: idea@sbm.net.sa, Jeddah 21441, Saudi Arabia.

ZAIN AL ABEDIN (Habib, Mustafa), Saudi administrator. **Born** in 1943 in Mecca, Saudi Arabia. **Married**, 3 daughters. **Educ.:** University of Hanover, West Germany; University of Essen, West Germany. **Dipl.:** M.Sc. and Ph.D. in Civil Engineering. **Career:** Civil Engineer, Ministry of Housing (1971); Member of the Board of Directors of Construction Research Institute, University of Essen, West Germany (1972-); Member of the Board of Directors of Arab Saudi Society for Measuring (1976-); **Deputy** Minister, Ministry of Housing and Public Works (1978). **Prof. Addr.:** P.O.Box 11151, Riyadh, Saudi Arabia.

ZAINAL (Mohamad, Abdallah Rida), Saudi businessman. **Born** in Saudi Arabia. **Son** of Abdallah Rida **Zainal. Educ.:** Secondary. **Career:** Vice-President "Hage Abdallah Ali Rida and Co.", former Chairman of the Chamber of Commerce and Industry. **Addr.:** Jeddah, Saudi Arabia.

ZAINALABEDIN (Hassan), Bahraini businessman. **Born** in 1942 in Bahrain. **Son** of Mohamad Zainalabedin. **Married** in 1972, 1 son, 2 daughters. **Educ.:** Cairo University. **Dipl.:** B.Econ. (1966-67). **Career:** Chairman, Syscon Trading and Mechanical Services; Director, Bahrain Kuwait Insurance Co.; Continental Bank Ltd.; Managing Director and President, Bahrain Investment Co. BSC, Manama, Bahrain. **Hobbies:** Football and reading. **Addr.:** P.O.Box 5808, Tel.: 250053, Telex: 8937 A/B INVEST BN, Manama, Bahrain.

ZAINI (Mahmud Hassan), Saudi academic. **Born** in 1939 in Mecca, Saudi Arabia. **Dipl.:** Ph.D. (Arabic language and Literature). **Career:** Demonstrator (1963) and later Lecturer (1970), Umm al-Qura University; Chairman, Arabic Department (1972-74), and Associate Professor, later Vice Dean, Faculty of Shari'a, Umm al-Qura University, Makkah (1974-77); Editor in Chief, Bulletin of the Faculty of Shari'a and Islamic Studies, Makkah; member, the Permanent Committee of King Faisal International Prize in Arabic Literature; founding member, Makkah Literary Club; participated in the International Conference of Scholars of Oriental Studies, Pakistan, 1972, and various national and international conferences organized by the Muslim and Arab Leagues respectively: First Conference of Saudi Men of Letters (Mecca 1974), Teachers' Training Conference (Mecca 1974); Director General, World Center for Islamic Education. **Publications:** Several research articles on both Islamic and Arabic Literature. **Prof. Addr.:** Umm al-Qura University, Faculty of Shari'a, **Priv. Addr.:** P.O.Box 1034, Mecca, Saudi Arabia.

ZAIWAR (Ali), Egyptian journalist, army officer. **Born** in 1922 in Cairo, Egypt. **Married**, two sons. **Career:** General in the Armed Forces, retired (1974); held various posts in the Army dealing with sports; Secretary General, Army Sports' Union for eight consecutive years; Secretary of Football Studies, Egyptian Football Union (1960-62); Editor, Sports Section of various Egyptian newspapers (since 1958); Editor, sports section of the "Akhbar al-Yaum" organisation, Cairo; Manager, al-Ahli Football Team; Radio Sports Commentator (1958); Television Sports Commentator (1960). **Medals:** Various military decorations and orders. Honorary **member** of the Gezira Sporting Club, of the Aviation Club, of al-Ahli Club. **Sports:** Walking, swimming, table tennis. **Prof. Addr.:** 57

al-Hejaz Street, Masr al-Gedida, Tel.: 930643, Cairo, Egypt. **Priv. Addr.:** Tel.: 867449, Cairo, Egypt.

ZAKARI (Yahia, Makki), Saudi academic. **Born** in 1941 at Sabya. **Son** of Makki Zakari. **Dipl.:** B.Sc., M.Sc: and Ph.D (in Agronomy). **Career:** Demonstrator, King Saud University (1965); Assistant Professor, King Saud University (1967); Vice Dean, Faculty of Agriculture King Saud University (1977); Dean Faculty of Agricultural and Food Sciences (1980). **Member** King Faisal University Council, the Saudi Biological Society and the American Society of Agronomy; has attended several conferences related to his career; has conducted several agricultural consultive projects. **Publications:** Several research papers on Crop Physiology. **Hobbies:** Reading, music, sports. **Address:** Riyadh, Saudi Arabia.

ZAKARIA (Ghassan, Wasfi), Syrian journalist. **Born** in 1931 in Damascus, Syria. **Married,** 3 daughters. **Educ.:** American University of Beirut, Lebanon. **Dipl.:** B.A. in the Ancient History of the East. **Career:** Managing Director of "Kabas" newspaper, Damascus (1956-58); Assistant Director of the Egyptian Company for Transport and Engineering, Damascus (1958-61); Correspondent for "al-Hasna" magazine, Damascus (1961-67); Director of Afamya Organization (1967-68); General Director of al-Yamama Wa Zahrat al-Shark Hotels (1969); Director of "al-Siyasa" newspaper, Beirut (1970-74); Director of the Information Centre of "al-Hawadess" Beirut; Political Editor of "al-Destour" magazine, London (1980-82); London Correspondent, "al-Siyasa" newspaper (1982-83); Member of the Board of Sourakia Ltd. (1982-); Editor in Chief of "Sourakia" magazine, London (1983-). **Publ.:** "Cyprus: Between Reality and History" (1973), "Leaders who Unified the Fertile Crescent" (1980). **Hobby:** horse riding. **Prof. Addr.:** 46-47 Pall Mall, London SWI, United Kingdom; 49 Itani Street, Beirut, Lebanon.

ZAKI (Abdul Rahman, Muhammad), Sudanese lawyer, **Born** in 1939 in Delgo, Sudan. **Married,** 3 daughters. **Dipl.:** LL.B., LL.M. **Educ.:** in London, UK. **Career:** Legal Assistant, Attorney General's Chambers (1962-64); Assistant Legal Council, Attorney General's Chambers (1964-67); Legal Council (1967-71); Advocate (1972); Provincial Judge (1972-73); Deputy Advocate General (1973-74); Legal Counsel to the People's Assembly (1974-75); Under Secretary, Attorney General's Chambers (1975-76), Attorney General (1976). **Hobbies:** table-tennis, picnics, psychology. **Addr.:** Khartoum, Sudan.

ZAKI (Hassan, Abbas), Egyptian politician and economist. **Born** on January 2, in 1917 in Port Said, Egypt. **Son** of Abbas Zaki. **Married,** 3 children: Sawsan, Mona and Nadia. **Educ.:** Cairo University, Egypt; American University, Washington. **Dipl.:** B.A. in Economics; Higher Studies, American University, USA. **Career:** Government Representative, Alexandria Stock Exchange; Commercial Secretary, Egyptian Embassy (1953); Director-General, Currency Control Administration (1955); Minister of the Treasury (1958); Minister of Economy and Supply (1961); Minister of Economy and Trade (1966-71); Adviser to HH the President of the United Arab Emirates; Member, Board of the Abu Dhabi Fund for Arab Economic Development; member, Board of Abu Dhabi National Oil Company (ADNOC); Member, Board of Abu Dhabi Investment Organization; Chairman: Arab International Com. for Hotels, Vice-Chairman of the Board, Arab International Bank, Egypt; Currently Chairman, Société Arabe Internationale de Banque. **Awards:** from Egypt, Yugoslavia, Greece, Roumania, Somalia, Italy. **Publ.:** Several articles on monetary, International trade and cotton policies. **Hobbies:** Social studies, sufism, economics. **Member:** Banking Club. **Addr.:** 12 Saleh Ayoub St., Zamalek, Tel.: 3401754, 3418343, Cairo, Egypt and Société Arabe Internationale de Banque, 56, Gameat el-Dowal al-Arabia Street, Giza, P.O.Box 124 al-Mohandeseen, Tel.: 3602605, 3606526, Giza, Egypt.

ZAKI (Hussain, Abbas), Egyptian dentist. **Born in 1932** in Alexandria, Egypt. **Married,** 4 daughters. **Educ.:** University of Minnesota, USA. **Dipl.:** Master of Public Health and Maste of Science in Dentistry. **Career:** Associate Professor, University of Minnesota, USA (1968-83); Member of the American Dental Association (1975-83); Professor of Dentistry, King Faisal University, Saudi Arabia (1983-). **Hobbies:** swimming, chess. **Addr.:** al-Saray al-Jazira, Zamalek, Cairo, Egypt.

ZAKI (Hussain, Mohamad), Egyptian businessman. **Born** in 1914 in Cairo, Egypt. **Married,** 2 daughters. **Educ.:** Cairo University, Egypt; Purdue University, USA. **Dipl.:** B.Sc. and M.Sc. in Engineering. **Career:** Technical Manager of Tractor & Engineering Company (1950-54); Secretary General (1954-62), General Manager (1962-67), Chairman of the Board (1967-74); Director of newtrend Company Ltd. (1967-74); Partner and Director of Modern Management Methods Company (1967-74); Partner and Director of Wellcon Company Ltd. (1967-74); Member of Egyptian Business Association (1975-); Member of US Business Council (1975-). **Member:** Automobile Club of Egypt, Gezira Sporting Club. **Prof. Addr.:** 6 el-Gezira al-Wousta Street, Zamalek, Cairo, Egypt; **Priv. Addr.:** 8 Bahgat Ali Street, Zamalek, Cairo, Egypt.

ZAKI (Mahmoud, Hassan Abdel Ghaffar), Egyptian executive banker. **Born** in 1951 in Cairo, Egypt. **Son** of Hassan Abdel Ghaffar Zaki **and** Mrs., née Amal Aly Helmy. **Married** in 1980 in England to Miss Stella Zaki. Two children. **Educ.:** B.Comm. (Accountancy) from Alexandria Faculty of Commerce, Alexandria University, Egypt. **Career:** Trainee at the National Bank of Egypt, Alexandria (1976-77); Accounts Officer, Loan Admin. Officer, Assistant Manager and Manager at European Arab Bank (1977-82); Arab African International Bank,

London Representative, Manager Credit and Marketing and currently Branch Manager for West Branch (since 1982). **Sports:** Squash and swimming. **Member of:** Arab Bankers Association, London, the Lombard Association, London. **Credit Cards:** Amex, Diners, Barclaycard and Access. **Priv. Addr.:** Tel.: 01-942 5417, London.

ZAKI (Mohamad Sabry, Dr.), Egyptian politician. **Educ.:** Faculty of Medicine, Cairo University. **Career:** Joined the Egyptian Armed Forces as medical officer, 1947; Director General of medical services, Military Factories; Secretary, Ministry of Health, in charge of curative medicine department, follow up and People's Assembly Affairs; contributed to the preparatory stages of the October 1973 war between Egypt and Israel, as representative of the Ministry of Health; supervisor of the medical department, Insurance Authority; chairman of the Board of Directors, Health Insurance Authority (1974); set up comprehensive clinics in all governorates; appointed governor of Aswan Governorate (May 1981); Minister of Health (1982). **Address:** Cairo, Egypt.

ZAKI (Sayed Ali), Sudanese economist and former minister. **Born** in 1944 in Bara, Sudan. **Son** of Ahmad Zaki (Trader) **and** Mrs., née Aisha Adam Hassan. **Married** in 1973 to Miss Eisa Omdurman, 4 children: Elsiddig, Bashaer, Shoug and Asawir. **Educ.:** Bara Elementary School; Elobeid Intermediate School; Khortaggat Secondary School; University of Khartoum, Sudan; Michigan State University, USA. **Dipl.:** B.Sc (Honors) (1967); M.Sc. (Rural Econ.) (1967); M.A. (Economic) (1977); Ph.D. (Agric. Econ.), Michigan State University (1988). **Career:** Agricultural Planning Director (1970); Deputy Under Secretary Planning (1980); Undersecretary of Planning (1983); Executive Director, Islamic Development Bank (1989); Minister of Finance and Economic Planning, Sudan (1989). **Sport:** Basketball. **Prof. Addr.:** P.O.Box 29092, Tel.: 77003, Khartoum, Sudan. **Priv. Addr.:** P.O.Box 833, Tel.: 757, Omdurman, Sudan.

ZAKI (Shukri, Saleh), Iraqi former statesman. **Born** in Iraq. **Educ.:** Secondary and Higher. **Career:** Minister of Commerce (1963); Ambassador to Egypt (1963-64); Minister of Education (1964-65); Member Egypt-Iraq Unified Political Command in 1964; Minister of Economy, Minister of Finance and Petroleum in the Cabinet of Mr. Abdurrahman al-Bazzaz (1965). **Addr.:** Baghdad, Iraq.

ZALZALAH (Abdulhassan, Ali), Iraqi statesman. **Born** on December 28, 1927 in Amarah (Iraq). **Son** of Ali Zalzalah **and** Mrs. Najyiah Kubbah. **Married** to Nabiha Zalzalah on January 25, 1952, 4 children: Lith, Lu'ay, Rand and Naghum. **Educ.:** College of Law, (Baghdad); Indiana College, Indiana (U.S.A.), **Dipl.:**.Bachelor of Law (1948), Master of Arts, Doctor of Philosophy (1957). **Career:** Director, Loans and Investments Dept., Central Bank of Iraq (1957); Director, Foreign Exchange Dept. (1957); Acting Director, Statistics and Economic Research Dept. (1959-62); Deputy Governor Central Bank (1962-63); Chairman, Board of Administration, Central Bank (1962-63); Ambassador to Iran (1963-64); Minister of Industry (June 1964); Minister of Planning (Nov. 1964); Acting Minister of Finance (Aug. 1965); Ambassador to Austria (1965); Ambassador to Egypt, Somalia (Nov. 1966); Ministry of Foreign Affairs (Oct. 1968); Governor, Central Bank (January 1969- May 1973); Ambassador to Canada (1973-76); Assistant Secretary General of the League of Arab States For Economic Affairs (1976). **Vice Chairman** of the Association of Iraqi Economists. **Addr.:** Baghdad, Iraq.

ZALZALAH (Hadi), Arab-American engineer. **Born** in 1936 in Baghdad, Iraq. **Married**, 2 children. **Educ.:** Purdue University, Indiana, USA, postgraduate studies, Indiana University, USA, Institute of Technology, Roosevelt University, USA. **Dipl.:** BS. **Career:** Project Engineer, Ingersol Milling Machine Company, Rockford, Illinois, USA (1961-65); Vice President of Electro Corporation, a design and manufacturing company for machine tools (1965-66); Chief Electronics Engineer, Pratt and Whitney machine Tool Division, Cudahy, California, USA (1967-). **Prof. Addr.:** 8420 Atlantic Avenue, Cudahy CA 90201, USA. **Priv. Addr.:** 31281 Ganado Drive, Palos Verdes Peninsula, CA 902704, USA.

ZAMAKHSHARY (Taher, Abdul Rahman), Saudi leading poet and prose writer. **Born** in 1914 in Mecca, Saudi Arabia. **Educ.:** Received general education in Al Falah School. **Career:** Clerk, Statistical Department; various positions in the Government Press; Secretary, Secretariat of the Holy Capital; Teacher Orphanage; returned to Government Press; Secretary, Customs Secretariat, Riyadh Municipality; Radio and TV service; member of al-Tawfir Co.; attended several literary symposia in Lebanon, Syria, Egypt and Tunisia. **Honours:** Republic Medal of Honour (third category), Republic Medal of Honour for Culture (second category) awarded by Government of Tunisia. **Publications:** Fourteen collections of poetry: Ahlamu'l Rabie (Spring Dreams, first collection of poetry published in contemporary Saudi literature), Hamasat (Whispers), and other eight collections (under publication); several prose writing; some novels and short stories. **Address:** Waqf al-Zakaria, Flat 2, Sharafia, Tel.: 6431947, Jeddah, Saudi Arabia.

ZAMEL (Youssef, al), Saudi Economist. **Born** on September 15, 1954. **Son** of Abdullah Al-Zamel (Trader) **and** Mrs. Muneirah Al-Shubaili. **Married** in January 1980 to Fawziyah Alfaris. **Educ.:** King Saud University, Indiana University, University of Colorado. **Dipl.:** B.A. Economics, Administrative Sciences, M.A. Economics, Ph.D. Economics. **Career:** Teaching Assistant (1978-1986); Assistant Professor, Economics (1987); Dean, Associate (1989); Assistant Professor, Economics (1988- present). **Sport:**

Swimming. **Hobbies:** Reading, Social Activities. **Member:** American Express. **Priv. Addr.:** Tel.: 364-8816, Saudi Arabia.

ZAMIL (Abdul Kareem ben Saleh, al), Saudi official. **Born** in 1922 at Ha'el, Saudi Arabia. **Dipl.:** High School. **Career:** former Director of Finance (1937-49); Secretary at the Ministry of Foreign Affairs (1960); Vice-Consul in Jerusalem until 1964; Consul 1965 in Basrah, Iraq; attended the Ambassadors' Conference in Jeddah; Vice-President, Sasi Orphanage, Damascus. **Address:** Riyadh, Saudi Arabia.

ZAMIL (Abdulaziz, Abdallah, al), Saudi former minister and businessman. **Born** in 1942 in Bahrain. **Dipl.:** M.Sc. (Industrial Engineering). **Career:** Industrial Estate Expert, and Director of Technical Services Department and Deputy Director General of the Industrial Studies and Development Centre (ISDC), Riyadh; Chairman, the Arabian Petrochemical Company (PETRO-KEMYA) and the Saudi Methanol Company (AR-RAZI); Vice Chairman, Saudi Petrochemical Company (SADAF), Saudi Yanbu Petrochemical Industries Company (GPIC); Director of al-Zamil and Sons, al-Khobar, (1958-62); Director, of Dammam Central Hospital (1974-76); Chairman of Saudi Basic Industries Corporation (SABIC); member of the Board, Arabian Refrigeration Industries Ltd., Zamil Aluminium Factory, Zamil Soule Steel Building Company Ltd., Zamil Great Ways Food Industries Ltd., Zamil Marine Services Company and the Arabian Gulf Construction Company; Minister of Industry and Electricity (until August 1995). **Hobbies:** Reading, football, numismatics. **Address:** Riyadh, Saudi Arabia.

ZAMIL (Abdulrahman, A., al), Saudi official. **Born** in 1942, at Onaizah, Saudi Arabia. **Dipl.:** BLL, M.A., and Ph.D. (International Relations). **Career:** Assistant Professor, King Fahad University of Petroleum and Minerals, Dean of Educational Services, KFUPM (1974-77); Deputy Governor, Electricity Corporation (1977-80); Deputy Minister of Commerce; Chairman of Saudi Consolidated Electric Company in the Southern Province; member of the Board, Saudi Industrial Development Fund, Saudi Consolidated Electric Company in the Middle Province, General Ports Authority, Saudi Public Transport Co., National Gas and Industries Co., Saudi Hotels and Resort Areas Co. and the Saudi Arabian Standards Organization; member of related activities conferences, seminars and Symposia. **Publications:** Arab Information Crisis (a textbook). **Hobbies:** Sports, reading. **Address:** Ministry of Commerce, P.O.Box 1774, Tel.: (1) 401-2222, Riyad, Saudi Arabia.

ZAMIL (Hamed, Abdallah, al), Prominent Saudi businessman. **Born** on February 15, 1941 in Onaizah, Saudi Arabia. **Educ.:** B.Sc. (Business Management); M.Sc. (Hospital Administration). **Current Positions:** President and Vice-Chairman: A.H. al-Zamil Group of Companies. Chairman of: Zamil Birla Technical Services Co. Ltd.; United Carton Industries Co. Ltd. Director of: Saudi Formaldehyde Chemical Co. Ltd. Board Member: Saudi Arabian Airlines; Bahraini Saudi Bank; Dhahran International Exhibition Center; Tihama Advertising Co.; Saudi Diabetes & Endocrine Association; Tourism Enterprises Co. (SHAMS). **Represented Saudi Arabia in:** First Conference of Hospital Administrators, Cairo (1974); Trade & Investment Seminar between Arab Gulf States & India, in Doha, Qatar (1987); 7th General Assembly of the Islamic Chamber in Cairo (1988). Was Director, Dammam Central Hospital Prior to entering business. **Hobbies:** Reading, Football and Numismatics. **Address:** A.H. al-Zamil Group of Companies, P.O.Box 9, al-Khobar 31952, Saudi Arabia, Tel.: 966-3-8842552, Fax: 966-3-894336, Telex: 870132 ZAMIL SJ.

ZAMIL (Ibrahim, A., al), Saudi educator. **Born** in 1945 at Onaizah, Saudi Arabia. **Dipl.:** Ph.D. **Career:** Member, several welfare societies, the American Society of Public Administration (ASPA) and the American Association of University Professors; Associate Professor, King Fahad, University of Petroleum and Minerals, Dhahran, the Irish Management Association, the American Management Association, the American-Arab Anti-Discrimination Committee. Co-author of books dealing with management fields. **Publications:** Several research articles and a Ph.D. thesis. **Hobbies:** Reading, swimming, jogging. **Address:** King Fahad University of Petroleum and Minerals, No.87, P.O.Box 144, Tel.: 8602680, Dhahran 31261, Saudi Arabia.

ZAMIL (Khalid Abdallah, al), Saudi engineer. **Born** in 1948 at al-Khobar, Saudi Arabia. **Dipl.:** B.S. (Civil Engineering), 1972. **Career:** Engineer, Industrial Studies and Development Centre (1972-74); General Manager, Arabian Refrigerating Industries (Fredrich Airconditioners) (1974-76); Vice President, al-Zamil Group Companies; President of Zamil-Soule; President, Eastern Province Chamber of Commerce. Chairman, Council of Saudi Chambers of Commerce and Industry, Riyadh. **Hobbies:** football, squash. **Address:** P.O.Box 270, Tel.: 8571479, Dhahran Airport, Saudi Arabia.

ZAMIL (Mohamed, Abdulla, al), Bahraini executive. **Born** in 1936 in Manama, Bahrain. **Son** of Abdulla Hamad Al-Zamil (Businessman). **Married,** 2 sons, 3 daughters. **Educ.:** Higher Secondary studies, Bahrain. **Career:** Chairman and President of Al-Zamil Group of Companies since 1960. Chairman of Grindlays Bahrain Bank. Member of the Board of Investcorp, Bahrain Islamic Bank, G.O.S.I., Gulf Union Insurance and Reinsurance Co., Saudi Cement Co., Al-Bustan Commercial Center, Cairo, IFA Banque S.A., Paris. **Sports:** Football, tennis. **Hobbies:** Reading, watching sports and games. **Member:** Marina Club; Al-Ahli Sports Club; Alumni Club. **Prof. Addr.:** A.H. Al-Zamil Group of Companies, P.O.Box 285, Tel.: 223071,

223009, Manama, Bahrain.

ZAMZAMI (Awatif, Ahmad Hussein, Miss), Saudi lecturer. **Born** in 1951 in Mecca, Saudi Arabia. **Dipl.:** M.A. (Psychology). **Career:** lecturer, Department of Psychology and Supervisor of Girls' University Library, Umm al-Qura University, Mecca. **Address:** Women's Section, Umm al-Qura University, Tel.: 5433406 (Home), Mecca, Saudi Arabia.

ZAMZAMI (Siraj, Jamil), Saudi academic. **Born** in 1938 in Mecca, Saudi Arabia. **Dipl.:** B.A. 1964, University of Perugia, Italy; M. Phil, 1972, Reading University, England, Ph.D. (International Relations), Clairmont University. **Career:** Began his career as a civil servant in the Ministry of Education, Riyadh; Assistant Cultural Attache, Saudi Arabian Embassy, England (1968-73); Associate Professor and Chairman, Department of Political Science, King Abdulaziz University, Jeddah. **Publications:** A book in English language entitled "The League of the Arab States", co-author of another book in English named "International Organizations". **Hobbies:** Classical Arabic Poetry, Gardening. **Address:** Jeddah, Saudi Arabia.

ZANDO (Ahmad), Egyptian economist. **Born** in 1917. **Educ.:** B.Com. Cairo University, Egypt (1938). **Career:** Taught for sometime at Commercial Institute in Alexandria; formed State Audit Department (1942); later Controller General of this Department; Director General of Exchange Control (1958); Director General of the Budget Department, Ministry of Economy; Under Secretary at the Treasury; member of the Board of Directors of the Economic Development Organisation; Director ofthe Office of the Minister of Treasury; member of the Board of Directors of the Economic Development Organisation; Director of the Office of the Minister of Treasury (1961); Deputy Minister (1962); Minister of Economy and member of the Egyptian Executive Council (1962); Governor of the Central Bank (1964-67); Planning Adviser to the President (1967) with responsibility for the National Planning Institute; Governor of the Central Bank (1971); presently Governor Faisal Islamic Bank of Egypt. **Addr.:** P.O.Box 2446, Cairo, Egypt.

ZAQZOUK (Mahmoud, Hamdy, Dr.), Egyptian Politician. **Born** on December 27, 1933 in Dakahleya. **Married** one daughter. **Educ.:** Secondary School, Al-Mansoura Religious Institute; Graduated, Faculty of Language, Al-Azhar University (1959); M.A. Teaching Al-Azhar University (1960); Ph.D. Philosophy, Munich University, Germany (1968). **Career:** Dean, Faculty of Fundamentals of Islam; Vice-President, Al-Azhar University; Head, Islamic Thought Committee, Supreme Council for Islamic Affairs; Member Islamic Research Academy; Chairman, Egyptian Society of Philosophy; attended several international conferences and symposia as a representative of the Grand Imam of Al-Azhar, particularly in relation to dialogue among religions, tolerance of Islam and its high status among religions. Presently Minister of Awqaf. **Publ.:** Author Researcher of many works on philosophy, ethics, islamic thought and orientalist studies. **Address:** Ministry of Awqaf, Sharia Sabri Abul Alam, bab al-Louk, Cairo, Egypt.

ZARIFA (Salem, Shukri), Egyptian mechanical engineer. **Born** on December 3, 1923 in Cairo. **Son** of Shukri Zarifa (manufacturer) **and** Mrs. Bahia Seraphim. **Married** to Sylvie Hury on October 1950, 2 children: Shukri and Myriam. **Educ.:** Sainte Famille College (1928-41); Cairo University, Faculty of Engineering (1942-48). **Dipl.:** Secondary Certificate (1941); Bachelor of Science in Engineering (1948). **Career:** Partner, International Engineering and Trading Bureau, Cairo; Technical Director, Egyptian Diesel and Components Industries, Cairo; Consulting and Manufacturers Adviser. **Sports:** Swimming, tennis, horseriding and fencing. **Member:** The Gazira Sporting Club; Cairo Engineers Association, Cairo. **Remark:** Special Interest in Mechanical Research Work. **Priv. Addr.:** 32, Shagaret ad-Dorr Street, Zamalek, Tel. 804410, Cairo, Egypt.

ZARROUK (Neziha Mehoud), Tunisian Politician. **Born** on December 12, 1946 in Jemmal. **Married,** three children. **Educ.:** Degree, Arab Language and Literature. **Career:** Vice President, Youth Committee, International Council of Women; Teacher; Treasurer, Regional Federation, Democratic Constitutional Rally (RCD), Ariana; Member, Central Committee, (1988); Executive Officer, National Union of Tunisian Women (1989); Permanent secretary Responsible for Women's Affairs, RCD (1992); Member Politburo and Assistant Secretary General in charge of Women's Affairs RCD (1993); Member, High Commission for Bosniac Women (1996); Minister of Women's and Family Affairs (1995-to date). **Decor:** Grand Officer of the Order of the Republic; The 7th of November Medal; Commander of the Order of November 7th. **Address:** Ministry of Women and Family Affairs, Place du Gouvernement, La Kasbah, 1008 Tunis, Tunisia.

ZAWAWI (Omar Bin Abdulmunim, al, Dr.), Omani businessman. **Born** in 1930 in Circa. **Son** of Abdul Munim al-Zawawi. **Educ.:** Cairo University, Egypt. **Dipl.:** M.D. **Career:** Founder, Walled Associates Trading Agency (1970); Assistant Political and Economic Adviser to H.E. the Sultan; Director, European Arab Holding SA (Luxembourg), Luxembourg; Director, Zawawi Trading Co., Oman. Director, Société Arabe Internationale de Banque (SAIB); Arab International Bank Cairo, Egypt; Director Omar National Insurance Co. SAO; Director Kassara Transport Co.; Chairman, Oman International Bank SAO; Chairman, Oman Mechanical Services Co. Ltd.; Chairman, Oman Services & Supply Organization; Chairman Omar Zawawi Est., P.O.Box 879; Chairman, Qurum Contractors LLC; Chairman Walid Associates; Chairman,

Zawawi Power Engineering LLC; Director, Zawawi Trading Co. **Addr.:** P.O.Box 58, Tel.: 602408, Telex: 3232 A/B ZAWAWI MB, Muscat, Oman and P.O.Box 879, Muscat, Oman.

ZAYADINE (Fawzi, Ibrahim), Jordanian academic. **Born** in 1938 in Jordan. **Married. Educ.:** Sorbonne, Paris, Ecole du Louvre. **Dipl.:** Ph.D. **Career:** Assistant, Jerusalem Bib. & Arch. French School (1959-61); Head of Sebastia Excavations, Jordan Department of Antiquities (1965-67); Inspector of Antiquities, Kerak (1967-68). Member of French Arch. Institute of Beirut, Lebanon (1968-71); Assis. Director of Antiquities (1976-). **Publ.:** "Quseir "Amra", Amman, 1977. Contributions: Petra und das Königreich der Nabatäer", Munich, 1989, Neue Ausgrabungen und Entdeckungen, Munich, 1986. Editor: Jerash Archaeological Project, Amman, 1986; Petra and the Caravan Cities, Amman, 1990. **Member:** Institute for Advanced Study, Princeton, N.J., ICOMOS, Jordan Writers' Association, ICCROM, UNESCO. **Decor.:** Order of Merit, France; Chevalier des Arts et Lettres (1987). **Prof. Addr.:** P.O.Box 88, Amman, Jordan. **Priv. Addr.:** Jebel Amman, Othman B. Affän Str., Jordan, 51.

ZAYANI (Rashid, Abdelrahman, al), Bahraini businessman, banker. **Born** in 1915. **Married. Career:** Private enterprise; Chairman of Bank of Bahrain and Kuwait; Chairman of ALUBAF Arab International Bank; member of Constituent Assembly (1972-73); Director A.A. Zayani & Sons, Bahrain. **Addr.:** Bank of Bahrain and Kuwait, P.O.Box 597, Tel.: 253388, Telex: 8919 BAHKUBANK BN, Manama, Bahrain.

ZAYANI (Yousuf, A. Rahman, al), Bahraini previous registrar. **Born** in 1953 in Manama, Bahrain. **Son** of Mohamed A. Rahman al-Zayani (Businessman) **and** Mrs. Mariam Ahmad al-Zayani. **Married** on March 1988 in Bahrain to Aysha al-Shaer, two children: Abdullah (Dec. 12, 1988), Latifa (July 21, 1990). **Educ.:** King Saud University, Riyadh, Saudi Arabia; University of Leeds, U.K.; University of Bradford, U.K. **Dipl.:** B.Sc., Electrical Engineering (1982), King Saud University, Riyadh; M.Sc., Computer Sc. (1989), Leeds University, U.K.; Ph.D.; Computer Sc. (Expected 1993), Bradford University, U.K. **Career:** University Registrar (1983-93); Member, Arabic Association for Collgate Registrar's and Admissions Officers (since 1984); Member, American Association for Collgate Registrar's and Admissions Officers (1984-); President, Arabic Ass. for Collgate Registrars and Admissions Officers (1986-87); Member, Executive Commission Arabic A.C.R.A.O. (1984-88); Member, National Commission for Academic Credentials Evaluations. Developed Computer Software Package for Student Information System (Registration, Records, Admissions) to support the needs of the University of Bahrain (since 1984-); Many Computerization Consultancies. **Award:** Golden Medal for Post Graduate Studies, (Dec. 1991), Government of Bahrain. **Credit Card:** Master Card. **Priv. Addr.:** 194, A. Rahman al-Dakhil Avenue, Tel.: 973-713884, Telefax: 973-742960, Manama 321, Bahrain.

ZAYED (Abdallah ben Abdallah ben Obaid, al), Saudi academic. **Born** in 1932 at al-Aflaj. **Dipl.:** B.A. (Islamic Law). **Career:** Director, General Administration, Islamic University, 1961; teacher, Scientific Institute, 1966; teaching staff member, Faculty of Shari'a (Islamic Law), Riyadh, 1969; Vice President of the Higher Institute of Jurisdiction, Riyadh, 1974; Chairman of Higher Institute for Islamic Da'wa (Advocation), 1976; member of the Board, Supreme Council of Imam Muhammad Ibn Saud Islamic University; Vice-Chancellor, Islamic University of Medina. **Publ.:** Author of "Tabi'atul Jihad Fil Islam" (The Nature of Jihad "Holy Struggle" in Islam); "Ibn Ham al-Ossoli" (Fundamental Ibn Hazm). **Hobbies:** Reading, writing, travel, gymnastics. **Addr.:** Tel.: 8222297 (Home), Medina, Saudi Arabia.

ZAYED (Georges), Egyptian university professor. **Born** in Cairo. **Educ.:** Secondary in Cairo and Higher in France. **Dipl.:** Doctor in letters from the University of Paris (La Sorbonne). **Career:** Professor at the University of Alexandria; contributed to the "Revue d'Histoire Littéraire de la France" (edited in Paris). **Publ.:** Author of "Lettres Inédites de Paul Verlaine à Charles Morice" (1963). **Addr.:** University of Alexandria, Alexandria City, Egypt.

ZAYNOUN (Shafik, T.), Lebanese geophysicist. **Born** on February 12, 1943 in Lebanon. **Son** of Towfik Zaynoun (Pharmacist) **and** Mohiba Zaynoun. **Married** on January 30, 1982 in Cairo to Naheda Nassar, 3 children: Nada, Ghassan and Samy. **Educ.:** Brummana High School; American University of Beirut, Beirut. **Dipl.:** B.Sc.; B.A. **Career:** Worked for Geophysical Service Inc. (GSI) in oil exploration from 1969 till 1989 in several countries including Lebanon, Abu Dhabi, U.S.A., U.K., Oman and Egypt in the following positions: Data Processing Seismologist (1969-72); Party Chief (1973-74); Technical Supervisor (1974-75); General Manager for Oman (1976-77); General Manager for the Near East-Area (1978-89). Worked for Halliburton Geophysical Services (HGS) in oil exploration as General Manager for the Near East Area (1990-94). From 1995 till the present date: Representative of Arab Geophysical Services Company (AGESCO) in Egypt and owner of United Consultants. **Sport:** Swimming, jogging. **Hobbies:** Chess, backgammon, reading. **Member:** Heliopolis Sporting Club, Cairo. **Credit Card:** American Express. **Prof. Addr.:** United Consultants, 7, Al-Athary Mahmoud Akoush St., Al-Golf Heliopolis, Tel.: (202) 4186796, Cairo, Egypt. **Priv. Addr.:** 7, el-Athary Mahmoud Akoush St., Al-Golf, Heliopolis, Tel.: (202) 2919616, Cairo, Egypt.

ZAYYAT (Fuad), Syrian businessman. **Born** in 1941 in Damascus, Syria. **Married,** three children. **Educ.:** Law,

University of Damascus, Syria. **Career:** Chairman, GENVICO Group of Companies with branches in Damascus, Geneva, London, Nicosia, Beirut, Washington. **Hobby:** Music. **Addr.:** Damascus, Syria.

ZAYYAT (Latifa, al), Egyptian academic, writer. **Born** in 1926 in Egypt. **Career:** Assistant Professor, English Department, Ain Shams University, Cairo, Egypt. **Publ.:** Several collections of short stories and novels, including "The Open Door"; literary studies of T.S. Eliot and Ford Madox Ford. **Addr.:** Ain Shams University, Faculty of Arts, English Department, Cairo, Egypt.

ZAYYAT (Mohamad, Abdul Salaam, al), Egyptian politician. **Born** in 1917. **Career:** elected to Chamber of Deputies in the last elections before the July 1952 Revolution and subsequently a Member of the National Assemblies (1957, 1964 and 1969); Secretary to the Provisional Committee to supervise elections to the Arab Socialist Union (ASU) (1968); elected Secretary General of the National Congress (1968); elected secretary General of the Fourth ASU National Congress (1970); Member of the Presidential Secretariat of the newly formed ASU Central Committee in 1971; Adviser for Political Affairs to the President with the rank of Deputy Prime Minister (1971); Deputy Prime Minister without Portfolio (1972); Member of the Foreign Relations Commitee of the People's Assembly; Chairman, Egyptian-Soviet Friendship Society. **Prof. Addr.:** The People's Assembly, al-Kasr al-Aini, Cairo, Egypt.

ZAYYAT (Mohamad, Hassan, al), Egyptian diplomat. **Born** on February 14, 1915 in Damietta Province. **Son** of Hassan al-Zayyat **and** Badia Abboud. **Married** to Miss Amina Taha Hussain on June 12, 1948, 3 children: Hassan, Sawsan and Mona Badia. **Educ.:** Cairo University (1939), Oxford University (1947). **Dipl.:** Bachelor of Arts (1939), Master of Arts (1942), Diploma Institute Oriental Studies (Cairo 1942), Doctor of Philosophy (1947). **Career:** Assistant Lecturer Middle Eastern Studies and Civilization, Cairo University (1940); Lecturer, Associate Professor Middle East, Alexandria (1942-50); Cultural Attache, Egyptian Embassy, Washington (1950-54); Visiting Associate Professor of Government Columbia University, New York (1945); also Counsellor Egyptian Embassy, Washington; Chargé d'Affaires of Egyptian Embassy in Teheran (1955-56); Egyptian Representative to United Nations Advisory Council for Somaliland (1957-60); Head, Department Arab Affairs, Ministry Foreign Affairs; also Permanent Representative Arab Republic of Egypt to Arab League (Cairo 1960-62); Ambassador to India and to Napal (1964-65); alternate Permanent Representative of Egypt to United Nations (1962-64); Under Secretary of State, Ministry of Foreign Affairs (1965-67); President, State Information Service to and Official Spokesman for Egypt (1967-69); Permanent Representative to United Nations (1969-72), Minister of State for Information (Jan. 1972); Minister of Foreign Affairs (Sept. 1972-73); President Sadat's Special Adviser on Foreign Affairs (1973-75); retired 1975; Visiting Prof. Alexandria University and UCLA; California. Elected deputy for Damietta National Assembly (since 1984); President of Immigration, Culture and Tourism Commission, National Assembly, Cairo (since 1984). **Member** of the "Institut d'Egypte", Cairo; formerly, representative of Egypt on the Council at the League of Arab States, and on ten council of ministers of the organes action of African states, and on the council of ministers of the non aligned countries, formerly member of the Daf Hammerdield Committee on the Congo, of the U.N. eighteen states committee for disarmament, Geneva, and of the U.N. Trusteeship council, and of the U.N. Security council, member of delegation to the U.N.E.S. Co. conference in montevedios also representative of the League of Arab States on special mission to the united states. **Awards:** Recipient decorations Government of Grand Cordon Order of the Nile (Egypt), Somaliland and decorations from Lebanon, Mauritania, Tunis. Somalia, Chad, Italy, Poland, Brazil, Austria, Thailand and Iran. **Addr.:** 7 Hassan Sabry. St., Zamalek, Cairo, Egypt.

ZAZA (Hassan, Mohamad Tewfik), Egyptian university professor. **Born** on 23 June 1919 in Cairo (Egypt). **Married** to Barriol Andrée Marie-Annette Thérèse in 1955, 2 children. **Educ.:** Primary and Secondary Government schools in Cairo; Faculty of Arts, Cairo University; The Hebrew University of Jerusalem; Ecole des Hautes Etudes (Sorbonne, Paris); Ecole du Louvre, Paris. **Dipl.:** B.A. (Hons) Cairo (1941), M.A. Jerusalem (1944); Diplôma de l'Ecole des Hautes Etudes, Sorbonne, Paris (1952); Diplôme de l'Ecole des Langues Orientales, Paris (1952); Ph.D. (Doctorat d'Etat) La Sorbonne (1958). **Career:** Lecturer, Associate Professor then Professor, Alexandria University, Egypt since 1943; Visiting Professor and Council Member, University of Rabat, Morocco (1963-64); Visiting Professor, Arab University of Beirut (Lebanon) (1964-68); now Professor, Faculty of Arts, King Saud University (Saudi Arabia). **Publ.:** The Religious Thought of Israel (1971); The Institute of Arabic Studies, Cairo; Language and Man (Published by Dar el-Maaref, Cairo); The Language of the Arabs (Dar el-Maaref, Cairo) and other titles. **Hobbies:** Music and Poetry, Plastic Arts. **Prof. Addr.:** Faculty of Arts, King Saud University, Dept. of Arabic, P.O.Box 2456, Riyadh 11451, Saudi Arabia. **Priv. Addr.:** 23 Port Said street, Chatby, Alexandria, Tel.: 4028979, Egypt.

ZEBAN (Akasha, al), Jordanian politician. **Born** in 1927 in Jordan. **Married. Educ.:** Military studies at Cadets College; Staff College UK. **Career:** Training officer; section and battalion Commander; infantry battalion staff officer; Talal Divisional Staff Officer (1952-54); commander of infantry and armoured battalion; Head of Royal Bodyguard (3 times); Founder and Commander of Royal Armoured Force; Assistant Commander of War Operations (1964); Jordanian Ambassador to Kuwait (1964); Deputy Director of Public Security for irbid (1969); retired with rank of Governor in Ministry of Interior (1970); Governor of Salt and Minister of Defence (1970). retired; **Publ.:** various books on military and historal subjects. **Medal:** Renaissance Medal (1st Class), Independence Medal (1st Class), Military Bravery Medal, **Decor.:** Star of Jordan (1st Class) and various other orders. **Hobbies:** swimming, reading, riding, hunting. **Addr.:** Jabal Hussein, Amman, Jordan.

ZEBDANI (Abdul Aziz), Algerian politician. **Born** in 1934 in Canrobert, Algeria. **Married. Career:** Political Commissioner of Wilaya I, Aures; later Private Secretary to Krim Belkacem; entered Ministry of Foreign Affairs of Provisional Government (1961); Deputy for Batna in National Assembly (1962), re-elected in 1964; President of National Assembly Economic Commission; Director of "Le Peuple" newspaper and former regular contributor to "Révolution Africaine"; elected Member of National Liberation Front Central Committee April 1964 Congress and helped draft the Algerian Charter; Minister of Labour (1965-67); currently a practising lawyer. **Addr.:** al-Chaab, 1 Place Maurice Audin, Algiers, Algeria.

ZEBDI (Kamil), Moroccan administrator. **Born** in 1927 in Rabat, Morocco. **Educ.:** Diploma, l'Ecole du Louvre, Paris, France. **Career:** Curator of museums; Clutural Attaché, Embassy to France; Cultural Attaché, Embassy to Denmark; now ethnographer, Ministry of Cultural Affairs of Morocco. **Publ.:** "Le Cri du Royaume" (1960); "Kyrielle" (1967); "Echelle pour le Futur du Maroc" (1974); "Seve" (1981). **Decor.:** Award from l'Académie Française (1960). **Addr.:** P.O.B. 99, Rabat, Morocco.

ZEDAN (Fereed M.H.), Saudi educator. **Born** in 1945 in Makkah, Saudi Arabia. **Educ.:** Engineering, University of Karlsruhe, West Germany; University of Southern California, U.S.A. **Dipl.:** Electrical Engineering (1970); Ph.D. in Electrical Engineering (1979). **Career:** Electrical Engineer (1970-73); Graduate Assistant, King Fahd University of Petroleum and Minerals, Dhahran, Saudi Arabia (1973-74); later Assistant Professor (1979-83), Associate Professor (1983), Professor (1990); Chairman, EE Dept. (1981-87) at the above University; Chairman of the Board, Tabuk Electric Co. (1982-86); Chairman of the Arabian Gulf Cooperation Regional Committee CIGRE (1986-87); Project Manager Arab Gulf Countries' Power System Interconnection; Principal Advisor to Board of Directors: Saudi Electricity Company, Consultant to the Ministry of Industry and Electricity, Member of the Board of Directors, Riyadh Bank. **Publ.:** of various articles, papers and research reports. **Addr.:** P.O.Box 20516, Al-Khobar 31952, Saudi Arabia.

ZEERA (Mohamed Akram, al), Bahraini businessman. **Born** on December 1, 1959 in Manama, Bahrain. **Son** of late Issa Abdulnabi al-Zeera **and** late Mrs. Fakhr el-Hajeeh Abdul-Majeed. **Married** on December 8, 1988 in Bahrain to Miss Bucheeri, Three children: Fatima, Hussain, Hussam. **Educ.:** American University of Beirut; Texas Tech. University Lubbouck Texas; University of Texas at Arlington. **Dipl.:** Bachelor of Business Administration. **Career:** Managing Director Oriental Press, since 1981. **Prof. Addr.:** Oriental Press, 17 Tijjar Avenue, P.O.Box 161, Manama 304, Bahrain.

ZEGHARI (Mohamad), Moroccan former financial official and statesman. **Born** in Morocco. **Educ.:** Secondary and Higher. **Career:** Governor of Banque du Maroc (Central Bank); Minister of State (1965); Vice-President of the Council of Ministers; Minister of Agriculture and Agrarian Reform and Economy (1967); Governor of Banque du Maroc (1967). **Addr.:** Rabat, Morocco.

ZEID (Abdulrazzak, al-Khalid, al), Kuwaiti businessman. **Son** of al-Khalid al-Zeid. **Educ.:** Cairo University, Egypt. **Career:** Private enterprise; represented Kuwait at labour conferences in Geneva. Founding member of the Kuwait Chamber of Commerce and Industry (1952); Honorary Treasurer of the Chamber. **Sports:** Walking, swimming. **Addr.:** Kuwait Chamber of Commerce and Industry, P.O.Box 775, Tel.: 2435801, Telex: 22198 GURFTIGARA KT, Safat, Kuwait.

ZEIN (Izzeddine, al), Syrian dean of faculty. **Born** in Syria. **Educ.:** Secondary and Higher. **Dipl.:** Doctor in Pharmacy. **Career:** Professor and former Dean of Faculty of Pharmacy at the Syrian University of Damascus, also Professor of Pharmacology at the said university. **Addr.:** University of Damascus, Tel.: 115100, Damascus, Syria.

ZEITOUNI (Elias), Lebanese financial controller. **Born** in 1949 in Beirut, Lebanon. **Son** of Hares Zeitouni. **Married** in 1975, 1 son, 1 daughter. **Dipl.:** B.A. (Accounting); Diploma of Superior Banking and Finance; Banking Association, Advanced Banking Courses, U.S. (1978). **Career:** Manager, Arab Shipping Co., Beirut (1969-72); Senior Accountant, Byblos Bank SAL, Beirut (1972-76); International Officer, Citizens Southern National Bank, USA (1976-80); Financial Controller, Middle East Operations, Arab European Investment Corp. Ltd., Cayman Islands (1980-). **Member:** Atlanta Driving Club. **Hobbies:** Sports and Reading. **Addr.:** P.O.Box 1588, Tel.: 6870361, 6885786, Telex: 40041/2 A/B ZTRJ SJ, Jeddah, Saudi Arabia.

ZEMMAMA (Faycal), Moroccan bank executive. **Born** in 1940 in Oujda, Morocco. **Son** of Hadj Mohamad Zemama. **Married** in 1967, 1 son, 2 daughters. **Dipl.:** B.A. (Econ.) (1963). **Career:** Credit Populaire du Maroc, Morocco (1963); Manager, Banque Populaire de Fès (1968-75); Manager, Banque Populaire de Casablanca (1969-75); Manager, Banque Centrale Populaire, Casablanca, Morocco (1976-). **Addr.:** 101, Zerktouni Blvd., Tel.: 270540, Casablanca, Morocco.

ZEMMOURI (Hassan), Moroccan politician. **Born** in 1930 in Tedders. **Educ.:** in Khemisset and Azrou; Institut des Sciences Politiques; Ecole Internationale d'Administration. **Dipl.:** Law Degree. **Career:** Participated in Independence Movement; Director, private office of Minister of Labour and Social Affairs (Moulay Abdallah Ibrahim) (1957); Director, Rural Affairs; Under-Secretary of State, Ministry of Interior; Minister of Agriculture (1960); President, Casablanca Chamber of Commerce and Industry (1961); President, Casablanca Municipal Council (1969); Minister of Town Planning, Housing and Environment in Lamrani Government (April 1972-74); Minister of Town-Planning. Housing, Environmental and Tourism (1977-Oct. 1977). **Addr.:** Rabat, Morocco.

ZENTAR (Mehdi, Mrani), Moroccan diplomat. **Born** on September 6, 1929 in Meknes (Morocco). **Married** in January 1959 to Milouda Abbas, one daughter; Mouna. **Educ.:** Moulay Idriss College (Fès), Lycée Peomireau (Meknes), Faculty of Law, University of Rabat (Morocco); Faculty of Law, University of Paris. **Dipl.:** L.L.B. **Career:** Director, African Affairs, Cabinet of the Minister of State for Foreign Affairs, Ministry of Foreign Affairs, Rabat; Consul General, Paris; Director, American Affairs and International Organisations, Ministry of Foreign Affairs; Director, Office of National Tourism, Rabat; Legal Adviser, Ministry of Foreign Affairs, Rabat; Ambassador, Director of Political Affairs, Morocco; Ambassador to Algeria (1963); Ambassador to Yugoslavia (1964); Ambassador to Egypt; Ambassador, Permanent Representative of Morocco, New York (1971); Ambassador to Italy (1974); Ambassador to Nigeria (1978); Ambassador, Permanent Representative to United Nations, New York (1980). **Awards:** Officer of the Throne Order (Morocco), Grand Cordon Yugoslav Order. **Sports:** Swimming, tennis and motoring. **Hobbies:** Music, travelling and reading. **Addr.:** Ministry of Foreign Affairs, Rabat, Morocco.

ZERAFFA (Michel), Tunisian novelist and essayist. **Born** in 1918 in Tunis. **Educ.:** Secondary and Higher. **Career:** Novelist and Essayist (in French Laguage). **Publ.:** Author of "Temps des Rencontres" (1949), "L'Ecume et le Sel" (1950), "Le Commerce des Hommes", "Les Derniers Sacrements", "Les Doublures" (1958), "L'histoire" (1964). **Prof. & Priv. Addr.:** Paris, France.

ZERGUINI (Mohamad), Algerian colonel and former minister. **Married,** 4 children. **Career:** Served in French Army; during Independence fought in Frontier Army of Morocco; Deputy Chief, General Staff, after Independence; Commander, Fourth Military Region (Ouargla) (1968); Commander, Third Military Region (Bechar) (1970); promoted Colonel (1973); Minister of Posts, Telegraphs and Telecommunications (April 1977- March 1979), re-appointed (8 March 1979-82). **Addr.:** Algiers, Algeria.

ZEROUAL (Liamine, Maj.Gen. Ret)), Former President of Algeria. **Born** on July 3, 1941 in Batna. **Married,** 3 children. **Educ.:** Military school, Moscow War College, Paris. **Career:** Joined F.L.N. (Front de Libération Nationale) (1957); War of Independance (1960-62); Holding various posts, active in F.L.N.; Commandant, Batna Military School (1974-75); Brigade Commander (1975-79) Head, Southern Sector (1979-80); Commander, Airborne Troops (1980-81); Commandant, Churchill Military Academy (1981-82); Commander, 5th Military Region (1982-83); 3rd Military Region (1983-87); 5th Military Region (1987-90); Army Chief of Staff (1989); Ambassador to Romania (1990-91); Minister of National Defence (sept. 1992 - Nov. 1995); Elected President of Algeria (Nov. 1995 - April 1999). **Address:** Algiers, Algeria.

ZGHAL (Houssine), Tunisian international civil servant. **Born** in 1933 in Tunis (Tunisia). **Married,** children. **Educ.:** Institute of Higher Studies of Tunis (1955); Institute of Statistics, University of Paris (1957); School of Statistics and Economic Administration, Paris (1958); Faculty of Science, University of Paris. **Dipl.:** Certificate of Mathematics; Certificate of Statistical Methods; Degree of Statistician; Certificate of Probability Theory; Diploma of Statistics. **Career:** Statistical Officer (1958-60); Head, Office of Government Accounts (1960-62); Head, National Accounts Department (1962-66); Assistant Director for Programming & Research, Government of Tunisia (1966-68); Member, Executive Board, African Institute for Economic Development & Planning, Dakar (Senegal, 1964-68); Representative of Tunisia, African Planners Conference (1964-70); Head, Planning Division (1968-69); Director of Sector Programming, Tunis (1969-71); Projects Director, Government of Tunisia (1970-71); Counsellor, Economic & Social Council of Tunis (1970-79); Director, National Institute of Statistics, Tunis since 1971; Director general of Central Administration, Government of Tunisia (1971-75); Member UN Statistical Commission, National Institute of Statistics, Tunis, since 1974; Expert, Arab League (since 1980). **Member:** Board of Governors, Central Bank of Tunisia (1970-77); Executive Board, National Fisheries Office (1971-78); Tunisian Insurance and Reinsurance Co. (1971-78); Chairman General Manager (1976-79) of Société Industrielle d'Acide Phosphorique et d'Engrais (SLAPE) and "Social NPK Engrais" **Addr.:** Tunis, Tunisia.

ZGHAL (Mohamad), Tunisian official. **Born** in 1929 in Sfax, Tunisia. **Married. Educ.:** Sorbonne, University of Paris, France. **Dipl.:** Degree in Science. **Career:** became first Director of Information after Independence; Head of Tunisian Press Agency (TAP); Head of State Phosphate Company; Director of Information (1969); Chef de Cabinet, Ministry of Information (1970-71); Chef de Cabinet,

Ministry of the Interior (1971); Secretary of State for Education (1971); **Addr.:** Tunis, Tunisia.

ZGOLLI (Taieb), Tunisian engineer. **Born** in 1946. **Married**, 2 daughters. **Educ.:** studied in France. **Dipl.:** graduated as an Electronics Engineer, RFA. **Career:** Public sector employment until 1983; Manager of AZEL SA (1983-). **Prof. Addr.:** AZEL, Rue du 9 Avril, 8070 Korba, Tunisia.

ZHIRI (Qassem, al), Moroccan diplomat. **Born** on March 25, 1920. **Educ.:** Institute of Higher Studies, Rabat. **Career:** Detained for activities in Moroccan Independence Movement (1936, 1944); Exiled and detained (1952); Manager, al-Maghreb and al-Alam daily newspapers; Director-General, Moroccan Broadcasting Station (1956-59); Ambassador to Senegal (1960-61); Ambassador to Yugoslavia (1961-64); Director of Information, Ministry of Foreign Affairs (1966); Permanent Delegate, League of Arab States to UN, Geneva (1966-68); Minister of Secondary and Technical Education (1968-69); Ambassador to People's Republic of China (1972-73); Founder, Free School, el-Jedida. **Awards:** Moroccan and Yugoslav decorations. **Publ.:** Biography of Mohammed V (1962); The Gold of Sons (novel); political commentaries and social and historical studies. **Addr.:** Rabat, Morocco.

ZIADE (Nicolas, Abdo), Academic. **Born** on 2 December 1907 in Damascus, Syria. **Son** of Abdo Ziadé **and** Mrs., née Hélène Assaad. **Married** to Miss Marguerite Shahwan, 2 children: Riad and Bassem. **Educ.:** Men's training College (1921-24), Research student at the School of Oriental and African Studies (London University) (1947-48). **Dipl.:** Teacher's diploma (The Arab College, 1924), Teacher's Higher Certificate Examination (Palestine Government, 1931), B.A. with honours in the classical history of London University (University College, 1939), Ph.D. London University (1950) (thesis 1200-1400 A.D. Urban Life in Syria). **Career:** teacher in Saint John Acre secondary schools (Palestine 1925-35), lecturer at Arab Government College (Jerusalem 1939-47), lecturer Middle East Arabic Studies Centre (Jerusalem 1944-45), lecturer Faculty of Oriental Languages (Cambridge University 1948-49), assistant director of studies (Cyrenaica 1949), Professor of Arab Modern History at the American University of Beirut since 1949, Visiting Professor at Harvard University (1957, 1962, 1963), chairman Committee of University Publications (1961-62, 1963-65), president History and Archaeology Department at AUB since 1965, secretary general Social Sciences Research Council for the Mediterranean Zone. **Publ.:** author of 20 works in Arabic including: "Mediaeval travellers of the Arab World" (Cairo, 1943), "Nationalism and Arabism" (Jerusalem, 1945), revised editions "Arabism in the Balance of Nationalism", Beirut (1950), "The Rise of Arabs to Power" (Jerusalem 1945), "al-Hisba wal Nuhtasib fil Islam" (Beirut 1963), "Arab Cities" (Beirut 1965), and 7 books in English including "Urban Life in Syria under the Early Mamluks" (Beirut 1953), "Syria and Lebanon" (New York, 1957), "Sanusiyah" (Holland 1958), "Damascus under the Mamluks", (Norman, 1964), as well as a number of studies and articles in Arabic and English. **Priv. Addr.:** Mme Curie Street/Koreitem, face Hariri Palace, Dar al Khadra Bldg., 9th Floor, Tel.: 807557, 03-382169, Beirut, Lebanon.

ZIADEH (Farhat, J.), Arab-American professor and lawyer. **Born** on April 8, 1917, in Ramallah, Palestine. **Son** of Jacob (Ya'qub) Ziadeh (businessman) **and** Mrs. Nimeh née Farah. **Married** on 24 July 1949 to Suad Salem in Jacksonsville, Florida, five daughters: Shireen, Suzan, Rhonda, Deena and Reema. **Educ.:** American University of Beirut; University of London. **Dipl.:** B.A., LL.B., Barrister-at-Law. **Career:** Magistrate, Government of Palestine (1947-48); Lecturer, Princeton University (1948-54); Assistant Professor of Arabic & Islamics, Princeton University (1954-58); Associate Professor of Arabic and Islamics, Princeton University (1958-66); Professor of Arabic and Islamics, University of Washington (1966-87); Adjunct Professor of Law (1978-87); Professor Emeritus (since 1987); Chairman, Department of Near Eastern Languages and Civilization (1970-82); Chairman of Near East Interdisciplinary Program (1966-82); Director, Center for Arabic Study Abroad (1983-89). **Author of:** Reader in Modern Literary Arabic, Princeton and Oxford Universities Presses (1964); University of Washington Press (1984); Lawyers, the Rule of Law and Liberalism in Modern Egypt; Hoover Institution, Stanford University (1968); Property Law in the Arab World, Graham and Trotman, London (1979); Editor, al-Khassaf's Adab al-Qadi, American University in Cairo Press (1979). **Member:** Middle East Studies Association (President 1980); American Research Center in Egypt; Advisory Editor; Editorial Boards of Arab Law Quarterly, London, and Islamic Law and Society, Leiden. **Prof. Addr.:** Dept. of Near Eastern Languages and Civilization University of Washington, Box 353120; Seattle, Tel.(206) 543-4959, Washinton 98195, U.S.A. **Priv. Addr.:** 3919 48th Ave. N.E. Seattle, Tel. (206) 523-2093 Washington 98105, USA.

ZIDI (Makki), Tunisian engineer. **Born** in 1929 in Thala, Tunis. **Married**, 4 children. **Educ.:** Ecole Polytechnique, Paris, France; Ecole des Mines. **Dipl.:** graduated as a Metallurgical and Mining Engineer. **Career:** Steel Work, al-Fouladh, Bizerta, Tunisia; President of Steel Works and Director of Mines (1967-70); Secretary of State, Ministry of National Economy (1970-75); President, Office National des Mines, Tunis (1975-84). **Addr.:** Tunis, Tunisia.

ZIMAITY (Muhammad, Abdul Maguid), Egyptian aviation official. **Born** in 1922. **Married**, 1 son. **Educ.:** Associate Fellow, Royal Aeronautical Society, London; Council of Engineering Institutions, London. **Dipl.:** B.Sc. in Aero-Engineering, Chartered Engineer. **Career:** Egyptian Airforce (1948-56); General Manager of Societe

Aeronavale Mediterraneenne SAM, Cairo Airport (1956-57); Adviser, Vocational Training Centre (1958-60); General Manager, Procurement and Supply, United Arab Airlines (1961-69); Technical Director General, United Arab Airlines (1970); Director General, of General Organization for International Exhibitions and Fairs (1973-75); Vice President of Egypt Air, Corporate Planning (1975-80); Adviser to the Chairman, Egypt Air; Member of the Scientific Rresearch Academy and the Transport Research Council; Reporter for different scientific and technical semiras, workshops, symposia; External Examiner, Faculty of Commerce, Ain Shams and Cairo Universities, for M.Sc. in Business Administration and Air Transport Economics. **Publ.:** Editor and Compiler of "Dictionary of Technical Terms" (1962), reprinted several times (in English and Arabic); Compiler and editor of "Technical Directory, Aeronautical Engineering" (1976), published by Leipzig, as well as articles in the "Engineering Magazine" on aviation science and technology. **Decor.:** Order of Liberation, Order of Merit (1st Class) (1980). **Hobbies:** music, writing, reading, editing, translation, techno-economics and feasibility studies, science and technology, literature and organising seminars. **Addr.:** 41 Nakhla Metei Street, Heliopolis, Egypt.

ZINE (Abdallah, Yahia), Yemeni official. **Born** in 1943 in Sanaa, Yemen. **Married**, 2 children. **Educ.:** Université d'Alger, Algeria; Sorbonne, University of Paris, France. **Dipl.:** Diploma, Licence and Doctorate en Sciences de l'Information. **Career:** Director General of Yemen News Agency; Assistant to the General Secretary of the National Assembly; Director General of Yemen Radio and Television Office; Director of Information and Culture at the Presidency. **Publ.:** "Le Yemen et ses Moyens d'information, Etude Historique, Politique, Juridique, Sociale et Critique 1982-1974" (1978) published by SNED. **Hobbies:** tennis, table tennis, swimming. **Addr.:** Sanaa, Yemen.

ZINTANI (Abdulwahab, Mohamad, al), Libyan diplomat, engineer. **Born** in 1936 in Zintan, Libya. **Son** of Mohamad al-Zintani. **Married**, seven children. **Educ.:** B.Sc. in Electrical Sciences; Diploma in Engineering; Diploma in Wireless Engineering. **Career:** Officer and Teacher of Wireless Engineering and Electricity (1959-69); Chief of Benghazi Municipality (1971); Mayor of Benghazi (1973); Ambassador to Cyprus, Lebanon, USSR, Finland, Sweden. **Publ.:** Articles in al-Hagiga and al-Amal newspapers (1970); "Radio and Television Engineering"; "The Slide Rule"; "The Revolution of jungles"; "Document of the Unity"; "The Middle East War"; "The Fairytale of the Iran Curtain". **Sports:** Football, tennis, swimming, horeseriding. **Hobby:** Scientific writing. **Addr.:** Tripoli, Libya.

ZNINED (Abdeslam), Moroccan politician. **Born** on December 15, 1934 at Wizzan. **Educ.:** Faculty of Letters (Bordeaux) (1958) and the Sorbonne, Paris; Institut des Hautes-Etudes Internationales, Geneva (1961-62). **Dipl.:** Licence ès-Lettres. **Career:** Ministry of Foreign Affairs: Head of Personnel (1959-60); Economic Division (1960-61); African Division (1963); attached to Prime Minister's Cabinet (1964); Chef de Cabinet (Sept. 1964); Director of Cabinet, Minister of Agriculture and Agrarian Reform; Secretary-General, Ministry of Information (1967-72); Director of General Affairs, Prime Minister's Office (Nov. 1972); Secretary of State, Prime Minister's Office for General Affairs (April 1974); concurrently for Saharan Affairs (Dec. 1974); re-appointed (October 1977); Appointed on March 14, 1998 Minister-Delegate in charge of Maghreb, Arab and Islamic Affairs. **Addr.:** Rabat, Morocco.

ZOGHBI (Elie, H.E. Mgr.), Egyptian archbishop. **Born** in Cairo. **Educ.:** Primary at Patriarchal College (Cairo), Secondary and Theology at St. Anne Seminary of Jerusalem (1927-35). **Career:** Ordained to the Priesthood (1936), Professor at St. Anne Junior Seminary (1937-41), Parish Priest in Egypt (1941-49), in Alexandria (1949-51), Archimandrite (1951), Sacred Bishop Titular and Patriarchal Vicar-General for Egypt and the Sudan (1954-68), Archbishop of Baalbeck Diocese since September 1968. **Publ.:** Founder of "The Sap", Review, "God's Gift", "Gibrane Khalil Gibrane" (Harissa 1959). **Resid.:** P.O.Box 50076, Beirut, Lebanon.

ZOUAYEN (Yusuf), Syrian physician and former statesman. **Born** in 1931 in Abou Kamal (Euphrates District). **Educ.:** Damascus Faculty of Medicine. **Dipl.:** Doctor of Medicine. **Career:** Physician; Minister of Agrarian Reform in the Cabinet of General Amine al-Hafez (November 12, 1963); Member of the Presidential Council (October 3, 1964- September 2, 1965); Member of the Regional Directorate of the Baath Party; President of the Ministers Council of the Syrian Arab Republic (4 times) (1964-69). **Addr.:** Damascus, Syria.

ZOUBI (Farouk, Nasser, al), Jordanian businessman. **Born** in 1937 in Alramtha, Jordan. **Married**, 3 children. **Educ.:** Cairo University, Egypt. Pittsburgh University USA. **Dipl.:** London School of Economics, England. **Career:** Secretary, Ministry of Defence (1962-66); Deputy Director General of Jordan Radio (1966-73); Administrative Director of Youth Organisation (1968-69); Administrative Director of "el-Rai'" daily newspaper (1969-70); Assistant Director of Jordan Television (1973-75); Deputy Director General (1981-83); Member of the Board of Al-Jeser Co. and Friends of Children Club; Member of the Royal Society of Nature Conservation; Director General of "al-Shaab" daily newspaper (1985-); Vice-Chairman Director General Media Consultants. The International Herald Tribune Representative in Jordan. **Hobbies:** gardening, swimming, Cooking. **Addr.:** P.O.Box 811738, Code 11181 Jabal Amman 3rd Circle, Insurance Building 4th floor, Amman, Jordan.

ZOUHEIRI (Bachir), Syrian executive. **Born** in 1927 in Damascus, Syria. **Son** of Ali Zouheiri. **Married** in 1955, 4 sons, 1 daughter. **Educ.:** University of Cairo; **Dipl.:** Diploma in Commercial Finance (1953). **Career:** Controller, Arab Bank; Controller and Deputy Manager, Rafidain Bank; (1945-52); Manager, Office des Changes, Damascus, Syria (1952-54); Chief, Commissariat du Gouvernment Aupres des Banques, Damascus (1955-56); Manager and Inspector, Central Bank of Syria (1957-60); General Manager and Board Member, Arab World Bank, Syria (1960-66); Technical Adviser, Central Bank of Jordan (1968-69); Technical Adviser, Ministry of Finance, Algeria (1969-71); Chairman and General Manager, Commercial Bank of Syria (1971); General Manager, European Arab Bank, Belgium (1978). Board Advisor, Arab Bankers' Association, London; Vice-Chairman, The Arab-Belgian Luxembourgeoise Chamber of Commerce, Brussels. **Member:** Union of Chartered Accountants, Damascus; International Bankers Association, Washington, USA. **Hobbies:** Billiards and Chess. **Addr.:** 107 Cheapside, Tel.: 016066099, Telex: 8956287 A/B EURAB UK, London EC2V 6DT, UK.

ZOUMAN (Saleh Mohamad), Saudi businessman. **Born** in 1936 at Buraidah, Saudi Arabia. **Career:** Businessman: general trade, travel and tourism, airlines agents; Owner Dar al-Atfal Exhibition. **Hobbies:** sports, travel. **Address:** P.O.Box 1514, Tel.: 6533770 (Office), and 6604441 (Home), Jeddah, Saudi Arabia.

ZUBAIR (Mohamad), Omani businessman. **Born** in 1939 in Husn, Oman. **Married**, 7 children. **Dipl.:** Degree in Public Administration. **Career:** worked with petroleum Development in Oman; established Muscat Trading Company in 1967 Chairman Oman International Development & Investment and Zubair Enterprises with many subsidiary companies (1974-). **Prof. Addr.:** Zubair Enterprises, P.O.Box 4127, Ruwi, Muscat, Oman.

ZUBAIR (Mohamad, Omar), Saudi educator. **Born** on 1 September 1936. **Dipl.:** M.A., Ph.D. (Economics), 1971. **Career:** Dean of the Faculty of Economics and Public Administration, King Abdulaziz University and Head of the Economics Department; Vice Rector, King Abdulaziz University; Ex-Rector, King Abdulaziz University; Head of the Economics Department, Ministry of Finance; Chairman of King Abdulaziz University Council; member of Supreme Council of Saudi Universities; attended UN Conference of Trade and Development, Islamic Conference, London, 1975, International Conference of Islamic Economics, Makkah, 1976 (sponsored by King Abdulaziz University). **Publications:** several research papers on Islamic economics. **Hobbies:** travel, reading. **Address:** Tel.: 6433708 (Home), Jeddah, Saudi Arabia.

ZUBEAR (Mohamed Kheir, Ahmed, Al, Dr.), Sudanese, Minister of Finance and National, Economy. **Born** in 1945 at Shambat, Sudan. **Son** of Ahmed Al Zubear (Farmer) **and** Mrs. née Amna Abdul Mageed. **Married** in 1976 in Shambat to Afaf Al Zubear, 5 children: Sara (1980), Muhtadi (1983), Amna (1986), Ala (1988), Ahmed (1995). **Educ.:** Khartoum Secondary School (1964); Faculty of Economy, University of Khartoum (BSc. Economics, 1968), University of Wales U.K. (MSc. Economics, 1976), University of Wales U.K. (Ph.D. Economics, 1983). **Career:** 1968-78 - Economist Ministry of Finance; 1978-89 - Director Foreign Aid Administration, Ministry of Planning; 1989-92 - Undersecretary for Planning, Ministry of Finance & Economic Planning; 1992-96 - Minister of State, Ministry of Finance; 1996-97 - Chairman & Managing Director, Sudan Development Corporation; 1997-1999 - Minister of State for Finance; Jan. 2000 - to date Minister of Finance and National Economy. **Sports Practised:** Soccer. **Clubs.:** Shambat Sports Club. **Prof. Addr.:** Ministry of Finance & National Economy, P.O.Box 298 Khartoum, Tel.: 777563, Telex 776081, Khartoum, Sudan. **Priv. Addr.:** Shambat, Khartoum North, Tel.: Home 313464, Sudan.

ZU'BI (Hatim, Sharif), Jordanian banker, lawyer, statesman. **Born** in 1927 in Nazareth, Palestine. **Son** of Sharif Zu'bi. **Married**, four sons. **Educ.:** LL.B. (Hons), University College, University of London, England (1949); Barrister at Law, Lincoln's Inn (1950). **Career:** Legal Adviser, Ministry of Finance, Saudi Arabia (1950-54); Visiting Law Lecturer, American University of Beirut, Lebanon (1954); Manager, Banque du Caire, Amman, Jordan (1956-60); Director: Jordan Hotels and Tourism Company (1956-65); Jordan Phosphate Mines Co. S.A.; Director and Deputy General Manager, Cairo Amman Bank, Amman, Jordan (1960-65); Jordan's Minister of National Economy (1965-69); and in addition at times: Acting Minister of Foreign Affairs; Minister of Communications; Acting Minister of Finance, Minister of State for Cabinet Affairs; Chairman of Jordan Electricity Authority; Chairman of Agricultural Marketing Board; Governor for Jordan at the World Bank; Member of Arab Economic Council, Arab League; Director and Deputy Manager of Cairo Amman Bank, Amman (1970-71); from 1971 Legal Consultant and Attorney, International Legal Practice, Amman, Bahrain (1983 Al Mahmood & Zu'bi), Abu Dhabi, Dubai, Sharjah and Doha, Eastem Province, Saudi Arabia; Fellow of the Chartered Institute of Arbitrators, London; Member of the Bar Association; Middle East Chair, Committee 'O' Litrigation of the International Bar Association; Member of the International Court of Commercial Arbitration at the International Chamber of Commerce, Paris. **Decorations:** Order of the Jordanian Star, 1st Class; Order of the Tunisian Republic, 1st Class; Order of the National Order of the Cedar, 1st Class, Lebanon; Hon. GBE Knight Grand Cross of the Most Excellent Order of the British Empire; Grand Ufficial nell Ordinario al Merito della Republica Italiana. **Hobbies:** Shooting, fishing, stamp collection. **Sports:** Horse-riding, swimming, tennis, **Addr.:**

Hatim S. Zu'bi, P.O.Box 502, Manama, Bahrain. Tel.: 0973 225151, Fax: 0973 224744 E.mail: almazubi@batelco.com.bh.

ZUBI (Yusif, Mohamad), Jordanian aviation official. **Born** in 1946 in Salt, Jordan. **Married. Educ.:** Damascus University, Syria; McGill University, Montreal, Canada. **Dipl.:** LL.B., LL.M., Diploma in Air Space Laws. **Career:** Chief of International Affairs, Jordan Civil Aviation (1971-73); Chief of Bilateral Agreements, Jordan Civil Aviation (1973-75); Chief of Air Transport, Jordan Civil Aviation (1975-78); Deputy Director of Air Transport, Jordan Civil Aviation (1978-81); Member of Air and Space Association, McGill University, Montreal; Director of Air Transport, Arab Civil Aviation Council (ACAC), Rabat, Morocco (1981-82). **Hobbies:** reading, travelling. **Addr.:** Aman, Jordan.

ZUHAIR (Assaad, al), Saudi diplomat. **Born** in 1932. **Educ.:** military Flying School, Taif; Hamble, UK. **Dipl.:** A and B Licences with Air Service Training followed by RAF training. **Career:** Director of the Royal Saudi Air Force; Air Attache, Embassy to USA; Armed Forces Attache, Embassy to Pakistan (1966-71); Commander of the Royal Saudi Air Force (1972); Lieutenant General (1974); Ambassador, Ministry of Foreign Affairs (1979); Ambassador to the Republic of China in Taiwan (1980). **Decor.:** Order of King Abdul-Aziz (3rd Class), Order of Resplendent Banner with Plaque, Republic of China, Order of National Security Merit (Tong II Medal) Republic of Korea, Order of the Cedar Degree of Commander), Lebanon, Legion of Merit (Degree of Commander) USA, Orden de Mayo al-Mérito Naval Gran Official Class, Argentina. **Medal:** Medal of the Hawk for Flying (1st Class), Medal of the Holy Mosque. **Hobbies:** reading, swimming, tennis. **Prof. Addr.:** Ministry of Foreign Affairs, Jeddah, Saudi Arabia.

ZUHAIR (Harb, Salih, al), Saudi engineer, businessman. **Born** in 1938 in Zubair, Iraq. **Son** of Salih al-Zubair. **Married**, three children. **Educ.:** Civil Engineering, Portsmouth College of Technology, Portsmouth, UK (1961); Diploma of Technology. **Career:** Civil Engineer, Ministry of Communications, Saudi Arabia (1961-68); Chief of Maintenance and Rural Road Department; Deputy Chief Engineer of the Roads Department; Director of Planning, Ministry of Communicaations for Posts Telephones Telegraphs, Roads and Ports; resigned from Ministry of Communications (1968); Managing Director of family company SADCO (1968); Chairman, Electronic Equipment Marketing Co., Modern Arab Contractors, Saudi Arabia, Trust Investment and Development Est. Holding Co., Riyadh, Saudi Arabia; Partner and Director, Societe Bancaire Arabe, Paris, France. **Sports:** Swimming, tennis, sailing. **Hobbies:** Reading, music, hunting. **Addr.:** P.O.B. 3750, Riyadh 21481, Saudi Arabia.

ZUHAIR (Latifa), Tunisian broadcasting official. **Born** in 1933. **Married**, 2 children. **Dipl.:** Degree in Modern Literature, M.A. in Literature. **Career:** two years of journalism; broadcaster on Tunisian Radio; Director of International Programmes on Radio-Télévision-Tunisienne (1970); Member of the Higher Information Council. **Publ.:** "La Littérature maghrebine d'expression française" essay in French; broadcast literary criticism. **Decor.:** Order of the Tunisian Republic (1974). **Hobbies:** music, reading, swimming, tennis. **Addr.:** 53 Rue du 1er Juin, Tunis, Tunisia.

ZURAYQ (Constantin, Qaysar), Syrian former rector of university, dean of faculty, writer. **Born** on April 18, 1909 in Damascus. **Son** of Qaysar Zurayq. **Married** to Miss Najla Qortas, 4 children: Ilham, Houda, Afaf and Hanan. **Educ.:** American University of Beirut, Universities of Chicago and Princeton. **Dipl.:** Bachelor of Arts (1928), Master of Arts (1929), Doctor of Philosophy (1930). **Career:** Assistant Professor of History at the American University of Beirut (1930-42); Associate Professor (1942-45); Counsellor at the Syrian Legation in Washington (1945-46); Minister Plenipotentiary of Syria to the United States of America (1946-47); Syrian Delegate to the General Assembly of the United Nations (1947); Vice-President and Professor of History at the American University of Beirut (1947-49); Rector of the Syrian University of Damascus (1949-52); Vice-President at the American University of Beirut (1952-54); Acting President (1954-57); Full Professor at the said University since 1956. **Publ.:** Author of several publications, including "al-Wa'y al-Qawmi", "Ma'nal Nakba", "Ayyu Ghaden", "Nahnu wal Tarikh", "al-Yaxidiyah Qadiman wa Hadithan", "Ibn al-Furat". **Awards:** Commander, Order of Cedar (Lebanon); Medal, Order of Cedar (Lebanon), Medal Order of Merit (Syria); Medal of Education (Lebanon). **Member:** of the Arabic Academies of Damascus and Baghdad, president of the "Association des Amis du Livre" (Lebanon); President of the "International Association of Universities"; member of the Alumni Club. **Prof. Addr.:** American University of Beirut, Bliss Street, Tel.: 340460, Beirut. **Priv. Addr.:** Makdissi Street, Dr. Yenikomuchian Bldg., Tel.: 343174 Beirut, Lebanon.

ZURAYK (Huda, C.), Academic. **Born** on 7 November, 1943 in Beirut. **Daughter** of Constantin Zurayk (Professor of History) **and** Mrs. née Najla Cortas. **Educ.:** Ahliah Girls School, Beirut; American University of Beirut (1961-65); Harvard University (1965-66); Johns Hopkins University (1971-74). **Dipl.:** B.A. in Statistics (1965), M.A. in Statistics (1966), Ph.D. in Biostatistics (1974). **Career.:** Assistant Statistician, Statistical Office, United Nations Secretariate, New York (June 1966- March 1967); Computer Programmer, Computer Center, United Nations Relief and Works Agency, Beirut (March 1968 - Dec. 1968); Instructor (part-time), Department of Mathematics, American University of Beirut (Oct. 1968 - June 1969); Senior Reserach Assistant (part-time) Department of Maternal and Child

Health, A.U.B. (Jan. 1969 - June 1969); Instruct Department of Epidemiology and Biostatistics, A.U.B. (July 1969 - June 1971), Assistant Professor, Department of Epidemiology and Biostatistics, A.U.B (July 1974 - June 1979); Associate Professor, (July 1979 - June 1985); Professor and Chairman, Department of Epidemiology and Biostatistics, A.U.B (July 1985 - August 1987); Acting Dean, Faculty of Health Sciences, A.U.B (August 1986- August 1987); Senior Representative Designate, Population Council Regional Office, for West Asia and North Africa in Cairo (September 1987 - February 1988); Senior Representative, Population Council Regional Office for West Asia and North Africa in Cairo (1 March 1988 - to December 1990); Senior Associate, Population Council Regional Office for West Asia and North Africa in Cairo (January 1991- July 1998); Dean, Faculty of Health Sciences, American University of Beirut (September 1999- to present). **Sports:** Tennis, swimming, skiing. **Hobbies:** reading, sports. **Credit Card:** American Express. **Prof. Addr.:** c/o Faculty of Health Sciences, American University of Beirut, Beirut, Lebanon; P.O.Box 115 Dokki, Cairo, Egypt.

ZWAI (Mohamad, Abdul Qassem), Libyan Politician. **Career:** Under-Secretary, Ministry of Information and Culture; Minister of State without Portfolio (November 1974-77); Secretary for Information and General People's Committee (March 1977-80); Secretary for Justice (1981-82). **Addr.:** Tripoli, Libya.

PART II
WHO'S WHO
of companies and institutions

UNITED ARAB EMIRATES
GENERAL POSTAL AUTHORITY

دولة الامارات العربية المتحدة
الهيئة العامة للبريد

* MUMTAZ POST Service — خدمة البريد الممتاز
* Pick-Up and Delivery Service — خدمة التسليم و الاستلام
* Postage Paid Service — خدمة خالص الأجرة
* Postal Agencies Service — خدمة الوكالات البريدية
* Postal Parcel Service — خد مة الطرود البريدية
* Private Bags Service — خدمة الأكياس البريدية المغلقة

العالم بين يديك

ص.ب ٨٨٨٨ دبي-الامارات العربية المتحدة , تلفون ٢٦٢٢٢٢٢-٠٤ , فاكس ٢٦٦٢٩٢٩-٠٤
P. O. Box 8888, Dubai - UAE, Tel. : 04 - 2622222, Fax : 04 - 2662929

SHOPPING FROM A TO Z

ABC is Lebanon's largest department store, having consistently maintained its leadership position throughout the years. It offers men, women, and children with different interests a wide choice of products varying from clothes, to accessories, shoes, jewellery, cosmetics and household appliances.

The flagship ABC store is located in Dbayeh, just 10 km north of Beirut. It spans an area of 20,000m2 -including a parking lot for 1000 cars- all dedicated to the shopping pleasure of young and old alike. With a staff of over 785, ABC has also opened its doors in Hamra, Furn el Chebbak, Kaslik, Tripoli, Zahlé, Taanayel.

HISTORY

ABC was established in 1936 by a group of students and professors at the American University of Beirut. Today, commemorating over six decades of customer satisfaction, ABC has become a public share holding company. The majority of shares belong to Maurice Fadel, the Chairman and General Manager.

ABC GETS A MAKEOVER

Any recent visitor to ABC will tell you of the great new changes taking place in Lebanon's favourite department store. Several departments have been completely renovated to offer shoppers a more enjoyable shopping experience. In addition, the Blue Card, ABC's own credit card helps to make shopping here even easier.

MEET OUR SHOPPERS

ABC clients generally identify with the upper and middle socio-economic groups. ABC has also become an important stop for tourists, the expatriate community and other non-Lebanese patrons.

THE QUEST FOR EXCELLENCE

ABC is constantly working to improve its internal environment. That is why it has taken steps to update its administrative department and initiate intensive training programs for newly recruited personnel. Training programs include basic familiarity with the company, its principles, its values, and above all its commitment to customer service.

Department Store

Tel.: 01 416000 402376

The origin of our insurance organization dates back to the early days of the century. At that time, the late Mr. M. Hanemoglou, founder of Ets. M. Hanemoglou, started his relations with l'UNION, Compagnie d'Assurances, a french insurance company. These firms developed each in its territory and time passing by, they became UAP-UNION DES ASSURANCES DE PARIS and SOCIETE MARCEL HANEMOGLOU & CIE (NASNAS & HANEMOGLOU) the latter being the General Agent and Legal Representative of UAP.

In 1974, and jointly with UAP, the Group NASNAS & HANEMOGLOU established a local insurance company under the name of SLF - SOCIETE LIBANO-FRANÇAISE D'ASSURANCES ET DE REASSURANCES SAL. Then, in March 1992, the Group took full control of SLF which became totally owned by Mr. Roger Nasnas (Chairman & CEO), Mr. Maurice Hanemoglou (Deputy Chairman & Deputy CEO) and Mr. Elie Nasnas (Director and Deputy CEO). SLF with a paid up capital of LBP 6,000,000,000 (approx US.$ 4,000,000) consolidated its activities in securing prudent and steady growth maintaining a leadership position in its field. Further, and through its two affiliated companies MEDNET Liban sal and CLPC sal (Compagnie Libanaise pour la Protection du Credit), SLF developed in Medical Covers and TPA and Credit Insurance.

From July 98 onwards and as a result of the restructuration that took place all over the world following the merge on a global level in Nov. 96 between UAP and AXA described as the merge of the century, the portfolio of UAP was transfered to SLF who has been nominated as the AXA Group Correspondent in Lebanon. In its time, a special communiqué was published in the local newspapers.

Uninterruptedly present in the market, even during the worst days of the war, owned and managed by the third generation of the founders, the organization operates directly through its offices in Beirut, Jal El Dib, Tripoli, Saïda, Chtaura and Zahleh. It is ran by a team of 100 experienced professionals, managing a porfolio of 25000 policies generating over U.S. $ 20 mios premium income, having developed a large and diversified network of old-established clientele, enjoying privileged connections and relations locally and internationally in all fields of business activities and writing all classes of business such as Engineering Risks, Special Risks, Consequential Loss, Marine, Fire, Liabilities, Life, Hospitalization, Motor, Workers Compensation, as well as Travel Assistance with AXA Assistance.

Recently, in july 1999, AXA and SLF signed a partnership contract whereby AXA acquired 51% of SLF's capital and the Nasnas Hanemoglou Group the remaining 49%, to better promote and develop their insurance and reinsurance activities in Lebanon and the region. Then, in May 2000 this new entity took the name of AXA MIDDLE EAST S.A.L. whose chairmanship was entrusted to Mr. Roger Nasnas. This even was widely relayed in its time in the local media.

Here are some key figures of the AXA Group:

- US. $ 72 billion in premium income
- US. $ 789 billion in assets under management
- 140 000 men and women in over 60 countries
- 40 million assured.

AXA MIDDLE EAST S.A.L.

Société Anonyme au Capital de LBP 6.000.000 entièrement versé - RCB 34145

ADRESSE COURRIER: B.P. 11-550 Beyrouth, Liban - E-Mail: axa-middleeast@inco.com.lb

ADRESSE VISITEURS: Jal El Dib: Autoroute, Imm Zard Zard, Tél: (+ 961.4) 716333/716444/716555, Fax (+ 961. 4) 716562

Beyrouth: Rue Maamari (wardieh). Imm SOLICLEM. Tél: (+ 961.1) 373630/31/32. Fax (+ 961.1) 361431

Tripoli: Rue Maarad, Centre Tripoli. Tél: (961.6) 430465/442340. Fax: (+ 961.6) 442341 Saïda: Rue Hussam Hariri, Golden Tower. Tél et Fax: (+ 961.7) 734655/6

Jdita: Route Nationale Chtaura, Centre Bassel. Tél: (+ 961.8) 540532/541147. Fax: (+ 961.8) 541147 - Zahleh: Centre Fakhoury. Tél: (+ 961.8) 800339/805190, Fax: (+ 961.8) 805190

Inscrite au Registre des Sociétés d'Assurances au Liban en date du 13/6/1975 sous le N° 156 et soumise aux dispositions de la loi Libanaise, Décret N° 9812 du 4/5/1968

INTERNATIONAL

MECICO (MIDDLE EAST COMMERCIAL INFORMATION CENTER), was established in 1967 in Beirut, Lebanon, as the first Credit Information Agency in Lebanon and in the Middle East. It does also Debt Collections. It has an affiliated Company under the name of MECICO-KUWAIT in Kuwait-City and another one under the name of MECICO-MAROC in Casablanca, Morocco. Slowly and surely, during 30 years, it expanded to many other countries and it is now covering all the countries of the world, listed as follows:

Countries covered by our Debt Collection and Credit Reporting Services

A
Afghanistan
Albania
Algeria
American Samoa
Andorra
Angola
Anguilla
Antarctica
Antigua and Barbados
Argentina
Armenia
Aruba
Australia
Austria
Azerbaidjan

B
Bahamas
Bahrain
Bangladesh
Barbados
Belarus
Belgium
Belize
Benin
Bermuda
Bhutan
Bolivia
Bosnia
Botswana
Bouvet Island
Brazil
British Indian Ocean Territory
Brunei
Bulgaria
Burkina Faso
Burma
Burundi
Byelorussian Republic

C
Cambodia
Cameroon
Canada
Cape Verde
Cayman Islands
Central African Republic
Chad
Chile
China
Christmas Island
Cocos (Keeling) Islands
Colombia
Comoros
Congo
Cook Islands
Costa Rica
Côte D'Ivoire
Croatia
Cuba
Cyprus
Czech Republic

D
Denmark
Djibouti
Dominica
Dominican Republic

E
East Timor
Ecuador
Egypt
El Salvador
England
Equatorial Guinea
Estonia
Ethiopia

F
Faeroe Islands
Falkland Islands (Malvinas)
Fiji
Finland
France
French Guyana
French Polynesia
French Southern Territories

G
Gabon
Gambia
Georgia
Germany
Ghana
Gibraltar
Great Britain
Greece
Greenland
Grenada
Guadeloupe
Guam
Guatemala
Guinea
Guinea-Bissau
Guyana

H
Haiti
Heard and McDonnell Islands
Honduras
Hong Kong
Hungary

I
Iceland
India
Indonesia
Iran
Iraq
Ireland
Italy
Ivory Coast

J
Jamaica
Japan
Jordan

K
Kampuchea
Kazakhstan
Kenya
Kiribati
Korea, Democratic People's Rep.
Korea, Republic of
Kroatia
Kuwait
Kyrgyzstan

L
Laos
Latvia
Lebanon
Lesotho
Liberia
Libya
Liechtenstein
Lithuania
Luxembourg

M
Macao
Macedonia
Madagascar
Malawi
Malaysia
Maldives
Mali
Malta
Mariana Islands
Marshall Islands
Martinique
Mauritania
Mauritius
Mexico
Micronesia
Moldova
Monaco
Mongolia
Montenegro
Montserrat
Morocco
Mozambique
Myanmar

N
Namibia
Nauru
Nepal
Netherlands
Netherlands Antilles
Neutral Zone (Between Saudi Arabia and Iraq)
New Caledonia
New Zealand
Nicaragua
Niger
Nigeria
Nlue
Norfolk Island
Northern Mariana Islands
Norway

O
Oman

P
Pakistan
Palo
Panama
Papua New Guinea
Paraguay
Peru
Philippines
Pitcalm
Poland
Portugal
Puerto Rico

Q
Qatar

R
Reunion
Romania
Rwanda
Russia

S
St. Helena
St. Kitts-Nevis
St. Lucia
St. Pierre et Miquelon
St. Vincent and the Grenadines
Samoa
San Marino
Sao Tome and Principe
Saudi Arabia
Senegal
Serbia
Seychelles
Sierra Leone
Singapore
Slovekia
Slovenia
Solomon Islands
Somalia
South Africa
Spain
Sri Lanka
Sudan
Suriname
Svalbard and Jan Mayan Islands
Swaziland
Sweden
Switzerland
Syria

T
Taiwan
Tajikistan
Tanzania
Thailand
Togo
Takelau
Tonga
Trinidad and Tobago
Tunisia
Turkey
Turkmenistan
Turks and Calcos Islands
Tuvalu

U
Uganda
Ukrania
United Arab Emirates
United Kingdom
United States of America (USA)
U.S. Minor Outlying Islands
Uruguay
Uzbekistan

V
Vanuatu
Vatican
Venezuela
Vietnam
Virgin Islands, British
Virgin Islands, U.S.

W
Wallis and Futuna Islands
Westem Sahara

Y
Yemen
Yugoslavia

Z
Zaire
Zambia
Zimbabwe

Remarks: -For Countries not listed, please refer to our international Division.
-We reserve the right to withdraw our service in any country, if we deem it necessary, without any prior notice.

MECICO International. Gedeon House 139-141 John Kennedy Street, Jisr el-Bacha. P.O.Box 166142. Beirut-LEBANON. Tel.: 01-495401/2/3. Fax: 01-493330. E-Mail: mecico@dm.net.lb

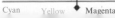

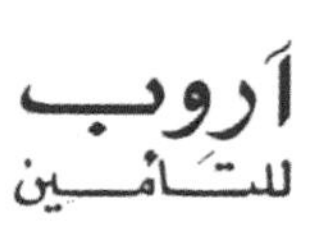

AROPE
INSURANCE

OUR PROFILE

Establishment

Founded in 1974 by Banque du Liban et d'Outre-Mer S.A.L., the largest bank in Lebanon, and SCOR reassurance, the first French Reinsurer, Arope Insurance has maintained constant growth and financial stability since the very beginning. In 1999 Arope was among the first insurance companies in Lebanon to fully comply with all the requirements of the Ministry of Economy concerning the new insurance law legislation.

Major Shareholders

Banque du Liban et d'Outre-Mer s.a.l.	29.77%
SCOR Reassurance (FRANCE)	9.67%
BLOM Shareholders	60.23%
Others	0.33%

General Management

Mr. Samer AZHARI	Chairman & General Manager
Mr. Fateh BEKDACHE	General Manager
Ms. Faten DOUGLAS	Senior Manager

Board of Directors

Mr. Samer AZHARI	Chairman
Mr. Serge OSOUF	Vice Chairman
SCOR Re. (FRANCE)	represented by Mr. Patrick LOISY
Mr. Rami HOURIE	
Mr. Rami GHANDOUR	
Mr. François NEGRIER	
Mr. Habib RAHAL	
Mr. Marwan JAROUDI	

Main Reinsurers

	Rating
• SCOR RE	AA-
• MUNICH RE	AAA
• HANNOVER RE	AA+
• ERC FRANKONA	AAA
• ARAB RE	BBpi

source: Standard &Poor's

Auditors

SEMAAN, GHOLAM & Co.

OUR ADDRESSES

Head Office

- Verdun - Sanayeh Crossing - Monte Marina Center
- P.O.Box: 113-5686 Beirut - Lebanon
- Tel: (961)1 747444 (24hrs)
- Fax: (961) 1 344012
- E-mail: arope@arope.com
- Domain: www.arope.com

Branches

Dora
Main Road - Cebaco Center - Bloc B
- Tel: (961)1 251378/9

Saida
Riad Solh Street - Fakhoury Bldg.
- Tel: (961) 7 725303

Tripoli
Al Tall Street - Byssar Bldg.
- Tel.: (961) 6 446877

MAJOR ACHIEVEMENTS

- www.arope.com:

Due to a growing demand from customers for quick access to services and information, and with the **worldwide technological development** in the business world towards e-commerce, Arope was the **first insurance company in Lebanon to launch a website** for its clients allowing them to be informed about all products and services and even order their policy online.

- New products:

Further to the prominent accomplishments, Arope has launched, in conjunction with BLOM, two innovative plans: **Damanati**, the ideal saving plan for retirement and **Waladi**, a saving plan that ensures a child's future school and university education.

OUR SERVICES

To allow customers optimum services at any hour, one may call Arope's **24-hour hotline service** at (961) 1 747444, in order to inquire about products and policies:

Life, Hospitalization, Personal Accident, Travel Insurance

Motor, Marine (Cargo & Hull), Fire, Burglary, Engineering

Workmen's Compensation, General Third Party Liability

Cash in Transit/ in Safe, Fidelity Guarantee

Contractors All Risks, Credit Insurance, Bancassurance

MISSION STATEMENT

SAFETY AND FINANCIAL STRENGTH TO ASSURE DEDICATED SERVICE AND CONTINUOUS GROWTH.

FINANCIAL HIGHLIGHT - 1999

	IN L.P
• CAPITAL	4.800.000.000
• REAL ESTATE INVESTMENT	3.611.408.706
• PROFIT	711.596.275
• ADDITIONAL PROVISIONS	614.436.718
• DEBTORS	3.375.351.493
• CASH & BANKS	6.997.221.110
• WRITTEN PREMIUM	8.319.634.808

GOALS & STRATEGIES

Arope's vision and strategy is to constantly identify customers' needs and create the required solutions that satisfy them on both general and individual basis by always aiming for:

- DEVELOPMENT OF NEW PRODUCTS
- MAINTAINING A CAUTIOUS UNDERWRITING STRATEY
- DEVELOPMENT OF OUR CUSTOMER SERVICE DEPARTMENT TO ASSURE GLOBAL PRESENCE AND DEDICATED SERVICES

LibanCell sal, was incorporated in Beirut in November 1994, following the award by the Lebanese's Ministry of Post and Telecommunications, of a 12 years BOT contract (Build, Operate and Transfer) for implementing a GSM 900 MHz cellular network covering Lebanon.

Since its start of operations, **LibanCell** aimed at providing the Lebanese community with the most advanced telecommunication innovations, and welcomed subscribers and customers to the convenience, versatility and freedom offered bar its GSM network.

LibanCell elected to foster its network capabilities not only in terms of capacity and coverage, but also in providing advanced and sophisticated value-added services. The value-added services offered by **LibanCell** were on a par and even outclassed those available from well-established worldwide GSM operators.

In spite of all the start-up challenges, ranging from the lack of infrastructure services, the country's topography, unforeseen customer demand, and the usage patterns of the Lebanese subscriber, **LibanCell** succeeded in building its network and providing services to more than 50,000 subscribers in its first year of operations. This performance was achieved through building the local human resources as well as partnering with leading international telecommunications firms.

LibanCell has ascertained its leadership in the provision of cellular services in Lebanon by introducing prepaid services in September 1997, achieving a 100% growth in its customer base within 8 months and taking a 54% marketshare lead.

LibanCell serves currently around 240,000 subscribers, employs 270 people, manages a network comprising around 200 radio base stations and five switching elements and a full overlay microwave network, and has over 90 international roaming partners covering all the globe. **LibanCell** is well present on the international scene, participates in various seminars and conferences and is an active member of the GSM Memorandum of Understanding (MoU) and of the GSM Arab Interest Group community.

Aggressive marketing programs made **LibanCell "Talk of the Town"**, and **"Premiere"** a highly recognized brand. **LibanCell** looks ahead to continue developing products and services to meet the needs of the different market sectors through superior engineer ing competence and excellent customer service.

Address: **LibanCell Building, Charles Helou Ave.**
P.O.Box 136406, Beirut, Lebanon
Tel + 961 3 792000, Fax + 961 3 792020

Contact: **Mr. Hussein Rifai, Chairman – General Manager**
Me. Nabil Feghali - Deputy General Manager

Murr Television was launched by the end of 1990. It is held by shareholders owning a maximum of 10% of the company. Major shareholders are the Murr family, the Chairman is Michel Gabriel EL MURR.

Thanks to a dynamic and creative crew of 250 persons, all of young graduates, **MTV** has always been a forerunner in the Lebanese audiovisual sector, and it launched its News Bulletin on March 31st 1995.

Its challenge was to innovate and its programs are the best proof of its success:
MTV was the first station to have a live political debate: AL HAKE BAYNATA
MTV was the first to produce a TV-Shopping program
MTV has the most-watched comedy program in Lebanon (S.L.CHI)
MTV was the first to produce a computerized TV Game (OUA TENSA)
MTV was the first to fix the duration of the NEWS to 30 minutes.

In addition to a very important local production, including programs as Tlet Banet, Khallik Maana, Ciné Cinéphile, Ministudio, Maraya, **MTV** also broadcasts major American series and worldwide hits: X-files, Friends, Superman, E.R., Baywatch...
MTV is the exclusive representative of TF1 in Lebanon, and broadcasts top French programs.
MTV is one of the few stations that covers all Lebanon, as well as some of the neighboring countries. Its next goal is to launch a Satellite Broadcasting Station over the Middle East.

RML is one of the first radios which broadcast in Lebanon. It has kept from the 6th of December 1979 its very specific image of popular songs radio.
RML is the only radio which broadcasts all kinds of music, french, english, spanish, brazilian, italian, and even westernized arabic.
RML it's 24h/24 of music. At any moment, night and day, wherever you are, **RML** keeps you company.
RML it's varied music, during all the day: funk and dance music, rap or rave, rock and new wave...
RML it's the best coverage all over Lebanon and some of the neighboring countries, Cyprus, Syria, Egypt, Jordan, Palestine and the south coast of Turkey on 99, 100.3 and 100.5.
RML is the radio which launches hits, all the new songs of the world are first broadcast on **RML**.
RML it's the speaking Lebanese broadcasters of the FM. It is Joumana, Raya, John and Gilles in French. It is also Alain, Chris Mahne, George Edwards, Jihad and Laura in English, as well as the best international broadcasters ever: Casey Kasem, Rick Dees and PhilJay.
RML it's a young and dynamic team, which spares no effort to satisfy its listeners.
RML it's a variety of programs conceived and prepared to reach everybody. However, the programs are mainly aimed at a young audience, who feels like having fun.

Nostalgie started broadcasting on the 6th of February 1998, and was officially launched in Lebanon in February 1995, in the presence of Mr. Didier Gouzien, General Manager of "Nostalgie International Network", Top Model Vanessa Demouy, and the water skiing champion, Patrice Martin.

Nostalgie obtained its broadcasting license as a Western and apolitical music radio. This license was granted by the Lebanese government on the 24th of July 1997.
Nostalgie is a member of "NOSTALGIE INTERNATIONAL NETWORK", same marketing applied in Lebanon.
Nostalgie is rated first music radio in Lebanon. It covers all Lebanon on 88 and 90,4 FM. The audience of **Nostalgie** includes persons from all sociocultural classes and all ages. **Nostalgie** broadcasts French and English "Oldies" which please all the listeners.
Nostalgie has organized many concerts in Lebanon, among them the concert of Engelbert Humperdinck, Hervé Villard, Philippe Lavil, Marc Lavoine, Bernard Sauvat, and was also the media partner in the concerts of El Chato, Pierre Bachelet, Claude Barzotti, Santa Esmeralda, Gilbert Montagné, Gérard Lenorman and others.
The policy of **Nostalgie** is to broadcast hits and nothing but hits, without programs with hosts, so that listeners can enjoy music and nothing but music.

GEDEON BUSINESS FORMS (MIDDLE EAST) S.A.L.

Continuous Stationery and Systems

G E D E O N

B U S I N E S S

FORMS

(MIDDLE EAST) S.A.L.

Continuous Stationery and Systems

Firm established in 1962 in Beirut, Lebanon. It was the first company to introduce in the Middle East the printing of continuous stationery forms under the brand GBF.

It was also the first to introduce the register for continuous invoices.

It started in Lebanon by the Gedeon Family who started printing in Lebanon in 1868.

The firm extended its activities to Iran and established in that country the first printing plant for continuous stationery forms. The name of the firm in Teheran was: BUSINESS FORMS IRAN.

Then it moved to Saudi Arabia and established the: ARABIAN BUSINESS FORMS wll in Alkhobar. This firm is still operating.

All these Gedeon Firms produce continuous Stationery Forms, Snap-Out-Forms, Continuous Cheques,Continuous Invoices, etc.

GEDEON BUSINESS FORMS (Middle East) SAL is one of the most important plants in that field of activity.

GEDEON BUSINESS FORMS (MIDDLE EAST) SAL. Gedeon House, 141 John Kennedy Street, P.O.Box 11-4203. Beirut-LEBANON. Tel.: 01-494941/2/3. Fax: 01-493330. E-Mail: chgedeon@dm.net.lb

Founded over 70 years ago, DANTZIGUIAN is one of Lebanon's leading manufacturers in aluminium and steel works. The company and factory are located in Mkalles, at the outskirts of Beirut, Lebanon. During all these years, the company policy has been to form its own teams for the construction and installation in order to ensure a job of high quality and value.

Our extensive experience guarantees that DANTZIGUIAN meets the highest demands - from the selection of raw materials to the quality of production. For your private, as well as commercial use, we offer complete construction finishing and decorative solutions.

DANTZIGUIAN know-how in manufacturing and production has opened up expanding new fields of activity. The distribution and trade of a variety of construction finishing products in the Lebanese market is the basis of our success in the import of innovative and quality products which have long been used in our own production. Today, we are making these internationally famous products available to the retailers and distributors on the local market.

Steel works such as the manufacturing of decorative balustrades, doors, windows, gates, staircases, and general structural steel executions were the starting point of the company.

DANTZIGUIAN has been the first firm to introduce aluminum as construction material into the Middle East in 1954. Special DANTZIGUIAN aluminum profiles are extruded, anodised or powder coated in Lebanon. The Company's work force also excels in the manufacturing and installing of curtain wall structures, glazing and sandwich panels for high-rise buildings.

DANTZIGUIAN has also developed with today's architectural novelties and demands to include special features within its aluminium range. Arcade windows, curved sliding bays, lift and slide panels, tilt and swing windows, wood interior aluminium exterior framed French style windows, curved-glass balustrades, skylights and winter gardens. For these works, the company cooperates with a multitude of European suppliers such as TECHNAL/ALCAN, France, FARAONE, Italy and SYKON, Germany.

The electromechanical section started in the 60's and is essentially concerned with the supply, manufacturing, installation, and maintenance of electromechanical systems for doors, gates, windows, or other entrances. The line includes automatic door operators, swing and sliding type gates, electrical parking barriers electrical rolling shutters. A variety of control units are available for different uses.

DANTZIGUIAN'S electrical team has been trained at our suppliers factories SEA in Italy and BESAM Sweden for the installation and maintenance of all operators. The service we offer extends our suppliers' products warranty.

Completing its range, DANTZIGUIAN has developed an ironmongery division which supplies fittings for aluminium, wood and glass doors and windows mainly of German origin.

PAPER CONVERTING COMPANY (Middle East) S.A.L.

PAPER CONVERTING COMPANY
(Middle East) S.A.L.

This firm was established in 1966 in Beirut, Lebanon. It is specialized in the production of telex rolls, fax rolls, cash register rolls, self-adhesive labels, printed rolls, etc.

It was the first manufacturer in the Middle East of one time carbon paper which is currently used for continuous stationery forms and snap-out-forms. It exports its products to some countries of the Middle East, under the brand name PCC

PAPER CONVERTING COMPANY (MIDDLE EAST) SAL. P.O.Box 11-6465. Beirut - LEBANON. Tel.: 01-492001. Fax: 01-493330. E-Mail: mecico@dm.net.lb

DRIVE CAREFULLY,

SURF FAST

www.sodetel.net.lb

YOUR ULTIMATE INTERNET PARTNER

e-mail: sodetel@sodetel.net.lb 01.868041-2-3/868370-1

As-Safir

(Means in Arabic the ambassador)

Date of foundation: March 26th, 1974

Owner, publisher and editor: Talal Salman
General Manager: Yasser Nehmeh
Deputy editor in chief: Mohamed Mashmoushi & Joseph Samaha

Content: Local pages including political, educational, environmental, etc.
International pages
Cultural section
Editor's Opinion
Sports page
Economical page
Distribution: All over the Arab World & Europe

Offices abroad: Washington tel. 1.703.4253879
Paris tel. 45245097
Berlin tel. 49.30.2414967 fax 49.30.2412974
Damascus tel. 96311.2238350

Correspondents abroad: Cairo, Amman, Moscow and Rome

Lebanon's offices: Tripoli tel. 06.432560
Junieh tel. 09.931660
Sidon tel. 07.721744
Tyre tel. 07.343431
Shtoura tel. 08.542354
Baalbek tel. 08.371928

Advertisement: Regiemedia tel.353056, 577000

Internet homepage: http://www.assafir.com
Email: coordinator @assafir.com
Telefax: 9611.349430
Telex: Safir 21484 LE

Address: Beirut, Lebanon, Hamra, Mneimneh str.
Telephones: 350080/1/2/3 – 353106/7 – 350001/2

Distributor: The Lebanese Co. for Distribution
Beirut tel. 9611.36067

AS-SAFIR

The Voice of those who have no Voice

Lebanon's Newspaper to the Arab World

Arab World's Newspaper to Lebanon

Shell
IN THE MIDDLE EAST

now online!

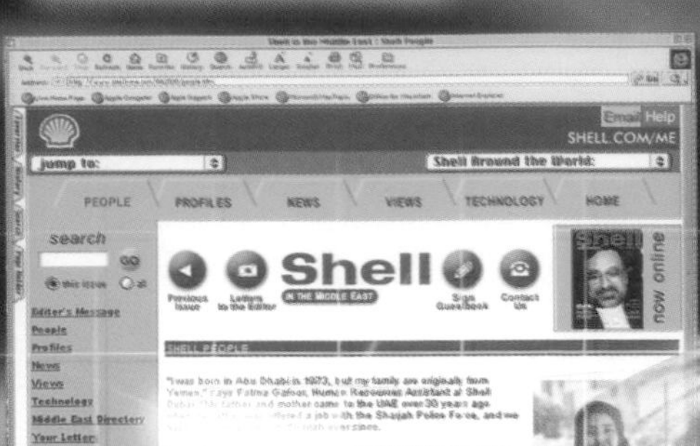

http://www.shell.com/me

As part of Shell's commitment to communicate, to listen and to respond "Shell in the Middle East" magazine, Shell's flagship publication for customers and partners in the Middle East region, is now online. The magazine, which is the primary source of up to date information about Shell and about the energy sector in the Middle East, is now just a click away. A powerful search facility allows you to find all you want to know both from the current edition of the magazine and also from all the previous editions. This means that the website is a regularly updated and comprehensive archive of events, people, technology and latest news on the region's most important and most dynamic business sector.

The website also invites you to go give us your views on Shell by making an entry in the online "Guestbook"... So visit http://www.shell.com/me now!

Partners with people and planet

PART III

SURVEY OF THE 19 ARAB COUNTRIES

1 - ALGERIA
2 - BAHRAIN
3 - DJIBOUTI
4 - EGYPT
5 - IRAQ
6 - JORDAN
7 - KUWAIT
8 - LIBYA
9 - MAURITANIA
10 - MOROCCO
11 - OMAN
12 - QATAR
13 - SAUDI ARABIA
14 - SOMALIA
15 - SUDAN
16 - SYRIA
17 - TUNISIA
18 - UNITED ARAB EMIRATES
19 - YEMEN

ALGERIA
(The Republic of Algeria)

ALGERIA

Head of State : Abdelaziz BOUTEFLIKA
Capital : Algiers
Area : 2,381,748 sq. Km.
Population : 29.2 million (Est. 1998)
Currency : Algerian Dinar, divided into 100 centimes.
Denominations in circulation
Notes : 5-10-50 and 100 dinars
Coins : 1 dinar; 1, 2, 5, 20 and 50 centimes
Exchange Rate = Dinars per US $ = 58.74 Algerian Dinars (AD) (Dec. 1998)

Geography

Algeria occupies an area of 2,381,748 sq. km. lying, between Morocco and Tunisia, in the centre of that stretch of the North African coast which lies between Tangier and Cape Bon. Algeria lies high, having an average altitude of 3,000 feet.

From north to south, the country is divided into two natural regions; one is the Tell, and the other the Steppes of the High Plateaux. The great desert, the Sahara, extends southwards from the foot of the Saharan Atlas.

The Tell is a Mediterranean land; it has a regular annual rainfall of over 16 inches, but this is very irregularly divided between autumn and spring.

The steppes of the High Plateaux, at a greater altitude, has a more continental and a drier climate.

South of this plateau region lies the main ridge of the Atlas mountains, cutting across the country diagonally from north-east to south-west. From these mountains several rivers run to the Algerian coast, the chief of which is the Chelif, 435 miles long, and teeming with fish.

CLIMATE

Along the coast the climate is temperate. The four summer months from June to September are generally warm and humid, the day temperature registering between 27–32 degrees C (80–90F), but rising when the hot dry "siroco" wind blows from the south for brief periods.

Further south in the Sahara desert it is hot not arid, the daytime temperature in the summer reaches 43 degrees C (110 degrees F).

PUBLIC HOLIDAYS

New Year's Day (1 January); Mulid al Nabi-birthday of the Prophet (16 December); Labour Day (1 May); National Day (19 June); Independence Day (5 July); Eid Al Fitr (11-13 July); Eid al Adha, Feast of the Sacrifice (17-20 September); Revolution Day (1 November); Muslim New Year (7 October); Ashoura-martyrdom of Imam Hussein, day of mourning for Shiite Muslims (16 October).

LANGUAGE & RELIGION

The official language is Arabic but French is still the language of business. English is gradually gaining ground among the younger generations.

The Algerians, Arabs and Berbers are Moslems. There are also Roman Catholic and Protestant minorities.

History

The Prehistoric period of Algeria remains a mystery. All that we learn from the discovery of stone tools is that there were men in Algeria between the tenth and fifth centuries B.C. It would appear that the Berbers of today are the product of a complicated racial mixture due to a succession of invasions and cross-breedings.

Though the pagan and Christian civilizations of Rome were at work in the Berber lands of North Africa for nearly 800 years, they have few traces, apart from the ruins of their cities.

In the middle of the seventh century, fifteen years after the death of the Prophet of Islam, Arab horsemen appeared in the Berber lands for the first time.

A second Arab invasion, that of the Beni Hilal, who came from Upper Egypt in the middle of the eleventh century, devastated the Maghreb. This invasion, like the first, failed to turn the Berbers of present-day Algeria into Arabs by race.

At the beginning of the sixteenth century the Spaniards occupied several Algerian ports, including Mersa al-Kebir, Oran, and Bougie and besieged Algiers itself.

They were followed in 1830 by the French.

FRENCH OCCUPATION

The French soon found the temperate and hilly coastal belt suitable for commercial agriculture, and nearly a million French and other Europeans settled in Algeria. Fourfifths of the Europeans lived in towns, but 45,000 European farmers owned a third of all arable land, through widespread confiscation especially after the unsuccessful rebellion of 1871.

From then until the end of the nineteenth century Algeria was the scene of considerable economic progress. A feature of the period was the growth of large scale agricultural and industrial enterprises, from which the Muslim population had benefited little owing to settlers opposition.

The years between World War I and 1953 were marked by a movement of independence.

In 1954, the rebel FLN (Front de Libération Nationale) launched a guerilla revolt; it was soon pinning down a French army of 450,000. The FLN was supported by the Arab states; the war embittered French relations with them, and French resentment at Egyptian actions contributed to the 1956 Suez entanglement.

In 1958 frustration over failure to suppress the rebellion produced the overthrow of the French Government by a revolt among the settlers, backed by the army in Algeria and by French supporters of the claim that Algeria was part of France.

LIBERATION

A referendum was held in Metropolitan France and Algeria between 6-8 January 1961 to decide on Algerian self-determination as proposed by President de Gaulle. His proposals were approved by 15,200,073 against 4,996,474 votes in Metropolitan France, and by 1,749,969 against 676,546 votes in Algeria.

A cease-fire agreement was concluded between the French Government and the representatives of the Algerian Nationalists on 18 March 1962. On 7 April a provisional executive of 7 members was set up, under the chairmanship of Abderrahman Fares, as provided by the Evian agreements which put an end to French rule in Algeria.

In May the Government abrogated some 60 mining concessions, all or most of which were believed to have been effectively abandoned by their owners since independence. This was followed in May 1966 by the nationalisation of 11 working iron, zinc, lead and copper mines, mostly owned by French companies.

Between May 1966 and May 1968, the Government took over all banking and insurance operations, as well as 41 French firms in the mechanical, fertilizer, building materials, food and chemical industries.

On February 24, 1971, the Algerian Government nationalised 51% of all the activities of the French petroleum companies. SONATRACH -the State-owned company-took over 51% of all shares, rights and interests of the oil concessions belonging to the French companies operating in Algeria, and brought up to 51% its shares in other companies owned by other foreign interests where these shares were less than 51%.

All natural gas fields, and allied installations were 100% nationalised. The State also took over completely rights to the associated gas that came out from producing oil wells. All non-Algerian interests with respect to transportation of gas or oil by pipelines were completely nationalised.

In 1973 and early 1974 the Foreign Ministers of Algeria and France were busy mending fences between the two countries caused by the nationalisation of French petroleum interests and other issues.

In April 1975, President Valery Giscard d'Estaing visited Algiers, the first visit since independence by a French President.

On the home front President Boumedienne started what was in effect a quest for internal legitimisation for his regime, following the publication by two former Presidents of the wartime government-in-exile, Ferhat Abbas and Ben Yussef Ben Khedda, accusing Boumedienne of totalitarian rule and personality cult.

The President's response was to issue a National Charter which set out three aims: consolidation of national independence, development of agriculture and industry, and decentralisation. The National Charter was approved by referendum (98.5%). This was followed in February 1977 by the election of a 261-member National Assembly, which would henceforth constitute the basic structure of government power.

Meanwhile, Algeria's relations with its neighbours, Morocco and Mauritania, deteriorated towards the end of the year as the case of the Spanish Sahara moved towards crisis. Algeria, while not claiming any part of the territory, actively supported self-determination for the Saharans and provided a base for the independence movement, the Frente Polisario. Its concern for the future of the territory was strongly expressed at the United Nations and in Madrid, and Algerian-Spanish commercial relations were threatened when Spain announced its intention to leave the Sahara.

Under President Boumedienne's leadership, Algeria maintained close links with the Soviet Union and other East European States. It staunchly supported Arab unity, the non-aligned movement, third world affairs, and was among the principal initiators of the declaration and programme of action on the establishment of a new international economic order for which a special session of the UN General Assembly had been convened in 1974.

DEATH OF BOUMEDIENNE

Mr Houari Boumedienne, the President of Algeria for 13 of its 16 years of independence, died in hospital in Algiers on Dec. 27, 1978, having on the previous six weeks been in a coma brought on by a rare blood disease known as Waldenstrom's syndrome. The state funeral on Dec. 29 was attended by representatives of some 60 countries.

PRESIDENT CHADLI

In accordance with the Constitution of 1976, the National Assembly thereupon appointed its Speaker, Mr. Rabah Bitat, as interim President, who was obliged to call presidential elections within 45 days, Elections were accordingly held on Feb. 7,1979 when Col. Benjedid Chadli, was unanimously elected as the new head of state.

GROWING SOCIAL UNREST

During the first half of 1981 mounting discontent with poor social and economic conditions in Algeria gave rise to a series of strikes, demonstrations and sporadic outbreaks of violence involving in particular students and other young people. (Of Algeria's total population of some 27.9 million an estimated 60 per cent were under the age of 21, a substantial proportion of them being unemployed). The main grievances were with continually rising prices, critical housing problems and social inequalities, such conditions providing an ideal recruiting environment for extremist groups, notably the Moslemfundamentalists.

While a number of incidents of agitation in Algerian cities in the first months of 1981 involved Moslem fundamentalists, many disturbances were connected with demands for greater recognition of the Berber language and culture.

RELATIONS WITH FRANCE

Relations between Algeria and France improved in 1981, boosted by the election of a socialist Government in France in May-June, and a series of interministerial meetings were held between July and November in preparation for the visit of President Mitterrand to Algiers which took place on Nov. 30-Dec. 1.

In November 1983, President Chadli visited Paris, the first visit since Independence by an Algerian President.

POLITICAL PARTIES

Algeria had only one permitted political party, the National Liberation Front (FLN).

The FLN has its representatives in most walks of Algerian life, from workers' and students' unions and such organisations as those for journalists, youth, and women, to offices in each town.

However in July 1989 the Algerian Government authorized formation of new political parties, and by mid 1991, besides the FLN, several political parties have emerged. The most important are: Front Islamique du Salut (officially dissolved in March 1992), Parti Social Démocrate, Mouvement pour la Démocratie en Algérie, Parti Islamique Démocratique d'Unité Arabe, Etc.

SITUATION

Algeria was ruled by President Bendjedid Chadli since 1979. In the elections held in January 1984, he was confirmed in office for a further five years, polling 95.4% of the votes cast. President Chadli was reelected in December 1989 for another term.

However, on January 11,1992 President Chadli resigned as Head of State, and on January 15,1992, a "High Council of State" was formed of five members and headed by Mohamed Boudiaf. The other four members were Khaled Nezzar, Ali Kafi, Tijani Haddam and Ali Haroun. The chairman, Mohamed Boudiaf assassinated in June 1992, was replaced by Ali Kafi. On January 31,1994, Ali Kafi passed on the presidency to Brig. Gen. Liamine ZEROUAL. Elections took place in November 1995 and his excellency Mr. Liamine ZEROUAL has been elected President of Algeria. On April 15, 1999 new elections were held and Mr. Abdelaziz Bouteflika has been elected President.

The Cabinet

(Dec. 1999)

Prime Minister: Ahmed BENBITOUR
Minister of Foreign Affairs: Youcef YOUSIF
Minister of the Interior and Local Communities: Yazid ZERHOUNI
Minister of State for Justice: Ahmad OUYAHIA
Minister of Finance: Abdellatif BENACHENHOU
Minister of Water Resources: Salim SAADI
Minister of Small and Medium-sized Enterprises: Noureddine BOUKROUH
Minister of Energy and Mines: Chakib KHELIL
Minister of National Education: Boubeker BENBOUZID
Minister of Culture and Communications: Abdelmadjid TEBBOUNE
Minister of Higher Education and Scientific Research: Ammar SAKHRI
Minister of Youth and Sports: Abdelmalek SELLAL
Minister of Commerce: Mourad MEDELCI
Minister of Posts and telecommunications: Mohamed MAGHLAOUI
Minister of Vocational Training: Karim YOUNES
Minister of Religious Affairs: Boudellah GHLAMALLAH
Minister of Housing: Abdelkader BOUNEKRAF
Minister of Industry and Reconstruction: Abdelmadjid MENSARA
Minister of Labour and Social Protection: Soltani BOUGUERRA
Minister of National Solidarity: Djamel Ould ABBES
Minister of War Veterans: Mohamed Cherif ABBES
Minister of Agriculture: Said BERKAT
Minister of Relations with the Parliament: Abdelwahab DERBAL
Minister of Health and Population: Amara BENYOUNES
Minister of Public Works, Territorial Management, Environment and Urban Planning: Mohamed Ali BOUGHAZI
Minister of Tourism and Handicraft: Lakhdar DORBANI
Minister of Transport: Hamid LOUNAOUCI
Minister of Fisheries and Marine Resources: Omar GHOUL
Minister of Prime Minister's Office in charge of Algiers Governorate: Cherif RAHMANI
Minister of Participation and Coordination of Reforms: : Hamid TEMMAR
Secretary General of the Government: Ahmed NOUI

Foreign Embassies

Angola: 14 rue Curie, El-Biar, Algiers
Argentina: 26 rue Finaltiori, El-Biar, Algiers
Austria: Les Vergers, Villa 136, Bir Mourad, Algiers
Belgium: 22 Chemin Youcef Tayebi, El-Biar, Algiers
Benin: 36 Lot du Stade, Birkhadem, Algiers
Brazil: P.O.Box 186, Algiers
Bulgaria: 13 Blvd. Col. Bougara, Tel. 2-230014, Algiers
Burkina Faso: 10 rue du Vercors, Air de France, al-Hammadia, Algiers
Cameroon: 34 rue Yahia Mazoumi, 16011 El-Biar, Algiers
Canada: 27 bis rue Frères Benhafid, B.P. 225, Hydra, Algiers
Chad: Villa No. 18, Cité DNC, Chemin Ahmed Kara, Hydra, Algiers
China, People's Republic: 34 Blvd. des Martyrs, Algiers

Congo: 111 Parc Ben Omar Kouba, Algiers
Congo, Democratic Republic: 5 rue St. Georges, Djenane Ben Oumar Kouba, Algiers
Côte d'Ivoire: Immeuble "Le Bosquet", Le Paradou, B.P. 710 Hydra, Algiers
Cuba: 22 rue Larbi Alik, Hydra, Algiers
Czech: Villa Koudia, 7 Chemin Zyriab, B.P. 358, Algiers
Denmark: 12 Ave. Emile Marquis, Lot. Djenane El-Malik, 16035 Hydra, Algiers
Egypt: B.P. 297, 16300, Algiers
Finland: B.P. 256, 16035 Hydra, Algiers
France: Rue Abdelkader Gadouche, Hydra, Algiers
Gabon: 21 rue Hadj Ahmed Mohamed, Hydra, Algiers
Germany: 165, Chemin Sfindja, B,P, 664, Algiers
Ghana: 62 Rue des Frères Bénali Abdellah, Hydra, Algiers
Greece: 60 blvd. Col. Bougara, Algiers
Guinea: 43, Central Said Hamdine Blvd., Hydra, Algiers
Guinea-Bissau: Cité DNC, Rue Ahmad Kara, Hydra, Algiers
Holy See: 1 Rue Noureddine Mekiri, 16090 Bologhine, Algiers
Hungary: 18 Ave des Frères Oughlis, B.P. 68 El-Mouradia, Algiers
India: 14 rue des Abbassides, Algiers
Indonesia: B.P. 62 El-Mouradia, Algiers
Iraq: 4, Rue Areski Abri, Hydra, Algiers
Italy: 18 Rue Muhammad Ouidir Amellal, El-Biar, Algiers
Japan: 1 Chemin El-Bakri, El-Biar, Algiers
Jordan: 6 Rue Chenoua, Algiers
Korea, Democratic People's Republic: 49 rue Hamlia, Bologhine, Algiers
Korea Republic: 12 rue Chemin des Crêtes, Hydra, Algiers
Kuwait: Chemin Abdelkader Gaaddouche, Hydra, Algiers
Lebanon: 9 rue Kaid Ahmed, El-Biar, Algiers
Libya: 15 Chemin Cheikh Bachir Ibrahimi, Algiers
Madagascar: 22 Rue Abdelkader Aouis, Bologhine, Algiers
Mali: Villa No. 15, Cité DNC-ANP, Chemin du Kaddous, Algiers
Mauritania: B.P. 276 El-Mouradia, Algiers
Mexico: P.O.Box 329, 21 rue du Commandant Amar Azzouz, El-Biar, Alger-Gare, Algiers
Morocco: 8 rue des Cèdres, El-Mouradia, Algiers
Netherlands: B.P. 72, El-Biar, Algiers
Niger: 54 rue Vercors Rostamia Bouzareah, Algiers
Nigeria: B.P. 629, 27 bis rue Blaise Pascal, Algiers
Oman: 53 rue Djamaleddine El-Afghani, Algiers
Pakistan: B.P. 404 Hydra, Algiers
Poland: 37 rue Mustapha Ali Khoja, El-Biar, Algiers
Portugal: 7 rue Mohamed Khoudi, El-biar, Algiers
Qatar: 25 Allée Centrale, Clairval, B.P. 118, Algiers
Romania: 24, rue Si Areski, Hydra, Algiers
Russia: 7 Chemin du Prince d'Annam, El-Biar, Algiers
Saudi Arabia: 62 rue Med. Drafini, Chemin de la Madeleine, Hydra, Algiers
Senegal: B.P. 379, Alger-Gare, Algiers
Slovakia: B.P. 84, 7 chemin du Zyriab, Didouche Mourad, 16006 Algiers
Spain: 10, rue Azil Ali, Algiers
Sudan: 8 Sharia Baski Brond, el-Yanabia, Bir Mourad Rais, Algiers
Sweden: rue Olof Palme, Nouveau Paradou, Hydra, Algiers
Switzerland: 27 Blvd. Zirout Youcef DZ-1600 Alger-Gare, Algiers
Syria: Domaine Tamzali, Chemin A. Gadouche, Hydra, Algiers
Tunisia: 11 Rue du Bois de Boulogne, Hydra, Algiers
Turkey: Villa Dar Al-Ouard, Chemin de la Rochele, Blvd. Col. Bougara, Algiers
United Arab Emirates: B.P. 454 El-Mouradia, Algiers
United Kingdom: B.P. 43, Résidence Cassiopée, Bâtiment B, 7 Chemin des Glycines, DZ-16000 Alger-Gare, Algiers
U.S.A.: P.O.Box 549, 4 Chemin Cheikh Bachir Brahimi, Alger-Gare, 16000 Algiers
Venezuela: P.O.Box 297, 3 Impasse Ahmed Kara, Algiers
Viet-Nam: 30, Rue Chenoua, Hydra, Algiers
Yemen Villa 19, Cité DNC, rue Ahmed Kara, Hydra, Algiers
Yugoslavia: 7 Rue des Frères Benhafid, B.P. 366 Hydra, Algiers

The Economy

HYDROCARBONS

Production of Crude Oil began commercially in 1958. The principal producing centres are in central Algeria, north east of the Sahara and near the Libyan frontier.

In 1998, Algeria produced 820.000 barrels per day. Algeria's proven reserves are estimated at 9.2 billion barrels by end 1998. Gas reserves are estimated at end 1998 at 3.700 billion cubic meters.

OTHER MINERALS

The country has extensive deposits of highgrade iron ore, mainly at Ouenza, and poorer quality ore at Gara Djebilet, near Tindouf. Deposits of nonferrous metal ores are small and widely scattered. There are, however, sizable deposits of zinc and lead at el-Abed on the Moroccan border near Tlemcen, and mercury at Ismail. Traces of nickel, tin, cobalt, chrome and uranium have been found, and there are high hopes of finding tungsten, gold, platinum, and diamonds.

Reserves of phosphate deposits are estimated at about 1,000,000,000 tons, and are mining about 800 thousand tons of rock phosphate per year.

INDUSTRY

The 1980-84 plan envisaged non-hydrocarbon industrial investment of AD 91.5 billion, some 38% of total investment and 32% in the 1985-89 plan. Greater priority was accorded to light industry, food processing, construction materials, paper and textiles. Cement production capacity is about 9 million tons.

Heavy industry, includes steel, fertilisers and petrochemicals complexes. Present annual steel capacity is approx. 1.8 million tons, while studies for a new works provide for additional 2 million tons. Fertilisers capacity is being expanded to produce a surplus for export.

AGRICULTURE

Agriculture is an important sector in the economy employing about 25 per cent of Algeria's labour force. The most important crop is grapes. Other crops are dates, figs, wheat, barley, sorghum, citrus fruits, olives, tobacco and rice. Important investments are made to reduce imports. The aim is to achieve over 75 per cent self sufficiency.

ECONOMY

Aims at liberalizing the economy to encourage more foreign investments in the country, is pursued dynamically alongside promotion of the other sectors of industry and agriculture.

A series of economic reforms were introduced in an attempt to reduce state control of the economy, to boost productivity and to stimulate non-hydrocarbon production. Large investments and various programs were introduced to encourage farmers and increase agricultural output, in order to reduce the high level of food imports; and further steps are taken to control expenditure. Special measures are taken to liberalize more and more the economy, and encourage foreign investments in the country. In August 1995 plans were announced to privatize more than 1200 state companies. However, Hydrocarbons remain the main foreign currency earner.

Algeria's total foreign debt at end 1998 was estimated to total US$ 30.47 billion. The 1995 budget published in June 1995 set revenue at Algerian Dinars 568.5 billion and expenditure at 734.9 billion, leaving a deficit of A.D. 166.4 billion. The 1996 budget was approved on December 30, 1995. It estimates revenue at Algerian Dinars 749.2 billion and expenditure projected at 848.6 billion, leaving a deficit of 99.4 billion Dinars. The projected 1997 budget estimated revenue at A.D. 829.4 billion and expenditure at A.D. 914.1 billion leaving a deficit of A.D. 84.7 billion.

The 1998 budget set revenues at A.D. 901.5 billion and expenditure at A.D. 980.2 billion. The 1999 budget set expenditure at A.D. 1,098 billion and revenues at A.D. 937.1 billion. The 2000 budget was set at expenditure A.D. 1,252 billion and revenues at A.D. 1,032 billion.

The Banking System

The Algerian banking system comprises the Central Bank and deposit money banks.

The Central Bank of Algeria 38 ave Franklin Roosevelt, Algiers; Tel. (2)60-10-44; Established by Law No. 62-144 of December 13,1962, and commenced operations in January 1963 by assuming the issue functions formerly undertaken by the French nationalised bank, Bank of Algeria. It maintains agencies in Oran, Constantine, Annaba, Skikda, Tizi-Ouzou, Setif, Batna, Blida, El-Asnam, Mostaganem, Tiaret, Tlemcen, and Side-Bel-Abbes. Capital: 40 million Algerian dinars.

Its board of directors determines the rules and regulations that govern the internal administration of the bank, and it has broad powers over credit and money policies.

Al-Baraka Bank of Algeria: Est. 1991, 12 blvd. Col Amirouche, Tel. (2)69-32-76, Algiers.

Banque Algérienne de Développement: Est. 1963, 12 blvd. Col Amirouche, Tel. (2)73-89-50, Algiers.

Banque de l'Agriculture et du Développement Rural: Est. 1982, 17 blvd. Col Amirouche, Tel. (2)64-72-64, P.O.Box 484, Algiers.

Banque de Développement Local: Est. 1985, 5 Rue Gaci Amar Staouéli, Tel. (2)39-28-01, Wilaya de Tipaza.

Banque Extérieure d'Algérie: Est. 1967, 11 blvd. Col Amirouche, Tel. (2) 71-12-52, P.O.Box 344, Algiers.

Banque du Maghreb Arabe pour l'Investissement et le Commerce: 21 blvd. des Frères Bouaddou, Bir Mourad Rais, Tel. (2) 56-04-46, Algiers.

Banque Nationale d'Algérie: Est. 1966, 8 blvd. Ernesto Ché Guévara, Tel. (2) 71-55-64, P.O.Box 713, Alger-Gare, 1600 Algiers.

Crédit Populaire d'Algérie: Est. 1966, B.P. 1031, 2 blvd Col Amirouche, Tel. (2)71-78-78, 1600 Algiers.

Transport

To meet the demands of a rapidly growing economy, investments for the improvement and extension of the transportation system have been sharply increased.

ROADS

A total of 100,000 km of road includes 26,000 km of national roads, about 24,000 km of provincial roads, and 21,000 km of local roads. A trans-Saharan road is under way ensuring connections between Algeria, Niger and Mali.

RAILWAYS

The railroad system consisting of almost 4,200 km of track, is operated by the National Corporation of Railway Transport. It connects all major cities in the north and extends to Tunisia and Morocco. There are five lines to the south, of which the most important is the Djebel-Onk-Annaba line for the transportation of iron ore and phosphates to the industrial centre of Annaba.

SHIPPING & PORTS

There are 6 well-equipped and 14 secondary ports in Algeria. The port of Algiers handles most of the country's general cargo imports and exports. Most of the other ports are specialised: Arzew, for exports of crude oil and liquified natural gas; Bedjaia, for crude oil; Annaba for steel and iron ore exports; and Skikda, for exports of ammonia, refined petroleum products, crude oil, and liquified natural gas.

CIVIL AVIATION

Algeria's main international airport is situated about 20 km from Algiers. Smaller airports are at Annaba, Constantine, Tlemcen and Oran.

Air Algérie – Est. 1946. 1, Place Maurice Audin, Algiers, Telephone (2)742428.

There are also regular services operated by other international airlines.

Radio – Television – Cinema and Press

RADIO – TELEVISION

Radiodiffusion Télévision Algérienne – RTA building, 21, Boulevard des Martyrs, Algiers. Tel. (2)590700, (2)602300. Public Corporation.

THE PRESS

A. – Newspapers – Weeklies

Al Chaab: Est. 1962, 1, Place Maurice Audin Algiers, Arabic.

Algérie - Actualités: Est. 1965, 2, rue Jacques Cartier, Tel. (2)63-54-20, 16000 Algiers, French.

Al Hadef: Est. 1972, Zone Industrielle, La Palma, Tel. (4) 93-92-16, P.O.Box 388, Constantine.

Horizons: Est. 1985, 20 rue de la Liberté, Tel. (2) 73-67-25, Algiers, French.

El Moujahed: Est. 1965, 20 rue de la Liberté, Algiers, French and Arabic.

Al Nasr: Est. 1963, Zone Industrielle, La Palma, Tel. (4)93-92-16, Constantine, Arabic.

Thakafa: Est. 1971, 2 Place Cheikh Ben Badis, Tel. (2) 62-20-73, P.O.Box 96, Algiers.

B. – News Agencies

Algérie Press Service (APS): Est. 1962, 4 rue Zoueiche, Kouba, Tel. (2) 77-79-28, Algiers.

Universities

Université d'Alger
Est. 1879; 2 Didouche Mourad Str., Tel.: 64-69-70, Algiers

Université des Sciences et de la Technologie Houari Boumedienne
Est. 1974; El Alia, Bab Ezzouar, P.O.Box 32, Tel.: 75-12-85, Algiers

Université d'Annaba
Est. 1975; El Hadjar, P.O.Box 12, Tel.: 83-34-29, Annaba

Université de Blida
Est. 1981: Route de Soumaa Blida, P.O.Box 270, Tel.: (3) 41-10-00, Blida

Université de Boumerdes
Est. 1981; Boumerdes

Université de Constantine
Est. 1969; Route d'Ain El Bey, Tel.: 69-73-85, Constantine

Université d'Oran
Est. 1965; Colonel Lotti Str., P.O.Box 1524, Es Senia, Tel.: 38-71-44, Oran

Université des Sciences et de la Technologie d'Oran
Est. 1975; P.O.Box 1505, El Menaouer, Tel.: 35-06-05, Oran

Université de Sétif
Est. 1978; Route de Scipion, Tel.: 90-88-93, Sétif

Université de Tlemcen
Est. 1974; Immeuble Administratif F.G. Pasteur, P.O.Box 119, Tel.: 20-09-22, 1300 Tlemcen.

Museums

Musée de Préhistoire et d'Ethnographie du Bardo: Est. 1928-3, Avenue Franklin Roosevelt.

Musée du Mont Riant (Algiers) –

Musée National des Antiquités: Est. 1897, Algiers. Parc de la Liberté.

Musée National des Beaux Arts d'Alger: Est. 1930, Algiers. Jardin d'Essai.

Musée de Cirta: Est. 1853; Blvd de la République, Constantine.

Tourism

Algeria has many advantages which give it a great potential for tourism; a Mediterranean coast of over 620 miles, desert oases, a highly developed transportation system, and proximity to large tourist markets in Europe. Although promotional activity and investments in this sector have received secondary priorities, the improvement in basic infrastructure and the transport system indirectly has benefited the tourist sector, as has also the Government's considerable investment in hotels. Sizeable investments have been made with about 70 to 75 percent of the expansion located on the seashore and the balance mostly in the urban centres. The number of hotels have been increased since, and now total more than 700. Tourists visiting Algeria have increased during the last decade and were estimated at about 700,000 yearly but have fallen since 1995 to about 100,000.

Two public agencies are in charge of the tourist sector:

a) **Opérateur National Algérien du Tourisme** (National Tourist Bureau) responsible for the study and implementation of hotel projects. 25-27 rue Khelifa Boukhalfa, Algiers.
b) **Office National de Tourisme** charged with the management and operation of hotels, 8 rue Ismail Kerrar, Algiers.

BAHRAIN
(State of Bahrain)

BAHRAIN

Head of State	: H.M. Sheikh Hamad Bin Issa Bin Salman al-KHALIFA
Crown Prince	: Sheikh Salman Bin Hamad Bin Issa al-KHALIFA
Capital	: Manama
Area	: 691 Square Km
Population	: 0.62 million (1997 estimate)
Currency	: The basic unit is the Bahrain dinar (BD.) divided into 1000 fils. Denominations: a) Notes 100 fils; ¼, ½, 1,5 and 10 dinars. b) Coins 1, 5, 10, 25, 50, 100 and Notes of 500 fils.
Exchange Rate	: US $1=0.376 Bahraini Dinars (May. 1999)

Geography

Bahrain is an archipelago lying in the entrance to the Gulf of Salwa, 20 miles from the Hasa Province of Saudi Arabia and 18 from the Qatar Peninsula. The main island is pear-shaped running north and south with the broader end at the north. It is about 10 miles wide here, and its length is about 30 miles.

The greater part of the main island is desert and at its southern end tails off into a spit of sand. All round the center of the island there is an escarpment, like a huge crater where there is a sudden drop, in some places precipitous of about a hundred feet. The ground then rises again in a sort of dome, reaching a height of 450 feet at the Jabal Dukhan in the very center of the island. It is in this area that oil is found.

Off its northeast corner, and joined to it by a causeway one and a half miles long, lies the island of Muharraq. Further south, on the east side, are the small circular islands of Nabi Salih, completely covered with date orchards, and the larger island of Sitral.

Off the northwest corner of the main island there are three islands: Umm al-Sb'an, Jiddah island and Umm al Na'san. There are a number of smaller islands in the archipelago, most of them on the side of the main island.

URBAN CENTRES

The two main centres of population are the towns of Manama and Muharraq.

Manama is the business centre.

Muharraq, of truly Arab appearance has electricity and a pipe water supply. Hiss, the third town, is sited at the southeast end of Muharraq island.

However, the most important development in recent years is Isa town which boasts the most imaginative housing scheme in the Middle East, incorporating the complete range of urban services; municipal offices, police and firefighting stations, mosques, schools for boys and girls, outpatient clinics, a traffic-free shopping centre and a sports stadium.

RELIGION

The overwhelming majority of the population in Bahrain are Muslims whose religion permeates every aspect of their daily life. The two main sects are the Shia, which originated in Arabia, and the Sunni, or Orthodox Sect.

PUBLIC HOLIDAYS

Mulid al Naby-birthday of the Prophet; Eid al Fitr, end of Ramadan, Muslim month of fasting and self-purification; Eid al Adha, feast of the Sacrifice; Muslim New Year, Ashura, day of mourning for shi'ite Muslims.

History

The recorded history of Bahrain goes back to the third millineum BC, when Sargon of Akkad, the great Semetic king, conquered Dilmun, by which Bahrain is thought to have been known. Dilmun figures in many Mesopotamian writings as a major trading centre serving as the half-way house between the civilisations of Mesopotamia and the Indus valley. In the 8th century B.C., it was seized by another Sargon, this time the Assyrian king of that name.

This was one of the first areas ouside the Arabian Peninsula to accept the religion of Islam (in the 7th century AD). Subsequently the Bahrain islands had a chequered career, being at times independent and at times under the domination or rulers from the mainland of Arabia. There were two brief spells of foreign control: the Portuguese exercising fitful rule from 1522 to 1602; to be replaced by the Persians whose control was equally tenuous. In 1782 the first of the al-Khalifa sheikhs - Ahmed- seized Bahrain from the Persians.

During the second half of the 19th century, the rulers of Bahrain signed a number of agreements with Britain by virtue of which Britain undertook to defend Bahrain against aggression.

INDEPENDENCE

Bahrain made its debut on the world stage in the early 1960's when contacts were made with many States, notably those of the Arab World. Formal international recognition of its independence was declared in May 1970 by unanimous vote of the Security Council.

Bahrain was admitted to membership of the Arab League and the United Nations in 1971.

The Constitution

In June 1973 a 108-article constitution was ratified. It states that "all citizens are equal before the law" and guarantees "freedom of speech, of the press, of conscience and worship". The constitution also provides for a financial comptroller answerable to the National Assembly, for free primary education and free medical care.

The National Assembly was dissolved in August 1975.

In late 1992, however a 30 member Consultative Council has been appointed. On September 1996, a new 40 member Consultative Council were appointed and presided by Ibrahim Hassan Humeidan.

POLITICAL SITUATION

The Amir, who succeeded his father in March 1999, holds executive power and is assisted by a Cabinet in which many of the key ministries are occupied by members of the Khalifa family. There is currently no directly elected national decision-making body and political participation takes the form of the traditional majlis – informal meetings at which any citizen can present petitions to the ruler. In 1981, Bahrain, with five Arab states, established the Gulf Co-operation Council (GCC). The grouping seeks to promote regional coordination of industry, agriculture, transport, energy and defence policy.

The Cabinet

(June 1999)

Prime Minister: Sheikh Khalifa Bin Salman AL KHALIFA
Minister of Justice and Islamic Affairs: Sheikh Abdullah bin Khalid AL KHALIFA
Minister of Foreign Affairs: Sheikh Mohamed Bin Mubarak Bin Hamad AL KHALIFA
Minister of Interior: Sheikh Mohamed Bin Khalifa Bin Hamad AL KHALIFA
Minister of Transport, Civil Aviation: Sheikh Ali Bin Khalifa Bin Salman AL KHALIFA
Minister of State: Jawad Salim Al ARRAYEDH
Minister of Housing, Municipalities and Environment: Sheikh Khaled Bin Abdullah Bin Khaled AL KHALIFA
Minister of Public Works, Agriculture: Ali Al MAHROOS
Minister of Finance and National Economy: Abdullah Hassan SAIF
Minister of Defence: Maj. Gen. Sheikh Khalifa Bin Ahmad AL KHALIFA
Minister of Cabinet, Information: Mohamed Ibrahim AL MUTAWA
Minister of Oil and Industry: Sheikh Issa Bin Ali Bin Hamad AL KHALIFA
Minister of Commerce: Ali Saleh Abdullah AL SALIH
Minister of Education: Brig. Gen. Abdul Aziz Mohamed AL FADHIL
Minister of Health: Faisal Radhi AL MOOSAWI
Minister of Power and Water: Sheikh Daij Bin Khalifa Bin Mohamed AL KHALIFA
Minister of Labour and Social Affairs: Abdul Nabi AL SHULA
Minister of Amiri Court Affairs: Sheikh Ali Bin Issa AL KHALIFA

Foreign Embassies

Algeria: P.O.Box 26402, Adiliya 336, Villa 579, Rd. 3622, Manama.
Bangladesh: P.O.Box 26718, House 159, Area 320, Hoora.
China, People's Republic: P.O.Box 3150, Villa 379, Rd 1912, Area 319, Al-Hoora, Manama.
Egypt: P.O.Box 818, Adiliya, Tel. 720005.
France: P.I.Box 11134, King Faisal Rd., Tel. 291734, Manama.
Germany: P.O.Box 10306, Dipl. Area 317, Al-Hassan Bldg. Manama.
India: P.O.Box 26106, Bldg. 182, Rd. 2608, Area 326, Adiliya, Manama.
Iran: P.O.Box 26365, Tel. 722400, Manama.
Japan: P.O.Box 23720, House 403, Rd. 915, Salmaniya, Tel. 243364, Manama.
Jordan: P.O.Box 5242, Villa 43, Rd. 1901, Al-Fatih Ave., Manama.
Korea Republic: P.O.Box 11700, King Faisal Rd., Tel. 291629, Manama.
Kuwait: P.O.Box 786, Diplomatic Area, 76 Rd. 1703, Tel. 242330, Manama.
Morocco: P.O.Box 26229, Villa 58, Rd 3404, Area 334, Mahooz, Manama.
Oman: P.O.Box 26414, Diplomatic Area, Bldg. 37, Rd. 1901, Manama.
Pakistan: P.O.Box 563, House 75, Rd. 3403, Mahooz, Tel. 712470, Manama.
Philippines: P.O.Box 26681, Bldg. 81, Rd 3902, Block 339, Umm Al-Hassan, Manama.
Russia: P.O.Box 26612, House 111, al-Shabab Ave, Rd 40, Juffair, Manama.
Saudi Arabia: P.O.Box 1085, Bldg. 1450, Rd. 4043, Jufair, Manama.
Tunisia: P.O.Box 26911, Al-Mahouz, Te. 721431, Manama.
Turkey: P.O.Box 10821, Flat 10, Bldg 81, Rd 1702, Area 317, Manama.
United Kingdom: P.O.Box 114, 21 Government Rd., Tel. 534404, Manama.
U.S.A.: P.O.Box 26431, Off Sheikh Issa Rd., Tel. 714151, Manama.
Yemen: P.O.B 26193, House 1048, Rd 1730, Area 517, Saar, Manama.

Justice

Justice is administered in accordance with Sharia (Islamic Canon Law), and for almost two decades now various legislative texts have been promulgated in replacement of British legal jurisdiction which was terminated in 1971.

Bahrainis and foreign residents alike are under the jurisdiction of the Bahrain courts.

Education

The modern system of education in Bahrain dates back to 1919 when the Khalifa School was opened in Muharraq to be followed, nine years later, by the inauguration in Manama of Bahrain's first Girls' School.
Education is free. From the ages of six to twelve boys and girls attend primary school. Intermediate stage lasts two years and is followed by a three-year secondary state. Higher education is provided either at home or abroad.

Universities

Arabian Gulf University
Est. 1980; P.O.Box 26671, Tel.: 440044, Manama
University of Bahrain
Est. 1986; P.O.Box 32038, Tel.: 682748, Issa Town

Colleges

a) Gulf Technical College: Isa Town; f.1968.
b) Men's Teacher Training College (Est. 1966)
c) Women's Teacher Training College (Est. 1968)
Bahrain Writers and Literators Association: P.O.Box 1010, Manama; f.1969 to promote the literary movement in Bahrain.
British Council: P.O.B. 452, Al Mathaf Square, Manama; f.1967
College of Health Sciences: f. 1976; P.O.Box 12, Bahrain.

Cultural Societies

Bahrain Historical and Archæological Society: f. 1953, organizes film shows, lectures, discussions and visits to archæological sites in Bahrain.
Bahrain Society of Engineers: P.O.B. 835, Manama; f.1972.

Museum

Bahrain Museum: P.O.B. 43, Manama; f.1970; archæological research; collections of remains and artefacts from the Middle Stone Age to the 7th century A.D.; graphic presentation of principal Sumerian legends relating to Dilmun.

The Economy

Possessing limited and diminishing oil reserves, Bahrain set in motion a process of diversification shortly after independence, setting up heavy industries and a ship repair yard (mostly on the basis of consortia involving other Arab countries) and encouraging the growth of a substantial offshore banking sector. These developments have reduced the impact of the weakness in the price of oil over the last few years to some extent, but nonetheless oil-related activities continue to predominate, contributing over 80% of export earnings and providing around 60% of budgetary receipts. The consequent reduction in government finance has led to expenditure being kept on a tight rein, with a package of austerity measures introduced since 1985.

However, the opening of the causeway between Bahrain and Saudi Arabia has given a boost not only to industry but to tourism, which the government is keen to promote. A number of hotels and other facilities are being improved, and new attractions were planned to capitalise on the country's good location and cultural heritage. The fact that the industry is labour-intensive, and that the government is to take steps to ensure more jobs in future go to indigenous Bahrainis, is important in view of the comparatively high population growth rate. At the same time, however, the direct link with the mainland has exposed the economy to much sterner competition, forcing traders to reduce prices after its opening.

Provided a permanent settlement can be reached, the recent ending of the Gulf War, provide Bahrain with many opportunities. The banking system looks set to benefit from a growth in trade and project finance resulting from increased confidence in the region, while industry, particularly aluminium and iron, should benefit from the reconstruction work in the area. Expansion in the island's heavy industry and petrochemical plants had been planned well before the ceasefire came into effect, placing Bahrain in an advantageous position compared with its competitors in the region. In 1989 a Stock Exchange opened in an attempt to encourage inflows of private capital.

OIL DEVELOPMENTS

Oil and Gas:
Bahrain proven oil reserves at the end of 1997 were estimated at 200 million barrels. Oil production averaged 40000 barrels per day (b/d) in 1997, output being refined at the 250,000 b/d capacity refinery at Sitra. The Bahrain Petroleum Company (BAPCO), which operates the refinery, is preparing a modernisation programme to increase the capacity.

Natural gas is gaining importance by virtue of the fact that reserves are expected to last longer than those of oil – the estimated 140 billion cu m should last well into the next 20 years at current production levels.

ECONOMIC DIVERSIFICATION

Since the late 1960s Bahrain has implemented development projects to diversify the economy, thereby reducing the country's heavy dependence on petroleum and also providing employment opportunities for the Bahraini population. An Aluminium smelter began operation in April 1971. The smelter, produced little over 450,000 tons in 1995.

Aluminium is imported from Australia and most of the

production is exported. Three ancillary industries use aluminum either in molten or ingot form as the basic raw material: an aluminum atomizer, an extrusion plant, and a cable factory.

OPENING OF CAUSEWAY LINK WITH SAUDI ARABIA

The Saudi-financed "King Fahd Causeway" linking Bahrain and Saudi Arabia, under construction since 1981 and originally sheduled for opening in December 1985, was officially opened on Nov.26, 1986, by King Fahd ibn Abdul Aziz of Saudi Arabia and the then ruler of Bahrain, Shaikh Isa bin Sulman al-Khalifa. More than 4 million people use it yearly.

THE BUDGET

The budget for the two calendar years 1986 and 1987 was approved by the government on Jan. 13, 1986. It provided for total expenditure over those two years of 1,110 million Bahraini dinars, with revenue estimated at the same amount (US$1.00 = BD 0.3769 as at Jan. 13, 1987). Total expenditure during 1984-85 was estimated to have reached BD 1,043 million. Oil income during 1986 totalled BD 335 million, down 5.7 per cent from the previous year's total. It was anticipated that gross domestic product (GDP), having fallen by 7 per cent in 1985, would fall by 14 per cent in 1986, largely because of the decline in oil prices.

The Finance Ministry in early February 1986 announced that treasury bills would be issued to help finance the budget. The first batch of bills, worth a total of BD 26 million, each with a face value of BD 10,000 and a life of 91 days, was issued in early December.

The Finance Minister, Mr Ibrahim Abdel Karim Mohammed, warned in an interview with the Gulf Daily News in late June 1986 that falling oil prices would result in the postponement of a number of large projects, including construction work on government buldings and the expansion of the water and electricity system.

The Cabinet in August 1986 approved plans for the creation of an official stock exchange, to replace the present unofficial "telephone market" conducted by licensed brokers. The plans were endorsed by an Amiri decree in early March 1987, which specified that the exchange would trade in 20 domestic stocks.

The Budget for the two calendar years 1988 and 1989 provided for total expenditure over those two years of 1,100 million Bahraini dinars, with revenue estimated at the same amount (US$ 1.00 = BD 0.376 as at Nov. 1989).

BUDGET AND TRADE

Bahraini economy continued to face difficulties during 1987–88 due to declining revenues from oil exports.

During 1986 oil earnings had fallen by 34 per cent to 247,200,000 Bahraini dinars (US$1.00 = BD 0.3769 as at Dec. 31, 1986) from the 1985 figure of BD 375,000,000; state revenue overall fell by 12.3 per cent to BD 176,600,000. Despite a reduction in government expenditure of 4.7 percent to BD 487,100,000, there was a budgetary deficit of BD 10,500,000 contrasting with the previous year's surplus of BD 24,700,000). The deficit was financed by government cash balances, including those raised by the sale of treasury bills (introduced in December 1986). The revenue shortfall continued during the first half of 1987, with a deficit of BD 11,700,000 being recorded over the first six months.

The government announced in mid-August 1987 that the value of the weekly issue of treasury bills was to be increased to BD 2,700,000 from BD 2,000,000 to meet heavy demand.

The trade deficit for 1986 totalled BD 31,200,000, compared with BD 78,900,000 in 1985, largely as a result of government measures to limit imports.

In 1989 revenue totalled BD 496,000,000 and expenditure was BD 438,000,000 resulting in a deficit of BD 58,000,000 mostly financed by treasury bonds issues.

In 1990 government revenue totalled BD 498,000,000 and estimated expenditure of BD 536,000,000.

In 1991 revenue stood at BD 427,000,000 and the deficit in the budget reached BD 118,000,000 which were mostly financed by bond issues.

In 1992 revenue was BD 465.4 million and expenditure BD 548.7 million. In 1993 revenue was estimated at BD 580 million and expenditure at BD 643 million. However, more recently the budgets for 1995 and 1996 approved in November 1994 are set at revenue (1995) BD 520 million and expenditure at 642 million and (1996) BD 530 million for revenue and 644 million for expenditure. Leaving a deficit for the years 1995 and 1996 BD 122 million and BD. 114 million respectively. The budgets for 1997 and 1998 were revenue BD 1245 million and expenditure BD 1395 million. The 1999-2000 budget forcast revenue at BD 1138 million and expenditure at BD 1458 million.

Banking System

By 1995 the financial and banking system in Bahrain consisted of the Bahrain Monetary Agency, 20 commercial banks, and 44 reporting offshore banking units, 31 representative offices of foreign banks, 18 investment banks, 21 insurance companies, 6 money brokers, 17 money changers, a state pension fund and a social insurance fund.

The Bahrain Monetary Agency, established in 1973, has all the usual powers of a Central Bank, such as the licensing, inspection and supervision of financial institutions, stipulation of reserve requirements, open market operations, regulation of credit, and service as the Government's banker.

THE BANKING SYSTEM

Bahrain Monetary Agency: Est. 1973, P.O.Box 27, Tel. 535535, Manama

ABN AMRO Bank NV: P.O.Box 350, Tel. 255420, Manama

Al Ahli Commercial Bank BSC: Est. 1977, P.O.Box 5941,

Tel. 224333, Manama

Al Baraka Islamic Investment Bank BSC: Est 1984, P.O.Box 1882, Tel. 274488, Manama

Arab Bank PLC.: Manama Centre, P.O.Box 395, Tel. 212255, Manama

Bahrain Development Bank: Est. 1992, P.O.Box 20501, Tel. 537007, Manama

The Housing Bank: Est 1979, Diplomatic Area, P.O.Box 5370, Tel. 534443, Manama

Bahrain Islamic Bank BSC: Est. 1979, P.O.Box 5240, Tel. 223402, Manama

Bahrain Middle East Bank EC: Est. 1982, P.O.Box 797, Tel. 532345, Manama

Bahraini Saudi Bank BSC: Est. 1983, P.O.Box 1159, Tel. 211010, Manama

Bank of Bahrain and Kuwait BSC: Est. 1971, P.O.Box 597, Tel. 223388, Manama

Bank Melli Iran: Government Road, P.O.Box 785, Tel. 259910, Manama

Bank Saderat Iran: P.O.Box 825, Tel. 210003, Manama

Banque du Caire: P.O.Box 815, Tel. 257454, Manama

Banque Paribas FCB: P.O.Box 5241, Tel. 225275, Manama

British Bank of the Middle East: P.O.Box 57, Tel. 242555, Manama

Citibank NA: P.O.Box 548, Tel. 223344, Manama

Faisal Islamic Bank of Bahrain: Est. 1982, Chamber of Commerce Bldg., King Faisal Rd., P.O.Box 2820, Tel. 211373, Manama

Grindlays Bahrain Bank BSC: P.O.Box 793, Tel. 225599, Manama

Gulf International Bank BSC: Est. 1975, 3 Palace Ave, Al-Dowali Bldg., P.O.Box 1017, Tel. 534000, Manama

Habib Bank Ltd: Est. 1941, Manama Centre, P.O.Box 566, Tel. 227118, Manama

Investcorp Bank EC: Est, 1982, P.O.Box 5340, Diplomatic Area, Tel. 532000, Manama

National Bank of Bahrain BSC: Est. 1957, Government Rd., P.O.Box 106, Tel. 228800, Manama

Rafidain Bank: Est. 1979, P.O.Box 607, Tel. 255796, Manama

Standard Chartered Bank: Est. 1920, P.O.Box 29, Tel. 255946, Manama

United Bank Ltd: Government Rd., P.O.Box 546, Tel. 224032, Manama

THE PRESS

Newspapers – Weeklies

Al Adhwaa: Est. 1965, P.O.Box 250, Tel. 291226, Manama, Arabic

Akhbar al Khalij: Est. 1976, P.O.Box 5300, Tel. 620111. Manama, Arabic

Al Ayam: Est. 1989, P.O.Box 3232, Tel. 727111, Manama

Al Bahrain: P.O.Box 26005, Tel. 731888, Isa Town, Arabic

Al Mawakif: Est. 1973, P.O.Box 1083, Tel. 231231, Manama, Arabic

Gulf Construction: Exhibition Ave., P.O.Box 224, Tel. 293131, Manama, English

Gulf Daily News: Est. 1978, P.O.Box 5300, Tel. 620222, Manama, English

Gulf Economic Monitor: Exhibition Ave., P.O.Box 224, Tel. 293131, Manama, English

Oil and Gas News: Exhibition Ave., Bldg., 149, P.O.Box 224, Tel. 293131, Manama, English

Sada al Usbou: Est. 1969, P.O.Box 549, Tel. 291234, Bahrain, Arabic

DJIBOUTI
(Republic of Djibouti)

REPUBLIC OF DJIBOUTI

Head of State	: Ismael Omar GUELLEH
Capital	: Djibouti
Area	: 23,200 sq. Km.
Population	: 635.000 (1997 estimate)
Currency	: 100 Centimes = 1 Djibouti Franc. Notes 500,1000 and 5000 Djibouti Francs. Coins: 1, 2, 5, 10, 20, 50 and 100 Djibouti Francs.
Exchange Rate	: US $ 1=177.721 Djibouti Francs. (Dec. 1998)

History

INDEPENDENCE

The former French territory of the Afars and Issas became the independent Republic of Djibouti at midnight on June 26,1977, following approval of the relevant legislation by the French Parliament earlier in the month.

The achievement of independence was celebrated on June 27 at a ceremony organised by the "Ligue Populaire Africaine Pour l'Indépendance", the ruling party representing mainly the Issas (the country's majority ethnic group, akin to the Somalis), and in the presence of M. Robert Galley, the French Minister of Cooperation, and M. Olivier Stirn, French Secretary of State for Overseas Departments and Territories, both having been invited by Mr. Hassan Gouled Aptidon, the leader of the LPAI.

Mr. Hassan Gouled Aptidon who was at that time also Premier and in charge of Cooperation had, on June 24, by acclamation, been elected President of the Republic by the territorial Chamber of Deputies. The new President subsequently declared that the country's official language would be Arabic, and that the Republic of Djibouti would be non-aligned and remain committed to free enterprise.

The new Republic was immediately recognised by numerous countries, among them, Britain, China, Ethiopia, Saudi Arabia (and many other Arab countries), Somalia and the Soviet Union.

Furthermore on June 27, the Government of President Gouled applied for admission to the Organisation of African Unity and to the Arab League.

A French proposal to recommend to the UN General Assembly for the admission of the Republic of Djibouti to the United Nations was approved unanimously by the UN Security Council on July 7.

The territory of the Afars and Issas, formerly known as French Somaliland, had been a French possession for 115 years. It covered an area of some 9,000 square miles consisting mainly of desert country. In the absence of natural resources its population, apart from nomads, was economically dependent on the port of Djibouti, the coastal terminal of the Addis Ababa-Djibouti railway line, which had been completed in 1917. The line had been the property of the French-owned France-Ethiopia Railway Company until 1959, when President de Gaulle ceded 50% of its capital to the Ethiopian state and it became a company under Ethiopian law, with its head office in Addis Ababa.

Until May 1977 it carried about 60% of Ethiopia's imports and 40% of its exports, the remainder being handled by the Eritrean ports of Assab and Massawa.

The Republic of Djibouti, formerly known as the French Territory of Affars and Issas, became independent in June 1977 and was ruled since its independence by President Hassan Gouled Aptidon who was reelected in June 1981, April 1987 and for a fourth six year term in May 1993. He is the leader of the Rassemblement Populaire pour le Progrés (RPP). His party has won a confortable majority in the country's first multi-party parliamentary elections held on December 18 1992, following a referendum held in September 1992 which voted in favour of a multiparty constitution. In April 1999, Mr. Ismael Omar Guelleh was elected President. Legislative power is vested in a 65-member Chamber of Deputies elected for a five years term. The Cabinet is composed of the two main ethnic groups, the Affars and the Issas.

The Cabinet

(August 1999)

Prime Minister: Barkad Gourad HAMADOU

Minister of Justice, Muslim and Penal Affairs, and Human Rights: Ibrahim Idriss DJIBRIL

Minister of the Interior: Abdallah Abdillahi MIGUIL

Minister of Defence: Ougoureh Kifleh AHMED

Minister of Foreign Affairs, International Cooperation and Parliamentary Relations: Ali Abdi FARAH

Minister of Economy, Finance and Privatization: Yacin Elmi BOUH

Minister of Trade, Industry and Handicrafts: Elmi Obsieh WA'AYS

Minister of Agriculture, Livestock and Fishing: Ali Mohamed DAOUD

Minister of Communication and Culture, in charge of Post and Telecommunications, and Government Spoksman: Rifki Abdulkader BAMAKHRAMA

Minister of Education: Abdi Ibrahim ABSIEH

Minister of Employment and National Solidarity: Mohamed Barkat ABDILLAHI

Minister of Energy and Natural Resources: Mohamed Ali MOHAMED

Minister of Equipment and Transportation: Osman Idriss DJAMA

Minister of Health: Mohamed Dini FARAH

Minister of Presidential Affairs, in charge of Investment Promotion: Osman Ahmed MOUSSA

Minister of Urban Planning, Housing, the Environment

and National and Regional Development: Souleiman Omar OUDINE
Minister of Youth, Sports, Leisure and Tourism: Dini Abdallah BILILIS
Minister-Delegate to the Prime Minister in charge of Decentralization: Ahmed Guirreh WABERI
Minister-Delegate to the Prime Minister in charge of Mosque Properties and Muslim Affairs: Cheik Mogueh DIRIR
Minister-Delegate to the Prime Minister in charge of the Promotion of Women's, Family and Social Affairs: Hawa Ahmed YOUSSOUF

Foreign Embassies

China, People's Republic: Tel. 352246, Djbouti
Egypt: P.O.Box 1989, Tel. 351231, Djibouti
Ethiopia: P.O.Box 230, Tel. 350718, Djibouti
France: 45 Bldv. du Maréchal Foch, P.O.Box 2039, Tel. 350963, Djibouti
Iraq: P.O.Box 1983, Tel. 353469, Djibouti
Libya: P.O.Box 2073, Tel. 350202, Djibouti
Oman: P.O.Box 1996, Tel. 350852, Djibouti
Saudi Arabia: P.O.Box 1921, Tel. 351645, Djibouti
Somalia: P.O.Box 549, Tel. 353521, Djibouti
Sudan: P.O.Box 4259 Tel. 351404, Djibouti
Russia: P.O.Box 1913, Tel. 352051, Djibouti
U.S.A.: Villa Plateau du Serpent, Blvd. Maréchal Joffre, P.O.Box 185, Djibouti
Yemen: P.O.Box 194, Tel. 352975, Djibouti

Political Parties

Rassemblement Populaire pour le Progrès: formed in 1979,
Front pour la Restauration de l'Unité et de la Démocratie (FRUD): formed in 1991,
Parti du Renouveau Démocratique (PRD): Formed in 1992; Abdillahi Hamareite.
Parti National Démocratique: Formed in 1992; President Aden Robleh AWALLEH.

Religion

Protestants – Eglise Evangélique Française à l'Extérieur. Avenue de la République, P.O.Box 416, Djibouti.
Orthodox – There are about 500 Greek Orthodox.
Islam – Almost the entire population are Muslims.
Roman Catholic - Secretariat of the Bishopric, P.O.Box 94, Djibouti. There are about 9,000 Roman Catholics.

Banks

Banque Al Baraka: P.O.Box 2607, Tel. 355046, Djibouti.
Banque Nationale de Djibouti: Est. 1977, P.O.Box 2118, Tel. 352751, Djibouti.
Banque Indosuez (Mer Rouge): Est. 1908, 10 Place Lagarde, P.O.Box 88, Tel. 353016, Djibouti
Banque pour le Commerce et l'Industrie (Mer Rouge): Est. 1977, Place Lagarde, P.O.Box 2122, Tel. 350857, Djibouti
Banque de Développement de Djibouti: Est. 1983, P.O.Box 520, Tel. 353391, Djibouti

Transport

Railway

Compagnie du Chemin de Fer Djibouti-Ethiopien: P.O.Box 2116, Djibouti.

Roads

Over 3,000 km of roads, of which over 400km are surfaced.

Civil aviation

Air Djibouti: (Red Sea Airlines): P.O.Box 505, Djibouti.

Radio & Television and Press

The Press

Carrefour Africain: P.O.Box 393, Djibouti
La Nation: P.O.Box 32, Djibouti.
Radiodiffusion – Télévision de Djibouti (RTD)
P.O.Box 97, Djibouti; established in 1956; daily programmes in French, Afar, Somali and Arabic

Tourism

Office Nationale du Tourisme et de l'Artisanat: P.O.Box 1938, Place du 27 Juin, Tel. 353790, Djibouti

EGYPT
(Arab Republic of Egypt)

ARAB REPUBLIC OF EGYPT

Head of State : Mr Hosni MUBARAK
Area : 1,001,449 sq. Km.
Population : 62.9 million (mid 1996 estimate)
Exchange Rate : US$ 1=3.39 Egyptian pounds (£E) (May. 1998)

Geography

LAND AREA

The area of the Arab Republic of Egypt is about one million square kilometers, or nearly 238 million feddans (a feddan is slightly more than one acre, being 1.038 acre), of which only about 5,967,600 feddans (2.55) are cultivated.

The total area under cultivation in Lower Egypt is 3,478, 993 feddans as against 2,394,862 feddans in Upper Egypt and 93,745 feddans in other areas. However as the average rate of cropping per feddan is 1.68 crops per year, this gives the country an equivalent of 10,001,030 feddans of cropped area. It is important, in this respect, to distinguish between the two terms, the cultivated area and the cropped area.

The cultivated area is the number of feddans actually planted, whereas the cropped area (also expressed in feddans) is the cultivated area multiplied by the number of crops sown annually under perennial irrigation when several crops can be planted in rotation on the same land in the same area. The area that can be cultivated wholly depends on the level of the land in relation to the nearest supply of water. On the basis that the economic lift for water is at present limited to 20 meters, the total cultivable area is estimated at 10 million feddans.

CLIMATE

Basically, the A.R.E. can be divided into two climatic zones. The first comprises the Mediterranean coastal areas, including the Delta. The climate of this zone is of Mediterranean type, which is characterised by a mild rainy winter and a hot dry summer. The second zone covers the rest of Egypt south of Cairo. This is of the desert type, characterised by a winter with very little rain, warm during the day and cold during the night, and a dry summer, hot by day and mild during the night.

POPULATION

The population of the A.R.E. in 1996 totalled 62 million. Statistics also show that about two-thirds of the country's active labour force are engaged in agriculture and allied activities.

Population density has increased by more than 63 percent over the last 43 years, moving from 446 people to the square kilometre in 1937 to 763 people in 1980, according to the Egyptian Gazette daily newspaper of April 4, 1980 quoting the last special report of the Egyptian Central Statistical Agency.

RELIGION

Of a total population of 62,000,000 about 90 per cent are Sunni Muslims of the Hanafi and Shafi's sects, Islam being the official religion of the State.

The Christian communities, including Greeks, Italians, and other Europeans, and also Syrians and Lebanese have seen their numbers thinned down following the sweeping nationalisation measures of 1961.

The other Middle Eastern Christian communities (Greek Orthodox and Greek Catholic, Syrian Orthodox and Syrian Catholic and Maronite), enjoy a fairly stable position, though emigration to Canada and Australia has drained away the younger generations.

The long-resident Egyptian-Jewish community has been greatly diminished by emigration to Israel, since the 1956 Suez War.

The Copts, variously estimated at between 8,000,000 and 10,000,000, mainly peasants but also landowners and town-dwellers are authentic Egyptians with no other home or allegiance. The majority of Copts have kept their ancient faith (monophysite Christianity), minorities have accepted protestantism, others Catholicism, while conversions to Islam are not infrequent.

PUBLIC HOLIDAYS

Union Day (22 February); Sinai Day (25 April) — Labour Day (1 May); Sham El Nessim (Spring Day) (9 May); Evacuation Day (18 June); Eid al Fitr; Revolution Day (23 July); Wafa El Nil (15 August); Eid al Adha; Armed Forces Day (6 October); Muslim New Year. Suez city and Popular Resistance Day (24 October); Prophet's Birthday; Victory Day (23 December); New Year (Gregorian Calendar) (1 January).

REMARK

The Muslim year has only 354 days, so Muslim dates and holidays fall 10 to 12 days earlier each year on the Gregorian calendar.

History

FOREIGN INVADERS

From 30 B.C. to A.D. 639 Egypt was a Province of the Roman Empire, but in A.D. 640 the Christian inhabitants were subjugated by Moslem invaders, and Egypt became a province of the Eastern Caliphate. In 1517, the country was incorporated in the Ottoman Empire and was governed by Pashas sent from Constantinople until the beginning of the 18th century, when for about 100 years the ruler was chosen from among the Mamelukes, or bodyguard. Muhammad Ali, who was proclaimed Pasha in 1795, exterminated the Mamelukes in 1811 and was eventually made hereditary governor of Egypt and the Sudan by a firman from the Sultan on June 1, 1841.

In 1882, a military revolt, headed by an officer of the Egyptian Army (Ahmad Orabi Pasha) assumed alarming proportions and a British expedition was despatched to reestablish the authority of the Khedive. Meanwhile a revolt had broken out in the southern provinces, headed by Shaikh Muhammad Ahmad of Dongola, who proclaimed himself a Mahdi of Islam, and the British expeditionary force, sent to quell the rebellion of 1882, remained in the country as an army of occupation, until 1936.

BRITISH OCCUPATION

During the war of 1914-18 a British Protectorate over Egypt was declared (December 18, 1914) and the Khedive Abbas Hilmi was deposed. He was succeeded by Prince Hussein Kamel with the title of Sultan, and died on October 9, 1917 being suceeded by his brother, Prince Ahmad Fuad.

On the outbreak of war in 1914, Egypt was immediately and for ever severed from her long but now meaningless Turkish connection, and became a Sultanate under declared British protection, a status which Egyptian politicians strongly resented. After the war period, in which Egypt served as an important Allied base and entrepot, its future status became in 1919-22 a burning question which led to a series of demands and refusals, demonstrations and imprisonments, diplomatic missions and outbreaks of violence. Finally in 1922 a unilateral declaration by Britain confirmed the country's formal independence, as a constitutional monarchy.

In the Second World War Egypt took no part save that, again, of Allied base, a role which, in selfdefence, compelled the British to a measure of interference in Egyptian affairs.

THE KING ABDICATES

On July 23, 1952, following a military coup d'Etat, King Farouk was forced to abdicate and left the country on July 26. His property was sequestrated. The King's infant son Ahmad Fuad II became King of Egypt, and a Regency Council was appointed August 5,1952.

On June 18, 1953, the Council of Revolution deposed the young king, and declared Egypt a Republic, and Bikbashi (Lieutenant-Colonel) Gamal Abdel Nasser assumed the premiership.

THE SUEZ CONFLICT (1956)

In July 1956, after America and Britain had withdrawn their offers to help finance Egypt's Aswan Dam project, President Nasser summarily expropriated the Suez Canal Company. On October 29th the Israelis invaded Sinai, advancing to points near the Suez Canal. Britain and France demanded that both belligerents cease fire and allow them to occupy key places along the Canal. Egypt refused, and on November 5th British and French troops seized Port Said. Egypt blocked the Canal by sinking ships in it. Only a few hours after the Port Said landing all four parties ceased fire. The United Nations Assembly demanded almost unanimously that Britain, France and Israel withdraw from Egyptian soil, and an international UN force was sent to the Canal and Sinai to help prevent further conflicts.

DEATH OF PRESIDENT NASSER

On September 28, 1970, President Gamal Abdel Nasser died in Cairo at the age of 52 due to coronary thrombosis. His death occurred only 24 hours after the ending of the Cairo summit meeting which had succeeded in bringing to an end the civil war in Jordan.

Following Nasser's death, Mohamed Anwar Sadat became acting president and after the unanimous approval of his candidature for the presidency by the National Assembly his election was confirmed by a national referendum on October 15 in which 90.04% of the votes cast were affirmative.

SOVIET MILITARY ADVISERS WITHDRAWN FROM EGYPT

In an entirely unexpected and unanticipated development President Sadat announced the immediate departure from Egypt of all Soviet military advisers and experts in the country, and their replacement by Egyptian personnel. (Western sources estimated the number of Soviet advisers and experts in Egypt to be in the region of 20,000).

DESEQUESTRATION

On April 19, 1972, a parliamentary committee recommended that millions of pounds worth of property arbitrarily seized from Egyptian citizens since 1964 should be returned to their owners.

Other reforms announced by the President on Sept. 16 included: 1) a rise in minimum wages;2) the setting up of an Egyptian Bank for Foreign Trade;3) the creation of "technical bureaux" consisting of experts serving under the President's advisers;4) the reinstatement of 112 judges who had been transferred or retired by President Nasser as a disciplinary measure;5) the restoration of full political rights to some 12,000 persons who had been under political restrictions since 1962.

THE FOURTH ARAB-ISRAELI WAR

The fourth war between the Arab states and Israel since 1948 broke out on Oct. 6,1973, when a powerful Egyptian offensive was launched across the Suez Canal and an equally strong Syrian offensive on the Golan Heights.

After some of the bitterest and bloodiest fighting since the Second World War, marked by great tank battles and heavy losses of men and material on both sides, Egypt and Israel agreed to a cease-fire on Oct. 22 in response to a resolution of the UN Security Council, and after the truce had been broken, agreed on Oct. 24 to cease hostilities in response to a second Security Council resolution.

WAR AFTERMATH

A number of important developments took place in Egypt following the fourth Arab-Israel war of October 1973, notably the drafting and adoption in a referendum, of a far-reaching plan for economic, social and political reforms for the transformation of Egypt into a completely modern society by the end of the 20th century.

The main points of this programme were: (1) the rapid economic development of the country during the last quarter of the century, envisaging economic development at a faster rate than hitherto and with priority for the reconstruction of the war devastated towns of the Suez Canal; (2) an "open door" financial policy designed to attract foreign investors by establishing industrial free zones, giving investors liberal terms for the repatriation of their profits, and assuring them of protection against nationalization and confiscation; (3) non-alignment in foreign affairs; (4) an "open society" in which the rights of all citizens would be protected by the courts against police interference and bureaucracy: (5) systematic planning for social development, and for the application of science, technology and cultural progress based upon both science and the Islamic religion; (6) a pledge to maintain the public sector of the economy while at the same time creating a new free-enterprise sector to complement it.

SADAT'S PEACE INITIATIVE

Historic development in Arab-Israeli relations took place in the latter part of 1977 when President Sadat visited Jerusalem on November 19 which led to normalisation of relations between the two countries under the provisions of the Camp David peace treaty. Several agreements were signed on cultural, economic, transport and tourism matters.

ASSASSINATION OF PRESIDENT SADAT

President Anwar el Sadat of Egypt was assassinated on Oct.6 1981 in an attack mounted during a military parade in Cairo by an army officer and three men who were later found to be members of the country's Islamic fundamentalist movement.

PRESIDENT HOSNI MUBARAK

In accordance with the Egyptian Constitution, effective political power passed to Vice-President Hosni Mubarak, who was nominated as President by the People's Assembly on Oct.6. He was sworn in as Head of the State on Oct. 14. In his inaugural address he pledged to continue all aspects of President Sadat's domestic and international policies, including the peace process with Israel.

President Hosni Mubarak was sworm in for a second six-year term as President on Oct. 12, 1987. He had become President on Oct. 14, 1981, following the assassination of President Anwar el-Sadat.

His uncontested renomination by the ruling National Democratic Party had been approved by the People's Assembly (parliament) on July 6,1987, and was approved by slightly more than 97 per cent of the valid votes cast in a national referendum held on Oct. 5, 1987.

President Mubarak has been sworn in for a third six-year term in July 1993 by 439 out of 448 in the People's Assembly. He was sworn in for a fourth term of six years on Oct. 5,1999

RELATIONS WITH ISRAEL - LINKS WITH ARAB COUNTRIES

President Mubarak attended the seventh United Nations Conference on trade and development in Geneva on July 9,1987, during which he held two hours of talks with the Israeli Foreign Minister, Mr. Shimon Peres. It was reported that they discussed a US "working paper" on the prospects for an international peace conference on the Middle East. President Mubarak and Mr. Peres had previously met in Cairo in February 1987.

On July 13, 1987, the director-general of the Israeli Foreign Ministry, Mr. Abraham Tamir visited Cairo to discuss peace efforts in the Middle East. This was followed on July 20, 1987, by a three-day visit to Israel by the Egyptian Foreign Minister, Dr. Ahmed Esmat Abdel Meguid, who discussed similar matters with Mr. Peres. This was the first such visit since the Israeli invasion of Lebanon in 1982.

Egypt had been expelled from the Arab League in 1979, following the Egypt's signing of the 1978 Camp David agreements and of a peace treaty with Israel.

The Summit meeting of the Arab Heads of States in Casablanca on 23-26, 5, 1989 readmitted Egypt to the Arab League.

In March 1990 the Arab States agreed to return the Arab League's headquarters from Tunis to Cairo.

In August 1990, following Iraq's invasion of Kuwait, an emergency summit conference of the Arab League was held. 12 members approved a resolution demanding the withdrawal of Iraq forces from Kuwait, impose economic sanctions on Iraq and send troops for an Arab defensive force in Saudi Arabia.

In 1991 following the League's Return to Cairo, Egypt regained its status as the country to be accounted for in the Arab World.

In 1992 and 1993 fundamentalist actions have become more active and tourists facilities became targets of terrorists attacks. However, measures were taken by the government to combat violent activism in the country.

Egypt is actively involved in bringing about Arab reconciliation and the settlement of the Arab-Israeli dispute.

Political Parties

- **National Democratic Party (NDP)** Founded in August 1979 by Egyptian President Sadat; vice-president of NDP: President Hosni Mubarak; secretary-general: Dr. Yousuf Amin WALI.
- **Socialist Labour Party (SLP)** Founded in August 1978 Leader Ibrahim Shukri.
- **New Wafd Party** re-established in February 1978 under the leadership of Fuad Serageddin.
- **National Progressive Unionist Party (NPUP)** led by Khaled Mohiedin.

— **Liberal Socialist Party,** Founded 1976, leader Mustapha Kamel Murad.

The Cabinet

(Oct. 1999)

Prime Minister: Dr. Atef Mohamad OBAID
Deputy Prime Minister: Dr. Yusuf Amin WALLY
Minister of Defence and Military Production: Field Marshal Mohamed Hussein TANTAWI
Minister of Foreign Affairs: Amr MOUSSA
Minister of the Interior: Abed al ADLI
Minister of Information: Mohamed Safwat Mohamed Yusuf al SHARIF
Minister of Public Business Sector: Dr. Mukhtar KHATTAB
Minister of Education: Hussein Kamel BAHAEDDINE
Minister of Transport: Dr. Ibrahim DAMIRI
Minister of Communications: Dr. Ahmed NAZIF
Minister of Electricity and Energy: Ali SAIDI
Minister of Justice: Farouk Mahmoud Seif al NASR
Minister of Finance: Dr. Medhat HASSANEIN
Minister of Awqaf: Mahmoud ZAKZOUK
Minister of Supply and Trade: Dr. Hassan KHODOR
Minister of Petroleum and Mineral Wealth: Dr. Sameh FAHMI
Minister of Culture: Farouk HOSNI
Minister of Social Insurance and Social Affairs: Dr. Amina JUNDI
Minister of Economy: Yusuf Boutros GHALI
Minister of Rural Development: Mahmoud Sayed Ahmed SHARIF
Minister of Health: Ismail Awadallah SALAM
Minister of State for People's Assembly and Shura Council: Kamal SHAZLI
Minister of Planning and International Cooperation: Dr. Ahmed DARDACH
Minister of Public Works and Water Resources: Mahmoud Abdelhalim ABU ZEID
Minister of Industry and Technology Development: Dr. Mustafa RIFAI
Minister of Higher Education and Scientific Research: Mufid Mahmoud SHEHAB
Minister of State for Military Production: Dr. Said MASHAAL
Minister of Manpower and Employment: Ahmad Ahmad al AMMAWI
Minister of Housing and Utilities: Mohamed Ibrahim SOLEIMAN
Minister of State for Environment: Nadia Makram OBEID
Minister of State for Administrative Development: Mustafa ABDELKADER
Minister of Tourism: Mamdouh Ahmad BALTAGI
Minister of Youths: Dr. Ali Eddine HILAL

Foreign Embassies

Albania: 29 Ismail Mohamed, Str., Tel. (02)3415651, Zamalek, Cairo
Algeria: 14 Bresil Str., Zamalek, Cairo; Tel: (02)3418527
Angola: 12 Midan an-Nasr, Tel. (02)707602, Dokki, Cairo
Argentina: 8 As-Saleh Ayoub, Str., Tel. (02)3401501, Zamalek Cairo
Australia: Corniche, en-Nil, Cairo Plaza Annexe, South Bldg., 5th Floor, Tel. (02)777900, Cairo
Austria: En-Nil Str., Cnr of Wissa Wassef Str., Tel (02)5702975, Giza, Cairo
Bahrain: 8 Gamiet an-Nisr Str., Tel. (02)706202
Bangladesh: 47 Sharia Ahmed Hesmat, Tel. (2)3412642, Zamalek, Cairo
Belgium: 20 Kamel esh-Shennawi Str., Tel. (02)3547494, Garden City, Cairo
Bolivia: Tel. (02)3546390, Cairo
Brazil: 1125 Corniche en-Nil, Tel. (02)756938, Maspiro, 11561 Cairo
Brunei: 11 Sharia Amer Tel. (2) 3485903, Dokki, Cairo
Bulgaria: 141 Tahrir, Str., Tel. (02)982691, Dokki, Cairo
Burkina Faso: 3 Abdel-Khawi Ahmed Str., Ramses Centre, P.O.Box 306, Tel. (02)3440301, Cairo
Burundi: 13 el-Israa Str., Madinet el-Mohandessin, Tel. (02)3419940, Dokki, Cairo
Cameroon: 15 el-Israa Str., Madinet el-Mohandessin, P.O.Box 2061, Tel. (02)341101, Dokki, Cairo
Canada: 6 Muhammad Fahmy eld-Sayed Str., Tel. (02)3543110, Garden City, Cairo
Central African Republic: 13 Chehab Str., Madinet eld-Mohandessin, Tel. (02)713291, Dokki, Cairo
Chad: 12 Midan ar-Refaï, P.O.Box 1869, Tel. (02)703232, Dokki, Cairo
Chile: 5 Shagaret Ad-Dorr Str., Tel. (02)3408711, Zamalek, Cairo
China People's Republic: 14 Bahgat Ali Str., Tel. (02)3417691, Zamalek, Cairo
Colombia: 20/A Gamal-Eddine Aboul-Mahassen, Tel. (02)3546152, Garden City, Cairo
Cuba: 6 Fawakeh Str., Madinet el-Mohandessin, Tel. (02)710525, Dokki, Cairo
Cyprus: 23 Ismail Mohamed Str., Tel. (02)3411288, Zamalek, Cairo
Czech: 4 Dokki Str., Tel. (02)3485531, Giza, Cairo
Denmark: 12 Hassan Sabri Str., Tel. (02)3407411, Zamalek, Cairo
Djibouti: 157 Sudan Str., Madinet el-Mohandessin, Tel. (02)709787, Dokki, Cairo
Ecuador: 4 Sharia Ibn Kasir, Suez Canal Bldg., Tel. (2) 3496782, Giza, Cairo
Ethiopia: 3 Sharia Ismail Osman, Mohandessin, Tel. (2) 3477805, Dokki, Cairo
Finland: 3 Abu el Feda Str., Tel. (02)3411487, Zamalek, Cairo
France: 29 Ave en-Nil, Tel. (02)728346, Giza, Cairo

Gabon: 15 Mossadek Str., Tel. (02)702963, Dokki, Cairo
Germany: 8 Hassan Sabri Str., Tel. (02)3410015, Zamalek, Cairo
Ghana: 24 Batal Ahmad Abdelaziz Str., Tel. (02)704275, Dokki, Cairo
Greece: 18 Aicha et-Taimouria Str., Tel. (02)3550443, Garden City, Cairo
Guatemala: 8 Muhammad Fahmi el-Mohdar St., Primer Zone, P.O.Box 8062, Tel. (2) 2611813, Madinet Nasr, Cairo
Guinea: 46 Mohamed Mazhar Str., Tel. (02)3411088, Zamalek, Cairo
Guinea-Bissau: 37 Lebanon Str., Madinet el-Mohandessin, Dokki, Cairo
Holy See: Apostolic Nunciature, 5 Mohamed Mazhar Str., Tel. (02)3402250, Zamalek, Cairo
Hungary: 29 Mohamed Mazhar Str., Tel. (02)3400653, Zamalek, Cairo
India: 5 Aziz Abaza Str., Tel. (02)3413051, Zamalek, Cairo
Indonesia: 13 Aicha et-Taimouria Str., P.O.Box 1661, Tel. (02)3547200, Garden City, Cairo
Ireland: 3 Abu el-Feda Str., P.O.Box 2681, Tel. (02)3408264, Zamalek, Cairo
Israel: 6 Ibn el-Malek Str., Tel. (02)729329, Giza, Cairo
Italy: 15 Abderrahman Fahmi Str., Tel. (02)3543974, Garden City, Cairo
Ivory Coast: 39 el-Kods esh-Sherif Str., Madinet el-Mohandessin, Tel. (02)699009, Dokki, Cairo
Japan: 2 Abdel Kadr Hamza Str., Cairo Centre Bldg., 3rd Floor, Tel. (02)3551477, Cairo
Jordan: 6 Juhaini Str., Tel. (02)982766, Cairo
Kenya: 7 el-Mohandess Galal St., P.O.Box 362, Tel. (2) 3453907, Dokki, Cairo
Korea Democratic People's Republic: 6 Saleh Ayoub Str., Tel. (02)650970, Zamalek, Cairo
Korea Republic: 3 Sharia Boolos Hanna, Tel. (2) 3611234, Dokki, Cairo
Kuwait: 12 Nabil el-Wakkad Str., Tel. (02)701611, Dokki, Cairo
Lebanon: 5 Ahmad Nessim Str., Tel. (02)728454, Giza, Cairo
Liberia: 11 Brazil Str., Tel. (02)3419864, Zamalek, Cairo
Libya: 7 es-Saleh Ayoub, Zamalek, Cairo; Tel: (02)3401864
Malaysia: 7 Wadi en-Nil Str., Mohandessin, Tel. (02)699162, Agouza, Cairo
Mali: 3 al-Kawsar Str., Tel. (02)701641, Dokki, Cairo
Mauritania: 31 Syria Str., Tel. (02)707229, Dokki, Cairo
Mauritius: 72 Abdel-Moneim Riad Str., Tel. (02)3470929, Agouza, Cairo
Mexico: 5 Dar es-Shifa Str., Tel. (02)988457, Cairo
Mongolia: 3 Midan en-Nasr, Tel. (02)650060, Dokki, Cairo
Morocco: 10 Salah Eddine Str., Zamalek, Cairo; Tel: (02)3409849
Myanmar: 24 Mohamed Mazhar Str., Tel. (02)3404176, Zamalek, Cairo
Nepal: 9 Tiba Str., Tel. (02)704447, Dokki, Cairo
Netherlands: 18 Hassan Sabri Str., Tel. (02)3406434, Zamalek, Cairo
Niger: 28 Pahlaw Str., Tel. (02)987740, Dokki, Cairo
Nigeria: 13 Gabalaya Str., Tel. (02)3406042, Zamalek, Cairo
Norway: 8 Gezireh Str., Tel. (02)3403340, Zamalek, Cairo
Oman: 30 el-Montazah Str., Tel. (02)3407811, Zamalek, Cairo
Pakistan: 8 es-Salouli Str., Tel. (02)3487677, Dokki, Cairo
Panama: 5 Shagaret Ad-Dorr Str., Tel. (02)3411093, Zamalek, Cairo
Peru: 8 Kamel esh-Shennawi Str., Tel. (02)3411754, Garden City, Cairo
Philippines: 6 Ibn el-Walid Str., Tel. (02)3480396, Dokki, Cairo
Poland: 5 el-Aziz Osman Str., Tel. (02)3409583, Zamalek, Cairo
Portugal: 15 A Mansour Mohamed Str., Tel (02)3405583, Zamalek, Cairo
Qatar: 10 ath-Thamar Str., Midan an-Nasr, Madinet el-Mohandessin, Tel. (02)704537, Cairo
Romania: 4 Sharia Aziz Abaza, Tel. (02)3410107, Zamalek, Cairo
Russia: 95 Giza Str., Tel. (02)731416, Giza, Cairo
Rwanda: 9 Ibrahim Osman Str., P.O.Box 485, Tel. (02)361079, Cairo
Saudi Arabia: 12 al-Kamel Mohamed Str., Tel. (02)819111, Zamalek, Cairo
Senegal: 46 Abdel-Moneim Riad Str., Mohandessin, Tel. (02)3458479, Dokki, Cairo
Singapore: 40 Babel Str., P.O.Box 356, Tel. (02)704744, Dokki, Cairo
Slovakia: 3 Sharia Adel Hussein Rostom, Tel. (2) 718240, Giza, 12511 Cairo
Somalia: 28 Abdel-Moneim Riad Str., Tel. (02)704038, Dokki, Cairo
Spain: 9 Hod el-Laban, Tel. (02)3547069, Garden City, Cairo
Sri Lanka: 8 Sri Lanka Str., P.O.Box 1157, Tel. (02)3417138, Zamalek, Cairo
Sudan: 4 el-Ibrahimi Str., Tel. (02)3549661, Garden City, Cairo
Sweden: 13 Mohamed Mazhar Str., P.O.Box 131, Tel. (02)3414132, Zamalek, Cairo
Switzerland: 10 Abdel Khalek Sarwat Str., P.O.Box 633, Tel. (02)758133, Cairo
Syria: 14 Ahmad Hechmar Str., Zamalek, Cairo
Tanzania: 9 Abdel-Hamid Lotfi Str., Tel. (02)704155, Dokki, Cairo
Thailand: 2 al-Malek al-Afdal Str., Tel. (02)3408356, Zamalek, Cairo
Tunisia: 26 el-Jazirah Str., Tel. (02)3404940, Zamalek, Cairo
Turkey: Ave. en-Nil, Tel. (02)726115, Giza, Cairo
Uganda: 9 Midan el-Messaha, Tel. (02)3485544, Dokki, Cairo
United Arab Emirates: 4 Ibn Sina Str., Giza, Cairo; Tel: (02)729955

United Kindgom: Ahmad Raghab Str., Tel. (02)3540852, Garden City, Cairo

U.S.A.: 8 Sharia Kamal ed-Dine, Tel. (02)3557371, Garden City, Cairo

Uruguay: 6 Lotfallah Str., Tel. (02)3415137, Zamalek, Cairo

Venezuela: 15A Mansour Mohamed Str., Tel. (02)3413517, Zamalek, Cairo

Viet-Nam: 39 Sharia Kambiz, Tel. (02) 701494, Dokki, Cairo

Yemen: 28 Amin Rifai Str., Dokki, Cairo; Tel. (02)3604806

Yugoslavia: 33 Mansour Mohamed Str., Tel. (02)3404061, Zamalek, Cairo

Zaire: 5 Mansour Mohamed Str., Tel. (02)3403662, Zamalek, Cairo

Zambia: 6 Abd ar-Rahman Hossein, Mohandessin, P.O.Box 253, Dokki, Tel. (02) 3610282, 12311 Cairo.

Zimbabwe: 36 Wadi an-Nil Str., Mohandessin, Cairo; Tel. (02)3471217

The Economy

In 1987, there were improvements both in the domestic economy and on the external account. Real growth in GDP reached an estimated 3.7%, accompanied by an increase in exports of some 17% and an increase in imports of only 6%, following an estimated fall expected to remain so over the medium term. Only marginal growth of 0.4% is estimated to have taken place in investment and consumption with the latter, both public and private, being held back by cuts in government subsidies. Investment was low as a result of reduced government expenditure, and a credit squeeze was imposed on banks throughout most of the year. Despite tight monetary policies which limited money supply growth (M2) to around 17%, prices rose by over 20%, reflecting higher import costs and increased charges for several basic industrial and consumer goods. Analysed by sector, services are estimated to have made the strongest recovery with an expansion of some 5% which is mainly to be credited to an upsurge in tourism which stimulated the hotel, recreation and retail trades. The industrial sector grew by 3.0%, after an estimated contraction of 2.8% in 1986, and agriculture by 2.3%

The improvement in economic performance continued into 1988. Although oil prices were weaker, revenues from tourism continued to increase. The reforms in the financial and exchange rate regimes contributed to a more buoyant investment outlook and the competitive exchange rate encouraged further export growth. Real GDP growth for 1988 was around 3.5%. Inflation remained high, however, partly as a result of currency depreciation and partly reflecting the impact of the continued removal of subsidies on domestic prices.

The five-year plan for the fiscal years 1 July-30 June 1987/88 - 1991/92 aimed at an annual average GDP growth of 5.8% and stresses structural changes with a view to making industry the dominant sector in the Egyptian economy. Production of goods and services was promoted at the expense of private consumption, which is planned to expand by 4.4% a year. Investments totalling £E 46.5 billion increased output by over 30% during the course of the plan.

The 1987 budget reduced the deficit from 20% to 13% of GDP through an increase in revenues. Austerity measures included further elimination of subsidies, price increases, and higher taxes and customs duties. Further measures suggested by the IMF included raising interest rates from their level of 11% – 13% to around 20%, taking significant steps towards removing structural imbalances in the government budget, and tax reform.

In 1989 government revenue was £E 22.6 million and expenditure stood at £E 23.91 billion.

The July 1991/June 1992 budget was estimated et Egyptian Pounds 54,341 million expenditure and revenue et £E 45,083 million. The 1992/93 budget estimates were £E 62,533 million expenditure and £E 53,389 million revenue.

In 1994 the budget figures were at £E 61.98 billion revenue and £E 70.54 billion for expenditure.

In 1995 the government budget for the fiscal year 1995–96 starting July 1995 was unveiled by the Minister of Finance on April 11. The revenue projected is £E 66.195 billion and expenditure £E 71.492 billion.

The 1996/97 government budget figures were £E 77.4 billion for expenditure and a revenue of £E 71.4 billion. As for the year 1997/98 the budget was set at an expected expenditure of £E 83.8 billion and a revenue of £E 76.4 billion, and the 1998/99 budget approved in May 1999 was £E 91.8 billion expenditure and £E 83.2 revenue.

The Banking System

Central Bank of Egypt: Est. 1961, 31 Kasr el-Nil Str., Tel. (02)3931514, Cairo

Alexandria Commercial and Maritime Bank: Est. 1981, 85 Ave. el-Houriya, P.O.Box 2376, Tel. (03)4921556, Alexandria

Alwatany Bank of Egypt: Est. 1980, P.O.Box 63, Tel. (02)3379134, Cairo

Arab African International Bank: Est. 1964, 5 Midan es-Saray el-Koubra, P.O.Box 60, Garden City, Tel. (02)3545094, 11516 Cairo

Arab International Bank: Est. 1971, 35 Abdel-Khalek Sarwat Str., P.O.Box 1563, Tel. (02)3916120, Cairo

Bank of Alexandria SAE: Est. 1957, 6 Salah Salem Str., Tel. (03)4836073, Alexandria

Bank of Commerce and Development: Est. 1980, 13 Midan 26 July, Sphinx, Mohandessin, Tel. (02)3479461, Cairo

Banque du Caire, SAE: Est. 1952, 30 Roushdy Str., P.O.Box 1495, Tel. (02)3904554, Cairo

Banque du Caire Barclays International, SAE: Est. 1957, 12 Midan Sheikh Yousuf, P.O.Box 10, Tel. (02)3542195, Garden City, Cairo

Banque du Caire et de Paris: Est. 1977, 3 Latin America Str., P.O.Box 2441, Tel. (02)3548323, Cairo

Banque Misr: Est. 1920, 151 Mohamed Farid Str. Tel. (02)3912150, Cairo

Cairo Far East Bank: Est. 1978, 104 Corniche en-Nil, P.O.Box 757, Tel. (02)3362516, Cairo

Commercial International Bank (Egypt), SAE: Est. 1975, Nile Tower Bldg., 21-23 Giza Str., P.O.Box 2430, Tel. (02)5701949, Giza, Cairo

Credit Foncier Egyptien: Est. 1880, el-Mashadi Str., P.O.Box 141, Tel. (02)3911977, Cairo

Credit International d'Egypte: Est. 1977, 46 El Batal Ahmed Abdelaziz Str. Tel. (02)712823, Cairo

Delta International Bank: Est. 1978, 1113 Corniche en-Nil, P.O.Box 1159, Tel. (02)5753484, Cairo

Egypt Arab African Bank: Est. 1982, 5 Midan es-Saray el-Koubra, P.O.Box 61, Tel. (02)3550948, Garden City, Cairo

Egyptian American Bank: Est. 1976, 4 Hassan Sabri Str., P.O.Box 1825, Tel. (02)3416150, Zamalek, Cairo

Egyptian Export Development Bank: Est. 1983, 10 Talaat Harb Str., Evergreen Bldg., Tel. (02)5782584, Cairo

Egyptian Gulf Bank: Est. 1981, 8-10 Ahmad Nessim Str., P.O.Box 56, Tel. (02)3606457, Giza, Cairo

Egyptian Saudi Finance Bank: Est. 1980, 12 Ittihad el-Mohameen el-Arab Str., Tel. (02)3546208, Garden City, Cairo

Faisal Islamic Bank of Egypt: Est. 1979, 1113 Corniche en-Nil, P.O.Box 2446, Tel. (02)5753109, Cairo

Egyptian British Bank: Est. 1982, 3 Abu el-Feda Str., Abu el-Feda Bldg., P.O.Box 126, Tel. (02)3404849, Zamalek, Cairo

Housing and Development Bank: Est. 1979, 26 Syria Str. P.O.Box 234, Tel. (02)3492013, Dokki, Cairo

Islamic International Bank for Investment and Development: Est. 1980, 4 Ali Ismail Str., Mesaha Sq., P.O.Box 180, Tel. (02)3489973, Cairo

Misr-America International Bank: Est. 1977,5 Midan es-Seraya el-Koubra, P.O.Box 1003, Tel. (02)3554359, Garden City, Cairo

Misr Exterior Bank, SAE: Est. 1981, Corniche en-Nill, Cairo Plaza Bldg., P.O.Box 272, Tel. (02)778552, Cairo

Misr International Bank, SAE: Est. 1975, 54 El Batal Ahmed Abdelaziz Str., P.O.Box 218, Tel. (02)3497091, Cairo

Misr Iran Development Bank: Est. 1975, 21 Giza Str., The Nile Tower, P.O.Box 219, Tel. (02)5727311, el-Orman, Cairo

Misr-Romanian Bank, SAE: Est. 1977, 15 Abu el-Feda Str., P.O.Box 35, Tel. (02)3419275, Zamalek, Cairo

Mohandes Bank: Est. 1979, 30 Ramses Str., P.O.Box 170, Tel. (02)3362760, Cairo

Nasser Social Bank: Est. 1971, 35 Kasr el-Nil Str., P.O.Box 2552, Te. (02)744377, Cairo

National Bank for Development: Est. 1980, 5 el-Borsa e7l-Gedida Str., P.O.Box 647, Tel. (02)3563505, Cairo

National Bank of Egypt: Est. 1898, P.O.Box 11611, Tel. (02)5749101, Cairo

National Investment Bank: 18 Abdel-Meguid Remaly Str., Bad el-Louk, Tel. (02)3541336, Cairo

National Société Générale Bank, SAE: Est. 1978, 4 Talaat Harb Str., P.O.Box 2664, Tel. (02)5747396, Cairo

Nile Bank, SAE: Eskt. 1978, 35 Ramses Str., P.O.Box 2741, Tel. (02)5741417, Cairo

Principal Bank for Development and Agricultural Credit: Est. 1976, 110 Kasr el-Eini Str., P.O.Box 11669, Tel. (02)3551204, Cairo

Société Arabe Internationale de Banque: Est. 1976, 56 Gamet ed-Dowal al-Arabia Str., P.O.Box 124, Tel. (02)3499460, Giza, Cairo

Suez Canal Bank: Est. 1978, 11 Mohamed Sabry Abu Alam Str., P.O.Box 2620, Tel. (02)3931033, Cairo.

STOCK EXCHANGES

Alexandria Stock Exchange: Est. 1861, 11 Talaat Harb Str., Tel. (03)4835432, Alexandria

Cairo Stock Exchange: Est. 1904, 4 Sherifein Str., Tel. (02)3921447, Cairo

Capital Market Authority: Est. 1979, 20 Emadeddine Str., Tel. (02)726626, Cairo

Trade Unions

Egyptian Trade Union Federation: Est. 1957, 90 Galaa Str., Tel. (02)5740362, Cairo, 23 affiliated Unions, about 5 million members. Affiliated to the International Confederation of Arab Trade Unions and to the Organization of Africa Trade Union.

General Trade Union of Air Transport: 5 Ahmad Sennan Str., Fatima, Heliopolis, Cairo

General Trade Union of Banks and Insurance: 2 Kadi el-Fadel Str., Cairo

General Trade Union of Building Workers: 9 Emadeddine Str., Cairo

General Trade Union of Chemical Workers: 90 Galaa Str., Cairo

General Trade Union of Commerce: Est. 1903, 70 Goumhouriya Str., Tel. (02)914124, Cairo

General Trade Union of Food Industries: 3 Hosni Hadaek el-Koba Str., Cairo

General Trade Union of Health Services: 22 Sheikh Kamar Sakakiny Str., Cairo

General Trade Union of Maritime Transport: 36 Sherif Str., Cairo

General Trade Union of Military Production: 90 Galaa Str., Cairo

General Trade Union of Mine Workers: 5 Ali Sharawi Str., Hadaek el-Koba, Cairo

General Trade Union of Petroleum Workers: 5 Ali Sharawi Str., Cairo

General Trade Union of Postal Workers: 90 Galaa Street, Cairo

General Trade Union of Press, Printing and Information: 90 Galaa Str., Tel. (02)740324, Cairo

General Trade Union of Public and Administrative

Workers: 2 Mohamed Haggag Str., Midan el-Tahrir, Tel. (02)742134, Cairo

General Trade Union of Public Utilities: 22 Sherif Str., Cairo

General Trade Union of Railway Workers: 15 Emadeddine Str., P.O.Box 84, Tel. (02)5930305, Cairo

General Trade Union of Road Transport: 90 Galaa Str., Tel. (02)5754919, Cairo

General Trade Union of Textile Workers: 327 Shoubra Str., Cairo

General Trade Union of Hotels and Tourism Workers: 90 Galaa Str., Cairo

General Trade Union of Workers in Engineering, Metal and Electrical Industries: 90 Galaa Str., Tel. (02)742519, Cairo

General Trade Union of Teleconnumications Workers: P.O.Box 651, Cairo

Transport

RAILWAYS

Egyptian Railways: Est. 1851; Midan Ramses, Cairo.

Cairo Metro: Kasr al Aini Streeet, Cairo.

Cairo Transport Authority: P.O.Box 254, Nasr City, Cairo.

Alexandria Passenger Transport Authority: P.O.Box 466, 2 Aflaton Street, Alexandria.

Lower Egypt Railways: Est. 1898, Mansura, Lower Egypt.

ROADS

Egypt has well asphalted roads connecting Cairo (the capital) to various important cities as Alexandria, Tanta, Damanhour, Benha, Suez, Ismailia and Port Said. A road tunnel beneath the Suez Canal, with a length of 1600 meters connecting Egypt with Sinai is also operating since end 1980.

SHIPPING

The principal ports in Egypt are Alexandria, Port Said, Suez and Damietta.

The Suez Canal is an important link between the Mediterranean and the Red Sea. About 15000 ships used this waterway in 1995.

Alexandria Port Authority: 66 Gamal Abdel-Nasser Ave., Alexandria.

Suez Canal Authority: Est. 1956, Ismailia, Tel. (64)330000, 6 Lazoghli Str., Garden City, Cairo

Civil Aviation

The main Airports in Egypt are at Heliopolis near Cairo, and at Alexandria.

Egyptair: Est. 1932; Cairo international airport Heliopolis, Cairo.

Egyptian Civil Aviation Authority: 31, 26th July Street, Cairo.

Radio, Television and Press

RADIO & TELEVISION

Egyptian Radio & Television Union - Corniche el Nil street, P.O.Box 11511, Cairo. Est. 1928.

THE PRESS

The Egyptian press is well developed. The leading publishers are:

Dar el Ahram: Est. 1875, Galaa Str., Tel. (02)576069, Cairo; (publications: Al Ahram, daily Arabic newspaper; Al Ahram Al Iktissadi, Arabic Weekly).

Dar Akhbar el Yom: Est. 1944, 6 Sahafa Str., Cairo; (publications: (Akhbar el Yom Arabic weekly; al Akhbar, Arabic daily; Akher Saa, Arabic weekly).

Dar al-Goumhouriya: 24 Zakaria Ahmad Str., Cairo; (publications: Al Goumhouriya and Al Masaa, Arabic dailies; Egyptian Gazette, English daily; Progrès Egyptien, French daily).

Dar Al Hilal: Est. 1892, Mohamed Ezz el Arab Str., Tel. (02)20610, Cairo; (publications: Al Moussawar, Hawaa, Kawaqeb, Samir, Mickey-weeklies; Al Hilal, Tabibak-monthlies).

Dar al Kitab al Masri: Est. 1929, 33 Kasr el Nil Str., P.O.Box 156, Tel. (02)3922168, Cairo

Dar al Maaref: Est. 1890, 1119 Corniche en Nil Str., Tel. (02)7770777, Cairo

General Egyptian Book Organization: Est. 1961, 117 Corniche en Nil Str., Tel. (02)775000, Cairo

Tahrir Printing and Publishing House: Est. 1953, 24 Zakaria Ahmad Str., Tel. (02)5781010, Cairo

Universities

Aïn Shams University
Est. 1950; Kasr el Zaafaran, Abbasiya, Tel.: 820230, Cairo

Alexandria University
Est. 1942; El Sgeish Ave., El Shatby, Tel.: 71675/8, Alexandria

Al Azhar University
Est. 970; Tel. 904051, 706097, 906154, Cairo

American University in Cairo
Est. 1919; 113 Kasr El Aini Str., P.O.Box 2511, Tel.: 3542969, Cairo

Assiut University
Est. 1957; Tel.: 324040, Assiut

Cairo University
Est., 1908; Tel. (2)5729584, Orman, Giza, Cairo

Helwan University
Est. 1975; 96 Ahmed Ouraby Str., Mohandissen, Tel.: 3446441, Cairo

Mansoura University
Est. 1973; P.O.Box 305516, Tel.: 5347054, Mansoura

Menia University
Est. 1976; Tel.: 2498, Menia

Menoufia University
Est. 1976; Tel.: (48)224155, Shebeen El Kom

Suez Canal University
Est. 1976; El Sheikh Zayed, Tel.: 229976, Ismailia
Tanta University
Est. 1972; Tel.: 327929, Tanta
Zagazig University
Est. 1974; Tel.: (55) 322417, Zagazig

Tourism

Ministry of Tourism Est. 1965; Abbassia Square, Misr Travel Tower, Tel. (02)2828430, Cairo.

Egyptian General Company for Tourism and Hotels. Est. 1961; 4 Latin America Str., Garden City, Tel. (02)3026470, Cairo.

IRAQ
(Iraqi Arab Republic)

Iraq

Head of State	: SADDAM HUSSAIN TAKRITI
Area	: 438,317 sq. Km.
Population	: 20.4 million (mid 1995 estimate)
Currency	: Iraqi Dinar, which is divided into 1,000 fils.
Denominations	: a) Note: ¼ – ½ – 1 – 5 – 10 – 25 – 50 – 100 – 250 dinars b) Coins: 1 – 5 – 10 – 25 – 50 – 100 fils
Exchange Rate	: Us Dollars per Dinar = 0.311 dinars (Dec. 1998)

Geography

Iraq is bordered on the north by Turkey, on the east by Iran, on the south and southwest by the Arabian Gulf, Kuwait and Saudi Arabia, on the west by Jordan and on the northwest by Syria.

By its topography, Iraq is divided into three distinct geographical zones: the desert in the west and southwest, the plains, and the highlands of Kurdistan in the northeast which rise to well over 10.000 feet.

The desert zone is an upland region with altitudes varying from 2 to 3,000 feet, declining gently towards the Euphrates river.

From earliest times to the present day, the peoples of Iraq have had to construct irrigation works and dams to control the great rivers and the recurrent floods, for both the Euphrates and the Tigris often changed their courses and abandoned channels combined with frequent floods to complicate their control.

Today's flood control policy is based on the following four projects:

1 – The barrage at Samara, which has a potential storage capacity of 30 milliard cubic meters.

2 – The Dokan Dam-storage capacity = 6,300 million cubic meters.

3 – The Derbenki Khan Dam-storage capacity = 3,250 million cubic meters.

4 – The Habbaniyah Reservoir

Economically the richest, the plains area is dominated by the river systems of the Tigris and Euphrates. At Qarmal Ali, just above Basra, the two rivers combine and form the Shatt al Arab, a broad navigable waterway through which ocean-going vessels enter the harbour of Basra.

For thousands of years these rivers have been the source of both life and misery for their riverain inhabitants. Even today all the large towns are on the rivers, for until the arrival of the railway and the lorry, the only way to carry goods in bulk was by water. From Ramadi and Samarra southwards in the flat alluvial plain that makes the country's land surface, agriculture depends on irrigation from the rivers. The traveller who arrives at Baghdad by air at any season except spring sees little to relieve the flat monotony of the dusty landscape except the Tigris, meandering in extravagant loops to the horizon. Over most of its length the bare cracked desert comes right to the bank. There is no strip of bright green, as there is along the Nile in Egypt.

CLIMATE

Iraq's climate is sub-tropical.

In Baghdad and in most inland areas the heat is dry and the nights comparatively cool, but in Basra the himidity is generally high throughout the summer and the nights are hot.

POPULATION

There are important racial and cultural distinctions among the population of Iraq, with the major difference between the Arabs and the Kurds. The Arabs are a markedly homogenous group, and occupy most of the centre, west and south of Iraq. The Kurds are racially akin to the Iranians, and form another, smaller homogenous group located mainly in the north and east.

PRINCIPAL CITIES & TOWNS

Baghdad is the capital of Iraq and its largest city. It is situated on the Tigris about 275 miles from Basra. The population is predominantly Arab Muslim with sizeable Christian and Kurdish minorities.

Basra is situated on the Shatt-al-Arab in the date growing region in south Iraq. It is Iraq's second largest city and its only general port.

Mossul lies on the Tigris about 250 miles north of Baghdad, in an agriculturally rich region (cereals and livestock) which depends on natural rainfall.

Kirkuk lies 190 miles north of Baghdad, and south east of Mossul, in the main oil producing area of Iraq.

Suleimaniya is about 250 miles north-east of Baghdad in the mountainous and principally Kurdish region.

Kut lies 120 miles south of Baghdad on the Tigris. It is a grain centre which also boasts a poultry project, fish breeding farm and textile factories.

PUBLIC HOLIDAYS

New Year's Day (1 January); Army Day (6 January); Mouled el Nabi (Birthday of the Prophet); Now Ruz (Spring Festival) (21 March); Anniversary of founding Arab Baath Socialist Party (7 April); Labour Day (1 May); Republic Day & 1st day of Ramadan, National Day (1968 Revolution) (17 July); Id el Fitr; Id al Adha (feast of the Sacrifice); Muslim New Year (7 October).

LANGUAGE

Arabic, the official language is the most widely spoken. Kurdish and Turkish dialects are common in the north.

RELIGION

The majority of the Arab population are Shi'ah Muslims as

are 60% of the Kurds. There are also small Christian groups, who live mainly in the north, around Mossul, or in the larger towns.

History

After the first world war England gets a mandate from the League of Nations up to 1932 when Iraq was granted her independence and as an independent power joins the League of Nations. In 1955, a pact was formed between Turkey, Iran, Iraq and England called the Pact of Baghdad.

On 14 July 1958 the Republic of Iraq was declared by a group of army Officers after a coup d'état in which the reigning King Faisal II and his uncle, the ex-Regent the Emir Abul Illah, and the Prime Minister, lost their lives. For the next 4 years the country was under the control of General Kassim, who was executed on February 9, 1963. The Baath Party takes over for a little while and is in turn overthrown by Marshal Abdusslam Muhammad Aref.

Under Aref, who initiated a policy of closer relations with Egypt, martial law, in force since 1958, was brought to an end in January 1965, and a purely civilian Government was inaugurated. In March 1966, President Aref was killed in an air accident, and was succeeded by his brother Abdul Rahman Mohammed Aref whose presidency was abruptly terminated by the Baath Party in 1968. General Hassan al Bakr, a former Prime Minister, then assumed power both as President and Prime Minister.

The regime adopted stiffer policies at home and abroad; fighting was resumed against the Kurdish rebels in the northeast.

Relations with Iran deteriorated since April 1969 following a dispute over the Shatt-el-Arab waterway which forms the frontier; Iran was further accused of complicity in an abortive coup in Baghdad in January 1970.

The Kurdish war virtually ended in March 1970, the Kurds were granted autonomy, and five Kurdish ministers were invited to join the Baghdad cabinet.

In July 1979 Saddam Hussein became President of Iraq and Chairman of the Revolutionary Command Council.

IRAQI ARMED FORCES ATTACK IRAN

Following a series of border skirmishes in late September 1980, Iraqi armour and ground forces moved into Iran attacking Iranian border posts with heavy mortar fire. Because there had been no formal declaration of war, most military experts thought that hostilities between the two countries would flare out within days.

As the Iraqi troops penetrated deeper into enemy territory they met with increasingly stiff resistance, notably outside several Iranian cities. The invaders fought at close quarters in the port city of Khoramshahr, shelled the big refinery at Abadan (admittedly the world's largest) and launched a devastating barrage of Soviet-made missiles at the towns of Dezful and Andimeshk.

The Iraqi drive was aimed at three principal targets: the oil refinery centre of Abadan, Khuzistan's capital of Ahwaz and the important communications junction of Dezful, 150 miles north of Khoramshahr.

Iran fought back with concentrated air raids on Baghdad, Kirkuk, Mosul and a number of industrial installations, including the nuclear station under construction with French technical assistance.

Iraqi warplanes retaliated by bombing several factories on the edge of Tehran International Airport, a refinery at Tabriz and the oil-loading terminal a Kharg Island.

But for all the bitter fighting, neither side could land a killing blow, although by mid-October both Abadan and Khoramshahr were totally encircled and virtually in Iraqi hands.

However, by September 1981 the front line created by the Iraqi advance into Iranian territory had been pushed back by up to 25 miles, when Iranian forces lifted the siege of Abadan and went on to launch a new military offensive, capturing the town of Bostan in November. Althouth by early 1982 the conflict seemed to have reached a stalemate, the military initiative subsequently appeared to pass to Iran, which responded to a series of Iraqi counter-attacks in February 1982 by launching a further major offensive in mid-March, which by mid-May had succeeded in driving the Iraqi forces back to the border.

By July 1985 the toll of dead and wounded was estimated at more than 500,000 Despite approaches by the UN and various governments (Egypt, Saudi Arabia and Syria among them), Iran refused to negotiate with Iraq, insisting that nothing less than the removal of the regime of Saddam Hussein, the withdrawal of Iraqi troops from Iranian territory and agreement to pay reparations for war damages could bring hostilities to an end.

According to the Cairo newspaper Al Ahram, Iran set damages in the amount of 300 billion dollars, at the end of January 1987.

During the first half of 1988, Iraq regained much of the territory which it has lost to Iran. In July 1988, Iran agreed to accept Resolution 598 and a cease-fire was proclaimed. The cease-fire came into force on 20 August, after which Iran accepted direct talks with Iraq.

In August 1990, and in an abrupt change in policy, Iraq made peace with Iran dropping all its previous claims, and resumption of diplomatic relations were formally agreed upon in September 1990. On August 2, following territorial disputes, oil pricing and debt to Kuwait, Iraq invaded neghbouring Kuwait and controlled the whole country within a short time, in spite of prior efforts by the Arab Countries to avoid tension and military action. The Security Council adopted several resolutions for the unconditional withdrawal of Iraqi forces; and U.S. troops were dispatched to Saudi Arabia for its defence, and by the end of January 1991 several countries have sent troops to the Gulf area. Tensions grew in the following months in 1990 and early 1991 and after many initiatives and proposals for the resolution of the conflict through political and diplomatic means have failed, culminating with UN Secretary General visit to Baghdad on January

10, 1991, coalition forces led by the United States launched a ground offensive on Feb. 23, following intensive aerial bombardments for several days, to liberate Kuwait. Iraqi troops were defeated and Iraq accepted the cease fire terms dictated by the multinational forces on March 3. After the conflict, an armed rebellion broke in the South and the North of the country but the Iraqi Army crushed the rebellion in the South and the Kurdish insurrection in the North has been ineffective and Kurdish guerillas have withdrawn to an enclave in the far North.

The Cabinet

(Dec. 1997)

Prime Minister: H.E. Saddam HUSSEIN

Deputy Prime Ministers: Tareq AZIZ, Taha Yassine RAMADAN, Mohamed Hamza ZUBAIDI

Minister of Foreign Affairs: Mohamed Said Kazim SAHHAF

Deputy Prime Minister, Minister of Finance: Hikmat Mizban IBRAHIM

Minister for Oil: Gen. Amer Mohamed RACHID

Minister of Industry and Minerals: Adnane Abdelmajid JASSEM

Minister of Labour and Social Affairs: Gen. Saadi Tuma ABBAS

Minister of Agriculture: Abdel Ilah Hamid Mohamed SALEH

Minister of Irrigation: Mahmoud Diab AHMED

Minister of Transport and Communications: Ahmad Mortada Ahmad KHALIL

Minister of Wakf: Abdelmoneim Ahmad SALEH

Minister of the Interior: Mohamed Zammam ABDEL-RAZZAK

Minister of Defence: Gen. Sultan Hashem AHMED

Minister of Planning: Samal Majid FARAJ

Minister of Trade: Mohamed Mahdi SALEH

Minister of Information and Culture: Hamam ABDEL GHAFFAR

Minister of Justice: Shabib Lazem MALKI

Minister of Education: Fahed Salem SHAKRA

Minister of Health: Umeed Madhat MUBARAK

Minister of Higher Education and Scientific Research: Abdeljaber Tawfic MOHAMED

Minister of Housing and Construction: Maan Abdallah SARSAM

Minister of State for Military Affairs: Gen. Abduljabbar Khalil SHANSHAL

Minister of State: Arshad Mohamed Ahmed ZIBARI

Minister of State: Abdel Wahhab Omar Mirza AL ATRUSHI

Foreign Embassies

Afghanistan: Maghrib Str., al Difa'ie, 27/1/12 Waziriya, Tel.: 5560331, Baghdad

Algeria: Shawaf Sq., Karradat Mariam, Tel.: 5372181, Baghdad

Argentina: Hay al Jamia District 915, Str., 24 No.142, P.O.Box 2443, Tel.: 776-8140, Baghdad

Austria: Hay Babel 929/2/5 Aqaba bin Nafis Sq., Masbah, P.O.Box 294, Tel.: 719-9033, Baghdad

Bangladesh: 75/17/929 Hay Babel, Tel.: 7196367, Baghdad

Belgium: 929/27/25 Hay Babel, Tel.: 719-8297, Baghdad

Brazil: 609/16 al Mansour, Houses 62/62-1, Tel.: 5411365, Baghdad

Bulgaria: Ameriya, New Diplomatic Quarter, P.O.Box 28022, Tel.: 556-8197, Baghdad

Central African Republic: 208/406 Al Zawra, Harthiya, Tel.: 551/6520, Baghdad

Chad: 97/4/4 Karradat Mariam, P.O.Box 8037, Tel.: 537-6160, Baghdad

China, People's Republic: New Embassy Area, International Airport Rd., Tel.: 556-2740, Baghdad

Cuba: St. 7, District 929 Hay Babel, Masbah Arrasat al Hindi, Tel.: 719-5177, Baghdad

Czech: Dijlaschool Str., No. 37, Mansoor, Tel.: 541-7136, Baghdad

Denmark: Zukaka No. 34 Mahallat 902, Hay Al-Wahda, House No. 18/1, P.O.Box 2001, Alwiyah, Tel.: 719-3058, Baghdad

Djibouti: P.O.Box 6223 al Mansour, Tel.: 551-3805, Baghdad

Finland: P.O.Box 2041, Alwiyah, Tel.: 776/6271, Baghdad

Germany: Zuqaq 2, Mahala 929, Hay Babel, Masbah Sq., Tel.: 719-2037, Baghdad

Greece: 63/3/913 Hay al Jamia, al Jadriya, Tel.: 776-9511, Baghdad

Holy See: Saadoun Str. 904/2/46, P.O.Box 2090, Tel.: 719-5183, Baghdad

Hungary: Abu Nuwas Str., Al Zuwiya, P.O.Box 2065, Tel.: 776-5000, Baghdad

India: Taha Str., Najib Pasha, Adhamiya, Tel.: 422-2014, Baghdad

Indonesia: 906/2/77 Hay al Wahda, Tel.: 719-8677, Baghdad

Ireland: 913/28/101 Hay al Mamia, Tel.: 7768661, Baghdad

Japan: 929/17/70 Hay Babel, Masbah, Tel.: 719-5156, Baghdad

Jordan: House No.1, Str. 12, District 609, al Mansour, P.O.Box 6314, Tel.: 541-2892, Baghdad

Korea, Republic: 915/22/278 Hay al Jamia, Tel.: 7765496, Baghdad

Libya: Baghdad

Malaysia: 6/14-929 Hay Babel, Tel.: 7762622, Baghdad

Malta: 2/1 Zuqaq 49, Mahalla 503, Hay al Nil, Tel.: 7725032, Baghdad

Mauritania: Al Mansour, Tel.: 551-8261, Baghdad

Mexico: 601/11/45 al Mansour, Tel.: 719-8039, Baghdad

Morocco: Hay al Mansour, P.O.Box 6039, Tel.: 552-1779, Baghdad

Netherlands: 19/35/915 Jadiriya, P.O.Box 2064, Tel.: 776-7616, Baghdad

Nigeria: 2/3/603 Mutanabi, al Mansour, P.O.Box 5933, Tel.: 5421750, Baghdad
Norway: 20/3/609 Hay al Mansour, Tel.: 5410097, Baghdad
Oman: 213/36/15 al Harthiya, P.O.Box 6180, Tel.: 551-8198, Baghdad
Pakistan: 14/7/609 al Mansour, Tel.: 541-5120, Baghdad
Philippines: Hay Babel, Tel.: 719-3228, Baghdad
Poland: 30 Zuqaq 13, Mahalla 931, Hay Babel, P.O.Box 2051, Tel.: 719-0296, Baghdad
Portugal: 66/11 al Karada al Sharqiva, Hay Babel, Sector 925, Str., 25, No. 79, P.O.Box 2123 Alwiyah, Tel.: 776-4953, Baghdad
Romania: Arassat al Hindia, Hay Babel, Mahalla 929, Zukak 31, No.452/A, Te.: 7762860, Baghdad
Senegal: 569/5/10, Hay al Mansour, Tel.: 5420806, Baghdad
Somalia: 603/1/5 al Mansour, Tel.: 5510088, Baghdad
Spain: Riyadh Quarter, District 908, Str., No. 1,No. 21, P.O.Box 2072, Alwiyah, Tel.: 719-2852, Baghdad
Sri Lanka: 07/80/904 Hay al Wahda, P.O.Box 1094, Tel.: 719-3040, Baghdad
Sudan: 38/15/601 al Imarat, Tel.: 542-4889, Baghdad
Sweden: 15/41/103 Hay al Nidhal, Tel.: 719-5361, Baghdad
Switzerland: Hay Babel, House No.41/5/929, P.O.Box 2107, Tel.: 719-3091, Baghdad
Thailand: 1/4/609, P.O.Box 6062 al Mansour, Tel.: 5418798, Baghdad
Tunisia: Mansour 34/2/4, P.O.Box 6057, Tel.: 551-7786, Baghdad
Uganda: 41/1/609 al Mansour, Tel.: 551-3594, Baghdad
Russia.: 4/5/605 al Mutanabi, Tel.: 541-4749, Baghdad
Venezuela: Al Mansour, House No. 12/79/601, Tel.: 552-0965, Baghdad
Viet-Nam: 29/611 Hay al Andalus, Tel.: 551-1388, Baghdad
Yemen (Republic of): Jadiriya 923/28/29, Tel.: 776-0647, Baghdad
Yugoslavia: 16/35/923 Hay Babel, Jadiriyah, P.O.Box 2061, Tel.: 776-7887, Baghdad

The Economy

Oil Production is the cornestone of the economy with earnings being used to finance development of agriculture, industry and resources such as sulphur and phosphate. Iraq's petroleum Industry is highly dependent on pipelines through neighbouring territory or to the Gulf coast.

Iraqi exports are directed via a pipeline across Turkey, by a fleet to road tankers to port facilities in Turkey and Jordan and via a line linking the country's southern oil field to Saudi Arabia's Petro-line. Completion of a 500,000 b/d pipeline system from Iraq's oilfields near Basra in the south-east to the Kirkuk fields in the north-east will allow an existing expanded pipeline to carry oil exports to Ceyhan in Turkey; and another pipeline through Saudi Arabia with a capacity of 1.5 million b/d. Iraq's proven oil reserves stand at about 112 billion barrels.

In addition to oil, there are extensive deposits of phosphate and sulphur.

The mandatory sanctions imposed on Iraq by the United Nations Security Council in 1990 placed the Iraqi economy in isolation.

Main Oil Pipelines

Route	Diameter (in inches)	Length (in miles)
Kirkuk – Tripoli	12	532
Kirkuk – Tripoli	30–32	532
Kirkuk – Baniyas	30–32	555
Ain – Zalah/K3	12	134
Zubair – Fao	24	65
Zubair – Fao	30-32	65
Fao-Khor al Amaya	32	28
Khanaqin – Daura	12	81
Khanaqin – Beedjee	16	—
Beedjee – Daura	12	197
Kirkuk – Turkey	40	600

Main Pipelines for Natural Gas

Route	Diameter (in inches)	Length (in miles)
Kirkuk – T/4	16	421
Jambour – Kirkuk	20	32
Bai Hassan – Kirkuk	12	20
Zubair – Fao	12 – 16	65
Rumaila – Basrah	18	17
Kirkuk – Baghdad	16	186
Kirkuk – Baghdad	16	186
	8	186

AGRICULTURE AND INDUSTRY

Agriculture, the mainstay of the economy until oil production began on a large scale, which occupied 50% of the labour force in the 1960s, has decreased at present to about 20%. The sector is comparatively well developed with finance being directed towards controlling salinity and improving drainage with a view to producing a surplus for export. In the light of their disappointing performance, the state farms have been offered to the private sector for sale or lease. The principal crops are, by order of importance, barley, wheat, tomatoes, grapes, watermelons, dates, cucumbers, melons, potatoes, rice, oranges, apples, sugar cane, etc; and livestock mainly sheep, cattle and goats.

Iraq's previously promising industrial sector has suffered severely from the war and many projects have had to be shelved. Nevertheless, a number of important projects are planned or under way, including new power stations, a petrochemical complex and plant for producing iron and steel, building materials and fertilisers. Output of wool and cotton clothing and electrical and mechanical goods is also to be stepped up. Among the sector's main problems, however, are a lack of advanced technology and an acute shortage of technicians as well

The consequences of the war in 1991 were economically devastating to Iraq. The cost of rebuilding the economic infrastructure (bridges, roads, industries, communications, oil installations, etc.) runs into billions of dollars, and is expected to take several years particularly in the absence of oil revenues as a result to the United Nations Sanctions.

The Banking System

Central Bank of Iraq: Est. 1947; P.O.Box 64, Rashid Street, Tel. 8865171, Baghdad, Branches in Mosul and Basra cities.

Agricultural Cooperative Bank of Iraq: Est. 1936; P.O.Box 5112, Rashid Street, Tel. 8889081, Baghdad. 32 branches.

Industrial Bank of Iraq: Est. 1940; P.O.Box 5825, Khullani Square, Tel. 8872181, Baghdad. 5 branches.

Rafidain Bank: Est. 1941, P.O.Box 11360, Al Massarif Street, Tel. 8870521, Baghdad. 215 branches in Iraq and many branches Internationally.

Real Estate Bank of Iraq: Est. 1949; P.O.Box 14145, Yafa Street, Salhiya, Tel. 5375165, Baghdad. 27 branches.

Transport

Increasing modernisation is reflected in changes of emphasis given to different parts of the transport system. Until the mid – 20th century, transport was either by water or by animal. River transport had developed over the centuries to transmit goods and personnel, particularly from central to southern Iraq. The use of animals – camels, horses and horse-drawn carts - complemented this system. Both of these modes are adequate for a traditional economy, but increasing commercialisation and industrialisation and the increasing scale of economic interaction between Iraq and its neighbours brought about fundamental changes.

ROADS

There are about 46,000 km of roads in Iraq, over 70 percent of which are paved. Also, the desert land is sufficiently hard to allow cars, trucks, and buses to travel across it. The most developed parts of the road system are in central, northern and southern Iraq.

RAILWAYS

They are divided into three main lines radiating from Baghdad:

1. Baghdad – Ma'qil (Basra) Metre Gauge Line, a distance of 569 Kilometres, with branch lines, one at Al-Hindiyah Junction for the holy city of Kerbala (a distance of 38 kms) and the other at Ur-Junction (Ur of the Chaldees) for An-Nassiriyah. The line serves the Liwas of Kerbala, Al-Hilla, Ad-Diwaniyah, Nassiriya and Basra, famous for its world renowned dates. On this line travellers can visit the ancient places of Babylon, Al-Ukhaidher, Eridu (Warka) and Ur of the Chaldees and Holy Shrines at Kerbala.

2. Baghdad-Kirkuk – Erbil Metre gauge line, a distance of 427 kilometres with a branch line at Juloula'Junction, for Khanaqin City, a distance of about 28 kms. The line serves the Liwas of Diyala, Kirkuk and Erbil. On this section travellers can visit the famous oilfields at Kirkuk (Baba Gurgur) and ancient Castle at Erbil.

3. Baghdad – Mosul – Tel Kotchek standard gauge line, a distance of 531 kilometres. The line serves the Liwas of Baghdad and Mosul. On this section travellers can visit Samarrah, the ruins of Hatra, Nirmud, and Ninevah, the famous capital of the Assyrian Empire and other historical places. The Baghdad – Tel Kotchek line offers direct connection to Aleppo, Beirut, Ankara, Istanbul and with the Simplon-Orient Express from Istanbul to Rome, Paris and London via Nice, Belgrade, Zagreb, Trieste and Milan.

SHIPPING

The port of Basra is the commercial gateway of Iraq. It is connected by various ocean routes with all parts of the world, and constitutes the natural distributing centre for overseas supplies.

The port of Basra has five wharves of reinforced concrete and is provided with modern cargo handling equipment. Other Ports are at Umm Kasr, Khor Amaya and Faw.

CIVIL AVIATION

Iraqi Airways: I.R.R. Saddam International Airport Baghdad; Founded 1945.

Education

I – Universities

Mustansiriya University
Est. 1963, P.O.Box 14022, Waziriya, Tel.: 4168501, Baghdad

Saddam University for Engineering and Science
Est. 1988; P.O.Box 47077, Jadiriya, Tel.: 7765679, Baghdad

University of Baghdad
Est. 1957; P.O.Box 12, Jadiriya, Tel.: 93091, Baghdad

University of Basrah
Est. 1964; Tel.: 417914, Basrah

University of Mosul
Est. 1967; Tel.: 812611, Mosul

University of Salahaddin

Est. 1968; Tel.: (0566) 21422, Arbid
University of Technology
Est. 1975; P.O.Box 745, Baghdad
University of Tikrit
Est. 1987; P.O.Box 42, Te.: (021) 824531, Tikrit

II – Institutes

There are nineteen specialised institutes providing courses of university level, among which:

Institute of Technology: Est. 1972, Baghdad.

Technical Institute: Est. 1975, Basrah.

Technical Institute of Agriculture: Est. 1964, Baghdad.

Technical Institute of Medicine: Est. 1966, Baghdad.

Technical Institute of Medical Technology: Est. 1973, Sulaimaniya.

Institute of Administration: Est. 1964, Baghdad.

Institute of Applied Arts: Est. 1969, Baghdad.

Technical Institute of Mosul: Est. 1976.

Technical Institute of Kirkuk: Est. 1976.

Technical Institute of Agriculture: Est. 1976, Aski-Kalak (Arbil).

Institute of Administration of Karh: Est. 1976, Baghdad.

Institute of Administration in Hilla: Est. 1976.

Radio, Television and Press

RADIO

Iraqi Broadcasting and Television Est: Salihiya Baghdad. Broadcasts in Arabic, Kurdish, Syriac, Turkoman and foreign service in French, German, English, Russian, Persian, Turkish...

Izaat Baghdad: 22 hours of broadcasting daily. Est. 1936.

Izaat Sawt al-Jamahir: 24 Hours of broadcasting daily. Est. 1970

TELEVISION

Baghdad Television: Public corporation (Ministry of Information). Est. 1956. Operating 7 hours daily

Kirkuk Television: Est. 1967. Public corporation. Operating 6 hours daily.

Mosul Television: Est. 1968. Public corporation. Operating 6 hours daily.

Basrah Television: Est. 1968. Public corporation. Operating 6 hours daily.

Missan Television: Est. 1974. Public corporation. Operating 6 hours daily.

Kurdish Television: Est. 1974. Public corporation. Operating 6 hours daily.

THE PRESS

A. NEWSPAPERS

Baghdad Observer: (English) P.O.Box 624, Baghdad. Est. 1967. State-sponsored.

Al-Iraq: (Kurdish) P.O.Box 5717, Baghdad. Est. 1976. Organ of the National Progressive Front.

Al-Jumhuriya: (Arabic) Waziriya, Baghdad. Est. 1963.

Al Thawra: (Arabic) Aqaba bin Nafi's Square, P.O.Box 2009, Baghdad. Est. 1968. Organ of the Baath Party.

B. NEWS AGENCY

Iraqi News Agency (INA): P.O.Box 3084, Baghdad Est. 1959.

Museum

Baghdad Museum

Seven separate sections depict prehistoric civilisations, Sumerian, Babylonian, Chaldean, Assyrian, Parthic, Sassanid and Islamic.

Its Library comprising no less than 70,000 specialised volumes and some 5,000 manuscripts, most of which unpublished, is equipped with rooms for recording, photography and the preservation of art objects.

A study laboratory, a moulding shop and a photography section complete the administrative buildings.

JORDAN
(Hashemite Kingdom of Jordan)

Jordan

Head of State : King ABDALLAH Ibn Hussein II
Area : 97,740 sq. Km.
Population : 5.4 million (1995 estimate)
Currency : Jordanian Dinar (JD)
Currency Units per US Dollar: 0.709 (May. 1997)

Geography

The Hashemite Kingdom of Jordan is bounded on the North by Syria, on the North-East by Iraq, on the East and South by Saudi Arabia, on the West by Israel.

The major agricultural region is the eastern uplands from the Irbib plateau South to Madada where rainfall is lighter and more variable.

The Jordan Valley has an average annual rainfall of less than 200 mm.

The eastern uplands South of Madada constitute the region where altitude ranges between 900 and 1,500 meters. Rainfall is therefore variable, exceeding 300 mm only on two patches of land around Karak and Shaubak.

The remainder of the country lying East of the uplands is a desert plateau sloping away towards Iraq and Saudi Arabia.

As it is, the bulk of the agricultural districts in Jordan lie West of the Hedjaz railway line where the hillsides are terraced, fruit-trees planted and irrigation developed.

Jordan's main towns are: Amman, the capital, seat of Government and business centres; Zarka; Irbid.

LOCAL ADMINISTRATION

The kingdom is divided into ten districts or "Liwa", these in turn divided into sub-districts "Qada", governed by district governors "Muhafez" and sub-district governors "Quaem Makam". In some subdistricts there are in addition "Nahiyas", smaller administrative units, governed by "Mudirs". All these administrative divisions are under the jurisdiction of the Ministry of the Interior.

PUBLIC HOLIDAYS

Labour Day (1 May); Independence Day (25 May); King Abdallah Accession to throne (9 June); Mulid al Nabi birthday of the Prophet; first day of Ramadan, month of Muslim fasting and self-purification; Eid al fitr, end of Ramadan; Eid al Adha, feast of the Sacrifice; Muslim New Year; Ashura day, day of mourning for Shi'te Muslims.

RELIGION AND LANGUAGE

Nearly 80 per cent of the population are Sunni Moslems, but the Constitution recognizes freedom of worship and Christian churches of all denominations are allowed to hold religious services.

Arabic is the State's official language, but most educated Jordanians speak fluent English.

History

The country has seen the empires of Egypt, Assyria, and Persia; it has also been the battlefield of the Roman eagles and their Byzantine successors. Within it occurred the birth of Christianity. Jordan is an Arab country. Arabs had been living in this area since before the Christian era, and the Arab conquest of Syria and Palestine in the seventh century A.D. established them as the dominant group. But for the period of the Crusader Kingdom (1099 to 1187), it remained under Arab rule until the beginning of the 16th century, when all the Middle Eastern countries were conquered by the Turks. In 1916, the Arab Revolt against the Ottoman Rule was led by the late King Hussain of the Hedjaz. After the 1914-18 War, Jordan became part of the Arab Kingdom of Syria with Faisal of Arabia as King. When he was forced to leave Syria in 1920 the Transjordan districts of Ajlun, Amman, Balqa, Karak and Ma'an formed an independent state under British Mandate with the Emir Abdallah, Faisal's brother, at its head. In 1946 Jordan attained independence as a Kingdom, with the Emir Abdallah as its King.

The first six months of 1971, like the closing weeks of 1970, were marked by continued clashes at frequent intervals between the Jordanian Army and the Palestinian guerrilla forces in Jordan. Eventually, the Jordanian Army launched a powerful military offensive in July against the guerrilla forces in northern Jordan-their last stronghold in the country-which was claimed in Amman to have achieved complete success and to have resulted in the destruction of the guerrilla organisation in Jordanian territory.

King Hussain travelled abroad widely. He visited Britain, Romania, the United States, Moscow, Australia, Japan, Singapore, Canada, and made extensive tours of the Arab world, both to put over his views on the Palestine question and the Middle East and to drum up financial support for Jordan's economy from the oil-rich states on the Arab side of the Gulf.

On July 25, 1994 Jordan and Israel signed a joint declaration in Washington formally ending the state of conflict. On 26 October, a peace treaty was signed by King Hussein and Itzhak Rabin, Prime Minister of Israel, on their respective borders in Wadi Araba. The treaty has been ratified in the Israeli Knesset. The National Assembly in Jordan ratified the treaty on November 6, 1994. On February, 7, 1999 King Hussain Ibn Talal, after a long illness, passed away. Before his death he appointed his son Prince Abdallah as his successor.

The Constitution

THE STATE AND THE GOVERNMENT

The Hashemite Kingdom of Jordan is an Arab independent and sovereign State. Its territory is indivisible and no portion of it may be ceded. The Government of the country is a hereditary monarchy, parliamentary in form. Islam is the religion of the State and Arabic its official language. The capital of the Kingdom is the city of Amman, but it may be changed to another locality by a special law.

THE AUTHORITIES

The Throne of the Hashemite Kingdom of Jordan is hereditary in the family of King Abdallah Ibn-ul-Hussain and shall devolve on his male heirs in direct line through males.

I – The King declares war, concludes peace and international treaties. Treaties of peace, alliance, trade, navigation and treaties involving territorial changes of entrenchment on sovereignty of embodying the general or private right of citizens shall not become executory until they have been ratified by the National Assembly.

The King may grant special Pardon and may reduce sentences. No death sentence shall be executed until it has been confirmed by the King.

II – The Council of Ministers shall comprise the Prime Minister as President and a number of Ministers, determined according to circumstances and need.

The Council of Ministers shall be responsible for the direction of all internal and external affairs of the State, with exception of such affairs as may be delegated to another person or body by the Constitution or by law.

The Prime Minister and his Ministers are collectively responsible to the Chamber of Deputies for the general policy of the State; and every Minister is responsible to the Chamber for the affairs of his Ministry.

III – The National Assembly shall consist of two bodies: the Senate and the Chamber of Deputies. The Senate shall comprise a number of Notables including the President, which shall not exceed one half of the number of members of the chamber of Deputies. The term of office in the Senate is four years. The Chamber of Deputies shall consist of members elected by universal secret and direct suffrage in accordance with the electoral law.

The term of the Chamber of Deputies is four solar years, but the King shall have the right to extend the duration of Parliament by Royal Irada.

The Cabinet

(Jan. 2000)

Prime Minister, Minister of Defence: Abdel Raouf RAWABDEH
Deputy Prime Minister: Ayman MAJALI
Minister of Foreign Affairs: Abdul Ilah AL KHATIB
Minister of the Interior: Nayef AL QADI
Minister of Finance: Michel MARTO
Minister of Industry and Trade and Planning: Mohamad AL HALAIQA
Minister of Justice: Khalaf MASAADEH
Minister of Municipal and Rural Affairs, and the Environment: Tawfiq KHREISHAN
Minister of Tourism and Antiquities: Akel BALTAJI
Minister of Labour: Eid FAYEZ
Minister of Education: Izzat JARADAT
Minister of Agriculture: Hashem SHBOUL
Minister of Energy and Minerals: Wael SABRI
Minister of Posts and Telecommunication: Abdullah TOUKAN
Minister of Transport: Issa AYOUB
Minister of Awqaf and Islamic Affairs: Abul Salam AL ABBADI
Minister of Water and Irrigation: Kamel Kamel MAHADIN
Minister of Social and Administrative Development: Mohamad Jumma AL WAHSH
Minister of Health: Musleh AL TARAWNEH
Minister of Public Works and Housing: Hosni ABU GHAIDA
Minister of Youth and Sports: Saed SHUQUM
Minister of Culture and Information: Saleh KALLAB
Chief of Royal Court: Fayez TARAWNEH

Foreign Embassies

Algeria: Jabal Amman, 3rd Circle, Tel. (6)5641271, Amman
Australia: Jabal Amman, 4th Circle, P.O.Box 35201, Tel. (6)5931260, Amman
Austria: P.O.Box 815368, Tel. (6)4644635, Amman
Bahrain: Tel. (6)5664148, Amman
Belgium: Tel. (6)5675683, Amman
Brazil: P.O.Box 5497, Tel. (6)4642183, Amman
Bulgaria: P.O.Box 950578, Tel. (6)5699391, Amman
Canada: Pearl of Shmeisani Bldg., P.O.Box 815403, Tel. (6)5666124, Shmeisani, Amman
Chile: Tel. (6)5924263, Shmeisani, Amman
China, People's Republic: Tel. (6)5666139, Shmeisani, Amman
Egypt: Jabal Amman, Zahran Str., 3rd Circle, P.O.Box 35178, Tel. (6)5605175, Amman
France: Jabal Amman, P.O.Box 374, Tel. (6)4641273, Amman
Germany: 25 Benghazi Str., Jabal Amman, P.O.Box 183, Tel. (6)593051, Amman
Greece: Jabal Amman, P.O.Box 35069, Tel. (6)5672331, Amman
Hungary: P.O.Box 3441, Tel. (6)5925614, Amman
India: Jabal Amman, 1st Circle, P.O.Box 2168, Tel. (6)4622098, Amman
Iran: Jabal Amman, P.O.Box 173, Tel. (6)5641281, Amman
Iraq: Jabal Amman, 1st. Circle, P.O.Box 2025, Tel. (6)5639331, Amman
Italy: Jabal Luweibdeh, P.O.Box 9800, Tel. (6)4638185, Amman
Japan: Jabal Amman, P.O.Box 2835, Tel. (6)5672486, Amman

Korea, Democratic People's Republic: Tel. (6)5666349, Amman

Korea, Republic: Jabal Amman, 3rd Circle, Abu Tammam Str., P.O.Box 3060, Tel. (6)5930745, Amman

Lebanon: Jabal Amman, 2nd Circle, Tel. (6)5641381, Amman

Morocco: Jabal Amman, Tel. (6)5641451, Amman

Oman: Tel. (6)5661131, Amman

Pakistan: Tel. (6)5611633, Amman

Philippines: Jabal Amman, 2nd Circle, Abbas Aqad Str., P.O.Box 925107, Amman

Poland: Jabal Amman, 1st Circle, P.O.Box 2124, Tel. (6)4637153, Amman

Qatar: Tel. (6)5644331, Amman

Romania: Tel. (6)5667738, Amman

Russia: Tel. (6)5641158, Amman

Saudi Arabia: Jabal Amman, 5th Circle, P.O.Box 2133, Tel. (6)5644154, Amman

Spain: Jabal Amman, Tel. (6)4614166, Amman

Sudan: Jabal Amman, Tel. (6)5624145, Amman

Sweden: Jabal Amman, 4th Circle, P.O.Box 830536, Tel. (6)5931177, Amman

Switzerland: Jabal Amman, Tel. (6), Tel. 5931416, Amman

Syria: Jabal Amman, 4th Circle, P.O.Box 1377, Tel. (6)5641935, Amman

Tunisia: Jabal Amman, Tel. (6)5674307, Amman

Turkey: Jabal Amman, 2nd Circle, Queen Zein ash-Sharaf Str., P.O.Box 2062, Tel. (6)5641251, Amman

United Arab Emirates: Jabal Amman, Tel. (6)5644369, Amman

United Kingdom: P.O.Box 87, Tel. (6)5923100, Abdoun, Amman

U.S.A.: Jabal Amman, P.O.Box 354, Tel. (6)5920101, Amman

Yemen (Republic of): Tel. 5642381, Amman

Justice

The judiciary is constitutionally independent, though judges are appointed and dismissed by royal decree. There are three categories of courts. The first category consists of regular courts, including magistrates courts, courts of first instance, and courts of appeals and cassation in Amman, which hear appeals passed on from lower appeals courts. The constitution also provides for a Special Council, which interprets the laws and passes on their constitutionality. The second category consists of Shari'ah Muslim courts and other religious courts for non-Muslims; these exercise jurisdiction over matters of personal status. The third category consists of special courts, such as land, government, property, municipal, tax, and customs courts.

The Economy

The budget for 1988, approved by parliament in December 1987, projected a rise of 11% in domestic revenue to JD611 million and a decline of JD22 million in foreign borrowing and aid to JD371 million. With total expenditure set at JD1075 million, of which two-fifths is earmarked for development, the budget deficit is targeted at JD67 million compared with the outturn deficit of JD89 million in 1987. 1989 and 1990 were economically difficult years for Jordan and foreign debt was estimated at over US $ 8 billion. The effects of the prewar tension period in the Gulf was to deprive Jordan from remittances of thousands of Jordanian Nationals in Iraq and Kuwait and from the transit trade with those two countries and the decline in transit goods through the Port of Aqaba, during the Naval blockade. As tensions further grew and Iraq invaded Kuwait, thousands of Jordanian Nationals lost their jobs and or returned to Jordan creating more economic difficulties. The United Nations Sanctions on Iraq also deprived Jordan from its main source of oil supply. In 1991 the Government has taken steps to assist in the recovery of the important economic sectors which have been damaged during the Gulf crisis.

However, the massive return of some 250,000 persons expelled from Kuwait and the Gulf, brought money in the country, which generated an economic boom in 1992 mainly in the construction sector. The 1993 budget presented by the government in December 1992 projected an expenditure of J.D. 1,328 million and revenue of J.D. 1,273 million leaving a deficit of J.D. 55 million. In 1992 revenues were J.D. 1,353 million and J.D. 1,204 million.

In November 1994 the Cabinet approved the budget figures for the year 1995 with revenue at J.D. 1.62 billion and expenditure at J.D. 1.67 billion.

The 1996 budget figures were, expenditure JD 1.79 billion with revenue at JD 1.63 billion and in 1997 were JD 1.91 billion expenditure and revenue set at JD 1.86 billion.

In 1998 the budget figures were expenditure JD 1.950 billion and revenue at JD 1.913 billion and the budget for 1999 was JD 2.160 billion.

Jordan's main exports are phosphates, potash, fertilizers, chemicals, cement, vegetables and fruits.

MINING AND INDUSTRY

The mining sector is largely based on the extraction and processing of phosphates and potash, although there is some potential for developing production of other resources such as uranium, vanadium and copper. Phosphate reserves are estimated at 2,000 million tonnes.

Political Parties

All political parties were banned since 1963.

A general election to the House of Representatives took place in November 1989, and in April 1990 a Royal Commission was formed to draft a charter to regulate political activity in the Country. Approved in June 1991, it lifted the ban on political parties. In August 1992, the House of Representatives approved legislation which permitted the formation of political parties. By September 1993, about 20 parties were registered and approved by the government. Elections to the 80-member House of Representatives took place on November 8, 1993, which elected Mr. Saad Hayel Srour as its Speaker; and on November 18 King Hussein appointed a 40-member Senate with Mr. Abdelhadi AL MAJALI at its Head.

The Banking System

Central Bank of Jordan: Est. 1964; P.O.Box 37, Amman; Tel. (6)4630301/9 Telex 21250.

Agricultural Credit Corporation: Est. 1960; P.O.Box 77, Amman; Tel. (6)5661105 Amman (16 branch offices in Jordan).

Arab Bank, PLC: Est. 1930; King Faisal street; P.O.Box 950544, Amman; Tel. (6)5607115; Telex: 23091. Subsidiaries: Arab Bank (Overseas) Ltd; Arab Bank (Nigeria) Ltd. Branches throughout the Arab countries.

Bank of Jordan PLC: Est. 1960; Jabal Amman, 3rd Circle, Amman; P.O.Box 2140; Tel. (6)5644327.

Cairo Amman Bank: Est. 1960; Prince Hassan street; P.O.Box 950661 Amman; Tel. (6)5616910; Telex 24049.

Industrial Development Bank: Est. 1965; P.O.Box 1982 Amman. Tel. (6)5642216;

British Bank of the Middle East: P.O.Box 925286 Amman; Main office: King Hussein street, Amman. Tel. (6)5607471

ANZ Grindlays Bank: P.O.Box 9997 Amman; Tel. (6)5607210

Jordan National Bank: Est. 1956; P.O.Box 3103, Amman; Tel. (6)5702282.

Transport

ROADS

Jordan has a main, secondary, and rural road network about 4700 km long. This roadway system, maintained by the Ministry of Public Works, links the major cities and towns and also links the kingdom with neighbouring countries. Within cities, towns, and villages, however, the local authorities are responsible for road upkeep. One of the main traffic arteries is the Amman – Jarash – Ramtha highway, which links Jordan with Syria to the north. The route from Amman via Ma'an to the port of al-'Aqabah is the principal route to the sea. From Ma'an, the Desert Highway passes through al-Mudawwarah, linking Jordan with Saudi Arabia.

RAILWAYS

In the early sixties Jordan, Saudi Arabia, and Syria reached agreement on the rehabilitation of the Hedjaz Railway which runs between Damascus and Medina and crosses Jordan from north to south.

The line between Ma'an and Saudi Arabia is now operational together with a 15-km extension into Saudi Arabia as far as Haret Ammar station.

Since 1975 a 115-km extension to Aqaba, is now mainly used for transporting phosphates for export.

SHIPPING

The Port of Aqaba is Jordan's only outlet to the sea. Present installations include 20 modern berths, and one container terminal, storage facilities for phosphates and other goods, mechanical handling equipment, and power generation.

CIVIL AVIATION

There are two International Airports in Jordan, situated in Amman and Akaba.

Royal Jordanian Airline: Head Office, Housing Bank commercial Centre, Shmeisani, P.O.Box 302, Amman Established in December 1963 with joint ownership between the Government and the private sector. The company became completely state-owned in March 1968. Services throughout the Middle East, Europe, Far East and U.S.A.

Education

There are three types of schools in Jordan - government schools, private and missionary schools, and the UNRWA schools for refugee children. The Ministry of Education supervises all schools, establishes the curricula, teachers' qualifications, and state examinations; it also distributes free books to students in government schools and enforces compulsory education to the age of 14. Almost 70 percent of the students attend government schools.

Universities

University of Jordan
Est. 1962; P.O.Box 1682, Tel.: 844595, Amman

Jordan University of Science and Technology
Est. 1986; P.O.Box 3030, Tel.: (962) 2-295111, Irbid

Mutah University
Est. 1981; Al Karak, P.O.Box 7, Mutah; Amman Office: P.O.Box 5076, Tel.: 629545, Amman

Quds Open University
Est. 1985; P.O.Box 77, Tel.: 822561, Um Summaq, Amman; Tel.: (6)822561

Yarmouk University
Est. 1976; P.O.Box 566, Irbid; Amman Office: P.O.Box 20184, Tel.: (02)271100, 271115, Amman

CULTURAL AND RESEARCH INSTITUTES

Goethe Institut:
Ibn Sina St. P.O.B. 1676, Amman; f. 1961; German cultural institute and library, language courses.

British Council:
Amman Centre, Jebel Amman, Amman; library.

Department of Agricultural and Scientific Research and Extension:
P.O.B. 226 and P.O.B. 2178, Amman; f. 1958; covers all branches of agricultural research, information and extension.

Radio, Television and Press

RADIO – TELEVISION

Jordan Radio and Television Corporation: P.O.Box 1041, Amman; Est. 1968. Broadcasting time: 85-90 hours weekly.

THE PRESS

Al-Dustour: P.O.Box 591, Amman; Est. 1967; Arabic; Daily.

Al-Rai: P.O.Box 6710, Amman; Est. 1971, Arabic; Daily.

The Jordan Times: P.O.Box 6710, Amman; Est. 1975; English; Daily

Al-Akhbar: P.O.Box 62420, Amman; Est. 1976; Arabic; Daily

Akhbar al-Usbu: Est. 1959; P.O.Box 605, Amman , Arabic; Weekly

Al-Aqsa: P.O.Box 1957 Amman; armed forces magazine; weekly

Huda al Islam: Est. 1956; P.O.Box 659, Amman; Monthly

Jordan: P.O.Box 224, Amman; Est. 1982; quarterly, Jordan Information Bureau, Washington

Sharia: P.O.Box 585, Amman; Est. 1959; fortnightly; Islamic Affairs

The Star: P.O.Box 9313, Amman, Arabic, Weekly

NEWS AGENCIES

Jordanian News Agency (PETRA): P.O.Box 6845, Amman; Est. 1965.

KUWAIT
(State of Kuwait)

Kuwait

Head of State	: H.H. Jaber al-Ahmad al-Jaber as SABAH
Crown Prince	: Shaikh Saad al Abdullah as Salim as SABAH
Capital	: Kuwait City.
Area	: 17.818 sq. km.
Population	: 1.7 million (1995 estimate)
Currency	: Kuwait Dinar (KD) divided into, 1,000 fils
Denominations	: a) Notes: ¼, ½, 1, 5, 10 dinars
	: b) Coins: 1,5,10,20,50 and 100 fils
Exchange rate	: US Dollar: 0.3 Kuwait Dinars (May 1998)

Geography

Kuwait is situated on the northwestern shore of the Arabian Gulf, being the most northerly, the largest and the most populous of the Arab Shaikhdoms and communities of the area.

It is bounded on the east by the Gulf, on the north and west by Iraq and on the south west by Saudi Arabia. The area of the State proper is approximately 6,000 square miles, or somewhat less than that of New Jersey or Wales. The country is roughly rectangular in shape, 130 miles East to West and with a maximum North-South dimension of about 115 miles. The State includes a number of offshore islands the larger of which are Budiyan, Failakah, and Warbah. Only Failakah, the site of an ancient Greek Temple built by Alexander's forces, is permanently inhabited. Kuwait bay is the only prominent coastal feature. It indents the shoreline about 25 miles and provides protection for the port of Kuwait. Half of the shoreline of the country lies on Kuwait Bay, Kuwait City and its immediate environs, plus the oil town of Amadi and adjacent Fahaheel a few miles of the south, contain all but a few thousand of the State's population, numbering 1.71 million in mid-1985. Apart from a small Bedouin population and oil field workers. The Neutral Zone is uninhabited.

Kuwait's climate and physical aspect are, of course, typical of the region. Mean annual rainfall is 4 to 5 inches and average daytime summer temperatures well exceed 110 degrees F. The entire area is semi-arid to arid. There are no springs or streams on the surface. Scarcity of fresh water is thus the major physical problem. The only usable water, in addition to that distilled from the sea, is found trapped in sub-surface sedimentary beds.

PUBLIC HOLIDAYS

Mulid al Nabi - birthday of the Prophet; Eid al Fitr, end of Ramadan; Eid al Ahda, (Feast of the Sacrifice); Muslim New Year; Ashura, day of mourning for Shi'ite Muslims.

LANGUAGE & RELIGION

The official language is Arabic; English is used as a second language.

Islam is the religion of the State, but there is a number of Christian churches of various denominations (Anglicans, Roman Catholics, Armenian, Greek, Coptic and Syrian Orthodox churches).

History

Recent archeological investigations undertaken on the island of Failakah have shown that Kuwait's history as a centre of trade and commerce extends back into the 3rd millenium before Christ.

The island of Failakah is located about 32 kms. northeast of Kuwait City, and has been host since 1958 to Danish archeologists who have unearthed a number of temples, fortresses, residential quarters, seals, statues and inscriptions. These show that Failakah during the Bronze Age, had trade relations with many other countries and possessed a high level of technical achievement in building and domestic crafts. It is the opinion of some that Failakah is one of the possible sites of the «Dilmun» culture, often mentioned in Sumerian inscriptions.

THE TRADE CENTRE

During the early Islamic period, the centre of life in Kuwait shifted to a small peninsula located at the head of Kuwait Bay near the present town of Jahra: Kazimah.

Because of its attraction for the desert Arab, in search of water and forage for his flocks and merchants and traders, because of its natural harbour, Kazimah became an important trading centre, where pilgrims and travellers stopped on their way to and from Mecca and other towns in the Arabian peninsula.

Kazimah has attracted the interest of Danish archeologists. Preliminary surveys along the nothern shore of Kiwait Bay, and particularly the Kazimah area, have shown four areas to be of special interest. The discovery of hard stone tools indicates that the area was the home of past civilizations, while more recent historical records would indicate that the once flourishing city itself is worthy of further research and excavation. Kuwait grew from a settlement on the site of Kuwait City about the beginning of the 18th century, when a number of families of the Anaiza tribe migrated from the interior to the shore of the Gulf. The ruling families of Kuwait, Saudi Arabia and Bahrain step from this tribe.

KUWAIT AND BRITAIN

In 1756 the head of the as-Sabah family was selected Amir, or Ruler. The need for security and for representation in dealings with the Ottoman Government probably prompted the selection of a leader. as-Sabah has been Ruler of Kuwait since then.

Relations with the British began as a result of the transfer by the East India Company of the southern terminal of its overland mail route (through Aleppo) from

Basra to Kuwait when the former was captured by the Persians during the Turkish-Persian war of 1776.

In 1899 the Ruler, Shaikh Moubarak the Great, sought British protection, which was granted under a treaty similar to those Britain made with other Gulf Shaikhdoms in the 1890s.

Under the treaty the Shaikhdom's foreign relations were handled through the British Foreign Office. In 1904 the British Political Agency was established.

An American Consulate was opened shortly after World War II. In 1941, the British formally agreed that Kuwait was an independent principality under British protection.

STATEHOOD

Government power, though vested with the Ruler and his family, derived its main support until the end of World War II from the Kuwaiti merchant families which were the sources of the Shaikhdoms' modest prosperity and contributed, directly or indirectly, the major part of its limited government revenue.

After World War II the material needs of oil exploration and oil production and the feverish development of governmental and private activities in the fields of construction, transport, banking, trade and public services caused a stream of immigration, mainly from Arab countries.

In the 1950's the primary source of prosperity shifted from the merchants to Government, which dispensed the oil revenues. Thus the ruling family, and particularly its head, the Ruler, became more important.

In January 1961, the Government announced that Kuwait was now fully responsible for her foreign relations. In June 1961, the 1899 agreement was replaced by a treaty of friendship and consultation with the United Kingdom.

Since the new treaty with Britain, Kuwait has been moving rapidly toward democratic government. A constitution has been promulgated and a National Assembly elected to which the ministers heading the various ministries of the Government are responsible, although they continue to be appointed by the Ruler.

EVENTS IN 1965 – 1977

The Ruler of Kuwait, Emir Abdallah as-Salem as-Sabah, died on 24 November 1965, aged 70, and was succeeded by the Crown Prince Shaikh Sabah as-Salem as-Sabah who was Prime Minister until his accession.

A new University of Kuwait was inaugurated on 27 November 1966, with faculties of Arts, Science, and Education.

THE ARAB-ISRAELI WAR

Shortly after the news was received in Kuwait of the outbreak of hostilities in the A.R.E. and Jordan, the Emir declared in a broadcast statement that Kuwait was putting all its resources into the struggle.

In 1967, Kuwait joined the Arab oil embargo on exports to Great Britain and the USA.

Kuwait was in 1974 in the forefront in measures to increase oil companies' interests, and preserve its natural resources by cutting back production and keeping more of its oil wealth under the ground.

CROWN PRINCE JABER

Following the death on Dec. 31, 1977, of the Amir (Ruler) of Kuwait, Shaikh Sabah as Salim as Sabah (63), the Crown Prince and Prime Minister, Shaikh Jaber al Ahmad al Jaber as Sabah (49), a cousin of the late Amir, became the country's new ruler in accordance with the constitution.

Following a 40-day period of mourning for the late ruler, the Amir, on Feb. 8, appointed the new Heir Apparent as Prime Minister and charged him form a new government.

CENSUS RESULTS

The final results of a national census carried out in April 1985, as published in May 1987, gave Kuwait's total population as 1,697,301, of whom only 681,288 were Kuwaiti citizens. Of the remainder, 642,814 were from other Arab countries and 355,947 were from countries further east. Europeans and North Americans accounted for 14,857. The proportion of naturalized Kuwaitis had declined from 48 per cent in 1975 to 40 per cent at the time of the census. The country's total workforce amounted to 667,535, of whom 543,975 were expatriates. As of Dec. 1995 the population was estimated at 1.7 million.

THE GULF CRISIS

The end of the Iranian-Iraqi war in August 1988 brought a certain stability in the Gulf region and an increase of economic activity in Kuwait, and in 1989 relations with Iran were normalized. Internally a programme to train Kuwaitis to take over jobs hitherto held by foreigners met with some success mainly in the public administrations. However, in July relations with Iraq deteriorated over several issues mainly oil production quotas, Iraq's war debt, and disputed borders. The Arab World's leaders attempted several mediations but their efforts met with no success. Iraq began deploying its military forces on the borders with Kuwait at the end of July. An ultimate meeting was held in Saudi Arabia between representatives of Iraq and Kuwait and after the collapse of negotiations Kuwait was invaded by neighbouring Iraq on August 2.

Iraqi troops estimated at 100,000 crossed the border and occupied the country. On August 4, Iraq formed a provisional government (short lived), and on August 8, Kuwait was officially declared the 19th province of Iraq.

During and after the invasion, thousands of expatriates fled the country to Jordan and Saudi Arabia. Others less fortunate were detained in Kuwait.

During the invasion The Emir and Members of the Government of Kuwait have managed to escape and set up provisional headquarters in Taef, Saudi Arabia, to direct the country's affairs from there.

Foreigners trapped in Kuwait for several months were not allowed to leave the country but following continous interventions were finally authorized by the Iraqis to leave in early December.

During these months there were reports of plundering, looting, torture and executions. Many installations were removed to Iraq, and by the end of the year troops in the country and bordering Saudi Arabia were roughly estimated to have reached 400,000. Condemning the invasion, the UN Security Council immediately adopted resolution 660 demanding the withdrawal of Iraqi forces from Kuwait. Further resolutions were adopted to impose a trade embargo on Iraq (661) and in November resolution 678 authorized the multinational force in Saudi Arabia and the Gulf to use all means to liberate Kuwait setting the deadline to January 15, 1991.

On the other hand, on the 7th of August, the Saudi Government requested the U.S. to send troops to defend its borders from an eventual Iraqi attack. Other military support came from the European Community (particularly Britain and France) and some Arab States.

Meanwhile intensive diplomatic attempts, proposals and initiatives were undertaken to avoid a military confrontation until the last minute, but they were unsuccessful. Back to Taef, the Kuwait Government in exile has been active in every field by establishing committees for military, political, social and financial matters and looking for the urgent needs of the exiled population and back a resistance movement in Kuwait. On January 17, 1991 the multinational force began its military operations to liberate Kuwait, by an intensive aerial bombardment followed by a land offensive on February 24. Within a few days Kuwait was liberated. However, before retreating the Iraqis have ignited over 600 oilwells out of the 950 causing considerable damage to the economy and the environment.

In March Iraq accepted UN resolution 686 for a permanent cease fire.

The Emir and members of the Government returned to Kuwait soon after liberation and on the 20th the Government resigned. A new Government was formed in April headed by Crown Prince Saad Al Abdullah Al Salim Al Sabah. The government was formed in October 1992 with minor changes in January 1993, and more recently in April 1994. On October 16, 1996 a new government was formed.

The Cabinet

(Dec. 1999)

Prime Minister: Sheikh Saad al-Abdallah al-Salem AL SABAH

First Deputy Prime Minister, Minister of Foreign Affairs: Shaikh Sabah al-Ahmad al-Jabir AL SABAH

Deputy Prime Minister, Minister of Defence: Shaikh Salem Sabah al-Salem AL SABAH

Deputy Prime Minister, Minister of State for National Assembly Affairs: Mohamad Dhaifallah SHARAR

Minister of the Interior: Sheikh Mohamed Khalid al-Hamad AL-SABAH

Minister of Finance and Communications: Shaikh Ahmad Abdullah al-Ahmad AL-SABAH

Minister of Justice, Waqf and Islamic Affairs: Saad Jassem Yussef AL-HASHEL

Minister of Oil: Shaikh Saud Nasir Saud AL-SABAH

Minister of State for Foreign Affairs: Suleiman Majed AL-SHAHEEN

Minister of Information: Saadi Mohamad Bin Tefiah AL-AJMI

Minister of Commerce, Industry, Labour and Social Affairs: Abdel Wahab Mohammad AL-WAZZAN

Minister of Public Works: Eid Hathal Saud AL-RASHIDI

Minister of Electricity and Water, and Minister of State for Housing Affairs: Adel AL-SABIH

Minister of Health: Mohamad Ahmad AL-JARALLAH

Minister of Planning and Minister of State for Administrative Development Affairs: Mohamad Bteihan AL-DWEIHEES

Minister of Education and Higher Education: Yussef Hamad AL-IBRAHIM

Foreign Embassies

Afghanistan: 7 Mishref St., Block 1, P.O.Box 33186, Rawdah 73452, Tel. 5396916, Kuwait City

Algeria: Istiqlal St., P.O.Box 578, Tel. 2519987, Safat 13006, Kuwait City

Austria: P.O.Box 15013, Rawdah 73453, Tel. 2552532, Kuwait City

Bahrain: Jabriya, Plot 10, Parcel 312, P.O.Box 196, Safat 13002, Tel. 5318530, Kuwait City

Bangladesh: Jabriya, Block 11, House 181, P.O.Box 22344, Safat 13084, Tel. 5330546, Kuwait City

Belgium: Salmiya, Baghdad Str., Block 8, Plot 1, P.O.Box 3280, Safat 13033, Tel. 5722014, Kuwait City

Bhutan: Mishref Str., Block 15, St. 14, Villa 19, Rd. 55, P.O.Box 1510, Safat 13016, Tel. 5382873, Kuwait City

Bulgaria: Salwa, Parcel 10, Plot 312, P.O.Box 12090, Shamiya, 71651, Tel. 5643877, Kuwait City

Canada: Daiya, Block 4, Al-Motawakel St., Villa 4, P.O.Box 25281, Tel. 2563025, Safat 13113, Kuwait City

China, People's Republic: Jabriya, Block 12, P.O.B. 2346, Safat 13024, Kuwait City

Czech: Nuzha, Block 3, St. 34, House 13, P.O.Box 1151, Safat 13012, Tel. 2548206, Kuwait City

Egypt: Istiklal Str., P.O.Box 11252, Desmah 35153, Tel. 2561297, Kuwait City

Finland: Dasman Sq., White House 2, P.O.Box 26699, Safat 13127, Tel. 5312890, Kuwait City

France: Jabriya, Block 12, Parcel 156-158, P.O.Box 1037, Safat 13011, Tel. 5312000, Kuwait City

Germany: Plot 1, St. 14, Villa 13, Tel. 2520857, Kuwait City

Greece: Block 2, Str. 2, House 21, Surra, P.O.Box 23812,

Safat 13099, Tel. 5335861, Kuwait City

Hungary: Shamiya, Block 8, Str. 84, Villa 6, P.O.Box 23955, Safat 13100, Tel. 4814080, Kuwait City

India: 34 Istiqlal Str., P.O.Box 1450, Safat 13015, Tel. 2530600, Kuwait City

Indonesia: Nuzha Main Str., Block 3, P.O.Box 21560, Safat 13076, Tel. 2514588, Kuwait City

Iran: 24 Istiqlal Str., P.O.Box 4686, Safat 13047, Tel. 2533220, Kuwait City

Italy: F. Omar Ben Khattab Str., Mulla Bldg., Villa 6, P.O.Box 4453, Safat 13045, Tel. 2445120, Kuwait City

Japan: Jabriya, Block 9, Plot 486, P.O.Box 2304, Safat 13024, Tel. 5312870, Kuwait City

Jordan: Istiqlal Str., Embassies Area, P.O.Box 15314, 35305 Diiyah, Tel. 2533500, Kuwait City

Korea, Republic: Nuzha, Damascus Str., Block 2, Div. 42, Villa 12, P.O.Box 4272, Safat 13043, Tel. 2531816, Kuwait City

Lebanon: 31 Istiklal Str., P.O.Box 253, Safat 13003, Tel. 2619765, Kuwait City

Malaysia: Faiha, Block 7, Villa 1, Str. 70, P.O.Box 4105, Safat 13042, Tel. 2546022, Kuwait City

Mauritania: Mishrif, Parcel 6, Villa 37, P.O.Box 23784, Safat 13098, Tel. 5384849, Kuwait City

Morocco: Shuwaikh B, Block 5, House 5, P.O.Box 784, Safat 13008, Tel. 4813912, Kuwait City

Netherlands: Jabriya, Block 9, Parcel 40A, P.O.Box 21822, Safat 13079, Tel. 5312650, Kuwait City

Niger: Salwa, Area 10, Plot 447, P.O.Box 44451, Hawalli 32059, Tel. 5652639, Kuwait City

Nigeria: Surra, Area 1, Str. 14, House 25, P.O.Box 6432, Hawalli 32039, Tel. 5320794, Kuwait City

Oman: Undailia, Block 3, Parcel 123, House 25, P.O.Box 21975, Safat 13080, Tel. 2561962, Kuwait City

Pakistan: Diiyah, Hamza Str., Villa 29, P.O.B. 988, Safat 13010, Tel. 2532101, Kuwait City

Paraguay: Shuwaikh, P.O.Box 886, Safat 13009, Tel. 4814462, Kuwait City

Philippines: Rawdah, Str. 34, Area 3, Villa 24, P.O.Box 26288, Safat 13123, Tel. 5329316, Kuwait City

Poland: Rawdah, Block 4, 3rd Ring Rd., Villa 13, P.O.Box 5066, Safat 13051, Tel. 2510355, Kuwait City

Qatar: Istiqlal Str., Diiyah, P.O.Box 1825, Safat 13019, Tel. 2513599, Kuwait City

Romania: Dasmah, 35152 Kifan, Zone 4, Mouna Str., House 34, P.O.Box 11149, Tel. 843419, Kuwait City

Russia: Baghdad Str., Midan-Hawalli, House 6, P.O.Box 1765, Safat 13018, Tel. 5642711, Kuwait City

Saudi Arabia: Arabian Gulf Str., P.O.Box 20498, Safat 13065, Tel. 2531155, Kuwait City

Senegal: Rawdah, Parcel 3, Str. 35, House 9, P.O.B. 23892, Safat 13099, Tel. 2542044, Kuwait City

Spain: Abdullah Salem District, Str. 12, Bldg. 2, P.O.Box 22207, Safat 13083, Tel. 2512722, Kuwait City

Sri Lanka: House 381, ST 9, Block 5, Salwa, P.O.Box 13212, 71952 Keifan, Tel. 5612261, Kuwait City

Sweden: Faiha, Parcel 7, Shahba Str., House 3, P.O.Box 21448, Safat 13075, Tel. 2523588, Kuwait City

Switzerland: Udailia, Str. 32, Area 3, House 12, P.O.Box 23954, Safat 13100, Tel. 2551872, Kuwait City

Syria: Rawdah, Str., 43, Plot 4, Villa 5, P.O.Box 25600, Safat 13115, Tel. 2531164, Kuwait City

Thailand: Surra, Area 3, Block 49, Ali Ben Taleb Str., P.O.Box 66647, Bayan 43757, Tel. 5314870, Kuwait City

Tunisia: Faiha, Plot 9, Str. 91, Villa 10F, P.O.Box 5976, Safat 13060, Tel. 2542144, Kuwait City

Turkey: Istiklal Str., Block 16, Plot 10, P.O.Box 20627, Safat 13067, Tel. 2531785, Kuwait City

United Arab Emirates: Istiqlal Str., Plot 70, P.O.Box 1828, Safat 13019, Tel. 2518381, Kuwait City

United Kingdom: Arabian Gulf Str., P.O.Box 2, Safat 13001, Tel. 2403334, Kuwait City

U.S.A.: Arabian Gulf Str., P.O.Box 77, Safat 13001, Tel. 5395307, Kuwait City

Venezuela: Surra, Parcel 2, 11 Ali bin Abi Taleb Str., P.O.Box 24440, Safat 13105, Tel. 5334578, Kuwait City

Yugoslavia: Shuwaikh, «B», al Mansour Str., Villa 15, P.O.Box 20511, Safat 13066, Tel. 4813140, Kuwait City

Justice

Justice in Kuwait is administered as follows: a) by Magistrates' Courts which have jurisdiction in criminal matters and contraventions; b) by Criminal Assizes which deal with felonies; and c) by Misdemeanour Courts which hear appeals in cases of misdemeanour.

Civil cases are adjudicated by a General Court within which are specialised chambers (commerce, personal status, summary jurisdiction, etc...)

Appeal is made to a High Appeal Court, but a Higher Appeal Court (Known as Court of Cassation) administers justice in personal status disputes.

The Economy

The oil sector plays a dominant role in the economy with Kuwait possessing some of the largest reserves in the world. Earnings from hydrocarbons generate over 90% of export receipts, provide the bulk of government revenue and directly contribute just under one half of GDP. Moreover, much of the non-oil economy is dependent upon oil-derived government revenues which have been deployed in infrastructural development, the provision of comprehensive social services and the promotion of industrial diversification.

Although the economy remains adversely affected by unfavourable conditions in the international oil market, by the collapse of the unofficial stock-market in 1982 and by the loss of transit trade due to the Gulf war, sizeable investment income is generated by the country's substantial holdings of overseas assets. Nevertheless, as a consequence of the collapse of the unofficial stock market, the Souq al-Manakh, which has seriously interfered with the normal course of business, the state has had to continue to provide financial support to maintain activity and confidence. Intervention has included the purchase of shares as well as support for the banking system. Recently, however the authorities have taken a more stringent approach, insisting on extensive loan loss provision by the banks as well as restricting financial support to key financial and business institutions.

Since the early 1980s the economy has been adversely affected by the depressed international oil market conditions which have resulted in lower oil-derived government revenues and a more cautious fiscal policy which in turn has contributed to subdued growth rates. Most sectors in the economy experienced difficulties in 1985, with the construction industry in particular recording a large reduction in output. Moreover, as a consequence of the halving of international oil prices since the beginning of 1986 government revenues will be far short of originally anticipated levels and further economic retrenchment can be expected. Local Kuwaiti employment, however, has so far remained largely unaffected due to the country's heavy dependence on expatriate labour which is contracting as foreign workers leave. Furthermore, a very high per capita income, combined with the widespread provision of social services has given Kuwait nationals one of the highest standards of living in the world.

Proven reserves of hydrocarbon are estimated to be around 95 billion barrels, second only to Saudi Arabia in the Middle East and sufficient to last over 150 years at current rates of extraction.

And while crude oil sales still account for a significant proportion of total hydrocarbons output, Kuwait remains firmly committed to its long-term strategy of increasing the proportion of more profitable refined products in its overall sales. Largely through an expansion of the two main oil refineries at Mina al-Ahmadi and Mina Abdullah, in addition to the third refinery at Shuaiba, domestic refining capacity was in early 1997 approximately 900.000 b/d.

ECONOMIC INDICATORS

The Kuwaiti economy was strengthened during 1987 by increased oil exports, which rose by 13.3 per cent to a value of KD2, 100 million over the year. Gross domestic product (GDP) increased by 5 per cent. Inflation for the year averaged 0.6 per cent (down from 1 per cent in 1986).

The budget for fiscal year 1988/89 (ending June 30, 1989), as announced by Finance and Economy Minister Mr Jassim Mohammed al Kharafi on Jude 25, 1988, provided for a deficit of KD 1,350 million (including the allocation to the Reserve Fund for Future Generations). Expenditure (which excluded reserve allocations) was set at KD 3,190 million, with revenue estimated as KD 2,050 million, of which oil earnings accounted for KD 1,790 million (a planned increase of 3.7 per cent on the previous year's budget).

The final deficit for 1987-88 was expected to be much lower than the estimated KD 1,179 million, due to improved oil revenue.

To provide for the increased spending involved in its major arms procurement programme, the government announced in June 1988 that 1,532 million Kuwaiti dinars were to be transferred from the reserve fund to boost the defence budget (US$1.00= KD 0.2771 as at June 27, 1988).

The budget for fiscal year 1990/91 expenditures were KD 3,634 million. The 1991/92 budget expenditures were raised to KD 6,087 million mainly in allocations for defence. The 1992/93 budget was deficitary by an estimated KD 1.8 billion whereas the 1993/94 approved budget is expected to reduce the deficit to KD 1.2 billion.

In 1994/95 budget was set at revenue KD 2.637 billion and expenditure at KD 4.403 billion. The 1995/96 budget approved by the National Assembly on August 22, 1995 projected revenues at KD 2.910 billion and expenditure at KD 4.230 billion.

The 1996/97 budget was estimated at revenues of KD 3.000 billion and expenditure at KD 4.210 billion.

The 1997/98 budget estimated expenditures at KD 4.378 million and revenue at KD 3.105; The 1998/99 budget set expenditure at KD 4.362 million and revenue at KD 2.443 and 1999/2000 KD 4.250 expenditure and KD 2.224 revenue.

The Banking System

Central Bank of Kuwait: Est. 1969, Abdullah Salem Str., P.O.Box 526, Safat 13006, Tel. 2449200, Kuwait City

Bank of Bahrain and Kuwait BSC: Ahmad al Jaber Str., P.O.Box 24396, Safat 13104, Tel. 2417140, Kuwait City

Bank of Kuwait and the Middle East KSC: Darwazat Abderrazak, P.O.Box 71, Safat 13001, Tel. 2459771, Kuwait City

Burgan Bank SAK: Est. 1975; Ahmad al Jaber Str., P.O.Box 5389; Safat, Kuwait City.

Commercial Bank of Kuwait: Est. 1960; Mubarak al-Kabir Str., P.O.Box 2861, Safat 13029, Tel. 2411001, Kuwait City

Gulf Bank KSC.: Est. 1960; Mubarak al-Kabir Str., P.O.Box 3200, Safat 13032, Tel. 2449501, Kuwait City

Industrial Bank of Kuwait: Est. 1973, Joint Banking Center, Commercial Area 9, P.O.Box 3146, Safat 13032, Kuwait City

Kuwait Real Estate Bank KSC: Est. 1973; Darwazat Abderrazak, West - Tower - Joint Banking Center, P.O.Box 22822, Safat 13089, Tel. 2458177, Kuwait City

National Bank of Kuwait SAK (NBK): Est. 1952, Abdullah Salem Str., P.O.Box 95, Safat 13001, Tel. 2422011, Kuwait City

Education

Education is free from kindergarten through postgraduate levels, both at home and abroad. Among the perquisites all students enjoy are free books, free school meals, free uniforms, free transportation between home and school and, of course, free medical and dental services.

Although Kuwait University now offers doctoral programmes, so great is the need and absorptive capacity of the Kuwait economy for technologists, engineers and other professionals that large numbers of recent graduates go abroad, for advanced study.

Kuwait University

Est. 1962; P.O.Box 5969, Safat 13060, Tel.: 4811188, Kuwait

EDUCATION 1995/1996

	Schools	Teachers	Students
Kindergarten	143	2,530	37,00
Primary	175	6,990	94,000
Intermediate	157	7,450	87,000
Secondary	111	7,800	64,000
Religious Institutes	6	250	1,500
Special Training Intitutes	30	470	1,600

Transport

ROADS

Both metalled and roads cover a total of 4270 km.

There is a good road between Basra (Iraq) and Kuwait and Saudi Arabia.

In Kuwait itself there are two good roads between Kuwait City and Ahmadi, which is the Kuwait Oil Company's centre of operation and also the other main centres of population in Kuwait. Regular bus services are provided by the Kuwait Transport Co., S.A.K.

PORTS

Kuwait Port at Shuwaikh, comprises 21 deep water berths.
Shuaiba Port, south of Kuwait City, comprises 20 berts.
Mina Al Ahmadi, south of Kuwait City, for oil exports.

CIVIL AVIATION

The main international airport is situated about 10 miles from the centre of Kuwait City, and the road journey takes about 20 minutes.

Kuwait Airways Corporation: Est. 1954; has services in operation to principal Middle Eastern points, to Asia, Africa and Europe.

Radio, Television, Cinema and Press

A. – RADIO

Kuwait Broadcasting Station: P.O.Box 397; Est. 1951.

B. - TELEVISION

Television of Kuwait: P.O.Box 193, 13002 Safat, Kuwait; Public corporation (Est. 1961).

THE PRESS

A – DAILIES, WEEKLIES AND PERIODICALS

Al-Anbaa: P.O.Box 23915, Kuwait; Est. 1976; Arabic; Daily

Al-Qabas: P.O.Box 21800, Kuwait: Est 1972; Arabic; Daily.

Al Ray al-Aam: P.O.Box 695, Kuwait; Est. 1961; Arabic; Political, social and cultural; Daily.

Al-Siyassa: P.O.Box 2270, Kuwait; Est. 1965; Arabic; Political; Daily

Al-Watan: P.O.Box 1142, Kuwait; Est. 1962; Arabic; Political; Daily

Kuwait Times: P.O.Box 1301, Safat Kuwait; Est. 1961; English, Political; Daily

Kuwait al-Yawm: P.O.Box 193, Kuwait; Est. 1954; published by Ministry of Information

Al-Arabi: P.O.Box 748, Kuwait; Est. 1958; Arabic; Arts, History and Science; monthly; published by the Ministry of Information

Al-Hadaf: P.O.Box 1142, Safat Kuwait; Est. 1961; Arabic; Social Political; Weekly

Al-Yaqza: P.O.Box 6000, Kuwait; Est. 1966; Political, Economic, Social and General; Weekly

Hayatuna: P.O.Box 1708, Kuwait; Est. 1968; Arabic; Medicine and Hygiene; Fortnightly

Saut al-Khalij: P.O.Box 659, Kuwait; Est. 1962; Political; Weekly

Mejallat al-Kuwait: P.O.Box 193, Kuwait; Arabic; fortnightly; published by Ministry of Information

Osrati: P.O.Box 2995, Kuwait; Arabic Women's magazine; Weekly

B – NEWS AGENCIES

Kuwait News Agency (KUNA): Al-Nakib Bldg., Fahd Al-Salem St., Kuwait; Tel. 2412040, P.O.Box 24063 Est. 1976

Middle East News Agency (MENA); Fahd Salem Str., P.O.Box 1927, Safat, Kuwait City

Reuters Middle East Ltd.: P.O.Box 5616, Safat 13057, Tel. 2431920, Kuwait City

LIBYA
(The Great Socialist People's Libyan Arab Jamahiriya)

Libya

(The Great Socialist People's Libyan Arab Jamahiriya)

Leader	: Colonel Moammar al-QADDAFI
Capital	: Tripoli
Area	: 1,775,500 sq. km.
Population	: 5.4 million (1995 estimate)
Currency	: Libyan Dinar divided into 1,000 dirhams. The Dinar succeeded the Libyan Pound which ceased to be the unit of currency on 31 August 1971.
Denominations	: a) Notes: ¼, ½, 1,5 and 10 Libyan Dinars. b) Coins: 1,5, 10,20,50 and 100 milliemes dirhams.
Exchange Rate	: US $ per Dinar = 0.469 Libyan Dinars (Apr. 1999)

Geography

The Great Socialist People's Libyan Arab Jamahiriya consists of two fertile strips on the Mediterranean and of a vast desert hinterland, studded with oases. The coast stretches from Tunisia to Egypt. The western boundary marches with Tunisia and southern Algeria, until it finally reaches West Africa about 700 miles from the Mediterranean. The eastern boundary runs for an equal distance down to Djebel Oweinat, at the junction of Egypt and the Republic of the Sudan, and then follows the Sudan frontier for a further 250 miles to its junction with the boundary of Equatorial Africa in the foothills of the Erdi region.

The Mediterranean coastline of Libya is about 1,200 miles long, though the distance as the crow flies is only 800. The area of the country is approximately 1,775,500 square Km. while the fertile coastal strips are nowhere broader than 50 miles. Their continuity is broken round the barren and forbidding Gulf of Sirte where the desert comes right down to the sea and separates the settled areas of the **Eastern Provinces** (formerly Cyrenaica) from those of the **Western Provinces** (formerly Tripolitania) by a barrier 3000 miles wide. In the southern desert the distances between the oases are too great to allow casual movement between them except within the group of oases known as the **Southern Provinces** (formerly Fezzan).

N.B. In 1969 the three regions of Tripolitania, Cyrenaica and the Fezzan have been renamed Western Provinces, Eastern Provinces and Southern Provinces respectively.

CLIMATE

In terms of climate Libya can be divided into three zones. The coastal strip is predominantly well watered and has a warm Mediterranean climate. In it are found the principal towns and villages, and an overwhelming majority of the population. Rainfall is somewhat irregular and occurs mostly from October to March. No rain falls in June, July or August. Further to the south is the second zone, which is too arid for permanent villages though it provides grazing for nomadic tribes who also grow barley, rainfall permitting. The third zone is absolute desert, apart from the Eastern Provinces oases groups of Jalo, Marda, Kufra and the Southern Provinces.

PRINCIPAL CITIES & TOWNS

Tripoli (capital), Benghazi, Misurata, Azzawiya, Al Beida, Agedabia, Darna, Sebha, Tubruk, Al Marj and Zeleten.

Arabic is the official language.

RELIGION

The Libyan population are Sunni Moslems and there are minority groups of Italians, Greeks and Maltese, of different Christian denominations.

PUBLIC HOLIDAYS

Anniversary of Libyan Revolution (1 September); Anniversary of Evacuation of Fascist Settlers (7 October); Anniversary of Evacuation of British troops (31 March); Anniversary of Evacuation of American troops (11 June); Anniversary of Egyptian Revolution (23 July); Mulid al Nabi-birthday of the Prophet; Eid al Fitr, end of Ramadan, month of Muslim fasting and prayer; Eid al Adha, feast of the Sacrifice; Muslim New Year, Ashura, day of mourning for Shi'it Muslims.

GENERAL PEOPLE'S COMMITTEE

(March 2000)

Secretary General of People's Committee: Mubarak SHAMIKH

Secretary for African Unity: Ali Abdessalam TRIKI

Secretary for Foreign Liaison: Abdelrahman SHALGHAM

Secretary for Justice and General Security: Mohamed Bengacem ZWAI

Secretary for Finance: Mohamed BEIT EL MAL

Secretary for Information: Mrs. Fawzia CHLABI

Foreign Embassies

Afghanistan: Mozhar el-Aftas Str., P.O.Box 4245, Tripoli

Algeria: 12 Kairawan Str., Tel. (21)4440025, Tripoli

Argentina: Ibn Mufarrej Str., P.O.Box 932, Tripoli

Austria: Khaled Ben Walid Str., Garden City, P.O.Box 3207, Tel. (21)4443379, Tripoli

Bangladesh: Hadaba el-Khadra, Villa Omran al-Wershafani, P.O.Box 5086, Tripoli

Belgium: Abu Ubaida ben Jaraj No.1 Str., P.O.Box 91650, Tel. (21)3350117

Benin: P.O.Box 6676, Tripoli

Brazil: Ben Ashur Str., P.O.Box 2270, Tel. (21)3614894, Tripoli

Bulgaria: Murad Agha 1-3 Str., P.O.Box 2945, Tel. (21)3609988, Tripoli

Burundi: Ras Hassan Str., P.O.Box 2817, Tripoli

Chad: Mohammed Mussadeq 25 Str., P.O.Box 1078, Tel. (21)4443955, Tripoli

China People's Republic: Gargaresh M. 86, P.O.Box 5329, Tripoli

Cuba: Ben Ashur Str./ Essagrah Str., P.O.Box 83738, Tripoli

Czech: Ahmad Lotfi Sayed Str., Ben Ashur Area, P.O.Box 1097, Tripoli

Egypt: The Grand Hotel, Fax: (21)4445959, Libya

Finland: P.O.Box 2508, Tel. (21)4831132, Tripoli

France: P.O.Box 312, Tel. (21)4774892, Tripoli

Germany: Hassan al-Marshai Str., P.O.Box 302, Tel. (21)3330554, Tripoli

Ghana: Sway Khetumi Str., P.O.Box 4169, Tel. (21)4772366, Tripoli

Greece: Jala Bayar 18 Str., Tel. (21)3336978, Tripoli

Guinea: Andalous, P.O.Box 10657, Tripoli

Hungary: Talha ben Abdullah Str., P.O.Box 4010, Tripoli

India: 18 Mahmoud Shaltut Str., P.O.Box 3150, Tel. (21)4441835, Tripoli

Iran: Gargaresh Str., Andalous, Tripoli

Iraq: Ben Ashur Str., Tripoli

Italy: Uahran 1 Str., P.O.Box 912, Tel. (21)3334131, Tripoli; Section: Uahran Str., P.O.Box 4206, Te. (21)3331191, Tripoli

Korea, Democratic people's Republic: Tripoli

Korea, Republic: Gargaresh 6 kn, Travito Project, P.O.Box 4781, Tel. (21)4831322, Tripoli

Kuwait: Omar ben Yaser Str., Garden City, P.O.Box 2225, Tel. (21)4440281, Tripoli

Lebanon: Omar ben Yaser 20 Str., P.O.Box 927, Tel. 3333733, Tripoli

Malaysia: Andalous, P.O.Box 6309, Tripoli

Mali: Jaraba Saniet Zarrouk Str., Tel. (21)4444924, Tripoli

Malta: Ubei ben Kaab Str., P.O.Box 2534, Tel. (21)3611180, Tripoli

Mauritania: Aissa Wokwak Str., Tel. (21)4443223, Tripoli

Morocco: Bashir Ibrahim Str., Garden City, Tel. (21)4445757, Tripoli

Netherlands: Jelal Bayar 20 Str., P.O.Box 3801, Tel. (21)4441549, Tripoli

Nicaragua: Beach Hotel, Andalous, Tripoli

Niger: Fachloun Area, P.O.Box 2351, Tripoli

Nigeria: Bashir Ibrahim Str., P.O.Box 4417, Tripoli

Pakistan: Abdelkarim el-Khattabi 16 Str., Midan al-Qadasia, P.O.Box 2169, Tripoli

Philippines: Dul Str., P.O.Box 12508, Tripoli

Poland: Ben Ashur Str., P.O.Box 519, Tripoli

Qatar: Ben Ashur Str., P.O.Box 3506, Tripoli

Romania: Ahmad Lotfi Sayed Str., P.O.Box 5085, Tel. (21)3615295, Tripoli

Rwanda: Villa Ibrahim Musbah Missalati, Andalous, P.O.Box 6677, Tripoli

Saudi Arabia: Kairawan 2 Str., Tripoli

Spain: Amir Abdelkader el-Jazairi 36 Str., P.O.Box 2302, Tel. (21)3336797, Tripoli

Sudan: Tripoli

Sweden: Ahmad ash-Sharif 30 Str., Soufraki's Bldg., P.O.Box 437, Tripoli

Switzerland: Jeraba Str., P.O.Box 439, Tripoli

Syria: Mohamed Rashid Reda 4 Str., P.O.Box 4219, Tel. (21)3331783, Tripoli

Togo: Khaled ben Walid Str., P.O.Box 3420, Tel. (21)3332423, Tripoli

Tunisia: Bashir Ibrahimi Str., P.O.Box 613, Tel. (21)3331051, Tripoli

Turkey: Jeraba Str., P.O.Box 947, Tel. (21)3337717, Tripoli

Uganda: Jeraba Str., P.O.Box 10987, Tel. (21)4831602, Tripoli

Russia: Mustapha Kamel Str., Tel. (21)3330545, Tripoli

Venezuela: Abdulrahman Kwakby Str., P.O.Box 2584, Tel. (21)3600408, Tripoli

Viet-Nam: Talha ben Abdullah Str., P.O.Box 587, Tripoli

Yemen: Ubei ben Kaab 36 Str., P.O.Box 4839, Tripoli

Yugoslavia: Turkia No. 14 Str., Tel. (21)3334114, Tripoli

Zaire: Aziz al-Masri Str., P.O.Box 5066, Tripoli

GENERAL

Proven oil reserves are estimated at 29.5 billion barrels, equivalent to over 56 years of production at current rates of output. Libya supplies high quality oil and possesses fields for exploration which are potentially among the most lucrative in the world. Reserves of natural gas at the beginning of 1999 were estimated at over 1,300 billion tons cu. m.

Many large projects are operating or developped such as the Great Man-made River, heavy industry in the form of large steel complexes at Misurata, refineries, petro-chemicals, gas facilities, besides processing agricultural products, and manufacture of tobacco, wood, glassware, electric cables, clothing, textiles, shoes.

Agriculture is given strong support. The objective is to achieve self sufficiency in food. Several contracts were awarded for reclamation and irrigation works in various areas. Examples Kufra Oasis, Tawurgha, Sarir, Jebel al Akhdar, Jefara, Wadi Qatara. The most important project is the "Great Man-made River" project. The main crops are cereals, barley, wheat, olives, citrus fruits, almonds, tomatoes, beans, groundnuts, potatoes, dates, figs, apples and grapes.

Animal husbandry is also being developped in breeding of cattle for dairy produce, milk production and a major increase in poultry. Other important livestock are sheep, goats and camels.

Fish is also plentiful in the offshore waters, especially

tuna and sardines. Important sponge-beds are also exploited. The fishing industry is also being expanded.

THE GREAT MAN MADE RIVER PROJECT

This project commenced on the 28 April, 1984 aims at creating self sufficiency in food and water. It calls for a building of a man made river with pipelines of 4000 km and a water carrying capacity of 6 million cubic meters per day from natural underground reservoirs in the South-east of the Sahara Desert at Tazerbo and Sarir to Sirte, Benghazi, Tobruc, Tripoli and all the Mediterranean coast cities in Libya, as well as irrigation of about 250000 hectars of land. The project is composed of five stages at a cost of over 25 billion dollars.

The first phase of the project was completed and inaugurated on the lst September 1991 by Colonel Qaddafi.

The achievement was that 141 wells were drilled at Sarir and 120 wells at Tazerbo and construction of 2 pipelines of 957 and 918 kilometers long each to a great reservoir at Agedabia, supplying 2 million cubic meters of water per day to the towns of Sirte (402 kms from Agadebia) and Benghazi (147 kms from Agadebia) with the aim of irrigating some 280000 hectares in established modern farms.

The second stage of the project is to build water carrying pipelines 660 kms long from Fezzan, South, to Tripoli North. Work has already began in the second half of 1990.

Three additional stages are planned. The extention of the first phase southwards to Kutra oasis by doubling the water piping capacity to 4 million cu m per day; and the construction of pipelines to serve the north-eastern coast town of Tubruk from Agedabia, and to link the eastern and western systems of the first two stages along the coast to Tripoli and Sirte.

The Banking System

Central Bank of Libya: Est. 1955; Malik Seoud Str., P.O.Box 1103, Tel. (21)3333591, Tripoli

Jamahiriya Bank: Est. 1969; Martyr Str. P.O.Box 65155, Tel. (41) 3610594, Ghariar, Tripoli

Libyan Arab Foreign Bank: Est. 1972; Thatul Imad Administrative Complex, P.O.Box 2542, Tel. (21)3350155, Tripoli

National Commercial Bank SAL: Est. 1970; Shuhada Square, P.O.Box 543, Tel. (21)3612267, Tripoli

Sahara Bank: Est. 1964; 10 1 September Str., P.O.Box 270, Tel. (21)3339804, Tripoli

Umma Bank SAL: Est. 1969; 1 Giaddat Omar Mukhtar, P.O.Box 685, Tel. (21)3334031 Tripoli

Wahda Bank: Est. 1970; Fadiel Abu Omar Sq., El-Berkha, P.O.Box 452, Tel. (61)24709, Benghazi

National Companies

PETROLEUM

National Oil Corporation (NOC), P.O.B. 2655, Tripoli, was established in 1970: Corporation to undertake Joint ventures with foreign companies; to build and operate refineries, storage tanks, petrochemical facilities, pipelines and tankers; to participate in general planning of oil installations in Libya

Agip Oil, Co. (North Africa and Middle East, Libyan Branch Ltd): P.O.B. 346, Tripoli

Arabian Gulf Oil Co: P.O.B. 263, Benghazi

Brega Oil Marketing Co.: P.O.B. 402, Tripoli

Oasis Oil Co.: P.O.B. 395, Tripoli

Ras Lanouf Oil and Gas Processing Co.: P.O.Box 2323, Tripoli

Sirte Oil Co.: P.O.Box 385, Tripoli

Umm Al-Jawaby Petroleum Co: P.O.B. 693, Tripoli

Zuweitina Oil Co.: P.O.Box 2134; Tripoli

Foreign Companies

PETROLEUM

Aquitaine Libya: P.O.Box 282, Tripoli

Wintershall-Libya: P.O.Box 469 and 905, Tripoli.

Education

Public education is free and primary education is compulsory for both boys and girls.

The school system is composed of a six-year primary level, a three-year intermediate and vocational level, and a three-year secondary and advanced vocational level.

Higher education is offered by the several universities in the country.

Universities

Al Fateh University
Est. 1973; P.O.Box 13040, Tel.: 36010/8, Tripoli

Arab Medical University
Est. 1970; P.O.Box 18251, Tel.: (061) 25007, Benghazi

Bright Star University of Technology
Est. 1981; P.O.Box 858, Tel.: (021) 600184, Mersa El Brega

Sebha University
Est. 1983; P.O.Box 18758, Tel.: (71) 21575, Sebha

University of Garyounis
Est. 1955; P.O.Box 1308, Tel.: (061)87462, Benghazi

Transport

ROADS

A modern road system links the towns of the coast and the centers of the interior. Even the far oases of the Southern provinces are connected by motorable roads which have

been subsequently widened.
All the towns and villages in the Great Socialist People's Libyan Arab Jamahiriya are accessible by roads.

SHIPPING

The principal ports are at Tripoli, Benghazi, Mersa Brega, Misurata, Tubruk and As-Sider, Zueitina, Ras Lanouf, Mersa Hariga, Darna.

CIVIL AVIATION

Libya's two main airports are Tripoli International, which is 21 miles from Tripoli, and Benina, which is 13 miles from Benghazi. Other airports are at Sebha and Misurata.

Jamahiriya Libyan Arab Airlines: P.O.Box 2555, Haiti Str. Tripoli; operates flights from Tripoli and Benghazi to Europe, Asia and Africa.

Radio, Television and Press

RADIO AND TELEVISION

Great Socialist People's Libyan Arab Jamahiriya Broadcasting Corporation: P.O.Box 3731, Tripoli; P.O.Box 119, Al Beida; Est. 1957, Radio and a National Television service (since 1968)

THE PRESS
DAILIES, PERIODICALS

Al-Fajr al Jadid: P.O.Box 2303, Tripoli; Est. 1969; published by JANA (Jamahiriya News Agency) since 1978

Al-Amal: Social, for children; weekly; published by the Press Service

Economic Bulletin: P.O.Box 2303, Tripoli, Monthly; published by JANA

Al-Jarida al-Rasmiya: Official State Gazette

Al-Thaqafa al-Arabiya: P.O.Box 4587, Tripoli; Est. 1973; cultural; weekly

NEWS AGENCY

Jamahiriya News Agency (JANA): P.O.Box 2303, Tripoli; Branches throughout Libya and correspondents abroad.

Tourism

Department of Tourism and Fairs: Est. 1964; P.O.Box 891, Omar Mukhtar Str., Tripoli

MAURITANIA
(The Islamic Republic of Mauritania)

Mauritania

Head of State : Col. Mouawiah Ould Sid Ahmed TAYA.
Population : 2.35 million (1996 estimate).
Capital : Nouakchott
Area : 1,030,700 sq. km.
Currency : Ouguiya
Exchange Rate : US$ 1=151.85 Ouguiya (1997)

Geography

The Islamic Republic of Mauritania, on the Atlantic coast of Northwest Africa, is bounded on the Northwest by the former Spanish Sahara, on the northeast by Algeria, on the east by the Republic of Mali, and on the south by the Republic of Senegal. Nouakchott is the capital.

The country covers an area of 1,030,700 sq. Km. Most of Mauritania is low-lying desert, with ridges and cliff-like projections between areas of lower and higher altitude. The Senegal River on the southern border is the only waterway. The coastline is generally unidented.

CLIMATE

Though the climate is generally desertic, three climate regions can be distinguished. Southern Mauritania has a Saharan climate; there is one rainy season, with rainfall less than 700 mm. (27.5 inches) a year, and only one or two months with more than 50 mm. (2 inches) of rain. Temperature and humidity have wide seasonal and daily variations.

The strip of land along the coast is marked by a sub-Canarian climate, again with only one rainy season and an annual rainfall less than 700 mm (27.5 inches).

Port-Etienne, in the sub-Canarian climatic zone, has an average maximum temperature for the months of January, April, July, and October of approximately 26°, 28°, 29°, and 32° C. (79°, 82°, 84°, and 90°F.) respectively.

RELIGION

The state religion is Islam, though religious freedom is assured in the constitution. About 99% of the population is Muslim. Mauritania has for centuries been a fountain head of Koranic scholarship, not only in West Africa but throughout the Muslim world.

LANGUAGE

The official language is Arabic, and French is widely used.

PUBLIC HOLIDAYS

Labour Day (May 1); African Liberation Day (May 25); Korite-Eid al Fitr, end of Ramadan, the Muslim month of fasting and self purification; Tabaski-Eid al Adha, feast of the Sacrifice; Muslim New Year's Day; National Day (November 20); Prophet's birthday.

History

Before the arrival of Europeans in the 15th century, the history of the area that is now Mauritania was marked by successive invasions of Arabs and Berbers, who pressed down from the north toward the Senegal River valley. Negro-Africans who lived in the path of the invaders were pushed south. A Berber tribe, the Lemtouna, destroyed the great Sudanese empire of Ghana in the 11th century, and turned northward, conquering North Africa and then Spain.

The Portuguese were the first Europeans to arrive, attracted in the 15th century by the gum trade. They set up trading posts (escalles) along the Senegal River. Competition was keen among Portuguese, French, Dutch, and English traders. The issue of control was resolved in 1815, when Senegal was given to France in the post-Napoleonic War settlement. One Frenchman Xavier Coppolani, played a key role in the extension of French influence in the area. He exploited Arab-Berber rivalries and persuaded many tribes of the need for French protection. By 1903 he was in control of Trarza, the Moors' main base for raids on the river tribes. Coppolani was killed in 1905, and his work was completed by Colonel Gouraud. The territory of Mauritania was established as an administrative unit in 1920, and its capital established in Saint Louis in Senegal. In 1946 a Mauritania territorial assembly was established, with some control over internal affairs, and Mauritania elected representatives to the French Parliament and the Assembly of the French Union. Between 1946 and 1956, increasing political power passed to local political leaders. Mauritania voted in favor of the constitution of the Fifth French Republic at the referendum of 28 September 1958. As a result it became a self-governing member of the French Community, and the Islamic Republic of Mauritania was established by a constituent assembly in March 1959. The country obtained its complete independence in November 1996.

GENERAL

The Government of President Mokhtar Ould Dadah was overthrown on July 10, 1978 in a bloodless coup led by Lieut. Colonel Mustapha Ould Mohamed Salek, the Chief of Staff of the Armed Forces.

On June 3, 1979 Col. Ould Salek handed in his resignation as President of Mauritania and as President of the Military Committee for National Salvation (CMSN).

He was replaced in both posts by Lt.-Col. Mohamed Mahmoud ould Ahmed Louly hiherto Minister of Public Services. At the same time Lt-Col. Haidalla announced the formation of a new Government. In early January 1980, Lt.-Col. Haidalla, the former prime minister, replaced Lt-Col. Mohamed Louly as head of state. He is the fourth head of state since July 1978 when, a military coup ousted the civilian regime of President Mokhtar

Ould Daddah. President Khouna Ould Haidalla was deposed on Dec. 12 1984 during his absence by Lt.-Col. Mouaouia Ould Sidi Ahmed Taya (Army Chief of Staff since March 1984 and previously Prime Minister from 1981) and was arrested on his return to Mauritania on Dec. 13. In the January 1992 elections Col. Taya was elected as President, and reelected in December 1997.

The Constitution

Mauritania's constitution was approved by a national referendum on July 12, 1991.

According to the constitution the "Islamic Republic of Mauritania" stipulates:

– The establishment of a multi-party political system.

– The President of the Republic is elected by universal suffrage, for a period of six years.

– Legislative power is vested in a national assembly which is elected by universal suffrage for five years; and a senate elected by municipal leaders for a six years period.

– The President of the Republic appoints the head of government.

– Establishment of a Constitutional Council, Supreme Islamic Council (both inaugurated in 1992), Economic and Social Council.

– The official language is arabic.

POLITICAL PARTIES

By the end of 1993 there were several parties officially recognized. Among which:

Democratic and Social Republic Party (DSRP): Est. 1991

Mauritanian Party for Renewal (MPR): Est. 1991

Rally for Democracy and National Unity (RDNU): Est. 1991

Socialist and Democratic People's Union (SDPU): Est. 1991

Union for Democracy and Progress (UDP): Est. 1993

The Cabinet

(May. 1999)

Prime Minister: Cheikh El Afia Ould Mohamed KHOUNA

Minister Counsellor to the Presidency: Ahmed Ould Sidi BABA

Minister Counsellor to the Presidency: Hamdi Ould MOUKNASS

Minister of Foreign Affairs and Cooperation: Ahmed Ould SID AHMED

Minister of Defence: Kaba Ould ELEWA

Minister of Justice: Mohamed Salem Ould MERZOUG

Minister of the Interior, Posts and Telecommunications: Dah Ould ABDELJELIL

Minister of Finance: Kamara Ali GUELADIO

Minister of Fisheries and Marine Economy: Mohamed El Moctar Ould ZAMEL

Minister of Economic and Development Affairs: Mohamed Ould ANNAI

Minister of trade, Handicrafts and Tourism: Mohamed Ould HAMADY

Minister of National Education: Sghair Ould MBARECK

Minister of Industry and Mines: Ishag Ould RAJEL

Minister of Equipment and Transport: N'Gaidé Lamine KAYOU

Minister of Culture and Islamic Affairs: Isselmou Ould Sidi MOUSTAPHA

Minister of Civil Service, Labour, Youth and Sports: Baba Ould SIDI

Minister of Water and Energy: Cheikh Ahmed Ould EZZAHAF

Minister of Rural Development and the Environment: Mohamed Ould Sid Ahmed Ould LEKHAL

Minister of Health and Social Affairs: Diye BA

Minister of Communication and Relations with Parliament: Rachid Ould SALEH

Minister, Secretary-General of the Presidency: Sidi Mohamed Ould BOUBACAR

Minister, Secretary-General with the Government: Ba SILEYE

Foreign Embassies

Algeria: P.O.Box 625 Nouakchott

China: P.O.Box 196, Nouakchott

Congo (Democratic Republic): P.O.Box 487, Tel. 52836, Nouakchott

Egypt: P.O.Box 176, Nouakchott

France: Ahmed Ould Mohamed Str., P.O.Box 231, Tel. 51740, Nouakchott

Gabon: P.O.Box 38; Tel. 52919, Nouakchott.

Germany: P.O.Box 372, Tel. 51729, Nouakchott

Korea: P.O.Box 324, Tel. 53786, Nouakchott

Morocco: P.O.Box 621, Tel. 51411, Nouakchott

Nigeria: P.O.Box 367, Nouakchott

Russia: P.O.Box 251, Tel. 51973, Nouakchott

Saudi Arabia: P.O.Box 498 Nouakchott

Spain: P.O.Box 232, Tel. 52080, Nouackchott

Tunisia: P.O.Box 681, Tel. 52871, Nouakchott

U.S.A.: P.O.Box 222, Tel. 52660, Nouakchott

The Economy

Mauritania's gross National Product was estimated by the World Bank at slightly over US$ 1.1 billion in 1997. The Country's gross domestic product growth in the year 1993 was 5.5 per cent and averaged 4.7 in 1994, 1995, 1996, 4.5 in 1997 and 5.0 in 1998.

The economy is characterised by a large traditional farming sector alongside a modern sector dominated by mining and a fishing industry.

Agricultural output is highly dependent on weather.

However, irrigation programmes in the south, mainly the Senegal River Development Scheme and the Gorgol Noir Irrigation Project, helped to protect agriculture from future droughts. The main crops are millet, sorghum, rice, pulses and dates, wheat.

Livestock accounts for about 10% of gross national product (1.3 million herds of cattle, 9.1 million sheep and goats and 0.9 million camels), as estimated in 1997.

Mining is also another source of income. Reserves of iron ore and copper are mainly exploited in the Guelbs region and a production level of 11.7 million tons was registered in 1997. Mauritania's coastal zone is rich with fish and is the main source of income. It is estimated that annual potential is about 600,000 tons. As a result of large-scale investment in the fishing industry, production increased rapidly and became the leading currency earner ahead of iron-ore. Despite this impressive performance, as yet Mauritania has not obtained full benefit from its fishing resources. The bulk of fishing has been carried out by foreign vessels which landed only a minute proportion of their catch in Mauritania itself. To rectify the situation, new emphasis have been placed on the industry; a 200-mile exclusive economic zone has been declared and new agreements including joint ventures have been drawn up with several countries to ensure a steady supply of fish to domestic canning plants.

Mauritania has limited natural resources and its economy is subject to climatic uncertainties and prices for its raw materials. Development is dependent on continued inflow of foreign assistance.

Insurance

NASR: Est. 1974. 12 Gamal Abdel Nasser St., B.P. 163, Nouakchott; state monopoly.

The Banking System

Banque Centrale de Mauritanie: Est. 1973; Head Office: Avenue de l'Indépendance, P.O.Box 623, Nouakchott

Banque Al Baraka Mauritanienne Islamique: Est. 1985; Avenue du Roi Faisal, P.O.B. 650; Nouakchott

Banque Mauritanienne pour le Commerce International: Est. 1974; Head Office: Gamal Abdel Nasser Str., P.O.Box 622, Nouakchott

Banque Nationale de Mauritanie: Est. 1988; P.O.Box 614, Nouakchott

Transport

RAILWAY

A railway connecting Nouadhibou and Akjouit with the iron ore fields at Zouérate is 670 km-long, and other smaller extention service Al Rhein and Mhaoudat.

ROADS

There are some 7,500 km of roads and tracks, Several roads now connect Kaédi to Kiffa, Nouakchott to Rosso, and Nouakchott to Akjouit, and Nouakchott to Néma.

SHIPPING

Several shipping companies serve Nouadhibou and Nouakchott, the most important two ports in Mauritania.

CIVIL AVIATION

Mauritania is served by its national airline Air Mauritanie B.P. 41, Nouakchott-Est. 1974. The country's two main International Airports are located at Nouadhibou and Nouakchott, respectively, another airport is at Néma in the east of the country.

Development and Trade Organizations

GEMAK: Est. 1991; P.O.Box 9; Akjoujt.

Société Algéro-Mauritanienne des Pêches (ALMAP): Est. 1974; P.O.Box 321; Nouadhibou

Société Arabe du Fer et de l'Acier (SAFA): Est. 1984; P.O.Box 114; Nouadhibou

Société Arabe Mauritano-Libyenne de Développement Agricole (SAMALIDA): Est. 1980; P.O.Box 658; Nouakchott

Société de Construction et de Gestion Immobilière de Mauritanie (SOGOGIM): Est. 1974; P.O.Box 28, Nouakchott

Société Mauritanienne de Commercialisation du Poisson (SMCP): Est. 1984; P.O.Box 259; Nouadhibou.

Naftal S.A. Est. 1981, P.O.Box 73; Nouadhibou

Société Nationale d'Eau et d'Electricité (SONELEC): Est. 1968; P.O.Box 355; Nouakchott

Naftec sa: Est. 1980; B.P. 89; Nouakchott

Compagnie Mauritano-Coréenne de Pêche (COMACOP): Est. 1997; B.P. 527; Nouakchott

Société Arabe de Fer et de l'Acier (SAFA): Est. 1984; B.P. 114; Nouadhibou

Société Arabe des Industries Métallurgiques Mauritano-Koweitienne (SAMIA): Est. 1974; B.P. 1248; Nouakchott

Société Arabe Libyenne-Mauritanienne des Resources Maritimes (SALIMAUREM): Est. 1978; B.P. 75, Nouadhibou

Société Arabe des Mines d'Inchiri (SAMIN): Est. 1981; B.P. 9; Akjoujt

Société de Construction et de Gestion Immobilière de Mauritanie (SOCOGIM): Est. 1974; B.P. 28; Nouakchott

Société Nationale pour le Developpement Rural (SONADER): B.P. 321; Nouakchott

Société Nationale Industrielle et Minière (SNIM): Est. 1972; B.P. 42; Nouadhibou

Radio, Television and Press

RADIO - TELEVISION

Radio de Mauritanie: Est. 1958: P.O.Box 200; Nouakchott
Télévision de Mauritanie: P.O.Box 5522; Nouakchott

THE PRESS

Ach-Chaab: P.O.Box: 371, Nouakchott; daily Arabic.

Journal Officiel: Ministry of Justice, P.O.Box 350, Nouakchott

Tourism

Direction du Tourisme: P.O.Box 246, Nouakchott

MOROCCO
(Kingdom of Morocco)

Morocco

Sovereign	: King MOHAMED VI
Capital	: Rabat (pop. 1,400,000)
Area	: 710.850 sq. Km.
Population	: 27.00 million (1995 estimate)
Currency	: 1 Dirham = 100 centimes
Exchange Rate	: US Dollar = 9.60 Dirhams (Dec. 1998)

Geography

Situated at the north-west corner of the African continent, the present Kingdom of Morocco is shaped like an irregular quadrilateral. Its sides are formed by 620 miles of Atlantic coast, by 290 miles in the Straits of Gibraltar and on the Mediterranean, 310 miles of frontier with Algeria, and 680 miles of frontier with the Sahara. Morocco falls within latitudes 28 and 36 north and between the 2nd and 11th longitudes west of Greenwich.

The land frontiers are not indicated by definite geographical features such as mountain ranges or rivers.

Morocco's geographical position gives her a special and privileged place among the countries of North Africa, to which she definitely belongs since there is no break in continuity between Morocco and Algeria in the spheres of geography, climate, botany, or the human way of life.

In the north, Morocco projects in the form of the Tangier peninsula as if reaching out to meet Europe and the Iberian peninsula at the point of Tarifa, only nine miles away across the sea.

Geologically, the soil of Morocco has been divided into three principal zones; these differ in age and structure. Northern Morocco is a detached fragment of Europe, and the Rif an Alpine range which prolongs the Andalusian Cordillera.

The country has a strongly marked relief. Several peaks in the High Atlas reach 13,000 feet while Tubkal (13,694) is the highest in all North Africa. It has been pointed out that if the level of the sea were to be raised by 1,000 feet the general outline of the country would still be the same. High plains and plateaux work their way into the heart of the main ranges.

The latter are like a jaw, opening towards the west. The more northerly branch, the Rif, which is prolonged by the Beni Anassen mountains to the east of the Muluya, runs along the Mediterranean. The lower branch is separated from the former on the east by the narrow Taza Corridor, forms the circle of an arc, north-east and south-west, and ends at the edge of the Atlantic. This branch is more complex than the other. Three ranges can be distinguished: The high Atlas, which runs beside and then accompanies the Middle Atlas range to the north, beyond the valley of the upper Muluya; and in the south the Anti-Atlas, by the footbridge-like Sirma mountain.

This mountain framework has had important consequences some of them happy, others less so. Morocco lies wide open to the ocean to whose beneficent influences she is subject. The two arms of the pincers enfold the fertile plains of the Gharb, the Chaouis, and the Sus, which are the heart and the wealth of the country. Almost all the great cities are to be found there; **Fez, Meknes, Rabat, Casablanca, Marrakesh,** The Rif on the other hand cuts Morocco off from the Mediterranean which has only played a substantial part in the life of the country by means of the Straits. In the north, **Tangier and Tetuan** are the only large cities.

CLIMATE

The average temperature during the winter months (November to May) is 15°C (60°F).

At no time of the year is the climate extreme except in the interior during the summer.

PUBLIC HOLIDAYS

New Year's Day (1 January); Fête du Trône (3 March); Fête du Travail (Labour day) (1 May); Masirat al Khadra (Green March) (6 November); Independence Day (18 November).

MUSLIM HOLIDAYS

Mulid al Nabi – birthday of the prophet; Lailat al Miraj - ascension of the prophet; first month of Ramadan, month of fasting and self-purification; Eid al Fitr, Eid al Adha Muslim New Year.

History

Man seems to have been present in Morocco from the Chellean age.

The country was inhabited by Berbers. All that is known of the history of ancient Morocco, is that of the foreign settlements. The Phoenicians were the first to land on the coasts of Morocco, in the twelfth century.

In the fifteenth century the Spanish began to assault the Moroccan coast and by the sixteenth century were masters of Ceuta, Tangier and Arcila, and had founded Agadir and Mazagan and had captured Safi and Azemmoun on the Atlantic.

THE FRENCH PROTECTORATE

In 1904 France succeeded in obtaining the recognition by Great Britain of her preponderance in Morocco. On the 30th of March 1912, the Treaty of Fez was signed with Moulay Abdul Hafiz, by which a French Protectorate was established over Morocco.

THE INDEPENDENCE

In 1947 the affiliation of Morocco with the Arab world was proclaimed in Tangiers and legitimate national aspirations were demanded to be satisfied.

By the Declaration of La Celle St. Cloud in November 1955 France undertook to terminate the protectorate and recognize the independence of Morocco. Morocco gained its independence in 1956.

In 1969 Morocco laid claim to the Rio de Oro, in the Spanish province of Ifni. On January 4, 1969 an agreement for the cession of Ifni, on the Moroccan Atlantic coast was signed at Fez by the Moroccan Foreign Minister, M. Ahmad Laraki, and the Spanish Ambassador.

King Hassan II has reigned over Morocco for 37 years. In July 1999, he passed away and H.M. King Mohamed VI acceded to the throne on 23.7.1999.

INTERNAL STRIFE

After five years of direct rule by decree, King Hassan II decided in 1970 that Morocco should return to a modified form of parliamentary Government. On July 24 a revised Constitution, strengthening the authority of the King, was approved by 98.7% of the 4.5 million voters in a national referendum. In 1971, the Moroccan monarchy suffered-but survived-the only serious threat to its existence since full independence in 1956.

The attempted coup was staged during a royal birthday party at the sea side of Skhirat. Trainees from the Ahermoumou military training school fired wildly at the royal guests, killing several ministers, army generals, civilian officials, and one foreign diplomat.

Thirteen months after the attempted coup by army officers of July 1971, attacks were carried out on August 16,1972, by Moroccan Air Force fighters on King Hassan's personal aircraft and, later the same day, on both Rabat airport and the royal palace in Rabat. The King escaped unharmed in spite of serious damage to his aircraft which landed safely, enabling some of the royal group to take refuge in the summer palace at Skhirat.

The trial of those accused of complicity in the attack on King Hassan on August 16 opened on October 17 before a military court at Kenitra.

In its verdict on November 7, the Court condemned 11 men to death, 5 men were sentenced to 20 years imprisonment, one to 10 years, three to five years, and 23 to three years, the remaining 177 being acquitted.

THE WESTERN SAHARA

On 17 November, 1975 the 20th anniversary of Moroccan independence, King Hassan of Morocco was able to claim "our Sahara has been returned to us".

Under an agreement concluded on 14 November, Spain undertook to hand over the territory to joint Moroccan – Mauritanian control by the end of February 1976.

The last Spanish troops left the Sahara on February 26; the division of the territory between Morocco and Mauritania was formalised in April; and by September the Moroccan Army claimed total control of its sector.

On 8 March, 1979, however King Hassan announced the formation of a National Defence Council to deal with the Saharan crisis, a clear indication that the King had no intention of giving way on the Saharan issue, preferring instead to tighten support within Morocco.

By early 1982 little progress had been made towards holding the referendum in Western Sahara which had been proposed by King Hassan of Morocco at the Nairobi summit meeting of the Organization of African Unity (OAU) on June 26, 1981. The major problem facing the special implementation committee which had been established under an OAU resolution to arrange a referendum was Morocco's refusal to engage in direct negotiations with the Polisario Front, the guerrilla organization fighting for the independence of the self-proclaimed Saharan Arab Democratic Republic (SADR).

A new military dimension was given to the Western Sahara conflict when Polisario in late 1981 and early 1982 carried out attacks against Moroccan positions in Western Sahara using sophisticated tanks, and also shot down four Moroccan aircraft with what Morocco alleged were advanced Soviet-made SAM-6 surface-to-air missiles.

A deep rift appeared in the OAU after a delegation of SADR was seated for the first time at the 38th Council of Ministers meeting in Addis Ababa on Feb. 22-28, in protest against which the Moroccan delegation immediately walked out of the conference and was followed over the next two days by the following 18 countries: Cameroon, Central African Republic, Comoros, Djibouti, Equatorial Guinea, Gabon, the Gambia, Guinea (which announced on March 2 that it was suspending participation in the OAU), Ivory Coast, Liberia, Mauritius, Niger, Senegal, Somalia, Sudan Tunisia, Upper Volta and Zaire. Morocco also claimed to have the tacit support of Egypt, Nigeria, Sierra Leone and Togo.

Military operations in the Western Sahara resumed in mid-1983 after a year of relative peace, with both the Polisario Front guerillas and Moroccan forces staging offensives and claiming major victories. Polisario forces, however, failed to pierce the Moroccan "wall" of defensive fortifications enclosing the so-called "useful triangle" of the north-western portion of the territory (where almost all the population and economic activity were concentrated).

Diplomatic efforts to solve the conflict mounted by the OAU (Organisation of African Unity) appeared by the end of 1983 to have failed as a result of the Moroccan government's refusal to hold direct negociations with the Polisario Front which had in 1976 proclaimed the independence of the Western Sahara as the Saharan Arab Democratic Republic (SADR). By the end of 1998 the Referendum for autonomy had been postponed.

Political Parties

Front des Forces Démocratiques (FFD): Est. 1997, Rabat
Istiqlal: Est. 1955, Rabat
Mouvement Démocratique et Social: Est. 1996
Mouvement National Populaire (MNP): Est. 1991
Mouvement Populaire: Est. 1959, Rabat

Mouvement Populaire Constitutionnel et Démocratique (MPCD): Est. 1967, Rabat
Organisation de l'Action Démocratique et Populaire (OADP): Est. 1983, Casablanca
Parti de l'Action: Est. 1974, Rabat
Parti Démocratique pour l'Indépendance: Est. 1946, Casablanca
Parti National Démocrate (PND): Est. 1981, Rabat
Parti Socialiste Démocratique (PSP): Est. 1996, Salé
Rassemblement National des Indépendants (RNI): Est. 1978, Rabat
Union Constitutionelle (UC): Est. 1983, Rabat
Union Nationale des Forces Populaires (UNFP): Est. 1959, Casablanca
Union Socialiste des Forces Populaires (USFP): Est. 1959, Rabat

GENERAL

New elections were held on November 14, 1997 for a 325 seats Assembly:

	Total
Union Constitutionnelle	50
Mouvement Populaire	40
Parti National Démocrate	10
Mouvement National Populaire	19
Union Socialiste des Forces Populaires	57
Istiqlal	32
Parti du Progrès et du Renouveau	9
Organisation de l'Action Démocratique et Populaire	4
Rassemblement National des Indépendents	46
Parti Démocratique pour l'Indépendence	1
Parti de l'Action	2
Mouvement Populaire Constitutionnel et Démocratique	9
Front des Forces Démocratiques	9
Parti Socialiste Démocratique	5
Mouvement Démocratique et Social	32
	325

The Cabinet

(March. 1998)

Prime Minister: Abderrahmane AL YOUSIFI
Minister of Stater for Foreign Affairs and Cooperation: Mohamed BENAISSA
Minister of State for the Interior: Ahmed MIDAOUI
Minister of Justice: Omar AZZIMANE
Minister of Awqafs and Islamic Affairs: Abdelkebir Mdhaghri ALAOUI
Minister of Territorial Administration, Environment, Urban Planning and Housing: Mohamed ALYAZGHI
Minister of Economy and Finance: Fathallah OUALALOU
Minister of Agriculture, Rural Development and Fishing: Habib MALKI
Minister of Industry, Commerce and Traditional Industries: Alami TAZI
Minister of Social Development, Solidarity, Employment and Professional Training, Official Spokesman of the Government: Khaled ALIOUA
Minister of Tourism: Hassan SEBBAR
Minister of Equipment: Bouamar TIGHOUANE
Minister of Transport and Merchant Marine: Mustapha MANSOURI
Minister of Energy and Mines: Youssef TAHIRI
Minister of National Education: Ismail ALAOUI
Minister of Higher Education, Graduate Training and Scientific Research: Najib ZEROUALI
Minister of Parliamentary Relations: Mohamed BOUZOUBOUAA
Minister of Human Rights: Mohamed AOUJAR
Minister of Cultural Affairs: Mohamed ACHAARI
Minister of Health: Abdelwahed AL FASSI
Minister of Youth and Sports: Ahmad MOUSSAOUI
Minister of Communication: Larbi MESSARI
Minister of Administrative Reform: Aziz HUSSEIN
Minister of Public Sector and Privatization: Rachid FILALI
Minister Delegate to the Prime Minister in charge of Administration of National Defence: Abderahmane SBAI
Minister Delegate to the Prime Minister in charge of General Affairs of the Government: Ahmed LAHLIMI
Minister Delegate to the Prime Minister in charge of Economic Provision and Planning: Abdelhamid AOUAD
Minister Delegate to the Prime Minister in charge of Maghreb, Arab and Islamic World Affairs: Abdeslam ZNINAD
Minister Delegate to the Prime Minister in charge of Fishing: Thami KHIARI
Minister Delegate to the Prime Minister in charge of Water and Forests: Said CHBAATOU
Secretary General of the Government: Abdessadek RABI

Foreign Embassies

Algeria: 46 Blvd. Ben Ziad, Tel. 765474, Rabat
Argentina: 12 Mekki Bitaouri Souissi Str., Tel. 755120, Rabat
Austria: 2 Zankat Tiddas, P.O.Box 135, Tel. 764003, Rabat
Belgium: 6 Ave. Marrakech, P.O.Box 163, Tel. 764746, Rabat
Brazil: 1 Marrakech Str., Tel. 765522, Rabat
Bulgaria: 4 Ave. Meknes, Tel. 764082, Rabat
Canada: 13 Jaafar As Sadik Str., P.O.Box 709, Tel. 772880, Agdal, Rabat
Central African Republic: Villa 42, Ave. Pasteur, Tel. 770203, Agdal, Rabat

China, People's Republic: 16 Fahs Str., Tel. 754056, Rabat
Congo, Democratic Republic: 34 Ave. an-Nasr, P.O.Box 537, Tel. (7)734862, 10002 Rabat
Czech Republic: Zankat Ait Melloul, P.O.Box 410, Tel. 755420, Souissi, Rabat
Denmark: 4 Khemisset Str., P.O.Box 203, Tel. 769293, Rabat
Egypt: 31 Zankat Al Jazair, Tel. 731833, Rabat
Equatorial Guinea: 30 United Nations Ave. P.O.Box 723, Tel. 774205, Agdal, Rabat
Finland: 18 Khemisset Str., Tel. 762352, Rabat
France: 3 Sahnoun Str., Tel. 777822, Rabat
Gabon: Zaër's Ave., Tel. 751968, Rabat
Germany: 7 Zankat Madnine, P.O.Box 235, Tel. 769662, Rabat
Greece: 23 Oujda Str., Tel. 723839, Rabat
Guinea: 2 Zankat Mokla, Orangers, Tel. 674148, Rabat
Holy See: Beni Mtir Str., P.O.Box 1303, Tel. 772277, Souissi, Rabat
Hungary: P.O.Box 5026 Tel. 754123, Rabat
Indonesia: 63 Beni Boufram Str., Tel. 757860, Rabat
Iraq: 39 Beni Iznassen Str., Tel. 754466, Souissi, Rabat
Italy: 2 Zankat Idriss el Azhar, P.O.Box 111, Tel. 766597, Rabat
Ivory Coast: 21 Zankat Tiddas, P.O.Box 192, Tel. 763151, Rabat
Japan: 70 United Nations Ave., Tel. 674163, Agdal, Rabat
Jordan: Villa al Wafae, Souissi 11, Tel. 759270, Rabat
Korea, Republic: 41 Beni Iznassen Ave., Tel. 751767, Souissi, Rabat
Kuwait: Rm 413 Imam Malik Str., Tel. 756423, Rabat
Lebanon: 19 Ave. Fes, Tel. 766667, Rabat
Libya: 1 Chouaib Doukkali Str., P.O.Box 225, Tel. 768828, Rabat
Mauritania: 9 Taza Str., Souissi, Rabat
Mexico: 6 rue Cadi Mohamed Brebi, Souissi, Tel. (7)631969, Rabat
Netherlands: 40 Tunis Str., P.O.Box 329, Tel. 733512, Rabat
Nigeria: 70 Ave. Omar ben Khatttab, P.O.Box 347, Tel. 671856, Agdal, Rabat
Oman: 21 Hamza Str., Tel. 771064, Agdal, Rabat
Pakistan: 2 Blvd. Soomat Hassan, Tel. 762402, Rabat
Peru: 16 Ifrane Str., Tel. 723236, Rabat
Poland: 23 Zankat Oqbah, P.O.Box 425, Tel. 771791, Agdal, Rabat
Portugal: 5 Thami Lamdouar Str., Souissi, Tel. 756446, Rabat
Qatar: 4 Tarik ben Ziad Str., P.O.Box 1220, Tel. 765681, Rabat
Romania: 10 Ouezzane Str., Tel. 738611, Rabat
Russia: Zaër's Str., Tel. 753509, Rabat
Saudi Arabia: 43 Place de l'Unité Africaine, Tel. 730171, Rabat
Senegal: 17 ben Hamadi Senhaji Str., Souissi, Tel. 754171, Rabat
South Africa: 34 Rue des Saadiens, Tel. (7) 706760, Rabat
Spain: 3 Zankat Madnine, Tel. 707600, Rabat
Sudan: 5 Ave. Ghomara, Souissi, Tel. 752863, Rabat
Sweden: 159 Ave. John Kennedy, P.O.Box 428, Tel. 759303, Rabat
Switzerland: Berkane Sq., P.O.Box 169, Tel. 706974, Rabat
Tunisia: 6 ave. Fes, Tel. 730636, Rabat
Turkey: 7 Ave Fes, Tel. 762605, Rabat
United Arab Emirates: 11 Ave. Alaouines, Tel. 730975, Rabat
United Kingdom: 17 Blvd. Hassan Tower, P.O.Box 45, Tel. 720905, Rabat
U.S.A.: 2 Marrakech Str., Tel. 762265, Rabat
Yemen: 11 Abou Hanifa Str., Tel. 774363, Agdal, Rabat
Yugoslavia: 23 Ave. Beni Iznassen, Souissi, P.O.Box 5014, Tel. 752201, Rabat

The Economy

The agricultural sector employs about 40% of the working population, generating about 18% of GDP. The principal crops are wheat, barley, maize, citrus fruits, olives, beans, tomatoes, potatoes, sugar beet and cane. Fishing is also important. The fishing sector expanded strongly in the previous years. Total catch in 1996 was 638,000 tons. Mining accounted for 2% of GDP in 1996, most of which comes from phosphates of which Morocco has 70% of world supply. Commercial production attained 23 million tons in 1997. Production of other minerals barely reached 1 million tons. The manufacturing sector is geared to exports based mainly on foodstuffs, textiles, leather, shoes and paper pulp.Tourism is also an important sector in Morocco. In 1998 over 2 million tourists have visited the country.

The Banking System

Banque al Maghrib: Est. 1959; 277 Ave. Mohamed V, P.O.Box 445, telex: 31006, Rabat. bank of issue.
Banque National pour le Developpement Economique: Est. 1959; 12 place des Alouites, P.O.Box 407, telex 31942, Rabat.
ABN Amro Bank S.A.: Est. 1948; Place du 16 November, P.O.Box 13478, Casablanca.
Arab Bank Maroc: Est. 1975; 174 Blvd. Mohammed V, P.O.Box 13810, telex 22942, Casablanca.
Banque Commerciale du Maroc SA.: Est. 1911; Blvd. Moulay Yousuf et 2 angle Rue d'Alger, P.O.Box 11141, Casablanca.
Banque Marocaine du Commerce Extérieur: Est. 1959; 140 Ave. Hassan II, P.O.Box 13425, telex 21635, Casablanca.
Banque Marocaine pour l'Afrique et l'Orient: Est. 1975; 1 place Bandoeng, P.O.Box 880, telex 26720, Casablanca.
Banque Marocaine pour le Commerce et l'Industrie SA: Est. 1964; 26 Place Mohammed V, P.O.Box 573, telex 21967, Casablanca.

Crédit du Maroc S.A.: Est. 1963; 48-58 Blvd. Mohamed V, P.O.Box 13579, telex 46678, Casablanca.

Société Générale Marocaine de Banques: Est. 1962; 55 Blvd. Moumen, P.O.Box 13090, telex 24898, Casablanca.

Société Marocaine de Dépôt et Crédit: Est. 1974; 79 Ave. Hassan II; P.O.Box 296, telex 21013, Casablanca.

Wafabank: Est. 1964; 163 Ave. Hassan II, P.O.Box 13057, telex 21051, Casablanca.

Transport

OFFICE NATIONAL DES TRANSPORTS:

10 Rue Alfadila, Quartier Industriel, B.P. 596 Rabat-Chellah

RAILWAYS

Office National des Chemins de Fer du Maroc: 8 bis Rue Abderrahman Al Ghafiki, Rabat-Agdal

ROADS

Compagnie de Transports au Maroc "Lignes Nationales" (CTM-LN) 23 Rue Léon L'Africain, Casablanca

SHIPPING

The chief ports of Morocco are Casablanca, Safi, Mohammedia, Tangier, Kenitra and Agadir. Casablanca is the principal freight port; Tangier is the principal passenger service port.

CIVIL AVIATION

The main International airports are at: Casablancca, Marrakesh, Agadir, Rabat, Oujda, Tangier and Fez.

Royal Air Maroc

Est. 1953; majority of shares owned by government

Aéroport International Casablanca-Anfa; domestic flights and services to Europe, America (South and North), etc.. Tel. (2)912000

FOREIGN AIRLINES

Air Afrique, Air Algérie, Air France, Air Mali, Balkan, Iberia, KLM, Lufthansa, TWA, Sabena, Saudia, Swissair...

Radio, Television and Press

RADIO & TELEVISION

Radiodiffusion Télévision Marocaine:

Government Station; 1 Zenkat al Brihi, P.O.Box 1042 Rabat

Radio: Broadcasts in Arabic, French, English, Berber and Spanish

Television: f. 1962: service in Arabic and French; over 40 hours weekly

THE PRESS

Achorta: B.P. 437, Rabat; Arabic; Monthly

Al Aklam: B.P. 2229, Rabat; Arabic; Monthly

Al Alam: Est. 1946; 11 Ave. Allal Ben Abdullah, Rabat; Arabic; Daily

Al Anbaa: Est. 1970; 21 Rue Patrice Lumumba, Rabat; Arabic; Daily

Al Bayane: 62 Blvd. de la Gironde, B.P. 13152, Casablance; Arabic and French; Daily

Al Irchad: Ministry of Waqfs, Rabat; Arabic; Monthly

Al Ittihad ul Watani: 28-30 Rue Magellan, Casablance; Arabic; Weekly

Al Maghreb: Est. 1977; 6 Rue, Laos, Rabat; French; Daily

Annidal: Est. 1973; 10 Rue Cols Bleus, Sidi Bousmara, Medina Kedima, Casablanca; Weekly

Cedies Informations: 23 Blvd. Mohamed Abdouh, Casablanca; weekly; French

Construire: Est. 1946; 25 Rue d'Azilal, Imm. Ortiba, Casablanca; French; weekly

Le Journal de Tanger: 11 Ave. Abdalaziz, B.P. 420; Tangier; Weekly

Le Matin du Sahara: Est. Nov. 1971; 28 Blvd Mohamed V, Casablanca; French; Daily

Les Echos Africains: Est. 1972; B.P. 13140, Casablanca; French; Monthly

L'Opinion: Est. 1965; 11 Ave. Allal Ben Abdullah, Rabat; French; Daily

Maroc Soir: Est. Nov. 1971; 34 Rue Mohamed Smiha, Casablanca; French; Daily

Revue Mensuelle de la Chambre de Commerce et d'Industrie de Casablanca: B.P. 423, Casablanca; French; Monthly

NEWS AGENCIES

Agence France Presse: 2 Bis Rue du Caire, B.P. 118, Rabat; French

Reuters: 509 Avenue Hassan II, Rabat; British

Wikalat Al Maghreb Al Arabi: Est. 1959; 122 Ave. Allal ben Abdallah, B.P. 1049, Rabat; Government owned

Education

Enrolment at all levels of education in Morocco has grown considerably in the last decade. There are about 40000 institutions with an enrolment of about 5,200,000 in the primary and secondary level and over 242,000 in Universities.

Universities

Université Cadi Ayyad

Est. 1978; Ave. Prince May Abdallah, P.O.Box S 511, Tel.: (04)348-13, Marakech

Université Hassan II

Est. 1975; 19 Tariq Ben Ziad Str., P.O.Box 9167, Tel.: 27-37-37, Casablancaa

Université Ibnou Zohr

Est. 1989; Agadir

Université Mohamed I

Est. 1978; P.O.Box 524, Oujda

Université Mohammed V

Est. 1957; 3 Michlifen Str., Agdal, P.O.Box 554, Tel.: 713-18, Rabat

Université Quaraouyine

Est. 859; P.O.Box 60, Fès

Université Sidi Mohamed Ben Abdellah

Est. 1974; Ave. des Almohades, P.O.Box 2626, Tel.: 255-85, Fès. Branch: Est. 1982; P.O.Box 4009, Tel.: (05)24929, Meknès

Cultural and Research Institutes

African Centre for Administrative Training and Research for Development: 31, Rue de Grenade, B.P. 310, Tangier; Founded 1964; research and training for adopting public administration to development problems; Economic Commission for Africa: library of 2,000 vols.

British Council: 288, Avenue Muhammad V,B.P. 427, Rabat.

Centre d'Etudes et d'Informations Economiques et Sociales (Cedies): 25, Rue Dupleix; Casablanca.

Centro Cultural Espagnol: 8, Rue Capitaine Allardet, Rabat.

Comité national de Géographie du Maroc: Institut Scientifique Chérifien, Rabat; Founded 1974; 12 sections; Pres. The Minister of Education; Publication: Atlas du Maroc.

Goethe Institute: 3, Boulevard Muhammad V, Casablanca; 10, Rue Djebli, Rabat.

Institut Pasteur: Tangier; Founded 1912.

Institut Scientifique Chérifien: Avenue Moulay-Chérif, Rabat; Founded 1920 for the pratical study of nature; the Institute has a collection of animals and an herbarium in its building at Rabat, as well as petrographic and palaeontological collections; the Station de Biologie at Ifrane (Moyen Atlas), the Station de Recherches Présahariennes at Aouinet Torkoz (Dra), and the observatory at Berrechid also belong to the Institute.

Attached Institutes

Station de Recherches Présahariennes: Aouinet-Torkoz.

Station de Seismologie: Ifrane.

Instituto Espagnol en Tangier (Spanish Institute in Tangier): Tangier.

Mission Universitaire et Culturelle Française au Maroc: (French University and Cultural Mision in Morocco): rue Michaux – Bellaire, Rabat; examination courses, cultural and artistic visits and exhibitions, lectures, libraries, Rabat, Casablanca and other large towns.

Observatoire de Seimologie Averroes: Berrechid.

Service de Physique du Globe et de Météorologie: 2, Rue de Foucauld, Casablanca; Founded 1933; research on meteorology climatology, ionosphere, seismology terrestrial magnetism, surge, etc. Publication: Annales.

Société de Géographie du Maroc (Université de Rabat): Rabat; Founded 1916; 500 members; Publication: Revue de Géographie du Maroc (twice yearly).

Société de Préhistoire du Maroc: Syndicat d'Initiative, Blvd. de la Gare, Casablanca; Founded 1926; Publication: Bulletin (biannually).

Société des Sciences Naturelles et Physiques du Maroc: Institut Scientifique Chérifien, Rabat; Founded 1921. Publications: Mémoires, Bulletins, Comptes-rendus, Variétés scientifiques, Travaux de la Section de Pédologie.

Sociétés d'Etudes Economiques Sociales et Statistiques du Maroc: Recette Postale, Rabat.

Société d'Horticulture et d'Acclimatation du Maroc: P.O.Box 854, Casablanca; Founded 1914. Publication: Bulletin (quarterly).

Station de Biologie: Ifreane.

U.S. Information Centres: 6, Rue Branly, Casablanca. Salaj, N°. 15, Batha, Fez. 43, Avenue de L'Allal B. Abdallah, Rabat, Blvd. 37 Pasteur, Tangier.

Libraries and Archives

CASABLANCA

Bibliothèque Municipale: Avenue Général-d'Amade.

FEZ

Al Qarawiyin University Library: Contains about 16,000 ancient and precious MSS. of famous Muslim teachers and thinkers.

RABAT

Bibliothèque Générale et Archives: Avenue Moulay Charif, Rabat; Founded 1920; 180,000 vols. 9,361 MSS.

Bibliothèque de L'Institut Scientifique Chérifien: Avenue Moulay Charif; Founded 1920; 25,000 vols, 1,257 periodicals.

TANGIER

Bibliotica Publica Espanola: Consulado General de Espana, 26, Avenida de Espana, Tangier: Founded 1941; the library is divided into Arabic and European Sections; 20,000 vols.

TETUAN

The official libraries and archives are covered by the **Directorate of Archives and Libraries,** Carretera de Tanger, Tetuan.

Archivo Fotografico: Founded 1948; 45,000 photographs.

Archivo General: Founded 1943; 4,000 vols of administrative documents.

Archivo Historico: Founded 1945; 20,000 Arab documents.

Biblioteca General: Founded 1939; 55,000 vols, including

1,000 Arab MSS.

Homeroteca (newspaper-library): Founded 1939; 4,700 vols.

Officina de distribution intercambio de publicaciones: (Office for the distribution and Exchange of Publications): Tetuan; Founded 1953.

Theatres

Théâtre Municipal de Casablanca: Est. 1922, reorganized in 1934 and 1949; maintained by the Casablanca Municipality.

Théâtre National Mohammed V: Est. 1961; Rabat; Morocco's national theatre sponsored by the State.

Orchestras

Orchestre Symphonique de Conservatoire National de Musique: Rabat

Orchestre du Conservatoire de Tétouan: Tetuan (Arabic music)

Orchestre du Conservatoire Dar Adyel: Fez (Traditional music)

Museums

Archeological Museum: Tetuan; Founded 1940; Prehistoric, Carthaginian, Roman and Islamic collections.

Direction des Musées et des Antiquités: Ministère de L'Information, du Tourisme, de l'Artisanat et des Beaux-Arts, 23 Rue Pierre Parent, Rabat.

Musée des Oudaïa: Rabat.

Musée des Antiquités: Rabat.

Musée du Dar Batha: Fez.

Musée d'Armes du Bordj Nord: Fez.

Musée de la Kasbah: Tangier.

Musée du Dar Jamaï: Meknès.

Musée Dar Si Said: Marrakesh.

Musée de Tetuan: Tetuan.

Musée Archéologique: Tetuan.

Musée des Antiquités: 23, Rue Pierre Parent, Rabat; Founded 1917; prehistoric and Roman exhibits; annexes at Tetuan (Musée Archéologique), Tangier (Musée de la Kasbah).

Tourism

Office National Marocain du Tourisme: Est. 1946; B.P. 19, 31 Angle Ave. Abtal et rue Oved Fas, Rabat

BALANCE OF TRADE

In million US dollars

	1991	1992	1993	1994	1995	1996	1997
Exports	4,278	3,956	4,936	5,541	6,871	6,886	7,039
Imports	6,257	6,692	7,001	7,648	9,268	9,080	8,903
Balance	–1,979	–2,736	–2,065	–2,107	–2,397	–2,482	–1,864

OMAN
(Sultanate of Oman)

Oman

Head of State	: Sultan Qaboos Bin Saïd TAYMOUR
Area	: 300.000 sq. Km.
Population	: 2.4 million (1997 estimate)
Capital	: Muscat
Currency	: In May 1970 the Sultan introduced a new currency, the Riyal Saidi (RS), (renamed the Riyal Omani (RO) in 1972) divided into 1,000 baizas
Denominations	: a) Notes: 100-250 and 500 baizas; 1-5-10 Riyal Omani b) Coins: 2-10-25-50 and 100 baizas
Exchange Rate:	: US $ 1 = 0.3845 Riyal Omani (May 1998)

Geography

The Sultanate of Oman lies south of the Straits of Hormuz and is outside the Gulf. It has, however, a separate territory at the tip of the Musandam Peninsula overlooking the entrance to the Gulf, and its geographical and historical links with the United Arab Emirates are very close. In size it is much the largest of the states in the Gulf area, covering some 120,000 square miles with an estimated population of 2.4 million. Neighbouring countries, all to the west, are the Gulf Emirates, Saudi Arabia and the former People's Democratic Republic of Yemen. The coastline, which is over 1000 miles long, faces the Gulf of Oman and the Arabian Sea.

The Sultanate generally is arid and barren but there are four relatively fertile areas - the Batina coast, which stretches north-west of Muscat towards the Musandam Peninsula, the valleys of the Jebel Akhdar (Green Mountain), other parts of the Hajar range behind the coastal strip, and the Salalah plain in the south-west of Oman. The mountains in the Dhofar region trap the monsoon rains and this small area was celebrated in ancient times as the only known source of frankincense in the world.

PUBLIC HOLIDAYS

Mulid al Nabi – birthday of the Prophet; Eid al Fitr, end of Ramadan, month of fasting and self - purification, Eid al Adha, feast of the Sacrifice, Muslim New Year's Day; Ashura, day of mourning for Shi'ite Muslims (16 October).

RELIGION

About three-quarters of the population are Idahi Muslims, one of the strictest Muslim sects; the rest are Sunni Muslims.

The Idahis are small little people with the characteristic hawk-like nose and fine features, intensely tribal and independent, and in the past given to fierce tribal battles.

History

In the Middle Ages the seafarers of Oman were renowned, and Sohar, on the Batina coast, was the advance base of Gulf merchants trading in the Indian Ocean and with China. When the Portuguese rounded the Cape and sought to monopolize Indian Ocean trade, one of the first points they seized was Muscat, which they held for the best part of 150 years until driven out by the Omani Arabs in 1650. In the next century the Omanis resisted Persian invasions and conquered various Portuguese settlements in the Indian Ocean including Zanzibar, Mogadishu and Mombasa. The dynasty now ruling the Sultanate, the Said family, was established in the mid-18th century. The British entered into the first of successive treaties of friendship with Oman in 1798 when they decided that Napoleon was too interested in the Sultanate as a possible stepping stone to India. Soon after this the long reign of the great Sultan Said bin Sultan began. He died in 1856, and a subsequent dispute between two sons was settled by the Canning Award of 1861 - an arbitration by the British Government which gave Oman to one son and Zanzibar to the other.

POLITICAL SITUATION

The Sultan has ruled since 1970 with the help of an appointed executive Council of Ministers and, since 1983, a 55-man Council Assembly, replaced by a 59-member Consultative Council in November 1991 and again increased to 82 in 1997. In December 16, 1997, a new Council of State of 41 members have been appointed which act in conjonction with the Consultative Council. Relations with neighbouring states have been strengthened by the establishment in 1981 of the Gulf Co-operation Council (GCC) by Bahrain, Kuwait, Oman, Qatar, Saudi Arabia and the United Arab Emirates to promote regional Co-ordination of Industry, agriculture, transport and energy as well as defence.

The Cabinet

(Dec. 1998)

Prime Minister and Minister of Foreign Affairs, Defence and Finance: Sultan Qaboos Ben SAID

Deputy Prime Minister for Cabinet Affairs: Sayed Fahd Ben Mahmoud AL SAID

Special Representative of the Sultan: Sayyid Thuwainy Ben Shihab AL SAID

Minister for Legal Affairs: Mohamed Ben Ali Ben Nasir AL ALAWI

Minister of Justice: Mohamed Ben Abdullah Ben Zahir AL HINAI

Minister Responsible for Defence: Sayed Badre Ben Saud Ben Hareb AL BUSAIDI

Minister of Waqfs and Islamic Affairs: Abdullah Ben Mohamed AL SALAMI
Minister of Information: Abdula Aziz Ben Mohamed AL ROWAS
Minister of State for Foreign Affairs: Youssef Ben Alawi Ben ABDULLAH
Minister of Telecommunications: Sheikh Suhail Ben Mustahil Ben Salem Beit CHAMAS
Minister of Communications and Housing: Malek Ben Soleiman AL MUAMMARI
Minister of Education and Youth Affairs: Sayed Saud Ben Ibrahim Ben Saud ALBUSAIDI
Minister of Higher Education: Yahya Ben Mahfouz AL MUNZIRI
Minister of Social Affairs and Labour: Sheikh Amir Ben Shuwain AL HOSNI
Minister of National Economy: Ahmed Ben Abd An Nabi MAKKI
Minister of National Heritage and Culture: Sayyid Faisal Ben Ali AL SAID
Minister of the Interior: Ali Ben Hamud Ben Ali AL BUSAIDI
Minister of Petroleum and Minerals: Mohamed Ben Hamad Ben Seif AL RAMHI
Minister of Agriculture and Fisheries: Ahmed Ben Khalfan Ben Mohamed RAWAHI
Minister of Commerce and Industry: Maqbool Ben Ali Ben SULTAN
Minister of Civil Service: Abdulaziz Ben Matar AL AZIZI
Minister of Water Resources: Hamid Ben Said AL AUFI
Minister of Regional Municipalities and of the Environment: Khamis Ben Mubarak Ben Issa AL ALAWI
Minister of Health: Ali Ben Mohamed Ben Moussa AL RAISSI
Minister of Electricity and Water: Sheikh Mohamed Ben Ali AL QOTUBI
Govenor of Muscat and Minister of State: Sayed Al Mutassim Ben Hamoud AL BUSAIDI
Governor of Dhofar and Minister of State: Sayed Mussallam Ben Ali AL BUSAIDI
Minister of Royal Court Affairs: Sayyid Sayf Ben Hamed Ben SAUD
Minister of Palace Office: Maj. Gen. Ali Ben Majid AL MAAMARI

Foreign Embassies

Algeria: P.O.Box 50216, Tel. 601698, Madinat Qaboos
Austria: P.O. Box 2070, Tel. 793135, Ruwi
Bangladesh: P.O.Box 3959, Tel. 703155, Ruwi
China People's Republic: P.O.Box 3315, Tel. 696782, Muscat
Egypt: P.O. Box 5225, Tel. 600411, Ruwi
France: P.O. Box 50208, Tel. 604310, Muscat
Germany: P.O.Box 3128, Tel. 702482, Ruwi
India: P.O.Box 4727, Tel. 702957, Ruwi
Iran: P.O.Box 6155, Tel. 696944, Ruwi
Iraq: P.O.Box 4848, Tel. 701349, Muscat
Italy: P.O.Box 6727, Tel. 560968, Muscat
Japan: P.O.Box 6511, Tel. 603464, Ruwi
Jordan: P.O.Box 5281, Tel. 602561 Ruwi
Korea, Republic: P.O.Box 5220, Tel. 702322, Ruwi
Kuwait: P.O.Box 4798, Tel. 706444, Muscat
Malaysia: P.O.Box 6939, Tel. 698329, Ruwi
Morocco: P.O.Box 6125, Tel. 701977, Ruwi
Netherlands: P.O.Box 6302, Tel. 705410, Ruwi
Pakistan: P.O.Box 4302, Tel. 603439, Ruwi
Qatar: P.O.Box 802, Tel. 701802, Muscat
Russia: P.O.Box 3080, Ruwi
Saudi Arabia: P.O.Box 4411, Tel. 701111, Muscat
Somalia: P.O.Box 1767, Tel. 701355, Ruwi
Sri Lanka: P.O.Box 95, Ruwi
Sudan: P.O. Box 6971, Tel. 708790, Ruwi
Sweden: P.O.Box 3001, Tel. 708693, Ruwi
Syria: P.O.Box 85, Muscat
Thailand: P.O.Box 6367, Tel. 602684, Ruwi
Tunisia: P.O.Box 220, Tel. 704574, Ruwi
Turkey: P.O.Box 8511, Tel. 697050, Mutrah
United Arab Emirates: P.O.Box 1551, Tel. 600302, Muscat
United Kingdom: P.O.Box 300, Tel. 738501, Muscat
U.S.A.: P.O.Box 50202, Tel. 698989, Medinat Qaboos
Yemen: P.O. Box 50105, Tel. 700091, Muscat

Justice

Justice is administered in accordance with Sharia (Canon Law of Islam) by local judges or "Cadis". Proceedings for appeal are filed with the Court of Appeal at Muscat.

The Economy

Oman is one of the smaller Arab oil-producing nations and as such is not a member of OPEC, though it has attempted broadly to match its pricing with the organisation's policy. In 1998 the rate of extraction rose to an estimated 900,000 barrels per day (b/d). The 1996 production rate was about 895000 b/d.

Reflecting continuing exploration, proven reserves of oil in 1998 were estimated at 5.3 billion barrels, considerably above the end-1982 estimate and equivalent to approximately 16 year's supply at the current extraction rate. The bulk of production is undertaken by Petroleum Development Oman (PDO), in which the government has a majority share, in the south and in offshore explorations.

Production of natural gas is being encouraged in order to release greater quantities of petroleum for export by using gas to fuel power stations, boost oil recovery and as an energy supply for all main towns. In early 1998 reserves were estimated at 28.4 trillion cubic feet (cu.ft).

Petroleum accounts for around 80% of government revenues.

Meanwhile the contribution of agriculture and fishing to the economy has fallen sharply since the development of the hydrocarbons sector. Most agriculture is devoted to subsistence farming, while around a half of the cultivated area supports date palms; other crops include alfalfa, limes, melons, bananas and coconuts. Dates, bananas and dried limes constitute a large partof Oman's traditional non-oil exports, especially to neighbouring states.

The sea off Oman's long coastline is rich in a variety of fish, but at present most fishing is carried out for subsistence rather than commercially and the catch is many times below its potential. The total catch has been estimated at 121,000 tons in 1998.

The government is concentrating on development of agriculture and the fishing industry.

Oman is comparatively well-endowed with minerals, though so far only copper and chromite (chromium ore) have been discovered in sufficiently large quantities to warrant exploitation.

Exploration for lead, zink and gold are also underway.

The budget for 1998 was expenditure Omani Rials 2,307 billion and revenue Omani Rials 2,012 billion compared with 1997 for expenditure 2,266 and 2,003 revenue. The budget for 1999 was expenditure 2,156 and revenue 1,525.

he Banking System

With the large expansion in government financial operations and the accompanying growth of the domestic economy, the number of commercial banks rose from 4 in 1972 to 21 in 1998; the number of bank branches has reached 330.

Central Bank of Oman: Est. 1974; P.O.Box 1161, Tel. 702222, Ruwi; 2 branches

Alliance Housing Bank: Est. 1997; P.O.Box 545, Mina al-Fahl 116; Tel. 568568

Bank of Baroda: Est. 1976; P.O.Box 231, Tel. 714549, Mutrah

Bank Dhofar al-Omani al-Fransi SAOC: Est. 1990; P.O.Box 1507, Tel. 790466, Ruwi 112

Bank Melli Iran: Est. 1974; P.O.Box 2643, Tel. 701579, Ruwi

Bank of Muscat International SAO.: Est. 1982; P.O.Box 134, Tel. 703044, Ruwi; 14 branches

Bank Saderat Iran: P.O.Box 1269, Tel. 793923, Ruwi

Banque Banorabe: Est. 1981; P.O.Box 1608, Tel. 702274, Ruwi

HSBC Middle East: Est. 1948; P.O.Box 3240, Tel. 799920, Ruwi, 4 branches

Citibank N.A.: Est. 1975; P.O.Box 8994, Tel. 795705, Ruwi

Commercial Bank of Oman Ltd. SAO.: Est. 1976; P.O.Box 1976, P.O.Box 1696, Tel. 793229, Ruwi; 23 branches.

Habib Bank Ltd.: Est. 1972; P.O.Box 3538; Tel. 705276, Ruwi; 22 branches.

Industrial Bank of Oman: Est. 1997; P.O.Box 2613, Tel. 706786, Ruwi 112

Majan International Bank: Est. 1998; P.O.Box 2717; Tel. 780388, Ruwi 112

National Bank of Abu Dhabi: Est. 1976; P.O.Box 2293, Tel. 798842, Ruwi

National Bank of Oman SAO.: Est. 1973; P.O.Box 3751, Tel. 708894, Ruwi; 49 branches

Oman Arab Bank SAO.: Est. 1984; P.O.Box 2010, Tel. 700161, Ruwi; 14 branches

Oman Development Bank SAO.: Est. 1976; P.O.Box 309, Tel. 738577, Muscat

Oman Housing Bank SAO.: Est. 1977; P.O.Box 2555, Tel. 704444, Ruwi

Oman International Bank: Est. 1979; P.O.Box 1727, Tel. 682500, Ruwi; 38 branches

Standard Chartered Bank: Est. 1968; P.O.Box 2353, Tel. 703999, Ruwi; 4 branches

Insurance

Al Ahlia Insurance Co. S.A.O.: Est. 1985; P.O.Box 1463, Tel. 709331, Ruwi

Oman National Insurance Co. S.A.O.: Est. 1978; P.O.Box 5254, Tel. 795020, Ruwi

Oman United Insurance Co. S.A.O.: Est. 1985; P.O.Box 1522, Tel. 703990, ruwi

Transport

ROADS

There are some 6000 km of asphalted roads and about 20000 km of gravelled ones.

SHIPPING

Muscat is the largest seaport with a good natural harbour.

Matrah, Marbat, Sohar, Kaburah are minor ports for small craft only.

In Dhofar a new port has been constructed at Raysut, 20 Km., west of Salalah. With berthage for small trading vessels, Raysut port came into use in 1975, and expansion to meet increasing seaborne trade was completed in 1980.

Port Services Corporation Ltd.: P.O.Box 133, Muscat.

CIVIL AVIATION

The Seeb International Airport, located 30 kms from Muscat, was opened in 1973. With its 3500 metre long runway, it can handle the biggest commerical aircraft.

The second international airport is located at Salalah and was opened in 1978.

Gulf Aviation Ltd. (Gulf Air): P.O.Box 138, Bahrain; founded in 1950. Services linking Oman to the Arab Peninsula, Asia, Europe.

Oman Aviation Services: P.O.Box 1058, Seeb International Airport, Oman.

Radio, Television and Press

RADIO AND TELEVISION

Radio Oman: Est. 1970 for Arabic and Dhofari programmes.

Radio Salalah: Est. 1970. Daily transmission 15 hours.

Oman Television: P.O.Box 600, Muscat.

THE PRESS

Al Watan (The Nation): P.O.Box 463, Muscat; Arabic; Daily.

Oman Daily Observer: P.O.Box 3303, Ruwi, English; Daily.

Times of Oman: P.O.Box 3770, Ruwi, Muscat; English; daily.

Al-Akidah: P.O.Box 4001, Ruwi, Arabic weekly.

Al Mawared al Tabeiah: Ministry of Agriculture, Fisheries, Petroleum and Minerals, P.O.Box 551, Muscat; English and Arabic.

Al Nahda: P.O.Box 979, Muscat; weekly Arabic.

Al Usra: P.O.Box 7440, Mutrah; weekly Arabic.

Jund Oman: P.O.Box 113, Muscat; monthly.

QATAR

QATAR

Head of State	: Shaikh Hamad Bin Khalifa Bin Hamad AL THANI
Crown prince	: Sheikh Jassim Bin Hamad Bin Khalifa AL-THANI
Capital	: Doha
Area	: 11,437 sq. Km.
Population	: 600.000 (1994 estimate)
Currency	: Qatar Riyal (QR) divided into 100 dirhams.
Denominations	: a) Notes: 1-5-10-25-50, 100 and 500 Riyals b) Coins: 1-5-10-25-50 Dirhams.
Rate of Exchange	: US $ 1 = 3.64 Qatari Riyals (Dec. 1997)

Geography

Qatar occupies a peninsula of approximately 4,400 square miles that projects through north into the Arabian Gulf for about 1000 miles and has an approximate maximum width of 55 miles.

There are also some small offshore islands. Those permanently settled include Halul, important as the storage centre and tanker terminal for two seabed oil-fields.

Qatar's landward frontiers at the neck of the peninsula lie with the Kingdom of Saudi Arabia to the west and the Shaikhdom of Abu Dhabi to the east. Riyadh, the northern Saudi capital, lies 250 miles due west behind the Jafura Desert, and Abu Dhabi port 150 miles to the south-east where the equally vast Rub al-Khali Desert (the so-called Empty Quarter') runs to the Gulf along an ill-defined shore of shallow inlets, reefs and shoals.

The State's nearest seaward neighbour is the Bahrain Islands to the north. Their capital, Manama is 100 miles from Doha, although only 20 miles separate the two territories at the narrowest part of the channel running between them in the Gulf of Salwah. The eastern Iranian shore of the Gulf is 120 miles off Qatar's rounded northern extremity, and the nearest Iranian port, Bushire, is 250 miles from Doha.

The Peninsula is, for the most part, flat and barren, but with special beauty of a desert landscape and the sea nowhere very far away. Along the southern half of the western coastline a chain of low limestone hills marks the "Dukhan anticline", Qatar's oilfield. Such natural vegetation as there is appears mainly in the north, around wells and small wadis. In the south of the Peninsula a topographical feature is the string of salt flats across the neck of land from Salwa to Khor al Odeid. This suggests that Qatar may have been an island at some time in the remote past.

CLIMATE

Qatar lies outside the area of the south-western monsoons and its seasons generally conform with those of the temperate zone lands. The weather in the winter months of December, January, February and March is relatively cold for the latitude. But humidity is frequently excessive.

TOWNS

Doha (pop. 218,000), the capital, is the seat of the Qatar Government and the commercial and financial head-quarters of the State. Two decades or so ago it was a sleepy fishing village; now it is a thriving town with wide and well-lit streets crowded with traffic under automatic light control, modern airconditioned shops, parks and gardens, and numerous public buildings.

Qatar's second town is Khor, overlooking a narrow and deeply indented bay about 28 miles due north of the capital and linked to it by a metalled road.

PUBLIC HOLIDAYS

Eid al Fitr; Independence Day (3 September), Eid al Adha; Islamic New Year Prophet's Birthday; Accession of Shaikh Khalifa (22 February).

RELIGION

Islam is the dominant religion of the population, indegenous and migratory alike.

Most Qatari are Sunni Moslems of the Wahabi sect, the more numerous and most orthodox of the two main Islamic streams, and as such regard exact obedience to the tenets of the "Koran" (The Moslem Holy Book) as a sufficient guide for moral and social purposes.

LANGUAGE

The official language of the State is Arabic, although much Government business is conducted in English and most senior Qatari departmental officials are fluent in that language.

History

Qatar had few visitors from the European world until well on into the present century. The Danish traveller Carsten Niebuhr has "Gattar" on his mid-18th century map but the detail is quite inaccurate. The first European to have travelled into the interior seems to have been the German, Hermann Burchardt, in 1904. The British expelled an Ottoman garrison from Doha early in the First World War, and Qatar entered into treaty relations with Britain in 1916 whereby Shaikh Abdallah Ben Jassim al-Thani, the then Ruler, agreed not to enter into relations with other foreign powers nor to alienate Qatari territory without British consent. He abdicated in 1949, just when the Shaikhdom was first gaining its new wealth. He was succeeded by his son, Shaikh Ali ben Abdallah al-Thani, whose rule of little more than 10 years ended in 1960 - again by abdication, with the agreement of the ruling family. In his turn, Shaikh Ahmad bin Aly bin Abdallah al

Thani, was deposed in a bloodless coup by his cousin, Shaikh Khalifa bin Hamad al Thani – on February 22, 1972. On June 27, 1995, in a bloodless coup Shaikh Khalifa bin Hamad al-Thani was deposed by his son Shaikh Hamad bin Khalifa al-Thani, present Ruler of Qatar.

Constitution

(April 2, 1970)

A provisional Constitution was promulgated on April 2, 1970. It comprises 77 articles under five chapter heads - the Form of Government, Essential Guiding Principles of State Policy, Public Rights and Duties, the Authorities, (General Provisions, the Head of State, the Council of Ministers, the Advisory Council and the Judiciary) and General and Transitional Provisions.

All fundamental democratic rights are guaranteed: sanctity of the home, freedom of publication and the press, individual and collective ownership of property, etc.

THE POLITICAL SITUATION: The present Amir Sheikh Hamad bin Khalifa al-Thani who has replaced his father Shaikh Khalifa bin Hamad al-Thani on June 27, 1995, combines the role with that of Prime Minister. Under the terms of the Provisional Constitution, executive power is vested in the Amir, who appoints a Council of Ministers.

Qatar joined the Gulf Co-operation Council (GCC) when it was set up in 1981, to foster economic co-operation and integration and to increase regional security. The other member states are Bahrain, Kuwait, Oman, Saudi Arabia and the United Arab Emirates.

Qatar is a full member of the Organisation of Petroleum Exporting Countries (OPEC), the Organisation of Arab Union of Broadcasting Services, and the Arab Union of Tourism; and an associate member of the World Health Organisation (WHO), the International Bureau of Education in Geneva, Unesco, and the United Nations Food and Agricultural Organisation.

The Cabinet

(June. 1999)

Amir, Minister of Defence and Commander-in-Chief of the Armed Forces: Maj. Gen. Sheikh Hamad Bin Khalifa AL THANI

Prime Minister and Minister of Interior: Sheikh Abdullah Bin Khalifa AL THANI

Minister of Foreign Affairs: Sheikh Hamad Bin Jasim Bin Jaber AL THANI

Minister of Finance, Economy and Trade: Yousuf Hussein KAMAL

Minister of Waqfs (Religious Endowments) and Islamic Affairs: Ahmad Bin Abdullah Salem AL MARRI

Minister of Municipal Affairs and Agriculture: Ali Mohamed AL KHATIR

Minister of Communications and Transport: Sheikh Ahmed Bin Nasser AL THANI

Minister of Education, Culture and Higher Education: Mohamed Abdel Rahim KAFOUD

Minister of Justice: Hassan Bin Abdallah AL GHANEM

Minister of Energy and Industry: Abdullah Bin Hamad AL ATTIYA

Minister of Public Health: Abdel Rahman al-Salem al-Hajr Bin Ahmad HAJR

Minister of Housing and the Civil Service: Sheikh Falah Bin Jasim AL THANI

Minister of State for Foreign Affairs: Ahmad Abdullah AL MAHMOUD

Minister of State for Cabinet Affairs: Ali Bin Saad AL KAWARI

Minister of State for the Interior: Sheikh Abdullah Bin Khaled AL THANI

Ministers of State without Portfolio: Sheikh Ahmed Bin Saif AL THANI, Sheikh Hassan Bin Abdullah Bin Mohamed AL THANI, Sheikh Hamad Bin Sahim AL THANI, Sheikh Hamad Bin Abdullah AL THANI, Sheikh Mohamed Bin Khalid AL THANI

Foreign Embassies

Algeria: P.O.Box 2494, Tel. 662900, Doha

Bangladesh: P.O.Box 2080, Tel. 671927, Doha

Bosnia and Herzegovina: P.O.Box 876, Tel. 670194, Doha

China, People's Republic: P.O.Box 17200, Tel. 824200, Doha

Cuba: P.O.Box 12017, Tel. 672072, Doha

Egypt: P.O.Box 2899, Tel. 832555, Doha

France: P.O.Box 2669, Tel. 832281, Doha

Germany: P.O.Box 3064, Tel. 876959, Doha

India: P.O.Box 2788, Tel. 672021, Doha

Iran: P.O.Box 1633, Tel. 835300, Doha

Italy: P.O.Box 4188, Tel. 436842, Doha

Iraq: P.O.Box 1526, Tel. 672237, Doha

Japan: P.O.Box 2208, Tel. 831224, Doha

Jordan: P.O.Box 2366, Tel. 832204, Doha

Korea, Republic: P.O.Box 3727, Tel. 832238, Doha

Kuwait: P.O.Box 1177, Tel. 832111, Doha

Lebanon: P.O.Box 2411, Tel. 444468, Doha

Libya: P.O.Box 574, Tel. 429546, Doha

Mauritania: P.O.Box 3132, Tel. 836003, Doha

Morocco: P.O.Box 3242, Tel. 831885, Doha

Oman: P.O.Box 1525, Tel. 670744, Doha

Pakistan: P.O.Box 334, Tel. 832535, Doha

Philippines: P.O.Box 24900, Tel. 831585, Doha

Romania: P.O.Box 22511, Tel. 426740, Doha

Russia: P.O.Box 15404, Tel. 329117, Doha

Saudi Arabia: P.O.Box 1255, Tel. 832030, Doha

Somalia: P.O.Box 1948, Tel. 832181, Doha

Sudan: P.O.Box 2999, Tel. 423007, Doha

Syria: P.O.Box 1257, Tel. 831844, Doha

Tunisia: P.O.Box 2707, Tel. 832645, Doha
Turkey: P.O.Box 1977, Tel. 835553, Doha
United Arab Emirates: P.O.Box 3, Tel. 421991, Doha
United Kingdom: P.O.Box 3, Tel. 421991, Doha
U.S.A.: P.O.Box 2399, Tel. 864701, Doha
Yemen: P.O.Box 3318, Tel. 432555, Doha

The Economy

OUTLOOK

The development of the massive natural gas reserves in the North Field should generate another period of growth in the Qatari economy.

The hydrocarbon sector remains the lynchpin of the Qatari economy, accounting for the vast majority of export earnings and the bulk of government revenues. Earnings from petroleum have been used to provide the country with an advanced infrastructure and a number of basic industries, and have also generated one of the highest per capita income levels in the world. Recession followed the fall in oil prices at the start of 1986 with the country's external and budgetary positions both weakening markedly. Much of the momentum of recovery is expected to be created by the exploitation of the North Field natural gas reserves over the next few years.

Qatar, with oil reserves estimated at 3.7 billion barrels at the end of 1998 has produced over 800,000 barrels per day (b/d) of crude petroleum and 800 million cubic feet of natural gas, and development is underway to increase the capacity to 2 trillion cubic feet. Two refineries have been built, both at Umm Said, with a total capacity of 62,000 b/d, making Qatar self-sufficient in refined products and generating a surplus for export. The larger of the two refineries has been designed so as to simplify further expansion to meet anticipated growth in local consumption. Qatar remains heavily dependent on earnings from export of oil, despite the construction of several heavy industrial plants and is therefore especially vulnerable to fluctuations in the world price of oil. This makes the development of the estimated 150 trillion cubic feet of reserves of natural gas in the North Field – about 4% of the world total and the largest gas field in the world – all the more attractive. Drilling for the start of phase one started in August 1988, and was completed in 1991.

Several heavy industries, utilising gas as a fuel of feedstock, have been established, often on the basis of joint venture capital with overseas concerns. The first major plant to be founded was the Qatar Fertiliser Company, commenced production in 1973. The Qatar Iron and Steel Company, began operations in 1978, processing imported ore and local scrap principally for export. The last of the three major schemes is the Qatar Petrochemicals Company which commissioned its facilities in 1980 and 1981. The plant, produces ethylene, low-density polyethylene and sulphur; smaller ventures have also been set up.

Although agriculture constitutes only about 1% of GDP, production has risen such that Qatar is now virtually self-sufficient in vegetables. Other crops grown include fruit, cereals and dates. Fishing has suffered from declining catch size in recent years but still meets the bulk of local demand. Government is encouraging fishermen with interest-free loans for modernization. Total catch in 1996 was over 4,700 tons.

The Qatar budget approved in May 1995 was set at revenue QR 9,204 million and expenditure at QR 12,735 million with a deficit of QR 3,531 million for the fiscal year 1995/96 commencing in April. The 1994/95 budget was revenue QR 8.359 million and expenditure 11,830 million and a deficit of 3,471 million. The 1995/96 budget was revenue QR 9,204 million and expenditured QR 12,735 with a deficit of QR 3,531. The 1996/97 budget was set at revenue QR 10,800 million and expenditure at QR 13,750 with a deficit of QR 2,950 million. The 1997/98 budget was set at revenue QR 13,390 million and expenditure at QR 16,380 million with a deficit of QR 2,900 million. The 1998/1999 budget set expenditure at QR 15,660 billion and revenue QR 12,350 billion with a deficit of QR 3,310 billion. The 1999/2000 budget was set at expenditure QR 14,136 billion and revenue at QR 10,530 billion with a deficit of QR 3,606 billion.

INFRASTRUCTURE

The pace of development is impressive. Health and education have become major priorities.

There are several government hospitals with a total of about 1100 beds and 23 new clinics were built. Physicians in good numbers are available, assisted by supporting health personnel including pharmacists, dentists, midwives and nurses.

Meanwhile, expansion of the university is under way and there are plans to increase the number of schools.

The housing crisis has been effectively solved by the extensive construction of prefabricated units.

Port delays have been virtually eliminated as a result of a major expansion programme.

Demand for electricity, which is free to Qataris has been increasing.

The Banking System

Qatar Central Bank: Est. 1966; P.O.Box 1234, Tel. 456456, Doha

Qatar National Bank, S.A.Q.: Est. 1965; P.O.Box 1000, Tel. 407407, Doha

Al Ahli Bank of Qatar, Q.S.C.: Est. 1984; P.O.Box 2309, Tel. 326611, Doha

ANZ Grindlays Bank PLC (UK): Est. 1956; Rayyan Rd., P.O.Box 2001, Tel. 418222, Doha

Arab Bank PLC (Jordan): Est. 1957; P.O.Box 172, Tel. 437979, Doha

Bank Saderat Iran: Est. 1970; P.O.Box 2256, Tel. 414646, Doha

Banque Paribas (France): Est. 1973; P.O.Box 2636, Tel. 433844, Doha

British Bank of the Middle East: Est. 1954; P.O.Box 57, Tel. 335222, Doha

Commercial Bank of Qatar Ltd. Q.S.C.: Est. 1975; Grand Hamad Ave., P.O.Box 3232, Tel. 490222, Doha

Doha Bank Ltd.: Est. 1979; P.O.Box 3818, Tel. 456600, Doha

Qatar Islamic Bank, S.A.Q.: Est. 1983; P.O.Box 559, Tel. 409409, Doha

Standard Chartered Bank (UK): Est. 1950; P.O.Box 29, Tel. 414252, Doha

United Bank Ltd. (Pakistan): Est. 1970; P.O.Box 242, Tel. 416930, Doha

Insurance

Al Khaleej Insurance Co., S.A.Q.: Est. 1978; P.O.Box 4555, Tel. 414151, Doha

Qatar General Insurance and Reinsurance Co., S.A.Q.: Est. 1979; P.O.Box 4500, Tel. 417800, Doha

Qatar Insurance Co., S.A.Q.: Est 1964; P.O.Box 666, Tel. 490490, Doha

Petroleum Industry

Qatar General Petroleum Corporation: Est. 1974; P.O.Box 47, Tel. 402400, Doha

Qatar Liquified Gas Co.: Est. 1984; P.O.Box 22666, Tel. 327121, Doha

Qatar Petrochemicals Co.: Est. 1974; P.O.Box 756, Tel. 321105, Doha

National Oil Distribution Co.: P.O.Box 50033, Tel. 776555, UM Said

Transport

ROADS

The peninsula contains a network of over 2000 km of main all-weather roads springing from Doha. The Salwa road links the Qatar capital with the trans-Arabian highway network; a 260-mile highway links Doha to Abu Dhabi; a 70-mile motorway from Doha to Ruwais in the extreme north.

SHIPPING

Qatar National Navigation & Transport Co Ltd - P.O.Box 153 Doha. Shipping agents for all dry-cargo vessels and passenger liners; chartering agents; stevedores; clearance and forwarding agents; truckers; lighterage contractors; owners of slipway; travel agency.

CIVIL AVIATION

An international airport equipped to receive all kinds of aircraft is located 3½miles southeast of Doha.

Gulf Air Co. Ltd.: P.O.Box 3394, Doha. Owned Jointly by the governments Bahrain, Oman, Qatar, U.A.E.

Gulf Helicopters P.O.Box 811, Doha.

Qatar Airways: P.O.Box 22550, Doha

Foreign Airlines: Operating scheduled flights to Doha include: Air France, Alia, BA, Egyptair, Iranian Airways, of, Saudia, MEA.

Education

The per capita cost of Qatari education is among the highest in the world. The Government is wholly responsible for tuition and maintenance up to and including university courses abroad. Books, school meals and transportation, clothing and shoes, holidays and boarding facilities are provided free. Cash grants are available to needy parents to encourage regular attendance by their children at the key primary stage; and other, more selective incentives apply to the preparatory and secondary stages.

Specialised courses are offered by:

Doha Technical College (opened in 1956/57)
The Secondary Commercial College (1967)
The Teacher Training Institute (1967)
The Institute of Religious Studies (1957)
The Institute of Management (1957)
The Higher Training College (1974)
The Faculty of Education (1973)

Universities

University of Qatar
Est. 1973; P.O.Box 2713, Tel.: 83-2222, Doha

Radio, Television and Press

RADIO

Qatar Broadcasting Service: Est. 1968; P.O.Box 3939; Public Corporation; In Arabic and English, French and Urdu)

TELEVISION

Qatar Television: Est. 1970; P.O.Box 1944, Doha

THE PRESS

Al Jawhara: Est. 1977; P.O.Box 2531, Tel. 414575, Doha; Arabic; Monthly

Arrayah: Est. 1979; P.O.box 3464, Tel. 466555, Doha; Arabic; daily and Weekly

Al Ourouba: Est. 1957; P.O.Box 663, Doha; Tel. 325874 publ. daily Arabic newspaper "Al Arab" and weekly magazine "Al-Ourouba"

Gulf Times: Est. 1978. P.O.Box 2888, Doha Tel. 350478; English; daily and Weekly

Library

Qatar Public Library: Est. 1963; P.O.Box 205, Doha; 40,900 volumes in Arabic; 7,000 volumes in English; 109 periodicals

Museum

National Museum: Doha. Est. 1975 sited in 10 old houses restored to traditional style, and two new galleries; collection of ethnographical, archaeological, ecologica-land historical material; includes man-made lagoon on which are exhibited six Gulf sailing craft; also Museum of the sea and aquarium.

SAUDI ARABIA
(Kingdom of Saudi Arabia)

Saudi Arabia

Sovereign	: King Fahd Ibn Abdul Aziz AL SAUD
Crown Prince	: Abdullah Ibn Abdul Aziz AL SAUD
Royal Capital	: Riyad
Administration Capital:	Jeddah
Area	: 2,150,000 sq. Km.
Population	: 19.0 million (1996 estimate)
Currency	: Saudi Riyal (SR) sub-divided into 20 Qirsh and the Qirsh is sub-divided into 5 halalahs (the halalah is used for accounting purposes).
Denominations	: a) Notes: 1-5-10-50-100-500 SR b) Coins: 1-2-4 Qirsh c) Halalah coins do exist but are not in general use.
Exchange rate	: SR per US dollar = 3.745 (May 1997)

Geography

The Kingdom of Saudi Arabia comprises about nine-tenths of the Arabian Peninsula in the extreme south-west of Asia. On the north, it is bounded by the Gulf of Aqaba, Jordan, Iraq and Kuwait; two neutral areas along the northern frontier are administered jointly. The Southern neighbours are Yemen, and Oman; except for a mountain ridge on the Yemenite border, the boundary is not marked. On the east are the Arabian Gulf, Qatar and Oman. The Red Sea provides the boundary on the west.

Estimates vary between 500,000 and 895,000 square miles depending on how much is included of Rub al Khali, the Empty Quarter or Great Sandy Desert in the south. The forbidding desert wastes reduce the habitable area of the country by between 150,000 and 250,000 square miles.

REGIONS

Saudi Arabia is divided into four main geographical divisions: Najd, high country is the heart of Saudi Arabia; al-Hijaz, an elongated shelf region along the upper Red Sea coast; Asir, in the southern Red Sea-Yemen border area; al-Hasa, or Eastern province, the sandy and eastern part of the country.

THE CAPITAL

The capital of the Kingdom of Saudi Arabia is Riyad, the seat of the House of Saud since the destruction of the family's old capital of ad-Dir'iyah, which stood a little farther up Wadi Hanifah, by the army of Muhammad Ali of Egypt in the early nineteenth century. A virtually new city has evolved from and been superimposed upon the old fortified town and Riyad's new palaces, public buildings, mosques, schools, hospitals, boulevards and parks are rapidly replacing mudbrick buildings and narrow lanes.

THE HOLY CITY

Mecca, the holiest city in Islam, has been the capital of the Hijaz for many years. The city contains the sanctuary of the Ka'bah, toward which all Muslims face at prayer. Mecca was the birthplace of the Prophet Muhammad and the scene of his earliest preaching. In addition, Mecca is a flourishing commercial centre.

THE ILLUMINATED CITY

Sharing with Mecca the honour of being one of the Holy cities of Islam is **Medina,** the full name of which is al Madinah al Munawwarah (the Illuminated City). The original name of the city was Yathrib. After the Prophet migrated from Mecca and set up the government of the Islamic state there, it became pre-eminently "The City" and received its new name, which it has retained ever since. Medina was the southern terminus of the Hijaz Railway, built in the days of the Ottoman Empire before the First World War.

THE RED SEA PORT

The port of Jeddah, situated on the Red Sea, less than 50 miles from Mecca, is the most important commercial centre in western Arabia. Most Pilgrims to Mecca and most imports into the Hijaz enter the Kingdom through Jeddah. Many business concerns, including foreign consultants and banks, have offices there. The city has a modern seaport and a modern airport, both of which attract much international traffic.

THE SUMMER CAPITAL

North of Jeddah on the Red Sea is the town of **Yunbu',** which serves as a port for Medina. Scattered up and down the coast are other ports, of which Jaizan, near the Yemen border, is probably the most active. High up in the mountains above Mecca is Tayif, a very old town and a popular summer resort. The Royal Court usually spends a part of the summer at Ta'if. At that time this spot becomes a second capital.

THE LARGEST OASIS

Probably the largest oasis in Saudi Arabia is al-Hasa, in the Eastern Province, which has sixty or more springs, four of them very large, and which is famous for the quality of its dates. There are approximately 200,000 inhabitants in al-Hasa, about 100,000 of them in the town of Hofuf, about 55,000 in the town of al-Mubarraz, and the remainder in over fifty villages and hamlets. Hofuf used to be the capital of eastern Arabia, and is still an important administrative centre.

Dammam, about 10 miles north of Dhahran, is the eastern terminus of the Saudi Government Railroad. Most of the construction materials and heavy machinery destined for Riyad are imported through Dammam. Since 1953 Dammam has been the capital of the Eastern Province.

Ten miles up the coast from Dammam is the **Qatif** oasis, with an estimated population of 50,000. The town of

Qatif, has a port, now little used except by fishermen, and a population of approximately 10,000. Farther northwest along the coast of the Arabian Gulf, between Ras Tanura and Ras al-Mish'ab, is the port of **Jubail,** which was the first headquarters of the Aramco geologists in their search for oil.

THE OIL CENTRES

The oil industry has established three large centres at Dhahran, Abqaiq and Ras Tanura, as well as several smaller ones. Dhahran, the headquarters of Saudi Aramco, is centrally located in the Dammam oil field. Dhahran is also the location of the largest international airport in Saudi Arabia. The Abqaiq community, about 40 miles southwest of Dhahran, lies in the great oil fields of the same name. The peninsula of Ras Tanura, which is the site of the Company's refinery and oil shipping terminal is about 25 miles by air and 45 miles by road north of Dhahran.

THE TRADE CENTRE

Seven miles east of Dhahran is the trade centre of **Al Khobar.** The town's merchants and craftsmen cater to the Western tastes of Saudi Aramco employees, who find there a large variety of American and European clothing, household goods and luxury articles.

POPULATION

The great majority of the inhabitants are Arabs although there are small ethnic groups especially those who have entered the country on pilgrimages or to work in the expanding oil industry.

Almost all Saudi Arabs, regardless of their racial origins, have at least two characteristics in common: they speak Arabic and they are Muslims.

Not all Arabs meet the genealogical qualification of a blood line traceable back through the ages to one or the other of two ancestors. The Bedouins of the desert are regarded commonly as the chief repository of this pure stock.

The coastal towns and the oil industry's installations have the highest proportion of foreign elements in Saudi Arabia. Mecca, where pious Muslims from all over the world have chosen to live and die, also has a very heterogeneous population.

THE BEDOUINS

The life of the Bedouins naturally differs from that of their settled countrymen. Their occupations as herdsmen keeps them moving back and forth over the desert. Their homes are tents, because of the need for a portable shelter, but the design of these tents provides a maximum of shade and ventilation.

Under the Faysal Model Settlement Scheme launched in 1965 by the Ministry of Agriculture the Bedouins are expected to be gradually brought round to a more settled way of life on reclaimed land irrigated by artesian wells and distribution canals. Early in 1971 the scheme received its first batch of settlers after the network of asphalt roads, linking production and marketing centres, had been opened to traffic.

CLIMATE

Saudi Arabia has a desert climate. In Jeddah, it is warm and humid for most of the year. Temperatures seldom rise above 38 degrees C (100 degrees F) but the high humidity, which can often exceed 90% (particularly in September) can be very tiring.

OFFICIAL PUBLIC HOLIDAYS

The weekly holiday is Friday although many retail shops remain open on that day. The following public holidays are observed when all Government and business offices are closed.

Id al-Adha
Id al-Fitr
Muslim New Year
Birthday of the Prophet

The Constitution

Saudi Arabia is an independent monarchy under the predominant religious influence of the Sunnite Wahabi sect of Islam. Its only formal written constitutional law is a set of Organic Instructions established for the governing of al-Hijaz in 1926 and a decree of October 1935, amplified by later regulations, setting up a Council of Ministers.

The monarch is the centre of the Saudi government. In essence the government is based on traditional forms of law and institutions and it operates according to principles deeply embedded in the consciousness and understanding of the people. Such institutions and principles function as a constitution in a broad sense and tend to give greater strength and stability to the existing order than could be achieved through lip service to a formal constitution.

The principles of government are justice, consultation and equality in accordance with Islamic law.

In August 1993 a decree was issued announcing the members (60 members and a chairman increased to 90 in 1997) of the Consultative Council); and in September details of a new provincial system of government. (13 Regions and 103 Governorates).

Region	Capital	Governor
Riyadh	Riyadh	Prince Salman Ibn ABDU-LAZIZ
Mecca	Mecca	Prince Majed Ibn ABDULA-ZIZ
Medina	Medina	Prince Abdulmajeed Ibn AB-DULAZIZ
Qassim	Brida	Prince Faisal Ibn Bandar Ibn ABDULAZIZ
Eastern Region	Dammam	Prince Mohamed Ibn FAHD
Asir	Abha	Prince Khaled AL FAISAL

Tabuk	Tabuk	Prince Fahd Ibn Sultan Ibn ABDULAZIZ
Hail	Hail	Prince Muqren Ibn ABDULAZIZ
Northern Border	Arar	Prince Abdullah Ibn Abdulaziz Ibn Musaed Ibn JILUWI
Jizan	Jazan	Prince Mohamed Ibn Turki Ibn AL SUDAIRI
Narjan	Narjan	Prince Fahd Ibn Khaled AL SUDAIRI
Baha	Baha	Prince Mohamed Ibn Saud Ibn ABDULAZIZ
Jouf	Sakaka	Prince Sultan Ibn Abdulrahman AL SUDAIRI

The Cabinet

(June. 1999)

Prime Minister: H.M. King Fahad Ibn ABDULAZIZ AL SAUD

First Deputy Prime Minister and Commander of National Guard: H.R.H. Prince Abdullah Ibn ABDULAZIZ AL SAUD

Second Deputy Prime Minister and Minister of Defence and Civil Aviation: H.R.H. Prince Sultan Ibn ABDULAZIZ AL SAUD

Minister of Public Works and Housing: Prince Muteb Ibn ABDULAZIZ AL SAUD

Minister of Interior: Prince Nayef Ibn ABDULAZIZ AL SAUD

Minister of Foreign Affairs: Prince Saud AL FAISAL Ibn ABDULAZIZ AL SAUD

Minister of Justice: Abdullah Ibn Mohamed Ibn Ibrahim AL SHEIKH

Minister of Higher Education: Khalid Ibn Mohamed AL ANQARI

Minister of Islamic Affairs, Endowments, Call and Guidance: Sheikh Saleh Ibn Abdulaziz Ibn Mohamed Ibn Ibrahim AL SHEIKH

Minister of Finance and National Economy: Ibrahim Ibn Abdulaziz AL ASSAF

Minister of Planning: Khaled Ibn Mohamed AL GOSEIBI

Minister of Pilgrimage: Ayad Ibn Amin MADANI

Minister of Commerce: Osama Ibn Jaafar Ibn Ibrahim AL FAQUIH

Minister of Health: Osama Ibn Abdul Majid SHOBOKSHI

Minister of Agriculture and Water Resources: Abdullah Ibn Abdulaziz Ibn MUAMMAR

Minister of Oil and Mineral Resources: Ali Ibrahim AL NUAIMI

Minister of Telegraphs, Posts and Telecommunications: Khaled Ibn Mohamed AL GOSEIBI

Minister of Information: Fouad Ibn Abdul Salam Ibn Mohamed FARISI

Minister of Municipal and Rural Affairs: Mohamed Ibn Ibrahim AL JARALLAH

Minister of Education: Mohamed Ibn Ahmed AL RASHEED

Minister of Labour and Social Affairs: Ali Ibn Ibrahim AL NAMLEH

Minister of Civil Services: Mohamed Ibn Ali FAYEZ

Minister of Transport: Nasir Ibn Mohamed AL SALLUM

Minister of Industry and Electricity: Hashem Ibn Abdullah Ibn Hashem YAMANI

Ministers of State: Prince Abdulaziz Ibn Fahd Ibn Abdulaziz AL SAUD, Mutlib Ibn Abdullah AL NAFISA, Abdulaziz Ibn Ibrahim AL MANIE, Musaed Ibn Mohamed AL AYBAN, Madani Ibn Abdulkader ALAQI, Mohamed Ibn Abdelaziz AL SHEIKH, Abdulaziz Abdullah AL KHUWEITER

Foreign Embassies

Afghanistan: Tariq al-Madina, Kilo No.3, Jeddah; tel. (2)53142.

Algeria: POB 94388, Riyadh 11693; tel. (1)488-7171

Argentina: POB 94369, Riyadh 11693, tel. (1)465-2600

Australia: POB 94400. Riyadh 11693; tel. (1)488-7788

Austria: POB 94373, Riyadh 11693; tel. (1)477-7445

Bahrain: POB 94371, Riyadh 11693; tel. (1)488-0013

Bangladesh: POB 94395, Riyadh 11693; tel. (1)465-5300

Belgium: POB 94396, Riyadh 11693; tel. (1)488-2888

Bosnia and Herzegovina: P.O.Box 94301, Riyadh 11693; Tel. (1)4544360

Brazil: POB 94348, Riyadh 11693; tel. (1)488-0018

Burkina Faso: POB 94300, Riyadh 11693; tel. (1)465-2244

Burundi: POB 94355, Riyadh 11693; tel. (1)464-1155

Cameroon: POB94336, Riyadh 11693; tel. (1)488-0203

Canada: POB 94321, Riyadh 11693; tel. (1)488-2288

Chad: POB 94374, Riyadh 11693; tel. (1)465-7702

China, People's Republic: P.O.Box 75231, Riyadh 11578; Tel. (1)4824246

Côte d'Ivoire: P.O.Box 94301, Riyadh 11693; Tel. (1)4825582

Denmark: POB 94398, Riyadh 11693; tel. (1)488-0101

Djibouti: POB 94340, Riyadh 11693; tel. (1)454-3182

Egypt: POB 94333, Riyadh 11693; tel. (1)465-8425

Ethiopia: POB 94341, Riyadh 11693; tel. (1)477-5285

Finland: POB94363, Riyadh 11693; tel. (1)488-1515

France: POB 94367, Riyadh 11693; tel. (1)488-1255

Gabon: POB 94325, Riyadh 11693; tel. (1)463-2664

Gambia: POB 94322, Riyadh 11693; tel. (1)465-1320

Germany: POB 8974, Riyadh 11492; tel. (1)488-0700

Ghana: POB 94339, Riyadh 11693; tel. (1)464-1383

Greece: POB 94375, Riyadh 11693; tel. (1)465-9094

Guinea: POB 94326, Riyadh 11693; tel. (1)488-1121

India: POB 94387, Riyadh 11693; tel. (1)488-4144

Indonesia: POB 94343, Riyadh 11693; tel. (1)488-2800

Iran: POB 94394, Riyadh 11693; tel. (1)488-1916

Ireland: POB 94349, Riyadh 11693; tel. (1)488-2300

Italy: POB 94389, Riyadh 11693; tel. (1)488-1212

Japan: POB 4095, Riyadh 11491; tel. (1)488-1100

Jordan: Riyadh 11693; tel. (1)488-0071
Kenya: POB 94358, Riyadh 11693; tel (1)488-2484
Korea, Republic: POB 94399, Riyadh 11693; tel. (1)488-2211
Kuwait: POB 2166, Riyadh 11451; tel. (1)488-3500
Lebanon: POB 94350, Riyadh 11693; tel. (1)465-1000
Libya: POB 94365, Riyadh 11693; tel. (1)454-4511
Malaysia: POB 94335, Riyadh 11693; tel. (1)488-7100
Mali: POB 94331, Riyadh 11693; tel. (1)465-8900
Malta: POB 94361, Riyadh 11693; tel. (1)463-2345
Mauritania: POB 94354, Riyadh 11693; tel. (1)465-6313
Mexico: POB 94391, Riyadh 11693; tel. (1)482-8218
Morocco: POB 94392, Riyadh 11693; tel. (1)481-1858
Nepal: POB 94384, Riyadh 11693; tel. (1)402-4758
Netherlands: POB 21683, Riyadh 11485; tel. (1)488-0011
New Zealand: POB 94397, Riyadh 11693; tel. (1)476-6602
Niger: POB 94334, Riyadh 11693; tel. (1)464-3116
Nigeria: POB 94386, Riyadh 11693; tel. (1)482-3024
Norway: POB 94380, Riyadh 11693; tel. (1)488-1904
Oman: POB 94381, Riyadh 11693; tel. (1)465-0010
Pakistan: POB 6891, Riyadh 11452; tel. (1)476-7266
Philippines: POB 94366, Riyadh 11693; tel. (1)454-0777
Portugal: POB 94328, Riyadh 11693; tel. (1)464-4853
Qatar: POB 94353, Riyadh 11461; tel. (1)482-5544
Russia: POB 94308, Riyadh 11693; Tel. (1)4811875
Rwanda: POB 94383, Riyadh 11693; tel. (1)454-0808
Senegal: POB 94352, Riyadh 11693; tel. (1)454-2144
Sierra Leone: POB 94329, Riyadh 11693; tel. (1)463-3149
Singapore: POB 94378, Riyadh 11693; tel. (1)465-7007
Somalia: POB 94372; Riyadh 11693; tel. (1)454-0111
South Africa: POB 94006, Riyadh 11693; Tel. (1)4543723
Spain: POB 94347, Riyadh 11693; tel. (1)488-0606
Sri Lanka: POB 94360, Riyadh 11693; tel. (1)463-4200
Sudan: POB 94337, Riyadh 11693; tel. (1)482-9666
Sweden: POB 94382, Riyadh 11693; tel. (1)488-3100
Switzerland: POB 9265, Riyadh 11413; tel. (1)488-1291
Syria: POB 94323, Riyadh 11693; tel. (1)465-3800
Tanzania: POB 94320, Riyadh 11693; tel. 454-2839
Thailand: POB 94359, Riyadh 11693; tel. (1)482-6002
Tunisia: POB 94368, Riyadh 11693; tel. (1)465-4585
Turkey: POB 94390, Riyadh 11613; tel. (1)464-8890
Uganda: POB 94344, Riyadh 11693; tel. (1)454-4910
United Arab Emirates: POB 94385, Riyadh 11693; tel. (1)482-6303
United Kingdom: POB 94351, Riyadh 11693; tel. (1)488-0077
USA: POB 9041, Riyadh 11413, tel. (1)488-3800
Uruguay: POB 94346, Riyadh 11693; tel. (1)455-0146
Venezuela: POB 94364, Riyadh 11693; tel. (1)476-7867
Yemen: POB 94356, Riyadh 11693; tel. (1)464-2116

The Economy

The economy remains heavily dependent on the oil sector and consequently continues to be vulnerable to developments in the international oil market. The government's efforts to diversify the economy have brought about some modifications. However an increasingly large contribution is expected from trade, agriculture and especially manufacturing.

The government's "Fourth Development Plan" (1985-1990) included the following objectives: further diversification of the economy – especially in terms of industry and additional services – stimulation of the private sector, agricultural development, and education and training with a view to ensuring an adequate supply of Saudi manpower.

In the Fifth Development Plan (1990–1995) government expenditure will total 753 billion Saudi Riyals, of which the civilian sector will account for almost 500 billion Saudi Riyals. Military spending will absorb about 34 per cent of the total. The target annual economic growth rate is 3.2% and the Plan will focus on stimulating private enterprise, creating new jobs and reducing the government deficit.

The oil industry will continue to constitute around one third of General Domestic product and over 80% of export earnings. As a result, price movements on the world oil market will continue to have a major impact on economic performance. Agricultural production, (which contributes about 8% of gross domestic product), which is subsidised, and the non-oil sector grew rapidly, with output rising by 11.3% and 10.4% respectively.

On July 3, 1995, the Council of Ministers approved the "Sixth Development plan" (1995–2000). One of the major objectives is to increase the private sector's contribution to the national economy by diversifications and creation of new jobs. It forcasts an average yearly economic rate of 3.8 per cent.

On December 1997, the 1998 budget announced was set at expenditure 196 Billion riyals and revenue at 178 billion Riyals.

On December 28, 1998, the 1999 budget announced was set at expenditure 165 billion Riyals and revenue at 121 billion Riyals.

HYDROCARBONS

At 261.5 barrels, Saudi Arabia's proven oil reserves at the end of 1998 were equal to a quarter of the world's total known reserves. In 1985 annual production of crude oil was 3,6m b/d. Having abandoned its role as swing producer, Saudi Arabia raised its oil production in 1986 to 5.2m b/d. However, because of the precipitous decline in prices, oil export revenues that year fell to a low of US$ 18.3 billion. In 1987, output was 4.36 b/d, 1988 output was 5.26m b/d and in 1989 5.2m b/d and in 1990 production averaged 6.4m b/d and in 1991 due to the abscence of Iraqi and Kuwaiti oil, Saudi Arabia increased its production to an averaqge 8.2m b/d. In 1992 average production was 8.38m b/d and in 1993 8.13m b/d. In 1994 production was 8.00m b/d, in 1995 8.02m b/d and in 1996 8.15m b/d. In 1997 production was 8.35m b/d and in 1998 7.44m b/d. Proven gas reserves were estimated at 5.790 billion cubic meters at the end of 1998. Production is gaining in importance as an energy supply for domestic industry, and is increasingly used in the production of fertilizers, methanol and liquid petroleum gas (LPG); LPG is largely exported.

The Banking System

Saudi Arabian Monetary Agency: Est. 1952; Airport Road, P.O.Box 2992, Tel. (1)463-3000, Riyadh

Al-Bank Al-Saudi Al-Fransi: Est. 1977; P.O.Box 56006, Tel. (1)401-0288, Riyadh 11554

Al-Bank Al-Saudi Al-Hollandi: Est. 1977; P.O.Box 1467, Tel. (1)406-7888, Riyadh 11431

Al Rajhi Banking and Investment Co.: Est. 1988; P.O.Box 28, Tel. (1)405-4244, Riyadh 11411

Arab Investment Co. S.A.A.: Est. 1974; P.O.Box 4009, Tel. (1)476-0601, Riyadh 11491

Arab National Bank: Est. 1980; P.O.Box 56921, Tel. (1)402-9000, Riyadh 11564

Bank al-Jazira: P.O.Box 6277, Tel. (2)631-8070, Jeddah 21442

National Commercial Bank: Est. 1954; P.O.Box 3555, Tel. (2)644-6644, Jeddah 21481

Riyadh Bank Ltd.: Est. 1957; Old Airport Road, P.O. Box 22622, Tel. (1)401-3030, Riyadh 11416

Saudi American Bank: P.O.Box 833, Tel. (1)477-4770, Riyadh 11421

Saudi Arabian Agricultural Bank: Est. 1963; P.O.Box 11126, Tel. (1)402-2361, Riyadh

Saudi British Bank: P.O.Box 9084, Tel. (1)405-0677, Riyadh 11413

Saudi Credit Bank: Est. 1973; P.O.Box 3401, Tel. (1)402-9128, Riyadh

Saudi Investment Bank: Est. 1976; P.O.Box 3533, Tel. (1)477-8433, Riyadh 11481

United Saudi Bank: Est. 1987; P.O.Box 25895, Tel. (1)478-4200, Riyadh 11476

Transport

RAILWAYS

Saudi Railways Organization: P.O.Box 36, Dammam.

Independent Organization with a Board of Directors headed by the Minister of Communications

ROADS

Existing network of asphalted roads is over 150,000 Km. Several new roads are planned for construction.

National Transport Company of Saudi Arabia: P.O.Box 7280, Jeddah.

Shipping - The ports of Jeddah (principal port) Dammam (second largest port), Yanbu (cargo port) Jizan and Jubail, as well as minor ports are under the management of the Ports Authority.

Civil Aviation - Saudi Arabian Airlines: Est. 1945; Saudia Building. P.O.Box 620, Jeddah; regular international services with the USA, Europe Africa and Asia.

Airports: Some 25 airports are in operation, of which three are international airports, namely King Abdul Aziz International Airport, in Jeddah, King Khalid International Airport in Riyad, and the Eastern Province King Fahd International Airport in Dhahran.

Universities

Islamic University of Imam Muhammad Ibn Saud
Est. 1953; P.O.Box 5701, Tel.: 4054448, Riyadh

Islamic University
Est. 1961; P.O.Box 170, Tel.: 8224080, Medina

King Abdulaziz University
Est. 1967; P.O.Box 1540, Tel.: 6879033, Jeddah 21441

King Fahad University of Petroleum and Minerals
Est. 1963; Dhahran, Tel.: 860-0000, Dhahran 31261

King Faisal University
Est. 1975; P.O.Box 1982, Dammam

King Saud University
Est. 1957; P.O.Box 2454, Tel.: 476-0000, Riyadh 11451

Umm Al Qura University
Est. 1979; P.O.Box 407/715, Tel.: (02)5564770, Mecca

Umm Al Qura University, Taif Campus
Est. 1981; Al Saddad Rd., Shihar, Tel.: 7469008, Taif

Radio, Television and the Press

RADIO

Saudi Arabian Broadcasting Service: Ministry of Information, Airport Rd., Jeddah; programmes in Arabic and English and for overseas services in Urdu, Indonesian, French, Persian, Swahili and Somali.

Saudi Aramco Radio: P.O.Box 96, Dhahran; music and programmes in English.

TELEVISION

Saudi Arabian Government Television Service: Ministry of Information, P.O.Box 570, Riyadh; broadcasts in Arabic and English.

Saudi Aramco TV (Dhahran-HZ-22-TV): Room 300, Administration Bldg. Dhahran: non-commercial; film-chain operation only.

THE PRESS

Arab News: Est. 1976; P.O.Box 4556, Jeddah; English; Daily

Al-Bilad: Est. 1934; P.O.Box 7095, King Abdul Aziz St., Jeddah; Arabic; Daily

Al-Jazirah: P.O.Box 354, Riyadh; Arabic; Daily

Al-Madina al-Munawara: Est 1937; P.O.Box 807, Jeddah; Arabic; Daily

Al-Nadwah: Est. 1958; P.O.Box 5803 Mecca; Arabic; Daily

Okaz: Est. 1960; P.O.Box 1508, Jeddah; Arabic; Daily

Al-Riyadh: P.O.Box 2943, Riyadh; Arabic; Daily

Saudi Review: Est. 1966; P.O.Box 4288, Jeddah; English; monthly.

Saudi Gazette: Est. 1975; Mina Rd., P.O.Box 5576, Jeddah; English; Daily

Al-Yaum: Est. 1964; P.O.Box 565, Dammam

Saudi Economic Survey: Est. 1976; P.O.Box 1989, Jeddah

Al-Manhal: 44 Shahrah Arafet, P.O.Box 2925, Jeddah; Arabic; Monthly

Majallat al-Iqtisad wal Edara: P.O.Box 1540, Centre of Research and Development, King Abdul Aziz Univ., Jeddah; Monthly

Al-Sharkiah-Elle: P.O.Box 6, Riyadh; Arabic; Monthly

Al-Tijarah: Est. 1960; P.O.Box 1264, Jeddah; pub. by Jeddah Chamber of Commerce and Industry

Ahlan Wa Sahlan: P.O.Box 4288, Jeddah; pub. by Saudi Arabian Airlines. (SAUDIA)

NEWS AGENCY

Saudi Press Agency: Est. 1970; P.O.Box 7186 Riyadh.

SOMALIA
(Somali Democratic Republic)

SOMALIA

Capital	: Mogadishu
Area	: 637.657 sq. Km.
Population	: 9.3 million (1995 estimate)
Currency	: Somali Shilling which is divided into 100 Centisimi
Coins	: ½ , 1 Somali Shilling Coins: 1, 5, 10 Centisimi; Notes: 5, 10, 20, 100 Somali Shillings.

Geography

As whole, the country presents a harsh environment, part of it being semidesert. The northern coastal plains, which stretch from the Gulf of Tadjoura (Tajura) along the Gulf of Aden into Mijirtein region, are particularly arid, and from their scorched appearance in the dry seasons are known locally as guban («burned»). Inland this barren coastal strip gives place to the maritime range, the Ogo Highland (Surud Ad) near Erigavo, 7,894 ft. (2,406m), running from Afars and Issas parallel with the coast and descending gradually southward into the vast tilting Haud Plateau. This plateau has an average height of 3,000 ft. (900 m) in the centre but rises much higher in the Harar highlands to the west into Ethiopia. The highlands slope gradually and fairly regularly from the northwest and are intersected by lowlying plains and valleys are much more widely spaced in the south than in the precipitate north. The Juba River and the Webi Shbeli contain water all the year round and provide the main river system of the whole area. Both rivers descend from the Ethiopian highlands.

POPULATION

The Somali population is estimated at 9.30 million. The main cities are Mogadishu, Hargeisa, Kismayu, Berbera and Merca.

CLIMATE

From June to September, especially, the northern coast is unbearably hot and virtually deserted. Berbera and Bender Kassim have average maximum temperatures of 42°C (108°F) and 40° (104°), respectively, with a minimum of 21° (70°).

The largest towns are: Mogadishu, capital of the republic; Merca or Merka and Hargeisa and Berbera, capital and port of the Northern regions, respectively.

RELIGION

Islam is the State Religion

PUBLIC HOLIDAYS

Labour Day (May 1st); Independence Day (June 26); Foundation of the Republic (July 1st); Id al Fitr, end of Ramadan; Id al Adha, Feast of the Sacrifice National Day, anniversary of military coup in 1969 (Ocotber 21); United Nations Day (Oct. 24); Mouloud, Birth of the Prophet.

LANGUAGE

The 2 official languages are Somali and Arabic.

History

From their connection with the Ethiopian hinterland, their proximity to Arabia, and their export of precious gums, ostrich feathers, ghee (clarified butter), and other animal produce, as well as slaves from farther inland, the northern and eastern Somali coasts have for centuries been open to the outside world. This area probably formed part of Punt, "the land of aromatics and incense", mentioned in ancient Egyptian writings. Between the 7th and 10th centuries of trading posts along the Gulf of Aden and Indian Ocean coasts. Many of the early Arab geographers mentioned these and the sultanates that grew out of them, but they rarely described the interior of the country in detail. In fact intensive exploration really began only after the occupation of Aden by the British in 1839 and the ensuing scramble for Somali possessions by Britain, France, and Italy.

THE IMPERIAL PARTITION

About the middle of the 19th century the Somali Peninsula became a theatre of competition between Great Britain, Italy, and France. On the African continent itself Egypt was also involved and later Ethiopia, expanding and consolidating its realm under the guiding genius of Emperor Menelika II. Britain's interest in the northern Somali coast followed the establishment (1839) of the British coaling station at Aden or the short route to India. The Aden garrison relied upon the import of meat from the adjacent Somali coast. France sought its own coaling station and obtained Obock on the Danakil coast in 1862, later thrusting eastward and developing the Somali port of Djibouti. Farther north, Italy opened a station in 1869 at Aseb. Stimulated by these European maneuvers, Egypt revived Turkey's ancient claims to the Red Sea coast. In 1870 the Egyptian flag was raised at Bulhar and Berbera, but with the disorganization caused by the revolt in the Sudan, however, Egypt was obliged to curtail its colonial responsibilities, and evacuate Marar and its Somali possessions in 1885.

ESTABLISHMENT OF THE SOMALIA REPUBLIC

During World War II the British Protectorate was evacuated (1940) but was recaptured with Italian Somalia in 1941 when Ethiopia was also liberated. With the exception of French Somali land, all the Somali territories were then united under British military administration. In 1948 the Protectorate reverted to the Colonial Office; the

Ogaden and the Haud were gradually surrendered to Ethiopia; and in 1950 the Italians returned to Somalia with ten years to prepare the country for independence under a United Nations trusteeship.

Taking advantage of the modest progress which the British military administration had effected, the Italians rapidly pursued social and political advancement, although economic development proved much more difficult. The effect of these changes was naturally felt also in the British Protectorate, which, in the event, became independent on June 26, 1960. On July 1 Somalia followed suit and the two territories joined to form the Somali Republic. On July 12 Abdirashid Ali Shermarke was nominated prime minister.

In 1967 Shermarke (replaced as prime minister by Abdirazak Hajj Husain in 1964) was elected to the Presidency and Muhammad Hajj Ibrahim Egal became prime minister. The new government achieved a detente with Ethiopia and Kenya in disputes caused on the one hand by the Somali government's refusal to recognize Ethiopia's rights to the Ogaden and to grazing lands as set out in the Anglo - Ethiopian Treaty of 1897 and the agreement of 1954, and, on the other hand, by the failure of the independent government of Kenya to accede to the wish of Somali tribesmen in the north-eastern area of Kenya to join.

A further general election in March 1969 led to the entrenchment of the government's Somali Youth League, with Muhammad Hajj Ibrahim Egal reappointed as prime minister. This result left many people dissatisfied, and led to a situation of increasing public unrest accompanied by increasingly autocratic acts on the part of the president and the government. On Oct. 15, 1969, the president, Shermarke, was assassinated by a policeman while on a tour of the Northern Region. The ensuing rushed attempts by the prime minister to secure the election to the presidency of his candidate formed the immediate background against which the army and the police seized power on Oct. 21. Ministers and a number of other prominent people (including the former commander of the police) were placed under arrest, and parliament was dissolved. A supreme Revolutionary Council was then set up and announced that it would replace corruption and tribal nepotism with justice and restore to the republic its democratic heritage while securing real social and economic progress. The republic's name was also changed to the Somali Democratic Republic.

Relations between Somalia and Kenya, which had deteriorated following the signing in December 1980 of a joint Ethiopian – Kenyan communiqué on "Somali expansionism", improved in June 1981 when President Siyad Barre and President Arap Moi of Kenya signed a co-operation accord which ended several years of hostility between the two countries.

The improvement in relations between the two countries was preceded by a Somali offer of economic co-operation, made by Dr. Hussein Abdulkadir Quasim, then Somali Minister of Mineral Resources and Water Development, who was reported by Mogadishu radio on June 17 as having told Kenyan television that Somalia was prepared to participate in economic cooperation between the countries of the Horn of Africa.

Other developments in Somalia's foreign relations included (i) a tour of West Africa by President Siyad Barre in June 1981, which included the signing on June 5 of a co-operation agreement with Nigeria (covering economic, scientific, technical, cultural and educational fields), and visits to Benin, Ivory Coast and Sudan; (ii) an announcement by Signor Emilio Colombo, the Italian Foreign Minister, on Aug. 6, 1981, that Italy would provide over $ 200,000,000 in aid to Somalia (the package including a new three-year economic and technical co-operation agreement and an increase in food aid); (iii) an announcement on Feb. 1, 1982, that Portugal and Somalia had established diplomatic relations at ambassadorial level.

In the 1980s there was widespread discontent and the country was faced with many difficulties, economic, social, political. Moreover there were several political parties all struggling and fighting each other for control of the country, (to cite some of the most important, Democratic Front for the Salvation of Somalia (DFSS), Somali Democratic Movement, Somali National Movement, Somali Patriotic Movement (SPM) until in the years 1989 and 1990 it led to open fighting between rebel groups active all over the country and government troops. The rebels controlled Mogadishu the capital in January 1991, President Syad Barre fled the capital, and a new government was formed on 20 January headed by Omar Arteh Ghaleb, and Ali Mahdi Mohamed was appointed as temporary President for a period of two years. However in the second half of 1991 a sudden Coup d'Etat took place and President Ali Mahdi Mohamed was replaced by Mohamed Farah Idid.

In May 1991 leaders in the northern parts of the country declared unilateral independence and formed the Republic of Somaliland. However, so far they have not been recognised internationally as an independent state.

By the end of 1991 the country was close to anarchy, and a large part of the population was threatened with famine.

In mid 1992 relief agencies intensified their distribution of food aids, and by September UN peace-keeping forces were deployed. Many armed incidents took place, and following increasing international criticism of the UN operation, several nations participating in the operation have expressed their wish to withdraw their troops in early 1994.

In early March 1995 the last UN personnel were evacuated from Somalia. At the same time no political progress has been made to bring about a solution among the faction leaders in the country.

Political Parties

Democratic Front for the Salvation of Somalia: Est. 1981; Mogadishu, Somalia

United Front of Somalia: Est. 1989; Mogadishu, Somalia
Somali Democratic Alliance: Est. 1989; Mogadishu, Somalia
Somali Patriotic Movement: Est. 1989; Mogadishu, Somalia
United Somali Congress: Est. 1989

Foreign Embassies

Algeria: P.O.Box 2850, Tel. 81696, Mogadishu
Bulgaria: Hodan District, Km 5, off Via Afgoi, P.O.Box 1736, Tel. 81820, Mogadishu
China, People's Republic: P.O.Box 548, Tel. 20805, Mogadishu
Cuba: Mogadishu
Djibouti: Mogadishu
Egypt: Via Makka al Mukarrama, Km 4, P.O.Box 76, Tel. 80781, Mogadishu
Ethiopia: P.O.Box 368, Mogadishu
France: Corso Primo Luglio, P.O.Box 13, Tel. 21715, Mogadishu
Germany, Federal Republic: Via Mahmoud Harbi, P.O.Box 17, Tel. 20547, Mogadishu
India: Via Jigjiga, Shingrani, P.O.Box 955, Tel. 21262, Mogadishu
Iran: Via Makka al Mukarrama, P.O.Box 1166, Tel. 80881, Mogadishu
Iraq: Via Makka al Mukarrama, P.O.Box 641, Tel. 80821, Mogadishu
Italy: Via Alto Giuba, P.O.Box 6, Tel. 20544, Mogadishu
Kenya: Via Mecca, P.O.Box 618, Tel. 80857, Mogadishu
Korea, Democratic Republic: Via Km 5, Mogadishu
Kuwait: First Medina Rd., Km 5, P.O.Box 1348, Mogadishu
Libya: Via Medina, P.O.Box 125, Mogadishu
Nigeria: Via Km 5, Tel. 81362, Mogadishu
Oman: Via Afgoi, P.O.Box 2992, Tel. 81658, Mogadishu
Pakistan: Via Afgoi, Km 5, P.O.Box 339, Tel. 80856, Mogadishu
Qatar: Via Km 4, P.O.Box 1744, Tel. 80746, Mogadishu
Romania: Via Lido, P.O.Box 651, Mogadishu
Russia: Via Republica, P.O.Box 607, Mogadishu
Saudi Arabia: Via Benadir, P.O.Box 603, Tel. 22087, Mogadishu
Sudan: Via Mecca, P.O.Box 552, Mogadishu
Syria: Via Medina, P.O.Box 986, Mogadishu
Turkey: Via Km 6, P.O.Box 2833, Tel. 81975, Mogadishu
United Arab Emirates: Via Afgoi, Km 5, Tel. 23178, Mogadishu
United Kingdom: Hassan Geedi Abtow, P.O.Box 1036, Tel. 20288, Mogadishu
U.S.A.: Km 5, P.O.Box 574, Tel. 39959, Mogadishu
Yemen, Republic of: Via Km 5, P.O.Box 493, Mogadishu
Yugoslavia: Via Mecca, P.O.Box 952, Mogadishu
Zimbabwe: Mogadishu
Note: Most of the foreign diplomats have let the country since early 1995

The Economy

Somalia's centrally planned economy is based on livestock rearing which provides a subsistence livelihood for some three-quarters of the population and the major share of export earnings. Bananas, the second largest export earner, are grown on riverside plantations. Other products are cotton, other fruit, frankincense, of which Somalia is the world's leading producer, and subsistence maize and sorghum. The possible construction of a dam at Badhera on the Juba river has been under discussion for several years. Development of fishing is negligible. Somalia has a number of minerals, including uranium, gypsum, iron ore, coal, granite and zinc; exploration for oil has so far proved disappointing. Industry is small-scale, based on agricultural products, and some-recently completed ventures have been idle because of lack of foreign exchange for imported input. The economy has virtually collapsed because of the civil war, and the country faces enormous obstacles to its development. Foreign aid will be required for many years, even after peace is restored.

LIVESTOCK (In thousand head)

	1990	1991	1992	1993	1994	1995
Cattle	3,800	2,000	1,000	1,500	4,900	5,100
Sheep	12,000	9,500	6,000	6,500	13,800	13,400
Pigs	10	7	2	6	6	9
Asses	25	25	20	23	24	24
Mules	24	23	18	20	21	21

The Banking System

Central Bank of Somalia: Est. 1960; P.O.Box 11, Mogadishu; central bank and currency issuing authority.
Commercial Bank of Somalia: Est. 1990; P.O.Box 203, Mogadishu; branches throughout the country.
Somali Development Bank: Est. 1968; P.O.Box 1079, Mogadishu; branches in Hargeisa and Kismayo.

Insurance

State Insurance Company of Somalia: Est. 1974; P.O.Box 902, Mogadishu; Branches throughout Somalia.
Cassa per le Assicurazioni Sociali della Somalia: Est. 1950; P.O.Box 123, Mogadishu.

Trade and Development Organizations

National Agency of Foreign Trade: P.O.Box 602, Magadishu; state owned; Branches throughout the country.

Agricultural Development Corporation: Est. 1971; P.O.Box 930, Mogadishu.

Livestock Development Agency: P.O.Box 1759, Mogadishu; branches throughout the country.

Water Development Agency: P.O.Box 525, Mogadishu

Somali Oil Refinery Agency: P.O.Box 1241, Mogadishu

Transport

RAILWAYS

There are no railways in Somalia

ROADS

International associations (World Bank, International Development Association, the United Arab Emirates and China) helped building new roads and highways: 216 km. road project between Afgoi and Baidoia; highway between Belet-Uen and Burao; 110 km road between Berbera and Burao,... In all there are 23,600 Km of roads.

SHIPPING

Mogadishu (new port), Merca, Berbera and Kismayu are the chief ports.

CIVIL AVIATION

Mogadishu has an International airport. There are airports at Hargeisa and Baidoa.

Somali Airlines: Est. 1964; P.O.Box 726, Mogadishu; cargo, internal and international flights to Italy, Arabian Peninsula, and countries in Africa, (suspended in 1991)

Radio and The Press

Radio Hargeisa: Hargeisa.

Radio Mogadishu: Mogadishu.

THE PRESS

Heegan: Mogadishu, English; weekly.

Horseed: Mogadishu; Italian and Arabic; weekly.

Xiddigta Oktobar: Mogadishu; Daily newspaper

NEWS AGENCY

Sonna: Mogadishu: National News agency, P.O.B.: 1748, Mogadishu

SUDAN

(Republic of Sudan)

Sudan

President	: Brig. Gen. Omar Hassan Ahmed EL BACHIR
Capital	: Khartoum
Area	: 2,506,805 sq. Km.
Population	: 28.1 million (1995 estimate)
Currency	: 1 Sudanese Pound (£s) = 100 piastres = 1000 milliemes

Geography

The Republic of the Sudan is the largest country in Africa with an area of 2.5 million square kilometres, or 8.3% of the area of Africa and 1.7% of the land area of the world. It extends from the Egyptian border at lat. 220 North over a distance of approximately 1,400 miles, as far south as lat. 40 North. The east-west distance is about 1,200 miles. On the east the Sudan has boundaries with Ethiopia, and on the south Congo, while on the west it has common border with Chad, the Central African Republic and Libya. Its coastline extends over 400 miles.

The Sudan is watered by the Nile, which is formed by the confluence at Khartoum of the White Nile from Lake Victoria and the Blue Nile from Lake Tana. The northern part of the country starting just below the Tropic of Cancer down to some 300 kilometers south of Khartoum has a rainfall of less than 180 mm per annum and agriculture of all kinds is dependent upon irrigation. Further south the annual average rainfall increases to 500 mm or more, so that crops can be grown after the summer rains.

URBAN CENTRES

The Sudan is a very lightly urbanised country, having about 12% of its population living in towns and cities. The bulk of the country urban population is concentrated in a few principal cities of which the "Three Towns" are the most important.

Foremost as an urban centre is **Khartoum,** which has come to dominate the Sudan only really in the last century and a half. Before 1800 it was very small indeed, but its growth arises from a central position in what is now by far the richest zone of the country – the Central Clay Plains – and centre of routes by rail, road, river and air.

Across the river from Khartoum is **Omdurman,** larger in size than Khartoum and traditionally more of an "Islamic" centre and a focus of nationalist interests, this deriving to some extent from the presence of the Mahdi and his political supporters. Whilst Omdurman, longer established as a large town, became increasingly residential, Khartoum became the centre of British rule, and drew in, because of its better communications, a number of industrial and commercial activities.

The next larger town is **Port Sudan,** which has grown from tiny beginnings since about 1900. Previously, Suakin was the main sea outlet for the Sudan, but a restricted harbour site and difficult seaward approach through coral reefs led to the decision to create a new port some 65 kilometres further north. Port Sudan is on a well developed "sharm".

POPULATION

With a rate of natural increase of about 2.8% per year, the Sudan has one of the fastest growing population of the world. If the present rate of growth is to be maintained, the population of the Sudan is expected to double within the next 30 years.

The population is divided into three main categories: Sudanese, foreigners with Sudanese nationality, and aliens.

The Sudan comprises Arabs (40%), Nilotic or negroid peoples (20%), Western tribesmen (14%), Beja (including the Hadendowa 6%), Nuba (Arab negroid 5.5%), Nilo-Hamitic peoples, including Ethiopians (5%), and Sudanic peoples, a negroid group (5%).

RELIGION

No census of religion has yet been taken in the Sudan. The population of the six northern provinces is almost entirely Muslim (Sunni) apart from a few small areas of pagans and from the Christian communities, mostly in the towns. In the three southern provinces there are Christians and Muslims, but the majority are pagans.

The Christian elements are not numerically imposing, they include about 250,000 Catholics of Latin or the various oriental rites, a few thousand each of Greek Orthodox, Armenians, and Copts, perhaps 100,000 Protestants.

OFFICIAL HOLIDAYS

Independence Day; Bairam; New Year (A.H.); Martyrs Day (March 29); Ach-Sharikein (April 11); Sham an-Nassim (April 19); May Day (May 1); Prophet's Birth; 25 May Revolution (May 25); 21 October Revolution (October 21); Id al-Fitr; Christmas (December 25).

History

Man has lived in the Sudan for at least one million years and the valley of the Nile which wanders more than 4,000 miles from the lakes of Central Africa to the Mediterranean, may well be the cradle of civilisation, rather than the Euphrates. About four centuries before Christ the ox-driven waterwheel which still plays a vital role in the country's economy, was introduced to the Sudan. At the same time came camels, brought with them by the Persians when Cambyses invaded Egypt in 525 BC.

Homer knew of the Sudan and his countrymen visited it, to barter cloth, wine and trinkets for gum arabic, spices and slaves. Nero sent a reconnaissance expedition far up the river but the commander's experience with the "sudd" (Arabic for obstruction), a vast and impenetrable papyrus swamp in the southern Sudan, dissuaded the emperor from any thought of conquest. During the reign of Justinian, many Sudanese kingdoms were converted to Christianity and churches dotted the sweep of the Nile until the spread of Islam in the XVIth century.

Modern Sudanese history owes much to Napoleon. It was the victory in 1797, at the battle of the Pyramids which shook the power of the Mamelukes, the Caucasian ruling class of Egypt, and paved the way for the rise to power of the Albenian soldier of fortune Muhammad Ali.

Muhammad Ali sent his third son Ismail at the head of 10,000 men across the desert and, by 1821, all of north and central Sudan was his. For the first time, the Sudan- the name means "Land of Blacks" - began to take shape as a political entity.

Salvation was to come from the desert. Muhammad Ahmad, the son of a Dongola boat-builder, was born in 1844. He grew into a soft-spoken mystic and soon retired to Aba Island, 150 miles south of Khartoum, to live the life of a religious recluse, proclaiming himself in 1881 to be the Mahdi, the second great prophet. The tribes of the west rallied to the Mahdi's call for a war against the infidels and despots and, early in 1884, the Mahdi was master of all Sudan save Khartoum.

Britain, who meanwhile had moved into Egypt, resolved that the Sudan could not be held and sent General Charles Gordon to evacuate Khartoum. No man could have been more ill-fitted for the job, and after 317 days the Mahdi's dervish hordes overran the city's defences and razed Khartoum.

Five months after the fall of Khartoum, the Mahdi died of typhus; he was succeeded by Khalifa Abdallah. Hardly had he come to power when the Sudan was plunged in a series of civil wars.

In September 1898 the Anglo-Egyptian force led by General Herbert Kitchener met the Khalifa's 60,000 warriors on an open plain outside Omdurman, the new Sudanese city built across the Nile. Khalifa's casualties comprised 10,800 killed and 16.000 wounded, and Kitchener entered Omdurman as a conqueror.

On January 19, 1899 Britain and Egypt signed a condominium agreement under which the Sudan was to be administered jointly. In the twelve ensuing years, the Sudan's revenue had increased seventeenfold, its expenditure tripled, and its budget reached a balanced state which was to be maintained until 1960.

Mounting Egyptian nationalism in the period after World War I culminated in 1924 in the assassination in the streets of Cairo of Sir Lee Stack, Governor - General of the Sudan; British reaction resulted in the expulsion of all Egyptian officials from the Sudan.

After the Anglo-Egyptian "entente" of 1936, a few Egyptians were allowed to return to the country in minor posts. But the signing of the 1936 agreement stimulated Sudanese nationalists who objected both to the return of the Egyptians and to the fact that other nations were deciding their destiny. Expression of this feeling was seen in the formation of the Graduates' Congress, under the leadership of Ismail al-Azhari.

POLITICAL PARTIES

By 1945, two political parties had emerged. The National Unionist Party led by al-Azhari, demanded union of the Sudan and Egypt; it had the support of Sayed Sir Ali al-Mirghani, head of a powerful religious sect. The Umma Party, backed by Sayed Sir Abdur-Rahman al-Mahdi demanded unqualified independence and no links with Egypt.

END OF CONDOMINIUM

On February 12, 1953, Britain and Egypt signed an accord ending the condominium arrangement and agreeing to grant Sudan selfgovernment within three years. The agreement also provided for a senate for the Sudan, a Council of Ministers, and a House of Representatives, elections to which was to be supervised by an international commission.

The elections, which were held during November and December 1953, resulted in victory for the NUP, and its leader, Ismail al-Azhari, became the Sudan's first Prime Minister in January 1954. The replacement of British and Egyptian officers in the Sudanese civil service by Sudanese nationals followed rapidly.

INDEPENDENCE

On December 19, 1955, the Parliament voted unanimously that the Sudan should become "a fully independent sovereign state". British and Egyptian troops left the country on January 1, 1956; the same day a five-man Council of State was appointed to take over the powers of the governor-general until a new constitution was agreed.

Two years, later, on 17 November 1958 a bloodless army coup led by General Ibrahim Abboud toppled the Government of al-Azhari. On his assuming power, General Abboud declared that he would rule through a thirteen member army junta and that democracy was being suspended in the Sudan in the name of "honesty and integrity".

TROUBLE IN THE SOUTH

In 1966, Sadik al-Mahdi, the 30 year old President of the Umma Party, took over as Prime Minister. Internally the security situation in the southern Sudan continued to cause anxiety; successive Prime Ministers visited the South in April and October but neither threats nor blandishments succeeded in curbing the rebels.

The Ministry for Southern Affairs sought to restore normal life to those parts of the southern provinces under government control, but there was little or no security in Equatoria Province and the armed forces launched a major offensive against the rebel camps there in October 1970.

The war ended officially in March 1972, when Colonel Numeiry signed a peace pact with Major-General Lagu, the Leader of the Anya-Nya rebels in the south.

INTERNAL TURMOIL

In July 1976, President Numeiry survived the most serious threat so far to his eight-year-old regime. A coup attempt, masterminded by former finance minister Hussein al-Hindi and former prime minister Sadik al-Mahdi, both in exile, involved the infiltration of some 2,000 heavily armed civilians into Khartoum and Omdurman. The rebels caused much destruction, including the immobilisation of Sudan's Air Force on the ground.

Retribution was quick and severe; 98 were executed for their part in the plot, and several hundred were imprisoned. The July coup attempt brought Sudan closer to its two most powerful neighbours. A mutual defence pact was signed with Egypt immediately after the attempt, and this was followed by tripartite talks with Egypt and Saudi Arabia.

INDUSTRIAL UNREST (1981)

Industrial unrest in Sudan in 1981 included a national strike by the country's 43,000 railway and river transport workers in early June in support of a pay claim. After the SSU secretariat had on June 14 condemned the strike as politically motivated and as a "conspiracy directed from abroad".

On June 16, President Numeiry ordered the security forces to arrest the "saboteurs" responsible for the strike and decreed new measures to ban work stoppages and to bring all trade unions under the closer "supervision" of the SSU (Sudan Socialist Union).

Since 1971 Sudan has moved from close friendship with the USSR towards firmer ties with the West and the Arab world. This new direction in external relations has been matched by a change in internal economic policy. Nationalisation of private and foreign-owned businesses was reversed in 1973 with many confiscated businesses being returned to private ownership.

INTRODUCTION OF ISLAMIC LAW

President Jaafer Mohammed al-Numeiry announced on Sept.8, 1983 that the penal code had been revised in order to link it "organically and spiritually" with Islamic Law (Sharia). Theft, adultery, murder and related offences would henceforth be judged according to the Koran, and alcohol and gambling were both prohibited; non-Moslems, however, would be exempt from Koranic penalties except when convicted of murder or theft.

The inauguration of the new code was marked by a ceremony in the capital, Khartoum, on Sept.23, presided over by President Numeiry, in which stocks of alcohol were dumped in the river Nile.

The introduction of the new code followed a thorough reform of the judicial system announced by President Numeiry in June 1983.

STRIKES

Schools in Khartoum were closed on Aug.28 1983 following student protests concerning social conditions in the capital, which had suffered a series of power cuts throughout August.

A strike by doctors began on March 1, 1984, in protest over low pay and the deteriorating situation in the health service. All 2,000 of the country's doctors tendered their resignation on March 8 to be effective from March 24. The government rejected the resignations, however, and declared the doctors' union to be illegal. The union was subsequently reinstated.

TIME OF CHANGE

When a rising tide of refugees briefly provoked rioting in the city of Port Sudan in 1982, Sudanese President Gaafar Numeiry came under mounting pressure from some members of his government to close his nation's borders. Numeiry would have none of it. During a climatic Cabinet debate on the issue, he dramatically invoked the ancient Arab tradition of hospitality toward strangers. "They are the guests of Sudan", he said.

By February 1985 there were about 1 million refugees in the country, and their number could swell beyond 2 million, in 1986, according to relief officials. A spokesman for the United Nations High Commissioner of Refugees has described the situation as rapidly becoming "a disaster of major proportions".

By March 1985, some 500 metric tons of relief goods have been airlifted into Eastern Sudan on flights financed or provided by the United States of America, Sweden and by the United Nations High Commissioner for Refugees. Items delivered include 20,000 tents, 83,000 blankets, 19,000 water containers, 7 water tanks, 6 water storage tanks (50,000 litre capacity), 61,000 doses of oral rehydration salts, disinfectants, 10 emergency relief kits (to cover the needs of 100,000 persons for three months), refrigerators for medicines, 100,000 doses of measles vaccine, 3,500 drums of fuel, 65 tons of high protein/energy foods, 3 pre-fabricated warehouses and 10 additional vehicles. Further items have been made available in kind, particularly by agencies currently working in Sudan.

On the basis of the present caseload estimates, the United Nations High Commissioner for Refugees's financial requirements (other than basic food) for the relief programme amounted as of 11 January 1985 to US$ 14,526,000.

Once regarded as the potential breadbasket of the Arab world, Sudan has in four years gone from being an exporter to an importer of its sorghum, a grainlike staple crop. Through a combination of bad weather and over-grazing of arable land production fell from 3.4 million tons in 1981 to 1.3 million tons in 1984. The result has been bread shortages throughout the country, even in the capital of Khartoum.

In the troubled southern Sudan, guerilla war waged by the members of the Southern Sudan People's Liberation Army has spread from the Upper Nile and Bahr El Ghazal regions to Equatoria. The rebels, who are mostly Christians and animists, have chafed under domination for years. In 1983, Sharia Law replaced existing law; abolished in 1987 and reinstated in 1991 with the exception of the southern provinces.

Their major victory has so far been to interrupt, by killing, or by capturing non-Sudanese workers, two major economic projects: oilfields under exploration by Chevron Oil Co., and the Jonglei Canal in southern Sudan.

In early 1985 discontent with Numeiry's regime had been growing and in April while in visit to the USA, he was deposed in a military coup led by Lt. Gen. Swar Al Dahab, who after a period, passed the reigns of government to civilian rule, headed by Sadiq Al Mehdi. Again in 1988 and early 1989 following further discontent in the country and within the military, another bloodless coup d'Etat took place on June 30, 1989 led by Brig. Omar Hassan Ahmed El Bashir who formed a 15 member Revolutionary Command Council for National Salvation. Head of State, Prime Minister and Minister of Defence, he quickly dismantled civilian rule, constitution was suspended, and the National Assembly and all political institutions were dissolved. In mid October 1993 Brig. Omar Hassan Ahmed El Bashir dissolved the Revolutionary Command Council; and on October 30 announced the formation of a new government. In March 1996, elections were held and a National Assembly of 400 seats have been elected and presided by Dr. Hassan Turabi. In April 1998 a new constitution was approved by the National Assembly.

The Cabinet

(Jan. 2000)

Prime Minister: Brig. Gen. Omar Hassan Ahmad EL BACHIR
Minister of the Presidency: Maj. Gen. Bakri Hassan SALEH
Minister of Cabinet Affairs: Abdella Hassan AHMED
Minister of Defence: Mustafa Osman Ismail SIR-EL-KHATIM
Minister of Foreign Affairs: Mustafa Osman ISMAIL
Minister of the Interior: Maj. Gen. Abdelrahim Mohamed HUSSEIN
Minister of Justice: Ali Mohamed Osman YASSIN
Minister of Finance and National Economy: Mohamed Khair AL ZUBAIR
Minister of Culture and Information: Ghazi Salaheddin ATABANI
Minister of Federal Relations: Ahmad Ibrahim AL-TAHIR
Minister of Energy and Mining: Awad Ahmed AL-JAZ
Minister of Social Planning: Qutbi al-Mahdi AHMAD
Minister of National Industry and Investment: Abdelhalim Ismail AL MUTAAFI
Minister of Agriculture and Forestry: Hajj Adam YUSUF
Minister of Foreign Trade: Mekki Ali BALAYIL
Minister of Higher Education and Scientific Research: Zubair Bashir TAHA
Minister of Education: Abdelbasit ABDELMAJID
Minister of Roads and Telecommunications: Mohamed Taher ILA
Minister of Tourism and Environment: Maj. Gen. AL-TIJANI Adam AL TAHIR
Minister of Survey, Construction and Development: Joseph MALWAL
Minister of Animal Resources: Abdullah Mohamed SID AHMAD
Minister of Irrigation and Water Resources: Kamal Ali MOHAMED
Minister of Manpower: Maj. Gen. Allison Manami MAGAYA
Minister of Health: Abulqasim Mohamed IBRAHIM
Minister of Transport: Lam Akol AJAWIN
Minister of Aviation: Lt-Gen. Ibrahim Sulaiman HASSAN

Foreign Embassies

Algeria: Str. 31, New Extension, P.O.Box 80, Tel. (11)741954, Khartoum
Chad: 21 Str. 17, New Extension, P.O.Box 1514, Tel. (11)742545, Khartoum
China, People's Republic: 93, Str. 22, P.O.Box 1425, Tel. (11)222036, Khartoum
Czech: 39, Str. 39, P.O.Box 1047, Tel. (11)743448, Khartoum
Denmark: Gamhouria Str., Nazer Bldg., P.O.Box 2758, Tel. 80489, Khartoum
Egypt: el Gamma Str., P.O.Box 1126, Tel. (11)772836, Khartoum
Ethiopia: 6,11A Str., 3, New Extension, P.O.Box 844, Khartoum
France: Junction 19th and Ali Dinar Str., Bloc 6H, East Plot 2, P.O.Box 377, Tel. (11)225608, Khartoum
Germany: Baladia Str., Block No. 8DE, P.O.Box 970, Khartoum
Greece: Gamhouria Str., Block 5, No.30, P.O.Box 1182, Khartoum
Holy See: Kfouri, Belgravia, P.O.Box 623, Khartoum
Hungary: Block 12AE, House 1, Str. 1 New Extension, P.O.Box 1029, Khartoum
India: 61 Africa Rd., P.O.Box 707, Khartoum
Iran: House No. 8, Square 2, Mogran, Tel. (11)748843, Khartoum
Italy: Str. 39, P.O.Box 793, Tel. 45326, Khartoum
Japan: 24, Block AE, Str. 3, New Extension, P.O.Box 1649, Khartoum
Jordan: 25, Str. 7, New Extension, Tel. 43264, Khartoum
Kenya: P.O.Box 8242, Khartoum
Korea, Democratic People's Republic: House No.59, 1 Str. 31, New Extension, P.O.Box 332, Khartoum
Korea, Republic: House 2, Str. 1, New Extension, P.O.Box 2414, Khartoum
Kuwait: Africa Ave., P.O.Box 1457, Khartoum
Lebanon: 60, Str. 49, P.O.Box 1407, Khartoum
Libya: 50 Africa Rd., P.O.Box 2091, Khartoum

Morocco: 22, Str. 19, New Extension, P.O.Box 2024, Khartoum

Netherlands: Str. 47, House No.47, P.O.Box 391, Khartoum

Niger: Str. 1, New Extension, P.O.Box 1283, Khartoum

Nigeria: Str. 17, el Mek Nimr Str., P.O.Box 1538, Khartoum

Oman: Str. 49, New Extension, P.O.Box 2839, Khartoum

Pakistan: House No.6 Block 12AE, Str. 3, New Extension, P.O.Box 1178, Khartoum

Poland: 73 Africa Rd., P.O.Box 902, Khartoum

Qatar: Str. 15, New Extension, P.O.Box 223, Khartoum

Romania: House 20, Block AE, Str. 3, New Extension, P.O.Box 1494, Khartoum

Saudi Arabia: Str. 29, New Extension, P.O.Box 258, Khartoum

Somalia: Str. 23-25, New Extension, P.O.Box 1857, Khartoum

Spain: Str. 3, New Extension, P.O.Box 2621, Khartoum

Switzerland: New Aboulela Bldg., P.O.Box 1707, Khartoum

Syria: Str. 3, New Extension, P.O.Box 1139, Khartoum

Tanzania: House No.6, Sq. 42, P.O.Box 6080, Khartoum

Tunisia: 18 Baladiya Ave., P.O.Box 8270, Khartoum

Turkey: 31, Str. 29, New Extension, P.O.Box 771, Khartoum

Uganda: Plot No.9, Block 9L, Str. 35, P.O.Box 2676, Khartoum

Russia: B1, A10 Str., New Extension, P.O.Box 1161, Khartoum

Unite Arab Emirates: St. 10, off Baladia St, P.O.Box 801, Tel. (11)777105, Khartoum

United Kingdom: New Aboulela Bldg., P.O.Box 801, Khartoum

U.S.A.: Ali Abdellatif Ave., P.O.Box 699, Khartoum

Yemen: Str. 35, New Extension, P.O.Box 1010, Khartoum

Yugoslavia: Str. 31, 79A, P.O.Box 1180, Khartoum 1

Justice

Civil justice is administrated through the High Court of Justice in Khartoum, province courts, and district judges. There is a body of civil law; where there is no special enactment. Cases are decided according to "justice, equity, and good conscience". The criminal code is based upon the Indian Penal Code and is dispensed in major, minor, and magistrate's courts. There are also people's courts that try a substantial proportion of civil and.criminal cases in accordance with popular custom. Islamic law was reintroduced in 1991, but was not applied in the three southern provinces.

The Economy

Sudan, the largest country in Africa covering over 2 1/2 million square kilometres, remains largely undeveloped and the majority of the population lives at subsistence level. Agriculture is the mainstay of the economy generating about 40% of Gross Domestic Product (GDP), and more than (90%) of exports and half of government revenues. Although the private sector is expanding, the public sector nevertheless continues to account for around half of employment and investment and nearly 80% of export earnings.

Whilst investment, particularly in the public sector, has picked up in recent years, economic development is constrained by a number of factors including inadequate transport, communications and services, and shortages of both unskilled and skilled labour. In addition, a shortage of foreign exchange and the consequent need to curtail imports has meant that capital equipment and spare parts have been in short supply.

A major factor in the present economic malaise is difficulty in fiscal policy. In the absence of external funds, for example, Arab finance has not been as forthcoming as expected, the government has been forced to borrow from the domestic banking system to finance large budget deficits.

INDUSTRIAL & MINERAL DEVELOPMENT

Industry, which a decade ago was virtually non-existent, now accounts for some 18% of GDP and provides employment for around 2% of the population. In the main, industrial establishments are either small-or medium-scale utilising indigenous agricultural products and producing for the domestic market. Activities include textiles and footwear manufacture, food processing, sugar refining and the production of cement.

Mining, although presently small-scale, is expanding rapidly with the aid of foreign capital. Various programmes are underway for the exploration and exploitation of minerals thought to be available in commercially-viable quantities, including copper, gypsum, gold, magnesite, asbestos, iron, mica, chromite, marble, limestone, kaolin, talc and manganese. Deposits of oil and natural gas were discovered in early 1981 in the south of the country by the (US) Chevron oil company who ceded its concession to a local company. The government is actively seeking to develop the oil sector.

AGRICULTURE

Successful exploitation of the immense agricultural potential is regarded as the key to economic development. The Sudan has over 200 million acres suitable for agriculture although only around 15 million are currently cultivated, mostly on a subsistence basis. The Arab oil states, who wish to reduce their dependence on western industrial countries for food, see the country as a future "breadbasket of the Arab World". Towards this end, a 25-year programme, which in the coming years will form part of overall development planning, has been drawn up by the Arab Fund for Economic and Social Development, based in Kuwait. A total of 100 agricultural and infrastructural projects are to be undertaken in the first ten years at a cost of some US$6 1/2 billion. The plan has not been implemented.

Of the considerable number of projects to develop both arable and pastoral farming, the Gezira irrigated farming project is perhaps the most successful, producing 75% of total cotton output. Other important projects include the Rahad irrigation scheme, the first phase of which was opened in December 1977, the Kenana Sugar Estate, which however, has faced rapidly rising costs and falling international sugar prices, and the Jonglei canal project in the South, which aims at providing irrigation and a navigable waterway and parallel road.

Although the stage is set for a swing from cotton to other agricultural products as major exports by the end of next decade, cotton will nevertheless remain of considerable economic importance. In recent years, world demand has switched from favouring the long variety (once the bulk of Sudanese output) to the medium staple. In response, Sudanese cotton growers have increased the area set aside for this variety, and in 1996 it represented 22 per cent of total exports. Other important agricultural products are groundnuts, gum arabic, sesame, sugar cane, sorghum and millet.

Livestock (cattle, sheep, goats) also accounted for about 13% of exports value.

The Banking System

Bank of Sudan: Est. 1960; Gamma Ave., P.O.Box 313, Tel. (11)778064, Khartoum

Al Baraka Bank: Est. 1984; Hashim Hago Bldg., P.O.Box 3583, Tel. (11)780688, Khartoum

Agricultural Bank of Sudan: Est. 1957; P.O.Box 1363, Tel. (11)779410, Khartoum

Bank of Khartoum: Est. 1913; 8 Gamhouria Ave., P.O.Box 1008, Tel. 772880, Khartoum

Blue Nile Bank Ltd.: Est. 1983; Zubeir Pasha Ave., P.O.Box 984, Tel. 778925, Khartoum

Faisal Islamic Bank (Sudan): Est. 1978; Ali Abdellatif Ave., P.O.Box 10143, Tel. 781848, Khartoum

Habib Bank: Est. 1982; Baladia Ave., P.O.Box 8246, Tel. 781498, Khartoum

Nilein Industrial Bank of Sudan: Est. 1961; United Nations Sq., P.O.Box 1722, Tel. 780929, Khartoum

Islamic Cooperative Development Bank: Est. 1983; P.O.Box 62, Tel. 780223, Khartoum

Mashreq Bank PSC: Baladia St, P.O.Box 371, Tel. (11)772969, Khartoum

Middle East Bank Ltd.: Est. 1982; Al Qasr Ave., P.O.Box 1950, Tel. 773696, Khartoum

National Bank of Abu Dhabi: Est. 1976; Atbara Str., P.O.Box 2465, Tel. 774870, Khartoum

National Bank of Sudan: Kronfli Bldg., al Qasr Ave., P.O.Box 1183, Tel. 778153, Khartoum

Omdurman National Bank: Est. 1993; P.O.Box 11522, Tel. (11)770400, Khartoum

People's Cooperative Bank: P.O.Box 922, Tel. 773555, Khartoum

Saudi Sudanese Bank: Est. 1986; Baladia St., P.O.Box 1773, Tel. (11)776700, Khartoum

Sudan Commercial Bank: Est. 1960; al Qasr Ave., P.O.Box 1116, Tel. 779836, Khartoum

Sudanese Estates Bank: Est. 1967; Baladia Ave., P.O.Box 309, Tel. 777917, Khartoum

Sudanese French Bank: Est. 1978; Zubair Basha St., P.O.Box 2775, Tel. (11)776542, Khartoum

Sudanese Savings Bank: Est. 1974; P.O.Box 159, Tel. (11)772000, Khartoum

Trade Organizations

Aboulela Cotton Ginning Co. Ltd.: P.O.Box 121, Tel. 770020, Khartoum

AGIP (Sudan) Ltd.: Est. 1959; P.O.Box 1155, Tel. 780253, Khartoum

Agricultural Research Corporation: P.O.Box 126, Wadi Medani

Animal Production Public Corporation: P.O.Box 624, Tel. 778555, Khartoum

Automobile Corporation: P.O.Box 221, Tel. 778555, Khartoum

Bata (Sudan) Ltd.: Est. 1950; P.O.Box 88, Tel. 732240, Khartoum

The Blue Nile Brewery: Est. 1954; P.O.Box 1408, Khartoum

Cement and Building Materials Sector Coordination Office: P.O.Box 2241, Tel. 774269, Khartoum

The Central Desert Mining Co. Ltd.: Est. 1946; P.O.Box 20, Port Sudan

Engineering Equipment Corporation: P.O.Box 97, Tel. 773731, Khartoum

Food Industries Corporation: P.O.Box 2341, Tel. 775463, Khartoum

Gum Arabic Co.: Est. 1969; P.O.Box 857, Tel. 777288, Khartoum

Industrial Production Corporation: P.O.Box 1034, Tel. 771278, Khartoum

Kenana Sugar Co. Ltd.: Est. 1971; P.O.Box 2632, Tel. 744297, Khartoum

Khartoum Commercial and Shipping Co.: P.O.Box 221, Tel. 778555, Khartoum

Leather Trading and Manufacturing Co. Ltd.: Est. 1986; P.O.Box 1639, Tel. 778187, Khartoum

Mechanized Farming Corporation: P.O.Box 2482, Khartoum

National Cotton and Trade Co. Ltd.: P.O.Box 1552, Khartoum

Port Sudan Cotton Trade Co. Ltd.: P.O.Box 261, Port Sudan

Public Agricultural Production Corporation: P.O.Box 538, Khartoum

Public Corporation for Building and Construction: P.O.Box 2110, Tel. 774544, Khartoum

Public Corporation for Irrigation and Excavations: P.O.Box 619, Tel. 780167, Khartoum

Public Corporation for Oil Products and Pipelines: P.O.Box 1704, Tel. 778290, Khartoum

Public Electricity Corporation: P.O.Box 1380, Khartoum

Rahad Corporation: P.O.Box 2523, Tel. 81381, Khartoum

Spinning and Weaving General Co. Ltd.: Est. 1975; P.O.Box 765, Tel. 774306, Khartoum

The State Trading Corporation: P.O.Box 211, Tel. 775175, Khartoum

Sudan Cotton Co. Ltd.: Est. 1970; P.O.Box 1672, Tel. 771567, Khartoum

Sudan Development Corporation: Est. 1974; 21 el Amarat, P.O.Box 710, Tel. 472151, Khartoum

Sudan Gezira Board: HQ Barakat Wadi Medani, Gezira Province; P.O.Box 884, Tel. 740145, Khartoum

Sudan Oilseeds Co. Ltd.: Est. 1974; Parliament Ave., P.O.Box 167, Tel. 780120, Khartoum

Sudan Tobacco Co. Ltd.: P.O.Box 87, Khartoum

Transport

RAILWAYS

Sudan Railways Corporation: P.O.Box 1812, Khartoum and P.O.Box 65, Atbara

The total length of line open to traffic is estimated at approx. 5,000 km. The main railway lines run from: Khartoum to Al-Obeid (689 km); Ar-Rahad to Nyala (698 km); Sennar Junction to Kassala (455 km); Kassala to Port Sudan (550 km); Khartoum to Wadi Halfa (924 km); Abou Hamad to Karima (248 Km); Atbara to Haiya Junction (270 km); Ad-Daein-Way (630 Km).

ROADS

National Transport Corporation: P.O.Box 723, Khartoum

Public Corporation for Roads and Bridges: P.O.Box 756, Khartoum; Est. 1976

INLAND WATERWAYS

River Transport Corporation: P.O.Box 284, North Khartoum

River Navigation Corporation: Khartoum; Est. 1970; jointly owned by the Sudanese and the Egyptian Governments.

SHIPPING

Port Sudan and Suakin are the only ports on the Red Sea.

CIVIL AVIATION

Sudan Airways Co. Ltd: Amarat str. P.O.Box 19, Khartoum; Est. 1946; Government owned; internal and international services

Foreign airlines serving Sudan: Aeroflot, Air France, Alitalia, British Airways. Egyptair, Ethiopian Airlines, Interflug, Libyan Arab Airlines, MEA, Saudi Arabian Airlines, Yemen Airways.

Radio, Television and the Press

RADIO

Sudan National Broadcasting Service: P.O.Box 572, Omdurman; government controlled radio with daily broadcasts in Arabic, English, Somali.

TELEVISION

Sudan Television Service: P.O.Box 1094, Omdurman; Est. 1962; Daily programmes of news, educational and entertainment features.

THE PRESS

The Press in the Sudan was nationalized in 1970, and since 1989 only one weekly newspaper was permitted.

El Guwat El Musallaha: Est. 1969; armed forces publication: weekly newspaper

The two main Publishing houses are: El Ayam and El Sahafa; they publish most of the newspapers and magazines.

El Ayam: Est. 1953; P.O.Box 363, Khartoum

El Sahafa: Est. 1961; P.O.Box 1228, Khartoum

NEWS AGENCY

Sudan News Agency (SUNA): P.O.Box 1506, Gamhouria Ave., Khartoum

Foreign Bureaux:

Middle East News Agency (MENA); Iraqi News Agency; Xinhua;

Universities

Ahfad University for Women
Est. 1966; P.O.Box 167, Omdurman

Nilein University
Est. 1955; P.O.Box 1055, Khartoum

Omdurman Ahlia University
Est. 1986; P.O.Box 785, Tel.: 51489, Omdurman

Omdurman Islamic University
Est. 1912; P.O.Box 382, Tel.: 54220, Omdurman

University of Gezira
Est. 1975; P.O.Box 20, Wad Medani, 2667 Khartoum

University of Juba
Est. 1975; P.O.Box 82, Juba

University of Khartoum
Est. 1956; P.O.Box 321, Tel.: 775100, Khartoum

Museums

Ethnographical Museum: P.O.Box 178, Khartoum

Sudan Natural History Museum: P.O.Box 321, Khartoum

Sudan National Museum: P.O.Box 178, Khartoum

Tourism

Tourism and Hotels Corporation: P.O.Box 7104, Khartoum

SYRIA

(Syrian Arab Republic)

Syria

President	:	Lieutenant General Bachar Hafez al-ASSAD
Capital	:	Damascus (pop. 1.400.000)
Area	:	185,180 sq. km.
Population	:	14.6 million (1996 estimate)
Currency	:	Syrian Pound which is divided into 100 piastres
Exchange rate	:	US Dollar 1= 11.225 Syrian Pounds (May 1999

Geography

Syria is bounded by the Mediterranean and the Lebanese Republic on the West, by Israel and Jordan on the south, by Iraq on the east and by Turkey on the north. The frontier between Syria and Turkey (Nisibin - Jeziret ibn Omar) was settled by the Franco - Turkish agreement of June 1929.

There is plenty of land available in Syria but water severely limits its utilisation. Fortunately, rainfall is supplemented by the water brought down from the mountains by its rivers. The principal of these is the Euphrates which has its headwaters in Turkey and flows in a generally southeasternly direction across Syria into Iraq. Together with its most important tributary, the Khabour, which also rises in Turkey, it accounts for about 90% of the total annual flow of all Syrian rivers. In the west, the largest river is the Orontes which is fed by springs from the Lebanon and Anti-Lebanon ranges and flows northwards through the marshy area known as the Ghab into Turkey. Farther south the Barada river, rising in the Anti-Lebanon, supplies lifegiving water to the fertile Ghouta oasis around Damascus. In the extreme south the Yarmuk river flows along the Jordan river.

CLIMATE

The climate varies from region to region. The eastern and southern zones are almost rainless, the north has a deposit normally sufficient to support light vegetation and crops, the west enjoys up to 40 inches of rain in the mountains, with less but adequate amounts in the plains, valleys and coast.

POPULATION

Population growth has been steady over the last twenty-six years, almost doubling in number from a total of 2,649,058 in 1940 to 6,471,074 in 1969. 7,410,000 in 1975, before reaching 14.6 million in 1996.

Syria has been known through history to be the Mecca of Immigrants. Foreign elements who have settled in the country since the Arab Conquest in A.D. 636 are as numerous as they are variegated: Turks (VIIIth century), Circassians (XIIIth century), Tsherkess (1878), Albanians (1910), Armenians (1922), Kurds (XXIth century), and Palestinians (1967).

RELIGION

The religious groups within the population are the Sunni Muslims, Ismailis, Alawites and other Shi'its, Druzes and Christians.

PUBLIC HOLIDAYS

New year (1 January); Union Day (22 February); Revolution Day (8 March); Arab League Day (2 March); Easter; Independence Day (17 April); International Labour Day (1 May); Martyr's Day (6 May); Union of Arab Republics Day (1 September); Corrective Movement Day (16 November); Mulid al Nabi - birthday of the Prophet; Eid al Fitr, end of Ramadan, month of Muslim fasting and self - purification; Eid al Adha, feast of Sacrifice; Muslim New year, Ashura, day of mouring for Shi'ite Muslims.

History

Syria from the earliest times was successively invaded by the Canaanites, the Phoenicians, the Aramaens and the Nomad Tribes, the Egyptians, the Hittites, the Persian and the Macedonian Greeks.

Moslem invaders by their decisive victory in 636 on the Yarmuk, ruled all of Syria in the time of the Umayyad dynasty till the year 730. In 1098, the first Crusaders conquered Antioch but not the other towns and in 1174, Salah Eddine had control over Damascus and conquered Allepo in 1183. Salah Eddin destroyed the Kingdom of Jerusalem which was established by the Crusaders by his victory over them in 1187 at Hittin. The Crusaders regained control over the coasts of Syria after Salah Eddine's death.

After the First World War, Syria was brought under the influence of the French by a secret agreement negotiated between England, France and Russia (1916). In 1920 Syrian Nationalists called their country "The Independent State of Great Syria", but again in July 1920 French troops occupied Damascus as the San Remo Conference had given France a mandate for the whole of Syria.

INDEPENDENCE ACHIEVED

Following the capitulation of France soon after the beginning of World War II, the British and Free French stated to the Syrians and Lebanese "From henceforth you will be sovereign and independent peoples and you will be able either to form yourselves into separate states or to unite into a single state".

Independent Syria suffered teething trouble. In March 1949, the civilian government headed by Shukri al-Kuwatli came to an end when Col. Husni az-Zaim assumed power in a bloodless coup. Zaim was himself overthrown in August by Col. Sami al-Hinnawi. A third coup, led by Col. Fawzi Salu in conjunction with Col. Adib ash-Shishakli, followed in December; by November 1951 Shishakli had removed his associate by a fourth coup. Shishakli was overthrown in February 1954.

UNION WITH EGYPT

The years that followed the overthrow of Shishakli in Syria saw the rise of Pres. Gamal Abdel Nasser of Egypt to uncontested leadership of the pan-Arab unity movement. The continued interference of pro-western Iraq in Syrian affairs forced Syria to give up its sovereignty in Feb. 1958 to become, for the next three and one-half years, the "Northern Province" of the United Arab Republic (UAR) of which Nasser was President. The Union of Syria with Egypt proved a bitter disappointment. In September 1961 a coup led by Syrian army officers, re-established Syria as a sovereign and independent state.

In 1963 the National Council of the Revolution seized control in March, and in July Maj. Gen. Amin EL Hafez became President of the Council; and in 1964 became Head of the State. In 1970 Ahmed Khatib became acting President, and in March 1971 Gen. Hafez Assad was elected President for a period of Seven years. Reelected in February 1978, February 1985, and for a Fourth term in December 1991, and for a fifth term in February 1999.

VOTE OF CONFIDENCE

Syria gave its leader, President al-Assad, a big vote of confidence and concentrated even more power in his hands in a referendum on March 12, 1973 when 97.6 per cent of the voters approved a Constitution.

Under the new Constitution, the President will not only be Head of the State but commander-in-chief of the armed forces, secretary-general of the ruling Baath Socialist Party and President of the National Progressive Front which links minority groups with the Baathists.

THE FOURTH ARAB-ISRAELI WAR (OCT. 1–1973)

The Syrian Front – While the Egyptian armed forces were crossing the Suez Canal, the Syrian Army launched an offensive with some 1,400 tanks aimed at the recapture of the Golan Heights, which had been lost in the 1967 war. During the first three or four days the Syrians-who in the initial stages greatly outnumbered the Israelis on this front succeeded in driving more than 15 miles into Israeli-occupied territory, recapturing the "ghost town" of Quneitra which had been lost to the Israelis in 1967 and had been deserted by its inhabitants, and advancing across the Golan Heights to within a few miles of Israel proper; much of which they subsequently lost. A disengagement agreement was signed in May 1974.

OTHER DEVELOPMENTS

Implementing the "Taef Agreement", a treaty of fraternity, co-operation and co-ordination, was signed with Lebanon in May 1991. In July Syria accepted to participate in a Middle East peace conference based on UN Security Council Resolutions 242 and 338.

On December 3, 1991 and February 1999, President Hafez Assad was re-elected for a fourth and fifth term in a universal suffrage by an overwelming majority.

In January 1994 President Assad met U.S. President Bill Clinton in Geneva to discuss the Middle East peace process; and in October during a tour in the Middle East, President Clinton visited Damascus and held talks with President Assad in a attempt to break the impasse in the Syrian-Israeli negotiations. Negotiations were resumed in Washington and Sheperdstown on 15th December 1999 and the Syrian delegation was headed by H.E. the Foreign Minister Farouk Al Sharah. The second round of negotiations was held in Sheperdstown on January 3, 2000 but were later discontinued. A summit meeting between President Assad and President Clinton was held in Geneva on March 23, 2000 to revive the Peace Process.

On June 10, 2000 President Hafez al-Assad passed away and on June 25, 2000, Lieutenant General Bachar al-Assad has been nominated by the People's Assembly as the next President of Syria.

The Constitution

The Constitution defines Syria as a socialist popular democracy. Under its terms, the President has the power to appoint and dismiss his vice-president, Premier and Government Ministers, and also becomes C-in-C of the armed forces, secretary-general of the Baath Socialist party, and President of the National Progressive Front.

Legislative power is vested in the People's Assembly, whose members are elected by universal adult suffrage.

The Cabinet

(March 2000)

Prime Minister: Dr. Mohamed Mustafa MIRO

Deputy Prime Minister, Minister of Defence: Gen. Mustafa TLASS

Deputy Prime Minister for Public Services: Eng. Mohamed Naji ITRI

Deputy Prime Minister for Economic Affairs: Dr. Khaled RAAD

Minister of Foreign Affairs: Farouq AL SHARAH

Minister of Interior: Dr. Mohamed HARBEH

Minister of Economy and Foreign Trade: Dr. Mohamed EL IMADI

Minister of State for Foreign Affairs: Nasser KADDOUR

Minister of Finance: Dr. Mohamed Khaled AL MAHAINY

Minister of Health: Dr. Mohamed Ayad AL SHATTI

Minister of Agriculture and Agrarian Reform: Assaad MUSTAFA

Minister of Transport: Eng. Radwan MARTINI

Minister of Housing and Utilities: Eng. Housam AL SAFADI

Minister of Electricity: Eng. Mounib Bin Assaad SAEM

AL-DAHER
Minister of Waqfs: Mohamed Ben Abdelraouf ZIADEH
Minister of Petroleum and Mineral Resources: Mohamed Maher Ben Husni JAMAL
Minister of Local Administration: Salam AL-YASSIN
Minister of Information: Adnan OMRAN
Minister of Presidential Affairs: Haitham DHOUAIHI
Minister of Culture: Dr. Maha KNOUT
Minister of Tourism: Kassem MOKDAD
Minister of Education: Dr. Mahmoud AL SAYED
Minister of State for the Environment: Dr. Farouk AL ADLI
Minister of Justice: Nabil AL KHATIB
Minister of State for Planning: Dr. Issam AL ZAIM
Minister of Higher Education: Dr. Hassan RICHEH
Minister of Transport: Eng. Makram OBEID
Minister of State for Council of Ministers Affairs: Mohamed Mofdi SAIFO
Minister of Labour and Social Affairs: Dr. Bariah AL KODSI
Minister of Supply and Internal Trade: Dr. Ousama MAE'EL-BARED
Minister of Industry: Eng. Ahmad HEMMO
Minister of Irrigation: Taha AL ATRACHE
Minister of Construction: Nouhad MCHANTAT
Ministers of State: Dr. Hassan AL NOURI, Dr. Ihsan CHRAITEH, Makhoul ABOU HAMDAH

Foreign Embassies

Afghanistan: P.O.Box 12217; Tel. (11)6112910, Damascus
Algeria: Noss Bldg., Raouda, Damascus
Argentina: P.O.Box 116; Tel. (11)3334167, Damascus
Australia: Dakkak Bldg., 128A Farabi Str., East Villas, Mezzeh; Tel. (11)6664317, Damascus
Austria: Mohamed Naim al-Deker, 152A Farabi Str., East Villas, Mezzeh; Tel. (11)6116730, Damascus
Belgium: Syndicat des Medecins Bldg., al-Jalaa Str., Abou Roumaneh; Tel. (11)3332821, Damascus
Brazil: P.O.Box 2219; Tel. (11)333770, Damascus
Bulgaria: 4 Chahbandar Str., Damascus
Canada: P.O.Box 3394; Tel. (11)6116692, Damascus
Chile: P.O.Box 3561; Tel. (11)3331563, Damascus
China, People's Republic: 83 Ata Ayoubi Str., Damascus
Cuba: Oustwani and Charabati Str., 40 al-Rachid Str., Tel. (11)3339624, Damascus
Cyprus: P.O.Box 9269; Tel. (11)6130812, Damascus
Czech Republic: P.O.Box 2249; Tel. (11)3331383, Damascus
Denmark: P.O.Box 2244; Tel. (11)3331008, Damascus
Egypt: Tel. (11)3330756, Damascus
Finland: P.O.Box 3893; Tel. (11)3338809, Damascus
France: P.O.Box 769; Tel. (11)3338632, Damascus
Germany: P.O.Box 2237; Tel. (11)3323800, Damascus
Greece: Pharaon Bldg., 1 Farabi Str., East Villas, Mezzeh; Tel. (11)6113035, Damascus
Holy See: P.O.Box 2271; Tel. (11)3327550, Damascus
Hungary: P.O.Box 2607; Tel. (11)6110787, Damascus
India: P.O.Box 685; Tel. (11)3739081, Damascus
Indonesia: P.O.Box 3530; Tel. (11)6119630, Damascus
Iran: Mezzeh Highway, near al-Razi Hospital, Damascus
Italy: 82 al-Mansour Ave., Damascus
Japan: 15 al Jalaa Ave., Tel. (11)339421, Damascus
Jordan: Abou Roumaneh Str., Damascus
Korea, Democratic People's Republic: Fares al-Khouri-Jisr Tora Str., Damascus
Kuwait: Ibrahim Hanano Str., Damascus
Libya: Abou Roumaneh, Damascus
Mauritania: al-Jalaa, ave., Karameh Str., Damascus
Morocco: Farabi Str., East Villas, Mezzeh; Tel. (11)6110451, Damascus
Netherlands: P.O.Box 72; Tel. (11)3335119, Damascus
Norway: P.O.Box 7703; Tel. (11)3322072, Damascus
Oman: P.O.Box 9635; Tel. (11)6110408, Damascus
Pakistan: P.O.Box 9284; Tel. (11)6132694, Damascus
Panama: P.O.Box 2548; Tel. (11)224743, Damascus
Qatar: P.O.Box 4188; Tel. (11)336717, Damascus
Romania: P.O.Box 4454; Tel. (11)3327570, Damascus
Russia: Aleppo Str., Boustan al-Kouzbari, Damascus
Saudi Arabia: al-Jalaa ave., Damascus
Slovakia: P.O.Box 33115; Tel. (11)6132114, Damascus
Somalia: Ata Ayoubi ave., Damascus
Spain: P.O.Box 392, Damascus
Sudan: Tel. (11)6111405, Damascus
Sweden: P.O.Box 4266; Tel. (11)3327261, Damascus
Switzerland: P.O.Box 234; Tel. (11)6111972, Damascus
Tunisia: P.O.Box 4114; Tel. (11)660356, Damascus
Turkey: 56-58 Ziad ben Abou Soufian ave., Tel. (11)3331370, Damascus
United Arab Emirates: Housami Bldg., 62 Raouda Str., Damascus
United Kingdom: P.O.Box 37; Tel. (11)3712561, Damascus
USA.: P.O.Box 29; Tel. (11)3333232, Damascus
Venezuela: P.O.Box 2403; Tel. (11)3335356, Damascus
Viet-Nam: 9 Malki ave., Tel. (11)333008, Damascus
Yemen: Abou Roumaneh, Charkassieh, Damascus
Yugoslavia: P.O.Box 739; Tel. (11)3336222, Damascus

The Economy

Having a greater diversity of resources than many Middle Eastern countries – oil, gas, phosphates, a good river system and large agricultural area, a position on the east-west trade route, a strong commercial tradition and a relatively well-educated population – the Syrian economy has considerable potential.

AGRICULTURE

Farming employs about 32% of the labour force and contributes about 26% to GDP. About 45% of the land is arable, of which about three-quarters is cultivated, other land is used for nomadic animal husbandry, while the remainder is desert and mountain.

Extensive irrigation programmes, notably in the Euphrates basin have eased the problem of periodic droughts and consequent fluctuations in agricultural production.

Cotton was traditionaly the main export earner but has taken second place to oil since 1974 despite a rising volume of cotton exports. Development of improved strains of cotton seed has increased in the area planted. The cotton crop in 1997 was estimated at 1.000.000 tons, followed by sugar beet.

Grain crops, notably of wheat and barley, are of considerable importance, occupying about two-thirds of arable land. Tobacco, fruits (grapes, apricots, apples, plums, figs, watermelons) and vegetables (tomatoes, onions, potatoes, lentils) are significant. Stock raising is also important with herds of over 800,000 cattle, 1 million goats and 13 million sheep.

INDUSTRY

Most of the manufacturing industry is in the public sector, though a significant section remains in private hands and has government approval and contributes about 27% of gross domestic product. State industry is divided into six main groupings covering food, engineering, sugar, textiles, chemicals and building materials; the private sector is active in textiles, food products, leather, paper, chemicals, machinery and electrical goods, as well as in traditional crafts.

Cement production has grown fast following construction of several plants.

There has also been an expansion in fertilizer productions; production is based partly on the country's phosphate reserves and partly on feedstock from the Homs oil refinery.

The iron and steel industry has expanded in recent years with the addition of a new smelter and a steel pipe plant, and a rolling mill.

Mining of phosphates started in 1972 with production reaching 2 million tons in 1987. Further expansion by the state-owned company is expected to bring output considerably higher by the year 2000. While development of port facilities at Tartous should facilitate exports.

It is believed that substantial deposits of uranium are associated with the phosphate deposits and there are tentative plans for a nuclear power station if these resources can be exploited.

OIL AND GAS

Proven oil reserves at the end of 1998 of 2,500 million barrels are expected to last 12 years at present rates of production. Gas reserves of 1,260 billion cubic feet have been identified and major gas development projects are in progress. As a part of the oil produced is heavy and has a high sulphur content it is mixed with lighter blends before being refined. Refining capacity at the Homs refinery and the opening of a second refinery at Banias, give a total capacity of 11.4 million tons a year.

BUDGET

The 1993 budget was approved by the National Assembly on May 9, 1993, Expenditure was set at 123,018 million Syrian Pounds.

In 1994 the budget provided for total expenditure of 144,162 million Syrian Pounds. The People's Assembly in April 1995 approved the budget for 1995 setting expenditure at 162,040 million Syrian Pounds. The 1996 budget's total expenditure is 187,450 million Syrian Pounds and the 1997 budget estimated at 211,125 million Syrian Pounds. The 1998 budget was set at 237,300 million Syrian Pounds and the 1999 budget provided for a total expenditure of 255,000 million Syrian Pounds.

Syria's principal trading partners in 1994 were: exports to Italy, France, Russia, Spain, Saudi Arabia, Lebanon, Germany, Romania and the United Kingdom. Imports from France, Germany, USA, Turkey, Italy, Japan and Belgium, United Kingdom.

The Banking System

Central Bank of Syria: Est. 1956; P.O.Box 2254, Tel. (11)2212642, Damascus: 9 branches

Agricultural Bank: Est. 1924; P.O.Box 5325, Damascus; 55 branches

Commercial Bank of Syria: Est. 1967; Youssef el Azmeh Sq., P.O.Box 933, Tel. (11)2219390, Damascus; 37 branches

Industrial Bank: Est. 1959; P.O.Box 7578, Tel. (11)2228200, Damascus, 13 branches

Popular Credit Bank: Est. 1967; P.O.Box 2841, Tel. (11)2227604, Damascus; 43 branches

Real Estate Bank: Est. 1966; Al Furat Str., P.O.Box 2339, Tel. (11)2218602, Damascus, 13 branches.

Insurance

Syrian General Organization for Insurance: Est. 1953; nationalized company; Tajheez St., P.O.Box 2279, Damascus; operates throughout Syria

Transport

RAILWAYS

The Syrian railways system, total over 2000 Km.:

Syrian Railways: Est. 1897; P.O.Box 182, Tel. 2213900, Aleppo

General Organization for the Hejaz Syrian Railway: P.O.Box 134, Tel. (11)2215815, Damascus

ROADS

Four main networks of roads and highways link Syria to Lebanon, Jordan, Iraq and Turkey.

SHIPPING

Maritime traffic in Syria is handled through three harbours: Latakia, Banias, Tartus.

Latakia, the main harbour, is served by foreign shipping lines operating passenger-cargo vessels.

Syrian General Authority for Maritime Transport: P.O.Box 730, Tel. (11)2226350, Damascus

CIVIL AVIATION

The International Airport of Damascus is served by:

Syrian Arab Airlines: Est. 1946; P.O.Box 417, Social Insurance Bldg., Jabri Str. Damascus; international services to Europe, Africa and the Arabic Peninsula

FOREIGN AIRLINES

Air France, Alitalia, Aeroflot, Kuwait Airways, Lufthansa, Malev, PIA, Qantas, SAS, Saudia and Swissair etc...

Radio, Television and The Press

Directorate-General of Broadcasting and Television: Est. 1946, Omayad Square Damascus

RADIO

Service in Arabic, French, English, Russian, German, Spanish, Hebrew, Turkish, Bulgarian and Polish.

TELEVISION

Services started in 1960.

THE PRESS

Al-Baath: Est. 1946; P.O.Box 9389, Mezze Highway, Damascus; Arabic; organ of the Baath Arab Socialist Party; daily

Al-Thawrah: P.O.Box 2448, Damascus; Arabic; Political; daily

Al-Jamahir Al Arabia: Aleppo; Political; Arabic; daily

Al-Fida: Rue Kuwatly, Hama; Arabic; daily

Tishrin: P.O.Box 5452, Damascus; Arabic; daily

Jaysh al-Shaab: P.O.Box 3320, Blvd. Palestine, Damascus; army magazine; Arabic weekly

al-Masira: Damascus; political; weekly

Al-Nass: P.O.Box 926, Aleppo; Arabic; weekly

Al-Kanoun: Ministry of Justice, Damascus; Arabic; monthly

Al-Maarifa: Ministry of Culture, Damascus; literary, Arabic; monthly

Al-Majalla al-Toubiya al-Arabiya: Al-Jalla's St., Damascus; Medical; Arabic; monthly

Monthly Survey of Arab Economics: P.O.Box 2306, Damascus; English and French; monthly

Al-Shourta: Directorate of Public Affairs and Moral Guidance, Damascus; Arabic; Monthly

Al-Yakza: Sisi St., Al Yaksa Association, Aleppo; monthly

PRESS AGENCIES

Agence Arabe Syrienne d'Information: Est. 1966; Damascus

Foreign Bureaux: Agencia EFE (Spain); Agenzia Nationale Stampa Associata (ANSA) (Italy); Agence France-Press (AFP), etc.

Universities

Al Baath University
Est. 1979; P.O.Box 77, Tel.: 31440, Homs

University of Aleppo
Est. 1960; Tel.: (21)236130, Aleppo

University of Damascus
Est. 1903; Tel.: (11)2215100, Damascus

Tishreen University
Est. 1971; Tel.: (431)236311, Lattakia

Tourism

Ministry of Tourism: Est. 1972; Victoria St., Damascus

Middle East Tourism: Est. 1966; P.O.Box 201, Fardoss Str., Damascus; 7 branches.

TUNISIA
(Republic of Tunisia)

Tunisia

Head of State	: Zain el Abidine BIN ALI
Capital	: Tunis (pop. 700,000)
Area	: 164,150 sq. Km.
Population	: 9.20 million (1997 estimate)
Currency	: The official unit of currency is the Tunisian dinar (D) divided into 1,000 milliemes (m). The following denominations are in circulation: Notes ½ -1 - 5 - 10 - 20 Dinars Coins 1 - 2 - 5 - 10 - 20 - 50 - 100 - 500
Exchange Rate	: Dinars per US $ = 1.156 (May 1998)

Geography

Geographically, Tunisia occupies a key position between the eastern and western basins of the Mediterranean: the Sicilian Channel between Cape Bon (Tunisia) and Sicily is only 80 miles wide and is therefore one of the busiest stretches of water in the world.

While it is only some 63,000 square miles in area, Tunisia has a long seaboard, stretching for 745 miles. This is the main feature distinguishing Tunisia from its neighbour Algeria, where the Tell Atlas barrier stops the valuable influence of the sea, too close to the coast, and from Morocco, which is partly in the Sahara though it looks towards the Atlantic. The whole of Tunisia lies open to the Mediterranean.

Traditionally, Tunisia is divided into four main natural regions:

The North, crossed from west to east by the continuations of the Atlas Mountains (Kroumirian Mountains), is the area with the highest rainfall: 23 to 31 inches annually. Essentially it is an agricultural region and the Medjerda Valley, situated in it, is one of the richest plains in the country.

The Sahel : is a coastal zone stretching from Cape Bon to south of Sfax. Conditions there are ideal for growing olive trees which, with the local fisheries and intensive handicraft production, constitute the main source of wealth of the region, after tourism.

The Centre is a zone of steppe country separated from the North by a range of hills (Djebel Shambi 5,065 feet), where the influence of the sea can no longer be felt. Irrigation possibilities are relatively limited and the rainfall is less than 16 inches. The region is well-suited for stock-breeding.

The South is a pre-desert zone with rainfall of less then 8 inches. Its principal resources are in the oases, where certain crops (vegetables and dates mostly) can be grown and livestock raised.

CLIMATE

In the north, including the city of Tunis, the climate is **Mediterranean.** From May to mid-October temperatures **average** 30 degrees centigrade to 37 degrees centigrade; there is little rainfall except during the second half of September and in October.

In April and early May and from mid-October to mid-November, the weather is warm but unreliable.

PRINCIPAL CITIES AND TOWNS

Tunis, population 700,000, is the centre of Government and business, and, together with La Goulette, is the chief port.

Sfax, population 300,000, is the chief town of southern Tunisia, the second port and the centre for export of phosphates and olive oil.

Souss, population 130,000, and **Bizerte,** population 100,000, are ports and industrial and administrative centres. There is also a special petroleum port at La Skhira.

Kairouan, population 100,000, is an administrative centre and Islamic holy place.

Nearly all important business is handled through Tunis. With the exception of Sfax, none of the other towns is of any commercial importance.

LANGUAGE

Arabic, is the official language but for all commercial and technical needs French is more useful. English is only very rarely understood.

PRINCIPAL RELIGIONS

The majority of the people are Moslem, mostly Sunnis. The largest Christian community is Roman Catholic. There are also Protestant, Greek Orthodox and Jewish minorities.

PUBLIC HOLIDAYS

New Year's Day (1 January); Revolution Day (18 January); Mulid al Nabi-birthday of the Prophet; Independence Day (20 March); Martyrs' Day (9 April); Labour Day (1 May); Victory Day (1 June); Republic Day (25 July); Women's Day (13 August); Eid al Fitr - end Ramadan (2 days); Memorial Day - commemoration of the foundation of the Party in 1934 (3 September); Evacuation of Bizerta (15 October); Eid Al Adha (2 days); Muslim New Year.

History

Carthage founded in Tunisia the first empire recorded in history. In 534 Tunisia becomes part of the Byzantine Empire and by the end of the 10th century the Hillalian invasion brings the whole country under complete Arab domination. From a Spanish Protectorate in 1534, Tunisia became a Turkish province. In 1881 LE BARDO Treaty gave France responsability for Tunisia's defence and external relations and LA MARSA convention in 1883 formally established a french protectorate over Tunisia. In the ensueing years a large number of French settlers landed in Tunisia. In 1920 internal events in the protectorate lead to the formation of a Tunisian nationalist movement, and in 1934 the Neo-Destour Party was created. In June 1955, through negotiations with France, Tunisia achieved statehood. On 20 March 1956 a protocol agreement between France and Tunisia formally, recognized the country's independence and right to conduct her own foreign policy and to form an army. On 25 July 1957 the Tunisian Republic was proclaimed. Mr. Habib Bourguiba became its President. On 7 November 1987 Zine el Abidine BEN ALI was sworn in as its next President, re-elected March 20, 1994, reelected in October 1999 and sworn in as Presiden on 15 November 1999.

The Constitution

Tunisia became a republic in 1957. The Neo-Destour Party, the only one represented in the National Assembly or Majlis al Ummah, drew up the republican constitution of 1959, and was amended on 12 July 1988.

Main provisions: Legislative power is exercised by the National Assembly which is elected every five years by direct universal suffrage. All citizens who have attained the age of 20 have the right to vote.

The President is elected by Universal suffrage for a five year term which is renewable twice, consecutively, must have at least 40 years of age and not more than 70. The government may be censured by the National Assembly.

The Cabinet

(Nov. 1999)

Prime Minister: Mohammed GHANNOUCHI
Minister of State; Special Adviser to the President: Abdelaziz Ben DHIA
Secretary General to the Presidential Office: Slaheddine CHERIF
Secretary General to the Government: Abdallah KAABI
Minister Delegate to the Prime Minister in charge of Human Rights, Communications and Relations with the National Assembly: Dali JAZY
Minister of the Interior: Abdallah KALLEL
Minister of Defence: Mohamed JEGHAM
Minister of Foreign Affairs: Habib Ben YAHIA
Minister of Women's and Family Affairs: Neziha ZARROUK
Minister of Justice: Bechir TAKALI
Minister of Religious Affairs: Jelloul JRIBI
Minister of Social Affairs: Chedi NEFFATI
Minister of Agriculture: Sadok RABAH
Minister of Vocational Training and Employment: Moncer ROUISSI
Minister of Public Health: Hedi MHENNI
Minister of State Properties and Real Estate: Ridha GRIRA
Minister of Higher Education: Sadok CHAABANE
Minister of Communications: Ahmed FRIAA
Minister of International Cooperation and Foreign Investment: Fethi MERDASSI
Minister of Trade: Mondher ZENAIDI
Minister of Tourism and Handicrafts: Slaheddine MAAOUI
Minister of Finance: Tawfik BACCAR
Minister of Industry: Moncef Ben ABDALLAH
Minister of Culture: Abdelbaki HERMASSI
Minister of Youth, Children and Sports: Raouf NAJAR
Minister of Transport: Hassine CHOUK
Minister of Equipment and Housing: Slaheddine BELAID
Minister of Environment and Land Use Management: Faiza KEFI
Minister of Economic Development: Abdellatif SADDAM
Minister of Education: Ahmed Eyadh OUEDERNI

Foreign Embassies

Algeria: 18 rue de Niger, Tel. 783-166, Tunis.
Argentina: 10 rue Hassan et Hussain, al Menzah IV, Tel. 231-222, Tunis
Austria: 16 rue Ibn Hamdiss, al Menzah, B.P. 23, Tel. 751091, 1004 Tunis
Bahrain: 72 rue Moawia Ibn Abi Soufiane, al Menzah 6, Tel. 750865, Tunis
Belgium: 47 rue du 1er Juin, B.P. 1002, Tel. 792797, Tunis
Brazil: 37 Ave. d'Afrique, al Menzah, V, B.P. 64, Tel. 232-538, 1004 Tunis
Bulgaria: 5 rue Ryhane, Cité Mahragène, Tel. 798962, Tunis
Canada: 3 rue du Sénégal, Place Palestine, Belvédère, Tel. 796577, Tunis.
China, People's Republic: 41 Ave. Jugurtha, Tel. 282-090, Tunis
Cuba: 6 rue Yahia Ibn Omat, Mutuelleville, Tel. 712844, Tunis
Czech: 98 rue de Palestine, Belvédère, B.P. 53, Tel. 780456, Tunis
Denmark: 5 rue de Mauritanie, Place d'Afrique, B.P. 451, Tel. 792600, 1025 Tunis
Djibouti: 5 rue Fatma al Fahria, Mutuelleville, B.O. 71, Tel. 890-589, Tunis
Egypt: 16 Ave al Soyoubi, al Menzah, Tel. 792233, Tunis
France: Place de l'Indépendance, Tel. 860033, Tunis
Germany: 1 rue Hamra, Mutuelleville, Tel. 786-455, Tunis
Greece: 3 rue al Birouni, Mutuelleville, al Menzah, B.P. 58, Tel. 288-890, Tunis.
Hungary: 8 rue al Jahedh, al Menzah 1, Tel. 751987, Tunis
India: 4 Place Didon, Notre Dame, Tel. 891-006, Tunis
Indonesia: 117 Ave. Jugurtha, Mutuelleville, Tel. 893-127, 1002 Tunis
Iraq: Ave. Tahar B. Achour, route X2 m. 10, Mutuelleville, Tel. 890-633, Tunis
Italy: 37 rue Gamal Abdel Nasser, Tel. 321811, Tunis

Ivory Coast: 84 Ave. Hédi Chaker, Tel. 796601, Tunis
Japan: 10 rue Mahmoud al Matri, Belvédère, B.P. 95, Tel. 285-937, Tunis
Jordan: 87 Ave. Juguartha, Mutuelleville, Tel. 288-401, Tunis
Korea, Democratic People's Republic: 10 rue Holima Saodia, al Menzah, Tel. 231-715, Tunis
Korea, Republic: 16 rue Caracalla, Notre Dame, Tel. 894-357, 1002 Tunis
Kuwait: 40 route Ariane, al Menzah, Tel. 236-811, Tunis
Libya: 48 bis rue du 1er Juin, Tel. 236-666, Tunis
Mauritania: 17 rue Fatma Ennechi, al Menzah, B.P. 62, Tel. 234-935, Tunis
Morocco: 39 Ave. du 1er Juin, Tel. 782-775, Tunis
Netherlands: 6-8 rue Meycen, Belvédère, B.P. 449, Tel. 797724, 1025 Tunis
Pakistan: 7 rue Ali Ibn Abi Taleb, al Menzah, Tel. 234-366, Tunis.
Poland: 4 rue Sophonisbe, Notre Dame, Tel. 795118, Tunis
Portugal: 2 rue Sufetula, Belvédère, Tel. 893-981, 1002 Tunis
Qatar: 2 rue Dr. Burnet, Belvédère, Tel. 285-600, Tunis
Romania: 22 rue Dr. Burnet, Belvédère, Tel. 766926, Tunis
Russia: 31 rue du 1er Juin, Tel. 882446, Tunis.
Saudi Arabia: 16 rue d'Autriche, Belvédère, Tel. 281-295, Tunis
Sénégal: 122 Ave. de la Liberté, Tel. 282-544, Tunis
Somalia: 6 rue Hadramout, Mutuelleville, Tel. 289-505, Tunis
Spain: 22 Ave. Dr. Ernest Counseil, Cité Jardin, Tel. 782217, Tunis
Sudan: 30 Ave. d'Afrique, Tunis
Sweden: 87 Ave. Taieb Mhiri, Tel. 860580, Tunis
Switzerland: 10 rue Chenkiti, Mutuelleville, B.P. 501, Tel. 793997, 1025 Tunis
Syria: Cité al Manor III, No.119, Tel. 235-577, Tunis
Turkey: 47 Ave. Mohamed, V, Tel. 750668, Tunis
United Arab Emirates: 15 rue du 1er Juin, Mutuelleville, Tel. 783-522, Tunis
United Kingdom: 5 Place de la Victoire, Tel. 341444, Tunis.
U.S.A.: 144 Ave. de la Liberté, Tel. 782-566, Tunis
Venezuela: 30 rue de Niger, Tel. 285-075, Tunis
Yemen (Republic of): Rue Moawia Ibn Soufiane, al Menzah 6, Tel. 237-933, Tunis
Yugoslavia: 4 rue du Libéria, Tel. 783057, Tunis

Political Parties

Mouvement de l'Unité Populaire: Tunis
Mouvement des Démocrates Socialistes: Tunis
Parti Social Liberal: Est. 1988; Tunis
Parti de l'Unité Populaire: Tunis
Rassemblement Constitutionnel Démocratique-RCD: Est. 1934; Blvd. 9 Avril 1938, Tunis
Rassemblement Socialiste Progressiste: Est. 1983; Tunis
Union Démocratique Unioniste: Tunis

Justice

The Government has abolished the multiple jurisdictions of religious (shari'i and rabbinic) tribunals. These have been integrated into the civil courts so as to form a single three-level jurisdiction, courts of appeal and High Courts.

A Personal Status Code was promulgated on August 17, 1956, and applied to Tunisians from 1 January 1957. This raised the status of women, made divorce subject to court decision, abolished polygamy and decreed a minimum marriage age.

The Economy

ECONOMIC SITUATION

The Tunisian economy is relatively well diversified with an important oil sector, considerable phosphate deposits, a wide variety of manufacturing industries and a sizeable tourist sector. GDP rose by an average rate of 6% in real terms between 1973 and 1986 reflecting favourable international conditions, accelerated industrial development and expanding income from tourism.

Tunisia has traditionally encouraged a liberal economic environment. Since 1969, it has enacted measures to assist industries to establish themselves in the country as well as permitting the free transfer of profits and capital.

Tunisia's development plans serve as guidelines rather than as official policy. The aim of the sixth Economic and Development Plan for 1982-1986, envisaging economic growth of 6.3% a year with an investment of TD 8.2 billion, were not realised as several projects had to be cancelled as a result of financial constraints. Only a few large projects are included in the Five Year Plan for 1987-1991 which tends more toward a consolidation of previous achievements. The new projects aim to improve the transportation and communications infrastructure and to iron out the economic disparities between regions during this period substantial progress was made and the program was successful.

The 1992-96 Plan encourages private investment in agro-industrial projects to increase the export and food-processing potential. In 1996 GDP grew by 6.9% as against 3.5% in 1995 and 3.3% in 1994 and 2% in 1993. In 1997 GDP grew by 5.1% and in 1998 by 5%.

The agricultural sector provided jobs for a quarter of the labour force. A major programme of water development including the construction of dams for irrigation and flood prevention are being implemented. Cereals are cultivated mainly in the fertile valleys in the north, while citrus fruits, vines, fruit and vegetables predominate in the north east. Tunisia is the fourth largest producer in the world in olives and its exports account for almost half of total earning from agricultural exports.

The fishing industry mainly centered in Sfax employs over 50000 persons, and the total catch rose to about 90000 tons in 1997 from an average of 31000 tons in 1975.

As of January 1998, oil reserves amount to 0.4 billion

barrels. However, the reserves are only partially developed. Tunisia is also the world's fourth larger producer of phosphates. As a result to the liberal investment code, a growing number of foreign enterprises set up operations in Tunisia, thereby contributing to an expansion in manufacturing. Tunisia's exports of manufacturers include textiles, footwear, construction materials, mechanical and electrical products. Tourism is a principal source of foreign exchange, and contributes more than a fifth of total foreign exchange receipts. Over 4.2 million tourists visited Tunisia in 1997.

The Banking System

Banque Centrale de Tunisie: Est. 1958; 7 Rue Hedi Nouira, B.P. 369, Tel. 259-977, Tunis

Alubaf International Bank: Est. 1986; Belvédère, B.P. 51, Tel. 783500, Tunis.

Arab Tunisian Bank: Est. 1982; 9 Rue Hedi Nouira, Tel. 351-155, 1001 Tunis

Banque Arabe Tuniso-Libyenne pour le Développement et le Commerce Extérieur: Est. 1984; B.P. 102, Belvédère, Tel. 781-500, 1002 Tunis

Banque de Cooperation du Maghreb Arabe: Est. 1981; B.P. 46, Belvédère, Tel. 780-311, 1012 Tunis

Banque de Developpment Economique de Tunisie: Est. 1959; 34 rue 7050, el Menzah 1004, B.P. 48, Tel. 718-000, 1080 Tunis

Banque Internationale Arabe de Tunisie: Est. 1976; 70-72 Ave. du 7 Novembre, B.P. 520, Tel. 340-733, 1080 Tunis

Banque Nationale Agricole: Est. 1959; Hedi Nouira, Tel. 791000, 1001 Tunis

Banque du Sud: Est. 1968; 95 Ave. de la Liberté, Tel. 849-400, Tunis

Banque de Tunisie: Est. 1884; 3 Rue de Turquie, B.P. 289, Tel. 340-544, Tunis

Banque Tuniso-Koweitienne de Développement: Est. 1981; B.P. 49, Tel. 340-000, 1002 Tunis

Citibank N.A.: 3 Ave. Jugurtha, Belvédère, B.P. 72, Tel. 890-066, 1002 Tunis

Société Tunisienne de Banque: Est. 1958; Tel. 340-477, 1001 Tunis

Tunis International Bank: Est. 1982, 18 Ave. des Etats Unis, B.P. 81, Belvédère, Tel. 782411, 1002 Tunis

Union Bancaire pour le Commerce et l'Industrie: Est. 1961; B.P 829, Tel. 245-877, Tunis

Union Internationale de Banques: Est. 1963; 65 Ave. du 7 Novembre, B.P. 109, Tel. 247-000, Tunis

Transport

RAILWAYS

Société Nationale des Chemins de Fer Tunisiens (SNCFT): Est. 1957; 67 Ave. Farhat Hached, Tunis; State Organization; operates the entire railways system in Tunisia totalling over 2,200 kilometres

ROADS

There are about 24,000 km of roads, of which more than 6,000 km are main roads.

Société Régionale des Transports: Est. 1963; 1 Ave. Habib Bourguiba, Tunis, operates the buses system.

SHIPPING

The Port of Tunis-La Goulette is the major port of Tunisia. Bizerte, Sousse, Sfax and Gabès are less important. There is a special petroleum port at La Skhirra.

Compagnie Tunisienne de Navigation: P.O.Box 40, 5 avenue Dag Hammarshoeld, Tunis; with branches at Gabès, La Skhirra, La Goulette, Sfax, Sousse and Bizerte.

CIVIL AVIATION

There are international airports at Tunis-Carthage, Sfax Djerba, Monastir, Gafsa and Tozeur.

Tunis Air (Société Tunisienne de l'Air): Est. 1948; Tunis; majority of shares owned by the Government; operates flights to neighbouring countries in Africa, Asia, Europe.

Foreign airlines: Aeroflot, Air Afrique, Air Algérie, Air France, Air India, Alitalia, Austrian Airlines, CSA, JAT, KLM, LOT, Lufthansa, Malev, Royal Air Maroc, Sabena, SAS, Swissair, etc.

Radio, Television and The Press

Radiodiffusion Television Tunisienne: 71, Avenue de la Liberté, Tunis. Public corporation

RADIO

Broadcasting in Arabic, French and Italian.

TELEVISION

Hours of broadcasting: 43 per week.

THE PRESS

L'Action: Est. 1932, 15 Rue de Mars 1934, Tel. 264-899, Tunis; French, Organ of the Rassemblement Constitutionnel Démocratique; Daily

Akhbar: Est. 1984; 1 Passage Houdaybiyah, Tel. 344-100, Tunis; Weekly

Anouar at Tounisia: Est. 1981; 10 rue ach Cham, Tel. 331000, 1002 Tunis; weekly

Assabah: Est. 1951; 4 rue Ali Bach-Hamba, Tunis

Biladi: Est. 1974; 15 rue de Mars 1934, Tunis; Arabic; Weekly

Chourouk: 10 rue Ach Cham, Tel. 834-000, Tunis; Weekly

Fikr: Est. 1955; 13 rue Dar al Jel, B.P. 556, Tel. 260-237, Tunis; Arabic; Monthly

Journal Officiel: Est. 1860; Ave. Farhat Hached, 2040

Radès, Tel. 299-914, Tunis; official gazette; French and Arabic; twice weekly

Maraa: Est. 1961; 56 Blvd. Bab Benat, Tel. 560-178, Tunis; Arabic and French; every 2 months

Moussawar: 10 rue Ach Cham, Tel. 289-000, Tunis; Weekly

La Presse de Tunisie: Est. 1936; Tel. 341-066, Tunis; French; Daily

Al Rai: Est. 1977; 118 rue de Yougoslavie, Tel. 242-251, Tunis; Weekly

Le Temps: Est. 1975; 4 rue Ali Bach Hamba, Tel. 340-222, Tunis; French; Weekly

Tunis Hebdo: Est. 1973; 1 Passage Houdaybiyah, Tel. 344-100, Tunis; French; Weekly

NEWS AGENCIES

Tunis Afrique Presse: Est. 1961; 7 Ave. Slimane Ben Slimane, Al Manar, Tunis

FOREIGN AGENCIES

Agence France-Presse (AFP); Agenzia Nationale Stampa Associata (ANSA); Reuters; United Press International (UPI); Xinhua.

Universities

Université des Lettres des Arts et des Sciences Humaines (Tunis I)

Est. 1988; 29 Rue Asdrubal, Lafayette, Tel.: 788-068, 1002 Tunis

Université des Sciences, des Techniques et de Médecine de Tunis (Tunis II)

Est. 1988; 29 Rue Asdrubal, 1002 Tunis

Université de Droit, d'Economique et de Gestion (Tunis III)

Est. 1988; Campus Universitaire, Tunis

Université de Sfax

Est. 1986; Route de l'Aéroport, Tel.: 40200, Sfax

Université Zitouna

Est. 1988; Abou Zakaria El Hafsi, Montfleury, Tunis

Museums

All museums are placed under the control of the "Direction de Musées Nationaux", Tunis.

Musée National du Bardo: Est. 1888. Le Bardo, Tunis. Contains prehistoric collections; Punic, Greek and Roman art relics, ancient and modern Islamic art.

Other museums: Musée de Ribet, Monastir
Musée Classique de Sousse, Sousse
Musée Islamique de Ribat,
Musée des Arts Islamiques, Tunis
Musée Lapidaire, Tunis
Musée Antiquarium, Carthage (Utic, Punic and Roman)

Tourism

Office Nationale du Tourisme Tunisien: Est. 1958; 1 Av. Mohammed V, Tunis.

Tourism has been the fastest expanding sector of Tunisia's economy. The country's eastern coast, previously largely deserted, now has many hotels and other facilities for tourists. Tunisia also contains many monuments of Roman antiquity such as the Colosseum and the ruins of the city of Dugga between Tunis and the Algerian frontier. There is a fine Roman collection in the Bardo Museum in Tunis. From the Arab period the great mosque of Qairawan and the reservoirs of that city are notable.

UNITED ARAB EMIRATES

United Arab Emirates

Supreme Council	
President	: Shaikh Zayed Ben Sultan AL NAHAYAN
Vice-President	: Shaikh Maktum Bin Rashid AL MAKTUM
Area	: 77,700 square km.
Capital	: Abu Dhabi Town
Population	: 2.4 million (1996 estimate)
Currency	: Dirham
Denominations	: 1, 5, 10, 100 Dirhams
	100 fils = 1 Dirham

Exchange Rate: 3.67 Dirhams per US dollar (May 1998)

Geography

The United Arab Emirates, formerly known as the Trucial States, extend along the coast of the Gulf eastwards from the base of the Qatar peninsula to a short way beyond Ras al Khaimah. The Sheikhdoms which form the UAE are Abu Dhabi, Dubai, Sharjah, Ajman, Umm al Qaiwain, Ras al Khaimah and Fujairah. They cover an area of approximately 77,700 square km. Abu Dhabi is the largest and richest and has an area of about 26,000 square miles. The remaining Sheikhdoms, known for convenience as the "Northern Emirates", cover an area of about 8000 square miles and are situated in the northeast corner of the territory.

Six of the seven states have their capitals on the coast which sweeps northward and eastward from the border of Qatar to Cape Musandam on the Straits of Hormuz, the entrance of the Gulf. The seventh, Fujairah, is on the eastern side of the Musandam Peninsula, outside the Straits and facing the Gulf of Oman. The extreme tip of the Peninsula-wild, mountainous and forbidding — is inhabited by the Shihuh, a people quite distinct from those of the United Emirates, and is a dependency of the Sultanate of Oman. The mountains which form the backbone of the Musandam Peninsula are one of the geographical features of the UAE.

Important archaeological discoveries have been made at **Umm al Nar**, on the coast a little way to the east of Abu Dhabi. This is the site of a port dating from the period between 3000 and 2000 BC. Many examples have been found of pottery made in southern Baluchistan, of a type found also in Ur and other Sumerian sites in Iraq. A large stone house has been unearthed and also a number of stone graves of exceptionally fine masonry. There are relief carvings of various animals.

ABU DHABI

Abu Dhabi is the largest of the United Arab Emirates, covering an area of 26,000 square miles. The population in 1997 census was 1,000,000, including foreign residents. The town of Abu Dhabi is on an island separated from the mainland by a narrow creek. It was settled by the Bedu tribe of Beni Yas rather more than two centuries ago, when they discovered water there.

DUBAI

Dubai is Abu Dhabi's next door neighbour to the north and east, and it has the first of the splendid creeks which are a feature of the coast up to Cape Musandam and the Straits of Hormuz. The State occupies some 1500 square miles of flat and largely featureless coastal plain with a 45 mile seaboard on the Gulf. It has a cosmopolitan population estimated at 738,000 people, with sizeable communities of Indians, Pakistanis, Iranians, Europeans and Americans. All but a very small proportion are concentrated in the city area.

A significant event in Dubai's trading history was at the very start of this century, when the Persian port of Lingeh, on the other side of the Gulf, was an important rival. The activities of the Lingeh merchants led to heavy taxation and other official harassment. They decided to move, lock, stock and barrel to the freer and more congenial atmosphere of the Trucial Coast and they settled in Dubai.

Dubai's original prosperity came from trade, but it was the dicovery of oil in 1966 that provided funds to finance many of the State's major projects.

RELIGION

Islam is the principal religion.

There is an Anglican church and a Roman Catholic church in Abu Dhabi Town with resident chaplains; there is an Anglican and a Roman Catholic church in Dubai.

OFFICIAL PUBLIC HOLIDAYS

Friday is the weekly holiday; Saturday and Sunday are normal working days.

Main holidays are: Eid al Fitr; Eid al Adha, the feast of Sacrifice; The Prophet's birthday; Ashura-day of mourning for Shi'it Muslims; Muslim New Year Day

CLIMATE

During the summer the heat is intense along the lowlying coast of the Gulf. This, combined with the high humidity and hot, moist air drifting in from the sea can be extremely trying. Between July and September the temperature frequently rises to over 100° and 110° is not uncommon. By contrast, the climate during the six winter months from November to April is very pleasant with warm, sunny days.

History

The United Arab Emirates was formed in December 2, 1971 as a federation of the States of Abu Dhabi, Dubai, Sharjah, Um al Qaiwain, Ajman and Fujeirah. In February 1972 Ras al Khaimah joined the union.

The federation aproved a provisional constitution and at independence Sheikh Zayed Bin Sultan Al Nahayan, ruler of Abu Dhabi, became its first President.

The Constitution

(2 DECEMBER 1971)

The provisional Constitution of the United Arab Emirates promulgated on 2 December 1971 provides for the setting up of three basic government bodies: 1) the Supreme Council, 2) the Federal Council of Ministers and 3) Federal National Council.

Islam is declared the official religion, the Shariah a major source of legislation, and Arabic the official language.

"Equality, social justice, law, order and security, with equal opportunities for all citizens, all of whom shall be bound together with solidarity, charity and love", are the foundations of society, with the family at its base. Education, compulsory at the elementary stage, is free and health services are guaranteed to all.

The principal subjects over which the Federal Government has responsibility both for legislation and for execution are laid down in the Constitution as:

Foreign affairs: Federal armed forces and defence: Safeguarding the security of the Federation from within and without: Security, law and Government affairs in the permanent capital: Affairs of federal employees and the judiciary: Federal finance, taxes, fees and royalties: Federal general loans: Postal, Telegraph and wireless services: Road construction and maintenance where routes are envisaged as main highways: Air traffic control and licensing of aircraft and pilots: Education: Public health and medical services: Currency: Weights and measures: Electrical services: Federal nationality, passports, residence and immigration: Federal property: Statistics and census for federal purposes: Federal information.

The provisional Constitution is still in effect. It has been extended for further periods of five years, the last extention was in 1991, and became permanent in June 1996.

The Government

THE SUPREME COUNCIL

The Supreme Council has responsibility for general policy in all matters and for the ratification of federal laws. The Council is composed of the Rulers of the seven Emirates and, on matters of substance, decisions require the support of five members including the Rulers of Abu Dhabi and Dubai.

THE FEDERAL COUNCIL

The Federal Council of Ministers has executive authority, initiates federal laws and implements them, and is collectively responsible to the Supreme Council. The Prime Minister is appointed by the President, after consultation with his fellow-members of the Supreme Council, and the President also appoints the individual ministers, on the advice of the Prime Minister.

THE FEDERAL NATIONAL COUNCIL

The Federal National Council, which held its first meeting in February 1972 and began its full new session in November 1972, is empowered to discuss and, if necessary, propose amendments to federal laws tabled for approval by the Council of Ministers but it has also wide powers to debate other matters of public interest. The National Council's 40 members are chosen, for a two-year term.

GENERAL

The federation of the United Arab Emirates consisting of Abu Dhabi, Dubai, Sharjah, Ajman, Umm al-Qaiwan, Ras al-Khaimah and Fujairah was established under the terms of a provisional constitution in 1971.

The Supreme Council is the highest federal authority, comprising the rulers of the seven Emirates. It elects a president who, in turn, appoints a Council of Ministers which has executive powers. The Federal National Council – a consultative assembly made up of 40 members appointed by the Emirates – acts as a forum for debating government policy.

With the outbreak of the Gulf War in 1980, the UAE became vulnerable to external forces over which it has no control. Iran's repeated threats to close the Strait of Hormuz to traffic carrying exports of petroleum from Gulf countries represented a grave threat to states such as the UAE, which depends on revenues from petroleum. Partly in response to this threat, the UAE joined with six other Gulf states to form the Gulf Co-operation Council (GCC) in March 1981 to work towards economic, political and social integration in the Gulf.

Supreme Council of Rulers

Ruler of Sharjah: Sheikh Sultan Bin Muhammad AL-QASIMI

Ruler of Ras al Khaimah: Sheikh Saqr Bin Muhamad AL-QASIMI

Ruler of Umm al-Qaiwain: Sheikh Rashid Bin Ahmad AL-MUALLA

Ruler of Ajman: Sheikh Humaid Bin Rashid AL-NUAIMI

Ruler of Dubai: Sheikh Maktum Bin Rashid Bin Said AL-MAKTUM

Ruler of Abu Dhabi: Sheikh Zayed Bin Sultan AL-NAHAYAN

Ruler of Fujairah: Sheikh Hamad Bin Mohamad AL-SHARQI

The Cabinet

(Sept. 1998)

Prime Minister: Sheikh Maktoum Bin Rached AL MAKTOUM

Deputy Prime Minister: Sheikh Sultan Bin Zayed AL NAHAYAN

Minister of the Interior: Lt. Gen. Dr. Muhamed Said AL BADI
Minister of Foreign Affairs: Rashid Abdullah NUAIMİ
Minister of Finance and Industry: Sheikh Hamdan Bin Rashid AL MAKTOUM
Minister of Defence: Sheikh Mohamed Bin Rashid AL MAKTOUM
Minister of Defence: Sheikh Mohamed Bin Rashid AL MAKTOUM
Minister of Economy and Commerce: Sheikh Fahim Bin Sultan AL QASIMI
Minister of Information and Culture: Sheikh Abdullah Bin Zayed AL NAHAYAN
Minister of Communications: Ahmad Bin Humaid AL TAYER
Minister of Public Works and Housing: Rakkad Bin Salem bin RAKKAD
Minister of Higher Education and Scientific Research: Sheikh Nahayan Bin Mubarak AL NAHAYAN
Minister of Health: Hamad Abdelrahman AL MADFA
Minister of Electricity and Water: Humaid Bin Nasser AL-OWAIS
Minister of Labour and Social Affairs: Matir Humaid AL TAYER
Minister of Planning: Sheikh Humaid Bin Ahmad AL MUALLA
Minister of Petroleum and Mineral Resources: Obeid Bin Seif AL NASIRI
Minister of Agriculture and Fisheries: Said Muhamed AL RAQABANI
Minister of Education and Youth: Ali Abdelaziz AL SHARHA
Minister of Justice, Islamic Affairs and Waqfs: Mohamed Nakhira AL DHAHERI
Minister of State for Cabinet Affairs: Said Khalfan AL GHAITH
Minister of State for Finance and Industry: Mohamed Khalfan Bin KHARBASH
Minister of State for Foreign Affairs: Sheikh Hamdan Bin Zayed AL NAHAYAN
Minister of State for Affairs of the Supreme Council: Sheikh Majid Bin Said AL NAHAYAN

Foreign Embassies

Afghanistan: P.O.Box 5687, Tel. (2)661244, Abu Dhabi
Algeria: P.O.Box 3070, Tel. (2)48943, Abu Dhabi
Argentina: P.O.Box 3325, Tel. (2)436838, Abu Dhabi
Austria: P.O.Box 3095, Tel. (2)324103, Abu Dhabi
Bahrain: P.O.Box 3367, Tel. (2)312200, Abu Dhabi
Bangladesh: P.O.Box 2504, Tel. (2)668375, Abu Dhabi
Belgium: P.O.Box 3686, Tel. (2)319449, Abu Dhabi
Belize: P.O.Box 43432, Tel. (2)333554, Abu Dhabi
Bosnia and Herzegovina: P.O.Box 43362, Tel. (2)464235, Abu Dhabi
Brazil: P.O.Box 3027, Tel. (2)665352, Abu Dhabi
Brunei: P.O.Box 5836, Tel. (2)313739, Abu Dhabi
Canada: P.O.Box 6970, Tel. (2)263655, Abu Dhabi
China, People's Republic: P.O.Box 2741, Tel. (2)434276, Abu Dhabi
Croatia: P.O.Box 41227, Tel. (2)662878, Abu Dhabi
Czech Republic: P.O.Box 27009, Tel. (2)782800, Abu Dhabi
Denmark: P.O.Box 46666, Tel. (2)325900, Abu Dhabi
Egypt: P.O.Box 4026, Tel. (2)445566, Abu Dhabi
Eritrea: P.O.Box 2597, Tel. (2)331838, Abu Dhabi
Finland: P.O.Box 3634, Tel. (2)328927, Abu Dhabi
France: P.O.Box 4041, Tel. (2)435100, Abu Dhabi
Germany: P.O.Box 2591, Tel. (2)435630, Abu Dhabi
Greece: P.O.Box 5483, Tel. (2)654847, Abu Dhabi
Hungary: P.O.Box 44450, Tel. (2)660107, Abu Dhabi
India: P.O.Box 4090, Tel. (2)664800, Abu Dhabi
Indonesia: P.O.Box 7256, Tel. (2)454448, Abu Dhabi
Iran: P.O.Box 4080, Tel. (2)447618, Abu Dhabi
Italy: P.O.Box 46752, Tel. (2)435622, Abu Dhabi
Japan: P.O.Box 2430, Tel. (2)435969, Abu Dhabi
Jordan: P.O.Box 4024, Tel. (2)447100, Abu Dhabi
Kenya: P.O.Box 3854, Tel. (2)666300, Abu Dhabi
Korea, Republic: P.O.Box 3270, Tel. (2)435337, Abu Dhabi
Kuwait: P.O.Box 926, Tel. (2)446888, Abu Dhabi
Lebanon: P.O.Box 4023, Tel. (2)434722, Abu Dhabi
Libya: P.O.Box 5739, Tel. (2)450030, Abu Dhabi
Malaysia: P.O.Box 3887, Tel. (2)656698, Abu Dhabi
Mauritania: P.O.Box 2714, Tel. (2)462724, Abu Dhabi
Morocco: P.O.Box 4066, Tel. (2)433963, Abu Dhabi
Namibia: Abu Dhabi
Netherlands: P.O.Box 46560, Tel. (2)321920, Abu Dhabi
Norway: P.O.Box 47270, Tel. (2)211221, Abu Dhabi
Oman: P.O.Box 2517, Tel. (2)463333, Abu Dhabi
Pakistan: P.O.Box 846, Tel. (2)447172, Abu Dhabi
Philippines: P.O.Box 3215, Tel. (2)345664, Abu Dhabi
Poland: P.O.Box 2334, Tel. (2)465200, Abu Dhabi
Qatar: P.O.Box 3503, Tel. (2)435900, Abu Dhabi
Romania: P.O.Box 70416, (2)666346, Abu Dhabi
Russia: P.O.Box 8211, Tel. (2)721797, Abu Dhabi
Saudi Arabia: P.O.Box 4057, Tel. (2)445700, Abu Dhabi
Slovakia: P.O.Box 3382, Tel. (2)321674, Abu Dhabi
Somalia: P.O.Box 4155, Tel. (2)669700, Abu Dhabi
South Africa: P.O.Box 29446, Tel. (2)726200, Abu Dhabi
Spain: P.O.Box 46474, Tel. (2)213544, Abu Dhabi
Sri Lanka: P.O.Box 46534, Tel. (2)666688, Abu Dhabi
Sudan: P.O.Box 4027, Tel. (2)666788, Abu Dhabi
Switzerland: P.O.Box 46116, Tel. (2)343636, Abu Dhabi
Syria: P.O.Box 4011, Tel. (2)448768, Abu Dhabi
Thailand: P.O.Box 47466, Tel. (2)770797, Abu Dhabi
Tunisia: P.O.Box 4166, Tel. (2)661331, Abu Dhabi
Turkey: P.O.Box 3204, Tel. (2)655466, Abu Dhabi
Ukraine: P.O.Box 45714, Tel. (2)327586, Abu Dhabi
United Kingdom: P.O.Box 248, Tel. (2)326600, Abu Dhabi
USA.: P.O.Box 4009, Tel. (2)436691, Abu Dhabi
Yemen: P.O.Box 2095, Tel. (2)448454, Abu Dhabi
Zimbabwe: Abu Dhabi

The Economy

The exploitation of oil and gas has enabled the Emirates to enjoy one of the highest per capital incomes in the world. The population of approximately 380,000 in the 1960's has grown by the end of 1998 to 2.7 million.

As Abu Dhabi and Dubai are the most well-endowed in terms of hydrocarbon deposits, they have been the main centres of industrialisation; development of the other Emirates has been impeded by a lack of natural resources and have depended on federal assistance and direct transfers from Abu Dhabi to sustain their economic growth.

Proven oil reserves of some 100 billion barrels, of which Abu Dhabi possesses some 93%, will provide around 100 years of production at current output levels, thereby ensuring the UAE's status as a major oil exporter and the fourth within OPEC after Saudi Arabia, Iran and Venezuela in the long-term. Abu Dhabi is the main hydrocarbon producer, accounting for roughly two-thirds of the total, while Dubai is the second largest followed by Sharjah and Ras al-Khaima.

Despite excess capacity, exploration and development activity continues apace, especially in the northern Emirates. Proven gas reserves in the Emirates are estimated at 6 trillion cubic meters at end 1998. Sharjah has augmented its existing oil and gas capacity through the development of its Sajaa field. Natural gas from the field is being used to fuel local power stations and power plants in Ras al-Khaima. Umm al-Qaiwain is stepping up its oil exploration efforts, and Fujairah is carrying out its own exploitation programmes.

In the northern Emirates, industrial activity is concentrated on the manufacture of construction-related materials, cement manufacture, and plastic pipes. Ras al-Khaimah which has developed a valuable export business, based on sales of construction aggregates, established the first white cement factory in the Gulf and an explosives factory, and a pharmaceutical factory.

The 1998 budget set expenditure at Dirhams 21.393 billion and revenues at 19.635 billion as compared with the 1997 budget which set expenditure at Dirhams 19.860 and revenues at 18.870.

THE BANKING SYSTEM

An active banking industry has existed in the Gulf Emirates, especially Dubai, for many years, the present monetary system in the U.A.E. dates from the establishment of the Currency Board in May 1973 and the simultaneous issuance of the U.A.E.'s own currency the United Arab Emirates dirham (AED), to replace the Bahrain dinar and the Qatar-Dubai riyal previously in circulation.

A Central Bank was established in December 1980, in response to the need for a strong monetary authority. During its first year of operation, the Central Bank has sought to coordinate U.A.E. fiscal and monetary policies through the formation of a consultative committee composed of representatives from the Ministries of Finance and Planning and the Central Bank. Measures have also been taken to strengthen the commercial banking system. The number of branches of foreign banks, in view of the overbanked structure of the system, tightened its auditing provisions; and issued regulations regarding the minimum paid-up capital, the capital total assets ratio, and the reserve level of banks, as well as provisions for the licensing of money changers.

Central Bank of the United Arab Emirates: Est. 1973; P.O.Box 854, Tel. (2)652220, Abu Dhabi

Abu Dhabi Commercial Bank: Est. 1985; P.O.Box 939, Tel. (2)720000, Abu Dhabi

ABN-AMRO Bank N.V.: Est. 1975; Faraj Bin Hamoodah Bldg., Sheikh Hamdan Str., P.O.Box 2720, Tel. (2)335400, Abu Dhabi; P.O.Box 2567, Tel. (4)512233, Deira, Dubai; P.O.Box 1971, Tel. (6)594900, Sharjah

ANZ Grindlays Bank PLC: P.O.Box 241, Tel. (2)330876, Abu Dhabi; P.OBox 357, Sharjah; P.O.Box 4166, Tel. (4)285663, Dubai

Arab Bank for Investment and Foreign Trade: Est. 1975; P.O.Box 2484, Tel. (2)721900, Abu Dhabi

Arab Bank Ltd.: Est. 1970; P.O.Box 875, Tel. (2)334111, Abu Dhabi; P.O.Box 1650, Dubai; P.O.Box 130, Sharjah; P.O.Box 4972, Ras al Khaimah; P.O.Box 300, Fujairah; P.O.Box 17 Ajmam

Arab-African International Bank: Est. 1970; P.O.Box 1049, Tel. (4)223131, Dubai; P.O.Box 928, Tel. (2)323400, Abu Dhabi

Arab Emirate Investment Bank Ltd.: P.O.Box 5503, Tel. (4)222191, Dubai

Banca Commerciale Italiana: P.O.Box 3839, Tel. (2)324330, Abu Dhabi

Bank of Baroda (India): Est. 1974; P.O.Box 2303, Tel. (2)330244, Abu Dhabi

Bank Melli Iran: Est. 1969; P.O.Box 1894, Tel. (4)216777, Dubai

Bank Mashreq Ltd.: Est. 1967; P.O.Box 1250, Tel. (4)229131, Deira, Dubai

Bank Saderat Iran: P.O.Box 700, Tel. (2)335155, Abu Dhabi; P.O.Box 4182, Dubai; also Sharjah, Ajman, Ras al Khaimah, Fujairah and al Ain

Bank of Sharjah Ltd.: Est. 1973; P.O.Box 1394, Tel. (6)352111, Sharjah

Banque du Caire (Egypt): P.O.Box 533, Tel. (2)328700, Abu Dhabi; P.O.Box 1502, Dubai; P.O.Box 254, Sharjah; P.O.Box 618, Ras al Khaimah

Credit Agricole Indosuez (France): Est. 1975; P.O.Box 9256, Tel. (4)314211, Dubai; P.O.Box 46786, Tel. (2)338400, Abu Dhabi (Est. 1981)

Banque Libanaise pour le Commerce S.A.: P.O.Box 4207, Tel. (4)222291, Dubai; P.O.Box 854, Sharjah; P.O.Box 3771, Abu Dhabi; P.O.Box 771, Ras al Khaimah

Banque Banorabe: Est. 1974; P.O.Box 4370, Tel. (4)284655, Dubai

Banque Paribas: P.O.Box 2742, Tel. (2)267800, Abu Dhabi; P.O.Box 7233, Tel. (4)525929, Dubai

Barclays Bank PLC: P.O.Box 2734, Tel. (2)275313, Abu

Dhabi; P.O.Box 1891, Tel. (4)351551, Deira, Dubai; P.O.Box 1953, Tel. (4)355288, Sharjah

British Bank of the Middle East: Est. 1946; P.O.Box 66, Tel. (4)332200, Dubai

Citibank N.A. (U.S.A.): Est. 1963; P.O.Box 749, Tel. (4)522100, Dubai; P.O.Box 346, Sharjah; P.O.Box 999, Abu Dhabi; P.O.Box 294, Ras al Khaimah; P.O.Box 1430, al Ain

Commercial Bank of Dubai Ltd.: Est. 1969; P.O.Box 2668, Tel. (4)523355, Deira, Dubai

Commercial Bank International Plc: Est. 1991, P.O.Box 4449, Tel. (4)275265, Dubai

Dubai Islamic Bank PLC: Est. 1975; P.O.Box 1080, Tel. (4)214888, Deira Dubai

Emirates Bank International Ltd.: Est. 1977; P.O.Box 2923, Tel. (4)256256, Dubai

Emirates Industrial Bank: Est. 1982, P.O.Box 2722, Tel. (2)339700, Abu Dhabi

First Gulf Bank: Est. 1979; P.O.Box 414, Tel. (6)423450, Ajman

Habib Bank AG Zûrich (Switzerland): Est. 1974; P.O.Box 2681, Tel. (2)322838, Abu Dhabi; P.O.Box 1166, Sharjah; P.O.Box 3306, Dubai; P.O.Box 168, Ajman; P.O.Box 181, Umm al Qaiwain; P.O.Box 767 Ras al Khaimah

Habib Bank Ltd. (Pakistan): Est. 1967, P.O.Box 888, Dubai; Est. 1975, P.O.Box 897, Abu Dhabi

Invest Bank: Est. 1975; P.O.Box 1885, Tel. (6)355391, Sharjah

Janata Bank (Bangladesh): P.O.Box 2630, Tel. (2)344542, Abu Dhabi; P.O Box 3342, Dubai

Lloyds Bank PLC (UK): Est. 1977; P.O.Box 3766, Tel. (4)313005, Dubai

Middle East Bank Ltd.: Est. 1976; P.O.Box 5547, Tel. (4)220121, Deira, Dubai

National Bank of Abu Dhabi: Est. 1968; P.O.Box 4, Tel. (2)335262, Abu Dhabi

National Bank of Bahrain BSC: P.O.Box 46080. Tel. (2)333783, Abu Dhabi

National Bank of Dubai Ltd.: Est. 1963; P.O.Box 777, Tel. (4)222111, Dubai

National Bank of Fujairah: Est. 1982, P.O.Box 887, Tel. (9)224518, Fujairah

National Bank of Oman SAO: P.O.Box 3822, Tel. (2)325354, Abu Dhabi

National Bank of Ras al Khaimah PSC: Est. 1976; P.O.Box 5300, Tel. (7)221127, Ras al Khaimah

National Bank of Sharjah: Est. 1976, P.O.Box 4, Tel. (6)547745, Sharjah

National Bank of Umm al Qaiwain Ltd.: Est. 1982; P.O.Box 800, Tel. (6)655225, Umm al Qaiwain

Nilein Industrial Development Bank: P.O.Box 6013, Abu Dhabi

Rafidain Bank: Est. 1978; P.O.Box 2727, Abu Dhabi

Royal Bank of Canada: Est. 1976; P.O.Box 3614, Tel. (4)225226, Dubai

Standard Chartered PLC: P.O.Box 240, Tel. (2)330077, Abu Dhabi; P.O.Box 999, Tel. (4)520455, Dubai; P.O.Box 5, Tel. (6)357788, Sharjah; P.O.Box 1240, Tel. (3)641253, al Ain

Union National Bank: Est. 1983, P.O.Box 3865, Tel. (2)741600, Abu Dhabi

United Arab Bank: Est. 1975, P.O.Box 3562, Tel. (2)325000, Abu Dhabi

United Arab Emirates Development Bank: Est. 1974, Tel. (2)344986, Abu Dhabi

United Bank Ltd. (Pakistan): P.O.Box 1367, Tel. (4)552020, Dubai

Oil

Abu Dhabi Co. for Onshore Oil Operations: P.O.Box 270, Tel. (2)604400, Abu Dhabi

Abu Dhabi Drilling Chemicals and Products Ltd.: Est. 1975; P.O.Box 46121, Tel. (2)602900, Abu Dhabi

Abu Dhabi Gas Industries Co.: P.O.Box 665, Tel. (2)651100, Abu Dhabi

Abu Dhabi Gas Liquefaction Co.: Est. 1973; P.O.Box 3500, Tel. (2)606111, Abu Dhabi

Abu Dhabi Marine Operating Co.: P.O.Box 303, Tel. (2)606000, Abu Dhabi

Abu Dhabi National Oil Co.: Est. 1971; P.O.Box 898, Tel. (2)666000, Abu Dhabi.

Abu Dhabi National Oil Company for Oil Distribution: P.O.Box 4188, Tel. (2)771300, Abu Dhabi

Abu Dhabi Oil Co. Ltd. (Japan): P.O.Box 630, Tel. (2)661100,

Ajman National Oil Co.: Est. 1988; P.O.Box 410, Tel. (6)421218, Ajman

Amerada Hess Oil Corp. of Abu Dhabi: P.O.Box 2046, Tel. (2)779500, Abu Dhabi

Bunduq Oil Co.: Est. 1975; P.O.Box 46015, Tel. (2)779922, Abu Dhabi

Crescent Petroleum Co. Int'l: P.O.Box 2222, Tel. (6)543000, Sharjah

Dubai Natural Gas Company Ltd.: P.O.Box 4311, Tel. (4)46234, Dubai

Dubai Petroleum Co.: P.O.Box 2222, Tel. (4)846000, Dubai

Emirates General Petroleum Corp: Est. 1981; P.O.Box 9400, Tel. (4)444444, Dubai

Emirates National Oil Co. (ENOC): Est. 1993, P.O.Box 6442, Tel. (4)374400, Dubai

Emirates Petroleum Products Co. (Pvt) Ltd.: Est. 1980; P.O.Box 5589, Tel. (4)372131, Dubai

The Liquefied Gas Shipping Co. Ltd.: P.O.Box 3500, Tel. (2)333888, Abu Dhabi

National Drilling Company: P.O.Box 4017, Tel. (2)316600, Abu Dhabi

National Petroleum Construction Co. Ltd.: Est. 1973; P.O.Box 2058, Tel. (2)549000, Abu Dhabi

Sedco-Houston Oil Group: P.O.Box 702, Tel. (4)224141, Dubai

Sharjah Amoco-Oil Co.: P.O.Box 1191, Sharjah

Sharjah Liquefied Petroleum Gas Co.: Est. 1984;

P.O.Box 787, Tel. (6)543666, Sharjah

Total Abu Bukhoosh Oil Co. Ltd.: P.O.Box 4058, Tel. (2)785000, Abu Dhabi

Zakum Development Co.: P.O.Box 46808, Tel. (2)605000, Abu Dhabi

Insurance

Abu Dhabi National Insurance Co.: Est. 1973; Shaikha Mariam Bldg., Loewa St., P.O.Box 839, Abu Dhabi

Al Ahlia Insurance Co.: Est. 1977; P.O.Box 128, Ras al-Khaimah

Al Ain Ahlia Insurance Co.: P.O.Box 3077, Abu Dhabi; Est. 1975;

Dubai Insurance Co.: Est. 1970; P.O.Box 3027, Dubai

Sharjah Insurance and ReinsuranceCo.: Est. 1970; P.O.Box 792, Sharjah

Union Insurance Co.: P.O.Box 460, Umm al Qaiwain

Chambers of Commerce

Federation of UAE Chambers of Commerce and Industry: P.O.Box 3014, Tel. (2)214144, Abu Dhabi; and P.O.Box 8886, Tel. (4)212977, Dubai

Abu Dhabi Chamber of Commerce and Industry: P.O.Box 662, Tel. (2)214000, Abu Dhabi

Ajman Chamber of Commerce and Industry: P.O.Box 662, Tel. (6)422177, Ajman

Dubai Chamber of Commerce and Industry: P.O.Box 1457, Tel. (4)280000, Dubai

Fujairah Chamber of Commerce, Industry and Agriculture: P.O.Box 738, Tel. (9)222400, Fujairah

Ras al-Khaimah Chamber of Commerce, Industry and Agriculture: P.O.Box 87, Tel. (7)333511, Ras al-Khaimah

Sharjah Chamber of Commerce and Industry: P.O.Box 580, Tel. (6)541444, Sharjah

Umm Al-Qaiwain Chamber of Commerce and Industry: P.O.Box 436, Tel. (6)656915, Umm al-Qaiwain

Transport

ROADS

The United Arab Emirates has over 4500 km of paved roads linking the important towns.

SHIPPING & PORTS

Abu Dhabi National Tanker Company: P.O.Box 2977, Tel. (2)277733, Abu Dhabi

Dubai Drydocks Co.: P.O.Box 8988, Tel. (4)450626, Dubai

Fujairah Port: Est. 1982; P.O.Box 787, Tel. (9)228800, Fujairah

Jebel Ali Free Zone Authority: P.O.Box 17000, Tel. (4)815000, Dubai

Abu Dhabi Seaport authority: P.O.Box 279, Tel. (2)730600, Port Zayed, Abu Dhabi

Ahmad Bin Rashid Port and Free Trade Zone: P.O.Box 279, Tel. (6)655882, Umm al-Qaiwain

Dubai Ports Authority (DPA): P.O.Box 17000, Tel. (4)815000, Dubai

Mina Saqr Port Authority: P.O.Box 5130, Tel. (7)668444, Ras el-Khaimah

Jebel Dhanna Port: c/o ADCO, P.O.Box 270, Tel. (2)666100, Abu Dhabi

National Marine Services Co.: P.O.Box 7202, Tel. (2)339800, Abu Dhabi

Ras al Khaimah Port Services: P.O.Box 5130, Tel. (7)668444, Ras al Khaimah

Sharjah Ports and Customs: P.O.Box 510, Tel. (6)281666, Sharjah

Umm al Qaiwain Port: P.O.Box 225, Tel. (6)666126, Umm al Qaiwain

Port Zayed Authority: P.O.Box 422, (2)730600, Abu Dhabi

CIVIL AVIATION

The UAE has six international airports, at Abu Dhabi, Dubai, Fujairah, Ras al Khaimah Sharjah, and Al Ain

Abu Dhabi Aviation: P.O.Box 2723, Tel. (2)449100, Abu Dhabi

Emirates Airline: P.O.Box 686, Dubai

Falcon Express Cargo Airlines: P.O.Box 9372, Tel. (4)826886, Dubai

Gulf Air Dubai: P.O.Box 4410, Dubai

Gulf Air Co. GSC: P.O.Box 5015, Sharjah.

Radio, Television and the Press

RADIO - TELEVISION

Abu Dhabi Radio: Est. 1968; P.O.Box 63, Tel. (2)451000, Abu Dhabi

Abu Dhabi Television: P.O.Box 637, Tel. (2)452000, Abu Dhabi

Capital Radio: P.O.Box 63, Tel. (4)451000, Abu Dhabi

Dubai Radio and Colour Television: P.O.Box 1695, Tel. (4)370255, Dubai

Ras al Khaimah Broadcasting Station: P.O.Box 141, Tel. (7)851151, Ras al Khaimah

Sharjah Broadcasting Station: P.O.Box 155, Sharjah

Umm al Qaiwain Broadcasting Station: P.O.Box 444, Tel. (6)666044, Umm al Qaiwain

United Arab Emirates Radio and Television-Dubai: P.O.Box 1695, Tel. (4)370255, Dubai

THE PRESS

Abu Dhabi Chamber of Commerce Review: Est. 1969; P.O.Box 662, Tel. (2)214000, Arabic with some articles in English, Monthly

Akhbar Dubai: Est. 1965; P.O.Box 1420, Dubai; Arabic; Weekly

Akhbar Ras al Khaimah: P.O.Box 87, Ras al Khaimah; Arabic; Monthly

Azman al Arabia: P.O.Box 5823, Tel. 356034, Sharjah

Bayan: Est. 1980; P.O.Box 2710, Tel. (4)444400, Dubai; Arabic; Daily

Dhafra: P.O.Box 4288, Tel. (2)328103, Abu Dhabi; Arabic; Weekly

Emirates News: Est. 1975; P.O.Box 791, Tel. (2)451600, Abu Dhabi; English; Daily

Fajr: P.O.Box 505, Tel. (2)478300; Arabic; Daily

Gulf News: Est. 1980; P.O.Box 6519, Tel. (4)447100, Dubai; English; Daily

Ittihad: Est. 1972; P.O.Box 17, Tel. (2)461600, Abu Dhabi; Arabic; Daily and Weekly

Khaleej: Est. 1970; P.O.Box 30, Tel. (6)598777, Sharjah; Arabic; Daily

Khaleej Times: Est. 1978; P.O.Box 11243, Tel. (4)582400, Dubai, P.O.Box 3082, Tel. 336000, Abu Dhabi; English; Daily

Majed: P.O.Box 3558, Tel. (2)451804, Abu Dhabi; Arabic; Weekly

Ras al Khaimah Magazine: P.O.Box 200, Ras al Khaimah; Arabic; Monthly

Tijarah: Est. 1970; P.O.Box 580, Tel. (6)541444, Sharjah; Arabic and English; Monthly

Trade and Industry: Est. 1975; P.O.Box 1457, Tel. (4)221181, Dubai; Arabic and English; Monthly

U.A.E. and Abu Dhabi Official Gazette: P.O.Box 899, Abu Dhabi; Arabic

U.A.E. Press Service Daily News: Est. 1973; P.O.Box 2035, Tel. (2)44292, Abu Dhabi; English; Daily

U.A.E. Digest: P.O.Box 6872, Tel. (6)354633, Sharjah; English; Monthly

Al Wahdah: Est. 1973; P.O.Box 2488, Tel. (2)478400, Abu Dhabi; Arabic; Daily

What's On: P.O.Box 2331, Tel. (4)246060, Dubai; English; Monthly

Zahrat al Khaleej: P.O.Box 3342, Tel. (2)455555; Arabic Weekly

NEWS AGENCIES

Emirates News Agency (WAM): Est. 1977; P.O.Box 3790, Tel. (2)464600, Abu Dhabi.

Education

Good progress has been made in education in the past years in the Emirates that comprise the UAE.

The rapid expansion and development of education over a comparatively few years has brought problems, no least of which has been the provision of qualified teachers in sufficient numbers to meet the everincreasing demands of the newly created schools. In this respect teachers have been brought from other countries to supplement the native teaching staff.

School is free, and since July 1972 education has been compulsory for all children over the age of six.

Teacher's and vocational training schools are available in the more advanced areas of the UAE, and the more promising students are awarded scholarships for university education.

In the UAE there is only one university in Al-Ain, composed of eight faculties and an enrolment of over 9300 students and over 840 teachers.

United Arab Emirates University: P.O.Box 15551, Al-Ain.

Abu Dhabi
Cultural Centres, Libraries
Museum, University

Centre for Documentation and Research:
P.O.Box 2380; f. 1968; attached to the Ministry of Foreign Affairs collects manuscripts, documents, books, maps and articles relevant to the Arabian Gulf and the Arabian peninsula, and carries out research on subjects related to this area; library of 10,000 vols, in Arabic, English and other languages.

Archaeological Museum: Al Ain: archeological sites at Buraimi and Umm Al Nar Island.

Dubai

British Council: Abu Dhabi and Dubai; library of 10400 vols.

Dubai Public Library: P.O.Box 67, Dubai; 15,000 vols in Arabic, English and Urdu

National Archives: P.O.Box 2380, Abu Dhabi (current and historic records)

National Library: P.O.Box 2380, Abu Dhabi; 800,000 vols.

United Arab Emirates University: Est. 1976; P.O.Box 15551, Al Aïn

YEMEN
(Republic of Yemen)

Republic of Yemen

President	: Field Marshal Ali Abdallah SALEH
Vice President	: Abed Rabbu Mansur HADI
Capital	: Sanaa
Area	: 536,869 sq. km.
Population	: 15.9 million (1996 estimate)
	Coins: 50 fils, 25 fils, 1 fils
Currency	: Riyal which is divided into 100 fils
Denominations	: Coins: 1, 5, 10, 25 and 50 fils
	Notes: 1, 5, 10, 20 and 100 riyals
Exchange Rate	: US $1 = 133.8 Yemeni riyals (May 1998)

The **Republic of Yemen** was proclaimed on 22 May 1990 following a merger between the "People's Democratic Republic of Yemen" (Capital: Aden); and the "Yemen Arab Republic" (Capital: Sanaa).

The New **Republic of Yemen** now covers an area of 536,869 square kilometers and a population of approx. 15.9 million. Its new Capital is Sanaa (2175 meters above sea level).

The New Republic was formed as follows.

– The President Gen. Ali Abdullah Saleh (former head of State of the Yemen Arab Republic) and, the Vice President Ali Salem Al Baid (Secretary General of the Central Committee of the Yemen Socialist Party based in Aden, in the former People's Democratic Republic of Yemen).

– A "Presidential Council" of five members (including the President and Vice President); and an "Advisory Council" of 45 members from both former states.

– The Prime Minister Haidar Abu Bakr Al Attas (former President of the People's Democratic Republic of Yemen).

– All Ministries as well as Diplomatic representations and the Central Bank based in Sanaa.

– A "Presidential Council" of five members elected on 10 Oct. 1993 Ali Abdallah Saleh, Abdel Aziz Abdelghani, Ali Salim Al Baid, Salem Saleh Mohamed, Sheikh Abdelmajid Zindani Zindani.

Four years after unification in May 1990, a conflict has arisen between leaders of Sanaa and Aden which developped into an open military confrontation between the former "People's Democratic Republic of Yemen" Capital Aden, and the former "Yemen Arab Republic" Capital Sanaa.

Leaders of the former People's Democratic Republic of Yemen (Capital Aden) have unilaterally declared its separation from the Unity, and established, a new state "Democratic Republic of Yemen" headed by Ali Salim AL BAID, and announced the formation of a government on June 2,1994; However the above government was shortlived, war broke out and following the defeat of the former "People's Democratic Republic of Yemen", on July 7, 1994 the Unification was saved. In the meantime changes in the formation of the government of the unified Republic of Yemen took place.

On September 28, 1994, the House of Representatives (301 members) voted reforms to the unification constitution in force since May 1990. The amended Constitution described the political system as a multiparty democracy. It instituted Islamic Sharia law as the source of all legislation. It abolished the five-member Presidential Council and had re-elected (on October 1, 1994 and 23 September 1999) Gen. Ali Abdullah SALEH as President. In his turn, the President appointed Maj. Gen. Abed Rabbuh Mansur Hadi as Vice President.

The Unified Country's first budget in 1991 was set at riyals 50, 980 million and revenue at 35, 218 million riyals. In 1992 budget provided for expenditure 58, 114 million riyals and revenue at 45, 778 million riyals. There had been no official fiscal planning in 1993 and 1994.

However on April 30, 1995, the House of Representatives approved a budget for 1995 setting expenditure at 124,100 million riyals and revenue at 87,000 million riyals.

The 1996 budget was set at revenue 155,800 million riyals and expenditure at 181,400 million riyals and the 1997 budget set revenue at 301,222 million riyals and expenditure at 313,985 million riyals. The 1998 budget was set at expenditure 350 billion riyals and revenue at 336.6 billion riyals and the 1999 budget has been set at expenditure 335.5 billion riyals and revenue at 294.4. The 2000 budget has been set at expenditure 422.25 billion and revenue at 388.95.

former **People's Democratic Republic of Yemen**

Geography

The People's Democratic Republic of Yemen occupies an area of 130.000 square miles with a coastline that stretches eastward from Ras Murad, opposite the island of Perim on the borders of the Sultanate of Oman, more than six hundred miles to the east. The inland depth of the country varies from about a hundred miles in the vicinity of Aden to a greater depth in the Hadhramut.

With a coastline mainly consisting of arid plains and broken up by steep mountain slopes and wadis carving their way through the coastal hills to the sea, the physical characteristics of the country provide interesting variations. Oases of cultivation and farms of different sizes are found around those wadis, particularly in Lahej and Abyan only a few miles from Aden, Meifa, and Gheil Bawazeer. Inside the hinterland high mountain tops, elevated plateaux and serrated ranges are remarkable characteristics of most of the western regions.

One of the most prominent features in the granitic Kaur ranges running roughly west-south to eastnorth-east. The Kaur Alawathil rises to 6,500 feet with peaks of 8,000 and 9,000 feet. The Kaur Alawaliq to the east stretches over long ranges of barren hills.

The Wadi Hadhramut stands out as the main feature of the eastern territory and cuts in half the broad belt of limestone tableland which rises to 6,000 feet on the southern side of the main wadi, and to some 3,500 feet on the northern side. The limestone rises in a series of steppes with many shallow depressions where farming is possible with rain water collected in pools or shallow pits, and are intersected by deep wadis.

The Wadi Hadhramut and some of its main tributaries is considered the major source of economic prosperity. The Wadi extends 350 miles from its source in al-Abr, about 3,000 feet above sea level to its mouth near Saihout. It is rich in its subsoil water and in certain areas near the sea the water is perennial. The cleft in the coastal range where the wadi breaks through the sea is a remarkably striking feature of the coastline.

THE GOVERNORATES

For administrative purposes, the country is divided into six Governorates which now supersede the former "colony" and "protectorates". The six Governorates are:

1 – Aden,
2 – Lahej,
3 – Abyan
4 – Shabwah,
5 – Hadhramut,
6 – Mahra.

THE ISLANDS

Three islands fall under the administration of the first Governorate:

Socotra, which lies in the south-eastern side of Aden is the largest in size with an area of 1,500 square miles.

Socotra has a population of 20,000 to 30,000 people. The majority are of Arab descent.

Kamaran, situated on the Red Sea, has an area of eighty square miles and a population of 3,000. Most of the people are fishermen. In recent years, the export of dried fish has increased considerably.

Perim, which lies at the entrance of the southern tip of the Red Sea, was occupied by the French in the XVIIIth century and by the British in 1861. Ships used to call at the island, where they were supplied with coal. When, after 1920, oil replaced coal as fuel for ships the importance of the island dwindled by the rise of Aden as a bunkering port.

PRINCIPAL TOWNS

Aden: - With a population of 400,000, Aden is the capital and is situated on the coast approximately 70 miles east of the junction of the Indian Ocean and the entrance to the Red Sea.

Aden is made up of:

a – Crater, built in and around the site of an extinct volcano whose highest peak rises to a height of 1,725 feet.

b – Khormaksar, a residential area near the airport on the peninsula connecting Aden town to the mainland.

c – Steamer Point and Ma'alia - two residential business and shopping areas.

d – The Arab town and oasis of Shaikh Othman at the mainland end of the isthums, which is a busy trading centre.

e – Little Aden, a second extinct volcano forming the other head of the bay which is Aden Harbour. A.B.P. Refinery is situated here.

f – Madinat Ach-Sha'ab, the administrative capital of the country.

Mukalla, with a population of 60,000, is the only other town of any importance.

THE CLIMATE

The country is essentially hot but owing to the variety of its physical geography both extremes of temperature may be experienced. The coastal areas have a humid atmosphere and are liable to heavy dews and early morning mist without sufficient rainfall. The highlands and steppes are dry.

RELIGION

Most of the population are Moslem, but there are a large number of Hindus, some Parsees, and a minority of Christians. There are both Protestant and Catholic churches in Aden.

History

The ancient Kingdoms of Yemen were known to Greeks and the Romans chiefly because of the famous "incense route" which brought the luxury of the East to the West, passed through their land. The fact that ancient Yemenis found the "incense route" profitable venture is attested by the lavish construction of their ancient buildings, forts and temples.

Of all the ancient kingdoms of Yemen, the kingdom of Saba (biblical Sheba), was the most powerful and enduring.

Historians ascribe the decline of the Kingdom to the bursting of the Marib dam in the early Christian era, but the major causes were probably the diversion of the spice trade from the incense route in the area, a diversion which must have brought about radical changes in social, political and economic conditions.

The growth of steam navigation in the 19th century rendered it imperative to find a coaling station at the south end of the Red Sea. Negotiations were in progress for the purchase of Socotra when Captain Haines, who had orders to gain control of Aden against an annual payment, captured it from the Abdalis in 1839. The Sultan soon made peace and signed a treaty, being granted an annual stipend of 6,000 Maria Theresa dollars. From 1863 relations with Britain remained harmonious until 1958.

The establishment of the Aden Refinery brought vastly higher standards of living and attracted tribal immigrants; the population trebled in 15 years, over two-thirds being

Arabs, while many were Yemeni immigrants drawn by Aden's expanding economy.

With the prospect of a labour win in the 1964 elections in Britain, nationalist agitation increased but was contained, until the British Government's decision to abandon Aden was made public in February 1966.

INDEPENDENCE

Two rival political groups emerge: FLOSY (Front for the Liberation of Occupied South Yemen) was composed mostly of Adenese and western tribesmen; and NLF (National Liberation Front) which was led by discontended teachers, a class peculiarly susceptible to propaganda on Arabism and socialism.

Before leaving Aden, the British authorities under orders from London came to terms with the NLF rather than FLOSY, and in the bloody battle fought out between the tribal supporters of the two groups in Shaikh Othman, the NLF emerged as victors. The British withdrew on 29 November, and the NLF set up a government in Aden with Qahtan ach-Shaabi as its first president.

A draft Constitution approved by the ruling National Liberation Front and published on August 2 referred to South Yemen as a 'popular democratic republic' with Islam as its religion. Coming into effect on November 30, it provided for free and direct elections to a 101 member People's Supreme Council to be held before November 1971. On November 30 the country was officially named the People's Democratic Republic of Yemen.

In a bloodless coup in June 1969 Qahtan ash-Shaabi was deposed and replaced by a five-man Presidency Council, headed by Salim Rubai Ali. In July 1978 he was ousted from power and executed. Ali Nasir Mohamed became interim Head of State. Abdel Fattah Ismail who became Head of State following election of the Supreme People's Council, resigned on grounds of ill health and went into exile on April 20, 1980. Ali Nasir Mohamed resumed the presidency until January 1986, when he fled the country after a brief but intensive fighting. The then Prime Minister Haidar Abu Bakr Al Attas who was on mission outside the country, returned and assumed the posts of President of the Republic and Secretary General of the Yemen Socialist Party. In October 1986 following general elections to the Supreme People's Council, Mr. Attas was elected President for five years and Ali Salim Al Baid secretary General to the YSP, until unification with the Yemen Arab Republic in May 1990 was declared.

UNITY TALKS

The first session of the Yemen Council was held in Sana'a on Aug. 15-20 1983 to look into the findings of the Joint Ministerial Committee in a bid to speed up co-operation between North and South Yemen, as a first step towards their unification.

The committee had passed a number of resolutions including provisions (i) to facilitate movement between the two states with the establishment of joint border post, (ii) to formulate unified legislation to organise the function of Yemeni joint companies, (iii) to simplify trade between the two countries by cancelling all (customs) dues on products of Yemeni origin, and by setting up a unified technical committee for specifications and measures, and (iv) to form a "technical committee to... study co-operation and co-ordination in the field of agriculture". It culminated in the unity of both Yemen in May 1990.

The Economy

Prior to indepence in 1967, the economy of the People's Democratic Republic of Yemen was largely dominated by the trade and services sector. The position of Aden on the main shipping route from Europe to the Far East, India and East Africa via the Suez Canal had created favourable conditions for the development of a thriving entrepot trade and ship bunkering and servicing.

Economic conditions changed radically on the eve of independence as a result of the closure of the Suez Canal in June 1967, the withdrawal of the British troops in the same year, and the cessation of British budgetary aid. Consequently, the People's Democratic Republic of Yemen experienced a deep and protracted recession together with severe pressure on the budget and on the balance of payments.

However in the 1980's the economy improved by the discovery of oil in commercial quantities, increased productivity in manufacturing, agriculture and fisheries.

FISHING

The fish wealth of the People's Democratic Republic of Yemen is considered the country's most promising economic sector.

About 10,000 fishermen currently catch about 50,000 tons a year. However estimates indicate annual catches could be increased substantially without over-fishing.

To develop coastal fishing the Government initiated projects to construct shore facilities, improve the fishing fleet, improve fisheries administration and carry out studies for additional projects.

AGRICULTURE

Only 300,000 acres of land, or one per cent of the total area of the country is under cultivation at present, although the potential area of cultivation exceeds one and a half million acres, according to expert opinion including that of FAO experts.

The main crops are cotton, tobacco, coffee, vegetables, fruit (bananas and melons) and cereals (wheat, sorgum, millet and barley).

Hooka-type tobacco is grown in the coastal area, although the demand for this type has been limited. But experiments in the cultivation of tobaccos likely to attract foreign demand are planned under economic development plans.

The PDRY is almost self-sufficient in most kinds of vegetables and research on other varieties is continuing.

But the production of fruit does not come anywhere near the market requirements of the country, with the exception of bananas which is exported.

Food crops (sorghum, wheat, millet, barley and sesame) are well below the requirements of home consumption.

INDUSTRY

Industrial activity in the PDRY prior to independence was confined to the British Petroleum Refinery at Little Aden. The only industry which had expanded rapidly in the past was the bottling of soft drinks, with an average annual output of fifty million bottles.

Today there is a small ship repairing industry capable of building small craft up to 1500 tons per year. Other industries include the production of tiles, cement blocks, aluminium ware, paper bags, furniture.

Apart from handicraft and cottage industries there is one small tuna fish canning factory at Mukalla, two cotton ginneries at Adyan and Lahej, and sesame oil extraction plants.

LEATHER GOODS

Rough estimates put the number of sheep and goats in the country at four million head and the output of hides and skins at about 750,000 pieces a year which, if rationally processed, could put a ban on the import of leather and footwear.

COTTON SEED OIL

Annual output of cotton seeds amounts to an average of 7000-10000 tons. This should provide sufficient raw material to feed a cotton seed oil extraction plant with a crushing capacity of 18 tons per 24 hours. An oil extraction-soap-detergents industrial complex also provides employment to 400-500 hand.

former **Yemen Arab Republic**

Geography

The Yemen Arab Republic lies at the south end of the Red Sea between Asia and the Aden Protectorate. The country may be divided into 3 main topographical zones: the Tihama, the Central Highlands and the Eastern Plateau. The Tihama or coastal strip is narrow, hot, and dry, with the ports of Luhaiya, Hodaida and Mocha.

Most of the country is plateau with summits of 10,000 ft and more, and constitutes the most fertile part of Arabia, with intense terrace cultivation.

The area of the Yemen Republic is approximately 190,000 sq. km. and its population has been estimated at 9,000,000 as no census has ever taken place. The capital Sana'a, is gradually assuming the characteristics of a modern town, with a Municipal Corporation, metalled roads, hospitals, schools, and banks.

Climate varies with altitude. The coastal plain is extremely hot and humid in summer but more pleasant in winter.

Rainfall can be as high as 35 inches per year in the mountains.

POPULATION

Besides the Saidi majority, there are smaller groups of Sunni Moslems, and until 1950 a fairly considerable community of Oriental Jews. Since 1949 most Jews have emigrated to Israel

LANGUAGE AND RELIGION

Arabic is the official language but some Yemenis speak English through working or studying abroad. Very few speak French or German.

Islam is the State religion.

History

Like many areas in the Middle East, Yemen can look back on a long history of civilization and economic development. Assumed to be homeland of the legendary Queen of Sheba and known to the writers of antiquity as "Arabia Felix", it was famed in those days for its walled cities, lush fruit gardens and savoury spices.

The first historically documented large-scale political units in Yemen were the kingdoms of the Minaeans and Sabaeans. They were founded during the eighth century B.C. and existed simultaneously for some 500-600 years. At their height, they dominated much of Southern Arabia and controlled the Incense Trail, the routes over which Arabian frankincense, and Indian and East African goods were transported across or around the Arabian Peninsula to the Mediterranean Basin. Equally important, however, was the agricultural system that was created by the skill and ingenuity of these people. Terraced fields made possible the full utilization of scarce land and rainfall, while dams, the most famous of which was located at Marib on the eastern slope of the Yemeni mountain range, diverted and stored flood water for irrigation. It was the surplus production in agriculture that freed a relatively large part of the population to control and carry out trade, to build cities and to develop a flourishing artisan industry. The collapse of the two kingdoms came with the rise of the Himyarites (115 B.C.) who inherited the Minaeo-Sabaean culture and trade and founded a kingdom which endured until the sixth century A.D. Under the Himyarite rulers, however, the might of South Arabia began to decline. After the fall of Palmyra in the third century A.D., the Himyarites tried to extend their influence to Central and Northern Arabia, in an attempt to insure the safety of the Incense Trail. But this expansion invited Persian retaliation which drove back the Himyarites to the South. An important factor in the decline was the spread of Christianity and Judaism which served as a decisive influence in the Kingdom and encouraged the Christian Abyssinians (Ethiopians) to occupy the Kingdom in the year 525 A.D. The Abyssinians were later driven out by the Persians, who in turn were superseded by Islam. It was at this period of political decline that much of the agricultural system in Southern Arabia fell into disuse, and the last break up the Marib Dam around 570 A.D. signalled the end of a once great civilization.

It is only some 36 years ago that the stage was set for an economic revival of Yemen. In September 1962, units of the Yemeni Army occupied the palace of the Imam, the traditional ruler of the country. The revolutionary forces, supported by Egypt, rapidly gained control of Sana'a and other principal areas, and established the Yemen Arab Republic (YAR). Egypt sent troops and supplies to help combat the deposed Imam Badr, who had fled north where, with the help of Saudi Arabia and Jordan, he raised Royalist forces to oppose the Republic.

Almost at once the Egyptian supported regime of President Abdullah Al-Sallal was ousted and moderate republican leaders rallied to the defence of Sana'a against a final Royalist siege of the city. By 1968 the siege was broken and Republican leaders began a long, but eventually successful effort of reconciliation with Royalist tribes and their Saudi supporters.

Following the fall of President Abdullah Al Sallah, the reigns of the state were successively in the hands of Qadi Abdelrahman Al Iryani as head of a three-man Council in November 1967. Removed from Office, he was succeded by Lt. Col. Ibrahim Al Hamdi in 1973 who was murdered in October 1977, and replaced by Lt. Col. Ahmed Ibn Hussein Ghashmi. In his turn he was murdered on 24 June 1978. A temporary Presidential Council was formed under the chairmanship of the Speaker of the Constitutional Assembly, Qadi Abdelkarim Al Arshi, and nearly a month later the Assembly, by a large majority,. elected Lt. Col. Ali Abdullah Saleh as President.

Subsequent republican governments terminated Yemen's isolation from the rest of the world by opening the country to new social and economic concepts and values and to foreign products and techonologies.

More recently, especially since the quadrupling of international oil prices at the beginning of 1974, there has been an unprecedented increase in personal cash incomes based mainly on remittances by Yemenis who went to work in Saudi Arabia and the Gulf States. It is estimated that workers' remittances rose from some $ 40 million in 1969/70 to over $800 million in 1976/77 and $ 1,500 on average per annum since then. Largely as a result of these cash inflows YAR's per capita GNP has more than doubled in real terms since 1969/70 reaching a level of about $ 390 in 1976/77, $580 in 1978, before declining to $ 420 in 1979/80, and $ 650 by 1989.

STEPS TOWARDS UNIFICATION

Steps towards a merger of North Yemen and South Yemen, proposals for which had originally been made in October 1972 and had been revived in March 1979, were taken in late 1981, when a series of talks between President Ali Abdullah Saleh (North Yemen) and President Ali Nasser Mohammed (South Yemen) resulted in the compilation of statutes for the executive functioning of a united state and the draft of a constitution.

A meeting of the two presidents was held in TAIZ (North Yemen) on Sept. 14, following which a joint statement was issued referring to the "achievements and practical steps along the road of restoring Yemeni unity by peaceful and democratic means" already attained. Unification took place in May 1990.

The Economy

AGRICULTURE

The climate of Yemen makes possible the successful cultivation of different crops. Potential farmland amounts to about 12 million acres.

Possibilities of agricultural development are great as about 60 per cent of the Yemenis are shepherds and farmers. New trends in economic and agricultural development can result in a doubling of agricultural production.

Despite predominance of grains, the distinctly different ecological zones of the country permit the growing of a wide range of crops. In the Highlands, temperate zone crops like potatoes, grapes and deciduous fruits are grown successfully. Various legumes such as beans and pulses are grown extensively. In the sub-tropical climate and relatively ample rainfall of the southern Uplands, sorghum, millet, maize, barley and wheat are the principal crops. But a large variety of fruits and vegetables are also grown, including bananas, citrus fruits, tomatoes and onions. In the Tihama Plain with its tropical climate, warm winters, hot summers, high humidity and scant rainfull, millet is the staple crop.

Probably the most important cash crop in Yemen – and also the most controversial – is qat, a mildy narcotic plant which is widely consumed by the population. Although there are no statistics estimating the acreage planted to qat, the farm inputs used (e.g. water, fertilizer, labor) and the value of annual production, there is ample evidence suggesting that qat growing has expanded rapidly in recent years and that agricultural resources are increasingly diverted to this crop.

INDUSTRY

The five largest industrial operations in the country are the Spinning and Weaving Corporation in Sana'a the Yemen Company for Industry and Trades biscuit and sweet factory at Taiz the public sector Cement Corporation at Bajil and the National Tobacco and Matches Company. Other substantial operations are the Cotton Corporation's Hodeida ginnery, the Yemen Company for Industry and Trade's ghee substitute plant at Taiz, and aluminium products plant at Taiz, and three soft drinks plants, two at Hodeida, one at Taiz.

OIL

Petroleum has been discovered in 1984 and production

began in 1985 and following further discoveries of significant quantities of oil and gas, Yemen became an exporter. Yemen's proven oil reserves are estimated at 4 billion barrels.

The house of Representatives (elected in April 1993), abolished on 28 September 1994 the five-member Presidential Council, and elected Gen. Ali Abdullah Saleh as the country's President, and reelected him in 23 September 1999 for a further 5 years.

General elections were held in april 1997 for a new House of Representatives of 301 Members.

The Cabinet

(Sept. 1999)

Prime Minister: Dr. Abdel Karim AL IRYANI
Deputy Prime Minister and Minister of Foreign Affairs: Abdelkader BAJAMMAL
Minister of Petroleum and Mineral Resources: Mohamed Al Khadem AL WAJIH
Minister of State for Cabinet Affairs: Dr. Mutahar AL SAEEDI
Minister of Planning and Development: Ahmad Mohamed SUFAN
Minister of Labour and Vocational Training: Mohamed Mohamed AL TAYYIB
Minister of Supply and Trade: Abdelaziz AL KOMAIN
Minister of Local Administration: Sadiq Amin ABU RAS
Minister of the Interior: Brig.-Gen. Hussain Mohamed ARAB
Minister of Finance: Alawi Salih AL SALAMI
Minister of Justice: Ismail Ahmad AL WAZIR
Minister of Waqfs and Guidance: Sheikh Nasser AL SHAYBANI
Minister of Information: Abdelrahman Mohamed AL AKWA
Minister of Culture and Tourism: Abdelmalik MANSOUR
Minister of Transport: Brig.-Gen. Abdelmalik AL SAYYANI
Minister of Industry: Abdelrahman Mohamed Ali OTHMAN
Minister of Construction, Housing and Urban Planning: Abdullah Hussein AL DAFI
Minister of Health: Abdullah Abdulwali NASHIR
Minister of Agriculture and Water Resources: Ahmad Selim AL JABALI
Minister of Fisheries: Ahmad Musaed HUSSAIN
Minister of Defence: Col. Mohamed Daifallah MOHAMED
Minister of Social Security and social Affairs: Muhamed Abdullah AL BATTANI
Minister of Electricity and Water: Ali Hamid SHARAF
Minister of Parliamentary and Legal Affairs: Abdullah Ahmad GHANIM
Minister for the Civil Service and Administrative Reform: Mohamed Ahmad AL JUNAID
Minister of Communications: Ahmad Mohamed AL ANISI
Minister of Youth and Sport: Dr. Abdelwahab RAWIH
Minister of Education: Yahya Mohamed Abdullah AL SHUAIBI
Minister of Expatriate Affairs: Ahmad Ali AL BISHARI
Minister of State: Faisal Mahmoud Hassan ALI

Foreign Embassies

Algeria: 67 Amman Str. P.O.Box 509, Sanaa
Egypt: Gamal Abdel Nasser St., P.O.Box 1134 Sanaa
China, People's Republic: Zubairy Str., Sanaa
Czech Republic: Safiya Rd., P.O.Box 2501, Sanaa
Ethiopia: Haddah Rd., P.O.Box 234, Sanaa
France: Al Baonia, P.O.Box 1286, Sanaa
Germany: Outer Ring Rd., West Haddah, P.O.Box 41, Sanaa
Hungary: Safiya, Str. No.5, House No.6B, Sanaa
Iran: Haddah Str., P.O.Box 1437, Sanaa
Iraq: South Airport Rd., P.O.Box 498, Sanaa
Italy: Str. No.29, No.5 Bldg., P.O.Box 1152, Sanaa
Japan: Ring Rd., West Safiya, P.O.Box 817, Sanaa
Jordan: 60 South Str., Sakfiya, P.O.Box 2152, Sanaa
Korea, Democratic People's Republic: Al Hasaba, Mazda Rd., P.O.Box 1209, Sanaa
Kuwait: near Ring Rd.60, P.O.Box 3746, Sanaa
Lebanon: Haddah Str., P.O.Box 2283, Sanaa
Libya: Ring Rd., Str. No.8, House No.145, P.O.Box 1506, Sanaa
Morocco: West Safiya, P.O.Box 10236, Sanaa
Netherlands: Haddah Rd., P.O.Box 463, Sanaa
Oman: Aser area, Zubairy Str., P.O.Box 105, Sanaa
Pakistan: Ring Rd., P.O.Box 2848, Sanaa
Romania: Haddah Rd., P.O.Box 2169, Sanaa
Russia: 26 September Str., P.O.Box 1087, Sanaa
Saudi Arabia: Zuhara House, Haddah Rd., P.O.Box 1184, Sanaa
Somalia: Haddah Rd., P.O.Box 12277, Sanaa
Sudan: 82 Abou al Hassan al Hamadani Str., Sanaa
Syria: Haddah Rd., Str. No.1, P.O.Box 494, Sanaa
Tunisia: Diplomatic area, Str. No.22, P.O.Box 2561, Sanaa
Turkey: Safiya, P.O.Box 12450, Sanaa
United Arab Emirates: Ring Rd., P.O.Box 2250, Sanaa
United Kingdom: 129 Haddah Rd., P.O.Box 1287, Sanaa
U.S.A.: Saawan Str., P.O.Box 22347, Sanaa

The Banking System

Central Bank of Yemen: Est. 1971; Ali Abdel Mughni Str., P.O.Box 59, Sanaa
Arab Bank PLC.: Est. 1972; Zubairy Str., P.O.Box 475, Sanaa
Credit Agricole Indosuez: Qasr al Jumhuriya Str., P.O.Box 651, Sanaa

Cooperative and Agricultural Credit Bank: Est. 1976; Zubairy Str., P.O.Box 2015, Sanaa
Habib Bank Ltd.: Akhwa Hotel Bldg., P.O.Box 3927, Hodeida
Industrial Bank of Yemen: Est. 1976; Zubairy Str., P.O.Box 323, Sanaa
International Bank of Yemen: Est. 1979; 106 Zubairy Str., P.O.Box 2847, Sanaa
National Bank of Yemen: Est. 1970; Arwa Rd., Crater, P.O.Box 5, Aden
United Bank Ltd.: Ali Abdel Mughni Str., P.O.Box 1295, Sanaa
The Yemen Bank for Reconstruction and Development: Est. 1962; 26 September Str., P.O.Box 541, Sanaa
Yemen Commercial Bank: P.O.Box 19845, Tel. (1)213662, Sanaa

Insurance

Marib Yemen Insurance Co.: Est. 1974; Zubairy Str., P.O.Box 2284, Sanaa
National Insurance and Reinsurance Co.: Est. 1970; P.O.Box 456, Aden
United Insurance Co.: Est. 1981; Qasr al Jumhuriya Str., P.O.Box 1983, Sanaa
Yemen General Insurance Co.: Est. 1977; 25 al Thalatheen Str., YGI Bldg., P.O.Box 2709, Sanaa

Trade Organizations

Aden Refinery Co.: P.O.Box 3003, Tel. (2)76234, 110 Aden
General Corpn for Manufacturing and Marketing of Cement: P.O.Box 1920, Tel. (1)215691, Sanaa
National Co. for Foreign Trade: P.O.Box 90, Tel. (2)42793, Aden
National Co. for Home trade: P.O.Box 90, Tel. (2)41483, Aden
National Dockyards Co.: P.O.Box 1244, Tel. (2)23837, Aden
National Drug Corpn.: P.O.Box 192, Tel. (2)04912, Aden
Public Corpn for Building and Housing: P.O.Box 7022, Tel. (2)342296, Aden
Public Corpn for Maritime Affaire (PCMA): P.O.Box 19396, Tel. (1)41412, Sanaa
Yemen Co for Investment and Finance Ltd.: P.O.Box 2789, Tel. (1)276372, Sanaa
Yemen Drug Co. for Industry and Commerce: P.O.Box 40, Tel. (1)234250, Sanaa
Yemen Economioal Corpn: P.O.Box 1207, Tel. (1)262501, Sanaa
Yemen Free Zone Public Authority: Tel. (2)241210, Aden
Yemen Land Transport Corpn: P.O.Box 279, Tel. (1)262108, Sanaa
Yemen National Oil Co.: P.O.Box 5050, Aden
Yemen Trading and Construction: P.O.Box 1092, Tel. (1)264005, Sanaa

Transport

ROADS

The network of roads linking the principal centers of population consist of about 64000 Km. of roads running from Hodeida to Sanaa, Salif, Taiz, Ibb, Saada, Marib, Mafraq. Also highways run from Aden to Mukalla; Nisab to Naqubah; Naqubah to Wadi Beihan; Shihr to Sayhut.

SHIPPING

The main ports are Aden, Nishtun, Hodeida, Mocha and Salif

CIVIL AVIATION

Six Major Airports service domestic and international travel, at Khormaksar near Aden, Ganad near Taiz, Hodeida Mukalla, Seyun and Sanaa.
Yemen Airways: Airport Road, P.O.Box 1183, Sanaa.

Higher Education

Aden University: Est. 1975; P.O.Box 7039, Al Mansoora, Tel.: 82434, Aden
Faculty of Agriculture
Faculty of Commerce & Economics
Faculty of Medicine
Sanaa University: Est. 1970; P.O.Box 1247, Sanaa; (Arabic and English).
Higher College of Education: Est. 1970; Aden. Two-year diploma course for primary school teachers, and four-year course for secondary school teachers.

VOCATIONAL INSTITUTES

Military Academy, Sanaa
College of Aviation, Sanaa
Radio Communications College, Sanaa
Agricultural Institute, Sanaa

CULTURAL INSTITUTES

British Council: Est. 1974; P.O.Box 2175, Sinan Abou Luhum Bldg., Sanaa Library: 4,000 volumes, 26 periodicals.
Library of the Great Mosque of Sanaa: Est. 1925; Sanaa

Radio, Television and Press

Yemen Radio and Television Corporation: P.O.Box 2182, Sanaa, Est. 1990 to control Radio Stations and Televisions in operation

THE PRESS

Fanoon: Est. 1980; Tawahi 102, P.O.Box 1187, Aden; Arabic; Monthly
Gumhuryyah: Taiz; Arabic; Daily
Hikma: P.O.Box 4227, Crater, Aden; Arabic; Monthly
Marib: Dar al Qalam, Taiz; Arabic; Weekly

Qadiyat al Asr: Est. 1981; Aden; Arabic; Weekly
Rabi Ashar Min Uktubar: Est. 1968; P.O.Box 4227, Aden; Arabic; Daily
Ra'i al 'Am: P.O.Box 293, Sanaa; Weekly
Risalah: 26 September Str., Sanaa; Arabic; Weekly
Salam: Est. 1948; P.O.Box 181, Sanaa; Arabic; Weekly
Sawt al'Ummal: P.O.Box 4227, Crater, Aden; Arabic; Weekly
Thaqafat al Jadida: Est. 1970; Tawahi 102, P.O.Box 1187, Aden; Arabic; Monthly
Attijarah: P.O.Box 3370, Hodeida; Arabic; Monthly
Al Wahda al Watani: Est. 1982; P.O.Box 193, Sanaa; Monthy
Yemen: Est. 1971; P.O.Box 1081, Tel. (2)72376, Sanaa; Arabic

NEWS AGENCIES

Aden News Agency: Est. 1970; P.O.Box 1207, Yawabi, Aden; governement organization
Sanaa News Agency: Est. 1970; P.O.Box 1475 Sanaa

PART IV
OUTLINE OF THE ARAB WORLD

1 – GENERAL SURVEY
2 – THE LEAGUE OR ARAB STATES
3 – THE MAGHREB
4 – ARAB PETROLEUM
5 – THE SUEZ CANAL
6 – DEVELOPMENT OF ARAB BANKS AND FUTURE PROSPECTS
7 – THE PALESTINIAN PROBLEM
8 – GULF CO–OPERATION COUNCIL
9 – PEACE CONFERENCE ON THE MIDDLE EAST

1 - GENERAL SURVEY

- **History** of the Arabian Gulf
- **The** Early Arabs
- **The** rise of Islam and the Arab Empire
- **The** Golden Age of the Arabs

History of the Arabian Gulf

The lands on the western side of the Arabian Gulf, now the area of oil developments have held a place in history for thousands of years, going back almost to the beginning of civilization. They undoubtedly offer a field for archaeological exploration – a field, however, which remains virtually untouched except for brief surface surveys and some excavations at Jawan in Saudi Arabia and in Bahrain. The findings have been enlightening, but most presentday knowledge about the early peoples of this region comes from ancient historians.

There is little doubt that civilized man lived here at least as far back as the development of the art of seafaring, which was known in the Arabian Gulf by the dawn of recorded history about 4000 B.C.

It is very likely that the ancient Sumerians of Mesopotamia carried on an active trade with the peoples of the Arabian Gulf. Ancient cuneiform inscriptions refer to a land called Dilmun in Babylonian and Assyrian and named Niduk-ki in Sumerian. This land may have been the Bahrain Islands and a part of the Eastern Province of Saudi Arabia. Possibly the Sumerians at one time set up colonies in this area.

However that may have been, one of the most interesting features of Bahrain and parts of the Eastern Province is the presence of many large mounds or tumuli and tens of thousands of small ones, which were the tombs or sepulchers of the dead of an ancient people. Some of these may be seen today in the Dhahran area. The mound-building tradition in Arabia and Bahrain probably covered a considerable time span. It is certain that burial mounds were being built in this region down to the second century of the Christian era, but a date for the begining of this tradition has not yet been established.

Mounds of this type have been found also in other parts of Arabia, particularly at al-Karj and Yabrin, and by H. St. John B. Philby in the ancient home of the Sabeans in south western Arabia. The ancient Phoenicians followed a similar practice. A tomb complex at Jawan, near the road from Dhahran to Ras Tanura, has been excavated by a western archaeologist with the agreement of the Saudi Arabian Government. Objects found in the tomb belong to the late first or early second century A.D.

Greek and Roman geographers shed some light on eastern Arabia at the beginning of the Christian era and for a few centuries before that time. These geographers tell of the city of Gerra or perhaps its seaport, which may have been located near the present port of al'-Uqair, though this identification is not certain. Gerra was reported by the Greek geographer Strabo to have been a Chaldean colony, that is, a colony of Babylon. Strabo says:

"The merchants of Gerra generally carry the Arabian merchandise and aromatics by land; but Aristobulus says, on the contrary, that they frequently travel into Babylonia on rafts and thence sail up the Euphrates with their cargoes, but afterwards carry them by land to all parts of the country".

Gerra was apparently an important centre of trade with Babylonia in products not only from southwestern Arabia but also from Oman and India. The overland caravan journey from Hadhramaut to Gerra was said to take forty days. Speaking of Gerra's wealth, Strabo says, quoting earlier writers:

"By the trade both the Sabeans and Gerraei have become the richest of all tribes, and possess a great quantity of wrought articles in gold and silver, as couches, tripods, basins, drinking vessels, to which we must add the costly magnificence of their houses; for the doors, walls and roofs are variegated with inlaid ivory, gold, silver and precious stones".

Both Strabo and Pliny stated that the houses of Gerra were built of blocks of salt. It is more likely that they were constructed of bricks made out of salty mud from the sabkhahs (salt flats).

Pliny described the location of Gerra as being opposite Tylos (presumably Bahrain), which even then was "famous for the vast number of its pearls". He also referred to the region of Attene, 50 miles inland, which doutless was on or near the site of present-day Hofuf. The date gardens along the coast were probably much more extensive in Pliny's time than they are now, as sand dunes have been encroaching upon them.

In the first few centuries of the Christian era, many inhabitants of eastern Arabia became Christians. Darin, on Tarut Island, was a bishopric of the Nestorian Church. A number of gravestones found in the Qatif area, inscribed in the Sabean of Himyaritic alphabet, are thought to commemorate some long-forgotten Christians. Oriental Christian sources mention bishoprics here from the third Christian century. The region did not accept Muslim domination without a struggle. Following the death of the Prophet there was a rebellion which was put down only with the taking of Darin by Muslim troops who waded from the mainland to Tarut Island.

A few centuries later, at the end of the ninth century, much of the present Eastern Province and Bahrain was taken over by, and became the headquarters of violent Muslim sect known as the Carmanthians. The Carmanthians gained control over a large part of Arabia. They even took Mecca in 930 and carried off the sacred Black Stone of the Ka'bah to their capital in eastern Arabia, near what is now Hofuf. The Stone was soon restored to Mecca.

In the sixteenth century the Portuguese were active in the Arabian Gulf. On Bahrain Island they built a large fort, which is still standing. Bahrain also was for limited and temporary periods ruled by the Persians on several occasions. The present ruling family of Al-Khalifah took the Bahrain Islands from the Persians in 1783. Meanwhile the British, after forming the East India Company in 1600, had won control of the Gulf, first from the Portuguese and then from the Dutch.

Until the rise of the House of Sa'ud, eastern Arabia was at times under local leaders such as the chiefs of the tribe of Bani Khalid and at other times under Turkish provincial governors. Occasionally Arabian Gulf pirates used coastal points as bases for their operations. A recently demolished port at Damman was the lair of a notorious pirate during the early nineteenth century.

The Early Arabs

The better-watered and more arable lands bordering the north Arabian desert (that is, the valleys of the Tigris and Euphrates Rivers, the southern slopes of the Taurus Mountains and the eastern shores of the Mediterranean) have been aptly called the Fertile Crescent. It was largely within these lands that the ancient civilization of the Middle East flourished.

Throughout Middle Eastern history, the peoples of the vast Arabian Peninsula also have played important roles. The distinctive contribution of the people of the great Arabian deserts, however, has been to supply their neighbours with new blood and with the stimulation of their less sophisticated but fresher energies.

The Arabian Peninsula has also had its own ancient centres of civilization. It has always had its oasis gardens and its towns, which still are centres of culture, trade and leadership. But the desert tracts have been peopled, as they are today, by the Bedouins.

From the time of the earliest civilizations, the desert nomads frequently made raids upon their more prosperous neighbours within the Fertile Crescent. On occasion, when organized by leaders who arose among them, they attacked and conquered some of the great centres of civilization, bringing with them the simplicity and virility of the desert and infusing new blood and vitality into the communities of which they became masters. They, in turn, absorbed the culture of the conquered.

In other instances Semitic peoples seem to have migrated en masse to new lands which had not been developed fully – probably gathering Bedouin allies as they went. The Akkadians, the Amorites, the Assyrians, the Chaldeans, the Hebrews and the Arameans were all Semites who may have come out of the Syrian and the Arabian deserts. Semites also made incursions into the land of the Nile. At one time, in the eighteenth century B.C., they probably took part in setting up a dynasty there, that of the Hyksos, which controlled Egypt for nearly 200 years. Later, fired by the new faith of Islam, the people of the Arabian Peninsula surged forth from their deserts to conquer much of the known world.

Another important role played by the peninsular Arabs in the old civilizations of the Nile and the Fertile Crescent was in trade and commerce. Southern Arabia was then a populous and thriving area, known to the Romans as Arabia Felix or Happy Arabia. It was one of the principal sources of frankincense and myrrh, which were used extensively in unguents and perfumes, as incense for the many temples, and by the Romans in the cremation of royal and noble persons. Frankincense and myrrh are still produced in southern Arabia.

Southern Arabia was also a focal region for trade in spices, silks, ivory and other valuable goods destined for Egypt and other Mediterranean lands. The sources of these commodities – India, the Indies and East Africa – were apparently unknown to the consumer countries at first hand. Accordingly the Arabs had a practical monopoly of this highly profitable trade.

The Arabs are reported also to have supplied the more northern countries with gold, copper and precious stones. Some of the gold came from Arabia itself, where ancient mines existed. Copper may have come from the mountains of Oman. Western Arabia is still a source of semiprecious gems.

Radiating from southwestern Arabia were great caravan routes. One of these ran along the western side of the peninsula through Mecca and Yathrib (now Medina) and thence to Palestine or Damascus or around the head of the Gulf of Aqaba to Egypt. Another one ran to the Arabian Gulf seaport of Gerra, from which the goods from Arabia Felix were shipped to Babylonia and other areas. There were other important overland routes, and long trains of camels, carrying rich cargoes and no doubt heavily guarded, were a familiar part of the Arabian scene. The Points at which they halted, and the centres at which the goods were sold or redistributed by merchant middlemen, became thriving communities.

Some of the ancient caravans are still in use; others are still indicated by paths deeply worn by the tread of countless camels. Until replaced by airplanes and motor vehicles in recent years, camels carried pilgrims by the thousands to the Holy Cities.

ANCIENT ARABIAN CIVILIZATION

Arabia in ancient times was not merely an adjunct to the civilized countries farther north. It had its own centres of civilization, although they developed later than those in Mesopotamia or Egypt.

At one time, no doubt during the Ice Age, the whole of the Arabian Peninsula enjoyed a much more favourable climate than it does now. Evidence is found in the well-developed and well-entrenched water courses which could hardly have been formed under conditions existing today. Good examples for these water courses are al-Batin, which trends north-easterly from Najd past Kuwait, and as-Sahba, which runs easternly from the Tuwaiq Mountains south of the latitude of Riyad. These at some time must have been the valleys of rivers.

Stone artifacts or implements found sporadically throughout the Arabian Peninsula provide traces of cultural levels of Middle Paleolithic aspect in northern Arabia, along the area now traversed by the trans-Arabian pipeline system, and of late Paleolithic and Neolothic aspect in the western Rub' al-Khali. One hand axe from central Arabia and another from the western Rub' al-Kali can be classed as Early Paleolithic. At present, none of these cultural levels, which should be of great antiquity, can be dated accurately in the Peninsula.

The early traditions of the Arabs make a distinction between the Arabs of the north and the Arabs of the south. The distinction may have been partly due to the fact that many of those in the south lived in cities, while most of those in the north were nomads. As trade developed between the southern communities and the north, some mixing of the two types of Arabs took place. Before the time of the Prophet Muhammad, many Arabs of southern origin were already living in north Arabia. There, they figured in the tribal wars which inspired much of the pre-Islamic poetry belonging to the earliest period of Arabic literature. Many Arabs of both types also moved into the Fertile Crescent where they mingled with earlier settlers.

The mountains of the Yemen form a populous and relatively well-watered area which for many centuries has been somewhat isolated from the rest of the world. A wider region, comprising the southwestern and the central southern coast, was the scene of ancient kingdoms which engaged in international commerce.

The people of ancient south Arabia built dams to impound and conserve the floods of the rainy periods, and their system of irrigation seems to have provided their basic means of support. The control they acquired over what was then the main highway for trade between the East and the West was an important element in their prosperity.

Among the earliest states in southwestern Arabia, which rose to prominence in the first millennium B.C., were the Minean of Ma'in and the Sabean of Saba. The Queen of Sheba, who visited King Solomon in the tenth century B.C., may well have been an Arabian princess. However, she may have come from a Sabean colony in the northern part of the peninsula rather than from the land of Saba in the south.

Other kingdoms in southern Arabia were Ausan in the southwest corner nearest Aden, Qataban northeast of Ausan, and Hadhramaut east of Qataban. They fought many wars and experienced many changes in relative fortunes. This southern civilization in its later periods is often referred to as Hymyaritic rather than Minean or Sabean, after the southwestern tribe of Himyar, which grew increasingly powerful.

With the exception of a few scholars such as al-Hamdani in the tenth century A.D., the Arabs have largely neglected earlier Arabian history because of their pre-ocupation with Islamic civilization. Zealous believers, considering pre-Islamic culture to be of no consequence, destroyed many of its vestiges in their efforts to eradicate all traces of idolatry. Except for references in the writings of other ancient peoples and accounts by a few Arab authors, the Western world had no knowledge of the ancient cities of southwestern Arabia until the nineteenth century, when Western explorers visited the area. They found ruins of fine buildings, sculpture, canals, roads and wellplanned cities which revealed an advanced stage of culture.

Of particular importance was the great dam of Ma'rib, constructed of finely hewn limestone and so well-engineered that it compared favourably with the most ambitious structures in other ancient countries. This dam, which supplied an irrigation system adequate for a sizable population, fell into disuse between the time of Christ and the time of Muhammad.

Many inscriptions carved in stone in the Minean and Sabean alphabets have been found in southwestern Arabia. Knowledge of the ancient history of this area is increasing rapidly with the collection and interpretation of these inscriptions.

The Arabs of the north developed more slowly. The first settled communities in their midst appear to have been outposts or colonics of thc Mincans and Sabeans. Later, a local people known as the Nabateans assumed control of the northern portion of the rich trade route from thc south and built a rcmarkably beautiful city at Petra, where large buildings were carved out of red sandstone cliffs. Lying in a remote spot in present-day Jordan, it had become lost to the knowledge of the West until rediscovered by the Swiss traveller John Lewis Burckhardt in the early nineteenth century.

After the rise of Roman power, covetous eyes were turned upon the wealth and trade which Arabia Felix had so long enjoyed. An invasion based on Egypt was organized under the Roman general Aelius Gallus in 24 B.C. According to the Greek geographer Strabo, no difficulty was anticipated because "the Arabians, being engaged mostly in traffic and commerce, are not a war-like people". Strabo reported further that "the barbarians were entirely inexperienced in war and used their weapons unskillfully, which were bows, swords and slings; but the greater part of them used a double edged axe".

The invasion is said to have been aided and guided by a Nabatean official. After a difficult passage through the desert, Najaran was taken with ease. In a battle in the old Minean district of al-Jauf, 10,000 of the Arabs were said - most improbably- to have been killed with the loss of only two Romans. Running short of water, however, the Romans were forced to retire without having reached the incense country of Hadhramaut. By the time Aelius Gallus returned to Egypt, most of his army had perished from disease, starvation and thirst. Thus the first Western invasion of the Arabian Peninsula ended in failure.

The military threat, however, was not the only menace to the trade monopoly enjoyed by the Arabs. The Greeks and Romans acquired the Arabs' skill of navigating to India with the aid of the monsoon winds. There-after the economic decline of Arabia was only a question of time. The Arabs, for their part, attributed the decline to the breaking of the Ma'rib dam and the consequent ill effects on the agricultural economy.

A northward migration resulted from the southern decline. The kingdoms of al-Hirah in lower Iraq and

Ghassan in what is now Jordan were formed by the southern Arabs. Others, of the tribe of Kindah, formed a kingdom in northern Najd, but it was short-lived.

The Abyssinians or Ethiopians fought with the Sassanid Persians for control of southwestern Arabia. The former were largely Semitic in language as a result of earlier migrations from Arabia. The Abyssinians invaded and conquered areas of southwest Arabia in the fourth century A.D., and again in the sixth century. After the latter invasion, the Abyssinian Abraha made an unsuccessful expedition against Mecca in or about 570. His forces included at least one elephant, an animal singularly unsuited for desert warfare. Muhammad the Prophet was born in Mecca during the same year in which the Holy City was saved from danger.

During the rise of Islam in the seventh century, Sassanid Persia again held the Yemen. The Sassanids, who earlier had controlled a part of northeastern Arabia, looked with disdain upon the tribes of Arabia Desert. These same tribes, under the banner of Islam, soon conquered the Sassanid Empire.

The Rise of Islam and the Arab Empire

One of the most amazing episodes in the experience of mankind was the birth of a new faith, Islam. From humble beginnings it first enkindled the town and desert peoples of the Arabian Peninsula and then swept over most of the civilized world. It brought forth one of the most brilliant periods of art and culture that the world has known. It remains today the vital faith of some one billion people.

At the time of the birth of Muhammad at Mecca, about A.D. 570, the Western world was in a state of decadence and unrest. The Roman Empire, which had controlled the world in the first few centuries of the Christian era, had succumbed long since to the onslaught of European barbarians. Its successor, the Christian Byzantine Empire, centered at Constantinople, had been engaged with the Sassanid Empire of Persia in wars which had exhausted both. It was a disorganized world into which Muhammad was born. His teachings spread not only because they were propagated with zeal by his followers, but also because they offered a refreshing new outlook to many misgoverned and disheartened people.

Arabia had been in a state of anarchy, with constant tribal feuds and fights and occasional religious persecutions, such as that of the Christians by the Jews in the southwestern part of the country. The majority of the Arabs still worshipped pagan gods. Even before the rise of Islam, Mecca was a sacred city, the site of a temple: the Ka'bah. Large pilgrimages were made to this shrine, and at that time, as today, the pilgrimage was one of the sources of revenue for the residents of Mecca.

The Prophet Muhammad was born, according to tradition, in the year of the Elephant, so named because it was the year when Mecca was being threatened by the Abyssinian army accompanied by an elephant. Muhammad belonged to the clan of Hashim in the tribe of Quraish, whose members were custodians of the Ka'bah. Even before his birth there had been a rift between his clan and another Quraishite clan known as the Umayyads. This foreshadowed a great schism in the ranks of Islam after his death.

Muhammad was the son of 'Abd Allah ibn' Abd al-Muttalib of Mecca. His mother, Aminah, was a daughter of the tribe of Quraish. Little is known of the first forty years of his life except that he became an orphan at an early age, was reared by his grandfather and by an uncle, and at the age of twenty-five married a rich widow, Khadijah, fifteen years his senior, whose caravans he successfully managed. He spent a portion of his boyhood among the Bedouins and from them learned the simplicity of life and the purity of speech of the desert.

About the age of forty Muhammad began to have revelations. He became convinced that God had chosen him to perfect the religion earlier revealed to Abraham, the prophets of Israel and Jesus. Among his initial converts were his wife, his cousin Ali (later also his son-in-law), and another kinsman Abu Bakr (later also one of his fathers-in-laws), a leader among Quraish. Other leaders of Quraish were jealous and suspicious of Muhammad's teachings, which threatened their vested interest in the pilgrim trade.

Muhammad continued to make converts, mostly among poor people and slaves. The hostility against him twice grew to a point where he advised his followers to take refuge in Christian Abyssinia. At length his enemies plotted to murder him; but he was forewarned and, 'Ali, his cousin heroically, lay in Muhammad's bed feigning sleep when the would-be murderers arrived. Meanwhile Muhammad, accompanied by Abu Bakr, fled to a nearby mountain cave, and after two nights continued on to Medina, then known as Yathrib. The way had been prepared in the previous year by a compact between the Prophet and leaders of Medina.

The year of this transfer to Medina, the **Hijrah** (commonly written Hegira), was later taken as Anno Hegirae or A.H. 1 of the Muslim calendar (A.D. 622). At that time Muhammad was fiftyone.

Muhammad's teachings were widely accepted in his new home except by local Judaized Arabs. The new faith began to spread also to other parts of Arabia. The people of Mecca, however, remained hostile, and a number of battles were fought before they came to terms. In 629 Muhammad returned to Mecca as its master. By the time he died, in 632, large numbers of people in all parts of Arabia had embraced the faith of Islam.

Late in life Muhammad began thinking of extending his work beyond the borders of Arabia, and his followers proceeded to put this idea into effect. After quelling some rebellious elements in the country, including eastern Arabia, they started forth with an army of from 3,000 to 4,000 men on campaigns that were to lead to extensive conquests. As the movement gathered momentum, the numbers were swelled from newly converted populations outside Arabia.

Abu Bakr, the devoted companion of Muhammad, succeeded to the leadership of Islam and became the first Caliph (Khalifah or successor). Khalid ibn al-Walid was one of his most brilliant generals, and ranks among the foremost military men of history. Under Khalid's leadership the Muslim armies struck east toward Sassanid Persia and north towards the Eastern Roman or Byzantine province of Syria. Wherever the armies encountered resistance they offered three alternatives: embrace the religion of the true God, or surrender and pay tribute, or war. Often they were welcomed and converted large numbers of the conquered.

The Byzantine army was dealt a decisive defeat in 636 near the Yarmuk River, east of the sea of Galilee, and was forced subsequently to retreat north of the Taurus mountains.

The Sassanid Persian Emperor was given good cause to regret his scornful and insulting treatment of the first emissaries of Islam. The Muslims won all of Iraq and Persia between 637 and 650. Their greatest victories over the Persians were decivise battles at Qadisiyah, Ctesiphon (the Sassanid capital) and Nehavend.

After Abu Bakr died in 634, 'Umar, another of the Prophet's fathers-in-laws, became the second Caliph. He continued the conquests, and one country after another fell or surrendered. Jerusalem, the third holiest city in Islam, was taken in 638, and was visited by the pious Caliph himself. The Christians were permitted to retain their faith and their shrines. Egypt was won from the Byzantines in 640 and 641, and the city of Alexandria was retaken in 646 after a Byzantine counterattack. Fustat (later Cairo) in Egypt and Basra and Kufah in Iraq were founded as military encampments and afterwards became great cities.

The conquests continued for over 100 years. By 750 the Muslims had swept over North Africa and Spain and over central Asia toward China, but they had failed to conquer Constantinople or France.

Like the Prophet Muhammad, the earlier Caliphs were humble and democratic leaders inspired by a great faith. Thereafter, a complex series of rivalries developped for the Caliphate. They resulted in the principal division of the Muslim world into the Shi'ah (or Shi'ites) and the people of the Sunnah (or Sunnites).

The third Caliph, 'Uthman, was an old man by the time his rule began. He was from the Umayyad clan of the tribe of Quraish of Mecca. This clan had been rivals of the Hashimite clan even before the birth of the Prophet. 'Uthman aroused the displeasure of many by showing special favours to members of his own group. He was murdered in his house at the age of 80.

'Ali, the cousin and son-in-law of Muhammad, became the fourth Caliph. Another Umayyad, Mu'awiyah, the able Muslim governor of Syria, charged 'Ali with implication in the murder of 'Uthman and challenged his leadership. In a battle the forces of Ali were nearly victorious, but the followers of Mu'awiyah turned the tide by mounting copies of the Koran on their spears to signify that the issue should be decided by the holy word. Ali was impressed and agreed to arbitrate. The arbitration went against him, but since it was regarded as unfairly conducted he did not accept the decision.

'Ali continued as nominal Caliph. However, he was opposed by the followers of Mu'awiyah, and he lost many of his own supporters, who turned against him because he had agreed to arbitration. He put down a rebellion, but then was assassinated. Mu'awiyah thus gained the Caliphate.

Ever since that time Islam has been divided between the Shi'ites, who believe that the Caliphate should have descended to the heirs of Muhammad's daughter Fatimah and her husband Ali, and the Sunnites, who believe it was properly an elective office. A few years after the death of Ali, the Shi'ites attempted to place Hussain, the son of Ali, in the Caliphate, He and his followers were overcome and massacred at Karbala in Iraq, in the Arabic month of Muharram, A.H. 61 (October, 680). This tragic event is still mourned and commemorated by the Shi'ites during Muharram each year. Karbala and an Najaf, where Ali was buried, are important Shi'ite shrines.

Although Medina had been the original Islamic capital, even before the death of Ali the control of the new empire had passed from Arabia, which was left in the status of a province dignified chiefly by possession of the two Holy Cities. Mu'awiyah set up his Caliphate in Damascus. The Umayyad dynasty which he founded lasted until 750. It was then violently overthrown by descendants of al-Abbas, an uncle of Muhammad. Thus began the 'Abbasid dynasty, which retained the Caliphate until overwhelmed by the Mongols in 1258.

Such are the Highlights of the Muslim Caliphate down to the fall of the great Arab Empire. Thereafter, the Caliphate was merely an appendage of Mameluke rule in Egypt and later of the Ottoman Empire, until the last Caliph was deposed by the Republic of Turkey in 1922 and the office was abolished in 1924.

The Golden Age of the Arabs

After seizing the Caliphate in 750, the 'Abbasids moved their capital to Baghdad, the scene of the golden age of the Arabs. This age brought together the art, skill, philospy, learning, science and culture developed by many great civilizations.

On the material side, Baghdad became a fabulous city of mosques, palaces and mansions. Gold and silver, pearls, ivory, jewels, silk works of art, spices, and all types of luxurious goods and handicrafts poured into Baghdad from many parts of the world. Baghdad was not the only city to prosper. Cairo, Alexandria, Damascus, Aleppo and

Basra also became centres of wealth and luxury.

The accumulation of learning encouraged the Arabs to carry on energetic research in various fields of knowledge. They welcomed, sponsored and stimulated learned men, scientists, artists, musicians and poets from many places. They established schools in which the knowledge and wisdon of great scholars and philosophers could be studied. The works of such men – Greek, Roman, Syrian, Persian and Indian – were translated into Arabic, and thus were preserved for future civilizations. The Arabs also made new contributions of their own in medicine and other sciences and in literature, especially poetry. They invented algebra and chemistry, the names of which are derived from Arabic words. They greatly advanced the knowledge of astronomy.

While the evidence seems to be that Arabic numerals were brought to Baghdad from India, it was in the great days of Baghdad that the cipher was invented. This concept revolutionized and simplified numerical calculations by leading to the development of the decimal and place system – that is, the use of only ten numerals in an indefinite number of places (units, tens, hundreds, thousands, etc.)

The Arabs had an important role in advancing the manufacture and use of paper, originally devised in China. They introduced this more practical substitute for earlier writing materials, such as clay tablets, papyrus and parchment, through Spain into Europe in time to facilitate the rapid development of printing with movable type.

The tales *The Arabian Nights* provide an insight into the life and culture of the brilliant age of the Caliph Harun ar-Rashid. These tales are widely known in the Western world even though the real significance of those days has been largely forgotten: namely, that the Arabs not only brought to fruition the accumulated knowledge of world experience but also kept the torch of knowledge burning during the so-called Dark Ages in Europe.

Harun ar-Rashid died in 809. While the glories of his age continued with diminishing brightness long after his time, the empire of the Arabs weakened and decayed. Many areas became independent under separate dynasties. In Iraq several Caliphs fell under the power of Turkish mercenaries, and the capital was moved temporarily from Baghdad northward to Samarra. A militant revival occurred in the period 1055-1194 with the westward sweep of the Seljuk Turks, new converts to Islam, who wrested power from the Muslim Arabs and all others who stood in their path. It was during the Seljuk dominance that the Crusades occurred.

The Crusades, although highly dramatized in the West, did not have much effect upon the general course of events in the Middle East. They did not even stir up any great religious animosity among Muslims whose usual tolerance for other religions has been a commendable trait. One important result of the Crusades was to bring Europeans into contact with Middle Eastern civilization and culture, which contributed greatly to the Renaissance in Europe.

In 1258 the Arab empire was invaded by the Mongols or Tartars under Hulagu Khan, grandson of Genghis Khan, who ravaged Asia and terrorized Europe. The Mongols were probably the most ruthless warriors of all time. Their guiding creed was expressed by Genghis Khan in these words:

«The greatest joy is to conquer one's enemies, to pursue them, to seize their property, to see their families in tears, to ride their horses, to possess their daughters and wives».

When Hulagu Khan and his hordes swept down upon Baghdad, the powerless Abbasid Caliph surrendered after a weak defence. To show his scorn, Hulagu had him put in a sack and trampled to death. Although suffering less than some other cities, Baghdad was plundered, priceless libraries and works of art were destroyed, and many of the inhabitants were massacred. The Mongols continued their destruction elsewhere in Mesopotamia and Syria. What remained of the great system of irrigation, which had made this region fertile and prosperous for thousands of years, was ruined.

The Mongols were defeated near Nazareth by the Egyptian Mamelukes, and withdrew for a period of rule in Persia. The Mamelukes took over Palestine and Syria, ejected the last of the Crusaders in 1291, and joined these lands with Egypt until they themselves were conquered by the Ottoman Turks in 1517. The Middle East suffered another destructive invasion by the Mongols under Timur Lenk (Tamerlanc) between 1393 and 1402.

Meanwhile, the Ottoman Turks had come into Asia Minor in the wake of the Seljuks. Recovering from the blows by Tamerlanc, they ended the Byzantine Empire with the capture of Constantinople in 1453. Ottoman military power was feared throughout Europe for about two centuries thereafter. However, after the failure of the second Ottoman attempt to take Vienna in 1683, the empire declined — and with it the Middle Eastern lands under its inefficient rule.

About the time that Columbus discovered the New World, Portuguese seafarers and merchants were establishing footholds on the coasts of India and the Arabian Gulf. After them came the British and, temporarily, the Dutch. The British not only displaced the Portuguese but challenged the hold of the Turks at strategic points. These developments, however, had little effect upon the slumbering lands of the Middle East.

2 – THE LEAGUE OF ARAB STATES

- The League of Arab States
- Joint Defence Treaty
- Military Annex
- Economic Unity
- The Arab Common Market
- The Arab Fund for Economic and Social Development
- Cultural Activities
- Cultural Agreement with Unesco

The League of Arab States

(Founded in 1945)
Cairo-Egypt

The League of Arab States is a voluntary association of sovereign Arab States designed to strengthen the close ties linking them and to coordinate their policies and activities and direct them towards the common good of all the Arab countries.

CONCEPT OF THE LEAGUE

The concept of Arab cooperation in the field of international political manœuvering takes its roots in the early 30s. The emergence of Italy as a political power and the steps taken by Mussolini to extend Italian overseas possessions came as a rude awakening to a number of Arab States. It was borne home by the lesson of Abyssinia that imperialist penetration was to be regarded as by no means at an end, and though the further expansion of British and French power seemed unlikely at the end of World War II, the prevailing tendency towards Arab independence might be reversed, with other aggressive outsiders seeking to obtain colonial territories in the Middle East. Middle Eastern apprehensions had earlier materialised in the Treaty of Saadabad between Iran, Iraq, Turkey and Afghanistan.

Though the treaty had little positive results, the way had been pointed for further collaboration; and when four years later the Middle East had been drawn into the Second World War, and for the second time in twenty-five years opposing armies from Europe were fighting across Arab soil, the idea of political cooperation returned.

On this occasion Egypt took the lead and invitations were issued to a number of Arab States in order to discuss the possibility of advancing Arab interests by joint colaboration in measures designed to reduce foreign intervention. As a result, the Arab League was formed in 1945, with the States of Egypt, Iraq, the Lebanon, Saudi Arabia, Syria, Yemen and Transjordan as members.

At present they are 22 members with their date of admission:

PRESENT MEMBERS

The People's Democratic Republic of **Algeria** (1962)
Bahrain (1971)
The Federal Islamic Republic of the **Comoros** (1993)
The Republic of **Djibouti** (1977)
The Hashemite Kingdom of **Jordan** (1945)
The Republic of **Iraq** (1945)
Kuwait (1961)
The Republic of **Lebanon** (1945)
The Great Socialist People's **Libyan Arab Jamahiriya** (1953)
The Islamic Republic of **Mauritania** (1973)
The Kingdom of **Morocco** (1956)
The Sultanate of **Oman** (1971)
Qatar (1971)
The Kingdom of **Saudi Arabia** (1945)
Somali Democratic Republic (1974)
The Democratic Republic of the **Sudan** (1956)
The **Syrian** Arab Republic (1945)
The Republic of **Tunisia** (1958)
The Arab Republic of **Egypt** (1945)
The Republic of **Yemen** (1945)
Palestine (1964)
United Arab **Emirates** (1971)

The Council of the League of Arab States which is the supreme organ of the League consists of representatives of all the member States, each of which has one vote, and of a representative for Palestine. The Organisation for the Liberation of Palestine has been nominated to represent Palestine.

There are nine permanent committees for political, cultural, economic, social and legal affairs, information, communications, health, petroleum, human rights, all cooperating with the Secretariat General of the League.

I. — COUNCILS AND ORGANISATIONS

Economic Council: Established in 1953.
Joint Defence Council: Established in 1950.
Civil Aviation Council: Created in 1965.
The International Arab Organisation for Social Defence
Against Crime: Created in March 1965.
The Arab Organisation for Administrative Science.
Arab Agricultural Development Organisation.
Arab Cultural, Scientific and Educational Organisation.
Arab Organisation for Specifications & Standards.
Arab Labour Organisation.

UNIONS

Arab Scientific Union.
Arab Postal Union.
Arab Tourism Union.
Arab Telecommunications Union.
Arab Teachers Union.
Arab Universities Union.
Arab Air Transport Union.
Arab Veterinary Union.
Union of Arab Publishers.
Arab States Broadcasting Union.

INSTITUTES

Arab Manuscript Institute: Formed in April 1946. Object: to collect indices of Arab manuscript and mimeographs as many valuable Arab manuscripts as possible. Mimeographs of 1021 manuscripts have been received through Unesco.

Institute for Arab Studies and Research: Created in 1953 to further specialisation in Arab studies.

CENTRES

The Arab League Statistical Centre.
The Arab States Industrial Development Centre.

AGENCIES

Arab Youth Welfare Agency: Formed in 1954.
Israel Boycott Agency: Created in 1951.

DEPARTMENTS

Secretariat Department: Created in 1964.
Cultural Department: Created in 1945.
Social Affairs Department: Formed in 1946.
Legal Department: Formed on 4 April 1946.
Political Department: Formed on April 4 1946.
Economic Department.
Palestine Department.
Communications Department: Created in 1958.
Petroleum Department: Created in 1958.
Health Department: Formed on 19 September 1961.

Information Offices: New-York (with branches at Washington, Chicago, San Francisco, Dallas and Ottawa), Geneva, Bonn, Rio de Janeiro, London, New Delhi, Rome and Buenos Aires.

Publications: – daily Bulletin (Arabic) – New York Office: **Arab World** (monthly) and **News and Views** – Geneva Office: **Le Monde Arabe** (monthly) and **Nouvelles du Monde Arabe** (Weekly) – Buenos Aires Office: **Arabia Review** (monthly) – Rio de Janeiro Office: **Oriente Arabe** (monthly).

In accordance with the decision of the March 1979 Baghdad conference held in protest against the peace negotiations between Egypt and Israel, new headquarters for the Arab League were subsequently established in Tunis.

However on the 10th of March 1991 Ministers of Foreign Affairs of the Arab League agreed to transfer the League's headquarters back to Cairo.

Pact of the League of Arab States

(March 22, 1945)

His Excellency the President of the Syrian Republic;
His Royal Highness the Amir of Transjordan;
His Majesty the King of Iraq;
His Majesty the King of Saudi Arabia;
His Excellency the President of the Lebanese Republic;
His Majesty the King of Egypt.
His Majesty the King of Yemen;

Desirous of strengthening the close relations and numerous ties which link the Arab States; and anxious to support and stabilise these ties upon a basis of respect for the independence and sovereignty of these States, and to direct their efforts toward the common good of all the Arab countries, the security of their future, the realization of their aspirations and hopes; and responding to the wishes of Arab public opinion in all Arab lands have agreed to conclude a pact to that end.

Art. 1 – The League of Arab States is composed of independent Arab States which have signed this Pact.

Any independent Arab State has the right to become a member of the League. If it desires to do so, it shall submit a request which will be deposited with the Permanent Secretariat General and submitted to the Council at the first meeting held after submission of that request.

Art. 2 – The League has as its purpose the strengthening of the relations between the member States; the coordination of their policies in order to achieve cooperation between them and to safeguard their independence and sovereignty; and a general concern with the affairs of the Arab countries. It has also as its purpose the close cooperation of the member States, with due regard to the organization and circumstances of each State, on the following matters:

A – Economic and financial affairs, including trade relations, customs, currency, agriculture and industry;

B – Communications, including railways, roads, aviation, navigation, telegraph and post;

C – Cultural affairs;

D – Nationality, passports, visas, execution of judgements and extradition of criminals:

E – Social affairs;

F – Health problems.

Art. 3 – The League shall have a Council composed of the representatives of the member States of the League; each State shall have a single vote, irrespective of the number of its representatives.

It shall be the task of the Council to achieve the objectives of the League and to supervise the execution of agreements which the member States have concluded on the questions enumerated in the foregoing article, or on any other question.

Likewise it shall be the Council's task to decide upon the means by which the League is to co-operate with the international bodies to be created in the future in order to guarantee security and peace and regulate economic and social relations.

Art. 4 – For each of the questions listed in Article 2 there shall be set up a special committee in which the member States of the League shall be represented. These committees shall be charged with the task of laying down the principles and extent of cooperation. Such principles shall be formulated as draft agreements to be presented to the Council for examination preparatory to their submission to the aforementioned States.

Representatives of the other Arab countries may take part in the work of the aforesaid committees. The Council shall determine the conditions under which these representatives may be permitted to participate and the rules governing such participation.

Art. 5 – Any resort to force in order to resolve disputes arising between two or more member States of the League is prohibited. If there should arise among them a difference which does not concern a State's independence, sovereignty, or territorial integrity, and if the parties to the disputes have recourse to the Council for the settlement of this dispute, the decision of the Council shall then be enforceable and obligatory.

In such a case, the States between whom the difference has arisen shall not participate in the deliberations and decisions of the Council.

The Council shall mediate in all differences which threaten to lead to war between two member States, or a member State and a third State, with a view to bringing about their reconciliation.

Decisions of arbitration and mediation shall be taken by majority vote.

Art. 6 — In case of aggression or threat of aggression by one State against a member State, the State which has been attacked or threatened with aggression may demand the immediate convocation of the Council.

The Council shall by unanimous decision determine the measures necessary to repel aggression. If the aggressor is a member State, his vote shall not be counted in determining unanimity.

If as a result of the attack, the government of the State attacked finds itself unable to communicate with the Council, that State's representative on the Council shall have the right to request the convocation of the Council for the purpose indicated in the foregoing paragraph. In the event that his representative is unable to communicate with the Council, any member State of the League shall have the right to request the convocation of the Council.

Art. 7 — Unanimous decisions of the Council shall be binding upon all member States of the League; majority decisions shall be binding only upon those States which have accepted them.

In either case the decision of the Council shall be enforced on each member State according to its respective basic laws.

Art. 8 — Each member State shall respect the systems of government established in the other members States and regard them as exclusive concerns of those States. Each shall pledge to abstain from any action calculated to change established systems of government.

Art. 9 — States of the League which desire to establish closer co-operation and stronger bonds than are provided by this Pact may conclude agreements to that end.

Treaties and agreements already concluded or to be concluded in the future between a member State and another State shall not be binding or restrictive upon other members.

Art. 10 — The permanent seat of the League shall convene in ordinary session twice a year, in March and September. It shall convene in extraordinay session upon the request of two member States of the League whenever the need arises.

Art. 11 — The League shall have a permanent Secretariat-General which shall consist of a Secretary-General, Assistant Secretaries, and an appropriate number of officials.

Art. 12 — The Secretary-General shall prepare the draft budget of the League and submit it to the Council for approval before the beginning of each fiscal year.

The Council shall fix the share of the expenses to be borne by each State of the League. This share may be reconsidered if necessary.

Art. 13 — The members of the Council of the League as well as the members of the committees and the officials who are to be designated in the administrative regulation shall enjoy diplomatic privileges and immunity when engaged in the exercice of their functions.

The buildings occupied by the League shall be inviolable.

Art. 14 — The Council shall be convened on the first occasion at the instance of the Head of the Egyptian Government, and subsequently at the instance of the Secretary-General.

Art. 15 — A majority opinion shall suffice for the Council to make effective decisions of the following matters:

(i) personnel — (ii) approval of the League budget — (iii) the internal organisation of the Council, committees and General Secretariat — (iv) the termination of sessions.

Art. 16 — Texts of all the treaties and agreements which member States may conclude shall be deposited with the General Secretariat.

Art. 17 — Should any of the League States contemplate withdrawal from the League, notice of its decision to withdraw shall be given to the Council, one calendar year before withdrawal takes effect. Failure by any State to fulfill the obligations of this Pact may be regarded by the Council that such State has ceased to belong to the League.

Art. 18 — This Pact may be amended by agreement of two-thirds of the member States. Any State which does not accept the amendment may withdraw on the amendment becoming effective.

Art. 19 — The instruments of ratification of the present Pact shall be deposited with the general Secretariat, and the Pact shall have effect with those who have ratified it, 15 clear days after the Secretary-General has received the instruments of ratification from four States.

The present Pact was drawn up in Arabic in Cairo, on the 8th of Rabi al Thani 1364 (22 March 1945) in a single text which shall be preserved in the General Secretariat.

A copy true to the original shall be delivered to each of the member States.

Joint Defence Treaty

Art. 1 — The Contracting States, in an effort to maintain and stabilize peace and security, hereby confirm their desire to settle their international disputes by peaceful means, whether such disputes concern relations among themselves or with other Powers.

Art. 2 — The Contracting States consider any (act of) armed aggression made against any one or more of them or their armed forces, to be directed against them all, Therefore, in accordance with the right of self-defence, individually and collectively, they undertake to go without delay to the assistance of the State or States against which such an act of aggression is made, and immediately to take, individually and collectively, all steps available, including the use of armed force, to repel the agression and restore security and peace. In conformity with Article 6 of the Arab League Pact and Article 51 of the United Nations Charter, the Arab League Council and the UN Security Council shall be notified of such act of aggression and the means and procedure taken to check it.

Art. 3 — At the invitation of any one of the signatories of this Treaty, the Contracting States shall hold consultations whenever there are reasonable grounds for the belief that the territorial integrity, independence or security of any of the parties is threatened. In the event of the threat of war or the existence of an international emergency, the Contracting States shall immediately proceed to unify their plans and defensive measures, as the situation may require.

Art. 4 — The Contracting States, desiring to implement fully the foregoing obligations and effectively carry them out shall cooperate in consolidating and coordinating their armed forces, and shall participate according to their resources and needs in preparing individual and collective means of defence to repulse aggressions.

Art. 5 — A Permanent Military Commission composed of representatives of the General Staffs of the armies of the Contracting States shall be formed to draw up plans of joint defence and their implementation. The duties of the Permanent Military Commission which are set in an annex attached to this Treaty, include the drafting of necessary reports on the methods of co-operation and participation referred to in Article 4. The Permanent Military Commission shall submit to the Joint Defence Council provided here under Article 6, reports dealing with questions within its province.

Art. 6 — A Joint Defence Council under the supervision of the Arab League Council shall be formed to deal with all matters concerning the implementation of the provisions of Articles 2,3,4 and 5 of this Treaty. It shall be assisted in the performance of its task by the Permanent Military Commission referred to in Article 5. The Joint Defence Council shall consist of the Foreign Ministers and the Defence Ministers of the Contracting States or their representatives. Decisions taken by a two-thirds majority shall be binding on all the Contracting States.

Military Annex

1. The Permanent Military Commission provided for under Article 5 of the Joint Defence Treaty between the States of the Arab League shall undertake the following:

a) in co-operation with the Joint Defence Council, prepare plans to deal with any anticipated dangers or armed aggression that may be launched against one or more of the Contracting States or their armed forces, such plans to be based on the principles determined by the Joint Defence Council;

b) submit proposals for the organization of the forces of the Contracting States, stipulating the minimum force for each in accordance with military exigencies and the potentialities of each State;

c) submit proposals for increasing the effectiveness of the forces of the Contracting States in so far as their equipment, organization and training are concerned, so that they may keep pace with modern military methods and developments, and for the unification and co-ordination of all such forces;

d) submit proposals for the exploitation of natural, agricultural and industrial resources of all Contracting States in favour of the inter-Arab military effort and Joint Defence

e) organize the exchange of training missions between the Contracting States for the preparation of plans, participation in military exercises and manœuvres and the study of their results, recommendations for the improvement of methods to ensure close cooperation in the field, and for the general improvement of the forces of all the Contracting States;

f) prepare the necessary data on the resources and military preparedness of each of the Contracting States and the part to be played by the forces of each in the joint military effort;

g) discuss the facilities and various contributions which each of the Contracting States, in conformity with the provisions of this Treaty, might be asked to provide, during a state of war, on behalf of the armies of such other Contracting States as might be operating on its territory.

2. The Permanent Military Commission may form temporary or permanent subcommittees from among its own members to deal with any of the matters within its jurisdiction. It may also seek the advice of any experts whose views on certain questions are deemed necessary.

3. The Permanent Military Commission shall submit detailed reports on the results of its activities and studies to the Joint Defence Council provided for in Article 6 of this Treaty, as well as an annual report giving full particulars of its work and studies during the year.

4. The Permanent Military Commission shall establish its headquarters in Cairo but may hold meetings in any other place the Commission may specify. The Commission shall elect its Chairman for a period of two years: he may be re-elected. Candidates for the chairmanship shall hold at least the rank of a high commanding officer. Each member of the Commission must have as his original nationality that of the Contracting State he represents.

5. In the event of war, the Supreme Command of the joint forces shall be entrusted to the Contracting State possessing the largest military force taking part in actual field operations, unless by unanimous agreement, the

Commander-in-Chief is selected otherwise. The Commander-in-Chief shall be assisted in directing military operations by a Joint Staff.

Economic Unity

Agreement for Economic Unity among the Arab League States

The Governments of:
1 — The Hashemite Kingdom of Jordan
2 — The Tunisian Republic
3 — The Republic of Sudan
4 — The Iraqi Republic
5 — The Saudi Arabian Kingdom
6 — The Syrian Arab Republic
7 — The Lebanese Republic
8 — The United Libyan Republic
9 — The Yemenite Kingdom
10 — The Kingdom of Morocco
11 — The State of Kuwait

Declare that it is their ardent desire to organise economic relations among the Arab League States, to strengthen these relations on such bases as shall suit the existing natural and historical ties among them to realise the best conditions for the development of their economies, to exploit their wealth, and to secure the welfare of their countries.

They agree to establish a complete unity among themselves and to implement it gradually in the shortest possible time that will guarantee the transfer of their countries from present to future conditions without harming fundamental interests, in accordance with the following provisions.

OBJECTIVES AND MEANS

Art. 1 — A complete economic unity shall be established among the Arab League states to guarantee in particular, for these states and for their citizens on the basis of complete equality:

1. — freedom of movement of men and capital,

2. — freedom of exchange of national and foreign products and goods,

3. — freedom of residence, work, employment, and the practice of economic activity,

4. — freedom of transport and transit and the use of the means of transport, ports, and civil airports,

5. — the rights of ownership, donation and inheritance.

Art. 2 — To achieve the realization of the unity specific in the foregoing article, the contracting parties agree:

1. — to consider their countries a unified customs region subject to a unified administration; and to unify the customs tariffs, legislations, and regulations applied in each of them,

2. — to unify the policy and systems of import and export.

3. — to unify the transport and transit policies,

4. — to conclude trade and payments agreements with other countries collectively,

5. — to co-ordinate policy regarding agriculture, industry and internal trade and to unify economic legislation in such a manner as shall guarantee equal opportunities for citizens of the contracting countries engaged in agriculture, industry and trade, and the professions,

6. — to co-ordinate legislation concerning labour and social security,

7. — a) to co-ordinate legislation regarding government taxation and municipal dues, and all other kinds of taxations and duties on agriculture, industry, immovable property, and capital investment in such a way as shall guarantee the principle of equal opportunity for all,

b) to prevent double taxation and duties on the citizens of the contracting states,

8. — to co-ordinate financial and monetary policies and regulations in the countries of the contracting parties with a view to unify currency in them all,

9. — to unify methods of statistical tabulations and classifications,and,

10. — to take any other necessary measures for the implementation of the objectives specified in Art. 1 and 2.

It is possible to disregard the principle of unification in certain cases and countries provided the approval of the Council of Arab Economic Unity is secured. Art. 3 of this agreement stipulates the formation of this Council.

MANAGEMENT

Art. 3 — A permanent body to be called "The Council of Arab Economic Unity" shall be established. Its duties and powers are determined in accordance with the provisions of this agreement.

Art. 4 — 1) The Council shall be formed of one or more full time representatives of each of the contracting parties.

2) Cairo shall be the permanent seat for the Council of Arab Economic Unity. The Council has the right to convene at any other place it shall determine.

3) The term of office of the Chairman of the Council shall be for one year and in a rotating order among the contracting parties.

The Council shall pass its resolutions by a two-thirds majority vote. Each contracting country has one single vote.

Art. 5 — 1) The Council shall be helped in its duties by economic and administrative committees which function permanently or temporarily under its supervision. The Council determines their duties.

2) The following permanent committees shall be preliminarily formed:

a) the Customs committee to consider the techinal and administrative Customs affairs,

b) the Monetary and Financial committee to consider matters relating to currency, banking, taxation, rates and other financial questions;

c) the Economic committee to consider matters relating to agriculture, industry, trade, transport and communications; labour and social security;

The Council shall have the right to form other committees when necessary and in accordance with the requirements of the situation.

3) Each of the contracting parties shall appoint its representatives on the above – mentioned permanent committees. Each party shall have one single vote.

Art. 6 — 1) A Permanent Technical Advisory Office shall be established for the Council of Arab Economic Unity. It shall be made of experts appointed by the Council and shall function under its supervision.

2) The Permanent Technical Office shall execute the study and research work in matters referred to it by the Council or any of its committees. The Office shall submit research work and recommendations that will guarantee harmony and co-ordination in matters within the jurisdiction of the Council.

3) The Council shall establish a central office for statistics. This office shall gather and analyse statistics and publish them when necessary.

Art. 7 — 1) The Council of Arab Economic Unity, together with its subsidiary organs shall constitute one single unit enjoying financial and administrative independence and having its own budget.

2) The Council shall draft its own regulations and those of its subsidiary organs.

Art. 8 — During a period not exceeding one month of the date of implementation of this agreement, the governments of the Contracting Parties shall nominate their representatives on the Council and on the committees specified in paragraph (2) of Art. 5 of this agreement, and the Council shall carry out its functions immediately upon its formation. Also, the Council shall immediately form its subsidiary organs.

Art. 9 — The Council of Arab Economic Unity shall carry out, in general, all the duties and powers specified in this agreement and its appendices which it shall deem necessary for its implementation. In particular, the Council shall:

IN ADMINISTRATION

a) Implement the provisions of this agreement and its appendices and all the regulations and resolutions issued for the implementation of this agreement and its appendices;

b) Supervise the working of the committees and the subsidiary organs;

c) Appoint the staff and experts for the Council and its subsidiary organs, in accordance with the provisions of this agreement.

IN ORGANIZATION AND LEGISLATION

a) Draft tariffs, laws and regulations which aim at the establishment of an Arab unified Customs zone and subsequently introduce whaterver alterations may be deemed essential;

b) Co-ordinate foreign trade policies with a view to streamline the economy of the region in relation to world economy, and to attain the objectives of economic unity as specified in this agreement. The signing of trade and payments agreements with other countries shall take place with the approval of the Council of Arab Economic Unity;

c) Co-ordinate economic development activities and draft plans for the execution of common Arab development projects;

d) Co-ordinate policies regarding agriculture, industry, and domestic trade;

e) Co-ordinate financial and monetary policies as a mean of achieving monetary unity;

f) Draft unified transport regulations in the Contracting Countries as well as transit regulations and co-ordinate common policy;

g) Draft unified labour and social security legislations and modifying them;

h) Co-ordinate taxation and rates laws:

i) Draft other legislations concerning matters specified in this agreement and its appendices which are essential to the implementation of this agreement and its appendices;

j) Draft and approve the budget of the Council and its subsidiary organs.

Art. 10 — Expenditures of the Council and its subsidiary organs shall be drawn from common revenues. During the period before the realization of such revenues, governments shall participate to these expenditures according to rates fixed by the Council.

Art. 11 — The common revenues of the Council shall be distributed among the governments of the Contracting Parties by agreement among them on the basis of the studies carried out by the Council of Economic Unity. These studies shall be made before the realization of the Customs unity.

Art. 12 — The Council shall perform these and other powers vested in it by this agreement and its appendices by resolutions to be adopted and implemented by the member states in accordance with their own constitutional principles.

Art. 13 — The Governments of the Contracting Parties undertake not to issue in their respective territories any laws, regulations or administrative orders contradictory to this agreement or its appendices.

TRANSITIONAL RULES

Art. 14 — 1) The implementation of this agreement shall take place in successive stages and in the shortest possible time.

2) The Council of Arab Economic Unity shall, upon its formation, draft a practical plan indicating the stages of implemention and determining the legislative, administrative, and technical measures necessary for each step, taking into consideration the appendix concerning "... the necessary steps for the realization of Arab Economic Unity..." attached to this agreement and constituting an integral part of it.

3) On exercising its duties as specified in this

agreement the Council shall take into consideration certain specific circumstances existing in some contracting countries. This shall not undermine the objectives of the Arab Economic Unity.

4) The Council, as well as the Contracting Parties, shall carry out the measures specified in Paragraph (2) of this article according to the terms of this agreement.

Art. 15 — Any two or more of the Contracting Parties shall have the right to conclude economic agreements among themeselves with the object of realizing a unity, wider in range, than that stipulated by this agreement.

RATIFICATION, MEMBERSHIP AND WITHDRAWAL

Art. 16 — This agreement shall be ratified by the Signatory States according to their constitutional systems in the shortest time possible. Documents of ratification shall be deposited with the Secretariat General of the Arab League who shall prepare the necessary minutes regarding the ratification documents of each state and who shall inform the other Contracting States accordingly.

Art. 17 — States of the Arab League which are not party to this agreement can apply for membership through the Secretary-General of the Arab League who shall announce their membership to the other Contracting States.

Art. 18 — Arab countries which are not members in the League of Arab States can subscribe to this agreement subject to the approval of the Contracting States. Such countries shall apply for membership to the Secretary-General of the League of Arab States who shall advise the Contracting States accordingly for their approval.

Art. 19 — Any of the Contracting Parties can withdraw from this agreement after five calendar years from the end of the transitional period. The withdrawal shall be effective after the lapse of one year from the date of application for withdrawal to the Secretary-General of the League of Arab States.

Art. 20 — This agreement shall go into force three months from the date of deposit of the ratification documents by three of the Signatory States. Regarding other States, the agreement shall go into force one month after the date of deposit of their ratification documents or their application for membership.

In confirmation of the foregoing stipulation, the delegated members, whose names are listed hereinafter, have signed this agreement on behalf and in the name of their governments.

The Arab Common Market

In accordance with the provisions of the agreement for Economic Unity among the Arab League States, the Council of Arab Economic Unity, desirous of achieving social progress and economic prosperity for the Contracting Parties and of establishing economic unity on the sound foundations of continuous and harmonious economic development in keeping with the natural and historical links that exist between them; wishing to achieve economic integration among the Contracting Countries and to consolidate their efforts for the attainment of the most favourable environment for the development of their resources, the raising of their standard of living and the improvement of living conditions, had decided to establish the Arab Common Market with the aim accomplishing the following:

1 — freedom of movement of persons and capital,

2 — freedom of exchange of national and foreign commodities,

3 — freedom of residence, work, employment and the undertaking of economic activities,

4 — freedom of transport and transit as well as the use of means of transport, seaports and civil airports.

In accordance with the following provision:

DEFINITIONS AND TERMINOLOGY

Art. 1 — The following definitions wherever they occur, shall mean:

1 — Contracting Parties: These are the member States of the Council of Arab Economic Unity.

2 — Restrictions: These are the administrative restrictions imposed by any one of the Contracting Parties on its imports and exports and include the prohibition of importation and exportation, quotas, licences and all other similar restrictions on trade.

3 — Customs and other duties: Customs duties are those duties embodied in the schedule of customs tariffs, while other duties are all duties and taxes, whatever their nomenclature, imposed on imported goods. The following shall not be considered as duties or taxes:

a) all duties, taxes or payments in return for services

b) all duties or taxes imposed on products, imported from Contracting Parties where similar domestic products or raw materials are subjected to the same duties and taxes.

4 — Agriculture and animal products and natural resources: These are the products and resources which originate from one of the Contracting Countries and which are imported in their natural form.

5 — Manufactured goods: These are the goods manufactured in any of the Contracting Countries and whose domestic cost of production is not less than 40 per cent of their total cost. Materials imported from any of the Contracting Countries shall be deemed a part of the domestic cost of production.

GENERAL PRINCIPLES

Art. 2 — There shall be freedom of exchange of agricultural and animal products, natural resources and manufactured goods between the Contracting Parties in accordance with the principles and provisions of the following articles.

Art. 3 — Restrictions, duties and taxes on imports and exports — at present in force in the Contracting Countries — shall remain unaltered. None of the said countries shall introduce new duties, taxes or restrictions on agricultural and animal products, natural resources and manufactured goods exchanged between themselves.

Art. 4 — The governments of the Contracting Parties shall apply "the most favoured Nation" principle as between themselves where this treatment is accorded to countries which are not members of the Agreement for Economic Unity, provided that the provisions of this article shall not apply to existing agreements.

Art. 5 — The governments of the Contracting Parties shall not impose duties or excise taxes on agricultural and animal products, natural resources and manufactured goods exchanged between themselves which exceed the duties or excise taxes imposed on similar domestic products or on the raw materials used in the manufacture of such products.

Art. 6 — No export duties shall be levied on agricultural and animal products, natural resources and manufactured goods exchanged between the Contracting Countries.

Art. 7 — 1) The re-exportation, outside the Market, of agricultural and animal products, of natural resources and manufactured goods, which have been exchanged between the Contracting Countries, shall be prohibited, unless permission from the exporting country has been obtained and provided that the said products, resources and goods have not undergone any manufacturing process which has given them the characteristics of domestically manufactured goods in the importing country.

2) The re-exportation, to any Contracting Country, of agricultural and animal products, natural resources and domestically manufactured goods which have been exchanged between the Contracting Countries shall be prohibited where the said products, resources and goods have been subsidized and there exists similar domestic production in the country to which these products have been re-exported.

Art. 8 — Subsidization: Contracting Countries shall not grant any subsidy whatsoever to domestic products exported to other Contracting Parties, where similar products exist in the importing countries.

Art. 9 — Concessions and monopolies in existence in the Contracting Countries shall not obstruct the application of the provisions of the Arab Common Market.

EXCHANGE OF AGRICULTURE AND ANIMAL PRODUCTS AND NATURAL RESOURCES.

Art. 10 — The following provisions shall apply until a technical committee, formed by the Council of Economic Unity, has prepared more detailed tables for the Arab Common Market:

1 — Agricultural and animal products and natural resources listed in Table A, which is annexed to the Treaty for the Facilitation of Trade and Organization of Transit Trade and its first three amendments, concluded between the Arab League States, and which originate from one of the Contracting Parties, shall be exempt from customs and other duties and taxes when exchanged between the Contracting Countries. As regards agricultural and animal products and natural resources which are not included in the aforementioned table, these shall enjoy a reduction of 20 per cent per annum, in all duties and taxes as from the beginning of 1965.

2 — All Contracting Countries shall endeavour to remove restrictions on the said products at the rate of 20 per cent of such products, in five annual stages, as from the beginning of 1965.

The process was completed in 1971.

The Arab Fund for Economic and Social Development

After the Israeli attack against neighbouring Arab countries in June 1967, closer Arab cooperation became urgent. This obvious fact was submitted by the Kuwaiti Government to the Conference of Arab Ministers of Finance, Economy and Petroleum held in Baghdad on 15 August 1967. An agreement was signed on 16 May 1968 by the member countries of the Arab League, together with Abu Dhabi, Bahrain and Qatar for the establishment of the "Arab Fund for Economic and Social Development", to act within the framework of the economic cooperation provided by the Charter of the Arab League.

According to the agreement, the Fund would be an autonomous legal body, located in Kuwait, which would be empowered to establish agencies or branch offices elsewhere. All properties and assets of the Fund wherever located would be immune from restriction, requisition, confiscation, expropriation and any other similar act.

Membership of the Arab Fund would be confined to member States of the Arab League and other Arab countries who would have subscribed to the Fund's capital before July 1,1968. However, membership could also be extended to any other Arab country on the approval of the Board of Governors.

THE FUND'S CAPITAL

The Fund's authorised capital of Kuwait Dinar (KD) 100 million (KD x 2.48823 grammes of fine gold) is divided into 10,000 shares of 10,000 dinars each. In case of change in the value of the Kuwaiti Dinar in terms of gold, the capital would be revalued so as to equal at all times to 248828 kg of fine gold (increased to 400 million in 1975 and to 800 million in 1982). Each member country is required to pay 10 per cent of its subscription when the instruments of ratification are deposited, and another 10 per cent when the agreement goes into force. The balance would be paid in six equal annual instalments, starting one year after the Fund commences operations. Stockholding would not be pledged or encumbered in any manner whatsoever, and would not be transferable except to the Fund. Other countries that might join the Fund after the agreement comes into force would pay a percentage of their subscriptions equal to what founder members would have paid at any time.

During the thirteenth session of the Arab Economic Council, member countries had fixed their subscriptions with the exception of December 1991 Saudi Arabia, Morocco, Bahrain together with Abu Dhabi and Qatar — which, however, have determined their subscriptions of late. Up to the end of December 1991, subscriptions so far promised by various members of the Fund's authorised capital reached the equivalent of KD 694.8 million subscribed as follows:

Kuwait = KD 169.7 million, Saudi Arabia 159.07, Algeria 64.78, Iraq 63.52, Libya 59.85, Egypt 40.50, United Arab Emirates 28, Syria 24, Jordan 17.3, Oman 17.28, Morocco 16, Sudan 11.06, Qatar 6.75, Yemen 4.25, Bahrain 2.16, Lebanon 2, PLO 1.1, and Somalia 0.21. The capital might be increased by the absolute majority of voting members, to meet the entry of new members, or otherwise by no less than 75 per cent of the total voting power; and in such a case each member country would have the right to subscribe with its quota in the Fund's capital.

In addition to the paid-in capital and reserves, the Fund would be able to augment its ordinary resources by borrowings whether through the issue of bonds, or through credits opened by Arab nationals and Arab public and private institutions, as well as by international organisations. The value of the bonds to be issued by the Fund would not exceed twice its capital unless agreement has been reached by a special decision taken by two thirds voting majority of the Board of Governors.

The agreement provides that 10 per cent of the annual net profit would be allocated to build up a general reserve fund. The Board of Governors might allocate another portion for the formation of a supplementary reserve. The remaining balance would then be distributed among member countries in accordance with their subscriptions.

BOARD MEETINGS AND QUORUM

The Fund would be managed by a Board of Governors, a Board of Directors, a president, and such officers and staff as might be considered necessary. The Board of Governors which is vested with all managerial powers, would consist of a governor and a deputy, appointed by each member country for a period of five years, and would be presided over by a chairman, to be elected for one year from among the Governors. The Board would meet at least once a year or whenever requested to do so by three members having 25 per cent of the total voting power. Apart from certain powers (including notably the admission of new members, the increase of the authorised capital, the suspension of members and the termination of the Fund's operations), the Board of Governors might delegate other powers to the Board of Directors. Each member country would have 200 votes plus one vote for each share of its holding of the capital stock.

The Board of Directors, composed of four elected members — other than governors or their deputies — for a renewable period of two years, would be generally responsible for conducting the Fund's operations. The Board of Governors would appoint, from outside the two Boards, a general manager who presides over the Board of Directors with no voting right except in the case of a tie, and would be responsible for all the Fund's business under the supervision of the Board of Directors.

A majority of the Directors would constitute a quorum for any meeting of the Board, provided such majority represents no less than two-thirds of the total voting power of the members.

Unless otherwise explicitly provided for in the agreement, all matters submitted to the Board of Directors would be decided by a majority of the voting power represented at the meeting.

Cultural Activities

Although the Arab States were inspired, in the organization of their league, by a community of political, economic and social interests, the Arabs have always been knit together by a unity of ideals and by a spiritual and intellectual affinity which, above all things, make for mutual co-operation, sympathy and understanding.

How to regulate, direct and consolidate these ties was one of the questions that confronted the Arab Congress Preparatory Committee, whose task it was to lay the foundations of the Arab League. A Cultural Committee was created to frame the rules for a uniform cultural policy to achieve close collaboration and consolidation of efforts throughout the Arab World. The outcome was a Cultural Treaty derived, from the experience of progressive nations, which designated the main cultural activities and prescribed the best methods and policies. On November 27th 1945, the treaty, with a few alterations was ratified by the Arab League Council.

THE TEXT OF THE CULTURAL TREATY

Art. 1 — The Member States of the League do hereby agree to establish each in its respective country, a local organization whose function shall be the promotion and development of cultural cooperation between Arab States. Each State shall have full freedom to choose the way in which such organization is to be formed.

Art. 2 — Member States agree to the exchange of professors and teachers between their respective schools and institutions in accordance with such general or individual conditions as shall be agreed upon between them. The duration of service of exchanged professors or teachers who are Government officials, shall be reckoned as part of their Government service, entitling them to retain their original Government posts with the consequent rights to promotion and pension.

Art. 3 — Member States agree to the exchange of students and pupils between their schools and institutions. These shall be admitted to the classes for which they are fitted, within the limits of the places available, due regard being paid to regulations governing such schools and institutions. To facilitate such an exchange, the Member

States, with due observance of the fundamental educational principles applied in their respective countries, shall endeavour to standardize educational stages and certificates. Such procedure shall be governed by specific agreements concluded between the respective States

Each Member State shall also extend to the country or countries concerned all possible facilities for the establishment of residential quarters for the accommodation of their respective pupils.

Art. 4 — Member States shall endeavour to encourage cultural tours as well as scouting and sport excursions, to those areas of their countries to which access is allowed by their respective Governments. They shall also encourage the holding of cultural and educational conferences for the benefit of students, and extend all possible facilities for such purposes, particularly with regard to travel and the reduction of travelling expenses.

Art. 5 — Member States agree to the establishment in their respective countries of educational and scientific institutes by any other Member State.

Art. 6 — Member States shall co-operate with one another for the revival, preservation and dissemination of the Arabs' legacy to Art and Literature, so as to make such legacy available to all scholars.

Art. 7 — To keep pace with the world's intellectual movement, the Member States shall encourage the translation from foreign languages of works of famous authors, classical or modern, and coordinate all efforts exerted in this direction.

They shall also encourage intellectual production in the Arab countries by diverse methods such as the establishment of Library and scientific research institutes amongst writers and authors, awarding prizes for the best achievements in Literature, Science and Art.

Art. 8 — Member States shall undertake to enact legislation safeguarding literary, scientific and art copyright in their respective countries.

Art. 9 — Member States shall endeavour to unify scientific expressions and terms through the medium of joint congresses, conferences and committees to be organized for the purpose, and through bulletins to be published by these bodies. They shall also endeavour to develop and promote the Arabic language so as to make it capable of rendering all modern literary and scientific expressions, and to make Arabic the medium for teaching all subjects in all educational stages throughout the Arab countries.

Art. 10 — Member States shall endeavour to strengthen relations between public libraries, and scientific, historical and art museums in their respective countries by various means such as the exchange of literary works, indexes, replicas of ancient relics, and facsimiles. They shall also endeavour to exchange technical and scientific co-operation between scientific experts and excavation missions by means of agreements to be concluded between the respective States.

Art. 11 — Member States agree to strengthen relations and facilitate co-operation between scientists, scholars, journalists, people engaged in free professions, and persons connected with the stage, the cinema, music and broadcasting — wherever these may exist — through the organization of visits from one country to another.

They shall also encourage, for the same purpose, the holding of cultural, educational and scientific conferences, the placing of adequately equipped research centres and laboratories belonging to the various scientific institutions of each country at the disposal of the scientists and scholars of other countries for the conducting and demonstration of scientific researches, and the publication of periodic bulletins on all works written and researches made in all Arab countries.

They shall make it obligatory for all authors and publishers to present copies of all publications issued by them to the Cultural Committee of the League for preservation in its library and for distribution to public libraries in each State.

Art. 12 — Member States agree to introduce into the educational syllabuses for their respective countries literary, geographical and historical subjects sufficient to enable students to form a clear idea about the life and civilisation of the other Arab countries. They shall also endeavour to establish an Arabic Library for pupils in each State.

Art. 13 — Member States shall endeavour to acquaint their nationals with the cultural, social, economic and political conditions of the other Arab States through the medium of radio, the theatre, the cinema, the press and any other media, also through the foundation of museums for Arab culture and civilisation, adequately equipped by them and by other Member States to ensure success, and through the organization of periodic art and literary exhibitions and school festivals in the different Arab countries.

Art. 14 — Member States shall encourage the establishment of Arab cultural and social clubs in their respective countries.

Art. 15 — Member States shall adopt all measures necessary to ensure the closest similarity possible in matters of legislation. They shall also endeavour to unify their laws, whenever that is practicable, and to introduce comparative legal study of Arab countries into the syllabuses of their respective educational institutions.

Art. 16 — This Treaty shall be ratified by the undersigned States in accordance with their respective constitutional regulations at the earliest possible date. The instruments of ratification shall be entrusted for safe custody to the Secretariat-General of the League which shall draw up a separate report registering the deposit of the ratification instrument of each country and shall communicate the fact to other Member States.

Art. 17 — Other Arab countries may join this Treaty by notifying such a desire to the Secretary-General of the League, who shall in turn communicate the fact to Member States.

Art. 18 — The Treaty shall come into force one month after the deposit of the ratification instruments by two

Member States. The same applies to the other States that ratify the Treaty after it has come into force.

Art. 19 — Any State bound by the obligations of this Treaty may withdraw therefrom by notifying the Secretary-General to that effect. Withdrawal shall take effect six months after the despatch of such a notice.

Cultural Agreement with Unesco Co-operation

The United Nations Educational, Scientific and Cultural Organization and the League of Arab States agree to co-operate with each other through their appropriate bodies.

This co-operation shall extend to all matters that arise in the field of education, science and culture and are connected with those tasks and activities of the two Organizations that are in harmony.

MUTUAL CONSULTATION

The United Nations Educational, Scientific and Cultural Organization and the League of Arab States shall consult each other regularly on matters of common interest, with a view to co-ordinating their efforts to accomplish those of their tasks and activities which are in harmony.

The United Nations Educational, Scientific and Cultural Organization shall inform the League of Arab States of any proposals which, owing to their nature and the cultural region in which they are to be carried out, appear likely to be of direct interest to the League of Arab States, and shall consider any observations on such proposals which may be conveyed to it by the League of Arab States with a view to establishing effective coordination between the two Organizations.

Similarly, the League of Arab States shall inform the United Nations Educational, Scientific and Cultural Organization of any proposals for the development of its activities in matters of interest to the United Nations Educational, Scientific and Cultural Organization and shall consider any observations on such proposals which may be conveyed to it by the United Nations Educational, Scientific and Cultural Organization with a view to establishing effective coordination between the two Organizations.

The United Nations Educational, Scientific and Cultural Organization and the League of Arab States shall, after consulting with each other, take all appropriate steps to ensure that the organs of each of them are kept fully informed concerning relevant activities of the other Organization when these organs are considering questions which have a bearing on these activities.

The appropriate steps referred to in paragraph 3 may also include invitation to the Organization concerned to be represented at meetings when matters relating to its activities are to be discussed.

henever circumstances so require, consultation shall take place between the representatives of the two Organizations to determine jointly the most effective methods of dealing with particular problems of interest to both Organizations.

These methods may, for instance, include the establishment of joint committees.

JOINT ACTION

The United Nations Educational, Scientific and Cultural Organization and the League of Arab States may, through special agreements, together decide upon joint action with a view to attaining objects of common interest.

These special agreements shall define the ways in which each of the two Organizations shall participate in such action and shall specify the financial commitments that each is to assume.

REGIONAL ARAB UNIONS

1) **Cooperation Council for the Arab States of the Gulf** Est. 25 May 1981 (Bahrain, Kuwait, Oman, Qatar, Saudi Arabia, United Arab Emirates).
2) **Arab Maghreb Union** Est. 1989 (Morocco, Mauritania, Algeria, Tunisia, Libya).

3 — The MAGHREB

The Maghreb

Once called the Barbary Coast, North West Africa, is now restrictively known by its Arabic name "al-Maghrib". It is composed of five Arab States joined by a Community Pact: Libya, Algeria, Morocco, Mauritania and Tunisia.

Geographically, the eastern limit of North West Africa can be taken as the Libyan-Egyptian and Libyan Sudanese frontiers. In the North the area is limited by the Mediterranean sea, in the west by the Atlantic, in the South by the Sahara.

As in the rest of the Arab World, the fertile inhabited areas of North West Africa are really islands, set not in the sea but in the desert or between the desert and the sea. Apart from the scattered oases of the South, there is in the West and in the North a long, narrow coastal strip of about 2,600 miles long and rarely more than 50-100 miles deep, though it widens out a little on the Atlantic coast where the Moroccan plains are cut off from the desert by the lofty ranges of the Atlas Mountains.

The majority of the Maghreb belongs to the Mediterranean world which was at one time the home of Greco-Roman civilization, and formed part of the Roman Empire.

Roughly three-quarters of the population of the whole area speak Arabic as their mother-tongue, and one-quarter Berber. A knowledge of French is common among the Muslim upper and middle classes in Algeria, Tunisia and the former French zone of Morocco; Italian and English in Libya. In Arabic which is the mother-tongue of the people who are now resuming control of North West Africa, the area is known as the "al-Maghrib al-Arabi".

Fundamental change in the history of the Maghreb was brought about by the coming of the Arabs; these first appeared in Libya in 642 A.D., only nine years after the death of the Prophet Muhammad.

During 800 years of Arab rule, four dynasties succeeded one another in North West Africa.

EUROPEAN RULE

French rule was established in Algeria in 1830 in a colonized way, with no hope whatsoever of equal citizenship, with a terrible contrast in the standards of living of European and of Arab communities. The country was not conquered but became a protectorate, retaining its monarchy and something of its former administration, though in practice all authority was soon in the hands of French officials. The next stage in the European occupation of North Africa was the Italian invasion of Libya in 1911 which was presented as a liberation from Turkish government. Finally Morocco in 1912 was occupied jointly by France (Treaty of Fez) and Spain.

In 1934, which saw the completion of the occupation, began in Tunisia the birth of a dynastic new nationalist party, the Neo-Destour, under the leadership of the President of Independent Tunisia Habib Bourguiba.

In Morocco, a significant nationalist demonstration because of a visit by Muhammad V to Fez led to the termination of the French protectorate within twenty-five years.

THE MAGHREB AND THE ARAB LEAGUE

Libya, Morocco, Tunisia, Mauritania and Algeria entered the Arab League because of a powerful bond of sentiment which binds them to the Arab world in general. Another Pact which reunited the five countries of the Maghreb was formed in 1989.

ARAB MAGHREB UNION

(Founded 1989)

Members

Algeria | **Morocco**
Libya | **Tunisia**
Mauritania

aiming at economic cooperation and creation of a one market economy

4 — ARAB PETROLEUM

- **Arab Oil and the World Oil Industry Today**
- **Natural Gas**
- **Organization of Arab Petroleum Exporting Countries**
- **Statistics**

Arab Oil and the World Oil Industry Today

The last few years have witnessed major and unprecedented changes in the world oil industry characterised by feverish search for new oilfields to supplement production from traditional suppliers. Strikes in numerous regions in the Arab World, e.g. in Libya, U.A.E., Syria and Yemen and Oman have very substantially boosted proven reserves to which the new North Sea finds must be added.

But rising world demand and the widening gap between energy production and consumption in a number of major industrialised countries have set a premium on oil as a source of energy.

Capital investments in the oil industry are equally impressive.

The international oil companies find themselves up against increasing difficulties. On the one hand, they have to satisfy demands from host Governments calling for a larger share in production and profit, and, on the other, overcome competition from national oil corporations set up by these Governments, but which may be a matter for concern, especially at a time when other problems claim the attention of the oil companies, notably stepping up output in existing concessions or diversifying their sources of supply.

ARAB CONTRIBUTION

The industrialised world's growing dependence on Arab oil to meet its energy needs is dictated by the logic of geography and economics. In addition to the relative ease and low cost at which Arab oil is produced, the potential of increasing oil production is greater in the Arab world than elsewhere. The Arab world's abundant reserves will supply the world with oil for many years. Out of a total of approximately, 1,053 billion barrels published proven world oil reserves at the end of 1998, the Arab Countries' share alone is 631 billion barrels. In 1997, OAPEC (Organization of Arab Petroleum Exporting Countries) produced 25.9% of total world petroleum production.

REFINING

Although the Arab countries control more than half the world's crude oil reserves and produce 25% of world output their share in non-communist world refining capacity still stands at less than 4%. Even after the completion of new refineries and the expansion of others, the Arab share would remain at less than 9%.

In contrast to the years immediately preceding World War II, when refineries were located in producing areas, the oil companies have sited new refineries in the consuming countries, preferring to limit imports from the Arab States to crude oil. These policies are in conformity with the strategy of industrialised countries to reap the added value accruing to crude oil processing and to promote their own welfare, technological development and employment, plus to guarantee oil supplies by diversifying sources of crude oil imports and concentrating refining capacity in their own states.

The problem requiring attention at present is not only limited to the need of raising Arab refining output within the framework of a plan for gradually shifting from exports of crude oil to exports to refined products. It also concerns the need for a joint Arab policy on investment in export refining capacity and the exporting of products. Western European countries,' share is approximately 35% of total world refining capacity.

Natural Gas

A change is taking place in the energy supply potential of the crude oil-producing countries — not least the Arab countries of the Middle East and North Africa - as a result of the new status of natural gas. These countries have now, in effect, four saleable energy products available directly or indirectly from their oilfields: crude oil, petroleum products, natural gas and liquified petroleum gases. Middle East and North African Arab Countries account for more than one third of total proven reserves of natural gas.

The coming-of-age of natural gas which is now occuring is due partly to technological advance in the transport of gas to overseas markets, and partly to overall economic progress creating local markets for gas in the countries where it is produced. Natural gas already, of course, for decades previously was a significant contributor to energy requirements in the United States and in a few other countries. But, predominantly, natural gas reserves have been discovered in places such as the Arab oil countries which are far distant from the world's main energy - consuming areas. Only recently have these areas been brought potentially within economic reach, by the development of techniques for transporting refrigerated gases – both liquified natural gas and liquified petroleum gases – long distances by sea. Almost simultaneously the economic progress of some of the oil and gas-producing countries has created opportunities for the large scale local utilisation of this valuable natural resource.

At present there are several instances in the Arab countries, of an actual functioning programme of liquified natural gas supplies. One is Algeria's pipeline to Italy via Tunisia for the export of natural gas.

In the Western Hemisphere Phillips – Marathon supply natural gas from Alaska to the Tokyo Gas Co. in Japan.

An altogether simpler and less costly operation is the ocean transport of refrigerated LPG's available in considerable volumes from associated gas in the oilfields.

The other avenue for natural gas development in the Arab oil-producing countries is through the encouragement of the local markets. In Kuwait, for example, the petrochemical facilities, the Kuwait National Petroleum Company's refinery and other industrial facilities at Shuaiba promoted by the government, require more than 200 million cu. ft. daily of natural gas. In Saudi Arabia, likewise, vigorous efforts are being made to initiate petrochemical production as well as other industrial activity which would utilise natural gas. The other major crude oil exporting nation in the Middle East is Iraq; and here also plans are being actively pursued to increase the local use of natural gas.

These are the initial stages of a long - term development which over the next 20 years or so should witness a very substantial expansion of natural gas demand in the Arab oil-producing countries, representing a major stimulus to their economic growth.

FLARING OF GAS

The problem of gas flared due to lack of market outlets is a big one which has caused anxiety for many years. Significant inroads on it are now at last beginning to be made, where it has proved practical and desirable from an engineering viewpoint to undertake major reinjection schemes with the dual purpose of increasing the ultimate recovery of oil and of conserving gas.

Throughout the Middle East efforts are being made to develop industrial activities which will be founded on natural gas, including petrochemical facilities requiring gas as raw material as well as fuel.

BASIC HANDICAP

Natural gas suffers from the handicap that although it can now technically be transported long distances by sea it is inherently more costly to transport than oil. This is due essentially to the fact that calories in the form of gas, even when liquified, occupy larger volume than in the form of oil, entirely apart from the costly problem of insulation, etc... In round figures an LNG tanker of the same deadweight tonnage as an oil tanker costs approximately twice as much to build but can carry only about half the therms that the oil tanker can. Thus per therm transported, the capital cost is roughly four times greater for gas than for oil.

In addition to the high cost natural-gas transport by sea, costly facilities are required for liquifaction, deliquifaction and storage of the gas. An overriding factor is the limited number of markets potentially able to absorb substantial supplies of imported gas.

Taking all these factors into account it is unlikely that many new viable projects for LNG will come forward in the next few years. In the long-term, however, the position may be quite different. On the one hand continuing advances in the techniques of transporting and storing LNG — including the use of bigger LNG tankers, for instance — appreciably reduced the costs of LNG supply. On the other hand, the markets for gas will be much bigger. During the next ten to twenty years Western Europe will become increasingly gas - oriented, basing its sharply rising use of gas on the very big Slochteren gasfields in the Netherlands, on discoveries in the North Sea and other fields in the Netherlands, Germany and elsewhere, some already discovered, some yet to be found.

Western Europe, of course, will not be the only prospective market for LNG in the long-term. The other principal possibilities lie in Japan, where a phenomenal rate of expansion of energy requirements may be confidently predicted.

LPG EXPORT

More immediately there may be scope for further increasing the Arab oil countries's export of LPG (liquified petroleum gases), which are generally present in significant quantities in oilwell gas.

On the debit side the distance factor is again important. LPG from the oilfields must compete both with other energy products which are less costly to transport, store and handle, and also with LPG from local refineries in the marketing areas.

One issue of particular interest is the location of nationally-owned refineries. The international oil companies have concentrated most of their refinery construction in recent years in the oil importing countries. They have done this for a variety of reason; but one major reason is the cheapness of bulk crude transport in very large tankers to a single point of import compared with the higher costs of moving refined products in smaller loads to more numerous import terminals. Presently most Arab Countries have their own refineries.

Organisation of Arab Petroleum Exporting Countries

P.O.Box 20501 Safat
Kuwait City, Kuwait

In the field of Arab oil cooperation, an important agreement was concluded on 9th January 1968 in Beirut providing for the creation of the "Organisation of Arab Petroleum Exporting Countries".

Signed initially by Libya, Saudi Arabia and Kuwait, the agreement is open to other Arab countries producing a large proportion of Arab oil and which depend primarily on oil revenues as a source of income, in a bid to further cooperation and the coordination of oil policies of member states (later joined by Algeria, Bahrain, Egypt, Iraq, Qatar, Syria, and the United Arab Emirates). Its objectives are, therefore, complementary to those of the Organisation of Petroleum Exporting Countries, established in Vienna, (OPEC) and not inconsistent as had been feared.

The relationship between the objectives of the two Organisations was stressed when the acting Secretary General of the Organisation of Arab Petroleum Exporting Countries stated that while OPEC's activities are directed primarily towards price stabilisation, those of the new Arab Organisation are geared towards achieving the principle of partnership in all stages of the oil industry so as to enable member countries to embrace the oil sector within the framework of the national economy instead of being an external factor as it is at the present moment.

MAIN OBJECTIVE

The main objective of the Organisation is the cooperation of its members in various forms of economic activity in the petroleum industry, the realization of the closest ties among them in this field, the determination of ways and means of safeguarding the legitimate interests of its members in this industry, individually and collectively, the unification of efforts to ensure the flow of petroleum to its consumption markets on equitable and reasonable terms and the creation of suitable climate for the capital and expertise invested in the petroleum industry of the member countries.

PROJECTS

OAPEC founding agreement has provided that its main objective is to take such measures as may be deemed necessary to achieve closer cooperation among its member states. Within this perspective four main joint Arab projects have been established:

1 — Arab Petroleum Investments Corporation (APICORP).

The incorporation of APICORP was announced on November 23, 1975. its present authorised capital of US$ 1,200 million will be used to finance petroleum projects and industries and fields of activity which are related, ancillary or complementary to such projects and industries, priority being given to joint Arab ventures.

2 — Arab Petroleum Services Company (APSC)- Incorporated in 1977 with an authorised capital of 100 million Libyan Dinars, to provide petroleum services, including the supply of trained manpower.

3 — Arab Maritime Petroleum Transport Company (AMPTC).

Formed in 1973 with an authorized and subscribed capital of US$ 200 million) operate a fleet of tankers

4 — Arab Shipbuilding and Repair Yard Company (ASRY).

Formed in 1974 with an authorised capital of US $ 340 million, ASRY started operations in Bahrain in 1974, with the declared object of training and qualifying member states in ship-building, repair and maintenance. Its drydock, completed in 1977 and built on a man-made island, is fully equipped with the most sophisticated mechanical installations to cope with the needs of super-tankers.

PRESENT PROVEN RESERVES AND DISCOVERED RESERVES IN THE ARAB PETROLEUM PRODUCING COUNTRIES (billion barrels)

	Reserves 1/1/1986	Present reserves 1/1/1999
Eastern Arab Countries		
U.A.E.	33.0	97.7
Bahrain	–	0.2
Iraq	65.0	112.5
Kuwait	92.5	96.5
Neutral zone (Kuwait/Saudi Arabia)	–	5.0
Qatar	3.3	3.7
Saudi Arabia	171.5	261.5
Syria	1.4	2.5
Oman	4.0	5.3
Yemen	–	4.0
Total	**370.7**	**588.9**
North African Arab Countries		
Algeria	8.8	9.2
Egypt	3.9	3.5
Libyan Jamahiriya	21.3	29.5
Tunisia	1.8	0.3
Total	**35.8**	**42.5**
Grand Total	**406.5**	**631.4**

Note: World reserves amounted to about 1052.9 billion barrels of oil as at 1 January 1999.

5 - THE SUEZ CANAL

The Suez Canal

The Suez Canal is a one way Canal. The northbound convoy and southbound convoys meet at Ballah derivation and at the Bitter Lakes.

The Suez Canal offers the shortest navigable route between the Eastern and Western hemispheres. The distance saved varies according to the route followed by the vessels. Thus a ship sailing from the Persian Gulf and making for a North American Atlantic port would have to travel 12,000 miles by the route around the Cape of Good Hope against 8,500 miles via the Suez Canal, whereas for a ship going from the Persian Gulf to a Mediterranean port these figures are 10,700 miles against 4,500 miles.

The Suez Canal was nationalized on July 26, 1956, when the operation, maintenance and improvement of this vital waterway became the responsibility of the Suez Canal Authority, an Arab organization formed specially for this purpose.

A vast programme was then prepared for the improvement of the Canal, based on extensive studies and scientific researches covering actual and future necessities of world navigation and shipbuilding.

The improvement projects executed after the nationalization have resulted in the following.

1. – Increase of the permissible draught from 33 to 38 feet and in 1993 to 56 feet.

2. – Increase of the number of ships transiting the Canal to 80 ships per day.

RESPONSE TO NEW SHIPPING PATTERNS

Since its reopening in 1975, following an eight-year closure due to the 1967 and 1973 Arab-Israeli wars, the Suez Canal Authority has devoted all its efforts first to re-establishing international confidence in the waterway and second to responding to the changes that had taken place in the patterns of world trade during that period.

The initial part of that response was more visible by the end of 1980 when the US $ 2 billion expansion programme was completed.

Until the end of 1980 the largest vessel able to use the canal fully loaded was limited to 60,000 dwt, but during the first six months of 1981 that capacity was gradually increased to vessels of 150,000 dwt fully loaded, ships of 200,000 dwt partially loaded and tankers of up to 370,000 dwt in ballast In 1993 vessels of 170,000 dwt fully loaded were allowed passage.

A new management system has also been introduced. Today, the position of each ship is individually monitored through a complex system of radars, radios and nine mini computers, enabling the control centre in Ismalia to be immediately aware of any difficulties.

The Canal development programme had a significant international impact. World shipping benefited from the shorter routes, and consignors and recipients may benefit from reduced freight rates. The shortening of some major trade routes will allow for more productive use of capital invested in shipping, a reduction in operating costs and in the energy use for oil shipping.

Suez Canal Authority: Irshad Building, Tel. 20001, Tlx: 63238, Ismailia, Egypt.

Cairo Office: 6 Lazoghli str; Garden City, Cairo

SUEZ CANAL TRAFFIC

	Number of ships	Merchandise ('000 tons)	Number of Passengers
1980	20.759	89.729	28.852
1981	21.577	102.532	30.166
1982	22.545	106.588	29.744
1983	22.224	115.703	17.181
1984	21.361	109.491	18.176
1985	19.991	105.695	n.a.
1986	18.403	262.452	12.000
1987	17.541	256.935	11.000
1988	18.190	259,494	—
1989	17,628	265,819	—
1990	17,664	271,881	—
1991	18,326	272,542	—
1992	16,629	275,027	—
1993	17,317	296,914	—
1994	16,370	289,955	—
1995	15,051	293,124	—
1996	14,731	282,015	—
1997	14,430	369,000	—

6 - DEVELOPMENT OF ARAB BANKS AND FUTURE PROSPECTS

Extent of their Present Operations

Since the second major oil price increase of 1979-80, concern has been expressed as to whether funds from the surplus oil exporting countries can by recycled smoothly and efficiently to those countries that are running persistent deficits. Fears that international banks would be unable, because of binding capital constraints and fully extended country limits, to undertake the intermediary role have, in the event, proved unfounded. One reason is that a new group of banks, the Arab banks, has become increasingly active in the international capital markets.

ORIGINS AND DEVELOPMENT

Arab banking has developed in four distinct stages. The first stage includes the colonial period and the period up to the early 1960s when small local banks were established. These banks were chiefly concerned with domestic business and coexisted alongside the traditional money changers. Trade transactions during this period were financed mostly by branches of foreign banks in the Middle East. Indigenous Banks such as the National Commercial Bank of Saudi Arabia, the Rafidain Bank of Iraq, and the Arab Bank of Jordan, which later grew into sizable domestic banks, were established during this period.

The second stage, covering the 1960s and the early 1970s, was one of great significance. This period was characterized by the emergence of the Arab countries as major participants in world trade and finance seeking to develop their economies and to make fuller use of their resources. The need for banking development was complementary to the other aspects of the development process. In a number of countries, especially the major oil producing countries, national commercial banks were set up, some with large-scale branch banking networks. The National Bank of Kuwait, the National Commercial Bank of Libya, the Qatar National Bank, the Bank of Oman, and the National Bank of Dubai are examples of banks established during this stage.

The third stage, which lasted from about the time of the first major oil price in 1973-74 to the onset of the second in 1979, witnessed a rapid growth of Arab institutions and the setting up of new national money and capital markets. International banking markets evolved in Bahrain and the United Arab Emirates, while Kuwait opened up its capital market for the issuance of foreign bonds denominated in Kuwaiti dinars. Furthermore, a new group of Arab Banks flourished by setting up joint ventures with Western banks. A number of these joint ventures, which enabled Western banking know-how to be combined with the plentiful supply of capital available to the oil producing Arab countries, registered strong growth during this period. Examples of the new joint-venture banks are the Union de Banques Arabes et Françaises and the Banque Arabe et Internationale d'Investissement, both based in Paris and both jointly Arab and French owned; the European Arab Bank in Brussels and the Arab Latin American Bank operating out of Peru, both owned by consortia of Arab Banks and, respectively, European and Latin American Banks, and the Saudi International Bank, based in London, which is half owned by the Saudi Arabian Monetary Agency and half by a group of International banks.

The fourth stage of development – from the second oil price rise of 1979-80 to the present time – was one in which the Arab oil producing countries again accumulated substantial oil revenues. During this period, however, there was a change in attitude on the part of the Arab oil producers toward both the placement of their surplus funds and the development of Arab banking institutions. The enlarged surpluses of investable funds quickened the process of porfolio diversification across countries, and types of assets. As part of this process, the banking industry itself was seen as a profitable business for investing capital.

This change in attitude has resulted in increased investment in banks, particularly in wholly Arab-owned banks. For instance, in 1996 the capital base of the Bahrain-based Gulf International Bank, which is owned by seven Arab governments, was increased to US$ 450 million and total assets US$ 8,983 million. In January 1980 a new bank, the Arab Banking Corporation jointly owned by Kuwait, Libya, and Abu Dhabi, was set up in Bahrain; its capital and reserves at end 1996 were US$ 1,657 million, with total assets at US$ 22,988 million.

Another manifestation of the change in attitude is reflected in the development of the Islamic banking concept. The first Islamic Commercial Bank was set up in Egypt during the 1960s, and others have recently been established in the Middle East and abroad. These banks are run according to Islamic principles. As payment of interest (riba) is forbidden in Islam, the Islam banks base their business on an alternative form of compensation for depositors. The concept of profit is, by contrast, acceptable, and so these institutions operate along the lines of a mutual fund – that is, the depositor gains the right to a share in the profits of the institutions. The most significant recent development in this context has been the establishment in Geneva of a highly capitalized ($ 1 billion authorized capital – Paid up $ 316 million) Islamic bank – Dar-al-Maal al Islami – which undertakes international banking operations. Since, many other Islamic banks have been operating in Bahrain, Jordan, Kuwait, Qatar, Malaysia, Saudi Arabia and Sudan.

CENTRES OF INTERNATIONAL ARAB BANKING

The three main centers of Arab banking are the Middle East, Paris, and London. There is, however, much evidence to suggest that both the older and the newly established banks are actively seeking to expand into other banking centers. Singapore and New York are but two current examples.

International banking activity in the Middle East has been centered in Bahrain. Bahrain developed as an international financial center through the establishment of offshore banking units. Its growth since the mid-1970s, however, has been slower than expected, although some banks (notably the Gulf International Bank and the Arab Banking Corporation) are now using Bahrain as a base for a strong expansion into international lending. Japanese banks have also opened offshore banking units in Bahrain and seem destined to become a significant banking force in the area.

In Paris there are 35 wholly or partly Arab-owned banks, the large number reflecting the-standing French-Arab connection, which was cemented further during the late 1960s. Many of the important new banks were set up in Paris late in the second and third stage of Arab banking development.

In London, there are some 29 Arab banks and investment institutions. London became the home for the Arab Bankers Association – an international association of bankers set up to foster interest in Arab banking affairs, publish research studies, and organize training courses for Arab bankers.

In USA there are at present more than 11 Arab banks among which Abu Dhabi International Bank Inc., Arab Bank PLC, Arab Banking Corporation, Bahrain Middle East Bank, Bank of Oman Ltd, Commercial Bank of Kuwait, Riyad Bank, Bank Audi.

SIZE OF ARAB BANKS

The largest Arab banks are those that were set up in the first stage of Arab banking development; banks from Saudi Arabia, Kuwait, and Algeria are among the largest 20. The banks established in the fourth stage of development have accomplished the fastest rates of growth in assets, however.

GROWTH OF ARAB BANKING BUSINESS

The process of external intermediation of banking business that occurred among the banks of North America, Europe, and Japan in the 1970s is clearly taking place in the Arab banking world now.

In the first and second stages of Arab banking, activity was almost entirely confined to the domestic market. In these periods, banking services were extended in regions which were, by Western standards, underbanked. Building on their stronger domestic bases, several of these banks – the National Commercial Bank, and the Arab Bank, for instance – are now playing a growing role in international markets.

The newer banks, founded late in the third stage and in the fourth stage, were oriented toward international business from the outset. Trade financing was one area of growth, but several banks have become established names in the foreign and international bond markets. The newest banks – the Arab Banking Corporation, the Gulf International Bank, and the Saudi International Bank — are quickly establishing themselves in the highly visible syndicated Eurocurrency lending market, an area of banking activity that does not require a well-established and highly sophisticated banking structure.

FUTURE PROSPECTS

A number of factors will influence the growth of Arab banks in the future, including capitalization and managerial capacity. Since many of these banks are already highly capitalized, the availability of capital is unlikely to be a constraint in the short term. However, a shortage of skilled banking personnel, particularly staff of Arab origin, might limit the pace and nature of the expansion.

Most Arab banks have not been direct recipients of large volumes of funds from the Organization of Petroleum Exporting Countries. Hitherto, the Arab banks have generally sought funding from a range of primary depositors and have also tapped the inter-bank money markets. As confidence grows in Arab institutions, Arab depositors begin to place a higher proportion of their funds with them.

To summarize, banks established in the fourth stage appear to be set for a period of sound growth, while many of the larger banks established in the first and second stage will also continue to increase their operations in international markets. For some of the consortia of Arab and Western banks created in the third stage, the next few years may be a period of change and consolidation. Others, mindful that they do not have the capacity for large-scale lending, may seek steadier growth by diversifying into a wider range of banking functions.

LEADING ISLAMIC BANKING GROUPS

A) DAR AL-MAL AL-ISLAMI
Established 1981 in Switzerland
Authorised capital: one billion US dollars
Paid-up capital: 316 million US dollars with over 20 subsidiaries operating in Bahamas, Bahrain, Guinea, Niger, Senegal, Sudan, Switzerland and the United Arab Emirates.

B) AL BARAKA
Established 1982 in Jeddah
Paid-up capital: 1,500 million US dollars.
Operates in Bahrain, Saudi Arabia, Sudan, Tunisia, Turkey, UK, Jordan, Lebanon.

C) ISLAMIC DEVELOPMENT BANK
Established 1975 in Jeddah
Authorized capital: 2.2 billion US dollars

Arab Banks
Listed in chronological order

	Founded		
National Bank of Egypt	1898	Wahda Bank	1970
Misr Bank	1920	National Commercial Bank	1970
Arab Bank	1930	Bank of Kuwait and the Middle East	1971
Rafidain Bank	1941	Arab International Bank	1971
National Bank of Kuwait	1952	Bank of Bahrain and Kuwait	1971
Banque du Caire	1952	Libyan Arab Foreign Bank	1972
Riyad Bank	1957	European Arab Holding	1972
Bank of Alexandria	1957	Banque Arabe et Internationale d'Investissement	1973
Banque Nationale du Commerce Extérieur	1959		
Gulf Bank	1960	Gulf International Bank	1975
Commercial Bank of Kuwait	1961	Saudi International Bank	1975
National Bank of Dubai	1963	Banque Internationale Arabe	1975
Arab African International Bank	1964	Burgan Bank	1975
Qatar National Bank	1965	Union Méditerranéenne de Banques	1975
Crédit Populaire d'Algérie	1966	Saudi Investment Banking Corporation	1976
United Bank of Kuwait	1966	Bank Al-Jazira	1976
Commercial Bank of Syria	1967	UBAF Arab American Bank	1976
Alahli Bank of Kuwait	1967	Al Bank Al Saudi Al Fransi	1977
Banque Extérieure d'Algérie	1967	Al Bank Al Saudi Al Hollandi	1977
Bank of Oman	1967	Saudi British Bank	1978
National Bank of Abu Dhabi	1968	Saudi Cairo Bank	1979
Jamahiriya Bank	1969	Saudi American Bank	1980
Union des Banques Arabes et Françaises	1970	Arab Banking Corporation	1980

7- THE PALESTINIAN PROBLEM

The Palestinian Problem

At the turn of the century, there were only about 500,000 people living in Palestine; most were Arab peasants, but 35,000 were Jews, who owned less than 1% of the land. In 1917 the British, in an effort to gain Jewish support during World War I, issued the Balfour Declaration. That document, prepared by Foreign Secretary Arthur Balfour, endorsed the Zionist dream of establishing a Jewish homeland in Palestine, though it contended that such a homeland should not "prejudice" the rights of its Arab inhabitants.

Historically, the Palestinians have lived in the same general region on the eastern shore of the Mediterranean since ancient times. They trace their ancestry to the Canaanites, though it was the Philistines from whom the name of latter-day Palestine is derived. In Arabic, the country is called Filastine. The region has been ruled by a seemingly endless procession of conquerors, including the Ottoman Turks, who held it from the 16th century until World War I. For 30 years thereafter, Britain governed Palestine, which included the present territory of Israel, Jordan, the West Bank and Gaza, under a League of Nations mandate.

On November 29th 1947, the United Nations proposed the division of the present area of Israel, the West Bank and Gaza into separate Jewish and Arab states; Jerusalem was to have a special status as an internationalized city. Most Jewish leaders in Palestine accepted the partition; the Arabs did not. Fearful of impending civil war, 300,000 Arabs living in Palestine fled their homeland in the weeks before the declaration of the state of Israel on May 15, 1948; when Arab armies attacked the new country, another 350,000 took flight or were forced to leave, abandoning homes, farms, orchards and shops.

At first these 650,000 refugees rejected all attempts to resettle them. They even refused to leave their UNRWA tents, fearing that their transfer to the concrete huts offered them would be taken as a sign that they had accepted their dispersal. Other Arabs gave minimal support to the refugees, on the ground that the West had created the problem by recognizing Israel's existence. However the attitude has since changed and Arab Countries have largely participated in the ever growing deficit of UNRWA.

Since the Six-Day war of 1967, Israelis have bought, expropriated or taken over roughly 30% of the West Bank's 2,200 sq. mi., including some of the most fertile farm-land in the Jordan Valley. In many instances, land has been seized in the name of defence. Housing projects for Israelis were constructed since the 1967 war.

Of the world's 4 million Palestinians, according to the United Nations Relief and Works Agency (UNRWA), which assists in running the refugee camps, there were approx. 3,574,000 registered Palestinian refugees at end 1998; but only about 1,160,000 of them lived in 59 camps, scattered throughout Lebanon (367600), Syria (370100), Jordan (1,488,300), the West Bank and Gaza (1,348,000). The UNRWA budget in 1999 amounted to US$ 353 million. The great majority of the world's Palestinians still live in the Middle East, mainly in Jordan, the West Bank and Gaza, Israel and Lebanon, but there are also sizable communities in the Gulf states, Egypt and Saudi Arabia, and Syria.

Most are still peasant farmers or workers, but a surprising number are doctors, lawyers, industrialists, bankers and poets. Remittances from foreign workers, mostly Palestinians in the Gulf (before the Gulf War), added more than US $.800 million a year to Jordan's economy. The Palestinians still demonstrate an extraordinary drive for education. In 1978, in fact, according to one survey, there were 80,000 Palestinians enrolled in universities throughout the world, a remarkably high rate for an impoverished people.

Meanwhile, the P.L.O. has been active on more than one front: military against Israel; social and diplomatic in a bid to earn the respect and recognition of the outside world, notably in Arab and Western capitals.

It runs hospitals and clinics, dispenses social security benefits, sponsors trade unions and even association for writers, poets and painters. It maintains factories that produce clothing, blankets, furniture and toys, and others.

On the diplomatic front it has opened 82 offices around the world, and appointed representatives in every Arab country as well as in non-Arab states, including USA, Russia, China, Cuba, Yugoslavia, Switzerland and Britain and France. On November 22nd, 1974 it was granted permanent observer status at the General Assembly of the UN and at international conferences sponsored by the UN. In September 1976, the P.L.O. became a full member of the League of Arab States.

As it is, it has tranformed itself, in effect, into a government in exile with a legislature (the Council), and a Cabinet (the executive committee).

The Palestine National Charter

The following are extracts from the 33-article Palestine National Charter, or "Covenant", originally adopted at the inaugural meeting of the Palestine National Council held in East Jerusalem in May-June 1964 at which the decision was taken to form the PLO, as amended by the PNC in July 1968 and reaffirmed by the 13th PNC session held in Cairo in March 1977.

ARTICLE 1

Palestine is the homeland of the Palestinian Arab people, it is an indivisible part of the Arab homeland, and the Palestinian people are an integral part of the Arab nation.

ARTICLE 2

Palestine, with the boundaries it had during the British mandate (from 1922 to 1948), is an indivisible territorial unit.

ARTICLE 3

The Palestinian Arab people possess the legal right to their homeland and have the right to determine their destiny after achieving the liberation of their country in accordance with their wishes and entirely of their own accord and will.

ARTICLE 5

The Palestinians are those Arab nationals who, until 1947, normally resided in Palestine regardless of whether they were evicted from it or have stayed there. Anyone born, after that date, of a Palestinian father whether inside Palestine or outside it-is also a Palestinian.

ARTICLE 6

The Jews who had normally resided in Palestine until the beginning of the Zionist invasion will be considered Palestinians.

ARTICLE 8

The phase in their history, through which the Palestinian people are now living, is that of national struggle for the liberation of Palestine. Thus the conflicts among the Palestinian national forces are secondary, and should be ended for the sake of the basic conflict that exists between the forces of Zionism and of imperialism on the one hand, and the Palestinian Arab people on the other. On this basis the Palestinian masses, regardless of whether they are residing in the national homeland or in diaspora constitute-both their organizations and the individuals-one national front working for the retrieval of Palestine and its liberation through armed struggle.

ARTICLE 9

Armed struggle is the only way to liberate Palestine. Thus it is the overall strategy, not merely a tactical phase. The Palestinian Arab people assert their absolute determination and firm resolution to continue their armed struggle and to work for an armed popular revolution for the liberation of their country and their return to it. They also assert their right to normal life in Palestine and to exercise their right to self-determination and sovereignty over it.

ARTICLE 11

The Palestinians will have three mottoes; national unity, national mobilization and liberation.

ARTICLE 12

The Palestinian people believe in Arab unity. In order to contribute their share towards the attainment of that objective, however, they must, at the present stage of their struggle, safeguard their Palestinian identity and develop their consciousness of that identity, and oppose any plan that may dissolve or impair it.

ARTICLE 15

The liberation of Palestine, from an Arab viewpoint, is a national duty, and it attempts to repel the Zionist and imperialist aggression against the Arab homeland, and aims at the elimination of Zionism in Palestine.

Absolute responsibility for this falls upon the Arab nation-peoples and governments-with the Arab people of Palestine in the vanguard. Accordingly the Arab nation must mobilize all its military, human, moral and spiritual capabilities to participate actively with the Palestinian people in the liberation of Palestine. It must, particularly in the phase of the armed Palestinian revolution, offer and furnish the Palestinian people with all possible help, and material and human support, and make available to them the means and opportunities that will enable them to continue to carry out their leading role in the armed revolution, until they liberate their homeland.

ARTICLE 16

The liberation of Palestine, from a spiritual point of view, will provide the Holy Land with an atmosphere of safety and tranquility, which in turn will safeguard the country's religious sanctuaries and guarantee freedom of worship and of visit to all, without discrimination of race, colour, language, or religion. Accordingly, the people of Palestine look to all spiritual forces in the world for support.

ARTICLE 17/19

The Liberation of Palestine, from a human point of view, will restore to the Palestinian individual his dignity, pride and freedom. Accordingly the Palestinian Arab people look forward to the support of all those who believe in the dignity of man and his freedom in the world.

The partition of Palestine in 1947 and the establishment of the state of Israel are entirely illegal, regardless of the passage of time, because they were contrary to the will of the Palestinian people and to their natural right in their homeland, and inconsistent with the principles embodied in the Charter of the United Nations, particularly the right to self-determination.

ARTICLE 20

The Balfour Declaration (issued by the then British Foreign Secretary in November 1917, viewing "with favour the establishment in Palestine of a National Home for the Jewish people" but including a provision that "nothing shall be done which may prejudice the civil and religious rights of existing non-Jewish communities in Palestine"), the (British) mandate for Palestine and everything that has been based upon them, are deemed null and void. Claims of historical of religious ties of Jews with Palestine are incompatible with the facts of history and the true conception of what constitutes statehood. Judaism, being a religion, is not an independent nationality. Nor do Jews constitute a single nation with an identity of its own; they are citizens of the states to which they belong.

ARTICLE 21

The Palestinian Arab people, expressing themselves by the armed Palestinian revolution, reject all solutions which are substitutes for the total liberation of Palestine and reject all proposals aiming at the liquidation of the Palestinian problem, or its internationalization.

ARTICLE 22

Zionism is a political movement organically associated with international imperialism and antagonistic to all action for liberation and progressive movements in the world. It is racist and fanatic in its methods. Israel is the instrument of the Zionist movement, and a geographical base for world imperialism placed strategically in the midst of the Arab homeland to combat the hopes of the Arab nation for liberation, unity and progress. Israel is a constant source of threat vis-a-vis peace in the Middle East and the whole world. Since the liberation of Palestine will destroy the Zionist and imperialist presence and will contribute to the establishment of peace in the Middle East, the Palestinian people look for the support of all the progressive and peaceful forces and urge them all, irrespective of their affiliations and beliefs, to offer the Palestinian people all aid and support in their just struggle for the liberation of their homeland.

ARTICLE 23

The demands of security and peace, as well as the demands of right and justice, require all states to consider Zionism an illegitimate movement, to outlaw its existence, and to ban its operations, in order that friendly relations among peoples may be preserved, and the loyalty of citizens to their respective homelands safeguarded.

ARTICLE 26

The Palestine Liberation Organisation, representative of the Palestinian revolutionary forces, is responsible for the Palestinian Arab people's movement in its struggle to retrieve its homeland, liberate and return to it and exercise the right of self determination in it-in all military, political and financial fields and also for whatever may be required by the Palestine cause on the inter-Arab and international levels.

ARTICLE 28

The Palestinian Arab people assert the genuineness and independence of their national revolution and reject all forms of intervention, trusteeship and subordination.

ARTICLE 29

The Palestinian people possess the fundamental and genuine legal right to liberate and retrieve their homeland. The Palestinian people determine their attitude towards all states and forces on the basis of the stands they adopt vis-a-vis the Palestinian cause and the extent of the support they offer to the Palestinian revolution to fulfil the aims of the Palestinian people.

ARTICLE 33

The Charter shall not be amended save by (vote of) a majority of two-thirds of the total membership of the National Council of the Palestine Liberation Organization (taken) at a special session convened for that purpose.

UN CONFERENCE ON PALESTINE

An "International Conference on the Question of Palestine", held under United Nations auspices in Geneva, Switzerland, on Aug. 28-Sept. 7,1983, passed a number of resolutions calling inter alia for the creation of an independent Palestinian state.

In the opening speech, Sr Javier Pérez de Cuellar, the UN Secretary-General, set out three conditions for Middle East peace as follows: (i) the withdrawal of Israeli forces from the occupied territories; (ii) respect for and acknowledgement of the sovereignty, territorial integrity and independence of every state in the region; and (iii) a just settlement based upon the legitimate rights of the Palestinian people, including self-determination.

The "Programme of Action" adopted by the conference called on all states to "alleviate the economic and social burdens" imposed on the Palestinians by Israeli occupation by ensuring that the United Nations Relief and Works Agency (UNRWA) for Palestine Refugees in the Near East had sufficient funds to meet all essential needs. It also demanded that Palestinians held in Israeli detention after the war in Lebanon should be accorded prisoner of war status under the Geneva Convention. Finally, the programmes called for the observance of the International Day of Solidarity with the Palestinian People on November 29 each year.

Meeting in Algiers in 1983, the 16th session of the PNC (Palestine National Council), made no changes in the PLO Charter. It rejected the "Reagan Plan" and stated that the Fez Plan was the minimum acceptable to the PLO. The 17th session of the PNC, meeting in Amman in November 1984, delegated the PLO Executive committee to examine King Hussein's proposals for a joint Jordanian-Palestinian position on a Middle East peace settlement. The formal establishment of the joint negotiating platform was endorsed by the PLO Executive Committee in February 1985, on the condition that it received full Arab support.

In November 1988 Mr. Yasser Arafat, President of the Executive Committee of the Palestinian Liberation Organisation, has proclaimed the establishment of a Palestinian State on the Palestinian Soil with Holy Jerusalem as its capital at the meeting of the Palestinian National Council held in Algiers. The Palestinian National Council has accepted Resolution 242 of the security council of the United Nations with guarantees to national rights of the Palestinian people on the basis of negociations towards peace.

In 1991 the Palestinians have accepted to join in the Peace Conference on the Middle East. under the joint Chairmanship of the United States of America and Russia., which opened in Madrid, Spain, on 30 October 1991.

They were represented by:
Haidar ABDEL SHAFI – Saeb ORAIKAT – Abdelrahman HAMAD – Nabil KASSIS – Sami KILANI – Nabil JAABARI
Elias FREIGE – Zakaria AGHA – Freige ABOU MADINE – Mamdouh ACAR – Samih KANAAN – Moustapha NATSHEH – Samir ABDALLAH
Advisors: Faisal HUSSEINI – Rashid KHALIDI – Sirry NUSAIBAH – Anis KASSEM – Kamil MANSOUR – Hanane ASHRAWI – Zahia KAMAL

The West Bank and Gaza Strip
Area: West Bank 5633 sq. km
Gaza Strip 364 sq. km
Total Palestinian Population: estimated at end 1997 2,896,000
Main Economic Activity: Industry, Agriculture (olives, citrus fruits, vegetables, potatoes), live stock, fishing and tourism.

The Cabinet

(sept. 1999)

Chairman: Yasser ARAFAT
Minister of Civil Affairs: Jamil AL TARIFI
Minister of the Interior: Ahmad TAMIMI
Minister of Planning and International Cooperation: Nabil SHAATH
Minister of Finance: Mohamed Zihdi AL NASHASHIBI
Minister of Justice: Furayh ABU MIDAYN
Minister of Culture and Information: Yasser ABED RABBUH
Minister of Local Government: Dr. Saeb UREIKAT
Minister of Social Affairs: Intisar AL WAZIR
Minister of Housing: Abdelrahman HAMAD
Minister of Posts and Telecommunications: Imad AL FALLOULI
Minister of Public Works: Azzam AL AHMAD
Minister of Supply: Abdelaziz CHAHINE
Minister of Health: Riyad AL ZAANOUN
Minister of Higher Education: Munzer SALAH
Minister of Transport: Ali AL KAWASMEH
Minister of Economy and Trade: Maher AL MASRI
Minister of Industry: Saadi AL KARNAZ
Minister of Labour: Rafic AL NATSHA
Minister of Tourism and Antiquities: Metri ABU ATTIA
Minister of Agriculture: Hekmat ZAID
Minister of Bethlehem 2000 Affairs: Nabil QAIS
Minister of Parliamentary Affairs: Nabil AMR
Minister of State for Prisoners' Affairs: Hisham ABDEL-RAZZAK
Minister of State for Jerusalem Affairs: Ziad ABU ZIAD
Minister of State for the Environment: Yousuf ABU SAFIEH
Ministers of State: Hassan ASFOUR, Talal SADR, Salah AL TAMARI

8 – GULF CO-OPERATION COUNCIL

Gulf Co-operation Council

Acting upon an idea reportedly conceived at an Islamic summit conference held in Taif (Saudi Arabia) in late January 1981, the Gulf states of Bahrain, Kuwait, Oman, Qatar, Saudi Arabia and the United Arab Emirates (UAE) agreed at a meeting of their Foreign Ministers in Riyad (Saudi Arabia) on Feb. 4-5 to establish a Cooperation Council of the Arab Gulf States which would provide a framework for the co-ordination of all government policies between the member countries with a view to safeguarding security and stability in the Gulf.

Following a further meeting of the Foreign Ministers in Muscat (Oman) on March 9-10, the heads of state of the member countries of the new Cooperation Council held their first summit meeting in Abu Dhabi (UAE) on May 25-26. On the first day of their summit the rulers approved the statutes of the New Council, in accordance with which the aims of the organization were defined as follows:

"(i) To achieve co-ordination, integration and co-operation among the member states in all fields in order to bring about their unity; (ii) to deepen and strengthen the bonds of co-operation existing among their peoples in all fields; (iii) to draw up similar systems in all fields... including economic and financial, trade, customs and transport, educational and cultural, health and social, information and tourism, and judicial and administrative; and (iv) to promote scientific and technical progress in the fields of industry, minerals, agriculture, sea wealth and animal wealth and to establish scientific research centres and collective projects and to encourage the private sector's cooperation for the good of the peoples of the member states".

The six countries stated that they had agreed to form the Council out of their "awareness of their special ties and common characteristics and the similarity of the regimes governing them on the basis of the Islamic faith", their "belief in the common destiny and aim uniting their peoples", their "desire to achieve co-ordination, integration and co-operation" which they believed would serve "the sublime objective of the Arab nation", and "a desire to continue efforts in all vital fields concerning their peoples and to achieve their aspirations for a better future and unity".

It was agreed that the Council, the headquarters of which were to be in Riyadh, would be composed of a Supreme Council, a Ministerial Council and a General Secretariat, these three bodies being able to establish auxiliary organs as required.

In an appendix to a final statement agreed by the member countries on May 26 it was stated that committees had been set up with responsibility for (i) economic and social planning; (ii) financial, economic and trade co-operation; (iii) industrial co-operation; (iv) oil; and (v) social and cultural services.

With regard to the oil committee, which would comprise the Foreign, Oil and Finance Ministers of the member countries (which together provided over a quarter of the non-communist world's oil supplies), its duties would be to "co-ordinate the policies of the Council's members in the field of oil industry in all stages of drilling, refining, marketing and pricing", as well as "transporting and exploiting natural gas and developing sources of energy". In addition, the oil committee would draw up a "unified oil policy and joint stands towards the outside world and international organizations". One of the first projects of the Cooperation Council was the setting-up, of a $2,100 million joint investment fund the Gulf Investment Corporation.

On June 8 the Finance Ministers met in Riyadh to draw up a collective co-operation pact aimed inter alia at abolishing all trade and customs barriers among the member countries, unifying financial and banking regulations and encouraging private capital for investment projects.

The member countries of the Co-operation Council emphasized generally that the role of the new organization would, for the most part, be restricted to economic and social issues, pointing out at the same time that such co-operation had existed for some time and that the Council had been formed merely to provide an administrative framework to put this into effect. It was, however, widely accepted that the defence and security of the Gulf and of the oil installations there had been a key factor in the establishment of the Council.

In particular, the Gulf countries had repeatedly expressed fears of super-power rivalry in the Gulf area, their anxieties in this respect being heightened by the desire of the United States to increase its military presence in the region to counter what it viewed as a growing Soviet encroachment in the Gulf. In this connection the Council members-with exception of Oman, which was co-operating militarily with the United States-had consistently expressed their opposition to the presence of foreign troops in the area, in particular to the deployment of Western forces within the framework of the US rapid deployment force (set up by President Carter in 1980), and declared their determination to provide their own security.

In their final statement, the heads of state reaffirmed that "the region's security and stability are the responsibility of its peoples and countries". and that "this Council expresses the will of these countries and their right to defend their security and independence". They also recorded their "absolute rejection of any foreign interference in the region from whatever source" and called for the entire region to be kept "free of international conflicts, and particularly the presence of military fleets and foreign bases", in order to "safeguard their interests and the interests of the world".

In October 1990 GCC Countries agreed to support regional banks affected by the crisis, following the invasion of Kuwait; and in July 1991 central Banks agreed to cooperate in reducing the risks in banks operating within their countries, and in May 1992 formulated their objective of establishing a common market by the end of this century. In November 1981 the Council agreed to include defence cooperation to the original charter, and in 1984 agreed to form a Shield Force under a central command. Following the invasion of Kuwait in 1990 this combined force was put on alert to counter any possible invasion of Saudi Arabia. Later this force became part of the United Nations coalition in the Gulfwar.

In March 1991 the Gulf cooperation Council together with Egypt and Syria announced Plans, "Declaration of Damascus", to establish a peace keeping force in the region.

In December 1993 the 14th summit held on the 20-22nd December was attended by all six member countries to study oil production, joint security, relations with Iran, the peace process in the Middle East.

The 15th summit was held in Manama, Bahrain on December 1994 with all six members present. Border disputes and security were the main concern.

The 16th summit was held in Muscat, Oman on December 4, 1995 the main topic was internal security issues and foreign policy.

The 17th summit took place in Doha, Qatar on December 7,1996. The issues dealt with were the Middle East peace process, condemnation of terrorism, economic and military cooperation.

The 18th summit was hosted by Kuwait on December 20, 1997.

The 19th summit took place in Abu Dhabi on 7th December 1998, and Sheikh Jamil al-Hojeilan was re-appointed as Gulf Cooperation Council Secretary General for a further three years term.

The 20th summit was held in Riyadh, Saudi Arabia on November 27, 1999. The main topic was customs unions.

9 – PEACE CONFERENCE ON THE MIDDLE EAST

PEACE CONFERENCE ON THE MIDDLE EAST

Arab Israeli Conflict

After the war in the Gulf, the United States of America, together with the U.S.S.R. and E.E.C. countries have taken steps to bring about a solution to the 44 years old Arab-Israeli Conflict. After several months of hard and unrelenting negotiations by the United States of America and the U.S.S.R., and mainly by the U.S. Secretary of State Mr. James Baker, with the parties in conflict, the Arab Countries and Israel have accepted the proposals for a Peace Conference to end the enemity between them.

The Conference was held in Madrid, Spain, on the 30th October 1991 under the joint Chairmanship of the United State of America and the U.S.S.R., and attended by delegations of the following Countries.

a) The United States of America
b) The U.S.S.R.
c) EEC Countries (as participants in negotiations)
d) The United Nations (as observers)
e) The Gulf Cooperation Council (as observers)
f) The Arab Maghreb Union (as observers)
g) The parties in conflict: Syria – Egypt – Jordan – Lebanon – Palestinians on the one hand, and Israel on the other.

The Arab delegations were:

Syria: Farouk Sharaa – Muwaffac Allaf – Zakaria Ismail – Dia Allah Fattal – Nasrat Mulla Haidar – Mohamed Khodr – Walid Moallem – Majdi Jazzar – Ahmed Fathi Masri – Adnan Tayara – Saber Falhout – Ahmed Arnus – Rizcallah Elias – Zuheir Accad.

Egypt: Amro Mussa – Alae Barakat – Mahmoud Abu Nasr – Wagih Hamawi – Rida Shehata – Ahmed Aboul Gaith – Nabil Fahmi – Ahmed Fakhr – Lutfi Kholi – Yunan Labib Rizk – Saleh Omar – Ayaleddin Halal.

Jordan: Kamal Abu Jaber – Abdel Salam Majali – Awwad Khalidi – Talal Al Hassan – Mohamed Adwan – Fuad Ayoub – Adnan Najieh – Aoun Hassouni – Ghassan Jurdi – Mohamed Bani Hani – Moussa Breizat – Abdelhafez Merhi – Walid Khalidi – Anwar Khatib.

Lebanon: Farès Boueiz – Zafer Hassan – Mahmoud Hammoud – Abbas Hamieh – Samir Moubarak – Jihad Mourtada – Naji Abou Assi – Jaafar Maawi – Antoine Kheir – Ghassan Salameh.

Palestinians: Haidar Abdel Shafi – Saeb Oreikat – Abdelrahman Hamad – Nabil Kassis – Sami Kilani – Nabil Jaabari – Elias Freige – Zakaria Agha – Freige Abou Madine – Mamdouh Acar – Samih Kanaan – Moustafa Natsheh – Samir Abdallah.

Advisors: Faisal Husseini – Rashid Khalidi – Sirry Nusseibah – Anis Kassem – Kamil Mansour – Hanan Ashrawi – Zahira Kamal.

Following the peace conference held in Madrid at the end of October 1991 bilateral talks began on the 3rd of November in Madrid.

The second round of negociations was held in Washington (where all following negociations took place), on 10 December 1991. The talks ended on December 18 with no progress having been achieved.

The third round of talks was held on 13 January 1992 until the 16th.

Simultaneously multilateral talks were held in Moscow on January 28-29.

The object is to tackle regional matters on water sharing economic development, the environment etc. The Palestinian delegation boycotted the meeting and Syria and Lebanon declined to attend. The conference established five committees. The economic cooperation committee chaired by the EC, would meet in Brussels; the environment committee, chaired by Japan, would meet in Tokyo; the refugee committee, chaired by Canada, would meet in Ottawa; the water sharing committee, chaired by the USA, would meet in Turkey or Austria; and the ams control committee, chaired by Russia, would meet in Washington.

The fourth round of bilateral negotiations opened on February 24. The ten-day talks made little progress.

The fifth Middle East peace talks took place on April 27th, and the 6th round on 24th August 1992. In the meantime multilateral sessions were held in May, on regional economic cooperation in Brussels, regional arms control in Washington, on refugees in Ottawa, water sharing in Vienna, environmental protection in Tokyo. Finally a meeting was held in Lisbon of the steering committe and an agreement was reached on the venues of future meetings. The regional economic cooperation multilateral negotiations were held in Paris on October 29-30 1992, and on refugees in Ottawa on November 11-12, 1992 and the meeting on water sharing and economic cooperation were held in late April in Geneva and Rome, and the refugees and arms control committees in Norway and Washington respectively. The refugees committee held a further meeting in Tunisia on October 12-14 and the water sharing committe in China on October 26 28. The regional economic cooperation committe was held on November 8th and 9th in Copenhagen and agreed on a number of studies covering transport, energy, tourism, financial markets, trade, and other sections.

The seventh round took place on 21 October and ended on November 19, and the 8th round was opened in Washington on December 7.

In 1993 the ninth round took place on April 27 and finished on May 13 with a deadlock, (the first session since the inauguration of US President Bill Clinton).

The tenth round of bilateral talks which was held from June 15 to July 1 also ended in a deadlock. On August 30, it was announced that Israel and the Palestine Liberation Organization had secretly negociated a draft peace agreement. News of the agreement completely overshadowed the 11th round of peace talks in Washington in the first two weeks of September where no progress was reported. On September 10 Israel and the PLO formally recognised each other. Shortly after the declaration of mutual recognition,

US President Bill Clinton announced that the USA would renew its contacts with the PLO which had been suspended in June 1990. The Israeli-PLO agreement officially called a "Declaration of Principles" was signed in Washington on September 13 by Shimon Peres and Mahmoud Abbas in a ceremony attended by Clinton, Arafat and Rabin, and some 3000 guests.

The timetable of the peace plan was set as follows:

Oct. 13, 1993. Declaration becomes effective. Israeli military administration begins to transfer authority in West Bank and Gaza to "authorized Palestinians"

Dec. 13, 1993. Israel and Palestinians to have agreed protocol on withdrawal of Israeli forces form Gaza Strip and Jericho area. Military withdrawal to begin upon signing.

April 13, 1994. Israel to have completed military withdrawal from Gaza and Jericho area. Israel to transfer powers to nominated Palestinian authority. Beginning of the five-year period of interim self-government to a permanent settlement begins.

July 13, 1994. Elections to a Palestinian Council to have been held. Elections to be followed by inauguration of Council and the dissolution of Israeli military-run civil administration in the occupied territories.

April 13, 1996. Israel and the Palestinians to have begun negociations on a permanent settlement.

April 13, 1999. Permanent settlement to be in force.

In October 1993 Israeli and PLO delegation began talks for implementation of the agreement by holding a number of meetings in Egypt.

Until the end of January 1994 no further bilateral negotiations were held. An event of dimension, however, is the proposed meeting in Geneva between US President Bill Clinton and Syrian President Hafez Assad, with a view to enhance the Peace process in the Middle East.

The Meeting took place in Geneva on January 16, 1994.

The 12th bilateral talks opened in Washington on January 24 1994 between Israel, Jordan, Syria and Lebanon and were temporarily suspended by the Arab States on February 27, 1994. On October 27, during a Middle East tour, US President Clinton visited Damascus and held talks with President Assad, in an attempt to break the impasse on the Syrian/Israeli negotiating tract. Resumption of talks between Syrian and Israeli officials took place in March 1995, and in June 27-29 both countries chiefs of staff held a round of talks in Washington. Further peace talks took place on December 27-29 at Wye Plantation in Maryland U.S.A., and a further round of talks on January 3, 1996.

Peace talks were resumed in Washington and Sheperdstown on 15 December 1999 with Clinton, Sharaa and Barak and a second round of talks took place in Sheperdstown, Virginia on 3 January, 2000, but were later discontinued.

On the Palestinian side, Israel and the PLO began to implement the Declaration of Principles agreement which they had signed on September 13 1993, by holding a meeting between Rabin/Arafat on October 6,1993 in Cairo, and committees have beeb established, On May 4,1994, Prime Minister Rabin and Chairman Yasser Arafat signed an agreement in Cairo, in the presence of President Hosni Mubarak and US Secretary of State Warren Christopher providing for Palestinian self-rule in the Gaza Strip and Jericho after seven months of negotiations. The agreement represented the first stage of the "Declaration of Principles" accord.

And in May, a Palestinian Cabinet was appointed to manage the affairs in the self-rule areas of Gaza-Jericho.

On June 28 Palestinian and Israeli officials began talks aimed at extending the Palestinian self-rule area.

On July 6, 1994, Arafat and Prime Minister Rabin met again in Paris to discuss further implementation of the next phase of the "Declaration of Principles" peace accord. A further meeting was held on August 10 at the border crossing between Israel and Gaza. Other meetings took place between Arafat and Rabin on September 25, November 8, 1994, January 19, 1995 and February 9, 1995 to discuss further transfer of authority to the West Bank.

Israeli and Palestinian negotiators finally agreed on the expansion of Palestinian self-rule in the occupied West Bank, and was formally signed in Washington on September 28, 1995 and endorsed by Arafat and Rabin.

It stipulates that Israel would withdraw its forces from several towns and villages in the West Bank, and transfer civic authority and Palestinian responsability for public order in the 440 villages of the West Bank and Palestinian elections to take place in the West Bank and Gaza.

Elections were held in Gaza and the West Bank on 20th January 1996. Yasser Arafat was elected as Chairman of the Palestinian self-rule Authority and an Assembly of 88 members.

Further negotiations took place in 1996 and a summit was held in Washington in October with Arafat, Hussein and Netanyahu, in 1997, and in early 1998 the US Secretary of State Madeleine Albright toured the Middle East in an attempt to enhance the Middle East Process.

In mid October 1998 a summit was convened in the U.S. and the Wye River Memorandum was signed on 23 October 1998.

In August 1999, Israelis and Palestinians met to reactivate the memorandum, agreed upon in October and early September 1999. Ehud Barak and Yasser Arafat signed at Sharm el Sheikh the memorandum on the implementation time table on oustanding commitments and the Resumption of Permanent status negotiations.

The Camp David Middle East talks which started on 11th July, 2000 (Clinton/ Barak/ Arafat) for the final Status of a Palestinian/ Israeli Peace Agreement, have been going on in the presence of President Clinton until he left to Japan for the G8 meeting during which time Secretary of State Mrs. Madeleine Albright headed the American side. On Mr. Clinton's return from Japan on the 23rd July, 2000, he resumed the talks with both Barak and Arafat in order to reach a final solution. The discussions ended in a failure to reach an agreement. Both Middle East Leaders have left the United States, with an understanding however, that further discussions will continue until such a time that a final solution is reached. Hereafter is the White House communique issued in this respect:

"Both Parties, the Israelis and the Palestinians, agree on the principles to be followed for further Talks:

a) The object of the negotiations is to put an end to the conflict and to reach a just and permanent peace.

b) Both Parties agree to make further efforts to solve, as soon as possible, all issues leading to a final solution.

c) Both parties agree that the negotiations based on United Nations resolutions 242 and 338, will be the only way to reach such an agreement and, both are committed to create a peaceful environment for discussions away from all pressure and violence.

d) Both Parties understand the importance of any unilateral action which might jeopardise any negotiations and, to solve their problems only by peaceful means.

e) Both sides agree that the United States should remain an essential partner to attain peace, by maintaining their contacts with President Bill Clinton and Secretary of State Madeleine Albright".

On the Jordanian side, a joint declaration was signed on 25 July 1994 in Washington, between Jordan and Israel which formally ended their state of conflict. The declaration was signed by King Hussein, Prime Minister Itshak Rabin and witnessed by President Bill Clinton. High level bilateral negotiations continued in August and September and October, which culminated on October 26 in a peace treaty between both countries and signed at Wadi Araba some 13 km north of Akaba, by King Hussein of Jordan and Itshak Rabin Prime Minister of Israel in the presence of US President Bill Clinton and thousands of guests. The main points of the treaty were, establishment of peace, international boundary, security, diplomatic relations, water, economic relations, refugees, historical and religious shrines, navigation, etc...

The Israeli legisture approved the treaty in October, and the Jordanian National Assembly formally ratified it on November 6, 1994 and the Jordanian Senate on November 9. On February 9, 1995, Israel completed its full withdrawal from Jordanian territories.

The Multilateral talks took place in April 6-7 1994 in the Netherlands on environment, in Oman in April 17-19 on water, and May 3-5 in Qatar on arms control and regional security, and in Egypt on May 10-12 on refugees, in Morocco on June 14-16 on regional economic development. The steering committee met in Tunisia on July 12-13 and agreed on a study of the Middle East what it might look in the next few years. Another meeting on environment was held in Bahrain, on October 24-25 1994. The committee of disarmament in the Middle East was convened in Jordan on November 8-10, and on water issues in late June 1995.

INDEX OF BIOGRAPHIES

BY PROFESSION AND BY COUNTRY

ALGERIA

ARTS (Literature, Music, Journalism, Painting, Sculpting)
ALLOUACHE Merzak
BOUDIA Mohamad
DIB Mohamad
MAHIUT Rabah
OUZEGAN Omar
YASSIN Kateb

BUSINESS (Banking, Economics, Finance, Industry)
ABDALLA KHODJA Kamil
AOUFI Mahfud
ASHAHNU Abdullatif Bin
BELGUEDJ Mourad
BENAMARA Abdelkader
BENRAHMOUN Ahmad, Hashemi
BERRABAH, Belkacem
DAHLAB Saad
HARBI Jamal
KADA Mohamad
KHELEF Abdelaziz
KHELEF Yehia
MAHRUG Smail
YAKER Layachi

CIVIL SERVANTS (Officials and diplomats)
ABERKANE Muhammad
AISSA Brahim
AKBI Abdulghani
ALLAHOUM Abdelmajid
BEKKA Abdennour
BELAID Abdessalam
BENAHMAD Mohamad
BENAMAR Mustafa
BENCHENEB Rachid, Mohammad
BENNIKOUS Abdelkader
BITAT Rabah
BOUTAIBA Belgasim Saad
DJOUDI Hocine
FELLAGUE-ARIOUAT-Mustafa
GUELLAL Charif
GUENNEZ Mahmoud
HAMDANI Ismail
HARBI Mousseddine
HESHMAOUI Mustafa
HOUM Abdelmajid al
IBRAHIMI Lakhdar
JAZAIRY Idriss
KAFI Ali Hussain
KELLOU Mohamad, Massoud
KHALIFA Larouissi
MAHSAS Ahmad, Ali
MAOUI Abdul Aziz
MEHRI Abdalhamid
MENTOURI Muhammad Salah
NABI Mohamad
NOURANI Abdelmalek
OULD KHALIFA Muhammad Larbi
OUSSEDIK Omar
RAHAL Abdullatif
SAID Mazzouzi Mohamad
SEKFALI Zine Eddine
SHANDIRLI Abdulkadir
SHELAL Ait
TALEB Choaïb
TOBBAL Lakhdar Bin
YAHYAWI Mohamad, Salah
YAZID Mohamad

EDUCATION
AZZI Abderrahmane
BEBBOUCHI Rashid
BENAISSA Hanafi
BENBOUZID BOUBAKEUR
BOUMAHDI Ali
DJEBAR Assia
KRIM Fateh
MAZOUNI Muhammad, Halim
METALTA Ahmad, Ammar
TOURI Rashid

ENGINEERING
ABDALLAQUI AISSA
BENDJEBBOUR Abdulkarim, Kaddour
LIASSINE Mohamad

LAW
BEDJAOUI Mohamad
DERBAL AbdelWahab
KECHOUD Mohamed
MAHI-BAHI Abdelhamid
MAHIEDDIN Mohamad, N.
MERAD Rouchdi

MEDICINE
ABDELMOUMENE Mohamed
BUDJELLAB Omar

MILITARY
BENSALEM Abdul Rahman
LATRECHE Lieutenant Colonel Abdulhamid
ZERGUINI Mohamad
ZEROUAL Liamine, Maj. Gen., Ret.

POLITICS
ABDULGHANI Colonel Mohamad Ben Ahmad
AIT-MESSAOUDENE Said
ATTAF Ahmed
AZZOUZ Amar
BELAYAT Abderrahman
BELHOUCHET Abdallah
BELKACEM Nabi
BEN BELLA Ahmad
BENCHERIF Ahmad

BENFREIHA Ahmad
BENHABYLES Abdelmalek
BEN HAMOUDA Boualem
BENLOUCIF Mostafa
BENZAZA Mustaf
BESSAIAH Boualem
BOUCHEMA Kamel
BOUCHEMA Kamel
BOUHARA Abdulrazak
BOUTEFLIKA Abdelaziz
BRAHIMI Abdelhamid
BRAHIMI Brahim
BREHRI Abdelhak
CHALI Colonel Benjedid
CHIBANE Abdelrahman
GHOZALI Sid-Ahmed Ali
HAMROUCHE Mouloud
HOUHOU Djamel Eddine
IBRAHIMI Ahmed, Taleb
KAID Ahmad
KHERROUBI Mohamad, Cherif
MALIK Rida, Ahmad
MESSAADIA Muhamad, Cherif
MESSAOUDENE Said Ait
MEZIANE Abdulmajid
NABI Belkacem
NAIT BELKACEM Mouloud, Kassim
NEMMICHE Bekhti, Djelloul
OUNISI Z'hor
ROUIGHI Mohamad
ROUIS Bachir
SAADI Selim
SAHNOUN Mohamad
ZEBDANI Abdulaziz

BAHRAIN

ARTS (Literature, Music, Journalism, Painting, Sculpting)
ALWANI Abdul Wahed, Al
MARDI Mahmoud, al
SAYAR Ali, Abdallah

BUSINESS (Banking, Economics, Finance, Industry)
ABUL Hamad, Abdallah
AKHTARZADEH Mohamed
ALWAN Faisal, Mansoor, al
ASHRAF Anwar
BAHARNA Taqi, Mohamad, al
BASSAM Abdul Aziz, Sulaiman Al
BASSAM Khalid Suleiman, al
BORSHAID Isa Abdullah al
BSEISU Adnan, Noureddine
BUZIZI Mohamed, Jassim
DAWAWI Abdul Hussain, Khalil
FALAH Hassan, Ali
GHARABALLY Ahmad, Sayed Hachem, al
HASSAN Abdul Razzak, Abdalla
HASSAN Mohamad Ahmad
JALAL Mohamad Bin Yusuf
al, JALLABI Ebrahim M.
JANAHI Abdul Latif, Abdul Rahim
JAWAD Faisal, Hassan
JAWAD Jawad, Habib
JUMA Hassan Ali
KAIKSOW Salman, Ahmad
KANOO Abdul Latif, Jasim, Dr.
KANOO Ahmad, Ali
KANOO Yusuf, Ahmed
KATCHADURIAN K.J.A.
KHAJAH Fareed, al
KHALAF Essam A.
MAHMOUD Ali Hassan
MAHMOUD A.K. AL Nouri
MASKATI Hussein Mahdi Al
MASKATI Khalid, al
MOAYYED Farouk, Yousuf, al
MOAYED Nabeel, al
MOAYYED Sabbah, al
MOAYYED Yusuf, Khalil, al
MOHAMAD Ahmad, Mahmoud
MOHAMAD Y, Yacoob
MUDHAFFAR Ismail Ali
MURAD Murad Ali
MUSAWI Ghazi, Radhi al
MUSAWI Salman, Radhi, al
NAQI Abdulrahim H.
NOORUDDIN Nooruddin, Abdalla
RABIA Ali Qassim
SALMAN R. Moosawi, al
SHEHABI Ali, Saleh, Al
SHEHABI Mahmoud
SHEROOQUI Salem
SHO'ALA Abdulnabi, Abdalla, al
SOUFI Mahmood, Al
YATEEM Hussain Ali
YATEEM Shahrazad, Hussain
ZAINALABEDIN Hassan
ZAMIL Mohamed Abdulla al
ZAYANI Rashid, Abdelrahman al
ZEERA Mohamed Akram Al

CIVIL SERVANTS (Officials and diplomats)
ABSY Salim R.
ALMOAYED Tariq, Abdul Rahman
BAHARNA Hussain Mohamad, al
BINALI Abdul Aziz M. Al Rashid
BUALLAY Kassim, Muhammad
BUALY Abdul Aziz, Abdul Rahman
FULAYFIL Rashid, Ali
KASSIM Habib Ahmad
KHALIFA Shaikh Abdullah Bin Khalid, al
KHALIFA Shaikh Abdul Rahman Bin Mohamed, al
KHALIFA Shaikh Daij Bin Khalifa, al
KHALIFA Shaikh Khaled bin Abdallah, al
KHALIFA Mohamad, Atiyattulah, al
KHALIFA Sheikh Rashid Bin Khalifa, al
KHOZAI Mohamad, A. al
MAHROOS Ali, Ibrahim, al
MOUSAWI Faisal Radhi, al
SABBAGH Hussein Rashid, al
SAFFAR Salman, Mohamad, al
SHAKAR Karim, Ebrahim, al
SULAYTI Hamad, Ali

EDUCATION
AL-ARRAYED Dr. Jalil, Ibrahim
ARRAYID Jalil, Mansour
HASHIMI Alawi Hashim Hussain, al
MEHRI Hassan, al
SALEH Faiqa, Saeed Miss al
SARHAN Mansour, Mohamed
ZAYANI Yousuf, A. Rahman al

ENGINEERING
ABU HAMAD WILLIAM, Yousef
JUMA Abdulla, Mohammed
MANNAI Salem Abdallah, al

LAW
KHALIFA Shaikh Mohamad Bin Sulman, al

MEDICINE
FAKHRO Abdul Rahman, E.
FAKHRO Ali, Mohamad
MATAR Ali Mohamed
NASIR, Faisal Abdullatif, Al

MILITARY
KHALIFA (Brig. Gen. Shaikh Abdullah Bin Salman Bin Khalid)

POLITICS
ABDUL KARIM Ibrahim
ARAYED Jawad, Salim
HUMAIDAN Ibrahim Mohamed
JISHI Majid, Jawad al
KHALIFA Shaikh Hamad, Bin Issa al
KHALIFA Shaikh Khalifa Bin Sulman, al
KHALIFA Shaikh Mohamad, Bin Khalifa Bin Hamad, al
KHALIFA Shaikh Mohamad Bin Mubarak Bin Hamad, al
SHIRAWI Yusuf, Bin Ahmad, al

DJIBOUTI (REPUBLIC OF)

ARTS
FARAH Idriss, Harbi
MOHAMED Mohamed, Dileita

BUSINESS (Banking, Economics, Finance, Industry)
ADEN Mohamed
ATTEYEH Abchir, Hassan
AWAD Ali, Mohamed
BARKOUKY Mohamed Adel, El
CHIRDON Djama, Aouled
COUBECHE Said, Ali
DOUALEH Houssein, Aden
HOUMED Gadito, Hassanle

CIVIL SERVANTS (Officials and diplomats)
ABDILLAHI Mohamed, Barkat
ABDOULKADER Mohamed, Daoud
ALI Ibrahim, Ali
ALI Idriss, Arnaoud
DAWALEH Youssouf, Moussa
DILEITA Abdoulkader, Mohamed
DIRANEH Dirir, Miguil
DJIBRIL Ibrahim, Idriss
FARAH Ali Abdi
FARAH DIRIR Saleh Hadji
FARAH Mohamed, Dini
GUEDI Ahmed, Djama
GUERKALA Abdallah, Dabaleh
HAMADOU Ibiro, Ahmed
HASSAN Moussa, Ismail
HASSAN Said, Mohamed
ILTIREH Omar, Farah
KAWALIEH Houssein, Omar
KOCHIN Abdi, Mahmoud
LOITA Habib, Mohamed
MICHEL Antoine
MIGUIL Hassan, Farah
MOHAMED Abdi, Ibrahim
MOHAMED Chehem, Ahmed
MOHAMED Houmed, Daoud
MOHAMED Mohamed, Kamil
RAYALEH Meraneh, Boudine
ROBLEH Doualeh, Mohamed
SAID Omar, Aden
SILAY Silay, Mohamed
WABERI Ahmed Guirreh
WABERI Mohamed, Aden
WAIS Ahmed Aouled
WAIS Elmi, Obsieh
YOUSSOUF Mohamed, Ahmed

EDUCATION
RAYALEH Abdourahman, Hassan

LAW
ABDOULKADER Ali Dini

MEDICINE
ABOU Abbate, Ebo, Dr.
HASSAN Ahmed, Mohamed

POLITICS
AHMED Ougoureh, Kifleh
ALI Souleiman, Miyir
BADOUL Said Ibrahim
BOUH Robleh, Obsieh
DAOUD Ali, Mohamed
DAOUD Moussa, Baragoita
DJAMA Djama, Djilil
DIJIBRIL Abdalla, Chirwa
DINI AHMED Ahmed
DOUALEH Aden, Warsama
DOUALEH YOUSSOUF, Dideh
GUELDON Hassan, Elmi
HAMADOU Ali, Moussa
HAMADOU Barkat, Gourad
HAMADOU Gourad, Mohamed
IDRISS Moussa, Ahmed
MOHAMAD FAMIL Abdallah
MOHAMED Fahmi, Ahmed
MOHAMED Mohamed, Abdoulkader
MOHAMED Mohamed, Ali
MOUHOUMED Ahmed, Abdillahi
YOUSSOUF Mohamed, Adoyta

EGYPT (ARAB REPUBLIC OF)

ARTS (Literature, Music, Journalism, Painting, Sculpting)
ABDA IBRAHIM Fahmi, Abdul Hamid
ABDALLAH Abdulsami
ABDEL BARI Abdalla
ABDULMUNIM Mohamed
ABDULNABI Hidayat
ABU ZAID Othman, Mahmud
ADIB Abdul Hary
ALAMI Muhammad Yahyia, Abdel Raouf, al
AMR Mohamed
AQUILINA Nelly, Joseph
ATALLAH Mursi
AZZAM André-Mounir, Afif
BADAWI Mohamed Badawi Ismail
BADR-KHAN Ali, Ahmad
BAHAEDDIN Ahmad
BASILIOUS Nagi, Moussa
BIALI Mohamad, al
DAHABI Mahir, Antoun, al
DAOUD Raafat, Georges
DARWISH Mustafa
DEIF Chawqi
DEMERDASH Ahmad, Nour el Deen Muhammad al
DIA Dia Azeez
DIAB Mahmoud
ELFATOUN Inji, Hassan
ELMOALLIM Mohamed
FARID Morris, Nazmi
FAYYAD Sulaiman
GALAL Mohamad, Nadir
GAZZAR Abdel Hadi, el
GHADBANE Adel, al
GHANIM Ahmed, Kamel
GHONEIM Hassan, Bahjat Ghonein
GIBALI Hussain, Mahmoud al
GUINDY Hosny
HAIKAL Kawthar, Mohamed Ali
HAIKAL Mohamad, Hassanein
HAIKAL Nabil, Ismail
HALIM Tahia, Muhammad, Ahmad
HAMAMA Faten
HAMZA Raouf, Abdul Majid
HAWARI Ahmad, Mahmood
HEGAZI Ahmad
HENEIN Naguib, Elias
HUSSEIN Mustafa, Mahmoud
IBRAHIM Sun'allah
JAMIL Sana'
KAMAL Madiha, Sami
KAMI Hassan, Mohamad Aly
KHAFAGY Mohamed Abdel Moneim
KHALIL Khairy, Aziz
KHARRAT Edward, al
MAHFOUZ Naguib
MAKKAWI Amal Abbas, al
MALLAKH Kamal, al
MANSOUR Anis, Mohamed
MANSOUR Sami
MANSOUR Sanaa, Ali
MASOUD Salahiddin Abu-Saif
MATOUK Amal, Bishara
MEGALLI Nabila
MISTIKAWI Mohamad, Naguib, al
MITWALLI Sami
MOHAMAD Mohsen
MOHAMAD Najwa, Ibrahim
MONEIM Mohamad Abdul
MOUNTASSER Muhammad Salah Al Deen
MURSI Al Sayyid Abdulwahab
MUSTAFA Ali
MUSTAFA Niazi
NAAMAN Abdulmagid
NAFIE Ibrahim, Abdel Fattah
NASER Samira, Hafiz khairi
NESSIM Magdy, Adib
NIL Zakaria, Mustafa
OKASHA Sarwat
RATEB Gamil
SAADIDDIN Mursi, Abdulhamid
SABRI Musa
SADEK Adel
SADEK Hassan, Sadek
SAID Amina, al
SAID Fuad
SALEH Ibrahim, Mahmoud
SALMAWY Mohamad
SAMMAN Ali, al
SAWI Abdel Moneim, al
SAYED AHMAD, Mohamad, al
SHAFEI Tharwat
SHAFIQ Dorai, Ahmad
SHAMIYA Shafick
SHARAF Abdulaziz Mohamad
SHARIF Omar, ach (Chalhoub Michel)
SHARQAWI Abdulrahman, al
SHAWAN Aziz, al
SHAWQI Farid, Mohamad Abdo
SHIHATA Mrs-Shirine Hamza
SHUKRALLAH Ibrahim
SIRRY Gazbia Hassan
SONBOL Said
TAWFIK Ruhiyah, Mohamad Tawfiq
TOBIA Maguid
VASSILIADES Lambros, Prodromos
WISSA Zikry, Philippe
YASSA Ramzi, Nagui
YASSIN Sayed, Mohamad
ZAIWAR Ali
ZAYYAT Latifa, al

BUSINESS (Banking, Economics, Finance, Industry)
ABAZA Mohamed Magid, Hussain
ABD Omar, el

NOUR Mohamad, Abdellatif
NOUR Tariq Mahmoud, Abdal-Fattah
OBEID Said Fekri Makram
ONSI Mahmoud Bahir
ORABI Mohamed, Zaki, El
OWEISS Ibrahim, Mohamad
OZALP Mohamad
QANDIL Abdulhamid
RAAFAT Sherif Hassan, Waheed
RABBAT Joseph
RABBAT Wagdi, Yusuf
RADWAN Abdel Aziz, Mohamad
RADWAN Samir, Mohamad
RIFAAT Mohamad, Ali
RIZK George Kamel
ROUSHDI Abdul-Munim Negib
ROUSHDI Mustafa, Sayid
ROUSHDI Subhi, Khalil
RUWAIDAR Ahmad, Said
SAADEDDIN Dr. Ibrahim
SAADI Miazi, Mounir
SABBOUR Sameh S'a adiddin
SABRI Isamil Baligh
SADEK Hatem, Ali
SADEK Dr. Medhat, Abdel Hamid
SADEK Mustafa, al
SADEK Yehia, al
SAID Mohamed, Helmi Tawfik, al
SALAMA Anis Mustafa
SALEM Hussain
SALEM Sami, Ali
SAMI Sherif Mahmoud Murad
SARKI Ahmed, Rushdi, Mohamed, Yusif
SAWI Tawfic, al
SAYEH Hamid Abdullatif, al
SHADI Mohamad, Fuad
SHARIF Mohamad, Sami Abdelmajid
SHATHLY el Shathly Mohamad, al
SHENOUDA Hilmy, Said
SHIHATA Ibrahim
SHUKRI Adel, Mohamad
SIRAGEDDINE Jamil
SIRAGEDDINE Yassine
SISI Abdul Kader, Abdul Rahman, al
SULAIMAN Mustafa, Dawud
SULTAN Ahmed Mustafa Hussein
SULTAN Fuad, Abdel Latif
TAHER Samir
TATAWY Dr. Nawal, Abdel-Moneim, El
TAWFIK Abdel Fattah, Zakaria
TAYMUR Emad Al-Deen
TOUTOUNJI Lucien, Sami
TURK Mohamed Abdel Moneim Ibrahim
WAHDAN Dr. Samir, Sayed
WAKIL Abdulwahid, al
YACOUBIAN Philip
YARED Michel, Youssef
ZAKI Hassan, Abbas
ZAKI Hussain Mohamad
ZAKI Mahmoud, Hassan Abdel Ghaffar
ZANDO Ahmad

CIVIL SERVANTS (Officials and diplomats)

ABAZA Mohamed Maher
ABDEL WAHAB Mohamed, Farag
ABDUL AKHAR Ahmad, Mustafa
ABDUL FATTAH Abdallah, Mahmoud
ABDULHAFEZ Mahmoud
ABDULHAMID Shafie
ABDULKADIR Yahia
ABDULLATIF al-Hussaini
ADULMEGUID Dr. Ahmad Esmat
ABUGHAZALA Fouad
ABUL NASR Mahmoud
ABUTALEB Youssef Sabry
ABUZAID Mohamad, Hamdi
ABUZAID Mustafa Fahmi
AFRA Saad, Abdallah
AHMAD Ahmad, Mohamad
ALI Abdul Halim Mohamad
AMIN Mohamed, Ahmad
AMMAWI Ahmad, al-
ANWAR Mohamad Samih
ARIAN Abdalla, al
ATALLAH Gen, Tharwat Taha
ATIYAH Ahmed Mamdouh
BADAWI Abdel Halim
BADR Maj. Gen. Zaki
BAKR Mohamad Bakr
BARAKAT Gamaleddine
BARAKAT Muhammad Rushdi
BASHEER Tahseen, Mohamad
BAZ Oussama, al
BELTAGUI Mahmoud, Ahmad, al-
BOGHDADI Abdullatif, Mahmoud, al
BOUTROS-GHALI Boutros
BOUTROS-GHALI Dr. Youssef
DAOUD Diaeddine
DA'OUR Muhammad Salah Al-Deen Muhammad al
DAW Hussain, Talaat
DESSUKI Salah
DIB Mohammad Khalil al
DIWANI Mustapha Kamal Ibrahim al
EKIANE Abdallah, al
ELAMLY Abdelkader, Mohamad
ELARABY Nabil
ELSALAWY Ahmed Nabil
ERIANE Abdallah, al
FAHMY Abdulazim
FAHMY Ismail
FAKHR Ahmad, Ismail
FARNAWANI Taha, Muhammad, al
GABALLAH el-Sayyid, Sayyid
GALAL Mohamed, Noman
GHALEB Mourad
GHARIB Muhieddine, al-, Dr.

EDUCATION

BALBAA Chafiq
BOCTOR Samuel, Matta
CHARIF Saad, Mahmoud
EL-ETR Mohamed Kamal Ahmed
ELNAGHY Mohamed, Abdelwahab, Prof. Dr.
FARID-MESSIHA Kamal
FARID Samir, Muhammad
FARRAG Abdelmegid M.
FATHI Sayed, Abdulrahim
FAWZI Samiha al-Sayyid
FUAD Naamat, Ahmad
GALAL Osman, Mahmoud
GAMALEDIN Awad, Aly
GHALI Yusuf, Iskandar
GHANNAM Mohamad, Ahmad, al
GHUNEIM Sayyid, Muhammad
GOHAR Mohamad, Abdulhamid
GOWHARY Yousry, Abdel Razik, El, Prof. Dr.
HADARY Mahmoud el Sayed el
HAIKAL Fayzrah, Mohamed Hussein
HAMED FAHMI Noha Al-Sayyid
HASHIM Malik, Mohamad
HASSAN Farkhonda
HASSAN Mahmoud, Yousry
HASSANEIN Sayed Hanafi
HEFNY Anissa, Mahmoud al
HUSSEIN Hussain, Mustafa
HUSSEIN Mohamad, Taha
HUSSEIN Mrs. Aishah Ahmad al
IBRAHIM Izziddin
ISSA Husam, Muhammad
ISSAWI Charles Philippe, Elias
JABR Sami
JUNDI Mohamad Mumtaz, Sayed Ahmad
KADI Hamid, M. Roushdy, Dr. al
KAMEL Raafat Wassef, Kamel
KATIB Saif El Deen, Abdalla al
KAZEM Muhamad, Ibrahim
KHADEM Hassan, Saad
KHADRAWY Mohsen, Prof. Dr. el
KHOLY Ussama, Amin, al
LOZA Sarah, Fahim
MARSOT Afaf Lutfi al-Sayyid
MASRI Yusuf, Helmi, al
MEKKAWAY Fawzy
METAWEH Ibrahim, Esmat
MORSI Salah E.
MOURAD Mohamad Helmi
MUKHTAR Muhammad Gamaliddin
MURSI Mohamad Khairi
MUSTAFA Ahmad Farid
NAAMAN Antoine
NADI Mohamad, Abdulmaqsoud
NAGUIB Mohamad, Ibrahim
NASR Mohamad Saad, Ahmad Mohamad
OBAID Mohamad, Abdul Fattah
OSMAN Mohamad, Mohamad
OSMANA Amin
QAZIM Mohamad, Ibrahim
RAMADAN Abdulazim
RAZZAZ Mustafa, Farid
SAATI Hassan, Abdulaziz, al
SABAT Dr. Khalil, Yusuf
SADEK Amal, Ahmed M.
SAKR Sakr, Ahmed
SAYED Mohamad, Lutfi, al
SAYED Mustafa, Amr, el
SHAHAT Mahmoud, Abdul Hamid, al
SHAZLI K., Abdussalam Mohamad, al
SHEHAB Ibrahim, Khalil
SHUCRI Ibrahim, Mohamad
TAHA S.A.
TUNI Sayed Mohamad
WAHBA Magdi, Mourad
WASSIF Kamal M., Dr.
YASSIN Aziz, Ahmad, Prof.
YASSIN Sayed
YOUSEF Ibrahim M.
ZAQZOUK Mahmoud, Hamdy, Dr.
ZAHRAN Hamdia, M. Prof. Dr.
ZAYED Georges
ZAZA Hassan, Mohamad Tewfik

ENGINEERING

ABD Medhat, Mohamed, al
ABDEL SALAM Mohamed El-Hosseiny
ABUTALEB Mohamad, Gamal
ALFI Mahmoud Amr al
AMER Hamad, Hassanein
AMIN Mahmoud
AMLY Abdul Kader al
ARNAOUT Zaki, Mahmoud
BABLI Rafic, Muhammad al
BANBI Hamdi Ali, Abdelwahab, al-
BELTAGY Adel S., El
DAGHISTANI Ali, Mahmoud, Fahmi'al
DAOUD Mahmoud, Mohamad, Dr.
DIAB Salaheddine, Ahmad
EFFAT Ahmad M.
EFFAT Kamal-Eddine, Ahmad
FADL Mohamad, Fathi al
GOFAIL Abdulmagid
HADIDI Taher, Abdel Razzak, el
HALAWA Nabil
HALFAWY Mohamad, al
HAMZA Mohamad Abdulmalek
HIDAYAT Salahuddin
HIFNAWI Mustafa, Mitwalli al
HILAL Ahmad, Ezzedin
ISMAIL Ahmad, Sultan
ISMAIL Hassan, Mohamed
KASHIF Ali, Fahmi, Mahmoud al
MAHMOUD Galal Eddine
MAHMOUD Talaat
MAREI Hassan
METWALLI Suleiman

LAW

MEDICINE

NAAMAN Ahmad, Abdulmagid Sallam
NASR Anis, Naguib
OSMAN Ahmad, Mahmoud
ROFAEL Nazmy
ROUSHDI Jamaleddin Sayid
SAADAWI Nawal, el
SABBA Hassouna, Mahmoud
SALEM Mohamad, Nabil Ahmad
SALLAM Ismail A.
SALMAN Mohamad, Mahmoud
SAMRA Khairi, Ahmad
SEKLA Kamat, Yusuf
SHAALAN Abdel Karim Mohamad
SHAHBANDAR Salah Abdulrahman
SHAHIN Faroud Mohammad
SIDKI Izziddin
SIMAIKA Samir, Mahfouz
SOUELEM Nadir, Mohamed
SULEIMAN Yahia
TARRAF Noureddine
YACOUB Magdi
ZAKI Hussain, Abbas

MILITARY
ABUGHAZALA Field Marshal Mohammad Abdul Halim
AFIFI Major General Hilmi al-Bar
ARABI Abdulmu'ti, al
FAHMY General Mohamad Ali
GAMASSY Mohamad, Abdulghani, al
GOMAA Chaaraoui
HINNAWI Mustafa Chalabi, Mahjoob, al
MAGDUB General Taha, Muhamad, al
MOAZ Gen, Mohamad, Fauzi
MORTAGUA Mohamad, Abdulhamid
MUHIEDDINE Zakaria, Abdulmagid
NUR Abdul Mohsen, Abou, al
SADEK Mohamad, Ahmad
SHAZLI Abdulmoneim, al
SHAZLI Gen. Saad, Mohamad El Husseiny, al
TAHRI Izzedine, al

POLITICS
ABAZA Sami Abdallah
ABAZA Sarwat
ABDEL RAHMAN Ibrahim, Hilmi
ABU ALI Sultan
ABU BASHA Hassan
ABU ISMAIL Tewfick
ABULATTA Abdul Azim Abdallah
ABULMAGD Ahmad, Kamal
ABULNOUR Mohamad el Ahmadi
ABUTALEB Sufi Hassan
ABU ZAID Hikmat
AHMAD Saad Mohamed
ALI Fathy, Mohamed
ALI General Kamal Hassan
BULTIA Abdul Latif Miligi
CHALABI Raouf
EBAID Dr. Atef, Mohamed
FAIEK Mohamad, Mohamad
GANZOURY Dr. Kamal, Ahmed, el
GHARIB Salahuddin, Muhammad
GHAROURI Mohamad, Sayed, al
HADIDI Helmi el
HAIKAL Ahmed Abdel Maksoud
HATEM Mohamad Abdulqader
HUSSEIN Mansour, Ibrahim
IBRAHIM Hassan
ISMAIL Mohamad, Othman
KAFRAWY Hasaballah el
KAISSOUNI Abdel Monein
LABIB Abdel Rahman
MAHMOUD Mohamad, Hamid
MOHAMAD Dr. Abdul Hamid Hassan
MOURAD Mustafa Kamil
MUBARAK Mohamad Hosni
MUHIEDDINE Khaled
NAZER Ali Gamal, al
NOUH Ahmad Ahmad
OBAID Fikri, Makram
OTEIFI Dr. Gamal, al
RADWAN Abdel Hamid
SAID Rushdi, Farag
SALEM Mamdouh Mohamad
SAYED Gamal, el
SHAFEI Hussain, Mahmoud, al
SHAKER Amir, Mustafa
SHATLI Dr. Mohamad Nagui
SHENDY Wagih
SHUKRI Ibrahim
SIDKI Atef
SIDKI Aziz
SOROUR Ahmed Fathi
SULEIMAN Magdi Ahmad
SULEIMAN Mohamad Sedqi
TAKLA Laila, I.
TALAWY Farouk, Dr., al
TAWFIK Ahmad, Talaat
WALLY Dr. Yusuf Amin
ZAKI Dr. Mohamad Sabry
ZAYYAT Mohamad, Abdul Salaam, al

RELIGION
ABDULNOOR Yusef, the Rev
ANTAKI H.E. Mgr, Paul
CHENOUDA III. H.E. Nasri Gayeb
DOUEK Maurice-Haim
GABRIEL Nabil, Aziz
HADDAD Pierre, Naaman
GHATTAS Stephanos II, H.E.
SARKIS Paul, Antoine
SHEA Leo Joseph
SOURIAL Rev. Dr. Samuel Habib
ZOGHBI Elie, H.E. Mgr.

IRAQ (IRAQ ARAB REPUBLIC)

EDUCATION
ABDALLAH Jalal Mohamed Salih
ANI Abdullah Najim al
ANI Badri, Ahmad al
ATTAR Nawzar Ahmad Amin, al
BASSAM Mohamad Ali, Abdul Amir Ali, al
BIATI Abdul Jabbour Toufiq Mohamed, al
DABBAGH Abdussattar, Yunes
DABBAGH Riyadh Hamid, al
DOURI Abdulaziz, ad
HAIDAR Mohamad Abdul Rahman, al
HANTUCH Mahdi, Saleh
HASSO Abdul Rahman, Abdullah al
HILMI Mahdi, Ibrahim
IZZIDIN Yusuf
JANABI Nawal, Yusif, al
JIBOURI Nadhima, Abdul Jabbar al
JUMAH Hassan, Fahmi
KARAGHOULI Saleh al
KHAFAGY Abbas, Nasser Hussin, al
KHALIL Najih, Muhammad
KHALIS Salah Abdul Rahman
KHYATAT Talal, M. Nuri, al
MAHDI Abdul Wahab Rauf
MAHDI Mohsin, Sayyid
MUSAWI Muhsin, Jassim al
NAAMA Mustafa Rajab, al
NAJJAR Mustafa, Abdelkader, al
NASSER Mohamad
OMAR Farouk
OMARI Farouq, Sunaallah
QAISI Nuri, Hamudi, al
QAZZAZ Ayad, al
SAADI Mohamad Ali, al
SHAIKHLY Abdul Qadir Jassim, al
SHALI Khusruw, Ghani
SHAMMA' Khalil al
SHAMSA Mohamad, Sadiq, Bakir
SHAWI Mundhir, al
SHAWI Nazar Nadhif, al
WAKIL Saleh, Jawad
ZAHID Mohamad Wasil Ahmad

ENGINEERING
ARAJI Ali, Mouhieddine, al
BAYATI Mohamad, Abdulhussain, al
CJADIRJI Rifat Kamil
DANNO Severius
GARABET Samir, Noori
IRHAYIM Tarik, al
KASHIF ALGHITA Bakir, Ahmad
KHUDAYRI Tariq, Shamel al
MADFAI Husham Hassan Fahmi al
MADFAI Kahtan Hassan Fahmi al
MAKKIYAH Mohamed Saleh Aziz
MALAIKA Jamil
NAIMI Taha Tayih, Al
OMARI Tariq, Nassib, al
RIFAI Rashid Mohamed Said, al
TAI Muhibiddin, al

LAW
ABBAS Abbas, Khadhair
OMARI Mumtaz, al
TARAZI Fuad, Philip

MEDICINE
ABDULGHAFUR Adil, Salim
ALOUSI Khalil, Ibrahim Akif, al
ARIF Awni al Din
CHALABI Abdulwahab, al
CHALABI Talal, Saleem, al
GHAIB Muklis, Mouloud
HAMID Abdul Mun'im
KAISSI Ahmad Izzat
MAHMOUD Mohamad, Saleh
QASSAB Khalid, Abdulaziz, al

MILITARY
ANSARI Faisal, al
FARHAN Abdulqarim
GHAIDAN Gen. Saadoun
SAID Brigadier Mohamad Farhi, Ali
SHANSHAL General Abduljabbar Khalil

POLITICS
ABDULBAKI Murtada Said
ABDULKARIM Tayih
ALWAN Hamia
AMIRI Hassan Ali, al
ANI Tahir, Tawfiq, al
AQRAWI Hashim, Hassan
AZIZ Tareq
AZZAWI Hikmat Ibrahim, al
DOURI Izzat, Ibrahim Khalil, al
HADITHI Anwar, Abdul Qadir, al
HAMDANI Adnan Hussain, al
HUSSEIN General Saddam
JIBOURI Hamid, Alwan, al
MAHJOUB Mohamad
MALKI Shebib, Lazim, al
MA'RUF Taha, Muhyiddin
MUHIEDDINE Abdurrazzaq
PESHDARI Babekr, Mahmoud, al
RAMADAN Taha, Yassin
SABRI Adnan, Ayub
SHAKER Mahmoud Saadoun
SHARIF Abdul Sattar Tahir
TAWFIK Taher

RELIGION
BIDAWID H.E. Mgr. Raphael I

JORDAN (HASHEMITE KINGDOM OF JORDAN)

MAKKIYAH Taher, Darwish
MARTO Dr. Michel Issa
MASRI Mohamad, Qahtan Rafiq, al
MASRI Munib, Rashid, al
MOUASHER Anis
MOUASHER Rajai, S
NABULSI Hamdallah, Farid
NABULSI Mohamad, Said
NAHAWI Noreddin Salah
NASSER Hayat Mohamed
NIMR Rifaat, Sidqi al
NUOUL Elia, Costandi
ODEH Dr. Hanna
OMARI Mahmud, Ali, al
QADOUMI Ghazi, R.
QADISHI Hani, Salem
QASIM Qasim Mohamed
QUTUB Dawud, Yacub
RASHID Lieutenant General Nadir
SABBAGH Hashim Mohamad Ali, al
SAKET Bassam, Khalil
SALEM Dr. Khalil
SALTI Amer
SALTI Sami
SAMMAN Nabil, Abdullatif
SAQQAF Mohamed, Hashim, al
SARHAN Khalid, Mohamed
SARTAWI Sufian, Ibrahim
SATI Iklil
SHAIR Wahib, Abdo
SHAQWARA Yahya, Ali
SHARABI Burhan S.
SHARABI Nazim, Bishara
SHARAIHA Wadih J.
SHAASHA Jawdat, Rouhi
SHATIT Ghassan
SHIHADEH Musa, Abdel-Aziz
SHOCAIR Amin, Khalil
SHOMAN Abdel Hamid
SHOMAN Abdulmajeed
SHOMAN Issa
SHOMAN Khalid, A.H.
SHOURBAJI Mohammad, Mounir Tarek
SHRYDEH Borhan, Najib
SHUKRI Dr. Maher, Ganj
SOUSSA Antoine, Michel
SUKKAR Yusuf, Y.
TABBAH Tawfik
TAHER Thabet, Abdul Rauf, al
TARQAN Abdalla Mohamed Said
TEVAL Shehadeh
TOUKAN Mohamad, Abdul Rahman
WAKED Maher, A.
YASSIN Sufian, Ibrahim
ZU'BI Farouk, Nasser, al
ZU'BI Hatim, Sharif

CIVIL SERVANTS (Officials and diplomats)
ABU GHAZALA Dawud, Sulaiman
ABUJABER Kamel, Saleh
ABUNAWAR Ma'an
ABU OBEID Awad Muhsen
ABU Odeh Adnan, Said
ABURABAH Abdulrahman
ABU ZAID Salah
ADWAN Dr. Mohammad Affash
AKRUSH Anwar, Atallah
ANNAB Ziad Radhi
ARRAR Sulaiman, Atallah
ASFOUR Khalil Mohamad Ibrahim
ASSAD Nassereddine, Mohamad, al
ASSAD Shuja' Mohamad, al
ATALLAH Nasri, Fuad
AYOUB Fouad
AYOUB Sami
BADRAN Adnan, M. Dr.
BARAKAT Ghaleb, Zaki
BATAYNEH Aref S. Dr.
BATTIKHI Anwar, Munir, Dr.
BAYOUN Adnan, Adel
BILBEISSI Mo'atasim, Ismail
BURGAN Salih Khalil
DAHMAN Zuhair
DAJANI Abdul Salim
DAJANI Ali, Taher, ad
DAJANI Said, al
DAQHAN Omar, Abdullah
ELKHATIB Numan
FARRA Mohamad, Hussain, al
HAMARNEH Michael, Yacub
HAYARI General Ali, Ahmad al
HAZAIMAH Rifai
HIJAZI Ismail
HIKMAT Yanal, Omar
HOMOOD Kamal al
HUSSEINI Muhieddine M. al
IBRAHIM Hassan
IZZIDDIN Ibrahim
JARRAR Abdul Rahim, Ibrahim
JOURY Yacoub
JUMAA Madhat
JUMAA Salah, Mohamad
JUMAYAN Mikhael
KAILANI Mohammad Rasul
KASWANI Salim, Yusuf al
KEILANI Dr. Musa al
AL KHALDI Awwad
KHATIB Abdulilah, el-
KHATIB Hisham
KHLEIFAT Awad, Mohamad
LAWZI Salim, Abdulkarim
MADADHA Khaled, Falah
MAJALI Nasouh, Salem
NASSER Sharif, Ghazi Rakan
NUSEIBEH Hazem

EDUCATION

ENGINEERING

LAW

TARAWNAH Naji, Hussain

MEDICINE

ABU QURA Ahmad, Salih
AFIFI Kamil, Faeq, al
AKASHEH Farid Abdallah
BAKRI Maawiya, Mahmoud al
HADDADIN Muwaffaq
HAMZEH Zaid
HANANIA Daoud
HIJAZI Sa'ad Sliman
KAMHAWI Walid
KHAIRI Ishaq, Najati al
KILANI Fuad, Zeid
MAANI Walid, Al
MALHAS Abdul Rahim, Dr.
MARAQA Muhammad, Isaac Abdul Haye
SHAIR Jamal, Abdul, al
TOUKAN Ala Uddine, Dr.

MILITARY

ABUNAWAR Ali, Abdulqader
ABU Taleb Lt, Gen. Fathi
MAJALI Habès, al
SHAKER Field Marshal Sharif Zaid Bin

POLITICS

ABDELNABI Hafiz, Abdel Ghani
BADRAN Mudar Mohamad
DUDIN Marwan
FAYEZ Akef, Mithkal, al
FAYYAD Khalid, Abdallah, al
HASSAN IBN TALAL
HASSAN Khalid al Haj
HINDAWI Doukhan, Salim
HUSSEIN HM Queen Nour, al
HUSSEIN HH Prince Raad Bin Zeid, El
HUSSEIN Amin, Yunis al
JAZI Rakan, Inad, al
KAKISH Fuad
KAYED Hassan Ali
KHAMMACHE Amer
KHATIB Mohamad, al
LAWZI Ahmed Abdel Karim
MAJALI Abdulwahab, al
MAJALI Rakan, Mohamad
MASRI Awni, Fuad el
MASRI Taher
MASSADEH Salem
MOHAMMAD BIN TALAL (HRH Prince)
MUMNI Hassan Ahmad al
NABULSI Omar
OBAIDAT Ahmad, Abdul Majid
QADHAT Salman, Muhammad, al
RAWABDEH Abdur-Ra'uf
SHARARI Hesham, Fayez, al
SHARI Saduk, al
SHARIF Kamel, Ismail
SUHEIMAT Ali, Mohamad
TARAWNAH Ahmad, Mahmud, al
THEWAYB Muhammad, Ahmad, al
ZEBAN Akasha, al

RELIGION

NAJJAR Mgr. Rauf, Salim
SAYEGH Bishop Salim Wahban

KUWAIT (STATE OF KUWAIT)

TAMMAR Abdul Wahab, al
TARKAIT Salah, Abdul Wahab, al
THUWAINI Abdel Muhsin Faisal
YAHYA Mohamad, Abdulrahman, al
YASEEN Badr, Bazie, al
YOUSEF Saleh Mohamed, al
ZEID Abdulrazzak, al-Khalid, al

CIVIL SERVANTS (Officials and diplomats)
ABDALLAH Seif, Abbas
ADASANI Mohamad, Yusuf, al
AL EBRAHIM Ahmad, A.
AL SALLAL Mohammad, Saad
AWADI Abdul Raman A., al, Dr.
AYAR Hamad Mubarak, al
BAHAR Abdullatif, A.R., al
BARGES Barges, Hamud
BISHARA Abdallah, Yacoub
DABBAGH Hassan Ali, al
FUHAID Khaled, Massud, al
GHUNEIM Abdul Rahman, Khalid, al
GHUNEIM Khalifa, Khaled, al
HAMAD Issa, Ahmad, al
HOUTY Abdul Rahman, Ibrahim
HUSSEIN Abdul Aziz
JAAFAR Ezzat, Mohamad
JAAFAR Khaled, Mohamad
AL-JASSIM Ahmed, Abdulaziz
KHALED Faisal, al
KHALED Sulaiman, Humud al-Zaid, al
KHAMIS Abdul Razzak, al
KHARAFI Jasim Mohamed, al
MUFFARIJ Abdallah, Ibrahim, al
MUTAWA Faisal, Saleh, al
NOURI Anwar, Abdallah, al
RAYES Ghazi, al
RQOBAH Homoud Abdulla, al
SABAH Shaikh Ali, al-Khalifa, al-Athbi, al
SABAH Shaikh Jaber al-Ali Salem, al
SABAH Shaikh Jabir al-Athbi, al
SABAH Shaikh Nawaf, al-Ahmad, al-Jaber, al
SABAH Shaikh Sabah al-Ahmad al-Jaber, al
SABAH Shaikh Salem al-Sabah al-Salem, al
SABAH Shaikh Saud Nasir Saud, al
SANOUSSI Mohamad, Nasir, al
SARHAN Ahmad, Zeid
SHAHIN Sulaiman, Majid
SHAMMAS Said, Yacoub
SHATTI Ibrahim, al
THUWAINI Major General Abdullatif Faisal, al

EDUCATION
ABDUL SALAM Jassem M.
AL AQEEL Adnan H.
ALIKHAN Abbas, Abdullatif
SHATTI Mohamad, Abdelkarim, al
SHEHABIDDIN Adnan

ENGINEERING
ADASANI Mahmoud, Khaled, al
MUFARREJ Mufarrej Ibrahim, al
OBAIDAN Abdallah, Abdel Aziz, al
RAYES Sabah, Mohammed Amin, al
SALEH Abdalla, Essa, al
SHAHIN Ibrahim, Majid
SHUAIB Hamid, Abdussalam
YAHYA Mahmoud Yahia Abdulla, al

LAW
AWADI Dr. Badria Abdullah, al

MEDICINE
MULLA HUSSAIN Nazar Abdel Rahman

MILITARY
SABAH Shaikh Misha'al Ahmad al-Jaber, al
SABAH Mubarak, al-Abdallah al-Jaber, al
SABAH Major General Shaikh al-Mohamad, al

POLITICS
ATEEQI Abdul Rahman Salem, al
FULAIJ Abdul Latif, al
GHUNEIM Yacoub, Yusuf, al
KAZEMI Abdul Muttaleb, al
MARZOOQ Jasim Khalid
MARZOOQ Salim, Khalid, al
NAFISI Abdul Wahab, Yusuf, al
NISF Muhammad, Yusuf, al
RASHID Rashid Abdulaziz, al
SABAH Nasser Mohammed al-Ahmad, al-
SABAH Shaikh Jaber, Abdallah, Jaber, al
SABAH H.H. Shaikh Jaber al-Ahmad al-Jaber, al
SABAH Shaikh Saad al-Abdallah al-Salem, al

LIBYA (LIBYAN ARAB JAMAHIRIYA)

ARTS (Literature, Music, Journalism, Painting, Sculpting)
TILLISI Khalifa, Mohamad

BUSINESS (Banking, Economics, Finance, Industry)
ABDULLA A. Saudi
ATTIGA Ali, Ahmad
BREISH Abdulmagid
BRENI Ageli
DAJANI Aziz, Awni
FEZZANI Mohamed Ali, Hussein
FIGHI Hadi Mohamad
HAFIZ Ibrahim
KARAH Bashir Abdel Majid
KHUSHAIBI Hassan, Ahmed, al
LAYAS Mohamed
NAHAISI Mohamad Hassan
OMAR Mohamad
SAID Giuma, Said
SALEM Mohamad, Omeish
SWAYEH Omar
TARBAGHIA Mansour, Saleh
TARBAGHIA Nabil M.

CIVIL SERVANTS (Officials and diplomats)
ABU FURAYWAH Musa, Ahmad
AZZABI Ayyad, Muhammad
FAITURI Muhammad, Abdul Salam, al
FINAISII Mohamad
KUAIBA Muftah Mohamed
MAGHRABI Mahmoud Sulaiman
MANQOUSH Mohamad Ahmad, al
MUNTASSER Omar, Mustafa
MURSI Ibrahim, Guider
OBAIDI Abdul Ati, al
OSMAN Assaïd Mohamad
QA'UD Abdul Mcjid, al
SHERLALA Kassem Mohamad
SWEDAN Daw, A.
ZINTANI Abdulwahab, Mohamad, al

EDUCATION
BUERA Abubakr, Mustafa
DAGHMAN Abdulmoula, Khalil
DAW Khalifa, Ali
MEHRIK Yusuf, Ibrahim, al
SHARAFEDDIN Abdallah, Mustafa
SHEBANI Omar
SUBHI Shaikh Mahmoud, Mohamed, Abdulsalam

ENGINEERING
HADI Omar, Ramadan, al
TARBAGHIA Tarek M.

LAW
MABROUK Ezzedin, al, Dr.
GHANEM Shokri

MILITARY
IDRIS Lieutenant Colonel Jumaa Awadh
YOUNES Brig, Gabir Abu Bakr

POLITICS
BADR Mansour, Mohamad
BIN Amir Taha Sharif
DORDA Abu Zeid Umar
JALLUD Abdul Salam Ahmad
JIDDI Muhammad, Ali, al
MAGIIOUR Kamal, IIassan
MAGSABI Omar Ahmad, al
OMAR Miftah al-Usta, Dr.
RAJAB Mohamad, Zaruk
SHARIF Abubakr, Ali, al
SHARIF Mohamad Ahmad, al
SMAILA Milad, Abdulsalam
TALHI Jadallah Azzuz, al
TIBBU Mohamad Ali
ZWAI Mohamad, Abdul Qassem

MAURITANIA (THE ISLAMIC REPUBLIC OF)

ARTS
HAMADY Mohamed, Ould

BUSINESS (Banking, Economics, Finance, Industry)
HACEN Moctar Ould Mohamed, El
MALOUM Zeine, Ould

CIVIL SERVANTS (Officials and diplomats)
ABDALLAH Ahmadou, Ould
ABDALLAHI Sidi Ould Sheikh
AMAR Ahmad Ben
BARO Abdoulaye
BRAHAM Maloum, Ould
DADDAH Abdallahi, Ould
DAHI Abdel Wedoud Ould
DIAGANA Sidi, Mohamad
DIDI Hasni Ould
HASSEN Mulay al
MOHAMEDOU Ould Mohamed Mahmoud
MOUKNASS Hamdi
SALL Abdul Aziz

ENGINEERING
BEYAH Mohamed Khalifa, Ould
HEYINE Mohamed Saleck Ould
RAJEL Ishac, Ould

LAW
HACHEME Abdou, al

MILITARY
HUSSEIN Ahmad Mahmoud, Ould al

POLITICS
BAALASSANE Mamadou
BABBAH Mohamad, Ould
BAH Abdallah, Ould
DADDAH Moukkar, Ould
DIOP Mamadou, Amadou
MOHAMAD SALAH Ahmad, Ould
SIDI-BABA Ahmad, Ould
SOUMARE Diaramouna
TAYA Col. Maawiya Ould Sid Ahmed

MOROCCO (KINDGOM OF MOROCCO)

IBRAHIM Moulay, Abdallah
JADIDI Arsalan
JETTOU Driss
JORIO Maati
KABBAJ Mohamad
KERSTEN Jean Hendrik Jr.
KHALIS Abdul Latif
LALLA AICHA H.R.H. Princess
MANSOUR Ben Ali
MAZZIANE Mohamad
MEKOUAR Muhammad
MEKOUAR Tahar, Ahmad
NEKROUF Younes
OSMAN Ahmad
OUAZZANI Maitre Thami, al
SAADI Moussa
SALHI Abderrahim Mahdi
SANOUSSI Ahmad
SANOUSSI Badriddine
SBIHI Abdul Hadi
SEBTI Zine el Abidine
SHORFI Abdallah
SIDI BABA Ould Dey
SIJELMASSI Mohamad
SKALLI Ali
SLAWI Idriss
TAZI Abdurrahman, Hamad, al
TAZI Ahmed
WARZAZI Halima, Embarek
ZAHIDI Moulay Zine
ZEBDI Kamil
ZEMMOURI Hassan
ZENTAR Mehdi, Mrani
ZHIRI Qassem, al

EDUCATION
ABDULQADIR Gaguig, Salih
AHMADI Mohamad, Bin Mussa, al
ALAMI Muhammad, Ahmad Al Idrissi
AMRANI Mohamed Raja
AYADI Mohammed, el
AZIZ OUAZZANI Kacem
BENABDALLAH Abdulaziz
BENALLAL Mohamad
BENNIS Mohamad Abdulwahid
BENYAKLEF Mustafa, Mohamad
BOUCHOUK Elmostapha
BOUGHALI Mohamed
CHAFIK Mohamad, Binali
DERRIJ Mohamad
ELMANDJRA Mahdi
FELLOUSE Rachid, al
GERMOUNI Muhammad
JARARI Abdullah, Al-Abbas al
KETTANI Hamza al
KETTANI Idris
KHATIB Ismail, Muhamad al Arabi, al
KHIYARI Allal, al
KHLEF Mustafa, Muhammad, Bin
LAHBABI Mohamad, Aziz
LAKHDAR Ghazal, Ahmad
LAMRHILI Ahmad, Mohamad
LAROUI Doctor Abdallah, Mohamad
LAROUI Rkia Mrs.
MANSOUR Mohamed, el
OUFARA Saadia, Mrs.
SALAHDINE Mohamed
TOURI Abdelaziz

ENGINEERING
AMRAWI Omar Abdul Aziz
BACHIRI Mohamad Mamoun
BASTOS Mohamed
BELHAJ Mohamed
BENABDERRAZIK Abderrahman
BENNIS Mohamad
BENZEKRI Mehdi, Muhammad
BERRADA ALLAM Tayib
BOURI Abdul Rahman, Al Tohami al
DAOUDI Abdel Jawad, Muhammad al
DRISSI QEYTONI Bennacer
LADRISSI Muhammad, Bin Issa Ifrata
LAHLOU Abdallah
LASKY Ahmad
MOULINE Larbi
MOUSSAOUI Ahmed
NAJIOULLAH Bouchaib, Muhammad
NASSER Mohamad
OUAZZANI TOUHAMI Tayib
RAHALI Sidi, Muhammad
SHAMI Hassan
TADLAOUI Muhammad, al
VERDUGA Claude
VOTOAN Cong

LAW
AZZIMAN Omar
BENJELLOUN Ahmed, Majid
BENNOUNA Mohamed
BENSAID Mohamad
BENSLAMA Abdel Rahim Abdel Salem
CHOUFANI Abdulmagid
DAHAK Driss, Jelloul al
FILALI Abdullaziz, al
SHUKRI Ahmad al-Sibai

MEDICINE
BENMANSOUR Noureddin
BENNIS Abdurrahim
BERRADA Mohamad, Jadj
BOUCETTA Dr. Hadj Omar
CHRAIBI Dr. Larbi
KERDOUDI-KOLALI Abdeslam, Habib
LAHBABI Driss
LAHBABI Hassan
RAHALI Rahal, Dr.

OMAN (SULTANATE OF OMAN)

ARTS (Literature, Music, Journalism, Painting, Sculpting)
ABDOWANI Sadek
KATHIRI Said, Samhan al

BUSINESS (Banking, Economics, Finance, Industry)
AL-YOUSEF Mohammed Bin Musa Abdullah
AMEIR Ahmad, Mohamad Bin
BOUSAIDI Riad, Abdalla al
FADHIL Murtada Mohammed
HASHAR Khamis, al
KHALILI Shaikh Saud bin Ali, al
NASIB Yahya Mohammed
OMAR Yahia
RIKAISHY Ahmad, Bin Nassir, el
SALEH Maqbool, Hameed Mohammed, Al
SALEM Mubarak, Khalfan
ZAWAWI Omar, Bin Abdulmunim al
ZUBAIR Mohamad

CIVIL SERVANTS (Officials and diplomats)
ALAWI BINABDULLAH Yusuf Binal
ANSI Saudi Salim Hassan al
AZIZI Abdul Aziz bin Matar, al, H.E.
BOUSAIDI Salim, Bin Nasr, al
BUALY Nassir, Seif, el
HABIB Malallah, Ali
HARTHY Mohamad, Sulaiman al
JAMALI Dr. Assim
MAKKI Ahmad, Abd Nabi
MAKKI Munir
RAJAB Abdulhafidh Salem
SAID Sayyid Faisal Bin Ali, al
SAID HH Sayyid Shabib bin Taimur, al
SAID Sayyid Thuwainy Bin Shihab, al
SHANFARI Said Ahmad, al
WOHAIBI Khalfan Bin Nasser, al

POLITICS
HARIMI Karim, Ahmad al
KHADDURI Mubarak, Salih al
QABOOS HM Sultan Qaboos bin Taymour Bin Said
SAID Sayyid Fahad Bin Mahmoud, al

PLO (Palestine Liberation Organization) and Occupied Palestinian Territories

QATAR

ARTS (Literature, Music, Journalism, Painting, Sculpting)
KAABI Muhammad, Rashid, al
NAAMA Khalid, Abdullah

BUSINESS (Banking, Economics, Finance, Industry)
ALDARWISH Yousuf, Jassim
ALI Hassan, bin Ali
ALI Mohammad, J. al
ALI Mohamed Yusuf, al
ANSARI Salem Hassan, al
FAKHROO Abdallah, Darwish
FAKHROO Nasser, Ahmad Abidan
FAKHROO Qassem Darwish
JAIDAH Ali, Mohamad
KAWARI Issa, Ghanem, al
KAWARI Mohamad, Yusuf
KHALFAN Maqbool, Habib Jaffar
MANNAI Ahmed, Abdulla
MARRI Dr. Jaber, Abdulhadi, al
MESHAL Mohamad, Said Khalil, al
MOHANNADI Hamad, Rashid, al
NAAMA Abdulla Hussein
QADI Abdul Kadir, al
THANI Hamad Bin Jassim Bin Jaber, H.E. Shaikh
THANI Shaikh Nasir, Bin Khalid, al
THANI Shaikh Rashed, Awaida, al
THANI Shaikh Suhaim Bin Hamad, al

CIVIL SERVANTS (Official and diplomats)
AMERI Abdul Qadir, Braik, al
ANSARI Ali, Ahmad, al
DAFFA Khattab, Omar, al
JAMAL Jasim, Yousif
KAWARI Hamad, Abdelaziz, al
MANA Abdulla, Saleh, al
NI'MAH Dr. Hassan, Ali Hussain, Al
SUBAIE Abdulaziz, Abdallah, Turki, al

EDUCATION
KAFOUD Mohamed, Abdul Rahim

ENGINEERING
QADOUMI Hisham

LAW
BEHZAD Behzad Youssef

POLITICS
ATIYAH Shaikh Khalid Bin Abdallah
THANI Shaikh Abdulaziz Bin Khalifa, al
THANI Shaikh Ahmad Bin Saif, al
THANI Shaikh Hamad Bin Khalifa, al
THANI H.H. Shaikh Khalifa Bin Hamad, al

SAUDI ARABIA (KINGDOM OF)

ATTAR Omar Saddiq
ATTAS Hussein Ibn Hashim, al
AZZI Bah'a Ibn Hussein
BADKOOK Mohamad Mohamad
BADR Mansour Ibrahim Yusuf
BADRAH Abdul Rasheed Ahmad
BAGHDADY Bakr Ahmad
BAHARETH Abdul Rahman Saleh
BAHARETH Mohamad Slaeh
BAKHSH Abdalla Taha
BAKHSH Adnan, Taha
BALKHAIR Ya'rub Abdullah
BAMUJALLY Ahmad ben Mohsin
BAMUJALLY Mohsin Mujalli Ahmad
BAMOGADDAM Abdallah Ali
BANAJAH Mohamad Said
BANAWI Ali Mohamad
BANYAN Abdallah Saleh, al
BARAJA Abdallah Saleh
BAROOM Abdallah Mohamad el-Sayed
BASHRAHEEL Mohamad Saleh
BASSAM Abdul Hamid, Abdul Rahman, al
BASSAM Abdullah al-Ali, al
BATTERJEE Abdul Jaleel Ibrahim
BATTERJEE Abdul Majeed
BATTERJEE Abdul Raoof Ibrahim
BAWARDI Mohamad al-Saad, al
BAYAZID Ali Mohamad
BEN LADEN al-Fadhl Abdul Kadir Mohamad
BEN LADEN Salem Mohamed
BINZAGH Wahib
BOGARY Mohamad Ahmad
BOKHARI Abdul Hameed Mohamed Zaker
BUBSHAIT Abdulla, Fouad
BUBSHAT Ahmad, Ibrahim
CHAPRA Mohamad, Omar
DAGHISTANI Jafar Abdul Hamid
DAHLAN Mohamad Bakry
DAHLAWI Sheikh Hassan, al
DAHLAWI Sheikh Mohamed Amin, al
DARDEER Hassan Mohamad
DEHLAWI Ahmad Ismail
DEHLAWI Ismail Haroon
DEHLAWI Sami Ismail
DHULAYMI Talal Taha
DUBAISHY Ali Ibrahim
DUKHEIL Abdulaziz M., al
ELIAS Mohamad Atta'Allah Hassan
EMAM Hani, Shafik
ENANY Fuad Mohamad Khalil
ENANY Hassan Mohamad Khalil
EZZAT H.H. Princess Fawzia Hussein
EZZI Wasfi Hussein
FADL Abdulkader M., al
FADL Othman Ibrahim, al
FAQIH Abdul Rahman, Abdul Qadir
FARSY Mohamad Aly Hassan
FATANI Khaled
FAYEZ Khaled, Mohamed, al
FAYEZ Mohamad, Hamed H.
FOUAD Fouad, Abdulla
GAIN Abdelrazag, Abdallah, al
GAZZAZ Hassan Abdul Haye
GHAMDY Ali Saeed S., al
GHAMDY Mohamad Ibn Ibrahim A., al
GHORDAN Said Ali
GOSAIBY Abdulaziz Hamad, al
GOSAIBI Fahad, A.R., al
GOSAIBI Khalid, Mohamed, al
HAFFAR Bishr, Lutfi
HAKIM Rida Talib
HAMAD Riad Ahmad Mohamad ben
HAMDAN Yusuf Hamdan, al
HAMRANI Mohamad, Ali, al
HARBI Abdallah Salih, al
HARTHI Hussain, Mohsin, al
HASHIM Abdallah Hashim
HASHIM Major General Hashim Said
HASSOUN Mohamad Abdallah, al
HEID Mohamad Ibrahim, al
HIMD Riyad, Ahmad Mohamad, bin
HIMDY Fuad, Amin
HOKAIL Abdelaziz Mohamad, al
HOSHAN Ahmad Hamad, al
HUDAITHI Abdullah I., al
HUGAIL Abdallah, Mohamad, al
HUSSEIN Abdelkader, Muhammad
IDRIS Abdulgader
ISSA Abdulrahman Abdullatif Ali, al
ISSA Ibrahim Abdullatif Ali, al
ISSA Ibrahim Mohamed, al
JALAL Mahsoun
JAMAL Adel Mahmoud
JAMAL Saleh Mohamad
JAMEEL Yousef Abdullatif
JAMJOOM Ahmad Salah
JAMJOOM Hisham Mohamad Nour
JAMJOOM Mohamad, Abdul Wahid
JAMJOOM Yusuf Salah
JARBOU Abdulaziz S., al
JAWA Jamal Hassan
JERAISY Abdulrahman, Ali, al
JISHI Jamil Abdallah, al
JOMAIH Mohammed, Abdullah, al
JOUKHDAR Mohamed Saleh
JUFFALI Ahmad
JUFFALI, Ali, Abdallah, al
KAKI Ahmed, Saleh
KAMEL Omar A.
KAMEL Saleh, Abdullah
KANDIEL Asa'ad M.
KANOO Abdulla Ali
KANOO Abdulaziz, Qassim
KASHMIRY Mohamad Abdul Rahman
KASSIM Tarek, Jamal
KAYAL Rashad Abdallah

SUDAIRY Abdulrahman Ahmad Mohamad, al
SUDAIRY Faisal Abdulrahman, al
SUKKARY Ali Hassan
SULEIMAN Abdul Aziz Abdallah, al
SULEIMAN Abdul Mohsem Abdul Rahman, al
SULEIMAN Ahmad al-Abdallah, al
SULEIMAN Fahad al-Abdallah, al
SULEIMAN Fahd Abdul Rahman, al
SULEIMAN Ghassan Abdul Rahman, al
SULTAN Mahmoud Abdullah
SWAILEM Shaikh Abdul Mohsen, al
TAMER Farouk Mohamad Said
TAMER Maamoun Mohamad Said
TARIQI Abdallah
TASHKANDY Ahmad Mohamad
THANAYAN Abdallah Sheikh, al
TUNISSI Abdallah B.
TUNISSI Mohamad al-Taib, al
TURKI Abdul Rahman, Ali, al
TURKI Mansour, I., al
TWAIJRY Ahmad, Saleh, al
TWAIJRY Yusuf, Saleh, al
ZAHID Abdul Majid
ZAHID Erahim, Mahmoud
ZAHID Yusuf, Mahmoud
ZAIDAN Ahmad Mohamad
ZAINAL Mohamad, Abdallah Rida
ZAMIL Abdulaziz Abdallah, al
ZAMIL Hamed Abdullah, al
ZOUMAN Saleh Mohamad

CIVIL SERVANTS (Officials and diplomats)
ABALKHAIL Abdul Rahman Abdullah
ABALKHAIL Mohamad Ali
ABDAL al-Sharif Sharaf Nasser, al
ABDULGHAFFAR Mansour Mahmoud
ABDULJABBAR Sheikh Ahmad Khalil
ABDULKADER Abdulrahman Abdulmohsen, al
ABDUL MAJEED Amin Abdel Razzaq
ABDULWAHAB Sheikh Ahmad
ABDULWASIE Abdul Wahhab Ahmad
ABED Hamza, Mohamad
ABU AL-ELA Ali Hassan
ABU Hussein Hassan Hamza Ali Marzouqi
ABUL NAJA Abdallah, Siraj
ABU MILHA Mohamad Abdulaziz
ABU RASHID Abdul Razzag Rashid
ABU SOLAIMAN Jamil, Ahmad Mohamad
AHMAD Ahmad Sulaiman, al
AHMAD Othman, I., al
AJROOSH Mohamad al-Saad, al
AJROOSH Saleh, al-Ali, al
AKHDAR Farouq M.
ALAKI Mohamad, Abdul Kader
AL MUBARAK Issam
AL TORKI Khaled, N., H.E.
ALGOSAIBI Ghazi
ALI Zailaie, Ali
ALIREZA Abdallah, Mohamad
ALIREZA Sheikh Ali Abdallah
ALSHAREEF Fahied Fahad
AMEEL Mohamad Iben Saleh, al
AMOUDI Muhammad Said
ANBARI Saleh Abdul Muhsen, al
ANQARY Khalid Ibn Mohamad, al-, Dr.
ANQARY Ibrahim, Abdallah, al
ANSARI Nasser, Abdallah, al
ASHY Abdul-Ghany Mahmoud
ASKARI Hussein Mohamad Hussein, al
ASSAD Mohamad, Qussay Walliyuddin
ASSAF Ibrahim Ibn Abdulaziz, al-, Dr.
ATTAS Amin Akil
AYOUBI Mohamad, Zuhair bin Abdul Wahab, al
BADR Fayez Ibrahim
BAFAQIH Fadhl, Abdalah
BAHABRY Mohamad Sultan
BAKHOTMAH M. Saleh
BAKR Ibrahim, Salih
BAKR Mohamad Abdul Karim
BALTO Omar, Mohamad
BAMUFLEH Salem
BANAJAH Samir Hamid
BANGASH Ibrahim Abdallah
BANGASH Mohamad, Ali
BASALEEM Mohamad, Ali
BASRAWY Mohamad Said
BATTERJEE Abdul-llah H.
BATTERJEE Shahir Abdul Raouf
BAZ Mohamad ben Abdul Rahman, al
BILAIHID Abdallah ben Mohamad ben Abdallah, al
BOGAMI Tami Hudaif
BOGIS Abdalla Abdul Muttalib
BUKHARI Dr. Atif Y.
CHARARA Mohamad
DABBAGH Ammar, Tahir, al
DABBAGH Zein el-Abidin
DAGHISTANI Abdulaziz Mohamad
DAHLAN Rabea Sadiq
DERHALLY Abdul Hamid, Said
DIALDIN Ali M.
DUGHAITHER Taha Ali al-Rashid
ELEHADAN Saleh Ibn Saad
ENANY Farida Mohamad Khalid, Miss
EZZI Fakhry Hussein
FADL Abdallah Ibn Saleh, al
FAKI Mohamad Mohamad Hassan
FAKIEH Omar Abdul Kader, Mohamad
FAQIH Abdallah Ibn Saleh, al
FAQUIH Osama J.
FARSY Fouad Abdul Salam, al
FARSY Mohamad Said Hassan
FATANI Zakariya, Yahya Abdallah
FAYEZ Mohamad Ali, al
FRAYAN Hamad, Bin Mohamed, al
FUAD Ibrahim Amine
FUHAID Mohamad Abdallah al-Mutlaq, al

QASSEM Mohamad Abdulaziz, al
QOSAIMY Mohamad Dakkayl, al
QURAISHI Abdul Aziz, al
QUTUB Ahmad Hassan
RABIAH Othman, Abdul Azi, al
RABIE Abdulaziz Mohamad Ali, al
RAJHI Nasser Hamad, al
RASHEED Ali, al
RASHOUDY Ali Ibrahim, al
RASHOUDY Hamad Ibrahim Ali, al
RIDA Abdallah Mohamad
ROUQI Mutlag al-Diyabi, al
SAAD Ali, Rashid, al
SAADI Hani Jameel, al
SAADI Mohamad Ali Amin, al
SABBAN Shaikh Mohamad, Serour, al
SADHAN Abdul Rahman M., al
SAFAR Mahmoud Mohamad
SAGR Abdulaziz N., al
SAID Hassan, bin Saad, bin
SAIF A. Jaleel
SAJA Fahad Mohamad, al
SALEH Mohamad Uthman
SALEH Zaki Abdul Rahman, al
SALLOUM Hamad Ibrahim Mohamad, al
SALLOUM Nasser Mohamad, al
SAMMAN Abdul Mohsin M.
SAMMAN Nizar Hassan
SAMMAN Yasser Shahir, al
SAUD H.R.H. Prince Abdallah Ibn Abdulaziz, al
SAUD H.R.H. Prince Ahmad Ibn Abdulaziz, al
SAUD H.R.H. Badr Ibn Abdulaziz, al
SAUD H.H. Prince Bandar Ibn Abdallah Ibn Abdulrahman, al
SAUD H.R.H. Prince Bandar Ibn Sultan Ibn Abdulaziz, al
SAUD H.R.H. Prince Fahad Ibn Sultan, Ibn Abdulaziz, al
SAUD H.R.H. Prince Khaled al-Faisal, Ibn Abdulaziz, al
SAUD H.R.H. Prince Mohamad Ibn Saud, Ibn Abdulaziz, al
SAUD H.R.H. Prince Mut'ed Ibn Abdulaziz, al
SAUD H.R.H. Prince Nayef, Ibn Abdulaziz, al
SAUD H.R.H. Prince Salman Ibn Abdulaziz, al
SAUD H.R.H. Prince Saud Ibn Abdul Mohsen, Ibn Abdulaziz, al
SAUD H.R.H. Prince Saud Ibn Faisal, Ibn Abdulaziz, al
SAUD H.R.H. Prince Sultan Ibn Abdulaziz, al
SAWA Tajuldin Mohamad ben Ali
SAYARI Sheikh Hamad Saud, al
SAYARI Sulaiman Abdulaziz
SAYED Ibrahim Ahmad, al
SEJINI Hussain, Abdullah
SHAER Ali Hassan, al
SHAIBANI Mohamad, Bin Abdul Rahman, al
SHALLAL Abdullah ben Ali, al
SHAMI Abdul Hamid Mohamad Yahya, al
SHARIE Abdallah al-Nafie, al
SHARIEF Farooq, A.M.
SHATA Bakri, Salih
SHEHABI Samir Sobhi
SHEIKH Dr. Abdulrahman Ibn Abdulaziz, al
SHEIKH Abid, Mohamad Saleh
SHEIKH Hassan ben Abdallah ben Hassan, al
SHEIKH Ibrahim Ibn Mohamad Ibn Ibrahim, al
SHENAIBER Abdul Aziz Abdulah, al
SHIBEL Abdul Rahman Saleh
SHIBRY Mohamad Sad, al
SHIHAIL Faisal Mohamad Abdulaziz, al
SHIQDAR Hashim Noor
SHUBAILI Abdulrahman Abdulaziz, al
SHUBAILI Abdul Rahman Saleh
SHUWAIMAN Abdul Kareem Mohamad, al
SIMAIRI Abdul Mahain Salma Abdul Rahman, al
SINDI Abdul Aziz Mohamad
SINDI Kamil A.
SINDI Mohamad Bakor
SINDI Zuhair Farid
SIRAJ Ahmad Abdul Rahman
SIRAJ Ahmad A.
SOBAIHI Mohamad Ahmad, al
SOLAIM Soliman Abdul Aziz, al
SOWAINE Ali Sulaiman
SUDAIRY Abdelmuhsin Mohamad, al
SUDAIRY Saad-el-Nasser, al
SUDAIRY Salman Ibn Turkey Ibn Naseer, al
SUDAIRY Sultan Abdul Rahman, al
SUDAIRY Sultan Ibn Abdulaziz Ibn Ahmad, al
SUDAIRY Turki ben Khalid, al
SUHAIL Faisal Mohamad, al
SULEIMAN Abdallah Ghati, al
SULEIMAN Jameel Ahmad Mohamad Abdu
SULTAN Ghazi Hashim
SULTAN Ibrahim Mohamad, al
SUNBUL Salim
SUQAIR Saleh Abdallah, al
TAHER Abdulhady Hassan
TAIBA Mahmoud
TALLAB Ra'fat Hashim
TASSAN Ibrahim Abdulrahman, al
TAWAIL Mohamed, al
TAWFIK Farouk M. Omar
TAWFIQ Nizar Ibrahim
TAWFIK Tawfik Ibrahim
TERAIQY Abdulaziz
THANAYAN Abdulaziz, al
THANAYAN Muayyad Abdallah, al
TIBAH Mustafa Abdallah
TURKI Abdulaziz Abdallah, al
TURKI Hilmi Qasim
TWAIJRI Abdul Aziz, Ibn Abdul Mohsin ben Mohamad, al
TWAIJRI Abdulaziz Ibn Ali, al
TWAIJRY Abdul Aziz ben Saleh ben Sulaiman al-Fahd
YAGHMOUR Mohamad Ahmed ben Mohamad Kazem
YAHYA Ahmad Hamad, al
YAMANI Hashem Ibn Abdallah Ibn Hashem, al-, Dr.
YASSIN Anas, Yusuf

EDUCATION

FI'ER Mohamad Hussein, al
FOZAN Ibrahim Fozan, al
FURAIH Ibrahim, Salih, al
FURAIH Othman, Salih, al
GAIN Abdulbar, al
GANDOUL Said, Abdul Aziz, al
GHAMDY Ali Abdallah Mughram, al
GHAMDI Ali Ahmad Ali, al
GHANIM Abdallah Mohamad, al
GHANNAM Soliman Mohamad, al
GHATHAMI Abdallah Mohamad, al
GHOFAILY Ibrahim Fahad, al
GHONEIM Samir, A.
GUBLAN Yusuf, Muhammad, al
GWAIZ Abdul Aziz, al
HABIB Fayez, Ibrahim, al
HADLAQ Mohamad Abdulrahman, al
HAFIZ Faisal Abdallah
HAFIZ Omar Z.A.
HAKIM Muntazar
HALAWANI Seham Abdul Rahman Saleh, Mrs.
HAMDAN Abdallah al-Aqeel al-Soleiman, al
HAMIDY Abdul Rahman Ibn Saad, al
HAMMAD Mohamad, Abdalla Mohamad, al
HAMMOUDA Mona, Tareq, Mrs.
HAMZA Abdulrazzak, Mohamad
HARBI Abdallah Ibn Abdallah Ibn Ebeid al-Zayed, al
HARTHI Fahad al-Orabi, al
HASSAN Bakr Ahmad Dr.
HASSAN Layla, al, Mrs.
HAZMI Ahmad Saad F., al
HAZIMI Mansour Ibrahim, al
HENAIDY Hamid Mohamad
HIBSHI Hashim Bakor
HIBSHI Mohamad Ali
HOMIEDAN Abdullah, Hamad
HULABY Abdul Aziz S., al
HUMAIDAN Humaidan Abdallah, al
IDRIS Abdallah, bin Abdul Aziz
ISLAM Samira, Ibrahim
ISMAIL Mohamad A.
ISSA Mohamad Ali Ahmad
JABOUR Abdullah Sulaiman, al
JAD Ali Bakor
JADO Ahmad Ismail
JAMAL Ahmad, Mohamad
JAMJOOM Shihab Mohamad
JANDOOL Said ben Abdul Aziz, al
JARALLAH Mohamad Ibrahim, al
JERASH Mohamad al-Abdallah, al
JOHANY Ali Ibn Talal, al
JURUF Radwan S., al
JUSTINYYAH Darwish Saddiq, Dr.
KABBAA Abdallah Saud
KABLY Reda Ali
KADI Munir Ahmad, al
KAHTANI Abdul-Mohsen Farraj Saif, al
KAHTANI Mohamad Said Abdul Rahman, al
KARAMI Mohamad Salih
KHAFAJY Hassan Ali
KHALEDI Adnan Mohamad Tahir, al
KHALIFA Mohamad Saleh, al
KHATEEB Mohammad Shahhat, H.
KHATIB Farouk S.
KHATIB Mohamed Khedr
KHATIB Yassir Abdul-Hameed, al
KHATRAWI Mohamad, al-Eid, al
KHATTAB Ezzat Abdul Majid
KHAYAL Abdul Malik A., al
KHAYAT Abdeiah Ismail Abdul Rahman, Mrs.
KHEREIJI Abdallah al-Mohamad, al
KHIDR Abdulfattah
KHODAIR Mohamad Abdallah Abdul Rahman, al
KHOJAH Talaat Mohamad
KHOWAITER Soliman Hammad al
KHOMAIS Yusuf Abdallah, al
KORDI Khalil Abdulfattah
KURNAS Salim Sultan
LEMEILEN Abdulaziz Mohamad, al
MADANI Ghazi Obaid
MADANI Hamza Ali S., al
MAGBOOL Gadi M., Dr.
MAGHRIB Yusuf Mohamad Saleh
MAHBOUB Abdallah Abdul Karim
MAHDI Kamis Amer
MAKOSHI Abdallah A., al
MALAK Mohamad Ali
MALIBARI Salem, Ahmed
MANAA Ibrahim M. Abdallah
MANDILY Fatma Abdalla, Mrs.
MANDURAH Ruqayah Abdul Latif, Mrs.
MANNIE Mohamad Abdallah, al
MANSOUR Saleh Abdul Aziz, al
MARGHALANY Yousuf Abdul Mannan
MARHOUN Mohamad Ali, al
MARZOOQ Abdus-Sabour
MASOUD Abdul Aziz Abdallah, al
MATROUDI Mohamad Ibrahim, al
MESHAL Ibrahim Abdulrahman, al
MESHARI Abdulaziz Ali, al
MILIANI Rajaa Mahmoud Mohamad
MOAJIL Abdallah Hamad, al
MOMENA Fuad Mohamad
MONSHI Mahmoud A. Saleemuddin
MOSHRIF Mohamad A., Dr.
MOURAD Farouk Abdul Rahman
MOUSA Jaber Salem
MUBARAK Rashid Ibn Abdulaziz, al
MUFADDA Mohamad Abdul Rahman, al
MUHTADY Farid Jalal, al
MUJAHID Abdulaziz Mohamad, al
MURSHID Ali al-Murshid ben Mohamad, al
MURSHID Samir Asad
MURSHID Talal Asad
MUSTAJEL Sadaka Y.
NAFIE Abdallah, al

WEDYANI Sulaiman, al
YAHYA Abdul Rahman Ibrahim, al
YAHYA Ali M.
YAMANI Mohamad Abdu
YUSUF Mohamad, Saleh, al
ZABIDI Saud Abdul Aziz
ZAFAR Jamil Ahmad
ZAFER Mohamad Ismail
ZAHRAN Fuad Mustafa
ZAID Abdallah Mohamad, al
ZAID Abdulaziz Mohamad, al
ZAINI Mahmud Hassan
ZAKARI Yahia, Makki
ZAMEL Youssef, al
ZAMIL Ibrahim A., al
ZAMZAMI Awatif Ahmad Hussein, Miss
ZAMZAMI Siraj Jamil
ZAYED Abdallah ben Abdallah ben Obaid, al
ZEDAN Fereed M.H.
ZUBAIR Mohamad Omar

ENGINEERING

ABU GHAZALA Hani Fouad
ABU AL HAMAYEL Habib A.
ALIREZA Mohamad, Ahmad Y.Z.
BAKR Abdallah Yusuf
BALEELA Mustafa M.
BASHIN Yusuf Abdulrahman
BASUNBUL Islam A.
BATTERJEE Sobhi, A.
DARWISH Essam A.
FARSY Zaky Mohamad Aly
FAYEZ Zuhair, Hamid
GHAMDY Ali G. Maadhah, al
HANAFI Abdul Aziz Abdallah
JAMJOOM Muhammad Omar
JANAIDY Abdul Rahman A., al
JAWHAR Saud, Obaysan, al
KASMEERI Nouri A.
KHOSHAIM Bakr Hamza
KOSHAK Yahya, Hamza
LINJAWY Osman Abdllah
MANSOURI Abdul Wahab Hassan
MANSOURI Tareq, Ahmad
MOJADDIDY Muhamad Moussa, al
MOKRIN Zamil A.R., al
MUBARAK Ahmad I
MUDBIL Abdulaziz Hamad, al
NAIM Mohamad Salih
NAQSHABANDI Mohamad A.
OSAIMI Ayed E.
RAJHI Hamad Nasser, al
RASHID Nasir Ibn Ibrahim, al
SAIF Abdullah Saif, al
SALLOUM Ahmed, Mohamed, al
SEHAIMI Mansour, A., al
SHAWLY Abdul Aziz Abdallah
TASHKANDY Farhat Khourshid
WISHAHI Hussein, Ali
ZAIN AL-ABEDIN Habib, Mustafa
ZAMIL Khalid Abdallah, al
ZUHAIR Harb, Salih, al

LAW

ALAMOUDI Abdallah
BASERAIN Mohamad Abdul Rahman
DHAHRI Mohamad Ibn Omar Ibn Abdul Rahman Ibn Aqeel
DURAIB Saud Ibn Saad, al
HEJAILAN Salah Ibrahim, al
HOSHAN Mohamad, H., al
ISSA Abdulaziz Ibn Ibrahim Ibn Abdulaziz, al
MANEI Abdallah Ibn Soliman Ibn Mohamad, al
NAAMY Hashim Said Ali, al
NAZER Ismail
SAIM AL-DAHR Sami Bakor
SAKKA Jawad Omar, al
SAWAF Mohamad Mahmoud, al
SAYED Hussain, Mohamad, al
TURKI Ali Mohamad al-Ali
YAMANI Ahmad Zaki

MEDICINE

ABDULGHAFFAR Hashim Hassan
AL-SIBAI M. Hisham N.
AMRI Abdul Rahman Omar, al
ASSAAD Omar Abdul Mohsin
BAKHSH Abdul Rahman, Taha, Dr.
BASALAMAH Abdullah, Hussain
DABBAGH Hasheem, Salih
FARSY Mansour Mohamad Hassan
GAZZAZ Abbas Ahmad
GEZAIRY Hussein Abdul-Razzaq
GOHARY Hassan Abbas Salem, al
HABBAL Adnan Mohamad Adib, al
HAJERI Yusuf
HARASANY Hamid Mohamad
ISLAM Samer M. Saleh
JAMAL-ELLAIL Nawal Mahjoob, Mrs.
JAMJOOM Abdullatif Mohamed Salah
JAMJOOM Adnan Mohamad Rashid
JAN Mohamad Yunis Yacob
JEFRY Safi Aqeel
KAMEL Hassan Abdallah, Dr.
KHOQAIR Isam, Mohamad
KORDI Mahmoud Taher
MALAIKA Siraj Saleh
MESHARI Abdul Rahman, al
MIRA Siraj A., Dr.
MOKHTAR Ahmad Mohamad Abbas
MUDARRIS Abdulaziz M.S.
MUTABAGANI Hamed
NASEEF Hassan Yusuf
QARMALLI Hassan, Bahaeddin
QASAH Arif Mohamad Salem
QAZNA Mohamad Farjallah

MILITARY

POLITICS

RELIGION

SOMALIA (ISLAMIC REPUBLIC OF)

BUSINESS (Banking, Economics, Finance, Industry)
HUSSEIN Abdillahi
MOHAMOUD Abdulkadir, Mohamed

CIVIL SERVANTS (Officials and diplomats)
ADEN Mohamad, Ali
ARTEH GHALIB Omar
FARAH Abdulrahim Abi
GOULED Ahmad Haji Aden
HUSSEIN Abdirizak, Haji
JAMA Rabile, God
NUR ELMI Hussein
OSMAN Abdillahi Said
SHARIF Salem, Mohamad Dr.

EDUCATION
FIDO Abdullahi, Ali

MILITARY
ISMAIL Ali, Abukar, Gen.

POLITICS
EGAL Mohamed Ibrahim
SAMATER Lt. Gen. Mohamed, Ali

SUDAN (REPUBLIC OF SUDAN)

NOUR Mohamed, Abdalla
ODUHO Joseph
OMER Al Fadil Al-Obeid
ORAT ADOR Peter
OSMAN Dr. Mohamad Khair
QASSEM Osman, al
RAHAMA Mubarak, Othman
RIAL Cleto, Hassan
SAID Kamil, Mohamad
SALEH Galobawi, Muhammad
SAWI Amir, al
SHAAR Mohamad, Sayid, al
SHIBEIKA Izzeddine Makki
SHUMMO Ali Mohamad
TUHAMI Mohamad Sharif
YASSIN Mohamad, Osman
ZUBEAR Mohamed Kheir, Ahmed, Al, Dr.

EDUCATION

ABDULKARIM Bakri, Musa, Dr.
ABUSALIM Mohamad, Ibrahim
ABUSHAMA Faisal, Tageldine
AKALWIN Natali, Olwak
BAKR Kamel, Mohamad al-Wali Ismail, al
BILI Osman, Sid Ahmad Isamil, Al
BURHAN Hamid, othman
DEIFALLAH an-Nazer
GASIM Awn Sahrif al
HABASHI Wadi
HAGE Ali Nasr, al
IBRAHIM Abdul Aziz al-Tayib
IBRAHIM Saad, Ahmad
ISHAK Mustafa, Hassan
KHEIR Yahya, Muhammad, al
KHOGALI Ali
MUSTAFA Mukhtar, Ahmad, Dr.
QASSEM Awn al-Sharif, Dr.
SAAD Chawqi

ENGINEERING

ABBADI Beshir, Ahmad B.
ABDEL MAGUID Abbas
AGEEB Osman A.A.
ALI Abdulaziz Mohamad
ELAMIN Mohamed, Abdelrahman Ali
HAMID Ibrahim, Mahmoud
IBRAHIM Murtada, Ahmad
IDRIS Azzam
ISSA Omar Saleh
JAK Dr. Mohamad Hassan, al
KAROURI Muhammad, Othman al-Hassan al
SALEH Saleh, Muhammad

LAW

ABU KHEIR Osman, Haga
AHMED Dr. Hassan Omer
BAKR Babikir, Abdallah
GAI Martin Majier
GASM ELSEED Elamin Dafalla, Prof.
IDRIS Kamil, E. Dr.
KHALED Mansour
KHALFALLAH Khalfallah al Rashid Mohamad Ahmad
MAKKAWI Makkawi, Awad, al
MOHAMMAD Al Bushra A. Hamid
MOHAMMAD Mohamad, Yusuf
RASHEED Khalafalla, al
ZAKI Abdul Rahman, Muhammad

MEDICINE

AROP Justin, Jac
BAHSIR Mustafa, Badawi
BASHIR Taha, Ahmad
DAFALLAH Nazir, Dr.
FADL Ali, Mohamad
HASSAN Ahmad, Mohamad al
TAHA Elzubeir, Beshir

MILITARY

ABDULGADER Major General Mohamad Abdul Aziz
ABU ZAID Major Ma'Moon, Awad
AWAD General Khalafalla Amir
BAGHIR Ahmad, Mohamad, Gen., el
BASHIR Lieutenant General Mohamed, Ali
BISHARA Al-Fatih Mohamad Bashir
DAHAB Gen. Abdul-Rahman Swar al
FATIH Mohamad Beshara, al
KADR Abdel Mohamad
KHALIFA Mohamed Elamin
LAGU Major-General Joseph
MAQBUL General Taj al-Sirr Ahmad
MARDI Colonel al-Tayib, al
MOUSA Omar, El-Hag
OMAR Mohamad Abdul Gadir

POLITICS

ABDALLAH Abdul Rahman
ABDULGADER Zain al Mohamad Ahmad
ABDULHALIM Mohamed
ABDULMAJEED Yahia
ABULQADIR al-Mardhy al-Tayib
ABULGASIM Major Mohamad Ibrahim
ABUSAQ Mohamad, Othman
ABUSINEINA Amin
AMIN Nafisa, Ahmad al
AWAD Karamallah
AYIK Arop, Yor
DAFALLAH Gizouli
DENG Francis Mading
DIREJJ Ahmad, Ibrahim
FAISAL Muhammad Abdul Rahman
GAAFAR Mohamad Ali Bakhit
GARANG Enok, Madling De
GUAL Peter Gatkuouth
HADI Mahdi, Mustafa, al
HAG Musa Ismail, al
HASSAN Mustafa Othman

RELIGION

SYRIA *(SYRIAN ARAB REPUBLIC)*

ARTS (Literature, Music, Journalism, Painting, Sculpting)
BAHNASSI Afif, Rafiq
ISSA Sulaiman, al
KARKOUTI Mustapha
LAHHAM Duraid
MUDARRIS Assaad
MUSTAFA Chaker, Ahmad
NABAA Nazir
NEDHAMEDDIN Arfan, Abdul Kader
ORSAN Ali Okla
QADDAMA Ahmad, Mohamad Badawi
QATTINIS Julien
RAFAIAH Yassine
RAYES Riad, Najib, al
RIDA Ismat
SAKAKINI Wadad
SALEM Georges
SAMMAN Ghada, Wagih, al
TADMORI Ahmad Jalal, al
TALEB Bassam
YAZBEK Qassem
ZAKARIA Ghassan, Wasfi
ZURAYK Constantin, Kaysar

BUSINESS (Banking, Economics, Finance, Industry)
ABUASSALI Dib
ACCAD Rifaat
AIDI Osman
AKHRAS Mohamed, Chafic
ARABI Issam
ATASSI Safwan
AZHARI Naaman, al
AZMEH Dr. Abdallah, al
BITAR Muhammad
CHADAREVIAN Henri
CHATTI Bourhan Eddine
DARKAZALLY Maamoun
DARWICH Samir
HADDAD Adham K.
HAIKAL Walid, Hasan
HAKIM Moh. Riad
HILAL Fouad
HISHAM Awad
HOMSI Naoom, Victor
HORANIEH George
HUSSAMI Argan
HUSSAMI Mazhar
IMADY Mohamad, Al
JALLAD Jaber I.
KHALIL Hilal
KHALIL Fakhruddin
KHAYATA Dr. Abdul Wahab
KUTUBI Orfan, Kader, al
KWEIDER Mohamed, Rateb
MAHAYNI Thabit, Ghalib
MAKDISI Faiz
MERHEJ Michel
MISKAL Mahmoud Nadim
MOHAMAD Mousto
NOUDARARRI Nicolas, Soubhi
MOUKAYED Assad, Major General
OMARI Mohamad Eyad
OSMANI Khaled
RABBAT Walid B.
SAADI Majed
SABEH Samir
SAFADI Hassan
SAFADI Hisham, J.
SAWAF Abdulaziz, al
SAYED HASSAN Muwaffaq, al
SHAHBANDAR Mustafa
SHALLAH Rateb, Dr.
SHARIF Mohamed, al
SHASH Mohamad, M., al
SIBA'I Nouhad
TERMANINI Radwan
TRABOULSI Hassan
USAMA Malluhi
YASSINE Soufian A.F.
ZAYYAT Fuad
ZOUHEIRI Bachir

CIVIL SERVANTS (Officials and diplomats)
ADEL Fouad Rachad, al
ADLI Ibrahim
ARMANAZI Ghaith, Najib
AYOUBI Mahmoud, al
AZHARI Ryad
BAGHAJATI Adnan
BAKJAJI Dr. Sabah El Deen
CHAYA Jamil
DAWOUDI Adib
DROOBI Sami, Misbah
FATTAL Dia Allah el
HADDAD Soubhi
HAIRAT Taha Mohamad
HAMADA Anwar
HAMAWI Maamoun, al
HAMMOUDA M. Faruk
HANNUSH Basim, Abdulmasih
ISMAIL Mohamad, Zakaria
JABBOUR Georges
JABER Mamdouh
KADI Ismail, Al
KATKHOUDA Louay
KEICHE Sulaiman, al
KHAIRAT Taha
KILANI Haitham al
KODMANI Nazem
KOTAITE Abdullatif
MAHAYNI Mohammd Khaled, al
MANSOUR Abdel Hamid
MASRI Ahmad Fathi, al

MOUNAYER H.E. Mgr. Eustache Joseph
NIJMEH H.E. Mgr. Elias
RAI H.E. Mgr. Pierre
SCHELHOTH H.E. Mgr. George
ZIADE Nicolas, Abdo

TUNISIA (REPUBLIC OF TUNISIA)

KLIBI Ridha
LADGHAM Salah
LAOUANI Othman
MAAMDOURI Mahmoud
MABROUK Hedi
MAHERZI Mohamad, al
MASMOUDI Mohamad, Mohamad
MASMOUDI Mustafa
MESTIRI Ahmad
MESTIRI Mahmoud
MOKADDEM Sadeq
MOKADDEM Youssef
NASSER Mohamad, an
NOUIRA Habib
RIAHI Lamine
ROUISI Moncer, Dr.
SAHBANI Tayeb
SAID Rafik
SAYAH Mohamad, Melki
SELMI Saida Bin Abid
SHAKER Abdul Magid
SLIM Taeib
SOUDANI Ferid
TURKI Ibrahim
ZARROUK Neziha, Mehoud
ZGHAL Houssine
ZGHAL Mohamad

EDUCATION
AYED Ahmad, al
AZIZA Muhammad, Sadeq
BASTI Abderraouf Mohamed
BECHRAOUI Mohamad Taher
BEN AHMED Mohamed
BOUMIZA Salem
BOURICHA Abdelrazzak
CHABAANE Mahmoud
CHARFI Abdelmajid Ahmad
DJAIT Hichem
FAYALA Mohamad
HASSOUMI Ali, al
KALLAL Zuhair
KTARI Mohamed, Hedi
MAAMOURI Muhammad
MAHJOU Bechir, Mohamad
MILI Ali, Fredje

ENGINEERING
AMAMI Salahiddin, al
AZZABI Ali, Ridha
BELAID Slaheddine
BENABDESSELEM Muhammad, Muncef
BENSAID Abdussalam
CHAKER Moncef
CHOUK Houcine
ENNABLI Nouriddin
FURATI Malik
KHATTECH Hichem
KHOUADJA Brahim
MADANI Bouraoui
MA'MAR Mukhtar
MILI Mohamad
RABAH Sadok
SAID Hashim
SASSI M. Abdulhamid
ZGOLLI Taieb
ZIDI Makki

LAW
ESSEBSI Slahiddin
FITOURI Mohamad
JAZI Dali
MALKI Abdul Hamid

MEDICINE
BOUCHOUCHA Sadeq
KAROUI Hamed, Dr.
MESTIRI Said, Mohamed, Tahar
MIHENNI Hedi

MILITARY
MASHTA Lieutnant Colonel Tuham

POLITICS
AMMAR Ferdjani Ben Hadj
AMMAR Moncef, Belhadj
BELLAGHA Bachir
BEN ALI Zine el Abidine
BENOSMAN Lassaad
BOUZIRI Najib
CHEDLY Muhammad, Fredj Muhammad
ESSEBSI Begi, Qaid
FEKIH Mungi
HADDAD Radhia
HENABLIA Dhaoui
KEFI Abdelrrazak Jilani
KHALED Ahmad
KHELIL Ismail
KOOLI Mongi
LASRAM Abdelaziz
M'BAZA Fuad
MELLAKH Larbi
MEZGHANI Ridha, Ahmad
MOALLA Mansour
MZALI Mohamad
SFAR Rachid
TLILI Ahmad

RELIGION
TERZI Shaikh Kamel

UNITED ARAB EMIRATES (7 STATES)

EDUCATION
AL-JASSIM Sulaiman, Moosa, Dr.
BUHUSSAIN Ahmad, Abdallah
MUSTAFA Izzidin, Ibrahim
SALMAN Saeed, Abdullah, Dr.
SHARBAN Ali, Abdulaziz, al-, Dr.
SHOMALI Ahmad Abdulaziz

LAW
AZRAQ Abdulwahab, al
DWEIK Yusuri
FARAH Salih
MAKTOUM Shaikh Mohamad Bin Hasher, al

MILITARY
MAKTOUM Shaikh Ahmad Bin Rashid Bin Said, al
NAHAYAN Shaikh Sultan Bin Ziad, al

POLITICS
BAKR Mohamad, Abdulrahman, al
GHAITH Saeed, al
GHOBASH Said, Ahmed
HAMILI Sultan Ghanoum al
JARWAN Sayf Ali al
KINDI Mohamad Khalifa, al
MAKTOUM Shaikh Hamdan Bin Rashid, al
MAKTOUN Shaikh Maktoum Bin Rashid, al
MAKTOUM Shaikh Mohamad Bin Rashid Bin Said, al
MADFA Hamad, Abdul Rahman, al
MUALLA Mohamad, Said, al
MUALLA H.H. Shaikh Rashid bin Ahmad al
MUALLA Shaikh Sultan Bin Ahmad, al
NAHAYAN Shaikh Hamdan Bin Mohamad, al
NAHAYAN Shaikh Khalifa Bin Zayed
NAHAYAN Shaikh Mubarak Bin Mohamad, al
NAHAYAN HH Shaikh Zayed Bin Sultan, al
NUAIMI Shaikh Humaid Bin Rashid, al
OTAIBA Maneh, Said, al
QASIMI Shaikh Abdul Aziz Bin Humaid, al
QASIMI Shaikh Khalid Bin Saqr., al
QASSEMI Shaikh Mohamad Bin Salem Bin, Sultan, al
QASIMI Shaikh Saqr Bin Mohamad, al
QASIMI Shaikh Sultan Bin Saqr, al
QASSEMI Shaikh Sultan Bin Mohamad, al
RAQABANI Said Mohamed al
SHARQI HH Shaikh Hamad Bin Mohamad, al
SUWEIDI Ahmad Khalifa, al
TARYAM Abdullah, Omran

YEMEN (REPUBLIC OF)

BUSINESS (Banking, Economics, Finance, Industry)
ADDAILAMY Yahia Abdullah
AMER Hussain, Qassim
ANAM Abduljabbar Hail Said
ASWADY Fateh Abdulrahman, al
BAHR, Ali, Abdulrahman, al
BAZARA Omar Salim
GHALEB Mohamad, Anaam
IDD Zuhair, Ali
IRYANI Abdallah, Hassan, al
KIRSHY Abbas Muhammad al
LUQMAN Ali Muhammad Ali
NUSEIF Ali, al
OMAYA Mohamad, Ali
SAID Abdulsamad Mutahar
SANABANI Abdallah, Mohamad, al
SULTAN Amin Kassim Mohamed
UWAIDH Ahmad Abdallah
WATAARY Hussein, al
ZABARAH Abdulmalik, Ali

CIVIL SERVANTS (Officials and diplomats)
ABDULGHANI Major Abdul Aziz
ABDULHAMID Abdulwahab, Mahmoud
ABURAS Sadek, Amin
ABU RIJAL Ali Ahmed
ABU SAID Ahmad
ABU SHAWARIB Lieutenant-Colonel Mujahid Yehya
AFIF Ahmad, Jaber
AINI Mohsen
AKWAA Ismail, Ali
AMRI Hussain al
ARASHI Yahya, Hussain Ahmad al
ASHTAL Abdallah Saleh al
ASNAJ Abdallah, Abdulmajid, al
ATTAR Dr. Mohamad Said, al
ATTAS Faisal al
AULAQI Shaikh Mohamad Farid, al
AWAD Mohamad Hadi
BAID Ali, Salim, al
BAIDAR Lieutenant Colonel Hamud Mohamed
BARKAT Abdallah, Hussein
BATANI Mohammed, Abdullah, Al
BAYOUMI Hussain, Ali, al
BUKAIR Abdallah Ahmad
CHAABI Faisal, Abdullatif, ach
CHAMLANE Faisal
DAFA'I Hussain, al
DHAIFALLAH Abdullatif, Mohamed, H.E.
DHALI Seif Ahmad, ad
FUTAIH Abdulaziz, al
GEGHMAN Yahya Hamoud
GHAFARI Lieutenant Colonel Hussain Muhammad
HABORY Ali, Hamoud al
HADDAD Ahmad, Ali, al
HADI Abdul Hamid, Saif Manih al
HAGI Mohamad Ibn Ismail Ibn Yusuf, al
HALLALI Abdullah, Hussain, al
IRYANI Mohamad, Abdulla, al
ISMAIL Abdulmalek
JAMIL Ghalib, Ali
KURSHUMI Abdallah, Hussain Ahmad, al
MASRI Salah, Ahmad, al
MOKBIL Saeed, Taleb
MUTAWAKIL Muhammad Abdul Malik Abdul Karim al
MUTAWAKEL Yahia Mohamad, al
NAAMAN Ismail, Saïd
SAIDI Sharaf al-Deen Saleh, al
SALAMI Ali, Ahmad, Nasir
SAMMAN Qadi, Ali, bin Ali, al
SARY Ahmad M.
SHAMI Ahmad, al
TAYIB Abdul Malik, al
THABET Rashed, Mohamed
WAZIR Muhammad, Abdul Koddos, al
ZINE Abdallah, Yahia

EDUCATION
MUTAHAR Mohamad, Bin Mohamad, al

ENGINEERING
ALAWI Ali Jaber
ALI Mohamed, Othman
KUAIB Ali, Ghanim

LAW
ABDALLAH AWAD AHMAD Ahmad
ABDULKHALIQ Dr. Mustafa
AHMAD Abdallah, Awadh

MEDICINE
ABDULLAH (Abdul Melik, Muhammad)
GHANEM Najeeb Saeed, Dr.
WADUD Mohamad, al

MILITARY
AKWAA Brigadier Mohamad Ali, al
BISHI Ali, Ahmad Nasr al
DAHLEH Seif
DEIFALLAH Abdullatif
SHAYBA Ali, al

POLITICS
ABBAS Salih, Mohammad
ANAM Ali Mohamad Said
ARASHI Qadi, Abdul Karim, al
ATTAS Haidar, Abu Bakr, al
BADIB Ali Abdul Razzak
BARAKAT Ahmad Kaid
BASINDWAH Mohamad, bin Salim
CHAABI Kahtane, ach
DAHMASH Ahmad, Qassim
HAKIM Said, Mouhammad al

HUBAISHI Hussein Ali, al
IRYANI Abdul Karim, al
JUNAID Mohamad Ahmad, al
KHAMIS Mohamad Hamoud
KHAMRI Abdullah, al
MAKDAMI Hussein, Abdallah, al
MAKKI Dr. Hassan Mohamad
MIDHI Mahmoud, Said
MOHAMAD Ali, Nassir
MOHSEN Mohamad, Said Abdallah
MUTI Mohamad Saleh Abdallah
NASHER Abdul Aziz Abdul Wali
NUBAN Said, Abdul Khair, al
OTHMAN Abdu, Ali
RAINI Ahmad Saleh, al
SAID Ahmad, Abdu
SALEH Col. Ali Abdullah
SALLAL Abdallah
SHU ABI Major Salih Muslih Qasim Majdul
THOR Ali, Lutfi, al
URAISH Mahmud, Abdallah
WAJIH Mohamad Khadim, al
YAHYA Anis, Hassan
YUSUFI Muhsim, Abdullah, al

RELIGION

ANSI Abd al-Karim

ARAB & OTHER NATIONALS RESIDING IN & OUTSIDE THE ARAB COUNTRIES

MULLANE Terence John
NIXON Patrick, Michael
PELLETREAU Robert H.
ROSS Christopher W.S.
SCHLINGENSIEPEN Dr. Georg Hermann
VAN STEENBERGS Ignace
VOLES IVAN

EDUCATION
AL-HASHIM Dhia, Dawod
AL-MARAYATI Abid A.
ATIYEH George, Nicholas
BADAWI Mohamed Mustafa
BOOLAKY Ibrahim
DABBAGH Hussein, Mohamad Ali, al
DAJANI Jarir, Subhi
DIA Amir
FARAH Caesar E.
GHAITH Muhammad, Ahmad
HADDAD Robert, M.
HATTAR Michael, Mizyad
JIBURY Falik, Khidir al
KHALEDI Walid
KHOLY Hussein, A. al
KHOURI Nicola Najib
LANGHADE Jacques
LINDERS Albert, Frederikus
MABRO Robert, Emile
MAGHRABY Salahiddin, al
MAKDISI George
MANZER Bruce Monroe
MAZZAWI Musa
MUSTAFA Mohamad Eid
NAJJAR Fawi M.
PEDERSEN Dr. Richard F.
PRATT Leighton
SUCCARI Owais, R.
SULEIMAN Michael, Wadie
TAMIMI Hamdi A.
TAWASHI Rashad, Kamel, al
TUMA Elias, H.
WAKIL Mohamad, al
YAQUB Adel, Mohamad
YUNIS Adil, Assad

ENGINEERING
ALAMI Zuheir
AWAR Arif Mahmoud al
BAZ Farouk, El
JOSEPH Pazhunnan Verghese
KAMAL Munir, Mark
KARARA Dr. Houssam, Mahmoud
KHAZEN Farid, F., al
NUSEYBEH Azmi, Izzat
SHAH Rajnikant C.
TABARI Hisham, R.
TARAMAN Khalil Shawki
TAYARD Carol, Youssef
ZALZALAH Hadi
ZAYNOUN Shafik T.

LAW
HABIB Mustafa, Salman
MAHSHIE George, T.
ZIADEH Farhat, J.

MEDICINE
BANOOB Samir Nagib
DIB Edward
HADDAD Farid, Sami
HATOUM Platon, Assad
HIJAZI Miss Narryman Asaad
MOLLA Abdul Majid
NAHAS Gabriel Georges, Bechara
SHAKHASHIR Radi, Shukri
SHEIKH Fazal-ur-Rahman Amir Bakhsh
SUKI Wadi, Najib

POLITICS
BAKR Ibrahim

RELIGION
CARTY John Alston
MANOUKIAN H.E. Mgr. Ardag
NURUL ALAM Shah Sufi Mohammad
PETROS VII, His Beatitude
RAYA Mgr. Joseph
SALAMA Mgr. Joseph
TEISSIER Henri-Antoine-Marie
YOUAKIM Saba, H.E. Mgr.
ZOGHBI Elie, H.E. Mgr.

SELECT BIBLIOGRAPHY

BOOKS ON THE MIDDLE EAST

- ATYIAH, EDWARD, The Arabs (Baltimore, 1955).
- BAER, GABRIEL, Population and Society in the Arab East (Routledge, London, 1964).
- BELYAEV, J.C (ed). Arabs, Islam and the Arab Caliphate in the early Middle Ages (Pall Mall Press, London, 1969).
- BERQUE, JAQUES AND CHARNAY, J.P. Normes et Valeurs dans l'Islam Contemporain (Payot, Paris, 1966)
- MIDWELL'S GUIDES TO GOVERNMENT MINISTERS, Vol. II, The Arab World 1900-1972. Compiled and edited by Robin Bidwell (Frank Cass, London, 1973)
- BINDER, LEONARD. The Ideological Revolution in the Middle East (New York, 1964).
- BROCKELMANN, C. History of The Islamic Peoples (New York and London, 1974-48).
- BULLOCH, JOHN. The Making of a War: The Middle East from 1967-1973 (Longman, London, 1974).
- CARRERE D'ENCAUSSE, HELENE. La Politique Sovietique au Moyen-Orient, 1955-1975 (Presses de la Fondation Nationale des Sciences Politiques, Paris, 1976).
- CATTAN, HENRY, Palestine and International Law: The Legal aspects of the Arab-Israeli Conflict (Longman, London, 1973).
- COOK, M.A. (ed.) Studies in the Economic History of the Middle East (Oxford University Press, 1970).
- COSTELIO, V.F. Urbanisation in the Middle East (Cambridge University Press, 1977).
- DE VORE, RONALD M. (ed). The Arab-Israeli Conflict; A Historical, Political, Social and Military Bibliograhpy (Clio Press, Oxford, 1977).
- ENCYCLOPAEDIA OF ISLAM, THE, 4 vols, and supplement (Leiden, 1913, 38).
- FARIS, N.A. (ed.) The Arab Heritage (Princeton, N.J., Princeton University Press, 1944).
- FISHER S.N. Social Forces in the Middle East (Cornell University Press Ithaca, N.Y., 1955).
  The Middle East: A History (Alfred Knoph, New York, 6th edition, 1971).
- GLUBB, LT., Gen Sir John. A Short History of the Arab peoples (Hodder and Stoughton, London, 1969).
- GOMMA, AHMED M. The Foundation of the League of Arabe States (Longman, London, 1977).
- HAIM, SYLVIA G. Arab Nationalism: An Anthology (Berkeley, Calif, 1962).
  HATEM, M. ABDEL-KADER, Information and the Arab Cause (Longman, London, 1974).
- HAZARD, Atlas of Islamic History (Oxford University Press, 1951).
- HITTI, PHILIP K, History of the Arabs (London, 1940, 10th edn, 1970).
  A Short History of the Near East (New York, 1966).
  Makers of Arab History (Macmillan. London, 1968).
  Islam. A Way of Life (Oxford University Press, London, 1971).
- HOURANI, A.H. Minorities in the Arab World (London, 1947).
  A Vision of History (Beirut, 1961).
  Arabic Thought in The Liberal Age 1798-1939 (Oxford Univ, Press, 1962).
- INSIGHT ON THE MIDDLE EAST WAR (André Deutsch, London, 1974) (Sunday Times team of writers)
- ISSAWI, CHARLES (ed.). The Economic History of the Middle East, 1800-1914 (University of Chicago Press, 1966).
- KEDOURIE, ELIE, England and The Middle East (London 1956).
  The Chatham House Version and other Middle-Eastern Studies (Weindenfeld and Nicolson, London, 1970).
  Arabic Political Memoirs and other Studies (Frank Cass, London, 1974).
- KHALIL, MUHAMMAD. The Arab States and the Arab League (historical document Khayat's Beirut).
- KHAYAT, M.K. and KEATINGE, M.C. Food from the Arab World (Beirut, 1959).
- KHOURI, FRED J. The Arab-Israeli Dilemma (Syracuse/New York, 1968).
- LAHBABI, MOHAMED AZIZ. Le Personnalisme Musulman (Press Universitaires de France, Paris, 1964).
- POLIAK, A.N. Feudalism in Egypt, Syria, Palestine, and the Lebanon, 1250-1900 (London, Lusac, for the Royal Asiatic Society 1939).
- PORATH, Y. The Emergence of the Palestinian Arab Movement 1918-1929 (Frank Cass, London, 1974).
- ROUHANI, FUAD. A History of OPEC (Pall Mall Press, London 1972).
- SAYIGH, YUSIF, The Determinants of Arab Economic Development (Croom Helm, London, 1977).
- SHARABI, H.B. Governments and Politics of the Middle East in the Twentieth Century (Van Nostrand, New York, 1962).
- SID-AHMED, MUHAMMAD, After the Guns Fell Silent (Croom Helm, London, 1976).
- WATT, W, MONTGOMERY, Muhammad at Mecca (Clarendon Press, Oxford, 1953).
  Muhammad at Medina (Clarendon press, Oxford, 1956).

Muhammad, Prophet and Statesman (Oxford University Press 1961).
Muslim Intellectual-Al Ghazari (Edinburgh University Press, 1962).
Islamic Philosophy and Theology (Edinburgh University Press, 1963).
- Islamic. Political Thought: The Basic Concepts: Edinburgh University Press, 1968).
- WILSON, RODNEY, Trade and Investment in the Middle East (Macmillan Press, 1977).
- ZEINE, Z.N. The Struggle for Arab Independence (Beirut, 1960).
- ABC-CLIO'S Middle Eastern Political Dictionary.

Printed in Lebanon
by S.I.E.L. (Société d'Impression et d'Edition Libanaise) – Beirut – Tel.: (01)250545 - 883152